ROGET'S
21ST CENTURY THESAURUS
Second Edition

ROGET'S
—21ST—
CENTURY
THESAURUS

Second Edition

IN DICTIONARY FORM

*The Essential Reference for Home,
School, or Office*

EDITED BY THE PRINCETON LANGUAGE INSTITUTE
BARBARA ANN KIPFER, PH.D., HEAD LEXICOGRAPHER

Produced by The Philip Lief Group, Inc.

Delta

A Delta Book
Published by
Dell Publishing
a division of
Random House, Inc.
1540 Broadway
New York, New York 10036

Published by arrangement with
The Philip Lief Group, Inc.

ISBN: 0-7394-0609-4

Manufactured in the United States of America

Published simultaneously in Canada

CONTENTS

PREFACE

More than ever before, our language and our ideas about language are changing as rapidly as the world around us. Our Information Age has been made possible, of course, by the ever-expanding technology of computers and the extraordinary explosion of information from the Internet and World Wide Web. We are receiving more information than we had ever imagined possible.

But how do we process this information—and articulate it in speech and writing? With expanded research and development of artificial intelligence systems, we have been able to examine more closely the complex cognitive relationships human beings form between their ideas and the words they choose. We now know more about how this process works, and how it can be re-created. Learning from this, current lexicographical research must go beyond traditional methods and techniques to develop effective and contemporary reference materials for students, linguists, and writers.

Most people learn a new word by guessing, based on context, what that word means. Recent studies on students' ability to develop reference skills bear this out. Combining this proven pattern with the advanced theories of language gained through electronic media, we have arrived at an "onomasiological" approach to understanding American English. That is, we are capable of traveling successfully from a meaning to a word instead of the straightforward dictionary approach of going from word to meaning. Onomasiologically, readers move from the concepts of "yellow" and "flower" to a selection of words that describe the combination, or from the notion of a "positive state of mind" to its qualities, actions, and conditions.

We have searched for a method of presenting this lexical theory in a format that provides diversified access to words within one resource. In *Roget's 21st Century Thesaurus, Second Edition,* the text is designed to do just that: allowing users to search both from word to meaning and from meaning to word. The dictionary format is familiar to use, and the Concept Index provides helpful links between words as it illustrates the language's semantic structure. The A to Z listings further amplify the resonances between words with their parts of speech and different sense divisions.

This second edition of *Roget's 21st Century Thesaurus* has almost 3,000 new headwords reflecting the dynamic changes in our language and the fabric of our lives. It continues as the most complete and comprehensive selection of synonyms published in print media today.

BARBARA ANN KIPFER, PH.D.

INTRODUCTION

The history of *Roget's Thesaurus* is a long and fascinating one. It began in 1805, when P. M. Roget, a British surgeon and inventor, took up a peculiar hobby: the classification of words according to ideas. He hoped to create a kind of verbal catalogue that would assist writers and linguists in their search for the right expression. His work was perhaps inspired by two earlier texts: the ancient Sanskrit *Amarakosha,* arguably the first arrangement of words by subject, and the French *Pasigraphie* (published in 1797), which was an attempt to order words so they could be understood universally, without translation. Roget called his own work a "thesaurus"—a Latin word meaning "treasury" or "storehouse of knowledge."

Gradually, Roget's casual pastime became his lifelong passion. In 1852, some forty-seven years of work culminated in the publication of Roget's *Thesaurus of English Words and Phrases, Classified and Arranged so as to Facilitate the Expression of Ideas and Assist in Literary Composition.* This new reference book (published when Roget was seventy-three) became enormously popular, and a second edition was published only a year after the first. By the time of his death in 1869, there had been twenty-eight editions and printings. Today, his name is literally "synonymous" with the thesaurus.

RENOVATING THE ORIGINAL THESAURUS

Although Roget's original idea was brilliant, his thesaurus assumed that all users shared the compiler's ideas about language. Its classifications and indexes presented a labyrinth of possibilities in which each route could end in a disappointing or inappropriate selection of synonyms. The classification of terms made the text almost impenetrable and forced the reader to rely on the index, which did not even include every synonym. All too often, the right word remained elusive, or the thesaurus remained on the shelf. And today, Roget's nineteenth-century thesaurus is difficult for many twenty-first-century readers to use or even understand.

For over a century, thesaurus editors have strived to redefine the nature and function of the thesaurus. Essentially, their goal has been to present accurate information in a highly usable format. Attempts to improve Roget's thesaurus began with Roget's own son, John Lewis, who expanded the selection of synonyms. Later, Thomas Y. Crowell acquired publishing rights to the thesaurus. His 1886 edition of *Roget's* provided a clearer page design and format that enhanced the book's readability. Subsequent generations of Crowells have added Americanisms, foreign expressions, slang and nonstandard speech, prefixes, suffixes, and quotations. Although these changes were indeed improvements, *Roget's* original structure of categories, cross-references, and indexes actually became *more* complicated by the addition of an elaborately conceived type design, boldface entries, numbered paragraphs, and a decimal system that required an explanatory diagram.

One of the most important breakthroughs in the evolution of the thesaurus came in the early twentieth century when C. O. Sylvester Mawson attempted to simplify and reorganize

Roget's Thesaurus into a dictionary-like format. Roget's original work and the early revisions had not been arranged alphabetically. In 1911, Mawson radically changed the book's organization by issuing his alphabetical presentation of the famous Roget system. Twentieth-century editors quickly followed his lead, eager to find an easier method for frustrated thesaurus users.

Even with this improvement, the thesaurus still lacked something, for it did not suggest any relationships between words beyond the simple group of synonyms listed with a main entry. Although it did offer a more straightforward presentation than the index-reliant *Roget's,* it neither helped users organize thoughts nor provided broad conceptual links between ideas as expressed through language in words.

A THESAURUS FOR THE NEW MILLENNIUM

Roget's 21st Century Thesaurus achieved what no other thesaurus has been able to do: combine the simplicity of the dictionary format with the utility of arranging words according to ideas. This revolutionary design has become the new standard for thesaurus users. It is, simultaneously, a fast and efficient handbook for writers and a medium to facilitate the expression of ideas—both of Roget's original objectives brought forward and reinterpreted for the twenty-first-century user.

This second edition of *Roget's 21st Century Thesaurus* has been electronically compiled using state-of-the-art techniques. It lists approximately 20,000 main entries, or headwords, in alphabetical order. These generate over 500,000 synonyms— more than any other thesaurus in dictionary form.

Reflecting the most recent changes in language, *Roget's 21st Century Thesaurus, Second Edition* is the most contemporary and useful thesaurus in history. The final selection of main entry words and synonyms was derived with today's practices of speaking and writing in mind. Reflecting contemporary usage, obsolete terms have been replaced by timely words and phrases. You will find terms from all areas of our experience, particularly the high-tech world of computers (such as "hacker," "computerese," "on-line," and "artificial intelligence"), the Internet and World Wide Web ("cyberpunk," "chat room"), video and multimedia ("telecast," "digital library"), medicine ("AIDS," "attention deficit disorder"), political and civil spheres ("politically correct," "affirmative action," "out of the closet"), the environment ("ecosystem"), and money and business ("mutual fund," "desk jockey"). A nonsexist, nonracist approach to language replaces outmoded epithets. Foreign words and phrases that reflect our global consciousness have been included ("au pair," "schlemiel"), as well as hundreds of Americanisms ("psyched," "rubberneck"). Synonyms that represent colloquial or slang terms are marked with an asterisk.

Roget's 21st Century Thesaurus, Second Edition is not just ultra-contemporary but also eminently usable. Drawing upon computer technology and recent innovations in typesetting and design, the pages are printed in a highly readable and contemporary format so the reader can make quick and effective choices. The synonym lists are not littered with cross-references, usage labels, or abbreviations, all of which can come between the user and the words themselves. Like main entries, the synonym lists are arranged in alphabetical order, completely objective, and not prescriptive, leaving the user to choose from the wealth of synonym choices available.

USING *ROGET'S 21st CENTURY THESAURUS, SECOND EDITION*

The book's sensible format ensures swift access to the right alternatives. For quick identification, each headword in the A to Z listing is printed in boldface; its part of speech follows in bracketed italics. Some headwords have more than one listing; separate entries are included for each different part of speech—adjectives, nouns, and verbs, as well as adverbs, conjunctions, and prepositions. "Pass," for example, has thirteen entries—four noun forms and nine verb forms. Each sense of the word "pass" is treated individually to help writers pinpoint the precise sense of the word desired.

Concise definitions accompany the headwords, supplying users with a basic reference point and helping them to evaluate synonym choices. Semicolons sometimes appear within definitions to denote fine points of sense for a word's particular usage when the differences are too subtle to warrant a separate entry.

Remember that no two words mean exactly the same thing. No two words are directly interchangeable. It is the subtle nuance and flavor of particular words that give the English language its rich and varied texture. We turn to a thesaurus to find different, more expressive ways of speaking and writing, but we must turn to a dictionary, a sophisticated semantic tool, to determine meaning. Always consider synonyms in their desired context and consult a dictionary if you have any doubt about the application of a word or phrase.

USING THE CONCEPT INDEX

The entries in *Roget's 21st Century Thesaurus, Second Edition* are enriched by directing users to related concepts in the Concept Index. This unique index offers users an up-to-the-minute language hierarchy that bridges the gap between thought and expression. The Concept Index actually helps writers organize their thoughts by generating possibilities for millions of word choices—far beyond the capabilities of a traditional thesaurus.

Each of the book's approximately 20,000 headwords is referenced to at least one of the 837 individually numbered concepts in the index. The words "SEE CONCEPT(S)" appear in small caps at the end of a main entry, followed by the numbers for all relevant concepts for that word. When an initial search does not yield the desired results, the Concept Index automatically provides users with alternative places to look.

For example, if none of the synonyms listed with the word "scintillating" seems appropriate, the Concept Index directs the writer to concepts #401, "attributes of behavior"; #529, "cognitive qualities"; and #617, "visual brightness." Each concept gathers together scores of headwords that share the same characteristics. Persistent writers or linguists can turn back to the A to Z listing to find the synonyms for any of these headwords, allowing them to locate even more word choices.

The Concept Index follows the alphabetical listing of headwords and begins with a reference key. The concepts appear in the index in numerical order and are divided into ten overarching categories of interest: Actions, Causes, Fields of Human Activity, Life Forms, Objects, The Planet, Qualities, Senses, States, and Weights and Measures. All headwords grouped under a specific concept are ordered alphabetically and by different parts of speech, if applicable.

The most advanced theories of communication and learning available have been used to determine concept names and classifications. The word hierarchies in *Roget's 21st Century Thesaurus, Second Edition* have been streamlined into categories that reflect contemporary ways of thinking. It is clear what concepts mean and how they are organized. Whether performing a speedy search through the concepts or entering the index with just a vague notion in mind, users will find the Concept Index to be a fast and reliable research tool.

A CLASSIC FOR TODAY AND TOMORROW

In the minds of writers and linguists, Roget has always been the trademark of a dependable thesaurus. As we enter an era unimagined by P. M. Roget two hundred years ago, *Roget's 21st Century Thesaurus, Second Edition* upholds that reputation. Adapting Roget's thesaurus to reflect today's concerns, this new text represents a fresh and vital reference of American English.

ROGET'S
21ST CENTURY THESAURUS
Second Edition

A

aback [*adv*] *taken unawares*
confused, surprised, thrown off, thrown off guard*; SEE CONCEPT *403*

abaft [*adj*] *to the rear*
astern, back, behind, rearward; SEE CONCEPTS *586,820*

abandon [*n*] *careless disregard for consequences*
disregard, freedom, impulse, licentiousness, recklessness, spontaneity, thoughtlessness, uninhibitedness, unrestraint, wantonness, wildness; SEE CONCEPTS *633,645*

abandon [*v1*] *leave behind, relinquish*
abdicate, back out, bail out*, bow out*, chicken out*, cop out*, cut loose*, desert, discard, discontinue, ditch*, drop, drop out, duck*, dump*, dust*, flake out*, fly the coop*, give up the ship*, kiss goodbye*, leave, leg it*, let go, opt out, pull out, quit, run out on, screw*, ship out, stop, storm out*, surrender, take a powder*, take a walk*, throw over*, vacate, walk out on, wash hands of*, withdraw, yield; SEE CONCEPT *195*

abandon [*v2*] *leave in troubled state*
back out, desert, disown, forsake, jilt, leave, leave behind, quit, reject, renounce, throw over*, walk out on; SEE CONCEPTS *7,19,195*

abandoned [*adj1*] *left alone, deserted*
alone, cast aside, cast away, deserted, discarded, dissipated, dropped, dumped, eighty-sixed*, eliminated, empty, forgotten, forsaken, given up, godforsaken*, jilted, left, left in the cold*, left in the lurch*, neglected, on the rocks*, outcast, passed up*, pigeon-holed*, rejected, relinquished, shunned, sidelined*, side-tracked*, unoccupied, vacant, vacated; SEE CONCEPT *577*

abandoned [*adj2*] *free from moral restraint; uninhibited*
corrupt, depraved, dissolute, immoral, incontinent, incorrigible, licentious, profligate, shameless, sinful, uncontrolled, unprincipled, unrestrained, wanton, wicked, wild; SEE CONCEPT *545*

abase [*v*] *deprive of self-esteem, confidence*
belittle, debase, degrade, demean, diminish, disgrace, dishonor, humble, humiliate, lower, mortify, reduce, shame; SEE CONCEPTS *7,19*

abasement [*n*] *disgrace*
degradation, dishonor, downgrade, humiliation, shame; SEE CONCEPT *388*

abashed [*adj*] *exhibiting mental discomfort, ill at ease*
ashamed, bewildered, bugged*, chagrined, confounded, confused, crushed, discombobulated*, disconcerted, embarrassed, fazed*, fuddled, humbled, humiliated, in a tizzy*, mortified, rattled, shamed, taken aback; SEE CONCEPT *403*

abate [*v*] *lessen, grow or cause to grow less*
allay, chill out*, coast*, cool, cool it*, decline, decrease, diminish, dull, dwindle, ebb, go with the flow*, hang easy*, hang loose*, lay back*, let go, let it all hang out*, let up, mellow out*, moderate, quell, recede, reduce, slacken, slow, subdue, subside, take it easy*, taper, taper off, unlax*, wane; SEE CONCEPTS *240,698*

abbey [*n*] *building that houses monks, nuns, or priests; church*
cloister, convent, friary, ministry, monastery, nunnery, priory, temple; SEE CONCEPTS *368,439*

abbreviate [*v1*] *shorten*
abridge, abstract, boil down*, clip, compress, condense, contract, cut, cut back, cut down, cut off, cut out, digest, encapsulate, get to the meat*, pare, prune, put in a nutshell*, reduce, summarize, take out, trim; SEE CONCEPTS *236,247*

abbreviate [*v2*] *cut short an activity*
abort, curtail, restrict, stop short, truncate; SEE CONCEPT *234*

abbreviation [*n*] *something shortened*
abridgement, abstract, abstraction, clipping, compendium, compression, condensation, contraction, digest, outline, precis, reduction, sketch, summary, syllabus, synopsis; SEE CONCEPTS *283,652*

abdicate [*v*] *give up a right, position, or power*
abandon, abjure, abnegate, bag it*, bail out*, cede, demit, drop, forgo, give up, leave, leave high and dry*, leave holding the bag*, leave in the lurch*, opt out*, quit, quitclaim, relinquish, renounce, resign, retire, sell out*, step down, surrender, vacate, waive, withdraw, yield; SEE CONCEPTS *133,298*

abdomen [*n*] *the stomach and area directly below in an animate being*
bay window*, belly, bowels, breadbasket*, corporation, gut*, guts, intestines, middle, midriff, midsection, paunch, pot*, potbelly*, spare tire*, tummy, venter, viscera; SEE CONCEPT *393*

abdominal [*adj*] *concerning the stomach and the area below it*
belly, duodenal, gastric, intestinal, stomachic, ventral, visceral; SEE CONCEPT *393*

abduct [*v*] *take by force and without permission*
carry off, dognap*, grab, kidnap, make off with, put the snatch on*, remove, seize, shanghai*, snatch, sneeze*, spirit away*; SEE CONCEPT *139*

abducted [*adj*] *taken away by force*
appropriated, kidnapped, seized, snatched, stolen; SEE CONCEPTS *90,139*

abduction [*n*] *taking away by force*
appropriation, kidnapping, rape, seizure, theft; SEE CONCEPTS *90,139*

abend [*n*] *abnormal end of task*
abort, crash, loss; SEE CONCEPTS *658,674*

aberrant [*adj*] *not normal; varying from the usual*
abnormal, atypical, bizarre, deviant, different, flaky*, mental*, nonstandard, odd, off-base, off-color, out of line*, peculiar, psycho*, strange, unusual, weird; SEE CONCEPT *547*

aberration [*n1*] *state of abnormality*
delusion, eccentricity, oddity, peculiarity, quirk, strangeness, weirdness; SEE CONCEPT *647*

aberration [*n2*] *different from that expected*
departure, deviation, difference, distortion, divergence, diversion, irregularity, lapse, straying, wandering; SEE CONCEPT *665*

abet [*v*] *assist, help in wrongdoing*
advocate, back, condone, egg on*, encourage, endorse, goad, incite, instigate, prod, promote, provoke, sanction, spur, support, urge; SEE CONCEPTS *14,110*

abettor [*n*] *assistant*
accessory, accomplice, co-conspirator, confederate, cooperator, helper, partner in crime*, second, supporter; SEE CONCEPT *348*

abeyance [*n*] *being inactive or suspended temporarily*
deferral, discontinuation, dormancy, inactivity,

intermission, latency, postponement, quiescence, recess, remission, suspension, waiting; SEE CONCEPTS *681,705*

abhor [v] *regard with contempt or disgust*
abominate, be allergic to*, be down on*, be grossed out by*, despise, detest, hate, have no use for*, loathe, scorn; SEE CONCEPT *29*

abhorrence [n] *disgust*
detestation, enmity, hate, hatred, horror, loathing, malice, odium, repugnance, revulsion; SEE CONCEPTS *410,720*

abhorrent [adj] *disgusting*
despicable, detestable, execrable, loathsome, offensive, repulsive, revolting; SEE CONCEPTS *485,548*

abide [v1] *submit to, put up with*
accept, acknowledge, bear, bear with*, be big about*, concede, consent, defer, endure, hang in*, hang in there*, hang tough*, live with*, put up with*, receive, sit tight*, stand, stand for, stomach, suffer, swallow, take, tolerate, withstand; SEE CONCEPTS *23,35*

abide [v2] *live in a certain place*
bide, bunk*, bunk out*, crash*, dwell, hang out*, inhabit, lodge, nest, perch, reside, room, roost, settle, squat, stay; SEE CONCEPT *226*

abide [v3] *remain or continue in a state*
continue, endure, keep on, last, persevere, persist, remain, survive; SEE CONCEPTS *23,239*

abide [v4] *stop temporarily and wait for*
anticipate, bide, expect, linger, pause, remain, rest, sojourn, stay, stick around*, stop, tarry, wait; SEE CONCEPTS *119,681*

abiding [adj] *continuing or existing for an indefinite time*
constant, continuing, enduring, eternal, everlasting, fast, indissoluble, lasting, permanent, perpetual, persistent, persisting, steadfast, steady; SEE CONCEPT *551*

ability [n1] *power to act, perform*
aptitude, capability, capacity, competence, competency, comprehension, dexterity, endowment, facility, faculty, intelligence, might, potentiality, qualification, resourcefulness, skill, strength, talent, understanding; SEE CONCEPT *630*

ability [n2] *natural or acquired power in a particular activity*
adeptness, adroitness, bent, capability, cleverness, command, craft, deftness, expertise, expertness, finesse, flair, genius, gift, handiness, ingenuity, knack, know-how, mastery, mind for, proficiency, savvy, skill, skillfulness, strength, talent, the goods*, the right stuff*, what it takes*; SEE CONCEPT *706*

abject [adj] *hopeless and downtrodden*
base, contemptible, degraded, dejected, deplorable, dishonorable, fawning, forlorn, groveling, hangdog, humiliated, low, miserable, outcast, pitiable, servile, submissive, worthless, wretched; SEE CONCEPT *571*

abjure [v] *give up*
abstain from, forswear, recant, renege, renounce, retract, take back, withdraw; SEE CONCEPTS *30,54,195*

ablate [v] *wear away*
erode, evaporate, melt, vaporize; SEE CONCEPTS *252,469*

ablaze [adj1] *on fire*
afire, aflame, alight, blazing, burning, conflagrant, fiery, flaming, flaring, ignited, lighted; SEE CONCEPTS *485,605*

ablaze [adj2] *very excited*
afire, angry, aroused, enthusiastic, fervent, frenzied, fuming, furious, heated, impassioned, incensed, intense, on fire, passionate, raging, stimulated, vehement; SEE CONCEPT *550*

ablaze [adj3] *brightly illuminated*
aflame, aglow, brilliant, flashing, gleaming, glowing, incandescent, luminous, radiant, refulgent, sparkling; SEE CONCEPT *617*

able [adj1] *capable of performing; having an innate capacity*
adept, adequate, adroit, agile, alert, apt, bright, capable, competent, cunning, deft, dexterous, easy, effortless, endowed, equipped, facile, fitted, good, intelligent, knowing, powerful, ready, smart, strong, worthy; SEE CONCEPTS *402,527*

able [adj2] *able to perform well; having a proven capacity*
accomplished, adroit, agile, artful, au fait, brilliant, capable, clever, deft, dexterous, effective, effectual, efficient, equal to, experienced, expert, facile, gifted, ingenious, intelligent, keen, know backwards and forwards*, know one's onions*, know the ropes*, learned, masterful, masterly, powerful, practiced, prepared, proficient, qualified, responsible, savvy, sharp, skilled, skillful, smart, talented, there*, trained, up to it*, up to snuff*, up to speed*, with it*; SEE CONCEPTS *402,528*

able-bodied [adj] *physically strong and capable*
firm, fit, hale, hardy, healthy, hearty, lusty, powerful, robust, staunch, stout, strapping*, sturdy, vigorous; SEE CONCEPTS *314,489*

ablution [n] *washing*
bath, cleansing, decontamination, lavation, purification, shower, showering; SEE CONCEPTS *161,165*

ably [adv] *capably*
adroitly, capably, competently; SEE CONCEPT *527*

abnegate [v] *renounce*
abstain, decline, forbear, forgo, give up, refrain, reject; SEE CONCEPTS *30,54,195*

abnegation [n] *denial, renouncement of something*
abandonment, abstinence, eschewal, forbearance, giving up, nixing, refusal, rejection, relinquishment, renunciation, sacrifice, self-denial, stonewall*, surrender, temperance; SEE CONCEPTS *18,25*

abnormal [adj] *different from standard or norm*
aberrant, anomalistic, anomalous, atypical, bizarre, curious, deviant, deviate, deviating, divergent, eccentric, exceptional, extraordinary, fantastic, funny, grody*, gross, heteroclite, heterodox, heteromorphic, irregular, odd, off-base, off-color, out of line, peculiar, preternatural, queer, screwy*, spastic*, strange, uncommon, unexpected, unnatural, unorthodox, unusual, weird; SEE CONCEPT *547*

abnormality [n] *being different from standard or norm*
aberrancy, aberration, anomalism, anomaly, atypicalness, bizarreness, deformity, deviance, deviancy, deviation, eccentricity, exception, extraordinariness, flaw, irregularity, oddity, peculiarity, preternaturalness, singularity, strangeness, uncommonness, unnaturalness, unusualness, weirdness; SEE CONCEPT *647*

aboard [adj] *on or in a transportation object*
boarded, consigned, embarked, en route, in transit, loaded, on, on board, traveling; SEE CONCEPT *583*

abode [n] *building or place where one resides*
address, apartment, base, casa, condo, co-op, crash pad*, crib*, den, digs*, domicile, dwelling, flat, flop*, habitat, haunt, headquarters, hearth, hole*, home, homestead, house, joint*, lodging, pad, quarters, residence, roost*, sanctuary, seat; SEE CONCEPT *515*

abolish [v] *do away with or put an end to*
abate, abrogate, annihilate, annul, call off, cancel, destroy, disestablish, dissolve, end, eradicate, erase, expunge, extinguish, extirpate, finish, inhibit, invalidate, kill, negate, nix, nullify, obliterate, overthrow, overturn, prohibit, put an end to, put kibosh on*, put the kibosh on*, quash, repeal, repudiate, rescind, revoke, scrub*, set aside, squelch, stamp out, subvert, supersede, suppress, terminate, undo, vacate, vitiate, void, wipe out, zap*; SEE CONCEPTS *121,252,298*

abolition [n] *formal act of putting an end to, annulling*
abolishment, abrogation, annihilation, annulment, cancellation, destruction, dissolution, elimination, end, ending, eradication, extirpation, invalidation, negation, nullification, obliteration, overthrow, overturning, quashing, repeal, repudiation, rescinding, rescindment, rescission, revocation, subversion, suppression, termination, voiding, wiping out, withdrawal; SEE CONCEPTS *121,252,298*

abolitionist [n] *person wanting something ended*
activist, advocate, opponent, revolutionary; SEE CONCEPT *366*

A-bomb [n] *atomic bomb*
nuclear bomb, nuclear weapon, physics package*, thermonuclear bomb; SEE CONCEPT *500*

abominable [adj] *awful, detestable*
abhorrent, atrocious, awful, bad, base, beastly, contemptible, cursed, despicable, disgusting, foul, grim, grody*, gross*, hairy*, hateful, heinous, hellish, horrible, horrid, loathsome, lousy, nauseating, obnoxious, odious, offensive, repellent, reprehensible, repugnant, repulsive, revolting, rotten, sleazy*, stinking, terrible, vile, wretched; SEE CONCEPTS *29,544,571*

abominate [v] *detest*
abhor, despise, dislike, hate, loathe; SEE CONCEPT *29*

abomination [n1] *object of extreme dislike, hate*
anathema, aversion, bother, curse, detestation, evil, horror, nuisance, plague, shame, torment; SEE CONCEPTS *29,666*

abomination [n2] *wrongdoing*
crime, offense, wrong; SEE CONCEPT *691*

aboriginal [adj] *belonging to one, existing in a place since prehistory*
ancient, earliest, endemic, first, indigenous, native, original, primary, primeval, primitive, primordial; SEE CONCEPT *549*

aborigine [n] *first inhabitant*
aboriginal, autochthon, bushman*, indigene, native, primitive; SEE CONCEPT *413*

abort [v1] *stop or cancel something*
arrest, break off, call it quits*, call off, check, cut off, drop, end, fail, halt, interrupt, knock it off*, lay off*, nullify, scrap, scratch, scrub*, terminate; SEE CONCEPT *121*

abort [v2] *terminate or fail to complete pregnancy*
miscarry; SEE CONCEPTS *121,304,308*

abortion [n1] *expulsion of fetus*
aborticide, feticide, misbirth, miscarriage, termination; SEE CONCEPTS *230,699*

abortion [n2] *failure*
disappointment, disaster, fiasco, misadventure, premature delivery; SEE CONCEPTS *304,308,674*

abortive [adj] *failing to achieve a goal*
failed, failing, fruitless, futile, ineffective, ineffectual, miscarried, unavailing, unproductive, unsuccessful, useless, vain, worthless; SEE CONCEPT *528*

abound [v] *exist in abundance*
be alive with, be all over the place*, be knee deep in*, be no end to*, be plentiful, be thick with*, be up to one's ears in*, crawl with*, crowd, flourish, flow, have a full plate*, infest, overflow, proliferate, swarm, swell, teem, thrive; SEE CONCEPT *141*

abounding [adj] *plentiful*
abundant, bountiful, copious, filled, flush, plenteous, prodigal, profuse, prolific, replete, teeming; SEE CONCEPTS *762,781*

about [adv1] *in an opposite direction*
around, back, backward, in reverse, round; SEE CONCEPT *581*

about [adv2] *lying anywhere without order, arrangement*
anyhow, any which way*, around, here and there; SEE CONCEPT *583*

about [prep1] *near an amount, quantity*
almost, approximately, in general, in the ball park*, in the neighborhood*, nearly, practically, pretty nearly, roughly; SEE CONCEPT *771*

about [prep2] *concerning, relating to*
apropos, as concerns, as respects, dealing with, in connection with, in relation to, in respect to, referring to, regarding, relative to, touching, touching on; SEE CONCEPT *532*

about [prep3] *near or close to in position*
adjacent, beside, nearby; SEE CONCEPTS *586,778*

about [prep4] *on every side, in every direction*
around, encircling, round, surrounding, through, throughout; SEE CONCEPT *586*

about-face [n] *change in direction*
changeabout, double, doubleback, reversal, reverse, turn, turnabout, volte-face; SEE CONCEPT *697*

above [prep1] *higher in position*
aloft, atop, beyond, high, on high, on top of, over, overhead, raised, superior, upon; SEE CONCEPT *752*

above [prep2] *more, higher in amount, degree*
beyond, exceeding, greater than, larger than, over; SEE CONCEPT *793*

above [prep3] *superior to*
before, beyond, exceeding, prior to, superior to, surpassing; SEE CONCEPT *567*

aboveboard [adj] *candid*
forthright, frank, honest, open, overt, right on*, square, straight, straightforward, straight from shoulder*, true, trustworthy, truthful, up front*, veracious; SEE CONCEPT *404*

aboveboard [adv] *candidly*
frankly, honestly, on the up and up*, openly, overtly, truly, truthfully, veraciously; SEE CONCEPT *404*

ab
ab

above suspicion [*adj*] *innocent*
above reproach, blameless, guiltless, having clean hands*, inculpable, irreproachable, scrupulous, sinless; SEE CONCEPT *545*

abracadabra [*n*] *magic word*
hocus-pocus, incantation, invocation, mumbo jumbo, open sesame, spell; SEE CONCEPTS *370,673,689*

abrade [*v*] *scrape*
chafe, erode, grate, rub, rub off, scuff, triturate, wear, wear down; SEE CONCEPTS *165,186,215*

abrasion [*n1*] *scraped area*
chafe, injury, scrape, scratch, scuff; SEE CONCEPT *309*

abrasion [*n2*] *scraping or wearing down by friction*
abrading, chafing, erosion, grating, rubbing, scratching, scuffing; SEE CONCEPT *186*

abrasive [*adj1*] *irritating in manner*
annoying, biting, caustic, cutting, galling, hard to take*, hateful, hurtful, nasty, rough, rubbing the wrong way*, sharp, spiky*, unpleasant; SEE CONCEPT *404*

abrasive [*adj2*] *scraping or wearing*
cutting, erosive, grinding, polishing, rough, scratching, scratchy, scuffing, sharpening, smoothing; SEE CONCEPT *606*

abreast [*adv1*] *next to, alongside*
beside, equal, in alignment, in line, level, opposite, shoulder to shoulder, side by side; SEE CONCEPT *586*

abreast [*adv2*] *up-to-date*
acquainted, au courant, au fait, contemporary, familiar, informed, in touch, knowledgeable, up*, versed; SEE CONCEPT *402*

abridge [*v*] *shorten*
abbreviate, abstract, blue pencil*, chop, clip, compress, concentrate, condense, contract, curtail, cut, decrease, digest, diminish, downsize, lessen, limit, narrow, put in nutshell*, reduce, restrict, slash, snip*, summarize, trim, truncate; SEE CONCEPTS *236,247*

abridgement [*n*] *shortening, summary*
abbreviation, abstract, brief, compendium, condensation, conspectus, contraction, curtailment, cutting, decrease, digest, diminishment, diminution, lessening, outline, precis, reducing, reduction, synopsis; SEE CONCEPTS *283,652*

abroad [*adj*] *in a foreign country*
away, elsewhere, in foreign lands, in foreign parts, out of the country, overseas, touring, traveling; SEE CONCEPT *583*

abrogate [*v*] *formally put an end to*
abate, abolish, annul, cancel, dissolve, do in*, end, finish off*, invalidate, knock out*, negate, nix, nullify, quash, reject, renege, repeal, retract, revoke, scrub*, torpedo*, undo, vacate, vitiate, void; SEE CONCEPT *121*

abrogation [*n*] *cancellation*
annulment, discontinuation, ending, invalidation, quashing, repudiation, rescission, retraction, reversal, voiding, withdrawal; SEE CONCEPT *119*

abrupt [*adj1*] *rude or brief in manner*
blunt, brusque, crude, crusty, curt, direct, discourteous, gruff, impetuous, impolite, matter-of-fact, rough, short, snappy, snippy, uncivil, ungracious; SEE CONCEPT *542*

abrupt [*adj2*] *happening suddenly and unexpectedly*
hasty, hurried, jerky, precipitate, precipitous, quick, rushing, sudden, surprising, unanticipated, unceremonious, unexpected, unforeseen; SEE CONCEPT *820*

abscess [*n*] *swelling*
boil, carbuncle, pustule, ulcer; SEE CONCEPTS *306,309*

abscond [*v*] *run away, depart secretly*
beat it*, bolt*, break, clear out*, cut and run*, decamp, disappear, dog it*, duck out, escape, fade*, flee, fly the coop*, get, go AWOL*, go south*, hightail*, jump*, leave, make a break*, make off, make scarce*, pull out, quit, run off, scram*, skedaddle*, skip out*, slip, sneak away, split*, steal away, take off*, vamoose*, vanish; SEE CONCEPTS *102,195*

absconder [*n*] *person who escapes*
absentee, bolter, escapee, quitter, truant; SEE CONCEPTS *403,583*

absence [*n1*] *state of not being present*
absenteeism, AWOL*, cut*, French leave*, hooky*, nonappearance, nonattendance, no show*, truancy, vacancy; SEE CONCEPT *746*

absence [*n2*] *state of lacking something needed or usual*
dearth, deficiency, drought, inadequacy, insufficiency, lack, need, omission, privation, unavailability, void, want; SEE CONCEPT *646*

absent [*adj1*] *not present*
astray, away, AWOL*, elsewhere, ghost, gone, hooky*, missing, nobody home*, no-show*, removed, vanished; SEE CONCEPT *583*

absent [*adj2*] *deficient in something needed or usual*
bare, blank, devoid, empty, hollow, lacking, minus, missing, nonexistent, omitted, unavailable, vacant, vacuous, wanting; SEE CONCEPT *546*

absentee [*adj*] *not being present*
absent, distant, oblivious, remote; SEE CONCEPTS *403,583*

absenteeism [*n*] *state of not being present*
absence, defection, desertion, skipping, truancy; SEE CONCEPT *746*

absent-minded [*adj*] *unaware of events, surroundings*
absent, absorbed, abstracted, airheaded*, bemused, daydreaming, distracted, distrait, dreaming, dreamy, engrossed, faraway, forgetful, goofing off*, heedless, inattentive, inconscient, lost, mooning*, moony*, oblivious, out to lunch*, pipe dreaming*, preoccupied, remote, removed, space cadet*, spacey*, unconscious, unheeding, unmindful, unobservant, unthinking, withdrawn, woolgathering*; SEE CONCEPT *403*

absent-mindedness [*n*] *preoccupation*
absorption, abstraction, distraction, dreaminess, forgetfulness, heedlessness, inattention; SEE CONCEPTS *293,410,532,690*

absolute [*adj1*] *without limit*
complete, consummate, downright, entire, flat out*, free, full, infinite, no catch*, no fine print*, no holds barred*, no ifs ands or buts*, no joke*, no strings attached*, outright, plenary, pure, sheer, simple, straight out, supreme, thorough, total, unabridged, unadulterated, unconditional, unlimited, unqualified, unrestricted, utter; SEE CONCEPT *546*

absolute [*adj2*] *in control or complete authority*
absolutist, arbitrary, authoritarian, autocratic, autonomous, despotic, dictatorial, full, monocratic,

preeminent, sovereign, supreme, totalitarian, tyrannical, tyrannous; SEE CONCEPT *536*

absolute [*adj3*] *certain*
actual, categorical, conclusive, consummate, decided, decisive, definite, exact, factual, fixed, genuine, infallible, positive, precise, sure, unambiguous, undeniable, unequivocal, unmitigated, unquestionable; SEE CONCEPT *535*

absolute [*adj4*] *excellent, perfect*
categorical, complete, faultless, flawless, ideal, impeccable, thorough, ultimate, unblemished, unflawed, untarnished; SEE CONCEPT *574*

absolutely [*adv1*] *certainly, without question*
actually, categorically, come hell or high water*, conclusively, decidedly, decisively, definitely, doubtless, easily, exactly, for sure*, no ifs ands or buts*, no strings attached*, on the button*, on the money*, on the nose*, positively, precisely, really, right on*, straight out*, sure as can be*, sure as hell*, sure enough*, surely, sure thing*, the very thing*, truly, unambiguously, unconditionally, unquestionably; SEE CONCEPT *535*

absolutely [*adv2*] *in a complete manner, degree*
completely, consummately, entirely, fully, thoroughly, utterly, wholly; SEE CONCEPT *531*

absolution [*n*] *forgiveness*
acquittal, amnesty, compurgation, exculpation, forgiveness, mercy, pardon, release; SEE CONCEPTS *685,689*

absolve [*v*] *free from responsibility, duty*
acquit, bleach, blink at, clear, discharge, exculpate, excuse, exempt, exonerate, forgive, free, go easy on, launder*, let off*, let off easy*, let off the hook*, let up on*, liberate, lifeboat*, loose, pardon, release, relieve, sanitize*, set free, spare, spring*, vindicate, whitewash, wink at*, wipe it off*, wipe the slate clean*, write off*; SEE CONCEPTS *83,317*

absorb [*v1*] *physically take in a liquid*
blot, consume, devour, drink in, imbibe, ingest, ingurgitate, osmose, soak up, sop up*, sponge up*, suck in*, swallow, take in; SEE CONCEPT *256*

absorb [*v2*] *mentally take in information*
assimilate, comprehend, digest, follow, get, get into*, grasp, incorporate, latch onto, learn, sense, soak up, take in, understand; SEE CONCEPT *31*

absorb [*v3*] *occupy complete attention*
captivate, concern, consume, employ, engage, engross, fascinate, fill, hold, immerse, involve, monopolize, obsess, preoccupy, rivet; SEE CONCEPT *17*

absorbed [*adj*] *being completely occupied mentally*
captivated, consumed, deep in thought, engaged, engrossed, fascinated, fixed, gone*, head over heels*, held, immersed, intent, involved, lost, preoccupied, rapt, really into*, up to here*, wrapped up*; SEE CONCEPT *403*

absorbent [*adj*] *capable of physically taking in a liquid*
absorptive, bibulous, dry, imbibing, penetrable, permeable, porous, pregnable, retentive, spongy, thirsty; SEE CONCEPT *603*

absorbing [*adj*] *holding one's attention*
arresting, captivating, consuming, engrossing, enthralling, exciting, fascinating, gripping, interesting, intriguing, monopolizing, preoccupying, riveting, spellbinding; SEE CONCEPT *403*

absorption [*n1*] *assimilation, incorporation*
consumption, digestion, drinking in, exhaustion, fusion, imbibing, impregnation, ingestion, inhalation, intake, osmosis, penetration, reception, retention, saturation, soaking up, suction, taking in; SEE CONCEPTS *169,256*

absorption [*n2*] *total attention toward something*
captivation, concentration, engagement, engrossment, enthrallment, fascination, hang-up*, holding, immersion, intentness, involvement, occupation, preoccupation, raptness; SEE CONCEPT *410*

abstain [*v*] *hold back from doing*
abjure, abnegate, avoid, cease, constrain, curb, decline, deny oneself, do without, eschew, evade, fast, fence-sit*, forbear, forgo, give the go by*, give up, go on the wagon*, keep from, pass, pass up, quit, refrain, refuse, renounce, shun, sit on one's hands*, sit on the fence*, sit out, spurn, starve, stop, take the cure*, take the pledge*, withhold; SEE CONCEPTS *25,121*

abstemious [*adj*] *restraining behavior or appetite*
abstinent, ascetic, austere, continent, frugal, moderate, moderating, restrained, self-denying, self-restrained, sober, sparing, temperate; SEE CONCEPT *401*

abstention [*n*] *refraining*
abstaining, abstinence, avoidance, non-indulgence, self-control, self-denial, self-restraint, sobriety; SEE CONCEPT *633*

abstinence [*n*] *restraint from desires, especially physical desires*
abnegation, abstaining, abstemiousness, asceticism, avoidance, chastity, continence, fasting, forbearance, frugality, moderation, refraining, renunciation, self-control, self-denial, self-restraint, soberness, sobriety, teetotalism, temperance; SEE CONCEPT *633*

abstract [*adj*] *conceptual, theoretical*
abstruse, complex, deep, hypothetical, ideal, indefinite, intellectual, nonconcrete, philosophical, recondite, transcendent, transcendental, unreal; SEE CONCEPT *582*

abstract [*n*] *short document prepared from a longer one*
abridgment, brief, compendium, condensation, conspectus, digest, outline, precis, résumé, summary, synopsis; SEE CONCEPT *283*

abstract [*v1*] *take away from*
detach, disconnect, disengage, dissociate, extract, isolate, part, remove, separate, steal, take out, uncouple, withdraw; SEE CONCEPTS *135,211*

abstract [*v2*] *prepare short document from longer one*
abbreviate, abridge, condense, digest, outline, review, shorten, summarize; SEE CONCEPTS *79,236,247*

abstracted [*adj*] *preoccupied*
absent-minded, daydreaming, inattentive, lost in thought, out in space*, out to lunch*, remote, withdrawn; SEE CONCEPT *403*

abstraction [*n*] *state of being lost in thought*
absorption, aloofness, brooding, cogitation, consideration, contemplation, daydreaming, detachment, engrossment, entrancement, musing, pensiveness, pondering, preoccupation, reflecting, reflection, remoteness, reverie, ruminating, thinking, trance; SEE CONCEPT *410*

ab
ab

abstruse [adj] *difficult to understand*
abstract, clear as dishwater*, complex, complicated, deep, enigmatic, esoteric, Greek to me*, heavy*, hidden, incomprehensible, intricate, involved, muddy, obscure, perplexing, profound, puzzling, recondite, subtle, unfathomable, vague; SEE CONCEPTS *402,562*

absurd [adj] *ridiculous, senseless*
batty, campy, crazy, daffy, dippy*, flaky*, fooling around, foolish, for grins*, freaky, gagged up*, goofy*, idiotic, illogical, inane, incongruous, irrational, jokey, joshing, laughable, loony, ludicrous, nonsensical, nutty, off the wall*, preposterous, sappy*, screwy*, silly, stupid, tomfool, unreasonable, wacky; SEE CONCEPTS *544,552,558*

absurdity [n] *ridiculous situation or behavior*
applesauce*, BS*, bull*, crap*, craziness, farce, flapdoodle*, folly, foolishness, hot air*, idiocy, illogicality, illogicalness, improbability, inanity, incongruity, insanity, irrationality, jazz*, jive*, ludicrousness, ridiculousness, senselessness, silliness, stupidity, unreasonableness; SEE CONCEPTS *650,656*

abundance [n] *great amount or supply*
affluence, ampleness, bounty, copiousness, fortune, myriad, opulence, plenitude, plenty, plethora, profusion, prosperity, prosperousness, riches, thriving, wealth; SEE CONCEPTS *710,767*

abundant [adj] *plentiful, large in number*
abounding, ample, bounteous, bountiful, copious, crawling with*, cup runs over with*, eco-rich, exuberant, filled, full, generous, heavy, lavish, liberal, lousy with*, luxuriant, mucho*, no end of*, overflowing, plate is full of*, plenteous, plenty, profuse, rich, rolling in*, stinking with*, sufficient, teeming; SEE CONCEPT *781*

abuse [n1] *wrong use*
corruption, crime, debasement, delinquency, desecration, exploitation, fault, injustice, misapplication, misconduct, misdeed, mishandling, mismanage, misuse, offense, perversion, prostitution, sin, wrong, wrongdoing; SEE CONCEPT *156*

abuse [n2] *physical hurting, injuring*
crime, damage, defilement, harm, hurt, impairment, injury, malevolence, maltreatment, manhandling, misdeed, offense, pollution, violation, wrongdoing; SEE CONCEPT *246*

abuse [n3] *verbal attack*
bad-mouthing*, blame, castigation, censure, curse, curses*, defamation, derision, hosing*, insults, invective, kicking around*, knifing*, libel, obloquy, opprobrium, pushing around*, put-down, quinine*, reproach, revilement, scolding, signifying, slander, swearing, tirade, upbraiding, vilification, vituperation; SEE CONCEPT *54*

abuse [v1] *physically hurt or injure*
bang up*, beat up*, bung up*, corrupt, cut up*, damage, defile, deprave, desecrate, harm, hose*, ill-treat, impair, maltreat, mar, mess up*, mishandle, mistreat, misuse, molest, oppress, persecute, pollute*, roughhouse, rough up, ruin, shake up*, spoil, taint, total*, victimize, violate, wax*; SEE CONCEPT *246*

abuse [v2] *use wrongly*
dissipate, exhaust, misemploy, mishandle, misuse, overburden, overtax, overwork, prostitute, spoil, squander, taint, waste; SEE CONCEPT *156*

abuse [v3] *attack with words*
backbite, bad-mouth, bash, belittle, berate, blow off*, calumniate, cap*, castigate, cuss out*, cut down*, cut to the quick*, decry, defame, derogate, discount, do a number on*, dump on*, give a black eye*, hurl brickbat*, insult, knock*, minimize, nag, offend, oppress, persecute, pick on, put down*, rag on*, reproach, revile, ride*, rip up*, run down*, scold, signify, slam*, slap*, sling mud*, smear*, sound*, swear at*, tear apart*, trash*, upbraid, vilify, vituperate, zing*; SEE CONCEPTS *52,54*

abuse [v4] *take advantage of*
do an injustice to, exploit, impose on, use, wrong; SEE CONCEPTS *156,384*

abusive [adj] *exhibiting unkind behavior or words*
calumniating, castigating, censorious, contumelious, defamatory, derisive, disparaging, insolent, insulting, invective, libelous, maligning, obloquious, offensive, opprobrious, reproachful, reviling, rude, sarcastic, scathing, scolding, scurrilous, sharp-tongued, slanderous, traducing, upbraiding, vilifying, vituperative; SEE CONCEPT *267*

abut [v] *touch or be next to something*
adjoin, be adjacent to, border on, butt against, join, neighbor; SEE CONCEPT *749*

abutment [n] *masonry mass*
arch end, bridge end, end piece, jutting piece, support, vault end; SEE CONCEPTS *745,827,833*

abysmal [adj1] *great extent; immeasurable*
bottomless, boundless, complete, deep, endless, extreme, illimitable, incalculable, infinite, profound, thorough, unending, unfathomable, vast; SEE CONCEPTS *772,793*

abysmal [adj2] *extending deeply*
bottomless, fathomless, plumbless, plummetless; SEE CONCEPT *777*

abyss [n] *something very deep, usually a feature of land*
abysm, chasm, crevasse, depth, fissure, gorge, gulf, hole, pit, void; SEE CONCEPTS *509,514*

academia [n] *scholarly world*
academe, academic community, academicians, college, savants, school; SEE CONCEPTS *287,288,289*

academic [adj1] *relating to schooling, learning*
bookish, book-learned, college, collegiate, erudite, intellectual, learned, pedantic, scholarly, scholastic, studious, university; SEE CONCEPT *536*

academic [adj2] *relating to theories, philosophy*
abstract, closet, conjectural, formalistic, hypothetical, notional, speculative, theoretical; SEE CONCEPTS *402,529*

academic [n] *scholar or university/college teacher*
academician, lecturer, professor, pupil, scholar, scholastic, student, tutor; SEE CONCEPT *350*

academy [n1] *school, especially for higher education*
boarding school, brainery*, finishing school, halls of ivy*, institute, military school, preparatory school, prep school, secondary school, seminary; SEE CONCEPT *289*

academy [n2] *society or institution interested in learning*
alliance, association, circle, council, federation,

foundation, fraternity, institute, league; SEE CONCEPT *288*

accede [*v*] *agree or consent*
accept, acquiesce, admit, allow, assent, be game for*, cave in*, comply, concede, concur, cooperate, cry uncle*, endorse, enter into, fold, give the go-ahead*, give the green light*, go along with, grant, let, okay, permit, play ball*, roll over and play dead*, subscribe, throw in the towel*, yield; SEE CONCEPTS *8,50,82,88*

accelerate [*v*] *increase speed, timing*
advance, drive, dust*, expedite, fire up*, forward, further, gun*, hammer on*, hasten, hurry, impel, lay a patch*, lay rubber*, make tracks*, nail it*, open up*, peel rubber*, precipitate, put on afterburners*, put pedal to metal*, quicken, railroad*, rev, rev up, roll*, speed up, spur, step on gas*, step up, stimulate, tool*; SEE CONCEPTS *234,242*

acceleration [*n*] *increasing speed, timing*
dispatch, expedition, hastening, hurrying, quickening, speeding up, spurring, stepping up, stimulation; SEE CONCEPT *234*

accent [*n1*] *importance, emphasis*
significance, stress, weight; SEE CONCEPT *668*

accent [*n2*] *stress or pitch in pronunciation*
accentuation, articulation, beat, cadence, emphasis, enunciation, force, inflection, intonation, meter, modulation, pronunciation, rhythm, stroke, timbre, tonality, tone; SEE CONCEPT *77*

accent [*v*] *place emphasis, importance*
accentuate, draw attention to, emphasize, highlight, intensify, stress, underline, underscore; SEE CONCEPTS *69,243*

accept [*v1*] *receive something given physically*
acquire, gain, get, obtain, secure, take, welcome; SEE CONCEPT *124*

accept [*v2*] *allow into group*
admit, receive, welcome; SEE CONCEPT *384*

accept [*v3*] *believe the goodness, realness of something*
acknowledge, affirm, approbate, approve, buy*, countenance, fancy, favor, go for*, hold, hold with, like, recognize, relish, swallow*, take as gospel truth*, take stock in*, trust; SEE CONCEPT *12*

accept [*v4*] *put up with*
acknowledge, acquiesce, agree, assent, bear, bear with, bow, capitulate, defer to, don't make waves*, don't rock the boat*, endure, fit in, go along with, live with, play the game*, recognize, respect, sit still for*, stand, stand for, stomach, submit to, suffer, swallow, take, tolerate, yield to; SEE CONCEPT *23*

accept [*v5*] *receive by agreeing, consenting*
accede, acknowledge, acquiesce, admit, adopt, affirm, agree to, approve, assent, assume, avow, bear, buy, check out*, comply, concur with, cooperate with, give stamp of approval*, give the go-ahead*, give the green light*, give the nod*, go for*, lap up*, okay, recognize, rubberstamp*, set store by*, sign, sign off on*, take on*, take one up on*, thumbs up*, undertake; SEE CONCEPTS *8,82*

acceptable [*adj*] *satisfactory, agreeable*
adequate, admissible, all right, A-OK*, average, big*, common, cooking with gas*, cool*, copacetic, decent, delightful, fair, hep*, hip*, hunky-dory*, in the swim*, kosher*, large, okay, on the ball*, on the beam*, passable, peachy keen*, pleasant, pleasing, respectable, right on*, standard, sufficient, swell*, tolerable, trendy, unexceptional, unobjectionable, up to code*, up to snuff*, welcome; SEE CONCEPTS *533,558*

acceptance [*n1*] *agreement, taking*
accepting, acknowledging, acquiring, admission, approval, assent, compliance, consent, cooperation, gaining, getting, go-ahead*, green light*, nod*, obtaining, okay, permission, receipt, receiving, reception, recognition, securing, taking on, undertaking, yes; SEE CONCEPTS *8,124*

acceptance [*n2*] *belief in goodness of something*
accedence, accession, acknowledgment, acquiescence, admission, adoption, affirmation, agreement, approbation, approval, assent, concession, concurrence, favor, recognition, seal of approval; SEE CONCEPTS *12,32*

accepted [*adj*] *generally agreed upon*
accustomed, acknowledged, allowed, approved, arrived at, authorized, card-carrying*, chosen, confirmed, conventional, credited, current, customary, endorsed, established, fashionable, in vogue, kosher*, legit*, normal, okayed, orthodox, passed, popular, preferred, received, recognized, regular, sanctioned, standard, straight*, time-honored, touted, universal, unopposed, usual, welcomed; SEE CONCEPTS *547,558*

access [*n*] *admission, means of entry, approach*
admittance, approach, avenue, connection, contact, course, door, entrance, entree, entry, in, ingress, introduction, key, open arms*, open door*, passage, path, road, route, way; SEE CONCEPTS *501,631*

accessible [*adj*] *approachable; ready for use*
attainable, available, door's always open*, employable, exposed, getatable, handy, near, obtainable, open, operative, possible, practicable, public, reachable, susceptible, unrestricted, usable; SEE CONCEPT *576*

accession [*n1*] *something that augments, adds to*
accretion, addition, augmentation, enlargement, extension, increase, increment, raise, rise; SEE CONCEPTS *700,775*

accession [*n2*] *coming to power*
assumption, attainment, inauguration, induction, investment, succession, taking on, taking over; SEE CONCEPTS *133,298*

accession [*n3*] *agreement*
accedence, acceptance, acquiescence, assent, concurrence, consent; SEE CONCEPTS *8,410*

accessorize [*v*] *add ornament*
accent, add on, adorn, equip, supplement; SEE CONCEPTS *162,177*

accessory [*n1*] *ornament; accompanying item; supplementary part*
accent, addition, adjunct, adornment, appendage, appendix, appliance, appurtenance, attachment, component, decoration, extension, extra, frill, help, supplement, trim, trimming; SEE CONCEPT *834*

accessory [*n2*] *person peripherally involved in illegal activity*
abettor, accomplice, aid, aide, assistant, associate, co-conspirator, colleague, confederate, conspirator, helper, insider, partner, plant*, ringer*, shill*, stall*, subordinate; SEE CONCEPT *412*

accident [*n1*] *unexpected, undesirable event; often physically injurious*
blow, calamity, casualty, collision, crack-up*, disaster, fender-bender*, fluke*, hazard, misad-

venture, misfortune, mishap, pileup*, rear ender*, setback, smash*, smashup*, stack-up*, total*, wrack-up*; SEE CONCEPT *674*

accident [*n2*] *chance event*
adventure, circumstance, contingency, fate, fluke*, fortuity, fortune, happening, luck, occasion, occurrence, turn; SEE CONCEPT *679*

accidental [*adj*] *happening unexpectedly*
adventitious, casual, chance, coincidental, contingent, fluky*, fortuitous, inadvertent, incidental, random, uncalculated, unexpected, unforeseen, unintended, unintentional, unplanned; SEE CONCEPTS *530,552*

accidentally [*adj*] *by chance*
by mistake, fortuitously, haphazardly, unintentionally, unwittingly; SEE CONCEPTS *548,552*

accident-prone [*adj*] *clumsy*
all thumbs*, bungling, inept, klutzy*, two left feet*; SEE CONCEPTS *401,402,584*

acclaim [*n*] *expression of approval*
acclamation, acknowledgment, applause, approbation, celebration, cheering, clapping, commendation, eulogizing, exaltation, honor, kudos, pat on the back*, pat on the head*, plaudits, PR, praise, puff, pumping up*, rave, recognition, strokes*, stroking*; SEE CONCEPT *69*

acclaim [*v*] *give approval*
applaud, approve, blow horn*, boost, celebrate, cheer, clap, commend, complement, eulogize, exalt, extol, give a bouquet*, give a posy*, give kudos*, hail, hand it to*, hear it for*, honor, laud, praise, puff up*, push*, rave, recommend, root, salute, stroke*; SEE CONCEPT *69*

acclaimed [*adj*] *praised*
cheered, extolled, hailed, lauded, renowned; SEE CONCEPTS *568,574*

acclamation [*n*] *enthusiastic expression of approval*
acclaim, adulation, applause, approbation, big hand*, cheer, cheering, cheers, hand, honor, jubilation, laudation, ovation, plaudits, salutation, standing O*, tribute; SEE CONCEPTS *69,377*

acclimate [*v*] *make or become adjusted, adapted*
acclimatize, accommodate, acculture, accustom, climatize, conform, get used to, habituate, harden, season, toughen; SEE CONCEPTS *202,701*

accolade [*n*] *strong praise, recognition of achievement*
approval, award, badge, decoration, distinction, honor, kudos*, laurels; SEE CONCEPT *69*

accommodate [*v1*] *make room, lodging available*
board-contain, domicile, entertain, furnish, harbor, hold, house, put up*, quarter, receive, rent, shelter, supply, take in, welcome; SEE CONCEPT *226*

accommodate [*v2*] *make, become suitable for something*
accord, accustom, adapt, adjust, agree, attune, bend over backwards*, comply, compose, conform, coordinate, correspond, don't make waves*, don't rock the boat*, fit, go by the book*, go with the flow*, harmonize, integrate, make consistent, modify, play the game*, proportion, reconcile, settle, shape up*, suit, tailor, tailor-make, tune; SEE CONCEPTS *23,126*

accommodate [*v3*] *perform service*
afford, aid, arrange, assist, avail, benefit, bow, comfort, convenience, defer, favor, furnish, gratify, help, humor, indulge, oblige, pamper, please,

provide, serve, settle, submit, suit, supply, support, sustain, yield; SEE CONCEPT *136*

accommodating [*adj*] *willing to help*
considerate, cooperative, friendly, generous, handy, helpful, hospitable, kind, neighborly, obliging, on deck*, on tap*, polite, unselfish, user friendly*; SEE CONCEPTS *542,555*

accommodation [*n*] *adjustment for different situation, circumstances*
adaptation, compliance, composition, compromise, conformity, fifty-fifty deal*, fitting, modification, reconciliation, settlement; SEE CONCEPT *697*

accommodations [*n*] *place of residence, usually temporary*
apartment, board, boardinghouse, crash pad*, crib*, digs*, hotel, house, housing, lodging, motel, pad*, quarters, roof, room and board, rooming house, rooms, shelter; SEE CONCEPT *516*

accompaniment [*n1*] *necessary part or embellishment*
accessory, adjunct, appendage, appurtenance, attachment, attendant, attribute, augmentation, complement, concomitant, enhancement, enrichment, supplement; SEE CONCEPTS *834,835*

accompaniment [*n2*] *music that supports a theme or performer in a composition*
back, background, backing, back-up, harmony, instrument, part; SEE CONCEPT *262*

accompany [*v1*] *go or be with something*
associate with, attend, chaperon, come along, conduct, consort, convoy, date, dog*, draft*, drag*, escort, follow, go along, guard, guide, hang around with*, hang out*, keep company, lead, look after, shadow, shlep along*, show about, show around, spook, squire, stick to*, string along*, tag along*, tailgate*, take out, usher; SEE CONCEPTS *113,224*

accompany [*v2*] *occur with something*
add, appear with, append, be connected, belong to, characterize, coexist, coincide with, come with, complete, co-occur, follow, go together, happen with, join with, occur with, supplement, take place with; SEE CONCEPT *643*

accomplice [*n*] *helper, especially in committing a crime*
abettor, accessory, aid, aide, ally, assistant, associate, co-conspirator, collaborator, colleague, confederate, conspirator, insider, partner, plant*, stall*; SEE CONCEPT *412*

accomplish [*v*] *succeed in doing*
achieve, arrive, attain, bring about, bring off, carry out, conclude, consummate, do, do a bang-up job*, do justice*, do one proud*, do the trick*, effect, finish, fulfill, gain, get someplace*, get there*, hit*, make hay*, make it, manage, nail it*, perform, produce, pull off*, put it over*, rack up*, reach, realize, score*, sew up*, take care of, win; SEE CONCEPTS *91,706*

accomplished [*adj*] *skilled in activity*
able, adept, brainy, consummate, cool*, cultivated, expert, gifted, hep*, hip*, masterly, polished, practiced, proficient, savvy, sharp, skillful, talented, wised up*, with it*; SEE CONCEPTS *326,528*

accomplishment [*n*] *something successfully done, completed*
ability, achievement, act, art, attainment, bringing about, capability, carrying out, completion, conclusion, consummation, coup, deed, effect-

ing, effort, execution, exploit, feat, finish, fulfillment, performance, production, proficiency, realization, skill, stroke, talent, triumph; SEE CONCEPT *706*

accord [n] *agreement, mutual understanding (often written)*
10-4*, accordance, concert, concord, concurrence, conformity, congruence, correspondence, deal, good vibes*, good vibrations*, harmony, okay, pact, rapport, reconciliation, sympathy, treaty, unanimity; SEE CONCEPT *684*

accord [v1] *give approval, grant*
accede, acquiesce, admit, allow, award, bestow, concede, confer, endow, give, present, render, tender, vouchsafe; SEE CONCEPTS *50,83,88*

accord [v2] *come to agreement*
affirm, agree, assent, be in tune, concur, conform, correspond, fit, harmonize, jibe, match, square, suit, tally; SEE CONCEPTS *8,664*

accordant [adj] *in agreement*
agreeing, conforming, congruous, harmonious, in concert; SEE CONCEPTS *558,563*

accordingly [adv] *in an appropriate, suitable way*
appropriately, as a consequence, as a result, consequently, correspondingly, duly, equally, ergo, fitly, hence, in consequence, in respect to, in that event, properly, proportionately, respectively, resultantly, so, subsequently, suitably, then, therefore, thus, under the circumstances; SEE CONCEPT *558*

accordion [n] *musical instrument*
concertina, groanbox*, melodeon, squeezebox*, stomach Steinway*, windbox*; SEE CONCEPTS *463,499*

accost [v] *approach for conversation or solicitation*
address, annoy, bother, brace*, buttonhole*, call, challenge, confront, cross, dare, entice, face, flag, greet, hail, proposition, run into, salute, welcome, whistle for*; SEE CONCEPTS *48,51*

account [n1] *written description of past events*
ABCs*, annal, blow by blow*, bulletin, chronicle, detail, explanation, history, lowdown*, make*, narration, narrative, play by play*, recital, report, run-down, score, story, tab, take, tale, the picture*, the whole picture*, version; SEE CONCEPT *282*

account [n2] *record of finances, fees, or charges*
bad news*, balance, bill, book, books, charge, check, computation, cuff*, grunt*, inventory, invoice, IOU*, ledger, reckoning, record, register, report, score, statement, tab, tally; SEE CONCEPTS *331,332*

account [n3] *basis or consideration for action*
cause, ground, grounds, interest, justification, motive, rationale, rationalization, reason, regard, sake; SEE CONCEPT *229*

accountability [n] *responsibility*
answerability, blameworthiness, liability; SEE CONCEPT *645*

accountable [adj] *responsible for having done*
answerable, charged with, culpable, liable, obligated, obliged, on the hook*; SEE CONCEPT *527*

accountant [n] *person who maintains financial accounts of a business*
actuary, analyst, auditor, bookkeeper, calculator, cashier, clerk, comptroller, CPA, examiner, public accountant, reckoner, teller; SEE CONCEPTS

348,353

account for [v] *offer reason, explanation*
answer for, clarify, elucidate, explain, illuminate, justify, rationalize, resolve; SEE CONCEPT *57*

accounting [n] *keeping financial accounts*
auditing, balancing the books*, bookkeeping, calculating, computing, reckoning; SEE CONCEPTS *28,764*

accredit [v1] *attribute responsibility or achievement*
ascribe, assign, charge, credit, refer; SEE CONCEPTS *49,69*

accredit [v2] *give authorization or control*
appoint, approve, authorize, certify, commission, empower, enable, endorse, entrust, guarantee, license, okay, recognize, sanction, vouch for; SEE CONCEPTS *50,88*

accretion [n] *gradual growth, addition*
accession, accumulation, augmentation, build-up, increase, increment, raise, rise; SEE CONCEPT *780*

accrual [n] *growth*
accumulation, amassing, amassment, buildup, increase; SEE CONCEPTS *432,780*

accrue [v] *increase by addition or growth, often financial*
accumulate, amass, build up, collect, enlarge, flow, gather, grow, increase; SEE CONCEPTS *763,780*

acculturation [n] *adjustment to culture*
acclimatization, assimilation, culture shock, nationalization, naturalization; SEE CONCEPTS *202,701*

accumulate [v] *gather or amass something*
accrue, acquire, add to, agglomerate, aggregate, amalgamate, assemble, bring together, cache, clean up*, collect, collocate, compile, concentrate, cumulate, draw together, expand, gain, gather, grow, heap, heap together, hoard, incorporate, increase, load up*, lump*, make a bundle*, make a killing*, mass, pile*, pile up*, procure, profit, rack up*, roll up*, round up*, scare up*, stack up, stockpile, store, store up, swell, unite; SEE CONCEPTS *236,245*

accumulation [n] *gathering or amassing*
accession, accretion, addition, agglomeration, aggrandizement, aggregation, amassment, augmentation, build-up, chunk, collecting, collection, conglomeration, enlargement, gob, growth, heap, hoarding, hunk, increase, inflation, intensification, mass, multiplication, pile, quantity, stack, stock, store, trove, up, upping; SEE CONCEPTS *432,780*

accuracy [n] *precision or correctness*
accurateness, carefulness, certainty, closeness, definiteness, definitiveness, definitude, efficiency, exactitude, exactness, faultlessness, incisiveness, mastery, meticulousness, preciseness, sharpness, skill, skillfulness, strictness, sureness, truthfulness, veracity, verity; SEE CONCEPTS *638,654*

accurate [adj1] *precise*
authentic, careful, close, concrete, correct, defined, definite, deft, detailed, discriminating, discriminative, distinct, exact, explicit, factual, faithful, genuine, judicious, just, literal, matter-of-fact, methodical, meticulous, on the button*, on the money*, on the nose*, particular, proper, punctilious, punctual, regular, right, rigid, rigorous, scientific, scrupulous, severe, sharp, skillful,

solid, specific, strict, systematic, true, ultraprecise, unerring, unmistakable, veracious; SEE CONCEPT 535

accurate [adj2] *correct, without error*
absolute, actual, authentic, authoritative, certain, conclusive, definite, definitive, errorless, exact, factual, faultless, final, flawless, genuine, infallible, irrefutable, official, perfect, right, straight, strict, true, truthful, undeniable, undisputed, unimpeachable, unquestionable, unrefuted, valid, veracious; SEE CONCEPT 557

accurately [adv] *correctly*
exactly, flawlessly, meticulously, precisely, scrupulously, veraciously; SEE CONCEPTS 535,557

accursed [adj] *cursed*
bedeviled, condemned, damned, done for*, doomed, hexed, ill-fated, star-crossed, unfortunate; SEE CONCEPTS 548,571

accusation [n] *charge of wrongdoing, fault*
allegation, arraignment, attribution, beef*, blast*, bum rap*, censure, citation, complaint, denunciation, dido, exposé, gripe, impeachment, imputation, incrimination, indictment, insinuation, recrimination, roar*, rumble*, slur, squawk*, stink*; SEE CONCEPT 54

accuse [v] *place blame for wrongdoing, fault*
allege, apprehend, arraign, arrest, attack, attribute, betray, blame, blow the whistle*, brand, bring charges, censure, charge, cite, complain, criminate, denounce, file claim, finger*, frame, hang something on*, hold accountable, impeach, implicate, impute, incriminate, inculpate, indict, lay at door*, let have it*, libel, litigate, lodge complaint, name, pin on*, point finger at*, prosecute, recriminate, serve summons, slander, slur, sue, summon, tax; SEE CONCEPT 44

accuser [n] *person laying blame*
indicter, informer, prosecutor, rat*, tattletale*; SEE CONCEPTS 412,423

accustom [v] *get used to*
acclimatize, acculturate, acquaint, adapt, familiarize, habituate, season; SEE CONCEPTS 35,202

accustomed [adj1] *be or become prepared, used to*
acclimatized, acquainted, adapted, addicted, confirmed, disciplined, familiar, familiarized, given to, grooved*, habituated, habituated in, in the habit, inured, seasoned, settled in, trained; SEE CONCEPT 403

accustomed [adj2] *normal, usual*
accepted, chronic, common, conventional, customary, established, everyday, expected, general, habitual, ordinary, orthodox, regular, routine, set, traditional, typical; SEE CONCEPT 547

AC-DC [adj] *bisexual*
ambidextrous, androgynous, bi*, double-gaited, epicene, gay, gynandrous, hermaphroditic, hits both ways*, intersexual, monoclinous, swings both ways*, switch-hitting*; SEE CONCEPT 372

ace [adj] *exhibiting expertise in some activity*
brilliant, champion, distinguished, excellent, expert, first-rate, great, master, outstanding, superb, virtuoso; SEE CONCEPT 528

ace [n] *expert in some activity*
champion, genius, master, pro, star, virtuoso, winner, wizard; SEE CONCEPT 416

ace in the hole [n] *secret weapon*
card up one's sleeve, reserve; SEE CONCEPTS

274,340

acerbate [v] *exasperate*
aggravate, annoy, disturb, perturb, provoke, rattle one's cage*; SEE CONCEPTS 7,19

acerbic [adj] *bitter, sharp, or sour*
acidic, acrid, astringent, caustic, harsh, sharp, tart; SEE CONCEPT 613

acerbity [n1] *bitterness of taste*
acidity, asperity, astringency, mordancy, sourness, tartness; SEE CONCEPTS 462,613

acerbity [n2] *harsh speech, behavior*
acrimoniousness, causticity, ill temper, irritability, rancor, rudeness, sarcasm, sarcasticness, vitriolicism; SEE CONCEPTS 267,401

aces [adj] *great*
excellent, fabulous, peachy, wonderful; SEE CONCEPTS 527,528,574

ache [n] *sore feeling; dull pain*
anguish, hurt, misery, pang, pounding, smarting, soreness, spasm, suffering, throb, throbbing, throe, twinge; SEE CONCEPTS 316,410,728

ache [v] *feeling soreness or dull pain, often physical*
be sore, hurt, pain, pound, smart, suffer, throb, twinge; SEE CONCEPTS 13,17,303,308,313

achievable [adj] *doable*
attainable, feasible, obtainable; SEE CONCEPTS 528,552,558

achieve [v] *bring to successful conclusion; reach a goal*
accomplish, acquire, actualize, attain, bring about, bring off*, bring to pass, cap, carry out, carry through, close, complete, conclude, consummate, deliver, discharge, dispatch, do, earn, earn wings*, effect, effectuate, enact, end, execute, finish, follow through, fulfill, gain, get, get done, manage, negotiate, obtain, perfect, perform, procure, produce, rack up*, reach, realize, resolve, score, seal, see through, settle, sign, solve, win, wind up, work out; SEE CONCEPT 706

achievement [n] *something completed successfully; goal reached*
accomplishment, acquirement, acquisition, act, actualization, attainment, completion, conquest, consummation, contrivance, creation, deed, effectuation, effort, enactment, encompassment, execution, exploit, feat, fulfillment, hit, masterpiece, performance, production, realization, stroke, success, tour de force, triumph, victory; SEE CONCEPT 706

Achilles' heel [n] *vulnerability*
chink in the armor*, deficiency, frailty, handicap, soft underbelly*, susceptibility, weakness; SEE CONCEPTS 101,230,411,580

acid [adj1] *bitter, sour in taste*
acerbic, acidulous, biting, piquant, pungent, sharp, tart, vinegarish, vinegary; SEE CONCEPT 613

acid [adj2] *having acidic, corrosive properties*
acerbic, acidulous, acrid, anti-alkaline, biting, bleaching, corroding, disintegrative, dissolvent, eating away, eroding, erosive, oxidizing, rusting; SEE CONCEPT 485

acid [adj3] *bitter in words or behavior*
acerbic, biting, caustic, cutting, dry, harsh, hateful, hurtful, mordant, nasty, offensive, sarcastic, sharp, stinging, trenchant, vitriolic; SEE CONCEPTS 267,401

acid [n] *lysergic acid diethylamide, LSD*
black tabs*, blotter*, blue acid*, blue dot*, blue

Owsley*, California sunshine*, candy*, cubes*, dot*, electric Kool Aid*, green dragon*, hallucinogen, instant Zen*, Lucy in the sky with diamonds*, magic mushrooms, mescalin, microdots*, mushrooms, orange sunshine*, Owsley's acid*, peyote, purple haze*, strawberry fields*, sugar cubes*, yellow sunshine*; SEE CONCEPT *307*

acidity [*n*] *bitterness*
acerbity, acridness, astringency, causticity, pungency, sourness, tartness; SEE CONCEPT *614*

acid test [*n*] *test of value, genuineness*
proof, proving ground, substantiation, trial, verification; SEE CONCEPTS *87,290,291*

acidulous [*adj1*] *bitter, sour*
acerb, acerbic, acetose, dry, piquant, sharp, tart; SEE CONCEPT *613*

acidulous [*adj2*] *bitter in speech*
biting, cutting, ironical, mocking, sarcastic; SEE CONCEPT *267*

acknowledge [*v1*] *verbally recognize authority*
accede, accept, acquiesce, agree, allow, approve, attest to, certify, defend, defer to, endorse, grant, own, ratify, recognize, subscribe to, support, take an oath, uphold, yield; SEE CONCEPTS *8,50,88*

acknowledge [*v2*] *admit truth or reality of something*
accede, accept, acquiesce, allow, avow, come clean*, come out of closet*, concede, confess, cop a plea*, crack*, declare, fess up*, get off chest*, grant, let on*, open up*, own, profess, recognize, yield; SEE CONCEPTS *12,49*

acknowledge [*v3*] *verbally recognize receipt of something*
address, answer, greet, hail, notice, react, remark, reply, respond, return, salute, thank; SEE CONCEPTS *38,45,51,60*

acknowledgment [*n1*] *act of recognizing authority or truth of something*
acceptance, accession, acquiescence, admission, admitting, affirmation, allowance, allowing, assent, assertion, asseveration, avowal, compliance, conceding, concession, concurrence, confession, confirmation, corroboration, declaration, profession, ratification, realization, recognition, yielding; SEE CONCEPTS *8,50,88*

acknowledgment [*n2*] *physical symbol of recognition*
acclamation, addressing, answer, apology, applause, appreciation, bestowal, bow, card, confession, contract, credit, gift, gratitude, greeting, guarantee, hail, hailing, letter, nod, notice, reaction, receipt, reply, response, return, salutation, salute, signature, statement, support, thanks, token; SEE CONCEPTS *595,628*

acme [*n*] *pinnacle of achievement or physical object*
apogee, capstone, climax, culmination, height, highest point, high point, meridian, optimum, peak, summit, top, ultimate, vertex, zenith; SEE CONCEPTS *706,836*

acne [*n*] *blemishes*
blackheads, pimples, pizza-face*, pustules, rosacea, skin inflammation, whiteheads, zits*; SEE CONCEPT *580*

acolyte [*n*] *attendant, usually in a church*
aid, assistant, follower, helper; SEE CONCEPT *361*

acoustic [*adj*] *sound*
audile, audio, auditory, aural, hearing, phonic;

SEE CONCEPTS *591,594*

acoustics [*n*] *sound quality*
echo, noise, sound, sound properties, sound transmission; SEE CONCEPT *595*

acquaint [*v*] *inform oneself or another about something new*
accustom, advise, apprise, bring out, clue, come out with*, disclose, divulge, enlighten, familiarize, fill in, fix up*, get together*, habituate, inform, intro*, introduce, knock down*, let know, make familiar, notify, post, present, reveal, tell, warn; SEE CONCEPTS *31,60*

acquaintance [*n1*] *a person known informally*
associate, association, colleague, companion, contact, friend, neighbor; SEE CONCEPT *423*

acquaintance [*n2*] *knowledge of something through experience*
awareness, cognizance, conversance, familiarity, fellowship, grasp, intimacy, ken, relationship, understanding; SEE CONCEPT *409*

acquainted [*adj*] *aware*
abreast, advised, apprised of, clued in*, conversant, enlightened, familiarized, familiar with, informed, in the know*, versed in; SEE CONCEPT *402*

acquiesce [*v*] *agree with some reluctance*
accede, accept, accommodate, adapt, adjust, agree, allow, approve, bow to, buy, cave in*, come across, come around, comply, concur, conform, consent, cry uncle*, cut a deal*, ditto*, give in, give out, go along, jibe*, okay, pass, play ball*, reconcile, roll over and play dead*, say uncle*, set, shake on, submit, subscribe, yes, yield; SEE CONCEPTS *8,10,23,82*

acquiescence [*n*] *reluctant agreement*
acceptance, accession, approval, assent, compliance, concurrence, conformity, consent, giving in, obedience, permission, resignation, submission, submissiveness, yielding; SEE CONCEPTS *8,10*

acquire [*v*] *obtain or receive*
access, achieve, amass, annex, attain, bring in, buy, catch, collect, cop*, corral*, earn, gain, gather, get, get hands on, get hold of, grab, have, hustle, land, latch onto, lock up, pick up, procure, promote, rack up*, scare up*, secure, snag*, take, take possession of*, wangle*, win; SEE CONCEPTS *120,124,142*

acquisition [*n1*] *obtaining or receiving*
accretion, achievement, acquirement, acquiring, addition, attainment, buy, gain, gaining, learning, obtainment, possession, prize, procuration, procurement, procuring, property, purchase, pursuit, recovery, redemption, retrieval, salvage, winning; SEE CONCEPTS *120,124,142*

acquisition [*n2*] *something obtained, received*
accomplishment, achievement, allowance, annuity, award, benefit, bonus, commission, dividend, donation, earnings, fortune, gain, gift, grant, income, increment, inheritance, net, premium, prize, proceeds, profit, remuneration, return, reward, riches, salary, security, wages, wealth, winnings; SEE CONCEPTS *120,337,710*

acquisitive [*adj*] *eager to obtain knowledge or things*
avaricious, avid, covetous, demanding, desirous, grabbing, grabby, grasping, greedy, predatory, prehensile, rapacious; SEE CONCEPT *542*

acquit [*v1*] *announce removal of blame*
absolve, blink at*, clear, deliver, discharge, dis-

culpate, exculpate, excuse, exonerate, free, let go, let off, let off the hook*, liberate, release, relieve, vindicate, whitewash*, wink at*, wipe off*; SEE CONCEPTS *50,83,88,317*

acquit [*v2*] *behave some way*
act, bear, carry, comport, conduct, deport, perform; SEE CONCEPT *633*

acquittal [*n*] *declaration removing blame*
absolution, acquitting, amnesty, clearance, deliverance, discharge, discharging, dismissal, dismissing, exculpation, exemption, exoneration, freeing, letting off, liberation, pardon, release, releasing, relief from, reprieve, vindication; SEE CONCEPTS *127,317,318*

acre [*n*] *piece of land, unit of area*
acreage, bit, estate, grounds, manor, plot, property; SEE CONCEPT *792*

acreage [*n*] *land*
back forty*, expanse, holding, parcel, plot, property, real estate; SEE CONCEPTS *509,513*

acrid [*adj1*] *bitter, sour to taste*
acid, amaroidal, astringent, biting, burning, caustic, harsh, irritating, pungent, sharp, stinging; SEE CONCEPT *613*

acrid [*adj2*] *nasty in behavior or words*
acrimonious, austere, biting, bitter, caustic, cutting, harsh, mordant, sarcastic, sharp, trenchant, vitriolic; SEE CONCEPTS *267,401*

acrimonious [*adj*] *nasty in behavior, speech*
acerbic, acid, angry, astringent, belligerent, biting, bitter, caustic, censorious, churlish, crabby, cranky, cross, cutting, indignant, irascible, irate, ireful, mad, mordant, peevish, petulant, rancorous, sarcastic, sharp, spiteful, splenetic, tart, testy, trenchant, wrathful; SEE CONCEPTS *267,401*

acrimony [*n*] *nasty behavior, speech*
acerbity, animosity, antipathy, asperity, astringency, belligerence, bitterness, churlishness, crankiness, harshness, ill will, irascibility, malevolence, malice, mordancy, peevishness, rancor, rudeness, sarcasm, spite, tartness, unkindness, virulence; SEE CONCEPTS *633,657*

acrobat [*n*] *performer who does tricks, physical feats*
aerialist, artist, athlete, balancer, clown, contortionist, dancer, funambulist, gymnast, performer, stunt person, trapezist, tumbler; SEE CONCEPT *352*

acrobatics [*n*] *athletic floor exercises*
balancing, feats, gymnastics, somersaults, stunts, tumbling; SEE CONCEPT *363*

across [*prep*] *traversing a space, side to side*
athwart, beyond, cross, crossed, crosswise, opposite, over, transversely; SEE CONCEPT *581*

across-the-board [*adj*] *all*
all-inclusive, blanket, complete, comprehensive, everything, sweeping, total; SEE CONCEPTS *513,772*

act [*n1*] *something done*
accomplishment, achievement, action, deed, doing, execution, exploit, feat, move, operation, performance, step, thing, undertaking; SEE CONCEPT *1*

act [*n2*] *legislative document*
amendment, announcement, bill, clause, code, commitment, decree, edict, enactment, judgment, law, measure, order, ordinance, resolution, statute, subpoena, summons, verdict, warrant, writ; SEE CONCEPTS *271,318*

act [*n3*] *part of a performance*

bit*, curtain, epilogue, gag*, introduction, number, piece, prologue, routine, scene, schtick*, show, sketch, spot, turn; SEE CONCEPT *264*

act [*n4*] *pretended behavior*
affectation, attitude, bit*, chaser*, dissimulation, fake, false front*, feigning, front, performance, phony, pose, posture, pretense, put-on, sham, show, shuck and jive*, simulation, soft soap*, stall, stance, stunt, sweet talk*; SEE CONCEPT *633*

act [*v1*] *do something*
accomplish, achieve, begin, carry on, carry out, consummate, cook, create, develop, do, do a number*, do one's thing*, enforce, execute, function, get in there*, go about, go for broke*, go for it*, go in for*, go that route*, go to town*, intrude, knock off*, labor, make progress, maneuver, move, officiate, operate, percolate*, perk*, perpetrate, persevere, persist, practice, preside, pursue, respond, serve, take effect, take part, take steps, take up, transort, undertake, work out; SEE CONCEPTS *1,4*

act [*v2*] *behave in a certain way*
appear, behave, carry, carry oneself, carry out, comport, conduct, do, enact, execute, exert, function, give the appearance, go about, impress as, operate, perform, play part, react, represent oneself, seem, serve, strike, take on; SEE CONCEPT *633*

act [*v3*] *entertain by playing a role*
be on*, bring down the house*, burlesque, characterize, do a turn*, dramatize, emote, enact, feign, go on, go over, ham*, ham it up*, impersonate, lay an egg*, make debut, mime, mimic, mug, parody, perform, personate, personify, play, play act, play gig, play part, play role, portray, pretend, put it over*, rehearse, represent, say one's piece*, simulate, star, stooge*, strut*, take part, tread the boards*; SEE CONCEPT *292*

acting [*adj*] *substituting in a role*
ad interim, adjutant, alternate, assistant, delegated, deputy, interim, pro tem, pro tempore, provisional, surrogate, temporary; SEE CONCEPT *560*

acting [*n*] *entertaining, performing*
assuming, characterization, depiction, dramatics, dramatizing, enacting, enactment, feigning, hamming*, histrionics, imitating, imitation, impersonation, improvisation, mime, mimicry, pantomime, performance, play acting, playing, portrayal, portraying, posing, posturing, pretending, pretense, putting, rendition, seeming, showing off, simulating, stagecraft, stooging*, theatre, theatricals; SEE CONCEPT *292*

action [*n1*] *something done*
activity, agility, alacrity, alertness, animation, bag*, ballgame*, big idea*, bit*, business, bustle, commotion, dash, deal, energy, enterprise, flurry, force, functioning, game, going, happening, haste, hoopla*, hopper*, industry, in the works, life, liveliness, motion, movement, occupation, operation, plan, power, process, proposition, racket*, reaction, response, rush, scene, spirit, stir, stunt, trip, turmoil, vigor, vim, vitality, vivacity; SEE CONCEPT *1*

action [*n2*] *individual deed*
accomplishment, achievement, act, blow, commission, dealings, doing, effort, enterprise, execution, exercise, exertion, exploit, feat, handiwork, maneuver, manipulation, move, op-

eration, performance, procedure, step, stroke, thrust, transaction, undertaking; SEE CONCEPTS *91,706*

action [*n3*] *a legal process*
case, cause, claim, lawsuit, litigation, proceeding, prosecution, suit; SEE CONCEPT *317*

action [*n4*] *an aggressive military deed*
battle, combat, conflict, contest, encounter, engagement, fight, fighting, fray, skirmish, warfare; SEE CONCEPT *320*

activate [*v*] *initiate something; start a function*
actify, actuate, arouse, call up, energize, impel, mobilize, motivate, move, prompt, propel, rouse, set in motion, start, stimulate, stir, switch on, take out of mothballs*, trigger, turn on; SEE CONCEPT *234*

active [*adj1*] *having movement*
alive, astir, at work, bustling, effective, efficacious, exertive, flowing, functioning, going, hasty, impelling, in force, in play, in process, mobile, movable, moving, operating, operative, progressive, pushing, rapid, restless, rolling, running, rushing, rustling, shifting, simmering, speeding, speedy, streaming, swarming, traveling, turning, walking, working; SEE CONCEPT *542*

active [*adj2*] *very involved in activity*
aggressive, agile, alert, alive, animated, assiduous, bold, brisk, bustling, busy, chipper, daring, dashing, determined, dexterous, diligent, dynamic, eager, energetic, engaged, enlivened, enterprising, enthusiastic, eventful, fireball*, forceful, forcible, fresh, frisky, hard-working, high-spirited, hyper*, industrious, intense, inventive, jumping, keen, lively, nimble, on the move, perky, persevering, purposeful, pushing, quick, rapid, ready, resolute, sharp, sprightly, spry, whiz*, zealous; SEE CONCEPTS *401,542*

activism [*n*] *action for change*
advocacy, boycotting, championing, effecting change, influence peddling, involvement, logrolling, militancy, moving and shaking*, picketing, striking; SEE CONCEPT *689*

activity [*n1*] *state of being active*
action, activeness, animation, bustle, enterprise, exercise, exertion, hustle, labor, life, liveliness, motion, movement; SEE CONCEPTS *1,748*

activity [*n2*] *special interest or pursuit*
act, avocation, bag*, ballgame*, bit*, deed, endeavor, enterprise, entertainment, game, hobby, job, labor, occupation, pastime, project, racket, scene*, scheme, stunt, task, trip, undertaking, venture, work, zoo*; SEE CONCEPT *32*

act of God [*n*] *natural disaster*
accident, earthquake, freak accident, hurricane, tornado, unforeseen event; SEE CONCEPTS *674,675*

actor [*n*] *person who performs, entertains by role-playing*
amateur, artist, barnstormer, bit player, character, clown, comedian, entertainer, extra, foil, ham*, hambone*, headliner, idol, impersonator, ingénue, lead, mime, mimic, pantomimist, performer, play-actor, player, soubrette, stand-in, star, stooge*, straight person, thesp*, thespian, trouper, understudy, ventriloquist, villain, walk-on; SEE CONCEPT *352*

actress [*n*] *woman actor*
diva, ingenue, leading lady, prima donna, starlet, thespian; SEE CONCEPT *352*

actual [*adj1*] *truly existing, real*

absolute, authentic, categorical, certain, concrete, confirmed, definite, factual, for real*, genuine, hard, honest injun*, honest to God*, indisputable, indubitable, kosher*, physical, positive, realistic, substantial, substantive, sure enough*, tangible, true, truthful, undeniable, unquestionable, verified; SEE CONCEPT *582*

actual [*adj2*] *existing at the present time*
current, exact, existent, extant, live, living, original, prevailing; SEE CONCEPT *799*

actuality [*n*] *something that truly exists, is real*
achievement, actualization, attainment, brass tacks*, fact, materiality, materialization, reality, real world*, straight stuff*, substance, substantiality, truth, what it is*; SEE CONCEPT *725*

actualize [*v*] *make real*
accomplish, bring about, engineer, produce, realize; SEE CONCEPT *91*

actually [*adj*] *truly real, existent*
absolutely, as a matter of fact, de facto, genuinely, indeed, in fact, in point of fact, in reality, in truth, literally, really, veritably, very; SEE CONCEPT *582*

actuate [*v*] *start a function or action, motivate*
activate, animate, arouse, cause, drive, egg on*, energize, excite, fire up*, impel, incite, induce, influence, inspire, instigate, key up*, mobilize, motivate, move, prompt, propel, put up to*, quicken, rouse, spur, stimulate, turn on*, work into lather*, work up*; SEE CONCEPTS *221,234*

act up [*v*] *misbehave*
act out*, carry on, raise hell*, rebel, sow one's wild oats*; SEE CONCEPTS *106,633*

acumen [*n*] *ability to understand and reason*
acuity, acuteness, astuteness, awareness, brains, brilliance, cleverness, comprehension, cunning, discernment, discrimination, farsightedness, good taste, grasp, guile, ingenuity, insight, intellect, intelligence, intuition, judgment, keenness, perception, percipience, perspicacity, perspicuity, refinement, sagacity, sensitivity, sharpness, shrewdness, smartness, smarts*, understanding, vision, wisdom, wit; SEE CONCEPT *409*

acute [*adj1*] *deeply perceptive*
astute, canny, clever, discerning, discriminating, incisive, ingenious, insightful, intense, intuitive, judicious, keen, observant, penetrating, perspicacious, piercing, quick-witted, sensitive, sharp, smart, subtle; SEE CONCEPT *402*

acute [*adj2*] *very important*
afflicting, critical, crucial, dangerous, decisive, desperate, dire, essential, grave, serious, severe, sudden, urgent, vital; SEE CONCEPT *568*

acute [*adj3*] *severe, intense*
cutting, distressing, excruciating, exquisite, fierce, keen, overpowering, overwhelming, piercing, poignant, powerful, racking, severe, sharp, shooting, stabbing, sudden, violent; SEE CONCEPT *569*

acute [*adj4*] *having a sharp end or point*
acicular, aciculate, acuminate, acuminous, cuspate, cuspidate, knifelike, needle-shaped, peaked, piked, pointed, sharpened, spiked; SEE CONCEPT *485*

adage [*n*] *saying or proverb*
aphorism, apothegm, axiom, byword, dictum, maxim, motto, precept, saw; SEE CONCEPT *276*

adamant [*adj*] *unyielding*
determined, firm, fixed, hanging tough*, hard-nosed, immovable, inexorable, inflexible, insis-

ac
ad

tent, intransigent, obdurate, pat*, relentless, resolute, rigid, set, set in stone*, standing pat*, stiff, stubborn, unbendable, unbending, uncompromising, unrelenting, unshakable, unswayable; SEE CONCEPT *401*

adamant [*adj2*] *hard like rock*
adamantine, flinty, impenetrable, indestructible, rock-hard, tough, unbreakable; SEE CONCEPT *604*

adapt [*v*] *adjust to a different situation or condition*
acclimate, accommodate, accustom, alter, change, come around, comply, conform, familiarize, fashion, fit, get act together*, get used to, grow used to, habituate, harmonize, make, match, modify, play the game*, prepare, qualify, readjust, reconcile, remodel, revise, roll with punches*, shape, shape up*, square, suit, tailor; SEE CONCEPTS *232,697*

adaptable [*adj*] *able and usually willing to change*
AC-DC*, adjustable, all around, alterable, cando*, changeable, compliant, conformable, convertible, ductile, easy-going, flexible, hanging loose*, malleable, modifiable, moldable, plastic, pliable, pliant, resilient, supple, switch-hitting, tractable, variable, versatile; SEE CONCEPTS *550,576*

adaptation [*n1*] *act of adapting*
adjustment, adoption, alteration, conversion, modification, refitting, remodeling, reworking, shift, transformation, variation; SEE CONCEPT *697*

adaptation [*n2*] *condition of something resulting from change*
acclimatization, accustomedness, agreement, compliance, correspondence, familiarization, habituation, naturalization; SEE CONCEPT *230*

adaptive [*adj*] *adjusting*
flexible, modifying, robust; SEE CONCEPTS *314,489,613*

add [*v1*] *simple arithmetical process of increase; accumulation*
calculate, cast, compute, count, count up, do addition, enumerate, figure, reckon, reckon up, sum, summate, tally, tot*, total, tote*, tot up*; SEE CONCEPT *764*

add [*v2*] *adjoin, increase; make further comment*
affix, annex, ante, append, augment, beef up*, boost, build up, charge up, continue, cue in*, figure in, flesh out*, heat up*, hike, hike up*, hitch on*, hook on*, hook up with*, include, jack up*, jazz up*, join together, pad, parlay, piggyback*, plug into*, pour it on*, reply, run up*, say further, slap on*, snowball*, soup up*, speed up, spike, step up, supplement, sweeten*, tack on*, tag; SEE CONCEPTS *51,113,236,245*

addendum [*n*] *something conjoined, added*
addition, adjunct, appendage, appendix, attachment, augmentation, codicil, extension, extra, postscript, rider, supplement; SEE CONCEPTS *270,827*

addict [*n*] *person who has compulsion toward activity, often injurious*
aficionado, buff, devotee, enthusiast, fan, fanatic, fiend, follower, freak*, habitué, hound*, junkie*, nut, practitioner, zealot; SEE CONCEPTS *412,423*

addicted [*adj*] *dependent on something, compulsive*
absorbed, accustomed, attached, dependent, devoted, disposed, fanatic, fond, given over to, given to, habituated, hooked, hyped*, imbued,

inclined, obsessed, predisposed, prone to, spaced out*, strung out*, under the influence, used to, wedded to; SEE CONCEPT *542*

addiction [*n*] *a habit of activity, often injurious*
bag*, bent, craving, dependence, enslavement, fixation, hang-up*, hook, inclination, jones*, kick*, monkey*, monkey on back*, obsession, shot*, sweet tooth*, thing*; SEE CONCEPTS *20,316,709*

addictive [*adj*] *habit-forming*
enslaving, hooking, obsessive; SEE CONCEPTS *530,547*

addition [*n1*] *process of conjoining, adding*
accession, adding, adjoining, affixing, annexation, attachment, augmentation, enlargement, extension, inclusion, increasing; SEE CONCEPTS *236,245*

addition [*n2*] *something conjoined to or enlargement of something*
accession, accessory, accretion, accrual, addendum, additive, adjunct, aggrandizement, annex, appendage, appendix, attachment, augmentation, bonus, boost, commission, dividend, enhancement, enlargement, expansion, extension, extra, gain, hike, increase, increment, option, profit, raise, reinforcement, rise, supplement, wing; SEE CONCEPTS *640,835*

addition [*n3*] *arithmetical process of augmentation*
accretion, accruing, adding, computing, counting, enlarging, expanding, increasing, reckoning, summation, summing, tabulating, totaling, toting*; SEE CONCEPT *764*

additional [*adj*] *extra, supplementary*
added, affixed, appended, further, increased, more, new, on the side, option, other, over-and-above, padding, perk, spare, supplementary; SEE CONCEPT *771*

addled [*adj*] *confused*
balled up*, befuddled, bewildered, fouled up*, gone*, mixed up, out of it, punchy, rattled, shaken, shook, shook up, slap-happy, thrown, unglued*, woozy*; SEE CONCEPT *403*

address [*n1*] *place of residence or business where one can be contacted*
abode, box number, direction, domicile, dwelling, headquarters, home, house, living quarters, location, lodging, number, place of business, place of residence, street, whereabouts, zip code; SEE CONCEPT *516*

address [*n2*] *speech given to formal gathering*
chalk talk*, discourse, dissertation, lecture, oration, pep talk*, pitch, sermon, soapbox*, spiel*, talk; SEE CONCEPT *278*

address [*v1*] *write directions for delivery*
consign, dispatch, forward, inscribe, label, mark, postmark, remit, route, send, ship, superscribe, transmit; SEE CONCEPTS *60,79*

address [*v2*] *speak to a formal gathering*
approach, bespeak, call, deliver speech, deliver talk, discourse, discuss, get on a soapbox*, give speech, give talk, greet, hail, lecture, memorialize, orate, pitch, pontificate, root for, sermonize, spiel*, spout, stump*, take the floor, talk; SEE CONCEPTS *60,266,285*

address [*v3*] *devote effort to something*
apply oneself to, attend to, concentrate on, devote oneself to, dig, direct, engage in, focus on, give, go at*, go for*, hammer away*, have a go at*, have at*, knuckle down to*, peg away*,

pitch into*, plug away at*, take care of, take up, throw oneself into, try, turn, turn to, undertake; SEE CONCEPT *100*

adduce [*v*] *affirm*
cite, illustrate, point out, prove, show; SEE CONCEPTS *49,50,88*

adept [*adj*] *very able*
accomplished, ace*, adroit, brainy, capable, clean*, crack*, crackerjack*, deft, dexterous, expert, hot*, hotshot*, know stuff*, masterful, masterly, nobody's fool*, no dummy*, no slouch*, on the ball*, on the beam*, practiced, proficient, quick, savvy, sharp, sharp as a tack*, skilled, skillful, slick, smooth, there*, up to speed*, versed, whiz*, wizard; SEE CONCEPTS *402,527*

adequacy [*n*] *ability, competency in some action*
capability, capacity, commensurateness, competence, enough, fairness, plenty, requisiteness, satisfactoriness, sufficiency, suitableness, tolerableness; SEE CONCEPTS *636,656*

adequate [*adj*] *enough, able*
acceptable, all right, capable, comfortable, commensurate, competent, decent, equal, fair, passable, requisite, satisfactory, sufficient, sufficing, suitable, tolerable, unexceptional, unobjectionable; SEE CONCEPTS *533,558*

adequately [*adv*] *sufficiently*
abundantly, acceptably, appropriately, capably, competently, copiously, decently, fairly well, fittingly, modestly, pleasantly enough, presentably, satisfactorily, sufficiently, suitably, to an acceptable degree, tolerably, well enough; SEE CONCEPTS *558,560*

adhere [*v1*] *conform to or follow rules exactly*
abide by, be attached, be constant, be devoted, be devoted to, be faithful, be loyal, be true, cleave to, comply, follow, fulfill, heed, keep, maintain, mind, obey, observe, practice, respect, stand by, support; SEE CONCEPTS *87,636*

adhere [*v2*] *stick or become stuck to, either physically or mentally*
attach, cement, cleave, cling like ivy*, cohere, fasten, fix, freeze to*, glue, hold fast, hold on like bulldog*, paste, stay put, stick like a barnacle*, stick like glue*, unite; SEE CONCEPTS *85,113,160*

adherent [*n*] *supporter or follower*
advocate, aficionado, backer, believer, card-carrying member*, devotee, disciple, enthusiast, fan, hanger-on; SEE CONCEPTS *352,366,423*

adhesion [*n*] *holding fast*
adherence, adhesiveness, attachment, bond, cling, grip, stickiness, sticking; SEE CONCEPTS *85,160*

adhesive [*adj*] *sticking*
adherent, adhering, agglutinant, attaching, clinging, clingy, gelatinous, glutinous, gooey, gummed, gummy, holding, hugging, mucilaginous, pasty, resinous, sticky, tenacious, viscid, viscous, waxy; SEE CONCEPTS *488,606*

ad hoc [*adj*] *for a specific purpose*
impromptu, provisional, special, specific, specified; SEE CONCEPTS *535,557,564*

adieu [*n*] *parting remark or action*
adios*, congé, farewell, goodbye, leave-taking, parting, so long, valediction; SEE CONCEPT *276*

ad infinitum [*adj*] *neverending*
ceaselessly, endlessly, forever, perpetually; SEE

CONCEPT *798*

adjacent [*adj*] *next to, abutting*
adjoining, alongside, beside, bordering, close, close by, contiguous, near, neighboring, next door, touching; SEE CONCEPT *586*

adjective [*n*] *word that modifies a noun*
accessory, additional, adjunct, adnoun, attribute, attributive, dependent, descriptive, identifier, modifier, qualifier; SEE CONCEPT *275*

adjoin [*v1*] *be next to*
abut, approximate, be adjacent to, border, butt, communicate, connect, join, lie, lie beside, link, neighbor, touch, verge; SEE CONCEPT *747*

adjoin [*v2*] *attach*
add, affix, annex, append, combine, connect, couple, interconnect, join, link, unite; SEE CONCEPTS *85,113,160*

adjoining [*adj*] *being next to*
abutting, adjacent, approximal, bordering on, connecting, conterminous, contiguous, coterminous, impinging, interconnecting, joined, joining, juxtaposed, near, neighboring, next door, touching, verging; SEE CONCEPT *586*

adjourn [*v*] *stop a proceeding*
curb, defer, delay, discontinue, hold off, hold over, hold up, postpone, prorogue, put off, recess, restrain, shelve, stay, suspend; SEE CONCEPTS *121,234*

adjournment [*n*] *discontinuation or delay of a proceeding*
break, deferment, deferral, intermission, interruption, pause, postponement, prorogation, putting off, recess, stay, suspension; SEE CONCEPTS *121,703*

adjudicate [*v*] *formally judge*
adjudge, arbitrate, decide, determine, mediate, referee, settle, umpire; SEE CONCEPTS *18,317*

adjudication [*n*] *judgment*
conclusion, decision, determination, finding, pronouncement, ruling, settlement, verdict; SEE CONCEPTS *103,689*

adjunct [*n*] *addition; help*
accessory, addendum, appendage, appendix, appurtenance, associate, auxiliary, complement, detail, partner, subordinate, supplement; SEE CONCEPTS *484,835*

adjure [*v*] *command*
beseech, charge, entreat, implore, obligate, order, require, supplicate; SEE CONCEPT *53*

adjust [*v1*] *become or make prepared, adapted*
acclimatize, accommodate, accustom, adapt, alter, arrange, compose, conform, dispose, do as Romans do*, doctor*, fiddle with*, fine-tune, fit, fix, fix up, get act together*, get it together*, grin and bear it*, habituate, harmonize, make conform, modify, order, quadrate, reconcile, rectify, redress, regulate, remodel, settle, suit, swim with the tide*, tailor, tailor-make, tune; SEE CONCEPTS *35,232,697*

adjust [*v2*] *mechanically alter, especially to improve*
accommodate, align, balance, bring into line, calibrate, connect, correct, fine-tune, fit, fix, focus, grind, improve, mend, overhaul, polish, put in working order, readjust, rectify, regulate, renovate, repair, service, set, sharpen, square, tighten, troubleshoot, tune up; SEE CONCEPTS *202,212*

adjust [*v3*] *bring into agreement or to a standard*
accord, allocate, arrange, clarify, conclude, con-

form, coordinate, doctor*, fiddle with*, fine-tune, fix up, grade, methodize, modify, organize, reconcile, regulate, settle, sort, standardize, straighten, systematize, tally; SEE CONCEPTS *84,117*

adjustable [*adj*] *alterable*
accommodating, adaptable, changeable, conformable, flexible, malleable, modifiable, pliable, tractable; SEE CONCEPT *534*

adjustment [*n1*] *adaptation*
acclimation, acclimatization, alteration, arrangement, balancing, conformance, correcting, fitting, fixing, improvement, mending, modification, ordering, organization, organizing, orientation, readjustment, redress, regulating, regulation, repairing, setting, shaping, standardization, turning; SEE CONCEPT *697*

adjustment [*n2*] *financial retribution, payment of claim*
agreement, allotment, apportionment, benefit, compensation, compromise, pay, reconciliation, reimbursement, remuneration, settlement, share, stake, stipulation; SEE CONCEPT *332*

adjutant [*n*] *assistant*
aide, auxiliary, helper; SEE CONCEPT *348*

ad-lib [*adj*] *improvised*
extemporaneous, extempore, extemporized, impromptu, made-up, off-the-cuff*, spontaneous, unprepared, unrehearsed; SEE CONCEPT *267*

ad-lib [*adv*] *in an improvised manner*
extemporaneously, extempore, impromptu, off the cuff*, off the top of one's head*, spontaneously, without preparation, without rehearsal; SEE CONCEPT *267*

ad-lib [*v*] *improvise speech*
extemporize, invent, make up, speak extemporaneously, speak impromptu, speak off the cuff*; SEE CONCEPT *266*

administer [*v1*] *manage an organization or effort*
administrate, be in the driver's seat*, be in the saddle*, boss*, carry out, conduct, control, crack the whip*, direct, execute, govern, head, head up*, hold the reins*, oversee, pull the strings*, pull the wires*, render, ride herd on*, run, run the show*, sit on top of*, superintend, supervise; SEE CONCEPTS *117,298*

administer [*v2*] *dispense something needed*
apply, apportion, authorize, bring, contribute, deal, deliver, disburse, distribute, dole out, execute, extend, furnish, give, impose, inflict, issue, measure out, mete out, offer, perform, portion, proffer, provide, regulate, serve, supply, tender; SEE CONCEPTS *108,136*

administration [*n1*] *management of an organization or effort*
administering, agency, application, authority, charge, command, conduct, conducting, control, directing, direction, dispensation, disposition, distribution, enforcement, execution, governing, government, guidance, handling, jurisdiction, legislation, order, organization, overseeing, oversight, performance, policy, power, provision, regulation, rule, running, strategy, superintendence, supervision, surveillance; SEE CONCEPTS *117,298*

administration [*n2*] *human or group who manages effort of an organization*
admiral, advisers, board, bureau, cabinet, chair, chairperson, chargé d'affaires, command, commander, committee, consulate, department, directors, embassy, executive, executives, feds*, front office*, general, governing body, headquarters, legislature, management, ministry, officers, officials, powers, presidency, president, presidium, stewards, superintendents, supervisors, top brass*, upstairs*; SEE CONCEPT *299*

administration [*n3*] *period during which a particular human group is in power*
dynasty, incumbency, presidency, regime, reign, stay, tenure, term; SEE CONCEPTS *298,816*

administrative [*adj*] *involved in managing or using power*
authoritative, bureaucratic, central, commanding, controlling, deciding, decisive, departmental, directing, directive, directorial, executive, governing, governmental, in charge, in control, jurisdictional, legislative, managerial, official, organizational, policy-making, presiding, regulative, regulatory, ruling, superintending, supervising, supervisory; SEE CONCEPTS *319,536*

administrator [*n*] *person who manages organization*
ambassador, authority, boss, bureaucrat, captain, CEO, chair, chairperson, chief, commander, consul, controller, custodian, dean, director, exec*, executive, front office*, governor, head, head honcho*, head person*, inspector, judge, leader, manager, mayor, minister, officer, official, organizer, overseer, person upstairs*, premier, president, prez*, producer, superintendent, supervisor; SEE CONCEPTS *347,354*

admirable [*adj*] *held in great respect*
A-1*, ace*, A-OK*, attractive, best ever, cat's pajamas*, choice, commendable, cool*, copacetic*, crackerjack*, deserving, dream*, estimable, excellent, exquisite, fine, good, great, greatest, hunky dory*, keen*, laudable, meritable, meritorious, neat*, out of sight*, out of this world*, peachy*, praiseworthy, rare, solid, super, super-duper*, superior, unreal*, valuable, wicked*, wonderful, worthy, zero cool*; SEE CONCEPTS *572,574*

admiration [*n*] *great respect*
account, adoration, affection, applause, appreciation, approbation, approval, deference, delight, esteem, estimation, favor, fondness, glorification, homage, honor, idolatry, idolization, liking, love, marveling, obeisance, pleasure, praise, prizing, recognition, regard, reverence, valuing, veneration, wonder, wonderment, worship; SEE CONCEPT *32*

admire [*v*] *hold in high regard*
adore, applaud, appreciate, approve, be crazy about*, be crazy for*, be crazy over*, be mad about*, be nuts about*, be stuck on*, be sweet on*, be wild about*, cherish, commend, credit, delight in, esteem, eulogize, extol, fall for*, get high on*, glorify, go for*, groove on*, hail, hold in respect, honor, idolize, laud, look up to, marvel at, moon over*, pay homage to, praise, prize, rate highly, respect, revere, take pleasure in, think highly of, treasure, value, venerate, wonder at, worship; SEE CONCEPT *32*

admirer [*n*] *person who holds someone in high regard*
adherent, beau, believer, booster, boyfriend, buff, bug*, cat*, devotee, disciple, enthusiast, fan, fancier, fiend*, follower, freak*, girlfriend,

groupie*, hound*, junkie*, lover, nut*, partisan, patron, rooter*, suitor, supporter, swain, sweetheart, wooer, worshiper; SEE CONCEPT *423*

admissible [adj] *able or deserving of consideration; allowable*
acceptable, allowed, applicable, appropriate, concedable, fair, fitting, just, justifiable, lawful, legal, legitimate, licit, likely, logical, not impossible, not unlikely, okay, passable, permissible, permitted, pertinent, possible, probable, proper, rational, reasonable, relevant, right, suitable, tolerable, tolerated, warranted, worthy; SEE CONCEPT *533*

admission [n1] *entering or allowing entry*
acceptance, access, admittance, certification, confirmation, designation, door, entrance, entree, ingress, initiation, introduction, permission, reception, recognition, way, welcome; SEE CONCEPTS *83,159*

admission [n2] *confession or acknowledgment*
accession, admittance, affidavit, affirmation, allowance, assent, assertion, attestation, averment, avowal, concession, confirmation, declaration, deposition, disclosure, divulgence, profession, revelation, statement, testimonial, testimony; SEE CONCEPT *57*

admit [v1] *allow entry or use*
accept, be big on*, bless, buy, concede, enter, entertain, give access, give the nod*, give thumbs up*, grant, harbor, house, initiate, introduce, let, let in, lodge, okay, permit, receive, shelter, sign*, sign off on*, suffer, take, take in; SEE CONCEPT *83*

admit [v2] *confess, acknowledge*
accept, accord, acquiesce, adopt, affirm, agree, allow, approve, avow, bare, bring to light*, communicate, concede, concur, confide, confirm, consent, cop a plea*, credit, declare, disclose, divulge, enumerate, expose, go into details*, grant, indicate, let, let on, make known, narrate, number, open up, own, own up*, permit, proclaim, profess, recite, recognize, relate, reveal, spill*, subscribe to, talk, tell, tolerate, uncover, unveil, yield; SEE CONCEPTS *57,82*

admittance [n] *permission to enter*
access, entrance, entrée, entry, ingress, pass, passage, reception; SEE CONCEPTS *388,685*

admixture [n] *blending*
amalgamation, blend, combination, commixture, compound, fusion, melange, mingling, mixture; SEE CONCEPT *432*

admonish [v] *warn, strongly criticize*
advise, berate, call down, call on the carpet*, censure, check, chide, come down hard on*, counsel, ding*, draw the line*, enjoin, exhort, forewarn, give a going over*, give a piece of one's mind*, glue*, growl*, hoist*, jack up*, notice, rap*, rap on knuckles*, rebuke, reprimand, reprove, scold, sit on, slap on wrist*, speak to, talk to, tell a thing or two*, tell off*, upbraid, warn; SEE CONCEPTS *52,78*

admonition [n1] *caution*
advice, apprisal, counsel, forewarning, warning; SEE CONCEPTS *78,274*

admonition [n2] *scolding*
berating, dressing down*, rebuke, reprimand, reproach, reproval, talking to*, upbraiding; SEE CONCEPTS *44,52*

ad nauseam [adv] *to the point of illness*
more than one can stomach, to a sickening degree, too much; SEE CONCEPTS *529,571*

ado [n] *fuss*
bother, confusion, excitement, flurry, hubbub, to-do*, travail, trouble, turmoil; SEE CONCEPTS *46,106,388,633*

adolescence [n] *state of puberty, preadulthood*
boyhood, girlhood, greenness, juvenility, minority, pubescence, spring, teens, youth, youthfulness; SEE CONCEPT *817*

adolescent [adj] *preadult or immature*
boyish, girlish, growing, juvenile, pubescent, puerile, teen, teenage, young, youthful; SEE CONCEPTS *401,578,797*

adolescent [n] *person in puberty, preadulthood*
juvenile, minor, stripling, sweet sixteen*, teen, teenager, teenybopper*, youngster, youth; SEE CONCEPT *424*

adopt [v1] *choose or take something as one's own*
accept, adapt, affiliate, affirm, appropriate, approve, assent, assume, borrow, embrace, endorse, espouse, follow, go down the line*, go in for*, imitate, maintain, mimic, opt, ratify, seize, select, support, take on, take over, take up, tap, use, utilize; SEE CONCEPT *18*

adopt [v2] *legally care for another's child*
choose, foster, naturalize, pick, raise, select, take in; SEE CONCEPT *317*

adoption [n1] *choosing or taking something as one's own*
acceptance, approbation, appropriation, approval, assumption, choice, confirmation, embracement, embracing, enactment, endorsement, espousal, following, maintenance, ratification, selection, support, taking on, taking over, taking up; SEE CONCEPT *18*

adoption [n2] *legal taking of another's child*
adopting, fosterage, fostering, naturalizing, raising, taking in; SEE CONCEPT *317*

adorable [adj] *cute, lovable*
ambrosial, appealing, attractive, captivating, charming, cute, darling, dear, delectable, delicious, delightful, dishy*, dreamy*, fetching, heavenly, hot*, luscious, pleasing, precious, sexy, suave; SEE CONCEPTS *579,589*

adoration [n] *intense love*
admiration, amore, ardor, attachment, crush, devotion, esteem, estimation, exaltation, glorification, hankering, honor, idolatry, idolization, infatuation, pash*, passion, puppy love*, reverence, shine*, veneration, weakness*, worship, worshipping, yen*; SEE CONCEPT *32*

adore [v] *love intensely*
admire, be crazy about*, be gone on*, be mad for*, be nuts about*, be serious about*, be smitten with*, be stuck on*, be sweet on*, be wild about*, cherish, delight in, dig*, dote on, esteem, exalt, fall for, flip over*, glorify, go for*, honor, idolize, prize, revere, reverence, treasure, venerate, worship; SEE CONCEPT *32*

adorn [v] *decorate*
array, beautify, bedeck, deck, doll up*, dress up, embellish, enhance, enrich, fix up, furbish, garnish, grace, gussy up*, ornament, spruce up, trim; SEE CONCEPTS *162,177*

adornment [n1] *decorating, enhancing*
beautification, decoration, embellishment, gilding, ornamentation, trimming; SEE CONCEPTS *162,177*

adornment [n2] *a decoration*

ad
ad

accessory, dingbat, doodad, embellishment, fandangle*, floss*, frill, frippery, furbelow*, gewgaw*, jazz*, ornament, thing, trimming; SEE CONCEPTS *446,484*

adrift [*adv1*] *floating out of control*
afloat, drifting, loose, unanchored, unmoored; SEE CONCEPT *488*

adrift [*adv2*] *without purpose*
aimless, directionless, goalless, purposeless; SEE CONCEPT *542*

adrift [*adv3*] *off course*
amiss, astray, erring, wrong; SEE CONCEPT *581*

adroit [*adj*] *very able or skilled*
adept, apt, artful, clean, clever, crack*, crackerjack*, cunning, cute, deft, dexterous, expert, foxy*, good, handy, hot tamale*, ingenious, masterful, neat*, nifty*, nimble, on the ball*, on the beam*, proficient, quick on the trigger*, quick on the uptake*, quick-witted, savvy, sharp, skillful, slick, smart, up*, up to speed*, whiz*, wizard; SEE CONCEPT *527*

adulate [*v*] *flatter*
apple polish*, brown-nose*, fall all over*, fawn, gush, kiss feet*, praise, worship; SEE CONCEPTS *59,69*

adulation [*n*] *overenthusiastic praise*
applause, audation, blandishment, bootlicking*, commendation, fawning, flattery, sycophancy, worship; SEE CONCEPTS *32,69*

adult [*adj*] *being mature, fully grown*
developed, grown, grown-up, of age, ripe, ripened; SEE CONCEPT *406*

adult [*n*] *a mature, fully grown person*
gentleperson, grownup, man, person, woman; SEE CONCEPTS *394,424*

adulterate [*v*] *alter or debase, often for profit*
alloy, amalgamate, attenuate, blend, cheapen, commingle, contaminate, cook, corrupt, cut*, defile, degrade, denature, depreciate, deteriorate, devalue, dilute, dissolve, doctor*, doctor up*, falsify, impair, infiltrate, intermix, irrigate, lace*, make impure, mingle, mix, phony up*, plant*, pollute, shave*, spike*, taint, thin, transfuse, vitiate, water down*, weaken; SEE CONCEPTS *240,254*

adulterated [*adj*] *debased or dirty*
attenuated, blended, contaminated, corrupt, defiled, degraded, depreciated, deteriorated, devalued, diluted, dissolved, impaired, mixed, polluted, tainted, thinned, vitiated, watered down, weakened; SEE CONCEPT *485*

adulterous [*adj*] *unfaithful*
cheating, double-crossing*, extracurricular*, fast and loose*, illicit, immoral, moonlighting*, speedy*, two-faced*, two-timing*, unchaste; SEE CONCEPT *372*

adultery [*n*] *extramarital affair*
affair, carrying on*, cheating, extracurricular activity*, fling, fornication, hanky-panky*, immorality, infidelity, matinee*, playing around*, relationship, thing*, two-timing*; SEE CONCEPT *633*

advance [*adj*] *ahead in position or time*
beforehand, earlier, early, first, foremost, forward, in front, in the forefront, in the lead, leading, previously, prior; SEE CONCEPTS *583,585,799*

advance [*n1*] *forward movement*
advancement, headway, impetus, motion, progress, progression; SEE CONCEPTS *152,208*

advance [*n2*] *improvement, progress in development*
advancement, amelioration, betterment, boost, break*, breakthrough, buildup, development, enrichment, furtherance, gain, go-ahead*, growth, headway, increase, progress, promotion, rise, step, up, upgrade, upping; SEE CONCEPTS *700,704*

advance [*n3*] *money given beforehand*
accommodation, allowance, bite*, credit, deposit, down payment, floater*, front money*, hike, increase, loan, prepayment, retainer, rise*, score, stake, take*, touch*; SEE CONCEPTS *340,344*

advance [*v1*] *move something forward, often quickly*
accelerate, achieve, bring forward, come forward, conquer, continue ahead, continue on, dispatch, drive, elevate, forge ahead, gain ground, get ahead, get green light*, get there*, get with it*, go ahead, go forth, go forward, go great guns*, go places*, go to town*, hasten, launch, make headway, make the scene*, march, move on, move onward, move up, press on, proceed, progress, promote, propel, push ahead, push on, quicken, send forward, skyrocket*, speed, step forward, storm; SEE CONCEPTS *152,208,704*

advance [*v2*] *promote or propose an idea*
adduce, allege, ballyhoo, beat the drum for, benefit, boost, cite, encourage, foster, further, get ink for*, hype*, introduce, lay forward, make a pitch for*, offer, plug*, present, proffer, puff*, push, put forward, put on the map*, serve, set forth, splash, spot, submit, suggest, throw spotlight on*, urge; SEE CONCEPTS *49,60,68*

advance [*v3*] *give money beforehand*
furnish, lend, loan, pay, provide; SEE CONCEPT *341*

advance [*v4*] *increase in amount, number, or position*
boost, break the bank*, develop, elevate, enlarge, get fat*, get rich*, grade, grow, hit pay dirt*, hit the jackpot*, improve, magnify, make a killing*, make out*, multiply, pan out*, prefer, prosper, raise, strike gold*, strike it rich*, thrive, up, upgrade, uplift; SEE CONCEPTS *236,244,245*

advanced [*adj*] *ahead in position, time, manner*
avant-garde, breakthrough, cutting-edge*, excellent, exceptional, extreme, first, foremost, forward, higher, late, leading, leading-edge*, liberal, precocious, progressive, radical, state-of-the-art*, unconventional; SEE CONCEPTS *574,578,585,797*

advancement [*n1*] *promotion, progress*
advance, amelioration, betterment, elevation, gain, growth, headway, improvement, preference, preferment, prelation, rise, upgrading; SEE CONCEPTS *700,704*

advancement [*n2*] *forward movement*
advance, anabasis, gain, headway, march, progress, progression; SEE CONCEPTS *152,208*

advance(s) [*n4*] *desirous pursuit of someone*
approach, move, overture, proposal, proposition, suggestion; SEE CONCEPTS *20,384*

advantage [*n*] *benefit, favored position or circumstance*
aid, ascendancy, asset, assistance, authority, avail, blessing, boon, break, choice, comfort, convenience, dominance, edge, eminence, expe-

diency, favor, gain, good, gratification, help, hold, improvement, influence, interest, lead, leeway, leg-up*, leverage, luck, mastery, odds, position, power, precedence, pre-eminence, preference, prestige, prevalence, profit, protection, recognition, resources, return, sanction, starting, superiority, support, supremacy, upper hand*, utility, wealth; SEE CONCEPT *574*

advantageous [*adj*] *favorable*
auspicious, beneficial, expedient, for the best, fortunate, helpful, opportune, profitable, propitious, worthwhile; SEE CONCEPTS *537,558,572*

advent [*n*] *beginning or arrival of something anticipated*
appearance, approach, arrival, coming, entrance, occurrence, onset, visitation; SEE CONCEPTS *119,159*

adventure [*n*] *risky or unexpected undertaking*
chance, contingency, emprise, endangerment, enterprise, experience, exploit, feat, happening, hazard, incident, jeopardy, occurrence, peril, scene, speculation, trip, undertaking, venture; SEE CONCEPTS *384,386*

adventurer [*n*] *person who takes risks*
charlatan, daredevil, entrepreneur, explorer, fortune-hunter, gambler, globetrotter, hero, heroine, madcap, mercenary, opportunist, pioneer, pirate, romantic, speculator, stunt person, swashbuckler, traveler, venturer, voyager, wanderer; SEE CONCEPT *423*

adventurous [*adj*] *daring, risk-taking*
adventuresome, audacious, bold, brave, courageous, dangerous, daredevil, enterprising, foolhardy, hazardous, headstrong, intrepid, rash, reckless, risky, temerarious, venturesome, venturous; SEE CONCEPTS *404,542*

adverb [*n*] *word modifying a verb*
limiter, modifier, qualifier; SEE CONCEPT *275*

adversary [*n*] *opponent*
antagonist, attacker, bad person, bandit, competitor, contestant, enemy, foe, match, opposer, opposite number*, oppugner, rival; SEE CONCEPT *412*

adverse [*adj*] *unfavorable, antagonistic*
allergic to*, conflicting, contrary, detrimental, disadvantageous, down on*, down side*, have no use for*, inimical, injurious, inopportune, negative, opposed, opposing, opposite, oppugning, ornery*, reluctant, repugnant, stuffy*, unfortunate, unfriendly, unlucky, unpropitious, unwilling; SEE CONCEPT *570*

adversity [*n*] *bad luck, situation*
affliction, bad break*, bummer*, calamity, can of worms*, catastrophe, clutch, contretemps, crunch*, difficulty, disaster, distress, downer*, drag*, evil eye*, hard knocks*, hardship, hard times, hurting, ill fortune, jam, jinx, kiss of death*, misery, misfortune, mishap, on the skids*, pain in the neck*, poison*, reverse, sorrow, suffering, the worst*, tough luck*, trial, trouble; SEE CONCEPT *674*

advertise [*v*] *publicize for the purpose of selling or causing one to want*
acquaint, advance, advise, announce, apprise, ballyhoo*, beat the drum for*, bill, blazon, boost*, build up, circularize, communicate, declare, disclose, display, divulge, drum*, endorse, exhibit, expose, flaunt, get on soapbox for*, hard sell, herald, hype*, inform, make a pitch*, make known, notify, pitch, plug, press agent*, proclaim, promote, promulgate, puff*, push, put on the map*, reveal, show, soft sell, splash*, sponsor, spot, tout, uncover, unmask; SEE CONCEPTS *60,324*

advertisement [*n*] *public notice of sale*
ad, announcement, bill, blurb, broadcast, circular, classified ad, commercial, communication, declaration, display, endorsement, exhibit, exhibition, flyer, literature, notice, notification, placard, plug, poster, proclamation, promotion, promulgation, propaganda, publication, publicity, squib, throwaway, want ad; SEE CONCEPTS *270,277,278,280*

advertising [*n*] *public notice of sale; notices to increase consumer desire*
announcement, announcing, ballyhoo*, billing, blasting*, broadcasting, buildup, displaying, exhibiting, exhibition, exposition, hard sell, hoopla*, hype*, pitch, plug, posting, PR, proclamation, promo*, promoting, promotion, publicity, puff*, screamer*, spread, squib; SEE CONCEPTS *97,138,324*

advice [*n*] *recommendation*
admonition, advisement, advocacy, aid, bum steer*, caution, charge, consultation, counsel, directions, dissuasion, encouragement, exhortation, forewarning, guidance, help, information, injunction, input, instruction, judgment, lesson, news, opinion, persuasion, prescription, proposal, proposition, recommendation, steer, suggestion, teaching, telltale, tidings, tip, tip-off*, two cents' worth*, view, warning, word, word to the wise*; SEE CONCEPTS *75,274*

advisable [*adj*] *recommended, wise*
appropriate, apt, commendable, desirable, expedient, fit, fitting, judicious, politic, prudent, seemly, sensible, sound, suggested, suitable, tactical; SEE CONCEPT *574*

advise [*v1*] *offer recommendation*
admonish, advocate, caution, charge, commend, counsel, direct, dissuade, encourage, enjoin, exhort, forewarn, give a pointer*, give a tip*, guide, instruct, kibitz*, level with*, move, opine, point out, preach, prepare, prescribe, prompt, put bug in ear*, put in two cents*, recommend, steer, suggest, tout, update, urge, warn; SEE CONCEPT *75*

advise [*v2*] *offer information*
acquaint, apprise, clue*, clue in*, fill in, give the word*, inform, keep posted*, lay it out*, let in on*, make known, notify, post*, put next to*, put on the line*, put on to*, report, show, tell, tip off*, update, warn; SEE CONCEPT *60*

advisedly [*adv*] *with due consideration*
carefully, cautiously, consciously, deliberately, discreetly, intentionally, prudently, thoughtfully; SEE CONCEPT *544*

adviser/advisor [*n*] *person who recommends, teaches, or otherwise helps*
aide, attorney, authority, backseat driver*, buttinski*, clubhouse lawyer*, coach, confidant, consultant, counsel, counselor, director, doctor, Dutch uncle*, expert, friend, guide, helper, instructor, judge, kibitzer*, lawyer, mentor, monitor, partner, priest, quarterback*, referee, righthand person, second-guesser, teacher, tutor; SEE CONCEPTS *348,350*

advisory [*adj*] *able, authorized to recommend*
advising, consultative, consultive, counseling,

helping, recommending; SEE CONCEPT 537

advocacy [n] *support for an idea or cause*
advancement, aid, assistance, backing, campaigning for, championing, defense, encouragement, justification, pleading for, promotion, promulgation, propagation, proposal, recommendation, upholding, urging; SEE CONCEPT 689

advocate [n] *person supporting an idea or cause publicly*
apostle, attorney, backer, campaigner, champion, counsel, defender, exponent, expounder, lawyer, pleader, promoter, proponent, proposer, speaker, spokesperson, supporter, upholder; SEE CONCEPTS 359,423

advocate [v] *support idea or cause publicly*
advance, advise, argue for, back, be in corner*, bless, bolster, boost*, brace up*, build up, campaign for, champion, countenance, defend, encourage, favor, further, get on bandwagon*, give a leg up*, give a lift*, go for, go to bat for*, go with, hold with, justify, plead for, plug*, plump for*, press for, promote, propose, push, recommend, ride shotgun for*, root for*, run interference for*, say so*, side, speak for, spread around*, stump for*, support, tout, uphold, urge, vindicate; SEE CONCEPTS 10,49,75

aegis [n] *protection*
auspices, backing, patronage, shelter, sponsorship, wing*; SEE CONCEPTS 94,376

aerial [adj] *occurring in the air*
aeriform, aeronautical, airy, atmospheric, birdlike, ethereal, flying, lofty, pneumatic, up above, vaporous; SEE CONCEPT 583

aerobics/aerobic [n/adj] *exercise regime designed to increase heart and lung activity while toning muscles*
aquarobics, dance workout, drill, exercise, high impact, low impact, slimnastics, step, warm-up, workout; SEE CONCEPT 363

aesthetic/esthetic [adj] *beautiful or artful*
artistic, creative, gorgeous, inventive; SEE CONCEPTS 485,579

afar [adv] *a great distance away*
distant, far away, far off, remote; SEE CONCEPT 778

affable [adj] *friendly*
amiable, amicable, approachable, benevolent, benign, breezy, civil, clubby*, congenial, cordial, courteous, genial, gentle, good-humored, good-natured, gracious, kindly, mild, nice, obliging, pleasant, polite, sociable, urbane, warm; SEE CONCEPT 401

affair [n1] *matter or business to be taken care of; happening activity*
assignment, avocation, calling, case, circumstance, concern, duty, employment, episode, event, hap, happening, incident, interest, job, mission, obligation, occupation, occurrence, office function, proceeding, profession, project, province, pursuit, question, realm, responsibility, subject, task, thing*, topic, transaction, undertaking; SEE CONCEPTS 2,349,362

affair [n2] *illicit sexual relationship*
affaire, amour, carrying on*, extracurricular activity*, fling, goings-on*, hanky-panky*, intimacy, intrigue, liaison, love, playing around*, relationship, rendezvous, romance, thing together*, two-timing*; SEE CONCEPTS 32,375

affair [n3] *party or celebration*
do, entertainment, function, gathering, reception,

shindig, soiree; SEE CONCEPTS 377,383

affect [v1] *influence, affect emotionally*
act on, alter, change, disturb, impinge, impress, induce, influence, inspire, interest, involve, modify, move, overcome, perturb, prevail, regard, relate, stir, sway, touch, transform, upset; SEE CONCEPTS 7,19,22,228

affect [v2] *pretend, imitate*
act, adopt, aspire to, assume, bluff, contrive, counterfeit, do a bit*, fake, feign, lay it on thick, make out like*, playact, put on, put up a front*, sham*, simulate, take on; SEE CONCEPT 59

affectation [n] *pretended behavior to make an impression*
air, airs, appearance, artificiality, facade, false front*, front, going Hollywood*, imitation, insincerity, mannerism, pose, pretense, pretension, pretentiousness, put-on, putting on airs*, sham*, show, showing off, simulation; SEE CONCEPT 633

affected [adj1] *deeply moved or hurt emotionally*
afflicted, altered, changed, compassionate, concerned, damaged, distressed, excited, grieved, impaired, impressed, influenced, injured, overwhelmed, overwrought, sorry, stimulated, stirred, sympathetic, tender, touched, troubled, upset; SEE CONCEPT 403

affected [adj2] *changed in a bad or artificial way*
apish, artificial, assumed, awkward, campy*, chichi*, conceited, contrived, counterfeit, counterfeited, faked, false, feigned, fraud*, gone Hollywood*, ham*, hammy*, high falutin'*, hollow, imitated, insincere, melodramatic, ostentatious, overdone, pedantic, phony, playacting, pompous, precious, pretended, pretentious, put-on*, schmaltzy*, self-conscious, shallow, sham*, simulated, spurious, stiff, stilted, studied, superficial, theatrical, unnatural; SEE CONCEPTS 401,570

affection [n] *strong fondness*
amore, ardor, attachment, care, case*, closeness, concern, crush, desire, devotion, emotion, endearment, feeling, friendliness, friendship, good will, hankering*, heart, inclination, itch*, kindness, liking, love, passion, predilection, propensity, puppy love*, regard, sentiment, shine*, soft spot*, solicitude, tenderness, warmth, weakness*, yen*; SEE CONCEPT 32

affectionate [adj] *having or showing fondness*
all over*, attached, caring, crazy over*, dear, devoted, doting, fond, friendly, huggy*, kind, lovey-dovey*, loving, mushy*, nutty about*, partial, soft on*, sympathetic, tender, warm, warmhearted; SEE CONCEPTS 401,403

affective [adj] *concerning feelings and intuition*
emotional, emotive, feeling, intuitive, noncognitive, perceptual, visceral; SEE CONCEPT 529

affidavit [n] *written legal declaration*
affirmation, oath, sworn statement, testimony; SEE CONCEPTS 271,318

affiliate [n] *organization that is associated with another*
affil*, associate, branch, offshoot, partner, sibling; SEE CONCEPT 381

affiliate [v] *associate or be associated with a larger organization*
ally, amalgamate, annex, associate, band together, combine, come aboard, confederate, connect, form connection, go partners*, hook up*, incorporate, join, line up*, plug into*, relate*, team up, throw in with*, tie up, unite; SEE CON-

CEPTS *113,114*

affiliation [*n*] *association with an organization*
alliance, amalgamation, banding together, bunch, cahoots*, clan, coalition, combination, confederation, conjunction, connection, crew, crowd, gang, hookup*, incorporation, joining, league, merging, mob, outfit, partnership, relationship, ring, syndicate, tie-in, union; SEE CONCEPT *381*

affinity [*n1*] *liking or inclination toward something*
affection, attraction, closeness, compatibility, cotton*, cup of tea*, druthers*, fondness, good vibrations*, leaning, partiality, rapport, same wavelength, simpatico, sympathy, thing*, weakness*; SEE CONCEPTS *20,32,709*

affinity [*n2*] *similarity*
alikeness, alliance, analogy, association, closeness, connection, correspondence, kinship, likeness, relation, relationship, resemblance, semblance, similitude; SEE CONCEPT *670*

affirm [*v*] *declare the truth of something*
assert, asseverate, attest, aver, avouch, avow, certify, cinch, clinch, confirm, cross heart, declare, guarantee, have a lock on*, ice*, insist, lock up*, maintain, nail down*, okay, predicate, profess, pronounce, put on ice*, ratify, repeat, rubber-stamp*, say so, set, state, swear, swear on bible*, swear up and down*, testify, vouch, witness; SEE CONCEPTS *49,50,88*

affirmation [*n*] *declaration of the truth of something*
affidavit, assertion, asseveration, attestation, averment, avouchment, avowal, certification, confirmation, declaration, green light*, oath, okay, pronouncement, ratification, stamp of approval*, statement, sworn statement, testimonial, testimony; SEE CONCEPT *49*

affirmative [*adj*] *being agreeable or assenting*
acknowledging, acquiescent, affirmatory, affirming, approving, complying, concurring, confirmative, confirmatory, confirming, consenting, corroborative, endorsing, favorable, positive, ratifying, supporting; SEE CONCEPTS *542,572*

affirmative action [*n*] *equal rights policy*
anti-discrimination, equal opportunity, fair hiring, fair treatment, quota system, reverse discrimination; SEE CONCEPTS *388,645,667*

affix [*v*] *attach or stick*
add, annex, append, bind, fasten, glue, hitch on*, join, paste, put on, rivet, slap on*, subjoin, tack, tack on*, tag, tag on*; SEE CONCEPTS *85,113,160*

afflict [*v*] *cause or become hurt*
agonize, annoy, beset, bother, burden, crucify, distress, grieve, harass, harrow, harry, irk, lacerate, martyr, oppress, pain, pester, plague, press, rack, smite, strike, torment, torture, trouble, try, vex, worry, wound; SEE CONCEPTS *7,19,246,313*

affliction [*n*] *hurt condition; something that causes hurt*
adversity, anguish, calamity, cross, crux, depression, difficulty, disease, disorder, distress, grief, hardship, illness, infirmity, misery, misfortune, ordeal, pain, plague, plight, scourge, sickness, sorrow, suffering, torment, trial, tribulation, trouble, woe; SEE CONCEPTS *306,309,674,728*

affluence [*n*] *wealth*
abundance, fortune, luxury, opulence, plenty, prosperity, riches, wealthiness; SEE CONCEPTS

340,710

affluent [*adj1*] *wealthy*
flush*, loaded*, moneyed*, opulent, prosperous, rich, stinking rich*, upper class, upscale, well-off, well-to-do; SEE CONCEPT *334*

affluent [*adj2*] *plentiful*
abundant, bountiful, copious, full, plenteous; SEE CONCEPT *771*

afford [*v1*] *able to have or do; within financial means*
allow, be able to, bear, be disposed to, have enough for, have the means for, incur, manage, spare, stand, support, sustain; SEE CONCEPTS *335,713*

afford [*v2*] *give, produce*
bestow, furnish, grant, impart, offer, provide, render, supply, yield; SEE CONCEPTS *108,143*

affront [*n*] *an insult*
abuse, backhanded compliment*, brickbat*, dirty deed*, indignity, injury, left-handed compliment*, offense, outrage, provocation, put-down*, slap*, slap in the face*, slight, slur, vexation, wrong; SEE CONCEPTS *7,19,44,54*

affront [*v*] *insult or involve in entanglement*
abuse, anger, annoy, confront, criticize, displease, dispraise, dump on*, encounter, face, give a zinger*, give the cold shoulder*, hit where one lives*, meet, offend, outrage, pique, provoke, put down*, slander, slight, taunt, vex; SEE CONCEPTS *7,19,44,54*

aficionado [*n*] *fan*
connoisseur, devotee, enthusiast, fanatic; SEE CONCEPTS *352,366,423*

afraid [*adj1*] *fearful*
abashed, aghast, alarmed, anxious, apprehensive, aroused, blanched, cowardly, cowed, daunted, discouraged, disheartened, dismayed, distressed, disturbed, faint-hearted, frightened, frozen, have cold feet*, horrified, in awe, intimidated, nervous, panic-stricken, perplexed, perturbed, petrified, rattled, run scared*, scared, scared stiff*, scared to death*, shocked, spooked, startled, stunned, suspicious, terrified, terror-stricken, timid, timorous, trembling, upset, worried; SEE CONCEPTS *403,690*

afraid [*adj2*] *reluctant, regretful*
averse, backward, disinclined, hesitant, indisposed, loath, reluctant, sorry, uneager, unhappy, unwilling; SEE CONCEPT *529*

afresh [*adj*] *new or repeated*
again, anew, de novo, lately, newly, of late, once again, once more, over, over again, recently; SEE CONCEPTS *578,797*

Afro [*n*] *frizzy hairstyle*
curly hair, fro; SEE CONCEPT *718*

after [*adj*] *following in position or time*
afterwards, back, back of, behind, below, ensuing, hind, hindmost, in the rear, later, next, posterior, postliminary, rear, subsequential, subsequently, succeeding, thereafter; SEE CONCEPTS *586,820*

afterlife [*n*] *life after death*
eternity, heaven, hereafter, immortality, the great beyond*; SEE CONCEPTS *370,410,435*

aftermath [*n*] *situation following an event, occurrence*
after-effects, causatum, chain reaction*, consequences, end, eventuality, flak*, impact, issue, outcome, payoff*, remainder, residual, residuum,

results, upshot, waves*; SEE CONCEPT 230

afternoon [n] *period after 12 noon and before sunset*
cocktail hour, P.M., post meridian, siesta, teatime; SEE CONCEPTS 801,806,810

afterthought [n] *idea that occurs after it is timely*
reconsideration, review, second thought; SEE CONCEPT 529

afterward/afterwards [adv] *following a time, event*
after, another time, at a later time, a while later, behind, by and by, ensuingly, eventually, in a while, intra, late, later, latterly, next, on the next day, soon, subsequently, then, thereafter, thereon, ultimately; SEE CONCEPT 799

again [adv1] *another time; repeated*
afresh, anew, anon, bis, come again, encore, freshly, newly, once more, one more time, over, over and over, recurrently, reiteratively, repeatedly; SEE CONCEPTS 553,799

again [adv2] *in addition*
additionally, also, besides, further, furthermore, moreover, on the contrary, on the other hand, then; SEE CONCEPT 577

against [prep] *opposite to*
across, adjacent, contra, contrary to, counter to, facing, in contrast to, in opposition to, opposed to, opposing, versus; SEE CONCEPT 564

age [n1] *period of animate existence*
adolescence, adulthood, boyhood, childhood, dotage, elderliness, girlhood, infancy, life, lifetime, majority, maturity, middle age, milestone, old age, senility, seniority, wear and tear*, youth; SEE CONCEPTS 816,817

age [n2] *a period of time*
aeon, blue moon*, century, date, day, duration, epoch, era, generation, interim, interval, life, lifetime, millennium, span; SEE CONCEPT 807

age [v] *become older*
decline, deteriorate, develop, get along, grow, grow feeble, grow old, grow up, mature, mellow, push, put mileage on*, ripen, wane; SEE CONCEPT 105

aged [adj] *old*
age-old, ancient, antediluvian, antiquated, antique, been around*, creaky*, elderly, getting on*, gray, moth-eaten*, oldie*, over the hill*, passé*, rusty*, senescent, senior citizen, shot*, timeworn, venerable, worn, worse for wear*; SEE CONCEPTS 578,797

ageism [n] *age-based discrimination*
age bias, generation gap; SEE CONCEPT 689

agency [n1] *organization, often business-related*
bureau, company, department, firm, office; SEE CONCEPTS 325,381,441

agency [n2] *power, instrumentality*
action, activity, auspices, channel, efficiency, force, influence, instrument, instrumentality, intercession, intervention, means, mechanism, mediation, medium, operation, organ, vehicle, work; SEE CONCEPTS 376,658

agenda [n] *list of things to do*
calendar, card, diary, docket, lineup, plan, program, schedule, timetable; SEE CONCEPT 283

agent [n1] *person representing an organization or person in business*
abettor, actor, advocate, ambassador, assignee, assistant, attorney, broker, commissioner, delegate, deputy, doer, emissary, envoy, executor, factor, factotum, functionary, go-between, handler, intermediary, lawyer, mediary, middleperson, minister, mover, negotiator, officer, operative, operator, principal, proctor, promoter, proxy, representative, salesperson, servant, steward, substitute, surrogate, ten percenter*, worker; SEE CONCEPT 348

agent [n2] *power, instrument for achievement*
cause, channel, factor, force, means, medium, organ, power, vehicle; SEE CONCEPTS 376,658

agent provocateur [n] *instigator*
agitator, goad, incendiary, rabble-rouser, troublemaker; SEE CONCEPT 412

agglomeration [n] *collection*
cluster, heap, jumble, load, mass, pile; SEE CONCEPTS 432,786

aggrandize [v] *cause something to seem or be greater, bigger*
acclaim, applaud, augment, beef up*, boost, commend, dignify, distinguish, enlarge, ennoble, expand, extend, glorify, heighten, hike, hike up*, honor, hype, increase, intensify, jack up*, jump, magnify, multiply, parlay, praise; SEE CONCEPTS 50,69,88,236,245

aggravate [v1] *annoy*
be at*, be on the back of*, bother, bug, bum*, dog, drive up the wall*, exasperate, gall, get, get on one's nerves, get to, give a hard time, grate, hack, irk, irritate, nag, needle, nettle, peeve, pester, pick on, pique, provoke, tease, vex, wig*; SEE CONCEPTS 7,19

aggravate [v2] *cause to become worse*
complicate, deepen, enhance, exacerbate, exaggerate, heighten, increase, inflame, intensify, magnify, mount, rise, rouse, worsen; SEE CONCEPT 240

aggravation [n1] *annoyance*
affliction, aggro*, bother, botheration*, difficulty, distress, exasperation, hang-up*, headache*, irksomeness, irritation, pain, pain in the neck*, pet peeve*, provocation, teasing, vexation, worry; SEE CONCEPT 410

aggravation [n2] *worsening of a situation, condition*
deepening, exacerbation, exaggeration, heightening, increase, inflaming, inflammation, intensification, magnification, sharpening, strengthening, worsening; SEE CONCEPT 240

aggregate [adj] *forming a collection from separate parts*
accumulated, added, amassed, assembled, collected, collective, combined, composite, corporate, cumulative, heaped, mixed, piled, total; SEE CONCEPT 781

aggregate [n] *collection*
accumulation, agglomerate, agglomeration, all, amount, assemblage, body, bulk, combination, conglomerate, conglomeration, gross, heap, lump, mass, mixture, pile, quantity, sum, the works*, total, totality, whole, whole ball of wax*, whole enchilada*, whole schmear*, whole shooting match*; SEE CONCEPT 432

aggregate [v] *combine into a collection*
accumulate, add up, amass, amount, assemble, collect, combine, come, heap, mix, number, pile, sum, total; SEE CONCEPT 109

aggression [n1] *attack, often military*
assailment, assault, blitz, blitzkrieg, encroachment, injury, invasion, offense, offensive, onset,

onslaught, push, raid; SEE CONCEPTS *86,320*

aggression [*n2*] *hostile or forceful behavior, attitude*
aggressiveness, antagonism, belligerence, blitz, combativeness, destructiveness, fight, hostility, pugnacity, push; SEE CONCEPTS *29,411*

aggressive [*adj1*] *belligerent, hostile*
advancing, antipathetic, assailing, attacking, barbaric, bellicose, combative, contentious, destructive, disruptive, disturbing, encroaching, hawkish, intruding, intrusive, invading, martial, militant, offensive, pugnacious, quarrelsome, rapacious, threatening, warlike; SEE CONCEPT *550*

aggressive [*adj2*] *assertive*
assertory, bold, brassy*, cheeky*, cocky*, come on*, domineering, dynamic, energetic, enterprising, flip*, forceful, fresh*, get up and go*, go after, hard sell, imperious, masterful, militant, nervy*, pushing, pushy, sassy, shooting from the hip*, smart*, smart alecky*, strenuous, tough, vigorous, zealous; SEE CONCEPTS *404,542*

aggressor [*n*] *attacker*
assailant, initiator, instigator, intruder, invader, provoker, raider, trespasser; SEE CONCEPT *412*

aggrieved [*adj*] *very distressed*
afflicted, depressed, disturbed, grieving, harmed, hurt, injured, oppressed, pained, peeved, persecuted, saddened, unhappy, woeful, wronged; SEE CONCEPT *403*

aghast [*adj*] *horrified; very surprised*
afraid, agape, agog, alarmed, amazed, anxious, appalled, astonished, astounded, awestruck, confounded, dismayed, dumbfounded, frightened, horror-struck, overwhelmed, shocked, startled, stunned, terrified, thunderstruck; SEE CONCEPTS *403,690*

agile [*adj*] *physically or mentally nimble, deft*
active, acute, alert, athletic, brisk, buoyant, bustling, clever, dexterous, easy-moving, energetic, fleet, frisky, limber, lithe, lively, mercurial, prompt, quick, quick on the draw*, quick on the trigger*, quick-witted, rapid, ready, sharp, spirited, sportive, spright, sprightly, spry, stirring, supple, swift, twinkle toes*, vigorous, vivacious, winged, zippy; SEE CONCEPTS *485,527,588*

agility [*n*] *physical or mental nimbleness, deftness*
activity, acuteness, adroitness, alacrity, alertness, briskness, celerity, cleverness, dexterity, dispatch, expedition, fleetness, friskiness, litheness, liveliness, promptitude, promptness, quickness, quickwittedness, sharpness, sprightliness, spryness, suppleness, swiftness; SEE CONCEPTS *410,630,748*

aging [*n*] *becoming older*
crumbling, declining, developing, fading, fermenting, getting along*, getting on*, maturing, mellowing, senescent, slumping, stale, waning, wearing out*; SEE CONCEPT *701*

agitate [*v1*] *shake physically*
beat, churn, concuss, convulse, disturb, rock, rouse, stir, toss; SEE CONCEPT *152*

agitate [*v2*] *disturb, trouble someone*
alarm, argue, arouse, bug*, bug up*, burn up*, confuse, craze*, debate, discompose, disconcert, discuss, dispute, disquiet, distract, disturb, egg on*, examine, excite, ferment, flurry, fluster, get to*, incite, inflame, make flip*, move, perturb, psych*, push buttons*, rouse, ruffle, spook, stim-

ulate, stir, trouble, turn on*, unhinge*, upset, ventilate*, work up*, worry; SEE CONCEPTS *7,19,46*

agitation [*n*] *shaking, mixing*
churning, commotion, discomposure, disturbance, rocking, stirring, tizzy, tossing, turbulence, turmoil, unrest, upheaval; SEE CONCEPTS *158,170*

agitator [*n*] *person who disturbs, causes trouble*
adjy, advocate, agent, anarchist, champion, demagogue, disrupter, dissident, dogmatist, fighter, firebrand*, fomenter, heretic, incendiary, inciter, instigator, leftist, malcontent, mover, partisan, propagandist, provocateur, pusher, rabble-rouser, radical, reactionary, rebel, reformer, revisionist, revolutionary, ringleader, sparkplug*, troublemaker, wave maker*, zealot; SEE CONCEPT *412*

agnostic [*n*] *person unsure that God exists*
doubter, freethinker, materialist, skeptic, unbeliever; SEE CONCEPT *361*

ago [*adv*] *in the past*
ages ago, back, back when, before, from way back, from year one*, gone, since, since God knows when*, time was; SEE CONCEPT *820*

agog [*adj*] *enthralled*
anxious, avid, breathless, eager, enthusiastic, excited, expectant, impatient, in suspense, on tenterhooks; SEE CONCEPTS *401,542*

agonize [*v*] *suffer or cause another to suffer*
afflict, bleed, carry on, crucify, distress, disturb, eat heart out*, excruciate, harrow, hurt, labor, lament, martyr, pain, rack, sing the blues*, squirm, stew over, strain, strive, struggle, take it badly*, torment, torture, try, wince, worry, writhe; SEE CONCEPTS *7,19,410*

agonizing [*adj*] *difficult and painful, suffering*
disturbing, excruciating, extreme, fierce, harrowing, intense, racking, struggling, tearing, tormenting, tortuous, torturing, vehement, violent; SEE CONCEPTS *403,565*

agony [*n*] *suffering, pain*
affliction, anguish, distress, dolor, misery, pangs, passion, throes, torment, torture, woe; SEE CONCEPTS *410,728*

agrarian [*adj*] *concerning land, farming*
agricultural, natural, peasant, rural, rustic, uncultivated, undomesticated; SEE CONCEPT *536*

agree [*v1*] *be in unison, assent with another*
accede, acknowledge, acquiesce, admit, allow, be of the same mind*, bury the hatchet*, buy into*, check, clinch the deal*, come to terms, comply, concede, concur, consent, cut a deal*, engage, give blessing*, give carte blanche*, give green light*, give the go-ahead*, go along with, grant, make a deal*, okay, pass on, permit, play ball*, recognize, see eye to eye*, set, settle, shake on*, side with, sign*, subscribe, take one up on*, yes*; SEE CONCEPTS *8,10,45,235*

agree [*v2*] *be similar or consistent*
accord, answer, attune, be in harmony, blend, click, cohere, coincide, concert, concord, concur, conform, consort, correspond, equal, fall in with*, fit, get along with, go hand in hand*, go together, go well with, harmonize, jibe, match, parallel, square, suit, synchronize, tally; SEE CONCEPTS *118,656,670*

agreeable [*adj1*] *pleasing*
acceptable, dandy, delicious, delightful, enjoyable, fair, fine, gratifying, hunky-dory*, mild, nice, peach*, peachy*, pleasant, pleasurable,

pleasureful, pussycat*, ready, satisfying, spiffy*, swell*, to one's liking, to one's taste, welcome; SEE CONCEPT *572*

agreeable [*adj2*] *appropriate, in keeping* befitting, compatible, congruous, consistent, consonant, fitting, proper; SEE CONCEPT *558*

agreeable [*adj3*] *willing to be in unison, assent* acquiescent, amenable, approving, complying, concurring, congenial, consenting, favorable, grateful, in accord, responsive, sympathetic, well-disposed, willing; SEE CONCEPTS *401,542*

agreeably [*adv*] *willingly, assenting; pleasantly; in keeping* affably, affirmatively, amiably, amicably, appropriately, benevolently, charmingly, cheerfully, convivially, favorably, genially, good-humoredly, good-naturedly, graciously, happily, kindly, mutually, obligingly, peacefully, pleasingly, politely, satisfactorily, sympathetically, well, wonderfully; SEE CONCEPTS *401,572*

agreement [*n1*] *concurrence* acceding, accession, accommodation, accord, accordance, acknowledging, adjustment, affiliation, affinity, alliance, amity, approving, arbitration, arrangement, assenting, authorizing, bargaining, compatibility, compliance, complying, compromise, concert, concession, concord, concordance, concurring, conformity, congruity, consistency, correspondence, endorsing, granting, harmony, mediation, ratifying, reconciliation, similarity, suitableness, sympathy, understanding, union, unison, verification, verifying; SEE CONCEPT *684*

agreement [*n2*] *document of concurrence, contract* acknowledgment, adjudication, affidavit, approval, arrangement, assent, avowal, bargain, bond, cartel, charter, codicil, compact, compromise, confirmation, covenant, deal, indenture, lease, negotiation, note, oath, okay, pact, piece of paper*, protocol, recognition, settlement, stipulation, the nod*, transaction, treaty, understanding, writ; SEE CONCEPTS *271,331*

agricultural [*adj*] *concerning farming, land* aggie*, agronomical, arboricultural, floricultural, gardening, horticultural, ranch, rural, rustic; SEE CONCEPTS *536,583*

agriculture [*n*] *farming, crop production* agronomics, agronomy, cultivation, culture, horticulture, husbandry, tillage; SEE CONCEPTS *205,257*

aground [*adv*] *on the bottom of* ashore, beached, disabled, foundered, grounded, high and dry*, marooned, reefed, shipwrecked, stranded, stuck, swamped, wrecked; SEE CONCEPT *583*

ahead [*adv*] *in front or advance of* advanced, advancing, ahead, along, ante, antecedently, at an advantage, at the head, before, beforehand, earlier, first, fore, foremost, forward, forwards, in the foreground, in the lead, leading, on, onward, onwards, precedent, precedently, preceding, previous, progressing, to the fore; SEE CONCEPTS *586,632,820*

aid [*n1*] *help, support* advancement, advice, advocacy, alleviation, allowance, assist, assistance, attention, backing, backup, benefaction, benefit, benevolence, bounty, care, charity, comfort, compensation, cooperation, deliverance, encouragement, endowment, favor, furtherance, gift, giving, guidance, hand, handout, leg up*, lift, ministration, ministry, patronage, promotion, reinforcement, relief, rescue, reward, salvation, service, shot in the arm*, subsidy, sustenance, treatment; SEE CONCEPT *110*

aid [*v*] *help, support* abet, alleviate, assist, bail out, befriend, benefact, encourage, favor, go to bat for*, go with*, lend a hand*, lighten, mitigate, open doors for*, promote, relieve, serve, stick up for*, straighten out*, subsidize, sustain; SEE CONCEPT *110*

aid/aide [*n2*] *person who helps* abettor, adjutant, aide-de-camp, assistant, attendant, coadjutant, coadjutor, crew, deputy, helper, lieutenant, second, supporter; SEE CONCEPT *348*

AIDS [*n*] *immunological disorder* acquired immune deficiency syndrome, HIV, HIV-positive, sexually transmitted disease, STD, virus; SEE CONCEPT *306*

ail [*v*] *hurt* afflict, annoy, bother, distress, pain, sicken, trouble, upset; SEE CONCEPTS *14,246*

ailing [*adj*] *not feeling well* below par, debilitated, diseased, down, down with, enfeebled, feeble, feeling awful, ill, indisposed, rocky*, run down*, sick, sick as a dog*, sickly, under the weather*, unwell, wasting, weak; SEE CONCEPT *314*

ailment [*n*] *mild sickness* ache, bug, complaint, condition, disease, disorder, dose*, flu, illness, indisposition, infirmity, malady, syndrome; SEE CONCEPTS *306,316*

aim [*n*] *goal* ambition, aspiration, course, desideratum, design, desire, direction, end, intent, intention, mark, object, objective, plan, purpose, scheme, target, where one is heading*, wish; SEE CONCEPT *659*

aim [*v*] *point or direct at a goal* address, angle, aspire, attempt, cast, concentrate, contemplate, covet, design, direct, endeavor, essay, fix, focus, intend, level, mean, plan, propose, purpose, set one's sights on*, sight, slant, steer, strive, target, train, try, want, wish, zero in on, zoom in; SEE CONCEPTS *20,41,201*

aimless [*adj*] *having no goal* accidental, any which way*, bits-and-pieces*, blind, capricious, careless, casual, chance, desultory, directionless, drifting, erratic, fanciful, fickle, fits and starts*, flighty, fortuitous, frivolous, goalless, haphazard, heedless, hit-or-miss*, indecisive, indiscriminate, irresolute, objectless, pointless, purposeless, random, shiftless, stray, thoughtless, unavailing, undirected, unguided, unplanned, unpredictable, vagrant, wandering, wanton, wayward; SEE CONCEPTS *401,535,544*

air [*n1*] *gases forming the atmosphere* blast, breath, breeze, draft, heavens, ozone, puff, sky, stratosphere, troposphere, ventilation, waft, whiff, wind, zephyr; SEE CONCEPT *437*

air [*n2*] *distinctive quality or character; style* address, affectation, ambience, appearance, atmosphere, aura, bearing, comportment, demeanor, deportment, effect, feel, feeling, flavor, impression, look, manner, mannerism, mien, mood, pose, presence, property, quality, semblance, tone; SEE CONCEPTS *644,673*

air [*n3*] *musical tune* aria, descant, lay, melody, song, strain, theme;

SEE CONCEPTS *77,595*
air [*v1*] *put into the atmosphere; freshen*
aerate, aerify, air-condition, circulate, cool, eject, expel, expose, fan, open, oxygenate, purify, refresh, ventilate; SEE CONCEPT *255*
air [*v2*] *express opinion publicly*
broadcast, circulate, communicate, declare, disclose, display, disseminate, divulge, exhibit, expose, make known, make public, proclaim, publicize, publish, put, reveal, speak, state, tell, utter, ventilate, voice; SEE CONCEPTS *51,52*
aircraft [*n*] *airplane*
airliner, airship, balloon, blimp, chopper*, dirigible, flying machine, flying saucer, helicopter, jet, UFO, zeppelin; SEE CONCEPT *504*
airplane [*n*] *vehicle that transports cargo or passengers through the air*
aeroplane, airbus, aircraft, airliner, airship, cab*, crate*, jet, kite*, plane, ramjet*, ship*; SEE CONCEPT *504*
airport [*n*] *center for transportation by air*
aerodrome, airdrome, airfield, airstrip, hangar, helipad, heliport, home plate*, installation, landing strip, runway, strip; SEE CONCEPTS *325,439*
airs [*n*] *affectation; pretended behavior*
affectedness, arrogance, false front, front, haughtiness, hauteur, mannerism, ostentation, pomposity, pose, pretense, pretension, pretentiousness, put-on*, show, superciliousness; SEE CONCEPT *633*
airtight [*adj1*] *sealed*
closed, impenetrable, impermeable, shut; SEE CONCEPTS *483,490*
airtight [*adj2*] *certain*
incontestable, indisputable, invulnerable, irrefutable, unassailable; SEE CONCEPT *535*
airy [*adj1*] *open to the atmosphere*
aerial, atmospheric, blowy, breezy, drafty, exposed, fluttering, fresh, gaseous, gusty, light, lofty, out-of-doors, uncluttered, vaporous, ventilated, well-ventilated, windy; SEE CONCEPT *583*
airy [*adj2*] *delicate or ethereal*
dainty, diaphanous, flimsy, fragile, frail, frivolous, illusory, imaginary, immaterial, intangible, light, rare, rarefied, tenuous, thin, vaporous, visionary, volatile, weightless, wispy; SEE CONCEPTS *490,582*
airy [*adj3*] *buoyant, light, or lively in nature*
animated, blithe, bouncy, cheerful, cheery, effervescent, elastic, fanciful, flippant, frolicsome, gay, graceful, happy, high-spirited, jaunty, light, light-hearted, merry, nonchalant, resilient, sprightly, volatile, whimsical; SEE CONCEPTS *404,550*
aisle [*n*] *passageway dividing something*
alley, artery, avenue, clearing, corridor, course, egress, gangway, hallway, ingress, lane, opening, passage, path, walk, way; SEE CONCEPTS *440,513,830*
ajar [*adj/adv*] *slightly open*
open, unclosed, unlatched, unshut; SEE CONCEPT *586*
akin [*adj*] *related or connected*
affiliated, agnate, alike, allied, analogous, cognated, comparable, connate, consonant, corresponding, incident, kindred, like, parallel, similar; SEE CONCEPTS *487,563,573*
alacrity [*n*] *liveliness; promptness*
alertness, avidity, briskness, cheerfulness, dispatch, eagerness, enthusiasm, expedition, fervor,

gaiety, hilarity, joyousness, promptitude, quickness, readiness, speed, sprightliness, willingness, zeal; SEE CONCEPTS *633,657*
alarm [*n1*] *feeling of sudden fear*
anxiety, apprehension, cold feet*, consternation, dismay, distress, dread, fright, horror, nervousness, panic, scare, strain, stress, tension, terror, trepidation, unease, uneasiness; SEE CONCEPTS *410,690*
alarm [*n2*] *warning, signaling device*
alert, bell, blast, buzzer, call, caution, clock, cry, drum, flap*, flash*, forewarning, gong, high sign*, horn, Mayday*, nod*, scramble*, scream, shout, sign, signal, siren, SOS, squeal, tip, tip off*, tocsin, trumpet, warning, whistle, wink*, yell; SEE CONCEPTS *269,463*
alarm [*v*] *upset*
amaze, astonish, chill, daunt, dismay, distress, frighten, give a turn*, make jump*, panic, scare, scare silly*, scare stiff*, scare to death*, spook, startle, surprise, terrify, unnerve; SEE CONCEPTS *7,14,19,42*
alarmist [*n*] *person who spreads alarm*
Cassandra, Chicken Little*, pessimist, scaremonger, voice of doom*; SEE CONCEPTS *412,423*
albatross [*n*] *burden*
cross to bear, disgrace, load, millstone, misery, woe; SEE CONCEPTS *532,690*
album [*n*] *blank book for collecting; holder*
anthology, collection, depository, index, memento, memory book, miscellany, notebook, portfolio, register, registry, scrapbook; SEE CONCEPTS *271,446*
alchemy [*n*] *medieval science*
black arts, black magic, hermetics, magic, pseudo science, sorcery, thaumaturgy, witchcraft, wizardry; SEE CONCEPTS *367,370,689*
alcohol [*n*] *intoxicating, flammable liquid*
alky*, booze*, canned heat*, cocktail, drink, ethanol, firewater*, hard stuff*, hootch*, intoxicant, liquor, methanol, moonshine*, palliative*, red-eye*, rotgut*, sauce*, smoke*, spirits, tipple*, toddy*; SEE CONCEPTS *454,467*
alcoholic [*adj*] *intoxicating*
brewed, distilled, fermented, hard, inebriant, inebriating, sprituous, vinous; SEE CONCEPT *462*
alcoholic [*n*] *drunk*
bar fly*, boozer*, dipsomaniac, hard drinker, inebriate, lush*, problem drinker, sot, souse, substance abuser, tipper, wino; SEE CONCEPT *423*
alcoholism [*n*] *alcohol abuse*
addiction, alcohol addiction, alcohol dependence, crapulence, dipsomania, drunkenness, methomania, problem drinking, substance abuse, vinosity; SEE CONCEPTS *20,316,709*
alcove [*n*] *nook, secluded spot*
anteroom, bay, bower, compartment, corner, cubbyhole, cubicle, niche, recess, study; SEE CONCEPTS *440,448,513*
ale [*n*] *intoxicating, fermented beverage*
beer, brew, hops, malt, suds*; SEE CONCEPT *454*
alert [*adj*] *attentive, lively*
active, all ears*, bright, cagey*, careful, circumspect, clever, fast on the draw*, good hands*, heads up*, heedful, hip, intelligent, jazzed*, observant, on guard*, on one's toes*, on the ball*, on the job*, on the lookout*, on the qui vive*, perceptive, psyched up*, quick, ready, sharp, spirited, switched on*, vigilant, wary, watchful, wide-awake, wired*, wise, with it*; SEE CON-

CEPTS *402,403*
alert [*n*] *warning*
admonition, alarm, flap*, high sign*, Mayday*, sign, signal, siren, SOS, tip off, wink*; SEE CONCEPTS *78,278,595,628*
alert [*v*] *warn*
alarm, flag, forewarn, give the high sign*, inform, notify, put on guard, signal, tip, tip off, wave flag*; SEE CONCEPT *78*
algae [*n*] *rootless, leafless plants living in water*
dulse, kelp, scum, seaweed; SEE CONCEPT *429*
alias [*adv*] *otherwise known as*
also called, also known as, otherwise; SEE CONCEPT *582*
alias [*n*] *false name*
AKA, anonym, assumed name, handle*, moniker, nickname, nom de guerre, nom de plume, pen name, pseudonym, stage name, summer name*; SEE CONCEPT *683*
alibi [*n*] *defense against charges of wrongdoing; evidence of absence*
account, affirmation, airtight case*, allegation, answer, assertion, assurance, avowal, case, copout*, cover, declaration, excuse, explanation, fish story*, justification, plea, pretext, profession, proof, reason, reply, retort, song and dance*, stall, statement, vindication; SEE CONCEPT *661*
alien [*adj*] *foreign*
conflicting, contrary, estranged, exotic, extraneous, extrinsic, inappropriate, incompatible, incongruous, opposed, remote, separate, unusual; SEE CONCEPT *564*
alien [*n*] *foreign being*
blow in*, floater*, foreigner, greenhorn*, guest, immigrant, incomer*, interloper, intruder, invader, migrant, newcomer, noncitizen, outsider, refugee, settler, squatter, stranger, visitor, weed*; SEE CONCEPT *423*
alienate [*v*] *cause unfriendliness, hostility*
break off, come between, disaffect, disunite, divide, divorce, estrange, make indifferent, part, separate, set against, turn away, turn off, wean, withdraw the affections of; SEE CONCEPTS *7,19,231*
alienation [*n*] *unfriendliness*
breach, breaking off, coolness, disaffection, diverting, division, divorce, estrangement, indifference, remoteness, rupture, separation, setting against, turning away, variance, withdrawal; SEE CONCEPT *410*
alight [*v*] *land*
come down, debark, descend, disembark, dismount, get off, light, perch, settle, touch down; SEE CONCEPTS *159,181*
align [*v1*] *line up, arrange next to*
adjust, allineate, coordinate, even, even up, fix, make parallel, order, range, regulate, straighten; SEE CONCEPT *158*
align [*v2*] *join; bring to agreement*
affiliate, agree, ally, associate, cooperate, enlist, follow, join sides, sympathize; SEE CONCEPTS *8,114*
alignment [*n*] *lining up*
adjustment, arrangement, calibration, order, positioning, sequence, sighting; SEE CONCEPTS *721,727*
alike [*adj*] *similar*
akin, allied, analogous, approximate, associated,

carbon copy*, cognate, comparable, concurrent, correspondent, corresponding, dead ringer*, ditto*, double, duplicate, equal, equivalent, even, facsimile, identical, indistinguishable, kindred, like, look-alike, matched, matching, mated, parallel, proportionate, related, resembling, same, same difference*, similar, spitting image*, undifferentiated, uniform, Xerox*; SEE CONCEPTS *487,566,573*
alike [*adv*] *similarly*
analogously, comparably, comparatively, consonantly, correspondingly, equally, equivalently, evenly, identically, in accordance with, in common, in the same degree, in the same manner, likewise, similarly, the same way, uniformly; SEE CONCEPTS *487,566,573*
alimentary [*adj*] *digestive*
comestible, dietary, digestible, nourishing, nutrient, nutritional, nutritious, nutritive, peptic, salutary, sustaining, sustentative; SEE CONCEPTS *406,485*
alimony [*n*] *money paid in support of a former spouse*
keep, livelihood, living, maintenance, provision, remittance, subsistence, sustenance, upkeep; SEE CONCEPT *344*
alive [*adj1*] *being animately existent*
animate, around, awake, breathing, cognizant, conscious, dynamic, existing, extant, functioning, growing, knowing, live, living, mortal, operative, running, subsisting, viable, vital, working, zoetic; SEE CONCEPT *539*
alive [*adj2*] *being active, full of life*
abounding, alert, animated, awake, brisk, bustling, cheerful, dynamic, eager, energetic, lively, overflowing, quick, ready, replete, rife, sharp, spirited, sprightly, spry, stirring, swarming, teeming, vigorous, vital, vivacious, zestful; SEE CONCEPTS *401,542*
alkali [*n*] *soluble base; opposite of an acid*
antacid, caustic soda, salt; SEE CONCEPT *472*
alkaline [*adj*] *being basic, not acid (chemically)*
acrid, alkalescent, alkali, antacid, bitter, caustic, neutralizing, salty, soluble; SEE CONCEPT *472*
all [*adj1*] *whole quantity*
complete, entire, full, greatest, gross, outright, perfect, total, utter; SEE CONCEPT *771*
all [*adj2*] *each; every one of a class*
any, bar none*, barring no one, complete, each and every, entire, every, every bit of, every single, sum, total, totality, whole; SEE CONCEPT *772*
all [*adj3*] *exclusively*
alone, nothing but, only, solely; SEE CONCEPT *554*
all [*adv*] *completely, without exception*
all in all, altogether, entirely, exactly, fully, just, purely, quite, totally, utterly, wholly; SEE CONCEPTS *771,772*
all [*n*] *whole; totality*
accumulation, across the board, aggregate, aggregation, collection, ensemble, entirety, everyone, everything, gross, group, integer, jackpot*, lock stock and barrel*, mass, quantity, sum, sum total, total, unit, utmost, wall to wall*, whole ball of wax*, whole enchilada*, whole nine yards*, whole schmear*, whole shooting match*, whole show*, works; SEE CONCEPTS *787,837*
all-around [*adj*] *multifaceted*
comprehensive, diverse, inclusive, versatile; SEE

CONCEPTS *527,542*

allay [v] *reduce something, usually a pain or a problem*
abate, alleviate, assuage, calm, compose, cool out*, decrease, ease, lessen, lighten, make nice*, mitigate, moderate, mollify, pacify, play up to*, pour oil on*, quiet, square, take the bite out*, take the sting out*; SEE CONCEPTS *7,22,244*

allegation [n] *assertion placing blame*
accusation, affirmation, asseveration, avowal, charge, claim, declaration, deposition, overment, plea, profession, statement; SEE CONCEPT *49*

allege [v] *assert; claim*
adduce, advance, affirm, asservate, aver, avouch, avow, charge, cite, declare, depose, lay, maintain, offer, plead, present, profess, put forward, recite, recount, state, testify; SEE CONCEPT *49*

alleged [adj] *asserted, often doubtful*
averred, declared, described, dubious, ostensible, pretended, professed, purported, questionable, so-called, stated, supposed, suspect, suspicious; SEE CONCEPT *552*

allegiance [n] *loyalty*
adherence, ardor, consecration, constancy, dedication, deference, devotion, duty, faithfulness, fealty, fidelity, homage, honor, obedience, obligation, piety; SEE CONCEPT *689*

allegorical [adj] *symbolic*
emblematic, figurative, illustrative, metaphorical, parabolic, symbolizing, typifying; SEE CONCEPT *582*

allegory [n] *indirect representation, storytelling*
apologue, emblem, fable, figuration, moral, myth, parable, story, symbol, symbolism, symbolization, tale, typification; SEE CONCEPT *282*

allergen [n] *irritant*
antigen, dander, dust mite, foreign substance, immune trigger, irritant, pollen, ragweed; SEE CONCEPT *478*

allergic [adj] *having a reaction to food, material, etc.*
affected, averse to, dyspathetic, hypersensitive, immune sensitive, sensitive, sensitized, susceptible; SEE CONCEPTS *403,542*

allergy [n] *reaction to certain food, material, etc.*
allergic reaction, aversion, hay fever, hypersensitivity, sensitivity, susceptibility, vulnerability; SEE CONCEPTS *405,410*

alleviate [v] *relieve; lessen*
allay, assuage, ease, lighten, mitigate, mollify, pacify, pour oil on*, soft-pedal*, take the bite out*, take the edge off*, take the sting out*; SEE CONCEPTS *7,22,110,236,247*

alley [n] *narrow passage*
alleyway, back street, lane, passageway, path, pathway, walk; SEE CONCEPT *501*

alliance [n] *friendly association, agreement*
accord, affiliation, affinity, betrothal, bond, coalition, coherence, collaboration, collusion, combination, communion, compact, concord, concurrence, confederacy, confederation, congruity, conjunction, connection, consanguinity, cooperation, engagement, entente, federation, fraternization, friendship, interrelation, kinship, league, marriage, matrimony, membership, mutuality, pact, participation, partnership, relation, support, tie, treaty, union; SEE CONCEPTS *301,423,684*

allied [adj] *friendly; united*
affiliated, agnate, akin, amalgamated, associated, bound, cognate, combined, confederate, connate, connected, incident, in league, joined, joint, kindred, linked, married, related, unified, wed; SEE CONCEPTS *555,563*

allocate [v] *assign; divide among*
admeasure, allot, apportion, appropriate, budget, cut, designate, dish out*, divvy*, earmark, give, mete, set aside, share, slice; SEE CONCEPTS *41,98,108,129*

allocation [n] *distribution*
allotment, apportionment, appropriation, portion, quota, ration, share; SEE CONCEPT *835*

allot [v] *assign; give portion*
admeasure, allocate, appoint, apportion, appropriate, assign, budget, cut, cut the pie*, designate, distribute, divvy*, dole, earmark, mete, set aside, share, shell out*, slice, split up; SEE CONCEPTS *41,108*

allotment [n] *portion assigned or given*
allocation, allowance, apportionment, appropriation, bite, chunk, cut, cut of pie*, end, grant, lot, measure, part, piece, piece of the action*, quota, rake off*, ration, share, slice, split, stint*; SEE CONCEPT *835*

all-out [adj] *complete*
absolute, determined, entire, exhaustive, full, full-blown, full-fledged, full-scale, maximum, optimum, resolute, supreme, thorough, total, undivided, unlimited, utmost, utter; SEE CONCEPTS *531,772*

allow [v1] *admit; acknowledge*
acquiesce, avow, concede, confess, grant, let on, own; SEE CONCEPTS *60,82*

allow [v2] *permit an action*
accord, accredit, admit, approve, authorize, bear, be big*, be game for*, brook, certify, commission, consent, empower, endorse, endure, favor, free up*, give a blank check*, give carte blanche, give leave, give permission, give the go-ahead, give the green light*, go along with, grant permission, hear of, hold with, indulge, let, license, live with*, oblige, okay, pass, pass on, put up with, recognize, release, sanction, sit still for*, stand, suffer, support, take kindly to, tolerate, warrant; SEE CONCEPTS *83,99*

allow [v3] *set aside*
admeasure, allocate, allot, apportion, assign, deduct, give, grant, lot, mete, provide, remit, spare; SEE CONCEPTS *41,108*

allowance [n1] *amount of money or other supply*
aid, alimony, allocation, allotment, annuity, apportionment, bequest, bite*, bounty, commission, contribution, cut, endowment, fee, fellowship, gift, grant, honorarium, inheritance, interest, legacy, lot, measure, part, pay, pension, piece, portion, prize, quantity, quota, ration, recompense, remittance, salary, scholarship, share, slice, stint, stipend, subsidy, taste, wage; SEE CONCEPTS *337,340*

allowance [n2] *discount; concession*
accommodation, adaptation, adjustment, admission, advantage, cut, deduction, rebate, reduction, sanction, sufferance, toleration; SEE CONCEPT *775*

alloy [n] *mixture, usually of two metals*
admixture, adulterant, adulteration, amalgam, amalgamation, blend, combination, composite, compound, debasement, denaturant, fusion, hybrid, intermixture, reduction; SEE CONCEPTS

al
al

260,476
alloy [*v1*] *mix metals*
admix, amalgamate, blend, combine, compound, fuse, intermix, mix; SEE CONCEPTS *109,113*
alloy [*v2*] *adulterate*
debase, denature, devalue, diminish, impair, reduce; SEE CONCEPT *240*
all right [*adj1*] *satisfactory*
acceptable, adequate, appropriate, average, decent, fair, fit, fitting, good, hunky-dory*, okay, okey-dokey*, passable, proper, satisfying, standard, sufficient, swell*, tolerable, unexceptional, unobjectionable; SEE CONCEPTS *547,558*
all right [*adj2*] *in good condition or health*
hale, healthy, safe, sound, unharmed, unhurt, unimpaired, well, whole; SEE CONCEPT *572*
all right [*adj3*] *correct; excellent*
accurate, exact, good, great, precise, right; SEE CONCEPTS *557,574*
all right [*adv1*] *satisfactorily*
acceptably, adequately, okay, passably, tolerably, unobjectionably, well enough; SEE CONCEPTS *547,558*
all right [*adv2*] *yes*
agreed, certainly, definitely, of course, okay, positively, surely, very well, without a doubt; SEE CONCEPT *572*
all-time [*adj*] *unsurpassed and permanent*
best, champion, enduring, everlasting, perpetual; SEE CONCEPTS *574,798*
allude [*v*] *hint at*
advert, bring up, imply, insinuate, intimate, point, refer, suggest; SEE CONCEPTS *60,66*
allure [*n*] *appeal*
attraction, bedroom eyes*, charisma, charm, come-hither look*, come-on*, enchantment, enticement, glamor, inveiglement, lure, magnetism, seductiveness, temptation, the jazz*; SEE CONCEPTS *673,720*
allure [*v*] *entice*
attract, bait, beguile, bewitch, cajole, captivate, charm, coax, come on*, decoy, draw, enchant, entrap, fascinate, hook*, inveigle, lead on, lure, magnetize, persuade, pull, seduce, suck in*, sweep off feet*, tempt, turn on*, wile, win over; SEE CONCEPTS *7,22*
alluring [*adj*] *attractive*
beguiling, bewitching, captivating, charming, enticing, magnetic, seductive, tempting, winning; SEE CONCEPTS *529,579*
allusion [*n*] *indirect reference; hint*
casual remark, charge, citation, connotation, denotation, figure of speech, implication, imputation, incidental mention, indication, inference, innuendo, insinuation, intimation, mention, play on words, quotation, remark, statement, suggestion; SEE CONCEPTS *60,274*
ally [*n*] *something united with another, especially by treaty*
accessory, accomplice, associate, coadjutor, collaborator, colleague, confederate, co-worker, friend, helper, partner; SEE CONCEPTS *299,322,354,359*
alma mater [*n*] *school from which one has graduated*
academy, college, institution, old school, place of graduation, place of matriculation, university; SEE CONCEPTS *288,289*
almanac [*n*] *document containing information for a year*
annual, calendar, chronicle, ephemeris, journal, record, register, registry, yearbook; SEE CONCEPTS *280,801,809,823*
almighty [*adj1*] *having complete power, control*
absolute, all-powerful, invincible, mighty, omnipotent, puissant, supreme, unlimited; SEE CONCEPT *540*
almighty [*adj2*] *godlike*
all-knowing, all-seeing, boundless, celestial, deathless, deific, divine, enduring, eternal, everlasting, godly, heavenly, illimitable, immortal, infinite, omnipotent, omnipresent, omniscient, pervading; SEE CONCEPT *539*
almighty [*adj3*] *severe*
awful, desperate, enormous, excessive, extreme, great, intense, loud, terrible; SEE CONCEPT *569*
almost [*adv*] *nearly, very nearly*
about, about to, all but, approximately, around, as good as, bordering on, close to, close upon, essentially, for all practical purposes, for the greatest part, in effect, in the neighborhood of, in the vicinity of, just about, most, much, near to, nigh, not far from, not quite, on the brink of, on the edge of, on the point of, on the verge of, practically, pretty near, relatively, roughly, substantially, virtually, well-nigh, within sight of; SEE CONCEPTS *531,586,799*
alms [*n*] *handout*
aid, assistance, benefaction, charity, contribution, dole, donation, offering; SEE CONCEPTS *337,657*
alone [*adj1*] *separate; apart*
abandoned, batching it*, by itself/oneself, companionless, deserted, desolate, detached, forlorn, forsaken, friendless, hermit, individual, in solitary*, isolated, lone, lonely, lonesome, me and my shadow*, me myself and I*, onliest*, only, on one's own, shag*, single, sole, solitary, solo, stag, traveling light*, unaccompanied, unaided, unassisted, unattached, unattended, unescorted, unmarried, widowed; SEE CONCEPTS *577,583*
alone [*adj2*] *to the exclusion of; unique*
incomparable, matchless, peerless, singly, singular, solely, unequalled, unique, unmatched, unparalleled, unrivaled, unsurpassed; SEE CONCEPTS *556,653*
along [*adv1*] *ahead*
forth, forward, on, onward; SEE CONCEPT *581*
along [*adv2*] *together with*
accompanying, additionally, also, as companion, as well, at same time, besides, coupled with, furthermore, in addition to, likewise, moreover, side by side, simultaneously, too, with; SEE CONCEPT *577*
along [*adv3*] *near*
adjacent, at, by; SEE CONCEPT *586*
alongside [*prep*] *close, near side of*
along the side of, apace with, at the side of, beside, by, by the side of, close at hand, close by, equal with, in company with, next to, parallel to, side by side; SEE CONCEPT *586*
aloof [*adj*] *remote*
above, apart, casual, chilly, cold, cold fish*, cool, detached, distant, forbidding, hard-boiled*, hardhearted, haughty, incurious, indifferent, laid back*, loner*, lone wolf*, offish*, on ice*, putting on airs*, reserved, secluded, solitary, standoffish*, stuck up*, supercilious, thick-skinned*, unapproachable, unconcerned, un-

friendly, uninterested, unresponsive, unsociable, unsympathetic, uppity*, withdrawn; SEE CONCEPTS **401,542**

aloud [*adv*] *in a spoken voice, usually not softly*
audibly, clearly, distinctly, intelligibly, loudly, lustily, noisily, out loud, plainly, vociferously; SEE CONCEPT **594**

alphabet [*n*] *letters of a writing system*
ABCs, characters, elements, fundamentals, graphic representation, hieroglyphs, ideograph, morphemes, phonemes, pictograph, rune, signs, syllabary, symbols; SEE CONCEPT **276**

alphabetical [*adj*] *in ascending order of a writing system*
A to Z, consecutive, graded, indexed, logical, ordered, progressive; SEE CONCEPT **585**

alphabetize [*v*] *place in order of a writing system*
index, order, systematize; SEE CONCEPT **84**

alpine [*adj*] *mountaintop; high altitude*
aerial, elevated, high, high-reaching, in the clouds, lofty, montane, mountainous, rangy, snowcapped, soaring, towering; SEE CONCEPTS **779,836**

already [*adv*] *before expected time*
as of now, at present, before, before now, but now, by now, by that time, by then, by the time mentioned, by this time, earlier, even now, formerly, heretofore, in the past, just now, now, once, previously, then, up to now; SEE CONCEPT **799**

also [*adv*] *in addition to*
additionally, again, along, along with, and, as well, as well as, besides, conjointly, further, furthermore, including, in conjunction with, in like manner, likewise, more, moreover, more than that, on top of, over and above, plus, still, to boot*, together with, too, withal; SEE CONCEPT **577**

altar [*n*] *church table, pedestal*
chantry, font, reredos, retable, shrine, tabernacle; SEE CONCEPT **443**

alter [*v1*] *change*
adapt, adjust, amend, change, convert, cook, correct mid-course*, develop, dial back*, diversify, doctor, fine tune*, make different, metamorphose, modify, mutate, phony up*, recalibrate, recast, reconstruct, refashion, reform, remodel, renovate, reshape, revamp, revise, shift, transform, transmute, turn, vary; SEE CONCEPT **232**

alter [*v2*] *sterilize animal*
caponize, castrate, change, desexualize, emasculate, fix, geld, mutilate, neuter, spay, unsex; SEE CONCEPTS **310,375**

alteration [*n*] *change*
about-face, accommodation, adaptation, adjustment, amendment, conversion, correction, difference, diversification, exchange, fixing, flip-flop*, metamorphosis, mid-course correction*, modification, mutation, reformation, remodeling, reshaping, revision, shift, switch, switch-over*, transformation, transmutation, turn, variance, variation; SEE CONCEPT **701**

altercation [*n*] *fight, often verbal*
argument, beef*, bickering, blowup*, bone of contention*, brawl*, brush*, combat, contest, controversy, dispute, embroilment, flap*, fracas*, fuss, go*, hassle, quarrel, row, rumble*, run-in*, set-to*, squabbling, tiff*, words*, wrangle; SEE CONCEPTS **46,106**

altered [*adj*] *changed*

adapted, adjusted, amended, converted, cooked, corrected, diversified, doctored, fitted, fixed, modified, qualified, redone, refitted, reformed, remade, remodeled, renovated, reshaped, retailored, revised, spiked, transformed, turned, updated; SEE CONCEPT **564**

alter ego [*n1*] *other side to personality*
doppelganger, evil twin*, second self; SEE CONCEPTS **410,423**

alter ego [*n2*] *companion*
buddy, chum, confidante, counterpart, doppelganger*, pal, soul mate; SEE CONCEPT **423**

alternate [*adj1*] *every other*
alternating, every second, intermittent, periodic, recurrent, recurring, rotating; SEE CONCEPT **553**

alternate [*adj2*] *substitute*
alternative, another, backup, different, interchanging, makeshift, second, surrogate, temporary; SEE CONCEPT **566**

alternate [*n*] *substitute*
backup, double, equivalent, fill-in, proxy, replacement, stand-in, sub*, surrogate; SEE CONCEPT **667**

alternate [*v*] *take turns, change back and forth*
act reciprocally, alter, blow hot and cold*, change, come and go, exchange, fill in for, fluctuate, follow, follow in turn, interchange, intersperse, oscillate, relieve, rotate, seesaw, shift, shilly-shally*, substitute, sway, vacillate, vary, waver, yo-yo*; SEE CONCEPTS **13,104,232,701**

alternative [*adj*] *other, alternate*
another, back-up, different, flipside, other side, second, substitute, surrogate; SEE CONCEPT **564**

alternative [*n*] *possible choice*
back-up, druthers*, opportunity, option, other, other fish in sea*, other fish to fry*, pick, preference, recourse, redundancy, selection, sub*, substitute, take it or leave it*; SEE CONCEPT **529**

although [*conj*] *even though*
admitting, albeit, despite, despite the fact, even if, even supposing, granting, granting all this, in spite of, much as, notwithstanding, still, supposing, though, when, whereas, while; SEE CONCEPT **544**

altitude [*n*] *height in the sky*
apex, distance, elevation, eminence, loftiness, peak, summit; SEE CONCEPTS **739,752,791**

altogether [*adv1*] *as a whole*
all, all in all, all things considered, all told, bodily, by and large, collectively, conjointly, en masse, everything considered, everything included, for the most part, generally, in all, in sum, in toto, on the whole, taken together; SEE CONCEPT **771**

altogether [*adv2*] *completely*
absolutely, fully, perfectly, quite, thoroughly, totally, utterly, well, wholly; SEE CONCEPT **531**

altruism [*n*] *unselfish concern*
benevolence, charity, humanitarianism, kindness, magnanimity, philanthropy, public spirit, selflessness, social conscience; SEE CONCEPT **633**

altruistic [*adj*] *unselfish*
all heart*, benevolent, big*, big-hearted*, bleeding heart*, charitable, considerate, generous, good, good scout, human, humane, humanitarian, kind, magnanimous, openhanded, philanthropic, Robin Hood*, self-sacrificing; SEE CONCEPT **404**

alumnus/alumna [*n*] *graduate*

alum, old grad*, postgraduate; SEE CONCEPT *350*

always [*adv*] *forever; continually*
consistently, constantly, eternally, ever, everlastingly, evermore, forevermore, for keeps, in perpetuum, invariably, perpetually, regularly, repeatedly, till blue in the face*, till cows come home*, till hell freezes over*, unceasingly, without exception; SEE CONCEPTS *551,798*

amalgam [*n*] *mixture*
admixture, alloy, amalgamation, blend, combination, combo*, composite, compound, fusion, mishmash*, soup; SEE CONCEPT *432*

amalgamate [*v*] *blend*
admix, alloy, ally, coalesce, combine, come together, compound, consolidate, fuse, hook up with*, incorporate, integrate, interface, intermix, join together, meld, merge, mingle, network, pool, team up*, tie in, tie up*, unite; SEE CONCEPT *113*

amass [*v*] *gather, accumulate*
aggregate, assemble, clean up*, collect, compile, corral*, garner, heap*, hoard, lay up*, make a killing*, make a pile*, pile, round up*, scare up*, stockpile, store; SEE CONCEPTS *109,120*

amateur [*n*] *casual participant*
abecedarian, apprentice, aspirant, beginner, bush leaguer*, dabbler, dilettante, greenhorn, ham*, hopeful, layperson, learner, neophyte, nonprofessional, novice, probationer, putterer, recruit, Sunday driver*, tenderfoot*, tyro; SEE CONCEPT *366*

amateurish [*adj*] *unprofessional*
bush-league*, incompetent, inept, inexperienced, inexpert, insipid, unskilled, untrained; SEE CONCEPTS *527,538*

amatory [*adj*] *affectionate, desirous*
admiring, amorous, aphrodisiac, ardent, attracted, devoted, doting, erotic, fervent, fond, languishing, lovesick, loving, passionate, rapturous, romantic, sentimental, tender, wooing, yearning; SEE CONCEPTS *372,403*

amaze [*v*] *surprise*
affect, alarm, astonish, astound, bewilder, blow away*, blow one's mind*, bowl over*, daze, dumbfound, electrify, flabbergast*, impress, move, perplex, put one away*, shock, stagger, startle, strike, stun, stupefy, touch*; SEE CONCEPT *42*

amazement [*n*] *state of surprise*
admiration, astonishment, awe, bewilderment, confoundment, confusion, marvel, one for the books*, perplexity, shock, something else*, stopper*, stunner*, stupefaction, wonder, wonderment; SEE CONCEPTS *230,410*

amazing [*adj*] *astonishing*
awesome, fascinating, incredible, marvelous, prodigious, shocking, stunning, surprising, unbelievable, wonderful; SEE CONCEPTS *547,572*

ambassador [*n*] *representative to a foreign country*
agent, consul, deputy, diplomat, emissary, envoy, minister, plenipotentiary; SEE CONCEPT *354*

amber [*n/adj*] *gold-colored*
brown, golden, tan, yellowish; SEE CONCEPT *618*

ambience [*n*] *environment*
ambient, atmosphere, climate, medium, surroundings; SEE CONCEPT *673*

ambiguity [*n*] *uncertainty of meaning*
double-entendre, double meaning, doubt, doubtfulness, dubiety, dubiousness, enigma, equivocacy, equivocality, equivocation, incertitude, inconclusiveness, indefiniteness, indeterminateness, obscurity, puzzle, tergiversation, uncertainty, unclearness, vagueness; SEE CONCEPTS *638,682*

ambiguous [*adj*] *having more than one meaning*
clear as dishwater*, cryptic, doubtful, dubious, enigmatic, enigmatical, equivocal, inconclusive, indefinite, indeterminate, inexplicit, muddy, obscure, opaque, puzzling, questionable, tenebrous, uncertain, unclear, unintelligible, vague; SEE CONCEPTS *267,535*

ambition [*n1*] *strong desire for success*
appetite, ardor, aspiration, avidity, craving, desire, drive, eagerness, earnestness, emulation, energy, enterprise, enthusiasm, fire in belly*, get up and go*, hankering*, hope, hunger, initiative, itch*, keenness, longing, love, lust, moxie*, passion, pretension, push, right stuff*, spirit, striving, thirst, vigor, yearning, zeal; SEE CONCEPT *20*

ambition [*n2*] *something desired*
aim, aspiration, desire, dream, end, enterprise, goal, hope, intent, mark, objective, purpose, target, wish; SEE CONCEPT *659*

ambitious [*adj1*] *desiring success*
aggressive, anxious, ardent, aspiring, avid, ball of fire*, bent upon, climbing, come on, come on strong, designing, desirous, determined, driving, eager, eager beaver*, earnest, energetic, enterprising, enthusiastic, fireball*, get up and go*, goal-oriented, go-getter*, hard ball*, high-reaching, hopeful, hungry, industrious, inspired, intent, longing, power-loving, purposeful, pushing, pushy*, resourceful, self-starting, sharp, soaring, striving, thirsty, vaulting, zealous; SEE CONCEPTS *326,542*

ambitious [*adj2*] *requiring great effort, ability*
arduous, bold, challenging, demanding, difficult, elaborate, energetic, exacting, formidable, grandiose, hard, impressive, industrious, lofty, pretentious, severe, strenuous, visionary; SEE CONCEPT *538*

ambivalent [*adj*] *conflicting*
clashing, contradictory, debatable, doubtful, equivocal, fluctuating, hesitant, inconclusive, irresolute, mixed, opposed, uncertain, undecided, unresolved, unsure, vacillating, warring, wavering; SEE CONCEPTS *534,564*

amble [*v*] *walk casually*
ankle*, boogie*, dawdle, drift, gander*, hoof it*, loiter, meander, mosey*, percolate*, ramble, sashay*, saunter, stroll, toddle*, wander; SEE CONCEPT *151*

ambulance [*n*] *emergency vehicle*
EMS, hospital wagon, rescue, transport; SEE CONCEPT *505*

ambulatory [*adj*] *changing position; able to move under own power*
ambulant, itinerant, nomadic, perambulant, perambulatory, peripatetic, roving, vagabond, vagrant; SEE CONCEPT *584*

ambush [*n*] *lying in wait; concealed position*
ambuscade, ambushment, camouflage, concealment, deception, hiding, hiding place, lurking, pitfall, shelter, trap, trick*, waiting, waylaying; SEE CONCEPTS *86,188*

ambush [*v*] *lie in wait; attack*
ambuscade, assail, assault, box in*, bushwhack*, decoy, dry gulch*, ensnare, entrap, hem in*,

hide, hook*, jap*, jump, lay for, lurk, net, set trap, surprise, surround, trap, wait, waylay; SEE CONCEPTS *86,188*

ameliorate [*v*] *make, become better*
alleviate, amend, help, improve, lighten, meliorate, mitigate, relieve, step up, upgrade; SEE CONCEPT *244*

amenable [*adj1*] *willing, cooperative*
acquiescent, agreeable, biddable, docile, influenceable, manageable, obedient, open, persuadable, pliable, responsive, susceptible, tractable; SEE CONCEPT *404*

amenable [*adj2*] *able to be judged; responsible*
accountable, answerable, chargeable, liable, subject; SEE CONCEPT *402*

amend [*v*] *improve, correct*
alter, ameliorate, better, change, elevate, enhance, fix, help, lift, make up for, mend, modify, pay one's dues*, raise, rectify, reform, remedy, repair, revise, right, square*; SEE CONCEPTS *126,244*

amendment [*n1*] *correction, improvement*
alteration, amelioration, betterment, change, correction, enhancement, improvement, mending, modification, rectification, reform, reformation, remedy, repair, revision; SEE CONCEPT *700*

amendment [*n2*] *addition to a document*
act, addendum, adjunct, alteration, attachment, bill, clarification, clause, codicil, measure, modification, motion, revision, rider, suggestion, supplement; SEE CONCEPT *270*

amends [*n*] *compensation*
apology, atonement, expiation, indemnification, indemnity, quittance, recompense, redress, reparation, reprisal, requital, restitution, restoration, satisfaction; SEE CONCEPTS *67,104,384*

amenity [*n1*] *pleasant thing*
advantage, betterment, comfort, convenience, enhancement, enrichment, excellence, extravagance, facility, frill, improvement, luxury, merit, quality, service, superfluity, virtue; SEE CONCEPT *712*

amenity [*n2*] *pleasing, agreeable behavior*
affability, agreeableness, amiability, attention, attractiveness, charity, charm, complaisance, cordiality, courtesy, delightfulness, enjoyableness, etiquette, gallantry, geniality, gentility, gratefulness, kindness, mildness, pleasantness, politeness, refinement, suavity, sweetness; SEE CONCEPT *633*

amiable [*adj*] *friendly, agreeable*
affable, amicable, attractive, benign, breezy, buddy-buddy*, charming, cheerful, clubby*, complaisant, cool*, copacetic*, cordial, cozy, delightful, downright neighborly*, easy, engaging, friendly, genial, good-humored, good-natured, gracious, home cooking*, kind, kindly, lenient, lovable, mellow, mild, obliging, palsy-walsy*, pleasant, pleasing, princely*, pussycat*, responsive, right, righteous, sociable, sweet-tempered, swell*, tight*, warm, warmhearted, winning; SEE CONCEPT *401*

amicable [*adj*] *friendly, especially regarding an agreement*
accordant, agreeing, amiable, civil, clubby*, concordant, cordial, courteous, cozy, empathic, good-humored, harmonious, kind, kindly, likeminded, mellow, neighborly, pacific, peaceable, peaceful, polite, regular, right nice*, sociable, square shooting*, sympathetic, understanding;

SEE CONCEPTS *529,542*

amid/amidst [*prep*] *in middle of; among*
amongst, between, during, in the midst of, in the thick of, mid, over, surrounded by, throughout; SEE CONCEPTS *586,820*

amiss [*adj*] *wrong; defective*
awry, bad, confused, crooked, erring, erroneous, fallacious, false, faulty, flawed, foul, glitched up*, haywire, imperfect, improper, inaccurate, inappropriate, incorrect, mistaken, out of order, sick, unfair, unlawful, unsuitable, untoward; SEE CONCEPT *570*

amiss [*adv*] *wrongly; defectively*
afield, afoul, badly, erringly, erroneously, faultily, improperly, inappropriately, incorrectly, mistakenly, out of turn, unfavorably, unsuitably; SEE CONCEPT *570*

amity [*n*] *friendship*
amicableness, benevolence, comity, concord, cordiality, friendliness, good vibrations*, goodwill, harmony, hitting it off*, kindliness, neighborliness, same wavelength*, simpatico*, togetherness*; SEE CONCEPT *388*

ammonia [*n*] *pungent gas, liquid*
alkali, salts, spirits, vapor; SEE CONCEPT *472*

ammunition [*n*] *projectiles for weaponry*
ammo*, armament, ball, bomb, buckshot, bullet, cannonball, cartridge, charge, chemical, confetti*, explosive, fuse, grenade, gunpowder, iron rations*, materiel, missile, munition, napalm, powder, rocket, round, shell, shot, shrapnel, torpedo; SEE CONCEPTS *498,500*

amnesty [*n*] *pardon, often by government*
absolution, condonation, dispensation, forgiveness, immunity, reprieve; SEE CONCEPTS *298,300*

among [*prep1*] *in the middle of; between*
amid, amidst, betwixt, encompassed by, in dispersion through, in the midst of, in the thick of, mid, surrounded by, with; SEE CONCEPT *586*

among [*prep2*] *in a group*
by all of, by the whole of, in association with, in connection with, in the class of, in the company of, mutually, out of, together with, with, with one another; SEE CONCEPT *785*

amorous [*adj*] *loving, affectionate*
amative, amatory, aphrodisiac, ardent, attached, boy crazy*, doting, enamored, erotic, fond, girl crazy*, have a crush on*, horny*, hot, hot and heavy*, impassioned, infatuated, in love, lovesick, lovey dovey*, lustful, passionate, romantic, sexy, sweet for*, sweet on*, tender, turned on*; SEE CONCEPTS *372,403,555*

amorphous [*adj*] *without definite shape, character*
baggy, blobby, characterless, formless, inchoate, indeterminate, irregular, nebulous, nondescript, shapeless, unformed, unshaped, unstructured, vague; SEE CONCEPTS *404,490*

amount [*n1*] *quantity*
aplenty, bags*, bulk, bundle, chunk, expanse, extent, flock, gob*, heap, hunk, jillion*, load, lot, magnitude, mass, measure, mess*, mint*, mucho*, number, oodles*, pack, passle, peck, pile, scads*, score, slat*, slew*, supply, ton*, volume, whopper*; SEE CONCEPTS *787,837*

amount [*n2*] *total*
addition, aggregate, all, bad news*, body, budget, cost, damage*, entirety, expense, extent, list, lot, net, outlay, output, price tag*, product, quantum, score, set-back*, sum, tab*, tidy sum*,

al
am

whole; SEE CONCEPTS *329,784,787*

amount [*n3*] *whole effect*
body, burden, core, full value, import, matter, purport, result, sense, significance, substance, thrust, upshot, value; SEE CONCEPT *676*

amount [*v*] *equal, add up to*
aggregate, approach, approximate, become, be equivalent to, be tantamount to, check with, come to, correspond, develop into, effect, extend, grow, match, mean, number, purport, reach, rival, sum, tally, total, touch; SEE CONCEPT *667*

amour [*n*] *romance*
affair, entanglement, liaison, love, love affair, passion, relationship; SEE CONCEPT *32*

amphetamine [*n*] *hard drug*
analeptic, benny*, crank*, crystal, dexy*, pep pill*, speed*, stimulant, STP*, tab*, upper*; SEE CONCEPT *307*

ample [*adj*] *more than necessary, sufficient*
abounding, abundant, big, bounteous, bountiful, broad, capacious, commodious, copious, enough, expansive, extensive, full, galore, generous, great, heavy, large, lavish, liberal, no end, plenteous, plentiful, plenty, profuse, rich, roomy, spacious, spare, substantial, unrestricted, voluminous, wide; SEE CONCEPTS *558,781*

amplification [*n*] *increase in size or effect*
addition, augmentation, boost, boosting, buildup, deepening, development, elaboration, enlargement, exaggeration, expansion, expatiation, extension, fleshing out, heightening, intensification, lengthening, magnification, padding, raising, strengthening, stretching, supplementing, upping, widening; SEE CONCEPTS *236,245,780*

amplify [*v*] *increase in size or effect*
add, augment, beef up*, boost, build up, deepen, develop, elaborate, enlarge, exaggerate, expand, expatiate, extend, flesh out*, heighten, hike up*, inflate, intensify, jack up*, lengthen, magnify, pad, pyramid, raise, soup up*, strengthen, stretch, supplement, swell, up, widen; SEE CONCEPTS *236,245*

amply [*adv*] *fully, sufficiently*
abundantly, acceptably, adequately, appropriately, bountifully, capaciously, completely, copiously, enough, extensively, fittingly, generously, greatly, lavishly, liberally, plenteously, plentifully, profusely, properly, richly, rightly, satisfactorily, substantially, suitably, thoroughly, well; SEE CONCEPTS *558,771*

amputate [*v*] *remove a limb*
cut away, cut off, dismember, eliminate, excise, lop, separate, sever, truncate; SEE CONCEPTS *176,211*

amuck [*adv*] *crazily*
berserk, destructively, ferociously, frenziedly, in a frenzy, insanely, madly, maniacally, murderously, savagely, uncontrollably, violently, wildly; SEE CONCEPT *401*

amulet [*n*] *charm*
fetish, lucky piece, ornament, talisman; SEE CONCEPTS *260,446*

amuse [*v*] *entertain; make laugh*
break one up*, charm, cheer, crack up*, delight, divert, fracture*, gladden, grab*, gratify, interest, kill*, knock dead*, make roll in the aisles*, occupy, panic*, please, put away*, regale, slay*, tickle, wow*; SEE CONCEPTS *9,292,384*

amusement [*n1*] *entertaining, making someone laugh*
action, ball*, beguilement, cheer, delight, diversion, enjoyment, entertainment, field day*, fun, fun and games*, gladdening, gratification, grins*, high time*, hilarity, hoopla*, laughs*, laughter, merriment, merry go round*, mirth, picnic*, play, pleasing, pleasure, regalement, whoopee*; SEE CONCEPT *292*

amusement [*n2*] *game, pastime*
distraction, diversion, entertainment, hobby, interest, joke, lark, play, prank, recreation, sport; SEE CONCEPT *364*

amusing [*adj*] *entertaining, funny*
agreeable, boffo*, camp, campy, charming, cheerful, cheering, comical, cut up*, delightful, diverting, droll, enchanting, engaging, enjoyable, entertaining, for grins*, fun, gladdening, gratifying, gut-busting*, humorous, interesting, jocular, jokey*, joshing*, laughable, lively, merry, pleasant, pleasing, priceless, screaming*, sidesplitting*, too funny for words*, witty; SEE CONCEPTS *267,548*

anachronism [*n*] *error in time placement*
chronological error, metachronism, misdate, misplacement, postdate, prolepsis, solecism; SEE CONCEPT *818*

analgesic [*n*] *pain remover*
anesthetic, anodyne, painkiller, soother; SEE CONCEPT *307*

analogous [*adj*] *agreeing, similar*
akin, alike, comparable, consonant, convertible, correspondent, corresponding, equivalent, homologous, interchangeable, kindred, like, parallel, related, resembling, undifferentiated, uniform; SEE CONCEPTS *487,573*

analogy [*n*] *agreement, similarity*
affinity, alikeness, comparison, correlation, correspondence, equivalence, homology, likeness, metaphor, parallel, relation, relationship, resemblance, semblance, simile, similitude; SEE CONCEPTS *278,670*

analysis [*n1*] *examination and determination*
assay, breakdown, dissection, dissolution, division, inquiry, investigation, partition, reasoning, resolution, scrutiny, search, separation, study, subdivision, test; SEE CONCEPTS *24,103*

analysis [*n2*] *statement of results from examination*
estimation, evaluation, finding, interpretation, judgment, opinion, outline, reasoning, report, study, summary; SEE CONCEPTS *271,274*

analyst [*n*] *person who examines and determines; psychoanalyst*
accountant, couch doctor*, examiner, guru*, head shrinker*, inquisitor, investigator, number cruncher*, psychiatrist, psychotherapist, questioner, shrink*, therapist; SEE CONCEPTS *348,357*

analytic/analytical [*adj*] *examining and determining*
cogent, conclusive, detailed, diagnostic, discrete, dissecting, explanatory, expository, inquiring, inquisitive, interpretive, investigative, judicious, logical, organized, penetrating, perceptive, perspicuous, precise, problem-solving, questioning, ratiocinative, rational, reasonable, scientific, searching, solid, sound, studious, subtle, systematic, testing, thorough, valid, well-grounded; SEE

CONCEPT *402*
analyze [*v1*] *examine and determine*
assay, beat a dead horse*, chew over*, confab*, consider, estimate, evaluate, figure, figure out, get down to brass tacks*, hash*, inspect, interpret, investigate, judge, kick around*, rehash, resolve, scrutinize, sort out, spell out, study, talk game*, test, think through; SEE CONCEPTS *24,37,103*

analyze [*v2*] *break down to components*
anatomize, break up, cut up, decompose, decompound, determine, disintegrate, dissect, dissolve, divide, electrolyze, hydrolyze, lay bare, parse, part, resolve, separate, x-ray; SEE CONCEPTS *135,310*

anarchist [*n*] *person who opposes the idea of government and laws*
agitator, insurgent, insurrectionist, malcontent, mutineer, nihilist, rebel, revolter, revolutionary, terrorist; SEE CONCEPTS *359,412*

anarchy [*n*] *lawlessness; absence of government*
chaos, confusion, disorder, disorganization, disregard, hostility, misrule, mob rule, nihilism, nongovernment, rebellion, reign of terror, revolution, riot, turmoil, unrest; SEE CONCEPTS *29,674*

anathema [*n1*] *something hated*
abomination, bane, bugbear, detestation, enemy, hate, pariah; SEE CONCEPT *529*

anathema [*n2*] *denouncement*
ban, censure, commination, condemnation, curse, damnation, denunciation, excommunication, execration, imprecation, malediction, proscription, reprehension, reprobation, reproof, taboo; SEE CONCEPT *278*

anatomy [*n1*] *study of animal, plant structure*
analysis, biology, cytology, diagnosis, dissection, division, embryology, etiology, examination, genetics, histology, inquiry, investigation, medicine, morphology, physiology, zoology; SEE CONCEPT *349*

anatomy [*n2*] *physical structure of animals, plants*
build, composition, figure, form, frame, framework, makeup, physique, shape; SEE CONCEPT *733*

ancestor [*n*] *predecessor in family*
antecedent, antecessor, ascendant, forebear, forefather, foregoer, foremother, forerunner, founder, precursor, primogenitor, progenitor; SEE CONCEPT *414*

ancestral [*adj*] *related to previous family or family trait*
affiliated, born with, congenital, consanguine, consanguineous, familial, genealogical, inborn, inbred, inherited, innate, in the family, lineal, maternal, old, past, paternal, running in the family, totemic, tribal; SEE CONCEPT *549*

ancestry [*n*] *family predecessors; family history*
ancestor, antecedent, antecessor, blood, breed, breeding, derivation, descent, extraction, forebear, forefather, foregoer, foremother, forerunner, genealogy, heritage, house, kindred, line, lineage, origin, parentage, pedigree, precursor, primogenitor, progenitor, race, source, stock; SEE CONCEPTS *414,648*

anchor [*n*] *something used to hold another thing securely*
ballast, bower, comfort, defense, fastener, foothold, grapnel, grappling iron, grip, hold, hook, kedge, mainstay, mooring, mud hook, pillar, protection, safeguard, security, staff, stay, support; SEE CONCEPTS *464,502,731*

anchor [*v*] *hold, be held securely*
attach, berth, catch, dock, drop, fasten, fix, imbed, make port, moor, plant, secure, stay, tie, tie up; SEE CONCEPTS *85,160,190*

ancient [*adj*] *old, often very old*
aged, age-old, antediluvian, antiquated, antique, archaic, back number*, been around*, bygone, creaky*, early, elderly, few miles on*, fossil*, hoary, lot of mileage*, moth-eaten*, obsolete, older, old-fashioned, old goat*, oldie*, outmoded, out-of-date, primal, primeval, primordial, relic, remote, rusty, superannuated, timeworn, venerable, worse for wear*; SEE CONCEPTS *578,797*

ancillary [*adj*] *extra; supplementary*
accessory, accompanying, additional, adjuvant, appurtenant, attendant, attending, coincident, collateral, concomitant, contributory, incident, satellite, secondary, subordinate, subservient, subsidary; SEE CONCEPT *835*

and [*conj*] *in addition to; plus*
along with, also, as a consequence, as well as, furthermore, including, moreover, together with; SEE CONCEPT *577*

androgynous [*adj*] *having male and female traits*
bisexual, cross-sexual, epicene, hermaphrodite, trans-sexual, unisexual; SEE CONCEPT *372*

anecdote [*n*] *interesting or amusing story*
chestnut*, episode, fairy tale*, fish story*, gag*, incident, long and short of it*, narration, narrative, old chestnut*, recital, relation, reminiscence, short story, sketch, tale, tall story*, tall tale*, yarn; SEE CONCEPT *282*

anemic [*adj*] *weak and pale*
bloodless, feeble, frail, infirm, pallid, sickly, wan, watery; SEE CONCEPTS *314,483,618*

anesthesia/anaesthesia [*n*] *induced sleep; induced absence of feeling*
analgesia, insentience, numbness, stupor, unconsciousness; SEE CONCEPTS *313,315,728*

anesthetic/anaesthetic [*n*] *sleep-inducing or numbing drug*
analgesic, anodyne, dope*, gas, hypnotic, inhalant, narcotic, opiate, pain-killer, shot, soporific, spinal; SEE CONCEPT *307*

anew [*adj/adv*] *fresh; again*
afresh, another time, come again, de novo, from scratch, from the beginning, in a different way, in a new way, lately, new, newly, once again, once more, one more time, over, over again, recently; SEE CONCEPT *820*

angel [*n1*] *attendant of God*
archangel, celestial being, cherub, divine messenger, God's messenger, guardian, heavenly being, holy being, seraph, spirit, spiritual being, sprite, supernatural being; SEE CONCEPTS *361,370*

angel [*n2*] *sweet, kind person*
beauty, darling, dear, dream, gem, ideal, jewel, paragon, saint, treasure; SEE CONCEPT *416*

angel dust [*n*] *phencyclidine, PCP*
angel hair*, angel mist*, aurora borealis*, black whack*, crystal*, cyclones*, devil dust*, dummy dust*, embalming fluid*, hallucinogen, horse tranquilizer*, jet fuel*, magic dust*, rocket fuel*, star dust*; SEE CONCEPT *307*

angelic [*adj*] *sweet, kind, and usually beautiful*

am
an

adorable, archangelic, beatific, beneficent, celestial, cherubic, devout, divine, entrancing, ethereal, godly, good, heavenly, holy, humble, innocent, lovely, otherworldly, pure, radiant, rapturous, righteous, saintly, self-sacrificing, seraphic, virtuous; SEE CONCEPT *572*

anger [*n*] *state of being mad, annoyed*
acrimony, animosity, annoyance, antagonism, blow up*, cat fit*, chagrin, choler, conniption, dander*, disapprobation, displeasure, distemper, enmity, exasperation, fury, gall, hatred, hissy fit*, huff, ill humor, ill temper, impatience, indignation, infuriation, irascibility, ire, irritability, irritation, mad, miff, outrage, passion, peevishness, petulance, pique, rage, rankling, resentment, slow burn*, soreness, stew, storm, tantrum, temper, tiff, umbrage, vexation, violence; SEE CONCEPTS *29,410*

anger [*v*] *make someone mad; become mad*
acerbate, affront, aggravate, agitate, annoy, antagonize, arouse, bait, blow up*, boil*, boil over*, bristle, burn, burn up, chafe, craze*, cross, displease, egg on*, embitter, enrage, exacerbate, exasperate, excite, fret, gall, get mad, get on one's nerves*, goad, incense, inflame, infuriate, irritate, lose one's temper, madden, make sore*, miff, nettle, offend, outrage, pique, provoke, raise hell*, rankle, rant, rave, rile, ruffle, seethe, steam up*, stew, stir up*, tempt, umbrage, vex; SEE CONCEPTS *7,19*

angle [*n1*] *shape formed by two lines meeting at a point*
bend, corner, crook, crotch, cusp, decline, divergence, dogleg, edge, elbow, flare, flection, flexure, fork, incline, intersection, knee, nook, notch, obliquity, point, slant, turn, turning, twist, V, Y; SEE CONCEPT *436*

angle [*n2*] *personal approach, purpose*
aim, approach, aspect, direction, hand, intention, outlook, perspective, plan, point of view, position, side, slant, standpoint, viewpoint; SEE CONCEPTS *660,661*

angle [*v*] *fish*
cast, dangle a line*, drop a line*; SEE CONCEPT *363*

angle for [*v*] *attempt to get*
aim for, be after, cast about for, connive, conspire, contrive, fish for, hint, hunt, invite, look for, maneuver, plan, plot, scheme, seek, solicit, strive, try for; SEE CONCEPTS *20,87*

angry [*adj*] *being mad, often extremely mad*
affronted, annoyed, antagonized, bitter, chafed, choleric, convulsed, cross, displeased, enraged, exacerbated, exasperated, ferocious, fierce, fiery, fuming, furious, galled, hateful, heated, hot, huffy, ill-tempered, impassioned, incensed, indignant, inflamed, infuriated, irascible, irate, ireful, irritable, irritated, maddened, nettled, offended, outraged, piqued, provoked, raging, resentful, riled, sore, splenetic, storming, sulky, sullen, tumultous/tumultuous, turbulent, uptight, vexed, wrathful; SEE CONCEPT *403*

angst [*n*] *feeling of anxiety*
agony, apprehension, blues, depression, dread, mid-life crisis*, misgiving, nervousness, uneasiness, Weltschmerz; SEE CONCEPTS *410,532,690*

anguish [*n*] *severe upset or pain*
affliction, agony, distress, dole, dolor, grief, heartache, heartbreak, hurting, misery, pang, rue, sorrow, suffering, throe, torment, torture, woe,

wretchedness; SEE CONCEPT *410*

angular [*adj1*] *bent*
akimbo, bifurcate, cornered, crooked, crossing, crotched, divaricate, forked, intersecting, jagged, oblique, sharp-cornered, skewed, slanted, staggered, V-shaped, Y-shaped, zigzag; SEE CONCEPT *486*

angular [*adj2*] *thin, especially referring to people*
awkward, bony, gangling, gaunt, lank, lanky, lean, rangy, rawboned, scrawny, sharp, skinny, spare; SEE CONCEPT *773*

animal [*adj*] *beastlike; carnal*
beastly, bestial, bodily, brute, brutish, corporeal, earthly, earthy, feral, fleshy, mammalian, muscular, natural, physical, sensual, untamed, wild, zoological; SEE CONCEPT *406*

animal [*n*] *animate being; mammal*
beast, being, brute, bum*, creature, critter, invertebrate, living thing, mutt*, pet, stray, varmint*, vertebrate, wild thing; SEE CONCEPT *394*

animate [*adj1*] *alive*
breathing, live, living, mortal, moving, viable, vital, zoetic; SEE CONCEPT *539*

animate [*adj2*] *lively*
activated, active, alert, animated, dynamic, energized, gay, happy, spirited, vivacious; SEE CONCEPT *401*

animate [*v*] *bring to life*
activate, arouse, cheer, embolden, encourage, energize, enliven, exalt, excite, fire, gladden, hearten, impel, incite, inform, inspire, inspirit, instigate, invigorate, kindle, liven, make alive, move, quicken, revive, revivify, rouse, spark, spur, stimulate, stir, urge, vitalize, vivify; SEE CONCEPTS *231,241*

animated [*adj*] *lively*
activated, active, alert, animate, ardent, brisk, buoyant, dynamic, ebullient, elated, energetic, energized, enthusiastic, excited, fervent, gay, happy, passionate, peppy, quick, snappy, spirited, sprightly, vibrant, vigorous, vital, vitalized, vivacious, vivid, zealous, zestful, zingy, zippy; SEE CONCEPT *401*

animation [*n*] *liveliness; activity*
action, ardor, bounce, brio, briskness, buoyancy, dash, dynamism, ebullience, élan, elation, energy, enthusiasm, esprit, excitement, exhilaration, fervor, gaiety, high spirits, life, oomph*, passion, pep*, sparkle, spirit, sprightliness, verve, vibrancy, vigor, vim, vitality, vivacity, zap*, zeal, zest, zing*, zip*; SEE CONCEPT *657*

animosity [*n*] *extreme dislike, hatred*
acrimony, animus, antagonism, antipathy, bad blood, bitterness, displeasure, enmity, hate, hostility, ill will, malevolence, malice, malignity, rancor, resentment, virulence; SEE CONCEPT *29*

ankle [*n*] *joint between leg and foot*
anklebone, astragalus, bone, talus, tarsus; SEE CONCEPTS *392,418*

annal(s) [*n*] *history, records*
account, archive, chronicle, journal, memorial, record, register; SEE CONCEPTS *271,281*

annex [*n*] *something added; extension*
addendum, addition, adjunct, affix, appendix, arm, attachment, ell, subsidiary, supplement, wing; SEE CONCEPTS *440,441,484*

annex [*v*] *join or add*
adjoin, affix, append, appropriate, associate, attach, connect, fasten, hitch on*, hitch up*, hook

on*, hook up*, link, slap on*, subjoin, tack on*, tag, tag on*, take on, take over, unite; SEE CONCEPTS *85,113,160*

annexation [*n*] *adding, joining*
addition, annexing, appropriation, attachment, grab, incorporation, increase, increment, merger, takeover; SEE CONCEPTS *113,324*

Annie Oakley [*n*] *complimentary ticket*
Chinese ducket*, free admission, freebie*, free pass, free seats, free ticket; SEE CONCEPTS *271,685*

annihilate [*v*] *destroy completely*
abate, abolish, abrogate, annul, blot out*, crush*, decimate, demolish, do in*, eradicate, erase, expunge, exterminate, extinguish, extirpate, finish off, invalidate, liquidate, massacre, murder, negate, nullify, obliterate, quash, quell, raze, root out*, rub out*, ruin, slaughter, take out*, undo, vitiate, wipe out*, wrack*, wreck; SEE CONCEPT *252*

anniversary [*n*] *yearly observance, celebration*
ceremony, commemoration, feast day, festival, holiday, jubilee, recurrence, red-letter day; SEE CONCEPTS *800,801,815,823*

annotate [*v*] *write explanatory notes*
comment, commentate, construe, define, elucidate, explain, expound, footnote, gloss, illustrate, interpret, note, remark; SEE CONCEPTS *51,57,79*

annotation [*n*] *explanatory note*
comment, commentary, definition, elucidation, exegesis, explanation, explication, footnote, gloss, glossary, illustration, interpretation, note, observation; SEE CONCEPTS *274,283*

announce [*v1*] *make a proclamation*
advertise, annunciate, blast, blazon, broadcast, call, communicate, declare, disclose, disseminate, divulge, drum*, give out, impart, intimate, issue, make known, make public, pass the word*, proclaim, promulgate, propound, publicize, publish, release, report, reveal, run off at mouth*, sound off*, spread around*, state, tell, trumpet; SEE CONCEPT *49*

announce [*v2*] *declare arrival*
augur, forebode, forecast, forerun, foreshow, foretell, harbinger, herald, indicate, portend, predict, presage, signal, signify; SEE CONCEPTS *60,70*

announcement [*n*] *proclamation, declaration*
advertisement, advice, briefing, broadcast, broadcasting, bulletin, communication, communiqué, disclosure, dissemination, divulgence, edict, exposing, exposition, expression, intimation, message, narration, news, notice, notification, prediction, promulgation, publication, publishing, recitation, release, report, reporting, revelation, statement; SEE CONCEPTS *49,274*

announcer [*n*] *media commentator*
anchorperson, broadcaster, communicator, deejay, disc jockey, DJ, leader of ceremonies, newscaster, reporter, rip and reader*, spieler*, talker, telecaster, veejay*, VJ; SEE CONCEPT *348*

annoy [*v*] *irritate, upset*
abrade, agitate, ask for it*, badger, be at*, bedevil, beleaguer, be on the back of*, bore, bother, break, bug, burn up, chafe, displease, distress, disturb, egg on*, exasperate, fire up*, gall, get, gnaw, harass, harry, heat up*, henpeck, hit where one lives*, irk, madden, make waves*, miff, nag, needle, nettle, nudge, peeve, perturb,

pester, plague, provoke, push button*, ride, rile, ruffle, tease, tick off*, T-off*, trouble, turn off*, vex, work on*, worry; SEE CONCEPTS *7,19*

annual [*adj1*] *occurring, done yearly*
anniversary, each year, every year, once a year, year end; SEE CONCEPTS *541,823*

annual [*adj2*] *lasting for a year*
a year's worth, yearlong; SEE CONCEPT *798*

annual [*n*] *book produced once a year*
annuary, report, summary, yearbook; SEE CONCEPT *271*

annually [*adv*] *occurring, done yearly*
by the year, each year, every year, once a year, per annum, per year, year after year; SEE CONCEPTS *541,823*

annul [*v*] *void an agreement*
abate, abolish, abrogate, annihilate, blot out, call off, cancel, countermand, declare, delete, discharge, dissolve, efface, erase, expunge, get off the hook*, invalidate, kill, negate, neutralize, nix, nullify, obliterate, quash, recall, render null and void, repeal, rescind, retract, reverse, revoke, scrub*, undo, vacate, vitiate, wipe out*; SEE CONCEPTS *252,297,317*

annulment [*n*] *voiding an agreement*
abatement, abolition, abrogation, annihilation, breakup, cancellation, countermanding, dedomiciling, deletion, discharge, dissolution, erasing, going phfft*, invalidation, negation, neutralization, nullification, obliteration, recall, repeal, rescinding, rescindment, rescission, retraction, reversal, revocation, split*, split up*, undoing*, vitiation, voiding; SEE CONCEPTS *297,317,691*

anoint [*v*] *bless, usually with oil or water*
bless, consecrate, daub, embrocate, grease, hallow, rub, sanctify, smear; SEE CONCEPT *367*

anomalous [*adj*] *deviating from normal, usual*
aberrant, abnormal, atypical, bizarre, divergent, eccentric, exceptional, foreign, heteroclite, incongruous, inconsistent, irregular, odd, peculiar, preternatural, prodigous, rare, strange, unnatural, unorthodox, unrepresentative, untypical, unusual; SEE CONCEPT *547*

anomaly [*n*] *deviation from normal, usual*
aberration, abnormality, departure, deviation, eccentricity, exception, incongruity, inconsistency, irregularity, oddity, peculiarity, rarity, unconformity, unorthodoxy; SEE CONCEPT *647*

anonymous [*adj*] *unknown, usually by choice*
bearding*, incognito, innominate, Jane/John Doe*, nameless, pseudo, pseudonymous, secret, so and so*, such and such*, unacknowledged, unattested, unavowed, unclaimed, uncredited, undesignated, undisclosed, unidentified, unnamed, unsigned, unspecified, whatchamacallit*, what's his/her name*, whatsis*, X*, you know who*; SEE CONCEPT *683*

anorexic [*adj*] *starving*
bulimic, emaciated, malnourished, sickly looking, thin, without appetite; SEE CONCEPTS *490,491*

another [*n*] *other person*
addition, a different person, one more, someone else, something else; SEE CONCEPT *423*

another [*prep/det*] *additional, different*
added, a distinct, a further, a separate, else, farther, fresh, further, more, new, one more, other, some other, that; SEE CONCEPT *564*

answer [*n*] *reply; reaction*

acknowledgment, antiphon, backcap*, back talk, band-aid*, close, comeback, comment, cooler*, counterclaim, crack, defense, disclosure, echo, elucidation, explanation, feedback, guff*, interpretation, justification, key, lip*, observation, parting shot*, pay dirt*, plea, quick fix*, rebuttal, refutation, rejoinder, remark, repartee, report, resolution, response, result, retort, return, riposte, sign, solution, statement, thank-you note*, the ticket*, topper*, vindication, wisecrack; SEE CONCEPTS *274,278*

answer [*v1*] *reply, react*
acknowledge, answer back, argue, back at you*, back talk, be in touch*, claim, comeback, contest, counterclaim, defend, deny, disprove, dispute, echo, explain, feedback, field the question*, get back at*, get back to*, give a snappy comeback*, parry, plead, rebut, refute, rejoin, remark, resolve, respond, retaliate, retort, return, sass*, say, settle, shoot back*, solve, squelch, talk back, top*; SEE CONCEPTS *45,266*

answer [*v2*] *solve; fulfill*
clarify, conform, correlate, correspond, crack*, deal with*, do*, dope, dope out*, elucidate, fill, fit*, lick*, measure up, meet, pass, qualify, satisfy, serve, suffice, suit, unzip*, work, work through; SEE CONCEPTS *87,664*

answerable [*adj*] *responsible*
accountable, amenable, bound, chargeable, compelled, constrained, liable, obligated, obliged, subject, to blame; SEE CONCEPT *545*

antagonism [*n*] *causing problem; opposition*
animosity, animus, antipathy, antithesis, clashing, competition, conflict, contention, contradistinction, contrariety, difference, disagreement, discord, dissension, enmity, friction, hatred, hostility, incongruity, oppugnancy, rancor, resistance, rivalry; SEE CONCEPT *29*

antagonist [*n*] *person causing problem*
adversary, angries*, bad person*, bandit*, competitor, contender, crip*, enemy, foe, match, opponent, opposer, opposite number*, oppugnant, rival; SEE CONCEPT *412*

antagonize [*v*] *cause problem; oppose*
alienate, anger, annoy, counteract, estrange, insult, irritate, neutralize, offend, repel, struggle, work against; SEE CONCEPTS *7,19,231*

antecedent [*adj*] *prior*
anterior, earlier, foregoing, former, past, precedent, preceding, precursory, preliminary, previous; SEE CONCEPT *820*

antecedent(s) [*n*] *predecessor(s) in family*
ancestor, ancestry, antecessor, blood, descent, extraction, forebears, forefather/mother, genealogy, line, primogenitor, progenitor, stock; SEE CONCEPT *414*

antedate [*v*] *occur or cause to occur earlier*
accelerate, anachronize, antecede, backdate, date back, forerun, misdate, pace, precede, predate; SEE CONCEPT *84*

antediluvian [*adj*] *out-of-date; prehistoric*
age-old, ancient, antiquated, antique, archaic, hoary, obsolete, old, old-fashioned, passé, primeval, primitive, primordial, timeworn, venerable; SEE CONCEPTS *578,797,799*

antenna [*n*] *appendages for sensing, usually on insects or electronics*
aerial, bird snapper*, bullwhip*, ears*, feelers*, rabbit ears, receiver, sky wire*, whip*, wire; SEE

CONCEPT *464*

anterior [*adj*] *beginning, prior*
antecedent, foregoing, former, past, precedent, preceding, previous; SEE CONCEPT *799*

anthem [*n*] *song*
canticle, chant, chorus, hymn, melody, paean; SEE CONCEPTS *263,595*

anthology [*n*] *literary collection*
album, analect, compendium, compilation, digest, garland, omnibus, selection, treasury; SEE CONCEPTS *280,432*

anthropology [*n*] *study of humans and their culture*
folklore, sociology; SEE CONCEPT *349*

antibiotic [*n*] *medicine*
amoxicillin, ampicillin, erythromycin, penicillin, streptomycin, sulfa drug, sulfonamide, tetracycline, wonder drug*; SEE CONCEPT *307*

antic [*n*] *funny act*
caper, dido, frolic, joke, lark, romp, shenanigan, tomfoolery, trick; SEE CONCEPT *292*

anticipate [*v1*] *expect; predict*
assume, await, bargain for*, be afraid*, conjecture, count chickens*, count on, cross the bridge*, divine, entertain*, figure, forecast, foresee, foretaste, foretell, have a hunch*, hope for, jump the gun*, look for, look forward to, plan on, prepare for, prevision, prognosticate, promise oneself, prophesy, see, see coming*, see in the cards*, suppose, visualize, wait, wait for; SEE CONCEPTS *26,70*

anticipate [*v2*] *act in advance of*
apprehend, beat someone to it*, be early, be one step ahead of*, block, delay, forestall, hinder, hold back, intercept, precede, preclude, prepare for, prevent, provide against; SEE CONCEPTS *100,121*

anticipation [*n1*] *expectation*
apprehension, awaiting, contemplation, expectancy, foresight, foretaste, high hopes, hope, impatience, joy, looking forward, outlook, preconception, premonition, preoccupation, prescience, presentiment, promise, prospect, trust; SEE CONCEPTS *26,689*

anticipation [*n2*] *readiness; forethought*
apprehension, awareness, foreboding, forecast, foreseeing, foresight, foretaste, forethought, inkling, intuition, preconception, premonition, prescience, presentiment, prevision, prior knowledge, realization; SEE CONCEPTS *409,410*

anticlimax [*n*] *ineffective conclusion*
bathos, comedown, decline, descent, disappointment, drop, letdown, slump; SEE CONCEPTS *230,674*

antidote [*n*] *counteracting agent*
antitoxin, antivenin, corrective, counteractant, counteragent, countermeasure, counterstep, cure, medicine, negator, neutralizer, nullifier, preventive, remedy; SEE CONCEPT *307*

antipathy [*n*] *strong dislike, disgust*
abhorrence, allergy, animosity, animus, antagonism, aversion, avoidance, bad blood*, contrariety, distaste, dyspathy, enmity, escape, eschewal, evasion, hate, hatred, hostility, ill will, incompatibility, loathing, opposition, rancor, repellency, repugnance, repulsion; SEE CONCEPT *29*

antiquarian [*adj*] *old, ancient*
aged, antique, archaic, hoary, obsolete, primitive, timeworn, venerable; SEE CONCEPTS *578,797*

antiquated [*adj*] *obsolete*

aged, ancient, antediluvian, antique, archaic, dated, elderly, fusty*, hoary, moldy, obsolescent, old, old-fangled, old-fashioned, old hat*, outmoded, out-of-date, outworn, superannuated; SEE CONCEPTS 530,578,797

antique [adj1] old
aged, ancient, elderly, obsolescent, obsolete, outdated, out-of-date, prehistoric, superannuated; SEE CONCEPTS 578,797

antique [adj2] old-fashioned
antiquarian, archaic, classic, obsolete, olden, outdated, vintage; SEE CONCEPTS 530,578,797

antique [n] old object, often of great value
antiquity, artifact, bygone, heirloom, monument, objet d'art, rarity, relic, ruin, vestige; SEE CONCEPTS 259,443

antiquity [n1] old object
antique, relic, ruin; SEE CONCEPT 259

antiquity [n2] oldness
age, ancientness, antiqueness, archaicism, archaism, elderliness, hoariness, old age, venerableness; SEE CONCEPT 715

antiquity [n3] distant past
ancient time(s), classical times, days of old, days of yore, former age, old days, olden days, remote time, time immemorial; SEE CONCEPT 807

antiseptic [adj] completely clean, uncontaminated; decontaminating
antibacterial, antibiotic, aseptic, bactericidal, clean, disinfectant, germ-destroying, germ-free, germicidal, hygienic, medicated, prophylactic, pure, purifying, sanitary, sterile, sterilized, sterilizing, unpolluted; SEE CONCEPT 485

antiseptic [n] decontaminating agent
bactericide, detergent, disinfectant, germicide, preservative, preventative, preventive, prophylactic, purifier, sterilizer; SEE CONCEPTS 307,472,492

antisocial [adj] nonparticipating; avoiding company
alienated, ascetic, asocial, austere, cold, cynical, eremetic, hermitlike, introverted, misanthropic, reclusive, remote, reserved, retiring, solitary, standoffish, uncommunicative, unfriendly, unsociable, withdrawn; SEE CONCEPT 555

antithesis [n1] exact opposite
antipode, antipole, contra, contradictory, contrary, contrast, converse, counter, flip side*, inverse, other side, reverse; SEE CONCEPT 665

antithesis [n2] contrast, opposition
antagonism, contradiction, contradistinction, contraposition, contrariety, inversion, opposure, reversal; SEE CONCEPTS 633,665

antithetical [adj] reverse
contradictory, contrary, contrasted, converse, counter, inverse, opposed, opposite, polarized, poles apart*; SEE CONCEPT 542

antitoxin [n] agent for negating the effect of an infection or poison
antibiotic, antibody, antipoison, antiseptic, antiserum, antivenin, counteractant, counteragent, medicine, neutralizer, preventive, serum, vaccine; SEE CONCEPT 307

antonym [n] word with opposite meaning to another word
opposite, reverse; SEE CONCEPT 275

antsy [adj] fidgety
anxious, edgy, impatient, on pins and needles*, restless; SEE CONCEPT 401

anxiety [n] worry, tension

all-overs*, angst, ants in pants*, apprehension, botheration*, butterflies*, care, cold sweat*, concern, creeps*, disquiet, disquietude, distress, doubt, downer*, drag*, dread, fidgets*, flap*, foreboding, fretfulness, fuss, goose bumps*, heebie-jeebies*, jitters, jumps*, misery, misgiving, mistrust, nail-biting*, needles*, nervousness, panic, pins and needles*, restlessness, shakes*, shivers*, solicitude, suffering, suspense, sweat*, trouble, uncertainty, unease, uneasiness, watchfulness, willies*, worriment; SEE CONCEPTS 410,532,690

anxious [adj1] worried, tense
afraid, aghast, antsy*, apprehensive, basket case*, bugged*, butterflies, careful, choked*, clutched*, concerned, disquieted, distressed, disturbed, dreading, fearful, fidgety, fretful, hacked*, hyper*, in a state*, in a tizzy*, in suspense*, jittery, jumpy, nervous, nervy, overwrought, restless, scared, shaking, shaky, shivery, shook up*, shot to pieces*, solicitous, spooked*, strung out*, sweating bullets*, taut, troubled, uneasy, unglued*, unquiet, uptight*, watchful, wired*, worried sick*, wreck*; SEE CONCEPTS 403,690

anxious [adj2] eager
agog, ardent, avid, breathless, desirous, enthusiastic, expectant, fervent, impatient, intent, itching*, keen, thirsty, yearning, zealous; SEE CONCEPTS 401,542

any [det] one, some; unspecified, indiscriminate
a bit, a little, all, each, each and every, either, in general, part of, several, whatever; SEE CONCEPT 762

anybody [n] one, some unspecified person or people
all, any of, anyone, anyone at all, any person, a person, each and every one, everybody, everyone, masses, one, public, whole world; SEE CONCEPT 417

anyhow [adv] by any means
about, anyway, any which way, around, at any rate, at random, haphazard, haphazardly, helter-skelter, however, in any case, in any respect, in any way, in either way, in one way or another, in whatever way, nevertheless, random, randomly, regardless, under any circumstances, whatever happens, willy-nilly; SEE CONCEPT 544

anyone [n] one, some unspecified person
all, anybody, anybody at all, any of, any person, a person, each and every one, everybody, everyone, masses, one, public, whole world; SEE CONCEPT 417

anyplace [n] unspecified area
all over, anywhere, everywhere, in any place, in whatever place, wherever; SEE CONCEPT 198

anything [n] unspecified object or event
all, any one thing, anything at all, everything, whatever; SEE CONCEPTS 2,433

anytime [n] unspecified moment, period
at all, at any moment, at one's convenience, every-time, no matter when, whenever, when one will; SEE CONCEPTS 807,819

anyway [adv] by any means
anyhow, at all, at any rate, ever, however, in any case, in any event, in any manner, nevertheless, once; SEE CONCEPT 544

anywhere [n] unspecified area
all over, anyplace, everywhere, in any place, in

whatever place, wherever; SEE CONCEPT *198*
apart [*adv*] *separate*
afar, alone, aloof, aside, away, by itself, cut off*, disassociated, disconnected, distant, distinct, divorced, excluded, exclusively, freely, independent, independently, individually, isolated, lone wolf*, separated, separately, singly, special, to itself, to one side; SEE CONCEPTS *586,785*
apartheid [*n*] *racial segregation*
discrimination, racism, separation; SEE CONCEPT *689*
apartment [*n*] *set of rooms for rent*
accommodation, cave*, chambers, cold-water*, condo, coop, cooperative, crash pad*, den*, digs*, dump*, flat, living quarters, lodging, pad*, penthouse, rental, residence, suite, walkup; SEE CONCEPTS *448,516*
apathetic [*adj*] *uncaring, disinterested*
blah*, callous, cold, cool, could care less*, couldn't care less*, don't give a damn*, draggy*, emotionless, flat, impassive, indifferent, insensible, laid-back*, languid, moony*, passive, stoic, stolid, unconcerned, unemotional, unfeeling, uninterested, unmoved, unresponsive, untouched, what the hell*, wimpy*; SEE CONCEPTS *401,403*
apathy [*n*] *uncaring attitude, lack of interest*
aloofness, coldness, coolness, detachment, disinterest, dispassion, disregard, dullness, emotionlessness, halfheartedness, heedlessness, indifference, insensibility, insensitivity, insouciance, lassitude, lethargy, listlessness, passiveness, passivity, stoicism, unconcern, unresponsiveness; SEE CONCEPTS *410,633*
ape [*v*] *mimic*
affect, caricature, copy, counterfeit, ditto*, do*, do like*, echo, emulate, go like*, imitate, impersonate, make like*, mirror, mock, parody, parrot, take off*, travesty; SEE CONCEPTS *111,171*
aperture [*n*] *hole*
breach, break, chasm, chink, cleft, crack, cut, eye, fissure, gap, gash, interstice, opening, orifice, outlet, passage, perforation, pinhole, puncture, rift, rupture, slash, slit, slot, space, vent; SEE CONCEPT *757*
apex [*n*] *top, high point*
acme, apogee, climax, crest, crown, culmination, cusp, greatest, height, max*, maximum, meridian, most*, ne plus ultra, peak, pinnacle, point, roof, spire, sublimity, summit, tip, tops, up there*, vertex, zenith; SEE CONCEPTS *706,836*
aphorism [*n*] *saying expressing a belief, often true*
adage, apothegm, axiom, dictum, maxim, moral, precept, proverb, rule, saw, saying, truism; SEE CONCEPTS *275,278,689*
aphrodisiac [*n/adj*] *seductive; inducing sex*
amative, amatory, amorous, erotic, love drug, popper*, Spanish fly*, turn-on*, wampole*; SEE CONCEPTS *372,537*
apiece [*adv*] *each*
all, a pop*, aside, for each, from each, individually, one by one, per, respectively, separately, severally, singly, successively, to each; SEE CONCEPT *762*
apocalypse [*n*] *mass destruction*
annihilation, Armageddon, cataclysm, catastrophe, decimation, devastation, end of the world, holocaust; SEE CONCEPT *674*
apocryphal [*adj*] *questionable; fake*
counterfeit, doubtful, dubious, equivocal, false,

fictitious, inaccurate, mythical, spurious, unauthenticated, ungenuine, unsubstantiated, untrue, unverified, wrong; SEE CONCEPTS *570,582*
apologetic [*adj*] *expressing remorse, regret*
atoning, attritional, compunctious, conciliatory, contrite, expiatory, explanatory, on one's knees*, penitent, penitential, propitiatory, regretful, remorseful, repentant, rueful, self-effacing, self-incriminating, sorry, supplicating; SEE CONCEPT *267*
apologize [*v*] *express remorse, regret*
admit guilt, ask pardon, atone, beg pardon, bow to*, clear oneself, confess, cop a plea*, cop out*, crawl*, excuse oneself, get down on knees*, give satisfaction*, make amends, make reparations, make up for, make up with, offer compensation, offer excuse, purge, retract, say one is sorry, square*, withdraw; SEE CONCEPTS *48,67*
apology [*n*] *offering of remorse, regret*
acknowledgment, admission, amends, atonement, concession, confession, defense, excuse, explanation, extenuation, justification, mea culpa, mitigation, plea, redress, reparation, vindication; SEE CONCEPTS *48,67*
apoplexy [*n*] *loss of consciousness from blockage in vein or artery*
occlusion, seizure, stroke, thrombosis; SEE CONCEPTS *316,720*
apostate [*n*] *traitor*
backslider, defector, deserter, dissenter, heretic, nonconformist, rat*, recreant, renegade, turncoat; SEE CONCEPTS *359,412*
apostle [*n*] *preacher; supporter*
advocate, champion, companion, converter, evangelist, follower, herald, messenger, missionary, pioneer, propagandist, proponent, proselytizer, witness; SEE CONCEPTS *359,361*
apotheosis [*n*] *glorification*
deification, elevation, idolization, immortalization; SEE CONCEPTS *69,367*
appall/appal [*v*] *horrify*
alarm, amaze, astound, awe, consternate, daunt, disconcert, dishearten, dismay, faze, frighten, get to*, gross out*, insult, intimidate, outrage, petrify, scare, shake, shock, terrify, throw, unnerve; SEE CONCEPTS *7,19,42*
appalling [*adj*] *horrifying*
alarming, astounding, awful, bad, daunting, dire, disheartening, dismaying, dreadful, fearful, formidable, frightening, frightful, ghastly, grim, grody*, gross*, harrowing, heavy*, hideous, horrible, horrid, horrific, intimidating, mean, petrifying, scaring, shocking, terrible, terrifying, the end*, unnerving; SEE CONCEPT *529*
apparatus [*n1*] *equipment with a purpose*
accoutrement, appliance, black box*, contraption, device, dingbat, doodad*, doohickey*, furnishings, gaff*, gear, gimcrack*, gimmick, gizmo*, grabber*, habiliments, idiot box*, implement, jigger*, job*, machine, machinery, means, mechanism, outfit, paraphernalia, provisions, setup, stuff, supplies, tackle, thingamajig*, tools, utensils, whatchamacallit*, whatsis*, whosis*, widget*; SEE CONCEPTS *260,463,499*
apparatus [*n2*] *organization or system*
bureaucracy, chain of command, hierarchy, network, setup, structure; SEE CONCEPTS *381,770*
apparel [*n*] *clothing; covering*
accoutrement, array, attire, clothes, costume,

drapery, dress, duds*, equipment, garb, garment, gear*, getup*, habiliment, habit, outfit, raiment, rig*, robe, suit, threads*, trapping, vestment; SEE CONCEPTS *451,473*

apparent [*adj1*] *seeming, not proven real*
credible, illusive, illusory, likely, ostensible, outward, plausible, possible, probable, semblant, specious, superficial, supposed, suppositious; SEE CONCEPTS *552,582*

apparent [*adj2*] *obvious*
barefaced, big as life*, clear, clear cut, conspicuous, crystal clear, discernible, distinct, evident, glaring, indubitable, make no bones*, manifest, marked, noticeable, observable, open, open and shut*, out in the open*, overt, palpable, patent, perceivable, plain, self-evident, transparent, unambiguous, under one's nose*, understandable, unequivocal, unmistakable, visible; SEE CONCEPTS *535,582*

apparently [*adv1*] *seemingly*
allegedly, as if, as though, at a glance, at first sight, in all likelihood, intuitively, it appears that, it seems that, most likely, on the face of it, ostensibly, outwardly, plausibly, possibly, probably, professedly, reasonably, reputably, speciously, superficially, supposedly, tangibly, to all appearances; SEE CONCEPTS *552,582*

apparently [*adv2*] *obviously*
clearly, conspicuously, evidently, expressly, indubitably, in plain sight, manifestly, officially, openly, overtly, palpably, patently, perceptibly, plainly, transparently, unmistakably; SEE CONCEPT *535*

apparition [*n*] *ghost*
bogeyman, bump in the night*, chimera, delusion, hallucination, haunt, illusion, phantasm, phantom, revenant, specter, spirit, spook, visitant; SEE CONCEPTS *370,689*

appeal [*n1*] *request for help*
address, adjuration, application, bid, call, claim, demand, entreaty, imploration, importunity, invocation, overture, petition, plea, prayer, proposal, proposition, question, recourse, requisition, solicitation, submission, suit, supplication; SEE CONCEPT *48*

appeal [*n2*] *power to attract, interest*
allure, attraction, attractiveness, beauty, charm, charmingness, engagingness, fascination, glamor, interestingness, pleasingness, seductiveness; SEE CONCEPTS *655,673*

appeal [*v1*] *request*
address, adjure, advance, apply, ask, beg, beseech, bid, call, call upon, claim, contest, crave, demand, entreat, hit on, implore, importune, petition, plead, pray, propose, proposition, question, refer, require, resort to, solicit, strike, submit, sue, supplicate, urge; SEE CONCEPT *48*

appeal [*v2*] *attract, interest*
allure, beguile, captivate, catch the eye, charm, enchant, engage, entice, fascinate, intrigue, invite, please, tantalize, tempt; SEE CONCEPTS *7,19,22,384*

appear [*v1*] *come into sight*
arise, arrive, attend, be present, be within view, blow in*, bob up*, break through, breeze in*, check in*, clock in*, come, come forth, come into view, come out, come to light*, crop up*, develop, drop in*, emerge, expose, issue, loom, make the scene*, materialize, occur, pop in*, pop up*, present, punch in*, punch the clock*,

recur, ring in*, rise, roll in*, show, show up, spring, surface, time in*, turn out, turn up; SEE CONCEPTS *159,261*

appear [*v2*] *seem*
have the appearance, look as if, look like, occur, resemble, sound, strike one as; SEE CONCEPTS *543,716*

appear [*v3*] *be obvious, clear*
be apparent, be evident, be manifest, be patent, be plain; SEE CONCEPT *725*

appear [*v4*] *be published; perform*
become available, be created, be developed, be invented, come into being, come into existence, come on, come on stage*, come out, enter, make an appearance, oblige, perform, play, play a part, present oneself, take part; SEE CONCEPTS *292,324*

appearance [*n1*] *coming into sight*
actualization, advent, appearing, arrival, coming, debut, display, emergence, entrance, exhibition, introduction, manifestation, materialization, presence, presentation, representation, rise, showing up, turning up, unveiling; SEE CONCEPTS *159,261*

appearance [*n2*] *outward aspect, characteristic*
air, attitude, bearing, blind, carriage, cast, character, condition, countenance, demeanor, dress, expression, face, fashion, feature, figure, form, front, guise, image, look, looks, manner, mannerism, mien, mode, outline, pose, presence, presentation, screen, semblance, shape, stamp; SEE CONCEPTS *543,716*

appearance [*n3*] *outward show; pretense*
aura, beard*, blind, countenance, dream, facade, front, guise, idea, illusion, image, impression, mirage, phenomenon, reflection, screen, seeming, semblance, sound, specter, vision; SEE CONCEPT *673*

appease [*v*] *satisfy, pacify*
allay, alleviate, assuage, be enough, blunt, calm, compose, conciliate, content, diminish, do*, ease, gratify, lessen, lull, make matters up, meet halfway, mitigate, mollify, patch things up, placate, propitiate, quell, quench, quiet, serve, soften, soothe, subdue, sweeten, tranquilize; SEE CONCEPTS *7,22,126*

appeasement [*n*] *satisfaction; pacification*
abatement, acceding, accommodation, adjustment, alleviation, amends, assuagement, blunting, compromise, concession, conciliation, easing, grant, lessening, lulling, mitigation, moderation, mollification, peace offering, placation, propitiation, quelling, quenching, quieting, reconciliation, reparation, restoration, settlement, softening, solace, soothing, tranquilization; SEE CONCEPTS *7,22,126*

appellation [*n*] *name*
designation, epithet, handle*, label, moniker*, nickname, sobriquet, title; SEE CONCEPTS *268,683*

append [*v*] *add, join*
adjoin, affix, annex, attach, conjoin, fasten, fix, hang, subjoin, supplement, tack on*, tag on*; SEE CONCEPTS *85,113,160*

appendage [*n*] *limb; accessory*
addendum, addition, adjunct, ancillary, annex, appendix, appurtenance, attachment, auxiliary, extremity, member, projection, protuberance, supplement; SEE CONCEPT *835*

appendix [*n*] *added material at end of document*
addendum, addition, adjunct, appendage, appur-

tenance, attachment, codicil, excursus, index, notes, postscript, rider, sample, supplement, table, verification; SEE CONCEPT *270*

appertain [*v*] *belong, be connected*
apply, bear, be characteristic of, be part of, be pertinent, be proper, be relevant, have to do with, pertain, refer, relate, touch upon, vest; SEE CONCEPT *532*

appetite [*n*] *desire for food, worldly goods*
appetence, appetency, appetition, big eyes*, craving, demand, fondness, gluttony, greed, hankering, hunger, inclination, itch*, liking, longing, lust, passion, penchant, proclivity, propensity, ravenousness, relish, soft spot*, stomach, sweet tooth*, taste, thirst, urge, voracity, weakness, willingness, yearning, yen, zeal, zest; SEE CONCEPTS *20,32*

appetizer [*n*] *snack before meal*
antipasto, aperitif, canapé, cocktail, dip, finger food, hors d'oeuvre, munchies*, relish, sample, spread, taste, tidbit; SEE CONCEPTS *457,828*

appetizing [*adj*] *tasting very good*
aperitive, appealing, delectable, delicious, delish*, divine*, flavorsome, heavenly, inviting, luscious, mouthwatering, palatable, saporous, savory, scrumptious, succulent, sugar-coated*, sweetened, tantalizing, tasty, tempting, toothsome, yummy*; SEE CONCEPT *613*

applaud [*v*] *clap for; express approval*
acclaim, approve, boost, cheer, commend, compliment, encourage, eulogize, extol, give a hand*, give ovation, glorify, hail, hear it for*, kudize*, laud, magnify, plug, praise, rave, recommend, root*; SEE CONCEPTS *10,69,189*

applause [*n*] *clapping; expression of approval*
acclaim, acclamation, accolade, approbation, big hand, bring down the house*, cheering, cheers, commendation, eulogizing, hand, hand-clapping, hurrahs, kudos, laudation, ovation, plaudits, praise, rooting, round, standing ovation; SEE CONCEPTS *69,189*

appliance [*n*] *machine, usually with domestic purpose*
apparatus, device, gadget, implement, instrument, mechanism, tool; SEE CONCEPT *463*

applicable [*adj*] *appropriate*
applicative, applicatory, apposite, apropos, apt, associable, befitting, felicitous, fit, fitting, germane, kosher, legit*, material, on target*, on the button*, on the nose*, pertinent, relevant, right on*, suitable, that's the idea*, that's the ticket*, to the point, to the purpose, useful; SEE CONCEPTS *558,563*

applicant [*n*] *person trying for position*
appellant, aspirant, candidate, claimant, hopeful, inquirer, petitioner, postulant, seeker, suitor, suppliant; SEE CONCEPTS *348,359*

application [*n1*] *use*
appliance, appositeness, employment, exercise, exercising, function, germaneness, operation, pertinence, play, practice, purpose, relevance, usance, utilization, value; SEE CONCEPTS *680,694*

application [*n2*] *request*
appeal, blank, claim, demand, draft, entreaty, form, inquiry, letter, paper, petition, requisition, solicitation, suit; SEE CONCEPT *48*

application [*n3*] *hard work*
assiduity, attention, attentiveness, busyness, commitment, concentration, consideration, dedication, deliberation, diligence, effort, industry,

perseverance, study, zeal; SEE CONCEPTS *91,410*

application [*n4*] *putting substance on another*
administering, administration, applying, creaming, dosing, oiling, rubbing, treatment; SEE CONCEPT *200*

applied [*adj*] *used*
activated, adapted, adjusted, brought to bear, correlated, devoted, enforced, exercised, practiced, related, tested, utilized; SEE CONCEPTS *538,546*

apply [*v1*] *put into use*
administer, assign, bring into play, bring to bear, employ, engage, execute, exercise, exploit, handle, implement, practice, utilize; SEE CONCEPT *225*

apply [*v2*] *be appropriate, relevant*
affect, allude, appertain, be applicable, bear upon, be pertinent, concern, connect, fit, involve, pertain, refer, regard, relate, suit, touch; SEE CONCEPT *532*

apply [*v3*] *put substance on another*
administer, affix, anoint, bestow, cover, fasten, join, lay on, massage, paint, place, put on, rub, smear, spread, touch; SEE CONCEPT *200*

apply [*v4*] *ask, request*
appeal, claim, demand, inquire, petition, put in, put in for, requisition, solicit, sue; SEE CONCEPT *48*

apply [*v5*] *work hard*
address, bear down, be diligent, be industrious, bend, buckle down*, commit, concentrate, dedicate, devote, dig, direct, give, give all one's got*, give best shot*, give old college try*, grind, hammer away*, hit the ball*, hustle*, knuckle down*, make effort, peg away*, persevere, plug*, pour it on*, pull out all stops*, scratch, study, sweat*, throw, try, turn; SEE CONCEPTS *87,100*

appoint [*v1*] *assign responsibility; decide*
accredit, allot, assign, choose, command, commission, decree, delegate, designate, determine, direct, elect, enjoin, establish, finger, fix, install, name, nominate, ordain, select, set, settle, tap; SEE CONCEPTS *41,50,88*

appoint [*v2*] *furnish*
arm, equip, fit, fit out, gear, outfit, provide, rig, supply, turn out; SEE CONCEPT *140*

appointment [*n1*] *arrangement for meeting; prearranged meeting*
assignation, assignment, blind date*, consultation, date, engagement, errand, gig, interview, invitation, meet, rendezvous, session, tryst, zero hour*; SEE CONCEPTS *324,384*

appointment [*n2*] *assignment of responsibility*
allotment, approval, assigning, authorization, certification, choice, choosing, commissioning, delegation, deputation, designation, election, empowering, installation, naming, nomination, ordination, promotion, selection; SEE CONCEPTS *41,50,88*

appointment [*n3*] *job, position of responsibility*
appointee, assignment, berth, candidate, delegate, employment, nominee, office, officeholder, place, post, representative, situation, station, work; SEE CONCEPT *349*

appointment [*n4*] *furnishing(s)*
accoutrement, appurtenance, equipage, fitting, fixture, gear, outfit, paraphernalia, trappings; SEE CONCEPT *475*

apportion [*v*] *divide into shares*

accord, admeasure, administer, allocate, allot, assign, bestow, cut, cut up, deal, dispense, distribute, divvy, divvy up, dole out, give, lot, measure, mete, parcel, part, partition, piece up, prorate, ration, slice, split, split up; SEE CONCEPTS *98,108*

appraisal [*n*] *judgment, estimation*
appraisement, assessment, estimate, evaluation, opinion, pricing, rating, reckoning, stock, survey, valuation; SEE CONCEPTS *18,328,766*

appraise [*v*] *judge, estimate*
adjudge, assay, assess, audit, calculate, check, check out*, deem, evaluate, examine, eye*, figure, figure in, figure out, gauge, guesstimate*, have one's number*, inspect, look over, peg, price, rate, read, review, set at, size, survey, take account of, valuate, value; SEE CONCEPTS *18,764*

appreciable [*adj*] *easily noticed; considerable*
apparent, ascertainable, clear-cut, definite, detectable, discernible, distinguishable, estimable, evident, goodly, good-sized, healthy, large, manifest, marked, material, measurable, noticeable, observable, obvious, perceivable, perceptible, plain, pronounced, recognizable, sensible, significant, sizable, substantial, tangible, visible; SEE CONCEPTS *619,781*

appreciate [*v1*] *be grateful, thankful*
acknowledge, be appreciative, be indebted, be obliged, enjoy, flip over*, freak out on*, get high on*, give thanks, groove on*, welcome; SEE CONCEPTS *12,32,76*

appreciate [*v2*] *increase in worth*
enhance, gain, grow, improve, inflate, raise the value of, rise; SEE CONCEPT *763*

appreciate [*v3*] *recognize worth*
acknowledge, apprehend, be aware of, be cognizant of, be conscious of, catch the drift, comprehend, dig, fathom, grasp, know, perceive, read, realize, recognize, savvy, see daylight*, sympathize with, take account of, understand; SEE CONCEPT *15*

appreciate [*v4*] *value highly*
admire, adore, applaud, apprise, cherish, enjoy, esteem, extol, honor, like, look up to, love, praise, prize, rate highly, regard, relish, respect, savor, treasure; SEE CONCEPTS *10,32*

appreciation [*n1*] *thankfulness*
acknowledgment, gratefulness, gratitude, indebtedness, obligation, recognition, testimonial, thanks, tribute; SEE CONCEPTS *12,32*

appreciation [*n2*] *increase in worth*
enhancement, gain, growth, improvement, inflation, rise; SEE CONCEPTS *346,763*

appreciation [*n3*] *recognition of worth*
admiration, aesthetic sense, affection, appraisal, assessment, attraction, awareness, cognizance, commendation, comprehension, enjoyment, esteem, estimation, grasp, high regard, knowledge, liking, love, perception, realization, recognition, regard, relish, respect, responsivenesss, sensibility, sensitiveness, sensitivity, sympathy, understanding, valuation; SEE CONCEPTS *15,409*

appreciative [*adj1*] *thankful*
beholden, grateful, indebted, obliged, responsive; SEE CONCEPT *403*

appreciative [*adj2*] *understanding, recognizing worth*
admiring, affectionate, alive, aware, cognizant, conscious, considerate, cooperative, cordial, enlightened, enthusiastic, favorable, friendly, generous, keen, kindly, knowledgeable, magnan-imous, mindful, perceptive, pleased, receptive, regardful, respectful, responsive, satisfied, sensitive, supportive, sympathetic, understanding; SEE CONCEPT *402*

apprehend [*v1*] *catch and arrest*
bag*, bust*, capture, collar, cop*, grab, nab, nail*, place under arrest, run in, seize, take in, take into custody, take prisoner; SEE CONCEPTS *90,191,317*

apprehend [*v2*] *understand*
absorb, accept, appreciate, believe, catch, comprehend, conceive, digest, fathom, get, get the picture*, grasp, have, imagine, know, perceive, read, realize, recognize, sense, think; SEE CONCEPT *15*

apprehension [*n1*] *anxiety, fear*
alarm, apprehensiveness, concern, disquiet, doubt, dread, foreboding, misgiving, mistrust, premonition, presage, presentiment, suspicion, trepidation, uneasiness, worry; SEE CONCEPTS *27,690*

apprehension [*n2*] *catching and arresting*
booking, capture, collaring, detention, seizure, taking; SEE CONCEPTS *90,317*

apprehension [*n3*] *understanding*
awareness, comprehension, grasp, idea, intellect, intelligence, judgment, ken, knowledge, notion, perception, perspicacity, thought; SEE CONCEPT *409*

apprehensive [*adj*] *anxious, fearful*
afraid, alarmed, biting nails*, butterflies*, concerned, disquieted, doubtful, feel in bones*, foreboding, frozen*, get vibes*, have a hunch*, have cold feet*, have funny feeling*, have stage fright*, hung up*, in a cold sweat*, in a dither*, in a sweat*, jellyfish*, jittery, jumpy, lily-livered*, mistrustful, running scared*, scaredy-cat*, shaky*, stiff, suspicious, troubled, uncertain, uneasy, uptight, weak, worried, worried sick*; SEE CONCEPT *403*

apprentice [*n*] *novice/learner of a trade*
amateur, beginner, flunky*, greenhorn*, heel*, neophyte, newcomer, new kid on block*, novitiate, probationer, pupil, rook*, rookie*, starter, student, tenderfoot*, tyro; SEE CONCEPTS *348,423*

apprise [*v*] *tell*
advise, brief, enlighten, fill in, inform, notify, tip off; SEE CONCEPTS *57,60,75*

approach [*n1*] *way, means of arriving*
access, accession, advance, advent, avenue, coming, drawing near, entrance, gate, landing, nearing, passage, path, reaching, road, way; SEE CONCEPTS *159,501*

approach [*n2*] *request, suggestion*
advance, appeal, application, offer, overture, proposal, proposition; SEE CONCEPT *278*

approach [*n3*] *plan of attack, resolution*
attitude, concept, course, crack, fling, go*, idea, lick, manner, means, method, mode, modus operandi, new wrinkle*, offer, procedure, program, shot, stab, style, technique, way, whack*, wrinkle*; SEE CONCEPTS *655,660*

approach [*v1*] *come nearer*
advance, approximate, bear, be comparable to, be like, belly up to*, border, buzz*, catch up, close in, come, come at, come close, compare with, contact, converge, correspond to, creep up, draw near, equal, gain on, go toward, impend, loom up, match, meet, move in on, move toward,

ap
ap

near, progress, reach, resemble, surround, take after, threaten, verge upon; SEE CONCEPTS *159,198,701*

approach [*v2*] *make request, suggestion*
accost, address, advise, appeal to, apply to, beseech, confer, consult, entreat, feel, feel one out*, give a play*, give a tumble*, greet, implore, make advance, make overture, make up to, plead, propose, sound out, speak to, supplicate, take aside, talk to, thumb, tumble; SEE CONCEPTS *48,75*

approach [*v3*] *begin*
commence, embark, set about, start, undertake; SEE CONCEPT *234*

approachable [*adj1*] *accessible*
attainable, come-at-able*, convenient, door's always open*, getable*, obtainable, reachable; SEE CONCEPT *576*

approachable [*adj2*] *friendly*
affable, agreeable, congenial, cordial, open, receptive, sociable; SEE CONCEPT *404*

approbation [*n*] *praise*
admiration, approval, bells*, consent, endorsement, esteem, favor, go-ahead*, high regard, okay, permission, recognition, sanction, support, the nod*; SEE CONCEPTS *10,69*

appropriate [*adj*] *suitable*
adapted, applicable, appurtenant, apropos, apt, becoming, befitting, belonging, congruous, convenient, correct, deserved, desired, due, felicitous, fit, fitting, germane, good, just, on the button*, on the nose*, opportune, pertinent, proper, relevant, right, rightful, seemly, tailor-made, true, useful, well-suited, well-timed; SEE CONCEPT *558*

appropriate [*v1*] *set aside; allocate*
allot, allow, appoint, apportion, assign, budget, devote, disburse, earmark, reserve, set apart; SEE CONCEPT *135*

appropriate [*v2*] *steal*
annex, borrow, clap*, confiscate, cop, embezzle, filch, get fingers on*, get hands on*, glom on to*, grab, grab hold of*, hijack, liberate, lift, misappropriate, moonlight requisition*, pilfer, pocket, secure, snatch, swipe*, take over, usurp; SEE CONCEPT *139*

appropriation [*n1*] *allocation, setting aside*
allotment, allowance, apportionment, assignment, budgeting, concession, donation, earmarking, endowing, funding, giving, grant, provision, setting apart, sponsoring, stipend, stipulation, subsidy; SEE CONCEPTS *135,340*

appropriation [*n2*] *stealing*
confiscation, embezzlement, expropriation, grab, misappropriation, pilfering, seizure, takeover, taking, usurpation; SEE CONCEPT *139*

approval [*n1*] *authorization*
acquiescence, assent, bells*, blessing, compliance, concurrence, confirmation, consent, countenance, endorsement, go-ahead*, green light*, leave, license, mandate, okay, permission, ratification, recommendation, sanction, support, the nod*, validation; SEE CONCEPTS *10,685*

approval [*n2*] *good opinion*
acclaim, admiration, applause, appreciation, approbation, commendation, esteem, favor, liking, pat on the back*, pat on the head*, PR*, praise, puff, pumping up, regard, respect, strokes, stroking, wow*; SEE CONCEPT *32*

approve [*v1*] *agree something is good*

accept, acclaim, admire, applaud, appreciate, approbate, be big on*, commend, countenance, esteem, face it, favor, go along with, grin and bear it*, handle, like, live with*, praise, put up with, regard highly, respect, roll with punches*, string along with*, take up on*, think highly of; SEE CONCEPT *10*

approve [*v2*] *allow, authorize*
accede, accept, accredit, acquiesce, advocate, affirm, agree, assent, authorize, back*, bless*, boost, buy, buy into*, certify, charter, concur, confirm, consent, dig*, empower, encourage, endorse, establish, get behind, give go-ahead*, go along with, groove*, hats off to*, lap up*, license, maintain, make law, make valid, mandate, okay, permit, pronounce, push for, ratify, recommend, sanction, seal, second, sign, sign off on, stump for, subscribe to, support, thumbs up*, uphold, validate; SEE CONCEPTS *50,83,88*

approximate [*adj1*] *almost accurate, exact*
almost, close, comparative, near, proximate, relative, rough; SEE CONCEPT *557*

approximate [*adj2*] *inexact*
estimated, guessed, imperfect, imprecise, loose, rough, surmised, uncertain, unprecise, unscientific; SEE CONCEPT *557*

approximate [*adj3*] *similar*
alike, analogous, close, comparable, like, matching, near, relative, resembling, verging on; SEE CONCEPTS *487,573*

approximate [*adj4*] *near*
adjacent, bordering, close together, contiguous, nearby, neighboring; SEE CONCEPT *586*

approximate [*v*] *come close*
approach, border on, come near, estimate, near, reach, resemble, touch, verge on; SEE CONCEPT *664*

approximately [*adv*] *nearly*
about, almost, around, ballpark figure*, bordering on, circa, closely, close to, comparatively, generally, in the ballpark*, in the neighborhood of, in the region of, in the vicinity of, just about, loosely, more or less, most, much, not far from, not quite, proximately, relatively, roughly, upwards of*, very close; SEE CONCEPT *566*

apropos [*adj*] *relevant, suitable*
applicable, apposite, appropriate, apt, befitting, belonging, correct, fit, fitting, germane, kosher*, legit*, material, on the button*, on the nose*, opportune, pertinent, proper, related, right, right on*, seemly; SEE CONCEPT *558*

apropos [*adv*] *relevantly, suitably*
appropriately, aptly, opportunely, pertinently, suitably, timely; SEE CONCEPT *558*

apropos [*prep*] *in respect of*
about, against, as for, as regards, as to, concerning, on the subject of, regarding, respecting, touching, toward, with reference to, with respect to; SEE CONCEPT *532*

apt [*adj1*] *suitable*
applicable, apposite, appropriate, apropos, befitting, correct, felicitous, fit, fitting, germane, happy, just, pertinent, proper, relevant, seemly, suitable, timely; SEE CONCEPT *558*

apt [*adj2*] *tending, inclined*
disposed, given, liable, likely, of a mind, prone, ready; SEE CONCEPT *542*

apt [*adj3*] *quick to learn*
able, adept, astute, bright, clever, expert, gifted, ingenious, intelligent, nobody's fool*, no

dummy*, not born yesterday*, prompt, quick on the trigger*, quick on the uptake*, ready, savvy, sharp, skilled, skillful, smart, talented, teachable; SEE CONCEPT *402*

aptitude [*n1*] *inclination*
bent, disposition, drift, leaning, predilection, proclivity, proneness, propensity, tendency; SEE CONCEPT *657*

aptitude [*n2*] *quickness at learning*
ability, capability, capacity, cleverness, competence, faculty, flair, gift, giftedness, intelligence, knack, proficiency, savvy, smarts, stuff*, talent, what it takes*; SEE CONCEPT *409*

aquarium [*n*] *fish tank*
aquatic museum, fishbowl, marine exhibit; SEE CONCEPTS *396,438,514*

aquatic [*adj*] *occurring in water*
amphibian, amphibious, floating, marine, maritime, natatory, oceanic, of the sea, sea, swimming, watery; SEE CONCEPTS *396,536*

aqueduct [*n*] *canal*
channel, conduit, course, duct, pipeline, water passage, waterworks; SEE CONCEPT *514*

arbiter [*n*] *person who settles dispute*
adjudicator, arbitrator, fixer, go-between, holdout, judge, maven, mediator, middleperson, moderator, referee, umpire; SEE CONCEPT *354*

arbitrary [*adj1*] *whimsical, chance*
approximate, capricious, discretionary, erratic, fanciful, frivolous, inconsistent, injudicious, irrational, irresponsible, offhand, optional, random, subjective, supercilious, superficial, unaccountable, unreasonable, unscientific, wayward, willful; SEE CONCEPTS *534,542*

arbitrary [*adj2*] *dictatorial*
absolute, autocratic, bossy, despotic, dogmatic, domineering, downright, flat out*, high-handed, imperious, magisterial, monocratic, no ifs ands or buts*, no joke*, overbearing, peremptory, straight out*, summary, tyrannical, tyrannous; SEE CONCEPT *401*

arbitrate [*v*] *achieve settlement*
adjudge, adjudicate, adjust, bring to terms, come to school, come to terms, conciliate, decide, determine, hammer out a deal*, interpose, intervene, judge, make a deal, mediate, meet halfway, negotiate, parley, pass judgment, placate, play ball*, reconcile, referee, settle, smooth, soothe, step in, straighten out, strike happy medium*, trade off, umpire, work out a deal; SEE CONCEPTS *126,300*

arbitration [*n*] *settlement of dispute*
adjudication, adjustment, agreement, compromise, decision, determination, judgment, mediation; SEE CONCEPTS *126,300*

arbitrator [*n*] *settler of a dispute*
adjudicator, arbiter, fixer, go-between, holdout, judge, maven, mediator, middleperson, referee, umpire; SEE CONCEPTS *348,359*

arc [*n*] *curve*
arch, bend, bow, crescent, curvation, curvature, half-moon, round; SEE CONCEPT *436*

arcade [*n*] *covered way*
cloister, colonnade, gallery, loggia, mall, passageway, piazza, portico, stoa, walkway; SEE CONCEPT *501*

arcane [*adj*] *hidden, secret*
cabalistic, esoteric, impenetrable, mysterious, mystic, occult, recondite, unaccountable, un-

knowable; SEE CONCEPT *576*

arch [*adj1*] *principal, superior*
accomplished, champion, chief, consummate, expert, finished, first, foremost, greatest, head, highest, leading, main, major, master, preeminent, premier, primary, top; SEE CONCEPT *574*

arch [*adj2*] *knowing, coy*
artful, frolicsome, mischievous, pert, playful, roguish, saucy, sly, waggish, wily; SEE CONCEPT *401*

arch [*n*] *curve, curved structure*
arc, archway, bend, bow, curvature, dome, semicircle, span, vault; SEE CONCEPT *436*

arch [*v*] *curve*
arc, bend, bow, bridge, camber, extend, form, hook, hump, hunch, round, shape, span, stretch; SEE CONCEPT *184*

archaeologist [*n*] *student of the physical remains of ancient cultures or eras*
archaeologian, classicist, excavator, paleologist, paleontologist, prehistorian; SEE CONCEPT *348*

archaeology [*n*] *study of the physical remains of ancient cultures or eras*
antiquarianism, excavation, paleohistory, paleology, paleontology, prehistory; SEE CONCEPT *349*

archaic [*adj*] *very old*
ancient, antiquated, antique, bygone, obsolete, olden, old-fashioned, outmoded, out of date, passé, primitive, superannuated; SEE CONCEPTS *578,797*

archetype [*n*] *typical example*
classic exemplar, form, ideal, model, original, paradigm, pattern, perfect specimen, prime example, prototype, standard; SEE CONCEPTS *636,686*

architect [*n*] *person who designs buildings*
artist, builder, creator, designer, draftsperson, engineer, inventor, maker, master builder, originator, planner, prime mover; SEE CONCEPT *348*

architecture [*n1*] *design of buildings*
architectonics, building, construction, engineering, planning; SEE CONCEPTS *349,439*

architecture [*n2*] *design, structure of something*
composition, constitution, construction, formation, framework, make-up, style; SEE CONCEPTS *660,733*

archive [*n*] *collection, usually of records*
annals, chronicles, clippings, documents, excerpts, extracts, files, papers, registers, roll, scrolls, writings; SEE CONCEPTS *271,281,432*

archives [*n*] *place where records are stored*
athenaeum, library, museum, office, registry, repository, storage, treasury, vault; SEE CONCEPT *439*

archway [*n*] *curved opening*
entrance, passage; SEE CONCEPT *440*

arctic [*adj*] *very cold*
chill, chilly, cool, freezing, frigid, frosty, frozen, gelid, glacial, icy, nippy, polar; SEE CONCEPT *605*

ardent [*adj1*] *very enthusiastic*
agog, avid, blazing, burning, desirous, eager, fervent, fervid, fierce, fiery, horny*, hot*, hungry, impassioned, intense, keen, lovey-dovey*, lusty, passionate, spirited, thirsty, vehement, warm, zealous; SEE CONCEPTS *401,404*

ardent [*adj2*] *loyal*
allegiant, constant, devoted, faithful, resolute, steadfast, true; SEE CONCEPT *404*

ardor [*n*] *enthusiasm*
avidity, devotion, eagerness, earnestness, feeling,

fervor, fierceness, fire, gusto, heat, intensity, jazz*, keenness, oomph*, passion, pep talk*, spirit, turn on*, vehemence, verve, warmth, weakness*, zeal, zest, zing; SEE CONCEPT *411*

arduous [adj] *difficult, hard to endure*
backbreaking, burdensome, exhausting, fatiguing, formidable, grueling, harsh, heavy, labored, laborious, murder, no picnic*, onerous, painful, punishing, rigorous, rough, severe, strenuous, taxing, tiring, toilsome, tough, troublesome, trying, uphill; SEE CONCEPT *565*

area [n1] *extent, scope of a surface*
breadth, compass, distance, expanse, field, operation, range, size, space, sphere, stretch, width; SEE CONCEPTS *651,792*

area [n2] *region, district*
belt, block, city, county, division, domain, dominion, enclosure, field, kingdom, locality, neck of the woods*, neighborhood, parcel, patch, plot, precinct, principality, quarter, section, sector, sphere, square, state, stretch, territory, township, tract, turf, vicinity, ward, zone; SEE CONCEPT *508*

arena [n1] *building or enclosure for entertainment or sports*
amphitheatre, boards*, bowl*, circus, coliseum, course, diamond, field, gridiron, ground, gym, gymnasium, hippodrome, ice, park, pit, platform, ring, rink, square, stadium, stage; SEE CONCEPT *438*

arena [n2] *area of activity*
battlefield, battleground, domain, field, province, realm, scene, sector, sphere, territory, theatre; SEE CONCEPT *198*

argot [n] *jargon*
cant, dialect, idiom, lingo, parlance, patois, slang, terminology, vernacular, vocabulary; SEE CONCEPT *276*

argue [v1] *verbally fight*
altercate, bandy, battle, bicker, break with, buck, bump heads, contend, cross, cross swords, disagree, dispute, face down, face off, feud, gang up on, get in one's face*, go one on one, hammer, hammer away, hash, hash over, hassle, have at each other, have at it, jump, jump on, knock around, lock horns*, mix it up*, pettifog, pick an argument, put up a fight, put up a struggle, quarrel, quibble, rehash, row, sass, set to, sock it to*, squabble, stick it to, talk back, wrangle; SEE CONCEPT *46*

argue [v2] *try to convince; present support*
appeal, assert, attest, claim, contend, controvert, defend, demonstrate, denote, display, elucidate, establish, evince, exhibit, explain, hold, imply, indicate, justify, maintain, manifest, persuade, plead, present, prevail upon, reason, show, suggest, talk into, testify, vindicate, warrant, witness; SEE CONCEPT *68*

argue [v3] *discuss*
agitate, canvass, clarify, debate, dispute, expostulate, hold, maintain, question, reason, remonstrate, talk about; SEE CONCEPTS *46,56*

argument [n1] *verbal fight*
altercation, beef, bickering, blowup, bone, bone of contention, bone to pick*, brannigan*, brawl, brush, clash, controversy, crusher*, debate, difference of opinion, disagreement, dispute, donnybrook, dustup*, exchange, face-off, falling, feud, finisher*, flap, fuss, gin*, go*, hassle, knockdown*, knock down and drag out*, out, quarrel, rhubarb*, romp, row, ruckus, ruction,

rumpus, run-in, scene, scrap, set-to, shindy*, spat, squabble, static*, stew*, talking heads*, tiff, words, wrangle; SEE CONCEPT *46*

argument [n2] *effort to convince; presentation of support*
argumentation, assertion, case, claim, contention, debate, defense, discussion, exchange, expostulation, grounds, line of reasoning, logic, plea, pleading, polemic, proof, questioning, reason, reasoning, remonstrance, remonstration; SEE CONCEPT *68*

argumentative [adj] *wanting to quarrel*
belligerent, combative, contentious, contrary, controversial, disputatious, factious, fire-eating, having a chip on one's shoulder*, litigious, opinionated, pugnacious, quarrelsome, salty, scrappy, spiky, touchy; SEE CONCEPT *401*

aria [n] *operatic solo*
descant, hymn, song; SEE CONCEPTS *263,595*

arid [adj1] *dry*
barren, bone-dry, desert, dry as a bone, dry as dust, dusty, moistureless, parched, thirsty, waterless; SEE CONCEPT *603*

arid [adj2] *uninterested, spiritless*
boring, colorless, drab, dreary, dry, dull, flat, insipid, lackluster, lifeless, tedious, unanimated, uninspired, vapid, wearisome; SEE CONCEPT *542*

arise [v1] *come into being; proceed*
appear, begin, come to light, commence, crop up, derive, emanate, emerge, ensue, flow, follow, happen, head, issue, occur, originate, result, rise, set in, spring, start, stem; SEE CONCEPT *105*

arise [v2] *get, stand, or go up*
ascend, climb, jump, mount, move upward, pile out*, rise, rise and shine*, roll out*, soar, stand, tower, turn out, wake up; SEE CONCEPTS *154,166*

aristocracy [n] *privileged class, government*
elite, gentility, gentry, haut monde, high society, nobility, noblesse, patricians, patriciate, peerage, society, upper class, upper crust*; SEE CONCEPTS *296,423*

aristocrat [n] *privileged person*
blueblood, gentleperson, lace curtain*, noble, patrician, peer, silk stocking, swell*, upper cruster*; SEE CONCEPT *423*

aristocratic [adj] *privileged, elegant*
aloof, blue-blooded, courtly, dignified, elegant, elite, fine, haughty, noble, patrician, polished, refined, snobbish, stylish, upper-class, well-born, well-bred; SEE CONCEPT *555*

arithmetic [n] *mathematics*
addition, calculation, computation, division, estimation, figuring, mathematics, reckoning, subtraction; SEE CONCEPTS *349,764*

arm [n1] *limb, appendage*
bender, bough, bow, branch, fin, flapper, flipper, handle, hook, member, offshoot, projection, prong, rod, stump, wing; SEE CONCEPTS *392,471*

arm [n2] *subdivision, annex*
affiliate, authority, block, branch, command, department, detachment, division, ell, extension, force, offshoot, power, projection, section, sector, wing; SEE CONCEPTS *824,835*

arm [n3] *narrow body of water*
branch, brook, channel, creek, estuary, firth, fjord, inlet, rivulet, sound, strait, stream, subdivision, tributary; SEE CONCEPT *514*

arm [v] *equip with weapon or power*
accouter, appoint, array, deck, equalize, fortify, furnish, gear, gird, guard, heel*, heel up*, issue,

load, load up, lug iron*, make ready, mobilize, outfit, pack, pack a rod*, prepare, prime, protect, provide, rig, rod up*, strengthen, supply, tote; SEE CONCEPTS *50,88,182*

armada [*n*] *group of ships or aircraft*
fleet, flotilla, force, navy, squadron; SEE CONCEPTS *432,504,506*

armament(s) [*n*] *weapon(s)*
ammunition, arms, defense, gun, hardware, heat*, material, materiel, munitions, ordnance, protection, security, weaponry; SEE CONCEPT *500*

armed [*adj*] *with weapon*
accoutered, equipped, fitted out, girded, loaded, outfitted, packing*, steeled, supplied; SEE CONCEPT *182*

armistice [*n*] *peace-establishing agreement*
ceasefire, suspension, treaty, truce; SEE CONCEPTS *230,684*

armor [*n*] *protective covering, often made of metal*
bulletproof vest, defense, guard, mail, plate, protection, security, sheath, shield; SEE CONCEPTS *451,476*

armory [*n*] *military building, usually for storing weapons*
arsenal, center, depot, dump, factory, headquarters, magazine, plant, range; SEE CONCEPTS *321,439*

arms [*n1*] *weaponry*
accoutrements, armaments, artillery, equipment, firearms, guns, munitions, ordnance, panoply, weapons; SEE CONCEPT *500*

arms [*n2*] *family crest*
blazonry, coat, emblazonry, emblem, ensign, escutcheon, heraldry, insignia, shield, signet; SEE CONCEPTS *284,625*

army [*n1*] *military force, usually for land*
armed force, artillery, battalion, battery, brigade, cavalry, column, command, company, corps, detail, division, flight, formation, infantry, legion, outfit, patrol unit, platoon, regiment, soldiers, soldiery, squad, troops, wing; SEE CONCEPT *322*

army [*n2*] *group resembling military force*
array, cloud, company, crowd, division, flock, horde, host, legion, mob, multitude, outfit, pack, regiment, scores, swarm, throng, unit; SEE CONCEPT *417*

aroma [*n*] *distinctive smell*
balm, bouquet, fragrance, incense, odor, perfume, redolence, scent, spice; SEE CONCEPT *599*

aromatic [*adj*] *distinctive smelling*
ambrosial, balmy, fragrant, odoriferous, perfumed, pungent, redolent, savory, scented, spicy, sweet, sweet-smelling; SEE CONCEPT *598*

around [*adv1*] *situated on sides, circumference, or in general area*
about, all over, any which way, encompassing, everywhere, in the vicinity, in this area, neighboring, over, throughout; SEE CONCEPT *581*

around [*adv2*] *close to a place*
about, almost, approximately, close at hand, near, nearby; SEE CONCEPT *586*

arouse [*v*] *excite, entice*
agitate, alert, animate, awaken, call, challenge, electrify, enliven, fire up, foment, foster, goad, heat up, incite, inflame, instigate, kindle, move, provoke, rally, rouse, send, spark, spur, stimulate, stir, thrill, turn on, waken, wake up, warm, whet, whip up, work up; SEE CONCEPTS *7,19,22*

arraign [*v*] *accuse*

blame, charge, criminate, hang on, incriminate, inculpate, indict, lay at one's door*, pin it on*, point the finger at*, summon; SEE CONCEPTS *44,317*

arrange [*v1*] *put in an order*
align, array, class, classify, clear the decks, dispose, file, fix up, form, group, line up, methodize, organize, police, police up, position, put in good shape*, put in order*, put to rights*, range, rank, regulate, sort, spruce, spruce up, systematize, tidy, whip into shape*; SEE CONCEPTS *84,158*

arrange [*v2*] *make plans, often involving agreement*
adapt, adjust, agree to, blueprint, chart, come to terms, compromise, concert, construct, contrive, decide, design, determine, direct, draft, establish, frame*, get act together*, get ready, hammer out a deal*, harmonize, iron out*, lay out, line up, make a connection, make ready, manage, map out, negotiate, organize, prepare, project, promote, provide, pull a wire, pull things together, quarterback*, resolve, schedule, scheme, set stage, settle, shape up, tailor, work out, work out a deal; SEE CONCEPTS *36,84*

arrange [*v3*] *prepare musical composition differently*
adapt, instrument, orchestrate, score; SEE CONCEPT *292*

arrangement [*n1*] *an understanding*
adjustment, agreement, compact, compromise, deal, frame-up*, game plan*, layout*, organization, package*, package deal*, plan, preparation, provision, schedule, settlement, setup, terms; SEE CONCEPT *684*

arrangement [*n2*] *something that has been ordered*
alignment, array, classification, combination, composition, design, display, disposition, distribution, form, grouping, lineup, method, ordering, organization, pattern, pecking order*, ranging, rank, sequence, setup, structure, system; SEE CONCEPTS *84,727*

arrangement [*n3*] *musical adaptation*
chart, composition, instrumentation, interpretation, lead sheet, orchestration, score, version; SEE CONCEPTS *262,595*

arrant [*adj*] *flagrant*
absolute, blatant, glaring, notorious, out-and-out, unmitigated, unregenerate; SEE CONCEPTS *401,545,576*

array [*n1*] *collection, considerable group*
arrangement, batch, body, bunch, bundle, clump, cluster, design, display, disposition, exhibition, formation, host, lineup, lot, multitude, order, parade, pattern, set, show, supply, throng; SEE CONCEPTS *432,769,787*

array [*n2*] *fine clothes*
apparel, attire, drapes*, dress, duds*, finery, full dress, garb, garments, getup*, rig*, threads*; SEE CONCEPT *451*

array [*v1*] *arrange in collection or order*
align, display, exhibit, form, group, line up, methodize, organize, parade, range, set, show, systematize; SEE CONCEPT *84*

array [*v2*] *dress in fine clothes*
attire, bedeck, clothe, deck, deck out, decorate, dog out*, drape, dud, dude up*, fit, fit out, garb, outfit, suit up, tog, try on, turn out, wrap; SEE

CONCEPT *167*
arrears [n] *debt*
back payment, balance due, claim, debit, deficiency, deficit, liability, obligation, unpaid bill; SEE CONCEPTS *332,335*
arrest [n1] *taking into custody*
accommodation, apprehension, appropriation, bag*, booby trap*, bust, captivity, capture, collar, commitment, confinement, constraint, crimp*, detention, drop*, fall*, gaff*, glom*, grab*, heat*, hook*, imprisonment, incarceration, jailing, mitt*, nab*, nail*, nick*, nip*, pickle*, pick up*, pinch*, preventive custody, protective custody, pull*, pull in*, restraining, run in*, sequestering, snare, sweep*; SEE CONCEPTS *90,317*
arrest [n2] *slowing or stopping*
blockage, cessation, check, checking, delay, end, halt, hindrance, inhibition, interruption, obstruction, prevention, restraining, restraint, stalling, stay, staying, stoppage, suppression, suspension; SEE CONCEPTS *121,234*
arrest [v1] *take into authorized custody*
apprehend, bag*, book, brace*, bust, capture, catch, collar, detain, drop*, gaff*, get*, glom*, grab*, hook*, imprison, incarcerate, jail, kick*, nab*, nail*, net*, nick*, pick up*, pinch*, pull*, pull in*, put the arm on*, put the cuffs on*, round up*, roust*, run in*, secure*, seize*, sidetrack*, snag*, tab*, tag*, take in, take prisoner, toss in jail*; SEE CONCEPTS *90,317*
arrest [v2] *stop or slow*
block, can, check, delay, drop, end, freeze, halt, hinder, hold, inhibit, interrupt, knock off, obstruct, prevent, restrain, restrict, retard, scrub*, shut down, stall, stay, suppress; SEE CONCEPTS *121,234*
arrest [v3] *get someone's attention*
absorb, catch, engage, engross, fascinate, grip; SEE CONCEPTS *7,19,22*
arrival [n1] *coming to a destination*
accession, advent, alighting, appearance, approach, arriving, debarkation, disembarkation, dismounting, entrance, happening, homecoming, influx, ingress, landing, meeting, occurrence, return; SEE CONCEPT *159*
arrival [n2] *something that makes it to a destination*
addition, arriver, caller, cargo, comer, conferee, delegate, delivery, entrant, envoy, freight, guest, mail, newcomer, package, parcel, passenger, representative, shipment, tourist, traveler, visitant, visitor; SEE CONCEPTS *337,423,712*
arrive [v1] *come to a destination*
access, alight, appear, attain, barge in, blow in, bob up*, breeze in*, bust in*, buzz*, check in*, clock in*, disembark, dismount, drop anchor, drop in, enter, fall by, fall in, get to, hit*, hit town*, land*, make it*, make the scene*, pop in*, pop up*, pull in*, punch the clock*, reach, report, roll in*, show, show up, sign in, sky in*, take place, turn up, visit, wind up at; SEE CONCEPT *159*
arrive [v2] *achieve recognition*
accomplish, become famous, flourish, make good, make it, make the grade, prosper, reach the top, score, succeed, thrive; SEE CONCEPT *706*
arrogance [n] *exaggerated self-opinion*
airs, aloofness, audacity, bluster, braggadocio, brass*, cheek*, chutzpah*, conceit, conceited-

ness, contemptuousness, crust*, disdain, disdainfulness, ego, egotism, gall, haughtiness, hauteur, high-handedness, hubris, imperiousness, insolence, loftiness, nerve, ostentation, overbearance, pomposity, pompousness, presumption, pretension, pretentiousness, pride, priggishness, scornfulness, self-importance, self-love, smugness, superciliousness, swagger, vanity; SEE CONCEPTS *411,633*
arrogant [adj] *having exaggerated self-opinion*
aloof, assuming, audacious, autocratic, biggety*, bossy, bragging, cavalier, cheeky, cocky, coldshoulder*, conceited, contemptuous, cool*, disdainful, domineering, egotistic, haughty, high and mighty*, high-handed, imperious, insolent, know-it-all*, lordly, on an ego trip*, overbearing, peremptory, pompous, presumptuous, pretentious, proud, puffed up*, scornful, self-important, smarty, smug, sniffy*, snippy*, snooty*, snotty*, stuck up*, supercilious, superior, swaggering, uppity*, vain, wise guy*; SEE CONCEPTS *401,404*
arrogate [v] *claim without justification*
accroach, appropriate, assume, commandeer, confiscate, demand, expropriate, preempt, presume, seize, take, usurp; SEE CONCEPTS *142,266*
arrow [n] *pointed weapon or symbol*
bolt, cursor, dart, indicator, missile, pointer, projectile, shaft; SEE CONCEPT *500*
arsenal [n] *storage of weapons*
armory, depository, depot, dump, factory, magazine, ordnance, plant, repository, stock, stockpile, store, storehouse, supply, warehouse; SEE CONCEPTS *432,439*
arson [n] *intentional burning*
firing, incendiarism, pyromania, setting fire, torching, touching off; SEE CONCEPT *249*
art [n1] *skill, creativity*
adroitness, aptitude, artistry, craft, craftsmanship, dexterity, expertise, facility, imagination, ingenuity, inventiveness, knack, know-how, knowledge, mastery, method, profession, trade, virtuosity; SEE CONCEPT *706*
art [n2] *cunning*
artfulness, artifice, astuteness, canniness, craftiness, deceit, duplicity, guile, slyness, trickery, wiliness; SEE CONCEPT *411*
art [n3] *creation meant to communicate or appeal to senses or mind*
abstraction, carving, description, design, illustration, imitation, modeling, molding, painting, pictorialization, portrayal, representation, sculpting, shaping, simulation, sketching, symbolization; SEE CONCEPT *349*
artery [n] *channel*
avenue, boulevard, canal, conduit, corridor, course, duct, highway, line, passage, pathway, road, route, sewer, thoroughfare, track, tube, way; SEE CONCEPT *501*
artful [adj] *skillful; cunning*
adept, adroit, clever, crafty, designing, dexterous, foxy*, ingenious, masterly, politic, proficient, resourceful, scheming, sharp, shrewd, slick*, sly, smart, smooth*, tricky, wily; SEE CONCEPTS *404,528*
article [n1] *item, object*
commodity, dojigger*, gizmo*, piece, substance, thing, thingamabob*, thingamajig*, unit; SEE CONCEPT *433*
article [n2] *piece of writing*

beat*, blurb*, column, commentary, composition, discourse, editorial, essay, exposition, feature, item, paper, piece, scoop*, spread, story, theme, think piece*, treatise, write-up; SEE CONCEPTS 270,271,280

article [n3] *section of document*
branch, chapter, clause, detail, division, element, head, heading, item, matter, paragraph, part, passage, piece, point, portion, provision; SEE CONCEPTS 270,318

articulate [adj] *clearly, coherently spoken*
clear, coherent, comprehensible, definite, distinct, eloquent, expressive, fluent, intelligible, lucid, meaningful, understandable, well-spoken; SEE CONCEPT 267

articulate [v1] *say clearly, coherently*
enunciate, express, mouth, pronounce, say, sound off*, speak, state, talk, utter, verbalize, vocalize, voice; SEE CONCEPTS 47,55

articulate [v2] *connect*
concatenate, couple, fit together, hinge, integrate, join, link; SEE CONCEPT 113

articulation [n1] *clear, coherent speech*
delivery, diction, enunciation, expression, pronunciation, saying, speaking, statement, talking, utterance, verbalization, vocalization, voicing; SEE CONCEPT 55

articulation [n2] *connection*
coupling, hinge, joining, joint, junction, juncture, unification, union; SEE CONCEPT 113

artifice [n1] *hoax; clever act*
con, contrivance, device, dodge, expedient, gambit, gimmick*, machination, maneuver, play, ploy, racket*, ruse, savvy, scam*, stratagem, subterfuge, tactic, wile; SEE CONCEPT 59

artifice [n2] *cunning; deception*
artfulness, chicanery, craftiness, dishonesty, duplicity, guile, scheming, slyness, trickery, wiliness; SEE CONCEPT 411

artifice [n3] *skill, cleverness*
ability, adroitness, deftness, facility, finesse, ingenuity, invention, inventiveness, know-how*, skill; SEE CONCEPT 630

artificial [adj1] *fake; imitation*
bogus, counterfeit, ersatz, fabricated, factitious, faked, false, falsie*, hyped up*, manufactured, mock, phony*, plastic, sham, simulated, specious, spurious, substitute, synthetic, unnatural, unreal; SEE CONCEPT 582

artificial [adj2] *pretended; affected*
assumed, contrived, false, feigned, forced, hollow, insincere, labored, mannered, meretricious, phony*, put-on, spurious, theatrical, unnatural; SEE CONCEPT 401

artificial intelligence [n] *development of "thinking" computer systems*
AI, expert system, natural language processing, neural network, robotics; SEE CONCEPTS 269,463

artillery [n] *weaponry or military unit*
arms, battery, bazooka, big guns*, cannon, cannonry, force, gunnery, heavy stuff*, munitions, ordnance, rainmakers*, stovepipe, weapons; SEE CONCEPTS 322,500

artist [n] *person skilled in creative activity*
artisan, artiste, authority, composer, craftsperson, creator, expert, handicrafter, inventor, painter, virtuoso, whiz*; SEE CONCEPT 352

artistic [adj1] *beautiful, satisfying to senses*
aesthetic, creative, cultivated, cultured, decorative, dramatic, elegant, exquisite, fine, graceful, grand, harmonious, ideal, imaginative, musical, ornamental, pictorial, picturesque, pleasing, poetic, refined, rhythmical, sensitive, stimulating, stylish, sublime, tasteful; SEE CONCEPT 579

artistic [adj2] *being skilled in creative activity*
accomplished, artful, artsy-craftsy*, arty, crafty, discriminating, gifted, imaginative, inventive, skillful, talented; SEE CONCEPT 527

artistry [n] *great skill in creative endeavors*
ability, accomplishment, artfulness, brilliance, craftship, creativity, finesse, flair, genius, mastery, proficiency, style, talent, taste, touch, virtuosity, workmanship; SEE CONCEPTS 630,655

artless [adj] *simple*
direct, genuine, guileless, honest, ingenuous, innocent, naive, natural, open, plain, pure, sincere, straight, straightforward, talking turkey*, true, unadorned, unaffected, uncontrived, unpretentious, unsophisticated, up front*; SEE CONCEPTS 267,562

arty [adj] *pretended expertise in art; affected interest*
affected, deceptive, ephemeral, false, flaunting, illusory, imitative, overblown, popular, popularized, pretentious, pseudo, tasteless; SEE CONCEPT 582

as [conj1] *while, when*
at the time that, during the time that, in the act of, in the process of, just as, on the point of; SEE CONCEPT 544

as [conj2] *in the way that; to a degree*
acting as, being, by its nature, comparatively, equally, essentially, for instance, functioning as, in the manner that, in the same manner with, just as, just for, like, serving as, similarly, such as; SEE CONCEPT 544

as [conj3] *because*
as long as, being, cause, considering, for, for the reason that, inasmuch as, now, seeing that, since, whereas; SEE CONCEPT 544

as [prep] *in the role of*
being, in the character of, under the name of; SEE CONCEPT 544

ascend [v] *go up*
arise, climb, escalate, float, fly, lift off, mount, move up, rise, scale, soar, sprout, take off, tower; SEE CONCEPTS 149,166

ascendancy/ascendency [n] *domination*
advantage, authority, command, control, dominance, dominion, edge, influence, jump*, leg up*, mastery, on top, power, predominance, preeminence, prepotence, prevalence, reign, rule, sovereignty, superiority, supremacy, sway, upper hand*, whip hand*; SEE CONCEPTS 376,671

ascension [n] *going up*
ascent, climbing, escalating, flying, mounting, rise, rising, scaling, soaring, towering; SEE CONCEPTS 149,166

ascent [n1] *upward movement*
ascendance, ascending, ascension, clambering, climb, climbing, lift, mounting, rise, rising, scaling, spring, take off; SEE CONCEPT 166

ascent [n2] *upward slope*
acclivity, grade, gradient, incline, ramp, rise; SEE CONCEPTS 738,757

ascertain [v] *make sure*
catch on, check, check out*, check up on*, confirm, determine, dig*, discover, divine, double-check*, establish, eye*, eyeball*, find out, figure out, get down cold*, get down pat*, get old...

it down*, get the hang of*, identify, learn, learn the ropes*, look-see*, make certain, make sure, peg*, pick up*, pick up on*, read, see, settle, size, size up*, tell, verify; SEE CONCEPTS 31,34,38

ascetic [adj] *self-denying*
abstaining, abstemious, abstinent, austere, disciplined, puritanical, Spartan, strict; SEE CONCEPT 401

ascribe [v] *assign to source*
accredit, attribute, charge, credit, hang on, impute, lay, pin on*, put down, refer, reference, set down; SEE CONCEPTS 39,49

ashamed [adj] *regretting, remorseful*
abashed, apologetic, bashful, blushing, chagrined, compunctious, conscience-stricken, contrite, crestfallen, debased, demeaned, discomfited, disconcerted, distraught, distressed, embarrassed, flustered, guilty, hesitant, humble, humbled, humiliated, meek, mortified, muddled, penitent, regretful, reluctant, repentant, shamed, shamefaced, sheepish, shy, sorry, stammering, stuttering, submissive; SEE CONCEPT 550

ashen [adj] *gray*
anemic, blanched, cadaverous, colorless, ghastly, gray, leaden, pale, pallid, pasty, sallow, wan, white; SEE CONCEPT 618

ash(es) [n] *remains of burning*
charcoal, cinders, dust, embers, powder, relics, remains, ruins, slag, soot; SEE CONCEPT 260

ashore [adv] *toward, onto land from water*
aground, beached, on dry land, on land, on shore, shorewards; SEE CONCEPT 583

aside [adv] *away from; to the side*
abreast, afar, alone, alongside, apart, away, beside, by oneself, down, in isolation, in reserve, near, nearby, neck and neck, out, out of the way, privately, separately, sidewise; SEE CONCEPT 586

aside [n] *confidential statement*
departure, digression, discursion, interpolation, interposition, parenthesis, tangent, throwaway*; SEE CONCEPT 51

asinine [adj] *senseless*
absurd, cretinous, daft, foolish, half-witted, idiotic, inane, moronic, silly, sophomoric, stupid; SEE CONCEPTS 402,548

ask [v1] *question*
buzz*, canvass, catechize, challenge, cross-examine, demand, direct, enjoin, examine, give the third degree*, go over, grill*, hit*, hunt for*, inquire, institute, interrogate, investigate, needle*, pick one's brains*, pop the question*, pry into, pump, put the screws to*, put through the wringer*, query, quiz, request, roast*, sweat*; SEE CONCEPT 48

ask [v2] *request*
angle, appeal, apply, beg, beseech, bite*, bum*, call for, charge, claim, command, contend for, crave, demand, entreat, file for, hit*, hustle*, implore, impose, knock*, levy, mooch*, order, petition, plead, pray, promote*, request, requisition, seek, solicit, sue, supplicate, touch*, urge; SEE CONCEPT 53

ask [v3] *invite*
bid, call upon, propose, suggest, summon, urge; SEE CONCEPT 75

askance [adv] *sideways*
_kew, disapprovingly, disdainfully, dubiously, _long, sideways, skeptically, suspi-

ciously; SEE CONCEPTS 581,583

askew [adj] *crooked*
askance, askant, aslant, awry, bent, buckled, catawampus*, cockeyed*, crookedly, curved, knotted, lopsided, oblique, obliquely, off-center, slanted, slanting, to one side, topsy-turvey*, turned, twisted, yaw ways*, zigzag*; SEE CONCEPT 586

asleep [adj] *unconscious*
catching some zzz's*, comatose, conked*, crashed*, dormant, dozing, dreaming, flaked out*, getting shut-eye*, hibernating, inactive, in dreamland*, inert, in repose, napping, on the kip*, out*, out cold*, out like a light*, out of it*, reposing, resting, sacked out*, sleeping, slumbering, snoozing, snoring, somnolent, taking forty winks*; SEE CONCEPTS 210,315,681

aspect [n1] *visible feature*
air, appearance, attitude, bearing, condition, countenance, demeanor, expression, face, facet, form, look, manner, mien; SEE CONCEPTS 434,628,673

aspect [n2] *element to consider*
angle, bearing, direction, facet, feature, gimmick, hand, outlook, perspective, phase, point of view, position, prospect, regard, scene, side, situation, slant, switch, twist, view, vista; SEE CONCEPT 668

asperity [n] *harshness; bad temper*
acerbity, acrimony, bitterness, churlishness, crabbiness, crossness, difficulty, disagreeableness, irascibility, irritability, meanness, moroseness, peevishness, roughness, sharpness, sourness, sullenness, tartness; SEE CONCEPT 633

aspersion [n] *verbal exhibition of bad temper*
abuse, animadversion, backbiting, backhanded compliment, black eye*, calumny, defamation, detraction, dirty dig*, hit*, invective, knock*, libel, obloquy, put-down*, rap*, slam*, slander, smear*, vituperation; SEE CONCEPTS 52,54,58

asphyxiate [v] *cut off air*
choke, drown, smother, stifle, strangle, strangulate, suffocate; SEE CONCEPTS 121,246

aspirant [n] *person with wish, dream*
applicant, candidate, competitor, contestant, hopeful, postulant, striver, wannabe; SEE CONCEPTS 366,423

aspiration [n] *goal, hope*
aim, ambition, ambitiousness, craving, desire, direction, dream, eagerness, endeavor, fire in the belly*, hankering, inclination, longing, object, objective, passion, pursuit, push, right stuff*, urge, vocation, wish, work, yearning; SEE CONCEPTS 20,659

aspire [v] *aim, hope*
be ambitious, be eager, crave, desire, dream, hanker, long, pursue, seek, strive, struggle, try, want, wish, yearn; SEE CONCEPT 20

aspiring [adj] *hopeful*
ambitious, aspirant, eager, eager beaver*, endeavoring, enthusiastic, impassioned, longing, on the make*, striving, wishful, would-be, zealous; SEE CONCEPT 403

ass [n] *stupid person*
blockhead*, dolt, donkey*, dope, dunce, fool, idiot, imbecile, jackass*, jerk*, nitwit*, numbskull*, simpleton*, twit*; SEE CONCEPT 412

assail [v] *attack, usually with words*
abuse, assault, bash, berate, beset, blast, blister, bust, charge, come at, criticize, encounter, have

at*, impugn, invade, lambaste, lay into*, malign, maltreat, molest, revile, set upon*, trash*, vilify, work over; SEE CONCEPTS 52,86

assailant [n] *attacker*
aggressor, antagonist, assaulter, bushwhacker*, enemy, foe, goon*, hit person, invader, mugger, opposite number*, trigger person; SEE CONCEPT 412

assassin [n] *murderer of prominent or important person*
butcher*, clipper*, dropper*, eliminator, enforcer, executioner, guerrilla*, gun*, gun person, hatchet person, hit person, killer, liquidator, piece person*, plugger*, slayer, soldier, torpedo*, trigger person; SEE CONCEPT 412

assassinate [v] *murder prominent or important person*
bump off*, do in*, eliminate, execute, gun down, hit, kill, knock off*, liquidate, slaughter, slay; SEE CONCEPT 252

assault [n] *attack*
advance, aggression, charge, incursion, invasion, offensive, onset, onslaught, rape, storm, storming, strike, violation; SEE CONCEPT 86

assault [v] *attack*
abuse, advance, assail, bash, beset, blast, blitz, bushwhack, charge, come down on*, go for, haul off on*, invade, jump, jump down one's throat*, jump on one's case*, lay into, let have it*, light into*, rape, ruin, set upon, shoot down, slam, slap around, storm, strike, trash, violate, work over, zap*; SEE CONCEPTS 52,86

assay [n] *analysis*
appraisal, assessment, estimation, evaluation, examination, inspection, investigation, measurement, rating, survey, test, trial, valuation; SEE CONCEPTS 24,103,290

assay [v] *analyze*
appraise, apprise, assess, check, check out, estimate, evaluate, examine, eyeball*, inspect, investigate, measure, peg*, prove, rate, read, see, size, size up*, survey, test, try, valuate, value, weigh; SEE CONCEPTS 24,103

assemblage [v] *gathering of people*
aggregation, assembly, association, collection, company, congregation, convergence, crowd, group, throng; SEE CONCEPT 417

assemble [v1] *congregate*
accumulate, agglomerate, amass, bring together, bunch, bunch up, call, call together, capture*, collect, come together, convene, convoke, corral*, flock, gang up*, gather, group, hang around*, hang out*, huddle, lump, make the scene*, meet, meet up, mobilize, muster, rally, reunite, round up, scare up*, summon, unite; SEE CONCEPT 114

assemble [v2] *put together*
compile, connect, construct, contrive, erect, fabricate, fashion, fit, form, join, make, manufacture, model, mold, piece together, produce, set up, shape, unite, weld; SEE CONCEPT 113

assembly [n1] *congregation*
accumulation, aggregation, assemblage, association, band, body, bunch, clambake*, cluster, coffee klatch*, collection, company, conclave, confab*, conference, convocation, council, crew, crowd, faction, flock, gathering, get-together*, group, huddle, mass, meet*, meeting, multitude, rally, sit-in*, throng, turnout*; SEE CONCEPTS

381,432

assembly [n2] *putting together*
adjustment, attachment, building, collection, connecting, construction, erection, fabrication, fitting together, joining, manufacture, manufacturing, modeling, molding, piecing together, setting up, shaping, welding; SEE CONCEPT 113

assent [n] *agreement*
acceptance, accession, accord, acknowledgment, acquiescence, admission, affirmation, approval, authorization, compliance, concurrence, consent, nod, permission, sanction; SEE CONCEPTS 8,684

assent [v] *agree*
accede, accept, accord, acquiesce, adopt, allow, approve, buy, cave in*, comply, concur, conform, consent, cut a deal*, defer, ditto*, embrace, espouse, give five*, give in, go along with, grant, knuckle under*, okay*, pass on*, permit, recognize, sanction, say uncle*, shake on*, subscribe; SEE CONCEPT 8

assert [v] *insist, declare, maintain*
advance, affirm, allege, argue, asservate, attest, aver, avouch, avow, butt in*, cite, claim, contend, defend, horn in, justify, mouth off*, pop off*, predicate, press, proclaim, profess, pronounce, protest, put forward, say, shoot off one's mouth*, shoot one's wad*, stand up for, state, stress, swear, uphold, vindicate, warrant; SEE CONCEPT 49

assertion [n] *declaration, positive statement*
affirmation, allegation, asservation, attestation, avowal, contention, defense, insistence, maintenance, mouthful, okay, predication, profession, pronouncement, report, say so*, stamp of approval, stressing, two cents' worth*, vindication; SEE CONCEPTS 49,278

assertive [adj] *aggressive*
absolute, assured, certain, confident, decided, decisive, demanding, dogmatic, domineering, emphatic, firm, forceful, forward, insistent, militant, overbearing, positive, pushy, self-assured, self-confident, strong-willed, sure; SEE CONCEPT 404

assess [v1] *evaluate, determine*
appraise, apprise, assay, check*, check out*, compute, determine, dig it*, estimate, figure*, fix, gauge, guess, judge, nick*, peg*, rate, reckon, set, size*, size up, survey, take measure*, valuate, value, weigh; SEE CONCEPT 24

assess [v2] *assign fee,*
amount charge, demand, evaluate, exact, fix, impose, levy, rate, tax, value; SEE CONCEPT 330

assessment [n1] *evaluation*
appraisal, computation, determination, estimate, estimation, judgment, rating, reckoning, valuation, value judgment; SEE CONCEPT 24

assessment [n2] *assignment of fee, amount*
appraisal, charge, demand, duty, estimate, fee, levy, rate, rating, tariff, tax, taxation, toll, valuation; SEE CONCEPT 332

asset [n1] *advantage*
aid, benefit, blessing, boon, credit, distinction, help, resource, service, treasure; SEE CONCEPT 661

asset(s) [n2] *property or money possessed*
ace in the hole*, ace up sleeve*, backing, bankroll, budget, capital, credit, equity, estate, funds, goods, holdings, kitty*, mattress*, money, nest egg*, nut*, possessions, rainy day, reserve(s), resources, riches, sock*, something aside, something put away, stake,

valuables, wealth; SEE CONCEPTS *332,340,710*

assiduous [*adj*] *hard-working*
active, attentive, busy, constant, diligent, eager beaver*, exacting, grinding, indefatigable, industrious, laborious, persevering, plugging, scrupulous, sedulous, steady, studious, unflagging, untiring, whiz, zealous; SEE CONCEPTS *538,542*

assign [*v1*] *select and give a responsibility*
accredit, allow, appoint, ascribe, attach, attribute, authorize, cast, charge, choice, commission, commit, credit, delegate, deputize, designate, downlink, download, draft, elect, empower, enroll, entrust, hang on*, hire, hold responsible, impute, name, nominate, ordain, pin on*, refer, reference, select, slot, tab, tag; SEE CONCEPTS *41,50,88*

assign [*v2*] *set apart for a reason*
allocate, allot, appoint, apportion, appropriate, consign, designate, detail, determine, dish out*, distribute, divide, earmark, fix, fork out*, give, grant, hand out*, hand over, indicate, mete, prescribe, relegate, shell out*, specify, stipulate; SEE CONCEPTS *129,135*

assignation [*n*] *clandestine meeting*
affair, appointment, date, engagement, heavy date*, illicit meeting, love nest*, one-night stand*, quickie*, rendezvous, secret meeting, tryst; SEE CONCEPTS *375,386*

assignment [*n1*] *responsibility, task*
appointment, beat, charge, chore, commission, drill, duty, homework, job, mission, position, post, practice, stint; SEE CONCEPT *362*

assignment [*n2*] *selecting or setting apart*
allocation, allotment, appointment, apportionment, appropriation, ascription, assignation, attribution, authorization, choice, consignment, delegation, designation, determination, distribution, giving, grant, nomination, selection, specification, stipulation; SEE CONCEPTS *41,129*

assimilate [*v1*] *absorb mentally*
comprehend, digest, grasp, incorporate, ingest, learn, osmose, sense, soak up, take in, take up, understand; SEE CONCEPT *15*

assimilate [*v2*] *become adjusted; adjust*
acclimatize, accommodate, acculturate, accustom, adapt, become like, become similar, blend in, conform, fit, go native*, homogenize, homologize, intermix, match, mingle, parallel, standardize; SEE CONCEPTS *232,701*

assist [*n*] *help*
abetment, aid, assistance, backing, benefit, boost, collaboration, comfort, compensation, cooperation, facilitation, furtherance, hand, helping hand, lift, reinforcement, relief, service, support; SEE CONCEPT *110*

assist [*v*] *help*
abet, aid, back, bail out, benefit, boost, collaborate, cooperate, do for*, expedite, facilitate, further, give a boost*, give a leg up*, give a lift*, go down the line for*, go for, go to bat for*, go with, grease the wheels*, hype*, lend a hand*, make a pitch for*, open doors*, plug*, puff*, put on the map*, reinforce, relieve, ride s*, root for*, run interference for*, serve, p for, stump*, support, sustain, take care np*, work for, work with; SEE CONCEPT

e [*n*] *help*
t, aid, assist, backing, benefit, boost, coln, comfort, compensation, cooperation,

facilitation, furtherance, hand, help, helping hand, lift, reinforcement, relief, service, support, sustenance; SEE CONCEPT *110*

assistant [*n*] *helper*
abettor, accessory, accomplice, adherent, adjunct, aide, ally, appointee, apprentice, associate, attendant, auxiliary, backer, backup*, coadjutant, coadjutor, collaborator, colleague, companion, confederate, cooperator, deputy, fellow worker, flunky*, follower, friend, gofer*, help, helpmate, mate, partner, patron, peon*, representative, right-hand person, secretary, subordinate, supporter, temp*, temporary worker; SEE CONCEPTS *348,423*

associate [*n*] *colleague*
accessory, accomplice, affiliate, aid, ally, assistant, auxiliary, branch, buddy, chum, clubber*, cohort, collaborator, companion, compatriot, comrade, confederate, consort, cooperator, coworker, crony, fellow, friend, helper, joiner, kissing cousin, mate, offshoot, one of the folks*, pal, pard*, partner, peer, playmate, sidekick; SEE CONCEPTS *348,423*

associate [*v1*] *connect in the mind*
affiliate, blend, bracket, combine, concord, conjoin, correlate, couple, group, identify, join, league, link, lump together, mix, pair, relate, think of together, unite, yoke; SEE CONCEPT *39*

associate [*v2*] *befriend*
accompany, amalgamate, be friends, be in cahoots*, buddy up, bunch up, come together, confederate, consort, fraternize, gang up, get in on, get into, get in with, get together, go along with, go partners*, hang around, hang out, hang out with*, hobnob, join, join up with, line up with, mingle, mix, pal up, play footsie with*, pool, run around with, run with, string along with, swing with, take up with, team up, throw in together, tie in, tie up, truck with, work with; SEE CONCEPTS *114,384*

association [*n1*] *group with common interest or pursuit*
affiliation, alliance, band, bunch, circle, clan, clique, club, coalition, combination, combo, company, confederacy, confederation, congress, cooperative, corporation, crew, crowd, family, federation, fellowship, fraternity, gang, guild, hookup*, league, mob, order, organization, outfit, partnership, pool, rat pack*, ring, society, sodality, sorority, syndicate, tie-in, tie-up, tribe, troops, troupe, union, zoo*; SEE CONCEPTS *323,325,387*

association [*n2*] *friendship*
acquaintance, acquaintanceship, affiliation, agreement, assistance, camaraderie, companionship, comradeship, conjunction, cooperation, familiarity, fellowship, fraternization, frequenting, friendliness, hookup*, intimacy, membership, participation, partnership, relation, relationship; SEE CONCEPTS *387,388*

association [*n3*] *mental connection*
bond, combination, concomitance, concordance, connotation, correlation, identification, impression, joining, juxtaposition, linkage, linking, lumping together, mixing, mixture, pairing, recollection, relation, remembrance, tie, train of thought, union; SEE CONCEPT *39*

assorted [*adj*] *various*
different, diverse, diversified, heterogeneous, hybrid, indiscriminate, miscellaneous, mixed, mot-

ley, sundry, varied, variegated; SEE CONCEPT *564*

assortment [*n*] *variety*
array, choice, collection, combination, combo, diversity, garbage, group, hodgepodge, jumble, kind, medley, mélange, miscellany, mishmash, mixed bag, mixture, potpourri, selection, sort; SEE CONCEPTS *432,665*

assuage [*v*] *soothe, relieve*
allay, alleviate, appease, calm, compose, conciliate, cool*, ease, fill, lessen, lighten, lull, make nice*, mitigate, moderate, mollify, pacify, palliate, placate, pour oil on*, propitiate, quench, quiet, sate, satisfy, soften, still, surfeit, sweeten, take the edge off*, take the sting out*, temper, tranquilize; SEE CONCEPTS *7,22,244*

assume [*v1*] *believe, take for granted*
accept, ascertain, be afraid, be inclined to think, conclude, conjecture, consider, count upon, deduce, deem, divine, estimate, expect, fall for, fancy, find, gather, get the idea*, guess, have a hunch*, have sneaking suspicion, hypothesize, imagine, infer, judge, posit, postulate, predicate, presume, presuppose, speculate, suppose, surmise, suspect, theorize, think, understand; SEE CONCEPTS *12,26*

assume [*v2*] *take, undertake*
accept, acquire, appropriate, arrogate, attend to, begin, confiscate, don, embark upon, embrace, enter upon, seize, set about, take on, take over, take up; SEE CONCEPTS *87,142*

assume [*v3*] *pretend*
act, adopt, affect, bluff, counterfeit, fake, feign, imitate, impersonate, mimic, pretend, put on, simulate; SEE CONCEPT *59*

assume [*v4*] *adopt, acquire*
annex, appropriate, arrogate, borrow, clap hands on*, commandeer, confiscate, expropriate, get fingers on*, get hands on*, glom onto*, grab, grab hold of*, hijack, kipe*, liberate, moonlight requisition*, preempt, seize, snatch, swipe, take over, usurp; SEE CONCEPTS *139,142*

assumed [*adj1*] *pretended*
affected, artificial, bogus, counterfeit, fake, false, feigned, fictitious, imitation, made-up, make-believe, phony, pretended, put-on, sham, simulated, spurious; SEE CONCEPT *582*

assumed [*adj2*] *expected*
accepted, conjectured, connoted, counted on, given, granted, hypothesized, hypothetical, inferred, postulated, presumed, presupposed, supposed, suppositional, surmised, tacit, taken as known, taken for granted, understood; SEE CONCEPTS *403,689*

assuming [*adj*] *presumptuous, arrogant*
bold, conceited, disdainful, domineering, egotistic, forward, haughty, imperious, overbearing, pushy, rude; SEE CONCEPT *404*

assumption [*n1*] *taking something for granted; something expected*
acceptance, accepting, assuming, belief, conjecture, expectation, fancy, guess, hunch, hypothesis, inference, posit, postulate, postulation, premise, presumption, presupposition, shot*, shot in the dark*, sneaking suspicion, stab, supposal, supposition, surmise, suspicion, theorization, theory; SEE CONCEPT *689*

assumption [*n2*] *assuming possession, power*
acceptance, accepting, acquisition, adoption, appropriation, arrogation, assuming, embracing, grab, seizure, shouldering, takeover, taking, taking on, taking up, undertaking, usurpation; SEE CONCEPTS *129,142*

assumption [*n3*] *arrogance*
brass*, chutzpah*, cockiness, conceit, imperiousness, insolence, nerve, presumption, pride, sass*, self-importance; SEE CONCEPT *411*

assurance [*n1*] *statement to relieve doubt*
affirmation, assertion, declaration, guarantee, insurance, lock*, lock on*, oath, pledge, profession, promise, rain or shine*, security, shoo-in*, support, sure thing*, vow, warrant, warranty, word, word of honor; SEE CONCEPTS *71,278*

assurance [*n2*] *confidence*
aggressiveness, aplomb, arrogance, assuredness, audacity, boldness, bravery, certainty, certitude, conviction, coolness, courage, effrontery, faith, firmness, impudence, nerve, poise, positiveness, presumption, security, self-confidence, self-reliance, sureness, surety, temerity, trust; SEE CONCEPT *410*

assure [*v1*] *convince, relieve doubt*
bag*, bet on*, comfort, encourage, hearten, inspire, persuade, reassure, satisfy, sell*, sell on*, soothe; SEE CONCEPT *68*

assure [*v2*] *promise*
affirm, attest, aver, brace up, buck up, certify, confirm, give one's word, guarantee, pledge, swear, vouch for, vow; SEE CONCEPT *71*

assure [*v3*] *make certain*
cinch, clinch, complete, confirm, ensure, guarantee, have a lock on*, ice*, insure, lock, lock on, lock up, make sure, nail down*, put on ice*, seal, secure, set; SEE CONCEPTS *36,91*

assured [*adj1*] *absolutely certain*
beyond doubt, cinched, clear-cut, clinched, confirmed, decided, definite, dependable, ensured, fixed, guaranteed, indubitable, insured, in the bag*, irrefutable, made certain, nailed down*, on ice*, pronounced, racked*, sealed, secure, set, settled, sewed up*, sure, surefire, undoubted, unquestionable; SEE CONCEPT *535*

assured [*adj2*] *confident*
assertive, audacious, bold, brazen, certain, cocksure*, collected, complacent, composed, confident, cool, gung ho*, gutsy*, high*, imperturbable, overconfident, poised, positive, puffed up*, pumped up*, pushy, rosy*, sanguine, secure, self-assured, self-confident, self-possessed, sure, unflappable, unhesitating, upbeat*; SEE CONCEPTS *401,404*

astern [*adv*] *backward*
abaft, aft, rear, rearward; SEE CONCEPT *581*

astonish [*v*] *surprise*
amaze, astound, bewilder, blow away*, blow one's mind*, boggle, bowl over*, confound, daze, dumbfound, flabbergast, floor*, knock over*, overwhelm, put one away*, shock, spring on, stagger, startle, stun, stupefy, take aback, throw a curve*; SEE CONCEPT *42*

astonishing [*adj*] *surprising*
amazing, astounding, bewildering, breathtaking, extraordinary, impressive, marvelous, miraculous, spectacular, staggering, startling, striking, stunning, stupefying, stupendous, wonderful, wondrous; SEE CONCEPTS *547,572*

astonishment [*n*] *state of surprise*
amazement, astoundment, awe, bewilderment, confusion, consternation, dumbfoundment, one

for the books*, shock, something else*, stunner, stupefaction, wonder, wonderment; SEE CONCEPTS *230,410*

astound [v] *amaze*
astonish, bewilder, blow away, bowl over*, confound, confuse, daze, dumbfound, flabbergast, knock over with feather*, overwhelm, shock, stagger, startle, stun, stupefy, surprise, take aback; SEE CONCEPT *42*

astounding [adj] *amazing*
astonishing, breathtaking, confounding, eye-popping*, mind-blowing*, mind-boggling*, overwhelming, shocking, startling, stupefying, surprising, wondrous; SEE CONCEPTS *548,571*

astray [adj] *off the path or right direction*
adrift, afield, amiss, awry, gone, lost, off, off course, off the mark, roaming, straying, vanished, wandering, wrong; SEE CONCEPTS *545,581*

astride [adj] *with a leg on either side*
astraddle, athwart, on the back of, piggyback, sitting on, straddling; SEE CONCEPT *583*

astringent [adj] *harsh*
acetic, acrid, biting, bitter, cutting, sharp, tonic; SEE CONCEPTS *598,613*

astrology [n] *prophesy of the future by observation of stars and planets*
astrometry, horoscope; SEE CONCEPT *70*

astronaut [n] *space explorer*
cosmonaut, moonwalker, pilot, rocketeer, rocket scientist, space person, star person; SEE CONCEPT *348*

astronomy [n] *study of the stars and planets other than Earth*
astrochemistry, astrography, astrolithology, astrometry, astrophysics, selenology, sky-watching, stargazing, uranology; SEE CONCEPT *349*

astute [adj] *perceptive*
adroit, brainy, bright, calculating, canny, clever, crafty, discerning, foxy, insightful, intelligent, keen, knowing, not born yesterday*, on the ball*, perspicacious, quick on the uptake*, sagacious, savvy, sharp, sharp as a tack*, shrewd, sly; SEE CONCEPT *402*

asunder [adv] *apart; into pieces*
disconnected, disjoined, divided, in half, loose, separated, split, torn, to shreds; SEE CONCEPT *785*

asylum [n1] *refuge*
cover, den, harbor, haven, hideaway, hideout, hole, ivory tower*, port, preserve, refuge, retreat, safe house, safety, sanctuary, security, shelter; SEE CONCEPTS *435,515*

asylum [n2] *psychiatric hospital*
institution, loony bin*, madhouse*, mental hospital, mental institution, sanatorium; SEE CONCEPTS *312,439,516*

asymmetrical [adj] *uneven*
awry, crooked, disproportional, gibbous, lacking correspondence, not proportionate, not uniform, unbalanced, unequal, unsymmetrical; SEE CONCEPTS *480,566,606*

at [prep] *about; in the direction of*
appearing in, by, found in, in the vicinity of, near to, on, placed at, situated at, through, toward; SEE CONCEPTS *581,583,799*

atheism [n] *belief that no God exists*
disbelief, doubt, freethinking, godlessness, heresy, iconoclasm, impiety, infidelity, irreligion, irreverence, nihilism, nonbelief, paganism,

skepticism, unbelief; SEE CONCEPT *689*

atheist [n] *nonbeliever*
agnostic, free thinker, heathen, infidel, irreligionist, pagan, skeptic; SEE CONCEPTS *361,423*

athlete [n] *person involved in sports*
amateur, animal, challenger, competitor, contender, contestant, games player, gorilla*, iron person*, jock, jockey, muscle person*, player, professional, shoulders, sport, sportsperson, superjock*; SEE CONCEPT *366*

athletic [adj1] *agile; prepared to participate in sports*
able-bodied, active, brawny, energetic, fit, lusty, muscular, powerful, robust, strapping, strong, sturdy, vigorous; SEE CONCEPTS *406,489*

athletic [adj2] *relating to sports*
competitive, contesting, exercise-related, recreational, sporting, team; SEE CONCEPT *536*

athletics [n] *sports*
contest, drill, events, exercises, games, practice, races, recreation, workout; SEE CONCEPT *363*

atmosphere [n1] *gases around the earth*
air, envelope, heavens, pressure, sky, substratosphere, troposphere; SEE CONCEPT *437*

atmosphere [n2] *general feeling or mood*
air, ambience, aura, background, character, climate, color, environment, feel, feeling, flavor, impression, local color, medium, mood, place, property, quality, scene, semblance, sense, space, spirit, surroundings, taste, tone; SEE CONCEPT *673*

atom [n] *smallest part of something*
bit, crumb, dot, fragment, grain, iota, jot, minimum, mite, modicum, molecule, morsel, mote, ounce, particle, scintilla, scrap, shred, smidgen, speck, spot, tittle, trace, whit; SEE CONCEPT *831*

atom bomb [n] *nuclear weapon*
A-bomb, backpack nuke*, doomsday machine*, fission bomb, H-bomb, hydrogen bomb, neutron bomb, nuclear bomb, nuke*, thermonuclear weapon; SEE CONCEPT *500*

atomic [adj1] *tiny*
diminutive, fragmentary, granular, microscopic, minute; SEE CONCEPT *773*

atomic [adj2] *nuclear*
atom-powered, fissionable, thermonuclear; SEE CONCEPT *485*

atone [v] *compensate; make amends for former misdoing*
absolve, answer, apologize, appease, balance, correct, counterbalance, do penance, expiate, make amends, make redress, make reparation, make up for, offset, outweigh, pay, pay one's dues*, propitiate, recompense, reconcile, redeem, redress, repair, set off, square, take one's medicine*; SEE CONCEPTS *108,126*

atonement [n] *compensation*
amends, expiation, indemnification, payment, penance, propitiation, recompense, redemption, redress, reparation, restitution, satisfaction; SEE CONCEPTS *126,337*

atrocious [adj1] *outrageous; widely condemned*
awful, bad, barbaric, beastly, desperate, diabolical, fiendish, flagrant, godawful*, grody*, gross*, hairy*, heinous, lousy, monstrous, nefarious, rotten, scandalous, shocking, villainous, wicked; SEE CONCEPTS *545,571*

atrocious [adj2] *offensive*
appalling, awful, bad, beastly, detestable, disgusting, dreadful, execrable, foul, godawful*,

grody*, gross*, horrible, horrid, horrifying, icky*, loathsome, noisome, obscene, repulsive, rotten, sickening, terrible; SEE CONCEPTS 548,571

atrocity [n1] outrageous behavior

atrociousness, barbarity, barbarousness, enormity, fiendishness, heinousness, horror, monstrousness, nefariousness, shockingness, villianousness, wickedness; SEE CONCEPTS 411,657

atrocity [n2] cruelness, offensiveness; widely condemned action

abomination, barbarity, brutality, crime, enormity, evil, horror, infamy, inhumanity, iniquity, monstrosity, offense, outrage, ruthlessness, savagery, viciousness, wrong; SEE CONCEPTS 29,645

atrophy [n] wasting away, disintegration

decline, degeneracy, degeneration, deterioration, diminution, downfall, downgrade; SEE CONCEPTS 674,698

attach [v1] join, fasten

add, adhere, affix, annex, append, bind, connect, couple, fix, hitch on, hitch up, hook on, hook up, latch onto, link, make fast, prefix, rivet, secure, slap on*, stick, tag on*, tie, unite; SEE CONCEPTS 85,113,160

attach [v2] socially join

accompany, affiliate, associate, become associated with, combine, enlist, join forces with, latch onto*, sign on with, sign up with, unite with; SEE CONCEPT 114

attach [v3] attribute, ascribe

allocate, allot, appoint, assign, associate, connect, consign, designate, detail, earmark, impute, invest with, lay, name, place, put, second, send; SEE CONCEPTS 62,73

attachment [n1] fastening

adapter, bond, clamp, connection, connector, coupling, fastener, joint, junction, link, tie; SEE CONCEPT 471

attachment [n2] something joined, fastened to another

accessory, accoutrement, adapter, addition, adjunct, annex, appendage, appurtenance, auxiliary, extension, extra, fitting, fixture, part, supplement; SEE CONCEPT 824

attachment [n3] affection, high regard

affinity, amore, attraction, bond, case, crush, devotion, fidelity, fondness, friendship, hankering*, liking, love, loyalty, partiality, possessiveness, regard, shine*, tenderness, weakness, yen*; SEE CONCEPT 32

attack [n1] physical assault

advance, aggression, assailing, assailment, barrage, blitz, blitzkrieg, charge, defilement, dirty deed*, drive, encounter, encroachment, foray, incursion, initiative, inroad, intervention, intrusion, invasion, irruption, mugging, offense, offensive, onrush, onset, onslaught, outbreak, push, raid, rape, rush, skirmish, storming, strike, thrust, violation, volley; SEE CONCEPT 86

attack [n2] verbal assault

abuse, aggression, belligerence, blame, calumny, censure, combativeness, criticism, denigration, denunciation, impugnment, libel, pugnacity, slander, vilification; SEE CONCEPTS 52,54

attack [n3] sudden dysfunction or disorder

access, ailment, bout, breakdown, convulsion, disease, failure, fit, illness, paroxysm, relapse, seizure, spasm, spell, stroke, throe; SEE CONCEPT

308

attack [v1] assault physically

advance, aggress, ambush, assail, assault, bash, bat, bean*, beat, beset, besiege, biff*, blast, blister, boff*, bombard, boot*, bop*, brain*, bust, charge, chop down, clip, clock*, club, combat, cook*, harm, hit, hurt, infiltrate, invade, jump, kick, knock block off*, knock cold*, knock for a loop*, larrup*, lay siege to, light into*, molest, mug, overwhelm, pounce upon, punch, raid, rush, set upon, slog, soak, stab, storm, strike, take the offensive, turn on, wallop*, whop*; SEE CONCEPT 86

attack [v2] assault verbally

abuse, berate, blame, blitz, censure, criticize, impugn, jump down one's throat*, jump on one's case*, lay into, malign, refute, reprove, revile, shoot down*, stretch, vilify; SEE CONCEPTS 52,54

attack [v3] set to work

buckle down*, deal with, dive into, plunge into, set to, start in on, tackle, take up, tear into*; SEE CONCEPT 112

attacker [n] aggressor

assailant, assaulter, mugger, raider, traducer; SEE CONCEPT 412

attain [v] achieve, accomplish

accede to, acquire, arrive, arrive at, bring off, come through, complete, cop*, earn, effect, fulfill, gain, get*, get fat*, get hands on, get there, glom onto*, grasp, hit, latch onto, make it, obtain, procure, promote, pull off*, rack up, reach, realize, reap, score, secure, snag, succeed, unzip*, win; SEE CONCEPTS 120,706

attainable [adj] within reach; achievable

accessible, accomplishable, at hand, available, cherry pie*, duck soup*, easy, feasible, gettable, likely, no problem*, no sweat*, obtainable, piece of cake*, possible, potential, practicable, probable, procurable, reachable, realizable, securable; SEE CONCEPTS 528,552

attainment [n] achievement, accomplishment

acquirement, acquisition, arrival, completion, feat, finish, fulfillment, gaining, getting, obtaining, procurement, reaching, realization, reaping, securing, succeeding, winning; SEE CONCEPT 706

attempt [n] try, effort

all one's got*, attack, bid*, crack*, dry run*, endeavor, exertion, experiment, fling, go, header*, lick*, one's all, one's darnedest*, one's level best*, pursuit, shot, stab, striving, struggle, trial, try, tryout, undertaking, venture, whack*, workout; SEE CONCEPT 87

attempt [v] try, make effort

aim, attack, do level best*, endeavor, essay, exert oneself, experiment, give a fling*, give a whirl*, give best shot*, give it a go*, give it a try*, give old college try*, go the limit*, have a crack*, have a go at*, make a run at*, pursue, push, seek, shoot the works*, solicit, strive, tackle, take a stab at*, take best shot*, take on, try one's hand at*, undertake, venture; SEE CONCEPT 87

attend [v1] be present at

appear, be a guest, be at, be present, be there, bob up*, catch, check in, clock in*, come to light*, drop in, frequent, go to, haunt, make an appearance, make it*, make the scene*, pop up*, punch in*, punch the clock*, ring in*, show, show up, sit in on, time in, turn up, visit; SEE CONCEPT 114

attend [v2] care for

be in the service of, doctor, do for, look after, mind, minister to, nurse, serve, take care of, tend, wait upon, watch, work for; SEE CONCEPT *110*

attend [*v3*] *pay attention; apply oneself*
catch, concentrate on, devote oneself, follow, get a load of*, hear, hearken, heed, keep one's eye on*, lend an ear*, listen, listen up*, look after, look on, mark, mind, note, notice, observe, occupy oneself with, pay heed, pick up, regard, see to, watch; SEE CONCEPTS *34,596,623*

attend [*v4*] *accompany*
bear, be associated with, be connected with, catch, follow, issue from, make the scene, occur with, result from; SEE CONCEPT *714*

attend [*v5*] *escort*
accompany, chaperon, companion, consort, convoy, escort, guard, squire, usher; SEE CONCEPTS *114,714*

attendance [*n1*] *being present*
appearance, attending, being in evidence, being there, participation, presence; SEE CONCEPT *388*

attendance [*v2*] *people present at event*
assemblage, assembly, audience, box office, company, congregation, crowd, draw, gate, gathering, gross, house, observers, onlookers, patrons, public, spectators, turnout, witnesses; SEE CONCEPT *417*

attendant [*adj*] *being present or related*
accessory, accompanying, ancillary, associated, attending, coincident, concomitant, consequent, incident; SEE CONCEPT *577*

attendant [*n*] *person who serves others*
aide, alarm clock*, assistant, auxiliary, baby sitter, bird dog, chaperon, companion, custodian, domestic, escort, follower, guide, helper, lackey, nurse, orderly, secretary, servant, understudy, usher, waitperson; SEE CONCEPT *348*

attention [*n1*] *concentration*
absorption, application, assiduity, consideration, contemplation, debate, deliberation, diligence, engrossment, heed, heedfulness, immersion, industry, intentness, mind, scrutiny, study, thinking, thought, thoughtfulness; SEE CONCEPT *409*

attention [*n2*] *consideration, care*
awareness, big rush*, brace, concern, consciousness, looking after, ministration, notice, observation, recognition, regard, spotlight, tender loving care, TLC*, treatment; SEE CONCEPTS *32,410*

attention deficit disorder [*n*] *learning disability*
ADD, ADHD, hyperactiveness, hyperactivity, short attention span; SEE CONCEPTS *403,542*

attention(s) [*n3*] *courtesy*
amenity, assiduities, care, civility, compliment, consideration, deference, gallantry, mindfulness, politeness, regard, respect, service; SEE CONCEPT *644*

attentive [*adj1*] *concentrating*
alert, all ears*, awake, aware, conscientious, enrapt, enthralled, fascinated, glued, hanging on every word*, heedful, hooked, immersed, intent, interested, listening, mindful, observant, on one's toes*, on the ball*, on the job*, on the lookout*, on the qui vive*, preoccupied, regardful, studious, vigilant, watchful; SEE CONCEPT *403*

attentive [*adj2*] *considerate*
accommodating, civil, courteous, devoted, gallant, gracious, kind, obliging, polite, respectful, solicitous, thoughtful; SEE CONCEPT *401*

attenuate [*v*] *weaken*
abate, constrict, contract, cripple, debilitate, deflate, disable, dissipate, enfeeble, extenuate, lessen, mitigate, sap, shrink, thin, undermine, vitiate; SEE CONCEPT *240*

attest [*v*] *affirm, vouch for*
adjure, announce, argue, assert, asseverate, authenticate, aver, bear out, bear witness, certify, confirm, corroborate, countersign, declare, demonstrate, display, exhibit, give evidence, indicate, prove, ratify, seal, show, substantiate, support, sustain, swear, testify, uphold, verify, warrant, witness; SEE CONCEPT *49*

attic [*n*] *space under the roof of a house*
garret, loft, sky parlor*, top floor; SEE CONCEPTS *440,448*

attire [*n*] *clothing*
accoutrements, apparel, array, bib and tucker*, clothes, costume, drapes, dress, duds*, garb, garments, gear, getup, habiliments, habit, outfit, raiment, things, threads*, togs, uniform, vestment, wear; SEE CONCEPT *451*

attire [*v*] *clothe*
accoutre, array, clad, costume, deck, deck out*, doll up*, drape, dress, dud*, dude up*, equip, fit out, outfit, suit up, tog, turn out; SEE CONCEPT *167*

attitude [*n1*] *mental outlook*
air, angle, approach, belief, bent, bias, character, demeanor, disposition, frame of mind, headset*, inclination, leaning, like it is*, mental state, mindset*, mindtrip*, mood, notion, opinion, perspective, philosophy, point of view, position, posture, predilection, prejudice, proclivity, reaction, routine, say so*, sensibility, sentiment, set, slant, stance, stand, standing, standpoint, temper, temperament, twist, view, where one is at*; SEE CONCEPTS *410,689*

attitude [*n2*] *stance*
aspect, bearing, carriage, manner, mien, pose, position, posture, stand; SEE CONCEPT *757*

attorney [*n*] *lawyer*
advocate, ambulance chaser*, barrister, counsel, counselor, DA, fixer, front, legal beagle*, legal eagle*, lip*, mouthpiece*, pleader*, proxy, spieler*; SEE CONCEPT *355*

attract [*v*] *draw attention*
allure, appeal to, bait, beckon, beguile, bewitch, bring, captivate, charm, come on*, court, drag, draw, enchant, endear, engage, enthrall, entice, entrance, exert influence, fascinate, freak out*, give the come-on*, go over big, grab, hook, induce, interest, intrigue, inveigle, invite, kill, knock dead*, knock out*, lure, magnetize, make a hit with*, mousetrap*, pull, rope in*, score, seduce, send*, slay*, solicit, spellbind, steer, suck in*, sweep off one's feet*, tempt, turn on, vamp, wile, wow*; SEE CONCEPTS *7,11,22*

attraction [*n*] *ability to draw attention; something that draws attention*
allure, allurement, appeal, attractiveness, bait, captivation, charm, chemistry, come-on*, courting, draw, drawing power, enchantment, endearment, enthrallment, enticement, fascination, gravitation, inclination, inducement, interest, invitation, it*, lure, magnetism, pull, seduction, solicitation, temptation, tendency; SEE CONCEPTS *14,676*

attractive [*adj*] *appealing, drawing attention*
adorable, agreeable, alluring, beautiful, beckoning, bewitching, captivating, charming, comely,

enchanting, engaging, enthralling, enticing, fair, fascinating, fetching, glamorous, good-looking, gorgeous, handsome, hunky*, interesting, inviting, looker*, lovely, luring, magnetic, mesmeric, pleasant, pleasing, prepossessing, pretty, provocative, seductive, stunning, taking, tantalizing, teasing, tempting, winning, winsome; SEE CONCEPTS *529,579*

attribute [n] *feature*
aspect, character, characteristic, facet, idiosyncrasy, indication, mark, note, particularity, peculiarity, point, property, quality, quirk, sign, speciality, symbol, trait, virtue; SEE CONCEPTS *411,673,834*

attribute [v] *ascribe, assign to source*
account for, accredit, apply, associate, blame, charge, connect, credit, fix upon, hang on, hold responsible, impute, lay, pin on, refer, reference, trace; SEE CONCEPT *73*

attrition [n1] *wearing down or away*
abrasion, attenuation, debilitation, depreciation, disintegration, erosion, grinding, rubbing, thinning, weakening, wear; SEE CONCEPTS *469,776*

attrition [n2] *regret*
contriteness, penance, penitence, remorse, remorsefulness, repentance; SEE CONCEPTS *410,689*

attune [v] *adjust*
acclimatize, accommodate, accord, accustom, adapt, balance, compensate, conform, coordinate, counterbalance, familiarize, harmonize, integrate, make agree, proportion, reconcile, regulate, tune; SEE CONCEPT *232*

atypical [adj] *nonconforming*
aberrant, abnormal, anomalous, deviant, different, divergent, exceptional, heteroclite, irregular, odd, peculiar, preternatural, strange, unnatural, unrepresentative; SEE CONCEPTS *547,564*

auburn [n] *reddish-brown color*
chestnut, copper, hazel, henna, nut, russet, rust, tawny, titian; SEE CONCEPT *622*

au courant [adj] *up-to-date*
aware, current, enlightened, hip*, informed, up to speed*, well-informed; SEE CONCEPTS *530,820*

auction [n] *competitive sale; sale by bid*
bargain, jam*, sell-off; SEE CONCEPTS *324,345*

audacious [adj1] *reckless, daring*
adventurous, aweless, bold, brassy, brave, cheeky*, courageous, daredevil, dauntless, enterprising, fearless, foolhardy, gutty*, intrepid, nervy, rash, resolute, risky, smart ass*, unafraid, uncurbed, undaunted, ungoverned, valiant, venturesome; SEE CONCEPT *401*

audacious [adj2] *arrogant, presumptuous*
assuming, bantam, bold, brash, brassy, brazen, cheeky*, defiant, disrespectful, forward, impertinent, impudent, insolent, nervy, rude, saucy, shameless; SEE CONCEPTS *401,404*

audacity [n1] *recklessness, daring*
adventurousness, audaciousness, boldness, bravery, courage, dauntlessness, enterprise, fearlessness, guts, intrepidity, nerve, rashness, valor, venturesomeness; SEE CONCEPT *633*

audacity [n2] *arrogance, presumptuousness*
assurance, audaciousness, brass, cheek*, chutzpah*, cockiness*, crust, defiance, disrespectfulness, effrontery, forwardness, gall, guts*, gutsiness, hardiness, impertinence, impudence, insolence, moxie, nerve, rudeness, shameless-

ness, spunk, stuff*, temerity; SEE CONCEPTS *411,633*

audible [adj] *able to be heard*
aural, auricular, clear, deafening, detectable, discernible, distinct, hearable, loud, loud enough, perceptible, plain, resounding, roaring, sounding, within earshot; SEE CONCEPTS *591,594*

audience [n1] *group observing an entertainment or sporting event*
admirers, assemblage, assembly, congregation, crowd, devotees, fans, following, gallery, gathering, hearers, house, listeners, market, moviegoers, onlookers, patrons, playgoers, public, showgoers, spectators, theatergoers, turnout, viewers, witnesses; SEE CONCEPT *417*

audience [n2] *hearing*
audition, conference, consideration, consultation, conversation, discussion, interview, meeting, reception; SEE CONCEPT *266*

audit [n] *inspection of financial records*
analysis, balancing, check, checking, examination, investigation, report, review, scrutiny, survey, verification, view; SEE CONCEPT *330*

audit [v] *inspect financial records*
analyze, balance, check, examine, go over, go through, investigate, report, review, scrutinize, sit in, survey, verify; SEE CONCEPTS *103,330*

audition [n] *test of ability*
audience, demo, hearing, reading, trial, try on, tryout; SEE CONCEPT *290*

auditor [n] *person who inspects financial records*
accountant, actuary, bookkeeper, cashier; SEE CONCEPT *348*

auditorium [n] *room, building for entertainment events*
amphitheater, assembly hall, barn*, concert hall, hall, movie house, music hall, opera house, playhouse, reception hall, theater; SEE CONCEPTS *293,439,448*

augment [v] *make greater; improve*
add to, aggrandize, amplify, beef up*, boost, build, build up, compound, develop, enhance, enlarge, expand, extend, grow, heighten, increase, inflate, intensify, magnify, mount, multiply, pad, piggyback*, progress, raise, reinforce, strengthen, sweeten, swell, tag on; SEE CONCEPTS *236,244,245*

augmentation [n] *making greater; improving*
accession, accretion, addition, amplification, beefing up*, boost, buildup, development, enhancement, enlargement, enrichment, expansion, extension, fleshing out, growth, heightening, hike, increase, increment, inflation, intensification, magnification, multiplication, raise, reinforcement, rise, strengthening, swelling, up, upping; SEE CONCEPTS *244,245*

augur [n] *predictor*
diviner, forecaster, harbinger, herald, oracle, prognosticator, prophet, seer, soothsayer; SEE CONCEPT *423*

augur [v] *predict; be an omen of*
adumbrate, bespeak, bode, call it*, call the shots*, crystal-ball, figure out, forecast, foreshadow, foretell, harbinger, have a hunch, herald, portend, presage, prognosticate, promise, prophesy, psych out*, read, signify, soothsay; SEE CONCEPT *70*

augury [n1] *omen*
auspice, boding, forerunner, foretoken, forewarning, harbinger, herald, portent, precursor,

presage, prognostication, promise, prophecy, sign, token, warning; SEE CONCEPT *284*

augury [*n2*] *prediction*
divination, prediction, prophecy, soothsaying; SEE CONCEPT *70*

august [*adj*] *dignified, noble*
baronial, brilliant, eminent, exalted, glorious, grand, grandiose, highfalutin'*, high-minded, high-ranking, honorable, imposing, impressive, lofty, lordly, magnificent, majestic, monumental, pompous, regal, resplendent, stately, superb, venerable; SEE CONCEPTS *404,567*

au pair [*n*] *live-in nanny*
babysitter, caregiver, day care provider, domestic servant, governess, housekeeper, live-in; SEE CONCEPT *295*

aura [*n*] *air, character*
ambience, appearance, aspect, atmosphere, background, emanation, feel, feeling, mood, quality, scent, semblance, suggestion, tone; SEE CONCEPT *673*

auspices [*n*] *protection; support*
advocacy, aegis, authority, backing, care, charge, control, countenance, guidance, influence, patronage, sponsorship, supervision; SEE CONCEPTS *94,376*

auspicious [*adj*] *encouraging; favorable*
advantageous, bright, favorable, felicitous, fortunate, golden, halcyon, happy, hopeful, lucky, opportune, promising, propitious, prosperous, rosy, timely, well-timed; SEE CONCEPT *572*

austere [*adj1*] *severe in manner*
ascetic, astringent, cold, earnest, exacting, forbidding, formal, grave, grim, hard, harsh, inexorable, inflexible, obdurate, rigid, rigorous, serious, sober, solemn, somber, stern, stiff, strict, stringent, unfeeling, unrelenting; SEE CONCEPT *550*

austere [*adj2*] *refraining; abstinent*
abstemious, ascetic, chaste, continent, economical, puritanical, self-denying, self-disciplined, sober, straightlaced, strict, subdued, unrelenting; SEE CONCEPT *401*

austere [*adj3*] *grim, barren*
bald, bare, bare-bones, bleak, clean, dour, plain, primitive, rustic, severe, simple, spare, spartan, stark, subdued, unadorned, unembellished, vanilla*; SEE CONCEPT *485*

austerity [*n1*] *severity*
acerbity, asperity, astringence, coldness, exactingness, exactness, formality, formalness, gravity, grimness, hardness, harshness, inclemency, inflexibility, obduracy, rigidity, rigor, seriousness, solemnity, sternness, stiffness, strictness, stringency; SEE CONCEPT *644*

austerity [*n2*] *refraining; abstinence*
abstemiousness, asceticism, chasteness, chastity, continence, determination, economy, prudence, puritanism, self-denial, self-discipline, sobriety, stoicism, strictness, temperance; SEE CONCEPT *633*

austerity [*n3*] *grimness, barrenness*
baldness, bareness, dourness, economy, plainness, primitiveness, rusticism, severity, simplicity, spareness, spartanism, starkness, unadornment; SEE CONCEPT *723*

authentic [*adj*] *real, genuine*
accurate, actual, authoritative, bona fide, certain, convincing, credible, creditable, dependable, fac-

tual, faithful, for real*, legit*, legitimate, official, original, pure, reliable, sure, true, trustworthy, trusty, twenty-four carat*, valid, veritable; SEE CONCEPT *582*

authenticate [*v*] *establish as real, genuine*
accredit, attest, authorize, bear out, certify, confirm, corroborate, endorse, guarantee, justify, prove, substantiate, validate, verify, vouch, warrant; SEE CONCEPTS *12,103*

author [*n*] *composer of written work*
biographer, columnist, composer, creator, essayist, ghost, ghostwriter, ink slinger*, journalist, originator, playwright, poet, producer, prose writer, reporter, scribbler*, scribe, scripter, word slinger*, wordsmith, work-for-hire*, writer; SEE CONCEPT *348*

authoritarian [*adj*] *domineering*
absolute, authoritative, autocratic, despotic, dictatorial, disciplinarian, doctrinaire, dogmatic, harsh, imperious, magisterial, rigid, severe, strict, totalitarian, tyrannical, unyielding; SEE CONCEPTS *319,401*

authoritarian [*n*] *domineering person*
absolutist, autocrat, despot, dictator, disciplinarian, tyrant; SEE CONCEPTS *354,412*

authoritative [*adj1*] *recognized as true, valid*
accurate, attested, authentic, authenticated, circumstantiated, confirmed, definitive, dependable, documented, factual, faithful, learned, legit*, proven, reliable, righteous, scholarly, sound, straight from horse's mouth*, supported, trustworthy, truthful, validated, verified, veritable; SEE CONCEPT *582*

authoritative [*adj2*] *domineering*
assertive, authoritarian, autocratic, commanding, confident, decisive, dictatorial, doctrinaire, dogmatic, dominating, imperative, imperious, imposing, masterly, officious, peremptory, self-assured; SEE CONCEPT *550*

authoritative [*adj3*] *official, authorized*
administrative, approved, bureaucratic, canonical, departmental, ex cathedra, executive, ex officio, imperial, lawful, legal, legitimate, magisterial, mandatory, ruling, sanctioned, sovereign, supreme; SEE CONCEPTS *319,536*

authority [*n1*] *power, control*
ascendancy, authorization, beef*, charge, clout*, command, credit, domination, dominion, edge, esteem, force, goods*, government, guts*, influence, juice*, jump, jurisdiction, leg up*, license, mastery, might, might and main*, permission, permit, pizzazz*, pow*, powerhouse, prerogative, prestige, punch, right, ropes*, rule, say, sayso*, steam, strength, strong arm*, stuff*, supremacy, sway, upper hand*, warrant, weight, what it takes*, whip hand*, word, zap*; SEE CONCEPTS *376,685,688*

authority [*n2*] *expert, animate or inanimate*
arbiter, aristocrat, bible, big cheese*, big shot*, big wig*, boss, brains*, brass*, buff*, CEO, city hall*, connoisseur, czar, egghead*, establishment*, exec*, executive, expert, feds*, front office*, governor, guru, ivory dome*, judge, kingfish*, kingpin*, law*, power elite, pro, professional, professor, pundit, scholar, specialist, textbook*, top brass*, top dog*, top hand*, upstairs*, veteran, virtuoso, whiz, wizard; SEE CONCEPTS *280,348,354*

authorize [*v1*] *give power or control*

accredit, bless, commission, empower, enable, entitle, give authority, give the go-ahead*, give the green light*, give the word*, invest, license, okay, rubber-stamp*, say the word*, vest; SEE CONCEPTS *50,88*

authorize [*v2*] *permit, allow*
affirm, approve, confirm, countenance, endorse, give leave, let, license, qualify, ratify, sanction, suffer, tolerate, warrant; SEE CONCEPTS *10,83*

autobiography [*n*] *written account of one's own life*
adventures, bio, biography, confession, diary, experience, journal, letter, letters, life, life story, memoir, personal history, reminiscences, self-portrayal; SEE CONCEPT *280*

autocracy [*n*] *government by one*
absolutism, czarism, despotism, dictatorship, monarchy, monocracy, oppression, totalitarian government, tyranny; SEE CONCEPTS *354,691*

autocrat [*n*] *dictator*
authoritarian, Caesar*, despot, Fascist, Hitler*, overlord, totalitarian, tyrant; SEE CONCEPT *354*

autocratic [*adj*] *holding power exclusively*
absolute, all-powerful, arbitrary, bossy, czarlike, despotic, dictatorial, domineering, driving, imperious, monocratic, pushing, tyrannical, tyrannous; SEE CONCEPTS *319,536*

autograph [*n*] *handwritten signature*
endorsement, handwriting, inscription, John Hancock*, seal, token, undersignature, writing; SEE CONCEPT *284*

autograph [*v*] *write signature*
endorse, engross, handwrite, ink, inscribe, pen, sign, signature, subscribe, write by hand; SEE CONCEPT *79*

automated [*adj*] *made or done by a machine*
automatic, computerized, electrical, electronic, mechanical, mechanized, motorized, programmed, robotic; SEE CONCEPTS *538,549*

automatic [*adj1*] *done or made by machine*
automated, electric, electronic, mechanical, mechanized, motorized, robotic, self-moving, self-regulating, self-starting; SEE CONCEPTS *538,549*

automatic [*adj2*] *done by habit*
autogenetic, habitual, impulsive, instinctive, instinctual, intuitive, involuntary, knee-jerk, mechanical, natural, perfunctory, reflex, routine, spontaneous, unconscious, unforced, unintentional, unmeditated, unthinking, unwilled; SEE CONCEPTS *403,538*

automatic [*adj3*] *occurring as natural consequence*
assured, certain, inescapable, inevitable, necessary, routine, unavoidable; SEE CONCEPTS *530,535*

automation [*n*] *machine control*
computerization, industrialization, mechanization; SEE CONCEPT *770*

automobile [*n*] *land vehicle; car*
auto, bucket of bolts*, bug*, buggy*, bus, clunker*, compact, convertible, crate*, four-wheeler*, gas guzzler*, go-cart*, hardtop, hatchback, heap*, jalopy*, junker*, lemon*, limousine, motor car, oil burner*, passenger car, pickup truck, ride*, sedan, sports car, station wagon, subcompact, taxi, transportation, truck, tub*, van, wheels*, wreck*; SEE CONCEPT *505*

autonomous [*adj*] *independent*

free, self-determining, self-governing, self-ruling, sovereign, uncontrolled; SEE CONCEPT *554*

autonomy [*n*] *independence*
freedom, liberty, self-determination, self-government, self-rule, sovereignty; SEE CONCEPT *652*

autopsy [*n*] *examination of dead body*
dissection, necropsy, pathological examination, postmortem; SEE CONCEPTS *103,310*

autumn [*n*] *season between summer and winter*
autumnal equinox, fall, harvest; SEE CONCEPT *814*

auxiliary [*adj*] *supplementary*
abetting, accessory, adjuvant, ancillary, appurtenant, backup, complementary, contributory, extra, reserve, secondary, spare, subordinate, subservient, subsidiary, supporting; SEE CONCEPTS *546,824*

auxiliary [*n*] *helper*
accessory, accomplice, adjutant, ally, assistant, associate, companion, confederate, crutch*, partner, reserve, subordinate, supporter; SEE CONCEPT *423*

avail [*n*] *use*
account, advantage, applicability, appropriateness, fitness, service, usefulness; SEE CONCEPT *680*

avail [*v*] *be of use; use*
account, advantage, answer, be adequate, benefit, fill, fulfill, meet, profit, satisfy, serve, suffice, work; SEE CONCEPTS *91,225*

available [*adj*] *ready for use*
accessible, achievable, applicable, at hand, at one's disposal*, attainable, come-at-able*, convenient, derivable from, feasible, free, getatable*, handy, obtainable, on deck*, on hand*, on tap*, open to, possible, prepared, procurable, purchasable, reachable, ready willing and able*, realizable, securable, serviceable, up for grabs*, usable, vacant; SEE CONCEPT *576*

avalanche [*n*] *falling large mass; sudden rush of large quantity*
barrage, deluge, flood, inundation, landslide, landslip, snowslide, torrent; SEE CONCEPTS *509,524,787*

avant-garde [*adj*] *unconventional, forward-looking*
beat*, experimental, head*, hip*, innovative, lead, leading-edge*, liberal, new, new wave, pioneering, progressive, radical, state-of-the-art, vanguard; SEE CONCEPTS *564,585*

avarice [*n*] *extreme greed*
avidity, close-fistedness*, covetousness, cupidity, frugality, grabbiness, greediness, miserliness, niggardliness, parsimony, penny-pinching*, penuriousness, rapacity, stinginess, thrift; SEE CONCEPTS *335,410*

avaricious [*adj*] *greedy*
covetous, gluttonous, hoarding, money-grubbing*, pleonectic, predatory, rapacious, selfish, tight*; SEE CONCEPTS *404,542*

avenge [*v*] *retaliate*
chasten, chastise, come back at, even the score, get back at, get even, payback, punish, redress, repay, requite, retribute, revenge, stick it to, take satisfaction, take vengeance, venge, vindicate; SEE CONCEPTS *122,126*

avenue [*n*] *street; path*
access, alley, approach, boulevard, channel, course, drive, entrance, entry, exit, outlet, park-

way, passage, pathway, promenade, road, route, thoroughfare, way; SEE CONCEPT *501*

average [*adj1*] *normal, typical*
boilerplate*, common, commonplace, customary, dime a dozen*, everyday, fair, fair to middling*, familiar, garden*, garden-variety*, general, humdrum*, intermediate, mainstream, mediocre, medium, middle of the road*, middling, moderate, nowhere*, ordinary, passable, plastic*, regular, run of the mill*, so-so*, standard, tolerable, undistinguished, unexceptional, usual; SEE CONCEPT *547*

average [*adj2*] *numerical mean*
intermediate, median, medium, middle; SEE CONCEPT *762*

average [*n*] *normal, typical amount*
mean, median, medium, middle, midpoint, norm, par, rule, standard, usual; SEE CONCEPTS *647,787*

average [*v*] *obtain numerical mean*
balance, equate, even out; SEE CONCEPT *764*

averse [*adj*] *opposing*
afraid, allergic, antagonistic, antipathetic, contrary, disinclined, disliking, having no use for*, hesitant, hostile, ill-disposed, indisposed, inimical, loath, nasty, perverse, reluctant, uneager, unfavorable, unfriendly, unwilling; SEE CONCEPTS *403,564*

aversion [*n*] *dislike; opposition*
abhorrence, abomination, allergy, animosity, antagonism, antipathy, detestation, disfavor, disgust, disinclination, disliking, displeasure, dissatisfaction, distaste, dread, hate, hatred, having no use for*, horror, hostility, indisposition, loathing, odium, reluctance, repugnance, repulsion, revulsion, unwillingness; SEE CONCEPT *29*

avert [*v*] *thwart; avoid by turning away*
avoid, deflect, deter, divert, fend off, foil, forestall, frustrate, halt, look away, preclude, prevent, rule out, shove aside, shunt, stave off, turn, turn aside, turn away, ward off; SEE CONCEPTS *121,623*

aviation [*n*] *flying an aircraft; study of flying aircraft*
aerodynamics, aeronautics, flight, navigation, piloting; SEE CONCEPTS *148,187,324*

aviator [*n*] *person who flies aircraft*
ace, aeronaut, airperson, barnstormer, bird legs*, eagle*, flier, hotshot*, jockey*, navigator, pilot; SEE CONCEPTS *348,366*

avid [*adj*] *enthusiastic*
ardent, athirst, avaricious, breathless, covetous, desirous, devoted, dying to*, eager, fanatical, fervent, gotta have*, grasping, greedy, hungry, impatient, insatiable, intense, keen, passionate, rapacious, ravenous, thirsty, voracious, zealous; SEE CONCEPTS *20,401,403*

avocation [*n*] *hobby*
amusement, diversion, kick*, occupation, pastime, recreation, schtick*, shot*, side interest, sideline, thing*; SEE CONCEPT *364*

avoid [*v*] *refrain or stay away from; prevent*
abstain, avert, bypass, circumlocute, circumvent, deflect, desist, ditch, divert, dodge, duck, elude, escape, eschew, evade, fake out*, fend off, flee, give the slip*, hide, hold off, jump, keep clear, lay low*, obviate, recoil, run for cover*, shake, shake and bake*, shake off, shirk, shrink from, shuffle off, shun, shy, sidestep, skip*, skip out on*, skip town*, skirt*, stay away, stay out, steer

clear of*, step aside, turn aside, ward off, weave, withdraw; SEE CONCEPTS *102,121*

avoidance [*n*] *eluding; preventing*
absention, circumvention, delay, departure, dodge, dodging, elusion, escape, escapism, eschewal, evasion, flight, forbearance, nonparticipation, parry, passive resistance, prevention, recession, recoil, restraint, retreat, run-around, self-restraint, shirking, shunning, steering clear of*; SEE CONCEPTS *102,121*

avow [*v*] *state; profess*
acknowledge, admit, affirm, allow, assert, aver, avouch, concede, confess, cross one's heart*, declare, grant, maintain, own up, proclaim, swear, swear on bible*, swear up and down*; SEE CONCEPTS *49,60,71*

avowal [*n*] *acknowledgment*
admission, affirmation, announcement, assertion, confession, declaration, oath, proclamation, testimony; SEE CONCEPTS *8,50,88*

await [*v*] *wait with expectation*
anticipate, attend, be prepared for, be ready for, cool one's heels*, count on, hang around*, hang in*, hang out*, hope, look for, look forward to, stay, sweat*, sweat it out*; SEE CONCEPT *26*

awake [*adj*] *conscious; alert*
alive, aroused, attentive, awakened, aware, cognizant, excited, heedful, knowing, observant, on guard, roused, vigilant, wakeful, waking, watchful; SEE CONCEPTS *402,406*

awake [*v1*] *become alert or cause to rise from sleep*
arise, awaken, call, gain consciousness, get up, roll out*, rouse, stir, wake, wake up; SEE CONCEPTS *250,315*

awake [*v2*] *become or make aware*
activate, alert, animate, arouse, awaken, call forth, enliven, excite, incite, kindle, provoke, revive, stimulate, stir up, vivify; SEE CONCEPT *231*

awaken [*v*] *make conscious or alert*
activate, animate, arouse, awake, call, enliven, excite, fan, incite, kindle, pile out*, provoke, rally, revive, rise and shine*, roll out*, rouse, show a leg*, stimulate, stir up, turn out*, vivify, wake; SEE CONCEPTS *7,19,22,105,231*

awakening [*n*] *making conscious or alert*
activation, animating, arousal, awaking, birth, enlivening, incitement, kindling, provocation, rebirth, renewal, revival, rousing, stimulation, stirring up, vivication, waking, waking up; SEE CONCEPTS *13,105,231*

award [*n*] *prize or reward*
accolade, adjudication, allotment, bestowal, citation, conferment, conferral, decision, decoration, decree, distinction, donation, endowment, feather in cap*, gift, gold, gold star*, grant, honor, order, presentation, scholarship, trophy, verdict; SEE CONCEPT *337*

award [*v*] *give prize or reward*
accord, adjudge, allocate, allot, apportion, assign, bestow, concede, confer, decree, dish out*, distribute, donate, endow, fork out*, gift, grant, hand out, present, render, reward, shell out*, sweeten the kitty*; SEE CONCEPT *132*

aware [*adj*] *knowledgeable*
acquainted, alert, alive, appraised, appreciative, apprehensive, apprised, attentive, au courant, awake, cognizant, conscious, cool*, enlightened, familiar, go-go*, groovy*, grounded*, heedful,

hip*, informed, in the know*, in the picture*, into*, know-how, knowing, know the score*, know what's what*, latched on*, mindful, on the beam*, on to*, perceptive, plugged in*, receptive, savvy, sensible, sentient, sharp, tuned in, up on, wise, wised up*, wise to*, with it*; SEE CONCEPT *402*

awareness [*n*] *knowledge*
acquaintance, acquaintanceship, alertness, aliveness, appreciation, apprehension, attention, attentiveness, cognizance, comprehension, consciousness, discernment, enlightenment, experience, familiarity, information, keenness, mindfulness, perception, realization, recognition, sensibility, sentience, understanding; SEE CONCEPT *409*

away [*adv1*] *in another direction; at a distance*
abroad, absent, afar, apart, aside, beyond, distant, elsewhere, far afield, far away, far off, far remote, forth, from here, hence, not present, off, out of, out of the way, over, to one side; SEE CONCEPTS *581,778*

away [*adv2*] *continuously*
endlessly, forever, incessantly, interminably, on and on, relentlessly, repeatedly, tirelessly, unremittingly, without break, without end, without rest, without stopping; SEE CONCEPT *553*

awe [*n*] *amazement*
admiration, apprehension, astonishment, consternation, dread, esteem, fear, fright, horror, regard, respect, reverence, shock, stupefaction, terror, veneration, wonder, wonderment, worship; SEE CONCEPTS *230,410*

awe [*v*] *amaze*
alarm, appall, astonish, blow away*, cow*, daunt, dazzle, flabbergast, frighten, grandstand, horrify, hotdog*, impress, intimidate, knock socks off*, overawe, scare, showboat*, startle, strike, stun, stupefy, terrify; SEE CONCEPTS *7,19,22,42*

awesome [*adj*] *amazing*
alarming, astonishing, awe-inspiring, awful, beautiful, breathtaking, daunting, dreadful, exalted, fearful, fearsome, formidable, frantic, frightening, grand, hairy*, horrible, horrifying, imposing, impressive, intimidating, magnificent, majestic, mean, mind-blowing*, moving, nervous, overwhelming, real gone*, shocking, something else*, striking, stunning, stupefying, terrible, terrifying, wonderful, wondrous, zero cool*; SEE CONCEPTS *537,572*

awful [*adj*] *very bad; terrible*
abominable, alarming, appalling, atrocious, deplorable, depressing, dire, disgusting, distressing, dreadful, fearful, frightful, ghastly, grody*, gross*, gruesome, grungy*, harrowing, hideous, horrendous, horrible, horrific, horrifying, nasty, offensive, raunchy, repulsive, shocking, stinking, synthetic, tough, ugly, unpleasant, unsightly; SEE CONCEPTS *570,571*

awfully [*adv1*] *badly*
clumsily, disgracefully, disreputably, dreadfully, inadequately, incompletely, poorly, reprehensibly, shoddily, unforgivably, unpleasantly, wickedly, wretchedly; SEE CONCEPTS *570,571*

awfully [*adv2*] *very*
badly, dreadfully, excessively, extremely, greatly, hugely, immensely, indeed, much, quite, terribly, truly, very much; SEE CONCEPT *569*

awhile [*adv*] *for a short period*
briefly, for a bit, for a little while, for a moment, for a spell, for a while, for the moment, momentarily, not for long, temporarily, transiently; SEE CONCEPT *798*

awkward [*adj1*] *clumsy, inelegant*
all thumbs*, amateurish, artless, blundering, bulky, bumbling, bungling, butterfingers*, coarse, floundering, gawky, graceless, green*, having two left feet*, having two left hands*, incompetent, inept, inexpert, klutzy*, lumbering, maladroit, oafish, rude, stiff, stumbling, uncoordinated, uncouth, unfit, ungainly, ungraceful, unhandy, unpolished, unrefined, unskilled, unskillful; SEE CONCEPTS *406,480,527*

awkward [*adj2*] *difficult to handle*
annoying, bulky, chancy, cramped, cumbersome, dangerous, disagreeable, discommodious, hard to use, hazardous, incommodious, inconvenient, perilous, risky, troublesome, uncomfortable, unhandy, unmanageable, unwieldy; SEE CONCEPTS *558,565*

awkward [*adj3*] *embarrassing*
compromising, delicate, difficult, embarrassed, ill at ease, inconvenient, inopportune, painful, perplexing, sticky*, thorny*, ticklish*, troublesome, trying, uncomfortable, unpleasant, untimely; SEE CONCEPT *555*

awkwardness [*n1*] *clumsiness; inelegance*
amateurishness, artlessness, boorishness, cloddishness, coarseness, crudeness, gawkiness, gracelessness, greenness*, ignorance, inability, incompetence, ineptitude, ineptness, inexpertness, maladroitness, oafishness, rudeness, tactlessness, uncoordination, uncouthness, ungainliness, unskillfulness; SEE CONCEPTS *405,630,717*

awkwardness [*n2*] *difficulty*
bulkiness, chanciness, cumbersomeness, danger, hazardousness, inconvenience, peril, perilousness, risk, troublesomeness, uncomfortableness, unhandiness, unmanageability, unwieldiness; SEE CONCEPTS *656,666*

awkwardness [*n3*] *embarrassment*
delicacy, difficulty, discomfort, inconvenience, inopportuneness, painfulness, stickiness*, thorniness*, ticklishness, trouble, uncomfortableness, unpleasantness, untimeliness; SEE CONCEPT *388*

awning [*n*] *canopy*
covering, door cover, marquee, protection, shade, shelter, sunshade, tent; SEE CONCEPTS *440,473*

awry [*adj*] *off course; amiss*
afield, askance, askew, aslant, astray, badly, bent, cockeyed, crooked, curved, slanting, turned, wrong, zigzag; SEE CONCEPTS *537,581*

ax/axe [*n*] *large cutting tool*
adz, chopper, hatchet, tomahawk; SEE CONCEPT *499*

ax/axe [*v1*] *cut with large blade*
chop, cut, cut down, fell, hew; SEE CONCEPT *176*

ax/axe [*v2*] *dismiss from service*
boot*, bounce*, can*, cancel, cut back, discharge, dispense with, eliminate, fire, get rid of, give a pink slip*, give the boot*, kick out, lay off, remove, sack*, terminate, throw out; SEE CONCEPT *351*

axiom [*n*] *principle*
adage, aphorism, apothegm, device, dictum, fundamental, law, maxim, moral, postulate, precept,

av
ax

proposition, proverb, saying, theorem, truism, truth; SEE CONCEPTS *278,688,689*

axiomatic [*adj*] *understood; aphoristic*
absolute, accepted, aphoristic, apothegmatic, assumed, certain, fundamental, given, indubitable, manifest, obvious, presupposed, proverbial, self-evident, unquestioned; SEE CONCEPT *529*

axis [*n*] *point around which something revolves*
arbor, axle, hinge, pivot, pole, shaft, spindle, stalk, stem, support, turning point; SEE CONCEPT *830*

axle [*n*] *shaft around which wheels rotate*
arbor, axis, gudgeon, mandrel, pin, pivot, pole, rod, shaft, spindle, stalk, stem, support; SEE CONCEPTS *464,830*

ax to grind [*n*] *hidden motive*
agenda, driving force, hidden agenda, incentive, motivation, motive, reason, score to settle*; SEE CONCEPTS *20,661,689*

B

babble [*n*] *trivial talk, often incessant*
blubbering, burble, chatter, clamor, drivel, gab, gabble, gibberish, gossip, gushing, idle talk, jabber, jabbering, jargon, murmur, muttering, prattle, ranting, tattling; SEE CONCEPTS *266,278*

babble [*v*] *talk trivially, often incessantly*
blab, blubber, blurt, burble, cackle, chat, chatter, gibber, go on, gossip, gush, jabber, mumble, murmur, mutter, patter, prate, prattle, rant, rave, run off at the mouth*, run on, spill the beans*, squeal*, talk foolishly, talk incoherently, talk nonsensically, tattle, trivialize, yak*, yakkety yak*; SEE CONCEPTS *51,266*

babe [*n*] *baby*
bairn, child, infant, little one, newborn, suckling; SEE CONCEPTS *414,424*

baby [*adj*] *miniature*
babyish, diminutive, dwarf, little, midget, mini*, minute, petite, small, tiny, wee, youthful; SEE CONCEPT *773*

baby [*n*] *infant*
angelface*, babe, bairn, bambino, bundle, buttercup*, button, cherub, chick, child, crawler*, deduction*, dividend*, dumpling*, kid, little angel*, little darling*, little doll*, little one*, newborn, nipper*, nursling, papoose, preemie*, suckling, tad*, toddler, tot, write-off*, youngster; SEE CONCEPTS *414,424*

baby [*v*] *treat like a child*
cater to, cherish, coddle, cosset, cuddle, dandle, dote on, foster, humor, indulge, nurse, overindulge, pamper, pet, please, satisfy, serve, spoil; SEE CONCEPTS *110,295*

babyhood [*n*] *period of infancy*
childhood, diaper days*, infanthood; SEE CONCEPT *817*

babyish [*adj*] *acting like an infant*
baby, childish, foolish, immature, infantile, juvenile, kid stuff, puerile, silly, sissy, spoiled; SEE CONCEPTS *401,550*

baby-sit [*v*] *care for a child*

guard, sit, take care, tend, watch; SEE CONCEPT *295*

bachelor [*n*] *unmarried man or woman*
available*, celibate, single*, single person, stag*, unattached; SEE CONCEPTS *415,419,423*

back [*adj1*] *end*
aback, abaft, aft, after, astern, back of, backward, behind, final, following, hind, hindmost, in the wake of, posterior, rear, rearmost, rearward, tail; SEE CONCEPTS *827,833*

back [*adj2*] *from earlier time*
delayed, elapsed, former, overdue, past, previous; SEE CONCEPT *820*

back [*n*] *end part*
aft, back end, backside, extremity, far end, hindpart, hindquarters, posterior, rear, reverse, stern, tail, tail end, tailpiece; SEE CONCEPTS *392,471,827,833*

back [*v1*] *support*
abet, abide by, advocate, ally, angel*, assist, bankroll, boost, champion, countenance, encourage, endorse, favor, finance, give a boost, give a leg up*, give a lift*, go to bat for*, grubstake, sanction, second, side with, sponsor, stake, stand behind, stick by, stick up for, subsidize, sustain, underwrite, uphold; SEE CONCEPTS *8,50,88*

back [*v2*] *put in reverse direction*
backtrack, drive back, fall back, recede, regress, repel, repulse, retire, retract, retreat, reverse, turn tail, withdraw; SEE CONCEPTS *195,208*

backbiting [*n*] *hateful talk*
abuse, aspersion, backstabbing*, belittlement, calumniation, calumny, cattiness, defamation, denigration, depreciation, detraction, disparagement, gossip, invective, lie, malice, obloquy, scandal, slander, spite, spitefulness, tale, traducement, vilification, vituperation; SEE CONCEPTS *54,58,63*

backbone [*n1*] *strength of character*
courage, determination, firmness, fortitude, grit, guts, hardihood, heart, intestinal fortitude*, mettle, moral fiber, nerve, pluck, resolution, resolve, spunk, stamina, steadfastness, tenacity, toughness, will, willpower; SEE CONCEPT *411*

backbone [*n2*] *spinal column of vertebrate*
base, basis, foundation, spine, support, vertebrae, vertebral column; SEE CONCEPTS *420,442*

backbreaking [*adj*] *strenuous*
arduous, exhausting, grueling, hard, laborious, punishing, taxing, toilsome, wearisome; SEE CONCEPT *538*

back door [*n*] *secretive or illicit method*
back entrance, back way, indirect access, means of entry, trap door; SEE CONCEPTS *274,631*

back down [*v*] *withdraw from agreement or statement*
abandon, accede, admit, back off, back out, back pedal*, backtrack, balk, beg off*, cancel, chicken out*, concede, cop out*, demur, give in, give up, go back on, hold back, recant, recoil, renege, resign, retreat, surrender, take back, withdraw, yield; SEE CONCEPTS *266,697*

backer [*n*] *supporter*
advocate, ally, angel*, benefactor, champion, endorser, follower, grubstaker, meal ticket*, money, patron, promoter, protagonist, sponsor, staker, underwriter, well-wisher; SEE CONCEPT *359*

backfire [*v*] *have an opposite effect*
backlash, boomerang, bounce back, disappoint,

fail, flop, miscarry, rebound, recoil, ricochet, spring back; SEE CONCEPTS *42,701*

background [*n*] *experience or circumstances* accomplishments, acquirement, actions, atmosphere, attainment, aura, backdrop, breeding, capacity, credentials, cultivation, culture, deeds, education, environment, framework, grounding, history, practice, preparation, qualification, rearing, seasoning, tradition, training, upbringing; SEE CONCEPTS *673,678,706*

backhanded [*adj*] *underhanded* ambiguous, double-edged, equivocal, sarcastic, sardonic, two-edged; SEE CONCEPTS *401,544*

backing [*n*] *support* abetment, accompaniment, adherence, advocacy, aegis, aid, assistance, auspices, championing, championship, encouragement, endorsement, funds, grant, help, patronage, reinforcement, sanction, secondment, sponsorship, subsidy; SEE CONCEPTS *110,332*

backlash [*n*] *adverse reaction* backfire, boomerang, counteraction, kickback, reaction, recoil, repercussion, resentment, resistance, response, retaliation, retroaction, tangle; SEE CONCEPT *230*

backlog [*n*] *uncompleted work; accumulation* excess, hoard, inventory, quantity, reserve(s), reservoir, resources, stock, stockpile, store, supply; SEE CONCEPTS *432,787*

back out [*v*] *withdraw* avoid, back down, back pedal*, beg off*, blow it off*, cancel, chicken out*, cop out*, get cold feet*, give up, go back on, recant, renege, resign, scratch, shy from, surrender, throw in the towel*, weasel out, welsh, wiggle out, worm out*; SEE CONCEPTS *50,88,121,266,697*

backpack [*n*] *sack carried on the back* haversack, knapsack, pack, rucksack; SEE CONCEPT *446*

backside [*n*] *rear end* behind, bottom, butt*, buttocks, derrière, fanny*, posterior, rear, rump*, seat*, tail*, tush*; SEE CONCEPT *392*

backslide [*v*] *go astray* apostatize, deviate, fall from grace, lapse, leave the straight and narrow*, relapse, revert, sin, slip; SEE CONCEPTS *195,665,697*

backstab [*v*] *attack indirectly* backbite, betray, double-cross*, play Judas*, sell down the river*, slander, smear; SEE CONCEPTS *54,192*

back talk [*n*] *nasty reply* cheek, guff, lip, mouth, sass; SEE CONCEPTS *46,278*

backup [*n*] *auxiliary* alternate, extra, substitute; SEE CONCEPTS *546,824*

backward [*adj1*] *toward the rear* astern, behind, inverted, rearward, regressive, retrograde; SEE CONCEPT *581*

backward [*adj2*] *bashful* afraid, averse, demure, diffident, disinclined, hesitant, hesitating, humble, indisposed, late, loath, modest, reluctant, reserved, retiring, shy, sluggish, tardy, timid, uneager, unwilling, wavering; SEE CONCEPT *401*

backward [*adj3*] *slow in growth* arrested, behind, checked, delayed, dense, dull, feeble-minded, imbecile, late, moronic, stupid, subnormal, underdeveloped, underprivileged, undeveloped; SEE CONCEPTS *402,562*

backward [*adv*] *toward the rear* aback, abaft, about, astern, back, behind, in reverse, inverted, rearward, turned around; SEE CONCEPT *581*

backwash [*n*] *repercussion* aftermath, result, wake; SEE CONCEPTS *230,674*

backwoods [*n/adj*] *forests; land distant from settled area* backcountry, boondocks*, frontier, hinterland, interior, isolation, outback, rural area, sticks*, timberland, woodland; SEE CONCEPT *509*

backyard [*n*] *expanse behind house* courtyard, garden, grass, lawn, patio, play area, terrace, yard; SEE CONCEPT *513*

bacteria [*n*] *microorganisms* bacilli, germs, microbes, organisms, pathogens; SEE CONCEPTS *306,393*

bad [*adj1*] *poor quality* abominable, amiss, atrocious, awful, bad news*, beastly, blah*, bottom out, bummer*, careless, cheap, cheesy*, crappy*, cruddy*, crummy*, defective, deficient, diddly*, dissatisfactory, downer*, dreadful, erroneous, fallacious, faulty, garbage, godawful*, grody*, gross*, grungy*, icky*, imperfect, inadequate, incorrect, inferior, junky*, lousy*, not good, off, poor, raunchy*, rough, sad, slipshod, stinking, substandard, synthetic, the pits*, unacceptable, unsatisfactory; SEE CONCEPT *571*

bad [*adj2*] *harmful* damaging, dangerous, deleterious, detrimental, hurtful, injurious, ruinous, unhealthy; SEE CONCEPTS *537,570*

bad [*adj3*] *immoral* base, corrupt, criminal, delinquent, evil, iniquitous, mean, reprobate, sinful, vicious, vile, villainous, wicked, wrong; SEE CONCEPT *545*

bad [*adj4*] *mischievous* disobedient, ill-behaved, misbehaving, naughty, unruly, wrong; SEE CONCEPT *401*

bad [*adj5*] *decayed* moldy, off, putrid, rancid, rotten, sour, spoiled; SEE CONCEPTS *485,613*

bad [*adj6*] *severe* disastrous, distressing, grave, harsh, intense, painful, serious, terrible; SEE CONCEPT *569*

bad [*adj7*] *sick* ailing, diseased, ill, in pain, unwell; SEE CONCEPT *314*

bad [*adj8*] *sorry* apologetic, conscience-stricken, contrite, crestfallen, dejected, depressed, disconsolate, down, downcast, downhearted, guilty, low, regretful, remorseful, sad, upset, woebegone; SEE CONCEPT *403*

bad [*adj9*] *distressing* adverse, disagreeable, discouraged, discouraging, displeasing, distressed, gloomy, grim, melancholy, troubled, troubling, unfavorable, unfortunate, unhappy, unpleasant; SEE CONCEPTS *403,529*

bad blood [*n*] *ill will* acrimony, anger, animosity, antagonism, bad feeling, bitterness, dislike, distrust, enmity, hard feelings, hatred, hostility, malevolence, malice, nastiness, odium, rancor, resentment, unfriendliness, venom; SEE CONCEPT *29*

bad form [*n*] *bad style*

ax
ba

barbarism, impropriety, indecorum, inelegance, infelicity, solecism; SEE CONCEPTS *275,633*

badge [*n*] *emblem worn*
brand, cordon, device, identification, insignia, mark, marker, medallion, motto, pin, ribbon, scepter, shield, sign, stamp, symbol, token; SEE CONCEPTS *260,284,476*

badger [*v*] *nag, bother*
annoy, bait, bug, bully, eat*, give the business*, goad, harass, harry, hassle, heckle, hound, importune, insist on, needle, nudge, pester, plague, ride, tease, torment, work on; SEE CONCEPTS *14,51*

bad luck [*n*] *adversity*
blow, hard luck, hard time, mischance, misfortune, reverse, setback; SEE CONCEPTS *388,674,679*

badly [*adv1*] *inadequately*
abominably, awkwardly, blunderingly, carelessly, clumsily, crudely, defectively, erroneously, faultily, feebly, haphazardly, imperfectly, incompetently, ineffectively, ineptly, maladroitly, negligently, poorly, shoddily, stupidly, unfavorably, unfortunately, unsatisfactorily, unskillfully, unsuccessfully, weakly, wrong, wrongly; SEE CONCEPT *571*

badly [*adv2*] *immorally*
criminally, evilly, improperly, naughtily, shamefully, unethically, wickedly; SEE CONCEPT *545*

badly [*adv3*] *very much; desperately*
acutely, deeply, exceedingly, extremely, gravely, greatly, hard, intensely, painfully, roughly, seriously, severely; SEE CONCEPT *569*

bad manners [*n*] *improper behavior*
boorishness, discourtesy, disrespect, impoliteness, inconsideration, unmannerliness; SEE CONCEPTS *29,633*

bad-mouth [*v*] *to denigrate*
belittle, criticize, cut down to size*, dis*, disparage, dump on*, find fault, knock*, malign, mudsling*, pan, pooh pooh*, put down*, rap, rip, roast*, run down*, slam, slander, take a dig at*, take down a peg*, tear down*, tear to pieces*; SEE CONCEPTS *52,54*

bad news [*n*] *trouble*
bind, bother, concern, danger, deep trouble, difficulty, dilemma, dire straits, disappointment, distress, grief, headache*, hindrance, hot water*, inconvenience, mess, misfortune, nuisance, pain, predicament, problem, struggle, torment, woe; SEE CONCEPTS *532,674,675,690,728*

bad scene [*n*] *misfortunate event*
bad trip*, bummer*, bum trip*, depressing experience, disaster, downer*, drag*, raw deal, rotten hand, unhappy situation, unpleasant experience, unpleasant situation; SEE CONCEPTS *674,675*

bad time [*n*] *agony*
going-over, grief, grilling, hard time, third degree, torture; SEE CONCEPTS *410,728*

bad trip [*n*] *unpleasant experience*
bad scene, bummer*, bum trip*, disaster, downer*, drag*, freak-out*, unhappy situation, unpleasant drug experience, unpleasant situation; SEE CONCEPTS *674,675*

baffle [*v1*] *perplex*
addle, amaze, astound, befuddle, bewilder, buffalo*, confound, confuse, daze, disconcert, dumbfound, elude, embarrass, faze, floor*, get, mix up, muddle, mystify, nonplus, puzzle, rattle,

stick*, stump*, stun, throw; SEE CONCEPTS *7,19,42*

baffle [*v2*] *hinder*
beat, block, check, circumvent, dash, defeat, disappoint, foil, frustrate, impede, obstruct, prevent, ruin, thwart, upset; SEE CONCEPT *121*

bag [*n1*] *container for one's possesions*
attaché, backpack, briefcase, carryall, carry-on, case, duffel, gear, handbag, haversack, holdall, kit, knapsack, pack, packet, pocket, pocketbook, poke, pouch, purse, rucksack, sac, sack, saddlebag, satchel, suitcase, tote; SEE CONCEPTS *339,450,494*

bag [*n2*] *special interest*
expertise, favorite activity, hobby, preference, speciality, thing*; SEE CONCEPTS *32,529*

bag [*v1*] *catch*
acquire, apprehend, capture, collar, gain, get, hook, kill, land, nab, nail, net, seize, shoot, take, trap; SEE CONCEPT *90*

bag [*v2*] *droop*
balloon, billow, bulge, flap, flop, hang, lop, sag, swell; SEE CONCEPTS *754,757*

baggage [*n*] *gear*
accoutrements, bags, belongings, carry-on, effects, equipment, fortnighter, gear, impedimenta, luggage, overnighter*, paraphernalia, parcels, slough, suitcases, things, tote, tote bag, trappings, two-suiter; SEE CONCEPT *494*

baggy [*adj*] *drooping*
billowing, bulging, droopy, flabby, floppy, ill-fitting, loose, oversize, roomy, sagging, slack, unshapely; SEE CONCEPTS *486,490*

bail [*n*] *money for assurance*
bond, collateral, guarantee, pawn, pledge, recognizance, security, surety, warrant, warranty; SEE CONCEPTS *318,332*

bail out [*v1*] *help*
aid, deliver, release, relieve, rescue, spring; SEE CONCEPT *110*

bail out [*v2*] *escape*
flee, quit, retreat, withdraw; SEE CONCEPT *102*

bait [*n*] *something for luring*
allurement, attraction, bribe, come-on*, drag, enticement, inducement, lure, seducement, shill, snare, temptation, trap; SEE CONCEPT *709*

bait [*v1*] *lure*
allure, attract, bedevil, beguile, draw, entice, fascinate, lead on, seduce, tempt; SEE CONCEPTS *9,14*

bait [*v2*] *needle*
anger, annoy, badger, bother, gall, harass, heckle, hound, irk, irritate, nag, persecute, provoke, tease, torment; SEE CONCEPTS *7,19*

bake [*v*] *cook in oven*
heat, melt, scorch, simmer, stew, warm; SEE CONCEPT *170*

baked [*adj*] *cooked in oven*
dried, heated, melted, scorched, simmered, stewed, warmed; SEE CONCEPT *462*

baker [*n*] *person who cooks baked goods*
chef, cook, dough puncher*, pastry maker; SEE CONCEPT *348*

bakery [*n*] *cooking business where baked goods are produced*
bake shop, confectionery, pastry shop, pâtisserie; SEE CONCEPTS *325,439,449*

balance [*n1*] *equilibrium*
antithesis, correspondence, counterbalance, equity, equivalence, evenness, even-steven*, hang,

harmony, parity, proportion, stasis, symmetry, tension; SEE CONCEPTS *664,667*

balance [*n2*] *composure*
equanimity, poise, self-control, self-possession, stability, steadfastness; SEE CONCEPT *633*

balance [*n3*] *money remaining in account*
difference, dividend, excess, profit, remainder, residue, rest, surplus; SEE CONCEPT *332*

balance [*v1*] *make equal; cause to have equilibrium*
accord, adjust, attune, cancel, collate, come out, come out even, compensate, correspond, counteract, counterbalance, equalize, equate, even, harmonize, level, make up for, match, neutralize, nullify, offset, oppose, pair off, parallel, poise, readjust, redeem, set, square, stabilize, steady, tie, weigh; SEE CONCEPTS *197,697*

balance [*v2*] *compare*
assess, consider, deliberate, estimate, evaluate, weigh; SEE CONCEPT *17*

balance [*v3*] *make equal numerically*
adjust, audit, calculate, compute, count, enumerate, equate, estimate, figure, settle, square, sum up, tally, total; SEE CONCEPT *764*

balanced [*adj1*] *equalized*
counterbalanced, equitable, equivalent, evened, fair, just, offset, proportional, stabilized, symmetrical, uniform; SEE CONCEPT *566*

balanced [*adj2*] *settled financially*
certified, confirmed, validated; SEE CONCEPT *334*

balance sheet [*n*] *financial statement including gains and losses for a period*
account, annual report, assets and liabilities, budget, ledger, report; SEE CONCEPTS *271,332*

balcony [*n*] *porch or structure above the ground*
balustrade, box*, catwalk, gallery, mezzanine, piazza, platform, porch, portico, stoop, terrace, veranda; SEE CONCEPT *440*

bald [*adj1*] *having no covering*
baldheaded, bare, barren, depilated, exposed, glabrous, hairless, head*, naked, shaven, skin head*, smooth, stark, uncovered; SEE CONCEPT *485*

bald [*adj2*] *simple, unadorned*
austere, bare, blunt, direct, downright, forthright, outright, plain, severe, straight, straightforward, unembellished; SEE CONCEPTS *485,589*

bale [*n*] *bunch*
bundle, package, parcel; SEE CONCEPT *432*

baleful [*adj*] *menacing*
calamitous, deadly, dire, evil, foreboding, harmful, hurtful, injurious, malevolent, malignant, noxious, ominous, pernicious, ruinous, sinister, threatening, venomous, vindictive, woeful; SEE CONCEPTS *537,570*

balk [*v1*] *stop short*
cramp, crimp, demur, desist, dodge, evade, flinch, hesitate, recoil, refuse, resist, shirk, shrink from, shy, turn down, upset apple cart*; SEE CONCEPTS *119,121,188*

balk [*v2*] *thwart*
baffle, bar, beat, check, circumvent, counteract, cramp, cramp one's style*, dash, defeat, disappoint, disconcert, foil, forestall, frustrate, hinder, obstruct, prevent, ruin, stall, stop, throw a curve*, throw monkey wrench in*, upset the apple cart*; SEE CONCEPT *121*

balky [*adj*] *uncooperative*
averse, contrary, hesitant, immovable, indis-

posed, inflexible, intractable, loath, negative, negativistic, obstinate, ornery, perverse, reluctant, stubborn, unbending, unmanageable, unpredictable, unruly; SEE CONCEPT *401*

ball [*n1*] *dance party*
hoedown, hoodang, hop, jump, mingle, prom, promenade, reception, shindig; SEE CONCEPT *386*

ball [*n2*] *globe, sphere*
apple, balloon, drop, globule, orb, pellet, pill, round, spheroid; SEE CONCEPT *436*

ballad [*n*] *narrative song*
carol, chant, ditty, serenade; SEE CONCEPT *595*

ballast [*n*] *something giving balance*
balance, brace, bracket, counterbalance, counterweight, equilibrium, sandbag, stability, stabilizer, support, weight; SEE CONCEPT *712*

ballet [*n*] *graceful, expressive dancing*
choreography, dance, toe dancing; SEE CONCEPT *263*

ballet dancer [*n*] *person who performs graceful dance*
company, coryphee, dancer, danseur, danseuse, figurant, figurante, hoofer*, prima ballerina; SEE CONCEPT *352*

balloon [*n*] *inflated material or vehicle*
airship, bladder, blimp, dirigible, zeppelin; SEE CONCEPTS *293,504*

balloon [*v*] *billow out; bloat*
belly, blow up, bulge, dilate, distend, enlarge, expand, inflate, puff out, swell; SEE CONCEPTS *208,756*

ballot [*n1*] *voting; recording of vote*
election, franchise, plebiscite, poll, polling, referendum, slate, tally, ticket; SEE CONCEPTS *300,301*

ballot [*n2*] *candidates from political party*
choice, lineup, slate, ticket; SEE CONCEPT *301*

balm [*n1*] *oily substance*
analgesic, application, balsam, cerate, compound, cream, demulcent, dressing, embrocation, emollient, formula, lotion, medicine, ointment, potion, poultice, preparation, prescription, salve, soother, soothing agent, unction, unguent; SEE CONCEPTS *307,466*

balm [*n2*] *something soothing*
alleviation, anodyne, assuagement, comfort, consolation, curative, cure, easement, mitigation, palliative, refreshment, relief, remedy, restorative, solace, soother; SEE CONCEPTS *337,529*

balmy [*adj1*] *comfortable with respect to weather*
mild, moderate, moist, pleasant, refreshing, summerlike, summery, temperate, tropical; SEE CONCEPTS *603,605*

balmy [*adj2*] *insane*
absurd, bugged out*, cracked*, crazed, crazy, daft, deranged, dotty*, foolish, harebrained*, idiotic, loony, mentally incompetent, moronic, nuts*, nutty*, odd, potty*, preposterous, silly, stupid, wacky; SEE CONCEPT *403*

bamboozle [*v*] *fool; cheat*
baffle, befuddle, bilk, con, confound, confuse, deceive, defraud, delude, dupe, flimflam*, hoax, hoodwink*, hornswoggle*, mystify, perplex, puzzle, stump, swindle, trick; SEE CONCEPT *59*

ban [*n*] *official forbiddance*
a thou-shalt-not*, boycott, censorship, don't*, embargo, injunction, interdiction, limitation, no-no*, off limits*, out of bounds*, prohibition,

ba
ba

proscription, refusal, restriction, stoppage, suppression, taboo; SEE CONCEPTS *50,88,121,688*

ban [*v*] *officially forbid*
banish, bar, blackball*, close down, close up, curse, declare illegal, disallow, enjoin, exclude, halt, ice out*, illegalize, inhibit, interdict, outlaw, pass by, pass up, prevent, prohibit, proscribe, restrict, shut out, suppress; SEE CONCEPTS *50,88,121*

banal [*adj*] *commonplace*
blah*, bland, bromidic, clichéd, common, conventional, cornball*, cornfed*, corny, dull as dishwater*, dumb, everyday, flat, hackneyed, ho hum*, hokey*, humdrum*, insipid, mundane, noplace, nothing, nowhere, old hat*, ordinary, pabulum*, pedestrian, platitudinous, square, stale, stereotyped, stock, stupid, tired, tripe, trite, unimaginative, unoriginal, vapid, watery, wishywashy*, zero*; SEE CONCEPT *530*

banality [*n*] *common saying*
adage, boiler*, buzzword, chestnut*, cliché, corn*, dullsville*, familiar tune*, high camp*, hokum*, old chestnut*, old saw*, plate*, platitude, prosaicism, prosaism, saw*, trite phrase, trivia, triviality, truism; SEE CONCEPT *275*

band [*n1*] *something which encircles*
bandage, bandeau, belt, binding, bond, braid, cable, chain, circle, circuit, copula, cord, fillet, harness, hoop, ligature, line, link, manacle, ribbon, ring, rope, sash, scarf, shackle, snood, stay, strap, string, strip, tape, tie, truss; SEE CONCEPTS *470,751*

band [*n2*] *group of people with same interest*
assembly, association, bevy, body, bunch, clique, club, cluster, collection, company, corps, coterie, covey, crew, gang, gathering, horde, menagerie, outfit, party, society, troop, troupe; SEE CONCEPTS *387,391,417*

band [*n3*] *musical group*
combo, ensemble, orchestra, philharmonic, symphony, troupe; SEE CONCEPT *294*

band [*v*] *group or join group*
affiliate, ally, amalgamate, belt, coadjute, combine, conjoin, consolidate, federate, gather, league, merge, team, unite; SEE CONCEPTS *113,114*

bandage [*n*] *covering for wound*
cast, compress, dressing, gauze, plaster; SEE CONCEPT *311*

bandage [*v*] *cover a wound*
bind, dress, swathe, truss, wrap; SEE CONCEPT *310*

bandanna [*n*] *colorful scarf*
handkerchief, kerchief, neckerchief, silk; SEE CONCEPT *450*

bandit [*n*] *thief*
brigand, criminal, crook, desperado, forager, gangster, gunperson, highwayperson, hijacker, holdup person, hooligan, marauder, mobster, outlaw, pillager, pirate, plunderer, racketeer, raider, ravager, robber, villain; SEE CONCEPT *412*

bandwidth [*n*] *frequency range*
high frequency, low frequency, radio band, radio bandwidth, transmission capacity; SEE CONCEPT *279*

bane [*n*] *cause of misery*
affliction, bête noir, blight, burden, calamity, curse, despair, destruction, disaster, downfall, fatal attraction, misery, nuisance, pest, plague,

poison, ruin, ruination, scourge, torment, trial, trouble, undoing, venom, woe; SEE CONCEPTS *529,674*

baneful [*adj*] *ruinous, injurious*
baleful, calamitous, deadly, deleterious, destructive, disastrous, evil, fatal, harmful, hurtful, malefic, noxious, pernicious, pestilent, pestilential, poisonous, venomous, wicked; SEE CONCEPTS *537,570*

bang [*adv*] *suddenly, with force*
abruptly, hard, headlong, head on, noisily, precisely, smack, straight, suddenly; SEE CONCEPT *540*

bang [*n1*] *explosive noise*
blast, boom, burst, clang, clap, clash, crack, detonation, discharge, howl, peal, pop, report, roar, roll, rumble, salvo, shot, slam, smash, sound, thud, thump, thunder, wham; SEE CONCEPT *595*

bang [*n2*] *loud hit or knock*
bash, bat, belt, blow, box, bump, collide, crack, cuff, punch, slam, smack, smash, sock, stroke, wallop, whack, whop; SEE CONCEPT *189*

bang [*n3*] *thrilling situation*
enjoyment, excitement, kick*, pleasant feeling, smash, wallop, wow*; SEE CONCEPT *230*

bang [*v1*] *hit or knock loudly*
boom, burst, clang, clatter, crash, detonate, drum, echo, explode, make noise, peal, rattle, resound, sound, thump, thunder; SEE CONCEPTS *65,189*

bang [*v2*] *moving by hitting hard*
bash, beat, bump, clatter, collide, crash, hammer, hit, knock, pound, pummel, rap, slam, smash, strike, thump, whack; SEE CONCEPT *189*

banish [*v*] *expel from place or situation*
ban, cast out, deport, discard, discharge, dislodge, dismiss, dispel, drive away, eject, eliminate, eradicate, evict, exclude, excommunicate, exile, expatriate, expulse, extradict, get rid of, isolate, ostracize, oust, outlaw, proscribe, relegate, remove, rusticate, sequester, shake off, shut out, transport; SEE CONCEPTS *121,217*

banister [*n*] *railing of stairs*
baluster, balustrade, handrail, rail, support; SEE CONCEPT *443*

bank [*n1*] *financial institution*
coffer, countinghouse, credit union, depository, exchequer, fund, hoard, investment firm, repository, reserve, reservoir, safe, savings, stock, stockpile, store, storehouse, thrift, treasury, trust company, vault; SEE CONCEPTS *333,339,439*

bank [*n2*] *ground bounding waters*
beach, cay, cliff, coast, edge, embankment, lakefront, lakeshore, lakeside, ledge, levee, oceanfront, reef, riverfront, riverside, seabank, seaboard, seafront, shore, strand, streamside, waterfront; SEE CONCEPT *509*

bank [*n3*] *row or tier of objects*
array, dashboard, group, line, rank, row, sequence, series, succession; SEE CONCEPT *464*

bank [*v1*] *collect money or advantage*
amass, deposit, heap, hill, hoard, invest, lay aside, lay away, mass, mound, pile, put by, salt away, save, sock away, speculate, squirrel, stash; SEE CONCEPTS *109,330*

bank [*v2*] *lean or tilt*
bend, camber, cant, incline, pitch, slant, slope; SEE CONCEPTS *148,213*

banker [*n*] *professional in financial institution*

broker, capitalist, croupier, dealer, financier, house, investor, manager, money-lender, officer, teller, treasurer, usurer; SEE CONCEPTS *347,348,353*

bank on [*v*] *depend upon*
assume, believe in, be sure about, bet on, build on, count on, gamble on, lean on, look to, reckon on, rely on, stake, trust, venture, wager; SEE CONCEPT *12*

bankrupt [*adj*] *unable to pay debts*
broke, depleted, destitute, exhausted, failed, impoverished, in Chapter 11*, insolvent, lacking, lost, out of business, ruined, spent, tapped out; SEE CONCEPT *334*

bankruptcy [*n*] *inability to pay debts*
Chapter 11*, defalcation, default, destituteness, destitution, disaster, exhaustion, failure, indebtedness, indigence, insolvency, lack, liquidation, loss, nonpayment, overdraft, pauperism, privation, repudiation, ruin, ruination; SEE CONCEPT *335*

banner [*adj*] *successful*
exceptional, foremost, leading, outstanding, redletter; SEE CONCEPT *528*

banner [*n1*] *flag, usually with message*
banderole, burgee, colors, emblem, ensign, gonfalon, heading, headline, pennant, pennon, standard, streamer; SEE CONCEPTS *270,277,278*

banner [*n2*] *ad on Web/Internet page*
advertisement, burst page, headline, streamer; SEE CONCEPTS *270,277,278,280*

banquet [*n*] *formal dinner, usually ceremonial*
feast, festivity, fete, meal, reception, regale, repast, spread, treat; SEE CONCEPTS *377,459*

bantam [*adj*] *small*
diminutive, little, petite, tiny; SEE CONCEPTS *491,773*

banter [*n*] *teasing*
badinage, chaff, chaffing, chitchat, derision, dissing*, exchange, fun, gossip, jeering, jesting, joking, joshing, kidding, mockery, persiflage, play, raillery, repartee, ribbing, ridicule, small talk; SEE CONCEPTS *59,278*

banter [*v*] *tease*
chaff, deride, fool, fun, jeer, jest, jive*, joke, josh, kid, make fun of, mock, rag*, razz*, rib, ridicule, satirize, taunt; SEE CONCEPTS *59,273*

baptism [*n*] *church rite; initiation*
ablution, baptismal, christening, debut, dedication, dunking, immersion, introduction, launching, lustration, purgation, purge, purification, rite of passage, ritual, sanctification, sprinkling; SEE CONCEPTS *367,377*

baptize [*v*] *initiate in church rite*
admit, asperse, besprinkle, call, christen, cleanse, denominate, dip, dub, entitle, immerse, name, purify, regenerate, sprinkle, term, title; SEE CONCEPT *367*

bar [*n1*] *rod; straight length of material*
batten, billet, boom, crossbar, crosspiece, ingot, lever, paling, pig, pole, rail, rib, rule, shaft, slab, spar, spoke, stake, stick, streak, strip, stripe, stroke; SEE CONCEPTS *470,471*

bar [*n2*] *barrier; blockage*
barricade, blank wall, block, clog, deterrent, encumbrance, fence, hindrance, hurdle, impediment, obstacle, obstruction, pale, rail, railing, restraint, road block, snag, stop, stumbling block, traverse, wall; SEE CONCEPTS *470,652,680*

bar [*n3*] *establishment serving alcohol*

alehouse, barroom, beer garden, bistro, canteen, cocktail lounge, drinkery, inn, lounge, pub, public house, rathskeller, saloon, tap, taproom, tavern, watering hole*; SEE CONCEPTS *325,439*

bar [*n4*] *legal system*
attorneys, barristers, bench, counsel, counselors, court, courtroom, dock, judgment, judiciary, jurists, law, law court, law practice, lawyers, legal profession, solicitors, tribunal; SEE CONCEPTS *318,381*

bar [*v1*] *secure, usually with a length of material*
barricade, block, blockade, bolt, caulk, clog, close, dam, deadbolt, dike, fasten, fence, jam, latch, lock, plug, seal, secure, trammel, wall; SEE CONCEPTS *121,130*

bar [*v2*] *prohibit*
ban, boycott, circumvent, condemn, debar, deny, disallow, discountenance, discourage, eliminate, enjoin, except, exclude, exile, forbid, freeze out, frustrate, hinder, interdict, interfere, keep out, limit, obstruct, ostracize, outlaw, override, preclude, prevent, refuse, reject, restrain, rule out, segregate, shut out, stop, suspend; SEE CONCEPTS *50,61,88*

barb [*n1*] *point*
arrow, bristle, dart, prickle, prong, quill, shaft, spike, spur, thistle, thorn; SEE CONCEPTS *434,836*

barb [*n2*] *pointed comment*
affront, criticism, cut, dig, gibe, insult, rebuff, sarcasm, scoff, sneer; SEE CONCEPTS *52,54*

barbarian [*adj*] *crude, savage*
barbaric, barbarous, boorish, brutal, coarse, cruel, inhuman, lowbrow, merciless, philistine, primitive, rough, rude, uncivil, uncivilized, uncouth, uncultivated, uncultured, unsophisticated, untamed, vicious, vulgar, wild; SEE CONCEPT *401*

barbarian [*n*] *crude, savage person*
beast, bigot, boor, brute, cannibal, clod, hooligan, hun, ignoramus, lout, monster, philistine, rascal, ruffian, troglodyte, vandal; SEE CONCEPT *412*

barbaric [*adj*] *crude, savage*
barbarian, barbarous, boorish, brutal, coarse, cruel, fierce, graceless, inhuman, lowbrow, primitive, rough, rude, tasteless, uncivilized, uncouth, vulgar, wild; SEE CONCEPT *401*

barbarism [*n*] *crudity, savagery, especially in speech*
atrocity, barbarity, brutality, catachresis, coarseness, corruption, cruelty, impropriety, inhumanity, localism, malapropism, misusage, misuse, primitive culture, provincialism, solecism, uncivilizedness, vernacularism, vernacularity, vulgarism; SEE CONCEPTS *275,633*

barbarity [*n*] *crudity, savagery*
boorishness, brutality, crudeness, cruelty, inhumanity, ruthlessness, savageness, viciousness, vulgarity; SEE CONCEPT *633*

barbarous [*adj*] *crude, savage*
atrocious, barbarian, barbaric, brutal, brutish, coarse, cruel, ferocious, heartless, ignorant, inhuman, inhumane, monstrous, primitive, rough, rude, ruthless, sadistic, truculent, uncivil, uncivilized, uncouth, uncultured, unsophisticated, vicious, vulgar, wicked, wild, wolfish; SEE CONCEPT *401*

barbecue [*n1*] *meal cooked on grill*
bake, clam bake, cookout, party, picnic, weinie

ba
ba

roast; SEE CONCEPT *459*
barbecue [*n2*] *grill for cookout*
broiler, charcoal grill, fireplace, gas grill, griddle, pit of coals, roaster, spit; SEE CONCEPT *493*
barbecue [*v*] *cook outside, usually on a grill*
broil, charcoal, fry, grill, rotisserie, sear; SEE CONCEPT *170*
barber [*n*] *hair cutter*
beautician, coiffeur, coiffeuse, cosmetologist, hairdresser, hair stylist, shaver, tonsorial artist; SEE CONCEPT *348*
bare [*adj1*] *without clothing*
bald, bareskinned, denuded, disrobed, divested, exposed, in one's birthday suit*, naked, nude, peeled, shorn, stripped, unclad, unclothed, uncovered, undressed, unrobed; SEE CONCEPT *485*
bare [*adj2*] *without covering or content*
arid, barren, blank, bleak, clear, desert, desolate, empty, lacking, mean, open, poor, scanty, scarce, stark, unfurnished, vacant, vacuous, void, wanting; SEE CONCEPT *490*
bare [*adj3*] *simple, unadorned*
austere, bald, basic, blunt, chaste, cold, essential, hard, literal, meager, mere, modest, scant, severe, sheer, simple, spare, stark, unembellished, unornamented; SEE CONCEPT *562*
bare [*v*] *reveal*
disclose, divulge, exhibit, expose, publish, show, uncover, unroll, unveil; SEE CONCEPTS *60,138*
barefaced [*adj*] *shameless; open*
apparent, arrant, audacious, blatant, blunt, bold, brash, brassy, brazen, candid, clear, flagrant, frank, glaring, immodest, impudent, insolent, manifest, naked, obvious, palpable, temerarious, transparent, unabashed, unconcealed; SEE CONCEPT *401*
barefoot [*adj*] *wearing no shoes*
barefooted, discalceate, discalced, shoeless, unshod; SEE CONCEPT *406*
barely [*adj*] *not quite*
almost, hardly, just, only just, scantily, scarcely; SEE CONCEPT *772*
bareness [*n*] *state of being unclothed*
dishabille, nakedness, nudity, starkness, unadornment, undress; SEE CONCEPT *453*
bargain [*n1*] *agreement*
arrangement, bond, business, compact, contract, convention, covenant, deal, engagement, negotiation, pact, pledge, promise, stipulation, transaction, treaty, understanding; SEE CONCEPT *684*
bargain [*n2*] *something bought at cheap price*
budget price, buy, closeout, deal, discount, giveaway, good buy, good deal, good value, low price, markdown, nominal price, reduction, steal, value; SEE CONCEPTS *332,338*
bargain [*v*] *negotiate terms of sale or agreement*
agree, arrange, barter, buy, compromise, confer, contract, covenant, deal, dicker, do business, haggle, make terms, palter, promise, sell, stipulate, trade, traffic, transact; SEE CONCEPTS *56,330*
bargain for [*v*] *expect*
aim for, anticipate, contemplate, count on, foresee, imagine, look for, plan on, reckon on; SEE CONCEPT *26*
barge [*n*] *large work boat*
ark, canal boat, dory, flatboat, freight ship, lighter, raft, scow; SEE CONCEPT *506*
barge in/barge into [*v*] *charge*
break in, burst in, collide, infringe, interrupt, intrude, muscle in, push, shove, stumble; SEE CON-

CEPTS *150,208*
bark [*n1*] *plant covering*
case, casing, coat, cortex, crust, husk, peeling, rind, shell, skin; SEE CONCEPT *428*
bark [*n2*] *animal yelp*
bay, growl, grunt, howl, roar, snarl, woof, yap, yip; SEE CONCEPT *64*
bark [*v1*] *yelp*
arf, bay, cry, gnarl, growl, howl, snap, snarl, woof, yap, yip; SEE CONCEPT *64*
bark [*v2*] *shout*
bawl, bellow, clamor, cry, growl, grumble, mutter, roar, snap, snarl, yell; SEE CONCEPT *77*
barn [*n*] *animal shelter*
farm building, outbuilding, shed; SEE CONCEPTS *439,517*
baroque [*adj*] *decorative, especially architecture*
bizarre, convoluted, elaborate, embellished, extravagant, flamboyant, florid, gilt, grotesque, ornamented, ornate, overdecorated, rich, rococo; SEE CONCEPTS *562,589*
barracks [*n*] *shelter for military*
billet, bivouac, camp, cantonment, dormitory, encampment, enclosure, garrison, headquarters, hut, prefab, quarters, Quonset hut, tent; SEE CONCEPTS *321,516*
barrage [*n1*] *weapon fire*
battery, blast, bombardment, broadside, cannonade, crossfire, curtain of fire, discharge, enfilade, fire, fusillade, gunfire, hail, salvo, shelling, shower, storm, volley; SEE CONCEPT *320*
barrage [*n2*] *profusion of something*
assault, attack, blast, bombardment, burst, deluge, hail, mass, onslaught, plethora, rain, shower, storm, stream, surge, torrent; SEE CONCEPT *787*
barrel [*n*] *cylindrical container*
butt, cask, cylinder, drum, firkin, hogshead, keg, pipe, receptacle, tub, tun, vat, vessel; SEE CONCEPT *494*
barren [*adj1*] *unable to support growth*
arid, depleted, desert, desolate, dry, effete, empty, fallow, fruitless, impotent, impoverished, infecund, infertile, parched, sterile, unbearing, uncultivable, unfertile, unfruitful, unproductive, waste; SEE CONCEPTS *485,527*
barren [*adj2*] *unprofitable*
dull, flat, fruitless, futile, lackluster, profitless, stale, uninspiring, unproductive, unrewarding, useless, vain, vapid; SEE CONCEPT *560*
barricade [*n*] *blocking object*
bar, barrier, blank wall, block, blockade, bulwark, fence, obstruction, palisade, rampart, roadblock, stockade, stop, wall; SEE CONCEPT *470*
barricade [*v*] *block, usually to protect*
bar, blockade, defend, fortify, obstruct, shut in; SEE CONCEPTS *130,201*
barrier [*n1*] *obstruction*
bar, barricade, blank wall, blockade, bound, boundary, confines, curtain, ditch, enclosure, fence, fortification, gully, hurdle, impediment, limit, moat, obstacle, pale, palisade, railing, rampart, roadblock, stop, trench, wall; SEE CONCEPTS *435,470,513*
barrier [*n2*] *obstruction to goal*
bar, check, difficulty, drawback, encumbrance, handicap, hindrance, hurdle, impediment, limitation, obstacle, pale, preventive, restraint, restriction, stumbling block; SEE CONCEPT *532*
barter [*v*] *trade goods or services*

bargain, exchange, haggle, swap, trade, traffic, truck; SEE CONCEPT *104*

base [*adj*] *vulgar, low*
abject, abominable, cheap, coarse, common, contemptible, corrupt, depraved, despicable, disgraceful, dishonorable, disreputable, foul, grovelling, humble, ignoble, immoral, indelicate, loathsome, lowly, mean, menial, offensive, paltry, pitiful, plebeian, poor, scandalous, servile, shameful, shoddy, sleazy, sordid, sorry, squalid, trashy, ugly, unworthy, vile, worthless, wretched; SEE CONCEPTS *542,570*

base [*n1*] *foundation*
basement, basis, bed, bedrock, bottom, foot, footing, ground, groundwork, infrastructure, pedestal, rest, root, seat, seating, stand, substratum, substructure, support, underpinning; SEE CONCEPT *442*

base [*n2*] *fundamental part*
authority, backbone, basis, chief constituent, core, essence, essential, evidence, foundation, fundamental, groundwork, heart, important part, infrastructure, key, origin, primary element, principal, principle, root, source, underpinning; SEE CONCEPT *826*

base [*n3*] *headquarters*
camp, center, depot, dock, field, garrison, hangar, harbor, home, port, post, settlement, site, starting point, station, strip, terminal; SEE CONCEPTS *435,449*

base [*v*] *build plan or opinion on*
construct, depend, derive, establish, found, ground, hinge, locate, plant, predicate, prop, rest, set up, station, stay; SEE CONCEPT *36*

baseless [*adj*] *without substantiation*
bottomless, flimsy, foundationless, gratuitous, groundless, reasonless, unconfirmed, uncorroborated, unfounded, ungrounded, unjustifiable, unjustified, unsubstantiated, unsupported, untenable, unwarranted; SEE CONCEPT *582*

basement [*n*] *room on lower floor of building*
bottom, cellar, crypt, excavation, furnace room, storage, substructure, subterranean room, underbuilding, understructure, vault; SEE CONCEPT *440*

bash [*n*] *party*
celebration, spree, wing-ding*; SEE CONCEPT *383*

bash [*v*] *hit*
clobber*, pop*, punch, slam, slug, smash, strike, whack; SEE CONCEPTS *189,200*

bashful [*adj*] *shy*
abashed, backward, blushful, blushing, chary, confused, constrained, coy, demure, diffident, embarrassed, humble, modest, nervous, overmodest, recoiling, reserved, reticent, retiring, self-conscious, self-effacing, shamefaced, sheepish, shrinking, silent, timid, timorous, unassertive; SEE CONCEPT *404*

bashing [*n*] *abuse against a group or individual based on identity or ideological beliefs*
assault, attack, beating, beating up, bias crime, censure, charge, condemnation, criticism, denigration, harassment, hate crime, hounding, jumping, offensive, persecution, strike, torment; SEE CONCEPT *86*

basic [*adj*] *elementary, fundamental*
basal, capital, central, chief, elemental, essential, indispensable, inherent, intrinsic, key, main, necessary, primary, primitive, principal, radical, substratal, underlying, vital; SEE CONCEPT *568*

basically [*adv*] *fundamentally*
at heart, at the bottom, essentially, firstly, in essence, inherently, in substance, intrinsically, mostly, primarily, radically; SEE CONCEPT *568*

basin [*n*] *container or area where water is held*
bay, bowl, concavity, depression, dip, ewer, gulf, hole, hollow, lagoon, pan, pool, pot, sag, sink, sinkage, sinkhole, tub, valley, vessel, watershed; SEE CONCEPTS *494,509,514*

basis [*n1*] *physical foundation*
base, bed, bottom, foot, footing, ground, groundwork, rest, resting place, seat, substructure, support; SEE CONCEPT *442*

basis [*n2*] *foundation for belief, action*
antecedent, assumption, authority, axiom, backbone, background, backing, base, bedrock, cause, center, chief ingredient, core, crux, data, dictum, essence, essential, evidence, explanation, footing, fundamental, hard fact, heart, infrastructure, justification, keynote, keystone, law, nexus, nucleus, postulate, premise, presumption, presupposition, principal element, principle, proof, reason, root, rudiment, sanction, security, source, substratum, support, theorem, theory, underpinning, warrant; SEE CONCEPTS *661,688,689*

bask [*v1*] *lie in sunlight*
laze, loll, lounge, relax, sun, sunbathe, swim in, toast oneself*, warm oneself; SEE CONCEPTS *162,210*

bask [*v2*] *lie in glory*
delight in, derive pleasure, enjoy, indulge, luxuriate, relish, revel, rollick, savor, take comfort, take pleasure, wallow, welter; SEE CONCEPT *32*

basket [*n*] *woven container*
bassinet, bin, box, bushel, cradle, crate, creel, hamper, nacelle, pannier; SEE CONCEPT *494*

basketball [*n*] *team sport*
ball, B-ball*, brownball*, hoops*; SEE CONCEPT *363*

bastard [*adj*] *illegitimate*
adulterated, baseborn, counterfeit, fake, false, imperfect, impure, inferior, irregular, misbegotten, misborn, mixed, mongrel, natural, phony, sham, spurious, suppositious, ungenuine; SEE CONCEPT *549*

bastardize [*v*] *debase*
adulterate, bestialize, brutalize, corrupt, debauch, declare illegitimate, degrade, demoralize, deprave, pervert, vitiate, warp; SEE CONCEPT *44*

baste [*v1*] *moisten during cooking*
brush with liquid, drip, grease, lard, season; SEE CONCEPT *170*

baste [*v2*] *sew temporarily*
catch, fasten, stitch, tack; SEE CONCEPT *218*

baste [*v3*] *pummel, thrash*
batter, beat, berate, blister, clobber, club, drub, lambaste, lash, maul, pelt, revile, scold, trounce, wallop, whip, whomp; SEE CONCEPTS *52,189*

bastion [*n*] *support; fortified place*
breastwork, bulwark, citadel, defense, fortification, fortress, mainstay, parapet, prop, protection, rock, stronghold, support, tower of strength; SEE CONCEPT *712*

bat [*n/v*] *a hit with a solid object*
bang, belt, blow, bop, crack, knock, rap, slam, smack, sock, strike, swat, thump, thwack, wallop, whack, whop; SEE CONCEPT *189*

batch [*n*] *group of same objects*
accumulation, aggregation, amount, array, as-

semblage, assortment, bunch, bundle, clump, cluster, clutch, collection, crowd, group, lot, pack, parcel, quantity, set, shipment, volume; SEE CONCEPTS *432,787*

bath [*n1*] *washing with water and, usually, soap*
ablution, cleansing, dip, douche, dousing, gargle, laving, scrubbing, shower, soak, soaking, soaping, sponging, tub, wash; SEE CONCEPTS *161,165*

bath [*n2*] *room for bathing*
bathroom, lavatory, powder room, restroom, sauna, shower, shower room, spa, steam room, toilet, washroom; SEE CONCEPT *448*

bathe [*v*] *wash with water and, usually, soap*
bath, clean, cleanse, dip, douse, dunk, flood, hose, imbathe, imbue, immerse, moisten, rinse, scour, scrub, shower, soak, soap, sponge, steep, submerge, suffuse, tub, water, wet; SEE CONCEPTS *161,165*

bathing suit [*n*] *clothing for swimming, sunning*
bathing costume, beach costume, bikini, maillot, one-piece, swimsuit, trunks, two-piece; SEE CONCEPT *451*

bathos [*n*] *sentimentality*
anticlimax, comedown, letdown, melodrama, mush, schmaltz*; SEE CONCEPTS *32,410,689*

bathroom [*n*] *room for bathing, toilet use*
bath, lavatory, powder room, restroom, sauna, shower, shower room, spa, steam room, toilet, washroom, water closet; SEE CONCEPT *448*

baton [*n*] *stick used for conducting or for protection*
billy, billy club, blackjack, club, cudgel, mace, nightstick, rod, staff, truncheon, wand; SEE CONCEPTS *262,470,500*

battalion [*n*] *military division*
army, brigade, company, contingent, corps, force, horde, host, legion, multitude, regiment, squadron, throng, unit; SEE CONCEPT *322*

batten [*v1*] *fasten securely*
board up, clamp down, cover up, fix, nail down, secure, tie, tighten; SEE CONCEPTS *85,160*

batten [*v2*] *grow fat*
burgeon, feed on, grow, prosper, thrive, wax; SEE CONCEPT *704*

batter [*n*] *mixture before baking*
concoction, dough, mix, mush*, paste, preparation, recipe; SEE CONCEPTS *457,466*

batter [*v*] *strike and damage*
assault, bash, beat, break, bruise, buffet, clobber, contuse, cripple, crush, dash, deface, demolish, destroy, disable, disfigure, drub, hurt, injure, lacerate, lambaste, lame, lash, mangle, mar, maul, mutilate, pelt, pommel, pound, pummel, punish, ruin, shatter, smash, thrash, wallop, wreck; SEE CONCEPTS *189,246,252*

battery [*n1*] *series of similar things*
array, batch, body, bunch, bundle, chain, clot, clump, cluster, group, lot, ring, sequence, set, suite; SEE CONCEPT *432*

battery [*n2*] *physical abuse*
assault, attack, beating, mayhem, mugging, onslaught, thumping, violence; SEE CONCEPTS *189,246*

battery [*n3*] *group of weapons*
artillery, cannon, cannonry, gunnery unit, guns; SEE CONCEPTS *321,500*

battle [*n1*] *military fight*
action, assault, attack, barrage, blitzkreig, bloodshed, bombing, brush, campaign, carnage, clash, combat, conflict, contention, crusade, encounter,

engagement, fighting, fray, havoc, hostility, onset, onslaught, press, ravage, scrimmage, significant contact, skirmish, sortie, strife, struggle, war, warfare; SEE CONCEPT *106*

battle [*n2*] *struggle*
agitation, campaign, clash, conflict, contest, controversy, crusade, debate, disagreement, dispute, strife; SEE CONCEPTS *46,106*

battle [*v*] *fight, struggle*
agitate, argue, clamor, combat, contend, contest, dispute, feud, oppugn, skirmish, strive, tug, war, wrestle; SEE CONCEPTS *46,106*

battlefield [*n*] *location of military fights*
arena, Armageddon, battleground, combat zone, field, front, front line, salient, theater of operations, theater of war; SEE CONCEPTS *198,321*

bawdy [*adj*] *vulgar, dirty*
blue, cheap, coarse, erotic, gross, indecent, indecorous, indelicate, lascivious, lecherous, lewd, libidinous, licentious, lustful, obscene, off-color, prurient, ribald, risqué, rude, salacious, suggestive; SEE CONCEPT *545*

bawl [*v1*] *yell*
bark, bellow, bluster, call, cheer, clamor, holler, howl, roar, rout, scream, screech, shout, shriek, vociferate; SEE CONCEPT *77*

bawl [*v2*] *cry*
blubber*, boohoo*, howl, shed tears, sob, squall, wail, weep, yowl; SEE CONCEPTS *77,185*

bay [*n1*] *shoreline indentation*
anchorage, arm, basin, bayou, bight, cove, estuary, fiord, firth, gulf, harbor, inlet, lagoon, loch, mouth, narrows, sound, strait; SEE CONCEPTS *509,514*

bay [*n2*] *alcove in wall*
bow window, compartment, niche, nook, opening, oriel, recess; SEE CONCEPT *440*

bay [*n3*] *howl*
bark, bellow, clamor, cry, growl, howl, ululation, wail, yelp; SEE CONCEPT *64*

bazaar [*n*] *fair; sale place*
exchange, exposition, fete, market, marketplace, mart; SEE CONCEPTS *345,438,449*

bboard [*n*] *electronic messaging system*
BBS, board, bulletin board, bulletin board system; SEE CONCEPTS *349,770*

be [*v1*] *exist*
abide, act, be alive, breathe, continue, do, endure, go on, have being, have place, hold, inhabit, last, live, move, obtain, persist, prevail, remain, rest, stand, stay, subsist, survive; SEE CONCEPT *407*

be [*v2*] *happen*
befall, come about, come to pass, occur, take place, transpire; SEE CONCEPT *2*

beach [*n*] *sandy area by body of water*
bank, coast, lakeshore, lakeside, littoral, margin, oceanfront, seaboard, seafront, seashore, seaside, shingle, shore, strand, waterfront; SEE CONCEPTS *509,514*

beached [*adj*] *grounded*
abandoned, aground, ashore, deserted, high and dry, marooned, stranded, wrecked; SEE CONCEPT *583*

beacon [*n*] *light used as signal, guide*
alarm, alert, balefire, beam, bonfire, flare, guidepost, heliograph, lamp, lantern, lighthouse, lodestar, pharos, radar, rocket, sign, signal fire, smoke signal, warning signal, watchtower; SEE CONCEPT *628*

bead [*n*] *droplet, blob*
bean, bubble, dab, dot, driblet, drop, globule, grain, particle, pea, pellet, pill, shot, speck, spherule, stone; SEE CONCEPT *436*

beads [*n*] *string of small, often round, objects*
chaplet, choker, necklace, necklet, pearls, pendant, rosary, wampum; SEE CONCEPTS *368,446*

beak [*n*] *nose of animal*
bill, mandible, muzzle, neb, nib, nozzle, pecker, proboscis, projection, prow, snout; SEE CONCEPT *392*

beam [*n1*] *length of material used as support*
axle, bail, balk, bolster, boom, brace, cantilever, column, crossbar, crosspiece, girder, jamb, joist, lath, lintel, pile, piling, pillar, plank, pole, post, prop, rafter, reach, scaffolding, scantling, shaft, sill, spar, stanchion, stay, stringer, strip, strut, stud, timber, transverse, trestle, two-by-four; SEE CONCEPTS *471,479*

beam [*n2*] *ray of light*
bar, beacon, chink, column, dartle, emission, finger, flicker, glare, gleam, glimmer, glint, glitter, glow, laser, radiation, ray, shaft, shimmer, shoot, sparkle, streak, stream, twinkle; SEE CONCEPTS *624,628*

beam [*v1*] *broadcast on air waves*
emit, give off, give out, glare, glimmer, glow, radiate, send, shed, shine, throw off, transmit; SEE CONCEPTS *519,624*

beam [*v2*] *smile broadly*
gleam, glow, grin, laugh, radiate, shine, smirk; SEE CONCEPT *185*

beam [*v3*] *shine, as a light*
burn, emit, glare, gleam, glitter, glow, radiate, yield; SEE CONCEPT *624*

beam [*v4*] *make electronic transfer*
emit, radiate, send out, transfer file, transmit, transmit signal; SEE CONCEPT *266*

beaming [*adj1*] *radiant; beautiful*
bright, brilliant, effulgent, flashing, fulgent, gleaming, glistening, glittering, glowing, incandescent, lambent, lucent, luminous, refulgent, scintillating, sparkling; SEE CONCEPT *617*

beaming [*adj2*] *very happy*
animated, cheerful, genial, grinning, joyful, radiant, shining, smiling, sparkling, sunny; SEE CONCEPT *401*

bean counter [*n*] *number cruncher*
accountant, actuary, analyst, auditor, bookkeeper, certified public accountant, comptroller, CPA, financial executive, statistician, treasurer; SEE CONCEPTS *348,353*

beanpole [*n*] *a tall, thin person*
beanstalk*, broomstick*, hatrack*, stick*, string bean*; SEE CONCEPT *417*

bear [*v1*] *bring*
buck, carry, convey, deliver, ferry, fetch, lug, move, pack, take, tote, transfer, transport; SEE CONCEPTS *108,143*

bear [*v2*] *support mentally*
cherish, entertain, exhibit, harbor, have, hold, hold up, maintain, possess, shoulder, sustain, uphold, weigh upon; SEE CONCEPTS *8,12*

bear [*v3*] *endure*
abide, admit, allow, brook, encounter, experience, permit, put up with, stomach, suffer, tolerate, undergo; SEE CONCEPTS *23,239*

bear [*v4*] *give birth*
be delivered of, beget, breed, bring forth, create, develop, engender, form, fructify, generate, invent, make, parturitate, produce, propagate, provide, reproduce, yield; SEE CONCEPTS *173,251,302,373*

bearable [*adj*] *endurable*
acceptable, admissible, allowable, livable, manageable, passable, satisfactory, sufferable, supportable, sustainable, tolerable; SEE CONCEPT *529*

beard [*n1*] *facial hair on human*
bristles, brush, five-o'clock shadow*, fuzz, goatee, imperial, muttonchops, Santa Claus*, stubble, Vandyke*; SEE CONCEPT *418*

beard [*n2*] *decoy*
false face, front, mask; SEE CONCEPT *716*

beard [*v*] *confront*
brave, face, oppose, stand up to; SEE CONCEPTS *46,96*

bearded [*adj*] *having facial hair*
barbate, beardy, bewhiskered, bristly, bushy, goateed, hairy, hirsute, shaggy, stubbled, stubbly, unshaven, whiskered; SEE CONCEPTS *406,485*

bear down [*v*] *close in on*
advance on, approach, converge on, near, press, weigh down; SEE CONCEPTS *152,208,704*

bearer [*n1*] *person who carries messages or deliveries*
agent, beast of burden*, carrier, conveyor, courier, drogher, emissary, envoy, internuncio, messenger, porter, runner, servant, shipper, transporter; SEE CONCEPT *348*

bearer [*n2*] *person who requests payment of bill*
beneficiary, casher, collector, consignee, payee; SEE CONCEPT *353*

bearing [*n1*] *person's conduct, posture*
address, air, aspect, attitude, behavior, carriage, comportment, demeanor, deportment, display, front, look, manner, mien, poise, port, pose, presence, set, stand; SEE CONCEPTS *411,633*

bearing [*n2*] *significance*
application, connection, import, meaning, pertinence, reference, relation, relevance, weight; SEE CONCEPT *668*

bearing/bearings [*n3*] *position, usually of water vehicle*
aim, course, direction, location, orientation, point of compass, position, situation, track, way, whereabouts; SEE CONCEPTS *739,746*

bear in mind [*v*] *be aware of*
be cognizant of, be mindful of, beware, consider, heed, mind, note, remember; SEE CONCEPTS *17,623*

bear on/bear upon [*v*] *concern*
affect, appertain to, apply, belong to, involve, pertain to, refer to, relate to, touch upon; SEE CONCEPT *532*

bear out [*v*] *substantiate*
authenticate, confirm, corroborate, endorse, justify, prove, substantiate, support, uphold, validate, verify, vindicate; SEE CONCEPTS *50,88,97*

bear up [*v*] *endure*
carry on, persevere, soldier on, suffer, withstand; SEE CONCEPT *23*

bear with [*v*] *tolerate*
be patient, endure, forbear, make allowance, put up with, suffer, wait; SEE CONCEPT *23*

bear witness [*v*] *vouch for*
attest, confirm, corroborate, demonstrate, depose, evidence, evince, prove, show, testify, testify to;

ba
be

SEE CONCEPTS *49,71,317*
beast [*n*] *large wild animal; brute*
barbarian, beastie*, creature, critter*, fiend, gargoyle, glutton, lower animal, monster, monstrosity, pig, quadruped, swine, varmint*; SEE CONCEPT *394*
beastly [*adv1*] *savage; vulgar*
abominable, animal, barbarous, base, bestial, boorish, brutal, brute, brutish, carnal, coarse, cruel, degraded, depraved, disgusting, feral, ferine, foul, gluttonous, gross, inhuman, irrational, loathsome, low, monstrous, obscene, piggish, prurient, repulsive, sadistic, swinish, unclean, vile; SEE CONCEPT *401*
beastly [*adv2*] *offensive*
awful, disagreeable, disgusting, foul, gross, mean, nasty, revolting, rotten, terrible, unpleasant, vile; SEE CONCEPTS *537,542*
beat [*adj*] *very tired*
dog tired*, exhausted, fatigued, kaput*, wearied, weary, worn out; SEE CONCEPTS *316,720*
beat [*n1*] *throbbing*
cadence, cadency, flow, flutter, measure, meter, oscillation, palpitation, pound, pressure, pulsation, pulse, quake, quiver, rhyme, rhythm, ripple, shake, surge, swell, swing, throb, thump, tick, undulation, vibration; SEE CONCEPTS *150,185*
beat [*n2*] *blow, stroke*
hit, lash, punch, shake, slap, strike, swing, thump; SEE CONCEPT *189*
beat [*n3*] *area of responsibility*
circuit, course, march, path, patrol, precinct, rounds, route, walk, way; SEE CONCEPTS *513,532*
beat [*v1*] *injure by striking*
bang, bash, bat, batter, belt, box, break, bruise, buffet, cane, castigate, clout, club, collide, crush, cudgel, drub, flagellate, flail, flog, hammer, hit, knock, lambaste*, lash, lick*, maltreat, mash, maul, pelt, pound, pummel, punch, punish, ram, rap, slap, slug, smack, spank, strike, swat, thrash, thresh, thump, thwack, trounce, wallop, whale*, whip; SEE CONCEPTS *189,246*
beat [*v2*] *defeat, surpass*
best, better, be victorious, conquer, exceed, excel, outdo, outplay, outrival, outrun, outshine, outstrip, overcome, overtake, overwhelm, shoot ahead of, subdue, top, transcend, triumph, vanquish, whip; SEE CONCEPTS *95,141*
beat [*v3*] *forge*
fashion, form, hammer, malleate, model, pound, shape, work; SEE CONCEPTS *137,175*
beat [*v4*] *throb*
agitate, alternate, bob, bounce, buffet, flap, flicker, fluctuate, flutter, heave, jerk, jounce, oscillate, palpitate, pitch, pound, pulsate, pulse, quake, quaver, quiver, ripple, shake, shiver, swing, thrill, throb, thump, tremble, twitch, undulate, vibrate, writhe; SEE CONCEPTS *150,185*
beat [*v5*] *mix*
stir, whip; SEE CONCEPT *170*
beaten [*adj1*] *defeated*
baffled, bested, circumvented, conquered, cowed, crushed, disappointed, discomfited, disheartened, frustrated, humbled, licked, mastered, overcome, overpowered, overthrown, overwhelmed, routed, ruined, subjugated, surmounted, thwarted, trounced, undone, vanquished, worsted; SEE CONCEPTS *403,674*
beaten [*adj2*] *forged*
formed, hammered, milled, pounded, rolled,

shaped, stamped, tamped, tramped, tramped down, trodden, worked; SEE CONCEPTS *486,490*
beaten [*adj3*] *mixed*
aerated, blended, bubbly, churned, creamy, foamy, frothy, meringued, stirred, whipped, whisked; SEE CONCEPTS *491,606*
beat it [*v*] *go away*
leave, scram, shoo, skedaddle, vamoose; SEE CONCEPT *195*
beatitude [*n*] *blessedness*
bliss, ecstasy, felicity, happiness, peace, serenity; SEE CONCEPT *410*
beatnik [*n*] *unconventional, free-sprited person*
beat, Bohemian, demonstrator, dropout, flower child*, hippie, iconoclast, maverick, nonconformist, peacenik*, protester, radical; SEE CONCEPT *423*
beat up [*v*] *assault*
attack, batter, do over, hammer, knock around, pulverize, thrash; SEE CONCEPTS *52,86*
beau [*n*] *boyfriend*
admirer, beloved, cavalier, escort, fiancé, flame, gentleman caller, gentleman friend, honey, inamorato, love, lover, paramour, squire, steady, suitor, swain, sweetheart, true love; SEE CONCEPT *423*
beautiful [*adj*] *physically attractive*
admirable, alluring, angelic, appealing, beauteous, bewitching, charming, classy, comely, cute, dazzling, delicate, delightful, divine, elegant, enticing, excellent, exquisite, fair, fascinating, fine, foxy*, good-looking, gorgeous, graceful, grand, handsome, ideal, lovely, magnificent, marvelous, nice, pleasing, pretty, pulchritudinous, radiant, ravishing, refined, resplendent, shapely, sightly, splendid, statuesque, stunning, sublime, superb, symmetrical, taking, well-formed, wonderful; SEE CONCEPTS *485,579,589*
beautifully [*adv*] *in an attractive or pleasing manner*
alluringly, appealingly, attractively, bewitchingly, celestially, charmingly, cutely, delightfully, divinely, elegantly, entrancingly, excellently, exquisitely, gorgeously, gracefully, handsomely, ideally, magnificently, prettily, seductively, splendidly, sublimely, superbly, tastefully, wonderfully; SEE CONCEPT *544*
beautify [*v*] *make more physically attractive*
adorn, array, bedeck, deck, decorate, dress up, embellish, enhance, garnish, gild, glamorize, grace, improve, make up, ornament, prettify, set off, trim; SEE CONCEPT *162*
beauty [*n1*] *physical attractiveness*
adorableness, allure, allurement, artistry, attraction, bloom, charm, class, comeliness, delicacy, elegance, exquisiteness, fairness, fascination, glamor, good looks, grace, handsomeness, loveliness, polish, pulchritude, refinement, shapeliness, style, symmetry, winsomeness; SEE CONCEPT *718*
beauty [*n2*] *good-looking person*
Adonis*, Apollo*, beaut*, charmer, dream, dreamboat*, enchanter, eyeful*, good-looker*, head turner*, looker*, ornament*, stunner*, Venus*, vision; SEE CONCEPT *424*
beauty [*n3*] *advantage*
asset, attraction, benefit, blessing, boon, excellent, feature, good thing, importance, merit, value, worth; SEE CONCEPT *668*
because [*conj/prep*] *on account of*

as, as a result of, as long as, as things go, being, by cause of, by virtue of, considering, due to, for, for the reason that, for the sake of, in as much as, in behalf of, in that, in the interest of, in view of, now that, on the grounds that, over, owing to, seeing, since, thanks to, through, whereas; SEE CONCEPT *676*

beckon [*v*] *call, signal, or lure*
allure, ask, attract, bid, coax, command, demand, draw, entice, gesticulate, gesture, invite, motion, nod, pull, sign, summon, tempt, wave; SEE CONCEPTS *7,22,53,74*

become [*v1*] *evolve into*
alter to, assume form of, be converted to, be reduced to, be reformed, be remodeled, be transformed into, change into, come, come to be, convert, develop into, emerge as, eventually be, grow into, incline, mature, metamorphose, pass into, ripen into, shift, turn into, turn out, wax; SEE CONCEPT *701*

become [*v2*] *enhance*
accord, adorn, agree, augment, be appropriate, belong to, display, embellish, enrich, fit, flatter, garnish, go together, go with, grace, harmonize, heighten, make handsome, match, ornament, set off, suit; SEE CONCEPT *244*

becoming [*adj1*] *flattering*
acceptable, agreeable, attractive, beautiful, comely, cute, effective, enhancing, excellent, fair, graceful, handsome, neat, nice, presentable, pretty, seemly, tasteful, welcome, well-chosen; SEE CONCEPTS *579,589*

becoming [*adj2*] *suitable; appropriate*
befitting, comme il faut, compatible, conforming, congruous, correct, decent, decorous, fit, fitting, in keeping, nice, proper, right, seemly, worthy; SEE CONCEPT *558*

bed [*n1*] *furniture for sleeping*
bassinet, bedstead, berth, bunk, chaise, cot, couch, cradle, crib, davenport, divan, mattress, pallet, platform, sack, trundle; SEE CONCEPT *443*

bed [*n2*] *patch of ground for planting*
area, border, frame, garden, piece, plot, row, strip; SEE CONCEPTS *509,513*

bed [*n3*] *base, foundation*
basis, bedrock, bottom, ground, groundwork, rest, seat, substratum, understructure; SEE CONCEPT *442*

bed [*v*] *plant*
base, embed, establish, fix, found, implant, insert, settle, set up; SEE CONCEPTS *234,257*

bedazzle [*v*] *captivate*
astound, bewilder, blind, confuse, daze, dazzle, dumbfound, enchant, overwhelm, stagger, stun; SEE CONCEPTS *7,22,42*

bedding [*n*] *covering for sleeping furniture*
bedclothes, bed linen, bedspread, blanket, comforter, cover, coverlet, eiderdown, electric blanket, linen, pillow, pillowcase, quilt, sheet, spread, thermal blanket; SEE CONCEPTS *444,473*

bedlam [*n*] *chaotic situation*
chaos, clamor, commotion, confusion, din, disquiet, disquietude, furor, hubbub, madhouse, maelstrom, noise, pandemonium, racket, shambles, tumult, turmoil, uproar; SEE CONCEPTS *230,674*

bedraggled [*adj*] *unkempt*
decrepit, dilapidated, dirty, disheveled, disordered, dowdy, drenched, dripping, faded, messy,

muddied, muddy, run-down, seedy, shabby, sloppy, slovenly, sodden, soiled, stained, sullied, tacky, tattered, threadbare, untidy, wet; SEE CONCEPT *589*

bedridden [*adj*] *sick in bed*
ailing, disabled, flat on one's back*, ill, incapacitated, infirm, invalid, laid up*, prostrate; SEE CONCEPTS *314,485,489*

bedroom [*n*] *place for sleeping*
bedchamber, bunk room, chamber, cubicle, guest room; SEE CONCEPT *448*

bedspread [*n*] *thick, often quilted, covering for bed*
bedcover, blanket, counterpane, cover, coverlet, spread; SEE CONCEPT *444*

bee [*n1*] *honey-making, stinging insect*
bumblebee, drone, honey bee, killer bee, queen bee; SEE CONCEPT *398*

bee [*n2*] *collective task*
communal gathering, harvest, party, social, work party; SEE CONCEPTS *362,386*

beef [*n1*] *strong physical makeup*
arm, brawn, flesh, force, heftiness, meat, might, muscle, physique, power, robustness, sinew, steam, strength, thew, vigor; SEE CONCEPT *757*

beef [*n2*] *complaint*
bickering, criticism, dispute, grievance, gripe, grouse, grumble, objection, protestation, quarrel, rhubarb*, squabble; SEE CONCEPT *52*

beep [*n*] *sound from electronic device*
bell sound, bleep, breedle, computer sound, ding, eep, feep, signal, tone, warning; SEE CONCEPTS *74,284,529,685*

beep [*v*] *call for electronically*
call, page, summon, track down, warn; SEE CONCEPT *74*

beer [*n*] *alcoholic beverage made from malted grain*
ale, amber brew*, barley pop*, brew, brewski*, brown bottle*, chill*, cold coffee*, cold one*, hops, lager, malt, malt liquor*, oil*, stout*, suds*; SEE CONCEPT *455*

befall [*v*] *happen to; take place*
action, bechance, betide, break, chance, come down, come off, come to pass, cook*, cook up a storm*, cook with gas*, develop, ensue, fall, fall out, follow, gel, go, go down, hap*, happen, jell*, materialize, occur, shake*, smoke*, supervene, transpire; SEE CONCEPT *4*

befitting [*adj*] *appropriate*
according to Hoyle*, apt, becoming, behooving, beseeming, comme il faut, conforming, correct, decent, decorous, felicitous, fit, fitting, happy, just, kosher*, nice, on the button*, on the nose*, proper, right, right on*, seemly, suitable, what the doctor ordered*; SEE CONCEPTS *533,558*

before [*adv*] *earlier*
afore, aforetime, ahead, ante, antecedently, anteriorly, back, before present, ere, fore, former, formerly, forward, gone, gone by, heretofore, in advance, in days of yore, in front, in old days, in the past, past, precendently, previous, previously, since, sooner, up to now; SEE CONCEPT *820*

before [*prep*] *earlier than*
ahead of, ante, antecedent to, anterior to, ere, in advance of, in front of, preceding, previous to, prior to, since; SEE CONCEPT *820*

beforehand [*adj/adv*] *early*

be
be

advanced, ahead, ahead of time, already, ante, antecedently, before, before now, earlier, fore, in advance, in anticipation, precedently, precocious, previous, previously, sooner; SEE CONCEPT *820*

befriend [*v*] *make social acquaintance; support*
advise, aid, assist, back, benefit, buddy up*, case out*, come on to*, cotton to*, encourage, favor, get chummy with, get in with*, help, hit it off*, patronize, side with, stand by, sustain, take under one's wing*, take up with, uphold, welcome; SEE CONCEPTS *110,384*

befuddle [*v*] *confuse*
addle, baffle, ball up*, bewilder, bother, daze, disorient, distract, dumbfound, fluster, inebriate, intoxicate, make punchy*, mix up, muddle, puzzle, shake, stupefy, throw off*; SEE CONCEPTS *7,19,42*

beg [*v1*] *request*
abjure, advocate, apply to, ask, beseech, besiege, call to, canvass, conjure, crave, desire, entreat, impetrate, implore, importune, invoke, nag, obsecrate, obtest, petition, plead, pray, press, requisition, solicit, sue, supplicate, urge, woo, worry; SEE CONCEPT *48*

beg [*v2*] *seek charity*
ask alms, benefit, bite*, brace, bum*, burn*, buzz*, cadge*, call on, call upon, chisel*, clamor for, dime up*, ding*, freeload*, hit up*, hustle, knock, live hand to mouth*, mendicate, mooch*, nick*, nickel up*, panhandle, pass the hat*, put the bite on*, put the touch on*, score*, scrounge, solicit charity, sponge*, sponge on*, tap, touch, want; SEE CONCEPT *53*

beget [*v*] *create, bear*
afford, breed, bring, bring about, cause, effect, engender, father, generate, get, give rise to, multiply, occasion, procreate, produce, progenerate, propagate, reproduce, result in, sire; SEE CONCEPTS *173,251,374*

beggar [*n1*] *person asking for charity*
asker, borrower, bum, deadbeat, hobo, mendicant, panhandler, rustler, scrounger, supplicant, supplicator, tramp, vagabond; SEE CONCEPTS *412,423*

beggar [*n2*] *person in financial trouble*
alms person, bankrupt, dependent, down-and-out*, guttersnipe*, indigent, mendicant, pauper, poor person, poverty-stricken person, street person*, suppliant, vagrant, ward of state; SEE CONCEPT *423*

begin [*v1*] *start*
activate, actualize, break ground, break the ice*, bring about, bring to pass, cause, commence, create, do, drive, effect, embark on, enter on, enter upon, establish, eventuate, found, generate, get going, give birth to, give impulse, go ahead, go into, impel, inaugurate, induce, initiate, instigate, institute, introduce, launch, lay foundation for, lead, make, make active, motivate, mount, occasion, open, originate, plunge into, prepare, produce, set about, set in motion, set up, trigger, undertake; SEE CONCEPTS *234,241*

begin [*v2*] *come into being; become functional*
appear, arise, be born, bud, come forth, come into existence, come out, commence, crop up, dawn, derive from, emanate, emerge, enter, germinate, get going, get show on road*, get under way, grow out of, happen, issue forth, kick off, make tick*, occur, originate, proceed from, re-

sult from, rise, sail, send off, set, spring, sprout, start, stem from, take off; SEE CONCEPTS *105,680*

beginner [*n*] *person unskilled in something*
abecedarian, amateur, apprentice, buckwheater*, catechumen, colt, fish*, fledgling, greenhorn, greenie*, initiate, learner, neophyte, newcomer, new kid on the block*, new person, novice, novitiate, probationer, recruit, starter, student, tenderfoot*, trainee, tyro; SEE CONCEPTS *423,424*

beginning [*n1*] *start of an event or action*
alpha, basis, birth, blastoff*, commencement, creation, dawn, dawning, day one*, genesis, inauguration, inception, induction, infancy, initiation, installation, introduction, kickoff, onset, opener, opening, origin, origination, outset, point of departure, preface, prelude, presentation, rise, root, rudiment, source, spring, square one*, starting point, takeoff, threshold, top; SEE CONCEPTS *815,833*

beginning [*n2*] *origin, cause*
antecedent, birth, conception, egg, embryo, font, fount, fountain, fountainhead, generation, genesis, germ, heart, principle, resource, root, seed, stem, well; SEE CONCEPT *229*

begrudge [*v*] *wish that someone did not have*
be jealous, be reluctant, be stingy, covet, eat one's heart out, envy, grudge, pinch, resent, stint; SEE CONCEPTS *17,21*

beguile [*v1*] *fool*
betray, bluff, burn*, cheat, chisel, con, deceive, delude, double-cross, dupe, entice, exploit, finesse, flimflam*, gyp*, have, hoodwink*, impose on, jockey, juggle, lure, manipulate, mislead, play, play for a sucker*, rook*, rope in*, scam, seduce, shave*, snow*, stick*, string along, suck in*, take, take in, trick; SEE CONCEPT *59*

beguile [*v2*] *charm*
amuse, attract, cheer, delight, distract, divert, engross, entertain, entice, knock dead, knock out, lure, occupy, seduce, send, slay, solace, sweep off one's feet, tickle, tickle pink*, tickle to death*, turn on, vamp, wow*; SEE CONCEPTS *7,19,22*

behalf [*n*] *personal interest*
account, advantage, aid, assistance, benefit, cause, concern, countenance, defense, encouragement, favor, furtherance, good, help, part, place, profit, recommendation, representation, sake, service, side, stead, support, welfare; SEE CONCEPTS *410,532*

behave [*v1*] *function*
act, operate, perform, react, run, take, work; SEE CONCEPTS *1,4*

behave [*v2*] *act reasonably, properly*
act correctly, act one's age, act with decorum, be civil, be good, be nice, be on best behavior*, be orderly, comport oneself, conduct oneself properly, control oneself, demean oneself, deport oneself, direct, discipline oneself, keep one's nose clean*, keep the peace, live up to, manage, manage oneself, mind one's manners*, mind one's p's and q's*, observe golden rule*, observe the law, play fair, shape up, toe the mark*, watch one's step*; SEE CONCEPT *633*

behavior [*n*] *manner of conducting oneself*
act, action, address, air, attitude, bag*, bearing, carriage, code, comportment, conduct, convention, course, dealings, decency, decorum, deed, delivery, demeanor, deportment, ethics, eti-

quette, expression, form, front, guise, habits, management, mien, mode, morals, nature, observance, performance, practice, presence, propriety, ritual, role, routine, savoir-faire, seemliness, social graces, speech, style, tact, talk, taste, tenue, tone, way, way of life, ways, what's done*; SEE CONCEPTS *633,655*

behead [*v*] *decapitate*
bring to the block, decollate, execute, guillotine, head, kill, neck; SEE CONCEPT *176*

behest [*n*] *order; personal decree*
bidding, charge, command, commandment, demand, dictate, direction, expressed desire, injunction, instruction, mandate, order, precept, prompting, request, solicitation, wish, word; SEE CONCEPTS *20,53*

behind [*adv1/prep1*] *position farther back; following*
abaft, after, afterwards, at the heels of*, at the rear of, back of, bringing up the rear*, eating the dust*, in the background, in the wake, later than, next, off the pace, subsequently, trailing; SEE CONCEPTS *586,820*

behind [*adv2*] *in debt; late*
backward, behindhand, behind schedule, behind time, belated, delayed, dilatory, have to play catch up*, in arrears, laggard, overdue, slow, sluggish, tardy; SEE CONCEPTS *334,799*

behind [*n*] *buttocks*
backside, bottom, breech, can*, derrière, fanny*, fundament, posterior, rear, rump, seat, tail, tush*; SEE CONCEPT *392*

behind [*prep2*] *being the reason for*
at the bottom of, causing, concerning the circumstances, initiating, instigating, responsible for; SEE CONCEPT *532*

behind [*prep3*] *in support*
backing, for, in agreement, on the side of, supporting; SEE CONCEPT *388*

behind one's back [*adv*] *deceitfully*
covertly, secretly, sneakily, sub rosa, surreptitiously; SEE CONCEPTS *267,548*

behind the times [*adj*] *old-fashioned*
antiquated, dated, obsolete, old hat*, outdated, outmoded, out of date, passe, square; SEE CONCEPTS *578,589,797,799*

behold [*v*] *regard; look at*
catch, consider, contemplate, descry, discern, distinguish, earmark, eye, eyeball*, feast one's eyes*, flash*, lay eyes on*, note, notice, observe, perceive, regard, scan, see, spot, spy, survey, view, watch, witness; SEE CONCEPTS *34,626*

beholden [*adj*] *indebted*
bound, grateful, in hock, into, obligated, obliged, on a string*, on the arm*, on the cuff*, on the tab*, owe one, owing, responsible, under obligation; SEE CONCEPT *403*

behoove [*v*] *be necessary, proper*
be expected, befit, be fitting, be incumbent upon, be needful, be one's obligation, be required, be requisite, be right, beseem, owe it to, suit; SEE CONCEPT *646*

beige [*n/adj*] *light brown color*
biscuit, buff, café au lait, camel, cream, ecru, fawn, khaki, mushroom, neutral, oatmeal, off-white, sand, tan, taupe; SEE CONCEPTS *618,622*

being [*n1*] *existence*
actuality, animation, journey, life, living, presence, reality, subsistence, vitality, world; SEE CONCEPT *407*

being [*n2*] *essential nature*
character, entity, essence, essentia, essentiality, individuality, marrow, personality, quintessence, self, soul, spirit, substance, texture; SEE CONCEPTS *411,673*

being [*n3*] *animate object*
animal, beast, body, conscious thing, creature, entity, human, human being, individual, living thing, mortal, organism, person, personage, soul, thing; SEE CONCEPT *389*

belabor [*v*] *dwell on*
beat a dead horse*, go on about, hammer home, overwork, pound, rehash, repeat; SEE CONCEPT *56*

belated [*adj*] *late, slow*
behindhand, behind time, delayed, long-delayed, overdue, remiss, tardy, unpunctual; SEE CONCEPT *820*

belch [*v*] *burp; spew*
discharge, disgorge, emit, eruct, eructate, erupt, give off, gush, hiccup, irrupt, repeat, ventilate, vomit; SEE CONCEPT *185*

beleaguer [*v*] *harass, besiege*
annoy, badger, bedevil, beset, blockade, bother, gnaw, harry, nag, persecute, pester, plague, put upon, set upon, siege, storm, tease, vex, worry; SEE CONCEPTS *7,19*

belfry [*n*] *tower; part of tower*
bell tower, campanile, carillon, clocher, cupola, dome, head, minaret, spire, steeple, turret; SEE CONCEPT *440*

belie [*v1*] *disprove*
confute, contradict, contravene, controvert, deny, disaffirm, disagree, explode, gainsay, negate, negative, oppose, repudiate; SEE CONCEPTS *54,58*

belie [*v2*] *deceive*
color, conceal, disguise, distort, falsify, garble, give the lie to, gloss over, hide, miscolor, mislead, misrepresent, misstate, pervert, trump up, twist, warp; SEE CONCEPT *63*

belief [*n1*] *putting regard in as true*
acceptance, admission, assent, assumption, assurance, avowal, axiom, certainty, conclusion, confidence, conjecture, conviction, credence, credit, deduction, divination, expectation, faith, fancy, feeling, guess, hope, hypothesis, idea, impression, intuition, judgment, knowledge, mind, mindset, notion, opinion, persuasion, position, postulation, presumption, presupposition, profession, reliance, supposition, surmise, suspicion, theorem, theory, thesis, thinking, trust, understanding, view; SEE CONCEPTS *410,529*

belief [*n2*] *something regarded as true*
assumption, concept, credence, credo, creed, doctrine, dogma, faith, fundamental, gospel, gospel truth*, hypothesis, idea, ideology, law, opinion, postulate, precept, principle, say-so*, tenet, theorem, theory; SEE CONCEPT *689*

believable [*adj*] *trustworthy*
aboveboard, acceptable, authentic, colorable, conceivable, convincing, credential, credible, creditable, fiduciary, honest-to-God*, imaginable, impressive, likely, persuasive, plausible, possible, presumable, presumptive, probable, rational, reasonable, reliable, satisfying, straight, supposable, tenable, tried, trusty, unquestionable, up front*; SEE CONCEPTS *403,582*

believe [*v1*] *trust, rely on*
accept, accredit, admit, affirm, attach weight to, be certain of, be convinced of, be credulous, be

be
be

of the opinion, buy*, conceive, conclude, consider, count on, credit, deem, fall for*, give credence to, have, have faith in, have no doubt, hold, keep the faith, lap up*, place confidence in, posit, postulate, presume true, presuppose, reckon on, regard, rest assured, suppose, swallow*, swear by, take as gospel*, take at one's word, take for granted, take it, think, trust, understand; SEE CONCEPT *12*

believe [*v2*] *assume or suppose*
conjecture, consider, credit, deem, expect, feel, gather, guess, hold, imagine, judge, maintain, postulate, presume, reckon, sense, speculate, suppose, suspect, take, think, understand; SEE CONCEPT *28*

believer [*n*] *person who has faith in something*
acceptor, adherent, apostle, canonist, convert, devotee, disciple, doctrinaire, dogmatist, follower, freak, orthodox, prophet, proselyte, religionist, religious person, supporter, upholder, zealot; SEE CONCEPTS *361,423*

belittle [*v*] *detract*
bad-mouth, blister, criticize, cut down to size*, cut to the quick*, decry, deprecate, depreciate, deride, derogate, diminish, discount, discredit, disparage, dispraise, downgrade, downplay, dump on*, knock*, lower, minimize, pan, pooh pooh*, poor mouth*, put down, rip*, roast*, run down, scoff at, scorch*, scorn, shoot down*, shoot full of holes*, slam*, smear, sneer at, sour grapes*, squash*, squelch, take a swipe at*, take down, take down a peg*, tear down*, underestimate, underrate, undervalue, write off; SEE CONCEPTS *52,54*

bell [*n*] *signaling object or sound*
alarm, buzz, buzzer, carillon, chime, clapper, curfew, ding-dong*, dinger*, gong, peal, ringer, siren, tintinnabulum, tocsin, toll, vesper; SEE CONCEPT *595*

belligerent [*adj*] *nasty, argumentative*
aggressive, antagonistic, ardent, at loggerheads*, battling, bellicose, cantankerous, combative, contentious, fierce, fighting, flip, have a bone to pick*, have chip on shoulder*, have it in for*, hostile, hot, hot-tempered, mean, militant, on the outs*, ornery, pugnacious, quarrelsome, scrappy, truculent, warlike; SEE CONCEPTS *401,404*

bellow [*v*] *holler*
bark, bawl, bay, beller, blare, bluster, bray, call, clamor, cry, howl, low, roar, rout, scream, shout, shriek, wail, whoop, yawp, yell, yelp; SEE CONCEPT *77*

bells and whistles [*n*] *added-value features*
accessories, added features, attractive features, chrome, dressing, extras, gongs, trappings; SEE CONCEPTS *386,829*

belly [*n*] *stomach*
abdomen, bay window*, beer belly*, breadbasket*, corporation*, front porch*, gut, insides, intestines, paunch, pelvis, pot*, pot belly*, solar plexus, spare tire*, tank, tummy, venter; SEE CONCEPT *393*

belong [*v1*] *be part of, be in proper place*
accord, agree, appertain, apply, associate, attach to, be a component, be a constituent, be akin to, be an adjunct of, be a part, bear, bear upon, become, be connected with, befit, be fitting, be linked with, be related, be relevant, chime, concern, correlate, correspond, exist, fit, go, go with, harmonize, have relationship to, have respect to,

have to do with, inhere, match, permeate, pertain, refer, regard, reside, set, suit, touch, vest; SEE CONCEPTS *532,543*

belong [*v2*] *be affiliated with*
be allied to, be a member, be a member of, be associated with, be classified among, be contained in, be included in, be one of, be one of the family, be part of, fit in, have a place, in, in with, owe allegiance, owe support, run with*, swing*, swing with*, take one's place with; SEE CONCEPTS *114,388*

belonging [*n*] *sense of security in friendship*
acceptance, affinity, association, attachment, inclusion, kinship, loyalty, rapport, relationship; SEE CONCEPTS *388,410*

belongings [*n*] *personal possessions*
accouterments, appurtenances, assets, chattels, effects, gear, goods, paraphernalia, personal property, property, stuff, things; SEE CONCEPTS *446,710*

belonging to [*adj*] *owned by*
affiliated with, associated with, essential to, held by, inherent in, intrinsic in, native to; SEE CONCEPTS *404,549*

beloved [*adj*] *adored*
admired, cared for, cherished, darling, dear, dearest, doted on, endeared, esteemed, fair-haired, favorite, hallowed, highly regarded, highly valued, idolized, loved, near to one's heart*, pet*, pleasing, popular, precious, prized, respected, revered, sweet, treasured, venerated, well-liked, worshiped; SEE CONCEPTS *568,572*

beloved [*n*] *someone adored*
baby*, beau, boyfriend, darling, dear, dearest, fiancé, flame, girlfriend, heartbeat*, heartthrob, honey, idol, inamorato, love, love of my life*, lover, number one*, numero uno*, object of affection, one and only, pet*, prize, rave*, significant other, steady, sugar*, sweetheart, tootsie*, treasure, true love; SEE CONCEPT *423*

below [*adv/prep*] *lower*
beneath, down, down from, under, underneath; SEE CONCEPTS *581,586,735*

below [*prep2*] *less than; beneath*
inferior, lesser, lower, subject, subordinate, unworthy; SEE CONCEPTS *567,771*

below par [*adj*] *second-rate in quality*
below average, imperfect, inferior, lacking, not oneself, off, off-form, poor, substandard, under the weather*, wanting; SEE CONCEPT *574*

below the belt [*adj/adv*] *nastily and unfairly*
cowardly, dirty, dishonest, foul, unjust, unscrupulous, unsportsmanlike; SEE CONCEPTS *411,674,732*

belt [*n1*] *supporting band*
cincture, cummerbund, girdle, ribbon, ring, sash, strap, string, waistband; SEE CONCEPT *450*

belt [*n2*] *strip of land with characteristic feature*
area, district, layer, region, stretch, territory, tract, zone; SEE CONCEPTS *513,517*

belt [*v*] *hit hard*
bash, bat, biff, blast, blow, bop, clobber, slam, slug, smack, smash, sock, strap, switch, wallop, whip, whop; SEE CONCEPT *189*

bemoan [*v*] *express sorrow*
beat one's breast*, bewail, complain, cry over spilled milk*, deplore, grieve for, lament, moan over, mourn, regret, rue, sing the blues*, weep for; SEE CONCEPTS *49,51*

bemuse [v] *confuse*
addle, amaze, bewilder, daydream, daze, gather wool*, moon, muddle, overwhelm, paralyze, perplex, pipe dream*, puzzle, stun, stupefy; SEE CONCEPTS *7,19,22*

bench [n1] *furniture for sitting*
bank, chair, form, lawn seat, pew, seat, settee, settle, stall; SEE CONCEPT *443*

bench [n2] *large table*
board, counter, desk, easel, ledge, shelf, trestle, workbench, work table; SEE CONCEPT *443*

bench [n3] *group of judges*
court, courtroom, judiciary, magistrate, the bar, tribunal, your honors; SEE CONCEPTS *318,355*

benchmark [n] *reference point*
criterion, gauge, measure, standard, touchstone, yardstick; SEE CONCEPT *688*

bend [n] *curve*
angle, arc, bending, bow, corner, crook, curvation, curvature, deflection, deviation, flection, flexure, hook, lean, loop, round, sag, shift, tack, tilt, turn, twist, yaw, zigzag; SEE CONCEPT *436*

bend [v1] *form or cause a curve*
angle away, angle off, arch, bow, buckle, camber, careen, circle, contort, crimp, crinkle, crook, crouch, curl, deflect, deform, detour, double, droop, flex, genuflect, hook, incline, incurvate, lean, loop, pervert, round, spiral, stoop, swerve, tilt, turn, twist, veer, verge, warp, waver, wilt, wind, yaw, zigzag; SEE CONCEPTS *149,184*

bend [v2] *persuade; influence*
change mind, compel, direct, mold, shape, subdue, submit, sway, yield; SEE CONCEPT *68*

beneath [adv] *in a lower place*
below, underneath; SEE CONCEPT *586*

beneath [prep] *inferior*
below, lesser, less than, lower than, subject, subordinate, unbefitting, under, underneath, unworthy of; SEE CONCEPT *567*

benediction [n] *closing prayer*
amen, approbation, approval, beatitude, benedictus, benison, blessing, consecration, favor, grace, gratitude, invocation, laying on of hands, okay, orison, praise, sanctification, thanks, thanksgiving; SEE CONCEPT *69*

benefactor [n] *donor*
aid, altruist, angel, assistant, backer, contributor, fairy godparent*, fan, good Samaritan, grubstaker, helper, humanitarian, mark*, patron, philanthropist, promoter, protector, Santa Claus*, sponsor, subscriber, subsidizer, supporter, wellwisher; SEE CONCEPTS *416,423*

beneficial [adj] *advantageous*
benign, constructive, favorable, favoring, gainful, good, good for what ails you*, healthful, helpful, profitable, propitious, salubrious, salutary, serviceable, toward, useful, valuable, what the doctor ordered*, wholesome, worthy; SEE CONCEPTS *567,572*

beneficiary [n] *person who gains, benefits*
almsperson, assignee, devisee, donee, grantee, heir, heiress, inheritor, legatee, payee, possessor, receiver, recipient, stipendiary, successor; SEE CONCEPTS *355,423*

benefit [n1] *advantage, profit*
account, aid, asset, assistance, avail, benediction, betterment, blessing, boon, cream*, egg in one's beer*, extras, favor, gain, godsend*, good, gravy*, help, interest, perk*, profit, prosperity,
use, welfare, worth; SEE CONCEPTS *337,346,661*

benefit [n2] *event to raise money*
ball, bazaar, charitable affair, charity performance, concert, dance, dinner, exhibit, exhibition, fair, pancake breakfast, raffle; SEE CONCEPT *386*

benefit [v] *help, enhance*
advance, advantage, aid, ameliorate, assist, avail, be good for, better, build, contribute to, do for one, do the trick, favor, fill the bill*, further, improve, make a killing*, make it*, pay, pay off*, profit, promote, relieve, serve, succor, work for; SEE CONCEPTS *110,244*

benevolence [n] *charity*
altruism, amity, comity, compassion, feeling, friendliness, friendship, generosity, gift, goodness, good will, humanity, kindheartedness, kindness, sympathy; SEE CONCEPT *633*

benevolent [adj] *charitable, kind*
all heart, altruistic, beneficent, benign, big, bighearted, bounteous, bountiful, caring, chivalrous, compassionate, considerate, generous, helpful, humane, humanitarian, kindhearted, liberal, magnanimous, philanthropic, tenderhearted, warmhearted, well-disposed; SEE CONCEPT *401*

benign [adj1] *kindly*
amiable, beneficent, benevolent, benignant, complaisant, congenial, favorable, friendly, generous, genial, gentle, good, goodhearted, gracious, kind, liberal, merciful, mild, obliging, sympathetic; SEE CONCEPT *542*

benign [adj2] *mild, especially describing weather*
auspicious, balmy, bright, favorable, fortunate, gentle, healthful, propitious, refreshing, temperate, warm; SEE CONCEPT *605*

benign [adj3] *advantageous*
auspicious, beneficent, benevolent, bright, charitable, dexter, encouraging, favorable, fortunate, good, lucky, merciful, propitious, salutary, smiling; SEE CONCEPTS *537,572*

benign [adj4] *not cancerous*
curable, early stage, harmless, limited, remediable, slight, superficial; SEE CONCEPT *314*

bent [adj1] *curved*
angled, arced, arched, arciform, bowed, contorted, crooked, curvilinear, doubled over, drooping, droopy, hooked, humped, hunched, inclined, limp, looped, round, rounded, sinuous, slouchy, slumped, stooped, twined, twisted, warped, wilted; SEE CONCEPT *486*

bent [adj2] *determined*
bound, decided, decisive, dedicated, disposed, firm, fixed, inclined, insistent, intent, leaning, predisposed, resolute, resolved, set, settled, tending; SEE CONCEPT *403*

bent [n] *inclination; talent*
ability, aim, aptitude, bag*, disposition, druthers*, facility, faculty, flair, forte, genius, gift, head-set*, inclining, knack, leaning, mindset*, nose, penchant, predilection, predisposition, preference, proclivity, propensity, set, tack, tendency, thing for*, tilt, turn, weakness for; SEE CONCEPTS *409,630*

bequeath [v] *give in a will*
bestow, commit, devise, endow, entrust, grant, hand down, hand on, impart, leave, leave to, legate, pass on, transmit, will; SEE CONCEPTS *108,317*

bequest [n] *something given in will*

bequeathal, bequeathment, bestowal, devisal, devise, dower, endowment, estate, gift, heritage, inheritance, legacy, settlement, trust; SEE CONCEPTS *318,337*

berate [*v*] *criticize hatefully*
bawl out*, blister, call down, castigate, censure, chew*, chew out*, chide, cuss out*, eat out*, give one hell*, give what for*, jaw*, jump all over*, rail at*, rake over the coals*, rate, rebuke, reprimand, reproach, reprove, revile, scold, scorch, tell off, tongue-lash, upbraid, vituperate; SEE CONCEPT *52*

bereavement [*n*] *death; loss*
affliction, deprivation, distress, misfortune, sorrow, tribulation; SEE CONCEPTS *230,674*

bereft [*adj*] *lacking; missing*
beggared, bereaved, cut off, deprived, destitute, devoid, dispossessed, divested, fleeced, impoverished, left without, minus, naked, parted from, robbed, shorn, stripped, wanting, without; SEE CONCEPTS *546,576*

berry [*n*] *small fruit*
bean, drupe, drupelet, grain, haw, hip, kernel, pome, seed; SEE CONCEPT *426*

berserk [*adj*] *crazed*
crazy, demented, deranged, insane, mad, maniacal, manic, violent; SEE CONCEPT *403*

berth [*n1*] *harbor; bunk*
anchorage, bed, bedroom, billet, compartment, cot, dock, hammock, haven, jetty, levee, pier, port, quay, slip, wharf; SEE CONCEPTS *513,516*

berth [*n2*] *position of responsibility*
appointment, billet, capacity, connection, employment, job, living, office, place, post, profession, situation, spot; SEE CONCEPTS *362,668*

beseech [*v*] *beg*
adjure, appeal, ask, call upon, crave, entreat, implore, importune, invoke, petition, plead, pray, solicit, sue, supplicate; SEE CONCEPT *48*

beset [*v*] *plague; hem in*
aggress, assail, attack, badger, bedevil, beleaguer, besiege, bug*, circle*, compass, dog*, drive up the wall*, embarrass, encircle, enclose, encompass, entangle, environ, fall on, fall upon, girdle, give a bad time*, give a hard time*, give one the business*, give the needle*, harass, harry, hassle, infest, invade, jump on one's case*, nag, nudge, overrun, perplex, pester, pick on, put the squeeze on*, ride, ring, start in on, storm, strike, surround; SEE CONCEPTS *7,19*

beside [*adv/prep*] *next to*
abreast of, adjacent to, adjoining, alongside, aside, a step from, at one's elbow, at the edge of, at the side of, bordering on, by, cheek by jowl*, close at hand, close to, close upon, connected with, contiguous to, fornent, in juxtaposition, near, nearby, neck and neck*, neighboring, next door to, nigh, opposite, overlooking, round, side by side, verging on, with; SEE CONCEPT *586*

beside oneself [*adj*] *very upset*
berserk, crazed, delirious, demented, distraught, frantic, frenetic, insane, mad, unbalanced, unhinged; SEE CONCEPTS *403,485,570*

besides [*adv*] *in addition; as well*
added to, additionally, along with, also, and all, apart from, aside from, as well as, beyond, conjointly, else, exceeding, exclusive of, extra, further, furthermore, in conjunction with, in distinction to, in excess of, in other respects, likewise, more, moreover, more than, not counting, on the side*, on top of everything, other than, otherwise, over and above, plus, secondly, supplementary to, to boot*, together with, too, what's more*, with the exception of, yet; SEE CONCEPT *772*

besides [*prep1*] *apart from*
aside from, bar, barring, beside, but, except, excepting, excluding, exclusive of, in addition to, other than, outside of, over and above, save, without; SEE CONCEPT *772*

besides [*prep2*] *in addition to*
added to, along with, as well as, beside, beyond, in excess of, more than, on top of, other than, over and above, plus, supplementary, together with; SEE CONCEPT *772*

beside the point [*adj*] *not important*
extraneous, immaterial, inapplicable, incidental, inconsequential, irrelevant, pointless, unimportant, unrelated; SEE CONCEPT *575*

besiege [*v1*] *surround; assault*
assail, attack, beleaguer, beset, blockade, come at from all sides, confine, congregate, encircle, encompass, environ, hem in, invest, lay siege to, shut in, trap, work on, work over; SEE CONCEPTS *86,90*

besiege [*v2*] *bother*
badger, beleaguer, bug*, buttonhole*, harass, harry, hound*, importune, nag, pester, plague, trouble; SEE CONCEPTS *7,19*

best [*adj1*] *most excellent*
10*, A-1*, ace, bad*, beyond compare, boss*, capital, champion, chief, choicest, cool*, culminating, finest, first, first-class, first-rate, foremost, greatest, highest, incomparable, inimitable, leading, matchless, nonpareil, number 1*, optimum, out-of-sight*, outstanding, paramount, peerless, perfect, preeminent, premium, prime, primo*, principal, sans pareil, second to none, super, superlative, supreme, terrific, tops, tough, transcendent, unequaled, unparalleled, unrivaled, unsurpassed; SEE CONCEPTS *568,572*

best [*adj2*] *correct, right*
advantageous, apt, desirable, golden, most desirable, most fitting, preferred, presentable; SEE CONCEPT *558*

best [*adj3*] *most*
biggest, bulkiest, greatest, largest; SEE CONCEPT *771*

best [*adv*] *most excellently*
advantageously, attractively, creditably, extremely, gloriously, greatly, honorably, illustriously, magnanimously, most deeply, most fortunately, most fully, most highly, sincerely; SEE CONCEPTS *568,572*

best [*n1*] *most outstanding thing in class*
choice, cream, cream of the crop*, elite, fat, favorite, finest, first, flower, gem, model, nonpareil, paragon, pick, prime, prize, select, top; SEE CONCEPT *668*

best [*n2*] *highest personal effort*
all one's got, best shot, hardest, highest endeavor, level best*, Sunday best*, utmost; SEE CONCEPT *411*

best [*v*] *defeat; gain advantage*
beat, beat up*, better, blank*, blast*, bulldoze*, clobber*, conquer, cream*, deck*, drub*, exceed, excel, flax*, floor*, get the better of, knock off*, KO*, lambaste, let have it*, lick*, master, outclass, outdo, outshine, outstrip, overcome,

prevail, put away, shoot down*, shut down*, surpass, take care of, take down*, tan*, thrash*, top, total, transcend, trash*, triumph, triumph over, trounce, wallop, waste*, wax*, whip*, whomp*, whop*, wipe*, wipe out, wipe the floor with*, zap*; SEE CONCEPT 95

bestow [v] *give, allot*
accord, apportion, award, bequeath, come through, commit, confer, devote, donate, entrust, favor, gift, give away, grant, hand out, honor with, impart, kick in, lavish, offer, present, put out, render to; SEE CONCEPTS 98,108

best-seller [n] *top-selling item*
a top ten, chart-buster, favorite, hit*, hot item*, hot seller, mover*, number one, record-breaker, success, winner; SEE CONCEPTS 423,446

best shot [n] *all-out try*
all one's got, best effort, best one can do, maximum effort, one's all, one's damnedest, optimum effort; SEE CONCEPTS 87,362,677,724

bet [n] *game of chance; money gambled*
action, ante, betting, chance, down on, hazard, long shot, lot, lottery, odds, odds on, parlay, play, pledge, plunge, pot, raffle, random shot, risk, shot, shot in the dark*, speculation, stake, sweepstakes, uncertainty, venture, wager; SEE CONCEPTS 28,293,329

bet [v] *gamble*
ante, buy in on, chance, dice, game, hazard, lay down, lay odds, play against, play for, play the ponies*, pledge, pony up*, put, put money on, risk, set, speculate, tempt fortune*, toss up, trust, venture, wager; SEE CONCEPTS 292,330

beta [adj] *being tested*
dubious, experimental, flaky, mostly working, new, pre-release, suspect, testing, unready; SEE CONCEPTS 529,582

bête noire [n] *trouble*
adversary, anathema, antagonist, bad news*, bane, curse, devil, enemy, pet hate, plague; SEE CONCEPTS 532,674,675,690,728

betray [v1] *be disloyal*
abandon, be unfaithful, bite the hand that feeds you*, blow the whistle*, bluff, break faith, break promise, break trust, break with, commit treason, cross, deceive, deliver up*, delude, desert, double-cross, finger*, forsake, go back on, inform against, inform on, jilt, knife*, let down, mislead, play false*, play Judas*, seduce, sell down the river*, sell out, stab in the back*, take in*, trick, turn in, turn informer, turn state's evidence, walk out on; SEE CONCEPT 384

betray [v2] *divulge, expose information*
blurt out, dime*, disclose, evince, fink on*, give away, inform, lay bare, let slip, make known, manifest, rat on*, reveal, show, sing*, snitch*, spill, squeal*, stool*, tattle, tell, tell on, turn in, uncover, unmask; SEE CONCEPTS 44,60

betrayal [n1] *exhibition of disloyalty*
deception, dishonesty, double-crossing, double-dealing, duplicity, falseness, giveaway, Judas kiss*, let-down, perfidy, sellout, treachery, treason, trickery, unfaithfulness; SEE CONCEPT 633

betrayal [n2] *divulgence of information*
blurting out, diming*, disclosure, giving away, ratting*, revelation, snitching*, spilling*, squealing*, tattling, telling; SEE CONCEPTS 44,60

betroth [v] *marry*
affiance, become engaged, bind, commit, contract, engage, espouse, give one's hand, make compact, plight faith, plight troth, promise, tie oneself to, vow; SEE CONCEPT 297

betrothal [n] *marriage*
affiancing, betrothing, engagement, espousal, plight, promise, troth, vow; SEE CONCEPT 297

better [adj1] *excelling, more excellent*
bigger, choice, exceeding, exceptional, finer, fitter, greater, higher quality, improved, larger, more appropriate, more desirable, more fitting, more select, more suitable, more useful, more valuable, preferable, preferred, prominent, sharpened, sophisticated, souped up*, superior, surpassing, worthier; SEE CONCEPTS 568,572

better [adj2] *improved in health*
convalescent, cured, fitter, fully recovered, healthier, improving, less ill, mending, more healthy, on the comeback trail*, on the mend, on the road to recovery*, out of the woods*, over the hump*, progressing, recovering, stronger, well; SEE CONCEPT 314

better [adj3] *larger*
bigger, greater, longer, more, preponderant, weightier; SEE CONCEPTS 771,773

better [adv] *in a more excellent manner*
finer, greater, in a superior way, more, more advantageously, more attractively, more competently, more completely, more effectively, more thoroughly, preferably, to a greater degree; SEE CONCEPTS 568,572

better [v] *improve performance; outdo*
advance, ameliorate, amend, beat, best, cap, correct, enhance, exceed, excel, forward, further, help, meliorate, mend, outshine, outstrip, promote, raise, rectify, refine, reform, revamp, surpass, top, transcend; SEE CONCEPTS 141,244

betterment [n] *improvement*
advancement, amelioration, mastery, melioration, progress, prosperity, upgrading; SEE CONCEPT 244

between [adv/prep] *middle from two points*
amid, amidst, among, at intervals, betwixt, bounded by, centrally located, enclosed by, halfway, in, inserted, interpolated, intervening, in the middle, in the midst of, in the seam, in the thick of, medially, mid, midway, separating, surrounded by, 'tween, within; SEE CONCEPTS 586,820

beverage [n] *liquid refreshment*
cooler, draft, drink, drinkable, libation, liquor, potable, potation; SEE CONCEPT 454

bevy [n] *swarm*
assembly, band, bunch, cluster, collection, company, covey, crew, crowd, flight, flock, gathering, group, pack, party, troupe; SEE CONCEPT 432

bewail [v] *cry over, lament*
bemoan, deplore, eat heart out*, express sorrow, grieve for, moan, mourn, regret, repent, rue, sing the blues*, take on, wail, weep over; SEE CONCEPT 266

beware [v] *be careful*
attend, avoid, be cautious, be wary, guard against, heed, keep eyes open*, keep one's distance, keep on one's toes*, look out, mind, mind p's and q's*, notice, refrain from, shun, steer clear of*, take care, take heed, walk on eggs*, watch one's step, watch out; SEE CONCEPT 34

bewilder [v] *confuse*
addle, baffle, ball up*, befuddle, bemuse, confound, daze, disconcert, distract, floor*, fluster,

be
be

mess with one's head*, mix up, muddle, mystify, perplex, puzzle, rattle, snow*, stump, stupefy, throw, upset; SEE CONCEPTS *14,42*

bewildered [*adj*] *confused*
addled, agape, aghast, agog, appalled, astonished, astounded, awed, awe-struck, baffled, befuddled, bowled over*, dazed, dazzled, disconcerted, dizzy, dumbfounded, dumbstruck, flabbergasted, flipped out*, floored*, flustered, giddy, in a dither*, lost, misled, muddled, mystified, perplexed, punchy*, puzzled, rattled, reeling, shocked, shook up, speechless, staggered, startled, stumped, stunned, stupefied, surprised, taken aback, thrown, thunderstruck*, uncertain, unglued*; SEE CONCEPTS *402,403*

bewilderment [*n*] *puzzlement*
bafflement, confusion, daze, discombobulation*, disorientation, perplexity, surprise; SEE CONCEPT *14*

bewitch [*v*] *charm*
allure, attract, bedevil, beguile, captivate, capture, control, dazzle, draw, enchant, enrapture, enthrall, entrance, fascinate, hex, hypnotize, knock dead*, knock out, put horns on*, put the whammy on*, put under magic spell*, send*, slay*, spell*, spellbind, sweep off one's feet*, take, tickle*, tickle pink*, tickle to death*, trick, turn on*, vamp, voodoo, wile, wow*; SEE CONCEPTS *7,22*

bewitched [*adj*] *charmed*
captivated, enamored, enchanted, enraptured, ensorcelled, entranced, fallen for, fascinated, gaga about*, have a bug in one's ear*, have a thing about*, head over heels*, hooked*, hung up*, mad about, mesmerized, possessed, spellbound, transformed, turned on*, under a spell; SEE CONCEPTS *32,403*

beyond [*adv/prep*] *further; outside limits*
above, after, ahead, apart from, as well as, at a distance, away from, before, behind, besides, beyond the bounds, clear of, farther, free of, good way off, hyper, in addition to, in advance of, long way off, moreover, more remote, on the far side, on the other side, out of range, out of reach, outside, over, over and above, over there, past, remote, superior to, without, yonder; SEE CONCEPTS *554,772,778*

bias [*n1*] *belief in one way; partiality*
bent, bigotry, chauvinism, disposition, favoritism, flash, head-set*, illiberality, inclination, intolerance, leaning, mind-set*, mind trip*, narrowmindedness, one-sidedness, penchant, preconception, predilection, predisposition, preference, prejudice, prepossession, proclivity, proneness, propensity, spin, standpoint, tendency, tilt, turn, unfairness, viewpoint; SEE CONCEPT *689*

bias [*n2*] *diagonal weave of fabric*
angle, cant, cross, incline, oblique, slant; SEE CONCEPT *606*

bias [*v*] *cause to favor*
distort, incline, influence, make partial, prejudice, prepossess, slant, sway, twist, warp, weight; SEE CONCEPTS *7,19*

bible [*n*] *holy book; authoritative book*
authority, creed, doctrine, guide, guidebook, handbook, manual, sacred writ, sacred writings, scripture, testament, text, the good news; SEE CONCEPTS *280,368*

bicker [*v*] *nastily argue*
altercate, brawl, caterwaul, cause a scene*, cavil, dig, disagree, dispute, fall out, fight, hassle, pick at, quarrel, quibble, row, scrap, scrape, spar, spat, squabble, tiff, trade zingers*, wrangle; SEE CONCEPT *46*

bicycle [*n*] *pedal-driven recreational vehicle*
bike, cycle, tandem, two-wheeler, velocipede, wheels; SEE CONCEPTS *364,505*

bid [*n1*] *offering of money or services*
advance, amount, declaration, feeler, hit, invitation, offer, pass, price, proffer, proposal, proposition, request, submission, suggestion, sum, summons, tender; SEE CONCEPTS *67,330*

bid [*n2*] *endeavor*
attempt, crack, effort, essay, try, venture; SEE CONCEPT *87*

bid [*v1*] *offer money or services*
present, proffer, propose, render, submit, tender, venture; SEE CONCEPTS *67,330*

bid [*v2*] *say*
call, greet, tell, wish; SEE CONCEPT *266*

bid [*v3*] *ask for; command*
call, charge, demand, desire, direct, enjoin, instruct, invite, make a pass at*, make a pitch*, make a play for*, order, proposition, request, require, solicit, summon, tell, warn; SEE CONCEPT *53*

bidding [*n1*] *command*
behest, call, charge, demand, dictate, direction, injunction, instruction, invitation, mandate, order, request, summons, word; SEE CONCEPT *53*

bidding [*n2*] *offering of money, services*
advance, auction, invitation, offer, proffering, proposal, proposition, request, submission, suggestion, tender; SEE CONCEPTS *67,330*

bide [*v*] *wait*
abide, attend, await, continue, dwell, hang around, hang in*, hang out*, hold the phone*, lie in wait*, linger, live, remain, reside, sit tight*, stay, stick around, sweat it*, tarry, watch for; SEE CONCEPT *681*

big [*adj1*] *large, great*
ample, awash, a whale of a*, brimming, bulky, bull*, burly, capacious, chock-full*, colossal, commodious, considerable, copious, crowded, enormous, extensive, fat, full, gigantic, heavy-duty*, heavyweight, hefty, huge, hulking, humongous*, husky, immense, jumbo, mammoth, massive, mondo*, monster*, oversize, packed, ponderous, prodigious, roomy, sizable, spacious, strapping, stuffed, substantial, super colossal*, thundering, tremendous, vast, voluminous, walloping, whopper, whopping; SEE CONCEPTS *771,773*

big [*adj2*] *important*
big league*, big-time*, consequential, considerable, eminent, heavy-duty*, heavyweight, influential, leading, main, major league*, material, meaningful, momentous, paramount, popular, powerful, prime, principal, prominent, serious, significant, substantial, super, super colossal*, valuable, weighty; SEE CONCEPT *568*

big [*adj3*] *grown*
adult, elder, full-grown, grown-up, mature, tall; SEE CONCEPTS *578,797*

big [*adj4*] *generous*
altruistic, benevolent, bighearted, chivalrous, considerate, free, gracious, greathearted, heroic, liberal, lofty, magnanimous, noble, princely, un-

selfish; SEE CONCEPT *404*
big [*adj5*] *arrogant*
arty, boastful, bragging, conceited, flamboyant, haughty, high-sounding, imperious, imposing, inflated, overblown, pompous, presumptuous, pretentious, proud; SEE CONCEPT *401*
big deal [*n*] *something or someone important*
big cheese*, big enchilada*, big fish*, biggie*, big gun*, big shot*, big wheel*, bigwig*, boss, boss man*, head honcho*, hotshot*, important person, top dog*, tycoon, very important person, VIP; SEE CONCEPT *347*
big-hearted [*adj*] *very kind*
altruistic, benevolent, compassionate, generous, giving, gracious, noble; SEE CONCEPTS *404,542*
big league [*adj*] *important*
big-time, chief, critical, crucial, exceptional, four-star, front-page*, grave, great, heavy, high-power, major-league, playing hard ball*, professional, serious, strictly business; SEE CONCEPTS *567,568*
bigmouth [*n*] *a loudmouth*
bag of wind*, big talker*, blowhard*, blusterer, boaster, brag, braggart, bragger, bull artist*, bull-thrower*, gasbag*, gossiper, grandstander, know-it-all, show-off, swelled head*, trumpeter*, windbag*; SEE CONCEPTS *412,423*
bigot [*n*] *intolerant, prejudiced person*
chauvinist, diehard, doctrinaire, dogmatist, enthusiast, extremist, fanatic, fiend, maniac, monomaniac, opinionated person, partisan, persecutor, puritan, racist, sectarian, segregationist, sexist, stickler, superpatriot, zealot; SEE CONCEPTS *359,423*
bigoted [*adj*] *intolerant, prejudiced*
biased, chauvinistic, conservative, dogmatic, illiberal, narrow, narrow-minded, obstinate, opinionated, partial, partisan, sectarian, slanted, small-minded, twisted, unfair, warped; SEE CONCEPTS *403,555*
bigotry [*n*] *intolerance, prejudice*
bias, conservatism/conservativism, discrimination, dogmatism, fanaticism, injustice, Jim Crowism*, narrow-mindedness, partiality, provincialism, racialism, racism, sectarianism, sexism, unfairness; SEE CONCEPTS *388,410*
big shot [*n*] *important person*
big cheese*, big gun*, big wheel*, bigwig*, celebrity, dignitary, heavy-hitter*, heavyweight*, mogul, personage, somebody, VIP; SEE CONCEPT *423*
big win [*n1*] *overwhelming success or victory*
coup, coup d'etat, obliteration; SEE CONCEPT *706*
big win [*n2*] *desirable chance discovery*
accidental discovery, chance discovery, good fortune, luck, serendipity; SEE CONCEPT *693*
bilateral [*adj*] *having two sides*
mutual, reciprocal, respective, two-sided; SEE CONCEPT *562*
bilk [*v*] *cheat*
bamboozle*, beat, circumvent, con, deceive, defraud, disappoint, do*, fleece*, flimflam*, foil, frustrate, gyp*, overreach, rook*, ruin, snow*, swindle, thwart, trick; SEE CONCEPTS *59,139*
bill [*n1*] *account of charges; money owed*
bad news*, check, chit, damage*, debt, invoice, IOU, itemized account, knock*, note, reckoning, request for payment, score, statement, statement of indebtedness, tab; SEE CONCEPTS *329,332*

bill [*n2*] *list; circular*
advertisement, affiche, agenda, bulletin, card, catalogue, flyer, handbill, handout, inventory, leaflet, listing, notice, placard, playbill, poster, program, roster, schedule, syllabus; SEE CONCEPTS *280,283*
bill [*n3*] *piece of legislation*
act, draft, measure, projected law, proposal, proposed act; SEE CONCEPTS *271,318*
bill [*n4*] *piece of paper money*
bank note, buck, certificate, currency, dollar, greenback*, long green*, skin*; SEE CONCEPT *340*
bill [*n5*] *beak of animal*
mandible, neb, nib, pecker, projection; SEE CONCEPT *399*
bill [*v1*] *charge money for goods, services*
bone, chase, debit, draw upon, dun, figure, invoice, put the arm on*, put the bite on*, put the squeeze on*, reckon, record, render, solicit; SEE CONCEPTS *330,342*
bill [*v2*] *advertise*
announce, book, give advance notice, post; SEE CONCEPTS *60,292*
billow [*n*] *surging mass*
beachcomber, breaker, crest, roller, surge, swell, tide, wave; SEE CONCEPTS *437,514*
billow [*v*] *surge*
balloon, belly, bloat, bounce, bulge, ebb and flow, heave, pitch, puff up, ripple, rise and fall, rise up, rock, roll, swell, toss, undulate, wave; SEE CONCEPTS *159,208*
billowy [*adj*] *surging*
bouncing, bouncy, bulgy, distended, ebbing and flowing, heaving, puffy, rippled, rippling, rising, rising and falling, rolling, swelling, swirling, swollen, undulating, waving, wavy; SEE CONCEPTS *486,584*
bind [*n*] *predicament*
between a rock and a hard place*, crunch*, difficulty, dilemma, hot water*, no-win situation*, nuisance, pickle*, predicament, quandary, sticky situation*, tight situation, tight spot*; SEE CONCEPTS *230,674*
bind [*v1*] *fasten, secure*
adhere, attach, bandage, border, chain, cinch, clamp, connect, constrict, cover, dress, edge, encase, enchain, enfetter, fetter, finish, fix, fold, furl, glue, hamper, handcuff, hem, hitch, hitch on, hobble, hook on, hook up, lace, lap, lash, leash, manacle, moor, muzzle, paste, peg down, pin, pin down, pinion, put together, restrain, restrict, rope, shackle, stick, strap, swathe, tack on, tether, tie, tie up, trammel, trim, truss, unite, wrap, yoke; SEE CONCEPTS *85,160*
bind [*v2*] *obligate; restrict*
compel, confine, constrain, detain, engage, enslave, force, hamper, hinder, hogtie*, indenture, lock up, necessitate, oblige, prescribe, put half nelson on*, put lock on*, require, restrain, restrict, yoke; SEE CONCEPTS *14,130*
binding [*adj1*] *necessary*
bounden*, compulsory, conclusive, counted upon, essential, imperative, incumbent on, indissoluble, irrevocable, mandatory, obligatory, required, requisite, unalterable; SEE CONCEPT *546*
binding [*adj2*] *confining*
attached, enslaved, fastened, indentured, limiting, restraining, tied, tying; SEE CONCEPT *554*
binding [*n*] *cover; something which fastens*

be
bi

adhesive, belt, fastener, jacket, tie, wrapper; SEE CONCEPT *475*

binge [*n*] *spree*
affair, bender, blind*, bout*, carousal, compotation, drunk*, fling, jag*, orgy*, toot*; SEE CONCEPT *386*

biography [*n*] *account of person's life*
adventures, autobiography, bio, biog, close-up, confessions, diary, experiences, journal, letters, life, life history, life story, memoir, personal account, personal anecdote, personal narrative, personal record, picture, profile, résumé, saga, sketch, vita; SEE CONCEPTS *280,282*

bird [*n*] *flying animal*
feathered creature, fowl, game; SEE CONCEPT *395*

birds of a feather [*n*] *two of a kind*
Bobbsey twins, close friends, compadres, comrades, friends, two minds thinking as one; SEE CONCEPT *423*

birth [*n1*] *becoming alive*
bearing, beginning, birthing, blessed event*, childbearing, childbirth, creation, ct of God, delivery, labor, nascency, natality, nativity, parturition, producing, travail, visit from stork*; SEE CONCEPTS *302,373*

birth [*n2*] *beginning*
commencement, dawn, dawning, emergence, fountainhead, genesis, onset, opening, origin, outset, rise, source, start; SEE CONCEPT *119*

birth [*n3*] *heritage*
ancestry, background, blood, breeding, derivation, descent, extraction, forebears, genealogy, heritance, legacy, line, lineage, parentage, pedigree, position, race, rank, station, status, stock, strain; SEE CONCEPTS *296,648*

birth control [*n*] *method of preventing pregnancy*
abstinence, condom, contraception, contraceptive, diaphragm, IUD, pill, planned parenthood, rhythm method, rubber, safety*, tied tubes, vasectomy; SEE CONCEPTS *121,375*

birth defect [*n*] *congenital defect*
abnormality, congenital malformation, deformity; SEE CONCEPT *580*

birthmark [*n*] *blemish one is born with*
angioma, beauty mark, hemangioma, mole, mother's mark, nevus, port wine stain; SEE CONCEPT *580*

bisect [*v*] *divide in two*
bifurcate, branch off, cleave, cross, cut across, cut in half, cut in two, dichotomize, dimidiate, divaricate, divide in two, fork, furcate, halve, hemisect, intersect, separate, split, split down the middle; SEE CONCEPTS *98,137,176*

bisexual [*adj*] *having relations with either gender*
AC-DC*, androgynous, bi*, epicene, gynandrous, hermaphroditic, intersexual, monoclinous, swings both ways*; SEE CONCEPT *372*

bistro [*n*] *drinkery with food*
bar, lounge, restaurant, tavern; SEE CONCEPTS *439,448,449*

bit [*n1*] *tiny piece*
atom, butt, chicken feed*, chip, chunk, crumb, dab, dash, division, dollop, dose, dot, driblet, droplet, end, excerpt, flake, fraction, fragment, grain, iota, item, jot, lick*, lump, mite, modicum, moiety, molecule, morsel, niggle, parcel, part, particle, peanuts*, pinch, portion, sample, scale, scintilla, scrap, section, segment, shard, share, shaving, shred, slice, sliver, smidgen, snatch, snip, snippet, specimen, speck, splinter, sprinkling, stub, stump, taste, tittle, trace, trickle; SEE CONCEPTS *831,835*

bit [*n2*] *short period of time*
instant, jiffy, little while, minute, moment, second, space, spell, stretch, tick, while; SEE CONCEPT *807*

bit [*n3*] *computer information*
0, 1, binary digit, binary unit, data; SEE CONCEPT *274*

bite [*n1*] *injury from gripping, tearing*
chaw*, chomp*, gob*, itch*, laceration, nip, pain, pinch, prick, smarting, sting, tooth marks*, wound; SEE CONCEPT *309*

bite [*n2*] *mouthful of food*
brunch, drop, light meal, morsel, nibble, nosh*, piece, refreshment, sample, snack, sop*, taste; SEE CONCEPTS *457,459*

bite [*n3*] *pungency; stinging sensation*
burn, edge, guts*, kick, piquancy, punch, spice, sting, zap*, zip*; SEE CONCEPT *614*

bite [*n4*] *allotment*
allowance, cut, lot, part, piece, portion, quota, share, slice; SEE CONCEPT *835*

bite [*v1*] *grip or tear with teeth*
champ, chaw, chaw on, chew, chomp, clamp, crunch, crush, cut, eat, gnaw, hold, lacerate, masticate, munch, nibble, nip, pierce, pinch, rend, ruminate, seize, sever, snap, take a chunk out of*, taste, tooth, wound; SEE CONCEPTS *185,616*

bite [*v2*] *corrode, eat away*
burn, consume, decay, decompose, deteriorate, dissolve, eat into, engrave, erode, etch, oxidize, rot, rust, scour, sear, slash, smart, sting, tingle, wear away; SEE CONCEPTS *215,250*

bite [*v3*] *take a chance*
be victim, get hooked*, nibble, risk, volunteer; SEE CONCEPT *384*

bite the bullet [*v*] *take it*
be forced, bow to fate, face the music*, have no choice, know no alternative, pay the piper*, stand up and take it, swallow the pill*, take one's medicine*, take the rap; SEE CONCEPTS *23,96*

biting [*adj1*] *piercing, sharp*
bitter, bleak, blighting, cold, crisp, cutting, freezing, harsh, nipping, penetrating, raw; SEE CONCEPTS *569,605*

biting [*adj2*] *sarcastic*
acerbic, acrimonious, bitter, caustic, cutting, incisive, mordant, scathing, severe, sharp, stinging, trenchant, withering; SEE CONCEPT *267*

bitter [*adj1*] *pungent, sharp*
absinthal, absinthian, acerb, acerbic, acid, acrid, amaroidal, astringent, harsh, sour, tart, unsweetened, vinegary; SEE CONCEPT *613*

bitter [*adj2*] *hostile, nasty*
acrimonious, alienated, antagonistic, begrudging, biting, caustic, crabby, divided, embittered, estranged, fierce, freezing, hateful, intense, irreconcilable, morose, rancorous, resentful, sardonic, severe, sore, sour, stinging, sullen, virulent, vitriolic, with chip on shoulder*; SEE CONCEPTS *267,404*

bitter [*adj3*] *painful, distressing*
afflictive, annoying, bad, brutal, calamitous, cruel, dire, disagreeable, displeasing, distasteful, disturbing, galling, grievous, hard, harsh, heartbreaking, hurtful, inclement, intemperate, in-

tense, merciless, offensive, poignant, provoking, rigorous, rugged, ruthless, savage, severe, sharp, stinging, unpalatable, unpleasant, vexatious, woeful; SEE CONCEPT *537*

bitterness [n1] *sourness*
acerbity, acidity, acridity, astringency, brackishness, brininess, piquancy, pungency, sharpness, tartness, vinegariness; SEE CONCEPT *614*

bitterness [n2] *agony*
acrimoniousness, anguish, asperity, distress, grievousness, harshness, hostility, mordancy, pain, painfulness, sarcasm, venom, virulence; SEE CONCEPTS *410,633*

bizarre [adj] *strange, wild*
bugged out*, camp*, comical, curious, eccentric, extraordinary, fantastic, far-out*, freakish, grody*, grotesque, kooky, ludicrous, odd, oddball, offbeat, off the wall*, outlandish, outré, peculiar, queer, ridiculous, singular, unusual, way-out*, weird; SEE CONCEPTS *547,564*

blab [v] *gossip*
babble, betray, blather, blurt out, chatter, disclose, divulge, gab, gabble, give away, go on, jabber, let out, let slip, mouth, peach*, prattle, reveal, run off at the mouth*, run on, shoot the breeze*, spill*, spill the beans*, squeal*, talk through one's hat*, tattle, tell, tell on, yak*, yakkety-yak*; SEE CONCEPTS *55,60*

blabbermouth [n] *someone who talks too much*
babblemouth, babbler, bag of wind*, bigmouth, blabber, blabberer, blowhard*, chatterbox, chatterer, gabber, gasbag*, gossiper, gossipmonger, jabberer, loudmouth, motor-mouth, squealer*, tattletale, windbag*, yapper; SEE CONCEPTS *412,423*

black [adj1] *dark, inky*
atramentous, brunet, charcoal, clouded, coal, dingy, dusky, ebon, ebony, inklike, jet, livid, melanoid, murky, obsidian, onyx, piceous, pitch, pitch-dark, raven, sable, shadowy, slate, sloe, somber, sombre, sooty, starless, stygian, swart, swarthy; SEE CONCEPT *618*

black [adj2] *hopeless*
atrocious, bleak, depressing, depressive, dismal, dispiriting, distressing, doleful, dreary, foreboding, funereal, gloomy, horrible, lugubrious, mournful, ominous, oppressive, sad, sinister, sombre, threatening; SEE CONCEPTS *529,570*

black [adj3] *dirty*
dingy, filthy, foul, grimy, grubby, impure, nasty, soiled, sooty, spotted, squalid, stained, unclean, uncleanly; SEE CONCEPT *589*

black [adj4] *angry*
enraged, fierce, furious, hostile, menacing, resentful, sour, sullen, threatening; SEE CONCEPT *403*

black [adj5] *evil*
bad, diabolical, iniquitous, mean, nefarious, villainous, wicked; SEE CONCEPT *545*

black [n] *African-American*
African, Afro-American, Negro; SEE CONCEPT *380*

blackball [v] *expel from group*
ban, blacklist, debar, exclude, ostracize, oust, reject, repudiate, snub, veto; SEE CONCEPTS *25,384*

blacken [v1] *darken*
befoul, begrime, blot, cloud, deepen, ebonize, grow dark, grow dim, ink, make dark, shade, smudge, soil; SEE CONCEPT *250*

blacken [v2] *malign; smear*

asperse, attack, bad-mouth*, blot, blotch, calumniate, decry, defame, defile, denigrate, dishonor, do a number on*, give a black eye*, knock*, libel, malign, rip*, rip up and down*, slander, slur, smudge, stain, sully, taint, tarnish, traduce, vilify; SEE CONCEPT *54*

black hole [n] *abyss*
great void, supernova, theoretical mass, void; SEE CONCEPTS *509,514*

blacklist [v] *ban*
banish, bar, blackball, boycott, debar, exclude, expel, hit list*, ostracize, preclude, proscribe, put on hit list*, reject, repudiate, snub, thumbs down*, vote against; SEE CONCEPT *25*

black magic [n] *sorcery*
diabolism, magic, necromancy, voodoo, witchcraft, wizardry; SEE CONCEPTS *370,689*

blackmail [n] *intimidation for money; money to quiet informer*
bribe, bribery, exaction, extortion, hush money*, milking*, payoff, protection, ransom, slush fund*, tribute; SEE CONCEPTS *123,192*

blackmail [v] *intimidating for money*
badger, bleed, coerce, compel, demand, exact, extort, force, hold to ransom, milk*, put the shake on*, ransom, shake*, shake down*, squeeze*, threaten; SEE CONCEPTS *192,342*

black market [n] *illegal sales*
bootleg market, underground, underground market, underworld market; SEE CONCEPT *323*

black out [v1] *delete; cover*
batten, conceal, cover up, cross out, cut off, darken, eclipse, eradicate, erase, hold back, make dark, obfuscate, rub out, shade, squash, squelch; SEE CONCEPT *250*

black out [v2] *faint*
collapse, crap out*, draw a blank*, go out like a light*, lose consciousness, pass out*, slip into coma, swoon*, zone out*; SEE CONCEPT *303*

black sheep [n] *disgraceful person*
ne'er-do-well, outcast, pariah, prodigal, reject, reprobate; SEE CONCEPT *423*

blade [n] *cutting tool*
brand, cutlass, edge, épée, knife, shank, sword; SEE CONCEPTS *495,499*

blah [adj] *dull, lifeless*
banausic, bland, boring, dim, dreary, humdrum, monotone, monotonous, pedestrian, plodding, yawn producing*; SEE CONCEPT *544*

blame [n1] *condemnation*
accusation, animadversion, arraignment, attack, attribution, castigation, censure, charge, chiding, complaint, criticism, denunciation, depreciation, diatribe, disapprobation, disapproval, disfavor, disparagement, expostulation, exprobation, impeachment, implication, imputation, incrimination, inculpation, indictment, invective, objurgation, obloquy, opposition, rebuke, recrimination, remonstrance, reprehension, reprimand, reproach, reprobation, reproof, repudiation, slur, tirade; SEE CONCEPT *54*

blame [n2] *responsibility*
accountability, answerability, burden, culpability, fault, guilt, incrimination, liability, onus, rap*; SEE CONCEPTS *639,661*

blame [v] *accuse; place responsibility*
admonish, ascribe, attribute, blast, blow the whistle on*, censure, charge, chide, climb all over*, condemn, criticize, denounce, denunciate,

bi
bl

disapprove, express disapprobation, find fault with, finger*, frame, hold responsible, impute, indict, jump all over*, jump down one's throat*, knock*, lay a bad trip on*, lay at one's door*, lay to*, let one have it*, lower the boom*, pass the buck*, point the finger*, rap, rebuke, reprehend, reproach, reprove, roast*, saddle, skin*, stick it to*, tax, upbraid; SEE CONCEPT 44

blameless [adj] *not responsible*
above suspicion, clean, clean-handed, clear, crimeless, exemplary, faultless, good, guilt-free, guiltless, immaculate, impeccable, inculpable, innocent, in the clear*, irreprehensible, irreproachable, not guilty, perfect, pure, righteous, stainless, unblemished, unimpeachable, unoffending, unspotted, unsullied, untarnished, upright, virtuous; SEE CONCEPT 555

blanch [v] *become afraid*
flinch, pale, recoil, shrink, start, wince; SEE CONCEPT 27

bland [adj1] *tasteless; undistinctive*
banal, blah*, boring, dull, dull as dishwater*, flat, flavorless, ho hum*, humdrum, insipid, milk-and-water*, monotonous, nerdy*, nothing, pabulum*, sapless*, tame, tedious, unexciting, uninspiring, uninteresting, unstimulating, vanilla*, vapid, waterish, watery, weak, wimpy*, wishy-washy*, zero*; SEE CONCEPTS 589,613

bland [adj2] *friendly, gracious*
affable, amiable, civilized, congenial, courteous, gentle, good-natured, ingratiating, oily, pleasant, smooth, suave, unctuous, unemotional, urbane; SEE CONCEPT 401

bland [adj3] *mild, temperate*
balmy, calm, calmative, clear, lenient, mollifying, nonirritant, nonirritating, smooth, soft, soothing; SEE CONCEPTS 485,605

blank [adj1] *clear*
bare, barren, clean, empty, fresh, new, pale, plain, spotless, uncompleted, unfilled, unmarked, untouched, unused, vacant, vacuous, virgin, virginal, void, white; SEE CONCEPTS 485,562

blank [adj2] *expressionless*
deadpan, dull, empty, fruitless, hollow, immobile, impassive, inane, inexpressive, inscrutable, lifeless, masklike, meaningless, noncommittal, poker-faced, stiff, stupid, uncommunicative, unexpressive, vacant, vacuous, vague; SEE CONCEPT 406

blank [adj3] *dumbfounded*
at a loss, awestruck, bewildered, confounded, confused, dazed, disconcerted, muddled, nonplussed, stupefied, uncomprehending, wonderstruck; SEE CONCEPT 402

blank [adj4] *absolute, utter*
complete, downright, out-and-out, outright, perfect, regular, sheer, straight-out, thorough, total, unconditional, unqualified; SEE CONCEPT 531

blank [n] *empty space*
abyss, cavity, chasm, emptiness, gap, gulf, hiatus, hole, hollow, hollowness, interstice, interval, lacuna, nihility, nothingness, nullity, omission, opening, preterition, pretermission, skip, tabula rasa, vacancy, vacuity, vacuum, void, womb; SEE CONCEPT 513

blank check [n] *carte blanche*
free hand, free rein, license, permission, permit, say-so, the run of, total freedom, unconditional authority, unconditional right; SEE CONCEPT 376

blanket [adj] *comprehensive*

absolute, across-the-board, all-inclusive, overall, powerful, sweeping, unconditional, wide-ranging; SEE CONCEPT 772

blanket [n] *cover, covering*
afghan, carpet, cloak, coat, coating, comforter, covering, coverlet, envelope, film, fleece, layer, mat, puff, quilt, rug, sheath, sheet, throw, wrapper; SEE CONCEPTS 473,475

blanket [v] *cover*
bury, cloak, cloud, coat, conceal, crown, eclipse, envelop, hide, mask, obscure, overcast, overlay, overspread, suppress, surround; SEE CONCEPT 172

blare [v] *make loud noise*
bark, bellow, blast, boom, bray, clamor, clang, honk, hoot, peal, resound, roar, scream, shout, shriek, sound out, toot, trumpet; SEE CONCEPTS 65,77

blarney [n] *flattery*
adulation, a line*, baloney*, blandishment, cajolery, coaxing, compliments, exaggeration, eyewash*, fawning*, honey*, incense, ingratiation, inveiglement, oil*, overpraise, soft soap*, soft words, sweet talk*, wheedling; SEE CONCEPT 69

blasé [adj] *nonchalant*
apathetic, been around twice*, bored, cloyed, cool*, disenchanted, distranced, done it all*, fed up*, glutted, indifferent, jaded, knowing, laid-back*, lukewarm*, mellow*, mundane, offhand, satiated, sick of, sophisticate, sophisticated, surfeited, unconcerned, unexcited, uninterested, unmoved, weary, worldly, world-weary; SEE CONCEPT 404

blasphemous [adj] *irreverent*
cursing, disrespectful, godless, impious, insulting, irreligious, profanatory, profane, sacrilegious, swearing, ungodly; SEE CONCEPT 545

blasphemy [n] *irreverence*
abuse, cursing, cussing, desecration, execration, heresy, impiety, impiousness, imprecation, indignity, lewdness, profanation, profaneness, profanity, reviling, sacrilege, scoffing, scurrility, swearing, vituperation; SEE CONCEPT 645

blast [n1/v1] *loud sound; make loud sound*
bang, blare, blow, burst, clang, clap, crack, din, honk, peal, roar, scream, slam, smash, toot, trumpet, wail, wham; SEE CONCEPTS 65,521,595

blast [n2] *explosion*
bang, blow-up, burst, crash, detonation, discharge, dynamite, eruption, outbreak, outburst, salvo, volley; SEE CONCEPTS 179,521

blast [n3] *gust of wind*
blow, draft, gale, squall, storm, strong breeze, tempest; SEE CONCEPTS 437,524

blast [n4] *fun time*
amusement, bash*, blow out*, excitement, good time, great time, party, riot*; SEE CONCEPT 386

blast [v2] *explode*
annihilate, blight, blow up, bomb, break up, burst, damage, dash, demolish, destroy, detonate, dynamite, injure, kill, ruin, shatter, shrivel, spoil, stunt, torpedo, wither, wreck; SEE CONCEPTS 86,179

blast [v3] *lambaste; defeat mentally*
attack, beat, castigate, clobber*, criticize, drub*, flay, lash out at, lick*, rail at, shellac*, whip*; SEE CONCEPT 52

blatant [adj1] *obvious; brazen*
arrant, bald, barefaced, brassy, clear, conspicuous, crying, flagrant, flashy, flaunting, garish,

gaudy, glaring, glitzy, impudent, loud, meretricious, naked, obtrusive, ostentatious, outright, overbold, overt, plain, prominent, pronounced, protrusive, screaming, shameless, sheer, showy, snazzy, unabashed, unblushing, unmitigated; SEE CONCEPTS 540,569

blatant [adj2] *deafening*
boisterous, clamorous, crying, ear-splitting, harsh, loud, loudmouthed, noisy, obstreperous, obtrusive, piercing, screaming, scurrilous, strident, vociferant, vociferous, vulgar; SEE CONCEPTS 592,594

blaze [n1] *fire*
bonfire, burning, combustion, conflagration, flame, flames, holocaust, wildfire; SEE CONCEPTS 478,521

blaze [n2] *flash of light*
beam, brilliance, burst, flare, glare, gleam, glitter, glow, radiance; SEE CONCEPT 628

blaze [n3] *torrent*
blast, burst, eruption, flare-up, flash, fury, outbreak, outburst, rush, storm; SEE CONCEPT 673

blaze [v] *burn brightly*
beam, burst out, coruscate, explode, fire, flame, flare, flash, flicker, fulgurate, glare, gleam, glow, illuminate, illumine, incandesce, jet, light, radiate, scintillate, shimmer, shine, sparkle; SEE CONCEPT 249

bleach [v] *whiten*
achromatize, blanch, blench, decolor, decolorize, etiolate, fade, grow pale, lighten, make pale, peroxide, wash out; SEE CONCEPT 250

bleachers [n] *seating for watching event*
benches, boxes, grandstand, Ruthville*, seats, stands; SEE CONCEPTS 440,443

bleak [adj1] *barren*
austere, bare, blank, blighted, bombed, bulldozed, burned, chilly, cleared, cold, deforested, desert, deserted, desolate, dreary, exposed, flat, gaunt, grim, open, raw, scorched, stripped, unpopulated, unsheltered, weather-beaten, wild, windswept; SEE CONCEPT 490

bleak [adj2] *depressing*
black, cheerless, comfortless, dark, discouraging, disheartening, dismal, drear, dreary, funereal, gloomy, grim, hard, harsh, hopeless, joyless, lonely, melancholy, mournful, oppressive, sad, somber, unpromising; SEE CONCEPTS 403,537

bleed [v1] *cause blood to flow*
drain, exude, gush, hemorrhage, leech, ooze, open vein, phlebotomize, run, seep, shed, spurt, trickle, weep; SEE CONCEPT 185

bleed [v2] *extort*
blackmail, confiscate, deplete, drain, exhaust, extract, fleece, impoverish, leech*, milk*, mulct, overcharge, pauperize, put the screws to*, rook*, sap*, skin*, squeeze*, steal, stick*, strong-arm; SEE CONCEPTS 192,342

bleed [v3] *grieve*
agonize, be in pain, che, feel for, pity, suffer, sympathize; SEE CONCEPTS 12,17

blemish [n] *flaw*
beauty spot, birthmark, blackhead, blister, bloom*, blot, blotch, blot on the landscape*, blur, brand, bruise, bug*, catch, chip, cicatrix, defacement, defect, deformity, dent, discoloration, disfigurement, disgrace, dishonor, eyesore, fault, freckle, hickey*, imperfection, impurity, lentigo, lump, macula, maculation, mark, mole, nevus, nodule, patch, pimple, pock,

pockmark, scar, second, sight, smudge, snag, speck, speckle, spot, stain, stigma, taint, tarnish, vice, wart, whitehead, zit*; SEE CONCEPT 580

blemish [v] *flaw, disfigure*
blot, blotch, blur, damage, deface, distort, harm, hurt, impair, injure, maim, mangle, mar, mark, mutilate, pervert, prejudice, scar, smudge, spoil, spot, stain, sully, taint, tarnish, twist, vitiate, wrench; SEE CONCEPTS 54,246

blend [n] *composite, mix*
alloy, amalgam, amalgamation, brew, combination, commixture, composite, compound, concoction, fusion, interfusion, intermixture, mixture, synthesis, union; SEE CONCEPT 432

blend [v1] *mix*
amalgamate, cement, coalesce, combine, commingle, commix, compound, fuse, integrate, interblend, intermix, meld, merge, mingle, synthesize, unite, weld; SEE CONCEPT 109

blend [v2] *harmonize*
arrange, complement, fit, go well, go with, integrate, orchestrate, suit, symphonize, synthesize, unify; SEE CONCEPT 656

bless [v1] *sanctify*
absolve, anoint, baptize, beatify, canonize, commend, confirm, consecrate, cross, dedicate, enshrine, eulogize, exalt, extol, give thanks to, glorify, hallow, honor, invoke benefits, invoke happiness, laud, magnify, make holy, offer, offer benediction, ordain, panegyrize, praise, pray for, pronounce holy, sacrifice, sign, sprinkle, thank; SEE CONCEPTS 69,367

bless [v2] *grant, bestow*
celebrate, endow, favor, give, glorify, grace, laud, magnify, praise, provide; SEE CONCEPTS 50,88

blessed [adj1] *sanctified*
adored, among the angels, beatified, consecrated, divine, enthroned, exalted, glorified, hallowed, holy, inviolable, redeemed, resurrected, revered, rewarded, sacred, sacrosanct, saved, spiritual, unprofane; SEE CONCEPTS 536,568

blessed [adj2] *happy*
blissful, content, contented, endowed, favored, fortunate, glad, granted, joyful, joyous, lucky; SEE CONCEPT 404

blessing [n1] *sanctification*
absolution, benedicite, benediction, benison, commendation, consecration, dedication, divine sanction, grace, invocation, laying on of hands, thanks, thanksgiving; SEE CONCEPT 367

blessing [n2] *good wishes, approval*
approbation, backing, concurrence, consent, favor, Godspeed, leave, okay*, permission, regard, sanction, support, valediction; SEE CONCEPTS 10,50,88

blessing [n3] *advantage*
asset, benediction, benefit, boon, bounty, break, favor, gain, gift, godsend, good, good fortune, good luck, help, kindness, lucky break, manna from heaven*, miracle, profit, service, stroke of luck*, windfall; SEE CONCEPTS 230,679

blight [n] *disease; plague*
affliction, bane, blot on the landscape*, canker, contamination, corruption, curse, decay, dump, evil, eyesore, fungus, infestation, mildew, pest, pestilence, pollution, rot, scourge, sight, withering, woe; SEE CONCEPTS 306,674

blight [v] *ruin, destroy*
annihilate, blast, crush, damage, dash, decay,

disappoint, foul up*, frustrate, glitch up*, injure, mar, mess up*, nip in the bud*, nullify, shrivel, spoil, taint, trash*, wither, wreck; SEE CONCEPT 252

blimp [n] *airship*
aircraft, dirigible, zeppelin; SEE CONCEPT 504

blind [adj1] *sightless*
amaurotic, blind as a bat*, dark, destitute of vision, eyeless, groping, in darkness, purblind, typhlotic, undiscerning, unseeing, unsighted, visionless; SEE CONCEPT 619

blind [adj2] *indifferent*
careless, heedless, ignorant, imperceptive, inattentive, inconsiderate, indiscriminate, injudicious, insensitive, myopic, nearsighted, neglectful, oblivious, thoughtless, unaware, unconscious, undiscerning, unmindful, unobservant, unperceiving, unreasoning, unseeing; SEE CONCEPT 402

blind [adj3] *uncontrolled*
hasty, heedless, impetuous, inconsiderate, irrational, mindless, rash, reckless, senseless, shortsighted, thoughtless, unseeing, unthinking, violent, wild; SEE CONCEPT 544

blind [adj4] *hidden or covered*
blocked, closed, closed at one end, concealed, dark, dead-end, dim, disguised, impassable, leading nowhere, obscured, obstructed, secluded, unmarked, without egress, without exit; SEE CONCEPTS 490,576

blind [n] *screen, covering*
blinder, blindfold, blinker, camouflage, cloak, cover, curtain, facade, front, mask, trap, veil; SEE CONCEPT 716

blindly [adv1] *without direction, purpose*
aimlessly, at random, confusedly, frantically, in all directions, indiscriminately, instinctively, madly, pell-mell, purposelessly, wildly; SEE CONCEPT 542

blindly [adv2] *carelessly*
foolishly, heedlessly, impulsively, inconsiderately, obtusely, passionately, purblindly, recklessly, regardlessly, senselessly, thoughtlessly, tumultuously, unreasonably, unreasoningly, willfully, without rhyme or reason*; SEE CONCEPT 401

blindness [n] *sightlessness*
amaurosis, anopsia, astigmatism, cataracts, darkness, defect, myopia, presbyopia, purblindness, typhlosis; SEE CONCEPT 629

blind-side [v] *attack by surprise*
bushwhack, catch unaware, hit unexpectedly, sucker-punch; SEE CONCEPTS 86,189,200

blink [v1] *wink of eye; twinkle*
bat, flash, flicker, flutter, glimmer, glitter, nictate, nictitate, scintillate, shimmer, sparkle, squint; SEE CONCEPTS 185,624

blink [v2] *ignore*
bypass, condone, connive, cushion, discount, disregard, fail, forget, neglect, omit, overlook, overpass, pass by, slight, turn a blind eye*; SEE CONCEPT 30

bliss [n] *ecstasy*
beatitude, blessedness, cool*, euphoria, felicity, gladness, gone*, happiness, heaven*, joy, paradise, rapture; SEE CONCEPTS 32,230

blissful [adj] *happy*
beatific, cool*, crazy, delighted, dreamy, ecstatic, elated, enchanted, enraptured, euphoric, floating*, flying*, gone*, heavenly, in ecstasy, in seventh heaven*, in the twilight zone*, joyful, joyous, mad*, on cloud nine*, rapturous, sent*, spaced-out*, turned-on*; SEE CONCEPT 403

blister [n] *swelling*
abscess, blain, bleb, boil, bubble, bulla, burn, canker, carbuncle, cyst, furuncle, pimple, pustule, sac, sore, ulcer, vesication, vesicle, wale, weal, welt, wheal; SEE CONCEPT 309

blithe [adj] *happy*
animated, buoyant, carefree, cheerful, cheery, chirpy, gay, gladsome, gleeful, jaunty, jocund, jolly, jovial, joyful, lighthearted, merry, mirthful, sprightly, sunny, vivacious; SEE CONCEPT 404

blitz [n] *heavy attack*
assault, blitzkrieg, bombardment, bombing, lightning attack, offensive, onslaught, raid, shelling, strike; SEE CONCEPTS 86,320

blizzard [n] *snow storm*
blast, gale, precipitation, snowfall, squall, tempest, whiteout; SEE CONCEPT 526

bloat [v] *blow up like a balloon*
balloon, belly, bilge, billow, dilate, distend, enlarge, expand, inflate, puff up, swell; SEE CONCEPTS 184,208

block [n1] *mass of material*
bar, brick, cake, chunk, cube, hunk, ingot, loaf, lump, oblong, piece, section, segment, slab, slice, solid, square; SEE CONCEPTS 470,471

block [n2] *obstruction*
bar, barrier, blank wall, blockage, chunk, clog, hindrance, impediment, jam, mass, obstacle, obstruction, roadblock, snag, stop, stoppage, wall; SEE CONCEPTS 470,652

block [v] *obstruct*
arrest, bar, barricade, blockade, block out, brake, catch, charge, check, choke, clog, close, close off, close out, congest, cut off, dam, deter, fill, halt, hang up*, hinder, hold up, impede, intercept, interfere with, occlude, plug, prevent, shut off*, shut out, stall, stonewall, stop, stopper, stop up*, stymie, tackle, take out of play*, thwart; SEE CONCEPTS 121,130

blockade [n] *barrier*
bar, barricade, blank wall, clog, closure, embolus, encirclement, hindrance, impediment, infarct, infarction, obstacle, obstruction, restriction, roadblock, siege, snag, stop, stoppage, wall; SEE CONCEPTS 470,652

block out [v1] *plan course*
arrange, chart, map out, outline, prepare, sketch; SEE CONCEPT 36

block out [v2] *try to forget*
close, conceal, cover, hide, obscure, obstruct, screen, shroud, shut off, shut out; SEE CONCEPT 40

blond/blonde [adj] *having light-colored hair*
albino, auricomous, bleached, champagne, fair, fair-haired, flaxen, golden-haired, light, pale, pearly, platinum, sallow, sandy-haired, snowy, straw, strawberry, towheaded*, washed-out, yellow-haired; SEE CONCEPT 618

blood [n1] *red body fluid*
claret, clot, cruor, gore, hemoglobin, juice, plasma, sanguine fluid, vital fluid; SEE CONCEPTS 393,420

blood [n2] *ancestry*
birth, consanguinity, descendants, descent, extraction, family, kindred, kinship, line, lineage, origin, pedigree, relations, stock; SEE CONCEPT 296

bloodless [*adj1*] *unfeeling*
anesthetic, cold, coldhearted, dull, impassive, indolent, insensible, insensitive, languid, lazy, lifeless, listless, passionless, slow, sluggish, spiritless, torpid, unemotional, unkind; SEE CONCEPT *404*

bloodless [*adj2*] *pale*
anemic, ashen, cadaverous, chalky, colorless, ghostly, lifeless, pallid, pasty, sallow, sickly, wan, watery; SEE CONCEPT *618*

bloodthirsty [*adj*] *murderous*
barbaric, cruel, homicidal, inhuman, ruthless, sanguinary, savage, slaughterous; SEE CONCEPT *401*

bloody [*adj1*] *bleeding*
blood-soaked, blood-spattered, bloodstained, crimson, ensanguined, gaping, gory, grisly, hematic, hemic, imbrued, open, raw, sanguinary, sanguine, unstaunched, unstopped, wounded; SEE CONCEPT *485*

bloody [*adj2*] *hard-fought*
bloodthirsty, cruel, cutthroat, decimating, ferocious, fierce, gory, grim, heavy, homicidal, murderous, sanguinary, sanguine, savage, slaughterous; SEE CONCEPTS *540,569*

bloom [*n*] *flower*
blossom, blossoming, bud, efflorescence, floret, flourishing, flower, floweret, opening; SEE CONCEPT *425*

bloom [*v*] *flower; flourish*
bear fruit, be in flower, blossom, blow, bud, burgeon, burst, develop, effloresce, fare well, fructify, germinate, grow, open, prosper, sprout, succeed, tassel out, thrive, wax; SEE CONCEPTS *427,706*

blooper [*n*] *blunder*
boner*, boo-boo*, bungle, error, faux pas, fluff*, gaffe, impropriety, indecorum, lapse, mistake, slip, solecism, trip*; SEE CONCEPTS *384,674*

blossom [*n*] *flower*
bloom, bud, efflorescence, floret, floweret, inflorescence, posy, spike; SEE CONCEPT *425*

blossom [*v1*] *flower*
bloom, blow, burgeon, burst, effloresce, leaf, open, outbloom, shoot, unfold; SEE CONCEPT *427*

blossom [*v2*] *flourish*
batten, bloom, develop, grow, mature, progress, prosper, succeed, thrive; SEE CONCEPT *706*

blot [*n*] *mark; flaw*
black eye*, blemish, blotch, blur, brand, defect, discoloration, disgrace, fault, odium, onus, patch, slur, smear, smudge, speck, spot, stain, stigma, taint; SEE CONCEPTS *230,580*

blot [*v1*] *disgrace, disfigure*
bespatter, blemish, dirty, discolor, mark, smudge, smut, soil, spoil, spot, stain, sully, tarnish; SEE CONCEPT *240*

blot [*v2*] *soak up*
absorb, dry, take up; SEE CONCEPT *211*

blotch [*n*] *smudge*
acne, blemish, blot, breakout, eruption, mark, mottling, patch, splash, spot, stain, stigma; SEE CONCEPT *580*

blouse [*n*] *shirt for woman*
bodice, bodysuit, middy, pullover, shell, slipover, T-shirt, turtleneck, V-neck; SEE CONCEPT *451*

blow [*n1*] *blast, rush of air, wind*
draft, flurry, gale, gust, hurricane, puff, squall, strong breeze, tempest, typhoon; SEE CONCEPT *526*

blow [*n2*] *hard hit*
bang, bash, bat, belt, biff, blindside, bop*, buffet, bump, clip, clout, clump, collision, concussion, crack, cut, ding*, impact, jab, jar, jolt, kick, knock, knockout, knuckle sandwich*, KO*, lick, percussion, poke, pound, punch, rap, shock, slam, slap, slug, smack, smash, sock, strike, stroke, swat, swing, swipe, thrust, thump, thwack*, uppercut, wallop, whack, whomp*, zap*; SEE CONCEPT *189*

blow [*n3*] *catastrophe*
affliction, balk, bolt from the blue*, bombshell*, calamity, casualty, chagrin, comedown, debacle, disappointment, disaster, disgruntlement, frustration, jolt, letdown, misadventure, misfortune, mishap, reverse, setback, shock, tragedy, upset; SEE CONCEPT *674*

blow [*v1*] *blast, rush of air, wind*
breathe, buffet, drive, exhale, fan, flap, flow, flutter, gasp, heave, huff, inflate, pant, puff, pump, ruffle, rush, stream, swell, swirl, waft, wave, whiff, whirl, whisk, whisper, whistle; SEE CONCEPTS *185,526*

blow [*v2*] *make sound, usually with instrument*
blare, blast, honk, mouth, pipe, play, sound, toot, trumpet, vibrate; SEE CONCEPT *65*

blow [*v3*] *leave suddenly*
depart, go, hit the road*, split*, take a hike*, take a powder*; SEE CONCEPT *195*

blow [*v4*] *ruin chance*
fail, flounder, goof*, miscarry, miss; SEE CONCEPT *699*

blow [*v5*] *use up money*
dissipate, lay out, pay out, spend, squander, waste; SEE CONCEPT *341*

blowout [*n1*] *explosion; something exploded*
blast, break, burst, detonation, eruption, escape, flat tire, leak, puncture, rupture, tear; SEE CONCEPT *179*

blowout [*n2*] *wild party*
bash, binge, feast, riot*, shindig, spree; SEE CONCEPT *383*

blow over [*v*] *disappear slowly*
cease, die down, dissipate, end, finish, fizzle out, pass, peter out*, subside, vanish; SEE CONCEPT *699*

blow up [*v1*] *inflate*
billow, bloat, distend, enlarge, expand, fill, inflate, puff up, pump up, swell; SEE CONCEPTS *208,236,245*

blow up [*v2*] *explode*
blast, bomb, burst, detonate, dynamite, erupt, go off, mushroom, rupture, shatter; SEE CONCEPTS *179,320*

blow up [*v3*] *magnify importance*
enlarge, exaggerate, heighten, overstate; SEE CONCEPTS *49,59*

blow up [*v4*] *burst with anger*
become angry, become enraged, erupt, go off the deep end*, hit the roof*, lose control, lose temper, rage, rave; SEE CONCEPTS *29,44*

blue [*adj1*] *sky, sea color*
azure, beryl, cerulean, cobalt, indigo, navy, royal, sapphire, teal, turquoise, ultramarine; SEE CONCEPT *618*

blue [*adj2*] *sad*
dejected, depressed, despondent, disconsolate, dismal, dispirited, downcast, downhearted, down in the dumps*, fed up*, gloomy, glum, low,

bl
bl

melancholy, moody, unhappy, woebegone; SEE
CONCEPT *403*

blue [*adj3*] *vulgar*
bawdy, dirty, indecent, lewd, naughty, obscene,
off-color, racy, risqué, salty, shady, smutty,
spicy, suggestive, wicked; SEE CONCEPT *545*

blueprint [*n*] *plan*
archetype, architectural plan, design, draft, game
plan, layout, master plan, model, prototype,
rendering, scheme, sketch; SEE CONCEPTS
268,271,625

blues [*n*] *depression*
dejection, despondency, doldrums, dumps*,
gloom, gloominess, glumness, heavy heart*, low
spirits, melancholy, moodiness, mournfulness,
sadness, the dismals*, the mopes*, unhappiness;
SEE CONCEPT *410*

bluff [*adj*] *abrupt*
barefaced, bearish, blunt, blustering, breviloquent, brief, brusque, candid, crusty, curt, direct,
downright, forthright, frank, gruff, hearty, honest, laconic, no-nonsense, open, outspoken,
plain-spoken, rough, rude, short, short-spoken,
sincere, snippety, snippy, straightforward, tactless, tart, terse, unceremonious; SEE CONCEPT
267

bluff [*n1*] *boast; deceit*
bluster, braggadocio, bragging, bravado, deception, delusion, facade, fake, false colors, false
front, feint, fraud, front, humbug*, jiving*, lie,
pretense, pretext, ruse, sham, show, snow*, stall,
subterfuge, trick; SEE CONCEPTS *58,59*

bluff [*n2*] *precipice*
bank, cliff, crag, escarpment, headland, hill,
mountain, peak, promontory, ridge, rock; SEE
CONCEPT *509*

bluff [*v*] *deceive*
affect, beguile, betray, bunco*, con, counterfeit,
defraud, delude, double-cross, fake*, fake out*,
feign, fool, humbug*, illude, jive*, juggle, lie,
mislead, pretend, psych out*, put on*, sham*,
shuck*, simulate, snow*, take in*, trick; SEE
CONCEPTS *58,59*

blunder [*n*] *mistake*
blooper*, boner*, boo-boo*, bungle, dumb
move*, dumb thing to do*, error, fault, faux pas,
flub*, flub-up*, fluff*, gaffe, goof*, howler*, impropriety, inaccuracy, indiscretion, lapse, muff*,
oversight, slip, slip-up, solecism, trip*; SEE CON-
CEPTS *101,230*

blunder [*v*] *make mistake*
ball up*, blow, bobble, botch, bumble, bungle,
confuse, drop the ball*, err, flounder, flub*, foul
up, fumble, gum up*, louse up, mess up, misjudge, screw up*, slip up, stumble; SEE CONCEPT
101

blunt [*adj1*] *not sharp*
dull, dulled, edgeless, insensitive, obtuse, pointless, round, rounded, unsharpened; SEE CON-
CEPTS *485,486*

blunt [*adj2*] *straightforward*
abrupt, bluff, brief, brusque, candid, crusty, curt,
discourteous, explicit, forthright, frank, gruff,
impolite, matter-of-fact, outspoken, plain-spoken, rude, short, snappy, snippy, tactless, trenchant, unceremonious, uncivil, unpolished; SEE
CONCEPT *267*

blunt [*v*] *make dull*
attenuate, benumb, cripple, dampen, deaden, de-

bilitate, desensitize, disable, enfeeble, numb, obtund, sap, soften, take the edge off, undermine,
water down, weaken; SEE CONCEPT *240*

blur [*v1*] *cloud, fog*
becloud, bedim, befog, blear, blind, darken,
daze, dazzle, dim, glare, make hazy, make indistinct, make vague, mask, muddy, obscure, shade,
soften; SEE CONCEPT *627*

blur [*v2*] *make dirty*
besmear, blemish, blot, discolor, smear, smudge,
spot, stain, taint, tarnish; SEE CONCEPT *254*

blush [*n*] *pink coloring*
bloom, blossom, burning, color, flush, flushing,
glow, glowing, mantling, pink tinge, reddening,
redness, rosiness, rosy tint, ruddiness, scarlet;
SEE CONCEPT *622*

blush [*v*] *become colored, pinken*
color, crimson, flush, glow, have rosy cheeks,
mantle, redden, rouge, turn red, turn scarlet; SEE
CONCEPT *250*

bluster [*n*] *bullying, intimidation*
bluff, boasting, boisterousness, bombast, braggadocio, bragging, bravado, crowing, rabidity,
rampancy, swagger, swaggering; SEE CONCEPT
633

bluster [*v*] *bully, intimidate*
badger, boast, brag, brazen, browbeat, bulldoze*,
cow*, crow*, domineer, gloat, hector, rant, rave,
ride the high horse*, roar, roister, shoot off one's
mouth*, show off, storm, strut, swagger, swell,
talk big*, vapor*, vaunt, yap*; SEE CONCEPTS
49,78

board [*n1*] *piece of wood*
lath, panel, plank, slat, strip, timber; SEE CON-
CEPT *479*

board [*n2*] *meal*
daily bread*, eats*, fare, food, keep*, mess, provisions, victuals; SEE CONCEPT *459*

board [*n3*] *group of advisers*
advisers, advisory group, brass, cabinet, committee, conclave, council, directorate, directors,
execs*, executives, executive suite, front office*,
jury, panel, trustees, upstairs*; SEE CONCEPTS
323,333,417

board [*v1*] *embark on vehicle*
catch, climb on, embus, emplane, enter, entrain,
get on, hop on, mount; SEE CONCEPTS *159,195*

board [*v2*] *provide food and sleeping quarters*
accommodate, bed, canton, care for, feed, harbor, house, let crash*, lodge, put up, quarter,
room; SEE CONCEPT *136*

boast [*n*] *brag; source of pride*
avowal, bluster, bombast, braggadocio, bravado,
exaggeration, gasconade, grandiloquence, heroics, joy, pretension, pride, pride and joy, self-satisfaction, swank, treasure, vaunt; SEE CONCEPTS
410,710

boast [*v1*] *brag*
advertise, aggrandize, attract attention, blow,
blow one's own horn*, blow smoke*, bluster,
bully, cock-a-doodle-doo*, con, congratulate
oneself, crow, exaggerate, exult, fake, flatter
oneself, flaunt, flourish, gasconade, give a good
account of oneself, gloat, glory, grandstand*,
hug oneself*, jive*, lay on thick*, prate, preen,
psych*, puff*, shoot*, shovel*, showboat*, show
off, shuck*, sling*, sound off, strut, swagger,
talk big*, triumph, vapor*; SEE CONCEPT *49*

boast [*v2*] *to have advantage*
be proud of, claim, exhibit, have in keeping,

own, possess, pride oneself on, show off; SEE CONCEPT *261*

boastful [*adj*] *bragging*
arrogant, big, big-headed, bombastic, cocky, conceited, crowing, egotistic, egotistical, exultant, full of hot air*, hifalutin*, hot stuff*, know-it-all, loudmouth, on ego trip*, pompous, pretentious, puffed-up, self-aggrandizing, self-applauding, smart-alecky*, snooty, strutting, stuck-up, swaggering, swanky, swollen-headed, too big for one's britches*, vainglorious, vaunting, windbag*; SEE CONCEPTS *267,404*

boat [*n*] *vehicle for water travel*
ark, barge, bark, bateau, bottom, bucket, canoe, catamaran, craft, dinghy, dory, hulk, ketch, launch, lifeboat, pinnace, raft, sailboat, schooner, scow, ship, skiff, sloop, steamboat, tub, yacht; SEE CONCEPT *506*

boating [*n*] *travel, recreation in water*
canoeing, cruising, drifting, paddling, rowing, sailing, sculling, trawling, yachting; SEE CONCEPT *363*

bob [*v*] *bounce up and down*
bow, duck, genuflect, hop, jerk, jounce, leap, nod, oscillate, quaver, quiver, ricochet, seesaw, skip, waggle, weave, wobble; SEE CONCEPT *147*

bodily [*adj*] *concerning animate structure*
actual, animal, carnal, corporal, corporeal, fleshly, gross, human, material, natural, normal, organic, physical, sensual, somatic, substantial, tangible, unspiritual; SEE CONCEPT *406*

bodily [*adv*] *totally*
absolutely, altogether, as a body, as a group, collectively, completely, en masse, entirely, fully, wholly; SEE CONCEPTS *531,772*

body [*n1*] *physique*
anatomy, bag of bones*, beefcake*, bod*, boody*, build, carcass, chassis, constitution, embodiment, figure, form, frame, makeup, mortal part, protoplasm, shaft, shape, tenement, torso, trunk; SEE CONCEPT *405*

body [*n2*] *corpse*
ashes, bones, cadaver, carcass, carrion, clay, corpus delicti, dead body, deceased, dust, relic, remains, stiff*; SEE CONCEPT *390*

body [*n3*] *human being*
being, creature, human, individual, mortal, party, person, personage, soul; SEE CONCEPT *389*

body [*n4*] *bulk; central portion*
assembly, basis, bed, box, chassis, core, corpus, crux, essence, frame, fuselage, gist, gravamen, groundwork, hull, main part, majority, mass, material, matter, pith, skeleton, staple, substance, substructure, sum, tenor, total, trunk, whole; SEE CONCEPT *829*

body [*n5*] *crowd*
array, batch, bunch, bundle, clump, cluster, group, horde, lot, majority, mass, mob, multitude, parcel, party, set, society, throng; SEE CONCEPTS *417,432*

body [*n6*] *main part of written work*
argument, burden, core, discourse, dissertation, evidence, exposition, gist, heart, material, meat, pith, sense, substance, text, thesis, treatise, upshot; SEE CONCEPT *270*

bodyguard [*n*] *protector*
bouncer, escort, guardian, minder, muscle*, praetorian, security guard; SEE CONCEPT *348*

bog [*n*] *swamp*
fen, lowland, marsh, marshland, mire, morass, moss, peat, quag, quagmire, slough, sump, wetlands; SEE CONCEPT *509*

bog down [*v*] *stick; become stuck*
decelerate, delay, detain, halt, hang up, impede, retard, set back, sink, slacken, slow down, slow up, stall; SEE CONCEPT *121*

bogus [*adj*] *counterfeit*
artificial, dummy, ersatz, fake, false, fictitious, forged, fraudulent, imitation, not what it is cracked up to be*, phony, pretended, pseudo, sham, simulated, spurious; SEE CONCEPT *582*

bohemian [*n*] *nonconformist*
artist, beatnik*, dilettante, flower child*, free spirit, gypsy, hippie*, iconoclast, writer; SEE CONCEPT *423*

boil [*n*] *blister*
abscess, blain, blister, carbuncle, excrescence, furuncle, pimple, pustule, sore, tumor, ulcer; SEE CONCEPT *309*

boil [*v1*] *heat to bubbling*
agitate, bubble, churn, coddle, cook, decoct, effervesce, evaporate, fizz, foam, froth, parboil, poach, seethe, simmer, smolder, steam, steep, stew; SEE CONCEPTS *170,255*

boil [*v2*] *be angry*
be indignant, blow up, bristle, burn, flare, foam at the mouth*, fulminate, fume, rage, rave, sputter, storm; SEE CONCEPT *29*

boiling [*adj1*] *very hot*
baking, blistering, broiling, burning, fiery, hot, red-hot, roasting, scalding, scorching, sizzling, torrid, tropical, warm; SEE CONCEPT *605*

boiling [*adj2*] *angered*
angry, enraged, fuming, furious, incensed, indignant, infuriated, mad, raging; SEE CONCEPT *403*

boisterous [*adj*] *noisy and mischievous*
bouncy, brawling, clamorous, disorderly, effervescent, impetuous, loud, obstreperous, rambunctious, raucous, riotous, rollicking, rowdy, strident, tumultous/tumultuous, unrestrained, unruly, uproarious, vociferant, vociferous, wild; SEE CONCEPT *401*

bold [*adj1*] *brave*
adventurous, assuming, audacious, aweless, bantam, courageous, daring, dauntless, enterprising, fearless, forward, gallant, heroic, intrepid, resolute, unafraid, undaunted, valiant, valorous; SEE CONCEPT *401*

bold [*adj2*] *brazen, insolent*
assuming, audacious, barefaced, brash, brassy, cheeky, coming on strong*, confident, forward, fresh, gritty, gutsy, immodest, impudent, insolent, nervy, pert, presumptuous, rude, sassy, saucy, shameless, smart, smart-alecky*, spunky; SEE CONCEPTS *401,404*

bold [*adj3*] *bright, striking*
clear, colorful, conspicuous, definite, evident, eye-catching, flashy, forceful, lively, loud, manifest, plain, prominent, pronounced, showy, spirited, strong, vivid; SEE CONCEPTS *589,617,618*

bolster [*v*] *help*
aid, assist, bear up, boost, brace, buck up, bulwark, buoy, buttress, carry, cushion, help, hold up, maintain, pick up, pillow, prop, reinforce, shore up, stay, strengthen, support, sustain, uphold; SEE CONCEPT *110*

bolt [*n1*] *lock; part of lock*
bar, brad, catch, coupling, dowel, fastener, lag,

latch, lock, nut, padlock, peg, pin, pipe, rivet, rod, screw, skewer, sliding bar, spike, stake, staple, stud; SEE CONCEPTS *470,471,680*

bolt [*n2*] *flash; projectile*
arrow, dart, fulmination, missile, shaft, thunderbolt, thunderstroke; SEE CONCEPTS *624,687*

bolt [*n3*] *large roll of material*
coil, curl, cylinder, package, spindle, spiral, twist; SEE CONCEPT *432*

bolt [*v1*] *run quickly away*
abscond, bail out*, bound, cop out*, cut loose*, cut out*, dart, dash, ditch*, drop out*, dump*, escape, flee, flight, fly, hightail*, hotfoot*, hurtle, jump, kiss goodbye*, leap, leave flat*, leave high and dry*, leave holding the bag*, leave in the lurch*, make a break for it*, make off*, make tracks*, opt out*, run like scared rabbit*, run out on, rush, scamper, scoot, skedaddle*, skip, split*, spring, sprint, start, startle, step on it*, take flight, take off*, walk out on; SEE CONCEPTS *150,195*

bolt [*v2*] *fasten securely*
bar, deadbolt, latch, lock, secure; SEE CONCEPT *225*

bolt [*v3*] *eat very fast*
consume, cram, devour, englut, gobble, gorge, gulp, guzzle, ingurgitate, inhale, scarf*, slop, slosh, stuff, swallow whole, wolf*; SEE CONCEPT *169*

bomb [*n*] *exploding weapon*
atom bomb, bombshell, charge, device, explosive, grenade, hydrogen bomb, mine, missile, Molotov cocktail, nuclear bomb, projectile, rocket, shell, ticker*, torpedo; SEE CONCEPT *500*

bomb [*v1*] *detonate weapon*
attack, blast, blitz, blow up, bombard, cannonade, destroy, napalm, prang, raid, rain destruction*, rake, shell, strafe, torpedo, wipe out*, zero in*; SEE CONCEPTS *86,252*

bomb [*v2*] *fail miserably*
blow it*, flop, flummox, go out of business, lose, wash out*, wipe out*; SEE CONCEPT *699*

bombard [*v*] *assault, attack*
assail, barrage, batter, beset, besiege, blast, blitz, bomb, cannonade, catapult, fire upon, harass, hound, launch, open fire, pester, pound, shell, strafe, strike; SEE CONCEPTS *7,19,86*

bombastic [*adj*] *pompous, grandiloquent*
aureate, balderdash, big-talking*, declamatory, euphuistic, flowery, full of hot air*, fustian, grandiose, highfalutin*, high-flown, histrionic, inflated, loudmouthed, magniloquent, orotund, ostentatious, overblown, ranting, rhapsodic, rhetorical, sonorous, stuffed shirt*, swollen, tumid, turgid, verbose, windbag*, windy, wordy; SEE CONCEPT *267*

bona fide [*n*] *genuine*
actual, authentic, honest, kosher, legitimate, real, true, valid; SEE CONCEPT *582*

bonanza [*n*] *windfall*
cash cow*, gold mine, treasure trove; SEE CONCEPTS *332,337,446,710*

bond [*n1*] *binder or fastener*
band, binding, chain, connection, cord, fastening, fetter, gunk, handcuff, hookup, irons, ligature, link, linkage, manacle, network, nexus, rope, shackle, stickum*, tie, tie-in, wire; SEE CONCEPT *497*

bond [*n2*] *association, relation*
affiliation, affinity, attachment, connection, connective, friendship, hookup, interrelationship, liaison, link, marriage, network, obligation, relationship, restraint, tie, tie-in, union; SEE CONCEPT *388*

bond [*n3*] *guarantee; contract*
agreement, bargain, certificate, collateral, compact, convention, covenant, debenture, guaranty, obligation, pact, pledge, promise, security, transaction, warrant, warranty, word; SEE CONCEPTS *318,684*

bond [*v*] *fasten; stick*
bind, connect, fix, fuse, glue, gum, paste, stickum*; SEE CONCEPTS *85,160*

bondage [*n*] *slavery*
chains, enslavement, helotry, peonage, serfage, serfdom, servility, servitude, subjection, subjugation, thrall, thralldom, villenage, yoke; SEE CONCEPTS *136,652*

bone [*n*] *piece of animate skeleton*
bony process, cartilage, ossein, osseous matter; SEE CONCEPTS *393,420*

boner [*n*] *a mistake*
blooper*, blunder, bonehead play, boo-boo*, bungle, error, false move, faux pas*, flub, flummox, foulup, gaffe, goof-up, miscalculation, miscue, misstep, muddle, muff, oversight, screw-up, slipup*, snafu*, whoops; SEE CONCEPTS *101,230,410*

boneyard [*n*] *burial ground*
boot hill*, catacomb, cemetery, charnel, charnel house, churchyard, city of the dead*, crypt, eternal home*, funerary grounds, garden, God's acre*, Golgotha, grave, graveyard, marble town*, memorial park, mortuary, necropolis, ossuary, polyandrium, potter's field, resting place, sepulcher, tomb, vault; SEE CONCEPTS *305,368*

bonfire [*n*] *large prepared fire*
beacon, conflagration, feu de joie, pyre; SEE CONCEPTS *478,521*

bonus [*n*] *unexpected extra*
additional compensation, benefit, bounty, commission, dividend, fringe benefit, frosting*, gift, golden parachute*, goody*, gratuity, gravy*, hand-out*, honorarium, ice*, perk*, plus*, premium, prize, reward, special compensation, tip; SEE CONCEPT *337*

boo boo [*n1*] *small hurt*
black and blue mark, bruise, cut, injury, laceration, scratch, sore; SEE CONCEPTS *309,728*

boo boo [*n2*] *small mistake*
blunder, error, gaffe, goof*, misstep, oversight, screw-up*, slip; SEE CONCEPTS *101,230,410*

book [*n1*] *published document*
album, atlas, bestseller, bible, booklet, brochure, codex, compendium, copy, dictionary, dissertation, edition, encyclopedia, essay, fiction, folio, handbook, hardcover, leaflet, lexicon, magazine, manual, monograph, nonfiction, novel, octavo, offprint, omnibus, opus, opuscule, pamphlet, paperback, periodical, portfolio, preprint, primer, publication, quarto, reader, reprint, roll, scroll, softcover, speller, text, textbook, thesaurus, tome, tract, treatise, vade mecum, volume, work, writing; SEE CONCEPT *280*

book [*n2*] *account; diary*
agenda, album, list, notebook, pad, record, register, roster; SEE CONCEPTS *271,331*

book [*v1*] *register, arrange for*
bespeak, bill, charter, engage, enroll, enter, hire,

line up*, make reservation, order, organize, pencil in*, preengage, procure, program, reserve, schedule, set up, sew up*; SEE CONCEPT *36*

book [*v2*] *arrest*
accuse, charge, prefer charges, take into custody; SEE CONCEPT *317*

booking [*n*] *engagement*
gig, performance date, play date, tour date; SEE CONCEPT *384*

boom [*n1*] *loud sound; crash*
bang, barrage, blare, blast, burst, cannonade, clap, crack, drumfire, explosion, reverberation, roar, rumble, slam, smash, thunder, wham; SEE CONCEPTS *521,595*

boom [*n2*] *prosperity*
advance, boost, development, expansion, gain, growth, improvement, increase, inflation, jump, prosperousness, push, rush, spurt, upsurge, upswing, upturn; SEE CONCEPTS *230,335,700*

boom [*v1*] *crash; make loud sound*
bang, blast, burst, clap, crack, drum, explode, resound, reverberate, roar, roll, rumble, slam, smash, sound, thunder, wham; SEE CONCEPT *65*

boom [*v2*] *prosper*
appreciate, bloom, develop, enhance, expand, flourish, flower, gain, grow, increase, intensify, rise in value, spurt, strengthen, succeed, swell, thrive; SEE CONCEPTS *700,704*

boom box [*n*] *portable music machine*
audio system, CD player, ghetto blaster*, ghetto box*, radio, stereo, tape player; SEE CONCEPT *463*

boomerang [*v*] *backfire*
backlash, bounce back, come back, come home to roost*, kick back, react, rebound, recoil, return, reverse, ricochet; SEE CONCEPTS *242,695*

boon [*n*] *advantage*
benefaction, benefit, benevolence, blessing, break, compliment, donation, favor, gift, godsend, good, good fortune, grant, gratuity, help, largess, present, windfall; SEE CONCEPTS *337,661*

boor [*n*] *clod*
barbarian, bear, boob*, brute, buffoon, cad, churl, dork*, goon*, lout, oaf, peasant, philistine, rube*, vulgarian; SEE CONCEPT *423*

boorish [*adj*] *crude, awkward*
bad-mannered, barbaric, bearish, cantankerous, churlish, cloddish, clodhopping*, clownish, clumsy, coarse, countrified, gross*, gruff, ill-bred, ill-mannered, impolite, inurbane, loud, loutish, lowbred, oafish, ornery, out-of-line, out-of-order, provincial, rough, rude, rustic, swinish, tasteless, ugly, uncivilized, uncouth, uncultured, uneducated, ungracious, unpoised, unpolished, unrefined, vulgar; SEE CONCEPT *404*

boost [*n1*] *increase*
addition, advance, breakthrough, expansion, hike, improvement, increment, jump, lift, raise, rise, step-up, up, upgrade, wax; SEE CONCEPTS *700,780*

boost [*n2*] *encouragement*
aid, assistance, backup, buildup, goose*, hand*, handout, help, helping hand, improvement, leg*, leg up*, lift, praise, promotion, shot in the arm*, support; SEE CONCEPT *110*

boost [*n3*] *push, usually up*
advance, goose*, heave, hoist, lift, raise, shove, thrust; SEE CONCEPTS *196,208*

boost [*v1*] *further, improve*
advance, advertise, assist, encourage, foster, in-

spire, plug, praise, promote, push, support, sustain; SEE CONCEPT *244*

boost [*v2*] *push, usually up*
advance, elevate, heave, heighten, hoist, lift, raise, shove, thrust, upraise, uprear; SEE CONCEPTS *196,208*

boost [*v3*] *increase*
add to, aggrandize, amplify, augment, beef up*, develop, enlarge, expand, extend, heighten, hike, jack up*, jump, magnify, multiply, put up, raise, up; SEE CONCEPTS *236,245*

boot [*n*] *heavy, often tall, shoe*
brogan, footwear, galoshes, mukluk, oxford, snow shoes, waders, waters*; SEE CONCEPT *450*

boot [*v1*] *kick; oust*
ax, bounce, can*, chase, chuck*, cut, discharge, dismiss, drive, dropkick*, eighty-six*, eject, evict, expel, extrude, fire, heave, kick out, knock, punt*, sack*, shove, terminate, throw out; SEE CONCEPTS *180,189*

boot [*v2*] *start operating system*
bootstrap, cold boot, load, reboot, reset, restart, start, start computer, warm boot; SEE CONCEPT *221*

booth [*n*] *small enclosure or building*
berth, box, carrel, compartment, coop, corner, cote, counter, cubbyhole, cubicle, dispensary, hut, hutch, nook, pen, pew, repository, shed, stall, stand; SEE CONCEPTS *439,440,443*

booty [*n*] *loot*
boodle, gain, goods, haul*, pickings*, plunder, spoils, swag, takings*; SEE CONCEPTS *337,710*

border [*n1*] *outermost edge, margin*
bound, boundary, bounds, brim, brink, circumference, confine, end, extremity, fringe, hem, limit, line, lip, outskirt, perimeter, periphery, rim, selvage, skirt, trim, trimming, verge; SEE CONCEPTS *484,827*

border [*n2*] *boundary; frontier*
beginning, borderline, door, edge, entrance, line, march, marchland, outpost, pale, perimeter, sideline, threshold; SEE CONCEPTS *484,513*

border [*v*] *bound on; be on the edge*
abut, adjoin, be adjacent to, bind, circumscribe, communicate, contour, decorate, define, delineate, edge, encircle, enclose, flank, frame, fringe, hem, join, line, march, margin, mark off, neighbor, outline, rim, set off, side, skirt, surround, touch, trim, verge; SEE CONCEPT *747*

borderline [*adj*] *inexact*
ambiguous, ambivalent, doubtful, dubitable, equivocal, indecisive, indefinite, indeterminate, marginal, open, problematic, uncertain, unclassifiable, unclear, undecided, unsettled; SEE CONCEPT *534*

border on [*v*] *come close to; approximate*
abut, adjoin, approach, be like, be similar to, come near, compare, connect, contact, echo, impinge, join, lie near, lie next to, march, match, near, neighbor, parallel, resemble, touch, verge on; SEE CONCEPTS *667,749*

bore [*n*] *nuisance*
bother, bromide, bummer*, creep*, deadhead*, downer*, drag*, drip*, dull person, flat tire*, headache, nag, nudge, pain, pain in the neck*, pest, pill*, soporific, stuffed shirt*, tedious person, tiresome person, wet blanket*, wimp*, yawn*; SEE CONCEPT *423*

bore [*v1*] *drill hole*
burrow, gouge out, mine, penetrate, perforate,

bo
bo

pierce, pit, prick, punch, puncture, ream, riddle, sink, tunnel; SEE CONCEPT *178*

bore [*v2*] *cause weariness, disinterest*
afflict, annoy, bend one's ear*, be tedious, bother, burn out, cloy, discomfort, drag, exhaust, fatigue, irk, irritate, jade, pall, pester, put to sleep*, send to sleep*, talk one's ear off*, tire, trouble, turn one off*, vex, wear, wear out, weary, worry; SEE CONCEPTS *7,19*

boredom [*n*] *disinterest; weariness*
apathy, detachment, disgust, distaste, doldrums, dullness, ennui, fatigue, flatness, incuriosity, indifference, irksomeness, jadedness, lack of interest, lassitude, lethargy, listlessness, monotony, pococurantism, sameness, taedium vitae, tediousness, tedium, tiresomeness, unconcern, world-weariness, yawn; SEE CONCEPT *410*

boring [*adj*] *uninteresting*
arid, bomb*, bromidic, bummer*, characterless, cloying, colorless, commonplace, dead*, drab, drag*, drudging, dull, flat*, ho hum*, humdrum, insipid, interminable, irksome, lifeless, monotonous, moth-eaten*, mundane, nothing, nowhere, platitudinous, plebeian, prosaic, repetitious, routine, spiritless, stale, stereotyped, stodgy, stuffy, stupid, tame, tedious, threadbare, tiresome, tiring, trite, unexciting, uninteresting, unvaried, vapid, wearisome, well-worn, zero*; SEE CONCEPT *529*

born [*adj*] *innate*
built-in, congenital, constitutional, deep-seated, essential, inborn, inbred, ingenerate, inherent, intrinsic, natural; SEE CONCEPTS *549,550*

borrow [*v1*] *take for temporary use*
accept loan of, acquire, beg, bite, bum, cadge*, chisel*, give a note for*, hire, hit up*, lift, mooch*, negotiate, obtain, pawn, pledge, raise money, rent into debt, scrounge, see one's uncle*, soak, sponge, take on loan, tap, touch, use temporarily; SEE CONCEPT *89*

borrow [*v2*] *adopt from another source; appropriate*
acquire, adopt, assume, copy, filch, imitate, make one's own, obtain, pilfer, pirate, plagiarize, simulate, steal, take, use, usurp; SEE CONCEPT *225*

bosom [*n1*] *breast*
bust, chest, rib cage, teats; SEE CONCEPT *418*

bosom [*n2*] *heart; core*
affections, center, circle, conscience, emotions, feelings, inside, interior, sentiments, soul, spirit, sympathies; SEE CONCEPTS *410,826*

boss [*adj*] *great*
awesome*, bang-up*, capital, champion, excellent, fine, first-rate, fly*, top, whiz-bang*, wonderful; SEE CONCEPT *572*

boss [*n*] *manager over other employees*
administrator, big cheese*, big gun*, big person*, chief, chieftain, controller, director, dominator, employer, exec*, executive, foreperson, head, head honcho*, helmer, honcho*, leader, overseer, owner, person in charge, superintendent, supervisor, taskperson, top dog*, wheel*; SEE CONCEPT *347*

boss [*v*] *control; command*
administer, administrate, chaperon, direct, employ, manage, overlook, oversee, quarterback*, run, superintend, supervise, survey, take charge; SEE CONCEPT *117*

boss around [*v*] *bully*

browbeat, bulldoze, dominate, domineer, dragoon, oppress, order around, push around, tyrannize; SEE CONCEPT *14*

bossy [*adj*] *domineering*
authoritarian, commanding, controlling, despotic, dictatorial, high-handed, imperious, ironhanded, oppressive, overbearing, overpowering, pushy, strict, tyrannical; SEE CONCEPTS *401,404*

botany [*n*] *study of plants*
anatomy, cytology, dendrology, ecology, floristics, genetics, horticulture, morphology, natural history, paleobotany, pathology, physiology, phytogeography, phytology, pomology, study of flora, study of vegetation, taxonomy; SEE CONCEPT *349*

botch [*v*] *blunder*
blow*, bobble*, boggle*, bollix*, boot, bumble, bungle, butcher*, distort, err, fall down*, flounder, flub*, fumble, goof up*, gum up*, louse up*, mar, mend, mess, mess up*, misapply, miscalculate, miscompute, misconjecture, misconstrue, mishandle, misjudge, mismanage, muck up*, muddle, muff, mutilate, patch, pull a boner*, ruin, screw up*, spoil, stumble, wreck; SEE CONCEPT *101*

both [*det*] *two together*
one and the other, the couple, the pair, the two, twain; SEE CONCEPT *714*

bother [*n*] *trouble, inconvenience*
ado, aggravation, annoyance, anxiety, bellyache*, botheration, bustle, care, concern, difficulty, distress, drag*, exasperation, flurry, fuss, headache*, irritant, irritation, molestation, nudge, nuisance, pain, pain in the neck*, perplexity, pest, plague, pother*, pressure, problem, strain, to-do*, trial, trouble, vexation, worriment, worry; SEE CONCEPT *532*

bother [*v1*] *harass, annoy; give trouble*
afflict, aggravate, agitate, alarm, badger, bedevil, bore, browbeat, carp at, concern, cross, discommode, disconcert, disgust, dismay, displease, disquiet, distress, disturb, eat, embarrass, exacerbate, exasperate, goad, grate on, grieve, harry, hinder, hurt, impede, inconvenience, insult, intrude upon, irk, irritate, molest, nag, needle, nudge, pain, perplex, perturb, pester, pick on, plague, provoke, pursue, put out, ride, scare, spite, tantalize, taunt, tease, torment, trouble, upset, vex, worry; SEE CONCEPTS *7,19*

bother [*v2*] *take the trouble*
be concerned about, concern oneself, exert oneself, fuss over, go out of one's way*, make a fuss about*, make an effort, put oneself out*, take pains, try, worry about; SEE CONCEPT *87*

bothersome [*adj*] *troubling*
aggravating, annoying, distressing, disturbing, exasperating, incommodious, inconvenient, irritating, rebarbative, remote, tiresome, troublesome, vexatious, vexing; SEE CONCEPT *529*

bottle [*n*] *container, usually for liquids*
canteen, carafe, cruet, dead soldier*, decanter, ewer, flagon, flask, glass, jar, jug, phial, soldier, urn, vacuum bottle, vial; SEE CONCEPT *494*

bottleneck [*n*] *obstacle*
barrier, block, blockage, clog, congestion, hindrance, hold-up, impediment, jam, obstruction, snag, traffic jam; SEE CONCEPTS *470,532,666,674*

bottle up [*v*] *keep feeling inside oneself*
box up, check, collar, contain, coop up, corner,

cramp, curb, keep back, restrain, restrict, shut in, suppress, trap; SEE CONCEPT *35*

bottom [*adj*] *lowest; fundamental*
basal, base, basement, basic, foundational, ground, last, lowermost, lowest, meat-and-potatoes*, nethermost, primary, radical, rock-bottom, underlying, undermost; SEE CONCEPTS *585,586,735,799*

bottom [*n1*] *foundation*
base, basement, basis, bed, bedrock, belly, deepest part, depths, floor, foot, footing, ground, groundwork, lowest part, nadir, nether portion, pedestal, pediment, rest, seat, sole, substratum, substructure, support, terra firma, underbelly, underneath, underside; SEE CONCEPT *442*

bottom [*n2*] *base, core*
basis, bottom line, cause, essence, essentiality, ground, heart, mainspring, marrow, origin, pith, principle, quintessence, root, soul, source, stuff, substance, virtuality; SEE CONCEPTS *648,826*

bottom [*n3*] *rear end*
backside, behind, breech, bum*, butt*, buttocks, derriere, fanny*, fundament, posterior, rear, rump, seat, tail, tush*; SEE CONCEPT *418*

bottom feeder [*n*] *lowlife*
base person, bottom fish, hungry puppy, lowest common denominator, riffraff, scum*, slopsucker; SEE CONCEPT *412*

bottomless pit [*n*] *extremely hopeless situation*
abysm, abyss, chasm, crevasse, fire and brimstone*, gulf, Hades, Hell, infernal regions; SEE CONCEPTS *370,435,674*

bottom line [*n*] *conclusion*
determination, final decision, income, last word, loss, main point, net, profit; SEE CONCEPT *230*

bough [*n*] *branch*
arm, fork, limb, offshoot, shoot, sprig, sucker; SEE CONCEPT *428*

boulevard [*n*] *street, often lined with trees*
artery, avenue, drag, highway, passage, path, road, thoroughfare, track, way; SEE CONCEPT *501*

bounce [*n*] *spring*
animation, bound, dynamism, elasticity, energy, give, go, life, liveliness, pep, rebound, recoil, resilience, springiness, vigor, vitality, vivacity, zip; SEE CONCEPTS *150,411*

bounce [*v1*] *spring up; rebound*
backlash, bob, boomerang, bound, buck, bump, carom, fly back, glance off, hop, hurdle, jerk up and down*, jounce, jump, kick back, leap, rebound, recoil, resile, ricochet, saltate, snap back, spring back, thump, vault; SEE CONCEPTS *150,194*

bounce [*v2*] *evict*
ax*, boot out*, can*, discharge, dismiss, eightysix*, eject, fire, give one notice, give the heave ho*, heave*, kick out*, oust, sack*, terminate, throw; SEE CONCEPTS *211,351,384*

bound [*adj*] *obligated; destined*
apprenticed, articled, bent, bounden, certain, coerced, compelled, constrained, contracted, doomed, driven, duty-bound, enslaved, fated, firm, forced, having no alternative, impelled, indentured, intent, made, necessitated, obligated, obliged, pledged, pressed, required, restrained, sure, under compulsion, under necessity, urged; SEE CONCEPT *554*

bound [*v1*] *jump, bounce*
bob, caper, frisk, gambol, hop, hurdle, leap, pounce, prance, recoil, ricochet, saltate, skip,

spring, vault; SEE CONCEPT *194*

bound [*v2*] *restrict*
circumscribe, confine, define, delimit, delimitate, demarcate, determine, encircle, enclose, hem in, limit, mark, mark out, measure, restrain, restrict, surround, terminate; SEE CONCEPT *130*

boundary [*n*] *outer limit*
abuttals, ambit, barrier, beginning, border, borderland, borderline, bounds, brink, circumference, circumscription, compass, confines, edge, end, environs, extent, extremity, frame, fringe, frontier, hem, horizon, limits, line, line of demarcation, march, margin, mark, mere, mete, outline, outpost, pale, perimeter, periphery, precinct, purlieus, radius, rim, side, skirt, terminal, termination, terminus, verge; SEE CONCEPTS *5,484,745*

bound/bounds [*n*] *farthest limit*
boundary, compass, confine, edge, end, environs, extremity, fringe, limit, limitation, line, march, margin, pale, periphery, precinct, purlieus, rim, term, termination, verge; SEE CONCEPTS *484,788*

bounded [*adj*] *limited, confined*
belted, bordered, boundaried, circumscribed, compassed, contiguous, defined, definite, delimited, determinate, edged, encircled, enclosed, encompassed, enveloped, fenced, finite, flanked, fringed, girdled, hedged, hog-tied*, limitary, restricted, rimmed, ringed, surrounded, walled; SEE CONCEPTS *554,772*

boundless [*adj*] *endless, without limit*
great, illimitable, immeasurable, immense, incalculable, indefinite, inexhaustible, infinite, limitless, measureless, no catch*, no end of, no end to, no holds barred*, no strings*, no strings attached*, tremendous, unbounded, unconfined, unending, unlimited, untold, vast, wide open; SEE CONCEPTS *554,772*

bountiful [*adj*] *abundant*
ample, aplenty, bounteous, copious, crawling with*, dime a dozen*, exuberant, free, galore*, generous, handsome, lavish, liberal, luxuriant, magnanimous, munificent, no end of*, plenteous, plentiful, plenty, prolific, stink with*, unsparing; SEE CONCEPT *771*

bounty [*n*] *bonus; compensation*
donation, gift, grant, gratuity, largess, pay, premium, present, prize, recompense, reward; SEE CONCEPTS *337,344*

bouquet [*n1*] *flower arrangement*
boutonniere, buttonhole, corsage, festoon, garland, lei, nosegay, posy, pot, spray, vase, wreath; SEE CONCEPTS *425,429*

bouquet [*n2*] *aroma*
aura, balm, fragrance, incense, odor, perfume, redolence, savor, scent, smell, spice; SEE CONCEPT *599*

bourgeois [*adj*] *commonplace*
common, conservative, conventional, hidebound, illiberal, materialistic, middle-class, old-line, Philistine, traditional, Victorian; SEE CONCEPTS *530,589*

bout [*n1*] *period of time in which something occurs*
course, fit*, go*, round, run, session, shift, spell, stint, stretch, tear, term, tour, trick*, turn; SEE CONCEPT *807*

bout [*n2*] *competitive fight*
bat, battle, boxing match, competition, contest, encounter, engagement, go, match, round, set-to, struggle; SEE CONCEPTS *92,106*

boutique [*n*] *shop*
booth, concession, exclusive shop, franchise, gift store, specialty shop, store; SEE CONCEPTS *441,448,449*

bow [*n1*] *bend from waist*
angle, arc, arch, bend, bending, bob, curtsy, curvation, curvature, curve, flection, flexure, genuflection, inclination, kowtow*, nod, obeisance, round, salaam, turn, turning; SEE CONCEPTS *154,201*

bow [*n2*] *front of boat*
beak, bowsprit, fore, forepart, head, nose, prow, stem; SEE CONCEPT *502*

bow [*v1*] *bend over*
arch, bob, cower, crook, curtsy, curve, debase, dip, do obeisance, droop, duck, genuflect, hunch, incline, nod, round, stoop; SEE CONCEPT *213*

bow [*v2*] *submit, concede*
accept, acquiesce, bend, be servile, capitulate, cave, comply, defer, give in, knuckle*, knuckle under*, kowtow*, relent, succumb, surrender, yield; SEE CONCEPT *23*

bowels [*n*] *insides*
belly, core, deep, depths, entrails, guts, hold, innards, interior, intestines, penetralia, recesses, viscera, vitals; SEE CONCEPTS *393,830*

bowl [*n*] *hollow, concave container*
basin, boat, casserole, crock, deep dish, dish, porringer, pot, saucer, tureen, urn, vessel; SEE CONCEPTS *493,494*

bowl [*v*] *roll a ball down a lane*
fling, hurl, pitch, play duckpins, play tenpins, revolve, rotate, spin, throw, trundle, whirl; SEE CONCEPT *363*

bowl over [*v*] *amaze*
astonish, astound, dumbfound, flabbergast, floor, stagger, startle, stun, surprise; SEE CONCEPT *42*

box [*n*] *container, often square or rectangular*
bin, carton, case, casket, chest, coffer, crate, pack, package, portmanteau, receptacle, trunk; SEE CONCEPT *494*

box [*v1*] *place in square or rectangular container*
case, confine, crate, encase, pack, package, wrap; SEE CONCEPT *209*

box [*v2*] *punch competitively*
buffet, clout, cuff, duke*, exchange blows, hit, mix, scrap, slap, slug, sock, spar, strike, wallop, whack*; SEE CONCEPTS *106,189*

boxing [*n*] *punching competition*
battle, glove game*, mill*, prelim*, prizefighting, pugilism, slugfest*, sparring, the ring*; SEE CONCEPTS *92,363*

boy [*n*] *young man*
buck, cadet, chap, child, dude*, fellow, gamin, guy, half-pint*, junior, lad, little guy*, little shaver*, master, punk*, puppy*, runt*, schoolboy, shaver*, small fry*, sonny*, sprout*, squirt*, stripling, tadpole*, whippersnapper*, youngster, youth; SEE CONCEPTS *419,424*

boycott [*v*] *ban; refrain from using*
avoid, bar, blackball*, blacklist, brush off, cut off, embargo, exclude, hold aloof from, ice out*, ostracize, outlaw, pass by*, pass up*, prohibit, proscribe, refuse, reject, shut out*, snub, spurn, strike, withhold patronage; SEE CONCEPTS *25,130*

boyfriend [*n*] *male acquaintance or romantic companion*
admirer, beau, companion, confidant, date, escort, fiancé, flame*, follower, friend, intimate, partner, soul mate, steady, suitor, swain, sweetheart, young man; SEE CONCEPTS *419,423*

brace [*n*] *support*
arm, band, bar, bearing, block, bolster, boom, bracer, bracket, buttress, cantilever, clamp, girder, grip, guy, lever, mainstay, peg, prop, rafter, reinforcement, rib, shore, skid, splice, splint, staff, stanchion, stave, stay, stirrup, strengthener, strut, sustainer, truss, underpinning, vice; SEE CONCEPTS *470,475,499*

brace [*v*] *support*
bandage, bind, bolster, buttress, fasten, fortify, gird, hold up, prepare, prop, ready, reinforce, shove, steady, steel, strap, strengthen, support, tie, tighten, uphold; SEE CONCEPT *191*

bracelet [*n*] *wrist jewelry*
arm band, armlet, bangle, circlet, manacle, ornament, trinket, wristlet; SEE CONCEPT *446*

bracing [*adj*] *brisk; exhilarating*
animating, chilly, cool, crisp, energizing, exhilarative, fortifying, fresh, invigorating, lively, quickening, refreshing, restorative, reviving, rousing, stimulating, stimulative, tonic, vigorous; SEE CONCEPTS *537,605*

brag [*v*] *talk boastingly*
blow one's own horn*, bluster*, boast, crow*, exult, gasconade, gloat, grandstand*, hotdog*, jive*, mouth*, pat oneself on the back*, prate, puff*, rodomontade, showboat*, shuck*, swagger, vaunt; SEE CONCEPTS *49,51*

braggart [*n*] *person who talks boastingly*
bag of wind*, bigmouth, big talker*, big-timer*, blowhard*, blusterer, boaster, brag, braggadocio, bragger, egotist, exhibitionist, gasbag*, gascon*, grandstander*, hotshot*, know-it-all, peacock*, ranter, raver, show-off, strutter, swaggerer, swashbuckler*, swelled head*, trumpeter*, windbag*; SEE CONCEPTS *412,423*

braid [*n*] *interwoven hair style*
pigtail, plait, ponytail, queue; SEE CONCEPTS *418,716*

braid [*v*] *interweave*
complect, cue, entwine, interknit, interlace, intertwine, lace, mesh, pigtail, plait, ravel, twine, twist, weave; SEE CONCEPTS *184,202*

brain [*n1*] *very smart person*
academician, doctor, egghead*, Einstein*, genius, highbrow, intellect, intellectual, mastermind, prodigy, pundit, sage, scholar; SEE CONCEPT *350*

brain [*n2*] *mind, intelligence*
cerebellum, cerebrum, encephalon, gray matter*, head, intellect, medulla oblongata, mentality, upper story*, wit; SEE CONCEPTS *393,409,420*

brain drain [*n*] *loss of important personnel*
departure, mass exodus, turnover; SEE CONCEPT *195*

brainstorm [*v*] *problem-solve*
analyze, conceive, conceptualize, conjure up, create, deliberate, dream up, invent, plan, ponder, put heads together*, rack brains*, share ideas, think; SEE CONCEPTS *35,173,251*

brainwash [*v*] *force to believe or do things*
alter, catechize, condition, convert, convince, educate, indoctrinate, influence, instill, persuade, proselytize, teach; SEE CONCEPT *14*

brainy [*adj*] *intelligent*
bright, brilliant, clever, intellectual, sapient, smart; SEE CONCEPT *402*

brake [*n*] *stopping device; check*

anchor, binders, cinchers, constraint, control, curb, damper, deterrent, discouragement, hamper, hindrance, hurdle, obstacle, rein, restraint, retarding device; SEE CONCEPTS *130,463*

brake [v] *check; stop*
bar, block, dam, decelerate, halt, hinder, impede, moderate, obstruct, reduce speed, slacken, slow, slow down, stop; SEE CONCEPT *121*

bramble [n] *thorny bush*
brier, burr, catch weed, cleaver, furze, goose grass, gorse, hedge, nettle, prick, prickly shrub, shrub, spray, thistle, thistle sage, thorn; SEE CONCEPT *429*

branch [n1] *department*
annex, arm, bureau, category, chapter, classification, connection, dependency, derivative, division, extension, local, member, office, outpost, part, portion, section, subdivision, subsection, subsidiary, tributary, wing; SEE CONCEPTS *325,378*

branch [n2] *arm, limb*
bough, branchlet, bug, detour, divergence, extension, fork, growth, offshoot, prong, scion, shoot, spray, sprig, wing; SEE CONCEPTS *392,428,471,835*

branch off/branch out [v] *extend beyond main part*
add to, develop, diverge, diversify, divide, enlarge, expand, extend, fork, grow, increase, multiply, part, proliferate, ramify, separate, spread out; SEE CONCEPT *756*

brand [n1] *type, kind*
cast, character, class, description, grade, make, quality, sort, species, variety; SEE CONCEPT *378*

brand [n2] *distinctive label, mark*
brand name, emblem, hallmark, heraldry, imprint, logo, logotype, marker, sign, stamp, symbol, trademark, welt; SEE CONCEPT *284*

brand [n3] *stigma*
bar sinister, black eye, blot, blur, disgrace, infamy, mark, mark of Cain, odium, onus, reproach, slur, smirch, spot, stain, stigma, taint; SEE CONCEPT *388*

brand [v] *label negatively*
disgrace, mark, stigmatize, taint; SEE CONCEPTS *62,79*

brandish [v] *flaunt, swing around*
come on strong*, display, disport, exhibit, expose, flash, gesture, parade, raise, shake, show, show off, sport, swing, threaten, throw weight around*, trot out*, warn, wield; SEE CONCEPT *261*

brash [adj] *impulsive, brazen*
audacious, bold, brazenfaced, cheeky*, cocksure, cocky*, effervescent, flip, foolhardy, forward, hasty, headlong, heedless, hotheaded, ill-advised, impertinent, impetuous, impolitic, imprudent, incautious, inconsiderate, indiscreet, insolent, madcap, maladroit, nervy, precipitate, presuming, presumptuous, pushing, rash, reckless, rude, self-asserting, self-assertive, tactless, thoughtless, undiplomatic, untactful, uppity, vivacious; SEE CONCEPTS *401,404*

brass [n] *impulsiveness; nerve*
assumption, audacity, brashness, cheek*, chutzpah*, confidence, effrontery, gall, impertinence, impudence, insolence, presumption, rudeness; SEE CONCEPT *633*

brassy [adj] *vulgar, loud to the senses*
arrant, barefaced, blaring, blatant, bold, brash, brazen, flashy, flirtatious, forward, garish, gaudy, grating, hard, harsh, impudent, insolent, jarring, jazzy, loudmouthed, noisy, obtrusive, overbold, pert, piercing, rude, saucy, shameless, showy, shrill, strident, unabashed, unblushing; SEE CONCEPTS *401,589,592,594*

brat [n] *spoiled child*
devil*, enfant terrible*, holy terror*, impudent child, kid, punk*, rascal, unruly child, urchin, whippersnapper*, wild one*, youngster; SEE CONCEPT *424*

bravado [n] *boastfulness*
blowing, bluff, bluster, boasting, bombast, braggadocio, bragging, bullying, crowing*, fancy talk*, fuming*, gasconade, grandiosity, guts*, hot air*, pomposity, pretension, raging, railing, rant, selfglorification, storming, swaggering, swelling, talk, tall talk*; SEE CONCEPTS *49,51*

brave [adj] *bold*
adventurous, audacious, chin-up*, chivalrous, confident, courageous, daring, dashing, dauntless, defiant, doughty, fearless, firm, foolhardy, forward, gallant, game, gritty, gutsy, hardy, heroic, herolike, imprudent, indomitable, intrepid, lionhearted, militant, nervy, plucky, reckless, resolute, spirited, spunky, stalwart, stout, stouthearted, strong, unabashed, unafraid, unblenching, undauntable, undaunted, undismayed, unfearful, valiant, valorous, venturesome; SEE CONCEPT *401*

brave [v] *endure bad situation*
bear, beard, challenge, confront, court, dare, defy, face, face off, fly in the face of*, go through, outdare, risk, stand up to, suffer, support, take on, venture, withstand; SEE CONCEPT *23*

bravery [n] *boldness*
courage, daring, dauntlessness, fearlessness, fortitude, gallantry, grit, guts, hardiness, heroism, indomitability, intrepidity, mettle, pluck, pluckiness, spirit, spunk, valor; SEE CONCEPTS *411,633*

brawl [n] *nasty fight*
affray, altercation, argument, battle, battle royal*, bickering, broil, clash, disorder, dispute, donnybrook, duke out*, feud, fight, fracas, fray, free-for-all*, fuss, hassle, melee, quarrel, rhubarb*, riot, ruckus*, rumble*, rumpus, scrap, scuffle, squabble, tumult, uproar, wrangle; SEE CONCEPTS *46,106*

brawl [v] *fight nastily*
altercate, argue, battle, bicker, buck*, caterwaul, dispute, kick up a row*, quarrel, raise Cain*, roughhouse*, row, rumble*, scrap, scuffle, spat, squabble, tussle, wrangle, wrestle; SEE CONCEPTS *46,106*

brawn [n] *muscular strength and breadth*
beef, beefiness, clout, energy, flesh, kick, meat, might, moxie*, muscle, muscularity, power, punch, robustness, sinews, sock, steam, thew, vigor; SEE CONCEPTS *723,732*

brawny [adj] *muscular, strong*
able-bodied, athletic, beefy, bulky, burly, fleshy, hardy, hefty, husky, powerful, robust, sinewy, stalwart, strapping, sturdy, thewy, tough, vigorous, vital; SEE CONCEPTS *485,489*

brazen [adj] *brash, unashamed*
audacious, barefaced, blatant, bold, brassy, cheeky, cocky, contumelious, defiant, flashy, flip, forward, gritty, gutsy, hotshot*, immodest, impertinent, impudent, indecent, insolent, loud,

**bo
br**

meretricious, nervy, overbold, pert, saucy, shameless, smart-alecky*, smart-ass*, spunky, tawdry, unabashed, unblushing; SEE CONCEPTS *267,401*

breach [*n1*] *gap*
aperture, break, chasm, chip, cleft, crack, discontinuity, fissure, hole, opening, rent, rift, rupture, slit, split; SEE CONCEPT *513*

breach [*n2*] *violation of a law*
contravention, delinquency, dereliction, disobedience, disregard, infraction, infringement, neglect, noncompliance, nonobservance, offense, transgression, trespass, violation; SEE CONCEPT *192*

breach [*n3*] *change from friendly to unfriendly relationship*
alienation, break, difference, disaffection, disagreement, discord, disharmony, dissension, disunity, division, estrangement, falling-out, fissure, fracture, parting of the ways*, quarrel, rent, rift, rupture, schism, secession, separation, severance, split, strife, variance, withdrawal; SEE CONCEPT *388*

bread [*n1*] *daily food*
aliment, bed and board, comestibles, diet, fare, feed, grub*, necessities, nourishment, nurture, nutriment, provender, provisions, shingle*, staff of life*, subsistence, sustenance, viands, victuals; SEE CONCEPT *457*

bread [*n2*] *money*
cabbage*, cash, coin, dollars, dough*, finance, funds, greenbacks*, mazuma*, scratch*; SEE CONCEPT *340*

breadth [*n1*] *width*
broadness, diameter, distance across, latitude, span, spread, wideness; SEE CONCEPT *760*

breadth [*n2*] *extent*
amplitude, area, compass, comprehensiveness, dimension, expanse, extensiveness, fullness, gamut, greatness, inclusiveness, largeness, magnitude, measure, orbit, range, reach, scale, scope, size, space, spread, stretch, sweep, vastness; SEE CONCEPTS *651,756,788*

break [*n*] *fissure, opening*
breach, cleft, crack, discontinuity, disjunction, division, fracture, gap, gash, hole, rent, rift, rupture, schism, split, tear; SEE CONCEPTS *230,757*

break [*n2*] *interruption of activity*
blow, breather, breathing space, caesura, coffee break, cutoff, downtime*, halt, hiatus, interlude, intermission, interval, lacuna, layoff*, letup*, lull, pause, recess, respite, rest, suspension, ten*, time off, time out; SEE CONCEPT *807*

break [*n3*] *change from friendly to unfriendly relationship*
alienation, altercation, breach, clash, difference of opinion, disaffection, dispute, divergence, estrangement, fight, misunderstanding, rift, rupture, schism, separation, split, trouble; SEE CONCEPT *388*

break [*n4*] *lucky happening*
accident, advantage, chance, favorable circumstances, fortune, good luck, luck, occasion, opening, opportunity, shot, show, stroke of luck, time; SEE CONCEPT *679*

break [*v1*] *destroy; make whole into pieces*
annihilate, batter, burst, bust, bust up, crack, crash, crush, damage, demolish, disintegrate, divide, eradicate, finish off, fracture, fragment,

make hash of*, make mincemeat of*, part, pull to pieces, rend, separate, sever, shatter, shiver, smash, snap, splinter, split, tear, torpedo, total, trash*; SEE CONCEPT *252*

break [*v2*] *violate law*
breach, contravene, disobey, disregard, infract, infringe, offend, renege on, transgress, violate; SEE CONCEPT *192*

break [*v3*] *weaken, cause instability*
bankrupt, bust, confound, confute, controvert, cow, cripple, declass, degrade, demerit, demoralize, demote, disconfirm, dispirit, disprove, downgrade, enervate, enfeeble, humiliate, impair, impoverish, incapacitate, pauperize, rebut, reduce, refute, ruin, subdue, tame, undermine; SEE CONCEPT *240*

break [*v4*] *stop an action*
abandon, cut, discontinue, give up, interrupt, pause, rest, suspend; SEE CONCEPT *121*

break [*v5*] *tell news*
announce, come out, communicate, convey, disclose, divulge, impart, inform, let out, make public, pass on, proclaim, reveal, tell, transmit; SEE CONCEPT *60*

break [*v6*] *better a performance*
beat, cap, exceed, excel, go beyond, outdo, outstrip, surpass, top; SEE CONCEPT *141*

break [*v7*] *emerge, happen*
appear, befall, betide, burst out, chance, come forth, come off, come to pass, develop, erupt, go, occur, transpire; SEE CONCEPT *4*

break [*v8*] *run away*
abscond, bust out*, clear out*, cut and run*, dash, decamp, escape, flee, fly, get away, get out; SEE CONCEPTS *102,195*

break [*v9*] *cushion something's effect*
diminish, lessen, lighten, moderate, reduce, soften, weaken; SEE CONCEPT *110*

breakable [*adj*] *easily hurt or destroyed*
brittle, crisp, crispy, crumbly, delicate, flimsy, fracturable, fragile, frail, frangible, friable, shatterable, shattery, splintery, vitreous, weak; SEE CONCEPTS *489,606*

break away [*v*] *depart*
escape, flee, fly, leave, part company*, quit, run away, split*; SEE CONCEPT *195*

breakdown [*n1*] *nervous collapse*
basket case*, crackup*, disintegration, disruption, failure, mishap, nervous prostration, neurasthenia, neurosis, psychasthenia; SEE CONCEPT *410*

breakdown [*n2*] *account of finances or other business*
analysis, categorization, classification, detailed list, diagnosis, dissection, itemization, resolution; SEE CONCEPT *283*

break even [*v*] *be or become equal*
balance books, equalize, experience no loss, recover cost, recover expense; SEE CONCEPTS *126,232*

break in [*v1*] *intrude*
barge in, breach, break and enter, burglarize, burgle, burst in*, butt in*, interfere, interject, interrupt, intervene, invade, meddle, raid, rob, steal, trespass; SEE CONCEPTS *139,192*

break in [*v2*] *train in new skill*
accustom, condition, educate, gentle, get used to, habituate, initiate, instruct, prepare, tame; SEE CONCEPT *285*

break off [*v1*] *snap off something*
detach, disassemble, divide, part, pull off, separate, sever, splinter, take apart; SEE CONCEPT *211*
break off [*v2*] *end activity*
cease, desist, discontinue, end, finish, halt, pause, stop, suspend, terminate; SEE CONCEPT *234*
break out [*v1*] *happen, emerge*
appear, arise, begin, burst forth, commence, erupt, explode, occur, set in, spring up, start; SEE CONCEPT *701*
break out [*v2*] *escape*
abscond, bolt, break loose, burst out, bust out*, depart, flee, get free, leave; SEE CONCEPTS *102,195*
break the ice [*v*] *be friendly and talkative*
lead the way, oil the works*, set at ease, socialize, start the ball rolling; SEE CONCEPT *384*
breakthrough [*n*] *advance, progress*
boost, development, discovery, find, finding, gain, hike, improvement, increase, invention, leap, progress, quantum leap*, rise, step forward; SEE CONCEPT *704*
breakup [*n*] *end of relationship*
breakdown, breaking, crackup*, disintegration, dispersal, dissolution, divorce, ending, parting, rift, separation, split, splitsville*, splitting, termination, wind-up; SEE CONCEPT *385*
break up [*v*] *end relationship, activity*
adjourn, disassemble, disband, dismantle, disperse, disrupt, dissolve, divide, divorce, end, halt, part, put an end to, scatter, separate, sever, split, stop, sunder, suspend, take apart, terminate; SEE CONCEPT *234*
break with [*v*] *part ways*
ditch, drop, jilt, reject, renounce, separate; SEE CONCEPTS *21,30,180*
breast [*n1*] *front of upper body*
bosom, bust, chest, front, mammary glands, mammilla, nipple, teat, udder; SEE CONCEPT *418*
breast [*n2*] *feelings, conscience*
being, bosom, character, core, emotions, essential nature, heart, mind, psyche, seat of affections, sentiments, soul, spirit, thoughts; SEE CONCEPTS *410,529*
breath [*n1*] *respiration*
animation, breathing, eupnea, exhalation, expiration, gasp, gulp, inhalation, inspiration, insufflation, pant, wheeze; SEE CONCEPT *163*
breath [*n2*] *wind or something in the air*
aroma, faint breeze, flatus, flutter, gust, odor, puff, sigh, smell, vapor, waft, whiff, zephyr; SEE CONCEPTS *437,599*
breath [*n3*] *respite, break*
blow*, breather, breathing space*, instant, moment, pause, rest, second, ten*; SEE CONCEPT *807*
breath [*n4*] *hint, suggestion*
dash, murmur, shade, soupçon, streak, suspicion, touch, trace, undertone, whiff, whisper; SEE CONCEPTS *278,831*
breathe [*v1*] *take air in and let out*
draw in, exhale, expire, fan, gasp, gulp, inhale, insufflate, open the floodgates*, pant, puff, respire, scent, sigh, sniff, snore, snort, use lungs, wheeze; SEE CONCEPTS *163,601*
breathe [*v2*] *inspire action*
imbue, impart, infuse, inject, instill, transfuse; SEE CONCEPT *242*
breathe [*v3*] *tell information*
articulate, confide, express, murmur, say, sigh,

utter, voice, whisper; SEE CONCEPT *60*
breathless [*adj1*] *unable to respire normally*
asthmatic, blown, choking, emphysematous, exhausted, gasping, gulping, out of breath, panting, short of breath, short-winded, spent, stertorous, wheezing, winded; SEE CONCEPT *406*
breathless [*adj2*] *astounded*
agog, anxious, avid, eager, excited, flabbergasted, open-mouthed, thunderstruck, with bated breath; SEE CONCEPT *403*
breathtaking [*adj*] *beautiful, awesome*
amazing, astonishing, awe-inspiring, exciting, hair-raising, heart-stirring, heart-stopping, impressive, magnificent, moving, overwhelming, spine-tingling, stunning, thrilling; SEE CONCEPT *529*
breed [*n*] *kind, class*
brand, character, extraction, family, feather, genus, ilk, likes, line, lineage, lot, nature, number, pedigree, progeny, race, sort, species, stamp, stock, strain, stripe, type, variety; SEE CONCEPT *378*
breed [*v1*] *generate, bring into being*
bear, beget, bring about, bring forth, cause, create, deliver, engender, give birth to, give rise to, hatch, impregnate, induce, make, multiply, originate, procreate, produce, progenerate, propagate, reproduce; SEE CONCEPTS *173,251,302,373*
breed [*v2*] *raise, nurture*
bring up, cultivate, develop, discipline, educate, foster, instruct, nourish, rear; SEE CONCEPTS *285,295*
breeding [*n*] *cultivation of person*
ancestry, civility, conduct, courtesy, culture, development, gentility, grace, lineage, manners, nurture, polish, raising, rearing, refinement, schooling, training, upbringing, urbanity; SEE CONCEPT *388*
breeze [*n*] *light wind*
air, airflow, breath, current, draft, flurry, gust, puff, waft, whiff, zephyr; SEE CONCEPTS *437,524*
breeze [*v*] *work quickly through task*
cruise, flit, glide, hurry, move, pass, sail, sally, skim, slide, slip, sweep, trip, waltz, zip; SEE CONCEPT *704*
breezy [*adj1*] *windy*
airy, blowing, blowy, blusterous, blustery, drafty, fresh, gusty, squally, stormy; SEE CONCEPT *525*
breezy [*adj2*] *easy, lighthearted*
airy, animated, blithe, buoyant, carefree, casual, cheerful, debonair, easy-going, effervescent, free and easy*, gay, informal, jaunty, light, lively, low-pressure, peppy, racy, relaxed, sparkling, spicy, spirited, sprightly, sunny, unconstrained, vivacious; SEE CONCEPT *544*
brevity [*n*] *shortness, briefness*
conciseness, concision, condensation, crispness, curtness, economy, ephemerality, impermanence, pithiness, pointedness, succinctness, terseness, transience, transitoriness; SEE CONCEPTS *730,804*
brew [*n*] *concoction*
beverage, blend, broth, compound, distillation, drink, fermentation, hash, hodgepodge*, infusion, instillation, liquor, melange, miscellany, mishmash*, mixture, potpourri, preparation; SEE CONCEPTS *260,454,457*
brew [*v1*] *prepare by boiling*
boil, concoct, cook, ferment, infuse, mull, seethe,

br
br

soak, steep, stew; SEE CONCEPT *170*

brew [*v2*] *plan, devise*
breed, compound, concoct, contrive, develop, excite, foment, form, gather, hatch, impend, loom, mull, plot, project, scheme, start, stir up, weave; SEE CONCEPT *36*

bribe [*n*] *payoff to influence illegal or wrong activity*
allurement, bait, blackmail, buyoff, compensation, contract, corrupting gift, corrupt money, enticement, envelope*, feedbag*, fringe benefit, gift, goody*, graft, gratuity, gravy*, grease*, hush money*, ice*, incentive, inducement, influence peddling, kickback, lagniappe, lure, payola*, perk*, perquisite, present, price, protection*, remuneration, reward, sop*, sweetener*, sweetening*, take; SEE CONCEPTS *192,329*

bribe [*v*] *request silence, action, or inaction for money*
approach, buy, buy back, buy off, coax, corrupt, do business*, entice, fix*, get at, get to, grease palm*, influence, instigate, lubricate, lure, make a deal, oil palm*, pay off, pervert, reward, seduce, soap*, square, suborn, sugar, sweeten the pot*, take care of, tamper, tempt, tip; SEE CONCEPTS *53,192*

bridal [*adj*] *concerning marriage*
conjugal, connubial, epithalamic, espousal, hymeneal, marital, matrimonial, nubile, nuptial, pre-wedding, prothalamic, spousal; SEE CONCEPT *536*

bride [*n*] *female marriage partner*
helpmate, mate, newly married woman, newlywed, old woman*, spouse, wife; SEE CONCEPTS *296,415*

bridegroom [*n*] *male marriage partner*
benedict, groom, helpmate, husband, mate, newlywed, old man*, spouse; SEE CONCEPTS *296,419*

bridge [*n*] *structure or something that makes connection*
arch, bond, branch, catwalk, connection, extension, gangplank, link, overpass, platform, pontoon, scaffold, span, tie, transit, trestle, viaduct, wing; SEE CONCEPTS *501,721*

bridge [*v*] *connect, extend*
arch over, attach, bind, branch, couple, cross, cross over, go over, join, link, reach, span, subtend, traverse, unite; SEE CONCEPTS *113,756*

bridle [*n*] *restraining device*
check, control, curb, deterrent, hackamore, halter, headstall, leash, rein, restraint, trammels; SEE CONCEPT *497*

bridle [*v*] *check, hold back*
constrain, control, curb, govern, inhibit, keep in check, master, moderate, repress, restrain, rule, subdue, suppress, withhold; SEE CONCEPT *121*

brief [*adj1*] *short, compressed*
abrupt, bluff, blunt, boiled down*, breviloquent, brusque, compendiary, compendious, concise, crisp, curt, hasty, laconic, limited, little, pithy, sharp, short and sweet*, skimpy, small, snippy, succinct, surly, terse, to the point; SEE CONCEPTS *267,773*

brief [*adj2*] *short in time*
concise, curtailed, ephemeral, fast, fleeting, hasty, instantaneous, little, meteoric, momentary, passing, quick, short-lived, short-term, swift, temporary, transient, transitory; SEE CONCEPT *798*

brief [*n*] *abridgment*

abstract, argument, boildown*, case, condensation, conspectus, contention, data, defense, digest, epitome, outline, précis, sketch, summary, synopsis; SEE CONCEPTS *283,318*

brief [*v*] *inform of facts*
abridge, advise, apprise, edify, enlighten, epitomize, explain, fill in, give rundown*, give the lowdown*, inform, initiate, instruct, let in on*, orient, prepare, prime, recapitulate, show the lay of the land*, show the ropes*, summarize, tip off*, update; SEE CONCEPT *60*

briefcase [*n*] *carrier for work papers*
attaché, bag, baggage, case, dispatch, folder, portfolio, valise; SEE CONCEPTS *446,494*

briefing [*n*] *preparation by informing of facts*
background meeting, conference, directions, discussion, guidance, information, initiation, instruction, meeting, preamble, priming, rundown, update; SEE CONCEPT *60*

brigade [*n*] *fleet of trained people*
army, band, body, company, contingent, corps, crew, detachment, force, group, organization, outfit, party, posse, squad, team, troop, unit; SEE CONCEPTS *322,381*

bright [*adj1*] *shining, glowing in appearance*
ablaze, aglow, alight, argent, auroral, beaming, blazing, brilliant, burning, burnished, coruscating, dazzling, effulgent, flashing, fulgent, fulgid, glaring, gleaming, glistening, glittering, glossy, golden, illuminated, illumined, incandescent, intense, irradiated, lambent, light, lighted, limpid, luminous, lustrous, mirrorlike, moonlit, phosphorescent, polished, radiant, relucent, resplendent, scintillating, shimmering, shiny, silvery, sparkling, sunlit, sunny, twinkling, vivid; SEE CONCEPT *617*

bright [*adj2*] *sunny, clear (weather)*
clement, cloudless, fair, favorable, limpid, lucid, mild, pellucid, pleasant, translucent, transparent, unclouded; SEE CONCEPT *525*

bright [*adj3*] *intelligent*
acute, advanced, alert, astute, aware, brainy, brilliant, clear-headed, clever, discerning, eggheaded*, Einstein*, having smarts*, ingenious, inventive, keen, knowing, precocious, quick, quick-witted, sharp, smart, whiz kid*, wideawake; SEE CONCEPT *402*

bright [*adj4*] *hopeful, promising*
airy, auspicious, benign, breezy, cheering, encouraging, excellent, favorable, golden, good, optimistic, palmy, propitious, prosperous, rosy; SEE CONCEPT *537*

bright [*adj5*] *cheerful*
alert, animated, gay, genial, glad, happy, jolly, joyful, joyous, keen, lighthearted, lively, merry, optimistic, sanguine, spirited, sprightly, vivacious; SEE CONCEPT *404*

bright [*adj6*] *famous, outstanding*
distinguished, eminent, glorious, illustrious, magnificent, prominent, remarkable, splendid; SEE CONCEPT *568*

bright [*adj7*] *vivid in color*
brave, brilliant, clear, colored, colorful, deep, flashy, fresh, gay, glitzy*, hued, intense, psychedelic, razzle-dazzle, rich, ruddy, sharp, showy, tinged, tinted; SEE CONCEPT *618*

brighten [*v1*] *make shine or glow*
buff up, burnish, clear up, enliven, gleam, grow

sunny, illuminate, illumine, intensify, kindle, lighten, light up, polish, punch up*, spiff up*; SEE CONCEPTS 244,250

brighten [v2] *make happy, feel better*
become cheerful, buck up, buoy up, cheer, cheer up, clear up, encourage, enliven, gladden, hearten, improve, look up, perk up; SEE CONCEPTS 7,22

brilliant [adj1] *shining, glowing in appearance*
ablaze, bright, coruscating, dazzling, effulgent, flashy, fulgent, gleaming, glittering, glossy, incandescent, intense, lambent, lucent, luminous, lustrous, radiant, refulgent, resplendent, scintillating, showy, sparkling, vivid; SEE CONCEPT 617

brilliant [adj2] *famous, outstanding*
celebrated, distinguished, eminent, excellent, exceptional, glorious, illustrious, magnificent, prominent, splendid, superb; SEE CONCEPT 568

brilliant [adj3] *very intelligent*
accomplished, acute, astute, brainy, bright, clever, discerning, eggheaded*, Einstein*, expert, genius, gifted, ingenious, intellectual, inventive, knowing, knowledgeable, masterly, penetrating, profound, quick, quick-witted, sharp, smart, talented, whip, whiz kid*; SEE CONCEPT 402

brim [n] *edge of object, usually the top*
border, brink, circumference, fringe, hem, lip, margin, perimeter, periphery, rim, skirt, verge; SEE CONCEPT 836

brim [v] *flow over the top*
fill, fill up, hold no more, overflow, run over, spill, swell, teem, well over; SEE CONCEPT 740

brimming/brimful [adj] *overflowing; up to the top*
awash, chock-full, crammed, crowded, filled, flush, full, full to the top, jammed, level with, loaded, overfull, packed, running over, stuffed, topfull; SEE CONCEPTS 481,771,774

brine [n] *salt solution*
alkali, blue, brackish water, deep, drink, marinade, ocean, pickling solution, preservative, saline, salt water, sea water, sodium chloride solution, vinegar; SEE CONCEPT 514

bring [v1] *transport or accompany*
attend, back, bear, buck*, carry, chaperon, companion, conduct, consort, convey, deliver, escort, fetch, gather, guide, gun*, heel*, import, lead, lug, pack, pick up, piggyback*, ride, schlepp*, shoulder, take, take along, tote, transfer, transport, truck, usher; SEE CONCEPT 143

bring [v2] *cause; influence*
begin, compel, contribute to, convert, convince, create, dispose, effect, engender, force, induce, inflict, lead, make, move, occasion, persuade, prevail on, prevail upon, produce, prompt, result in, sway, wreak; SEE CONCEPT 242

bring [v3] *command a price*
afford, bring in, draw, earn, fetch, gross, net, produce, return, sell for, take, yield; SEE CONCEPTS 330,335

bring [v4] *file charges in court*
appeal, arraign, cite, declare, indict, initiate legal action, institute, prefer, serve, sue, summon, take to court; SEE CONCEPT 317

bring about [v] *cause success*
accomplish, achieve, beget, bring to pass, compass, create, do, draw on, effect, effectuate, engender, generate, give rise to, make happen,

manage, occasion, produce, realize, secure, succeed; SEE CONCEPTS 244,706

bring around [v] *convince, induce*
argue, convert, draw, get, indoctrinate, persuade, prevail upon, prompt, prove, talk into, win over; SEE CONCEPT 68

bring down [v] *reduce or hurt*
abase, cut down, damage, drop, fell, floor, injure, knock down, KO*, lay low, level, lower, mow down, murder*, overthrow, overturn, prostrate, pull down, shoot down, slay*, throw down, tumble, undermine, upset, wound; SEE CONCEPTS 7,19,252

bring in [v] *make a profit*
accrue, acquire, bear, be worth, bring, cost, earn, fetch, gain, get, gross, make, pay, produce, realize, return, sell, yield; SEE CONCEPTS 124,330

bring off [v] *accomplish*
achieve, bring home the bacon*, bring to pass, carry off, carry out, discharge, effect, effectuate, execute, perform, pull off, realize, succeed; SEE CONCEPTS 704,706

bring on [v] *provoke*
accelerate, advance, cause, expedite, generate, give rise to, induce, inspire, lead to, occasion, precipitate, prompt; SEE CONCEPTS 7,19

bring out [v] *draw out*
bring to light, emphasize, expose, highlight, introduce, publish, utter; SEE CONCEPTS 49,57

bring up [v1] *raise youngster*
breed, cultivate, develop, discipline, educate, feed, form, foster, nourish, nurture, provide for, rear, school, support, teach, train; SEE CONCEPT 295

bring up [v2] *initiate, mention in conversation*
advance, advert, allude to, broach, discuss, introduce, moot, move, offer, point out, propose, put forward, raise, raise a subject, refer, submit, tender, touch on, ventilate*; SEE CONCEPT 51

brink [n] *edge of an object or area*
border, boundary, brim, fringe, frontier, limit, lip, margin, perimeter, periphery, point, rim, skirt, threshold, verge; SEE CONCEPTS 484,513

brisk [adj1] *fast-moving; active*
adroit, agile, alert, animated, bustling, busy, energetic, lively, nimble, quick, speedy, sprightly, spry, vigorous, vivacious, zippy; SEE CONCEPTS 542,584

brisk [adj2] *chilly, refreshing (weather)*
biting, bracing, crisp, exhilarating, fresh, invigorating, keen, nippy, sharp, snappy, stimulating; SEE CONCEPT 605

bristle [n] *short, prickly hair*
barb, feeler, fiber, point, prickle, quill, spine, stubble, thorn, vibrissa, whisker; SEE CONCEPT 418

bristle [v] *become upset, excited*
be angry, be infuriated, be maddened, blow up*, boil, boil over, bridle, flare, flare up, fume, get one's dander up*, rage, rise, ruffle, see red*, seethe, spit*, stand on end*, swell; SEE CONCEPT 410

brittle [adj1] *fragile*
breakable, crisp, crumbling, crumbly, delicate, frail, frangible, friable, inelastic, shatterable, shivery, vitreous, weak; SEE CONCEPTS 488,606

brittle [adj2] *tense*
curt, edgy, irritable, nervous, prim, short, stiff, stilted; SEE CONCEPT 401

br
br

broach [v1] *bring up a topic*
advance, approach, bring up, hint at, interject, interpose, introduce, mention, moot, move, offer, open up, propose, raise subject, speak of, submit, suggest, talk of, touch on, ventilate*; SEE CONCEPT *51*

broach [v2] *open, pierce*
begin, crack, decant, draw off, puncture, start, tap, uncork; SEE CONCEPTS *142,225*

broad [adj1] *wide physically*
ample, capacious, deep, expansive, extended, extensive, full, generous, immense, large, latitudinous, outspread, outstretched, roomy, spacious, splay, squat, thick, vast, voluminous, widespread; SEE CONCEPTS *773,796*

broad [adj2] *extensive*
all-embracing, all-inclusive, comprehensive, copious, encyclopedic, expansive, extended, far-flung, far-reaching, general, inclusive, nonspecific, scopic, sweeping, ubiquitous, undetailed, universal, unlimited, wide, wide-ranging, widespread; SEE CONCEPT *772*

broad [adj3] *full, obvious*
apparent, clear, explicit, open, plain, straightforward, undisguised, unequivocal; SEE CONCEPT *576*

broad [adj4] *liberal-minded*
advanced, cultivated, experienced, open, open-minded, permissive, progressive, radical, tolerant, unbiased, wide; SEE CONCEPT *403*

broad [adj5] *vulgar*
blue, coarse, dirty, gross, improper, indecent, indelicate, low-minded, off-color, purple, racy, risqué, salty, saucy, smutty, spicy, suggestive, unrefined, unrestrained, wicked; SEE CONCEPT *545*

broad [n] *a woman*
babe*, bimbo*, chick*, dame, dish, doll*, doxy, female, floozy, gal, girl, honey*, lady, lassie, miss, moll, skirt*, sweet thing*, tootsie*; SEE CONCEPTS *414,415*

broadcast [n] *information on electronic media*
advertisement, air time, announcement, newscast, performance, program, publication, radiocast, show, simulcast, telecast, transmission; SEE CONCEPTS *274,293*

broadcast [v1] *put forth on electronic media*
air, announce, beam, be on the air, cable, circulate, colorcast, communicate, get out*, go on the air, go on the airwaves, put on the air, radio, radiograph, relay, send, show, simulcast, telecast, telegraph, telephone, televise, transmit; SEE CONCEPTS *60,292*

broadcast [v2] *make public*
advertise, announce, annunciate, blare, blazon, circulate, communicate, declare, disseminate, distribute, proclaim, promulgate, publish, report, sow, spread, strew, troll; SEE CONCEPT *60*

broadcasting [n] *informing via electronic media*
airing, air time, announcing, auditioning, newscasting, performing, posting online, putting on program, radio, reporting, telecasting, television, transmission, transmitting; SEE CONCEPTS *263,293*

broaden [v] *extend, supplement*
augment, breadthen, develop, enlarge, expand, fatten, grow, increase, open up, ream, spread, stretch, swell, widen; SEE CONCEPT *239*

broad-minded [adj] *liberal*

advanced, catholic, cosmopolitan, dispassionate, flexible, free-thinking, indulgent, liberal, open, open-minded, permissive, progressive, radical, receptive, responsive, tolerant, unbiased, unbigoted, undogmatic, unprejudiced, wide; SEE CONCEPT *403*

brochure [n] *short, printed document*
advertisement, booklet, circular, flyer, folder, handbill, handout, leaflet, pamphlet; SEE CONCEPT *280*

broil [v] *cook under direct heat*
burn, melt, roast, scorch, sear, swelter; SEE CONCEPT *170*

broiling [adj] *very hot*
baking, burning, fiery, on fire, red-hot, roasting, scalding, scorching, sizzling, sweltering, torrid; SEE CONCEPT *605*

broke [adj] *without money*
bankrupt, beggared, bust*, cleaned out*, destitute, dirt poor*, flat broke*, impoverished, in Chapter 11*, in debt, indebted, indigent, insolvent, needy, penniless, penurious, poor, ruined, stone broke*, strapped*, tapped out; SEE CONCEPT *334*

broken [adj1] *destroyed; made into pieces from a whole*
burst, busted, collapsed, cracked, crippled, crumbled, crushed, damaged, defective, demolished, disintegrated, dismembered, fractured, fragmentary, fragmented, hurt, injured, in pieces, mangled, mutilated, pulverized, rent, riven, ruptured, separated, severed, shattered, shivered, shredded, slivered, smashed, split; SEE CONCEPT *485*

broken [adj2] *discontinuous*
disconnected, disturbed, erratic, fragmentary, incomplete, intermittent, interrupted, irregular, spasmodic, spastic; SEE CONCEPT *482*

broken [adj3] *mentally defeated*
beaten, browbeaten, crippled, crushed, defeated, demoralized, depressed, discouraged, disheartened, heartsick, humbled, oppressed, overpowered, subdued, tamed, vanquished; SEE CONCEPT *403*

broken [adj4] *not working*
busted, coming unglued, coming unstuck, defective, disabled, down, exhausted, fallen apart, faulty, feeble, gone, gone to pieces*, gone to pot*, haywire, imperfect, in disrepair, in need of repair, inoperable, in the shop*, kaput*, not functioning, on the blink*, on the fritz*, on the shelf*, out, out of commission*, out of kilter*, out of order, out of whack*, ruined, run-down, screwed up*, shot, spent, unsatisfactory, weak, wracked*, wrecked; SEE CONCEPTS *485,560*

broken [adj5] *forgotten, ignored (promise)*
abandoned, dishonored, disobeyed, disregarded, ignored, infringed, isolated, retracted, traduced, transgressed, violated; SEE CONCEPT *544*

broken [adj6] *stuttering in speech*
disjointed, halting, hesitant, hesitating, imperfect, incoherent, mumbled, muttered, stammering, unintelligible, weak; SEE CONCEPT *267*

brokenhearted [adj] *devastated*
crestfallen, crushed, desolate, despairing, despondent, disappointed, disconsolate, grief-stricken, grieved, heartbroken, heartsick, heartsore, inconsolable, miserable, mournful, prostrated, sorrowful, wretched; SEE CONCEPT *403*

broker [*n*] *financial expert*
agent, business person, dealer, entrepreneur, factor, financier, go-between, interagent, interceder, intercessor, intermediary, intermediate, mediator, merchant, middleperson, negotiator, stockbroker; SEE CONCEPTS *348,353*

bronze [*adj*] *coppery-brown color*
brownish, burnished, chestnut, copper, copper-colored, metallic brown, reddish-brown, reddish-tan, russet, rust, tan; SEE CONCEPT *618*

brooch [*n*] *ornamental pin*
bar pin, breastpin, clip, cluster, jewelry; SEE CONCEPT *446*

brood [*n*] *cluster of children*
begats, breed, chicks, clutch, descendants, family, flock, hatch, infants, issue, litter, offspring, posterity, progeniture, progeny, scions, seed, young; SEE CONCEPT *296*

brood [*v*] *agonize over*
be in brown study*, bleed, chafe inwardly*, consider, daydream, deliberate, despond, dream, dwell upon, eat one's heart out*, fret, gloom, grieve, lament, languish, meditate, mope, mull over, muse, ponder, reflect, repine, ruminate, sigh, speculate, stew over*, sulk, sweat out*, sweat over*, think about, think upon, worry; SEE CONCEPT *17*

brook [*n*] *stream of water*
beck, branch, burn, creek, rill, rindle, river, rivulet, run, runnel, streamlet, watercourse; SEE CONCEPT *514*

brook [*v*] *endure, accept*
abide, allow, bear, be big*, countenance, go, hang in, hang in there*, hear of, live with, put up with, sit tight*, stand, stomach, suffer, support, swallow, take, tolerate, withstand; SEE CONCEPT *23*

broom [*n*] *device for cleaning floors*
besom, carpet sweeper, feather duster, floor brush, mop, swab, sweeper, whisk; SEE CONCEPT *499*

broth [*n*] *soup, usually clear*
borscht, bouillon, bowl, brew, chowder, concoction, consommé, decoction, dishwater*, distillation, elixir, fluid, gumbo, hodge-podge*, olio, porridge, potage, potpourri, pottage, puree, splash, stock, vichyssoise; SEE CONCEPTS *457,467*

brothel [*n*] *house of prostitution*
bagnio, bawdy house*, bordello, call house*, cathouse*, den of iniquity*, house of assignation, house of ill repute, house with red doors*, massage parlor, red-light district, whorehouse; SEE CONCEPT *449*

brother [*n1*] *male sibling*
blood brother, kin, kinsperson, relation, relative, twin; SEE CONCEPTS *414,419*

brotherhood [*n*] *association*
affiliation, alliance, clan, clique, community, comradeship, confederacy, coterie, fellowship, fraternity, guild, kinship, league, society, union; SEE CONCEPTS *387,388*

brow [*n*] *forehead*
countenance, eyebrow, face, frons, front, mien, temple, top; SEE CONCEPT *418*

browbeat [*v*] *castigate, nag*
badger, bludgeon, bluster, bulldoze*, bully, coerce, cow, despotize, domineer, dragoon, frighten, harass, hector, intimidate, lean on*, lord it over*, oppress, overawe, overbear, put heat on*, put the chill on*, put through the wringer*, threaten, tyrannize; SEE CONCEPTS *14,52*

brown [*adj*] *dark, burnished color*
amber, auburn, bay, beige, bister, brick, bronze, buff, burnt sienna, chestnut, chocolate, cinnamon, cocoa, coffee, copper, drab, dust, ecru, fawn, ginger, hazel, henna, khaki, mahogany, nut, ochre, puce, russet, rust, sepia, snuff-colored, sorrel, tan, tawny, terra-cotta, toast, umber; SEE CONCEPT *618*

brownnose [*v*] *suck up to*
apple-polish, back-scratch, bootlick, curry favor, fawn on, flatter, get on the right side of, kiss ass, scratch one's back, suck up to, toady; SEE CONCEPTS *59,69*

brownnoser [*n*] *sycophant, toady*
apple-polisher, ass-kisser, backscratcher*, backslapper*, bootlicker*, brownnose*, doter, fawner, flatterer, flunky*, kiss-ass, kowtower, lackey, minion, teacher's pet, yes-man, yes-person; SEE CONCEPT *423*

browse [*v*] *look around; look through*
check over, dip into*, examine cursorily, feed, flip through, get the cream*, give the once over*, glance at, graze, hit the high spots*, inspect loosely, leaf through, nibble*, once over lightly*, pass an eye over*, peruse, read, read here and there, riffle through, riff through, run through, scan, skim, skip through, survey, thumb through wander; SEE CONCEPT *623*

browser [*n*] *Internet /Web viewing software*
display program, gateway, Internet service provider, portal, search engine, web directory, web crawler, web spider; SEE CONCEPTS *349,770*

bruise [*n*] *black and blue mark under skin*
black eye, black mark, blemish, boo-boo*, contusion, discoloration, injury, mark, mouse*, swelling, wale, wound; SEE CONCEPT *309*

bruise [*v*] *break blood vessel; discolor*
bang up, batter, beat, black, blacken, blemish, bung up*, contuse, crush, damage, deface, do a number on*, injure, mar, mark, pound, pulverize, wound, zing*; SEE CONCEPTS *137,246,250*

brunette/brunet [*adj*] *dark hair and/or skin*
bistered, brown, dusky, pigmented, swart, swarthy, tanned, tawny; SEE CONCEPTS *406,618*

brunt [*n*] *bad end of a situation*
burden, force, full force, impact, pressure, shock, strain, stress, tension, thrust, violence; SEE CONCEPT *674*

brush [*n1*] *tool with bristles for cleaning*
besom, broom, hairbrush, mop, polisher, sweeper, toothbrush, waxer, whisk; SEE CONCEPT *499*

brush [*n2*] *fight*
clash, conflict, confrontation, encounter, engagement, fracas, rub, run-in, scrap, set-to, skirmish, tap, touch, tussle; SEE CONCEPT *106*

brush [*n3*] *scrappy bushes*
boscage, bracken, brushwood, chaparral, coppice, copse, cover, dingle, fern, gorse, grove, hedge, scrub, sedge, shrubbery, spinney, thicket, undergrowth, underwood; SEE CONCEPT *429*

brush [*v1*] *touch lightly*
caress, contact, flick, glance, graze, kiss, scrape, shave, skim, smooth, stroke, sweep, tickle; SEE CONCEPT *612*

brush [*v2*] *clean, prepare by whisking*
buff, clean, paint, polish, sweep, wash, whisk, wipe; SEE CONCEPTS *165,202*

brush aside/brush off [v] *ignore; refuse*
boycott, cold-shoulder*, contradict, cut, deny, disclaim, dismiss, disown, disregard, get rid of, have no time for*, ostracize, override, rebuff, reject, repudiate, scorn, send away, slight, snub, spurn, sweep aside; SEE CONCEPT *30*

brush up [v] *improve condition*
clean up, cram, go over, look over, polish up, read up, refresh one's memory, refurbish, relearn, renovate, reread, retouch, review, revise, study, touch up; SEE CONCEPTS *202,244*

brusque [adj] *curt, surly*
abrupt, bluff, blunt, brief, crusty, discourteous, gruff, hasty, impolite, sharp, short, snappy, snippy, tart, terse, unmannerly; SEE CONCEPTS *267,401*

brutal [adj1] *cruel, remorseless*
barbarous, bloodthirsty, callous, ferocious, gruff, hard, harsh, heartless, impolite, inhuman, insensitive, merciless, pitiless, remorseless, rough, rude, ruthless, savage, severe, uncivil, uncivilized, unfeeling, unmannerly, unmerciful, vicious; SEE CONCEPT *401*

brutal [adj2] *crude, rough*
animal, bearish, beastly, bestial, brute, brutish, carnal, coarse, feral, ferine, inhuman, inhumane, rude, savage, swinish, unfeeling; SEE CONCEPT *544*

brutality [n] *cruel treatment*
atrocity, barbarism, barbarity, bloodthirstiness, brutishness, choke hold*, cruelty, ferocity, fierceness, grossness, inhumanity, ruthlessness, sadism, savageness, savagery, third degree*, unfeelingness, viciousness; SEE CONCEPTS *14,86*

brutally [adv] *cruelly, without remorse*
atrociously, barbarically, barbarously, brutishly, callously, demoniacally, diabolically, ferally, ferociously, fiercely, hardheartedly, heartlessly, in cold blood, inexorably, inhumanely, inhumanly, meanly, mercilessly, murderously, pitilessly, relentlessly, remorselessly, ruthlessly, savagely, something fierce, something terrible, unkindly, unrelentingly, viciously; SEE CONCEPT *544*

brute [adj] *very strong; animal-like*
animal, beastly, bestial, bodily, carnal, feral, ferine, fleshly, instinctive, mindless, physical, senseless, swinish, unthinking; SEE CONCEPTS *489,540*

brute [n] *barbarian*
animal, beast, cannibal, creature, critter*, degenerate, devil, fiend, lout, monster, ogre, ruffian, sadist, savage, swine, wild animal; SEE CONCEPTS *394,423*

bubble [n] *globule of air*
air ball*, balloon, barm, bead, blister, blob, drop, droplet, effervescence, foam, froth, lather, sac, spume, vesicle; SEE CONCEPT *437*

bubble [v] *foam, froth up, especially with sound*
boil, burble, churn, eddy, effervesce, erupt, fester, fizz, gurgle, gush, issue, moil, murmur, percolate, ripple, seep, seethe, simmer, smolder, sparkle, spume, stir, swash, trickle, well; SEE CONCEPTS *179,469*

buck [n] *male animal*
bull, stag; SEE CONCEPTS *394,419*

buck [v] *resist, kick off*
bound, combat, contest, dislodge, dispute, duel, fight, jerk, jump, leap, oppose, prance, repel, start, throw, traverse, trip, unseat, vault, withstand; SEE CONCEPTS *180,222*

bucket [n] *container, often for liquids, with handle*
brazier, can, canister, cask, hod, kettle, pail, pot, scuttle, vat; SEE CONCEPT *494*

buckle [n] *fastener with long pin*
catch, clamp, clasp, clip, fastening, fibula, harness, hasp; SEE CONCEPT *450*

buckle [v] *contort, warp*
bend, bulge, cave in, collapse, crumple, distort, fold, twist, yield; SEE CONCEPT *702*

buckle down [v] *concentrate on*
address, apply oneself, attend to, bend, dedicate oneself to, devote oneself to, exert oneself, give, give oneself over to, keep close to, keep one's mind on, launch into, occupy oneself with, pitch in, set to, throw, turn; SEE CONCEPTS *17,87*

bucolic [adj] *rural or rustic*
agrarian, agricultural, Arcadian, countrified, country, pastoral; SEE CONCEPTS *536,583*

bud [n] *new sprout on plant*
bloom, blossom, embryo, floret, germ, incipient flower, nucleus, shoot, spark; SEE CONCEPT *428*

bud [v] *sprout*
burgeon, burst forth, develop, grow, pullulate, shoot; SEE CONCEPT *427*

budding [adj] *developing, flowering*
beginning, blossoming, burgeoning, bursting forth, embryonic, fledgling, fresh, germinal, germinating, growing, incipient, maturing, nascent, opening, potential, promising, pubescent, pullulating, shooting up, sprouting, vegetating, young; SEE CONCEPT *490*

buddy [n] *friend*
associate, chum, co-mate, companion, comrade, confidant, co-worker, crony, intimate, mate, pal, peer, sidekick; SEE CONCEPT *423*

budge [v] *dislodge from staid position*
bend, change, change position, convince, give way, inch, influence, locomote, move, persuade, propel, push, remove, roll, shift, slide, stir, sway, yield; SEE CONCEPTS *68,147*

budget [n] *financial plan*
account, aggregate, allocation, allowance, bulk, cost, estimated expenses, finances, fiscal estimate, funds, means, planned disbursement, quantity, quantum, resources, spending plan, statement, total; SEE CONCEPT *332*

budget [v] *plan money or action*
allocate, apportion, calculate, compute, cost, estimate, predict, ration; SEE CONCEPTS *36,330*

buff [adj] *sandy color*
bare, blonde, canary, ecru, lemon, light brown, nude, ochre, straw, tan, tawny, yellow-brown, yellowish; SEE CONCEPT *618*

buff [n] *enthusiast*
addict, admirer, aficionado, connoisseur, devotee, expert, fan, fiend*, freak*, habitué, hound, lover, votary; SEE CONCEPTS *352,423*

buff [v] *polish to a shine*
brush, burnish, furbish, glaze, gloss, pumice, rub, sandpaper, scour, shine, smooth; SEE CONCEPTS *202,215*

buffer [n] *safeguard*
bulwark, bumper, cushion, defense, fender, intermediary, screen, shield, shock absorber; SEE CONCEPTS *484,729*

buffet [n] *meal set out on table for choosing*

café, cafeteria, cold table, counter, cupboard, lunch wagon, salad bar, shelf, sideboard, smorgasbord, snack bar; SEE CONCEPTS *443,459*

buffet [*v*] *hit repeatedly*
bang, batter, beat, blow, box, bump, clobber, cuff, flail, jolt, knock, pound, pummel, push, rap, shove, slap, smack, spank, strike, thrash, thump, wallop; SEE CONCEPT *189*

buffoon [*n*] *clownlike person*
antic, bozo*, clown, comedian, comic, droll, fool, harlequin, jester, joker, merry-andrew, wag, zany; SEE CONCEPT *423*

bug [*n1*] *bacterium, microorganism*
bacillus, disease, germ, infection, microbe, virus; SEE CONCEPT *306*

bug [*n2*] *insect*
ant, beetle, cootie, flea, gnat, louse, pest, vermin; SEE CONCEPT *398*

bug [*n3*] *obsession*
craze, enthusiasm, fad, mania, rage, zeal; SEE CONCEPT *532*

bug [*n4*] *computer glitch*
breakdown, computer malfunction, defect, error, failure, fault, flaw, hitch, problem, something wrong, trouble; SEE CONCEPTS *580,674*

bug [*v1*] *bother, disturb*
abrade, annoy, badger, chafe, gall, get on someone*, harass, irk, irritate, needle, nettle, pester, plague, provoke, vex; SEE CONCEPTS *7,19*

bug [*v2*] *listen to without permission*
eavesdrop, listen in, overhear, spy, tap, wiretap; SEE CONCEPTS *192,596*

bugle [*n*] *musical horn*
clarion, cornet, misery pipe*, trumpet; SEE CONCEPT *262*

build [*n*] *physical structure, form*
body, conformation, constitution, figure, frame, habit, habitus, physique, shape; SEE CONCEPT *757*

build [*v1*] *construct structure*
assemble, bring about, carpenter, cast, compile, compose, contrive, engineer, erect, evolve, fabricate, fashion, fit together, forge, form, frame, jerry-build, knock together*, make, manufacture, model, prefabricate, produce, put together, put up, raise, rear, reconstruct, sculpture, set up, superstruct, synthesize, throw together*, throw up*; SEE CONCEPT *168*

build [*v2*] *initiate, found*
base, begin, constitute, establish, formulate, inaugurate, institute, originate, set up, start; SEE CONCEPT *234*

build [*v3*] *increase, accelerate*
aggrandize, amplify, augment, boost, compound, develop, enlarge, escalate, expand, extend, heighten, improve, intensify, magnify, mount, multiply, strengthen, swell, wax; SEE CONCEPTS *236,245*

builder [*n*] *construction worker*
architect, artisan, constructor, contractor, craftsperson, erector, fabricator, framer, inventor, maker, manufacturer, mason, originator, producer; SEE CONCEPT *348*

building [*n*] *constructed dwelling*
architecture, construction, domicile, edifice, erection, fabric, framework, home, house, hut, pile, superstructure; SEE CONCEPTS *439,441*

buildup [*n*] *development; accumulation*
accretion, advertising, enlargement, escalation, expansion, gain, growth, heap, hype, increase,

load, mass, plug, promotion, publicity, puff*, stack, stockpile, store; SEE CONCEPTS *230,704,787*

build up [*v*] *amplify, advertise*
add to, boost, develop, enhance, expand, extend, fortify, heighten, hype, improve, increase, intensify, plug*, promote, publicize, puff*, reinforce, spotlight, strengthen; SEE CONCEPTS *236,245,266*

built-in [*adj*] *included*
congenital, constitutional, deep-seated, essential, implicit, inborn, inbred, in-built, incorporated, indwelling, ingrained, inherent, innate, inseparable, integral, part and parcel*; SEE CONCEPT *549*

bulb [*n*] *globular object*
ball, bunch, corm, corn, globe, head, knob, nodule, nub, protuberance, swelling, tube, tumor; SEE CONCEPT *436*

bulge [*n*] *swollen object*
appendage, bagginess, blob, bump, bunch, bunching, convexity, dilation, distention, excess, excrescence, gibbosity, growth, hump, intumescence, jut, lump, nodulation, nodule, outgrowth, outthrust, projection, prominence, promontory, protrusion, protuberance, sac, sagging, salience, salient, superfluity, swelling, tuberosity, tumefaction, tumor, wart; SEE CONCEPTS *436,470*

bulge [*v*] *project outward*
bag, balloon, beetle, belly, bilge, billow, bloat, blob, bug out, dilate, distend, enlarge, expand, extrude, jut, overhang, poke, pop out, pouch, protrude, protuberate, puff out, sag, stand out, stick out, swell; SEE CONCEPTS *208,780*

bulk [*n1*] *size, largeness*
aggregate, amount, amplitude, bigness, dimensions, extent, immensity, magnitude, mass, massiveness, quantity, quantum, substance, total, totality, volume, weight; SEE CONCEPT *730*

bulk [*n2*] *main part, most*
best part, better part, biggest share, body, generality, greater number, greater part, gross, lion's share*, majority, major part, mass, nearly all, plurality, predominant part, preponderance, principal part; SEE CONCEPTS *635,829*

bulky [*adj*] *huge*
awkward, beefy, big, colossal, cumbersome, cumbrous, enormous, gross, heavy, hefty, high, hulking, immense, large, long, mammoth, massive, ponderous, substantial, unhandy, unmanageable, unwieldy, voluminous, weighty; SEE CONCEPT *781*

bulldoze [*v1*] *demolish*
drive, elbow, flatten, force, jostle, level, press, propel, push, raze, shove, thrust; SEE CONCEPTS *208,252*

bulldoze [*v2*] *bully, intimidate*
bludgeon, bluster, browbeat, coerce, cow, dragoon, harass, hector; SEE CONCEPT *14*

bullet [*n*] *small missile*
ammo*, ammunition, ball, bolt, cap, cartridge, dose*, lead, love letter*, pellet, projectile, rocket, round, shot, slug, trajectile; SEE CONCEPT *500*

bulletin [*n*] *message, notification*
account, announcement, break, calendar, communication, communiqué, dispatch, flash*, handout, hot wire*, item, list, news, news flash*, notice, program, publication, release, report, scoop*, skinny*, statement, the dope*, what's going down*, what's happening*; SEE CONCEPTS *271,274*

br
bu

bulletin board [*n*] *electronic messaging system*
bboard, BBS, board, bulletin board system; SEE
CONCEPTS *349,770*
bully [*n*] *domineering person*
annoyer, antagonizer, browbeater, bulldozer, co-
ercer, harrier, hector, insolent, intimidator, oppressor, persecutor, pest, rascal, rowdy, ruffian,
tease, tormenter, tough; SEE CONCEPT *423*
bully [*v*] *intimidate, push around*
bludgeon, bluster, browbeat, buffalo, bulldoze,
coerce, cow, despotize, domineer, dragoon, enforce, harass, hector, lean on, menace, oppress,
overbear, persecute, ride roughshod*, showboat*, swagger, terrorize, threaten, torment, torture, turn on the heat*, tyrannize, walk heavy*;
SEE CONCEPT *14*
bulwark [*n*] *fortification, support*
barrier, bastion, buffet, buttress, citadel, defense,
embankment, fort, fortress, guard, mainstay, out-
work, parapet, partition, protection, rampart, redoubt, safeguard, security, stronghold, vallation;
SEE CONCEPTS *96,729*
bum [*n*] *beggar*
bindle*, black sheep*, derelict, drifter, floater,
gutterpup*, guttersnipe*, hobo, stiff*, tramp,
transient, vagabond, vagrant; SEE CONCEPTS
412,423
bummer [*n*] *bad experience*
disappointment, disaster, downer*, drag*, misfortune; SEE CONCEPTS *674,679*
bump [*v1*] *collide, hit, usually with sound*
bang, bounce, box, buck, bunt, butt, carom, clap,
clatter, crack, crash, impinge, jar, jerk, jolt, jostle, jounce, knock, pat, plop, plunk, pound,
punch, rap, rattle, shake, slam, slap, smack,
smash into, strike, thud, thump, thunder, thwack,
whack; SEE CONCEPT *189*
bump [*v2*] *move over, dislodge*
budge, displace, remove, shift; SEE CONCEPT *213*
bump [*v3*] *increment*
increase, raise, step up; SEE CONCEPTS
236,245,780
bump into [*v*] *happen upon*
chance upon, come across, encounter, hit, light,
light upon, luck, meet, meet up with, run across,
run into, stumble, tumble; SEE CONCEPT *114*
bumpy [*adj*] *rough*
choppy, corrugated, jarring, jerky, knobby,
lumpy, potholed*, rugged, rutted, uneven; SEE
CONCEPTS *485,606*
bum rap [*n*] *rotten deal*
bad break*, bad deal, bad rap*, bum deal*, bummer*, drag*, frame-up, lousy deal, misfortune,
raw deal, stroke of bad luck*, the shaft*; SEE
CONCEPTS *674,679*
bun [*n*] *baked roll*
bread, cruller, Danish, doughnut, eclair, muffin,
pastry, scone, sweet roll; SEE CONCEPT *457*
bunch [*n*] *collection of something*
agglomeration, assemblage, assortment, band,
batch, bevy, blob, bouquet, bundle, caboodle*,
chunk, clump, cluster, covey, crew, crowd, fasci-
cle, flock, galaxy, gang, gathering, group, heap,
host, hunk, knot, lot, mass, mess, mob, multitude, number, oodles*, pack, parcel, party, passel*, pile, quantity, sheaf, shebang*, shock,
shooting match*, spray, stack, swarm, team,
thicket, troop, tuft; SEE CONCEPT *432*
bunch [*v*] *gather in group*
assemble, bundle, cluster, collect, congregate,

cram, crowd, flock, group, herd, huddle, mass,
pack; SEE CONCEPT *109*
bundle [*n*] *accumulation, package of something*
array, assortment, bag, bale, batch, box, bunch,
carton, clump, cluster, collection, crate, group,
heap, lot, mass, pack, package, packet, pallet,
parcel, pile, quantity, roll, set, stack, wad; SEE
CONCEPTS *432,787*
bundle [*v*] *accumulate, package*
bale, bind, clothe, fasten, pack, palletize, tie,
truss, wrap; SEE CONCEPTS *158,202*
bungle [*v*] *blunder, mess up*
ball up*, boggle, botch, butcher*, drop the ball*,
err, flub, foul up*, fudge*, fumble, goof up*,
gum up*, louse up*, make a mess of, mar, mess
up, miscalculate, mishandle, mismanage, muff*,
ruin, screw up*, spoil; SEE CONCEPT *101*
bungler [*n*] *person who blunders*
addlebrain*, blockhead*, blunderer, bonehead*,
botcher*, bumbler, butcher*, butterfingers*,
clod, clumsy oaf*, dolt, donkey*, duffer*, dunce,
featherbrain*, fool, foul-up*, fumbler*, goofball*, goof off*, harebrain*, idiot, ignoramus, incompetent, klutz*, mismanager, muddler,
muffer*, numskull*, screw up*, spoiler; SEE
CONCEPTS *412,423*
bunk [*n1*] *nonsense*
applesauce*, balderdash, baloney*, bilge*, claptrap, eyewash*, flimflam*, garbage*, hogwash*,
hooey*, horsefeathers*, jazz*, piffle*, poppycock, rot*, rubbish, tomfoolery*, tommyrot*,
trash*, twaddle*; SEE CONCEPTS *63,278*
bunk [*n2*] *twin bed, usually stacked; place to
sleep*
berth, cot, doss, hay, kip, pallet, sack; SEE CON-
CEPT *443*
bunt [*v*] *hit half-heartedly*
butt, lay it down*, meet, sacrifice, throw, toss;
SEE CONCEPTS *189,363*
buoy [*n*] *floating device*
beacon, drift, float, guide, marker, signal; SEE
CONCEPT *628*
buoyancy/buoyance [*n1*] *lightness in weight*
airiness, ethereality, floatability, levity, weight-
lessness; SEE CONCEPT *734*
buoyancy/buoyance [*n2*] *lightness in spirit*
animation, bounce, cheerfulness, cheeriness,
ebullience, effervescence, exuberance, gaiety,
good feeling, good humor, happiness, high spirits, jollity, liveliness, pep, spiritedness, sunniness, vim and vigor*, zing*, zip; SEE CONCEPTS
410,411
buoyant [*adj1*] *light in weight*
afloat, airy, bouncy, floatable, floating, resilient,
supernatant, unsinkable, weightless; SEE CON-
CEPT *491*
buoyant [*adj2*] *light in spirit*
animated, blithe, bouncy, breezy, bright, carefree, cheerful, debonair, effervescent, elastic, expansive, full of zip, gay, happy, invigorated,
jaunty, jovial, joyful, laid back*, lighthearted,
lively, peppy, resilient, sunny, supple, vivacious;
SEE CONCEPTS *403,404*
buoy (up) [*v*] *make light, encourage*
bolster, boost, buck up, cheer, cheer up, encourage, hearten, keep afloat, lift, prop, raise, support, sustain, uphold; SEE CONCEPTS *7,22*
burden [*n*] *mental weight; stress*
accountability, affliction, albatross*, anxiety,

ball and chain*, blame, care, charge, clog, concern, deadweight, difficulty, duty, encumbrance, excess baggage*, grievance, hardship, Herculean task, hindrance, load, millstone, misfortune, mishap, obstruction, onus, punishment, responsibility, sorrow, strain, task, tax, thorn in one's side*, trial, trouble, weary load, work, worry; SEE CONCEPTS *532,690*

burden [*v*] *encumber, strain*
afflict, bear down on, bother, crush, cumber, depress, dish it out*, dish out*, dump on*, encumber, give it to, hamper, handicap, hinder, impede, lade, load, make heavy, obligate, oppress, overcharge, overload, overwhelm, pile, press, saddle with, snow*, snow under*, stick it to, strain, tax, trouble, try, vex, weigh down, worry; SEE CONCEPTS *7,14,19*

burdensome [*adj*] *troublesome*
carking, crushing, demanding, difficult, disturbing, exacting, exigent, heavy*, irksome, onerous, oppressive, superincumbent, taxing, tough, trying, wearing, wearying, weighty; SEE CONCEPT *529*

bureau [*n1*] *branch of an organization*
agency, authority, board, commission, committee, department, division, front office*, office, salt mines*, service, setup, shop, store; SEE CONCEPTS *325,441,449*

bureau [*n2*] *chest of drawers*
chiffonier, commode, desk, dresser, highboy, sideboard, writing desk; SEE CONCEPT *443*

bureaucracy [*n*] *system which controls organization*
administration, authority, beadledom*, city hall*, civil service, directorate, government, management, ministry, officialdom, officials, powers that be*, red tape*, regulatory commission, the Establishment*, the system*; SEE CONCEPTS *325,770*

bureaucrat [*n*] *government official*
administrator, civil servant, desk-jockey*, functionary, office-holder, pencil-pusher*, politician, public servant; SEE CONCEPTS *347,354*

burglar [*n*] *person who steals*
cat burglar, crook, filcher*, housebreaker, midnighter*, owl*, picklock*, pilferer*, porchclimber*, prowler, robber, safecracker, sneakthief*, thief; SEE CONCEPT *412*

burglary [*n*] *stealing from residence, business*
break-in, breaking and entering, caper, crime, filching, heist, housebreaking, larceny, owl job*, pilferage, prowl, robbery, safecracking, second-story work*, sting, theft, thieving; SEE CONCEPT *139*

burial [*n*] *laying in of dead body*
burying, deep six*, deposition, entombment, exequies, funeral, inhumation, interment, last rites, obsequies, sepulture; SEE CONCEPT *367*

burlesque [*adj*] *farcical*
caricatural, comic, ironical, ludicrous, mock, mocking, parodic, satirical, travestying; SEE CONCEPT *555*

burlesque [*n*] *bawdy show; vaudeville*
burly*, caricature, farce, lampoon, lampoonery, mock, mockery, parody, pastiche, peep show, revue, satire, send-up, spoof, strip, takeoff, travesty, vaudeville; SEE CONCEPT *263*

burly [*adj*] *husky*
able-bodied, athletic, beefcake*, beefy*, big, brawny, bruising, bulky, gorillalike, hefty, hulk-

ing, hulky, hunk, muscular, portly, powerful, stocky, stout, strapping, strong, sturdy, thickset, well-built; SEE CONCEPT *773*

burn [*v1*] *be on fire; set on fire*
bake, be ablaze, blaze, brand, broil, calcine, cauterize, char, combust, conflagrate, cook, cremate, enkindle, flame, flare, flash, flicker, glow, heat, ignite, incinerate, kindle, light, melt, parch, reduce to ashes, rekindle, roast, scald, scorch, sear, set a match to, singe, smoke, smolder, toast, torch, wither; SEE CONCEPT *249*

burn [*v2*] *feel stinging pain*
bite, hurt, pain, smart, sting, tingle; SEE CONCEPT *590*

burn [*v3*] *be excited about; yearn for*
be angry, be aroused, be inflamed, be passionate, be stirred up, blaze, boil, breathe fire*, bristle, desire, eat up*, fume, lust, rage, seethe, simmer, smoulder, tingle, yearn; SEE CONCEPTS *20,29,34*

burn [*v4*] *cheat*
beat, bilk, chisel, cozen, deceive, defraud, gyp, overreach, ream, swindle, take, trick, use; SEE CONCEPTS *59,142*

burning [*adj1*] *blazing, flashing*
afire, aflame, alight, blistering, broiling, conflagrant, enkindled, fiery, flaming, flaring, gleaming, glowing, heated, hot, ignited, illuminated, incandescent, in flames, kindled, on fire, oxidizing, red-hot*, scorching, searing, sizzling, smoking, smouldering, torrid, white-hot*; SEE CONCEPTS *485,605*

burning [*adj2*] *fervent, excited*
all-consuming, ardent, blazing, eager, earnest, fervid, feverish, frantic, frenzied, heated, hectic, impassioned, intense, passionate, red-hot*, vehement, white-hot*, zealous; SEE CONCEPT *403*

burning [*adj3*] *stinging, painful*
acrid, biting, caustic, irritating, painful, piercing, prickling, pungent, reeking, sharp, smarting, tingling; SEE CONCEPTS *314,537*

burning [*adj4*] *important*
acute, clamant, clamorous, compelling, critical, crucial, crying, dire, essential, exigent, imperative, importunate, instant, pressing, significant, urgent, vital; SEE CONCEPT *568*

burnish [*v*] *polish, brighten*
buff, furbish, glance, glaze, gloss, luster, patina, put on a finish, rub, sheen, shine, smooth, wax; SEE CONCEPTS *202,215*

burrow [*n*] *hole dug by animal*
couch, den, hovel, lair, retreat, shelter, tunnel; SEE CONCEPT *517*

burrow [*v*] *dig a hole*
delve, excavate, hollow out, scoop out, tunnel, undermine; SEE CONCEPT *178*

burst [*n*] *blow-up, blast*
access, bang, barrage, blowout, bombardment, breach, break, cannonade, crack, discharge, eruption, explosion, fit, flare, fusillade, gush, gust, outbreak, outpouring, round, rupture, rush, sally, salvo, shower, spate, split, spurt, storm, surge, torrent, volley; SEE CONCEPTS *86,179,208*

burst [*v*] *blow up, break out*
barge, blow, break, crack, detonate, discharge, disintegrate, erupt, explode, fly open, fracture, fragment, gush forth, perforate, pierce, pop, prick, puncture, rend asunder, run, rupture, rush, shatter, shiver, splinter, split, spout, tear apart; SEE CONCEPTS *179,252*

bu
bu

bury [v1] *lay to rest after death*
consign to grave, cover up, deposit, embalm, ensepulcher, enshrine, entomb, hold last rites for*,
hold services for, inearth, inhume, inter, inurn,
lay out, mummify, plant*, put away*, put six feet
under*, sepulcher, sepulture, tomb; SEE CONCEPT
367
bury [v2] *conceal, cover*
cache, cover up, ensconce, enshroud, hide, occult, plant, screen, secrete, shroud, stash, stow
away; SEE CONCEPTS *172,188*
bury [v3] *plant in ground*
drive in, embed, engulf, implant, sink, submerge;
SEE CONCEPTS *172,257*
bury [v4] *engross oneself*
absorb, concentrate, engage, immerse, interest,
occupy, rivet, throw oneself into; SEE CONCEPT
24
bush [n] *shrubs; woodland*
backcountry, backwoods, boscage, bramble,
briar, brush, chaparral, creeper, forest, hedge,
hinterland, jungle, outback, plant, scrub, scrub-
land, shrubbery, the wild, thicket, vine, wilderness; SEE CONCEPT *429*
bush-league [adj] *second-rate*
minor league*, small potatoes*; SEE CONCEPTS
334,567,574
bushy [adj] *shaggy, unkempt*
bristling, bristly, disordered, feathery, fluffy,
fringed, full, furry, fuzzy, hairy, heavy, hirsute,
leafy, luxuriant, nappy, prickly, rough, rumpled,
spreading, stiff, thick, tufted, unruly, wiry,
woolly; SEE CONCEPTS *406,606*
busily [adv] *actively; intently*
agilely, animatedly, ardently, arduously, assiduously, briskly, carefully, diligently, eagerly,
earnestly, energetically, enthusiastically, expeditiously, fervently, hastily, hurriedly, indefatigably, industriously, laboriously, like all get out*,
like the devil*, like the dickens*, nimbly,
painstakingly, perseveringly, persistently, purposefully, restlessly, seriously, speedily, spiritedly, strenuously, studiously, unremittingly,
unweariedly, vigilantly, vigorously, vivaciously,
zealously; SEE CONCEPT *544*
business [n1] *job, profession*
bag*, biz*, calling, career, craft, dodge*, employment, field, function, game, line, livelihood,
métier, occupation, pursuit, racket*, specialty,
trade, vocation, what one is into*, work; SEE
CONCEPT *360*
business [n2] *company, enterprise*
cartel, concern, corporation, establishment, factory, firm, fly-by-night operation*, house, institution, market, megacorp*, mill, Mom and Pop*,
monopoly, organization, outfit, partnership,
setup, shoestring operation*, shop, store, syndicate, trust, venture; SEE CONCEPTS *325,449*
business [n3] *commerce, trade*
affairs, bargaining, barter, buying and selling,
capital and labor, commercialism, contracts,
deal, dealings, exchange, free enterprise, game,
industrialism, industry, manufacturing, market,
merchandising, production and distribution,
racket*, sales, selling, trading, traffic, transaction, undertaking; SEE CONCEPTS *325,770*
business [n4] *personal concern*
affair, assignment, beeswax*, carrying on, duty,
function, goings-on*, hanky-panky*, happening,

interest, issue, lookout, matter, palaver, point,
problem, question, responsibility, subject, task,
topic; SEE CONCEPT *532*
businesslike [adj] *efficient, professional*
accomplished, careful, concentrated, correct,
diligent, direct, disciplined, earnest, effective,
enterprising, expeditious, hardworking, industrious, intent, matter-of-fact, methodical, orderly,
organized, painstaking, practical, practiced, purposeful, regular, routine, sedulous, serious, skillful, systematic, thorough, well-ordered,
workaday; SEE CONCEPTS *326,544*
businessperson [n] *professional working person*
baron, big-time operator*, big wheel*, capitalist,
dealer, employer, entrepreneur, executive, financier, franchiser, gray flannel suit*, industrialist, manager, merchandiser, merchant, operator,
organization person, small potatoes*, storekeeper, suit*, the bacon*, tradesperson, trafficker, tycoon, wheeler-dealer*; SEE CONCEPTS
347,348
bust [n1] *chest of human*
bosom, breast, chest, front; SEE CONCEPT *392*
bust [n2] *arrest for illegal action*
apprehension, arrest, capture, cop, detention,
nab, pickup, pinch, raid, search, seizure; SEE
CONCEPTS *298,317*
bust [v1] *ruin, impoverish*
become insolvent, break, crash, fail, fold up, go
bankrupt, go into Chapter 11*, pauperize; SEE
CONCEPT *330*
bust [v2] *arrest for illegal action*
apprehend, catch, collar, cop*, detain, nab, pick
up, pinch, pull in, raid, run in, search; SEE CON-
CEPTS *298,317*
bust [v3] *physically break*
burst, fold, fracture, rupture; SEE CONCEPT *252*
bustle [n] *quick and busy activity*
ado, agitation, clamor, commotion, do*, excitement, flurry, furor, fuss, haste, hubbub, hurly-
burly*, hurry, pother, rumpus, stir, to-do*,
tumult, turmoil, uproar, whirl, whirlpool, whirlwind; SEE CONCEPT *386*
bustle [v] *move around quickly, busily*
bestir, dash, dust, flit, flutter, fuss, hasten, hum,
hurry, hustle, run, rush, scamper, scramble,
scurry, scuttle, stir, tear, whirl, whisk; SEE CON-
CEPT *150*
busy [adj1] *engaged, at work*
active, already taken*, assiduous, at it*, buried,
diligent, employed, engaged, engrossed, having a
full plate*, having enough on one's plate*, having fish to fry*, having many irons in the fire*,
hustling, in a meeting, in conference, industrious, in someone else's possession*, in the field,
in the laboratory, occupied, on assignment, on
duty, on the go, overloaded, persevering, slaving,
snowed*, swamped*, tied up, unavailable, up to
one's ears*, with a customer, working; SEE CON-
CEPTS *326,544,555*
busy [adj2] *active, on the go*
bustling, busy as a beaver*, energetic, full, fussy,
hectic, humming*, hustling, lively, popping*,
restless, strenuous, tireless, tiring; SEE CONCEPT
542
busy [adj3] *nosy, impertinent*
butting in, curious, forward, inquisitive, interfering, intrusive, meddlesome, meddling, nebby,
obtrusive, officious, prying, pushy, snoopy, stirring, troublesome; SEE CONCEPT *404*

busybody [n] *nosy, impertinent person*
backseat driver*, butt-in*, buttinsky*, eavesdropper, fink*, fussbudget, gossip, intermeddler, intruder, meddler, newsmonger*, nosey parker*, rubberneck*, scandalmonger*, sidewalk superintendent*, snoop, snooper, tattletale, troublemaker, yenta*; SEE CONCEPT *423*

butcher [n] *meat killer, seller*
boner*, meatmarket person, meat person, processor, skinner*, slaughterer, slayer*; SEE CONCEPT *348*

butcher [v1] *slay and prepare animal for meat*
beef up, carve, clean, cure, cut, cut down, dress, joint, liquidate, salt, slaughter, smoke, stick; SEE CONCEPTS *170,252*

butcher [v2] *ruin*
bollix up*, botch, destroy, goof up*, louse up*, make a mess of*, mutilate, screw up*, spoil, wreck; SEE CONCEPT *101*

butt [n1] *end, shaft*
base, bottom, edge, extremity, fag end, foot, fundament, haft, handle, hilt, shank, stock, stub, stump, tail, tip; SEE CONCEPT *827*

butt/buttocks [n2] *animate rear end*
back end, backside, behind, bottom, bum*, derrière, fanny*, fundament, gluteus maximus, haunches, hindquarters, posterior, rear, rump, seat, tush*; SEE CONCEPT *392*

butt [n3] *object of joking*
chump*, clay pigeon*, derision, dupe*, easy mark*, fall guy, fool, goat, jestee*, joke, laughingstock, mark, patsy, pigeon*, sap, setup*, sitting duck*, softie*, subject, sucker, target, turkey, victim; SEE CONCEPT *423*

butt [n4] *cigarette*
cancer stick*, cig*, coffin nail*, fag*, smoke*, tobacco; SEE CONCEPT *293*

butt [v1] *bang up against with head*
batter, buck, buffet, bump, bunt, collide, gore, hook, horn, jab, knock, poke, prod, punch, push, ram, run into, shove, smack, strike, thrust, toss; SEE CONCEPT *189*

butt [v2] *touch, adjoin*
abut, border, bound, communicate, join, jut, meet, neighbor, project, protrude, verge; SEE CONCEPTS *113,747*

butterfingers [n] *a clumsy person*
bull in a china shop*, bungler, clod, clumsy oaf*, clunker, dolt, duffer*, foozle, fumbler, klutz, lummox, muffer*, schlep; SEE CONCEPTS *412,423*

butt in [v] *meddle*
barge in, bother, burst in, charge in, chisel in*, cut in, disturb, get into the act*, interject, interrupt, intrude, muscle in, pester, poke one's face in*, pry, put one's two cents in*; SEE CONCEPTS *14,159,208,266,384*

button [n1] *fastener*
catch, clasp, fastening, frog, knob, stud; SEE CONCEPTS *445,471*

button [n2] *pushbutton*
adjuster, dial, knob, on/off, power switch, switch, toggle, tuner; SEE CONCEPT *201*

buttress [n] *brace, support*
abutment, column, mainstay, pier, prop, reinforcement, shore, stanchion, stay, strut, underpinning; SEE CONCEPT *440*

buttress [v] *support, bolster*
back up, beef up*, brace, build up, bulwark, carry, jack up, jazz up*, prop, reinforce, shore, step up, strengthen, sustain, uphold; SEE CONCEPT *250*

buxom [adj] *bosomy*
ample, built, busty, chubby, comely, curvaceous, curvy, full-bosomed, full-figured, healthy, hearty, lusty, plump, robust, shapely, stacked*, voluptuous, well-made, well-proportioned, wellrounded, zaftig*; SEE CONCEPT *406*

buy [n] *something purchased*
acquisition, bargain, closeout, deal, good deal, investment, purchase, steal, value; SEE CONCEPT *710*

buy [v1] *purchase*
acquire, bargain for, barter for, contract for, get, get in exchange, go shopping, invest in, market, obtain, pay for, procure, purchase, redeem, score, secure, shop for, sign for, take; SEE CONCEPT *327*

buy [v2] *bribe*
corrupt, fix, grease palm*, have, land, lubricate, oil palm*, ransom, reach, redeem, sop*, square, suborn, tamper; SEE CONCEPTS *192,341*

buyer [n] *someone who purchases*
client, consumer, customer, easy make*, emptor, end user, patron, prospect, purchaser, representative, shopper, sucker*, user, vendee; SEE CONCEPT *348*

buzz [n1] *droning sound*
drone, fizz, fizzle, hiss, hum, murmur, purr, ring, ringing, sibilation, whir, whisper; SEE CONCEPT *595*

buzz [n2] *gossip*
comment, cry, grapevine*, hearsay, news, report, rumble*, rumor, scandal, scuttlebutt, talk, whisper; SEE CONCEPT *274*

buzz [v1] *make droning sound*
bombinate, bumble, drone, fizz, fizzle, hum, murmur, reverberate, ring, sibilate, whir, whisper, whiz; SEE CONCEPT *65*

buzz [v2] *gossip*
call, chatter, inform, natter, rumor, tattle; SEE CONCEPT *60*

buzzword [n] *popular word or phrase*
argot, cant, doublespeak, fuzzword, jargon, lingo, mediaspeak, phraseology, policyspeak, slang; SEE CONCEPT *275*

by [adv] *near*
aside, at hand, away, beyond, close, handy, in reach, over, past, through, to one side; SEE CONCEPT *586*

by [prep1] *next to*
along, alongside, beside, by way of, close to, near, nearby, nigh, over, past, round, via; SEE CONCEPT *586*

by [prep2] *by means of*
at the hand of, in the name of, on, over, supported by, through, through the agency of, through the medium of, under the aegis of, with, with the assistance of; SEE CONCEPT *544*

bygone [adj] *in the past*
ancient, antiquated, archaic, belated, dated, dead, defunct, departed, down memory lane*, erstwhile, extinct, forgotten, former, gone, gone by, in oblivion, late, lost, of old, of yore, olden, oldfangled, old-fashioned, old-time, one-time, outof-date, previous, quondam, sometime, vanished, water over the dam*, water under the bridge*; SEE CONCEPT *820*

by hand [v] *manually*
arduously, laboriously, strenuously, the hard way, tooth and nail; SEE CONCEPT *544*

bu
by

by-product [n] *side product*
after-effect, consequence, fall-out, offshoot, outgrowth, repercussion, result, side effect, spinoff; SEE CONCEPTS *230,260*

bystander [n] *person who watches*
eyewitness, gaper*, kibitzer*, looker-on, observer, onlooker, passerby, spectator, viewer, watcher, witness; SEE CONCEPT *423*

byte [n] *unit of computer memory*
data, eight bits, unit; SEE CONCEPT *274*

byword [n] *saying*
adage, aphorism, apophthegm, axiom, catchphrase, catchword, dictum, epithet, gnome, gnomic saying, handle, maxim, motto, nickname, precept, proverb, saw, shibboleth, slogan, standing joke; SEE CONCEPT *275*

C

cab [n] *car for hire*
carriage, hack, hackney, jitney, taxi, taxicab, tourist car; SEE CONCEPT *505*

cabaret [n] *nightclub with musical performances*
after-hours joint*, bar, café, disco, discothèque, dive, hideaway, hot spot*, nightery, night spot, speakeasy, supper club, tavern, watering hole*; SEE CONCEPTS *447,449*

cabin [n] *tiny house; lodging*
berth, box, caboose, camp, chalet, compartment, cot, cottage, crib, deckhouse, home, hovel, hut, lodge, log house, quarters, room, shack, shanty, shed, shelter; SEE CONCEPT *516*

cabinet [n1] *cupboard for storage*
case, chiffonier, closet, commode, container, depository, dresser, escritoire, locker, repository, wardrobe; SEE CONCEPTS *443,494*

cabinet [n2] *executives serving a leader*
administration, administrators, advisers, assembly, assistants, authority, brain trust*, bureau, bureaucracy, committee, council, counselors, department heads, governing body, government, kitchen cabinet*, ministry, official family; SEE CONCEPT *299*

cabin fever [n] *claustrophobia*
climbing the walls*, distress, neurosis, restlessness, SAD, seasonal affective disorder, temporary insanity, winter blues; SEE CONCEPTS *410,657,748*

cache [n] *hidden supply*
accumulation, assets, drop, drop joint, drop-off, fund, hideout, hiding place, hoard, kitty*, nest egg*, plant, repository, reserve, shade, stake, stash, stockpile, store, storehouse, supplies, treasure, treasury, wealth; SEE CONCEPTS *446,710*

cache [v] *hide a supply of something*
accumulate, bury, conceal, cover, ditch, duck, ensconce, lay away, maintain, park, plant, put away, put in the hole*, save, screen, secrete, squirrel*, squirrel away*, stash, stash away, store; SEE CONCEPT *188*

cackle [n] *a loud laugh*
chortle, chuckle, cluck, crow, gibber, giggle, gobble, guffaw, quack, snicker, snigger, titter; SEE CONCEPT *77*

cackle [v] *laugh irritatingly*
babble, blather, burble, chortle, chuckle, cluck, crow, gibber, giggle, gobble, jabber, quack, snicker, snigger, titter; SEE CONCEPT *77*

cacophonous [adj] *harsh sounding*
clinking, discordant, disharmonic, dissonant, grating, ill-sounding, immusical, inharmonious, jangly, jarring, noisy, raucous, sour, strident, unmusical; SEE CONCEPTS *592,594*

cad [n] *sly, dastardly person*
boor, bounder*, clown, creep, cur*, dog*, heel, louse, lout, rake, rascal, rat*, rotter*, rounder*, scoundrel, stinker, worm; SEE CONCEPT *412*

cadaver [n] *dead body*
body, cage, carcass, corpse, deceased, mort*, remains, skeleton, stiff*; SEE CONCEPT *390*

cadaverous [adj] *pale, corpselike*
ashen, bag of bones, blanched, bloodless, consumptive, dead, deathlike, deathly, emaciated, exsanguinous, gaunt, ghastly, ghostly, haggard, pallid, peaked, peaky, sallow, shadowy, sick, skeletal, skeletonlike, skin and bones*, spectral, thin, wan, wasted; SEE CONCEPTS *406,491,618*

cadence [n] *rhythm*
accent, beat, count, inflection, intonation, lilt, measure, meter, modulation, pulse, rhythmus, swing, tempo, throb; SEE CONCEPT *65*

cadre [n] *nucleus of effort*
core, force, framework, infrastructure, key group, officers, organization, personnel, staff; SEE CONCEPTS *417,432*

café [n] *small, informal restaurant*
bistro, burger joint, cafeteria, cake shop, chophouse, coffee bar, coffee shop, diner, eating house, grease joint*, greasy spoon*, hash house*, luncheonette, lunchroom, noshery*, pit stop*, quick-lunch, snack bar, soup house, tearoom; SEE CONCEPT *449*

cafeteria [n] *restaurant*
café, commissary, lunch counter, lunchroom, snack bar, tea room; SEE CONCEPT *449*

cage [n] *enclosure with bars*
coop, corral, crate, enclosure, fold, jail, mew, pen, pinfold, pound; SEE CONCEPT *494*

cage [v] *hold in enclosure*
close in, confine, coop up, enclose, envelop, fence in, hem, immure, impound, imprison, incarcerate, jail, lock up, mew, pen, restrain, shut in, shut up; SEE CONCEPT *191*

cagey [adj] *tricky*
cagey, careful, circumspect, crafty, cunning, leery, secretive, shrewd, sly, wary, wily; SEE CONCEPTS *401,545*

cahoots [n] *conspiracy*
alliance, collusion, league, partnership; SEE CONCEPTS *114,660*

cajole [v] *attempt to coax; flatter*
apple polish*, argue into, banter, beguile, blandish*, bootlick*, brownnose*, build up, butter up*, con, crowd, deceive, decoy, delude, dupe, entice, entrap, get around, get next to*, hand a line*, induce, influence, inveigle, jolly, lay it on thick*, lure, make up to, maneuver, massage, mislead, oil*, play up to, push, rub the right way*, seduce, snow*, soap*, soften, soft-soap*, spread it on*, stroke, suck up to*, sweeten up*, sweet-talk*, tantalize, tempt, urge, wheedle, work on, work over*; SEE CONCEPTS *59,68,75*

cake [*n*] *bar of something*
block, brick, loaf, lump, mass, slab; SEE CONCEPT *470*

calamitous [*adj*] *disastrous; tragic*
adverse, afflictive, blighting, cataclysmic, catastrophic, deadly, deplorable, devastating, dire, fatal, grievous, harmful, heartbreaking, lamentable, messy, pernicious, regrettable, ruinous, unfavorable, unfortunate, woeful; SEE CONCEPT *537*

calamity [*n*] *disaster; tragedy*
adversity, affliction, blue ruin*, cataclysm, catastrophe, collapse, cross, curtains, distress, downfall, hardship, holy mess*, misadventure, mischance, misfortune, mishap, reverse, ruin, scourge, the worst*, trial, tribulation, unholy mess*, visitation, waterloo*, woe, wreck, wretchedness; SEE CONCEPTS *674,675*

calculable [*adj*] *able to be computed or estimated*
accountable, ascertainable, computable, countable, discoverable, estimable, foreseeable, measurable, predictable, reckonable; SEE CONCEPTS *402,762*

calculate [*v1*] *compute or estimate amount*
account, add, adjust, appraise, assay, cast, cipher, consider, count, determine, divide, dope out*, enumerate, figure, forecast, foretell, gauge, guess, judge, keep tabs*, measure, multiply, number, rate, reckon, size up, subtract, sum, take account of, tally, tot, tote up*, value, weigh, work out; SEE CONCEPT *764*

calculate [*v2*] *plan on*
aim, anticipate, assume, bank on, build, count on, depend on, design, intend, judge, plan, reckon, rely on, suppose, think likely, trust; SEE CONCEPTS *26,36*

calculating [*adj*] *scheming to manipulate*
artful, canny, careful, cautious, chary, circumspect, considerate, contriving, crafty, cunning, designing, devious, discreet, gingerly, guarded, guileful, intelligent, Machiavellian, manipulative, politic, premeditating, safe, scheming, sharp, shrewd, sly, wary, wily; SEE CONCEPTS *401,403*

calculation [*n1*] *computing, estimating amount*
adding, arithmetic, ciphering, computation, counting, dividing, estimate, estimation, figuring, forecast, judgment, multiplying, prediction, reckoning, subtracting, summation, totaling; SEE CONCEPTS *28,764*

calculation [*n2*] *computed or estimated amount*
answer, computation, divination, estimate, estimation, figuring, forecast, judgment, prediction, prognosis, prognostication, reckoning, reply; SEE CONCEPT *787*

calculation [*n3*] *forethought*
canniness, caution, circumspection, contrivance, deliberation, discretion, foresight, planning, precaution, prudence, thought; SEE CONCEPT *660*

calculator [*n*] *adding machine*
computer, number cruncher*, PDA, personal digital assistant; SEE CONCEPTS *269,463*

calendar [*n*] *schedule of events*
agenda, almanac, annal, bulletin, card, chronology, daybook, diary, docket, journal, lineup, list, log, logbook, menology, pipeline, program, record, register, sked, system of reckoning, tab, table, time, timetable; SEE CONCEPTS *274,281,809*

calf [*n1*] *leg between knee and ankle*
foreleg, shin; SEE CONCEPT *392*

calf [*n2*] *baby cow*
dogie, freemartin, heifer, maverick, veal, yearling, young bull, young cow; SEE CONCEPT *394*

caliber [*n1*] *capacity; character*
ability, appetency, capability, competence, constitution, dignity, distinction, endowment, essence, faculty, force, gifts, habilitation, merit, nature, parts, power, quality, scope, stature, strength, talent, value, virtue, worth, worthiness; SEE CONCEPT *411*

caliber [*n2*] *size of ammunition*
bore, class, diameter, gauge, grade, length, measure, measurement, quality, striking power, weight; SEE CONCEPT *730*

call [*n1*] *yelled statement*
alarm, calling, command, cry, hail, holler*, scream, shout, signal, whoop, yawp, yell; SEE CONCEPT *278*

call [*n2*] *demand, announcement*
appeal, bidding, command, invitation, notice, order, plea, proposal, request, solicitation, subpoena, summons, supplication, visit; SEE CONCEPT *53*

call [*n3*] *need, cause for action*
claim, excuse, grounds, justification, necessity, obligation, occasion, reason, right, urge; SEE CONCEPT *709*

call [*n4*] *normal sound of animal*
cheep, chirp, cry, note, peep, roar, shriek, song, tweet, twitter, warble; SEE CONCEPT *64*

call [*v1*] *yell declaration*
announce, arouse, awaken, bawl, bellow, cry, cry out, exclaim, hail, holler*, hoot, howl, proclaim, roar, rouse, scream, screech, shout, shriek, vociferate, waken, whoop, yawp*, yoo hoo*, yowl; SEE CONCEPTS *47,266*

call [*v2*] *arrange meeting*
ask, assemble, bid, collect, contact, convene, convoke, gather, invite, muster, phone*, rally, request, ring up, subpoena, summon, telephone; SEE CONCEPT *114*

call [*v3*] *entitle*
address, baptize, christen, denominate, describe as, designate, dub, label, name, style, term, title; SEE CONCEPT *62*

call [*v4*] *demand or announce action*
appeal to, appoint, ask, challenge, charge, claim, command, declare, decree, elect, entreat, exact, ordain, order, postulate, pray to, proclaim, require, requisition, set apart, solicit, summon; SEE CONCEPT *53*

call [*v5*] *estimate, consider*
adumbrate, approximate, augur, forecast, foretell, guess, judge, make rough guess, place, portend, predict, presage, prognosticate, prophesy, put, reckon, regard, think, vaticinate; SEE CONCEPTS *28,70*

call [*v6*] *attempt to communicate by telephone*
beep, blast*, bleep, buzz, contact, get back to*, phone, ring, telephone; SEE CONCEPTS *74,266*

call [*v7*] *visit at residence or business*
come by, come over, crash, drop by, drop in, fall by, fall down, hit, look in on, look up, play, pop in*, run in, see, stop by, stop in, swing by; SEE CONCEPT *227*

call for [*v*] *demand; entail*
ask for, inquire, involve, lack, necessitate, need,

occasion, request, require, suggest, want; SEE CONCEPT *646*

calling [*n*] *chosen profession*
art, business, career, craft, day gig*, do*, dodge*, employment, gig*, go*, handicraft, hang*, life's work, lifework, line, métier, mission, nine-to-five*, occupation, play, province, pursuit, racket*, rat race*, slot*, swindle*, trade, vocation, walk of life, work; SEE CONCEPT *360*

call off [*v*] *discontinue*
abandon, abort, break off, cancel, desist, drop, kill*, postpone, scrub*, withdraw; SEE CONCEPTS *18,211,234*

callous [*adj*] *cruel, insensitive*
apathetic, blind to, careless, case-hardened, cold, cold-blooded, deaf to, hard, hard-bitten, hard-boiled, hardened, hardhearted, heartless, impassive, impenitent, indifferent, indurated, inflexible, insensate, insensible, insensitive, insentient, inured, obdurate, soulless, spiritless, stiff, stony, stubborn, thick-skinned, torpid, tough, toughened, unaffected, unbending, uncaring, uncompassionate, unconcerned, unfeeling, unimpressionable, unresponsive, unsusceptible, unsympathetic; SEE CONCEPT *404*

callow [*adj*] *immature*
crude, green, guileless, inexperienced, infant, jejune, jellybean*, juvenile, kid, low tech*, naive, not dry behind ears*, puerile, raw, sophomore, tenderfoot, unbaked, unfledged, unripe, unsophisticated, untrained, untried, young; SEE CONCEPTS *578,678,797*

calm [*adj1*] *peaceful, quiet (inanimate)*
at a standstill, at peace, bland, bucolic, cool, halcyon, harmonious, hushed, inactive, in order, low-key, mild, motionless, pacific, pastoral, placid, quiescent, reposeful, reposing, restful, rural, serene, slow, smooth, soothing, still, stormless, tranquil, undisturbed, unruffled, waveless, windless; SEE CONCEPTS *544,705*

calm [*adj2*] *composed, cool (animate)*
aloof, amiable, amicable, civil, collected, cool as cucumber*, cool-headed, detached, disinterested, dispassionate, equable, gentle, impassive, imperturbable, inscrutable, kind, laid-back*, levelheaded, listless, moderate, neutral, patient, placid, pleased, poised, relaxed, restful, satisfied, sedate, self-possessed, serene, still, temperate, unconcerned, undisturbed, unemotional, unexcitable, unexcited, unflappable, unimpressed, unmoved, unruffled, untroubled; SEE CONCEPTS *401,404*

calm [*n*] *quietness, composure*
calmness, dispassion, doldrums, hush, impassivity, imperturbation, lull, patience, peace, peacefulness, peace of mind, placidity, quiet, repose, rest, restraint, serenity, silence, stillness, stoicism, tranquility; SEE CONCEPTS *388,411,720*

calm [*v*] *make composed, quiet*
allay, alleviate, appease, assuage, balm, becalm, compose, cool, cool it*, cool out*, hush, lay back*, lull, mitigate, mollify, pacify, placate, quiet, quieten, relax, relieve, sedate, settle, simmer down, soft-pedal*, soothe, steady, still, stroke, take it easy*, take the edge off*, tranquilize; SEE CONCEPT *231*

camaraderie [*n*] *friendship*
cheer, companionability, companionship, comradeship, conviviality, esprit de corps, fellow-

ship, gregariousness, intimacy, jollity, sociability, togetherness; SEE CONCEPT *388*

camera [*n*] *photographic equipment*
camcorder, Kodak*, 35mm, Polaroid*, video camera; SEE CONCEPTS *446,463*

camouflage [*n*] *disguise*
beard*, blind, cloak, concealment, cover, coverup, deceit, deceptive marking, dissimulation, faking, false appearance, front, guise, mask, masking, masquerade, mimicry, paint, plain brown wrapper*, protective coloring, red herring*, screen, shade, shroud, smokescreen, veil; SEE CONCEPT *260*

camouflage [*v*] *disguise, cover*
beard*, becloud, befog, cloak, conceal, cover up, deceive, dim, dissemble, dissimulate, dress up, hide, mask, obfuscate, obscure, screen, throw on makeup, veil; SEE CONCEPTS *172,188*

camp [*adj*] *consciously affecting the unfashionable, weird, or bizarre*
affected, arch, artificial, avant-garde, Daliesque*, far out*, in*, mannered, mod, ostentatious, pop, posturing, wild; SEE CONCEPT *544*

camp [*n*] *site for outdoor living*
bivouac, campfire, campground, camping ground, caravansary, chalet, cottage, encampment, hut, lean-to, lodge, log cabin, shack, shanty, shed, summer home, tent, tent city, tepee, tilt, wigwam; SEE CONCEPTS *198,516*

campaign [*n*] *attempt to win; attack*
crusade, drive, expedition, fight, movement, offensive, operation, push, warfare; SEE CONCEPTS *87,320*

campaign [*v*] *attempt to win political election*
agitate, barnstorm, canvass, contend for, contest, crusade, electioneer, go to grass roots*, hit the trail*, lobby, mend fences*, muckrake, mudsling*, politick, press the flesh*, ring doorbells*, run, run for, shake hands and kiss babies*, solicit votes, stand for, stump*, tour, whistle-stop*; SEE CONCEPT *300*

camper [*n*] *mobile home*
recreational vehicle, RV, tin can*, Winnebago*; SEE CONCEPT *503*

campus [*n*] *school grounds*
dorm, grounds, quad, quadrangle, square, yard; SEE CONCEPT *509*

can [*n1*] *container, usually metallic*
aluminum, bottle, bucket, canister, cannikin, gunboat*, gutbucket*, jar, package, pop top*, receptacle, tin, vessel; SEE CONCEPTS *476,494*

can [*n2*] *toilet*
head*, john*, johnny*, latrine, lavatory, litter box*, outhouse, pot*, potty*, privy, restroom, sandbox*, throne*, washroom, water closet; SEE CONCEPT *443*

can [*n3*] *buttocks*
backside, behind, butt*, derrière, fanny*, fundament, gluteus maximus, hind end, posterior, rump, seat, tush*; SEE CONCEPT *418*

can [*v1*] *preserve fruit, vegetable*
bottle, keep, put up; SEE CONCEPT *170*

can [*v2*] *be able*
be capable of, be equal to, be up to, be within one's area, be within one's control, can do*, commit, could, cut the mustard*, have it made*, lie in one's power, make it*, make out, make the grade*, manage, may, take care of; SEE CONCEPT *630*

can [v3] *fire from job*
ax*, boot*, bounce*, cashier, discharge, dismiss, expel, give the heave ho*, kick out*, let go, sack*, terminate; SEE CONCEPT *351*

canal [n] *waterway*
aqueduct, bottleneck, channel, choke point, conduit, course, cove, ditch, duct, estuary, firth, trench, water, watercourse; SEE CONCEPT *514*

cancel [v1] *call off; erase*
abolish, abort, abrogate, annul, ax, black out, blot out, break, break off, countermand, cross out, cut, deface, delete, destroy, do away with, do in, efface, eliminate, eradicate, expunge, finish off*, go back on one's word*, kill, obliterate, off*, omit, quash, remove, render invalid, repeal, repudiate, rescind, revoke, rub out, scratch out, scrub*, sink*, smash, squash, stamp across, strike out, torpedo*, total*, trash*, trim*, undo, wash out*, wipe out*, wipe slate clean*, X-out*, zap*; SEE CONCEPTS *18,211,234*

cancel [v2] *equal out*
abort, abrogate, annul, balance out, call off, compensate for, counteract, counterbalance, countercheck, countermand, counterpoise, declare invalid, discard, discharge, frustrate, ignore, invalidate, make up for, negate, neutralize, nullify, offset, overthrow, put an end to, recall, recant, redeem, redress, refute, render inert, render null and void, repeal, repudiate, rescind, retract, revoke, rule out, set aside, suppress, vacate, void; SEE CONCEPTS *232,667*

cancellation [n] *calling off; erasure*
abandoning, abandonment, abolishing, abolition, abrogation, annulment, canceling, deletion, dissolution, dissolving, elimination, invalidating, invalidation, nullification, overruling, quashing, recall, recalling, repeal, repudiation, retirement, retracting, retraction, reversal, reversing, revocation, revoking, undoing, withdrawing; SEE CONCEPT *119*

cancer [n] *malignant growth*
big C*, C*, canker, carcinoma, corruption, disease, long illness, malignancy, sickness, tumor; SEE CONCEPT *306*

candid [adj] *honest*
aboveboard, bluff, blunt, equal, equitable, fair, forthright, frank, free, frontal, genuine, guileless, impartial, ingenuous, just, objective, open, outspoken, plain, right up front*, scrupulous, sincere, straightforward, talking turkey*, telling it like it is*, truthful, unbiased, uncolored, unequivocal, unprejudiced, unpretended, up front*, upright; SEE CONCEPT *267*

candidate [n] *person desiring political office, job*
applicant, aspirant, bidder, claimant, competitor, contender, contestant, dark horse*, entrant, favorite son*, handshaker*, hopeful*, job-hunter, nominee, office-seeker, petitioner, possibility, possible choice, pothunter*, runner, seeker, solicitant, stumper*, successor, suitor, whistle-stopper*, write-in*; SEE CONCEPT *359*

candlestick [n] *holder for candles*
candelabra, candelabrum, menorah, pricket, sconce, taper holder; SEE CONCEPT *444*

candor [n] *complete honesty*
artlessness, directness, fairness, forthrightness, frankness, glasnost, guilelessness, honesty, impartiality, ingenuousness, naïveté, openness, outspokenness, probity, simplicity, sincerity, straightforwardness, truthfulness, unequivocalness, uprightness, veracity; SEE CONCEPT *411*

candy [n] *confection*
bonbon, confectionery, confit, hokum*, jawbreaker*, sweet, sweetmeat; SEE CONCEPT *457*

cane [n] *stick to aid walking of disabled*
pikestaff, pole, rod, staff, vade mecum, walking stick; SEE CONCEPT *479*

canker [n] *blistered infection*
bane, blight, blister, boil, cancer, corrosion, corruption, lesion, rot, scourge, smutch, sore, ulcer; SEE CONCEPT *306*

canker [v] *blight, corrupt*
animalize, bestialize, consume, corrode, debase, debauch, demoralize, deprave, embitter, envenom, inflict, pervert, poison, pollute, rot, ruin, scourge, sore, stain, ulcer, vitiate; SEE CONCEPT *240*

cannibal [n] *beast, beastlike human*
aborigine, anthrophagite, anthropophaginian, anthropophagus, brute, bush dweller, cruel person, head-hunter, ogre, ogress, primitive, ruffian, savage; SEE CONCEPT *412*

cannon [n] *large gun*
Big Bertha*, heavy artillery, howitzer, Long Tom*, mortar, ordnance; SEE CONCEPT *500*

canny [adj] *clever, artful*
able, acute, adroit, astute, cagey, careful, cautious, circumspect, cunning, dexterous, discreet, foxy*, frugal, having fancy footwork*, hep*, ingenious, intelligent, judicious, knowing, nimble-witted, perspicacious, prudent, quick, quick-witted, sagacious, shrewd, skillful, slick, slippery*, sly, smart, smooth*, street smart*, streetwise*, subtle, wary, watchful, wise, with it*, worldly-wise; SEE CONCEPT *402*

canoe [n] *light, paddled boat*
coracle, dugout, kayak, outrigger, piragua, pirogue; SEE CONCEPT *506*

can of worms [n] *troublesome problem*
complication, difficulty, entanglement, Gordian knot, hot water*, Pandora's box, predicament, quagmire, quandary, trouble; SEE CONCEPTS *532,674,690*

canon [n1] *rule, edict*
assize, catalogue, command, commandment, criterion, declaration, decree, decretum, dictate, doctrine, dogma, formula, law, list, maxim, order, ordinance, precept, principle, regulation, roll, screed, standard, statute, table, tenet, touchstone, yardstick; SEE CONCEPTS *318,688*

canon [n2] *a body of the most important, influential or superior works in music, literature, or art*
ana, analects, anthology, chrestomathy, classics, collected works, delectus, library, miscellanea, oeuvre, works; SEE CONCEPTS *280,432*

canonical [adj] *accepted, recognized*
approved, authoritative, authorized, lawful, legal, official, orthodox, received, sanctioned, sound, statutory; SEE CONCEPTS *319,535*

canonize [v] *sanctify; idolize*
apotheosize, beatify, besaint, bless, consecrate, dedicate, deify, glorify, idolatrize, love, put on a pedestal*, saint, worship; SEE CONCEPTS *32,367*

canopy [n] *overhanging covering*
awning, baldachin, cover, marquee, shade, sunshade, umbrella; SEE CONCEPTS *440,444*

cant [n1] *hypocritical statement*
affected piety, deceit, dishonesty, humbug, hypocrisy, hypocriticalness, insincerity, lip ser-

ca
ca

vice*, pecksniffery, pharisaicalness, pious platitudes, pomposity, pretense, pretentiousness, sanctimoniousness, sanctimony, sham holiness, show; SEE CONCEPT 63

cant [n2] *jargon*
argot, dialect, diction, idiom, language, lingo, patois, patter, phraseology, slang, vernacular, vocabulary; SEE CONCEPTS 275,278

cant [v] *lean, slant*
angle, bevel, careen, grade, heel, incline, list, recline, rise, slope, tilt, tip; SEE CONCEPTS 154,201

cantankerous [adj] *difficult, crabby*
bad-tempered, bearish, captious, choleric, contrary, cranky, critical, cross, crotchety*, crusty*, disagreeable, dour, grouchy*, grumpy*, huffy*, ill-humored, ill-natured, irascible, irritable, morose, obstinate, ornery*, peevish, perverse, petulant, prickly, quarrelsome, snappish, sour, stuffy*, testy, vinegarish, vinegary; SEE CONCEPT 401

canteen [n1] *portable kitchen*
chuck wagon, mobile kitchen, snack bar, snack shop; SEE CONCEPT 449

canteen [n2] *container for liquids, used in travels*
bota, bottle, flacon, flask, flasket, jug, thermos, water bottle; SEE CONCEPT 494

canvas [n1] *coarse material*
awning cloth, duck, fly, sailcloth, shade, tarp, tarpaulin, tenting; SEE CONCEPT 473

canvas [n2] *painting on coarse material*
art, artwork, oil, picture, piece, portrait, still life, watercolor; SEE CONCEPT 259

canvass [v] *poll; discuss issues*
agitate, analyze, apply, argue, campaign, check, check over, consult, debate, dispute, electioneer, examine, inspect, investigate, review, run, scan, scrutinize, sift, solicit, study, survey, ventilate; SEE CONCEPTS 24,48,56,300

canyon [n] *gulf in mountain area*
coulee, glen, gorge, gulch, gully, ravine, valley; SEE CONCEPTS 509,513

cap [n] *small hat*
beanie*, beret, bonnet, dink*, fez, pillbox, skullcap, tam, tam o'shanter; SEE CONCEPT 450

cap [v] *outdo a performance*
beat, best, better, button down*, button up*, can*, clinch*, cob*, complete, cover, crest, crown, do to a T*, eclipse, exceed, excel, finish, outshine, outstrip, pass, put the lid on*, surmount, surpass, top, top it off*, transcend, trump, wrap up*; SEE CONCEPT 141

capability [n] *ability to perform*
adequacy, aptitude, art, capacity, competence, craft, cunning, effectiveness, efficacy, efficiency, facility, faculty, means, might, potency, potential, potentiality, power, proficiency, qualification, qualifiedness, skill, wherewithal; SEE CONCEPT 630

capable [adj] *able to perform*
able, accomplished, adapted, adept, adequate, apt, au fait, clever, competent, dynamite, efficient, experienced, fireball*, fitted, gifted, good, green thumb*, has what it takes*, having knowhow*, having the goods*, having the right stuff*, intelligent, knowing the ropes*, knowing the score*, like a one-man band*, like a pistol*, masterly, old hand*, old-timer*, on the ball*, proficient, proper, qualified, skillful, suited, talented, there*, up*, up to it*, up to snuff*, up to speed*, veteran; SEE CONCEPT 527

capacious [adj] *ample, extensive*
abundant, broad, comfortable, commodious, comprehensive, dilatable, distensible, expandable, expansive, extended, generous, liberal, plentiful, roomy, sizable, spacious, substantial, vast, voluminous, wide; SEE CONCEPTS 481,772,773,774

capacity [n1] *volume; limit of volume held*
accommodation, amplitude, bulk, burden, compass, contents, dimensions, expanse, extent, full, holding ability, holding power, latitude, magnitude, mass, measure, proportions, quantity, range, reach, retention, room, scope, size, space, spread, standing room only*, sufficiency, sweep; SEE CONCEPTS 736,774,794

capacity [n2] *ability; competency*
adequacy, aptitude, aptness, bent, brains, caliber, capability, cleverness, compass, competence, efficiency, facility, faculty, forte, genius, gift, inclination, intelligence, knack, might, power, qualification, readiness, skill, stature, strength, talent, the goods*, up to it*, what it takes*; SEE CONCEPTS 409,630

cape [n1] *promontory into water*
arm, beak, bill, chersonese, finger, foreland, head, headland, jetty, jutty, mole, naze, neck, ness, peninsula, point, tongue; SEE CONCEPTS 509,514

cape [n2] *sleeveless coat*
bertha, capote, cardinal, cloak, cope, dolman, fichu, gabardine, manteau, mantelletta, mantilla, mantle, overdress, paletot, pelerine, pelisse, poncho, shawl, tabard, talma, tippet, Vandyke, victorine, wrap, wrapper; SEE CONCEPT 451

caper [n] *antic, lark*
escapade, gag*, gambol, high jinks*, hop, hot foot*, jest, joke, jump, leap, mischief, monkeyshines*, practical joke, prank, put on*, revel, rib*, rollick, shenanigan*, sport, stunt, tomfoolery*, trick; SEE CONCEPT 386

caper [v] *frolic, cavort*
blow the lid off*, bounce, bound, cut capers*, cut loose*, dance, frisk, gambol, go on a tear*, hop, horse around*, jump, kick up one's heels*, leap, let loose*, play, raise hell*, rollick, romp, skip, spring, whoop it up*; SEE CONCEPT 384

capital [adj1] *main, essential*
basic, cardinal, central, chief, controlling, dominant, first, foremost, fundamental, important, leading, major, number one*, outstanding, overruling, paramount, predominant, preeminent, primary, prime, principal, prominent, underlying, vital; SEE CONCEPTS 546,568,829

capital [adj2] *superior*
best, champion, choice, crack, dandy, delightful, deluxe, excellent, famous, fine, first, first-class*, first-rate*, five-star*, fly, great, prime, splendid, superb, top, top-notch*, world-class*; SEE CONCEPT 574

capital [n1] *financial assets*
business, cash, CD, estate, finances, financing, fortune, funds, gold, interests, investment, IRA, kitty*, means, money, nest egg*, principal, property, resources, savings, stake, stock, substance, treasure, ways and means*, wealth, wherewithal; SEE CONCEPTS 332,710

capital [n2] *city of governmental seat*
control, county seat, metropolis, municipality, political front, principal city, the Hill*; SEE CONCEPTS 507,512

capital [n3] *upper case written symbol*
cap, initial, majuscule, small cap, uncial; SEE CONCEPT *284*

capitalism [n] *economic system of private ownership*
commercialism, competition, democracy, free enterprise, free market, industrialism, laissez faire economics, mercantilism, private enterprise; SEE CONCEPTS *299,689,770*

capitalist [n] *person engaged in private ownership of business*
backer, banker, bourgeois, businessperson, entrepreneur, financier, investor, landowner, moneybags*, one who signs the checks*, plutocrat, the boss*, the money*; SEE CONCEPT *347*

capitalize [v] *benefit from situation*
avail oneself of, exploit, gain, make capital of, obtain, profit, realize, subsidize, take advantage of; SEE CONCEPT *120*

capitol [n] *building or buildings housing chief governmental offices*
Capitol Hill, center, dome, legislative hall, political scene*, seat of government, statehouse; SEE CONCEPTS *299,449*

capitulate [v] *give in*
bow, buckle under, cave in, cede, come across, come to terms, concede, defer, fold, give away the store*, give out, give up, knuckle under, put out, relent, submit, succumb, surrender, yield; SEE CONCEPTS *35,83*

capitulation [n] *giving in*
accedence, bowing, buckling, conceding, giving up, knuckling under, relenting, resignation, submission, succumbing, surrender, yielding; SEE CONCEPTS *83,410*

caprice [n] *sudden change of behavior*
bee*, caper*, changeableness, contrariety, crotchet, fad, fancy, fickleness, fitfulness, fool notion*, freak, gag*, humor, impulse, inconsistency, inconstancy, jerk, kink, mood, notion, peculiarity, perversity, put on*, quirk, rib*, temper, thought, vagary, vein, whim, whimsy; SEE CONCEPTS *13,410*

capricious [adj] *given to sudden behavior change*
any way the wind blows*, arbitrary, blowing hot and cold*, careless, changeful, contrary, crotchety, effervescent, erratic, every which way*, fanciful, fickle, fitful, flaky*, flighty, freakish, gaga*, helter-skelter*, humorsome, impulsive, inconstant, kinky*, lubricious, mercurial, moody, mutable, notional, odd, picky*, punchy*, queer, quirky, temperamental, ticklish, unpredictable, unreasonable, unstable, up and down*, vagarious, variable, volatile, wayward, whimsical, yo-yo*; SEE CONCEPT *401*

capsize [v] *overturn*
invert, keel over, roll, tip over, turn over, turn turtle*, upset; SEE CONCEPTS *150,152*

capsule [adj] *shortened form*
abridged, canned, condensed, epitomized, pocket, potted, tabloid; SEE CONCEPTS *531,773*

capsule [n] *tablet, usually medicine*
bolus, cap, dose, lozenge, pellet, pill, troche; SEE CONCEPTS *260,307*

captain [n] *chief of vehicle, effort*
authority, boss, cap, CEO, CFO, chieftain, commander, director, exec*, executive, four-striper*, guide, head, head honcho*, higher up*, leader, master, mistress, number one*, officer, operator, owner, pilot, royalty, skip*, skipper*, top*, top dog*; SEE CONCEPT *347*

caption [n] *heading; short description*
explanation, head, inscription, legend, rubric, subtitle, title, underline; SEE CONCEPT *283*

captious [adj] *very critical*
acrimonious, cantankerous, carping, caviling, cavillous, censorious, contrary, crabby, cross, demanding, deprecating, disparaging, exacting, exceptive, fault-finding, finicky, hypercritical, irritable, nagging, nit-picking, overcritical, peevish, perverse, petulant, sarcastic, severe, testy, touchy; SEE CONCEPTS *267,404*

captivate [v] *attract, enchant*
allure, beguile, bewitch, charm, dazzle, delight, draw, enamour, enrapture, enslave, ensnare, entertain, enthrall, entrance, fascinate, gratify, grip, hold, hook, hypnotize, infatuate, intrigue, lure, magnetize, make a hit with*, mesmerize, please, rope in*, seduce, spellbind, sweep off one's feet*, take, turn one on, vamp, wile, win; SEE CONCEPTS *7,22*

captive [adj1] *physically held by force*
bound, caged, confined, enslaved, ensnared, imprisoned, incarcerated, incommunicado, in custody, jailed, locked up, penned, restricted, subjugated, under lock and key*; SEE CONCEPTS *536,554*

captive [adj2] *mentally enchanted, held*
beguiled, bewitched, charmed, delighted, enraptured, enthralled, fascinated, hypnotized, infatuated; SEE CONCEPT *403*

captive [n] *person held physically*
bondman, bondservant, bondwoman, con, convict, detainee, hostage, internee, prisoner, prisoner of war, slave; SEE CONCEPTS *412,423*

captivity [n] *physical detention by force*
bondage, committal, confinement, constraint, custody, durance, duress, enslavement, enthrallment, entombment, impoundment, imprisonment, incarceration, internment, jail, limbo, restraint, serfdom, servitude, slavery, subjection, thralldom, vassalage; SEE CONCEPTS *191,652*

capture [n] *catching, forceful holding*
abduction, acquirement, acquisition, apprehension, appropriating, appropriation, arrest, bag*, bust*, catch, collar, commandeering, confiscation, drop*, ensnaring, fall, gaining, grab*, grasping, hit the jackpot*, hook*, imprisonment, knock off*, laying hold of*, nab*, nail*, obtaining, occupation, pick up*, pinch*, pull*, run in*, securing, seizing, seizure, snatching*, sweep*, taking, taking captive, taking into custody, trapping, trip, winning; SEE CONCEPT *90*

capture [v] *catch and forcefully hold*
apprehend, arrest, bag*, bust*, catch, collar, conquer, cop, gain control, get, grab*, hook*, land, nab*, nail*, net, occupy, overwhelm, pick up*, pinch*, prehend, pull in, put the cuffs on*, round up*, run in*, secure, seize, snare, snatch, take, take captive, take into custody, take prisoner, trap, tumble; SEE CONCEPT *90*

car [n] *vehicle driven on streets*
auto, automobile, bucket*, buggy*, bus, clunker*, compact, convertible, conveyance, coupe, gas guzzler*, hardtop, hatchback, heap*, jalopy*, jeep, junker*, limousine, machine, motor, motorcar, pickup, ride*, roadster, sedan, station wagon, subcompact, touring car, truck, van, wagon, wheels*, wreck*; SEE CONCEPT *505*

ca
ca

caravan [n] *group traveling together*
band, camel train, campers, cavalcade, convoy, expedition, procession, safari, train, troop; SEE CONCEPTS *432,503*

carbohydrate [n] *organic compound composed of carbon, hydrogen, and oxygen*
cellulose, dextrin, dextrose, disaccharide, fructose, galactose, glucose, glycogen, lactose, maltose, monosaccharide, polysaccharide, starch, sucrose, sugar; SEE CONCEPT *478*

carcass/carcase [n] *dead body; framework, base structure*
body, cadaver, corpse, framework, hulk, mort*, remains, shell, skeleton, stiff*; SEE CONCEPTS *390,434*

carcinogen [n] *cancer-causing agent*
deadly chemical, health hazard, killer*, mutagen, poison, toxin; SEE CONCEPT *675*

card [n] *piece of paper, often with purposeful writing*
agenda, badge, billet, calendar, cardboard, check, docket, fiberboard, identification, label, pass, poster, program, schedule, sheet, square, tally, ticket, timetable, voucher; SEE CONCEPTS *260,271*

cardiac arrest [n] *heart stoppage*
coronary thrombosis, heart attack, heart failure, myocardial infarction; SEE CONCEPT *308*

cardinal [adj] *important, key*
basal, basic, central, chief, constitutive, essential, first, foremost, fundamental, greatest, highest, indispensable, leading, main, overriding, overruling, paramount, pivotal, preeminent, primary, prime, principal, ruling, vital; SEE CONCEPTS *568,574*

care [n1] *personal interest, concern*
affliction, aggravation, alarm, anguish, annoyance, anxiety, apprehension, bother, burden, chagrin, charge, consternation, discomposure, dismay, disquiet, distress, disturbance, encumbrance, exasperation, fear, foreboding, fretfulness, handicap, hardship, hindrance, impediment, incubus, load, misgiving, nuisance, onus, oppression, perplexity, pressure, responsibility, solicitude, sorrow, stew, strain, stress, sweat, tribulation, trouble, uneasiness, unhappiness, vexation, woe, worry; SEE CONCEPTS *410,532*

care [n2] *carefulness, attention to detail*
alertness, caution, circumspection, concentration, concern, conscientiousness, consideration, diligence, direction, discrimination, effort, enthusiasm, exactness, exertion, fastidiousness, forethought, heed, interest, management, meticulousness, nicety, pains, particularity, precaution, prudence, regard, scrupulousness, solicitude, thought, trouble, vigilance, wariness, watchfulness; SEE CONCEPT *657*

care [n3] *custody of person, usually child*
administration, aegis, auspices, charge, control, direction, guardianship, keeping, management, ministration, protection, safekeeping, superintendence, supervision, trust, tutelage, ward, wardship; SEE CONCEPTS *285,295,388*

care [v1] *tend to*
attend, baby sit, consider, foster, keep an eye on*, keep tabs on*, look after, mind, mind the store*, minister, mother, nurse, nurture, pay attention to, protect, provide for, ride herd on*, sit,

take pains, tend, treasure, wait on, watch, watch over; SEE CONCEPTS *110,295*

care [v2] *regard highly*
be crazy about*, be fond of*, cherish, desire, enjoy, find congenial, hold dear, like, love, prize, respect, take to, want; SEE CONCEPTS *20,32*

careen [v] *tilt; move wildly down path*
bend, lean, lurch, pitch, sway, tilt; SEE CONCEPT *147*

career [n1] *occupation*
bag*, calling, course, dodge*, employment, field, game*, job, lifework, livelihood, number*, pilgrimage, profession, pursuit, racket*, specialty, thing*, vocation, work; SEE CONCEPTS *349,360*

career [n2] *course, path*
course, orbit, passage, pilgrimage, procedure, progress, race, walk; SEE CONCEPTS *501,678,692*

carefree [adj] *lighthearted, untroubled*
airy, at ease, blithe, breezy, buoyant, calm, careless, cheerful, cheery, cool, easy, easy-going, feelgood*, happy, happy-go-lucky, insouciant, jaunty, jovial, laid back*, radiant, secure, sunny, unanxious, unbothered; SEE CONCEPT *404*

careful [adj] *cautious; painstaking*
accurate, alert, apprehensive, assiduous, attentive, chary, choosy, circumspect, concerned, conscientious, conservative, cool, deliberate, discreet, exacting, fastidious, finicky, fussy, going to great lengths*, guarded, heedful, judicious, leery, meticulous, mindful, observant, particular, playing safe*, precise, prim, protective, provident, prudent, punctilious, regardful, religious, rigorous, scrupulous, selfdisciplined, shy, sober, solicitous, solid, thorough, thoughtful, vigilant, wary; SEE CONCEPTS *326,542*

carefully [adv] *cautiously; painstakingly*
anxiously, attentively, circumspectly, concernedly, conscientiously, correctly, deliberately, delicately, dependably, discreetly, exactly, faithfully, fastidiously, fully, gingerly, guardedly, heedfully, honorably, in detail, laboriously, meticulously, particularly, precisely, providently, prudently, punctiliously, regardfully, reliably, rigorously, scrupulously, solicitously, thoroughly, thoughtfully, trustily, uprightly, vigilantly, warily, watchfully, with forethought, with reservations; SEE CONCEPT *542*

caregiver [n] *person caring for child*
au pair, babysitter, caretaker, custodian, father, governess, mother, nanny, nurse, parent; SEE CONCEPT *348*

careless [adj1] *without sufficient attention*
absent-minded, abstracted, casual, cursory, disregardful, forgetful, hasty, heedless, improvident, imprudent, inaccurate, inadvertent, incautious, inconsiderate, indifferent, indiscreet, indolent, injudicious, irresponsible, lackadaisical, lax, loose, mindless, napping, negligent, nonchalant, oblivious, offhand, perfunctory, pococurante, reckless, regardless, remiss, slipshod, sloppy, thoughtless, uncircumspect, unconcerned, unguarded, unheeding, unmindful, unobservant, unreflective, unthinking, wasteful; SEE CONCEPT *542*

careless [adj2] *artless*
casual, modest, naive, natural, nonchalant, simple, unstudied; SEE CONCEPT *557*

caress [n] *loving touch*
cuddle, embrace, endearment, feel, fondling,

hug, kiss, pat, pet, petting, snuggle, squeeze, stroke; SEE CONCEPTS *375,590*

caress [v] *touch lovingly*
bear hug*, brush, buss, clinch, clutch, coddle, cosset, cuddle, dandle, embrace, feel, fondle, graze, handle, hug, kiss, make love, massage, mug, neck, nestle, nuzzle, pat, pet, play around*, rub, squeeze, stroke, toy; SEE CONCEPTS *375,612*

caretaker [n] *person who maintains something*
baby sitter, concierge, curator, custodian, house-sitter, janitor, keeper, porter, sitter, super*, superintendent, supervisor, warden, watchperson; SEE CONCEPT *348*

cargo [n] *baggage; something to be delivered*
burden, consignment, contents, freight, goods, haul, lading, load, merchandise, payload, shipload, shipment, tonnage, ware; SEE CONCEPTS *338,446*

caricature [n] *exaggerated description in writing, drawing*
burlesque, cartoon, distortion, farce, imitation, lampoon, libel, mimicry, mockery, parody, pasquinade, pastiche, put-on*, ridicule, satire, send-up*, sham, takeoff*, travesty; SEE CONCEPTS *271,386,625*

carillon [n] *set of bells*
angelus, chimes, glockenspiel, gong, lyra, peal, tintinnabulation, tocsin; SEE CONCEPT *595*

carnage [n] *massacre*
annihilation, blitz, blood, blood and guts*, blood bath*, bloodshed, butchering, butchery, crime, extermination, gore, havoc, hecatomb, holocaust, homicide, killing, liquidation, manslaughter, mass murder, murder, offing*, rapine, search and destroy*, shambles, slaughter, slaying, taking out*, warfare, wasting; SEE CONCEPT *252*

carnal [adj] *erotic, sensual*
animal, bodily, corporal, corporeal, earthly, fleshly, genital, impure, lascivious, lecherous, lewd, libidinous, licentious, lustful, physical, prurient, salacious, sensuous, temporal, unchaste, venereal, voluptuous, vulgar, wanton, worldly; SEE CONCEPTS *372,403*

carnival [n] *outdoor celebration*
amusement park, bacchanal, carny*, carousal, circus, conviviality, exposition, fair, feasting, festival, fete, fiesta, frolic, gala, grind show*, heyday, jamboree, jollification, jubilee, Mardi Gras, masquerade, merrymaking, orgy, ragbag*, revelry, rout, saturnalia, side show, spree, street fair; SEE CONCEPTS *377,386*

carnivorous [adj] *eating animal flesh*
cannibal, flesh-eating, hungry, omnivorous, predatory, rapacious; SEE CONCEPT *401*

carol [n] *joyful hymn*
ballad, canticle, canzonet, chorus, Christmas song, ditty*, lay, madrigal, noel, song, strain; SEE CONCEPTS *263,595*

carouse [v] *make merry, often with liquor*
booze, drink, frolic, go on a spree*, have fun, imbibe, paint the town*, paint the town red*, play, quaff, raise Cain*, revel, riot, roister, wassail, whoop it up*; SEE CONCEPT *384*

carp [v] *nag*
bother, cavil, censure, complain, criticize, find fault, fuss, grumble, hypercriticize, knock, nitpick*, objurgate, pan, peck*, pick at, quibble, reproach; SEE CONCEPT *52*

carpal tunnel syndrome [n] *wrist irritation*
repetitive motion disorder, repetitive motion injury, sensorimotor disorder; SEE CONCEPT *306*

carpenter [n] *person who works with wood*
artisan, builder, cabinetmaker, carps*, chips*, craftsperson, joiner, laborer, mason, woodworker, worker; SEE CONCEPT *348*

carpet [n] *nappy floor covering*
carpeting, matting, rug, runner, tapestry, throw rug, wall-to-wall*; SEE CONCEPT *473*

carriage [n1] *delivery of freight*
carrying, conveyance, conveying, delivering, freight, transit, transport, transportation; SEE CONCEPTS *148,217*

carriage [n2] *posture, physical and mental*
air, aspect, attitude, bearing, behavior, cast, comportment, conduct, demeanor, deportment, gait, look, manner, mien, pace, posture, presence, stance, step; SEE CONCEPTS *633,720*

carry [v1] *transport physical object*
backpack*, bear, bring, cart, channel, conduct, convey, convoy, displace, ferry, fetch, freight, funnel, give, haul, heft, hoist, import, lift, lug*, move, pack, pipe, portage, relay, relocate, remove, schlepp*, shift, shoulder*, sustain, take, tote, traject, transfer, transmit, transplant, truck, waft; SEE CONCEPTS *148,217*

carry [v2] *win; accomplish*
affect, be victorious, capture, drive, effect, gain, get, impel, impress, influence, inspire, move, prevail, secure, spur, strike, sway, touch, urge; SEE CONCEPTS *68,706*

carry [v3] *broadcast electronically*
air, bear, communicate, conduct, convey, display, disseminate, give, offer, pass on, publish, relay, release, send, transfer, transport; SEE CONCEPTS *217,266*

carry on [v1] *continue activity*
achieve, endure, hang on, keep going, last, maintain, perpetuate, persevere, persist, proceed; SEE CONCEPT *239*

carry on [v2] *manage operations*
administer, conduct, direct, engage in, keep, operate, ordain, run; SEE CONCEPT *117*

carry on [v3] *lose control emotionally*
act up, be indecorous, blunder, cut up, lose it*, make a fuss*, misbehave, rage, raise Cain*; SEE CONCEPT *633*

carry out [v] *complete activity*
accomplish, achieve, carry through, consummate, discharge, effect, effectuate, execute, finalize, fulfill, implement, meet, perform, realize; SEE CONCEPT *706*

cart [n] *small attachment for transporting*
barrow, buggy, curricle, dolly, dray, gig, gurney, handcart, palanquin, pushcart, rickshaw, tilbury, truck, tumbrel, two-wheeler, wagon, wheelbarrow; SEE CONCEPTS *499,505*

cart [v] *carry*
bear, bring, convey, ferry, haul, move, schlepp*, take, tote; SEE CONCEPTS *148,217*

carte blanche [n] *full power, authority*
blank check, freedom, free hand, free rein, license, permission, power of attorney, prerogative, sanction, say, say-so, unconditional right; SEE CONCEPT *376*

cartel [n] *group which shares business interest*
bunch*, chain, combine, conglomerate, consortium, corporation, crew*, crowd*, gang*, holding company, megacorp*, mob*, monopoly,

ca
ca

multinational*, outfit*, plunderbund*, pool, ring*, syndicate, trust; SEE CONCEPTS *323,325*

carton [n] *box for holding items*
bin, case, casket, chest, coffer, container, corrugated box, crate, pack, package, packet; SEE CONCEPT *494*

cartoon [n] *funny drawing, often with dialogue or caption*
animation, caricature, comic strip, drawing, lampoon, parody, representation, satire, sketch, take-off; SEE CONCEPTS *280,625*

cartoonist [n] *person who draws cartoons*
artist, caricaturist, comic artist, gag person*, gagster*, illustrator, social critic; SEE CONCEPT *348*

carve [v] *cut carefully with sharp instrument*
block out, chip, chisel, cleave, dissect, dissever, divide, engrave, etch, fashion, form, grave, hack, hew, incise, indent, insculpt, model, mold, mould, pattern, rough-hew, sculpt, shape, slash, slice, stipple, sunder, tool, trim, whittle; SEE CONCEPTS *137,176,184*

carved in stone [adj] *fixed*
established, etched in stone*, firm, immutable, permanent, set in concrete*, set in stone*, unchangeable; SEE CONCEPTS *488,551,583,649,798*

cascade [n] *something falling, especially water*
avalanche, cataract, chute, deluge, downrush, falls, flood, force, fountain, outpouring, precipitation, rapids, shower, spout, torrent, watercourse, waterfall; SEE CONCEPTS *514,787*

cascade [v] *fall in a rush*
descend, disgorge, flood, gush, heave, overflow, pitch, plunge, pour, spew, spill, spit up, surge, throw up, tumble, vomit; SEE CONCEPT *179*

case [n1] *container; items in container*
bag, baggage, basket, bin, box, cabinet, caddy, caisson, canister, capsule, carton, cartridge, casing, casket, chamber, chassis, chest, coffer, compact, cover, covering, crate, crating, crib, drawer, envelope, folder, grip, holder, integument, jacket, receptacle, safe, scabbard, sheath, shell, suitcase, tray, trunk, wallet, wrapper, wrapping; SEE CONCEPT *494*

case [n2] *circumstance, conditions*
context, contingency, crisis, dilemma, event, eventuality, fact, incident, occurrence, plight, position, predicament, problem, quandary, situation, state, status; SEE CONCEPT *696*

case [n3] *example*
case history, exemplification, illustration, instance, occasion, occurrence, representative, sample, sampling, specimen; SEE CONCEPT *686*

case [n4] *matter brought before a court*
action, argument, cause, claim, dispute, evidence, lawsuit, litigation, petition, proceedings, process, proof, suit, trial; SEE CONCEPT *318*

case [v] *check something in detail*
canvass, check out, check over, check up, examine, inspect, scrutinize, study, view; SEE CONCEPT *103*

cash [n] *money; assets*
banknote, bread*, buck*, bullion, cabbage*, chicken feed*, coin, coinage, currency, dinero*, dough*, funds, green stuff*, investment, legal tender, lot, mazumah*, note, payment, pledge, principal, ready assets, refund, remuneration, reserve, resources, riches, savings, scratch*, security, skins*, stock, supply, treasure, wampum*, wherewithal; SEE CONCEPTS *340,710*

cash [v] *exchange for real money*
acknowledge, break a bill*, change, discharge, draw, honor, liquidate, make change, pay, realize, redeem; SEE CONCEPT *330*

cashier [n] *bank worker*
accountant, banker, bursar, clerk, collector, paymaster, purser, receiver, teller, treasurer; SEE CONCEPT *348*

cashier [v] *discard, expel*
ax*, boot*, bounce, break, can*, cast off, discharge, dismiss, displace, drum out*, fire, give a pink slip*, give the heave ho*, heave*, remove, sack*, terminate; SEE CONCEPTS *211,324*

casing [n] *covering*
hull, jacket, sheath, skin, wrapper; SEE CONCEPTS *484,750*

casino [n] *gambling establishment*
bank, betting house, big store*, club, clubhouse, dance hall, dice joint*, dive, gambling den, hall, honky-tonk, house, joint, Monte Carlo, pool hall, roadhouse, rotunda, saloon, track; SEE CONCEPT *447*

cask [n] *rounded container for liquids*
barrel, barrelet, butt, firkin, hogshead, keg, pipe, tun, vat; SEE CONCEPT *494*

casket [n] *burial box*
bin, carton, case, chest, coffer, crate, funerary box, pine box, pinto, sarcophagus, wood overcoat*; SEE CONCEPTS *368,494*

casserole [n] *dish consisting of a combination of cooked food*
covered dish, goulash, hash, meat pie, pot pie, pottage, stew, stroganoff; SEE CONCEPT *457*

cast [n1] *a throw to the side*
casting, ejection, expulsion, fling, flinging, heave, heaving, hurl, hurling, launching, lob, lobbing, pitch, pitching, projection, propulsion, shooting, sling, slinging, thrust, thrusting, toss, tossing; SEE CONCEPT *222*

cast [n2] *appearance; shade of color*
air, complexion, countenance, demeanor, embodiment, expression, face, hue, look, manner, mien, semblance, stamp, style, tinge, tint, tone, turn, visage; SEE CONCEPTS *622,716*

cast [n3] *actors in performance*
actors, actresses, artists, characters, company, dramatis, list, parts, personae, players, roles, troupe; SEE CONCEPT *294*

cast [n4] *molded structure*
conformation, copy, duplicate, embodiment, facsimile, figure, form, mold, plaster, replica, sculpture, shape; SEE CONCEPTS *470,475*

cast [v1] *throw aside*
boot, bung*, chuck*, drive, drop, fire*, fling, heave, hurl, impel, launch, lob, peg, pitch, project, shed, shy, sling, thrust, toss; SEE CONCEPT *222*

cast [v2] *emit, give*
aim, bestow, deposit, diffuse, direct, distribute, point, radiate, scatter, shed, spatter, spray, spread, sprinkle, strew, train; SEE CONCEPTS *108,624*

cast [v3] *calculate*
add, compute, count, figure, foot, forecast, number, reckon, sum, summate, tot, total; SEE CONCEPT *764*

cast [v4] *select for activity*
allot, appoint, arrange, assign, blueprint, chart, choose, decide upon, delegate, design, designate,

detail, determine, devise, give parts, name, pick, plan, project; SEE CONCEPT *41*

caste [*n*] *social class*
cultural level, degree, estate, grade, lineage, order, position, race, rank, social order, species, sphere, standing, station, status, stratum; SEE CONCEPTS *378,388*

castigate [*v*] *criticize severely*
baste, bawl out*, beat, berate, blister, cane, censure, chasten, chastise, chew out*, come down on*, correct, criticize, discipline, drag over the coals*, dress down*, drub, excoriate, flay, flog, jump down one's throat*, lambaste, lash, lay out*, lean on*, penalize, pummel, punish, rail, rate, read the riot act*, ream, rebuke, reprimand, scarify, scathe, scold, scorch, scourge, thrash, tongue-lash*, upbraid, whip; SEE CONCEPT *52*

castle [*n*] *magnificent home, often for royalty*
acropolis, alcazar, château, citadel, donjon, estate house, fasthold, fastness, fort, fortification, fortress, hold, keep, manor, mansion, palace, peel, safehold, seat, stronghold, tower, villa; SEE CONCEPT *516*

castrate [*v*] *remove sexual organs*
alter, asexualize, caponize, change, cut, deprive of virility, desexualize, emasculate, eunuchize, fix, geld, mutilate, neuter, spay, sterilize, unsex; SEE CONCEPT *310*

casual [*adj1*] *chance, random*
accidental, adventitious, by chance, contingent, erratic, extemporaneous, extempore, fluky, fortuitous, impromptu, improvised, impulsive, incidental, infrequent, irregular, occasional, odd, offhand, serendipitous, spontaneous, uncertain, unexpected, unforeseen, unintentional, unplanned, unpremeditated; SEE CONCEPTS *541,544*

casual [*adj2*] *nonchalant, relaxed in manner*
aloof, apathetic, blasé, breezy, cool*, cursory, detached, down home*, easygoing, folksy*, homey*, incurious, indifferent, informal, insouciant, lackadaisical, laid-back*, loose*, low-pressure, mellow, offhand, perfunctory, pococurante, purposeless, remote, unconcerned, unfussy, uninterested, withdrawn; SEE CONCEPTS *401,542,589*

casualty [*n1*] *accident*
blow, calamity, catastrophe, chance, contingency, debacle, disaster, misadventure, misfortune, mishap; SEE CONCEPT *674*

casualty [*n2*] *victim*
dead, death toll, fatality, injured, killed, loss, missing, prey, sufferer, wounded; SEE CONCEPTS *407,423*

casuistry [*n*] *overgeneral reasoning*
chicanery, deception, deceptiveness, delusion, equivocation, evasion, fallacy, lie, oversubtleness, sophism, sophistry, speciousness, spuriousness, trick; SEE CONCEPTS *54,63*

cat [*n*] *feline animal, sometimes a pet*
bobcat, cheetah, cougar, grimalkin, jaguar, kitten, kitty, leopard, lion, lynx, malkin, mouser, ocelot, panther, puma, puss, pussy, tabby, tiger, tom, tomcat; SEE CONCEPTS *394,400*

cataclysm [*n*] *disaster*
calamity, cataract, catastrophe, collapse, convulsion, crunch*, curtains*, debacle, deluge, disturbance, double trouble*, flood, flooding, holy mess*, inundation, misadventure, ruin, torrent, tragedy, unholy mess*, upheaval, waterloo*, woe; SEE CONCEPTS *674,675*

catalog/catalogue [*n*] *written or printed matter featuring a selection of objects*
archive, brief, bulletin, calendar, cartulary, charts, classification, compendium, directory, docket, draft, enumeration, gazette, gazetteer, hit list*, index, inventory, list, prospectus, record, register, roll, roster, schedule, slate, specification, syllabus, synopsis, table; SEE CONCEPTS *271,280*

catalyst [*n*] *something which incites activity*
adjuvant, agitator, enzyme, goad, impetus, impulse, incendiary, incentive, incitation, incitement, motivation, radical stimulus, reactant, reactionary, spark plug*, spur, stimulant, synergist, wave maker*; SEE CONCEPT *712*

catapult [*n*] *implement for shooting weapon*
arbalest, ballista, heaver, hurler, pitcher, propeller, shooter, sling, slingshot, tosser, trebuchet; SEE CONCEPTS *463,500*

catastrophe [*n*] *calamity; unhappy conclusion*
accident, adversity, affliction, alluvion, bad luck, bad news*, blow, calamity, casualty, cataclysm, contretemps, crash, culmination, curtains*, debacle, denouement, desolation, devastation, disaster, emergency, end, failure, fatality, fiasco, finale, grief, hardship, havoc, ill, infliction, meltdown*, misadventure, mischance, misery, misfortune, mishap, reverse, scourge, stroke, termination, the worst*, tragedy, trial, trouble, upshot, waterloo*, wreck; SEE CONCEPT *674*

catatonic [*adj*] *unaware*
comatose, confused, hung, suspended, unconscious, wedged; SEE CONCEPT *402*

catcall [*n*] *heckle*
boo, Bronx cheer*, derision, gibe, hiss, hoot, jeer, raspberry*, shout, whistle; SEE CONCEPTS *44,47*

catch-22 [*n*] *no-win situation*
contradiction, dilemma, lose-lose, paradox, quagmire; SEE CONCEPT *532*

catch [*n1*] *fastener*
bolt, buckle, clamp, clasp, clip, hasp, hook, hook and eye, latch, snap; SEE CONCEPT *497*

catch [*n2*] *trick, hidden disadvantage*
Catch-22, conundrum, deception, decoy, drawback, fly in the ointment*, hitch, joke, puzzle, puzzler, snag, stumbling block, trap; SEE CONCEPTS *674,679*

catch [*v1*] *ensnare, apprehend*
arrest, bag, bust*, capture, clasp, claw, clench, clutch, collar, cop, corral, entangle, entrap, get one's fingers on*, glom, glove, grab, grasp, grip, hook, lasso, lay hold of, nab, nail, net, pick, pluck, pounce on, prehend, secure, seize, snag, snare, snatch, take, take hold of, trap; SEE CONCEPT *90*

catch [*v2*] *find out, discover*
descry, detect, encounter, expose, hit upon, meet with, spot, surprise, take unawares, turn up, unmask; SEE CONCEPT *31*

catch [*v3*] *contract an illness*
become infected with, break out with, come down with, develop, fall ill with, fall victim to, get, incur, receive, sicken, succumb to, suffer from, take; SEE CONCEPTS *93,308*

catch [*v4*] *come from behind and grab*
board, climb on, come upon, cotch, get, go after, grab, hop on, jump, make, overhaul, overtake, pass, ram, reach, run down, take; SEE CONCEPT *164*

ca
ca

catch [v5] *hear and understand*
accept, apprehend, comprehend, discern, feel, follow, get, grasp, perceive, recognize, see, sense, take in, understand; SEE CONCEPT *15*

catching [adj] *contagious (disease)*
communicable, dangerous, endemic, epidemic, epizootic, infectious, infective, miasmatic, pandemic, pestiferous, pestilential, taking, transferable, transmittable; SEE CONCEPT *314*

catchword [n] *motto*
byword, catchphrase, household word, maxim, password, refrain, shibboleth, slogan, watchword; SEE CONCEPTS *275,278*

catchy [adj] *captivating, addictive*
fetching, haunting, having a good hook*, memorable, popular; SEE CONCEPT *544*

catechize [v] *instruct and question*
ask, cross-examine, drill, educate, examine, grill, inquire, interrogate, query, quiz, teach, train; SEE CONCEPTS *48,285*

categorical [adj] *explicit, unconditional*
absolute, all out*, certain, clear-cut, definite, definitive, direct, downright, emphatic, express, flat out*, forthright, no holds barred*, no strings attached*, positive, specific, straight out, sure, ultimate, unambiguous, unequivocal, unmitigated, unqualified, unreserved; SEE CONCEPT *535*

categorize [v] *sort by type, classification*
assort, button down*, class, classify, group, identify, peg*, pigeonhole*, put down as, rank, tab, typecast; SEE CONCEPT *39*

category [n] *classification, type*
class, department, division, grade, group, grouping, head, heading, kind, league, level, list, order, pigeonhole*, rank, section, sort, tier; SEE CONCEPT *378*

cater [v] *provide, help*
baby, coddle, cotton, furnish, gratify, humor, indulge, minister to, outfit, pamper, pander to, procure, provision, purvey, spoil, supply, victual; SEE CONCEPT *136*

caterwaul [v] *make screeching, crying noise*
bawl, bicker, howl, quarrel, scream, screech, shriek, squall, wail, yell, yowl; SEE CONCEPT *77*

catharsis [n] *purging, purification*
ablution, abreaction, cleansing, expurgation, lustration, purgation, purification, release; SEE CONCEPTS *13,165,230*

cathedral [n] *large church*
basilica, bishop's seat, chancel, holy place, house of God, house of prayer, house of worship, minster, place of worship, sanctuary, temple; SEE CONCEPTS *368,439*

catholic [adj] *all-embracing, general*
all-inclusive, broad-minded, charitable, comprehensive, cosmic, cosmopolitan, diffuse, eclectic, ecumenical, extensive, generic, global, inclusive, indeterminate, large-scale, liberal, open-minded, planetary, receptive, tolerant, unbigoted, universal, unprejudiced, unsectarian, whole, wide, world-wide; SEE CONCEPTS *557,772*

cattle [n] *bovine animals*
beasts, bovid mammals, bulls, calves, cows, dogies*, herd, livestock, longhorn*, moo cows*, oxen, shorthorns, stock, strays; SEE CONCEPT *394*

catty [adj] *nasty, malicious*
backbiting, evil, hateful, ill-natured, malevolent, mean, rancorous, spiteful, venomous, vicious, wicked; SEE CONCEPT *404*

caucus [n] *group gathered to make decision*
assembly, conclave, convention, council, gathering, get-together, meeting, parley, session; SEE CONCEPTS *301,417*

cause [n1] *agent, originator*
account, agency, aim, antecedent, author, basis, beginning, causation, consideration, creator, determinant, doer, element, end, explanation, foundation, genesis, ground, grounds, incitement, inducement, instigation, leaven, mainspring, maker, matter, motivation, motive, object, occasion, origin, prime mover, principle, producer, purpose, root, source, spring, stimulation; SEE CONCEPTS *229,661*

cause [n2] *belief; undertaking for belief*
attempt, conviction, creed, enterprise, faith, goal, ideal, intention, movement, object, objective, plan, principles, purpose; SEE CONCEPT *689*

cause [v] *bring into being; bring about*
be at the bottom of*, begin, brainstorm*, break in*, break the ice*, breed, bring to pass, come out with*, compel, cook up*, create, dream up*, effect, elicit, engender, evoke, fire up*, generate, get things rolling*, give rise to, hatch, incite, induce, introduce, kickoff*, kindle, lead to, let, make, make up, motivate, muster, occasion, open, originate, precipitate, produce, provoke, result in, revert, secure, sow the seeds, start the ball rolling*, think up, work up; SEE CONCEPTS *228,231,241*

cause célèbre [n] *controversial issue*
bone of contention, celebrated case, controversy, debate, grist for the gossip mill*, hot potato*, moot point, political football*, scandal, war of words; SEE CONCEPTS *46,278,665*

caustic [adj1] *burning, corrosive*
abrasive, acerbic, acid, acrid, alkaline, astringent, biting, corroding, erosive, keen, mordant, pungent, tart; SEE CONCEPT *485*

caustic [adj2] *sarcastic*
acerb, acerbic, acrimonious, bitter, cutting, harsh, incisive, pithy, pungent, rough, salty, satiric, scathing, severe, sharp, stinging, trenchant, virulent; SEE CONCEPT *267*

caution [n1] *alertness, carefulness*
attention, canniness, care, circumspection, deliberation, discreetness, discretion, Fabian policy, foresight, forethought, heed, heedfulness, providence, prudence, vigilance, watchfulness; SEE CONCEPT *410*

caution [n2] *warning*
admonition, advice, bug in one's ear*, caveat, commonition, counsel, forewarning, hint, injunction, monition, notice, omen, premonition, sign, tip*, tip-off*; SEE CONCEPTS *78,274*

caution [v] *warn, advise*
admonish, alert, exhort, flag, forewarn, give the high sign*, give the lowdown on*, pull one's coat*, put one wise*, tip*, tip off*, urge, wave a red flag*, wise one up*; SEE CONCEPT *78*

cautionary tale [n] *event illustrating a hazard*
admonition, advisory, caveat, message, omen, portent, red flag*, sign of things to come*, wake-up call*, warning, word to the wise*; SEE CONCEPTS *78,274*

cautious [adj] *careful, guarded*
alert, all ears*, cagey, calculating, chary, circumspect, considerate, discreet, forethoughtful, gingerly, hedging one's bets*, heedful, judicious, keeping one's toes*, leery, on the lookout*,

playing it cool*, playing safe*, politic, provident, prudent, pussyfoot*, safe, shrewd, taking it easy, taking it slow*, tentative, thinking twice*, vigilant, walking on eggs*, wary, watchful, watching one's step*, watching out, with one's eyes peeled*; SEE CONCEPTS *401,403*

cavalcade [*n*] *parade*
array, drill, march-past, procession, promenade, review, spectacle, train; SEE CONCEPT *432*

cavalier [*adj*] *arrogant*
condescending, curt, disdainful, haughty, high-and-mighty*, insolent, lofty, lordly, offhand, overbearing, proud, scornful, snooty*, snotty*, supercilious, superior; SEE CONCEPT *401*

cavalry [*n*] *troops riding horses*
army, bowlegs*, chasseurs, cuirassiers, dragoons, horse, horse soldiers, hussars, lancers, mounted troops, Mounties, rangers, squadron, uhlans; SEE CONCEPT *322*

cave [*n*] *hole in land formation*
cavern, cavity, den, grotto, hollow, pothole, rock shelter, subterrane, subterranean area; SEE CONCEPT *509*

caveat [*n*] *warning*
admonition, alarm, caution, commonition, forewarning, monition, sign; SEE CONCEPTS *78,274*

cavern [*n*] *hollow in land formation*
cave, grotto, hole, pothole, subterrane, subterranean area; SEE CONCEPT *509*

cavernous [*adj*] *hollow and large*
alveolate, broad, chambered, chasmal, commodious, concave, curved inward, deep, deep-set, echoing, gaping, huge, resonant, reverberant, roomy, sepulchral, socketed, spacious, sunken, vast, wide, yawning; SEE CONCEPTS *490,773,796*

cavity [*n*] *sunken or decayed area*
atrium, basin, caries, chamber, crater, decay, dent, depression, gap, hole, hollow, pit, pocket, sinus, socket, vacuity, void; SEE CONCEPT *513*

cavort [*v*] *frolic, prance*
caper, caracole, carry on*, cut loose*, cut up*, dance, fool around*, frisk, gambol, go places and do things*, horse around*, horseplay, monkey around*, play, revel, rollick, romp, roughhouse*, sport; SEE CONCEPTS *114,384*

cease [*v*] *stop, conclude*
back off, break off, bring to an end, call it a day*, call it quits*, close, close out, come to an end, culminate, cut it out*, desist, die, discontinue, drop, end, fail, finish, give over, halt, intermit, knock off*, leave off, pack in*, quit, quit cold turkey*, refrain, shut down, stay, surcease, terminate, wind up*; SEE CONCEPT *234*

cease-fire [*n*] *stop in fighting*
armistice, suspension of hostilities, truce; SEE CONCEPTS *230,298,684*

ceaseless [*adj*] *never-ending*
amaranthine, constant, continual, continuous, day and night*, endless, eternal, everlasting, incessant, indefatigable, interminable, nonstop, on a treadmill*, perennial, perpetual, round the clock*, unceasing, unending, uninterrupted, unremitting, untiring, world-without-end*; SEE CONCEPT *798*

cede [*v*] *abandon, surrender*
abalienate, abdicate, accord, alien, alienate, allow, capitulate, come across with*, communicate, concede, convey, deed, drop, fold*, fork over*, give in*, give up, grant, hand over*, leave, make over, part with, relinquish, remise, renounce, resign, sign over, throw in the sponge*, throw in the towel*, transfer, vouchsafe, waive, yield; SEE CONCEPTS *108,127*

ceiling [*n1*] *top of a room*
baldachin, beam, canopy, covert, dome, fan vaulting, groin, highest point, housetop, plafond, planchement, plaster, roof, roofing, timber, topside covering; SEE CONCEPT *440*

ceiling [*n2*] *maximum*
legal price, record, superiority, top; SEE CONCEPT *836*

celebrate [*v*] *commemorate occasion, achievement*
beat the drum*, bless, blow off steam*, carouse, ceremonialize, commend, consecrate, dedicate, drink to, eulogize, exalt, extol, feast, fete, glorify, hallow, have a ball*, honor, jubilate, keep, kick up one's heels*, laud, let loose*, lionize, live it up*, make merry, make whoopee*, mark with a red letter*, memorialize, observe, paint the town red*, party*, perform, praise, proclaim, publicize, raise hell*, rejoice, revel, revere, ritualize, signalize, solemnize; SEE CONCEPT *377*

celebrated [*adj*] *distinguished, famous*
acclaimed, big*, eminent, famed, glorious, great, high-powered, illustrious, immortal, important, large, laureate, lionized, notable, number one*, numero uno*, outstanding, popular, preeminent, prominent, renowned, revered, storied, up there*, well-known, w. k.*; SEE CONCEPT *568*

celebration [*n*] *commemoration of occasion, achievement*
anniversary, bash*, birthday, blast*, blowout*, carousal, ceremony, conviviality, festival, festivity, fete, frolic, gaiety, gala, glorification, hilarity, honoring, hoopla, hullabaloo*, jollification, joviality, jubilation, jubilee, keeping, magnification, memorialization, merriment, merrymaking, observance, party, performance, recognition, remembrance, revelry, saturnalia, solemnization, spree, triumph, wingding*; SEE CONCEPT *377*

celebrity [*n1*] *dignitary*
ace, big cheese*, big deal*, big gun*, big name*, big shot*, big stuff*, bigwig*, celeb*, cynosure, famous person, figure, heavyweight, hero, hotshot*, immortal, lion*, luminary, magnate, mahatma, major leaguer*, name, notable, personage, personality, somebody, someone, star, superstar, the cheese*, VIP, worthy; SEE CONCEPT *423*

celebrity [*n2*] *fame, notoriety*
distinction, éclat, eminence, glory, honor, notability, popularity, preeminence, prestige, prominence, renown, reputation, repute, stardom; SEE CONCEPTS *388,668*

celerity [*n*] *swiftness*
alacrity, briskness, dispatch, expedition, expeditiousness, fleetness, gait, haste, hurry, hustle, legerity, promptness, quickness, rapidity, speed, speediness, swiftness, velocity, vivacity; SEE CONCEPT *755*

celestial [*adj*] *heavenly*
angelic, astral, beatific, blessed, divine, elysian, empyral, empyrean, eternal, ethereal, godlike, hallowed, holy, immortal, Olympian, otherworldly, seraphic, spiritual, sublime, supernal, supernatural, transcendental, transmundane; SEE CONCEPTS *536,673*

ca
ce

celibacy [n] *abstinence from sexual activity*
abstention, chastity, continence, frigidity, impotence, maidenhood, purity, singleness, virginity, virtue; SEE CONCEPT 388

celibate [adj] *abstaining from sexual activity*
chaste, continent, pure, virgin, virginal, virtuous; SEE CONCEPT 372

cell [n1] *smallest living organism*
bacterium, cellule, corpuscle, egg, embryo, follicle, germ, haematid, microorganism, spore, unit, utricle, vacuole; SEE CONCEPTS 389,478

cell [n2] *small room, container*
alcove, antechamber, apartment, bastille, booth, burrow, cage, cavity, chamber, cloister, closet, compartment, coop, crib, crypt, cubicle, den, dungeon, hold, hole, keep, lockup, nook, pen, receptacle, recess, retreat, stall, tower, vault; SEE CONCEPTS 448,494,513

cellar [n] *underground story of building*
apartment, basement, subbasement, subterrane, underground room, vault; SEE CONCEPTS 440,448

cement [n] *gluing, binding material*
adhesive, binder, birdlime, bond, concrete, epoxy, glue, grout, gum, gunk*, lime, lute, mortar, mucilage, mud*, paste, plaster, putty, rubber cement, sand, sealant, size, solder, stickum*, tar; SEE CONCEPT 475

cement [v] *attach securely, often with sticky material*
bind, blend, bond, cohere, combine, connect, fasten, fuse, glue, gum, join, merge, mortar, paste, plaster, seal, solder, stick together, unite, weld; SEE CONCEPTS 85,160

cemetery [n] *burial ground*
boot hill*, catacomb, charnel, charnel house, churchyard, city of the dead*, crypt, eternal home*, funerary grounds, garden, God's acre*, Golgotha, grave, graveyard, marble town*, memorial park, mortuary, necropolis, ossuary, polyandrium, potter's field, resting place, sepulcher, tomb, vault; SEE CONCEPTS 305,368

censor [v] *forbid, ban; selectively remove*
abridge, blacklist, black out*, bleach, bleep*, blue-pencil*, bowdlerize, clean up, conceal, control, cork*, criticize, cut, decontaminate, delete, drop the iron curtain*, edit, examine, excise, expurgate, exscind, inspect, launder*, narrow, oversee, prevent publication, purge, purify, put the lid on*, refuse transmission, repress, restrain, restrict, review, revile, sanitize, scissor out*, squelch, sterilize, strike out, supervise communications, suppress, withhold; SEE CONCEPTS 121,266

censorious [adj] *very critical*
accusatory, captious, carping, caviling, cavillous, chiding, complaining, condemnatory, condemning, critical, culpatory, denouncing, disapproving, disparaging, fault-finding, hypercritical, overcritical, reprehending, reproaching, severe; · SEE CONCEPT 267

censorship [n] *forbiddance; ban*
blackout*, blue pencil*, bowdlerization, control, forbidding, hush up*, infringing on rights, iron curtain*, restriction, suppression, thought control*; SEE CONCEPTS 376,388

censure [n] *severe criticism*
admonishment, admonition, blame, castigation, condemnation, disapproval, dressing down, objection, obloquy, rebuke, remonstrance, reprehension, reprimand, reproach, reproof, stricture; SEE CONCEPTS 52,410

censure [v] *condemn; criticize severely*
abuse, admonish, animadvert, asperse, attack, backbite, berate, blame, carp at, castigate, cavil, chastise, chide, contemn, cut up*, denigrate, denounce, deprecate, disapprove, discipline, disparage, exprobate, find fault with, get after, impugn, incriminate, judge, knock, lecture, look askance, ostracize, pick apart, pull apart, read out*, rebuff, rebuke, remonstrate, reprehend, reprimand, reproach, reprove, scold, take to task*, tear apart*, tell off, upbraid; SEE CONCEPT 52

census [n] *head count*
demographics, demography, enumeration, poll, population tally, statistics, stats; SEE CONCEPTS 283,786

center [adj] *middle*
at halfway point, centermost, deepest, equidistant, inmost, inner, innermost, inside, intermediary, intermediate, internal, mean, medial, mid, middlemost, midpoint, midway; SEE CONCEPTS 583,585,830

center [n1] *middle point*
axis, bull's-eye, centrality, centriole, centrum, core, cynosure, equidistance, essence, focal point, focus, gist, heart, hotbed, hub, inside, interior, intermediacy, kernel, mainstream*, marrow, middle of the road*, midpoint, midst, nave, navel, nucleus, omphalos, pith, pivot, place, polestar, quick, radial point, root, seat; SEE CONCEPT 830

center [n2] *point of attraction for visitors, shoppers, travelers*
capital, city, club, concourse, crossroads, focal point, focus, heart, hub, mall, market, marketplace, mart, meeting place, metropolis, nerve center, plaza, polestar, shopping center, social center, station, town, trading center; SEE CONCEPTS 435,438,507

center [v] *concentrate, draw together*
attract, bring to a focus, bring together, centralize, close on, collect, concenter, consolidate, converge upon, focalize, focus, gather, intensify, join, medialize, meet, unify; SEE CONCEPTS 35,84

central [adj] *main, principal; in the middle*
axial, basic, cardinal, center, centric, centroidal, chief, dominant, equidistant, essential, focal, foremost, fundamental, important, inmost, inner, interior, intermediate, key, leading, master, mean, median, mid, middle, middlemost, midmost, midway, nuclear, outstanding, overriding, paramount, pivotal, predominant, primary, prime, radical, ruling, salient, significant, umbilical; SEE CONCEPTS 567,583,830

centralize [v] *concentrate, draw toward a point*
accumulate, amalgamate, assemble, compact, concenter, condense, consolidate, converge, focus, gather, incorporate, integrate, organize, rationalize, streamline, systematize, unify; SEE CONCEPTS 35,84

centrifugal [adj] *radiating from a central point*
deviating, diffusive, divergent, diverging, eccentric, efferent, outward, radial, spiral, spreading; SEE CONCEPTS 581,584

cereal [n] *edible grain*
bran, breakfast food, corn, grain, oats, rice, rye, wheat; SEE CONCEPTS 428,831

cerebral [*a*] *using one's brain*
analytical, brainy, deep, erudite, intellectual, intelligent, recondite, scholarly, smart; SEE CONCEPT *402*

ceremonial [*adj*] *ritual, formal*
august, conventional, imposing, liturgical, lofty, mannered, ritualistic, solemn, stately, studied, stylized; SEE CONCEPT *548*

ceremonious [*adj*] *ritual, formal*
civil, courteous, courtly, decorous, deferential, dignified, exact, grandiose, impressive, majestic, moving, precise, proper, punctilious, seemly, solemn, starchy, stately, stiff, striking; SEE CONCEPT *548*

ceremony [*n1*] *ritual; celebratory observation*
ceremonial, commemoration, custom, formality, function, liturgy, observance, ordinance, parade, rite, sacrament, service, show, solemnity, tradition; SEE CONCEPT *386*

ceremony [*n2*] *etiquette*
ceremonial, conformity, decorum, form, formal courtesy, formalism, formality, nicety, politeness, pomp, preciseness, prescription, propriety, protocol, strictness, usage; SEE CONCEPT *388*

certain [*adj1*] *confident*
assertive, assured, believing, calm, cocksure, convinced, positive, questionless, sanguine, satisfied, secure, self-confident, sure, unconcerned, undisturbed, undoubtful, undoubting, unperturbed, untroubled; SEE CONCEPT *403*

certain [*adj2*] *undoubtable, valid*
absolute, ascertained, authoritative, clear, conclusive, confirmable, definite, demonstrable, destined, determined, establishable, evident, firm, fixed, genuine, guaranteed, having down pat*, incontrovertible, indubitable, infallible, in the bag*, irrefutable, known, on ice*, plain, positive, predestined, provable, real, reliable, safe, salted away*, set, sound, supreme, sure, sure thing*, true, trustworthy, unambiguous, undeniable, undoubted, unequivocal, unerring, unmistakable, verifiable; SEE CONCEPTS *535,582*

certain [*adj3*] *fixed*
assured, bound, certified, concluded, decided, definite, determined, ensured, established, guaranteed, insured, set, settled, stated, stipulated, sure, warranted; SEE CONCEPT *535*

certain [*adj4*] *referring to a specifically known amount*
a couple, a few, defined, divers, express, individual, many, marked, numerous, one, particular, precise, regular, several, singular, some, special, specific, specified, sundry, upwards of, various; SEE CONCEPT *557*

certainly [*adv*] *without doubt*
absolutely, assuredly, cert*, exactly, for a fact, of course, positively, posolutely*, right on*, surely, unquestionably, without fail; SEE CONCEPT *535*

certainty [*n1*] *positive assurance*
all sewn up*, authoritativeness, belief, certitude, cinch, confidence, conviction, credence, definiteness, dogmatism, faith, firmness, indubitableness, inevitability, lock*, lockup*, open and shut case*, positiveness, positivism, rain or shine*, setup, shoo-in*, staunchness, steadiness, stock, store, sure bet*, surefire*, sureness, sure thing*, surety, trust, validity, wrap-up; SEE CONCEPTS *638,725*

certainty [*n2*] *fact, resulting truth*
consequence, foregone conclusion, inevitable result, reality, sure thing*, surety; SEE CONCEPT *230*

certificate [*n*] *authorizing document*
affidavit, affirmation, attestation, authentication, authorization, certification, coupon, credential, deed, diploma, docket, documentation, endorsement, guarantee, license, paper, pass, permit, receipt, record, sheepskin*, shingle, testament, testification, testimonial, testimony, ticket, voucher, warrant, warranty; SEE CONCEPTS *271,685*

certify [*v*] *declare as true*
accredit, approve, ascertain, assure, attest, authenticate, authorize, aver, avow, commission, confirm, corroborate, endorse, guarantee, license, notify, okay, profess, reassure, rubber-stamp*, sanction, show, state, swear, testify, validate, verify, vouch, witness; SEE CONCEPTS *50,88*

cessation [*n*] *ending*
abeyance, arrest, break, break-off*, breather*, cease, ceasing, close, conclusion, cutoff*, desistance, discontinuance, downtime*, end, finish, freeze*, grinding halt, halt, halting, hiatus, intermission, interruption, interval, layoff*, let-up*, pause, recess, remission, respite, rest, screaming halt*, standstill, stay, stop, stoppage, suspension, termination, time off, time-out*; SEE CONCEPT *119*

chafe [*v1*] *rub, grind against*
abrade, bark, corrode, damage, erode, excoriate, gall, grate, graze, hurt, impair, inflame, irritate, peel, ruffle, scrape, scratch, skin, wear; SEE CONCEPT *215*

chafe [*v2*] *annoy*
abrade, anger, annoy, bother, exasperate, excise, fret, fume, gall, grate, harass, incense, inflame, irk, irritate, itch, offend, provoke, rage, rasp, rub, ruffle, scrape, scratch, vex, worry; SEE CONCEPTS *7,19*

chaff [*n*] *waste*
crust, debris, dregs, husks, pod, refuse, remains, rubbish, shard, shell, trash; SEE CONCEPT *679*

chaff [*v*] *joke, ridicule*
banter, deride, fun, jeer, jolly, josh, kid, mock, rag*, rally, razz*, rib*, scoff, taunt, tease; SEE CONCEPT *273*

chagrin [*n*] *displeasure*
annoyance, balk, blow, crushing, discomfiture, discomposure, disgruntlement, dismay, disquiet, dissatisfaction, embarrassment, fretfulness, frustration, humiliation, ill-humor, irritation, letdown, mortification, peevishness, shame, spleen, upset, vexation; SEE CONCEPTS *410,674*

chagrin [*v*] *cause displeasure*
abash, annoy, confuse, crush, discomfit, discompose, disconcert, disgrace, dismay, displease, disquiet, dissatisfy, embarrass, humiliate, irk, irritate, mortify, peeve, perturb, shame, upset, vex; SEE CONCEPTS *7,19*

chain [*n1*] *succession, series*
alternation, catena, concatenation, conglomerate, consecution, continuity, group, order, progression, row, sequence, set, string, syndicate, train, trust; SEE CONCEPTS *432,727,769*

chain [*n2*] *connected metal links; jewelry made of such links*
bond, bracelet, cable, clinker*, connection, coupling, fetter, iron, lavaliere, link, locket, manacle, pendant, shackle, trammel; SEE CONCEPTS *446,476,499*

ce
ch

chain [v] *manacle in metal*
attach, bind, confine, connect, enslave, fetter, handcuff, hold, moor, restrain, shackle, tether, tie up, trammel; SEE CONCEPTS *85,160*

chair [n1] *single-seat furniture*
armchair, bench, cathedra, recliner, rocker, sling*; SEE CONCEPT *443*

chair [n2] *person in or position of authority*
captain, chairperson, director, fellowship, helm, instructorship, leader, monitor, position of control, principal, professorate, professorship, throne, tutor, tutorship; SEE CONCEPTS *348,376*

chairperson [n] *person in charge of proceedings*
administrator, captain, chair, director, introducer, leader, moderator, monitor, president, presider, principal, prolocutor, speaker, spokesperson, symposiarch; SEE CONCEPTS *348,376*

challenge [n] *dispute, question*
claiming, confrontation, dare, defiance, demanding, demur, interrogation, objection, protest, provocation, remonstrance, summons to contest, test, threat, trial, ultimatum; SEE CONCEPTS *53,532*

challenge [v] *dispute, question*
accost, arouse, ask for, assert, beard, brave, call for, call out, claim, confront, cross, dare, defy, demand, denounce, exact, face down, face off, face the music*, fly in the face of*, hang in*, impeach, impose, impugn, inquire, insist upon, investigate, invite competition, make a point of, make a stand, object to, provoke, query, reclaim, require, search out, stand up to, stick it out, stimulate, summon, tax, test, throw down the gauntlet*, try, vindicate; SEE CONCEPT *53*

chamber [n1] *small compartment, room*
alcove, antechamber, apartment, bedchamber, bedroom, box, case, cavity, cell, chest, container, cubicle, enclosure, flat, hall, hollow, lodging, pocket, room, socket; SEE CONCEPTS *448,494*

chamber [n2] *legislative body*
assembly, council, legislature, organization, representatives; SEE CONCEPT *299*

champion [adj] *best, excellent*
blue-ribbon, boss*, capital, chief, choice, cool, dandy, distinguished, first, greatest, head, illustrious, out of sight*, out of this world*, outstanding, premier, prime, principal, prize-winning, splendid, super, superior, tip top*, top drawer*, topflight*, top-notch*, tops*, unbeaten, undefeated, world class*; SEE CONCEPT *574*

champion [n] *defeater in competition; preeminent supporter*
advocate, ally, backer, challenger, champ, conqueror, defender, endorser, exponent, expounder, guardian, hero, heroine, medalist, nonpareil, number one*, numero uno*, paladin, partisan, patron, proponent, protector, supporter, sympathizer, the greatest*, titleholder, top dog*, upholder, vanquisher, victor, vindicator, warrior, winner; SEE CONCEPT *366*

champion [v] *advocate, support*
back, battle, contend, defend, espouse, fight for, go to bat for*, patronize, plead for, promote, put in a good word for*, ride shotgun for*, side with, stand behind, stand up for, support, thump for, uphold; SEE CONCEPTS *10,69*

championship [n] *contest for ultimate victor*
crown, crowning achievement, elimination, playoffs, showdown, title match, tournament, winner takes all*; SEE CONCEPT *363*

chance [adj] *accidental, unforeseeable*
adventitious, at random, casual, contingent, fluky, fortuitous, fortunate, happy, inadvertent, incidental, lucky, odd, offhand, unforeseen, unintentional, unlooked for, unplanned; SEE CONCEPT *552*

chance [n1] *possibility, probability*
break, contingency, fair shake*, fighting chance*, indications, liability, likelihood, long shot*, look-in, occasion, odds, opening, opportunity, outlook, prospect, scope, shot*, show, squeak, time, wager; SEE CONCEPT *650*

chance [n2] *fate, luck*
accident, advantage, adventure, bad luck, break, cast, casualty, coincidence, contingency, destination, destiny, doom, even chance, fluke, fortuity, fortune, future, gamble, good luck, hap*, haphazard, happening, hazard, heads or tails*, hit*, in the cards*, kismet, lot, lottery, luck out*, lucky break, misfortune, occurrence, odds, outcome, peradventure, peril, providence, risk, stroke of luck*, throw of the dice*, toss-up*, turn of the cards*, way the cookie crumbles*, wheel of fortune*; SEE CONCEPT *679*

chance [n3] *gamble, risk*
bet, craps game*, fall of the cards*, hazard, jeopardy, lottery, raffle, speculation, stake, throw of the dice*, try, venture, wager; SEE CONCEPT *363*

chance [v1] *risk, endanger*
attempt, cast lots, draw lots, gamble, go out on a limb, have a fling at, hazard, jeopardize, play with fire*, plunge, put eggs in one basket*, put it on the line*, roll the dice*, run the risk, skate on thin ice*, speculate, stake, stick one's neck out*, take shot in the dark*, tempt fate*, tempt fortune*, toss up*, try, venture, wager, wildcat; SEE CONCEPT *87*

chance [v2] *happen*
arrive, befall, be one's fate, betide, blunder on, break, bump, come, come about, come off, come to pass, fall out, fall to one's lot, go, hap*, hit upon, light, light upon, luck, meet, occur, stumble, stumble on, transpire, tumble, turn up; SEE CONCEPT *4*

chancy [adj] *dangerous, risky*
capricious, contingent, dicey, erratic, fluctuant, fluky, hazardous, iffy*, incalculable, precarious, problematic, problematical, rocky, speculative, ticklish, touchy, tricky, uncertain, unpredictable, unsound, whimsical; SEE CONCEPTS *552,587*

chandelier [n] *light hanging from ceiling*
candelabrum, candleholder, corona, crown, electrolier, gasolier, light fixture, luster; SEE CONCEPT *444*

change [n1] *something made different; alteration*
about-face*, addition, adjustment, advance, break, compression, contraction, conversion, correction, development, difference, distortion, diversification, diversity, innovation, metamorphosis, modification, modulation, mutation, novelty, permutation, reconstruction, refinement, remodeling, reversal, revision, revolution, shift, surrogate, switch, tempering, transformation, transition, transmutation, turn, turnover, variance, variation, variety, vicissitude; SEE CONCEPTS *230,260,701*

change [n2] *substitution; replacement*
conversion, exchange, flip-flop*, interchange, swap, switch, trade, turnaround; SEE CONCEPT *128*

change [*n3*] *smaller currency in exchange for larger*
chicken feed*, coins, copper, dimes, nickels, pennies, pin money*, pocket money, quarters, silver, spending money; SEE CONCEPT *340*

change [*v1*] *make or become different*
accommodate, adapt, adjust, alter, alternate, commute, convert, diminish, diverge, diversify, evolve, fluctuate, make innovations, make over, merge, metamorphose, moderate, modify, modulate, mutate, naturalize, recondition, redo, reduce, reform, regenerate, remake, remodel, renovate, reorganize, replace, resolve, restyle, revolutionize, shape, shift, substitute, tamper with, temper, transfigure, transform, translate, transmute, transpose, turn, vacillate, vary, veer, warp; SEE CONCEPTS *228,232,235,701*

change [*v2*] *substitute, replace*
alternate, barter, convert, displace, exchange, interchange, invert, remove, reverse, shift, supplant, swap, switch around, trade, transmit, transpose; SEE CONCEPT *128*

changeable [*adj*] *erratic*
agitated, capricious, changeful, commutative, convertible, fickle, fitful, flighty, fluctuating, fluid, impulsive, inconstant, indecisive, irregular, irresolute, irresponsible, kaleidoscopic, mercurial, mobile, movable, mutable, permutable, protean, restless, reversible, revocable, shifting, skittish, spasmodic, transformable, transitional, uncertain, unpredictable, unreliable, unsettled, unstable, unsteady, vacillating, vagrant, variable, variant, varying, versatile, volatile, wavering, whimsical; SEE CONCEPT *534*

channel [*n1*] *pathway, usually containing water*
approach, aqueduct, arroyo, artery, avenue, canal, canyon, carrier, chamber, chase, conduit, course, dig, ditch, duct, fluting, furrow, gouge, groove, gully, gutter, main, means, medium, pass, passage, pipe, raceway, route, runway, sewer, slit, sound, strait, tideway, trough, tube, tunnel, vein, watercourse, way; SEE CONCEPTS *501,514*

channel [*n2*] *means*
agency, agent, approach, avenue, course, instrument, instrumentality, instrumentation, medium, ministry, organ, route, vehicle, way; SEE CONCEPTS *6,660,770*

channel [*v*] *direct, guide*
carry, conduct, convey, funnel, pipe, route, send, siphon, traject, transmit, transport; SEE CONCEPTS *187,217*

chant [*n*] *chorus of song*
carol, croon, hymn, incantation, intonation, lilt, melody, psalm, shout, singing, song, trill, tune, warble; SEE CONCEPTS *263,595*

chant [*v*] *sing simple song or song part*
cantillate, carol, chorus, croon, descant, doxologize, drone, intone, recite, shout, tune, vocalize, warble; SEE CONCEPTS *65,77*

chaos [*n*] *utter confusion*
anarchy, ataxia, bedlam, clutter, disarray, discord, disorder, disorganization, entropy, free-for-all*, holy mess*, lawlessness, misrule, mix-up, mobocracy, muddle, pandemonium, rat's nest*, snarl, topsy-turviness*, tumult, turmoil, unruliness; SEE CONCEPTS *230,674*

chaotic [*adj*] *utterly confused*
anarchic, deranged, disordered, disorganized, every which way*, harum-scarum*, helter-skel-

ter*, lawless, purposeless, rampageous, riotous, topsy-turvy*, tumultuous, turbid, turbulent, uncontrolled; SEE CONCEPT *548*

chaperon [*n*] *person who accompanies for supervision*
alarm clock*, babysitter*, bird dog*, companion, escort; SEE CONCEPT *423*

chaperon [*v*] *accompany for supervision*
attend, carry, conduct, consort with, convoy, escort, guide, oversee, protect, safeguard, shepherd, supervise, watch over; SEE CONCEPTS *114,714*

chaplain [*n*] *minister in church*
cleric, member of clergy, pastor, preacher, priest, rabbi, turn-around collar*; SEE CONCEPT *361*

chapter [*n*] *section of book or group of items*
affiliate, branch, clause, division, episode, member, offshoot, part, period, phase, stage, topic, unit, wing; SEE CONCEPTS *270,382,832*

char [*v*] *scorch, sear*
burn, carbonize, cauterize, singe; SEE CONCEPT *249*

character [*n1*] *individuality*
appearance, aspect, attribute, badge, bent, caliber, cast, complex, complexion, constitution, crasis, disposition, emotions, estimation, ethos, frame, frame of mind, genius, grain, habit, humor, kind, makeup, mettle, mood, morale, mystique, nature, personality, quality, record, reputation, repute, sense, set, shape, singularity, sort, specialty, spirit, standing, streak, style, temper, temperament, tone, trait, turn, type, vein; SEE CONCEPT *411*

character [*n2*] *integrity*
courage, fame, honor, intelligence, mind, name, place, position, rank, rectitude, rep, report, reputation, repute, standing, station, status, uprightness; SEE CONCEPT *668*

character [*n3*] *odd person*
card*, case*, clown, crank*, customer*, duck*, eccentric, figure, freak, nut, oddball, oddity, original*, personage, personality, queer, spook*, wack*, weirdo, zombie*; SEE CONCEPTS *412,423*

character [*n4*] *written symbol*
cipher, device, emblem, figure, hieroglyph, letter, logo, mark, monogram, number, numeral, rune, sign, type; SEE CONCEPT *284*

character [*n5*] *portrayal of another*
impersonation, part, personification, role; SEE CONCEPTS *263,352*

characteristic [*adj*] *typical; distinguishing*
appropriate, diagnostic, differentiating, discriminating, discriminative, distinctive, distinguishing, emblematic, especial, essential, exclusive, fixed, idiosyncratic, inborn, inbred, indicative, individual, individualistic, individualizing, ingrained, inherent, innate, local, marked, native, normal, original, particular, peculiar, personal, private, proper, regular, representative, singular, special, specific, symbolic, symptomatic, unique; SEE CONCEPTS *542,547,550*

characteristic [*n*] *typical feature, trait*
affection, aspect, attribute, badge, bag, bearing, bent, caliber, cast, complexion, component, differentia, disposition, distinction, earmark, endowment, essence, essential, faculty, flavor, frame, idiosyncrasy, inclination, individuality, lineament, mannerism, mark, mood, nature, originality, particularity, peculiarity, personality, point, property, quality, singularity, specialty,

ch
ch

streak, stripe, style, symptom, temperament, tendency, thing, thumbprint, tinge, tone, trademark, turn, virtue; SEE CONCEPT *411*

characterize [*v*] *typify, distinguish*
belong to, brand, button down*, constitute, define, delineate, describe, designate, differentiate, discriminate, feature, identify, indicate, individualize, individuate, inform, make up, mark, outline, peculiarize, peg, personalize, pigeonhole*, portray, represent, signalize, singularize, stamp, style, symbolize, tab, typecast; SEE CONCEPT *644*

charade [*n*] *pretense*
deception, disguise, fake, farce, make-believe, mimicry, pageant, pantomime, parody, pretension, pretentiousness, put-on, travesty, trick; SEE CONCEPT *59*

charge [*n1*] *accusation*
allegation, beef*, complaint, gripe, imputation, indictment, plaint, stink*; SEE CONCEPTS *44,317*

charge [*n2*] *attack*
assault, blitz, blitzkrieg, invasion, mugging, onset, onslaught, outbreak, push, rush, sortie; SEE CONCEPT *86*

charge [*n3*] *burden*
care, commitment, committal, concern, custody, deadweight, duty, millstone, must, need, obligation, office, onus, ought, responsibility, right, safekeeping, task, tax, trust, ward, weight; SEE CONCEPTS *532,709*

charge [*n4*] *price asked for something*
amount, bad news*, bite, cost, damage, expenditure, expense, nick, outlay, payment, price, price tag, rate, squeeze, tab, tariff, tick; SEE CONCEPT *329*

charge [*n5*] *command*
behest, bidding, dictate, direction, exhortation, injunction, instruction, mandate, order, precept, word; SEE CONCEPTS *53,274*

charge [*n6*] *supervisory responsibility*
care, conduct, custody, handling, intendance, management, oversight, running, superintendence, superintendency, supervision, ward; SEE CONCEPT *117*

charge [*v1*] *accuse*
arraign, blame, blow the whistle on*, censure, criminate, drag into court*, finger*, hang something on*, impeach, impugn, impute, incriminate, inculpate, indict, involve, peg, point the finger at*, reprehend, reproach, tax, turn on, whistle-blow*; SEE CONCEPTS *44,317*

charge [*v2*] *attack*
assail, assault, blindside, bolt, buck, bushwhack*, chase, dash, invade, jump on, lunge, mug, rush, smash, stampede, storm, tear; SEE CONCEPT *86*

charge [*v3*] *load, tax*
afflict, burden, choke, clog, commit, cram, crowd, cumber, encumber, entrust, fill, heap, impregnate, instill, lade, pack, penetrate, permeate, pervade, pile, ram, saddle, saturate, suffuse, transfuse, weigh; SEE CONCEPTS *107,156,740*

charge [*v4*] *order something done*
adjure, ask, bid, command, direct, enjoin, entrust, exhort, instruct, request, require, solicit, tell, warn; SEE CONCEPTS *53,78*

charge [*v5*] *ask a price*
demand, fix price at, impose, levy, price, require, sell for; SEE CONCEPTS *330,345*

charge [*v6*] *pay with credit card*
book, buy on credit, chalk up, cuff, debit, encumber, go into hock*, incur debt, nick*, paste*, put on account, put on one's card, put on the cuff, put on the tab, receive credit, run up; SEE CONCEPTS *327,330*

charisma [*n*] *great personal charm*
allure, animal magnetism*, appeal, dazzle, drawing power, fascination, flash, glamour, it*, magnetism, pizzazz*, something*, star quality, witchcraft, witchery; SEE CONCEPT *411*

charismatic [*adj*] *charming*
alluring, appealing, hypnotic, larger than life*, magnetic, mesmerizing, poised; SEE CONCEPTS *529,537*

charitable [*adj1*] *giving, generous*
accommodating, all heart, altruistic, beneficent, benevolent, benign, big*, bighearted*, bountiful, eleemosynary, good, helpful, humane, humanitarian, kind, kindly, lavish, liberal, obliging, philanthropic, sympathetic; SEE CONCEPTS *334,542*

charitable [*adj2*] *kind, lenient*
all heart*, benevolent, big*, bighearted*, broadminded, clement, considerate, easy, favorable, forbearing, forgiving, gracious, humane, indulgent, kindly, lenient, magnanimous, merciful, sympathetic, thoughtful, tolerant, understanding; SEE CONCEPT *404*

charity [*n1*] *generosity, gift*
alms, alms-giving, assistance, benefaction, beneficence, contribution, dole, donation, endowment, fund, gifting, hand*, hand-out, helping hand*, largesse, oblation, offering, philanthropy, relief, write-off; SEE CONCEPTS *337,657*

charity [*n2*] *kindness, compassion*
affection, agape, altruism, amity, attachment, benevolence, benignity, bountifulness, bounty, caritas, clemency, fellow feeling, generosity, goodness, goodwill, grace, humaneness, humanity, indulgence, kindliness, lenity, love, magnanimity, mercy, tenderheartedness; SEE CONCEPTS *32,411*

charlatan [*n*] *swindler*
cheat, con, con artist, fake, fraud, imposter, mountebank, phony, pretender, quack, rip-off artist*, sham; SEE CONCEPTS *260,412*

charm [*n1*] *enchantment, allure*
agreeableness, allurement, appeal, attraction, attractiveness, beauty, bewitchery, charisma, chemistry, conjuration, delightfulness, desirability, fascination, glamour, grace, it*, lure, magic, magnetism, pizzazz*, something*, sorcery, spell, star quality, witchery; SEE CONCEPTS *411,673*

charm [*n2*] *talisman*
amulet, fetish, good-luck piece, juju, lucky piece, madstone, mascot, phylactery, rabbit's foot, trinket, zemi; SEE CONCEPTS *284,446*

charm [*v*] *enchant*
allure, attract, beguile, bewitch, cajole, captivate, delight, draw, enamor, enrapture, ensorcell, enthrall, entrance, fascinate, grab, hex, hypnotize, inveigle, kill*, knock dead*, knock out*, magnetize, mesmerize, please, possess, put under a spell*, send*, slay*, spell*, sweep off feet*, take*, tickle, tickle pink*, transport, turn on*, vamp, voodoo, wile, win, win over, wow*; SEE CONCEPTS *7,22*

charming [*adj*] *captivating*
absorbing, alluring, amiable, appealing, attractive, bewitching, charismatic, choice, cute, dainty, delectable, delicate, delightful, desirable,

electrifying, elegant, enamoring, engaging, engrossing, enthralling, entrancing, eye-catching, fascinating, fetching, glamorous, graceful, infatuating, inviting, irresistible, likable, lovable, lovely, magnetizing, nice, pleasant, pleasing, provocative, rapturous, ravishing, seducing, seductive, sweet, tantalizing, tempting, titillating, winning, winsome; SEE CONCEPT *404*

chart [*n*] *map, plan*
blueprint, diagram, graph, outline, plat, plot, rough draft, scheme, sketch, table, tabulation; SEE CONCEPTS *625,660*

chart [*v*] *plan, map out*
arrange, block out, blueprint, cast, delineate, design, devise, draft, graph, lay out, outline, plot, project, shape, sketch; SEE CONCEPTS *36,174*

charter [*n*] *treaty, agreement*
allotment, bond, code, concession, constitution, contract, conveyance, deed, document, endowment, franchise, grant, indenture, license, pact, patent, permit, prerogative, privilege, right, settlement; SEE CONCEPTS *684,685*

charter [*v*] *reserve, commission*
allow, authorize, borrow, contract, employ, engage, hire, lease, let, license, permit, rent, sanction; SEE CONCEPTS *48,50,88,89*

chary [*adj*] *careful, cautious*
cagey, calculating, canny, circumspect, considerate, constrained, discreet, economical, fastidious, frugal, gingerly, guarded, heedful, hesitant, inhibited, leery, loath, miserly, particular, prudent, reluctant, restrained, safe, scrupulous, sparing, stingy, suspicious, thrifty, uneasy, wary, watchful; SEE CONCEPTS *401,587*

chase [*n*] *pursuit*
hunt, hunting, quest, race, venery; SEE CONCEPT *207*

chase [*v*] *run after, pursue*
bird-dog*, charge, chivy, course, drive, drive away, expel, follow, go after, hound, hunt, run down, rush, seek, shag*, speed, take off after*, tear, track, track down, trail; SEE CONCEPT *207*

chasm [*n*] *gap, abyss*
abysm, alienation, arroyo, blank, breach, cavity, cleavage, cleft, clough, clove, crater, crevasse, fissure, flume, gorge, gulch, gulf, hiatus, hole, hollow, omission, opening, oversight, preterition, ravine, rent, rift, schism, skip, split, void, yawn; SEE CONCEPT *513*

chaste [*adj*] *pure, incorrupt*
austere, celibate, clean, continent, controlled, decent, decorous, elegant, immaculate, impotent, inexperienced, innocent, intemerate, modest, monogamous, moral, neat, platonic, proper, prudish, quiet, refined, restrained, simple, spotless, stainless, subdued, unaffected, unblemished, uncontaminated, undefiled, unstained, unsullied, unwed, vestal, virginal, virtuous, wholesome; SEE CONCEPTS *372,404*

chasten [*v*] *correct, humiliate*
abase, admonish, afflict, berate, call down, castigate, chastise, chide, cow, curb, discipline, exprobate, fulminate against, have on the carpet*, humble, objurgate, penalize, punish, rake over the coals*, rebuke, reprehend, repress, reprimand, reproach, reprove, restrain, scold, scourge, soften, subdue, take to task, tame, tongue-lash*, try, upbraid; SEE CONCEPTS *52,122*

chastise [*v*] *scold, discipline*
baste, beat, berate, castigate, censure, chasten,

chew out*, climb all over*, correct, ferule*, flog*, lash*, lay into*, lean on*, pummel, punish, ream, scourge, skelp, slap down*, spank, thrash, upbraid, whip; SEE CONCEPTS *52,122*

chastity [*n*] *celibacy, purity*
abstemiousness, abstinence, chasteness, cleanness, continence, decency, demureness, devotion, honor, immaculacy, innocence, integrity, modesty, monogamy, morality, naïveté, restraint, singleness, sinlessness, spotlessness, temperance, uprightness, virginity, virtue; SEE CONCEPT *633*

chat [*n*] *talk, often short*
babble, bull session, chatter, conversation, converse, gab*, gas*, gossip, heart-to-heart*, hot air*, jabber*, palaver, prattle*, rap*, rap session*, tête-à-tête, visit, yak*; SEE CONCEPT *278*

chat [*v*] *talk, gossip*
babble, blab*, burble, cackle, chatter, chew the fat*, chew the rag*, converse, gab*, go on*, jaw*, prate, prattle*, run on*, shoot the breeze*, yap*; SEE CONCEPT *266*

chat room [*n*] *interaction via computer*
data communication channel, live discussion, net event, room; SEE CONCEPTS *349,770*

chatter [*n*] *constant or rapid talk*
babble, blather, chat, chitchat, gas*, gossip, jabber*, palaver, prattle*, twaddle, yakking*; SEE CONCEPTS *266,278*

chatter [*v*] *speak fast and non-stop*
babble, blab*, blather, cackle, chat, chitchat, clack, gab*, gabble, gas*, gibber, go on and on, gossip, jabber, jaw*, natter, palaver, prate, prattle*, tattle, twaddle, twiddle, yak*; SEE CONCEPT *266*

chatty [*adj*] *talkative*
colloquial, communicative, conversational, familiar, friendly, gabby, garrulous, gossipy, informal, intimate, loose-lipped, loquacious, multieloquent, spontaneous, talky; SEE CONCEPT *267*

chauvinism [*n*] *extreme devotion to a belief or nation*
bellicism, ethnocentricity, fanatical patriotism, fanaticism, jingoism, narrowness, nationalism, zealotry; SEE CONCEPT *689*

cheap [*adj1*] *inexpensive*
at a bargain, bargain, bargain-basement*, bargain-counter, bought for a song*, budget, buy, cheapo*, competitive, cost next to nothing*, cut-price, cut-rate, depreciated, dime a dozen*, easy on the pocketbook*, economical, half-priced, irregular, low-cost, lowered, low-priced, low tariff, marked down, moderate, nominal, on sale, popularly priced, real buy*, reasonable, reduced, sale, slashed, standard, steal, uncostly, undear, utility, worth the money*; SEE CONCEPT *334*

cheap [*adj2*] *inferior, low in quality*
bad, base, bogus, catchpenny, cheesy, common, commonplace, crappy*, cruddy, dud, flashy, garbage, garish, glitzy*, junky*, lousy, mangy, mean, mediocre, meretricious, no bargain*, no good, ordinary, paltry, poor, ratty, raunchy, rinky-dink*, rotten, rubbishy, scroungy, secondrate, shoddy, sleazy, small-time*, tatty, tawdry, terrible, trashy, trumpery, two-bit, valueless, white elephant*, worthless; SEE CONCEPT *589*

cheap [*adj3*] *low, vulgar*
abject, base, beggarly, contemptible, despicable,

ch
ch

dirty, dishonest, mean, pitiable, scurvy, shabby, sordid, sorry, tawdry, vile; SEE CONCEPT 542

cheap [adj4] *concerned with saving money*
mean, mingy, miserly, penny-pinching, stingy, thrifty, tight*, tight-wad*; SEE CONCEPT 332

cheapen [v] *diminish worth*
abase, beat down, belittle, corrupt, damage, debase, decline, decry, degrade, demean, denigrate, depreciate, derogate, devalue, discredit, disparage, downgrade, drop, fall, lose value, lower, mar, mark down, minimize, reduce, render worthless, ruin, spoil, undervalue, write off; SEE CONCEPT 240

cheat [n1] *person who fools others*
bluff, charlatan, chiseler, con artist, confidence operator, conniver, cozener, crook, deceiver, decoy, defrauder, dodger, double-crosser*, double-dealer*, enticer, fake, hypocrite, impostor, inveigler, jockey, masquerader, pretender, quack, rascal, rogue, scammer*, shark, sharper, shyster, swindler, trickster; SEE CONCEPT 412

cheat [n2] *trick*
artifice, baloney, bamboozlement*, bill of goods*, bunco, chicanery, con, con game, cover up, cozening, deceit, deception, dirty pool*, dirty trick*, dodge, double-dealing*, fake, fast one, fast shuffle*, fix, flimflam, frame, fraud, gyp, hanky-panky*, hoax, hoaxing, humbug, hustle, imposture, jazz, jive, plant, put-on, racket, rip-off, run around, scam, sell, shady deal, sham, shell game, snow job*, spoof, sting, stunt, swindle, trickery, whitewash, wrong; SEE CONCEPT 59

cheat [v1] *defraud, fool*
bamboozle*, beat, beguile, bilk, bleed, bunco, burn, caboodle, chisel, con, cozen, crib, cross, deceive, defraud, delude, diddle*, do*, do a number on*, double-cross, double-deal, dupe, fast talk, finagle, fleece, flimflam, fudge*, give bum steer*, gouge, gyp*, hoodwink, hose, jerk around, milk, mislead, pull one's leg*, ream*, rip off*, rook*, rope in*, sandbag, scam, screw, shaft, short, shuck, skin, snow, stiff, sucker, swindle, take, take for a ride*, take in, take out, trick, trim, two-time, victimize; SEE CONCEPTS 59,139,192

cheat [v2] *frustrate, thwart*
baffle, check, defeat, deprive, foil, prevent; SEE CONCEPT 121

check [n1] *inspection, examination*
analysis, audit, checkup, control, inquiry, investigation, poll, rein, research, review, scrutiny, test; SEE CONCEPT 103

check [n2] *restraint, hindrance*
blow, constraint, control, curb, damper, disappointment, frustration, grunt, harness, holdup, impediment, inhibition, limitation, obstruction, rebuff, rejection, restrainer, reversal, reverse, setback, stoppage, trouble; SEE CONCEPTS 121,130,230

check [n3] *symbol for ticking off*
cross, dot, line, mark, score, sign, stroke, tick, X*; SEE CONCEPT 284

check [n4] *pattern of squares*
checkerboard, patchwork, plaid, quilt, tartan; SEE CONCEPT 436

check [v1] *inspect, examine*
analyze, ascertain, audit, balance account, candle, case, compare, confirm, correct, count, enquire about, eyeball*, find out, frisk, go through, investigate, keep account, look at, look over, look see*, make sure, monitor, note, overlook, probe, prove, quiz, review, scout out, scrutinize, study, take stock, tell, test, try, verify; SEE CONCEPTS 24,103

check [v2] *hinder, restrain*
arrest, baffle, bar, bit, bottleneck*, bridle, checkmate, choke, circumvent, constrain, control, counteract, curb, cut short, delay, discourage, foil, frustrate, halt, harness, hold, hold back, hold down, hold in, impede, interrupt, keep back, limit, moderate, neutralize, nip in the bud*, obstruct, obviate, pause, play for time, preclude, prevent, rebuff, reduce, rein in, repress, repulse, retard, slacken pace, slow down, snub, squelch, stay, stop, suppress, tame, terminate, thwart, withhold; SEE CONCEPTS 121,130

checkered [adj] *patterned*
checky, diversified, motley, mutable, patchwork, plaid, quilted, spotted, variegated; SEE CONCEPT 486

cheek [n1] *side of human face*
chop*, choppers*, gill, jowl; SEE CONCEPT 418

cheek [n2] *audacity, boldness*
brashness, brass*, brazenness, chutzpah*, confidence, disrespect, effrontery, gall, impertinence, impudence, insolence, lip*, nerve*, presumption, rudeness, sauce*, temerity; SEE CONCEPT 633

cheeky [adj] *impudent*
audacious, ballsy*, bold, brash, brazen, disrespectful, forward, impertinent, insolent, insulting, nervy, saucy; SEE CONCEPTS 401,404

cheep [v] *vocalize as a bird*
chip, chipper, chirp, chirrup, peek, tweedle, tweet, twitter; SEE CONCEPT 64

cheer [n1] *happiness*
animation, buoyancy, cheerfulness, cheeriness, comfort, delight, encouragement, exuberance, gaiety, geniality, gladness, glee, good cheer, hilarity, hopefulness, jauntiness, jocundity, joy, joyousness, lightheartedness, liveliness, merriment, merry-making, mirth, optimism, solace; SEE CONCEPT 410

cheer [n2] *applause, supportive yell*
acclamation, approbation, approval, cry, encouragement, hurrah, hurray, huzzah, ovation, plaudits, roar, shout; SEE CONCEPTS 69,77

cheer [v1] *make someone feel happier*
animate, brace up, brighten, buck up*, buoy, comfort, console, elate, elevate, embolden, encourage, enliven, exhilarate, give a lift*, gladden, hearten, help, incite, inspirit, let the sun shine in*, perk up, pick up, put on cloud nine*, put on top of the world*, snap out of it*, solace, steel, strengthen, uplift, upraise, warm; SEE CONCEPTS 7,22

cheer [v2] *encourage in activity*
acclaim, applaud, clap, hail, hurrah, plug*, rise to, root, salute, sound off for, support, yell; SEE CONCEPT 69

cheerful [adj] *happy*
airy, animated, blithe, bouncy, bright, bucked, buoyant, cheery, chipper, chirpy, contented, effervescent, enlivening, enthusiastic, full of pep, gay, glad, gladsome, good-humored, good-natured, hearty, high, hilarious, hopeful, in good spirits, in high spirits, jaunty, jocund, jolly, joyful, lighthearted, lively, merry, optimistic, peppy, perky, pleasant, roseate, rosy, sanguine, snappy, sparkling, sprightly, sunny, sunny side up*, up*,

upbeat, vivacious, winsome, zappy, zingy, zippy; SEE CONCEPTS *403,404*

cheering [*adj*] *encouraging*
auspicious, bright, comforting, heartening, hopeful, promising, propitious; SEE CONCEPT *529*

cheerless [*adj*] *depressing, unhappy*
austere, black, bleak, blue, comfortless, dark, dejected, dejecting, depressed, desolate, despondent, disconsolate, dismal, dispiriting, dolorous, drab, draggy, drearisome, dreary, dull, forlorn, funereal, gloomy, grim, in the dumps*, jarring, joyless, melancholy, miserable, mopey, mournful, oppressive, sad, somber, sorrowful, sullen, tenebrific, uncomfortable, wintry, woebegone, woeful; SEE CONCEPT *403*

chef [*n*] *cook*
chief cook and bottle washer*, cuisinier, culinary artist, gourmet chef, hash slinger*, sous chef; SEE CONCEPT *348*

chemical [*adj*] *concerned with atom and molecule change*
actinic, alchemical, enzymatic, synthesized, synthetic, synthetical; SEE CONCEPT *536*

cherish [*v*] *care about deeply*
admire, adore, appreciate, apprize, care for, clasp, cleave to, cling to, coddle, comfort, cosset, cultivate, defend, dote on, embrace, encourage, enshrine, entertain, fancy, fondle, foster, guard, harbor, hold dear, hold in high esteem, honor, hug, idolize, like, love, nourish, nurse, nurture, pet, preserve, prize, revere, reverence, safeguard, shelter, shield, support, sustain, treasure, value, venerate, worship; SEE CONCEPT *32*

cherry [*adj*] *bright red color*
blooming, blushing, bright red, cerise, claret, crimson, dark red, erubescent, incarnadine, reddish, rosy, rubescent, rubicund, ruddy; SEE CONCEPT *618*

cherry-picker [*n*] *truck with raisable boom*
boom, cable truck, telephone truck, utility truck; SEE CONCEPT *505*

chest [*n1*] *box for storage*
bin, bureau, cabinet, carton, case, casket, chiffonier, coffer, commode, crate, exchequer, pyxis, receptacle, reliquary, strongbox, treasury, trunk; SEE CONCEPT *494*

chest [*n2*] *upper front of body*
bosom, breast, bust, heart, mammary glands, peritoneum, pulmonary cavity, rib cage, ribs, thorax, upper trunk; SEE CONCEPT *392*

chew [*v1*] *grind with teeth*
bite, champ, chaw, chomp, crunch, dispatch, feast upon, gnaw, gulp, gum, manducate, masticate, munch, nibble, rend, ruminate, scrunch; SEE CONCEPTS *169,185*

chew [*v2*] *think about deeply*
consider, deliberate, meditate, mull, mull over, muse on, ponder, reflect upon, ruminate, weigh; SEE CONCEPT *24*

chew out [*v*] *scold*
bawl out, carpet*, criticize, dress down, jaw, revile, tell off, tongue-lash*, vituperate, wig, yell at; SEE CONCEPT *52*

chic [*adj*] *fashionable*
chichi*, clean*, current, dap*, dapper, dashing, elegant, exclusive, faddish, last word*, latest thing*, mod*, modern, modish, natty, sharp, smart, stylish, swank, trendy, voguish, with-it*; SEE CONCEPT *589*

chicanery [*n*] *deception, trickery*
artifice, cheating, chicane, deviousness, dishonesty, dodge, double-crossing, double-dealing*, duplicity, feint, fourberie, fraud, furtiveness, gambit, hanky-panky*, intrigue, machination, maneuver, plot, ploy, ruse, sharp practice, skullduggery, sophistry, stratagem, subterfuge, surreptitiousness, underhandedness, wiles; SEE CONCEPTS *59,660*

chicken [*n1*] *person afraid to try something*
coward, craven, dastard, funk, poltroon, quitter, recreant, scaredy cat*, yellow belly*; SEE CONCEPT *423*

chicken [*n2*] *farm fowl*
banty, barnyard fowl, biddy, capon, chick, cock, cock-a-doodle-do*, cockalorum, cockerel, gump*, heeler, hen, poultry, pullet, rooster; SEE CONCEPTS *394,395*

chicken feed [*n*] *small amount of money*
coins, nickles and dimes*, paltry sum, peanuts*, pin money*, pocket money, small change, small potatoes*, spending money; SEE CONCEPT *340*

chicken out [*v*] *back out*
avoid, back down, back pedal*, beg off*, blow it off*, cancel, chicken out*, cop out*, get cold feet*, give up, go back on, recant, renege, resign, scratch, shy from, surrender, throw in the towel*, turn yellow*, weasel out, welsh, wiggle out, withdraw, worm out*; SEE CONCEPTS *50,88,121,266,697*

chide [*v*] *criticize, lecture*
admonish, berate, blame, call down*, call on the carpet*, castigate, censure, check, condemn, exprobate, find fault, flay, give a hard time*, lesson, monish, rate, rebuke, reprehend, reprimand, reproach, reprove, scold, slap on the wrist*, speak to, take down*, take down a peg*, talk to, tell off*, tick off*, upbraid; SEE CONCEPT *52*

chief [*adj*] *most important, essential*
arch, capital, cardinal, central, champion, consequential, controlling, crucial, effective, especial, first, foremost, grand, head, highest, key, leading, main, major, momentous, number one*, outstanding, paramount, potent, predominant, preeminent, premier, primal, primary, prime, principal, ruling, significant, star, stellar, superior, supreme, telling, uppermost, vital, weighty; SEE CONCEPTS *568,574,829*

chief [*n*] *person in charge*
big cheese*, big gun*, big wheel*, bigwig*, boss, captain, chieftain, commander, dictator, director, foreperson, general, governor, head, head honcho*, head person*, honcho*, key player*, leader, manager, monarch, overlord, overseer, president, principal, proprietor, ringleader, ruler, sovereign, superintendent, supervisor, suzerain, top brass*, top cat*; SEE CONCEPTS *347,376*

chiefly [*adv*] *most importantly*
above all, especially, essentially, in general, in the first place, in the main, largely, mainly, mostly, on the whole, overall, predominantly, primarily, principally, usually; SEE CONCEPTS *567,772*

child [*n*] *very young person*
adolescent, anklebiter*, babe, baby, bairn, bambino, brat, cherub, chick, cub, descendant, dickens*, imp, infant, innocent, issue, juvenile, kid, kiddie*, lamb*, little angel*, little darling*, little doll*, little one, minor, mite, moppet, neonate, nestling, newborn, nipper, nursling, offspring,

ch
ch

preteen, progeny, pubescent, shaver, small fry*, sprout, squirt, stripling, suckling, tadpole, teen, teenager, teenybopper*, toddler, tot, tyke, urchin*, whippersnapper*, young one, youngster, youth; SEE CONCEPTS *414,424*

childbirth [*n*] *giving birth*
accouchement, bearing children, blessed event*, childbed, confinement, delivering, delivery, labor, lying-in, nativity, parturience, parturition, procreation, producing, propagation, reproduction, travail, visit from the stork*; SEE CONCEPTS *302,373*

childhood [*n*] *period of being young*
adolescence, babyhood, cradle, immaturity, infancy, juniority, juvenility, minority, nonage, nursery, puberty, pupilage, schooldays, teens, tender age, youth; SEE CONCEPTS *816,817*

childish [*adj*] *immature, silly*
adolescent, baby, babyish, callow, childlike, foolish, frivolous, green, infantile, infantine, innocent, jejune, juvenile, kid stuff*, naive, puerile, unsophisticated, young, youthful; SEE CONCEPTS *401,402,424,578,797*

childlike [*adj*] *innocent, naive*
artless, childish, credulous, guileless, immature, ingenuous, natural, simple, spontaneous, trustful, trusting, unaffected, unfeigned; SEE CONCEPT *404*

chill [*adj1*] *cold, raw*
arctic, biting, bleak, brisk, chilly, cool, freezing, frigid, frosty, gelid, glacial, icy, nippy, sharp, wintry; SEE CONCEPT *605*

chill [*adj2*] *unfriendly, aloof*
cool, depressing, discouraging, dismal, dispiriting, distant, emotionless, formal, frigid, glacial, hateful, hostile, icy, indifferent, reserved, solitary, standoffish, stony, uncompanionable, unemotional, ungenial, unhappy, unresponsive, unwelcoming, wintry, withdrawn; SEE CONCEPTS *401,404*

chill [*n*] *cold conditions*
bite, coldness, coolness, crispness, frigidity, gelidity, iciness, nip, rawness, rigor, sharpness; SEE CONCEPT *524*

chill [*v1*] *make cold*
air-condition, congeal, cool, freeze, frost, ice, refrigerate; SEE CONCEPTS *255,521*

chill [*v2*] *discourage*
cloud, dampen, dash, deject, demoralize, depress, dishearten, dismay, disparage, dispirit; SEE CONCEPTS *7,19*

chilly [*adj1*] *cold*
arctic, biting, blowy, breezy, brisk, cool, crisp, drafty, freezing, fresh, frosty, glacial, hawkish, icebox, icy, nippy, penetrating, sharp, snappy, wintry; SEE CONCEPT *605*

chilly [*adj2*] *unfriendly, aloof*
cold, frigid, hostile, unfriendly, unresponsive, unsympathetic, unwelcoming; SEE CONCEPT *404*

chime [*v*] *ring, peal*
bell, bong, boom, clang, dong, jingle, knell, sound, strike, tinkle, tintinnabulate, toll; SEE CONCEPT *65*

chimera [*n*] *dream, fantasy*
bogy, bubble, delusion, fabrication, fancy, fata morgana, figment, fool's paradise*, hallucination, ignis fatuus, illusion, mirage, monster, monstrosity, pipe dream*, rainbow*, snare, specter, virtual reality; SEE CONCEPT *529*

chimney [*n*] *smokestack for building*
chase, chimney pot, chimney stack, fireplace, flue, funnel, furnace, hearth, pipe, smokeshaft, stack, vent, ventilator; SEE CONCEPT *440*

chin [*n*] *area under mouth*
button, jaw, jawbone, mandible, mentum, point; SEE CONCEPT *399*

china [*n*] *dishes, often valuable*
ceramics, crockery, porcelain, pottery, service, stoneware, tableware, ware; SEE CONCEPT *493*

chink [*n*] *opening*
aperture, cleft, crack, crevice, cut, fissure, gap, hole, rift, slit, slot, space; SEE CONCEPT *513*

chintzy [*adj*] *cheap-looking*
cheap, frowzy, schlocky*, shabby, sleazy, tacky; SEE CONCEPT *485*

chip [*n*] *shard, flaw*
dent, flake, fragment, gobbet, nick, notch, paring, part, scrap, scratch, shaving, slice, sliver, wafer, wedge; SEE CONCEPTS *580,831*

chip [*v*] *knock a piece out of*
break, chisel, chop, clip, crack, crack off, crumble, cut away, cut off, damage, flake, fragment, gash, hack, hackle, hew, incise, nick, notch, shape, shear, slash, slice, sliver, snick, snip, splinter, split, whack, whittle; SEE CONCEPTS *137,189,246,250*

chip in [*v*] *contribute*
ante up*, break in*, chime in*, come through*, conate, go Dutch*, interpose, interrupt, pay, pitch in, subscribe; SEE CONCEPT *110*

chipper [*adj*] *happy*
alert, animate, animated, bright, brisk, gay, in good spirits, keen, lively, spirited, sprightly, vivacious; SEE CONCEPT *403*

chips [*n*] *substitute for money; money*
coin, currency, markers, play money, scratch; SEE CONCEPT *340*

chirp [*v*] *peep, cheep*
call, chip, chipper, chirrup, lilt, pipe, purl, quaver, roll, sing, sound, trill, tweedle, tweet, twitter, warble; SEE CONCEPT *64*

chisel [*n*] *shaping tool*
adze, blade, edge, gouge, knife; SEE CONCEPTS *495,499*

chisel [*v*] *cut, wear away*
carve, hew, incise, roughcast, roughhew, sculpt, sculpture, shape; SEE CONCEPTS *137,176,184*

chivalrous [*adj*] *valiant*
benevolent, big, bold, brave, considerate, courageous, courteous, courtly, gallant, gentlemanlike, great-hearted, heroic, high-minded, honorable, intrepid, lofty, magnanimous, manly, nobleminded, polite, quixotic, spirited, sublime, true, valorous; SEE CONCEPT *401*

chivalry [*n*] *valor, gallantry*
courage, courtesy, courtliness, fairness, politeness, valiance; SEE CONCEPT *633*

choice [*adj*] *best, superior*
10*, A-1*, elect, elite, excellent, exceptional, exclusive, exquisite, fine, first-class, hand-picked, 24-karat*, nice, popular, precious, preferential, preferred, prime, prize, rare, select, solid gold*, special, top-drawer*, uncommon, unusual, valuable, winner; SEE CONCEPT *574*

choice [*n*] *power to select; selection*
alternative, appraisal, choosing, cull, cup of tea*, decision, determination, discretion, discrimination, distinction, druthers*, election, evaluation, extract, favorite, finding, free will, judgment, op-

portunity, option, pick, preference, rating, say, substitute, variety, verdict, volition, vote, weakness; SEE CONCEPTS *41,376*

choke [v] *smother, block*
asphyxiate, bar, check, clog, close, congest, constrict, dam, die, drown, fill, gag, garrote, gasp, gibbet, kill, noose, obstruct, occlude, overpower, retard, squeeze, stifle, stop, stopper, strangle, strangulate, stuff, stunt, suffocate, suppress, throttle, wring; SEE CONCEPTS *121,219*

choose [v] *pick, select*
accept, adopt, appoint, call for, cast, commit oneself, co-opt, crave, cull, decide on, designate, desire, determine, discriminate between, draw lots, elect, embrace, espouse, excerpt, extract, fancy, favor, feel disposed to, finger, fix on, glean, judge, love, make choice, make decision, make up one's mind, name, opt for, predestine, prefer, see fit, separate, set aside, settle upon, sift out, single out, slot, sort, tab, tag, take, take up, tap, want, weigh, will, winnow, wish, wish for; SEE CONCEPT *41*

choosy [adj] *fussy, discriminating*
dainty, eclectic, exacting, fastidious, finical, finicky, nice, overparticular, particular, persnickety*, picky, prissy, select, selective; SEE CONCEPT *404*

chop [v] *cut up with tool*
axe, cleave, clip, cube, dice, divide, fell, fragment, hack, hackle, hash, hew, lop, mangle, mince, sever, shear, slash, truncate, whack; SEE CONCEPT *176*

choppy [adj] *wavy*
inclement, ripply, rough, uneven, violent, wild; SEE CONCEPT *488*

chore [n] *task*
assignment, burden, devoir, duty, effort, errand, grind, housework, job, KP*, routine, scutwork, stint, trial, tribulation, workout; SEE CONCEPT *362*

chortle [v] *laugh gleefully*
cackle, chuckle, crow, giggle, guffaw, hee-haw*, snicker, sniggle, snort, teehee*, titter; SEE CONCEPT *77*

chorus [n1] *group of singers*
carolers, choir, chorale, choristers, ensemble, glee club, singing group, vocalists, voices; SEE CONCEPT *294*

chorus [n2] *refrain*
bob, burden, chorale, main section, melody, motif, music, recurrent verse, response, ritornelle, song, strain, theme, tune, undersong; SEE CONCEPT *264*

chorus [n3] *agreement*
accord, concert, concord, consonance, harmony, tune, unison; SEE CONCEPTS *673,684*

chosen [adj] *preferred*
called, conscript, elect, exclusive, got the nod*, named, pegged, pick, picked, popular, preferential, select, selected, tabbed; SEE CONCEPTS *546,567,574*

christen [v] *named in religious rite*
asperse, baptize, bless, call, dedicate, denominate, designate, dub, entitle, godparent, immerse, sprinkle, style, term, title; SEE CONCEPTS *62,367*

chronic [adj] *incessant, never-ending*
abiding, ceaseless, confirmed, constant, continual, continuing, continuous, deep-rooted, deep-seated, enduring, ever-present, fixed, habitual, inborn, inbred, incurable, ineradicable, in-grained, inveterate, lasting, lifelong, lingering, long-lived, long-standing, obstinate, perennial, persistent, persisting, prolonged, protracted, recurrent, recurring, rooted, routine, settled, stubborn, sustained, tenacious, unabating, unmitigated, unyielding, usual; SEE CONCEPTS *534,551,798*

chronicle [n] *account, narrative*
annals, archives, diary, history, journal, narration, prehistory, recital, record, recountal, register, report, story, version; SEE CONCEPTS *271,282*

chronicle [v] *report, recount*
enter, narrate, record, register, relate, set down, tell; SEE CONCEPTS *60,79*

chronological [adj] *in consecutive time order*
archival, chronographic, chronologic, chronometric, chronometrical, chronoscopic, classified, dated, historical, horological, horometrical, in due course, in due time, in order, in sequence, junctural, ordered, progressive, sequent, sequential, tabulated, temporal; SEE CONCEPTS *548,585*

chubby [adj] *slightly fat*
ample, bearish, big, butterball*, buxom, chunky, fatty, flabby, fleshy, full-figured, hefty, husky, pleasingly plump*, plump, plumpish, podgy, portly, pudgy, roly-poly*, rotund, round, stout, tubby, zaftig*; SEE CONCEPTS *491,773*

chuck [v] *throw aside, throw away, throw out*
abandon, can, cast, desert, discard, ditch, eighty-six*, eject, fire, fling, flip, forsake, give the heave ho*, heave, hurl, jettison, junk, launch, pitch, quit, reject, relinquish, renounce, scrap, shed, shy, sling, slough, toss; SEE CONCEPTS *180,222*

chuckle [v] *giggle*
cackle, chortle, crow, exult, guffaw, hee-haw*, laugh, smile, snicker, snigger, sniggle, teehee*, titter; SEE CONCEPT *77*

chug [v] *drink quickly*
chug-a-lug, down, drink in one draft; SEE CONCEPT *169*

chum [n] *friend*
associate, bro*, buddy, co-mate, companion, comrade, crony, mate, pal, playmate, sis*; SEE CONCEPT *423*

chummy [adj] *friendly*
affectionate, buddy-buddy*, close, confidential, constant, cozy, familiar, intimate, pally*, palsy-walsy*, thick*; SEE CONCEPTS *401,555*

chunk [n] *mass, slab of something*
block, clod, dollop, glob, gob, hunk, lump, nugget, part, piece, portion, wad; SEE CONCEPT *471*

chunky [adj] *fat, plump*
beefy, chubby, dumpy, heavyset, husky, rotund, scrub, squat, stocky, stout, stubby, thick-bodied, thickset; SEE CONCEPTS *491,773*

church [n1] *religious institution, building*
abbey, basilica, bethel, cathedral, chancel, chantry, chapel, fold, house of God, house of prayer, house of worship, Lord's house, minster, mission, mosque, oratory, parish, sacellum, sanctuary, shrine, synagogue, tabernacle, temple; SEE CONCEPTS *368,449*

church [n2] *religious belief, group*
affiliation, body, chapter, communion, congregation, connection, creed, cult, denomination, doctrine, faction, faith, gathering, ism, order, persuasion, religion, schism, sect, society; SEE CONCEPTS *369,689*

ch
ch

churl [n] *rude and ill-bred, a boor; person overly concerned with saving money*
beast, chuff, clodhopper*, miser, mucker*, niggard*, oaf, peasant, provincial, rustic, tightwad, yokel; SEE CONCEPT *423*

churlish [adj] *crude, boorish*
base, blunt, brusque, cantankerous*, cloddish, clodhopping*, crabbed, crude, crusty, curt, cussed*, discourteous, dour, grouchy, gruff, grumpy, harsh, ill-tempered, impolite, loutish, lowbred, mean, miserly, morose, oafish, ornery*, rude, rustic, snippy*, sullen, surly, touchy*, ugly, uncivil, uncivilized, uncultured, unmannerly, unneighborly, unpolished, unsociable, vulgar; SEE CONCEPT *404*

churn [v] *mix up, beat*
agitate, boil, bubble, convulse, ferment, foam, froth, jolt, moil, seethe, simmer, stir up, swirl, toss; SEE CONCEPTS *147,170*

chute [n] *ramp, slope*
channel, course, fall, gutter, incline, rapid, runway, slide, trough; SEE CONCEPTS *440,471*

chutzpah [n] *fearlessness*
arrogance, audacity, backbone*, balls*, boldness, brass, gall, nerve, spine*; SEE CONCEPT *633*

cinch [n] *easy accomplishment*
breeze, cakewalk, child's play*, duck soup*, no sweat*, piece of cake*, snap; SEE CONCEPT *693*

cinder [n] *hot ash*
clinker, ember, hot coal, soot; SEE CONCEPT *260*

cinema [n] *movie industry; movie arena*
big screen*, bijou, cine, drive-in, film, flicks*, motion pictures, movie house, movie theater, moving pictures, nabes*, photoplay, pictures, picture show, playhouse, show, silver screen*; SEE CONCEPTS *293,349*

cipher [n] *zero; nothingness*
blank, diddly squat*, goose egg*, insignificancy, nada*, naught, nil, nobody, nonentity, nothing, nought, nullity, squat, zilch, zip, zippo*, zot*; SEE CONCEPTS *668,787*

cipher [v] *figure out code*
break, calculate, clear up, compute, count, decipher, estimate, figure, reckon, resolve, solve, unravel; SEE CONCEPT *37*

circa [prep] *approximately*
about, around, close on, in the region of, near, nearby, nigh, roughly; SEE CONCEPT *820*

circle [n1] *orb, loop, round figure*
amphitheater, aureole, band, belt, bowl, bracelet, circlet, circuit, circumference, circus, cirque, coil, colure, compass, cordon, corona, crown, cycle, disc, disk, ecliptic, enclosure, equator, full turn, globe, halo, hoop, horizon, lap, meridian, orbit, parallel of latitude, perimeter, periphery, record, revolution, ring, ringlet, round, sphere, stadium, tire, turn, vortex, wheel, wreath, zodiac; SEE CONCEPT *436*

circle [n2] *group of close friends, associates*
assembly, bunch, cabal, camarilla, camp, clan, class, clique, club, companions, company, comrades, coterie, crew, cronies, crowd, crush, fraternity, gang, mob, outfit, party, posse, ring, school, set, society, sorority; SEE CONCEPTS *387,417*

circle [v] *go around, circumnavigate*
begird, belt, cincture, circuit, circulate, circumduct, circumscribe, coil, compass, curve, embrace, encircle, enclose, encompass, ensphere, envelop, gird, girdle, gyrate, gyre, hem in, loop,

mill around, pivot, revolve, ring, roll, rotate, round, spiral, surround, tour, wheel, whirl, wind about; SEE CONCEPT *758*

circuit [n] *revolution, track, boundary*
ambit, area, bounds, circle, circling, circulation, circumference, circumnavigation, circumscription, circumvolution, compass, course, cycle, district, gyration, gyre, journey, lap, limit, line, orbit, perambulation, perimeter, periphery, range, region, round, route, tour, tract, turn, turning, twirl, way, wheel, whirl, wind, winding, zone; SEE CONCEPTS *484,501,770*

circuitous [adj] *going around, indirect*
back road*, by way of, circular, collateral, complicated, devious, labyrinthine, long way*, long way around*, meandering, oblique, rambling, roundabout, tortuous, winding around; SEE CONCEPTS *544,581*

circular [adj] *going around*
annular, circling, disklike, indirect, oblique, orbicular, round, rounded, spheroid; SEE CONCEPT *486*

circular [n] *handbill*
advertisement, booklet, broadside, brochure, flyer, handout, insert, leaflet, literature, notice, pamphlet, poster, publication, throwaway*; SEE CONCEPT *271*

circulate [v1] *make known*
bring out, broadcast, diffuse, disperse, disseminate, distribute, exchange, interview, issue, promulgate, propagate, publicize, publish, radiate, report, spread, strew, troll; SEE CONCEPTS *60,138*

circulate [v2] *flow*
actuate, circle, fly about, get about, get around, go about, gyrate, mill around, mobilize, move around, radiate, revolve, rotate, set off, travel, wander; SEE CONCEPT *147*

circulation [n1] *distribution*
apportionment, currency, dissemination, spread, transmission; SEE CONCEPTS *631,651*

circulation [n2] *moving circularly*
circling, circuit, circumvolution, current, flow, flowing, gyration, gyre, motion, revolution, rotation, round, turn, twirl, wheel, whirl; SEE CONCEPTS *147,738*

circumference [n] *edge, perimeter*
ambit, border, boundary, bounds, circuit, compass, confines, extremity, fringe, girth, limits, lip, margin, outline, periphery, rim, verge; SEE CONCEPT *484*

circumlocution [n] *indirect speech*
beating around the bush*, circumambages, diffuseness, discursiveness, euphemism, gassiness, indirectness, periphrase, periphrasis, pleonasm, prolixity, roundabout, tautology, verbal evasion, verbality, verbiage, wordiness; SEE CONCEPTS *51,266*

circumscribe [v] *mark off, delimit*
bar, bound, confine, define, delineate, demarcate, encircle, enclose, encompass, environ, girdle, hamper, hem in*, limit, nail down*, outline, prelimit, restrain, restrict, surround, trammel; SEE CONCEPTS *18,130*

circumspect [adj] *cautious, discreet*
attentive, cagey, calculating, canny, careful, chary, considerate, deliberate, discriminating, gingerly, guarded, heedful, judicious, meticulous, observant, politic, prudent, punctilious, safe, sagacious, sage, scrupulous, vigilant, wary, watchful; SEE CONCEPTS *403,544*

circumstance [n] *situation, condition*
accident, action, adjunct, affair, article, case, cause, coincidence, concern, contingency, crisis, destiny, detail, doom, element, episode, event, exigency, fact, factor, fate, feature, fortuity, go, happening, happenstance, incident, intervention, item, juncture, kismet, lot, matter, Moira, occasion, occurrence, particular, phase, place, point, portion, proviso, respect, scene, status, stipulation, supervention, thing, time, where it's at*; SEE CONCEPT *696*

circumstances [n] *state of affairs in one's life*
assets, capital, chances, class, command, degree, dowry, financial status, footing, income, lifestyle, lot, means, net worth, outlook, position, precedence, prestige, property, prospects, prosperity, rank, rating, resources, situation, sphere, standing, state, station, status, substance, times, way of life, worldly goods; SEE CONCEPTS *335,388*

circumstantial [adj] *incidental*
amplified, coincidental, concomitant, concurrent, conjectural, contingent, detailed, environmental, fortuitous, inconclusive, indirect, inferential, presumptive, provisional, uncertain; SEE CONCEPTS *556,582,653*

circumvent [v] *fool, mislead*
avoid, beat, beguile, bilk, bypass, circumnavigate, cramp, crimp, deceive, detour, disappoint, dodge, dupe, elude, ensnare, entrap, escape, evade, foil, frustrate, get around, hoodwink, outflank, outwit, overreach, prevent, queer, ruin, shun, sidestep, skirt, stave off, steer clear of*, stump, stymie, thwart, trick, ward off; SEE CONCEPTS *59,102,121*

circus [n] *fair with entertainment*
bazaar, big top, festival, gilly*, hippodrome, kermis, show, spectacle, three-ring*; SEE CONCEPT *293*

citadel [n] *top, tower*
bastion, blockhouse, castle, fastness, fort, fortification, fortress, keep, manor, redoubt, stronghold; SEE CONCEPTS *321,836*

citation [n1] *excerpt*
example, illustration, mention, passage, quotation, quote, quoting, reference, saying, source; SEE CONCEPT *283*

citation [n2] *award*
bidding, charge, commendation, encomium, mention, panegyric, reward, salutation, summons, tribute; SEE CONCEPTS *69,337*

cite [v1] *note, quote*
adduce, advance, allege, allude to, appeal to, enumerate, evidence, excerpt, exemplify, extract, get down to brass tacks*, give as example, illustrate with, indicate, instance, lay, mention, name, number, offer, point out, present, recite, recount, reference, refer to, rehearse, remember, reminisce, repeat, specify, spell out, tell; SEE CONCEPT *57*

cite [v2] *subpoena*
arraign, call, command, name, order, summon; SEE CONCEPT *317*

citizen [n] *person native of country*
aborigine, burgess, burgher, civilian, commoner, cosmopolite, denizen, dweller, freeman/woman, householder, inhabitant, John/Jane Q. Public*, member of body politic, member of community, national, native, naturalized person, occupant, resident, settler, subject, taxpayer, townsperson, urbanite, villager, voter; SEE CONCEPT *413*

city [adj] *metropolitan*
burghal, citified, civic, civil, interurban, intraurban, megalopolitan, municipal, urban; SEE CONCEPT *536*

city [n] *large town*
apple*, boom town, borough, burg, capital, center, conurbation, downtown, megalopolis, metropolis, metropolitan area, municipality, place, polis, port, urban place, urbs*; SEE CONCEPT *507*

civic [adj] *community*
borough, civil, communal, local, metropolitan, municipal, national, public, urban; SEE CONCEPTS *536,583*

civil [adj1] *civic, community*
civilian, domestic, governmental, home, interior, local, municipal, national, political, public; SEE CONCEPTS *536,583*

civil [adj2] *obliging, kind*
accommodating, affable, civilized, complaisant, cordial, courteous, courtly, cultivated, diplomatic, formal, genteel, gracious, mannerly, polished, polite, politic, refined, suave, urbane, well-bred, wellmannered; SEE CONCEPT *401*

civilian [adj] *nonmilitary*
noncombatant, noncombative, nonmilitant, not in armed forces, pacificist, private, unhostile; SEE CONCEPT *555*

civilian [n] *nonmilitary person*
citizen, civ*, civvie*, commoner, noncombatant, private citizen, subject; SEE CONCEPT *423*

civilization [n1] *culture, sophistication*
acculturation, advancement, breeding, civility, cultivation, development, edification, education, elevation, enlightenment, illumination, polish, progress, refinement, social well-being; SEE CONCEPT *388*

civilization [n2] *society*
civilized life, community, customs, literate society, modern humanity, mores, nation, people, polity, way of life; SEE CONCEPTS *388,417*

civilize [v] *make cultured; develop*
acculturate, acquaint, advance, better, cultivate, edify, educate, elevate, enlighten, ennoble, enrich, ethicize, foster, help forward, humanize, idealize, improve, indoctrinate, inform, instruct, polish, promote, reclaim, refine, sophisticate, spiritualize, tame, uplift; SEE CONCEPTS *244,385*

civilized [adj] *polished*
advanced, civil, cultured, educated, enlightened, humane, refined, sophisticated, urbane; SEE CONCEPT *562*

civil rights [n] *freedoms of citizens*
civil liberties, constitutional rights, freedom of religion, freedom of speech, freedoms, God-given rights, rights; SEE CONCEPT *376*

claim [n] *property, right demanded or reserved*
affirmation, allegation, application, assertion, birthright, call, case, counterclaim, declaration, demand, dibs, due, entreaty, interest, lien, part, petition, plea, postulation, prerogative, pretense, pretension, privilege, profession, protestation, reclamation, request, requirement, requisition, suit, title, ultimatum; SEE CONCEPTS *278,318,376,709*

claim [v] *demand, maintain property or right*
adduce, advance, allege, ask, assert, believe, call for, challenge, collect, declare, defend, exact, have dibs on something*, hit, hit up*, hold, hold

out for*, insist, justify, knock, lay claim to, need, pick up, pop the question*, postulate, pretend, profess, pronounce, require, requisition, solicit, stake out, take, uphold, vindicate; SEE CONCEPTS *53,129*

clairvoyance [*n*] *intuition*
acumen, discernment, ESP*, feeling, foreknowledge, insight, omen, penetration, perception, precognition, premonition, psyche, sixth sense*, telepathy; SEE CONCEPTS *409,410*

clairvoyant [*adj*] *intuitive, psychic*
clear-sighted, discerning, extrasensory, farseeing, far-sighted, fey, judicious, long-sighted, new age*, oracular, penetrating, perceptive, prescient, prophetic, second-sighted, sibylline, spiritualistic, telepathic, vatic, visionary; SEE CONCEPTS *402,403*

clairvoyant [*n*] *person who is psychic*
augur, channeller, diviner, fortune-teller, haruspex, horoscopist, medium, oracle, palm reader, prophet, seer, sibyl, soothsayer, telepath, telepathist, visionary, voodoo doctor*; SEE CONCEPT *423*

clam [*n*] *bivalve living in ocean*
cherrystone, littleneck, mollusk, quahog; SEE CONCEPT *394*

clammy [*adj*] *damp*
close, dank, drizzly, moist, mucid, mucous, muculent, pasty, slimy, soggy, sticky, sweating, sweaty, wet; SEE CONCEPT *603*

clamor [*n*] *loud cry; commotion*
agitation, babel, blare, brouhaha*, bustle, buzz, clinker, complaint, convulsion, din, discord, exclamation, ferment, hassle, hoo-ha*, hubba-hubba*, hubbub, hullabaloo*, hurly-burly*, lament, noise, outcry, pandemonium, protesting, racket, remonstrance, row, ruckus, shout, shouting, to-do, tumult, turmoil, upheaval, uproar, vociferation; SEE CONCEPTS *386,595,674*

clamor [*v*] *cry out, make commotion*
agitate, bark, bawl, bellow, bluster, claim, debate, demand, dispute, holler, put up a howl*, raise Cain*, raise the roof*, roar, rout, shout; SEE CONCEPTS *77,106*

clamp [*n*] *fastener*
bracket, catch, clasp, grip, hold, lock, nipper, press, snap, vice; SEE CONCEPT *499*

clamp [*v*] *fasten*
brace, clench, clinch, fix, impose, make fast, secure; SEE CONCEPTS *85,160*

clan [*n*] *family, clique*
association, band, bunch, club, coterie, crew, crowd, crush, faction, folks, gang, group, house, insiders, kinfolks, mob, moiety, organization, outfit, race, ring, sect, set, society, sodality, stock, tribe; SEE CONCEPTS *296,387*

clandestine [*adj*] *secret, sly*
artful, cloak-and-dagger, closet, concealed, covert, foxy, fraudulent, furtive, hidden, hush-hush*, illegitimate, illicit, in holes and corners*, on the Q. T.*, on the quiet, private, sneaky, stealthy, surreptitious, undercover, underground, underhand, under-the-counter*, under wraps*; SEE CONCEPTS *555,576*

clank [*n*] *metallic noise*
bang, bong, clash, clink, jangle, ring; SEE CONCEPT *595*

clank [*v*] *clang, clatter*
bong, clash, clink, jangle, make noise, resound, reverberate, ring, toll; SEE CONCEPT *65*

clannish [*adj*] *exclusive, select*
akin, alike, associative, cliquish, close, insular, like, narrow, related, reserved, restricting, restrictive, sectarian, unfriendly, unreceptive; SEE CONCEPT *555*

clap [*n*] *loud hitting noise*
applause, bang, blast, boom, burst, crack, crash, handclap, pat, slam, slap, smash, strike, thrust, thunder, thunderclap, thwack, wallop, whack, wham; SEE CONCEPTS *189,595*

clap [*v*] *applaud; slap with approbation*
acclaim, approve, bang, cheer, give a big hand*, give a hand*, hear it for*, pat, praise, slap, strike gently, thwack, whack; SEE CONCEPTS *185,189*

clarification [*n*] *explanation*
description, elucidation, exposition, illumination, interpretation, resolution, simplification, solution, unravelment, vivification; SEE CONCEPTS *57,274*

clarify [*v1*] *explain, make clear*
analyze, break down, clear up, define, delineate, draw a picture, elucidate, formulate, illuminate, illustrate, interpret, make perfectly clear, make plain, resolve, settle, shed light on*, simplify, spell out*, straighten out, throw light on; SEE CONCEPT *57*

clarify [*v2*] *purify*
clean, cleanse, depurate, distill, filter, rarefy, refine; SEE CONCEPT *165*

clarion [*adj*] *clear, stirring sound*
blaring, definite, inspiring, loud, ringing, sharp, shrill, strident; SEE CONCEPTS *562,592,594*

clarity [*n*] *clearness*
accuracy, articulateness, brightness, certainty, cognizability, comprehensibility, conspicuousness, decipherability, definition, directness, distinctness, evidence, exactitude, exactness, explicability, explicitness, intelligibility, legibility, limpidity, limpidness, lucidity, manifestness, obviousness, openness, overtness, palpability, penetrability, perceptibility, perspicuity, plainness, precision, prominence, purity, salience, simplicity, tangibility, transparency, unambiguity, unmistakability; SEE CONCEPTS *409,638*

clash [*n1*] *disagreement or fight, often brief*
affray, argument, battle, brawl, break, broil, brush, bump, collision, concussion, conflict, confrontation, crash, difference of opinion, discord, discordance, disharmony, dispute, donnybrook*, embroilment, encounter, engagement, fracas, fray, have a go at each other*, impact, jam, jar, jolt, jump, melee, misunderstanding, mix up, opposition, rift, riot, row, rumpus, run-in, rupture, scrap, scrimmage, set-to, shock, showdown, skirmish, smash, wallop; SEE CONCEPTS *46,106*

clash [*v1*] *hit with a loud noise*
bang, bump, clang, clank, clatter, collide, crash, grate, grind, jangle, jar, jolt, prang, rattle, scrap, scrimmage, shock, smash, wallop; SEE CONCEPTS *65,189*

clash [*v2*] *fight about, often verbally*
argue, bang heads*, battle, brawl, buck, combat, conflict, contend, cross swords*, differ, disagree, encounter, feud, fret, gall, grapple, grate, mix it up*, quarrel, raise Cain*, row, try, war, wrangle; SEE CONCEPTS *46,106*

clash [*v3*] *do not match*
be dissimilar, conflict, contrast, differ, disaccord, discord, disharmonize, mismatch, not go with; SEE CONCEPTS *655,664*

clasp [*n*] *fastener; hold on something*
brooch, buckle, catch, clamp, clench, clinch, clip, clutch, embrace, fastening, fibula, grapple, grasp, grip, hasp, hold, hook, hug, pin, safety pin, snap; SEE CONCEPTS *497,641*

clasp [*v*] *grab tightly*
attack, bear hug*, buckle, clamp, clinch, clip, clutch, coll, concatenate, connect, embrace, enfold, fasten, glom onto*, grapple, grasp, grip, hold, hug, pin, press, seize, snatch, squeeze, take; SEE CONCEPTS *85,160,191,219*

class [*adj*] *stylish; with panache*
chic, classy, dashing, fashionable, fine, fly*, foxy*, sharp; SEE CONCEPT *589*

class [*n1*] *kind, sort, category*
branch, brand, breed, cast, caste, character, classification, collection, color, degree, denomination, department, description, designation, distinction, division, domain, estate, family, feather, frame, genre, genus, grade, grain, grouping, hierarchy, humor, ilk, kidney, league, make, mold, name, nature, order, origin, property, province, quality, range, rank, rate, school, sect, section, selection, set, source, species, sphere, standing, status, stripe, style, suit, temperament, value, variety; SEE CONCEPT *378*

class [*n2*] *societal group, background*
ancestry, birth, bourgeoisie, breed, caliber, caste, circle, clan, clique, club, company, condition, connection, coterie, cultural level, degree, derivation, descent, estate, extraction, family, genealogy, grade, hierarchy, influence, intelligentsia, league, lineage, moiety, nobility, origin, pecking order*, pedigree, pigeonhole*, place, position, prestige, quality, sect, social rank, source, sphere, standing, state, station, status, stock, strain, stratum, the right stuff*, tier, title; SEE CONCEPTS *296,387,388,417*

class [*n3*] *group in school*
academy, colloquium, course, course of study, division, form, grade, homeroom, lecture group, line, quiz group, recitation, room, round table, section, seminar, seminary, session, study, study group, subdivision, subject; SEE CONCEPTS *286,287,288,289*

class [*v*] *categorize*
account, allot, appraise, assess, assign, assort, brand, classify, codify, consider, designate, divide, evaluate, gauge, grade, group, hold, identify, judge, mark, part, pigeonhole*, rank, rate, reckon, regard, score, separate; SEE CONCEPTS *39,135*

classic [*adj2*] *characteristic, regular*
prototypal, prototypical, representative, simple, standard, time-honored, typical, usual, vintage; SEE CONCEPTS *533,547*

classic [*n*] *model*
chef d'oeuvre, exemplar, magnum opus, paradigm, prototype, standard, tour de force; SEE CONCEPTS *259,655,686*

classical [*adj1*] *concerning ancient culture*
academic, Attic, Augustan, belletristic, bookish, canonic, canonical, classic, classicistic, Doric, Grecian, Greek, Hellenic, Homeric, humanistic, Ionic, Latin, Roman, scholastic, Virgilian; SEE CONCEPTS *536,549*

classical [*adj2*] *simple, chaste*
classic, elegant, harmonious, pure, refined, restrained, symmetrical, understated, well-proportioned; SEE CONCEPT *589*

classic/classical [*adj*] *best, model*
archetypal, capital, champion, consummate, definitive, distinguished, esthetic, excellent, exemplary, famous, fine, finest, first-rate, flawless, ideal, master, masterly, paradigmatic, paramount, perfect, prime, quintessential, ranking, standard, superior, top, top-notch, vintage, well-known; SEE CONCEPT *574*

classicism [*n*] *simple style; regularity, restraint*
aesthetic principle, Atticism, balance, Ciceronianism, clarity, class, classicalism, conventional formality, dignity, elegance, excellence, finish, formality, formal style, grandeur, grand style, Hellenism, high art, lucidity, majesty, neoclassicism, nobility, objectivity, polish, proportion, propriety, pure taste, purity, rationalism, refinement, rhythm, severity, simplicity, sobriety, sublimity, symmetry; SEE CONCEPT *655*

classification [*n*] *categorization*
allocation, alloting, allotment, analysis, apportionment, arrangement, assignment, assortment, cataloguing, categorizing, codification, collocation, consignment, coordination, denomination, department, designation, disposal, disposition, distributing, distribution, division, echelon, gradation, grade, grading, graduation, group, grouping, kind, order, ordering, ordination, organization, pigeonholing*, regulation, sizing, sorting, systematization, tabulating, taxonomy, typecasting; SEE CONCEPTS *18,39,135,378*

classified [*adj*] *top-secret*
confidential, private, restricted, secret; SEE CONCEPTS *267,576*

classify [*v*] *categorize*
allocate, allot, alphabetize, analyze, arrange, assort, brand, break down, button down*, catalogue, class, codify, collocate, coordinate, correlate, dispose, distinguish, distribute, divide, docket, embody, file, grade, group, incorporate, index, label, match, name, number, order, organize, peg*, pigeonhole*, put away, put down as, put down for, range, rank, rank out, rate, regiment, segregate, size, size up, sort, systematize, tab, tabulate, tag, take one's measure, ticket, type, typecast; SEE CONCEPTS *18,39,135*

classy [*adj*] *stylish, having panache*
chic, dashing, elegant, exclusive, fashionable, high-class, in, in vogue, mod, modish, posh, select, sharp, superior, swank, swanky, tony, uptown; SEE CONCEPT *589*

clatter [*n*] *loud noise*
ballyhoo*, bluster, clack, clangor, hullabaloo*, pandemonium, racket, rattle, rumpus, shattering, smashing; SEE CONCEPTS *181,189,595*

clatter [*v*] *crash; make racket*
bang, bluster, bump, clang, clank, clash, hurtle, noise, rattle, roar, shatter, smash; SEE CONCEPTS *65,181,189*

clause [*n*] *provision in document*
article, catch*, chapter, codicil, condition, fine print*, heading, item, joker*, kicker*, limitation, paragraph, part, passage, point, provision, proviso, requirement, rider, section, small print*, specification, stipulation, string attached to something*, ultimatum; SEE CONCEPTS *270,275*

claw [*n*] *nail of animal; tool shaped like nail of an animal*
barb, cant hook, clapperclaw, crook, fang, fingernail, grapnel, grappler, hook, manus, nail claw,

cl
cl

nipper, paw, pincer, retractile, spur, talon, tentacle, unguis, ungula; SEE CONCEPT *392*

claw [*v*] *using sharp nail*
break, dig, graze, hurt, itch, lacerate, mangle, maul, open, rip, scrabble, scrap, scrape, scratch, tear; SEE CONCEPTS *178,214,220*

clay [*n*] *workable earth material*
adobe, argil, argillaceous earth, bole, brick, china material, clunch, earth, kaolin, loam, loess, marl, mud, porcelain material, pottery, slip, terra cotta, till, wacke; SEE CONCEPT *509*

clean [*adj1*] *not dirty; uncluttered*
apple-pie order*, blank, bright, cleansed, clear, delicate, dirtless, elegant, faultless, flawless, fresh, graceful, hygienic, immaculate, laundered, neat, neat as a button*, neat as a pin*, orderly, pure, sanitary, shining, simple, snowy, sparkling, speckless, spic and span*, spotless, squeaky, stainless, taintless, tidy, trim, unblemished, unpolluted, unsmudged, unsoiled, unspotted, unstained, unsullied, untarnished, vanilla*, washed, well-kept, white; SEE CONCEPT *485*

clean [*adj2*] *sterile*
antiseptic, aseptic, clarified, decontaminated, disinfected, hygienic, pure, purified, sanitary, sterilized, unadulterated, uncontaminated, uninfected, unpolluted, unsullied, wholesome; SEE CONCEPTS *314,485*

clean [*adj3*] *chaste, virtuous*
blameless, crimeless, decent, exemplary, faultless, good, guiltless, honorable, inculpable, innocent, modest, moral, respectable, sinless, undefiled, unguilty, unsullied, upright, wholesome; SEE CONCEPT *404*

clean [*adj4*] *precise, sharp*
clear, clear-cut, correct, definite, distinct, legible, neat, plain, readable, simple, trim, uncluttered; SEE CONCEPT *535*

clean [*adj5*] *complete, thorough*
absolute, conclusive, decisive, entire, final, perfect, total, unimpaired, whole; SEE CONCEPT *531*

clean [*v*] *make undirty, uncluttered*
absterge, bath, bathe, blot, brush, cauterize, clarify, cleanse, clear the decks*, clear up, deodorlze, depurate, deterge, disinfect, do up*, dredge, dust, edulcorate, elutriate, erase, expunge, expurgate, flush, hackle, launder, lave, mop, neaten, pick, pick up, polish, purge, purify, rake, rasp, refine, rinse, rout out, sanitize, scald, scour, scrape, scrub, shake out, shampoo, soak, soap, sponge, spruce up*, sterilize, straighten up, swab, sweep, tidy up, vacuum, wash, whisk, winnow, wipe; SEE CONCEPTS *161,165*

clean-cut [*adj*] *neat, clearly outlined*
categorical, chiseled, clear, definite, definitive, etched, explicit, express, sharp, specific, unambiguous, well-defined; SEE CONCEPTS *490,535*

cleanse [*v*] *make undirty; wash*
absolve, clarify, clean, clear, depurate, disinfect, expurgate, launder, lustrate, purge, purify, refine, restore, rinse, sanitize, scour, scrub, sterilize; SEE CONCEPT *165*

cleanser [*n*] *strong disinfectant, solvent*
abrasive, abstergent, antiseptic, cathartic, deodorant, detergent, fumigant, lather, polish, purgative, purifier, scourer, soap, soap powder, suds; SEE CONCEPT *492*

clear [*adj1*] *cloudless, bright*
clarion, crystal, fair, fine, halcyon, light, luminous, pleasant, rainless, shining, shiny, sunny,

sunshiny, unclouded, undarkened, undimmed; SEE CONCEPTS *525,617,627*

clear [*adj2*] *understandable, apparent*
apprehensible, audible, clear-cut, coherent, comprehensible, conspicuous, crystal, definite, distinct, evident, explicit, express, graspable, incontrovertible, intelligible, knowable, legible, loud enough, lucent, lucid, manifest, obvious, open and shut*, palpable, patent, perceptible, perspicuous, plain, precise, pronounced, readable, recognizable, sharp, simple, spelled out*, straightforward, transparent, transpicuous, unambiguous, unblurred, uncomplicated, unequivocal, unmistakable, unquestionable; SEE CONCEPTS *402,562*

clear [*adj3*] *open, unhindered*
bare, empty, free, smooth, stark, unhampered, unimpeded, unlimited, unobstructed, vacant, vacuous, void; SEE CONCEPT *490*

clear [*adj4*] *transparent*
apparent, cloudless, crystal, crystal clear, crystalline, glassy, limpid, pellucid, pure, see-through, thin, tralucent, translucent, translucid; SEE CONCEPTS *618,619*

clear [*adj5*] *not guilty*
absolved, blameless, clean, cleared, discharged, dismissed, exculpated, exonerated, guiltless, immaculate, innocent, pure, sinless, stainless, unblemished, uncensurable, undefiled, untarnished, untroubled; SEE CONCEPTS *319,404*

clear [*adj6*] *certain in one's mind*
absolute, confirmed, convinced, decided, definite, positive, resolved, satisfied, sure; SEE CONCEPT *403*

clear [*v1*] *clean, clear away*
ameliorate, break up, brighten, burn off, clarify, cleanse, disencumber, disengage, disentangle, eliminate, empty, erase, extricate, free, lighten, loosen, lose, meliorate, open, purify, refine, rid, rule out, shake off, sweep, throw off, tidy, unblock, unburden, unclog, unload, unloose, unpack, untie, vacate, void, wipe; SEE CONCEPTS *165,211*

clear [*v2*] *liberate; free from uncertainty*
absolve, acquit, clarify, defog*, discharge, disculpate, emancipate, exculpate, exonerate, explain, find innocent, let go, let off, let off the hook*, release, relieve, set free, vindicate; SEE CONCEPTS *7,22,127*

clear [*v3*] *pass over, often by jumping*
hurdle, leap, miss, negotiate, overleap, surmount, vault; SEE CONCEPT *194*

clear [*v4*] *profit*
accumulate, acquire, clean up*, earn, gain, gather, get, glean, make, net, obtain, pick up, realize, reap, receive, secure, win; SEE CONCEPTS *129,342*

clearance [*n1*] *permission for activity*
approval, authorization, consent, endorsement, go-ahead*, green light*, leave, okay, sanction, say-so*; SEE CONCEPT *376*

clearance [*n2*] *gap above something*
allowance, assart, defoliated area, empty space, expanse, gap, headroom, margin, opening, open space; SEE CONCEPT *513*

clear-cut [*adj*] *definite*
assured, categorical, crystalline, decided, definitive, distinct, evident, explicit, express, indubitable, lucent, lucid, obvious, plain, precise, pronounced, sharp-cut, specific, straightforward,

unambiguous, undisputed, undoubted, unequivocal, unquestioned, well-defined; SEE CONCEPT *535*

clearing [*n*] *gap in area*
allowance, assart, clearance, defoliated area, dell, empty space, expanse, gap, glade, headroom, margin, opening, open space; SEE CONCEPT *513*

clearly [*adv*] *without any doubt*
acutely, apparently, audibly, beyond doubt, certainly, conspicuously, decidedly, definitely, discernibly, distinctly, evidently, incontestably, incontrovertibly, indubitably, lucidly, manifestly, markedly, noticeably, obviously, openly, overtly, patently, penetratingly, perceptibly, plainly, positively, precisely, prominently, purely, recognizably, seemingly, sharply, sonorously, surely, translucently, transparently, undeniably, undoubtedly, unmistakably; SEE CONCEPTS *535,552*

clear out [*v1*] *empty something*
clean out, dispose of, eliminate, exhaust, get rid of, remove, sort, tidy up; SEE CONCEPT *211*

clear out [*v2*] *leave, often quickly*
beat it*, begone, decamp, depart, go, hightail*, kite*, make oneself scarce*, remove oneself, retire, scram, skedaddle*, split*, take a hike*, take off, vamoose*, withdraw; SEE CONCEPT *195*

clear up [*v1*] *explain; resolve*
answer, cipher, clarify, decipher, dissolve, elucidate, figure out, illuminate, illustrate, make plausible, make reasonable, puzzle out, resolve, solve, straighten out, tidy, unfold, unravel; SEE CONCEPTS *37,57*

clear up [*v2*] *become improved*
become fair, become sunny, blow over, brighten, die away, die down, improve, lapse, lift, pick up, run its course*; SEE CONCEPT *700*

cleavage [*n*] *gap*
break, chasm, cleft, discontinuity, divide, division, fracture, hole, rift, schism, separation, severance, split, valley; SEE CONCEPT *513*

cleave [*v1*] *divide, split*
carve, chop, crack, cut, dissect, dissever, disunite, divorce, hack, hew, open, part, pierce, rend, rip, rive, separate, sever, slice, stab, sunder, tear asunder, whack; SEE CONCEPTS *98,137,176*

cleave [*v2*] *stand by, stick together*
abide by, adhere, agree, associate, attach, be devoted to, be true with*, be true*, cling, cohere, combine, freeze to*, hold, join, link, remain, stay put, unite; SEE CONCEPTS *8,113*

cleft [*adj*] *separated, split*
broken, cloven, cracked, crannied, crenelated, parted, perforated, pierced, rent, riven, ruptured, separated, sundered, torn; SEE CONCEPT *490*

cleft [*n*] *break, gap*
aperture, arroyo, breach, canyon, chasm, chink, cleavage, clough, clove, crack, cranny, crevasse, crevice, fissure, fracture, gorge, gulch, opening, ravine, rent, rift, rima, rimation, rime, schism, slit; SEE CONCEPT *513*

clemency [*n*] *forgiveness*
caritas, charity, compassion, endurance, equitableness, fairness, forbearance, gentleness, grace, humanity, indulgence, justness, kindness, lenience, leniency, lenity, lifesaver, mercifulness, mercy, mildness, moderation, soft-heartedness, sufferance, tenderness, tolerance, toleration; SEE CONCEPTS *410,644*

clement [*adj1*] *calm, mild (weather)*
balmy, clear, fair, fine, moderate, peaceful, temperate, warm; SEE CONCEPT *525*

clement [*adj2*] *forgiving*
benevolent, benign, benignant, charitable, compassionate, easy, forbearing, gentle, humane, humanitarian, indulgent, kind, kind-hearted, kindly, lenient, merciful, mild, soft-hearted, sympathetic, tender, tolerant; SEE CONCEPTS *404,550*

clench [*v*] *grasp*
clamp, clasp, clinch, clutch, constrict, contract, double up, draw together, grapple, grip, hold; SEE CONCEPT *191*

clergy [*n*] *ministry of church*
canonicate, canonry, cardinalate, churchpersons, clerics, conclave, deaconry, diaconate, ecclesiastics, first estate, holy order, pastorate, prelacy, priesthood, rabbinate, the cloth, the desk, the pulpit; SEE CONCEPT *369*

clergyperson [*n*] *minister of church*
abbey, archbishop, bishop, blackcoat*, cardinal, cassock, chaplain, churchperson, cleric, clerk, curate, dean, divine, ecclesiast, ecclesiastic, evangelist, father, missionary, monsignor, padre, parson, pastor, person of God, person of the cloth, pontiff, preacher, predicant, priest, primate, pulpitarian, pulpiteer, rabbi, rector, reverend, sermonizer, shepherd, vicar; SEE CONCEPT *361*

clerical [*adj1*] *secretarial*
accounting, bookkeeping, clerkish, clerkly, office, pink collar*, scribal, stenographic, subordinate, typing, white collar*, written; SEE CONCEPT *536*

clerical [*adj2*] *concerning clergy*
apostolic, canonical, churchly, cleric, ecclesiastic, ecclesiastical, episcopal, holy, ministerial, monastic, monkish, papal, parsonical, parsonish, pastoral, pontifical, prelatic, priestly, rabbinical, sacerdotal, sacred, theocratical; SEE CONCEPT *536*

clerk [*n*] *assistant*
agent, amanuensis, auditor, bookkeeper, cashier, copyist, counter jumper*, counterperson, employee, notary, office helper, operator, paper pusher*, paper shuffler*, pencil pusher*, pen pusher*, receptionist, recorder, registrar, salesperson, secretary, seller, shopperson, stenographer, teller, transcriber, white collar*, worker; SEE CONCEPT *348*

clever [*adj*] *bright, ingenious*
able, adept, adroit, alert, apt, astute, brainy, brilliant, cagey, canny, capable, competent, crackerjack*, cunning, deep, dexterous/dextrous, discerning, egghead*, expert, foxy*, gifted, good, handy, intelligent, inventive, keen, knowing, knowledgeable, many-sided, nimble, nobody's fool*, pretty, pro, qualified, quick, quick on trigger*, quick-witted, rational, resourceful, sagacious, savvy, sensible, sharp, shrewd, skilled, skillful, slick, sly, smart, sprightly, talented, versatile, wise, witty; SEE CONCEPT *402*

cleverness [*n*] *brightness, ingenuity*
ability, adroitness, astuteness, brains, calculation, canniness, dexterity, discernment, flair, gift, gumption, intelligence, quickness, quick wit, resourcefulness, sagacity, sense, sharpness, shrewdness, skill, smartness, talent, wisdom, wit; SEE CONCEPT *409*

cl
cl

cliché [n] *overused, hackneyed phrase*
adage, banality, boiler plate*, bromide, buzzword, chestnut*, commonplace, corn*, counterword, familiar tune, motto, old story*, platitude, potboiler, prosaism, proverb, rubber stamp*, saying, shibboleth, slogan, stale saying, stereotype, threadbare phrase, triteness, trite remark, triviality, truism, vapid expression; SEE CONCEPTS *275,278*

click [n/v1] *metallic sound*
bang, beat, clack, snap, tick; SEE CONCEPTS *65,595*

click [v2] *fall into place*
become clear, be compatible, be on same wavelength*, come off*, feel a rapport*, get on*, go, go off well*, go over, hit it off*, make a hit*, make sense, match, meet with approval, pan out*, prove out, succeed, take to each other*; SEE CONCEPT *704*

client [n] *customer*
applicant, believer, buyer, chump, consumer, dependent, disciple, follower, front, habitué, head, mark, patient, patron, protégé, protégée, purchaser, shopper, walk-in, ward; SEE CONCEPT *348*

clientele [n] *customers of business*
audience, business, clientage, clientry, clients, constituency, cortege, dependents, following, market, patronage, patrons, public, regulars, trade; SEE CONCEPTS *325,417*

cliff [n] *overhang on hill or mountain*
bluff, crag, escarpment, face, precipice, rock face, rocky height, scar, scarp, steep rock, wall; SEE CONCEPT *509*

cliffhanger [n] *something suspenseful*
close call, close shave*, narrow escape, shocker, spine-chiller, thriller, white knuckle; SEE CONCEPTS *410,679*

climactic/climacteric [adj] *decisive*
acute, climactical, critical, crucial, desperate, dire, paramount, peak; SEE CONCEPT *567*

climate [n1] *weather of region*
altitude, aridity, atmospheric conditions, characteristic weather, clime, conditions, humidity, latitude, meteorological character, meteorologic conditions, temperature; SEE CONCEPT *524*

climate [n2] *mood of situation*
ambience, ambient, atmosphere, disposition, environment, feeling, medium, milieu, mise-enscène, mood, surroundings, temper, tendency, trend; SEE CONCEPT *673*

climax [n] *peak, culmination*
acme, apex, apogee, ascendancy, capsheaf, capstone, climacteric, crest, crowning point, extremity, head, height, highlight, high spot, intensification, limit, maximum, meridian, ne plus ultra, orgasm, payoff*, pinnacle, pitch, summit, tiptop, top, turning point, utmost, zenith; SEE CONCEPTS *706,836*

climax [v] *come to top; culminate*
accomplish, achieve, break the record*, cap, come, come to a head*, conclude, content, crown, end, finish, fulfill, hit high spot, orgasm, peak, please, reach a peak, reach the zenith, rise to crescendo*, satisfy, succeed, terminate, top, tower; SEE CONCEPTS *375,704,706*

climb [v] *crawl, move up*
ape up*, ascend, clamber, escalade, escalate, go up, mount, rise, scale, soar, top; SEE CONCEPT *166*

clinch [v1] *secure a goal*
assure, cap, conclude, confirm, decide, determine, seal, seize, set, settle, sew up, verify; SEE CONCEPT *706*

clinch [v2] *hold securely; grab*
bolt, clamp, clasp, clench, clutch, cuddle, embrace, enfold, fasten, fix, grab hold of, grapple, grasp, grip, hug, lay hands on, make fast, nail, press, rivet, secure, seize, snatch, squeeze; SEE CONCEPTS *191,219*

clincher [n] *settling event*
capper, closer, coup de grâce, crowning blow*, culmination, deathblow*, deciding moment, finisher, finishing touch; SEE CONCEPTS *230,635,676*

cling [v] *attach to*
adhere, be true to, cherish, clasp, cleave to, clutch, cohere, continue, embrace, endure, fasten, freeze to, grasp, grip, hang in, hang onto, hold fast, hug, last, linger, squeeze, stay put, stick, stick like glue*; SEE CONCEPTS *85,160,190*

clinic [n] *medical center*
dispensary, hospital, infirmary, sick bay, surgery center; SEE CONCEPTS *312,439,449*

clinical [adj] *dispassionate*
analytic, antiseptic, cold, detached, disinterested, emotionless, impersonal, objective, scientific, unemotional; SEE CONCEPT *404*

clink [n/v] *bang against, ring*
chink, clang, jangle, jingle, sound, tingle, tinkle; SEE CONCEPTS *65,595*

clip [v1] *cut short*
bob, crop, curtail, cut, cut back, decrease, dock, lower, mow, pare, prune, reduce, shave, shear, shorten, skive, slash, snip, trim, truncate; SEE CONCEPTS *137,176*

clip [v2/n] *punch*
blow, box, clout, cuff, knock, punch, smack, sock, thump, wallop, whack; SEE CONCEPT *189*

clique [n] *group of friends*
bunch, cabal, camarilla, camp, circle, clan, club, coterie, crew, crowd, crush, faction, gang, ingroup, insiders, lobby, Mafia, mob, organization, outfit, pack, posse, ring, set, society; SEE CONCEPTS *387,417*

cloak [n] *cover; coat*
beard, blind, camouflage, cape, capote, disguise, facade, face, front, guise, manteau, mantle, mask, pretext, semblance, shawl, shield, show, veneer, wrap; SEE CONCEPTS *451,475,680*

cloak [v] *disguise*
blanket, camouflage, coat, conceal, cover, curtain, dissemble, dissimulate, dress up, hide, mask, obscure, pretext, screen, shroud, veil; SEE CONCEPT *188*

clobber [v] *hit, beat*
belt, blast, drub, lambaste*, lick, shellac*, slam, slug, smash, smear, smother, thrash, trim, wallop, whip; SEE CONCEPTS *189,252*

clock [n] *timekeeping device*
alarm, Big Ben*, chroniker*, chronograph, chronometer, digital watch, hourglass, pendulum, stopwatch, sundial, tattler, ticker*, ticktock*, timekeeper, timemarker, timepiece, timer, turnip*, watch; SEE CONCEPTS *463,819*

clockwork [n] *being on time; precision*
accuracy, consistency, perfect timing, regularity, smoothness; SEE CONCEPT *818*

clod [n] *stupid person*
blockhead*, boor, chump, clown, dimwit*, dolt,

dope*, dumbbell, dummy, dunce, fool, imbecile, lame-brain*, lout, oaf, simpleton; SEE CONCEPTS *412,423*

clog [*n*] *blockage*
bar, block, blockade, burden, cumbrance, dead weight, drag, encumbrance, hindrance, impedance, impediment, obstruction, snag; SEE CONCEPTS *121,674*

clog [*v*] *block, hinder*
burden, choke, close, congest, curb, dam up, encumber, entrammel, fetter, fill, glut, hamper, impede, jam, leash, obstruct, occlude, plug, seal, shackle, stopper, stop up, stuff, tie, trammel; SEE CONCEPTS *121,130,190*

cloister [*n*] *secluded religious place*
abbey, cell, chapter house, convent, friary, hermitage, house, lamasery, monastery, nunnery, order, priorate, priory, religious community, retreat, sanctuary; SEE CONCEPTS *368,516*

cloistered [*adj*] *secluded*
cloistral, confined, hermitic, hidden, insulated, recluse, reclusive, restricted, secluse, seclusive, sequestered, sheltered, shielded, shut off, withdrawn; SEE CONCEPTS *554,583*

clone [*n*] *exact duplicate*
act-alike, copy, double, duplicate, look-alike computer, reproduction, twin; SEE CONCEPTS *664,667,716*

clone [*v*] *copy exactly*
copy, duplicate, repeat, replicate, reproduce; SEE CONCEPTS *91,171*

close [*adj1*] *near, nearby*
abutting, across the street, adjacent, adjoining, approaching, around the corner, at hand, contiguous, convenient, give or take a little*, handy, hard by, immediate, imminent, impending, in spitting distance*, in the ball park*, near-at-hand, nearest, nearly, neighboring, next, nigh, proximate, under one's nose*, warm; SEE CONCEPT *586*

close [*adj2*] *dense, cramped*
circumscribed, close-grained, compact, confined, confining, congested, consolidated, cropped, crowded, firm, impenetrable, impermeable, jam-packed, narrow, packed, restricted, short, solid, substantial, thick, tight; SEE CONCEPTS *481,483,774*

close [*adj3*] *accurate, precise*
conscientious, exact, faithful, lifelike, literal, resembling, similar, strict; SEE CONCEPTS *535,563*

close [*adj4*] *intimate*
attached, buddy-buddy*, chummy, confidential, cozy with, dear, devoted, familiar, inseparable, kissing cousins*, loving, making it with*, on top of each other*, palsy-walsy*, private, related, thick*, thick as thieves*, thick with*; SEE CONCEPTS *372,555*

close [*adj5*] *oppressive, humid*
airless, breathless, choky, confined, fusty, heavy, moldy, motionless, muggy, musty, stagnant, stale, stale-smelling, sticky, stifling, stuffy, suffocating, sultry, sweltering, sweltry, thick, tight, uncomfortable, unventilated; SEE CONCEPTS *525,605*

close [*adj6*] *secret, reserved*
buttoning one's lip*, buttoning up*, clamming up*, close-lipped, closemouthed, hidden, hush-hush*, mum's the word*, on the Q. T.*, private, reticent, retired, secluded, secretive, silent, taciturn, tight chops*, tight-lipped*, uncommunica-

tive, unforthcoming, zipping one's lips*; SEE CONCEPTS *267,576*

close [*adj7*] *stingy*
chintzy*, closefisted, illiberal, mean, mingy, miserly, narrow, niggardly, parsimonious, penny-pinching, penurious, skimpy, skinflint*, tight, tight-fisted, ungenerous; SEE CONCEPTS *334,404*

close [*n*] *ending*
adjournment, cease, cessation, completion, conclusion, culmination, denouement, desistance, end, finale, finish, period, stop, termination, windup; SEE CONCEPTS *119,832*

close [*v1*] *obstruct, seal*
bang, bar, block, bolt, button, caulk, choke, clap, clench, clog, confine, congest, cork, dam, exclude, fasten, fill, lock, occlude, plug, prevent passage, put to, retard flow, screen, secure, shut, shut off, shutter, slam, stopper, stop up, stuff, turn off; SEE CONCEPTS *113,121,201*

close [*v2*] *complete, finish, stop*
button down*, button up*, call it a day*, call off, cap, cease, clear, clinch, conclude, consummate, culminate, cut loose, determine, discontinue, do, drop the curtain*, end, fold, fold up, halt, pack it in*, put a lid on*, put to bed*, sew up*, shut down, shutter, terminate, ultimate, wind down*, wind up*, wrap up*; SEE CONCEPT *234*

close [*v3*] *join, unite*
agree, bind, chain, coalesce, come together, connect, couple, encounter, fuse, grapple, inclose, meet, put together, tie, tie up; SEE CONCEPT *113*

close call [*n*] *narrow escape*
cliffhanger, close shave*, heart stopper*, near miss, photofinish, squeaker*, white-knuckler*; SEE CONCEPT *102*

closed [*adj1*] *shut, out of service*
bankrupt, dark, fastened, folded, gone fishing*, locked, not open, out of business*, out of order*, padlocked, sealed, shut down; SEE CONCEPT *576*

closed [*adj2*] *finished, terminated*
concluded, decided, ended, final, over, resolved, settled; SEE CONCEPT *548*

closed [*adj3*] *exclusive, independent*
restricted, self-centered, self-contained, self-sufficient, self-sufficing, self-supported, self-supporting, self-sustained, self-sustaining; SEE CONCEPT *550*

closely [*adv*] *approximately, carefully*
by the skin of one's teeth*, exactly, firmly, hard, heedfully, in conjunction with, intently, intimately, jointly, meticulously, mindfully, minutely, nearly, punctiliously, scrupulously, searchingly, sharply, similarly, strictly, thoughtfully; SEE CONCEPTS *487,557,573*

closemouthed [*adj*] *silent, reserved*
buttoned up*, clammed up*, close, close-lipped, dummied up, have tight chops*, hush-hush, on the Q. T.*, quiet, reticent, sedate, taciturn, tight-lipped, uncommunicative, zipped one's lips*; SEE CONCEPT *267*

closet [*n*] *storage cupboard, usually tall*
ambry, bin, buffet, cabinet, chest of drawers, clothes room, cold storage, container, depository, locker, receptacle, recess, repository, room, safe, sideboard, vault, walk-in, wardrobe; SEE CONCEPT *440*

closure [*n1*] *conclusion*
cease, cessation, close, closing, desistance, end,

cl
cl

ending, finish, stop, stoppage, termination; SEE
CONCEPT *119*

closure [n2] *plug, seal*
blockade, bolt, bung, cap, cork, fastener, latch,
lid, obstruction, occludent, occlusion, padlock,
stop, stopper, stopple, tampon, tap; SEE CON-
CEPTS *471,680*

clot [n] *blockage, mass of coagulation*
array, batch, battery, body, bulk, bunch, bundle,
clotting, clump, cluster, coagulum, coalescence,
conglutination, consolidation, curd, curdling,
embolism, embolus, glob, gob, group, grume,
lump, occlusion, precipitate, set, thickness,
thrombus; SEE CONCEPTS *432,466,470*

clot [v] *coagulate*
clabber, coalesce, congeal, curdle, gel, gelate,
gelatinize, glop up*, jell, jellify, jelly, lopper*,
lump, set, solidify, thicken; SEE CONCEPT *469*

cloth [n] *fabric*
bolt, calico, cotton, dry goods, goods, material,
stuff, synthetics, textiles, tissue, twill, weave,
yard goods; SEE CONCEPT *473*

clothe [v] *cover with apparel*
accouter, apparel, array, attire, bedizen, bedrape,
breech, bundle up, caparison, cloak, coat, costume, dandify, deck, disguise, dizen, do up*,
drape, dress, dress up, dud*, endow, endue, enwrap, equip, fit, fit out, garb, gown, guise, habili-
tate, habit, invest, jacket, livery, mantle, outfit,
primp, raiment, rig, robe, spruce, suit up, swaddle, swathe, tog, turn out, vest; SEE CONCEPT *167*

clothes/clothing [n] *personal attire*
accouterment, apparel, array, caparison,
civvies*, costume, covering, drag*, drapery,
dress, duds*, ensemble, equipment, finery, frippery, frock, full feather*, garb, garments, gear,
get-up*, habiliment, habit, hand-me-downs, livery, mufti, outfit, overclothes, panoply, rags*,
raiment, regalia, rigging*, sack*, sportswear,
Sunday best*, tailleur, tatters*, things*, threads*,
toggery*, togs, tout ensemble, trappings,
trousseau, underclothes, vestment, vesture,
vines*, wardrobe, wear, weeds*, zoot suit*; SEE
CONCEPT *451*

cloud [n1] *mass of water particles in air*
billow, brume, darkness, dimness, film, fog, fogginess, frost, gloom, haze, haziness, mare's tail*,
mist, murk, nebula, nebulosity, obscurity, ol'
buttermilk sky*, overcast, pea soup*, pother,
puff, rack, scud, sheep, smog, smoke, smother,
steam, thunderhead, vapor, veil, woolpack; SEE
CONCEPTS *437,524*

cloud [n2] *crowd*
army, dense mass, flock, horde, host, legion,
multitude, rout, scores, shower, swarm, throng;
SEE CONCEPTS *417,432*

cloud [v1] *become foggy or obscured*
adumbrate, becloud, befog, blur, darken, dim,
eclipse, envelop, fog, gloom, mist, obfuscate,
overcast, overshadow, shade, shadow, veil; SEE
CONCEPTS *469,526*

cloud [v2] *confuse*
addle, becloud, befuddle, disorient, distort, distract, impair, muddle, muddy, obscure, perplex,
puzzle; SEE CONCEPTS *7,19*

cloudy [adj] *hazy; darkened*
blurred, confused, dark, dense, dim, dismal, dull,
dusky, emulsified, foggy, gloomy, heavy, indefinite, indistinct, leaden, lowering, misty, mucky,
muddy, murky, mushy, nebulous, nontranslu-

cent, nontransparent, not clear, nubilous, obscure, opaque, overcast, somber, sullen, sunless,
vaporous; SEE CONCEPT *525*

clout [n] *power*
authority, influence, prestige, pull*, standing,
sway, weight; SEE CONCEPT *686*

clout [v] *hit*
blow, box, clip, clobber, cuff, rap, slap, smack,
sock, strike, thump, wallop, whack; SEE CON-
CEPTS *189,200*

clown [n1] *joking person*
antic, buffoon, comedian, comic, cut-up*, dolt,
droll, farceur, fool, funnyperson, funster, gag-
man*, gagster*, harlequin, humorist, jester,
joker, jokesmith, jokester, life of the party*,
madcap, merry-andrew, merrymaker, mime,
mountebank, mummer, picador, pierrot,
prankster, punch, punchinello*, quipster, ribald,
wag, wisecracker, wit*, zany*; SEE CONCEPT *423*

clown [n2] *stupid, ignorant person*
blockhead*, boor, bucolic, buffoon, bumpkin*,
chuff, churl, clodhopper*, gawk, hayseed*,
hick*, hind, jake, lout, mucker*, oaf, peasant,
rube, rustic, swain, yahoo*, yokel; SEE CONCEPTS
412,423

clown [v] *joke*
act crazy, act the fool*, bug out*, cut up*, fool
around, have fun, jest, kid around; SEE CONCEPT
386

cloy [v] *overfill*
disgust, fill, glut, gorge, jade, nauseate, pall, sate,
satiate, satisfy, sicken, stall, stodge, suffice, surfeit, weary; SEE CONCEPT *740*

club [n1] *bat, stick*
baton, billy*, blackjack, bludgeon, business*,
conk buster*, convincer*, cosh, cudgel, hammer,
hickory, mace, mallet, nightstick, persuader*,
quarterstaff, rosewood, sap, shill, shillelagh,
staff, swatter, truncheon, works*; SEE CONCEPTS
470,499

club [n2] *social organization*
affiliation, alliance, association, bunch, circle,
clique, company, crew, faction, gang, guild,
hangout*, league, lodge, meeting, mob, order,
outfit, ring, set, society, sodality, stamping
ground*, union; SEE CONCEPTS *387,439*

club [n3] *golfing tool*
brassie, cleek, driver, iron, mashie, midiron, nib-
lick, putter, spoon, stick, wedge, wood; SEE CON-
CEPT *364*

club [v] *hit hard with object*
bash, baste, batter, beat, blackjack, bludgeon,
clobber, clout, cosh, cudgel, fustigate, hammer,
pommel, pound, pummel, strike, whack; SEE
CONCEPT *189*

clue [n] *hint, evidence*
cue, dead giveaway*, hot lead*, indication,
inkling, intimation, key, lead, mark, notion,
pointer, print, proof, sign, solution, suggestion,
suspicion, telltale, tip, tip-off*, trace, track,
wind; SEE CONCEPT *274*

clue [v] *give information*
acquaint, advise, apprise, fill in, give the low-
down*, give the skinny on*, hint, indicate, inform, intimate, lead to, leave evidence, leave
trace, leave tracks, notify, point to, post, suggest,
tell, warn, wise up; SEE CONCEPT *60*

clump [n1] *mass of something*
array, batch, blob, body, bunch, bundle, chunk,
cluster, clutter, gob, group, hodgepodge, hunk,

jumble, knot, lot, lump, nugget, parcel, set, shock, wad; SEE CONCEPTS *432,470*

clump [*n2*] *thumping noise*
clatter, clomp, galumph, scuff, stomp, stumble, thud; SEE CONCEPT *595*

clump [*v*] *make thumping noise*
barge, bumble, clatter, clomp, galumph, hobble, limp, lumber, plod, scuff, stamp, stomp, stumble, stump, thud, thump, tramp; SEE CONCEPTS *65,595*

clumsy [*adj*] *not agile; awkward*
all thumbs*, blundering, blunderous, bulky, bumbling, bungling, butterfingered*, clownish, crude, elephantine, gauche, gawkish, gawky, graceless, ham-handed*, heavy, heavy-handed, helpless, hulking, ill-shaped, incompetent, inelegant, inept, inexperienced, inexpert, lubberly, lumbering, lumpish, maladroit, oafish, ponderous, splay, stumbling, unable, unadept, uncoordinated, uncouth, undexterous, uneasy, ungainly, unhandy, unskillful, untactful, untalented, untoward, unwieldy, weedy; SEE CONCEPTS *401,402,584*

cluster [*n*] *group of something*
array, assemblage, band, batch, bevy, blob, body, bunch, bundle, chunk, clump, clutch, collection, covey, crew, gathering, hunk, knot, lot, pack, party, set; SEE CONCEPT *432*

cluster [*v*] *assemble, group*
accumulate, aggregate, associate, bunch, bunch up, bundle, collect, crowd around, cumulate, flock, gang around, gather, package, parcel, round up; SEE CONCEPT *109*

clutch [*n*] *strong hold*
clamp, clasp, clench, clinch, connection, coupling, grapple, grasp, grip, gripe, link; SEE CONCEPT *190*

clutch [*v*] *grab, snatch*
catch, cherish, clasp, clench, clinch, cling to, collar, embrace, fasten, glom*, grapple, grasp, grip, harbor, hold, hook, keep, nab, nail*, put the snare on*, seize, snag, snatch, take; SEE CONCEPTS *190,191*

clutches [*n*] *personal power*
claws, control, custody, grasp, grip, hands, keeping, possession, sway; SEE CONCEPTS *388,641,710*

clutter [*n*] *disarray, mess*
ataxia, chaos, confusion, derangement, disorder, hodgepodge, huddle, jumble, litter, medley, melange, muddle, rummage, scramble, shuffle, tumble, untidiness; SEE CONCEPTS *432,674*

clutter [*v*] *cause mess, disarray*
dirty, jumble, litter, muddle, scatter, snarl, strew; SEE CONCEPT *254*

coach [*n1*] *instructor, usually in recreation*
drill instructor, educator, mentor, physical education instructor, skipper, teacher, trainer, tutor; SEE CONCEPTS *350,366*

coach [*n2*] *carriage*
bus, car, chaise, charabanc, fourwheeler, gocart, perambulator, stage, tallyho*, train, vehicle, victoria; SEE CONCEPT *505*

coach [*v*] *instruct, usually in recreation*
break in*, cram, drill, educate, hone, lay it out for*, lick into shape*, prepare, pull one's coat*, put through the grind*, put through the mill*, ready, school, teach, train, tutor; SEE CONCEPTS *285,363*

coagulate [*v*] *clot*
clabber, coalesce, compact, concentrate, concrete, condense, congeal, consolidate, curdle, dry, gel, gelate, gelatinize, glop up*, harden, inspissate, jell, jellify, jelly, lopper*, set, solidify, thicken; SEE CONCEPT *469*

coagulation [*n*] *clotting*
agglomeration, caseation, concentration, concretion, condensation, congelation, consolidation, curdling, embolism, gelatination, incrassation, inspissation, jellification, thickening; SEE CONCEPT *469*

coalesce [*v*] *blend, come together*
adhere, amalgamate, associate, bracket, cleave, cling, cohere, combine, commingle, commix, conjoin, connect, consolidate, fuse, hook up with*, incorporate, integrate, join, join up with, link, merge, mingle, mix, relate, stick, tie in with*, unite, wed; SEE CONCEPTS *112,113*

coalition [*n*] *allied group, association*
affiliation, alliance, amalgam, amalgamation, anschluss, bloc, coadunation, combination, combine, compact, confederacy, confederation, conjunction, consolidation, conspiracy, faction, federation, fusion, integration, league, melding, mergence, merger, merging, party, ring, unification, union; SEE CONCEPT *381*

coarse [*adj1*] *not fine, rude*
base, bawdy, blue*, boorish, brutish, cheap, common, crass, crude, dirty, earthy, filthy, foul, foul-mouthed, gross, gruff, immodest, impolite, improper, impure, incult, indelicate, inelegant, loutish, low, lowbred, lowdown and dirty*, mean, nasty, obscene, off-color, offensive, raffish, raunchy, raw, ribald, rough, roughneck*, rude, scatological, smutty*, tacky, uncivil, uncouth, uncultivated, uncultured, unrefined, vulgar, vulgarian; SEE CONCEPTS *401,545*

coarse [*adj2*] *rough, unrefined*
chapped, coarse-grained, crude, grainy, granular, harsh, homespun, impure, inferior, loose, lumpy, mediocre, particulate, poor quality, rough-hewn, rugged, unfinished, unpolished, unprocessed, unpurified; SEE CONCEPTS *574,606*

coarseness [*n*] *rudeness, vulgarity*
bawdiness, boorishness, callousness, crassness, crudity, earthiness, harshness, indelicacy, offensiveness, poor taste, rawness, ribaldry, roughness, smut*, smuttiness*, uncouthness, unevenness, unrefinement; SEE CONCEPTS *633,645*

coast [*n*] *border by water*
bank, beach, coastline, littoral, margin, seaboard, seacoast, seashore, seaside, shore, shoreline, strand; SEE CONCEPTS *509,514*

coast [*v*] *glide along without much effort*
cruise, drift, float, freewheel, get by*, ride on current, sail, skate, slide, smooth along*, taxi; SEE CONCEPTS *150,704*

coastal [*adj*] *bordering the water*
along a coast, littoral, marginal, marshy, riverine, seaside, skirting; SEE CONCEPT *583*

coat [*n1*] *animal hair*
crust, ectoderm, epidermis, felt, fleece, fur, hide, husk, integument, leather, membrane, pelage, pellicle, pelt, peltry, protective covering, rind, scale, scarfskin, shell, skin, wool; SEE CONCEPT *399*

coat [*n2*] *covering*
bark, coating, crust, finish, glaze, gloss, lacquer,

cl
co

lamination, layer, overlay, painting, plaster, priming, roughcast, set, tinge, varnish, wash, whitewashing; SEE CONCEPTS *259,475*

coat [*n3*] *personal outerwear*
cape, cloak, cutaway, flogger, frock, greatcoat, jacket, mackinaw, mink, overcoat, pea, raincoat, slicker, suit, tails, threads, topcoat, trench, tux, tuxedo, ulster, windbreaker, wrap; SEE CONCEPT *451*

coat [*v*] *cover with layer of material*
apply, cover, crust, enamel, foil, glaze, incrust, laminate, paint, plaster, plate, smear, spread, stain, surface, varnish; SEE CONCEPTS *172,202*

coating [*n*] *covering*
blanket, bloom, coat, crust, dusting, encrustation, film, finish, glaze, lamination, layer, membrane, patina, sheet, skin, varnish, veneer; SEE CONCEPT *475*

coax [*v*] *persuade*
allure, argue into, arm-twist*, barter, beguile, blandish, blarney, butter up*, cajole, come on, con, decoy, entice, flatter, get, hook, importune, induce, influence, inveigle, jawbone*, lure, pester, plague, press, prevail upon, rope in*, soft-soap*, soothe, sweet-talk, talk into, tease, tempt, urge, wangle, wheedle, work on, worm; SEE CONCEPT *68*

cobweb [*n*] *entanglement; filament*
fiber, gossamer, labyrinth, mesh, net, network, snare, tissue, toil, web, webbing; SEE CONCEPTS *517,674*

cocaine [*n*] *illegal drug*
blow*, coke*, controlled substance, crack*, crystal*, freebase*, happy dust*, ice*, joy powder*, mojo*, narcotic, nose candy*, poison*, snort*, snow*, speedball*, stardust*, stuff*, sugar*, white horse*, white lady*, wings*; SEE CONCEPT *307*

cock [*n*] *rooster*
capon, chanticleer, chicken, cock-a-doodle-doo*, cockalorum, cockerel; SEE CONCEPT *394*

cock [*v*] *aim up toward*
erect, hump, perk up, pile, prick, raise, stack, stand erect, stand up, stick up; SEE CONCEPT *201*

cockeyed [*adj*] *crooked, askew*
absurd, askance, askant, asymmetrical, awry, cam, canted, crazy, crooked, cross-eyed, lop-sided, ludicrous, nonsensical, preposterous, squint, strabismic; SEE CONCEPT *586*

cocky/cocksure [*adj*] *self-assured, full of oneself*
arrogant, brash, bumptious, certain, conceited, confident, egotistical, hotdogging*, hotshot*, hubristic, know-it-all*, lordly, nervy, overconfident, overweening, positive, presumptuous, self-confident, smart aleck*, smart guy*, smarty*, smarty pants*, sure, swaggering, swollen-headed, vain, wise guy*; SEE CONCEPTS *401,404*

cocoon [*v*] *protect with covering*
cushion, encase, envelop, insulate, pad, swaddle, swathe, truss, wrap; SEE CONCEPTS *130,134*

coddle [*v1*] *indulge, pamper*
baby, caress, cater to, cosset, cotton, favor, humor, make much of, make over, mollycoddle, nurse, pet, play up to, spoil; SEE CONCEPTS *110,295*

coddle [*v2*] *boil lightly, usually eggs*
brew, cook, poach, simmer, steam; SEE CONCEPT *170*

code [*n1*] *secret language system*
cipher, cryptograph; SEE CONCEPTS *276,284*

code [*n2*] *law, rule*
canon, charter, codex, constitution, convention, custom, digest, discipline, ethics, etiquette, manners, maxim, method, regulation, system; SEE CONCEPTS *318,688*

co-dependent [*adj*] *unhealthy psychological reliance of one person on another*
addicted, attached, hooked, interconnected, interdependent, mutually dependent, slavish trust, unhealthy confidence; SEE CONCEPTS *404,542*

codicil [*n*] *added part to document*
addendum, addition, appendix, postscript, rider, supplement; SEE CONCEPT *270*

codify [*v*] *systematize*
arrange, catalogue, classify, code, collect, condense, digest, order, organize, summarize, tabulate; SEE CONCEPTS *39,84*

coerce [*v*] *compel, press*
beset, browbeat, bulldoze*, bully, concuss, constrain, cow, dragoon, drive, force, high pressure*, hinder, impel, intimidate, lean on, make, make an offer they can't refuse*, menace, oblige, pressurize, push, put the squeeze on*, repress, restrict, shotgun*, strong-arm, suppress, terrorize, threaten, twist one's arm*, urge; SEE CONCEPTS *14,68*

coercion [*n*] *compulsion, pressure*
browbeating, bullying, constraint, duress, force, intimidation, menace, menacing, persuasion, restraint, strong-arm tactic*, threat, threatening, violence; SEE CONCEPTS *14,68*

coexistence [*n*] *happening or being at same time, place*
accord, coetaneousness, coevality, coincidence, concurrence, conformity, conjunction, contemporaneousness, harmony, order, peace, simultaneousness, synchronicity; SEE CONCEPT *407*

coffee [*n*] *hot beverage made from beans of a tree*
battery acid*, brew, café, café au lait, café noir, cappuccino, decaf, decoction, demitasse, espresso, forty weight*, hot stuff*, ink*, jamocha*, java*, joe*, mocha*, mud*, perk*, varnish remover*; SEE CONCEPT *454*

coffer [*n*] *large box*
case, casket, chest, exchequer, repository, strongbox, treasure chest, treasury, war chest*; SEE CONCEPT *494*

coffin [*n*] *box for dead person*
casket, catafalque, crate, funerary box, pall, pine box, pine drape*, sarcophagus; SEE CONCEPTS *368,479,494*

cog [*n*] *main part of device*
cogwheel, differential, fang, gear, pinion, prong, rack, ratchet, tine, tooth, transmission, tusk, wheel; SEE CONCEPT *464*

cogency [*n*] *effectiveness*
bearing, concern, connection, conviction, convincingness, force, forcefulness, pertinence, point, potency, power, punch, relevance, strength, validity, validness; SEE CONCEPTS *376,676*

cogent [*adj*] *effective*
apposite, apt, compelling, conclusive, consequential, convictive, convincing, fitting, forceful, forcible, inducing, influential, irresistible, justified, meaningful, momentous, persuasive, pertinent, potent, powerful, puissant, relevant, satisfactory, satisfying, significant, solid, sound,

strong, suasive, telling, urgent, valid, weighty, well-grounded; SEE CONCEPT *537*

cogitate [v] *think deeply about*
brainstorm*, cerebrate, chew the cud*, conceive, consider, contemplate, deliberate, envisage, envision, figure, flash on*, imagine, kick around*, meditate, mull over, muse, noodle around*, ponder, reason, reflect, ruminate, speculate, stew over*; SEE CONCEPTS *17,24*

cogitation [n] *deep thought*
brainwork, cerebration, consideration, contemplation, deliberation, meditation, reflection, rumination, speculation; SEE CONCEPT *410*

cognate [adj] *alike, associated*
affiliated, agnate, akin, allied, analogous, comparable, connate, connatural, connected, consanguine, general, generic, incident, kindred, like, related, same, similar, universal; SEE CONCEPTS *487,573*

cognizance/cognition [n] *understanding*
acknowledgment, apprehension, attention, awareness, comprehension, discernment, insight, intelligence, knowledge, mind, need, note, notice, observance, observation, perception, percipience, reasoning, recognition, regard; SEE CONCEPT *409*

cognizant [adj] *aware*
acquainted, alive, apprehensive, au courant, awake, conscious, conversant, down with, familiar, grounded, hep to*, hip to*, informed, in on, in the know, in the picture*, judicious, knowing, knowledgeable, observant, on the beam*, on to*, perceptive, plugged in, savvy, sensible, sentient, tuned in*, up on*, versed, wise to*, with it*, witting; SEE CONCEPT *402*

cohabit [v] *live together*
be roommates with, conjugate, couple, have relations, live illegally, live with, mingle, play house*, room together, shack up*, share address, take up housekeeping*; SEE CONCEPTS *226,375,384*

cohere [v1] *stick to, cling*
adhere, associate, bind, blend, cleave, coalesce, combine, connect, consolidate, fuse, glue, hold, join, merge, unite; SEE CONCEPTS *85,113,160*

cohere [v2] *agree, conform*
accord, be connected, be consistent, check, check out, comport, conform, correspond, dovetail, fit in, go, hang together, harmonize, hold, hold water, make sense, relate, square; SEE CONCEPTS *8,636,667*

coherence [n] *agreement*
adherence, attachment, bond, cementation, cling, clinging, comprehensibility, concordance, conformity, congruity, connection, consistency, consonance, construction, continuity, correspondence, inseparability, inseparableness, integrity, intelligibility, rationality, relations, solidarity, stickage, tenacity, union, unity; SEE CONCEPTS *388,684*

coherent [adj] *understandable*
articulate, comprehensible, consistent, identified, intelligible, logical, lucid, meaningful, orderly, organized, rational, reasoned, sound, systematic; SEE CONCEPT *402*

cohort [n] *partner in activity*
accomplice, adherent, aide, ally, assistant, associate, companion, company, comrade, confrere, consociate, contingent, disciple, follower, friend, hand, legion, mate, myrmidon, pal, partisan, regiment, satellite, sidekick, stall, supporter; SEE CONCEPT *423*

coiffure [n] *hairstyle*
afro, beehive, blow dry*, braids, corn rows, crew cut, DA*, dreadlocks, dreads, flip, fuzz cut*, hair, hair-comb, haircut, hairdo, permanent, pigtails, plait, ponytail, razor cut*, tail, tease, trim, wave; SEE CONCEPTS *418,718*

coil [n] *thread that curls*
bight, braid, circle, convolution, corkscrew, curlicue, gyration, helix, involution, lap, loop, ring, roll, scroll, spiral, tendril, turn, twine, twirl, twist, whorl, wind; SEE CONCEPT *436*

coil [v] *curl around, entwine*
convolute, convolve, corkscrew, fold, intertwine, intervolve, lap, loop, make serpentine, rotate, scroll, sinuate, snake, spiral, spire, turn, twine, twist, wind, wrap around, wreathe, writhe; SEE CONCEPTS *201,758*

coin [n] *metallic money*
bread*, cash, change, chicken feed*, chips*, coinage, copper, currency, dough, gold, jack*, legal tender, meter money*, mintage, money, piece, scratch*, silver, small change*, specie; SEE CONCEPT *340*

coin [v] *create, invent*
brainstorm*, compose, conceive, contrive, counterfeit, dream up, fabricate, forge, formulate, frame, head trip*, make up, make up off the top of one's head*, manufacture, mint, mold, originate, spark, spitball*, stamp, strike, think up, trump up*; SEE CONCEPTS *36,173*

coincide [v] *go along with; coexist*
accompany, accord, acquiesce, agree, be concurrent, befall, be the same, come about, concert, concur, correspond, equal, eventuate, harmonize, identify, jibe, match, occur simultaneously, quadrate, square, sync, synchronize, tally; SEE CONCEPTS *667,714*

coincidence [n1] *agreement; coexistence*
accompaniment, accord, accordance, collaboration, concomitance, concurrence, conformity, conjunction, consonance, correlation, correspondence, parallelism, synchronism, union; SEE CONCEPTS *667,684,714*

coincidence [n2] *accidental happening*
accident, chance, eventuality, fate, fluke, fortuity, happening, happy accident, incident, luck, stroke of luck; SEE CONCEPTS *4,230*

coincident [adj] *concurring, happening together*
ancillary, attendant, attending, coinciding, collateral, concomitant, consonant, contemporaneous, contemporary, coordinate, correspondent, incident, satellite, simultaneous, synchronous; SEE CONCEPTS *548,820*

coincidental [adj] *accidental*
casual, chance, circumstantial, fluky, fortuitous, incidental, unintentional, unplanned; SEE CONCEPT *548*

cold [adj1] *chilly, freezing*
algid, arctic, below freezing, below zero, benumbed, biting, bitter, blasting, bleak, boreal, brisk, brumal, chill, chilled, cool, crisp, cutting, frigid, frore, frosty, frozen, gelid, glacial, have goose bumps*, hawkish, hiemal, hyperborean, icebox, iced, icy, inclement, intense, keen, nipping, nippy, numbed, numbing, one-dog night*, penetrating, piercing, polar, raw, rimy, severe, sharp, shivery, Siberian, sleety, snappy, snowy,

CO
CO

stinging, two-dog night*, wintry; SEE CONCEPT **605**

cold [*adj2*] *aloof, unresponsive*
apathetic, cold-blooded, cool, dead, distant, emotionless, frigid, frosty, glacial, icy, impersonal, imperturbable, indifferent, inhibited, inhospitable, joyless, lukewarm, matter-of-fact, passionless, phlegmatic, reserved, reticent, spiritless, standoffish, stony, unconcerned, undemonstrative, unenthusiastic, unfeeling, unimpassioned, unmoved, unresponsive, unsympathetic; SEE CONCEPT **404**

cold [*n*] *frigid conditions*
ague, algidity, algor, chill, chilliness, coldness, congelation, draft, freeze, frigidity, frost, frostbite, frostiness, frozenness, gelidity, gelidness, glaciation, goose flesh, iciness, inclemency, rawness, refrigeration, shivering, shivers, snow, wintertime, wintriness; SEE CONCEPTS **524,610**

cold-blooded [*adj*] *cruel, heartless*
barbarous, brutal, callous, cold, dispassionate, hard-boiled, hardened, hard-hearted, imperturbable, inhuman, matter-of-fact, merciless, obdurate, pitiless, relentless, ruthless, savage, steely, stony-hearted, uncompassionate, unemotional, unfeeling, unmoved; SEE CONCEPT **542**

cold feet [*n*] *fear of carrying out an activity*
anxiety, fear, reservations, second thoughts, timidity; SEE CONCEPT **27**

cold fish [*n*] *unemotional person*
aloof person, iceberg*, unfeeling person; SEE CONCEPT **412**

cold shoulder [*n*] *snub*
aloofness, brush-off, coldness, dismissal, disregard, iciness; SEE CONCEPTS **30,633**

coliseum [*n*] *arena for events*
amphitheater, bowl, hippodrome, open-air theater, stade, stadium, theater; SEE CONCEPT **438**

collaborate [*v*] *work together*
be in cahoots*, coact, cofunction, collude, come together, concert, concur, conspire, cooperate, coproduce, do business with, get together, glue oneself to*, go partners*, hook on, hook up*, interface, join forces, join together, join up with, participate, team up, throw in together*, throw in with*, tie in, work with; SEE CONCEPTS **100,351,384**

collaborator [*n*] *person who works with another*
assistant, associate, colleague, confederate, co-worker, fellow traveller, helper, partner, quisling, running dog, teammate, team player*; SEE CONCEPTS **348,423**

collage [*n*] *mixture of pictures*
abstract composition, found art, photomontage; SEE CONCEPT **259**

collapse [*n*] *downfall, breakdown*
bankruptcy, basket case*, cataclysm, catastrophe, cave-in, conk out*, crackup*, crash, debacle, destruction, disintegration, disorganization, disruption, exhaustion, failure, faint, flop, prostration, ruination, ruining, smash, smashup, subsidence, undoing, wreck; SEE CONCEPTS **230,316,410,674**

collapse [*v*] *fall apart, break down*
belly up*, bend, break, cave in, conk out*, crack up*, crumple, deflate, disintegrate, droop, drop, exhaust, fail, faint, fall down, flag, flake out, fold, founder, give, give in, give out, give way, go*, go to pieces*, keel over, languish, shatter,

subside, succumb, tire, topple, weaken, weary, wilt, yield; SEE CONCEPTS **252,469,702**

collar [*n*] *neck attire*
bertha, choker, dicky, Eton, fichu, fraise, frill, jabot, neckband, ruff, torque, Vandyke; SEE CONCEPTS **450,452**

collar [*v*] *apprehend*
abduct, appropriate, arrest, bag, capture, catch, cop*, corner, get, grab, hook, lay hands on, nab, nail*, prehend, secure, seize, take, tree; SEE CONCEPTS **90,317**

collate [*v*] *sort collection*
adduce, analogize, assemble, bracket, collect, compare, compose, contrast, examine, gather, group, match, order, relate, verify; SEE CONCEPTS **84,158**

collateral [*adj*] *indirect, secondary*
accessory, accompanying, added, adjunctive, adjuvant, ancillary, appurtenant, attendant, auxiliary, circuitous, coincident, complementary, concomitant, concurrent, confirmatory, coordinate, corresponding, corroborative, dependent, incident, lateral, not lineal, parallel, related, roundabout, satellite, side, sub, subordinate, subservient, subsidiary, supporting, tributary, under; SEE CONCEPTS **546,567,831**

collateral [*n*] *monetary deposit*
assurance, bond, endorsement, guarantee, pledge, promise, security, surety, warrant, wealth; SEE CONCEPT **344**

colleague [*n*] *associate, fellow worker*
aide, ally, assistant, auxiliary, buddy, chum, coadjutor, cohort, collaborator, companion, compatriot, compeer, comrade, confederate, confrere, co-worker, crony, friend, helper, pal, partner, teammate, workmate; SEE CONCEPTS **348,423**

collect [*v1*] *accumulate, come together*
aggregate, amass, array, assemble, cluster, compile, congregate, congress, convene, converge, convoke, corral, flock, flock together, gather, get hold of, group, heap, hoard, muster, rally, rendezvous, round up, save, scare up, stockpile; SEE CONCEPTS **109,114**

collect [*v2*] *obtain (money)*
acquire, dig up, muster, pass the hat*, raise, requisition, secure, solicit; SEE CONCEPT **342**

collected [*adj*] *composed, calm*
confident, cool, easy, easygoing, levelheaded, nonchalant, peaceful, placid, poised, possessed, quiet, sanguine, self-possessed, serene, still, sure, temperate, together, tranquil, unflappable, unperturbable, unperturbed, unruffled; SEE CONCEPT **401**

collection [*n*] *group, accumulation*
accumulating, acquiring, acquisition, agglomeration, amassing, amassment, anthology, assemblage, assembling, assembly, assortment, batch, bringing together, caboodle, clump, cluster, collation, combination, company, compilation, congeries, congregation, convocation, crowd, cumulation, digest, gathering, heap, hoard, kit, levy, lot, mass, medley, mess, miscellany, mobilization, muster, number, obtaining, omnibus, pile, quantity, securing, selection, set, stack, stock, stockpile, store; SEE CONCEPTS **109,432**

collective [*adj*] *composite*
aggregate, assembled, collated, combined, common, compiled, concentrated, concerted, conjoint, consolidated, cooperative, corporate, cumulative, gathered, grouped, heaped, hoarded,

joint, massed, mutual, piled, shared, unified, united; SEE CONCEPT *585*

college [*n*] *institution of higher education*
alma mater, association, brainery*, halls of ivy*, halls of knowledge*, institute, lyceum, organization, seminary, university; SEE CONCEPTS *287,288,289*

college student [*n*] *person studying at institution of higher education*
first year student, grad student*, graduate student, junior, senior, sophomore, undergrad*, undergraduate student; SEE CONCEPT *350*

collide [*v*] *slam into*
bang, beat, break up, bump, clash, conflict, crash, crunch*, disagree, fender-bend*, fragment, hit, jolt, meet head-on*, pile up*, plow into*, pulverize*, scrap*, shatter, sideswipe, smash, splinter, strike, wrack up*; SEE CONCEPTS *189,248*

collision [*n*] *accident*
blow, bump, butt, concussion, contact, crash, demolishment, destruction, dilapidation, encounter, fender bender*, head-on*, hit, impact, jar, jolt, knock, percussion, pileup*, rap, ruin, shock, sideswipe, slam, smash, strike, thud, thump, wreck; SEE CONCEPTS *189,230,674*

collocate [*v*] *compile*
accumulate, assemble, collect, collimate, gather, parallel; SEE CONCEPT *84*

colloquial [*adj*] *particular, familiar to an area, informal*
chatty, common, conversational, demotic, dialectal, everyday, idiomatic, jive*, popular, street*, vernacular; SEE CONCEPT *267*

colloquy [*n*] *conversation, debate*
buzz session, chat, chinfest*, chitchat, clambake*, colloquium, confab*, confabulation, conference, converse, dialogue, discourse, discussion, flap*, gab fest*, gam*, groupthink*, huddle*, palaver, parley, powwow*, rap*, rap session*, seminar, talk, talkfest*; SEE CONCEPT *266*

collusion [*n*] *secret understanding, often with intent to defraud*
bait and switch*, bill of goods*, bunco*, cahoots*, complicity, con game*, connivance, conspiracy, craft, deceit, diddling*, dodge, double-cross, fast shuffle, flam*, flimflam*, fradulent artifice, graft, guilt, guiltiness, gyp, intrigue, plot, racket, scam, scheme, shell game*, skunk*, sting*, trick, whitewash; SEE CONCEPTS *114,660*

cologne [*n*] *fragrance product*
fragrance, perfume, scent, toilet water; SEE CONCEPTS *599,600*

colonial [*adj*] *pioneering, relating to a nonindependent or new territory*
crude, dependent, dominion, early American, emigrant, frontier, immigrant, new, outland, pilgrim, pioneer, prerevolutionary, primitive, provincial, puritan, territorial, transplanted, uncultured, unsettled, unsophisticated, wild; SEE CONCEPTS *549,799*

colonization [*n*] *settlement of area*
clearing, establishment, expanding, expansion, founding, immigration, migration, opening up, peopling, pioneering, populating, settlement, settling, squatting, transplanting; SEE CONCEPTS *198,298*

colony [*n*] *community*
antecedents, clearing, dependency, dominion, mandate, new land, offshoot, outpost, possession, protectorate, province, satellite, settlement, subject state, swarm, territory; SEE CONCEPTS *379,512*

color [*n1*] *pigment, shade*
blush, cast, chroma, chromaticity, chromatism, chromism, colorant, coloration, coloring, complexion, dye, glow, hue, intensity, iridescence, luminosity, paint, pigmentation, polychromasia, saturation, stain, tinct, tincture, tinge, tint, undertone, value, wash; SEE CONCEPT *622*

color [*n2*] *deceptive appearance*
deception, disguise, excuse, facade, face, false show, front, guise, mask, plea, pretense, pretext, put-on, semblance, show; SEE CONCEPTS *59,716*

color [*v1*] *make pigmented; shade*
adorn, blacken, bloom, blush, burn, chalk, crayon, crimson, darken, daub, dye, embellish, emblazon, enamel, enliven, flush, fresco, gild, glaze, gloss, illuminate, imbue, infuse, lacquer, paint, pigment, pinken, redden, rouge, stain, stipple, suffuse, tinge, tint, tone, variegate, wash; SEE CONCEPTS *250,469*

color [*v2*] *distort, exaggerate*
angle*, belie, cook up*, disguise, doctor*, embroider*, fake, falsify, fudge*, garble, gloss over, magnify, misrepresent, misstate, overstate, pad*, pervert, prejudice, slant*, taint, twist*, warp*; SEE CONCEPTS *49,63*

colored [*adj1*] *not white*
dyed, flushed, glowing, hued, shaded, stained, tinged, tinted, washed; SEE CONCEPT *618*

colored [*adj2*] *distorted*
angled, biased, false, falsified, jaundiced, misrepresented, one-sided, partial, partisan, perverted, prejudiced, prepossessed, tampered with, tendentious, warped; SEE CONCEPT *582*

colorful [*adj1*] *brilliant, intensely hued*
bright, chromatic, flashy, florid, gaudy, gay, hued, intense, jazzy, kaleidoscopic, loud, motley, multicolored, picturesque, prismatic, psychedelic, rich, showy, splashy, variegated, vibrant, vivid; SEE CONCEPTS *617,618*

colorful [*adj2*] *full of life, interesting*
brave, characterful, distinctive, flaky*, gay, glamorous, graphic, jazzy, lively, picturesque, rich, stimulating, unusual, vivid; SEE CONCEPT *404*

colorless [*adj1*] *without hue*
achromatic, achromic, anemic, ashen, ashy, blanched, bleached, cadaverous, doughy, drab, dull, faded, flat, ghastly, livid, lurid, neutral, pale, sickly, uncolored, wan, washed out, waxen, white; SEE CONCEPT *618*

colorless [*adj2*] *unlively, uninteresting*
characterless, dreary, dull, insipid, lackluster, lifeless, prosaic, run-of-the-mill*, tame, unmemorable, unpassioned, vacuous, vapid; SEE CONCEPT *404*

colossal [*adj*] *very large*
barn door*, behemothic, blimp*, cyclopean, elephantine, enormous, gargantuan, giant, gigantic, huge, humongous*, immense, jumbo, mammoth, mondo*, monstrous, mountainous, super, titanic, vast; SEE CONCEPT *781*

colossus [*n*] *giant thing*
behemoth, Cyclops, Gargantua, giant, Godzilla, Goliath, Hercules, leviathan, mammoth, Samson, titan; SEE CONCEPT *424*

CO
CO

colt [n] *young horse*
filly, fledgling, foal, rookie, sapling, yearling, youngling, youngster; SEE CONCEPT *394*

column [n1] *line, procession*
cavalcade, company, file, list, platoon, queue, rank, row, string, train; SEE CONCEPTS *432,727*

column [n2] *pillar*
brace, buttress, caryatid, colonnade, cylinder, mast, minaret, monolith, monument, obelisk, pedestal, peristyle, pier, pilaster, post, prop, pylon, shaft, standard, stay, stele, support, totem, tower, underpinning, upright; SEE CONCEPT *440*

coma [n] *deep unconsciousness*
blackout, dullness, faint, hebetude, insensibility, lethargy, oblivion, sleep, slumber, somnolence, stupor, swoon, syncope, torpidity, torpor, trance; SEE CONCEPT *315*

comatose [adj] *unconscious*
cold, dead, dead to the world*, dopey, drowsy, drugged, hebetudinous, inconscious, insensible, lethargic, out, out cold*, out to lunch*, senseless, sleepy, sluggish, slumberous, somnolent, soporose, stupefied, stupid, stuporous, torpid, vegged out*; SEE CONCEPT *539*

comb [v1] *arrange hair*
adjust, card, cleanse, curry, disentangle, dress, groom, hackle, hatchel, lay smooth, rasp, scrape, separate, smooth, sort, straighten, tease, untangle; SEE CONCEPT *162*

comb [v2] *search by ransacking*
beat, beat the bushes*, examine, finecomb*, forage, go through with fine-tooth comb*, grub, hunt, inspect, investigate, leave no stone unturned*, look high and low*, probe, rake, ransack, rummage, scour, screen, scrutinize, search high heaven*, sift, sweep, turn inside out*, turn upside down*; SEE CONCEPT *216*

combat [n] *battle*
action, affray, battle royal*, brush, brush-off, conflict, contest, encounter, engagement, fight, flap, fray, jackpot*, mix-up*, run-in*, service, shoot-out*, skirmish, struggle, war, warfare; SEE CONCEPTS *86,106*

combat [v] *fight*
battle, buck, clash, contend, contest, cope, cross swords with*, defy, dispute, do battle with, duel, engage, fight, go up against, oppose, put up a fight*, repel, resist, shoot it out*, strive, struggle, traverse, war, withstand; SEE CONCEPTS *86,106*

combatant [n] *fighter*
adversary, antagonist, assailant, attacker, battler, belligerent, contender, enemy, foe, serviceman, soldier, warrior; SEE CONCEPT *358*

combative [adj] *aggressive*
antagonistic, bellicose, belligerent, cantankerous, contentious, cussed, energetic, fire-eating*, gladiatorial, hawkish, militant, ornery*, pugnacious, quarrelsome, ructious, scrappy, strenuous, trigger-happy*, truculent, warlike, warring; SEE CONCEPTS *401,404*

combination [n1] *mixture, blend*
aggregate, amalgam, amalgamation, blending, brew, coalescence, combo, composite, compound, connection, consolidation, everything but kitchen sink*, fusion, junction, medley, merger, miscellany, mishmash*, mix, olio, order, sequence, solution, soup, stew, succession, synthesis, unification, union; SEE CONCEPT *432*

combination [n2] *alliance, association*
affiliation, bloc, cabal, cahoots, camarilla, cartel, circle, clique, club, coadunation, coalition, combine, compound, confederacy, confederation, conjunction, connection, consolidation, consortium, conspiracy, coterie, faction, federation, gang, guild, hookup*, mafia, melding, mergence, merger, merging, partnership, party, pool, ring, set, syndicate, tie-up*, trust, unification, union; SEE CONCEPT *381*

combine [v] *connect, integrate*
amalgamate, associate, band, bind, blend, bond, bracket, bunch up, coadjute, coalesce, commingle, compound, conjoin, cooperate, couple, dub, fuse, get together, glue oneself to, hitch on*, hook on*, incorporate, interface, join, league, link, marry, merge, mingle, mix, network, plug into, pool, put together, relate, slap on*, stand in with, synthesize, tack on*, tag on*, team up with*, throw in together*, tie up with*, unify, unite, wed; SEE CONCEPT *113*

combustible [adj] *able to be exploded*
burnable, comburent, combustive, explosive, fiery, firing, flammable, ignitable, incendiary, inflammable, kindling, volatile; SEE CONCEPTS *485,537*

combustion [n] *explosion; on fire*
agitation, candescence, disturbance, flaming, ignition, kindling, oxidization, thermogenesis, tumult, turmoil; SEE CONCEPTS *521,676,724*

come [v1] *advance, approach*
appear, arrive, attain, be accessible, be at disposal, become, be convenient, be handy, be obtainable, be ready, blow in*, bob up, breeze in*, burst, buzz*, check in*, clock in*, close in, draw near, drop in, enter, fall by, fall in, flare*, get, get in, happen, hit, hit town*, make it, make the scene*, materialize, move, move toward, near, occur, originate, pop in*, pop up*, punch in*, punch the clock*, reach, ring in*, roll in*, show, show up, sign in, sky in*, spring in, turn out, turn up, wind up at; SEE CONCEPT *159*

come [v2] *happen*
befall, betide, break, chance, come to pass, develop, fall, hap*, occur, take place, transpire, turn out; SEE CONCEPT *4*

come [v3] *extend, reach*
add up, aggregate, amount, become, come over, develop, expand, get, go, grow, join, mature, number, run, run into, spread, stretch, sum to, total, turn, wax; SEE CONCEPTS *239,701*

come about [v] *happen*
arise, befall, come to pass, occur, result, take place, transpire; SEE CONCEPT *701*

come across [v] *encounter, find*
bump into, chance upon, discover, happen upon, hit upon, light upon, meet, notice, stumble upon, uncover, unearth; SEE CONCEPTS *38,183*

come along [v] *progress, develop*
do well, get on, improve, mend, perk up, pick up, rally, recover, recuperate, show improvement; SEE CONCEPT *700*

come at [v1] *reach, attain*
accomplish, achieve, discover, feel for, find, grasp, succeed, touch, win; SEE CONCEPTS *34,706*

come at [v2] *attack*
assail, assault, charge, fall upon, fly at, go for, invade, light into*, rush; SEE CONCEPT *86*

comeback [n1] *recovery, triumph*
improvement, rally, rebound, resurgence, return, revival, victory, winning; SEE CONCEPT *706*

comeback [n2] *snappy retort*
answer back, quip, rejoinder, repartee, reply, response, retaliation, riposte; SEE CONCEPT *278*

come back [v] *return*
come again, do better, reappear, recover, recur, re-enter, remigrate, resume, triumph; SEE CONCEPT *239*

come between [v] *alienate*
divide, estrange, interfere, interpose, interrupt, intervene, meddle, part, put at odds, separate; SEE CONCEPTS *14,386*

come by [v1] *acquire*
get, lay hold of, obtain, procure, secure, take possession of, win; SEE CONCEPTS *124,129*

come by [v2] *visit someone*
call, come over, drop by, drop in, look in, look up, meet, pay a call, pop in, run in, see, step in, stop by, visit; SEE CONCEPT *227*

come clean [v] *acknowledge information*
admit, confess, explain, make clean breast*, own up, reveal; SEE CONCEPTS *49,57*

comedian [n] *funny person, often professional*
actor, banana*, card*, clown, comic, cutup, droll, entertainer, farceur, humorist, jester, joker, jokester, laugh, merry-andrew, million laughs*, quipster, stand-up comic, stooge*, top banana*, wag, wisecracker, wit*, zany*; SEE CONCEPTS *352,423*

comedown [n] *letdown, blow*
anticlimax, blow, collapse, comeuppance, crash, cropper*, decline, defeat, deflation, demotion, descent, disappointment, discomfiture, dive, down, downfall, failure, fall, flop*, humiliation, pratfall*, reverse, ruin, setback, undoing, wreck; SEE CONCEPTS *674,699*

come down [v] *worsen*
decline, decrease, degenerate, descend, deteriorate, fail, fall, go downhill, reduce, suffer; SEE CONCEPT *698*

come down on [v] *criticize strongly*
attack, dress down, jump on, land on, rebuke, reprimand, scold; SEE CONCEPT *52*

come down with [v] *contract illness*
be stricken with, catch, contract, fall ill, fall victim to, sicken, take, take sick; SEE CONCEPTS *93,303*

comedy [n] *funny entertainment*
ball*, burlesque, camp, chaffing, comicality, comicalness, comic drama, drollery, drollness, facetiousness, farce, field day*, fun, fun and games*, funnies*, funniness, gag show, grins, high camp*, high time, hilarity, hoopla, humor, humorousness, interlude, jesting, joking, laughs, light entertainment, merry-go-round*, picnic, play on, satire, schtick*, send-up, sitcom*, slapstick, takeoff, travesty, vaudeville, wisecracking, witticism, wittiness; SEE CONCEPTS *263,293*

come forward [v] *volunteer services*
appear, make proposal, offer services, present oneself, proffer oneself; SEE CONCEPT *67*

come from [v] *arise, emanate*
accrue, derive from, ejaculate, emerge, end up, flow, hail from, issue, originate, proceed, result, rise, spring, stem, turn out; SEE CONCEPTS *105,179*

come in [v] *enter place*
alight, appear, arrive, cross threshold, disembark, finish, immigrate, intrude, land, pass in, reach, set foot in, show up; SEE CONCEPT *159*

come in for [v] *be eligible for something*
acquire, bear brunt, endure, get, receive, suffer; SEE CONCEPTS *23,124*

comely [adj] *beautiful*
a ten*, attractive, beauteous, becoming, blooming, buxom, fair, fine, good-looking, gorgeous, graceful, handsome, nice, pleasing, pretty, pulchritudinous, stunning, wholesome, winsome; SEE CONCEPT *579*

come off [v] *transpire*
befall, betide, break, chance, click, come about, develop, go, go off, go over, hap*, happen, occur, pan out, prove out, succeed, take place; SEE CONCEPT *4*

come on [v1] *advance, progress*
develop, gain, improve, increase, make headway, proceed; SEE CONCEPT *704*

come on [v2] *appear, enter*
begin, come across, come into, come upon, encounter, meet, pass in, set foot in*, take place; SEE CONCEPT *119*

come out [v1] *make public*
appear, be announced, be brought out, be disclosed, be divulged, be exposed, be issued, be made known, be promulgated, be published, be released, be reported, be revealed, break*, debut, get out, leak*, out, transpire; SEE CONCEPT *60*

come out [v2] *conclude*
end, result, terminate, transpire; SEE CONCEPT *119*

come out with [v] *disclose information*
acknowledge, bring out, chime in*, come clean, declare, deliver, divulge, lay open, own, own up, say, state, tell, throw out, utter; SEE CONCEPT *60*

come through [v1] *accomplish goal*
achieve, be successful, be victorious, carry out, chip in, contribute, kick in, pitch in, prevail, score, succeed, triumph, win; SEE CONCEPT *706*

come through [v2] *survive bad situation*
endure, live through, persist, pull through, ride, ride out, survive, weather storm*, withstand; SEE CONCEPT *23*

come unglued [v] *go to pieces*
break down, come apart at the seams*, come unstuck, come unwrapped, disintegrate, fall apart, fall to bits*, fall to pieces*, malfunction; SEE CONCEPTS *252,469*

come up [v] *happen suddenly*
arise, crop up, occur, rise, spring up, turn up; SEE CONCEPT *119*

come upon [v] *happen upon*
bump into*, chance, come across, encounter, meet; SEE CONCEPTS *38,384*

come up to [v] *meet expectations*
admit of comparison with, approach, arrive, bear comparison with, come near, compare with, equal, extend, get near, match, measure up to, rank with, reach, resemble, rival, stand comparison with; SEE CONCEPT *667*

come up with [v] *suggest, create*
advance, bring forth, compose, detect, discover, find, furnish, invent, offer, originate, present, produce, propose, provide, recommend, stumble upon, submit, uncover; SEE CONCEPTS *75,173*

comfort [n1] *good feeling; ease*
abundance, alleviation, amenity, assuagement, bed of roses*, cheer, cheerfulness, complacency, contentment, convenience, coziness, creature comforts*, enjoyment, exhilaration, facility, gratification, happiness, luxury, opulence, peace-

fulness, pleasure, plenty, poise, quiet, relaxation, relief, repose, rest, restfulness, satisfaction, snugness, succor, sufficiency, warmth, well-being; SEE CONCEPTS *230,410,720*

comfort [*n2*] *aid, help*
alleviation, assist, compassion, compensation, consolation, encouragement, hand, lift, pity, relief, secours, solace, succor, support, sympathy; SEE CONCEPTS *337,712*

comfort [*v*] *make to feel better*
abate, aid, allay, alleviate, ameliorate, assist, assuage, bolster, buck up*, calm, cheer, commiserate with, compose, condole, confirm, console, delight, divert, ease, encourage, enliven, free, gladden, grant respite, hearten, help, inspirit, invigorate, lighten burden, make well, mitigate, nourish, put at ease, quiet fears, reanimate, reassure, refresh, relieve, remedy, revitalize, revive, salve, soften, solace, soothe, strengthen, stroke, succor, support, sustain, sympathize, uphold, upraise; SEE CONCEPTS *7,22,572*

comfortable [*adj1*] *good feeling*
adequate, agreeable, appropriate, at rest, cared for, cheerful, complacent, contented, convenient, cozy, delightful, easy, enjoyable, enjoying, gratified, hale, happy, healthy, hearty, loose, loose-fitting, made well, pleasant, pleased, protected, relaxed, relaxing, relieved, rested, restful, restored, satisfactory, satisfying, serene, sheltered, snug, snug as a bug in a rug*, soft, soothed, strengthened, untroubled, useful, warm, well-off; SEE CONCEPT *572*

comfortable [*adj2*] *affluent, wealthy*
ample, easy, enough, prosperous, substantial, sufficient, suitable, well-heeled*, well-off, well-to-do; SEE CONCEPT *334*

comfortable [*adj3*] *more than adequate*
ample, commodious, cushy, luxurious, palatial, rich, roomy, spacious; SEE CONCEPT *485*

comfort food [*n*] *satisfying food*
home cooking, meat and potatoes, Mom's food, plain food, prepackaged food; SEE CONCEPTS *457,460,461*

comforting [*adj*] *cheering*
abating, allaying, alleviating, analeptic, assuaging, consolatory, consoling, curing, encouraging, freeing, health-giving, heart-warming, inspiriting, invigorating, lightening, mitigating, reassuring, refreshing, relieving, remedying, restoring, revitalizing, revivifying, softening, solacing, soothing, succoring, sustaining, tranquilizing, upholding, warming; SEE CONCEPT *529*

comic [*n*] *funny person, often professional*
banana*, buffoon*, card*, clown, comedian, droll, humorist, jester, joker, jokester, life of the party*, million laughs*, quipster, stand-up comic, stooge*, top banana*, wag*, wit*; SEE CONCEPTS *352,423*

comic/comical [*adj*] *amusing*
absurd, batty, boffo*, camp*, comical, crazy, dippy, diverting, dizzy, droll, entertaining, facetious, farcical, flaky*, fool, foolheaded, for grins*, freaky, funny, gelastic, goofus*, goofy, gump*, horse's tail*, humorous, ironic, jerky, jocular, joking, joshing, laughable, light, loony, ludicrous, Mickey Mouse*, nutty, off the wall*, priceless, ridiculous, risible, schtick*, screwy, side-splitting, silly, wacky, waggish, whimsical, witty; SEE CONCEPTS *401,529*

coming [*adj*] *approaching, promising*
about to happen, advancing, almost on one, anticipated, aspiring, at hand, certain, close, converging, deserving, docking, drawing near, due, en route, eventual, expected, fated, foreseen, forthcoming, future, gaining upon, getting near, immediate, imminent, impending, in prospect, instant, in store, in the offing, in the wind*, in view, marked, near, nearing, next, nigh, oncoming, ordained, predestined, preparing, progressing, prospective, pursuing, running after, subsequent, to be, up-and-coming; SEE CONCEPTS *537,799*

coming [*n*] *arrival*
accession, advent, approach, landing, reception; SEE CONCEPTS *119,159*

command [*n1*] *directive, instruction*
act, adjuration, ban, behest, bidding, call, canon, caveat, charge, citation, commandment, decree, demand, devoir, dictate, dictation, dictum, direction, duty, edict, enactment, exaction, fiat, imperative, imposition, injunction, interdiction, law, mandate, notification, obligation, order, ordinance, precept, prescript, proclamation, prohibition, proscription, regulation, request, requirement, requisition, responsibility, rule, subpoena, summons, ultimatum, warrant, will, word, writ; SEE CONCEPTS *274,662*

command [*n2*] *rule, power*
ability, absolutism, aplomb, authority, authorization, charge, coercion, compulsion, constraint, control, despotism, domination, dominion, expertise, expertism, expertness, government, grasp, grip, hold, jurisdiction, know-how*, leadership, management, might, prerogative, primacy, restraint, right, royalty, skill, sovereignty, strings*, supervision, supremacy, sway, tyranny, upper hand*; SEE CONCEPT *376*

command [*v1*] *demand*
adjure, appoint, authorize, ban, bar, beckon, bid, call, call for, call on, call the signals*, call upon, charge, check, cite, compel, debar, dictate, direct, enact, enjoin, exact, forbid, force upon, give directions, give orders, grant, impose, inflict, inhibit, instruct, interdict, lay down the law, mark out, oblige, ordain, order, ordinate, proclaim, prohibit, put foot down*, require, requisition, restrain, rule out, send for, set, subpoena, summon, take charge, take lead, task, tell, warn; SEE CONCEPT *53*

command [*v2*] *rule, have power*
administer, boss, charge, check, coach, coerce, compel, conduct, conquer, constrain, control, curb, determine, dictate, direct, dominate, domineer, exact, exercise power, force, govern, guide, have authority, head, hinder, hold office, influence, lead, manage, officiate, oppress, overbear, override, predominate, prescribe, preside over, prevail, push, regulate, reign, reign over, repress, restrain, run, stop, subdue, superintend, supervise, sway, take over, tyrannize, wield; SEE CONCEPTS *133,298*

commandeer [*v*] *seize, take over*
accroach, activate, annex, appropriate, arrogate, assume, confiscate, conscript, draft, enslave, expropriate, grab, hijack, liberate, moonlight requisition*, preempt, requisition, sequester, sequestrate, snatch, take, usurp; SEE CONCEPTS *90,142*

commander [*n*] *leader of military or other organization*
administrator, big cheese*, boss, captain, chief, CO*, commandant, czar, director, don, exec, guru, head, head honcho*, head person, higher up, high priest/priestess*, kingfish*, kingpin*, lead-off person*, mastermind, officer, point person*, ruler, skipper, top banana*, top brass*, top dog*; SEE CONCEPTS *347,358*

commanding [*adj*] *superior, authoritative*
advantageous, arresting, assertive, autocratic, bossy, compelling, controlling, decisive, dictatorial, dominant, dominating, forceful, imperious, imposing, impressive, in charge, lofty, peremptory, striking; SEE CONCEPTS *536,574*

commemorate [*v*] *honor, observe occasion*
admire, celebrate, immortalize, keep, memorialize, monument, monumentalize, observe, pay tribute to, perpetuate, remember, salute, solemnize; SEE CONCEPTS *69,377,384*

commemoration [*n*] *honoring, observance*
celebration, ceremony, custom, memorial service, monumentalization, recognition, remembrance, tribute; SEE CONCEPT *377*

commemorative [*adj*] *in honor of something*
celebratory, commemoratory, dedicatory, in memory, in remembrance, memorial, observing; SEE CONCEPT *555*

commence [*v*] *start action*
arise, begin, come into being, come into existence, embark on, enter upon, get cracking*, get going, get one's feet wet*, get show on road*, hit the ground running*, inaugurate, initiate, jump into, kick off*, launch, lead off, open, originate, start the ball rolling*, take up, tear into; SEE CONCEPTS *119,234*

commencement [*n*] *ceremony marking the beginning of stage*
admission, alpha, birth, bow, celebration, convocation, countdown, curtain-raiser*, dawn, dawning, genesis, graduation, initiation, kickoff*, onset, opener, opening, outset, proem, services, start, starting point, tee off*; SEE CONCEPT *377*

commend [*v1*] *recommend, praise*
acclaim, accredit, advocate, applaud, approve, boost, build, build up, compliment, countenance, endorse, eulogize, extol, give a posy*, gold star*, hail, hand it to*, hats off to*, hear it for*, kudize, laud, pat on the back*, puff up, sanction, speak highly of, stroke, support; SEE CONCEPTS *69,75*

commend [*v2*] *hand over with confidence*
assign, commit, confer, confide, consign, deliver, entrust, proffer, relegate, resign, tender, trust, turn over, yield; SEE CONCEPTS *108,132*

commendable [*adj*] *praiseworthy*
admirable, creditable, deserving, estimable, excellent, exemplary, laudable, meritable, meritorious, praisable, thankworthy, worthy; SEE CONCEPTS *527,572*

commendation [*n*] *giving of praise; acclaim*
acclamation, approbation, approval, award, bouquet, Brownie points*, credit, encomium, encouragement, good opinion, honor, panegyric, pat on the back*, pat on the head*, pay, plum, points*, posy, PR*, puff, pumping up*, rave, recommendation, shot in the arm*, stroke, stroking, tribute; SEE CONCEPTS *69,337*

commensurate [*adj*] *adequate, corresponding*
appropriate, coextensive, comparable, compatible, consistent, due, equal, equivalent, fit, fitting, in accord, proportionate, sufficient, symmetrical; SEE CONCEPTS *563,566*

comment [*n*] *statement of opinion; explanation*
animadversion, annotation, backtalk*, buzz*, comeback*, commentary, crack*, criticism, dictum, discussion, editorial, elucidation, exposition, footnote, gloss, hearsay, illustration, input, judgment, mention, mouthful, note, obiter, observation, opinion, remark, report, review, two cents' worth*, wisecrack*; SEE CONCEPTS *51,278*

comment [*v*] *make statement of opinion, explanation*
affirm, animadvert, annotate, assert, bring out, clarify, commentate, conclude, construe, criticize, disclose, elucidate, explain, explicate, expound, express, gloss, illustrate, interject, interpose, interpret, mention, note, notice, observe, opine, pass on, point out, pronounce, reflect, remark, say, state, touch upon; SEE CONCEPTS *51,57*

commentary [*n*] *analysis*
annotation, appreciation, comment, consideration, criticism, critique, description, discourse, exegesis, explanation, exposition, gloss, narration, notes, obiter dictum, observation, remark, review, treatise, voice-over; SEE CONCEPTS *51,278*

commentator [*n*] *reporter*
analyst, annotator, announcer, correspondent, critic, expositor, interpreter, observer, pundit, reviewer, sportscaster, writer; SEE CONCEPT *356*

commerce [*n*] *buying and selling*
business, dealing, dealings, economics, exchange, industry, marketing, merchandising, merchantry, retailing, trade, traffic, truck, wholesaling; SEE CONCEPTS *325,770*

commercial [*adj1*] *concerning business, marketing*
across the counter*, bartering, commissary, economic, exchange, financial, fiscal, for sale, in demand, in the market, market, marketable, mercantile, merchandising, monetary, pecuniary, popular, profitable, profit-making, retail, retailing, saleable, sales, supplying, trade, trading, wholesale, wholesaling; SEE CONCEPT *536*

commercial [*adj2*] *intended for financial gain*
exploited, for profit, investment, materialistic, mercenary, monetary, money-making, pecuniary, profitmaking, venal, Wall Street*; SEE CONCEPT *334*

commercialize [*v*] *prepare for saleability*
advertise, cheapen, degrade, depreciate, develop as business, lessen, lower, make bring returns, make marketable, make pay, make profitable, make saleable, market, sell; SEE CONCEPT *324*

commingle [*v*] *blend*
amalgamate, combine, commix, compound, inmix, integrate, intermingle, intermix, join, merge, mingle, unite; SEE CONCEPT *109*

commiserate [*v*] *listen to woes of another*
ache, compassionate, condole, console, feel, feel for, have mercy, pity, share sorrow, sympathize; SEE CONCEPTS *110,596*

commission [*n1*] *task, duty*
agency, appointment, authority, brevet, certificate, charge, consignment, delegation, deputation, diploma, embassy, employment, errand, function, instruction, legation, mandate, mission, obligation, office, permit, power of attorney, proxy, trust, warrant, work; SEE CONCEPT *362*

CO
CO

commission [*n2*] *share of a profit*
allowance, ante, bite*, bonus, brokerage, chunk, compensation, cut, cut-in*, discount, end*, factorage, fee, indemnity, juice, pay, payment, percentage, piece, piece of the action*, rake-off*, remuneration, royalty, salary, slice*, stipend, taste, vigorish; SEE CONCEPTS *329,344*

commission [*n3*] *group working together toward goal*
board, commissioners, committee, delegation, deputation, representative; SEE CONCEPT *381*

commission [*v*] *authorize or delegate task*
accredit, appoint, assign, bespeak, bid, charge, command, commit, confide to, consign, constitute, contract, crown, depute, deputize, dispatch, employ, empower, enable, engage, enlist, enroll, entrust, hire, inaugurate, induct, instruct, invest, license, name, nominate, ordain, order, select, send; SEE CONCEPTS *50,88,324,351*

commit [*v1*] *perform an action*
accomplish, achieve, act, carry out, complete, contravene, do, effectuate, enact, execute, go for broke*, go in for*, go out for*, offend, perpetrate, pull, pull off*, scandalize, sin, transgress, trespass, violate, wreak; SEE CONCEPTS *6,87*

commit [*v2*] *deliver, entrust*
allocate, allot, apportion, authorize, charge, commend, commission, confer trust, confide, consign, convey, delegate, deliver, depend upon, deposit, depute, deputize, destine, dispatch, employ, empower, engage, give, give to do, grant authority, hand over, hold, ice, imprison, institutionalize, intrust, invest, leave to, make responsible for, move, offer, ordain, promise, put away, put in the hands of, relegate, rely upon, remove, send, shift, submit, transfer, turn over to, vest; SEE CONCEPTS *108,143,217*

commitment [*n*] *assurance; obligation*
charge, committal, devoir, duty, engagement, guarantee, liability, must, need, ought, pledge, promise, responsibility, undertaking, vow, word; SEE CONCEPTS *71,271,274*

committee [*n*] *group working on project*
board, bureau, cabinet, chamber, commission, consultants, convocation, council, investigators, jury, panel, representatives, task force, trustees; SEE CONCEPT *381*

commodious [*adj*] *ample, spacious*
big, capacious, comfortable, convenient, expansive, extensive, large, loose, roomy, wide; SEE CONCEPTS *773,781*

commodity [*n*] *merchandise, possession*
article, asset, belonging, chattel, goods, line, material, object, produce, product, property, specialty, stock, thing, vendible, ware; SEE CONCEPTS *338,710*

common [*adj1*] *average, ordinary*
accepted, banal, bourgeois, casual, characteristic, colloquial, comformable, commonplace, conventional, current, customary, daily, everyday, familiar, frequent, general, habitual, hackneyed, homely, humdrum, informal, mediocre, monotonous, natural, obscure, passable, plain, prevailing, prevalent, prosaic, regular, routine, run-of-the-mill*, simple, stale, standard, stereotyped, stock, trite, trivial, typical, undistinguished, universal, unvaried, usual, wearisome, workaday, worn-out; SEE CONCEPT *547*

common [*adj2*] *generally known; held in common*
accepted, coincident, collective, communal, communistic, community, commutual, congruous, conjoint, conjunct, constant, corporate, correspondent, customary, general, generic, in common, intermutual, joint, like, mutual, popular, prevailing, prevalent, public, reciprocal, shared, social, socialistic, united, universal, usual, well-known, widespread; SEE CONCEPT *530*

common [*adj3*] *low, coarse*
baseborn, characterless, cheap, colorless, crass, declassé, hack, hackneyed, impure, inferior, low-grade, mean, middling, nondescript, passable, pedestrian, Philistine, plebeian, poor, prosy, raffish, second-class, second-rate, shoddy, sleazy, stale, trite, undistinguished, vulgar; SEE CONCEPTS *401,545*

commonly [*adv*] *usually*
as a rule, by ordinary, frequently, generally, more often than not, ordinarily, regularly; SEE CONCEPTS *530,541*

commonplace [*adj*] *usual, everyday*
boiler plate*, characterless, clichéd, colorless, conventional, corny*, customary, dime-a-dozen*, familiar, familiar tune, garden variety*, hackneyed, humdrum, lowly, mainstream, matter-of-course, mediocre, middle-of-the-road*, middling, mundane, natural, normal, obvious, ordinary, pedestrian, plebeian, prevalent, prosaic, run-of-the-mill*, stale, starch, stereotyped, threadbare, trite, typical, uneventful, unexceptional, uninteresting, unnoteworthy, vanilla*, widespread, workaday, worn-out; SEE CONCEPT *530*

commonplace [*n*] *clichéd saying or idea*
banality, bromide*, chestnut*, cliché, corn*, inanity, motto, platitude, prosaicism, prosaism, prose, rubber stamp*, shallowness, shibboleth, stereotype, tag, triteness, triusm, triviality; SEE CONCEPTS *278,689*

common-sense [*adj*] *reasonable*
astute, commonsensical, cool, down-to-earth, hard-headed, judicious, levelheaded, matter-of-fact, practical, rational, realistic, sane, sensible, shrewd, sound; SEE CONCEPT *402*

common sense [*n*] *good reasoning*
acumen, cool, good sense, gumption, horse sense*, intelligence, levelheadedness, practicality, prudence, reasonableness, sense, sound judgment, soundness, wisdom, wit; SEE CONCEPT *409*

commonwealth [*n*] *political or geographic area*
body politic, citizenry, citizens, commonality, democracy, federation, nation, people, polity, republic, society; SEE CONCEPTS *301,512*

commotion [*n*] *clamor, uproar*
ado, agitation, annoyance, backwash, ballyhoo*, bedlam, big scene*, big stink*, brouhaha, bustle, clatter, combustion, confusion, convulsion, discomposure, disquiet, dither, excitement, ferment, fermentation, flap, flurry, furor, fuss, hell broke loose*, hubbub, hurly-burly, insurgence, insurrection, lather*, mutiny, outcry, pandemonium, perturbation, pother, racket, rebellion, revolt, riot, rumpus, stew, stir, to-do, tumult, turbulence, upheaval, uprising, upset, upturn, vexation, welter, whirl; SEE CONCEPTS *388,674*

communal [*adj*] *collective; shared*
common, communistic, community, conjoint,

conjunct, cooperative, general, intermutual, joint, mutual, neighborhood, public; SEE CONCEPTS *536,708*

commune [*n*] *group living together*
collective, commonage, commonality, community, cooperative, family, kibbutz, municipality, neighborhood, rank and file, village; SEE CONCEPT *379*

commune [*v*] *communicate, experience with another*
confer, confide in, contemplate, converse, discourse, discuss, mediate, muse, parley, ponder, reflect; SEE CONCEPTS *17,266*

communicable [*adj*] *able to be contracted*
catching, communicative, contagious, expansive, infectious, pandemic, taking, transferable, transmittable; SEE CONCEPT *314*

communicate [*v1*] *give or exchange information, ideas*
acquaint, advertise, advise, announce, be in touch, betray, break, broadcast, carry, connect, contact, convey, correspond, declare, disclose, discover, disseminate, divulge, enlighten, get across, get through, hint, impart, imply, inform, interact, interface, keep in touch, let on, let out, make known, network*, pass on, phone, proclaim, publicize, publish, raise, reach out, relate, report, reveal, ring up, signify, spread, state, suggest, tell, touch base*, transfer, transmit, unfold, write; SEE CONCEPT *266*

communicate [*v2*] *mutually exchange information*
answer, associate with, be close to, be in touch, be near, buzz, cable, chat, commune with, confabulate, confer, converse, correspond, discourse, drop a line*, drop a note*, establish contact, get on the horn*, give a call, give a ring*, have confidence of hear from, reach, reply, talk, telephone, wire, write; SEE CONCEPTS *56,266*

communication [*n1*] *giving, exchanging information, ideas*
advice, advisement, announcing, articulation, assertion, communion, connection, contact, conversation, converse, correspondence, corresponding, declaration, delivery, disclosing, dissemination, elucidation, expression, intelligence, interchange, intercommunication, intercourse, link, making known, mention, notifying, publication, reading, reception, revelation, talk, talking, telling, transfer, translating, transmission, utterance, writing; SEE CONCEPT *266*

communication [*n2*] *information transmitted*
account, advice, announcement, briefing, bulletin, communiqué, conversation, converse, declaration, directive, disclosure, dispatch, excerpt, goods*, hot story*, ideas, info*, information, inside story*, intelligence, language, lowdown, message, missive, news, note, pipeline, poop*, precis, prophecy, publicity, report, revelation, scoop*, skinny*, speech, statement, summary, tidings, translation, utterance, warning, word, work; SEE CONCEPT *274*

communications [*n*] *systems of information exchange*
information technology, means, media, publicity, public relations, route, telecommunications, transport, travel; SEE CONCEPTS *349,770*

communicative [*adj*] *informative*
candid, chatty, communicable, conversable, conversational, demonstrative, effusive, enlightening, expansive, forthcoming, frank, garrulous, gushing, loquacious, open, outgoing, talkative, unreserved, voluble; SEE CONCEPT *267*

communion [*n1*] *affinity, agreement*
accord, association, closeness, close relationship, communing, concord, contact, converse, fellowship, harmony, intercommunication, intercourse, intimacy, participation, rapport, sympathy, togetherness, unity; SEE CONCEPT *684*

communion [*n2*] *sacrament in church; body of believers sharing a sacrament*
breaking of bread, church, creed, denomination, Eucharist, faith, Lord's Supper, Mass, persuasion, religion, sacrament; SEE CONCEPT *367*

communism [*n*] *socialist government*
Bolshevism, collectivism, Leninism, Marxism, rule of the proletariat, socialism, state ownership, totalitarianism; SEE CONCEPT *301*

community [*n1*] *society, area of people*
association, body politic, center, colony, commonality, commonwealth, company, district, general public, hamlet, locality, nation, neck of the woods*, neighborhood, people, populace, public, residents, society, state, stomping ground*, territory, turf; SEE CONCEPTS *379,512*

community [*n2*] *agreement, similarity*
affinity, identity, kinship, likeness, sameness, semblance; SEE CONCEPTS *664,670*

commute [*v1*] *travel to work*
drive, go back and forth, take the bus/subway/train; SEE CONCEPT *224*

commute [*v2*] *reduce punishment*
alleviate, curtail, decrease, mitigate, modify, remit, shorten, soften; SEE CONCEPTS *236,247, 317*

commute [*v3*] *exchange, trade*
barter, change, convert, interchange, metamorphose, substitute, switch, transfer, transfigure, transform, translate, transmogrify, transmute, transpose; SEE CONCEPTS *104,232*

commuter [*n*] *daily traveler, usually for work*
city worker, driver, straphanger*, suburbanite, traveler; SEE CONCEPT *348*

compact [*adj1*] *condensed*
appressed, bunched, close, compressed, crowded, dense, firm, hard, impenetrable, impermeable, packed, pressed, solid, thick, tight; SEE CONCEPTS *481,483,774*

compact [*adj2*] *short, brief*
boiled down, compendious, concise, epigrammatic, in a nutshell*, laconic, make a long story short*, marrowy, meaty, pithy, pointed, short and sweet*, succinct, terse, to the point; SEE CONCEPTS *773,798*

compact [*n*] *agreement*
alliance, arrangement, bargain, bond, concordat, contract, convention, covenant, deal, engagement, entente, indenture, pact, settlement, stipulation, transaction, treaty, understanding; SEE CONCEPTS *271,684*

compact [*v*] *make condensed*
combine, compress, concentrate, condense, consolidate, contract, cram, integrate, pack, set, solidify, stuff, unify, unite; SEE CONCEPTS *137,208,250*

compact disc [*n*] *recording of music or speech*
album, CD, cut*, cylinder, demo, digital recording, disk, laser disk, record, release, track; SEE CONCEPT *262*

CO
CO

companion [n] *helper, friend*
accompaniment, accomplice, aide, ally, assistant, associate, attendant, buddy, chaperon, colleague, comate, complement, comrade, concomitant, confederate, consort, convoy, counterpart, cousin, co-worker, crony, cuz*, double, escort, guide, match, mate, nurse, pal, pard*, partner, playmate, protector, roomie*, safeguard, sidekick; SEE CONCEPT *423*

companionable [adj] *friendly*
affable, amicable, buddy buddy*, clubby*, complacent, congenial, conversable, convivial, cordial, cozy, cozy with, familiar, genial, good-natured, gregarious, intimate, mellow, neighborly, outgoing, pally, palsy*, sociable, social, tight, tight with*; SEE CONCEPT *555*

companionship [n] *friendship, accompaniment*
affiliation, alliance, amity, camaraderie, company, comradeship, conviviality, esprit de corps, rapport, society, togetherness, union; SEE CONCEPT *388*

company [n1] *crowd of people*
aggregation, assemblage, assembly, association, band, body, circle, clan, clique, club, collection, community, concourse, congregation, convention, corps, cortege, coterie, crew, ensemble, gang*, gathering, group, horde, jungle*, league, mob*, muster, order, outfit, pack, party, retinue, ring, ruck, set, team, throng, troop, troupe, turnout, zoo*; SEE CONCEPT *417*

company [n2] *business concern*
association, business, concern, corporation, enterprise, establishment, firm, house, megacorp*, multinational, outfit, partnership, syndicate; SEE CONCEPT *325*

company [n3] *social friend, guest*
boarder, caller, companionship, cortege, party, presence, retinue, society, visitor; SEE CONCEPTS *417,423*

comparable [adj1] *worthy of comparison*
a match for, as good as, commensurable, commensurate, equal, equipollent, equipotential, equivalent, in a class with, on a par, proportionate, tantamount; SEE CONCEPT *566*

comparable [adj2] *corresponding, similar*
agnate, akin, alike, analogous, cognate, consonant, corresponding, like, parallel, related, relative, undifferenced, uniform; SEE CONCEPTS *487,573*

comparative [adj] *approximate, close to*
allusive, analogous, approaching, by comparison, comparable, conditional, connected, contingent, contrastive, correlative, corresponding, equivalent, in proportion, like, matching, metaphorical, near, not absolute, not positive, parallel, provisional, qualified, related, relative, restricted, rivaling, similar, vying, with reservation; SEE CONCEPTS *487,566,573*

compare [v1] *examine in contrast*
analyze, approach, balance, bracket, collate, confront, consider, contemplate, contrast, correlate, divide, equal, examine, hang, hold a candle to*, inspect, juxtapose, match, match up, measure, observe, oppose, parallel, place in juxtaposition, ponder, rival, scan, scrutinize, segregate, separate, set against, set side by side, size up, stack up against*, study, touch, weigh, weigh against another; SEE CONCEPTS *24,103*

compare [v2] *liken, equate*
allegorize, approach, approximate to, assimilate,

balance, bear comparison, be in the same class as*, be on a par with*, bring near, come up to, compete with, connect, correlate, distinguish between, draw parallel, equal, equate, hold a candle to*, identify with, link, make like, match, notice similarities, parallel, put alongside, relate, resemble, show correspondence, stack up with*, standardize, tie up, vie; SEE CONCEPT *39*

comparison [n] *contrasting; corresponding*
allegory, analogizing, analogy, analyzing, association, balancing, bringing together, collating, collation, comparability, connection, contrast, correlation, discrimination, distinguishing, dividing, estimation, example, exemplification, identification, illustration, juxtaposition, likeness, likening, measuring, metaphor, observation, opposition, paralleling, ratio, relating, relation, resemblance, segregation, separation, similarity, testing, weighing; SEE CONCEPTS *24,39,529*

compartment [n] *section, subdivision*
alcove, area, bay, berth, booth, carrel, carriage, category, cell, chamber, corner, cubbyhole, cubicle, department, division, hole, locker, niche, nook, part, piece, pigeonhole, place, portion, slot, stall; SEE CONCEPT *434*

compass [n] *boundary, periphery*
ambit, area, bound, circle, circuit, circumference, circumscription, confines, domain, enclosure, environs, expanse, extent, field, limit, limitation, orbit, perimeter, precinct, purlieus, purview, radius, range, reach, realm, restriction, round, scope, sphere, stretch, sweep, zone; SEE CONCEPTS *484,651,788*

compass [v1] *enclose*
beset, besiege, blockade, circle, circumscribe, encircle, encompass, environ, gird, girdle, hem in, ring, round, surround; SEE CONCEPT *758*

compass [v2] *achieve, get*
accomplish, annex, attain, bring about, effect, execute, fulfill, gain, have, land, obtain, perform, procure, realize, secure, win; SEE CONCEPTS *142,706*

compassion [n] *tender feeling*
benevolence, charity, clemency, commiseration, compunction, condolence, consideration, empathy, fellow feeling, grace, heart, humaneness, humanity, kindness, lenity, mercy, softheartedness, softness, sorrow, sympathy, tenderheartedness, tenderness, yearning; SEE CONCEPTS *410,633*

compassionate [adj] *having tender feelings*
all heart, being big*, benevolent, bleeding heart*, charitable, commiserative, forbearing, going easy on*, humane, humanitarian, indulgent, kindhearted, kindly, lenient, living with, merciful, old softie*, piteous, pitying, responsive, softhearted, soft shell*, sparing, sympathetic, tender, tenderhearted, understanding, warm, warmhearted; SEE CONCEPTS *401,403*

compatibility [n] *harmony in relationship*
affinity, agreeableness, agreement, amity, congeniality, congruity, consonance, empathy, fit, like-mindedness, rapport, single-mindedness, sympathy, unity; SEE CONCEPT *388*

compatible [adj] *agreeable, in harmony*
accordant, adaptable, appropriate, congenial, congruent, congruous, consistent, consonant, cooperative, cotton to*, fit, fitting, getting along with, harmonious, having good vibes*, hitting it off*, in keeping, in sync with*, in the groove*, like-minded, meet, on the same wavelength*,

proper, reconcilable, simpatico, suitable, sympathetic, together; SEE CONCEPT *555*

compel [*v*] *force to act*
bulldoze*, coerce, concuss, constrain, crack down, dragoon, drive, enforce, exact, hustle, impel, make, make necessary, necessitate, oblige, put the arm on*, put the chill on*, restrain, shotgun*, squeeze, throw weight around*, turn on the heat*, urge; SEE CONCEPTS *14,384*

compendious [*adj*] *abridged*
abbreviated, breviloquent, brief, close, compact, compendiary, comprehensive, concise, condensed, contracted, curt, inclusive, laconic, short, short and sweet*, succinct, summarized, summary, synoptic; SEE CONCEPTS *773,789*

compendium [*n*] *abridgment*
abstract, aperçu, brief, conspectus, digest, epitome, essence, guide, handbook, manual, overview, pandect, precis, sketch, summary, survey, syllabus, sylloge; SEE CONCEPT *283*

compensate [*v1*] *make restitution*
atone, come down with*, commit, guerdon, indemnify, make good*, pay, pay up, plank out*, pony up*, recompense, recoup, refund, reimburse, remunerate, repay, requite, reward, satisfy, shell out*, take care of, tickle the palm*; SEE CONCEPTS *108,126,341*

compensate [*v2*] *offset, make up for*
abrogate, annul, atone for, balance, better, cancel out, counteract, counterbalance, counterpoise, countervail, fix, improve, invalidate, make amends, negate, negative, neutralize, nullify, outweigh, redress, repair, set off; SEE CONCEPTS *126,212*

compensation [*n*] *repayment; rectification*
advantage, allowance, amends, atonement, benefit, bonus, bread*, consideration, counterclaim, coverage, damages, defrayal, deserts*, earnings, fee*, gain, honorarium, indemnification, indemnity, meet, pay, payment, payoff, premium, profit, quittance, reciprocity, reckoning, recompense, recoupment, redress, reimbursement, remittal, remittance, remuneration, reparation, reprisal, requital, restitution, reward, salary, salt, satisfaction, scale, settlement, shake, stipend, take*, take-home*, wage; SEE CONCEPTS *337,344*

compete [*v*] *go up against in contest*
attempt, bandy, battle, be in the running*, bid, challenge, clash, collide, contend, contest, cope with, emulate, encounter, essay, face, fence, fight, go after, go for*, go for broke*, go for the gold*, grapple, in the hunt*, jockey for position*, joust, lock horns*, match strength, match wits*, oppose, participate in, pit oneself against*, play, rival, run for, scramble for*, seek prize, spar, strive, struggle, take on, take part, tilt, try, tussle, vie, wrestle; SEE CONCEPT *92*

competence [*n*] *ability*
adequacy, appropriateness, capability, capacity, competency, cutting it*, cutting the mustard*, expertise, fitness, hacking it*, know-how, makings, making the grade*, might, moxie, proficiency, qualification, qualifiedness, savvy, skill, suitability, the goods*, the right stuff*, what it takes*; SEE CONCEPT *630*

competent [*adj*] *able*
adapted, adequate, all around, appropriate, au fait, being a pistol*, capable, clever, complete, crisp, decent, dynamite, efficient, endowed, enough, equal, fireball*, fit, fool, good, know ins and outs*, know one's business*, know one's stuff*, know the answers*, know the ropes*, know the score*, no slouch*, on the ball*, paid one's dues*, pertinent, polished, proficient, qualified, satisfactory, savvy, skilled, sufficient, suitable, there*, up to it, up to snuff*, up to speed*, wicked*; SEE CONCEPT *527*

competition [*n*] *contest*
antagonism, athletic event, bout, candidacy, championship, clash, concours, contention, controversy, counteraction, dog eat dog*, do or die*, emulation, encounter, engagement, event, fight, game, go for it, go for the gold*, horse race*, jungle*, match, matchup, meeting, one on one*, one-upping, opposition, pairing off, puzzle, quiz, race, racing, rat race*, rivalry, run, sport, strife, striving, struggle, tilt, tournament, trial, tug-of-war, warfare; SEE CONCEPTS *92,363*

competitive [*adj*] *willing to oppose*
aggressive, ambitious, antagonistic, at odds, combative, competing, cutthroat, dog-eat-dog*, emulous, killer*, killer instinct*, opposing, rival, streetwise, vying; SEE CONCEPT *542*

competitor [*n*] *person willing to enter contest*
adversary, antagonist, challenger, competition, contestant, corival, dark horse*, emulator, favorite, opponent, opposition, rival; SEE CONCEPTS *366,423*

compilation [*n*] *assemblage*
accumulating, accumulation, aggregating, anthology, assembling, assortment, collecting, collection, collocating, combining, compiling, consolidating, garner, garnering, gathering, incorporating, joining, treasury, unifying; SEE CONCEPTS *109,432*

compile [*v*] *assemble, accumulate*
abridge, amass, anthologize, arrange, assemble, bring together, collate, collect, colligate, collocate, compose, concentrate, congregate, consolidate, cull, draw together, edit, garner, gather, get together, glean, group, heap up, marshal, muster, organize, put together, recapitulate, unite; SEE CONCEPTS *79,84,109*

complacent [*adj*] *contented*
conceited, confident, easy-going, egoistic, egotistic, gratified, happy, obsequious, pleased, satisfied, self-assured, self-contented, self-pleased, self-possessed, self-righteous, self-satisfied, serene, smug, unconcerned; SEE CONCEPTS *401,403*

complain [*v*] *grumble about*
accuse, ascribe, attack, beef*, bellyache*, bemoan, bewail, bitch, carp, cavil, charge, contravene, criticize, defy, demur, denounce, deplore, deprecate, differ, disagree, disapprove, dissent, expostulate, find fault, fret, fuss, gainsay, grieve, gripe, groan, grouse, growl, grumble, impute, indict, kick up a fuss*, lament, lay, look askance, make a fuss, moan, nag, object, oppose, protest, refute, remonstrate, repine, reproach, snivel, sound off, take exception to, wail, whimper, whine, yammer; SEE CONCEPT *52*

complaint [*n1*] *statement of disagreement, discontent*
accusation, annoyance, beef*, cavil, CC*, charge, clamor, criticism, dissatisfaction, expostulation, fault-finding, grievance, gripe, grouse, grumble, guff*, jeremiad, kick, lament, moan, objection, plaint, protest, protestation, rap, remonstrance, remonstration, representation, re-

CO
CO

proach, rumble*, squawk, stink, trouble, wail, whine; SEE CONCEPTS *52,689*

complaint [*n2*] *illness, affliction*
affection, ailment, condition, disease, disorder, ill, indisposition, infirmity, malady, sickness, syndrome, upset; SEE CONCEPTS *306,316*

complaisance [*n*] *agreeableness*
accommodativeness, acquiescence, compliance, courtesy, deference, friendliness, kindness, obligingness, politeness, respect; SEE CONCEPT *633*

complaisant [*adj*] *agreeable*
accommodating, amiable, compliant, conciliatory, deferential, easy, easy-going, friendly, generous, good-humored, good-natured, good-tempered, indulgent, lenient, mild, obliging, polite, solicitous, submissive; SEE CONCEPT *401*

complement [*n*] *companion, counterpart*
accompaniment, addition, aggregate, augmentation, balance, capacity, completion, consummation, correlate, correlative, counterpart, enhancement, enrichment, entirety, filler, finishing touch, makeweight, pendant, quota, remainder, rest, rounding-off*, supplement, total, totality; SEE CONCEPTS *635,824*

complement [*v*] *complete*
accomplish, achieve, cap, clinch, conclude, consummate, crown, finish, fulfill, integrate, perfect, round off, top off; SEE CONCEPTS *91,119,234*

complementary [*adj*] *filling, completing*
commutual, complemental, completing, complectory, conclusive, correlative, correspondent, corresponding, crowning, equivalent, fellow, integral, integrative, interconnected, interdependent, interrelated, interrelating, matched, mated, paired, parallel, reciprocal; SEE CONCEPTS *577,824*

complete [*adj1*] *total, not lacking*
all, entire, exhaustive, faultless, full, full-dress, gross, hook line and sinker*, imperforate, intact, integral, integrated, lock stock and barrel*, organic, outright, plenary, replete, the works*, thorough, thoroughgoing, unabbreviated, unabridged, unbroken, uncondensed, uncut, undiminished, undivided, undocked, unexpurgated, unimpaired, unitary, unreduced, whole, whole enchilada*, whole-hog*, whole-length, whole nine yards*; SEE CONCEPT *531*

complete [*adj2*] *finished*
accomplished, achieved, all-embracing, all-inclusive, all over, all over but the shouting*, attained, compassed, concluded, consummate, done, done with, down, effected, ended, entire, executed, fini*, finished off, full, full-fledged, home free*, perfect, plenary, realized, sweeping, terminated, that's it*, through; SEE CONCEPT *528*

complete [*adj3*] *utter, absolute*
blank, blanket, categorical, consummate, downright, dyed-in-the-wool*, flawless, impeccable, out-and-out, outright, perfect, positive, sheer, thorough, thoroughgoing, total, unblemished, unconditional, unmitigated, unqualified, whole; SEE CONCEPTS *531,535*

complete [*v*] *carry out action*
accomplish, achieve, actualize, bring to fruition, bring to maturity, call it a day*, cap, carry off, close, conclude, consummate, crown, determine, develop, discharge, do, do thoroughly, effect, effectuate, elaborate, end, equip, execute, fill, fi-

nalize, finish, fulfill, furnish, get through, go the limit*, go through with, go whole hog*, halt, make good*, make up, perfect, perform, put to bed*, realize, refine, round off, round out, settle, sew up*, supplement, terminate, ultimate, wind up*, wrap up*; SEE CONCEPT *91*

completely [*adv*] *entirely*
absolutely, all the way*, altogether, competently, comprehensively, conclusively, effectively, en masse, exclusively, exhaustively, extensively, finally, from A to Z*, from beginning to end*, fully, heart and soul*, hook line and sinker*, in all, in entirety, in full, in toto*, on all counts*, painstakingly, perfectly, quite, solidly, thoroughly, totally, to the end, to the limit, to the max*, to the nth degree*, ultimately, unabridged, unanimously, unconditionally, undividedly, utterly, wholly, without omission; SEE CONCEPT *531*

completion [*n*] *accomplishment, finishing*
achievement, attainment, close, conclusion, consummation, culmination, curtains*, dispatch, end, expiration, finalization, finis, finish, fruition, fulfillment, hips*, integration, perfection, realization, swan song*, windup*, wrap-up; SEE CONCEPTS *119,706*

complex [*adj1*] *involved, intricate*
circuitous, complicated, composite, compound, compounded, confused, conglomerate, convoluted, elaborate, entangled, heterogeneous, knotty, labyrinthine, manifold, mingled, miscellaneous, mixed, mixed-up, mosaic, motley, multifarious, multiform, multiple, multiplex, tangled, tortuous, variegated; SEE CONCEPT *562*

complex [*adj2*] *difficult to understand*
abstruse, bewildering, Byzantine, circuitous, complicated, confused, convoluted, crabbed, cryptic, Daedalean, discursive, disordered, disturbing, enigmatic, entangled, excursive, Gordian, hidden, impenetrable, inscrutable, interwoven, intricate, involved, jumbled, knotted, knotty, labyrinthine, mazy, meandering, mingled, mixed, muddled, obscure, paradoxical, perplexing, puzzling, rambling, recondite, roundabout, sinuous, snarled, sophisticated, tangled, tortuous, undecipherable, unfathomable, winding; SEE CONCEPTS *402,529*

complex [*n1*] *composite, aggregate*
association, compound, conglomerate, ecosystem, entanglement, group, network, organization, scheme, structure, syndrome, synthesis, system, totality; SEE CONCEPTS *432,770*

complex [*n2*] *psychological problem*
anxiety, a thing about something*, exaggerated reaction, fear, fixation, fixed idea, hang-up*, idée fixe, insanity, mania, neurosis, obsession, phobia, preoccupation, repression; SEE CONCEPT *410*

complexion [*n1*] *skin coloring, appearance*
cast, color, coloration, coloring, flush, front, glow, hue, looks, mug*, phiz*, pigmentation, skin, skin tone, texture, tinge, tint, tone; SEE CONCEPTS *405,622*

complexion [*n2*] *someone's character*
appearance, aspect, cast, countenance, disposition, guise, humor, ilk, individualism, individuality, kind, light, look, make-up, nature, personality, seeming, semblance, sort, stamp, style, temper, temperament, type; SEE CONCEPT *411*

complexity [*n*] *complicatedness*
complication, convolution, elaboration, entanglement, intricacy, involvement, multiplicity, ramification; SEE CONCEPT *663*

compliance [*n*] *agreement*
acquiescence, amenability, assent, complaisance, concession, concurrence, conformity, consent, deference, docility, obedience, observance, passivity, resignation, submission, submissiveness, tractibility, yielding; SEE CONCEPTS *411,684*

complicate [*v*] *confuse, make difficult*
add fuel to fire*, bedevil, clog, combine, confound, convolute, derange, disarrange, disorder, elaborate, embroil, entangle, fold, foul up*, handicap, impede, infold, interfuse, interrelate, interweave, involve, jumble, make intricate, make waves*, mix up, muck up*, muddle, multiply, obscure, open can of worms*, perplex, ravel, render unintelligible, screw up*, snafu*, snag, snarl up*, tangle, twist, upset; SEE CONCEPTS *7,19*

complicated [*adj*] *difficult, complex*
abstruse, arduous, Byzantine, can of worms*, convoluted, Daedalean, difficult, elaborate, entangled, fancy, gasser*, Gordian, hard, hi-tech*, interlaced, intricate, involved, knotty, labyrinthine, mega factor*, mixed, perplexing, problematic, puzzling, recondite, sophisticated, troublesome, various, wheels within wheels*; SEE CONCEPTS *562,565*

complication [*n*] *difficult situation*
aggravation, complexity, confusion, development, difficulty, dilemma, drawback, embarrassment, entanglement, factor, intricacy, obstacle, problem, snag, web; SEE CONCEPTS *230,674*

complicity [*n*] *conspiracy*
abetment, agreement, collaboration, collusion, complot, concurrence, confederacy, connivance, engineering, guilt, guiltiness, implication, intrigue, involvement, machination, manipulation, partnership; SEE CONCEPTS *388,660*

compliment [*n*] *praise, flattery*
acclaim, acclamation, admiration, adulation, applause, appreciation, approval, blessing, bouquet*, buttering up*, cajolery, commendation, comp, confirmation, congratulations, courtesy, encomium, endorsement, eulogy, favor, felicitation, good word, homage, honor, kudo, laud, laudation, laurels, notice, orchid*, ovation, panegyric, pat on the back*, posy*, regard, respects, sanction, sentiment, tribute, veneration, warm fuzzy*; SEE CONCEPTS *69,278*

compliment [*v*] *praise, flatter*
acclaim, adulate, applaud, butter up*, cajole, celebrate, charm, cheer, commemorate, commend, congratulate, endorse, eulogize, exalt, extol, fawn upon, felicitate, give bouquet*, glorify, hail, hand it to*, honor, ingratiate oneself with, kudize*, laud, magnify, make much of, panegyrize, pat on the back*, pay respects, pay tribute to, please, puff up*, recommend, roose, salute, sanction, satisfy, sing praises of, soothe, speak highly of, take off hat to*, toast, trade last*, wish joy to, worship; SEE CONCEPT *69*

complimentary [*adj1*] *flattering*
adulatory, appreciative, approbative, approbatory, approving, celebrating, commendatory, congratulatory, courtly, encomiastic, encomiastical, eulogistic, fair-spoken, fawning, highly favorable, honeyed, honoring, laudatory,

panegyrical, plauditory, polite, praiseful, respectful, sycophantic, unctuous, well-wishing, with highest recommendation, with high praise; SEE CONCEPT *267*

complimentary [*adj2*] *free*
as a perk*, chargeless, comp, costless, courtesy, donated, free lunch*, free of charge, gratis, gratuitous, honorary, on the house*; SEE CONCEPT *334*

comply [*v*] *abide by, follow agreement or instructions*
accede, accord, acquiesce, adhere to, agree to, cave in, come around, conform to, consent to, cry uncle*, defer, discharge, ditto*, don't make waves*, don't rock the boat*, fit in, fold, fulfill, give in, give out, go along with, go with the flow*, keep, knuckle to*, knuckle under*, mind, obey, observe, perform, play ball*, play the game*, put out, quit, respect, roll over and play dead*, satisfy, shape up, stay in line*, straighten up, submit, throw in towel*, toss it in*, yes one*, yield; SEE CONCEPTS *8,35,91*

component [*adj*] *constituent*
basic, composing, elemental, fundamental, inherent, integral, intrinsic, part and parcel of*, part of; SEE CONCEPTS *546,567*

component [*n*] *part, element*
constituent, factor, fixings, ingredient, item, making, makings, peripheral, piece, plug-in, segment, unit; SEE CONCEPTS *831,834*

compose [*v1*] *be part of construction*
be an adjunct, be an element of, belong to, be made of, build, compound, comprise, consist of, constitute, construct, enter in, fashion, form, go into, make, make up, merge in; SEE CONCEPTS *168,642*

compose [*v2*] *create writing, artwork, or music*
author, bang out*, cast, clef*, coin a phrase, comp, conceive, contrive, cook up*, design, devise, discover, draw up, dream up, fabricate, forge, form, formulate, frame*, fudge together*, ghost*, ghostwrite, imagine, indite, invent, knock off*, knock out*, make up, note down, orchestrate, originate, pen, poetize, produce, push pencil*, put down, put pen to paper*, score, scribble, script, set type, set up, time, turn out, whip up*, write; SEE CONCEPTS *79,173,174*

compose [*v3*] *calm, bring under control*
adjust, allay, appease, arrange, assuage, balm, becalm, check, collect, comfort, console, contain, control, cool, ease, ease up, hold in, lessen, let up, lull, mitigate, moderate, modulate, pacify, placate, quell, quiet, re-collect, reconcile, regulate, rein, relax, repress, resolve, restrain, settle, simmer down, slacken, smother, soften, solace, soothe, still, suppress, temper, tranquilize, tune down; SEE CONCEPTS *7,22,117*

composed [*adj*] *calm, collected*
at ease, calmed, clearheaded, commonsensical, confident, cool, cool as cucumber*, disimpassioned, dispassionate, easy, easygoing, have one's act together*, imperturbable, keeping a stiff upper lip*, keeping one's shirt on*, levelheaded, nonchalant, not turn a hair*, placid, poised, possessed, quieted, relaxed, repressed, sedate, self-assured, self-possessed, sensible, serene, serious, soothed, staid, suppressed, sure of oneself, temperate, together, tranquil, unflappable, unruffled, untroubled; SEE CONCEPT *401*

CO
CO

composite [*adj*] *combined, mixed*
blended, complex, compound, conglomerate, melded, synthesized; SEE CONCEPT *490*

composite [*n*] *combination, mixture*
amalgam, amalgamation, blend, combo, commixture, complex, compost, compound, conglomerate, fusion, immixture, intermixture, medley, mix, olio, pasteup*, stew*, synthesis, union; SEE CONCEPTS *260,432*

composition [*n1*] *structure, arrangement*
agreement, architecture, balance, beauty, combination, concord, configuration, consonance, constitution, content, design, distribution, form, formation, harmony, layout, make-up, placing, proportion, relation, rhythm, spacing, style, symmetry, weave; SEE CONCEPTS *733,757*

composition [*n2*] *written or musical creation*
arrangement, article, chart, concerto, dissertation, drama, essay, exercise, exposition, fiction, getup*, literary work, manuscript, melody, music, novel, number, opus, paper, piece, play, poetry, rhapsody, romance, score, setup*, short story, song, stanza, study, symphony, theme, thesis, tune, verse, work, writing; SEE CONCEPTS *259,260,263,271*

compost [*n*] *organic material*
admixture, blend, commixture, composition, compound, fertilizer, fusion, humus, manure, mix, mixture, mulch, ordure, pile; SEE CONCEPT *509*

composure [*n*] *calmness, collectedness*
accord, aplomb, assurance, balance, calm, contentment, control, cool*, cool head*, coolheadedness, coolness, dignity, dispassion, ease, equanimity, equilibrium, evenness, even temper, fortitude, harmony, imperturbability, inexcitability, levelheadedness, moderation, nonchalance, peace of mind, placidity, poise, polish, presence of mind, quiet, quietude, repose, sang-froid, sedateness, self-assurance, self-control, self-possession, serenity, sobriety, stability, tranquility; SEE CONCEPT *410*

compound [*n*] *combination, mixture*
admixture, aggregate, alloy, amalgam, amalgamation, blend, combo, commixture, composite, composition, compost, conglomerate, fusion, goulash, medley, mishmash*, soup, stew, synthesis, union; SEE CONCEPTS *260,432*

compound [*v1*] *mix, combine*
admix, amalgamate, associate, blend, bracket, coagment, coalesce, commingle, commix, concoct, connect, couple, fuse, immix, intermingle, join, link, make up, meld, mingle, synthesize, unite; SEE CONCEPTS *109,113*

compound [*v2*] *make difficult; complicate*
add to, aggravate, augment, confound, confuse, exacerbate, extend, heighten, intensify, magnify, make complex, make intricate, multiply, worsen; SEE CONCEPTS *231,240*

comprehend [*v1*] *understand*
appreciate, apprehend, assimilate, capiche*, catch, click, cognize, conceive, dig*, discern, envisage, envision, fathom, get*, get the picture*, gotcha*, grasp, have, know, make out*, perceive, read, savvy*, see, take in, tumble*; SEE CONCEPT *15*

comprehend [*v2*] *include*
comprise, contain, embody, embrace, enclose, encompass, have, involve, subsume, take in; SEE CONCEPT *118*

comprehensible [*adj*] *understandable*
apprehensible, clear, coherent, comprehendible, conceivable, explicit, fathomable, graspable, intelligible, knowable, lucid, luminous, plain; SEE CONCEPTS *402,529*

comprehension [*n*] *understanding*
aha*, apperception, apprehension, awareness, capacity, cognizance, conception, discernment, double take*, grasp, intelligence, judgment, ken, knowledge, perception, prehension, realization, sense, slow take*, take*; SEE CONCEPT *409*

comprehensive [*adj*] *inclusive*
absolute, across the board*, all-embracing, all-inclusive, blanket, broad, catholic, compendious, complete, comprising, containing, discursive, encircling, encyclopedic, exhaustive, expansive, extensive, far-reaching, full, general, global, in depth, infinite, lock stock and barrel*, of great scope, overall, sweeping, synoptic, the big picture*, the whole shebang*, the works*, thorough, umbrella, wall-to-wall*, whole, wide, widespread; SEE CONCEPTS *531,772*

compress [*v*] *compact, condense*
abbreviate, abridge, abstract, bind, boil down, coagulate, concentrate, consolidate, constrict, contract, cram, cramp, crowd, crush, decrease, dehydrate, densen, densify, epitomize, force into space, make brief, narrow, pack, press, press together, ram, reduce, restrict, shorten, shrink, shrivel, squash, squeeze, stuff, summarize, syncopate, telescope, tighten, wedge, wrap; SEE CONCEPTS *208,236,247*

comprise [*v*] *make up, consist of*
add up to, amount to, be composed of, be contained in, compass, compose, comprehend, constitute, contain, cover, embody, embrace, encircle, enclose, encompass, engross, form, hold, include, incorporate, involve, span, subsume, sum up, take in; SEE CONCEPT *643*

compromise [*n*] *agreement, give-and-take*
accommodation, accord, adjustment, arrangement, bargain, compact, composition, concession, contract, copout*, covenant, deal, fifty-fifty*, half and half, half measure, happy medium*, mean, middle course, middle ground, pact, sellout, settlement, trade-off, understanding, win-win situation*; SEE CONCEPTS *230,684*

compromise [*v1*] *give and take*
adjust, agree, arbitrate, compose, compound, concede, conciliate, find happy medium*, find middle ground*, go fifty-fifty*, make a deal, make concession, meet halfway, negotiate, play ball with*, settle, split the difference*, strike balance, trade off; SEE CONCEPT *8*

compromise [*v2*] *put in jeopardy*
blight, cop out*, discredit, dishonor, embarrass, endanger, explode, expose, give in, hazard, imperil, implicate, jeopardize, mar, menace, peril, prejudice, put under suspicion, risk, ruin, sell out, spoil, weaken; SEE CONCEPTS *101,240*

compulsion [*n*] *drive, obligation*
coercion, constraint, demand, drive, driving, duress, duty, engrossment, exigency, force, hang-up, have on the brain*, monkey*, necessity, need, obsession, preoccupation, prepossession, pressure, tiger by the tail*, urge, urgency; SEE CONCEPTS *410,532*

compulsive [*adj*] *driving, obsessive*
besetting, compelling, enthusiastic, irresistible,

overwhelming, passionate, uncontrollable, urgent; SEE CONCEPT *401*

compulsory [*adj*] *binding*
compulsatory, de rigueur, forced, imperative, imperious, mandatory, necessary, obligatory, required, requisite; SEE CONCEPT *546*

compunction [*n*] *regret, sorrow*
attrition, conscience, contrition, misgiving, penitence, penitency, pity, punctiliousness, qualm, reluctance, remorse, repentance, rue, ruth, second thoughts, shame, stab of conscience, sympathy; SEE CONCEPT *410*

computation [*n*] *performing arithmetic*
calculation, ciphering, computing, counting, data processing, estimating, estimation, figuring, gauge, guess, reckoning, summing, totalling; SEE CONCEPT *764*

compute [*v*] *calculate, estimate*
add up, cast up, cipher, count, count heads, count noses, cut ice*, dope out*, enumerate, figure, figure out, gauge, keep tabs*, measure, rate, reckon, run down, size up, sum, take account of, take one's measure, tally, tot*, total, tote*, tote up*; SEE CONCEPT *764*

computer [*n*] *calculating, data processing machine*
abacus, adding machine, analog, artificial intelligence, brain*, calculator, clone, CPU, data processor, digital, electronic brain*, laptop*, MAC, mainframe, micro*, microcomputer, mini*, minicomputer, number cruncher*, PC, personal computer, thinking machine*; SEE CONCEPTS *269,463*

computerese [*n*] *computer technical language*
computer jargon, computer terminology, computer terms, hacker talk, tech talk; SEE CONCEPTS *275,276*

computer geek [*n*] *computer expert*
computer specialist, engineer, guru, hacker, programmer, techie; SEE CONCEPT *348*

comrade [*n*] *ally*
associate, bosom buddy, buddy, chum, colleague, comate, companion, compatriot, compeer, confederate, confidant, confidante, co-worker, crony, friend, intimate, mate, pal, partner, sidekick; SEE CONCEPT *423*

con [*n*] *trick*
bluff, cheat, crime, deception, double-cross, dupe, fraud, gold brick*, graft, mockery, swindle, take in; SEE CONCEPT *59*

con [*v*] *deceive, defraud*
bamboozle*, bilk, cajole, cheat, chicane, coax, double-cross, dupe, flimflam*, fool, hoax, hoodwink, hornswoggle*, humbug, inveigle, mislead, rip off*, rook, sweet-talk*, swindle, trick, wheedle; SEE CONCEPT *59*

concatenation [*n*] *connection, sequence*
chain, connecting, continuity, integration, interlocking, link, linking, nexus, series, succession, uniting; SEE CONCEPTS *721,727*

concave [*adj*] *curved, depressed*
biconcave, cupped, dented, dimpled, dipped, excavated, hollow, hollowed, incurvate, incurvated, incurved, indented, round, rounded, sagging, scooped, sinking, sunken; SEE CONCEPT *486*

conceal [*v*] *hide, disguise*
beard, burrow, bury, cache, camouflage, cloak, couch, cover, cover up, dissemble, ditch, duck, ensconce, enshroud, harbor, hole up*, keep dark, keep secret, lie low*, lurk, mask, masquerade,

obscure, plant*, put in a hole*, screen, secrete, shelter, skulk, slink, sneak, stash, stay out of sight, stow, tuck away, veil, wrap; SEE CONCEPT *188*

concealed [*adj*] *hidden, secret*
buried, cached, camouflaged, covered, covered up, covert, enshrouded, guarded, holed up, hushed up, hush-hush*, incog*, incognito, inconspicuous, masked, obscure, obscured, on the Q. T.*, perdu, planted, privy, put in the hole*, recondite, screened, secreted, shrouded, stashed, tucked away, ulterior, under wraps*, unseen, veiled; SEE CONCEPTS *576,619*

concealment [*n*] *hiding, secrecy*
beard, blind, camouflage, cover, covering, cover-up, curtain, disguise, dissimulation, fig leaf*, front, hideaway, hide-out, laundromat, mask, obliteration, obscuration, occultation, privacy, red herring*, secretion, smoke screen*, veil, wraps*; SEE CONCEPTS *188,631*

concede [*v*] *acknowledge, give in*
accept, accord, admit, allow, avow, award, bury the hatchet*, capitulate, cave in, cede, confess, cry uncle*, ditto*, fess up*, fold, give up, go along with, go with the flow*, grant, hand over, knuckle under, let on, own, own up, play ball with*, quit, relinquish, say uncle*, surrender, throw in the towel*, waive, yes one*, yield; SEE CONCEPTS *35,57,82,235*

conceit [*n*] *egotism*
amour-propre, arrogance, complacence, complacency, consequence, immodesty, narcissism, outrecuidance, pomposity, pride, self-admiration, self-exaltation, self-importance, self-love, self-regard, smugness, snottiness, stuffiness, swagger, swelled head*, vainglory, vainness, vanity; SEE CONCEPT *411*

conceited [*adj*] *egotistical*
arrogant, bigheaded*, big talking, cocky, conceity, full of hot air*, gall, ham*, hot stuff*, immodest, know-it-all, loudmouth, narcissistic, overweening, phony, puffed up*, self-important, smart-alecky*, snotty*, stuck up*, swollen-headed*, vain, vainglorious, windbag*; SEE CONCEPT *404*

conceivable [*adj*] *reasonable, easy to understand*
believable, convincing, credible, earthly, imaginable, likely, mortal, possible, probable, supposable, thinkable; SEE CONCEPTS *529,552*

conceive [*v1*] *understand*
accept, appreciate, apprehend, assume, believe, catch, compass, comprehend, deem, dig, envisage, expect, fancy, feel, follow, gather, get, grasp, imagine, judge, perceive, realize, reckon, suppose, suspect, take, twig; SEE CONCEPT *15*

conceive [*v2*] *create*
become pregnant, brainstorm, cogitate, consider, contrive, cook up*, depicture, design, develop, devise, dream up, envisage, envision, fancy, feature, form, formulate, head trip*, image, imagine, make up, meditate, originate, ponder, produce, project, purpose, realize, ruminate, spark, speculate, spitball, think up, trump up*, visualize; SEE CONCEPTS *35,173,251*

concentrate [*v1*] *think about closely*
apply, attend, be engrossed in, bring to bear, brood over, center, consider closely, contemplate, crack one's brains*, direct attention, establish, examine, fixate, fix attention, focus, focus attention, get on the beam*, give attention, ham-

CO
CO

mer*, hammer away at*, head trip*, intensify, knuckle down, meditate, muse, need, occupy thoughts, peruse, ponder, pour it on*, put, put mind to, rack one's brains*, rivet, ruminate, scrutinize, set, settle, study, sweat, think hard, weigh; SEE CONCEPT *17*

concentrate [*v2*] *gather, collect*
accumulate, agglomerate, aggregate, amass, assemble, bunch, center, centralize, cluster, coalesce, collect, combine, compact, compress, congest, conglomerate, congregate, consolidate, constrict, contract, converge, cramp, crowd, draw together, eliminate, embody, focalize, focus, forgather, garner, get to the meat*, heap, heap up, hoard, huddle, integrate, intensify, localize, mass, muster, narrow, pile, reduce, salt away, store, strengthen, swarm, unify, zero in*; SEE CONCEPTS *84,109*

concentrated [*adj*] *condensed, reduced*
boiled down, complete, crashed*, entire, evaporated, fixed, full-bodied, lusty, potent, rich, robust, straight, strong, stuffed*, telescoped*, thick, thickened, total, unadulterated, undiffused, undiluted, undivided, unmingled, unmixed, whole; SEE CONCEPTS *483,554*

concentrated [*adj2*] *intense*
all-out, deep, desperate, exquisite, fierce, furious, hard, intensive, terrible, vehement, vicious; SEE CONCEPTS *326,569*

concentration [*n1*] *consolidation of effort*
absorption, amassing, application, assembly, bringing to bear, centering, centralization, close attention, clustering, coalescing, combination, compacting, compression, concern, congregation, consolidation, convergence, converging, debate, deliberation, fixing, flocking, focusing, heed, huddling, intensification, massing, narrowing, need, single-mindedness, study, unity; SEE CONCEPT *677*

concentration [*n2*] *aggregation*
accumulation, army, array, audience, band, cluster, collection, company, concourse, convergence, flock, group, herd, horde, mass, miscellany, mob, party; SEE CONCEPT *432*

concept [*n*] *idea*
abstraction, apprehension, approach, big idea*, brainchild*, brain wave*, conceit, conception, conceptualization, consideration, fool notion*, hypothesis, image, impression, intellection, notion, perception, slant, supposition, theory, thought, twist, view, wrinkle; SEE CONCEPTS *532,689*

conception [*n1*] *understanding; idea*
apperception, appreciation, apprehension, clue, cogitating, cognition, communing, comprehension, conceit, concentrating, concept, consideration, considering, deliberating, design, dreaming, envisaging, explanation, exposition, fancy, fancying, image, imagining, impression, inkling, intellection, interpretation, meditating, meditation, mental grasp, musing, notion, perception, philosophizing, picture, plan, realization, representation, speculating, speculation, thought, version; SEE CONCEPTS *409,410,689*

conception [*n2*] *beginning, birth*
fertilization, formation, germination, impregnation, inception, initiation, insemination, invention, launching, origin, outset, start; SEE CONCEPTS *119,302,373,375*

concern [*n1*] *business, responsibility*
affair, burden, care, charge, company, corporation, deportment, entanglement, enterprise, establishment, field, firm, house, interest, involvement, job, jungle*, matter, megacorp*, mission, multinational, occupation, organization, outfit, shooting match*, task, thing, transaction, worry, zoo*; SEE CONCEPTS *325,362,532*

concern [*n2*] *interest; anxiety*
apprehension, attention, bearing, care, carefulness, concernment, consideration, disquiet, disquietude, distress, heed, heedfulness, important matter, matter, reference, regard, relation, relevance, solicitude, tender loving care, unease, worry; SEE CONCEPTS *410,690*

concern [*v1*] *affect personally*
apply to, bear on, become involved, be relevant to, bother, disquiet, distress, disturb, interest, involve, make anxious, make uneasy, pertain to, perturb, regard, take pains, touch, trouble, worry; SEE CONCEPTS *7,19,22*

concern [*v2*] *relate to, have reference to*
answer to, appertain to, apply to, be about, be applicable to, bear on, bear upon, be connected with, be dependent upon, be interdependent with, belong to, be pertinent to, be well taken, deal with, depend upon, have a bearing on, have connections with, have implications for, have relation to, have significance for, have to do with, involve, pertain to, refer to, regard; SEE CONCEPT *532*

concerned [*adj1*] *worried*
anxious, biting one's nails*, bothered, butterflies in stomach*, distressed, disturbed, exercised, in a stew*, on pins and needles*, perturbed, tied up in knots*, troubled, uneasy, upset, uptight, worried sick*; SEE CONCEPT *403*

concerned [*adj2*] *involved with*
active, affected, attentive, caring, down with, implicated, in on, interested, mixed up, privy to, solicitous; SEE CONCEPTS *401,403*

concerning [*prep*] *having to do with*
about, anent, apropos of, as regards, germane to, in regard to, in the matter of, pertaining to, re, regarding, relating to, relevant to, respecting, touching, with reference to, with regard to; SEE CONCEPT *563*

concert [*n1*] *musical performance*
gig, jam session, musical, musicale, recital, rockfest, selections, show; SEE CONCEPT *263*

concert [*n2*] *agreement, harmony*
accord, chorus, collaboration, concord, concordance, consonance, joint, league, togetherness, tune, unanimity, union, unison; SEE CONCEPTS *388,684*

concerted [*adj*] *coordinated*
agreed upon, collaborative, combined, joint, mutual, planned, prearranged, united; SEE CONCEPT *538*

concession [*n*] *yielding, adjustment*
acknowledgment, admission, allowance, assent, authorization, boon, buyback, compromise, confession, copout*, deal, giveback, giving in, grant, indulgence, permission, permit, privilege, rollback, sellout, surrender, trade-off, warrant; SEE CONCEPTS *13,50,67,88*

conciliatory [*adj*] *placid, yielding*
appeasing, assuaging, calm, civil, disarming, irenic, mollifying, pacific, peaceable, placating,

placatory, propitiative, quiet, willing; SEE CONCEPT **401**

concise [adj] *short, to the point*
abridged, boiled down*, breviloquent, brief, compact, compendiary, compendious, compressed, condensed, curt, epigrammatic, in a nutshell*, laconic, lean, marrowy, meaty, pithy, short and sweet*, succinct, summary, synoptic, terse; SEE CONCEPTS **773,798**

conclave [n] *secret meeting*
assembly, buzz session*, cabinet*, confab*, conference, council, encounter, gathering, get-together, huddle, meet, parley, powwow*, private meeting, session; SEE CONCEPTS **324,384**

conclude [v1] *finish, come to an end*
achieve, bring down curtain*, call it a day*, cease, cinch, clinch, close, close out, complete, consummate, crown, desist, draw to close, end, halt, knock off, put the lid on*, put to bed*, round off, stop, terminate, top off, ultimate, wind up, wrap up; SEE CONCEPTS **119,234**

conclude [v2] *decide, deduce*
add up to, adjudge, analyze, assume, be afraid, boil down to*, collect, derive, draw, figure, gather, have a hunch*, infer, intuit, judge, make, make out, presume, ratiocinate, reason, reckon, sum up, suppose, surmise, the way one sees it*; SEE CONCEPTS **18,37**

conclude [v3] *settle, resolve*
accomplish, achieve, bring about, carry out, clinch, confirm, decide, determine, effect, establish, fix, pull off, rule, work out; SEE CONCEPTS **18,91,126**

conclusion [n1] *end*
cease, cessation, close, closure, completion, consequence, culmination, denouement, desistance, development, ending, end of the line*, eventuality, finale, finish, issue, outcome, payoff, period, result, stop, termination, upshot, windup, wrap; SEE CONCEPTS **119,832**

conclusion [n2] *judgment, decision*
agreement, conviction, corollary, deduction, determination, illation, inference, opinion, ratiocination, resolution, resolve, sequitur, settlement, verdict; SEE CONCEPT **689**

conclusive [adj] *definite, final*
absolute, all out*, clear, clinching, cogent, compelling, convincing, deciding, decisive, demonstrative, determinant, determinative, flat out*, incontrovertible, indisputable, irrefragable, irrefrangible, irrefutable, irrevocable, litmus test*, precise, resolving, revealing, settling, straight out, telling, ultimate, unambiguous, unanswerable, unarguable, unconditional, undeniable, unmistakable, unquestionable, what you see is what you get*; SEE CONCEPT **535**

concoct [v] *formulate, think up*
ad lib, batch*, brew*, compound, contrive, cook up, create, design, devise, discover, dream up, envisage, envision, fabricate, frame*, hatch, invent, make up, mature, originate, plan, plot, prefab*, prepare, project, scheme, slap together*, throw together*, vamp; SEE CONCEPTS **36,173,251**

concoction [n] *creation, blend*
brew, combination, compound, contrivance, intention, medley, mixture, plan, preparation, project, solution; SEE CONCEPTS **260,432,660**

concomitant [adj] *contributing, accompanying*
accessory, adjuvant, agreeing, ancillary, associated with, associative, attendant, attending, belonging, coefficient, coetaneous, coeval, coexistent, coincident, coincidental, collateral, complementary, concordant, concurrent, conjoined, conjoined with, connected, contemporaneous, contemporary, coordinate, corollary, coterminous, coupled with, fellow, incident, in tempo, in time, isochronal, isochronous, joint, satellite, synchronal, synchronous, synergetic, synergistic; SEE CONCEPT **577**

concord [n1] *unity, harmony*
accord, agreement, amity, calmness, chime, comity, concert, concordance, consensus, consonance, friendship, goodwill, peace, placidity, rapport, serenity, tranquility, tune, unanimity, understanding, unison; SEE CONCEPT **388**

concord [n2] *agreement, treaty*
compact, concordat, contract, convention, entente, pact, protocol; SEE CONCEPTS **271,684**

concourse [n1] *passageway*
avenue, boulevard, entrance, foyer, hall, highway, lobby, lounge, meeting place, path, rallying point*, road, street; SEE CONCEPTS **440,501**

concourse [n2] *crowd, group*
assemblage, assembly, collection, concursion, confluence, convergence, crush, gang, gathering, joining, junction, linkage, meeting, mob, multitude, rout, throng; SEE CONCEPT **432**

concrete [adj1] *actual, factual*
accurate, corporeal, definite, detailed, explicit, material, objective, particular, precise, real, sensible, solid, specific, substantial, tangible; SEE CONCEPTS **535,582**

concrete [adj2] *hardened*
caked, calcified, cemented, compact, compressed, congealed, conglomerated, consolidated, dried, firm, indurate, monolithic, petrified, poured, precast, set, set in stone*, solid, solidified, steeled, strong, unyielding; SEE CONCEPT **604**

concur [v] *agree, approve*
accede, accord, acquiesce, assent, band, be consonant with, be in harmony, coadjute, coincide, collaborate, combine, come together, consent, cooperate, cut a deal*, equal, harmonize, jibe*, join, league*, meet, okay*, pass on*, shake on*, unite; SEE CONCEPTS **8,10,82**

concurrent [adj1] *simultaneous*
circumstantial, coeval, coexisting, coincident, concerted, concomitant, contemporaneous, incidental, in sync, parallel, synchronal, synchronous; SEE CONCEPT **799**

concurrent [adj2] *agreeing, converging*
allied, at one, centrolineal, coinciding, compatible, concerted, confluent, consentient, consistent, convergent, cooperating, coterminous, harmonious, in agreement, in rapport, joined, likeminded, meeting, mutual, of the same mind, unified, uniting; SEE CONCEPT **563**

concussion [n] *collision, shaking*
blast, blow, buffeting, bump, clash, clout, crack, crash, hit, impact, injury, jar, jarring, jolt, jolting, jounce, pounding, punch, shock, trauma; SEE CONCEPTS **189,309,521**

condemn [v] *blame, convict*
adjudge, belittle, blow whistle on*, call down*, castigate, censure, chide, come down on*, criticize, damn, decry, denounce, denunciate, deprecate, depreciate, disapprove, disparage, doom, find fault with, find guilty, frame, hang some-

CO
CO

thing on*, judge, knock, lay at one's door*, let have it*, name, pass sentence on*, pin it on*, point finger at*, pronounce, proscribe, punish, put away, put down, reprehend, reproach, reprobate, reprove, send up, send up the river*, sentence, skin, thumbs down on*, upbraid; SEE CONCEPTS *44,52,317*

condemnation [*n*] *blaming, conviction*
accusation, blame, censure, damnation, denouncement, denunciation, disapproval, doom, judgment, proscription, reproach, reprobation, reproof, sentence, stricture; SEE CONCEPTS *44,52,317*

condensation [*n1*] *abridgment*
abstract, boildown*, breviary, brief, compendium, compression, concentration, consolidation, conspectus, contraction, curtailment, digest, epitome, essence, précis, reduction, summary, synopsis; SEE CONCEPTS *283,730*

condensation [*n2*] *water buildup*
condensate, crystallization, deliquescence, dew, distillation, liquefaction, precipitate, precipitation, rainfall; SEE CONCEPT *514*

condense [*v*] *abridge*
abbreviate, blue pencil*, boil down, chop, coagulate, compact, compress, concentrate, constrict, contract, curtail, cut, cut down, decoct, densen, digest, edit, encapsulate, epitomize, inventory, precipitate, précis, press together, put in a nutshell*, reduce, shorten, shrink, snip, solidify, sum, summarize, summate, synopsize, telescope, thicken, trim; SEE CONCEPTS *236,247*

condescend [*v*] *stoop, humble oneself*
accommodate, accord, acquiesce, agree, be courteous, bend, come down off high horse*, comply, concede, degrade oneself, deign, demean oneself, descend, favor, grant, high hat*, lower oneself, oblige, see fit, submit, talk down to, toss a few crumbs*, unbend, vouchsafe, yield; SEE CONCEPT *633*

condescending [*adj*] *snobby, lordly*
arrogant, complaisant, disdainful, egotistic, ladee-da*, lofty, patronizing, snobbish, snooty*, snotty*, supercilious, superior, uppish, uppity; SEE CONCEPT *401*

condescension [*n*] *disdain, superiority*
airs, civility, deference, haughtiness, loftiness, lordliness, patronage, patronizing attitude, superciliousness, toleration; SEE CONCEPT *633*

condiment [*n*] *flavoring*
catsup, dressing, gravy, horseradish, ketchup, mustard, pepper, relish, salsa, salt, sauce, seasoning, spice, zest; SEE CONCEPTS *457,461*

condition [*n1*] *circumstances*
action, ballgame*, case, estate, happening, how it goes*, how things are*, how things stack up*, lay of the land*, like it is*, mode, order, plight, position, posture, predicament, quality, rank, repair, reputation, riff, scene, shape, situation, size of it*, sphere, spot, standing, state, state of affairs, status, status quo, trim, way things are*, way things shape up*, where it's at*; SEE CONCEPTS *639,696*

condition [*n2*] *requirement, limitation*
arrangement, article, catch, codicil, contingency, demand, essential, exception, exemption, fine print*, kicker*, modification, must, necessity, postulate, precondition, prerequisite, provision, proviso, qualification, requisite, reservation, rule,

sine qua non, small print*, stipulation, strings*, terms; SEE CONCEPTS *270,688*

condition [*n3*] *physical shape, fitness*
appearance, aspect, build, constitution, fettle, form, health, kilter, mint, order, phase, repair, state, status, tone, trim; SEE CONCEPTS *316,757*

condition [*n4*] *illness*
affection, ailment, complaint, disease, ill, infirmity, malady, predicament, problem, syndrome, temper, weakness; SEE CONCEPT *306*

condition [*v*] *adapt, prepare*
accustom, brainwash, build up, educate, equip, habituate, inure, loosen up, make ready, modify, practice, program, ready, shape up, sharpen, tone up, toughen up, train, warm up, whip into shape*, work out, work over; SEE CONCEPTS *35,202*

conditional [*adj*] *dependent*
codicillary, contingent, depending on, fortuitous, granted on certain terms, guarded, iffy*, incidental, inconclusive, limited, modified, not absolute, obscure, provisional, provisory, qualified, relative, reliant, relying on, restricted, restrictive, subject to, tentative, uncertain, with grain of salt*, with reservations, with strings attached*; SEE CONCEPT *554*

condolence [*n*] *sympathy*
comfort, commiseration, compassion, condolement, consolation, fellow feeling, solace; SEE CONCEPT *633*

condom [*n*] *birth control*
contraceptive, French letter*, johnnie*, johnny*, prophylactic, protection, raincoat*, rubber*, safe, sheath; SEE CONCEPTS *307,446*

condominium [*n*] *tenant-owned apartment house*
apartment, condo, co-op, timeshare, townhouse; SEE CONCEPT *516*

condone [*v*] *make allowance for*
buy*, disregard, excuse, forget, forgive, give green light*, go along with, ignore, lap up*, let it come*, let it go by*, let pass*, look the other way*, nod at*, okay, overlook, pardon, pass over, remit, wink at*; SEE CONCEPTS *10,23*

conducive [*adj*] *favorable for*
accessory, calculated to produce, contributive, contributory, helpful, leading, productive of, promotive, tending, useful; SEE CONCEPT *542*

conduct [*n1*] *administration*
care, carrying on*, channels, charge, control, direction, execution, guidance, handling, intendance, leadership, management, manipulation, organization, oversight, plan, policy, posture, red tape*, regimen, regulation, rule, running, strategy, superintendence, supervision, tactics, transaction, treatment, wielding; SEE CONCEPT *117*

conduct [*n2*] *behavior*
address, attitude, bearing, carriage, comportment, demeanor, deportment, manner, manners, mien, posture, stance, tenue, ways; SEE CONCEPT *633*

conduct [*v1*] *administer*
accompany, attend, call the tune*, carry on*, chair, chaperon, control, convey, direct, engineer, escort, govern, guide, handle, head, keep, lead, manage, operate, ordain, order, organize, oversee, pilot, preside over, regulate, ride herd on*, rule, run, run things, shepherd, steer, supervise, trailblaze*, usher, wield baton*; SEE CONCEPT *117*

conduct [*v2*] *comport oneself*
acquit, act, bear, behave, carry, demean, deport, go on, quit; SEE CONCEPT *384*

conduct [*v3*] *transport*
accompany, attend, bring, carry, chaperon, companion, convoy, escort, guide, lead, move, pass on, pilot, route, send, shepherd, show, steer, transfer; SEE CONCEPT *187*

conductor [*n*] *leader*
director, guide, maestro, manager, marshal, master, supervisor; SEE CONCEPTS *347,350,354*

conduit [*n*] *passage*
aqueduct, cable, canal, channel, conductor, course, culvert, duct, flow, flume, gully, gutter, lead-in, lead-out, main, pipe, pipeline, race, sewer, spout, trough, tube, watercourse; SEE CONCEPTS *499,501*

cone [*n*] *circular-shaped object with pointed end*
conoid, pyramid, raceme, strobile, strobiloid; SEE CONCEPT *436*

confection [*n*] *sweet food*
cake, candy, dainty, jam, pastry, sweet; SEE CONCEPT *457*

confederacy [*n*] *coalition*
alliance, anschluss, bond, compact, confederation, conspiracy, covenant, federation, government, league, organization, union; SEE CONCEPTS *299,301*

confederate [*adj*] *allied*
amalgamated, associated, combined, corporate, federal, federated, in alliance, incorporated, leagued, organized, syndicated, unionized; SEE CONCEPT *536*

confederate [*n*] *abettor*
accessory, accomplice, ally, associate, coconspirator, collaborator, colleague, conspirator, fellow, fellow traveler, partner; SEE CONCEPT *412*

confer [*v1*] *discuss, deliberate*
advise, argue, bargain, blitz*, brainstorm*, breeze*, collogue, confab*, confabulate, consult, converse, deal, debate, discourse, flap*, gab*, get heads together*, give meeting*, groupthink*, huddle, jaw, kick ideas around*, negotiate, parley, pick one's brain*, powwow*, speak, talk, toss ideas around*, treat; SEE CONCEPT *56*

confer [*v2*] *giving honor, award*
accord, allot, award, bestow, donate, gift with, give, grant, lay on, present, provide, sweeten the kitty*, vouchsafe; SEE CONCEPT *132*

conference [*n1*] *convention, colloquium*
appointment, argument, chat, colloquy, confabulation, conferring, congress, consultation, conversation, convocation, deliberation, discussion, forum, gabfest*, groupthink*, huddle, interchange, interview, meeting, palaver, parley, powwow*, round robin, round table, seminar, symposium, talk, think-in*, ventilation; SEE CONCEPTS *56,324,386*

conference [*n2*] *league of athletic teams*
association, athletic union, circuit, league, loop, organization, ring; SEE CONCEPT *365*

confess [*v*] *admit, confirm*
acknowledge, affirm, allow, assert, attest, aver, avow, blow, blurt out, chirp, clue in, come clean*, come out, concede, confide, declare, disclose, divulge, dump on*, evince, finger*, fink*, grant, humble oneself, leak*, let on*, level with, make clean breast of*, manifest, narrate, open one's heart*, own, own up, post, profess, prove, rat on*, recognize, relate, reveal, sing*, snitch*,

sound off*, spill the beans*, spit out*, squeal*, tip hand*, unload*, vent, weasel*; SEE CONCEPT *60*

confession [*n*] *admittance of information*
acknowledgment, admission, affirmation, allowance, assenting, assertion, avowal, concession, declaration, disclosing, disclosure, divulgence, enumeration, exposé, exposure, making public, narration, owning up, proclamation, profession, publication, recitation, relation, revealing, revelation, song*, squawk*, squeal*, statement, story, telling, unbosoming, utterance; SEE CONCEPTS *60,274*

confidant [*n*] *close friend*
acquaintance, adherent, adviser, alter ego, bosom buddy, companion, crony, familiar, intimate, mate, pal; SEE CONCEPT *423*

confide [*v1*] *divulge information*
admit, bend an ear*, breathe, buzz*, confess, crack to, disclose, hint, impart, insinuate, intimate, lay it on*, lay the gaff*, let in on*, reveal, spill to*, suggest, tell, unload on*, whisper; SEE CONCEPT *57*

confide [*v2*] *entrust*
bestow, charge, commend, commit, consign, delegate, hand over, present, relegate, trust; SEE CONCEPT *108*

confidence [*n1*] *belief in oneself*
aplomb, assurance, backbone, boldness, brashness, certainty, cool, courage, daring, dash, determination, elan, faith in oneself, fearlessness, firmness, fortitude, grit, hardihood, heart, impudence, intrepidity, mettle, morale, nerve, pluck, poise, presumption, reliance, resoluteness, resolution, self-possession, self-reliance, spirit, spunk, sureness, tenacity; SEE CONCEPT *411*

confidence [*n2*] *belief in something*
assurance, credence, dependence, faith, hope, reliance, stock, store, sure bet*, trust; SEE CONCEPT *689*

confident [*adj1*] *certain, assured*
bet on*, bold, brave, cocksure, convinced, counting on, courageous, dauntless, depending on, expectant, expecting, fearless, having faith in, high*, hopeful, intrepid, positive, presuming, presumptuous, puffed up*, pushy, racked, sanguine, satisfied, secure, self-assured, self-reliant, self-sufficient, sure, trusting, unafraid, undaunted, upbeat, uppity*, valiant; SEE CONCEPTS *403,404*

confidential [*adj*] *secret*
arcane, backdoor, classified, closet, hushed, hush-hush*, inside, intimate, off the record*, private, privy; SEE CONCEPTS *267,576*

confidentially [*adv*] *in secret*
behind closed doors*, between ourselves, between us, between you and me*, covertly, don't breathe a word*, hushedly, in confidence, in on the ground floor*, off the cuff*, off the record*, personally, privately, sub rosa; SEE CONCEPTS *267,576*

configuration [*n*] *arrangement*
composition, contour, disposition, figure, form, Gestalt, outline, shape, structure; SEE CONCEPTS *84,727*

confine [*v*] *enclose, limit*
bar, bind, bound, cage, circumscribe, constrain, cool, cool down, cramp, delimit, detain, enslave, fix, hem in, hinder, hog-tie*, hold back, ice*, immure, imprison, incarcerate, intern, jail, keep,

CO
CO

put a lid on*, put away, put on ice*, repress, restrain, restrict, send up, shorten, shut up; SEE CONCEPTS *121,130*

confined [*adj*] *limited, enclosed*
bedfast, bedridden, bottled up, bound, chilled, circumscribed, compassed, cooped up, cramp, cramped, detained, flattened out, grounded, hampered, held, hog-tied*, iced*, immured, imprisoned, incarcerated, in chains, incommodious, indisposed, in jail, invalided, jailed, laid up, locked up, on ice*, pent, restrained, restricted, sealed up, shut in, sick; SEE CONCEPT *554*

confinement [*nl*] *imprisonment; restriction*
bonds, bounding, bounds, check, circumscription, coercion, constrainment, constraint, control, cramp, curb, custody, delimitation, detention, immuration, incarceration, internment, jail, keeping, limitation, repression, safekeeping, trammels; SEE CONCEPTS *90,191*

confines [*n*] *boundaries*
borders, bounds, circumference, compass, country, dimension, edge, end, environs, extent, limits, orbit, periphery, precinct, proportions, purlieus, purview, radius, range, reach, region, scope, sweep, term, terrain, territory; SEE CONCEPTS *484,745,788*

confirm [*v1*] *ratify, validate, prove*
affirm, approve, attest, authenticate, back, bear out, bless, buy, certify, check, check out, circumstantiate, corroborate, debunk, double-check, endorse, establish, explain, give green light*, give high sign*, give stamp of approval*, give the go-ahead*, give the nod*, justify, lap up, make good*, make sure, okay, rubber-stamp*, sanction, settle, sign, sign off on*, size up, subscribe, substantiate, support, thumbs up*, underpin, uphold, verify, vouch, warrant, witness; SEE CONCEPTS *57,103*

confirm [*v2*] *reinforce*
assure, buttress, clinch, establish, fix, fortify, invigorate, make firm, settle, strengthen; SEE CONCEPTS *244,250*

confirmation [*n*] *ratification, validation, proof*
acceptance, accepting, accord, admission, affirmation, affirming, agreement, approval, assent, attestation, authenticating, authentication, authorization, authorizing, avowal, consent, corroborating, corroboration, endorsement, evidence, go ahead*, green light*, nod, okay, passage, passing, proving, recognition, sanction, sanctioning, stamp of approval*, substantiation, support, supporting, testament, testimonial, testimony, validating, verification, verifying, visa, witness; SEE CONCEPTS *661,685*

confirmed [*adj*] *habitual; rooted*
accepted, accustomed, chronic, deep-rooted, deep-seated, dyed-in-the-wool*, entrenched, firmly established, fixed, habituated, hardened, hard-shell*, ingrained, inured, inveterate, long-established, proved, seasoned, settled, staid, valid, worn; SEE CONCEPTS *542,798*

confiscate [*v*] *steal; seize*
accroach, annex, appropriate, arrogate, assume, commandeer, confisticate, expropriate, glom on to*, grab, hijack, impound, liberate, moonlight requisition*, possess oneself of, preempt, sequester, sequestrate, swipe, take, take over, usurp; SEE CONCEPTS *139,142*

conflagration [*n*] *large fire*
blaze, bonfire, burning, flaming, holocaust, inferno, rapid oxidation, up in smoke*, wildfire; SEE CONCEPTS *249,478*

conflict [*nl*] *fight, warfare*
battle, clash, collision, combat, competition, contention, contest, emulation, encounter, engagement, fracas, fray, rivalry, set-to, strife, striving, struggle, tug-of-war, war; SEE CONCEPTS *106,320*

conflict [*n2*] *disagreement, discord*
affray, animosity, antagonism, bad blood*, brush, competition, concours, contention, contest, dance, difference, disaccord, dispute, dissension, dissent, dissidence, disunity, divided loyalties, faction, factionalism, flap, fray, friction, fuss, hassle, hostility, interference, meeting, opposition, row, ruckus, run-in, set-to, strife, variance; SEE CONCEPTS *106,388,674*

conflict [*v*] *be at odds*
brawl, bump heads with*, clash, collide, combat, contend, contest, contrast, cross swords with, differ, disaccord, disagree, discord, disharmonize, disturb, fight, interfere, jar, lock horns with*, mismatch, oppose, romp, run against tide*, scrap, slug, square off with, strive, struggle, tangle, vary; SEE CONCEPTS *46,106*

conflicting [*adj*] *contradictory*
adverse, antagonistic, antipathetic, at odds with, clashing, contrariant, contrary, disconsonant, discordant, discrepant, dissonant, incompatible, incongruent, incongruous, inconsistent, inconsonant, opposed, opposing, paradoxical, unfavorable, unmixable; SEE CONCEPTS *542,570*

confluence [*n*] *coming together*
assemblage, assembly, concourse, concurrence, concursion, conflux, convergence, crowd, gathering, host, junction, meeting, mob, multitude, union; SEE CONCEPTS *109,114*

conform [*v1*] *adjust, adapt*
accommodate, attune, be guided by, clean up act*, comply, coordinate, don't make waves*, don't rock the boat*, fall in with, fit, follow, follow beaten path*, follow the crowd, go by the book*, go with the flow*, harmonize, integrate, keep, make room, meet halfway, mind, move over, obey, observe, play the game*, proportion, quadrate, reconcile, reconciliate, roll with punches*, run with the pack*, shape up, square, straighten up, suit, tailor, tailor-make*, toe the line*, tune, yield; SEE CONCEPT *13*

conform [*v2*] *correspond, match*
accord, agree, assimilate, be regular, dovetail, fit in, fit the pattern, go, harmonize, jibe, square, suit, tally; SEE CONCEPT *664*

conformable [*adj*] *appropriate; matching*
adapted, agreeable, alike, amenable, applicable, assorted, comparable, compliant, consistent, docile, fitted, fitting, harmonious, in agreement, like, matched, obedient, orderly, proper, regular, resembling, similar, submissive, suitable, suited, tractable, unified, useable, well-regulated; SEE CONCEPTS *487,558,563,573*

conformation [*n*] *shape*
anatomy, arrangement, build, cast, configuration, figure, form, formation, frame, framework, outline, structure, symmetry, type; SEE CONCEPTS *754,757*

conformist [*n*] *person in agreement*
Babbit, bourgeois, brick in a wall*, conventionalist, emulator, follower, one of the herd*, rubber stamp*, sheep*, traditionalist, yes man*; SEE CONCEPTS *361,423*

conformity [*n1*] *compliance*
acquiescence, allegiance, assent, consent, conventionality, docility, obedience, observance, orthodoxy, resignation, submission, willingness; SEE CONCEPTS *13,689*

conformity [*n2*] *correspondence, harmony*
accord, affinity, agreement, coherence, conformance, congruity, consistency, consonance, likeness, resemblance, similarity; SEE CONCEPT *664*

confound [*v*] *confuse*
abash, amaze, astonish, astound, baffle, befog, bewilder, blend, bug*, commingle, confute, discombobulate*, discomfit, discountenance, dumbfound, embarrass, faze, fiddle, flabbergast, jumble, metagrobolize, misidentify, mix, mix up*, mystify, nonplus, perplex, pose, puzzle, rattle, screw up*, startle, surprise, throw*; SEE CONCEPTS *16,42*

confront [*v*] *challenge*
accost, affront, beard, brave, call one's bluff*, come up against*, dare, defy, encounter, face down*, face up to*, face with*, flout, front, go one-on-one*, go up against*, make my day*, meet, meet eyeball-to-eyeball*, oppose, repel, resist, scorn, stand up to, tell off, withstand; SEE CONCEPTS *46,52,54*

confrontation [*n*] *conflict*
affray, battle, contest, crisis, dispute, encounter, fight, meeting, set-to, showdown, strife; SEE CONCEPTS *46,106*

confuse [*v1*] *bewilder someone*
abash, addle, amaze, astonish, baffle, becloud, bedevil, befuddle, bemuse, cloud, clutter, complicate, confound, darken, daze, demoralize, discomfit, discompose, disconcert, discountenance, disorient, distract, embarrass, faze, fluster, fog, frustrate, fuddle, involve, lead astray, mess up*, misinform, mislead, mortify, muddle, mystify, nonplus, obscure, perplex, perturb, puzzle, rattle, render uncertain, shame, stir up, stump, throw off, throw off balance*, trouble, unhinge, unsettle, upset, worry; SEE CONCEPT *16*

confuse [*v2*] *mix up; involve*
bedlamize, blend, clutter, confound, disarrange, disarray, discombobulate*, discreate, disorder, disorganize, embroil, encumber, entangle, intermingle, involve, jumble, litter, mess up*, mingle, mistake, muddle, muss up, rumple, snarl up, tangle, tousle, tumble; SEE CONCEPT *112*

confused [*adj1*] *disoriented mentally*
abashed, addled, at a loss*, at sea*, at sixes and sevens*, baffled, befuddled, bewildered, come apart*, dazed, discombobulated*, disconcerted, disorganized, distracted, flummoxed, flustered, fouled up*, glassy-eyed*, gone*, misled, mixed up, muddled, nonplussed, not with it*, out to lunch*, perplexed, perturbed, punch-drunk*, punchy*, puzzled, screwy*, shook up*, shot to pieces*, slaphappy, spaced out*, stumped, taken aback, thrown, thrown off balance*, unglued*, unscrewed*, unzipped*; SEE CONCEPT *403*

confused [*adj2*] *mixed up, disordered*
anarchic, blurred, chaotic, disarranged, disorderly, disorganized, haywire, in a muddle, in disarray, involved, jumbled, messy, miscalculated, miscellaneous, mistaken, misunderstood, obscured, out of order, snafu*, snarled, topsy-turvy, unsettled, untidy; SEE CONCEPT *585*

confusion [*n1*] *disorientation*
abashing, abashment, addling, agitation, befud- dlement, befuddling, bemusement, bewilderment, blurring, chagrin, cluttering, commotion, confounding, demoralization, disarranging, discomfiting, discomfiture, disorientation, distraction, disturbing, dither, dumbfounding, embarrassing, embarrassment, embroiling, flap, fluster, lather, mixup mystification, obscuring, perplexing, perplexity, perturbation, pother, puzzlement, stew, stirring up, tangling, tumult, turbulence, turmoil, unsettling, upsetting; SEE CONCEPT *14*

confusion [*n2*] *disoriented state*
abashment, ado, anarchy, astonishment, bustle, chaos, clutter, commotion, complexity, complication, consternation, daze, difficulty, disarray, discomposure, dislocation, disorganization, distraction, emotional upset, ferment, fog, fracas, haze, hodge-podge, imbroglio, intricacy, jumble, labyrinth, mess, mixture, muddle, mystification, pandemonium, perturbation, racket, riot, row, shambles, stir, stupefaction, surprise, tangle, trouble, tumult, turmoil, untidiness, upheaval, uproar, wilderness; SEE CONCEPTS *410,727*

confute [*v*] *disprove, refute*
blow sky high*, break, bring to naught, confound, contradict, controvert, defeat, demolish, dismay, disprove, expose, invalidate, knocks props out from under*, negate, oppugn, overcome, overthrow, overturn, overwhelm, parry, prove false, prove wrong, put down, rebut, set aside, shut up, silence, subvert, tap, upset, vanquish; SEE CONCEPTS *46,95*

congeal [*v*] *coagulate*
cake, clabber, clot, concrete, condense, curdle, dry, freeze, gel, gelate, gelatinate, gelatinize, glob up*, harden, indurate, jell, jellify, jelly, refrigerate, set, solidify, stiffen, thicken; SEE CONCEPTS *250,469*

congenial [*adj*] *friendly, compatible*
adapted, affable, agreeable, amical, clubby, companionable, compatible, complaisant, congruous, consistent, consonant, conversable, convivial, cooperative, cordial, delightful, favorable, fit, genial, good-humored, gracious, happy, harmonious, jovial, kindly, kindred, like-minded, mellow, pleasant, pleasing, regular fellow, right neighborly, sociable, social, suitable, sympathetic, well-suited; SEE CONCEPT *555*

congenital [*adj*] *inborn*
complete, connate, connatural, constitutional, inbred, indigenous, indwelling, ingrained, inherent, inherited, innate, intrinsic, inveterate, latent, native, natural, thorough, unacquired, utter; SEE CONCEPTS *314,549*

congested [*adj*] *blocked, clogged*
chock-full, choked, closed, crammed, crowded, filled, glutted, gorged, gridlocked, jam-full, jammed, jam-packed, massed, mobbed, obstructed, occluded, overcrowded, overfilled, overflowing, packed, packed like sardines*, plugged, stopped, stoppered, stuffed, stuffed-up, teeming, up to the rafters*; SEE CONCEPTS *481,483,774*

congestion [*n*] *blockage*
bottleneck*, clogging, crowdedness, crowding, excess, jam, mass, overcrowding, overdevelopment, overpopulation, press, profusion, rubbernecking*, snarl-up*, surfeit, surplus, traffic jam; SEE CONCEPTS *230,432*

CO
CO

conglomerate [*adj*] *composite*
amassed, assorted, blended, clustered, heterogeneous, indiscriminate, massed, melded, miscellaneous, mixed, motley, multifarious, promiscuous, varied, variegated; SEE CONCEPTS *490,589*

conglomerate [*n*] *composite organization*
agglomerate, agglomeration, aggregate, aggregation, cartel, chain, combine, conglomeration, group, multinational, pool, syndicate, trust; SEE CONCEPTS *323,325*

conglomeration [*n*] *accumulation, potpourri*
agglomeration, aggregate, aggregation, amassment, assortment, collection, combination, combo*, composite, cumulation, everything but the kitchen sink*, hoard, hodge-podge, mass, medley, miscellany, mishmash*, mixed bag*, trove; SEE CONCEPT *432*

congratulate [*v*] *compliment on achievement, luck*
applaud, bless, boost, felicitate, give a big cigar*, give bouquet*, give regards, gold star*, hand it to*, hear it for*, laud, pat on back, praise, rejoice with, salute, stroke*, toast, wish happy returns*, wish joy to, wish one well; SEE CONCEPTS *51,69*

congratulations [*n*] *complimentation on achievement, luck*
best wishes, compliments, felicitations, give a " hear-hear"*, good going*, good wishes, good work, greetings, hail; SEE CONCEPTS *69,278*

congregate [*v*] *assemble, come together*
besiege, bunch up*, collect, concentrate, congress, convene, converge, convoke, corral, flock*, forgather, gang around, gang up, gather, hang out*, make the scene*, mass, meet, meet up, muster, pack, raise, rally, rendezvous, round up, swarm, teem, throng; SEE CONCEPTS *109,114*

congregation [*n*] *assembled group, especially concerned with church-going*
aggregation, assemblage, assembly, audience, churchgoers, collection, company, confab*, crowd, disciples, flock, following, gathering, get-together, group, host, laity, meet, meeting, multitude, muster, parish, parishioners, public, sit-in, throng, turnout; SEE CONCEPTS *369,387,417*

congress [*n*] *delegation of representatives*
assembly, association, caucus, chamber, club, committee, conclave, conference, convention, convocation, council, delegates, government, guild, league, legislative body, legislature, meeting, order, parliament, senate, society, the Hill, the house, union; SEE CONCEPTS *299,387*

congruent [*adj*] *agreeable, harmonious*
coinciding, compatible, concurring, conforming, consistent, corresponding, identical, in agreement; SEE CONCEPT *563*

congruous [*adj*] *corresponding, suitable*
accordant, appropriate, apt, becoming, coincidental, compatible, concordant, congruent, consistent, consonant, correspondent, fit, fitting, harmonious, meet, proper, seemly, sympathetic; SEE CONCEPTS *558,563*

conical/conic [*adj*] *shaped cylindrically and with a point*
coned, cone-shaped, conoid, conoidal, funnel-shaped, pointed, pyramidal, sharp, strobilate, strobiloid, tapered, tapering; SEE CONCEPT *486*

conjectural [*adj*] *speculative*
academic, assumed, doubtful, figured, guessing, guesstimated*, hypothetical, on a hunch*, on a long shot*, putative, reputed, supposed, suppositional, suppositious, suppositive, surmised, surmising, suspect, tentative, theoretical, uncertain, unresolved; SEE CONCEPT *582*

conjecture [*n*] *speculation, assumption*
conclusion, fancy, guess, guesstimate*, guesswork, hunch, hypothesis, inference, notion, opinion, perhaps, presumption, shot in the dark*, sneaking suspicion, stab in the dark*, supposition, surmise, theorizing, theory; SEE CONCEPTS *28,274,689*

conjecture [*v*] *speculate*
assume, believe, conceive, conclude, deem, estimate, expect, fancy, feel*, figure, gather, glean, guess, guesstimate*, hazard a guess*, hypothesize, imagine, infer, judge, presume, pretend, suppose, surmise, suspect, take a shot*, take a stab*, take for granted, theorize, think; SEE CONCEPTS *28,51*

conjugal [*adj*] *marital*
bridal, connubial, hymeneal, married, matrimonial, nuptial, spousal, wedded; SEE CONCEPT *555*

conjunction [*n*] *combination*
affiliation, agreement, alliance, association, cahoots, coincidence, concomitance, concurrence, congruency, conjointment, hookup*, juxtaposition, parallelism, partnership, tie-up*, union; SEE CONCEPTS *388,714*

conjure [*v1*] *appeal to, implore*
adjure, ask, beg, beseech, brace, crave, entreat, importune, pray, supplicate, urge; SEE CONCEPT *48*

conjure [*v2*] *cast spell*
bewitch, call upon, charm, enchant, ensorcel, entrance, exorcise, fascinate, invoke, levitate, play tricks, raise, rouse, summon, voodoo; SEE CONCEPT *14*

conjure up [*v*] *bring to mind*
call, contrive, create, evoke, materialize, produce as by magic, recall, recollect, remember, review, summon, urge; SEE CONCEPT *38*

connect [*v*] *combine, link*
affix, ally, associate, attach, bridge, cohere, come aboard, conjoin, consociate, correlate, couple, equate, fasten, get into, hitch on, hook on, hook up, interface, join, join up with, marry, meld with, network with, plug into, relate, slap on, span, tack on, tag, tag on, tie in, tie in with, unite, wed, yoke; SEE CONCEPTS *85,113,160*

connected [*adj*] *related, affiliated*
akin, allied, applicable, associated, banded together, bracketed, coherent, combined, consecutive, coupled, in on with*, joined, linked, pertinent, undivided, united; SEE CONCEPTS *482,577*

connection [*n1*] *person who aids another in achieving goal*
acquaintance, agent, ally, associate, association, contact, friend, go-between, intermediary, kin, kindred, kinship, mentor, messenger, network, reciprocity, relation, relative, sponsor; SEE CONCEPTS *348,423*

connection [*n2*] *something that connects, links*
affiliation, alliance, association, attachment, bond, combination, conjointment, conjunction, coupling, fastening, hookup, joining, joint, junction, juncture, link, linkage, network, partnerhip, seam, tie, tie-in, tie-up, union; SEE CONCEPTS *499,720*

connection [*n3*] *something that communicates, relates*
affinity, application, association, bearing, bond, commerce, communication, correlation, correspondence, intercourse, interrelation, kinship, link, marriage, nexus, partnership, reciprocity, relation, relationship, relevance, tie-in, togetherness; SEE CONCEPTS *388,664*

connive [*v*] *plot, scheme*
angle, be in cahoots with*, cabal, cogitate, collude, conspire, contrive, cook up, devise, diddle*, finagle, frame, frame up, intrigue, machinate, operate, promote, wangle, wire, work hand in glove*; SEE CONCEPT *36*

connoisseur [*n*] *authority*
adept, aesthete, aficionado, appreciator, arbiter, bon vivant, buff*, cognoscente, critic, devotee, dilettante, epicure, expert, fan, freak*, gourmet, judge, maven*, nut*, one into*, savant, specialist; SEE CONCEPTS *352,376*

connotation [*n*] *implication*
association, coloring, essence, hint, meaning, nuance, overtone, significance, suggestion, undertone; SEE CONCEPTS *682,689*

connote [*v*] *imply*
add up to, betoken, denote, designate, evidence, express, hint at, import, indicate, insinuate, intend, intimate, involve, mean, signify, spell, suggest; SEE CONCEPTS *75,118*

connubial [*adj*] *marital*
conjugal, hymeneal, married, matrimonial, nuptial, spousal, wedded; SEE CONCEPT *555*

conquer [*v1*] *defeat, overcome*
beat, bring to knees*, checkmate, circumvent, clobber, control, cream*, crush, discomfit, drub, foil, frustrate, get the better of*, humble, lick, master, outwit, overmaster, overpower, override, overthrow, prevail, quell, reduce, rout, shut down, subdue, subjugate, succeed, surmount, throw, thwart, total*, trample underfoot, trash, triumph, vanquish, whip, wipe off map*, worst, zap*; SEE CONCEPT *95*

conquer [*v2*] *win; obtain*
achieve, acquire, annex, best, master, occupy, overcome, overrun, prevail, seize, succeed, triumph; SEE CONCEPTS *90,141,706*

conqueror [*n*] *champion*
conquistador, defeater, hero, subduer, subjugator, vanquisher, victor, winner; SEE CONCEPTS *354,358*

conquest [*n1*] *defeat, victory*
acquisition, annexation, appropriation, big win*, clean sweep*, conquering, coup, defeating, discomfiture, grand slam*, invasion, killing*, occupation, overthrow, rout, routing, score, splash*, subdual, subjection, subjugation, success, takeover, triumph, vanquishment, win; SEE CONCEPTS *95,706*

conquest [*n2*] *enchantment; person enchanted*
acquisition, adherent, admirer, captivation, catch, enthralment, enticement, fan, feather in cap*, follower, prize, seduction, supporter, worshiper; SEE CONCEPTS *410,423*

consanguinity [*n*] *family relationship*
affiliation, affinity, agnate, blood-relationship, brotherhood, cognate, connection, family tie, filiation, kin, kindred, kindredship, kinship, lineage, race, sisterhood, strain; SEE CONCEPTS *296,388*

conscience [*n*] *moral sense*
censor, compunction, demur, duty, inner voice,

morals, principles, qualms, right and wrong, scruples, shame, small voice*, squeam, still small voice*, superego; SEE CONCEPTS *645,689*

conscientious [*adj1*] *thorough, careful*
complete, diligent, exact, exacting, faithful, fastidious, fussy, hanging in*, hanging tough*, heart and soul into*, heedful, meticulous, minding p's and q's*, painstaking, particular, playing safe, punctilious, punctual, reliable, tough, walking on eggs*; SEE CONCEPTS *531,538*

conscientious [*adj2*] *moral, upright*
conscionable, high-minded, high-principled, honest, honorable, incorruptible, just, pious, principled, responsible, right, scrupulous, straightforward, strict, true; SEE CONCEPT *545*

conscious [*adj1*] *alert, awake*
able to recognize, acquainted, aesthetic, alive to, apperceptive, apprised, assured, attentive, au courant, aware, certain, cognizant, conversant, discerning, felt, hep to*, informed, in on*, in right mind, keen, knowing, known, mindful, noticing, noting, observing, on to*, perceiving, percipient, recognizing, remarking, responsive, seeing, sensible, sensitive to, sentient, supraliminal, sure, understanding, vigilant, watchful, wise to*, with it*, witting; SEE CONCEPTS *402,539*

conscious [*adj2*] *intentional*
affected, calculated, deliberate, knowing, mannered, premeditated, rational, reasoning, reflective, responsible, self-conscious, studied, willful; SEE CONCEPTS *403,535*

consciousness [*n*] *knowledge*
alertness, apprehension, awareness, care, carefulness, cognizance, concern, heed, heedfulness, mindfulness, realization, recognition, regard, sensibility; SEE CONCEPT *409*

consecrate [*v*] *hold in high religious regard*
anoint, beatify, bless, dedicate, devote, exalt, hallow, honor, ordain, sanctify, set apart, venerate; SEE CONCEPTS *69,367*

consecutive [*adj*] *in sequence*
after, chronological, connected, constant, continuing, continuous, ensuing, following, going on, increasing, in order, in turn, later, logical, numerical, one after another, progressive, running, sequent, sequential, serial, serialized, seriate, seriatim, succedent, succeeding, successional, successive, understandable, uninterrupted; SEE CONCEPTS *585,799*

consensus [*n*] *general agreement*
accord, concord, concurrence, consent, harmony, unanimity, unison, unity; SEE CONCEPTS *684,689*

consent [*n*] *agreement; concession*
accord, acquiescence, allowance, approval, assent, authorization, blank check*, blessing, carte blanche*, compliance, concurrence, go-ahead*, green light*, leave, okay*, permission, permit, right on*, sanction, say so*, stamp of approval*, sufferance, understanding, yes; SEE CONCEPTS *684,685*

consent [*v*] *agree*
accede, accept, acquiesce, allow, approve, assent, bless, comply, concede, concur, fold, give in, give the nod*, give up, knuckle under, let, make a deal, okay*, permit, roll over, sanction, say uncle*, say yes, sign off on*, subscribe, throw in the towel*, yes*, yield; SEE CONCEPTS *8,50,88*

consequence [*n1*] *result, outcome of action*
aftereffect, aftermath, bottom line*, can of

CO
CO

worms*, chain reaction*, effect, end, event, fallout, follow through, follow-up, issue, outgrowth, payback, reaction, repercussion, sequel, sequence, spin-off, upshot, waves*; SEE CONCEPT *230*

consequence [*n2*] *importance, significance*
account, concern, exigency, fame, honor, import, interest, magnitude, moment, momentousness, need, note, pith, portent, renown, reputation, repute, signification, value, weight, weightiness; SEE CONCEPT *668*

consequence [*n3*] *person's status*
cachet, dignity, distinction, eminence, notability, position, prestige, rank, repute, standing, state, stature, status; SEE CONCEPT *388*

consequent [*adj*] *resultant*
consistent, ensuing, following, indirect, inferable, intelligent, logical, rational, reasonable, resulting, sensible, sequential, sound, subsequent, successive, understandable; SEE CONCEPTS *537,548*

consequential [*adj*] *significant*
big, considerable, eventful, far-reaching, grave, important, material, meaningful, momentous, serious, substantial, weighty; SEE CONCEPT *568*

conservation [*n*] *preservation*
attention, care, cherishing, conservancy, conserving, control, custody, directing, economy, governing, guardianship, guarding, keeping, maintenance, management, managing, preserval, preserving, protecting, protection, safeguarding, safekeeping, salvation, saving, stewardship, storage, supervising, supervision, sustentation, upkeep; SEE CONCEPTS *134,257*

conservationist [*n*] *environmental activist*
environmentalist, green*, guardian, preservationist, tree hugger*; SEE CONCEPTS *414,423*

conservative [*adj*] *cautious, moderate, tending to preserve the status quo*
bourgeois, constant, controlled, conventional, die-hard, fearful, firm, fogyish*, fuddy-duddy*, guarded, hard hat*, hidebound, holding to, illiberal, in a rut*, inflexible, middle-of-the-road*, not extreme, obstinate, old guard*, old line*, orthodox, quiet, reactionary, redneck*, right, right of center*, right-wing, sober, stable, steady, timid, Tory*, traditional, traditionalistic, unchangeable, unchanging, uncreative, undaring, unimaginative, unprogressive, white bread*; SEE CONCEPT *542*

conservative [*n*] *person who is cautious, moderate; an opponent of change*
bitter-ender*, classicist, conserver, conventionalist, diehard, hard hat*, middle-of-the-roader*, moderate, moderatist, obstructionist, old guard*, old liner*, preserver, reactionary, redneck*, right, rightist, right-winger, silk-stocking*, standpat, stick-in-the-mud*, Tory*, traditionalist, unprogressive; SEE CONCEPT *359*

conservator [*n*] *caretaker of collection*
curator, custodian, guardian, keeper, protector, restorer; SEE CONCEPT *348*

conservatory [*n*] *greenhouse*
cold frame, glasshouse, hot house, nursery; SEE CONCEPTS *439,449,517*

conserve [*v*] *save, protect*
cut back, cut down on, go easy on*, hoard, keep, maintain, nurse, preserve, safeguard, scrimp, skimp, sock away*, squirrel*, squirrel away*,

stash, steward, store up, support, sustain, take care of, use sparingly; SEE CONCEPT *134*

consider [*v1*] *turn over in one's mind*
acknowledge, allow for, assent to, chew over*, cogitate, concede, consult, contemplate, deal with, deliberate, dream of, envisage, examine, excogitate, favor, flirt with*, grant, inspect, keep in mind, look at, meditate, mull over, muse, perpend, ponder, provide for, reason, reckon with, recognize, reflect, regard, revolve, ruminate, scan, scrutinize, see, see about, speculate, study, subscribe to, take into account, take under advisement, take up, think out, think over, toss around*; SEE CONCEPTS *17,24*

consider [*v2*] *regard a certain way*
analyze, appraise, bear in mind, believe, care for, count, credit, deem, estimate, feel, hold, hold an opinion, judge, keep in view, look upon, make allowance for, reckon with, reflect, remember, respect, sense, set down, suppose, take for, take into account, think, think of, view; SEE CONCEPT *12*

considerable [*adj1*] *abundant, large*
ample, appreciable, astronomical, big, bountiful, comfortable, commodious, extensive, goodly, great, hefty, huge, large-scale, lavish, major, marked, much, noticeable, plentiful, pretty, reasonable, respectable, sizable, substantial, tidy, tolerable; SEE CONCEPT *781*

considerable [*adj2*] *important*
big, consequential, distinguished, doozie*, dynamite, essential, fab*, fat, influential, material, meaningful, momentous, mondo*, noteworthy, renowned, significant, solid gold*, something, something else*, substantial, super, superduper*, to the max*, unreal*, venerable, weighty; SEE CONCEPT *568*

considerably [*adv*] *significantly*
appreciably, far, greatly, markedly, noticeably, quite, rather, remarkably, somewhat, substantially, very much, well; SEE CONCEPT *569*

considerate [*adj*] *respectful of others*
accommodating, amiable, attentive, benevolent, big, charitable, chivalrous, circumspect, compassionate, complaisant, concerned, cool, discreet, forbearing, generous, kind, kindly, like a sport*, magnanimous, mellow, mindful, obliging, patient, polite, solicitous, sympathetic, tactful, tender, thoughtful, unselfish, warmhearted; SEE CONCEPT *401*

consideration [*n1*] *mental analysis*
application, attention, cogitation, concentration, contemplation, debate, deliberation, discussion, examination, forethought, heed, reflection, regard, review, scrutiny, study, thinking, thought; SEE CONCEPT *24*

consideration [*n2*] *concern; something mentally examined*
development, difficulty, emergency, estate, evidence, exigency, extent, factor, fancy, idea, incident, issue, items, judgment, magnitude, minutiae, notion, occasion, occurrence, particulars, perplexity, plan, point, problem, proposal, puzzle, scope, situation, state, thought, trouble; SEE CONCEPT *532*

consideration [*n3*] *high regard*
attentiveness, awareness, concern, considerateness, esteem, estimation, favor, forbearance, friendliness, heed, heedfulness, kindliness, kindness, mercy, mindfulness, respect, solicitude,

tact, thoughtfulness, tolerance; SEE CONCEPTS
32,410
consideration [*n4*] *payment*
baksheesh, commish*, commission, fee*, payback, percentage, perk, perquisite, recompense,
remuneration, reward, salary, something to
sweeten pot*, tip, wage; SEE CONCEPT *344*
considered [*adj*] *deliberate, thought-out*
advised, aforethought, contemplated, designed,
designful, examined, express, given due consideration, gone into, intentional, investigated, me-
diated, premeditated, prepense, studied, studious,
thought-about, thought-through, treated, voluntary, weighed, well advised, well chosen, willful;
SEE CONCEPTS *402,529*
considering [*adj*] *taking everything in mind*
all in all, all things considered, as, as long as, because, everything being equal, for, forasmuch as,
inasmuch as, in consideration of, in light of, in-
somuch as, in view of, now, pending, seeing,
since, taking into account; SEE CONCEPT *529*
consign [*v*] *entrust, hand over for care*
address, appoint, assign, authorize, commend to,
commission, commit, confide, convey, delegate,
deliver, deposit with, dispatch, forward, give,
issue, put in charge of, relegate, remit, route,
send, ship, transfer, transmit, turn over; SEE CON-
CEPTS *108,143,217*
consignment [*n1*] *entrusting, handing over*
assignment, committal, dispatch, distribution,
relegation, sending shipment, transmittal; SEE
CONCEPTS *108,143,217*
consignment [*n2*] *something entrusted to an-*
other's care
batch, delivery, goods, shipment; SEE CONCEPT
338
consist [*v*] *exist, reside*
abide, be, be contained in, be expressed by, be
found in, dwell, inhere, lie, repose, rest, subsist;
SEE CONCEPT *539*
consistency [*n1*] *thickness*
bendability, bendableness, compactness, density,
elasticity, fabric, firmness, flexibility, frangibil-
ity, hardness, limberness, moldability, organization, plasticity, pliability, softness, solidity,
suppleness, texture, viscidity, viscosity, viscous-
ness; SEE CONCEPTS *611,722*
consistency [*n2*] *constancy, regularity*
accord, agreement, apposition, appropriateness,
aptness, coherence, cohesion, compatibility, concord, concurrence, conformability, congruity,
consonance, correspondence, evenness, fitness,
harmony, homogeneity, invariability, likeness,
proportion, similarity, stability, steadfastness,
steadiness, suitability, symmetry, uniformity,
union, unity; SEE CONCEPTS *637,656,670*
consistent [*adj1*] *constant, regular*
dependable, even, expected, homogeneous, invariable, logical, of a piece, persistent, rational,
same, steady, true, true to type, unchanging, undeviating, unfailing, uniform, unvarying; SEE
CONCEPT *534*
consistent [*adj2*] *agreeing, compatible*
accordant, according to, agreeable, all of a piece,
coherent, conforming with, congenial, congruous, consonant, equable, harmonious, like, logical, matching, sympathetic; SEE CONCEPT *563*
consist of [*v*] *made up of*
amount to, be composed of, comprise, contain,

embody, include, incorporate, involve; SEE CON-
CEPT *643*
consolation [*n*] *relief, comfort*
alleviation, assuagement, cheer, comfort, compassion, ease, easement, encouragement, fellow
feeling, help, lenity, pity, solace, succour, support, sympathy; SEE CONCEPTS *32,410*
console [*v*] *relieve, comfort*
animate, assuage, buck up*, calm, cheer, condole
with, encourage, express sympathy, gladden, inspirit, lift, solace, soothe, tranquilize, untrouble,
upraise; SEE CONCEPTS *7,22*
consolidate [*v*] *combine; make firm*
add to, amalgamate, amass, band, bind, blend,
build up, bunch up, cement, centralize, compact,
compound, concatenate, concentrate, condense,
conjoin, connect, densen, develop, federate, fortify, fuse, harden, hitch, hitch on, hook up with,
incorporate, join, league, mass, meld, mix, plug
into, pool, reinforce, render solid, secure, set,
slap on, solidify, stabilize, strengthen, tack on,
tag on, team up with*, thicken, throw in together*, tie in, tie up with, unify; SEE CONCEPTS
109,250
consolidation [*n*] *combination, fortification*
alliance, amalgamation, association, coadunation, coalition, compression, concentration, condensation, federation, fusion, incorporation,
melding, mergence, merger, merging, reinforcement, solidification, strengthening, unification;
SEE CONCEPTS *109,469*
consonance [*n*] *agreement, consistency*
accord, chime, chorus, concert, concord, conformity, congruence, congruity, correspondence,
harmony, suitableness, tune; SEE CONCEPT *664*
consonant [*adj*] *agreeing, consistent*
accordant, according, agnate, akin, alike, analogous, blending, coincident, comfortable, comparable, compatible, concordant, congenial,
congruous, correspondent, corresponding, harmonious, in agreement, in rapport, like, parallel,
similar, suitable, sympathetic, uniform; SEE CON-
CEPT *563*
consort [*n*] *associate, partner*
accompaniment, companion, concomitant,
friend, husband, mate, spouse, wife; SEE CON-
CEPT *423*
consort [*v1*] *be friendly with; fraternize*
accompany, associate, attend, bear, befriend,
bring, carry, chaperon, chum together*, chum
with*, clique with, company, conduct, convoy,
gang up with*, go around with, hang around
with*, hang out with*, hang with*, join, keep
company, mingle, mix, pal, pal around with, pal
with, run around with*, run with, take up with,
tie up with; SEE CONCEPTS *114,384*
consort [*v2*] *agree*
accord, coincide, comport, concur, conform, correspond, dovetail, harmonize, march, square,
tally; SEE CONCEPT *664*
conspicuous [*adj1*] *obvious, easily seen*
apparent, clear, discernible, distinct, evident,
manifest, noticeable, open-and-shut*, patent,
perceptible, plain, visible; SEE CONCEPT *619*
conspicuous [*adj2*] *important, prominent*
arresting, arrestive, blatant, celebrated, commanding, distinguished, eminent, famed, famous, flagrant, flashy, garish, glaring, glitzy*,
illustrious, influential, jazzy, loud, marked, notable, noted, notorious, outstanding, pointed,

CO
CO

rank, remarkable, renowned, salient, screaming, showy, signal, splashy, stick out like sore thumb*, striking, tony*, well-known; SEE CONCEPTS *542,567*

conspiracy [n] *collusion in plan*
cabal, complot, confederacy, connivance, countermine, counterplot, covin, disloyalty, fix, frame*, game, hookup*, intrigue, league, little game*, machination, perfidy, plot, practice, put-up job*, scheme, sedition, treacherousness, treachery, treason, trick, trickery; SEE CONCEPT *660*

conspirator [n] *schemer*
accomplice, backstabber*, betrayer, caballer, collaborator, colluder, highbinder, plotter, subversive, traitor; SEE CONCEPT *412*

conspire [v1] *plot, scheme with someone*
be in cahoots*, cabal, cogitate, collogue, collude, confederate, connive, contrive, cook up*, cooperate, devise, get in bed with*, hatch, intrigue, machinate, maneuver, operate, promote, put out a contract*, wangle, wire, work something out*; SEE CONCEPTS *36,192*

conspire [v2] *agree, concur*
cabal, colleague, combine, complot, conduce, consort, contribute, cooperate, join, tend, unite, work together; SEE CONCEPT *8*

constancy [n] *fixedness*
abidingness, adherence, allegiance, ardor, attachment, certainty, decision, dependability, determination, devotedness, devotion, doggedness, eagerness, earnestness, endurance, faith, fealty, fidelity, firmness, honesty, honor, integrity, love, loyalty, permanence, perseverance, principle, regularity, resolution, stability, staunchness, steadfastness, steadiness, surety, tenacity, trustiness, trustworthiness, truthfulness, unchangeableness, unfailingness, uniformity, zeal; SEE CONCEPTS *32,410,637*

constant [adj1] *fixed*
connected, consistent, continual, equable, even, firm, habitual, homogeneous, immutable, invariable, like the Rock of Gibralter*, monochrome, monophonic, monotonous, nonstop, of a piece, permanent, perpetual, regular, regularized, solid as rock*, stabile, stable, standardized, steadfast, steady, together, unalterable, unbroken, unchanging, unflappable, unfluctuating, uniform, uninterrupted, unvarying; SEE CONCEPT *534*

constant [adj2] *neverending*
abiding, ceaseless, chronic, continual, continuous, endless, enduring, eternal, everlasting, incessant, interminable, lasting, nonstop, perpetual, persistent, persisting, relentless, sustained, unending, uninterrupted, unrelenting, unremitting; SEE CONCEPTS *649,798*

constant [adj3] *loyal, determined*
allegiant, attached, dependable, devoted, dogged, faithful, fast, persevering, resolute, staunch, tried-and-true, true, trustworthy, trusty, unfailing, unflagging, unshaken, unwavering; SEE CONCEPT *542*

consternation [n] *dismay, distress*
alarm, amazement, anxiety, awe, bewilderment, confusion, distraction, dread, fear, fright, horror, muddle, muddlement, panic, perplexity, shock, stupefaction, terror, trepidation, trepidity, wonder; SEE CONCEPT *230*

constituency [n] *voting public*
balloters, body of voters, body politic, citizenry,

city, county, district, electorate, electors, faction, nation, people, precinct, state, system, voters, voting area, ward; SEE CONCEPT *379*

constituent [adj1] *component, part*
basic, combining, composing, constituting, division, elemental, essential, factor, forming, fraction, fundamental, ingredient, integral, portion; SEE CONCEPTS *826,834,835*

constituent [adj2] *voting*
balloter, citizen, electing, electoral, official, overruling; SEE CONCEPT *536*

constituent [n] *element*
board, component, division, essential, factor, fixins*, fraction, ingredient, makings, part, part and parcel*, plug-in*, portion, principle, unit; SEE CONCEPTS *826,834*

constitute [v1] *comprise, form*
aggregate, complement, complete, compose, compound, construct, cook up*, create, develop, dream up*, embody, enact, establish, fill out, fix, flesh out*, found, frame, fudge together*, incorporate, integrate, make, make up, set up; SEE CONCEPTS *173,184,251*

constitute [v2] *authorize*
appoint, commission, decree, delegate, depute, deputize, designate, draft, empower, enact, establish, legislate, make, name, nominate, ordain, order; SEE CONCEPTS *50,88*

constitution [n1] *physical make-up and health*
architecture, build, character, composition, construction, content, contents, design, disposition, essence, form, formation, frame, habit, habitus, nature, physique, structure, temper, temperament, type, vitality; SEE CONCEPT *757*

constitution [n2] *establishment*
charter, code, composition, custom, formation, lawmaking, legislation, organization, written law; SEE CONCEPTS *271,318*

constitutional [adj1] *inherent*
built-in, congenital, deep-seated, essential, inborn, inbred, ingrained, innate, intrinsic, natural, organic, vital; SEE CONCEPT *549*

constitutional [adj2] *provided for by law*
approved, chartered, democratic, ensured, lawful, legal, representative, statutory, vested; SEE CONCEPT *319*

constitutional [n] *walk*
airing, ambulation, footwork, legwork, perambulation, ramble, saunter, stroll, turn, walk; SEE CONCEPT *149*

constrain [v] *force; restrain*
ban, bar, bind, bottle up, bridle, chain, check, coerce, compel, concuss, confine, constrict, cool off*, cork, curb, deny, deprive, disallow, drive, hem in*, hog-tie*, hold back, hold down, hold in, immure, impel, imprison, incarcerate, inhibit, intern, jail, keep lid on*, make, necessitate, oblige, pressure, pressurize, put half nelson on*, shotgun*, stifle, urge, withhold; SEE CONCEPTS *14,121,130*

constraint [n1] *force*
a must*, coercion, compulsion, driving, duress, goad, hang-up*, impelling, impulsion, monkey*, motive, necessity, no-no*, pressure, repression, restraint, spring, spur, suppression, violence; SEE CONCEPTS *14,121*

constraint [n2] *shyness*
bashfulness, diffidence, embarrassment, hangup*, humility, inhibition, modesty, repression,

reservation, reserve, restraint, timidity; SEE CONCEPT *411*

constraint [*n3*] *restriction*
arrest, captivity, check, circumscription, confinement, constrainment, cramp, curb, damper, detention, deterrent, hindrance, limitation, restraint; SEE CONCEPTS *130,652*

constrict [*v*] *inhibit*
astringe, choke, circumscribe, clench, compress, concentrate, condense, confine, constringe, contract, cramp, curb, draw together, limit, narrow, pinch, restrain, restrict, shrink, squeeze, strangle, strangulate, tauten, tense, tighten, tuck; SEE CONCEPTS *130,191,219*

constriction [*n*] *blockage*
binding, choking, compression, constraint, contraction, cramp, impediment, limitation, narrowing, pressure, reduction, restriction, squeezing, stenosis, stricture, tightness; SEE CONCEPTS *130,191,219*

construct [*v*] *assemble, build*
build up, cobble up*, compose, compound, constitute, cook up*, create, design, dream up*, elevate, engineer, envision, erect, establish, fabricate, fashion, forge, form, formulate, found, frame, fudge together*, hammer out*, hoke up*, imagine, invent, make, manufacture, organize, prefab*, produce, put out, put together, put up, raise, rear, set up, shape, throw together, throw up*, trump up*, uprear, whip up*; SEE CONCEPTS *168,173,251*

construction [*n1*] *creation, building*
architecture, arrangement, assembly, build, cast, composition, conception, constitution, contour, cut, development, disposition, edifice, elevation, erecting, erection, fabric, fabricating, fabrication, figuration, figure, form, format, formation, foundation, improvisation, invention, makeup, making, manufacture, mold, origination, outline, plan, planning, prefab, prefabrication, putting up, raising, rearing, roadwork, shape, structure, system, systematization, turn, type; SEE CONCEPTS *168,439,757*

construction [*n2*] *explanation*
apprehension, construal, definition, exegesis, explication, exposé, exposition, inference, interpretation, reading, rendering, rendition, translation, version; SEE CONCEPT *274*

constructive [*adj*] *helpful*
effective, positive, practical, productive, useful, valuable; SEE CONCEPT *401*

construe [*v*] *deduce; explain*
analyze, decipher, define, explicate, expound, figure it to be*, infer, interpret, one's best guess*, parse, read, render, spell out, take, translate, understand; SEE CONCEPTS *37,57*

consul [*n*] *representative*
delegate, emissary, envoy, lawyer, legate; SEE CONCEPTS *354,355*

consulate [*n*] *embassy*
consular office, government office, ministry; SEE CONCEPTS *439,449*

consult [*v*] *ask, confer*
argue, ask advice of, be closeted with, brainstorm*, call in, cogitate, collogue, commune, compare notes, confab, confabulate, consider, debate, deliberate, discuss, examine, flap*, groupthink*, huddle, interrogate, interview, kick ideas around*, negotiate, parlay, pick one's brains*, powwow*, put heads together*, question, refer to, regard, respect, review, seek advice, seek opinion of, take account of, take a meeting*, take counsel, talk over, toss ideas around*, treat, turn to; SEE CONCEPTS *17,48,56*

consultant [*n*] *professional advisor*
advisor, authority, counsel, expert, freelancer, guide, master, maven, mentor, pro*, specialist, veteran; SEE CONCEPTS *348,350*

consultation [*n*] *asking, conference*
appointment, argument, buzz session*, clambake*, confab*, conference, council, deliberation, dialogue, discussion, examination, groupthink*, hearing, huddle, interview, meeting, powwow*, second opinion*, session; SEE CONCEPTS *48,114,324*

consume [*v1*] *use up*
absorb, apply, avail oneself of, deplete, devour, dissipate, dominate, drain, drivel, eat up, employ, engross, exhaust, expend, finish, finish up, fritter away, frivol away, go, go through, have recourse to, lavish, lessen, monopolize, obsess, preoccupy, profit by, put away, put to use, run out of, run through, spend, squander, throw away, trifle, utilize, vanish, wash up, waste, wear out; SEE CONCEPT *225*

consume [*v2*] *eat, drink*
absorb, bolt, chow down*, devour, down, eat up, feed, gobble*, gorge, gulp, guzzle, hoover*, ingest, ingurgitate, inhale, meal, mow*, nibble, partake, polish off*, punish, put away*, put down*, scarf*, snack, stuff one's face*, swallow, swill, take, toss down*, wolf*; SEE CONCEPT *169*

consume [*v3*] *destroy*
annihilate, crush, decay, demolish, devastate, eat up, exhaust, expend, extinguish, lay waste, overwhelm, ravage, raze, ruin, suppress, waste, wreck; SEE CONCEPT *252*

consumer [*n*] *person who buys merchandise, services*
buyer, customer, end user, enjoyer, purchaser, shopper, user; SEE CONCEPT *348*

consummate [*adj*] *ultimate, best*
able, absolute, accomplished, complete, conspicuous, downright, faultless, finished, flawless, gifted, ideal, immaculate, inimitable, matchless, out-and-out*, peerless, perfect, perfected, polished, positive, practiced, ripe, skilled, superb, superlative, supreme, talented, thoroughgoing, total, trained, transcendent, unmitigated, unqualified, unsurpassable, utter, virtuosic, whole; SEE CONCEPTS *528,572*

consummate [*v*] *achieve, finish*
accomplish, button down*, call a day*, can*, carry out, clean up, clinch, close, come, come through, compass, complete, conclude, crown, drop curtain*, effectuate, end, fold up, get it together*, go the distance*, halt, knock off, mop up, perfect, perform, polish off*, put away*, put finishing touch on*, put lid on*, put to bed*, sew up, sign, take care of, terminate, top it off, ultimate, wind up, wrap, wrap up; SEE CONCEPTS *234,704,706*

consummation [*n*] *achievement, fulfillment*
cleanup, completion, culmination, doing it to a T*, end, mop-up, payoff, perfection, realization, to a finish, wind-up*, wrap, wrap-up*; SEE CONCEPT *706*

consumption [*n*] *devouring; use*
burning, consuming, damage, decay, decrease, depletion, desolation, destruction, devastation,

CO
CO

diminution, dispersion, dissipation, drinking, eating, exhaustion, expenditure, loss, misuse, ruin, swallowing, using up, utilization, waste, wear and tear; SEE CONCEPTS *156,169,225,252*

contact [*n1*] *form of communication*
acquaintance, association, channel, commerce, communion, companionship, connection, influence, intercourse, junction, meeting, network, touch, union, unity; SEE CONCEPTS *278,388,687*

contact [*n2*] *touching*
approximation, closeness, collision, connection, contiguity, contingence, hit, impingement, junction, juxtaposition, nearness, propinquity, proximity, relation, strike, taction, touch, union; SEE CONCEPT *747*

contact [*v*] *communicate with*
approach, be in touch with, buzz*, call, check with, connect, get, get ahold of, get in touch with, interact, interface, network*, phone, reach, reach out, relate, speak to, talk, telephone, touch base*, visit, write to; SEE CONCEPT *266*

contagion [*n*] *infection*
bane, contamination, corruption, illness, miasma, pestilence, plague, poison, pollution, taint, transmission, venom, virus; SEE CONCEPT *306*

contagious [*adj*] *communicable*
catching, deadly, endemic, epidemic, epizootic, impartible, infectious, inoculable, pestiferous, pestilential, poisonous, spreading, taking, transmissible, transmittable; SEE CONCEPT *314*

contain [*v1*] *include, hold*
accommodate, be composed of, comprehend, comprise, consist of, embody, embrace, enclose, encompass, have, have capacity for, hold, incorporate, involve, seat, subsume, take in; SEE CONCEPTS *112,736,742*

contain [*v2*] *hold back, control*
bottle up*, check, collect, compose, cool*, cork*, curb, harness, hog-tie*, hold in, keep back, keep lid on*, put half nelson on*, rein, repress, restrain, restrict, simmer down, smother, stifle, stop; SEE CONCEPTS *94,191*

container [*n*] *holder for physical object*
alembic, bag, beaker, bin, bottle, bowl, box, bucket, bunker, caisson, can, canister, canteen, capsule, carafe, carton, cask, casket, cauldron, chamber, chest, churn, cistern, cradle, crate, crock, dish, ewer, firkin, flask, hamper, hod, hopper, humidor, hutch, jar, jeroboam, jug, kettle, magnum, package, packet, pail, pit, pod, poke, pot, pottery, pouch, purse, receptacle, reliquary, repository, sac, sack, scuttle, stein, storage, tank, tub, utensil, vase, vat, vessel, vial; SEE CONCEPT *494*

contaminate [*v*] *adulterate*
alloy, befoul, corrupt, debase, debauch, defile, deprave, desecrate, dirty, harm, infect, injure, muck up, pervert, poison, pollute, profane, radioactive, soil, spoil, stain, sully, taint, tarnish, vitiate; SEE CONCEPTS *252,254*

contamination [*n*] *adulteration*
contagion, corruption, decay, defilement, dirtying, disease, epidemic, filth, foulness, impurity, infection, pestilence, plague, poisoning, pollution, radioactivation, rottenness, spoliation, taint; SEE CONCEPTS *230,306,674*

contemplate [*v1*] *think about seriously; plan*
aim, aspire to, brood over, chew over, consider, cool out*, deliberate, design, envisage, excogitate, expect, foresee, intend, kick around*, mean,

meditate on, mind, mull over, muse over, observe, percolate, perpend, ponder, propose, purpose, reflect upon, ruminate, size up, speculate, study, take in, think of, weigh; SEE CONCEPTS *17,36*

contemplate [*v2*] *gaze at*
audit, behold, consider, examine, eye, inspect, notice, observe, peer, penetrate, peruse, pierce, pore over, probe, pry, regard, scan, scrutinize, see, stare at, study, survey, view, witness; SEE CONCEPT *623*

contemplation [*n1*] *deep thought; planning*
ambition, cogitation, consideration, deliberation, design, intention, meditation, musing, plan, pondering, purpose, reflection, reverie, rumination, study; SEE CONCEPT *410*

contemplation [*n2*] *gazing at*
examination, inspection, looking at, observation, scrutiny, survey, viewing; SEE CONCEPT *623*

contemplative [*adj*] *deep in thought*
attentive, cogitative, in brown study*, intent, introspective, lost, meditative, musing, pensive, pondering, rapt, reflecting, reflective, ruminative, speculative, thinking, thoughtful; SEE CONCEPTS *402,403*

contemporary [*adj1*] *modern*
abreast, à la mode*, au courant, contempo*, current, existent, extant, hot off press*, in fashion, instant, in vogue, just out*, latest, leading-edge*, mod*, new, newfangled, now, present, present-day, recent, red-hot*, state-of-the-art*, today*, topical, ultramodern, up*, up-to-date, up-to-the-minute, voguish, with it*; SEE CONCEPTS *578,589,797*

contemporary [*adj2*] *existing, occurring at same time*
accompanying, associated, attendant, coetaneous, coeval, coexistent, coexisting, coincident, concomitant, concurrent, connected, contemporaneous, current, linked, present, related, simultaneous, synchronal, synchronic, synchronous; SEE CONCEPT *820*

contempt [*n1*] *disdain, disrespect*
antipathy, audacity, aversion, condescension, contumely, defiance, derision, despisal, despisement, despite, disesteem, disregard, distaste, hatred, indignity, malice, mockery, neglect, recalcitrance, repugnance, ridicule, scorn, slight, snobbery, stubbornness; SEE CONCEPT *29*

contempt [*n2*] *state of disgrace*
discredit, disesteem, disfavor, dishonor, disrepute, humiliation, ignominy, infamy, insignificancy, opprobrium, shame, stigma; SEE CONCEPTS *388,674*

contemptible [*adj*] *despicable, shameful*
abhorrent, abject, abominable, bad, base, beggarly, cheap, crass, currish, degenerate, despisable, detestable, dirty, disgusting, hateful, heel, ignoble, ignominious, inferior, low, low-down*, lowest, mean, odious, outcast, paltry, pitiable, pitiful, poor, sad, scummy*, scurvy*, shabby, sordid, sorry*, swinish, unworthy, vile, worthless, wretched; SEE CONCEPT *550*

contemptuous [*adj*] *arrogant, insolent*
audacious, bold, cavalier, cheeky, cold-shoulder, condescending, contumelious, cool, derisive, derisory, disdainful, disrespectful, dog it*, hard, hard-nosed, haughty, high and mighty*, high hat*, insulting, on high horse*, opprobrious, sardonic, scornful, sneering, snippy, snobbish,

snooty*, snotty*, supercilious, temperamental, uppity, upstage; SEE CONCEPT *401*

contend [*v1*] *compete, fight*
argue, battle, clash, confront, contest, controvert, cope, dispute, emulate, encounter, face, give all one's got*, give one's all*, go after, go for, go for broke*, go for it*, go for jugular*, grapple, have at*, jockey for position*, jostle, knock oneself out*, litigate, lock horns*, make play for*, meet, mix it up with*, oppose, oppugn, push, push for, resist, rival, scramble for, shoot at, shoot for, skirmish, stand, strive, struggle, tangle with, tug, vie, withstand; SEE CONCEPTS *92,106*

contend [*v2*] *argue*
affirm, allege, assert, aver, avow, blast, charge, claim, come at, cross, debate, defend, dictate, dispute, enjoin, fly in face of*, gang up on, go at, have at*, have bone to pick*, hold, insist, jump on, justify, lace into*, lay into*, let have it*, light into*, lock horns with*, maintain, mix, mix it up*, prescribe, put up argument, report, rip*, say, set to, sock it to one*, stick it to*, take on, tell, urge, vindicate, warrant, zap*; SEE CONCEPT *46*

content [*adj*] *happy, agreeable*
appeased, at ease, can't complain*, comfortable, complacent, contented, fat dumb and happy*, fulfilled, gratified, pleased as punch*, satisfied, smug, tickled pink*, willing; SEE CONCEPT *403*

content [*n1*] *comfort, happiness*
contentment, ease, gratification, peace, peace of mind, pleasure, satisfaction; SEE CONCEPT *410*

content [*n2*] *essence, meaning*
burden, composition, constitution, gist, idea, matter, significance, subject, subject matter, substance, text, thought; SEE CONCEPT *682*

content [*n3*] *capacity, volume*
filling, load, measure, packing, size; SEE CONCEPTS *719,740*

content [*v*] *please*
appease, bewitch, captivate, charm, delight, enrapture, gladden, gratify, humor, indulge, make happy, mollify, placate, reconcile, satisfy, suffice, thrill, tickle; SEE CONCEPTS *7,22*

contented [*adj*] *at ease; happy*
at peace, cheerful, comfortable, complacent, content, glad, gratified, pleased, satisfied, serene, thankful; SEE CONCEPT *403*

contention [*n1*] *competition*
altercation, argument, battle, beef*, belligerency, bone of contention*, bone to pick*, combat, conflict, contest, controversy, difference, disaccord, discord, dispute, dissension, dissent, dissidence, disunity, enmity, feuding, fight, flak*, hassle, hostility, quarrel, rivalry, run-in, scene, scrap, set-to*, squabble, static, strife, struggle, variance, war, wrangle, wrangling; SEE CONCEPTS *92,106*

contention [*n2*] *argument for idea*
advancement, affirmation, allegation, assertion, asseveration, avowal, belief, charge, claim, contestation, declaration, demurrer, deposition, discussion, explanation, ground, hurrah, hypothesis, idea, maintaining, opinion, plea, position, predication, profession, rumpus, stand, thesis, view; SEE CONCEPTS *46,278,689*

contentious [*adj*] *quarrelsome*
antagonistic, argumentative, belligerent, combative, disagreeable, factious, perverse, petulant, querulous, testy; SEE CONCEPTS *401,542*

contentment [*n*] *comfort, happiness*
complacency, content, contentedness, ease, equanimity, fulfillment, gladness, gratification, peace, pleasure, repletion, satisfaction, serenity; SEE CONCEPT *410*

contents [*n*] *elements of larger object*
capacity, cargo, chapters, connotation, constituents, details, divisions, essence, filling, freight, furnishing, gist, guts, implication, ingredients, innards, inside, lading, load, meaning, nub, packing, shipment, significance, size, space, stuffing, subject matter, subjects, substance, sum, text, themes, topics, volume; SEE CONCEPT *835*

contest [*n1*] *competition*
challenge, concours, discussion, game, match, meet, meeting, proving, rencounter, sport, testing, tournament, trial, trying; SEE CONCEPTS *92,363*

contest [*n2*] *fight, struggle*
action, affray, altercation, battle, battle royal*, beef*, brawl, brush, combat, conflict, controversy, debate, discord, dispute, emulation, encounter, engagement, fray, go*, hassle, rivalry, row, rumble*, run-in, scrap, set-to*, shock, skirmish, static, strife, striving, tug-of-war, warfare, wrangle; SEE CONCEPTS *106,320*

contest [*v1*] *argue, challenge*
blast, call in question, debate, dispute, doubt, give it one's all*, go for it*, go for jugular*, jockey for position*, jump on, litigate, mix it up with*, object to, oppose, push, question, scramble for, shoot for*, stand up for, tangle; SEE CONCEPT *46*

contest [*v2*] *fight*
altercate, attack, battle, brawl, break with, buck, compete, conflict, contend, cross, defend, duel, feud, fight over, gang up on, hassle, knuckle with, lay a finger on*, lay out, put on gloves*, put up dukes*, quarrel, repel, rival, row, rumpus, scrap, scuffle, set to, sock*, square off, strike, struggle, take on, tilt, traverse, vie, withstand, wrangle; SEE CONCEPT *106*

contestant [*n*] *competitor*
adversary, antagonist, aspirant, battler, candidate, challenger, combatant, contender, contester, dark horse*, disputant, entrant, favorite, hopeful, member, participant, player, rival, scrapper*, team member, warrior; SEE CONCEPT *366*

context [*n*] *framework, circumstances*
ambience, background, conditions, connection, frame of reference, lexicon, relation, situation, substance, text, vocabulary; SEE CONCEPTS *682,696*

contiguous [*adj*] *adjacent, in contact*
abutting, adjoining, approximal, beside, bordering, close, contactual, conterminous, juxtaposed, juxtapositional, meeting, near, near-at-hand, nearby, neighboring, next, next door to, next to, touching; SEE CONCEPTS *586,778*

continence [*n*] *self-restraint*
abstemiousness, abstinence, asceticism, celibacy, chastity, forbearance, moderation, refraining, self-control, sobriety, temperance, virtue; SEE CONCEPT *633*

continent [*adj*] *chaste, pure*
abstemious, abstentious, abstinent, ascetic, austere, bridled, celibate, curbed, inhibited, modest, restrained, self-restrained, sober, temperate; SEE CONCEPT *550*

CO
CO

contingency [*n*] *chance happening; possibility*
accident, break, chance, crisis, crossroads, emergency, event, eventuality, exigency, fortuity, happening, if it's cool*, incident, juncture, likelihood, occasion, odds, opportunity, pass, pinch, predicament, probability, strait, turning point, uncertainty, zero hour*; SEE CONCEPTS *650,679,693*

contingent [*adj*] *conditional; possible*
accidental, casual, chance, controlled by, dependent, fluky, fortuitous, haphazard, incidental, likely, odd, probable, probably, random, subject to, unanticipated, uncertain, unexpected, unforeseeable, unforeseen, unpredictable; SEE CONCEPT *552*

contingent [*n*] *group of followers*
batch, body, bunch, deputation, detachment, disciples, mission, quota, sect, section, set; SEE CONCEPT *417*

continual [*adj*] *constant, incessant*
aeonian, around-the-clock, ceaseless, connected, consecutive, continuous, dateless, endless, enduring, eternal, everlasting, frequent, interminable, oft-repeated, permanent, perpetual, persistent, persisting, recurrent, regular, relentless, repeated, repetitive, running, staying, steady, timeless, unbroken, unceasing, unchanging, unending, unfailing, unflagging, uninterrupted, unremitting, unvarying, unwaning; SEE CONCEPTS *534,798*

continuance [*n*] *duration*
constancy, continuation, endurance, extension, guts*, longevity, period, permanence, perpetuation, protraction, run, survival, term, vitality; SEE CONCEPTS *637,804,807*

continuation [*n*] *addition; maintenance*
assiduity, augmenting, continuance, continuing, continuity, duration, endurance, enduring, extension, furtherance, going on, increase, increasing, line, maintaining, perpetuating, perpetuation, persisting, postscript, preservation, preserving, producing, production, prolongation, prolonging, propagation, protracting, protraction, sequel, succession, supplement, sustaining, sustenance, tenacity; SEE CONCEPTS *640,651,804*

continue [*v1*] *persist, carry on*
abide, advance, carry forward, draw out, endure, extend, forge ahead, get on with it*, go on, hang in*, keep at, keep on, keep on truckin'*, keep the ball rolling*, keep up, last, lengthen, linger, live on, loiter, maintain, make headway, move ahead, never cease, outlast, outlive, perdure, persevere, persist in, press on, progress, project, prolong, promote, pursue, push on, reach, remain, rest, ride, run on, stand, stay, stay on, stick at, stick to, survive, sustain, uphold; SEE CONCEPT *239*

continue [*v2*] *begin again; resume*
begin over, begin where one left off, carry on, carry over, go on with, pick up, proceed, recapitulate, recommence, reestablish, reinstate, reinstitute, renew, reopen, restart, restore, return to, take up; SEE CONCEPT *234*

continuity [*n*] *progression*
chain, cohesion, connection, constancy, continuance, continuousness, continuum, dovetailing, durability, duration, endurance, extension, flow, interrelationship, linking, perpetuity, persistence, prolongation, protraction, sequence, stability, stamina, succession, survival, train, uniting, unity, vitality, whole; SEE CONCEPT *721*

continuous [*adj*] *constant, unending*
connected, consecutive, continued, day and night*, endless, everlasting, extended, for ever and ever, interminable, looped, no end of*, no end to, on a treadmill*, perpetual, prolonged, regular, repeated, stable, steady, timeless, unbroken, unceasing, undivided, unfaltering, uninterrupted; SEE CONCEPTS *482,798*

contort [*v*] *disfigure, distort*
bend, convolute, curve, deform, gnarl, knot, misshape, torture, twist, warp, wind, wrench, writhe; SEE CONCEPTS *147,184*

contortion [*n*] *distortion, mutilation*
anamorphosis, crookedness, deformation, deformity, dislocation, grimace, malformation, misproportion, misshapement, pout, twist, ugliness, unsightliness, wryness; SEE CONCEPTS *436,580*

contour [*n*] *outline, profile*
curve, delineation, figuration, figure, form, lineament, lines, relief, shape, silhouette; SEE CONCEPT *436*

contraband [*adj*] *black-market; unlawful*
banned, bootleg, bootlegged, disapproved, excluded, forbidden, hot*, illegal, illicit, interdicted, prohibited, proscribed, shut out, smuggled, taboo, unauthorized, verboten; SEE CONCEPTS *319,545*

contraband [*n*] *black-market production*
bootlegging, counterfeiting, crime, dealing, goods*, moonshine*, piracy, plunder, poaching, rum-running*, smuggling, stuff, swag, theft, trafficking, violation, wetbacking*; SEE CONCEPTS *192,338*

contraceptive [*n*] *birth control method*
armor, barrier method, coil, condom, diaphragm, foam, hormone, intrauterine device, IUD, jelly, loop, pill, planned parenthood, preventative, preventive medicine, prophylactic, rhythm method, ring, rubber, safety, shield, spermicidal cream, sponge, vaginal suppository; SEE CONCEPTS *307,446*

contract [*n*] *agreement, deal*
arrangement, bargain, bond, commission, commitment, compact, concordat, convention, covenant, deposition, dicker*, engagement, evidence, guarantee, handshake*, indenture, liability, mise, obligation, pact, paper, pledge, promise, proof, record, settlement, stipulation, treaty, understanding; SEE CONCEPTS *271,684*

contract [*v1*] *condense*
abate, abbreviate, abridge, become smaller, clench, compress, confine, constrict, consume, curtail, decline, decrease, deflate, draw in, dwindle, ebb, edit, epitomize, evaporate, fall away, fall off, grow less, lessen, lose, narrow, omit, purse, recede, reduce, shrink, shrivel, subside, syncopate, take in, tighten, wane, waste, weaken, wither, wrinkle; SEE CONCEPTS *169,236,247*

contract [*v2*] *come to terms*
accept offer, adjust, agree, arrange, assent, bargain, become indebted, bound, buy, circumscribe, clinch, close, come around, commit, consent, covenant, dicker*, engage, enter into, firm a deal*, give one's word, go along with*, hammer out deal*, initial*, ink*, it's a deal*, limit, make terms, negotiate, obligate, owe, pact, pledge, promise, put in writing, set, settle, shake hands on it*, sign for, sign papers, sign up, stipulate, swear to, undertake, work out details*; SEE CONCEPTS *8,50,88*

contract [*v3*] *catch disease*
acquire, afflict, be afflicted with, become infected with, be ill with, bring on, cause, come down with, decline, derange, develop, disorder, fall, fall victim to, get, go down with, incur, indispose, induce, obtain, sicken, sink, succumb to, take, take one's death, upset, weaken; SEE CONCEPTS *93,308*

contraction [*n*] *drawing in; shortening*
abbreviating, abbreviation, abridging, abridgment, compression, condensation, condensing, confinement, confining, constriction, curtailing, curtailment, cutting down, decrease, decreasing, deflating, deflation, diminishing, diminution, drawing together, dwindling, elision, evaporating, evaporation, lessening, lopping, narrowing, omission, omitting, receding, recession, reducing, reduction, shrinkage, shrinking, shrivelling, tensing, tightening, withdrawal, withdrawing; SEE CONCEPTS *469,776*

contradict [*v*] *be at variance with*
belie, buck, call in question*, challenge, confront, contravene, controvert, counter, counteract, cross, dare, deny, differ, disaffirm, disclaim, disprove, dispute, fly in the face of*, gainsay, have bone to pick*, impugn, negate, negative, oppose, refuse to accept, repudiate, take on, thumbs down*, traverse; SEE CONCEPTS *46,54,665*

contradiction [*n*] *variance to something*
bucking, conflict, confutation, contravention, defiance, denial, difference, disagreement, discrepancy, dispute, dissension, gainsaying, incongruity, inconsistency, negation, opposite, opposition; SEE CONCEPTS *46,278,665*

contradictory [*adj*] *antagonistic*
adverse, against, agin, anti, antipodal, antipodean, antithetic, antithetical, con, conflicting, contrary, converse, counter, counteractive, diametric, discrepant, incompatible, incongruous, inconsistent, irreconcilable, negating, no go*, nullifying, opposing, opposite, ornery*, paradoxical, polar, repugnant, reverse; SEE CONCEPT *542*

contraption [*n*] *device*
apparatus, appliance, contrivance, doohickey*, gadget, gizmo*, machine, mechanism, rig, Rube Goldberg device*, thingamajig*, widget; SEE CONCEPTS *463,499*

contrary [*adj*] *antagonistic; opposite*
adverse, anti, antipathetic, antipodal, antipodean, antithetical, balky, clashing, conflicting, contradictory, contrariant, contumacious, converse, counter, diametric, discordant, dissentient, dissident, froward, headstrong, hostile, inconsistent, inimical, insubordinate, intractable, negative, nonconforming, nonconformist, obstinate, opposed, ornery*, paradoxical, perverse, rebellious, recalcitrant, recusant, refractory, restive, reverse, stubborn, unruly, wayward, wrongheaded; SEE CONCEPT *401*

contrast [*n*] *difference*
adverse, antithesis, comparison, contradiction, contradistinction, contraposition, contrariety, converse, differentiation, disagreement, disparity, dissimilarity, dissimilitude, distinction, divergence, diversity, foil, heterogeneity, incompatibility, incongruousness, inconsistency, inequality, inverse, oppositeness, opposition, reverse, unlikeness, variance, variation; SEE CONCEPTS *561,665*

contrast [*v*] *compare, differ*
balance, be a foil to*, be contrary to, be dissimilar, be diverse, be unlike, be variable, bracket, collate, conflict, contradict, depart, deviate, differentiate, disagree, distinguish, diverge, hang, hold a candle to*, match up, mismatch, oppose, separate, set in opposition, set off, stack up against*, stand out, vary, weigh; SEE CONCEPTS *39,561,665*

contravene [*v*] *go against, contradict*
abjure, breach, break, combat, conflict with, counteract, cross, defy, disaffirm, disobey, encroach, exclude, fight, gainsay, hinder, impugn, infract, infringe, interfere, interpose, intrude, negate, offend, oppose, overstep, refute, reject, repudiate, resist, spurn, thwart, transgress, traverse, trespass, violate; SEE CONCEPTS *46,106,121,192*

contribute [*v1*] *donate, provide*
accord, add, afford, ante up, assign, bequeath, bestow, chip in, come through, commit, confer, devote, dispense, dole out*, dower, endow, enrich, furnish, give, give away, go Dutch*, grant, hand out, kick in*, pitch in*, pony up*, present, proffer, sacrifice, share, subscribe, subsidize, supply, sweeten the kitty*, tender, will; SEE CONCEPTS *108,140*

contribute [*v2*] *be partly responsible for*
add to, advance, aid, assist, augment, be conducive, be instrumental, conduce, do one's bit*, finger in the pie**, fortify, get in the act*, have a hand in*, help, lead, put in two cents*, redound, reinforce, sit in on, strengthen, supplement, support, tend, uphold; SEE CONCEPTS *83,110,244*

contribution [*n*] *gift, offering*
addition, a hand, alms, augmentation, benefaction, beneficence, bestowal, charity, donation, do one's part*, gifting, grant, handout, helping hand, improvement, increase, input, present, significant addition, subscription, supplement, write-off*; SEE CONCEPTS *337,340*

contrite [*adj*] *regretful*
apologetic, attritional, chastened, compunctious, conscience-stricken, humble, penitent, penitential, remorseful, repentant, sorrowful, sorry; SEE CONCEPT *403*

contrition [*n*] *regret*
attrition, compunction, contriteness, humiliation, penance, penitence, penitency, remorse, repentance, rue, ruth, self-reproach, sorrow; SEE CONCEPT *410*

contrivance [*n1*] *plan, fabrication*
angle, artifice, brainchild, coinage, design, dodge, expedient, formation, gimmick, intrigue, invention, inventiveness, machination, measure, plot, project, ruse, scheme, slant, stratagem, switch, trick, twist; SEE CONCEPT *660*

contrivance [*n2*] *gadget*
apparatus, appliance, brainchild, coinage, contraption, convenience, creation, device, discovery, engine, equipment, gear, gimcrack*, harness, implement, instrument, invention, machine, material, mechanism, tackle, thingamabob*, thingamajig*, tool, utensil, whatsis*, widget*; SEE CONCEPTS *260,463,499*

contrive [*v1*] *invent, design*
come up with, concoct, construct, cook up, create, devise, dream up*, engineer, fabricate, fashion, forge, form, formulate, frame*, handle, hatch, improvise, make, make up*, manipulate,

CO
CO

manufacture, move, plan, plot, project, rig*, scheme, throw together*, trump up*, vamp, wangle, whip up*; SEE CONCEPTS *36,173*

contrive [*v2*] *bring about, succeed with difficulty* achieve, angle, arrange, carry out, cogitate, collude, compass, concoct, connive, develop, devise, effect, elaborate, engineer, execute, finagle*, hatch, hit upon, intrigue, jockey*, machinate, manage, maneuver, manipulate, mastermind, negotiate, pass, plan, play games*, plot, project, scheme, shift, swing, work out, wrangle; SEE CONCEPTS *36,91,94*

contrived [*adj*] *overly planned* affected, artificial, elaborate, fake, false, forced, labored, manipulated, overdone, phony, recherché, strained, unnatural, unspontaneous; SEE CONCEPTS *564,582*

control [*n*] *command, mastery* ascendancy, authority, bridle, charge, check, clout, containment, curb, determination, direction, discipline, domination, dominion, driver's seat*, force, government, guidance, inside track, juice, jurisdiction, limitation, management, manipulation, might, oversight, predomination, qualification, regimentation, regulation, restraint, restriction, ropes, rule, strings*, subjection, subordination, superintendence, supervision, supremacy, sway, upper hand*, weight, wire pulling*; SEE CONCEPT *376*

control [*v1*] *have charge of* administer, administrate, advise, be in saddle*, boss, bully, call, call the signals*, command, conduct, deal with, direct, discipline, dominate, domineer, govern, guide, handle, head, head up*, hold purse strings*, hold sway over*, hold the reins*, instruct, lead, manage, manipulate, overlook, oversee, pilot, predominate, push buttons*, quarterback*, regiment, regulate, reign over, rule, run*, run the show*, run things*, steer, subject, subjugate, superintend, supervise; SEE CONCEPT *117*

control [*v2*] *curb, hold back* adjust, awe, bridle, check, collect, compose, constrain, contain, cool, corner, cow, limit, monopolize, quell, regulate, rein in, repress, restrain, simmer down*, smother, subdue; SEE CONCEPT *130*

controversial [*adj*] *at issue* arguable, argumentative, contended, contentious, contestable, controvertible, debateable, disputable, disputatious, disputed, doubtable, doubtful, dubious, dubitable, in dispute, litigious, moot, open to discussion*, open to question*, polemical, questionable, suspect, uncertain, under discussion; SEE CONCEPTS *535,546*

controversy [*n*] *debate, dispute* altercation, argument, beef*, bickering, brush, contention, difference, discussion, disputation, dissention, embroilment, falling-out*, flak, fuss, hurrah, miff, polemic, quarrel, row, rumpus, scene, scrap, squabble, strife, tiff*, words, wrangle, wrangling; SEE CONCEPTS *46,278,665*

controvert [*v*] *oppose, argue* break, challenge, confound, confute, contest, contradict, counter, debate, deny, disconfirm, discuss, disprove, dispute, oppugn, question, rebut, refute, wrangle; SEE CONCEPTS *21,46*

contumacious [*adj*] *headstrong, obstinate* alienated, contrary, disaffected, estranged, factious, froward, haughty, inflexible, insubordinate,

insurgent, intractable, intransigent, irreconcilable, mutinous, obdurate, perverse, pig-headed, rebellious, recalcitrant, refractory, seditious, stubborn, unyielding; SEE CONCEPT *401*

contusion [*n*] *bruise, injury* bang, bump, cut, discoloration, knock, mouse, swelling, wale, wound; SEE CONCEPT *309*

conundrum [*n*] *puzzle* brain-teaser, closed book*, enigma, mystery, mystification, poser*, problem, puzzlement, riddle, why*; SEE CONCEPTS *532,666,690*

convalescent [*adj*] *improving, recuperating* ambulatory, discharged, dismissed, gaining strength, getting better, getting over something*, getting well, healing, mending, on the mend*, past crisis, perked up*, rallying, recovering, rejuvenated, rejuvenating, released, restored, strengthening; SEE CONCEPT *314*

convene [*v*] *bring together; meet* assemble, call, call in, collect, come together, congregate, convoke, corral, gather, get together, hold meeting, muster, open, rally, round up, scare up*, sit, summon, unite; SEE CONCEPTS *60,114,324*

convenience [*n1*] *availability, usefulness; useful thing* accessibility, accessory, accommodation, advancement, advantage, agreeableness, aid, amenity, appliance, appropriateness, assistance, avail, benefit, comfort, comforts, contribution, cooperation, decency, ease, enjoyment, facility, fitness, furtherance, handiness, help, life, luxury, means, ministration, ministry, openness, opportuneness, promotion, receptiveness, relief, satisfaction, service, serviceability, succor, suitability, suitableness, support, time saver, use, utility; SEE CONCEPTS *658,712*

convenience [*n2*] *spare time* chance, freedom, hour, leisure, liberty, occasion, one's own sweet time*, opportunity, place, preference, spare moment*, suitable time, whenever; SEE CONCEPT *807*

convenient [*adj*] *appropriate, useful* acceptable, accommodating, adaptable, adapted, advantageous, agreeable, aiding, assisting, available, beneficial, comfortable, commodious, conducive, contributive, decent, favorable, fit, fitted, good, handy, helpful, in public interest, opportune, proper, ready, roomy, seasonable, serviceable, suitable, suited, timely, time-saving, user-friendly*, well-planned*; SEE CONCEPT *560*

convenient [*adj2*] *nearby* accessible, adjacent, adjoining, all around, at elbows*, at fingertips*, at hand, available, central, close, close at hand, close-by, contiguous, easy to reach, handy, immediate, in neighborhood, next, next door, nigh, on deck*, on tap*, under one's nose*, within reach; SEE CONCEPT *586*

convent [*n*] *nunnery* abbey, cloister, monastery, religious community, retreat, school; SEE CONCEPTS *368,516*

convention [*n1*] *conference* assemblage, assembly, clambake, confab*, congress, convocation, council, delegates, delegation, get together, meet*, meeting, members, powwow*, rally, representatives, show; SEE CONCEPTS *114,324,417*

convention [*n2*] *practice, tradition* canon, code, covenance, custom, etiquette, fashion, form, formality, habit, law, percept, precept, propriety, rule, understanding, usage; SEE CONCEPT *688*

convention [*n3*] *agreement*
bargain, bond, compact, concord, concordat, contract, covenant, pact, protocol, stipulation, transaction, treaty; SEE CONCEPTS *271,684*

conventional [*adj1*] *common, normal*
accepted, accustomed, button-down, commonplace, correct, current, customary, decorous, everyday, expected, fashionable, formal, general, habitual, in established usage, ordinary, orthodox, plain, popular, predominant, prevailing, prevalent, proper, regular, ritual, routine, square, standard, stereotyped, straight, traditional, tralatitious, typical, usual, well-known, wonted; SEE CONCEPTS *530,547*

conventional [*adj2*] *unoriginal*
bigoted, bourgeois, commonplace, conforming, conservative, demure, doctrinal, dogmatic, drippy, hackneyed, hidebound, humdrum, illiberal, inflexible, in rut, insular, isolationist, lame, literal, moderate, moral, narrow, narrow-minded, not heretical, obstinate, parochial, pedestrian, prosaic, puritanical, rigid, routine, rube*, run-of-the-mill, sober, solemn, square, stereotyped, straight, straight-laced, strict, stuffy, uptight; SEE CONCEPT *550*

converge [*v*] *gather*
assemble, coincide, combine, come together, concenter, concentrate, concur, encounter, enter in, focalize, focus, join, meet, merge, mingle, rally, unite; SEE CONCEPTS *113,114*

conversant [*adj*] *experienced, familiar with*
abreast, acquainted, alive, apprehensive, au courant, au fait, aware, cognizant, comprehending, conscious, cool*, down with*, hep*, hip*, informed, into, kept posted, knowing, knowledgeable, learned, on the beam*, perceptive, percipient, plugged in*, practiced, proficient, sensible, sentient, skilled, up*, up-to-date, versant, versed, well-informed, witting; SEE CONCEPT *402*

conversation [*n*] *dialogue, discourse*
chat, colloquy, comment, communication, communion, confab*, confabulation, conference, consultation, converse, debate, discussion, exchange, expression, gab*, gossip, hearing, intercourse, jive*, observation, palaver, parley, pillow talk*, powwow*, questioning, remark, repartee, speech, talk, talkfest*, tête-à-tête*, ventilation*, visit, yak*; SEE CONCEPT *266*

converse [*adj*] *opposite*
antipodal, antipodean, antithetical, contradictory, contrary, counter, counterpole, different, reverse, reversed, transposed; SEE CONCEPT *564*

converse [*n*] *opposite*
antipode, antipole, antithesis, contra, contrary, counter, counterpole, inverse, obverse, other side, reverse; SEE CONCEPT *665*

converse [*v*] *talk*
chat, chew the fat*, chitchat*, commune, confer, discourse, exchange, gab*, parley, rap*, schmooze*, speak, use, yak*; SEE CONCEPT *266*

conversion [*n*] *change, adaptation*
about-face*, alteration, born again*, change of heart*, changeover, exchange, flip-flop*, flux, growth, innovation, metamorphosis, metanoia, metasis, modification, novelty, passage, passing, permutation, progress, proselytization, qualification, reclamation, reconstruction, reformation,

regeneration, remodelling, reorganization, resolution, resolving, reversal, see the light*, switch, transfiguration, transformation, translation, transmogrification, transmutation, turning, turning around; SEE CONCEPTS *232,701*

convert [*n*] *new believer*
catechumen, disciple, follower, neophyte, novice, novitiate, proselyte; SEE CONCEPT *361*

convert [*v1*] *change; adapt*
alter, apply, appropriate, commute, downlink, download, interchange, make, metamorphose, modify, remodel, reorganize, restyle, revise, switch, switch over, transfigure, transform, translate, transmogrify, transmute, transpose, turn; SEE CONCEPTS *232,701*

convert [*v2*] *change belief, especially regarding religion*
actuate, alter conviction, assimilate to, baptize, be born again*, bend, bias, brainwash, bring, bring around, budge, cause to adopt, change into, change of heart*, convince, create anew, impel, incline, lead, lead to believe, make over, move, persuade, proselyte, proselytize, redeem, reform, regenerate, save, see the light*, sway, turn; SEE CONCEPTS *12,14,35*

convex [*adj*] *rounded, curving outward*
arched, bent, biconvex, bulged, bulging, bulgy, gibbous, outcurved, protuberant, raised; SEE CONCEPT *486*

convey [*v1*] *transport*
back, bear, bring, carry, channel, conduct, dispatch, ferry, fetch, forward, funnel, grant, guide, hump, lead, lug, move, pack, pipe, ride, schlepp*, send, shoulder, siphon, tote, traject, transfer, transmit, truck; SEE CONCEPTS *187,217*

convey [*v2*] *express message*
break, carry, communicate, conduct, disclose, impart, make known, pass on, project, put across, relate, reveal, send, tell, transmit; SEE CONCEPT *60*

conveyance [*n*] *transport*
car, carriage, carrying, communication, machine, movement, transfer, transference, transmission, transportation, vehicle; SEE CONCEPTS *143,501,503*

convict [*n*] *criminal*
captive, con, culprit, felon, jailbird*, long-termer*, loser*, malefactor, prisoner, repeater*; SEE CONCEPT *412*

convict [*v*] *find guilty*
adjudge, attaint, bring to justice, condemn, declare guilty, doom, frame, imprison, pass sentence on, pronounce guilty, put away, put the screws to*, rap*, send up*, send up the river*, sentence, throw the book at*; SEE CONCEPTS *18,317*

conviction [*n1*] *belief, opinion*
confidence, creed, doctrine, dogma, eye, faith, feeling, judgment call, mind, persuasion, principle, reliance, say so*, sentiment, slant, tenet, view; SEE CONCEPT *689*

conviction [*n2*] *guilty sentence; assurance*
assuredness, certainty, certitude, condemnation, condemning, confidence, determining guilt, earnestness, fall, fervor, firmness, rap, reliance, sureness, surety, unfavorable verdict; SEE CONCEPTS *317,410*

convince [*v*] *gain the confidence of*
argue into, assure, brainwash, bring around,

CO
CO

bring home to*, bring to reason*, change, demonstrate, draw, effect, establish, get, hook*, induce, make a believer*, overcome, persuade, prevail upon, prompt, prove, put across, refute, satisfy, sell*, sell one on*, sway, talk into, turn, twist one's arm*, win over; SEE CONCEPT *68*

convincing [*adj*] *persuasive*
acceptable, authentic, believeable, cogent, conclusive, credible, dependable, faithful, hopeful, impressive, incontrovertible, likely, moving, plausible, possible, powerful, presumable, probable, rational, reasonable, reliable, satisfactory, satisfying, solid, sound, swaying, telling, trustworthy, trusty, valid; SEE CONCEPTS *267,537,552*

convivial [*adj*] *fun-loving*
back-slapping*, cheerful, clubby*, companionable, conversible, entertaining, festal, festive, friendly, gay, genial, glad-handering*, happy, hearty, hilarious, holiday, jocund, jolly, jovial, lively, merry, mirthful, pleasant, sociable, vivacious; SEE CONCEPTS *401,404*

convocation [*n*] *assembly*
assemblage, conclave, concourse, confab*, conference, congregation, congress, convention, council, diet, get-together, meet, meeting, pow-wow*, synod, turnout; SEE CONCEPT *114*

convolution [*n*] *loop, spiral*
coil, coiling, complexity, contortion, curlicue, flexing, gyration, helix, intricacy, involution, serpentine, sinuosity, sinuousness, snaking, swirl, tortuousness, twist, undulation, winding; SEE CONCEPT *436*

convoy [*n*] *guard, escort*
attendance, attendant, companion, protection; SEE CONCEPT *423*

convoy [*v*] *protect, escort*
accompany, attend, bear, bring, chaperon, companion, company, conduct, consort, defend, guard, pilot, safeguard, shepherd, shield, usher, watch; SEE CONCEPTS *96,110*

convulsion [*n1*] *muscle spasm*
algospasm, attack, contortion, contraction, cramp, epilepsy, fit, paroxysm, seizure, throe, tremor; SEE CONCEPT *308*

convulsion [*n2*] *disturbance*
agitation, cataclysm, clamor, commotion, disaster, ferment, furor, outcry, quaking, rocking, seism, shaking, shock, tottering, trembling, tumult, turbulence, upheaval, upturn; SEE CONCEPTS *152,748*

cook [*n*] *person who prepares food*
baker, chef, hash slinger*, mess sergeant, servant, sous chef; SEE CONCEPT *348*

cook [*v*] *prepare food, usually using heat*
bake, barbecue, blanch, boil, braise, brew, broil, brown, burn, coddle, curry, decoct, deep fry, devil, doctor*, escallop, fix, French fry, fricassee, fry, griddle, grill, heat, imbue, melt, microwave, mull, nuke*, panfry, parboil, parch, percolate, poach, pressure-cook, reduce, roast, ruin*, sauté, scald, scorch, sear, seethe, simmer, sizzle, spoil*, steam, steep, stew, toast, warm up; SEE CONCEPT *170*

cook up [*v*] *devise*
arrange, concoct, contrive, dream up, fabricate, falsify, formulate, frame, hatch, improvise, invent, make up, plan, plot, prepare, scheme, vamp; SEE CONCEPTS *17,36*

cool [*adj1*] *cold, nippy*
air-conditioned, algid, arctic, biting, chill, chilled, chilling, chilly, coldish, frigid, frore, frosty, gelid, hawkish, nipping, refreshing, refrigerated, shivery, snappy, wintry; SEE CONCEPT *605*

cool [*adj2*] *calm, collected*
assured, composed, coolheaded, deliberate, detached, dispassionate, impassive, imperturbable, levelheaded, nonchalant, philosophical, phlegmatic, placid, quiet, relaxed, self-controlled, self-possessed, serene, stolid, together, tranquil, unagitated, unemotional, unexcited, unflappable, unruffled; SEE CONCEPT *401*

cool [*adj3*] *aloof, disapproving*
annoyed, apathetic, distant, frigid, impertinent, impudent, incurious, indifferent, insolent, lukewarm, offended, offhand, offish, procacious, reserved, solitary, standoffish, unapproachable, uncommunicative, unenthusiastic, unfriendly, uninterested, unresponsive, unsociable, unwelcoming, withdrawn; SEE CONCEPT *404*

cool [*adj4*] *excellent*
boss*, dandy, divine, glorious, hunky-dory*, keen, marvelous, neat, nifty, sensational, swell; SEE CONCEPT *572*

cool [*v1*] *chill*
abate, air-condition, air-cool, ally, calm, freeze, frost, infrigidate, lessen, lose heat, mitigate, moderate, reduce, refrigerate, temper; SEE CONCEPT *255*

cool [*v2*] *take a break; abate*
allay, assuage, calm, calm down, chill, compose, control, dampen, lessen, mitigate, moderate, quiet, reduce, rein, repress, restrain, simmer down, suppress, temper; SEE CONCEPTS *240,384*

cooperate [*v*] *aid, assist*
abet, advance, agree, back up, band, befriend, be in cahoots*, chip in, coadjute, coincide, collaborate, combine, comply with, concert, concur, conduce, conspire, contribute, coordinate, espouse, forward, further, go along with, help, join forces, join in, league*, lend a hand*, participate, partner, pitch in*, play ball*, pool resources, pull together, second, share in, show willingness, side with, stick together, succor, take part, unite, uphold, work side by side, work together; SEE CONCEPTS *110,112*

cooperation [*n*] *mutual effort*
aid, alliance, assistance, cahoots*, coaction, coadjuvancy, coalition, collaboration, combination, combined effort, communion, company, concert, concurrence, confederacy, confederation, confunction, conspiracy, doing business with, esprit de corps, federation, fusion, give-and-take, harmony, help, helpfulness, logrolling*, participation, partisanship, partnership, playing ball*, reciprocity, responsiveness, service, society, symbiosis, synergism, synergy, teaming, teamwork, unanimity, union, unity; SEE CONCEPTS *110,112,388,677*

cooperative [*adj1*] *joint, unified*
agreeing, coacting, coactive, coadjuvant, coefficient, collaborating, collaborative, collective, collegial, collusive, combined, combining, common, concerted, concurring, coordinated, hand in glove*, harmonious, in league, interdependent, joining, participating, reciprocal, shared, symbiotic, synergetic, synergic, team, united, uniting; SEE CONCEPT *538*

cooperative [*adj2*] *helpful*
accommodating, companionable, obliging, re-

sponsive, sociable, supportive, useful; SEE CONCEPTS *538,555*

co-opt [v] *to assimilate in order to take over or appropriate*

absorb, accept, admit, adopt, bring in, bring into line, bring into the fold, connaturalize, convert, draw in, elect, embrace, encompass, enfold, homogenize, homologize, include, incorporate, make one's own, take in, take over; SEE CONCEPTS *232,701*

coordinate [adj] *equivalent*

alike, coequal, correlative, correspondent, counterpart, equal, equalized, like, parallel, same, tantamount; SEE CONCEPT *566*

coordinate [v] *match, relate*

accommodate, adjust, agree, atune, combine, conduce, conform, correlate, get it together*, get one's act together*, harmonize, integrate, mesh, organize, pool, proportion, pull together, quarterback*, reconcile, reconciliate, regulate, shape up, synchronize, systematize, team up; SEE CONCEPTS *36,84,158*

cop [n] *policeperson*

deputy, flatfoot, fuzz*, lawman, officer of the law, patrolman, patrolwoman, peace officer, policeman, police officer, policewoman, sheriff, the man*; SEE CONCEPTS *299,354*

cope [v] *manage, contend*

battle with, buffet, carry on, confront, deal, dispatch, encounter, endure, face, get a handle on*, get by, grapple, hack*, hack it*, handle, hold one's own*, live with, make go of it*, make it*, make out*, make the grade*, pit oneself against*, rise to occasion, struggle, struggle through, suffer, survive, tangle, tussle, weather, wrestle; SEE CONCEPTS *23,35*

copious [adj] *abundant*

alive with, a mess of*, ample, aplenty, bounteous, bountiful, coming out of ears*, crawling with*, extensive, exuberant, full, galore, generous, heavy, lavish, liberal, lush, luxuriant, no end*, overflowing, plenteous, plentiful, plenty, profuse, prolix, replete, rich, superabundant, thick with, verbose, wordy; SEE CONCEPT *771*

copiousness [n] *abundance*

affluence, amplitude, bountifulness, bounty, cornucopia, exuberance, fullness, horn of plenty*, lavishness, luxuriance, plentifulness, plenty, richness, superabundance; SEE CONCEPT *767*

cop out [v] *abandon, quit*

back down, back off, back out, backpedal, desert, dodge, excuse, give the slip*, have alibi, rationalize, renege, renounce, revoke, skip, use pretext, welsh, withdraw; SEE CONCEPTS *121,156*

copulate [v] *have sexual relations*

be carnal, bed, breed, cohabit, conjugate, couple, do it*, fool around*, fornicate, go all the way*, go to bed*, have coition, have relations, have sex, lay*, lie with, make it*, make love, make out*, mate, sleep together, sleep with, unite; SEE CONCEPT *375*

copy [n] *duplicate, imitation*

archetype, carbon, carbon copy*, cast, clone, counterfeit, counterpart, ditto*, ectype, effigy, ersatz, facsimile, forgery, hard copy, image, impersonation, impression, imprint, likeness, microfiche, mimeograph, miniature, mirror, model, offprint, parallel, pattern, photocopy, photograph, photostat, portrait, print, reflection, replica, replication, representation, reprint, re-

production, rubbings, similarity, simulacrum, simulation, study, tracing, transcript, transcription, type, Xerox*; SEE CONCEPTS *269,667,716*

copy [v1] *duplicate*

carbon, cartoon, clone, counterfeit, delineate, depict, ditto, draw, dupe, engrave, engross, fake, forge, imitate, knock off*, limn, manifold, mimeo, mirror, mold, paint, paraphrase, photocopy, photostat, picture, plagiarize, portray, reduplicate, reflect, repeat, replicate, represent, reproduce, rewrite, sculpture, simulate, sketch, stat, trace, transcribe, Xerox*; SEE CONCEPT *171*

copy [v2] *imitate*

act like, ape, burlesque, do, do a take-off*, do like*, echo, embody, emulate, epitomize, fake, follow, follow example, follow suit, go like*, illustrate, incarnate, knock off*, make like*, mimic, mirror, mock, model, parody, parrot, personify, phony, pirate, play a role, prefigure, repeat, sham, simulate, steal, take leaf out of book*, take off*, travesty, typify; SEE CONCEPTS *59,139,242*

coquet [v] *tease*

dally, flirt, fool, gold-dig*, lead on, make eyes at*, operate, philander, string along, titillate, toy, trifle, vamp, wanton, wink at*; SEE CONCEPTS *375,384*

cord [n] *rope*

bond, connection, cordage, fiber, line, link, string, tendon, tie, twine; SEE CONCEPTS *470,680*

cordial [adj] *friendly, sociable*

affable, affectionate, agreeable, amicable, buddy-buddy*, cheerful, clubby, companionable, congenial, convivial, cozy, earnest, genial, glowing, gracious, happy, heartfelt, heart-to-heart, hearty, invigorating, jovial, mellow, neighborly, palsy-walsy*, polite, red-carpet*, responsive, sincere, social, sympathetic, tender, warm, warmhearted, welcoming, wholehearted; SEE CONCEPT *401*

cordiality [n] *friendliness, sociability*

affability, agreeability, agreeableness, amenity, amiability, approbation, approval, earnestness, enjoyableness, favor, geniality, gratefulness, heartiness, mutuality, pleasantness, reciprocity, responsiveness, sincerity, sweetness and light*, sympathy, understanding, warmth, wholeheartedness; SEE CONCEPT *633*

core [n] *center, gist*

amount, base, basis, body, bottom line, bulk, burden, consequence, corpus, crux, essence, focus, foundation, heart, import, importance, kernel, main idea, mass, meat*, meat and potatoes*, middle, midpoint, midst, nitty gritty*, nub, nucleus, origin, pith, pivot, purport, quick, root, significance, staple, substance, thrust, upshot; SEE CONCEPTS *442,668,826*

corner [n1] *angle*

bend, branch, cloverleaf, crook, crossing, edge, fork, intersection, joint, junction, projection, ridge, rim, shift, V*, veer, Y*; SEE CONCEPTS *436,484,513*

corner [n2] *niche*

angle, cavity, compartment, cranny, hideaway, hide-out, hole, indentation, nook, recess, retreat; SEE CONCEPTS *440,471,513*

corner [n3] *predicament*

box, difficulty, dilemma, distress, fix, hole, impasse, impediment, jam, knot, pickle, plight, scrape, tight spot; SEE CONCEPTS *674,675*

CO
CO

corner [v] *trap*
bottle, bring to bay, capture, catch, collar*, fool, get on ropes*, have up a tree*, mousetrap*, nab, put out, seize, tree, trick, trouble; SEE CONCEPTS *59,90*

cornerstone [n] *vital element*
anchor, base, essential, foundation, key element, keystone, linchpin, main ingredient, mainspring, mainstay, pillar; SEE CONCEPTS *442,826*

corny [adj] *trite, clichéd*
banal, commonplace, dull, feeble, hackneyed, mawkish, melodramatic, old-fashioned, old hat*, sentimental, shopworn, stale, stereotyped, stupid, tired, warmed-over; SEE CONCEPT *550*

corollary [n] *conclusion, deduction*
aftereffect, analogy, consequence, culmination, effect, end, end product, induction, inference, issue, precipitate, result, sequel, sequence, upshot; SEE CONCEPTS *230,410,529*

corporal [adj] *bodily, physical*
anatomical, carnal, corporeal, fleshly, fleshy, gross, human, material, objective, phenomenal, sensible, somatic, substantial, tangible; SEE CONCEPT *542*

corporate [adj] *allied*
amalgamated, associated, collaborative, collective, combined, common, communal, concerted, incorporated, joint, pooled, shared, united; SEE CONCEPTS *563,577*

corporation [n] *business organization, usually large*
association, bunch, business, clan, company, corporate body, crew, crowd, enterprise, gang, hookup*, jungle*, legal entity, megacorp*, mob, multinational, octupus*, outfit, partnership, ring, shell, society, syndicate, zoo*; SEE CONCEPT *325*

corporeal [adj] *bodily, physical*
anatomical, carnal, corporal, fleshly, fleshy, human, material, mortal, objective, phenomenal, sensible, somatic, substantial, tangible; SEE CONCEPT *542*

corps [n] *group trained for action*
band, body, brigade, company, contingent, crew, detachment, division, outfit, party, posse, regiment, squad, squadron, team, troop, troupe, unit; SEE CONCEPTS *294,322,417*

corpse [n] *dead body*
body, bones*, cadaver, carcass, carrion, deceased, departed, mort*, remains, stiff*; SEE CONCEPTS *390,417*

corpulent [adj] *fat, chubby*
baby elephant*, beefy*, blimp*, bulky, burly, embonpoint, fat, fleshy, gross, having a bay window*, having a spare tire*, heavy, hefty, husky, large, lusty, obese, overblown, overweight, plump, portly, roly-poly*, rotund, stout, tubby, weighty, well-padded*; SEE CONCEPTS *406,491,773*

corpus [n] *body of text*
bulk, collection, compilation, complete works, core, entirety, extant works, mass, oeuvre, opera omnia, staple, substance, whole; SEE CONCEPT *271*

correct [adj1] *accurate, exact*
according to Hoyle*, actual, amen*, appropriate, cooking with gas*, dead on*, equitable, factual, faithful, faultless, flawless, for sure, free of error, impeccable, just, legitimate, nice, okay, on target*, on the ball*, on the beam*, on the button*, on the money*, on the nose*, on track*, perfect, precise, proper, regular, right, right as rain*, righteous, right on*, right stuff*, rigorous, stone, strict, true, undistorted, unmistaken, veracious, veridical; SEE CONCEPTS *542,557,574*

correct [adj2] *proper, appropriate*
acceptable, becoming, careful, comme il faut, conforming, conventional, decent, decorous, diplomatic, done, fitting, meticulous, nice, okay, punctilious, right, right stuff*, scrupulous, seemly, standard, suitable; SEE CONCEPTS *401,558*

correct [v1] *fix, adjust*
alter, ameliorate, amend, better, change, clean up, clean up act*, cure, debug*, doctor*, do over, edit, emend, fiddle with, fix up, get with it*, go over, help, improve, launder, make over, make right, make up for, mend, pay dues*, pick up, polish, put in order, reclaim, reconstruct, rectify, redress, reform, regulate, remedy, remodel, reorganize, repair, retouch, review, revise, right, scrub*, set right, set straight, shape up, straighten out, touch up, turn around, upgrade; SEE CONCEPT *126*

correct [v2] *discipline, chastise*
administer, admonish, castigate, chasten, chide, penalize, punish, reprimand, reprove; SEE CONCEPTS *52,122*

correction [n1] *adjustment; fixing*
alteration, amelioration, amending, amendment, changing, editing, emendation, improvement, indemnification, mending, modification, rectification, redress, reexamination, remodeling, repair, reparation, rereading, revisal, revising, righting; SEE CONCEPTS *126,700*

correction [n2] *discipline*
admonition, castigation, chastisement, punishment, punition, reformation, reproof, rod; SEE CONCEPT *122*

corrective [adj] *healing, curing*
antidotal, counteracting, curative, disciplinary, palliative, penal, punitive, reformatory, rehabilitative, remedial, restorative, therapeutic; SEE CONCEPT *537*

correctly [adv] *right*
accurately, befittingly, decently, decorously, fitly, fittingly, justly, nicely, perfectly, precisely, properly, rightly, to a T*, well; SEE CONCEPT *558*

correctness [n1] *accuracy*
definiteness, definitiveness, definitude, exactitude, exactness, faultlessness, fidelity, preciseness, precision, regularity, truth; SEE CONCEPTS *638,654*

correctness [n2] *propriety*
bon ton, civility, correctitude, decency, decorousness, decorum, fitness, good breeding, order, orderliness, properness, rightness, seemliness; SEE CONCEPTS *633,656*

correlate [v] *equate, compare*
associate, be on same wavelength*, connect, coordinate, correspond, have good vibes*, interact, parallel, relate mutually, tie in*, tune in on*; SEE CONCEPT *39*

correlation [n] *equating, equivalence*
alternation, analogue, complement, correspondence, correspondent, counterpart, interaction, interchange, interconnection, interdependence, interrelation, interrelationship, match, parallel, pendant, reciprocity, relationship; SEE CONCEPTS *388,667*

correspond [*v1*] *agree, complement*
accord, amount, approach, assimilate, be consistent, be identical to, be similar to, coincide, compare, conform, correlate, dovetail, equal, fit, harmonize, lip sync, match, partake of, reciprocate, resemble, rival, square, tally, touch; SEE CONCEPT *664*

correspond [*v2*] *communicate in writing*
answer, drop a kite*, drop a line*, drop a note*, epistolize, exchange letters, have pen pal, hear from, keep in touch, pen, put pen to paper*, reply, scribble, send letter, send word, write; SEE CONCEPTS *79,266*

correspondence [*n1*] *agreement*
accord, analogy, coherence, coincidence, comparability, comparison, concurrence, conformity, congruity, consistency, correlation, equivalence, fitness, harmony, likeness, match, regularity, relation, resemblance, similarity, symmetry; SEE CONCEPT *664*

correspondence [*n2*] *communication by writing*
exchange of letters, letters, mail, messages, post, reports, writing; SEE CONCEPTS *79,277,278*

correspondent [*n*] *person communicating in writing*
contributor, epistler, epistolarian, freelancer, gazetteer, journalist, letter writer, pen pal, reporter, stringer*, writer; SEE CONCEPTS *348,423*

corresponding [*adj*] *equivalent, matching*
agnate, akin, alike, analogous, answering, comparable, complementary, consonant, correlative, correspondent, coterminus, identical, interrelated, kin, kindred, like, parallel, reciprocal, similar, synonymous, undifferentiated; SEE CONCEPT *566*

corridor [*n*] *hallway*
aisle, couloir, entrance hall, entranceway, foyer, hall, ingress, lobby, passage, passageway; SEE CONCEPT *440*

corroborate [*v*] *back up information, story*
approve, authenticate, bear out, certify, check on, check out, check up, confirm, declare true, document, double check, endorse, establish, give nod*, justify, okay, prove, ratify, rubber-stamp*, strengthen, substantiate, support, sustain, validate, verify; SEE CONCEPTS *49,57*

corrode [*v*] *wear away; eat away*
bite, canker, consume, corrupt, destroy, deteriorate, erode, gnaw, impair, oxidize, rot, rust, scour, waste; SEE CONCEPTS *156,169,186,250*

corrosion [*n*] *disintegration*
decay, decomposition, degeneration, deterioration, erosion, oxidation, rust, wear; SEE CONCEPTS *309,720*

corrosive [*adj*] *consuming, wearing; bitter*
acerb, acerbic, acrid, biting, caustic, corroding, cutting, destructive, erosive, incisive, sarcastic, strongly acid, trenchant, venomous, virulent, wasting; SEE CONCEPT *537*

corrugated [*adj*] *ridged, grooved*
channelled, creased, crinkled, crumpled, flexed, fluted, folded, furrowed, puckered, roughened, rumpled, wrinkled; SEE CONCEPTS *485,606*

corrupt [*adj1*] *dishonest*
base, bent, bribable, crooked, debauched, double-dealing, exploiting, extortionate, faithless, fast and loose*, fixed, foul, fraudulent, gone to the dogs*, inconstant, iniquitous, knavish, mercenary, nefarious, on the take*, open, padded*, perfidious, praetorian, profiteering, racket up*, reprobate, rotten, shady, snide, suborned, tainted, treacherous, two-faced, underhanded, unethical, unfaithful, unprincipled, unscrupulous, untrustworthy, venal, wide open*; SEE CONCEPT *545*

corrupt [*adj2*] *debased, vicious*
abandoned, abased, baneful, boorish, degenerate, degraded, deleterious, depraved, dishonored, dissolute, evil, flagitious, infamous, loose, low, miscreant, monstrous, nefarious, perverse, profligate, rotten, villainous; SEE CONCEPTS *401,545*

corrupt [*adj3*] *adulterated, rotten*
altered, contaminated, decayed, defiled, distorted, doctored, falsified, foul, infected, noxious, polluted, putrescent, putrid, tainted; SEE CONCEPTS *485,613*

corrupt [*v*] *pervert; pollute*
abase, abuse, adulterate, animalize, bastardize, blemish, blight, bribe, contaminate, damage, debase, debauch, decay, decompose, deface, defile, deform, degrade, demean, demoralize, deprave, depreciate, despoil, disfigure, disgrace, dishonor, fix, grease palm*, harm, hurt, ill-treat, impair, infect, injure, lower, lure, maltreat, mar, mistreat, misuse, outrage, pull down, putrefy, ravage, reduce, rot, ruin, spoil, square, stain, suborn, subvert, taint, undermine, violate, vitiate, warp, waste; SEE CONCEPTS *14,240*

corruption [*n1*] *dishonesty*
breach of trust, bribery, bribing, crime, crookedness, demoralization, exploitation, extortion, fiddling, fraud, fraudulency, graft, jobbery, malfeasance, misrepresentation, nepotism, on the take*, payoff, payola*, profiteering, racket*, shadiness*, shady deal*, shuffle, skimming, squeeze*, unscrupulousness, venality; SEE CONCEPT *645*

corruption [*n2*] *baseness*
atrocity, decadence, degeneration, degradation, depravity, evil, immorality, impurity, infamy, iniquity, looseness, lubricity, perversion, profligacy, sinfulness, turpitude, vice, viciousness, vulgarity, wickedness; SEE CONCEPTS *633,645*

corruption [*n3*] *adulteration*
debasement, decay, defilement, distortion, doctoring, falsification, foulness, infection, noxiousness, pollution, putrefaction, putrescence, rot, rottenness; SEE CONCEPT *723*

cosmetic [*adj*] *beautifying; relating to appearance*
corrective, gooky*, improving, makeup, nonessential, painted, remedial, restorative, superficial, surface, touching-up; SEE CONCEPT *579*

cosmic [*adj*] *limitless; universal*
catholic, cosmogonal, cosmogonic, cosmopolitan, ecumenical, empyrean, global, grandiose, huge, immense, infinite, measureless, planetary, vast, worldwide; SEE CONCEPT *772*

cosmopolitan [*adj*] *worldly-wise*
catholic, cultivated, cultured, ecumenical, global, gregarious, metropolitan, planetary, polished, public, smooth, sophisticated, universal, urbane, well-travelled, worldly, worldwide; SEE CONCEPT *589*

cosmos [*n1*] *universe*
creation, galaxy, macrocosm, macrocosmos, megacosm, nature, solar system, star system, world; SEE CONCEPTS *511,770*

CO
CO

cosmos [*n2*] *ordered system*
harmony, order, organization, scheme, structure; SEE CONCEPTS *727,770*

cost [*n1*] *expense; price paid*
amount, arm and a leg*, bad news*, bite*, bottom dollar*, bottom line*, charge, damage*, disbursement, dues, expenditure, figure, line, nick*, nut*, outlay, payment, price, price tag, rate, score*, setback*, squeeze*, tab, tariff, ticket, toll, top dollar*, value, worth; SEE CONCEPTS *328,336*

cost [*n2*] *penalty, sacrifice*
damage, deprivation, detriment, expense, forfeit, forfeiture, harm, hurt, injury, loss, suffering; SEE CONCEPTS *676,679*

cost [*v1*] *command a price of*
amount to, be asked, be demanded, be given, be marked at, be needed, be paid, be priced at, be received, be valued at, be worth, bring in, come to, mount up, move back, nick*, rap*, require, sell at, sell for, set back, take, to the tune of*, yield; SEE CONCEPTS *328,336*

cost [*v2*] *harm; exact a penalty*
do disservice to, expect, hurt, infuriate, lose, necessitate, obligate, require; SEE CONCEPT *246*

cost-effective [*adj*] *economical*
practical, profitable, worthwhile; SEE CONCEPT *542*

costly [*adj1*] *expensive*
an arm and leg*, cher*, dear, excessive, executive, exorbitant, extortionate, extravagant, fancy, high, highly priced, high-priced, inordinate, precious, premium, pricey, steep, stiff*, top, valuable; SEE CONCEPT *334*

costly [*adj2*] *priceless*
gorgeous, inestimable, invaluable, lavish, luxurious, opulent, precious, rich, splendid, sumptuous, valuable; SEE CONCEPT *567*

costly [*adj3*] *harmful, damaging*
catastrophic, deleterious, disastrous, loss-making, ruinous, sacrificial; SEE CONCEPT *537*

costume [*n*] *set of clothes*
apparel, attire, clothing, dress, duds*, ensemble, fashion, garb, getup*, guise, livery, mode, outfit, rig*, robes*, style, suit, uniform, wardrobe; SEE CONCEPT *451*

cot [*n*] *temporary bed*
army bed, berth, bunk, camp bed, folding bed, gurney, small bed, trundle; SEE CONCEPT *443*

cottage [*n*] *tiny house; lodging*
box, bungalow, cabana, cabin, caboose, camp, carriage house, chalet, cot, home, hut, lean-to, lodge, ranch, shack, shanty, small house; SEE CONCEPT *516*

couch [*n*] *sofa; long, upholstered furniture*
bed, chair, chaise longue, chesterfield, davenport, daybed, divan, lounge, love seat, ottoman, resting place, settee; SEE CONCEPT *443*

couch [*v*] *express in particular way*
formulate, frame, phrase, put, set forth, utter, word; SEE CONCEPT *51*

couch potato [*n*] *inactive person*
bystander, goof-off*, idler, laggard, lazy person, loafer, lotuseater*, lounger, observer, slouch, sluggard, spectator, televiewer*, TV viewer, viewer; SEE CONCEPT *423*

cough [*n*] *expelled air with sound*
ahem, bark, cold, croup, frog in throat*, hack, hem, tickle in throat*, whoop; SEE CONCEPTS *65,316*

cough [*v*] *expelling air with sound*
bark, choke, clear throat, convulse, expectorate, hack, hawk, hem, spit up, vomit, whoop; SEE CONCEPTS *65,308*

council [*n*] *people assembled for purpose*
assembly, board, body, brain trust*, cabinet, chamber, clan, committee, conclave, confab*, conference, congregation, congress, convention, convocation, diet, directorate, gang, gathering, governing body, groupthink*, huddle*, kitchen cabinet*, meet, ministry, mob, official family, outfit, panel, parliament, powwow*, ring, senate, synod; SEE CONCEPTS *299,325,381*

counsel [*n1*] *guidance*
admonition, advice, advisement, caution, consideration, consultation, deliberation, direction, forethought, information, instruction, kibitz*, recommendation, steer, suggestion, tip, tip-off*, two cents' worth*, warning, word to the wise*; SEE CONCEPTS *75,274*

counsel [*n2*] *legal representative*
adviser, advocate, attorney, barrister, bomber*, counselor, legal adviser, legal beagle*, legal eagle*, lip*, mouthpiece*, patch*, shyster*, solicitor; SEE CONCEPT *355*

counsel [*v*] *give advice*
admonish, advise, advocate, caution, charge, confab*, direct, enjoin, exhort, give pointer, give two cents*, guide, huddle*, inform, instruct, keep posted, kibitz*, order, prescribe, prompt, put bug in ear*, put heads together*, put on to, recommend, reprehend, show the ropes*, steer, suggest, teach, tip, tip off*, tout, urge, warn, wise one up*; SEE CONCEPTS *75,317*

counselor [*n*] *legal representative; adviser*
advocate, ambulance chaser*, attorney, counsel, front*, guide, instructor, legal beagle*, legal eagle*, lip*, mentor, mouthpiece*, pleader, solicitor, squeal*, teacher*; SEE CONCEPT *355*

count [*n*] *tally; number*
calculation, computation, enumeration, numbering, outcome, poll, reckoning, result, sum, toll, total, whole; SEE CONCEPT *766*

count [*v1*] *add, check in order*
add up, calculate, cast, cast up, cipher, compute, enumerate, estimate, figure, foot, keep tab, number, numerate, reckon, run down, score, sum, take account of, tally, tell, tick off, total, tot up; SEE CONCEPT *764*

count [*v2*] *consider, deem*
await, esteem, expect, hope, impute, judge, look, look upon, rate, regard, think; SEE CONCEPTS *18,43*

count [*v3*] *have importance*
carry weight, cut ice*, enter into consideration, import, matter, mean, militate, rate, signify, tell, weigh; SEE CONCEPT *668*

count [*v4*] *include*
await, expect, hope, look, number among, take into account, take into consideration; SEE CONCEPTS *26,112*

countenance [*n1*] *appearance, usually of the face*
aspect, biscuit*, cast, demeanor, expression, face, features, gills*, kisser*, look, looks, map*, mask, mien, mug*, phizog*, physiognomy, poker face*, potato*, puss*, visage; SEE CONCEPTS *716,718*

countenance [*n2*] *self-control*
calmness, composure, presence of mind, self-composure; SEE CONCEPT *633*

countenance [*v*] *approve, support*
abet, accept, advocate, aid, applaud, approbate, back, bear with, champion, commend, condone, confirm, cope, encourage, endorse, favor, get behind, give green light*, give stamp of approval*, give the nod*, go along with, go for, grin and bear it*, handle, help, hold with, invite, live with*, nod at, okay*, put John Hancock on*, put up with, sanction, sign off on*, sit still for*, smile on*, stand for, stomach something*, swallow*, thumbs up*, uphold; SEE CONCEPTS *10,50,88*

counter [*adj*] *opposite, opposing*
adverse, against, antagonistic, anti, antipodal, antipodean, antithetical, conflicting, contradictory, contrary, contrasting, converse, diametric, hindering, impeding, obstructive, obverse, opposed, polar, reverse; SEE CONCEPTS *544,581*

counter [*adv*] *contrary, reverse*
against, at variance with, contrarily, contrariwise, conversely, in defiance of, opposite, versus; SEE CONCEPTS *544,581*

counter [*v*] *answer, respond in retaliation*
backtalk, beat, bilk, buck, circumvent, contravene, counteract, counterwork, cross, dash, disappoint, fly in the face of*, foil, frustrate, have bone to pick*, hinder, hit back, match, meet, offset, oppose, parry, pit, play off, resist, respond, retaliate, return, ruin, take on, thumbs down*, vie, ward off; SEE CONCEPTS *45,121*

counteract [*v*] *do opposing action*
annul, buck, cancel, cancel out, check, contravene, correct, counterbalance, countercheck, countervail, counterwork, cross, defeat, fix, foil, frustrate, go against, halt, hinder, invalidate, negate, negative, neutralize, offset, oppose, prevent, rectify, redress, resist, right, thwart; SEE CONCEPTS *87,96,126*

counterbalance [*v*] *offset an action*
amend, atone for, balance, cancel, compensate, correct, counteract, counterpoise, countervail, equalize, make up for, outweigh, rectify, redeem, set off; SEE CONCEPTS *87,96,126*

counterfeit [*adj*] *fake, simulated*
affected, assumed, bent, bogus*, brummagem, copied, crock, deceptive, delusive, delusory, ersatz, faked, false, feigned, fictitious, fishy*, forged, framed, fraudulent, Hollywood*, imitation, misleading, mock, not genuine, not kosher*, phony*, pirate, plant*, pretended, pretentious, pseudo, put-on*, queer, sham, snide, soft shell*, spurious, suppositious, two-faced*, won't fly*, wrong; SEE CONCEPTS *549,582*

counterfeit [*n*] *fake, forgery*
actor, bogus*, bum, copy, deceit, deception, dummy, facsimile, fraud, gyp, hoax, humbug, imitation, imposture, junque*, phony, pseudo, put-on*, reproduction, sell*, sham, simulacrum; SEE CONCEPTS *648,725*

counterfeit [*v*] *make deceitful imitation*
act like, affect, ape, assume, bluff, carbon, cheat, circulate bad money, clone, coin, copy, defraud, delude, ditto, do, do like*, dupe, fabricate, fake, feign, forge, go like*, imitate, impersonate, knock off*, make like*, make money, mimeo, mimic, mint, phony*, phony up*, pretend, put

on*, sham, simulate, stat, Xerox*; SEE CONCEPTS *59,171*

countermand [*v*] *annul, cancel a command*
override, recall, repeal, rescind, retract, retreat, reverse, revoke; SEE CONCEPTS *50,53,88*

counterpart [*n*] *match; identical part or thing*
analogue, carbon copy*, complement, copy, correlate, correlative, correspondent, dead ringer*, ditto*, doppelganger, duplicate, equal, equivalent, fellow, like, look alike, mate, obverse, opposite, opposite number, peas in a pod*, pendant, ringer*, spit and image*, spitting image*, supplement, tally, twin, two of a kind; SEE CONCEPTS *667,834*

countless [*adj*] *innumerable*
bags of*, endless, gobs*, heap*, immeasurable, incalculable, infinite, innumerous, jillion*, legion, limitless, loads*, lots of, many, measureless, mess*, mint*, mucho*, multitudinous, myriad, numberless, oodles*, passel of*, peck, pile, raft*, scads*, slew*, stack*, tidy sum, umpteen*, uncountable, uncounted, untold, wad*, whole slew*, zillion*; SEE CONCEPTS *762,781*

count on/count upon [*v*] *depend on; rely*
aim for, bank on, bargain for, believe, believe in, bet bottom dollar*, bet on, expect from, heed, lean on, pin faith on, place confidence in, plan on, reckon on, rest on, score, stake on, swear by, tab, take as gospel truth*, take for granted, take on trust, trust; SEE CONCEPTS *12,26*

count out [*v*] *disregard, exclude*
bar, bate, debar, eliminate, except, get rid of, leave out, leave out of account, mark off, pass over, rule out, suspend; SEE CONCEPT *25*

country [*adj*] *rural, pastoral*
agrarian, agrestic, Arcadian, bucolic, campestral, countrified, georgic, homey, out-country, outland, provincial, rustic, uncultured, unpolished, unrefined, unsophisticated; SEE CONCEPTS *401,536,589*

country [*n1*] *political territory; nation*
citizenry, citizens, commonwealth, community, constituents, electors, grass roots, homeland, inhabitants, kingdom, land, native land, patria, people, polity, populace, public, realm, region, society, soil, sovereign state, state, terrain, voters; SEE CONCEPTS *379,508,510*

country [*n2*] *rural area; area away from city*
back country, backwoods, boondocks*, boonies*, bush, countryside, cow country*, farmland, farms, forests, green belt*, hinterland, middle of nowhere*, outback, outdoors, province, sticks*, up country*, wide open space*, wilderness, wilds, woodlands, woods; SEE CONCEPTS *508,513*

country mile [*n*] *long distance*
far piece, good way, great distance; SEE CONCEPTS *651,739,790*

county [*n*] *province or district of area*
canton, constituency, division, shire; SEE CONCEPTS *508,513*

coup [*n*] *achievement, often by maneuver*
accomplishment, action, coup de maître, coup d'état, deed, exploit, feat, overthrow, plot, revolution, stratagem, stroke, stroke of genius*, stunt, successful stroke, tour de force, upset; SEE CONCEPT *706*

coup de grâce [*n*] *finishing blow*
blow, clincher*, comeuppance, deathblow, d

CO
CO

feat, final blow, final stroke, kill, knockout, mercy stroke, mortal blow, quietus; SEE CONCEPTS 95,252

coup d'état [n] *violent seizure*
coup, overthrow, palace revolution, power play*, putsch*, rebellion, revolt, revolution, takeover; SEE CONCEPTS 86,90,320

couple [n] *pair of things*
brace, couplet, deuce*, doublet, duo, dyad, husband and wife, item, newlyweds, set, span, team, twain, twosome, yoke; SEE CONCEPTS 432,766

couple [v] *join two things*
bracket, bring together, buckle, clasp, coalesce, cohabit, come together, conjoin, conjugate, connect, copulate, harness, hitch, hook up, link, marry, match, pair, unite, wed, yoke; SEE CONCEPTS 113,114,297,375

coupon [n] *discount ticket*
advertisement, box top*, card, certificate, credit slip, detachable portion, order blank, premium certificate, ration slip, redeemable part, redemption slip, slip, token, voucher; SEE CONCEPT 331

courage [n] *boldness, braveness*
adventuresomeness, adventurousness, audacity, backbone, bravery, bravura, daring, dash, dauntlessness, determination, élan, endurance, enterprise, fearlessness, firmness, fortitude, gallantry, gameness, grit, guts, hardihood, heroism, intrepidity, lion-heartedness, mettle, nerve, pluck, power, prowess, pugnacity, rashness, recklessness, resolution, spirit, spunk, stoutheartedness, temerity, tenacity, valor, venturesomeness; SEE CONCEPTS 411,633

courageous [adj] *brave, bold*
adventuresome, adventurous, assured, audacious, cool, daredevil, daring, dauntless, doughty, fearless, fiery, fire-eating*, gallant, game, gritty*, gutsy*, hardy, heroic, high-spirited, impavid, indomitable, intrepid, lionhearted, martial, nervy, plucky*, red-blooded*, resolute, Spartan, stalwart, stand tall*, stouthearted, strong, tenacious, tough, Trojan*, unafraid, undaunted, valiant, valorous, venturesome, venturous; SEE CONCEPTS 401,404

courier [n] *messenger*
bearer, carrier, dispatcher, emissary, envoy, express, go-between, gofer*, gopher*, herald, intelligencer, internuncio, runner; SEE CONCEPT 348

course [n1] *progress, advance*
advancement, chain, channels, consecution, continuity, development, flow, furtherance, line, manner, march, movement, order, plan, policy, polity, procedure, program, progression, red tape*, row, scheme, sequel, sequence, series, 'ring, succession, system, unfolding, way; SEE \CEPTS 704,727

e [n2] *path, channel*
aqueduct, boards, byway, canal, circuit, direction, duct, flow, groove, itinerary, ʹmovement, orbit, passage, range, road, rut, scope, stream, tack, track, trail, ʹatercourse, way; SEE CONCEPTS

ʹ₁ *of action*
ʹ, lapse, passage, passing, ʹ₁, time; SEE CONCEPT 804

ʹdy
ʹculum, discussion group, ʹre, matriculation, meet-ʹeparation, procedure, pro-

gram, regimen, schedule, seminar, session, speciality, subject; SEE CONCEPT 287

course [v] *flow; run*
career, chase, dart, dash, follow, gallop, gush, hasten, hunt, hurry, hustle, pursue, race, rush, scamper, scoot, scurry, speed, spring, stream, surge, tumble; SEE CONCEPTS 150,152

court [n1] *yard, garden of building*
cloister, close, compass, courtyard, curtilage, enclosure, forum, patio, piazza, plaza, quad, quadrangle, square, street; SEE CONCEPTS 509,513

court [n2] *ruler's attendants*
castle, cortege, entourage, hall, lords and ladies, palace, retinue, royal household, staff, suite, train; SEE CONCEPTS 296,348

court [n3] *judicial system*
bar, bench, court of justice, forum, judge, justice, kangaroo court*, law court, magistrate, seat of judgment, session, tribunal; SEE CONCEPTS 299,318

court [n4] *building for legal proceedings*
bar, bench, city hall, county courthouse, courthouse, courtroom, federal building, hall of justice, justice building, law court, municipal building, tribunal; SEE CONCEPTS 318,439

court [n5] *wooing*
address, attention, homage, love, respects, suit; SEE CONCEPT 32

court [v] *fawn over, pay attention to*
allure, ask in marriage, attract, beseech, bid, bootlick, captivate, charm, chase, cultivate, curry favor, date, entice, entreat, flatter, follow, gallant, go out with, go steady, go together, go with, grovel, importune, invite, keep company with, make love to, make overture, make time with*, pander to, pay addresses to, pay court to, please, pop the question*, praise, propose, pursue, run after*, seek, seek the hand of, serenade, set one's cap*, solicit, spark, spoon*, sue, sweetheart, take out, woo; SEE CONCEPTS 32,384

courteous [adj] *gentle, mannerly*
affable, attentive, ceremonious, civil, civilized, complaisant, considerate, courtly, cultivated, debonair, elegant, gallant, genteel, gracious, polished, polite, refined, respectful, soft-spoken, suave, thoughtful, urbane, well-behaved, well-bred, well-mannered, well-spoken; SEE CONCEPTS 267,401

courtesy [n1] *good manners*
address, affability, amenities, amiability, attentiveness, ceremony, chivalry, civility, comity, complaisance, consideration, cordiality, courteousness, courtliness, cultivation, culture, deference, elegance, familiarity, favor, friendliness, gallantness, gallantry, generosity, geniality, gentleness, good behavior, good breeding, graciousness, indulgence, kindness, polish, politeness, refinement, respect, reverence, solicitude, suavity, sympathy, tact, thoughtfulness, urbanity; SEE CONCEPTS 633,644

courtesy [n2] *favor, indulgence*
accommodation, benevolence, bounty, charity, chivalry, compassion, consent, consideration, dispensation, generosity, kindness, liberality, service, unselfishness; SEE CONCEPTS 337,388, 633

courtly [adj] *refined manner*
adulatory, affable, aristocratic, august, ceremonious, chivalrous, civil, civilized, complimentary, conventional, cultured, decorous, dignified, ele-

gant, flattering, formal, gallant, gracious, high-bred, imposing, lofty, obliging, polished, polite, preux, prim, refined, stately, studied, urbane; SEE CONCEPT *401*

courtship [*n*] *dating, romance*
courting, engagement, keeping company*, love, lovemaking, pursuit, suit, wooing; SEE CONCEPT *388*

cove [*n*] *inlet, small niche*
anchorage, arm, bay, bayou, bight, cave, cavern, creek, estuary, firth, frith, gulf, harbor, hole, lagoon, nook, retreat, slough, sound, wash; SEE CONCEPT *509*

covenant [*n*] *pact, promise*
agreement, arrangement, bargain, bond, commitment, compact, concordat, contract, convention, deal, deed, dicker*, handshake*, papers, stipulation, transaction, treaty, trust; SEE CONCEPT *684*

covenant [*v*] *agree*
bargain, concur, contract, engage, pledge, plight, promise, stipulate, swear, undertake, vow; SEE CONCEPTS *8,71,317*

cover [*n1*] *wrapping, cover-up*
awning, bark, binding, camouflage, canopy, canvas, cap, caparison, case, ceiling, cloak, clothing, coating, covering, coverlet, disguise, dome, dress, drop, envelope, facade, false front*, fig leaf, front, guise, hood, integument, jacket, lid, marquee, mask, masquerade, overlay, paint, parasol, polish, pretense, put-on*, roof, screen, seal, semblance, sheath, sheet, shroud, smoke screen*, spread, stopper, tarp, tarpaulin, tegument, tent, top, umbrella, varnish, veil, veneer, window-dressing, wrapper, wraps; SEE CONCEPTS *484,750*

cover [*n2*] *hiding place*
asylum, camouflage, concealment, covert, defense, drop, front, guard, harbor, harborage, haven, port, protection, refuge, retreat, safety, sanctuary, screen, security, shelter; SEE CONCEPT *198*

cover [*v1*] *wrap, hide*
blanket, board up, bury, bush up, cache, camouflage, canopy, cap, carpet, cloak, clothe, coat, conceal, cover up, crown, curtain, daub, disguise, do on the sly*, dress, eclipse, encase, enclose, enfold, ensconce, enshroud, envelop, hood, house, invest, layer, mantle, mask, obscure, overcast, overlay, overspread, protect, put on, screen, secrete, set on, shade, shield, shroud, stash*, superimpose, superpose, surface, veil; SEE CONCEPTS *172,188*

cover [*v2*] *protect, guard*
bulwark, defend, fend, house, reinforce, safeguard, screen, secure, shelter, shield, watch over; SEE CONCEPT *96*

cover [*v3*] *include, contain*
be enough, comprehend, comprise, consider, deal with, embody, embrace, encompass, examine, incorporate, involve, meet, provide for, reach, refer to, suffice, survey, take account of; SEE CONCEPT *643*

cover [*v4*] *describe in published writing*
broadcast, detail, investigate, narrate, recount, relate, report, tell of, write up; SEE CONCEPTS *60,79*

cover [*v5*] *fill in for, compensate*
balance, counterbalance, double for, insure, make good, make up for, offset, relieve, stand in

for*, substitute, take over, take the rap for*; SEE CONCEPTS *110,126*

cover [*v6*] *travel across area*
cross, do, journey over, pass over, pass through, range, track, traverse, trek; SEE CONCEPT *224*

covert [*adj*] *clandestine, underhanded*
buried, camouflaged, cloaked, concealed, disguised, dissembled, furtive, hidden, hush-hush*, incog*, incognito, masked, obscured, private, privy, QT*, secret, shrouded, stealthy, sub rosa, surreptitious, ulterior, undercover, underhand, under-the-table*, under wraps*, unsuspected, veiled; SEE CONCEPTS *544,548*

covertly [*adv*] *clandestine, underhandedly*
by stealth, clandestinely, furtively, hush-hush*, in camera, in holes and corners*, on the QT*, on the quiet, on the sly, privately, secretly, slyly, stealthily, sub rosa, surreptitiously, undercover, under wraps*, wildcat*; SEE CONCEPTS *544,548*

cover-up [*n*] *concealment*
burial*, camouflage, closeting, complicity, conspiracy, disguising, dissimulation, evasion, front, masking, pretense, smoke-screen, whitewash; SEE CONCEPTS *188,631*

covet [*v*] *desire strongly*
aspire to, begrudge, choose, crave, desiderate, envy, fancy, hanker for*, have eye on*, have hots for*, itch for*, long for, lust after, spoil for, thirst for, want, wish for, yearn for, yen for*; SEE CONCEPT *20*

covetous [*adj*] *greedy; very desirous*
acquisitive, avaricious, avid, close-fisted, eager, ensurient, envious, gluttonous, grabby, grasping, green-eyed*, grudging, hogging, itchy*, jealous, keen, mercenary, piggish*, prehensile, rapacious, ravenous, selfish, swinish*, voracious, yearning; SEE CONCEPT *401*

cow [*v*] *browbeat, intimidate*
abash, appall, awe, bludgeon, bluster, buffalo, bulldoze, bully, daunt, discomfit, disconcert, dishearten, dismay, dragoon, embarrass, enforce, faze, frighten, hector, lean on*, overawe, push around*, rattle, scare, showboat*, strong-arm*, subdue, terrorize, turn on the heat*, unnerve, walk heavy*; SEE CONCEPTS *7,19,52*

coward [*n*] *person who is scared, easily intimidated*
alarmist, baby*, caitiff, chicken*, chicken heart*, chicken liver*, craven, cur, dastard, deserter, faintheart, faint-of-heart, fraidy-cat, funk, gutless*, invertebrate*, jellyfish*, liver, malingerer, mouse*, pessimist, poltroon, quitter, rabbit*, recreant, scaredy cat*, shirker, skulker, sneak, weakling, white liver, wimp*, yellow*, yellow belly*; SEE CONCEPT *423*

cowardice [*n*] *timidity*
cold feet*, faintheartedness, fear, fearfulness, funk, gutlessness, mousiness, pusillanimity, wimpiness; SEE CONCEPT *27*

cowardly [*adj*] *fearful*
afraid, anxious, apprehensive, backward, base, caitiff, chicken-hearted, cowering, cowhearted, craven, dastardly, diffident, dismayed, fainthearted, frightened, gutless, having the willies*, jittery, lacking courage, lily-livered*, nervous, no guts, panicky, paper tiger*, pigeonhearted*, pusillanimous, recreant, retiring, running scared, scared, shrinking, shy, soft*, spineless*, timid,

timorous, weak, weak-kneed*, worthless, yellow*, yellow-bellied*; SEE CONCEPT 401

cowboy [n] *mounted cattle hand*
bronco, bronco-buster, buckaroo, cattle herder, cattleman, cowhand, cowpoke, cowpuncher, drover, gaucho, herdsman, rancher, stockman, vaquero, wrangler; SEE CONCEPT 258

cower [v] *hide, hover in fear*
apple-polish*, blench, bootlick*, brownnose*, cringe, crouch, draw back, fawn, flinch, grovel, honey*, kowtow*, quail*, recoil, shrink, skulk, sneak, toady*, tremble, truckle, wince; SEE CONCEPTS 188,384

coy [adj] *very modest*
backward, bashful, blushing, coquettish, demure, diffident, evasive, flirtatious, humble, kittenish, overmodest, prudish, rabbity, reserved, retiring, self-effacing, shrinking, shy, skittish, timid, unassertive; SEE CONCEPTS 401,404

cozy [adj] *comforting, soft, warm*
comfortable, comfy, cuddled up, cushy, easeful, in clover, intimate, in velvet*, on bed of roses*, restful, safe, secure, sheltered, snug, snug as bug in rug*, snuggled down, tucked up; SEE CONCEPTS 485,605,606

crabby/crabbed [adj] *in a bad mood*
acid, acrid, acrimonious, awkward, bad-tempered, blunt, brusque, captious, choleric, churlish, cranky*, cross, crotchety, crusty*, cynical, difficult, dour, fretful, gloomy, glum, grouchy*, harsh, huffy, ill-humored, ill-tempered, irascible, irritable, misanthropic, morose, nasty-tempered, peevish, perverse, petulant, prickly, saturnine, snappish, snappy, sour, splenetic, sulky, sullen, surly, tart, testy, tough, trying, unsociable; SEE CONCEPTS 401,403

crack [adj] *super, first-rate*
able, ace, adept, best, capital, choice, crackerjack*, deluxe, elite, excellent, expert, first-class, handpicked, pro*, proficient, skilled, skillful, superior, talented; SEE CONCEPTS 528,542,574

crack [n1] *break, crevice*
breach, chink, chip, cleft, cranny, crevasse, cut, discontinuity, division, fissure, fracture, gap, interstice, interval, rent, rift, rima, rimation, split; SEE CONCEPTS 469,513

crack [n2] *loud sound, usually from hitting*
bang, bash, belt, blast, blow, boom, buffet, burst, clap, clip, clout, crash, cuff, explosion, go, noise, pop, report, shot, slam, slap, smack, smash, snap, spattering, splitting, stab, stroke, thump, whack, wallop, whack, wham; SEE CONCEPTS 595

crack [n3] *attempt to do something*
fling, go, opportunity, pop, shot, stab, try, whack, whirl; SEE CONCEPT 87

crack [n4] *joke*
dig, funny remark, gag, insult, jest, jibe, quip, remark, return, smart remark, wisecrack, witticism; SEE CONCEPT 273

crack [v1] *break, usually into parts*
burst, chip, chop, cleave, crackle, crash, damage, detonate, explode, fracture, hurt, impair, injure, pop, ring, rive, sever, shiver, snap, splinter, split; SEE CONCEPT 248

crack [v2] *lose self-control*
become deranged, become insane, blow one's mind*, blow up, break down, bug out*, collapse, flip*, give way*, go bonkers*, go crazy, go to

pieces*, lose it*, succumb, yield; SEE CONCEPT 13

crack [v3] *hit very hard*
bash, buffet, clip, clout, cuff, slap, thump, thunder, wallop, whack; SEE CONCEPT 189

crack [v4] *discover meaning, answer*
break, cryptanalyze, decipher, decode, decrypt, fathom, figure out, get answer, solve, work out; SEE CONCEPTS 37,38

crackdown [n] *restraint*
clampdown, crush, end, repression, stop, strike, suppression; SEE CONCEPTS 240,832

cracker [n] *hard, often salted, baked wafer*
biscuit, bun, cookie, hardtack, pretzel, rusk, saltine; SEE CONCEPT 457

crack up [v] *break down mentally*
become demented, become psychotic, blow a fuse*, collapse, come apart at seams*, decline, derange, deteriorate, fail, flip out*, freak out*, go bonkers*, go crazy, go nuts, go off deep end*, go off rocker*, go out of mind*, go to pieces*, have breakdown, schizz out*, sicken; SEE CONCEPT 13

cradle [n1] *small bed for baby*
baby bed, bassinet, cot, crib, hamper, Moses basket, pannier, trundle bed; SEE CONCEPT 443

cradle [n2] *early childhood; origins*
babyhood, beginning, birthplace, fount, fountain, fountainhead, infancy, nativity, nursery, origin, source, spring, ultimate cause, wellspring; SEE CONCEPTS 648,817

cradle [v] *hold in arms; nurture*
lull, nestle, nourish, nurse, rock, support, tend, watch over; SEE CONCEPTS 190,295

craft [n1] *expertise, skill*
ability, adeptness, adroitness, aptitude, art, artistry, cleverness, competence, cunning, dexterity, expertness, ingenuity, knack, know-how*, proficiency, technique; SEE CONCEPTS 409,706

craft [n2] *deceit, scheme*
art, artfulness, artifice, cageyness, canniness, contrivance, craftiness, cunning, disingenuity, duplicity, foxiness, guile, ruse, shrewdness, slyness, stratagem, strategy, subterfuge, subtlety, trickery, wiles, wiliness; SEE CONCEPTS 645,660

craft [n3] *business, discipline*
art, calling, career, employment, handicraft, line, métier, occupation, profession, pursuit, trade, vocation, work; SEE CONCEPT 360

craft [n4] *water or air vehicle*
aircraft, airplane, air ship, barge, blimp, boat, bottom, plane, ship, shipping, spacecraft, vessel, watercraft, zeppelin; SEE CONCEPTS 504,506

craftsperson [n] *person skilled in art*
artificer, artisan, journeyperson, machinist, maker, manufacturer, mechanic, skilled worker, smith, specialist, technician, wright; SEE CONCEPT 348

crafty [adj] *clever, scheming*
adroit, artful, astute, cagey, calculating, canny, crazy like fox*, cunning, deceitful, deep, designing, devious, disingenuous, duplicitous, foxy*, fraudulent, guileful, insidious, intelligent, keen, knowing, sharp, shrewd, slick, slippery*, sly, smart, smooth, street smart*, streetwise*, subtle, tricky, vulpine, wily; SEE CONCEPT 401

craggy [adj] *jagged*
asperous, broken, cragged, harsh, precipitous, rock-bound, rocky, rough, rugged, scabrous, scraggy, stony, uneven, unlevel, unsmooth; SEE CONCEPTS 490,606

cram [*v1*] *fill to overflowing; compress*
charge, chock, choke, compact, crowd, crush, devour, drive, force, gobble, gorge, guzzle, heap, ingurgitate, jam, jam-pack*, load, overcrowd, overeat, overfill, pack, pack 'em in*, pack in, pack it in*, pack like sardines*, press, ram, sardine*, satiate, shove, slop, slosh, squash, squeeze, stive, stuff, tamp*, thrust, wedge, wolf*; SEE CONCEPTS 208,740

cram [*v2*] *study intensely*
burn midnight oil*, heavy booking*, hit the books*, megabook*, mug up*, read, review, revise; SEE CONCEPT 17

cramp [*n*] *muscle spasm*
ache, charley horse*, circumscription, confinement, constipation, contraction, convulsion, crick, hindrance, impediment, kink, obstruction, pain, pang, restriction, shooting pain, stiffness, stitch, stricture, twinge; SEE CONCEPTS 308,728

cramp [*v*] *hinder, restrain*
bottle up*, box up*, check, circumscribe, clamp, clasp, clog, confine, constrain, coop up*, encumber, fasten, grip, hamper, hamstring, handicap, impede, inhibit, limit, object, obstruct, restrict, shackle, stymie, thwart; SEE CONCEPTS 130,191

cramped [*adj*] *congested, overcrowded*
awkward, circumscribed, close, closed in, confined, crabbed, crowded, hemmed in*, illegible, incommodious, indecipherable, irregular, jammed in, little, minute, narrow, packed, pent, restricted, small, squeezed, tight, tiny, tucked up, two-by-four*, uncomfortable; SEE CONCEPTS 483,773

cranky [*adj*] *in bad mood*
bad-humored, bearish, cantankerous, choleric, crabby, cross, crotchety, cussed, disagreeable, got up on wrong side of bed*, grouchy, grumpy, hot-tempered, ill-humored, irascible, irritable, like a bear*, mean, ornery*, out of sorts, perverse, quick-tempered, ratty, snappish, tetchy, ugly, vinegary; SEE CONCEPTS 401,403

cranny [*n*] *nook, opening*
breach, byplace, chink, cleft, crack, crevice, fissure, gap, hole, interstice, niche; SEE CONCEPTS 440,513

crappy [*adj*] *poor*
cheap, inferior, junky, lousy, shoddy, sub-par, trashy, useless, worthless; SEE CONCEPT 571

crapshoot [*n*] *big chance*
iffy proposition, risk, risky business, shot in the dark*, spin of the roulette wheel*; SEE CONCEPTS 675,693

crash [*n1/v1*] *bang; banging sound*
blast, boom, burst, clang, clap, clash, clatter, clattering, crack, din, peal, racket, slam, smash, smashing, sound, thunder, thunderclap, wham; SEE CONCEPTS 65,521,595

crash [*n2*] *collision, accidental hitting*
accident, bump, collapse, concussion, crack-up*, crunch, debacle, ditch, fender bender*, fender tag*, impact, jar, jolt, percussion, pileup, ram, rear-ender*, shock, sideswipe, smash, smashup*, splashdown*, stack-up*, thud*, thump*, total*, washout*, wreck; SEE CONCEPT 189

crash [*n3*] *computer system failure*
abend, head crash, program crash, program error, program failure, system crash, system error; SEE CONCEPTS 699,706

crash [*v2*] *break into pieces*
bang into, crack up, crunch, dash, disintegrate,
fracture, fragment, pile up, shatter, shiver, sideswipe, smash, smash up, splinter, total*, wrack up*; SEE CONCEPT 248

crash [*v3*] *fall*
bite the dust*, bump, collapse, collide, crashland, ditch, dive, drive into, drop, fall flat*, fall headlong, fall prostrate, give way, go in*, hurtle, lurch, meet, overbalance, overturn, pancake*, pitch, plough into*, plunge, prang, slip, smash, splash down, sprawl, topple, tumble, upset, washout*; SEE CONCEPT 181

crass [*adj*] *coarse, insensitive*
asinine, blundering, boorish, bovine, churlish, dense, doltish, gross, indelicate, inelegant, loutish, lowbrow, lumpish, oafish, obtuse, Philistine, raw, rough, rude, stupid, uncouth, unrefined, vulgar, witless; SEE CONCEPT 401

crate [*n*] *wooden container*
box, cage, carton, case, chest, package; SEE CONCEPT 494

crave [*v1*] *desire intensely*
ache for, covet, cry out for, die for*, dream, eat one's heart out*, fancy, give eyeteeth for*, hunger for*, itch for*, long for, lust after, need, pine for*, require, sigh for, spoil for, suspire, thirst for*, want, yearn for, yen for*; SEE CONCEPT 20

crave [*v2*] *beg*
ask, beseech, call for, demand, entreat, implore, necessitate, petition, plead for, pray for, require, seek, solicit, supplicate, take; SEE CONCEPTS 48,53

craven [*adj*] *weak, timid*
chicken*, cowardly, dastardly, fearful, gutless, lily-livered*, mean-spirited, poltroonish, pusillanimous, scared, timorous, weak-kneed*, wimpish*, wimpy*, wussy*, yellow*, yellow-bellied*; SEE CONCEPTS 401,550

craven [*n*] *timid person*
caitiff, chicken*, coward, dastard, fraidy cat*, nebbish, poltroon, quitter, recreant, scaredy cat*, weakling, wheyface, wimp*, wuss*, yellow belly*; SEE CONCEPT 423

craving [*n*] *strong desire*
appetite, appetition, hankering, hunger, hurting, itch*, longing, lust, munchies*, need, passion, thirst, urge, yearning, yen*; SEE CONCEPTS 20,709

crawl [*v1*] *move very slowly*
clamber, creep, drag, drag oneself along, go on all fours, go on belly, grovel, hang back, inch, lag, loiter along, lollygag*, move at snail's pace*, move on hands and knees, plod, poke, pull oneself along, scrabble, slide, slither, squirm, worm, wriggle, writhe; SEE CONCEPT 151

crawl [*v2*] *humble oneself*
abase oneself, apple-polish*, brownnose*, cringe, fawn, grovel, toady, truckle; SEE CONCEPTS 35,48

craze [*n*] *fad, strong interest*
chic, cry, enthusiasm, fashion, fever, furor, infatuation, in thing*, kick*, mania, mode, monomania, newest wrinkle*, novelty, passion, preoccupation, rage, the last word*, the latest thing*, trend, vogue, wrinkle; SEE CONCEPTS 532,690

craze [*v*] *make insane*
bewilder, confuse, dement, derange, distemper, distract, drive mad, enrage, frenzy, infatuate, in-

flame, madden, unbalance, unhinge; SEE CONCEPTS 7,19

crazy [*adj1*] *mentally strange*
ape, barmy, batty, berserk, bonkers*, cracked, crazed, cuckoo, daft, delirious, demented, deranged, dingy*, dippy*, erratic, flaky, flipped*, flipped out*, freaked out*, fruity*, idiotic, insane, kooky, lunatic, mad, maniacal, mental*, moonstruck*, nuts, nutty, nutty as fruitcake*, of unsound mind, out of one's mind, out of one's tree*, out to lunch*, potty*, psycho*, round the bend*, schizo*, screwball*, screw loose*, screwy*, silly, touched*, unbalanced, unglued*, unhinged*, unzipped*, wacky; SEE CONCEPT 403

crazy [*adj2*] *unrealistic, fantastic*
absurd, balmy, beyond all reason, bizarre, cockeyed, derisory, eccentric, fatuous, foolhardy, foolish, goofy*, half-baked*, harebrained*, idiotic, ill-conceived, impracticable, imprudent, inane, inappropriate, insane, irresponsible, loony, ludicrous, nonsensical, odd, out of all reason, outrageous, peculiar, preposterous, puerile, quixotic, ridiculous, senseless, short-sighted, silly, strange, unworkable, weird, wild; SEE CONCEPT 529

crazy [*adj3*] *infatuated, in love*
ardent, beside oneself*, devoted, eager, enamored, fanatical, hysterical, keen, mad, passionate, smitten, wild, zealous; SEE CONCEPT 403

creak [*v*] *grind, grate with high noise*
chirr, crepitate, groan, rasp, scrape, scratch, screech, sound, squeak, squeal; SEE CONCEPTS 65,186,215

cream [*n1*] *lotion, oil*
cerate, chrism, cosmetic, demulcent, emulsion, essence, jelly, liniment, moisturizer, ointment, paste, salve, unction, unguent; SEE CONCEPTS 466,467,468

cream [*n2*] *the best*
choice, crème de la crème*, elite, fat, favorite, finest, flower, pick, pride, prime*, prize, skim*, top; SEE CONCEPT 668

creamy [*adj*] *smooth, buttery*
creamed, feathery, fluffy, gloppy*, gooey, gooky*, goopy*, greasy, gunky, luscious, lush, milky, oily, rich, soft, velvety; SEE CONCEPT 606

crease [*n*] *fold, wrinkle*
bend, bulge, cockle, corrugation, furrow, groove, line, overlap, pleat, plica, pucker, ridge, rimple, rivel, ruck, rugosity, tuck; SEE CONCEPTS 452,757

crease [*v*] *fold, rumple*
bend, cockle, corrugate, crimp, crinkle, crumple, dog-ear*, double up, plait, pleat, pucker, purse, ridge, ruck up, screw up*, wrinkle; SEE CONCEPTS 158,219

create [*v*] *develop in mind or physically*
actualize, author, beget, bring into being, bring into existence, bring to pass, build, cause to be, coin, compose, conceive, concoct, constitute, construct, contrive, design, devise, discover, dream up, effect, erect, establish, fabricate, fashion, father, forge, form, formulate, found, generate, give birth to, give life to, hatch, imagine, initiate, institute, invent, invest, make, occasion, organize, originate, parent, perform, plan, procreate, produce, rear, set up, shape, sire, spawn, start; SEE CONCEPTS 173,239,251

creation [*n1*] *development of entity*
conception, constitution, establishment, formation, formulation, foundation, generation, genesis, imagination, inception, institution, laying down, making, nascency, nativity, origination, procreation, production, setting up, siring; SEE CONCEPT 173

creation [*n2*] *all living things*
cosmos, life, living world, macrocosm, macrocosmos, megacosm, nature, totality, universe, world; SEE CONCEPTS 389,429

creation [*n3*] *invention, concoction*
achievement, brainchild, chef-d'oeuvre, concept, handiwork, magnum opus, opus, piece, pièce de résistance, production, work, work of genius; SEE CONCEPTS 259,260

creative [*adj*] *artistic, imaginative*
clever, cool*, demiurgic, deviceful, fertile, formative, gifted, hip*, ingenious, innovational, innovative, innovatory, inspired, inventive, leading-edge*, original, originative, productive, prolific, stimulating, visionary, way out*; SEE CONCEPT 402

creativity [*n*] *artistry*
cleverness, genius, imagination, imaginativeness, ingenuity, inspiration, inventiveness, originality, resourcefulness, talent, vision; SEE CONCEPTS 409,410

creator [*n*] *inventor; God*
architect, author, begetter, brain, deity, designer, founder, framer, generator, initiator, maker, originator, prime mover, producer, sire; SEE CONCEPTS 348,352,361

creature [*n*] *being, beast*
animal, body, brute, creation, critter*, fellow, individual, living being, living thing, lower animal, man, mortal, party, person, personage, quadruped, soul, varmint*, woman; SEE CONCEPT 389

credence [*n*] *trust, acceptance*
accepting, admission, admitting, assurance, belief, certainty, confidence, credit, dependence, faith, reliance, stock, store; SEE CONCEPT 689

credentials [*n*] *references, attestation*
accreditation, authorization, card, certificate, character, deed, diploma, docket, document, documentation, endorsement, letter of credence, letter of introduction, license, missive, papers, passport, proof, recommendation, sanction, testament, testimonial, title, token, voucher, warrant; SEE CONCEPTS 271,685

credibility [*n*] *believeableness*
believability, chance, integrity, likelihood, plausibility, possibility, probability, prospect, reliability, satisfactoriness, solidity, solidness, soundness, tenability, trustworthiness, validity; SEE CONCEPTS 650,725

credible [*adj*] *believable*
aboveboard, colorable, conceivable, conclusive, creditable, dependable, determinative, honest, honest to God*, imaginable, likely, plausible, possible, probable, probably, rational, reasonable, reliable, satisfactory, satisfying, seeming, sincere, solid, sound, straight, supposable, tenable, thinkable, trustworthy, trusty, up front*, valid; SEE CONCEPTS 552,582

credit [*n1*] *recognition; trust*
acclaim, acknowledgment, approval, attention, belief, Brownie points*, commendation, confidence, credence, distinction, faith, fame, glory, honor, kudos*, merit, notice, pat on the back*,

points*, praise, reliance, strokes*, thanks, tribute; SEE CONCEPTS *69,410*

credit [*n2*] *reputation, status*
authority, character, clout, esteem, estimation, fame, good name, influence, position, prestige, regard, renown, repute, standing, weight; SEE CONCEPT *388*

credit [*n3*] *deferred payment arrangement; assets*
balance, bond, capital outlay, continuance, debenture, extension, installment buying, installment plan, lien, loan, mortgage, on account, on the arm*, on the cuff*, plastic*, respite, securities, stock, surplus cash, tab, trust, wealth; SEE CONCEPT *335*

credit [*v1*] *believe, depend on*
accept, bank on, buy, consider, deem, fall for*, feel, hand it to one, have faith in, hold, pat on back, rely on, sense, swallow*, take as gospel truth*, take stock in*, think, trust; SEE CONCEPT *12*

credit [*v2*] *accredit, assign to*
ascribe to, attribute to, chalk up to, charge to, defer, impute, lay, refer; SEE CONCEPT *18*

creditable [*adj*] *praiseworthy*
admirable, batting a thousand*, believeable, commendable, decent, deserving, estimable, excellent, exemplary, honest, honorable, laudable, meritorious, nasty*, not too shabby*, organic, palmary, reputable, reputed, respectable, salt of the earth*, satisfactory, suitable, well-thought-of, worthy; SEE CONCEPT *542*

credulous [*adj*] *gullible, naive*
accepting, believing, born yesterday*, dupable, easy mark*, falling for*, green, overtrusting, simple, swallow whole, taken in, trustful, trusting, uncritical, unquestioning, unsophisticated, unsuspecting, unsuspicious, unwary; SEE CONCEPT *404*

creed [*n*] *belief, principles*
articles of faith, canon, catechism, church, confession, conviction, cult, doctrine, dogma, faith, ideology, persuasion, profession, religion, tenet, weltanschauung; SEE CONCEPTS *688,689*

creek [*n*] *stream of water*
brook, brooklet, burn, crick, ditch, race, rill, rindle, river, rivulet, run, runnel, spring, streamlet, tributary, watercourse; SEE CONCEPT *514*

creep [*v*] *crawl along, usually on ground*
approach unnoticed, crawl on all fours, edge, glide, grovel, gumshoe*, inch, insinuate, lurk, pussyfoot, scrabble, scramble, skulk, slink, slither, snake*, sneak, squirm, steal, tiptoe, worm, wriggle, writhe; SEE CONCEPT *151*

creepy [*adj*] *nasty, scary*
awful, direful, disgusting, disturbing, dreadful, eerie, frightening, ghoulish, gruesome, hair-raising, horrible, itching, itchy, macabre, menacing, nightmarish, ominous, shuddersome, sinister, terrifying, threatening, unpleasant, weird; SEE CONCEPT *570*

crescendo [*n*] *increase to climax*
apex, ascension, building, climb, crest, critical mass, culmination, elevation, escalation, intensification, peak, pinnacle, rise, summit, surge, upsurge, zenith; SEE CONCEPT *836*

crescent [*adj*] *sickle-shaped*
bowed, bow-shaped, concave, convex, crescentic, crescentiform, curved, falcate, semicircular; SEE CONCEPT *486*

crescent [*n*] *sickle-shaped object*
bow, concave figure, convex figure, cresentoid, curve, demilune, half-moon, horned moon, lune, meniscus, new moon, old moon, sickle; SEE CONCEPT *436*

crest [*n1*] *highest point*
acme, apex, apogee, climax, crescendo, crown, culmination, fastigium, head, height, noon, peak, pinnacle, ridge, roof, summit, top, vertex; SEE CONCEPT *836*

crest [*n2*] *emblem, symbol*
badge, bearings, charge, device, insignia; SEE CONCEPT *284*

crest [*n3*] *topknot on head of animal*
aigrette, caruncle, chine, cockscomb, comb, crown, feather, hogback, mane, panache, plume, ridge, tassel, tuft; SEE CONCEPT *399*

crestfallen [*adj*] *disappointed*
ass in a sling*, blue, cast down, chapfallen, dejected, depressed, despondent, disconsolate, discouraged, disheartened, dispirited, down, downcast, downhearted, down in the dumps*, in a funk*, inconsolable, low, sad, singing the blues*, taken down*; SEE CONCEPT *403*

cretin [*n*] *obnoxious stupid person*
creep, fool, idiot, imbecile, loser, moron; SEE CONCEPTS *350,423*

crevice/crevasse [*n*] *crack, gap*
abyss, chasm, chink, cleft, crack, cranny, cut, division, fissure, fracture, hole, interstice, opening, precipice, rent, rift, slit, split; SEE CONCEPTS *509,513*

crew [*n*] *group working together*
aggregation, assemblage, band, bevy, bunch, cluster, collection, company, complement, congregation, corps, covey, crowd, faction, gang, hands, herd, horde, lot, mob, organization, pack, party, posse, retinue, sailors, sect, set, squad, swarm, team, troop, troupe, workers, working party; SEE CONCEPTS *381,417*

crib [*n*] *baby bed*
bassinet, bin*, box*, bunk, cot, cradle, manger, Moses basket*, rack*, stall*, trundle bed; SEE CONCEPT *443*

crick [*n*] *muscle spasm*
ache, charley horse*, convulsion, cramp, jarring, kink, pain, stitch, twinge, wrench; SEE CONCEPTS *308,728*

crime [*n*] *offense against the law*
abomination, antisocial behavior, atrocity, breach, break, caper, case, corruption, criminality, delict, delictum, delinquency, depravity, dereliction, enormity, evil, evil behavior, fast one*, fault, felony, hit, illegality, immorality, infraction, infringement, iniquity, job, lawlessness, malefaction, malfeasance, misconduct, misdeed, misdemeanor, mortal sin, outrage, racket, scandal, sneak, tort, transgression, trespass, unlawful act, vice, villainy, violation, wickedness, wrong, wrongdoing; SEE CONCEPT *192*

criminal [*adj*] *lawless, felonious*
bent, caught, corrupt, crooked, culpable, deplorable, dirty, heavy, hung up*, illegal, illegitimate, illicit, immoral, indictable, iniquitous, nefarious, off base*, out of line*, peccant, racket, scandalous, senseless, shady*, smoking gun*, unlawful, unrighteous, vicious, villainous, wicked, wildcat*, wrong; SEE CONCEPT *545*

criminal [*n*] *person who breaks the law*
bad actor*, blackmailer, black marketeer, con,

convict, crook, culprit, delinquent, desperado, deuce, evildoer, ex-con, felon, fugitive, gangster, guerilla, heavy*, hood*, hoodlum, hooligan*, hustler, inside person*, jailbird, lawbreaker, malefactor, mobster, mug, muscle*, offender, outlaw, racketeer, repeater, scofflaw, sinner, slippery eel*, thug*, transgressor, trespasser, wrongdoer, yardbird*; SEE CONCEPT 412

crimp [v] *fold or curl*
coil, crease, crimple, crinkle, crisp, crumple, flow, frizz, pleat, rimple, ruck, screw, scrunch, set, swirl, undulate, wave, wrinkle; SEE CONCEPTS 137,213,250

cringe [v] *flinch, recoil from danger*
blench, cower, crawl, crouch, dodge, draw back, duck, eat dirt, grovel, kneel, quail, quiver, shrink, shy, start, stoop, tremble, wince; SEE CONCEPTS 188,195

crinkle [v] *crumple, ruffle*
cockle, coil, crackle, crease, crimp, crimple, curl, fold, hiss, pucker, ruck, rumple, rustle, scallop, screw, scrunch, seam, swish, twist, whisper, wind, wreathe, wrinkle; SEE CONCEPTS 65,137,213,250

cripple [v1] *disable; make lame*
attenuate, blunt, debilitate, disarm, dislimb, dismember, enfeeble, hamstring*, hurt, immobilize, incapacitate, injure, lame, maim, mangle, mutilate, palsy, paralyze, prostrate, sap, sideline*, stifle, undermine, unstrengthen, weaken; SEE CONCEPT 246

cripple [v2] *hinder action, progress*
bring to standstill, cramp, damage, destroy, halt, hamstring*, impair, put out of action*, ruin, spoil, stifle, vitiate; SEE CONCEPT 121

crippled [adj] *disabled*
bedridden, broken, damaged, defective, deformed, enfeebled, game, gimp*, halt, hamstrung*, handicapped, harmed, hog-tied*, housebound, impaired, incapacitated, laid up*, lame, maimed, mangled, marred, mutilated, out of commission*, paralyzed, sidelined*; SEE CONCEPTS 314,485

crisis [n] *critical situation*
big trouble*, catastrophe, change, climacteric, climax, confrontation, contingency, corner, crossroad, crunch*, crux, culmination, deadlock, dilemma, dire straits*, disaster, embarrassment, emergency, entanglement, exigency, extremity, height, hot potato*, hour of decision*, imbroglio, impasse, juncture, mess, moment of truth*, necessity, pass, perplexity, pickle*, pinch*, plight, point of no return*, predicament, pressure, puzzle, quandary, situation, stew, strait, trauma, trial, trouble, turning point, urgency; SEE CONCEPT 674

crisp [adj1] *brittle, dry*
crispy, crumbly, crunchy, crusty, firm, fresh, friable, green, plump, ripe, short, unwilted; SEE CONCEPT 606

crisp [adj2] *fresh, chilly*
bracing, brisk, clear, cloudless, invigorating, refreshing, stimulating; SEE CONCEPTS 525,605

crisp [adj3] *short, curt in presentation*
abrupt, biting, brief, brusque, clear, clear-cut, cutting, incisive, penetrating, piquing, pithy, provoking, stimulating, succinct, tart, terse; SEE CONCEPT 267

crisp [adj4] *smart, snappy in appearance*
clean-cut, neat, orderly, spruce, tidy, well-groomed, well-pressed; SEE CONCEPT 579

criterion [n] *test, gauge for judgment*
archetype, basis, benchmark, canon, example, exemplar, fact, foundation, law, measure, model, norm, opinion, original, paradigm, pattern, point of comparison, precedent, principle, proof, prototype, rule, scale, standard, touchstone, yardstick; SEE CONCEPTS 290,688

critic [n1] *analyst, interpreter*
analyzer, annotator, arbiter, authority, caricaturist, cartoonist, commentator, connoisseur, diagnostic, evaluator, expert, expositor, judge, pundit, reviewer, sharpshooter*; SEE CONCEPT 348

critic [n2] *faultfinder, detractor*
aristarch, attacker, backseat driver*, belittler, blamer, carper, caviler, censor, censurer, complainant, complainer, defamer, disapprover, disparager, disputer, doubter, fretter, hypercritic, maligner, muckraker, mud-slinger*, nagger*, nit-picker*, panner*, quibbler, reviler, scolder, sidewalk superintendent*, slanderer, vilifier, worrier, zapper*; SEE CONCEPT 412

critical [adj1] *fault-finding, detracting*
analytical, belittling, biting, calumniatory, captious, carping, caviling, cavillous, censorious, censuring, choleric, condemning, critic, cutting, cynical, demanding, demeaning, derogatory, diagnostic, disapproving, discerning, discriminating, disparaging, exacting, exceptive, finicky, fussy, hairsplitting, humbling, hypercritical, lowering, nagging, niggling, nit-picking*, overcritical, particular, penetrating, reproachful, sarcastic, satirical, scolding, severe, sharp, trenchant, withering; SEE CONCEPT 267

critical [adj2] *urgently important*
acute, all-important, climacteric, conclusive, consequential, crucial, dangerous, deciding, decisive, desperate, determinative, dire, exceptive, grave, hairy*, hazardous, high-priority, integral, momentous, perilous, pivotal, precarious, pressing, risky, serious, significant, strategic, urgent, vital, weighty; SEE CONCEPT 568

critical mass [n] *crisis point*
critical point, critical stage, crossroads*, crunch time, do or die time*, high noon*, irreversible momentum, moment of truth, point of no return, sink or swim time*, the Rubicon, turning point; SEE CONCEPT 674

criticism [n1] *interpretation, analysis*
appraisal, appreciation, assessment, comment, commentary, critique, elucidation, essay, estimate, evaluation, examination, exposition, judgment, notice, observation, opinion, pan*, rating, rave*, review, reviewal, scorcher, sideswipe*, sleighride*, study, write-up; SEE CONCEPTS 271,277,278

criticism [n2] *verbal disapproval*
animadversion, aspersion, bad press*, blast, brickbats, Bronx cheer*, call down*, carping, cavil, caviling, censure, critical remarks, cut*, denunciation, disparagement, faultfinding, flak*, hit*, knock*, nit-picking, objection, opprobrium, pan, panning, put down, quibble, rap on knuckles*, reproof, roast*, slam*, slap*, slap on wrist*, static, stricture, swipe*, vitriol, zapper*; SEE CONCEPT 52

criticize [v1] *disapprove, judge as bad*
animadvert on, bash, blame, blast, blister, carp, castigate, censure, chastise, chide, clobber, come down on, condemn, cut down*, cut to bits*, cut

up*, denounce, denunciate, disparage, do a number on*, dress down*, excoriate, find fault, fluff*, fulminate against, fustigate, give bad press*, hit, jump on*, knock*, lambaste*, nag at, nit-pick, pan, pick at, rap*, reprehend, reprimand, reprobate, reprove, rip*, roast*, scathe, scorch*, skin*, skin alive*, slam*, slog*, slug*, take down*, trash*, trim*, zap*; SEE CONCEPT 52

criticize [v2] *analyze, interpret*
appraise, assess, comment upon, evaluate, examine, give opinion, judge, pass judgment on, probe, review, scrutinize, study; SEE CONCEPTS 37,103

critique [n] *analysis, essay*
appraisal, assessment, comment, commentary, criticism, editorial, examination, exposition, flak*, judgment, notice, pan*, putdown*, rap*, rave*, review, reviewal, slam*, slap*, study, takedown*, write-up, zapper*; SEE CONCEPTS 51,52,271

croak [v] *make husky, squawking noise*
caw, crow, gasp, grunt, quack, squawk, utter huskily, utter throatily, wheeze; SEE CONCEPT 77

crony [n] *ally, companion*
accomplice, acquaintance, associate, bosom buddy*, buddy, chum, colleague, comate, comrade, confidant, friend, good buddy*, intimate, mate, pal, partner, sidekick*; SEE CONCEPT 423

crook [n] *criminal, thief*
cheat, filcher, knave, pilferer, purloiner, racketeer, robber, rogue, scoundrel, shark*, shyster*, swindler, villain; SEE CONCEPT 412

crook [v] *bend, angle*
bow, curve, flex, fork, hook, meander, notch, round, slither, snake, wind, zigzag; SEE CONCEPTS 213,738

crooked [adj1] *bent, angled*
agee, anfractuous, angular, asymmetric, awry, bowed, catawampus*, circuitous, cockeyed*, contorted, crippled, curved, curving, deformed, deviating, devious, disfigured, distorted, errant, gnarled, hooked, incurving, indirect, irregular, kinky, knurly, lopsided, meandering, misshapen, not straight, oblique, out of shape, rambling, roundabout, screwy*, serpentine, sinuous, skewed, slanted, snaky, spiral, tilted, topsyturvy*, tortile, tortuous, twisted, twisting, uneven, warped, winding, zigzag; SEE CONCEPTS 486,490,581

crooked [adj2] *evil, corrupt*
crafty, criminal, deceitful, devious, dishonest, dishonorable, double-dealing, dubious, fraudulent, illegal, indirect, iniquitous, lying, nefarious, questionable, ruthless, shady, shifty, suborned, treacherous, underhand, unlawful, unprincipled, unscrupulous, untruthful; SEE CONCEPT 545

crop [n] *harvest of fruit, vegetable*
annual production, byproduct, crops, fruitage, fruits, gathering, gleaning, output, produce, product, reaping, season's growth, vintage, yield; SEE CONCEPT 429

crop [v] *cut, trim off*
chop, clip, curtail, detach, detruncate, disengage, hew, lop, mow, pare, pollard, prune, reduce, shave, shear, shorten, skive, slash, snip, top, truncate; SEE CONCEPT 176

cross [adj] *very angry; in a bad mood*
annoyed, cantankerous, captious, caviling, choleric, churlish, crabby*, cranky, crotchety*, crusty, disagreeable, faultfinding, fractious, fretful, grouchy, grumpy, ill-humored, ill-tempered, impatient, irascible, irritable, jumpy, out of humor, peeved, peevish, pettish, petulant, put out*, querulous, quick-tempered, ratty, short, snappy, splenetic, sullen, surly, testy, tetchy, touchy, vexed, waspish; SEE CONCEPTS 401,403

cross [v1] *traverse an area*
bridge, cruise, cut across, extend over, ford, go across, meet, move across, navigate, overpass, pass over, ply, sail, span, transverse, voyage, zigzag; SEE CONCEPTS 159,224

cross [v2] *intersect, lie across*
bisect, crisscross, crosscut, decussate, divide, intercross, intertwine, lace, lie athwart of, rest across; SEE CONCEPTS 738,747

cross [v3] *hybridize, mix*
blend, crossbreed, cross-fertilize, cross-mate, cross-pollinate, interbreed, intercross, mingle, mongrelize; SEE CONCEPTS 250,257

cross [v4] *betray, hinder*
backtalk, block, bollix, buck, crab, cramp, crimp, deny, double-cross, flummox, foil, foul up*, frustrate, have bone to pick*, impede, interfere, knock props out*, louse up*, obstruct, oppose, resist, sell*, sell out*, snafu*, stab in the back*, stonewall*, stump, stymie, take on, take wind out of sails*, thwart; SEE CONCEPTS 7,19,59,121

cross-examine [v] *ask pointed questions*
catechize, check, cross-question, debrief, examine, grill, interrogate, investigate, pump, put the screws to*, question, quiz, sweat, third-degree*; SEE CONCEPTS 48,53,317

crossing [n] *pathway to traverse larger path*
bridge, cloverleaf, crossroad, crosswalk, crossway, decussation, exchange, grade crossing, grating, gridiron, interchange, intersection, junction, loop, network, overpass, passage, screen, traversal, traverse, underpass; SEE CONCEPTS 501,513

crosswise/crossways [adj] *across, at an angle*
angular, aslant, athwart, at right angles, awry, contrariwise, crisscross, cross, crossing, diagonally, from side to side, horizontally, longways, on the bias, over, perpendicular, sideways, thwart, transversal, transverse, transversely, traverse, vertically; SEE CONCEPT 581

crotchety [adj] *irritable, often due to old age*
awkward, bad-tempered, bearish, cantankerous, contrary, crabby*, cranky, cross, cross-grained, crusty, curmudgeonly, difficult, disagreeable, eccentric, fractious, grouchy, grumpy, irritable, obstinate, obstreperous, odd, ornery*, peevish, queer, surly, testy, unusual, vinegary*, waspish, waspy; SEE CONCEPTS 401,403

crouch [v] *stoop low; cringe*
bend, bend down, bow, cower, dip, duck, grovel, huddle, hunch, hunker down, kneel, quail, quat, scrooch down, squat, stoop, wince; SEE CONCEPT 213

crow [v] *brag, exult*
babble, blow, bluster, boast, cackle, caw, cock-a-doodle-doo*, cry, flourish, gas, gloat, glory in, gurgle, jubilate, mouth, prate, puff, rodomontade, squawk, strut, swagger, triumph, vaunt, whoop; SEE CONCEPT 49

crowd [n1] *large assembly*
army, array, blowout, bunch, cattle, circle, clique, cloud, cluster, company, concourse, con-

fluence, conflux, congeries, congregation, coterie, crew, crush, deluge, drove, faction, flock,
flood, gaggle, great unwashed*, group, herd,
horde, host, jam, legion, lot, mass, masses, meet,
mob, multitude, muster, organization, pack,
party, people, posse, press, rabble, rank and file*,
scores, sellout, set, stream, surge, swarm, throng,
troupe, tumult; SEE CONCEPTS *381,417*

crowd [*n2*] *special group of friends*
bunch, circle, clique, coterie, faction, group, in-
crowd, lot, posse, push, set; SEE CONCEPTS
387,417

crowd [*v*] *cram, press into area*
bear, bunch, bundle, chock, cluster, congest,
congregate, crush, deluge, elbow, flock, gather,
huddle, jam, jam-pack*, justle, mass, muster,
overcrowd, pack, pack 'em in*, pack like sardines*, pile, push, ram, sardine*, shove, squash,
squeeze, squish*, stream, surge, swamp, swarm,
throng, top off, troop; SEE CONCEPTS *208,740*

crowded [*adj*] *busy, congested*
awash, brimful, brimming, chock-full, clean,
close, compact, crammed, cramped, crushed,
dense, elbow-to-elbow*, filled to the rafters*, fit
to bust*, full, full house*, full up*, huddled,
jammed, jam-packed*, loaded, lousy with*,
massed, mobbed, mob scene*, overflowing,
packed, populous, sardined*, sold out, SRO*,
standing room only*, stiff with*, stuffed, swarming, teeming, thick, thickset, thronged, tight,
topped off, up to here*, up to the hilt*, wall-to-
wall*; SEE CONCEPTS *481,483,774*

crown [*n1*] *top; best*
acme, apex, climax, crest, culmination,
fastigium, head, meridian, peak, perfection, pinnacle, roof, summit, tip, top, ultimate, vertex,
zenith; SEE CONCEPTS *706,836*

crown [*n2*] *tiara for royalty*
chaplet, circlet, coronal, coronet, diadem, garland, headband, headdress, wreath; SEE CONCEPT
452

crown [*n3*] *royalty*
crowned head, monarch, monarchy, potentate,
ruler, sovereign, sovereignty, supreme ruler, the
throne; SEE CONCEPT *422*

crown [*v1*] *reward, dignify*
adorn, arm, authorize, commission, coronate,
delegate, determine, dower, enable, endow,
endue, ennoble, enthrone, erect, establish, exalt,
festoon, fix, heighten, honor, inaugurate, induct,
install, invest, raise, sanction, settle, set up, stabilize, strengthen; SEE CONCEPTS *50,69,88*

crown [*v2*] *be the culmination of*
cap, climax, complete, consummate, crest, finish,
fulfill, perfect, put finishing touch on, round off,
surmount, terminate, top, top off; SEE CONCEPTS
234,706

crown [*v3*] *hit, usually on head*
biff, box, cuff, knock, punch, smite, strike; SEE
CONCEPT *189*

crowning [*adj*] *climactic*
consummate, culminating, excellent, final, paramount, principal, sovereign, supreme, ultimate;
SEE CONCEPTS *531,548*

crucial [*adj*] *critical, important*
acute, central, clamorous, climacteric, climatic,
compelling, deciding, decisive, desperate, dire,
essential, hanging by thread*, high-priority, imperative, insistent, momentous, necessary, on
thin ice*, pivotal, pressing, searching, show-

down*, touch and go*, touchy, urgent, vital; SEE
CONCEPT *568*

crucify [*v1*] *execute; torture near to death*
excruciate, hang, harrow, kill, martyr, martyrize,
nail to cross, persecute, rack, torment, torture;
SEE CONCEPT *252*

crucify [*v2*] *browbeat, destroy with words*
afflict, agonize, bedevil, bother, harrow, ill-treat,
lampoon, pan, ridicule, smite, tear to pieces*,
torment, torture, try, wipe the floor with*; SEE
CONCEPTS *7,19,52*

crude [*adj1*] *vulgar, unpolished in manner*
awkward, backward, barnyard*, boorish, cheap,
cloddish, clumsy, coarse, crass, dirty, earthy,
filthy, foul, grody*, gross*, ignorant, ill-bred, indecent, indelicate, inelegant, insensible, lewd,
loud, loud-mouthed, loutish, lowbred, oafish, obscene, raunchy*, raw, rough, rude, savage,
smutty*, tacky*, tactless, uncouth, unenlightened, ungainly, unskillful; SEE CONCEPTS
267,401

crude [*adj2*] *unrefined, natural*
amateurish, callow, coarse, green, harsh, homemade, homespun, immature, impure, inexpert, in
the rough*, makeshift, outline, prentice, primitive, raw, rough, rough-hewn, rude, rudimentary,
rustic, simple, sketchy, thick, undeveloped, unfinished, unformed, ungraded, unmatured, un-
milled, unpolished, unprepared, unprocessed,
unproficient, unsorted, untaught, untrained, un-
worked,   unwrought;   SEE   CONCEPTS
562,578,589,797

cruel [*adj*] *vicious, pitiless; causing pain*
atrocious, barbarous, bestial, bitter, bloodthirsty,
brutal, brutish, callous, cold-blooded, degenerate, demoniac, depraved, evil, excruciating, ferocious, fierce, flinty, hard, hard-hearted, harsh,
hateful, heartless, hellish, implacable, inexorable, inhuman, inhumane, malevolent, merciless, monstrous, painful, pernicious, poignant,
rancorous, relentless, revengeful, ruthless, sadistic, sinful, spiteful, tyrannical, unfeeling, unkind,
unnatural, unrelenting, vengeful, vicious, virulent, wicked; SEE CONCEPTS *401,570*

cruelty [*n*] *brutality, harshness*
animality, barbarism, barbarity, bestiality, bloodthirstiness, brutishness, callousness, coarseness, coldness, depravity, despotism, ferocity,
fiendishness,   fierceness,   hard-heartedness,
heartlessness, inhumanity, insensibility, insensi-
tiveness,   malice,   malignity,   masochism,
mercilessness, murderousness, persecution, rancor, ruthlessness, sadism, savageness, savagery,
severity, spite, spitefulness, torture, truculence,
unfeelingness, unkindness, venom, viciousness,
wickedness; SEE CONCEPT *633*

cruise [*n*] *sailing expedition*
boat trip, crossing, jaunt, journey, sail, sailing,
sea trip, voyage; SEE CONCEPTS *224,292,363*

cruise [*v*] *sail*
boat, coast, drift, fare, gad, gallivant, go, hie,
jaunt, journey, keep steady pace, meander, navigate, pass, proceed, push on, repair, travel, voyage, wander about, wend; SEE CONCEPTS
147,151,159,224

crumb [*n*] *tiny bit, morsel*
atom, dab, dash, dram, drop, grain, iota, jot,
mite, ounce, particle, pinch, scrap, seed, shred,
sliver, smidgen, snippet, soupçon, speck; SEE
CONCEPT *831*

crumble [v] *break or fall into pieces*
break up, collapse, crumb, crush, decay, decompose, degenerate, deteriorate, disintegrate, dissolve, fragment, go to pieces, granulate, grind, molder, perish, powder, pulverize, putrefy, triturate, tumble; SEE CONCEPTS *181,248,469*

crumbly [*adj*] *brittle*
breakable, corroded, crisp, crunchy, decayed, degenerated, deteriorated, deteriorating, disintegrated, eroded, fragile, frail, frangible, friable, oxidized, perishing, powdery, pulverizable, rotted, rotten, rusted, shivery, short, soft, worn; SEE CONCEPTS *485,606*

crummy [*adj*] *lousy*
cheap, contemptible, crappy*, grotty, inferior, miserable, pathetic, poor, rotten, second-rate, shabby, sub-par, third-rate, useless, worthless; SEE CONCEPT *571*

crumple [v] *make or become wrinkled*
break down, buckle, cave in, collapse, crease, crimp, crimple, crinkle, crush, fall, fold, give way, go to pieces, pucker, rimple, ruck, rumple, screw, scrunch, shrivel, wad, wrinkle; SEE CONCEPTS *184,208,252*

crunch [n] *crucial point*
crisis, critical point, crux, difficulty, emergency, hour of decision*, moment of truth*, problem, test, trouble, trying time*; SEE CONCEPTS *388,674,675*

crunch [v] *grind, chew*
beat, bite, champ, chaw, chomp, crush, gnaw, masticate, munch, ruminate, scrunch; SEE CONCEPTS *169,186*

crunchy [*adj*] *brittle*
chewy, crackling, crisp, crispy, crumbly, crusty; SEE CONCEPT *606*

crusade [n] *campaign for cause*
cause, demonstration, drive, evangelism, expedition, holy war, jihad, march, movement, push; SEE CONCEPT *300*

crush [n1] *crowd of animate beings*
drove, gathering, horde, huddle, jam, multitude, party, press, push, throng, tumult; SEE CONCEPTS *417,432*

crush [n2] *infatuation*
beguin, desire, flame, love affair, passion, puppy love*, torch; SEE CONCEPT *20*

crush [v1] *compress, smash*
beat, bray, break, bruise, buck, comminute, contriturate, contuse, crease, crowd, crumble, crunch, embrace, enfold, express, hug, jam, kablooey*, mash, pound, powder, press, pulverize, push, romp, rumple, squash, squeeze, squish, total*, trample, tread, triturate, wrinkle; SEE CONCEPTS *208,219,246,252*

crush [v2] *defeating soundly*
annihilate, bear down, beat, blot out*, blow away*, conquer, defeat, demolish, extinguish, force down, ice*, kill, obliterate, overcome, overpower, overwhelm, quelch, quell, reduce, ruin, squelch, stamp out*, strangle, subdue, subjugate, suppress, vanquish, wreck; SEE CONCEPTS *95,252*

crush [v3] *humiliate*
abash, browbeat, chagrin, dispose of, dump, hurt, mortify, overwhelm, put away*, put down*, quash, quell, shame, suppress; SEE CONCEPTS *7,19*

crust [n] *stiff outer layer; coating*
band, bloom, border, caking, coat, concretion, covering, edge, encrustation, film, hull, incrustation, integument, layer, outside, rind, scab, shell, skin, surface, verge; SEE CONCEPT *484*

crusty [*adj1*] *irritable, often due to old age*
abrupt, bluff, blunt, brief, brusque, cantankerous, captious, choleric, crabbed, crabby*, cranky, cross, curt, dour, gruff, harsh, ill-humored, irascible, peevish, prickly, sarcastic, saturnine, scornful, short, short-tempered, snappish, snarling, snippety, snippy, splenetic, surly, testy, touchy, vinegary*; SEE CONCEPT *401*

crusty [*adj2*] *brittle on outside*
crisp, crispy, crunchy, friable, hard, short, well-baked, well-done; SEE CONCEPTS *462,606*

crux [n] *most important part*
body, bottom line*, core, decisive point, essence, gist, heart, kernel, matter, meat*, meat and potatoes*, nitty-gritty, nub, pith, purport, substance, thrust; SEE CONCEPTS *668,826*

cry [n1] *weeping and making sad sounds*
bawl, bawling, bewailing, blubber, blubbering, howl, howling, keening, lament, lamentation, mourning, shedding tears, snivel, snivelling, sob, sobbing, sorrowing, tears, the blues*, wailing, weep, whimpering, yowl; SEE CONCEPTS *77,469*

cry [n2] *calling out; yelling*
acclamation, bark, bawl, bay, bellow, cackle, call, caw, chatter, cheer, clack, clamor, cluck, coo, crow, ejaculation, exclamation, expletive, fuss, gobble, groan, grunt, hiss, holler, hoot, howl, hullabaloo, hurrah, meow, mewling, moo, motto, nicker, note, outcry, pipe, quack, report, roar, ruckus, scream, screech, shout, shriek, song, squall, squawk, squeak, trill, uproar, vociferation, wail, whine, whinny, whistle, whoop, yammer, yawp*, yell, yelp, yoo-hoo; SEE CONCEPTS *47,77,278*

cry [v1] *weep and make sad sounds*
bawl, bemoan, bewail, blub, blubber, boohoo*, break down, burst into tears*, caterwaul, choke up, complain, crack up*, deplore, dissolve in tears*, fret, grieve, groan, howl, keen, lament, let go, let it all out*, mewl, moan, mourn, put on the weeps*, regret, ring the blues*, shed bitter tears*, shed tears, sigh, sniff, snivel, sob, sorrow, squall, turn on waterworks*, wail, weep, whimper, whine, yammer, yowl; SEE CONCEPTS *77,469*

cry [v2] *call out, yell*
bark, bawl, bay, bellow, bleat, cackle, call, caw, chatter, cheer, clack, clamor, cluck, coo, croak, crow, ejaculate, exclaim, gabble, growl, grunt, hail, hiss, holler, holler out, hoot, howl, low, meow, moo, nicker, pipe, quack, roar, scream, screech, shout, shriek, sing out, snarl, squawk, trill, tweet, twitter, vociferate, whinny, whistle, whoop, yawp*, yelp; SEE CONCEPTS *47,77*

cry [v3] *advertise*
announce, bark*, broadcast, build up, hawk, hype*, press-agent*, proclaim, promulgate, publicize, publish, puff*, trumpet*; SEE CONCEPT *324*

crybaby [n] *malcontent*
bellyacher, cissy, complainer, critic, faultfinder, griper, grumbler, moaner, softy*, whiner, wimp*, wuss*; SEE CONCEPT *412*

crypt [n] *burial place*
catacomb, cave, cavern, cell, chamber, compartment, grave, grotto, mausoleum, room, sepulcher, tomb, undercroft, vault; SEE CONCEPT *305*

cr
cr

cryptic [*adj*] *secret; obscure in meaning*
abstruse, ambiguous, apocryphal, arcane, cabbalistic, dark, Delphian, Delphic, enigmatic, equivocal, esoteric, evasive, hidden, incomprehensible, inexplicable, murky, mysterious, mystic, mystical, mystifying, occult, opaque, oracular, perplexing, puzzling, recondite, secretive, strange, tenebrous, unclear, unfathomable, uninformative, vague, veiled; SEE CONCEPTS *267,576,682*

crystal [*adj*] *clear, transparent*
clear-cut, limpid, lucent, lucid, luminous, pellucid, translucent, transpicuous, unblurred; SEE CONCEPTS *617,618*

cubicle [*n*] *office compartment*
booth, cell, chamber, cubbyhole, desk, nook, office, pigeonhole, room, stall, work area; SEE CONCEPT *434*

cuddle [*v*] *hold fondly, closely*
bundle, burrow, caress, clasp, cosset, curl up, dandle, embrace, enfold, feel up*, fondle, huddle, hug, kiss, love, nestle, nuzzle, pet, snug, snuggle, touch; SEE CONCEPTS *190,375*

cuddly [*adj*] *huggable, embraceable*
caressible, cuddlesome, kissable, lovable, plump, snuggly, soft, warm; SEE CONCEPT *485*

cudgel [*n*] *baton for hitting*
bastinado, bat, billy*, billyclub, birch, blackjack, bludgeon, cane, club, cosh*, ferule, mace, nightstick, paddle, rod, sap, shill, shillelagh, spontoon, stick, switch, truncheon; SEE CONCEPT *500*

cue [*n*] *signal to act*
catchword, clue, hint, hot lead*, idea, indication, inkling, innuendo, in the wind*, intimation, job, key, lead, mnemonic, nod, notion, prod, prompt, prompting, reminder, sign, suggestion, telltale*, tip-off, warning; SEE CONCEPTS *278,284,628*

cuff [*n*] *beating with hands*
belt, biff, box, buffet, chop, clip, clout, hit, knock, poke, punch, rap, slap, smack, sock, thump, wallop, whack; SEE CONCEPT *189*

cuff [*v*] *beat with hands*
bat, belt, biff, box, buffet, clap, clobber*, clout, hit, knock, pummel, punch, slap, smack, spank, thump, whack; SEE CONCEPT *189*

cuisine [*n*] *food*
cooking, dishes, eats*, fare, grub*, meal, menu; SEE CONCEPT *459*

cull [*v1*] *pick out for reason*
choose, discriminate, elect, extract, glean, mark, optate, opt for, pluck, prefer, select, sift, single out, take, thin, thin out, winnow; SEE CONCEPTS *41,142*

cull [*v2*] *gather*
accumulate, amass, collect, extract, garner, glean, pick up, round up; SEE CONCEPT *109*

culminate [*v*] *come to a climax*
cap, climax, close, come to a head*, conclude, crown, end, end up, finish, go over the mountain*, go the route*, rise to crescendo, round off, shoot one's wad*, terminate, top off*, wind up*; SEE CONCEPT *119*

culmination [*n*] *conclusion; climactic stage*
acme, all the way*, apex, apogee, blow off*, capper*, climax, completion, consummation, critical mass, crown, crowning touch, finale, finish, height, limit, maximum, meridian, ne plus ultra, noon, payoff, peak, perfection, pinnacle, punch line*, summit, top, zenith; SEE CONCEPTS *230,635,676*

culpable [*adj*] *responsible for action*
amiss, answerable, at fault, blamable, blameful, blameworthy, caught, caught in the act*, caught red-handed*, censurable, demeritorious, dirty, found wanting, guilty, hung up, impeachable, indictable, in the wrong, liable, off base, out of line*, punishable, reprehensible, responsible, sinful, smoking gun*, to blame, unholy, wrong; SEE CONCEPTS *404,545*

culprit [*n*] *person responsible for wrongdoing*
con, convict, criminal, delinquent, evildoer, excon, felon, fugitive, guilty party, jailbird*, malefactor, miscreant, offender, rascal, sinner, transgressor, wrongdoer, yardbird*; SEE CONCEPT *412*

cult [*n1*] *group sharing belief*
band, body, church, clan, clique, creed, denomination, faction, faith, following, party, persuasion, religion, school, sect; SEE CONCEPTS *369,387*

cult [*n2*] *worship; form of ceremony*
admiration, ceremony, craze, creed, cultus, devotion, faddism, faith, idolization, liturgy, persuasion, religion, reverence, rite, ritual, veneration; SEE CONCEPTS *410,689*

cultivate [*v1*] *develop land for growing*
breed, crop, dress, farm, fertilize, garden, harvest, labor, manage, mature, plant, plow, prepare, propagate, raise, ripen, seed, tend, till, work; SEE CONCEPTS *253,257*

cultivate [*v2*] *enrich situation; give special attention*
advance, ameliorate, better, bolster, bring on, brownnose*, butter up*, cherish, civilize, court, develop, discipline, elevate, encourage, enrich, foster, further, get in with*, get next to*, get on good side of*, improve, nourish, nurse, nurture, play up to*, polish, promote, refine, run after, seek friendship, shine up to*, suck up to*, take pains with, train; SEE CONCEPTS *244,384*

cultivate [*v3*] *nurture, take care of*
aid, ameliorate, better, cherish, devote oneself to, educate, encourage, forward, foster, further, help, improve, instruct, nurse, patronize, promote, pursue, raise, rear, refine, support, teach, train; SEE CONCEPTS *110,295*

cultivation [*n1*] *development of land for growing*
agrology, agronomics, agronomy, farming, gardening, horticulture, planting, plowing, tillage, tilling, working; SEE CONCEPT *257*

cultivation [*n2*] *culture, sophistication, education*
advancement, aestheticism, breeding, civility, civilization, delicacy, discernment, discrimination, enlightenment, gentility, good taste, grounding, improvement, learning, letters, manners, polish, progress, refined taste, refinement, schooling, taste; SEE CONCEPTS *411,655,673*

cultivation [*n3*] *nurture, help*
advancement, advocacy, development, encouragement, enhancement, fostering, furtherance, patronage, promotion, support; SEE CONCEPTS *110,657*

cultural [*adj*] *educational, enlightening*
adorning, advancing, artistic, beautifying, beneficial, broadening, civilizing, constructive, corrective, developmental, dignifying, disciplining, edifying, educative, elevating, ennobling, enriching, expanding, glorifying, helpful, humane, humanizing, influential, inspirational, instructive,

learned, liberal, liberalizing, nurturing, ornamenting, polishing, promoting, raising, refined, refining, regenerative, socializing, stimulating, uplifting, widening; SEE CONCEPTS *537,555,589*

culture [*n1*] *breeding, education, sophistication*
ability, accomplishment, address, aestheticism, art, capacity, civilization, class, courtesy, cultivation, delicacy, dignity, discrimination, dress, elegance, elevation, enlightenment, erudition, experience, fashion, finish, gentility, good taste, grace, improvement, kindness, learning, manners, nobility, perception, polish, politeness, practice, proficiency, refinement, savoir-faire, science, skill, tact, training, urbanity; SEE CONCEPTS *388,633,678*

culture [*n2*] *ideas, values of a people*
arts and sciences, civilization, convention, customs, development, ethnology, folklore, folkways, grounding, habit, humanism, knowledge, lifestyle, mores, society, the arts, way of life; SEE CONCEPTS *388,689*

culture [*n3*] *development of land*
agriculture, agrology, agronomics, agronomy, cultivation, farming, gardening, raising, tending; SEE CONCEPT *257*

cultured [*adj*] *well-bred, experienced*
able, accomplished, advanced, aesthetic, appreciative, au courant, blue-stocking*, chivalrous, civilized, courteous, cultivated, distingue, educated, elegant, enlightened, erudite, gallant, genteel, highbrow*, high-class, informed, intellectual, intelligent, knowledgeable, lettered, liberal, literary, literate, mannerly, polished, polite, refined, savant, scholarly, sensitive, sophisticated, tasteful, tolerant, traveled, understanding, up-to-date, urbane, versed, well-informed; SEE CONCEPT *550*

culvert [*n*] *ditch for flow of water*
canal, channel, conduit, drain, duct, gutter, pipe, watercourse; SEE CONCEPT *509*

cumbersome [*adj*] *clumsy, awkward*
bulky, burdensome, clunker, clunking, clunky, cumbrous, embarrassing, galumphing, heavy, hefty, incommodious, inconvenient, leaden, massive, oppressive, ponderous, tiresome, unhandy, unmanageable, unwieldy, wearisome, weighty; SEE CONCEPTS *544,773*

cumulative [*adj*] *accruing; growing in size or effect*
accumulative, additive, additory, advancing, aggregate, amassed, augmenting, chain, collective, heaped, heightening, increasing, increscent, intensifying, magnifying, multiplying, snowballing*, summative; SEE CONCEPTS *540,548,786*

cunning [*adj1*] *devious*
acute, artful, astute, cagey, canny, crafty, crazy like fox*, deep, fancy footwork*, foxy, guileful, insidious, keen, knowing, Machiavellian, sharp, shifty, shrewd, slick, slippery, sly, sly boots*, smart, smarts, smooth, street-smart*, streetwise*, subtle, tricky, wary, wily; SEE CONCEPTS *401,545*

cunning [*adj2*] *imaginative*
able, adroit, canny, clever, crackerjack*, deft, dexterous, ingenious, intelligent, masterful, skillful, slighty, sly, smart, smooth, subtle, well-laid, well-planned; SEE CONCEPT *402*

cup [*n*] *container for drinking*
beaker, bowl, cannikin, chalice, cupful, demitasse, draught, drink, goblet, grail, mug, potion,

stein, taster, teacup, tumbler, vessel; SEE CONCEPT *494*

cupboard [*n*] *storage cabinet*
buffet, closet, depository, facility, locker, press, repository, sideboard, storeroom, wardrobe; SEE CONCEPT *443*

cupidity [*n*] *greed, strong desire*
acquisitiveness, avarice, avariciousness, avidity, covetousness, craving, eagerness, graspingness, greediness, hunger, infatuation, itching*, longing, lust, passion, possessiveness, rapaciousness, rapacity, voracity, yearning; SEE CONCEPTS *20,709*

cur [*n1*] *rotten, lowly animate being*
blackguard, black sheep*, bum, cad, coward, dog*, good-for-nothing*, heel*, hound*, ne'er-do-well*, rat*, riffraff*, scoundrel, scum*, skunk*, snake*, stinker*, toad*, villain, worm*, wretch, yellow dog*; SEE CONCEPTS *389,412*

cur [*n2*] *animal of mixed breed*
crossbreed, hybrid, mongrel, mutt; SEE CONCEPT *394*

curable [*adj*] *able to be improved, fixed*
amenable, capable, correctable, corrigible, healable, improvable, mendable, not hopeless, not too bad, reparative, restorable, subject to cure; SEE CONCEPTS *314,485*

curative [*adj*] *healing, health-giving*
alleviative, beneficial, corrective, curing, healthful, helpful, invigorating, medicable, medicative, medicinal, pick-me-up*, remedial, remedying, restorative, salutary, sanative, shot in the arm*, therapeutic, tonic, vulnerary, what the doctor ordered*, wholesome; SEE CONCEPTS *314,537*

curator [*n*] *caretaker of collection*
administrator, conservator, custodian, director, guardian, keeper, manager, steward; SEE CONCEPT *348*

curb [*n*] *restraining device; check*
barrier, border, brake, bridle, chain, control, deterrent, edge, harness, hindrance, ledge, limitation, lip, rein, restrainer, restraint, restriction, rim; SEE CONCEPTS *376,497,652,745*

curb [*v*] *repress, restrict*
abstain, bit, bottle up*, box in, bridle, bring to screeching halt*, check, clog, constrain, contain, control, cook*, cool down, cool off, deny, entrammel, fetter, hamper, hinder, hobble, hogtie*, hold back, hold down, hold in, ice*, impede, inhibit, keep lid on*, keep tight rein on*, leash, manacle, moderate, muzzle, refrain, rein in, restrain, retard, scrub*, send up, shackle, subdue, suppress, tame, tie, tie up, withhold; SEE CONCEPTS *121,130*

curdle [*n*] *sour; change into coagulated substance*
acerbate, acidify, acidulate, clabber, clot, coagulate, condense, congeal, curd, ferment, go off, spoil, thicken, turn, turn sour; SEE CONCEPT *456*

cure [*n*] *solution to problem, often health*
aid, alleviation, antidote, assistance, catholicon, corrective, counteractant, counteragent, countermeasure, drug, elixir, elixir vitae, fix, healing, healing agent, help, medicament, medicant, medication, medicine, nostrum, panacea, pharmacon, physic, placebo, proprietary, quick fix*, recovery, redress, remedy, reparation, restorative, therapeutic, treatment; SEE CONCEPTS *110,307,311*

cr
cu

cure [*v1*] *heal, ease bad situation*
alleviate, ameliorate, attend, better, cold turkey*, correct, doctor, dose, dress, dry out*, help, improve, kick, kick the habit*, make better, make healthy, make whole, medicate, mend, minister to, nurse, palliate, quit cold*, rectify, redress, rehabilitate, relieve, remedy, repair, restore, restore to health, right, shake, sweat it out*, treat; SEE CONCEPTS *126,244,310*

cure [*v2*] *cook, age food*
dry, fire, harden, keep, kipper, pickle, preserve, salt, smoke, steel, temper; SEE CONCEPT *170*

curio [*n*] *knickknack*
antique, bauble, bibelot, bygone, collectible, collector's item, objet d'art, toy, trifle, trinket, whatnot; SEE CONCEPT *446*

curiosity [*n1*] *intense desire to know, understand*
concern, eagerness, inquiring mind, inquiringness, inquisitiveness, interest, interestingness, intrusiveness, investigation, meddlesomeness, meddling, mental acquisitiveness, nosiness, officiousness, prying, questioning, regard, searching, snoopiness, snooping, thirst for knowledge; SEE CONCEPTS *20,410*

curiosity [*n2*] *odd item*
anomaly, bibelot, bygone, conversation piece, curio, exoticism, freak, knickknack, marvel, monstrosity, nonesuch, objet d'art, oddity, peculiar object, prodigy, rarity, singular object, trinket, unusual object, wonder; SEE CONCEPT *260*

curious [*adj1*] *desiring knowledge, understanding*
analytical, disquisitive, examining, impertinent, inquiring, inquisitive, inspecting, interested, interfering, intrusive, investigative, meddlesome, meddling, nosy, peeping, peering, prurient, prying, puzzled, questioning, scrutinizing, searching, snoopy*, tampering; SEE CONCEPTS *403,542*

curious [*adj2*] *very odd*
bizarre, exotic, extraordinary, marvelous, mysterious, novel, oddball, peculiar, puzzling, quaint, queer, rare, remarkable, singular, strange, unconventional, unexpected, unique, unorthodox, unusual, weird, wonderful; SEE CONCEPTS *547,564*

curl [*n*] *loop, ringlet, curve*
coil, crimp, crispation, curlicue, flourish, frizz, kink, quirk, spiral, swirl, twist, wave, whorl; SEE CONCEPTS *418,436*

curl [*v*] *bend, loop*
buckle, coil, contort, convolute, corkscrew, crimp, crinkle, crisp, crook, curve, entwine, fold, form into ringlets, frizz, indent, kink, lap, meander, ringlet, ripple, roll, scallop, snake, spiral, swirl, turn, twine, twirl, twist, undulate, wave, wind, wreathe, writhe, zigzag; SEE CONCEPTS *147,184,213*

curly [*adj*] *looping, forming ringlets*
coiled, convoluted, corkscrew, crimped, crimpy, crinkling, crinkly, crisp, curled, curling, frizzed, frizzy, fuzzy, kinky, looped, permed, spiralled, waved, waving, wavy, winding, wound; SEE CONCEPTS *406,486*

currency [*n*] *paper and coin money of a country*
almighty dollar*, bills, bread*, cabbage*, cash, chicken feed*, coinage, coins, cold cash*, dinero*, dough*, folding money, green stuff*, legal tender, medium of exchange, moolah*, notes, piece of change*, roll*, specie, wad*; SEE CONCEPT *340*

current [*adj*] *contemporary; common*
accepted, accustomed, afoot, circulating, common knowledge, customary, cutting-edge*, doing, existent, extant, fad, fashionable, general, going around, hot*, in, in circulation, in progress, instant, in the mainstream, in the news, in use, in vogue, leading-edge*, mod*, modern, now*, on front burner*, ongoing, popular, present, present-day, prevailing, prevalent, rampant, regnant, rife, ruling, state-of-the-art, swinging, topical, trendy, up-to-date, widespread; SEE CONCEPTS *530,820*

current [*n*] *flow of something, usually water*
course, draught, drift, ebb and flow, flood, flux, jet, juice, progression, river, run, rush, spate, stream, tidal motion, tide; SEE CONCEPTS *514,519,738*

curse [*n1*] *hateful, swearing remark*
anathema, ban, bane, blaspheming, blasphemy, commination, cursing, cussing*, cuss word*, damning, denunciation, dirty name*, dirty word*, double whammy*, execration, expletive, four-letter word*, fulmination, imprecation, malediction, malison, naughty words*, no-no*, oath, objuration, obloquy, obscenity, profanation, profanity, sacrilege, swearing, swear word, vilification, whammy*; SEE CONCEPTS *54,278*

curse [*n2*] *misfortune wished upon someone*
affliction, bane, burden, calamity, cancer, cross, disaster, evil, evil eye*, hydra, jinx, ordeal, pestilence, plague, scourge, torment, tribulation, trouble, vexation, voodoo; SEE CONCEPTS *674,675*

cursed [*adj1*] *damned, doomed for bad ending*
accursed, bedeviled, blankety-blank*, blasted, blessed, blighted, cast out, confounded, doggone*, excommunicate, execrable, fey, foredoomed, hell fire*, ill-fated, infernal, snakebit*, star-crossed, unholy, unsanctified, villainous, voodooed*; SEE CONCEPTS *548,571*

cursed [*adj2*] *detestable, hateful*
abominable, accursed, atrocious, damnable, devilish, disgusting, execrable, fiendish, flatitous, heinous, infamous, infernal, loathsome, odious, pernicious, pestilential, vile; SEE CONCEPTS *404,571*

cursory [*adj*] *casual, hasty*
brief, careless, depthless, desultory, fast, half-assed*, half-baked*, haphazard, hit or miss*, hurried, offhand, passing, perfunctory, quick, random, rapid, shallow, short, sketchy, slapdash, slight, sloppy, speedy, summary, superficial, swift, uncritical; SEE CONCEPTS *562,588,589*

curt [*adj*] *abrupt, rude*
blunt, breviloquent, brief, brusque, churlish, compendiary, compendious, concise, crusty, gruff, imperious, laconic, offhand, peremptory, pithy, sharp, short, short and sweet, snappish, snippety, snippy, succinct, summary, tart, terse, unceremonious, uncivil, ungracious; SEE CONCEPT *267*

curtail [*v*] *cut short; abridge*
abbreviate, boil down, chop, clip, contract, cramp, cut, cut back, decrease, diminish, dock, downsize, get to meat*, halt, lessen, lop, minify, pare down, put in nutshell*, reduce, retrench, roll back, shorten, slash, trim, truncate; SEE CONCEPTS *130,236,247*

curtain [*n*] *window covering*
blind, decoration, drape, drapery, film, hanging,

jalousie, oleo, portiere, rag, roller, screen, shade, shield, shroud, shutter, valance, veil, Venetian blind; SEE CONCEPT *444*

curtains [*n*] *the end*
bitter end, death, end of life, end of the line*, exit, extinction, lights out*, taps*; SEE CONCEPTS *195,304*

curvaceous [*adj*] *voluptuous, full-figured*
bosomy, buxom, curvesome, curvilinear, curvy, rounded, shapely, statuesque, well-developed, well-proportioned, well-rounded, zaftig*; SEE CONCEPTS *406,490*

curvature [*n*] *rounded part of thing, usually body part*
arc, arch, arching, bend, bow, curve, curving, curvity, deflection, flexure, incurvation, round, shape; SEE CONCEPTS *754,757*

curve [*n*] *arched, rounded line or object*
ambit, arc, arch, bend, bight, bow, camber, catenary, chord, circle, circuit, circumference, compass, concavity, contour, crook, curlicue, curvation, curvature, ellipse, festoon, flexure, hairpin, half-moon, helix, horseshoe, hyperbola, incurvation, incurvature, loop, meniscus, ogee, parabola, quirk, rondure, round, sinuosity, sweep, swerve, trajectory, turn, vault, whorl; SEE CONCEPT *436*

curve [*v*] *bending in a shape or course*
arc, arch, bend, bow, buckle, bulge, coil, concave, convex, crook, crumple, curl, deviate, divert, gyrate, hook, incurve, inflect, loop, round, skew, snake, spiral, stoop, swerve, turn, twist, veer, wind, wreathe; SEE CONCEPTS *147,184,213,738*

curved [*adj*] *bowed, bent*
arced, arched, arciform, arrondi, biflected, circular, compass, crooked, curly, curvaceous, curvilinear, declinate, elliptical, enbowed, humped, incurvate, incurved, looped, loopy, round, rounded, serpentine, sigmoid, sinuous, skewed, snaky, S-shaped, sweeping, swirly, turned, twisted, twisting, twisty, wreathed; SEE CONCEPTS *486,490*

cushion [*n*] *pillow, pad*
beanbag, bolster, buffer, bumper, fender, hassock, headrest, mat, rest, seat, sham, squab, woolsack; SEE CONCEPTS *444,464,484*

cushion [*v*] *pad, protect from blow*
bolster, buttress, cradle, dampen, deaden, insulate, muffle, pillow, seclude, soften, stifle, support, suppress; SEE CONCEPT *680*

cushy [*adj*] *lush, comfortable*
agreeable, comfy*, easy, pleasant, plum, soft*, undemanding; SEE CONCEPT *334*

custodian [*n*] *caretaker, maintenance person*
baby sitter, bodyguard, cerebus, claviger, cleaner, cleaning person, concierge, curator, escort, guardian, housesitter, keeper, maintenance person, manager, overseer, protector, sitter, steward, super*, superintendent, supervisor, swamper*, warden, watchdog, watchperson; SEE CONCEPT *348*

custody [*n1*] *supervision, charge of something*
aegis, auspices, care, conservation, custodianship, guardianship, keeping, management, observation, preservation, protection, safekeeping, salvation, superintendence, trusteeship, tutelage, ward, wardship, watch; SEE CONCEPTS *117,376,710*

custody [*n2*] *confinement, jailing*
arrest, detention, duress, imprisonment, incarceration, jail, keeping; SEE CONCEPTS *90,691*

custom [*n1*] *habitual action*
addiction, beaten path*, characteristic, consuetude, daily grind*, fashion, form, grind*, groove, habit, habitude, hang-up*, into*, manner, matter of course, mode, observance, practice, praxis, precedent, procedure, proprieties, routine, rule, second nature*, shot, swim, thing, trick, usage, use, way, wont; SEE CONCEPT *633*

custom [*n2*] *ritual, traditional action*
attitude, canon, ceremony, character, convention, conventionalism, design, dictates, established way, etiquette, fashion, folkways, form, formality, inheritance, manner, matter of course, method, mode, mold, mores, observance, observation, pattern, performance, policy, practice, praxis, precedent, precept, rite, routine, rule, second nature*, style, system, taste, type, unwritten law, unwritten rule, usage, use, vogue, way; SEE CONCEPTS *644,688*

customarily [*adv*] *ordinarily; as a rule*
as a matter of course, as usual, commonly, consistently, conventionally, frequently, generally, habitually, naturally, normally, regularly, routinely, traditionally, usually, wontedly; SEE CONCEPTS *530,547*

customary [*adj*] *usual, established*
accepted, according to Hoyle*, accustomed, acknowledged, by the numbers*, chronic, common, confirmed, conventional, established, everyday, familiar, fashionable, frequent, general, habitual, household, in a rut*, in the groove*, normal, ordinary, orthodox, playing it safe*, popular, prescriptive, recognized, regular, regulation, routine, same old*, SOP*, standard, standard operating procedure*, stipulated, traditional, understood, universal, wonted; SEE CONCEPTS *530,547*

customer [*n*] *buyer of goods, services*
client, clientele, consumer, habitué, patron, prospect, purchaser, regular shopper; SEE CONCEPT *348*

cut [*n1*] *incision*
carving, chip, chop, cleavage, cleft, dissection, fissure, furrow, gash, graze, groove, intersection, kerf, laceration, mark, nick, nip, notch, opening, passage, penetration, pierce, prick, rabbet, rent, rip, scarification, sculpture, section, shave, slash, slit, slot, snip, stab, stroke, trench, trim, wound; SEE CONCEPT *309*

cut [*n2*] *reduction, diminution*
cutback, decrease, decrement, downsize, economy, fall, lessening, lowering, reduction, saving; SEE CONCEPTS *698,776*

cut [*n3*] *portion of profit*
allotment, allowance, bite, chop*, division, kickback*, lot, member, moiety, part, partage, percentage, piece, quota, section, segment, share, slice; SEE CONCEPT *344*

cut [*n4*] *style, shape of clothing*
configuration, construction, fashion, figure, form, look, mode; SEE CONCEPTS *655,754*

cut [*n5*] *insult*
abuse, hateful remark, indignity, offense; SEE CONCEPT *52*

cut [*n6*] *type, kind*
cast, description, feather, ilk, lot, mold, sort, stamp; SEE CONCEPT *378*

CU
CU

cut [*v1*] *sever, chop with sharp instrument; incise*
amputate, behead, bisect, bite, carve, chine, chip, chisel, cleave, clip, crop, curtail, decussate, dice, dispatch, dissect, dissever, divide, facet, fell, flitch, gash, guillotine, hack, hash, hew, hew, intersect, lacerate, lay open, level, lop, lop, massacre, mince, mow, mow, mow down, nick, notch, part, penetrate, perforate, pierce, prune, puncture, quarter, rabbet, raze, reap, rend, rip, rive, saber, saw, scarify, scissor, score, scythe, separate, shave, shear, sickle, skive, slash, slaughter, slay, slice, slit, sliver, snip; SEE CONCEPT *252*

cut a deal [*v*] *make a deal*
bargain, barter, bicker, dicker*, do business, hammer out a deal*, negotiate, trade, work out a deal*; SEE CONCEPT *324*

cutback [*n*] *decrease*
abatement, belt-tightening, curtailment, decline, decrement, economy, lessening, lowering, reduction, reversal; SEE CONCEPT *698*

cute [*adj*] *perky, attractive*
adorable, beautiful, charming, dainty, delightful, pleasant, pretty; SEE CONCEPTS *404,579*

cut in [*v*] *interrupt*
break in, butt in*, chisel in*, horn in*, interfere, interpose, intervene, intrude, move in, obtrude; SEE CONCEPT *234*

cut off [*v1*] *prevent; interrupt*
block, break in, bring to end, catch, close off, disconnect, discontinue, halt, insulate, intercept, intersect, intervene, intrude, isolate, obstruct, renounce, segregate, separate, sequester, suspend; SEE CONCEPT *234*

cut off [*v2*] *disinherit in will*
cut out of will, disown, renounce; SEE CONCEPT *317*

cut out [*v*] *excise, remove*
carve, cease, delete, displace, eliminate, exclude, exsect, extirpate, extract, give up, oust, pull out, refrain from, sever, stop, supersede, supplant, usurp; SEE CONCEPT *211*

cut out for [*adj*] *adapted*
adequate, competent, designed, equipped, fit, fitted, good for, qualified, suitable, suited; SEE CONCEPT *558*

cut short [*v*] *bring to an end; leave unfinished*
abbreviate, abort, abridge, break off, check, diminish, end, finish, halt, hinder, intercept, interrupt, postpone, quit, shorten, stop, terminate; SEE CONCEPTS *121,234*

cutthroat [*adj*] *ruthless*
barbarous, bloodthirsty, cruel, dog-eat-dog*, ferocious, hard as nails*, merciless, pitiless, relentless, savage, unprincipled, vicious; SEE CONCEPTS *401,404*

cutting [*adj*] *nasty, hateful*
acerbic, acid, acrimonious, barbed, biting, bitter, caustic, clear-cut, crisp, hurtful, incisive, ingoing, malicious, penetrating, piercing, pointed, probing, raw, sarcastic, sardonic, scathing, severe, sharp, stinging, trenchant, wounding; SEE CONCEPT *267*

cutting edge [*n*] *newest technology*
advancement, avant-garde, fore, forefront, front line, innovation, invention, leading edge, new wave, point, vanguard; SEE CONCEPT *668*

cut up [*v1*] *make fun of; criticize*
censure, condemn, crucify, denounce, give a rough time*, knock, pan*, rap, reprehend, reprobate, ridicule, skin, vilify; SEE CONCEPT *52*

cut up [*v2*] *be rowdy*
act up, caper, carry on*, cavort, clown, fool around, joke, misbehave, play, play jokes, romp, roughhouse, show off, whoop it up*; SEE CONCEPT *384*

cut up [*v3*] *chop, mince*
carve, dice, divide, slice; SEE CONCEPT *176*

cybernetics [*n*] *science studying brain function to design analagous mechanical systems*
artificial intelligence, automatic technology, automation, autonetics, electronic communication, radiodynamics, robotization, telemechanics; SEE CONCEPTS *274,349*

cyberpunk [*n*] *computer hacker*
computer nerd, engineer, geek, hacker, programmer; SEE CONCEPT *348*

cyberspace [*n*] *computer world*
communications, computer network, data bank, data network, electronic highway, electronic mail, email, global village, infobahn*, information space, information superhighway*, information technology, Internet, online community, virtual community, virtual library, virtual reality, Web, World Wide Web, WWW; SEE CONCEPTS *349,770*

cycle [*n*] *era, phase*
aeon, age, alternation, chain, circle, circuit, course, eon, isochronism, loop, orbit, period, periodicity, revolution, rhythm, ring, rotation, round, run, sequel, sequence, series, succession, wheel; SEE CONCEPTS *816,817*

cynic [*n*] *nonbeliever*
carper, caviler, detractor, disbeliever, doubter, doubting Thomas*, egoist, egotist, flouter, misanthrope, misanthropist, misogamist, misogynist, mocker, pessimist, questioner, satirist, scoffer, skeptic, sneerer, unbeliever; SEE CONCEPTS *361,423*

cynical [*adj*] *nonbelieving; doubtful*
contemptuous, derisive, ironic, misanthropic, misanthropical, mocking, pessimistic, sarcastic, sardonic, scoffing, scornful, skeptical, sneering, suspicious, unbelieving, wry; SEE CONCEPTS *267,403*

cyst [*n*] *unusual growth*
bag, bleb, blister, injury, pouch, sac, sore, vesicle, wen; SEE CONCEPTS *306*

D

dab [*n*] *small quantity*
bit, blob, dollop, drop, fleck, flick, pat, peck, smidgen, smudge, speck, spot, stroke, tap, touch; SEE CONCEPT *835*

dab [*v*] *blot up; touch lightly*
bedaub, besmear, daub, pat, peck, plaster, smear, smudge, stipple, swab, tap, wipe; SEE CONCEPT *612*

dabble [*v*] *play at; tinker*
amuse oneself with, be amateur, dally, dillydally*, fiddle with*, flirt with*, horse around*, idle, kid around*, mess around*, monkey*, monkey around*, muck around*, not be serious*,

play, play around*, play games with, toy with, trifle, trifle with, work superficially; SEE CONCEPT 87

dabbler [n] *amateur*
abecedarian, beginner, dilettante, loafer, nonprofessional, novice, potterer, pretender, smatterer, tinkerer, trifler, tyro, uninitiate; SEE CONCEPTS 348,366

dad [n] *father*
daddy*, old man*, pa*, papa*, pappy*, parent, pop; SEE CONCEPTS 394,400,414,419,423

daffy [adj] *silly, crazy*
clownish, crackers*, daft, demented, deranged, dotty, foolish, goofy* loony*, nuts, nutty*; SEE CONCEPT 403

daft [adj] *stupid; crazy*
absurd, asinine, bedlamite, bonkers, cracked*, crackers*, daffy*, demented, deranged, dopey*, flaky*, foolish, fried*, giddy, half-baked*, idiotic, inane, insane, in the ozone*, lunatic, mad, mental*, nuts, nutty*, off the wall*, out of one's gourd*, ridiculous, screwy*, silly, simple, touched, unbalanced, unhinged*, unsound, wacky, whacko*, witless; SEE CONCEPT 403

dagger [n] *knife*
anlace, bayonet, blade, bodkin, cutlass, dirk, poniard, sidearm, skean, stiletto, stylet, switchblade, sword; SEE CONCEPTS 495,499

daily [adj] *occurring every day; during the day*
circadian, common, commonplace, constantly, cyclic, day after day, day by day, day-to-day, diurnal, everyday, from day to day, often, once a day, once daily, ordinary, per diem, periodic, quotidian, regular, regularly, routine; SEE CONCEPTS 541,801

dainty [adj1] *delicate, fragile, fine*
airy, attractive, beautiful, bonny, charming, choice, comely, cute, darling, delectable, delicious, delightful, diaphanous, elegant, ethereal, exquisite, fair, feeble, frail, graceful, lacy, light, lovely, neat, nice, palatable, petite, pleasing, precious, pretty, rare, recherché, refined, savory, select, soft, subtle, superior, sweet, tasteful, tasty, tender, thin, toothsome, trim, well-made; SEE CONCEPTS 490,491,606

dainty [adj2] *finicky, particular*
acute, choosy, delicate, fastidious, finical, finicking, fussy, mincing, nice, perceptive, persnickety*, refined, scrupulous, tasteful; SEE CONCEPT 404

dairy [n] *producer of milk products*
buttery, cow barn, creamery, dairy farm, factory, farm, pasteurizing plant; SEE CONCEPTS 449,517

dalliance [n1] *dawdling*
dabbling, delay, delaying, dilly-dallying*, frittering, frivoling, idling, loafing, loitering, playing, poking*, procrastinating, procrastination, puttering, toying, trifling; SEE CONCEPTS 151,210,681

dalliance [n2] *love affair*
affair, a little on the side*, amorous play, carrying on*, fling, fooling around*, frolicking, hanky-panky*, messing around*, relationship, seduction, toying*, working late at office*; SEE CONCEPTS 114,375,388

dally [v1] *dawdle, delay*
boondoggle*, drag, fool around, fool with, fritter away, hang about*, horse around*, idle, jerk off*, lag, linger, loiter, lollygag*, play around*, play games with*, procrastinate, put off, putter,

tarry, trail, trifle with, waste time, while away; SEE CONCEPTS 151,210,681

dally/dally with [v2] *have love affair*
be insincere with, carry on, cosset, fool around*, frivol, frolic, gambol, have a fling, lead on, play around*, rollick, romp, tamper, wanton; SEE CONCEPTS 114,375

dam [n] *embankment, wall*
bank, barrage, barrier, dike, ditch, gate, grade, hindrance, levee, milldam, millpond, obstruction, weir; SEE CONCEPT 470

dam [v] *hold back; block*
bar, barricade, brake, check, choke, clog, close, confine, hinder, hold in, impede, obstruct, repress, restrain, restrict, retard, slow, stop up, suppress; SEE CONCEPTS 130,191

damage [n1] *injury, loss*
accident, adulteration, adversity, affliction, bane, blemish, blow, breakage, bruise, casualty, catastrophe, cave-in, contamination, corruption, debasement, depreciation, deprivation, destruction, deterioration, detriment, devastation, disservice, disturbance, evil, hardship, harm, hurt, illness, impairment, infliction, knockout, marring, mischief, mishap, mutilation, outrage, pollution, ravage, reverse, ruin, ruining, spoilage, stroke, suffering, waste, wound, wreckage, wrecking, wrong; SEE CONCEPTS 309,674

damage [v] *cause injury, loss*
abuse, bang up*, batter, bleach, blight, break, burn, contaminate, corrode, corrupt, crack, cripple, deface, defile, dirty, discolor, disfigure, disintegrate, dismantle, fade, gnaw, harm, hurt, impair, incapacitate, infect, injure, lacerate, maim, maltreat, mangle, mar, mutilate, pollute, ravage, rot, ruin, rust, scathe, scorch, scratch, smash, split, spoil, stab, stain, tamper with, tarnish, tear, undermine, vitiate, weaken, wear away, wound, wreak havoc on*, wreck, wrong; SEE CONCEPTS 246,252

damaged [adj] *broken, not working*
beat-up, bent, blemished, busted, dinged, down, flawed, flubbed*, fouled up, glitched*, gone, hurt, impaired, imperfect, injured, in need of repair, in poor condition, in smithereens*, kaput*, loused up*, marred, messed up*, mucked up*, no go*, on the blink*, on the fritz*, out of action*, out of kilter*, out of whack*, run-down, screwed up*, shot, snafued*, spoiled, sunk*, totaled*, unsound; SEE CONCEPTS 485,560

damage(s) [n2] *cost for problem*
amends, bill, charge, compensation, expense, fine, forfeit, indemnity, reimbursement, reparation, satisfaction, total; SEE CONCEPTS 123,329

damaging [adj] *hurtful to reputation*
bad, deleterious, detrimental, disadvantageous, evil, harmful, injurious, mischievous, nocent, nocuous, prejudicial, ruinous; SEE CONCEPT 537

damn [v] *condemn, denounce*
abuse, anathematize, attack, ban, banish, blaspheme, blast, castigate, cast out, censure, complain of, confound, convict, criticize, cry down, curse, cuss*, darn, denunciate, doom, drat, excommunicate, excoriate, execrate, expel, flame, fulminate against, imprecate, inveigle against, jinx, object to, objurgate, pan*, penalize, proscribe, punish, revile, sentence, slam, swear, thunder against*; SEE CONCEPTS 52,54

damnable [adj] *atrocious, horrible*
abhorrent, abominable, accursed, blamed,

blessed, culpable, cursed, dang*, darn, depraved, despicable, detestable, dratted, execrable, hateful, odious, offensive, outrageous, wicked; SEE CONCEPTS 545,570

damnation [n] *everlasting punishment*
condemnation, doom, hell, perdition, suffering, torment; SEE CONCEPT 679

damned [adj] *hateful, unwelcome*
accursed, all-fired*, anathematized, bad, blankety-blank*, blasted, blessed*, bloody*, blooming*, condemned, confounded, cursed, cussed*, damnable, dang*, darn*, darned*, despicable, detestable, doggone*, done for*, doomed, dratted*, execrable, gone to blazes*, infamous, infernal*, loathsome, lost, lousy, reprobate, revolting, unhappy, voodooed*; SEE CONCEPTS 545,570

damp [adj] *wet, humid*
clammy, cloudy, dank, dewy, drenched, dripping, drippy, drizzly, irriguous, misty, moist, muggy, oozy, saturated, soaked, soaking, sodden, soggy, sopping, steam bath*, steamy, sticky, vaporous, waterlogged, wettish; SEE CONCEPT 603

dampen [v1] *make wet*
bedew, besprinkle, dabble, humidify, moisten, rinse, spray, sprinkle, water, wet; SEE CONCEPT 256

dampen [v2] *spoil spirits*
allay, check, chill, cloud, cool, curb, dash, deaden, deject, depress, diminish, discourage, dismay, dispirit, dull, humble, inhibit, moderate, muffle, mute, restrain, stifle; SEE CONCEPTS 7,19

damsel [n] *maiden*
colleen, lady, lass, lassie, miss, virgin, woman, young girl, young woman; SEE CONCEPTS 414,415

dance [n1/v] *moving feet and body to music*
bob*, boogie, boogie down*, bunny hop, caper, careen, cavort, Charleston, conga, cut a rug*, disco, flit*, foot it*, foxtrot, frolic, gambol, get down*, hoof it*, hop, hustle, jig, jitter*, jitterbug, jive*, jump, leap, one-step, prance, promenade, rhumba, rock, rock 'n' roll, samba, shimmy, skip, spin, step, strut, sway, swing, tango, tap, tread, trip, trip the light fantastic*, twist, two-step, waltz, whirl; SEE CONCEPTS 292,363

dance [n2] *party for moving to music*
ball, brawl, disco, formal, hoedown, hop, jump, masquerade, mingle, prom, promenade, shindig, social, sock hop; SEE CONCEPT 383

dancer [n] *ballerina*
ballet dancer, belly-dancer, chorus girl, coryphee, danseur, danseuse, go-go dancer, hoofer*, line-dancer, prima ballerina, show girl, tap-dancer; SEE CONCEPT 352

dandle [v] *caress, cuddle*
amuse, cosset, cradle, dance, fondle, love, nuzzle, pet, play, ride on knee, rock, sport, toss, toy*, toy with*; SEE CONCEPTS 147,190

dandruff [n] *scurf*
flakes, seborrhea; SEE CONCEPT 831

dandy [adj] *fine, excellent*
capital, cool*, exemplary, famous, first-class, first-rate, five-star*, fly*, glorious, grand, great, groovy*, hunky-dory*, keen, marvelous, model, neat, nifty, paragon, peachy*, prime, splendid, superior, swell, terrific; SEE CONCEPT 574

danger [n] *hazard, troublesome situation*
clouds, crisis, double trouble*, dynamite, emergency, endangerment, exigency, exposure, hot potato*, insecurity, instability, jeopardy, menace, peril, pitfall, possibility, precariousness, precipice, probability, risk, risky business*, slipperiness, storm, thin ice*, threat, uncertainty, venture, vulnerability; SEE CONCEPT 675

dangerous [adj] *hazardous, troubling*
alarming, bad, breakneck*, chancy, critical, dangersome, deadly, delicate, dynamite, exposed, fatal, formidable, hairy*, heavy*, hot*, impending, impregnable, insecure, jeopardous, loaded, malignant, menacing, mortal, nasty, on collision course*, parlous, perilous, portentous, precarious, pressing, queasy, risky, serious, serpentine, shaky, speculative, terrible, thorny*, threatening, ticklish*, touch-and-go*, touchy, treacherous, ugly*, unhealthy, unsafe, unstable, urgent, viperous, vulnerable, wicked; SEE CONCEPT 548

dangerously [adv] *precariously*
alarmingly, carelessly, critically, daringly, desperately, gravely, harmfully, hazardously, perilously, precariously, recklessly, riskily, seriously, severely, unsafely, unsecurely; SEE CONCEPT 548

dangle [v] *suspend*
brandish, depend, droop, entice, flap, flaunt, flourish, hang, hang down, lure, sling, sway, swing, tantalize, tempt, trail, wave; SEE CONCEPTS 153,190

dank [adj] *clammy*
chilly, close, damp, dewy, dripping, humid, moist, muggy, slimy, soggy, steamy, sticky, wet, wettish; SEE CONCEPT 603

dapper [adj] *well-groomed, neat*
bandbox, brisk, chic, chichi, classy, clean, dainty, dashing, doggy*, dressed to kill*, dressed to nines*, jaunty, natty, nice, nifty, nimble, nobby, posh, prim, rakish, ritzy, sassy, sharp, showy, smart, snazzy*, snug, spiff, spiffy, spruce, spry, stylish, swank, swanky, swell, trim, turned out, well turned out; SEE CONCEPT 579

dappled [adj] *mottled, freckled*
brindle, brindled, checkered, discolored, flecked, motley, multicolor, multicolored, multihued, parti-colored, piebald, pied, speckled, spotted, stippled, varicolored, variegated, versicolor, versicolored; SEE CONCEPT 618

dare [n] *challenge, defiance*
cartel, defy, provocation, stump, taunt; SEE CONCEPTS 53,87

dare [v1] *challenge, defy someone*
beard, brave, bully, call one's bluff, confront, cope, denounce, disregard, face, face off, front, goad, insult, knock chip off shoulder*, laugh at, make my day*, meet, mock, muster courage, oppose, outdare, provoke, resist, run the gauntlet, scorn, spurn, square off, step over the line, take one on, taunt, threaten, throw down gauntlet; SEE CONCEPTS 14,53

dare [v2] *take a risk; be courageous*
adventure, attempt, be bold, brave, endanger, endeavor, gamble, go ahead, hazard, make bold, pluck up, presume, risk, run the risk, speculate, stake, take a chance, take heart, try, try one's hand*, undertake, venture; SEE CONCEPTS 35,87

daredevil [n] *thrill-seeker*
adventurer, hotdog*, madcap, risk-taker, showoff, stuntman, stuntperson, stuntwoman; SEE CONCEPT 423

daring [*adj*] *adventurous*
adventuresome, audacious, bold, brassy*, brave, cheeky, cocky, courageous, crusty, fearless, fire eating*, foolhardy, forward, game, go for broke*, gritty, gutsy*, gutty*, hot shot*, impudent, impulsive, intrepid, nervy, obtrusive, out on a limb*, plucky, rash, reckless, salty*, smart, smart-alecky*, spunky*, temerarious, valiant, venturesome; SEE CONCEPT **401**

dark [*adj1*] *lack of light*
aphotic, atramentous, black, blackish, caliginous, Cimmerian, clouded, cloudy, crepuscular, darkened, dim, dingy, drab, dull, dun, dusk, dusky, faint, foggy, gloomy, grimy, ill-lighted, indistinct, inky, lightless, lurid, misty, murky, nebulous, obfuscous, obscure, opaque, overcast, pitch-black, pitch-dark, pitchy, rayless, shaded, shadowy, shady, somber, sooty, stygian, sunless, tenebrous, unlighted, unlit, vague; SEE CONCEPT **617**

dark [*adj2*] *shaded complexion, hair*
adumbral, bistered, black, brunet, brunette, dark-complexioned, dark-skinned, dusky, ebon, ebony, sable, swart, swarthy, tan; SEE CONCEPTS **406,618**

dark [*adj3*] *hidden, secret*
abstruse, anagogic, arcane, cabalistic, complicated, concealed, cryptic, deep, Delphian, enigmatic, esoteric, intricate, knotty, mysterious, mystic, mystical, mystifying, not known, obscure, occult, puzzling, recondite; SEE CONCEPTS **402,576,582**

dark [*adj4*] *grim, hopeless*
bleak, cheerless, dismal, doleful, drab, foreboding, gloomy, joyless, morbid, morose, mournful, ominous, sinister, somber, unpropitious; SEE CONCEPT **548**

dark [*adj5*] *evil, satanic*
atrocious, bad, corrupt, damnable, foul, hellish, horrible, immoral, infamous, infernal, nefarious, sinful, sinister, vile, wicked; SEE CONCEPT **545**

dark [*adj6*] *ignorant*
benighted, uncultivated, unenlightened, unlettered, unread; SEE CONCEPT **402**

dark [*adj7*] *angry, upset*
dour, forbidding, frowning, glowering, glum, ominous, scowling, sulky, sullen, threatening; SEE CONCEPT **401**

dark [*n1*] *place, time without light*
caliginosity, darkness, dead of night, dimness, dusk, duskiness, evening, gloom, midnight, murk, murkiness, night, nightfall, nighttime, obscurity, opacity, semidarkness, shade, shadows, twilight, witching hour; SEE CONCEPTS **620,810**

dark [*n2*] *ignorance; mystery*
concealment, denseness, inscrutability, seclusion, secrecy, thickness; SEE CONCEPTS **409,410**

darken [*v*] *become shaded, unlit*
becloud, bedim, blacken, cloud over, cloud up, deepen, dim, eclipse, fog, gray, haze, make dim, murk, obfuscate, obscure, overcast, overshadow, shade, shadow, tone down*; SEE CONCEPTS **250,469**

dark horse [*n*] *long shot*
hundred-to-one shot, improbability, outside chance, sleeper, small chance, underdog, unexpected winner, unknown, unlikelihood, unlikely winner; SEE CONCEPTS **366,423**

darkness [*n1*] *place, time that is unlit*
black, blackness, blackout, brownout, caliginosity, Cimmerian shade, cloudiness, crepuscule, dark, dimness, dusk, duskiness, eclipse, gloom, lightlessness, murk, murkiness, nightfall, obscurity, pitch darkness, shade, shadiness, shadows, smokiness, tenebrosity, twilight; SEE CONCEPT **620**

darkness [*n2*] *ignorance; mystery*
blindness, concealment, denseness, inscrutability, isolation, privacy, seclusion, secrecy, unawareness; SEE CONCEPTS **409,410**

darling [*n*] *sweetheart, favorite person*
angel*, apple of one's eye*, baby*, beloved, boyfriend, dear, dearest, dearie*, dear one, fair-haired boy*, flame, friend, girlfriend, heart's desire*, honeybunch, lamb*, light of my life*, love, lover, one and only*, pet*, precious, sugar*, sweetie, treasure*, truelove; SEE CONCEPT **423**

darn [*interj*] *damn*
confound it, cripes, damn it, dang*, darnation, doggone, drat*, gosh-darn; SEE CONCEPTS **52,54**

dart [*v*] *race away; propel*
bound, career, cast, course, dash, flash, fling, flit, float, fly, gallop, hasten, heave, hurry, hurtle, launch, move quickly, pitch, plunge, run, rush, sail, scamper, scoot, scud, scurry, shoot, skim, speed, spring, sprint, spurt, start, tear, throw, thrust, whiz; SEE CONCEPTS **150,195,222**

dash [*n1*] *fast race for short distance*
birr, bolt, dart, haste, onset, run, rush, sortie, sprint, spurt, zip; SEE CONCEPT **150**

dash [*n2*] *flair, style*
animation, birr, brio, éclat, élan, energy, esprit, flourish, force, impressiveness, intensity, life, might, oomph*, panache, power, spirit, strength, vehemence, verve, vigor, vim, vivacity, zing, zip; SEE CONCEPTS **411,655,673**

dash [*n3*] *small amount; suggestion*
bit, drop, few drops, flavor, grain, hint, lick, little, part, pinch, scattering, seasoning, smack, smidgen, soupçon, sprinkle, sprinkling, squirt, streak, suspicion, taste, tincture, tinge, touch, trace, trifle, zest; SEE CONCEPT **831**

dash [*v1*] *run very fast for short distance*
boil, bolt, bound, career, charge, chase, course, dart, fly, gallop, get on it*, haste, hasten, hurry, lash, make a run for it*, make it snappy*, race, rush, rush at, scamper, scoot, scurry, shoot, speed, spring, sprint, tear; SEE CONCEPT **150**

dash [*v2*] *break by hitting or throwing violently*
beat, bludgeon, cast, charge, crash, cudgel, destroy, fling, hit, hurl, hurtle, lunge, plunge, shatter, shiver, slam, sling, smash, splash, splatter, splinter, throw; SEE CONCEPTS **189,222,248**

dash [*v3*] *discourage, frustrate*
abash, baffle, balk, beat, bilk, blast, blight, chagrin, chill, circumvent, cloud, confound, dampen, disappoint, discomfort, dismay, dispirit, foil, nip, ruin, spoil, thwart; SEE CONCEPTS **7,19,121**

dashboard [*n*] *instrument panel*
control panel, indicator panel, instrument board; SEE CONCEPTS **463,499**

dashing [*adj*] *bold, flamboyant*
adventurous, alert, animated, chic, dapper, daring, dazzling, debonair, elegant, exclusive, exuberant, fashionable, fearless, gallant, gay, jaunty, keen, lively, modish, plucky, rousing, showy, smart, spirited, sporty, stylish, swank, swash-

da
da

buckling, swish, vivacious; SEE CONCEPTS *404,589*

dastardly [*adj*] *rotten*
base, contemptible, cowardly, craven, despicable, low, mean, pusillanimous, underhanded, vile; SEE CONCEPTS *404,545,570,571,574*

data [*n*] *information in visible form*
abstracts, brass tacks*, chapter and verse*, circumstances, compilations, conclusions, details, documents, dope, dossier, evidence, experiments, facts, figures, goods, info, input, knowledge, materials, measurements, memorandums, notes, picture, proof, reports, results, scoop, score, statistics, testimony, whole story*; SEE CONCEPT *274*

data bank [*n*] *database*
computerized information, data processing, storage; SEE CONCEPT *274*

data processor [*n*] *computer*
calculator, CPU, laptop, MAC, Macintosh, mainframe, microcomputer, number cruncher, PC, personal computer, word processor; SEE CONCEPTS *269,463*

date [*n1*] *point in time; particular day or time*
age, century, course, day, duration, epoch, era, generation, hour, juncture, moment, period, quarter, reign, span, spell, stage, term, time, while, year; SEE CONCEPTS *800,801,802,815*

date [*n2*] *social engagement*
appointment, assignation, call, interview, meeting, rendezvous, tryst, visit; SEE CONCEPTS *114,386*

date [*n3*] *person accompanying another socially*
blind date, boyfriend, companion, escort, friend, girlfriend, lover, partner, steady, sweetheart; SEE CONCEPT *423*

date [*v1*] *assign a time*
affix a date to, belong to, carbon-date, chronicle, come from, determine, exist from, fix, fix the date of, isolate, mark, measure, originate in, put in its place, record, register; SEE CONCEPTS *18,37*

date [*v2*] *see person socially*
associate with, attend, consort with, court, deuce it*, escort, fix up, go around together*, go around with*, go out with, go steady, go together, keep company, make a date, see, step around, take out, woo; SEE CONCEPT *114*

date [*v3*] *become obsolete*
antiquate, archaize, obsolesce, obsolete, outdate, show one's age; SEE CONCEPT *105*

dated [*adj*] *out-of-date*
antiquated, archaic, behind the times, obsolescent, obsolete, old-fashioned, old hat, outdated, outmoded, out of style, passé, unfashionable; SEE CONCEPTS *530,578,797*

daub [*v*] *coat; make dirty*
begrime, besmear, bespray, blur, cover, dab, deface, dirty, fleck, grime, paint, plaster, slap on, smear, smirch, smudge, spatter, speckle, splatter, spot, spread, stain, sully, variegate, varnish; SEE CONCEPTS *172,250*

daughter [*n*] *female child*
female offspring, girl, offspring, woman; SEE CONCEPTS *415,424*

daunt [*v*] *frighten, alarm*
appall, baffle, browbeat, bully, consternate, cow, deter, discourage, dishearten, dismay, dispirit, foil, horrify, intimidate, overawe, put off*, scare, shake, subdue, terrify, thwart; SEE CONCEPTS *7,19*

dauntless [*adj*] *bold, courageous*
aweless, brave, daring, doughty, fearless, gallant, game, heroic, indomitable, intrepid, invincible, lionhearted, resolute, stouthearted, unafraid, unconquerable, undaunted, unfearing, unflinching, valiant, valorous; SEE CONCEPT *401*

davenport [*n*] *sofa; small desk*
chesterfield, convertible sofa, couch, daybed, futon, secretary, sofa bed, writing desk; SEE CONCEPT *443*

dawdle [*v*] *delay; waste time*
amble, bum around*, dally, diddle-daddle*, dilly-dally*, drag, fool around*, fritter away*, get no place fast*, goof off*, hang around*, hang out*, idle, lag, laze, lazy, loaf, loiter, loll, lounge, mosey*, poke*, procrastinate, put off, saunter, scrounge around, shlep along*, sit around*, sit on one's butt*, stay, stroll, tarry, toddle, trifle, wait, warm a chair*; SEE CONCEPTS *210,681*

dawn [*n1*] *beginning of day*
aurora, break of day, bright, cockcrow, crack of dawn, dawning, daybreak, daylight, day peep, early bright, first blush, first light, light, morn, morning, sunrise, sunup, wee hours*; SEE CONCEPTS *810,815*

dawn [*n2*] *a beginning*
advent, alpha, birth, commencement, dawning, emergence, foundation, genesis, head, inception, onset, opening, origin, outset, outstart, rise, source, start, unfolding; SEE CONCEPT *832*

dawn [*v*] *start*
appear, begin, develop, emerge, glimmer, initiate, lighten, loom, open, originate, rise, show itself, unfold; SEE CONCEPT *119*

day [*n1*] *light part of every 24 hours*
astronomical day, bright, dawn-to-dark, daylight, daytime, diurnal course, early bright, light, light of day, mean solar day, nautical day, sidereal day, sunlight, sunrise-to-sunset, sunshine, working day; SEE CONCEPTS *801,803,810,821*

day [*n2*] *era*
age, ascendancy, cycle, epoch, generation, height, heyday, period, prime, term, time, years, zenith; SEE CONCEPTS *802,816*

daybook [*n*] *journal*
album, datebook, diary, Filofax®, ledger, log, logbook, memo pad, notebook, record, scrapbook; SEE CONCEPTS *280,283*

daybreak [*n*] *beginning of light hours*
aurora, break of day, bright, cockcrow, crack of dawn, dawn, dawning, daylight, day peep, dayspring, early bright, first light, morn, morning, sunrise, sunup; SEE CONCEPTS *810,815*

daycare [*n*] *child care center*
babysitter, kindergarten, nursery school, playgroup, pre-K, pre-school; SEE CONCEPT *295*

daydream [*n*] *fantasy thought of when awake*
castle in the air*, conceiving, dream, fancy, fancying, figment of imagination, fond hope, fool's paradise*, head trip*, imagination, imagining, in a zone*, mind trip*, musing, phantasm, phantasy, pie in the sky*, pipe dream, reverie, stargazing, trip*, vision, wish, woolgathering; SEE CONCEPT *529*

daydream [*v*] *make up fantasy*
build castles in air*, conceive, dream, envision, fancy, fantasize, hallucinate, imagine, moon, muse, pipe dream*, stargaze, trip out*, woolgather; SEE CONCEPTS *17,36*

daylight [n] *light part of 24 hours*
aurora, dawn, day, daybreak, daytime, during the day, light, light of day, sunlight, sunrise, sunshine; SEE CONCEPT *810*

daze [n] *confusion*
befuddlement, bewilderment, distraction, gauze, glaze, haze, lala-land*, maze, muddledness, nadaville*, narcosis, shock, stupefaction, stupor, trance; SEE CONCEPT *410*

daze [v] *confuse, shock*
addle, amaze, astonish, astound, befog, befuddle, benumb, bewilder, blind, blur, confound, dazzle, disorder, distract, dizzy, dumbfound, flabbergast, fuddle, mix up, muddle, mystify, numb, overpower, overwhelm, paralyze, perplex, petrify, puzzle, rock, stagger, startle, stun, stupefy, surprise; SEE CONCEPTS *16,42*

dazzle [v] *confuse, amaze*
astonish, awe, bedazzle, blind, blur, bowl over*, daze, excite, fascinate, glitz*, hypnotize, impress, overawe, overpower, overwhelm, razzle-dazzle, strike dumb*, stupefy, surprise; SEE CONCEPTS *16,42*

dazzling [adj] *radiant*
beaming, bright, brilliant, flashy, glaring, glittering, ravishing, resplendent, sensational, shining, sparkling, splendid, stunning; SEE CONCEPT *617*

deacon [n] *clergyperson*
church officer, cleric, elder, priest; SEE CONCEPT *361*

deactivate [v] *decommission*
demilitarize, disband, make inactive, shut down, shut off; SEE CONCEPTS *25,121,188*

dead [adj1] *no longer alive*
asleep, bereft of life, bloodless, bought the farm*, breathless, buried, cadaverous, checked out*, cold, cut off, deceased, defunct, departed, done for*, erased, expired, extinct, gone, gone to meet maker*, gone to reward*, inanimate, inert, late, lifeless, liquidated, mortified, no more, not existing, offed*, out of one's misery*, passed away, perished, pushing up daisies*, reposing, resting in peace, spiritless, stiff, unanimated, wasted; SEE CONCEPT *539*

dead [adj2] *indifferent, cold*
anesthetized, apathetic, asleep, boring, callous, deadened, dull, flat, frigid, glazed, inert, insensitive, insipid, lukewarm, numb, numbed, paralyzed, senseless, spiritless, stagnant, stale, still, tasteless, torpid, unfeeling, uninteresting, unresponsive, vapid, wooden; SEE CONCEPT *550*

dead [adj3] *not working*
barren, bygone, defunct, departed, exhausted, extinct, gone, inactive, inoperable, inoperative, lost, obsolete, spent, stagnant, sterile, still, tired, unemployed, unprofitable, useless, vanished, wearied, worn, worn out; SEE CONCEPT *560*

dead [adj4] *complete, total*
absolute, bloody, downright, entire, final, out-and-out*, outright, perfect, sure, thorough, unconditional, unmitigated, unqualified, utter, whole; SEE CONCEPT *531*

dead [adv] *completely, totally*
absolutely, direct, directly, due, entirely, exactly, right, straight, straightly, undeviatingly, wholly; SEE CONCEPTS *531,772*

deadbeat [n] *freeloader*
bum, debtor, leech, loafer, moocher, parasite, sponge; SEE CONCEPTS *412,423*

deaden [v] *diminish, muffle, quiet*
abate, alleviate, anesthetize, benumb, blunt, check, chloroform, consume, cushion, damp, dampen, depress, deprive, desensitize, destroy, devitalize, dim, dope, drown, dull, etherize, exhaust, freeze, frustrate, gas, hush, impair, incapacitate, injure, knock out, KO*, lay out, lessen, mute, numb, paralyze, put out of order*, put to sleep, quieten, reduce, repress, retard, slow, smother, soften, stifle, stun, stupefy, suppress, tire, tone down, unnerve, weaken; SEE CONCEPTS *130,240*

dead end [n] *cul-de-sac; deadlock*
blank wall, blind alley, Catch-22, corner, draw, impasse, nowhere to turn, obstacle, road block, stalemate, standoff, stumbling block; SEE CONCEPT *674*

deadline [n] *due date*
bound, cutoff, limit, period, target date, time frame, time limit, zero hour; SEE CONCEPTS *513,745,815,832*

deadlock [n] *stalemate, impasse*
box*, Catch-22*, cessation, checkmate, corner, dead end, dead heat, dilemma, draw, full stop, gridlock, halt, hole, pause, pickle, plight, posture, predicament, quandary, standoff, standstill, tie, wall*; SEE CONCEPT *674*

deadly [adj1] *causing end of life*
baleful, baneful, bloodthirsty, bloody, cannibalistic, carcinogenic, cruel, dangerous, death-dealing, deathly, deleterious, destroying, destructive, fatal, grim, harmful, homicidal, injurious, internecine, killing, lethal, malignant, mortal, mortiferous, murderous, noxious, pernicious, pestiferous, pestilent, pestilential, poisonous, ruthless, savage, slaying, suicidal, toxic, unrelenting, venomous, violent, virulent; SEE CONCEPT *537*

deadly [adj2] *ghostly*
ashen, corpselike, dead, deadened, deathful, deathlike, deathly, ghastly, pallid, wan, white; SEE CONCEPT *539*

dead-on [adj] *accurate*
by the book, dead-center, definite, direct, exact, on the button*, on the mark*, on the money*, on the nose*, precise, to the point; SEE CONCEPT *535*

deadpan [adj] *expressionless*
blank, impassive, nobody home*, poker-faced, serious, stony, straight-faced, unreadable, vacant, wooden; SEE CONCEPT *406*

deaf [adj1] *without hearing*
deafened, earless, hard of hearing, stone deaf*, unable to hear; SEE CONCEPT *591*

deaf [adj2] *unwilling*
bullheaded*, headstrong, indifferent, intractable, mulish*, oblivious, obstinate, pertinacious, perverse, pigheaded*, self-willed, strong-willed, stubborn, to listen blind, unaware, unconcerned, unhearing, unmoved; SEE CONCEPT *401*

deafening [adj] *very loud*
at full volume, blaring, booming, ear-piercing*, ear-popping*, ear-splitting*, noisy, ringing, roaring, rowdy, screaming, thunderous, turned up, vociferous; SEE CONCEPTS *592,594*

deal [n1] *agreement, bargain*
accord, arrangement, buy, compromise, conception, contract, pact, pledge, prearrangement, transaction, understanding; SEE CONCEPT *684*

deal [n2] *amount, share*
abundance, degree, distribution, extent, plenty,

da
de

plethora, portion, quantity, shake, superabundance, transaction; SEE CONCEPTS *344,787,835*

deal [*n3*] *distribution of playing cards*
appointment, chance, cut and shuffle*, fresh start, game, hand, opportunity, round; SEE CONCEPT *363*

deal [*v2*] *do business*
bargain, barter, bicker, buy and sell, dicker*, hammer out deal*, handle, horse trade*, knock down price*, negotiate, sell, stock, swap, trade, traffic, treat, work out deal; SEE CONCEPT *324*

deal [*v3*] *distribute*
administer, allot, apportion, assign, bestow, come across with*, deliver, disburse, dish out*, dispense, disperse, disseminate, divide, divvy*, dole out*, drop, fork out*, fork over*, give, hand out, impart, inflict, measure, mete out, partake, participate, partition, render, reward, share, strike; SEE CONCEPTS *108,140*

deal/deal with [*v1*] *handle, manage*
act, approach, attend to, behave, behave toward, clear, concern, conduct oneself, consider, control, cope with, direct, discuss, get a handle on something*, hack it*, handle, have to do with, live with*, make a go of it*, make it*, oversee, play, review, rid, see to, serve, take, take care of, treat, unburden, use; SEE CONCEPTS *94,117*

dealer [*n*] *business owner*
banker, bursar, businessperson, chandler, changer, dispenser, marketer, merchandiser, merchant, retailer, trader, tradesperson, trafficker, vendor, wholesaler; SEE CONCEPT *347*

dealings [*n*] *business relations*
affairs, balls in air*, business, commerce, concerns, doings, intercourse, irons in fire*, matters, proceedings, ropes*, sale, strings*, things, trade, traffic, transactions, truck, wire pulling*, wires*; SEE CONCEPT *324*

dean [*n*] *leader of institution*
administrator, authority, dignitary, doyen, ecclesiastic, guide, lead, legislator, pilot, president, principal, professor, senior, tack; SEE CONCEPT *350*

dear [*adj1*] *beloved, favorite*
cherished, close, darling, doll face, endeared, esteemed, familiar, intimate, loved, pet, precious, prized, respected, treasured; SEE CONCEPTS *555,567*

dear [*adj2*] *very expensive*
an arm and a leg*, at a premium, cher*, costly, fancy, high, high-priced, out of sight*, overpriced, pretty penny*, pricey*, prized, steep, stiff*, valuable; SEE CONCEPT *334*

dear [*n*] *beloved person*
darling, favorite, heartthrob, honey, love, loved one, lover, pet, precious, sweetheart, treasure; SEE CONCEPT *423*

dearly [*adv1*] *extremely*
greatly, profoundly, to a great extent, very, very much; SEE CONCEPT *772*

dearly [*adv2*] *lovingly*
affectionately, devotedly, fondly, tenderly, yearningly; SEE CONCEPT *403*

dearth [*n*] *insufficiency, scarcity*
absence, default, defect, deficiency, exiguousness, famine, inadequacy, infrequency, lack, meagerness, miss, need, paucity, poverty, privation, rareness, scantiness, scantness, shortage, slim pickings*, sparsity, uncommonness, want; SEE CONCEPTS *646,674,709*

death [*n*] *end of life*
afterlife, annihilation, bereavement, casualty, cessation, curtains*, darkness, decease, demise, departure, destruction, dissolution, downfall, dying, end, ending, eradication, eternal rest, euthanasia, exit, expiration, extermination, extinction, fatality, finis*, finish, grave, grim reaper*, heaven, loss, mortality, necrosis, obliteration, oblivion, paradise, parting, passing, passing over, quietus, release, repose, ruin, ruination, silence, sleep, termination, tomb; SEE CONCEPT *304*

deathly [*adj1*] *suggesting end of life*
appalling, cadaverous, corpselike, deathlike, defunctive, dreadful, gaunt, ghastly, grim, gruesome, haggard, horrible, macabre, pale, pallid, wan, wasted; SEE CONCEPTS *579,618*

deathly [*adj2*] *fatal*
deadly, extreme, intense, lethal, mortal, mortiferous, noxious, pestilent, pestilential, terrible; SEE CONCEPT *537*

debacle [*n*] *catastrophe*
beating, blue ruin*, breakdown, collapse, crackup*, crash, defeasance, defeat, devastation, disaster, dissolution, downfall, drubbing, failure, fiasco, havoc, licking, overthrow, reversal, rout, ruin, ruination, shellacking*, smash, smashup, trouncing, vanquishment, washout, wreck; SEE CONCEPT *674*

debase [*v1*] *degrade, shame*
abase, bemean, cast down, cheapen, corrupt, cripple, debauch, debilitate, demean, demoralize, deprave, devaluate, devalue, disable, disgrace, dishonor, drag down*, dump on*, enfeeble, fluff off*, humble, humiliate, lower, put away, put down, reduce, sap, shoot down, sink, take down*, take down a peg*, undermine, weaken; SEE CONCEPTS *7,19,52,54*

debase [*v2*] *adulterate*
abase, animalize, bastardize, bestialize, contaminate, corrupt, damage, defile, depreciate, doctor, dope up*, impair, load, pervert, pollute, sophisticate, spoil, taint, vitiate, weight, worsen; SEE CONCEPTS *240,250*

debatable [*adj*] *controversial*
arguable, between rock and hard place*, between sixes and sevens*, betwixt and between*, bone of contention*, borderline, chancy*, contestable, disputable, doubtful, dubious, iffy*, in dispute, moot, mootable*, open to question, problematic, problematical, questionable, the jury's out*, touch and go*, uncertain, undecided, unsettled, up for discussion; SEE CONCEPTS *267,535*

debate [*n*] *discussion of issues; consideration*
agitation, altercation, argument, argumentation, blah-blah*, cogitation, contention, contest, controversy, controverting, deliberation, dialectic, disputation, dispute, forensic, hassle, match, meditation, mooting, polemic, rebutting, reflection, refuting, tiff, words, wrangle; SEE CONCEPTS *56,532*

debate [*v*] *argue, discuss*
agitate, altercate, answer, bandy, bicker, bump heads*, canvass, chew the fat*, cogitate, confab*, confute, consider, contend, contest, controvert, cross swords*, deliberate, demonstrate, differ, discept, disprove, dispute, hammer away at*, hash over*, hassle, have at it*, kick around*, knock around*, lock horns*, moot, oppose, pettifog, pick a bone*, prove, put up argument, ques-

tion, reason, rebut, refute, rehash, set to, talk back*, talk game*, thrash out*, toss around*, wrangle; SEE CONCEPTS *24,56*

debauch [v] *deprave, corrupt*
abuse, bastardize, bestialize, betray, brutalize, debase, defile, deflower, demoralize, fornicate, fraternize, go bad*, go to hell*, intrigue, inveigle, lead astray*, live in the gutter*, lure, pervert, pollute, ravish, ruin, seduce, subvert, tempt, violate, vitiate, warp; SEE CONCEPTS *14,240,375*

debauched [adj] *violated, corrupted*
abandoned, corrupt, debased, defiled, degenerate, degraded, depraved, deteriorated, dissipated, dissolute, fast, gone bad*, gone to the dogs*, immoral, in the gutter*, licentious, perverted, profligate, reprobate, vitiate, vitiated, wanton, wicked; SEE CONCEPT *545*

debauchery [n] *immoral self-indulgence*
bender*, binge, blowout*, burning candle at both ends*, bust, carousal, depravity, dissipation, dissoluteness, drunk*, excess, fast living*, fornication, gluttony, incontinence, indulgence, intemperance, intimacy, la dolce vita*, lasciviousness, lechery, lewdness, license, licentiousness, life in fast lane*, lust, orgy, overindulgence, revel, revelry, seduction, sensuality, sybaritism, tear*; SEE CONCEPTS *633,645*

debenture [n] *certificate of debt*
bond, I.O.U., promise to pay, voucher; SEE CONCEPTS *318,684*

debilitate [v] *incapacitate*
attenuate, blunt, cripple, devitalize, disable, enervate, enfeeble, eviscerate, exhaust, extenuate, harm, hurt, injure, mar, prostrate, relax, sap, spoil, unbrace, undermine, unstrengthen, weaken, wear out; SEE CONCEPTS *240,246*

debility [n] *incapacity, weakness*
decrepitude, disease, enervation, enfeeblement, exhaustion, faintness, feebleness, frailty, infirmity, languor, malaise, sickliness, unhealthiness; SEE CONCEPT *316*

debonair [adj] *charming, elegant*
affable, buoyant, casual, cheerful, courteous, dashing, detached, happy, jaunty, lighthearted, nonchalant, pleasant, refined, smooth, sprightly, suave, urbane, well-bred; SEE CONCEPT *401*

debrief [v1] *question*
ask questions, cross-examine, examine, gather intelligence, give the third degree*, grill, interrogate, interview, investigate, probe, put through the wringer*, quiz, work over; SEE CONCEPTS *48,53*

debrief [v2] *silence*
censor, dummy up*, gag, hold one's tongue*, hush up, mute, muzzle, put the lid on, quash, say nothing, shut up, sit on*, soft-pedal*, squelch, stifle, suppress; SEE CONCEPT *266*

debris [n] *litter, waste*
bits, crap*, detritus, dregs, dross, fragments, garbage, junk, offal, pieces, refuse, remains, riffraff, rubbish, rubble, ruins, trash, wreck, wreckage; SEE CONCEPT *260*

debt [n] *money owed to others*
albatross*, arrearage, arrears, bad news*, baggage*, below the line*, bill, bite*, capital, check, chit*, claim, commitment, credit, cuff*, damage*, dead horse*, debenture, debit, deficit, due, dues, duty, encumbrance, indebtedness, in hock*, in the hole*, in the red*, invoice, IOU, liability, manifest, mortgage, note, obligation, outstandings*, price tag*, promissory note, receipt, reckoning, red ink*, responsibility, score, tab, tally, voucher; SEE CONCEPTS *329,344*

debug [v] *troubleshoot*
adjust, correct, fix, iron out, remedy, remove errors, repair, sort out, straighten out, unravel, unscramble, untangle, work the bugs out of; SEE CONCEPTS *126,212*

debunk [v] *disprove, ridicule*
cut down to size*, deflate, demystify, discover, disparage, expose, lampoon, mock, puncture, show up*, uncloak, unmask, unshroud; SEE CONCEPTS *49,60*

debut [n] *first public appearance*
admission, appearance, beginning, bow, coming out*, coming out party*, entrance, entree, first step*, graduating, graduation, inauguration, incoming, initiation, introduction, launching, opener, presentation; SEE CONCEPT *386*

debutante [n] *young woman*
deb, teenage girl, young girl, young lady; SEE CONCEPTS *415,424*

decadence [n] *perversion; deterioration of morality*
corruption, debasement, decay, declension, decline, degeneracy, degeneration, degradation, devolution, dissipation, dissolution, downfall, downgrade, evil, excess, fall, gluttony, incontinence, intemperance, lasciviousness, lechery, lewdness, licentiousness, regression, sensuality, sybaritism; SEE CONCEPT *645*

decadent [adj] *corrupt, self-indulgent*
debased, debauched, decaying, declining, degenerate, degraded, depraved, dissolute, effete, evil, gone bad, gone to the dogs*, immoral, lost, moribund, overripe, perverted, wanton, wicked; SEE CONCEPT *545*

decal [n] *sticker*
advertisement, decalcomania, decorative picture, emblem, symbol, token; SEE CONCEPTS *259,284,625*

decamp [v] *depart suddenly*
beat it, bolt, break camp, clear out, depart, disappear, escape, evacuate, flee, head for the hills*, hightail*, hit the road*, make a break for it, make oneself scarce*, make tracks*, run away, scram, skedaddle*, slip away, vamoose; SEE CONCEPTS *102,150,195*

decanter [n] *vessel*
bottle, canteen, carafe, container, cruet, flask, jug, magnum, pitcher, wine bottle; SEE CONCEPT *494*

decapitate [v] *behead*
ax, bring to the block*, chop off one's head, decollate, execute, guillotine; SEE CONCEPT *176*

decay [n] *breaking down, collapse*
adulteration, atrophy, blight, caries, cariosity, consumption, corrosion, crumbling, decadence, decline, decomposition, decrease, decrepitude, degeneracy, degeneration, depreciation, deterioration, dilapidation, disintegration, disrepair, dissolution, downfall, dying, extinction, fading, failing, gangrene, impairment, mortification, perishing, putrefaction, putrescence, putridity, putridness, rot, rotting, ruin, ruination, rust, senescence, spoilage, spoilation, wasting, wasting away, withering; SEE CONCEPTS *230,674,716*

decay [v] *deteriorate, crumble*
atrophy, become contaminated, be impaired, blight, break up, collapse, corrode, curdle, de-

cline, decompose, defile, degenerate, depreciate, discolor, disintegrate, dissolve, dry-rot, dwindle, fade, fail, get worse, go bad, go to seed*, go to the dogs*, hit rock bottom*, hit the skids*, lessen, mildew, mold, molder, mortify, pejorate, perish, pollute, putrefy, putresce, reach depths, rot, sap, shrivel, sicken, sink, slump, spoil, suppurate, turn, wane, waste away, weaken, wear away, wither; SEE CONCEPTS 240,246,469

decayed [*adj*] *rotten, falling apart*
addled, bad, carious, carrion, corroded, decomposed, effete, gangrenous, moldered, overripe, perished, putrefied, putrescent, putrid, rank, riddled, rotted, ruined, spoiled, wasted, withered; SEE CONCEPT 485

decease [*n*] *death*
buying the farm*, curtains*, defunction, demise, departure, dissolution, dying, grim reaper*, passing, passing away, passing over, quietus, release, silence, sleep, taps*, the end; SEE CONCEPT 304

decease [*v*] *pass away; expire*
buy a one-way ticket*, call off all bets*, cease, check out*, cool off*, croak*, deep six*, depart, die, drop, go, pass, pass away, pass on, pass over, perish, succumb; SEE CONCEPT 304

deceased [*adj*] *dead*
asleep, bit the dust*, cold*, defunct, departed, exanimate, expired, extinct, finished, former, gave up the ghost*, gone, inanimate, kicked the bucket*, late, lifeless, lost, passed on, pushing up daisies*; SEE CONCEPT 539

deceit [*n1*] *practice of misleading*
ambidexterity, ambidextrousness, artifice, cheating, chicane, chicanery, cozening, craft, craftiness, cunning, deceitfulness, deception, defrauding, dirty dealing*, dirty pool*, dishonesty, dissemblance, dissimulation, double-dealing, duplicity, entrapping, fraud, fraudulence, guile, hypocrisy, imposition, overreaching, pretense, slyness, smoke and mirrors*, trapping, treachery, trickery, trickiness, two-timing*, underhandedness; SEE CONCEPTS 59,633

deceit [*n2*] *particular type of trick, misleading*
artifice, blind, cheat, chicanery, crocodile tears*, deception, dirty trick*, dirty work*, duplicity, fake, feint, flimflam*, fraud, fraudulence, hoax, humbug, imposture, misrepresentation, pretense, ruse, sell, sellout, sham, shift, smoke and mirrors*, snow job*, soft soap*, spoof, stratagem, subterfuge, sweet talk*, swindle, trick, whitewash*, wile; SEE CONCEPTS 59,660

deceitful [*adj*] *dishonest, insincere*
artful, astucious, astute, beguiling, clandestine, counterfeit, crafty, cunning, deceiving, deceptive, delusive, delusory, designing, disingenuous, double-dealing, duplicitous, fallacious, false, feline, foxy, fraudulent, furtive, guileful, hypocritical, illusory, impostrous, indirect, insidious, knavish, lying, mendacious, misleading, rascal, roguish, shifty, slick, sly, sneaky, stealthy, subtle, treacherous, tricky, two-faced*, underhand, underhanded, untrustworthy, untruthful, wily; SEE CONCEPT 401

deceive [*v*] *mislead; be dishonest*
bamboozle*, beat, beat out of, beguile, betray, bilk, buffalo*, burn, cheat, circumvent, clip, con, cozen, cross up, defraud, delude, disappoint, double-cross, dupe, ensnare, entrap, fake, falsify, fleece, fool, gouge, gull, hoax, hoodwink, hook*, humbug, impose upon, lead on, outwit, play joke

on, pull fast one*, put on, rob, scam, screw, sell, skin, suck in*, swindle, take advantage of, take for, take for ride*, take in, take to cleaners*, trick, victimize; SEE CONCEPTS 7,19,59

decency [*n*] *respectable behavior*
appropriateness, ceremoniousness, civility, conventionality, correctness, courtesy, decorum, dignity, etiquette, fitness, fittingness, formality, good form, good manners, honesty, modesty, propriety, respectability, righteousness, seemliness, virtue; SEE CONCEPT 633

decent [*adj1*] *respectable, appropriate*
approved, becoming, befitting, chaste, clean, comely, comme il faut, conforming, continent, correct, decorous, delicate, ethical, fit, fitting, good, honest, honorable, immaculate, mannerly, modest, moral, nice, noble, on the up and up*, polite, presentable, proper, prudent, pure, reserved, right, seemly, spotless, stainless, standard, straight, straight arrow*, straight shooting*, suitable, trustworthy, unblemished, undefiled, untarnished, upright, virtuous, worthy; SEE CONCEPTS 401,558

decent [*adj2*] *kind, generous*
accommodating, courteous, friendly, gracious, helpful, obliging, thoughtful, virtuous; SEE CONCEPTS 404,542

decent [*adj3*] *sufficient, tolerable*
acceptable, adequate, all right, ample, average, comfortable, common, competent, enough, fair, fair to middling*, good, mediocre, middling, moderately good, passable, presentable, reasonable, respectable, right, satisfactory, sufficing, unexceptional, unimpeachable, unobjectionable; SEE CONCEPTS 533,558,572

deception [*n1*] *misleading; being dishonest*
beguilement, betrayal, blarney*, boondoggle*, cheat, circumvention, cozenage, craftiness, cunning, deceit, deceitfulness, deceptiveness, defraudation, dirt, disinformation, dissimulation, double-dealing, dupery, duplicity, equivocation, falsehood, fast one*, flimflam*, fraud, fraudulence, guile, hokum*, hypocrisy, imposition, insincerity, juggling, legerdemain, lying, mendacity, pretense, prevarication, snow job*, sophism, treachery, treason, trickery, trickiness, trumpery, untruth; SEE CONCEPTS 7,19,59

deception [*n2*] *trick*
artifice, bilk, bluff, catch, cheat, chicane, con, confidence game, con game*, cover-up, crock, decoy, device, dodge, fallacy, fast one*, fast shuffle*, feint, fib, fraud, gimmick, hoax, hogwash*, hustle, illusion, imposture, jive*, lie, malarkey*, mare's-nest*, pretext, ride*, ruse, scam, sham, shift, shuck, snare, snow job*, stall, sting, story, stratagem, subterfuge, swindle, trap, trick, whitewash*, wile, wrinkle*; SEE CONCEPTS 59,230

deceptive [*adj*] *dishonest*
ambiguous, astucious, beguiling, bum*, catchy, crafty, cunning, deceitful, deceiving, deluding, delusive, delusory, designing, disingenuous, fake, fallacious, false, fishy, foxy, fraudulent, illusory, impostrous, indirect, insidious, lying, misleading, mock, oblique, off*, phony, plausible, rascal, roguish, scheming, seeming, serpentine, shifty, slick, slippery, sly, sneaky, snide, specious, spurious, subtle, treacherous, tricky, two-faced*, underhand, underhanded, unreliable, wily; SEE CONCEPTS 401,582

decide [v] *make a determination; settle an issue*
adjudge, adjudicate, agree, arrive at conclusion, award, call shots*, cast the die*, choose, cinch, clinch, come to agreement, come to conclusion, come to decision, commit oneself, conclude, conjecture, decree, determine, draw a conclusion, elect, end, establish, figure, fix upon, form opinion, gather, go down line*, guess, have final word*, judge, make a decision, make up mind, mediate, opt, pick, poll, purpose, reach decision, resolve, rule, select, set, surmise, take a stand, tap, vote, will; SEE CONCEPT *18*

decided [adj1] *certain, definite*
absolute, assured, categorical, cinched, clear, clear-cut, clinched, destined, determined, distinct, emphatic, explicit, express, fated, for sure*, indisputable, in the bag*, nailed*, on ice*, positive, prearranged, predetermined, pronounced, resolved, runaway*, settled, sure, unalterable, unambiguous, undeniable, undisputed, unequivocal, unmistakable, unquestionable; SEE CONCEPT *535*

decided [adj2] *determined, strong-willed*
assertive, bent, certain, cocksure, decisive, deliberate, earnest, emphatic, established, firm, fixed, inflexible, intent, iron-jawed*, mulish, positive, purposeful, resolute, resolved, serious, set, settled, strong-minded, sure, unbending, unfaltering, unhesitating, unwavering, unyielding; SEE CONCEPTS *401,403*

decidedly [adv] *certainly*
absolutely, bloody*, by all means, clearly, decisively, determinedly, distinctly, downright, emphatically, flat out*, for a fact*, in spades*, no catch*, no holds barred*, no ifs ands or buts*, no mistake*, no strings attached*, of course, positively, powerful, real, really, right, straight out, strongly, sure, surely, terribly, terrifically, unequivocally, unmistakably; SEE CONCEPT *535*

deciding [adj] *determining*
chief, conclusive, critical, crucial, decisive, important, influential, key, necessary, prime, principal, significant; SEE CONCEPTS *546,568*

decimate [v] *destroy*
annihilate, butcher*, commit genocide, execute, exterminate, kill off, massacre, obliterate, slaughter, stamp out, wipe out; SEE CONCEPT *252*

decipher [v] *figure out, understand*
analyze, break, break down, bring out, cipher, construe, crack, decode, deduce, disentangle, dope out, elucidate, encipher, explain, expound, find the key, interpret, make clear, make out, puzzle out, read, render, reveal, solve, spell, translate, unfold, unravel, unriddle; SEE CONCEPTS *15,31,37*

decision [n1] *conclusion; resolution reached*
accommodation, accord, adjudication, adjudicature, adjustment, agreement, arbitration, arrangement, choice, compromise, declaration, determination, end, finding, judgment, opinion, outcome, prearrangement, preference, reconciliation, resolution, result, ruling, selection, sentence, settlement, showdown, the call, the nod, understanding, verdict; SEE CONCEPTS *278,689*

decision [n2] *strength of mind or will*
backbone, decidedness, decisiveness, determination, doggedness, earnestness, firmness, fortitude, grit, iron will, obstinacy, obstinance, perseverance, persistence, pluck*, purpose, purposefulness, purposiveness, resoluteness, resolu-

tion, resolve, seriousness, spine, stubbornness, volition, will, will power; SEE CONCEPTS *410,411*

decisive [adj] *definite*
absolute, all out*, assured, bent, certain, conclusive, crisp, critical, crucial, decided, definitive, determined, fateful, final, firm, flat out*, forceful, imperative, imperious, incisive, influential, intent, litmus test*, momentous, peremptory, positive, resolute, resolved, set, settled, significant, straight out*, strong-minded, trenchant; SEE CONCEPT *535*

deck [v] *put on clothing, usually nice*
accouter, adorn, appoint, array, attire, beautify, bedeck, clothe, decorate, dress, dress up, embellish, festoon, garland, garnish, grace, gussy up*, ornament, prettify, primp, slick, trim; SEE CONCEPT *167*

declaim [v] *proclaim; get on a soapbox*
attack, bloviate, blow hot air*, declare, decry, denounce, harangue, hold forth, inveigh, lecture, mouth, orate, perorate, pile it on*, proclaim, rail, rant, recite, soapbox*, speak, spiel*, spout*, talk big*; SEE CONCEPTS *49,51*

declaration [n1] *assertion of belief or knowledge*
acknowledgment, admission, advertisement, affirmation, allegation, announcement, answer, attestation, averment, avowal, bomb*, broadcast, communication, deposition, disclosure, enunciation, explanation, exposition, expression, hot air*, information, notice, notification, oath, pitch, presentation, profession, promulgation, protestation, publication, remark, report, revelation, saying, say so*, spiel*, statement, story, testimony, two cents' worth*, utterance; SEE CONCEPTS *49,274,278*

declaration [n2] *official proclamation*
acclamation, affidavit, allegation, announcement, article, attestation, bulletin, canon, charge, confirmation, constitution, credo, creed, denunciation, deposition, document, edict, gospel, indictment, manifesto, notice, notification, plea, proclamation, profession, promulgation, pronouncement, pronunciamento, resolution, testament, testimony, ultimatum; SEE CONCEPTS *271,274,278*

declare [v1] *make known clearly or officially*
acknowledge, advance, advocate, affirm, allegate, allege, announce, argue, assert, asservate, attest, aver, avow, be positive, blaze, bring forward, certify, cite, claim, confess, confirm, contend, convey, demonstrate, disclose, enunciate, give out, inform, insist, maintain, manifest, notify, pass, proclaim, profess, promulgate, pronounce, propound, publish, put forward, reaffirm, reassert, render, repeat, reveal, set forth, show, sound, state, stress, swear, tell, testify, validate, vouch; SEE CONCEPTS *49,60*

declare [v2] *claim as possession*
acknowledge, admit, avouch, avow, confess, convey, disclose, divulge, impart, indicate, manifest, notify, own, profess, represent, reveal, state, swear; SEE CONCEPTS *57,60*

declassify [v] *open to the public*
display, exhibit, make available, make public, publicize, show; SEE CONCEPT *261*

decline [n1] *lessening*
abatement, backsliding, comedown, cropper*, decay, decrepitude, degeneracy, degeneration, descent, deterioration, devolution, diminution, dissolution, dive, downfall, downgrade, down-

de
de

turn, drop, dwindling, ebb, ebbing, enfeeblement, failing, failure, fall, falling off, flop, lapse,
on the skids*, pratfall, recession, relapse, senility, skids*, slump, wane, waning, weakening,
worsening; SEE CONCEPTS *674,698,699*
decline [*n2*] *downward change in value, position*
declivity, decrease, depression, descent, dip,
downslide, downswing, downtrend, downturn,
drop, drop-off, fall-off, hill, incline, lapse, loss,
lowering, pitch, sag, slide, slip, slope, slump; SEE
CONCEPTS *336,346,738*
decline [*v1*] *say no*
abjure, abstain, avoid, balk, beg to be excused,
bypass, demur, deny, desist, disapprove, dismiss,
don't buy*, forbear, forgo, gainsay, nix*, not accept, not hear of, not think of, pass on*, refrain,
refuse, reject, renounce, reprobate, repudiate,
send regrets, shy, spurn, turn down, turn thumbs
down*; SEE CONCEPTS *45,51*
decline [*v2*] *lessen, become less*
abate, backslide, cheapen, decay, decrease, degenerate, depreciate, deteriorate, diminish, disimprove, disintegrate, droop, drop, dwindle, ebb,
fade, fail, fall, fall off, flag, go downhill*, go to
pot*, go to the dogs*, hit the skids*, languish,
lapse, lose value, lower, pine, recede, relapse,
retrograde, return, revert, rot, sag, settle, shrink,
sink, slide, subside, wane, weaken, worsen; SEE
CONCEPTS *240,698*
decline [*v3*] *descend*
dip, droop, drop, fall, go down, lower, sag, set,
settle, sink, slant, slope; SEE CONCEPTS *151,181*
decode [*v*] *decipher*
break, clear up, crack, crack the code, decrypt,
figure out, find the solution, interpret, make
clear, read, solve, translate, unravel, unriddle,
unscramble, untangle, work out; SEE CONCEPTS
15,31,37
decommission [*v*] *withdraw from active service*
deactivate, demilitarize, make inactive, retire,
shut down, shut off; SEE CONCEPTS *25,121,188*
decompose [*v1*] *rot, break up*
break down, crumble, decay, disintegrate, dissolve, fall apart, fester, molder, putrefy, putresce,
spoil, taint, turn; SEE CONCEPT *469*
decompose [*v2*] *analyze by taking apart*
anatomize, atomize, break down, break up, decompound, disintegrate, dissect, dissolve, distill,
resolve, separate; SEE CONCEPTS *24,103*
decomposition [*n*] *rot, breakdown*
atomization, corruption, decay, disintegration,
dissipation, dissolution, division, putrefaction,
putrescence, putridity; SEE CONCEPTS *230,674*
deconstructionist [*n/adj*] *exposing a text's multiple meanings*
critical, debunking, demystifying, demythifying,
hermeneutical, reinterpretative, revisionist; SEE
CONCEPT *268*
decontaminate [*v*] *clean*
antiseptize, cleanse, disinfect, fumigate, make
sterile, purify, sanitize, sterilize, wash; SEE CON-
CEPTS *161,165*
decor [*n*] *colors, furnishings of a place*
adornment, color scheme, decoration, interior
design, ornamentation; SEE CONCEPTS *622,723*
decorate [*v1*] *beautify, embellish*
add finishing touches, adorn, bedeck, bedizen,
brighten, burnish, color, deck, do up*, dress
out*, dress up*, enhance, enrich, festoon, finish,
fix up, frill, furbish, garnish, gild, grace, gussy

up*, idealize, illuminate, jazz up*, ornament,
paint, perfect, prank, renovate, spruce up*, trim;
SEE CONCEPTS *162,177*
decorate [*v2*] *honor and give medal*
cite, laureate, pin medal on, plume; SEE CONCEPT
132
decoration [*n1*] *beautification, embellishment*
adornment, beautifying, bedecking, bedizen-
ment, designing, elaboration, enhancement, enrichment, festooning, flounce, flourish, frill,
furbelow, garnish, garnishing, illumination, improvement, ornament, ornamentation, redecorat-
ing, spangle, trimming; SEE CONCEPTS *162,177*
decoration [*n2*] *particular type of embellishment*
appliqué, arabesque, bauble, braid, color,
curlicue, design, dingbat*, doodad*, extravagance, fandangle*, festoon, filigree, finery,
flounce, flourish, fretwork, frill, frippery, furbelow, fuss, garbage*, garnish, garniture, gew-
gaws, gilt, gimcracks*, gingerbread, inlay, jazz*,
lace, ornament, parquetry, plaque, ribbon, scroll,
sequin, spangle, thing*, tinsel, tooling, trimming,
trinket, wreath; SEE CONCEPTS *259,260*
decoration [*n3*] *medal of honor*
accolade, award, badge, bays, citation, colors,
cross, distinction, emblem, garter, kudos, laurels,
medal, mention, order, Purple Heart, ribbon, star;
SEE CONCEPT *337*
decorative [*adj*] *beautifying*
adorning, cosmetic, embellishing, enhancing,
fancy, florid, nonfunctional, ornamental, prettify-
ing, pretty; SEE CONCEPT *579*
decorous [*adj*] *appropriate, suitable*
au fait, becoming, befitting, ceremonial, ceremonious, civilized, comely, comme il faut, conforming, conventional, correct, decent, demure,
de rigueur, dignified, done, elegant, fit, fitting,
formal, good, mannerly, meet, moral, nice, polite, prim, proper, punctilious, refined, respectable, right, seasonable, sedate, seemly,
staid, well-behaved; SEE CONCEPTS *401,558*
decorum [*n*] *appropriate behavior, good manners*
breeding, civility, conduct, convenance, convention, correctitude, correctness, courtliness, decency, demeanor, deportment, dignity, etiquette,
form, formality, gentility, good grace, gravity,
habits, order, orderliness, politeness, politesse,
properness, propriety, protocol, punctilio, respectability, seemliness, tact, usage; SEE CON-
CEPT *633*
decoy [*n*] *bait, trap*
allurement, attraction, beard*, blind, blow off*,
booster, camouflage, catch, chicane, chicanery,
come-on, deception, drawing card, ensnarement,
enticement, facade, fake, front, imitation, inducement, inveiglement, lure, nark, plant, pretense, seducement, shill, sitting duck*, snare,
stick, stoolie*, stool pigeon*, temptation, trick,
trickery; SEE CONCEPTS *59,230,680*
decoy [*v*] *bait, entrap*
allure, come on, con, deceive, delude, egg one
on*, ensnare, ensorcell, entice, fascinate, inveigle, lead on*, lead up garden path*, lure, mislead, mousetrap*, rope in*, seduce, shill, steer,
suck in*, tempt, toll, tout, trap, wile; SEE CON-
CEPTS *16,59*
decrease [*n*] *diminishing, lessening*
abatement, compression, condensation, constriction, contraction, cutback, decline, declining, de-

crescence, depression, diminution, discount, downturn, dwindling, ebb, falling off, loss, reduction, shrinkage, striction, subsidence, waning; SEE CONCEPT 698

decrease [v] *grow less or make less*
abate, calm down, check, contract, crumble, curb, curtail, cut down, decay, decline, degenerate, depreciate, deteriorate, devaluate, die down, diminish, droop, drop, drop off, dry up, dwindle, ease, ebb, evaporate, fade, fall off, lessen, let up, lighten, lose edge, lower, modify, narrow down, peter out, quell, quiet, reduce, restrain, run low, settle, shrink, shrivel, sink, slacken, slack off, slash, slow down, slump, subside, tail off, wane, waste, weaken, wear away, wear down, wither; SEE CONCEPTS 240,698

decree [n] *mandate, legal order*
act, announcement, behest, bidding, charge, charging, command, commandment, declaration, decretum, dictum, direction, directive, edict, enactment, injunction, instruction, judgment, law, order, ordinance, precept, prescript, proclamation, promulgation, pronouncement, rap*, regulation, rule, ruling, say, statute, the riot act*, the word*, ukase; SEE CONCEPTS 318,685

decree [v] *order rule or action*
announce, command, compel, constrain, decide, declare, demand, determine, dictate, enact, force, impose, lay down the law*, oblige, ordain, prescribe, proclaim, pronounce, put one's foot down*, read the riot act*, require, rule, set; SEE CONCEPTS 50,53,81,88,317

decrepit [adj] *deteriorated, debilitated, especially as a result of age*
aged, anile, antiquated, battered, bedraggled, broken-down, creaky, crippled, dilapidated, doddering, effete, feeble, flimsy, fragile, frail, haggard, incapacitated, infirm, insubstantial, old, quavering, ramshackle, rickety, run-down, seedy, senile, shabby, shaking, superannuated, tacky, threadbare, tired, tottering, tumble-down, unsound, used, wasted, weak, weakly, weatherbeaten, worn, worn-out; SEE CONCEPTS 406,485

decriminalize [v] *legalize*
allow, declare lawful, legitimize, make legal, permit, regulate, sanction; SEE CONCEPTS 298,317

decry [v] *criticize, blame*
abuse, asperse, bad-mouth*, belittle, calumniate, censure, condemn, cry down, defame, denounce, depreciate, derogate, detract, devalue, diminish, discount, discredit, disgrace, disparage, do a number on*, downgrade, dump on*, hit*, knock*, lower, malign, mark down, minimize, opprobriate, pan*, poor-mouth*, put down, rail against, rap, reprehend, reprobate, run down, slam*, take away, take swipe at*, throw stones at*, traduce, underestimate, underrate, undervalue, vilify, write off; SEE CONCEPTS 44,52

dedicate [v1] *donate, set aside for special use*
address, allot, apply, apportion, appropriate, assign, commit, consign, devote, give, give over to, inscribe, offer, pledge, restrict, surrender; SEE CONCEPTS 18,50,88,135

dedicate [v2] *sanctify*
anoint, bless, consecrate, hallow, set apart; SEE CONCEPTS 69,367

dedicated [adj] *loyal, hard-working*
committed, devoted, enthusiastic, faithful, given over to, old faithful*, purposeful, single-hearted, single-minded, sworn, true blue*, true to the end*, wholehearted, zealous; SEE CONCEPTS 404,542

dedication [n1] *faithfulness, loyalty*
adherence, allegiance, commitment, devotedness, devotion, single-mindedness, wholeheartedness; SEE CONCEPTS 411,657

dedication [n2] *speech of praise; sanctification*
address, celebration, consecration, devotion, envoy, glorification, hallowing, inscription, message; SEE CONCEPTS 69,367

deduce [v] *figure out, understand*
add up, analyze, assume, be afraid, boil down, cogitate, collect, conceive, conclude, consider, deduct, deem, derive, draw, fancy, figure, gather, glean, have a hunch*, imagine, infer, judge, make, make out, presume, presuppose, ratiocinate, read into, reason, regard, surmise, take to mean; SEE CONCEPTS 15,24

deducible [adj] *understandable*
a priori, consequent, deductive, derivable, dogmatic, following, inferable, inferential, provable, reasoned, traceable; SEE CONCEPTS 402,529

deduct [v] *take away or out; reduce*
abstract, allow, bate, cut back, decrease by, diminish, discount, dock, draw back, knock off, lessen, rebate, reduce, remove, roll back, subtract, take, take from, take off, withdraw, write off; SEE CONCEPTS 236,247,330

deduction [n1] *conclusion, understanding*
answer, assumption, cogitation, concluding, consequence, consideration, contemplation, corollary, deliberation, derivation, finding, illation, inference, inferring, judgment, meditation, mulling, musing, opinion, pondering, ratiocination, reasoning, reflection, result, rumination, sequitur, speculation, thinking, thought; SEE CONCEPTS 15,24,689

deduction [n2] *something subtracted*
abatement, abstraction, allowance, credit, cut, decrease, decrement, depreciation, diminution, discount, dockage, excision, rebate, reduction, removal, subtraction, withdrawal, write-off; SEE CONCEPTS 763,776

deed [n1] *achievement*
accomplishment, act, action, adventure, ballgame, big idea*, bit, byplay, cause, commission, crusade, do, enterprise, exploit, fact, feat, follow through, game, happenin'*, performance, plan, quest, reality, securing, stunt, thing*, tour de force, truth, winning; SEE CONCEPTS 4,706

deed [n2] *legal paper assigning property; contract*
agreement, bargain, certificate, charter, compact, conveyance, covenant, document, indenture, instrument, lease, papers, proof, record, release, security, title, transaction, voucher, warranty; SEE CONCEPTS 271,318

deem [v] *regard, consider*
account, allow, appraise, assume, be afraid, believe, calculate, conceive, conjecture, credit, daresay, divine, esteem, estimate, expect, feel, guess, hold, imagine, judge, know, presume, reckon, sense, set store by, suppose, surmise, suspect, think, understand, view; SEE CONCEPTS 12,28

deep [adj1] *extending very far, usually down*
abysmal, abyssal, below, beneath, bottomless, broad, buried, deep-seated, distant, downreaching, far, fathomless, immersed, inmost, low, pro-

found, rooted, subaqueous, submarine, submerged, subterranean, sunk, underground, unfathomable, wide, yawning; SEE CONCEPTS *737,777*

deep [*adj2*] *abstract, complicated in meaning*
abstruse, acute, arcane, complex, concealed, Delphic, difficult, discerning, esoteric, hard to understand, heavy*, hermetic, hidden, incisive, intricate, learned, mysterious, obscure, occult, Orphic, penetrating, profound, recondite, sagacious, secret, serious, Sibylline, wise; SEE CONCEPTS *402,529*

deep [*adj3*] *scheming, devious*
acute, artful, astute, canny, contriving, crafty, cunning, designing, foxy, guileful, insidious, intriguing, keen, knowing, plotting, sharp, shrewd, sly, tricky, wily; SPEAK CONCEPT *404*

deep [*adj4*] *absorbed, engrossed in activity*
abstracted, centered, concentrated, enfolded, engaged, fixed, focused, immersed, intent, into, lost, musing, preoccupied, rapt, set, wrapped, wrapped up; SEE CONCEPT *542*

deep [*adj5*] *intense in effect on senses*
bass, booming, dark, extreme, full-toned, grave, great, hard, low, low-pitched, low-toned, profound, resonant, rich, sonorous, strong, vivid; SEE CONCEPTS *537,594,618*

deep [*n*] *the sea*
blue*, brine, briny*, Davy Jones's locker*, drink*, main, middle, ocean, Poseidon's realm*, the high seas; SEE CONCEPT *514*

deepen [*v1*] *make depth greater*
dig, dig out, dredge, excavate, expand, extend, hollow, scoop out, scrape out; SEE CONCEPT *250*

deepen [*v2*] *make more intense*
aggravate, develop, enhance, expand, extend, grow, heighten, increase, intensate, intensify, magnify, mount, redouble, reinforce, rise, rouse, strengthen; SEE CONCEPTS *236,245,697*

deeply [*adv*] *completely, intensely*
acutely, affectingly, distressingly, feelingly, genuinely, gravely, intensely, mournfully, movingly, passionately, profoundly, sadly, seriously, severely, surely, thoroughly, to the quick; SEE CONCEPTS *531,772*

deep-seated [*adj*] *ingrained*
built-in, chronic, confirmed, deep down, deeply felt, deep-rooted, dyed-in-the-wool, established, fixed, habitual, inborn, inbred, inherent, lodged in one's brain*, longstanding, longtime, subconscious; SEE CONCEPTS *535,549*

deep space [*n*] *region beyond Earth's solar system*
intergalactic space, interplanetary space, interstellar space, outer space; SEE CONCEPTS *370,511*

deface [*v*] *mar, mutilate*
blemish, contort, damage, deform, demolish, destroy, dilapidate, disfigure, distort, harm, impair, injure, mangle, misshape, obliterate, ruin, scratch, spoil, sully, tarnish, trash*, vandalize, wreck; SEE CONCEPTS *246,252*

de facto [*adv*] *in reality*
actual, actually, existing, genuinely, in effect, in fact, real, really, tangible, truly, veritably; SEE CONCEPT *582*

defamation [*n*] *libel, slander*
aspersion, backbiting, backstabbing, belittlement, black eye*, calumny, character assassination, cheap shot*, denigration, depreciation, detraction, dirt, dirty laundry*, disparagement,

dump*, dynamite, hit, knock, lie, low-down dirty*, mud, obloquy, opprobrium, scorcher, slam*, slap in face*, slime, slur, smear, tale, traducement, vilification; SEE CONCEPT *54*

defamatory [*adj*] *libelous, slanderous*
abusive, calumnious, contumelious, denigrating, derogatory, detracting, detractive, disparaging, injurious, insulting, maligning, opprobrious, traducing, vilifying, vituperative; SEE CONCEPTS *267,537*

defame [*v*] *inflict libel or slander*
asperse, bad-mouth*, belie, besmirch, blacken, blister, calumniate, cast aspersions on, cast slur on, denigrate, detract, discredit, disgrace, dishonor, disparage, do a number on*, knock, malign, pan*, put zingers on*, roast, scandalize, scorch, slam, smear, speak evil of*, stigmatize, throw mud at*, traduce, vilify, villainize, vituperate; SEE CONCEPTS *7,19,54*

default [*n*] *failure; want*
absence, blemish, blunder, dearth, defect, deficiency, delinquency, dereliction, disregard, error, fault, imperfection, inadequacy, insufficiency, lack, lapse, miss, neglect, nonpayment, offense, omission, overlooking, oversight, privation, shortcoming, slight, transgression, vice, weakness, wrongdoing; SEE CONCEPTS *335,699,709*

default [*v*] *dodge payment*
bilk, defraud, dishonor, evade, fail, leave town*, meet under arch*, neglect, put on the cuff*, rat*, repudiate, run out on*, see in the alley, shirk, skate*, skip, skip out on*, stiff*, swindle, welch, welsh; SEE CONCEPTS *59,63,330*

defeat [*n1*] *overthrow, beating*
ambush, annihilation, beating, blow, break, breakdown, check, collapse, conquest, count, debacle, defeasance, destruction, discomfiture, downthrow, drubbing*, embarrassment, extermination, failure, fall, insuccess, killing*, KO*, lacing, licking, loss, massacre, mastery, nonsuccess, paddling, rebuff, repulse, reverse, rout, ruin, scalping, setback, shellacking*, slaughter, subjugation, thrashing, trap, trashing, trimming, triumph, trouncing, vanquishment, waxing, whaling, whipping, whitewashing*; SEE CONCEPT *95*

defeat [*n2*] *frustration*
disappointment, discomfiture, downfall, failure, foil, loss, rebuff, repulse, reversal, reverse, setback, thwarting; SEE CONCEPT *410*

defeat [*v1*] *conquer in military manner*
ambush, annihilate, bar, bear down, beat, best, block, butcher, crush, decimate, demolish, discomfit, drown, entrap, finish off, halt, hinder, impede, lick, mow down, obliterate, obstruct, outflank, outmaneuver, overpower, overrun, overthrow, overwhelm, parry, prevail over, quell, reduce, repel, repress, repulse, roll back, rout, route, sack, scatter, shipwreck, sink, slaughter, smash, subdue, subjugate, suppress, surmount, swamp, torpedo*, trample, trash, upset, vanquish, whip, wipe out; SEE CONCEPTS *95,320*

defeat [*v2*] *conquer in athletic contest*
beat, bust*, clobber*, cream*, deck*, drop*, drub*, edge, flax*, flog*, floor*, knock out*, KO*, lambaste*, lick, outhit, outjump, outplay, outrun, overpower, plow under*, pommel*, pound*, powder*, pulverize*, run roughshod over*, skin*, steamroll*, take, take it all*, take to

cleaners*, tan*, thrash, total, trounce, wallop*, whack*, whomp*, win, work over*, zap*; SEE CONCEPTS 95,363

defeat [v3] *frustrate*
baffle, balk, beat down*, beat the system*, blank, block, bury, cast down, cause setback, checkmate, circumvent, confound, contravene, cook*, counterplot, cross, disappoint, discomfit, disconcert, disprove, edge out*, foil, invalidate, neutralize, nonplus, nose out*, nullify, outwit, overturn, put end to*, puzzle, quell, reduce, refute, ruin, scuttle, shave*, shellac*, skunk*, spoil, squash, stump, subdue, subjugate, surmount, take wind out of sails*, throw for loop*, thwart, undo, victimize; SEE CONCEPTS 14,121

defect [n] *blemish, imperfection*
birthmark, blot, blotch, break, bug, catch, check, crack, deficiency, deformity, discoloration, drawback, error, failing, fault, flaw, foible, frailty, gap, glitch, gremlin, hole, infirmity, injury, irregularity, kink, knot, lack, mark, marring, mistake, patch, rift, rough spot, scar, scarcity, scratch, seam, second, shortage, shortcoming, sin, speck, spot, stain, taint, unsoundness, vice, want, weakness, weak point; SEE CONCEPTS 309,580,646

defect [v] *break from belief, faith*
abandon, abscond, apostatize, back out, break faith*, change sides, depart, desert, fall away from, forsake, go, go back on, go over, go over the fence*, lapse, leave, pull out, quit, rat*, rebel, reject, renege, renounce, revolt, run out, schism, sell out*, spurn, take a walk*, tergiversate, tergiverse, turn, turn coat*, walk out on, withdraw; SEE CONCEPTS 198,367

defection [n] *abandonment*
alienation, apostasy, backsliding, deficiency, dereliction, desertion, disaffection, disloyalty, disownment, divorce, estrangement, failing, failure, faithlessness, forsaking, lack, parting, rebellion, recreancy, rejection, repudiation, retreat, revolt, separation, severance, sundering, tergiversation, withdrawal; SEE CONCEPTS 195,198, 367

defective [adj] *broken, not working*
abnormal, amiss, blemished, damaged, deficient, faulty, flawed, impaired, imperfect, inadequate, incomplete, injured, insufficient, lacking, on the bum*, out of order, poor, seconds, sick, subnormal, unfinished, unhealthy, unsound, wanting; SEE CONCEPTS 560,565

defend [v1] *protect*
avert, battle, beat off, bulwark, care for, cherish, conserve, contend, cover, entrench, espouse, fend off, fight, fight for, fortify, foster, garrison, guard, guard against, hedge, hold, hold at bay, house, insure, keep safe, look after, maintain, mine, nourish, oppose, panoply, preserve, prevent, provide sanctuary, repel danger, resist, retain, safeguard, save, screen, secure, shelter, shield, stave off, sustain, take in, uphold, war, ward off, watch, watch over, withstand; SEE CONCEPTS 96,110

defend [v2] *show support for*
advocate, aid, apologize for, argue, assert, back, back up, bear one out*, befriend, champion, come to defense of, cover for, endorse, espouse, exculpate, exonerate, explain, go to bat for*, guarantee, justify, maintain, plead, prove a case, put in a good word*, rationalize, recommend,

ride shotgun for*, say in defense, second, speak up for, stand by, stand up for, stick up for, stonewall*, support, sustain, thump for, uphold, vindicate, warrant; SEE CONCEPTS 10,49

defendant [n] *accused*
appellant, litigant, offender, prisoner, suspect; SEE CONCEPT 412

defense [n1] *armament; protection system*
aegis, armor, arms, barricade, bastille, bastion, bulwark, buttress, citadel, cover, deterrence, dike, embankment, fastness, fence, fort, fortification, fortress, garrison, guard, immunity, munitions, palisade, parapet, position, protection, rampart, redoubt, resistance, safeguard, security, shelter, shield, stockade, stronghold, trench, wall, ward, warfare, weaponry, weapons; SEE CONCEPTS 321,322,500

defense [n2] *explanation, justification*
answer, apologetics, apologia, apologizing, apology, argument, cleanup, copout*, exculpation, excuse, excusing, exoneration, explaining, extenuation, fish story*, jive, off-time*, plea, rationalization, rejoinder, reply, response, retort, return, song and dance*, story, vindication, whitewash*; SEE CONCEPTS 57,278

defenseless [adj] *powerless, vulnerable*
caught, endangered, exposed, hands tied*, helpless, indefensible, in line of fire*, like a clay pigeon*, like a sitting duck*, naked*, on the line*, on the spot*, open, out on limb*, pigeon*, poor, unarmed, unguarded, unprotected, up the creek*, weak, wide open*; SEE CONCEPTS 555,576

defensible [adj] *justifiable*
condonable, defendable, excusable, fit, logical, pardonable, permissible, plausible, proper, tenable, valid, vindicable, warrantable; SEE CONCEPT 528

defensive [adj] *protective, watchful*
arresting, averting, balking, checking, conservative, coping with, defending, foiling, forestalling, frustrating, guarding, in opposition, interrupting, opposing, preservative, preventive, protecting, resistive, safeguarding, thwarting, uptight*, warding off, withstanding; SEE CONCEPTS 401,550

defer [v1] *hold off, put off*
adjourn, block, delay, detain, extend, give rain check*, hang fire*, hinder, hold up, impede, intermit, lay over, lengthen, obstruct, postpone, procrastinate, prolong, prorogue, protract, put on back burner*, put on hold*, put on ice*, remit, retard, set aside, shelve, slow, stall, stay, suspend, table, waive; SEE CONCEPTS 121,130

defer [v2] *yield*
accede, accommodate, acquiesce, adapt, adjust, admit, agree, assent, bow, buckle, capitulate, cave, comply, concede, cringe, fawn, give in to, knuckle*, knuckle under*, kowtow*, obey, submit, succumb, truckle; SEE CONCEPT 83

deference [n1] *obedience, compliance*
acquiescence, capitulation, complaisance, condescension, docility, obeisance, submission, yielding; SEE CONCEPT 633

deference [n2] *attention, homage*
acclaim, civility, consideration, courtesy, esteem, honor, obeisance, politeness, regard, respect, reverence, thoughtfulness, veneration; SEE CONCEPTS 10,410

deferential [adj] *respectful, considerate*
civil, complaisant, courteous, disarming, du-

de
de

teous, dutiful, ingratiating, ingratiatory, insinuating, insinuative, obedient, obeisant, obsequious, polite, regardful, reverential, saccharine, silken, silky, submissive; SEE CONCEPT *401*

deferment/deferral [n] *postponement*
adjournment, delay, holdover*, moratorium, pause, putting off*, stay, suspension; SEE CONCEPTS *121,130*

deferred [adj] *put off till a later time*
adjourned, assessed, charged, delayed, funded, held up, indebted, in waiting, negotiated, on hold*, on the shelf*, pigeonholed*, postponed, prolonged, protracted, remanded, renegotiated, retarded, scrubbed*, stalled, staved off, temporized; SEE CONCEPT *820*

defiance [n] *disobedience, disregard*
affront, audacity, back talk*, big talk*, boldness, bravado, brazenness, call, cartel, challenge, command, confrontation, contempt, contrariness, contumacy, dare, defy, effrontery, enjoinder, factiousness, gas*, guts*, hot air*, impudence, impugnment, insolence, insubordination, insurgence, insurgency, intractableness, lip*, muster*, opposition, order, perversity, provocation, rebellion, rebelliousness, recalcitrance, revolt, sass*, spite, stump, summons, temerity, throwing of the gauntlet*, unruliness; SEE CONCEPTS *633,657*

defiant [adj] *disobedient, disregardful*
aggressive, audacious, bold, challenging, contumacious, daring, gutsy*, insolent, insubmissive, insubordinate, mutinous, obstinate, provocative, rebellious, recalcitrant, reckless, refractory, resistant, resistive, sassy*, truculent; SEE CONCEPT *401*

deficiency [n] *imperfection, inadequacy*
absence, bug*, dearth, defalcation, default, defect, deficit, demerit, dereliction, failing, failure, fault, flaw, frailty, glitch*, inability to hack it*, insufficience, insufficiency, lack, loss, need, neglect, paucity, privation, scantiness, scarcity, shortage, shortcoming, sin, want, weakness; SEE CONCEPTS *635,666,674*

deficient [adj] *imperfect, inadequate*
amiss, bad, damaged, defective, exiguous, faulty, flawed, found wanting, impaired, incomplete, inferior, infrequent, injured, insufficient, lacking, marred, meager, not cut out for*, not enough, not make it*, not up to scratch*, outta gas*, rare, scant, scanty*, scarce, second fiddle*, second string, short, shy, sketchy, skimpy, third string*, unassembled, unequal, unfinished, unsatisfactory, wanting, weak; SEE CONCEPTS *531,565*

deficit [n] *shortage of something needed, required*
arrears, dead horse*, defalcation, default, deficiency, due bill, dues, inadequacy, in hock*, insufficience, insufficiency, in the hole*, in the red, lack, loss, paucity, red ink*, scantiness, shortcoming, shortfall, underage; SEE CONCEPTS *335,646*

deficit spending [n] *paying out in excess of income*
debt, debt explosion, deficit financing, in the red, megadebt, negative cash flow, no assets, overspending; SEE CONCEPTS *324,330,344*

defile [v] *corrupt, violate*
abuse, adulterate, befoul, besmirch, contaminate, debase, deflower, degrade, desecrate, dirty, discolor, disgrace, dishonor, hurt, maculate, make foul, mess up*, molest, muck up*, pollute, profane, rape, ravish, scuzz up*, seduce, shame, smear, soil, stain, sully, taint, tar, tarnish, trash, vitiate; SEE CONCEPTS *54,156,246*

defiled [adj] *corrupted, violated*
besmirched, common, cooked, desecrated, dirty, dishonored, exposed, impure, mucked up*, polluted, profaned, ravished, spoilt, tainted, trashed*, unclean, vitiated; SEE CONCEPT *570*

define [v1] *give description*
ascertain, assign, call a spade a spade*, characterize, construe, decide, delineate, denominate, denote, describe, designate, detail, determine, dub, elucidate, entitle, etch, exemplify, explain, expound, formalize, illustrate, interpret, label, lay it out*, nail it down*, name, prescribe, represent, specify, spell out, tag, translate; SEE CONCEPTS *55,57,62*

define [v2] *delimit, outline*
belt, border, bound, circumscribe, compass, confine, curb, delineate, demarcate, distinguish, edge, encircle, enclose, encompass, envelop, establish, fence in, fix, flank, gird, girdle, limit, mark, mark out, rim, set, set bounds to, settle, stake out, surround, verge, wall in; SEE CONCEPTS *18,60,758*

definite [adj1] *exact, clear*
audible, bold, categorical, clean-cut, clear-cut, clearly defined, complete, crisp, definitive, determined, distinct, distinguishable, downright, explicit, express, fixed, forthright, full, graphic, incisive, marked, minute, not vague, obvious, palpable, particular, plain, positive, precise, pronounced, ringing, severe, sharp, silhouetted, specific, straightforward, tangible, unambiguous, undubitable, unequivocal, unmistakable, visible, vivid, well-defined, well-grounded, well-marked; SEE CONCEPT *557*

definite [adj2] *fixed, certain, positive*
assigned, assured, beyond doubt, circumscribed, convinced, assured, decided, defined, determinate, determined, established, guaranteed, limited, narrow, precise, prescribed, restricted, set, settled, sure; SEE CONCEPT *535*

definitely [adv] *certainly*
absolutely, beyond any doubt, categorically, clearly, decidedly, doubtless, doubtlessly, easily, explicitly, expressly, far and away*, finally, indubitably, no ifs ands or buts about it*, obviously, plainly, positively, specifically, surely, undeniably, unequivocally, unmistakably, unquestionably, without doubt, without fail, without question; SEE CONCEPTS *535,552*

definition [n] *description*
analogue, annotation, answer, characterization, clarification, clue, comment, commentary, cue, delimitation, delineation, demarcation, denotation, determination, diagnosis, drift, elucidation, exemplification, explanation, explication, exposition, expounding, fixing, formalization, gloss, individuation, interpretation, key, outlining, rationale, rendering, rendition, representation, settling, signification, solution, statement of meaning, terminology, translation; SEE CONCEPTS *274,278,689*

definitive [adj] *authoritative*
absolute, actual, categorical, clear-cut, closing, complete, completing, concluding, conclusive, decisive, definite, determining, downright*, ending, exhaustive, express, final, finishing, flat

out*, last, limiting, nailed down, perfect, plain, precise, real, reliable, settling, specific, straight out, terminal, terminating, ultimate, unambiguous; SEE CONCEPTS *531,535,574*

deflate [*v1*] *reduce or cause to contract*
collapse, decrease, depreciate, depress, devalue, diminish, empty, exhaust, flatten, puncture, shrink, squash, void; SEE CONCEPTS *236,247,776*

deflate [*v2*] *humiliate*
chasten, cut down to size*, dash, debunk, disconcert, dispirit, humble, kick in the teeth*, knock down*, let down easy*, let wind out of sails*, mortify, puncture balloon*, put down*, shoot down*, take down*; SEE CONCEPTS *7,19*

deflect [*v*] *bounce off; turn aside*
avert, bend, cover up, curve, deviate, disperse, diverge, divert, fend, glance off, hold off, hook, keep off, parry, pivot, ricochet, sheer, shy, sidetrack, slew, slip, swerve, twist, veer, volte-face, wheel, whip, whirl, wind; SEE CONCEPTS *147,189,194*

deflower [*v*] *ravish; take away beauty*
assault, defile, deflorate, depredate, desecrate, despoil, devour, force, harm, have, mar, molest, outrage, possess, ravage, ravish, ruin, seduce, spoil, violate; SEE CONCEPT *375*

deforestation [*n*] *clear-cutting*
denuding, desertification, erosion, logging; SEE CONCEPTS *252,257,698*

deform [*v*] *distort, disfigure*
batter, blemish, buckle, contort, cripple, damage, deface, flaw, gnarl, grimace, impair, injure, knot, maim, malform, mangle, mar, misshape, mutilate, ruin, skew, spoil, twist, warp, wince; SEE CONCEPTS *246,250*

deformed [*adj*] *disfigured, distorted*
askew, awry, bent, blemished, bowed, buckled, contorted, cramped, crippled, crooked, curved, damaged, disjointed, gnarled, grotesque, humpbacked, hunchbacked, ill-made, irregular, knotted, maimed, malformed, mangled, marred, misproportioned, misshapen, out of shape, scarred, twisted, ugly, warped; SEE CONCEPTS *485,486*

deformity [*n*] *disfigurement, distortion*
aberration, abnormality, asymmetry, buckle, contortion, corruption, crookedness, damage, defacement, defect, depravity, evil, grossness, hideousness, impairment, injury, irregularity, knot, malconformation, malformation, misproportion, misshape, misshapenness, repulsiveness, ugliness, unattractiveness, unnaturalness, unsightliness, warp; SEE CONCEPT *580*

defraud [*v*] *cheat, bilk*
bamboozle, beguile, burn, chouse, circumvent, clip, con, cozen, deceive, delude, do, do number on*, do out of*, dupe, embezzle, fleece, flimflam, foil, hoax, jive*, milk*, outwit, pilfer, pull fast one*, rip off*, rob, shaft*, shuck*, stick*, sucker into*, swindle, take*, take in*, take to the cleaner's*, trick, victimize; SEE CONCEPT *59*

defray [*v*] *pay*
bear the cost*, chip in*, cover cost, finance, foot the bill*, fund, pay for, pick up the bill*, pick up the check*, pick up the tab*, settle; SEE CONCEPTS *108,115,327,341,351*

deft [*adj*] *agile, clever*
able, adept, adroit, apt, crack, crackerjack*, cute, dexterous, expert, fleet, handy, having good hands, having know-how, ingenious, neat, nimble, proficient, prompt, quick, ready, skilled, skillful; SEE CONCEPT *527*

defunct [*adj*] *extinct, not functioning*
asleep, bygone, cold, dead, deceased, departed, done for*, down the drain*, exanimate, expired, gone, had it*, inanimate, inoperative, invalid, kaput*, late, lifeless, lost, nonexistent, obsolete, out of commission*, vanished; SEE CONCEPTS *539,560*

defuse [*v*] *disarm; smooth over*
alleviate, cripple, deactivate, demilitarize, diminish, disable, lessen, moderate, mollify, pacify, pad, restrain, soften, soothe, subdue, weaken; SEE CONCEPTS *7,22,142,211,320*

defy [*v*] *challenge, frustrate*
baffle, beard, brave, confront, contemn, dare, defeat, deride, despise, disregard, elude, face, flout, fly in face of*, foil, front, gibe*, hang tough*, hurl defiance at, ignore, insult, make my day*, mock, oppose, outdare, provoke, repel, repulse, resist, ridicule, scorn, slight, spurn, stick*, stick fast*, take one on*, thwart, venture, violate, withstand; SEE CONCEPTS *78,87*

degeneracy [*n1*] *corruption*
abasement, decadence, degradation, depravity, dissoluteness, downfall, immorality, inferiority, meanness, poorness; SEE CONCEPT *645*

degeneracy [*n2*] *decay, deterioration*
atrophy, debasement, declination, decline, decrease, depravation, devolution, downfall, downgrade; SEE CONCEPTS *230,469*

degenerate [*adj*] *corrupt, deteriorated*
base, debased, debauched, decadent, decayed, degenerated, degraded, demeaned, depraved, dissolute, effete, failing, fallen, flatitious, immoral, infamous, low, mean, miscreant, nefarious, overripe, perverted, retrograde, retrogressive, rotten, sinking, unhealthy, vicious, villainous, vitiated, wicked, worsen; SEE CONCEPTS *545,570*

degenerate [*v*] *decay, deteriorate*
backslide, come apart at seams*, corrode, corrupt, decline, decrease, deprave, descend, die on vine*, disimprove, disintegrate, fall off, go downhill*, go to pieces*, go to the dogs*, lapse, lessen, regress, retrogress, return, revert, rot, sink, slip, vitiate, worsen; SEE CONCEPTS *469,698,702*

degradation [*n*] *depravity, shame*
abasement, debasement, decadence, decline, degeneracy, degeneration, demotion, derogation, deterioration, discredit, disgrace, dishonor, downgrading, evil, humiliation, ignominy, mortification, perversion, reduction; SEE CONCEPTS *230,410*

degrade [*v*] *shame, humiliate*
abase, belittle, bemean, bench, break, bump, bust, canker, cast down, cheapen, corrupt, cut down to size*, debase, debauch, declass, decry, degenerate, demean, demote, depose, deprave, derogate, deteriorate, detract, diminish, disbar, discredit, disgrace, dishonor, disparage, downgrade, humble, impair, injure, lessen, lower, mudsling*, pan*, pervert, put down, reduce, rule out, run down*, shoot down*, sink, slam, take down*, take down a peg*, tear down*, vitiate, weaken; SEE CONCEPTS *7,19,240*

degrading [*adj*] *debasing*
cheapening, demeaning, derogatory, disgraceful, downgrading, humiliating, lowering; SEE CONCEPTS *267,555,570*

degree [*n1*] *unit of measurement*
amount, amplitude, caliber, dimension, division, expanse, extent, gauge, gradation, grade, height, intensity, interval, length, limit, line, link, mark, notch, period, plane, point, proportion, quality, quantity, range, rate, ratio, reach, rung, scale, scope, severity, shade, size, space, stage, stair, standard, step, stint, strength, tenor, term, tier; SEE CONCEPTS *651,783,792*

degree [*n2*] *recognition of achievement; rank or grade of position*
approbation, approval, baccalaureate, caliber, class, compass, credentials, credit, dignification, dignity, distinction, eminence, grade, height, honor, level, magnitude, order, pitch, point, position, potency, qualification, quality, quantity, range, rank, reach, scope, sheepskin, shingle, sort, stage, standard, standing, station, status, strength, testimonial, testimony; SEE CONCEPTS *388,706*

dehydrate [*v*] *take moisture out of*
cotton-mouth, desiccate, drain, dry, dry out, dry up, evaporate, exsiccate, parch, sear; SEE CONCEPTS *250,469*

deify [*v*] *elevate, glorify*
adore, apotheosize, consecrate, ennoble, enthrone, exalt, extol, idealize, idolize, immortalize, venerate, worship; SEE CONCEPTS *69,367*

deign [*v*] *lower oneself*
condescend, consent, deem worthy, patronize, see fit*, stoop, think fit*, vouchsafe; SEE CONCEPT *35*

deity [*n*] *god, worshiped being*
celestial, celestial being, creator, divine being, divinity, goddess, godhead, idol, immortal, supreme being; SEE CONCEPTS *368,370*

déjà vu [*n*] *already seen or experienced*
familiarity, past-life experience, recall, recognition, remembrance; SEE CONCEPTS *40,529*

dejected [*adj*] *depressed, blue*
abject, all torn up*, atrabilious, black, bleak, broody, bummed out*, cast down, cheerless, clouded, crestfallen, dampened, dashed, despondent, disconsolate, discouraged, disheartened, dismal, dispirited, doleful, down, downcast, downhearted, down in the dumps*, down in the mouth*, dragged, drooping, droopy, gloomy, glum, heavyhearted, hurting*, in the pits*, low, low-spirited, melancholy, miserable, moody, mopey*, mopish*, morose, sad, sagging, shot down*, spiritless, woebegone, wretched; SEE CONCEPT *403*

delay [*n*] *deferment, interruption*
adjournment, bind, check, cooling-off period*, cunctation, dawdling, demurral, detention, discontinuation, downtime*, filibuster, hangup*, hindrance, holding, holding pattern*, hold-up*, impediment, interval, jam, lag, lingering, logjam*, loitering, moratorium, obstruction, postponement, problem, procrastination, prorogation, putting off*, remission, reprieve, retardation, retardment, setback, showstopper*, stall, stay, stop, stoppage, surcease, suspension, tarrying, tie-up, wait; SEE CONCEPTS *121,130,666*

delay [*v*] *cause stop in action*
adjourn, arrest, bar, bide time, block, check, choke, clog, confine, curb, dawdle, defer, detain, deter, dilly-dally*, discourage, drag, encumber, filibuster, gain time, hamper, hold, hold over, impede, inhibit, interfere, intermit, keep, keep back,

lag, lay over, linger, loiter, obstruct, postpone, prevent, procrastinate, prolong, prorogue, protract, put off, remand, repress, restrict, retard, shelve, slacken, stall, stave off, stay, suspend, table, tarry, temporize, withhold; SEE CONCEPTS *121,130,237*

delectable [*adj*] *delicious, enjoyable*
adorable, agreeable, ambrosial, appetizing, charming, choice, dainty, darling, delicate, delightful, delish, divine, enticing, exquisite, gratifying, heavenly, inviting, luscious, lush, palatable, pleasant, pleasurable, rare, sapid, satisfying, savory, scrumptious, tasty, toothsome, yummy; SEE CONCEPTS *574,579,613*

delegate [*n*] *representative, often governmental*
agent, alternate, ambassador, appointee, catchpole*, commissioner, consul, deputy, emissary, envoy, factor, front*, legate, member, member of congress, minister, mouthpiece, nominee, people's choice, pinch hitter*, plenipotentiary, proxy, regent, rep*, replacement, senator, spokesperson, stand-in, substitute, surrogate, vicar, viceroy; SEE CONCEPT *354*

delegate [*v1*] *give authority; empower*
accredit, appoint, assign, authorize, cast, charge, choose, commission, constitute, depute, deputize, designate, elect, give nod, invest, license, mandate, name, nominate, ordain, place trust in, select, swear in, warrant; SEE CONCEPTS *50,88*

delegate [*v2*] *assign responsibility*
authorize, consign, devolve, entrust, give, hand over, hold responsible for, parcel out*, pass on*, relegate, send on errand, send on mission, shunt, transfer; SEE CONCEPTS *50,88,143*

delegation [*n1*] *assignment of responsibility*
appointment, apportioning, authorization, charge, commissioning, committal, consigning, consignment, conveyance, conveying, deputation, deputization, deputizing, devolution, entrustment, giving over, installation, investiture, mandate, nomination, ordination, reference, referring, relegation, sending away, submittal, submitting, transferal, transference, transferring, trust; SEE CONCEPTS *50,88,143,685*

delegation [*n2*] *group of representatives*
commission, contingent, deputation, embassy, envoys, gathering, legation, mission, organization; SEE CONCEPTS *299,301*

delete [*v*] *erase, remove*
annul, black out, bleep, blot out, blue-pencil*, cancel, clean, clean up, cross out, cut, cut out, decontaminate, destroy, drop, edit, efface, eliminate, exclude, expunge, obliterate, omit, pass up, rub, rub out, rule out, sanitize, snip, squash, squelch, sterilize, strike out, trim, wipe out, X-out*; SEE CONCEPT *211*

deleterious [*adj*] *harmful, damaging*
bad, destroying, destructive, detrimental, hurtful, injurious, mischievous, nocent, nocuous, pernicious, prejudicial, prejudicious, ruining, ruinous; SEE CONCEPTS *537,570*

deliberate [*adj*] *intentional*
advised, aforethought, calculated, careful, cautious, cold-blooded, conscious, considered, cut-and-dried*, designed, designful, done on purpose, express, fixed, intended, judged, meticulous, planned, pondered, prearranged, predesigned, predeterminate, predetermined, premeditated, prepense, projected, provident, prudent, purposed, purposeful, purposive, rea-

soned, resolved, schemed, scrupulous, studied, studious, thoughtful, thought out, voluntary, wary, weighed, willful, with forethought, witting; SEE CONCEPTS *401,542*

deliberate [v] *think about seriously; discuss* argue, bat it around*, cerebrate, chew over*, cogitate, consider, consult, contemplate, debate, excogitate, hammer away at*, judge, kick around, knock around, meditate, mull over, muse, ponder, pour it on*, put on thinking cap*, rack brains*, reason, reflect, revolve, roll, ruminate, run up a flagpole*, speculate, stew over*, study, sweat over*, talk over, turn over, weigh; SEE CONCEPTS *17,24,56*

deliberately [adv] *intentionally* advisedly, after consideration, apurpose, by design, calculatingly, consciously, designed, determinedly, emphatically, freely, in cold blood, independently, knowingly, meaningfully, on purpose, pointedly, premeditatively, prepensely, purposely, purposively, resolutely, studiously, to that end, voluntarily, willfully, with a view to, with eyes wide open*, with malice aforethought*, without qualms, wittingly; SEE CONCEPTS *401,542*

deliberation [n] *serious thought, discussion* application, attention, brainwork, calculation, care, carefulness, caution, cerebration, circumspection, cogitation, confabulation, conference, consideration, consultation, debate, forethought, heed, meditation, prudence, purpose, rap, ratiocination, reflection, speculation, study, ventilation, wariness; SEE CONCEPTS *17,24,56*

delicacy [n1] *daintiness, fineness of structure* airiness, debility, diaphaneity, elegance, etherealness, exquisiteness, fragility, frailness, frailty, gossameriness, infirmity, lightness, slenderness, smoothness, softness, subtlety, tenderness, tenuity, translucency, transparency, weakness; SEE CONCEPTS *611,733*

delicacy [n2] *delicious, gourmet food* ambrosia, banquet, bonne bouche, dainty, delight, dessert, feast, goody, indulgence, luxury, morsel, nectar, pleasure, rarity, regale, relish, savory, special, sweet, tidbit, treat; SEE CONCEPT *457*

delicate [adj1] *dainty, weak* aerial, balmy, breakable, choice, delectable, delicious, delightful, elegant, ethereal, exquisite, faint, filmy, fine, fine-grained, finespun, flimsy, fracturable, fragile, frail, frangible, gauzy, gentle, gossamery, graceful, hairline, mild, muted, nice, pale, pastel, rare, recherché, select, shatterable, shattery, slight, soft, subdued, subtle, superior, tender; SEE CONCEPTS *490,574,606*

delicate [adj2] *sickly* ailing, debilitated, decrepit, feeble, flimsy, fragile, frail, infirm, shatterable, shattery, slender, slight, susceptible, tender, unhealthy, weak; SEE CONCEPT *314*

delicate [adj3] *fussy, discriminating* alert, careful, critical, dainty, fastidious, finical, finicking, finicky, gentle, nice, particular, persnickety, prudish, pure, refined, scrupulous, sensitive, squeamish, thin-skinned; SEE CONCEPT *404*

delicate [adj4] *difficult, sticky (situation)* critical, hair-trigger*, precarious, sensitive, ticklish, touchy, tricky, uncertain, unpredictable, volatile; SEE CONCEPT *565*

delicate [adj5] *careful, tactful* accurate, adept, cautious, considerate, deft, detailed, diplomatic, discreet, expert, foresighted, heedful, masterly, minute, politic, precise, proficient, prudent, sensitive, skilled, tactical, wary; SEE CONCEPTS *401,542*

delicately [adv] *carefully* beautifully, cautiously, daintily, deftly, elegantly, exquisitely, fastidiously, finely, gracefully, lightly, precisely, sensitively, skillfully, softly, subtly, tactfully; SEE CONCEPTS *542,544*

delicatessen [n] *eatery* café, cafeteria, charcuterie, deli, restaurant, sandwich shop, subway shop; SEE CONCEPT *449*

delicious [adj] *pleasing, especially to the taste* adorable, ambrosial, appetizing, choice, dainty, darling, delectable, delightful, delish*, distinctive, divine, enjoyable, enticing, exquisite, fit for king*, good, gratifying, heavenly, luscious, lush, mellow, mouthwatering, nectarous, nice, palatable, piquant, pleasant, rare, rich, sapid, savory, scrumptious, spicy, sweet, tasteful, tasty, tempting, titillating, toothsome, well-prepared, well-seasoned, yummy*; SEE CONCEPTS *572,613*

delight [n] *enjoyment, happiness* contentment, delectation, ecstasy, enchantment, felicity, fruition, gladness, glee, gratification, hilarity, jollity, joy, joyance, mirth, pleasure, rapture, relish, satisfaction, transport; SEE CONCEPT *410*

delight [v] *make happy; experience happiness* allure, amuse, arride, attract, be the ticket*, charm, cheer, content, delectate, divert, enchant, enrapture, entertain, exult, fascinate, freak out, gladden, glory, go over big*, gratify, groove*, hit the spot*, jubilate, knock dead*, knock out*, please, pleasure, ravish, rejoice, satisfy, score, send, slay, thrill, tickle pink*, tickle to death*, turn on, wow; SEE CONCEPTS *7,22*

delighted [adj] *very happy* captivated, charmed, ecstatic, elated, enchanted, entranced, excited, fulfilled, gladdened, gratified, joyous, jubilant, overjoyed, pleasantly surprised, pleased, thrilled; SEE CONCEPT *403*

delightful [adj] *pleasant, charming* adorable, agreeable, alluring, ambrosial, amusing, attractive, beautiful, captivating, cheery, clever, congenial, darling, delectable, delicious, enchanting, engaging, enjoyable, entertaining, fair, fascinating, gratifying, heavenly, ineffable, lovely, luscious, lush, pleasing, pleasurable, rapturous, ravishing, refreshing, satisfying, scrumptious, thrilling, yummy*; SEE CONCEPTS *401,404*

delight in [v] *take pleasure from* admire, adore, amuse oneself, appreciate, be content, be pleased, cherish, dig*, eat up*, enjoy, feast on, get a kick out of*, get high on*, get off on*, get in, groove on*, indulge in, like, live a little*, live it up*, love, luxuriate in, relish, revel in, savor; SEE CONCEPTS *32,410*

delineate [v] *describe; outline* characterize, chart, define, depict, detail, draft, draw, figure, lay out, limn, mark, plot, portray, represent, sketch out, trace; SEE CONCEPTS *36,55,174*

delinquency [n] *misconduct* crime, default, dereliction, failure, fault, lapse, misbehavior, misdeed, misdemeanor, neglect, nonobservance, offense, oversight, weakness, wrongdoing; SEE CONCEPTS *192,645*

de
de

delinquent [*adj*] *irresponsible, defaulting*
behind, blamable, blameworthy, careless, censurable, criminal, culpable, defaultant, derelict, disregardful, faulty, guilty, lax, neglectful, negligent, offending, overdue, procrastinating, redhanded*, remiss, reprehensible, shabby, slack, tardy, unpaid; SEE CONCEPTS *401,570*

delinquent [*n*] *criminal, often young*
behind, blackguard, black sheep*, culprit, dawdler, deadbeat*, deadhead*, debtor, defaulter, derelict, desperado, evader, fallen angel*, felon, hoodlum*, jailbird*, JD*, juvenile delinquent, juvie*, lawbreaker, loafer, lounger, malefactor, miscreant, neglecter, no show*, offender, outlaw, punk*, recreant, reprobate, sinner, wrongdoer, young offender; SEE CONCEPT *412*

delirious [*adj1*] *mentally imbalanced*
aberrant, bewildered, confused, crazed, crazy, demented, deranged, deviant, deviate, disarranged, disordered, distracted, disturbed, flipped*, flipped out*, hallucinatory, incoherent, insane, irrational, lightheaded, lunatic, mad, maniac, maniacal, manic, off one's head*, out of one's head*, out of one's skull*, rambling, raving, unhinged, unreasonable, unsettled, wandering; SEE CONCEPTS *402,403*

delirious [*adj2*] *excited; very happy*
beside oneself*, carried away*, corybantic, crazy, delighted, drunk*, ecstatic, enthused, frantic, frenetic, frenzied, furious, hysterical, intoxicated, mad, overwrought, rabid*, rapturous, thrilled, transported, wild; SEE CONCEPTS *401,403*

delirium [*n*] *madness*
aberration, ardor, dementia, derangement, ecstasy, enthusiasm, fervor, fever, frenzy, furor, fury, hallucination, hysteria, insanity, lunacy, mania, passion, rage, raving, transport, zeal; SEE CONCEPT *410*

deliver [*v1*] *transfer, carry*
bear, bring, cart, come across with*, convey, dish out*, distribute, drop, fork over*, gimme*, give, hand, hand-carry, hand over, pass, put on, put out, remit, transport, truck; SEE CONCEPTS *108,217*

deliver [*v2*] *relinquish possession*
abandon, cede, commit, give up, grant, hand over, let go, resign, surrender, transfer, turn over, yield; SEE CONCEPTS *116,131*

deliver [*v3*] *free, liberate*
acquit, discharge, emancipate, loose, ransom, redeem, release, rescue, save, unshackle; SEE CONCEPT *127*

deliver [*v4*] *announce, proclaim*
address, bring out, broach, chime in, come out with, communicate, declare, express, give, give forth, impart, present, pronounce, publish, read, say, state, tell, throw out, utter, vent, voice; SEE CONCEPTS *51,60*

deliver [*v5*] *administer; throw*
aim, deal, direct, dispatch, fling, give, hurl, inflict, launch, pitch, send, strike, transmit; SEE CONCEPTS *217,222*

deliver [*v6*] *discharge, give forth*
accouch, bear, birth, born, dispense, feed, find, hand, hand over, produce, provide, release, supply, turn over; SEE CONCEPTS *179,374*

deliverance [*n*] *liberation*
acquittal, delivery, emancipation, extrication,

freeing, redemption, release, rescue, salvation, saving; SEE CONCEPT *134*

delivery [*n1*] *transfer, transmittal*
carting, commitment, consignment, conveyance, dispatch, distribution, drop, freighting, giving over, handing over, impartment, intrusting, mailing, parcel post, portage, post, rendition, shipment, surrender, transmission; SEE CONCEPTS *108,217*

delivery [*n2*] *articulation of message*
accent, diction, elocution, emphasis, enunciation, inflection, intonation, modulation, pronunciation, speech, utterance; SEE CONCEPTS *47,595*

delivery [*n3*] *childbirth*
accouchement, bearing, birth, birthing, bringing forth, Caesarian section, childbearing, confinement, geniture, labor, lying-in, parturition, travail; SEE CONCEPTS *302,373,374*

delivery [*n4*] *giving of freedom*
deliverance, emancipation, escape, freeing, liberation, pardon, release, rescue, salvage, salvation; SEE CONCEPT *127*

delivery room [*n*] *birthing room*
birthing center, hospital room; SEE CONCEPTS *312,439,449*

delude [*v*] *deceive, fool*
beguile, betray, bluff, caboodle*, cheat, con, cozen, disinform, do a number on*, doublecross, dupe*, gull*, hoax*, hoodwink*, illude, impose on, jive*, juggle*, lead up garden path*, misguide, mislead, mousetrap*, outfox, play trick on, snow*, string along, sucker*, take in, trick; SEE CONCEPT *59*

deluge [*n*] *downpour, flood of something*
avalanche, barrage, cataclysm, cataract, drencher, flux, inundation, niagara, overflowing, overrunning, pour, rush, spate, torrent; SEE CONCEPTS *432,524,787*

deluge [*v1*] *inundate with water*
douse, drench, drown, engulf, flood, flush, gush, overflow, overrun, overwhelm, pour, sluice, soak, sop, souse, stream, submerge, swamp, wet, whelm; SEE CONCEPT *256*

deluge [*v2*] *overwhelm*
abound, crowd, engulf, flood, glut, inundate, overcome, overcrowd, overload, overrun, oversupply, snow*, snow under*, swamp, teem; SEE CONCEPTS *42,140*

delusion [*n*] *misconception, misbelief*
apparition, blunder, casuistry, chicanery, daydream, deception, deceptiveness, dream, eidolon, error, fallacy, false impression, fancy, fantasy, figment*, fool's paradise*, ghost, hallucination, head trip*, ignis fatuus, illusion, lapse, mirage, misapprehension, mistake, optical illusion, oversight, phantasm, phantom, pipe dream*, selfdeception, shade, speciousness, spuriousness, trickery, trip, vision; SEE CONCEPTS *409,410,689*

delusive [*adj*] *deceptive*
apparent, beguiling, chimerical, deceiving, deluding, fallacious, false, fanciful, fantastic, illusive, illusory, imaginary, misleading, ostensible, quixotic, seeming, specious, spurious, visionary; SEE CONCEPT *582*

deluxe [*adj*] *superior, plush*
choice, costly, dainty, delicate, elegant, exclusive, expensive, exquisite, first-class, grand, luscious, lush, luxuriant, luxurious, opulent, palatial, posh, rare, recherché, rich, ritzy, select,

special, splendid, sumptuous, super, swank, swanky; SEE CONCEPT 574

delve [v] *dig into task, action*
burrow, dig, dredge, examine, excavate, explore, ferret out*, go into, gouge out, inquire, investigate, jump into, leave no stone unturned*, look into, probe, prospect, ransack, really get into*, research, rummage, scoop out, search, seek, shovel, sift, spade, trowel, turn inside out*, unearth; SEE CONCEPTS 87,103,216

demagogue [n] *agitating person*
agitator, fanatic, firebrand*, fomenter, haranger, hothead*, incendiary, inciter, inflamer, instigator, politician, rabble-rouser*, radical, rebel, revolutionary, soapbox orator*, troublemaker; SEE CONCEPTS 359,412

demand [n] *question, request*
appeal, application, arrogation, bid, bidding, call, call for, charge, claim, clamor, command, counterclaim, entreatment, entreaty, exaction, impetration, imploration, importunity, imposition, inquiry, insistence, interest, interrogation, lien, necessity, need, occasion, order, petition, plea, prayer, pursuit, requirement, requisition, rush, sale, search, solicitation, stipulation, suit, supplication, trade, ultimatum, use, vogue, want; SEE CONCEPT 662

demand [v1] *ask strongly for something*
abuse, appeal, apply, arrogate, badger, beg, beseech, besiege, bid, challenge, charge, cite, claim, clamor for, coerce, command, compel, constrain, counterclaim, direct, dun, enjoin, entreat, exact, expect, force, hit, hit up, impetrate, implore, importune, inquire, insist on, interrogate, knock, nag, necessitate, oblige, order, pester, petition, postulate, pray, press, question, request, require, requisition, solicit, stipulate, sue for, summon, supplicate, tax, urge, whistle for; SEE CONCEPT 53

demand [v2] *require*
ask, call for, command, crave, cry out for, fail, involve, lack, necessitate, need, oblige, take, want; SEE CONCEPTS 26,646

demanding [adj] *challenging, urgent*
ambitious, backbreaker*, bothersome, clamorous, critical, dictatorial, difficult, exacting, exhausting, exigent, fussy, grievous, hard, imperious, importunate, insistent, nagging, onerous, oppressive, pressing, querulous, strict, stringent, taxing, tough, troublesome, trying, wearing, weighty; SEE CONCEPTS 542,565

demarcation [n] *boundary, division*
bound, confine, delimitation, differentiation, distinction, enclosure, limit, margin, separation, split, terminus; SEE CONCEPT 745

demean [v] *humble, humiliate*
abase, bad-mouth*, belittle, bemean, cast down, contemn, cut down to size*, cut rate, debase, decry, degrade, derogate, descend, despise, detract, dis*, disparage, dump on*, knock down*, lower, pan*, poor-mouth*, scorn, sink, stoop*; SEE CONCEPTS 7,19,54

demeanor [n] *behavior, manner*
address, air, attitude, bearing, carriage, comportment, conduct, deportment, disposition, mien, poise, port, presence, set; SEE CONCEPTS 411,633

demented [adj] *crazy, insane*
bananas*, bemused, crackbrained*, daft, deliri-

ous, deranged, distracted, distraught, flipped out*, foolish, frenzied, fruity*, hysterical, idiotic, in the ozone*, lunatic, mad, maniac, maniacal, manic, non compos mentis, nutty as a fruitcake*, out of one's gourd*, out of one's tree*, psycho, psychopathic, psychotic, schitzy*, schizoid*, unbalanced, unglued*, unhinged*, unsound, whacko*; SEE CONCEPT 403

dementia [n] *senility*
Alzheimer's disease, derangement, insanity, madness, mental decay, mental deterioration, mental disorder, personality change, softening of the brain*, unbalance; SEE CONCEPTS 316,410

demise [n] *fate, usually death*
annihilation, collapse, curtains, decease, departure, dissolution, downfall, dying, end, ending, expiration, extinction, failure, fall, final thrill*, last out*, last roundup*, lights out*, number's up*, passing, quietus, ruin, silence, sleep, termination; SEE CONCEPTS 105,304,679

democracy [n] *government in which people participate*
commonwealth, egalitarianism, emancipation, equalitarianism, equality, freedom, justice, liberal government, representative government, republic, suffrage; SEE CONCEPTS 299,688,689

democratic [adj] *representative, self-governing*
autonomous, common, communal, constitutional, egalitarian, equal, free, friendly, individualistic, informal, just, libertarian, orderly, popular, populist, self-ruling, socialist; SEE CONCEPTS 319,536

demography [n] *study of human population*
anthropology, census-taking, population analysis, population density, population growth, population size, population studies, population vital statistics; SEE CONCEPT 349

demolish [v] *destroy; consume*
annihilate, break, bulldoze, burst, crack, crush, decimate, defeat, devastate, devour, dilapidate, dismantle, eat, flatten, gobble up, knock down, level, obliterate, overthrow, overturn, pulverize, put away, put in toilet*, raze, ruin, sink, smash, take apart, take out, tear down, torpedo*, total*, trash*, undo, wax*, wipe off map*, wrack, wreck; SEE CONCEPTS 169,252

demolition [n] *destruction*
annihilation, bulldozing, explosion, extermination, knocking down, leveling, razing, wrecking; SEE CONCEPT 252

demon [n] *evil, devilish being or influence*
archfiend, beast, brute, fiend, goblin, hellion, imp, incubus, little devil*, malignant spirit, monster, rascal, rogue, Satan, succubus, vampire, villain; SEE CONCEPTS 370,412

demonic [adj] *evil*
aroused, bad, crazed, demoniac, demoniacal, devilish, diabolic, diabolical, fiendish, fired, frantic, frenetic, frenzied, hellish, impious, infernal, insane, inspired, mad, maniacal, manic, possessed, satanic, serpentine, unhallowed, violent, wicked; SEE CONCEPTS 404,545

demonstrable [adj] *provable, evident*
ascertainable, attestable, axiomatic, certain, conclusive, deducible, evincible, incontrovertible, indubitable, inferable, irrefutable, obvious, palpable, positive, self-evident, undeniable, unmistakable, verifiable; SEE CONCEPTS 529,535

de
de

demonstrate [v1] *display, show*
authenticate, determine, establish, evidence, evince, exhibit, expose, flaunt, indicate, make evident, make out, manifest, prove, roll out*, show and tell*, test, testify to, trot out*, try, validate; SEE CONCEPT 97

demonstrate [v2] *explain, illustrate*
confirm, debunk, describe, express, give for instance, make clear, ostend, proclaim, set forth, show how, teach, testify to, walk one through*; SEE CONCEPT 57

demonstrate [v3] *display or take public action for a cause*
exhibit, fast, lie in, manifest, march, march on, parade, picket, protest, rally, sit in, stage walkout, strike, walkout; SEE CONCEPTS 261,300

demonstration [n1] *display of proof*
affirmation, confirmation, description, evidence, exhibition, explanation, exposition, expression, illustration, induction, manifestation, presentation, proof, show, spectacle, substantiation, test, testimony, trial, validation; SEE CONCEPT 261

demonstration [n2] *display of belief in cause by taking public action*
fast, lie-in*, love-in*, march, mass lobby, parade, peace march, picket, picket line, protest, rally, sit-in*, strike, teach-in*, walkout; SEE CONCEPTS 261,300

demonstrative [adj1] *expressive, communicative*
affectionate, candid, effusive, emotional, evincive, expansive, explanatory, expository, frank, gushing, histrionic, illustrative, indicative, loving, open, outgoing, outpouring, outspoken, plain, profuse, symptomatic, tender, unconstrained, unreserved, unrestrained, warmhearted; SEE CONCEPTS 267,401

demonstrative [adj2] *conclusive*
authenticating, certain, convincing, decisive, definite, final, proving, showing, specific, validating; SEE CONCEPTS 531,537

demonstrator [n] *protester*
agitator, boycotter, disrupter, dissenter, marcher, objector, picketer, radical, revolter, revolutionary, rioter, striker, troublemaker; SEE CONCEPT 412

demoralize [v1] *depress, unnerve*
abash, blow out, blow up, chill, cripple, damp, dampen, daunt, debilitate, deject, disarrange, disconcert, discountenance, discourage, dishearten, disorder, disorganize, disparage, dispirit, disturb, embarrass, enfeeble, get to*, jumble, muddle, nonplus, psych out*, rattle, sap, send up*, shake, snarl, take apart*, take steam out*, undermine, unglue*, unman, unsettle, unzip*, upset, weaken; SEE CONCEPTS 7,19

demoralize [v2] *corrupt, pervert*
bastardize, bestialize, brutalize, debase, debauch, deprave, lower, vitiate, warp; SEE CONCEPT 14

demote [v] *downgrade, lower in rank*
bench*, break, bump, bust, declass, degrade, demean, demerit, dismiss, disrate, hold back, kick downstairs*, lower, reduce, relegate, set back; SEE CONCEPTS 233,351

demur [v] *disagree*
balk, cavil, challenge, combat, complain, deprecate, disapprove, dispute, doubt, fight, hem and haw*, hesitate, object, oppose, pause, protest, pussyfoot*, refuse, remonstrate, resist, scruple, shy, stick, stickle, strain, take exception*, vacillate, wait and see*, waver; SEE CONCEPTS 46,54

demure [adj] *reserved, affected*
backward, bashful, blushing, close, coy, decorous, diffident, earnest, humble, modest, nice, prim, prissy, proper, prudish, reticent, retiring, sedate, serious, shy, silent, skittish, sober, solemn, staid, strait-laced, timid, unassertive, unassuming, unassured; SEE CONCEPTS 401,404

den [n1] *cavern, hideaway*
atelier, burrow, cave, cloister, couch, cubbyhole, haunt, hideout, hole, hotbed, lair, lodge, nest, retreat, sanctuary, sanctum, shelter, snuggery, study; SEE CONCEPTS 448,513

den [n2] *room for relaxation or informal entertaining*
family room, library, media room, playroom, recreation room, rec room*, rumpus room, studio, TV room; SEE CONCEPTS 440,448

denial [n] *dismissal, refusal of belief in statement*
abnegation, abstaining, adjuration, brush-off, cold shoulder*, contradiction, controversion, declination, disallowance, disapproval, disavowal, disclaimer, dismissing, disproof, dissent, forswearing, gainsaying, nay, negation, negative, nix*, nonacceptance, noncommittal, no way*, prohibition, protestation, rebuff, rebuttal, refraining, refusing, refutal, refutation, rejecting, rejection, renegement, renouncement, renunciation, repudiating, repudiation, repulse, retraction, turndown, veto; SEE CONCEPTS 45,54

denigrate [v] *belittle, malign*
asperse, bad mouth*, besmirch, blacken, blister, calumniate, decry, defame, dis*, disparage, give black eye*, impugn, knock*, libel, mudsling*, put down*, revile, rip up*, roast*, run down*, scandalize, slander, tear down*, traduce, vilify; SEE CONCEPTS 52,54

denizen [n] *resident*
citizen, dweller, habitant, indweller, inhabitant, inhabiter, liver, national, native, occupant, resider, subject; SEE CONCEPT 413

denomination [n1] *religious belief*
church, communion, connection, creed, cult, faith, group, persuasion, religion, school, sect; SEE CONCEPTS 368,689

denomination [n2] *classification*
body, category, class, grade, group, size, type, unit, value; SEE CONCEPT 378

denomination [n3] *name*
appellation, appellative, brand, cognomen, compellation, designation, flag, handle, identification, label, moniker, nomen, slot, style, surname, tab, tag, term, title; SEE CONCEPT 683

denotation [n] *meaning, description*
designation, explanation, implication, indication, signification, specification; SEE CONCEPTS 268,682

denote [v] *designate, mean*
add up, announce, argue, bespeak, betoken, connote, evidence, express, finger, flash, hang sign on*, imply, import, indicate, insinuate, intend, make, mark, peg, prove, put down for, put finger on*, show, signify, spell, stand for, symbolize, tab, tag, typify; SEE CONCEPTS 55,682

denouement [n] *the end result*
climax, close, completion, conclusion, culmination, end, final curtain*, finale, last act*, resolution, windup*; SEE CONCEPT 832

denounce [v] *condemn, attack*
accuse, adjudicate, arraign, blacklist, blame, boycott, brand, castigate, censure, charge, charge

with, criticize, damn, declaim, decry, denunciate, derogate, dress down, excoriate, expose, finger*, hang something on*, impeach, implicate, impugn, incriminate, indict, inveigh against, knock, ostracize, proscribe, prosecute, rap, rat*, rebuke, reprehend, reprimand, reproach, reprobate, reprove, revile, scold, show up, skin*, smear, stigmatize, take to task, threaten, upbraid, vilify, vituperate; SEE CONCEPTS 44,52

dense [adj1] *compressed, thick*
close, close-knit, compact, condensed, crammed, crowded, heaped, heavy, impenetrable, jammed, jam-packed*, massed, opaque, packed, packed like sardines*, piled, solid, substantial, thickset; SEE CONCEPT 483

dense [adj2] *slow, stupid*
blockheaded*, boorish, doltish, dull, dumb, fatheaded*, ignorant, imbecilic, impassive, lethargic, numskulled*, oafish, obtuse, phlegmatic, simple, slow-witted, sluggish, stolid, thick, torpid; SEE CONCEPT 402

density [n] *bulk, mass*
body, closeness, compactness, concretion, consistency, crowdedness, denseness, frequency, heaviness, impenetrability, massiveness, quantity, solidity, substantiality, thickness, tightness; SEE CONCEPT 722

dent [n] *depression, scrape, chip*
cavity, concavity, crater, crenel, cut, dimple, dint, dip, embrasure, furrow, hollow, impression, incision, indentation, nick, notch, pit, scallop, score, scratch, sink, trough; SEE CONCEPT 580

dent [v] *chip, scrape, depress*
dig, dimple, dint, furrow, gouge, hollow, imprint, indent, make concave, mark, nick, notch, perforate, pit, press in, push in, ridge, scratch; SEE CONCEPTS 176,189,208,246

dentures [n] *false teeth*
artificial teeth, bridge, choppers*, dental plate, implants, partial, set of teeth; SEE CONCEPT 393

denude [v] *strip*
bare, disrobe, expose, fleece, lay bare*, peel, uncover, undress; SEE CONCEPT 211

denunciation [n] *condemnation, criticism*
accusation, arraignment, blame, castigation, censure, charge, cursing, damning, denouncement, derogation, dressing down*, fulmination, incrimination, indictment, invective, knock*, obloquy, rap*, reprehension, reprimand, reprobation, smearing, stigmatization, upbraidment, vilification; SEE CONCEPT 52

deny [v] *disagree, renounce, decline*
abjure, abnegate, ban, begrudge, call on, contradict, contravene, controvert, curb, disacknowledge, disallow, disavow, disbelieve, discard, disclaim, discredit, disown, disprove, doubt, enjoin from, eschew, exclude, forbid, forgo, forsake, gainsay, hold back, keep back, negate, negative, not buy, nullify, oppose, rebuff, rebut, recant, refuse, refute, reject, repudiate, restrain, revoke, sacrifice, say no to, spurn, taboo, take exception to, turn down, turn thumbs down*, veto, withhold; SEE CONCEPTS 46,49,52

deodorant [n] *something that freshens*
air freshener, antiperspirant, cleanser, cosmetic, deodorizer, disinfectant, fumigant, fumigator, smoke screen*; SEE CONCEPT 492

depart [v1] *leave, retreat*
abandon, abdicate, absent, beat it*, blast off*, cut and run*, cut out*, decamp, desert, disappear,

emigrate, escape, evacuate, exit, get away, git*, go, go away, go forth, hit the bricks*, hit the road*, hit the trail*, make a break*, march out, migrate, move on, move out, part, perish, pull out, quit, remove, retire, sally forth*, say goodbye*, scram*, secede, set forth, shove off*, slip away*, split*, start, start out, take leave, tergiversate, troop*, vacate, vanish, withdraw; SEE CONCEPT 195

depart [v2] *diverge from normal, expected*
abandon, cast, desert, deviate, differ, digress, disagree, discard, dissent, excurse, forsake, ramble, reject, repudiate, stray, swerve, turn aside, vary, veer, wander; SEE CONCEPTS 665,697

departed [adj] *dead*
bought the farm*, buried, deceased, expired, gone, in the grave*, laid to rest*, late, passed away, pushing up daisies*, six feet under*, stiff; SEE CONCEPT 539

department [n1] *section of organization, area*
administration, agency, area, arena, beat, board, branch, bureau, canton, circuit, commission, commune, constituency, division, force, office, parish, precinct, quarter, range, staff, station, subdivision, territory, tract, unit, ward; SEE CONCEPTS 381,440,508

department [n2] *area of interest, expertise*
activity, administration, assignment, avocation, bailiwick, berth, bureau, business, capacity, class, classification, domain, dominion, duty, field, function, incumbency, jurisdiction, line, niche, occupation, office, province, realm, responsibility, slot, specialty, sphere, spot, station, vocation, walk of life, wing; SEE CONCEPT 349

department store [n] *retail store*
anchor store, chain store, dime store, discount store, five-and-dime store, outlet store, shop, store; SEE CONCEPTS 325,439,448,449

departure [n1] *leaving*
abandonment, adieu, bow out*, congé, decampment, desertion, egress, egression, embarkation, emigration, escape, evacuation, exit, exodus, expatriation, farewell, flight, getaway*, going, going away, goodbye*, hegira, migration, parting, passage, powder*, quitting, recession, removal, retirement, retreat, sailing, separation, setting forth, setting out, stampede, start, takeoff, taking leave, taking off, vacation, vanishing act*, walkout, withdrawal, withdrawing; SEE CONCEPT 195

departure [n2] *deviation from normal, expected*
aberration, branching off, branching out, change, declination, deflection, difference, digression, divergence, diversion, innovation, in thing*, last word*, latest thing*, new wrinkle*, novelty, rambling, shift, straying, turning, variance, variation, veering, wandering; SEE CONCEPTS 665,697

depend [v1] *count on, rely upon*
bank on*, bet bottom dollar on*, bet on*, build upon, calculate on, confide in, gamble on*, lay money on*, lean on*, reckon on, trust in, turn to; SEE CONCEPT 26

depend [v2] *be contingent on*
be at mercy of, be based on, be conditioned, be connected with, be determined by, be in control of, be in the power of, be subject to, be subordinate to, bottom, found, ground, hang, hang in suspense, hang on, hinge on, pend, rest, rest on, rest with, revolve around, revolve on, stand on, stay, trust to, turn on; SEE CONCEPT 711

de
de

dependable [*adj*] *reliable, responsible*
always there, carrying the load*, certain, constant, faithful, good as one's word*, loyal, rocklike*, secure, stable, staunch, steadfast, steady, sturdy, sure, to be counted on, tried, tried-and-true, true, trustworthy, trusty, unfailing; SEE CONCEPTS *542,560*

dependence/dependency [*n1*] *confidence, reliance*
assurance, belief, credence, expectation, faith, hope, interdependence, responsibility, responsibleness, stability, steadiness, stock, trust, trustiness, trustworthiness; SEE CONCEPTS *410,689*

dependence/dependency [*n2*] *addiction, need*
attachment, contingency, habit, helplessness, hook, inability, security blanket, servility, subjection, subordination, subservience, vulnerability, weakness, yoke; SEE CONCEPTS *20,709*

dependent [*adj1*] *weak, helpless*
abased, clinging, counting on, debased, defenseless, humbled, immature, indigent, inferior, lesser, minor, poor, reliant, relying on, secondary, subordinate, tied to apron strings*, under, under thumb*, unsustaining, vulnerable; SEE CONCEPTS *404,574*

dependent [*adj2*] *contingent, determined by*
accessory to, ancillary, appurtenant, conditional, controlled by, counting, depending, incidental to, liable to, provisory, reckoning, regulated by, relative, reliant, relying, subject to, subordinate, subservient, susceptible, sustained by, trusting, under control of; SEE CONCEPT *546*

depict [*v*] *describe, render in drawing or writing*
characterize, delineate, design, detail, illustrate, image, interpret, limn, narrate, outline, paint, picture, portray, relate, report, represent, reproduce, sculpt, sketch, state; SEE CONCEPTS *79,174*

depiction [*n*] *description, rendering*
delineation, drawing, illustration, image, likeness, outline, picture, portraiture, portrayal, presentment, representation, sketch; SEE CONCEPTS *259,268*

deplete [*v*] *consume, exhaust supply*
bankrupt, bleed*, decrease, dig into, diminish, drain, draw, dry up, empty, evacuate, expend, finish, impoverish, lessen, milk*, reduce, sap, spend, squander, suck dry*, undermine, use up, wash up, waste, weaken; SEE CONCEPTS *142,169,225*

depleted [*adj*] *consumed, exhausted*
all in*, bare, bleary*, collapsed, decreased, depreciated, destitute, devoid of, drained, effete, emptied, far-gone*, in want, kaput*, lessened, out of, pooped out*, reduced, sapped, short of, sold, sold out, spent, sucked out*, used, used up, vacant, washed out, wasted, weakened, without resources, worn, worn out; SEE CONCEPTS *576,771*

deplorable [*adj*] *unfortunate, shameful*
afflictive, awful, blameworthy, bummer*, calamitous, dire, dirty, disastrous, disgraceful, dishonorable, disreputable, distressing, dolorous, downer*, dreadful, execrable, faulty, godawful*, grievous, grim, heartbreaking, heartrending, horrifying, intolerable, lamentable, lousy, melancholy, miserable, mournful, opprobrious, overwhelming, pitiable, poor, regrettable, reprehensible, rotten, sad, scandalous, sickening, stinking, terrible, tragic, unbearable, unsatisfac-

tory, woeful, wretched; SEE CONCEPTS *529,570, 574*

deplore [*v*] *regret; condemn*
abhor, be against, bemoan, bewail, carry on, censure, complain, cry, denounce, deprecate, disapprove of, eat one's heart out*, grieve for, hate, hurt, lament, moan, mourn, object to, repent, rue, sing the blues*, sorrow over, take on, weep; SEE CONCEPTS *21,29*

deploy [*v*] *redistribute, station troops or weapons*
arrange, display, dispose, expand, extend, fan out, form front, open, position, put out patrol, set out, set up, spread out, take battle stations, unfold, use, utilize; SEE CONCEPTS *158,213,320*

deport [*v*] *banish*
cast out, dismiss, displace, exile, expatriate, expel, expulse, extradite, oust, relegate, ship out, transport; SEE CONCEPTS *198,211,217*

deportation [*n*] *banishment*
displacement, eviction, exile, expatriation, expulsion, extradition, ostracism, relegation, removal, transportation; SEE CONCEPTS *198,211, 217*

deportment [*n*] *carriage, manner of person*
actions, address, air, appearance, aspect, bearing, behavior, cast, comportment, conduct, demeanor, mien, port, posture, set, stance; SEE CONCEPT *633*

depose [*v*] *oust from position*
boot out, bounce, break, can*, cashier, chuck, degrade, demote, dethrone, discrown, dismiss, displace, downgrade, drum out, eject, freeze out*, give heave-ho*, impeach, kick out*, overthrow, remove from office, ride out on rail*, run out of town*, send packing*, subvert, throw out, throw out on ear*, uncrown, unfrock, unmake, unseat, upset; SEE CONCEPTS *133,298,320*

deposit [*n1*] *down payment; money saved*
drop, installment, money in the bank, partial payment, pledge, retainer, security, stake, warranty; SEE CONCEPTS *340,344*

deposit [*n2*] *accumulation of solid*
alluvium, delta, deposition, dregs, drift, grounds, lees, precipitate, precipitation, sediment, settlings, silt; SEE CONCEPTS *432,470,471*

deposit [*v*] *locate, put in place for safekeeping*
accumulate, amass, bank, collect, commit, deliver, ditch, drop, entrust, garner, give in trust, hoard, install, invest, keep, lay, lay away, park, place, plant*, plop*, plunk*, plunk down*, precipitate, put aside, put by, repose, rest, salt away*, save, settle, sit down, sock away*, squirrel away*, stash, stock up, store, stow, transfer, treasure; SEE CONCEPTS *134,201,330*

deposition [*n1*] *dethroning, ousting*
degradation, discharge, dismissal, displacement, ejection, impeachment, overthrow, removal, unfrocking; SEE CONCEPTS *133,298,320*

deposition [*n2*] *attestation of truth, especially in legal matters*
affidavit, affirmation, allegation, announcement, declaration, evidence, sworn statement, testimony; SEE CONCEPTS *271,318*

depository [*n*] *storage place*
archive, arsenal, bank, bunker, cache, collection, depot, gallery, magazine, museum, repertory, repository, safe, safe-deposit box, store, storehouse, tomb, vault, warehouse; SEE CONCEPT *435*

depot [*n*] *storage place; station*
annex, armory, base, depository, destination,

garage, halting-place, haven, junction, loft, lot, magazine, office, repository, stopping-place, store, storehouse, storeroom, terminal, terminus, waiting room, warehouse, yard; SEE CONCEPTS *435,449*

deprave [*v*] *corrupt, lead astray*
bastardize, bestialize, brutalize, debase, debauch, degrade, demoralize, pervert, seduce, subvert, vitiate, warp; SEE CONCEPT *14*

depraved [*adj*] *corrupt, immoral*
abandoned, bad, base, debased, debauched, degenerate, degraded, dirty*, dirty-minded, dissolute, evil, fast*, filthy*, flagitous, gone to the dogs*, kinky*, lascivious, lewd, licentious, low, mean, miscreant, nefarious, perverted, profligate, putrid, rotten, shameless, sinful, twisted, unhealthy, unnatural, vicious, vile, villainous, vitiate, vitiated, wanton, warped, wicked; SEE CONCEPT *545*

depravity [*n*] *corruption, immorality*
abandonment, baseness, contamination, criminality, debasement, debauchery, degeneracy, degradation, depravation, evil, iniquity, lewdness, licentiousness, perversion, profligacy, sensuality, sinfulness, vice, viciousness, vitiation, wickedness; SEE CONCEPT *645*

deprecate [*v*] *belittle, condemn*
cut down to size*, depreciate, derogate, detract, disapprove of, discommend, discountenance, disesteem, disfavor, disparage, expostulate, frown, mudsling*, not go for*, object, poohpooh*, poor mouth*, protest against, put down*, rip*, run down*, take dim view of, take down, take exception to; SEE CONCEPTS *7,19,52*

depreciate [*v1*] *devalue, lose value*
abate, cheapen, decay, decrease, decry, deflate, depress, deteriorate, devalorize, diminish, downgrade, drop, dwindle, erode, fall, lessen, lower, mark down, reduce, soften, underrate, undervalue, worsen, write down, write off; SEE CONCEPTS *698,776*

depreciate [*v2*] *belittle, ridicule*
abuse, asperse, attack, calumniate, censure, clamor against, condemn, contemn, decry, defame, denigrate, denounce, deprecate, deride, derogate, detract, discount, discountenance, discredit, disgrace, disparage, dispraise, fault, find fault with, humble, knock, look down on*, lower, malign, minimize, put down, rap, revile, roast*, run down*, scoff at, scorn, slam, slander, slight, slur, smear, sneer at, spurn, take down a peg*, traduce, underestimate, underrate, undervalue, vilify; SEE CONCEPTS *7,19,52*

depreciation [*n*] *devaluation*
accounting allowance, deflation, fall, loss of value, reduction, slump; SEE CONCEPTS *137,236, 240,247,698*

depredation [*n*] *devastation, destruction*
burglary, crime, desecration, desolation, despoiling, laying waste, marauding, pillage, plunder, ransacking, rapine, ravaging, robbery, sacking, spoliation, stealing, theft, wasting; SEE CONCEPTS *192,252*

depress [*v1*] *deject, make despondent; exhaust*
abase, afflict, ail, bear down, beat, beat down*, bother, bug*, bum out*, cast down, chill*, cow*, damp, dampen, darken, daunt, debase, debilitate, degrade, desolate, devitalize, discourage, dishearten, dismay, dispirit, distress, disturb, drag*, drain, dull, enervate, faze, keep under, lower,

mock, mortify, oppress, perturb, press, put down*, reduce, reduce to tears*, run down*, sadden, sap*, scorn, slow, throw cold water on*, torment, trouble, try, turn one off*, upset, weaken, weary, weigh down*; SEE CONCEPTS *7,19,240*

depress [*v2*] *devalue*
cheapen, debase, depreciate, diminish, downgrade, impair, lessen, lower, reduce; SEE CONCEPTS *240,330*

depress [*v3*] *push down*
couch, demit, dip, droop, flatten, let down, level, lower, press down, settle, sink, smoosh, squash; SEE CONCEPT *208*

depressant [*n*] *sedative*
calmant, downer, intoxicant, relaxant, tranquilizer; SEE CONCEPTS *7,22,310*

depressed [*adj1*] *discouraged*
bad, bleeding*, blue*, bummed out*, cast-down, crestfallen, crummy*, dejected, despondent, destroyed, disconsolate, dispirited, down, down and out*, downcast, downhearted, down in the dumps*, down in the mouth*, dragged*, fed up*, glum, grim, hurting, in a blue funk*, in pain*, in the dumps*, in the pits*, in the toilet*, let down, low, low-down, low-spirited, lugubrious, melancholy, moody, morose, on a downer*, pessimistic, ripped, sad, sob story*, spiritless, taken down*, torn up*, unhappy, weeping, woebegone; SEE CONCEPT *403*

depressed [*adj2*] *concave, pushed down*
hollow, indented, recessed, set back, sunken; SEE CONCEPT *490*

depressed [*adj3*] *disadvantaged*
cheapened, depreciated, deprived, destitute, devalued, distressed, ghetto, ghost, impaired, needy, poor, poverty-stricken, run-down, shanty, skid row*, underprivileged, weakened; SEE CONCEPTS *334,555*

depressing [*adj*] *discouraging, upsetting*
black, bleak, daunting, dejecting, disheartening, dismal, dispiriting, distressing, dreary, funereal, gloomy, heartbreaking, hopeless, joyless, melancholic, melancholy, mournful, oppressive, sad, saddening, somber; SEE CONCEPT *529*

depression [*n1*] *low spirits; despair*
abasement, abjection, abjectness, blahs*, bleakness, blue funk*, bummer, cheerlessness, dejection, desolation, desperation, despondency, disconsolation, discouragement, dispiritedness, distress, dole, dolefulness, dolor, downheartedness, dreariness, dullness, dumps, ennui, gloom, gloominess, heaviness of heart, heavyheartedness, hopelessness, lowness, lugubriosity, melancholia, melancholy, misery, mortification, qualm, sadness, sorrow, the blues*, trouble, unhappiness, vapors*, woefulness, worry; SEE CONCEPT *410*

depression [*n2*] *economic decline*
bad times*, bankruptcy, bear market*, big trouble*, bottom out*, bust, crash, crisis, deflation, dislocation, downturn, drop, failure, hard times*, inactivity, inflation, overproduction, panic, paralysis, rainy days*, recession, retrenchment, sag, slide, slowness, slump, stagflation, stagnation, unemployment; SEE CONCEPTS *324,330,335*

depression [*n3*] *concavity, cavity*
basin, bowl, crater, dent, dimple, dip, excavation, hole, hollow, impression, indentation, pit,

pocket, sag, scoop, sink, sinkage, sinkhole, vacuity, vacuum, valley, void; SEE CONCEPT *513*

deprivation [*n*] *taking, keeping away; need*
denial, deprival, destitution, detriment, disadvantage, dispossession, distress, divestiture, divestment, expropriation, hardship, loss, privation, removal, seizure, want, withdrawal, withholding; SEE CONCEPTS *121,142,709*

deprive [*v*] *keep or take away something wanted, needed*
bankrupt, bare, bereave, denude, despoil, disinherit, dismantle, dispossess, disrobe, divest, dock, expropriate, hold back, lose, oust, rob, seize, skim, stiff, strip, wrest; SEE CONCEPTS *121,142*

depth [*n1*] *distance down or across*
base, bottom, declination, deepness, draft, drop, expanse, extent, fathomage, intensity, lower register, lowness, measure, measurement, pit, pitch, profoundness, profundity, remoteness, sounding; SEE CONCEPTS *737,790*

depth [*n2*] *insight, wisdom*
acuity, acumen, astuteness, brain, discernment, intellect, intelligence, keenness, penetration, profoundness, profundity, sagacity, sense, sharpness, weightiness; SEE CONCEPT *409*

deputy [*n*] *assistant, agent*
aide, ambassador, appointee, assembly member, backup, commissioner, councilor, delegate, dogcatcher*, factor, legate, lieutenant, minister, proxy, regent, replacement, representant, representative, second-in-command, sub, subordinate, substitute, surrogate; SEE CONCEPTS *348,354*

derange [*v*] *make crazy; confuse*
confound, craze*, dement, disarrange, disarray, discommode, discompose, disconcert, disorder, disorganize, displace, distract, disturb, drive mad, frenzy, madden, make insane, mess up*, misplace, muss*, perplex, ruffle, rummage, unbalance, unhinge*, unsettle, upset; SEE CONCEPTS *16,84*

deranged [*adj*] *crazy, insane*
ape*, baked*, bananas*, berserk, cracked*, crazed, delirious, demented, disarranged, disconcerted, disordered, displaced, distracted, dotty*, flipped*, flipped out*, frantic, frenzied, fried*, irrational, loco*, lunatic, mad, maddened, maniac, maniacal, nuts*, perplexed, schizzo*, unbalanced, unglued*, unhinged*, unscrewed*, unsettled, unsound, unzipped*, whacko*; SEE CONCEPT *403*

deregulate [*v*] *remove imposed controls on a system*
decontrol, denationalize, leave be, let alone, not interfere, not meddle, not tamper; SEE CONCEPTS *94,117*

deregulation [*n*] *the removal of imposed controls on a system*
disinvolvement, free competition, free enterprise, free trade, isolationism, laissez-faire, liberalism, noninterference, nonintervention, self-regulating market; SEE CONCEPT *299*

derelict [*adj1*] *careless, negligent*
behindhand, delinquent, disregardful, irresponsible, lax, regardless, remiss, slack, undependable, unreliable, untrustworthy; SEE CONCEPT *542*

derelict [*adj2*] *deserted, forsaken*
abandoned, castoff, desolate, dilapidated, dingy, discarded, faded, lorn, neglected, ownerless, relinquished, ruined, run-down, seedy, shabby, solitary, threadbare, uncouth; SEE CONCEPT *560*

derelict [*n*] *destitute or down-and-out person*
beggar, bum, castaway, dawdler, drifter, floater, grifter, hobo, ne'er-do-well*, outcast, renegade, skidrow bum, stiff, stumblebum*, tramp, vagabond, vagrant; SEE CONCEPTS *412,423*

deride [*v*] *make fun of; insult*
banter, chaff, contemn, detract, dis*, disdain, disparage, do a number on*, dump on*, flout, gibe, jeer, jolly, kid, knock, laugh at, lout, mock, pan, pooh-pooh*, put down*, quiz, rag*, rally, razz*, rib*, ridicule, roast*, scoff, scorn, slam, sneer, taunt, twit; SEE CONCEPTS *52,54*

de rigeur [*adj*] *proper, right*
au fait, becoming, comme il faut, conventional, correct, decent, decorous, done, fitting, necessary, required; SEE CONCEPT *558*

derision [*n*] *insult, disrespect*
backhanded compliment*, brickbat*, Bronx cheer*, butt*, comeback, contempt, contumely, crack, dig*, disdain, disparagement, dump*, jab, jest, joke, laughingstock, laughter, mockery, object of ridicule, parting shot, pilgarlic, put-down, raillery, ridicule, satire, scoffing, scorn, slam*, slap, sneering; SEE CONCEPTS *52,278,689*

derisive [*adj*] *ridiculing*
cheeky*, cocky, contemptuous, crusty, disdainful, flip*, fresh, gally, insulting, jeering, mocking, nervy, out-of-line, rude, sarcastic, sassy, scoffing, scornful, smart*, smart-alecky*, taunting; SEE CONCEPT *267*

derivable [*adj*] *deducible*
a priori, attributable, available, determinable, dogmatic, extractable, inferable, likely, obtainable, reasoned, resultant, traceable; SEE CONCEPT *529*

derivation [*n*] *root, source*
ancestry, basis, beginning, descent, etymology, foundation, genealogy, inception, origin, provenance, provenience, spin-off, well, wellspring, whence it came; SEE CONCEPT *648*

derivative [*adj*] *borrowed, transmitted from source*
acquired, ancestral, caused, cognate, coming from, connate, copied, evolved, hereditary, imitative, inferential, inferred, not original, obtained, plagiaristic, plagiarized, procured, rehashed, secondary, secondhand, subordinate, uninventive, unoriginal; SEE CONCEPT *549*

derivative [*n*] *product, descendant*
by-product, offshoot, outgrowth, spin-off, wave; SEE CONCEPT *260*

derive [*v*] *deduce a conclusion*
acquire, arrive, assume, collect, determine, develop, draw, educe, elaborate, elicit, evolve, excogitate, extract, follow, formulate, gain, gather, get, glean, infer, judge, make, make out, obtain, procure, put together, reach, receive, trace, work out; SEE CONCEPTS *15,18*

derive from [*v*] *come from; arise*
descend, emanate, flow, head, issue, originate, proceed, rise, spring from, stem from; SEE CONCEPT *648*

dernier cri [*n*] *the latest thing*
fad, look, the last word*, the newest fashion, vogue; SEE CONCEPT *655*

derogatory [*adj*] *offensive, uncomplimentary*
aspersing, belittling, calumnious, censorious, contumelious, critical, damaging, decrying,

defamatory, degrading, demeaning, deprecatory, depreciative, despiteful, detracting, disdainful, dishonoring, disparaging, fault-finding, humiliating, injurious, malevolent, malicious, maligning, minimizing, opprobrious, reproachful, sarcastic, scornful, slanderous, slighting, spiteful, unfavorable, unflattering, vilifying; SEE CONCEPTS 267,570

derriere [n] backside
ass, bottom, buns, buttocks, can, cheeks, fanny, heinie, keister, posterior, rear, rear end, seat; SEE CONCEPT 392

descend [v1] move down, lower a
cascade, cataract, cave in*, coast, collapse, crash, crouch, decline, deplane, detrain, dip, disembark, dismount, dive, dribble*, drop, fall, fall prostrate, get down, get off, go down, gravitate, ground, incline, light, light, lose balance, penetrate, pitch, plop, plummet, plunge, prolapse, set, settle, sink, slant, slide, slip, slope, slough off, slump, stoop, stumble, submerge, subside, swoop, toboggan, topple, trickle, trip, tumble, weep; SEE CONCEPTS 147,181,213

descend [v2] condescend
abase oneself, concede, degenerate, deteriorate, humble oneself, lower oneself, patronize, stoop; SEE CONCEPTS 23,35

descend [v3] trace ancestry from; be passed or handed down
arise, derive, issue, originate, proceed, spring; SEE CONCEPT 108

descendant [n] person in line of ancestry
brood, child, children, chip off old block*, get*, heir, issue, kin, offshoot, offspring, posterity, product, progeniture, progeny, scion, seed, spinoff*; SEE CONCEPTS 296,414

descent [n1] moving down; lowering
cave-in, coast, coming down, crash, declension, declination, decline, declivity, dip, downgrade, droop, drop, drop-off, fall, falling, grade, gradient, header, hill, inclination, incline, landslide, plummeting, plunge, plunging, precipitation, prolapse, sag, settlement, sinkage, sinking, slant, slide, slip, slope, swoop, tailspin, topple, tumble; SEE CONCEPTS 147,181,213,738

descent [n2] line of ancestry
blood, extraction, family, family tree, genealogy, heredity, lineage, origin, parentage, pedigree, relationship; SEE CONCEPT 296

descent [n3] deterioration
abasement, anticlimax, cadence, comedown, debasement, decadence, decline, degradation, discomfiture, down, downcome, downfall, lapse, pathos, slump; SEE CONCEPTS 230,674

descent [n4] assault, attack
advance, foray, incursion, invasion, pounce, raid, swoop; SEE CONCEPTS 86,320

describe [v] explain in speech, writing
call, characterize, chronicle, communicate, construe, convey image, define, delineate, depict, detail, distinguish, draw, elucidate, epitomize, exemplify, explicate, expound, express, illuminate, illustrate, image, impart, interpret, label, limn, make apparent, make clear, make sense of, make vivid, mark out, name, narrate, outline, paint, particularize, picture, portray, recite, recount, rehearse, relate, report, represent, sketch, specify, state, tell, term, trace, transmit, write up; SEE CONCEPT 55

description [n1] account in speech, writing
ABCs*, blow by blow, brief, characterization, chronicle, confession, declaration, definition, delineation, depiction, detail, explanation, explication, fingerprint, information, make, monograph, narration, narrative, picture, portraiture, portrayal, presentment, recital, recitation, record, recountal, rehearsal, report, representation, rundown, sketch, specification, statement, story, summarization, summary, tale, version, vignette, writeup, yarn; SEE CONCEPT 268

description [n2] class, kind
brand, breed, category, character, classification, feather, genre, genus, ilk, kidney, nature, order, sort, species, stripe, type, variety; SEE CONCEPT 378

descriptive [adj] explanatory
anedotic, characteristic, characterizing, circumstantial, classificatory, clear, definitive, delineative, depictive, describing, designating, detailed, eloquent, explicative, expository, expressive, extended, graphic, identifying, illuminating, illuminative, illustrative, indicative, interpretive, lifelike, narrative, particularized, pictorial, picturesque, revealing, specific, true to life, vivid; SEE CONCEPTS 267,557

desecrate [v] abuse, violate
befoul, blaspheme, commit sacrilege, contaminate, defile, depredate, desolate, despoil, devastate, devour, dishonor, make lose face*, mess up*, pervert, pillage, pollute, profane, prostitute, ravage, sack*, spoil, spoliate, waste; SEE CONCEPTS 246,252

desecration [n] violation, abuse
blasphemy, debasement, defilement, impiety, irreverence, profanation, sacrilege; SEE CONCEPTS 246,252

desegregate [v] eliminate segregation
abolish segregation, commingle, give equal access, integrate, open, unify; SEE CONCEPTS 113,114

desensitize [v] dull
anesthetize, benumb, deaden, make inactive, make less sensitive, numb, render insensible; SEE CONCEPTS 130,240

desert [adj] barren, uncultivated
arid, bare, desolate, infertile, lonely, solitary, sterile, uninhabited, unproductive, untilled, waste, wild; SEE CONCEPT 560

desert [n] wasteland; dry area
arid region, badland, barren, barren land, flats, lava bed, Sahara, sand dunes, solitude, wild, wilderness, wilds; SEE CONCEPTS 508,517

desert [v] abandon, defect
abscond, apostatize, bail out*, beach, betray, bolt, check out*, chuck, cop out*, crawl out of, decamp, depart, duck*, escape, flee, fly, forsake, give up, go, go AWOL*, go back on, go over the hill*, go west*, jilt, leave, leave high and dry*, leave in the lurch*, leave stranded, light, maroon, opt out, play truant, pull out, quit, relinquish, renounce, resign, run out on*, sneak off*, split*, strand, take a hike*, take off, tergiversate, throw over, vacate, violate oath, walk; SEE CONCEPTS 195,297

deserted [adj] abandoned, unoccupied
bare, barren, bereft, cast off, derelict, desolate, empty, forlorn, forsaken, godforsaken*, isolated, left, left in the lurch*, left stranded, lonely, lorn,

de
de

neglected, relinquished, solitary, uncouth, uninhabited, vacant; SEE CONCEPTS *485,577*

deserter [*n*] *fugitive from responsibility*
absconder, apostate, AWOL*, backslider, betrayer, criminal, defector, delinquent, derelict, escapee, escaper, hookey player*, lawbreaker, maroon, no-show*, recreant, refugee, renegade, runaway, shirker, slacker, traitor, truant; SEE CONCEPTS *358,412,423*

desertion [*n*] *abandonment*
abrogation, absconding, apostasy, avoidance, backsliding, betrayal, castoff, defecting, departing, departure, derelict, dereliction, disaffection, disavowal, disavowing, divorce, elusion, escape, evasion, falling away, falseness, flight, forsaking, going back on*, leaving, marooning, perfidy, recreancy, rejection, relinquishment, renunciation, repudiation, resignation, retirement, retreat, running out on*, secession, tergiversation, treachery, truancy, withdrawal; SEE CONCEPTS *195,297*

deserts [*n*] *what is due one*
chastening, chastisement, comeuppance, compensation, deserving, discipline, disciplining, due, get hers*, get his*, guerdon, lumps*, meed, merit, payment, penalty, punishment, recompense, requital, retribution, return, revenge, reward, right, talion, what is coming to one*, what one is asking for*; SEE CONCEPTS *129,710*

deserve [*v*] *be entitled to*
be given one's due*, be in line for*, be worthy of, demand, earn, gain, get, get comeuppance*, get what is coming to one*, have it coming*, have the right to, justify, lay claim to, merit, procure, rate, warrant, win; SEE CONCEPT *129*

deserving [*adj*] *worthy, meritorious*
admirable, commendable, due, estimable, fitting, laudable, needy, praisable, praiseworthy, righteous, rightful, thankworthy; SEE CONCEPT *404*

desiccate [*v*] *take moisture out of*
anhydrate, dehydrate, deplete, devitalize, divest, drain, dry, dry up, evaporate, exsiccate, parch, sear, shrivel, wither, wizen; SEE CONCEPTS *137,250*

design [*n1*] *sketch, draft*
architecture, arrangement, blueprint, chart, comp, composition, conception, constitution, construction, delineation, depiction, diagram, doodle, drawing, dummy, form, formation, idea, layout, makeup, map, method, model, outline, paste-up, pattern, perspective, picture, plan, scheme, study, tracery, tracing, treatment; SEE CONCEPTS *268,625,660*

design [*n2*] *artful conception*
arrangement, configuration, construction, depiction, device, doodle, drawing, figure, form, illustration, motif, motive, organization, painting, pattern, picture, portrait, shape, sketch, style; SEE CONCEPT *259*

design [*n3*] *intention*
action, aim, angle, animus, big picture*, brainchild*, child*, conation, conspiracy, deliberation, end, enterprise, game plan*, gimmick, goal, intendment, intrigue, lay of the land*, machination, meaning, notion, object, objective, picture, pitch, plan, play, plot, point, project, proposition, purport, purpose, recipe, reflection, scenario, scene, schema, scheme, setup, story, target, thinking, thought, trick, undertaking, view, volition, what's cooking*, will; SEE CONCEPTS *410,660*

design [*v1*] *plan, outline*
accomplish, achieve, arrange, block out, blueprint, cast, chart, construct, contrive, create, delineate, describe, devise, diagram, dope out, draft, draw, effect, execute, fashion, form, frame, fulfill, invent, lay out, perform, produce, project, set out, sketch, sketch out, trace, work out; SEE CONCEPT *36*

design [*v2*] *create, conceive*
compose, contrive, cook up*, devise, dream up*, fabricate, fashion, form, frame, invent, make up, originate, produce, think up; SEE CONCEPTS *43,173*

design [*v3*] *intend, mean to do*
aim, contemplate, contrive, destine, devise, make, mind, plan, prepare, project, propose, purpose, scheme, tailor; SEE CONCEPTS *35,36*

designate [*v1*] *name, entitle*
baptize, call, christen, cognominate, denominate, dub, label, nickname, nominate, style, term, title; SEE CONCEPT *62*

designate [*v2*] *specify as selection*
allocate, allot, appoint, apportion, appropriate, assign, authorize, button down*, characterize, charge, choose, commission, connote, constitute, define, delegate, denote, depute, deputize, describe, dictate, earmark*, elect, evidence, favor, finger*, indicate, individualize, make, mark, mete, name, nominate, opt, peg*, pick, pin down, pinpoint, prefer, put down for*, reseve, set apart, set aside, show, single, slot, stipulate, tab*, tag*, tap*; SEE CONCEPTS *41,129*

designation [*n1*] *name, label, mark*
appellation, appellative, class, classification, cognomen, compellation, denomination, description, epithet, identification, key word, moniker, nickname, nomen, style, title; SEE CONCEPT *683*

designation [*n2*] *delegation, selection*
appointment, classification, identification, indication, pigeonhole*, recognition, specification; SEE CONCEPT *41*

designedly [*adv*] *intentionally*
apurpose, by design, calculatedly, deliberately, knowingly, on purpose, prepensely, purposedly, purposely, purposively, studiously, willfully, wittingly; SEE CONCEPTS *402,535*

designing [*adj*] *plotting, crafty*
artful, astute, conniving, conspiring, crooked, cunning, deceitful, devious, heedful, intriguing, Machiavellian, observant, scheming, sharp, shrewd, sly, treacherous, tricky, unscrupulous, wily; SEE CONCEPT *542*

desirable [*adj1*] *attractive, seductive*
adorable, alluring, beautiful*, charming, covetable, enticing, fascinating, fetching, sexy; SEE CONCEPTS *372,579*

desirable [*adj2*] *advantageous, good*
acceptable, advisable, agreeable, beneficial, covetable, eligible, enviable, expedient, grateful, gratifying, helpful, pleasing, preferable, profitable, useful, welcome, worthwhile; SEE CONCEPTS *560,572*

desire [*n1*] *want, longing*
admiration, ambition, appetite, ardor, aspiration, attraction, avidity, concupiscence, covetousness, craving, craze, cupidity, devotion, doting, eagerness, fancy, fascination, fervor, fondness, frenzy, greed, hankering*, hunger, inclination, infatua-

tion, itch*, lasciviousness, lechery, libido, liking, love, lust, mania, motive, need, passion, predilection, proclivity, propensity, rapaciousness, rapture, ravenousness, relish, salacity, solicitude, thirst, urge, voracity, will, wish, yearning; SEE CONCEPTS *20,709*

desire [*n2*] *request*
appeal, entreaty, hope, importunity, petition, solicitation, supplication, want, wish; SEE CONCEPT *662*

desire [*v1*] *want, long for*
aim, aspire to, be smitten, be turned on by*, choose, cotton to, covet, crave, desiderate, die over*, enjoy, fall for*, hanker after*, have eyes for*, have the hots for*, hunger for, like, lust after, make advances to, partial to, pine, set heart on*, spoil for, sweet on*, take a liking to*, take a shine to*, take to*, thirst, wish for, yearn for; SEE CONCEPT *20*

desire [*v2*] *ask, request*
beg, bespeak, entreat, importune, petition, seek, solicit; SEE CONCEPT *48*

desirous [*adj*] *aspiring, hopeful*
acquisitive, ambitious, amorous, anxious, avid, covetous, craving, desiring, eager, enthusiastic, grasping, greedy, hot*, itchy*, keen, longing, lustful, passionate, prehensile, ready, stimulated, turned on*, willing, wishful, wishing, yearning; SEE CONCEPT *529*

desist [*v*] *stop, refrain from*
abandon, abstain, avoid, break off, cease, discontinue, end, forbear, give over, give up, halt, have done with*, knock off*, leave off, not do, pause, quit, relinquish, resign, surcease, suspend, yield; SEE CONCEPTS *119,234*

desk [*n*] *table*
counter, davenport, escritoire, lectern, reading stand, rolltop, school desk, secretary, workspace, writing desk; SEE CONCEPT *443*

desk jockey [*n*] *an office worker*
clerical worker, desk worker, pencil driver, pencil pusher, pen pusher, white-collar worker; SEE CONCEPT *348*

desktop publishing [*n*] *producing publications with computer software*
desktop*, electronic publishing, formatting, outputting, typesetting; SEE CONCEPT *277*

desolate [*adj1*] *unused, barren*
abandoned, bare, bleak, derelict, desert, destroyed, dreary, empty, forsaken, godforsaken*, isolated, lonely, lonesome, lorn, ruined, solitary, unfrequented, uninhabited, unoccupied, vacant, waste, wild; SEE CONCEPTS *485,560*

desolate [*adj2*] *depressed, despondent*
abandoned, acheronian, bereft, black, bleak, blue, cheerless, comfortless, companionless, dejected, disconsolate, dismal, dolorous, down, downcast, forlorn, forsaken, funereal, gloomy, hurting, in a blue funk*, inconsolable, joyless, lonely, lonesome, lorn, melancholy, miserable, somber, tragic, wretched; SEE CONCEPT *403*

desolate [*v*] *ravage, destroy*
depopulate, depredate, desecrate, despoil, devastate, devour, lay low, lay waste, pillage, plunder, ruin, sack, spoliate, waste; SEE CONCEPT *252*

desolation [*n1*] *uninhabited area; barrenness*
bareness, bleakness, desert, devastation, dissolution, extinction, forlornness, isolation, loneliness, ruin, solitariness, solitude, waste, wildness, wreck; SEE CONCEPTS *517,710*

desolation [*n2*] *distress, unhappiness*
anguish, dejection, despair, gloom, gloominess, loneliness, melancholy, misery, mourning, sadness, sorrow, woe, wretchedness; SEE CONCEPT *410*

despair [*n*] *depression, hopelessness*
anguish, dashed hopes, dejection, desperation, despondency, discouragement, disheartenment, forlornness, gloom, melancholy, misery, ordeal, pain, sorrow, trial, tribulation, wretchedness; SEE CONCEPT *410*

despair [*v*] *give up hope*
abandon, be hopeless, despond, destroy, drop, flatten, give way, have heavy heart*, let air out*, lose faith, lose heart, relinquish, renounce, resign, surrender, take down, yield; SEE CONCEPT *21*

despairing [*adj*] *upset, despondent*
anxious, at end of one's rope*, blue, brokenhearted, can't win*, cynical, dejected, depressed, desperate, disconsolate, downcast, forlorn, frantic, grief-stricken, hopeless, inconsolable, in pain*, in the dumps*, in the pits*, in the soup*, melancholic, melancholy, miserable, not a prayer*, no-win*, oppressed, pessimistic, sad, shot down*, strabilious, suicidal, sunk*, weighed down*, wretched; SEE CONCEPT *403*

desperado [*n*] *criminal*
bandit, convict, cutthroat, gangster, hoodlum, lawbreaker, mugger, outlaw, ruffian, thug; SEE CONCEPT *412*

desperate [*adj1*] *reckless, outrageous*
atrocious, audacious, bold, careless, dangerous, daring, death-defying, determined, devil-may-care, foolhardy, frantic, frenzied, furious, hasty, hazardous, headlong, headstrong, heinous, impetuous, incautious, madcap, monstrous, precipitate, rash, risky, scandalous, shocking, venturesome, violent, wild; SEE CONCEPT *401*

desperate [*adj2*] *extreme, intense*
acute, climacteric, concentrated, critical, crucial, dire, drastic, exquisite, fierce, furious, great, terrible, urgent, vehement, very grave, vicious, violent; SEE CONCEPTS *537,540,569*

desperate [*adj3*] *hopeless*
at end of one's rope*, back to the wall*, can't win*, dead duck*, despairing, despondent, desponding, downcast, forlorn, futile, gone*, goner*, hard up*, inconsolable, in the soup*, in the toilet*, irrecoverable, irremediable, irretrievable, no-chance*, no-way*, no-win*, running out of time*, sad, sunk*, up against it*, up the creek*, useless, vain, wretched; SEE CONCEPT *548*

desperately [*adv1*] *severely*
badly, carelessly, dangerously, dramatically, fiercely, gravely, greatly, harmfully, hysterically, like crazy*, like mad*, perilously, seriously; SEE CONCEPT *569*

desperately [*adv2*] *frightfully*
appallingly, fearfully, hopelessly, shockingly; SEE CONCEPT *403*

desperation [*n1*] *hopelessness*
agony, anguish, anxiety, concern, dejection, depression, desolation, despair, despondency, discomfort, disconsolateness, distraction, distress, fear, gloom, grief, heartache, melancholy, mis-

ery, pain, pang, sorrow, torture, trouble, unhappiness, worry; SEE CONCEPT *410*

desperation [*n2*] *rashness*
carelessness, defiance, foolhardiness, frenzy, heedlessness, impetuosity, madness, recklessness; SEE CONCEPT *633*

despicable [*adj*] *hateful; beyond contempt*
abject, awful, base, beastly, cheap, contemptible, degrading, detestable, dirty, disgraceful, disreputable, down, ignominious, infamous, insignificant, loathsome, low, low-life*, mean, no-good*, pitiful, reprehensible, shameful, slimy*, sordid, vile, worthless, wretched; SEE CONCEPTS *404,570*

despise [*v*] *look down on*
abhor, abominate, allergic to*, contemn, deride, detest, disdain, disregard, eschew, execrate, feel contempt for, flout, hate, have no use for*, loathe, look down nose at*, misprize, neglect, put down*, reject, renounce, repudiate, revile, scorn, shun, slight, snub, spurn, undervalue, wipe out*; SEE CONCEPT *29*

despite [*prep*] *in spite of, regardless of*
against, although, even though, even with, in contempt of, in defiance of, in the face of, notwithstanding, undeterred by; SEE CONCEPT *544*

despoil [*v*] *ravage, destroy*
denude, depopulate, depredate, deprive, desecrate, desolate, devastate, devour, dispossess, divest, loot, maraud, pillage, plunder, raid, rifle, rob, sack, spoil, spoliate, strip, vandalize, waste, wreak havoc, wreck; SEE CONCEPT *252*

despondent [*adj*] *depressed*
all torn up*, blue*, bummed-out*, cast-down, dejected, despairing, disconsolate, discouraged, disheartened, dispirited, doleful, down, downcast, downhearted, forlorn, gloomy, glum, grief-stricken, grieving, hopeless, in a blue funk*, in despair, in the pits*, low, low-spirited, melancholy, miserable, morose, mourning, sad, shot down*, sorrowful, woebegone, wretched; SEE CONCEPT *403*

desposition [*n*] *absolute power*
authoritarianism, autocracy, dictatorship, tyranny; SEE CONCEPTS *133,299,641*

despot [*n*] *dictator*
autocrat, Hitler*, monocrat, oppressor, slave-driver, tyrant; SEE CONCEPTS *354,412*

destination [*n*] *goal; place one wants to go*
aim, ambition, design, end, harbor, haven, intention, journey's end, landing-place, object, objective, purpose, resting-place, station, stop, target, terminal, terminus; SEE CONCEPTS *198,659*

destine [*v*] *predetermine, ordain*
allot, appoint, assign, consecrate, decide, decree, dedicate, design, determine, devote, doom, doom to, earmark*, fate, foreordain, intend, mark out, predestine, preform, preordain, purpose, reserve; SEE CONCEPT *18*

destined [*adj1*] *bound for, fated in near future*
at hand, brewing*, certain, closed, coming, compelled, compulsory, condemned, designed, directed, doomed, foreordained, forthcoming, hanging over*, impending, ineluctable, inescapable, inevitable, inexorable, in prospect, instant, in store, intended, in the cards*, in the wind*, looming, meant, menacing, near, ordained, overhanging, predesigned, predestined, predetermined, que sera sera*, sealed, settled, stated, that is to be, that will be, threatening, to come, unavoidable, way the ball bounces*; SEE CONCEPTS *537,820*

destined [*adj2*] *en route, on the road to*
appointed, appropriated, assigned, bent upon, booked, bound for, chosen, consigned, delegated, designated, determined, directed, entrained, heading, ordered to, prepared, routed, scheduled, specified; SEE CONCEPT *584*

destiny [*n*] *fate*
afterlife, break*, breaks*, certainty, circumstance, conclusion, condition, constellation, course of events, cup, design, divine decree, doom, expectation, finality, foreordination, fortune, future, happenstance, hereafter, horoscope, inevitability, intent, intention, karma, kismet*, lot, luck, Moirai, objective, ordinance, portion, predestination, predetermination, prospect, serendipity, the stars*, way the ball bounces*, way the cookie crumbles*, what is written*, wheel of fortune*, world to come*; SEE CONCEPT *679*

destitute [*adj*] *down and out; wanting*
bankrupt, beggared, bereft, busted, dead broke*, deficient, depleted, deprived of, devoid of, dirt poor*, divested, drained, empty, exhausted, flat*, flat broke*, impecunious, impoverished, indigent, in need of, insolvent, lacking, moneyless, necessitous, needy, on the breadline*, on the rocks*, penniless, penurious, pinched, played out*, poor, poverty-stricken, stony, strapped, stripped, totaled, wiped out*, without; SEE CONCEPT *334*

destroy [*v*] *demolish, devastate*
abort, annihilate, annul, axe*, blot out, break down, butcher*, consume, cream*, crush, damage, deface, desolate, despoil, dismantle, dispatch, end, eradicate, erase, exterminate, extinguish, extirpate, gut*, impair, kill, lay waste, level, liquidate, maim, mar, maraud, mutilate, nuke*, nullify, overturn, quash, quell, ravage, ravish, raze, ruin, sabotage, shatter, slay, smash, snuff out*, spoliate, stamp out, suppress, swallow up*, tear down, torpedo*, total, trash*, vaporize, waste, wax*, wipe out, wreck, zap*; SEE CONCEPT *252*

destruction [*n*] *demolition, devastation*
abolishing, abolition, annihilation, assassinating, bane, carnage, crashing, crushing, disintegrating, disrupting, dissolving, downfall, elimination, end, eradication, extermination, extinction, extinguishing, extirpation, havoc, invalidating, invalidation, liquidation, loss, massacre, murder, overthrow, ravaging, ruin, ruination, sacking, shattering, slaughter, slaying, subjugation, subversion, subverting, undoing, wreckage, wrecking; SEE CONCEPTS *230,252*

destructive [*adj1*] *injurious, devastating*
annihilative, baleful, baneful, calamitous, cancerous, cataclysmic, catastrophic, consumptive, cutthroat, damaging, deadly, deleterious, detrimental, dire, disastrous, eradicative, evil, extirpative, fatal, fell, harmful, hurtful, internecine, lethal, lethiferous, mortal, noisome, noxious, pernicious, pestiferous, pestilential, ruinous, slaughterous, suicidal, toxic, venomous, wrackful, wreckful; SEE CONCEPT *537*

destructive [*adj2*] *hurtful, disparaging*
abrasive, adverse, antagonistic, cankerous, caustic, contrary, corrosive, deleterious, derogatory, detrimental, discouraging, discrediting, erosive,

hostile, injurious, invalidating, negative, offensive, opposed, troublesome, undermining, vicious; SEE CONCEPTS *267,537*

desultory [*adj*] *random*
aimless, chance, chaotic, deviating, erratic, haphazard, orderless, rambling, unmethodical, unstable, unsystematic, without purpose; SEE CONCEPTS *535,548,557*

detach [*v*] *disconnect, cut off*
abstract, disaffiliate, disassemble, disassociate, disengage, disentangle, disjoin, dismount, dissociate, disunite, divide, divorce, free, isolate, loose, loosen, part, remove, segregate, separate, sever, sunder, take apart, tear off, uncouple, unfasten, unfix, unhitch, withdraw; SEE CONCEPT *135*

detached [*adj1*] *disconnected*
alone, apart, discrete, disjoined, divided, emancipated, free, isolate, isolated, loose, loosened, removed, separate, severed, unaccompanied, unconnected; SEE CONCEPT *490*

detached [*adj2*] *aloof, disinterested; neutral*
abstract, apathetic, casual, cool*, dispassionate, distant, impartial, impersonal, incurious, indifferent, laid-back*, objective, out of it*, poker-faced*, remote, removed, reserved, spaced-out, spacey*, staid, stolid, unbiased, uncommitted, unconcerned, uncurious, uninvolved, unpassioned, unprejudiced, withdrawn; SEE CONCEPTS *401,404*

detachment [*n1*] *disconnection*
disengagement, disjoining, dissolution, disunion, division, divorce, divorcement, partition, rupture, separation, severing, split-up; SEE CONCEPTS *388,747*

detachment [*n2*] *aloofness*
brown study*, coldness, coolness, disinterestedness, dreaminess, impartiality, incuriosity, indifference, neutrality, nonpartisanship, objectivity, preoccupation, remoteness, reverie, unconcern, woolgathering*; SEE CONCEPT *633*

detachment [*n3*] *military troop*
army, body, detail, division, force, organization, party, patrol, special force, squad, task force, troupe, unit; SEE CONCEPT *322*

detail [*n1*] *feature, specific aspect*
ABCs*, accessory, article, brass tacks*, chapter and verse*, circumstantiality, component, count, cue, design, dope*, element, fact, factor, fine point, fraction, item, meat and potatoes*, minor point, minutia, nicety, nitty-gritty*, nuts and bolts*, part, particular, peculiarity, plan, point, portion, respect, schedule, singularity, specialty, specification, structure, technicality, thing, trait, trivia, triviality; SEE CONCEPT *831*

detail [*n2*] *military troop*
army, assignment, body, detachment, duty, fatigue, force, kitchen police, KP*, organization, party, special force, squad, unit; SEE CONCEPT *322*

detail [*v1*] *specify, make clear*
analyze, catalog, circumstantiate, communicate, delineate, depict, describe, designate, elaborate, embellish, enumerate, epitomize, exhibit, fly speck*, get down to brass tacks*, individualize, itemize, lay out, narrate, particularize, portray, produce, quote chapter and verse*, recapitulate, recite, recount, rehearse, relate, report, reveal, set forth, show, specialize, spell out, spread, stipulate, summarize, sweat details*, tell, uncover; SEE CONCEPTS *55,57,60*

detail [*v2*] *assign specific task*
allocate, appoint, charge, commission, delegate, detach, send; SEE CONCEPTS *50,88*

detailed [*adj*] *itemized, particularized*
abundant, accurate, all-inclusive, amplified, at length, blow-by-blow*, circumstantial, circumstantiated, clocklike, complete, complicated, comprehensive, copious, definite, described, developed, disclosed, elaborate, elaborated, enumerated, exact, exhausting, exhaustive, finicky*, full, fussy*, individual, individualized, intricate, meticulous, minute, narrow, nice, point-by-point, precise, seriatim, specific, specified, thorough, unfolded; SEE CONCEPT *557*

detain [*v*] *hold, keep back; arrest*
apprehend, bog down*, bust*, buttonhole*, check, confine, constrain, decelerate, delay, hang up*, hinder, hold up*, ice*, impede, inhibit, intern, jail, mire, nab*, pick up, pinch*, pull in*, put away*, reserve, restrain, retard, run in, send up, set back, slow down, slow up, withhold; SEE CONCEPTS *191,317*

detect [*v*] *discover*
ascertain, catch, descry, dig up*, disclose, distinguish, encounter, espy, expose, find, hit on*, hit upon*, identify, meet, meet with, nose out*, note, notice, observe, recognize, reveal, scent, see, smell out*, smoke out*, spot, stumble on, track down, tumble into, turn up, uncover, unmask, wise up to*; SEE CONCEPTS *38,183*

detection [*n*] *discovery*
apprehension, disclosure, espial, exposé, exposure, ferreting out, find, revelation, strike, tracking down, uncovering, unearthing, unmasking; SEE CONCEPTS *38,183*

detective [*n*] *investigator of crime*
agent, analyst, bird dog*, bloodhound*, bull*, constable, cop, dick*, eavesdropper, eye*, fed*, fink*, flatfoot*, gumshoe*, informer, nark*, peeper*, P. I.*, plainclothes officer, police officer, private eye, private investigator, prosecutor, reporter, roper, scout, sergeant, shadow*, shamus*, Sherlock Holmes*, shoofly*, sleuth, slewfoot*, snoop*, spy, tail*; SEE CONCEPT *348*

détente [*n*] *peace*
amity, cooling off, equal power, harmony, relaxation, relief, tranquility, truce; SEE CONCEPTS *388,691*

detention [*n*] *confinement, imprisonment*
apprehension, arrest, arrestation, bust*, custody, delay, detainment, hindrance, holding back, holding pen*, immurement, impediment, incarceration, internment, keeping in, nab, pen*, pickup, pinch*, quarantine, restraint, retention, time up the river*, withholding; SEE CONCEPTS *191,317*

deter [*v*] *check, inhibit from action*
act like a wet blanket*, avert, block, caution, chill, cool, damp, dampen, daunt, debar, disadvise, discourage, dissuade, divert, forestall, forfend, frighten, hinder, impede, intimidate, obstruct, obviate, preclude, prevent, prohibit, put a damper on, put off, restrain, rule out, scare, shut out, stave off, stop, talk out of, throw cold water on*, turn off, warn; SEE CONCEPT *121*

detergent [*n*] *soap*
cleaner, solvent; SEE CONCEPT *492*

deteriorate [*v*] *decay, degenerate*
adulterate, alloy, become worse, be worse for wear*, break, corrode, corrupt, crumble, debase, debilitate, decline, decompose, degrade, deprave, depreciate, descend, disimprove, disintegrate, ebb, fade, fail, fall apart, flag, go downhill*, go to pieces*, go to pot*, go to the dogs*, hit the skids*, impair, injure, languish, lapse, lessen, lose it, lose quality, lower, mar, pervert, regress, retrograde, retrogress, rot, sink, skid, slide, spoil, undermine, vitiate, weaken, wear away, worsen; SEE CONCEPT *698*

deterioration [*n*] *decay, degeneration*
abasement, adulteration, atrophy, corrosion, crumbling, debasement, decadence, decaying, declension, declination, decline, decomposition, degradation, degringolade, depreciation, descent, devaluation, dilapidation, disintegration, dislocation, disrepair, downfall, downgrade, downturn, drop, fall, lapse, lessening, perversion, retrogression, rotting, ruin, slump, spoiling, vitiation, worsening; SEE CONCEPTS *230,698*

determination [*n1*] *perseverance*
assurance, backbone*, boldness, bravery, certainty, certitude, constancy, conviction, courage, dauntlessness, decision, dedication, doggedness, dogmatism, drive, energy, fearlessness, firmness, fortitude, grit, guts*, hardihood, heart*, independence, indomitability, intrepidity, nerve*, obstinacy, persistence, pluck*, purpose, purposefulness, resoluteness, resolution, resolve, self-confidence, single-mindedness, spine*, spunk*, steadfastness, stiff upper lip*, stubbornness, tenacity, valor, willpower; SEE CONCEPTS *411, 657*

determination [*n2*] *conclusion*
decision, judgment, measurement, opinion, perception, purpose, resolution, resolve, result, settlement, solution, verdict, visualization; SEE CONCEPTS *685,689*

determine [*v1*] *conclude, decide*
actuate, arbitrate, call the shots*, cinch, clinch, complete, dispose, drive, end, figure, finish, fix upon, halt, impel, incline, induce, move, nail down*, opt, ordain, persuade, pin down*, predispose, regulate, resolve, rule, settle, take a decision, tap, terminate, ultimate, wind up*, wrap up*; SEE CONCEPTS *18,35,234*

determine [*v2*] *discover, find out*
add up to*, ascertain, boil down to*, catch on, certify, check, demonstrate, detect, divine, establish, figure, figure out, have a hunch*, hear, learn, make out, see, size up, tell, tumble, unearth, verify, work out; SEE CONCEPTS *15,31*

determine [*v3*] *choose, decide*
destine, doom, elect, establish, fate, finger*, fix, foreordain, make up mind, predestine, predetermine, preform, preordain, purpose, resolve, settle; SEE CONCEPT *18*

determine [*v4*] *dictate, govern, regulate*
affect, bound, circumscribe, command, condition, control, decide, delimit, devise, direct, impel, impose, incline, induce, influence, invent, lead, limit, manage, mark off, measure, modify, plot, rule, shape; SEE CONCEPT *94*

determined [*adj*] *driven, persistent*
bent, bent on, buckled down*, constant, decided, decisive, dogged, earnest, firm, fixed, hard-as-nails*, hardboiled*, intent, mean business*, obstinate, on ice*, pat, persevering, purposeful, resolute, resolved, serious, set, set on, settled, single-minded, solid, steadfast, strong-minded, strong-willed, stubborn, tenacious, unfaltering, unflinching, unhesitating, unwavering; SEE CONCEPTS *404,542*

deterrent [*n*] *impediment, restraint*
bridle, check, curb, defense, determent, discouragement, disincentive, hindrance, leash, obstacle, preventative, preventive, rein, shackle; SEE CONCEPT *680*

detest [*v*] *hate; feel disgust toward*
abhor, abominate, be allergic to, despise, dislike intensely, down on, execrate, feel aversion toward, feel hostility toward, feel repugnance toward, have no use for*, loathe, recoil from, reject, repudiate; SEE CONCEPT *29*

detestable [*adj*] *loathsome, abominable*
abhorred, abhorrent, accursed, atrocious, awful, despicable, disgusting, execrable, godawful*, grody*, gross*, hateable, hateful, heinous, horrid, lousy, low-down, maggot, monstrous, obnoxious, odious, offensive, outrageous, repugnant, repulsive, revolting, rotten, shocking, sorry, vile; SEE CONCEPTS *529,542*

dethrone [*v*] *oust*
degrade, depose, discrown, dismiss, displace, uncrown, unmake; SEE CONCEPTS *298,320*

detonate [*v*] *set off bomb*
bang, blast, blow up, burst, discharge, explode, fulminate, kablooey*, let go, mushroom*, push the button*, shoot off, touch off, va-voom*; SEE CONCEPT *179*

detonation [*n*] *explosion*
bang, blast, blowout, blow-up, boom, discharge, ignition; SEE CONCEPTS *179,320,521*

detour [*n*] *indirect course*
alternate route, back road, branch, bypass, by-path, byway, circuit, circuitous route, circumbendibus*, circumnavigation, circumvention, crotch, deviation, divergence, diversion, fork, roundabout way, runaround, secondary highway, service road, substitute, temporary route; SEE CONCEPT *501*

detract [*v*] *take away a part; lessen*
backbite*, belittle, blister, cheapen, cut rate, decrease, decry, depreciate, derogate, devaluate, diminish, discount, discredit, disesteem, draw away, knock*, laugh at, lower, minimize, misprize, reduce, subtract from, underrate, undervalue, vilipend, withdraw, write off; SEE CONCEPTS *52,54,236,247*

detraction [*n*] *misrepresentation; slander*
abuse, aspersion, backbiting*, backstabbing*, belittlement, calumny, damage, defamation, denigration, deprecation, derogation, disesteem, disparagement, harm, hit, hurt, injury, injustice, innuendo, insinuation, knock*, libel, libeling, lie, maligning, minimization, muckraking*, obloquy, pejorative, revilement, ridicule, running down*, scandal, scandalmongering, scurrility, slam, smear campaign*, tale, traducement, traducing, vilification, vituperation, wrong; SEE CONCEPTS *52,54,63*

detriment [*n*] *disadvantage*
damage, disability, disservice, drawback, handicap, harm, hurt, impairment, injury, liability, loss, marring, mischief, prejudice, spoiling; SEE CONCEPTS *309,674*

detrimental [*adj*] *damaging, disadvantageous*
adverse, bad, baleful, deleterious, destructive,

disturbing, evil, harmful, hurtful, ill, inimical, injurious, mischievous, negative, nocuous, pernicious, prejudicial, unfavorable; SEE CONCEPTS *537,570*

detritus [*n*] *debris*
deposit, fragments, grains, leavings, rubble, scree, sediment, shavings; SEE CONCEPT *260*

devalue [*v*] *depreciate*
cheapen, cut rate, debase, decrease, decry, devalorize, devaluate, knock off, lower, mark down, nose dive, revalue, take down, underrate, undervalue, write down, write off; SEE CONCEPTS *330,335*

devastate [*v*] *demolish, destroy*
depredate, desecrate, desolate, despoil, devour, do one in*, lay waste, level, pillage, plunder, raid, ravage, raze, ruin, sack, smash, spoil, spoliate, stamp out*, take apart, total*, trash*, waste, wipe off map*, wreck; SEE CONCEPTS *246,252*

devastation [*n*] *destruction*
confusion, defoliation, demolition, depredation, desolation, havoc, loss, pillage, plunder, ravages, ruin, ruination, spoliation, waste; SEE CONCEPT *674*

develop [*v1*] *cultivate, prosper*
advance, age, enroot, establish, evolve, expand, flourish, foster, grow, grow up, maturate, mature, mellow, progress, promote, ripen, thrive; SEE CONCEPTS *253,427,704*

develop [*v2*] *expand, work out*
actualize, advance, amplify, augment, beautify, broaden, build up, cultivate, deepen, dilate, elaborate, enlarge, enrich, evolve, exploit, extend, finish, heighten, improve, intensify, lengthen, magnify, materialize, perfect, polish, promote, realize, refine, spread, strengthen, stretch, unfold, widen; SEE CONCEPTS *700,775*

develop [*v3*] *begin; occur*
acquire, arise, befall, betide, break, break out, breed, chance, come about, come off, commence, contract, ensue, establish, follow, form, generate, go, happen, invest, originate, pick up, result, start, transpire; SEE CONCEPT *119*

develop [*v4*] *unfold; be made known*
account for, acquire, actualize, disclose, disentangle, elaborate, evolve, exhibit, explain, explicate, foretell, form, materialize, produce, reach, realize, recount, state, uncoil, uncover, unfurl, unravel, unroll, untwist, unwind; SEE CONCEPTS *60,261*

developer [*n*] *real estate developer*
builder, planner, real estate investor; SEE CONCEPT *348*

development [*n1*] *growth*
adding to, addition, adulthood, advance, advancement, advancing, augmentation, augmenting, boost, buildup, developing, elaborating, enlargement, evolution, evolvement, evolving, expansion, flowering, hike, improvement, increase, increasing, making progress, maturation, maturing, maturity, ongoing, perfecting, progress, progression, reinforcement, reinforcing, ripening, spread, spreading, unfolding, unraveling, upgrowth, upping; SEE CONCEPTS *700,704,775*

development [*n2*] *happening, incident*
change, circumstance, conclusion, denouement, event, eventuality, eventuation, issue, materialization, occurrence, outcome, phenomenon, re-

sult, situation, transpiration, turn of events, upshot; SEE CONCEPT *3*

deviant [*adj*] *abnormal, different*
aberrant, anomalous, atypical, bent, devious, divergent, freaky, heretical, heteroclite, irregular, kinky, off-key, perverse, perverted, preternatural, queer, twisted, unorthodox, unrepresentative, untypical, variant, varying, wandering, wayward, weird; SEE CONCEPT *564*

deviate [*v*] *stray from normal path*
aberrate, angle off, avert, bear off, bend, bend the rules*, break pattern, circumlocate, contrast, deflect, depart, depart from, differ, digress, divagate, diverge, drift, edge off*, err, get around, go amiss, go haywire*, go off on tangent*, go out of control*, go out of way, leave beaten path*, not conform, part, shy, swerve, swim against stream*, take a turn, turn, turn aside, vary, veer, wander; SEE CONCEPTS *195,665,697*

deviation [*n*] *change, departure*
aberration, alteration, anomaly, breach, crotch, deflection, detour, difference, digression, discrepancy, disparity, divergence, diversion, fluctuation, fork, hereticism, inconsistency, irregularity, modification, shift, transgression, turning, variance, variation; SEE CONCEPTS *665,697,738*

device [*n1*] *instrument, tool*
accessory, agent, apparatus, appliance, arrangement, article, construction, contraption, contrivance, creation, doohickey*, equipment, expedient, gadget, gear, gimmick, implement, invention, machine, makeshift, material, means, mechanism, medium, outfit, resort, resource, rigging*, Rube Goldberg invention*, shift, tackle, thingamabob*, utensil, whatchamacallit*, whatnot*, whatsit*; SEE CONCEPTS *463,499*

device [*n2*] *ploy, scheme, maneuver*
artifice, cabal, chicanery, clever move, craft, craftiness, cunningness, design, dodge, evasion, expedient, fake, feint, finesse, gambit, game, gimmick, improvisation, loophole*, machination, method, pattern, plan, plot, project, proposition, purpose, racket, ruse, shift, stratagem, strategy, stunt, subterfuge, trap, trick, wile; SEE CONCEPT *660*

device [*n3*] *symbol, emblem*
badge, colophon, crest, design, ensign, figure, insignia, logo, motif, motto, pattern, scroll, sign, slogan, token; SEE CONCEPT *284*

devil [*n*] *demon*
adversary, archfiend, beast, Beelzebub, bête noire, brute, common enemy, dastard, diablo, djinn, dybbuk, enfant terrible*, evil one, fiend, genie, hellion, imp, knave, Lucifer, Mephistopheles, monster, ogre, Prince of Darkness, rogue, Satan, scamp, scoundrel, the dickens*, the Erinyes, the Furies, villain; SEE CONCEPTS *370,412*

devilish [*adj*] *wicked*
accursed, atrocious, bad, brutish, cloven-footed, cursed, damnable, demoniac, demonic, detestable, diabolic, diabolical, evil, execrable, fiendish, hellborn, hellish, infernal, inhuman, iniquitous, Mephistophelian, nefarious, satanic, serpentine, unhallowed, villainous; SEE CONCEPT *545*

devil's advocate [*n*] *mediator*
apologist, pleader, polemicist, sophist; SEE CONCEPTS *348,423*

de
de

devious [adj1] *dishonest, crafty*
artful, calculating, crooked, deceitful, double-dealing, duplicitous, errant, erring, evasive, faking one out*, fishy*, foxy*, fraudulent, guileful, indirect, insidious, insincere, not straightforward, oblique, obliquitous, playing games, playing politics*, put on, roundabout, scheming, shady, shifty, shrewd, sly, sneaking, sneaky, surreptitious, treacherous, tricky, underhanded, wily; SEE CONCEPTS *401,404*

devious [adj2] *crooked; indirect*
ambiguous, bending, circuitous, confounding, confusing, curving, detouring, deviating, digressing, digressory, diverting, errant, erratic, excursive, flexuous, misleading, obscure, out-of-the-way, rambling, remote, removed, roundabout, serpentine, straying, tortuous, twisting, wandering; SEE CONCEPT *581*

devise [v] *conceive, dream up*
ad-lib, arrange, blueprint*, brainstorm*, cast, chart, cogitate, come up with, concoct, construct, contrive, cook up*, craft, create, design, discover, dope out*, fake it, forge, form, formulate, frame*, get off*, hatch, head trip*, imagine, improvise, intrigue, invent, machinate, make up, mastermind*, plan, play it by ear*, plot, prepare, project, scheme, shape, spark, think up, throw together, trump up*, vamp, whip up*, work out; SEE CONCEPTS *36,43*

devoid [adj] *empty, wanting*
bare, barren, bereft, deficient, denuded, destitute, free from, innocent, lacking, needed, sans*, unprovided with, vacant, void, without; SEE CONCEPTS *483,485*

devote [v] *commit one's energies, thoughts*
allot, apply, apportion, appropriate, assign, bestow, bless, concern oneself, confide, consecrate, consign, dedicate, donate, enshrine, entrust, give, give away, hallow, hand out, occupy oneself, pledge, present, reserve, sanctify, set apart, vow; SEE CONCEPTS *17,108,112*

devoted [adj] *committed, loyal*
adherent, affectionate, ardent, behind one, caring, concerned, consecrated, constant, crazy about*, dear, dedicated, devout, doting, dutiful, faithful, fervid, fond, gone on*, lovesome, loving, staunch, steadfast, stuck on*, thoughtful, true, true-blue*, wild about*, zealous; SEE CONCEPT *542*

devotee [n] *ardent supporter; fan*
addict, adherent, admirer, aficionado, amateur, believer, booster, buff, disciple, enthusiast, fanatic, fancier, fiend, follower, groupie, habitué, junkie, lover, rooter, supporter, votarient, votary; SEE CONCEPT *423*

devotion [n] *commitment; loyalty*
adherence, adoration, affection, allegiance, ardor, attachment, consecration, constancy, dedication, deference, devotedness, devotement, devoutness, earnestness, enthusiasm, faithfulness, fealty, fervor, fidelity, fondness, intensity, love, observance, passion, piety, reverence, sanctity, service, sincerity, spirituality, worship, zeal; SEE CONCEPTS *32,657*

devour [v] *swallow, consume*
absorb, annihilate, appreciate, be engrossed by, be preoccupied, bolt, bolt down*, chow down*, cram*, delight in, destroy, dispatch, do compulsively, do voraciously, drink in, eat, enjoy, exhaust, feast on, feed on, gloat over, gobble, gorge*, go through, gulp, guzzle, hoover*, imbibe, ingest, inhale, partake of, pig out*, polish off*, ravage, rejoice in, relish, revel in, scarf down*, spend, stuff, take, take in, use up, waste, wipe out, wolf*, wolf down*; SEE CONCEPTS *169,225*

devout [adj] *sincerely believing; devoted*
adherent, adoring, ardent, deep, earnest, faithful, fervent, fervid, genuine, godly, goody-goody*, goody two-shoes*, heart-and-soul, heartfelt, holy, intense, orthodox, passionate, pietistic, pious, prayerful, profound, religious, reverent, revering, serious, sincere, venerating, worshiping, zealous; SEE CONCEPT *542*

dew [n] *moisture*
condensation, water droplets; SEE CONCEPTS *467,524*

dewy-eyed [adj] *innocent*
dovelike, green, inexperienced, naïve, pure, sinless, uncorrupted, undefiled, unworldly, wide-eyed; SEE CONCEPTS *404,542*

dexterity [n] *aptitude, ability*
address, adroitness, aptness, art, artistry, cleverness, craft, cunning, deftness, effortlessness, expertise, expertness, facility, finesse, handiness, ingenuity, knack, know-how, mastery, neatness, nimbleness, proficiency, readiness, skill, skillfulness, smoothness, tact, touch; SEE CONCEPTS *409,630*

dexterous [adj] *ingenious, proficient*
able, active, acute, adept, adroit, agile, apt, artful, canny, clever, crack*, crackerjack*, deft, effortless, expert, facile, handy, having the know-how*, masterly, neat, nimble, nimble-fingered, prompt, quick, savvy, skilled, skillful, slick, sly, smooth; SEE CONCEPTS *402,527*

diabolic [adj] *evil, fiendish*
atrocious, cruel, damnable, demoniac, demonic, devilish, hellish, impious, infernal, Mephistophelian, monstrous, nasty, nefarious, satanic, serpentine, shocking, unhallowed, unpleasant, vicious, vile, villainous, wicked; SEE CONCEPT *545*

diagnose [v] *identify problem, disease*
analyze, determinate, determine, diagnosticate, distinguish, interpret, investigate, pinpoint, place, pronounce, recognize, spot; SEE CONCEPTS *38,310*

diagnosis [n] *identification of problem, disease*
analysis, conclusion, examination, interpretation, investigation, opinion, pronouncement, scrutiny, summary; SEE CONCEPTS *283,689*

diagonal [adj] *angled*
askew, bevel, beveled, bias, biased, cater-cornered, catty-cornered, cornerways, cross, crossways, crosswise, inclining, kitty-cornered*, oblique, skewing, slanted, slanting, transversal, transverse; SEE CONCEPT *581*

diagonally [adv] *at an angle*
askew, aslant, cater-corner, catty-corner, cornerwise, crosswise, kitty-corner*, obliquely, on a slant, on the bias, slantingways, slantways, slantwise, slaunchways; SEE CONCEPT *581*

diagram [n] *drawing, sketch of form or plan*
big picture*, blueprint, chart, description, design, draft, figure, floor plan, game, game plan, ground plan, layout, outline, perspective, representation, rough draft; SEE CONCEPTS *625,660*

dial [v] *tune to desired position*
punch, ring, rotate, turn, twist, wheel, zero in on*; SEE CONCEPT *201*

225 **DIALECT / DIE**

dialect [n] *local speech*
accent, argot, can, idiom, jargon, language, lingo, localism, patois, patter, pronunciation, provincialism, regionalism, slang, terminology, tongue, vernacular, vocabulary; SEE CONCEPT *276*

dialectic [adj] *logical, rational*
analytic, argumentative, controversial, dialectical, persuasive, polemical, rationalistic; SEE CONCEPT *529*

dialectic [n] *logic, reasoning*
argumentation, contention, debate, deduction, discussion, disputation, forensic, logical argument, mooting, persuasion, polemics, question-and-answer method, ratiocination; SEE CONCEPT *37*

dialogue/dialog [n] *talk, exchange of ideas*
chat, colloquy, communication, confab*, confabulation, conference, conversation, converse, discourse, discussion, duologue, interlocution, lines*, parlance, parley, powwow, remarks, repartee, script, sides, small talk*; SEE CONCEPTS *56,278*

diameter [n] *measurement across object*
bore, breadth, broadness, caliber, module, width; SEE CONCEPT *760*

diametric/diametrical [adj] *opposed, conflicting*
adverse, antipodal, antipodean, antithetical, contradictory, contrary, contrasting, converse, counter, facing, opposite, polar, reverse; SEE CONCEPT *564*

diaphanous [adj] *fine, see-through*
chiffon, clear, cobweblike, delicate, filmy, flimsy, gauzy, gossamer, light, pellucid, pure, sheer, thin, translucent, transparent; SEE CONCEPTS *490,606*

diarrhea [n] *loose bowels*
dysentery, flux, Montezuma's revenge*, the runs*, the trots*; SEE CONCEPT *306*

diary [n] *recounting of activities in writing*
account, agenda, appointment book, chronicle, daily record, daybook, engagement book, journal, log, minutes, notebook, record; SEE CONCEPT *283*

diaspora [n] *the spreading out of a group of people*
disbandment, dispersal, dispersion, dissolution, escape, exodus, mass exodus, refugee flow; SEE CONCEPT *195*

diatribe [n] *harangue, criticism*
abuse, castigation, denunciation, disputation, invective, jeremiad, objection, onslaught, philippic, reviling, screed, stricture, tirade, vituperation; SEE CONCEPT *52*

dibs [n] *claim*
dueness, entitlement, preemptive declaration, privilege, request, rights; SEE CONCEPTS *278,318, 376,709*

dicey [adj] *risky*
capricious, chancy, dangerous, difficult, erratic, fluctuant, iffy*, incalculable, ticklish, tricky, uncertain, unpredictable, whimsical; SEE CONCEPTS *535,552*

dichotomy [n] *division*
difference, difference of opinion, disagreement, disunion, separation, split; SEE CONCEPTS *98,135*

dicker [v] *bargain; argue about*
barter, buy and sell, chaffer, cut a deal*, haggle*, hammer out a deal*, huckster*, negotiate, palter, trade, work out a deal*; SEE CONCEPTS *46,330*

dictate [n] *command; rule*
behest, bidding, code, decree, dictum, direction, edict, fiat, injunction, law, mandate, order, ordinance, precept, principle, requirement, statute, ultimatum, word; SEE CONCEPTS *274,318,688*

dictate [v1] *command; give instructions*
bid, bulldoze*, call the play*, call the shots*, call the tune*, charge, control, decree, direct, enjoin, govern, guide, impose, instruct, lay down, lay down the law, lead, manage, ordain, order, prescribe, pronounce, put foot down*, read the riot act*, regiment, rule, set, take the reins*, walk heavy*; SEE CONCEPTS *53,60*

dictate [v2] *read out for the record*
compose, deliver, draft correspondence, emit, formulate, give account, give forth, interview, orate, prepare draft, say, speak, talk, transmit, utter, verbalize; SEE CONCEPTS *60,324*

dictator [n] *absolute ruler*
absolutist, adviser, authoritarian, autocrat, boss, chief, commander, despot, disciplinarian, fascist, Hitler*, leader, magnate, mogul, oligarch, oppressor, ringleader, slavedriver, totalitarian, tycoon, tyrant, usurper; SEE CONCEPT *354*

dictatorial [adj] *tyrannical, authoritarian*
absolute, arbitrary, arrogant, autocratic, bossy, clamorous, crack-the-whip*, despotic, dictative, doctrinaire, dogmatic, domineering, egotistic, firm, haughty, imperative, imperious, iron-handed, oppressive, overbearing, peremptory, pompous, proud, stern, throwing weight around, totalitarian, unlimited, unrestricted; SEE CONCEPT *542*

dictatorship [n] *absolute rule*
authoritarianism, autocracy, coercion, despotism, fascism, garrison state, Nazism, reign of terror*, totalitarianism, tyranny, unlimited rule; SEE CONCEPTS *133,299,641*

diction [n] *style of speech; articulation*
command of language, delivery, elocution, eloquence, enunciation, expression, fluency, gift of gab*, inflection, intonation, language, line, lingo, locution, oratory, parlance, phrase, phraseology, phrasing, pronunciation, rhetoric, usage, verbalism, verbiage, vocabulary, wordage, wording; SEE CONCEPTS *47,276*

dictionary [n] *book of word meanings*
concordance, cyclopedia, encyclopedia, glossary, language, lexicon, palaver, promptory, reference, terminology, vocabulary; SEE CONCEPT *280*

dictum [n1] *saying; proverb*
adage, aphorism, apothegm, axiom, brocard, gnome, maxim, moral, motto, precept, rule, saw, truism; SEE CONCEPTS *278,689*

dictum [n2] *decree, pronouncement*
affirmation, assertion, command, declaration, dictate, edict, fiat, order; SEE CONCEPT *278*

didactic [adj] *educational*
academic, advisory, donnish, edifying, enlightening, exhortative, expository, homiletic, hortative, instructive, moral, moralizing, pedagogic, pedantic, preachy, preceptive, schoolmasterist, sermonic, sermonizing, teacherish, teacherly, teachy; SEE CONCEPT *548*

die [v1] *pass away; stop living*
be no more*, be taken, breathe one's last*, cease to exist, conk*, croak*, decease, demise, depart, drop, drop off, drown, expire, finish, give up the ghost*, go way of all flesh*, kick the bucket*,

de
di

perish, relinquish life, rest in peace, succumb, suffocate; SEE CONCEPT *304*

die [*v2*] *wither, dwindle*
abate, bate, break down, crumble, decay, decline, degenerate, deteriorate, dilapidate, diminish, disappear, droop, ease off, ebb, end, expire, fade, fade away, fade out, fail, fall, fizzle out*, go bad*, go downhill*, halt, lapse, let up, lose power, melt away, moderate, molder, pass, peter out*, rankle, recede, retrograde, rot, run down, run low, run out, sink, slacken, stop, subside, vanish, wane, weaken, wear away, wilt; SEE CONCEPTS *469,698*

die-hard [*adj*] *uncompromising*
conservative, convinced, dyed-in-the-wool*, extremist, firm, fogyish, immovable, inflexible, intransigent, old-line*, orthodox, Philistine, reactionary, right, standpat, Tory*, traditionalistic, ultraconservative, unreconstructed; SEE CONCEPTS *404,542*

diehard [*n*] *overenthusiastic person*
bitter ender*, Bourbon*, dyed-in-the-wool*, extremist, fanatic, fogy, fundamentalist, intransigent, mossback*, old liner*, praetorian, pullback*, reactionary, right, rightist, rightwinger, standpat, standpatter, stick-in-the-mud*, Tory*, true blue*, ultraconservative, zealot; SEE CONCEPTS *359,423*

diet [*n1*] *abstinence from food*
dietary, fast, nutritional therapy, regime, regimen, restriction, starvation, weight-reduction plan; SEE CONCEPT *660*

diet [*n2*] *daily intake of food*
aliment, bite, comestibles, commons, daily bread, edibles, fare, goodies, grubbery, menu, nourishment, nutriment, nutrition, provisions, rations, snack, subsistence, sustenance, viands, victuals; SEE CONCEPTS *457,459*

diet [*v*] *abstain from food*
count calories*, eat sparingly, fall off, fast, go without, lose weight, reduce, skinny down*, slim, slim down, starve, tighten belt*, watch weight*; SEE CONCEPT *169*

differ [*v1*] *be dissimilar, distinct*
alter, bear no resemblance, be distinguished from, be off the beaten path*, be unlike, clash with, conflict with, contradict, contrast, depart from, deviate from, digress, disagree, divaricate from, diverge, diversify, jar with, lack resemblance, modify, not conform, not look like, qualify, reverse, run counter to, show contrast, sing a different tune*, stand apart, take exception, turn, vary; SEE CONCEPT *665*

differ [*v2*] *clash; hold opposing views*
bicker*, bump heads*, contend, debate, demur, disaccord, disagree, discept, discord, dispute, dissent, divide, fight, go after each other, go at it*, hit a clinker*, hit a sour note*, jar*, lock horns*, object, oppose, protest against, quarrel, squabble, take issue, vary, war; SEE CONCEPT *46*

difference [*n1*] *dissimilarity, distinctness*
aberration, alteration, anomaly, antithesis, asymmetry, change, characteristic, contrariety, contrariness, contrast, departure, deviation, digression, discongruity, discrepancy, disparity, dissemblance, distinction, divergence, diversity, exception, heterogeneity, idiosyncrasy, inequality, irregularity, nonconformity, opposition, particularity, peculiarity, separateness, separation, singularity, unconformity, unlikeness, unortho-

doxness, variance, variation, variety; SEE CONCEPT *665*

difference [*n2*] *opposing views*
argument, beef*, blowup*, bone to pick*, brannigan, brawl, brush*, brush-off*, catamaran, clash, conflict, contention, contrariety, contretemps, controversy, debate, disaccord, disagreement, discord, discordance, dispute, dissension, dissent, dissidence, disunity, dustup*, estrangement, hassle, quarrel, row*, run-in*, scrap*, setto*, spat*, strife, tiff*, variance, words*, wrangle; SEE CONCEPTS *46,388*

different [*adj1*] *dissimilar, unlike*
a far cry from*, altered, antithetic, at odds, at variance, changed, clashing, colorful, contradistinct, contradistinctive, contrary, contrasting, contrastive, deviating, differential, discrepant, disparate, distant, distinct, distinctive, divergent, divers, diverse, incommensurable, incomparable, inconsistent, individual, like night and day*, mismatched, mismated, offbeat, opposed, other, otherwise, particular, peculiar, poles apart*, single, unalike, unequal, unrelated, unsimilar, variant, various; SEE CONCEPTS *487,564,573*

different [*adj2*] *separate, distinct*
another, another story, atypical, bizarre, discrete, diverse, especial, express, extraordinary, individual, novel, original, other, out of the ordinary, particular, peculiar, rare, several, singular, something else, special, specialized, specific, startling, strange, uncommon, unconventional, unique, unusual, various; SEE CONCEPT *564*

different [*adj3*] *miscellaneous, various*
anthologized, assorted, asymmetrical, collected, disparate, dissonant, divergent, divers, diverse, diversified, diversiform, heterogeneous, incongruous, inconsistent, indiscriminate, jarring, manifold, many, multifarious, multiform, numerous, omnifarious, omniform, several, some, sundry, varicolored, varied, variegated, varietal, variform; SEE CONCEPT *772*

differentiate [*v1*] *make a distinction*
antithesize, characterize, comprehend, contrast, demarcate, discern, discrepate, discriminate, extricate, individualize, individuate, know, know what's what*, mark, mark off, redline*, separate, set apart, set off, sever, severalize, split hairs*, tell apart, understand; SEE CONCEPTS *15,38*

differentiate [*v2*] *change; make different*
adapt, alter, assort, convert, diversify, mismatch, mismate, modify, transform, variegate, vary; SEE CONCEPT *232*

differently [*adv*] *in another way; otherwise*
abnormally, adversely, antagonistically, antithetically, asymmetrically, conflictingly, contradictorily, contrarily, contrastingly, contrastively, discordantly, disparately, dissimilarly, distinctively, divergently, diversely, hostilely, in a different manner, incompatibly, incongruously, individually, negatively, nonconformably, on the contrary, on the other hand, oppositely, poles apart, separately, uniquely, unorthodoxly, unusually, variously, vice versa; SEE CONCEPT *564*

difficult [*adj1*] *hard on someone; hard to do*
ambitious, arduous, backbreaker*, bothersome, burdensome, challenging, crucial, demanding, difficile, easier said than done*, effortful, exacting, formidable, galling, Gargantuan*, hard-won, heavy, Herculean*, immense, intricate, irritating, labored, laborious, no picnic*, not easy, onerous,

operose, painful, problem, problematic, prohibitive, rigid, severe, stiff, strenuous, titanic, toilsome, tough, troublesome, trying, unyielding, uphill, upstream, wearisome; SEE CONCEPT *538*

difficult [*adj2*] *complicated; hard to comprehend*
abstract, abstruse, baffling, bewildering, complex, confounding, confusing, dark, deep, delicate, enigmatic, enigmatical, entangled, esoteric, formidable, hard to explain, hard to solve, hidden, inexplicable, intricate, involved, knotty, labyrinthine, loose, meandering, mysterious, mystical, mystifying, nice, obscure, obstinate, paradoxical, perplexing, problematical, profound, puzzling, rambling, subtle, tangled, thorny, ticklish, troublesome, unclear, unfathomable, unintelligible, vexing; SEE CONCEPT *529*

difficult [*adj3*] *unmanageable socially*
argumentative, bearish, boorish, dark, demanding, fastidious, finicky, fractious, fussy, grim, hard to please, impolite, intractable, irritable, oafish, obstreperous, perverse, picky, refractory, rigid, rude, tiresome, tough, troublesome, trying, unaccommodating, unamenable; SEE CONCEPTS *404,542,555*

difficulty [*n1*] *problem; situation requiring great effort*
adversity, arduousness, awkwardness, barricade, check, complication, crisis, crux, dead end, deadlock, deep water*, dilemma, distress, emergency, exigency, fix*, frustration, hardship, hazard, hindrance, hitch*, hot water*, impasse, knot*, labor, laboriousness, mess, misfortune, muddle, obstacle, obstruction, pain, painfulness, paradox, perplexity, pickle*, predicament, quagmire, quandary, scrape*, snag*, stew*, strain, strait, strenuousness, struggle, stumbling block*, tribulation, trouble; SEE CONCEPTS *674,677*

difficulty [*n2*] *mental burden*
ado, aggravation, annoyance, anxiety, bafflement, bother, care, charge, complication, crisis, depression, discouragement, distress, embarrassment, emergency, exigency, frustration, grievance, hangup, harassment, imbroglio, inconvenience, irritation, jam, maze, mess, millstone*, misery, oppression, perplexity, pickle*, pinch, predicament, pressure, puzzle, quandary, ramification, responsibility, scrape*, setback, strain, strait, stress, strife, struggle, to-do*, trouble, vicissitude, weight, worry; SEE CONCEPTS *410,532,690*

difficulty [*n3*] *argument*
altercation, beef*, bickering, controversy, dispute, falling-out*, fight, hassle, misunderstanding, quarrel, squabble, strife, trouble; SEE CONCEPT *46*

diffidence [*n*] *hesitancy; lack of confidence*
backwardness, bashfulness, constraint, doubt, fear, hesitation, humility, insecurity, meekness, modesty, mousiness, reluctance, reserve, self-consciousness, sheepishness, shyness, timidity, timidness, timorousness, unassertiveness; SEE CONCEPT *633*

diffident [*adj*] *hesitant; unconfident*
backward, bashful, blenching, chary, constrained, coy, demure, distrustful, doubtful, dubious, flinching, humble, insecure, meek, modest, mousy, rabbity, reluctant, reserved, retiring, self-conscious, self-effacing, sheepish, shrinking, shy, suspicious, timid, timorous, unassertive,

unassuming, unassured, unobtrusive, unpoised, unsure, withdrawn; SEE CONCEPT *401*

diffuse [*adj1*] *spread out*
broadcast, catholic, circulated, diluted, dispersed, disseminated, distributed, expanded, extended, general, prevalent, propagated, radiated, scattered, separated, strewn, thin, unconcentrated, universal, widespread; SEE CONCEPTS *530,583, 772*

diffuse [*adj2*] *wordy*
circumlocutory, copious, diffusive, digressive, discursive, dull, exuberant, lavish, lengthy, long, long-winded, loose, meandering, palaverous, profuse, prolix, rambling, random, redundant, vague, verbose, waffling, windy; SEE CONCEPT *267*

diffusion [*n*] *spread; wide distribution*
circulation, dispersal, dispersion, dissemination, dissipation, expansion, propaganda, propagation, scattering; SEE CONCEPTS *634,651*

dig [*n*] *insult*
crack, cut, cutting remark, gibe, innuendo, jeer, quip, slur, sneer, taunt, wisecrack; SEE CONCEPT *54*

dig [*v1*] *delve into; hollow out*
bore, break up, bulldoze, burrow, cat, channel, clean, concave, deepen, depress, dig down, discover, dredge, drill, drive, enter, excavate, exhume, fork out, go into, gouge, grub, harvest, hoe, investigate, mine, penetrate, pierce, pit, probe, produce, quarry, root, root out, rout, sap, scoop, scoop out, search, shovel, sift, spade, till, tunnel, turn over, uncover, undermine, unearth; SEE CONCEPT *178*

dig [*v2*] *thrust object into*
drive, gouge, jab, jog, nudge, plunge, poke, prod, punch, ram, sink, stab, stick; SEE CONCEPT *208*

dig [*v3*] *investigate; discover*
bring to light*, come across, come up with, delve, dig down, expose, extricate, find, go into, inquire, look into, probe, prospect, research, retrieve, root, search, search high and low*, shake down*, sift*, turn inside out*, turn upside down*, uncover, unearth; SEE CONCEPTS *31,103,216*

dig [*v4*] *enjoy, like*
appreciate, follow, go for*, groove*, love, mind, relish, understand; SEE CONCEPT *32*

dig [*v5*] *understand*
accept, apprehend, catch, comprehend, follow, grasp, recognize, see, take, take in; SEE CONCEPT *15*

digest [*n*] *abridgement of something written*
abstract, aperçu, brief, compendium, condensation, epitome, pandect, précis, résumé, short form, sketch, summary, survey, syllabus, sylloge, synopsis; SEE CONCEPT *271*

digest [*v1*] *assimilate food*
absorb, chymify, consume, dissolve, eat, incorporate, macerate, swallow, take; SEE CONCEPT *169*

digest [*v2*] *make shorter; abridge*
abbreviate, abstract, boil down, classify, codify, compress, condense, cut, cut down, cut to bone*, decrease, epitomize, get to the meat*, inventory, methodize, nutshell*, put in a nutshell*, reduce, shorten, sum, summarize, summate, sum up, survey, synopsize, systematize, tabulate, trim; SEE CONCEPTS *236,247*

di
di

digest [v3] *come to understand*
absorb, analyze, assimilate, consider, contemplate, deliberate, grasp, master, meditate, ponder, study, take in, think about, think over; SEE CONCEPT 15

digest [v4] *tolerate, endure*
abide, bear, brook, go, stand, stomach, swallow, take; SEE CONCEPT 23

dig in [v] *begin with enthusiasm*
bite, burrow, chew, commence, consume, delve, eat, rise, set about, spring, start eating; SEE CONCEPTS 100,169

digit [n1] *number*
arabic, chiffer, cipher, figure, integer, notation, numeral, symbol, whole number; SEE CONCEPTS 765,784

digit [n2] *small appendage of animate being*
claw, extremity, fang, feeler, finger, fork, hook, index finger, phalange, pinkie, pointer, ring finger, thumb, toe; SEE CONCEPT 392

digital library [n] *multimedia library*
digital object library, electronic library, information superhighway, national information infrastructure, virtual library; SEE CONCEPT 274

dignified [adj] *honorable*
aristocratic, august, courtly, decorous, distingué, distinguished, eminent, formal, grand, grave, great, highbrow*, highfalutin'*, imperial, imperious, lofty, magisterial, magnificent, nifty*, noble, proud, refined, regal, reserved, respected, solemn, somber, stately, superior, upright; SEE CONCEPTS 404,555,574

dignify [v] *make honorable; glorify*
adorn, advance, aggrandize, distinguish, elevate, ennoble, erect, exalt, grace, honor, magnify, prefer, promote, raise, sublime, uprear; SEE CONCEPTS 244,700

dignitary [n] *high ranking person*
big gun*, big kahuna*, bigshot*, bigwig*, celebrity, luminary, official, person of influence, star, top cat*, VIP*; SEE CONCEPTS 388,668

dignity [n] *excellence, nobility*
address, cachet, character, consequence, courtliness, culture, decency, decorum, distinction, elevation, eminence, ethics, etiquette, glory, grace, grandeur, gravity, greatness, hauteur, honor, importance, loftiness, majesty, merit, morality, nobleness, perfection, poise, prestige, propriety, quality, rank, regard, renown, respectability, seemliness, self-respect, significance, solemnity, splendor, standing, state, stateliness, station, stature, status, sublimity, virtue, worth, worthiness; SEE CONCEPTS 388,411,668

digress [v] *stray, deviate*
aberrate, beat about the bush*, be diffuse, circumlocute, depart, divagate, drift, excurse, get off the point, get off the subject, get sidetracked, go by way of*, go off on a tangent*, long way*, meander, ramble, roam, swerve, turn aside, veer, wander, wander away; SEE CONCEPTS 195,266, 697

digression [n] *deviation; straying*
apostrophe, aside, deflection, departure, detour, difference, discursion, divagation, divergence, diversion, drifting, episode, excursion, excursus, footnote, incident, note, obiter dictum, parenthesis, rambling, variation, wandering; SEE CONCEPTS 278,665,697

dilapidated [adj] *falling apart; in ruins*
battered, beat-up, broken-down, crumbling, crumbly, crummy*, damaged, decayed, decaying, decrepit, derelict, dingy, dog-eared*, faded, fallen-in, impaired, in a bad way*, injured, marred, neglected, old, ramshackle, ratty*, raunchy, rickety, rinky-dink*, run-down, seedy, shabby, shaky, slummy, tacky, threadbare, tumble-down, uncared for, unimproved, unkempt, used-up, worn-out; SEE CONCEPTS 485,560

dilate [v] *stretch, widen*
amplify, augment, be profuse, be prolix, broaden, develop, distend, enlarge, expand, expatiate, expound, extend, increase, inflate, lengthen, prolong, protract, puff out, spin off, swell; SEE CONCEPTS 57,236,245

dilatory [adj] *procrastinating*
backward, behindhand, dallying, delaying, deliberate, laggard, late, lax, lazy, leisurely, lingering, loitering, moratory, neglectful, negligent, putting off, remiss, slack, slow, sluggish, snail-like*, tardy, tarrying, time-wasting, unhasty, unhurried; SEE CONCEPTS 542,799

dilemma [n] *crisis*
bind*, box*, Catch-22*, corner, difficulty, double bind*, embarrassment, fix, hole, hooker*, impasse, jam, mess, mire, perplexity, pickle*, plight, predicament, problem, puzzle, quandary, scrape, spot, strait, tight corner*; SEE CONCEPTS 674,675

dilettante [adj] *amateurish*
artsy fartsy*, dabbling, green*, half-baked*, half-cocked*, rookie, tenderfoot*, unaccomplished, ungifted, unskilled; SEE CONCEPT 527

dilettante [n] *amateur*
abecedarian, aesthete, connoisseur, dabbler, dallier, greenhorn*, nonprofessional, rookie, smatterer, tenderfoot*, trifler, tyro, uninitiate; SEE CONCEPT 423

diligence [n] *perseverance in carrying out action*
activity, alertness, application, assiduity, assiduousness, attention, attentiveness, briskness, care, carefulness, constancy, earnestness, exertion, heed, heedfulness, industry, intensity, intent, intentness, keenness, laboriousness, pertinacity, quickness, sedulousness, vigor; SEE CONCEPTS 657,677

diligent [adj] *persevering, hard-working*
active, assiduous, attentive, busy, careful, conscientious, constant, eager, eager beaver*, earnest, grind*, indefatigable, industrious, laborious, occupied, operose, painstaking, persistent, persisting, pertinacious, plugging*, sedulous, steadfast, studious, tireless, unflagging, unrelenting, untiring; SEE CONCEPTS 326,538,542

dilly-dally [v] *waste time*
dawdle, delay, hem and haw*, hesitate, linger, loiter, meander, mosey, move slowly, procrastinate, vacillate; SEE CONCEPTS 151,210,681

dilute [v] *make thinner; weaken*
adulterate, alter, attenuate, cook, cut, decrease, deliquesce, diffuse, diminish, doctor*, doctor up*, irrigate, lace, lessen, liquefy, mitigate, mix, moderate, modify, needle*, phony up*, plant, qualify, reduce, shave*, spike, temper, water, water down; SEE CONCEPT 250

diluted/dilute [adj] *thinned, weakened*
adulterated, attenuated, cut, impaired, impoverished, laced, light, moderated, reduced, shaved*, spiked, tempered, washy, watered down, waterish, watery, wishy-washy*; SEE CONCEPTS 485,606

dim [*adj1*] *darkish*
blah, bleary, blurred, caliginous, cloudy, dark, dingy, dreary, dull, dusk, dusky, faded, faint, flat, fuzzy, gloomy, gray, ill-defined, indistinct, lack-luster, lightless, mat, monotone, monotonous, murky, muted, obscured, opaque, overcast, pale, poorly lit, shadowy, sullied, tarnished, tenebrous, unclear, unilluminated, vague, weak; SEE CONCEPT 617

dim [*adj2*] *unfavorable with regard to opinion*
depressing, disapproving, discouraging, gloomy, skeptical, somber, suspicious, unpromising; SEE CONCEPT 542

dim [*adj3*] *not very intelligent*
boorish, dense, dim-witted, doltish, dull, dumb, oafish, obtuse, slow, slow on uptake*, stupid, thick*, weak-minded; SEE CONCEPT 402

dim [*v*] *darken; obscure*
becloud, bedim, befog, blear, blur, cloud, dull, eclipse, fade, fog, haze, lower, muddy, obfuscate, pale, tarnish, turn down; SEE CONCEPTS 250,627

dimensions/dimension [*n*] *proportions; range*
admeasurement, ambit, amplitude, bigness, bulk, capacity, compass, depth, dimensionality, extension, extensity, extent, greatness, height, importance, largeness, length, magnitude, measure, measurement, reach, scale, scope, size, volume, width; SEE CONCEPTS 730,792

diminish [*v1*] *become or cause to be less*
abate, abbreviate, attenuate, become smaller, close, contract, curtail, cut, decline, decrease, depreciate, die out, drain, dwindle, ebb, extenuate, fade away, lessen, lower, minify, moderate, peter out, recede, reduce, retrench, shrink, shrivel, slacken, subside, taper, temper, wane, weaken; SEE CONCEPTS 698,776

diminish [*v2*] *belittle*
abuse, bad-mouth*, cheapen, cut down to size*, decry, demean, depreciate, derogate, detract from, devalue, dispraise, dump on*, give comeuppance*, knock off high horse*, minimize, pan*, poormouth*, put away*, put down*, run down*, tear down*; SEE CONCEPT 54

diminution [*n*] *lessening, reduction*
abatement, alleviation, contraction, curtailment, cut, cutback, decay, decline, decrease, deduction, retrenchment, weakening; SEE CONCEPTS 698, 776

diminutive [*adj*] *tiny, petite*
bantam, bitsy*, bitty*, button*, Lilliputian, little, midget, mini, miniature, minute, peewee*, pint-sized, pocket, pocket-sized, small, teensy*, teensy-weensy*, teeny*, teeny-weeny*, undersize, wee*, weeny*; SEE CONCEPT 789

dimwit [*n*] *a stupid person*
blockhead, bonehead, dolt, dullard, dunce, fool, idiot, ignoramus, imbecile, moron, numbskull, simpleton, twit; SEE CONCEPT 412

din [*n*] *loud, continuous noise*
babel, bedlam, boisterousness, brouhaha, buzz, clamor, clangor, clash, clatter, commotion, confusion, crash, disquiet, hoo-ha*, hubbub, hullabaloo*, hurly-burly*, jangle, music, outcry, pandemonium, percussion, racket, row, shout, sound, stridency, tintamarre*, tintinnabulation, tumult, uproar; SEE CONCEPT 595

dine [*v*] *eat, often formally*
banquet, breakfast, consume, do lunch*, eat

out*, fall to*, feast, feed on, lunch, sup, supper; SEE CONCEPT 169

diner [*n*] *casual restaurant with varied menu*
Automat*, bistro, booth, café, canteen, chuck wagon*, coffee shop, concession, dump*, eatery*, eating house, facility, fast-food outlet, greasy spoon*, grill, hash house*, ice-cream parlor, lunch counter, lunchroom, lunch wagon, mess hall, quick-lunch, saloon, sandwich shop, snack bar, tearoom; SEE CONCEPT 449

dingy [*adj*] *soiled, tacky*
bedimmed, broken-down, colorless, dark, darkish, dilapidated, dim, dirty, discolored, drab, dreary, dull, dusky, faded, gloomy, grimy, muddy, murky, obscure, run-down, seedy, shabby, smirched, somber, sullied, tarnished, threadbare, tired; SEE CONCEPTS 485,617

dinky [*adj*] *tiny, small*
bush-league*, dainty, insignificant, lesser, Lilliputian, mini, miniature, minor, minor-league*, neat, petite, secondary, second rate*, small-fry*, small-time*, trim; SEE CONCEPT 789

dinner [*n*] *evening meal*
banquet, blowout*, chow*, collation, din-din*, eats*, feast, feedbag*, fete, main meal, major munch*, potluck, principal meal, refection, regale, repast, ribs*, spread*, supper, table d'hôte; SEE CONCEPT 459

dip [*n1*] *submersion in liquid*
bath, dive, douche, drenching, ducking, immersion, plunge, soak, soaking, swim; SEE CONCEPT 256

dip [*n2*] *something for dunking*
concoction, dilution, infusion, mixture, preparation, solution, suffusion, suspension; SEE CONCEPTS 260,466

dip [*n3*] *depression; decline*
basin, concavity, declivity, descent, downslide, downswing, downtrend, drop, fall, fall-off, hole, hollow, inclination, incline, lowering, pitch, sag, sink, sinkage, sinkhole, slip, slope, slump; SEE CONCEPTS 513,697,738

dip [*v1*] *put into liquid*
baptize, bathe, douse, drench, duck, dunk, immerse, irrigate, lave, lower, moisten, pitch, plunge, rinse, slop, slosh, soak, souse, splash, steep, submerge, submerse, wash, water, wet; SEE CONCEPTS 201,256

dip [*v2*] *lower, descend*
bend, decline, disappear, droop, drop down, fade, fall, go down, incline, nose-dive, plummet, plunge, reach, recede, sag, set, settle, sheer, sink, skew, skid, slant, slip, slope, slue, slump, spiral, subside, swoop, tilt, tumble, veer, verge; SEE CONCEPT 181

dip [*v3*] *scoop, ladle*
bail, bale, bucket, decant, dish, draft off, draw, draw out, dredge, handle, lade, lift, offer, reach into, shovel, spoon, strain; SEE CONCEPTS 196,225

dip into [*v*] *try, sample*
appropriate, browse, dabble, flip through, get, glance at, glance over, leaf through, peruse, play at, rifle through*, run over, run through, scan, seize, skim, take, taste, thumb through*; SEE CONCEPTS 87,623

diploma [*n*] *certificate for achievement*
authority, award, charter, commission, confirmation, credentials, degree, honor, recognition,

di
di

sheepskin, shingle, voucher, warrant; SEE CONCEPTS *271,337*

diplomacy [*n*] *tact*
address, artfulness, craft, delicacy, delicatesse, discretion, expedience, finesse, negotiation, poise, politics, savoir-faire, skill, statecraft, subtlety; SEE CONCEPTS *388,633*

diplomat [*n*] *politician, consul*
agent, ambassador, attaché, cabinet member, chargé d'affaires, conciliator, emissary, envoy, expert, go-between, legate, mediator, minister, moderator, negotiator, plenipotentiary, public relations person, representative, tactician; SEE CONCEPTS *354,359*

diplomatic [*adj*] *politic, tactful*
adept, arch, artful, astute, bland, brainy, cagey, calculating, capable, clever, conciliatory, conniving, contriving, courteous, crafty, cunning, deft, delicate, dexterous, discreet, gracious, guileful, intriguing, opportunistic, polite, prudent, savvy, scheming, sensitive, sharp, shrewd, sly, smooth, strategic, suave, subtle, wily; SEE CONCEPTS *401,542*

dire [*adj1*] *urgent; crucial*
acute, burning, clamant, clamorous, climacteric, critical, crying, desperate, drastic, exigent, extreme, immoderate, imperative, importunate, instant, pressing; SEE CONCEPTS *546,568,799*

dire [*adj2*] *terrible, ominous*
afflictive, alarming, appalling, awful, black, calamitous, cataclysmic, catastrophic, cruel, deplorable, depressing, disastrous, dismal, distressing, dreadful, fearful, fierce, frightful, gloomy, grievous, grim, heartbreaking, horrible, horrid, lamentable, oppressing, portentous, redoubtable, regrettable, ruinous, scowling, shocking, terrific, ugly, unfortunate, woeful; SEE CONCEPTS *537,548,570*

direct [*adj1*] *honest*
absolute, bald, blunt, candid, categorical, downright, explicit, express, forthright, frank, matter-of-fact, open, outspoken, person-to-person, plain, plainspoken, point-blank, sincere, straight, straightforward, straight from the shoulder*, talk turkey*, unambiguous, unconcealed, undisguised, unequivocal, unreserved; SEE CONCEPT *267*

direct [*adj2*] *undeviating; uninterrupted*
beeline*, continuous, even, horizontal, in bee line*, in straight line, linear, nonstop, not crooked, point-blank, right, shortest, straight, straight ahead, straightaway, through, true, unbroken, unswerving; SEE CONCEPTS *482,581*

direct [*adj3*] *face-to-face; next to*
contiguous, firsthand, head-on, immediate, lineal, next, personal, primary, prompt, proximate, resultant, succeeding; SEE CONCEPTS *585,586*

direct [*v1*] *manage, oversee*
administer, advise, be in the driver's seat*, boss, call the shots*, carry on, conduct, control, control the affairs of, dispose, dominate, govern, guide, handle, have the say, head up*, influence, keep, lead, operate, ordain, preside over, quarterback*, regulate, rule, run, run the show*, run things*, shepherd, superintend, supervise, take the reins*; SEE CONCEPTS *94,117*

direct [*v2*] *give instructions; teach*
address, advise, bid, charge, command, deliver, dictate, enjoin, give directions, give orders, inform, instruct, lecture, order, read, tell, warn; SEE CONCEPTS *53,61*

direct [*v3*] *point in a direction; guide*
address, aim, beam, cast, conduct, escort, fix, focus, head, incline, indicate, intend, lay, lead, level, mean, move in, pilot, point, point the way, present, route, see, set, shepherd, show, sight, sight on, slant, steer, target, train, turn, zero in; SEE CONCEPTS *187,201*

direct [*v4*] *send, usually by mail system*
address, designate, inscribe, label, mail, mark, route, superscribe; SEE CONCEPT *217*

direct [*v5*] *put all of efforts toward*
address, aim, apply, bend, buckle down, devote, endeavor, fix, give, set, settle, strive, throw, try, turn; SEE CONCEPTS *87,677*

direction [*n1*] *management*
administration, charge, command, control, government, guidance, leadership, order, oversight, superintendence, supervision; SEE CONCEPTS *299,325*

direction [*n2*] *course, route*
aim, angle, area, aspect, bearing, beeline*, bent, bias, current, drift, end, inclination, line, objective, orientation, outlook, path, point of compass, proclivity, range, region, road, set, side, slant, spot, standpoint, stream, tack, tendency, that-a-way*, tide, track, trajectory, trend, viewpoint, way; SEE CONCEPTS *657,738*

direction(s) [*n3*] *instructions, guidance*
advice, advisement, assignment, briefing, directive, guidelines, indication, lowdown*, notification, plan, prescription, recommendation, regulation, sealed order, specification, specs*, steer*, summons, tip, word*; SEE CONCEPTS *271,274*

directive [*n*] *command, instruction*
charge, communication, decree, dictate, edict, injunction, mandate, memo, memorandum, message, notice, order, ordinance, regulation, ruling, ukase, word; SEE CONCEPTS *271,274,662*

directly [*adv1*] *the shortest route*
as a crow flies*, beeline*, dead, direct, due, exactly, plump, precisely, right, slam bang*, slap, smack, smack dab*, straight, straightly, undeviatingly, unswervingly, without deviation; SEE CONCEPTS *581,778*

directly [*adv2*] *as soon as possible*
anon, at once, contiguously, dead*, due, first off, forthwith, immediately, in a second, instantaneously, instanter, instantly, presently, promptly, pronto*, quickly, right away, shortly, speedily, straightway, straight off; SEE CONCEPT *820*

directly [*adv3*] *straightforwardly*
candidly, face-to-face, honestly, in person, literally, openly, personally, plainly, point-black, truthfully, unequivocally, verbatim, without prevarication, word for word; SEE CONCEPT *267*

director [*n*] *manager*
administrator, big person*, boss, chair, chief, controller, exec, executive, executive officer, governor, head, head honcho*, helmer, key player*, kingpin*, leader, organizer, overseer, person upstairs*, player, principal, producer, skipper*, supervisor, top dog*, top person*; SEE CONCEPTS *347,352*

directory [*n*] *reference book; guide*
agenda, almanac, atlas, blue book, book, catalogue, charts, gazeteer, hit list*, index, laundry list*, lineup, list, little black book*, record, regis-

ter, roster, scorecard, short list*, social register, syllabus, white pages*, who's who*, yellow pages*; SEE CONCEPTS *280,283*

direful [*adj*] *fearful; horrible*
apocalyptic, appalling, awful, baleful, baneful, calamitous, dreadful, fateful, ghastly, gloomy, horrid, ill-boding, inauspicious, ominous, shocking, terrible, terrific, unlucky, unpropitious; SEE CONCEPTS *537,570*

dirge [*n*] *sad song*
chant, coronach, cry, death march, death song, elegy, funeral song, hymn, jeremiad, keen, lament, march, monody, requiem, threnody; SEE CONCEPT *595*

dirigible [*n*] *airship*
blimp, hot-air balloon, zeppelin; SEE CONCEPT *504*

dirt [*n1*] *grime, impurity*
crud*, dreck, dregs, excrement, feculence, filth, filthiness, gook*, ground, gunk*, mire, muck, mud, rottenness, scuz*, sleaze, slime, smudge, smut, soil, stain, tarnish; SEE CONCEPT *509*

dirt [*n2*] *obscenity; immorality*
chicanery, double-dealing, filth, fourberie, fraud, indecency, lubricity, pornography, smut; SEE CONCEPT *645*

dirt [*n3*] *soil*
clay, dust, earth, loam, real estate, terra firma; SEE CONCEPT *509*

dirt [*n4*] *gossip*
buzz, intimate intelligence, juicy morsel, news, rumor, talk, the lowdown; SEE CONCEPTS *274,278*

dirty [*adj1*] *soiled, unclean*
bedraggled, begrimed, black, contaminated, cruddy*, crummy, defiled, disarrayed, dishabille, disheveled, dreggy, dungy, dusty, filthy, foul, fouled, greasy, grimy, grubby, grungy*, icky*, lousy, messy, mucky*, muddy, mung*, murky, nasty, pigpen*, polluted, raunchy, scummy*, scuzzy*, slatternly, slimy, sloppy, slovenly, smudged, smutty, sooty, spattered, spotted, squalid, stained, straggly, sullied, undusted, unhygienic, unkempt, unlaundered, unsanitary, unsightly, unswept, untidy, unwashed, yucky*; SEE CONCEPT *485*

dirty [*adj2*] *obscene, pornographic*
base, blue, coarse, contemptible, despicable, filthy, immoral, impure, indecent, lewd, low, mean, nasty, off-color, ribald, risqué, salacious, scatological, scurvy, smutty, sordid, squalid, unchaste, unclean, uncleanly, vile, vulgar; SEE CONCEPTS *542,545*

dirty [*adj3*] *dishonest*
below the belt*, cheating, corrupt, crooked, deceitful, double-dealing, foul, shabby, shady, shifty, sleazy, sneaky, sordid, underhanded, unethical, unscrupulous, untruthful; SEE CONCEPT *267*

dirty [*v*] *cause to be soiled*
begrime, besoil, blacken, blotch, blur, botch, coat, contaminate, corrupt, debase, decay, defile, discolor, draggle, encrust, foul, grime, make dusty, make impure, mess up, mold, muddy, pollute, rot, smear, smirch, smoke, smudge, smutch, spatter, spoil, spot, stain, sully, sweat, taint, tar, tarnish; SEE CONCEPT *254*

dirty old man [*n*] *pervert*
degenerate, lecher, sex maniac, sleazebag; SEE CONCEPT *412*

dirty tricks [*n*] *dishonest practices*
dirty pool*, funny business*, malicious tactics, monkey business*, shady business, skullduggery, unethical behavior; SEE CONCEPTS *59,633, 657*

disability [*n*] *disadvantage, restriction*
affliction, ailment, defect, detriment, disqualification, drawback, impairment, inability, incapacity, incompetency, inexperience, infirmity, injury, invalidity, lack, unfitness, weakness; SEE CONCEPTS *309,316,410,720*

disable [*v*] *render inoperative; cripple*
attenuate, batter, blunt, damage, debilitate, disarm, disenable, disqualify, enervate, enfeeble, exhaust, hamstring*, handicap, harm, hock*, hogtie*, hurt, immobilize, impair, incapacitate, invalidate, kibosh*, knock out*, maim, mangle, mar, mutilate, muzzle, paralyze, pinion, prostrate, put out of action*, render incapable, ruin, sabotage, sap, shatter, shoot down*, spoil, take out*, throw monkey wrench in*, total*, unbrace, undermine, unfit, unstrengthen, weaken, wreck; SEE CONCEPTS *130,246*

disabled [*adj*] *incapacitated*
broken-down, confined, decrepit, disarmed, hamstrung*, handicapped, helpless, hurt, incapable, infirm, laid-up, lame, maimed, out-of-action*, out-of-commission*, paralyzed, powerless, rundown, sidelined, stalled, weakened, worn-out, wounded, wrecked; SEE CONCEPTS *314,527*

disadvantage [*n2*] *hurt, loss*
damage, deprivation, detriment, disservice, harm, injury, prejudice; SEE CONCEPTS *230,309, 679*

disadvantaged [*adj*] *underprivileged*
deprived, discriminated against, handicapped, hindered, impaired, impoverished, poor; SEE CONCEPT *334*

disadvantageous [*adj*] *detrimental, inconvenient*
adverse, contrary, damaging, debit-side, deleterious, depreciative, depreciatory, derogatory, detracting, disparaging, downside, dyslogistic, harmful, hurtful, ill-timed, inexpedient, injurious, inopportune, objectionable, on the debit side, pejorative, prejudicial, slighting, uncomplimentary, unfavorable, unprofitable; SEE CONCEPTS *334,537,555*

disadvantage(s) [*n1*] *difficulty, trouble*
adverse circumstance, bar, blocking, burden, defect, deficiency, deprivation, detriment, disability, discommodity, drawback, failing, fault, flaw, fly in the ointment*, hamper, handicap, hardship, hindrance, impediment, imperfection, imposition, inadequacy, inconvenience, inutility, lack, liability, limitation, minus, nuisance, objection, obstacle, privation, problem, restraint, snag, stumbling block*, weakness, weak point; SEE CONCEPTS *666,674*

disaffect [*v*] *lose affection for, estrange*
agitate, alienate, antagonize, discompose, disquiet, disturb, disunify, disunite, divide, repel, upset, wean; SEE CONCEPTS *7,19,135,384*

disaffected [*adj*] *alienated, estranged*
antagonistic, discontented, disloyal, dissatisfied, hostile, indifferent, mutinous, rebellious, seditious, uncompliant, unfriendly, unsubmissive; SEE CONCEPTS *403,555*

disaffection [*n*] *alienation, estrangement*
animosity, antagonism, antipathy, aversion, breach, disagreement, discontent, dislike, disloy-

di
di

alty, dissatisfaction, hatred, hostility, ill will, repugnance, resentment, unfriendliness; SEE CON-
CEPTS *388,410*

disagree [*v1*] *be different*
be discordant, be dissimilar, clash, conflict, contradict, counter, depart, deviate, differ, discord,
disharmonize, dissent, diverge, run counter to,
vary, war; SEE CONCEPT *665*

disagree [*v2*] *argue; hold differing opinion*
altercate, battle, bicker, brawl, break with, bring
action, clash, contend, contest, controversialize,
controvert, debate, differ, disaccord, discept, discord, dispute, dissent, divide, fall out*, feud,
fight, go for the jugular*, haggle, have words*,
jump on*, lay into*, let have it, logomachize, object, oppose, palter, quarrel, quibble, rip, row,
scrap, set to, skirmish, spar, spat, sue, take issue,
take on, war, wrangle, zap*; SEE CONCEPTS *12,46*

disagree [*v3*] *be injurious*
be distasteful, be disturbing, be sickening, be unsuitable, bother, discomfort, distress, go against
the grain*, hurt, injure, make ill, nauseate,
sicken, trouble, upset; SEE CONCEPT *246*

disagreeable [*adj1*] *bad-tempered, irritable*
bellicose, brusque, cantankerous, churlish, contentious, contrary, cross, difficult, disobliging,
disputatious, eristic, grouchy, ill-natured, nasty,
obnoxious, offensive, out of sorts, peevish, pettish, petulant, querulous, rude, snappy, surly,
ugly, unfriendly, ungracious, unlikable, unpleasant, uptight, waspish, whiny; SEE CONCEPT *401*

disagreeable [*adj2*] *disgusting, offensive*
annoying, awful, bad, bothersome, displeasing,
distasteful, distressing, drag, nasty, objectionable, obnoxious, pain, repellent, repugnant, repulsive, rotten, sour, unhappy, uninviting,
unpalatable, unpleasant, unsavory, upsetting,
woeful; SEE CONCEPTS *537,548*

disagreement [*n1*] *dispute, quarrel*
altercation, animosity, antagonism, argument, at-
mospherics, bickering, breach, break, clash,
clashing, conflict, contention, contest, controversy, cross-purposes, debate, difference, discord, dissent, dissidence, disunion, disunity,
division, divisiveness, falling out, feud, fight,
friction, hassle, hostility, ill feeling, ill will, jarring, misunderstanding, opposition, rupture, spat,
split, squabble, strife, tension, variance, vendetta,
words, wrangle; SEE CONCEPTS *46,388*

disagreement [*n2*] *difference, unlikeness*
clash, disaccord, discordance, discrepancy,
disharmonism, disharmony, disparity, dissimilarity, dissimilitude, divergence, divergency,
diversity, incompatibility, incongruity, incongruousness, inconsistency, variance; SEE CONCEPT
665

disallow [*v*] *reject, prohibit*
abjure, cancel, censor, debar, deny, disacknowledge, disavow, disclaim, dismiss, disown, embargo, exclude, forbid, keep back, kill, nix*, pass
on, proscribe, put down, rebuff, refuse, repudiate, shut out, taboo*, veto, withhold, zing*; SEE
CONCEPTS *21,25,30*

disappear [*v*] *vanish; cease*
abandon, abscond, be done for, be gone, be lost,
be no more*, be swallowed up, cease to exist,
clear, come to naught, decamp, dematerialize,
depart, die, die out, disperse, dissipate, dissolve,
drop out of sight*, ebb, end, end gradually, escape, evanesce, evanish, evaporate, exit, expire,

fade, fade away, flee, fly, go, go south*, leave,
leave no trace, melt, melt away, pass, pass away,
perish, recede, retire, retreat, sink, take flight, vacate, vamoose*, wane, withdraw; SEE CONCEPTS
102,105,195

disappearance [*n*] *vanishing*
ceasing to exist, decline and fall, dematerialization, departure, desertion, disappearing act, disintegration, dispersal, dissipation, dissolution,
ebbing, eclipse, escape, evanescence, evaporation, exit, exodus, fading, flight, going, loss,
melting, passing, receding, recession, removal,
retirement, wane, wearing away, withdrawal; SEE
CONCEPTS *102,105,195*

disappoint [*v*] *sadden, dismay; frustrate*
abort, baffle, balk, bring to naught, bungle, cast
down, chagrin, circumvent, come to nothing,
dash, dash hopes*, deceive, delude, disconcert,
disenchant, disgruntle, dishearten, disillusion,
dissatisfy, dumbfound, embitter, fail, fall down
on, fall flat, fall short of, foil, founder, hamper,
hinder, leave in the lurch*, let down, miscarry,
mislead, not show, put out, ruin prospects, stand
up, tease, thwart, torment, vex; SEE CONCEPTS
7,19,699

disappointed [*adj*] *let down, saddened*
aghast, balked, beaten, chapfallen, complaining,
crestfallen, defeated, depressed, despondent, disconcerted, discontented, discouraged, disenchanted, disgruntled, disillusioned, dissatisfied,
distressed, down, downcast, downhearted, down
in the dumps*, foiled, frustrated, hopeless, objecting, shot down, taken down, thwarted, unhappy, unsatisfied, upset, vanquished, worsted;
SEE CONCEPT *403*

disappointment [*n1*] *saddening situation; let-*
down
bitter pill*, blind alley*, blow, blunder, bring-
down, bummer, bust*, calamity, defeat, disaster,
discouragement, downer*, downfall, drag, dud,
error, failure, false alarm*, faux pas*, fiasco, fizzle, flash in the pan*, impasse, inefficacy,
lemon*, miscalculation, mischance, misfortune,
mishap, mistake, obstacle, old one-two*, setback, slip, washout; SEE CONCEPTS *230,674*

disappointment [*n2*] *mental upset; displeasure*
adverse fate, adversity, bafflement, blow, chagrin, defeat, despondency, discontent, discouragement, disenchantment, disgruntlement,
disillusion, disillusionment, dissatisfaction, distress, failure, frustration, lack of success, letdown, mortification, nonsuccess, regret, setback,
the knocks*, unfulfillment; SEE CONCEPT *410*

disapproval [*n*] *condemnation*
blackball*, black list*, blame, boo*, boycott,
brickbat, call down, castigation, catcall*, censure, criticism, denunciation, deprecation,
disapprobation, discontent, disfavor, dislike, disparagement, displeasure, dissatisfaction, hiss*,
nix*, objection, opprobrium, ostracism, reproach, reproof, slap on wrist*, stricture, thumbs
down*, vitriol, zing*; SEE CONCEPTS *278,689*

disapprove [*v*] *condemn*
blame, censure, chastise, criticize, damn, decry,
denounce, deplore, deprecate, detract, disallow,
discommend, discountenance, disesteem, disfavor, dislike, dismiss, dispraise, expostulate, find
fault with, find unacceptable, frown on, look
askance at, look down on, nix*, object to, op-

pose, pan*, pass on, refuse, reject, remonstrate, reprehend, reprobate, reprove, set aside, slam, spurn, take dim view of, take exception to, turn down, veto, zing*; SEE CONCEPTS *18,21,52*

disarm [*v1*] *render defenseless*
conciliate, cripple, deactivate, debilitate, deescalate, demilitarize, demobilize, disable, disband, disqualify, incapacitate, invalidate, neutralize, occupy, pacify, paralyze, prostrate, skin, strip, subdue, subjugate, unarm, weaken; SEE CONCEPTS *142,211,320*

disarm [*v2*] *persuade*
allure, attract, bewitch, captivate, charm, coax, convince, enchant, fascinate, seduce, set at ease, unarm, urge, win over; SEE CONCEPTS *7,19,22,68*

disarmament [*n*] *reduction of weapons*
arms limitation, arms reduction, conquest, crippling, de-escalation, demilitarization, demobilization, disablement, disqualification, freeze, neutralizing, occupation, pacification, paralyzing, rendering powerless, subjugation; SEE CONCEPTS *142,211,320*

disarming [*adj*] *charming*
bewitching, convincing, deferential, ingratiating, ingratiatory, insinuating, insinuative, inveigling, irresistible, likable, persuasive, saccharine, seductive, silken, silky, winning; SEE CONCEPT *401*

disarrange [*v*] *disorder*
derange, discompose, disturb, get out of order, jumble, mess, mix up, ruffle, scramble, shuffle, unsettle, untidy; SEE CONCEPTS *240,250*

disarray [*n*] *disorder, confusion, mess*
anarchy, ataxia, chaos, clutter, disarrangement, discomposure, disharmony, dishevelment, disorganization, holy mess*, indiscipline, jumble, muddle, shambles*, snarl, tangle, topsy-turviness*, unholy mess*, unruliness, untidiness, upset; SEE CONCEPTS *230,727*

disaster [*n*] *accident, trouble*
act of God*, adversity, affliction, bad luck, bad news*, bale, bane, blight, blow, bust, calamity, casualty, cataclysm, catastrophe, collapse, collision, crash, debacle, defeat, depression, emergency, exigency, failure, fall, fell stroke*, fiasco, flood, flop, grief, hard luck, harm, hazard, holocaust, hot water*, ill luck, misadventure, mischance, misfortune, mishap, reverse, rock, rough, ruin, ruination, setback, slip, stroke, the worst*, tragedy, undoing, upset, washout*, woe; SEE CONCEPTS *674,675*

disaster area [*n*] *scene of destruction*
area of devastation, chaos, confusion, crisis zone, earthquake zone, emergency area, flood zone, havoc, hot spot, war zone; SEE CONCEPTS *230,674*

disastrous [*adj*] *detrimental, devastating*
adverse, calamitous, cataclysmal, cataclysmic, catastrophic, destructive, dire, dreadful, fatal, fateful, hapless, ill-fated, ill-starred, luckless, ruinous, terrible, tragic, unfavorable, unfortunate, unlucky, unpropitious, untoward; SEE CONCEPTS *537,548*

disavow [*v*] *reject*
abjure, contradict, deny, disacknowledge, disallow, disclaim, disown, drop out, forswear, gainsay, go back on word*, impugn, negate, negative, refuse, renege, renig, repudiate, wash hands of*, weasel out of*, welsh, worm out of*; SEE CONCEPTS *18,25*

disband [*v*] *break up*
demobilize, destroy, disperse, dissolve, fold, scatter, separate, thin out; SEE CONCEPT *234*

disbelief [*n*] *doubt, skepticism*
atheism, distrust, dubiety, incredulity, mistrust, nihilism, rejection, repudiation, spurning, unbelief, unbelievingness, unfaith; SEE CONCEPTS *21,689*

disbelieve [*v*] *doubt*
discount, discredit, distrust, eschew, give no credence to, mistrust, not accept, not buy, not credit, not swallow*, question, reject, repudiate, scoff at, scorn, scout, suspect, unbelieve; SEE CONCEPT *21*

disbelieving [*adj*] *suspicious, doubting*
aporetic, cagey, cynical, incredulous, leery, mistrustful, questioning, quizzical, show-me*, skeptical, unbelieving; SEE CONCEPT *403*

disburse [*v*] *spend money*
acquit, ante up*, come across, come through, come up with, contribute, cough up*, deal, defray, dispense, disperse, distribute, divide, divvy*, dole out*, expend, foot the bill*, give, lay out*, measure out, outlay, partition, pay out, pony up*, put out, shell out*, use; SEE CONCEPTS *108,341*

disbursement [*n*] *payment*
cost, disposal, expenditure, expense, outgoing, outlay, spending; SEE CONCEPT *344*

discard [*v*] *get rid of*
abandon, abdicate, abjure, adios*, banish, can*, cancel, cashier, cast aside, chuck, deep-six*, desert, dispatch, dispense with, dispose of, dispossess, ditch, divorce, do away with, drop, dump, eject, eliminate, expel, forsake, free of, give up, have done with, jettison, junk*, oust, part with, protest, put by, reject, relinquish, remove, renounce, repeal, repudiate, scrap, shake off, shed, sweep away, throw away, throw out, throw overboard*, toss aside, write off; SEE CONCEPT *180*

discern [*v*] *catch sight of; recognize and understand*
anticipate, apprehend, ascertain, behold, descry, detect, determine, difference, differentiate, discover, descrepate, discriminate, distinguish, divine, espy, extricate, figure out, find out, focus, foresee, get a load of*, get the picture*, get wise to, judge, know, make distinction, make out, note, notice, observe, perceive, pick out, read, remark, rubberneck*, secern, see the light*, see through, separate, severalize, spot, take in, view; SEE CONCEPTS *15,38*

discernible [*adj*] *recognizable; distinct*
apparent, appreciable, audible, clear, detectable, discoverable, distinguishable, noticeable, observable, obvious, palpable, perceivable, perceptible, plain, sensible, tangible, visible; SEE CONCEPTS *535,576,619*

discerning [*adj*] *discriminating*
acute, astute, bright, brilliant, clear-sighted, clever, critical, gnostic, ingenious, insighted, insightful, intelligent, judicious, knowing, knowledgeable, penetrating, perceptive, percipient, perspicacious, piercing, sagacious, sage, sensitive, sharp, shrewd, subtle, wise; SEE CONCEPT *402*

discharge [*n1*] *setting free*
acquittal, clearance, disimprisonment, exonera-

di
di

tion, liberation, pardon, parole, probation, release, remittance; SEE CONCEPT *127*

discharge [*n2*] *dismissal from responsibility*
ax, bounce, bum's rush*, congé, demobilization, ejection, gate, old heave ho*, pink slip*, the boot*, the door*, walking papers*; SEE CONCEPTS *324,351*

discharge [*n3*] *detonation*
barrage, blast, burst, explosion, firing, fusillade, report, salvo, shot, shower, volley; SEE CONCEPT *521*

discharge [*n4*] *pouring forth*
elimination, emission, emptying, excretion, exudation, flow, ooze, pus, secretion, seepage, shower, suppuration, vent, voiding; SEE CONCEPTS *179,748*

discharge [*n5*] *unloading*
disburdening, emptying, unburdening, unlading; SEE CONCEPT *211*

discharge [*n6*] *carrying out of responsibility*
accomplishment, achievement, execution, fulfillment, observance, performance; SEE CONCEPT *706*

discharge [*n7*] *payment of debt*
acquittal, disbursement, liquidation, satisfaction, settlement; SEE CONCEPTS *341,344*

discharge [*v1*] *set free*
absolve, acquit, allow to go*, clear, disimprison, dismiss, emancipate, exonerate, expel, liberate, loose, loosen, manumit, oust, pardon, release, unbind, unchain, unshackle; SEE CONCEPT *127*

discharge [*v2*] *dismiss from responsibility*
absolve, ax, boot out*, bounce, bump, bust, can*, cashier, disburden, discard, disencumber, dispense, displace, eject, excuse, exempt, expel, fire, freeze out*, give one notice, kick out, lay off, let go, let off, let one go, let out, lock out*, nix*, oust, privilege from, relieve, remove, replace, ride out on rail*, run out of town*, show the door*, spare, supersede, supplant, terminate, unload; SEE CONCEPTS *324,351*

discharge [*v3*] *detonate weapon*
blast, explode, fire, let off, set off, shoot, shoot off; SEE CONCEPT *179*

discharge [*v4*] *pour forth*
break out, disembogue, dispense, ejaculate, emit, empty, erupt, excrete, exude, give off, gush, leak, ooze, release, send forth, spew, void, vomit; SEE CONCEPTS *152,179*

discharge [*v5*] *unload*
carry away, disburden, empty, off-load, remove, remove cargo, send, take away, take off, unburden, unlade, unpack, unship, unstow; SEE CONCEPT *211*

discharge [*v6*] *carry out responsibility*
accomplish, achieve, do, execute, fulfill, meet, observe, perform; SEE CONCEPT *91*

discharge [*v7*] *pay, settle debt*
clear, honor, liquidate, meet, pay up, quit, relieve, satisfy, square up; SEE CONCEPT *341*

discharge [*v8*] *invalidate agreement*
abrogate, annul, cancel, dissolve, quash, render void, vacate, void; SEE CONCEPT *121*

disciple [*n*] *believer, follower*
adherent, apostle, attendant, booster, buff, bug*, catechumen, cohort, convert, devotee, enthusiast, fan, fanatic, fiend, freak, groupie, hound*, junkie*, learner, nut*, partisan, proselyte, pupil, rooter*, satellite, sectary, sectator, student, sup-

porter, votary, witness, zealot; SEE CONCEPTS *361,423*

disciplinarian [*n*] *person who makes others work hard*
authoritarian, bully, despot, drill sergeant, enforcer, formalist, master, sergeant, stickler, strict teacher, sundowner, teacher, trainer, tyrant; SEE CONCEPTS *350,354,423*

discipline [*n1*] *regimen, training*
conduct, control, cultivation, curb, development, domestication, drill, drilling, education, exercise, inculcation, indoctrination, limitation, method, orderliness, practice, preparation, regulation, restraint, self-command, self-control, self-government, self-mastery, self-restraint, strictness, subordination, will, willpower; SEE CONCEPTS *94,326,410*

discipline [*n2*] *punishment*
castigation, chastisement, comeuppance, correction, getting yours*, hell to pay*, punition, rod; SEE CONCEPTS *122,123*

discipline [*n3*] *field of study; subject of interest*
area, branch of knowledge, course, curriculum, specialty; SEE CONCEPT *349*

disc jockey [*n*] *radio personality*
announcer, broadcaster, deejay*, dj*, pancake turner*, radio performer, shock jock*, video jockey, vj*; SEE CONCEPT *348*

disclaim [*v*] *deny*
abandon, abjure, abnegate, belittle, contradict, contravene, criticize, decline, deprecate, disacknowledge, disaffirm, disallow, disavow, discard, disown, disparage, divorce oneself from, forswear, gainsay, minimize, negate, recant, refuse, reject, renounce, repudiate, retract, revoke, spurn, traverse, turn back on, wash hands of*; SEE CONCEPT *54*

disclaimer [*n*] *repudiation*
abjuration, abnegation, clause, denial, disavowal, dissociation, renunciation, retraction, waiver; SEE CONCEPTS *45,54*

disclose [*v*] *reveal, make public*
acknowledge, admit, avow, bare, betray, blab, bring to light*, broadcast, come out of the closet*, communicate, confess, discover, display, divulge, exhibit, expose, give away, impart, lay bare, leak, let slip, make known, mouth*, open, own, publish, relate, reveal, show, snitch*, spill, spill the beans*, squeal*, tell, uncover, unfurl, unveil, utter; SEE CONCEPT *60*

disclosure [*n*] *announcement, revelation*
acknowledgment, admission, advertisement, betrayal, blow-by-blow*, broadcast, confession, declaration, discovery, divulgation, divulgence, enlightenment, exposal, exposé, exposure, handout, impartance, impartation, leak, make, picture, publication, revealing, revealment, rundown, snitch*, squeal*, tip*, tip-off*, uncovering, unveilment, ventilation; SEE CONCEPT *274*

disco [*n*] *discotheque*
club, dance hall, nightclub, nightspot; SEE CONCEPTS *293,439,449*

discolor [*v*] *fading, dirtying of hue*
besmear, besmirch, blot, defile, mar, mark, rust, smear, soil, stain, streak, sully, tar, tarnish, tinge; SEE CONCEPTS *250,469*

discomfit [*v*] *defeat, frustrate; confuse*
abash, annoy, baffle, balk, beat, bother, checkmate, confound, demoralize, discompose, disconcert, discountenance, disturb, embarrass,

faze, fluster, foil, irk, outwit, overcome, perplex, perturb, prevent, rattle, ruffle, take aback, thwart, trump, unsettle, upset, vex, worry, worst; SEE CONCEPTS *7,19,95*

discomfiture [*n*] *embarrassment, frustration*
abashment, agitation, beating, chagrin, comedown, confusion, conquest, defeasance, defeat, demoralization, descent, disappointment, discomposure, disconcertion, disconcertment, disquiet, failure, humiliation, overthrow, perturbation, rout, ruin, shame, undoing, unease, uneasiness, upset, vanquishment, vexation; SEE CONCEPTS *410,674*

discomfort [*n*] *irritation, pain*
ache, annoyance, discomfiture, discomposure, displeasure, disquiet, distress, embarrassment, hardship, hurt, inquietude, malaise, nuisance, soreness, trouble, uneasiness, unpleasantness, upset, vexation; SEE CONCEPTS *410,728*

discomfort [*v*] *irritate; cause pain*
discomfit, discompose, disquiet, distress, disturb, embarrass, make uncomfortable, nettle, perturb, upset, vex; SEE CONCEPTS *7,19,246,313*

discommode [*v*] *annoy*
bother, burden, disoblige, disquiet, disturb, fluster, harass, incommode, inconvenience, irk, molest, perturb, put out, trouble, upset, vex; SEE CONCEPTS *7,19*

discompose [*v*] *provoke, agitate*
annoy, bewilder, bother, confuse, discombobulate, discomfit, disconcert, dismay, disorganize, displease, disquiet, disturb, embarrass, faze, flurry, fluster, harass, harry, irk, irritate, nettle, perplex, perturb, pester, plague, rattle, ruffle, unhinge, unsettle, upset, vex, worry; SEE CONCEPTS *7,19*

disconcert [*v*] *shake up; confuse*
abash, agitate, baffle, balk, bewilder, bug, confound, demoralize, disarrange, discombobulate, discomfit, discompose, discountenance, disturb, embarrass, faze, fluster, foul up, frustrate, get to, hinder, nonplus, perplex, perturb, psych out*, put off, puzzle, rattle, ruffle, take aback, throw off balance, trouble, unbalance, undo, unsettle, upset, upset apple cart*, worry; SEE CONCEPTS *7,16,19*

disconcerted [*adj*] *confused; shaken*
annoyed, bewildered, caught off balance, come apart, distracted, disturbed, embarrassed, fazed, flustered, in botheration, messed-up, mixed-up, nonplussed, out of countenance, perturbed, psyched-out*, rattled, ruffled, shook-up*, spaced-out*, taken aback, thrown, troubled, unglued, unsettled, unzipped*, upset; SEE CONCEPT *403*

disconnect [*v*] *take apart; uncouple*
abstract, break it off, break it up, cut off, detach, disassociate, disengage, disjoin, dissever, dissociate, disunite, divide, drop it, part, separate, sever, sideline, unfix; SEE CONCEPTS *98,135*

disconnected [*adj*] *confused; discontinuous*
broken, detached, disjointed, disordered, garbled, illogical, inchoate, incoherent, incohesive, interrupted, irrational, irregular, jumbled, loose, mixed-up, muddled, rambling, separated, uncontinuous, uncoordinated, unintelligible, wandering; SEE CONCEPTS *267,482*

disconsolate [*adj*] *depressed, unhappy*
bad, black, blue, cheerless, cold, comfortless, crestfallen, crushed, dark, dejected, desolate, despairing, destroyed, dispirited, distressed, dole-

ful, down, downcast, downhearted, dreary, forlorn, gloomy, grief-stricken, heartbroken, hopeless, hurting, inconsolable, in pain*, in the pits*, low, melancholy, miserable, ripped*, sad, somber, sorrowful, torn-up*, woebegone, woeful, wretched; SEE CONCEPT *403*

discontent [*n*] *dissatisfaction*
depression, discontentment, displeasure, envy, fretfulness, regret, restlessness, uneasiness, unhappiness, vexation; SEE CONCEPT *410*

discontented/discontent [*adj*] *unhappy, dissatisfied*
blue, complaining, crabby, disaffected, disgruntled, displeased, disquieted, disturbed, exasperated, fed up, fretful, griping, kvetching*, malcontent, malcontented, miserable, perturbed, picky, restless, ungratified, upset, vexed; SEE CONCEPT *403*

discontinuance [*n*] *stop, suspension of activity*
adjournment, alternation, cease, cessation, close, closing, desistance, desuetude, discontinuation, disjunction, disruption, ending, finish, intermission, interruption, separation, stopping, termination; SEE CONCEPT *119*

discontinue [*v*] *prevent activity from going on*
abandon, bag it*, blow off*, break off*, call it quits, cease, close, desist, disconnect, disjoin, dissever, disunite, drop, end, finish, give over, give up, halt, interpose, interrupt, intervene, kill, knock off*, leave off, part, pause, put an end to, quit, refrain from, scrub, separate, stop, surcease, suspend, terminate; SEE CONCEPTS *121,234*

discontinuous [*adj*] *broken; intermittent*
alternate, desultory, disconnected, disjointed, disordered, fitful, gaping, inchoate, incoherent, incohesive, interrupted, irregular, muddled, spasmodic, unconnected, unorganized; SEE CONCEPT *482*

discord [*n1*] *conflict, disagreement*
animosity, antagonism, antipathy, clash, clashing, collision, contention, difference, disaccord, discordance, discrepancy, disharmony, dispute, dissension, dissent, dissidence, dissonance, disunion, disunity, division, enmity, friction, fuss, hassle, hostility, incompatibility, incongruity, inharmony, lack of concord, mischief, opposition, polarization, rancor, row, ruckus, rupture, scene, spat, split, static, strife, variance, wrangling; SEE CONCEPT *388*

discord [*n2*] *noise*
cacophony, clamor, clinker, din, disharmony, dissonance, harshness, jangle, jarring, racket, sour note, tumult; SEE CONCEPT *595*

discordant [*adj*] *not in harmony; conflicting*
antagonistic, antipathetic, at odds, cacophonous, clashing, contradictory, contrarient, contrary, different, disagreeing, discrepant, dissonant, divergent, grating, harsh, incompatible, incongruous, inconsistent, inconsonant, inharmonious, jangling, jarring, on a sour note*, opposite, quarreling, strident, uncongenial, unharmonious, unmelodious, unmixable; SEE CONCEPTS *558,564, 592,594*

discount [*n*] *reduction in cost*
abatement, allowance, commission, concession, cut, cut rate, decrease, deduction, depreciation, diminution, drawback, exemption, knock-off*, markdown, modification, percentage, premium, qualification, rebate, remission, rollback, sal-

vage, something off, subtraction, tare; SEE CON-
CEPTS *335,763*

discount [*v1*] *lower, reduce cost*
abate, allow, deduct, depreciate, diminish, hold a
sale, knock off*, make allowance for, mark
down, modify, rebate, redeem, remove, sell at
discount, strike off, subtract, take away, take off,
undersell; SEE CONCEPTS *236,247,330*

discount [*v2*] *ignore; treat as insignificant*
belittle, blink at*, brush off*, depreciate, derogate, detract from, disbelieve, discredit, dispraise, disregard, doubt, fail, forget, minimize,
mistrust, neglect, omit, overlook, overpass, pass
over, question, reject, scoff at, scout, slight; SEE
CONCEPTS *21,30*

discountenance [*v1*] *reject, oppose*
condemn, count me out*, deprecate, disapprove,
discommend, discourage, disesteem, disfavor,
dispute, frown on*, hold no brief for*, not go
for*, not stand for*, object to, put down, resist,
take a dim view of*, take exception to*; SEE
CONCEPT *21*

discountenance [*v2*] *embarrass, disconcert*
abash, chagrin, confuse, discomfit, discompose,
faze, humiliate, rattle, shame; SEE CONCEPTS
7,19,54

discourage [*v1*] *dishearten, dispirit*
abash, afflict, alarm, appall, awe, beat down,
bother, break one's heart*, bully, cast down,
chill, confuse, cow, dampen, dash, daunt, deject,
demoralize, deprecate, depress, dismay, disparage, distress, droop, frighten, intimidate, irk,
overawe, prostrate, repress, scare, throw cold
water on*, trouble, try, unnerve, vex, weigh; SEE
CONCEPT *14*

discourage [*v2*] *deter, dissuade; restrain*
check, chill, control, curb, deprecate, disadvise,
discountenance, disfavor, disincline, divert,
frighten, hinder, hold back, hold off, impede, indispose, inhibit, interfere, keep back, obstruct,
prevent, put off, quiet, repress, scare, shake, talk
out of, throw cold water on*, turn aside, turn off,
warn, withhold; SEE CONCEPTS *68,121*

discouraged [*adj*] *disheartened*
beat, beat-down, blue, caved-in, come-apart,
crestfallen, dashed, daunted, depressed, deterred,
dismayed, dispirited, down, downbeat, downcast, down-in-mouth*, glum*, gone to pieces*,
in a funk*, in blue funk*, in the dumps*, lost
momentum, pessimistic, sad; SEE CONCEPT *403*

discouragement [*n1*] *despondency*
cold feet*, dejection, depression, despair, disappointment, discomfiture, dismay, downheartedness, hopelessness, loss of confidence, low
spirits, melancholy, pessimism, sadness, the
blues*; SEE CONCEPT *410*

discouragement [*n2*] *restraint*
bar, constraint, curb, damper, deterrent, disincentive, hindrance, impediment, obstacle, opposition, rebuff, setback; SEE CONCEPT *674*

discouraging [*adj*] *upsetting*
black, bleak, dampening, daunting, depressing,
depressive, deterring, disadvantageous, disappointing, disheartening, dismal, dismaying,
dispiriting, dissuading, dreary, gloomy, hindering, inopportune, off-putting, oppressive, re-
pressing, unfavorable, unpropitious; SEE
CONCEPTS *403,529*

discourse [*n*] *dialogue; dissertation*
address, article, chat, communication, conversa-

tion, converse, descant, discussion, disquisition,
essay, gabfest*, homily, huddle, lecture, memoir,
monograph, monologue, oration, paper, rhetoric,
sermon, speaking, speech, talk, thesis, tractate,
treatise, utterance, verbalization; SEE CONCEPT
266

discourse [*v*] *discuss, speak about*
argue, chew*, comment, commentate, confab*,
confer, converse, debate, declaim, descant, develop, dilate upon, dispute, dissert, dissertate,
elaborate, enlarge, expand, expatiate, explain,
expound, give a meeting, harangue, hold forth,
lecture, modulate, orate, perorate, remark, sermonize, talk, treat, voice; SEE CONCEPTS *51,56*

discourteous [*adj*] *rude, impolite*
abrupt, bad-mannered, boorish, brusque, cavalier, cheeky*, churlish, contumelious, crude,
crusty*, curt, disrespectful, flip, fresh, ill-bred,
ill-mannered, impertinent, inaffable, indelicate,
insolent, inurbane, oafish, offhand, rustic, sassy,
smart-alecky*, uncivil, uncouth, ungenteel, ungracious, unmannerly, unrefined; SEE CONCEPT
401

discover [*v*] *find, uncover*
ascertain, bring to light, catch, come across,
come upon, conceive, contrive, debunk, design,
detect, determine, devise, dig up, discern, disclose, distinguish, elicit, espy, explore, ferret
out*, get wind of*, get wise to*, glimpse, hear,
identify, invent, learn, light upon, locate, look
up, nose out*, notice, observe, originate, perceive, pick up on*, pioneer, realize, recognize,
reveal, see, sense, smoke out*, spot, think of,
turn up, unearth; SEE CONCEPTS *31,183*

discovery [*n1*] *finding, uncovering*
analysis, ascertainment, authentication, calculation, certification, detection, determination, diagnosis, discernment, disclosure, distinguishing,
empiricism, encounter, espial, experimentation,
exploration, exposition, exposure, feeling, hearing, identification, introduction, invention, learning, locating, location, origination, perception,
revelation, sensing, sighting, strike, unearthing,
verification; SEE CONCEPTS *31,183*

discovery [*n2*] *treasure; invention*
algorithm, bonanza*, breakthrough, conclusion,
contrivance, coup, data, design, device, find,
finding, formula, godsend*, innovation, law,
luck, luck out*, machine, method, principle,
process, result, secret, theorem, way; SEE CON-
CEPTS *260,532*

discredit [*v1*] *blame, detract from*
blow up*, bring into disrepute, bring to naught,
censure, defame, degrade, destroy, disconsider,
disesteem, disfavor, disgrace, dishonor, disparage, disprove, explode, expose, frown upon*,
knock bottom out of*, mudsling*, poke full of
holes*, pooh-pooh*, puncture, put down, reflect
on, reproach, ruin, run down, shoot, show up,
slander, slur, smear, take rug out from under*,
tear down*, vilify; SEE CONCEPTS *44,54*

discredit [*v2*] *doubt, question*
challenge, deny, disbelieve, discount, dispute,
distrust, mistrust, put under suspicion, reject,
scoff at; SEE CONCEPT *21*

discreet [*adj*] *cautious, sensible*
alert, attentive, awake, cagey, calculating, careful, chary, circumspect, civil, conservative, considerate, controlled, diplomatic, discerning,
discriminating, gingerly, guarded, having fore-

sight, heedful, intelligent, judicious, like a clam*, moderate, noncommittal, not rash, observant, on lookout*, politic, precautious, prudent, reasonable, reserved, restrained, safe, sagacious, strategic, tactful, temperate, thoughtful, vigilant, wary, watchful, wise, worldly-wise; SEE CONCEPT **401**

discrepancy [n] *conflict, disagreement*
alterity, contrariety, difference, discordance, disparity, dissemblance, dissimilarity, dissimilitude, dissonance, distinction, divergence, divergency, error, far cry*, incongruity, inconsistency, miscalculation, otherness, split, unlikeness, variance, variation; SEE CONCEPT **665**

discrepant [adj] *disagreeing*
at variance, conflicting, contradictory, contrary, different, differing, disconsonant, discordant, disparate, dissonant, divergent, diverse, incompatible, incongruent, incongruous, inconsistent, inconsonant, unmixable, varying; SEE CONCEPT **564**

discrete [adj] *individual*
detached, different, disconnected, discontinuous, distinct, diverse, separate, several, unattached, various; SEE CONCEPT **564**

discretion [n] *caution, judgment*
acumen, attention, calculation, canniness, care, carefulness, chariness, circumspection, concern, considerateness, consideration, deliberation, diplomacy, discernment, discrimination, foresight, forethought, good sense, gumption, heed, heedfulness, judiciousness, maturity, observation, perspicacity, precaution, presence of mind, providence, prudence, responsibility, sagacity, sense, shrewdness, solicitude, tact, thoughtfulness, vigilance, wariness, warning, watchfulness, wisdom; SEE CONCEPT **657**

discretionary [adj] *open to choice*
at the call*, elective, facultative, judge and jury, leftover, nonmandatory, nonobligatory, open, optional, unrestricted; SEE CONCEPT **546**

discriminate [v1] *show prejudice*
be bigot, be partial, contradistinguish, disfavor, favor, hate, incline, judge, segregate, separate, set apart, show bias, single out, treat as inferior, treat differently, victimize; SEE CONCEPTS **32,384**

discriminate [v2] *differentiate, distinguish*
assess, collate, compare, contradistinguish, contrast, difference, discern, discrepate, evaluate, extricate, judge, know, know what's what*, make out*, note, perceive, remark, segregate, separate, sever, severalize, sift, specify, split hairs*, tell apart, tell the difference; SEE CONCEPTS **15,38**

discriminating [adj] *critical*
acute, astute, careful, choicy, choosy, cultivated, discerning, distinctive, eclectic, fastidious, finical, finicky, fussy, individualizing, judicious, keen, opinionated, particular, persnickety*, picky, prudent, refined, select, selective, sensitive, tasteful, wise; SEE CONCEPTS **404,542**

discrimination [n1] *bias*
bigotry, favoritism, hatred, inequity, injustice, intolerance, partiality, prejudice, unfairness, wrong; SEE CONCEPTS **29,689**

discrimination [n2] *particularity in taste*
acumen, acuteness, astucity, astuteness, bias, clearness, decision, difference, differentiation, discernment, distinction, judgment, keenness, penetration, perception, percipience, perspicac-

ity, preference, refinement, sagacity, sense, separation, shrewdness, subtlety, taste, understanding; SEE CONCEPTS **32,410,655**

discursive [adj] *rambling*
deviating, digressive, erratic, excursive, long-winded, meandering, prolix, roaming, roving, spreading, wandering; SEE CONCEPT **267**

discuss [v] *talk over with another*
altercate, argue, bounce off*, canvass, compare notes, confabulate, confer, consider, consult with, contend, contest, converse, debate, deliberate, descant, discept, discourse about, dispute, dissert, dissertate, examine, exchange views on*, explain, figure, get together, go into, groupthink*, hash over*, hold forth, jaw*, kick about*, knock around*, moot, put heads together*, reason about, review, sift, take up, thrash out*, toss around*, ventilate, weigh; SEE CONCEPT **56**

discussion [n] *talk with another*
altercation, analysis, argument, argumentation, canvass, colloquy, confabulation, conference, consideration, consultation, contention, controversy, conversation, debate, deliberation, dialogue, discourse, disputation, dispute, dissertation, examination, exchange, excursus, groupthink*, huddle, interview, meet, meeting, powwow*, quarrel, review, scrutiny, symposium, ventilation, wrangling; SEE CONCEPT **56**

disdain [n] *hate; indifference*
antipathy, arrogance, aversion, contempt, contumely, derision, despisal, despisement, despite, dislike, disparagement, hatred, haughtiness, hauteur, insolence, loftiness, pride, ridicule, scorn, sneering, snobbishness, superbity, superciliousness; SEE CONCEPT **29**

disdain [v] *scorn*
abhor, be allergic to*, belittle, chill, contemn, deride, despise, disregard, hate, ignore, look down nose at*, look down on, misprize, pooh-pooh*, put down*, refuse, reject, scout, slight, sneer at, spurn, undervalue; SEE CONCEPTS **29,30**

disdainful [adj] *scornful*
aloof, antipathetic, arrogant, averse, cavalier, contemning, contemptuous, cool, derisive, despising, egotistic, haughty, high-and-mighty*, hoity-toity*, indifferent, insolent, lordly, overbearing, proud, rejecting, repudiating, scouting, sneering, snooty*, supercilious, superior, toplofty, unsympathetic, uppity*; SEE CONCEPT **401**

disease [n] *ailment, affliction*
ache, affection, attack, blight, breakdown, bug*, cancer, canker, collapse, complaint, condition, contagion, contamination, convulsions, debility, decrepitude, defect, disorder, distemper, endemic, epidemic, feebleness, fever, fit, flu, hemorrhage, ill health, illness, indisposition, infection, infirmity, inflammation, malady, misery, pathosis, plague, seizure, sickliness, sickness, spell, stroke, syndrome, temperature, unhealthiness, unsoundness, upset, virus, visitation; SEE CONCEPT **306**

diseased [adj] *unhealthy*
afflicted, ailing, indisposed, infected, infectious, infirm, rotten, sick, sickly, tainted, unsound, unwell, unwholesome; SEE CONCEPT **314**

disembark [v] *get off transportation*
alight, anchor, arrive, come ashore, debark, deplane, detrain, dismount, go ashore, land, put in, step out of; SEE CONCEPT **159**

di
di

disembowel [v] *gut*
clean, disbowel, draw, empty, eviscerate, exenterate, extract; SEE CONCEPTS *206,211*

disenchanted [adj] *let down*
blasé, cynical, disappointed, disenthralled, disentranced, disillusioned, embittered, indifferent, jaundiced, knowing, mondaine, out of love, sick of, sophisticate, sophisticated, soured, undeceived, worldly, worldly-wise; SEE CONCEPT *403*

disengage [v] *free from connection*
abstract, back off, back out, cut loose, cut out, detach, disassociate, disconnect, disentangle, disjoin, dissociate, disunite, divide, drop out, ease, extricate, liberate, loose, loosen, opt out, pull the plug, release, separate, set free, unbind, uncouple, undo, unfasten, unfix, unloose, untie, weasel out*, withdraw; SEE CONCEPT *135*

disentangle [v] *unwind, disconnect; solve*
bail one out*, clear up, detach, discumber, disembroil, disencumber, disengage, disinvolve, emancipate, expand, extricate, free, let go, let off, loose, open, part, resolve, separate, sever, simplify, sort out, sunder, unbraid, undo, unfold, unravel, unscramble, unsnarl, untangle, untie, untwine, untwist, work out; SEE CONCEPTS *127,135*

disfavor [n] *dislike; disgrace*
aversion, disapprobation, disapproval, discredit, disesteem, dishonor, disinclination, displeasure, disregard, disrepute, disrespect, dissatisfaction, distaste, distrust, doghouse*, indisposition, mistrust, shame, thumbs down*, unpopularity; SEE CONCEPTS *29,388*

disfigure [v] *make ugly*
blemish, damage, deface, defile, deform, disfashion, disfeature, distort, hurt, injure, maim, mangle, mar, mutilate, scar; SEE CONCEPTS *137,246,250*

disgorge [v] *vomit*
be sick*, discharge, lose one's lunch*, regurgitate, retch, spew, throw up, upchuck*; SEE CONCEPTS *179,185,308*

disgrace [n] *state of shame; bad reputation*
abasement, abuse, baseness, black eye*, blemish, blur, brand, comedown, contempt, contumely, corruption, culpability, debasement, debasing, defamation, degradation, derision, disbarment, discredit, disesteem, disfavor, dishonor, disrepute, disrespect, humbling, humiliation, ignominy, ill repute, infamy, ingloriousness, meanness, obloquy, odium, opprobrium, pollution, prostitution, put-down, reproach, scandal, scorn, slander, slight, slur, spot, stain, stigma, taint, tarnish, turpitude, venality; SEE CONCEPT *388*

disgrace [v] *bring shame upon*
abase, attaint, besmirch, blot, debase, defame, defile, degrade, depress, deride, derogate, desecrate, discredit, disfavor, dishonor, disparage, disregard, disrespect, expel, give a black eye*, humble, humiliate, libel, lose face*, lower, mock, put down, reduce, reproach, ridicule, slander, slur, snub, stain, stigmatize, sully, taint, take down a peg*, tar and feather*, tarnish; SEE CONCEPTS *14,54,384*

disgraceful [adj] *shameful, low*
blameworthy, contemptible, degrading, detestable, discreditable, dishonorable, disreputable, ignoble, ignominious, infamous, inglorious, mean, offensive, opprobrious, scandalous, shabby, shady, shocking, shoddy, unrespectable, unworthy; SEE CONCEPT *555*

disgruntled [adj] *unhappy; critical*
annoyed, bad tempered, bellyaching*, crabbing*, crabby, cranky, disappointed, discontent, discontented, displeased, dissatisfied, griping, grouchy, grousing, grumpy, irritable, irritated, kicking, kvetching*, malcontent, malcontented, peeved, peevish, petulant, put out, sulky, sullen, testy, uncontent, ungratified, vexed; SEE CONCEPTS *401,403*

disguise [n] *covering, makeup for deception*
beard, blind, camouflage, charade, cloak, color, coloring, concealment, costume, counterfeit, cover-up, dissimulation, dress, facade, face, faking, false front*, fig leaf*, front*, get-up, guise, illusion, make-believe, mask, masquerade, pageant, pen name, pretense, pretension, pretentiousness, pseudonym, put-on, red herring*, screen, semblance, smoke screen*, trickery, veil, veneer; SEE CONCEPTS *446,451,680*

disguise [v] *mask; misrepresent*
affect, age, alter, antique, assume, beard, belie, camouflage, change, cloak, color, conceal, counterfeit, cover, cover up, deceive, dissemble, dissimulate, doctor up*, dress up, fake, falsify, feign, front, fudge*, garble, gloss over, hide, make like, make up, masquerade, muffle, obfuscate, obscure, pretend, put on a false front*, put on a front*, put on an act*, put up a front*, redo*, screen, secrete, sham, shroud, simulate, touch up, varnish, veil, wear cheaters*, whitewash*; SEE CONCEPTS *59,137,172,188,202*

disguised [adj] *unrecognizable*
camouflaged, changed, cloaked, covered, covert, fake, false, feigned, hidden, incog, masked, pretend, undercover; SEE CONCEPTS *547,619*

disgust [n] *aversion; repulsion*
abhorrence, abomination, antipathy, detestation, dislike, distaste, hatefulness, hatred, loathing, nausea, nauseation, nauseousness, objection, repugnance, revolt, revulsion, satiation, satiety, sickness, surfeit; SEE CONCEPTS *410,720*

disgust [v] *cause aversion; repel*
abominate, be repulsive, bother, cloy on, disenchant, displease, disturb, fill with loathing, gross out*, insult, irk, make one sick*, nauseate, offend, offend morals of, outrage, pall, pique, put off, reluct, repulse, revolt, scandalize, shock, sicken, surfeit, turn off, turn one's stomach*, upset; SEE CONCEPTS *7,19*

disgusted [adj] *sickened; offended*
abhorred, appalled, displeased, fastidious, fed up*, full up*, grossed out*, had bellyful*, had enough*, had it*, nauseated, nauseous, outraged, overwrought, queasy, repelled, repulsed, revolted, satiated, scandalized, sick, sick and tired of*, sick of*, squeamish, teed off*, tired and turned off*, unhappy, up to here*, weary; SEE CONCEPT *403*

disgusting [adj] *sickening; repulsive*
abominable, awful, beastly, cloying, creepy, detestable, distasteful, foul, frightful, ghastly, grody*, gross*, gruesome, hateful, hideous, horrid, horrific, icky*, loathsome, lousy, macabre, monstrous, nasty, nauseating, nerdy*, noisome, objectionable, obnoxious, odious, offensive, outrageous, repellent, repugnant, revolting, rotten, satiating, scandalous, scuzzy*, shameless, shocking, sleazeball*, sleazy*, stinking, surfeiting,

vile, vulgar, yecchy*, yucky*; SEE CONCEPTS *485,548*

dish [*n1*] *eating receptacle*
bowl, casserole, ceramic, china, container, cup, mug, pitcher, plate, platter, porringer, pot, pottery, salver, saucer, tray, vessel; SEE CONCEPT *494*

dish [*n2*] *main part of meal*
course, eats*, entreé, fare, food, helping, recipe, serving; SEE CONCEPTS *457,460,461*

dish [*n3*] *attractive woman*
angel, babe*, bathing beauty, beauty queen, broad*, bunny*, centerfold, chick*, cover girl, cupcake*, cutie, cutie-pie*, doll*, dollface, dreamboat*, dream girl, fox*, glamor girl, good-looking woman, honey*, hot dish*, hot number*, peach*, pin-up, raving beauty, sex bunny*, sex kitten*, sex pot*, tomato*; SEE CONCEPTS *415,424*

disharmony [*n*] *conflict, discord*
clash, contention, difference, disaccord, dissension, dissonance, dissonancy, friction, inharmoniousness, strife, variance; SEE CONCEPTS *388,665*

dishearten [*v*] *depress, ruin one's hopes*
cast down, chill*, crush, damp, dampen, dash, daunt, deject, demoralize, deter, discourage, disincline, dismay, disparage, dispirit, get down*, humble, humiliate, indispose, put a damper on*, put down, shake, throw a pall over*; SEE CONCEPTS *7,19*

disheveled [*adj*] *wrinkled, unkempt in appearance*
bagged out*, beat up*, bedraggled, blowzy*, dirty, disarranged, disarrayed, disordered, frowzy*, grubby*, messed up, messy, mussed up*, mussy, ruffled, rumpled, scuzzy, slipshod, sloppy, slovenly, tousled, unbuttoned, uncombed, unfastidious, untidy, unzipped*; SEE CONCEPTS *485,579*

dishonest [*adj*] *lying, untruthful*
backbiting*, bent, bluffing, cheating, corrupt, crafty, crooked, cunning, deceitful, deceiving, deceptive, designing, disreputable, double-crossing, double-dealing, elusive, false, fraudulent, guileful, hoodwinking*, mendacious, misleading, perfidious, recreant, shady, shifty, sinister, slippery*, sneaking, sneaky, swindling, traitorous, treacherous, tricky, two-faced*, two-timing*, unctuous, underhanded, unfair, unprincipled, unscrupulous, untrustworthy, villainous, wily; SEE CONCEPT *267*

dishonesty [*n*] *lying; unwillingness to tell the truth*
artifice, bunk, cheating, chicane, chicanery, corruption, craft, criminality, crookedness, cunning, deceit, double-dealing, duplicity, faithlessness, falsehood, falsity, flimflam*, fourberie, fraud, fraudulence, graft, guile, hanky-panky*, hocuspocus*, improbity, infamy, infidelity, insidiousness, mendacity, perfidiousness, perfidy, racket, rascality, sharp practice*, slyness, stealing, swindle, treachery, trickery, trickiness, unscrupulousness, wiliness; SEE CONCEPTS *59,633,657*

dishonor [*n*] *state of shame*
abasement, abuse, affront, blame, degradation, discourtesy, discredit, disesteem, disfavor, disgrace, disrepute, ignominy, indignity, infamy, insult, obloquy, odium, offense, opprobrium, outrage, reproach, scandal, slight; SEE CONCEPT *388*

dishonor [*v*] *shame, degrade*
abase, attaint, blot, corrupt, debase, debauch, defame, defile, disconsider, discredit, disgrace, disoblige, give a black eye*, libel, make lose face*, reflect on, slander, sully; SEE CONCEPT *54*

dishonorable [*adj*] *shameful, corrupt*
base, blackguardly, contemptible, crooked, deceitful, despicable, devious, discreditable, disgraceful, disreputable, fraudulent, ignoble, ignominious, infamous, inglorious, low, miscreant, offensive, opprobious, putrid, scandalous, shabby, shady, treacherous, unprincipled, unrespectable, unscrupulous, untrustworthy; SEE CONCEPT *555*

dish out [*v*] *distribute*
allocate, deliver, dispense, dole out*, fork over*, furnish, give out, hand, hand out, hand over, inflict, ladle, mete out, present, produce, scoop, serve, serve up, spoon, supply, transfer, turn over; SEE CONCEPT *140*

disillusioned [*adj*] *disappointed*
blasé, broken, brought down to earth*, debunked, disabused, disenchanted, disenthralled, disentranced, embittered, enlightened, freed, indifferent, knowing, let-down, mondaine, out of love*, punctured, sadder and wiser*, shattered, sophisticated, undeceived, worldly, worldly-wise*; SEE CONCEPT *403*

disinclination [*n*] *unwillingness to do or believe something*
alienation, antipathy, aversion, demur, disfavor, dislike, disliking, displeasure, disrelish, dissatisfaction, distaste, hatred, hesitance, indisposition, lack of desire, lack of enthusiasm, loathness, objection, opposition, reluctance, repugnance, resistance; SEE CONCEPTS *29,410,657*

disinclined [*adj*] *unwilling*
afraid, antipathetic, averse, backward, balking, doubtful, dubious, hesitating, indisposed, loath, not in the mood*, objecting, opposed, protesting, reluctant, resistant, shy, shying, slow, sticking, uneager, unsympathetic; SEE CONCEPTS *403,542*

disinfect [*v*] *make clean, pure*
antisepticize, cleanse, decontaminate, deodorize, fumigate, purify, sanitize, sterilize; SEE CONCEPT *165*

disingenuous [*adj*] *insincere*
artful, crooked, cunning, deceitful, designing, dishonest, duplicitous, false, feigned, foxy, guileful, indirect, insidious, mendacious, oblique, shifty*, sly, tricky, two-faced*, uncandid, underhanded, unfair, unfrank, wily; SEE CONCEPTS *401,542*

disinherit [*v*] *cut off in will of bequeathal*
bereave, cut off without a cent*, deprive, disaffiliate, disown, dispossess, divest, evict, exclude, exheridate, neglect, oust, repudiate, rob; SEE CONCEPTS *25,317*

disintegrate [*v*] *fall apart; reduce to pieces*
atomize, break apart, break down, break up, come apart, crumble, decay, decline, decompose, degenerate, deliquesce, descend, detach, dilapidate, disband, disconnect, disimprove, dismantle, disorganize, disperse, disunite, divide, fade away, fall to pieces*, molder, pulverize, putrefy, rot, separate, sever, shatter, sink, splinter, spoil, taint, take apart, turn, turn to dust*, wash away, wash out, wither, worsen; SEE CONCEPTS *252,469*

di
di

disinterested [*adj*] *detached, uninvolved*
aloof, candid, casual, dispassionate, equitable, even-handed, impartial, impersonal, incurious, indifferent, just watching the clock*, lackadaisical, negative, neutral, nonpartisan, not giving a damn*, outside, perfunctory, remote, unbiased, unconcerned, uncurious, unprejudiced, unselfish, withdrawn; SEE CONCEPTS *401,403*

disjointed [*adj*] *loose, disconnected*
aimless, confused, cool, discontinuous, disordered, displaced, disunited, divided, far-out, fitful, fuzzy, inchoate, incoherent, incohesive, irrational, jumbled, muddled, out-of-it*, out-to-lunch*, rambling, separated, spaced-out*, spacey*, spasmodic, split, unattached, unconnected, unorganized; SEE CONCEPTS *267,482,585*

disk [*n*] *round object*
circle, disc, discoid, discoidal, discus, dish, flan, plate, platter, quoit, sabot, saucer, shell; SEE CONCEPT *436*

dislike [*n*] *antagonism, hatred toward something*
animosity, animus, antipathy, aversion, deprecation, detestation, disapprobation, disapproval, disesteem, disfavor, disgust, disinclination, displeasure, dissatisfaction, distaste, enmity, hostility, indisposition, loathing, objection, offense, opposition, prejudice, repugnance; SEE CONCEPT *29*

dislike [*v*] *be antagonistic toward something; hate*
abhor, abominate, antipathize, avoid, be allergic to*, bear malice toward, be averse to, be turned off to*, condemn, contemn, deplore, despise, detest, disapprove, disesteem, disfavor, disrelish, eschew, execrate, grossed out on*, have hard feelings*, have no stomach for*, have no taste for, loathe, look down on, lose interest in, make faces at*, mind, not appreciate, not care for, not endure, not feel like, not take kindly to, object to, regret, resent, scorn, shudder at, shun; SEE CONCEPT *29*

dislocate [*v*] *displace*
break, disarticulate, disconnect, disengage, disjoint, disorder, disrupt, disturb, disunite, divide, jumble, misplace, mix up, move, put out of joint, remove, rummage, separate, shift, transfer, unhinge, upset; SEE CONCEPTS *135,147,213*

dislocation [*n*] *displacement*
break, confusion, disarray, disarticulation, disconnection, discontinuity, disengagement, disorder, disorganization, disruption, disturbance, division, luxation, misplacement, unhinging; SEE CONCEPTS *316,720,727*

dislodge [*v*] *knock loose*
dig out, disentangle, dislocate, displace, disturb, eject, evict, extricate, force out, oust, remove, uproot; SEE CONCEPTS *147,213*

disloyal [*adj*] *unfaithful*
alienated, apostate, cheating, disaffected, double-crossing, estranged, faithless, false, perfidious, recreant, seditious, snaky*, subversive, traitorous, treacherous, treasonable, two-faced*, two-timing*, unloyal, unpatriotic, untrue, untrustworthy, wormlike*; SEE CONCEPT *401*

disloyalty [*n*] *unfaithfulness*
apostasy, bad faith, betrayal of trust, breach of trust, breaking of faith, deceitfulness, disaffection, double-dealing, faithlessness, falseness, falsity, inconstancy, infidelity, perfidiousness,

perfidy, recreancy, sedition, seditiousness, subversive activity, treachery, treason, untrueness, violation; SEE CONCEPT *633*

dismal [*adj*] *bleak, dreary, gloomy*
afflictive, black, boring, cheerless, cloudy, dark, depressed, depressing, desolate, despondent, dim, dingy, disagreeable, discouraging, disheartening, dispiriting, doleful, dolorous, dull, forlorn, frowning, funereal, ghastly, gruesome, hopeless, horrible, horrid, inauspicious, in the pits*, joyless, lonesome, lowering, lugubrious, melancholy, miserable, monotonous, morbid, murky, oppressive, overcast, sad, shadowy, somber, sorrowful, tedious, tenebrous, troublesome, unfortunate, unhappy; SEE CONCEPTS *525,536,548*

dismantle [*v*] *take apart*
annihilate, bankrupt, bare, break down, break up, decimate, demolish, denudate, denude, deprive, destroy, disassemble, dismember, dismount, disrobe, divest, fell, knock down, level, part out, pull down, raze, ruin, strike, strip, subvert, take down, take to pieces, tear down, undo, unrig, wrack, wreck; SEE CONCEPTS *135,168,252*

dismay [*n*] *disappointed feeling; distress*
agitation, alarm, anxiety, apprehension, blue funk*, blues*, bummer*, chagrin, cold feet*, consternation, discouragement, disheartenment, disillusionment, downer*, dread, dumps*, fear, fright, funk*, hassle, horror, letdown, panic, terror, the blahs*, trepidation, upset; SEE CONCEPTS *27,410,690*

dismay [*v*] *disappoint, fill with consternation*
abash, affright, agitate, alarm, appall, bewilder, bother, chill, confound, daunt, discomfit, discompose, disconcert, discourage, dishearten, disillusion, dispirit, disquiet, distress, disturb, dumbfound, embarrass, faze, flummox*, fluster, foul up*, frighten, get to, horrify, louse up*, mess up*, muck up*, mystify, nonplus, paralyze, perplex, put off, puzzle, rattle, scare, screw up*, shake, snafu*, take aback, terrify, terrorize, throw, throw into a tizzy*, unhinge*, unnerve, upset; SEE CONCEPTS *7,19*

dismember [*v*] *cut into pieces*
amputate, anatomize, cripple, disassemble, disjoint, dislimb, dislocate, dismantle, dismount, dissect, divide, maim, mutilate, part, rend, sever, sunder, take down; SEE CONCEPTS *98,135,176*

dismiss [*v1*] *send away, remove; free*
abolish, banish, boot*, brush off*, bundle, cast off*, cast out*, chase, chuck, clear, decline, deport, detach, disband, discard, dispatch, dispense with, disperse, dispose of, dissolve, divorce, do without, drive out, eject, expel, force out, have done with*, kick out*, let go, let out, lock out*, outlaw, push aside, push back, reject, release, relegate, relinquish, repel, repudiate, rid, send off, send packing*, shed, show out*, slough off, supersede, sweep away*, turn out; SEE CONCEPTS *127,217*

dismiss [*v2*] *remove from job, responsibility*
ax*, boot*, boot out*, bounce*, bump*, can*, cashier*, defrock, depone, depose, deselect, discharge, disemploy, disfrock, displace, disqualify, drop, fire, furlough, give notice to, give the ax*, give the gate*, give the heave-ho*, give walking papers*, give warning, impeach, kick out*, lay off, let go*, let out*, oust, pension, pink-slip*, put away*, recall, retire, sack*, send packing*,

shelve*, shut out*, suspend, terminate, turn away, unfrock, unseat, wash out*; SEE CONCEPTS 324,351

dismiss [v3] *put out of one's mind*
banish, contemn, deride, despise, discard, disdain, dispel, disregard, drop, flout, gibe, gird, jeer, kiss off*, laugh away*, lay aside, mock, pooh-pooh*, rally, reject, relegate, repudiate, repulse, ridicule, scoff, scorn, scout, set aside, shelve*, spurn, taunt, twit; SEE CONCEPT 35

dismissal [n] *release*
adjournment, banishment, bounce, brush-off, cold shoulder*, congé, deportation, deposal, deposition, discharge, dislodgment, displacement, dispossession, dissolution, door*, end, eviction, exile, exorcism, expatriation, expulsion, freedom, freeing, housecleaning*, kiss-off*, layoff, liberation, marching orders*, notice, old heaveho*, ostracism, ouster, permission, pink slip*, relegation, removal, suspension; SEE CONCEPTS 127,217,351

dismount [v] *get off something higher*
alight, debark, deplane, descend, detrain, disembark, get down, light; SEE CONCEPT 195

disobedience [n] *misbehavior; noncompliance with rules*
defiance, dereliction, disregard, indiscipline, infraction, infringement, insubmission, insubordination, insurgence, intractableness, mutiny, neglect, nonobservance, perversity, rebellion, recalcitrance, refractoriness, revolt, revolution, riot, sabotage, sedition, strike, stubbornness, transgression, unruliness, violation, waywardness; SEE CONCEPT 633

disobedient [adj] *defiant, mischievous*
contrary, contumacious, disorderly, fractious, froward, headstrong, insubordinate, intractable, naughty, noncompliant, nonobservant, obstreperous, perverse, recalcitrant, refractory, resistive, uncompliant, undisciplined, unruly, wayward, willful; SEE CONCEPT 401

disobey [v] *disregard rules; refuse to conform*
balk, be remiss, break rules, contravene, counteract, dare, decline, defy, desert, differ, disagree, evade, flout, fly in face of*, go counter to, ignore, infringe, insurrect, misbehave, mutiny, neglect, not heed, not listen, not mind, object, overstep, pay no attention to, rebel, recalcitrate, resist, revolt, revolution, revolutionize, riot, rise in arms*, run riot*, set aside, shirk, strike, take law into own hands*, transgress, violate, withstand; SEE CONCEPTS 30,192,384

disoblige [v] *displease, annoy*
affront, bother, discommode, disturb, incommode, inconvenience, insult, offend, put about, put out, slight, trouble, upset, vex; SEE CONCEPTS 7,19

disobliging [adj] *rude, annoying*
awkward, disagreeable, discourteous, ill-disposed, ill-natured, unaccommodating, unamiable, uncivil, uncongenial, uncooperative, unhelpful, unpleasant; SEE CONCEPT 401

disorder [n1] *chaos, clutter*
anarchy, ataxia, confusion, derangement, disarrangement, disarray, discombobulation, disorderliness, disorganization, huddle, irregularity, jumble, mess, muddle, rat's nest*, shambles, snarl, topsyturviness*, untidiness; SEE CONCEPT 230

disorder [n2] *social commotion; mental confusion*
agitation, anarchism, anarchy, brawl, bustle, chaos, clamor, complication, convulsion, discombobulation*, discord, disorganization, distemper, disturbance, dither, entanglement, fight, flap, fracas, fuss, hubbub, hullabaloo*, imbroglio, insurrection, lawlessness, mayhem, misrule, mob rule*, quarrel, rebellion, reign of terror*, revolution, riot, rioting, ruckus, rumpus, static, strike, terrorism, tizzy*, trouble, tumult, turbulence, turmoil, unrest, unruliness, uproar; SEE CONCEPTS 388,410

disorder [n3] *illness*
affliction, ailment, cachexia, complaint, disease, diseasedness, indisposition, infirmity, malady, sickness, unhealth, upset; SEE CONCEPT 306

disorder [v] *mix up, disarrange*
clutter, confound, confuse, derange, discompose, discreate, dishevel, disjoint, dislocate, disorganize, disrupt, distemper, disturb, embroil, jumble, mess up, muddle, muss up*, rummage, rumple, scatter, shuffle, tumble, unsettle, upset; SEE CONCEPTS 240,250

disordered [adj] *in a mess*
all over the place*, confused, deranged, disarranged, discombobulated, disconnected, discontinuous, disjointed, dislocated, disorganized, displaced, incoherent, in confusion, jumbled, mislaid, misplaced, molested, moved, muddled, out-of-place, removed, roiled, ruffled, rumpled, shifted, shuffled, stirred up, tampered-with, tangled, tossed, tousled, tumbled, unsettled, untidy; SEE CONCEPTS 485,535

disorderly [adj1] *messy, untidy*
all over the place*, chaotic, cluttered, confused, dislocated, disorganized, heterogeneous, indiscriminate, irregular, jumbled, mixed up, out-of-control*, out-of-line*, out-of-step*, out-of-whack*, scattered, scrambled, slovenly, topsy-turvy*, tumult, uncombed, undisciplined, unkempt, unmethodical, unrestrained, unsystematic, untrained; SEE CONCEPTS 485,535

disorderly [adj2] *causing trouble; unlawful*
boisterous, disobedient, disruptive, drunk, fractious, indisciplined, intemperate, noisy, obstreperous, off-base*, on-a-tear*, out-of-line*, out-of-order*, raucous, rebellious, refractory, riotous, rowdy, stormy, termagant, tumultous/tumultuous, turbulent, uncompliant, uncontrollable, ungovernable, unmanageable, unruly, wayward; SEE CONCEPTS 401,545

disorganization [n] *unordered situation or thing*
anarchy, chaos, confusion, derangement, disarray, disjointedness, disorder, disruption, dissolution, disunion, foul-up*, incoherence, mix-up, rat's nest*, screw-up*, unconnectedness, unholy mess*; SEE CONCEPTS 674,727

disorganize [v] *disrupt arrangement; make shambles of*
break down, break up, clutter, complicate, confound, confuse, demobilize, derange, destroy, disarrange, disarray, disband, discompose, discreate, dishevel, dislocate, disorder, disperse, disturb, embroil, jumble, litter, mess up, mislay, misplace, muddle, perturb, put out of order, scatter, scramble, shuffle, toss, turn topsy-turvy, unsettle, upset; SEE CONCEPTS 250,252,384

disorganized [adj] *unmethodical; messed up*
chaotic, confused, disordered, disorderly, hap-

di
di

hazard, jumbled, mixed up, muddled, screwed up*, shuffled, unsystematic; SEE CONCEPTS *485,585*

disoriented [*adj*] *confused, unstable*
adrift, all at sea*, astray, bewildered, discombobulated, lost, mixed-up, not adjusted, off-beam*, off-course, out-of-joint*, perplexed, unbalanced, unhinged, unsettled; SEE CONCEPT *403*

disown [*v*] *refuse to acknowledge*
abandon, abjure, abnegate, cast off, deny, disacknowledge, disallow, disavow, discard, disclaim, divorce oneself from, refuse to recognize, reject, renounce, repudiate, retract; SEE CONCEPTS *50,54,88*

disparage [*v*] *criticize; detract from*
abuse, belittle, chill*, cry down, decry, defame, degrade, deject, demoralize, denigrate, deprecate, depreciate, deride, derogate, dis*, discourage, discredit, disdain, dishearten, dismiss, dispirit, dispraise, downcry, dump on*, lower, malign, minimize, pan*, put down, put hooks in*, rap*, ridicule, roast*, run down*, scorch, scorn, slam*, slander, smear*, sour grapes*, tear down, traduce, underestimate, underrate, undervalue, vilify, write off; SEE CONCEPTS *7,19,52,54*

disparagement [*n*] *strong criticism; detraction*
aspersion, backbiting*, backstabbing*, belittlement, blame, calumny, censure, condemnation, contempt, contumely, debasement, degradation, denunciation, depreciation, derision, derogation, discredit, disdain, impairment, lessening, lie, prejudice, reproach, ridicule, scandal, scorn, slander, tale, underestimation; SEE CONCEPTS *52,54*

disparate [*adj*] *at odds, different*
at variance, contrary, contrasting, discordant, discrepant, dissimilar, distant, distinct, divergent, diverse, far cry, incommensurate, incompatible, inconsistent, inconsonant, like night and day*, poles apart, separate, unalike, unequal, unequivalent, uneven, unlike, unsimilar, various; SEE CONCEPT *564*

disparity [*n*] *difference*
alterity, discrepancy, disproportion, dissemblance, dissimilarity, dissimilitude, distinction, divergence, divergency, diverseness, gap, imbalance, imparity, incongruity, inequality, otherness, unevenness, unlikeness, variation; SEE CONCEPT *665*

dispassionate [*adj*] *unfeeling, impartial*
abstract, aloof, calm, candid, cold-blooded, coldfish*, collected, composed, cool, cool cat*, couldn't care less*, detached, disinterested, fair, iceberg*, impersonal, imperturbable, indifferent, judicial, just, laid back, moderate, neutral, nondiscriminatory, nonpartisan, objective, poker-faced*, quiet, serene, sober, temperate, tough, unbiased, unemotional, unexcitable, unexcited, unflappable, uninvolved, unmoved, unprejudiced, unruffled; SEE CONCEPTS *401,404*

dispatch [*n1*] *speed in carrying out action*
alacrity, celerity, expedition, expeditiousness, haste, hurry, hustle, precipitateness, promptitude, promptness, quickness, rapidity, rustle, speediness, swiftness; SEE CONCEPTS *755,818*

dispatch [*n2*] *communication*
account, bulletin, communiqué, document, instruction, item, letter, message, missive, news, piece, report, story; SEE CONCEPTS *271,277,278*

dispatch [*v1*] *hurry, send fast*
accelerate, address, consign, dismiss, express, forward, hand-carry, hasten, issue, quicken, railroad*, remit, route, run with, run with ball*, ship, speed, transmit, walk through; SEE CONCEPTS *152,217*

dispatch [*v2*] *finish; consume*
conclude, devour, discharge, dispose of, eat up, expedite, lay low, perform, polish off*, scarf down*, settle; SEE CONCEPTS *169,234*

dispatch [*v3*] *kill*
assassinate, bump off*, butcher*, destroy, eliminate, execute, finish, finish off*, murder, put away*, put end to, slaughter, slay, take out*; SEE CONCEPTS *238,252*

dispel [*v*] *drive away thought, belief*
allay, banish, beat off*, break it up*, break up*, bust up*, cancel, chase away, crumble, deploy, disband, disintegrate, dismiss, disperse, dissipate, distribute, eject, eliminate, expel, oust, repel, resolve, rout, scatter, scramble, split up*; SEE CONCEPTS *14,35*

dispensable [*adj*] *not necessary; able to be thrown away*
disposable, excessive, expendable, minor, needless, nonessential, removable, superfluous, trivial, unimportant, unnecessary, unrequired, useless; SEE CONCEPT *546*

dispensation [*n1*] *allocation of supply*
allotment, appointment, apportionment, award, bestowal, conferment, consignment, courtesy, dealing out, disbursement, distribution, dole, endowment, favor, indulgence, kindness, part, portion, quota, service, share; SEE CONCEPTS *140,337*

dispensation [*n2*] *management*
administration, direction, economy, plan, regulation, scheme, stewardship, system; SEE CONCEPTS *325,660,770*

dispensation [*n3*] *permission*
exception, exemption, immunity, indulgence, license, privilege, relaxation, relief, remission, reprieve; SEE CONCEPT *685*

dispense [*v1*] *dole out supply*
allocate, allot, apportion, assign, come across with, deal, deal out, disburse, dish out*, distribute, divide, divvy*, fork out*, furnish, give, give away, give with, hand out, hand over, lot, measure, mete out, partition, portion, prepare, prorate, share, shell out*; SEE CONCEPT *140*

dispense [*v2*] *operate, administer*
apply, carry out, command, direct, discharge, enforce, execute, handle, implement, manage, maneuver, manipulate, swing, undertake, wield; SEE CONCEPT *117*

dispense [*v3*] *exempt from responsibility*
absolve, discharge, except, excuse, exonerate, let off, privilege from, release, relieve, reprieve, spare; SEE CONCEPT *110*

dispense with [*v*] *omit; do away with*
abolish, abstain from, brush aside, cancel, dispose of, disregard, do without, forgo, get rid of, give up, ignore, pass over, relinquish, render needless, shake off, waive; SEE CONCEPT *30*

disperse [*v*] *distribute; scatter*
banish, besprinkle, break up, broadcast, cast forth, circulate, deal, diffuse, disappear, disband, disburse, discharge, dislodge, dismiss, dispel, disseminate, dissipate, dissolve, divvy*, dole out, eject, intersperse, measure out, partition,

propagate, radiate, rout, scatter, scramble, send off, separate, shed, sow, split up, spray, spread, strew, take off in all directions*, vanish; SEE CONCEPTS *135,217*

dispirited [*adj*] *dejected, sad*
blue*, bummed-out*, crestfallen, depressed, despondent, disconsolate, discouraged, disheartened, down*, downbeat, downcast, downhearted, dragged*, funky*, gloomy, glum, in the doldrums, low, melancholy, morose, shot-down*, spiritless, woebegone; SEE CONCEPT *403*

displace [*v1*] *move, remove from normal place*
change, crowd out, derange, disarrange, disestablish, dislocate, dislodge, displant, dispossess, disturb, eject, evict, expel, expulse, force out, lose, mislay, misplace, relegate, shift, transpose, unsettle, uproot; SEE CONCEPTS *147,213*

displace [*v2*] *remove from position of responsibility*
banish, can*, cashier*, cut out*, deport, depose, dethrone, discard, discharge, discrown, disenthone, dismiss, disthrone, exile, expatriate, fire, oust, relegate, remove, replace, sack*, step into shoes of*, succeed, supersede, supplant, take over, take the place of, transport, uncrown, unmake, usurp; SEE CONCEPTS *133,298,300*

display [*n*] *public showing; spectacle*
act, affectation, arrangement, array, arrayal, blaze, bravura, dash, demonstration, example, exhibit, exhibition, expo*, exposition, exposure, fanfare, flourish, for show, frame-up*, frippery, front, grandstand play*, layout, manifestation, ostentation, ostentatiousness, pageant, panorama, parade, pedantry, pomp, presentation, pretension, pretentiousness, revelation, sample, scheme, shine, showboat*, splash, splendor, splurge, spread, unfolding, vanity; SEE CONCEPTS *261,386*

display [*v*] *show for public viewing, effect*
advertise, arrange, bare, betray, boast, brandish, bring to view, demonstrate, disclose, emblazon, evidence, evince, exhibit, expand, expose, extend, feature, flash, flaunt, flourish, glaze, grandstand*, illustrate, impart, lay bare*, lay out, make clear, make known, manifest, model, open, open out, parade, perform, present, promote, promulgate, publish, represent, reveal, set out, showcase, show off, sport, spread out, stretch out, trot out*, uncover, unfold, unfurl, unmask, unroll, unveil, vamp; SEE CONCEPT *261*

displease [*v*] *make unhappy*
aggravate, anger, annoy, antagonize, bother, cap, chagrin, cool, curdle*, cut to the quick*, disappoint, discontent, disgruntle, disgust, disoblige, dissatisfy, enrage, exasperate, fret, frustrate, gall, hurt, incense, irk, irritate, nettle, offend, perplex, pique, play dirty, provoke, put out, repel, revolt, rile, roil, sound, turn off*, upset, vex, wing*, worry, zing*; SEE CONCEPTS *7,19*

displeasure [*n*] *unhappiness, anger*
annoyance, aversion, disapprobation, disapproval, discontentment, disfavor, disgruntlement, disinclination, dislike, disliking, disrelish, dissatisfaction, distaste, incensement, indignation, indisposition, irritation, offense, pique, resentment, umbrage, vexation, wrath; SEE CONCEPT *410*

disposal [*n1*] *parting with or throwing something away*
auctioning, bartering, chucking, clearance, conveyance, demolishing, demolition, destroying, destruction, discarding, dispatching, dispensa-

tion, disposition, dumping, ejection, jettison, jettisoning, junking, relegation, relinquishment, removal, riddance, sacrifice, sale, scrapping, selling, trading, transfer, transference, vending; SEE CONCEPT *180*

disposal [*n2*] *conclusion, settlement of situation*
action, allocation, arrangement, array, assignment, assortment, bequest, bestowal, consignment, control, conveyance, determination, dispensation, disposition, distribution, division, effectuation, end, gift, grouping, order, ordering, placing, position, provision, sequence, transfer, winding up; SEE CONCEPTS *119,230*

dispose [*v*] *place, order; deal with*
actuate, adapt, adjust, arrange, array, bend, bias, call the tune*, condition, determine, distribute, fix, govern, group, incline, induce, influence, lay down the law*, lead, locate, make willing, marshal, methodize, motivate, move, organize, predispose, prepare, promote, prompt, put, put one's foot down*, put to rights, range, rank, read the riot act*, regulate, ride herd on*, set, set in order, settle, shepherd, stand, sway, systematize, tailor, tempt; SEE CONCEPTS *84,117,158,180*

disposed [*adj*] *inclined to a type of behavior*
apt, at drop of hat*, biased, fain, game*, game for, given, liable, likely, minded, of a mind to*, partial, predisposed, prone, ready, subject, tending toward, willing; SEE CONCEPTS *542,552*

dispose of [*v1*] *throw away*
adios*, bestow, chuck*, deep six*, destroy, discard, dump, eighty-six*, eliminate, file in circular file*, get rid of, give, jettison, junk*, kiss*, kiss off*, make over, part with, relinquish, scrap, sell, transfer, unload; SEE CONCEPT *180*

dispose of [*v2*] *settle a matter*
chop, cut, cut off, deal with, decide, determine, do the trick*, end, finish, knock off*, polish off*, put away, take care of; SEE CONCEPTS *18,234*

disposition [*n1*] *personal temperament*
bag*, being, bent, bias, cast, character, complexion, constitution, cup of tea*, druthers*, emotions, flash, frame of mind, groove*, habit, humor, identity, inclination, individualism, individuality, leaning, make-up, mind-set*, mood, nature, penchant, personality, predilection, predisposition, proclivity, proneness, propensity, readiness, spirit, stamp, temper, tendency, tenor, thing*, tone, type, vein; SEE CONCEPT *411*

disposition [*n2*] *arrangement, management of a situation*
adjustment, classification, control, decision, direction, disposal, distribution, grouping, method, order, ordering, organization, placement, plan, regulation, sequence; SEE CONCEPTS *6,660*

dispossess [*v*] *deprive*
appropriate, eject, evict, expel, expropriate, oust, put out, throw into the street*; SEE CONCEPTS *121,142*

disproportion [*n*] *imbalance*
asymmetry, difference, discrepancy, disparity, imparity, inadequacy, inequality, insufficiency, irregularity, lopsidedness, unevenness, unsuitableness; SEE CONCEPTS *665,667*

disproportionate [*adj*] *out of balance*
asymmetric, excessive, incommensurate, inordinate, irregular, lopsided, nonsymmetrical, out of proportion, overbalanced, superfluous, too much, unequal, uneven, unreasonable, unsymmetrical; SEE CONCEPTS *564,566,771*

di
di

disprove [v] *prove false*
belie, blow sky high*, blow up*, break, confound, confute, contradict, contravene, controvert, deny, disconfirm, discredit, explode, expose, find unfounded, impugn, invalidate, knock bottom out of*, knock props out*, negate, negative, overthrow, overturn, poke holes in*, puncture, rebut, refute, set aside, shoot, shoot holes in*, tear down*, throw out, traverse, weaken; SEE CONCEPT 58

disputable [adj] *debatable; open to discussion*
arguable, controversial, doubtful, dubious, moot, mootable, problematic, questionable, uncertain; SEE CONCEPTS 529,535

disputation [n] *controversy*
argumentation, debate, dialectic, dispute, dissension, forensic, mooting, polemics; SEE CONCEPTS 278,532

disputatious [adj] *argumentative*
cantankerous, captious, caviling, contentious, controversial, dissentious, litigious, polemical, pugnacious, quarrelsome; SEE CONCEPTS 401,542

dispute [n] *argument*
altercation, beef*, bickering, bone of contention*, brawl, broil, brouhaha, commotion, conflict, contention, controversy, debate, difference of opinion, disagreement, discord, discussion, dissension, litigation, falling-out, feud, fireworks*, flare-up, fracas, friction, fuss, hubbub, miff*, misunderstanding, polemic, quarrel, row, rumpus*, squabble, squall, strife, tiff, uproar, variance, words, wrangle; SEE CONCEPTS 46,106,278

dispute [v] *argue*
agitate, altercate, bicker, brawl, bump heads*, canvass, challenge, clash, confute, contend, contest, contradict, controvert, debate, deny, disaffirm, discept, discuss, disprove, doubt, gainsay, hassle, have at*, impugn, jump on one's case*, kick around*, lock horns*, moot, negate, pick a bone*, quarrel, question, quibble, rebut, refute, squabble, take on, thrash out, toss around*, wrangle; SEE CONCEPT 46

disqualification [n] *disability; rejection for participation*
awkwardness, clumsiness, debarment, disenablement, disentitlement, elimination, exclusion, incapacitation, incapacity, incompetence, incompetency, ineligibility, ineptitude, lack, unfitness, unproficiency; SEE CONCEPT 630

disqualify [v] *be unfit for; be ineligible*
bar, bate, debar, disable, disenable, disentitle, disfranchise, eighty-six*, except, exclude, impair, incapacitate, invalidate, nix*, not make the cut*, paralyze, preclude, prohibit, rule out, suspend, unfit, weaken; SEE CONCEPTS 121,699

disquiet [n] *worry; mental upset*
ailment, alarm, angst, anxiety, care, concern, concernment, disquietude, distress, disturbance, fear, ferment, foreboding, fretfulness, inquietude, nervousness, restiveness, restlessness, solicitude, storm, trouble, turmoil, uneasiness, unrest; SEE CONCEPTS 410,532,690

disquiet [v] *worry; make uneasy*
agitate, annoy, bother, concern, discompose, distress, disturb, fluster, fret, harass, incommode, perplex, perturb, pester, plague, trouble, unhinge, unsettle, upset, vex; SEE CONCEPTS 7,19

disquieting [adj] *upsetting*
annoying, bothersome, disconcerting, distress-

ing, disturbing, irritating, perplexing, perturbing, troublesome, troubling, unnerving, unsettling, vexing, worrying; SEE CONCEPT 529

disregard [n] *ignoring*
apathy, brush-off*, contempt, disdain, disesteem, disfavor, disinterest, disrespect, forgetting, heedlessness, inadvertence, inattention, indifference, insouciance, lassitude, lethargy, listlessness, neglect, neglecting, negligence, oblivion, omission, omitting, overlooking, oversight, scorn, slight, slighting, the cold shoulder*, unconcern, unmindfulness; SEE CONCEPTS 30,633

disregard [v] *ignore; make light of*
blink at*, brush aside, brush away, brush off, cold-shoulder*, contemn, despise, discount, disdain, disobey, disparage, fail, forget, have no use for*, laugh off*, leave out of account, let go, let off easy*, let pass*, live with*, look the other way*, miss, neglect, omit, overlook, overpass, pass over, pay no attention to, pay no heed to, pay no mind*, pooh-pooh*, scorn, shut eyes to*, slight, snub, take no notice of, tune out*, turn a blind eye*, turn a deaf ear*, vilipend, wink at*; SEE CONCEPT 30

disrepair [adj] *broken; deteriorated*
busted*, damaged, dead, decayed, decrepit, down, kaput*, not functioning, on the blink*, on the fritz*, out of commission*, out of order, worn out, wracked*; SEE CONCEPT 485

disrepair [n] *state of deterioration*
collapse, decay, decrepitude, dilapidation, ruination; SEE CONCEPTS 230,674

disreputable [adj] *dishonorable, lowly*
abject, bad, base, beggarly, cheap, contemptible, derogatory, despicable, discreditable, disgraceful, disorderly, dissolute, ignominious, in bad, infamous, inglorious, in low esteem, in the doghouse*, lewd, libidinous, licentious, mean, no good*, notorious, opprobrious, pitiable, scandalous, scurvy, shabby, shady, shameful, shocking, shoddy, sordid, sorry, unprincipled, vicious, vile; SEE CONCEPT 404

disrepute [n] *dishonor, shame*
blemish, blot, brand, cloud, discredit, disesteem, disfavor, disgrace, ignominy, ill fame, ill favor, ill repute, infamy, ingloriousness, notoriety, obloquy, odium, opprobrium, reproach, scandal, scar, slur, smear, spot, stain, stigma, taint, unpopularity; SEE CONCEPT 411

disrespect [n] *disregard, rudeness toward someone*
boldness, coarseness, contempt, discourtesy, dishonor, flippancy, hardihood, impertinence, impiety, impoliteness, impudence, incivility, insolence, insolency, insolentness, irreverence, lack of respect, sacrilege, unmannerliness; SEE CONCEPTS 29,633

disrespectful [adj] *insulting, rude*
aweless, bad-mannered, blasphemous, bold, cheeky*, contemptuous, discourteous, disgracious, flip*, flippant, fresh, ill-bred, ill-mannered, impertinent, impious, impolite, impudent, insolent, irreverent, misbehaved, nervy*, out-of-line*, profanatory, profane, sacrilegious, sassy*, saucy*, smart-alecky*, snippy*, uncivil, unfilial, ungracious; SEE CONCEPTS 267,401

disrobe [v] *take off one's clothes*
bare, denudate, denude, deprive, dismantle, divest, doff, husk*, peel*, remove, shed, shuck*,

slip out of, strip, take it off, unbutton*, unclothe, uncover, undress; SEE CONCEPT *167*

disrupt [*v1*] *upset, disorganize*
agitate, bollix, confuse, disarray, discombobulate, discompose, disorder, disturb, mess up, mix up, muck up*, muddle, muddy the waters*, psych out*, put off, rattle, rattle one's cage*, rummage, screw up*, shake, spoil, throw, unsettle, upset the apple cart*; SEE CONCEPTS *16,84,234*

disrupt [*v2*] *break, interrupt*
breach, break into, break up, fracture, hole, interfere with, intrude, obstruct, open, rupture, unsettle, upset; SEE CONCEPTS *98,135*

disruptive [*adj*] *causing trouble, confusion*
disorderly, distracting, disturbing, obstreperous, off-base*, out-of-line*, out-of-order*, rowdy, troublemaking, troublesome, unruly, unsettling, upsetting; SEE CONCEPTS *401,537*

dissatisfaction [*n*] *discontent, unhappiness*
annoyance, anxiety, aversion, boredom, chagrin, complaint, desolation, disapproval, discomfort, discouragement, disfavor, disgruntlement, disinclination, dislike, disliking, dismay, displeasure, disquiet, disrelish, distaste, distress, ennui, envy, exasperation, fretfulness, frustration, heartburn, hopelessness, indisposition, irritation, jealousy, lamentation, malcontent, malcontentment, oppression, querulousness, regret, resentment, trouble, uneasiness, weariness, worry; SEE CONCEPTS *29,410*

dissatisfactory [*adj*] *unsatisfactory*
bad, damaged, deficient, disappointing, displeasing, distressing, inadequate, insufficient, junky*, lame, mediocre, no good, not satisfying, not up to par*, offensive, poor, rotten, unacceptable, unsatisfying, unsuitable, unworthy, useless; SEE CONCEPTS *529,558,570*

dissatisfied [*adj*] *discontented, unhappy*
annoyed, begrudging, bothered, complaining, crabby*, critical, disaffected, disappointed, disgruntled, displeased, ennuied, envious, faultfinding, fed-up*, fretful, fretting, frustrated, griping, grudging, grumbling, grumpy*, insatiable, irked, jaundiced, jealous, kvetching*, malcontent, malcontented, not satisfied, offended, picky, plaintive, put-out*, querulous, sniveling, sulky, sullen, unappeased, unassuaged, unfulfilled, ungratified, unsated, unsatisfied, vexed; SEE CONCEPT *403*

dissect [*v1*] *cut up; take apart*
anatomize, break up, cut, dichotomize, disjoin, disjoint, dislimb, dismember, dissever, divide, exscind, exsect, lay open, operate, part, prosect, quarter, section, sever, slice, sunder; SEE CONCEPTS *98,176*

dissect [*v2*] *analyze*
anatomize, break down, decompose, decompound, examine, explore, inquire about, inspect, investigate, resolve, scrutinize, study; SEE CONCEPT *24*

dissection [*n1*] *cutting up, particularly of a dead body*
anatomization, anatomy, autopsy, dismemberment, examination, necropsy, operation, postmortem, vivisection; SEE CONCEPTS *176,310*

dissection [*n2*] *thorough analysis*
breakdown, breakup, criticism, critique, examination, inquest, inspection, investigation, resolu-

tion, review, scrutiny, study; SEE CONCEPTS *24,290*

dissemble [*v*] *disguise, pretend*
affect, camouflage, cloak, conceal, counterfeit, cover, cover up, dissimulate, doublespeak*, double-talk*, dress up, fake, falsify, feign, four-flush*, hide, let on*, make like*, mask, pass, play possum*, pussyfoot*, put on a false front*, put on a front*, put on an act*, put up a front*, put up a smoke screen*, sham*, shroud, shuck and jive*, signify, simulate, stonewall*, whitewash*; SEE CONCEPTS *59,188,716*

disseminate [*v*] *distribute, scatter*
advertise, announce, annunciate, blaze, blazon, broadcast, circulate, declare, diffuse, disject, disperse, dissipate, proclaim, promulgate, propagate, publicize, publish, radiate, sow, spread, strew; SEE CONCEPTS *108,140,201,222*

dissemination [*n*] *distribution*
airing, broadcasting, circulation, diffusion, dissipation, promulgation, propagation, publication, publishing, spread; SEE CONCEPTS *651,746*

dissension [*n*] *conflict of opinion*
altercation, argument, bad vibes*, bickering, clinker*, contention, controversy, difference, disaccord, disagreement, discord, discordance, dispute, dissent, dissidence, disunity, faction, factionalism, flak*, friction, fuss, quarrel, scene, sour note*, static, strife, trouble, variance, wrangle; SEE CONCEPTS *46,278,665*

dissent [*n*] *disagreement, disapproval*
bone*, bone of contention*, bone to pick*, clinker*, conflict, contention, denial, difference, disaccord, discord, dissension, dissidence, disunity, far cry*, flak*, hassle, heresy, heterodoxy, misbelief, nonagreement, nonconcurrence, nonconformism, nonconformity, nope*, objection, opposition, poles apart*, protest, refusal, resistance, schism, sour note*, spat, split, strife, unorthodoxy, variance; SEE CONCEPTS *29,665,689*

dissent [*v*] *disagree*
argue, balk, break with, buck, contradict, decline, demur, differ, disaccord, discord, divide, fly in the face of*, object, oppose, pettifog, protest, put up a fight*, put up an argument, refuse, say not a chance*, say nothing doing*, say no way*, shy, stickle, vary, wrangle; SEE CONCEPTS *21,46*

dissertation [*n*] *scholarly thesis*
argumentation, commentary, critique, discourse, disputation, disquisition, essay, exposition, memoir, monograph, tractate, treatise; SEE CONCEPTS *271,287*

disservice [*n*] *unkindness*
bad turn, detriment, disfavor, harm, hurt, injury, injustice, insult, outrage, prejudice, wrong; SEE CONCEPTS *309,645,674*

dissidence [*n*] *difference of opinion*
bad vibes*, contention, disaccord, disagreement, discordance, disharmony, dispeace, dispute, dissension, dissent, feud, heresy, heterodoxy, misbelief, nonconformism, nonconformity, rupture, schism, sour note*, strife, unorthodoxy; SEE CONCEPTS *278,633,689*

dissident [*adj*] *disagreeing, differing*
discordant, dissentient, dissenting, heretical, heterodox, nonconformist, schismatic, sectarian, unorthodox; SEE CONCEPT *403*

dissident [*n*] *person who holds different belief*
agitator, dissenter, heretic, misbeliever, noncon-

di
di

formist, protester, rebel, recusant, schismatic, schismatist, sectary, separatist; SEE CONCEPTS *359,423*

dissimilar [*adj*] *not alike; not capable of comparison*
antithetical, antonymous, contradictory, contrary, different, disparate, distant, divergent, diverse, far cry*, heterogeneous, individual, like night and day*, march to a different drummer*, mismatched, mismated, not similar, offbeat, opposite, poles apart*, unequal, unique, unlike, unrelated, unsimilar, various, weird*; SEE CONCEPT *564*

dissimilarity [*n*] *unlikeness*
alterity, contrast, difference, discord, discordance, discrepancy, disparity, dissemblance, dissimilitude, distance, distinction, divarication, divergence, divergency, diversity, heterogeneity, incomparability, incongruity, inconsistency, inconsonance, nonuniformity, offset, otherness, separation, severance, unrelatedness, variance, variation; SEE CONCEPT *665*

dissimulate [*v*] *conceal, disguise*
beard*, camouflage, cloak, deceive, dissemble, dress up, fake, feign, hide, make-believe, mask, present a false face*, present a false front*, pretend; SEE CONCEPTS *59,172,188*

dissipate [*v1*] *expend, spend*
be wasteful with, blow*, burn up*, consume, deplete, dump*, fritter away, indulge oneself, kiss goodbye*, lavish, misspend, misuse, run through, squander, throw away, trifle away, use up, waste; SEE CONCEPTS *156,169*

dissipate [*v2*] *disappear*
dispel, disperse, dissolve, drive away, evanesce, evaporate, melt away, run dry, scatter, spread, vanish; SEE CONCEPTS *105,469*

dissipated [*adj1*] *used up*
blown, burnt out*, consumed, destroyed, exhausted, kaput*, played out*, scattered, spent, squandered, wasted; SEE CONCEPTS *560,576*

dissipated [*adj2*] *self-indulgent*
abandoned, corrupt, debauched, dissolute, gone bad*, gone to seed*, gone to the dogs*, hellbent*, intemperate, profligate, rakish, wicked; SEE CONCEPTS *401,545*

dissipation [*n1*] *amusement, entertainment, occasionally to excess*
bender*, binge, blow-out, bust*, celebration, circus, distraction, diversion, divertissement, gratification, party, recreation, self-indulgence, tear*, toot*, winging*; SEE CONCEPTS *363,386*

dissipation [*n2*] *wantonness*
abandonment, debauchery, dissoluteness, dissolution, drunkenness, evil, excess, extravagance, free-living, high-living*, indulgence, intemperance, lavishness, life in the fast lane*, prodigality, profligacy, self-gratification, squandering, to hell in handbasket*, waste; SEE CONCEPT *633*

dissipation [*n3*] *disappearance*
diffusion, disintegration, dispersal, dispersion, dissemination, dissolution, distribution, emission, extravagance, improvidence, radiation, scattering, spread, vanishing, wastage, waste; SEE CONCEPTS *230,651,720*

dissociate [*v*] *part company with; separate*
abstract, alienate, break off, detach, disassociate, disband, disconnect, disengage, disjoin, disperse, disrupt, distance, disunite, divide, divorce, estrange, isolate, quit, scatter, segregate, set apart, uncouple, unfix; SEE CONCEPTS *135,384*

dissociation [*n*] *detachment, separation*
break, disconnection, disengagement, disjunction, distancing, disunion, division, divorce, isolation, segregation, severance; SEE CONCEPT *388*

dissolute [*adj*] *lacking restraint, indulgent*
abandoned, corrupt, debauched, degenerate, depraved, dissipated, evil, fast*, fast and loose*, gone bad*, high living*, intemperate, in the fast lane*, lascivious, lax, lecherous, lewd, libertine, licentious, light, loose*, nighthawk*, night owl*, on the take*, open, player*, profligate, raffish, rakish, reprobate, slack, swift, sybaritic, unconstrained, unprincipled, unrestrained, vicious, wanton, wayward, wicked, wild; SEE CONCEPTS *401,545*

dissolution [*n1*] *separation, rupture*
breaking up, detachment, disintegration, disunion, division, divorce, divorcement, parting, partition, resolution, split-up; SEE CONCEPTS *230,388*

dissolution [*n2*] *death; destruction*
adjournment, conclusion, curtains, decay, decease, decomposition, defunction, demise, disappearance, disbandment, discontinuation, dismissal, dispersal, end, ending, evaporation, extinction, finish, liquefaction, melting, overthrow, passing, quietus, release, resolution, ruin, silence, sleep, solution, suspension, termination; SEE CONCEPTS *105,304,469,703*

dissolve [*v1*] *melt from solid to liquid; mix in*
defront, deliquesce, diffuse, fluidify, flux, fuse, liquefy, liquesce, render, run, soften, thaw, waste away; SEE CONCEPTS *469,702*

dissolve [*v2*] *disappear, disintegrate*
break down, break into pieces, break up, crumble, decline, decompose, diffuse, dilapidate, disband, disperse, dissipate, dwindle, evanesce, evaporate, fade, melt away, perish, separate, unmake, vanish, waste away; SEE CONCEPTS *105,469*

dissolve [*v3*] *annul, discontinue*
abrogate, adjourn, annihilate, break up, cancel, collapse, decimate, demolish, destroy, destruct, discharge, dismiss, disorganize, disunite, divorce, do away with, end, eradicate, invalidate, loose, overthrow, postpone, put an end to, quash, render void, repeal, resolve into, ruin, separate, sever, shatter, shoot, suspend, terminate, unmake, vacate, void, wind up, wrack, wreck; SEE CONCEPTS *121,234,252*

dissonance [*n1*] *disagreement*
antagonism, conflict, contention, controversy, difference, disaccord, discord, discrepancy, disharmony, disparity, dissension, dissidence, incongruity, inconsistency, strife, variance; SEE CONCEPTS *278,665,689*

dissonance [*n2*] *noise, discord*
cacophony, harshness, jangle, jarring, unmelodiousness; SEE CONCEPT *595*

dissonant [*adj1*] *different, conflicting*
anomalous, at variance, differing, disagreeing, disconsonant, discordant, discrepant, dissentient, incompatible, incongruent, incongruous, inconsistent, inconsonant, irreconcilable, irregular, sour note*, unmixable; SEE CONCEPT *564*

dissonant [*adj2*] *unharmonious*
cacophonic, cacophonous, discordant, disharmonic, disharmonious, grating, harsh, inhar-

monic, inharmonious, jangling, jarring, out of tune, raucous, strident, tuneless, unmelodious, unmusical; SEE CONCEPTS *592,594*

dissuade [*v*] *talk out of*
advise against, caution against, chicken out*, counsel, cry out against, deprecate, derail, deter, disadvise, discourage, disincline, divert, exhort, expostulate, faze, hinder, lean on*, persuade not to, prevent, prick, put off, remonstrate, throw a wet blanket on*, throw cold water on*, throw off, thwart, turn off*, urge not to, warn; SEE CONCEPTS *68,78*

distance [*n1*] *interval, range*
absence, ambit, amplitude, area, bit, breadth, compass, country mile*, expanse, extension, extent, farness, far piece*, gap, good ways*, heavens, hinterland, horizon, lapse, length, objective, orbit, outpost, outskirts, provinces, purlieu, purview, radius, reach, remoteness, remove, scope, separation, size, sky, space, span, spread, stretch, sweep, way, width; SEE CONCEPTS *651,739,790*

distance [*n2*] *aloofness*
coldness, coolness, frigidity, reserve, restraint, stiffness; SEE CONCEPT *633*

distance [*v*] *dissociate oneself; leave behind*
break away from the pack, outdo, outpace, outrun, outstrip, pass, put in proportion, separate oneself; SEE CONCEPT *195*

distant [*adj1*] *faraway*
abroad, abstracted, apart, a piece, arm's length*, asunder, away, backwoods, beyond range, far, far back, far-flung, far-off, farther, further, inaccessible, indirect, in the background, in the boonies*, in the distance, in the sticks*, isolated, middle of nowhere*, not home*, obscure, outlying, out of earshot*, out of range, out of reach, out-of-the-way, remote, removed, retired, secluded, secret, separate, sequestered, telescopic, unapproachable, ways*, wide of*, yonder*; SEE CONCEPTS *576,778*

distant [*adj2*] *aloof*
arrogant, ceremonious, cold, cool, formal, haughty, insociable, laid back, modest, offish, on ice*, proud, put on airs*, remote, reserved, restrained, reticent, retiring, shy, solitary, standoff, standoffish, stiff, stuck-up*, unapproachable, uncompanionable, unconcerned, unfriendly, unsociable, uppity*, withdrawn; SEE CONCEPTS *401,404*

distaste [*n*] *dislike, hate*
abhorrence, antipathy, aversion, detestation, disfavor, disgust, disinclination, displeasure, disrelish, dissatisfaction, hatred, horror, hostility, indisposition, loathing, repugnance, repulsion, revolt, revulsion; SEE CONCEPT *29*

distasteful [*adj*] *repulsive, unpleasant*
abhorrent, abominable, afflictive, bitter, detestable, disagreeable, dislikable, displeasing, flat, flavorless, galling, grievous, grody*, gross*, hateful, icky*, insipid, loathsome, nauseous, objectionable, obnoxious, odious, offensive, painful, repellent, repugnant, savorless, tasteless, unappetizing, undesirable, uninviting, unlikable, unpalatable, unsavory, yicky*, yucky*; SEE CONCEPTS *529,589,613*

distend [*v*] *bulge, swell*
amplify, augment, balloon, bloat, dilate, distort, enlarge, expand, increase, inflate, lengthen, puff, stretch, widen; SEE CONCEPTS *157,469,780*

distended [*adj*] *swollen*
bloated, bulging, enlarged, expanded, inflated, puffed out, puffy, stretched, tumescent, tumid, turgid; SEE CONCEPT *485*

distill [*v*] *make pure; draw out something*
boil down, brew, clarify, concentrate, condense, cook, cut, cut down, cut to the bone*, dribble, drip, drop, evaporate, express, extract, ferment, get to the meat*, infuse, precipitate, press, press out, purify, rarefy, rectify, refine, squeeze out, steam, sublimate, trickle, trim, vaporize, volatilize; SEE CONCEPTS *165,170,211,219*

distillation [*n*] *distillate*
cleansing, purification, refining; SEE CONCEPTS *165,367*

distinct [*adj1*] *apparent, obvious*
audible, categorical, clean-cut, clear, clear-cut, decided, definite, enunciated, evident, explicit, express, incisive, lucid, manifest, marked, noticeable, palatable, patent, perspicuous, plain, prescribed, recognizable, sharp, sharp-cut, specific, transparent, trenchant, unambiguous, unequivocal, unmistakable, well-defined; SEE CONCEPTS *535,591,619*

distinct [*adj2*] *different; unconnected*
detached, discrete, disparate, dissimilar, distinctive, disunited, divergent, diverse, especial, individual, offbeat, particular, peculiar, poles apart*, separate, separated, several, single, sole, special, specific, unassociated, unattached, unique, various; SEE CONCEPT *564*

distinction [*n1*] *differentiation; feature*
acumen, acuteness, alterity, analysis, characteristic, clearness, contrast, diagnosis, difference, differential, discernment, discrepancy, discreteness, discretion, discrimination, dissemblance, dissimilarity, dissimilitude, divergence, divergency, division, earmark, estimation, individuality, judgment, mark, marking, nicety, otherness, particularity, peculiarity, penetration, perception, qualification, quality, refinement, sensitivity, separation, sharpness, tact, unlikeness; SEE CONCEPTS *411,665*

distinction [*n2*] *prominence; achievement*
accolade, account, award, badge, bays, celebrity, consequence, credit, decoration, eminence, excellence, fame, flair, greatness, illustriousness, importance, kudos, laurels, manner, merit, name, note, perfection, preeminence, prestige, quality, rank, renown, reputation, repute, style, superiority, worth; SEE CONCEPTS *388,671,706*

distinctive [*adj*] *different, unique*
characteristic, cool, diacritic, diagnostic, discrete, distinguishing, excellent, extraordinary, far cry, gnarly*, idiosyncratic, individual, like night and day*, offbeat, original, outstanding, peculiar, perfect, poles apart*, proper, separate, single, singular, special, superior, typical, uncommon, unreal, weird, wicked; SEE CONCEPTS *564,574*

distinguish [*v1*] *tell the difference*
analyze, ascertain, categorize, characterize, classify, collate, decide, demarcate, determinate, determine, diagnose, diagnosticate, differentiate, discriminate, divide, estimate, extricate, figure out, finger*, identify, individualize, individuate, judge, know, label, make out, mark, mark off, name, part, pinpoint, place, qualify, recognize, select, separate, set apart, set off, sift, signalize, single out, singularize, sort out, specify, spot,

tag, tell apart, tell between, tell from; SEE CONCEPTS *15,18,38*

distinguish [v2] *discern, identify*
beam*, catch, descry, detect, dig, discover, discriminate, eye, eyeball*, flash*, focus, get a load of*, get an eyeful*, know, make out, mark, note, notice, observe, perceive, pick out, pick up on*, read, recognize, remark, see, spot, spy, take in, tell, view; SEE CONCEPTS *38,626*

distinguish [v3] *make famous*
acknowledge, admire, celebrate, dignify, honor, immortalize, pay tribute to, praise, signalize; SEE CONCEPT *69*

distinguished [adj] *famous, outstanding*
acclaimed, aristocratic, arresting, big name*, brilliant, celebrated, conspicuous, dignified, distingué, eminent, especial, esteemed, extraordinary, famed, foremost, glorious, great, highly regarded, honored, illustrious, imposing, marked, memorable, name, noble, nonpareil, notable, noted, noteworthy, peerless, prominent, remarkable, renowned, reputable, royal, salient, shining, signal, singular, special, stately, striking, superior, talked of, unforgettable, venerable, well-known; SEE CONCEPT *574*

distort [v] *deform; falsify*
alter, angle, belie, bend, bias, buckle, change, collapse, color, con, contort, crush, curve, deceive, decline, deteriorate, deviate, disfigure, doctor*, fake, fudge*, garble, gnarl, knot, lie, make out like, mangle, melt, misconstrue, misinterpret, misrepresent, misshape, pervert, phony up*, put one on, sag, scam*, slant, slump, snow*, torture, trump up*, twist, warp, whitewash*, wind, wrench, writhe; SEE CONCEPTS *63,137,232,250*

distortion [n] *deformity; falsification*
baloney*, bend, bias, BS*, buckle, coloring, contortion, crock, crookedness, exaggeration, intorsion, jazz*, jive*, lie, line, malconformation, malformation, misinterpretation, misrepresentation, misshape, misstatement, misuse, mutilation, perversion, slant, smoke*, story*, tall story*, torture, twist, twistedness, warp; SEE CONCEPTS *63,580*

distract [v] *divert attention; confuse*
abstract, addle, agitate, amuse, befuddle, beguile, bewilder, call away, catch flies*, confound, derange, detract, discompose, disconcert, disturb, divert, draw away, engross, entertain, fluster, frenzy, harass, lead astray*, lead away, madden, mislead, mix up, occupy, perplex, puzzle, sidetrack, stall, throw off*, torment, trouble, turn aside, unbalance, unhinge*; SEE CONCEPTS *14,16*

distraction [n] *having one's attention drawn away*
aberration, abstraction, agitation, amusement, beguilement, bewilderment, commotion, complication, confusion, disorder, dissipation, disturbance, diversion, divertissement, engrossment, entertainment, frenzy, game, interference, interruption, pastime, perplexity, preoccupation, recreation; SEE CONCEPTS *293,410,532,690*

distraught [adj] *very upset, worked-up*
addled, agitated, anxious, beside oneself, bothered, concerned, confused, crazed*, crazy, discomposed, distracted, distrait, distressed, flustered, frantic, harassed, hysterical, in a panic, like a chicken with its head cut off*, mad, muddled, nonplussed, nuts*, out of one's mind*,

overwrought, perturbed, rattled, raving, shook up, thrown*, tormented, troubled, unglued*, unscrewed*, unzipped*, wild, worried; SEE CONCEPTS *401,403,690*

distress [n1] *pain, agony*
ache, affliction, anguish, anxiety, bad news*, blues*, care, concern, cross, dejection, desolation, disappointment, discomfort, disquietude, dolor, embarrassment, grief, headache, heartache, heartbreak, irritation, malaise, misery, mortification, ordeal, pang, perplexity, sadness, shame, sorrow, stew, suffering, throe, torment, torture, trial, tribulation, trouble, twinge, unconsolability, unhappiness, vexation, visitation, woe, worriment, worry, wretchedness; SEE CONCEPTS *410,532,690,720,728*

distress [n2] *hardship, adversity*
bad luck, bummer*, calamity, can of worms*, catastrophe, crunch*, destitution, difficulty, disaster, downer*, drag*, exigency, hard knocks*, hard time*, holy mess*, hot water*, indigence, jam*, misfortune, need, pickle*, pinch*, poverty, privation, rigor, rotten luck*, scrape*, straits, throe, ticklish spot*, tough break*, tough luck*, trial, trouble, unholy mess*, vicissitude, want; SEE CONCEPT *674*

distress [v] *worry, upset*
afflict, aggrieve, agonize, ail, be on one's case*, bother, break, bug, burn up, depress, desolate, discombobulate*, disquiet, disturb, do a number on*, dog*, eat*, get*, get to*, give a hard time*, grieve, harass, harry, hound, hurt, injure, irk, irritate, make it tough for*, miff, nag, needle, nitpick, oppress, pain, peeve, perplex, pester, pick on, plague, push, push buttons*, rack, sadden, strain, strap, stress, tick off*, torment, torture, trouble, try, vex, weigh, wound; SEE CONCEPTS *7,19,313*

distressed [adj] *upset*
afflicted, agitated, all torn up*, antsy, anxious, basket case*, bothered, bugged, bummed out*, bundle of nerves*, concerned, cut up*, discombobulated*, disconsolate, distracted, distrait, distraught, dragged, exercised, fidgety, harassed, hyper*, in a stew*, in a tizzy*, inconsolable, jittery, jumpy, miffed, peeved, perturbed, ripped*, saddened, shaky, shook*, shook up*, shot down*, spooked*, strung out*, tormented, troubled, unconsolable, unglued*, up the wall*, uptight*, wired, worried, wrecked*, wretched; SEE CONCEPT *403*

distress signal [n] *alarm*
burglar alarm, call for help*, danger signal, fire alarm, mayday, SOS, warning signal; SEE CONCEPTS *269,463*

distribute [v1] *allocate, deliver, spread*
administer, allot, apportion, appropriate, assign, bestow, circulate, consign, convey, cut up, deal, deal out, diffuse, disburse, dish out*, dispense, disperse, dispose, disseminate, divide, divvy up*, dole out*, donate, endow, fork out*, give, give away, hand out, issue, lot out, measure out, mete, parcel, partition, pass out, pay out, present, prorate, radiate, ration, scatter, share, shell out*, slice up, sow, strew; SEE CONCEPTS *98,140,217*

distribute [v2] *classify*
arrange, assort, categorize, class, file, group, order; SEE CONCEPT *84*

distribution [n1] *allocation, dispersion*
administration, alloting, allotment, apportioning,

apportionment, assessment, assigning, circulating, circulation, dealing, delivery, diffusion, dispensation, dispersal, disposal, disposing, dissemination, dissipating, division, dole, handing out, handling, mailing, marketing, partition, partitioning, propagation, prorating, rationing, scattering, sharing, spreading, trading, transport, transportation; SEE CONCEPTS *98,140,217*

distribution [*n2*] *classification*
arrangement, assortment, disposal, disposition, grouping, location, order, ordering, organization, placement, sequence; SEE CONCEPTS *109,727*

distributor [*n*] *wholesaler*
dealer, jobber, merchandiser, middleperson, salesperson, trader; SEE CONCEPT *347*

district [*n*] *geographical area*
commune, community, department, locale, locality, neck of the woods*, neighborhood, parcel, parish, precinct, quarter, region, section, sector, stomping ground*, territory, turf*, vicinage, vicinity, ward; SEE CONCEPT *508*

distrust [*n*] *lack of faith in something*
disbelief, doubt, misdoubt, misgiving, mistrust, qualm, question, skepticism, suspicion, wariness; SEE CONCEPTS *21,689*

distrust [*v*] *be suspicious, skeptical of*
be wary of, disbelieve, discredit, doubt, misbelieve, mistrust, question, smell a rat*, suspect, wonder about; SEE CONCEPT *21*

distrustful [*adj*] *disbelieving*
been hit before*, cagey, cautious, chary, cynical, doubtful, doubting, dubious, fearful, jealous, leery, mistrustful, skeptical, suspicious, uneasy, uptight, wary; SEE CONCEPTS *403,542*

disturb [*v1*] *bother; upset*
afflict, agitate, ail, alarm, amaze, annoy, arouse, astound, badger, burn up*, complicate, confound, confuse, depress, discompose, dishearten, disrupt, distract, distress, excite, fluster, frighten, gall, grieve, harass, interfere, interrupt, intrude, irk, irritate, make uneasy, molest, muddle, outrage, pain, perplex, perturb, pester, pique, plague, provoke, puzzle, rattle, rouse, ruffle, shake, shake up*, startle, tire, trouble, unhinge*, unnerve, unsettle, vex, worry; SEE CONCEPTS *7,19*

disturb [*v2*] *disorder; dislocate*
confuse, derange, disarrange, disarray, discompose, disorganize, displace, distort, foul up*, interfere, jumble, louse up*, mess up, mix up, move, muddle, remove, replace, shift, tamper, unsettle, upset; SEE CONCEPTS *84,137,250*

disturbance [*n*] *commotion; upset*
agitation, annoyance, big scene*, big stink*, bother, brawl, brouhaha, clamor, confusion, convulsion, derangement, disarrangement, disorder, disruption, distraction, eruption, explosion, ferment, fisticuffs, flap, fracas, fray, fuss, hindrance, hubbub, hullabaloo*, insurrection, interruption, intrusion, molestation, perturbation, quake, quarrel, racket, rampage, restlessness, riot, ruckus, rumble, shock, spasm, stink*, stir*, storm, to-do*, tremor, tumult, turmoil, upheaval, uprising, uproar, violence; SEE CONCEPTS *388,410,674,720*

ditch [*n*] *gulley*
canal, channel, chase, cut, dike, drain, excavation, furrow, gutter, mine, moat, trench, watercourse; SEE CONCEPTS *509,513*

ditch [*v*] *get rid of*
abandon, desert, discard, dispose of, drop, dump*, eighty-six*, forsake, jettison, junk*, leave, reject, scrap*, throw away, throw out, throw overboard*; SEE CONCEPT *180*

ditsy [*adj*] *silly*
airbrained, airheaded, daffy*, dippy*, dipsy*, dizzy*, dopey, eccentric, empty, giddy, goofy*, inane, kooky*, rattlebrained, scatterbrained; SEE CONCEPTS *314,401*

ditto [*n*] *the same; duplicate*
clone, copy, double, duplication, facsimile, likewise, reproduction, the above, the very words*; SEE CONCEPTS *664,667,716*

ditty [*n*] *song*
ballad, composition, jingle, tune; SEE CONCEPT *595*

ditz [*n*] *scatterbrain*
airbrain, airhead, birdbrain*, dingbat*, fluffhead*, ninny, rattlebrain, silly person, space case; SEE CONCEPTS *412,423*

diva [*n*] *prima donna*
famous singer, lead singer, opera singer; SEE CONCEPT *352*

dive [*n1*] *descent, usually underwater*
belly flop*, dash, dip, duck, ducking, fall, header* headlong* jump, leap, lunge, nosedive, pitch, plunge, spring, submergence, submersion, swoop; SEE CONCEPTS *147,181,194*

dive [*n2*] *dirty, sleazy establishment*
bar, barroom, beer garden* cabaret, dump, flea trap*, flophouse*, hangout, hole, honky-tonk*, joint, lounge, night club, pool hall, pub, saloon, taproom, tavern; SEE CONCEPT *449*

dive [*v*] *descend, usually going underwater*
belly flop*, dip, disappear, drop, duck, fall, go headfirst, gutter, header*, jump, leap, lunge, nose-dive, pitch, plumb, plummet, plunge, spring, submerge, swoop, vanish, vault; SEE CONCEPTS *147,181,194*

diverge [*v1*] *go in different directions*
bend, bifurcate, branch, branch off, depart, deviate, digress, divagate, divaricate, divide, excurse, fork, part, radiate, ramble, separate, split, spread, stray, swerve, veer, wander; SEE CONCEPTS *195,738*

diverge [*v2*] *be different from; be at odds*
argue, conflict, contrast, depart, deviate, differ, digress, disagree, disapprove, dissent, oppose, stray, swerve, turn aside, vary, wander; SEE CONCEPTS *46,665*

divergence [*n*] *branching out; difference*
aberration, alteration, alterity, crotch, deflection, departure, detour, deviation, digression, disagreeing, discrepancy, disparity, dissemblance, dissimilarity, dissimilitude, distinction, divagation, divergency, diversity, division, fork, mutation, otherness, parting, radiation, ramification, separation, turning, unlikeness, variety, varying; SEE CONCEPTS *665,738*

divergent [*adj*] *differing*
aberrant, abnormal, anomalous, antithetical, atypical, conflicting, contradictory, contrary, deviating, different, disagreeing, disparate, dissimilar, dissonant, distant, diverging, diverse, factional, factious, irregular, off-key, opposite, poles apart*, separate, unlike, unequal, unlike, unnatural, unsimilar, untypical, variant, various; SEE CONCEPT *564*

di
di

diverse [*adj*] *different; various*
assorted, contradictory, contrary, contrasted, contrasting, contrastive, differing, discrete, disparate, dissimilar, distant, distinct, divergent, diversified, diversiform, incommensurable, like night and day*, manifold, miscellaneous, mixed bag*, multifarious, opposite, separate, several, sundry, unalike, unequal, unlike, varied, varying; SEE CONCEPTS *564,772*

diversify [*v*] *spread out; branch out*
alter, assort, change, expand, mix, modify, transform, variegate, vary; SEE CONCEPTS *232,697*

diversion [*n1*] *change in a course, path*
aberration, alteration, deflection, departure, detour, deviation, digression, divergence, fake out*, red herring*, turning, variation; SEE CONCEPTS *501,738*

diversion [*n2*] *entertainment, recreation*
amusement, ball, beguilement, delectation, delight, disport, dissipation, distraction, divertissement, enjoyment, field day*, frivolity, fun, fun and games*, game, gratification, grins*, high time*, hoopla*, laughs*, levity, merry-go-round*, pastime, picnic*, play, pleasure, relaxation, relish, sport, whoopee*; SEE CONCEPTS *292,363,386*

diversity [*n*] *variety, difference*
assortment, dissimilarity, distinction, distinctiveness, divergence, diverseness, diversification, heterogeneity, medley, mixed bag*, multeity, multifariousness, multiformity, multiplicity, range, unlikeness, variance, variegation, variousness; SEE CONCEPTS *651,665*

divert [*v1*] *turn a different direction*
alter, avert, change, deflect, modify, pivot, redirect, sheer, swerve, switch, turn aside, veer, volte-face, wheel, whip, whirl; SEE CONCEPTS *187,213*

divert [*v2*] *amuse, entertain*
beguile, break one up*, delight, fracture one*, get one's jollies*, gladden, gratify, knock 'em dead*, make happy, panic, please, put 'em away*, recreate, regale, relax, slay, tickle, wow; SEE CONCEPT *9*

divert [*v3*] *take attention away*
abstract, attract attention, bend the rules*, catch flies*, circumlocute, detach, deter, detract, disadvise, discourage, disengage, dissuade, distract, disturb, draw away, get around, lead astray, lead away, send on a wild-goose chase*, sidetrack, stall; SEE CONCEPTS *7,19,22*

divest [*v*] *dispossess; take off*
bankrupt, bare, bereave, bleed, denudate, denude, deprive, despoil, disinherit, dismantle, disrobe, ditch*, doff, dump, eighty-six*, lose, milk*, oust, plunder, remove, rob, seize, spoil, strip, take from, unclothe, uncover, undress, unload; SEE CONCEPTS *139,142,211*

divide [*v1*] *separate, disconnect*
abscind, bisect, branch, break, break down, carve, chop, cleave, cross, cut, cut up, demarcate, detach, dichotomize, disengage, disentangle, disjoin, dislocate, dismember, dissect, dissever, dissociate, dissolve, disunite, divorce, halve, intersect, isolate, loose, part, partition, pull away, quarter, rend, rupture, section, segment, segregate, sever, shear, split, subdivide, sunder, tear, unbind, undo; SEE CONCEPTS *98,135,137*

divide [*v2*] *distribute*
allocate, allot, apportion, articulate, cut, cut in*,

cut one in*, cut up, deal, deal out, disburse, dish out*, dispense, disperse, divvy up*, dole out*, factor, fork out*, go fifty-fifty*, hand out, hand over, lot out, measure out, parcel, partition, piece up, portion, prorate, quota, ration, share, shell out*, shift, slice, slice up, split up; SEE CONCEPTS *98,140*

divide [*v3*] *put in order; classify*
arrange, categorize, grade, group, separate, sort; SEE CONCEPT *84*

divide [*v4*] *disagree, alienate*
break up, cause to disagree, come between, differ, disaccord, dissent, disunite, estrange, part, pit against, separate, set against, set at odds*, sow dissension*, split, vary; SEE CONCEPTS *46,266*

dividend [*n*] *one's share, profit*
allotment, allowance, appropriation, bonus, carrot*, check, coupon, cut*, dispensation, divvy*, extra, gain, gravy*, guerdon, interest, lagniappe*, meed, pay, portion, premium, prize, proceeds, remittance, returns, reward, surplus, taste*; SEE CONCEPTS *337,344*

divination [*n*] *fortune-telling*
augury, clairvoyancy, horoscopy, occultism, palmistry, prediction, premonition, prognostication, prophecy, soothsaying; SEE CONCEPTS *70,278,689*

divine [*adj*] *godlike, perfect*
all-powerful, almighty, ambrosial, angelic, anointed, beatific, beautiful, blissful, celestial, consecrated, deific, deistic, eternal, exalted, excellent, glorious, godly, hallowed, heavenly, holy, immaculate, magnificent, marvelous, mystical, omnipotent, omnipresent, omniscient, rapturous, religious, sacramental, sacred, sacrosanct, sanctified, spiritual, splendid, superhuman, superlative, supernatural, supreme, theistic, transcendent, transcendental, transmundane, unearthly, wonderful; SEE CONCEPTS *568,574*

divine [*v*] *prophesy*
anticipate, apprehend, conjecture, deduce, discern, forebode, forefeel, foreknow, foresee, foretell, go out on a limb*, guess, infer, intuit, perceive, predict, previse, prognosticate, see, see in the cards*, suppose, surmise, suspect, take a shot*, take a stab*, understand, visualize; SEE CONCEPT *28*

divinity [*n*] *absolute being; divine nature*
celestial, deity, genius, god, goddess, godhead, godhood, godliness, godship, guardian spirit, higher power, holiness, lord, prime mover, sanctity, spirit; SEE CONCEPTS *368,370,689*

division [*n1*] *separation, disconnection*
analysis, apportionment, autopsy, bisection, breaking, breaking down, breaking up, carving, contrasting, cutting up, demarcation, departmentalizing, detaching, detachment, diagnosis, disjuncture, dismemberment, disparting, disseverance, dissolution, distinguishing, distribution, disunion, disuniting, dividing, divorce, parceling, parting, partition, reduction, rending, rupture, segmentation, selection, separating, severance, splitting up, subdivision, vivisection; SEE CONCEPTS *98,135*

division [*n2*] *something produced from separating*
affiliate, associate, border, boundary, branch, category, chunk, class, compartment, cut, degree,

demarcation, department, divide, dividend, divider, dividing line, divvy*, end, fraction, fragment, grouping, head, kind, lobe, lump, member, moiety, offshoot, parcel, partition, piece, piece of action*, portion, rake-off*, ramification, section, sector, segment, share, slice, sort, split, subdivision, wedge; SEE CONCEPTS *378,382,710,835*

division [*n3*] *breach, estrangement*
conflict, difference of opinion, difficulty, disaccord, disagreement, discord, disharmony, dispute, dissension, dissent, dissidence, dissonance, disunion, feud, rupture, split, trouble, variance, words; SEE CONCEPT *388*

divisive [*ad*] *dissenting*
alienating, at odds, discordant, disruptive; SEE CONCEPTS *401,537*

divorce [*n*] *split-up of marriage*
annulment, breach, break, breakup, decree nisi, dedomiciling, detachment, disparateness, dissociation, dissolution, disunion, division, divorcement, on the rocks*, parting of the ways*, partition, rupture, separate maintenance, separation, severance, split, splitsville*; SEE CONCEPT *297*

divorce [*v*] *split up a marriage*
annul, break up, cancel, disconnect, disjoin, dissever, dissociate, dissolve, disunite, divide, nullify, part, put away, separate, sever, split, sunder, unmarry; SEE CONCEPT *297*

divulge [*v*] *make known; confess*
admit, betray, blab, blow the whistle*, broadcast, communicate, cough up*, declare, disclose, discover, exhibit, expose, fess up*, give away, go public*, gossip, impart, leak, let hair down*, let slip*, mouth, open up*, own up*, proclaim, promulgate, publish, reveal, spill, spill the beans*, spring, tattle, tell, tip off*, uncover; SEE CONCEPT *60*

divvy up [*v*] *divide*
allocate, apportion, cut, cut up the pie*, dole out, go halves*, measure out, mete out, share, split; SEE CONCEPTS *98,140*

dizzy [*adj1*] *light-headed, confused*
addled, befuddled, bemused, bewildered, blind, blinded, dazed, dazzled, distracted, disturbed, dumb, dumbfounded, faint, gaga*, giddy, groggy*, hazy, light, muddled, off balance*, out of control*, punch-drunk*, punchy*, puzzled, reeling, shaky, slap-happy*, staggered, staggering, swimming*, tipsy, unsteady, upset, vertiginous, weak in the knees*, weak-kneed*, whirling, wobbly, woozy; SEE CONCEPTS *314,480*

dizzy [*adj2*] *flighty, scatterbrained*
capricious, changeable, crazy, empty-headed, fatuous, feather-brained, fickle, foolish, frivolous, giddy, harebrained, heady, inane, light-headed, silly, skittish, unstable; SEE CONCEPT *402*

DNA [*n*] *deoxyribonucleic acid*
chromosome, gene, genetic code, heredity, nucleic acid, RNA; SEE CONCEPT *648*

do [*v1*] *carry out*
accomplish, achieve, act, arrange, be responsible for, bring about, cause, close, complete, conclude, cook*, create, determine, discharge, do one's thing*, effect, end, engage in, execute, finish, fix, fulfill, get ready, get with it*, go for it*, look after, make, make ready, move, operate, organize, perform, prepare, produce, pull off*, see to, succeed, take care of business*, take on,

transact, undertake, wind up*, work, wrap up*; SEE CONCEPT *91*

do [*v2*] *be sufficient*
answer, avail, be adequate, be enough, be good enough for, be of use, be useful, give satisfaction*, pass muster*, satisfy, serve, suffice, suit; SEE CONCEPTS *646,656*

do [*v3*] *figure out, solve*
adapt, decipher, decode, interpret, puzzle out, render, resolve, translate, transliterate, transpose, work out; SEE CONCEPTS *15,37*

do [*v4*] *act, behave*
acquit oneself, appear, bear, carry, come on like*, comport, conduct, demean, deport, discourse, enact, fare, get along, get by, give, go on, impersonate, make out*, manage, muddle through*, operate, perform, personate, play, playact, portray, present, produce, put on*, quit, render the role, seem, stagger along*; SEE CONCEPT *633*

do [*v5*] *travel, visit*
cover, explore, journey, look at, pass through, stop in, tour, track, traverse; SEE CONCEPT *224*

do [*v6*] *cheat*
beat, bilk, chouse, con, cozen, deceive, defraud, dupe, fleece*, flimflam*, gyp*, hoax, overreach, swindle, take for a ride*, trick; SEE CONCEPT *59*

do away with [*v*] *get rid of; destroy*
abolish, bump off*, cancel, discard, discontinue, do in*, eliminate, exterminate, finish, kill, liquidate, murder, put an end to, put to death, remove, slaughter, slay, take away, wipe out*; SEE CONCEPTS *180,252*

docile [*adj*] *compliant, submissive*
accommodating, acquiescent, adaptable, agreeable, amenable, biddable, childlike, complacent, cool, docious, ductile, easily influenced, easy, easygoing, gentle, governable, humble, laid-back, manageable, meek, mellow, mild, obedient, obliging, orderly, pliable, pliant, quiet, resigned, soft, tame, teachable, tractable, usable, weak-kneed*, well-behaved, willing, yielding; SEE CONCEPTS *401,404*

dock [*n*] *waterfront*
berth, embarkment, harbor, jetty, landing, landing pier, levee, lock, marina, pier, quay, slip, wharf; SEE CONCEPT *439*

dock [*v*] *land on the waterfront*
anchor, berth, drop anchor, hook up, join, link up, moor, put in, rendezvous, tie up, unite; SEE CONCEPT *159*

docket [*n*] *program, agenda*
calendar, card, schedule, tab, tally, ticket, timetable; SEE CONCEPT *271*

doctor [*n*] *medical practitioner*
bones*, doc*, expert, general practitioner, healer, intern, MD, medic, medical person, medico, physician, professor*, quack*, scientist, specialist, surgeon; SEE CONCEPT *357*

doctor [*v1*] *fix up, treat*
administer, apply medication, attend, do up, fix, give treatment, medicate, mend, overhaul, patch up*, rebuild, recondition, reconstruct, repair, revamp, supply; SEE CONCEPTS *110,310*

doctor [*v2*] *adulterate, pervert*
add to, alter, change, cut, deacon, debase, dilute, disguise, dope up*, falsify, fudge*, gloss, load, misrepresent, mix with, sophisticate, spike*, tamper with, water down, weight; SEE CONCEPT *240*

di
do

doctrinaire [adj] *dogmatic, opinionated*
authoritarian, authoritative, biased, bigoted, bull-headed*, dictative, dictatorial, dogged, fanatical, impractical, inflexible, insistent, magisterial, mulish, obstinate, one-sided, pertinacious, pig-headed*, rigid, speculative, stiff-necked*, stubborn, unrealistic; SEE CONCEPTS *267,401*

doctrine [n] *opinion; principle*
article, article of faith, attitude, axiom, basic, belief, canon, concept, convention, conviction, credenda, creed, declaration, dogma, fundamental, gospel, implantation, inculcation, indoctrination, instruction, position, precept, pronouncement, propaganda, proposition, regulation, rule, statement, teaching, tenet, tradition, universal law, unwritten rule; SEE CONCEPTS *688,689*

document [n] *written communication*
archive, certificate, credentials, deed, diary, evidence, form, instrument, language, pages, paper, record, report, script, testimony, token; SEE CONCEPT *271*

documentary [n] *investigative report*
account, broadcast, docudrama, feature, film, information, narrative; SEE CONCEPTS *271,282*

dodder [v] *shake*
quiver, shiver, shudder, stagger, sway, teeter, totter, tremble, wobble; SEE CONCEPTS *150,152*

doddering [adj] *aged, feeble*
anile, decrepit, dotard, faltering, floundering, infirm, senile, shaky, tottering, trembling, unsteady, weak; SEE CONCEPTS *314,488,578,797*

dodge [n] *trick, feint*
contrivance, device, machination, method, plan, plot, ploy, ruse, scheme, stratagem, strategy, subterfuge, wile; SEE CONCEPT *660*

dodge [v] *avoid*
circumlocute, dark, deceive, ditch, duck, elude, equivocate, escape, evade, fence, fend off, fudge*, get around, get out of, give the slip*, hedge, juke, lurch, malinger, move to the side*, parry, pussyfoot*, put the move on*, shake, shake off*, shift, shirk, short-circuit, shuffle, sidestep, skip out on*, skirt, slide, slip, swerve, tergiversate, tergiverse, trick, turn aside, weasel*; SEE CONCEPTS *59,102*

doer [n] *go-getter*
achiever, busy person, dynamo*, energetic person, man of action, motivator, mover and shaker*, risk-taker, woman of action; SEE CONCEPT *706*

doff [v] *remove*
cast off, discard, disrobe, peel, put aside, shed, shuck, slip off, strip, take off, undress; SEE CONCEPTS *211,453*

do for [v1] *destroy*
defeat, deprive, finish, kill, ruin, shatter, slaughter, slay; SEE CONCEPTS *238,252*

do for [v2] *help*
abet, aid, assist, benefact, care for, help out, lend a hand*, look after, provide for, steady, support; SEE CONCEPT *110*

dog [n] *canine mammal*
bitch, bowwow*, cur, doggy, fido*, flea bag*, hound, man's best friend*, mongrel, mutt, pooch*, pup, puppy, stray, tail-wagger*, tyke; SEE CONCEPT *400*

dog [v] *chase after; bother*
bedog, haunt, hound, plague, pursue, shadow, tag, tail, track, trail, trouble; SEE CONCEPT *207*

dog-eat-dog [adj] *competitive*
aggressive, brutal, cutthroat, every person for themselves*, fierce, ruthless, vicious; SEE CONCEPT *542*

dogged [adj] *determined, persistent*
adamant, bullheaded*, firm, hanging tough*, hardheaded*, hard-nosed*, indefatigable, inexorable, inflexible, insistent, mulish, obdurate, obstinate, perseverant, perseverative, persevering, pertinacious, pigheaded*, relentless, resolute, rigid, single-minded, staunch, steadfast, steady, stubborn, tenacious, tough nut*, unbending, unflagging, unshakable, unyielding; SEE CONCEPTS *401,542*

dogleg [n] *bend*
curve, hairpin curve, sharp turn; SEE CONCEPT *436*

dogma [n] *belief, principle*
article, article of faith, canon, conviction, credenda, credo, creed, doctrine, gospel, opinion, persuasion, precept, rule, teachings, tenet, view; SEE CONCEPTS *688,689*

dogmatic [adj1] *dictatorial, opinionated*
arbitrary, arrogant, assertive, bigoted, bullheaded*, categorical, cocksure*, confident, definite, despotic, determined, dictative, doctrinaire, domineering, downright, egotistical, emphatic, fanatical, fascistic, formal, high and mighty*, imperious, intolerant, magisterial, narrow-minded, obdurate, obstinate, one-sided, overbearing, peremptory, pigheaded*, prejudiced, stiff-necked, stubborn, tenacious, tyrannical, unequivocal, wrong-headed; SEE CONCEPTS *267, 542*

dogmatic [adj2] *based on absolute truth*
a priori, as a matter of course, assertive, authoritarian, authoritative, axiomatic, by fiat, by natural law, by nature, canonical, categorical, deducible, deductive, derivable, doctrinaire, doctrinal, eternal, excathedra, formal, imperative, inevitable, on faith, oracular, orthodox, peremptory, positive, pragmatic, prophetic, reasoned, systematic, theoretical, unchangeable, unerring, unqualified; SEE CONCEPTS *530,567,582*

do-gooder [n] *idealist*
altruist, bleeding heart, good Samaritan, humanitarian, philanthropist, volunteer; SEE CONCEPTS *416,423*

do in [v] *destroy; exhaust*
assassinate, bankrupt, bump off*, butcher*, cool*, dilapidate, dispatch, do away with*, eliminate, execute, fatigue, finish, frazzle*, kill, knock out*, liquidate, murder, put away*, ruin, shatter, slaughter, slay, tire, wear out, weary, wreck; SEE CONCEPTS *137,250,252*

doing [n] *achievement*
accomplishing, accomplishment, achieving, act, action, carrying out, deed, execution, exploit, handiwork, implementation, performance, performing, thing; SEE CONCEPT *706*

doings [n] *actions*
acts, affairs, deal, deed, events, goings-on, happenings, matters, proceeding; SEE CONCEPT *1*

doldrums [n] *depression*
apathy, black mood*, blahs*, blue funk*, blues*, boredom, bummer*, dejection, disinterest, dismals, downer, dullness, dumps*, ennui, funk*, gloom, inactivity, indifference, inertia, lassitude, letdown, listlessness, malaise, mopes*, slump,

stagnation, stupor, tedium, torpor, yawn*; SEE CONCEPT *410*

dole [n] *allowance, allocation*
allotment, alms, apportionment, benefit, charity, dispensation, distribution, division, donation, gift, grant, gratuity, handout, living wage, mite, modicum, parcel, pittance, portion, quota, relief, share, subsistence, trifle; SEE CONCEPTS *337,344*

doleful [adj] *depressing*
afflicted, cast down, cheerless, crestfallen, dejected, depressed, dirgeful, dismal, dispirited, distressing, dolent, dolorous, down, downcast, downhearted, down in the mouth*, dreary, forlorn, funereal, gloomy, grieving, lamentable, lugubrious, melancholy, mournful, painful, piteous, pitiful, plaintive, rueful, sad, somber, sorrowful, woebegone, woeful, wretched; SEE CONCEPTS *403,529*

dole out [v] *allocate, distribute*
administer, allot, apportion, assign, deal, deal out, dispense, disperse, divide, divvy*, give, hand out, lot, measure, mete, mete out, parcel, partition, share, share out; SEE CONCEPTS *108,140*

doll [n1] *toy person*
baby, dolly, effigy, figure, figurine, manikin, marionette, model, moppet*, puppet; SEE CONCEPT *446*

doll [n2] *generous person*
darling, decent person, helpful person, honey*, prince*, sweetheart, sweetie; SEE CONCEPTS *296,423*

doll [n3] *attractive woman*
angel, babe*, bathing beauty, beauty queen, broad*, bunny*, centerfold, chick*, cover girl, cupcake*, cutie, cutie-pie*, dish*, dollface, dreamboat*, dream girl, fox*, glamour girl, good-looking woman, honey*, hot dish*, hot number*, peach*, pin-up, raving beauty, sex bunny*, sex kitten*, sexpot*, tomato*; SEE CONCEPTS *415,424*

dollar [n] *paper money*
ace*, bank note, bill, buck*, certificate, clam*, cucumber*, currency, folding money, greenback*, legal tender, note, one-spot*, single; SEE CONCEPT *340*

dollop [n] *lump*
bit, blob, glob, gob, mass, piece, portion; SEE CONCEPTS *432,786,835*

doll up [v] *beautify oneself; dress up*
deck out*, fix up, gussy up*, preen, primp, put on best clothes, smarten up*, spiff*, spruce up*; SEE CONCEPTS *162,167,202*

dolly [n] *handtruck*
carrier, cart, pushcart; SEE CONCEPTS *499,505*

dolor [n] *misery, anguish*
agony, distress, grief, heartache, heartbreak, passion, ruth, sadness, sorrow, suffering; SEE CONCEPT *410*

dolorous [adj] *miserable, anguished*
afflicted, afflictive, calamitous, deplorable, dire, distressing, doleful, dolent, dolesome, grievous, harrowing, heart-rending, lamentable, lugubrious, melancholy, mournful, painful, plaintive, regrettable, rueful, ruthful, sad, sorrowful, woebegone, woeful, wretched; SEE CONCEPTS *401,403*

dolt [n] *stupid person*
airhead*, blockhead*, boob*, chump*, dimwit*, dodo*, dope, dork*, dumbbell*, dumdum*, dunce, fool, goon*, idiot, ignoramus, lamebrain*, lunkhead*, meathead*, nitwit*, sap*, simpleton, stupid, yo-yo*; SEE CONCEPTS *412,423*

domain [n] *area of expertise, rule*
authority, bailiwick, concern, demesne, department, discipline, district, dominion, empire, estate, field, home park*, jurisdiction, land, neck of the woods*, occupation, orbit*, power, province, quarter, realm, region, scope, slot, specialty, sphere, stomping grounds*, terrain, territory, turf, walk, wing; SEE CONCEPTS *349,518,710*

dome [n] *arched part of ceiling*
arcade, arch, bubble, bulge, covering, cupola, mosque, roof, span, top, vault; SEE CONCEPT *440*

domestic [adj1] *household*
calm, devoted, domiciliary, family, home, homelike, home-loving, homely, indoor, pet, private, sedentary, settled, stay-at-home, subdued, submissive, tame, trained, tranquil; SEE CONCEPT *542*

domestic [adj2] *not foreign*
handcrafted, home-grown, homemade, indigenous, inland, internal, intestine, intramural, municipal, national, native; SEE CONCEPTS *536,549*

domesticate [v] *tame; habituate*
acclimatize, accustom, break, break in, breed, bring up, bust, corral, domiciliate, familiarize, gentle, herd, hitch, housetrain, naturalize, raise, reclaim, round up, subdue, teach, train, yoke; SEE CONCEPTS *202,285*

domesticity [n] *home life*
domestication, family life, staying at home; SEE CONCEPT *516*

domestic partner [n] *live-in significant other*
beneficiary, cohabitant, companion, housemate, longtime companion, lover, partner, spouse; SEE CONCEPT *414*

domicile [n] *human habitat*
abode, accommodation, apartment, castle, commorancy, condo*, condominium, co-op, crash pad*, dump, dwelling, habitation, home, house, joint, legal residence, mansion, pad*, rack*, residence, residency, roof over head*, roost*, settlement; SEE CONCEPTS *439,516*

dominance [n] *supremacy*
ascendancy, authority, command, control, domination, dominion, government, influence, paramountcy, power, preeminence, preponderance, prepotence, prepotency, rule, sovereignty, sway, upper hand, whip hand; SEE CONCEPTS *376,668*

dominant [adj1] *superior, controlling*
ascendant, assertive, authoritative, bossy, chief, commanding, demonstrative, despotic, domineering, effective, first, foremost, governing, imperative, imperious, leading, main, obtaining, outweighing, overbalancing, overbearing, overweighing, paramount, powerful, predominant, predominate, preeminent, preponderant, presiding, prevailing, prevalent, principal, regnant, reigning, ruling, sovereign, supreme, surpassing, transcendent; SEE CONCEPT *574*

dominant [adj2] *main, primary*
capital, chief, influential, major, number one*, outstanding, paramount, predominant, preeminent, prevailing, prevalent, principal, prominent, stellar; SEE CONCEPT *568*

dominate [v1] *govern, rule*
boss, call the shots*, command, control, detract from, dictate, direct, domineer, eclipse, handle,

do
do

have one's way*, have upper hand*, head, hold sway over*, influence, keep under thumb*, lay down the law*, lead, lead by the nose*, manage, monopolize, outshine, overbear, overrule, overshadow, play first fiddle*, predominate, preponderate, prevail, prevail over, reign, rule the roost*, run, run the show*, sit on top of*, subject, subjugate, superabound, sway, tyrannize; SEE CONCEPTS *94,117,298*

dominate [*v2*] *tower above*
bestride, look down upon, loom over, overlie, overlook, overtop, stand over, survey; SEE CONCEPTS *741,752*

domination [*n*] *control; subjection*
ascendancy, authority, command, despotism, dictatorship, dominance, dominion, influence, jurisdiction, might, oppression, power, preponderancy, prepotence, prepotency, repression, rule, sovereignty, strings*, subordination, superiority, suppression, supremacy, sway, tyranny; SEE CONCEPT *376*

domineer [*v*] *oppress; assume authority*
be in the saddle*, bend, bluster, boss around*, browbeat, bulldoze*, bully*, call the shots*, dominate, hector, henpeck*, in the driver's seat*, intimidate, keep under thumb*, kick around*, lead by the nose*, menace, overbear, predominate, preponderate, prevail, push the buttons*, reign, rule, rule the roost*, run the show*, run things*, swagger, threaten, throw weight around*, tyrannize; SEE CONCEPTS *14,94*

domineering [*adj*] *oppressive, authoritarian*
arrogant, autocratic, bossy, coercive, crack the whip*, despotic, dictatorial, egotistic, high-handed, imperative, imperial, imperious, in driver's seat*, insolent, iron-handed*, on high horse*, overbearing, peremptory, tyrannical; SEE CONCEPT *401*

dominion [*n*] *area of rule; authority*
ascendancy, authorization, bailiwick, command, commission, control, country, demesne, district, domain, dominance, domination, empire, enclave, field, government, jurisdiction, management, power, preeminence, prepotence, prepotency, prerogative, privilege, property, province, realm, regency, regiment, regimentation, region, reign, rule, seniority, sovereignty, sphere, state, stomping grounds*, supremacy, sway, terrain, territory, turf, walk; SEE CONCEPTS *198,376,710*

donate [*v*] *make a gift of*
accord, ante up*, award, bequeath, bestow, chip in*, confer, contribute, devote, dole out*, do one's part*, feed the kitty*, get in the act*, get it up*, give, give away, grant, hand out, lay on, pass the hat*, present, provide, subscribe, sweeten the pot*; SEE CONCEPT *108*

donation [*n*] *gift*
a hand*, aid, allowance, alms, appropriation, assistance, benefaction, beneficence, bequest, boon, charity, contribution, dole, do one's part*, endowment, gifting, grant, gratuity, handout, help, helping hand* largess, lump, offering, philanthropy, pittance, present, presentation, ration, relief, subscription, subsidy, subvention, write-off*; SEE CONCEPTS *337,340*

done [*adj1*] *accomplished, finished*
all in*, all over*, a wrap*, brought about, brought to pass, buttoned up*, compassed, complete, completed, concluded, consummated, de-

pleted, down, drained, effected, effete, ended, executed, exhausted, fixed, fulfilled, over, perfected, performed, realized, rendered, set, spent, succeeded, terminated, through, used up, wired, wrought; SEE CONCEPTS *528,531*

done [*adj2*] *thoroughly cooked*
baked, boiled, brewed, broiled, browned, crisped, fried, ready, stewed; SEE CONCEPTS *462,613*

done [*adj3*] *approved, agreed upon*
compacted, determined, okay, settled, you're on*; SEE CONCEPT *558*

done for [*adj*] *beaten, defeated*
broken, conquered, dashed, destroyed, doomed, finished, foiled, lost, ruined, through, undone, vanquished, washed-up*, wrecked; SEE CONCEPTS *537,570*

done in [*adj*] *exhausted*
all in*, bushed*, dead, depleted, done, effete, fagged, far-gone*, on last leg*, ready to drop*, spent, tired, used up, washed-out*, weary, worn-out; SEE CONCEPTS *314,485*

Don Juan [*n*] *ladies' man*
Casanova*, charmer, lady-killer*, libertine, lover, philanderer, playboy, Romeo*, seducer, skirt chaser, smooth operator, stud, woman chaser; SEE CONCEPT *423*

donkey [*n*] *small domestic horselike mammal*
ass, burro, horse, jackass, jennet, jenny, maud, moke, mule, neddy, pony, Rocky Mountain canary*; SEE CONCEPT *400*

donnybrook [*n*] *brawl*
battle royal, fight, fracas, fray, free-for-all, hoedown*, melee, rhubarb*, riot, row, rumble, shindig, slugfest*, turmoil, uproar; SEE CONCEPTS *46,106*

donor [*n*] *giver of gift*
almsgiver, altruist, angel*, backer, benefactor, benefactress, bestower, conferrer, contributor, donator, grantor, heavy hitter*, patron, philanthropist, presenter, Santa Claus*, savior, subscriber; SEE CONCEPTS *359,423*

do-nothing [*n*] *bum*
couch potato*, goof-off*, idler, lazybones, lazy person, loafer, moocher, slacker; SEE CONCEPTS *412,423*

doodad [*n*] *gadget*
contraption, contrivance, doohickey*, gismo, object, thing, thingamabob*, thingamajig*, whatchamacallit*, widget; SEE CONCEPTS *463, 499*

doohickey [*n*] *gadget*
contraption, contrivance, doodad*, gismo, object, thing, thingamabob*, thingamajig*, whatchamacallit*, widget; SEE CONCEPTS *463,499*

doom [*n*] *fate or decision, usually unpleasant*
annihilation, calamity, cataclysm, catastrophe, circumstance, conclusion, condemnation, death, decree, destination, destiny, destruction, disaster, downfall, end, fixed future, foreordination, fortune, handwriting on wall*, judgment, Judgment Day, karma, kismet, lap of the gods*, lot, Moira, opinion, portion, predestination, predetermination, ruin, sentence, tragedy, verdict, way the ball bounces*, way the cookie crumbles*; SEE CONCEPT *679*

doomed [*adj*] *condemned, hopeless*
bedeviled, bewitched, convicted, cursed, cut down, damned, dead duck*, destroyed, done,

done for*, fated, foreordained, ill-fated, ill-omened, in the cards*, kiss of death*, lost, luckless, menaced, overthrown, overwhelmed, predestined, que sera sera*, reprobate, ruined, sentenced, star-crossed, sunk, suppressed, threatened, thrown down, undone, unfortunate, unredeemed, wrecked; SEE CONCEPT 537

doomsayer [n] *alarmist*
Chicken Little, doom merchant, pessimist, scaremonger; SEE CONCEPTS 412,423

door [n] *entrance to room, building*
aperture, egress, entry, entryway, exit, gate, gateway, hatch, hatchway, ingress, opening, portal, postern, slammer; SEE CONCEPT 440

doorbell [n] *chime*
buzzer, door knocker, ringer; SEE CONCEPTS 74,284,529,685

do out of [v] *cheat*
balk, beat out of*, bilk, con, deceive, deprive, steal, swindle, trick; SEE CONCEPTS 59,139

doozy [n] *winner*
beauty, humdinger*, killer*, lulu*, smash hit, something; SEE CONCEPTS 366,416

dope [n1] *stupid person*
ass, blockhead*, dimwit*, dolt, donkey*, dunce, fool, idiot, lame-brain*, simpleton; SEE CONCEPTS 412,423

dope [n2] *drug*
narcotic, opiate, stimulant; SEE CONCEPT 307

dope [n3] *inside news*
account, details, developments, facts, info*, information, knowledge, lowdown*, tip*; SEE CONCEPT 274

dope [v] *drug someone*
adulterate, anesthetize, deaden, debase, inject, knock out*, load, narcotize, put to sleep, sedate, soak, sophisticate, stupefy; SEE CONCEPTS 156,310

dopey [adj] *stupid*
comatose, dense, dumb, foolish, heavy, hebetudinous, idiotic, lethargic, senseless, silly, simple, slow, sluggish, slumberish, thick, torpid; SEE CONCEPT 402

dormant [adj] *inactive; sleeping*
abeyant, asleep, closed down, comatose, down, fallow, hibernating, inert, inoperative, latent, lethargic, lurking, on the shelf*, out of action*, passive, potential, prepatent, quiescent, sidelined, slack, sluggish, slumbering, smoldering, suspended, torpid; SEE CONCEPT 539

dormitory [n] *living quarters*
bedroom, dorm, dorm room, sleeping quarters; SEE CONCEPT 448

dose [n] *portion of drug or other consumable*
application, dosage, dram, draught, fill, fix*, hit*, lot, measure, measurement, nip*, potion, prescription, quantity, share, shot*, slug*, spoonful; SEE CONCEPTS 307,835

dossier [n] *file*
archives, information, personal account, portfolio, profile, record, recorded information, report, summary; SEE CONCEPTS 271,281

dot [n] *tiny mark, drop*
atom, circle, dab, droplet, fleck, flyspeck, grain, iota, jot, mite, mote, particle, period, pinpoint, point, speck, spot, tittle; SEE CONCEPTS 284,831

dot [v] *make spot(s)*
bespeckle, dab, dabble, fleck, freckle, pepper, pimple, sprinkle, stipple, stud; SEE CONCEPTS 79,174

dotage [n] *feebleness, old age*
advanced age, decrepitude, elderliness, fatuity, imbecility, infirmity, second childhood*, senectitude, senility, weakness; SEE CONCEPTS 405,715

dote on/dote upon [v] *lavish affection on*
admire, adore, be fond of, be infatuated with, be sweet on*, cherish, enjoy, fancy, hold dear, idolize, like, love, pet, prize, treasure, worship; SEE CONCEPT 32

doting [adj] *indulgent; serving*
adoring, affectionate, devoted, fascinated, fatuous, fond, foolish, lovesick, lovesome, loving, silly, simple, struck; SEE CONCEPT 401

dotty [adj] *crazy*
absurd, daft, demented, disturbed, eccentric, foolish, goofy*, loony*, mentally unbalanced, nuts*, nutty, odd, peculiar, queer, ridiculous, strange, twisted, unconventional, weird; SEE CONCEPT 403

double [adj] *in a pair*
as much again, bifold, binary, binate, coupled, dual, dualistic, duple, duplex, duplicate, duplicated, geminate, paired, repeated, second, twice, twin, twofold, two times; SEE CONCEPT 771

double [n] *something which exactly resembles another*
angel, clone, companion, coordinate, copy, counterpart, dead ringer*, duplicate, image, impersonator, lookalike*, match, mate, picture, portrait, reciprocal, replica, ringer*, simulacrum, spitting image*, stand-in*, twin; SEE CONCEPTS 664,716

double [v] *make two of; make twice as large*
amplify, augment, dualize, dupe, duplicate, duplify, enlarge, fold, grow, increase, infold, loop, magnify, multiply, plait, pleat, plicate, redouble, repeat, replicate, supplement; SEE CONCEPTS 236,245

double back [v] *reverse path*
backtrack, circle, dodge, loop, retrace one's steps, return, turn; SEE CONCEPTS 224,232

double-cross [v] *betray*
beguile, bluff, cheat, con, cross, deceive, defraud, four-flush*, hoodwink*, humbug*, illude, juggle, mislead, sell, sell out*, split, swindle, take in, trick, two-time*; SEE CONCEPTS 7,19,59

double-dealing [adj] *cheating, deceitful*
ambidextrous, crooked, dishonest, double, duplicitous, fraudulent, hypocritical, insincere, left-handed*, lying, perfidious, sneaky, swindling, treacherous, tricky, two-faced*, two-timing*, underhanded, untrustworthy, wily; SEE CONCEPT 401

double-dealing [n] *betrayal, cheating*
bad faith, chicane, chicanery, deceit, deception, dishonesty, duplicity, foul play*, fourberie, fraud, hanky-panky*, hypocrisy, mendacity, perfidy, sharp practice*, treachery, trickery, two-timing*; SEE CONCEPT 59

double entendre [n] *play on words*
ambiguity, amphibiology, double meaning, equivocality, equivocation, equivoque, innuendo, joke, pun, tergiversation; SEE CONCEPTS 278,682

double standard [n] *contrasting principles*
contradictory standard, two sets of rules; SEE CONCEPTS 46,278,665

double-talk [n] *nonsense communicated*
amphibiology, balderdash, baloney*, bull*, dri-

do
do

vel, equivocation, flimflam*, gibberish, jazz*, mumbo jumbo*, rigmarole; SEE CONCEPT *278*

doubt [*n*] *lack of faith, conviction; questioning*
agnosticism, ambiguity, apprehension, confusion, demurral, difficulty, diffidence, dilemma, disbelief, discredit, disquiet, distrust, dubiety, dubiousness, faithlessness, faltering, fear, hesitancy, hesitation, incertitude, incredulity, indecision, irresolution, lack of confidence, misgiving, mistrust, perplexity, problem, qualm, quandary, rejection, reluctance, scruple, skepticism, suspense, suspicion, uncertainty, vacillation, wavering; SEE CONCEPTS *21,410,689,690*

doubt [*v*] *lack confidence in; question*
be apprehensive of, be curious, be dubious, be in a quandary, be puzzled, be uncertain, be undetermined, call in question, challenge, demur, disbelieve, discredit, dispute, distrust, fear, fluctuate, give no credence, harbor suspicion, have qualms, hesitate, imagine, impugn, insinuate, misdoubt, misgive, mistrust, not buy*, query, read differently, scruple, shilly-shally*, skepticize, smell a rat*, surmise, suspect, take dim view of, vacillate, waver, wonder at; SEE CONCEPT *21*

doubter [*n*] *person who does not believe*
agnostic, cynic, disbeliever, headshaker*, questioner, skeptic, unbeliever, zetetic; SEE CONCEPTS *361,423*

doubtful [*adj1*] *questionable, unclear*
ambiguous, borderline, chancy, clouded, contingent, debatable, dicey, disreputable, doubtable, dubious, dubitable, equivocal, far-fetched, fat chance, fishy*, hazardous, hazy, iffy*, impugnable, inconclusive, indecisive, indefinite, indeterminate, indistinct, insecure, long shot*, obscure, on thin ice*, open, pending, precarious, problematic, shady, sneaky*, speculative, suspect, suspicious, touch-and-go*, touchy, uncertain, unconfirmed, undecided, uneasy, unsettled, unstable, unsure, up for grabs*; SEE CONCEPTS *529,535*

doubtful [*adj2*] *not believing*
agnostic, baffled, confused, discomposed, disconcerted, distracted, distrustful, disturbed, doubting, dubious, equivocal, faithless, faltering, flustered, hesitant, hesitating, in a quandary, in clouds*, indecisive, in dilemma, irresolute, like doubting Thomas*, lost, not following, of two minds*, perplexed, puzzled, questioning, skeptical, suspicious, tentative, theoretical, troubled, uncertain, unconvinced, undecided, unresolved, unsettled, unsure, vacillating, wavering, without belief; SEE CONCEPTS *403,542*

doubting Thomas [*n*] *skeptic*
disbeliever, doubter, questioner, unbeliever; SEE CONCEPTS *361,423*

doubtless [*adv*] *certainly; most likely*
absolutely, apparently, assuredly, clearly, easily, for sure, indisputably, no ifs ands or buts*, of course, ostensibly, positively, precisely, presumably, probably, seemingly, supposedly, surely, truly, undoubtedly, unequivocally, unquestionably, without doubt; SEE CONCEPTS *535,552*

dough [*n*] *money*
beans*, boodle*, bread*, bucks*, cabbage*, cash, change, chips, clams*, coin, coinage, cold cash, currency, dinero, funds, greenback*, hard cash*, legal tender, lettuce*, loot, moola, pesos*, wealth; SEE CONCEPT *340*

doughnut [*n*] *sweet ring-shaped fried cake*
bun, cruller, danish, dunker*, pastry, sinker*, sweet roll; SEE CONCEPTS *457,461*

do up [*v*] *physically prepare; fix*
clean, doctor, enclose, finish, gift-wrap, launder, mend, overhaul, package, patch, rebuild, recondition, reconstruct, repair, revamp, wash, wrap; SEE CONCEPTS *126,165,182,202*

dour [*adj*] *gloomy, grim*
bleak, crabbed, dismal, dreary, forbidding, glum, hard, harsh, morose, saturnine, severe, sour, stringent, sulky, sullen, surly, ugly, unfriendly; SEE CONCEPTS *401,542*

douse [*v*] *drench, extinguish with liquid*
blow out, deluge, drown, duck, dunk, immerse, plunge, put out, quench, saturate, slop, slosh, smother, snuff, snuff out, soak, sop, souse, spatter, splash, splatter, squench, steep, submerge, submerse, wet; SEE CONCEPTS *250,256*

dovetail [*v*] *link, fit together*
accord, agree, check out, coincide, conform, correspond, go, harmonize, interlock, jibe, join, match, mortise, square, sync*, sync up*, tally, tenon, unite; SEE CONCEPTS *113,664*

dowdy [*adj*] *poorly dressed; old-fashioned*
antiquated, archaic, baggy, bedraggled, blowsy*, bygone, dated, dingy, drab, dull, frowzy*, frumpy*, homely, moldy, old hat*, outdated, outmoded, out-of-date, passé, plain, run-down, scrubby*, shabby, slatternly, sloppy, slovenly, stodgy, tacky, tasteless, unfashionable, unkempt, unseemly, unstylish, untidy, vintage, wrinkled; SEE CONCEPT *589*

do without [*v*] *get along without*
abstain from, dispense, endure, forgo, give up; SEE CONCEPTS *23,646*

down [*adj1/adv*] *below; physically lower*
bottomward, cascading, declining, depressed, descending, downgrade, downhill, downward, dropping, earthward, falling, gravitating, groundward, inferior, nether, precipitating, sagging, sinking, sliding, slipping, slumping, subjacent, to the bottom, under, underneath; SEE CONCEPTS *583,586,735*

down [*adj2*] *unhappy*
bad, blue*, cast down, chapfallen, crestfallen, dejected, depressed, disheartened, dispirited, downcast, downhearted, low, miserable, off, sad, slack, sluggish; SEE CONCEPT *403*

down-and-out [*adj*] *poverty-stricken*
beaten, beggared, defeated, derelict, destitute, finished, impoverished, needy, outcast, penniless, ruined, vagabond, vagrant; SEE CONCEPT *334*

downbeat [*adj*] *pessimistic*
cheerless, defeatist, dejected, dispirited, gloomy, hopeless, negative, unhappy, unhopeful; SEE CONCEPTS *403,548*

downcast [*adj*] *depressed, unhappy*
bad, blue, brooding, bummed out*, cast down, chapfallen, cheerless, crestfallen, daunted, dejected, despondent, disappointed, disconsolate, discouraged, disheartened, dismayed, dispirited, distressed, doleful, down, downhearted, down in the dumps*, down-in-the-mouth*, dragged*, droopy, dull, forlorn, gloomy, glum, heartsick, in pain, listless, low, low-spirited, miserable, moody, mopey*, morose, oppressed, sad, shot down*, singing the blues*, sunk*, troubled, weighed down*, woebegone; SEE CONCEPT *403*

downer [*n*] *depressing experience*
bad deal*, bad scene*, bad trip*, bummer*, drag*, misfortune, raw deal, rotten hand; SEE CONCEPTS *674,679*

downfall [*n*] *disgrace, ruin*
atrophy, bane, breakdown, cloudburst, collapse, comedown, comeuppance, debacle, decadence, declension, degeneracy, degeneration, deluge, descent, destruction, deterioration, devolution, discomfiture, down, drop, failure, fall, flood, on the rocks*, overthrow, rack and ruin*, road to ruin*, ruination, storm, the skids*, undoing; SEE CONCEPTS *674,679,699*

downgrade [*n*] *slope*
decline, declivity, descent, dip, hill, inclination, pitch; SEE CONCEPTS *509,738*

downgrade [*v*] *lower in opinion or rank*
abase, bench*, break*, bump*, bust*, declass, decrease, decry, degrade, demerit, demote, denigrate, depreciate, detract from, devalorize, devalue, disparage, disrate, humble, mark down, minimize, reduce, run down, set back, take down a peg*, undervalue, write off*; SEE CONCEPTS *7,19,54,240*

downhearted [*adj*] *depressed, unhappy*
blue*, chapfallen, crestfallen, dejected, despondent, disconsolate, discouraged, disheartened, dismayed, dispirited, down, downcast, low, lowspirited, sad, sorrowful, spiritless, woebegone; SEE CONCEPT *403*

downhill [*adj*] *descending*
declining, dipping, dropping, falling, sloping downward; SEE CONCEPTS *583,586,735*

downlink [*n*] *transmission path for data*
circuit, communications pathway, network, pathway, signal route; SEE CONCEPT *269*

download [*v*] *transfer data from one computer system to another*
boot up, compute, computerize, crunch numbers*, digitize, initialize, input, keyboard, key in, load, log in, log out, program, run; SEE CONCEPTS *211,217,223*

downplay [*v*] *minimize*
attach little importance to, deemphasize, devalue, give little weight to, lessen, make light of, play down, soften, think nothing of, whitewash; SEE CONCEPTS *54,240,247*

downpour [*n*] *tremendous pouring of rain*
cloudburst, deluge, drencher, flood, inundation, monsoon, rainstorm, storm, torrential rain; SEE CONCEPT *526*

downright [*adj*] *thorough, absolute*
blatant, blunt, categorical, certain, clear, complete, damned, explicit, flat, gross, honest, indubitable, open, out-and-out, outright, plain, positive, simple, sincere, straight, straightforward, sure, thoroughgoing, total, undisguised, unequivocal, unmitigated, unqualified, unquestionable, utter, whole; SEE CONCEPT *531*

downside [*n*] *a negative aspect of a situation*
defect, disadvantage, drawback, fault, flaw, inconvenience, minus, problem, trouble; SEE CONCEPTS *666,674*

downsize [*v*] *to decrease in size, especially of a workforce*
curtail, cut, cut back, cut down, decrease, deduct, diminish, phase down, phase out, reduce, retrench, roll back, roll down, scale back, scale down, shrink, step down, trim, trim away, tune down; SEE CONCEPTS *236,240,247*

downtime [*n*] *time during which an activity is stopped*
break, breathing spell, freedom, free time, halt, interim, interlude, intermission, letup, lull, pause, recess, repose, respite, rest, spare time, spell, stay, suspension, time on one's hands, time out, time to burn, time to kill; SEE CONCEPT *807*

down-to-earth [*adj*] *reasonable, practical*
common, commonsense, easy, hard, hardboiled, hardheaded, matter-of-fact, mundane, no-nonsense, plainspoken, pragmatic, rational, realistic, sane, sensible, sober, unfantastic, unidealistic, unsentimental; SEE CONCEPTS *402,558*

downtrodden [*adj*] *afflicted, abused*
abject, a slave to*, at one's beck and call*, at one's feet*, at one's mercy*, destitute, distressed, exploited, have-not, helpless, in one's clutches*, in one's pocket*, in one's power*, led by the nose*, maltreated, mistreated, needy, oppressed, overcome, persecuted, subjugated, subservient, suppressed, tyrannized, underdog*, underfoot*, under one's thumb*; SEE CONCEPT *542*

downturn [*n*] *drop*
decline, descent, deterioration, dip, downtick, fall, plunge, retreat, sinking, slide, slump; SEE CONCEPTS *336,346,738*

downy [*adj*] *fluffy*
featherlike, feathery, fleecy, fuzzy, light, plumate, plumose, pubescent, silky, soft, velutinous, velvety, woolly; SEE CONCEPTS *604,606*

doze [*n*] *light sleep*
catnap, drowse, forty winks*, nap, shut-eye*, siesta, slumber, snooze*; SEE CONCEPTS *315,681*

doze [*v*] *take a nap*
catch a wink*, catnap, cop some z's*, drift off*, drop off*, drowse, nod off*, sleep, sleep lightly, slumber, snooze; SEE CONCEPTS *315,681*

drab [*adj*] *dull, colorless*
arid, blah*, bleak, boring, brown, characterless, cheerless, desolate, dingy, dismal, dreary, dry, dull as dishwater*, faded, flat, gloomy, gray, grungy, lackluster, lusterless, muddy, murky, run-down, same, shabby, somber, subfuse, unchanging, uninspired, vapid, zero*; SEE CONCEPTS *536,617,618*

draconian [*adj*] *harsh*
brutal, cruel, drastic, exorbitant, extreme, heavyhanded, oppressive, rough, severe, strict, very severe; SEE CONCEPT *401*

draft [*n1*] *something formulated; plan*
abstract, blueprint, delineation, outline, preliminary form, rough sketch, version; SEE CONCEPTS *271,660*

draft [*n2*] *check for paying money*
bank draft, bill, bond, cheque, coupon, debenture, IOU, letter of credit, money order, order, promissory note, receipt, warrant; SEE CONCEPTS *332,344*

draft [*n3*] *gust of air*
breeze, current, eddy, puff, wind; SEE CONCEPT *437*

draft [*n4*] *military conscription*
allotment, assignment, call of duty, call-up*, greetings*, impressment, induction, letter from Uncle Sam*, levy, lottery, recruiting, registration, roll call*, selection, selective service; SEE CONCEPT *321*

do
dr

draft [*n5*] *drink of beverage*
drag*, drain, drench, glass, peg*, quaff, swallow, swig*, swill*; SEE CONCEPTS *169,454*

draft [*v1*] *formulate*
adumbrate, block out, characterize, compose, concoct, contrive, delineate, design, devise, draw, draw up, fabricate, fashion, forge, form, frame, invent, make, manufacture, outline, plan, prepare, project, rough, shape, skeleton, sketch; SEE CONCEPTS *36,79,173*

draft [*v2*] *select for military force*
call up, choose, conscribe, conscript, dragoon, enlist, enroll, impress, indite, induct, muster, press, recruit, sign on, sign up; SEE CONCEPTS *8,320*

drag [*n1*] *bad situation*
annoyance, bore, bother, burden, encumbrance, hang-up, hindrance, impediment, nuisance, pain, pest, pill, sway, trouble; SEE CONCEPT *674*

drag [*n2*] *a puff while smoking*
breathing, draw, inhalation, pull, smoke; SEE CONCEPT *185*

drag [*v1*] *haul something to a new place*
draw, hale, lug, magnetize, move, pull, schlepp*, tow, trail, transport, truck, tug, yank; SEE CONCEPTS *206,213*

drag [*v2*] *move very slowly*
be delayed, be quiescent, crawl, creep, dally*, dawdle*, delay, encounter difficulty*, hang*, inch*, lag, lag behind, limp along, linger, loiter, mark time*, poke*, procrastinate, put off*, sag, shamble, shuffle, slow down, stagnate, straggle, tarry, trail behind*, traipse; SEE CONCEPTS *151,681*

dragging [*adj*] *tiresome, monotonous*
boring, drawn-out, dull, going slowly, humdrum, lengthy, long, overlong, prolonged, protracted, tedious, wearisome; SEE CONCEPTS *482,798*

dragnet [*n*] *manhunt*
all points bulletin, chase, pursuit, search; SEE CONCEPT *207*

drag on/drag out [*v*] *extend time of action*
continue, draw out, endure, extend, go on slowly, keep going, lengthen, persist, prolong, protract, spin out, stretch out; SEE CONCEPT *239*

drag queen [*n*] *cross-dresser*
female impersonator, transvestite; SEE CONCEPT *412*

drain [*n*] *channel through which liquid runs off*
cesspool, cloaca, conduit, culvert, ditch, duct, outlet, pipe, sewer, sink, trench, watercourse; SEE CONCEPT *501*

drain [*v1*] *remove liquid; remove supply*
abate, bankrupt, bleed, bleed dry*, catheterize, consume, debilitate, decrease, deplete, devitalize, diminish, dissipate, divert, draft, draw off, drink up, dry, empty, evacuate, exhaust, expend, fatigue, filter off, finish, free from, get last drop*, get rid of, gulp down, impoverish, lessen, milk*, pump, pump out, quaff, reduce, sap, siphon, spend, strain, suck, suck dry*, swallow, tap, tax, tire out, use up, waste, wear, wear down, weary, withdraw; SEE CONCEPTS *142,211,225*

drain [*v2*] *seep, discharge liquid*
abate, decline, decrease, diminish, dwindle, effuse, exude, filter off, flow, flow out, leak, leave dry, ooze, osmose, percolate, reduce, run off, taper off, trickle, well; SEE CONCEPTS *179,698*

drained [*adj*] *used up; exhausted*
all in*, beat*, bleary, burned out*, dead, dead tired*, depleted, dragging, effete, far-gone, hacked*, pooped*, spent, washed-out, weary, wiped-out*, worn-out; SEE CONCEPTS *485,560*

drama [*n1*] *theatrical piece; acting*
boards*, Broadway*, climax, comedy, dramatic art, dramatization, dramaturgy, farce, footlights, histrionic art, melodrama, play, production, scene, show, show business, showmanship, stagecraft, stage show, tear-jerker*, theater, theatricals, thespian art, tragedy, vehicle*; SEE CONCEPTS *263,271,293*

drama [*n2*] *turmoil in real life*
climax, comedy, crisis, dramatics, emotion, excitement, farce, histrionics, melodrama, scene, spectacle, tension, theatrics, tragedy; SEE CONCEPT *674*

dramatic [*adj*] *exciting, moving*
affecting, breathtaking, climactic, comic, effective, electrifying, emotional, expressive, farcical, histrionic, impressive, melodramatic, powerful, sensational, startling, striking, sudden, suspenseful, tense, theatrical, thespian, thrilling, tragic, vivid; SEE CONCEPTS *537,548*

dramatization [*n*] *drama*
dramatics, entertainment, melodrama; SEE CONCEPTS *263,271,293*

dramatize [*v*] *make a performance of*
act, amplify, burlesque, enact, exaggerate, execute, farcialize, give color to, ham it up*, lay it on*, make a production of, melodramatize, overdo, overstate, perform, playact, play on heartstrings*, play to gallery, play up, present, produce, show, splash, stage, tragedize; SEE CONCEPTS *49,59,292*

drape [*v*] *hang over, adorn*
array, cloak, clothe, cover, dangle, display, don, dress, droop, drop, enclose, enswathe, envelop, enwrap, fold, hang, lean over, let fall, line, model, roll, sprawl, spread, spread-eagle, suspend, swathe, wrap; SEE CONCEPT *172*

drastic [*adj*] *severe, extreme*
desperate, dire, exorbitant, extravagant, forceful, harsh, immoderate, radical, strong; SEE CONCEPTS *537,569*

draw [*n*] *tie in competition*
dead end*, dead heat*, deadlock, even steven*, photo finish*, stalemate, standoff, tie; SEE CONCEPT *706*

draw [*v1*] *move something by pulling*
attract, bring, carry, convey, cull, draft, drag, drain, educe, elicit, evoke, extract, fetch, gather, haul, hook, jerk, lug, magnetize, pick, pluck, pump, rake, siphon, tap, tow, trail, trawl, tug, wind in, wrench, yank; SEE CONCEPT *206*

draw [*v2*] *create a likeness in a picture*
caricature, chart, compose, crayon, delineate, depict, describe, design, draft, engrave, etch, express, form, formulate, frame, graph, limn, map out, mark, model, outline, paint, pencil, portray, prepare, profile, sketch, trace, write; SEE CONCEPTS *79,174*

draw [*v3*] *deduce*
collect, conclude, derive, gather, get, infer, judge, make, make out, take; SEE CONCEPT *15*

draw [*v4*] *allure, influence*
argue into, attract, bewitch, bring around, bring forth, call forth, captivate, charm, convince, elicit, enchant, engage, entice, evoke, fascinate, get, induce, invite, lure, magnetize, persuade,

prompt, take, wile, win over; SEE CONCEPTS *7,19,22,68*

draw [*v5*] *take out, extend*
attenuate, choose, drain, elongate, extort, extract, lengthen, pick, pull out, respire, select, single out, stretch, suck, take; SEE CONCEPTS *142,163, 239*

drawback [*n*] *disadvantage*
check, defect, deficiency, detriment, difficulty, disability, evil, failing, fault, flaw, fly in the ointment*, handicap, hindrance, hitch, ill, impediment, imperfection, inconvenience, lack, nuisance, obstacle, shortcoming, snag, stumbling block*, trouble, weakness; SEE CONCEPTS *666,674*

draw back [*v*] *retract from position*
deduct, discount, pull back, recede, recoil, reel in, retreat, sheathe, shrink, start back, subtract, take away, withdraw; SEE CONCEPTS *195,213*

drawing [*n*] *illustration*
cartoon, commercial art, comp, delineation, depiction, design, doodle, etching, graphics, layout, likeness, outline, painting, picture, portrayal, representation, sketch, storyboard, study, tracing, work of art; SEE CONCEPT *625*

drawl [*v*] *lengthen, draw out*
chant, drag out, drone, extend, intone, nasalize, prolong, pronounce slowly, protract, utter; SEE CONCEPTS *77,239*

drawn [*adj*] *tense, fatigued*
fraught, haggard, harassed, harrowed, peaked, pinched, sapped, starved, strained, stressed, taut, thin, tired, worn; SEE CONCEPT *485*

draw on [*v*] *use to advantage*
effect, employ, exploit, extract, fall back on, have recourse to, make use of, rely on, require, take from; SEE CONCEPT *225*

draw out [*v*] *prolong*
attract, continue, drag, drag out, elongate, extend, lead on, lengthen, make longer, prolongate, protract, pull, spin, spin out*, stretch, string out*, tug; SEE CONCEPTS *236,239,245*

draw up [*v*] *draft document*
compose, formulate, frame, indite, make, prepare, write, write out; SEE CONCEPT *79*

dread [*adj*] *horrible, terrifying*
alarming, awe-inspiring, awful, creepy*, dire, frightening, frightful, shuddersome, terrible; SEE CONCEPT *537*

dread [*n*] *fear*
affright, alarm, apprehension, aversion, awe, cold feet*, consternation, creeps*, dismay, fright, funk*, goose bumps*, horror, jitters, panic, phobia, stage fright, terror, trepidation, trepidity, worriment; SEE CONCEPT *27*

dread [*v*] *anticipate with horror*
apprehend, be afraid, cringe, fear, have cold feet*, misdoubt, quake, shrink from, shudder, tremble; SEE CONCEPT *27*

dreadful [*adj*] *horrible, frightening*
abominable, alarming, appalling, atrocious, awful, bad, beastly, creepy*, dire, distressing, fearful, formidable, frightful, frozen, ghastly, godawful*, grievous, grim, grody*, gross*, hideous, horrendous, horrific, icky*, lousy, mean, monstrous, rotten, shameful, shocking, shuddersome, spooky, terrible, terrific, tragic, tremendous, wicked; SEE CONCEPTS *537,550*

dream [*n1*] *illusion, vision*
bubble*, castle in the air*, chimera, daydream, delusion, fancy, fantasy, hallucination, head trip*, idea, image, imagination, impression, incubus, mental picture, nightmare, pie in the sky*, pipe dream*, rainbow, reverie, specter, speculation, thought, trance, vagary, wraith; SEE CONCEPT *529*

dream [*n2*] *goal*
ambition, aspiration, design, desire, flight of fancy*, hope, notion, pipe dream*, wish; SEE CONCEPT *659*

dream [*v*] *conjure up scenario*
be delirious, be moonstruck, be up in clouds*, brainstorm, build castles in air*, conceive, concoct, cook up*, crave, create, daydream, devise, envisage, fancy, fantasize, formulate, hallucinate, hanker*, hatch*, have a flash*, have a nightmare*, have a notion*, have a vision, hunger, idealize, imagine, invent, long, lust, make up, picture, pine, search for pot of gold*, sigh, stargaze*, sublimate, think, think up, thirst, visualize; SEE CONCEPTS *17,529*

dreamer [*n*] *visionary*
daydreamer, escapist, fantasizer, idealist, romantic, star-gazer, theorizer, Walter Mitty*; SEE CONCEPTS *361,416*

dream up [*v*] *concoct plan*
contrive, cook up*, create, devise, frame, hatch*, imagine, invent, make up, spin*, think up; SEE CONCEPTS *17,36*

dreamy [*adj*] *illusory, romantic*
abstracted, astral, calming, chimerical, daydreaming, excellent, fanciful, fantastic, gentle, idealistic, imaginary, immaterial, impractical, intangible, introspective, introvertive, lulling, marvelous, misty, musing, mythical, nightmarish, otherworldly, out of this world*, pensive, phantasmagoric, phantasmagorical, preoccupied, quixotic, relaxing, shadowy, soothing, speculative, unreal, unsubstantial, utopian, vague, visionary, whimsical; SEE CONCEPT *582*

dreary [*adj*] *gloomy, lifeless*
black, blah, bleak, boring, cheerless, colorless, comfortless, damp, depressing, depressive, dingy, dismal, dispiriting, doleful, downcast, drab, dull, forlorn, funereal, glum, humdrum, joyless, lonely, lonesome, melancholy, monotonous, mournful, oppressive, pedestrian, raw, routine, sad, somber, sorrowful, tedious, uneventful, uninteresting, wearisome, windy, wintry, wretched; SEE CONCEPTS *525,544*

dredge [*v*] *deepen*
bring up, clean, dig up, raise, unearth, widen; SEE CONCEPT *178*

dregs [*n1*] *sediment*
deposits, dirt, draff, lees, residue, settlings, slag, waste; SEE CONCEPT *260*

dregs [*n2*] *bad person*
loser, outcast, rabble, riffraff, scum, trash; SEE CONCEPT *412*

drench [*v*] *wet thoroughly*
deluge, dip, douse, drown, duck, dunk, flood, imbrue, immerse, impregnate, inundate, pour, saturate, seethe, soak, sodden, sop, souse, steep, submerge, teem; SEE CONCEPT *256*

dress [*n*] *clothing; woman's garment*
accouterment, apparel, attire, attirement, civvies*, costume, covering, drape, dry goods, duds*, ensemble, evening clothes, frock, garb, gear, gown, guise, habiliment, habit, muumuu, outfit, raiment, robe, shift, skirt, smock, suit,

dr
dr

Sunday best*, things*, threads*, tog, toga, toggery, trappings, uniform, vestment, wardrobe; SEE CONCEPT *451*

dress [*v1*] *put on clothing*
adorn, apparel, array, attire, bedeck, bundle up, change, clad, clothe, costume, cover, deck, decorate, don, drape, embellish, fit out, furbish, garb, ornament, outfit, primp, put on, raiment, rig, robe, slip into, slip on, spruce up, suit up, trim, turn out, wear; SEE CONCEPT *167*

dress [*v2*] *physically prepare; groom*
adjust, align, arrange, comb, decorate, dispose, do up, fit, make ready, ornament, set, straighten, trim; SEE CONCEPT *202*

dress [*v3*] *cover a wound*
attend, bandage, bind, cauterize, cleanse, give first aid, heal, plaster, sew up, sterilize, treat; SEE CONCEPTS *172,310*

dress down [*v*] *scold*
bawl out, berate, carpet, castigate, censure, chew out*, lash, rail, rake over coals*, ream, rebuke, reprimand, reprove, tear into*, tell off*, tonguelash*, upbraid; SEE CONCEPT *52*

dresser [*n*] *chest of drawers*
bureau, cabinet, chiffonier, closet, highboy, wardrobe; SEE CONCEPT *443*

dressing-down [*n*] *severe scolding*
bawling-out, castigation, chiding, lambasting, reprimand, reproach, tongue-lashing, upbraiding; SEE CONCEPTS *123,278*

dress up [*v*] *put on one's best clothes*
array, attire, beautify, clothe, deck out*, embellish, fit out*, fix up, gussy up*, improve, overdress, preen, prettify, primp, prink, slick, smarten, spiff up*, spruce up*, titivate; SEE CONCEPT *167*

dressy [*adj*] *formal, fashionable*
chic, classy, dressed to kill*, dressed to the nines*, dressed up*, elaborate, elegant, fancy, in high feather*, looking sharp, ornate, ritzy, smart, stylish; SEE CONCEPTS *579,589*

dribble [*v*] *trickle*
distill, drip, drivel, drizzle, drool, drop, fall in drops, leak, ooze, run, salivate, seep, slaver, slobber, spout, squirt, trill, weep; SEE CONCEPTS *179,185*

drift [*n1*] *accumulation*
alluvion, bank, batch, bunch, bundle, clump, cluster, deposit, heap, hill, lot, mass, mound, mountain, parcel, pile, set, shock, stack; SEE CONCEPTS *432,524*

drift [*n2*] *meaning, significance of communication*
aim, design, direction, end, gist, implication, import, intention, object, progress, progression, purport, scope, significance, tendency, tenor; SEE CONCEPT *682*

drift [*v*] *move aimlessly*
accumulate, aim, amass, amble, be carried along, coast, dance, draw near, flicker, flit, flitter, float, flow, flutter, gad*, gallivant*, gather, go-that-a-way*, go with the tide*, gravitate, hover, kick around*, linger, malinger, meander, mosey*, muck*, ride, sail, saunter, scud, skim, slide, stray, stroll, tend, waft, wander, wash*; SEE CONCEPT *147*

drifter [*n*] *wanderer*
derelict, hobo, itinerant, nomad, rolling stone, tramp, transient, vagabond, vagrant; SEE CONCEPTS *412,423*

drill [*n1*] *practice, exercise*
assignment, call, conditioning, constitutional, daily dozen*, discipline, dress, drilling, dry run*, gym, homework, instruction, learning by doing, maneuvers, marching, preparation, repetition, run-through*, shakedown*, training, tryout, warm-up, workout; SEE CONCEPTS *87,290*

drill [*n2*] *tool for boring*
auger, awl, bit, borer, corkscrew, countersink, dibble, gimlet, implement, jackhammer, punch, riveter, rotary tool, trepan, trephine, wimble; SEE CONCEPT *499*

drill [*v1*] *train, discipline*
accustom, break, break in, exercise, get into shape, habituate, hone, instruct, lick into shape, practice, rehearse, teach, tune up, walk through, work out; SEE CONCEPTS *117,285*

drill [*v2*] *bore hole*
dig, penetrate, perforate, pierce, prick, punch, puncture, sink in; SEE CONCEPT *220*

drink [*n*] *beverage; alcoholic beverage*
alcohol, booze*, brew, cup, draft, glass, gulp, libation, liquid, liquor, potable, potation, potion, refreshment, shot, sip, slug*, spirits, spot*, swallow, swig, taste, thirst quencher*, toast; SEE CONCEPT *454*

drink [*v*] *take in liquid*
absorb, belt*, booze*, consume, dissipate, down, drain, gargle, gulp, guzzle*, hit the bottle*, imbibe, indulge, inhale, irrigate, lap*, liquor up*, nip*, partake of, put away, quaff, sip, slosh, slurp, soak up, sop, sponge, suck, sup, swallow, swig, swill, tank up*, thirst, tipple*, toast, toss off*, wash down*, wet whistle*; SEE CONCEPT *169*

drip [*v*] *drop, trickle*
dribble, drizzle, exude, filter, plop, rain, splash, sprinkle, trill, weep; SEE CONCEPT *181*

drive [*n1*] *journey by vehicle*
airing, commute, excursion, expedition, hitch, jaunt, joyride, lift, outing, pickup, ramble, ride, run, spin, Sunday drive*, tour, trip, turn, whirl; SEE CONCEPT *224*

drive [*n2*] *campaign for cause*
action, advance, appeal, crusade, effort, enterprise, get-up-and-go*, initiative, push, surge; SEE CONCEPTS *87,300*

drive [*n3*] *person's will to achieve*
ambition, clout, effort, energy, enterprise, fire in belly*, get-up-and-go, goods*, gumption*, guts*, impellent, impetus, impulse, initiative, momentum, motivation, motive, moxie*, pep, pressure, punch*, push*, right stuff*, spunk*, steam*, stuff*, vigor, vitality, what it takes*, zip*; SEE CONCEPTS *411,706*

drive [*v1*] *move or urge on*
actuate, act upon, animate, arouse, bulldoze*, chase, coerce, compel, constrain, dog*, egg on*, encourage, force, goad, goose*, harass, hasten, herd, hound*, hurl, hurry, hustle, impel, induce, inspire, instigate, kick, lean on*, make, motivate, nag, oblige, overburden, overwork, pound, press, pressure, prod, prompt, propel, provoke, push, put up to*, railroad*, ride herd on*, rouse, rush, send, shepherd, shove, spirit up, spur, steamroll*, stimulate, work on, worry; SEE CONCEPTS *68,147,208*

drive [*v2*] *moving, controlling a vehicle*
actuate, advance, bear down, bicycle, bike, burn rubber*, burn up the road*, coast, cruise, cycle,

dash, direct, drag, fire up*, floor it*, fly, guide, handle, impel, lean on it*, make sparks fly*, manage, mobilize, motor, operate, pour it on*, propel, push, ride, roll, run, send, speed, spin, start, steer, step on it*, step on the gas*, tailgate, tool*, transport, travel, turn, vehiculate*, wheel; SEE CONCEPTS *148,187*

drive [*v3*] *hit with heavy blow*
batter, beat, butt, dash, dig, hammer, jackhammer, knock, maul, plunge, pop, punch, ram, run, shoot, sink, smite, sock, stab, stick, strike, throw, thrust, thump, twack*, whack*, wham*; SEE CONCEPT *189*

drive at [*v*] *mean, suggest as meaning*
aim, allude to, contemplate, design, get at, have in mind, hint at, imply, indicate, intend, intimate, propose, refer to, signify; SEE CONCEPTS *73,682*

drivel [*n*] *foolish talk*
babble, balderdash*, blather, bunk*, double-talk, gibberish, gobbledygook*, Greek*, hogwash*, hooey*, jabber*, nonsense, poppycock*, prating, rot*, rubbish*, tripe*, twaddle*; SEE CONCEPT *278*

drivel [*v1*] *talk foolishly*
babble, blabber, blather*, blethe, gab, gabble, prate, prattle, ramble, twaddle*, waffle*; SEE CONCEPT *266*

drivel [*v2*] *drool*
dribble, salivate, slaver, slobber; SEE CONCEPTS *185,256*

driver [*n*] *person who engineers vehicle*
autoist, automobilist, cabbie, chauffeur, coach person, hack*, handler, jockey, leadfoot*, motorist, operator, road hog*, trainer, whip*; SEE CONCEPT *423*

driving [*adj*] *forceful*
active, compelling, dynamic, energetic, enterprising, galvanic, impellent, lively, propulsive, sweeping, urging, vigorous, violent; SEE CONCEPT *540*

drizzle [*v*] *fine rain*
dribble, drip, drop, mist, mizzle, shower, spit, spray, sprinkle; SEE CONCEPT *526*

droid [*n*] *robot*
android, clone, cyborg, drone; SEE CONCEPT *463*

droll [*adj*] *amusing, farcical*
absurd, camp, campy, clownish, comic, comical, crack-up, diverting, eccentric, entertaining, for grins*, funny, gagged up*, gelastic, humorous, jocular, joshing, laffer, laughable, ludicrous, odd, preposterous, quaint, queer, quizzical, ridiculous, riot, risible, waggish, whimsical; SEE CONCEPTS *267,548*

drone [*n1*] *person who is lazy*
idler, leech, loafer, lounger, parasite, slug, sluggard, sponger*; SEE CONCEPT *412*

drone [*n2*] *continuous noise*
buzz, hum, murmur, purr, sound, vibration, whirr; SEE CONCEPT *595*

drone [*v*] *making noise continuously*
bombinate, buzz, chant, drawl, hum, intone, nasalize, purr, sound, strum, thrum, vibrate, whirr; SEE CONCEPTS *65,77*

drool [*n*] *saliva*
drivel, expectoration, salivation, slaver, slobber, spit, spittle; SEE CONCEPT *467*

drool [*v*] *drivel*
dribble, lick one's chops*, salivate, slaver, slobber, water at the mouth; SEE CONCEPT *467*

drool [*v1*] *salivate*
dribble, drivel, froth, ooze, run, slabber, slaver, slobber, spit, water, water at the mouth; SEE CONCEPTS *185,256*

drool [*v2*] *desire, lust after*
dote on, enthuse, fondle, gush, lick chops*, make much of, pet, rave, rhapsodize, rhapsody, slobber over*, spoil, want; SEE CONCEPT *20*

droop [*v*] *hang down; languish*
bend, dangle, decline, depress, diminish, drop, fade, fail, faint, fall down, flag, lean, let down, loll, lop, sag, settle, sink, sling, slouch, slump, subside, suspend, weaken, wilt, wither; SEE CONCEPTS *181,699*

droopy [*adj*] *limp*
bent, drooping, flabby, floppy, languid, languorous, lassitudinous, pendulous, sagging, saggy, slouchy, stooped, wilting; SEE CONCEPT *485*

drop [*n1*] *globule*
bead, bit, bubble, crumb, dab, dash, dewdrop, driblet, drip, droplet, iota, molecule, morsel, nip, ounce, particle, pearl, pinch, sip, smidgen, speck, splash, spot, taste, tear, teardrop, trace, trickle; SEE CONCEPTS *467,468,831,835*

drop [*n2*] *steep decline; hole*
abyss, chasm, declivity, deepness, depth, descent, dip, fall, plunge, precipice, slope, tumble; SEE CONCEPTS *181,509*

drop [*n3*] *decrease*
cut, decline, descent, deterioration, dip, downfall, downslide, downswing, downtrend, downturn, fall, fall-off, landslide, lapse, lowering, precipitation, reduction, sag, slide, slip, slump, tumble, upset; SEE CONCEPTS *698,776*

drop [*v1*] *fall in globules*
bead, bleed, descend, distill, drain, dribble, drip, emanate, hail, leak, ooze, percolate, precipitate, seep, snow, splash, trickle, trill; SEE CONCEPT *179*

drop [*v2*] *let go of; fall*
abandon, bring down, cave in, collapse, decline, depress, descend, dive, duck, dump, fell, floor, flop, give up, go down, ground, keel over*, knock, loosen, lower, nose-dive*, pitch, plummet, plump, plunge, release, relinquish, shed, shoot, sink, slide, slip, slump, topple, tumble, unload; SEE CONCEPTS *181,200*

drop [*v3*] *abandon; ignore*
abort, adios*, be alienated from, break with, call off, cancel, cast off, cease, desert, discontinue, dismiss, disown, ditch*, divorce, dust off*, eighty-six*, end, forfeit, forget about, forsake, give up, have done with*, interrupt, jilt, kick*, leave, lose, part from, part with, quit, reject, relinquish, remit, renounce, repudiate, resign, sacrifice, scratch*, scrub*, separate, shake, stop, terminate, throw over, wash out*, waste one*, wipe out*, write off*; SEE CONCEPTS *30,121,195*

drop in [*v*] *visit*
blow in*, call, call upon, come by, come over, go and see*, look in on, look up, pop in*, run in*, stop, stop by, stop in, turn up; SEE CONCEPT *227*

drop in the bucket [*n*] *small amount*
bit, drop in the ocean*, not enough, pittance, small change*, small potatoes*, small quantity, speck, trivial amount; SEE CONCEPT *831*

drop off [*v1*] *decrease*
decline, diminish, dwindle, fall away, fall off,

lessen, sag, slacken, slide, slip, slump; SEE CONCEPTS *698,776*

drop off [*v2*] *deliver*
deposit, give, hand over, leave, let off, present, set down, unload; SEE CONCEPT *108*

drop off [*v3*] *fall asleep*
catnap, doze, doze off*, drowse, have forty winks*, nod, nod off*, snooze; SEE CONCEPTS *210,315*

drop out [*v*] *stop doing an activity*
abandon, back out, cease, forsake, give notice, give up, leave, quit, renege, retreat, withdraw; SEE CONCEPT *121*

droppings [*n*] *excrement*
cow pies*, cowplop*, crap, dung, feces, fertilizer, guano, manure, meadow muffin*, night soil*, ordure, poop*; SEE CONCEPT *260*

drought [*n*] *dryness; shortage of supply*
aridity, dearth, deficiency, dehydration, desiccation, dry spell, insufficiency, lack, need, parchedness, rainlessness, scarcity, want; SEE CONCEPTS *607,646*

drove [*n*] *large gathering*
collection, company, crowd, crush, drive, flock, herd, horde, mob, multitude, pack, press, rout, run, swarm, throng; SEE CONCEPTS *397,432*

drown [*v*] *submerge in liquid; submerge and die*
asphyxiate, deluge, dip, douse, drench, engulf, flood, go down, go under, immerse, inundate, knock over, obliterate, overcome, overflow, overpower, overwhelm, plunge, prostrate, sink, soak, sop, souse, stifle, suffocate, swamp, whelm, wipe out; SEE CONCEPTS *252,256*

drowsy [*adj*] *sleepy*
comatose, dazed, dopy, dozing, dozy, dreamy, drugged, half asleep, heavy, indolent, lackadaisical, languid, lazy, lethargic, lulling, napping, nodding, out of it*, restful, sluggish, slumberous, snoozy, somnolent, soothing, soporific, tired, torpid; SEE CONCEPTS *406,539*

drub [*v*] *thrash*
beat, cane, clobber, defeat, flog, hit, lash, pound, spank, strike, tan, trounce, wallop, whip; SEE CONCEPT *95*

drudge [*n*] *slave, very hard worker*
factotum, grind*, laborer, menial, nose to grindstone*, peon*, plodder*, servant, toiler, workaholic, worker, workhorse; SEE CONCEPT *348*

drudge [*v*] *work very hard*
back to the salt mines*, dig, grind*, hammer*, keep nose to grindstone*, labor, muck*, perform, plod, plow, plug away*, pound*, schlepp*, slave, slog, sweat, toil, travail; SEE CONCEPTS *87,100,324*

drudgery [*n*] *hard, tedious work*
backbreaker*, chore, daily grind*, elbow grease*, grind*, gruntwork*, labor, menial labor, rat race, slavery, struggle, sweat, toil, travail, workout; SEE CONCEPT *362*

drug [*n*] *medication*
biologic, cure, depressant, dope, essence, medicament, medicinal, medicine, narcotic, opiate, pharmaceutic, pharmaceutical, physic, pill, poison, potion, prescription, remedy, sedative, stimulant, tonic; SEE CONCEPT *307*

drug [*v*] *put under influence of medication*
analgize, anesthetize, benumb, blunt, deaden, desensitize, dope*, dope up, dose, dose up*, fix, hit, knock out*, medicate, narcotize, numb, poison, relax, sedate, stupefy, treat; SEE CONCEPT *310*

drugged [*adj*] *under the influence of medication*
benumbed, bombed, coked*, comatose, dazed, doped, dopey*, floating*, flying*, high*, junked-up*, loaded*, narcotized, on a trip*, out of it*, ripped*, smashed*, spaced-out*, stoned*, strung out*, stupefied, unconscious; SEE CONCEPT *314*

druggist [*n*] *pharmacist*
apothecary, pharmacologist, posologist; SEE CONCEPT *357*

drum [*v*] *beat, tap a beat*
boom*, pulsate, rap, reverberate, roar, strum, tattoo, throb, thrum, thunder*; SEE CONCEPTS *65,189*

drum into [*v*] *make a point strongly*
din into, drive home*, hammer away*, harp on*, instill, reiterate; SEE CONCEPTS *49,75*

drum up [*v*] *gather support for something*
attract, bid for, canvass, discover, obtain, petition, round up, solicit, succeed in finding; SEE CONCEPTS *68,300*

drunk [*adj*] *intoxicated by alcohol*
bashed, befuddled, boozed up*, buzzed*, crocked*, feeling no pain*, flushed*, flying*, fuddled, glazed*, groggy, high*, inebriated, juiced*, laced*, liquored up*, lit*, lush, muddled, plastered*, potted*, seeing double*, sloshed*, stewed*, stoned*, tanked*, three sheets to the wind*, tight*, tipsy, totaled*, under the influence, under the table*, wasted*; SEE CONCEPTS *314,545*

drunk/drunkard [*n*] *person who is inebriated*
alcoholic, boozer*, carouser*, dipsomaniac, drinker, guzzler*, inebriate, lush*, sot*, sponge*, wino*; SEE CONCEPT *423*

dry [*adj1*] *moistureless*
anhydrous, arid, athirst, baked, bald, bare, barren, dehydrated, depleted, desert, desiccant, desiccated, drained, dried-up, droughty, dusty, evaporated, exhausted, hard, impoverished, juiceless, not irrigated, parched, rainless, sapless, sapped, sear, shriveled, stale, thirsty, torrid, unmoistened, waterless; SEE CONCEPT *603*

dry [*adj2*] *dull, uninteresting*
apathetic, blah, boring, bromidic, draggy, dreary, dull as dishwater*, dusty, ho hum*, impassive, inelaborate, insipid, matter-of-fact, modest, monotonous, naked, phlegmatic, plain, simple, tedious, tiresome, trite, weariful, wearisome; SEE CONCEPT *529*

dry [*adj3*] *sarcastic, sharp-tongued*
acerbic, arcane, biting, caustic, cutting, cynical, deadpan, droll, harsh, humorous, ironical, keen, low-key, restrained, salty, sardonic, satirical, sharp, sly, sour, subtle, tart; SEE CONCEPT *267*

dry [*v*] *take moisture out of*
anhydrate, bake, blot, concentrate, condense, dehumidify, dehydrate, deplete, desiccate, drain, empty, evaporate, exhaust, exsiccate, freeze-dry, harden, kiln, mummify, parch, scorch, sear, shrivel, soak up, sponge, stale, swab, torrefy, towel, wilt, wipe, wither, wizen; SEE CONCEPTS *250,469*

dual [*adj*] *two-fold*
bifold, binal, binary, coupled, double, doubleheader, duple, duplex, duplicate, matched, paired, twin; SEE CONCEPTS *762,771*

dub [v] *name, label something*
baptize, bestow, call, christen, confer, denominate, designate, entitle, knight, nickname, style, tag, term, title; SEE CONCEPT *62*

dubious [*adj1*] *doubtful*
arguable, chancy, debatable, diffident, disputable, dubitable, equivocal, far-fetched, fishy*, fly-by-night*, hesitant, iffy*, improbable, indecisive, moot, mootable, open, perplexed, problematic, questionable, reluctant, shady, skeptical, suspect, suspicious, touch and go*, trustless, unassured, uncertain, unclear, unconvinced, undecided, undependable, unlikely, unreliable, unsure, untrustworthy, untrusty, wavering; SEE CONCEPT *552*

dubious [*adj2*] *vague, unclear*
ambiguous, debatable, disinclined, doubtful, equivocal, indefinite, indeterminate, mistrustful, obscure, open, problematic, problematical, undecided, unsettled; SEE CONCEPTS *535,576*

duck [v] *drop down; avoid*
bend, bob, bow, crouch, dip, dive, dodge, double, elude, escape, evade, fence, lower, lurch, move to side, parry, plunge, shirk, shun, shy, sidestep, stoop, submerge; SEE CONCEPTS *102,154,181*

duck soup [n] *easily accomplished task*
a breeze, a snap, cakewalk, child's play, easy thing, easy to do, piece of cake; SEE CONCEPT *693*

duct [n] *channel, pipe*
aqueduct, canal, conduit, course, funnel, passage, tube, vessel, watercourse; SEE CONCEPT *501*

ductile [*adj*] *pliant, flexible*
adaptable, amenable, biddable, docile, extensile, malleable, manageable, moldable, plastic, pliable, responsive, submitting, supple, tractable, yielding; SEE CONCEPTS *488,490*

dud [n] *failure*
bomb, bummer, bust, debacle, flop, lemon, loser, washout; SEE CONCEPT *674*

dude [*n1*] *friend*
buddy, chap, fellow, guy; SEE CONCEPT *423*

dude [*n2*] *dapper man*
Beau Brummel*, coxcomb, dandy, fancy Dan*, fashion plate, fine gentleman, fop, slicker*, stud; SEE CONCEPT *423*

duds [n] *clothes*
accouterment, apparel, array, civvies*, costume, covering, dress, finery, frippery, frock, garb, garments, habiliment, outfit, rags*, raiment, sportswear, Sunday best*, tatters*, threads*, wardrobe; SEE CONCEPT *451*

due [*adj1*] *unpaid; owing money*
chargeable, collectible, expected, in arrears, IOU, mature, not met, outstanding, overdue, owed, payable, receivable, scheduled, to be paid, unliquidated, unsatisfied, unsettled; SEE CONCEPT *334*

due [*adj2*] *appropriate, proper*
becoming, coming, condign, deserved, earned, equitable, fair, fit, fitting, good, just, justified, merited, obligatory, requisite, rhadamanthine, right, rightful, suitable; SEE CONCEPT *558*

due [*adv*] *directly*
dead, direct, exactly, right, straight, straightly, undeviatingly; SEE CONCEPTS *581,799*

due [n] *expected reward*
be in line for*, claim, comeuppance, compensation, deserts*, entitlement, guerdon, interest,

merits, need, payment, perquisite, prerogative, privilege, rate, recompense, repayment, reprisal, retaliation, retribution, revenge, right, rights, satisfaction, title, vengeance, what is coming to one*; SEE CONCEPTS *337,710*

duel [n] *fight*
affair of honor, bout, challenge, engagement, fencing, joust, shootout, single combat, sword fight; SEE CONCEPTS *53,532*

dues [n] *payment for membership*
ante, arrearage, assessment, charge, charges, collection, contribution, custom, debit, debt, duty, fee, kickback, levy, liability, obligation, pay, protection, rates, tax, toll; SEE CONCEPTS *344,679*

duff [n] *rear end*
ass, backside, behind, buns*, butt*, buttocks, cheeks*, derriere, fanny*, gluteus maximus, heinie*, keister, posterior, seat*; SEE CONCEPT *392*

dulcet [*adj*] *melodious*
agreeable, musical, pleasing to the ear, pleasurable, sweet, sweet-sounding; SEE CONCEPT *594*

dull [*adj1*] *unintelligent*
addled, backward, besotted, boring, brainless, daffy, daft, dense, dim, dim-witted, doltish, dumb, feeble-minded, half-baked, ignorant, imbecilic, indolent, insensate, low, moronic, not bright, numskulled, obtuse, scatterbrained, shallow, simple, simple-minded, slow, sluggish, stolid, stupid, tedious, thick, unintellectual, vacuous, wearisome, witless; SEE CONCEPT *402*

dull [*adj2*] *insensitive*
accustomed, apathetic, blank, boring, callous, colorless, dead, depressed, empty, even, flat, heavy, impassible, inactive, indifferent, inert, insensible, jejune, languid, lifeless, listless, lumpy, monotonous, passionless, placid, prosaic, quiet, regular, routine, slack, slow, sluggish, spiritless, stagnant, still, stolid, torpid, unexciting, unresponsive, unsympathetic, usual, vacuous; SEE CONCEPT *542*

dull [*adj3*] *boring, uninteresting*
abused, archaic, arid, big yawn*, blah, colorless, common, commonplace, dead, dismal, dreary, driveling, dry, familiar, flat, hackneyed, heavy, hoary, ho hum*, humdrum*, insipid, jejune, longwinded, monotonous, oft-repeated*, ordinary, out-of-date, plain, pointless, prolix, prosaic, prosy, repetitious, repetitive, routine, run-of-the-mill*, soporific, stale, stock, stupid, tame, tedious, tired, tiresome, trite, unimaginative, uninspiring, usual, usual thing, vapid, worn-out; SEE CONCEPTS *529,530*

dull [*adj4*] *not sharp*
blunt, blunted, edentate, edgeless, flat, not keen, obtuse, pointless, round, square, toothless, turned, unpointed, unsharpened; SEE CONCEPT *486*

dull [*adj5*] *uneventful*
accustomed, apathetic, blah, boring, dead, depressed, draggy*, even, falling off, flat, inactive, inert, languid, lifeless, listless, monotonous, placid, quiet, regular, routine, sitting tight*, slack, slothful, slow, sluggish, stagnant, still, stolid, tight, torpid, unexciting, unresponsive, usual, without incident, yawn; SEE CONCEPT *548*

dull [*adj6*] *drab, lackluster in effect on senses*
ashen, black, blind, cloudy, cold, colorless, dark, dead, dim, dingy, dismal, dun, dusky, faded, feeble, flat, grimy, hazy, indistinct, leaden, lifeless,

dr
du

low, matte, mousy, muddy, muffled, murky, muted, obscure, opaque, overcast, plain, shadowy, sober, soft, softened, somber, sooty, subdued, subfusc, toned-down, unlit; SEE CONCEPTS *594,617*

dullard [*n*] *dolt*
airhead*, blockhead*, boob*, dimwit, dope*, dork*, dumbbell*, dunce, fool, idiot, imbecile, lamebrain*, lunkhead*, meathead*, nitwit, simpleton, stupid person; SEE CONCEPTS *412,423*

dullsville [*adj*] *boring*
blah*, dead*, deadsville, dragsville, hicksville, tedious; SEE CONCEPTS *529,548*

duly [*adv*] *accordingly, properly*
appropriately, at the proper time, befittingly, correctly, decorously, deservedly, on time, punctually, rightfully, suitably; SEE CONCEPTS *558,799*

dumb [*adj1*] *unable to speak*
at a loss for words*, inarticulate, incoherent, mousy*, mum, mute, quiet, silent, soundless, speechless, tongue-tied, uncommunicative, voiceless, wordless; SEE CONCEPT *593*

dumb [*adj2*] *stupid, unintelligent*
dense, dim-witted, doltish, dull, feebleminded, foolish, moronic, simple-minded, thick*; SEE CONCEPT *402*

dumbbell [*n*] *stupid person*
dodo*, dolt, dullard, dumbo*, dumdum*, dummy, dunce, idiot, ignoramus, moron, simpleton; SEE CONCEPTS *412,423*

dumbfound [*v*] *astound, confuse*
amaze, astonish, bewilder, blow away*, blow one's mind*, boggle, bowl over*, confound, flabbergast, knock over with feather*, nonplus, overwhelm, puzzle, stagger, startle, stun, surprise, take aback, throw, throw into a tizzy*; SEE CONCEPTS *16,42*

dumbfounded [*adj*] *astounded, confused*
agape, aghast, amazed, astonished, bamboozled*, beat, bewildered, blown away*, bowled over*, breathless, buffaloed*, confounded, dismayed, dumb, flabbergasted, floored, knocked, licked, nonplused, overcome, overwhelmed, puzzled, shocked, speechless, staggered, startled, stuck, stumped, stunned, surprised, taken aback, thrown, thunderstruck*; SEE CONCEPT *403*

dumbstruck [*adj*] *shocked*
amazed, astonished, astounded, blown away, dumbfounded, flabbergasted, jolted, rendered speechless, startled, stunned, stupefied; SEE CONCEPT *42*

dummy [*n1*] *mannequin*
copy, counterfeit, duplicate, figure, form, imitation, manikin, model, ringer*, sham*, stand-in, sub, substitute; SEE CONCEPTS *436,716*

dummy [*n2*] *stupid person*
blockhead*, dimwit*, dolt*, dullard*, dunce, fool, idiot, ignoramus, moron, numbskull, oaf, simpleton; SEE CONCEPTS *412,423*

dump [*n1*] *junkyard*
ash heap*, cesspool, depot, dumping ground, garbage lot, junk pile*, magazine, refuse heap, rubbish pile, swamp; SEE CONCEPTS *438,449,680*

dump [*n2*] *slummy establishment*
hole, hovel, joint*, mess*, pigpen*, pigsty*, shack, shanty, slum, sty; SEE CONCEPTS *449,673*

dump [*v*] *drop, throw away*
cast, chuck, clear out, deep-six*, deposit, discard, discharge, dispose of, ditch, drain, eject, empty, evacuate, expel, exude, fling, fling down,

get rid of, jettison, junk, leave, let fall, scrap, throw down, throw out, throw overboard*, tip, unload, unpack; SEE CONCEPTS *180,181*

dumps [*n*] *depression*
blahs*, blues*, bummer, cheerlessness, doldrums, dreariness, gloom, gloominess, low spirits, melancholy, sulks, the blues*, trouble, unhappiness, woefulness; SEE CONCEPT *410*

dumpy [*adj*] *short and stout*
chubby, chunky, fat, homely, plump, podgy, pudgy, roly-poly, squat, stocky, stumpy, tubby; SEE CONCEPT *491*

dunce [*n*] *stupid person*
ass, birdbrain*, blockhead*, bonehead*, buffoon, dimwit*, dolt, donkey*, dope, dork*, drip*, dullard, dunderhead*, fool, goof, goof ball*, half-wit, idiot, ignoramus, imbecile, jerk, knucklehead*, lame-brain*, lightweight*, moron, nerd*, nincompoop*, ninny*, nitwit, numskull, oaf, pinhead*, scatterbrain*, schnook*, simpleton, twit*; SEE CONCEPTS *412,423*

dune [*n*] *hill*
hillock, hummock, knoll, ridge, sand drift, sand dune, sand pile; SEE CONCEPT *509*

dung [*n*] *excrement*
cow pies*, cowplop*, crap, droppings, feces, fertilizer, guano, manure, meadow muffin*, night soil*, ordure, poop*; SEE CONCEPT *260*

dungarees [*n*] *blue jeans*
denims, jeans, pants, trousers; SEE CONCEPT *451*

dungeon [*n*] *prison*
cell, oubliette, torture chamber, vault; SEE CONCEPTS *439,449,516*

dunk [*v*] *dip in liquid*
douse, duck, immerse, saturate, soak, sop, souse, submerge, submerse; SEE CONCEPT *256*

duo [*n*] *twosome*
brace, couple, doublet, dyad, pair; SEE CONCEPT *787*

dupe [*n*] *person who is fooled*
butt*, chump*, easy mark*, fish*, fool, mark*, patsy*, pigeon*, pushover*, sap*, sitting duck*, sucker, victim; SEE CONCEPT *423*

dupe [*v*] *fool someone*
baffle, bamboozle*, beguile, betray, catch, cheat, chicane, circumvent, con, cozen, deceive, defraud, delude, double-cross, dust*, flimflam*, gull, hoax, hoodwink*, hornswoggle, jerk around*, kid, mislead, outwit, overreach, pull one's leg*, pull something*, rip off*, rook*, rope in*, shaft, spoof, swindle, trick, victimize; SEE CONCEPT *59*

duplex [*adj*] *twofold*
double, paired, twin; SEE CONCEPT *771*

duplicate [*adj*] *matching*
alike, corresponding, dualistic, duple, duplex, equal, equivalent, identic, identical, indistinguishable, same, self-same, tantamount, twin, twofold, very same; SEE CONCEPTS *563,566*

duplicate [*n*] *copy, reproduction*
analogue, carbon, carbon copy*, chip off the old block*, clone, companion, coordinate, copycat*, correlate, counterfeit, counterpart, counterscript, dead ringer*, ditto*, double, dupe*, duplication, facsimile, fake, fellow, germination, imitation, knockoff*, likeness, lookalike, match, mate, obverse, parallel, phony, photocopy, photostat, pirate, reciprocal, recurrence, repetition, replica, replication, repro*, ringer*, second, similarity,

spitting image*, stat, twin, Xerox*; SEE CONCEPTS *664,667,716*

duplicate [v] *make a copy; repeat*
act like, clone, copy, counterfeit, ditto*, do again, do a takeoff*, do like*, double, dualize, dupe, echo, fake, go like*, imitate, knock off*, make like*, make replica, make twofold, manifold, mimeo, mirror, multiply, phony, photocopy, photostat, pirate*, redo, redouble, reduplicate, remake, replicate, repro, reproduce, rework, stat, take off as*, trace, Xerox*; SEE CONCEPTS *91,171*

duplicitous [adj] *deceptive*
cheating, deceitful, dishonest, double-dealing, shady, two-faced, two-timing; SEE CONCEPTS *401,582*

duplicity [n] *deception*
artifice, chicanery, cunning, deceit, dirty dealing*, dirty pool*, dirty trick, dirty work*, dishonesty, dissemblance, dissimulation, double-dealing, dualism, duality, faithlessness, falsehood, fraud, guile, hypocrisy, Judas kiss*, one-upmanship, perfidiousness, perfidy, skullduggery, stab in back*, treacherousness, treachery, two-facedness*, twoness; SEE CONCEPTS *59,63*

durability [n] *sturdiness over time*
backbone, constancy, durableness, endurance, grit, guts*, gutsiness, hard as nails*, heart*, imperishability, intestinal fortitude, lastingness, moxie*, permanence, persistence, stamina, starch*, staying power*, stick-to-itiveness*; SEE CONCEPTS *721,731,732*

durable [adj] *sturdy, long-lasting*
abiding, constant, dependable, diuturnal, enduring, fast, firm, fixed, impervious, lasting, long-continued, perdurable, perduring, permanent, persistent, reliable, resistant, sound, stable, stout, strong, substantial, tenacious, tough; SEE CONCEPTS *482,488,489*

duration [n] *length of action, event*
continuance, continuation, continuity, endurance, extent, period, perpetuation, persistence, prolongation, run, span, spell, stretch, term, tide, time; SEE CONCEPT *804*

duress [n] *threat, hardship*
bondage, captivity, coercion, compulsion, confinement, constraint, control, detention, discipline, force, imprisonment, incarceration, pressure, restraint, violence; SEE CONCEPTS *14,674*

during [prep] *concurrently with an activity, event*
all along, all the while, amid, as, at the same timeas, at the time, for the time being, in the course of, in the interim, in the meanwhile, in the middle of, in the time of, meanwhile, mid, midst, over, pending, the time between, the whole time, throughout, until, when, while; SEE CONCEPT *820*

dusk [n] *early evening*
dark, dimday, dimmet, eventide, gloaming, gloom, night, nightfall, sundown, sunset, twilight; SEE CONCEPT *810*

dusky [adj] *dark-hued; murky*
adusk, bistered, bleak, brunette, caliginous, cheerless, cloudy, crepuscular, dark, dark-complexioned, darkish, desolate, dim, dismal, dull, funereal, gloomy, joyless, lightless, obscure, overcast, sable, shadowy, shady, swart, swarthy, tenebrous, twilight, twilit, unilluminated, veiled; SEE CONCEPTS *617,618*

dust [n] *tiny particles in the air*
ashes, cinders, dirt, dust bunnies*, earth, filth, flakes, fragments, gilings, granules, grime, grit, ground, lint, loess, powder, refuse, sand, smut, soil, soot; SEE CONCEPT *437*

dust [v] *sprinkle tiny particles*
besprinkle, cover, dredge, powder, scatter, sift, spray, spread; SEE CONCEPTS *172,222*

dusty [adj] *filled with or covered with powdery particles*
arenaceous, arenose, chalky, crumbly, dirty, friable, granular, grubby, sandy, sooty, unclean, undusted, unswept, untouched; SEE CONCEPT *485*

dutiful [adj] *obedient*
binding, compliant, conscientious, deferential, devoted, docile, duteous, faithful, incumbent on, obligatory, punctilious, regardful, respectful, reverential, submissive; SEE CONCEPT *542*

duty [n1] *responsibility, assignment*
burden, business, calling, charge, chore, commission, commitment, committal, contract, devoir, dues, engagement, function, hook*, job, load, millstone*, minding the store*, mission, must, need, obligation, occupation, office, onus, ought*, pains, part, province, role, service, station, string*, taking care of business*, task, trouble, trust, undertaking, weight, work; SEE CONCEPTS *362,376,679*

duty [n2] *tax on foreign goods*
assessment, custom, customs, due, excise, impost, levy, rate, revenue, tariff, toll; SEE CONCEPT *329*

duty [n3] *moral obligation*
accountability, accountableness, allegiance, amenability, answerability, burden, call of duty, charge, conscience, deference, devoir, faithfulness, good faith, honesty, integrity, liability, loyalty, obedience, pledge, respect, reverence; SEE CONCEPT *388*

dwarf [adj] *miniature, tiny*
baby, diminutive, low, petite, pocket, small, undersized; SEE CONCEPT *773*

dwarf [n] *very small person*
bantam, dwarfling, homunculus, Lilliputian*, midget, Tom Thumb*; SEE CONCEPT *424*

dwarf [v] *minimize*
belittle, check, detract from, dim, diminish, dominate, hinder, look down upon, lower, make small, micrify, minify, overshadow, predominate, retard, rise above, stunt, suppress, tower above, tower over; SEE CONCEPTS *7,19,698,741*

dwell [v] *live in*
abide, bide, bunk*, continue, crash*, establish oneself, exist, flop*, hang one's hat*, hang out*, hole up*, inhabit, keep house, locate, lodge, make one's home, nest, occupy, park*, perch*, pitch tent*, quarter, remain, rent, reside, rest, room, roost*, settle, sojourn, squat*, stay, stop, tarry, tenant, tent; SEE CONCEPT *226*

dwelling [n] *home*
abode, castle, commoracy, den, digs*, domicile, dump*, establishment, habitat, habitation, haunt, hole in the wall*, house, lodging, pad, quarters, residence, residency; SEE CONCEPT *516*

dwell on/dwell upon [v] *linger over; be engrossed in*
consider, continue, elaborate, emphasize, expatiate, harp on*, involve oneself, tarry over; SEE CONCEPTS *17,239*

dwindle [v] *waste away; taper off*
abate, bate, become smaller, close, contract, decay, decline, decrease, die away, die down, die out, diminish, drain, drop, ebb, fade, fall, grow less, lessen, peter out*, pine, shrink, shrivel, sink, slack off*, subside, taper, wane, weaken, wither; SEE CONCEPTS **698,776**

dye [n] *coloring agent*
color, colorant, dyestuff, pigment, stain, tincture, tinge, tint; SEE CONCEPT **259**

dye [v] *change color with mixture*
impregnate, pigment, stain, tincture, tinge, tint; SEE CONCEPT **250**

dyed-in-the-wool [adj] *through and through*
absolute, complete, deep-down, deeply ingrained, deep-rooted, die-hard, entrenched, fixed, genuine, hardened, long-standing, to the core*, unchangeable, uncompromising; SEE CONCEPT **554**

dying [adj] *failing, expiring*
at death's door*, at end of rope*, decaying, declining, disintegrating, done for*, doomed, ebbing, fading, fated, final, giving up the ghost*, going, in extremis, moribund, mortal, one foot in grave*, on last leg*, passing, perishing, sinking, vanishing, withering; SEE CONCEPT **539**

dynamic [adj] *active, vital*
activating, aggressive, changing, charismatic, coming on strong*, compelling, driving, effective, electric, energetic, energizing, enterprising, forceful, forcible, go-ahead*, go-getter*, go-getting*, highpowered, hyped-up, influential, intense, lively, lusty, magnetic, peppy*, play for keeps*, play hard ball*, potent, powerful, productive, progressive, red-blooded*, strenuous, vehement, vigorous, vitalizing, zippy*; SEE CONCEPTS **404,540,542**

dynamite [n] *explosive*
gelignite, nitroglycerin, TNT, trinitrotoluene; SEE CONCEPT **500**

dynamo [n] *go-getter*
achiever, ball of fire*, bundle of energy*, busy person, doer, eager beaver*, energetic person, fireball*, generator, hard worker, hot shot, live wire*, mover and shaker*, pistol*, risk-taker, spark plug*, whiz kid*; SEE CONCEPT **706**

dynasty [n] *area of rule*
absolutism, ascendancy, dominion, empire, government, house, regime, sovereignty, sway; SEE CONCEPTS **435,508,710**

dysfunctional [adj] *socially impaired*
broken, debilitated, decayed, defective, deteriorated, flawed, inhibited, maladjusted, malfunctional, sick, undermined, unfit, wounded; SEE CONCEPT **314**

E

each [adj] *every*
all, any, exclusive, individual, one by one*, particular, personal, piece by piece*, respective, separate, several, single, specific, various, without exception; SEE CONCEPT **577**

each [adv] *apiece; for one*
all, a pop*, a shot*, aside, a throw*, by the,

every, individually, per, per capita, per head, per person, per unit, proportionately, respectively, separately, singly, without exception; SEE CONCEPT **577**

each [prep] *each one*
each and every one*, each other, every last one, every one, one, one and all*, one another; SEE CONCEPT **577**

eager [adj] *anxious, enthusiastic*
acquisitive, agog, ambitious, antsy, appetent, ardent, athirst, avid, breathless, champing at the bit*, covetous, craving, desiring, desirous, dying to, earnest, fervent, fervid, greedy, gung ho*, hankering, heated, hot*, hot to trot*, hungry*, impatient, intent, keen, longing, pining, rarin' to go*, ready and willing*, restive, restless, self-starting, solicitous, thirsty, vehement, voracious, warmblooded*, wild, wishful, yearning, zealous; SEE CONCEPTS **326,401,542**

eager beaver [n] *active person*
ambitious person, ball of fire*, busy bee*, busy person, doer, dynamo, fireball*, go-getter, hot shot, live wire*, pistol*, self-starter, spark plug*, workhorse; SEE CONCEPT **706**

eagerness [n] *enthusiasm, anxiousness*
alacrity, ambition, anticipation, ardor, avidity, earnestness, excitement, fervor, greediness, gusto, heartiness, hunger, impatience, impetuosity, intentness, keenness, longing, promptness, quickness, solicitude, thirst, vehemence, voracity, yearning, zeal, zest, zing*; SEE CONCEPTS **20,633,657**

eagle-eyed [adj] *keen-eyed*
clear-sighted, hawk-eyed, observant, perceptive, perspicacious, sharp-eyed, X-ray eye; SEE CONCEPTS **402,542**

ear [n] *attention*
appreciation, consideration, discrimination, hearing, heed, mark, mind, note, notice, observance, observation, perception, regard, remark, sensitivity, taste; SEE CONCEPT **532**

early [adj1] *in the beginning*
a bit previous, aboriginal, ancient, antecedent, antediluvian, antiquated, brand-new, budding, early bird*, fresh, initial, new, original, preceding, premier, prevenient, previous, primal, prime, primeval, primitive, primordial, prior, pristine, proleptical, raw, recent, undeveloped, young; SEE CONCEPTS **799,828**

early [adj2] *sooner than expected*
advanced, ahead of time, anticipative, anticipatory, before appointed time, beforehand, direct, immature, immediate, matinal, on short notice*, on the dot*, overearly, oversoon, preceding, precipitant, precocious, preexistent, premature, previous, prompt, pronto, punctual, quick, seasonable, soon, speedy, unanticipated, unexpected, untimely; SEE CONCEPT **820**

early [adv1] *sooner than expected*
a bit previous, ahead of time, anon, beforehand, before long, betimes, briefly, bright and early*, directly, early bird*, ere long, far ahead, immediately, in advance, in good time*, in the bud*, in time, on short notice*, on the dot*, oversoon, prematurely, presently, previous, promptly, pronto, proximately, quick, shortly, soon, too soon, unexpectedly, with time to spare*; SEE CONCEPT **820**

early [adv2] *immediately*
at once, betimes, directly, first, freshly, in a

jiffy*, in an instant*, in no time*, instantaneously, instantly, newly, presto, primitively, promptly, recently, right away, seasonably, soon, straightaway, summarily, thereon, thereupon, timely, without delay; SEE CONCEPTS *799,828*

earmark [*n*] *signature characteristic*
attribute, differential, distinction, feature, hallmark, label, marking, peculiarity, quality, stamp, tag, token, trademark, trait; SEE CONCEPT *644*

earmark [*v*] *reserve*
allocate, designate, keep back, label, maintain, mark out, name, set aside, slot, tab, tag; SEE CONCEPT *129*

earn [*v1*] *make money*
acquire, attain, be gainfully employed, be in line for*, bring home*, bring home the bacon*, bring home the groceries*, bring in, clean up*, clear*, collect, consummate, cop*, derive, draw, effect, gain, gather, get, gross, hustle, make, make fast buck*, make it big*, net, obtain, pay one's dues*, perform, pick up, procure, profit, pull*, pull down*, rate, realize, reap, receive, scare up*, score*, scrape together*, secure, snag*, sock*, turn, win, wrangle; SEE CONCEPTS *330,351*

earn [*v2*] *deserve a reward*
acquire, attain, bag, be entitled to, be worthy of, come by, gain, harvest, merit, net, rate, reap, score, warrant, win; SEE CONCEPTS *120,129*

earnest [*adj1*] *very enthusiastic*
ardent, busy, devoted, diligent, eager, fervent, fervid, heartfelt, impassioned, industrious, keen, passionate, perseverant, purposeful, sedulous, sincere, urgent, vehement, warm, wholehearted, zealous; SEE CONCEPTS *326,401,542*

earnest [*adj2*] *serious; very important*
close, constant, determined, firm, fixed, for real, grave, intent, mean business, meaningful, nofooling, no-nonsense, playing hard ball*, resolute, resolved, sedate, sincere, sober, solemn, somber, stable, staid, steady, thoughtful, weighty; SEE CONCEPT *568*

earnestness [*n*] *determination; seriousness*
absorption, ardor, attentiveness, concentration, decision, deliberation, devotion, doggedness, eagerness, engrossment, enthusiasm, fervor, firmness, gravity, intensity, intentness, keenness, passion, perseverance, persistence, purposefulness, resolution, resolve, serious-mindedness, sincerity, sobriety, solemnity, stress, tenacity, urgency, vehemence, warmth, zeal; SEE CONCEPTS *633,657*

earnings [*n*] *money for work performed*
balance, bottom line*, emolument, gain, gate, groceries*, income, in the black*, lucre, net, pay, payoff, piece of the pie*, proceeds, profit, receipts, remuneration, return, revenue, reward, salary, salt*, stipend, take-home*, takings, wages; SEE CONCEPT *344*

earsplitting [*adj*] *loud*
blaring, deafening, noisy, penetrating, piercing, ringing, shrill, strident, thunderous; SEE CONCEPTS *592,594*

Earth [*n1*] *the world*
apple*, big blue marble*, cosmos, creation, dust*, globe, macrocosm, orb, planet, sphere, star, sublunary world, terra, terra firma, terrene, terrestrial sphere, universe, vale; SEE CONCEPT *511*

earth [*n2*] *ground, soil*
alluvium, clay, clod, coast, compost, deposit, dirt, dry land, dust, fill, glebe, gravel, humus, land, loam, marl, mold, muck, mud, peat moss, sand, shore, sod, subsoil, surface, terra firma, terrain, terrane, topsoil, turf; SEE CONCEPT *509*

earthling [*n*] *human being*
earth dweller, humankind, man, person, tellurian, woman; SEE CONCEPT *417*

earthly [*adj1*] *physically concerning land or its inhabitants*
alluvial, carnal, corporeal, geotic, global, human, in all creation, material, mortal, mundane, nonspiritual, physical, profane, secular, subastral, sublunary, tellurian, telluric, temporal, terraqueous, terrene, terrestrial, uncelestial, under the sun*, unspiritual, worldly; SEE CONCEPT *536*

earthly [*adj2*] *conceivable*
feasible, imaginable, likely, mortal, possible, potential, practical, probable; SEE CONCEPT *552*

earthmover [*n*] *bulldozer*
backhoe, excavator, grader, heavy machinery, tracked vehicle; SEE CONCEPT *505*

earthquake [*n*] *tremor from inside the earth*
convulsion, fault, macroseism, microseism, movement, quake, quaker*, seimicity, seism, seismism, shake, shock, slip, temblor, trembler*, undulation, upheaval; SEE CONCEPTS *144,526*

earthy [*adj*] *unsophisticated*
bawdy, coarse, crude, down, down home*, down-to-earth*, dull, easygoing, folksy, funky*, hard-boiled*, home folk*, homely, homey, indelicate, lowbred, lusty, mundane, natural, pragmatic, ribald, robust, rough, simple, unidealistic, uninhibited, unrefined; SEE CONCEPT *542*

ease [*n1*] *peace, quiet; lack of difficulty*
affluence, ataraxia, bed of roses*, calm, calmness, comfort, content, contentment, easiness, enjoyment, gratification, happiness, idleness, inactivity, inertia, inertness, leisure, luxury, passivity, peace of mind*, prosperity, quietness, quietude, relaxation, repose, requiescence, rest, restfulness, satisfaction, security, serenity, supinity, tranquility; SEE CONCEPTS *388,410,673*

ease [*n2*] *facility, freedom*
adroitness, affability, aplomb, breeze, child's play*, cinch, cleverness, composure, dexterity, dispatch, duck soup*, easygoingness, efficiency, effortlessness, expertise, expertness, familiarity, flexibility, fluency, informality, insouciance, knack, liberty, naturalness, nonchalance, poise, pushover, quickness, readiness, relaxedness, setup, simplicity, skillfulness, smoothness, smooth sailing*, snap, unaffectedness, unconstraint, unreservedness; SEE CONCEPTS *376,388,630*

ease [*v1*] *alleviate, help*
abate, aid, allay, ameliorate, anesthetize, appease, assist, assuage, attend to, calm, cheer, clear the way*, comfort, cure, disburden, disengage, doctor, expedite, facilitate, forward, free, further, improve, lessen, let up on, lift, lighten, make easier, meliorate, mitigate, moderate, mollify, nurse, open the door*, pacify, palliate, promote, quiet, relax, release, relent, relieve, run interference for*, simplify, slacken, smooth, soften, soothe, speed, still, tranquilize, untighten; SEE CONCEPTS *110,310*

ease [*v2*] *guide, move carefully*
disentangle, edge, extricate, facilitate, handle,

dw
ea

inch, induce, insert, join, loose, loosen, maneuver, relax, remove, right, set right, slack, slacken, slide, slip, squeeze, steer, untighten; SEE CONCEPT *187*

easel [*n*] *stand*
frame, mount, tripod; SEE CONCEPTS *442,733,757*

easement [*n*] *right of way*
access, legal right, means of access, passage; SEE CONCEPTS *318,685*

easily [*adv1*] *without difficulty*
calmly, comfortably, competently, conveniently, coolly, dexterously, efficiently, effortlessly, evenly, facilely, fluently, freely, handily, hand over fist*, hands down*, just like that*, lightly, like nothing*, no sweat*, nothing to it*, piece of cake*, plainly, quickly, readily, regularly, simply, smoothly, steadily, surely, swimmingly, uncomplicatedly, well, with ease, with no effort, without a hitch*, without trouble; SEE CONCEPT *565*

easily [*adv2*] *without a doubt*
absolutely, actually, almost certainly, assuredly, beyond question, by far, certainly, clearly, decidedly, definitely, doubtless, doubtlessly, far and away, indeed, indisputably, indubitably, no doubt, plainly, positively, probably, really, surely, truly, undeniably, undoubtedly, unequivocally, unquestionably; SEE CONCEPTS *535,552*

easy [*adj1*] *not difficult*
accessible, apparent, basic, child's play*, cinch, clear, easily done, effortless, elementary, evident, facile, inconsiderable, light, little, manageable, manifest, mere, no bother*, no problem*, no sweat*, not burdensome, nothing to it*, no trouble*, obvious, painless, paltry, picnic*, piece of cake*, plain, plain sailing*, pushover*, royal, simple, simple as ABC*, slight, smooth, snap, straightforward, uncomplicated, undemanding, uninvolved, untroublesome, wieldy, yielding; SEE CONCEPT *565*

easy [*adj2*] *leisurely, relaxed*
at ease, calm, carefree, comfortable, comfy, commodious, composed, content, contented, cozy, cursive, cushy, easeful, effortless, flowing, fluent, forthright, gentle, in clover*, languid, light, mild, moderate, peaceful, pleasant, prosperous, quiet, running, satisfied, secure, serene, slow, smooth, snug, soft, spontaneous, substantial, successful, temperate, thriving, tranquil, undemanding, undistorted, unexacting, unhurried, untroubled, unworried, well-to-do; SEE CONCEPTS *542,544*

easy [*adj3*] *tolerant, permissive*
accommodating, amenable, benign, biddable, charitable, clement, compassionate, compliant, condoning, deceivable, deludable, dupable, easygoing, excusing, exploitable, fleeceable, flexible, forbearing, forgiving, gentle, gullible, humoring, indulgent, kindly, lax, lenient, liberal, light, merciful, mild, moderate, mollycoddling*, naive, pampering, pardoning, soft, spoiling, submissive, susceptible, sympathetic, temperate, tractable, trusting, unburdensome, unoppressive, unsuspicious; SEE CONCEPT *401*

easy [*adj4*] *good-humored*
affable, amiable, at ease, carefree, casual, complaisant, diplomatic, familiar, friendly, gentle, good natured, good-tempered, graceful, gracious, gregarious, informal, mild, natural, obliging, open, pleasant, polite, relaxed, secure,

smooth, sociable, suave, tolerant, unaffected, unanxious, undemanding, unforced, unpretentious, urbane; SEE CONCEPT *404*

easy as pie [*adj*] *very easy*
duck soup, easily done, easily managed, easy as can be, like falling off a log*, like shooting fish in a barrel*, like stealing candy from a baby*, no sweat, simple, simple as ABC; SEE CONCEPTS *527,565*

easygoing [*adj*] *complacent, permissive*
amenable, breezy, calm, carefree, casual, collected, complaisant, composed, devil-may-care*, even-tempered*, flexible, free and easy*, hang-loose*, happy-go-lucky*, indolent, indulgent, informal, insouciant, laid-back*, lazy, lenient, liberal, low-pressure, mild, moderate, nonchalant, offhand, outgiving, patient, placid, poised, relaxed, self-possessed, serene, tolerant, tranquil, unconcerned, uncritical, undemanding, unhurried, uninhibited; SEE CONCEPT *404*

eat [*v1*] *consume food*
absorb, attack, banquet, bite, bolt*, break bread*, breakfast, chew, chow down*, cram*, devour, digest, dine, dispatch, dispose of, fall to, feast upon, feed, gobble up*, gorge, gormandize, graze*, have a bite*, have a meal, have for, ingest, inhale*, lunch, make pig of oneself*, masticate, munch, nibble, nosh*, partake of, peck at*, pick, pig out*, polish off*, pork out*, put away*, ruminate, scarf*, scoff, snack, sup, swallow, take food, take in, take nourishment, wolf; SEE CONCEPT *169*

eat [*v2*] *erode, wear away; use up*
bite, condense, corrode, crumble, decay, decompose, disappear, disintegrate, dissipate, dissolve, drain, exhaust, gnaw, liquefy, melt, nibble, rot, run through, rust, spill, squander, vanish, waste away; SEE CONCEPTS *225,469*

eatable [*adj*] *able to be consumed*
appetizing, comestible, culinary, delicious, delish*, dietary, digestible, edible, esculent, fit, good, harmless, kosher*, nutritious, nutritive, palatable, piquant, safe, satisfying, savory, scrumptious, succulent, tasty, tempting, wholesome, yummy*; SEE CONCEPTS *462,613*

eat high on the hog [*v*] *live well*
be in fat city*, be in hog heaven*, be sitting pretty, have it good, have it made, sit pretty; SEE CONCEPTS *5539,544,589*

eating disorder [*n*] *unhealthy disturbance in eating behavior*
anorexia nervosa, bingeing, bulimarexia, bulimia, compulsive eating, hypheragia, pica, psychological disorder, purging; SEE CONCEPT *316*

eat up [*v*] *to accept*
buy, stand still for, swallow; SEE CONCEPT *12*

eavesdrop [*v*] *listen without permission*
be all ears*, bend an ear*, bug, ears into*, listen in, monitor, overhear, pry, snoop, spy, tap, tune in on*, wire, wiretap; SEE CONCEPTS *188,596*

ebb [*n*] *regression; decline*
abatement, backflow, decay, decrease, degeneration, depreciation, deterioration, diminution, drop, dwindling, fading away, flagging, going out, lessening, low tide, low water, outward flow, petering out*, recession, refluence, reflux, retreat, retrocession, retroflux, shrinkage, sinking, slackening, subsidence, sweep, wane, waning, weakening, withdrawal; SEE CONCEPTS *195,698*

ebb [v] *subside; decline*
abate, decay, decrease, degenerate, deteriorate, die down, die out, diminish, drop, dwindle, ease off, fade away, fall, fall away, fall back, flag, flow back, go out, languish, lessen, let up, melt, moderate, peter out, recede, relent, retire, retreat, retrocede, shrink, sink, slacken, wane, weaken, withdraw; SEE CONCEPTS *195,698*

ebullience [n] *enthusiasm*
agitation, animation, buoyancy, effervescence, effusiveness, elation, excitement, exhilaration, exuberance, exuberancy, ferment, gaiety, high-spiritedness, high spirits, liveliness, vitality, vivaciousness, vivacity, zest; SEE CONCEPT *633*

ebullient [adj] *enthusiastic*
agitated, bouncy, brash, buoyant, chipper*, chirpy*, effervescent, effusive, elated, excited, exhilarated, exuberant, frothy*, gushing, high-spirited, in high spirits*, irrepressible, vivacious, zestful, zippy*; SEE CONCEPT *401*

eccentric [adj] *bizarre, unusual*
aberrant, abnormal, anomalous, beat*, bent*, bizarre, capricious, characteristic, cockeyed, crazy, curious, droll, erratic, far out*, flaky, freak, freakish, funky*, funny, idiosyncratic, irregular, kooky, nutty, odd, oddball, offbeat, off-center, off the wall*, out in left field*, outlandish, peculiar, quaint, queer, quirky, quizzical, singular, strange, uncommon, unconventional, unnatural, way out*, weird, whimsical, wild; SEE CONCEPTS *547,564*

eccentric [n] *person who is bizarre, unusual*
beatnik, character, freak, hippie, kook, loner, maverick, nonconformist, nut*, oddball, oddity, odd person, original, queer duck*, rare bird*, three-dollar bill*, weirdo; SEE CONCEPT *423*

eccentricity [n] *bizarreness, unusualness*
aberration, abnormality, anomaly, caprice, capriciousness, foible, freakishness, hereticism, idiocrasy, idiosyncrasy, irregularity, kink, nonconformity, oddity, oddness, outlandishness, peculiarity, queerness, quirk, singularity, strangeness, unconventionality, unorthodoxness, waywardness, weirdness, whimsicality, whimsicalness; SEE CONCEPTS *647,665*

ecclesiastical [adj] *churchly*
clerical, diaconal, episcopal, holy, ministerial, orthodox, parochial, pastoral, religious, sectarian, spiritual; SEE CONCEPTS *536,582*

echelon [n] *class, level*
degree, file, grade, line, office, place, position, queue, rank, row, string, tier; SEE CONCEPTS *378,388*

echo [n] *repeat, copy*
answer, imitation, mirror, mirror image, onomatopoeia, parallel, parroting, rebound, reflection, reiteration, repercussion, repetition, reply, reproduction, reverberation, ringing, rubber stamp*; SEE CONCEPTS *595,695,716*

echo [v] *repeat, copy*
ape, ditto*, do like*, go like*, imitate, impersonate, make like*, mimic, mirror, parallel, parrot, react, recall, redouble, reflect, reiterate, reproduce, resemble, resound, respond, reverberate, ring, rubber-stamp*, second, vibrate; SEE CONCEPTS *91,171*

eclectic [adj] *comprehensive, general*
all-embracing, assorted, broad, catholic, dilettantish, diverse, diversified, heterogeneous, inclusive, liberal, many-sided, mingled, mixed,
multifarious, multiform, selective, universal, varied, wide-ranging; SEE CONCEPTS *537,772*

eclipse [n] *shadowing of the sun*
concealment, darkening, decline, diminution, dimming, extinction, extinguishment, obliteration, obscuration, occultation, penumbra, shading, shroud, veil; SEE CONCEPTS *522,624*

eclipse [v1] *obscure, veil*
adumbrate, becloud, bedim, blot out, cloud, darken, dim, extinguish, murk, overshadow, shadow, shroud; SEE CONCEPT *250*

eclipse [v2] *surpass achievement*
exceed, excel, outdo, outshine, overrun, surmount, tower above, transcend; SEE CONCEPT *141*

ecology [n] *environmental science*
bionomics, conservation, preservation; SEE CONCEPTS *134,257*

economic [adj] *business-related; financial*
bread-and-butter*, budgetary, commercial, fiscal, industrial, material, mercantile, monetary, money-making, pecuniary, productive, profitable, profit-making, remunerative, solvent, viable; SEE CONCEPTS *334,536*

economical [adj1] *conservative with resources; careful*
avaricious, canny, chary, circumspect, close, closefisted, cost-effective, curmudgeonly, efficient, frugal, meager, mean, methodical, miserly, money-saving, niggardly*, on the rims*, parsimonious, penny-pinching*, penny-wise*, penurious, practical, provident, prudent, prudential, saving, scrimping, skimping, spare, sparing, stingy, thrifty, tight, time-saving, unwasteful, watchful, work-saving; SEE CONCEPT *542*

economical [adj2] *inexpensive*
bought for a song*, cheap, cost next to nothing*, cost nothing, cut rate, dime a dozen*, dirt cheap*, dog cheap*, fair, low, low-priced, low tariff, marked down, moderate, modest, on sale, quite a buy*, reasonable, reduced, sound, steal*; SEE CONCEPT *334*

economize [v] *save money*
be frugal, be prudent, be sparing, conserve, cut back, cut corners*, cut down, keep within means, make ends meet*, manage, meet a budget, pay one's way*, pinch pennies*, retrench, run tight ship*, scrimp, shepherd, skimp, stint, stretch a dollar*, tighten one's belt*; SEE CONCEPT *330*

economy [n] *saving, frugality*
abridgement, austerity, care, carefulness, caution, curtailment, cutback, decrease, deduction, direction, discretion, husbandry, layoff, meanness, miserliness, moratorium, niggardliness, parcity, parsimony, providence, prudence, recession, reduction, regulation, restraint, retrenchment, rollback, scrimping, shrinkage, skimping, sparingness, stinginess, supervision, thrift, thriftiness; SEE CONCEPTS *117,330,335*

eco-rich [adj] *possessing an abundance of natural resources*
bountiful, clean, flowing, full, green, natural, plentiful, pure, rich; SEE CONCEPT *518*

ecosystem [n] *environment*
ecological community, environs; SEE CONCEPTS *515,673,696*

ecstasy [n] *bliss*
beatitude, blessedness, cool*, delectation, delight, delirium, ebullience, elation, enchantment, enthusiasm, euphoria, exaltation, felicity, fervor,

ea
ec

frenzy, gladness, happiness, heaven, inspiration, intoxication, joy, joyfulness, paradise, rapture, ravishment, rhapsody, seventh heaven*, trance, transport, twilight zone*; SEE CONCEPT *410*

ecstatic [*adj*] *very happy, blissful*
athrill, beatific, crazy, delirious, dreamy, elated, enraptured, enthusiastic, entranced, euphoric, fervent, floating, flying high*, frenzied, gone*, high*, in exaltation, in seventh heaven*, joyful, joyous, mad, on cloud nine*, out, overjoyed, pleased as punch*, rapturous, ravished, rhapsodic, sent*, sunny, thrilled, tickled pink*, tickled to death*, transported*, turned on*, upbeat, wild; SEE CONCEPT *403*

ecumenical [*adj*] *general*
all-comprehensive, all-inclusive, all-pervading, catholic, comprehensive, cosmic, cosmopolitan, global, inclusive, planetary, unifying, universal, worldwide; SEE CONCEPTS *537,772*

eddy [*n*] *current*
swirl, tide, vortex, whirlpool; SEE CONCEPT *514*

Eden [*n*] *Paradise*
Arcadia, garden, Garden of Eden, heaven, heaven on earth, promised land, Shangri-La, Utopia; SEE CONCEPTS *370,410,515*

edge [*n1*] *border, outline*
bend, berm, bound, boundary, brim, brink, butt, circumference, contour, corner, crook, crust, curb, end, extremity, frame, fringe, frontier, hem, hook, ledge, limb, limit, line, lip, margin, molding, mouth, outskirt, peak, perimeter, periphery, point, portal, rim, ring, shore, side, skirt, split, strand, term, threshold, tip, trimming, turn, verge; SEE CONCEPTS *484,513*

edge [*n2*] *advantage*
allowance, ascendancy, bulge, dominance, draw, handicap, head start, lead, odds, start, superiority, upper hand*, vantage; SEE CONCEPT *712*

edge [*v1*] *border, trim*
bind, bound, decorate, fringe, hem, margin, outline, rim, shape, skirt, surround, verge; SEE CONCEPTS *751,758*

edge [*v2*] *defeat narrowly*
creep, ease, inch, infiltrate, nose out*, sidle, slip by, slip past, squeeze by*, squeeze past*, steal, worm*; SEE CONCEPT *95*

edge [*v3*] *sharpen*
file, grind, hone, polish, sharpen, strop, whet; SEE CONCEPTS *137,250*

edgy [*adj*] *nervous*
anxious, critical, excitable, excited, high-strung, ill at ease, impatient, irascible, irritable, keyed up*, overstrung, restive, restless, skittish, tense, touchy, uneasy, uptight; SEE CONCEPT *401*

edible [*adj*] *able to be eaten*
comestible, digestible, eatable, esculent, fit, good, harmless, nourishing, nutritious, nutritive, palatable, savory, succulent, tasty, toothsome, wholesome; SEE CONCEPTS *462,613*

edict [*n*] *pronouncement, order*
act, canon, command, commandment, decree, decretum, dictate, dictum, directive, enactment, fiat, injunction, instrument, judgment, law, mandate, manifesto, ordinance, precept, prescript, proclamation, pronunciamento, regulation, rule, ruling, statute, ukase, writ; SEE CONCEPTS *278,662,688*

edification [*n*] *improvement, education*
betterment, elevation, elucidation, enhancement, enlightenment, guidance, illumination, informa-

tion, instruction, irradiation, knowledge, learning, nurture, schooling, teaching, tuition, uplifting; SEE CONCEPTS *31,287,700*

edifice [*n*] *structure*
building, construction, erection, habitation, house, monument, pile, rockpile*, skyscraper, towers; SEE CONCEPT *439*

edit [*v*] *rewrite, refine*
adapt, alter, amplify, analyze, annotate, arrange, assemble, assign, blue-pencil*, boil down*, butcher, censor, check, choose, compile, compose, condense, correct, cut, delete, discard, doctor, draft, emend, excise, feature, fine-tune, finish, fly speck*, go over, make up, massage*, polish, prepare, prescribe, proofread, publish, put together, rearrange, recalibrate, rectify, redact, regulate, rehash, rephrase, report, revise, scrub*, select, set up, strike out, style, tighten, trim, write over; SEE CONCEPTS *79,126,203*

edition [*n*] *issue of publication*
copy, impression, imprint, number, printing, program, publication, reissue, release, reprint, reprinting, version, volume; SEE CONCEPT *280*

editorial [*n*] *commentary*
article, critique, opinion, report, review; SEE CONCEPTS *51,278*

educate [*v*] *teach information, experience*
brainwash*, brief, civilize, coach, cultivate, develop, discipline, drill, drum into, edify, enlighten, exercise, explain, foster, improve, indoctrinate, inform, instruct, let in on, mature, nurture, put hip*, put through the grind*, rear, school, show the ropes*, train, tutor; SEE CONCEPTS *61,285*

educated [*adj*] *learned, experienced*
accomplished, acquainted with, brainy, civilized, coached, corrected, cultivated, cultured, developed, enlightened, enriched, erudite, expert, finished, fitted, formed, informed, initiated, instructed, intelligent, knowledgeable, lettered, literary, literate, nurtured, polished, prepared, professional, refined, scholarly, schooled, scientific, shaped, skilled, tasteful, taught, trained, tutored, versed in, well-informed, well-read, well-taught, well-versed; SEE CONCEPT *402*

education [*n*] *instruction, development of knowledge*
apprenticeship, background, book learning*, brainwashing*, breeding, catechism, civilization, coaching, cultivation, culture, direction, discipline, drilling, edification, enlightenment, erudition, finish, guidance, improvement, inculcation, indoctrination, information, learnedness, learning, literacy, nurture, pedagogy, preparation, propagandism, proselytism, reading, rearing, refinement, scholarship, schooling, science, study, teaching, training, tuition, tutelage, tutoring; SEE CONCEPTS *285,287,409*

educational [*adj*] *instructional*
academic, cultural, didactic, informational, informative, instructive, scholarly, scholastic, tutorial; SEE CONCEPT *536*

educator [*n*] *teacher*
coach, dean, department head, educationist, instructor, lecturer, mentor, monitor, professor, schoolteacher, trainer, tutor; SEE CONCEPT *350*

educe [*v*] *bring out, elicit*
come out, conclude, deduce, derive, develop, distill, drag, draw, draw out, evince, evoke, evolve, excogitate, extort, extract, gain, get,

infer, milk*, obtain, procure, pull, reason, secure, think out, wrest, wring; SEE CONCEPTS *37,142*

eerie [*adj*] *spooky*
awesome, bizarre, crawly, creepy, fantastic, fearful, frightening, ghostly, mysterious, scary, spectral, strange, supernatural, superstitious, uncanny, unearthly, weird; SEE CONCEPT *537*

efface [*v*] *erase*
blot out, blue-pencil, cancel, cross out, delete, destroy, edit, eliminate, expunge, fade, obliterate, rub out, scratch out, white out, wipe out; SEE CONCEPTS *211,215*

effect [*n1*] *result*
aftereffect, aftermath, backlash, backwash, can of worms*, causatum, chain reaction*, conclusion, consequence, corollary, denouement, development, end, end product, event, eventuality, fallout, flak*, follow through, follow-up, fruit, issue, outcome, outgrowth, precipitate, pursuance, ramification, reaction, reflex, repercussion, response, sequel, sequence, side effect, spin-off, upshot*, waves*; SEE CONCEPT *230*

effect [*n2*] *impact, impression*
action, clout, drift, effectiveness, efficacy, efficiency, enforcement, essence, execution, fact, force, implementation, import, imprint, influence, mark, meaning, power, purport, purpose, reality, sense, significance, strength, tenor, use, validity, vigor, weight; SEE CONCEPT *687*

effect [*v*] *carry out, accomplish*
achieve, actualize, actuate, begin, bring about, bring off, bring on, buy, carry through, cause, complete, conceive, conclude, consummate, create, do a number*, do one's thing*, do the job*, do the trick*, do to a T*, draw on, effectuate, enact, enforce, execute, fulfill, generate, get across, get to, give rise to, implement, induce, initiate, invoke, make, make it*, make waves*, perform, procure, produce, pull it off*, put across, realize, render, secure, sell, turn out, turn the trick*, unzip*, yield; SEE CONCEPTS *91,706*

effective [*adj1*] *productive, persuasive*
able, active, adequate, capable, cogent, compelling, competent, convincing, direct, effectual, efficacious, efficient, emphatic, energetic, forceful, forcible, having lead in pencil*, impressive, live, moving, on the ball*, operative, playing hardball*, potent, powerful, powerhouse*, practical, producing, resultant, serviceable, serving, sound, striking, sufficient, telling, trenchant, useful, valid, virtuous, wicked*, yielding; SEE CONCEPTS *537,540*

effective [*adj2*] *in use at the time*
active, actual, current, direct, dynamic, in effect, in execution, in force, in operation, operative, real; SEE CONCEPTS *560,582,799*

effectiveness [*n*] *influence*
capability, clout, cogency, effect, efficacy, efficiency, force, forcefulness, performance, point, potency, power, punch, strength, success, use, validity, validness, verve, vigor, weight; SEE CONCEPTS *676,687*

effects [*n*] *belongings*
accouterments, chattels, goods, holdings, paraphernalia, possessions, property, stuff, things, trappings; SEE CONCEPTS *446,710*

effectual [*adj*] *influential; authoritative*
accomplishing, achieving, adequate, binding, capable, conclusive, decisive, determinative, effecting, effective, efficacious, efficient, forcible,

fulfilling, in force, lawful, legal, licit, potent, powerful, practicable, productive, qualified, serviceable, sound, strong, successful, telling, useful, valid, virtuous, workable; SEE CONCEPTS *319,528,537*

effeminate [*adj*] *having female qualities*
epicene, feminine, womanish, womanlike, womanly; SEE CONCEPTS *401,404*

effervescence [*n1*] *fizz, foam*
bubbles, bubbling, ebullition, ferment, fermentation, froth, frothing, sparkle; SEE CONCEPTS *437,522*

effervescence [*n2*] *enthusiasm, vivacity*
animation, buoyancy, ebullience, excitedness, excitement, exhilaration, exuberance, exuberancy, gaiety, happiness, high spirits, joy, liveliness, vim, vitality, volatility, zing*; SEE CONCEPTS *633,657*

effervescent [*adj1*] *fizzing, foaming*
airy, boiling, bouncy, bubbling, bubbly, carbonated, elastic, expansive, fermenting, frothing, frothy, resilient, sparkling, volatile; SEE CONCEPTS *462,485*

effervescent [*adj2*] *enthusiastic, vivacious*
animated, bouncy, brash, bubbly, buoyant, ebullient, excited, exhilarated, exuberant, gleeful, happy, high-spirited, hilarious, in high spirits*, irrepressible, jolly, joyous, lively, merry, mirthful, sprightly, vital, zingy; SEE CONCEPTS *401,542*

effete [*adj1*] *spoiled, exhausted*
burnt out*, corrupt, debased, decadent, decayed, declining, decrepit, degenerate, dissipated, dissolute, drained, enervated, enfeebled, far-gone*, feeble, immoral, obsolete, overrefined, overripe, played out*, soft, spent, vitiated, washed-out*, wasted, weak, worn out; SEE CONCEPT *560*

effete [*adj2*] *unproductive*
barren, fruitless, impotent, infecund, infertile, sterile, unfruitful, unprolific; SEE CONCEPT *527*

efficacious [*adj*] *efficient, productive*
active, adequate, capable, competent, effective, effectual, energetic, influential, operative, potent, powerful, puissant, serviceable, strong, successful, useful, virtuous; SEE CONCEPTS *528,537*

efficacy [*n*] *efficiency; productiveness*
ability, adequacy, capability, capableness, capacity, competence, effect, effectiveness, efficaciousness, energy, force, influence, performance, potency, power, strength, success, sufficiency, use, vigor, virtue, weight; SEE CONCEPTS *641,676,706*

efficiency [*n*] *adeptness, effectiveness*
ability, abundance, adaptability, address, adequacy, capability, capableness, competence, competency, completeness, economy, effectualness, efficacy, energy, expertise, facility, faculty, know-how, performance, potency, power, powerfulness, productiveness, productivity, proficiency, prowess, quantity, readiness, resourcefulness, response, skill, skillfulness, suitability, suitableness, talent, thoroughness; SEE CONCEPTS *409,630,658*

efficient [*adj*] *adept, effective*
able, accomplished, active, adapted, adequate, apt, businesslike, capable, clever, competent, conducive, decisive, deft, dynamic, economic, economical, effectual, efficacious, energetic, equal to, experienced, expert, familiar with, fitted, good at, good for, handy, masterly, orga-

nized, potent, powerful, practiced, productive, proficient, profitable, qualified, ready, saving, shrewd, skilled, skillful, systematic, talented, tough, useful, valuable, virtuous, well-organized; SEE CONCEPTS *402,527,560*

effigy [*n*] *dummy*
figure, icon, idol, image, likeness, model, picture, portrait, puppet, representation, statue; SEE CONCEPT *436*

effort [*n*] *work, exertion*
accomplishment, achievement, act, aim, application, aspiration, attempt, battle, crack*, creation, deed, discipline, drill, elbow grease*, endeavor, energy, enterprise, essay, exercise, feat, fling*, force, go*, industry, intention, job, labor, old college try*, pains, power, product, production, pull, purpose, push, resolution, shot*, spurt, stab*, strain, stress, stretch, strife, striving, struggle, sweat, tension, toil, training, travail, trial, trouble, try, tug*, undertaking, venture, whack*; SEE CONCEPTS *87,362,677,724*

effortless [*adj*] *easy*
child's play*, cursive, duck soup*, facile, flowing, fluent, light, no problem*, no sweat*, offhand, painless, picnic*, piece of cake*, royal, running, simple, smooth, snap*, uncomplicated, undemanding, untroublesome; SEE CONCEPT *565*

effrontery [*n*] *nerve, boldness*
arrogance, assurance, audacity, backtalk, brashness, brass*, brazenness, cheek*, cheekiness, chutzpah*, crust*, disrespect, face, gall, guff, hardihood, impertinence, impudence, incivility, insolence, lip*, presumption, rudeness, sass, sauce*, self-assurance, self-confidence, shamelessness, smart talk, temerity; SEE CONCEPTS *411,633*

effulgent [*adj*] *glowing, luminous*
beaming, blazing, bright, brilliant, dazzling, flaming, fluorescent, incandescent, lambent, lucent, lustrous, radiant, resplendent, shining, splendid, vivid; SEE CONCEPT *617*

effusion [*n*] *outpouring*
address, diffusion, discharge, effluence, effluvium, efflux, emanation, emission, exudate, gush, gushing, ooze, outflow, pouring, shedding, stream, verbosity, wordiness; SEE CONCEPTS *179,266*

effusive [*adj*] *gushing, profuse*
all jaw*, big mouthed*, demonstrative, ebullient, enthusiastic, expansive, extravagant, exuberant, free-flowing, fulsome, gabby*, gushy*, lavish, outpouring, overflowing, prolix, talkative, unconstrained, unreserved, unrestrained, verbose, windbag*, windy*, wordy; SEE CONCEPTS *267,542*

egalitarian [*adj*] *equal*
democratic, equitable, even-handed, impartial, just, unbiased; SEE CONCEPTS *319,536*

egg [*n*] *seed, cell; embryo of an animal*
bud, cackle*, cackleberry*, germ, nucleus, oospore, ovum, roe, rudiment, spawn, yellow eye*; SEE CONCEPTS *389,392*

egghead [*n*] *intellectual*
bluestocking, bookworm*, brain*, geek*, genius, highbrow, know-it-all*, longhair*, rocket scientist*, scholar, thinker; SEE CONCEPTS *350,416*

egg on [*v*] *push to do something*
agitate, arouse, drive, encourage, excite, exhort, goad, incite, instigate, pique, prick, prod,

prompt, propel, rally, sic, spur, stimulate, stir up, urge, whip up; SEE CONCEPT *68*

ego [*n*] *personality*
character, psyche, self, self-admiration, selfdom, self-pride; SEE CONCEPT *411*

egocentric [*adj*] *thinking very highly of oneself*
conceited, egoistic, egoistical, egomaniacal, egotistic, egotistical, individualist, individualistic, megalomaniac, narcissistic, pompous, selfabsorbed, self-centered, self-concerned, selfindulgent, selfinterested, selfish, self-loving, self-serving, stuck-up, vainglorious, wrapped up in oneself; SEE CONCEPT *404*

egoism/egotism [*n*] *self-centeredness*
arrogance, assurance, boastfulness, boasting, bragging, conceit, conceitedness, egocentricity, egomania, gasconade, haughtiness, insolence, megalomania, narcissism, ostentation, overconfidence, preoccupation with self, presumption, pride, self-absorption, self-admiration, self-confidence, self-importance, self-interest, selfishness, self-love, self-possession, self-regard, self-worship, superiority, swellheadedness, vainglory, vanity, vaunting; SEE CONCEPT *411*

egotistic/egoistic [*adj*] *thinking very highly of oneself*
affected, aloof, autocratic, boastful, boasting, bragging, conceited, egocentric, egomaniacal, haughty, individualistic, inflated, inner-directed, intimate, intrinsic, introverted, isolated, narcissistic, obsessive, opinionated, personal, pompous, prideful, proud, puffed up*, self-absorbed, self-admiring, self-centered, self-important, snobbish, stuck on oneself*, stuck-up*, subjective, superior, swollen, vain, vainglorious; SEE CONCEPT *404*

egregious [*adj*] *outstandingly bad; outrageous*
arrant, atrocious, capital, deplorable, extreme, flagrant, glaring, grievous, gross*, heinous, infamous, insufferable, intolerable, monstrous, nefarious, notorious, outright, preposterous, rank, scandalous, shocking, stark; SEE CONCEPTS *545,548,570*

egress [*n*] *passage out*
departure, doorway, emanation, emergence, escape, exit, exiting, exodus, issue, opening, outlet, setting-out, vent, way out, withdrawal; SEE CONCEPTS *195,440*

ejaculate [*v*] *eject semen*
climax, come*, discharge, have an orgasm, spurt; SEE CONCEPTS *152,179*

eject [*v*] *throw or be thrown out*
banish, bounce*, bump, cast out, debar, disbar, discharge, disgorge, dislodge, dismiss, displace, dispossess, ditch, do away with*, drive off, dump*, eighty-six*, ejaculate, eliminate, emit, eradicate, eruct, erupt, evict, exclude, expel, expulse, extrude, fire, force out, get rid of, give the boot*, heave out*, irrupt, kick out*, kiss goodbye*, oust, reject, rout, sack, send packing*, show the gate to*, spew, spit out, spout, squeeze out, throw overboard*, turn out, unloose, vomit; SEE CONCEPTS *179,222*

ejection [*n*] *expulsion*
banishment, disbarment, discharge, dismissal, elimination, eviction, exile, ouster, removal, the boot*, the heave-ho*, the sack*, throwing out; SEE CONCEPTS *179,748*

eke out [*v*] *make something last*
barely exist, be economical with, be frugal with,

be sparing with, economize on, get by*, stretch out; SEE CONCEPT *239*

elaborate [*adj*] *intricate; involved*
busy, careful, complex, complicated, decorated, detailed, elegant, embellished, exact, extensive, extravagant, fancy, fussy, garnished, highly wrought, high tech*, imposing, knotty, labored, labyrinthine, luxurious, many-faceted, minute, ornamented, ornate, ostentatious, overdone, overworked, painstaking, perfected, plush, posh, precise, prodigious, refined, showy, skillful, sophisticated, studied, thorough, with all the extras*, with all the options*, with bells and whistles*; SEE CONCEPT *562*

elaborate [*v*] *make detailed; expand*
amplify, bedeck, clarify, comment, complicate, deck, decorate, develop, devise, discuss, embellish, enhance, enlarge, evolve, expatiate, explain, expound, flesh out, garnish, improve, interpret, ornament, particularize, polish, produce, refine, specify, unfold, work out; SEE CONCEPT *57*

élan [*n*] *vivacity*
animation, ardor, brio, dash, esprit, flair, impetuosity, impetus, life, oomph*, panache, spirit, style, verve, vigor, vim, zest, zing*; SEE CONCEPT *411*

elapse [*v*] *go by; slip away*
expire, flow, glide by, lapse, pass, pass away, pass by, roll by, roll on, run out, transpire, vanish; SEE CONCEPTS *6,144,818*

elastic [*adj1*] *pliant, rubbery*
adaptable, bouncy, buoyant, ductile, extendible, extensible, flexible, irrepressible, limber, lithe, malleable, moldable, plastic, pliable, resilient, rubberlike, springy, stretchable, stretchy, supple, tempered, yielding; SEE CONCEPTS *490,606*

elastic [*adj2*] *adaptable, tolerant*
accommodating, adjustable, airy, animated, bouncy, buoyant, complaisant, compliant, ebullient, effervescent, expansive, flexible, gay, high-spirited, lively, recuperative, resilient, soaring, spirited, sprightly, supple, variable, vivacious, volatile, yielding; SEE CONCEPT *404*

elated [*adj*] *very happy*
animated, aroused, blissful, cheered, delighted, ecstatic, elevated, enchanted, enraptured, euphoric, exalted, excited, exhilarated, exultant, fired up*, flying*, flying high*, gleeful, high, hopped up*, in heaven*, in high spirits*, in seventh heaven*, intoxicated, joyful, joyous, jubilant, looking good*, on cloud nine*, overjoyed, proud, puffed up*, roused, set up, transported, turned-on*; SEE CONCEPTS *22,403*

elation [*n*] *extreme happiness*
bliss, buoyancy, buzz, charge, cloud nine*, delight, ecstasy, enthusiasm, euphoria, exaltation, excitement, exhilaration, exultation, glee, high, high spirits, intoxication, jollies*, joy, joyfulness, joyousness, jubilation, kick*, kicks*, rapture, stars in one's eyes*, transport, triumph, up*, upper*; SEE CONCEPT *410*

elbow [*n*] *angular part of arm; angularly shaped item*
ancon, angle, bend, bow, corner, crazy bone*, crook, crutch, curve, fork, funny bone*, half turn, hinge, joint, turn; SEE CONCEPTS *418,436*

elbow [*v*] *push aside*
bend, bulldoze, bump, crowd, hook, hustle, jostle, knock, nudge, press, rough and tumble*, shoulder, shove; SEE CONCEPT *208*

elbow grease [*n*] *physical effort*
effort, exertion, labor, muscle, oomph*, strain, strength, sweat, toil; SEE CONCEPTS *87,100,351, 360,362*

elder [*adj*] *born earlier*
ancient, earlier, first-born, more mature, older, senior; SEE CONCEPTS *578,797*

elder [*n*] *older person*
ancestor, ancient, forebearer, golden ager*, matriarch, oldest, old fogey*, oldster*, patriarch, senior, senior citizen, superior, veteran; SEE CONCEPT *424*

elderly [*adj*] *in old age*
aged, aging, ancient, been around*, declining, gray*, hoary, long in tooth*, lot of mileage*, no spring chicken*, old, olden, on last leg*, over the hill*, retired, tired, venerable; SEE CONCEPTS *578,797*

elect [*v*] *select as representative; choose*
accept, admit, appoint, ballot, conclude, cull, decide upon, designate, determine, go down the line, judge, mark, name, nominate, optate, opt for, pick, pick out, prefer, receive, resolve, settle, settle on, single out, take, tap, vote, vote for; SEE CONCEPTS *41,300*

election [*n*] *choosing; voting*
alternative, appointment, ballot, balloting, choice, decision, determination, franchise, judgment, option, poll, polls, preference, primary, referendum, selection, ticket, vote-casting; SEE CONCEPTS *41,300*

electioneering [*n*] *campaigning*
barnstorming*, canvassing, polling, voting; SEE CONCEPTS *87,320*

elective [*adj*] *able to be chosen*
constituent, discretionary, electoral, facultative, nonobligatory, not compulsory, optional, selective, voluntary, voting; SEE CONCEPT *535*

electric/electrical [*adj*] *charged; energetic*
AC, DC, dynamic, electrifying, exciting, juiced*, magnetic, motor-driven, power-driven, rousing, stimulating, stirring, tense, thrilling, voltaic; SEE CONCEPT *540*

electricity [*n*] *energized matter, power*
AC, current, DC, electromagneticism, electron, galvanism, heat, hot stuff*, ignition, juice*, light, magneticism, service, spark, tension, utilities, voltage; SEE CONCEPT *520*

electrify [*v*] *thrill, stimulate*
amaze, animate, astonish, astound, charge, commove, disturb, dynamize, energize, enthuse, excite, fire, frenzy, galvanize, invigorate, jar, jolt, magnetize, power, provoke, rouse, send, shock, stagger, startle, stir, strike, stun, take one's breath away*, wire*; SEE CONCEPTS *7,22,42*

electronics [*n*] *electronic devices*
camcorders, CD players, computer chips, computers, electronic components, integrated circuitry, radios, stereos, televisions, transistors, VCRs, video cameras; SEE CONCEPTS *463,499*

elegance [*n*] *cultivated beauty, taste*
breeding, charm, class, courtliness, cultivation, culture, delicacy, dignity, discernment, distinction, exquisiteness, felicity, gentility, good taste, grace, gracefulness, grandeur, hauteur, lushness, luxury, magnificence, nicety, nobility, noblesse, ornateness, polish, politeness, poshness, propriety, purity, refinement, restraint, rhythm, sophistication, splendor, style, sumptuousness,

ef
el

symmetry, tastefulness; SEE CONCEPTS *655,671,718*

elegant [*adj*] *beautiful, tasteful*
affected, appropriate, apt, aristocratic, artistic, august, chic, choice, classic, clever, comely, courtly, cultivated, cultured, dainty, delicate, dignified, effective, exquisite, fancy, fashionable, fine, genteel, graceful, grand, handsome, ingenious, luxurious, majestic, modish, neat, nice, noble, opulent, ornamented, ornate, ostentatious, overdone, polished, rare, recherché, refined, rich, select, simple, stately, stuffy, stylish, stylized, sumptuous, superior, turgid, well-bred; SEE CONCEPTS *574,579,589*

elegiac [*adj*] *lamenting*
doleful, funereal, melancholy, mournful, sad, sorrowful, threnodial; SEE CONCEPT *403*

elegy [*n*] *dirge*
death song, funeral song, knell, lament, plaint, requiem, threnody; SEE CONCEPTS *262,293,595*

element [*n1*] *essential feature*
aspect, basic, basis, bit, component, constituent, detail, drop, facet, factor, fundamental, hint, ingredient, item, material, matter, member, part, particle, particular, piece, portion, principle, root, section, stem, subdivision, trace, unit, view; SEE CONCEPTS *668,826,829*

element [*n2*] *place where one feels comfortable*
domain, environment, field, habitation, medium, milieu, sphere; SEE CONCEPTS *198,516*

elementary [*adj*] *simple, basic*
ABCs, abecedarian, basal, beginning, child's play*, clear, duck soup*, easy, elemental, essential, facile, foundational, fundamental, initial, introductory, meat and potatoes*, original, plain, prefatory, preliminary, primary, primitive, primo*, rudimentary, simplest, simplex, simplified, straightforward, substratal, uncomplex, uncomplicated, underlying; SEE CONCEPTS *546,562*

elephantine [*adj*] *huge*
behemothic, big, colossal, enormous, extensive, gargantuan, giant, gigantic, grand, great, humongous, immense, jumbo*, large, mammoth, massive, monstrous, monumental, mountainous, titanic, towering; SEE CONCEPTS *771,773*

elevate [*v1*] *lift up*
erect, fetch up*, heighten, hike up*, hoist, jack up*, levitate, poise, pump, put up, pyramid*, raise, ramp, rear, shoot up*, stilt, take up, tilt, uphold, uplift, upraise; SEE CONCEPT *196*

elevate [*v2*] *promote; augment*
advance, aggrandize, appoint, boost, build up, dignify, enhance, ennoble, exalt, further, glorify, heighten, honor, increase, intensify, magnify, prefer, put up, skip, swell, upgrade; SEE CONCEPTS *69,351,700*

elevate [*v3*] *raise spirits*
animate, boost, brighten, bring up, buoy up*, cheer, elate, excite, exhilarate, glorify, hearten, inspire, lift up*, perk up*, refine, rouse, sublimate, uplift; SEE CONCEPTS *7,22*

elevated [*adj1*] *highly moral or dignified*
animated, big-time*, bright, elated, eloquent, eminent, ethical, exalted, exhilarated, formal, grand, grandiloquent, heavy, high, high-flown*, high-minded, honorable, inflated, lofty, noble, righteous, stately, sublime, superb, upright, upstanding, virtuous; SEE CONCEPTS *402,545,567*

elevated [*adj2*] *raised up*
aerial, high, high-rise, lifted, raised, stately, tall,

towering, upheaved, uplifted, upraised, uprisen; SEE CONCEPT *779*

elevation [*n1*] *height; high ground*
acclivity, altitude, ascent, boost, eminence, heave, hill, hillock, hoist, levitation, mountain, platform, ridge, rise, roof, top, uplift, upthrow; SEE CONCEPTS *509,741*

elevation [*n2*] *advancement, promotion*
aggrandizement, apotheosis, boost, deification, eminence, ennoblement, exaltation, exaltedness, glorification, grandeur, immortalization, lionization, loftiness, magnification, nobility, nobleness, preference, preferment, prelation, raise, sublimity, upgrading; SEE CONCEPTS *69,351,668*

elevator [*n*] *lift*
conveyor, dumbwaiter, escalator, hoist; SEE CONCEPT *196*

elf [*n*] *small, fairytale character*
brownie, elfin, fairy, fay, leprechaun, nisse, pixie; SEE CONCEPT *370*

elfin [*adj*] *mischievous; small*
delicate, devilish, disobedient, elfish, frolicsome, impish, little, minute, misbehaving, naughty, petite, playful, prankish, puckish, puny, rascally, slight, sprightly, tiny; SEE CONCEPTS *401,545*

elicit [*v*] *draw out*
arm-twist*, badger, bite*, bring, bring forth, bring out, bring to light*, call forth, cause, derive, educe, evince, evoke, evolve, exact, extort, extract, fetch, give rise to, milk*, obtain, put muscle on*, put the arm on*, rattle, shake, shake down*, squeeze, wrest, wring; SEE CONCEPTS *68,142*

eligible [*adj*] *fit, worthy*
acceptable, appropriate, becoming, capable of, desirable, discretionary, elective, employable, equal to, fitted, in line for*, in the running*, licensed, likely, preferable, privileged, proper, qualified, satisfactory, seemly, suitable, suited, trained, up to*, usable; SEE CONCEPTS *527,558*

eliminate [*v*] *remove, throw out*
annihilate, blot out*, bump off*, cancel, cast out, count out, cut out, defeat, discard, discharge, dismiss, dispense with, dispose of, disqualify, disregard, do away with, drive out, drop, eject, eradicate, erase, evict, exclude, expel, exterminate, get rid of, ignore, invalidate, kill, knock out*, leave out, liquidate, murder, omit, oust, phase out, put out, reject, rub out*, rule out, set aside, shut the door on*, slay, stamp out*, take out, terminate, waive, waste, wipe out*; SEE CONCEPTS *30,211*

elimination [*n*] *removal*
cut, destruction, discard, displacement, dropping, ejection, eradication, exclusion, expulsion, extermination, omission, rejection, riddance, taking away, weeding out, withdrawal; SEE CONCEPT *180*

elite [*adj*] *best, first-class*
aristocratic, choice, cool*, crack*, elect, exclusive, gilt-edged, greatest, noble, out of sight*, out of this world*, pick, selected, super, tip-top*, top, top drawer*, topflight, top-notch, upperclass, world-class; SEE CONCEPTS *555,574*

elite [*n*] *high-class persons*
aristocracy, beautiful people*, best, blue blood*, carriage trade*, celebrity, choice, country club set*, cream, crème de la crème*, crowd, elect, establishment, fast lane*, fat*, flower, gentility, gentry, glitterati, high society*, in-crowd*, jet-

set*, main line*, nobility, old money*, optimacy, pride, prime, prize, quality, select, society, top, upper class, upper crust*; SEE CONCEPTS 387,388,417

elitist [n] snob
highbrow, name-dropper, pompous ass, pompous person, philosopher, social climber, stiff, stuffed shirt; SEE CONCEPT 423

elixir [n] remedy
cure-all, elixir of life, extract, medicine, mixture, panacea, philosopher's stone, potion, principle, solution; SEE CONCEPTS 307,311,693,712

elliptical [adj] oval-shaped
egg-shaped, ellipsoidal, oblong, ovoid; SEE CONCEPT 486

elocution [n] articulation
declamation, delivery, diction, dramatic, eloquence, enunciation, expression, locution, oratory, pronunciation, public speaking, reading, rhetoric, speech, speechcraft, speechmaking, utterance, voice culture, voice production; SEE CONCEPT 47

elongate [v] make longer
drag one's feet*, drag out, draw, draw out, extend, fill, lengthen, let out, pad*, prolong, prolongate, protract, put rubber in*, spin out, stretch; SEE CONCEPTS 137,239,250

elongated [adj] lengthened
dragged out, drawn out, expanded, extended, increased, made longer, outstretched, prolonged, protracted, stretched, strung out; SEE CONCEPTS 482,779,798

elope [v] run away to be married
abscond, bolt, decamp, disappear, escape, flee, fly, go secretly, go to Gretna Green*, leave, run off, skip*, slip away, slip out, steal away; SEE CONCEPT 297

eloquence [n] skillful way with words
ability, appeal, articulation, command of language, delivery, diction, dramatic, expression, expressiveness, expressivity, facility, fervor, flow, fluency, force, forcefulness, gift of gab*, grandiloquence, loquacity, meaningfulness, mellifluousness, oration, oratory, passion, persuasiveness, poise, power, rhetoric, spirit, style, vigor, vivacity, volubility, wit, wittiness; SEE CONCEPTS 68,278,630

eloquent [adj] having a skillful way with words
affecting, ardent, articulate, expressive, facund, fervent, fervid, fluent, forceful, glib, grandiloquent, graphic, impassioned, impressive, indicative, magniloquent, meaningful, moving, outspoken, passionate, persuasive, poignant, potent, powerful, revealing, rhetorical, sententious, significant, silver-tongued*, smooth-spoken*, stirring, suggestive, telling, touching, vivid, vocal, voluble, well-expressed; SEE CONCEPT 267

elsewhere [adv] in another place
abroad, absent, away, formerly, gone, hence, not here, not present, not under consideration, otherwhere, outside, remote, removed, somewhere, somewhere else, subsequently; SEE CONCEPT 586

elucidate [v] explain in detail
annotate, clarify, clear, clear up, decode, demonstrate, draw a picture*, enlighten, exemplify, explicate, expound, get across*, gloss, illuminate, illustrate, interpret, make perfectly clear, make plain, make see daylight*, prove, shed light on*, spell out*, throw light on*, unfold; SEE CONCEPT 57

elude [v] avoid; escape
baffle, beat around the bush*, be beyond someone*, bilk, circumvent, confound, cop out*, ditch, dodge, double, duck, eschew, evade, flee, fly, foil, frustrate, get around, get away from, give the runaround*, give the slip*, give wide berth to*, hem and haw*, not touch, outrun, outwit, pass the buck*, pass up, puzzle, run around, shirk, shuck, shun, shy, stall, stay shy of*, steer clear of*, stonewall*, stump, thwart; SEE CONCEPTS 30,38,59,102

elusive [adj] evasive, mysterious
ambiguous, baffling, cagey, deceitful, deceptive, difficult to catch, elusory, equivocal, evanescent, fallacious, fleeting, fraudulent, fugacious, fugitive, greasy, illusory, imponderable, incomprehensible, indefinable, insubstantial, intangible, misleading, occult, phantom, puzzling, shifty, shy, slippery, stonewalling*, subtle, transient, transitory, tricky, unspecific, volatile; SEE CONCEPTS 529,542

emaciated [adj] undernourished; thin
anorexic, atrophied, attenuate, attenuated, bony, cadaverous, consumptive, famished, gaunt, haggard, lank, lean, like a bag of bones*, meager, peaked, pinched, scrawny, skeletal, skeletonlike, skin-andbones*, skinny, starved, thin as rail*, underfed, wasted, wizened; SEE CONCEPTS 490,491

E-mail [n] electronic mail
chat message, online correspondence, online mail, voice mail; SEE CONCEPT 266

emanate [v] come forth; give off
arise, birth, derive, discharge, egress, emerge, emit, exhale, exit, exude, flow, initiate, issue, originate, proceed, radiate, rise, send forth, spring, stem; SEE CONCEPTS 179,221,648

emanation [n] emergence, discharge
arising, beginning, derivation, drainage, effluence, effluent, efflux, effusion, ejaculation, emerging, emission, escape, exhalation, exudation, flow, flowing, gush, issuance, issuing, leakage, oozing, origin, origination, outflow, outpour, proceeding, radiation, springing, welling; SEE CONCEPTS 179,221,648

emancipate [v] set free
affranchise, deliver, discharge, disencumber, disenthral, enfranchise, liberate, loose, loosen, manumit, release, unbind, unchain, unfetter, unshackle; SEE CONCEPT 127

emancipation [n] freedom
deliverance, delivery, enfranchisement, independence, liberation, liberty, release, setting free; SEE CONCEPT 691

emasculate [v] weaken, deprive of force
alter, debilitate, devitalize, enervate, fix*, impoverish, vitiate; SEE CONCEPTS 240,250

embalm [v] preserve, immortalize
anoint, cherish, consecrate, conserve, enshrine, freeze, lay out, mummify, prepare, process, store, treasure, wrap; SEE CONCEPT 202

embargo [n] prohibition, restriction
ban, bar, barrier, blockage, check, hindrance, impediment, interdict, interdiction, proscription, restraint, stoppage; SEE CONCEPTS 119,130

embark [v] get on transportation object
board, commence, emplane, enter, entrain, go aboard ship, launch, leave port, plunge into, put on board, set about, set out, set sail, take on board, take ship; SEE CONCEPTS 159,195,224

el
em

embark on [*v*] *begin undertaking, journey*
broach, commence, engage, enter, get off, initiate, jump off, launch, open, plunge into, set about, set out, set to, start, take up, tee off*; SEE CONCEPTS *100,221*

embarrass [*v*] *cause mental discomfort*
abash, agitate, annoy, bewilder, bother, bug, catch one short*, chagrin, confuse, discombobulate*, discomfit, discompose, disconcert, discountenance, distract, distress, disturb, dumbfound, faze, fluster, give a bad time*, give a hard time*, hang up*, irk, let down*, make a monkey of*, mortify, nonplus, perplex, perturb, plague, put in a hole*, put in a spot*, put on the spot*, put out of countenance*, puzzle, rattle, shame, show up*, stun, tease, throw, throw into a tizzy*, upset; SEE CONCEPTS *7,19,54*

embarrassing [*adj*] *humiliating, shaming*
awkward, bewildering, compromising, confusing, delicate, difficult, disagreeable, discomfiting, discommoding, discommodious, disconcerting, distracting, distressing, disturbing, equivocal, exasperating, impossible, incommodious, inconvenient, inopportune, mortifying, perplexing, puzzling, rattling, sensitive, shameful, sticky, ticklish, touchy, tricky, troublesome, troubling, uncomfortable, uneasy, unpropitious, unseemly, upsetting, worrisome; SEE CONCEPTS *537,548*

embarrassment [*n*] *humiliation, shame*
awkwardness, awkward situation, bashfulness, bind, boo boo*, chagrin, clumsiness, complexity, confusion, destitution, difficulty, dilemma, discomfiture, discomposure, disconcertion, distress, egg on face*, faux pas, fix, hitch, hot seat*, hot water*, impecuniosity, indebtedness, indiscretion, inhibition, mess, mistake, mortification, pickle*, pinch, plight, poverty, predicament, puzzle, quandary, scrape, self-consciousness, shyness, snag, stew, strait, tangle, timidity, unease, uneasiness; SEE CONCEPTS *410,674*

embassy [*n*] *residence, offices of overseas representatives*
commission, committee, consular office, consulate, delegation, diplomatic office, legation, ministry, mission; SEE CONCEPTS *439,449,516*

embattle [*v*] *prepare for battle*
arm, array, equip, fortify, furnish, make ready, militarize, mobilize, prepare for combat, strengthen, supply; SEE CONCEPT *202*

embed [*v*] *sink, implant*
bury, deposit, dig in, drive in, enclose, fasten, fix, hammer in, impact, infix, ingrain, inlay, insert, install, lodge, pierce, plant, plunge, press, put into, ram in, root, set, stick in, stuff in, thrust in, tuck in; SEE CONCEPTS *178,188*

embellish [*v*] *make beautiful; decorate*
add bells and whistles*, adorn, amplify, array, beautify, bedeck, color, deck, dress up*, elaborate, emblaze, embroider, enhance, enrich, exaggerate, festoon, fix up*, fudge*, garnish, gild, give details, grace, gussy up*, magnify, ornament, overstate, spiff up*, spruce up*, trim; SEE CONCEPTS *49,162,177,700*

embellishment [*n*] *beautification; decorating*
adornment, coloring, decoration, doodad*, elaboration, embroidering, embroidery, enhancement, enrichment, exaggeration, fandangle*, floridity, flowery speech, frill, froufrou*, fuss*, garnish, gilding, gingerbread*, hyperbole, icing

on the cake*, jazz*, ornament, ornamentation, ostentation, overstatement; SEE CONCEPTS *177, 278,700,718*

embers [*n*] *hot ashes from fire*
ash, brand, cinders, clinkers, coals, firebrand, live coals, slag, smoking remnants, smoldering remains; SEE CONCEPTS *260,478*

embezzle [*v*] *steal money, often from employer*
abstract, appropriate, defalcate, filch, forge, loot, misapply, misappropriate, misuse, peculate, pilfer, purloin, put hand in cookie jar*, put hand in till*, skim, thieve; SEE CONCEPT *139*

embezzlement [*n*] *stealing money, often from employer*
abstraction, appropriation, defalcation, filching, fraud, larceny, misapplication, misappropriation, misuse, peculation, pilferage, pilfering, purloining, skimming, theft, thieving; SEE CONCEPT *139*

embitter [*v*] *upset, alienate*
acerbate, acidulate, aggravate, anger, annoy, bitter, bother, disaffect, disillusion, envenom, exacerbate, exasperate, irritate, make bitter, make resentful, poison, sour, venom, worsen; SEE CONCEPTS *7,14,19*

embittered [*adj*] *resentful*
bitter, disaffected, full of hate, irritated, rancorous, sore, spiteful; SEE CONCEPTS *267,404*

emblazon [*v*] *adorn*
add finishing touches, beautify, brighten, color, deck, decorate, do up*, embellish, fix up, gussy up*, jazz up*, ornament, paint, spruce up; SEE CONCEPTS *162,177*

emblem [*n*] *crest*
adumbration, arms, attribute, badge, banner, brand, character, coat of arms, colophon, colors, design, device, figure, flag, hallmark, identification, image, impress, insignia, logo, mark, marker, medal, memento, miniature, monogram, motto, pennant, regalia, reminder, representation, scepter, seal, sign, standard, symbol, token, trademark, type; SEE CONCEPTS *259,284,625*

embodiment [*n*] *representation, manifestation*
apotheosis, archetype, cast, collection, comprehension, conformation, embracement, encompassment, epitome, example, exemplar, exemplification, expression, form, formation, incarnation, inclusion, incorporation, integration, matter, organization, personification, prosopopoeia, quintessence, realization, reification, structure, symbol, systematization, type; SEE CONCEPTS *118,686*

embody [*v1*] *represent; materialize*
actualize, complete, concretize, demonstrate, emblematize, epitomize, evince, exemplify, exhibit, express, exteriorize, externalize, hypostatize, illustrate, incarnate, incorporate, manifest, mirror, objectify, personalize, personify, realize, reify, show, stand for, substantiate, symbolize, typify; SEE CONCEPT *118*

embody [*v2*] *include, integrate*
absorb, amalgamate, assimilate, blend, bring together, codify, collect, combine, comprehend, comprise, concentrate, consolidate, contain, embrace, encompass, establish, fuse, have, incorporate, involve, merge, organize, subsume, systematize, take in, unify; SEE CONCEPTS *112,113*

embolden [*v*] *encourage*
boost, buoy, cheer, energize, enhearten, exhilarate, give courage, give pep talk*, goad, inspire,

inspirit, invigorate, psyche up, push, rally, reassure, refresh, revitalize, spur, stir, sway; SEE CONCEPTS *7,22*

emboss [*v*] *imprint*
adorn, carve, decorate, etch, impress, punch, sculpt, stamp; SEE CONCEPT *79*

embrace [*v1*] *hold tightly in one's arms*
bear hug*, clasp, clinch, cling, clutch, cradle, cuddle, encircle, enfold, entwine, envelop, fold, fondle, grab, grasp, grip, hug, lock, nuzzle, press, seize, snuggle, squeeze, take in arms*, wrap; SEE CONCEPTS *190,191*

embrace [*v2*] *include in one's beliefs; take into account*
accept, accommodate, admit, adopt, avail oneself of, comprehend, comprise, contain, cover, deal with*, embody, enclose, encompass, espouse, get into*, go in for*, grab, have, incorporate, involve, make use of, provide for, receive, seize, subsume, take advantage of, take in, take on, take up, welcome; SEE CONCEPTS *12,15,112*

embroider [*v1*] *add fancy stitching, adornment*
beautify, bedeck, braid, color, cross-stitch, deck, decorate, embellish, fix up, garnish, gild, gussy up*, knit, ornament, pattern, quilt, spruce up*, stitch, weave pattern, work; SEE CONCEPTS *177,218*

embroider [*v2*] *exaggerate information*
aggrandize, amplify, blow-up*, build up, color, distend, dramatize, elaborate, embellish, enhance, enlarge, expand, falsify, fudge*, heighten, hyperbolize, lie, magnify, make federal case*, make mountain out of molehill*, overdo, overelaborate, overembellish, overemphasize, overestimate, overstate, pad*, play up*, puff*, romanticize, spread on thick*, stretch, stretch the truth*, yeast*; SEE CONCEPTS *58,63*

embroidery [*n*] *fancy stitching*
adornment, appliqué, arabesque, bargello, brocade, crewel, crochet, cross-stitch, decoration, lace, lacery, needlepoint, needlework, quilting, sampler, tapestry, tatting, tracery; SEE CONCEPTS *218,259*

embroil [*v*] *involve in dispute; complicate*
cause trouble, compromise, confound, confuse, derange, disorder, disturb, disunite, encumber, enmesh, ensnare, entangle, implicate, incriminate, involve, mire, mix up, muddle, perplex, snarl, tangle, trouble; SEE CONCEPTS *7,19,86*

embryonic [*adj*] *rudimentary*
beginning, developing, early, elementary, evolving, germinal, immature, incipient, undeveloped; SEE CONCEPTS *485,578,797*

emend [*v*] *correct*
alter, amend, better, edit, emendate, improve, polish, rectify, redact, retouch, revise, right, touch up; SEE CONCEPT *126*

emerge [*v*] *come out, arise*
appear, arrive, become apparent, become known, become visible, come forth, come into view, come on the scene, come to light, come up, crop up, dawn, derive, develop, egress, emanate, flow, gush, issue, loom, make appearance, materialize, originate, proceed, rise, show, spring, spring up, spurt, steam, stem, surface, transpire, turn up; SEE CONCEPTS *105,118*

emergency [*n*] *crisis, danger*
accident, climax, clutch*, compulsion, crossroad, crunch*, depression, difficulty, distress, exigency, extremity, fix, hole, impasse, juncture, meltdown*, misadventure, necessity, pass, pinch*, plight, predicament, pressure, push, quandary, scrape, squeeze, strait, tension, turning point, urgency, vicissitude, zero hour*; SEE CONCEPTS *674,675*

emergency room [*n*] *trauma center*
critical care facility, emergency clinic, ER, ICU, intensive care unit, triage room; SEE CONCEPTS *312,439,449*

emergent [*adj*] *resulting*
appearing, budding, coming, developing, efflorescent, emanant, emanating, issuing forth, outgoing, rising; SEE CONCEPT *537*

emigrant [*n*] *person who leaves his or her native country*
alien, colonist, departer, displaced person, émigré, evacuee, exile, expatriate, fugitive, migrant, migrator, outcast, pilgrim, refugee, traveler, wanderer, wayfarer; SEE CONCEPTS *413,423*

emigrate [*v*] *move to new country*
depart, migrate, move abroad, quit, remove, transmigrate; SEE CONCEPT *198*

émigré [*n*] *emigrant*
displaced person, DP, exile, expatriate, foreigner, migrant, refugee; SEE CONCEPT *413*

eminence [*n1*] *importance, fame*
authority, celebrity, credit, dignity, distinction, esteem, famousness, glory, greatness, honor, illustriousness, influence, kudos, loftiness, notability, note, power, preeminence, prepotency, prestige, prominence, prominency, rank, renown, reputation, repute, significance, standing, superiority, weight; SEE CONCEPTS *388,668,671*

eminence [*n2*] *high ground*
altitude, elevation, height, highland, highness, hill, hillock, knoll, loftiness, peak, project, prominence, promontory, raise, ridge, rise, summit, upland; SEE CONCEPTS *509,741*

eminent [*adj*] *very important; famous*
august, big-gun*, big-league*, big-name*, big-time*, celeb*, celebrated, celebrious, conspicuous, distinguished, dominant, elevated, esteemed, exalted, famed, grand, great, high, high-ranking, illustrious, lionlike, lofty, name, noble, notable, noted, noteworthy, of note, outstanding, page-oner*, paramount, preeminent, prestigious, prominent, redoubted, renowned, star, superior, superstar, VIP*, well-known; SEE CONCEPTS *555,568*

eminently [*adv*] *exceptionally; well*
conspicuously, exceedingly, extremely, greatly, highly, notably, outstandingly, prominently, remarkably, strikingly, suitably, surpassingly, very; SEE CONCEPT *574*

emir [*n*] *prince*
amir, chieftain, governor, leader, shah, sheik; SEE CONCEPTS *347,354*

emissary [*n*] *deputy*
agent, ambassador, bearer, carrier, consul, courier, delegate, envoy, front, go-between, herald, hired gun*, intermediary, internuncio, legate, messenger, rep*, representative, scout, spy; SEE CONCEPTS *348,423*

emission [*n*] *issuance, diffusion*
discharge, ejaculation, ejection, emanation, exhalation, exudation, issue, radiation, shedding, transmission, utterance, venting; SEE CONCEPT *179*

emit [*v*] *diffuse, discharge*
afford, beam, belch, breathe, cast out, disem-

bogue, drip, eject, emanate, erupt, evacuate, excrete, exhale, expectorate, expel, expend, expire, extrude, exude, give off, give out, give vent to, gush, issue, jet, let off, loose, ooze, pass, perspire, pour, pronounce, purge, radiate, reek, secrete, send forth, send out, shed, shoot, speak, spew, spill, spit, squirt, throw out, transmit, utter, vent, voice, void, vomit, yield; SEE CONCEPTS *108,179,266*

emollient [*adj*] *soothing*
balsamic, demulcent, healing, lenitive, palliative, relieving, remedial, softening; SEE CONCEPTS *7,22,110,384*

emollient [*n*] *lotion*
balm, cream, lenitive, liniment, moisturizer, oil, ointment, salve, soothing agent, unguent; SEE CONCEPTS *311,446,466*

emote [*v*] *express emotion*
act, dramatize, exaggerate, ham it up*, overact, overdramatize, overplay; SEE CONCEPT *292*

emoticon [*n*] *keyboard symbol code, :-)*
emotag, smiley, winkey; SEE CONCEPT *284*

emotion [*n*] *mental state*
affect, affection, affectivity, agitation, anger, ardor, commotion, concern, desire, despair, despondency, disturbance, drive, ecstasy, elation, empathy, excitability, excitement, feeling, fervor, grief, gut reaction, happiness, inspiration, joy, love, melancholy, passion, perturbation, pride, rage, remorse, responsiveness, sadness, satisfaction, sensation, sensibility, sensitiveness, sentiment, shame, sorrow, sympathy, thrill, tremor, vehemence, vibes, warmth, zeal; SEE CONCEPT *410*

emotional [*adj*] *demonstrative about feelings*
affecting, ardent, disturbed, ecstatic, emotive, enthusiastic, excitable, exciting, falling apart*, fanatical, feeling, fervent, fervid, fickle, fiery, heartwarming, heated, histrionic, hot-blooded*, hysterical, impassioned, impetuous, impulsive, irrational, moving, nervous, overwrought, passionate, pathetic, poignant, responsive, roused, sensitive, sentient, sentimental, spontaneous, stirred, stirring, susceptible, tear-jerking*, temperamental, tender, thrilling, touching, warm, zealous; SEE CONCEPTS *403,542*

emotionless [*adj*] *unfeeling, undemonstrative*
blank, chill, cold, cold-blooded*, cold fish*, cool, cool cat*, deadpan, detached, dispassionate, distant, flat, frigid, glacial*, heartless, icy, immovable, impassive, impersonal, in cold blood*, indifferent, laid back*, matter-of-fact, nonemotional, nowhere*, poker face*, remote, reserved, stony-eyed*, thick-skinned*, toneless, unemotional, unimpassioned, with straight face; SEE CONCEPTS *401,403,542*

empathize [*v*] *identify with*
comprehend, feel for, imagine, put oneself in another's place, relate to, share, stand in one's shoes, suffer with, sympathize, understand; SEE CONCEPTS *34,110*

empathy [*n*] *understanding*
affinity, appreciation, being on same wavelength*, being there for someone*, communion, community of interests, compassion, comprehension, concord, cottoning to*, good vibrations*, hitting it off*, insight, picking up on*, pity, rapport, recognition, responsiveness, soul, sympathy, warmth; SEE CONCEPTS *32,409,411*

emperor [*n*] *ruler*
czar, dictator, empress, king, monarch, prince, sovereign, sultan; SEE CONCEPTS *347,354*

emphasis [*n*] *importance, prominence*
accent, accentuation, attention, decidedness, force, headline, highlight, impressiveness, insistence, intensity, moment, positiveness, power, preeminence, priority, significance, strength, stress, underlining, underscoring, weight; SEE CONCEPTS *668,682*

emphasize [*v*] *stress, give priority to*
accent, accentuate, affirm, articulate, assert, bear down, charge, dramatize, dwell on, enlarge, enunciate, headline, highlight, hit*, impress, indicate, insist on, italicize, labor the point*, limelight*, maintain, make a point, make clear, make emphatic, make much of*, mark, pinpoint, play up*, point out*, point up*, press, pronounce, punctuate, put accent on*, reiterate, repeat, rub in*, spotlight*, underline, underscore, weight; SEE CONCEPTS *49,57*

emphatic [*adj*] *insistent, unequivocal*
absolute, accented, assertive, assured, categorical, certain, cogent, confident, decided, definite, definitive, determined, direct, distinct, dogmatic, dynamic, earnest, energetic, explicit, express, flat, for a face*, forceful, forcible, important, impressive, marked, momentous, no mistake*, pointed, positive, potent, powerful, pronounced, resounding, significant, sober, solemn, stressed, striking, strong, sure, telling, trenchant, unmistakable, vigorous; SEE CONCEPTS *267,535*

empire [*n*] *place ruled by sovereign; rule*
authority, command, commonwealth, control, domain, dominion, federation, government, people, power, realm, sovereignty, supremacy, sway, union; SEE CONCEPTS *198,299,376*

empirical/empiric [*adj*] *practical; based on experience*
experient, experiential, experimental, factual, observational, observed, pragmatic, provisional, speculative; SEE CONCEPTS *548,582*

employ [*v1*] *make use of*
apply, bestow, bring to bear*, engage, exercise, exert, exploit, fill, handle, keep busy*, manipulate, occupy, operate, put to use*, spend, take up*, use, use up*, utilize; SEE CONCEPT *225*

employ [*v2*] *give money in exchange for work performed*
bring on board*, come on board*, commission, contract, contract for, engage, enlist, hire, ink*, obtain, place, procure, put on*, retain, secure, sign on*, sign up*, take on, truck with*; SEE CONCEPT *351*

employed [*adj*] *working*
active, at it*, at work, busy, engaged, hired, in a job, in collar*, in harness*, inked*, in place, laboring, occupied, on board*, on duty*, on the job*, on the payroll*, operating, plugging away*, selected, signed*; SEE CONCEPTS *538,560*

employee [*n*] *person being paid for working for another or a corporation*
agent, apprentice, assistant, attendant, blue collar*, breadwinner*, clerk, cog*, company person, craftsperson, desk jockey*, domestic, hand, help, hired gun*, hired hand*, hireling, jobholder, laborer, member, operator, pink collar*, plug*, representative, sales help, salesperson, servant, slave, staff member, wage-earner, white

collar*, worker, working stiff*; SEE CONCEPT *348*

employer [*n*] *person, business who hires workers*
big cheese*, big shot*, boss, businessperson, capitalist, CEO*, chief, CO*, company, corporation, director, entrepreneur, establishment, executive, firm, front office, head, head honcho*, juice*, kingpin*, management, manager, manufacturer, meal ticket*, organization, outfit, overseer, owner, patron, president, proprietor, slavedriver*, superintendent, supervisor; SEE CONCEPT *347*

employment [*n1*] *working for a living; engagement in activity*
application, assignment, avocation, awarding, business, calling, carrying, commissioning, contracting, craft, employ, engaging, enlistment, enrollment, exercise, exercising, exertion, field, function, game*, hire, hiring, job, line, métier, mission, number, occupation, occupying, office, position, post, profession, pursuit, racket*, recruitment, retaining, service, servicing, setup, signing on*, situation, taking on, thing*, trade, using, vocation, what one is into*, work; SEE CONCEPTS *349,351,360*

employment [*n2*] *using something*
adoption, appliance, application, disposition, exercise, exercising, exertion, exploitation, handling, operation, play, purpose, usage, usance, use, utilization; SEE CONCEPTS *225,658,694*

emporium [*n*] *market*
bazaar, boutique, chain, co-op, cut-rate store*, discount store, five-and-dime*, flea market, galleria, mall, mart, outlet, outlet store, shop, shopping center, shopping plaza, stand, store, supermarket, thrift shop; SEE CONCEPT *449*

empower [*v*] *authorize, enable*
accredit, allow, capacitate, charge, commission, delegate, entitle, entrust, grant, invest, legitimize, license, okay, permit, privilege, qualify, sanction, vest, warrant; SEE CONCEPTS *50,88*

empress [*n*] *female ruler*
princess, queen, sovereign; SEE CONCEPTS *347,354*

emptiness [*n*] *void, bareness*
blank, blankness, chasm, depletedness, desertedness, desolation, destitution, exhaustion, gap, hollowness, inanition, vacancy, vacuity, vacuum, waste; SEE CONCEPTS *720,733*

empty [*adj1*] *containing nothing*
abandoned, bare, barren, blank, clear, dead, deflated, depleted, desert, deserted, desolate, despoiled, destitute, devoid, dry, evacuated, exhausted, forsaken, godforsaken*, hollow, lacking, stark, unfilled, unfurnished, uninhabited, unoccupied, vacant, vacated, vacuous, void, wanting, waste; SEE CONCEPTS *481,774,786*

empty [*adj2*] *fruitless, ineffective*
aimless, banal, barren, cheap, dead, deadpan, devoid, dishonest, dumb, expressionless, fatuous, flat, frivolous, futile, hollow, idle, ignorant, inane, ineffectual, inexpressive, insincere, insipid, jejune, meaningless, nugatory, otiose, paltry, petty, purposeless, senseless, silly, trivial, unintelligent, unreal, unsatisfactory, unsubstantial, vacuous, vain, valueless, vapid, worthless; SEE CONCEPTS *402,570,575*

empty [*adj3*] *hungry*
famished, ravenous, starving, unfed, unfilled; SEE CONCEPT *406*

empty [*v*] *remove contents*
clear, consume, decant, deplete, discharge, disgorge, drain, drink, dump, ebb, eject, escape, evacuate, exhaust, expel, flow out, gut, leak, leave, make void, pour out, purge, release, run out, rush out, tap, unburden, unload, use up, vacate, void; SEE CONCEPT *211*

empty-headed [*adj*] *flighty, scatterbrained*
brainless, dizzy, featherbrained, frivolous, giddy, harebrained, ignorant, illiterate, inane, knownothing, silly, skittish, stupid, uneducated, unschooled, untaught, vacant, vacuous; SEE CONCEPT *402*

emulate [*v*] *copy the actions of*
challenge, compete, compete with, contend, contend with, ditto*, do*, do like*, follow, follow in footsteps*, follow suit*, follow the example of*, go like*, imitate, make like*, mimic, mirror, outvie, pattern after*, rival, rivalize, take after*, vie with; SEE CONCEPTS *87,171*

enable [*v*] *allow, authorize*
accredit, approve, capacitate, commission, condition, empower, endow, facilitate, fit, give power, implement, invest, let, license, make possible, permit, prepare, provide the means*, qualify, ready, sanction, set up, warrant; SEE CONCEPTS *50,83,88,99*

enact [*v1*] *act out; accomplish*
achieve, appear as, depict, discourse, do, execute, go on*, perform, personate, play, playact, play the part of, portray, represent; SEE CONCEPTS *91,292*

enact [*v2*] *authorize, legislate*
accomplish, appoint, bring about, carry through, command, constitute, decree, determine, dictate, effect, effectuate, establish, execute, fix, formulate, get the floor*, institute, jam through*, make, make into law, make laws, ordain, order, pass, proclaim, put in force, put through, railroad*, railroad through*, ratify, sanction, set, steamroll*, transact, vote favorably*, vote in*; SEE CONCEPTS *50,88,298,317*

enactment [*n1*] *playacting*
achievement, acting, depiction, execution, impersonation, performance, personation, personification, playing, portrayal, representation; SEE CONCEPTS *263,292*

enactment [*n2*] *law; authorization*
command, commandment, decree, dictate, edict, execution, legislation, order, ordinance, proclamation, ratification, regulation, statute; SEE CONCEPTS *318,685*

enamel [*n*] *paint, often shiny*
cloisonné, coating, finish, glaze, gloss, japan, lacquer, polish, stain, topcoat, varnish, veneer; SEE CONCEPTS *259,260,467*

enamor [*v*] *fascinate, captivate*
attract, bewitch, charm, enchant, endear, enrapture, enthrall, entice, entrance, fall in love with*, grab, infatuate, make hit with*, please, slay*, sweep off feet*, turn on*; SEE CONCEPTS *7,22,375*

enamored [*adj*] *in love*
amorous, attracted, besotted, bewitched, captivated, charmed, crazy about*, devoted, dotty, enchanted, enraptured, entranced, fascinated, fond, gone*, has a thing about*, hooked*, infatuated, loving, nuts about*, silly about*, smitten, stuck on*, swept off one's feet*, taken*, wild about*; SEE CONCEPTS *32,403*

em
en

encampment [n] *camp*
bivouac, campground, campsite, rest area, site;
SEE CONCEPTS *198,516*

encapsulate [v1] *encase*
box, cover, enclose, envelop, sheathe, wrap; SEE
CONCEPTS *112,209,758*

encapsulate [v2] *epitomize*
abbreviate, abridge, capsulize, condense, cut, digest, precis, shorten, summarize, sum up, synopsize; SEE CONCEPTS *236,247*

enchant [v] *delight, mesmerize*
allure, beguile, bewitch, captivate, carry away*, cast a spell on*, charm, delectate, draw, enamor, enrapture, ensorcell, enthrall, entice, entrance, fascinate, grab, gratify, hex, hypnotize, kill*, knock dead*, magnetize, make a hit with*, make happy*, please, send*, slay*, spell, spellbind, sweep off feet*, take, thrill, turn on*, voodoo*, wile, wow*; SEE CONCEPTS *7,22*

enchanting [adj] *fascinating, delightful*
alluring, appealing, attractive, beguiling, bewitching, captivating, charming, delectable, endearing, enthralling, entrancing, exciting, glamorous, intriguing, lovely, pleasant, pleasing, ravishing, seductive, siren, sirenic, winsome; SEE
CONCEPTS *404,529*

enchantress [n] *sorceress*
charmer, diviner, femme fatale, seductress, siren, vamp, witch; SEE CONCEPTS *361,412,415*

encircle [v] *circumscribe*
band, begird, cincture, circle, circuit, compass, cover, enclose, encompass, enfold, enring, envelop, environ, gird in, girdle, halo, hem in*, inclose, invest, ring, surround, wreathe; SEE
CONCEPT *758*

enclose [v] *put inside, surround*
blockade, block off, bound, box up, cage, circle, circumscribe, close in, confine, coop, corral, cover, encase, encircle, encompass, enfold, enshroud, environ, fence, fence off*, hedge, hem in*, imbue, immure, implant, impound, imprison, include, induct, insert, intern, jail, limit, lock in*, lock up*, mew, mure, pen, restrict, set apart, shut in, veil, wall in, wrap; SEE CONCEPTS *112,209,758*

enclosure [n1] *area bounded by something*
asylum, aviary, bowl, building, cage, camp, cell, close, coliseum, coop, corral, court, courtyard, den, dungeon, garden, ghetto, hutch, jail, pale, park, patch, pen, place, plot, pound, precinct, prison, quad, quadrangle, region, room, stadium, stockade, sty, vault, walk, yard, zone; SEE CONCEPTS *439,448,513*

enclosure [n2] *something included with a letter*
check, circular, copy, document, form, information, money, printed matter, questionnaire; SEE
CONCEPT *271*

encode [v] *encrypt*
cipher, conceal, cryptograph, make secret, put into code; SEE CONCEPT *188*

encompass [v1] *surround, circumscribe*
beset, circle, compass, encircle, enclose, envelop, environ, gird, girdle, hem in, ring; SEE
CONCEPT *758*

encompass [v2] *include, contain*
admit, comprehend, comprise, cover, embody, embrace, have, hold, incorporate, involve, subsume, take in; SEE CONCEPT *112*

encore [n] *another round of applause; repeat*
acclamation, cheers, number, plaudits, praise,

reappearance, repeat performance, repetition, response, return; SEE CONCEPT *264*

encounter [n1] *chance meeting*
appointment, brush, concurrence, confrontation, interview, rendezvous; SEE CONCEPT *384*

encounter [n2] *fight, argument*
action, battle, bout, brush, clash, collision, combat, conflict, contention, contest, dispute, engagement, flap*, fray, hassle, quarrel, rumpus*, run-in*, scrap, set-to*, skirmish, velitation, violence; SEE CONCEPTS *46,86,106*

encounter [v1] *happen upon*
alight upon, bear, bump into, chance upon, close, come across, come upon, confront, cross the path*, descry, detect, espy, experience, face, fall in with*, find, front, hit upon, meet, meet up with, rub eyeballs*, run across, run into, run smack into*, suffer, sustain, turn up, undergo; SEE CONCEPTS *38,384*

encounter [v2] *fight, attack*
affront, battle, clash with, collide, combat, conflict, confront, contend, cross swords*, do battle*, engage, face, grapple, meet, strive, struggle; SEE CONCEPTS *86,106*

encourage [v1] *stimulate spiritually*
animate, applaud, boost, brighten, buck up*, buoy, cheer, cheer up, comfort, console, embolden, energize, enhearten, enliven, excite, hilarate, fortify, galvanize, give shot in arm*, gladden, goad, hearten, incite, inspire, inspirit, instigate, praise, prick, prop up*, psych up*, push, rally, reassure, refresh, restore, revitalize, revivify, rouse, spur, steel, stir, strengthen, sway; SEE CONCEPTS *7,22*

encourage [v2] *give support; help*
abet, advance, advocate, aid, approve, assist, back, back up, befriend, bolster, boost, brace, comfort, console, countenance, develop, ease, egg on*, endorse, favor, fortify, forward, foster, further, get behind, give a leg up*, go for*, improve, instigate, invite, pat on the back, prevail, promote, pull for*, push, reassure, reinforce, relieve, root for*, sanction, second, serve, side with*, smile upon*, solace, spur, strengthen, subscribe to, subsidize, succor, support, sustain, uphold; SEE CONCEPTS *8,110*

encouragement [n] *help, support*
advance, advocacy, aid, animation, assistance, backing, boost, cheer, comfort, confidence, consolation, consoling, easement, enlivening, faith, favor, firmness, fortitude, helpfulness, hope, incentive, incitement, inspiration, inspiritment, invigoration, optimism, promotion, reassurance, reassuring, refreshment, relief, relieving, reward, shot in the arm*, softening, solacing, stimulation, stimulus, succor, supporting, trust, urging; SEE CONCEPTS *7,22,110,410*

encroach [v] *invade another's property, business*
appropriate, arrogate, barge in*, butt in*, crash, elbow in*, entrench, horn in*, impinge, infringe, interfere, interpose, intervene, intrude, make inroads*, meddle, muscle in*, overstep, put two cents in*, squeeze in*, stick nose into*, trench, trespass, usurp, work in, worm in*; SEE CONCEPTS *7,19,86,159*

encumber [v] *bother, burden*
block, charge, clog, cramp, discommode, embarrass, hamper, handicap, hang up, hinder, hog-tie*, hold up, impede, incommode, inconvenience, lade, load, make difficult, obstruct, op-

press, overburden, overload, retard, saddle, saddle with*, slow down, tax, trammel, weigh down, weight; SEE CONCEPTS *121,130*

encumbrance [n] *burden*
albatross, ball and chain*, cross, debt, duty, guilt, handicap, hindrance, impediment, load, millstone, monkey on one's back*, obstruction, responsibility, saddle, thorn in one's side*, weight, worry; SEE CONCEPTS *532,690*

encyclopedic [adj] *comprehensive*
all-embracing, all-encompassing, all-inclusive, broad, catholic, complete, discursive, exhaustive, extensive, general, thorough, thorough-going, universal, vast, wide-ranging, widespread; SEE CONCEPTS *267,772*

end [n1] *extreme, limit*
borderline, bound, boundary, butt end, confine, cusp, deadline, edge, extent, extremity, foot, head, heel, limitation, neb, nib, point, prong, spire, stub, stump, tail, tail end, term, terminal, termination, terminus, tip, top, ultimate; SEE CONCEPTS *745,827,833*

end [n2] *completion, stop*
accomplishment, achievement, adjournment, attainment, bottom line*, cease, cessation, close, closing, closure, conclusion, consequence, consummation, culmination, curtain, denouement, desistance, desuetude, determination, discontinuance, execution, expiration, expiry, finale, finis, finish, fulfillment, issue, last word*, omega, outcome, payoff, perfection, realization, resolution, result, retirement, sign-off*, target, termination, terminus, upshot*, windup, wrap-up*; SEE CONCEPTS *119,230,832*

end [n3] *intention, aim*
aspiration, design, drift, goal, intent, mark, object, objective, point, purpose, reason, where one's heading*; SEE CONCEPT *659*

end [n4] *leftover part*
bit, butt end, dregs, fragment, leaving, lees, particle, piece, portion, remainder, remnant, residue, scrap, share, side, stub, tag end; SEE CONCEPT *835*

end [n5] *death, destruction*
annihilation, demise, dissolution, doom, expiration, extermination, extinction, finish, passing, ruin, ruination; SEE CONCEPT *304*

end [v1] *bring to an end*
abolish, abort, accomplish, achieve, break off, break up, call it a day*, call off*, cease, close, close out, complete, conclude, consummate, crown, culminate, cut short, delay, determine, discontinue, dispose of, dissolve, drop, expire, finish, get done, give up, halt, interrupt, pack it in*, perorate, postpone, pull the plug*, put the lid on*, quit, relinquish, resolve, settle, sew up*, shut down*, stop, switch off*, terminate, top off*, ultimate, wind up*, wrap, wrap up*; SEE CONCEPT *234*

end [v2] *die or kill*
abolish, annihilate, cease, depart, desist, destroy, die, expire, exterminate, extinguish, lapse, put to death, ruin, run out, wane; SEE CONCEPTS *252,304*

endanger [v] *put in jeopardy*
be careless, chance, chance it*, expose, hazard, imperil, lay on the line*, lay open*, leave defenseless, leave in the middle*, make liable, menace, peril, play into one's hands*, put at risk, put in danger, put on the spot*, risk, stick one's

neck out*, subject to loss, threaten, venture; SEE CONCEPTS *246,252,384*

endangered [adj] *imperiled*
at risk, facing extinction, in danger, threatened; SEE CONCEPTS *231,407*

endear [v] *attract attention*
attach, bind, captivate, charm, cherish, engage, prize, treasure, value, win; SEE CONCEPTS *7,22,32*

endearing [adj] *lovable*
adorable, captivating, charming, dear, irresistible, sweet, winning; SEE CONCEPT *404*

endeavor [n] *attempt to achieve something*
aim, all*, best shot*, crash project*, dry run*, effort, enterprise, essay, exertion, fling, full blast*, full court press*, full steam*, go, header*, labor, lick*, old college try*, one's all*, one's level best*, push, shot*, stab*, striving, struggle, toil, travail, trial, try, try-on*, undertaking, venture, whack*, whirl*, work; SEE CONCEPT *87*

endeavor [v] *attempt to achieve something*
address, aim, apply, aspire, assay, bid for, buck, determine, dig, do one's best*, drive at, essay, go for*, go for broke*, grind, hammer away*, hassle, have a crack*, have a shot at*, have a swing at*, hump*, hustle, intend, labor, make an effort, make a run at*, offer, peg away*, plug, pour it on*, purpose, push, risk, scratch, seek, strain, strive, struggle, sweat, take on, take pains*, try, undertake, venture; SEE CONCEPT *87*

endemic [adj] *native*
local, regional; SEE CONCEPT *536*

ending [n] *conclusion*
catastrophe, cessation, close, closing, closure, completion, consummation, coup de grace, culmination, denouement, desistance, dissolution, epilogue, expiration, finale, finish, lapse, omega, outcome, period, resolution, stop, summation, swan song*, termination, terminus, upshot, wane, windup; SEE CONCEPTS *119,230,832*

endless [adj] *not stopping, not finishing*
amaranthine, boundless, ceaseless, constant, continual, continuous, countless, deathless, enduring, eternal, everlasting, illimitable, immeasurable, immortal, incalculable, incessant, indeterminate, infinite, interminable, limitless, measureless, monotonous, multitudinous, never-ending, no end of, no end to, numberless, overlong, perpetual, self-perpetuating, unbounded, unbroken, undivided, undying, unending, unfathomable, uninterrupted, unlimited, unsurpassable, untold, without end; SEE CONCEPTS *482,551,798*

endorse [v1] *support, authorize*
accredit, advocate, affirm, approve, attest, authenticate, back, back up*, bless, boost, certify, champion, commend, confirm, countenance, defend, favor, give a boost to, give green light*, give one's word*, give the go-ahead*, give the nod*, go along with*, go to bat for*, go with, guarantee, lend one's name to, okay, praise, push, ratify, recommend, rubber-stamp*, sanction, second, stand behind, stand up for*, stump for*, subscribe to, sustain, underwrite, uphold, vouch for, warrant, witness; SEE CONCEPTS *10,50,69,88,300*

endorse [v2] *countersign a check*
add one's name to, authenticate, autograph, cosign, notarize, put John Hancock on*, put signature on, rubber-stamp*, say amen to*, sign, sign off on, sign on dotted line*, subscribe, su-

en
en

perscribe, undersign, underwrite; SEE CONCEPTS *50,79,88,330*

endorsement [*n*] *support, authorization*
advocacy, affirmation, approbation, approval, backing, championing, commercial, confirmation, countersignature, favor, fiat, go-ahead*, green light*, hubba-hubba*, okay, pat on back*, permission, qualification, ratification, recommendation, sanction, seal of approval, signature, stroke, subscription to, superscription, the nod*, warrant; SEE CONCEPT *685*

endow [*v*] *give large gift*
accord, award, back, bequeath, bestow, come through with, confer, contribute, donate, empower, enable, endue, enhance, enrich, establish, favor, finance, found, fund, furnish, grant, heighten, invest, lay on*, leave, make over*, organize, promote, provide, settle on, sponsor, subscribe, subsidize, supply, support, vest in, will; SEE CONCEPTS *108,341*

endowment [*n1*] *large gift*
award, benefaction, benefit, bequest, bestowal, boon, bounty, dispensation, donation, fund, funding, gifting, grant, gratuity, income, inheritance, largess, legacy, nest egg, pension, presentation, property, provision, revenue, stake, stipend, subsidy, trust; SEE CONCEPTS *337,340*

endowment [*n2*] *personal talent, ability*
aptitude, attribute, capability, capacity, faculty, flair, genius, gift, habilitation, power, qualification, quality, turn; SEE CONCEPTS *411,630*

end up [*v*] *become eventually; come to a close*
arrive finally, cease, come to a halt, finish, finish as, finish up, stop, turn out to be, wind up; SEE CONCEPT *119*

endurable [*adj*] *tolerable*
bearable, livable, sufferable, supportable, sustainable; SEE CONCEPT *548*

endurance [*n1*] *bearing hardship; staying power*
ability, allowance, backbone, bearing, capacity, continuing, cool, coolness, courage, enduring, forebearance, fortitude, grit, guts, gutsiness, heart*, holding up*, intestinal fortitude, mettle, moxie*, patience, perseverance, persistence, pertinacity, pluck, resignation, resistance, resolution, restraint, spunk, stamina, standing, starch*, strength, submission, sufferance, suffering, tenacity, tolerance, toleration, undergoing, vitality, will, withstanding; SEE CONCEPTS *411,633*

endurance [*n2*] *continuity, lastingness*
continuance, continuation, durability, duration, immutability, longevity, permanence, persistence, stability; SEE CONCEPT *804*

endure [*v1*] *bear hardship*
abide, accustom, allow, bear the brunt*, be patient with, brave, brook, cope with, countenance, eat, encounter, experience, face, feel, go through, grin and bear it*, hang in*, keep up, know, live out, live through, meet with, never say die*, permit, put up with, repress feelings, resign oneself, ride out*, sit through, stand, stick, stick it out*, stomach*, subject to, submit to, suffer, support, sustain, swallow*, take, take it*, take patiently, tolerate, undergo, weather, withstand; SEE CONCEPT *23*

endure [*v2*] *continue; be durable*
abide, be, be left, be long lived, be timeless, bide, carry on, carry through, cling, exist, go on, hang on*, have no end, hold, hold on, hold out, keep on, last, linger, live, live on, never say die*, outlast, outlive, perdure, persist, prevail, remain, ride out*, run on, stand, stay, stay on, stick to*, superannuate, survive, sustain, wear, wear on, wear well*; SEE CONCEPTS *239,407,804*

enemy [*n*] *someone hated or competed against*
adversary, agent, antagonist, archenemy, asperser, assailant, assassin, attacker, backbiter, bad person*, bandit, betrayer, calumniator, competitor, contender, criminal, defamer, defiler, detractor, disputant, emulator, falsifier, fifth column*, foe, guerrilla, informer, inquisitor, invader, murderer, opponent, opposition, other side*, prosecutor, rebel, revolutionary, rival, saboteur, seditionist, slanderer, spy, terrorist, traducer, traitor, vilifier, villain; SEE CONCEPTS *322,412*

energetic [*adj*] *full of life; forceful*
active, aggressive, animated, ball of fire*, breezy, brisk, demoniac, driving, dynamic, enterprising, forcible, fresh, hardy, high-powered, indefatigable, industrious, kinetic, lively, lusty, peppy, potent, powerful, red-blooded*, rugged, snappy, spirited, sprightly, spry, stalwart, strenuous, strong, sturdy, tireless, tough, unflagging, untiring, vigorous, vital, vivacious, zippy*; SEE CONCEPTS *404,542*

energize [*v*] *activate; give more life*
actify, activize, animate, arm, build up, electrify, empower, enable, enliven, excite, fortify, goose*, innervate, inspirit, invigorate, jazz up*, juice up*, liven up, motivate, pep up, prime, pump up*, put zip into*, quicken, reinforce, start up, stimulate, strengthen, sustain, switch on, trigger, turn on, vitalize, work up, zap*; SEE CONCEPTS *7,22,231,700*

energy [*n1*] *person's spirit and vigor*
activity, animation, application, ardor, birr, dash, drive, effectiveness, efficacy, efficiency, élan, endurance, enterprise, exertion, fire, force, forcefulness, fortitude, get-up-and-go*, go, hardihood, initiative, intensity, juice, life, liveliness, might, moxie*, muscle, operativeness, pep, pizzazz, pluck, potency, power, puissance, punch, spirit, spontaneity, stamina, steam, strength, toughness, tuck, vehemence, verve, vim, virility, vitality, vivacity, zeal, zest, zing, zip*; SEE CONCEPT *411*

energy [*n2*] *generated power*
application, burn, conductivity, current, dynamism, electricity, force, friction, gravity, heat, horsepower, juice, kilowatts, magnetism, potential, pressure, radioactivity, rays, reaction, response, service, steam, strength, voltage, wattage; SEE CONCEPT *520*

enervate [*v*] *tire, wear out*
debilitate, devitalize, disable, enfeeble, exhaust, fatigue, incapacitate, jade, paralyze, sap, unnerve, vitiate, weaken, weary; SEE CONCEPTS *156,225,250*

enervated [*adj*] *exhausted, worn out*
debilitated, deteriorated, devitalized, done in, enfeebled, fatigued, feeble, gone to seed*, incapacitated, lackadaisical, languid, languishing, languorous, limp, listless, on the ropes*, out of condition*, out of gas*, out of shape*, paralyzed, prostrate, prostrated, run-down, rusty, sapped, soft, spent, spiritless, tired, undermined, unnerved, vitiated, washed out, weak, weakened; SEE CONCEPTS *485,560*

enfeeble [*v*] *make very weak*
attenuate, blunt, cripple, debilitate, deplete, devitalize, diminish, disable, exhaust, fatigue, incapacitate, sap, undermine, unhinge, unnerve, weaken, wear out; SEE CONCEPTS *240,252*

enfold [*v*] *embrace, hug*
bear hug, cinch, clasp, clinch, clutch, cover, drape, encase, enclose, encompass, enshroud, envelop, envelope, enwrap, fold, girdle, grab, hold, invest, press, shroud, squeeze, surround, swathe, veil, wrap, wrap up; SEE CONCEPTS *191,219*

enforce [*v*] *put a rule, plan in force*
accomplish, administer, administrate, apply, carry out, coerce, commandeer, compel, constrain, crack down, demand, dictate, discharge, dragoon, drive, effect, egg on*, emphasize, exact, execute, exert, expect, extort, force upon, fortify, fulfill, goad, hound, impel, implement, impose, incite, insist on, invoke, lash, lean on, make, necessitate, oblige, perform, press, prosecute, put into effect, put screws to*, reinforce, require, sanction, spur, strain, stress, strong-arm, support, urge, whip, wrest; SEE CONCEPTS *50,88,133,298,317*

enforcement [*n*] *requirement to obey; implementation of rule(s)*
administration, application, carrying out, coercion, compulsion, compulsory law, constraint, duress, enforcing, exaction, execution, fulfilling, imposition, impulsion, insistence, lash, martial law, necessitation, obligation, prescription, pressure, prosecution, reinforcement, spur, whip; SEE CONCEPTS *133,298,317,685*

engage [*v1*] *hire for job, use*
appoint, bespeak, book, bring on board*, charter, come on board*, commission, contract, employ, enlist, enroll, ink*, lease, place, prearrange, put on, rent, reserve, retain, secure, sign on, sign up, take on, truck with*; SEE CONCEPTS *129,351*

engage [*v2*] *occupy oneself; engross*
absorb, allure, arrest, bewitch, busy, captivate, catch, charm, draw, embark on, employ, enamor, enchant, enter into, enthrall, fascinate, give a try*, give a whirl*, go for broke*, go in for*, go out for*, grip*, have a fling at*, have a go at*, have a shot at*, imbue, immerse, interest, involve, join, keep busy, monopolize, partake, participate, pitch in, practice, preengage, preoccupy, set about, soak, tackle*, take part, tie up, try on for size*, undertake; SEE CONCEPTS *87,363*

engage [*v3*] *promise to marry*
affiance, agree, betroth, bind, catch, commit, contract, covenant, give one's word*, guarantee, hook, obligate, oblige, pass, pledge, tie, troth, turn on*, undertake, vouch, vow; SEE CONCEPT *297*

engage [*v4*] *start a fight; attack*
assail, assault, combat, do battle with, encounter, face, fall on, give battle to, join battle with, launch, meet, strike, take on; SEE CONCEPTS *86,106,320*

engage [*v5*] *interconnect; bring into operation*
activate, apply, attach, dovetail, energize, fasten, get going, interact, interlace, interlock, intermesh, interplay, join, lock, mesh, switch on; SEE CONCEPTS *85,113,160,221*

engaged [*adj1*] *promised to be married*
affianced, asked for, betrothed, bound, committed, contracted, future, given one's word*, going steady*, hooked*, intended, matched, pinned, pledged, plighted, ringed, spoken for, steady; SEE CONCEPT *555*

engaged [*adj2*] *operating; busy*
absorbed, at work, committed, connected with, dealing in, deep, doing, employed, engrossed, immersed, in place, intent, interested, in use, involved, occupied, performing, practicing, preoccupied, pursuing, rapt, signed, tied up, unavailable, working, wrapped up*; SEE CONCEPTS *542,555,576*

engagement [*n1*] *pledge to marry*
assurance, betrothal, betrothing, betrothment, bond, commitment, compact, contract, espousal, match, oath, obligation, pact, plight, promise, troth, undertaking, vow, word; SEE CONCEPT *297*

engagement [*n2*] *meeting; date*
appointment, arrangement, assignation, blind date*, commission, commitment, date, errand, get-together, gig, going out*, interview, invitation, meet, seeing one*, stint, tryst, visit; SEE CONCEPT *384*

engagement [*n3*] *battle*
action, combat, conflict, confrontation, contest, encounter, fight, fray, skirmish; SEE CONCEPTS *106,320*

engaging [*adj*] *charming*
agreeable, alluring, appealing, attractive, bewitching, captivating, enchanting, enticing, entrancing, fascinating, fetching, glamorous, interesting, intriguing, inviting, likable, lovable, magnetic, mesmeric, pleasant, pleasing, prepossessing, siren, sweet, winning, winsome; SEE CONCEPT *404*

engender [*v*] *cause to happen; cause an action*
arouse, beget, breed, bring about, bring forth, create, develop, excite, foment, generate, give birth to, give rise to, hatch, incite, induce, instigate, lead to, make, muster, occasion, precipitate, procreate, produce, propagate, provoke, quicken, rouse, spawn, stimulate, stir, work up; SEE CONCEPTS *221,242*

engine [*n*] *device that drives a machine*
agent, apparatus, appliance, barrel, contrivance, cylinder, diesel, dynamo, fan, generator, horses*, implement, instrument, means, mechanism, motor, piston, pot*, powerhouse, power plant, power train, putt-putt*, rubber band*, tool, transformer, turbine, weapon, what's under the hood*; SEE CONCEPTS *463,464*

engineer [*n*] *person who puts together things*
architect, builder, contriver, designer, deviser, director, inventor, manager, manipulator, originator, planner, schemer, sights*, surveyor, techie, technie*; SEE CONCEPT *348*

engineer [*v*] *devise; bring about*
angle, arrange, cause, come up with, con, conceive, concoct, contrive, control, cook*, create, direct, doctor, effect, encompass, finagle*, jockey*, machinate, manage, maneuver, manipulate, negotiate, operate, organize, originate, plan, plant, play games*, plot, pull strings*, pull wires*, put one on*, put one over*, put over*, put through, rig*, scam, scheme, set up, superintend, supervise, swing, upstage, wangle, work; SEE CONCEPTS *36,173,251*

engrave [*v*] *carve letters or designs into*
bite, burn, chase, chisel, crosshatch, cut, diaper, embed, enchase, etch, fix, grave, hatch, impress, imprint, infix, ingrain, initial, inscribe, instill, in-

en
en

taglio, lithograph, lodge, mezzotint, ornament, print, scratch, stipple; SEE CONCEPTS *79,174,176*

engraving [*n*] *carving of letters or design into something*
blocking, chasing, chiselling, cutting, dry point, enchasing, etching, illustration, impression, inscribing, inscription, intaglio, lithograph, mezzotint, photoengraving, photogravure, print, rotogravure, scratch, woodcut; SEE CONCEPTS *79,174,176,625*

engross [*v*] *hold one's attention*
absorb, apply, arrest, assimilate, attract, become lost, be hung*, bewitch, busy, captivate, consume, corner, engage, engulf, enrapture, enthrall, fascinate, fill, grip, hog*, immerse, involve, monopolize, occupy, preoccupy, sew up*, soak, take up, up on*; SEE CONCEPTS *14,17*

engrossed [*adj*] *preoccupied; attentive to*
absorbed, all wound up*, assiduous, bugged*, busy, captivated, caught up, caught up in, consumed, deep, diligent, engaged, enthralled, fascinated, fiend for*, gone*, gripped, head over heels*, heavily into*, hooked, hung up, immersed, industrious, intent, into*, intrigued, lost, monopolized, occupied, rapt, really into*, riveted, sedulous, submerged, taken up with, tied up, turned on*, up to here in*, wrapped up*; SEE CONCEPTS *403,542*

engrossing [*adj*] *very interesting*
absorbing, all-consuming, captivating, compelling, consuming, controlling, enthralling, exciting, fascinating, gripping, intriguing, monopolizing, obsessing, preoccupying, provoking, riveting, stimulating; SEE CONCEPT *529*

engulf [*v*] *absorb, overwhelm*
bury, consume, deluge, drown, encompass, engross, envelop, flood, imbibe, immerse, inundate, overflow, overrun, overwhelm, plunge, submerge, swallow up, swamp, whelm; SEE CONCEPTS *169,172,256*

enhance [*v*] *improve, embellish*
add to, adorn, aggrandize, amplify, appreciate, augment, beautify, boom, boost, build up, complement, elevate, embroider, enlarge, exaggerate, exalt, flesh out*, heighten, increase, intensify, lift, magnify, pad*, pyramid*, raise, reinforce, strengthen, swell, upgrade; SEE CONCEPTS *162,177,244*

enigma [*n*] *mystery*
bewilderment, cliffhanger, conundrum, crux, cryptogram, Gordian knot*, grabber*, knot*, mind-boggler*, mind-twister*, mystification, parable, perplexity, problem, puzzle, puzzlement, puzzler, question, question mark, riddle, secret, sixty-four dollar question*, sphinx*, sticker, stickler, stumper, teaser, tough nut to crack*, twister, why*; SEE CONCEPT *532*

enigmatic/enigmatical [*adj*] *mysterious*
ambiguous, cryptic, dark, Delphian*, doubtful, equivocal, incomprehensible, indecipherable, inexplicable, inscrutable, obscure, occult, oracular, perplexing, puzzling, recondite, secret, Sibylline*, sphinxlike, stickling, stumping, teasing, uncertain, unfathomable, unintelligible; SEE CONCEPTS *529,576,582*

enjoin [*v1*] *order, command*
adjure, admonish, advise, appoint, bid, call upon, caution, charge, counsel, decree, demand, dictate, direct, forewarn, impose, instruct, ordain,

prescribe, require, rule, tell, urge, warn; SEE CONCEPTS *53,78*

enjoin [*v2*] *forbid*
ban, bar, deny, disallow, inhibit, interdict, outlaw, place injunction on, preclude, prohibit, proscribe, restrain, taboo; SEE CONCEPTS *50,53,88, 130*

enjoy [*v1*] *take pleasure in, from something*
adore, appreciate, be entertained, be fond of, be pleased, cotton to*, delight in, dig*, dote on*, drink in*, eat up*, fancy, flip over*, freak out on*, get a charge out of*, get a kick out of*, get high on*, go, have a ball*, have a good time, have fun, like, live a little*, live it up*, love, luxuriate in, mind, paint the town*, rejoice in, relish, revel in, savor, take joy in, thrill to; SEE CONCEPTS *32,384*

enjoy [*v2*] *have the benefit or use of*
be blessed, be favored, boast, command, experience, have, hold, maintain, occupy, own, possess, process, reap the benefits*, retain, use; SEE CONCEPT *710*

enjoyable [*adj*] *pleasing; to one's liking*
agreeable, amusing, clear sailing*, delectable, delicious, delightful, entertaining, fun, genial, gratifying, groovy*, just for grins*, just for kicks*, just for laughs*, just for the heck of it*, likable, lots of laughs*, pleasant, pleasurable, preferable, relishable, satisfying, welcome; SEE CONCEPTS *529,548*

enjoyment [*n1*] *delight in something*
amusement, delectation, diversion, enjoying, entertainment, fruition, fun, gladness, gratification, gusto, happiness, hedonism, indulgence, joy, loving, luxury, pleasure, recreation, rejoicing, relaxation, relish, satisfaction, savor, self-indulgence, sensuality, thrill, triumph, zest; SEE CONCEPTS *32,410*

enjoyment [*n2*] *possession; use of*
advantage, benefit, exercise, having, indulgence, ownership, spending, using; SEE CONCEPT *710*

enlarge [*v*] *make or grow bigger; increase*
add to, aggrandize, amplify, augment, beef up*, blow up*, boost, broaden, build, bulk, develop, diffuse, dilate, distend, elaborate, elongate, embroider, exaggerate, expand, expatiate, extend, give details, grow, grow larger, heighten, inflate, jack up*, jazz up*, lengthen, magnify, make larger, mount, multiply, pad*, pyramid*, rise, slap on*, snowball*, spread, stretch, swell, upsurge, wax, widen; SEE CONCEPTS *137,236,245, 780*

enlargement [*n*] *increase, expansion*
aggrandizement, amplification, augmentation, blow up, elongation, extension, growth, spread; SEE CONCEPT *780*

enlighten [*v*] *explain thoroughly; make aware*
acquaint, advise, apprise, brief, catechize, cause to understand, civilize, convert, counsel, direct, disclose, divulge, edify, educate, elucidate, give faith*, give the lowdown*, give the word*, guide, illume, illuminate, illumine, imitate, improve, inculcate, indoctrinate, inform, inspirit, instruct, let in on, open up, persuade, preach, put on to*, reveal, save, school, teach, tell, train, update, uplift; SEE CONCEPTS *57,60,75*

enlightened [*adj*] *informed, educated*
aware, broad-minded, civilized, cultivated, hip to*, instructed, in the picture*, knowing what's what*, knowledgeable, learned, liberal, literate,

open-minded, plugged in*, reasonable, refined, savvy, sharp, sophisticated, tuned in*, wised up*; SEE CONCEPT *402*

enlightenment [*n*] *awareness, understanding*
broad-mindedness, civilization, comprehension, cultivation, culture, edification, education, information, insight, instruction, knowledge, learning, literacy, open-mindedness, refinement, sophistication, teaching, wisdom; SEE CONCEPT *409*

enlist [*v*] *sign up for responsibility*
admit, appoint, assign, attract, call to arms, call up, conscribe, conscript, draft, embody, employ, engage, enroll, enter, enter into, gather, get, hire, hitch, incorporate, induct, initiate, inscribe, interest, join, join up, levy, list, mobilize, muster, oblige, obtain, place, press into service, procure, record, recruit, register, reserve, secure, serve, sign on, take on, volunteer; SEE CONCEPTS *8,320*

enliven [*v*] *inspire, vitalize*
animate, brace up, brighten, buck up, buoy, cheer, cheer up, divert, entertain, excite, exhilarate, fire, fire up, galvanize, give a lift, give life to, gladden, hearten, inspirit, invigorate, jazz up*, juice up*, let sunshine in*, pep up*, perk up*, pick up, put pep into, quicken, recreate, refresh, rejuvenate, renew, restore, rouse, snap out of it*, spark, spice, spice up*, stimulate, vivificate, vivify, wake up, work up*, zap*; SEE CONCEPTS *7,22*

en masse [*adj*] *all at once*
all in all, all together, altogether, as a body, as a group, as a whole, as one, bodily, by and large*, ensemble, generally, in a body, in a group, in a mass, jointly, on the whole, together; SEE CONCEPT *577*

enmesh [*v*] *involve in a situation*
box in, catch, drag into*, draw in, embroil, ensnare, entangle, entrap, hook, implicate, incriminate, lay a trap for*, lay for*, make party to*, net, snare, snarl, tangle, trammel, trap; SEE CONCEPTS *59,112*

enmity [*n*] *hatred, animosity*
acrimony, alienation, animus, antagonism, antipathy, aversion, bad blood*, bitterness, daggers*, detestation, dislike, hate, hostility, ill will, loathing, malevolence, malice, malignancy, malignity, rancor, spite, spleen, uncordiality, unfriendliness, venom; SEE CONCEPT *29*

ennui [*n*] *boredom*
apathy, blahs, blues, dejection, depression, dissatisfaction, doldrums, dumps*, fatigue, ho hums*, lack of interest, languidness, languor, lassitude, listlessness, melancholy, sadness, satiety, spiritlessness, surfeit, tedium, weariness, yawn*; SEE CONCEPT *410*

enormity [*n1*] *horribleness*
abomination, atrociousness, atrocity, crime, depravity, disgrace, evil, evilness, flagrancy, grossness, heinousness, horror, monstrosity, monstrousness, nefariousness, outrage, outrageousness, rankness, turpitude, vice, viciousness, vileness, villainy, wickedness; SEE CONCEPTS *645,666*

enormity [*n2*] *extreme largeness*
bigness, bulk, enormousness, greatness, hugeness, immensity, magnitude, massiveness, size, tremendousness, vastness; SEE CONCEPT *730*

enormous [*adj*] *very large*
astronomic, barn door*, blimp*, colossal, excessive, gargantuan, gigantic, gross, huge, humon-

gous, immense, jumbo*, mammoth, massive, monstrous, mountainous, prodigious, stupendous, super-colossal*, titanic*, tremendous, vast, whopping; SEE CONCEPT *773*

enough [*adj*] *plenty*
abundant, acceptable, adequate, all right already*, ample, bellyful*, bounteous, bountiful, comfortable, competent, complete, copious, decent, enough already*, fed up*, full, had it*, last straw*, lavish, plenteous, plentiful, replete, satisfactory, satisfying, sick and tired of*, sufficient, sufficing, suitable, unlimited, up to here*; SEE CONCEPTS *546,771*

enough [*adv*] *adequately*
abundantly, acceptably, admissibly, amply, averagely, barely, commensurately, decently, fairly, moderately, passably, proportionately, rather, reasonably, satisfactorily, so-so*, sufficiently, tolerably; SEE CONCEPTS *546,558,771*

enough [*n*] *plenty*
abundance, adequacy, ampleness, ample supply, competence, plenitude, right amount, sufficiency, sufficient; SEE CONCEPTS *646,767*

enquire [*v*] *ask about*
analyze, check, examine, explore, go over, inquire, inspect, investigate, look into, probe, pry, query, question, scrutinize, search, seek, seek an answer, want to know; SEE CONCEPTS *24,48*

enquiry [*n*] *inquest*
analysis, examination, exploration, inquiry, inquisition, inspection, interrogation, investigation, probe, query, questioning, research, study; SEE CONCEPTS *24,48,290*

enrage [*v*] *make very upset*
aggravate, anger, ask for it*, exasperate, get under skin*, hack*, incense, incite, inflame, infuriate, ire, irritate, madden, make blood boil*, make see red*, needle, provoke, rile, steam up*, T-off*, umbrage, whip up*; SEE CONCEPTS *7,14,19*

enraged [*adj*] *furious*
aggravated, angered, angry, boiling*, exasperated, fuming, incensed, inflamed, infuriated, irate, livid, mad, pushed too far*, riled, upset; SEE CONCEPT *403*

enrapture [*v*] *captivate*
allure, attract, beguile, bewitch, charm, delight, elate, enamor, enchant, enthrall, entrance, fascinate, gladden, gratify, please, ravish, rejoice, score, send, spellbind, transport; SEE CONCEPTS *7,22*

enrich [*v*] *improve, embellish*
adorn, aggrandize, ameliorate, augment, beef up*, better, build, build up, cultivate, decorate, develop, endow, enhance, figure in, flesh out*, grace, hike up*, hop up*, jack up*, jazz up*, make rich, ornament, pad, parlay, pour it on*, pyramid*, refine, run up*, soup up*, spike*, step up, supplement, sweeten*, up*, upgrade; SEE CONCEPTS *177,244*

enroll [*v1*] *sign up for membership*
accept, admit, become student, call up, employ, engage, enlist, enter, join, join up, matriculate, muster, obtain, recruit, register, serve, sign on, subscribe, take course, take on; SEE CONCEPTS *114,129*

enroll [*v2*] *list, record*
affix, bill, book, catalog, chronicle, engross, enlist, enter, file, fill out, index, inscribe, insert, in-

ventorize, mark, matriculate, note, poll, register, schedule, slate; SEE CONCEPTS *79,125*

enrollment [*n*] *registration for membership*
acceptance, accession, admission, conscription, engagement, enlistment, entrance, entry, induction, influx, listing, matriculation, rally, reception, record, recruitment, response, student body, students, subscription; SEE CONCEPTS *288,388, 417*

en route [*adj*] *on the way to destination*
advancing, along the way, bound, driving, entrained, en voyage*, flying, heading toward, in passage, in transit, making headway*, midway, on the road*, pressing on, progressing, traveling; SEE CONCEPTS *577,586*

ensconce [*v*] *hide; tuck away*
bury, cache, conceal, cover, curl up, ditch, establish, fix, install, locate, nestle, place, plant, protect, screen, seat, secrete, set, settle, shelter, shield, situate, snuggle up, stash, station; SEE CONCEPTS *188,201*

ensemble [*adv*] *at the same time*
all at once, altogether, as a body, as a group, as a whole, as one, at once, en masse, in concert; SEE CONCEPT *577*

ensemble [*n1*] *collection*
aggregate, assemblage, band, cast, choir, chorus, company, composite, entirety, gathering, glee club, group, octet, orchestra, organization, outfit, quartet, quintet, set, sextet, sum, total, totality, trio, troupe, whole; SEE CONCEPTS *294,432*

ensemble [*n2*] *clothing outfit*
coordinates, costume, garb*, get-up*, suit, togs*; SEE CONCEPT *451*

enshrine [*v*] *hold as sacred*
apotheosize, bless, cherish, consecrate, dedicate, embalm, exalt, hallow, idolize, preserve, revere, sanctify, treasure; SEE CONCEPTS *69,367*

enshroud [*v*] *cover*
cloak, conceal, hide, mask, pall, shroud; SEE CONCEPTS *172,188*

ensign [*n*] *flag*
banderole, banner, colors, emblem, gonfalon, insignia, pennant, standard, streamer, symbol; SEE CONCEPTS *284,473*

enslave [*v*] *make someone a servant*
bind, capture, chain, check, circumscribe, coerce, compel, confine, deprive, disenfranchise, disfranchise, dominate, enchain, enclose, enthrall, fetter, get hooks into*, hobble, hold, immure, imprison, incarcerate, indenture, jail, keep under thumb*, oppress, put in irons*, reduce, restrain, restrict, secure, shackle, shut in, subdue, subject, subjugate, suppress, tether, tie, yoke; SEE CONCEPTS *14,90,130,191*

ensnare [*v*] *trap*
bag*, bat eyes at*, capture, catch, cheat, come on, deceive, decoy, embroil, enmesh, entangle, entice, entrap, hook, inveigle, lure, mislead, net, rope in, snag, snare, snarl, suck in*, tangle, trick; SEE CONCEPTS *59,90*

ensue [*v*] *start to happen; come to pass*
appear, arise, attend, be consequent on, befall, be subsequent to, come after, come next, come up, derive, develop, emanate, eventualize, eventuate, flow, follow, issue, occur, proceed, result, stem, succeed, supervene, turn out, turn up; SEE CONCEPTS *119,242*

ensuing [*adj*] *resultant*
after, coming, coming up, consequent, conse-

quential, following, later, next, next off, posterior, postliminary, subsequent, subsequential; SEE CONCEPTS *548,820*

ensure [*v*] *guarantee; make secure*
arrange, assure, certify, cinch, clinch, confirm, effect, establish, guard, insure, lock on*, lock up*, make certain, make safe, make sure, nail down*, okay, protect, provide, put on ice*, safeguard, secure, set out, warrant; SEE CONCEPTS *71,96*

entail [*v*] *require; result in*
bring about, call for, cause, demand, encompass, entangle, evoke, give rise to, impose, involve, lead to, necessitate, occasion, require, tangle; SEE CONCEPTS *242,646*

entangle [*v*] *involve, mix up*
bewilder, burden, catch, clog, come on, complicate, compromise, confuse, corner, dishevel, duke in, embarrass, embrangle, embroil, enchain, enmesh, ensnare, entrap, fetter, hamper, hook, impede, implicate, intertangle, intertwine, interweave, jumble, knot, lead on, mat, muddle, perplex, puzzle, ravel, rope in, set up, snag, snare, snarl, swindle, tangle, trammel, trap, twist, unsettle; SEE CONCEPTS *59,90,112*

entanglement [*n*] *complication, predicament*
affair, association, cobweb, complexity, confusion, difficulty, embarrassment, embroilment, enmeshment, ensnarement, entrapment, imbroglio, intricacy, intrigue, involvement, jumble, knot, liaison, mesh, mess, mix-up, muddle, snare, tangle, tie-up, toil, trap, web; SEE CONCEPTS *666,674*

entente [*n*] *agreement*
accord, arrangement, deal, pact, settlement, treaty, understanding; SEE CONCEPTS *271,331*

enter [*v1*] *come, put into a place*
access, arrive, barge in*, blow in*, break in, breeze in*, burst in, bust in*, butt in*, come in, crack, crawl, creep, crowd in*, drive in, drop in, fall into, gain entree, get in, go in, horn in*, immigrate, infiltrate, ingress, insert, insinuate, introduce, intrude, invade, jump in, make an entrance, make way, move in, pass into, penetrate, pierce, pile in, pop in*, probe, rush in, set foot in, slip, sneak, work in, worm in*, wriggle; SEE CONCEPT *159*

enter [*v2*] *embark on; take part in*
become member, begin, commence, commit oneself, enlist, enroll, get oneself into*, inaugurate, join, join up, lead off, muster*, open, participate in, set about, set out on, set to, sign on, sign up, start, subscribe, take up, tee off*; SEE CONCEPTS *114,234*

enter [*v3*] *record, list*
admit, docket, inject, inscribe, insert, intercalate, interpolate, introduce, log, note, post, put in, register, set down, take down; SEE CONCEPT *125*

enterprise [*n1*] *adventure, undertaking*
action, activity, affair, attempt, baby*, bag*, ballgame*, biggie*, big idea*, bit*, business, campaign, cause, company, concern, crusade, deal, deed, do*, effort, endeavor, engagement, essay, establishment, firm, flier*, follow through*, game*, happening, hazard, house, move, operation, outfit, performance, pet project*, plan, plunge*, program, project, proposition, purpose, pursuit, risk, scheme, speculation, stake, striving, stunt, task, thing*, trade, try, venture, work; SEE CONCEPTS *87,324,325,362*

enterprise [*n2*] *resourcefulness, energy*
activity, adventurousness, alertness, ambition, audacity, boldness, courage, daring, dash, drive, eagerness, enthusiasm, force, foresight, get-up-and-go*, gumption, hustle, industry, initiative, inventiveness, pluck, push, readiness, resource, self-reliance, spirit, venturesomeness, vigor, zeal; SEE CONCEPTS *411,657*

enterprising [*adj*] *resourceful, energetic*
active, advancing, adventurous, aggressive, alert, ambitious, aspiring, audacious, bold, busy, coming on strong*, craving, daring, dashing, diligent, driving, eager, enthusiastic, go-ahead*, go-go*, gumptious, hard ball*, hardworking, hungry, hustling, industrious, intrepid, itching, keen, lively, lusting, peppy, progressive, pushing, ready, self-starting, snappy, spanking, spark plug*, spirited, stirring, take-over, up-and-coming*, venturesome, vigorous, yearning, zealous, zippy*; SEE CONCEPTS *326,404,542*

entertain [*v1*] *amuse*
absorb, beguile, captivate, charm, cheer, comfort, crack up*, delight, distract, divert, ecstasize, elate, engross, enliven, enthrall, gladden, grab, gratify, humor, indulge, inspire, inspirit, interest, knock dead*, make merry, occupy, pique, please, recreate, regale, relax, satisfy, slay, solace, stimulate, tickle; SEE CONCEPTS *9,292*

entertain [*v2*] *accommodate visitors*
admit, be host, board, chaperone, dine, do the honors*, feed, foster, give a party, harbor, have a do*, have a get-together*, have company, have guests, have visitors, house, invite, lodge, nourish, pick up the check*, pop for*, put up*, quarter, receive, recreate, regale, room, show hospitality, spring for*, throw a party*, treat, welcome, wine and dine*; SEE CONCEPTS *377,384*

entertain [*v3*] *think about seriously*
cherish, cogitate on, conceive, consider, contemplate, deliberate, foster, harbor, heed, hold, imagine, keep in mind, maintain, muse over, ponder, recognize, support, think over; SEE CONCEPT *17*

entertaining [*adj*] *amusing, pleasing*
absorbing, affecting, be a ball*, captivating, charming, cheerful, cheering, clever, compelling, delightful, diverting, droll, enchanting, engaging, engrossing, enjoyable, enthralling, enticing, entrancing, exciting, fascinating, fun, funny, gas*, gay, humorous, impressive, inspiring, interesting, lively, moving, piquant, pleasant, pleasurable, poignant, priceless, provocative, recreative, relaxing, restorative, riot, rousing, scream, side-splitting, stimulating, stirring, striking, thrilling, witty; SEE CONCEPTS *529,537*

entertainment [*n*] *amusement, pleasure*
ball*, bash*, big time*, blast*, blow out*, celebration, cheer, clambake*, delight, dissipation, distraction, diversion, divertissement, enjoyment, feast, frolic, fun, fun and games*, gaiety, game, good time*, grins*, high time*, laughs*, leisure activity, lots of laughs*, merriment, merrymaking, party, pastime, picnic, play, recreation, regalement, relaxation, relief, revelry, satisfaction, shindig*, sport, spree, surprise, treat, wingding*; SEE CONCEPTS *383,384,386,388*

enthrall [*v*] *captivate*
absorb, beguile, bewitch, charm, enchant, engage, enrapture, enslave, entrance, fascinate,

grab, grip, hold spellbound, hook, hypnotize, intrigue, mesmerize, preoccupy, rivet, spellbind, subdue, subject, subjugate; SEE CONCEPTS *7,19,22*

enthusiasm [*n*] *keen interest, excitement*
activity, ardency, ardor, avidity, conviction, craze, dash, devotion, eagerness, earnestness, ecstasy, elan, emotion, energy, exhilaration, fad, fanaticism, feeling, fervor, fever, fieriness, fire, flame, flare, frenzy, fury, gaiety, glow, go*, heat, hilarity, hobby, impetuosity, intensity, interest, joy, joyfulness, keenness, life, mania, mirth, nerve, oomph*, orgasm, passion, pep, rapture, red heat*, relish, snap, spirit, transport, vehemence, verve, vim, vivacity, warmth, zeal, zealousness, zest; SEE CONCEPTS *633,657*

enthusiast [*n*] *person active in interest*
addict, admirer, aficionado, believer, buff, bug*, bum*, devotee, eccentric, fan, fanatic, follower, freak, habitué, lover, maniac, monomaniac, nut*, optimist, participant, partisan, rooter, supporter, votary, worshiper, zealot; SEE CONCEPT *423*

enthusiastic [*adj*] *interested, excited*
agog, animated, anxious, ardent, athirst, attracted, avid, bugged*, concerned, crazy about*, devoted, dying to*, eager, earnest, ebullient, exhilarated, exuberant, fanatical, fascinated, fervent, fervid, forceful, gaga*, gone on*, gung ho*, hearty, intent, keen, keyed up*, lively, nutty*, obsessed, passionate, pleased, rabid, red-hot*, rhapsodic, spirited, tantalized, thrilled, titillated, unqualified, vehement, vigorous, wacky*, warm, wholehearted, willing, zealous; SEE CONCEPTS *401,542*

entice [*v*] *allure; persuade*
attract, bait, bat eyes at*, beguile, cajole, coax, decoy, draw, entrap, inveigle, lead on, lure, prevail on, seduce, tempt, toll, turn on*, wheedle; SEE CONCEPTS *7,19,22,68*

enticement [*n*] *allurement; persuasion*
attraction, bait, blandishment, cajolery, coaxing, come hither*, come-on*, decoy, fascination, inducement, inveiglement, lure, mousetrap*, promise, seduction, snare, sweetener*, sweetening, temptation, trap; SEE CONCEPTS *7,19,22,68*

entire [*adj*] *complete, whole*
absolute, all, choate, consolidated, continuous, full, gross, intact, integral, integrated, outright, perfect, plenary, sound, thorough, total, unbroken, undamaged, undiminished, undivided, unified, unimpaired, uninjured, unmarked, unmarred, unmitigated, unreserved, unrestricted, untouched; SEE CONCEPTS *482,531*

entirely [*adv*] *completely*
absolutely, alone, altogether, exclusively, fully, in every respect, only, perfectly, plumb, quite, reservedly, solely, thoroughly, totally, undividedly, uniquely, utterly, well, wholly, without exception, without reservation; SEE CONCEPTS *531,535*

entirety [*n*] *wholeness, whole*
absoluteness, aggregate, all, allness, collectiveness, collectivity, completeness, complex, comprehensiveness, ensemble, entireness, everything, fullness, gross, intactness, integrality, integrity, omneity, omnitude, oneness, perfection, plenitude, sum, sum total, the works*, total, totality, undividedness, unity, universality, whole ball of wax*, whole bit*, whole enchilada*, whole nine yards*; SEE CONCEPTS *635,837*

en
en

entitle [*v1*] *name, label*
baptize, call, characterize, christen, denominate, designate, dub, nickname, style, subtitle, term, title; SEE CONCEPT *62*

entitle [*v2*] *hold right to*
accredit, allow, authorize, be in line for*, confer a right, empower, enable, enfranchise, fit for, have coming*, let, license, make eligible, permit, qualify for, rate, warrant; SEE CONCEPTS *50,83,88,129*

entity [*n1*] *object that exists*
article, being, body, creature, existence, individual, item, material, matter, organism, presence, quantity, single, singleton, something, stuff, subsistence, substance, thing; SEE CONCEPT *433*

entity [*n2*] *nature of a being*
actuality, essence, existence, integral, integrate, quiddity, quintessence, reality, subsistence, substance, sum, system, totality; SEE CONCEPTS *411,644*

entomb [*v*] *bury*
embalm, ensepulcher, enshrine, hold last rites for*, hold services for*, inhume, inter, inurn, lay to rest*, put six feet under*, sepulcher, sepulture, tomb; SEE CONCEPT *367*

entourage [*n*] *followers*
associates, attendants, companions, company, cortege, court, courtiers, escort, following, groupies*, hangers-on*, retainers, retinue, staff, suite, sycophants, toadies*, train; SEE CONCEPTS *387,417*

entrails [*n*] *internal organs*
bowels, guts, innards, insides, internal parts, viscera, vitals; SEE CONCEPT *393*

entrance [*n1*] *a way into a place*
access, approach, archway, avenue, corridor, door, doorway, entry, entryway, gate, gateway, hall, hallway, ingress, inlet, lobby, opening, passage, passageway, path, porch, port, portal, portico, staircase, threshold, vestibule, way; SEE CONCEPT *440*

entrance [*n2*] *coming into a place; introduction*
access, accession, adit, admission, admittance, appearance, approach, arrival, baptism, beginning, commencement, debut, enlistment, enrollment, entree, entry, immigration, import, importation, inception, incoming, ingoing, ingress, ingression, initiation, invasion, outset, passage, penetration, progress, start, trespass; SEE CONCEPTS *119,159*

entrance [*v*] *captivate, hypnotize*
anesthetize, attract, bewitch, charm, delight, enchant, enrapture, enthrall, fascinate, gladden, mesmerize, please, put in a trance, ravish, rejoice, spellbind, transport; SEE CONCEPTS *7,14,22*

entrant [*n*] *person entering competition, starting new activity*
aspirant, beginner, candidate, competitor, contestant, convert, entry, incomer, initiate, neophyte, newcomer, new member, novice, participant, petitioner, player, probationer, rival, solicitor, tenderfoot*; SEE CONCEPTS *366,423*

entrap [*v*] *capture, involve*
allure, bag*, beguile, benet, box in*, catch, decoy, embroil, enmesh, ensnare, entangle, entice, hook, implicate, inveigle, lay for*, lead on, lure, net, reel in*, rope in*, seduce, set up, snare, suck in*, tempt, trap, trick; SEE CONCEPTS *59,90,112*

entreat [*v*] *plead with*
appeal to, ask, beg, beseech, blandish, coax, conjure, crave, enjoin, exhort, implore, importune, invoke, pester, petition, plague, pray, press, request, supplicate, urge, wheedle; SEE CONCEPTS *48,53*

entreaty [*n*] *plea*
appeal, application, imploration, imprecation, petition, prayer, request, suit, supplication; SEE CONCEPTS *318,662*

entrée [*n*] *admittance*
access, adit, admission, connection, contact, debut, door, entrance, entry, importation, in, incoming, induction, ingress, introduction, open arms*, open door*, way; SEE CONCEPTS *388,685*

entrench [*v1*] *establish, make inroads*
anchor, confirm, define, dig in, embed, ensconce, fence, fix, fortify, found, ground, hole up, implant, infix, ingrain, install, lodge, plant, protect, root, seat, set, settle, strengthen; SEE CONCEPTS *518,710*

entrench [*v2*] *trespass*
break in on, encroach, impinge, infringe, interfere, interlope, intervene, intrude, invade, make inroads*, stick nose into*; SEE CONCEPT *192*

entrepreneur [*n*] *person who starts a business alone*
administrator, backer, businessperson, contractor, executive, founder, impressario, industrialist, manager, organizer, producer, promoter, undertaker; SEE CONCEPT *347*

entropy [*n*] *deterioration*
breakup, collapse, decay, decline, degeneration, destruction, falling apart, worsening; SEE CONCEPTS *230,698*

entrust [*v*] *give custody, authority to*
allocate, allot, assign, authorize, bank, bend an ear*, charge, commend, commit, confer, confide, consign, count, delegate, deliver, depend, deposit with, hand over, impose, invest, leave with, reckon, relegate, rely, trust, turn over; SEE CONCEPTS *50,88,108*

entry [*n1*] *way in to a place*
access, adit, approach, avenue, door, doorway, entrance, foyer, gate, hall, ingress, ingression, inlet, lobby, opening, passage, passageway, portal, threshold, vestibule; SEE CONCEPT *440*

entry [*n2*] *introduction; permission to enter*
access, adit, admission, admittance, appearance, coming in, entering, entrance, entree, free passage*, ingress, initiation, introgression, way; SEE CONCEPTS *388,685*

entry [*n3*] *person participating in competition; effort*
attempt, candidate, competitor, contestant, entrant, participant, player, submission; SEE CONCEPT *366*

entry [*n4*] *listing in a record*
account, item, jotting, memo, memorandum, minute, note, registration; SEE CONCEPT *270*

entwine [*v*] *twist around*
braid, coil, corkscrew, curl, embrace, encircle, enmesh, entangle, interlace, interplait, intertwine, interweave, knit, lace, plait, spiral, surround, twine, weave, wind, wreathe; SEE CONCEPTS *147,201,754*

enumerate [*v*] *list, count*
add up, calculate, cite, compute, count noses*, detail, figure, identify, inventory, itemize, keep tabs*, mention, name, number, particularize,

quote, recapitulate, recite, reckon, recount, rehearse, relate, run down, run off*, specialize, specify, spell out, sum, take account of, tally, tell, tick off*, total; SEE CONCEPTS *57,125,764*

enunciate [*v*] *speak clearly*
affirm, announce, articulate, declare, deliver, develop, enounce, express, intone, lay down, modulate, outline, phonate, postulate, proclaim, promulgate, pronounce, propound, publish, say, show, sound, state, submit, utter, vocalize, voice; SEE CONCEPTS *47,51*

envelop [*v*] *encase, hide*
blanket, cage, cloak, conceal, contain, coop, corral, cover, drape, embrace, encircle, enclose, encompass, enfold, engulf, enshroud, enwrap, fence, gird, girdle, guard, hem, immure, invest, obscure, overlay, overspread, pen, protect, roll, sheathe, shield, shroud, shut in, superimpose, surround, swaddle, swathe, veil, wrap, wrap up; SEE CONCEPTS *172,188*

envelope [*n*] *wrapper*
bag, box, case, casing, cloak, coat, coating, container, cover, covering, enclosure, hide, jacket, pocket, pouch, receptacle, sheath, shell, skin, vesicle, wrapping; SEE CONCEPT *494*

enviable [*adj*] *desired, blessed*
advantageous, covetable, desirable, excellent, favored, fortunate, good, lucky, privileged, superior, welcome; SEE CONCEPT *574*

envious [*adj*] *jealous, resentful*
appetent, aspiring, begrudging, coveting, covetous, craving, desiring, desirous, distrustful, fain, grasping, greedy, green-eyed*, green with envy*, grudging, hankering, invidious, jaundiced, longing for, malicious, spiteful, suspicious, umbrageous, watchful, wishful, yearning; SEE CONCEPTS *401,403*

environment [*n*] *surroundings, atmosphere*
ambiance, aura, backdrop, background, circumstances, climate, conditions, context, domain, element, encompassment, entourage, habitat, hood*, jungle*, locale, medium, milieu, neck of the woods*, neighborhood, purlieus, scene, scenery, setting, situation, status, stomping ground*, surroundings, terrain, territory, turf, zoo*; SEE CONCEPTS *515,673,696*

environment [*n2*] *Earth's system of natural resources*
atmosphere, biosphere, ecosphere, ecosystem, environs, Gaia; SEE CONCEPTS *511,515*

environmentalist [*n*] *conservationist*
eagle freak*, ecologist, greenie*, naturalist, preservationist, tree-hugger*; SEE CONCEPTS *515,673,696*

environs [*n*] *neighborhood*
bound, boundary, compass, confine, district, fringes*, limits, locality, outskirts, precinct, purlieus, suburb, surroundings, territory, turf, vicinity; SEE CONCEPT *516*

envisage/envision [*v*] *picture in one's mind*
anticipate, behold, conceive, conceptualize, contemplate, externalize, fancy, feature, foresee, form mental picture of*, grasp, have a picture of*, image, imagine, look upon, materialize, objectify, predict, realize, regard, see, survey, think up, view, view in mind's eye*, vision, visualize; SEE CONCEPTS *17,43*

envoy [*n*] *deputy*
agent, ambassador, attaché, bearer, carrier, chargé d'affaires, consul, courier, delegate,

diplomat, emissary, intermediary, internuncio, legate, medium, messenger, minister, nuncio, plenipotentiary, representative, vicar; SEE CONCEPTS *348,354*

envy [*n*] *jealousy*
backbiting, coveting, covetousness, enviousness, evil eye*, green-eyed monster*, grudge, grudging, grudgingness, hatred, heartburn, ill will, invidiousness, jaundiced eye*, lusting, malevolence, malice, maliciousness, malignity, opposition, prejudice, resentfulness, resentment, rivalry, spite; SEE CONCEPT *410*

envy [*v*] *be jealous of another*
be envious, begrudge, covet, crave, desire, die over*, eat one's heart out*, grudge, hanker, have hard feelings*, hunger, long, lust, object to, resent, thirst, turn green*, want, yearn; SEE CONCEPTS *10,20*

eon [*n*] *an age*
aeon, ages, time period, years; SEE CONCEPT *807*

ephemeral [*adj*] *momentary, passing*
brief, episodic, evanescent, fleeting, flitting, fugacious, fugitive, impermanent, short, shortlived, temporary, transient, transitory, unenduring, volatile; SEE CONCEPTS *798,801*

epic [*n*] *long story*
heroic poem, legend, narrative, saga, tale; SEE CONCEPT *282*

epicure [*n*] *gourmet*
bon vivant, connoisseur, Epicurean, gastronome, gastronomer, gastronomist, gourmand; SEE CONCEPTS *348,423*

epicurean [*adj*] *loving food and finer things*
gluttonous, gourmandizing, gourmet, hedonistic, libertine, lush, luxurious, pleasure-seeking, self-indulgent, sensual, sensuous, sybaritic, voluptuous; SEE CONCEPT *401*

epicurean [*n*] *gourmet*
bon vivant, connoisseur, critic, epicure, gastronome, gastronomer, glutton, gourmand, hedonist, pleasure seeker, sensualist, specialist, sybarite; SEE CONCEPT *423*

epidemic [*adj*] *widespread*
catching, communicable, contagious, endemic, general, infectious, pandemic, prevailing, prevalent, rampant, rife, sweeping, wide-ranging; SEE CONCEPTS *314,537*

epidemic [*n*] *widespread disease*
contagion, endemic, growth, outbreak, pest, pestilence, plague, rash, scourge, spread, upsurge, wave, what's going around*; SEE CONCEPTS *306,316*

epigram [*n*] *witticism*
aphorism, bon mot, joke, motto, pithy saying, quip, quirk; SEE CONCEPT *278*

epilogue [*n*] *afterword*
coda, concluding speech, conclusion, ending, finale, follow-up, peroration, postlude, postscript, sequel, summation, swan song*; SEE CONCEPTS *264,270,278*

episode [*n*] *adventure; scene*
affair, business, chapter, circumstance, doings, event, experience, goings-on*, happening, incident, installment, interlude, matter, occasion, occurrence, part, passage, section, thing*, what's going down*; SEE CONCEPTS *3,4*

episodic [*adj*] *intermittent; composed of several tales*
anecdotal, digressive, disconnected, discursive, disjointed, incidental, irregular, occasional, pi-

en
ep

caresque, rambling, roundabout, segmented, soap opera*, sporadic, wandering; SEE CONCEPT *482*

epistle [*n*] *letter*
billet doux*, cannonball*, card, communication, dispatch, FYI*, get-well, invite, kite*, line*, love letter, memo, message, missive, note, poison pen*, postcard, scratch*, tab*, thank-you; SEE CONCEPT *271*

epitaph [*n*] *inscription on a gravestone*
commemoration, elegy, epigraph, eulogy, hic jacet, legend, memorial, monument, remembrance, requiscat in pacem, sentiment; SEE CONCEPT *278*

epithet [*n*] *nickname*
appellation, description, designation, name, sobriquet, tag, title; SEE CONCEPT *683*

epitome [*n1*] *perfect example*
apotheosis, archetype, embodiment, essence, exemplar, exemplification, illustration, last word*, personification, quintessence, representation, type, typification, ultimate; SEE CONCEPT *686*

epitome [*n2*] *abbreviation*
abridgment, abstract, brief, compendium, condensation, conspectus, contraction, digest, precis, recapitulation, résumé, summary, summation, syllabus, synopsis; SEE CONCEPT *283*

epitomize [*v1*] *typify*
characterize, embody, exemplify, illustrate, mean, model, personify, represent, stand for, symbolize; SEE CONCEPT *644*

epitomize [*v2*] *encapsulate*
abbreviate, abridge, capsulize, compress, condense, contract, cut, digest, reduce, shorten, summarize, sum up, synopsize; SEE CONCEPTS *236,247*

epoch [*n*] *period*
age, date, era, span, time; SEE CONCEPTS *807,822*

equable [*adj*] *steady, calm*
agreeable, composed, consistent, constant, easygoing, even, even-tempered, imperturbable, level-headed, methodical, orderly, placid, regular, serene, smooth, stabile, stable, systematic, temperate, tranquil, unchanging, unexcitable, unflappable, unfluctuating, uniform, unruffled, unvarying; SEE CONCEPTS *401,542,544*

equal [*adj1*] *alike*
according, balanced, break even, commensurate, comparable, coordinate, correspondent, corresponding, double, duplicate, equivalent, evenly matched, fifty-fifty*, homologous, identic, identical, indistinguishable, invariable, level, look-alike, matched, matching, one and the same, parallel, proportionate, same, same difference*, spit and image*, stack up with*, tantamount, to the same degree, two peas in pod*, uniform, unvarying; SEE CONCEPTS *487,566,573*

equal [*adj2*] *fair, unbiased*
dispassionate, egalitarian, equable, even-handed, impartial, just, nondiscriminatory, nonpartisan, objective, uncolored, unprejudiced, without distinction; SEE CONCEPTS *401,542*

equal [*n*] *peer*
alter ego, coequal, companion, compeer, competitor, complement, copy, counterpart, double, duplicate, equivalent, like, likeness, match, mate, parallel, rival, twin; SEE CONCEPT *423*

equal [*v*] *make even, be even with*
agree, amount to, approach, balance, be commensurate, be identical, be level, be tantamount,

break even, come up to, compare, comprise, consist of, coordinate, correspond, emulate, equalize, equate, equipoise, equiponderate, keep pace with*, level, live up to*, match, measure up, meet, parallel, partake of, rank with, reach, rise to, rival, run abreast, square with, tally, tie, touch; SEE CONCEPT *667*

equality [*n*] *similarity, balance; egalitarianism*
adequation, civil rights, commensurateness, coordination, correspondence, equal opportunity, equatability, equilibrium, equipoise, equivalence, evenness, fairness, fair play*, fair practice, fair shake*, homology, identity, impartiality, isonomy, likeness, par, parallelism, parity, sameness, tolerance, uniformity; SEE CONCEPTS *388,645,667*

equalize [*v*] *make the same; balance*
adjust, commeasure, communize, compare, coordinate, democratize, emulate, equal, equate, establish, even, even up, handicap, level, match, parallel, regularize, rival, smooth, socialize, square, standardize, trim; SEE CONCEPTS *126,232*

equanimity [*n*] *levelheadedness*
aplomb, assurance, ataraxia, ataraxy, calm, calmness, composure, confidence, cool, coolness, detachment, equability, imperturbability, patience, peace, phlegm, placidity, poise, presence of mind*, sangfroid, self-possession, serenity, steadiness, tranquillity; SEE CONCEPTS *410,633*

equate [*v*] *balance; think of together*
agree, assimilate, associate, average, be commensurate, compare, consider, correspond to, correspond with, equalize, even, hold, level, liken, make equal, match, offset, pair, paragon, parallel, regard, relate, represent, similize, square, tally, treat; SEE CONCEPTS *37,39,667*

equilibrium [*n*] *balance; evenness*
calm, calmness, composure, cool, coolness, counterbalance, counterpoise, equanimity, equipoise, poise, polish, rest, serenity, stability, stasis, steadiness, steadying, symmetry; SEE CONCEPTS *633,731*

equip [*v*] *make ready with supplies*
accouter, adorn, appoint, arm, array, attire, deck, deck out*, decorate, dress, endow, feather nest*, fit out, fix up, furnish, gear, gear up*, heel*, implement, line nest*, man, outfit, prep*, prepare, provide, qualify, ready, rig, set up, stake, stock, supply, turn out; SEE CONCEPTS *140,182*

equipment [*n*] *supplies, gear for activity*
accessories, accompaniments, accouterments, apparatus, appliances, appurtenances, articles, attachments, baggage, belongings, contraptions, contrivances, devices, equipage, facilities, fittings, fixtures, furnishings, furniture, gadgets, habiliments, impedimenta, kit and kaboodle*, machinery, material, materiel, miscellaneous, outfit, paraphernalia, provisioning, provisions, rig*, setup, shebang*, stock, store, stuff, tackle, things, tools, trappings, traps, utensils; SEE CONCEPTS *364,446,496*

equitable [*adj*] *impartial*
candid, cricket, decent, disinterested, dispassionate, due, ethical, even-handed, even-steven*, fair, fair and square*, fair shake*, fair-to-middling*, honest, impersonal, just, level, moral, nondiscriminatory, nonpartisan, objective, proper, proportionate, reasonable, right, rightful, square, square deal*, stable, unbiased, uncolored, unprejudiced; SEE CONCEPTS *542,545*

equity [n1] *impartiality*
disinterestedness, equitableness, even-handedness, fair-mindedness, fairness, fair play, honesty, integrity, justice, justness, nonpartisanship, piece, reasonableness, rectitude, righteousness, square deal*, uprightness; SEE CONCEPTS *645, 657*

equity [n2] *money invested in possession*
capital, investment, outlay; SEE CONCEPTS *332, 344*

equivalence [n] *sameness, similarity*
adequation, agreement, alikeness, compatibility, conformity, correlation, correspondence, equality, evenness, exchangeability, identity, interchangeability, interchangeableness, likeness, match, par, parallel, parity, synonym, synonymy; SEE CONCEPTS *667,670*

equivalent [adj] *same, similar*
agnate, akin, alike, analogous, carbon*, commensurate, comparable, convertible, copy, correlative, correspondent, corresponding, ditto*, duplicate, equal, even, homologous, identical, indistinguishable, interchangeable, like, of a kind, parallel, proportionate, reciprocal, same difference*, substitute, synonymous, tantamount; SEE CONCEPTS *487,566,573*

equivalent [n] *equal, counterpart*
carbon copy*, correspondent, dead ringer*, ditto, like, match, obverse, opposite, parallel, peer, reciprocal, same difference*, spitting image*, substitute, twin; SEE CONCEPTS *667,670*

equivocal [adj] *doubtful, uncertain*
ambiguous, ambivalent, amphibological, borderline, clear as mud*, clouded*, disreputable, dubious, evasive, fishy*, fuzzy*, hazy*, indefinite, indeterminate, indistinct, misleading, muddled, muzzy*, oblique, obscure, open, problematic, puzzling, questionable, suspect, suspicious, tenebrous, unclear, undecided, unexplicit, unintelligible, vague, with mixed feelings*; SEE CONCEPTS *529,535*

equivocate [v] *avoid an issue*
beat around the bush*, beg the question*, blow hot and cold*, cavil, cloud the issue*, con, cop a plea*, cop out*, cover up*, dodge, double-talk, elude, escape, eschew, evade, falsify, fence, fib, flip-flop*, fudge*, give run around*, hedge, hem and haw*, jive*, lie, mince words, palter, parry, pass the buck*, prevaricate, pussyfoot, quibble, run around, shuck, shuffle, sidestep, sit on the fence*, stonewall*, tell white lie*, tergiversate, tergiverse, waffle*, weasel*; SEE CONCEPTS *63,102*

equivocation [n] *avoidance of an issue*
ambiguity, amphibology, casuistry, coloring, con, cop out, cover, cover-up, deceit, deception, deceptiveness, delusion, dissimulation, distortion, double entendre, double meaning, double talk, doubtfulness, duplicity, equivocality, evasion, fallacy, fib, fibbing, hedging, lie, line*, lying, misrepresentation, prevarication, quibbling, routine, run-around, shuffling, song*, song and dance*, sophistry, speciousness, spuriousness, stall, stonewall*, tergiversation, waffle*; SEE CONCEPTS *63,278*

era [n] *time period in history*
aeon, age, cycle, date, day, days, eon, epoch, generation, stage, term, time; SEE CONCEPTS *807,816*

eradicate [v] *destroy; remove*
abate, abolish, annihilate, blot out*, demolish, deracinate, do away with, efface, eliminate, erase, expunge, exterminate, extinguish, extirpate, liquidate, mow down*, obliterate, off*, purge, raze, root out*, rub out*, scratch*, scrub, shoot down, squash, stamp out*, take out*, torpedo*, total, trash, unroot, uproot, wash out, waste, weed out*, wipe out*; SEE CONCEPTS *211,252*

erase [v] *remove; rub out*
abolish, annul, black out, blank, blot, blue pencil*, cancel, cross out, cut, cut out, delete, disannul, dispatch, efface, eliminate, excise, expunge, extirpate, gut, kill, launder*, negate, nullify, obliterate, scratch out*, stamp out*, strike, strike out, take out, trim, wipe out*, withdraw, X-out*; SEE CONCEPTS *211,215*

erect [adj] *straight up*
arrect, cocked, elevated, erectile, firm, perpendicular, raised, rigid, standing, stiff, upright, upstanding, vertical; SEE CONCEPTS *485,581,604*

erect [v] *build; establish*
assemble, bring about, cobble up*, cock, compose, construct, create, effect, elevate, fabricate, fashion, fit together, forge, form, found, frame, fudge together*, heighten, hoist, initiate, institute, join, knock together*, lift, make, make up, manufacture, mount, organize, pitch, plant, prefabricate*, produce, put together, put up, raise, rear, run up, set up, shape, stand, stand up, throw together*, throw up, upraise, uprear; SEE CONCEPTS *168,221*

ergo [adv] *for that reason*
accordingly, consequently, hence, in consequence, so, then, therefore, thereupon, thus, thusly; SEE CONCEPT *544*

ergonomics [n] *human engineering*
comfort design, functional design, human factors, user-friendly systems, workplace efficiency; SEE CONCEPT *349*

erode [v] *deteriorate; wear away*
abrade, bite, consume, corrode, crumble, destroy, disintegrate, eat, gnaw, grind down, scour, spoil, waste, wear down; SEE CONCEPTS *252,469*

erosion [n] *deterioration; wearing away*
abrasion, attrition, consumption, corrosion, decrease, desedimentation, despoliation, destruction, disintegration, eating away, grinding down, spoiling, washing away, wear, wearing down; SEE CONCEPTS *252,257,698*

erotic [adj] *sexy*
amative, amatory, amorous, aphrodisiac, bawdy, blue*, carnal, concupiscent, earthy, erogenous, fervid, filthy, fleshly, hot*, impassioned, kinky*, lascivious, lecherous, lewd, obscene, off-color*, prurient, purple*, raunchy, raw, romantic, rousing, salacious, seductive, sensual, sexual, spicy, steamy, stimulating, suggestive, titillating, venereal, voluptuous; SEE CONCEPTS *372,545*

erotica [n] *pornography*
adult literature, adult materials, dirt*, obscene art, obscene literature, porn, sexually explicit art, sexually explicit literature, smut, soft porn, X-rated materials; SEE CONCEPT *280*

eroticism [n] *sexual excitement*
arousal, libido, lust, stimulation, titillation; SEE CONCEPTS *20,709*

err [v] *make a mistake; do wrong*
be inaccurate, be incorrect, be in error, be mis-

ep
er

taken, blow*, blunder, bollix*, boo-boo*, deviate, drop the ball*, fall, flub*, foul up*, go astray, goof*, go wrong, lapse, louse up*, make a mess of*, mess up*, misapprehend, misbehave, miscalculate, misjudge, muff*, offend, screw up*, sin, slip up*, snafu*, snarl up, stray, stumble, transgress, trespass, wander; SEE CONCEPT *101*

errand [*n*] *task*
assignment, charge, commission, duty, job, message, mission; SEE CONCEPT *362*

errant [*adj*] *wrong; deviant*
aberrant, deviating, devious, drifting, errable, erratic, erring, fallible, heretic, meandering, misbehaving, mischievous, miscreant, naughty, offending, off straight and narrow*, rambling, ranging, roaming, roving, shifting, sinning, stray, straying, unorthodox, unreliable, wandering, wayward; SEE CONCEPTS *542,545,581*

erratic [*adj*] *unpredictable; wandering*
aberrant, abnormal, anomalous, arbitrary, bizarre, capricious, changeable, desultory, devious, dicey, directionless, dubious, eccentric, fitful, flaky*, fluctuant, idiosyncratic, iffy*, incalculable, inconsistent, inconstant, irregular, meandering, mercurial, nomadic, oddball*, peculiar, planetary, rambling, roving, shifting, spasmodic, strange, stray, uncertain, undirected, unnatural, unreliable, unstable, unusual, vagarious, variable, volatile, wayward, weird, whimsical; SEE CONCEPTS *535,542,581*

erroneous [*adj*] *wrong, incorrect*
all off*, all wet*, amiss, askew, awry, defective, fallacious, false, faulty, flawed, inaccurate, inexact, invalid, misguided, mistaken, off, specious, spurious, unfounded, unsound, untrue, way off, wrong number*; SEE CONCEPTS *267,570,582*

error [*n*] *mistake; wrong*
absurdity, bad job*, blunder, boner*, boo-boo*, delinquency, delusion, deviation, erratum, failure, fall, fallacy, falsehood, falsity, fault, faux pas, flaw, glitch, goof*, howler*, inaccuracy, lapse, misapprehension, misbelief, miscalculation, misconception, miscue, misdeed, misjudgment, mismanagement, miss, misstep, misunderstanding, offense, omission, oversight, screamer*, screw-up*, sin, slight, slip, slipup, solecism, stumble, transgression, trespass, untruth, wrongdoing, X*; SEE CONCEPTS *101,230, 674,699*

ersatz [*adj*] *artificial*
bogus, copied, counterfeit, fake, false, imitation, manufactured, phony, pretended, sham, simulated, spurious, substitute, synthetic; SEE CONCEPT *582*

erstwhile [*adj*] *former*
bygone, ex, late, old, once, one-time, past, preceding, previous, quondam, sometime; SEE CONCEPT *820*

erudite [*adj*] *well-educated, cultured*
brainy, cultivated, educated, highbrow, in the know, into*, knowledgeable, learned, lettered, literate, savvy, scholarly, scholastic, studious, well-read, wise up*; SEE CONCEPT *402*

erudition [*n*] *higher education*
bookishness, brains, cultivation, culture, enlightenment, intellectuality, knowledge, learnedness, learning, letters, literacy, lore, pedantry, refinement, savvy, scholarliness, scholarship, science, studiousness; SEE CONCEPTS *287,409*

erupt [*v*] *give forth, eject with force*
appear, belch, blow up, boil, break out, burst, cast out, detonate, discharge, emit, eruct, explode, extravasate, flare up*, go off*, gush, hurl, jet, pour forth, rupture, spew, spit, spout, spurt, throw off*, touch off*, vent, vomit; SEE CONCEPTS *179,222*

eruption [*n*] *ejection*
access, blast, blow-up, breakout, burst, discharge, explosion, flare-up, flow, gust, outbreak, outburst, sally, venting, vomiting; SEE CONCEPTS *179,467*

escalate [*v*] *increase, be increased*
amplify, ascend, broaden, climb, enlarge, expand, extend, grow, heighten, intensify, magnify, make worse, mount, raise, rise, scale, step up, widen; SEE CONCEPTS *236,245*

escapade [*n*] *adventure, usually lighthearted*
antic, caper, fling, folly, frolic, gag, high jinks, lark, mischief, monkeyshines*, prank, rib*, roguery, rollick, romp, scrape, shenanigans*, spree, stunt, trick, vagary; SEE CONCEPTS *384,386*

escape [*n*] *breaking away; getaway*
abdication, avoidance, AWOL*, beat, bolt, break, breakout, bypassing, circumvention, decampment, deliverance, departure, desertion, disappearance, dodging, ducking, elopement, elusion, elusiveness, eschewal, evasion, evasiveness, extrication, fadeout, flight, freedom, hegira, lam, leave, liberation, out, outbreak, powder, release, rescue, retreat, runaround, shunning, sidestepping, slip, spring, withdrawal; SEE CONCEPT *102*

escape [*v*] *break away from*
abscond, avoid, bail out*, bolt, burst out, circumvent, cut and run*, cut loose*, decamp, depart, desert, disappear, dodge, double, duck, duck out*, elope, elude, emerge, evade, flee, fly, fly the coop*, gafiate, get away with*, get off*, go scot-free*, leave, make getaway*, make off*, make oneself scarce*, pass, play hooky*, run, run away, run off*, run out on*, shun, skip, slip, slip away, steal away, take a powder*, take flight, take on the lam*, vanish, work out of, wriggle out*; SEE CONCEPT *102*

escapee [*n*] *fugitive*
defector, deserter, dodger, escaped prisoner, hunted person, jail-breaker, refugee, runaway; SEE CONCEPT *412*

eschew [*v*] *have nothing to do with*
abandon, abjure, abstain, avoid, double, duck, elude, evade, forgo, forswear, give up, have no truck with*, let well enough alone*, not touch, refrain, renounce, sacrifice, shun, shy, shy away from, steer clear of*, swear off*; SEE CONCEPTS *30,102*

escort [*n*] *protection; accompaniment*
alarm clock*, attendant, beau, bird dog*, bodyguard, cavalier, chaperon, companion, company, consort, convoy, convoyer, cortege, date, entourage, fellow, friend, gallant, guard, guide, partner, protector, retinue, safeguard, squire, train, warden*; SEE CONCEPTS *419,423*

escort [*v*] *act as a companion, guard*
accompany, attend, bear, bring, carry, chaperon, company, conduct, consort with, convoy, date, direct, drag, go with, guide, lead, partner, pilot, protect, route, see, shepherd, show, squire, steer, take out, usher; SEE CONCEPTS *114,384,714*

escrow [n] *collateral*
bond, deed, guarantee, insurance, pledge, security; SEE CONCEPTS *71,271,685*

esoteric [adj] *mysterious, obscure*
abstruse, acroamatic, arcane, cabbalistic, cryptic, deep, Delphic, heavy, hermetic, hidden, inner, inscrutable, mystic, mystical, occult, Orphic, private, profound, recondite, secret, Sibylline; SEE CONCEPTS *529,576,582*

especial [adj] *exceptional, particular*
chief, distinguished, dominant, exclusive, express, extraordinary, individual, marked, notable, noteworthy, outstanding, paramount, peculiar, personal, predominant, preeminent, preponderant, principal, private, set, signal, singular, special, specific, supreme, surpassing, uncommon, unique, unusual; SEE CONCEPTS *535,564,574*

especially [adv] *exceptionally, particularly*
abnormally, above all, before all else, chiefly, conspicuously, curiously, eminently, exclusively, expressly, extraordinarily, in particular, in specie, mainly, markedly, notably, oddly, outstandingly, peculiarly, preeminently, primarily, principally, remarkably, signally, singularly, specially, specifically, strangely, strikingly, supremely, unaccountably, uncommonly, uncustomarily, uniquely, unusually, wonderfully; SEE CONCEPTS *535,564,574*

espionage [n] *spying*
intelligence, reconnaissance, secret service, shadowing, tailing, undercover operations, undercover work, underground activities; SEE CONCEPTS *348,412*

esplanade [n] *promenade*
avenue, boardwalk, path, walk, walkway; SEE CONCEPTS *6,501*

espouse [v1] *stand up for; support*
accept, adopt, advocate, approve, back, champion, defend, embrace, get into*, go in for*, maintain, stand behind*, take on, take up, uphold; SEE CONCEPT *10*

espouse [v2] *marry*
betroth, catch, take as spouse, unite, wed; SEE CONCEPT *297*

esprit de corps [n] *group spirit*
camaraderie, common bond, cooperation, group loyalty, morale, solidarity, team spirit; SEE CONCEPTS *410,411*

essay [n1] *written discourse*
article, composition, discussion, disquisition, dissertation, explication, exposition, manuscript, paper, piece, study, theme, thesis, tract, treatise; SEE CONCEPT *271*

essay [n2] *try, attempt*
aim, bid, dry run*, effort, endeavor, exertion, experiment, hassle, labor, one's all*, one's level best*, shot*, striving, struggle, test, toil, travail, trial, try on*, tryout, undertaking, venture, whack*, work; SEE CONCEPT *87*

essay [v] *try, attempt*
aim, assay, endeavor, have a crack*, have a go*, have a shot*, have at it*, labor, make a run at*, offer, put to the test*, seek, strive, struggle, take a stab at*, take a whack at*, take on, test, toil, travail, try out, undertake, venture, work; SEE CONCEPT *87*

essence [n1] *heart, significance*
aspect, attribute, backbone, base, basis, be-all and end-all*, being, bottom, bottom line*, burden, caliber, character, chief constituent, constitution, core, crux, element, entity, essentia, essentiality, fiber, form, fundamentals, germ, grain, kernel, life, lifeblood, main idea, marrow, meaning, meat*, name of game*, nature, nitty-gritty*, nub, nucleus, pith, point, principle, property, quality, quiddity, quintessence, reality, root, soul, spirit, structure, stuff, substance, timber, vein, virtuality; SEE CONCEPTS *411,661,668,688*

essence [n2] *distillate, concentrate*
balm, cologne, drug, effusion, elixir, extract, fragrance, juice, liquor, perfume, potion, scent, spirits, tincture; SEE CONCEPTS *260,467*

essential [adj1] *important, vital*
capital, cardinal, chief, constitutive, crucial, foremost, fundamental, imperative, indispensable, leading, main, necessary, necessitous, needed, needful, prerequisite, principal, required, requisite, right-hand, wanted; SEE CONCEPT *567*

essential [adj2] *basic, fundamental*
absolute, basal, cardinal, cold, complete, congenital, connate, constitutional, deep-seated, elemental, elementary, ideal, inborn, inbred, inherent, innate, intrinsic, key, main, material, meat and potatoes*, name of the game*, nittygritty*, nub, perfect, primary, prime, primitive, principal, quintessential, substratal, underlying; SEE CONCEPTS *546,549*

essential [n] *necessity, basic*
ABCs*, bottom line*, brass tacks*, condition, element, essence, fire and ice*, fundamental, groceries*, guts*, heart, meat and potatoes*, must, name of the game*, nitty-gritty*, nuts and bolts*, part and parcel*, precondition, prerequisite, principle, quintessence, requirement, requisite, rudiment, sine qua non, stuff, substance, vital part, where one's at*; SEE CONCEPTS *646,661,826*

establish [v1] *set up, organize*
authorize, base, build, constitute, create, decree, domiciliate, enact, endow, ensconce, entrench, erect, fix, form, found, ground, implant, inaugurate, inculcate, install, institute, land, lay foundation, live, lodge, moor, originate, place, plant, practice, provide, put, ring in, rivet, root, secure, set down, settle, stabilize, start, start ball rolling*, station, stick; SEE CONCEPTS *168,173, 221,251*

establish [v2] *authenticate; demonstrate*
ascertain, authorize, base, certify, circumstantiate, confirm, constitute, corroborate, decree, determine, discover, enact, find out, formulate, learn, legislate, make, make out, predicate, prescribe, prove, ratify, rest, show, stay, substantiate, validate, verify; SEE CONCEPTS *49,50,88,97*

establishment [n1] *organization; creation*
enactment, endowment, formation, formulation, foundation, founding, inauguration, installation, institution, setting up; SEE CONCEPTS *173,221*

establishment [n2] *business, institution*
abode, building, company, concern, corporation, enterprise, factory, firm, foundation, house, institute, office, organization, outfit, plant, quarters, residence, setup, structure, system, workplace; SEE CONCEPTS *323,325,449*

establishment [n3] *ruling class; bureaucracy*
authority, city hall*, conservatives, diehards*, established order, Old Guard*, powers that be*, them, the system*; SEE CONCEPTS *347,354*

estate [n1] *extensive manor and its property*
acreage, area, country home, country place, demesne, domain, dominion, farm, finca, free-

er
es

hold, grounds, holdings, lands, parcel, plantation, quinta, ranch, residence, rural seat, territory, villa; SEE CONCEPT 516

estate [n2] *person's possessions, property, wealth*
assets, belongings, bequest, capital, chattels, devise, earthly possessions, effects, endowment, fortune, goods, heritage, inheritance, legacy, patrimony, substance; SEE CONCEPTS 340,710

estate [n3] *class, rank*
bracket, caste, category, classification, condition, echelon, footing, form, grade, level, lot, order, period, place, position, quality, repair, shape, situation, sphere, standing, state, station, status, stratum; SEE CONCEPTS 378,388

esteem [v1] *think highly of*
admire, appreciate, apprise, be fond of, cherish, consider, hold dear, honor, idolize, like, look up to*, love, prize, regard, regard highly, respect, revere, reverence, think the world of*, treasure, value, venerate, worship; SEE CONCEPT 32

esteem [v2] *consider, believe*
account, calculate, deem, estimate, hold, judge, rate, reckon, regard, think, view; SEE CONCEPT 12

estimable [adj] *honorable, worthy*
admirable, admired, appreciable, august, big name*, big time*, commendable, decent, deserving, esteemed, excellent, good, high-powered, honored, in limelight*, laudable, major league*, meretorious, meritable, name, noble, palmary, praisable, praiseworthy, reputable, reputed, respectable, respected, sterling, valuable, valued, venerable, well-thought-of*; SEE CONCEPTS 567,572

estimate [n] *approximate calculation; educated guess*
appraisal, appraisement, assay, assessment, ballpark figure*, belief, conclusion, conjecture, estimation, evaluation, gauging, guess, guesstimate*, impression, judgment, measure, measurement, mensuration, opinion, point of view, projection, rating, reckoning, sizing up*, stock, surmise, survey, thought, valuation; SEE CONCEPTS 28,37,689,784

estimate [v] *guess, try to value*
account, appraise, assay, assess, believe, budget, calculate roughly, cast, cipher, class, classify, compute, conjecture, consider, count, decide, deduce, determine, enumerate, evaluate, examine, expect, figure, form opinion, gauge, guess, guesstimate*, judge, look into, look upon, number, outline, plan, predict, prophesy, rank, rate, reason, reckon, regard, run over*, scheme, set a figure*, size up*, sum, suppose, surmise, suspect, tax, think, think through*; SEE CONCEPTS 28,37,764

estimation [n] *belief, guess*
admiration, appraisal, appreciation, arithmetic, assessment, calculating, ciphering, computation, consideration, considered opinion, credit, esteem, estimate, estimating, evaluation, favor, figuring, impression, judgment, opinion, predicting, reckoning, regard, respect, stock, valuation, veneration, view; SEE CONCEPTS 28,689

estrange [v] *destroy the affections of*
alien, alienate, antagonize, break up, disaffect, disunify, disunite, divert, divide, divorce, drive apart, leave, make hostile, part, put on the outs*, separate, set at odds*, sever, split, sunder, turn off*, wean, withdraw, withhold; SEE CONCEPTS 7,19,297,384

estrangement [n] *destruction of affections*
alienation, antagonization, breach, break-up, disaffection, disassociation, disunity, division, divorce, hostility, leave, leaving, parting, removal, schism, separation, split, withdrawal, withholding; SEE CONCEPTS 297,388

estuary [n] *mouth*
arm, creek, firth, fjord, inlet, tidewater, waterway; SEE CONCEPTS 509,514

et cetera [adj] *and so forth*
along with others, and all, and on and on, and others, and so on, and the like, and the rest, blah blah blah*, et al., whatever, whatnot; SEE CONCEPTS 267,577

etch [v] *carve*
compose, corrode, cut, define, delineate, depict, describe, eat into, engrave, erode, execute, furrow, grave, impress, imprint, incise, ingrain, inscribe, outline, picture, portray, reduce, represent, set forth, stamp; SEE CONCEPTS 174,176

etching [n] *art created by carving*
engraving, impression, imprint, inscription, mezzotint, photoengraving, photogravure, print, reproduction, rotogravure, transferring; SEE CONCEPT 259

eternal [adj] *without pause; endless*
abiding, ageless, always, amaranthine, boundless, ceaseless, constant, continual, continued, continuous, dateless, deathless, enduring, everlasting, forever, illimitable, immemorial, immortal, immutable, imperishable, incessant, indefinite, indestructible, infinite, interminable, lasting, never-ending, perdurable, perennial, permanent, perpetual, persistent, relentless, termless, timeless, unbroken, unceasing, undying, unending, unfading, uninterrupted, unremitting, without end; SEE CONCEPTS 482,798

eternally [adv] *endlessly*
always, continually, ever, evermore, forever, forevermore, for ever so long*, for keeps, in perpetuum, perpetually, regularly, till cows come home*; SEE CONCEPT 798

eternity [n] *forever*
aeon, afterlife, age, ages, blue moon*, dog's age*, endlessness, endless time, everlastingness, forever and a day*, future, immortality, imperishability, infiniteness, infinitude, infinity, kingdom come*, other world*, perpetuity, timelessness, time without end, wild blue yonder*, world without end*; SEE CONCEPTS 370,804,818

ethereal [adj] *delicate, heavenly*
aerial, airy, celestial, dainty, divine, empyreal, empyrean, exquisite, fairy, filmy, fine, gaseous, ghostly, gossamer, impalpable, insubstantial, intangible, light, rarefied, refined, spiritual, sublime, subtle, supernal, tenuous, unearthly, unsubstantial, unworldly, vaporous, vapory; SEE CONCEPTS 491,549,582,606

ethical [adj] *moral, righteous*
Christian, clean, conscientious, correct, decent, elevated, equitable, fair, fitting, good, high-principled, honest, honorable, humane, just, kosher*, moralistic, noble, principled, proper, respectable, right, right-minded, square, straight, true blue*, upright, upstanding, virtuous; SEE CONCEPT 545

ethics/ethic [n] *moral philosophy, values*
belief, conduct, conscience, convention, conventionalities, criteria, descency, ethos, goodness, honesty, honor, ideal, imperative, integrity, moral code, morality, mores, natural law, nature, practice, principles, right and wrong, rules of conduct, standard, standards, the Golden Rule*; SEE CONCEPTS *645,688,689*

ethnic [*adj*] *racial, cultural*
indigenous, national, native, traditional, tribal; SEE CONCEPT *549*

etiquette [n] *manners, politeness*
amenities, civility, code, convention, courtesy, customs, decency, decorum, deportment, dignity, form, formalities, good behavior*, mores, politesse, proper behavior, propriety, protocol, p's and q's*, rules, seemliness, social graces, suavities, usage; SEE CONCEPT *633*

eulogize [*v*] *praise, glorify*
acclaim, applaud, bless, celebrate, commend, compliment, cry up, exalt, extol, flatter, give a bouquet*, give a posy*, hymn, idolize, laud, magnify, panegyrize, pay tribute to, sing praises; SEE CONCEPT *69*

eulogy [n] *praise, acclamation*
acclaim, accolade, adulation, applause, citation, commendation, compliment, encomium, exaltation, glorification, laudation, paean, panegyric, plaudit, salutation, tribute; SEE CONCEPTS *69,278*

euphemism [n] *nice way of saying something*
circumlocution, delicacy, floridness, grandiloquence, inflation, pomposity, pretense, purism; SEE CONCEPTS *275,278*

euphonious [*adj*] *pleasing to the ear*
agreeable, clear, dulcet, harmonious, mellifluous, melodious, musical, rhythmic, smooth, sweet-sounding, tuneful, well-pitched; SEE CONCEPT *563*

euphoria [n] *extreme happiness*
bliss, dreamland, ecstasy, elation, exaltation, exhilaration, exultation, frenzy, glee, health, high spirits, intoxication, joy, joyousness, jubilation, madness, rapture, relaxation, transport; SEE CONCEPT *410*

euthanasia [n] *mercy killing*
assisted suicide, putting out of misery*; SEE CONCEPT *252*

evacuate [*v*] *clear an area; empty*
abandon, bail out*, cut out, decamp, depart, desert, discharge, displace, eject, expel, forsake, hightail, leave, move out, pack up, pull out, quit, relinquish, remove, run for the hills*, skidaddle*, vacate, withdraw; SEE CONCEPTS *179,195*

evade [*v*] *get away from*
avoid, baffle, balk, beat around bush*, beg the question*, bypass, cavil, circumvent, conceal, confuse, cop out, deceive, decline, dodge, double, duck, elude, equivocate, escape, eschew, fence, fend off*, flee, fly, fudge*, get around, give the runaround*, hedge, hide, keep distance*, lay low*, lead on a merry chase*, lie, parry, pass up, pretend, prevaricate, pussyfoot, put off, shift, shirk, shuck, shuffle, shun, shy, sidestep, slip out, sneak away*, steer clear of*, tergiversate, trick, waffle*, weasel*; SEE CONCEPTS *30,102*

evaluate [*v*] *judge*
appraise, assay, assess, calculate, check, check out, class, classify, criticize, decide, estimate, figure out, fiture, gauge, grade, guesstimate*, look over, peg*, price out, rank, rate, read, reckon, set at, size, size up*, survey, take account of, take measure, valuate, value, weigh; SEE CONCEPTS *18,24,103*

evaluation [n] *judgment*
appraisal, appraisement, assessment, calculation, decision, estimate, estimation, guesstimation*, interpretation, opinion, rating, stock, take, valuation; SEE CONCEPTS *24,103,689*

evanescent [*adj*] *transient*
brief, disappearing, fading, fleeting, momentary, passing, short-lived, temporary, tenuous, vanishing; SEE CONCEPTS *551,798*

evangelism [n] *preaching*
ministration, sermonizing, spreading the word, teaching; SEE CONCEPT *361*

evangelist [n] *preacher*
circuit rider, minister, missionary, pastor, religious teacher, revivalist, televangelist, television evangelist, television preacher, TV evangelist; SEE CONCEPT *361*

evaporate [*v*] *dry up, dissolve*
clear, concentrate, dehumidify, dehydrate, dematerialize, desiccate, disappear, dispel, disperse, dissipate, evanesce, evanish, fade, fade away, melt, parch, pass, vanish, vaporize, weaken; SEE CONCEPTS *469,698*

evaporation [n] *drying up; dissolution*
dehydration, dematerialization, desiccation, disappearance, dispelling, dispersal, dissipation, escape, evanescence, fading, melting, vanishing, vaporescence, vaporization; SEE CONCEPTS *469,607,698*

evasion [n] *escape, avoidance*
artifice, circumvention, cop-out*, cunning, ditch*, dodge*, dodging, elusion, equivocating, equivocation, eschewal, evading, evasiveness, excuse, fancy footwork*, fudging*, jive, lie, obliqueness, pretext, prevarication, quibble, routine, run-around, ruse, shift, shirking, shuffling, shunning, slip*, sophism, sophistry, stall, stonewall*, subterfuge, trick, trickery; SEE CONCEPTS *59,63,102*

evasive [*adj*] *deceitful, tricky*
ambiguous, cagey, casuistic, casuistical, cunning, deceptive, devious, dissembling, elusive, elusory, equivocating, false, fugitive, greasy, indirect, intangible, lying, misleading, oblique, prevaricating, shifty, shuffling, slippery, sly, sophistical, stonewalling*, unclear, vague; SEE CONCEPTS *267,401,542*

even [*adj1*] *flat, uniform*
alike, balanced, consistent, constant, continual, continuous, direct, equal, flush, homogenous, horizontal, level, matching, metrical, parallel, planate, plane, plumb, proportional, regular, right, same, smooth, square, stabile, stable, steady, straight, surfaced, true, unbroken, unchanging, undeviating, unfluctuating, uninterrupted, unvaried, unvarying, unwavering, unwrinkled; SEE CONCEPTS *480,490*

even [*adj2*] *calm, undisturbed*
composed, cool, equable, equanimous, even-tempered, imperturbable, peaceful, placid, serene, stable, steady, tranquil, unexcitable, unruffled, well-balanced; SEE CONCEPT *401*

even [*adj3*] *commensurate; having no advantage*
balanced, coequal, comparable, coterminous, drawn, equal, equalized, equivalent, even-steven*, exact, fifty-fifty*, horse to horse*, iden-

tical, level, matching, neck and neck*, on a par*, parallel, proportional, proportionate, same, similar, smack in the middle*, square, tied, uniform; SEE CONCEPT 566

even [adj4] *fair, impartial*
balanced, disinterested, dispassionate, equal, equitable, fair and square*, honest, just, matching, nonpartisan, square, straightforward, unbiased, unprejudiced; SEE CONCEPTS 267,542

even [adv] *still, yet*
all the more, despite, disregarding, indeed, in spite of, much, notwithstanding, so much as; SEE CONCEPT 544

even [v] *balance, make smooth*
align, equal, equalize, flatten, flush, grade, lay, level, match, pancake*, plane, regularize, roll, square, stabilize, steady, symmetrize, uniform; SEE CONCEPTS 231,757

even-handed [adj] *fair*
aboveboard, balanced, disinterested, equitable, honest, honorable, impartial, just, neutral, nonpartisan, objective, on the level*, on the up-and-up*, reasonable, square, straight, unbiased, unprejudiced, upright, virtuous; SEE CONCEPT 542

evening [n] *latter part of a day*
black, close, dark, decline, dim, dusk, duskiness, early black*, eve, even, eventide, late afternoon, nightfall, sundown, sunset, twilight; SEE CONCEPTS 801,806,810

event [n1] *occurrence, happening*
accident, act, action, advent, adventure, affair, appearance, business, calamity, case, catastrophe, celebration, ceremony, chance, circumstance, coincidence, conjuncture, crisis, deed, development, emergency, episode, experience, exploit, fact, function, holiday, incident, juncture, marvel, matter, milestone, miracle, misfortune, mishap, mistake, occasion, occurrence, pass, phase, phenomenon, predicament, proceeding, shift, situation, story, thing*, tide, transaction, triumph, turn, wonder; SEE CONCEPT 2

event [n2] *effect, result*
aftereffect, aftermath, case, causatum, chance, conclusion, consequence, end, end result, eventuality, fortuity, hap, happenstance, issue, offshoot, outcome, outgrowth, product, resultant, sequel, sequent, termination, upshot; SEE CONCEPT 230

event [n3] *performance, competition*
bout, contest, game, match, meet, tournament; SEE CONCEPTS 263,363

even-tempered [adj] *easygoing*
calm, collected, complacent, composed, cool, level-headed, patient, relaxed, stable, steady, unexcitable, unruffled; SEE CONCEPTS 401,404

eventful [adj] *significant, busy*
active, consequential, critical, crucial, decisive, exciting, fateful, full, historic, important, lively, memorable, momentous, notable, noteworthy, outstanding, remarkable, signal; SEE CONCEPT 548

eventual [adj] *future, concluding*
closing, conditional, consequent, contingent, dependent, down the pike*, down the road*, ending, endmost, ensuing, final, hindmost, indirect, inevitable, in the cards*, last, later, latter, overall, possible, prospective, resulting, secondary, succeeding, terminal, ulterior, ultimate, vicarious; SEE CONCEPTS 552,820

eventuality [n] *something that probably will happen*
aftereffect, aftermath, any case, case, chance, consequence, contingency, effect, event, godown*, goings-on*, happening, issue, likelihood, outcome, possibility, probability, result, sequel, toss-up, upshot*; SEE CONCEPTS 230,650

eventually [adv] *in the course of time*
after all, at last, at the end of the day*, finally, hereafter, in future, in the end, in the long run*, one day, someday, sometime, sooner or later*, ultimately, when all is said and done*, yet; SEE CONCEPTS 552,820

eventuate [v] *be a consequence*
be consequent, befall, come about, come to pass, end, ensue, eventualize, follow, happen, issue, occur, result, stop, take place, terminate; SEE CONCEPTS 2,242

ever [adv] *always, at any time*
anytime, at all, at all times, at any point, by any chance*, consistently, constantly, continually, endlessly, eternally, everlastingly, evermore, forever, for keeps, in any case*, incessantly, in perpetuum, invariably, on any occasion*, perpetually, regularly, relentlessly, till cows come home*, to the end of time*, unceasingly, unendingly, usually; SEE CONCEPTS 798,799

everlasting [adj] *infinite, never-ending*
abiding, amaranthine, boundless, ceaseless, constant, continual, continuous, deathless, endless, eternal, immortal, imperishable, incessant, indestructible, interminable, lasting, limitless, perdurable, permanent, perpetual, termless, timeless, unceasing, undying, unending, uninterrupted, unremitting; SEE CONCEPT 798

every [adj] *each, all*
each one, whole, without exception; SEE CONCEPT 531

everybody/everyone [n] *all involved, all human beings; the whole world*
all, all and sundry*, anybody, each one, each person, every person, generality, masses, people, populace, the public, the whole, young and old*; SEE CONCEPT 417

everyday [adj] *common*
accustomed, average, commonplace, conventional, customary, daily, dime a dozen*, dull, familiar, frequent, garden variety*, habitual, informal, lowly, mainstream, middle-of-the-road*, mundane, normal, ordinary, per diem, plain, prosaic, quotidian, routine, run-of-the-mill*, stock, unexceptional, unimaginative, unremarkable, usual, vanilla*, whitebread*, wonted, workaday; SEE CONCEPTS 530,547

everything [n] *entirety*
aggregate, all, all in all, all that, all things, business, complex, each thing, every little thing*, fixins'*, lock stock and barrel*, lot, many things, sum, the works*, total, universe, whole, whole ball of wax*, whole caboodle*, whole enchilada*, whole lot*, whole shebang*; SEE CONCEPTS 432,837

everywhere [adv] *in all places*
all around, all over, all over creation*, all over the map*, far and wide*, here and there*, here till Sunday*, high and low*, in all quarters, in each place, in every direction, in every place, inside and out, near and far*, omnipresent, overall, pole to pole*, the world over*, throughout, ubiq-

uitous, ubiquitously, universally, wherever; SEE CONCEPT *583*

evict [*v*] *throw out from residence*
boot out*, bounce*, chase, dislodge, dismiss, dispossess, eject, expel, extrude, force out, heave-ho*, kick out*, oust, out, put out, remove, send packing*, show out, show the door*, shut out, toss out on ear*, turn out; SEE CONCEPTS *122,198,211*

eviction [*n*] *throwing out of a residence*
boot*, bounce*, bum's rush*, clearance, dislodgement, dispossession, ejection, expulsion, kicking out*, ouster, removal, rush, the gate*, walking papers*; SEE CONCEPTS *123,198,211*

evidence [*n*] *proof*
affirmation, attestation, averment, cincher*, clincher*, clue, confirmation, corroboration, cue, data, declaration, demonstration, deposition, documentation, dope*, goods*, gospel, grabber*, grounds, index, indication, indicia, info*, information, manifestation, mark, sign, significant, smoking gun*, substantiation, symptom, testament, testimonial, testimony, token, witness; SEE CONCEPTS *274,318*

evidence [*v*] *prove*
attest, bespeak, betoken, confirm, connote, demonstrate, denote, designate, display, evince, exhibit, expose, illustrate, indicate, manifest, mark, ostend, proclaim, reveal, show, signify, testify to, witness; SEE CONCEPTS *57,97,317*

evident [*adj*] *apparent, clear*
axiomatic, barefaced*, clear-cut, conspicuous, crystal clear*, distinct, fact, incontestable, incontrovertible, indisputable, logical, manifest, noticeable, obvious, open-and-shut*, palpable, patent, perceptible, plain, plain as day*, reasonable, straightforward, tangible, unambiguous, unmistakable, visible; SEE CONCEPTS *529,535*

evidently [*adv*] *apparently, clearly*
doubtless, doubtlessly, incontestably, incontrovertibly, indisputably, it seems, it would seem, manifestly, obviously, officially, ostensibly, outwardly, patently, plainly, professedly, seemingly, to all appearances*, undoubtedly, unmistakably, without question; SEE CONCEPT *535*

evil [*adj*] *sinful, immoral*
angry, atrocious, bad, baneful, base, beastly, calamitous, corrupt, damnable, depraved, destructive, disastrous, execrable, flagitious, foul, harmful, hateful, heinous, hideous, iniquitous, injurious, loathsome, low, maleficent, malevolent, malicious, malignant, nefarious, no good, obscene, offensive, pernicious, poison, rancorous, reprobate, repugnant, repulsive, revolting, spiteful, stinking, ugly, unpleasant, unpropitious, vicious, vile, villainous, wicked, wrathful, wrong; SEE CONCEPTS *545,570*

evil [*n*] *badness, immorality; disaster*
affliction, baseness, blow, calamity, catastrophe, corruption, crime, criminality, curse, debauchery, depravity, devilry, diabolism, harm, hatred, heinousness, hurt, ill, impiety, indecency, infamy, iniquity, injury, knavery, lewdness, licentiousness, looseness, malevolence, malignity, meanness, mischief, misery, misfortune, obscenity, outrage, pain, perversity, ruin, sin, sinfulness, sorrow, suffering, turpitude, vice, viciousness, vileness, villainy, wickedness, woe, wrong, wrongdoing; SEE CONCEPT *645*

evildoer [*n*] *wrongdoer*
bad person, criminal, devil, evil person, felon, gangster, lawbreaker, murderer, psychopath, sinner, sociopath, troublemaker, villain; SEE CONCEPT *412*

evince [*v*] *manifest*
attest, declare, demonstrate, disclose, display, furnish, indicate, prove, reveal, show; SEE CONCEPTS *118,261*

evoke [*v*] *induce, stimulate*
arouse, awaken, call, call forth, conjure, educe, elicit, evince, evolve, excite, extort, extract, give rise to, invoke, milk*, provoke, raise, rally, recall, rouse, stir up, summon, waken; SEE CONCEPTS *228,242*

evolution [*n*] *development, progress*
change, enlargement, evolvement, expansion, flowering, growth, increase, maturation, natural process, progression, transformation, unfolding, working out; SEE CONCEPT *704*

evolve [*v*] *develop, progress*
advance, derive, disclose, educe, elaborate, emerge, enlarge, excogitate, expand, get, grow, increase, mature, obtain, open, result, ripen, unfold, work out; SEE CONCEPTS *236,245,704*

exacerbate [*v*] *infuriate; make worse*
add insult to injury*, aggravate, annoy, egg on*, embitter, enrage, envenom, exasperate, excite, fan the flames*, feed the fire*, go from bad to worse*, heat up*, heighten, hit on*, increase, inflame, intensify, irritate, madden, provoke, push one's button*, rattle one's cage*, rub salt in a wound*, vex, worsen; SEE CONCEPTS *7,19*

exact [*adj1*] *accurate, precise*
bull's-eye*, careful, clear, clear-cut, correct, dead on*, definite, distinct, downright, explicit, express, faithful, faultless, identical, literal, methodical, nailed down*, nice, on target*, on the button*, on the money*, on the numbers*, orderly, particular, perfect, right, right on*, rigorous, sharp, specific, true, unequivocal, unerring, veracious, verbal, verbatim; SEE CONCEPTS *535,557*

exact [*adj2*] *careful, painstaking*
conscientious, conscionable, demanding, exacting, finicky, fussy, heedful, meticulous, punctilious, punctual, rigorous, scrupulous, severe, strict; SEE CONCEPT *542*

exact [*v*] *demand, call for*
assess, bleed, call, challenge, claim, coerce, command, compel, constrain, extort, extract, force, gouge, impose, insist upon, lean on, levy, oblige, pinch, postulate, put on, require, requisition, shake down*, solicit, squeeze, wrench, wrest, wring; SEE CONCEPTS *53,142*

exacting [*adj*] *demanding*
burdensome, by the book*, careful, critical, difficult, exigent, finicky, fussy, grievous, hard, harsh, hypercritical, imperious, nit-picking, onerous, oppressive, painstaking, particular, persnickety, picky, precise, rigid, rigorous, severe, stern, strict, stringent, taxing, tough, trying, unsparing, weighty; SEE CONCEPTS *401,404*

exactly [*adv*] *accurately, particularly*
absolutely, altogether, bang*, carefully, completely, correctly, definitely, explicitly, expressly, faithfully, faultlessly, for a fact, for certain, for sure*, indeed, in every respect, just, literally, methodically, no mistake, on the dot*, on the money*, on the nail*, on the nose*, posi-

ev
ex

tively, precisely, quite, right, rigorously, scrupulously, severely, sharp, specifically, square, strictly, the ticket*, totally, truly, truthfully, unequivocally, unerringly, utterly, veraciously, wholly; SEE CONCEPTS 535,557

exactness [n] *accuracy, precision*
carefulness, correctness, definiteness, definitiveness, definitude, exactitude, faithfulness, faultlessness, nicety, orderliness, painstakingness, preciseness, promptitude, regularity, rigor, rigorousness, scrupulousness, strictness, truth, unequivocalness, veracity; SEE CONCEPTS 638,654

exaggerate [v] *overstate, embellish*
amplify, blow out of proportion*, boast, boost, brag, build up, caricature, color, cook up*, corrupt, distort, embroider, emphasize, enlarge, exalt, expand, fabricate, falsify, fudge*, go to extremes*, heighten, hike, hyperbolize, inflate, intensify, lay it on thick*, lie, loud talk*, magnify, make too much of*, misquote, misreport, misrepresent, overdo, overdraw, overemphasize, overestimate, pad*, pretty up*, puff, put on, pyramid*, romance, romanticize, scam, stretch, up*; SEE CONCEPT 63

exaggerated [adj] *overstated, embellished*
a bit thick*, abstract, amplified, artificial, bouncing, caricatural, distorted, embroidered, exalted, excessive, extravagant, fabricated, fabulous, false, fantastic, farfetched, hammy, highly colored, histrionic, hyperbolic, impossible, inflated, magnified, melodramatic, out of proportion, overblown, overdone, overestimated, overkill, overwrought, preposterous, pretentious, schmaltzy, sensational, spectacular, steep, strained, stylized, tall, too much*, too-too*, unrealistic; SEE CONCEPTS 267,542,562

exaggeration [n] *overstatement, embellishment*
aggrandizement, amplification, baloney*, boasting, caricature, coloring, crock*, elaboration, embroidery, emphasis, enlargement, exaltation, excess, extravagance, fabrication, falsehood, fancy, fantasy, figure of speech, fish story*, flight of fancy*, hogwash*, hyperbole, inflation, jazz*, line*, magnification, misjudgment, misrepresentation, overemphasis, overestimation, pretension, pretentiousness, rant, romance, stretch, tall story*, untruth, whopper*, yarn*; SEE CONCEPTS 63,278,663

exalt [v] *promote, praise*
acclaim, advance, aggrandize, apotheosize, applaud, bless, boost, build up*, commend, dignify, distinguish, ennoble, erect, eulogize, extol, glorify, halo, honor, idolize, intensify, laud, magnify, pay homage to, pay tribute to, raise, revere, set on pedestal*, sublime, transfigure, upgrade, uprear, worship; SEE CONCEPTS 10,69

exaltation [n1] *promotion, praise*
acclaim, acclamation, advancement, aggrandizement, apotheosis, applause, blessing, dignity, elevation, eminence, ennoblement, extolment, glorification, glory, grandeur, high rank, homage, honor, idolzation, laudation, lionization, loftiness, magnification, panegyric, plaudits, prestige, reverence, rise, tribute, upgrading, uplifting, worship; SEE CONCEPTS 69,278

exaltation [n2] *great joy*
animation, bliss, delectation, delight, ecstasy, elation, elevation, euphoria, excitement, exhilaration, exultation, inspiration, intoxication, joy-

ousness, jubilation, rapture, stimulation, transport, uplift; SEE CONCEPTS 32,410

exalted [adj] *praised; held in high esteem*
astral, august, dignified, elevated, eminent, exaggerated, excessive, first, grand, high, highest, highest-ranking, high-minded, high-ranking, honorable, honored, ideal, illustrious, immodest, imposing, inflated, intellectual, leading, lofty, magnificent, noble, number one, outstanding, overblown, pompous, prestigious, pretentious, proud, self-important, sublime, superb, superior, top-drawer*, top-ranking, uplifting; SEE CONCEPTS 404,529

examination [n1] *test, analysis*
assay, audit, battery, blue book*, breakdown, canvass, catechism, checking, checkup, cross-examination, diagnosis, dissection, exam, experiment, exploration, final, grilling, inquest, inquiry, inquisition, inspection, interrogation, investigation, legwork*, make-up, observation, once-over*, oral, perlustration, perusal, probe, quest, questioning, questionnaire, quiz, raid, reconnaissance, research, review, scan, scrutiny, search, study, survey, the eye*, third degree*, trial, tryout, view, written; SEE CONCEPT 290

examination [n2] *medical checkup*
autopsy, biopsy, exam, inquiry, observation, physical, postoperative, probe, test; SEE CONCEPTS 103,310

examine [v1] *analyze, test*
appraise, assay, audit, canvass, case, check, check out, chew over*, consider, criticize, delve into, dig into, explore, eye*, finger*, frisk, go into, go over, go through, gun*, inquire, inspect, investigate, look over, look see*, parse, pat down, peruse, pick at, ponder, pore over, probe, prospect, prove, read, reconnoiter, research, review, scan, scope, screen, scrutinate, scrutinize, search into, sift, size up*, study, survey, sweep, take stock of*, try, turn over*, vet, view, weigh, winnow*; SEE CONCEPTS 24,103

examine [v2] *ask questions pointedly*
catechize, check, cross-examine, experiment, give the third*, give the third degree*, grill, inquire, interrogate, judge, measure, pump, put through the wringer*, query, quiz, try, try out, weigh; SEE CONCEPT 48

example [n] *instance, model*
archetype, case, case history, case in point, citation, copy, excuse, exemplar, exemplification, for instance, ideal, illustration, kind of thing, lesson, object, original, paradigm, paragon, part, pattern, precedent, prototype, quotation, representation, sample, sampling, specimen, standard, stereotype, symbol; SEE CONCEPT 686

exasperate [v] *upset, provoke*
aggravate, agitate, anger, annoy, bug*, disturb, drive up the wall*, embitter, enrage, exacerbate, excite, gall, get*, get under one's skin*, incense, inflame, infuriate, irk, irritate, madden, make waves*, needle*, nettle, peeve, pique, rankle, rile, roil, rouse, T-off*, try the patience of, vex, work up; SEE CONCEPTS 7,19

exasperation [n] *upset, provocation*
aggravation, anger, annoyance, besetment, bother, botheration, displeasure, exacerbation, fury, ire, irritant, irritation, nuisance, passion, pest, pique, plague, rage, resentment, vexation, wrath; SEE CONCEPTS 29,410

excavate [v] *dig up*
burrow, cut, delve, empty, gouge, grub, hollow, mine, quarry, scoop, scrape, shovel, spade, trench, tunnel, uncover, unearth; SEE CONCEPT *178*

excavation [n] *site of digging; digging*
blasting, burrow, cavity, cut, cutting, dig, disinterring, ditch, dugout, exhuming, hole, hollow, mine, mining, pit, quarry, removal, scooping, shaft, shoveling, trench, trough, unearthing; SEE CONCEPTS *178,509,513*

excavator [n] *earthmover*
backhoe, bulldozer, digger, heavy machinery; SEE CONCEPT *505*

exceed [v] *be superior to; surpass*
beat, best, better, break record*, cap, distance, eclipse, excel, get upper hand*, go beyond, go by, have advantage, have a jump on*, have it all over*, out-distance, outdo, outpace, outreach, outrun, outshine, outstrip, overstep, overtake, overtax, pass, rise above*, run circles around*, surmount, top, transcend; SEE CONCEPT *141*

exceedingly [adv] *very; exceptionally*
awfully, enormously, especially, excessively, extraordinarily, extremely, greatly, highly, hugely, immoderately, in a marked degree, inordinately, powerful, really, remarkably, strikingly, superlatively, surpassingly, terribly, too much, unusually, vastly, vitally; SEE CONCEPT *569*

excel [v] *be superior; surpass*
beat, be good, be master of, be proficient, be skillful, best, be talented, better, cap, come through, eclipse, exceed, go beyond, go to town*, improve upon, make it, outdo, outrival, outshine, outstrip, pass, predominate, shine, show talent, surmount, take precedence, top, transcend, wax*; SEE CONCEPTS *141,671,706*

excellence [n] *superiority*
arete, class, distinction, éclat, eminence, excellency, fineness, goodness, greatness, high quality, merit, perfection, preeminence, purity, quality, superbness, supremacy, transcendence, virtue, worth; SEE CONCEPT *671*

excellent [adj] *superior, wonderful*
A-1*, accomplished, admirable, attractive, capital, certified, champion, choice, choicest, desirable, distinctive, distinguished, estimable, exceptional, exemplary, exquisite, fine, finest, first, first-class, first-rate, good, great, high, incomparable, invaluable, magnificent, meritorious, notable, noted, outstanding, peerless, piked*, premium, priceless, prime, select, skillful, sterling, striking, superb, superlative, supreme, tiptop*, top-notch, transcendent, world-class; SEE CONCEPT *574*

except [prep] *other than*
apart from, aside from, bar, barring, besides, but, excepting, excluding, exclusive of, exempting, if not, lacking, leaving out, minus, not for, omitting, outside of, rejecting, save, saving, short of, without, with the exception of; SEE CONCEPT *577*

except [v] *leave out*
ban, bar, bate, count out, debar, disallow, eliminate, exclude, exempt, expostulate, inveigh, object, omit, pass over, protest, reject, remonstrate, rule out, suspend, taboo; SEE CONCEPTS *25,30, 211*

exception [n1] *leaving out*
barring, debarment, disallowment, excepting, exclusion, excusing, expulsion, noninclusion, omission, passing over, rejection, repudiation, reservation; SEE CONCEPTS *25,30,211*

exception [n2] *special case; irregularity*
allowance, anomalism, anomaly, departure, deviation, difference, dispensation, eccentricity, exemption, freak, inconsistency, nonconformity, oddity, peculiarity, perquisitor, privilege, privileged person, quirk; SEE CONCEPTS *423,665*

exceptional [adj1] *irregular*
aberrant, abnormal, anomalous, atypical, deviant, distinct, extraordinary, inconsistent, infrequent, notable, noteworthy, odd, peculiar, phenomenal, rare, remarkable, scarce, singular, special, strange, uncommon, uncustomary, unheard-of, unimaginable, unique, unordinary, unprecedented, unthinkable, unusual; SEE CONCEPT *564*

exceptional [adj2] *excellent, wonderful*
brainy, extraordinary, fine, first-class, first-rate, good, high, marvelous, outstanding, phenomenal, premium, prodigious, remarkable, singular, special, superior, world-class; SEE CONCEPTS *572,574*

excerpt [n] *citation; something taken from a whole*
extract, fragment, notation, note, part, passage, pericope, piece, portion, quotation, quote, saying, section, selection; SEE CONCEPTS *270,274, 835*

excerpt [v] *take a part from a whole*
choose, cite, cull, extract, glean, note, pick, pick out, quote, select, single out; SEE CONCEPTS *41,142,211*

excess [n1] *overabundance of something*
balance, by-product, enough, exorbitance, exuberance, fat, fulsomeness, glut, inundation, lavishness, leavings, leftover, luxuriance, nimiety, overdose, overflow, overkill, overload, overmuch, overrun, oversupply, overweight, plenty, plethora, profusion, recrement, redundance, redundancy, refuse, remainder, residue, rest, spare, superabundance, supererogation, superfluity, surfeit, surplus, the limit, too much*, too much of a good thing*, waste, wastefulness; SEE CONCEPTS *787,824,835*

excess [n2] *overindulgence in personal desires*
debauchery, dissipation, dissoluteness, exorbitance, extravagance, extreme, extremity, immoderacy, immoderation, indulgence, inordinateness, intemperance, overdoing, prodigality, saturnalia, selfindulgence, unrestraint; SEE CONCEPTS *633, 645*

excessive [adj] *too much; overdone*
boundless, disproportionate, dissipated, dizzying, enormous, exaggerated, exorbitant, extra, extravagant, extreme, immoderate, indulgent, inordinate, intemperate, limitless, more, needless, over, overboard, overkill, overmuch, plethoric, prodigal, profligate, recrementitious, redundant, self-indulgent, sky-high*, steep, stiff, stratospheric*, super, superabundant, superfluous, supernatural, too many, towering, unbounded, unconscionable, undue, unmeasurable, unreasonable, way out*; SEE CONCEPTS *560,771,781*

exchange [n1] *trade; deal*
barter, buying and selling, castling, change, commerce, commutation, conversion, correspondence, dealing, interchange, interdependence, interrelation, network, quid pro quo, rearrangement, reciprocation, reciprocity, replacement, revision, shift, shuffle, shuffling, substitution,

ex
ex

supplanting, supplantment, swap, switch, tit for tat*, traffic, transaction, transfer, transposing, transposition, truck*; SEE CONCEPTS *104,324*

exchange [*n2*] *place where stocks are bought, sold*
curb, market, net, network, over the counter, stock exchange, store, the Big Board*, the Street*, Wall Street*; SEE CONCEPTS *325,449*

exchange [*v*] *trade*
alternate, bandy, bargain, barter, buy and sell, cash in, castle, change, change hands*, commute, contact with, convert into, correspond, deal in, displace, flip-flop*, give and take*, go over to*, hook up, horse trade, interchange, invert, link up, market, network, pass to, pay back, rearrange, reciprocate, replace, return the compliment*, reverse, revise, seesaw, shift, shuffle, shuttle, substitute, swap, swap horses*, switch, traffic, transact, transfer, transpose, truck*, turn the tables*; SEE CONCEPT *104*

excise [*n*] *tax on goods*
customs, duty, import tax, levy, surcharge, tariff, toll; SEE CONCEPT *329*

excise [*v*] *remove, delete*
amputate, black out, blot out*, blue pencil*, cross out, cut, cut off, cut out, cut up, destroy, edit, elide, eradicate, erase, expunge, exscind, exsect, exterminate, extirpate, extract, gut, knock off*, launder*, lop off*, resect, scissor out, scratch out, slash, stamp out*, strike, trim, wipe out, X out*; SEE CONCEPT *211*

excitable [*adj*] *easily upset or inspired*
agitable, alarmable, demonstrative, edgy, emotional, enthusiastic, fidgety, fierce, fiery, galvanic, hasty, high-strung, hot-headed, hot-tempered, hysterical, impatient, impetuous, impulsive, inflammable, intolerant, irascible, mercurial, moody, nervous, neurotic, overzealous, passionate, peevish, quick, quick-tempered, rash, reckless, restless, sensitive, short fused, skittish, susceptible, temperamental, testy, touchy, uncontrolled, uneasy, vehement, violent, volatile, volcanic; SEE CONCEPTS *401,404*

excite [*v*] *inspire; upset*
accelerate, agitate, amaze, anger, animate, annoy, arouse, astound, awaken, bother, chafe, delight, discompose, disturb, electrify, elicit, energize, evoke, feed the fire*, fire, fluster, foment, galvanize, goad, incite, induce, inflame, infuriate, instigate, intensify, irritate, jar, jolt, kindle, madden, mock, move, offend, precipitate, provoke, quicken, rouse, start, stimulate, stir up, taunt, tease, thrill, titillate, touch off, vex, waken, wake up, warm, whet, work up, worry; SEE CONCEPTS *7,14,19,22*

excited [*adj*] *inspired; upset*
aflame, agitated, animated, annoyed, aroused, awakened, beside oneself*, charged, delighted, discomposed, disconcerted, disturbed, eager, enthusiastic, feverish, fired up*, frantic, high*, hot*, hot and bothered*, hyperactive, hysterical, in a tizzy*, inflamed, juiced up*, jumpy*, keyed up*, moved, nervous, on edge*, on fire*, overwrought, passionate, piqued, provoked, roused, ruffled, steamed up*, stimulated, stirred, thrilled, tumultous/tumultuous, wild, wired*, worked up, zipped up*; SEE CONCEPTS *401,403*

excitement [*n*] *enthusiasm; incitement*
action, activity, ado, adventure, agitation, animation, bother, buzz*, commotion, confusion, dis-

composure, disturbance, dither*, drama, elation, emotion, excitation, feeling, ferment, fever, flurry, frenzy, furor, fuss, heat*, hubbub*, hullabaloo*, hurry, hysteria, impulse, instigation, intoxication, kicks*, melodrama, motivation, motive, movement, passion, perturbation, provocation, rage, stimulation, stimulus, stir, thrill, titillation, to-do*, trepidation, tumult, turmoil, urge, warmth, wildness; SEE CONCEPTS *388,410, 633*

exciting [*adj*] *inspiring, exhilarating*
agitative, animating, appealing, arousing, arresting, astonishing, bracing, breathtaking, commoving, dangerous, dramatic, electrifying, exhilarant, eye-popping*, far-out*, fine, flashy, groovy*, hair-raising*, heady*, hectic, impelling, impressive, interesting, intoxicating, intriguing, lively, melodramatic, mind-blowing, moving, neat, overpowering, overwhelming, provocative, racy, rip-roaring*, rousing, sensational, showy, spine-tingling*, stimulating, stirring, thrilling, titillating, wild, zestful; SEE CONCEPTS *529,542,548*

exclaim [*v*] *shout out*
assert, bellow, blurt, burst out, call, call aloud, call out, cry, cry out, declare, ejaculate, emit, figure, holler, proclaim, rend the air*, roar, say loudly, shout, state, utter, vociferate, yawp*, yell; SEE CONCEPTS *47,49*

exclamation [*n*] *shout; assertion*
bellow, call, clamor, cry, ejaculation, expletive, holler, interjection, outcry, roar, utterance, vociferation, yawp*, yell; SEE CONCEPTS *49,77*

exclude [*v*] *expel, forbid*
ban, bar, bate, blackball*, blacklist, block, bounce, boycott, close out, count out, debar, disallow, drive out, eject, eliminate, embargo, estop, evict, except, force out, get rid of, ignore, interdict, keep out, leave out, lock out, obviate, occlude, omit, ostracize, oust, pass over, preclude, prevent, prohibit, proscribe, put out, refuse, refuse admittance, reject, remove, repudiate, rule out, set aside, shut out, shut the door on*, sideline, suspend, throw out, veto, ward off; SEE CONCEPTS *25,30,121*

exclusion [*n*] *expulsion; forbiddance*
ban, bar, blackball*, blockade, boycott, coventry, cut, debarment, debarring, discharge, dismissal, ejection, elimination, embargo, eviction, exception, excommunication, interdict, interdicting, interdiction, keeping out, lockout, nonadmission, occlusion, omission, ostracism, ousting, preclusion, prevention, prohibition, proscription, refusal, rejection, relegation, removal, repudiation, segregation, separation, suspension, veto; SEE CONCEPTS *25,30,121*

exclusive [*adj*] *unshared, restricted*
absolute, aloof, aristocratic, chic, choice, chosen, circumscribed, clannish, classy, cliquish, closed, complete, confined, country club, discriminative, elegant, entire, exclusionary, exclusory, fashionable, full, independent, licensed, limited, narrow, only, particular, peculiar, posh, preferential, private, privileged, prohibitive, restrictive, ritzy, segregated, select, selfish, single, snobbish, socially correct, sole, swank, total, undivided, unique, upper crust*, whole; SEE CONCEPTS *554,567*

exclusively [*adv*] *particularly*
alone, but, completely, entirely, one and only,

onliest, only, singularly, solely, wholly; SEE CONCEPT *554*

exclusive of [*prep*] *except for*
aside from, bar, barring, bating, besides, but, debarring, excepting, excluding, leaving aside, not counting, omitting, outside of, restricting, ruling out, save; SEE CONCEPT *554*

excogitate [*v*] *think about seriously*
conceive, consider, contemplate, contrive, deliberate, derive, develop, devise, educe, evolve, frame, invent, mind, mull over, perpend, ponder, ruminate, study, think out, think up, weigh, work out; SEE CONCEPTS *17,24*

excommunicate [*v*] *banish*
anathematize, ban, cast out, curse, denounce, dismiss, eject, exclude, expel, oust, proscribe, remove, repudiate, unchurch; SEE CONCEPTS *317,367*

excoriate [*v1*] *scrape layers off*
abrade, chafe, flay, fret, gall, peel, rub, scarify, scratch, skin, strip; SEE CONCEPTS *211,215*

excoriate [*v2*] *denounce, criticize*
attack, berate, blister, castigate, censure, chastise, condemn, flay, lambaste, lash, rebuke, reproach, reprove, revile, scathe, scold, scorch, slash, tear into, upbraid, vilify; SEE CONCEPT *52*

excrement [*n*] *feces*
crap, droppings, dung, guano, manure, poop, sewage, stool, waste, waste matter; SEE CONCEPT *260*

excrete [*v*] *discharge, usually liquified substance*
defecate, egest, ejaculate, eject, eliminate, emanate, evacuate, exhale, expel, exudate, exude, give off, leak, pass, perspire, produce, remove, secrete, sweat, throw off, urinate, void; SEE CONCEPTS *179,185*

excruciating [*adj*] *torturous, painful*
acute, agonizing, burning, chastening, consuming, exquisite, extreme, grueling, harrowing, insufferable, intense, piercing, punishing, racking, rending, searing, severe, sharp, shooting, stabbing, tearing, tormenting, torturesome, torturing, unbearable, unendurable, violent; SEE CONCEPTS *314,548,609*

exculpate [*v*] *forgive*
absolve, acquit, amnesty, clear, condone, discharge, disculpate, dismiss, excuse, exonerate, explain, free, justify, let off*, pardon, rationalize, release, remit, vindicate, wipe slate clean*; SEE CONCEPTS *10,127,317*

excursion [*n*] *journey*
circuit, cruise, day trip, digression, expedition, jaunt, junket, outing, picnic, pleasure trip, ramble, round trip, safari, tour, trek, trip, walk, wandering; SEE CONCEPTS *224,384*

excusable [*adj*] *allowable*
all right, condonable, defensible, exculpatory, explainable, fair, forgivable, justifiable, minor, moderate, not too bad*, okay, pardonable, passable, permissible, plausible, reasonable, remittable, reprievable, slight, specious, temperate, tenable, trivial, understandable, venial, vindicable, vindicatory, warrantable, within limits; SEE CONCEPT *558*

excuse [*n*] *reason, explanation*
alibi, apology, cleanup*, cop-out*, cover*, cover story*, coverup, defense, disguise, evasion, expedient, extenuation, fish story*, grounds, jive*, justification, makeshift, mitigation, plea, pretext, rationalization, regrets, routine, semblance, shift,

song*, song and dance*, stall, stopgap*, story, substitute, subterfuge, trick*, vindication, whitewash*, why and wherefore*; SEE CONCEPTS *59,661*

excuse [*v*] *forgive, absolve; justify*
acquit, alibi, apologize for, appease, bear with, clear, condone, cover, defend, discharge, dispense from, exculpate, exempt, exempt from, exonerate, explain, extenuate, forgive, free, give absolution, grant amnesty, indulge, let go*, let off*, liberate, make allowances for, mitigate, overlook, pardon, pass over*, plead ignorance, pretext, purge, rationalize, release, relieve, remit, reprieve, shrive, shrug off*, spare, take rap for*, tolerate, vindicate, whitewash*, wink at*; SEE CONCEPTS *10,57,83*

execrable [*adj*] *horrible, sickening*
abhorrent, abominable, accursed, atrocious, confounded, cursed, damnable, defective, deplorable, despicable, detestable, disgusting, foul, hateful, heinous, horrific, loathsome, low, monstrous, nauseous, obnoxious, odious, offensive, repulsive, revolting, vile, wretched; SEE CONCEPT *542*

execrate [*v*] *hate*
abhor, abominate, accurse, anathematize, censure, condemn, curse, damn, denounce, deplore, despise, detest, excoriate, imprecate, loathe, objurgate, reprehend, reprobate, reprove, revile, vilify; SEE CONCEPT *29*

execration [*n*] *hating*
abhorrence, abomination, anathema, blasphemy, condemnation, contempt, curse, cursing, cussing, damnation, denunciation, detestation, detesting, excoriation, hatred, imprecation, loathing, malediction, odium, profanity, swearing, vilification; SEE CONCEPT *29*

execute [*v1*] *kill*
assassinate, behead, bump off*, do in*, electrocute, eliminate, finish, gas, guillotine, hang, knock off*, liquidate, murder, purge, put away*, put to death, shoot; SEE CONCEPT *252*

execute [*v2*] *carry out a task*
accomplish, achieve, act, administer, administrate, bring off, bring to fruition, cause, come through, complete, consummate, deal with, discharge, do, do the job*, do the trick*, do to a T*, earn wings*, effect, enact, enforce, finish, fulfill, get there*, govern, hack it*, hit*, implement, make it*, meet, percolate*, perform, play, polish off*, prosecute, pull off*, put into effect, put over*, put through, realize, render, sail through*, score*, take care of, take care of business*, transact; SEE CONCEPTS *91,706*

execution [*n1*] *killing*
beheading, capital punishment, contract killing*, crucifixion, decapitation, electrocution, gassing, guillotining, hanging, hit, impalement, lethal injection, necktie party*, punishment, rub out*, shooting, strangling, strangulation; SEE CONCEPT *252*

execution [*n2*] *carrying out of a task*
accomplishment, achievement, administration, completion, consummation, delivery, discharge, doing, effect, enactment, enforcement, fulfilling, implementation, nuts and bolts*, operation, performance, prosecution, realization, rendering, style; SEE CONCEPTS *91,706*

executive [*adj*] *administrative*
controlling, decision-making, directing, govern-

ex
ex

ing, managerial, managing, ruling; SEE CONCEPT 527

executive [n] *person who manages an organization*
administration, administrator, big wheel*, boss, brass, businessperson, CEO*, chief, CO*, commander, director, directorate, entrepreneur, exec*, government, governor, head, head honcho*, head person*, heavyweight*, hierarchy, higher-up*, industrialist, key player*, leader, leadership, management, manager, officer, official, skipper*, supervisor, top brass*, tycoon, VIP*; SEE CONCEPTS *347,354*

exemplar [n] *ideal*
archetype, copy, criterion, epitome, example, exemplification, illustration, instance, mirror, model, paradigm, paragon, pattern, prototype, specimen, standard, type; SEE CONCEPT *686*

exemplary [adj] *ideal*
admirable, batting a thousand*, blameless, bueno*, characteristic, classic, classical, commendable, correct, estimable, excellent, good, guiltless, honorable, illustrative, inculpable, innocent, irreprehensible, laudable, meritorious, model, neato*, not bad*, not too shabby*, paradigmatic, praiseworthy, prototypical, punctilious, pure, quintessential, representative, righteous, sterling, typical, virtuous, worthy; SEE CONCEPTS *404,572,574*

exemplify [v] *serve as an example*
body, cite, clarify, clear up, demonstrate, depict, display, elucidate, emblematize, embody, enlighten, epitomize, evidence, exhibit, illuminate, illustrate, instance, manifest, mirror, personify, quote, represent, show, spell out, symbolize, typify; SEE CONCEPTS *97,118*

exempt [adj] *freed from responsibility*
absolved, beat the rap*, clear, cleared, discharged, excepted, excluded, excused, favored, free, immune, let go*, let off*, liberated, not liable, not responsible, not subject, off the hook*, outside, privileged, released, set apart, spared, special, unbound, unchecked, unrestrained, unrestricted, unshackled, void of, walked*; SEE CONCEPTS *319,554*

exempt [v] *relieve, absolve*
clear, discharge, dispense, except, excuse, exonerate, free, go easy on*, grant immunity, let off*, let off the hook*, liberate, pass by, privilege from, release, spare, wipe the slate*, write off; SEE CONCEPTS *50,83,88,127*

exemption [n] *freedom from a responsibility*
absolution, discharge, dispensation, exception, exoneration, immunity, impunity, privilege, release; SEE CONCEPTS *652,685,691*

exercise [n1] *work, effort*
act, action, activity, calisthenics, constitutional*, daily dozen*, discharge, discipline, drill, drilling, examination, exercising, exertion, gym, labor, lesson, movement, occupation, operation, performance, problem, pursuit, recitation, schoolwork, study, task, test, theme, toil, training, warm-up, workout; SEE CONCEPTS *87,290,362,363*

exercise [n2] *accomplishment, use*
application, discharge, employment, enjoyment, exertion, fulfillment, implementation, operation, performance, practice, pursuit, utilization; SEE CONCEPTS *225,706*

exercise [v1] *put to use*
apply, bestow, bring to bear, devote, drill, employ, enjoy, execute, exert, exploit, handle, operate, practice, put into practice, rehearse, sharpen, use, utilize, wield; SEE CONCEPT *225*

exercise [v2] *do repeatedly, especially to improve*
break, break in, condition, cultivate, develop, discipline, drill, dry run*, exert, fix, foster, groom, habituate, hone, improve, inure, labor, lick into shape*, limber up, loosen up, maneuver, ply, practice, prepare, pump iron*, put out, put through grind*, put through mill*, rehearse, run through, set, strain, teach, train, tune up, walk through, warm up, work, work out; SEE CONCEPTS *87,363*

exercise [v3] *upset, worry*
abrade, afflict, agitate, annoy, bother, burden, chafe, distress, disturb, gall, irk, occupy, pain, perturb, preoccupy, provoke, trouble, try, vex; SEE CONCEPTS *7,19*

exert [v] *make use of*
apply, apply oneself, bring into play*, bring to bear*, dig*, employ, endeavor, exercise, expend, give all one's got*, give best shot*, labor, make effort, peg away*, plug*, ply, pour it on*, push, put forth, put out, strain, strive, struggle, sweat it*, throw, toil, try hard, use, utilize, wield, work; SEE CONCEPTS *87,225*

exertion [n] *hard work*
action, activity, application, attempt, effort, elbow grease*, employment, endeavor, exercise, hard pull*, industry, labor, long pull*, operation, pains, strain, stretch, striving, struggle, toil, travail, trial, trouble, use, utilization; SEE CONCEPTS *87,362,677*

exfoliate [v] *peel*
desquamate, doff, flake off, scale off, shed; SEE CONCEPTS *142,176,211*

exhale [v] *breathe out*
breathe, discharge, eject, emanate, emit, evaporate, expel, give off, issue, let out, respire, steam, vaporize; SEE CONCEPT *163*

exhaust [v1] *tire or wear out*
bankrupt, burn out*, conk out*, cripple, debilitate, disable, do in*, drain, draw, enervate, enfeeble, fag, fatigue, frazzle, impoverish, overdo, overexert, overextend, overfatigue, overtire, overwork, peter out*, poop*, poop out*, prostrate, run ragged*, sap*, suck dry*, tucker*, use up, weaken, wear down, weary; SEE CONCEPTS *250,469*

exhaust [v2] *consume, use up*
bankrupt, bleed dry*, deplete, devour, dispel, disperse, dissipate, drain, draw, dry, eat, eat up*, empty, expend, finish, impoverish, run out, run through, spend, squander, strain, suck dry*, take last of, void, wash up, waste; SEE CONCEPTS *169,225*

exhausted [adj1] *extremely tired*
all in*, beat*, bleary, bone-weary, bushed, crippled, dead*, dead tired*, debilitated, disabled, dog-tired*, done for*, done in*, drained, effete, enervated, frazzled, had it*, kaput*, limp, out on one's feet*, outta gas*, prostrated, ready to drop*, run-down, sapped*, shot*, spent, tired out, wasted*, weak, weakened, wearied, worn, worn out; SEE CONCEPTS *406,485*

exhausted [adj2] *used up*
all gone, at an end, bare, consumed, depleted, dissipated, done, drained, dry, empty, expended,

finished, gone, spent, squandered, void, washed-out, wasted; SEE CONCEPTS *560,771*

exhaustion [*n*] *tiredness*
burnout*, collapse, consumption, debilitation, debility, enervation, expenditure, fatigue, feebleness, lassitude, prostration, weariness; SEE CONCEPTS *410,720*

exhaustive [*adj*] *all-inclusive, complete*
all-embracing, all-encompassing, all-out, catholic, comprehensive, embracive, encyclopedic, extensive, far-reaching, from A to Z*, full, full-blown, full-dress*, full-scale, in-depth, intensive, no stone unturned*, out-and-out*, profound, radical, sweeping, the word, thorough, thoroughgoing, total, whole-hog*; SEE CONCEPTS *531,772*

exhibit [*n*] *viewing; presentation*
display, exhibition, exposition, fair, illustration, model, performance, show; SEE CONCEPTS *259,261*

exhibit [*v*] *put on view; present*
advertise, air, brandish, demonstrate, disclose, display, disport, evidence, evince, expose, express, feature, flash, flaunt, illustrate, indicate, let it all hang out*, make clear, make plain, manifest, mark, offer, ostend, parade, parade wares*, proclaim, reveal, roll out, show, show and tell*, showcase, show off, strut stuff*, trot out*, wave around*; SEE CONCEPT *261*

exhibition [*n*] *showing, demonstration*
advertisement, airing, an act*, a scene*, carnival, display, exhibit, expo, exposition, fair, fireworks, flash*, front*, manifestation, offering, pageant, performance, presentation, representation, show, sight, spectacle; SEE CONCEPTS *261,386*

exhibitionism [*n*] *attention-seeking behavior*
exposing oneself, flashing*, immodesty, indecent exposure, self-display, showing off; SEE CONCEPTS *261,386*

exhilarate [*v*] *make very happy*
animate, boost, buoy, cheer, commove, delight, elate, enliven, exalt, excite, gladden, inspire, inspirit, invigorate, juice*, lift, pep up*, perk up*, pick up, put zip into*, quicken, rejoice, send, snap up*, stimulate, thrill, turn on*, uplift, vitalize; SEE CONCEPTS *7,22*

exhilarating [*adj*] *stimulating, cheering*
animating, animative, bracing, breathtaking, electric, elevating, enlivening, exalting, exciting, exhilarant, exhilarative, exhilaratory, eye-popping*, gladdening, inspiring, inspiriting, intoxicating, invigorating, quickening, rousing, stimulative, stirring, thrilling, tonic, uplifting, vitalizing; SEE CONCEPTS *529,548*

exhilaration [*n*] *great happiness, excitement*
animation, a rush*, cheerfulness, delight, elation, electrification, elevation, enlivenment, euphoria, exaltation, excitation, firing, gaiety, galvanization, gladness, gleefulness, head rush*, high spirits*, hilarity, inspiration, invigoration, joy, joyfulness, liveliness, mirth, quickening, sprightliness, stimulation, uplift, vitalization, vivacity, vivification; SEE CONCEPT *410*

exhort [*v*] *urge, warn*
admonish, advise, beseech, bid, call upon, caution, counsel, egg on*, encourage, enjoin, entreat, goad, incite, insist, persuade, plead, preach, press, pressure, prick, prod, prompt, propel, spur, stimulate; SEE CONCEPTS *75,78*

exhortation [*n*] *warning, urging*
admonition, advice, beseeching, bidding, caution, counsel, encouragement, enjoinder, entreaty, goading, incitement, instigation, lecture, persuasion, preaching, sermon; SEE CONCEPTS *75,78,274*

exhume [*v*] *dig up, especially the dead*
disclose, disembalm, disentomb, disinhume, disinter, resurrect, reveal, unbury, uncharnel, unearth; SEE CONCEPT *178*

exigency/exigence [*n*] *difficulty; demand*
acuteness, constraint, contingency, crisis, criticalness, crossroad, demandingness, dilemma, distress, duress, emergency, extremity, fix, hardship, imperativeness, jam, juncture, necessity, need, needfulness, pass, pickle*, pinch, plight, predicament, pressingness, pressure, quandary, requirement, scrape*, stress, turning point*, urgency, vicissitude, want, wont, zero hour*; SEE CONCEPTS *646,674,709*

exigent [*adj1*] *urgent, pressing*
acute, burning, clamant, clamorous, constraining, critical, crucial, crying, imperative, importunate, insistent, instant, menacing, necessary, needful, threatening; SEE CONCEPTS *548,568*

exigent [*adj2*] *difficult, taxing*
arduous, burdensome, demanding, exacting, grievous, hard, harsh, onerous, oppressive, rigorous, severe, stiff, strict, stringent, superincumbent, tough, weighty; SEE CONCEPTS *537,542*

exiguous [*adj*] *scanty*
bare, confined, diminutive, inadequate, limited, little, meager, narrow, negligible, paltry, petty, poor, restricted, skimpy, slender, slight, small, spare, sparse, tenuous, thin, tiny; SEE CONCEPTS *771,789*

exile [*n1*] *deportation from a place*
banishment, diaspora, dispersion, displacement, exclusion, expatriation, expulsion, extradition, migration, ostracism, proscription, relegation, scattering, separation; SEE CONCEPT *298*

exile [*n2*] *person deported from a place*
deportee, displaced person, DP*, émigré, expatriate, expellee, fugitive, nonperson*, outcast, outlaw, person without country*, refugee; SEE CONCEPTS *354,412,423*

exile [*v*] *deport from place*
banish, cast out, displace, dispossess, drive out, eject, evacuate, expatriate, expel, expulse, extradite, ostracize, oust, outlaw, proscribe, relegate, transport, turn out; SEE CONCEPTS *122,198,298*

exist [*v1*] *be living*
abide, be, be extant, be latent, be present, breathe, continue, endure, happen, last, lie, live, move, obtain, occur, prevail, remain, stand, stay, subsist, survive; SEE CONCEPT *407*

exist [*v2*] *get along in life*
consist, dwell, eke out a living*, endure, get by*, go on, inhere, kick*, lie, live, make it*, reside, stay alive*, subsist, survive; SEE CONCEPTS *100,226*

existence [*n*] *life*
actuality, animation, being, breath, continuance, continuation, duration, endurance, entity, essence, hand one is dealt*, individuality, journey, lifing, permanence, perseverance, presence, rat race*, reality, real world*, something, subsistence, survival, the big game*, world; SEE CONCEPTS *407,639*

ex
ex

exit [n1] *way out of a place*
avenue, door, egress, fire escape, gate, hole, opening, outlet, passage out, vent; SEE CONCEPT *440*

exit [n2] *leaving*
adieu, death, demise, departure, egress, egression, evacuation, exodus, expiration, expiry, farewell, going, goodbye, leave-taking, offgoing, retirement, retreat, stampede, withdrawal; SEE CONCEPT *195*

exit [v] *leave a place*
bid farewell, blow*, depart, do vanishing act*, flake off*, get*, get away, get off, git*, go, go away, go out, issue, move, move out, quit, retire, retreat, say goodbye, split*, take a hike*, take one's leave*, withdraw; SEE CONCEPT *195*

exodus [n] *leaving*
departure, egress, egression, emigration, evacuation, exit, exiting, flight, going out, journey, migration, offgoing, retirement, retreat, withdrawal; SEE CONCEPT *195*

exonerate [v] *excuse, clear of responsibility or blame*
absolve, acquit, disburden, discharge, dismiss, except, exculpate, exempt, free, justify, let off*, let off hook*, liberate, pardon, release, relieve, sanitize, vindicate, whitewash*, wipe slate clean*; SEE CONCEPTS *10,127,317*

exorbitant [adj] *extravagant, excessive*
absonant, dear, enormous, exacting, expensive, extortionate, extreme, high, highway robbery*, immoderate, inordinate, out of sight*, outrageous, overboard, overmuch, over one's head*, preposterous, pricey, steep*, stiff*, towering, unconscionable, undue, unreasonable, unwarranted, up to here*, wasteful; SEE CONCEPTS *334,547, 558*

exorcise [v] *free from evil spirits*
cast out, dismiss, drive out, expel, purge, purify, remove; SEE CONCEPT *179*

exorcism [n] *expelling evil spirits*
casting out, ceremony, ejection, expulsion, purification, ritual; SEE CONCEPTS *165,367*

exotic [adj] *not native or usual; mysterious*
alien, alluring, avant garde, bizarre, colorful, curious, different, enticing, external, extraneous, extraordinary, extrinsic, far out*, fascinating, foreign, glamorous, imported, introduced, kinky*, outlandish, outside, peculiar, peregrine, romantic, strange, striking, unfamiliar, unusual, way out*, weird*; SEE CONCEPTS *542,549*

expand [v1] *extend, augment*
aggrandize, amplify, beef up*, bloat, blow up*, bolster, broaden, bulk up*, burgeon, detail, develop, diffuse, dilate, distend, elaborate, embellish, enlarge, explicate, fan out*, fatten, fill out, grow, heighten, hike, increase, inflate, lengthen, magnify, mount, multiply, mushroom, open, open out, outspread, pad, piggyback*, prolong, protract, puff up*, pyramid*, slap on*, soup up*, spread, spread out, stretch, stretch out, swell, tack on*, thicken, unfold, unfurl, unravel, unroll, upsurge, wax*, widen; SEE CONCEPTS *236,245*

expand [v2] *go into detail*
amplify, beef up*, build up, develop, dilate, discourse, drag out*, elaborate, embellish, enlarge, expatiate, expound, extend, flesh out*, spell out, sweeten; SEE CONCEPT *57*

expanse [n] *large space, usually open*
amplitude, area, belt, breadth, compass, distance, domain, extension, extent, field, immensity, latitude, length, margin, orbit, plain, radius, range, reach, region, remoteness, room, scope, span, sphere, spread, stretch, sweep, territory, tract, uninterrupted space, width, wilderness; SEE CONCEPTS *509,513,651,788*

expansion [n] *growth*
amplification, augmentation, breadth, development, diffusion, dilation, distance, distension, enlargement, evolution, expanse, extension, increase, inflation, magnification, maturation, multiplication, opening out, space, spread, stretch, swelling, unfolding, unfurling; SEE CONCEPTS *700,704,780*

expansionism [n] *growth*
development, economic expansion, imperialism, progress; SEE CONCEPTS *427,469,703,704,775*

expansive [adj1] *broad, comprehensive*
all-embracing, ample, big, dilatant, elastic, expanding, expansile, extensive, far-reaching, great, inclusive, large, scopic, scopious, stretching, thorough, unrepressed, unsuppressed, voluminous, wide, wide-ranging, widespread; SEE CONCEPT *772*

expansive [adj2] *talkative*
affable, communicative, demonstrative, easy, effervescent, effusive, extroverted, free, friendly, garrulous, generous, genial, gregarious, gushy, lavish, liberal, loquacious, open, outgoing, sociable, unconstrained, uninhibited, unreserved, unrestrained, warm; SEE CONCEPT *267*

expatriate [n] *person thrown out of a country*
departer, deportee, displaced person, emigrant, émigré, evacuee, exile, expellee, migrant, outcast, refugee; SEE CONCEPTS *354,412,423*

expatriate [v] *throw out of a country*
banish, deport, displace, exile, expel, expulse, ostracize, oust, proscribe, relegate, transport; SEE CONCEPTS *130,198,211*

expect [v1] *believe strongly; anticipate*
apprehend, assume, await, bargain for, bargain on, be afraid, calculate, conjecture, contemplate, count on, divine, envisage, feel, figure, forecast, foreknow, foresee, gather, hope, hope for, imagine, in the cards*, look, look ahead to, look for, look forward to*, predict, presume, presuppose, reckon, see coming*, sense, suppose, surmise, suspect, take, think, trust, understand, wait for, watch for; SEE CONCEPTS *12,26*

expect [v2] *want, wish*
call for, count on, demand, exact, insist on, look for, rely upon, require; SEE CONCEPT *20*

expectancy [n] *anticipation*
assumption, assurance, belief, calculation, confidence, conjecture, expectation, hope, likelihood, looking forward, outlook, prediction, presentation, presentiment, presumption, probability, prospect, reliance, supposition, surmise, suspense, trust, view, waiting; SEE CONCEPTS *410,689*

expectant [adj1] *anticipating*
alert, anticipative, anxious, apprehensive, awaiting, breathless, eager, expecting, hopeful, hoping, in suspense, looking for, on edge*, on tenterhooks*, prepared, raring*, ready, vigilant, waiting, waiting on, watchful, with bated breath*; SEE CONCEPTS *403,406*

expectant [adj2] *preparing to give birth*
enceinte, expecting, gravid, parturient, pregnant, with child*; SEE CONCEPT *485*

expectation [n] *belief, anticipation*
apprehension, assumption, assurance, calculation, chance, confidence, conjecture, design, expectancy, fear, forecast, hope, intention, likelihood, looking forward, motive, notion, outlook, possibility, prediction, presumption, probability, promise, prospect, reliance, supposition, surmise, suspense, trust, view; SEE CONCEPTS 410,689

expecting [adj] *pregnant*
carrying, expectant, in a family way*, with child*; SEE CONCEPTS 406,485

expediency/expedience [n1] *appropriateness; worth*
advantage, advantageousness, advisability, appositeness, aptness, benefit, convenience, desirability, effectiveness, efficiency, fitness, helpfulness, judiciousness, meetness, opportunism, opportunity, order, policy, practicality, pragmatism, profitability, profitableness, properness, propitiousness, propriety, prudence, rightness, suitability, usefulness, utilitarianism, utility; SEE CONCEPTS 656,658

expediency/expedience [n2] *resource*
band-aid*, contrivance, design, device, dodge, easy way out*, gimmick*, makeshift*, maneuver, means, measure, method, recourse, resort, scheme, shift, step, stopgap*, stratagem, strategy, substitute, surrogate, tactic, trick; SEE CONCEPTS 660,712

expedient [adj] *worthwhile, appropriate*
ad hoc, advantageous, advisable, beneficial, convenient, desirable, discreet, effective, feasible, fit, fitting, helpful, judicious, meet, opportune, politic, possible, practicable, practical, pragmatic, profitable, proper, prudent, seasonable, suitable, tactical, timely, useful, utilitarian, wise; SEE CONCEPTS 558,560

expedient [n] *resource*
contrivance, device, gency, instrument, instrumentality, makeshift, maneuver, means, measure, medium, method, recourse, refuge, resort, scheme, shift, stopgap, stratagem, substitute; SEE CONCEPTS 660,712

expedite [v] *make happen faster*
accelerate, advance, assist, cut the red tape*, dispatch, facilitate, fast track*, forward, grease wheels*, hand-carry, handle personally, handwalk*, hasten, hurry, precipitate, press, promote, quicken, railroad*, run interference*, run with the ball*, rush, shoot through*, speed, speed up, urge, walk it through*; SEE CONCEPT 242

expedition [n1] *journey; people on a journey*
campaign, caravan, cavalcade, company, crew, crowd, cruise, crusade, enterprise, entrada, excursion, exploration, explorers, fleet, jaunt, junket, mission, outing, party, patrol, peregrination, picnic, posse, quest, safari, squadron, swing, team, tour, travel, travellers, trek, trip, undertaking, voyage, voyagers, wayfarers; SEE CONCEPTS 224,417

expedition [n2] *speed; speeding up*
alacrity, celerity, dispatch, expeditiousness, goodwill, haste, hurry, hustle, promptitude, promptness, punctuality, quickness, rapidity, readiness, swiftness; SEE CONCEPTS 242,755

expeditious [adj] *immediate, speedy*
active, alert, breakneck, brisk, diligent, effective, effectual, efficient, fast, fleet, hasty, instant, nimble, prompt, punctual, quick, rapid, ready, swift; SEE CONCEPTS 542,588

expel [v1] *discharge*
belch, blow out, cast out, disgorge, dislodge, drive out, ejaculate, eruct, erupt, evacuate, exhaust, exudate, exude, get rid of, irrupt, pass, remove, spew, throw out, vomit; SEE CONCEPT 179

expel [v2] *throw out, banish*
ban, bar, blackball*, bust, cast out, chase, deport, discharge, dismiss, displace, dispossess, drum out, eject, eliminate, evict, exclude, exile, expatriate, expulse, fire, give the boot*, give the hook*, give walking papers*, kick out, oust, proscribe, send packing*, show the door*, suspend, throw out on ear*, turn out; SEE CONCEPTS 122,130,198

expend [v] *exhaust; spend*
ante up*, blow*, consume, disburse, dish out*, dispense, dissipate, distribute, employ, finish, foot the bill*, fork out*, give, go through*, lay out, outlay, pay, pay out, put out*, shell out*, splurge*, spring for*, throw money at*, use up, wash up*; SEE CONCEPTS 225,341

expendable [adj] *not important*
dispensable, disposable, excess, inessential, nonessential, replaceable, superfluous, unimportant; SEE CONCEPTS 546,575

expenditure [n] *payment*
amount, application, bottom line*, cash on barrelhead*, charge, come to*, consumption, cost, disbursement, dissipation, expense, figure, investment, kickback*, outgo, outlay, output, payoff, price, rate, setback*, spending, splurge, squander, throw*, tune*, use, valuation, value, waste; SEE CONCEPT 344

expense [n] *cost, payment*
amount, assessment, bite*, bottom line*, budget, charge, consumption, debit, debt, decrement, deprivation, disbursement, duty, expenditure, forfeit, forfeiture, insurance, investment, liability, loan, loss, mortgage, obligation, outdo*, outlay, out of pocket*, output, overhead, payroll, price, price tag, rate, responsibility, risk, sacrifice, spending, sum, surcharge, tariff, toll, upkeep, use, value, worth; SEE CONCEPTS 328,329,336, 344

expensive [adj] *high-priced*
an arm and a leg*, at a premium, big-ticket*, costly, dear, excessive, exorbitant, extravagant, fancy, high, highway robbery*, holdup*, immoderate, inordinate, invaluable, lavish, out of sight*, overpriced, plush, posh, pretty penny*, pricey*, rich, ritzy*, sky-high*, steep*, stiff*, swank*, too high, uneconomical, unreasonable, upscale*, valuable; SEE CONCEPT 334

experience [n1] *knowledge*
acquaintance, action, actuality, background, caution, combat, contact, doing, empiricism, evidence, existence, exposure, familiarity, forebearance, intimacy, involvement, inwardness, judgment, know-how*, maturity, observation, participation, patience, perspicacity, practicality, practice, proof, reality, savoir-faire, seasoning, sense, skill, sophistication, strife, struggle, training, trial, understanding, wisdom, worldliness; SEE CONCEPT 409

experience [n2] *happening, occurrence*
adventure, affair, encounter, episode, event, incident, ordeal, test, trial, trip; SEE CONCEPTS 2,696

ex
ex

experienced [*adj*] *knowledgeable, knowing*
accomplished, accustomed, adept, been around*, been there*, broken in*, capable, competent, cultivated, dynamite, expert, familiar, having something on the ball*, instructed, in the know*, knowing one's stuff*, knowing the score*, mature, matured, old, old hand*, practical, practiced, pro, professional, qualified, rounded, seasoned, skillful, sophisticated, sport, tested, the right stuff*, trained, tried, versed, vet, veteran, well-versed, wise, worldly, worldly-wise*; SEE CONCEPTS *402,527*

experiment [*n*] *investigation, test*
agreement, analysis, assay, attempt, check, dissection, dry run*, enterprise, essay, examination, exercise, experimentation, fling*, measure, observation, operation, practice, probe, procedure, proof, quiz, R and D*, rehearsal, research, research and development, scrutiny, search, speculation, study, trial, trial and error*, trial run*, try, try-on, tryout, undertaking, venture, verification; SEE CONCEPTS *103,290*

experiment [*v*] *investigate, test*
analyze, assay, diagnose, examine, explore, fool with*, futz around*, mess around*, play around with*, practice with, probe, prove, put to the test*, research, sample, scrutinize, search, shake down*, speculate, study, try, try on, try on for size*, try out, venture, verify, weigh; SEE CONCEPTS *24,87,103*

experimental [*adj*] *exploratory*
beginning, developmental, empirical, experiential, first stage, laboratory, momentary, on approval, pilot, preliminary, preparatory, primary, probationary, provisional, speculative, temporary, tentative, test, trial, trial-and-error, unconcluded, under probation, unproved; SEE CONCEPT *535*

expert [*adj*] *knowledgeable, proficient*
able, adept, adroit, apt, big league*, clever, crack, crackerjack*, deft, dexterous, experienced, facile, handy, practiced, professional, qualified, savvy, schooled, sharp, skilled, skillful, slick, trained, virtuoso; SEE CONCEPTS *402,527*

expert [*n*] *master, specialist*
ace*, adept, artist, artiste, authority, buff, connoisseur, doyen, graduate, guru*, hot shot*, old hand*, old pro*, phenomenon, pro, professional, proficient, shark*, virtuoso, whiz*, wizard; SEE CONCEPTS *348,350,416*

expertise/expertness [*n*] *knowledge, proficiency*
ability, ableness, adroitness, aptness, art, cleverness, command, competence, craft, cunning, deftness, dexterity, dodge*, facility, finesse, goods*, ingeniousness, judgment, knack*, know-how*, line*, makings*, oil*, one's thing*, prowess, readiness, savvy, sharpness, skill, skillfulness, stuff*; SEE CONCEPTS *409,630*

expiate [*v*] *make amends for*
absolve, amend, appease, atone, atone for, compensate, correct, do penance, excuse, forgive, pay one's dues*, rectify, redeem, redress, remedy, square things*; SEE CONCEPTS *67,126*

expiration [*n*] *finish, demise*
cessation, close, closing, conclusion, death, decease, departure, dying, elapsing, end, expiry, going, passing, termination, terminus; SEE CONCEPTS *119,304*

expire [*v1*] *come to an end*
bite the dust*, buy it*, cash in chips*, cease, close, conclude, croak*, decease, depart, die, elapse, end, finish, go, kick the bucket*, lapse, pass, pass away, pass on, pass over, perish, quit, run out, stop, strike out*, terminate, up and die*; SEE CONCEPTS *119,304*

expire [*v2*] *breathe out*
emit, exhale, expel; SEE CONCEPTS *163,185*

explain [*v*] *make clear; give a reason for*
account for, analyze, annotate, break down, bring out, clarify, clear up, construe, decipher, define, demonstrate, describe, diagram, disclose, elucidate, excuse, explicate, expound, get across*, go into detail, illustrate, interpret, justify, make plain*, manifest, paraphrase, point out, put across, put in plain English*, rationalize, read, refine, render, resolve, reveal, set right, solve, spell out*, teach, tell, throw light upon*, translate, unfold, unravel, untangle; SEE CONCEPT *57*

explanation [*n*] *clarification; reason*
account, annotation, answer, breakdown, brief, cause, comment, commentary, confession, definition, demonstration, description, details, display, elucidation, evidence, example, excuse, explication, exposition, expression, gloss, history, illustration, information, interpretation, justification, meaning, mitigation, motive, narration, note, recital, rendition, report, resolution, sense, showing, significance, specification, statement, story, summary, tale, talking, telling, vindication, writing; SEE CONCEPTS *271,274,661*

explanatory [*adj*] *descriptive*
allegorical, analytical, annotative, critical, declarative, demonstrative, diagrammatic, discursive, elucidatory, enlightening, exegetic, exegetical, explicative, expositional, expository, graphic, guiding, hermeneutic, illuminative, illustrative, informative, informing, instructive, interpretive, justifying, summary, supplementary; SEE CONCEPT *267*

expletive [*n*] *swear word; exclamation*
curse, cuss, cuss word, interjection, oath; SEE CONCEPT *275*

explicate [*v*] *clarify, expand*
amplify, clear up, construe, demonstrate, develop, dilate, elucidate, enlarge upon, enucleate, expatiate, explain, expound, give the big picture*, illustrate, interpret, make clear, make explicit, make plain*, run down, spell out*, tell why, unfold, untangle, work out; SEE CONCEPT *57*

explicit [*adj*] *specific, unambiguous*
absolute, accurate, categorical, certain, clean-cut, clear, clear-cut, correct, definite, definitive, direct, distinct, exact, express, frank, lucid, obvious, on the nose*, open, outspoken, patent, perspicuous, plain, positive, precise, stated, straightforward, sure, understandable, unequivocal, unqualified, unreserved; SEE CONCEPTS *267,529,535*

explode [*v1*] *blow up*
backfire, blast, blaze, blow to kingdom come*, break out, burst, collapse, convulse, detonate, discharge, erupt, flame up, flare up, fracture, jet, kablooey*, let go*, mushroom*, rupture, set off, shatter, shiver, split, thunder; SEE CONCEPTS *179,320*

explode [*v2*] *discredit*
belie, confute, debunk, deflate, discard, disprove, invalidate, puncture, refute, repudiate, shoot down*, shoot full of holes*; SEE CONCEPT *54*

exploit [*n*] *achievement*
accomplishment, adventure, attainment, coup, deed, do, effort, enterprise, escapade, feat, job, maneuver, performance, stroke, stunt, tour de force, venture; SEE CONCEPT *706*

exploit [*v*] *take advantage of; misuse*
abuse, apply, avail oneself of, bleed*, capitalize on, cash in on*, employ, exercise, finesse, fleece*, get mileage out of*, handle, impose upon, jockey*, make capital of, make use of, maneuver, manipulate, milk*, mine*, play*, play on, profit by, profit from, put to use, skin*, soak*, stick*, use, utilize, work; SEE CONCEPTS *156,225*

exploitation [*n*] *taking advantage*
bleeding*, profiteering, using; SEE CONCEPTS *156,225*

exploration [*n*] *investigation; survey*
analysis, examination, expedition, inquiry, inspection, probe, reconnaissance, research, scrutiny, search, study, tour, travel, trip; SEE CONCEPTS *216,224*

explore [*v*] *investigate; survey*
analyze, burrow, delve into, dig into, examine, go into*, have a look*, hunt, inquire into, inspect, leave no stone unturned*, look into, probe, prospect, question, reconnoitre, research, scout, scrutinize, search, seek, sift, test, tour, travel, traverse, try, turn inside out*; SEE CONCEPTS *103,216,224*

explorer [*n*] *trailblazer*
adventurer, experimenter, inquisitive person, pathfinder, pilgrim, pioneer, searcher, seeker, traveler; SEE CONCEPTS *348,413*

explosion [*n*] *eruption, discharge*
access, backfire, bang, blast, blowout, blowup, burst, clap, combustion, concussion, crack, detonation, firing, fit, flare-up, fulmination, gust, ignition, outbreak, outburst, paroxysm, percussion, pop, report, roar, salvo; SEE CONCEPTS *179,320, 521*

explosive [*adj*] *volatile, dangerous*
at the boiling point*, bursting, charged, consequential, convulsive, detonating, detonative, ebullient, eruptive, fiery, forceful, frenzied, fulminant, fulminating, hazardous, impetuous, meteoric, overwrought, perilous, raging, rampant, stormy, tense, touchy, ugly, uncontrollable, unstable, vehement, violent, wild; SEE CONCEPT *542*

explosive [*n*] *something that blows up*
ammunition, bomb, booby trap*, charge, detonator, dynamite, fireworks, grease*, grenade, gunpowder, mine, missile, mulligan, munition, nitroglycerin, pineapple*, powder, propellant, shell, shot, soup*, TNT*; SEE CONCEPT *500*

exponent [*n1*] *person who supports, advocates*
backer, booster, champion, defender, demonstrator, expositor, expounder, interpreter, partisan, promoter, propagandist, proponent, protagonist, second, seconder, spokesperson, supporter, upholder; SEE CONCEPT *423*

exponent [*n2*] *example*
denotation, exemplar, illustration, index, indication, model, representative, sample, sign, specimen, token, type; SEE CONCEPTS *284,686*

export [*v*] *sell or trade abroad*
consign, convey, dump, find market, find outlet, freight, send out, ship, smuggle, transport, transship; SEE CONCEPTS *217,324*

exposé [*n*] *disclosure*
betrayal, confession, construction, divulgence, exegesis, explanation, explication, exposal, exposition, exposure, interpretation, revelation, truth, uncovering; SEE CONCEPT *274*

expose [*v1*] *reveal*
advertise, air, bare, betray, brandish, bring to light*, broadcast, crack, debunk, denude, dig up*, disclose, display, disport, divulge, exhibit, feature, flash, flaunt, give away, lay bare*, lay open*, leak, let cat out of bag*, let out*, make known, manifest, open, open to view, parade, present, prove, publish, put on view, report, show, show off, smoke out*, spill, streak, tip off*, trot out*, unclothe, uncover, unearth, unfold, unmask, unshroud, unveil; SEE CONCEPTS *60,261*

expose [*v2*] *subject to danger*
endanger, hazard, imperil, jeopardize, lay open*, leave open*, make liable, make vulnerable, peril, put in harm's way*, risk; SEE CONCEPT *246*

exposed [*adj1*] *made public*
apparent, bare, bared, brought to light*, caught, clear, debunked, defined, denuded, disclosed, discovered, divulged, dug up*, evident, exhibited, for show, found out, laid bare*, made manifest, manifest, naked, on display, on the spot*, on view, open, peeled, resolved, revealed, shown, solved, stripped, unconcealed, uncovered, unhidden, unmasked, unprotected, unsealed, unsheltered, unveiled, visible; SEE CONCEPT *576*

exposed [*adj2*] *in danger*
accessible, in peril, laid bare*, laid open*, left open*, liable, menaced, open, prone, sensitive, subject, susceptible, threatened, unguarded, unprotected, vulnerable; SEE CONCEPTS *485,548*

exposition [*n1*] *written description*
account, analysis, annotation, article, comment, commentary, composition, construal, construction, critique, delineation, details, discourse, discussion, disquisition, dissertation, editorial, elucidation, enucleation, enunciation, essay, exegesis, explanation, explication, exposé, expounding, history, illustration, interpretation, monograph, paper, piece, position paper, presentation, report, review, statement, story, study, tale, text, theme, thesis, tract, tractate, treatise; SEE CONCEPTS *268,271*

exposition [*n2*] *fair*
bazaar, circus, county fair, demonstration, display, exhibition, expo, marketplace, mart, pageant, presentation, production, show, showing; SEE CONCEPT *386*

expository [*adj*] *descriptive*
critical, disquisitional, elucidative, exegetic, explanatory, explicative, explicatory, hermeneutic, illustrative, informative, interpretive; SEE CONCEPT *267*

expostulate [*v*] *reason with*
argue, dissuade, oppose, protest, remonstrate; SEE CONCEPT *46*

exposure [*n*] *uncovering; putting in view or danger*
acknowledgment, airing, baring, betrayal, confession, defenselessness, denudation, denuncia-

ex
ex

tion, disclosure, display, divulgence, divulging, exhibition, exposé, giveaway, hazard, introduction, jeopardy, laying open, liability, manifestation, nakedness, openness, peril, presentation, publicity, revelation, risk, showing, susceptibility, susceptiveness, susceptivity, unfolding, unmasking, unveiling, vulnerability, vulnerableness; SEE CONCEPTS *60,261*

expound [*v*] *talk about in great detail*
clarify, comment, construe, delineate, describe, discourse, elucidate, enucleate, exemplify, explain, explicate, express, illustrate, interpret, present, set forth, spell out, state, unfold; SEE CONCEPT *57*

express [*adj1*] *certain, precise*
accurate, categorical, clean-cut*, clear, clear-cut, considered, definite, definitive, deliberate, designful, direct, distinct, especial, exact, explicit, expressed, individual, intended, intentional, out-and-out*, outright, particular, plain, pointed, premeditated, set, singular, special, specific, unambiguous, unconditional, unmistakable, unqualified, uttered, voiced, voluntary, willing, witting; SEE CONCEPTS *535,556,653*

express [*adj2*] *direct, speedy*
accelerated, fast, high-speed, nonstop, quick, rapid, swift, velocious; SEE CONCEPTS *548,588*

express [*v1*] *articulate; signify, mean*
add up to*, air, assert, asseverate, bespeak, broach, circulate, communicate, connote, convey, couch, declare, denote, depict, designate, disclose, divulge, embody, enunciate, evince, exhibit, formulate, frame*, give, hint, import, indicate, insinuate, intend, intimate, make known, manifest, phrase, pop off*, proclaim, pronounce, put, put across, put into words*, represent, reveal, say, show, speak, spell, stand for, state, suggest, symbolize, tell, testify, utter, vent, ventilate, verbalize, voice, word; SEE CONCEPTS *51,682*

express [*v2*] *discharge by squeezing or force*
crush, dispatch, distill, expel, extract, force out, forward, press out, ship, squeeze out; SEE CONCEPT *179*

expression [*n1*] *verbalization*
announcement, argument, articulation, assertion, asseveration, choice of words, commentary, communication, declaration, definition, delivery, diction, elucidation, emphasis, enunciation, execution, explanation, exposition, formulation, idiom, interpretation, intonation, issue, language, locution, mention, narration, phrase, phraseology, phrasing, pronouncement, remark, rendition, set phrase, speaking, speech, statement, style, term, turn of phrase, utterance, vent, voice, voicing, word, writ; SEE CONCEPTS *47,268,276*

expression [*n2*] *facial appearance*
air, aspect, cast, character, contortion, countenance, face, grimace, grin, look, mien, mug*, pout*, simper, smile, smirk, sneer, visage; SEE CONCEPT *716*

expressionless [*adj*] *having a blank look on face*
dead*, deadpan, dull, empty, fish-eyed*, impassive, inexpressive, inscrutable, lackluster, lusterless, nobody home*, poker-faced*, stolid, straight-faced, stupid, unexpressive, vacant, vacuous, wooden; SEE CONCEPT *406*

expressive [*adj*] *telling, revealing*
alive, allusive, articulate, artistic, brilliant, colorful, demonstrative, dramatic, eloquent, emphatic,

energetic, forcible, graphic, indicative, ingenious, lively, masterly, meaningful, mobile, moving, passionate, pathetic, pictorial, picturesque, poignant, pointed, pregnant, representative, responsive, revelatory, showy, significant, silver-tongued*, spirited, stimulating, stirring, striking, strong, suggestive, sympathetic, tender, thoughtful, touching, understanding, vivid, warm; SEE CONCEPTS *267,537*

expressly [*adv1*] *purposely*
especially, exactly, in specie, intentionally, on purpose, particularly, precisely, specially, specifically; SEE CONCEPT *556*

expressly [*adv2*] *definitely, unambiguously*
absolutely, categorically, clearly, decidedly, directly, distinctly, explicitly, in no uncertain terms*, manifestly, outright, plainly, pointedly, positively, specifically, unequivocally, unmistakably; SEE CONCEPT *535*

expressway [*n*] *large, well-travelled road*
freeway, interstate, parkway, superhighway, thruway, turnpike; SEE CONCEPT *501*

expropriate [*v*] *seize*
accroach, annex, appropriate, arrogate, assume, commandeer, confiscate, deprive of property, dispossess, impound, preempt, requisition, sequester, take, take over; SEE CONCEPTS *90,142*

expulsion [*n*] *banishing*
banishment, boot*, bounce, debarment, deportment, discharge, dislodgment, dismissal, displacement, dispossession, driving out, ejection, eviction, exclusion, exile, expatriation, extrusion, forcing out, ostracism, ouster, ousting, proscription, purge, relegation, removal, rush, suspension; SEE CONCEPTS *130,211,298*

expunge [*v*] *destroy, obliterate*
abolish, annihilate, annul, black, black out*, blot out, blue pencil*, call all bets off*, call off, cancel, cut, delete, discard, drop, efface, eradicate, erase, exclude, exterminate, extinguish, extirpate, gut, kayo*, kill, knock off*, KO*, launder*, omit, raze, remove, scrub*, strike out, take out, trim, wipe out, X out*, zap*; SEE CONCEPTS *211,252*

expurgate [*v*] *censor, cut*
bleep*, bleep out*, blip*, blue pencil*, bowdlerize, cleanse, clean up, decontaminate, lustrate, purge, purify, sanitize, screen, scrub*, squash, sterilize; SEE CONCEPTS *165,232*

exquisite [*adj1*] *beautiful, excellent, finely detailed*
admirable, attractive, charming, choice, comely, consummate, cultivated, dainty, delicate, delicious, discerning, discriminating, elegant, errorless, ethereal, fastidious, fine, flawless, impeccable, incomparable, irreproachable, lovely, matchless, meticulous, outstanding, peerless, perfect, pleasing, polished, precious, precise, rare, recherché, refined, select, selective, splendid, striking, subtle, superb, superior, superlative; SEE CONCEPTS *574,579,589*

exquisite [*adj2*] *intense*
acute, concentrated, consummate, desperate, excruciating, extreme, fierce, furious, keen, piercing, poignant, sharp, terrible, transcending, vehement, vicious, violent; SEE CONCEPT *569*

extant [*adj*] *in existence*
actual, alive, around, being, contemporary, current, existent, existing, immediate, in current use, instant, living, not lost, present, present-day,

real, remaining, subsisting, surviving, undestroyed; SEE CONCEPTS *539,582*

extemporaneous/extemporary [*adj*] *unrehearsed, improvised*
ad hoc, ad lib, at first glance, automatic, by ear*, casual, expedient, extempore, free, immediate, impromptu, improv*, improvisatory, improviso, informal, jamming*, made-up, makeshift, offhand, off the cuff*, off the top of head*, on impulse, on-the-spot*, snap, spontaneous, spur-of-the-moment*, taking for ride*, thought out loud*, tossed off*, tossed out*, unplanned, unpremeditated, unprepared, unstudied, winging it*; SEE CONCEPTS *267,799*

extemporize [*v*] *improvise*
ad-lib, dash out, devise, do offhand*, improvisate, invent, knock off*, make up, play by ear*, toss off*; SEE CONCEPT *51*

extend [*v1*] *make larger, longer*
add to, aggrandize, amplify, augment, beef up*, boost, broaden, carry on, continue, crane, develop, dilate, drag one's feet*, drag out, draw, draw out, elongate, enhance, enlarge, expand, fan out, go on, heighten, increase, last, lengthen, let out, magnify, mantle, multiply, open, pad, prolong, prolongate, protract, run on, spin out, spread, spread out, stall, stretch, string out, supplement, take, unfold, unfurl, unroll, widen; SEE CONCEPTS *236,239,245*

extend [*v2*] *offer*
accord, advance, allocate, allot, award, bestow, bring forward, confer, donate, give, grant, hold out, impart, place at disposal, pose, present, proffer, put forth, put forward, reach out, stretch out, submit, tender, yield; SEE CONCEPTS *66,67*

extended [*adj1*] *lengthened*
continued, drawn-out, elongate, elongated, enlarged, lengthy, long, prolonged, protracted, spread, spread out, stretched out, unfolded, unfurled, very long; SEE CONCEPTS *782,798*

extended [*adj2*] *widespread, comprehensive*
broad, enlarged, expanded, expansive, extensive, far-flung, far-reaching, large-scale, outspread, scopic, scopious, spread, sweeping, thorough, wide; SEE CONCEPT *772*

extension [*n*] *enlargement, continuation*
addendum, addition, adjunct, amplification, annex, appendage, appendix, arm, augmentation, branch, broadening, compass, continuing, delay, development, dilatation, distension, drawing out, elongation, expansion, extent, increase, lengthening, orbit, postponement, production, prolongation, protraction, purview, radius, reach, scope, span, spreading out, stretch, stretching, supplement, sweep, widening, wing; SEE CONCEPTS *236,245,824*

extensive [*adj*] *far-reaching, thorough*
across the board*, all-encompassing, all-inclusive, big, blanket*, boundless, broad, capacious, commodious, comprehensive, comprising, considerable, expanded, extended, far-flung*, general, great, hefty, huge, inclusive, indiscriminate, large, large-scale, lengthy, long, major, pervasive, prevalent, protracted, roomy, scopic, scopious, sizable, spacious, sweeping, unexclusive, universal, unrestricted, vast, voluminous, wall to wall*, wholesale, wide, wide-ranging, widespread; SEE CONCEPTS *772,773*

extent [*n*] *range, magnitude*
admeasurement, ambit, amount, amplitude, area, bounds, breadth, bulk, capaciousness, compass, degree, dimensions, duration, elbowroom*, expanse, expansion, extension, intensity, leeway, length, limit, mass, matter, measure, neighborhood, orbit, order, period of time, play, proliferation, proportions, purview, quantity, radius, reach, scope, size, space, spaciousness, span, sphere, stretch, sweep, term, territory, time, tract, tune, vicinity, volume, wideness, width; SEE CONCEPTS *651,730,743,745,783,788,804*

extenuate [*v*] *lessen, mitigate*
decrease, diminish, downplay, excuse, justify, make allowances, minimize, moderate, palliate, qualify, reduce, soften; SEE CONCEPTS *247,698,776*

extenuating [*adj*] *serving as an excuse*
condoning, diminishing, justifying, lessening, mitigating, moderating, palliating, qualifying, reducing, sanitizing, softening, varnishing, whitewashing*; SEE CONCEPT *537*

exterior [*adj*] *outside*
exoteric, external, extraneous, extraterrestrial, extraterritorial, extrinsic, foreign, marginal, outdoor, outer, outermost, outlying, outmost, outward, over, peripheral, superficial, surface; SEE CONCEPT *583*

exterior [*n*] *visible part*
appearance, aspect, coating, cover, covering, exteriority, external, facade, face, finish, outside, polish, rind, shell, skin, superficies, superstratum, surface; SEE CONCEPT *484*

exterminate [*v*] *kill*
abolish, annihilate, blot out*, decimate, destroy, do away with*, eliminate, eradicate, erase, execute, extinguish, extirpate, finish off, massacre, obliterate, put an end to*, rub out*, send to kingdom come*, slaughter, stamp out*, wipe out*; SEE CONCEPT *252*

external [*adj*] *outside, extrinsic*
alien, apparent, exterior, extraneous, foreign, independent, out, outer, outermost, outmost, outward, over, peripheral, superficial, surface, visible; SEE CONCEPT *583*

extinct [*adj*] *dead, obsolete*
abolished, archaic, asleep, bygone, cold*, dead and gone*, deceased, defunct, departed, disappeared, done for*, doused, ended, exanimate, exterminated, extinguished, fallen, gone, inactive, late, lifeless, lost, no longer known, out, outmoded, passé, passed on, snuffed out*, superseded, terminated, unknown, vanished, vanquished, void; SEE CONCEPT *539*

extinction [*n*] *dying out*
annihilation, death, destruction, elimination, end of life, no life, obsolescence, thing of the past*; SEE CONCEPT *252*

extinguish [*v1*] *put out a fire*
blot out, blow out, choke, douse, drown, out, quench, smother, snuff out, stamp out, stifle, suffocate, trample; SEE CONCEPT *256*

extinguish [*v2*] *kill; quash*
abate, abolish, annihilate, blot out*, check, crush, destroy, eliminate, end, eradicate, erase, expunge, exterminate, extirpate, obliterate, obscure, put down, put the lid on*, quell, remove, squash, stamp out, suppress, wipe out*; SEE CONCEPTS *95,252*

extirpate [*v*] *destroy; uproot*
abate, abolish, annihilate, blot out*, cut out, demolish, deracinate, efface, eliminate, eradicate,

ex
ex

erase, excise, expunge, exsect, exterminate, extinguish, kill, raze, remove, root out, wipe out*; SEE CONCEPTS *211,252*

extol [v] *sing the praises of*
acclaim, applaud, bless, boost, brag about, celebrate, commend, cry up*, eulogize, exalt, give a boost to, give a bouquet*, glorify, hand it to*, hats off to*, hear it for*, hymn, laud, magnify, make much of, panegyrize, pay tribute to, praise, puff up*, push, rave, root, stroke*; SEE CONCEPT *69*

extort [v] *cheat; blackmail*
bleed*, bully, clip, coerce, demand, educe, elicit, evince, exact, extract, fleece, force, get, gouge, hold up*, ice*, make pay through nose*, milk*, obtain, pinch, pull one's leg*, put screws to*, put the arm on*, secure, shake down*, skin*, soak, squeeze, stick, sting, wrench, wrest, wring; SEE CONCEPTS *53,59,139,342*

extortion [n] *blackmail; cheating*
arm, badger, bite, coercion, compulsion, demand, exaction, force, fraud, oppression, payoff, payola*, pressure, protection, racket, rapacity, shake, shakedown*, squeeze, stealing, swindle, theft; SEE CONCEPTS *53,139,192,342*

extra [adj] *accessory; excess*
added, additional, ancillary, another, auxiliary, beyond, button*, extraneous, extraordinary, fresh, further, fuss*, gingerbread*, gravy*, ice*, in addition, inessential, in reserve, in store, lagniappe*, leftover, more, needless, new, one more, optional, other, over and above*, perk*, plus, redundant, reserve, spare, special, superfluous, supernumerary, supplemental, supplementary, surplus, tip, unnecessary, unneeded, unused; SEE CONCEPTS *546,771*

extra [adv] *particularly*
considerably, especially, exceptionally, extraordinarily, extremely, markedly, noticeably, rarely, remarkably, uncommon, uncommonly, unusually; SEE CONCEPTS *557,569*

extra [n] *accessory*
addendum, addition, adjunct, affix, appendage, appurtenance, attachment, bonus, complement, extension, supernumerary, supplement; SEE CONCEPT *824*

extract [n] *something condensed from whole*
abstract, citation, clipping, concentrate, cutting, decoction, distillate, distillation, elicitation, essence, excerpt, infusion, juice*, passage, quotation, selection; SEE CONCEPTS *270,835*

extract [v1] *physically remove, draw out*
avulse, bring out, catheterize, cull, derive, distill, eke out, elicit, eradicate, evoke, evulse, exact, express, extirpate, extort, extricate, garner, gather, get, glean, obtain, pick up, pluck, press out, pry, pull, reap, secure, select, separate, siphon, squeeze, take, tear, uproot, weed out*, withdraw, wrest, wring, yank; SEE CONCEPTS *206,211*

extract [v2] *select a quotation*
abridge, abstract, bring forth, choose, cite, condense, copy, cull, cut out, deduce, derive, educe, elicit, evolve, excerpt, glean, quote, shorten; SEE CONCEPTS *79,142,211*

extraction [n1] *removal from whole; distillation*
abstraction, derivation, drawing, elicitation, eradication, evocation, evulsion, expression, extirpation, extrication, pulling, separation, taking

out, uprooting, withdrawal, wrenching, wresting; SEE CONCEPT *211*

extraction [n2] *ancestry, origin*
birth, blood, derivation, descent, family, lineage, parentage, pedigree, race, stock; SEE CONCEPTS *296,648*

extradite [v] *send to another place by force*
abandon, apprehend, arrest, bring to justice, bring to trial, deliver, give up, release, surrender; SEE CONCEPTS *217,317*

extraneous [adj1] *unneeded; irrelevant*
accidental, additional, adventitious, beside the point, extra, foreign, immaterial, impertinent, inadmissible, inapplicable, inapposite, inappropriate, incidental, inessential, needless, nonessential, off the subject, peripheral, pointless, redundant, superfluous, supplementary, unconnected, unessential, unnecessary, unrelated; SEE CONCEPT *546*

extraneous [adj2] *foreign*
adventitious, alien, exotic, external, extrinsic, out of place, strange; SEE CONCEPT *549*

extraordinary [adj] *strange and wonderful*
amazing, bizarre, boss*, curious, exceptional, fab*, fantastic, flash*, gnarly*, heavy*, inconceivable, incredible, marvelous, odd, off beaten path*, out of the ordinary, outstanding, particular, peculiar, phenomenal, rare, remarkable, singular, special, strange, stupendous, surprising, terrific, uncommon, unfamiliar, unheard-of, unimaginable, unique, unprecedented, unthinkable, unusual, unwonted, weird, wicked*; SEE CONCEPTS *564,572*

extrapolate [v] *infer*
anticipate, assume, conclude, deduce, envision, figure, foresee, foretell, guess, hypothesize, make an educated guess*, predict, project, see ahead, theorize; SEE CONCEPTS *12,15,37*

extrasensory perception [n] *psychic powers*
clairvoyance, ESP, intuition, keen intuition, second sight, sixth sense, telepathy, vision; SEE CONCEPTS *409,410*

extraterrestrial [n] *alien*
E.T.*, little green man*, Martian, men from outer space*, space being, space inhabitant; SEE CONCEPT *423*

extravagance [n] *indulgence; waste*
absurdity, amenity, dissipation, exaggeration, excess, exorbitance, expenditure, folly, frill, icing on the cake*, immoderation, improvidence, lavishness, luxury, outrageousness, overdoing, overindulgence, overspending, preposterousness, prodigality, profligacy, profusion, recklessness, squander, squandering, superfluity, unreasonableness, unrestraint, unthrift, wastefulness, wildness; SEE CONCEPTS *335,337,787*

extravagant [adj] *indulgent, wasteful*
absurd, bizarre, costly, crazy, exaggerated, excessive, exorbitant, expensive, extortionate, extreme, fanciful, fancy, fantastic, flamboyant, flashy, foolish, garish, gaudy, grandiose, immoderate, implausible, improvident, imprudent, inordinate, lavish, ludicrous, nonsensical, ornate, ostentatious, outrageous, overpriced, preposterous, pretentious, prodigal, profligate, reckless, ridiculous, showy, silly, spendthrift, steep, unbalanced, unconscionable, unreasonable, unrestrained; SEE CONCEPTS *334,560,771*

extravaganza [n] *spectacle*
caricature, display, divertissement, flight of

fancy*, pageant, parody, show, spectacular; SEE CONCEPTS *263,293*

extreme [*adj1*] *very great*
acute, consummate, high, highest, intense, maximal, maximum, severe, sovereign, supreme, top, ultimate, utmost, uttermost; SEE CONCEPTS *569,771,781*

extreme [*adj2*] *beyond reason and convention*
absolute, desperate, dire, downright, drastic, egregious, exaggerated, exceptional, excessive, extraordinary, extravagant, fabulous, fanatical, flagrant, gross, harsh, immoderate, improper, imprudent, inordinate, intemperate, irrational, nonsensical, out-and-out*, out of proportion, outrageous, overkill, preposterous, rabid, radical, remarkable, rigid, severe, sheer, stern, strict, thorough, unbending, uncommon, uncompromising, unconventional, unreasonable, unseemly, unusual, utter, zealous; SEE CONCEPTS *547,558, 569*

extreme [*adj3*] *faraway*
far-off, farthest, final, furthermost, last, most distant, outermost, outmost, remotest, terminal, ultimate, utmost, uttermost; SEE CONCEPT *778*

extreme [*n*] *ultimate; limit*
acme, apex, apogee, bitter end, boundary, ceiling, climax, consummation, crest, crown, culmination, depth, edge, end, excess, extremity, height, inordinacy, maximum, nadir, nth degree*, peak, pinnacle, pole, termination, top, utmost, uttermost, zenith; SEE CONCEPTS *484,706, 745,836*

extremely [*adv*] *greatly, intensely*
acutely, almighty, awfully, drastically, exceedingly, exceptionally, excessively, exorbitantly, extraordinarily, highly, hugely, immensely, immoderately, inordinately, intensely, markedly, mortally, notably, over, overly, overmuch, parlous, plenty, powerful, prohibitively, quite, radically, rarely, remarkably, severely, strikingly, surpassingly, terribly, terrifically, to nth degree*, too, too much*, totally, ultra*, uncommonly, unduly, unusually, utterly, very*, violently, vitally; SEE CONCEPTS *569,771,781*

extremist [*n*] *person zealous about a belief*
agitator, die-hard, fanatic, radical, revolutionary, revolutionist, ultra, ultraist, zealot; SEE CONCEPTS *359,423*

extremity [*n1*] *ultimate; limit*
acme, acuteness, adversity, apex, apogee, border, bound, boundary, brim, brink, butt, climax, consummation, crisis, depth, dire straits, disaster, edge, end, excess, extreme, extremes, frontier, height, last, margin, maximum, nadir, outside, pinnacle, plight, pole, remote, rim, setback, terminal, termination, terminus, tip, top, trouble, verge, vertex, zenith; SEE CONCEPTS *484,706,745,836*

extremity [*n2*] *animate being's appendage*
backside, finger, flipper, foot, hand, leg, limb, paw, posterior, toe; SEE CONCEPT *392*

extricate [*v*] *get out of a situation; relieve of responsibility*
bail out*, clear, deliver, detach, difference, differentiate, disburden, discumber, disembarrass, disencumber, disengage, disentangle, disinvolve, extract, free, get off the hook*, get out from under*, let go, let off*, liberate, loose, loosen, pull out, release, remove, rescue, resolve, save

one's neck*, separate, sever, untie, withdraw, wriggle out of*; SEE CONCEPTS *102,127*

extrinsic [*adj*] *foreign*
acquired, alien, exotic, exterior, external, extraneous, gained, imported, outer, outside, outward, superficial; SEE CONCEPT *549*

extrovert [*n*] *sociable person*
character*, exhibitionist, gregarious person, life of the party*, showboat*, show-off*; SEE CONCEPT *423*

extroverted [*adj*] *outgoing*
congenial, cordial, demonstrative, friendly, gregarious, personable, sociable, social, unreserved; SEE CONCEPT *404*

extrude [*v*] *force out*
boot*, chase, dismiss, eject, evict, expel, kick out, press, project, squeeze*, throw out, thrust; SEE CONCEPTS *208,222*

exuberance [*n1*] *energy, enthusiasm*
abandon, animation, ardor, bounce, buoyancy, cheerfulness, eagerness, ebullience, effervescence, excitement, exhilaration, fervor, friskiness, gayness, get up and go*, high spirits, juice*, life, liveliness, pep, pepper*, spirit, sprightliness, vigor, vitality, zap*, zest*, zip*; SEE CONCEPT *633*

exuberance [*n2*] *profusion*
abundance, affluence, copiousness, effusiveness, exaggeration, excessiveness, fulsomeness, lavishness, lushness, luxuriance, plenitude, plenty, prodigality, richness, superabundance, superfluity, teemingness; SEE CONCEPTS *710,767*

exuberant [*adj1*] *energetic, enthusiastic*
animated, ardent, bouncy, brash, buoyant, cheerful, chipper, eager, ebullient, effervescent, elated, excited, exhilarated, feeling one's oats*, frolicsome, gay, high-spirited, lively, passionate, sparkling, spirited, sprightly, vigorous, vivacious, zappy*, zestful, zingy*, zippy*; SEE CONCEPT *401*

exuberant [*adj2*] *profuse*
abundant, affluent, copious, diffuse, effusive, exaggerated, excessive, fecund, fertile, fruitful, fulsome, lavish, lush, luxuriant, opulent, overdone, overflowing, plenteous, plentiful, prodigal, prolific, rampant, rich, riotous, superabundant, superfluous, teeming; SEE CONCEPT *781*

exude [*v*] *display, emit*
bleed, discharge, emanate, evacuate, excrete, exhibit, expel, flow out, give forth, give off, issue, leak, manifest, ooze, pass, percolate, radiate, secrete, seep, show, sweat, throw off, trickle, weep; SEE CONCEPTS *118,179*

exult [*v1*] *be joyful*
be delighted, be elated, be happy, be in high spirits*, be jubilant, be overjoyed, celebrate, cheer, jubilate, jump for joy*, make merry*, rejoice; SEE CONCEPTS *32,266*

exult [*v2*] *boast*
bluster, brag, bully, crow, gloat, glory, revel, show off, take delight in*, triumph, vaunt; SEE CONCEPT *49*

exultant [*adj*] *very happy*
blown away*, delighted, ecstatic, elated, exulting, flipping, flushed, flying, gleeful, high, joyful, joyous, jubilant, overjoyed, rejoicing, revelling, transported, triumphant, turned on*, wowed*; SEE CONCEPT *403*

exultation [*n*] *celebration, reveling*
crowing, delight, elation, glee, gloating, glory,

ex
ex

happiness, high spirits, joy, joyousness, jubilance, jubilation, merriment, rejoicing, satisfaction, transport, triumph; SEE CONCEPTS *32,410*

eye [*n1*] *judgment, opinion*
appreciation, belief, conviction, discernment, discrimination, eagle eye*, feeling, mind, perception, persuasion, point of view, recognition, scrutiny, sentiment, surveillance, tab, taste, view, viewpoint, watch; SEE CONCEPTS *411,689*

eye [*n2*] *optical organ of an animate being*
baby blue*, blinder*, eyeball*, headlight*, lamp*, ocular, oculus, optic, peeper*, pie*; SEE CONCEPT *392*

eye [*v*] *gaze at, scrutinize*
check out, consider, contemplate, eyeball*, gape, give the eye*, glance at, have a look, inspect, keep eagle eye on*, leer, look at, ogle, peruse, regard, rubberneck*, scan, size up*, stare at, study, survey, take a look, take in, view, watch; SEE CONCEPTS *17,623,626*

eye-catching [*adj*] *noticeable*
attractive, beautiful, can't miss it*, conspicuous, gorgeous, manifest, obvious, showy, spectacular, striking, stunning; SEE CONCEPTS *529,579*

eyeful [*n*] *spectacular-looking person*
beauty, dazzler*, knockout*, looker, lovely, show, spectacle, stunner*, vision; SEE CONCEPT *424*

eyeglasses [*n*] *glasses*
bifocals, cheaters*, contact lenses, contacts, goggles, lorgnette, monocle, pair of glasses, pince-nez, reading glasses, shades, specs*, spectacles, sunglasses, trifocals; SEE CONCEPT *446*

eyesight [*n*] *vision*
optics, perceiving, perception, range of view, seeing, sight, view; SEE CONCEPT *629*

eyesore [*n*] *mess, ugliness*
atrocity, blemish, blight, blot, blot on landscape*, deformity, disfigurement, disgrace, distortion, dump, horror, monstrosity, sight, ugly thing; SEE CONCEPTS *674,716*

eyewitness [*n*] *person who sees an event occur*
beholder, bystander, looker-on, observer, onlooker, passer-by, spectator, viewer, watcher, witness; SEE CONCEPT *423*

F

fable [*n*] *fantasy, story*
allegory, apologue, bestiary, bunk*, crock*, fabrication, fairy story, fairy tale, falsehood, fantasy, fib, fiction, figment, fish story*, hogwash*, invention, legend, lie, myth, old chestnut*, old saw*, one for the birds*, parable, romance, tale, tall story, untruth, white lie*, whopper*, yarn; SEE CONCEPT *282*

fabled [*adj*] *legendary*
fabulous, famed, famous, fanciful, fictional, mythical, mythological, storied, unreal; SEE CONCEPT *568*

fabric [*n1*] *cloth, material*
bolt, fiber, goods, stuff, textile, texture, web; SEE CONCEPT *473*

fabric [*n2*] *structure*
building, consistency, constitution, construction, foundation, frame, framework, infrastructure, make-up, mold, organization, stamp, substance, texture; SEE CONCEPTS *733,757*

fabricate [*v1*] *manufacture*
assemble, brainstorm, build, cobble up*, compose, concoct, construct, contrive, cook up*, create, devise, dream up, erect, fashion, fit together, form, formulate, frame, head trip*, invent, join, knock together*, make, make up, mix, organize, piece together, prefab*, produce, put together, shape, structure, think up, throw together*, throw up*, turn out, whip up*, whomp up*; SEE CONCEPTS *36,173,205,251*

fabricate [*v2*] *falsify, make up a story*
coin, concoct, contrive, counterfeit, devise, fake, feign, fib, forge, form, fudge*, invent, jive*, lie, make like*, misrepresent, pretend, prevaricate, trump up*; SEE CONCEPTS *58,63*

fabrication [*n1*] *lie*
artifact, concoction, deceit, fable, fairy story*, fake*, falsehood, fib, fiction, figment, forgery, hogwash*, invention, jazz*, jive*, line*, myth, opus, smoke*, song and dance*, untruth, work, yarn; SEE CONCEPTS *63,278*

fabrication [*n2*] *something manufactured*
assemblage, assembly, building, construction, creation, erection, product, production; SEE CONCEPTS *205,260,338*

fabulous [*adj*] *amazing, wonderful*
10*, A-1*, aces*, A-OK*, astonishing, astounding, awesome, best, breathtaking, cool*, doozie*, extravagant, fab*, fantastic, fictitious, first-class, greatest, groovy*, immense, inconceivable, incredible, legendary, marvelous, mind-blowing*, out-of-sight*, out-of-this-world*, outrageous, peachy*, phenomenal, primo*, prodigious, rad*, remarkable, spectacular, striking, stupendous, super, superb, terrific, top drawer*, tops*, turn-on*, unbelievable, unreal, wicked*; SEE CONCEPTS *529,572*

facade [*n*] *appearance, often deceptive*
beard*, bluff, color, disguise, exterior, face, fake, false colors*, false front*, front, frontage, guise, look, mask, phony, pretense, put-on*, semblance, show, veneer, window dressing*; SEE CONCEPT *716*

face [*n1*] *front of something; expression, exterior*
air, appearance, aspect, cast, clock, countenance, dial*, disguise, display, facet, features, finish, frontage*, frontal, frontispiece, frown, glower, grimace, guise, kisser*, light*, lineaments, look, makeup, map*, mask, mug*, obverse, paint*, physiognomy, pout, presentation, profile, scowl, seeming, semblance, show, showing, silhouette, simulacrum, smirk, surface, top, visage; SEE CONCEPTS *484,716,836*

face [*n2*] *pretense, nerve*
air, audacity, boldness, brass*, cheek*, chutzpah*, cloak, confidence, cover, disguise, effrontery, facade, false front*, front, gall, impertinence, impudence, mask, presumption, semblance, show, veil; SEE CONCEPTS *633,657*

face [*n3*] *authority, status*
dignity, honor, image, prestige, reputation, self-respect, social position, standing; SEE CONCEPT *388*

face [*v1*] *come up against a situation*
abide, accost, affront, allow, bear, beard, be confronted by, bit the bullet*, brace, brave, brook, challenge, confront, contend, cope with, counte-

nance, court, cross, dare, deal with, defy, encounter, endure, experience, eyeball*, fight, fly in face of*, go up against*, grapple with, make a stand*, meet, oppose, resist, risk, run into, square off*, stand, stomach*, submit, suffer, sustain, swallow*, take, take it, take on, take the bull by the horns*, tell off*, tolerate, venture, withstand; SEE CONCEPTS *23,35,117*

face [*v2*] *be opposite; look at*
be turned toward, border, confront, front, front onto, gaze, glare, meet, overlook, stare, watch; SEE CONCEPTS *623,747*

face [*v3*] *put paint or finish on*
clad, coat, cover, decorate, dress, finish, front, level, line, overlay, plaster, polish, redecorate, refinish, remodel, sheathe, shingle, side, skin, smooth, surface, veneer; SEE CONCEPTS *172,202*

face-lift [*n*] *beautification; cosmetic surgery*
new look, nose job, plastic surgery, renovation, repair, restoration, revival, rhytidectomy; SEE CONCEPT *162*

facet [*n*] *surface; aspect*
angle, appearance, character, face, feature, front, hand, level, obverse, part, phase, plane, side, slant, switch, twist; SEE CONCEPT *835*

face the music [*v*] *face up to*
be punished, bite the bullet*, grin and bear it*, pay the piper*, swallow the pill*, take one's lumps*, take one's medicine*; SEE CONCEPT *23*

facetious [*adj*] *tongue-in-cheek, kidding*
amusing, blithe, capering, clever, comic, comical, droll, dry, fanciful, farcical, flip*, flippant, frivolous, funny, gay, humorous, indecorous, ironic, irreverent, jesting, jocose, jocular, joking, joshing, laughable, ludicrous, merry, not serious, playful, pleasant, pulling one's leg*, punning, putting one on*, ridiculous, salty, sarcastic, satirical, smart, sportive, sprightly, waggish, whimsical, wisecracking, witty, wry; SEE CONCEPT *267*

facile [*adj*] *easy; easily mastered*
accomplished, adept, adroit, apparent, articulate, breeze, child's play*, cursory, deft, dexterous, easy as pie*, effortless, fast talk*, flip*, fluent, glib, hasty, light, obvious, picnic*, practiced, proficient, pushover*, quick, ready, shallow, simple, skillful, slick*, smooth, superficial, uncomplicated, untroublesome, voluble; SEE CONCEPTS *527,565*

facilitate [*v*] *assist the progress of*
aid, ease, expedite, forward, further, grease the wheels*, hand-carry*, help, make easy, open doors*, promote, run interference for*, simplify, smooth, speed, speed up, walk through*; SEE CONCEPTS *110,242*

facility [*n1*] *ease; ability*
address, adroitness, aptitude, bent, child's play*, competence, dexterity, efficiency, effortlessness, expertness, fluency, knack, leaning, lightness, poise, proficiency, propensity, quickness, readiness, skill, skillfulness, smoothness, smooth sailing*, spontaneity, tact, turn, wit; SEE CONCEPTS *630,666*

facility [*n2*] *convenience*
accommodation, advantage, aid, amenity, appliance, comfort, equipment, fitting, material, means, opportunity, resource, tool; SEE CONCEPTS *693,712*

facsimile [*n*] *reproduction*
carbon, carbon copy*, chip off old block*, clone, copy, copycat*, dead ringer*, ditto*, double,

dupe*, duplicate, knock-off*, likeness, lookalike, mimeo, miniature, mirror, photocopy, photostat, print, reduplication, replica, replication, repro*, ringer*, spitting image*, stat, transcript, twin, Xerox*; SEE CONCEPTS *271,625,716*

fact [*n1*] *verifiable truth; reality*
actuality, appearance, authenticity, basis, bottom line*, brass tacks*, case, certainty, certitude, concrete happening, dope*, evidence, experience, genuineness, gospel, gospel truth*, how it is*, intelligence, law, like it is*, matter*, naked truth*, palpability, permanence, scene, scripture, solidity, stability, substantiality, verity, what's what*; SEE CONCEPTS *688,725*

fact [*n2*] *event; detail of action*
accomplishment, act, action, actuality, adventure, affair, being, case, circumstance, conception, consideration, construction, creation, data, datum, deed, entity, episode, evidence, experience, factor, fait accompli, feature, happening, incident, information, item, manifestation, occurrence, organism, particular, performance, phenomenon, point, proceeding, specific, statistic, transaction, truism; SEE CONCEPTS *2,274,433*

faction [*n1*] *group sharing a belief or cause*
band, bloc, bunch, cabal, camp, caucus, cell, circle, clan, clique, club, coalition, combination, combine, combo, concern, conclave, confederacy, conspiracy, contingent, coterie, crew, crowd, design, division, entente, gang, guild, insiders, intrigue, junta, knot, lobby, machine, minority, mob, network, offshoot, outfit, partnership, party, pressure group, ring, schism, sect, section, sector, set, side, splinter group, team, unit, wing; SEE CONCEPTS *301,387*

faction [*n2*] *conflict, strife*
disagreement, discord, disharmony, dissension, disunity, division, divisiveness, friction, infighting, quarrelsomeness, rebellion, sedition, tumult, turbulence; SEE CONCEPTS *106,684*

factious [*adj*] *conflicting, warring*
alienated, belligerent, contending, contentious, contumacious, disaffected, disputatious, dissident, divisive, estranged, fighting, hostile, insubordinate, insurgent, insurrectionary, litigious, malcontent, mutinous, partisan, quarrelsome, rebellious, refractory, rival, sectarian, seditious, troublemaking, tumultous/tumultuous, turbulent; SEE CONCEPT *542*

factor [*n*] *determinant*
agency, agent, aid, antecedent, aspect, board, cause, circumstance, component, consideration, constituent, element, fixin's*, influence, ingredient, instrument, instrumentality, item, makin's*, means, part, part and parcel*, point, portion, thing; SEE CONCEPTS *831,835*

factory [*n*] *manufacturing plant*
branch, cooperative, firm, forge, foundry, industry, laboratory, machine shop, manufactory, mill, mint, salt mines*, shop, sweatshop*, warehouse, workroom, works, workshop; SEE CONCEPTS *439,441,449*

facts [*n*] *inside information*
bottom line*, brass tacks*, certainty, clue, cue, data, details, dope*, gospel, info*, inside dope*, like it is*, lowdown*, numbers, poop*, reality, scoop*, score*, story, whole story*; SEE CONCEPT *274*

factual [*adj*] *real, correct*
absolute, accurate, actual, authentic, card-carry-

ing*, certain, circumstantial, close, credible, descriptive, exact, faithful, genuine, hard, kosher*, legit*, legitimate, literal, objective, on the level*, positive, precise, righteous, specific, straight from horse's mouth*, sure, sure-enough*, true, true-to-life*, unadorned, unbiased, undoubted, unquestionable, valid, veritable; SEE CONCEPTS *535,582*

faculty [*n1*] *ability, skill*
adroitness, aptitude, aptness, bent, capability, capacity, cleverness, dexterity, facility, flair, forte, genius, gift, instinct, intelligence, knack, knowing way around*, leaning, nose*, peculiarity, penchant, pistol*, power, predilection, proclivity, propensity, property, quality, readiness, reason, right stuff*, sense, strength, talent, turn, what it takes*, wits; SEE CONCEPT *630*

faculty [*n2*] *teachers in educational institution*
academics, advisers, body, clinic, college, corps, department, employees, institute, instructors, lecturers, literati, mentors, organization, pedagogues, personnel, professorate, professors, profs*, researchers, scholars, society, staff, tutors, university, workers; SEE CONCEPTS *288,350*

fad [*n*] *craze*
affectation, amusement, caprice, chic, conceit, cry, custom, dernier cri, eccentricity, fancy, fantasy, fashion, fool notion*, frivolity, furor, hobby, humor, in, innovation, in thing*, kick, kink, latest word*, mania, mode, newest wrinkle*, new look*, passing fancy*, passion, quirk, rage, sport, style, thing, trend, vagary, vogue, whim, whimsy, wrinkle; SEE CONCEPT *655*

fade [*v1*] *lose color*
achromatize, become colorless, blanch, bleach, blench, clear, decolorize, dim, disappear, discolor, dissolve, dull, etiolate, evanish, evaporate, grow dim, lose brightness, lose luster, muddy, neutralize, pale, tarnish, tone down, vanish, wash out; SEE CONCEPTS *250,469,622*

fade [*v2*] *dwindle, die out*
abate, attenuate, clear, decline, deliquesce, deteriorate, die away, die on vine*, dim, diminish, disappear, disperse, dissolve, droop, ebb, etiolate, evanesce, evanish, evaporate, fag out*, fail, fall, flag, fold, hush, languish, lessen, melt, melt away, moderate, perish, peter out*, poop out*, quiet, rarefy, shrivel, sink, slack off*, taper, thin, tire, tucker out*, vanish, wane, waste away, weaken, wilt, wither; SEE CONCEPTS *105,698*

faded [*adj*] *bleached; used*
achromatic, ashen, bedraggled, dim, dingy, discolored, dull, etiolated, indistinct, lackluster, lusterless, murky, not shiny, pale, pallid, run-down, seedy, shabby, shopworn, tacky, tattered, threadbare, tired, wan, washed out, wasted, worn; SEE CONCEPTS *560,617,618*

fail [*v1*] *be unsuccessful*
abort, backslide, back wrong horse*, be defeated, be demoted, be found lacking*, be in vain*, be ruined, blunder, break down, come to naught, come to nothing, decline, deteriorate, fall, fall flat*, fall short*, fall through*, fizzle, flop, flounder, fold, founder, go astray*, go down*, go downhill*, go down swinging*, go up in smoke*, go wrong, hit bottom*, hit the skids*, lose control, lose out, lose status, meet with disaster, miscarry, miss, miss the boat*, play into, run aground*, slip, turn out badly; SEE CONCEPT *699*

fail [*v2*] *abandon, forsake*
abort, back out, blink, break one's word, desert, disappoint, discount, disregard, fault, forget, funk, go astray, ignore, let down, miscarry, neglect, omit, overlook, overpass, slight, slip; SEE CONCEPTS *7,19*

fail [*v3*] *lose money*
be cleaned out*, become insolvent, be in arrears, be ruined, be taken to the cleaners*, break, close, close down*, close one's doors*, crash, defalcate, default, dishonor, drop, drop a bundle*, end, finish, fold, go bankrupt, go belly up*, go broke*, go bust*, go into chapter 11*, go out of business*, go to the wall*, go under*, go up*, lose big*, lose one's shirt*, overdraw, repudiate, terminate; SEE CONCEPTS *330,335*

failing [*adj*] *not well, weak*
declining, defeated, deficient, faint, feeble, inadequate, insufficient, scant, scanty, scarce, short, shy, unavailing, unprosperous, unsuccessful, unsufficient, unthriving, vain, wanting; SEE CONCEPTS *485,489*

failing [*n*] *lapse, shortcoming*
blind spot*, defect, deficiency, drawback, error, failure, fault, flaw, foible, frailty, imperfection, infirmity, miscarriage, misfortune, vice, weakness, weak point*; SEE CONCEPTS *411,674*

fail-safe [*adj*] *guaranteed not to fail*
confident, covered, foolproof, protected, reliable, reliant, safeguarded, secure, sound, sure; SEE CONCEPTS *535,542,544*

failure [*n1*] *lack of success*
abortion, bankruptcy, bomb, botch*, breakdown, bungle*, bust, checkmate, collapse, decay, decline, defeat, deficiency, deficit, deterioration, downfall, failing, false step*, faux pas, fiasco, flash in the pan*, flop*, frustration, implosion, inadequacy, lead balloon*, lemon*, loser, loss, mess, misadventure, miscarriage, misstep, nonperformance, nonsuccess, overthrow, rout, rupture, sinking ship*, stalemate, stoppage, total loss, turkey*, washout*, wreck; SEE CONCEPTS *699,706*

failure [*n2*] *person who does not succeed*
also-ran*, bankrupt, beat*, born loser*, bum, castaway, deadbeat, defaulter, derelict, disappointment, dud*, flop, good-for-nothing*, has-been, incompetent, insolvent, loafer, loser, lumpy*, might-have-been*, moocher*, nobody, no-good, nonperformer, prodigal, turkey*, underachiever, washout*; SEE CONCEPTS *412,423*

faint [*adj1*] *having little effect on senses*
aside, bated, bland, bleached, blurred, breathless, deadened, deep, delicate, dim, distant, dull, dusty, faded, faltering, far-off, feeble, gentle, hazy, hoarse, hushed, ill-defined, imperceptible, inaudible, indistinct, lenient, light, low, low-pitched, mild, moderate, muffled, murmuring, muted, muttering, obscure, out of earshot*, padded, pale, piano, quiet, remote, shadowy, slight, smooth, soft, softened, soothing, stifled, subdued, tenuous, thin, unclear, vague, wan, weak, whispered; SEE CONCEPTS *537,594,617*

faint [*adj2*] *weak*
delicate, dizzy, drooping, enervated, exhausted, faltering, fatigued, feeble, fragile, languid, lethargic, lightheaded, slight, tender, unenthusiastic, woozy; SEE CONCEPTS *314,485*

faint [*n*] *unconsciousness*
blackout, collapse, dizziness, grayout, insensibil-

ity, knockout, stupor, swoon, syncope, vertigo; SEE CONCEPTS *308,316*

faint [v] *lose consciousness*
become unconscious, be overcome, black out, collapse, drop, fade, fail, fall, flicker, go out like light*, keel over, languish, pass out, succumb, swoon, weaken; SEE CONCEPTS *303,308*

fainthearted [adj] *timid*
afraid, cowardly, cowed, cowering, fearful, frightened, gutless, having cold feet*, intimidated, lily-livered*, meek, mousy, spineless, unassertive, weak, wimpy*, yellow*; SEE CONCEPT *401*

fair [adj1] *impartial, unprejudiced*
aboveboard, benevolent, blameless, candid, civil, clean, courteous, decent, disinterested, dispassionate, equal, equitable, even-handed, frank, generous, good, honest, honorable, impartial, just, lawful, legitimate, moderate, nonpartisan, objective, on the level*, on up-and-up*, open, pious, praiseworthy, principled, proper, reasonable, respectable, righteous, scrupulous, sincere, square, straight, straightforward, temperate, trustworthy, unbiased, uncolored, uncorrupted, upright, virtuous; SEE CONCEPT *542*

fair [adj2] *light-complexioned, light-haired*
argent, blanched, bleached, blond, blonde, chalky, colorless, creamy, faded, fair-haired, fair-skinned, flaxen-haired, light, milky, neutral, pale, pale-faced, pallid, pearly, sallow, silvery, snowy, tow-haired, tow-headed, white, whitish; SEE CONCEPTS *406,618*

fair [adj3] *mediocre, satisfactory*
adequate, all right, average, common, commonplace, decent, fairish, indifferent, intermediate, mean, medium, middling, moderate, not bad*, okay, ordinary, passable, pretty good*, reasonable, respectable, satisfactory, so-so*, tolerable, up to standard*, usual; SEE CONCEPT *530*

fair [adj4] *beautiful*
attractive, beauteous, bonny, charming, chaste, comely, dainty, delicate, enchanting, exquisite, good-looking, handsome, lovely, pretty, pulchritudinous, pure; SEE CONCEPT *579*

fair [adj5] *bright, cloudless (weather)*
balmy, calm, clarion, clear, clement, dry, favorable, fine, mild, placid, pleasant, pretty, rainless, smiling, sunny, sunshiny, tranquil, unclouded, undarkened, unthreatening; SEE CONCEPT *525*

fair [n] *exposition, carnival*
bazaar, celebration, centennial, display, exhibit, exhibition, expo*, festival, fete, gala, market, observance, occasion, pageant, show, spectacle; SEE CONCEPTS *377,386*

fairly [adv1] *somewhat*
adequately, averagely, enough, kind of, moderately, more or less, passably, pretty well, quite, rather, ratherish, reasonably, some, something, sort of, so-so*, tolerably; SEE CONCEPT *786*

fairly [adv2] *justly*
deservedly, equitably, honestly, honorably, impartially, objectively, properly, reasonably, without favor, without fear; SEE CONCEPT *542*

fairness [n] *justice*
candor, charitableness, charity, civility, consideration, courtesy, decency, decorum, disinterestedness, due, duty, equitableness, equity, exactitude, fair-mindedness, fair shake*, give and take*, good faith, goodness, honesty, honor, humanity, impartiality, integrity, justness, legitimacy, mod-

eration, open-mindedness, propriety, rationality, reasonableness, right, righteousness, rightfulness, rightness, seemliness, square deal*, suitability, tolerance, truth, uprightness, veracity; SEE CONCEPTS *645,657*

fairy [n] *supernatural being*
bogie, brownie, elf, enchanter, fay, genie, gnome, goblin, gremlin, hob, imp, leprechaun, mermaid, nisse, nymph, pixie, puck, siren, spirit, sprite, sylph; SEE CONCEPT *370*

fait accompli [n] *done deed*
accomplished fact, certainty, fact of life, hard facts, irreversible accomplishment, irreversible act, irreversible truth, matter of fact, reality, undeniable fact; SEE CONCEPTS *689,725*

faith [n1] *trust in something*
acceptance, allegiance, assent, assurance, belief, certainty, certitude, confidence, constancy, conviction, credence, credit, credulity, dependence, faithfulness, fealty, fidelity, hope, loyalty, reliance, stock, store, sureness, surety, troth, truth, truthfulness; SEE CONCEPT *689*

faith [n2] *belief in a higher being; community of believers*
canon, church, communion, confession, connection, conviction, credo, creed, cult, denomination, doctrine, dogma, doxy, gospel, orthodoxy, persuasion, piety, piousness, principle, profession, religion, revelation, sect, teaching, tenet, theism, theology, worship; SEE CONCEPTS *368,689*

faithful [adj1] *loyal, reliable*
affectionate, allegiant, ardent, attached, behind one, circumspect, confiding, conscientious, constant, dependable, devoted, dutiful, dyed-in-the-wool*, enduring, fast, firm, genuine, hard-core*, honest, honorable, incorruptible, loving, obedient, on the level*, patriotic, resolute, scrupulous, sincere, staunch, steadfast, steady, straight, string along with*, sure, tried, tried and true*, true, true-blue*, trustworthy, trusty, truthful, unchanging, unswerving, unwavering, upright, veracious; SEE CONCEPTS *401,545*

faithful [adj2] *authentic, accurate*
close, credible, exact, just, lifelike, precise, right, similar, strict, true, trusty, undistorted, veracious, veridical; SEE CONCEPTS *487,573*

faithfulness [n] *devotion*
adherence, adhesion, allegiance, ardor, attachment, care, constancy, dependability, duty, fealty, fidelity, loyalty, piety, trustworthiness, truth; SEE CONCEPTS *633,645,689*

faithless [adj] *disloyal*
capricious, changeable, changeful, cheating, deceitful, dishonest, double-crossing*, double-dealing*, doubting, dubious, false, fickle, fluctuating, inconstant, perfidious, recreant, skeptical, traitorous, treacherous, two-faced*, two-timing*, unbelieving, unconverted, unfaithful, unloyal, unreliable, unstable, untrue, untrustworthy, untruthful, wavering; SEE CONCEPTS *401,545*

faithlessness [n] *disloyalty*
betrayal, disbelief, dishonesty, doubt, falseness, fickleness, fraud, inconstancy, infidelity, perfidiousness, perfidy, skepticism, treacherousness, treachery, treason, unfaithfulness; SEE CONCEPTS *633,645*

fake [adj] *false, imitation*
affected, artificial, assumed, bogus, concocted,

fa
fa

counterfeit, fabricated, fictitious, forged, fraudulent, invented, make-believe, mock, phony, pretended, pseudo*, reproduction, sham, simulated, spurious; SEE CONCEPTS *401,582*

fake [*n*] *imposter, copy*
actor, bluffer, charlatan, cheat, counterfeit, deception, fabrication, faker, flimflam*, forgery, four-flusher*, fraud, gold brick*, hoax, imitation, imposition, imposture, junque, make-believe, mountebank, phony, plant*, pretender, pretense, pseudo*, put-on, reproduction, scam, sham*, sleight, spoof, swindle, trick; SEE CONCEPTS *260,412*

fake [*v*] *pretend*
act, affect, assume, bluff, copy, counterfeit, disguise, dissimulate, fabricate, feign, forge, put on, put on an act*, sham, simulate, spoof; SEE CONCEPT *59*

falderal [*n*] *folderol, foolishness*
absurdity, baloney, bunk*, craziness, garbage, gibberish, gobbledygook*, horse feathers*, lunacy, nonsense, stupidity, twaddle; SEE CONCEPT *633*

fall [*n1*] *descent; lowering*
abatement, belly flop*, cut, decline, declivity, decrease, diminution, dip, dive, downgrade, downward slope, drop, dwindling, ebb, falling off, header*, incline, lapse, lessening, nose dive*, plummet, plunge, pratfall*, recession, reduction, slant, slip, slope, slump, spill, tumble; SEE CONCEPTS *152,181,776*

fall [*n2*] *defeat, overthrow*
abasement, breakdown, capitulation, collapse, death, degradation, destruction, diminution, disaster, dive, downfall, drop, failure, humiliation, loss, resignation, ruin, surrender, tumble; SEE CONCEPTS *116,230,674,699*

fall [*v1*] *descend; become lower*
abate, backslide, be precipitated, break down, buckle, cascade, cave in, collapse, crash, decline, decrease, depreciate, diminish, dip, dive, drag, droop, drop down, dwindle, ease, ebb, flag, flop, fold up, go down, gravitate, hit the dirt*, keel over, land, lapse, lessen, nose-dive, pitch, plummet, plunge, recede, regress, relapse, settle, sink, slip, slope, slump, spin, stumble, subside, take a header*, tip over, topple, totter, trail, trip, tumble, wane; SEE CONCEPTS *152,181,776*

fall [*v2*] *be overthrown by an enemy; surrender*
back down, be casualty, be destroyed, be killed, be lost, bend, be taken, capitulate, defer to, die, drop, eat dirt*, fall to pieces*, give in, give up, give way, go down, go under, lie down, obey, pass into enemy hands*, perish, resign, slump, submit, succumb, yield; SEE CONCEPTS *116,699*

fall [*v3*] *happen*
arrive, become, befall, chance, come about, come to pass, occur, take place; SEE CONCEPT *119*

fallacious [*adj*] *false, wrong*
beguiling, deceiving, deceptive, deluding, delusive, delusory, erroneous, fictitious, fishy*, fraudulent, illogical, illusory, incorrect, invalid, irrational, mad, misleading, mistaken, off*, phony, reasonless, sophistic, sophistical, spurious, unfounded, ungrounded, unreal, unreasonable, unreasoned, unsound, untrue, way off*; SEE CONCEPTS *267,570,582*

fallacy [*n*] *illusion, misconception*
aberration, ambiguity, artifice, bias, casuistry,

cavil, deceit, deception, deceptiveness, delusion, deviation, elusion, equivocation, erratum, erroneousness, error, evasion, falsehood, faultiness, flaw, heresy, illogicality, inconsistency, inexactness, invalidity, misapprehension, miscalculation, misconstrual, misinterpretation, mistake, non sequitur, notion, paradox, perversion, preconception, prejudice, quibbling, quirk, solecism, sophism, sophistry, speciousness, subterfuge, untruth; SEE CONCEPTS *410,689,725*

fall back [*v*] *retreat*
back, draw back, give back, recede, recoil, retire, retrocede, retrograde, surrender, withdraw, yield; SEE CONCEPT *195*

fallen [*adj1*] *disgraced, ruined*
collapsed, decayed, dishonored, immoral, loose, ruinous, shaken, shamed, sinful, unchaste; SEE CONCEPTS *539,555*

fallen [*adj2*] *dead*
casualty, killed, lost, perished, slain, slaughtered; SEE CONCEPT *539*

fall for [*v*] *become infatuated with*
desire, fall in love with, flip over, go head over heels*, lose one's head over*, succumb; SEE CONCEPT *32*

fall guy [*n*] *scapegoat*
chopping block, dupe, patsy, pigeon, sacrifice, sap, schmuck, stooge, sucker, victim, whipping boy; SEE CONCEPT *412*

fallible [*adj*] *able or prone to err*
careless, deceptive, errable, errant, erring, faulty, frail, heedless, human, ignorant, imperfect, in question, liable, mortal, questionable, uncertain, unreliable, untrustworthy, weak; SEE CONCEPT *542*

falling-out [*n*] *disagreement*
altercation, argument, clash, dispute, exchange, feud, fight, friction, misunderstanding, quarrel; SEE CONCEPTS *46,388*

fall out [*v1*] *argue*
altercate, bicker, clash, differ, disagree, fight, quarrel, spar, squabble; SEE CONCEPT *46*

fall out [*v2*] *come to pass*
befall, chance, happen, occur, result, take place, turn out; SEE CONCEPT *4*

fallow [*adj*] *inactive*
dormant, idle, inert, neglected, quiescent, resting, slack, uncultivated, undeveloped, unplanted, unplowed, unproductive, unseeded, untilled, unused, vacant, virgin; SEE CONCEPTS *485,560*

fall to [*v*] *set about doing*
apply oneself to, begin, be up to, buckle down*, commence, jump in, pitch in*, start, undertake, wade into*; SEE CONCEPTS *100,221*

false [*adj1*] *wrong, made up*
apocryphal, beguiling, bogus, casuistic, concocted, contrary to fact, cooked-up*, counterfactual, deceitful, deceiving, delusive, dishonest, distorted, erroneous, ersatz*, fake, fallacious, fanciful, faulty, fictitious, fishy, fraudulent, illusive, imaginary, improper, inaccurate, incorrect, inexact, invalid, lying, mendacious, misleading, misrepresentative, mistaken, off the mark*, phony, sham, sophistical, specious, spurious, trumped up*, unfounded, unreal, unsound, untrue, untruthful; SEE CONCEPTS *267,570,582*

false [*adj2*] *dishonest, hypocritical*
apostate, base, beguiling, canting, corrupt, crooked, deceitful, deceiving, deceptive, deluding, delusive, devious, dishonorable, disloyal,

double-dealing*, duplicitous, faithless, false-hearted, forsworn, foul, lying, malevolent, malicious, mean, misleading, mythomaniac, perfidious, perjured, rascally, recreant, renegade, scoundrelly, traitorous, treacherous, treasonable, two-faced*, underhanded, unfaithful, unscrupulous, untrustworthy, venal, villainous, wicked; SEE CONCEPTS *267,401*

false [*adj 3*] *fake, counterfeit*
adulterated, alloyed, artificial, assumed, bent, bogus*, brummagem, bum*, colored, contrived, copied, crock*, deceptive, disguised, ersatz*, fabricated, factitious, feigned, fishy*, forged, framed*, hollow, imitation, made-up, make-believe, manufactured, meretricious, mock, ostensible, phony, pretended, pseudo*, seeming, shady, sham*, simulated, snide, so-called*, spurious, substitute, synthetic, unreal, wrong; SEE CONCEPT *582*

falsehood [*n*] *lie*
canard, cover-up, deceit, deception, dishonesty, dissimulation, distortion, equivocation, erroneousness, error, fable, fabrication, fakery, fallaciousness, fallacy, falseness, falsity, feigning, fib, fibbery, fiction, figment, fraud, half truth, hogwash*, line, mendacity, misstatement, perjury, pretense, prevarication, sham*, story, tale, tall tale*, untruism, untruth, untruthfulness, whopper*, yarn; SEE CONCEPTS *63,278*

falsely [*adv*] *deceitfully*
basely, behind one's back*, crookedly, dishonestly, dishonorably, disloyally, faithlessly, falseheartedly, malevolently, maliciously, perfidiously, roguishly, traitorously, treacherously, underhandedly, unfaithfully, unscrupulously; SEE CONCEPTS *267,401*

false teeth [*n*] *dentures*
artificial teeth, bridge, choppers*, dental plate, implants, partial, set of teeth; SEE CONCEPT *393*

falsies [*n*] *padded bra*
props, Wonderbra℗; SEE CONCEPT *451*

falsify [*v*] *alter, misrepresent*
adulterate, belie, change, color, con, contort, contradict, contravene, cook, counterfeit, deacon, deceive, deny, distort, doctor, dress up*, embroider, equivocate, exaggerate, fake, fake it, fib, forge, four-flush*, frame up*, garble, gloss, lie, misquote, misstate, palter, pervert, phony up*, prevaricate, promote, put on an act*, salt*, tamper with, traverse, trump up*, twist, warp; SEE CONCEPT *63*

falsity [*n*] *dishonesty, deception*
canard, cheating, deceit, deceptiveness, disingenuousness, double-dealing, duplicity, erroneousness, error, faithlessness, fake, fallacy, falsehood, fib, fraud, fraudulence, hypocrisy, inaccuracy, infidelity, insincerity, lie, mendacity, misrepresentation, perfidiousness, perfidy, prevarication, sham, story, tale, treachery, uncandidness, unfaithfulness, unreality, untruth; SEE CONCEPTS *278,645,725*

falter [*v*] *stumble, stutter*
be undecided, bobble, break, drop the ball*, flounder, fluctuate, fluff, halt, hem and haw*, hesitate, lurch, quaver, reel, rock, roll, scruple, shake, speak haltingly, stagger, stammer, stub toe*, teeter, topple, totter, tremble, trip up, vacillate, waver, whiffle, wobble; SEE CONCEPTS *18,147,266*

fame [*n*] *celebrity*
acclaim, acclamation, account, acknowledgment, character, credit, dignity, distinction, éclat, elevation, eminence, esteem, estimation, exaltation, favor, glory, greatness, heyday, honor, illustriousness, immortality, kudos, laurels, luster, majesty, name, nobility, note, notoriety, place, popularity, position, preeminence, prominence, public esteem, rank, recognition, regard, renown, rep*, report, reputation, repute, splendor, standing, stardom, station, superiority; SEE CONCEPT *388*

familiar [*adj 1*] *common, well-known*
accustomed, commonplace, conventional, customary, domestic, everyday, frequent, garden variety*, habitual, homespun, household, humble, informal, intimate, known, matter-of-fact, mundane, native, natural, old hat*, ordinary, plain, prosaic, proverbial, recognizable, repeated, routine, simple, stock, unceremonious, unsophisticated, usual, wonted, workaday; SEE CONCEPTS *530,547*

familiar [*adj 2*] *knowledgeable*
abreast, acquainted, apprised, at home with*, au courant, au fait, aware, cognizant, conscious, conversant, grounded*, informed, in on*, in the know*, introduced, kept posted*, mindful, no stranger to*, plugged in*, savvy, tuned in*, up*, up on*, versant, versed in, well up in*, with it*; SEE CONCEPT *402*

familiar [*adj 3*] *friendly, bold*
affable, amicable, buddy-buddy*, chummy*, close, comfortable, confidential, cordial, cozy, dear, easy, forward, free, free-and-easy*, fresh, genial, gracious, impudent, informal, intimate, intrusive, near, neighborly, nervy, obtrusive, officious, open, palsy, palsy-walsy*, presuming, presumptuous, relaxed, sassy*, smart, snug, sociable, thick, tight, unceremonious, unconstrained, unreserved, wise; SEE CONCEPT *555*

familiarity [*n 1*] *friendliness*
acquaintance, acquaintanceship, boldness, closeness, ease, fellowship, forwardness, freedom, freshness, friendship, informality, intimacy, liberty, naturalness, openness, presumption, sociability, unceremoniousness; SEE CONCEPT *388*

familiarity [*n 2*] *knowledgeableness*
acquaintance, awareness, cognition, comprehension, experience, feel, grasp, knowledge, sense, understanding; SEE CONCEPT *409*

familiarize [*v*] *make or become acquainted with, knowledgeable about*
accustom, adapt, adjust, awaken to, become adept in, become aware of, break the ice*, bring into use, case*, check out, coach, come to know, condition, enlighten, gain friendship, get in, get lay of land*, get lowdown on*, get together, get to know, get with it*, habituate, inform, instruct, inure, let down hair*, let know, let next to, make conversant, make used to, mix, naturalize, popularize, post, prime, put on to*, school, season, tip off*, train, use, wont; SEE CONCEPTS *15,38*

family [*n*] *kin, offspring; classification*
ancestors, ancestry, birth, blood, brood, children, clan, class, descendants, descent, dynasty, extraction, folk, forebears, genealogy, generations, genre, group, heirs and assigns, house, household, inheritance, in-laws, issue, kind, kindred, kith and kin, line, lineage, ménage, network, parentage, pedigree, people, progenitors, prog-

eny, race, relations, relationship, relatives, siblings, strain, subdivision, system, tribe; SEE CONCEPTS *296,378,397*

family tree [*n*] *family history*
ancestral tree, ancestry, bloodline, descent, genealogical chart, genealogy, heredity, lineage, pedigree; SEE CONCEPT *296*

famine [*n*] *hunger*
dearth, destitution, drought, misery, paucity, poverty, scarcity, starvation, want; SEE CONCEPTS *674,709*

famished [*adj*] *starving*
could eat a horse*, dog-hungry*, empty, flying light*, having the munchies*, hollow, hungering, hungry, ravening, ravenous, starved, starved to death*, voracious; SEE CONCEPTS *20,406,546*

famous [*adj*] *legendary, notable to many*
acclaimed, applauded, august, brilliant, celebrated, conspicuous, distinguished, elevated, eminent, exalted, excellent, extraordinary, foremost, glorious, grand, great, honored, illustrious, important, imposing, influential, in limelight*, in spotlight*, leading, lionized, memorable, mighty, much-publicized, noble, noted, noteworthy, notorious, of note, outstanding, peerless, powerful, preeminent, prominent, recognized, remarkable, renowned, reputable, signal, splendid, talked about*, well-known; SEE CONCEPT *568*

fan [*n1*] *blower of air*
air conditioner, blade, draft, flabellum, leaf, palm leaf, propeller, thermantidote, vane, ventilator, windmill; SEE CONCEPT *463*

fan [*n2*] *person enthusiastic about an interest*
addict, adherent, admirer, aficionado, amateur, buff, devotee, follower, freak*, groupie*, habitué, hound, lover, rooter, supporter, votary, zealot; SEE CONCEPTS *352,366,423*

fan [*v1*] *blow on*
aerate, air-condition, air-cool, cool, refresh, ruffle, spread, ventilate, wind, winnow; SEE CONCEPTS *199,208*

fan [*v2*] *provoke*
add fuel, agitate, arouse, enkindle, excite, expand, extend, impassion, increase, rouse, stimulate, stir up, whip up, work up; SEE CONCEPT *14*

fanatic [*n*] *person overenthusiastic about an interest*
activist, addict, bigot, bug*, crank*, crazy, demon, devotee, enthusiast, extremist, fiend*, fool, freak, maniac, militant, monomaniac, nut*, radical, ultraist, visionary, zealot; SEE CONCEPTS *352,359,366*

fanatical [*adj*] *overenthusiastic*
biased, bigoted, bugged*, burning*, contumacious, credulous, devoted, dogmatic, domineering, enthusiastic, erratic, extreme, fervent, feverish, fiery, frenzied, headstrong, high on*, immoderate, impassioned, impulsive, incorrigible, infatuated, mad, monomaniacal, narrow-minded, nuts for*, obsessed, obsessive, obstinate, opinionated, partial, partisan, passionate, possessed, prejudiced, rabid, radical, raving, single-minded, stubborn, turned on*, unruly, violent, visionary, wild, willful, zealous; SEE CONCEPT *401*

fanaticism [*n*] *overenthusiasm*
abandonment, arbitrariness, bias, bigotry, contumacy, dedication, devotion, dogma, enthusiasm, extremism, faction, frenzy, hatred, illiberality, immoderation, incorrigibility, infatuation, injustice, intolerance, madness, monomania, obsessiveness, obstinacy, partiality, partisanship, passion, prejudice, rage, single-mindedness, stubbornness, superstition, tenacity, transport, unfairness, unreasonableness, unruliness, violence, willfulness, zeal, zealotry; SEE CONCEPTS *633,689*

fanciful [*adj*] *imaginary, romantic*
absurd, aerial, bizarre, blue sky*, capricious, castles in the air*, chimerical, curious, dreamlike, extravagant, fabulous, fairy-tale, fancied, fantastic, fantastical, fictional, fictitious, fictive, flaky*, floating, ideal, illusory, imaginative, imagined, incredible, kinky*, legendary, mythical, notional, offbeat, on cloud nine*, pie in the sky*, pipe dream*, poetic, preposterous, shadowy, suppositious, unreal, visionary, whimsical, wild; SEE CONCEPTS *529,572*

fancy [*adj*] *extravagant, ornamental*
adorned, baroque, beautifying, chichi*, complicated, cushy, custom, decorated, decorative, deluxe, elaborate, elegant, embellished, fanciful, florid, frilly, froufrou*, garnished, gaudy, gingerbread*, intricate, lavish, ornate, ostentatious, resplendent, rich, rococo, showy, special, spiffy*, sumptuous, unusual; SEE CONCEPTS *562,579*

fancy [*n1*] *impulse, urge*
caprice, conceit, conception, contrariness, creation, cup of tea*, desire, druthers*, flash, fool's paradise*, groove*, humor, idea, image, imagination, impression, inclination, irrationality, liking, mind, notion, perverseness, pleasure, thing*, thought, vagary, velleity, visualization, weakness for, whim, will; SEE CONCEPTS *20,532*

fancy [*n2*] *liking, dream*
big eyes*, chimera, conception, daydream, delusion, envisagement, envisioning, eyes for*, fabrication, fantasy, figment, fondness, hallucination, hankering, idea, illusion, imagination, imaginativeness, inclination, invention, itch*, mirage, nightmare, notion, partiality, penchant, phantasm, picture, pie in the sky*, pipe dream*, predilection, preference, relish, reverie, romancing, sweet tooth*, vision, yearning, yen; SEE CONCEPTS *20,32,409*

fancy [*v1*] *imagine, create*
be inclined to think, believe, conceive, conjecture, dream up, envisage, envision, fantasize, feature*, guess, head trip*, image, infer, make up, make up off top of one's head*, phantom, picture, realize, reckon, spark, spitball*, suppose, surmise, think, think likely, think up, trump up*, vision, visualize; SEE CONCEPT *43*

fancy [*v2*] *love, desire*
approve, be attracted to, be captivated by, be enamored of, be in love with, care for, crave, crazy about*, desire, dream of, endorse, fall for, favor, like, long for, lust after, mad for*, prefer, relish, sanction, set one's heart on*, take a liking to*, take to, wild for*, wish for, yearn for; SEE CONCEPTS *17,20,32*

fanfare [*n*] *cheering*
alarum, array, ballyhoo*, demonstration, display, flourish, hullabaloo*, panoply, parade, pomp, shine, show, trump, trumpet call*; SEE CONCEPT *377*

fanny [*n*] *buttocks*
ass, backside, behind*, bottom*, buns*, butt*, cheeks*, derriere, gluteus maximus, heinie*,

hindquarters, posterior, rear end, rump*, seat*, tail; SEE CONCEPT *392*

fantasize [*v*] *dream about desires*
build castles in air*, daydream, envision, hallucinate, head trip*, imagine, invent, live in a dream world*, moon, romance, trip out*, woolgather*; SEE CONCEPT *17*

fantastic [*adj1*] *strange, different; imaginary*
absurd, artificial, capricious, chimerical, comical, crazy, eccentric, erratic, exotic, extravagant, extreme, fanciful, far-fetched, fictional, foolish, foreign, freakish, grotesque, hallucinatory, illusive, imaginative, implausible, incredible, insane, irrational, ludicrous, mad, misleading, nonsensical, odd, outlandish, out of sight*, peculiar, phantasmagorical, preposterous, quaint, queer, ridiculous, singular, suppositious, unbelievable, unlikely, unreal, wacky*, weird, whimsical; SEE CONCEPTS *564,582*

fantastic [*adj2*] *enormous*
cracking, extreme, great, huge, humongous, massive, monstrous, monumental, overwhelming, prodigious, severe, stupendous, towering, tremendous; SEE CONCEPT *781*

fantastic [*adj3*] *wonderful, excellent*
A-1*, awesome, best, best ever, cat's meow*, delicious, far out*, first-class, first-rate, great, like wow*, marvelous, out of sight*, out of this world*, primo*, sensational, superb, unreal*; SEE CONCEPTS *572,574*

fantasy [*n*] *imagination, dream*
air castle, apparition, appearance, Atlantis*, bubble*, chimera, conceiving, creativity, daydream, delusion, envisioning, externalizing, fabrication, fairyland*, fancy, fancying, fantasia, figment*, flight, flight of imagination, fool's paradise*, hallucination, head trip*, illusion, imaginativeness, imagining, invention, mind trip*, mirage, nightmare, objectifying, originality, rainbow*, reverie, trip, Utopia, vagary, vision; SEE CONCEPTS *20,529,689*

FAQ [*n*] *frequently asked questions*
common answers, common questions, listed questions and answers; SEE CONCEPTS *48,53*

far [*adj/adv1*] *at a great distance*
afar, a good way, a long way, bit, deep, distant, end of rainbow*, faraway, far-flung*, far-off, far piece*, far-removed, good ways*, long, middle of nowhere*, miles, outlying, out-of-the-way*, piece, remote, removed, stone's throw*, ways*; SEE CONCEPTS *586,778*

far [*adv2*] *considerably*
decidedly, extremely, greatly, incomparably, much, notably, quite, significantly, somewhat, very, very much, well; SEE CONCEPTS *772,781*

faraway [*adj*] *remote, distant*
absent, abstracted, beyond the horizon, distant, dreamy, far, far-flung*, far-off, far-removed, lost, outlying, preoccupied, quite a ways*, removed, well away; SEE CONCEPTS *586,778*

farce [*n*] *nonsense, satire*
absurdity, broad comedy, buffoonery, burlesque, camp, caricature, comedy, high camp*, horseplay*, interlude, joke, low camp*, mock, mockery, parody, play, pratfall comedy, ridiculousness, sham*, skit, slapstick, travesty; SEE CONCEPTS *263,293*

farcical [*adj*] *absurd*
amusing, camp, campy*, comic, comical, derisory, diverting, droll, for grins*, funny, gelas-

tic, joshing, laughable, ludicrous, nonsensical, outrageous, preposterous, ridiculous, risible, slapstick, stupid; SEE CONCEPTS *267,542*

fare [*n1*] *amount charged for transportation*
book, charge, check, expense, passage, price, slug, tariff, ticket, token, toll; SEE CONCEPT *329*

fare [*n2*] *food served at meals*
commons, diet, eatables, eats*, edibles, meals, menu, provision, rations, slop*, sustenance, swill*, table, victuals; SEE CONCEPTS *457,459*

fare [*v*] *get along; turn out*
advance, do, get by, get on, go, handle, happen, hie, journey, make headway, make out, manage, muddle through, pass, proceed, progress, prosper, prove, shift, stagger; SEE CONCEPTS *100,117,704*

farewell [*n*] *departing saying; departure*
adieu, adieus, adieux, adios, bye-bye, cheerio, ciao, goodbye, hasta la vista, have a nice day, leave-taking, parting, salutation, sendoff, so long, ta-ta, valediction; SEE CONCEPTS *195,278*

far-fetched [*adj*] *hard to believe*
bizarre, doubtful, dubious, eccentric, fantastic, fishy*, forced, hard to swallow*, illogical, implausible, improbable, incoherent, inconsequential, incredible, labored, preposterous, queer, recondite, strained, strange, suspicious, unbelievable, unconvincing, unlikely, unnatural, unrealistic; SEE CONCEPTS *529,552,582*

far-flung [*adj*] *wide-ranging*
comprehensive, distant, extensive, far-reaching, global, remote, spacious, widely distributed, widespread; SEE CONCEPTS *576,778*

farm [*n*] *land for agriculture or animal breeding*
acreage, acres, arboretum, claim, demense, enclosure, estate, farmstead, field, freehold, garden, grange, grassland, holding, homestead, lawn, meadow, nursery, orchard, pasture, patch, plantation, ranch, soil, vineyard; SEE CONCEPTS *258,449,509,517*

farm [*v*] *produce crops, raise animals*
bring under cultivation, crop, cultivate, direct, dress, garden, graze, grow, harrow, harvest, homestead, husband, landscape, look after, operate, pasture, plant, plow, ranch, reap, run, seed, sow, subdue, superintend, tend, till, till the soil, work; SEE CONCEPTS *117,253,324*

farmer [*n*] *person who produces crops, raises animals*
agriculturalist, agriculturist, agronomist, breeder, clodhopper*, cob*, country person, cropper, cultivator, feeder, gardener, gleaner, grazer, grower, harvester, hired hand, homesteader, horticulturist, laborer, peasant, planter, plower, producer, rancher, reaper, sharecropper, sower, tender, tiller, villein; SEE CONCEPTS *347,348*

farming [*n*] *producing crops, raising animals*
agriculture, agronomics, agronomy, breeding, crop-raising, cultivation, culture, feeding, fertilizing, gardening, geoponics, gleaning, grazing, growing, harvesting, homesteading, hydroponics, landscaping, operating, production, ranching, reaping, seeding, share-cropping, soil culture, threshing, tillage; SEE CONCEPTS *117, 253,324*

far-out [*adj*] *very unconventional*
boss*, cool*, deep*, excellent, fabulous, fantastic, groovy*, hip*, neat, nifty, rad*, sensational, strange, super, swell, trendy, unorthodox, way-out, weird, wild, wonderful; SEE CONCEPT *572*

far-reaching [*adj*] *broad, widespread*
extensive, far-ranging, important, momentous, pervasive, significant, sweeping, wide; SEE CONCEPT 772

far-sighted [*adj*] *looking ahead wisely*
acute, canny, cautious, clairvoyant, commonsensical, cool-headed*, discerning, judicious, level-headed, perceptive, politic, prescient, provident, prudent, sagacious, sage, shrewd, well-balanced, wise; SEE CONCEPT 402

fart [*n*] *flatulence*
gas, vapors, wind; SEE CONCEPT 465

fart [*v*] *expel gas*
break wind, cut one*, cut the cheese*, pass gas, rip one*, toot; SEE CONCEPT 465

farther [*adv*] *at a greater distance*
beyond, further, longer, more distant, more remote, remoter, yon, yonder; SEE CONCEPTS 586,778

farthest [*adv*] *most distant*
extreme, farthermost, furthermost, furthest, last, lattermost, outermost, outmost, remotest, ultimate, utmost, uttermost; SEE CONCEPTS 586,778

fascinate [*v*] *captivate, hold spellbound*
absorb, allure, animate, arouse, attach, attract, beguile, bewitch, charm, compel, delight, draw, enamor, enchant, engage, engross, enrapture, enslave, ensnare, enthrall, entice, entrance, excite, fire, gladden, hypnotize, infatuate, interest, intoxicate, intrigue, invite, kindle, lure, mesmerize, overpower, overwhelm, pique, please, provoke, ravish, rivet, seduce, spellbind, stimulate, stir, subdue, tantalize, tempt, thrill, titillate, transfix, transport, win; SEE CONCEPTS 7,11,22

fascinated [*adj*] *captivated, spellbound*
absorbed, aroused, attracted, beguiled, bewitched, charmed, dazzled, delighted, enamored, enchanted, engrossed, enraptured, enthralled, enticed, entranced, excited, fond of, hypnotized, infatuated, in love with, intoxicated, mesmerized, overpowered, seduced, sent, smitten, sold on*, stuck on*, tantalized, thrilled, titillated, transfixed, transported, under a spell*; SEE CONCEPTS 32,403

fascinating [*adj*] *interesting, spellbinding*
alluring, appealing, attractive, bewitching, captivating, charming, compelling, delectable, delightful, enchanting, engaging, engrossing, enticing, glamorous, gripping, intriguing, irresistible, ravishing, riveting, seducing, seductive, siren; SEE CONCEPT 529

fascination [*n*] *strong interest*
allure, appeal, attraction, bug*, charisma, charm, enchantment, enthrallment, glamour, grabber*, hang-up*, lure, magic, magnetism, obsession, piquancy, power, pull*, sorcery, spell, thing*, thing for*, trance, witchcraft, witchery; SEE CONCEPTS 20,32,532,690

fascism [*n*] *political system of dictatorship*
absolutism, authoritarianism, autocracy, bureaucracy, despotism, Nazism, one-party system, party government, racism, regimentation, totalitarianism; SEE CONCEPTS 299,301,689

fascist [*n*] *dictator*
authoritarian, autocrat, Nazi, totalitarian, tyrant; SEE CONCEPT 354

fashion [*n1*] *latest style, prevailing taste*
appearance, bandwagon*, chic, configuration, convention, craze, cry, cultism, cultus, custom, cut, dernier cri, fad, faddism, figure, form, furor, in thing*, last word*, latest*, latest thing*, line*, look, make, mode, model, mold, newest wrinkle*, pattern, rage, shape, thing*, tone, trend, usage, vogue; SEE CONCEPT 655

fashion [*n2*] *attitude, manner*
convention, custom, demeanor, device, etiquette, form, formality, formula, guise, method, mode, modus operandi, mores, observance, order, practice, precedent, prescription, prevalence, procedure, sort, style, system, technique, tendency, tone, trend, usage, vein, vogue, way; SEE CONCEPTS 644,657

fashion [*v*] *adjust, design, create*
accommodate, adapt, build, carve, construct, contrive, cook up*, cut, devise, dream up*, erect, fabricate, fit, forge, form, frame*, knock together*, make, manufacture, model, mold, plan, plot, produce, sculpture, shape, suit, tailor, throw together*, turn out*, work; SEE CONCEPTS 168,173,232

fashionable [*adj*] *stylish, up-to-date*
a go-go*, à la mode*, all the rage*, chic, chichi*, contemporary, current, customary, dashing, faddy*, favored, fly*, genteel, hot*, in style, in-thing*, in vogue, last word*, latest*, latest thing*, mod*, modern, modish*, natty*, new, newfangled, now, popular, prevailing, rakish, smart, swank, trendsetting, trendy, upscale*, up-to-the-minute*, usual, well-liked, with it*; SEE CONCEPTS 579,589

fast [*adj1*] *speedy*
accelerated, active, agile, blue streak*, breakneck*, brisk, chop-chop*, dashing, double-time*, electric, expeditious, expeditive, flashing, fleet, fleeting, flying, hairtrigger*, hasty, hot, hurried, hypersonic, in a jiffy*, in nothing flat*, lickety split*, like a bat out of hell*, like all get out*, like crazy*, like mad*, nimble, on the double*, PDQ*, posthaste, presto, pronto, quick, racing, rapid, ready, screamin'*, snap*, snappy*, speedball*, supersonic, swift, velocious, winged; SEE CONCEPTS 588,799

fast [*adj2*] *fixed, immovable*
adherent, ardent, attached, close, constant, constrained, durable, faithful, fastened, firm, fortified, glued, held, impregnable, indelible, inextricable, lasting, loyal, permanent, resistant, resolute, secure, set, sound, stable, staunch, steadfast, stuck, sure, tenacious, tight, true, true blue*, unwavering, wedged; SEE CONCEPTS 488,542

fast [*adj3*] *immoral, promiscuous*
bawdy, careless, debauched, depraved, devil-may-care*, dissipated, dissolute, easy, extravagant, flirtatious, frivolous, gadabout*, giddy, incontinent, indecent, intemperate, lascivious, lecherous, lewd, libertine, libidinous, licentious, light, loose, lustful, profligate, rakish, reckless, salacious, self-gratifying, self-indulgent, sportive, sporty, unchaste, wanton, wild; SEE CONCEPT 545

fast [*adv1*] *speedily*
apace, chop-chop*, expeditiously, flat-out*, fleetly, full tilt*, hastily, hurriedly, in a flash*, in haste, in nothing flat*, in short order*, like a flash*, like a shot*, like greased lightning*, like wildfire*, posthaste, presto, promptly, pronto, quick, quickly, rapidly, soon, swift, swiftly; SEE CONCEPTS 588,799

fast [*adv2*] *fixedly*
deeply, firm, firmly, hard, securely, solidly, soundly, steadfastly, tight, tightly; SEE CONCEPT *488*

fast [*n*] *abstention from eating*
abstinence, diet, fasting, xerophagy; SEE CONCEPT *169*

fast [*v*] *go without food*
abstain, deny oneself, diet, famish, forbear, go hungry, not eat, refrain, starve; SEE CONCEPT *169*

fasten [*v*] *make secure; join together*
adhere, affix, anchor, attach, band, bar, batten, belt, bind, bolt, bond, brace, button, catch, cement, chain, cleave, close, cohere, connect, couple, embed, establish, fix, freeze to*, girth, glue, grip, hitch, hitch on, hold, hook, hook up, implant, infix, jam, knot, lace, leash, link, lock, lodge, make firm, moor, mortise, nail, rivet, rope, screw, seal, set, settle, solder, stay put, stick, strengthen, string, tack on, tag, tie, tighten, truss, unite, wedge, weld; SEE CONCEPTS *85,113,160*

fastener [*n*] *holder*
bolt, buckle, button, catch, clasp, fastening, latch, lock, rivet, screw, snap; SEE CONCEPT *499*

fastidious [*adj*] *very careful, meticulous*
captious, choosy, critical, dainty, demanding, difficult, discriminating, easily disgusted, exacting, finical, finicky, fussbudgety*, fussy, hard to please*, hypercritical, nice, nit-picky, overdelicate, overnice, particular, persnickety*, picky, punctilious, queasy, squeamish, stickling; SEE CONCEPTS *542,550*

fat [*adj1*] *overweight*
beefy*, big, blimp, bovine, brawny, broad, bulging, bulky, bull, burly, butterball*, chunky*, corpulent, distended, dumpy, elephantine, fleshy, gargantuan, gross, heavy, heavyset*, hefty, husky, inflated, jelly-belly*, lard, large, meaty*, obese, oversize, paunchy, plump, plumpish, ponderous, porcine, portly, potbellied, pudgy*, roly-poly*, rotund, solid, stout, swollen, thickset*, weighty, whalelike*; SEE CONCEPT *491*

fat [*adj2*] *containing an oily substance*
adipose, fatlike, fatty, greasy, oleaginous, suety, unctuous; SEE CONCEPT *485*

fat [*adj3*] *productive, rich*
affluent, cushy, fertile, flourishing, fruitful, good, lucrative, lush, profitable, prosperous, remunerative, thriving; SEE CONCEPT *334*

fat [*n*] *overweight, adipose tissue*
blubber, bulk, cellulite, corpulence, excess, fatness, flab, flesh, grease, lard, obesity, overabundance, overflow, paunch, plethora, suet, superfluity, surfeit, surplus, tallow; SEE CONCEPTS *723,734*

fatal [*adj1*] *deadly, lethal*
baleful, baneful, calamitous, cataclysmic, catastrophic, deathly, destructive, disastrous, fateful, final, ill-fated, ill-starred, incurable, inevitable, killing, malefic, malignant, mortal, mortiferous, noxious, pernicious, pestilent, pestilential, poisonous, ruinous, terminal, virulent; SEE CONCEPTS *537,539*

fatal [*adj2*] *critical, very important*
crucial, decisive, destined, determining, doomed, fateful, final, foreordained, inevitable, predestined, unlucky; SEE CONCEPTS *531,568*

fatalism [*n*] *resignation to a fate*
acceptance, destinism, determinism, necessitari-anism, passivity, predestinarianism, predestination, stoicism; SEE CONCEPT *689*

fatality [*n*] *death, loss; ability to cause such*
accident, casualty, deadliness, destructiveness, disaster, dying, inevitability, lethality, lethalness, mortality, necrosis, noxiousness, poisonousness, virulence; SEE CONCEPTS *304,675*

fat chance [*n*] *no chance*
impossible, not a prayer, no way, snowball's chance in hell*, unthinkable, very little chance, when hell freezes over*; SEE CONCEPT *552*

fat city [*n*] *paradise*
cloud nine*, hog heaven*, pig heaven*; SEE CONCEPTS *370,410,515*

fate [*n*] *predetermined course*
break, chance, circumstance, consequence, cup*, destination, destiny, divine will*, doom, effect, end, ending, fortune, future, handwriting on the wall*, horoscope, inescapableness, issue, karma, kismet, lot, luck, Moirai, nemesis, outcome, portion, predestination, providence, stars*, termination, upshot, wheel of fortune*; SEE CONCEPT *679*

fated [*adj*] *governed by fate*
decided by fate, destined, doomed, foreordained, imminent, impending, inescapable, inevitable, in the stars*, predestined, predetermined, prejudged, preordained, unavoidable; SEE CONCEPTS *548,820*

fateful [*adj1*] *significant*
acute, apocalyptic, conclusive, critical, crucial, decisive, determinative, direful, doomful, eventful, important, inauspicious, momentous, ominous, portentous, resultful; SEE CONCEPT *568*

fateful [*adj2*] *deadly*
calamitous, cataclysmic, catastrophic, destructive, disastrous, fatal, lethal, mortal, ominous, ruinous; SEE CONCEPT *537*

father [*n1*] *male person who begets children*
ancestor, begetter, dad, daddy*, forebearer, origin, pa, padre, papa, parent, pop*, predecessor, procreator, progenitor, sire, source; SEE CONCEPTS *394,400,414,419,423*

father [*n2*] *priest*
abbé, clergyman, confessor, curé, ecclesiastic, minister, padre, parson, pastor, preacher, reverend; SEE CONCEPT *361*

father/mother [*n3*] *founder, inventor*
administrator, architect, author, builder, creator, dean, elder, encourager, generator, initiator, introducer, leader, maker, matriarch, motor*, mover, organizer, originator, patriarch, patron, prime mover*, promoter, promulgator, publisher, sire, sponsor, supporter; SEE CONCEPTS *347,423*

father [*v*] *sire*
beget, conceive, create, dream up, engender, establish, found, generate, invent, originate, procreate, produce, sow the seeds of*, spawn, trigger; SEE CONCEPTS *173,239,251*

fatherland [*n*] *homeland*
home, motherland, native land, the old country; SEE CONCEPTS *510,515,648*

fathom [*v*] *discern, understand*
appreciate, apprehend, catch, cognize, comprehend, dig, divine, estimate, figure out, follow, gauge, get, get to the bottom*, grasp, have, interpret, know, measure, penetrate, perceive, pierce, pinpoint, plumb, probe, recognize, savvy, sound, unravel; SEE CONCEPTS *15,38*

fa
fa

fatigue [*n*] *tiredness*
brain fag*, burnout*, debility, dullness, enervation, ennui, exhaustion, faintness, fatigation, feebleness, heaviness, languor, lassitude, lethargy, listlessness, overtiredness, weakness, weariness; SEE CONCEPTS *316,405*

fatigue [*v*] *tire, wear out*
bedraggle, burn out*, bush*, conk out*, debilitate, deplete, disable, drain, droop, drop, enervate, exhaust, fag, fizzle, flag, jade*, knock out*, languish, overtire, peter out*, poop*, poop out*, prostrate, sag, sink, succumb, take, tucker, weaken, wear down, weary; SEE CONCEPTS *137,225,240,250*

fatigued [*adj*] *tired*
all in*, beat*, bedraggled, blasé, burned out*, bushed*, dead*, dead-beat*, dead-tired*, dog-tired*, dog-weary*, done in*, droopy, dropping, enervated, exhausted, fagged out*, jaded*, languid, languorous, lassitudinous, listless, out of gas*, overtired, played out*, pooped*, prostrate, ready to drop*, spent*, tuckered*, washed out*, wasted*, weary, worn, worn-out, zonked*; SEE CONCEPT *485*

fatness [*n*] *overweight*
adiposity, breadth, bulkiness, corpulence, distension, flab*, flesh, fleshiness, girth, grossness, heaviness, heftiness, inflation, largeness, obesity, plumpness, portliness, protuberance, pudginess, rotundity, size, stoutness, tumidity, weight; SEE CONCEPT *734*

fatten [*v*] *grow or make bigger; nourish*
augment, bloat, broaden, build up, coarsen, cram, distend, expand, feed, fill, gain weight, increase, overfeed, plump, put flesh on*, put on weight, round out, spread, stuff, swell, thicken, thrive, wax; SEE CONCEPTS *236,245,250*

fatty [*adj*] *full of adipose tissue*
blubbery, fatlike, greasy, lardaceous, lardy, oily, oleaginous, rich, suety, unctuous; SEE CONCEPT *485*

fatuous [*adj*] *stupid*
absurd, asinine, birdbrained*, boneheaded*, brainless*, dense, dull, foolish, idiotic, imbecile, inane, insensate, jerky*, lamebrained*, ludicrous, lunatic, mad, mindless, moronic, puerile, sappy, silly, simple, vacuous, witless; SEE CONCEPT *402*

faucet [*n*] *spigot*
bibb, bibcock, hydrant, nozzle, spout, stopcock, tap, valve; SEE CONCEPTS *445,464,499*

fault [*n1*] *blame, sin; mistake*
accountability, answerability, blunder, crime, culpability, defect, delinquency, dereliction, error, evil doing, failing, flaw, foible, frailty, guilt, impropriety, inaccuracy, indiscretion, infirmity, lapse, liability, loss of innocence, malfeasance, malpractice, misconduct, miscue, misdeed, misdemeanor, negligence, offense, omission, onus, oversight, peccancy, responsibility, slip, slip-up*, solecism, transgression, trespass, vice, weakness, wrong, wrongdoing; SEE CONCEPTS *101,192,699*

fault [*n2*] *physical defect*
blemish, debility, deficiency, demerit, imperfection, infirmity, lack, pimple, shortcoming, weakness, weak point, zit*; SEE CONCEPT *580*

fault-finding [*adj*] *critical*
captious, carping, fussy, hairsplitting*, hard to please, hypercritical, nagging, niggling, nit-picking, overcritical, pettifogging, quibbling; SEE CONCEPT *267*

faultless [*adj*] *having nothing wrong with it*
above reproach, accurate, blameless, classic, clean, correct, crimeless, errorless, exemplary, exquisite, faithful, flawless, foolproof, guiltless, ideal, immaculate, impeccable, inculpable, innocent, intact, irreproachable, model, on target*, perfect, pure, right on*, sinless, spotless, stainless, supreme, textbook*, unblemished, unguilty, unspotted, unsullied, whole; SEE CONCEPTS *545,572*

faulty [*adj*] *not working; incorrect*
adulterated, amiss, awry, bad, below par, blamable, blemished, botched, broken, cracked, damaged, debased, defective, deficient, distorted, erroneous, fallacious, fallible, false, flawed, frail, impaired, imperfect, imprecise, inaccurate, inadequate, incomplete, inexact, injured, insufficient, invalid, lame, leaky, lemon, maimed, malformed, malfunctioning, marred, out of order, rank, sick, tainted, unfit, unreliable, unretentive, unsound, warped, weak, wrong; SEE CONCEPTS *560,570*

faux pas [*n*] *blunder in etiquette*
blooper*, boo-boo*, breach, break, bungle, error, flop, flub*, gaffe*, goof*, impropriety, indecorum, indiscretion, mess-up, misconduct, misjudgment, misstep, mistake, oversight, solecism; SEE CONCEPTS *101,384*

favor [*n*] *approval, good opinion; help*
accommodation, account, admiration, aid, approbation, assistance, backing, benediction, benefit, benevolence, benignity, bias, blessing, boon, championship, compliment, consideration, cooperation, courtesy, dispensation, encouragement, esteem, estimation, friendliness, gift, good turn*, good will*, grace, indulgence, kindness, largess, obligement, okay, partiality, patronage, present, regard, respect, service, support, token; SEE CONCEPTS *10,110,689*

favor [*v1*] *pamper, reward; help*
abet, accommodate, advance, aid, assist, befriend, be partial to, do a kindness, do right by*, esteem, facilitate, further, gratify, humor, indulge, make exception, oblige, play favorites*, promote, pull strings*, show consideration, side with, smile upon*, spare, spoil, treat well, value; SEE CONCEPT *110*

favor [*v2*] *prefer, like*
accept, advocate, appreciate, approbate, approve, back, be in favor of, be on one's side*, buck for*, champion, choose, commend, cotton to*, countenance, encourage, endorse, esteem, eulogize, fancy, flash on*, for, go for*, hold with, honor, incline, lean toward, look up to, opt for, patronize, pick, praise, prize, regard highly, root for, sanction, single out*, support, take a liking to*, take a shine to*, take to*, think well of, tilt toward*, value; SEE CONCEPT *32*

favor [*v3*] *look like*
be the image of*, be the picture of*, feature, resemble, simulate, take after*; SEE CONCEPT *716*

favorable [*adj1*] *approving, friendly*
acclamatory, affirmative, agreeable, amicable, approbative, approbatory, assenting, benevolent, benign, benignant, commending, complimentary, encouraging, enthusiastic, inclined, in favor of, kind, kindly, laudatory, okay, positive, praiseful, predisposed, reassuring, recommendatory, supportive, sympathetic, understanding, welcoming,

well-disposed, well-intentioned; SEE CONCEPT *401*

favorable [*adj2*] *good, timely, advantageous*
appropriate, auspicious, benefic, beneficial, benign, bright, cheering, convenient, encouraging, fair, fit, fortunate, full of promise, gratifying, happy, healthful, helpful, hopeful, kindly, lucky, nice, opportune, pleasant, pleasing, pleasurable, pleasureful, promising, propitious, prosperous, providential, reassuring, seasonable, suitable, toward, useful, welcome, well-timed, wholesome, worthy; SEE CONCEPTS *537,558,572*

favorably [*adv1*] *genially, in a kindly manner*
agreeably, amiably, approvingly, cordially, courteously, enthusiastically, fairly, generously, graciously, heartily, helpfully, positively, receptively, usefully, willingly, with approbation, with approval, without prejudice; SEE CONCEPT *401*

favorably [*adv2*] *opportunely, advantageously*
auspiciously, conveniently, fortunately, happily, profitably, prosperously, satisfyingly, successfully, swimmingly, to one's advantage, well; SEE CONCEPTS *537,558,572*

favored [*adj*] *popular*
advantaged, best-liked, blessed, chosen, elite, fair-haired*, lucky, pet*, preferred, privileged, recommended, selected, singled out, sweetheart, well-liked; SEE CONCEPTS *529,568*

favorite [*adj*] *preferred*
admired, adored, beloved, best-loved, cherished, choice, darling, dear, dearest, desired, especial, esteemed, favored, intimate, liked, main, number one*, personal, pet*, pleasant, popular, precious, prized, revered, sweetheart*, treasured, wished-for; SEE CONCEPTS *529,568*

favorite [*n*] *something or someone cherished, prized*
apple of eye*, beloved, chalk*, choice, darling, dear, fave*, front-runner*, ideal, idol, love, main, minion, number one*, paramour, pet*, pick, preference, shoo-in*, teacher's pet*; SEE CONCEPTS *423,446*

favoritism [*n*] *bias, partiality*
discrimination, inclination, inequity, nepotism, one-sidedness, partisanship, preference, preferential treatment, unfairness; SEE CONCEPTS *41,388,645*

fawn [*n*] *baby deer*
baby buck, baby doe, yearling; SEE CONCEPTS *394,400*

fawn [*v*] *ingratiate oneself to; serve*
abase, apple-polish*, be at beck and call*, be obsequious, be servile, blandish, bow, brownnose*, buddy up*, butter up*, cajole, cater to, cave in to*, cotton*, court, cower, crawl, creep, cringe, crouch, curry favor*, debase, defer, fall all over, fall on one's knees*, flatter, grovel, honey up*, invite, jolly, kneel, kowtow*, lay it on*, lick boots*, make up to, massage*, oil*, pander, pay court*, play up to*, scrape, slaver, snow*, stoop, stroke*, submit, toady*, truckle*, woo*, yield; SEE CONCEPTS *110,384*

fawning [*adj*] *deferential, groveling*
abject, adulatory, bootlicking*, bowing, brownnosing*, compliant, cowering, crawling, cringing, flattering, humble, ingratiating, kowtowing*, mealy-mouthed*, obsequious, parasitic, prostrate, scraping, servile, slavish, snivel-

ing, spineless, submissive, subservient, sycophant, sycophantic; SEE CONCEPT *401*

fax [*n*] *facsimile*
copy, duplicate, electronic message, reproduction, transmission; SEE CONCEPTS *269,667,716*

fax [*v*] *copy*
deliver, relay, send, transmit; SEE CONCEPTS *269,667,716*

faze [*v*] *embarrass*
abash, annoy, appall, bother, confound, confuse, daunt, discomfit, disconcert, discountenance, dismay, dumbfound, horrify, irritate, muddle, mystify, nonplus, perplex, puzzle, rattle, vex; SEE CONCEPTS *7,19*

fear [*n*] *alarm, apprehension*
abhorrence, agitation, angst, anxiety, aversion, awe, bête noire, chickenheartedness*, cold feet*, cold sweat*, concern, consternation, cowardice, creeps, despair, discomposure, dismay, disquietude, distress, doubt, dread, faintheartedness, foreboding, fright, funk*, horror, jitters, misgiving, nightmare, panic, phobia, presentiment, qualm, recreancy, reverence, revulsion, scare, suspicion, terror, timidity, trembling, tremor, trepidation, unease, uneasiness, worry; SEE CONCEPT *27*

fear [*v*] *feel alarm; be scared of*
anticipate, apprehend, avoid, be afraid, be anxious, be apprehensive, be disquieted, be frightened, be in awe, blanch, break out in a sweat*, cower, crouch, dare not, dread, expect, falter, feel concern, flinch, foresee, fret, have butterflies*, have qualms, lose courage*, quail, quaver, shrink, shudder, shun, shy, start, suspect, tremble, wilt, worry; SEE CONCEPT *27*

fearful [*adj1*] *alarmed, apprehensive*
aflutter, afraid, aghast, agitated, anxious, chicken, chickenhearted*, diffident, discomposed, disquieted, disturbed, fainthearted, frightened, goose-bumpy*, have cold feet*, hesitant, in a dither*, intimidated, jittery, jumpy, lily-livered*, mousy, nerveless, nervous, nervy, panicky, perturbed, phobic, pusillanimous, quivery, rabbity*, running scared*, scared, shaky, sheepish*, shrinking, shy, skittish, solicitous, spineless, tense, timid, timorous, tremulous, uneasy, unmanly, weak-kneed*, worried, yellow*; SEE CONCEPT *401*

fearful [*adj2*] *horrifying*
appalling, astounding, atrocious, awful, baleful, bloodcurdling, creepy, dire, distressing, dreadful, eerie, formidable, frightful, ghastly, ghoulish, grievous, grim, grisly, gruesome, hair-raising*, hideous, horrendous, horrible, horrific, lurid, macabre, monstrous, morbid, overwhelming, redoubtable, shocking, shuddersome, sinister, strange, sublime, terrible, tremendous, unearthly, unspeakable; SEE CONCEPTS *529,537,570*

fearless [*adj*] *brave, unafraid*
assured, aweless, bodacious, bold, brassy, cheeky, chesty*, cocky, confident, cool hand*, courageous, crack*, daring, dashing, dauntless, doughty, flip*, fresh*, gallant, game, gritty, gutsy, heroic, icy*, indomitable, intrepid, lionhearted, nervy, plucky, salty*, sanguine, sassy*, smart, spunky, sure, temerarious, unabashed, undaunted, unflinching, valiant, valorous, wise; SEE CONCEPT *401*

feasible [*adj*] *possible, doable*
achievable, advantageous, appropriate, attain-

able, beneficial, breeze, cinch, duck soup*, easy as pie*, expedient, fit, fitting, likely, no sweat*, performable, pie*, piece of cake*, practicable, practical, probable, profitable, pushover, realizable, reasonable, simple as ABC*, snap, suitable, viable, workable, worthwhile; SEE CONCEPTS *528,552,558*

feast [*n*] *banquet and celebration*
barbecue, big feed*, blow*, blowout*, carnival, carousal, clambake, dinner, entertainment, fest, festival, festivity, fete, fiesta, gala, jollification, merrymaking, picnic, refreshment, regale, repast, spread, treat, wassail; SEE CONCEPTS *377,459*

feast [*v*] *eat a great amount or very well*
banquet, dine, eat sumptuously, entertain, gorge, gormandize, indulge, overindulge, regale, stuff, stuff one's face*, treat, wine and dine*; SEE CONCEPT *169*

feat [*n*] *achievement*
accomplishment, act, action, adventure, attainment, conquest, consummation, coup, deed, effort, enterprise, execution, exploit, performance, stunt, tour de force, triumph, venture, victory; SEE CONCEPTS *1,706*

feather [*n*] *tuft of bird; plumage*
calamus, crest, down, fin, fluff, fringe, penna, pinion, pinna, plume, plumule, pompon, quill, shaft, spike, wing; SEE CONCEPT *399*

feature [*n1*] *characteristic*
affection, angle, article, aspect, attribute, character, component, constituent, detail, differential, earmark*, element, facet, factor, gag*, gimmick, hallmark, idiosyncrasy, individuality, ingredient, integrant, item, mark, notability, particularity, peculiarity, point, property, quality, savor, slant*, speciality, specialty, trait, twist*, unit, virtue; SEE CONCEPTS *831,834,835*

feature [*n2*] *highlight, special attraction*
big show*, crowd puller*, draw, drawing card*, headliner*, innovation, main item, peculiarity, prominent part, speciality, specialty; SEE CONCEPTS *386,829*

feature [*n3*] *special article in publication*
column, comment, item, piece, report, story; SEE CONCEPT *270*

feature [*v*] *give prominence to*
accentuate, advertise, blaze*, call attention to, emphasize, headline*, italicize, make conspicuous, mark, play up*, point up*, present, promote, set off*, spotlight*, star, stress, underline, underscore; SEE CONCEPT *60*

featureless [*adj*] *nondescript*
bland, characterless, faceless, forgettable, nameless, plain, stark, unadorned; SEE CONCEPTS *485,589*

features [*n*] *facial characteristics*
appearance, countenance, face, lineaments, looks, mien, mug*, physiognomy, puss*, visage; SEE CONCEPT *418*

featuring [*adj*] *giving prominence to*
calling attention to, displaying, drawing attention to, giving center stage to*, headlining*, highlighting, making much of*, pointing up*, presenting, promoting, pushing, recommending, showing, showing off*, starring, turning, turning the spotlight on*; SEE CONCEPT *292*

febrile [*adj*] *feverish*
delirious, fevered, fiery, flushed, hallucinatory, hot, inflamed, pyretic; SEE CONCEPTS *314,605*

feckless [*adj*] *without purpose*
aimless, carefree, careless, feeble, fustian, futile, good-for-nothing*, hopeless, incautious, incompetent, ineffective, ineffectual, irresponsible, meaningless, reckless, shiftless, uncareful, useless, weak, wild, worthless; SEE CONCEPTS *404, 542*

fecund [*adj*] *productive*
breeding, fertile, fructiferous, fruitful, generating, pregnant, proliferant, prolific, propagating, reproducing, rich, spawning, teeming; SEE CONCEPT *537*

federation [*n*] *partnership, organization*
alliance, amalgamation, association, bunch, coalition, combination, confederacy, crew, crowd, entente, family, federacy, gang, league, mob, outfit, pool, ring, syndicate, syndication, tribe, union; SEE CONCEPTS *323,381,417*

fed up [*adj*] *disgusted with*
annoyed, blasé, blue*, bored, depressed, discontented, dismal, dissatisfied, down, gloomy, glum, jaded, sated, satiated, sick and tired*, surfeited, tired, up to here*, weary; SEE CONCEPT *403*

fee [*n*] *charge for service or privilege*
account, ante*, bill, bite*, chunk*, commission, compensation, consideration, cost, cut*, emolument, end*, expense, gravy*, handle, hire, honorarium, house*, juice*, pay, payment, percentage, piece*, piece of the action*, price, rakeoff*, recompense, remuneration, reward, salary, share, slice*, stipend, take*, take-in*, toll, wage; SEE CONCEPTS *329,344*

feeble [*adj*] *not strong; ineffective*
aged, ailing, chicken*, debilitated, decrepit, delicate, doddering, dopey*, effete, emasculated, enervated, enfeebled, etiolated, exhausted, failing, faint, flabby*, flat, fragile, frail, gentle, helpless, impotent, inadequate, incompetent, indecisive, ineffectual, inefficient, infirm, insubstantial, insufficient, lame, languid, low, out of gas*, paltry, poor, powerless, puny, sapless, sickly, slight, strengthless, tame, thin, unconvincing, vitiated, weak, weakened, weakly, wimpy*, woozy*, zero*; SEE CONCEPTS *267,489,527*

feebleminded [*adj*] *mentally handicapped*
dim-witted, dull-witted, dumb, half-witted, imbecilic, moronic, retarded, simple, slow, soft in the head, stupid, unintelligent, weak-minded; SEE CONCEPTS *402,548*

feebleness [*n*] *lack of strength; ineffectiveness*
debility, decrepitude, delicacy, disease, effeteness, enervation, etiolation, exhaustion, flimsiness, frailness, frailty, inability, inadequacy, incapacity, incompetence, ineffectualness, infirmity, infirmness, insignificance, insufficiency, lameness, languor, lassitude, malaise, senility, sickliness, unhealthiness, weakness; SEE CONCEPTS *630,676,732*

feed [*n*] *food*
animal food, barley, corn, fodder, forage, grain, grass, grub, hay, meal, pasturage, provender, provisions, silage, straw, vittles; SEE CONCEPTS *457,460,461*

feed [*v*] *give nourishment; augment*
banquet, bolster, cater, cram, deliver, dine, dish out*, dispense, encourage, fatten, feast, fill, find, foster, fuel, furnish, give, gorge, hand, hand over, maintain, minister, nourish, nurse, nurture, provide, provision, regale, satisfy, stock,

strengthen, stuff, supply, support, sustain, victual, wine and dine*; SEE CONCEPTS *107,140*

feedback [*n*] *response*
answer, assessment, comeback, comment, criticism, evaluation, observation, reaction, rebuttal, reply, retaliation, sentiment; SEE CONCEPT *278*

feed on [*v*] *consume*
devour, eat, exist on, fare, feast, graze, have a bite*, ingest, live on*, meal, munch, nibble, nurture, partake, pasture*, peck*, pig out*, prey on, scarf*, snack, sponge, subsist, take, take nourishment; SEE CONCEPT *169*

feel [*n*] *texture; air*
ambience, atmosphere, aura, feeling, finish, impression, mood, palpation, quality, semblance, sensation, sense, surface, tactility, taction, touch, vibes; SEE CONCEPTS *611,673*

feel [*v1*] *touch, stroke*
apperceive, caress, clasp, clutch, explore, finger, fondle, frisk, fumble, grapple, grasp, grip, grope, handle, manipulate, maul, palm, palpate, paw, perceive, pinch, ply, poke, press, run hands over*, sense, squeeze, test, thumb, tickle, try, twiddle, wield; SEE CONCEPT *612*

feel [*v2*] *experience*
accept, acknowledge, appear, appreciate, be affected, be aware of, be excited, be impressed, be sensible of, be sensitive, be turned on to*, comprehend, discern, encounter, endure, enjoy, exhibit, get*, get in touch*, get vibes*, go through*, have, have a hunch, have funny feeling*, have vibes*, know, meet, note, notice, observe, perceive, receive, remark, resemble, savor, see, seem, sense, suffer, suggest, take to heart*, taste, undergo, understand, welcome; SEE CONCEPTS *15,34,38*

feel [*v3*] *believe*
assume, be convinced, be of the opinion, conclude, conjecture, consider, credit, deduce, deem, esteem, gather, guess, have a hunch*, have the impression*, hold, infer, intuit, judge, know, presume, repute, sense, suppose, surmise, suspect, think; SEE CONCEPT *12*

feeling [*n1*] *sensation, especially of touch*
activity, awareness, consciousness, enjoyment, excitability, excitation, excitement, feel, innervation, motility, motor response, pain, perceiving, perception, pleasure, reaction, receptivity, reflex, responsiveness, sense, sensibility, sensitivity, sensuality, tactility, tangibility, titillation; SEE CONCEPT *608*

feeling [*n2*] *idea, impression*
apprehension, belief, consciousness, conviction, eye*, hunch*, inclination, inkling, instinct, mind, notion, opinion, outlook, persuasion, point of view, presentiment, reaction, sense, sentiment, suspicion, thought, view; SEE CONCEPTS *532,689, 690*

feeling [*n3*] *a state of mind, often strong*
action, affection, appreciation, ardor, behavior, capacity, compassion, concern, cultivation, culture, delicacy, discernment, discrimination, emotion, empathy, faculty, fervor, fondness, heat, imagination, impression, intelligence, intensity, intuition, judgment, keenness, palpability, passion, pathos, pity, reaction, refinement, sensibility, sensitivity, sentiment, sentimentality, sharpness, spirit, sympathy, tangibility, taste, tenderness, understanding, warmth; SEE CONCEPTS *409,410*

feeling [*n4*] *ambience*
air, atmosphere, aura, impression, imprint, mood, quality, semblance; SEE CONCEPT *673*

feign [*v*] *pretend*
act, affect, assume, bluff*, counterfeit, devise, dissemble, dissimulate, do a bit*, fabricate, fake, forge, four-flush*, give appearance of, imagine, imitate, invent, make show of*, phony up*, play, play possum*, put on, put on act*, put up a front*, sham*, simulate, stonewall*; SEE CONCEPTS *59,63,292*

feigned [*adj*] *pretended*
affected, artificial, assumed, counterfeit, fabricated, fake, faked, false, fictitious, imaginary, imagined, imitation, insincere, phony, pretended, pseudo*, put-on*, sham*, simulated, spurious; SEE CONCEPTS *401,582*

feint [*n*] *pretense*
artifice, bait, blind, bluff, cheat, deceit, distraction, dodge, duck, expedient, fake, gambit, hoax, hoodwinking*, imposture, make-believe, maneuver, mock attack, play, ploy, pretension, pretext, ruse, sham*, shift, snare, stall, stratagem, subterfuge, trick, wile; SEE CONCEPTS *633,660,725*

feisty [*adj*] *spirited; touchy*
active, alive, bubbly, courageous, difficult, enthusiastic, excitable, fiery, frisky, full of pep, game, gritty, gutsy, gutty, high-strung, hotblooded, lively, mettlesome, ornery, peppy, quarrelsome, scrappy, sensitive, spunky, thinskinned, tough, truculent, zestful; SEE CONCEPTS *404,542*

felicitate [*v*] *congratulate*
commend, compliment, praise, recommend, rejoice with, salute, wish joy to; SEE CONCEPT *69*

felicitous [*adj*] *appropriate, suitable*
applicable, apposite, apropos, apt, convincing, fit, fitting, germane, happy, inspired, just, meet, neat, opportune, pat, pertinent, proper, propitious, relevant, seasonable, telling, timely, wellchosen, well-timed; SEE CONCEPTS *558,799*

felicity [*n1*] *happiness*
bliss, cheerfulness, contentment, delight, ecstasy, elation, enjoyment, euphoria, exhilaration, exuberance, glee, good spirits, joviality, joy, jubilation, merriment, mirth, pleasure, rapture, well-being; SEE CONCEPT *410*

felicity [*n2*] *appropriateness*
applicability, aptness, becomingness, suitability; SEE CONCEPT *558*

fell [*v*] *chop down*
blow down, bowl over*, bring down, cause to fall, cleave, cut, cut down, dash, demolish, down, drop, flatten, floor*, gash, ground, hack, hew, knock down, knock over, lay low*, level, mangle, mow down*, prostrate, pull down, raze, rive, sever, shoot, shoot down*, slash, split, strike down, sunder, throw down, tumble; SEE CONCEPTS *176,181*

fellow [*n2*] *male or female colleague, friend*
assistant, associate, cohort, companion, compeer, comrade, concomitant, confrere, consort, coordinate, counterpart*, coworker, double, duplicate, equal, instructor, lecturer, match, mate, member, partner, peer, professor, reciprocal, twin; SEE CONCEPTS *348,423*

fellowship [*n*] *sociability, association*
acquaintance, affability, alliance, amity, camaraderie, club, communion, companionability, companionship, company, comradeship, convivi-

fe
fe

ality, familiarity, friendliness, guild, intimacy, kindliness, league, order, society, sodality, togetherness; SEE CONCEPTS *387,388*

felon [*n*] *criminal*
con, convict, delinquent, ex-con*, jailbird*, lawbreaker, lifer*, loser*, malefactor, offender, outlaw, yardbird*; SEE CONCEPT *412*

felonious [*adj*] *criminal*
base, corrupt, evil, illegal, illicit, lawbreaking, villainous, wrongful; SEE CONCEPT *545*

felony [*n*] *crime*
arson, assault, burglary, criminal offense, foul play, murder, offense, rape, robbery, violation, wrongdoing; SEE CONCEPT *192*

female [*adj*] *having the qualities or characteristics of a woman*
effeminate, fecund, feminine, fertile, maternal, muliebrous, womanish, womanly; SEE CONCEPTS *371,408*

female [*n*] *woman*
daughter, femme, gal, gentlewoman, girl, grandmother, lady, madam, matron, Miss/Mrs./Ms., mother, she, sister; SEE CONCEPT *415*

femininity/feminine [*n/adj*] *womanly*
effeminate, effete, fertile, gender, gynic, womanhood, womanish, womanliness; SEE CONCEPTS *371,372,408,648*

femme fatale [*n*] *seductress*
attractive woman, dangerous woman, enchantress, enticing woman, siren, temptress, vamp; SEE CONCEPTS *361,412,415*

fence [*n*] *barrier used to enclose a piece of land*
backstop, balustrade, bar, barbed wire, barricade, block, boards, chains, Cyclone, defense, dike, guard, hedge, net, paling, palisade, pickets, posts, rail, railing, rampart, roadblock, shield, stakes, stockade, stop, wall; SEE CONCEPTS *260,476,479*

fence [*v1*] *enclose or separate an area*
bound, cage, circumscribe, confine, coop, corral, defend, encircle, fortify, girdle, guard, hedge, hem, immure, mew, mure, pen, protect, rail, restrict, secure, surround, wall; SEE CONCEPT *758*

fence [*v2*] *dodge; beat around the bush*
avoid, baffle, cavil, duck, equivocate, evade, feint, foil, hedge, maneuver, outwit, parry, prevaricate, quibble, shift, shirk, sidestep, stonewall*, tergiversate; SEE CONCEPTS *30,59*

fend [*v*] *defend*
bulwark, cover, dodge, guard, oppose, parry, protect, repel, resist, safeguard, screen, secure, shield; SEE CONCEPT *96*

fender [*n*] *piece protecting part of a vehicle*
apron, buffer, bumper, cover, curb, cushion, frame, guard, mask, mudguard*, protector, screen, shield, splashboard, ward; SEE CONCEPT *502*

fend for [*v*] *take care of*
eke out existence*, look after, make do, make provision for, provide for, stay alive*, subsist, support, survive, sustain; SEE CONCEPTS *100,117*

fend off [*v*] *keep at bay*
avert, avoid, beat off*, deflect, drive back*, hold at bay*, keep at a distance, keep at arm's length*, keep off, parry, rebuff, rebuke, rebut, refuse, reject, repel, repulse, resist, snub, spurn, stave off, turn aside, ward off; SEE CONCEPT *96*

feral [*adj*] *untamed*
animal, brutal, ferocious, fierce, raging, savage, tameless, uncultivated, undomesticated, wild; SEE CONCEPTS *401,542*

ferment [*n1*] *substance causing chemicals to split into simpler substances*
bacteria, bacterium, barm, ebullition, enzyme, fermentation agent, leaven, leavening, mold, seethe, simmer, yeast; SEE CONCEPT *478*

ferment [*n2*] *agitation, uprising*
ailment, brouhaha, clamor, commotion, convulsion, disquiet, disquietude, disruption, disturbance, excitement, fever, flap, frenzy, furor, fuss, heat, hell broke loose*, hubbub, imbroglio, outcry, restiveness, restlessness, row, rumble, scene, state of unrest, stew*, stink*, stir, storm, to-do*, tumult, turbulence, turmoil, unrest, upheaval, uproar, upturn; SEE CONCEPTS *106,674*

ferment [*v*] *split into simpler substances; be agitated*
acidify, be violent, boil, brew, bubble, churn, concoct, dissolve, effervesce, evaporate, excite, fester, fizz, foam, foment, froth, heat, incite, inflame, leaven, moil, overflow, provoke, ripen, rise, rouse, seethe, simmer, sour, sparkle, stir up, work; SEE CONCEPTS *7,19,22,250*

ferocious [*adj*] *violent, barbaric*
barbarous, bloodthirsty, brutal, brutish, cruel, fell, feral, fierce, frightful, grim, implacable, inhuman, inhumane, lupine, merciless, murderous, pitiless, predatory, rapacious, ravening, ravenous, relentless, ruthless, sanguinary, savage, tigerish, truculent, unmerciful, unrestrained, untamed, vehement, vicious, voracious, wild, wolfish; SEE CONCEPTS *401,542*

ferocity [*adj*] *fierceness*
barbarity, bloodthirstiness, brutality, cruelty, ferociousness, murderousness, savagery, viciousness, violence, wildness; SEE CONCEPTS *401,542*

ferret out [*v*] *trace, search out*
ascertain, be on to, bring to light*, chase, determine, dig up*, disclose, discover, drive out, elicit, extract, follow, get at*, hunt, learn, nose out*, penetrate, pick up on, pierce, probe, pry, pursue, quest, root out*, seek, smell out*, smoke out*, track down, trail, unearth; SEE CONCEPTS *183,216*

ferry [*n*] *transportation boat*
barge, ferryboat, packet, packet boat, passage boat; SEE CONCEPT *506*

ferry [*v*] *carry across*
bear, buck, carry, chauffeur, convey, lug*, move across, pack, run, schlepp*, send, ship, shuttle, tote*, transport; SEE CONCEPTS *187,217*

fertile [*adj*] *ready to bear, produce*
abundant, arable, bearing, black, bountiful, breeding, breedy, bringing forth, childing, fecund, feracious, flowering, flowing with milk and honey*, fruitful, generative, gravid, hebetic, loamy, lush, luxuriant, plenteous, plentiful, pregnant, procreant, producing, productive, proliferant, prolific, puberal, pubescent, rank, rich, spawning, teeming, uberous, vegetative, virile, with child*, yielding; SEE CONCEPTS *372,485*

fertility [*n*] *readiness to bear, produce*
abundance, copiousness, fecundity, feracity, fruitfulness, generative capacity, gravidity, luxuriance, plentifulness, potency, pregnancy, productiveness, productivity, prolifacacy, prolificity, puberty, pubescence, richness, uberty, virility; SEE CONCEPTS *372,723*

fertilize [v] *make ready to bear, produce*
beget, breed, compost, cover, dress, enrich, fecundate, feed, fructify, generate, germinate, impregnate, inseminate, lime, make fruitful, make pregnant, manure, mulch, pollinate, procreate, propagate, top-dress, treat; SEE CONCEPTS 257,374,375

fertilizer [n] *dressing to aid production of crops*
buffalo chips*, compost, cow chips*, dung, guano, humus, manure, maul*, mulch, peat moss, plant food, potash, top dressing*; SEE CONCEPTS 260,399,429

fervent/fervid [adj] *enthusiastic, excited*
animated, ardent, blazing, burning, devout, dying to*, eager, earnest, ecstatic, emotional, enthused, falling all over oneself*, fiery, glowing, go great guns*, heartfelt, hearty, hot*, hot-blooded*, impassioned, intense, passionate, perfervid, pious, religious, responsive, serious, sincere, unfeigned, vehement, warm, warmhearted, wholehearted, zealous; SEE CONCEPTS 401,542

fervor [n] *excitement, enthusiasm*
animation, ardency, ardor, devoutness, eagerness, earnestness, fervency, fire*, heartiness, heat*, hurrah, intensity, jazz*, love, oomph*, passion, pep talk*, piety, piousness, religiousness, seriousness, sincerity, solemnity, vehemence, warmth, weakness, wholeheartedness, zeal, zealousness; SEE CONCEPTS 633,657

fester [v] *intensify; become inflamed*
aggravate, blister, canker, chafe, decay, gall, gather, irk, maturate, putrefy, rankle, rot, smolder, suppurate, ulcer, ulcerate; SEE CONCEPTS 469,698

festival [n] *celebration*
anniversary, carnival, commemoration, competition, entertainment, fair, feast, festivities, fete, field day, fiesta, gala, holiday, jubilee, merrymaking, treat; SEE CONCEPT 377

festive [adj] *decorated, celebratory*
blithe, bouncy, carnival, cheery, chipper*, chirpy, convivial, festal, gala, gay, gleeful, go-go*, grooving, happy, hearty, holiday, jocund, jolly, jovial, joyful, joyous, jubilant, juiced up*, jumping, lighthearted, merry, mirthful, peppy*, perky, rocking*, snappy*, swinging, upbeat, zippy*; SEE CONCEPTS 403,548

festivity [n] *celebration, revelry*
amusement, bash*, blowout*, carousal*, clambake*, conviviality, do*, entertainment, festival, fun, fun and games*, gaiety, happiness, hilarity, hoopla, jamboree, jollity, joviality, joyfulness, levity, merriment, merrymaking, mirth, party, pleasure, revel, reveling, revelment, shindig*, sport, whoopee*, wingding*; SEE CONCEPTS 377,383

festoon [v] *decorate*
adorn, deck, drape, garnish, hang, trim, wreath; SEE CONCEPTS 162,177

fetch [v] *go get, bring in*
back, bear, be sold for, bring, bring back, bring to, buck, call for, carry, conduct, convey, deliver, draw forth, earn, elicit, escort, get, give rise to, go for, gun, heel, lead, lug*, make, obtain, pack, piggyback*, produce, realize, retrieve, ride, sell, sell for, shlep*, shoulder*, tote, transport, truck*, yield; SEE CONCEPTS 90,124,131

fetching [adj] *alluring, attractive*
beautiful, captivating, charming, cute, enchanting, enticing, fascinating, intriguing, luring,

pleasing, sweet, taking, tempting, winsome; SEE CONCEPTS 537,579

fete [n] *celebration, party*
ball, banquet, bazaar, do*, fair, festival, fiesta, gala; SEE CONCEPT 377

fete [v] *throw a party for someone*
celebrate, entertain, feast, festival, hold reception for, holiday, honor, lionize, make much of*, roll out the red carpet*, treat, wine and dine*; SEE CONCEPT 384

fetid [adj] *foul, rancid*
corrupt, fusty, grody*, gross*, icky*, loathsome, lousy, malodorous, mephitic, noisome, noxious, offensive, putrid, rank, reeking, repugnant, repulsive, revolting, rotten, smelly, stenchy, stinking, stinky, strong, yecchy*, yucky*; SEE CONCEPT 598

fetish [n1] *obsession*
bias, craze*, desire, fixation, golden calf*, idée fixe, leaning, luck, mania, partiality, penchant, periapt, predilection, prejudice, preoccupation, prepossession, proclivity, propensity, stimulant, thing*; SEE CONCEPTS 529,689

fetish [n2] *object believed to have supernatural powers*
amulet, charm, cult object, idol, image, juju*, mascot, phylactery, superstition, talisman, voodoo doll*, zemi; SEE CONCEPTS 446,687

fetter [v] *tie up, hold*
bind, chain, check, clog, confine, cuff, curb, drag feet, encumber, hamper, hamstring*, handcuff, hang up, hinder, hobble, hog-tie*, hold captive, leash, manacle, put straitjacket on*, repress, restrain, restrict, shackle, throw monkey wrench in*, trammel; SEE CONCEPTS 130,191

fetters [n] *bindings; bondage*
bilboes, bonds, captivity, chains, check, cuffs, curb, handcuffs, hindrance, irons, manacles, obstruction, restraint, shackles, trammels; SEE CONCEPTS 130,191,500

fettle [n] *spirits*
condition, emotional state, mental state, order, shape, sound condition, state of mind; SEE CONCEPTS 407,411

fetus [n] *unborn young*
blastosphere, blastula, developing infant, embryo, fertilized egg; SEE CONCEPTS 414,424

feud [n] *major argument; estrangement*
altercation, bad blood*, bickering, broil*, combat, conflict, contention, contest, controversy, disagreement, discord, dispute, dissension, enmity, faction, falling out*, fight, fracas, grudge, hostility, quarrel, rivalry, row, run-in*, squabble, strife, vendetta; SEE CONCEPTS 46,106,388

feud [v] *fight bitterly; fall out*
be at daggers with*, be at odds*, bicker, brawl, clash, contend, dispute, duel, quarrel, row, squabble, war; SEE CONCEPTS 46,106

fever [n] *state of high temperature or agitation*
burning up*, delirium, ecstasy, excitement, febrile disease, ferment, fervor, fire, flush, frenzy, heat, intensity, passion, pyrexia, restlessness, running a temperature*, the shakes*, turmoil, unrest; SEE CONCEPTS 410,610

feverish [adj1] *having a high temperature*
above normal*, aguey, burning, burning up*, febrile, fevered, fiery, flushed, having the shakes*, hectic, hot, inflamed, on fire, pyretic, running a temperature*; SEE CONCEPT 605

feverish [adj2] *excited, agitated*
burning, distracted, fervid, fevered, frantic, frenetic, frenzied, furious, heated, hectic, high-
strung*, impatient, keyed up*, nervous,
obsessive, overwrought, passionate, restless; SEE
CONCEPT *401*

few [adj] *hardly any*
exiguous, few and far between*, imperceptible,
inconsequential, inconsiderable, infrequent, insufficient, lean, less, meager, middling, minor,
minority, minute, negligible, not many, not too
many*, occasional, paltry, petty, piddling, rare,
scant, scanty, scarce, scarcely any, scattered,
scattering, seldom, semioccasional, short,
skimpy, slender, slight, slim, some, sparse, sporadic, stingy, straggling, thin, trifling, uncommon, unfrequent, widely spaced; SEE CONCEPTS
771,789

few [prep] *scarcely any*
not many, not too many*, scattering, several,
slim pickings*, small number, smatter, smattering, some, spattering, sprinkling; SEE CONCEPT
787

fiancé/fiancée [n] *person engaged to marry*
affianced person, betrothed, engaged person,
future*, husband-to-be, intended, prospective
spouse, steady*, wife-to-be; SEE CONCEPTS
414,423

fiasco [n] *catastrophe*
abortion, blunder, botched situation, breakdown,
debacle, disaster, dumb thing to do*, dumb
trick*, embarrassment, error, failure, farce, flap,
flop, mess, miscarriage, route, ruin, screwup*,
stunt, washout*; SEE CONCEPT *674*

fiat [n] *order, proclamation*
authorization, command, decree, dictate, dictum,
edict, endorsement, mandate, ordinance, permission, precept, sanction, ukase, warrant; SEE CON-
CEPT *685*

fib [n] *undetailed lie*
canard, crock*, equivocation, evasiveness, fabrication, fairy tale*, falsehood, falsity, fiction,
invention, jazz*, line*, mendacity, misrepresentation, prevarication, spinach*, story, tale, untruth, untruthfulness, white lie*, whopper*,
yarn*; SEE CONCEPTS *278,282*

fib [v] *tell an undetailed lie*
concoct, create fiction, equivocate, fabricate, falsify, invent, jive*, make up, palter, plant, prevaricate, promote, shovel*, speak with forked
tongue*, stretch the truth*, tell a little white lie*,
trump up*; SEE CONCEPT *63*

fiber [n1] *strand of material*
cilia, cord, fibril, filament, footlet, grain, grit,
hair, shred, staple, string, strip, tendril, thread,
tissue, tooth, vein, warp, web, woof; SEE CON-
CEPTS *392,428,611,831*

fiber [n2] *texture*
essence, fabric, feel, hand, nap, nature, pile,
spirit, substance; SEE CONCEPTS *411,682*

fibrous [adj] *stringy*
coarse, fibroid, hairy, muscular, pulpy, ropy,
sinewy, stalky, threadlike, tissued, veined, wiry,
woody; SEE CONCEPT *606*

fickle [adj] *vacillating, blowing hot and cold*
arbitrary, capricious, changeable, cheating, coquettish, double-crossing, faithless, fitful, flighty,
frivolous, inconstant, irresolute, lubricious,
mercurial, mutable, quicksilver, sneaking, temperamental, ticklish, two-timing, unfaithful, un-

predictable, unstable, unsteady, untrue, variable,
volatile, whimsical, yo-yo*; SEE CONCEPTS
401,534,545

fiction [n] *made-up story*
anecdote, best seller, book, cliff-hanger*,
clothesline*, concoction, crock*, drama, fable,
fabrication, falsehood, fancy, fantasy, fib, figment of imagination*, fish story*, hooey*, imagination, improvisation, invention, legend, lie,
misrepresentation, myth, narrative, novel, potboiler*, prevarication, romance, smoke*, storytelling, tale, tall story*, terminological
inexactitude, untruth, whopper*, work of imagination, yarn*; SEE CONCEPTS *63,271,280,282*

fictitious [adj] *untrue, made-up*
apocryphal, artificial, assumed, bogus*, chimerical, concocted, cooked-up*, counterfeit, created,
deceptive, delusive, delusory, dishonest, ersatz*,
fabricated, factitious, fake, faked, false, fanciful,
fantastic, fashioned, feigned, fictional, fictive,
figmental, hyped up*, illusory, imaginary, imagined, improvised, invented, made, make-believe,
misleading, mock, mythical, phony, queer, romantic, sham*, simulated, spurious, suppositious, supposititious, synthetic, trumped-up*,
unreal; SEE CONCEPTS *267,582*

fiddle [v] *mess with, tinker*
dabble, doodle, feel, fidget, finger, fool, handle,
interfere, mess, mess around*, monkey*, play,
potter, puddle, putter, tamper, touch, toy, trifle,
twiddle; SEE CONCEPTS *87,291*

fidelity [n1] *faithfulness in a relationship*
allegiance, ardor, attachment, constancy, dependability, devotedness, devotion, faith, fealty,
integrity, loyalty, piety, reliability, staunchness,
steadfastness, true-heartedness, trustworthiness;
SEE CONCEPTS *32,388*

fidelity [n2] *conformity to a standard*
accuracy, adherence, adhesion, attachment,
closeness, constancy, correspondence, exactitude, exactness, faithfulness, loyalty, naturalism,
preciseness, precision, realism, scrupulousness,
verism; SEE CONCEPT *636*

fidget [v] *move restlessly*
be antsy*, be hyper*, be nervous, be on pins and
needles*, be spooked*, be wired*, bustle, chafe,
fiddle, fret, fuss, hitch, jiggle, jitter, joggle, jump,
play, squirm, stir, toss, trifle, twiddle, twitch,
wiggle, worry; SEE CONCEPT *147*

fidgety [adj] *restlessly moving*
antsy*, apprehensive, high-strung*, hyper*, impatient, jerky, jittery, jumpy, nervous, nervous
wreck*, nervy, on edge*, on pins and needles*,
restive, restless, spooked*, spooky*, twitchy, uneasy, unrestful, up the wall*, wired*; SEE CON-
CEPT *401*

field [n1] *open land that can be cultivated*
acreage, cropland, enclosure, farmland, garden,
glebe, grassland, green, ground, lea, mead,
meadow, moorland, pasture, patch, plot, ranch-
land, range, terrain, territory, tillage, tract, vineyard; SEE CONCEPTS *509,517*

field [n2] *persons taking part in competition*
applicants, candidates, competition, competitors,
contestants, entrants, entries, nominees, participants, possibilities, runners; SEE CONCEPTS
325,365,417

field [n3] *sphere of influence, activity, interest,
study*
area, avocation, bailiwick, bounds, calling,

champaign, circle, compass, confines, cup of tea*, demesne, department, discipline, domain, dominion, environment, job, jurisdiction, limits, line, long suit*, margin, métier, occupation, orbit, precinct, province, purview, racket, range, reach, region, scope, speciality, specialty, sweep, terrain, territory, thing, vocation, walk, weakness, work; SEE CONCEPT *349*

field [*n4*] *arena with special use, as athletics*
amphitheater, battlefield, circuit, course, court, diamond, fairground, golf course, green, gridiron, grounds, landing strip, lot, park, playground, playing area, racecourse, race track, range, rink, stadium, terrain, theater, track, turf; SEE CONCEPTS *364,438,449*

field [*v*] *catch a hit or thrown object*
cover, deal with, deflect, handle, hold, occupy, patrol, pick up, play, retrieve, return, stop, turn aside; SEE CONCEPT *164*

field trip [*n*] *outing*
day trip, excursion, expedition, school outing, school trip; SEE CONCEPTS *224,386*

fiend [*n1*] *dastardly person*
barbarian, beast, brute, degenerate, demon, devil, diablo*, evil spirit, hellion, imp, little devil*, Mephistopheles, monster, ogre, Satan, savage, serpent, troll; SEE CONCEPT *412*

fiend [*n2*] *person overenthusiastic about interest*
addict, aficionado, bigot, devotee, enthusiast, fan, fanatic, freak, maniac, monomaniac, nut*, votarist, votary, zealot; SEE CONCEPT *423*

fiendish [*adj*] *diabolical*
atrocious, beastly, brutish, cruel, demonic, demonical, devilish, diabolic, evil, hellish, inhuman, malicious, nefarious, sadistic, satanic, savage, vicious, wicked; SEE CONCEPT *545*

fierce [*adj*] *violent, menacing*
angry, animal, ape, awful, barbarous, bloodthirsty, blustery, boisterous, bold, brutal, brutish, cruel, cutthroat*, dangerous, enraged, fell, feral, ferocious, fiery, flipped*, frightening, furious, horrible, howling, impetuous, infuriated, intense, malevolent, malign, murderous, passionate, powerful, primitive, raging, raving, relentless, savage, stormy, strong, tempestuous, terrible, threatening, tigerish, truculent, tumultous/tumultuous, uncontrollable, untamed, vehement, venomous, vicious, wild; SEE CONCEPTS *525,537,540*

fiercely [*adv*] *violently, menacingly*
angrily, awfully, boldly, brutally, ferociously, forcefully, forcibly, frantically, frenziedly, frighteningly, furiously, hard, horribly, impetuously, in a frenzy, irresistibly, like cats and dogs*, madly, maleficiently, malevolently, malignly, mightily, monstrous, no holds barred*, passionately, riotously, roughly, savagely, severely, stormily, tempestuously, terribly, threateningly, tigerishly, tooth and nail*, turbulently, uncontrollably, vehemently, venomously, viciously, wildly, with bared teeth*; SEE CONCEPTS *525,537,540*

fiery [*adj*] *passionate; on fire*
ablaze, afire, aflame, agitable, alight, blazing, burning, choleric, combustible, conflagrant, enthusiastic, excitable, febrile, fervid, fevered, feverish, fierce, flaming, flaring, flickering, flushed, glowing, heated, hot, hot-blooded, hotheaded*, hot-tempered*, igneous, ignited, impassioned, impetuous, impulsive, inflamed, in flames, intense, irascible, irritable, madcap, pep-

pery, perfervid, precipitate, red-hot*, spirited, unrestrained, vehement, violent; SEE CONCEPTS *401,542,605*

fiesta [*n*] *day of rest; religious celebration*
carnival, feast, festival, holiday, holy day, saint's day, vacation; SEE CONCEPTS *377,386*

fight [*n1*] *physical encounter*
action, affray, altercation, argument, battle, battle royal*, bout, brawl, broil, brush, clash, combat, conflict, confrontation, contention, contest, controversy, difficulty, disagreement, dispute, dissension, dogfight, duel, engagement, exchange, feud, fisticuffs*, fracas, fray, free-for-all*, fuss, hostility, joust, match, melee, quarrel, riot, rivalry, round, row, ruckus, rumble, scrap*, scrimmage, scuffle, set-to*, skirmish, sparring match, strife, struggle, tiff, to-do*, tussle, war, wrangling; SEE CONCEPT *106*

fight [*n2*] *courage, will to resist*
aggression, aggressiveness, attack, backbone, belligerence, boldness, combativeness, gameness, hardihood, mettle, militancy, pluck, pugnacity, resistance, spirit; SEE CONCEPT *411*

fight [*v1*] *engage in physical encounter*
altercate, assault, attack, bandy with*, battle, bear arms, bicker, box, brawl, brush with*, buck, carry on war, challenge, clash, contend, cross swords, dispute, do battle, duel, exchange blows, feud, flare up, go to war, grapple, joust, meet, mix it up*, oppugn, ply weapons, protect, quarrel, repel, resist, rowdy, scrap, scuffle, skirmish, spar, strive, struggle, take all comers*, take the field*, take up the gauntlet*, tiff*, tilt*, traverse, tug, tussle, wage war, war, withstand, wrangle, wrestle; SEE CONCEPT *106*

fight [*v2*] *oppose action, belief*
argue, bicker, buck*, buckle down*, carry on, combat, conduct, contest, continue, defy, dispute, effect, endure, engage in, exert oneself, fall out, force, further, hammer away*, hassle, lay into*, light into*, maintain, make a stand against*, oppose, persevere, persist, prosecute, push forward, put up an argument*, repel, resist, row, spare no effort*, squabble, stand up to*, strive, struggle, support, take on, take pains*, tangle with, toil on, travail, traverse, uphold, wage, withstand, wrangle; SEE CONCEPTS *46,100,384*

fight back/fight off [*v*] *defend oneself*
beat off*, bottle up*, check, contain, control, curb, fend off, hold at bay*, hold back, keep at bay*, oppose, put up fight, repel, reply, repress, repulse, resist, restrain, retaliate, stave off, ward off; SEE CONCEPTS *96,106*

fighter [*n*] *person engaged in hostile encounter*
aggressor, antagonist, assailant, battler, belligerent, boxer, brawler, bruiser*, bully, champion, combatant, competitor, contender, contestant, disputant, duelist, GI, gladiator, heavy*, jouster, mercenary, militant, opponent, person-at-arms, pugilist, punching bag*, rival, scrapper, serviceperson, slugger, soldier, tanker*, warrior, wildcat*; SEE CONCEPTS *358,366,412*

fighting [*adj*] *aggressive, warlike*
angry, argumentative, battling, bellicose, belligerent, boxing, brawling, combative, contending, contentious, determined, disputatious, disputative, fencing, ferocious, hawkish, hostile, jingoistic, jousting, martial, militant, militaristic, pugnacious, quarrelsome, ready to fight, resolute,

fe
fi

scrappy, skirmishing, sparring, tilting, truculent, unbeatable, under arms*, up in arms*, warmongering, wrestling; SEE CONCEPT *401*

fighting [*n*] *battle, encounter*
argument, battle royal*, beef*, bloodshed, blowup, bout, brannigan, brawling, brush, combat, conflict, contention, dispute, donnybrook*, exchange, flap*, fracas, free-for-all*, go, hassle, hell broke loose*, hostility, joust, match, melee, mix, punch out*, riot, roughhouse*, row, rowdy, rumble, rumpus, run-in*, scramble, scrap*, scrimmage, scuffle, set-to*, spat, strife, struggle, tiff, war, warfare, words, wrangle; SEE CONCEPT *106*

figment [*n*] *creation in one's mind*
bubble*, castle in the air*, chimera, daydream, dream, fable, fabrication, falsehood, fancy, fantasy, fiction, illusion, improvisation, invention, lie, nightmare, production; SEE CONCEPT *529*

figurative [*adj*] *not literal, but symbolic*
allegorical, denotative, descriptive, emblematic, emblematical, fanciful, florid, flowery, illustrative, metaphoric, metaphorical, ornate, pictorial, poetical, representative, signifying, typical; SEE CONCEPTS *267,582*

figure [*n1*] *numeral; numeric value*
amount, character, chiffer, cipher, cost, digit, integer, number, price, quotation, rate, sum, symbol, terms, total, worth; SEE CONCEPTS *784,787*

figure [*n2*] *form, shape; physical structure*
anatomy, appearance, attitude, bod*, body, build, carriage, cast, chassis*, configuration, conformation, constitution, delineation, development, frame, mass, measurements, outline, physique, pose, posture, proportions, shadow, silhouette, substance, torso; SEE CONCEPTS *733,754,757*

figure [*n3*] *object with design; depiction*
cast, composition, decoration, device, diagram, drawing, effigy, embellishment, emblem, illustration, image, model, mold, motif, motive, ornamentation, pattern, piece, portrait, representation, sketch, statue; SEE CONCEPTS *259,625*

figure [*n4*] *famous person*
celebrity, character, dignitary, force, leader, notability, notable, personage, personality, presence, somebody, worthy; SEE CONCEPTS *354,423*

figure [*v1*] *calculate, compute*
add, cast, cipher, count, count heads*, count noses*, cut ice*, dope out*, enumerate, estimate, fix a price, foot*, guess, keep tabs*, number, reckon, run down, sum, summate, take account of, tally, tot*, total, totalize, tote*, tot up*, work out; SEE CONCEPTS *197,764*

figure [*v2*] *understand; decide, infer*
catch on to, cipher, clear up, comprehend, conclude, crack, decipher, decode, determine, discover, disentangle, dope out*, fathom, follow, get*, make heads or tails of*, make out*, master, opine, puzzle out, reason, resolve, rule, see, settle, solve, suppose, think, think out, unfold, unravel, unriddle, unscramble, untangle; SEE CONCEPTS *15,18,37*

figurehead [*n*] *person who is leader in name only*
cipher, front*, mouthpiece*, nominal head, nonentity, nothing, puppet*, straw boss*, straw person, titular head, token; SEE CONCEPTS *354,423*

figure in [*v*] *contribute to*
act, appear, be conspicuous, be featured, be in-

cluded, be mentioned, have a place in, play a part*; SEE CONCEPT *112*

figure of speech [*n*] *communication that is not meant literally; stylistic device*
adumbration, allegory, alliteration, allusion, analogue, anaphora, anticlimax, antistrophe, antithesis, aposiopesis, apostrophe, asyndeton, bathos, comparison, conceit, echoism, ellipsis, euphemism, euphuism, exaggeration, hyperbole, image, imagery, irony, litotes, metaphor, metonymy, onomatopoeia, oxymoron, parable, paradox, parallel, personification, proteron, rhetoric, satire, simile, synecdoche, trope, tropology, turn of phrase, understatement; SEE CONCEPTS *275,278*

filch [*v*] *steal*
cop*, crib*, embezzle, hustle*, lift*, misappropriate, pilfer*, pinch*, purloin, rip off*, rob, scrounge, sneak, snipe, snitch*, swipe, take, thieve, walk off with*; SEE CONCEPTS *139,142*

file [*n1*] *system of order, placement for ease of use*
book, cabinet, case, census, charts, circular file*, data, directory, docket, documents, dossier, folder, index, information, list, notebook, pigeonhole*, portfolio, record, register, repository; SEE CONCEPTS *271,770*

file [*n2*] *line, queue*
column, echelon, list, parade, rank, row, string, tier, troop; SEE CONCEPT *727*

file [*v1*] *put in place, order*
alphabetize, arrange, catalog, catalogue, categorize, classify, deposit, docket, document, enter, index, list, pigeonhole*, record, register, slot, tabulate; SEE CONCEPTS *84,158*

file [*v2*] *rub down, grind*
abrade, burnish, erode, finish, furbish, grate, level, polish, rasp, raze, refine, scrape, shape, sharpen, smooth; SEE CONCEPTS *137,186,215,250*

filibuster [*n*] *obstruction of progress, especially in verbal argument*
delay, hindrance, holding the floor*, interference, opposition, postponement, procrastination, stonewalling*, talkathon*; SEE CONCEPT *298*

filigree [*n*] *ornamental art*
fretwork, interlace, lacework, lattice, ornamentation, tracery; SEE CONCEPT *473*

fill [*n*] *capacity*
all one wants, ample, enough, filler, padding, plenty, satiety, stuffing, sufficiency, sufficient; SEE CONCEPTS *719,736,794*

fill [*v1*] *to put in and occupy the whole of*
block, blow up, brim over, bulge out, charge, choke, clog, close, congest, cram, crowd, distend, fulfill, furnish, glut, gorge, heap, impregnate, inflate, jam-pack, lade, load, meet, overflow, overspread, pack, pack like sardines*, permeate, pervade, plug, puff up*, pump up, ram, ram in*, replenish, sate, satiate, satisfy, saturate, shoal, stock, stopper*, store, stretch, stuff, supply, swell, take up, top, top off*; SEE CONCEPTS *107,209*

fill [*v2*] *execute, fulfill*
answer, assign, carry out, discharge, dispatch, distribute, elect, engage, fix, hold, meet, name, occupy, officiate, perform, satisfy, take up; SEE CONCEPT *91*

fill in [*v1*] *answer in writing*
advise, apprise, clue, complete, fill out, inform,

insert, notify, post, sign, tell, warn, write in; SEE CONCEPTS *45,79*

fill in [*v2*] *act as substitute*
deputize, insinuate, interject, interpose, replace, represent, stand in, substract, take the place of, understudy; SEE CONCEPT *128*

filling/filler [*n*] *something that takes up capacity*
batting, bushing, cartridge, center, content, contents, cylinder, dressing, fill, guts*, impletion, inlay, innards, inside, layer, liner, mixture, pack, packing, pad, padding, refill, replenishment, shim, stuffing, wad, wadding; SEE CONCEPTS *826,830*

film [*n1*] *coating, tissue; mist*
blur, brume, cloud, coat, covering, dusting, fabric, foil, fold, gauze, haze, haziness, integument, layer, leaf, membrane, mistiness, nebula, obscuration, opacity, partition, pellicle, scum*, sheet, skin, transparency, veil, web; SEE CONCEPTS *478,524*

film [*n2*] *movie*
cinema, dailies*, flick*, footage, motion picture, moving picture, photoplay, picture, picture show, rushes, show, silent*, talkie*; SEE CONCEPT *293*

film [*v*] *take photographs*
photograph, put in the can*, record, roll, shoot, take, turn; SEE CONCEPTS *173,205*

filmy [*adj1*] *finespun, fragile*
chiffon, cobwebby*, dainty, delicate, diaphanous, fine, fine-grained, flimsy, floaty, gauzy, gossamer, insubstantial, see-through*, sheer, tiffany, transparent, wispy; SEE CONCEPT *606*

filmy [*adj2*] *covered with mist; blurry*
bleary, blurred, cloudy, dim, hazy, membranous, milky, misty, opalescent, opaque, pearly; SEE CONCEPTS *525,603*

filter [*v*] *separate to refine; seep through*
clarify, clean, distill, drain, dribble, escape, exude, filtrate, leak, metastasize, ooze, osmose, penetrate, percolate, permeate, purify, refine, screen, sieve, sift, soak through, strain, trickle, winnow; SEE CONCEPTS *135,165*

filth [*n*] *dirt, pollution*
carrion, contamination, corruption, crud*, defilement, dregs, dung, excrement, feces, feculence, filthiness, foul matter, foulness, garbage, grime, impurity, manure, mire, muck, mud, nastiness, ordure, putrefaction, putrescence, putridity, refuse, rottenness, sediment, sewage, silt, sleaze, slime, slop, sludge, slush, smut, trash, uncleanness; SEE CONCEPTS *260,674*

filthy [*adj1*] *dirty, polluted*
begrimed, black, blackened, cruddy*, crummy*, disheveled, fecal, feculent, foul, grimy*, gross*, grubby*, grungy*, impure, loathsome, miry, mucky*, muddy, nasty, obscene, offensive, putrid, repulsive, revolting, scummy, sleazy, slimy, slipshod, sloppy, slovenly, smoky, soiled, soily, sooty, squalid, unclean, uncleanly, unkempt, unwashed, verminous, vile, yecchy*; SEE CONCEPTS *485,570*

filthy [*adj2*] *vulgar, obscene*
base, bawdy, blue*, coarse, contemptible, corrupt, depraved, despicable, dirty-minded*, foul, foul-mouthed, impure, indecent, lewd, licentious, low, mean, nasty, offensive, pornographic, raunchy, scatological, scurvy, smutty, suggestive, vicious, vile; SEE CONCEPTS *267,545*

finagle [*v*] *maneuver*
cheat, contrive, deceive, manipulate, plot, scheme, swindle, trick, wheel and deal*; SEE CONCEPTS *36,59*

final [*adj1*] *ending, last*
closing, concluding, crowning, end, eventual, finishing, hindmost, lag, last-minute, latest, latter, supreme, terminal, terminating, ultimate; SEE CONCEPTS *531,820*

final [*adj2*] *conclusive, definitive*
absolute, decided, decisive, definite, determinate, determinative, finished, incontrovertible, irrefutable, irrevocable, settled, unanswerable, unappealable; SEE CONCEPT *535*

finale [*n*] *ending of an event*
afterpiece, blow-off*, button*, cessation, chaser*, climax, close, closer*, conclusion, consummation, crowning glory*, culmination, denouement, end, end piece, epilogue, finis, finish, last act, payoff*, peroration, summation, swan song*, termination, windup*; SEE CONCEPT *832*

finality [*n*] *definiteness, conclusiveness*
certitude, completeness, decidedness, decisiveness, entirety, finish, inevitableness, intactness, integrity, irrevocability, perfection, resolution, terminality, totality, unavoidability, wholeness; SEE CONCEPTS *635,638,832*

finalize [*v*] *finish, complete action*
agree, clinch*, conclude, consummate, decide, settle, sew up*, tie up*, work out, wrap up; SEE CONCEPT *91*

finally [*adv1*] *beyond any doubt*
assuredly, beyond recall*, beyond shadow of doubt*, certainly, completely, conclusively, convincingly, decisively, definitely, determinately, done with, enduringly, for all time*, for ever, for good*, in conclusion, inescapably, inexorably, irrevocably, lastly, once and for all*, past regret*, permanently, settled, with conviction; SEE CONCEPT *535*

finally [*adv2*] *in the end; after period of time*
after all, after a while, already, as a sequel, at last, at length, at long last*, at the end, at the last moment, belatedly, despite delay*, eventually, in conclusion, in spite of all*, in the eleventh hour*, in the long run*, lastly, someday, sometime, sooner or later*, subsequently, tardily, ultimately, yet; SEE CONCEPT *799*

finance [*n*] *economic affairs*
accounts, banking, business, commerce, economics, financial affairs, investment, money, money management; SEE CONCEPTS *360,770*

finance [*v*] *offer loan money; set up in business*
back, bank, bankroll, capitalize, endow, float*, fund, go for*, grubstake*, guarantee, juice*, lay on one*, loan shark*, patronize, pay for, pick up the check*, pick up the tab*, prime the pump*, promote, provide funds, provide security, put up money, raise dough*, sponsor, stake, subsidize, support, underwrite; SEE CONCEPTS *108,115,341*

finances [*n*] *person or corporation's money, property*
affairs, assets, balance sheet, budget, capital, cash, condition, funds, net, net worth, resources, revenue, wealth, wherewithal, worth; SEE CONCEPTS *340,710*

financial [*adj*] *having to do with money*
banking, budgeting, business, commercial, economic, fiscal, monetary, numbers*, numeric, pecuniary, pocket; SEE CONCEPT *334*

fi
fi

financier [n] *person who lends money, advises*
backer, banker, bankroller, broker, businessperson, capitalist, entrepreneur, fat cat*, grubstaker*, manipulator*, merchant, money, moneybags*, money lender, operator*, person who writes the checks*, rich person, Santa Claus*, speculator, sponsor, staker, stockbroker, tycoon, usurer; SEE CONCEPTS *347,348,353*

financing [n] *money for operating expenses*
costs, expenditure, funding, loan, matching funds, outgo, outlay, payment; SEE CONCEPTS *340,344*

find [n] *discovery*
acquisition, asset, bargain, boast, bonanza, catch, gem, good buy, jewel, one in a million*, pride, treasure, treasure trove; SEE CONCEPTS *337,712*

find [v1] *catch sight of, lay hands on*
arrive at, bring to light*, bump into*, chance upon, collar*, come across, come upon, come up with*, corral, descry, detect, dig up*, discern, discover, distinguish, encounter, espy, expose, fall in with*, ferret out, happen upon*, hit upon*, identify, lay fingers on, light upon*, locate, make out, meet, notice, observe, perceive, pinpoint, recognize, recover, run across, run into, scare up*, sight, smoke out*, spot, strike, stumble upon, track down, trip on*, turn up*, uncover, unearth; SEE CONCEPT *183*

find [v2] *achieve, win*
acquire, attain, be one's lot*, earn, fall to the lot*, gain, get, meet, meet with, obtain, procure; SEE CONCEPTS *124,706*

finding [n] *judgment, verdict*
award, conclusion, data, decision, decree, discovery, pronouncement, recommendation, sentence; SEE CONCEPT *685*

find out [v] *discover, learn*
ascertain, catch, catch on, detect, determine, disclose, divine, expose, hear, identify, note, observe, perceive, realize, reveal, see, uncover, unearth, unmask; SEE CONCEPTS *31,183*

fine [adj1] *excellent, masterly*
accomplished, aces*, admirable, attractive, beautiful, capital, choice, cool*, crack*, dandy*, elegant, enjoyable, exceptional, expensive, exquisite, fashionable, first-class, first-rate, first-string, five-star*, gilt-edged*, gnarly*, good-looking, great, handsome, lovely, magnificent, mean, neat*, not too shabby*, ornate, outstanding, pleasant, rare, refined, select, showy, skillful, smart, solid, splendid, striking, subtle, superior, supreme, top, top-notch, unreal*, well-made, wicked*; SEE CONCEPTS *528,574,579*

fine [adj2] *cloudless, sunny*
balmy, bright, clarion, clear, clement, dry, fair, pleasant, rainless, undarkened; SEE CONCEPT *525*

fine [adj3] *dainty, delicate; sheer*
diaphanous, ethereal, exquisite, filmy, fine-drawn, fine-grained, fine-spun, flimsy, fragile, gauzy, gossamer, gossamery, granular, impalpable, light, lightweight, little, loose, minute, porous, powdered, powdery, pulverized, quality, slender, small, thin, threadlike, transparent; SEE CONCEPTS *491,606*

fine [adj4] *discriminating, exact*
abstruse, acute, clear, critical, cryptic, delicate, distinct, enigmatic, esoteric, fastidious, fine-spun, hairline, hairsplitting, intelligent, keen, minute, nice, obscure, petty, precise, pure, quick, recondite, refined, sensitive, sharp, sterling,

strict, subtle, tasteful, tenuous, trifling, unadulterated, unpolluted; SEE CONCEPT *557*

fine [n] *penalty in money*
amends, amercement, assessment, damages, forfeit, mulct, punishment, reparation, rip; SEE CONCEPT *123*

fine [v] *penalize in monetary way*
alienate, amerce, confiscate, dock*, exact, extort, hit with*, levy, make pay, mulct, pay through the nose*, punish, sconce, seize, sequestrate, slap with*, tax, throw book at*; SEE CONCEPTS *122,342*

finery [n] *best clothing*
apparel, bib and tucker*, caparison, decoration, fancy dress, formals, frippery*, full dress, gear, regalia, splendor, suit, Sunday best* trappings, trimmings, trinkets; SEE CONCEPT *451*

finesse [n] *know-how, maneuver*
acumen, adeptness, adroitness, artfulness, artifice, big stick*, bluff, cleverness, competence, con, craft, craftiness, cunning, delicacy, diplomacy, discernment, discretion, feint, gimmick, grift, guile, polish, quickness, racket*, runaround*, ruse, savoir-faire, savvy, skill, sophistication, stratagem, subtlety, tact, trick, wile; SEE CONCEPTS *409,657*

finesse [v] *maneuver, manipulate*
angle, beguile, bluff, exploit, finagle*, jockey*, operate, play, play games*, pull strings*, pull wires*, rig*, wangle; SEE CONCEPTS *36,59*

fine-tune [v] *make small adjustments*
adjust, calibrate, make improvements, set, tune up, tweak; SEE CONCEPTS *202,212*

finger [n] *appendage of hand*
antenna*, claw, digit, extremity, feeler*, hook*, pinky*, pointer*, ring finger, tactile member, tentacle*, thumb; SEE CONCEPT *392*

finger [v1] *touch lightly*
feel, fiddle, grope, handle, manipulate, maul, meddle, palpate, paw, play with, thumb, toy with; SEE CONCEPT *612*

finger [v2] *choose, designate*
appoint, determine, identify, indicate, locate, make, name, nominate, pin down*, point out, specify, tap; SEE CONCEPT *41*

finicky [adj] *overparticular*
choosy, critical, dainty, difficult, fastidious, finical, finicking, fussbudget*, fussy, hard to please, nice, nit-picking, overnice, persnickety*, picky, scrupulous, squeamish, stickling; SEE CONCEPTS *401,404,556*

finish [n1] *conclusion; completion*
accomplishment, achievement, acquirement, acquisition, annihilation, attainment, cease, cessation, close, closing, culmination, curtain*, curtains*, death, defeat, denouement, desistance, end, ending, end of the line*, end of the road*, finale, finis, last, last stage, ruin, stop, termination, terminus, winding-up*, wind-up, wrap, wrap-up*; SEE CONCEPTS *119,832*

finish [n2] *coating; perfecting*
appearance, beauty, burnish, cultivation, culture, elaboration, glaze, grace, grain, lacquer, luster, patina, perfection, polish, refinement, shine, smoothness, surface, texture, veneer; SEE CONCEPTS *611,655*

finish [v1] *bring to a conclusion; get done*
accomplish, achieve, bag it*, break up, bring to a close, carry through, cease, clinch, close, complete, conclude, crown*, culminate, deal with,

determine, discharge, do, effect, end, execute, finalize, fold, fulfill, get out of the way*, halt,
hang it up*, have done with*, make, make short
work of*, mop up*, perfect, put finishing touches
on*, round off*, round up*, scratch, scrub, settle,
sew up*, shut down, shutter*, stop, terminate,
top off*, ultimate, wind up*, wrap, wrap up*;
SEE CONCEPTS *91,234,706*

finish [*v2*] *consume, use up*
deplete, devour, dispatch, dispose of, drain,
drink, eat, empty, exhaust, expend, go, run
through*, spend, use, wash up*; SEE CONCEPTS
169,225

finish [*v3*] *defeat; kill*
annihilate, assassinate, best*, bring down*, carry
off*, destroy, dispatch, dispose of, do in*, down,
execute, exterminate, get rid of*, liquidate, overcome, overpower, put an end to, put away*, rout,
rub out*, ruin, slaughter, slay, take off*, take
out*, vaporize, worst*; SEE CONCEPTS *95,252*

finish [*v4*] *put a coating on; perfect*
coat, develop, elaborate, face, gild, lacquer, polish, refine, smooth, stain, texture, veneer, wax;
SEE CONCEPTS *172,202*

finished [*adj1*] *cultivated, refined*
accomplished, all-around, classic, consummate,
cultured, elegant, expert, exquisite, flawless, impeccable, many-sided, masterly, perfected, polished, professional, proficient, skilled, smooth,
suave, urbane, versatile; SEE CONCEPTS *404,528*

finished [*adj2*] *complete, done*
accomplished, achieved, brought about, ceased,
closed, come to an end, compassed, concluded,
consummated, decided, discharged, dispatched,
disposed of, done for, done with, effected, effectuated, elaborated, ended, entire, executed, final,
finalized, fulfilled, full, in the past, lapsed, made,
over, over and done*, perfected, performed, put
into effect*, realized, resolved, satisfied, settled,
sewn up*, shut, stopped, terminated, through,
tied up*, worked out*, wound up*, wrapped up*;
SEE CONCEPTS *528,531*

finished [*adj3*] *consumed, used up*
bankrupt, devastated, done, done for*, done in*,
drained, empty, exhausted, gone, liquidated, lost,
played out*, ruined, spent, through, undone,
washed up*, wiped out*, wrecked*; SEE CON-
CEPTS *334,560*

finite [*adj*] *subject to limitations*
bound, bounded, circumscribed, conditioned,
confined, definable, definite, delimited, demar-
cated, determinate, exact, fixed, limited, precise,
restricted, specific, terminable; SEE CONCEPTS
535,554

fink [*n*] *informer*
canary*, narc, nark, rat*, scab, snake*, snitch,
squealer, stoolie, stool pigeon, tattletale, tipster,
weasel, whistle-blower; SEE CONCEPTS *412,423*

fire [*n1*] *burning*
blaze, bonfire, campfire, charring, coals, combustion, conflagration, devouring, element, embers, flame and smoke, flames, flare, glow,
hearth, heat, holocaust, hot spot*, incandescence,
inferno, luminosity, oxidation, phlogiston, pyre,
rapid oxidation, scintillation, scorching, sea of
flames*, searing, sparks, tinder, up in smoke*,
warmth; SEE CONCEPTS *478,521*

fire [*n2*] *barrage of projectiles*
attack, bombarding, bombardment, bombing,
cannonade, cannonading, crossfire, explosion,

fusillade, hail, round, salvo, shelling, sniping,
volley; SEE CONCEPTS *86,320*

fire [*n3*] *animation, vigor*
ardor, brio, calenture, dash, drive, eagerness,
élan, energy, enthusiasm, excitement, exhilaration, fervency, fervor, force, ginger*, gusto,
heartiness, heat, impetuosity, intensity, life, light,
liveliness, luster, passion, pep*, punch*, radiance, red heat*, scintillation, snap*, sparkle,
spirit, splendor, starch, verve, vim, virtuosity, vivacity, white heat*, zeal, zing, zip; SEE CONCEPT
411

fire [*v1*] *cause to burn*
enkindle, ignite, kindle, light, put a match to*,
set ablaze, set aflame, set alight, set fire to, set on
fire, start a fire, touch off*; SEE CONCEPT *249*

fire [*v2*] *detonate or throw a weapon*
cast, discharge, eject, explode, fling, heave, hurl,
launch, let off*, loose, pitch, pull trigger, set
off*, shell, shoot, toss, touch off*; SEE CONCEPTS
179,222

fire [*v3*] *excite, arouse*
animate, electrify, enliven, enthuse, exalt, galvanize, heighten, impassion, incite, inflame, inform, inspire, inspirit, intensify, intoxicate,
irritate, provoke, quicken, rouse, stir, thrill; SEE
CONCEPT *14*

fire [*v4*] *dismiss from responsibility*
ax*, boot*, can*, discharge, drop, eject, expel,
give bum's rush*, give marching orders*, give
one notice*, give pink slip*, give the sack*, hand
walking papers*, kick out*, lay off, let one go*,
oust, pink slip*, sack*, terminate; SEE CONCEPTS
50,88,351

fire alarm [*n*] *smoke detector*
danger signal, emergency alarm, fire bell, heat
sensor, siren, smoke alarm; SEE CONCEPTS
269,463

firearm [*n*] *gun*
handgun, heat*, musket, pistol, revolver, rifle,
shotgun, weapon; SEE CONCEPT *500*

firebrand [*n*] *agitator*
demonstrator, guerrilla, instigator, malcontent,
protester, rabble-rouser, rebel, revolutionist,
troublemaker; SEE CONCEPTS *359,412,423*

firecracker [*n*] *fireworks*
bottle rockets, bursts, cherry bomb, fire flowers,
illuminations, pyrotechnics, rockets, Roman candles, sparklers; SEE CONCEPT *293*

fireplace [*n*] *hearth for burning wood*
bed of coals, blaze, chimney, fireside, furnace,
grate, hearthside, hob, ingle, inglenook, ingle-
side, settle, stove; SEE CONCEPTS *440,443*

fireproof [*adj*] *resistant to burning*
asbestos, concrete, fire-resistant, incombustible,
noncandescent, noncombustible, nonflammable,
noninflammable; SEE CONCEPT *485*

fireworks [*n*] *pyrotechnic display at celebrations*
bottle rockets, bursts, firecrackers, fire flowers,
illuminations, rockets, Roman candles, sparklers;
SEE CONCEPT *293*

firm [*adj1*] *inflexible*
close, close-grained, compact, compressed, concentrated, concrete, condensed, congealed,
dense, fine-grained, hard, hardened, heavy, impenetrable, impermeable, impervious, inelastic,
jelled, nonporous, refractory, rigid, set, solid, solidified, stiff, sturdy, substantial, thick, tough,
unyielding; SEE CONCEPTS *604,606*

firm [*adj2*] *stable, unmoving*
anchored, bolted, braced, cemented, closed, durable, embedded, fast, fastened, fixed, immobile, immovable, motionless, mounted, nailed, petrified, riveted, robust, rooted, screwed, secure, secured, set, settled, soldered, solid, sound, spiked, stationary, steady, strong, sturdy, substantial, taut, tenacious, tight, tightened, unfluctuating, unshakable, welded; SEE CONCEPT *488*

firm [*adj3*] *unalterable, definite*
abiding, adamant, bent, bound, consistent, constant, dead set on*, determined, enduring, established, exact, explicit, fixed, flat, going, hang tough*, inflexible, intent, never-failing, obdurate, persevering, persistent, prevailing, resolute, resolved, set, settled, specific, stable, stand pat*, stated, staunch, steadfast, steady, stipulated, strict, strong, sure, tenacious, true, unbending, unchangeable, undeviating, unflinching, unqualified, unshakable, unshaken, unwavering, unyielding; SEE CONCEPTS *267,403,542*

firm [*n*] *business*
association, bunch, company, concern, conglomerate, corporation, crew, crowd, enterprise, gang, house, megacorp, mob, multinational, organization, outfit, partnership, ring; SEE CONCEPTS *323,325*

firmament [*n*] *heaven*
empyrean, lid*, sky, the blue*, the skies, vault, welkin, wild blue yonder*; SEE CONCEPT *437*

firmly [*adv1*] *immovably*
durably, enduringly, fast, fixedly, hard, inflexibly, like a rock*, motionlessly, rigidly, securely, solid, solidly, soundly, stably, steadily, stiffly, strongly, substantially, thoroughly, tight, tightly, unflinchingly, unshakeably; SEE CONCEPTS *488,489,604*

firmly [*adv2*] *with determination*
adamantly, constantly, decisively, doggedly, indefatigably, intently, obdurately, obstinately, perseveringly, persistently, pertinaciously, purposefully, resolutely, staunchly, steadfastly, stolidly, strictly, stubbornly, tenaciously, through thick and thin*, unchangeably, unwaveringly, with heavy hand*; SEE CONCEPTS *534,542*

firmness [*n1*] *stiffness*
compactness, density, durability, fixedness, hardness, impenetrability, impermeability, imperviousness, impliability, inelasticity, inflexibility, resistance, rigidity, solidity, temper, tensile strength, toughness; SEE CONCEPTS *722,726*

firmness [*n2*] *immovability*
durability, solidity, soundness, stability, steadiness, strength, substantiality, tautness, tension, tightness; SEE CONCEPTS *731,732*

firmness [*n3*] *resolution, resolve*
constancy, decidedness, decision, determination, fixedness, fixity, inflexibility, obduracy, obstinacy, purposefulness, purposiveness, staunchness, steadfastness, strength, strictness; SEE CONCEPTS *410,633*

first [*adj1*] *earliest in order*
aboriginal, ahead, antecedent, anterior, basic, beginning, cardinal, early, elementary, first off*, front, fundamental, head, headmost, inaugural, inceptive, incipient, initial, in the beginning, introductory, key, leading, lead off*, least, number one*, numero uno*, opening, original, pioneer, premier, primary, prime, primeval, primitive, primogenial, primordial, pristine, right up front*,

rudimentary, slightest, smallest; SEE CONCEPTS *585,632,820*

first [*adj2*] *highest in importance*
advanced, A-number-1*, arch, champion, chief, dominant, eminent, first-class, first-string*, foremost, greatest, head, head of the line*, leading, main, number one*, outstanding, paramount, predominant, preeminent, premier, primary, prime, primo*, principal, ranking, ruling, sovereign, supreme, top-flight*, top of the list; SEE CONCEPT *568*

first [*adv*] *at the beginning*
at the outset, before all else, beforehand, initially, in the first place, originally, to begin with, to start with; SEE CONCEPTS *585,820*

first-class/first-rate [*adj*] *superior, excellent*
capital, choice, dandy, fine, first-string*, five-star*, in class by itself*, prime*, shipshape, sound, supreme, tiptop*, top, top-notch*, very good; SEE CONCEPT *574*

firsthand [*adj*] *direct*
eyewitness, immediate, primary, straight, straight from the horse's mouth*; SEE CONCEPT *267*

fiscal [*adj*] *monetary*
budgetary, commercial, economic, financial, money, pecuniary, pocket; SEE CONCEPT *334*

fish [*v*] *throwing bait to catch seafood*
angle, bait, bait the hook*, bob, cast, cast one's hook*, cast one's net*, chum, extract, extricate, find, go fishing, haul out*, net, produce, pull out, seine, trawl, troll; SEE CONCEPT *363*

fisherman [*n*] *angler*
clam digger, fisher, lobsterman, piscator, rodman, trawler, troller; SEE CONCEPT *423*

fish for [*v*] *look for; hint*
angle, angle for, elicit, hope for, hunt for, invite, search for, seek, solicit, try to evoke; SEE CONCEPTS *20,75*

fishing [*n*] *angling*
fly-fishing, freshwater fishing, piscary, trawling, trolling; SEE CONCEPT *363*

fishy [*adj*] *doubtful, suspicious*
ambiguous, doubtable, dubious, dubitable, equivocal, far-fetched, funny, implausible, improbable, odd, problematic, queer, questionable, shady, suspect, uncertain, unlikely; SEE CONCEPT *552*

fission [*n*] *splitting*
atomic reaction, atom smashing, dividing, division, nuclear fission, parting, severance, splitting the atom, thermonuclear reaction; SEE CONCEPT *500*

fit [*adj1*] *suitable, appropriate*
able, adapted, adequate, advantageous, apposite, apt, becoming, befitting, beneficial, capable, comely, comme il faut, competent, conformable, convenient, correct, correspondent, deserving, desirable, due, equipped, equitable, expedient, favorable, feasible, felicitous, fitted, fitting, good enough, happy, just, likely, meet, opportune, practicable, preferable, prepared, proper, qualified, ready, right, rightful, seasonable, seemly, tasteful, timely, trained, well-suited, wise, worthy; SEE CONCEPT *558*

fit [*adj2*] *healthy, in good physical shape*
able-bodied, competent, fit as a fiddle*, hale, in good condition, muscled, robust, slim, sound, strapping*, toned, trim, up to snuff*, well,

wholesome, wrapped tight*; SEE CONCEPTS
314,485

fit [*n*] *seizure; sudden emotion*
access, attack, blow, bout, burst, caprice, conniption*, convulsion, epileptic attack, frenzy,
humor, jumps*, mood, outbreak, outburst, paroxysm, rage, rush, spasm, spate, spell, stroke,
tantrum, throe, torrent, turn, twitch, whim,
whimsy; SEE CONCEPTS *13,303*

fit [*v1*] *belong, correspond*
accord, agree, answer, apply, be apposite, be apt,
become, be comfortable, be consonant, befit, be
in keeping, click*, concur, conform, consist,
dovetail*, go, go together, go with, harmonize,
have its place, interlock, join, match, meet, parallel, relate, respond, set, suit, tally; SEE CONCEPT
664

fit [*v2*] *equip*
accommodate, accoutre, arm, fix, furnish, get,
implement, kit out*, make, make up, outfit, prepare, provide, ready, rig*; SEE CONCEPT *182*

fit [*v3*] *adapt, change*
adjust, alter, arrange, conform, dispose, fashion,
modify, place, position, quadrate, reconcile,
shape, square, suit, tailor, tailor-make*; SEE CON-
CEPT *232*

fitful [*adj*] *irregular, sporadic*
bits and pieces*, broken, capricious, catchy*,
changeable, desultory, disturbed, erratic, flickering, fluctuating, haphazard, herky-jerky*, hit-or-
miss*, impulsive, inconstant, intermittent,
interrupted, on-again-off-again, periodic, random, recurrent, restive, restless, shifting, spasmodic, spastic*, spotty, unstable, variable; SEE
CONCEPTS *482,534*

fitness [*n1*] *good condition*
fettle*, good health, health, kilter*, repair, robustness, shape, strength, trim, vigor; SEE CON-
CEPTS *316,723*

fitness [*n2*] *appropriateness*
accommodation, accordance, adaptation, adequacy, admissibility, agreeableness, applicability, appositeness, aptitude, aptness, assimilation, auspiciousness, compatibility, competence,
concurrency, congeniality, congruousness,
consistency, consonance, convenience, correspondence, decency, decorum, eligibility, expediency, harmony, keeping, order, patness,
pertinence, preparedness, propriety, qualification, readiness, relevancy, rightness, seasonable-
ness, seemliness, suitability, timeliness; SEE
CONCEPT *656*

fitted [*adj1*] *appropriate, right*
adapted, conformable, cut out for, equipped,
matched, proper, qualified, suitable, suited, tailor-made; SEE CONCEPT *558*

fitted [*adj2*] *equipped*
accoutered, appointed, armed, furnished, imple-
mented, outfitted, provided, rigged out*, set up,
supplied; SEE CONCEPTS *560,589*

fitting [*adj*] *appropriate, suitable*
applicable, apt, becoming, comme il faut, correct, decent, decorous, desirable, due, felicitous,
happy, just, just what was ordered*, meet, on the
button*, on the nose*, proper, right, right on*,
seemly, that's the ticket*; SEE CONCEPT *558*

fitting [*n*] *accessory*
accouterment, appointment, attachment, component, connection, convenience, equipment, extra,

furnishing, furniture, instrument, paraphernalia,
part, piece, trimming, unit; SEE CONCEPT *824*

fix [*n*] *difficult or ticklish situation*
box*, corner*, dilemma, embarrassment, hole*,
hot water*, jam*, mess*, pickle*, plight,
predicament, quandary, scrape, spot*; SEE CON-
CEPT *674*

fix [*v1*] *establish, make firm*
affix, anchor, attach, bind, catch, cement, congeal, connect, consolidate, couple, embed, entrench, fasten, freeze to*, glue, graft, harden,
implant, inculcate, infix, ingrain, install, instill,
link, locate, lodge, moor, nail down*, pin, place,
plant, position, rigidify, rivet, root, secure, set,
settle, solidify, stabilize, stay put, steady, stick,
stiffen, thicken, tie; SEE CONCEPTS *85,113,160,*
201

fix [*v2*] *determine, decide*
agree on, appoint, arrange, arrive at, conclude,
define, establish, limit, name, resolve, set, settle,
solve, specify, work, work out; SEE CONCEPT *18*

fix [*v3*] *mend, repair*
adjust, amend, correct, debug, doctor, do up*,
emend, face-lift*, fiddle with, overhaul, patch,
put to rights*, rebuild, recondition, reconstruct,
regulate, restore, retread, revamp, revise, see to*,
sort, tune up; SEE CONCEPTS *126,212*

fix [*v4*] *prepare, plan ahead*
arrange, dispose, frame, prearrange, precontrive,
predesign, preorder, preplan, put up, rig*, set up,
stack the deck*; SEE CONCEPT *36*

fix [*v5*] *focus on*
concenter, concentrate, direct, fasten, fixate,
level at, put, rivet; SEE CONCEPT *623*

fix [*v6*] *cook a meal*
fit, get, get ready, heat, make, make up, microwave, prepare, ready, warm, whip up*; SEE
CONCEPT *170*

fix [*v7*] *manipulate, influence an event*
bribe, buy, buy off, corrupt, fiddle*, have, lubricate, maneuver, pull strings*, reach, square, suborn, tamper with; SEE CONCEPTS *192,232*

fix [*v8*] *wreak vengeance on*
cook someone's goose*, get*, get even, get revenge, hurt, pay back, punish, take retribution;
SEE CONCEPT *86*

fixate [*v*] *focus*
become attached, center on, direct, haunt, infatuate, obsess, rivet one's eyes*, zero in on; SEE
CONCEPTS *17,623*

fixation [*n*] *obsession*
addiction, case, complex, craze, crush, fascination, fetish, hang-up*, idée fixe, infatuation,
mania, preoccupation, thing; SEE CONCEPTS
532,690

fixed [*adj1*] *permanent, steady*
anchored, attached, established, fast, firm,
hitched, hooked, immobile, immotile, immovable, located, locked, made fast, nailed*, quiet,
rigid, rooted, secure, set, settled, situated, solid,
stable, steadfast, stiff, still, tenacious, tight; SEE
CONCEPTS *488,551,583,649*

fixed [*adj2*] *intent, resolute; established*
abiding, agreed, arranged, certain, changeless,
circumscribed, confirmed, decided, defined, definite, definitive, determinate, enduring, firm, inalterable, inflexible, in the bag*, inveterate, level,
limited, narrow, never-failing, planned, prearranged, precise, resolved, restricted, rigged,
rooted, set, settled, set-up, stated, steadfast,

fi
fi

steady, still, stipulated, sure, unbending, unblinking, unchangeable, undeviating, unfaltering, unflinching, unmodifiable, unmovable, unqualified, unwavering; SEE CONCEPTS 535,554

fixed [*adj3*] *repaired*
back together, going, in order, in working order, mended, put right, rebuilt, refitted, sorted, whole; SEE CONCEPT 560

fixture [*n*] *fitting, appliance*
accessory, appendage, appurtenance, attachment, component, device, equipment; SEE CONCEPT 463

fix up [*v*] *prepare, beautify*
deck*, dress up, furnish, gussy up*, primp, provide, rehabilitate, repair, smarten, spiff*, spruce up*; SEE CONCEPTS 162,202

fizz [*v*] *bubble*
buzz, effervesce, fizzle, froth, hiss, seethe, sibilate, simmer, sparkle, sputter, whisper, whoosh; SEE CONCEPT 469

fizzle [*v*] *collapse, fall through*
abort, be a fiasco*, come to nothing*, die, end, end in defeat*, end in disappointment*, fail, fold, miscarry, misfire, miss the mark*, peter out*, wane; SEE CONCEPT 699

flabbergast [*v*] *surprise*
abash, amaze, astonish, astound, blow away*, bowl over*, confound, daze, disconcert, dumbfound, make speechless, nonplus, overcome, overwhelm, put away*, shock, stagger, stun, throw, throw for a loop*; SEE CONCEPT 42

flabby [*adj*] *baggy, fat*
drooping, enervated, flaccid, flexuous, floppy*, gone to seed*, hanging, irresilient, lax, limp, loose, out of condition*, out of shape*, pendulous, rusty, sagging, shapeless, slack, sloppy, soft, tender, toneless, unfit, yielding; SEE CONCEPTS 486,490

flaccid [*adj*] *drooping*
debilitated, emasculated, enervated, enfeebled, flabby, flimsy, inelastic, irresilient, lax, limp, loose, nerveless, quaggy, sapped, slack, soft, weak, weakened; SEE CONCEPTS 485,604

flag [*n*] *pennant, symbol*
banderole, banner, bannerol, burgee, colors, emblem, ensign, gonfalon, jack, pennon, standard, streamer; SEE CONCEPTS 284,473

flag [*v1*] *decline, fall off*
abate, deteriorate, die, droop, ebb, fade, fail, faint, languish, peter out*, pine, sag, sink, slump, succumb, taper off*, wane, weaken, weary, wilt; SEE CONCEPTS 698,699

flag [*v2*] *signal*
gesture, give a sign to, hail, indicate, motion, salute, warn, wave; SEE CONCEPT 74

flagrant [*adj*] *flaunting, blatant; without shame*
arrant, atrocious, awful, bare-faced*, bold, brazen, capital, conspicuous, crying, disgraceful, dreadful, egregious, enormous, flagitious, flaming, flashy*, glaring, grody*, gross*, hanging out*, heinous, immodest, infamous, noticeable, notorious, obvious, open, ostentatious, out-and-out*, outrageous, rank, scandalous, shameful, shameless, shocking, stick out like sore thumb*, striking, undisguised, wicked; SEE CONCEPTS 401,545,576

flagship [*n*] *leader*
bellwether, chief, crown jewel, flotilla leader, forerunner, front runner, head, lead ship, mother ship; SEE CONCEPTS 347,354

flail [*v*] *beat, strike*
bash, batter, club, flog, hit, knock, lash, maltreat, pummel, slug, smack, smash, sock, thrash, thwack, whale; SEE CONCEPTS 189,246

flair [*n*] *talent, style*
ability, accomplishment, aptitude, aptness, bent, chic, dash, elegance, faculty, feel, genius, gift, glamour, head, knack, mastery, panache, pizzazz*, presence, shine*, splash*, taste, turn, zip*; SEE CONCEPTS 630,706

flak [*n*] *complaint, criticism*
abuse, bad press*, brickbat*, censure, condemnation, disapprobation, disapproval, disparagement, fault-finding, hostility, knock*, opposition, pan*, rap*, swipe*; SEE CONCEPTS 52,278

flake [*n*] *scale, peel*
cell, disk, drop, foil, lamella, lamina, layer, leaf, membrane, pellicle, plate, scab, section, shaving, sheet, skin, slice, sliver, wafer; SEE CONCEPT 831

flake [*v*] *peel off*
blister, chip, delaminate, desquamate, drop, exfoliate, pare, scab, scale, shed, slice, sliver, trim, wear away; SEE CONCEPTS 157,469

flaky [*adj*] *eccentric*
birdy*, crazy, goofy*, half-cracked, haywire, nutty, odd, peculiar, queer, screwy, unconventional, wacky; SEE CONCEPTS 547,564

flamboyant [*adj*] *extravagant, theatrical*
baroque, bombastic, brilliant, camp, chichi*, colorful, dashing, dazzling, elaborate, exciting, flaky*, flaming, flashy, florid, gassy*, gaudy, glamorous, jazzy*, luscious, luxuriant, ornate, ostentatious, peacockish, pretentious, resplendent, rich, rococo, showy, splashy, sporty, swank*, swashbuckling*; SEE CONCEPTS 401,589

flame [*n1*] *fire*
blaze, brightness, conflagration, flare, flash, holocaust, light, rapid oxidation, wildfire; SEE CONCEPTS 478,521

flame [*n2*] *lover; passion*
affection, ardor, baby, beau, beloved, boyfriend, darling, dear, desire, enthusiasm, fervor, fire, girlfriend, heartthrob, honey, inamorata, inamorato, keenness, love, paramour, spark, steady, swain, sweetheart, sweetie, truelove; SEE CONCEPTS 32,423

flame [*n3*] *insulting e-mail message*
abusive e-mail message, abusive newsgroup message, abusive newsgroup posting, flamemail, flame war, insulting newsgroup message, insulting newsgroup posting; SEE CONCEPTS 52,54,278

flame [*v*] *burn*
blaze, coruscate, fire, flare, flare up, flash, glare, glint, glow, ignite, kindle, light, oxidize, shine; SEE CONCEPT 249

flaming [*adj1*] *burning*
ablaze, afire, aflame, alight, blazing, brilliant, conflagrant, fiery, flaring, glowing, ignited, in flames, raging, red, red-hot*; SEE CONCEPT 485

flaming [*adj2*] *very angry, vehement*
ardent, aroused, blazing, bright, burning, fervent, frenzied, hot, hot-blooded*, impassioned, intense, passionate, raging, red-hot*, scintillating, vivid, white-hot*; SEE CONCEPTS 267,403

flammable [*adj*] *easily set afire*
burnable, combustible, ignitable, incendiary, inflammable; SEE CONCEPT 485

flank [n] *haunch of an animate being*
ham, hand, hip, loin, pleuron, quarter, side, thigh, wing; SEE CONCEPT *392*

flap [n1] *winged or extended part of an object*
accessory, adjunct, appendage, apron, cover, drop, fly, fold, hanging, lapel, lobe, lug, overlap, pendant, pendulosity, ply, queue, skirt, strip, tab, tag, tail, tippet; SEE CONCEPTS *471,824*

flap [n2] *commotion*
agitation, banging, brouhaha, confusion, dither, fluster, flutter, fuss, lather*, panic, pother*, state*, stew*, sweat*, tizzy, to-do, tumult, turbulence, turmoil, twitter*; SEE CONCEPTS *230,674*

flap [v] *flutter*
agitate, beat, dangle, flail, flash, flop, hang, lop, shake, swing, swish, thrash, thresh, vibrate, wag, wave; SEE CONCEPT *149*

flare [v1] *erupt, blow*
blaze, boil over, break out, burn, burn up, burst, dart, dazzle, explode, fire up, flash, flicker, flutter, fume, glare, glow, go off, lose control, rant, seethe, shimmer, shoot, waver; SEE CONCEPTS *13,179,249*

flare [v2] *spread*
broaden, grow, splay, widen; SEE CONCEPT *469*

flare-up [n] *sudden outbreak*
blowup, epidemic, eruption, explosion, gush, outburst, rise; SEE CONCEPT *633*

flash [n1] *shimmer, flicker*
beam, bedazzlement, blaze, burst, coruscation, dazzle, flame, flare, glance, glare, gleam, glimmer, glint, glisten, glitter, glow, illumination, imprint, impulse, incandescence, luster, phosphorescence, quiver, radiation, ray, reflection, scintillation, shine, spark, sparkle, streak, stream, twinkle, twinkling, vision; SEE CONCEPTS *521,624*

flash [n2] *instant, split second*
breathing, burst, jiffy, minute, moment, outburst, shake, show, trice, twinkling; SEE CONCEPTS *808,821*

flash [n3] *demonstration*
burst, display, manifestation, outburst, show, sign, splash, swank; SEE CONCEPT *261*

flash [v1] *shimmer, flicker*
beam, bedazzle, blaze, blink, coruscate, dazzle, flame, flare, glance, glare, gleam, glimmer, glint, glisten, glitter, glow, incandesce, light, phosphoresce, radiate, reflect, scintillate, shine, shoot out, spangle, spark, sparkle, twinkle; SEE CONCEPT *624*

flash [v2] *move fast and display*
bolt, brandish, dart, dash, disport, exhibit, expose, flaunt, flit, flourish, fly, parade, race, shoot, show, show off, speed, spring, streak, sweep, trot out, whistle, zoom; SEE CONCEPTS *150,261*

flashback [n] *remembrance*
flash from the past*, hallucination, memory, nostalgia, recall, recollection, reliving, reminiscence, thoughts of the past*, voice from the past*; SEE CONCEPTS *40,529*

flash point [n] *crucial moment*
breaking point, crisis, critical moment, hour of decision, moment of truth, turning point, zero hour; SEE CONCEPT *674*

flashy [adj] *flamboyant, in poor taste*
blatant, brazen, catchpenny*, cheap, chintzy, flaunting, florid, garish, gaudy, glaring, glittering, glittery, glitzy, jazzy*, loud, meretricious, ornate, ostentatious, showy, snazzy, sparkling, tacky*, tasteless, tawdry, tinsel, vulgar; SEE CONCEPT *589*

flask [n] *small container for liquid*
alembic, ampulla, bag, beaker, bottle, canteen, carafe, caster, chalice, crock, cruel, crystal, decanter, demijohn, ewer, fiasco, flacon, flagon, flasket, glass, goblet, gourd, horn, jar, jug, noggin, phial, retort, tumbler, urn, vial; SEE CONCEPT *494*

flat [adj1] *level, smooth*
collapsed, complanate, decumbent, deflated, depressed, empty, even, extended, fallen, flush, horizontal, laid low, low, oblate, outstretched, pancake*, planar, planate, plane, procumbent, prone, prostrate, punctured, reclining, recumbent, splay, spread out, supine, tabular, unbroken; SEE CONCEPTS *486,490*

flat [adj2] *dull, lackluster to the senses*
banal, blah, bland, blind, boring, colorless, dead, dim, drab, draggy, flavorless, ho hum*, inane, innocuous, insipid, jejune, lead balloon*, lifeless, matte, monotonous, muted, pointless, prosaic, prosy, sapless, spiritless, stale, tasteless, tedious, uninteresting, unpalatable, unsavory, unseasoned, vanilla*, vapid, watery, weak, whitebread*; SEE CONCEPTS *529,537*

flat [adj3] *absolute, positive*
categorical, direct, downright, explicit, final, fixed, indubitable, out-and-out*, peremptory, plain, straight, unconditional, unequivocal, unmistakable, unqualified, unquestionable; SEE CONCEPT *535*

flat [n] *apartment*
chambers, condo, co-op*, crash pad*, floor-through, go-down, joint*, lodging, pad*, railroad apartment, rental, room, rooms, suite, tenement, walk-up; SEE CONCEPT *516*

flat-out [adv] *at top speed*
all-out, all the way, at a good clip*, for all one's worth*, full blast, head over heels*, in full gallop*, lickety-split, the whole nine yards*, to the max, unrestrainedly, wide open, without reservation; SEE CONCEPTS *574,762,781*

flatten [v] *level out*
abrade, beat down, compress, crush, debase, deflate, depress, even out, fell, floor, flush, grade, ground, iron out, knock down, lay, lay low, mow down, plane, plaster*, prostrate, raze, roll, smash, smooth, spread out, squash, straighten, subdue, trample; SEE CONCEPTS *137,250,469,702*

flatter [v1] *compliment excessively*
adulate, beslaver, blandish, bootlick*, brown-nose*, build up*, butter up*, cajole, cater to, charm, con, court, fawn*, get next to*, glorify, grovel, humor, inveigle, jolly, lay it on thick*, massage, oil*, overpraise, play up to*, praise, rub the right way*, salve, sell, snow*, soften*, soft-soap*, spread it on*, stroke, suck up to*, sweeten up*, sweet-talk*, toady*, wheedle, work on*, work over*; SEE CONCEPTS *59,69*

flatter [v2] *complement, enhance*
adorn, beautify, become, decorate, do something for*, embellish, enrich, finish, go with*, grace, ornament, perfect, put in best light*, set off, show to advantage, suit; SEE CONCEPTS *162,664*

flatterer [n] *complimenter*
apple polisher*, backscratcher, booster, bootlicker*, brownnose*, cajoler, charmer, fawner, flunkey, lackey, puffer*, sweet talker*, syco-

fi
fl

phant, teacher's pet, toady, yes-person*; SEE
CONCEPTS *59,69*

flattery [*n*] *false praise, compliments*
adulation, applause, approbation, blandishment,
blarney*, bootlicking*, cajolery, commendation,
encomium, eulogy, eyewash*, fawning*, flattering, flummery, fulsomeness, gallantry, gratification, hokum*, honeyed words, incense,
ingratiation, jive*, laud, mush*, obsequiousness,
palaver, plaudits, pretty speech, puffery*, servility, smoke*, snow*, snow job*, soft-soap*, soft
words, stroke*, sweet talk*, sycophancy, toady-
ism, tribute, truckling, unctuousness; SEE CON-
CEPTS *59,69*

flatulent [*adj*] *pretentious, long-winded*
bombastic, inflated, oratorical, overblown,
pompous, prolix, shallow, superficial, swollen,
tedious, tumescent, tumid, turgid, windy, wordy;
SEE CONCEPTS *267,404*

flaunt [*v*] *make an exhibition, show off*
advertise, air, boast, brandish, break out, broadcast, declare, disclose, display, disport, divulge,
expose, fan it*, flash, flash about, flourish, gasconade, grandstand*, hotdog*, let it all hang
out*, make a scene*, parade, proclaim, put on an
act*, reveal, roll out, show and tell, showcase,
smack with*, sport, spring on*, streak, throw
weight around*, trot out*, vaunt, wave around,
whip out*; SEE CONCEPT *261*

flavor [*n1*] *odor and taste*
acidity, aroma, astringency, bitterness, essence,
extract, gusto, hotness, piquancy, pungency, relish, saltiness, sapidity, sapor, savor, seasoning,
smack, sourness, spiciness, sweetness, tang, tartness, twang, vim, wallop, zest, zing; SEE CON-
CEPT *614*

flavor [*n2*] *aura, essence*
aspect, character, feel, feeling, property, quality,
soupçon, stamp, style, suggestion, tinge, tone,
touch; SEE CONCEPT *673*

flavor [*v*] *add seasoning*
add zing, add zip, ginger, hot it up*, imbue, impart, infuse, lace, leaven, pepper, pep up*, salt,
season, spice; SEE CONCEPT *170*

flavoring [*n*] *spice, extract added to food*
additive, condiment, distillation, essence, herb,
quintessence, relish, sauce, seasoning, spirit,
tincture, zest; SEE CONCEPT *428*

flaw [*n*] *imperfection*
blemish, bug, catch*, Catch-22*, defect, disfigurement, failing, fault, foible, glitch*, gremlin*,
pitfall, slipup, speck, spot, stain, typo*, vice,
wart*, weakness, weak spot; SEE CONCEPTS
580,674

flawless [*adj*] *spotless, intact*
absolute, entire, faultless, immaculate, impeccable, irreproachable, perfect, sound, unblemished,
unbroken, undamaged, unimpaired, unmarred,
unsullied, whole; SEE CONCEPTS *574,579*

fleck [*n*] *spot, pinpoint mark*
bit, dot, mite, mote, patch, pinpoint, speck,
speckle, stipple, streak, stripe; SEE CONCEPTS
284,831

fleck [*v*] *mark with spots*
bespeckle, besprinkle, dapple, dot, dust, maculate, mottle, speckle, stipple, streak, variegate;
SEE CONCEPT *79*

fledgling [*n*] *beginner in activity*
apprentice, chick, colt, greenhorn*, learner, neophyte, nestling, newcomer, novice, rookie, ten-

derfoot*, trainee, tyro*; SEE CONCEPTS
352,366,424

flee [*v*] *run away to escape*
abscond, avoid, beat a hasty retreat*, blow*,
bolt*, break, cut and run*, cut out*, decamp, depart, desert, elude, evade, fly, fly the coop*, get*,
get away, get the hell out*, hotfoot*, jump,
leave, make a getaway*, make off*, make oneself scarce*, make one's escape*, make quick
exit*, make tracks*, retreat, scamper, scoot,
scram*, skedaddle*, skip*, split*, step on it*,
step on the gas*, take a hike*, take flight, take
off, vamoose*, vanish; SEE CONCEPTS *102,150,*
195

fleece [*v*] *plunder, steal*
bleed*, burn*, cheat*, clip*, con, cozen, defraud,
despoil, flimflam*, gouge, hustle, jerk around*,
milk*, mulct, overcharge, pluck, rifle, rip off*,
rob, rook*, rope in*, run a game on*, sell a bill
of goods*, shaft*, strip, swindle, take for a ride*,
take to the cleaners*; SEE CONCEPTS *59,139,342*

fleecy [*adj*] *downy, woolly; like a lamb's coat*
floccose, flocculent, fluffy, hairy, hirsute, lanose,
pileous, pilose, shaggy, soft, whiskered; SEE
CONCEPT *606*

fleet [*adj*] *quick in movement*
agile, barreling, breakneck*, brisk, expeditious,
expeditive, fast, flying, hasty, in nothing flat*,
like greased lightning*, lively, mercurial, meteoric, nimble, nimble-footed, on the double*,
rapid, screaming, speedball*, speedy, swift,
winged; SEE CONCEPTS *584,588*

fleet [*n*] *group of ships*
argosy, armada, flotilla, formation, line, naval
force, navy, sea power, squadron, tonnage, vessels, warships; SEE CONCEPTS *322,432,506*

fleeting [*adj*] *brief, transient*
cursory, ephemeral, evanescent, fading, flash in
the pan*, flitting, flying, fugacious, fugitive, impermanent, meteoric, momentary, passing, short,
short-lived, sudden, temporary, transitory, vanishing, volatile; SEE CONCEPTS *551,798*

flesh [*n1*] *body tissue, skin*
beef, brawn, cells, corpuscles, fat, fatness, flesh
and blood, food, meat, muscle, plasm, plasma,
protoplasm, sinews, thews, weight; SEE CONCEPT
392

flesh [*n2*] *humankind*
animality, carnality, homo sapiens, humanity,
human nature, human race, living creatures, mortality, people, physicality, physical nature, race,
sensuality, stock, world; SEE CONCEPTS *407,417*

fleshly [*adv1*] *lecherous, desiring sex*
animal, animalistic, bodily, carnal, erotic, gross,
lascivious, lewd, lustful, profane, sensual, venereal, voluptuous; SEE CONCEPTS *372,529,545*

fleshly [*adv2*] *bodily*
corporal, corporeal, earthly, human, material,
mundane, of this world, physical, secular, somatic, terrestrial, worldly; SEE CONCEPT *536*

fleshy [*adj*] *overweight*
adipose, ample, beefy*, brawny, chubby*,
chunky*, corpulent, fat, gross, heavy, hefty,
husky, meaty*, obese, plump, porcine, portly,
pudgy*, pulpy, sarcous, stout, tubby*, weighty,
well-padded*, zaftig*; SEE CONCEPTS *406,491,*
773

flex [*v*] *bend*
angle, contract, crook, curve, lean, mold, ply,

spring, stretch, tighten, tilt, yield; SEE CONCEPTS *147,149*

flexibility [*n*] *elasticity, adaptability*
adjustability, affability, complaisance, compliance, docility, extensibility, flaccidity, flexibleness, give, limberness, litheness, plasticity, pliability, pliancy, resilience, springiness, suppleness, tensility, tractability; SEE CONCEPTS *652,731*

flexible [*adj1*] *pliable, bendable*
adjustable, bending, ductile, elastic, extensible, extensile, flexile, formable, formative, impressionable, like putty*, limber, lithe, malleable, moldable, plastic, pliant, soft, spongy, springy, stretch, stretchable, stretchy, supple, tensile, tractable, tractile, whippy*, willowy, yielding; SEE CONCEPTS *485,488*

flexible [*adj2*] *adaptable, responsive*
acquiescent, adjustable, amenable, biddable, complaisant, compliant, discretionary, docile, gentle, going every which way*, hanging loose*, like putty in hands*, manageable, open, rolling with punches*, tractable, variable; SEE CONCEPTS *401,542*

flick [*v*] *light touch*
dab, flicker, flip, hit, pat, snap, tap, tip, touch lightly; SEE CONCEPT *612*

flicker [*n*] *spark, glimmer*
beam, flare, flash, gleam, oscillation, quivering, ray, scintillation, twinkle, vibration; SEE CONCEPTS *145,624,831*

flicker [*v*] *sparkle, flutter*
blare, blaze, blink, burn, dance, flare, flash, flit, flitter, fluctuate, glance, gleam, glimmer, glint, glitter, glow, hover, oscillate, quaver, quiver, scintillate, shimmer, swing, tremble, twinkle, vibrate, waver; SEE CONCEPTS *152,624*

flier [*n*] *flyer, pilot*
ace*, aeronaut, air person, aviator, aviatrix, jet*, navigator; SEE CONCEPT *348*

flight [*n1*] *flying; journey*
aerial navigation, aeronautics, arrival, aviation, avigation, departure, gliding, hop, jump, mounting, navigation, shuttle, soaring, take-off, transport, trip, volitation, voyage, winging; SEE CONCEPT *224*

flight [*n2*] *fleeing; departure*
beat*, break*, breakout, escape, escapement, escaping, exfiltration, exit, exodus, fugue, getaway, getaway car*, lam, out*, powder*, retreat, retreating, running away, slip*, spring*; SEE CONCEPTS *102,195*

flightiness [*n*] *irresponsibility*
airheadedness*, capriciousness, changeability, dizziness, fickleness, flippancy, frivolity, giddiness, inconstancy, instability, levity, lightness, mercurialness, variability, volatility, whimsicality, whimsicalness; SEE CONCEPT *633*

flighty [*adj*] *fickle, irresponsible*
airheaded*, birdbrained*, bubbleheaded*, capricious, changeable, dingbat*, dingdong*, dizzy*, effervescent, empty-headed, featherbrained*, frivolous, gaga*, giddy, harebrained*, impetuous, impulsive, inconstant, lightheaded, lively, mercurial, scatterbrained, silly, thoughtless, twit, unbalanced, unstable, unsteady, volatile, whimsical, wild; SEE CONCEPT *401*

flimflam [*v*] *deceive, swindle*
bilk, burn*, cheat, chisel, con, defraud, diddle*, dupe*, fleece, fool, gip*, gull, gyp*, hose*, pull

a fast one*, rip off*, rook*, sandbag, scam, shaft, steal, take for a ride*, trick; SEE CONCEPTS *59,139,192*

flimsy [*adj1*] *not strong; light, thin*
chiffon, cut-rate*, decrepit, defective, delicate, diaphanous, feeble, fragile, frail, gauzy, gossamer, house of cards*, inadequate, infirm, insubstantial, meager, papery, rickety, rinkydink*, shaky, shallow, sheer, slapdash*, sleazy, slight, superficial, tacky, transparent, unsound, unsubstantial, weak, wobbly; SEE CONCEPTS *489,606*

flimsy [*adj2*] *unconvincing, implausible*
assailable, baseless, contemptible, controvertible, fallacious, false, feeble, frivolous, groundless, illogical, improbable, inadequate, inane, inconceivable, incredible, inept, lame, poor, puerile, superficial, thin, transparent, trifling, trivial, unbelievable, ungrounded, unpersuasive, unreasonable, unsatisfactory, unsubstantial, weak, weakly, wishful; SEE CONCEPT *267*

flinch [*v*] *shy away, wince*
avoid, balk, blanch, blench, blink, cower, cringe, crouch, draw back, duck, elude, escape, eschew, evade, flee, quail, recede, recoil, retire, retreat, shirk, shrink, shun, start, swerve, withdraw; SEE CONCEPTS *102,150*

fling [*n1*] *casual throw*
cast, chuck, firing, heave, hurl, launching, lob, peg, pitch, shot, slinging, toss; SEE CONCEPT *222*

fling [*n2*] *unrestrained behavior*
affair, attempt, binge, celebration, crack*, essay, fun, gamble, go*, good time, indulgence, orgy, party, rampage, shot*, splurge, spree, stab*, trial, try, venture, whirl; SEE CONCEPT *386*

fling [*v*] *throw with abandon*
cast, catapult, chuck*, dump, fire, heave, hurl, jerk, launch, let fly*, lob, peg*, pitch, precipitate, propel, send, shy*, sling, toss; SEE CONCEPT *222*

flinty [*adj*] *stern*
cruel, firm, hard, inflexible, rigid, steely, stony, unsympathetic, unyielding; SEE CONCEPT *604*

flip [*n/v*] *throw, jump with abandon*
cast, chuck, flick, jerk, pitch, snap, spin, toss, twist; SEE CONCEPTS *194,222*

flip-flop [*n*] *reversal*
about-face, change, change of heart, turn-around, U-turn; SEE CONCEPTS *674,679*

flip out [*v*] *lose one's cool*
blow a gasket*, blow one's mind*, blow one's stack*, blow one's top*, crack up*, fly off the handle*, freak out*, go ape*, go ballistic*, go berserk*, go crazy*, go haywire*, go nuts*, go off the deep end*, hit the ceiling*, lose control of oneself, lose it*, lose one's composure, lose one's mind, lose one's temper, wig out*; SEE CONCEPT *13*

flippancy [*n*] *irreverence*
archness, cheek, cheekiness, cockiness, disrespectfulness, flightiness, freshness, frivolity, impertinence, impishness, impudence, levity, lightness, mischievousness, pertness, playfulness, roguishness, rudeness, sauciness, volatility, waggishness; SEE CONCEPT *633*

flippant [*adj*] *irreverent*
brassy, breezy, cheeky*, cocky, disrespectful, flighty, flip*, fresh, frivolous, glib, impertinent, impudent, insolent, lippy*, nervy*, offhand, pert, playful, rude, sassy*, smart*, smart-alecky*, superficial; SEE CONCEPT *401*

flip side [*n*] *reverse side*
back, B-side*, contraposition, opposite side, other side, other side of the fence*; SEE CONCEPT *665*

flirt [*n*] *person who makes advances*
coquette, cruiser*, heartbreaker, operator*, philanderer, player, seducer, siren, swinger, tease, trifler, vamp, vixen, wanton, wolf*; SEE CONCEPT *423*

flirt [*v*] *make advances toward someone*
banter, bat eyes at*, come hither*, come on*, coquet, dally, disport, eyeball*, fool, gam*, hit on*, lead on, linger with, make a move*, make a pass*, ogle, philander, pick up*, pitch*, proposition, tease, wink at*; SEE CONCEPTS *375,384*

flirtation [*n*] *amorous advance*
amour, coquetry, courting, cruising, dalliance, flirting, intrigue, pickup*, romance, romancing, tease, teasing, toying*, trifling*; SEE CONCEPTS *32,375,384*

flirtatious [*adj*] *provocative, teasing*
amorous, arch, come-hither*, come-on*, coquettish, coy, dallying, enticing, flirty, libidinous, spoony*, sportive; SEE CONCEPTS *401,404*

flit [*v*] *flutter, move rapidly*
dance, dart, flash, fleet, flicker, float, fly, hover, hurry, pass, run, rush, sail, scud*, skim, speed, sweep, whisk, whiz, wing, zip; SEE CONCEPT *150*

float [*v*] *lie on the surface*
be buoyant, bob, drift, glide, hang, hover, move gently, poise, rest on water, ride, sail, skim, slide, slip along, smooth along, stay afloat, swim, waft, wash; SEE CONCEPT *153*

flock [*n*] *congregation*
army, assembly, bevy, brood, cloud, collection, colony, company, convoy, crowd, crush, drift, drove, flight, gaggle, gathering, group, herd, host, legion, litter, mass, multitude, pack, progeny, rout, scores, skein, throng; SEE CONCEPTS *391,432*

flock [*v*] *congregate*
collect, converge, crowd, gather, group, herd, huddle, mass, throng, troop; SEE CONCEPTS *109,384*

flog [*v*] *whip, lash*
beat, belt, cane, castigate, chastise, ferule, flagellate, flax, flay, give the cat o'nine tails*, hide, hit, larrup, lather, leather*, paddle, scourge, spank, strike, stripe, tan one's hide*, thrash, trounce, wax*, whack, whale*, whomp*, whop*; SEE CONCEPT *189*

flood [*n*] *overwhelming flow, quantity*
abundance, alluvion, bore, bounty, cataclysm, cataract, current, deluge, downpour, drencher, drift, eager, excess, flow, flux, freshet, glut, inundation, multitude, niagara, outgushing, outpouring, overflow, plenty, pour, profusion, rush, spate, stream, superabundance, superfluity, surge, surplus, tide, torrent, tsunami, wave; SEE CONCEPTS *179,524,787*

flood [*v*] *inundate or submerge*
brim over, choke, deluge, drown, engulf, fill, flow, glut, gush, immerse, overflow, oversupply, overwhelm, pour over, rush, saturate, surge, swamp, swarm, sweep, whelm; SEE CONCEPTS *179,209,740*

floor [*n*] *bottom of a room; level of a multistory building*
basement, boards, canvas, carpet, cellar, deck, downstairs, flat, flooring, ground, landing, lowest point, mat, mezzanine, nadir, rug, stage, story, tier, upstairs; SEE CONCEPT *440*

floor [*v*] *perplex, confound*
baffle, beat, bewilder, bowl over*, bring down*, bring up short*, conquer, defeat, discomfit, disconcert, down, drop, dumbfound, fell, flatten, ground, knock down, lay low*, level, nonplus, overthrow, prostrate, puzzle, stump, throw; SEE CONCEPTS *16,95*

floor it [*v*] *drive at full speed*
accelerate, barrel, gather momentum, go flat-out, nail it*, open the throttle, put the pedal to the metal*, sprint, step on it*, step on the gas; SEE CONCEPTS *234,242*

floozy [*n*] *sexually promiscuous woman*
bimbo, broad, doxy, easy make, hooker, moll, nympho, piece of tail*, prostitute, tramp, whore; SEE CONCEPTS *348,412,415,419*

flop [*n*] *miserable failure*
bomb, bust, debacle, disaster, dud*, fiasco, lemon*, loser, miscarriage, nonstarter, washout*; SEE CONCEPTS *674,699*

flop [*v1*] *fall limply, collapse*
dangle, droop, drop, flag, flap, flounder, flutter, hang, jerk, lop, quiver, sag, slump, stagger, teeter, topple, toss, totter, tumble, wave, wiggle; SEE CONCEPTS *144,181*

flop [*v2*] *fail miserably*
bomb*, close, come apart*, come to nothing*, fall flat*, fall short*, flummox, fold, founder, miscarry, misfire, wash out*; SEE CONCEPT *699*

flophouse [*n*] *cheap hotel*
fleabag, fleabox, fleahouse, fleatrap, flop joint, run-down boarding house, run-down hotel; SEE CONCEPTS *439,449,516*

floral [*adj*] *decorated with flowers*
blooming, blossoming, blossomy, botanic, decorative, dendritic, efflorescent, flower-patterned, flowery, herbaceous, sylvan, verdant; SEE CONCEPT *589*

florid [*adj1*] *very elaborate*
aureate, baroque, busy, decorative, embellished, euphuistic, figurative, flamboyant, flowery, fussy, garnished, grandiloquent, high-flown, luscious, magniloquent, ornamental, ornamented, ornate, overblown, pretentious, rhetorical, rich, sonorous; SEE CONCEPTS *267,589*

florid [*adj2*] *flushed, ruddy*
blowzy, flush, glowing, high-colored, pink, reddened, rubicund, sanguine; SEE CONCEPTS *406,618*

flotilla [*n*] *small fleet*
argosy, armada, group, navy, squadron, unit, vessels; SEE CONCEPTS *322,432,506*

flotsam [*n*] *floating debris*
cargo, castoffs, jetsam, junk, odds and ends, seadrift, wreckage; SEE CONCEPTS *260,674*

flounce [*v*] *bounce; intermittently move*
fling, jerk, mince, nancy, prance, sashay, spring, stamp, storm, strut, swish, throw, toss; SEE CONCEPT *149*

flounder [*v*] *struggle; be in the dark*
blunder, bobble, cast about, come apart at the seams*, drop the ball*, fall down, flop, flummox, foul up*, fumble, go at backwards*, go to pieces*, grope, labor, lurch, make a mess of, miss one's cue*, muddle, plunge, pratfall*, screw up*, slip up*, snafu*, strive, stub one's toe*, stumble, thrash, toil, toss, travail, trip up*, tumble, wallow, work at; SEE CONCEPTS *101,699*

flourish [n] *curlicue, decoration*
curl, embellishment, furbelow, garnish, ornamentation, plume, quirk, spiral, sweep, twist; SEE
CONCEPTS *259,284*

flourish [v1] *grow, prosper*
amplify, arrive, augment, batten, bear fruit, be on
top of heap*, bloom, blossom, boom, burgeon,
come along, develop, do well, expand, flower,
get ahead, get on*, go, go great guns*, hit it big*,
increase, live high on hog*, make out*, multiply,
score, succeed, thrive, wax; SEE CONCEPTS
141,704,706

flourish [v2] *wave about*
brandish, display, flaunt, flutter, shake, sweep,
swing, swish, twirl, vaunt, wag, wield; SEE CON-
CEPTS *147,152*

flourishing [adj] *prospering, going well*
blooming, burgeoning, doing well, expanding,
exuberant, going strong, growing, in full swing*,
in the pink*, in top form*, lush, luxuriant, mush-
rooming, profuse, prosperous, rampant, rank,
rich, roaring, robust, successful, thriving, vigorous; SEE CONCEPT *528*

flout [v] *show contempt for*
affront, defy, deride, disregard, gibe, gird, insult,
jeer, laugh at, mock, outrage, quip, repudiate,
ridicule, scoff, scorn, slight, sneer, spurn, taunt,
thumb nose at*; SEE CONCEPT *54*

flow [n] *issue, abundance*
breeze, continuance, continuation, continuity,
course, current, deluge, discharge, draft, draw,
dribble, drift, ebb, effusion, electricity, emanation, flood, flux, gush, juice, leakage, movement,
oozing, outflow, outpouring, plenty, plethora,
progress, progression, river, run, sequence, series, spate, spout, spurt, stream, succession, tide,
train, wind; SEE CONCEPTS *146,179,467,787*

flow [v] *issue, surge, run out*
abound, arise, brim, cascade, circulate, continue,
course, deluge, discharge, disembogue, dribble,
ebb, emanate, emerge, emit, exudate, exude,
flood, glide, gurgle, gush, inundate, jet, leak,
move, ooze, overflow, pass, percolate, pour, proceed, progress, pullulate, regurgitate, result, ripple, roll, rush, slide, sluice, smooth along, spew,
spill, splash, spring, spurt, sputter, squirt, stream,
sweep, swell, swirl, teem, trickle, tumble, void,
well forth; SEE CONCEPTS *146,179*

flowchart [n] *sequential diagram*
flow diagram, flow sheet; SEE CONCEPTS *625,660*

flower [n1] *bloom of a plant*
annual, blossom, bud, cluster, efflorescence, floret, floweret, head, herb, inflorescence, perennial,
pompon, posy, shoot, spike, spray, vine; SEE
CONCEPTS *425,428*

flower [n2] *best, choicest part*
cream, elite, finest point, freshness, greatest
point, height, pick, pride, prime, prize, top; SEE
CONCEPTS *668,829*

flower [v] *bloom, flourish*
batten, blossom, blow, burgeon, effloresce, mature, open, outbloom, prosper, thrive, unfold; SEE
CONCEPTS *253,704*

flowery [adj] *ornate, especially referring to
speech or writing*
aureate, baroque, bombastic, declamatory, diffuse, embellished, euphemistic, euphuistic,
fancy, figurative, florid, grandiloquent, high-
flown, magniloquent, ornamented, overwrought,
prolix, purple, redundant, rhetorical, rococo,

sonorous, swollen, verbose, windy, wordy; SEE
CONCEPTS *267,589*

flowing [adj] *gushing, abounding*
brimming, continuous, cursive, easy, falling,
flooded, fluent, fluid, fluidic, full, issuing, liquefied, liquid, overrun, pouring out, prolific, rich,
rippling, rolling, running, rushing, sinuous,
smooth, spouting, streaming, sweeping, teeming,
tidal, unbroken, uninterrupted; SEE CONCEPTS
482,584

fluctuate [v] *vacillate, change*
alter, alternate, be undecided, blow hot and
cold*, ebb and flow, flutter, go up and down*,
hem and haw*, hesitate, oscillate, rise and fall*,
seesaw*, shift, swing, undulate, vary, veer, vibrate, wave, waver, yo-yo*; SEE CONCEPTS
13,469,697

flue [n] *pipe*
channel, chimney, duct, exhaust pipe, passage,
smoke duct, tube, vent; SEE CONCEPT *440*

fluent [adj] *articulate*
chatty, cogent, copious, cursive, declamatory,
disputatious, easy, effortless, effusive, eloquent,
facile, flowing, garrulous, glib, liquid, loquacious, mellifluent, mellifluous, natural, persuasive, prompt, quick, ready, running,
silver-tongued*, smooth, smooth-spoken, talkative, verbose, vocal, voluble, well-versed,
wordy; SEE CONCEPTS *267,584*

fluff [n1] *down*
eiderdown, feathers, fleece, floss, fuzz, lint,
wool; SEE CONCEPT *606*

fluff [n2] *mistake*
blooper*, bungling, error, false step, flub*, fumble, miscalculation, miscue, miss, muddle, muff,
oversight, slip, slipup*, stumble; SEE CONCEPTS
101,230,410

fluffy [adj] *soft, furry*
creamy, downy, featherlike, feathery, fleecy,
flocculent, flossy, gossamer, linty, pile, silky, velutinous; SEE CONCEPT *606*

fluid [adj1] *liquid*
aqueous, flowing, fluent, in solution, juicy, liquefied, lymphatic, melted, molten, running, runny,
serous, uncongealed, watery; SEE CONCEPTS
603,757

fluid [adj2] *adaptable, changeable*
adjustable, changeful, flexible, floating, fluctuating, indefinite, malleable, mercurial, mobile, mutable, protean, shifting, unsettled, unstable,
unsteady, variable; SEE CONCEPTS *534,542*

fluid [n] *liquid*
agua, broth, chaser, cooler, goo*, goop*, juice,
liquor, solution, vapor; SEE CONCEPT *467*

fluke [n] *chance occurrence*
accident, blessing, break, contingency, fortuity,
fortunate, fortune, good fortune*, good luck, incident, lucky break*, odd chance, quirk, stroke
of luck*, windfall; SEE CONCEPTS *4,679,693*

fluky [adj] *chance*
accidental, casual, chancy, coincidental, contingent, fortuitous, incalculable, incidental, lucky,
odd, uncertain, variable; SEE CONCEPT *552*

flume [n] *chute*
channel, conduit, run, sluice, spillway; SEE CON-
CEPTS *501,514*

flurry [n] *commotion, burst*
ado, agitation, brouhaha, bustle, confusion, disturbance, excitement, ferment, flap*, flaw, fluster, flutter, furor, fuss, gust, haste, hurry,

fl
fl

outbreak, pother, spell, spurt, squall, stir*, to-do, tumult, turbulence, turmoil, whirl, whirlwind; SEE CONCEPTS *230,524*

flurry [*v*] *agitate, confuse*
bewilder, bother, bustle, discombobulate*, discompose, disconcert, disquiet, distract, disturb, excite, fluster, flutter, frustrate, fuss, galvanize, hassle, hurry, hustle, perplex, perturb, provoke, quicken, rattle, ruffle, stimulate, unhinge, unsettle, upset; SEE CONCEPTS *7,19*

flush [*adj1*] *flat*
even, horizontal, level, planate, plane, smooth, square, true; SEE CONCEPTS *486,490*

flush [*adj2*] *overflowing, abundant*
affluent, close, full, generous, lavish, liberal, opulent, prodigal, rich, wealthy, well-off; SEE CONCEPTS *334,771*

flush [*n*] *blush*
bloom, color, freshness, glow, pinkness, redness, rosiness, ruddiness; SEE CONCEPT *622*

flush [*v1*] *become or make pink or red*
blush, burn, color, color up, crimson, flame, glow, go red, mantle, pink, pinken, redden, rose, rouge, suffuse; SEE CONCEPTS *250,469*

flush [*v2*] *inundate with liquid*
cleanse, douche, drench, eject, expel, flood, hose, rinse, swab, wash; SEE CONCEPTS *165,179*

flushed [*adj*] *pink, glowing*
ablaze, animated, aroused, blushing, burning, crimson, elated, embarrassed, enthused, exhilarated, feverish, florid, full-blooded, high, hot, inspired, intoxicated, red, rosy, rubicund, ruddy, sanguine, thrilled; SEE CONCEPTS *401,403,618*

fluster [*n*] *perturbation, upset*
agitation, brouhaha, commotion, disturbance, dither, flap*, flurry, flutter, furor, ruffle, state*, to-do*, turmoil; SEE CONCEPT *410*

fluster [*v*] *upset, perturb*
addle, agitate, bewilder, bother, confound, confuse, craze*, discombobulate*, discompose, disquiet, distract, disturb, excite, flip*, flurry, frustrate, fuddle*, get to*, hassle, heat*, hurry, make nervous, make waves*, muddle, mystify, nonplus, perplex, psych*, puzzle, rattle, ruffle, spook*, stir up*, throw off balance*, unhinge*, work up*; SEE CONCEPTS *7,16,19*

flutter [*v*] *wave rapidly, flap*
agitate, bat, beat, dance, drift, flicker, flit, flitter, flop, fluctuate, hover, lop, oscillate, palpitate, pulsate, quaver, quiver, ripple, ruffle, shake, shiver, swing, throb, tremble, vibrate, wiggle, wobble; SEE CONCEPTS *150,152*

flux [*n*] *state of constant change*
alteration, change, flow, fluctuation, fluidity, instability, modification, motion, mutability, mutation, transition, unrest; SEE CONCEPT *697*

fly [*v1*] *take to the air, usually employing wings*
aviate, barnstorm*, bend the throttle*, buzz*, circle, circumnavigate, climb, control, cross, dart, dash, dive, drift, flat-hat*, fleet, flit, float, flutter, glide, hop, hover, hurry, jet, jet out, jet over, maneuver, mount, operate, pilot, reach, remain aloft, rush, sail, scud*, seagull*, shoot, skim, skirt, sky out*, soar, speed, swoop, take a hop*, take flight, take off, take wing, travel, whisk*, whiz*, whoosh*, wing*, wing in*, zip*, zoom*; SEE CONCEPTS *148,150,224*

fly [*v2*] *run or pass swiftly*
barrel, bolt, breeze, career, dart, dash, elapse, flee, flit, glide, go like the wind*, hasten, hurry,

hustle, make off*, pass, race, roll, run its course*, rush, scamper, scoot, shoot, slip away*, speed, sprint, tear, whiz*, zoom*; SEE CONCEPTS *150,818*

fly [*v3*] *escape, flee*
abscond, avoid, bolt, break, clear, clear out*, cut and run*, decamp, disappear, get away, hasten away, hide, hightail*, light out*, make a getaway*, make a quick exit*, make off, run*, run for it, run from, skedaddle*, skip, steal away, take flight, take off, withdraw; SEE CONCEPTS *102,195*

fly-by-night [*adj*] *undependable*
brief, cowboy*, dubious, here-today-gone-to-morrow*, impermanent, questionable, shady, shifty, short-lived, slimy*, slippery*, treacherous, trustless, unreliable, unsure, untrustworthy; SEE CONCEPTS *542,551*

flyer [*n*] *person who navigates an aircraft*
ace*, air person, aviator, flier, jet*, navigator, pilot; SEE CONCEPT *348*

flying [*adj*] *in the air, winged*
aerial, aeronautical, airborne, avian, drifting, express, flapping, fleet, floating, fluttering, gliding, hovering, mercurial, mobile, on the wing, plumed, soaring, speedy, streaming, swooping, volant, volar, volitant, waving, winging, zooming; SEE CONCEPT *584*

flying saucer [*n*] *spaceship*
extraterrestrial vessel, spacecraft, UFO, unidentified flying object; SEE CONCEPTS *504,506*

foam [*n*] *bubbles formed from a liquid*
cream, fluff, froth, head, lather, scum, spray, spume, suds, surf, yeast; SEE CONCEPT *260*

foam [*v*] *become bubbly*
aerate, boil, burble, effervesce, ferment, fizz, froth, gurgle, hiss, lather, seethe, simmer, sparkle; SEE CONCEPTS *170,469*

foamy [*adj*] *bubbly*
barmy, boiling, burbling, carbonated, creamy, ebullient, effervescent, fermented, fizzy, frothy, lathery, scummy*, seething, simmering, spumescent, spumous, spumy, sudsy, yeasty; SEE CONCEPT *485*

focus [*n*] *center of attraction*
bull's eye*, center, core, cynosure, focal point, headquarters*, heart, hub, limelight*, locus, meeting place, nerve center*, point of convergence, polestar, seat, spotlight, target; SEE CONCEPTS *532,826,829*

focus [*v*] *aim attention at*
adjust, attract, bring out, center, centralize, concenter, concentrate, convene, converge, direct, fasten, fix, fixate, get detail, home in*, home in on*, hone in*, join, key on*, knuckle down*, meet, move in, pinpoint, pour it on*, put, rivet, sharpen, spotlight*, sweat*, zero in*, zoom in*; SEE CONCEPTS *17,623*

fodder [*n*] *animal feed*
animal food, barley, corn, food, forage, grain, grass, grub, hay, meal, pasturage, provender, provisions, silage, straw, vittles; SEE CONCEPTS *457,460,461*

foe [*n*] *person who is an opponent*
adversary, antagonist, anti*, enemy, hostile party, rival; SEE CONCEPT *412*

fog [*n1*] *heavy mist that reduces visibility*
brume, cloud, effluvium, film, gloom, grease, ground clouds, haze, London fog, miasma, murk, murkiness, nebula, obscurity, pea soup*, smaze,

smog, smoke, smother, soup*, steam, vapor, visibility zero-zero*, wisp; SEE CONCEPTS *524,627*

fog [*n2*] *mental unclarity*
befuddlement, blindness, confusion, daze, haze, maze, mist, muddledness, muddlement, obscurity, perplexity, stupor, trance, vagueness; SEE CONCEPT *410*

fog [*v*] *muddle, obscure*
addle, becloud, bedim, befuddle, bewilder, blind, blur, cloud, confuse, darken, daze, dim, eclipse, mist, muddy, mystify, obfuscate, perplex, puzzle, steam up, stupefy; SEE CONCEPTS *250,526*

foggy [*adj*] *hazy, obscure*
blurred, ceiling zero*, closed in, clouded, cloudy, dark, dim, filmy, fogged in, fuzzy, gray, indistinct, misty, murky, mushy, nebulous, peasoupy*, smazy, smoggy, socked in*, soupy*, unclear, vague, vaporous, vapory, zero-zero*; SEE CONCEPTS *403,525*

foghorn [*n*] *warning signal*
alarm, danger signal, signal, siren; SEE CONCEPTS *269,463*

foible [*n*] *personal imperfection*
characteristic, defect, eccentricity, failing, fault, frailty, idiosyncrasy, infirmity, kink, mannerism, oddity, peculiarity, quirk, shortcoming, singularity, vice, weakness, weak point; SEE CONCEPTS *411,644*

foil [*n*] *contrast*
antithesis, background, complement, counterblow, defense, guard, setting; SEE CONCEPT *665*

foil [*v*] *circumvent, nip in the bud*
baffle, balk, beat, bilk, bollix*, buffalo*, check, checkmate, counter, crab, cramp, crimp, curb, dash, defeat, disappoint, disconcert, ditch, dodge, duck, elude, faze, foul up*, frustrate, get around*, give the run-around*, give the slip*, hang up*, hinder, juke, nullify, outwit, prevent, rattle, restrain, run circles around*, run rings around*, shake, shake off, shuffle off, skip, stop, stymie, throw monkey wrench in*, thwart, upset the apple cart*; SEE CONCEPTS *121,130*

foist [*v*] *force upon*
compel to accept, fob off, impose, insert fraudulently, palm off, pass off, pull a fast one*, ram down one's throat*, sneak in; SEE CONCEPT *14*

fold [*n*] *double thickness*
bend, circumvolution, cockle, convolution, corrugation, crease, crimp, crinkle, dog's ear*, flection, flexure, furrow, gather, gathering, groove, knife-edge*, lap, lapel, layer, loop, overlap, plait, pleat, plica, plication, plicature, ply, pucker, ridge, rimple, rivel, ruche, ruck, ruffle, rumple, shirring, smocking, tuck, turn, wrinkle; SEE CONCEPT *754*

fold [*v1*] *lay in creases*
bend, cockle, corrugate, crimp, crisp, crumple, curl, dog-ear*, double, double over, furrow, gather, groove, hem, intertwine, knit, lap, overlap, overlay, plait, pleat, plicate, pucker, purse, replicate, ridge, ruche, ruck, ruffle, telescope, tuck, turn under, wrinkle; SEE CONCEPT *184*

fold [*v2*] *encase, enclose*
do up, enfold, entwine, envelop, involve, wrap, wrap up; SEE CONCEPT *209*

fold [*v3*] *fail, close*
become insolvent, be ruined, break, bust, collapse, crash, crumple, give, go bankrupt, go bust, go into Chapter 11*, go under*, impoverish, pauper, pauperize, shut down, yield; SEE CONCEPTS *324,699*

folder [*n*] *paper envelope for holding items*
binder, case, file, pocket, portfolio, sheath, wrapper, wrapping; SEE CONCEPT *260*

foliage [*n*] *leaves*
frondescence, greenness, growth, herbage, leafage, umbrage, vegetation, verdure; SEE CONCEPT *428*

folk [*n*] *person's relations, acquaintances*
body politic, clan, community, confederation, culture group, ethnic group, family, general public, group, house, household, inhabitants, kin, kindred, lineage, masses, ménage, nation, nationality, people, population, proletariat, public, race, settlement, society, state, stock, tribe; SEE CONCEPTS *296,379*

folklore [*n*] *tales from the past*
ballad, custom, fable, folk story, legend, myth, mythology, mythos, oral literature, superstition, tradition, wisdom; SEE CONCEPT *282*

folks [*n*] *family*
brood, clan, horde, household, kin, parents, people, relatives, tribe; SEE CONCEPTS *296,378,397*

folksy [*adj*] *informal, simple*
cozy, down-to-earth*, homely, homey, low-key, modest, natural, plain, rustic, unassuming, unpretentious; SEE CONCEPTS *562,589*

follow [*v1*] *take the place of*
be subsequent to, chase, come after, come from, come next, displace, ensue, go after, go next, postdate, proceed from, pursue, replace, result, spring from, succeed, supersede, supervene, supplant; SEE CONCEPTS *128,242,813*

follow [*v2*] *trail, pursue physically*
accompany, attend, bring up the rear*, catenate, chase, come with, concatenate, convoy, dog*, dog the footsteps of*, draggle, escort, freeze, give chase, go after, go with, hound*, hunt, onto*, persecute, put a tail on*, run after, run down, schlepp along*, search, seek, shadow, shag*, spook*, stalk, stick to, string along, tag, tag after*, tag along*, tail, tailgate*, take out after, track; SEE CONCEPT *207*

follow [*v3*] *act in accordance with*
abide by, accord, adhere to, adopt, attend, be consistent with, be devoted to, be guided by, be in keeping, be interested in, comply, conform, copy, cultivate, do like, emulate, follow suit, give allegiance to, harmonize, heed, hold fast, imitate, keep, keep abreast of, keep an eye on, live up to, match, mimic, mind, mirror, model on, note, obey, observe, pattern oneself upon, reflect, regard, serve, string along*, support, take after, take as an example, watch; SEE CONCEPTS *8,91,171*

follow [*v4*] *understand*
accept, appreciate, apprehend, catch*, catch on*, comprehend, dig*, fathom, get*, get the picture*, grasp, realize, see, take in*; SEE CONCEPT *15*

follower [*n*] *person who believes or has great interest*
addict, adherent, admirer, advocate, apostle, attendant, backer, believer, bootlicker*, buff, client, cohort, companion, convert, copycat, devotee, disciple, fan, fancier, freak*, habitué, hanger-on*, helper, imitator, lackey*, member, minion, parasite, participant, partisan, patron, promoter, proselyte, protégé, pupil, representative, satellite, sectary, servant, sidekick, stooge*,

fl
fo

supporter, sycophant, toady*, vassal, votary, worshiper, zealot; SEE CONCEPTS *352,366,423*

following [*adj*] *happening, being next or after*
after a while, afterward, attendant, a while later, back, by and by, coming, coming after, coming next, consecutive, consequent, consequential, directly after, ensuing, henceforth, hinder, in pursuit, in search of, in the wake of, later, later on, latter, next, next off*, on the scent*, posterior, presently, proximate, pursuing, rear, resulting, sequent, sequential, serial, seriate, specified, subsequent, succeeding, successive, supervenient, then, trailing, when; SEE CONCEPTS *585,811,818, 820*

following [*n*] *persons of an interest or belief*
adherents, audience, circle, clientage, clientele, cortege, coterie, dependents, entourage, fans, group, groupies*, hangers-on*, patronage, patrons, public, retinue, rout, suite, support, supporters, train; SEE CONCEPTS *294,387,417*

follow through [*v*] *bring to a conclusion*
complete, conclude, consummate, pursue, see through; SEE CONCEPT *91*

follow up [*v*] *make inquiries*
check out, find out about, investigate, look into, make sure, pursue; SEE CONCEPT *103*

folly [*n*] *nonsense, ridiculous idea*
absurdity, craziness, daftness, dottiness, dumb thing to do*, dumb trick*, fatuity, foolishness, idiocy, imbecility, impracticality, imprudence, inadvisability, inanity, indiscretion, irrationality, lunacy, madness, obliquity, preposterousness, rashness, recklessness, senselessness, silliness, stupidity, triviality, unsoundness, vice, witlessness; SEE CONCEPTS *410,633*

foment [*v*] *instigate, provoke*
abet, agitate, arouse, brew, cultivate, encourage, excite, fan the flames*, foster, goad, incite, nurse, nurture, promote, quicken, raise, set, set on, sow the seeds*, spur, start, stimulate, stir up, whip up*; SEE CONCEPTS *14,221*

fond [*adj*] *have a liking or taste for*
addicted, adoring, affectionate, amorous, attached, caring, devoted, doting, enamored, indulgent, keen on, lovesome, lovey-dovey*, loving, mushy*, partial, predisposed, responsive, romantic, sentimental, silly over, sympathetic, tender, warm; SEE CONCEPTS *32,542*

fondle [*v*] *touch lovingly*
bear hug*, caress, clutch, cosset, cuddle, dandle, embrace, feel, fool around*, grab, grope, hug, love, make love to, neck, nestle, nuzzle, pat, paw, pet, play footsie*, snuggle, squeeze, stroke; SEE CONCEPTS *190,375*

fondness [*n*] *liking or taste for*
affection, attachment, devotion, fancy, kindness, love, partiality, penchant, predilection, preference, soft spot, susceptibility, tenderness, weakness; SEE CONCEPT *32*

font [*n1*] *source*
fount, fountain, genesis, origin, root, seed, wellspring; SEE CONCEPT *648*

font [*n2*] *print type*
face, typeface; SEE CONCEPTS *79,284*

food [*n*] *edible material*
aliment, bite*, board, bread, cheer, chow*, comestible, cookery, cooking, cuisine, diet, drink, eatable, eats*, entrée, fare, fast food, feed, fodder*, foodstuff, goodies*, grit*, groceries*, grub*, handout*, home cooking, keep, larder,

meal, meat, menu, mess*, moveable feast, nourishment, nutriment, nutrition, pabulum, provision, ration, refreshment, slop*, snack, store, subsistence, support, sustenance, table, take out, tuck, viand, victual, vittles*; SEE CONCEPTS *457,460,461*

food court [*n*] *public area where variety of food is sold*
cafe, counter, fast food, food festival, restaurant, smorgasbord; SEE CONCEPTS *439,448,449*

food poisoning [*n*] *poisoning caused by eating food*
botulism, ptomaine poisoning, salmonella; SEE CONCEPT *537*

fool [*n*] *stupid or ridiculous person*
ass, birdbrain*, blockhead*, bonehead*, boob*, bore, buffoon, clod*, clown, cretin*, dimwit*, dolt*, dope*, dumb ox*, dunce, dunderhead*, easy mark*, fair game*, fathead*, goose*, halfwit, idiot, ignoramus, illiterate, imbecile, innocent, jerk*, lamebrain*, lightweight*, loon*, moron, nerd*, nincompoop*, ninny*, nitwit, numskull*, oaf, sap*, schlemiel*, silly, simpleton, stooge*, sucker*, turkey*, twerp*, twit*, victim; SEE CONCEPTS *412,423*

fool [*v*] *trick, mislead*
bamboozle*, bluff, cheat, chicane, con, deceive, delude, diddle, dupe, fake out*, flimflam*, fox*, gull, hoax, hoodwink*, jive*, juke*, kid, lead on, make believe, outfox, play-act*, play a trick on, pretend, put on, put one over on*, scam*, snow*, spoof*, suck in*, take in*, trifle; SEE CONCEPT *59*

fool around [*v*] *waste time*
dawdle, hang around*, idle, kill time*, lark, mess around*, play around*; SEE CONCEPT *681*

fooled [*adj*] *tricked*
bamboozled*, conned, deceived, deluded, duped, flimflammed*, hornswoggled*, misled, outfoxed*, snowed*, sucked in*; SEE CONCEPT *537*

foolhardy [*adj*] *impetuous, rash*
adventuresome, adventurous, audacious, bold, breakneck*, daredevil, daring, devil-may-care*, harebrained*, headstrong, imprudent, incautious, irresponsible, madcap, off deep end*, out on limb*, precipitate, reckless, temerarious, venturesome, venturous, wide open; SEE CONCEPT *401*

fooling [*n*] *joking, tricks*
bluffing, buffoonery, clownishness, farce, frolicking, high jinks*, horseplay, jesting, joshing, kidding, making light*, mockery, nonsense, pretense, roughhouse*, roughhousing*, rowdiness, sham*, skylarking*, spoofing, teasing, trifling; SEE CONCEPT *59*

foolish [*adj*] *nonsensical, idiotic*
absurd, asinine, brainless, cockamamy*, crazy, daffy*, daft, dippy*, doltish*, dotty*, fantastic, fatuous, feebleminded*, half-baked*, half-witted*, harebrained*, ill-advised, ill-considered, imbecilic, imprudent, incautious, indiscreet, injudicious, insane, irrational, jerky*, kooky*, loony*, ludicrous, lunatic, mad, moronic, nerdy*, nutty*, preposterous, ridiculous, senseless, short-sighted, silly, simple, stupid, unintelligent, unreasonable, unwise, wacky*, weak, witless, zany*; SEE CONCEPTS *401,542,544*

foolishly [*adv*] *idiotic, without due consideration*
absurdly, ill-advisedly, imprudently, incautiously, indiscreetly, injudiciously, mistakenly,

short-sightedly, stupidly, unwisely; SEE CONCEPTS *401,542,544*

foolishness [*n*] *idiocy, nonsense*
absurdity, absurdness, bunk*, carrying-on*, claptrap*, craziness, dumb trick*, folly, foolery, fool trick, horse feathers*, impracticality, imprudence, inanity, indiscretion, insanity, insensibility, irrationality, irresponsibility, ludicrousness, lunacy, mistake, poppycock*, preposterousness, rubbish*, senselessness, silliness, stupidity, tommyrot*, twaddle, unreasonableness, unwiseness, weakness, witlessness; SEE CONCEPT *633*

foolproof [*adj*] *infallible*
certain, dependable, fail-safe, faultless, flawless, goofproof, guaranteed, idiot-proof*, never-failing, perfect, reliable, safe, sure, sure-fire, tested, tried, unassailable, unerring, unfailing; SEE CONCEPTS *535,582*

foot [*n1*] *extremity of an animate being*
hoof, pad, paw; SEE CONCEPT *392*

foot [*n2*] *base of an object*
bottom, foundation, lowest point, nadir, pier; SEE CONCEPT *442*

foot [*n3*] *twelve inches/30.48 centimeters measured*
cubic, square; SEE CONCEPTS *790,791*

footing [*n1*] *foundation, basis*
basement, bedrock, bottom, establishment, foot, foothold, ground, groundwork, infrastructure, installation, resting place, seat, seating, settlement, substratum, substructure, underpinning, understructure, warrant; SEE CONCEPTS *442,661*

footing [*n2*] *social status*
capacity, character, condition, grade, place, position, rank, relations, relationship, situation, standing, state, station, terms; SEE CONCEPT *388*

footloose [*adj*] *free*
easygoing, free and easy, go-as-you-please, loose, unattached, uncommitted, unengaged; SEE CONCEPTS *401,542*

footprint [*n*] *footmark*
footstep, hoofprint, impression, imprint, spoor, track, trail, tread; SEE CONCEPTS *513,628*

fop [*n*] *dandy*
beau, Beau Brummel, clotheshorse, coxcomb, dude, fashion plate, macaroni, peacock, popinjay; SEE CONCEPT *423*

for [*conj*] *in consequence of the fact that*
as, as long as, because, being, considering, inasmuch as, now, since, whereas; SEE CONCEPT *544*

for [*prep*] *in consideration of*
after, as, beneficial to, concerning, conducive to, during, for the sake of, in contemplation of, in exchange for, in favor of, in furtherance of, in order to, in order to get, in place of, in pursuance of, in spite of, in the direction of, in the interest of, in the name of, notwithstanding, on the part of, on the side of, pro, supposing, to, to counterbalance, to go to, to the amount of, to the extent of, toward, under the authority of, with a view to, with regard to, with respect; SEE CONCEPT *544*

forage [*v*] *search madly for*
beat, cast about, comb, explore, fine-tooth-comb*, grub, hunt, pilfer, plunder, raid, rake, ransack, ravage, rummage, scour, scrounge, seek; SEE CONCEPT *216*

foray [*n*] *incursion, attempt*
attack, depredation, descent, inroad, invasion, irruption, raid, reconnaissance, sally, sortie; SEE CONCEPTS *86,90,159*

forbear [*v*] *resist the temptation to*
abstain, avoid, bridle, cease, curb, decline, desist, escape, eschew, evade, forgo, go easy*, hold back*, inhibit, keep, keep from, omit, pause, refrain, restrain, sacrifice, shun, stop, withhold; SEE CONCEPTS *35,121,130,681*

forbearance [*n*] *resisting, avoidance*
abstinence, endurance, fortitude, going easy on*, living with*, longanimity, moderation, patience, patientness, refraining, resignation, restraint, self-control, temperance, tolerance; SEE CONCEPTS *410,633*

forbearing [*adj*] *tolerant*
being big*, charitable, clement, considerate, easy, forgiving, gentle, going easy on*, going easy with*, humane, humanitarian, indulgent, lenient, living with*, longanimous, long-suffering, merciful, mild, moderate, patient, soft-shell*, thoughtful; SEE CONCEPTS *404,542*

forbid [*v*] *outlaw, prohibit an action*
ban, block, cancel, censor, check, debar, declare illegal, deny, deprive, disallow, embargo, enjoin, exclude, forestall, forfend, freeze*, halt, hinder, hold up, impede, inhibit, interdict, lock up, nix*, obstruct, obviate, oppose, preclude, prevent, proscribe, put the chill on*, restrain, restrict, rule out, say no*, shut down*, shut out*, spike*, stop, stymie*, taboo*, veto, withhold; SEE CONCEPT *121*

forbidden [*adj*] *outlawed, prohibited*
banned, closed, closed-down*, closed-up*, contraband, no-no*, off limits, out of bounds, proscribed, refused, taboo*, verboten, vetoed; SEE CONCEPT *548*

forbidden fruit [*n*] *taboo*
desired object, golden apple, illicit love, no-no*, prohibition; SEE CONCEPTS *532,687*

forbidding [*adj*] *ominous, daunting*
abhorrent, disagreeable, dour, foreboding, frightening, glowering, grim, hostile, menacing, odious, offensive, off-putting, repellent, repulsive, sinister, threatening, tough, ugly, unapproachable, unfriendly, unpleasant; SEE CONCEPTS *537,550*

force [*n1*] *physical energy, power*
arm, brunt, clout, coercion, compulsion, conscription, constraint, draft, duress, dynamism, effort, enforcement, exaction, extortion, full head of steam*, fury, horsepower, impact, impetus, impulse, might, momentum, muscle, pains*, potency, potential, pow*, pressure, punch, push, sinew, sock*, speed, steam, stimulus, strain, strength, stress, strong arm*, stuff*, subjection, tension, trouble, velocity, vigor, violence, what it takes*; SEE CONCEPTS *641,724*

force [*n2*] *mental power, energy*
ability, authority, bite*, capability, coercion, cogency, competence, determination, dominance, drive, duress, effect, effectiveness, efficacy, emphasis, fierceness, forcefulness, gumption, guts*, impressiveness, influence, intensity, intestinal fortitude, obligation, persistence, persuasiveness, point, pressure, puissance, punch, push, requirement, sapience, stress, validity, validness, vehemence, vigor, willpower; SEE CONCEPTS *410,677*

force [*n3*] *military organization*
armed forces, army, battalion, body, cell, corps, crew, detachment, division, guard, horses, host, legion, patrol, regiment, reserves, shop, soldiers,

fo
fo

squad, squadron, troop, unit; SEE CONCEPTS *322,417*

force [*v1*] *obligate to do something*
apply, bear down, bear hard on, bind, blackmail, bring pressure to bear upon*, burden, cause, charge, choke, coerce, command, compel, concuss, conscript, constrain, contract, demand, draft, drag, dragoon*, drive, enforce, enjoin, exact, extort, fix, impel, impose, impress, inflict, insist, limit, make, move, necessitate, oblige, obtrude, occasion, order, overcome, pin down, press, pressure, pressurize, put screws to*, put squeeze on*, require, restrict, sandbag*, shotgun*, strong-arm*, urge, wrest, wring; SEE CONCEPT *14*

force [*v2*] *use violence upon*
assault, blast, break in, break open, burst, bust open, crack open, defile, extort, jimmy*, propel, pry, push, rape, ravish, spoil, squeeze, thrust, twist, undo, violate, wrench, wrest, wring; SEE CONCEPTS *156,208*

forced [*adj*] *compulsory, strained*
affected, artificial, begrudging, binding, bound, coerced, coercive, compelled, conscripted, constrained, contrived, enforced, factitious, false, grudging, inflexible, insincere, involuntary, labored, mandatory, obligatory, peremptory, rigid, slave, stiff, stringent, unnatural, unwilling, wooden*; SEE CONCEPTS *542,548*

forceful [*adj*] *effective, powerful*
ball of fire*, bullish*, cogent, coming on strong, commanding, compelling, constraining, convincing, dominant, dynamic, electric, elemental, energetic, forcible, gutsy*, mighty, persuasive, pithy, potent, powerhouse, puissant, punch, punchy*, steamroller*, stringent, strong, take-charge, take-over, telling, titanic, vehement, vigorous, violent, virile, weighty; SEE CONCEPTS *267,401,550*

forcible [*adj*] *powerful, aggressive*
active, armed, assertive, coercive, cogent, compelling, compulsory, drastic, effective, efficient, energetic, forceful, impressive, intense, mighty, militant, persuasive, potent, puissant, strong, telling, valid, vehement, vigorous, violent, weighty; SEE CONCEPTS *267,537*

forcibly [*adv*] *against one's will*
by force, coercively, compulsorily, effectively, energetically, hard, mightily, powerfully, strongly, under protest, vigorously; SEE CONCEPTS *544,548*

fore [*adv*] *in the front*
ahead, ante*, antecedently, before, beforehand, forward, in advance, near, nearest, precedently, previous; SEE CONCEPTS *585,820*

forebearer [*n*] *family predecessor*
ancestor, antecedent, ascendant, author, begetter, forerunner, founder, materfamilias, matriarch, originator, parent, paterfamilias, patriarch, precursor, primogenitor, procreator, progenitor, relative, sire; SEE CONCEPT *414*

forebode [*v*] *predict, warn*
augur, betoken, bode, divine, forecast, foresee, foreshadow, foretell, foretoken, forewarn, indicate, omen, portend, premonish, presage, prognosticate, promise; SEE CONCEPTS *70,78*

foreboding [*n*] *misgiving, bad omen*
anxiety, apprehension, apprehensiveness, augury, bad vibes*, chill, dread, fear, foreshadowing, foretoken, forewarning, funny feeling*,

handwriting on the wall*, portent, prediction, premonition, prenotion, presage, presentiment, prognostic, prophecy, sinking feeling*, vibes*, warning, wind change*; SEE CONCEPTS *78,689, 690*

forecast [*n*] *prediction, often of weather or business*
anticipation, augury, budget, calculation, cast, conjecture, divination, estimate, foreknowledge, foreseeing, foresight, foretelling, forethought, foretoken, guess, outlook, planning, precognition, prescience, prevision, prognosis, prognostication, projection, prophecy; SEE CONCEPTS *28,37,70,78*

forecast [*v*] *predict, guess*
adumbrate, anticipate, augur, calculate, call the turn*, conclude, conjecture, demonstrate, determine, divine, dope out*, estimate, figure, figure out*, foresee, foretell, gather, gauge, infer, in the cards*, plan, portend, predetermine, presage, prognosticate, prophesy, reason, see it coming*, soothsay, surmise, telegraph; SEE CONCEPTS *28,37,70,78*

forefather [*n*] *ancestor*
antecedent, ascendant, forebearer, patriarch, precursor, predecessor, primogenitor, procreator, progenitor; SEE CONCEPT *414*

forefront/foreground [*n*] *prominence*
beginning, center, cutting-edge*, focus, fore, forepart, front, lead, leading-edge*, limelight*, on the line*, spearhead*, state-of-the-art, vanguard; SEE CONCEPT *668*

foregoing [*adj*] *come before; previous*
above, aforementioned, aforesaid, aforestated, antecedent, anterior, former, past, precedent, preceding, prior; SEE CONCEPTS *585,820*

foreign [*adj1*] *from another country, experience*
adopted, alien, alienated, antipodal, barbarian, barbaric, borrowed, derived, different, distant, estranged, exiled, exotic, expatriate, external, extralocal, extraneous, extrinsic, far, faraway, far-fetched, far-off, from abroad, immigrant, imported, inaccessible, nonnative, nonresident, not domestic, not native, offshore, outlandish, outside, overseas, remote, strange, transoceanic, unaccustomed, unexplored, unfamiliar, unknown; SEE CONCEPTS *536,549*

foreign [*adj2*] *irrelevant*
accidental, adventitious, extraneous, extrinsic, heterogeneous, immaterial, impertinent, inapposite, incompatible, incongruous, inconsistent, inconsonant, irrelative, repugnant, unassimilable, uncharacteristic, unrelated; SEE CONCEPTS *267,537*

foreigner [*n*] *person from another country*
alien, fresh off the boat*, greenhorn*, immigrant, incomer, newcomer, outlander, outsider, stranger; SEE CONCEPT *413*

foremost [*adj*] *first in rank, order*
A-1*, A-number-1*, arch, at the cutting edge*, at the leading edge*, champion, chief, front, head, headmost, heavy, heavy stuff*, heavyweight*, highest, hotdog*, hotshot*, hot stuff*, inaugural, initial, leading, most important, number one*, original, paramount, preeminent, premier, primary, prime, primo*, principal, supreme; SEE CONCEPTS *568,585,799*

forensic [*adj*] *judicial, legal*
argumentative, debatable, dialectic, dialectical,

disputative, juridical, juristic, moot, polemical, rhetorical; SEE CONCEPTS *267,319*

foreordain [*v*] *doom, fate*
destinate, destine, foredoom, foreshadow, foretell, prearrange, predestine, predetermine, preform, preordain, reserve; SEE CONCEPT *70*

foreplay [*n*] *fondling*
action*, caress, cuddling, heavy petting, kissing, lovemaking, making out, necking, oral sex, petting, sex, sexual activity; SEE CONCEPTS *375,388*

forerunner [*n1*] *messenger, herald*
advertiser, advocate, ancestor, announcer, author, envoy, forebearer, foregoer, harbinger, initiator, originator, pioneer, precursor, progenitor, prognostic, prototype; SEE CONCEPTS *414,423*

forerunner [*n2*] *example, sign*
advertisement, announcement, antecedent, antecessor, augury, exemplar, foregoer, foreshadow, foretoken, forewarning, indication, mark, model, omen, pattern, portent, precursor, predecessor, premonition, presage, prognostic, prototype, sign, token, warning; SEE CONCEPT *529*

foresee [*v*] *anticipate, predict*
apprehend, call the turn*, crystal ball it*, discern, divine, dope out*, envisage, espy, expect, forebode, forecast, forefeel, foreknow, foretell, have a hunch*, perceive, preknow, presage, previse, prevision, prognosticate, prophesy, psych out*, see, see it coming*, understand, visualize; SEE CONCEPTS *26,70*

foreshadow [*v*] *indicate*
adumbrate, augur, be in the wind*, betoken, bode, forebode, foretell, hint, imply, omen, portend, predict, prefigure, presage, promise, prophesy, shadow, signal, suggest, telegraph; SEE CONCEPTS *70,75,261*

foresight [*n*] *mental preparedness*
anticipation, canniness, care, carefulness, caution, circumspection, clairvoyance, discernment, discreetness, discretion, economy, far-sightedness, foreknowledge, forethought, insight, long-sightedness, perception, precaution, precognition, preconception, premeditation, premonition, prenotion, prescience, prospect, providence, provision, prudence, sagacity; SEE CONCEPTS *409,410*

forest [*n*] *area with a large number of trees*
backwoods, brake, chase, clump, coppice, copse, cover, covert, grove, growth, jungle, park, shelter, stand, thicket, timber, timberland, weald, wildwood, wood, woodland, woodlot, woods; SEE CONCEPTS *509,517*

foretell [*v*] *predict, warn*
adumbrate, announce, anticipate, apprehend, augur, auspicate, betoken, bode, call, call it*, call the shot*, crystal ball it*, declare, disclose, divine, divulge, dope*, dope out*, figure, figure out*, forebode, forecast, foreknow, foreshadow, forewarn, make book*, portend, prefigure, presage, proclaim, prognosticate, prophesy, psych, read, reveal, see something coming*, signify, soothsay, tell; SEE CONCEPTS *70,78*

forethought [*n*] *mental preparedness*
anticipation, canniness, caution, deliberation, discreetness, discretion, far-sightedness, foresight, gumption, judgment, planning, precaution, premeditation, providence, provision, prudence, sense; SEE CONCEPT *410*

forever [*adj1*] *for all time; everlasting*
always, durably, endlessly, enduringly, eternally,

evermore, everything considered*, for always, forevermore, for good*, for keeps*, for life*, immortally, infinitely, in perpetuity, in perpetuum, interminably, lastingly, now and forever*, on and on*, permanently, perpetually, till blue in the face*, till death do us part*, till Doomsday*, till the cows come home*, till the end of time*, unchangingly, world without end*; SEE CONCEPTS *551,649,798,799*

forever [*adj2*] *not ceasing, continually*
all the time, constantly, endlessly, eternally, everlastingly, incessantly, interminably, perpetually, regularly, unendingly, unremittingly; SEE CONCEPTS *534,798*

forewarn [*v*] *caution that something may happen*
admonish, advise, alarm, alert, apprise, dissuade, flag, forbode, give fair warning*, give the high sign*, portend, premonish, pull one's coat*, put a bug in one's ear*, put one wise*, put on guard*, telegraph, tip, tip off, wave a red flag*; SEE CONCEPT *78*

foreword [*n*] *introduction to a document*
exordium, overture, preamble, preface, preliminary, prelude, prelusion, proem, prolegomenon, prologue; SEE CONCEPT *270*

forfeit [*n*] *something given as sacrifice*
cost, damages, fine, loss, mulct, penalty, relinquishment; SEE CONCEPT *123*

forfeit [*v*] *give up something in sacrifice*
abandon, be deprived of, be stripped of, drop, give over, lose, relinquish, renounce, sacrifice, surrender; SEE CONCEPT *116*

forge [*v1*] *counterfeit*
coin, copy, design, duplicate, fabricate, fake, falsify, fashion, feign, frame, imitate, invent, make, phony up*, pirate*, produce, reproduce, scratch, trace, transcribe, trump up*; SEE CONCEPTS *59,171*

forge [*v2*] *make something from scratch*
beat, build, construct, contrive, create, devise, fabricate, fashion, form, frame, hammer out*, invent, manufacture, mold, pound, put together, shape, turn out, work; SEE CONCEPTS *168,173, 175,205,251*

forgery [*n*] *counterfeiting; counterfeit item*
bogus*, carbon*, carbon copy, cheat, coining, copy, fabrication, fake, faking, falsification, fraudulence, imitating, imitation, imposition, imposture, lookalike, phony, pseudo, sham*, twin, workalike*; SEE CONCEPTS *59,171,716*

forget [*v1*] *not be able to remember*
blow, clean forget*, consign to oblivion*, dismiss from mind, disremember, draw a blank*, escape one's memory*, fail to remember, let slip from memory*, lose consciousness of, lose sight of*, misrecollect, obliterate, think no more of*; SEE CONCEPT *40*

forget [*v2*] *leave behind*
blink, discount, disregard, drop, fail, ignore, lose sight of*, neglect, omit, overlook, overpass, pass over, skip, slight, transgress, trespass; SEE CONCEPTS *30,116*

forgetful [*adj*] *tending to not remember*
absent, absent-minded, abstracted, airheaded*, amnemonic, amnesic, asleep on the job*, bemused, careless, distracted, dreamy, heedless, inattentive, lax, like an absent-minded professor*, looking out window*, mooning, moony*, neglectful, negligent, nirvanic, not on the job*, oblivious, out of it*, out to lunch*, pipe dream-

fo
fo

ing*, preoccupied, remiss, slack, sloppy, unmindful, unwitting, woolgathering*; SEE CON-
CEPTS *403,550*

forgetfulness [*n*] *consistent inability to remember*
absentmindedness, abstraction, amnesia, blackout, blank, blockout, carelessness, dreaminess,
fugue, heedlessness, hypomnesia, inattention,
lapse of memory, laxness, lethe, limbo, loss of
memory, negligence, nirvana, oblivion, obliviousness, paramnesia, repression, short memory,
suppression; SEE CONCEPTS *410,644*

forgive [*v*] *stop blame and grant pardon*
absolve, accept apology, acquit, allow for,
amnesty, bear no malice*, bear with, bury the
hatchet*, clear, commute, condone, dismiss from
mind, efface, exculpate, excuse, exempt, exonerate, extenuate, forget, kiss and make up*, laugh
off*, let bygones be bygones*, let it go*, let off*,
let off easy*, let pass*, let up on*, make allowance, overlook, palliate, pocket, purge, release, relent, remit, reprieve, respite, spring,
think no more of*, turn other cheek*, wink at*,
wipe slate clean*; SEE CONCEPTS *12,50,88*

forgiveness [*n*] *pardon; end of blame*
absolution, acquittal, amnesty, charity, clemency, compassion, condonation, dispensation,
exculpation, exoneration, extenuation, grace, immunity, impunity, indemnity, justification, lenience, lenity, mercy, overlooking, palliation,
purgation, quarter, quittance, remission, remittal,
reprieve, respite, vindication; SEE CONCEPTS
685,689

forgo [*v*] *give up, do without*
abandon, abdicate, abjure, abstain, cede, desist,
eschew, forbear, forsake, give in, go on the
wagon*, leave alone, leave out, pack in*, pass,
pass on, pass up, quit, refrain, relinquish, renounce, resign, resist, sacrifice, sit out*, surrender, swear off*, take the cure*, take the oath*,
waive, yield; SEE CONCEPTS *121,130,681*

forgotten [*adj*] *out of one's mind*
abandoned, blanked out*, blotted out*, blown
over*, buried, bygone, clean forgot*, consigned
to oblivion*, disremembered*, drew a blank*,
erased, fell between the cracks*, gone, lapsed,
left behind, left out, lost, obliterated, omitted,
past, past recollection, repressed, slipped one's
mind*, suppressed, unrecalled, unremembered;
SEE CONCEPTS *402,403,529*

fork [*v*] *go separate ways*
angle, bifurcate, branch off, branch out, divaricate, diverge, divide, part, split; SEE CONCEPTS
98,738

forked [*adj*] *going separate ways*
angled, bifid, bifurcate, bifurcated, branched,
branching, dichotomous, dichotonic, divaricate,
divided, furcate, furcated, pronged, split, tined,
tridented, zigzag; SEE CONCEPTS *485,581*

for keeps [*adv*] *forever*
for good, permanently, till hell freezes over*;
SEE CONCEPTS *551,649,798,799*

for kicks [*adv*] *for fun*
for mere pleasure, for no useful reason, for the
hell of it; SEE CONCEPTS *537,572*

forlorn [*adj*] *hopeless, inconsolable*
abandoned, alone, bereft, blue*, cheerless,
comfortless, cynical, defenseless, depressed,
deserted, desolate, despairing, desperate, despondent, destitute, destroyed, disconsolate, down

and out*, dragging*, forgotten, forsaken, friendless, fruitless, futile, godforsaken*, helpless,
homeless, in the dumps*, lonely, lonesome, lost,
miserable, oppressed, pathetic, pessimistic,
pitiable, pitiful, solitary, tragic, unhappy, vain,
weighed down, woebegone, wretched; SEE CON-
CEPT *403*

form [*n1*] *shape; arrangement*
anatomy, appearance, articulation, cast, configuration, conformation, construction, contour, cut,
design, die, embodiment, fashion, figure, formation, framework, mode, model, mold, outline,
pattern, plan, profile, scheme, silhouette, skeleton, structure, style, system; SEE CONCEPTS
184,660,754,757

form [*n2*] *animate body and its condition*
anatomy, being, build, condition, fettle*, figure,
fitness, frame, health, object, outline, person,
phenomenon, physique, shape, silhouette, thing,
torso, trim*; SEE CONCEPTS *316,389,720*

form [*n3*] *accepted procedure; ceremony*
behavior, by the book*, by the numbers*, canon,
ceremonial, channels*, conduct, convenance,
convention, custom, decorum, done thing*, etiquette, fashion, formality, habit, law, layout,
manner, manners, method, mode, practice, precept, proceeding, process, propriety, protocol,
regulation, rite, ritual, ropes*, rule, setup, style,
usage, way; SEE CONCEPT *688*

form [*n4*] *document that requires answers or information*
application, blank, chart, data sheet, letter, paper,
questionnaire, sheet; SEE CONCEPT *271*

form [*n5*] *type, kind*
arrangement, character, class, description, design, grade, guise, make, manifestation, manner,
method, mode, order, practice, rank, semblance,
sort, species, stamp, style, system, variety, way;
SEE CONCEPTS *6,378*

form [*n6*] *organization, arrangement*
format, framework, harmony, order, orderliness,
placement, plan, proportion, scheme, structure,
symmetry; SEE CONCEPT *727*

form [*v1*] *bring into existence; make, produce*
arrange, assemble, block out, bring about, build,
cast, complete, compose, conceive, concoct, constitute, construct, consummate, contrive, cook
up*, create, cultivate, cut, design, develop, devise, dream up, erect, establish, fabricate, fashion, finish, fix, forge, found, frame, hammer
out*, invent, knock off*, make up, manufacture,
model, mold, organize, outline, pattern, perfect,
plan, plot, project, put together, scheme, set, set
up, shape, structure, throw together, trace, turn
out*, work; SEE CONCEPTS *168,173,205,251*

form [*v2*] *come into being; arise*
accumulate, acquire, appear, become a reality,
become visible, condense, crystallize, develop,
eventuate, fall into place*, grow, harden, materialize, mature, rise, set, settle, shape up, show up,
take on character, take shape*; SEE CONCEPTS
105,704

form [*v3*] *educate, discipline*
breed, bring up, give character, instruct, rear,
school, teach, train; SEE CONCEPTS *285,295*

form [*v4*] *comprise, be a part of*
act as, compose, constitute, figure in, make,
make up, serve as; SEE CONCEPT *643*

formal [*adj1*] *established, orderly*
academic, approved, ceremonial, ceremonialis-

tic, ceremonious, confirmed, conventional, decorous, directed, explicit, express, fixed, formalistic, lawful, legal, methodical, official, precise, prescribed, pro forma, proper, punctilious, regular, rigid, ritual, ritualistic, set, solemn, stately, stereotyped, stereotypical, strict, systematic; SEE CONCEPTS *533,547*

formal [*adj2*] *stiff, affected, correct*
aloof, by the numbers*, ceremonious, conventional, decorous, distant, exact, nominal, playing the game*, polite, precise, prim, punctilious, reserved, seemly, sententious, starched*, stilted*, straight arrow*, stuffy*, unbending; SEE CONCEPT *401*

formality [*n1*] *convention, custom*
academism, ceremony, convenance, conventionality, form, gesture, liturgy, matter of form*, officialism, procedure, red tape*, rite, ritual, rituality, rubric, rule, service, solemnity, solemnness, stereotype, tradition; SEE CONCEPT *688*

formality [*n2*] *etiquette, protocol*
ceremoniousness, conventionalism, correctness, decorum, formalism, honors, mummery, politesse, propriety, p's and q's*, punctiliousness; SEE CONCEPT *633*

format [*n*] *layout, plan*
arrangement, composition, configuration, dimensions, figure, form, formation, formula, look, makeup, pattern, scheme, setup, shape, size; SEE CONCEPTS *625,660*

formation [*n*] *composition, establishment*
accumulation, architecture, arrangement, compilation, configuration, constitution, construction, creation, crystallization, deposit, design, development, dispersal, disposition, embodiment, evolution, fabrication, figure, forming, generation, genesis, grouping, induction, makeup, manufacture, order, organization, pattern, production, rank, structure, synthesis; SEE CONCEPTS *173,260*

formative [*adj*] *influential, impressionable*
determinative, developmental, immature, impressible, malleable, moldable, pliant, sensitive, shaping, susceptible; SEE CONCEPTS *534,537*

former [*adj*] *previous in time or order*
above, aforementioned, aforesaid, ancient, antecedent, anterior, bygone, departed, earlier, erstwhile, ex-*, first, foregoing, late, long ago*, long gone, of yore*, old, once, one-time, past, preceding, prior, quondam, sometime, whilom; SEE CONCEPTS *585,820*

formerly [*adv*] *previously in time or order*
aforetime, already, anciently, at one time, away back, a while back, back, back when*, before, before now, before this, down memory lane*, earlier, eons ago*, erewhile, erstwhile, heretofore, in former times, in the olden days*, in the past, lately, long ago, of old, of yore, olden days*, once, once upon a time*, radically, some time ago, time was*, used to be*, water under the bridge*; SEE CONCEPTS *585,820*

formidable [*adj1*] *horrible, terrifying*
appalling, awful, dangerous, daunting, dire, dismaying, dreadful, fearful, fierce, frightful, horrific, imposing, impregnable, intimidating, menacing, redoubtable, shocking, terrible, terrific, threatening; SEE CONCEPT *537*

formidable [*adj2*] *difficult, overwhelming*
all-powerful, arduous, awesome, ballbuster, challenging, colossal, dismaying, effortful, great, hard, impressive, indomitable, intimidating, la-

bored, laborious, mammoth, mighty, murder*, onerous, overpowering, powerful, puissant, rough*, rough go*, staggering, strenuous, tall order*, toilsome, tough*, tough proposition*, tremendous, uphill*; SEE CONCEPT *565*

formless [*adj*] *disorganized, vague*
amorphous, baggy*, blobby*, chaotic, crude, inchoate, incoherent, indefinite, indeterminate, indistinct, nebulous, obscure, orderless, raw, rough, rude, shapeless, unclear, undefined, unformed, unorganized; SEE CONCEPTS *485,535, 589*

formula [*n*] *set preparation; rule, recipe*
blueprint, canon, code, credo, creed, custom, description, direction, equation, form, formulary, maxim, method, modus operandi, precept, prescription, principle, procedure, rite, ritual, rote, rubric, specifications, theorem, way; SEE CONCEPTS *268,688*

formulate [*v*] *plan, specify systematically*
codify, coin, compose, concoct, contrive, cook up, couch, define, detail, develop, devise, draft, draw up*, dream up*, evolve, express, forge, frame, give form to, hatch, indite, invent, make, make up*, map, originate, particularize, phrase, prepare, put, set down*, systematize, vamp, work, work out; SEE CONCEPTS *36,173,202*

fornicate [*v*] *have sexual intercourse*
be promiscuous, commit adultery, philander, sleep around; SEE CONCEPTS *375,384*

fornication [*n*] *sexual intercourse*
coition, coitus, copulation, intimacy, lovemaking, relations, screwing around, sex, sleeping around; SEE CONCEPTS *375,384*

for openers [*adv*] *as a beginning*
first off, for starters, to begin with; SEE CONCEPTS *815,833*

forsake [*v*] *abandon, turn one's back on*
abdicate, cast off, change one's tune*, desert, disclaim, disown, drift away*, forgo, forswear, give up, have done with, jettison, jilt, kiss goodbye*, leave, leave flat*, leave high and dry*, quit, relinquish, renounce, repudiate, resign, run out on*, set aside, show the door*, spurn, surrender, take the oath*, throw over*, walk out on*, wash one's hands of*, yield; SEE CONCEPTS *30,195,384*

forsaken [*adj*] *abandoned*
cast off, derelict, deserted, desolate, destitute, disowned, forlorn, friendless, godforsaken*, ignored, isolated, jilted, left at the altar*, left behind, left in the lurch*, lonely, lorn, marooned, outcast, solitary, thrown over*; SEE CONCEPT *555*

for sure [*adv*] *definitely*
certainly, dead sure, for a fact, for certain, for real, no doubt, no question, no two ways about it, really, sure thing, unquestionably; SEE CONCEPTS *535,552*

forswear [*v*] *abandon, disavow*
abjure, deny, disclaim, disown, drop, forgo, forsake, give up, recall, recant, reject, renege, renounce, repudiate, retract, swear off, take back, withdraw; SEE CONCEPTS *44,54*

forte [*n*] *person's strong point*
ability, ableness, aptitude, competence, effectiveness, efficiency, eminency, faculty, gift*, long suit*, medium, métier, oyster*, speciality, strength, strong suit*, talent, thing*; SEE CONCEPTS *409,411*

fo
fo

fort/fortress [n] *stronghold*
acropolis, blockhouse, camp, castle, citadel, fast-ness, fortification, garrison, redoubt, station; SEE CONCEPTS *321,439*

forth [adv] *outward*
ahead, alee, along, away, first, forward, into, into the open*, on, onward, out; SEE CONCEPT *581*

forthcoming [adj] *expected, imminent*
accessible, anticipated, approaching, at hand, available, awaited, coming, destined, fated, fu-ture, impending, inescapable, in evidence, in-evitable, in preparation, in prospect, in store*, in the cards*, in the wind*, nearing, obtainable, on-coming, on tap*, open, pending, predestined, prospective, ready, resulting, upcoming; SEE CONCEPTS *548,799*

forthright [adj] *straightforward, honest*
aboveboard, bald, blunt, call a spade a spade*, candid, categorical, direct, directly, forward, frank, from the hip*, like it is*, no lie*, open, outspoken, plain, plainspoken, real, simple, sin-cere, straight, undisguised, up front*; SEE CON-CEPT *267*

forthwith [adv] *immediately*
abruptly, at once, away, directly, instantly, now, quickly, right away*, right now*, straightaway, suddenly, tout de suite, without delay; SEE CON-CEPTS *544,820*

fortification [n] *reinforced position*
barricade, barrier, bastion, battlement, block, blockhouse, breastwork, buffer, bulwark, castle, citadel, consolidation, defense, earthwork, em-battlement, entrenchment, fastness, fort, fortress, garrison, keep, outpost, parapet, preparation, presidio, protection, reinforcement, stockade, strengthening, stronghold, support, wall; SEE CONCEPTS *439,729*

fortify [v1] *make strong and secure; add to*
brace, build up, bulwark, buttress, charge up, consolidate, embattle, entrench, garrison, gird, prepare, prop, protect, punch up*, ready, rein-force, secure, shore up*, soup up*, steel*, step up, strengthen, support; SEE CONCEPT *202*

fortify [v2] *encourage, reassure*
arouse, brace, buck up*, build up, cheer, con-firm, embolden, energize, enliven, hearten, in-vigorate, pour it on*, punch up*, rally, refresh, reinforce, renew, restore, rouse, stiffen, stir, strengthen, sustain; SEE CONCEPTS *7,22*

fortitude [n] *strength of mind; guts*
backbone*, boldness, braveness, bravery, con-stancy, courage, courageousness, dauntlessness, determination, endurance, fearlessness, firmness, grit*, gutsiness, hardihood, heart, intrepidity, mettle, moxie, nerve, patience, perseverance, pith, pluck, resoluteness, resolution, spine*, spirit, spunk, stamina, starch, staying power, stick-to-itiveness*, stomach, stoutheartedness, tenacity, true grit*, valiancy, valor, valorousness, what it takes*; SEE CONCEPTS *410,411*

fortuitous [adj] *lucky, accidental*
arbitrary, casual, chance, contingent, fluke*, fluky*, fortunate, haphazard, happy, incidental, luck in*, luck out*, lucky-dog*, odd, providen-tial, random, serendipitous, unforeseen, un-planned; SEE CONCEPTS *548,552*

fortunate [adj] *having good luck*
advantageous, affluent, auspicious, blessed, born with a silver spoon*, bright, charmed, conve-nient, encouraging, favorable, favored, felicitous,

flourishing, fortuitous, gaining, get a break*, golden, happy, healthy, helpful, hopeful, in luck*, in the gravy*, lucky, on a roll*, oppor-tune, overcoming, profitable, promising, propi-tious, prosperous, providential, rosy, sitting pretty, successful, sunny side*, thriving, timely, triumphant, victorious, wealthy, well-off, well-to-do; SEE CONCEPTS *404,542,572*

fortunately [adv] *luckily*
auspiciously, by good luck, by happy chance*, favorably, happily, in good time*, in the nick of time*, opportunely, prosperously, providentially, satisfyingly, seasonably, successfully, swim-mingly, well; SEE CONCEPTS *537,544,572*

fortune [n1] *wealth, possessions*
affluence, capital, estate, gold mine*, inheri-tance, opulence, portion, property, prosperity, re-sources, riches, substance, treasure, worth; SEE CONCEPTS *335,710*

fortune [n2] *fate, lot in life*
accident, break*, certainty, chance, circum-stances, contingency, destiny, doom, expecta-tion, experience, fifty-fifty*, fighting chance*, fluke*, fortuity, fortunateness, good break, haz-ard, history, karma*, kismet*, life, luck, lucked into*, lucked out*, luckiness, lucky break*, lucky hit*, Moirai, portion, providence, roll of the dice*, run of luck*, star, streak of luck, suc-cess, way the ball bounces*, way the cookie crumbles*, wheel of fortune*; SEE CONCEPT *679*

fortune-teller [n] *person attempting to tell the future*
augur, clairvoyant, crystal ball gazer, diviner, medium, mind reader, oracle, palmist, palm reader, predicter, prophet, psychic, seer, sooth-sayer, spiritualist, tarot reader, tea-leaf reader; SEE CONCEPTS *348,423*

forward [adj1] *advancing, early*
ahead, forth, forward-looking, in advance, lead-ing, onward, precocious, premature, progressing, progressive, propulsive, well-developed; SEE CONCEPT *528*

forward [adj2] *in front, first*
advance, anterior, facial, fore, foremost, front, head, leading, ventral; SEE CONCEPTS *581,583, 585*

forward [adj3] *brash, impertinent*
aggressive, assuming, audacious, bantam, bare-faced, bold, brazen, cheeky*, coming on strong*, confident, familiar, fresh, impudent, nervy*, overassertive, overweening, pert, presuming, presumptuous, pushing, pushy*, rude, sassy*, saucy*, self-assertive, smart, smart-alecky*, up-pity*, wise; SEE CONCEPTS *401,404*

forward [adv] *toward the front in order, time*
ahead, alee, along, ante, antecedently, before, be-forehand, fore, forth, in advance, into promi-nence, into view, on, onward, out, precedently, previous, to the fore*, vanward; SEE CONCEPTS *581,585,799*

forward [v1] *aid, expedite*
advance, assist, back, champion, cultivate, en-courage, favor, foster, further, hasten, help, hurry, promote, serve, speed, support, uphold; SEE CONCEPTS *68,110*

forward [v2] *send, ship*
address, consign, deliver, dispatch, express, freight, post, remit, route, transmit, transport; SEE CONCEPT *217*

fossil [*n*] *organic remains of a previous time*
deposit, eolith, impression, neolith, paleolith, petrifaction, reconstruction, relic, skeleton, specimen, trace; SEE CONCEPTS *429,470,509*

foster [*v1*] *promote, support*
advance, back, champion, cherish, cultivate, encourage, feed, foment, forward, further, harbor, nurse, nurture, serve, stimulate, uphold; SEE CONCEPT *110*

foster [*v2*] *give care or accommodation to*
assist, bring up, care for, cherish, entertain, favor, harbor, help, house, lodge, minister to, nourish, nurse, oblige, raise, rear, serve, shelter, sustain, take care of; SEE CONCEPTS *110,140,295*

foul [*adj1*] *disgusting, dirty*
abhorrent, abominable, base, contaminated, despicable, detestable, disgraceful, dishonorable, egregious, fetid, filthy, gross*, hateful, heinous, horrid, icky*, impure, infamous, iniquitous, loathsome, malodorous, mucky*, nasty, nauseating, nefarious, noisome, notorious, offensive, pigpen*, polluted, putrid, rank*, raunchy*, repellent, repulsive, revolting, rotten, scandalous, shameful, squalid, stinking*, sullied, tainted, unclean, vicious, vile, wicked, yecchy*, yucky*; SEE CONCEPTS *485,529*

foul [*adj2*] *vulgar, offensive*
abusive, blasphemous, blue*, coarse, dirty, filthy, foul-mouthed, gross*, indecent, lewd, low, nasty, obscene, profane, raunchy, scatological, scurrilous, smutty*; SEE CONCEPT *267*

foul [*adj3*] *corrupt, dishonest*
caitiff, crooked, dirty, fraudulent, inequitable, monstrous, shady, underhand, underhanded, unfair, unjust, unscrupulous, vicious; SEE CONCEPTS *537,548*

foul [*n*] *infraction*
breach, encroachment, error, faux pas, infringement, offense, slip*, violation; SEE CONCEPTS *192,691*

foul [*v*] *make or become dirty*
befoul, begrime, besmear, besmirch, block, catch, choke, clog, contaminate, defile, desecrate, discolor, ensnare, entangle, fill, jam, pollute, profane, smear, smudge, snarl, soil, spot, stain, sully, taint, tarnish, twist; SEE CONCEPTS *250,469*

foul play [*n*] *treacherous action*
bad deed, corruption, crime, cruel act, dirty trick, dirty work, felony, fraud, funny business, lawbreaking, murder, violence, wrong; SEE CONCEPT *645*

foul up [*v*] *make a mess of*
botch, bungle, confuse, jumble, mismanage, mix up*, muck up*, muddle, screw up*, snafu*, snarl, tumble; SEE CONCEPTS *16,234*

found [*v1*] *bring into being*
begin, commence, constitute, construct, create, endow, erect, establish, fashion, fix, form, get going, inaugurate, initiate, institute, launch, organize, originate, plant, raise, ring in*, settle, settle up, start, start the ball rolling*, start up; SEE CONCEPT *221*

found [*v2*] *put on a base*
bottom, build, erect, establish, ground, predicate, raise, rear, rest, root, stay, support, sustain; SEE CONCEPTS *168,221*

foundation [*n1*] *basis for something physical or mental*
ABCs*, authority, base, basics, bed, bedrock, bottom, bottom line*, brass tacks*, foot, footing, ground, groundwork, guts*, heart*, infrastructure, justification, nitty-gritty*, nub*, nuts and bolts*, prop, reason, root, stay, substratum, substructure, support, underpinning, understructure; SEE CONCEPTS *442,826*

foundation [*n2*] *established institution*
association, charity, company, corporation, endowment, establishment, guild, inauguration, institute, organization, plantation, settlement, set-up, society, trusteeship; SEE CONCEPT *381*

founder [*n*] *person who establishes an institution*
architect, author, beginner, benefactor, builder, constructor, creator, designer, establisher, forebearer, framer, generator, initiator, institutor, inventor, maker, organizer, originator, patron, planner, prime mover*; SEE CONCEPTS *347,423*

founder [*v*] *go under, fail*
abort, be lost, break down, collapse, come to nothing, fall, fall through, go down, go lame, go to bottom, lurch, miscarry, misfire, sink, sprawl, stagger, stumble, submerge, submerse, trip; SEE CONCEPTS *181,699*

fountain [*n*] *source, often of liquid*
bubbler, cause, font, fount, geyser, gush, inception, inspiration, jet, lode, mainspring, mine, origin, play, provenance, provenience, pump, reservoir, root, spout, spray, spring, stream, well, wellhead, wellspring; SEE CONCEPTS *514,648*

fountainhead [*n*] *principal source; person who originates*
administrator, architect, author, builder, creator, father, fount, fountain, generator, initiator, leader, maker, mother, originator, spring, wellspring; SEE CONCEPTS *348,350*

foxy [*adj*] *shrewd*
artful, astute, canny, crafty, cunning, deceitful, deep, devious, dishonest, experienced, guileful, insidious, intelligent, knowing, retiary, sharp, slick, sly, subtle, tricky, vulpine, wily; SEE CONCEPTS *401,404*

foyer [*n*] *receiving area*
antechamber, anteroom, entrance hall, lobby, reception, vestibule; SEE CONCEPTS *440,441,448*

fracas [*n*] *disturbance, fight*
affray, altercation, battle, battle royal*, bickering, brawl, broil*, brouhaha, dispute, donnybrook*, feud, flap*, fray, free-for-all*, hassle, knock-down-drag-out*, melee, mix up*, quarrel, riot, row, ruction, ruffle, rumpus, run-in*, scrimmage, scuffle, set-to*, squabble, stew*, trouble, tumult, uproar, words*; SEE CONCEPTS *46,106*

fraction [*n1*] *part*
bite, chunk, cut, division, end, fragment, half, piece, portion, section, share, slice; SEE CONCEPT *835*

fraction [*n2*] *incomplete number*
bit, division, fragment, part, partial, piece, portion, quotient, ratio, section, segment, slice, subdivision; SEE CONCEPT *765*

fractional [*adj*] *partial*
apportioned, compartmental, compartmented, constituent, dismembered, dispersed, divided, fragmentary, frationary, incomplete, parceled, part, piecemeal, sectional, segmented; SEE CONCEPT *785*

fractious [*adj*] *grouchy, cross*
awkward, captious, crabby*, disorderly, fretful, froward, huffy*, indocile, indomitable, intractable, irritable, mean, ornery*, peevish, per-

fo
fr

verse, pettish, petulant, querulous, recalcitrant, refractory, restive, scrappy, snappish, testy, thin-skinned, touchy, uncompliant, undisciplined, unmanageable, unruly, wayward, wild; SEE CONCEPTS **267,401**

fracture [n] *break, rupture*
breach, cleavage, cleft, crack, discontinuity, disjunction, displacement, fissure, fragmentation, gap, mutilation, opening, rent, rift, schism, severance, splinter, split, wound; SEE CONCEPTS **309,513**

fragile [adj] *breakable, dainty*
brittle, crisp, crumbly, decrepit, delicate, feeble, fine, flimsy, fracturable, frail, frangible, friable, infirm, insubstantial, shatterable, shivery, slight, unsound, weak, weakly; SEE CONCEPTS **485,489**

fragment [n] *part, chip*
ace, atom, bit, bite, chunk, crumb, cut, end, fraction, gob*, grain, hunk, iota, job*, lump*, minim, morsel, particle, piece, portion, remnant, scrap, share, shiver, shred, slice, sliver, smithereen*; SEE CONCEPT **835**

fragment [v] *break into pieces*
burst, come apart, crumble, disintegrate, disunite, divide, rend, rive, shatter, shiver, smash, splinter, split, split up; SEE CONCEPTS **98,135, 137,246,469**

fragmentary [adj] *broken, incomplete*
bitty, disconnected, discrete, disjointed, fractional, incoherent, part, partial, piecemeal, scattered, scrappy, sketchy, unsystematic; SEE CONCEPT **785**

fragrance [n] *pleasant odor*
aroma, aura, balm, bouquet, incense, perfume, redolence, scent, smell, spice; SEE CONCEPT **600**

fragrant [adj] *smelling pleasant*
ambrosial, aromal, aromatic, balmy, delectable, delicious, delightful, odoriferous, odorous, perfumed, perfumy, redolent, savory, spicy, sweet, sweet-scented, sweet-smelling; SEE CONCEPT **598**

frail [adj] *breakable, weak*
brittle, dainty, decrepit, delicate, feeble, fishy, flimsy, fracturable, fragile, frangible, infirm, insubstantial, puny, sad, shatterable, shattery, sickly, slender, slight, slim, tender, tenuous, thin, unsound, unsubstantial, vulnerable, wimpy*, wishy-washy*, wispy; SEE CONCEPTS **485,489**

frailty [n] *weakness, flaw*
Achilles heel*, blemish, daintiness, debility, decrepitude, defect, deficiency, delicacy, error, failing, fallibility, fault, feebleness, flimsiness, foible, foil, imperfection, infirmity, peccability, peccadillo, shortcoming, solecism, suscept, weak point*; SEE CONCEPTS **101,230,411,580**

frame [n] *skeleton, casing*
anatomy, architecture, body, build, cage, carcass, construction, enclosure, fabric, flounce, form, framework, fringe, groundwork, hem, mount, mounting, outline, physique, scaffold, scaffolding, scheme, setting, shell, stage, structure, support, system, trim, trimming, truss, valance; SEE CONCEPTS **442,733,757**

frame [v1] *build*
assemble, back, border, constitute, construct, encase, enclose, erect, fabricate, fashion, forge, form, institute, invent, lath, make, manufacture, mat, model, mold, mount, panel, produce, put together, raise, set up, shingle; SEE CONCEPTS **168,758**

frame [v2] *compose, plan*
block out, conceive, concoct, contrive, cook up, design, devise, draft, draw up, dream up*, form, formulate, hatch, indite, invent, make, make up, map out, outline, prepare, shape, sketch, vamp, write; SEE CONCEPTS **36,173**

frame of mind [n] *state of mind*
attitude, constitution, disposition, emotions, inner nature, makeup, mentality, mood, nature, spirit, state, temperament; SEE CONCEPTS **410,689**

framework [n] *foundation, core*
bare bones*, cage, fabric, frame, frame of reference*, groundwork, plan, schema, scheme, shell, skeleton, structure; SEE CONCEPTS **439,479,733**

franchise [n] *authority, right*
authorization, ballot, charter, exemption, freedom, immunity, patent, prerogative, privilege, suffrage, vote; SEE CONCEPT **376**

frank [adj] *completely honest*
aboveboard, apparent, artless, bare-faced*, blunt, bold, brazen, call a spade a spade*, candid, direct, downright, easy, familiar, flat-out*, forthright, free, from the hip*, guileless, heart-to-heart*, ingenuous, lay it on the line*, like it is*, matter-of-fact, naive, natural, open, outright, outspoken, plain, plain-spoken, real, saying what one thinks*, scrupulous, sincere, straight, straightforward, transparent, truthful, unconcealed, undisguised, uninhibited, unreserved, unrestricted, up front*, upright; SEE CONCEPTS **267,582**

frankfurter [n] *cylindrical meat sausage*
bowwow*, Coney Island*, dog*, footlong*, frank, hot dog, link, weenie*, wiener, wienerwurst; SEE CONCEPTS **457,460**

frankly [adv] *very honestly*
bluntly, candidly, dead level*, dead on*, directly, forthrightly, freely, from the hip*, in truth, laid on the line*, level, on the level*, on the line*, openly, plainly, straight, straightforwardly, without reserve; SEE CONCEPT **267**

frantic [adj] *distressed, distracted*
agitated, angry, at wits' end*, berserk, beside oneself*, corybantic, crazy, delirious, deranged, distraught, excited, flipped out*, fraught, freaked out*, frenetic, frenzied, furious, hectic, hot and bothered*, hot under the collar*, hyper*, in a stew*, in a tizzy*, insane, keyed up*, mad, out of control, overwrought, rabid, raging, raving, shook up*, spazzed out*, unglued*, unscrewed*, unzipped*, violent, weird, weirded out*, wigged out*, wild, wired*, worked up*, zonkers*; SEE CONCEPTS **403,542**

fraternity [n] *brotherhood*
affiliation, camaraderie, club, fellowship, frat*, guild, house, kinship, order, sisterhood, society, sorority; SEE CONCEPTS **381,387**

fraternize [v] *associate with*
be friendly, be sociable with, club together, consort with, fall in with, go around with, hang out with, hobnob*, keep company with, make friends, mingle with, mix with, rub elbows with, rub shoulders with, run with, socialize with; SEE CONCEPTS **114,384**

fraud [n1] *trickery, deception*
artifice, bamboozlement*, blackmail, cheat, chicane, chicanery, con, craft*, deceit, double-dealing*, dupery, duping, duplicity, extortion, fake, fast one*, fast shuffle*, flimflam*, fourberie,

fraudulence, graft, guile, hanky-panky*, hoax, hocus-pocus*, hoodwinking*, hustle*, imposture, line, misrepresentation, racket, scam, sell, shakedown*, sham*, sharp practice*, skunk*, smoke*, song*, song and dance*, spuriousness, sting, string, swindle, swindling, treachery; SEE CONCEPTS *59,192,645*

fraud [*n2*] *person who is false, deceitful*
bastard, bluffer, charlatan, cheat, counterfeit, crook, deceiver, double-dealer*, fake, forger, four-flusher*, hoaxer, horse trader*, impostor, mechanic*, mountebank, phony, play actor*, pretender, quack*, racketeer, sham*, shark*, swindler; SEE CONCEPT *412*

fraudulent [*adj*] *deceptive, false*
bamboozling*, counterfeit, crafty, criminal, crooked, deceitful, devious, dishonest, dishonorable, double-dealing*, duplicitous, fake, forged, mock, phony, pseudo, sham*, spurious, swindling, treacherous, tricky; SEE CONCEPTS *545,582*

fraught [*adj*] *full of*
abounding, attended, bristling, charged, filled, heavy, laden, replete, stuffed; SEE CONCEPTS *483,771*

fray [*n*] *fight, battle*
affray, battle royal*, brawl, broil*, brouhaha*, clash, combat, conflict, contest, disturbance, donnybrook*, engagement, fracas, melee, quarrel, riot, row, ruckus, rumble, rumpus, scuffle, set-to*; SEE CONCEPTS *86,106*

fray [*v*] *shred, come apart*
become ragged, become threadbare, chafe, erode, frazzle, fret, ravel, rip, rub, tatter, tear, unravel, wear, wear away, wear thin; SEE CONCEPT *214*

frazzle [*n*] *exhaustion; something very worn*
collapse, enervation, lassitude, prostration, rag, remnant, shred; SEE CONCEPTS *410,720*

frazzle [*v*] *wear out*
exhaust, fray, knock out, poop*, prostrate, rip, shred, tear, tire, tucker*, wear; SEE CONCEPTS *156,186*

freak [*n1*] *something, someone very abnormal*
aberration, abortion, anomaly, chimera, curiosity, geek*, grotesque, malformation, miscreation, misshape, monster, monstrosity, mutant, mutation, oddity, queer, rarity, sport, weirdo*; SEE CONCEPTS *424,580*

freak [*n2*] *irregularity, whim*
caprice, conceit, crochet, fad, fancy, folly, humor, megrim, quirk, turn, twist, vagary, whimsy; SEE CONCEPT *679*

freak [*n3*] *person enthused about something*
addict, aficionado, buff, bug*, devotee, enthusiast, fan, fanatic, fiend*, maniac, nut*, zealot; SEE CONCEPTS *352,366,423*

freak [*v*] *become extraordinarily upset*
flip out*, go beserk, go insane, go mad, lose control, rave, unhinge*, wig out*; SEE CONCEPTS *7,19,80*

freakish [*adj*] *abnormal, unusual*
aberrant, arbitrary, bizarre, capricious, crazy, erratic, fantastic, far-out, freaky, grotesque, malformed, monstrous, odd, outlandish, outré, preternatural, queer, strange, unconventional, vagarious, wayward, weird, whimsical, wild; SEE CONCEPT *564*

freak out [*v*] *lose one's cool*
blow a gasket*, blow one's mind*, blow one's stack*, blow one's top*, break down, come

unglued, crack up*, flip out*, fly off the handle*, freak out*, go ape*, go ballistic*, go berserk*, go crazy*, go haywire*, go nuts*, go off the deep end*, hit the ceiling*, lose control of oneself, lose it*, lose one's composure, lose one's mind, lose one's temper, wig out*; SEE CONCEPTS *7,19,80*

freckle [*n*] *small discoloration on skin*
blemish, blotch, daisy, dot, lentigo, macula, mole, patch, pepper, pigmentation, pit, pock, pockmark, speck, speckle, sprinkle, stipple; SEE CONCEPT *392*

free [*adj1*] *without charge*
chargeless, comp*, complimentary, costless, for love*, for nothing*, freebie*, free of cost, free ride*, gratis, gratuitous, handout, on the cuff*, on the house*, paper*, unpaid, unrecompensed; SEE CONCEPT *334*

free [*adj2*] *unrestrained personally*
able, allowed, at large, at liberty, casual, clear, disengaged, easy, escaped, familiar, fancy-free*, footloose*, forward, frank, free-spirited, freewheeling, independent, informal, lax, liberal, liberated, loose, off the hook*, on one's own*, on the loose*, open, permitted, relaxed, unattached, uncommitted, unconfined, unconstrained, unengaged, unfettered, unhampered, unimpeded, unobstructed, unregulated, unrestricted, untrammeled; SEE CONCEPTS *401,542*

free [*adj3*] *unrestrained politically*
at liberty, autarchic, autonomic, autonomous, democratic, emancipated, enfranchised, freed, independent, individualistic, liberated, self-directing, self-governing, self-ruling, separate, sovereign, sui juris, unconstrained, unenslaved, unregimented; SEE CONCEPTS *319,536*

free [*adj4*] *not busy; unoccupied*
at leisure, available, clear, empty, extra, idle, loose, not tied down*, spare, unemployed, unengaged, unhampered, unimpeded, uninhabited, unobstructed, unused, vacant; SEE CONCEPT *485*

free [*adj5*] *generous, unsparing*
big, big-hearted*, bounteous, bountiful, charitable, eager, handsome, hospitable, lavish, liberal, munificent, open-handed*, prodigal, unstinging, willing; SEE CONCEPT *404*

free [*v1*] *liberate, let go*
absolve, acquit, bail, bail out*, clear, cut loose*, deliver, demobilize, discharge, disengage, disenthrall, disimprison, dismiss, emancipate, enfranchise, extricate, let loose*, let off*, let off the hook*, let out, loose, loosen, manumit, pardon, parole, put on the street*, ransom, redeem, release, relieve, reprieve, rescue, save, set free, spring*, turn loose, turn out, unbind, uncage, unchain, undo, unfetter, unfix, unleash, untie; SEE CONCEPT *127*

free [*v2*] *take burden from*
cast off, clear, cut loose, decontaminate, deliver, discharge, disembarrass, disencumber, disengage, disentangle, empty, excuse, exempt, extricate, put off, ransom, redeem, relieve, rescue, rid, unburden, undo, unlade, unload, unpack, unshackle; SEE CONCEPTS *110,211*

freebie [*n*] *something for nothing*
complimentary ticket, free lunch, free pass, gift, giveaway, handout; SEE CONCEPT *337*

freedom [*n1*] *independence, license to do as one wants*
abandon, abandonment, ability, bent, carte

blanche, compass, discretion, elbowroom*, exemption, facility, flexibility, free rein*, full play*, full swing*, immunity, indulgence, laissez faire, latitude, laxity, leeway, liberty, margin, opportunity, own accord*, play, plenty of rope*, power, prerogative, privilege, profligacy, rampancy, range, rein, right, rope*, scope, sweep, swing, unrestraint; SEE CONCEPT **693**

freedom [*n2*] *political independence*
abolition, abolitionism, autarchy, autonomy, citizenship, deliverance, delivery, democracy, discharge, disengagement, disimprisonment, emancipation, enfranchisement, exemption, extriction, franchise, home rule*, immunity, impunity, liberation, liberty, manumission, parole, prerogative, privilege, probation, redemption, release, relief, representative government, rescue, salvage, salvation, selfdetermination, self-government, sovereignty; SEE CONCEPT **691**

freedom [*n3*] *easy attitude*
abandon, boldness, brazenness, candor, directness, disrespect, ease, facility, familiarity, forthrightness, forwardness, frankness, impertinence, informality, ingenuousness, lack of reserve, lack of restraint, laxity, license, openness, overfamiliarity, presumption, readiness, spontaneity, unconstraint; SEE CONCEPT **633**

free-for-all [*n*] *fight*
affray, battle, brawl, broil*, brouhaha*, fracas, fray, knock-down-drag-out*, melee, riot, row, ruction; SEE CONCEPT **106**

freelance [*adj*] *independent*
free agent, non-staff, self-employed, unaffiliated; SEE CONCEPT **554**

freely [*adj1*] *without restriction*
advisedly, as you please*, at one's discretion, at one's pleasure, at will, candidly, deliberately, designedly, fancy-free*, frankly, intentionally, of one's own accord*, of one's own free will*, openly, plainly, purposely, spontaneously, unchallenged, unreservedly, voluntarily, willingly, without hindrance, without prompting, without reserve, without restraint, without urging; SEE CONCEPT **401**

freely [*adv2*] *easily, smoothly done*
abundantly, amply, as one pleases*, bountifully, cleanly, copiously, effortlessly, extravagantly, facilely, lavishly, liberally, lightly, like water*, loosely, open-handedly, readily, unhindered, unobstructedly, unstintingly, well, with a free hand*, without encumbrance*, without hindrance*, without restraint*, without stint*; SEE CONCEPT **544**

free spirit [*n*] *maverick*
bohemian, dissenter, eccentric, nonconformist, radical; SEE CONCEPT **359**

freeware [*n*] *free software*
public-domain software, shareware; SEE CONCEPTS **274,660**

freeway [*n*] *expressway*
artery, beltway, highway, interstate, parkway, road, superhighway, thoroughfare, thruway; SEE CONCEPT **501**

free will [*n*] *person's full intent and purpose*
assent, choice, consent, desire, determination, discretion, free choice, freedom, inclination, intention, mind, option, own say so*, own sweet way*, pleasure, power, say so*, velleity, volition, voluntary decision, willingness, wish; SEE CONCEPTS **20,410**

freeze [*v1*] *make cold enough to become solid*
benumb, bite, chill, chill to the bone*, congeal, frost, glaciate, harden, ice over, ice up, nip, pierce, refrigerate, solidify, stiffen; SEE CONCEPTS **255,521**

freeze [*v2*] *stop*
dampen, depress, discourage, dishearten, fix, hold up, inhibit, peg, suspend; SEE CONCEPTS **14,121**

freezer [*n*] *icebox*
cold storage, cooler, refrigerator; SEE CONCEPTS **202,255**

freezing [*adj*] *very cold*
arctic, biting, bitter, chill, chilled, chilly, cutting, frigid, frost-bound, frosty, gelid, glacial, hawkish, icy, nippy, numbing, one-dog night*, penetrating, polar, raw, shivery, Siberian*, snappy*, two-dog night*, wintry; SEE CONCEPT **605**

freight [*n*] *goods being shipped*
bales, ballast, bulk, burden, carriage, consignment, contents, conveyance, encumbrance, fardel, haul, lading, load, merchandise, pack, packages, payload, shipment, shipping, tonnage, transportation, wares, weight; SEE CONCEPT **338**

frenetic [*adj*] *maniacal*
corybantic, delirious, demented, distraught, excited, fanatical, frantic, frenzied, furibund, furious, hyper*, in a lather*, insane, lost it*, mad, obsessive, overwrought, phrenetic, rabid, unbalanced, unscrewed*, weirded out*, wigged out*, wild, wired*; SEE CONCEPT **403**

frenzied [*adj*] *uncontrolled*
agitated, berserk, convulsive, corybantic, delirious, distracted, distraught, excited, feverish, frantic, frenetic, furious, hysterical, mad, maniacal, nuts*, rabid, wild; SEE CONCEPTS **542,544**

frenzy [*n*] *uncontrolled state or situation*
aberration, agitation, blow, blow a fuse*, blow one's cork*, blow one's stack*, blow one's top*, bout, burst, conniption*, convulsion, craze, delirium, derangement, distemper, distraction, dithers*, excitement, ferment, fever, fit, flap*, flip one's lid*, free-for-all*, furor, fury, fuss, hell broke loose*, hysteria, insanity, lather, lunacy, madness, mania, outburst, paroxysm, passion, rage, row, ruckus, ruction, rumble, rumpus, seizure, spasm, stew, stir, to-do*, transport, turmoil, winging*; SEE CONCEPTS **230,410,674**

frequency [*n*] *commonness, repetitiveness*
abundance, beat, constancy, density, frequentness, iteration, number, oscillation, periodicity, persistence, prevalence, pulsation, recurrence, regularity, reiteration, repetition, rhythm; SEE CONCEPT **634**

frequent [*adj*] *common, repeated*
a good many*, commonplace, constant, continual, customary, everyday, expected, familiar, general, habitual, incessant, intermittent, iterated, manifold, many, monotonous, numberless, numerous, periodic, perpetual, persistent, pleonastic, profuse, recurrent, recurring, redundant, reiterated, reiterative, successive, thick, ubiquitous, usual, various; SEE CONCEPT **530**

frequent [*v*] *be a regular customer of*
affect, attend, attend regularly, be at home in*, be fraud at, be often in, drop in, go to, hang about*, hang around*, hang out at*, haunt*, hit*, infest, overrun, patronize, play*, resort, revisit, visit often; SEE CONCEPTS **227,384**

frequently [*adv*] *commonly, repeatedly*
again and again*, as a rule*, at regular intervals, at short intervals, at times, by ordinary, customarily, every now and then*, generally, habitually, in many instances*, in quick succession, intermittently, many a time*, many times, much, not infrequently, not seldom, oft, often, oftentimes, ofttimes, ordinarily, over and over, periodically, recurrently, regularly, spasmodically, successively, thick and fast*, time and again*, usually, very often; SEE CONCEPTS *530,544,799*

fresh [*adj1*] *new, just produced*
beginning, brand-new*, comer, contemporary, crisp, crude, current, different, gleaming, glistening, green*, hot*, hot off the press*, immature, just out*, late, latest, mint*, modern, modernistic, natural, neoteric, newborn, newfangled*, novel, now, original, radical, raw, recent, sparkling, state-of-the-art, the latest*, this season's*, unconventional, unprocessed, unseasoned, untouched, unusual, up-to-date, virginal, what's happening*, young, youthful; SEE CONCEPTS *578,797*

fresh [*adj2*] *additional*
added, another, auxiliary, else, extra, farther, further, increased, more, new, other, renewed, supplementary; SEE CONCEPTS *546,824*

fresh [*adj3*] *refreshing to the senses*
bracing, bright, brisk, clean, clear, colorful, cool, crisp, definite, fair, invigorating, not stale, pure, quick, sharp, spanking, sparkling, stiff, stimulating, sweet, uncontaminated, unpolluted, vivid; SEE CONCEPT *537*

fresh [*adj4*] *energetic, healthy*
active, alert, blooming, bouncing, bright, bright-eyed, bushy-tailed*, chipper*, clear, dewy, fair, florid, glowing, good, hardy, invigorated, keen, like new, lively, refreshed, rehabilitated, relaxed, relieved, rested, restored, revived, rosy, ruddy, sprightly, spry, stimulated, undimmed, unfaded, unused, unwearied, unwithered, verdant, vigorous, vital, wholesome, young; SEE CONCEPTS *485,542*

fresh [*adj5*] *inexperienced*
artless, callow, green*, natural, new, raw, tender-footed*, uncultivated, unpracticed, unskilled, untrained, untried, unversed, young, youthful; SEE CONCEPT *404*

fresh [*adj6*] *sassy, brazen*
bold, cheeky*, disrespectful, familiar, flip*, flippant, forward, impertinent, impudent, insolent, nervy*, pert, presumptuous, rude, saucy*, smart*, smart-alecky*, snippy*, wise; SEE CONCEPTS *267,401*

freshen [*v*] *make like new; revitalize*
activate, air, cleanse, enliven, invigorate, purify, refresh, restore, revive, rouse, spruce up, sweeten, titivate, ventilate; SEE CONCEPT *244*

freshman [*n*] *first-year student*
beginner, frosh*, greenhorn, novice, rookie, underclassman, undergrad*, undergraduate; SEE CONCEPTS *348,350,423*

freshness [*n*] *newness*
bloom, brightness, callowness, cleanness, clearness, dew, dewiness, glow, greenness, inexperience, innovativeness, inventiveness, novelty, originality, rawness, shine, sparkle, vigor, viridity, youth; SEE CONCEPT *715*

fret [*v1*] *worry, be annoyed*
affront, agonize, anguish, bleed, bother, brood, carp, carry a heavy load*, chafe, chagrin, distress oneself, eat one's heart out*, fume, fuss, get into a dither*, grieve, lose sleep over*, mope*, pother*, stew, sweat it out*, take on, torment, upset oneself; SEE CONCEPT *410*

fret [*v2*] *upset someone*
abrade, agitate, bother, displease, distress, disturb, gall, get on nerves*, goad, harass, irk, irritate, nag, nettle, peeve, pique, provoke, rile, ruffle, torment, trouble, vex; SEE CONCEPTS *7,19*

fret [*v3*] *rub hard*
abrade, chafe, corrode, erode, excoriate, fray, gall, riffle, ripple, wear away, wear threadbare; SEE CONCEPT *215*

fretful [*adj*] *irritable*
captious, carping*, caviling, complaining, contrary, crabby*, cranky*, critical, cross, crotchety*, edgy, faultfinding, fractious, huffy*, mean, ornery*, out of sorts*, peevish, perverse, petulant, querulous, short-tempered, snappish*, splenetic, testy, touchy, uneasy, worried, wreck*; SEE CONCEPTS *401,403*

friction [*n1*] *rubbing*
abrasion, agitation, attrition, chafing, erosion, filing, fretting, grating, grinding, irritation, massage, rasping, resistance, scraping, soreness, traction, trituration, wearing away; SEE CONCEPT *215*

friction [*n2*] *disagreement*
animosity, antagonism, bad blood*, bad feeling*, bickering, bone to pick*, conflict, counteraction, discontent, discord, disharmony, dispute, dissension, faction, factionalism, flak*, hassle, hatred, hostility, impedance, incompatibility, interference, opposition, quarrel, resentment, resistance, rivalry, row*, ruckus*, rumpus*, set-to*, sour note*, strife, trouble, wrangling*; SEE CONCEPTS *46,106,674*

friend [*n1*] *confidant, companion*
acquaintance, ally, alter ego, associate, bosom buddy*, buddy, chum*, classmate, cohort, colleague, companion*, compatriot, comrade, consort, cousin, crony, familiar, intimate, mate, pal, partner, playmate, roommate, schoolmate, sidekick, soul mate*, spare*, well-wisher; SEE CONCEPT *423*

friend [*n2*] *benefactor*
accomplice, adherent, advocate, ally, associate, backer, partisan, patron, supporter, well-wisher; SEE CONCEPT *348*

friendless [*adj*] *without companionship or confidant*
abandoned, adrift, alienated, all alone*, all by one's self*, alone, cut off*, deserted, estranged, forlorn, forsaken, isolated, lonely, lonesome, marooned*, ostracized, shunned, solitary, unattached, without ties; SEE CONCEPT *555*

friendliness [*n*] *companionability*
affability, amiability, amity, benevolence, camaraderie, comity, comradery, congeniality, conviviality, cordiality, friendship, geniality, goodwill, kindliness, kindness, neighborliness, open arms*, sociability, warmth; SEE CONCEPT *388*

friendly [*adj*] *intimate, companionable*
affable, affectionate, amiable, amicable, attached, attentive, auspicious, beneficial, benevolent, benign, buddy-buddy*, chummy*, civil, close, clubby, comradely, conciliatory, confiding, convivial, cordial, faithful, familiar, favor-

able, fond, genial, good, helpful, kind, kindly, loving, loyal, neighborly, on good terms*, outgoing, peaceable, peaceful, propitious, receptive, sociable, solicitous, sympathetic, tender, thick, welcoming, well-disposed*; SEE CONCEPT 555

friendship [n] *companionship*
accord, acquaintanceship, affection, affinity, agreement, alliance, amiability, amicability, amity, association, attachment, attraction, benevolence, closeness, coalition, comity, company, concord, consideration, consonance, devotion, empathy, esteem, familiarity, favor, favoritism, fondness, friendliness, fusion, good will, harmony, intimacy, league, love, pact, partiality, rapport, regard, sociability, society, sodality, solidarity, understanding; SEE CONCEPTS 388,714

fright [n1] *extreme apprehension*
alarm, cold sweat*, consternation, dismay, dread, fear, horror, panic, quaking, scare, shiver, shock, terror, trepidation, trepidity; SEE CONCEPT 410

fright [n2] *horrifying or unpleasant sight*
bother, eyesore*, frump*, mess, monstrosity, nuisance, scarecrow, ugliness; SEE CONCEPT 718

frighten [v] *shock, scare*
affright, agitate, alarm, appall, astound, awe, browbeat*, bulldoze*, chill, chill to the bone*, cow, curdle the blood*, daunt, demoralize, deter, disburb, discomfort, disconcert, discourage, dishearten, dismay, disquiet, faze, horrify, intimidate, make blood run cold*, make teeth chatter*, panic, perturb, petrify, repel, scare away, scare off, scare to death*, spook, startle, stiff, strike terror into*, terrify, terrorize, unhinge*, unnerve; SEE CONCEPTS 14,42

frightened [adj] *very scared*
abashed, affrighted, afraid, aghast, alarmed, anxious, butterflies*, chicken*, chicken-hearted*, cowed*, dismayed, fearful, frozen, have cold feet*, having kittens*, hung up*, in a cold sweat*, in a panic*, in a sweat*, jellyfish*, jittery, jumpy, lily-livered*, mousy*, numb, panicky, petrified, pushing the panic button*, rabbity*, running scared*, scared stiff*, shaky, shivery, sissy*, spooked, startled, terrified, terrorized, terror-stricken, unnerved, uptight, yellow*; SEE CONCEPTS 403,690

frightful [adj2] *offensive*
annoying, awful, bad, calamitous, disagreeable, dreadful, extreme, ghastly, great, hideous, horrible, insufferable, lewd, shocking, terrible, terrific, unpleasant, vile, wicked, wrong; SEE CONCEPTS 529,545

frightful/frightening [adj1] *scary, shocking*
alarming, appalling, atrocious, awesome, awful, chilling, daunting, dire, direful, dismaying, disquieting, dread, dreadful, fearful, fearsome, formidable, ghastly, grabber, grim, grisly, gruesome, hair-raising, hairy, harrowing, hideous, horrendous, horrible, horrid, horrifying, inconceivable, intimidating, lurid, macabre, menacing, morbid, ominous, petrifying, portentous, repellent, spooky, terrible, terrifying, traumatic, unnerving, unspeakable; SEE CONCEPTS 529,537

frigid [adj1] *extremely cold*
antarctic, arctic, chill, chilly, cool, freezing, frost-bound, frosty, frozen, gelid, glacial, hyperboreal, icebox*, ice-cold, icy, refrigerated, Siber-

ian*, snappy, three-dog night*, wintry; SEE CONCEPT 605

frigid [adj2] *unresponsive*
aloof, austere, chilly, cold, cold-hearted*, cold-shoulder*, cool, forbidding, formal, frosty, icy, impotent, indifferent, lifeless, passionless, passive, repellent, rigid, stiff, unapproachable, unbending, unfeeling, unloving; SEE CONCEPT 404

frill [n] *luxury, nice touch*
amenity, decoration, doodad*, extravagance, fandangle, flounce, foppery*, frippery*, fuss, garbage*, garnish, gathering, gimcrack*, gingerbread*, jazz*, lace, ruffle, superfluity, thing*, tuck; SEE CONCEPTS 646,655,824

fringe [n] *border, trimming*
binding, borderline, brim, brink, edge, edging, flounce, hem, limit, mane, march, margin, outside, outskirts, perimeter, periphery, rickrack, ruffle, skirt, tassel, verge; SEE CONCEPTS 484,825

frippery [n] *waste, nonsense*
adornment, bauble, decoration, fanciness, fandangle*, flashiness, frill, fussiness, gaudiness, knickknack, meretriciousness, ornament, ostentation, pretentiousness, showiness, tawdriness, toy, trinket; SEE CONCEPTS 655,824

frisk [v1] *cavort*
bounce, caper, dance, frolic, gambol, hop, jump, lark, leap, play, prance, rollick, romp, skip, sport, trip; SEE CONCEPT 384

frisk [v2] *search*
check, fan, inspect, run over, shake down; SEE CONCEPT 216

frisky [adj] *full of spirit*
active, antic, bouncy, coltish*, dashing, feeling one's oats*, frolicsome, full of beans*, gamesome, high-spirited, in high spirits*, jumpy, kittenish*, larkish, lively, peppy, playful, prankish, rollicking, romping, spirited, sportive, wicked, zesty, zippy; SEE CONCEPTS 401,542,555

fritter [v] *waste away*
be wasteful with, blow*, cast away, consume, dally, diddle away, dissipate, frivol, go through*, idle, lavish, misspend, run through*, spend like water*, squander, throw away, trifle; SEE CONCEPTS 156,341

frivolity [n] *silliness, childishness*
coquetting, dallying, flightiness, flippancy, flirting, flummery, folly, fribble, frippery, frivolousness, fun, gaiety, game, giddiness, jest, levity, lightheartedness, lightness, nonsense, play, puerility, shallowness, sport, superficiality, toying, trifling, triviality, volatility, whimsicality, whimsy; SEE CONCEPTS 388,633

frivolous [adj] *trivial, silly*
barmy*, childish, dizzy*, empty-headed*, facetious, featherbrained*, flighty, flip, flippant, foolish, gay, giddy*, harebrained*, idiotic, idle, ill-considered, impractical, juvenile, light, lightminded, minor, niggling*, nonserious, not serious, paltry, peripheral, petty, playful, pointless, puerile, scatterbrained*, senseless, shallow, sportive, superficial, tongue-in-cheek*, unimportant, unprofound, volatile, whimsical; SEE CONCEPTS 401,402,575

frock [n] *women's garment*
apron, clothing, dress, gown, habit, muumuu, robe; SEE CONCEPT 451

frog [n] *jumping amphibian*
bullfrog, croaker*, polliwog, toad; SEE CONCEPT 394

frolic [n] *amusement, revel*
antic, drollery, escapade, fun, fun and games*, gaiety, gambol, game, high jinks*, joke, joviality, lark, merriment, monkeyshines*, play, prank, romp, shenanigan*, skylarking*, sport, spree, tomfoolery*, trick; SEE CONCEPTS *59,386*

frolic [v] *have fun, make merry*
caper, carouse, cavort, cut capers, cut loose*, fool around*, frisk, gambol, go on a tear*, kick up one's heels*, lark, let go*, let loose*, play, prance, raise hell*, revel, riot, rollick, romp, sport, spree, whoop it up*; SEE CONCEPTS *384,386*

frolicsome [adj] *playful*
antic, coltish, frisky, fun, gamesome, gay, gleeful, happy, impish, jocular, jovial, kittenish, lively, merry, mischievous, roguish, rollicking, sportive, sprightly; SEE CONCEPT *542*

from [prep1] *outside of, separating*
against, in distinction to, out of possession of, taken away; SEE CONCEPT *583*

from [prep2] *arising out of*
beginning at, coming out of, deriving out of, originating at, starting with; SEE CONCEPT *549*

from scratch [adv] *from the very beginning*
from square one, from the ground up, from the top, initially; SEE CONCEPTS *585,799,828*

front [adj] *lead, beginning*
advanced, ahead, anterior, facial, first, fore, foremost, forward, frontal, head, headmost, in the foreground, leading, obverse, topmost, vanward, ventral; SEE CONCEPTS *567,583,585,632*

front [n1] *forward, beginning part of something*
anterior, bow, breast, brow, exterior, facade, face, facing, fore, foreground, forehead, forepart, frontage, frontal, frontispiece, front line, head, lead, obverse, proscenium, top, van, vanguard; SEE CONCEPTS *833,835,836*

front [n2] *appearance put on for show*
air, aspect, bearing, blind, carriage, coloring, countenance, cover, cover-up*, demeanor, disguise, display, expression, exterior, facade, face, fake, figure, manner, mask, mien, phony, port, presence, pretext, put-on*, show, veil, window dressing*; SEE CONCEPT *716*

front [v] *look out on to*
border, confront, cover, encounter, face, look over, meet, overlay, overlook; SEE CONCEPT *746*

frontier [n1] *boundary*
borderland, borderline, bound, confines, edge, limit, march, perimeter, verge; SEE CONCEPTS *513,745*

frontier [n2] *unexplored, unoccupied area of land*
backcountry, backwater, backwoods, boondocks*, boonies*, bush, hinterland, outback, outskirts, sticks*, unknown*; SEE CONCEPT *509*

front runner [n] *leader*
best bet*, favorite, first choice, forerunner, top seed; SEE CONCEPTS *347,354*

frost [n] *extreme cold*
blight, dip, drop, freeze, hoarfrost, ice, Jack Frost*, rime; SEE CONCEPTS *524,610*

frosting [n] *icing*
covering, glaze, spread, sugar coating, topping; SEE CONCEPTS *457,460,461*

frosty [adj] *very cold*
antarctic, arctic, chill, chilly, cool, frigid, frozen, gelid, glacial, hoar, ice-capped, icicled, icy, nippy*, rimy, shivery, wintry; SEE CONCEPT *605*

froth [n] *lather, bubbles*
barm, ebullition, effervescence, fizz, foam, head, scud, scum, spindrift, spray, spume, suds, yeast; SEE CONCEPTS *260,467,468*

frothy [adj] *bubbly*
barmy, bubbling, fermenting, fizzing, fizzy, foaming, foamy, soapy, spumescent, spumous, spumy, sudsy, with a head on*, yeasty; SEE CONCEPT *485*

frown [v1] *scowl*
cloud up*, do a slow burn*, give a dirty look*, give the evil eye*, glare, gloom, glower, grimace, knit brows*, look black*, look daggers*, look stern*, lower, pout, sulk; SEE CONCEPT *185*

frown [v2] *disapprove*
deprecate, discommend, discountenance, discourage, disesteem, disfavor, dislike, look askance at*, not take kindly to*, object, show displeasure, take a dim view of*; SEE CONCEPTS *21,29*

frozen [adj1] *very cold*
antarctic, arctic, chilled, frigid, frosted, ice-bound, ice-cold, ice-covered, iced, icy, numb, Siberian*; SEE CONCEPT *605*

frozen [adj2] *stopped*
fixed, pegged, petrified, rooted, stock-still, suspended, turned to stone; SEE CONCEPTS *534,584*

frugal [adj] *economical*
abstemious, canny, careful, chary, conserving, discreet, meager, meticulous, mingy*, niggardly*, parsimonious, penny-pinching*, penny-wise*, preserving, provident, prudent, saving, scrimping, sparing, Spartan*, stingy, thrifty, tight, tightwad*, unwasteful, wary; SEE CONCEPT *334*

frugality [n] *economizing*
avarice, avariciousness, carefulness, conservation, economy, forehandedness, good management, miserliness, moderation, niggardliness, parsimoniousness, parsimony, penuriousness, providence, prudence, saving, scrimping, stinginess, thrift, thriftiness; SEE CONCEPTS *330,335*

fruit [n1] *edible part of vegetative growth developed after flowering*
berry, crop, drupe, grain, harvest, nut, pome, produce, product, yield; SEE CONCEPTS *426,428*

fruit [n2] *result of labor*
advantage, benefit, consequence, effect, outcome, pay, profit, result, return, reward; SEE CONCEPTS *230,337*

fruitful [adj] *productive*
abounding, abundant, advantageous, beneficial, blooming, blossoming, breeding, childing, conducive, copious, effective, fecund, fertile, flourishing, flush, fructiferous, gainful, plenteous, plentiful, profitable, profuse, proliferant, prolific, propagating, reproducing, rewarding, rich, spawning, successful, useful, well-spent, worthwhile; SEE CONCEPTS *528,537,560*

fruition [n] *achievement, maturation*
accomplishment, actualization, attainment, completion, consummation, enjoyment, fulfillment, gratification, materialization, maturity, perfection, pleasure, realization, ripeness, satisfaction, success; SEE CONCEPTS *704,706*

fruitless [adj] *bringing no advantage, product*
abortive, barren, empty, futile, gainless, idle, ineffective, ineffectual, infertile, in vain, pointless, profitless, spinning one's wheels*, sterile, to no avail*, to no effect*, unavailable, unavailing, un-

fruitful, unproductive, unprofitable, unprolific, unsuccessful, useless, vain, wild goose chase*; SEE CONCEPTS *528,537,560*

frumpy [*adj*] *dowdy*
badly dressed, baggy, blowsy*, dingy, drab, dull, frumpish, homely, old-fashioned, outdated, plain, poorly dressed, shabby, sloppy, stodgy, unfashionable, unkempt, unstylish; SEE CONCEPT *589*

frustrate [*v*] *thwart, disappoint*
annul, arrest, baffle, balk, bar, beat, block, cancel, check, circumvent, confront, conquer, counter, counteract, cramp, cramp one's style*, crimp, dash, dash one's hope*, defeat, depress, discourage, dishearten, foil, forbid, forestall, foul up*, give the run around*, halt, hang up*, hinder, hold up, impede, inhibit, lick, negate, neutralize, nullify, obstruct, obviate, outwit, overcome, preclude, prevent, prohibit, render null and void*, ruin, stump*, stymie*, upset the applecart*; SEE CONCEPTS *7,19,121*

frustrated [*adj*] *disappointed, thwarted*
balked*, crabbed*, cramped, crimped, defeated, discontented, discouraged, disheartened, embittered, foiled, fouled up*, hung up on*, irked, resentful, stonewalled*, stymied*, through the mill*, ungratified, unsated, unslaked, up the wall*; SEE CONCEPT *403*

frustration [*n*] *disappointment, thwarting*
annoyance, bitter pill*, blocking, blow, bummer, chagrin, circumvention, contravention, curbing, defeat, disgruntlement, dissatisfaction, downer*, drag*, failure, fizzle, foiling, grievance, hindrance, impediment, irritation, letdown, nonfulfillment, nonsuccess, obstruction, old one-two*, resentment, setback, unfulfillment, vexation; SEE CONCEPTS *410,674*

fry [*v*] *cook in hot oil*
brown, french fry, fricassee, frizzle, pan fry, sauté, sear, singe, sizzle; SEE CONCEPT *170*

frying pan [*n*] *skillet*
fry pan, gridiron, spider, wok; SEE CONCEPTS *493,494*

fuddy-duddy [*n*] *fussy person*
fussbudget, fusspot*, old fogy*, old geezer*, old poop*, square*, stick-in-the-mud*, stuffed shirt*; SEE CONCEPT *423*

fudge [*v*] *fake, misrepresent*
avoid, color, cook up*, dodge, embellish, embroider, equivocate, evade, exaggerate, falsify, hedge, magnify, overstate, pad, patch, shuffle, slant, stall; SEE CONCEPTS *59,63*

fuel [*n*] *something providing energy*
ammunition, combustible, electricity, encouragement, food, gas, incitement, juice, material, means, nourishment, propellant, provocation; SEE CONCEPTS *467,520,523,661*

fuel [*v*] *give energy to*
charge, fan, feed, fill 'er up*, fill up, fire, gas, gas up*, incite, inflame, nourish, service, stoke up*, supply, sustain, tank up*; SEE CONCEPTS *107,140*

fugitive [*adj*] *fleeing, transient*
avoiding, brief, criminal, elusive, ephemeral, errant, erratic, escaping, evading, evanescent, fleeting, flitting, flying*, fugacious, hot*, impermanent, lamster, momentary, moving, on the lam*, passing, planetary, running away*, short*, short-lived, temporary, transitory, unstable, volatile, wandering, wanted; SEE CONCEPTS *551,584,798*

fugitive [*n*] *person escaping from law or other pursuer*
bolter, derelict, deserter, displaced person, dodger, émigré, escapee, escaper, evacuee, exile, fly-by-night*, hermit, hunted person, outcast, outlaw, recluse, refugee, runagate, runaway, stray, transient, truant, vagabond, waif, walkout; SEE CONCEPT *412*

fulfill [*v*] *bring to completion*
accomplish, achieve, answer, be just the ticket*, carry out, comply with, conclude, conform, discharge, do, effect, effectuate, execute, fill, fill the bill*, finish, hit the bull's-eye*, implement, keep, make it*, make the grade*, meet, obey, observe, perfect, perform, please, realize, render, satisfy, score*, suffice, suit; SEE CONCEPTS *7,22,91,706*

fulfilled [*adj*] *completed*
accomplished, achieved, actualized, attained, brought about, brought to a close, carried out, compassed, concluded, consummated, crowned, delighted, dispatched, effected, effectuated, executed, finished, gratified, made good*, matured, obtained, perfected, performed, pleased, put into effect, reached, realized, satisfied; SEE CONCEPTS *403,531*

fulfillment [*n*] *accomplishment, completion*
achievement, attainment, carrying out, carrying through, consummation, contentedness, contentment, crowning, discharge, discharging, effecting, end, gratification, implementation, just the ticket*, kick*, kicks* observance, perfection, realization, you got it*; SEE CONCEPTS *230,706*

full [*adj1*] *brimming, filled*
abounding, abundant, adequate, awash, big, bounteous, brimful, burdened, bursting, chockablock, chock-full, competent, complete, crammed, crowded, entire, extravagant, glutted, gorged, imbued, impregnated, intact, jammed, jammed full*, jam-packed*, laden, lavish, loaded, overflowing, packed, packed like sardines, padded, plenteous, plentiful, plethoric, profuse, replete, running over, sated, satiated, satisfied, saturated, stocked, stuffed, sufficient, suffused, surfeited, teeming, voluminous, weighted; SEE CONCEPTS *481,483,773,774,786*

full [*adj2*] *thorough*
absolute, abundant, adequate, all-inclusive, ample, blow-by-blow*, broad, choate, circumstantial, clocklike, complete, comprehensive, copious, detailed, entire, exhaustive, extensive, generous, integral, itemized, maximum, minute, particular, particularized, perfect, plenary, plenteous, plentiful, unabridged, unlimited, whole; SEE CONCEPT *531*

full [*adj3*] *deep in sound*
clear, distinct, loud, resonant, rich, rounded, throaty; SEE CONCEPT *594*

full [*adj4*] *satiated in hunger*
glutted, gorged, jaded, lousy with*, sated, satiate, stuffed, surfeited, up to here*; SEE CONCEPTS *406,481,774*

full-blooded [*adj*] *purebred; strong*
hardy, hearty, powerful, robust, sound, thoroughbred, unmixed, vigorous, virile, vital; SEE CONCEPTS *314,489,613*

full-bodied [*adj*] *robust*
concentrated, fruity, full-flavored, heady*, heavy, lusty, mellow, potent, redolent, rich, strong, well-matured; SEE CONCEPTS *489,613*

full-grown/full-fledged [*adj*] *developed, ripe, ready*
adult, full-blown*, grown, grown-up, in one's prime*, marriageable, mature, nubile, of age, perfected, prime, ripened; SEE CONCEPTS *558, 578,797*

fullness [*n*] *abundance, breadth*
adequateness, ampleness, amplitude, broadness, completeness, completion, comprehensiveness, congestion, copiousness, curvaceousness, dilation, distension, enlargement, entirety, extensiveness, fill, glut, plenitude, plenty, plenum, profusion, repletion, roundness, satiation, satiety, saturation, scope, sufficiency, surfeit, swelling, totality, tumescence, vastness, voluptuousness, wealth, wholeness, wideness; SEE CONCEPTS *635,730*

full-scale [*adj*] *total, all-out*
all-encompassing, comprehensive, exhaustive, extensive, full-blown*, full-dress*, full-out*, in-depth, major, proper, sweeping, thorough, thoroughgoing, total, unlimited, wide-ranging; SEE CONCEPTS *531,772*

fully [*adv1*] *completely, in all respects*
absolutely, all out*, all the way*, altogether*, entirely, every inch*, from A to Z*, from soup to nuts*, heart and soul*, intimately, outright, perfectly, positively, quite, royal*, thoroughly, through and through*, totally, utterly, wholly, without exaggeration; SEE CONCEPTS *531,772*

fully [*adv2*] *sufficiently, adequately*
abundantly, amply, comprehensively, enough, plentifully, satisfactorily, well; SEE CONCEPT *558*

fulminate [*v*] *criticize harshly*
animadvert, berate, blow up, bluster, castigate, censure, condemn, curse, declaim, denounce, denunciate, execrate, explode, fume, intimidate, inveigh against, menace, protest, rage, rail, reprobate, swear at, thunder, upbraid, vilify, vituperate; SEE CONCEPTS *52,54*

fulmination [*n*] *tirade, condemnation*
blast, curse, denunciation, diatribe, discharge, explosion, intimidation, invective, obloquy, outburst, philippic, reprobation, warning; SEE CONCEPTS *52,54,278*

fulsome [*adj*] *sickening or excessive behavior*
adulatory, bombastic, buttery*, canting, cloying, coarse, extravagant, fawning, flattering, glib, grandiloquent, hypocritical, immoderate, ingratiating, inordinate, insincere, magniloquent, mealy-mouthed*, nauseating, offensive, oily*, oleaginous, overdone, saccharine, sanctimonious, slick*, slimy*, smarmy*, smooth, suave, sycophantic, unctuous, wheedling*; SEE CONCEPTS *267,401*

fumble [*v*] *bumble, mess up*
bollix*, botch*, bungle*, err, feel, flounder, flub*, fluff*, goof*, grapple, grope, lose the handle*, louse up*, misfield, mishandle, mismanage, scrabble*, screw up*, spoil, stumble; SEE CONCEPTS *101,181*

fume [*v*] *get very upset about*
anger, blow up*, boil, bristle, burn, chafe, chomp at the bit*, get hot*, get steamed up*, rage, rant, rave, seethe, smoke*, storm*; SEE CONCEPTS *21,29,410*

fumes [*n*] *pollution, gas in air*
effluvium, exhalation, exhaust, haze, miasma, reek, smog, smoke, stench, vapor; SEE CONCEPTS *437,600*

fumigate [*v*] *disinfect, ventilate*
air out, antisepticize, circulate, decontaminate, deodorize, fan, freshen, purify, sanitize, sterilize, vaporize; SEE CONCEPTS *51,60*

fun [*adj*] *good, happy*
amusing, boisterous, convivial, diverting, enjoyable, entertaining, lively, merry, pleasant, witty; SEE CONCEPTS *537,572*

fun [*n*] *amusement, play*
absurdity, ball*, big time*, blast*, buffoonery, celebration, cheer, clowning, distraction, diversion, enjoyment, entertainment, escapade, festivity, foolery, frolic, gaiety, gambol, game*, good time*, grins*, high jinks*, holiday, horseplay*, jesting, jocularity, joke, joking, jollity, joy, junketing, laughter, living it up*, merriment, merrymaking, mirth, nonsense, pastime, picnic*, playfulness, pleasure, recreation, rejoicing, relaxation, riot, romp, romping, solace, sport, tomfoolery*, treat, whoopee*; SEE CONCEPTS *386, 388*

function [*n1*] *capacity, job*
action, activity, affair, behavior, business, charge, concern, duty, employment, exercise, faculty, goal, mark, mission, object, objective, occupation, office, operation, part, post, power, province, purpose, raison d'être*, responsibility, role, service, situation, target, task, use, utility, work; SEE CONCEPTS *362,659*

function [*n2*] *social occasion*
affair, celebration, do*, gathering, get-together*, meeting, party, reception; SEE CONCEPT *386*

function [*v*] *perform, work*
act, act the part*, behave, be in action, be in commission, be in operation, be running, cook, do, do duty*, do one's thing*, get with it*, go, go to town*, move, officialize, officiate, operate, percolate*, react, run, serve, take, take care of business*; SEE CONCEPTS *87,362*

functional [*adj*] *working*
handy, occupational, operative, practicable, practical, serviceable, useful, utile, utilitarian, utility; SEE CONCEPT *560*

fund [*n*] *repository, reserve*
armamentarium, capital, endowment, foundation, hoard, inventory, kitty*, mine, pool*, reservoir, source, stock, store, storehouse, supply, treasury, trust, vein; SEE CONCEPTS *332,340,710*

fund [*v*] *provide money for*
back, bankroll, capitalize, endow, finance, float, grubstake*, juice*, patronize, pay for, pick up the check*, pick up the tab*, promote, stake, subsidize, support; SEE CONCEPTS *115,341*

fundamental [*adj*] *basic, important*
axiological, axiomatic, basal, bottom, bottom-line*, cardinal, central, constitutional, constitutive, crucial, elemental, elementary, essential, first, foundational, grass-roots*, indispensable, integral, intrinsic, key, major, meat-and-potatoes*, necessary, organic, original, paramount, primary, prime, primitive, primordial, principal, radical, requisite, rudimentary, significant, structural, substratal, substrative, supporting, sustaining, theoretical, underived, underlying, vital; SEE CONCEPTS *546,567*

fundamental [*n*] *basic, essential part*
ABCs*, axiom, basis, bottom line*, brass tacks*, coal and ice*, component, constituent, cornerstone, element, factor, foundation, guts*, heart, law, nitty-gritty*, principium, principle, rock

fr
fu

bottom*, rudiment, rule, sine qua non*, theorem; SEE CONCEPTS *668,688,826,829*

fundraiser [n] *pledge drive*
appeal for funds, bazaar, charity event, charity sale, philanthropic enterprise, radiothon, telethon; SEE CONCEPTS *337,657*

funds [n] *cash reserve*
accounts receivable, affluence, assets, backing, bankroll, belongings, bread*, budget, capital, collateral, currency, dough*, earnings, finance, fluid assets, hard cash*, kitty*, lucre, means, money, money in the bank*, money on hand*, nest egg*, nut*, petty cash, pork barrel*, possessions, proceeds, profits, property, ready money*, resources, revenue, savings, scratch*, securities, specie, stakes*, store*, stuff*, substance, treasure, wealth, wherewithal*, winnings*; SEE CONCEPTS *340,710*

funeral [n] *ceremony for the dead*
burial, cremation, entombment, exequies, funeration, inhumation, interment, last rites, obit, obsequies, planting, requiem, sepulture, services, solemnities; SEE CONCEPTS *172,386*

funereal [adj] *depressing*
black, bleak, dark, deathlike, dirgelike, disheartening, dismal, doleful, dreary, elegiac, gloomy, grave, grim, lamenting, lugubrious, melancholy, mournful, oppressive, sad, sepulchral, serious, solemn, somber, woeful; SEE CONCEPTS *403,537, 542*

funk [n] *fear, depression*
alarm, cold sweat*, despondency, fright, gloom, misery, panic, trembling; SEE CONCEPTS *27,410*

funnel [v] *direct down a path*
carry, channel, conduct, convey, filter, move, pass, pipe, pour, siphon, traject, transmit; SEE CONCEPTS *187,217*

funny [adj1] *comical, humorous*
absurd, amusing, antic, blithe, capricious, clever, diverting, droll, entertaining, facetious, farcical, for grins*, gas*, gay, gelastic, good-humored, hilarious, humdinger, hysterical, jocose, jocular, joking, jolly, killing*, knee-slapper*, laughable, ludicrous, merry, mirthful, playful, priceless, rich, ridiculous, riot, riotous, risible, screaming, side-splitting*, silly, slapstick, sportive, waggish, whimsical, witty; SEE CONCEPTS *267,529, 537*

funny [adj2] *odd, peculiar*
bizarre, curious, dubious, fantastic, mysterious, perplexing, puzzling, queer, remarkable, strange, suspicious, unusual, weird; SEE CONCEPTS *552,564*

funny money [n] *counterfeit money*
bad currency, bad money, counterfeit currency, fake currency, fake money, false currency, false money, play money; SEE CONCEPTS *648,725*

fur [n] *hair on animals*
brush, coat, down, fluff, fuzz, hide, jacket, lint, pelage, pelt, pile, skin, wool; SEE CONCEPT *399*

furbish [v] *polish; renovate*
brighten, buff, burnish, clean, deck out*, fix up, glaze, gloss, gussy up*, improve, recondition, refurbish, rehabilitate, renew, restore, rub, shine, smarten up*, spruce up*; SEE CONCEPTS *162,165,700*

furious [adj1] *extremely angry, very mad*
bent*, bent out of shape*, beside oneself*, boiling*, browned off*, bummed out*, corybantic, crazed, demented, desperate, enraged, fierce, fit

to be tied*, frantic, frenetic, frenzied, fuming, hacked, hopping mad*, incensed, infuriated, insane, irrational, livid, maddened, maniac, on the warpath*, rabid, raging, smoking*, steamed, unreasonable, up in arms*, vehement, vicious, violent, wrathful; SEE CONCEPT *403*

furious [adj2] *stormy, turbulent*
agitated, blustering, blustery, boisterous, concentrated, excessive, exquisite, extreme, fierce, flaming, impetuous, intense, intensified, raging, rampageous, rough, savage, tempestuous, terrible, tumultous/tumultuous, ungovernable, unrestrained, vehement, vicious, violent, wild; SEE CONCEPTS *525,537,548*

furlough [n] *leave of absence*
layoff, leave, liberty, rest and recreation, rest and recuperation, rest and relaxation, R&R, sabbatical, shore leave, shutdown, vacation; SEE CONCEPTS *802,807*

furnace [n] *heating mechanism*
boiler, calefactor, cinerator, cremator, forge, Franklin stove, heater, heating system, incinerator, kiln, oil burner, smithy, stove; SEE CONCEPT *463*

furnish [v1] *decorate, supply*
accoutre, apparel, appoint, arm, array, clothe, endow, equip, feather a nest*, fit, fit out*, fix up*, gear, line a nest*, make habitable, outfit, provide, provision, purvey, rig, stock, store, turn out; SEE CONCEPTS *140,177,182*

furnish [v2] *give, reveal information*
afford, bestow, deliver, dispense, endow, feed, grant, hand, hand over, offer, present, provide, supply, transfer, turn over; SEE CONCEPTS *60,67,108*

furnishings [n] *appliances, furniture*
accessories, accouterments, appointments, décor, equipment, fittings, fixtures, gear, provisions, trappings; SEE CONCEPT *443*

furniture [n] *household property*
appliance, appointment, bed, bookcase, buffet, bureau, cabinet, chair, chattel, chest, commode, couch, counter, cupboard, davenport, desk, dresser, effect, equipment, fittings, furnishing, goods, highboy, hutch, movables, possession, sideboard, sofa, stool, table, thing, wardrobe; SEE CONCEPT *443*

furor [n] *disturbance, excitement*
ado*, agitation, big scene*, big stink*, bustle, commotion, craze, enthusiasm, fad, ferment, flap*, free-for-all*, frenzy, fury, fuss, hell broke loose*, hullabaloo*, hysteria, lunacy, madness*, mania, outburst, outcry, rage, row, ruckus, stir*, to-do*, tumult, uproar, whirl; SEE CONCEPTS *230,388,410*

furrow [n] *ditch*
channel, corrugation, crease, crinkle, crow's-foot*, dike, fluting, fold, groove, gutter, hollow, line, plica, rabbet, ridge, rimple, rivel, ruck, rut, seam, trench, wrinkle; SEE CONCEPT *513*

further [adj] *additional*
added, another, else, extra, farther, fresh, in addition, more, new, other, supplementary; SEE CONCEPT *771*

further [adv] *additionally*
again, also, as well as, besides, beyond, distant, farther, in addition, moreover, on top of*, over and above*, then, to boot, what's more*, yet, yonder; SEE CONCEPT *771*

further [v] *advance, lend support*
aid, assist, back up, bail out*, ballyhoo*, champion, contribute, encourage, engender, expedite, facilitate, forward, foster, generate, give a boost to*, go with, hasten, help, lend a hand*, open doors*, patronize, plug, promote, propagate, push, serve, speed, succor, take care of, work for; SEE CONCEPTS *69,87,110*

furtherance [n] *advancement*
advocacy, backing, boosting, carrying-out, championship, progress, progression, promotion, prosecution, pursuit; SEE CONCEPTS *110,704*

furthermore [adv] *in addition*
additionally, along, as well, besides, likewise, moreover, not to mention, to boot, too, what's more*, withal, yet; SEE CONCEPTS *577,824*

furthest [adj] *most distant*
extreme, farthest, most remote, outermost, outmost, remotest, ultimate, uttermost; SEE CONCEPTS *586,778*

furtive [adj] *sneaky, secretive*
artful, calculating, cautious, circumspect, clandestine, cloaked, conspiratorial, covert, crafty*, creepy*, cunning, disguised, elusive, evasive, foxy, guileful, hidden, hush-hush*, insidious, masked, scheming, shifty*, skulking, slinking*, sly, stealthy, sub-rosa*, surreptitious, tricky*, undercover, underhand, underhanded, under-the-table*, under wraps*, wily; SEE CONCEPTS *548,576*

fury [n] *anger, wrath*
acerbity, acrimony, asperity, boiling point*, conniption, energy, ferocity, fierceness, fire, flare-up, force, frenzy, furor, impetuosity, indignation, intensity, ire, madness, might, passion, power, rabidity, rage, rampancy, rise, savagery, severity, slow burn*, sore, stew*, storm*, tempestuousness, turbulence, vehemence, violence; SEE CONCEPTS *29,410*

fuse [v] *meld, intermix*
agglutinate, amalgamate, bind, blend, cement, coalesce, combine, commingle, deliquesce, dissolve, federate, flux, integrate, interblend, interfuse, intermingle, join, liquefy, liquesce, melt, merge, mingle, run, run together, smelt, solder, thaw, unite, weld; SEE CONCEPT *113*

fusillade [n] *rapid outburst*
barrage, broadside, burst of fire, hail, salvo, volley; SEE CONCEPT *633*

fusion [n] *melding; mixture*
admixture, alloy, amalgam, amalgamation, blend, blending, coadunation, coalescence, coalition, commingling, commixture, compound, federation, heating, immixture, integration, intermixture, junction, liquefaction, liquification, melting, merger, merging, smelting, soldering, synthesis, unification, union, uniting, welding; SEE CONCEPTS *113,260,432*

fuss [n] *disturbance, trouble*
ado, agitation, altercation, argument, bickering, bother, broil*, bustle, commotion, complaint, confusion, controversy, difficulty, display, dispute, excitement, falling-out*, fight, flap, flurry, flutter, fret, furor, hassle, kick-up*, objection, palaver, perturbation, quarrel, row, ruckus, scene, squabble, stew*, stink*, stir, storm, to-do*, turmoil, unrest, upset, wingding*, worry; SEE CONCEPTS *46,106,388,633*

fussy [adj] *meticulous, particular*
careful, choosy, conscientious, conscionable, dainty, difficult, discriminating, exact, exacting, fastidious, finical, finicky, fretful, fuddy-duddy*, hard to please*, heedful, nit-picking*, overfastidious, painstaking, persnickety, picky, picky-picky*, punctilious, punctual, querulous, scrupulous, squeamish, stickling; SEE CONCEPTS *401,404*

fustian [adj] *pompous*
arrogant, boastful, bombastic, conceited, flaunting, high and mighty*, highfalutin, lofty, ostentatious, pontifical, portentous, pretentious, puffed up*, ranting, self-centered, self-important, vain, vainglorious; SEE CONCEPTS *267,401,542*

futile [adj] *hopeless, pointless*
abortive, barren, bootless, delusive, empty, exhausted, forlorn, fruitless, hollow, idle, impracticable, impractical, ineffective, ineffectual, insufficient, in vain, no dice*, nugatory, on a treadmill*, otiose, out the window*, profitless, resultless, save one's breath*, sterile, to no avail*, to no effect*, to no purpose*, trifling, trivial, unavailing, unimportant, unneeded, unproductive, unprofitable, unreal, unsatisfactory, unsubstantial, unsuccessful, useless, vain, valueless, worthless; SEE CONCEPTS *528,548,560*

futility [n] *uselessness*
emptiness, frivolousness, fruitlessness, hollowness, idleness, ineffectiveness, ineffectuality, meaninglessness, pointlessness, senselessness, unprofitableness, worthlessness; SEE CONCEPT *560*

futon [n] *sofa bed*
convertible sofa, couch, davenport, daybed, sofa; SEE CONCEPT *443*

future [adj] *to come; expected*
approaching, booked, budgeted, close at hand*, coming, coming up, destined, down the line*, down the pike, down the road*, eventual, fated, final, forthcoming, from here in, from here on, from here to eternity*, from now on in*, imminent, impending, inevitable, in the cards*, in the course of time, in the offing*, just around the corner*, later, likely, looked toward, near, next, planned, prospective, scheduled, subsequent, to be*, ulterior, ultimate, unborn, unfolding, up; SEE CONCEPT *820*

future [n] *time to come*
aftertime, afterward, by and by*, destiny, eternity, expectation, fate, futurity, hereafter, infinity, life to come, millennium, morrow, offing, outlook, posterity, prospect, subsequent time, to be*, tomorrow, world to come*; SEE CONCEPTS *679,807,811,818*

futuristic [adj] *ahead of one's time*
advanced, cutting edge, innovative, modern, pioneering, revolutionary, visionary; SEE CONCEPTS *578,589,797*

fuzz [n] *fluff*
down, dust ball*, dust bunnies*, fiber, floss, fur, hair, lanugo, lint, nap, pile; SEE CONCEPT *260*

fuzzy [adj1] *fluffy*
down-covered, downy, flossy, frizzy, furry, hairy, linty, napped, pilate, velutinous, woolly; SEE CONCEPT *606*

fuzzy [adj2] *out of focus*
bleary, blurred, dim, distorted, faint, foggy, hazy, ill-defined, indefinite, indistinct, misty, muffled, murky, obscure, shadowy, unclear, unfocused, vague; SEE CONCEPT *619*

fu
fu

G

gab [*n*] *conversation*
blab*, blather*, chat, chitchat*, gossip, idle talk*, loquacity*, palaver*, prattle, small talk*, talk, tête-à-tête, tongue-wagging*, yak*, yakkety-yak*; SEE CONCEPT *278*

gab [*v*] *talk a lot*
blabber*, blather*, buzz*, chatter, gossip, jabber*, jaw*, prate, prattle, yak*, yakkety-yak*; SEE CONCEPT *266*

gabby [*adj*] *talkative*
chattering, chatty, effusive, garrulous, glib, gossiping, gushing, jabbering, long-winded*, loose-lipped*, loquacious, mouthy*, prattling, prolix, talky, verbose, voluble, windy*, wordy; SEE CONCEPT *267*

gad [*v*] *roam about*
cruise, gallivant, hit the road*, hit the trail*, jaunt, knock about*, knock around*, maunder, mooch*, ramble, range, rove, run around*, stray, traipse, wander; SEE CONCEPTS *149,224*

gadfly [*n*] *goad; nuisance*
annoyance, energizer, excitant, irritant, motivator, mover, pest, prod, spur, stimulator; SEE CONCEPTS *412,674*

gadget [*n*] *device, novelty*
apparatus, appliance, business, concern, contraption, contrivance, doodad*, doohickey*, gimmick, gizmo*, invention, object, thing*, thingamajig, tool, utensil, whatchamacallit*, widget*; SEE CONCEPTS *463,499*

gadgetry [*n*] *mechanism*
appliances, bells and whistles, contraptions, ingenious device, instrumentation, machinery, works; SEE CONCEPTS *463,499*

gaffe [*n*] *mistake, goof*
blooper*, blunder, boner*, boo-boo*, faux pas*, howler*, impropriety, indecorum, indiscretion, putting foot in mouth*, slip*, solecism; SEE CONCEPTS *101,230*

gag [*n*] *practical joke*
crack, drollery, hoax, jest, quip, ruse, trick, wile, wisecrack, witticism; SEE CONCEPT *59*

gag [*v1*] *silence, stop up*
balk, bottle up*, choke, constrain, cork*, cork up*, curb, deaden, demur, garrote, keep the lid on*, muffle, muzzle, obstruct, put the lid on*, quiet, repress, restrain, shut down, shy, squash*, squelch, stifle, still, stumble, suppress, tape up*, throttle*, tongue-tie*; SEE CONCEPTS *121,130*

gag [*v2*] *vomit, choke*
be nauseated, disgorge, gasp, heave, nauseate, pant, puke*, retch, sicken, spew, strain, struggle, throw up; SEE CONCEPTS *179,308*

gaiety [*n*] *happiness, celebration*
animation, blitheness, brightness, brilliance, cheer, color, colorfulness, conviviality, effervescence, elation, entertainment, exhilaration, festivity, frolic, fun, geniality, gladness, glee, glitter, good humor*, grins*, high spirits*, hilarity, joie de vivre, jollity, joviality, joyousness, lightheartedness, liveliness, merriment, merrymaking, mirth, pleasantness, radiance, revel, reveling, revelry, shindig*, showiness, sparkle, sport, sprightliness, vivacity, whoopee*, wingding*; SEE CONCEPTS *377,388*

gaily [*adv*] *happily, brightly*
blithely, brilliantly, cheerfully, colorfully, flamboyantly, flashily, gleefully, glowingly, joyfully, laughingly, lightheartedly, merrily, showily, sparklingly, spiritedly, splendidly, vivaciously, with élan*, with spirit*; SEE CONCEPTS *542,589*

gain [*n*] *acquisition, winnings*
accretion, accrual, accumulation, achievement, addition, advance, advancement, advantage, attainment, benefit, boost, buildup, cut, dividend, earnings, emolument, gravy*, growth, headway*, hike*, improvement, income, increase, increment, lucre, payoff, proceeds, produce, profit, progress, receipts, return, rise, share, take, up*, upping*, velvet*, yield; SEE CONCEPTS *337,344, 706,710*

gain [*v*] *acquire, win*
accomplish, achieve, advance, ameliorate, annex, attain, augment, benefit, boost, bring in, build up, capture, clear, collect, complete, consummate, earn, enlarge, enlist, expand, fulfill, gather, get, glean, grow, harvest, have, improve, increase, land, make, make a killing*, move forward, net, obtain, overtake, parlay, perfect, pick up, procure, produce, profit, progress, promote, rack up*, reach, realize, reap, score*, secure, succeed, win over; SEE CONCEPTS *120,124,129*

gainful [*adj*] *very productive, profitable*
advantageous, beneficial, fat, fruitful, generous, going, going concern*, good, in the black*, lucrative, lush, moneymaking, paid off, paying, remunerative, rewarding, rich, satisfying, substantial, sweet*, useful, well-paying, worthwhile; SEE CONCEPT *334*

gainsay [*v*] *contradict*
combat, contravene, controvert, cross, deny, disaffirm, disagree, disclaim, disprove, dispute, fight, impugn, negate, negative, oppose, refute, repudiate, resist, traverse, withstand; SEE CONCEPTS *52,54*

gait [*n*] *way an animal or person moves, walks*
amble, bearing, canter, carriage, clip, gallop, get along, lick, march, motion, movement, pace, run, speed, step, stride, tread, trot, walk; SEE CONCEPT *149*

gala [*adj*] *celebratory*
bright, colorful, convivial, festal, festive, gay, happy, jovial, joyful, merry; SEE CONCEPT *548*

gala [*n*] *festival*
affair, ball, bash, blast*, blowout*, carnival, celebration, clambake, dance, do, festivity, fete, fiesta, function, get-together*, hop, jamboree, moveable feast, pageant, party, prom, roast, shindig*, stag, to-do*, wingding*; SEE CONCEPTS *377,383*

galaxy [*n*] *nebula*
elliptical galaxy, irregular galaxy, island universe, Milky Way, spiral galaxy, star cluster, star system; SEE CONCEPTS *370,511*

gale [*n*] *violent storm*
blast, blow, burst, chinook, cyclone, hurricane, mistral, monsoon, outbreak, outburst, squall, tempest, tornado, typhoon, wind, windstorm; SEE CONCEPTS *524,526*

gall [*n*] *nerve, brashness*
acrimony, animosity, arrogance, bitterness, brass, brazenness, cheek*, chutzpah*, conceit, confidence, crust, cynicism, effrontery, guts*, haughtiness, hostility, impertinence, impudence, insolence, malevolence, malice, overbearance,

pomposity, presumption, rancor, sauciness, self-importance, spite, venom; SEE CONCEPTS *411, 633*

gall [*v1*] *upset, irritate*
aggravate, annoy, bedevil, bother, burn, chafe, chide, disturb, exasperate, fret, grate, harass, harry, inflame, irk, nag, peeve, pester, plague, provoke, rile, roil, rub, ruffle, scrape, torment, trouble, vex, worry; SEE CONCEPTS *7,19*

gall [*v2*] *rub raw*
abrade, bark, burn, chafe, corrode, erode, excoriate, file, fray, frazzle, fret, grate, graze, irritate, scrape, scratch, scuff, skin, wear; SEE CONCEPT *215*

gallant [*adj*] *brave, splendid*
attentive, bold, considerate, courageous, courteous, courtly, daring, dashing, dauntless, dignified, doughty, fearless, fire-eating*, game*, glorious, gracious, grand, gritty*, hairy*, heroic, honorable, intrepid, lionhearted*, lofty, magnanimous, noble, plucky*, polite, quixotic, stately, stouthearted, suave, thoughtful, urbane, valiant, valorous; SEE CONCEPTS *404,542*

gallantry [*n*] *bravery, civility*
address, attentiveness, audacity, boldness, courage, courageousness, courteousness, courtesy, daring, dauntlessness, deference, derring-do*, duty, elegance, fearlessness, graciousness, honor, intrepidity, mettle, nerve, nobility, pluck*, poise, politeness, prowess, resolution, reverence, savoir-faire, spirit, tact, urbanity, valiance, valor; SEE CONCEPTS *411,657*

gallery [*n1*] *balcony*
arcade, loggia, mezzanine, patio, porch, upstairs, veranda; SEE CONCEPT *440*

gallery [*n2*] *showplace for wares*
exhibit, exhibition room, hall, museum, salon, showroom, studio, wing; SEE CONCEPTS *448,449*

gallery [*n3*] *audience, usually seated high*
attendance, onlookers, peanut gallery*, public, spectators; SEE CONCEPTS *294,417*

galling [*adj*] *very upsetting*
acid, afflictive, aggravating, annoying, bitter, bothersome, distasteful, exasperating, grievous, harassing, humiliating, irksome, irritating, nettlesome, painful, plaguing, provoking, rankling, unpalatable, vexatious, vexing; SEE CONCEPTS *7,19*

gallivant [*v*] *run around, gad about*
cruise, jaunt, meander, mooch, ramble, range, roam, rove, stray, traipse, wander; SEE CONCEPTS *149,224*

gallop [*v*] *bolt, race with slight jumping motion*
amble, canter, career, course, dart, dash, fly, hasten, hurdle, hurry, jump, leap, lope, pace, rack, run, rush, shoot, speed, spring, sprint, stride, tear along, trot, zoom; SEE CONCEPTS *150,194*

galvanize [*v*] *inspire, stimulate*
animate, arouse, astonish, awaken, commove, electrify, energize, excite, fire*, frighten, innervate, invigorate, jolt, motivate, move, pique, prime, provoke, quicken, shock, spur, startle, stir, stun, thrill, vitalize, wake, zap*; SEE CONCEPTS *7,14,22*

gambit [*n*] *plan, plot*
artifice, design, device, gimmick, jig, maneuver, play, ploy, ruse, trick; SEE CONCEPT *660*

gamble [*n*] *chance, speculation*
action, bet, fling, leap*, long shot*, lottery, outside chance*, raffle, risk, shot in the dark*,

spec*, stab*, throw of the dice*, toss up*, uncertainty, venture, wager; SEE CONCEPTS *28,363*

gamble [*v*] *take a chance on winning*
back, bet, brave, buck the odds*, cast lots*, challenge, cut the cards, dare, defy, endanger, face, flip the coin*, game, go for broke*, hazard, imperil, jeopardize, lay money on*, lot, make a bet, play, plunge, put, put faith in, put trust in, risk, set, shoot the moon*, shoot the works*, speculate, stake, stick one's neck out*, take a flyer*, tempt fortune*, trust to luck, try one's luck, venture, wager; SEE CONCEPTS *28,363*

gambol [*v*] *tumble playfully*
bound, caper, carry on, cavort, cut, cut a caper*, cut loose*, fool around*, frisk, frolic, hop, horse around*, jump, kibitz around*, kick up one's heels*, lark, leap, play, prance, revel, roister, rollick, romp, skip, sport, spring, whoop it up*; SEE CONCEPTS *149,194,363*

game [*adj1*] *brave, willing*
bold, courageous, dauntless, desirous, disposed, dogged, eager, fearless, gallant, hardy, heroic, inclined, interested, intrepid, nervy*, persevering, persistent, plucky*, prepared, ready, resolute, spirited, spunky, unafraid, unflinching, up for*, valiant, valorous; SEE CONCEPT *404*

game [*adj2*] *debilitated*
ailing, bad, crippled, deformed, disabled, incapacitated, injured, lame, maimed, weak; SEE CONCEPTS *314,485*

game [*n1*] *entertainment*
adventure, amusement, athletics, business, distraction, diversion, enterprise, festivity, frolic, fun, jest, joke, lark, line, merriment, merrymaking, occupation, pastime, plan, play, proceeding, pursuit, recreation, romp, scheme, sport, sports, undertaking; SEE CONCEPTS *292,363*

game [*n2*] *individual sporting event*
competition, contest, match, meeting, round, tournament; SEE CONCEPT *364*

game [*n3*] *undomesticated animals chased for food*
chase, fish, fowl, kill, meat, prey, quarry, ravin, victim, wild animals; SEE CONCEPTS *394,457,460*

game [*n4*] *plot, trick*
butt, derision, design, device, hoax, joke, object of ridicule, plan, ploy, practical joke, prank, scheme, stratagem, strategy, tactic; SEE CONCEPTS *59,660*

gamely [*adv*] *bravely*
boldly, courageously, dauntlessly, eagerly, enthusiastically, fearlessly, stoutly, with one's head held high*; SEE CONCEPT *401*

gamut [*n*] *range*
area, catalogue, compass, diapason, extent, field, panorama, scale, scope, series, spectrum, sweep; SEE CONCEPTS *651,788*

gamy [*adj*] *ill-smelling; corrupt*
fetid, foul, malodorous, pungent, rancid, rank, reeking, seamy, sordid, strong-flavored, strong-smelling, strong-tasting, tainted; SEE CONCEPT *598*

gang [*n*] *group, mob of people*
assemblage, band, bunch, circle, clan, clique, club, cluster, combo*, company, coterie, crew, crowd, herd, horde, knot, lot, organization, outfit, pack, party, posse, ring, set, shift, squad, syndicate, team, tribe, troop, troupe, workers, zoo*; SEE CONCEPT *387*

ga
ga

gangling [adj] rangy
awkward, bony, gawky, lanky, leggy, long-legged, long-limbed, lumbering, skinny, spindly, tall, thin; SEE CONCEPTS 490,491

gangster [n] person involved in illegal activities
bandit, bruiser*, criminal, crook, dealer, desperado, goon*, hit person, hood, hoodlum, hooligan*, Mafioso*, member of the family, mobster, pusher, racketeer, robber, ruffian, soldier*, thug, tough; SEE CONCEPT 412

gap [n] break, breach
aperture, arroyo, blank, caesura, canyon, chasm, cleft, clove, crack, cranny, crevice, cut, defile, difference, disagreement, discontinuity, disparity, divergence, divide, division, fracture, gorge, gulch, gully, hiatus, hole, hollow, inconsistency, interlude, intermission, interruption, interspace, interstice, interval, lacuna, lull, notch, opening, orifice, pause, ravine, recess, rent, respite, rest, rift, rupture, separation, slit, slot, space, vacuity, void; SEE CONCEPTS 513,665

gape [v1] gawk
beam, bore, eye, eyeball*, focus, get a load of*, get an eyeful*, give the eye*, glare, gloat, goggle*, look, ogle, peer, rubberneck*, size up*, stare, take in*, wonder, yawp*; SEE CONCEPT 623

gape [v2] be wide open
cleave, crack, dehisce, divide, frondesce, gap, part, split, yaw, yawn; SEE CONCEPT 135

gaping [adj] wide open
broad, cavernous, chasmal, great, vast, yawning; SEE CONCEPTS 485,490

garage [n] storage building for vehicles, workplace
barn, carport*, car stall*, parking lot, parking space, repair shop, shop, storage; SEE CONCEPTS 439,449

garb [n] clothing
apparel, appearance, array, attire, clothes, costume, dress, duds*, feathers*, form, garment, gear, guise, habiliment, habit, outfit, rags*, raiment, robes*, semblance, things*, threads*, uniform, vestments, wear; SEE CONCEPT 451

garb [v] fit with clothes
apparel, array, attire, clad, clothe, cover, deck, deck out*, drape, dress, dud*, fit out*, garment, raiment, rig out*, rig up*, robe, suit up*, tog*, turn out*; SEE CONCEPT 167

garbage [n] refuse, litter
bits and pieces*, debris, detritus, dreck, dregs, dross, filth, junk, muck, odds and ends*, offal, rubbish, rubble, scrap, scrapings, sewage, slop*, sweepings, swill, trash, waste; SEE CONCEPT 260

garble [v] mix up, misrepresent
belie, color, confuse, corrupt, distort, doctor, falsify, jumble, misinterpret, mislead, misquote, misstate, mutilate, obscure, pervert, slant, tamper with, twist, warp; SEE CONCEPTS 59,63

garden [n] cultivated plants, flowers
back yard, bed, cold frame, conservatory, enclosure, field, greenhouse, hothouse, nursery, oasis, patch, patio, plot, terrace; SEE CONCEPTS 509,517

gargantuan [adj] very large
big, colossal, elephantine, enormous, giant, gigantic, heavyweight, huge, humongous, immense, jumbo, leviathan, mammoth, massive, monstrous, monumental, mountainous, prodigious, super-colossal*, super-duper*, titanic, towering, tremendous, vast, whopping*; SEE CONCEPTS 491,773

gargle [v] rinse the mouth with liquid
irrigate, swish, trill, use mouthwash; SEE CONCEPTS 169,308,616

garish [adj] flashy, tasteless
blatant, brassy, brazen, cheap, chintzy, flaunting, gaudy, glaring, glittering, kitschy*, loud, meretricious, ornate, ostentatious, overdone, overwrought, raffish, screaming*, showy, tawdry, tinsel, vulgar; SEE CONCEPT 589

garland [n] strand of material, usually hung
bays, chaplet, coronal, crown, festoon, honors, laurel, palm, wreath; SEE CONCEPTS 260,429

garment [n] article of clothing
apparel, array, attire, costume, covering, drapes*, dress, duds*, feathers*, garb, gear, get-up*, habiliment, habit, outfit, raiment, robe, things*, threads*, togs*, uniform, vestments, wear, weeds*; SEE CONCEPT 451

garner [v] collect, accumulate
amass, assemble, cull, cumulate, deposit, extract, gather, glean, harvest, hive, hoard, lay in*, lay up*, pick up, put by*, reap, reserve, roll up*, save, stockpile, store, stow away, treasure; SEE CONCEPTS 109,135

garnish [n] embellishment, improvement
adornment, decoration, enhancement, furbelow, gingerbread*, ornament, ornamentation, tinsel, trim, trimming; SEE CONCEPT 824

garnish [v] embellish, improve
adorn, beautify, bedeck, deck, decorate, dress up, enhance, fix up, grace, gussy up*, ornament, set off*, spiff up*, spruce up*, trim; SEE CONCEPT 244

garrison [n] military post, fort
barracks, base, camp, citadel, command post, encampment, fortification, fortress, stronghold; SEE CONCEPTS 321,439

garrulous [adj] talkative
babbling, blabbermouth*, chattering, chatty, effusive, flap jaw*, gabby, glib, gossiping, gushing, long-winded*, loose-lipped*, loose-tongued*, loquacious, motormouth*, mouthy, prating, prattling, prolix, prosy, running on at the mouth*, verbose, voluble, wind-bag*, windy*, wordy, yakkity*, yakky*; SEE CONCEPTS 267,404

gas [n] something not liquid or solid
effluvium, fumes, miasma, smoke, stream, vapor, volatile substance; SEE CONCEPT 465

gash [n] cut made by slicing
cleft, furrow, gouge, incision, laceration, mark, nip, notch, rent, slash, slit, split, tear, wound; SEE CONCEPT 309

gash [v] cut by slicing
carve, cleave, furrow, gouge, incise, injure, lacerate, lance, mark, nip, notch, pierce, rend, slash, slit, split, tear, wound; SEE CONCEPTS 137,176

gasket [n] seal
cap, covering, packing, stopper; SEE CONCEPTS 85,160

gasoline [n] fuel
diesel fuel, gasohol, juice*, oil, petrol, propellant; SEE CONCEPTS 467,520,523,661

gasp [n] sharply drawn breath
blow, ejaculation, exclamation, gulp, heave, pant, puff, wheeze, whoop; SEE CONCEPTS 163,595

gasp [v] draw breath in sharply
blow, catch one's breath, choke, convulse, fight for breath, gulp, heave, inhale, inspire, pant,

puff, respire, sniffle, snort, wheeze, whoop; SEE CONCEPT *163*

gate [*n*] *movable barrier at entrance*
access, bar, conduit, door, doorway, egress, exit, gateway, issue, lock, opening, passage, port, portal, revolving door, slammer*, turnstile, way, weir; SEE CONCEPTS *440,445*

gatekeeper [*n*] *watchperson*
doorkeeper, guard, lookout, monitor, protector, security officer, sentinel, sentry; SEE CONCEPT *348*

gather [*v1*] *come or bring together*
accumulate, aggregate, amass, assemble, associate, bunch up, capture, choose, close with, cluster, collect, concentrate, congregate, convene, converge, corral, crowd, cull, draw, draw in, flock, forgather, gang up, garner, get together, group, hang around*, hang out*, heap, herd, hoard, huddle, make the scene*, marshal, mass, meet, muster, pick, pile up, pluck, poke*, pour in, punch*, rally, reunite, round up*, scare up*, scrape together*, show up, stack up, stockpile, swarm, throng, unite; SEE CONCEPTS *109,114*

gather [*v2*] *be led to believe; infer*
assume, conclude, deduce, draw, expect, find, hear, imagine, judge, learn, make, presume, reckon, suppose, surmise, suspect, take, think, understand; SEE CONCEPT *15*

gather [*v3*] *harvest, pick out*
crop, cull, draw, extract, garner, glean, heap, ingather, mass, pick up, pile, pluck, reap, select, stack, take in; SEE CONCEPT *257*

gather [*v4*] *gain, increase*
build, deepen, enlarge, expand, grow, heighten, intensify, rise, swell, thicken, wax; SEE CONCEPT *780*

gathering [*n*] *assemblage, accumulation*
acquisition, affair, aggregate, aggregation, association, band, body, bunch, caucus, clambake*, collection, company, concentration, conclave, concourse, conference, congregation, congress, convention, convocation, crowd, crush, drove, flock, function, gain, get-together*, group, heap, herd, horde, huddle, junction, knot, levy, mass, meet, meeting, muster, parley, party, pile, powwow*, rally, roundup, social function, society, stock, stockpile, swarm, throng, turnout, union; SEE CONCEPTS *324,386,417*

gauche [*adj*] *tactless, unsophisticated*
awkward, bumbling, clumsy, crude, graceless, green, halting, ham-handed*, heavy-handed, ignorant, ill-bred, ill-mannered, inelegant, inept, insensitive, lacking, maladroit, oafish, uncouth, uncultured, unhappy, unpolished, wooden*; SEE CONCEPT *404*

gaudy [*adj*] *bright and vulgar*
blatant, brazen, brilliant, catchpenny*, chichi*, chintzy, coarse, crude, flashy, flaunting, florid, frou-frou*, garish, gay, glaring, gross, gussied up*, jazzy, kitschy*, loud, meretricious, obtrusive, ostentatious, pizzazz*, pretentious, putting on the ritz*, raffish, ritzy, screaming*, showy, snazzy, splashy, splendiferous, tasteless, tawdry, tinsel; SEE CONCEPTS *589,618*

gauge [*n*] *measure, standard*
barometer, basis, benchmark, bore, capacity, check, criterion, degree, depth, example, exemplar, extent, guide, guideline, height, indicator, magnitude, mark, meter, model, norm, pattern, rule, sample, scale, scope, size, span, test, thick-

ness, touchstone*, type, width, yardstick; SEE CONCEPTS *647,680,688,792*

gauge [*v*] *measure, judge*
adjudge, appraise, ascertain, assess, calculate, calibrate, check, check out, compute, count, determine, estimate, evaluate, eye*, figure, figure in, guess, guesstimate, have one's number*, look over, meter, peg*, quantify, quantitate, rate, reckon, scale, size, size up*, take account of, tally, value, weigh; SEE CONCEPTS *37,764*

gaunt [*adj*] *skinny*
angular, anorexic, attenuated, bare, bleak, bony, cadaverous, desolate, dismal, dreary, emaciated, forbidding, forlorn, grim, haggard, harsh, lank, lean, like a bag of bones*, meager, peaked, peaky, pinched, rawboned, scraggy, scrawny, skeletal, skeleton, skin and bones*, spare, thin, wasted; SEE CONCEPTS *406,490,491*

gauzy [*adj*] *see-through, gossamer in texture*
delicate, diaphanous, filmy, flimsy, insubstantial, light, lucid, pellucid, sheer, thin, tiffany, translucent, transparent; SEE CONCEPT *606*

gawk [*v*] *stare at in amazement*
bore*, eyeball*, gape, gaze, glare, gloat, goggle*, look, ogle, peer, rubberneck*, yawp*; SEE CONCEPT *623*

gawky [*adj*] *clumsy*
awkward, bumbling, clownish, gauche, loutish*, lumbering, lumpish*, lumpy, maladroit, oafish, rude, rustic, splay, uncouth, ungainly; SEE CONCEPTS *550,584*

gay [*adj1*] *happy*
alert, animate, animated, blithe, blithesome, bouncy, brash, carefree, cheerful, cheery, chipper*, chirpy, confident, convivial, devil-may-care*, festive, forward, frivolous, frolicsome, fun-loving, gamesome, glad, gleeful, hilarious, insouciant, jocund, jolly, jovial, joyful, joyous, keen, lighthearted, lively, merry, mirthful, playful, pleasure-seeking, presuming, pushy, rollicking, self-assertive, sparkling, spirited, sportive, sprightly, sunny, vivacious, wild, zippy*; SEE CONCEPTS *403,542*

gay [*adj2*] *colorful, vivid*
brave, bright, brilliant, flamboyant, flashy, fresh, garish, gaudy, intense, rich, showy; SEE CONCEPTS *589,618*

gay [*adj3*] *homosexual*
homoerotic, homophile, lesbian, Sapphic; SEE CONCEPT *372*

gaze [*n*] *long, fixed stare*
fish eye*, glaring, gun*, look, looking, ogling, peek, peep, rubbernecking*, scrutiny, seeing, survey, watching; SEE CONCEPT *623*

gaze [*v*] *stare at*
admire, beam*, bore*, contemplate, eye, eyeball*, gape, gawk, get a load of*, get an eyeful*, glare, gloat, inspect, lamp*, look, look fixedly, moon*, observe, ogle, peek, peep, peer, pin*, pipe*, regard, rubber*, rubberneck*, scrutinize, see, size up*, survey, take in*, view, watch, wonder; SEE CONCEPTS *623,626*

gazebo [*n*] *pavilion*
arbor, bandstand, belvedere, bower, kiosk, platform, rotunda, summerhouse; SEE CONCEPTS *440,443*

gear [*n1*] *equipment*
accessory, accouterment, adjunct, apparatus, appendage, appurtenance, baggage, belongings, contraption, effects, encumbrances, fittings, ha-

ga
ge

biliment, harness, impedimenta, instrument, kit, kit and kaboodle*, luggage, machinery, material, materiel, means, outfit, paraphernalia, possessions, rigging, setup, stuff, supply, tackle, things, tools, trappings; SEE CONCEPT *496*

gear [*n2*] *toothed part of wheel*
cog, cogwheel, gearwheel, pinion, ragwheel, sprocket, spurwheel; SEE CONCEPT *464*

gear [*n3*] *clothing*
apparel, array, attire, clothes, costume, drapes*, dress, duds*, feathers*, garb, garments, habit, outfit, rags*, threads*, toggery*, togs*, wear; SEE CONCEPT *451*

gear [*v*] *prepare, equip*
accouter, adapt, adjust, appoint, arm, blend, fit, fit out*, furnish, harness, match, organize, outfit, ready, regulate, rig*, suit, tailor, turn out; SEE CONCEPTS *182,202*

geek [*n*] *odd person; computer expert*
buffoon, computer specialist, curiosity, dolt, dork, freak, goon, guru, nerd, techie, weirdo; SEE CONCEPTS *352,366,423*

gelatinous [*adj*] *coagulated*
gluey, glutinous, gummy, jelled, jellied, jellylike, mucilaginous, pudding*, sticky, thick, viscid, viscous; SEE CONCEPT *606*

geld [*v*] *castrate*
alter*, emasculate, eunuchize, fix*, neuter, spay, sterilize, unman; SEE CONCEPTS *240,250*

gem [*n*] *precious stone; treasure*
bauble*, glass*, hardware*, jewel, jewelry, masterpiece, nonpareil, ornament, paragon, pearl, pick, prize, rock*, sparkler*, stone, trump*; SEE CONCEPTS *337,446,474*

gender [*n*] *grammatical rules applying to nouns that connote sex or animateness*
common, feminine, gender-specific, masculine, neuter; SEE CONCEPT *408*

genealogy [*n*] *person's family tree*
ancestry, blood line, derivation, descent, extraction, generation, genetics, heredity, history, line, lineage, parentage, pedigree, progeniture, stemma, stirps, stock, strain; SEE CONCEPT *296*

general [*adj1*] *common, accepted*
accustomed, broad, commonplace, conventional, customary, everyday, extensive, familiar, generic, habitual, humdrum, inclusive, matter-of-course*, natural, normal, ordinary, popular, prevailing, prevalent, public, regular, routine, run-of-the-mill*, typical, uneventful, universal, usual, wide, widespread, wonted; SEE CONCEPTS *530,547*

general [*adj2*] *inexact, approximate*
ill-defined, imprecise, inaccurate, indefinite, loose, not partial, not particular, not specific, uncertain, undetailed, unspecific, vague; SEE CONCEPT *557*

general [*adj3*] *comprehensive*
across-the-board*, all-around*, all-embracing*, all-inclusive*, ample, blanket, broad, catholic, collective, comprehending, diffuse, ecumenical, encyclopedic, endless, extensive, far-reaching, generic, global, inclusive, indiscriminate, infinite, limitless, miscellaneous, overall, panoramic, sweeping, taken as a whole, total, ubiquitous, unconfined, universal, unlimited, wide, worldwide; SEE CONCEPTS *537,772*

generality [*n*] *vague notion*
abstraction, abstract principle, generalization, half-truth, law, loose statement, observation,

principle, sweeping statement, universality; SEE CONCEPTS *688,689*

generalize [*v*] *make a sweeping assumption, statement*
be metaphysical, conclude, derive, discern, discover, establish, hypothesize, induce, observe, philosophize, postulate, speculate, stay in the clouds*, theorize, vapor; SEE CONCEPTS *37,49*

generally [*adv*] *mainly, in most cases*
about, all in all, almost always, altogether, approximately, as a rule, broadly, by and large, chiefly, commonly, conventionally, customarily, en masse, extensively, for the most part, habitually, largely, mostly, normally, on average, on the whole, ordinarily, overall, popularly, practically, predominantly, primarily, principally, publicly, regularly, roughly, roundly, thereabouts, typically, universally, usually, widely; SEE CONCEPTS *530,547,772*

generate [*v*] *produce, create*
accomplish, achieve, bear, beget, breed, bring about, bring to pass, cause, develop, effect, engender, form, found, get up, give birth to, give rise to, hatch, inaugurate, induce, initiate, institute, introduce, make, multiply, muster, occasion, originate, parent, perform, procreate, propagate, provoke, reproduce, set up, spawn, whip up*, work up; SEE CONCEPTS *173,205,251, 374*

generation [*n1*] *creation, production*
bearing, begetting, breeding, bringing forth, engenderment, formation, fructifying, genesis, multiplying, origination, procreation, propagation, reproduction, spawning; SEE CONCEPTS *173,205,374*

generation [*n2*] *era; age group*
aeon, breed, contemporaries, crop, day, days, eon, epoch, peers, period, rank, span, step, time, times; SEE CONCEPTS *807,816*

generic [*adj*] *common, general*
all-encompassing, blanket, collective, comprehensive, inclusive, nonexclusive, sweeping, universal, wide; SEE CONCEPT *530*

generosity [*n*] *spirit of giving*
all heart*, alms-giving, altruism, beneficence, benevolence, bounteousness, bounty, charitableness, charity, free giving, goodness, heart, highmindedness, hospitality, kindness, largesse, liberality, magnanimity, munificence, nobleness, openhandedness, philanthropy, profusion, readiness, unselfishness; SEE CONCEPTS *411,657*

generous [*adj1*] *giving, big-hearted*
acceptable, altruistic, beneficent, benevolent, big, bounteous, bountiful, charitable, considerate, easy, equitable, excellent, fair, free, good, greathearted, helpful, high-minded, honest, honorable, hospitable, just, kind, kindhearted, kindly, lavish, liberal, lofty, loose, magnanimous, moderate, munificent, noble, open-handed, philanthropic, prodigal, profuse, reasonable, soft-touch*, thoughtful, tolerant, ungrudging, unselfish, unsparing, unstinting, willing; SEE CONCEPTS *404,542*

generous [*adj2*] *plentiful*
abundant, affluent, ample, aplenty, bounteous, bountiful, copious, dime a dozen*, full, galore, handsome, large, lavish, liberal, luxuriant, no end*, no end in sight*, overflowing, plenteous, rich, stinking with*, unstinting, wealthy; SEE CONCEPTS *334,589,781*

genesis [n] *beginning, creation*
alpha, birth, commencement, dawn, dawning, engendering, formation, generation, inception, opening, origin, outset, propagation, provenance, provenience, root, source, start; SEE CONCEPTS *119,832*

genetic [adj] *coming from heredity*
abiogenetic, ancestral, digenetic, eugenic, genesiological, genital, hereditary, historical, matriclinous, patrimonial, phytogenetic, sprogenous, xenogenetic; SEE CONCEPTS *314,549*

genial [adj] *extremely nice and happy*
affable, agreeable, amiable, amicable, blithe, cheerful, cheering, cheery, chipper*, chirpy*, congenial, convivial, cordial, easygoing, enlivening, favorable, friendly, gentle, glad, good-natured, gracious, hearty, high, jocund, jolly, jovial, joyous, kind, kindly, merry, neighborly, perky, pleasant, sociable, sunny*, sunny side up*, up*, upbeat, upper*, warm, warm-hearted; SEE CONCEPTS *401,404*

geniality [n] *extreme niceness*
affability, agreeability, agreeableness, amenity, amiability, cheerfulness, cheeriness, congenialness, conviviality, cordiality, enjoyableness, friendliness, gladness, good cheer, good nature, gratefulness, happiness, heartiness, jollity, joviality, joy, joyousness, kindliness, kindness, mirth, pleasance, pleasantness, sunniness*, sweetness and light*, warmheartedness, warmth; SEE CONCEPTS *411,633*

genie [n] *mythical being*
demon, djinni, jinnee, jinni, spirit, wizard; SEE CONCEPT *361*

genius [n] *gift of high intellect*
ability, accomplishment, acumen, acuteness, adept, aptitude, aptness, astuteness, bent, brain, brilliance, capability, capacity, creativity, discernment, Einstein*, endowment, expert, faculty, flair, grasp, head, imagination, inclination, ingenuity, inspiration, intelligence, inventiveness, knack, mature, originality, percipience, perspicacity, power, precocity, prodigy, propensity, prowess, reach, sagacity, superability, talent, turn, understanding, virtuoso, wisdom; SEE CONCEPTS *350,409,416*

genocide [n] *mass extermination*
annihilation, carnage, decimation, ethnic cleansing, holocaust, massacre, mass execution, mass murder, race extermination, slaughter; SEE CONCEPT *252*

genre/genus [n] *type, class*
brand, category, character, classification, fashion, group, kind, school, sort, species, style; SEE CONCEPTS *378,388,655*

genteel [adj] *sophisticated, cultured*
affected, aristocratic, artificial, chivalrous, civil, confined, courteous, courtly, cultivated, distingué, elegant, fashionable, formal, graceful, hollow, intolerant, la-di-da*, mannerly, noble, ostentatious, polished, polite, pompous, precious, pretentious, priggish, prim, prissy, prudish, refined, respectable, straitlaced, stuffy*, stylish, urbane, well-behaved, well-bred, well-mannered; SEE CONCEPTS *401,404*

gentility [n] *sophistication, cultivation*
aristocracy, blue blood*, civility, courtesy, courtliness, culture, decorum, elegance, elite, etiquette, flower*, formality, gentle birth*, gentlefolk, gentry, good breeding*, good fam-

ily*, good manners*, high birth*, mannerliness, nobility, optimacy, polish, politeness, propriety, quality, rank, refinement, respectability, ruling class*, society, upper class, upper crust*, urbanity; SEE CONCEPTS *388,411*

gentle [adj1] *having a mild or kind nature*
affable, agreeable, amiable, benign, biddable, bland, compassionate, considerate, cool*, cultivated, disciplined, docile, domesticated, dovelike*, easy, genial, humane, kindly, laid back*, lenient, manageable, meek, mellow, merciful, moderate, pacific, peaceful, placid, pleasant, pleasing, pliable, quiet, soft, softhearted, sweet-tempered, sympathetic, tame, taught, temperate, tender, tractable, trained, warmhearted; SEE CONCEPTS *404,542*

gentle [adj2] *mild, temperate in effect on senses*
balmy, bland, calm, clement, delicate, easy, faint, feeble, gradual, halcyon, hushed, imperceptible, lenient, light, low, low-pitched, low-toned, mellow, mild, moderate, muted, peaceful, placid, quiet, sensitive, serene, slight, slow, smooth, soft, soothing, subdued, tender, tranquil, untroubled; SEE CONCEPTS *525,537,594*

gentle [adj3] *of noble birth*
aristocratic, blue-blooded*, Brahmin*, courteous, cultured, elegant, genteel, high-born, highbred, noble, polished, polite, refined, upper-class, well-born, well-bred; SEE CONCEPT *555*

gentleperson [n] *polite, well-mannered person*
aristocrat, brick*, good egg*, good person, nice person, noble, scholar; SEE CONCEPT *423*

genuine [adj1] *authentic, real*
absolute, accurate, actual, authenticated, bona fide, -carat*, 24-carat*, certain, certified, demonstrable, exact, existent, factual, for real*, good, hard, honest, honest-to-goodness*, indubitable, in the flesh*, kosher*, legit, legitimate, literal, natural, official, original, palpable, plain, positive, precise, proved, pure, real stuff*, sound, sterling, sure-enough*, tested, true, unadulterated, unalloyed, undoubted, unimpeachable, unquestionable, unvarnished, valid, veritable, very, whole; SEE CONCEPT *582*

genuine [adj2] *unaffected; honest*
actual, artless, candid, earnest, frank, heartfelt, known, natural, open, positive, real, reliable, righteous, sincere, true, trustworthy, undesigning, unfeigned, unimpeachable, unpretended, unquestionable, up front*, valid, well-established; SEE CONCEPTS *267,542*

geography [n] *the earth's features; study of land*
cartography, chorography, earth science, geology, geopolitical study, geopolitics, physiographics, physiography, topography, topology; SEE CONCEPTS *349,509*

germ [n1] *microscopic organism, often causing illness*
antibody, bacterium, bug*, disease, microbe, microorganism, parasite, pathogen, plague, virus, what's going around*; SEE CONCEPTS *306,392*

germ [n2] *beginning*
bud, cause, egg, embryo, inception, nucleus, origin, ovule, ovum, root, rudiment, seed, source, spark, spore, sprig, sprout; SEE CONCEPTS *392,648,826,832*

germane [adj] *appropriate*
ad rem, akin, allied, applicable, applicative, applicatory, apposite, apropos, apt, cognate, connected, fitting, kindred, kosher*, legit*, material,

on target*, on the button*, on the nose*, pertinent, proper, related, relating, relevant, right on*, suitable, that's the ticket*, to the point, to the purpose; SEE CONCEPT *558*

germinate [*v*] *grow*
bud, develop, generate, live, originate, pullulate, shoot, sprout, swell, vegetate; SEE CONCEPT *427*

gestation [*n*] *process of early development*
evolution, fecundation, gravidity, growth, incubation, maturation, pregnancy, reproduction, ripening; SEE CONCEPTS *316,704,809*

gesture [*n*] *motion as communication*
action, body language, bow, curtsy, expression, genuflection, gesticulation, high sign, indication, intimation, kinesics, mime, nod, pantomime, reminder, salute, shrug, sign, signal, sign language, token, wave, wink; SEE CONCEPTS *74,185*

gesture/gesticulate [*v*] *make signs, motions to communicate*
act out, flag, indicate, mime, pantomime, signal, signalize, use one's hands, use sign language, wave; SEE CONCEPT *74*

get [*v1*] *come into possession of; achieve*
access, accomplish, acquire, annex, attain, bag*, bring, bring in, build up, buy into, buy off, buy out, capture, cash in on*, chalk up*, clean up*, clear, come by, compass, cop*, draw, earn, educe, effect, elicit, evoke, extort, extract, fetch, gain, get hands on*, glean, grab, have, hustle*, inherit, land, lock up, make, make a buy, make a killing*, net, obtain, parlay, pick up, procure, pull, rack up*, realize, reap, receive, score, secure, snag*, snap up*, snowball*, succeed to, take, wangle*, win; SEE CONCEPTS *120,706,710*

get [*v2*] *fall victim to*
accept, be afflicted with, become infected with, be given, be smitten by, catch, come down with*, contract, get sick, receive, sicken, succumb, take; SEE CONCEPT *93*

get [*v3*] *seize*
apprehend, arrest, bag*, beat, capture, catch, collar*, defeat, grab, lay hold of*, lay one's hands on*, nab*, nail*, occupy, overcome, overpower, secure, take, trap; SEE CONCEPT *90*

get [*v4*] *come to be*
achieve, attain, become, come over, develop into, effect, go, grow, realize, run, turn, wax*; SEE CONCEPTS *697,706*

get [*v5*] *understand*
acquire, catch, catch on to, comprehend, fathom, figure out, follow, gain, get into one's head*, hear, know, learn, look at, memorize, notice, perceive, pick up*, receive, see, take in, work out; SEE CONCEPTS *15,31*

get [*v6*] *arrive*
advance, blow in*, come, come to, converge, draw near, land, make it, reach, show, show up, turn up; SEE CONCEPT *159*

get [*v7*] *contact for communication*
get in touch, reach; SEE CONCEPT *266*

get [*v8*] *arrange, manage desired goal*
adjust, contrive, dispose, dress, fit, fix, make, make up, order, prepare, ready, straighten, succeed, wangle*; SEE CONCEPT *202*

get [*v9*] *convince, induce*
argue into, beg, bring around, coax, compel, draw, influence, persuade, press, pressure, prevail upon, prompt, provoke, sway, talk into, urge, wheedle, win over; SEE CONCEPT *68*

get [*v10*] *have an effect on*
affect, amuse, arouse, bend, bias, carry, dispose, entertain, excite, gratify, impress, influence, inspire, move, predispose, prompt, satisfy, stimulate, stir, stir up, strike, sway, touch; SEE CONCEPTS *7,22*

get [*v11*] *produce offspring*
beget, breed, generate, procreate, produce, propagate, sire; SEE CONCEPT *374*

get [*v12*] *irritate, upset*
aggravate, annoy, bother, bug*, burn, exasperate, gall, get someone's goat*, irk, nettle, peeve, pique, provoke, put out*, rile, rub the wrong way*, try, vex; SEE CONCEPTS *7,19*

get [*v13*] *confuse*
baffle, beat, bewilder, buffalo*, confound, discomfit, disconcert, distress, disturb, embarrass, mystify, nonplus, perplex, perturb, puzzle, stick*, stump, upset; SEE CONCEPT *16*

get across [*v*] *communicate an idea*
bring home*, convey, get through to, impart, make clear, make understood, pass on, put over, transmit; SEE CONCEPT *60*

get ahead [*v*] *excel, succeed*
advance, be successful, climb, do well, flourish, get on, leave behind, make good, outdo, outmaneuver, overtake, progress, prosper, surpass, thrive; SEE CONCEPTS *141,706*

get a kick out of [*v*] *delight in*
be pleased, dig*, enjoy, get a bang out of*, get a charge out of*, get pleasure from, gloat over, take pleasure in; SEE CONCEPTS *32,384*

get along [*v1*] *make progress*
cope, develop, do, fare, flourish, get by*, get on*, make out, manage, muddle through*, prosper, shift, succeed, thrive; SEE CONCEPTS *117,704*

get along [*v2*] *depart*
advance, be off, go, go away, leave, march, move, move off, move on, proceed, progress, push along, take a hike*; SEE CONCEPT *195*

get along [*v3*] *be compatible*
agree, be friendly, get on*, harmonize, hit it off*; SEE CONCEPT *388*

get at [*v1*] *attain*
access, achieve, acquire, arrive, ascertain, gain access, get hold of, reach; SEE CONCEPT *120*

get at [*v2*] *mean, intend*
aim, hint, imply, lead up to, purpose, suggest; SEE CONCEPT *75*

getaway [*n*] *escape*
break, breakout, decampment, flight, lam, slip; SEE CONCEPT *102*

get back [*v1*] *regain*
reclaim, recoup, recover, repossess, retrieve, salvage; SEE CONCEPT *120*

get back [*v2*] *return*
arrive home, come back, come home, reappear, revert, revisit, turn back; SEE CONCEPT *159*

get back at [*v*] *settle a score*
be avenged, get even, pay back, retaliate, revenge, take vengeance; SEE CONCEPTS *14,246*

get by [*v*] *manage, survive*
contrive, cope, do, do well enough, exist, fare, flourish, get along, get on, make ends meet*, make out, muddle through*, prosper, shift, subsist, succeed, thrive; SEE CONCEPT *117*

get down [*v*] *dismount*
alight, bring down, climb down, come down, descend, disembark, get off, lower, step down; SEE CONCEPT *154*

get even [v] *to get revenge*
even the score, get back at, get square, settle the
score; SEE CONCEPTS *126,384*

get in [v] *infiltrate; find a way in*
alight, appear, arrive, blow in*, come, embark,
enter, gain ingress, get inside, include, insert, interpose, land, mount, penetrate, reach, show,
show up, turn up; SEE CONCEPT *159*

get off [v] *depart*
alight, blow*, descend, disembark, dismount, escape, exit, go, go away, leave, light, pull out,
quit, retire, withdraw; SEE CONCEPTS *154,195*

get off someone's back [v] *leave alone*
back off, get off someone's case, let someone
breathe, stop annoying, stop nagging; SEE CON-
CEPTS *30,83*

get on [v1] *mount*
ascend, board, climb, embark, enplane, entrain,
go up, scale; SEE CONCEPTS *159,166*

get on [v2] *cope, progress*
advance, do, do well enough, fare, get along, get
by, make out, manage, muddle through*, prosper, shift, succeed; SEE CONCEPTS *117,704*

get on [v3] *be compatible*
agree, be friendly, concur, get along, harmonize,
hit it off; SEE CONCEPT *388*

get on [v4] *put clothing on*
assume, attire, don, draw on, dress, slip into,
throw on, wear; SEE CONCEPT *167*

get out [v] *escape*
alight, avoid, beat it*, begone, be off, break out,
bug off*, buzz off*, clear out, decamp, depart,
dodge, duck, egress, evacuate, evade, exit, extricate oneself, flee, fly, free oneself, go, hightail*,
kite*, leave, make tracks*, run away, scram*,
shirk, shun, skedaddle*, split, take a hike*, take
off, vacate, vamoose*, withdraw; SEE CONCEPTS
102,195

get over [v] *recover*
come round, get better, mend, overcome, pull
through, recuperate, shake off, survive; SEE CON-
CEPT *35*

get the lead out [v] *hurry*
get a move on, get cracking*, get going, get it
on, hop to it, hustle, look alive, make it snappy,
shake a leg*, snap to it, step on it; SEE CONCEPTS
91,150

get together [v] *gather, accumulate*
assemble, collect, congregate, convene, converge, join, meet, muster, rally, unite; SEE CON-
CEPTS *109,113*

get up [v] *mount; get out of bed*
arise, ascend, awake, awaken, climb, increase,
move up, pile out*, rise, rise and shine*, roll out,
scale, spring out, stand, turn out, uprise, upspring; SEE CONCEPT *154*

geyser [n] *fountain*
gusher, hot spring, jet, spout, thermal spring; SEE
CONCEPTS *514,648*

ghastly [adj] *horrifying, dreadful; pale*
abhorrent, anemic, appalling, ashen, awful,
bloodless, cadaverous, corpselike, deathlike,
dim, disgusting, faint, frightening, frightful, funereal, ghostly, ghoulish, grim, grisly, gruesome,
haggard, hideous, horrendous, horrible, horrid,
livid, loathsome, lurid, macabre, mortuary, nauseating, offensive, pallid, repellent, repulsive,
sepulchral, shocking, sickening, spectral, supernatural, terrible, terrifying, uncanny, unearthly,

unnatural, unpleasant, wan, weak, wraithlike;
SEE CONCEPTS *485,529,537*

ghetto [n] *slum*
public squalor, rundown section of a city; SEE
CONCEPTS *334,485,570*

ghetto box [n] *large portable stereo*
boom box, ghetto blaster, radio; SEE CONCEPT
279

ghost [n] *spirit of the dead*
apparition, appearance, banshee, daemon,
demon, devil, eidolon, ethereal being, haunt, incorporeal being, kelpie, manes, phantasm, phantom, poltergeist, revenant, shade, shadow, soul,
specter, spook, vampire, vision, visitor, wraith,
zombie; SEE CONCEPT *370*

ghostly [adj] *spooky*
apparitional, cadaverous, corpselike, deathlike,
divine, eerie, eidolic, ghastly, haunted, holy, illusory, insubstantial, pale, phantasmal, phantom,
scary, shadowy, spectral, spiritual, supernatural,
uncanny, unearthly, vampiric, wan, weird,
wraithlike, wraithy; SEE CONCEPTS *485,537*

ghoul [n] *evil demon*
bogeyman, devil, evil spirit, fiend, grave robber,
monster; SEE CONCEPTS *370,412*

ghoulish [adj] *hideous, scary*
cruel, demonic, devilish, diabolical, eerie,
fiendish, frightening, ghastly, grim, grisly, gruesome, horrible, macabre, monstrous, morbid, revolting, spine-chilling, spooky, terrifying; SEE
CONCEPTS *529,548*

GI [n] *government issue; soldier*
army personnel, doughboy, enlisted person, GI
Joe, serviceperson; SEE CONCEPT *358*

giant [adj] *very large*
big, blimp*, brobdingnagian*, colossal, cyclopean, elephantine*, enormous, gargantuan, gigantic, gross*, Herculean*, huge, hulking,
humongous*, immense, jumbo*, mammoth,
monstrous*, mountainous, prodigious, super-
duper*, titanic, vast, whale of a*, whaling*; SEE
CONCEPTS *491,773,779,781*

giant [n] *extremely large person*
behemoth, bulk, colossus, cyclops, elephant*,
goliath, Hercules*, hulk, jumbo*, leviathan,
mammoth, monster*, mountain*, ogre, poly-
pheme, titan, whale*, whopper*; SEE CONCEPT
424

gibberish [n] *nonsense talk*
babble, balderdash*, blah-blah*, blather, chatter,
claptrap*, double talk*, drivel, gobbledygook*,
hocus-pocus*, jabber*, jargon, mumbo jumbo*,
palaver*, prattle, scat*, twaddle*, yammer*; SEE
CONCEPT *278*

gibe [n] *ridicule*
comeback, cutting remark, derision, dig*,
dump*, jab, jeer, joke, mockery, parting shot*,
put-down*, rank-out*, sarcasm, scoffing, slam*,
sneer, swipe, taunt; SEE CONCEPT *278*

gibe [v] *ridicule*
deride, dis*, disrespect, flout, jeer, make fun of*,
mock, poke fun at*, scoff, scorn, sneer, taunt;
SEE CONCEPTS *52,54*

giddy [adj] *silly, impulsive*
bemused, brainless, bubbleheaded*, capricious,
careless, changeable, changeful, ditzy*, dizzy,
empty-headed*, erratic, fickle, flighty*, flustered,
frivolous, gaga*, heedless, inconstant, irresolute,
irresponsible, lightheaded*, punchy*, reckless,
reeling, scatterbrained*, skittish*, slaphappy*,

ge
gi

swimming*, thoughtless, unbalanced, unsettled, unstable, unsteady, vacillating, volatile, whimsical, whirling, wild, woozy*; SEE CONCEPTS *314,401*

gift [*n1*] *something given freely, for no recompense*
allowance, alms, award, benefaction, benefit, bequest, bestowal, bonus, boon, bounty, charity, contribution, courtesy, dispensation, donation, endowment, fairing, favor, giveaway, goodie, grant, gratuity, hand, hand-me-down*, handout, honorarium, lagniappe, largesse, legacy, libation, oblation, offering, offertory, philanthropy, pittance, premium, present, presentation, provision, ration, relief, remembrance, remittance, reward, souvenir, subscription, subsidy, tip, token, tribute, write-off*; SEE CONCEPT *337*

gift [*n2*] *talent, aptitude*
ability, accomplishment, acquirement, aptness, attainment, attribute, bent, capability, capacity, endowment, faculty, flair, forte, genius, head*, instinct, knack, leaning, nose*, numen, power, propensity, set, specialty, turn; SEE CONCEPTS *409,630,706*

gifted [*adj*] *talented, intelligent*
able, accomplished, adroit, brilliant, capable, class act, clever, expert, got it*, have on the ball*, have smarts*, have the goods*, hot*, hotshot, ingenious, mad, masterly, phenomenal, shining at*, skilled, smart; SEE CONCEPTS *402,527,528*

gig [*n*] *show*
appearance, concert, employment, engagement, job, performance, recital; SEE CONCEPT *706*

gigantic [*adj*] *very large*
blimp, brobdingnagian*, colossal, cyclopean*, elephantine, enormous, gargantuan, giant, gross*, Herculean*, huge, immense, jumbo*, mammoth, massive, Moby*, monster, monstrous, prodigious, stupendous, super-colossal*, titan, tremendous, vast, whopping*; SEE CONCEPTS *491,773,779,781*

giggle [*n/v*] *snickering laugh*
cackle, chortle, chuckle, guffaw*, hee-haw*, snicker, snigger, teehee*, titter, twitter; SEE CONCEPT *77*

gigolo [*n*] *male escort*
Casanova, Don Juan, inamorato, ladies' man, lady-killer, Lothario, lover, male prostitute, seducer; SEE CONCEPT *423*

gild [*v*] *embellish, decorate*
adorn, aureate, aurify, beautify, bedeck, begild, brighten, coat, deck, dress up, embroider, engild, enhance, enrich, garnish, glitter, grace, ornament, overlay, paint, plate, tinsel, varnish, wash, whitewash*; SEE CONCEPTS *172,177,202*

gimcrack [*n*] *gewgaw*
bagatelle, bauble, curio, doodad*, knickknack, novelty, souvenir, trinket; SEE CONCEPT *446*

gimmick [*n*] *contrived object; scheme*
aid, apparatus, artifice, catch, concern, counterfeit, deceit, device, dodge*, fake, feint, fixture, fun, gadget, gambit, game, gizmo*, imposture, instrument, jest, maneuver, means, method, ploy, ruse, secret, shift, sport, stratagem, stunt, trick, widget*, wile; SEE CONCEPTS *59,260,660*

gingerly [*adj*] *careful*
calculating, cautious, chary, circumspect, considerate, dainty, delicate, discreet, fastidious, guarded, hesitant, reluctant, safe, squeamish, suspicious, timid, wary; SEE CONCEPTS *542,550*

gingerly [*adv*] *carefully*
cautiously, charily, circumspectly, daintily, delicately, discreetly, fastidiously, guardedly, hesitantly, reluctantly, safely, squeamishly, suspiciously, timidly, warily; SEE CONCEPTS *542,550*

gin mill [*n*] *barroom*
alehouse, beer garden, cocktail lounge, drinkery, pub, public house, saloon, taproom, tavern, watering hole; SEE CONCEPTS *439,448,449*

gird [*v1*] *encircle; strengthen*
band, belt, bind, block, blockade, bolster, brace, buttress, cincture, circle, enclose, encompass, enfold, environ, fasten, fortify, girdle, hem in*, make ready, pen, prepare, ready, reinforce, ring, round, secure, steel, support, surround; SEE CONCEPTS *250,758*

gird [*v2*] *make fun of*
deride, flout, fun at, gibe, jeer, jest, mock, poke, quip, ridicule, scoff, scorn, sneer, taunt; SEE CONCEPTS *52,54*

girder [*n*] *main support beam*
I-beam, joist, rafter, tiebeam, truss; SEE CONCEPTS *471,479*

girdle [*n*] *corset*
band, belt, sash, undergarment, underwear, waistband; SEE CONCEPT *451*

girl [*n*] *young female person*
adolescent, damsel, daughter, lady, lassie, mademoiselle, Ms, schoolgirl, she, teenager, young lady, young woman; SEE CONCEPTS *415,424*

girlfriend [*n*] *female acquaintance or romantic companion*
companion, confidante, date, financee, flame*, friend, intimate, partner, soul mate, steady, sweetheart; SEE CONCEPTS *415,423*

gist [*n*] *meaning, essence*
basis, bearing, bottom line*, burden, core, drift, force, heart, idea, import, kernel*, keynote, marrow, matter, meat*, name of the game*, nature of the beast*, nitty gritty*, nuts and bolts*, pith*, point, punch line, quintessence, score, sense, short, significance, soul, spirit, stuff*, subject, substance, summary, tenor, theme, thrust, topic, upshot*; SEE CONCEPT *682*

give [*v1*] *contribute, supply, transfer*
accord, administer, allow, ante up, award, bequeath, bestow, cede, come across, commit, confer, consign, convey, deed, deliver, dish out*, dispense, dispose of, dole out, donate, endow, entrust, fork over*, furnish, gift, grant, hand down, hand out, hand over, heap upon, lavish upon, lay upon, lease, let have, make over*, parcel out, part with, pass down, pass out, permit, pony up*, present, provide, relinquish, remit, sell, shell out*, subsidize, throw in, tip, transmit, turn over, vouchsafe, will; SEE CONCEPTS *108,223,243*

give [*v2*] *communicate*
air, announce, be a source of, broadcast, carry, deliver, emit, express, furnish, impart, issue, notify, present, pronounce, publish, put, read, render, state, supply, transfer, transmit, utter, vent, ventilate; SEE CONCEPTS *60,266*

give [*v3*] *demonstrate, proffer*
administer, bestow, confer, dispense, display, evidence, extend, furnish, hold out, indicate, issue, manifest, minister, offer, pose, present, produce,

provide, put on, render, return, set forth, show, tender, yield; SEE CONCEPTS *97,118*

give [*v4*] *yield, collapse*
allow, bend, bow to, break, cave, cede, concede, contract, crumble, crumple, devote, fail, fall, flex, fold, fold up, give way, go, grant, hand over, lend, open, recede, relax, relent, relinquish, retire, retreat, sag, shrink, sink, slacken, surrender, weaken; SEE CONCEPTS *13,469*

give [*v5*] *perform action*
address, apply, bend, buckle down, cause, devote, direct, do, engender, lead, make, occasion, produce, throw, turn; SEE CONCEPT *100*

give-and-take [*n*] *compromise*
adaptability, cooperation, exchange, reciprocity, swap, trade-off; SEE CONCEPTS *230,684*

give away [*v1*] *reveal*
betray, blab*, disclose, discover, divulge, expose, inform, leak, let out, let slip, mouth*, spill, tell, uncover; SEE CONCEPT *60*

give away [*v2*] *unselfishly transfer*
award, bestow, devote, donate, hand out, present; SEE CONCEPT *108*

give in/give up [*v*] *admit defeat*
abandon, back down*, bail out*, bow out*, buckle under*, capitulate, cave in*, cease, cede, chicken out*, collapse, comply, concede, cry uncle*, cut out, desist, despair, drop, drop like a hot potato*, fold, forswear, hand over, leave off, pull out, quit, relinquish, resign, stop, submit, surrender, take the oath*, throw in the towel*, waive, walk out on, wash one's hands of*, yield; SEE CONCEPTS *8,45,119,385*

given to [*adj*] *likely to*
accustomed, addicted, apt, disposed, habituated, inclined, in the habit of, inured, liable, obsessed, prone; SEE CONCEPT *542*

give off/give out [*v*] *discharge*
beam, belch, effuse, emanate, emit, exhale, exude, flow, give forth, issue, pour, produce, radiate, release, send out, smell of, throw out, vent, void; SEE CONCEPT *179*

give the cold shoulder [*v*] *snub*
act cool*, brush off*, disregard, eject, ignore, make unwelcome, neglect, ostracize, shun, turn up one's nose*, upstage; SEE CONCEPT *30*

gizmo [*n*] *gadget*
appliance, contraption, contrivance, device, doohickey, instrument, machine, mechanical device, thingamabob, thingamajig, tool, whatchamacallit, widget; SEE CONCEPTS *463,499*

glacial [*adj1*] *extremely cold*
antarctic, arctic, biting, bitter, chill, chilly, cool, freezing, frigid, frosty, frozen, gelid, icy, nippy, piercing, polar, raw, wintry; SEE CONCEPT *605*

glacial [*adj2*] *unfriendly*
aloof, antagonistic, chill, cold, cool, distant, emotionless, frigid, hostile, icy, inaccessible, indifferent, inimical, remote, reserved, seclusive, standoffish, unapproachable, unemotional, withdrawn; SEE CONCEPTS *401,404*

glacier [*n*] *mountain of ice, snow*
berg, floe, glacial mass, iceberg, icecap, ice field, ice floe, snow slide; SEE CONCEPT *509*

glad [*adj*] *happy, delightful*
animated, beaming, beautiful, blithesome, bright, can't complain*, cheerful, cheering, cheery, contented, exhilarated, felicitous, floating on air*, gay, genial, gleeful, gratified, gratifying, hilarious, jocund, jovial, joyful, joyous, lighthearted,

merry, mirthful, overjoyed, pleasant, pleased, pleased as punch*, pleasing, radiant, rejoicing, sparkling, tickled, tickled pink*, tickled to death*, up, willing; SEE CONCEPTS *403,529*

gladden [*v*] *please*
brighten, cheer, delight, elate, hearten, make happy, warm; SEE CONCEPTS *7,22*

gladiator [*n*] *combatant*
boxer, contender, fighter; SEE CONCEPTS *358,366,412*

gladly [*adv*] *happily*
acquiescently, ardently, beatifically, blissfully, blithely, cheerfully, cheerily, contentedly, cordially, delightedly, delightfully, ecstatically, enchantedly, enthusiastically, felicitously, freely, gaily, genially, gleefully, gratefully, heartily, jocundly, jovially, joyfully, joyously, lovingly, merrily, paradisiacally, passionately, pleasantly, pleasingly, pleasurably, rapturously, readily, sweetly, warmly, willingly, with good grace, with pleasure, with relish, zealously, zestfully; SEE CONCEPTS *403,538,542*

gladness [*n*] *happiness*
animation, blitheness, cheer, cheerfulness, delight, felicity, gaiety, glee, high spirits*, hilarity, jollity, joy, joyousness, mirth, pleasure; SEE CONCEPT *410*

glamorous [*adj*] *sophisticated in style*
alluring, attractive, bewitching, captivating, charismatic, charming, classy, dazzling, drop-dead gorgeous*, elegant, enchanting, entrancing, exciting, fascinating, flashy, foxy*, glittering, glossy, looking like a million*, lovely, magnetic, nifty, prestigious, righteous, seductive, siren, smart; SEE CONCEPTS *579,589*

glamour [*n*] *sophisticated style*
allure, allurement, animal magnetism, appeal, attraction, beauty, bewitchment, charisma, charm, color, enchantment, fascination, interest, magnetism, prestige, ravishment, razzle-dazzle*, romance, star quality; SEE CONCEPTS *655,718*

glance [*n1*] *brief look*
eye*, eyeball*, flash*, fleeting look, gander, glimpse, lamp*, look, look-see*, peek, peep, quick look, sight, slant*, squint, swivel*, view; SEE CONCEPT *623*

glance [*n2*] *reflection of light*
coruscation, flash, gleam, glimmer, glint, glisten, shimmer, sparkle, twinkle; SEE CONCEPTS *624,628*

glance [*v1*] *look at briefly*
browse, check out, dip into*, flash*, flip through, gaze, get a load of*, glimpse, leaf through, peek, peep, peer, riffle through*, run over, run through, scan, see, skim through*, take a gander*, take in, thumb through*, view; SEE CONCEPT *623*

glance [*v2*] *reflect light*
coruscate, flash, gleam, glimmer, glint, glisten, glitter, shimmer, shine, sparkle, twinkle; SEE CONCEPT *624*

glance [*v3*] *ricochet, hit off of something*
bounce, brush, careen, carom, contact, dart, graze, kiss*, rebound, scrape, shave*, sideswipe, skim, skip, slant, slide, strike, touch; SEE CONCEPT *189*

glare [*n1*] *very bright light, shine*
blaze, blinding light, brilliance, dazzle, flame, flare, glow; SEE CONCEPT *628*

glare [*n2*] *dirty look*
angry stare, bad eye*, black look*, evil eye*,

gi
gl

frown, glower, lower, scowl; SEE CONCEPTS *623,716*

glare [*v1*] *give a dirty look*
bore, do a slow burn*, fix, frown, gape, gawk, gaze, glower, look daggers*, lower, menace, peer, pierce, scowl, stare, stare angrily*, stare icily*, wither; SEE CONCEPT *623*

glare [*v2*] *shine very brightly*
beam, blare, blaze, blind, blur, daze, dazzle, flame, flare, glaze, glow, radiate; SEE CONCEPT *624*

glaring [*adj1*] *obvious, unconcealed*
audacious, blatant, brazen, capital, conspicuous, crying, egregious, evident, excessive, extreme, flagrant, gross, inordinate, manifest, noticeable, obtrusive, open, outrageous, outstanding, overt, patent, protrusive, rank, visible; SEE CONCEPTS *576,619*

glaring [*adj2*] *bright, dazzling; flashy*
blatant, blazing, blinding, brazen, chintzy, florid, garish, gaudy, glowing, loud, meretricious, shining, tawdry; SEE CONCEPTS *589,617*

glass [*n1*] *object that reflects an image*
looking glass, mirror, reflector, seeing glass; SEE CONCEPTS *260,470*

glass [*n2*] *object used for drinking liquids*
beaker, bottle, chalice, cup, decanter, goblet, highball, jar, jigger, jug, mug, pilsener, pony, snifter, tumbler; SEE CONCEPT *494*

glasses [*n*] *object worn to correct vision*
bifocals, blinkers*, cheaters*, contact lenses, eyeglasses, four eyes*, frames, goggles, lorgnette, pince-nez, rims*, shades*, specs*, spectacles, trifocals; SEE CONCEPT *446*

glassy [*adj1*] *polished, smooth*
burnished, clear, glazed, glazy, glossy, hyaline, hyaloid, icy, lustrous, shiny, sleek, slick, slippery, transparent, vitreous, vitric; SEE CONCEPT *606*

glassy [*adj2*] *expressionless, especially referring to eyes*
blank, cold, dazed, dull, empty, fixed, glazed, lifeless, stupid, vacant; SEE CONCEPTS *406,619*

glaze [*n*] *varnish, lacquer*
coat, enamel, finish, glint, gloss, luster, patina, polish, sheen, shine; SEE CONCEPTS *259,475*

glaze [*v*] *varnish, lacquer*
buff, burnish, coat, cover, enamel, furbish, glance, glass, gloss, incrust, make lustrous, make vitreous, overlay, polish, rub, shine, vitrify; SEE CONCEPTS *172,202,215*

gleam [*n*] *brightness, sparkle*
beam, brilliance, coruscation, flash, flicker, glance, glim, glimmer, glint, glitz, gloss, glow, luster, ray, scintillation, sheen, shimmer, splendor, twinkle; SEE CONCEPTS *620,624*

gleam [*v*] *sparkle*
beam, burn, coruscate, flare, flash, glance, glimmer, glint, glisten, glister, glitter, glow, radiate, scintillate, shimmer, shine, twinkle; SEE CONCEPTS *620,624*

glean [*v*] *pick out, collect*
accumulate, amass, ascertain, conclude, cull, deduce, extract, garner, gather, harvest, learn, pick, reap, select, sift, winnow; SEE CONCEPTS *31,135*

glee [*n*] *extreme happiness*
blitheness, cheerfulness, delectation, delight, elation, enjoyment, exhilaration, exuberance, exultation, fun, gaiety, gladness, hilarity, jocularity, jollity, joviality, joy, joyfulness, joyousness, liveliness, merriment, mirth, pleasure, sprightliness, triumph, verve; SEE CONCEPT *410*

gleeful [*adj*] *very happy*
blithe, blithesome, boon, cheerful, delighted, elated, exalted, exuberant, exultant, frolicsome, gay, gratified, hilarious, jocund, jolly, jovial, joyful, joyous, jubilant, lighthearted, merry, mirthful, overjoyed, pleased, triumphant; SEE CONCEPT *403*

glen [*n*] *valley*
canyon, combe, dale, dell, glade, gorge, vale; SEE CONCEPT *509*

glib [*adj*] *slick, smooth-talking*
artful, articulate, easy, eloquent, facile, fast-talking*, flip, fluent, garrulous, hot-air*, insincere, loquacious, plausible, quick, ready, silver-tongued*, slippery*, smooth operator*, smooth-spoken*, smooth-tongued*, suave, talkative, urbane, vocal, vocative, voluble; SEE CONCEPTS *267,404*

glide [*v*] *move smoothly and quickly on a surface*
coast, decline, descend, drift, flit, float, flow, fly, glissade, roll, run, sail, scud, shoot, skate, skim, skip, skirr, slide, slink, slip, slither, smooth along, soar, spiral, stream, trip, waft, wing; SEE CONCEPT *150*

glimmer [*n*] *flash, sparkle*
blink, coruscation, flicker, glance, gleam, glint, glow, grain, hint, inkling, ray, scintillation, shimmer, suggestion, trace, twinkle; SEE CONCEPTS *624,831*

glimmer [*v*] *sparkle*
blink, coruscate, fade, flash, flicker, glance, gleam, glint, glisten, glister, glitter, glow, scintillate, shimmer, shine, twinkle; SEE CONCEPT *624*

glimpse [*n*] *brief look*
eye, eyeball*, flash*, gander*, glance, glom*, gun*, impression, lamp*, look-see*, peek, peep, quick look, sight, sighting, slant, squint, swivel*; SEE CONCEPT *623*

glimpse [*v*] *look briefly*
catch sight of, check out, descry, espy, eye, flash, get a load of*, get an eyeful*, peek, sight, spot, spy, take a gander*, take in*, view; SEE CONCEPT *623*

glint [*n*] *sparkle*
flash, glance, gleam, glimmer, glitter, look, shine, trace, twinkle; SEE CONCEPTS *411,624,628*

glisten [*v*] *shimmer*
coruscate, flash, flicker, glance, glare, gleam, glimmer, glint, glister, glitter, glow, scintillate, shine, sparkle, twinkle; SEE CONCEPT *624*

glitch [*n*] *error*
bug*, defect, flaw, hitch, malfunction, misfire, mishap, problem, setback, snafu, snag, something wrong; SEE CONCEPTS *101,230,674,699*

glitter [*n*] *brilliance, sparkle*
beam, brightness, coruscation, display, flash, gaudiness, glamour, glare, gleam, glint, glisten, glister, glitz, luster, pageantry, radiance, scintillation, sheen, shimmer, shine, show, showiness, splendor, tinsel, twinkle, zap*; SEE CONCEPTS *620,655*

glitter [*v*] *sparkle*
coruscate, flash, glance, glare, gleam, glimmer, glint, glisten, glister, glow, scintillate, shimmer, shine, spangle, twinkle; SEE CONCEPT *624*

glitz [*n*] *showiness*
appeal, flashiness, gaudiness, glamour, ostentation, speciousness; SEE CONCEPT *261*

gloat [*v*] *exclaim triumph*
celebrate, crow*, exult, glory, rejoice, relish, rub it in*, triumph, vaunt, whoop*; SEE CONCEPT *49*

glob [*n*] *thick lump*
batch, blob, chunk, clump, gob, hunk, mass, wad; SEE CONCEPTS *432,470,471*

global [*adj*] *worldwide, all-encompassing*
all-around, all-inclusive, all-out, blanket, catholic, comprehensive, cosmic, cosmopolitan, earthly, ecumenical, encyclopedic, exhaustive, general, grand, international, mundane, overall, pandemic, planetary, spherical, sweeping, thorough, total, unbounded, universal, unlimited, world; SEE CONCEPTS *536,772*

globe [*n*] *Earth, sphere*
apple*, ball, balloon*, big blue marble*, map, orb, planet, rondure, round, spheroid, terrene, world; SEE CONCEPTS *436,511*

gloom [*n1*] *melancholy, depression*
anguish, bitterness, blue devils*, blue funk*, blues*, catatonia, chagrin, cheerlessness, dejection, desolation, despair, despondency, disconsolateness, discouragement, dismals, distress, doldrums, dolor, downheartedness, dullness, dumps*, foreboding, grief, heaviness, heavyheartedness, horror, low spirits*, malaise, misery, misgiving, mopes, morbidity, mourning, oppression, pensiveness, pessimism, sadness, saturninity, sorrow, unhappiness, vexation, weariness, woe; SEE CONCEPT *410*

gloom [*n2*] *darkness, blackness*
bleakness, cloud, cloudiness, dimness, dullness, dusk, duskiness, gloominess, murk, murkiness, obscurity, shade, shadow, twilight; SEE CONCEPTS *620,622,810*

gloomy [*adj1*] *dark, black*
bleak, caliginous, cheerless, clouded, cloudy, crepuscular, desolate, dim, dismal, dreary, dull, dusky, forlorn, funereal, lightless, murky, obscure, overcast, overclouded, sepulchral, shadowy, somber, tenebrous, unilluminated, unlit, wintry; SEE CONCEPTS *525,617,618*

gloomy [*adj2*] *feeling down, blue*
blue funk*, broody, chapfallen, cheerless, crabbed*, crestfallen, dejected, depressed, desolate, despondent, disconsolate, dismal, dispirited, dour, downcast, downhearted, down in the dumps*, down in the mouth*, dragged, forlorn, glum, in low spirits*, in the dumps*, joyless, low, melancholy, mirthless, miserable, moody, moping, mopish, morose, mournful, oppressed, pessimistic, sad, saturnine, solemn, sulky, sullen, surly, ugly, unhappy, weary, woebegone, woeful; SEE CONCEPT *403*

gloomy [*adj3*] *sad, depressing*
acheronian, acherontic, bad, black, bleak, cheerless, cold, comfortless, depressive, desolate, disconsolate, discouraging, disheartening, dismal, dispiriting, drab, dreary, dull, dusky, funereal, joyless, lugubrious, morose, oppressive, saddening, somber, tenebrific; SEE CONCEPTS *537,548*

glorify [*v1*] *praise*
acclaim, bless, boost, build up, celebrate, commend, cry up, eulogize, exalt, extol, hike, honor, hymn, laud, lionize, magnify, panegyrize, put on a pedestal*, put up, sing the praises of*; SEE CONCEPT *69*

glorify [*v2*] *adore, idolize*
adorn, aggrandize, apotheosize, augment, beatify, bless, canonize, deify, dignify, distinguish,

elevate, enhance, ennoble, enshrine, erect, exalt, halo*, honor, illuminate, immortalize, lift up, magnify, pay homage to, raise, revere, sanctify, transfigure, uprear, venerate, worship; SEE CONCEPT *12*

glorious [*adj*] *adored, idolized; divine*
august, beautiful, bright, brilliant, celebrated, dazzling, delightful, distinguished, effulgent, elevated, eminent, enjoyable, esteemed, exalted, excellent, famed, famous, fine, gorgeous, grand, gratifying, great, heavenly, heroic, honored, illustrious, immortal, magnificent, majestic, marvelous, memorable, noble, notable, noted, pleasurable, preeminent, radiant, remarkable, renowned, resplendent, shining, splendid, sublime, superb, time-honored, triumphant, venerable, well-known, wonderful; SEE CONCEPTS *568,574,579*

glory [*n1*] *fame, importance*
celebrity, dignity, distinction, eminence, exaltation, grandeur, greatness, honor, illustriousness, immortality, kudos, magnificence, majesty, nobility, praise, prestige, renown, reputation, splendor, sublimity, triumph; SEE CONCEPTS *388,668*

glory [*n2*] *great beauty*
brightness, brilliance, effulgence, fineness, gorgeousness, grandeur, luster, magnificence, majesty, pageantry, pomp, preciousness, radiance, resplendence, richness, splendor, sublimity, sumptuousness; SEE CONCEPTS *673,718*

glory [*v*] *boast, exult*
crow, gloat, jubilate, pride oneself, relish, revel, take delight, triumph; SEE CONCEPTS *12,49*

gloss [*n1*] *shine, sheen*
appearance, brightness, brilliance, burnish, facade, finish, front, glaze, gleam, glint, glossiness, luster, polish, shimmer, silkiness, sleekness, slickness, surface, varnish, veneer; SEE CONCEPTS *611,620*

gloss [*n2*] *definition*
annotation, comment, commentary, elucidation, explanation, footnote, interpretation, note, translation; SEE CONCEPT *268*

gloss [*v1*] *make shiny*
buff, burnish, finish, furbish, glance, glaze, lacquer, polish, rub, shine, varnish, veneer; SEE CONCEPTS *202,215*

gloss [*v2*] *conceal truth*
belie, camouflage, cover up, deacon, disguise, doctor, explain, extenuate, falsify, hide, justify, mask, misrepresent, palliate, rationalize, smooth over, soft-pedal, sugarcoat*, varnish, veil, veneer, white, whiten, whitewash*; SEE CONCEPTS *49,63*

gloss [*v3*] *define*
annotate, comment, construe, elucidate, explain, interpret, justify, translate; SEE CONCEPT *57*

glossary [*n*] *word list*
dictionary, lexicon, vocabulary, word index; SEE CONCEPT *280*

glossy [*adj*] *shiny*
bright, brilliant, burnished, glassy, glazed, gleaming, glistening, lustrous, polished, reflecting, silken, silky, sleek, slick, smooth; SEE CONCEPTS *606,617*

glove [*n*] *hand covering for warmth, protection*
gage, gauntlet, mitt, mitten, muff; SEE CONCEPT *451*

glow [*n*] *burning, brightness*
afterglow, bloom, blossom, blush, brilliance, ef-

gl
gl

fulgence, flush, glare, gleam, glimmer, glitter, gusto, heat, incandescence, intensity, lambency, light, luminosity, passion, phosphorescence, radiance, ray, splendor, vividness, warmth; SEE CONCEPTS *610,620,622,673*

glow [v] *burn, radiate*
be suffused, blare, blaze, blush, brighten, color, crimson, fill, flame, flare, flush, gleam, glimmer, glisten, glitter, ignite, kindle, light, mantle, pink, pinken, redden, rose, rouge, shine, smolder, thrill, tingle, twinkle; SEE CONCEPTS *249,469,624*

glower [v] *frown*
glare, gloom, look, look daggers*, lower, scowl, stare, sulk, watch; SEE CONCEPT *623*

glowing [adj1] *burning, bright*
aglow, beaming, flaming, florid, flush, flushed, gleaming, lambent, luminous, lustrous, phosphorescent, red, rich, rubicund, ruddy, sanguine, suffused, vibrant, vivid, warm; SEE CONCEPTS *617,618*

glowing [adj2] *very happy, enthusiastic*
adulatory, ardent, avid, blazing, burning, complimentary, desirous, eager, ecstatic, eulogistic, fervent, fervid, fierce, fiery, flaming, heated, hot-blooded, impassioned, keen, laudatory, panegyrical, passionate, rave, rhapsodic, zealous; SEE CONCEPTS *267,401*

glue [n] *adhesive*
cement, gum, gunk*, mucilage, paste, plaster, spit*, stickum*; SEE CONCEPT *475*

glum [adj] *sullen*
blue, bummed out, dejected, depressed, dismal, dispirited, down, gloomy, low, melancholy, morose, sad, sulky; SEE CONCEPT *403*

glut [n] *overabundance*
excess, nimiety, oversupply, plenitude, saturation, superfluity, surfeit, surplus, too much*; SEE CONCEPTS *740,787*

glut [v] *choke; oversupply*
burden, clog, cloy, congest, cram, deluge, devour, feast, fill, flood, gorge, hog*, inundate, jade, load, make a pig of*, overfeed, overload, overstock, overwhelm, pack*, pall, raven, sate, satiate, saturate, stuff, surfeit, wolf*; SEE CONCEPTS *140,169,209,740*

glutton [n] *person who overeats*
epicure, gorger*, gormandizer, gourmand, hefty eater, hog*, pig*, sensualist, stuffer*; SEE CONCEPT *412*

gluttonous [adj] *voracious*
covetous, devouring, edacious, gorging, gourmandizing, greedy, gross, hoggish*, insatiable, never full, omnivorous, piggish*, piggy*, prodigious, rapacious, ravening, ravenous, sating, starved, starving, unquenchable, wolfish*; SEE CONCEPTS *20,401*

gnarled [adj] *knotted*
bent, contorted, crooked, deformed, distorted, gnarly, knurled, leathery, out of shape, rough, rugged, tortured, twisted, weather-beaten, wrinkled; SEE CONCEPTS *485,486*

gnarly [adj] *cool, excellent*
boss*, finest, great, hairy*, keen, magnificent, marvelous, neat, nifty, sensational, superb, swell, wonderful; SEE CONCEPT *574*

gnash [v] *grind*
clamp, crush, grate, grit, rub; SEE CONCEPTS *186,204*

gnaw [v1] *bite, chew*
champ, chaw, chomp, consume, corrode, crunch, devour, eat, eat away, erode, gum, masticate, munch, nibble, wear; SEE CONCEPTS *169,185*

gnaw [v2] *be bothered, worried about*
annoy, bedevil, beleague, distress, eat at*, fret, harass, harry, haunt, irritate, nag, pester, plague, prey on one's mind*, rankle, tease, trouble, wear down; SEE CONCEPTS *17,34*

gnome [n] *troll*
elf, fairy; SEE CONCEPT *424*

go [n1] *spirit, vitality*
activity, animation, bang, birr*, drive, energy, force, get-up-and-go*, hardihood, life, moxie*, oomph*, pep, potency, push, snap*, starch*, tuck*, verve, vigor, vivacity, zest; SEE CONCEPT *411*

go [n2] *try, attempt*
bid, crack, effort, essay, fling, pop, shot, slap, stab, turn, whack, whirl; SEE CONCEPTS *87,677*

go [v1] *advance, proceed physically*
abscond, approach, beat it*, bug out*, cruise, decamp, depart, escape, exit, fare, flee, fly, get away, get going*, get lost, get off*, hie, hightail*, hit the road*, journey, lam, leave, light out*, make a break for it*, make for*, make one's way*, mosey*, move, move out, near, pass, progress, pull out, push off, push on, quit, repair, retire, run along, run away, set off, shove off*, skip out*, split*, take a hike*, take a powder*, take flight, take leave*, take off*, travel, vamoose*, wend, withdraw; SEE CONCEPTS *159,195*

go [v2] *operate, function*
act, carry on, click*, continue, flourish, maintain, make out, move, pan out*, perform, persist, prosper, run, score, succeed, thrive, work; SEE CONCEPTS *4,239*

go [v3] *span, stretch*
connect, cover, extend, fit, give access, lead, make, range, reach, run, spread, vary; SEE CONCEPTS *651,756*

go [v4] *contribute, work towards an end*
avail, befall, chance, come, concur, conduce, develop, eventuate, fall out, fare, happen, incline, lead to, occur, persevere, persist, proceed, result, serve, tend, transpire, turn, turn out, wax*, work out; SEE CONCEPTS *87,704*

go [v5] *agree, harmonize*
accord, be adapted for, be designed for, belong, blend, chime, complement, conform, correspond, dovetail*, enjoy, fit, jibe*, like, match, mesh, relish, set, square, suit; SEE CONCEPTS *8,664,714*

go [v6] *die, collapse*
bend, break, cave, conclude, consume, crumble, decease, decline, demise, depart, deplete, devour, dissipate, drop, exhaust, expend, expire, fail, finish, fold up, fritter, give, pass away*, pass on*, perish, run through*, spend, squander, succumb, terminate, use up, waste, weaken, worsen, yield; SEE CONCEPTS *105,698,699*

go [v7] *elapse*
be spent, expire, flow, lapse, pass, pass away, slip away, transpire, waste away; SEE CONCEPT *804*

go [v8] *endure*
abide, allow, bear, brook, consent to, let, permit, put up with*, stand, stomach*, suffer, swallow*, take, tolerate; SEE CONCEPT *23*

go about [v] *undertake*
approach, be employed, begin, devote oneself to,

engage in, get busy with, occupy oneself with, set about, tackle, work at; SEE CONCEPT *100*

goad [*n*] *stimulus*
catalyst, compulsion, desire, drive, impetus, impulse, impulsion, incentive, incitation, incitement, irritation, lash, lust, motivation, passion, pressure, prod, spur, urge, whip, zeal; SEE CONCEPTS *20,661*

goad [*v*] *egg on, incite*
animate, annoy, arouse, bully, coerce, drive, encourage, excite, exhort, fire up*, force, goose*, harass, hound, impel, inspirit, instigate, irritate, key up*, lash, move, needle*, press, prick*, prod, prompt, propel, provoke, push, put up to*, rowel, sic*, sound, spark*, spur, stimulate, sting*, tease, thrust, trigger, turn on*, urge, whip*, work up, worry; SEE CONCEPTS *14,68*

go-ahead [*adj*] *progressive*
ambitious, enterprising, entrepreneurial, go-getting*, gumptious*, pioneering, up-and-coming*; SEE CONCEPTS *538,542*

go-ahead [*n*] *authorization*
assent, consent, green light*, leave, okay, permission; SEE CONCEPT *685*

go ahead [*v*] *proceed*
advance, begin, continue, dash ahead, edge forward, go forward, go on, move on, progress, shoot ahead; SEE CONCEPTS *149,159,704*

goal [*n*] *aim, purpose of an action*
ambition, design, destination, duty, end, ground zero*, intent, intention, limit, mark, mission, object, objective, target, use, zero*; SEE CONCEPT *659*

go along/go along with [*v*] *agree, cooperate*
accompany, acquiesce, act jointly, assent, collaborate, concur, conspire, follow, share in, work together; SEE CONCEPTS *8,18*

goat [*n1*] *hollow-horned mammal*
billy, buck, kid; SEE CONCEPTS *394,400*

go back/go back on [*v*] *break promise; change one's mind*
abandon, betray, be unfaithful, desert, forsake, leave in the lurch*, renege, repudiate, retract, return, revert, run out on; SEE CONCEPTS *13,71*

go back to square one [*v*] *start all over*
begin again, go back to the drawing board, make a fresh start, make a new beginning, start from scratch, wipe the slate clean; SEE CONCEPTS *221,241*

gobble [*v*] *eat hurriedly*
cram*, devour, gorge, gulp*, guzzle, ingurgitate, scarf*, stuff*, suck up*, swallow, wolf*; SEE CONCEPT *169*

gobbledygook [*n*] *jargon*
balderdash*, baloney*, bosh, bull*, bunk*, cant, drivel, gibberish, hooey*, rigmarole, rubbish*; SEE CONCEPTS *275,276*

go-between [*n*] *person acting as an agent*
arbitrator, attorney, broker, dealer, delegate, deputy, emissary, entrepreneur, envoy, factor, interagent, interceder, intercessor, intermediary, intermediate, intermediator, liaison, matchmaker, mediator, medium, messenger, negotiator, proxy, referee, representative; SEE CONCEPTS *348,423*

goblin [*n*] *elf*
bogeyman, brownie, demon, fiend, gnome, gremlin, imp, kobold, nixie, pixie, spirit, sprite; SEE CONCEPT *370*

go by [*v1*] *elapse*
exceed, flow on, make one's way, move onward, pass, proceed; SEE CONCEPT *141*

go by [*v2*] *adopt, conform*
abide by, adjust to, agree, be guided by, comply, cooperate, fall in with, follow, heed, judge from, observe, take as guide; SEE CONCEPTS *8,18*

go crazy [*v*] *become insane*
blow a gasket*, blow one's mind*, blow one's stack*, blow one's top*, crack up*, flip one's lid*, flip out, fly off the handle*, freak out*, go ballistic*, go bananas*, go batty*, go berserk*, go bonkers*, go buggy*, go cuckoo*, go daffy*, go haywire*, go kooky*, go loco*, go loony*, go mental, go nuts*, go nutty*, go off, go off one's rocker*, go off the deep end*, go off the wall*, go psycho*, go wacko*, go wacky*, lose control of oneself, lose it*, lose one's cool, lose one's mind, wig out*; SEE CONCEPT *13*

god [*n*] *supernatural being worshipped by people*
Absolute Being, Allah, All Knowing, All Powerful, Almighty, Creator, daemon, deity, demigod, demon, Divine Being, divinity, Father, God, holiness, Holy Spirit, idol, Infinite Spirit, Jah, Jehovah, King of Kings, Lord, Maker, master, numen, omnipotent, power, prime mover, providence, soul, spirit, totem, tutelary, universal life force, world spirit, Yahweh; SEE CONCEPT *370*

God-fearing [*adj*] *religious*
churchgoing, dedicated, devoted, devout, ecclesiastical, faithful, godly, goody-goody*, holy, orthodox, pious, prayerful, reverent, righteous, sacred, spiritual, theological; SEE CONCEPTS *536,545*

godforsaken [*adj*] *desolate*
abandoned, backward, deserted, dismal, distant, empty, forgotten, forlorn, gloomy, isolated, lonely, miserable, neglected, out-of-the-way, remote, secluded, wicked; SEE CONCEPTS *485,560*

godless [*adj*] *without a god or divine faith*
adiamorphic, agnostic, atheistic, freethinking, iconoclastic, irreligious, nonbelieving, skeptical, undogmatic; SEE CONCEPT *542*

godly [*adj*] *religious*
angelic, born-again, celestial, charismatic, deific, devout, divine, god-fearing, good, holy, pietistic, pious, prayerful, righteous, saintlike, saintly, virtuous; SEE CONCEPT *542*

go down [*v*] *lose, fall*
be beaten, be defeated, cave in, collapse, crumple, decline, decrease, descend, droop, drop, fold, founder, go under, keel, lessen, make less, pitch, plunge, reduce, sag, set, sink, slump, submerge, submerse, submit, succumb, suffer defeat, topple, tumble; SEE CONCEPTS *181,698,699*

godsend [*n*] *gift, benefit*
advantage, benediction, blessing, boon, good, manna*, stroke of luck*, windfall; SEE CONCEPTS *337,679*

go far [*v*] *be successful*
achieve, advance, do well, get ahead, get on, make a name*, move up in the world*, progress, rise, succeed; SEE CONCEPTS *704,706*

gofer [*n*] *errand boy or girl*
bottom person on the totem pole*, gal Friday, go getter*, grunt, guy Friday, hired help, low person on the totem pole*, office boy, office girl, peon, scrub; SEE CONCEPT *348*

gl
go

go for [*v1*] *reach*
clutch at, fetch, obtain, outreach, seek, stretch for; SEE CONCEPT *149*

go for [*v2*] *like, choose*
accept, admire, approbate, approve, be attracted to, be fond of, care for, countenance, fancy, favor, hold with, prefer; SEE CONCEPTS *10,32*

go for [*v3*] *attack*
assail, assault, launch at, run at, rush, rush upon, set upon, spring at; SEE CONCEPT *86*

go for it [*v*] *take a risk*
bet the farm, bet the ranch, exert oneself, go all out, go for broke, pull out all the stops, put one's heart and soul into it, shoot the works, use every muscle; SEE CONCEPTS *87,100*

go into [*v1*] *take an interest in; participate*
be absorbed in, begin, develop, engage in, enter, get involved with, take on*, take up*, take upon oneself*, undertake; SEE CONCEPT *100*

go into [*v2*] *investigate*
analyze, consider, delve into, dig*, dig into*, discuss, examine, explore, inquire, look into, probe, prospect, pursue, review, scrutinize, sift, study; SEE CONCEPTS *24,103*

golden [*adj2*] *beautiful, advantageous*
auspicious, best, blissful, bright, brilliant, delightful, excellent, favorable, flourishing, glorious, happy, joyful, joyous, opportune, precious, promising, propitious, prosperous, resplendent, rich, rosy, shining, successful, valuable; SEE CONCEPTS *529,574*

gold/golden [*adj1*] *dark yellow*
aureate, auric, auriferous, aurous, aurulent, blond, blonde, caramel, dusty, flaxen, honeyed, mellow yellow, ochroid, straw, tan, tawny, wheat; SEE CONCEPT *618*

gold mine [*n*] *very profitable venture*
bonanza, cash cow*, golden goose*, goose that laid the golden egg*, gravy train*, license to print money*, mother lode, source of supply, vein; SEE CONCEPTS *334,537,572*

gone [*adj*] *not present, no longer in existence*
absent, astray, away, AWOL*, burned up*, consumed, dead, decamped, deceased, defunct, departed, disappeared, disintegrated, displaced, dissipated, dissolved, done, down the drain*, dried up, elapsed, ended, extinct, finished, flown, lacking, left, lost, missing, moved, no more, nonextant, not a sign of*, not here, out the window*, over, passed, past, quit, removed, retired, run-off, shifted, spent, split, taken a powder*, taken leave*, transferred, traveling, turned to dust*, vanished, withdrawn; SEE CONCEPTS *407,586*

gonzo [*adj*] *bizarre*
crazy, far-fetched, insane, odd, strange, unconventional, weird, wild; SEE CONCEPTS *547,564*

good [*adj1*] *pleasant, fine*
acceptable, ace*, admirable, agreeable, bad, boss*, bully, capital, choice, commendable, congenial, crack*, deluxe, excellent, exceptional, favorable, first-class, first-rate, gnarly*, gratifying, great, honorable, marvelous, neat*, nice, pleasing, positive, precious, prime, rad*, recherché*, reputable, satisfactory, satisfying, select, shipshape*, sound, spanking*, splendid, sterling, stupendous, super, superb, super-eminent, super-excellent, superior, tip-top*, up to snuff*, valuable, welcome, wonderful, worthy; SEE CONCEPTS *529,572*

good [*adj2*] *moral, virtuous*
admirable, blameless, charitable, dutiful, estimable, ethical, exemplary, guiltless, honest, honorable, incorrupt, inculpable, innocent, irreprehensible, irreproachable, lily-white*, obedient, praiseworthy, pure, reputable, respectable, right, righteous, sound, tractable, uncorrupted, untainted, upright, well-behaved, worthy; SEE CONCEPT *545*

good [*adj3*] *competent, skilled*
able, accomplished, adept, adroit, au fait, capable, clever, dexterous, efficient, expert, first-rate, proficient, proper, qualified, reliable, satisfactory, serviceable, skillful, suitable, suited, talented, thorough, trustworthy, useful; SEE CONCEPT *527*

good [*adj4*] *useful, adequate*
acceptable, advantageous, all right, ample, appropriate, approving, apt, auspicious, becoming, benefic, beneficial, benignant, brave, commendatory, commending, common, conformable, congruous, convenient, decent, desirable, favorable, favoring, fit, fitting, fruitful, healthful, healthy, helpful, hygienic, meet, needed, opportune, profitable, proper, propitious, respectable, right, salubrious, salutary, satisfying, seemly, serviceable, suitable, tolerable, toward, unobjectionable, wholesome; SEE CONCEPTS *537,558,560*

good [*adj5*] *reliable; untainted*
dependable, eatable, fit to eat, flawless, fresh, intact, loyal, normal, perfect, safe, solid, sound, stable, trustworthy, unblemished, uncontaminated, uncorrupted, undamaged, undecayed, unhurt, unimpaired, unspoiled, vigorous, whole; SEE CONCEPT *485*

good [*adj6*] *kind, giving*
altruistic, approving, beneficent, benevolent, charitable, considerate, friendly, gracious, humane, humanitarian, kindhearted, merciful, obliging, philanthropic, tolerant, well-disposed; SEE CONCEPTS *404,542*

good [*adj7*] *authentic, real*
bona fide, conforming, dependable, genuine, honest, justified, kosher*, legitimate, loyal, orthodox, proper, regular, reliable, sound, strict, true, trustworthy, valid, well-founded; SEE CONCEPT *582*

good [*adj8*] *well-behaved*
considerate, decorous, dutiful, kindly, mannerly, obedient, orderly, polite, proper, respectful, seemly, thoughtful, tolerant, tractable, well-mannered; SEE CONCEPT *401*

good [*adj9*] *considerable*
adequate, advantageous, ample, big, complete, entire, extensive, full, great, immeasurable, large, long, lucrative, much, paying, profitable, respectable, sizable, solid, substantial, sufficient, whole, worthwhile; SEE CONCEPTS *334,771,781*

good [*n1*] *advantage, benefit*
asset, avail, behalf, benediction, blessing, boon*, commonwealth, favor, gain, godsend, good fortune, interest, nugget*, plum*, prize, profit, prosperity, service, treasure, use, usefulness, welfare, well-being, windfall; SEE CONCEPTS *337,658,679*

good [*n2*] *morality*
class, dignity, excellence, ideal, merit, prerogative, probity, quality, rectitude, right, righteousness, straight, uprightness, value, virtue, worth; SEE CONCEPT *645*

goodbye [*n*] *farewell statement*
adieu, adios, bye-bye, cheerio, ciao, godspeed*, leave-taking, parting, so long*, swan song*, toodle-oo*; SEE CONCEPTS *195,278*

good-for-nothing [*n*] *person who is idle, worthless*
bad lot*, black sheep*, bum, loafer, ne'er-do-well*, no-good*, profligate, rapscallion, scalawag, scamp, tramp, vagabond, waster*, wastrel; SEE CONCEPT *412*

good-humored [*adj*] *funny, happy*
affable, amiable, buoyant, cheerful, cheery, complaisant, congenial, easy, genial, good-natured, good-tempered, lenient, merry, mild, obliging, pleasant, smiling; SEE CONCEPT *404*

good-looking [*adj*] *handsome*
attractive, beauteous, beautiful, clean-cut, comely, fair, impressive, lovely, pretty, pulchritudinous, righteous; SEE CONCEPT *579*

good-natured [*adj*] *easygoing, easily pleased*
acquiescent, agreeable, altruistic, amiable, benevolent, bighearted, breezy, charitable, complaisant, compliant, cordial, easy, even-tempered, friendly, good-hearted, good-humored, gracious, helpful, kind, kindly, lenient, marshmallow*, mild, moderate, nice, obliging, softie*, tolerant, warmhearted, well-disposed, willing to please; SEE CONCEPT *404*

goodness [*n*] *decency, excellence*
advantage, beneficence, benefit, benevolence, ethicality, friendliness, generosity, good will, grace, graciousness, honesty, honor, humaneness, integrity, kindheartedness, kindliness, kindness, mercy, merit, morality, nourishment, obligingness, probity, quality, rectitude, righteousness, rightness, superiority, uprightness, value, virtue, wholesomeness, worth; SEE CONCEPTS *411,645*

goods [*n*] *personal possessions*
appurtenances, belongings, chattels, effects, encumbrances, equipment, furnishings, furniture, gear, impedimenta, movables, paraphernalia, property, stuff, things, trappings; SEE CONCEPT *446*

goods [*n2*] *merchandise*
bolt, cargo, commodities, fabric, freight, line, load, materials, seconds, stock, stuff, textile, vendibles, wares; SEE CONCEPT *338*

good will/goodwill [*n*] *kindliness*
altruism, amity, benevolence, brownie points*, charity, comity, cordiality, favor, friendliness, friendship, generosity, good deed, good side of*, helpfulness, rapport, right side of*, sympathy, tolerance; SEE CONCEPTS *411,645*

goody-goody [*adj*] *straight-laced*
God-fearing, goody two-shoes*, holier-than-thou*, moral, nice, PC, pious, politically correct, priggish, prissy, prudish, Puritan, self-righteous, unctuous, Victorian, virtuous; SEE CONCEPT *401*

gooey [*adj*] *sticky, gummy*
adhesive, gluey, glutinous, mucilaginous, soft, tacky, viscous; SEE CONCEPT *606*

goof [*v*] *mistake*
blow it, blunder, botch*, bungle, err, flub*, foul up, get wrong, louse up, make a boner*, mess up, miscalculate, mix up, screw up*, slip, snarl; SEE CONCEPTS *101,230,410*

go off [*v1*] *explode*
befall, blow, blow up, burst, detonate, discharge, fire, happen, mushroom, occur, pass, take place; SEE CONCEPT *179*

go off [*v2*] *leave*
decamp, depart, exit, go away, move out, part, quit; SEE CONCEPT *195*

goof off [*v*] *avoid work*
bum around, coast, diddle, dog it*, doodle, drag one's feet*, featherbed, fiddle around, fluff off, fool around, hang around, hang out, horse around, lollygag, mess around, monkey around, putz around, screw off, shirk, slack, take it easy; SEE CONCEPTS *30,59,681*

goofy [*adj*] *silly*
crazy, daffy*, dippy*, ditzy*, dopey, dotty, empty-headed*, flaky*, foolish, idiotic, kooky*, nutty*, screwy, stupid, wacky*, weird; SEE CONCEPTS *401,403,542*

goon [*n*] *ruffian*
bozo*, bruiser*, dope, gorilla*, hood*, hooligan*, jerk, lummox, moron, nincompoop, ninny, sap, strong-arm, thug, tough guy*; SEE CONCEPTS *412,423*

go on [*v*] *continue*
act, advance, bear, behave, carry on, come about, comport, conduct, deport, endure, execute, go ahead, hang on, happen, hold on, keep on, last, occur, persevere, persist, proceed, ramble, stay, take place; SEE CONCEPTS *100,239*

go out [*v1*] *become extinguished*
become dark, burn out, cease, darken, die, die out, dim, expire, fade out, flicker, stop shining; SEE CONCEPTS *105,469*

go out [*v2*] *leave*
decamp, depart, exit, go on strike, walk out; SEE CONCEPT *195*

go over [*v1*] *review*
analyze, examine, inspect, investigate, look at, peruse, practice, read, rehearse, reiterate, repeat, revise, riffle through*, scan, skim, study, thumb through*; SEE CONCEPTS *24,103*

go over [*v2*] *succeed*
be impressive, be successful, click*, come off*, go, pan out*, prove; SEE CONCEPT *706*

gore [*n*] *bloodshed*
blood, carnage, slaughter; SEE CONCEPT *252*

gore [*v*] *pierce*
gouge, impale, lance, perforate, puncture, spear, stab, stick, wound; SEE CONCEPT *220*

gorge [*n*] *valley*
abyss, arroyo, canyon, chasm, cleft, clough, clove, crevasse, fissure, flume, gap, glen, gulch, pass, ravine; SEE CONCEPT *509*

gorge [*v*] *eat voraciously*
blimp out*, bolt*, cloy, congest, cram, devour, eat like a horse*, feed, fill, glut, gobble, gormandize, gulp, guzzle, hoover*, jade, jam, make a pig of*, overeat, overindulge, pack, sate, satiate, stuff*, surfeit, swallow, wolf*; SEE CONCEPT *169*

gorgeous [*adj*] *beautiful, magnificent*
attractive, beaut*, bright, brilliant, centerfold*, colorful, dazzling, delightful, dream, drop-dead*, easy on the eyes*, elegant, enjoyable, exquisite, fine, flamboyant, foxy*, gaudy, glittering, glorious, good-looking, grand, handsome, imposing, impressive, knockout*, lavish, lovely, lulu*, luxuriant, luxurious, opulent, ostentatious, pleasing, plush, pulchritudinous, ravishing, resplendent, showy, splendid, splendiferous, stunning, sublime, sumptuous, superb; SEE CONCEPTS *579,589*

go
go

gormandize [v] *gorge*
binge, devour, eat like a horse*, eat to excess, glut, gluttonize, gobble, gulp, guzzle, hoover*, overeat, overindulge, pig out*, stuff, wolf*; SEE CONCEPTS *169,225*

gory [adj] *bloody, horrible*
bleeding, blood-soaked, bloodstained, imbrued, murderous, offensive, sanguinary, sanguine; SEE CONCEPTS *314,537*

gospel [n] *fact, doctrine*
actuality, authority, belief, certainty, credo, creed, dogma, faith, last word, scripture, testament, truism, truth, veracity, verity; SEE CONCEPT *689*

gossamer [adj] *gauzy, thin*
airy, cobweb, delicate, diaphanous, fibrous, fine, flimsy, light, sheer, silky, tiffany, translucent, transparent; SEE CONCEPT *606*

gossip [n1] *talk about others; rumor*
account, babble, back-fence talk*, blather, blether, buzz*, calumny, chatter, chitchat*, chronicle, clothesline*, conversation, cry, defamation, dirty laundry*, dirty linen*, dirty wash*, earful*, grapevine*, hearsay, idle talk, injury, malicious talk, meddling, news, prate, prattle, report, scandal, scuttlebutt*, slander, small talk*, story, tale, talk, whispering campaign*, wire*; SEE CONCEPTS *274,278*

gossip [n2] *person who talks a lot, spreads rumors*
babbler*, blabbermouth*, busybody, chatterbox, chatterer, circulator, flibbertigibbet*, gossipmonger, informer, meddler, newsmonger, parrot*, prattler, rumormonger*, scandalizer*, scandalmonger*, snoop*, talebearer, tattler, telltale; SEE CONCEPT *412*

gossip [v] *talk about others; spread rumors*
babble, bad-mouth*, bend one's ear*, blab, blather, blether, chat, chatter, cut to pieces*, cut up*, dish, hint, imply, insinuate, intimate, jaw*, prate, prattle, rattle on*, repeat, report, rumor, schmoose*, spill the beans*, spread*, suggest, talk, talk idly, tattle, tell secrets*, tell tales*, wiggle-waggle*; SEE CONCEPTS *56,60*

go straight [v] *reform*
be honorable, go legit, mend one's ways*, turn over a new leaf*, walk the straight and narrow*; SEE CONCEPTS *35,110,126,202*

go through [v1] *endure*
bear, brave, experience, suffer, support, survive, swallow, tolerate, undergo, withstand; SEE CONCEPT *23*

go through [v2] *use up*
consume, deplete, exhaust, pay out, spend, squander; SEE CONCEPT *169*

go through [v3] *search*
audit, check, examine, explore, hunt, inspect, investigate, look, pass through; SEE CONCEPT *103*

go to bat for [v] *show support for*
back up, cover for, defend, endorse, go to the wall for*, recommend, stand behind, stand by, stand up for, stick up for, support; SEE CONCEPTS *10,49,110*

go together/go with [v1] *agree, match*
accompany, accord, become, befit, be suitable, blend, complement, concur, correspond, fit, go, harmonize, make a pair*, not clash, suit; SEE CONCEPT *664*

go together/go with [v2] *accompany socially*
attend, be with, court, date, escort, go out with*, go steady with*, keep company with*; SEE CONCEPT *384*

gouge [n] *groove, hole*
channel, cut, excavation, furrow, gash, hollow, notch, scoop, score, scratch, trench; SEE CONCEPT *220*

gouge [v] *cut, scoop*
burrow, claw, dig, dredge, excavate, gash, groove, scrape, scratch, shovel, tunnel; SEE CONCEPT *220*

go under [v] *fail, submerge*
bankrupt, default, die, drown, fall, fold, founder, go down, sink, submerse, submit, succumb, suffocate, surrender; SEE CONCEPTS *181,699*

gourmet [n] *person who likes, knows about food*
bon vivant, connoisseur, critic, epicure, epicurean, gastronome, gastronomer, gastronomist, gourmand; SEE CONCEPTS *348,423*

govern [v1] *take control; rule*
administer, assume command, be in power, be in the driver's seat*, call the shots*, call the signals*, captain*, carry out, command, conduct, control, dictate, direct, execute, exercise authority, guide, head, head up, hold dominion, hold office, hold sway, lay down the law*, lead, manage, occupy throne, order, overrule, oversee, pilot, pull the strings*, regulate, reign, render, run, serve the people*, steer, superintend, supervise, sway, tyrannize, wear the crown*; SEE CONCEPT *133*

govern [v2] *influence; hold in check*
boss, bridle, check, contain, control, curb, decide, determine, direct, directionalize, discipline, dispose, dominate, get the better of*, guide, handle, incline, inhibit, manage, predispose, regulate, restrain, rule, shepherd, steer, subdue, sway, tame, underlie; SEE CONCEPTS *7,19,22,130*

government [n] *management, administration*
authority, bureaucracy, command, control, direction, domination, dominion, empire, execution, executive, governance, guidance, influence, jurisdiction, law, ministry, patronage, political practice, politics, polity, power, powers-that-be*, predominance, presidency, regency, regime, regimentation, regulation, restraint, rule, sovereignty, state, statecraft, superintendence, superiority, supervision, supremacy, sway, the feds*, Uncle Sam*, union, Washington*; SEE CONCEPT *299*

governor [n] *person administrating government*
administrator, boss, chief, chief of state, commander, comptroller, controller, director, executive, gubernatorial leader, guv*, head, head honcho*, leader, manager, overseer, presiding officer, ruler, superintendent, supervisor; SEE CONCEPT *354*

go without [adj] *deny or be denied*
abstain, be deprived of, do without, fall short*, go short*, lack, need, want; SEE CONCEPT *646*

gown [n] *robe, dress*
clothes, costume, frock, garb, garment, habit; SEE CONCEPT *451*

grab [v] *latch on to*
capture, catch, catch hold of, clutch, collar*, corral*, get one's fingers on*, get one's hands on*, glom*, grapple, grasp, grip, hook, land, lay one's hands on*, nab, nail, pluck, seize, snag, snap up, snatch, take, take hold of; SEE CONCEPTS *90,190*

grace [n1] *charm, loveliness*
address, adroitness, agility, allure, attractiveness,

balance, beauty, breeding, comeliness, consideration, cultivation, decency, decorum, dexterity, dignity, ease, elegance, etiquette, finesse, finish, form, gracefulness, lissomeness, lithesomeness, mannerliness, manners, nimbleness, pleasantness, pliancy, poise, polish, propriety, refinement, shapeliness, smoothness, style, suppleness, symmetry, tact, tastefulness; SEE CONCEPTS *633,655,718*

grace [*n2*] *mercy, forgiveness*
benefaction, beneficence, benevolence, caritas, charity, clemency, compassion, compassionateness, favor, forbearance, generosity, goodness, good will, indulgence, kindliness, kindness, leniency, lenity, love, pardon, quarter, reprieve, responsiveness, tenderness; SEE CONCEPTS *278,657,685*

grace [*n3*] *prayer*
benediction, blessing, invocation, petition, thanks, thanksgiving; SEE CONCEPTS *278,368*

grace [*v*] *beautify, embellish*
adorn, bedeck, crown, deck, decorate, dignify, distinguish, elevate, enhance, enrich, favor, garnish, glorify, honor, laureate, ornament, set off; SEE CONCEPTS *202,700*

graceful [*adj*] *agile, charming, lovely*
adroit, aesthetic, artistic, balletic, beautiful, becoming, comely, controlled, curvaceous, dainty, decorative, delicate, dexterous, easy, elastic, elegant, exquisite, fair, fine, flowing, handsome, harmonious, limber, lissome, lithe, natural, neat, nimble, pleasing, pliant, poised, practiced, pretty, refined, rhythmic, seemly, shapely, skilled, slender, smooth, springy, statuesque, supple, symmetrical, tasteful, trim, willowy; SEE CONCEPTS *579,584,589*

graceless [*adj*] *clumsy, unsophisticated*
awkward, barbarian, barbaric, barbarous, boorish, clunky*, coarse, corrupt, crude*, forced, gauche, gawky*, ill-mannered, improper, indecorous, inelegant, inept, infelicitous, klutzy*, loutish, oafish, outlandish, rough, rude, shameless, tasteless, two left feet*, uncouth, uncultured, unfortunate, ungainly, unhappy, unmannered; SEE CONCEPTS *401,584*

gracious [*adj*] *kind, giving*
accommodating, affable, amiable, amicable, approachable, beneficent, benevolent, benign, benignant, big-hearted, bland, bonhomous, charitable, chivalrous, civil, compassionate, complaisant, congenial, considerate, cordial, courteous, courtly, easy, forthcoming, friendly, gallant, genial, good-hearted, good-natured, hospitable, indulgent, lenient, loving, merciful, mild, obliging, pleasing, polite, sociable, stately, suave, tender, unctuous, urbane, well-mannered; SEE CONCEPTS *401,542*

gradation [*n*] *classification, step*
arrangement, calibration, change, degree, difference, distinction, divergence, grade, grouping, level, mark, measurement, modification, notch, nuance, ordering, place, point, position, progression, rank, scale, sequence, series, shade, sorting, stage, succession, variation; SEE CONCEPTS *378,665,727,744*

grade [*n1*] *rank, step*
brand, caliber, category, class, classification, condition, degree, division, echelon, estate, form, gradation, group, grouping, league, level, mark, notch, order, pigeonhole*, place, position, qual-

ity, rung*, size, stage, standard, station, tier; SEE CONCEPTS *286,378,665,727,744*

grade [*n2*] *incline, slope*
acclivity, ascent, bank, cant, climb, declivity, descent, downgrade, elevation, embankment, gradient, height, hill, inclination, inclined plane, lean, leaning, level, obliquity, pitch, plane, ramp, rise, slant, tangent, tilt, upgrade; SEE CONCEPTS *738,757*

grade [*v*] *evaluate, rank*
arrange, assort, brand, class, classify, group, order, range, rate, sort, value; SEE CONCEPTS *103,291*

gradient [*n*] *slope*
acclivity, angle, bank, cant, declivity, grade, hill, inclination, incline, lean, leaning, pitch, ramp, rise, slant, tilt; SEE CONCEPTS *738,757*

gradual [*adj*] *happening slowly, evenly*
bit-by-bit*, by degrees, continuous, creeping, even, gentle, graduate, moderate, piecemeal, progressive, regular, slow, steady, step-by-step*, successive, unhurried; SEE CONCEPTS *544,588,799*

gradually [*adv*] *happening slowly, evenly*
bit by bit*, by degrees, by installments, constantly, continuously, deliberately, gently, imperceptibly, inch by inch*, increasingly, in small doses*, little by little*, moderately, perceptibly, piece by piece*, piecemeal, progressively, regularly, sequentially, serially, steadily, step by step*, successively, unhurriedly; SEE CONCEPTS *544,588,799*

graduate [*n*] *person who completes education, pursuit*
alum*, alumnus, baccalaureate, bachelor, collegian, diplomate, doctor, former student, grad, holder, licentiate, master, Ph.D., product, recipient; SEE CONCEPT *350*

graduate [*v1*] *complete education, pursuit*
be commissioned, certify, confer degree, earn, finish, get a degree, get out*, give sheepskin*, grant diploma, take a degree, win; SEE CONCEPT *234*

graduate [*v2*] *classify, grade*
arrange, calibrate, class, group, mark off, measure, measure out, order, proportion, range, rank, regulate, sort; SEE CONCEPTS *84,103*

graduation [*n*] *commencement*
commencement exercises, convocation; SEE CONCEPTS *119,706*

graffiti [*n*] *wall writing*
cave painting, defacement, doodles, scribbling; SEE CONCEPTS *79,284*

graft [*n1*] *transplant*
bud*, hybridization, implant, jointure, scion, shoot, slip, splice, sprout, union; SEE CONCEPTS *113,257*

graft [*n2*] *payoff for fraud*
bribe, corruption, gain, hat*, hush money*, juice*, money, money under the table*, pay, payola*, peculation, shake*, share, skimming*, squeeze*, thievery; SEE CONCEPTS *192,344*

graft [*v*] *transplant, splice*
affix, implant, ingraft, insert, join, plant, propagate, unite; SEE CONCEPTS *113,257*

grain [*n1*] *seed, piece*
atom, bit, cereal, corn, crumb, drop, fragment, granule, grist, iota, jot, kernel, mite, modicum, molecule, morsel, mote, ounce, particle, pellet,

go
gr

scintilla, scrap, scruple, smidgen, spark, speck, tittle, trace, whit; SEE CONCEPTS *428,831*

grain [*n2*] *texture of fabric*
character, current, direction, fiber, make-up, nap, pattern, staple, striation, surface, tendency, tissue, tooth, warp and woof, weave, weft; SEE CONCEPT *611*

grammar [*n*] *language rules*
ABCs*, accidence, alphabet, elements, fundaments, linguistics, morphology, principles, rudiments, sentence structure, stratification, structure, syntax, tagmemics; SEE CONCEPTS *275,276,770*

grand [*adj1*] *impressive, great*
admirable, ambitious, august, awe-inspiring, dignified, dynamite, elevated, eminent, exalted, excellent, fab*, fine, first-class, first-rate, glorious, grandiose, haughty, illustrious, imposing, large, lofty, luxurious, magnificent, majestic, marvelous, monumental, noble, opulent, ostentatious, outstanding, palatial, pompous, pretentious, regal, rich, smashing, something else*, splendid, stately, striking, sublime, sumptuous, super, superb, terrific, unreal, very good; SEE CONCEPTS *574,589,773*

grand [*adj2*] *most important*
chief, dignified, elevated, exalted, grave, head, highest, leading, lofty, main, majestic, mighty, noble, preeminent, principal, regal, supreme, transcendent; SEE CONCEPT *568*

grandeur [*n*] *great importance*
amplitude, augustness, beauty, breadth, brilliance, celebrity, circumstance, dignity, distinction, elevation, eminence, expansiveness, fame, fineness, glory, grandiosity, gravity, greatness, handsomeness, immensity, impressiveness, inclusiveness, loftiness, luxuriousness, magnificence, majesty, might, nobility, opulence, pomp, preeminence, richness, splendor, state, stateliness, sublimity, sumptuousness, superbity, sway, transcendency, vastness; SEE CONCEPT *668*

grandiloquent [*adj*] *pretentious, flowery (communication)*
aureate, big-talking*, bombastic, declamatory, euphistic, fustian, high-flown, histrionic, inflated, magniloquent, oratorical, orotund, overblown, pompous, purple*, rhetorical, sonorous, swollen, tall-talking*, verbose, windbag*, windy*; SEE CONCEPT *267*

grandiose [*adj*] *theatrical, extravagant*
affected, ambitious, august, bombastic, cosmic, egotistic, flamboyant, fustian, grand, high-falutin'*, high-flown, imposing, impressive, lofty, lordly, magnificent, majestic, monumental, noble, ostentatious, overwhelming, pompous, pretentious, purple*, royal, showy, splashy, stately, unfathomable, vast; SEE CONCEPTS *401,542,589*

grandstand [*v*] *show off*
be ostentatious, be vain, flaunt it*, hot dog*, parade, play to the crowd, prance, put on airs*, showboat*, strut, swagger; SEE CONCEPT *261*

grange [*n*] *farm*
acreage, farmstead, hacienda, manor, plantation, ranch; SEE CONCEPTS *258,516,517*

grant [*n*] *allowance, gift*
admission, allocation, allotment, alms, appropriation, assistance, award, benefaction, bequest, boon, bounty, charity, concession, contribution, dole, donation, endowment, fellowship, gratuity,

handout, lump, present, privilege, reward, scholarship, stipend, subsidy; SEE CONCEPTS *337,344*

grant [*v*] *authorize, allow*
accede, accept, accord, acknowledge, acquiesce, admit, agree to, allocate, allot, assign, assume, avow, award, bestow, bless, cede, come across, come around, come through, concede, confer, consent to, convey, donate, drop, gift with*, give, give in, give out, give the nod*, give thumbs-up*, go along with*, impart, invest, own, own up*, permit, present, profess, relinquish, shake on*, sign off on*, sign on*, stake, suppose, surrender, transfer, transmit, vouchsafe, yield; SEE CONCEPTS *8,50,82,83,88*

granted [*adv*] *allowed, accepted*
acknowledged, admitted, assumed, indeed, just so, yes; SEE CONCEPT *558*

granulate [*v*] *crush into tiny pieces*
atomize, comminute, crumble, crystallize, disintegrate, grate, grind, make coarse, make grainy, pound, powder, pulverize, triturate; SEE CONCEPT *186*

graphic [*adj1*] *clear, explicit*
colorful, compelling, comprehensible, concrete, convincing, definite, descriptive, detailed, distinct, eloquent, expressive, figurative, forcible, illustrative, incisive, intelligible, lively, lucid, moving, perspicuous, picturesque, precise, realistic, stirring, striking, strong, telling, unequivocal, vivid; SEE CONCEPTS *267,535,562*

graphic [*adj2*] *pictorial, visible*
blocked-out, delineated, depicted, descriptive, diagrammatic, drawn, engraved, etched, iconographic, illustrated, illustrational, illustrative, marked-out, outlined, painted, photographic, pictoric, pictured, portrayed, representational, seen, sketched, traced, visual; SEE CONCEPTS *576,589, 619*

graphics [*n*] *drawings*
artwork, computer graphics, illustrations, pictures, visuals; SEE CONCEPT *625*

grapple [*v*] *grab, wrestle*
attack, battle, catch, clash, clasp, close, clutch, combat, confront, contend, cope, deal with, do battle*, encounter, engage, face, fasten, fight, grasp, grip, hold, hook, hug, nab, nail, scuffle, seize, snatch, struggle, tackle, take, take on*, tussle; SEE CONCEPTS *106,191*

grasp [*n1*] *hold, grip*
butt, cinch, clamp, clasp, clench, clinch, clutches, embrace, grapple, lug, possession, purchase, tenure; SEE CONCEPTS *191,710*

grasp [*n2*] *understanding*
awareness, comprehension, ken, knowledge, mastery, perception, realization; SEE CONCEPT *409*

grasp [*v1*] *grab*
bag*, catch, clasp, clinch, clutch, collar*, corral, enclose, glom*, grapple, grip, hold, hook, land, seize, snatch, take, take hold of; SEE CONCEPTS *90,191*

grasp [*v2*] *understand*
accept, appreciate, apprehend, catch, catch on*, cognize, compass, comprehend, dig*, envisage, fathom, follow, get, get the drift*, get the picture*, have, know, latch on*, make, perceive, pick up*, realize, see, take, take in*; SEE CONCEPT *15*

grasping [*adj*] *greedy*
acquisitive, avaricious, avid, close-fisted, cov-

etous, desirous, extorting, extortionate, grabby*, itchy*, mean, miserly, niggardly*, penny-pinching*, penurious, prehensile, rapacious, selfish, stingy*, tightfisted*, usurious, venal; SEE CONCEPTS *326,334,542*

grass [n] *lawn*
barley, grama, hay, meadow, pasture, sod, turf, verdure; SEE CONCEPT *429*

grassland [n] *meadow*
campo, field, llano, pampas, pasture, plain, prairie, range, savanna, steep, sward, swarth, veldt; SEE CONCEPT *509*

grate [v1] *shred, grind down*
abrade, bark, bray, file, fray, gall, mince, pound, pulverize, rasp, raze, rub, scrape, scratch, scuff, skin, triturate; SEE CONCEPTS *186,215*

grate [v2] *irritate*
aggravate, annoy, burn, chafe, exasperate, fret, gall, get on one's nerves*, irk, nettle, peeve, pique, provoke, rankle, rile, rub the wrong way*, vex; SEE CONCEPTS *7,14,19*

grateful [adj1] *appreciative*
beholden, gratified, indebted, obliged, pleased, thankful; SEE CONCEPT *403*

grateful [adj2] *pleasing, nice*
acceptable, agreeable, comforting, congenial, consoling, delectable, delicious, delightful, desirable, favorable, good, gratifying, pleasant, pleasurable, pleasureful, refreshing, rejuvenating, renewing, restful, restorative, restoring, satisfactory, satisfying, solacing, welcome; SEE CONCEPTS *537,548,572*

gratification [n] *satisfaction*
delight, enjoyment, fruition, fulfillment, glee, hit, indulgence, joy, kicks*, luxury, pleasure, recompense, regalement, relish, reward, sure shock*, thrill; SEE CONCEPT *410*

gratify [v] *give pleasure; satisfy*
appease, arride, baby*, cater to, coddle, content, delectate, delight, do one proud*, do the trick*, enchant, favor, fill the bill*, fulfill*, get one's kicks*, gladden, hit the spot*, humor, indulge, make a hit*, make happy, oblige, pamper, please, recompense, requite, thrill; SEE CONCEPTS *7,22*

grating [adj] *irritating; scraping*
annoying, disagreeable, discordant, displeasing, dissonant, dry, grinding, harsh, harsh-sounding, hoarse, irksome, jarring, offensive, rasping, raucous, rough, shrill, squeaky, strident, stridulant, stridulous, unpleasant, vexatious; SEE CONCEPTS *529,592,594*

gratis [adj] *free*
as a gift, chargeless, complimentary, costless, for love*, for nothing, freebie*, freely given, free of charge, free ride*, gratuitous, on someone*, on the house*, unpaid for, without charge, without recompense; SEE CONCEPT *334*

gratitude [n] *appreciation*
acknowledgment, appreciativeness, grace, gratefulness, honor, indebtedness, obligation, praise, recognition, requital, response, responsiveness, sense of obligation, thankfulness, thanks, thanksgiving; SEE CONCEPTS *32,76,278,410*

gratuitous [adj1] *free*
chargeless, complimentary, costless, for nothing, gratis, spontaneous, unasked-for, unpaid, voluntary, willing; SEE CONCEPTS *334,542*

gratuitous [adj2] *not necessary*
assumed, baseless, bottomless, causeless, groundless, indefensible, inessential, needless,

reasonless, supererogatory, superfluous, uncalled-for, unessential, unfounded, unjustified, unmerited, unprovoked, unsupportable, unwarranted, wanton; SEE CONCEPT *546*

gratuity [n] *gift, tip*
alms, benefaction, bonus, boon, bounty, contribution, donation, fringe benefit, grease palm*, largesse, little something*, offering, perk*, perquisite, present, recompense, reward, salve*, sweetener*, token; SEE CONCEPTS *337,344*

grave [adj1] *serious; gloomy*
cold sober*, deadpan*, dignified, dour, dull, earnest, grim, grim-faced, heavy, leaden, long-faced, meaningful, muted, no-nonsense*, ponderous, quiet, sad, sage, saturnine, sedate, sober, solemn, somber, staid, strictly business*, subdued, thoughtful, unsmiling; SEE CONCEPT *401*

grave [adj2] *crucial, dangerous*
acute, afflictive, consequential, critical, deadly, destructive, dire, exigent, fatal, fell, grievous, hazardous, heavy*, important, killing*, life-and-death*, major, momentous, of great consequence, ominous, perilous, pressing, serious, severe, significant, threatening, ugly, urgent, vital, weighty; SEE CONCEPTS *537,548,567*

grave [n] *burial place*
catacomb, crypt, final resting place*, last home*, mausoleum, mound, permanent address*, place of interment, resting place, sepulcher, shrine, six feet under*, tomb, vault; SEE CONCEPT *305*

graveyard [n] *burial area*
boneyard*, burial ground, cemetery, charnel house, God's acre*, memorial park, necropolis; SEE CONCEPT *305*

gravitate [v] *be drawn toward; fall to*
approach, be attracted, be influenced, be pulled, descend, drift, drop, incline, lean, move, precipitate, settle, sink, tend; SEE CONCEPTS *34,159*

gravity [n1] *force of attraction*
force, heaviness, pressure, weight; SEE CONCEPT *641*

gravity [n2] *seriousness, importance*
acuteness, concern, consequence, exigency, hazardousness, momentousness, perilousness, severity, significance, solemnity, urgency, weightiness; SEE CONCEPT *668*

gray/grey [adj] *muted silver in color*
ash, ashen, battleship*, cinereal, clouded, dingy, dove, drab, dusky, dusty, granite, heather, iron, lead, leaden, livid, mousy, neutral, oyster, pearly, peppery, powder, sere, shaded, silvered, silvery, slate, smoky, somber, stone; SEE CONCEPT *618*

graze [v1] *touch*
abrade, brush, carom, chafe, glance off, kiss*, ricochet, rub, scrape, scratch, shave*, skim, skip; SEE CONCEPT *612*

graze [v2] *feed on*
bite, browse, champ, crop, crunch, eat, forage, gnaw, masticate, munch, nibble, pasture, ruminate, uproot; SEE CONCEPT *169*

grease [n] *fat*
animal oil, drippings, lard, lubricant, oil, tallow, vegetable oil; SEE CONCEPTS *723,734*

grease [v1] *lubricate*
anoint, butter, oil, slick; SEE CONCEPT *202*

grease [v2] *bribe*
buy off, corrupt, do business*, entice, fix*, influence, oil someone's palm*, pay off, take care of, tamper; SEE CONCEPTS *53,192*

gr
gr

greasy [*adj*] *slippery, oily*
anointed, creamy, daubed, fatty, lubricated, lubricious, oleaginous, pomaded, salved, slick, slimy*, slithery, smeared, swabbed, unctuous; SEE CONCEPT *606*

greasy spoon [*n*] *inexpensive restaurant*
beanery, bean wagon, cheap restaurant, dump*, eatery, grease pit*, hashery, hashhouse; SEE CONCEPTS *439,448,449*

great [*adj1*] *very large*
abundant, ample, big, big league*, bulky, bull, colossal, considerable, decided, enormous, excessive, extended, extensive, extravagant, extreme, fat, gigantic, grievous, high, huge, humongous, husky, immense, inordinate, jumbo*, lengthy, long, major league*, mammoth, mondo*, numerous, oversize, prodigious, prolonged, pronounced, protracted, strong, stupendous, terrible, titanic*, towering, tremendous, vast, voluminous; SEE CONCEPTS *773,781*

great [*adj2*] *important, celebrated*
august, capital, chief, commanding, dignified, distinguished, eminent, exalted, excellent, famed, famous, fine, glorious, grand, heroic, highly regarded, high-minded, honorable, idealistic, illustrious, impressive, leading, lofty, magnanimous, main, major, noble, notable, noted, noteworthy, outstanding, paramount, primary, principal, prominent, puissant, regal, remarkable, renowned, royal, stately, sublime, superior, superlative, talented; SEE CONCEPT *568*

great [*adj3*] *excellent, skillful*
able, absolute, aces*, adept, admirable, adroit, awesome, bad*, best, brutal, cold*, complete, consummate, crack*, downright, dynamite, egregious, exceptional, expert, fab*, fantastic, fine, first-class*, first-rate*, good, heavy*, hellacious*, marvelous, masterly, number one*, out-and-out*, out of sight*, out of this world*, perfect, positive, proficient, super-duper*, surpassing, terrific, total, tough, transcendent, tremendous, unmitigated, unqualified, utter, wonderful; SEE CONCEPTS *527,528,574*

greatly [*adv*] *considerably*
abundantly, by much, conspicuously, eminently, emphatically, enormously, exceedingly, exceptionally, extremely, famously, glaringly, highly, hugely, immeasurably, immensely, incalculably, incomparably, incredibly, indeed, infinitely, in great measure, inimitably, intensely, largely, markedly, mightily, most, much, notably, on a large scale, powerfully, remarkably, strikingly, superlatively, supremely, surpassingly, tremendously, vastly, very much; SEE CONCEPTS *537,569,772*

greatness [*n1*] *large size*
abundance, amplitude, bigness, bulk, enormity, force, high degree, hugeness, immensity, infinity, intensity, length, magnitude, mass, might, potency, power, prodigiousness, sizableness, strength, vastness; SEE CONCEPTS *730,767*

greatness [*n2*] *nobleness of character; eminence*
celebrity, chivalry, dignity, distinction, fame, generosity, glory, grandeur, heroism, high-mindedness, idealism, illustriousness, importance, loftiness, magnanimity, majesty, merit, morality, nobility, note, prominence, renown, stateliness, sublimity, worthiness; SEE CONCEPTS *411,645, 668*

greed [*n*] *overwhelming desire for more*
acquisitiveness, avarice, avidity, covetousness, craving, cupidity, eagerness, edacity, esurience, excess, gluttony, gormandizing, graspingness, hunger, indulgence, insatiableness, intemperance, longing, piggishness*, rapacity, ravenousness, selfishness, swinishness*, the gimmies*, voracity; SEE CONCEPT *20*

greedy [*adj*] *desiring excessively*
acquisitive, avaricious, avid, carnivorous, close, close-fisted*, covetous, craving, desirous, devouring, eager, edacious, esurient, gluttonous, gobbling, gormandizing, grabby, grasping, grudging, gulping, guzzling, hoggish*, hungry, impatient, insatiable, insatiate, intemperate, itchy*, miserly, niggardly, omnivorous, parsimonious, pennypinching*, penurious, piggish*, prehensile, rapacious, ravening, ravenous, selfish, stingy, swinish, tight*, tight-fisted*, voracious; SEE CONCEPTS *326,403,542*

green [*adj1*] *young, new, blooming*
bosky, budding, burgeoning, callow, developing, flourishing, foliate, fresh, grassy, growing, half-formed, immature, infant, juvenile, leafy, lush, maturing, pliable, puerile, pullulating, raw, recent, sprouting, supple, tender, undecayed, undried, unfledged, ungrown, unripe, unseasoned, verdant, verduous, visculent, youthful; SEE CONCEPTS *485,578,797*

green [*adj2*] *inexperienced*
callow, credulous, fresh, gullible, ignorant, immature, inexpert, ingenuous, innocent, naive, new, raw, tenderfoot*, unconversant, unpolished, unpracticed, unseasoned, unskillful, unsophisticated, untrained, unversed, wet behind the ears*, young, youthful; SEE CONCEPT *404*

green [*adj3*] *emerald in color*
apple, aquamarine, beryl, chartreuse, fir, forest, grass, jade, kelly, lime, malachite, moss, olive, pea, peacock, pine, sage, sap, sea, spinach, verdigris, vert, viridian, willow; SEE CONCEPT *618*

green [*adj4*] *referring to practices or policies that do not negatively affect the environment*
biodegradable, ecological, environmental, environmentally-safe, environment-friendly; SEE CONCEPT *485*

green [*n*] *square or park in center of town*
common, field, grass, grassplot, lawn, plaza, sward, terrace, turf; SEE CONCEPTS *509,513*

green around the gills [*adj*] *sick*
blah, crummy, miserable, nauseated, pale, queasy, shaky, sick as a dog*, sick to one's stomach, throwing up, under the weather, vomiting; SEE CONCEPT *314*

green card [*n*] *working card*
pass, passport, permit, visa; SEE CONCEPTS *271,376,685*

greenhorn [*n*] *inexperienced person*
amateur, apprentice, babe*, beginner, colt*, hayseed*, ingénue, learner, naif, neophyte, newcomer, new hand, novice, recruit, rube*, simpleton, tenderfoot*, tyro*, virgin; SEE CONCEPT *423*

greet [*v*] *welcome*
accost, acknowledge, address, approach, attend, bow, call to, compliment, curtsy, embrace, exchange greetings, extend one's hand, flag, hail, herald, highball*, high-five*, meet, move to, nod, pay respects, receive, recognize, roll out the red carpet*, salaam*, salute, say hello, say hi*,

shake hands, shoulder, speak to, stop, tip one's hat*, usher in*, whistle for; SEE CONCEPT *51*

greeting [*n*] *welcome; message of kindness*
accosting, acknowledgment, address, aloha*, attention, best wishes*, blow*, card*, ciao*, compellation, compliments, good wishes*, hail, hello, heralding, hi, highball*, high five*, how-do-you-do*, howdy*, letter*, nod, note, notice, ovation, reception, regards, respects, rumble, salaam*, salutation, salute, speaking to, testimonial, ushering in, what's happening*; SEE CONCEPT *51*

gregarious [*adj*] *friendly*
affable, clubby*, companionable, convivial, cordial, fun, outgoing, sociable, social; SEE CONCEPT *404*

gridlock [*n*] *traffic jam*
barrier, blockage, bottleneck, clog, congestion, impasse, logjam, obstacle, stoppage; SEE CONCEPTS *230,432*

grief [*n*] *mental suffering*
affliction, agony, anguish, bemoaning, bereavement, bewailing, care, dejection, deploring, depression, desolation, despair, despondency, discomfort, disquiet, distress, dole, dolor, gloom, grievance, harassment, heartache, heartbreak, infelicity, lamentation, lamenting, malaise, melancholy, misery, mortification, mournfulness, mourning, pain, purgatory, regret, remorse, repining, rue, sadness, sorrow, torture, trial, tribulation, trouble, unhappiness, vexation, woe, worry, wretchedness; SEE CONCEPTS *410,728*

grief-stricken [*adj*] *sad, sorrowful*
anguished, cheerless, dejected, depressed, despairing, devastated, distressed, down, heartbroken, heartsick, heavyhearted, hurting, inconsolable, melancholy, miserable, morose, overcome, troubled, unhappy, woebegone; SEE CONCEPT *403*

grievance [*n*] *complaint, gripe*
affliction, ax to grind*, beef*, bellyache*, big stink*, blast, case, cross*, damage, distress, flack*, grief, grouse*, hardship, holler*, hoo-ha*, howl*, injury, injustice, jeremiad*, kick, knock*, objection, outrage, pain, pain in the neck*, rap*, resentment, rigor, roar, rumble, sorrow, squawk*, stink*, trial, tribulation, trouble, unhappiness, violence, wrong, yell; SEE CONCEPTS *52,278,689*

grieve [*v1*] *mourn, feel deep distress*
ache, bear, bemoan, bewail, carry on, complain, cry, cry a river*, deplore, eat one's heart out*, endure, hang crepe*, keen, lament, regret, rue, sing the blues*, sorrow, suffer, take it hard*, wail, weep; SEE CONCEPTS *17,410*

grieve [*v2*] *upset, distress someone*
afflict, aggrieve, agonize, break the heart of*, constrain, crush, hurt, injure, pain, sadden, wound; SEE CONCEPTS *7,19*

grievous [*adj*] *severe, painful; serious*
afflicting, agonizing, appalling, atrocious, calamitous, damaging, deplorable, dire, dismal, disquieting, distressing, disturbing, dreadful, egregious, flagrant, glaring, grave, harmful, heart-rending, heavy*, heinous, hurtful, injurious, intolerable, lamentable, monstrous, mournful, offensive, onerous, oppressive, outrageous, pathetic, pitiful, sad, shameful, sharp, shocking, sorrowful, taxing, tough, tragic, troublesome,

unbearable, upsetting, villainous, weighty*, wounding; SEE CONCEPTS *537,544,548*

grift [*n*] *swindle*
cheating, confidence game, con game*, deceit, dirty pool*, double-dealing*, extortion, fix, fraud, racket*, rip-off*, scam, shady deal*, shell game*, stealing, sting, trickery; SEE CONCEPTS *59,139,192*

grill [*v1*] *broil food*
barbecue, burn, charcoal-broil, cook, cook over an open pit, roast, rotisserie, sear; SEE CONCEPT *170*

grill [*v2*] *ask questions aggressively*
catechize, cross-examine, give the third degree*, go over*, inquisition, interrogate, interview, put the pressure on*, put the screws to*, question, roast*, third degree*; SEE CONCEPTS *48,53*

grim [*adj*] *hopeless, horrible in manner, appearance*
austere, barbarous, bleak, cantankerous, churlish, crabbed*, cruel, crusty, dogged, ferocious, fierce, forbidding, foreboding, formidable, frightful, funereal, ghastly, gloomy, glowering, glum, grisly, grouchy, gruesome, grumpy*, harsh, hideous, horrid, implacable, inexorable, intractable, merciless, morose, ominous, relentless, resolute, ruthless, scowling, severe, shocking, sinister, somber, sour, splenetic, stern, stubborn, sulky, sullen, surly, terrible, truculent, unrelenting, unyielding; SEE CONCEPTS *534,544,570*

grimace [*n*] *scowling facial expression*
face, frown, moue, mouth, mouthing, mug*, scowl, smile, smirk, sneer, wry face; SEE CONCEPT *716*

grimace [*v*] *make a pained expression*
contort, deform, distort, frown, make a face, make a wry face, misshape, mouth, mug*, scowl, screw up one's face*, smirk, sneer; SEE CONCEPT *185*

grime [*n*] *dirt*
crud*, dust, film, filth, gook*, gunk*, muck*, smudge, smut*, soil, soot, tarnish; SEE CONCEPT *260*

grimy [*adj*] *dirty*
begrimed, besmirched, cruddy*, dingy*, filthy, foul, grubby*, grungy*, messy, mucky*, nasty, scuzzy*, sleazy*, smeared, smutty*, soiled, sooty, sordid, squalid, unclean; SEE CONCEPTS *485,621*

grin [*n/v*] *smile widely*
beam, crack, simper, smirk; SEE CONCEPTS *185,716*

grind [*n*] *tedious job*
chore, drudgery, groove*, grubwork*, hard work, labor, moil, pace, rote, routine, rut*, sweat*, task, toil, travail, treadmill*; SEE CONCEPT *362*

grind [*v1*] *crush, pulverize*
abrade, atomize, attenuate, beat, bray, chop up, comminute, crumble, crumple, disintegrate, file, granulate, grate, kibble*, levigate, mill, pestle, pound, powder, pulverize*, rasp, reduce, roll out*, scrape, shiver, triturate; SEE CONCEPTS *186,204*

grind [*v2*] *sharpen*
abrade, file, give an edge to, gnash, grate, grit, polish, rub, sand, scrape, smooth, whet; SEE CONCEPTS *186,215*

grind [*v3*] *oppress*
afflict, annoy, harass, hold down, hound, perse-

cute, plague, trouble, tyrannize, vex; SEE CONCEPTS *14,130*

grip [*n1*] *clasp, embrace*
anchor, brace, catch, cinch, cincture, clamp, clamping, clench, clinch, clutch, coercion, constraint, crushing, duress, enclosing, enclosure, fastening, fixing, grapnel, grapple, grasp, gripe, handclasp, handgrip, handhold, handshake, hold, hook, ligature, lug, purchase, restraint, snatch, squeeze, strength, tenure, vise, wrench; SEE CONCEPT *191*

grip [*n2*] *perception, understanding*
clutches*, comprehension, control, domination, grasp, hold, influence, keeping, ken, possession, power, tenure; SEE CONCEPT *409*

grip [*v1*] *hold tightly*
clap a hand on, clasp, clench, clinch, clutch, get one's hands on*, grasp, latch on to*, lay hands on, nab, seize, snag, snatch, take, take hold of; SEE CONCEPT *191*

grip [*v2*] *entrance, enchant*
catch up, compel, engross, enthrall, fascinate, hold, hypnotize, involve, mesmerize, rivet, spellbind; SEE CONCEPTS *7,11,22*

gripe [*n1*] *complaint*
ache, aching, affliction, disorder, distress, grievance, groan, grouse, grumble, illness, indisposition, infirmity, moan, objection, pain, pang; SEE CONCEPTS *52,278,313*

gripe [*n2*] *strong hold*
clamp, clasp, clench, clinch, clutch, crunch, grab, grapple, grasp, grip, tenure; SEE CONCEPT *191*

gripe [*v1*] *complain*
bellyache*, blow off*, carp, crab*, fuss, groan, grouch, grouse, grumble, kvetch*, moan, murmur, mutter, nag, squawk, take on*, whine, yammer*, yawp*; SEE CONCEPTS *44,52*

gripe [*v2*] *pain, annoy*
ache, bother, compress, cramp, disturb, hurt, irritate, pinch, press, squeeze, vex; SEE CONCEPTS *7,19,219,246*

grisly [*adj*] *horrifying*
abominable, appalling, awful, blood-stained, bloody, disgusting, dreadful, eerie, frightful, ghastly, grim, grody*, gross*, gruesome, hideous, horrible, horrid, lurid, macabre, sanguine, shocking, sick, sickening, terrible, terrifying, yucky*; SEE CONCEPTS *537,544,570*

grit [*n1*] *particles of dirt*
dust, foreign matter, gravel, lumps, pebbles, powder, sand; SEE CONCEPTS *260,831*

grit [*n2*] *courage, determination*
backbone, daring, doggedness, fortitude, gameness, guts*, hardihood, intestinal fortitude*, mettle, moxie*, nerve, perseverance, pluck, resolution, spine*, spirit, spunk, steadfastness, tenacity, toughness; SEE CONCEPTS *411,633*

gritty [*adj1*] *granular*
abrasive, branlike, calculous, crumbly, dusty, friable, grainy, gravelly, in particles, loose, lumpy, permeable, porous, powdery, pulverant, rasping, rough, sabulous, sandy, scratchy; SEE CONCEPT *606*

gritty [*adj2*] *brave*
courageous, determined, dogged, game*, hardy, mettlesome, plucky*, resolute, spirited, steadfast, tenacious, tough; SEE CONCEPTS *401,404*

groan [*n*] *moan, complaint*
cry, gripe, grouse, grumble, grunt, objection, sigh, sob, whine; SEE CONCEPTS *278,595*

groan [*v*] *moan, complain*
bemoan, cry, gripe, grouse, grumble, keen, lament, mumble, murmur, object, sigh, whine; SEE CONCEPTS *44,52,77*

grocery store [*n*] *supermarket*
bodega, convenience store, corner store*, food mart, food store, market, mom-and-pop store, retail food store; SEE CONCEPTS *323,333,449*

groggy [*adj*] *dizzy, stunned*
befuddled, confused, dazed, dopey*, drunken, faint, hazy, out of it*, punch-drunk*, punchy*, reeling, shaky, slaphappy*, staggering, stupefied, swaying, tired, unsteady, weak, whirling, wobbly, woozy*; SEE CONCEPT *314*

groom [*n1*] *man being married*
benedict, bridegroom, fiancé, husband, spouse, suitor; SEE CONCEPT *419*

groom [*n2*] *stable attendant; servant*
equerry, hostler, stable person; SEE CONCEPTS *348,419*

groom [*v*] *make ready, prepare physically*
brush, clean, coach, comb, curry, dress, drill, educate, lick into shape*, make attractive, make presentable, nurture, preen, prep*, pretty up*, prim, prime, primp, put through grind*, put through mill*, ready, refine, refresh, rub down, shape up, sleek, slick up*, smarten up*, spiff up*, spruce up*, tend, tidy, train, turn out; SEE CONCEPTS *162,202,285*

groove [*n1*] *channel, indentation*
canal, corrugation, crease, crimp, cut, cutting, depression, ditch, flute, fluting, furrow, gouge, gutter, hollow, incision, notch, pucker, rabbet, rut, scallop, score, scratch, slit, trench, valley; SEE CONCEPT *513*

groove [*n2*] *daily routine*
daily grind*, grind, pace, rote, rut*, same old stuff*, schtick*, slot*; SEE CONCEPTS *362,677*

groovy [*adj*] *cool, wonderful*
boss*, chic, deep*, excellent, fabulous, fantastic, far-out*, great, hip, neat*, nifty*, rad*, sensational, splendid, super, swell*, trendy, unorthodox, way-out, wild, with it; SEE CONCEPT *572*

grope [*v*] *feel about for*
cast about, examine, explore, feel blindly, finger*, fish*, flounder, fumble, grabble, handle, manipulate, poke, pry, root, scrabble, search, touch; SEE CONCEPTS *34,216,612*

gross [*adj1*] *large, fat*
adipose, big, bulky, chubby*, corpulent, dense, fleshy, great, heavy, hulking, husky, lumpish, massive, obese, overweight, porcine, portly, stout, thick, unwieldy, weighty; SEE CONCEPTS *773,781*

gross [*adj2*] *whole*
aggregate, all, before deductions, before tax, complete, entire, in sum, outright, total, whole ball of wax*, whole enchilada*, whole nine yards*, whole schmear*, whole shebang*; SEE CONCEPT *785*

gross [*adj3*] *crude, vulgar*
barnyard*, boorish, breezy, callous, carnal, cheap, coarse, corporeal, crass, dull, fleshly, foul, ignorant, improper, impure, indecent, indelicate, inelegant, insensitive, in the gutter*, lewd, loudmouthed, low, low-minded, lustful, obscene, offensive, rank, raunchy, raw, ribald, rough, rude, scatological, sensual, sexual, sleazy*, smutty*, swinish*, tasteless, ugly, uncouth, uncultured, undiscriminating, unfeeling, unrefined, un-

seemly, unsophisticated, voluptuous; SEE CON-
CEPTS *267,542,545*

gross [*adj4*] *obvious, apparent*
absolute, arrant, blatant, capital, complete,
downright, egregious, excessive, exorbitant, extreme, flagrant, glaring, grievous, heinous, immoderate, inordinate, manifest, out-and-out*,
outrageous, outright*, perfect, plain, rank, serious, shameful, sheer, shocking, unmitigated, unqualified, utter; SEE CONCEPTS *535,537*

gross [*n*] *total, whole*
aggregate, all, entirety, sum, sum total, totality;
SEE CONCEPTS *344,837*

gross [*v*] *bring in as total*
earn, make, take in; SEE CONCEPTS *330,351*

grotesque [*adj*] *ugly, misshapen*
aberrant, abnormal, absurd, antic, bizarre, deformed, distorted, eerie, extravagant, extreme,
fanciful, fantastic, flamboyant, freakish, grody*,
gross*, incongruous, ludicrous, malformed,
monstrous, odd, outlandish, perverted, preposterous, queer, ridiculous, strange, surrealistic,
uncanny, unnatural, weird, whimsical; SEE CON-
CEPTS *486,537,579*

grotto [*n*] *cave*
antre, cavern, cavity, chamber, den, hollow, rock
shelter, subterrane, underground chamber; SEE
CONCEPT *509*

grouch [*n*] *person who complains a lot*
bear*, bellyacher*, bug*, crab*, crank, crosspatch*, curmudgeon, faultfinder, griper, grouser,
growler, grumbler, grump*, kicker*, malcontent,
moaner, sorehead*, sourpuss*, whiner; SEE CON-
CEPTS *412,423*

grouch [*v*] *complain a lot*
bellyache*, carp, find fault, gripe, grouse, grumble, moan, murmur, mutter, scold, whine; SEE
CONCEPT *52*

grouchy [*adj*] *complaining, irritable*
cantankerous*, cross, crusty*, discontented,
grumbling, grumpy*, ill-tempered, irascible,
peevish, petulant, querulous, snappy, sulky,
surly, testy; SEE CONCEPTS *267,401*

ground [*n*] *earth, land*
arena, dirt, dust, field, landscape, loam, old sod,
park, real estate, sand, sod, soil, terra firma, terrain, turf; SEE CONCEPT *509*

ground [*v1*] *base, set; educate*
acquaint, bottom, coach, discipline, establish, familiarize, fit, fix, found, indoctrinate, inform, initiate, instruct, introduce, predicate, prepare,
prime, qualify, rest, settle, stay, teach, train,
tutor; SEE CONCEPTS *18,285*

ground [*v2*] *restrict; drop in place*
bar, beach, bring down, dock, down, fell, floor,
knock down, land, level, mow down*, prevent,
strand; SEE CONCEPTS *130,181*

groundbreaking [*adj*] *pioneering*
avant-garde, cutting-edge, innovating, innovative, leading-edge, radical, revolutionary, spear-
heading, trailblazing, trendsetting; SEE CONCEPTS
529,578,589,797

groundless [*adj*] *without reason, justification*
baseless, bottomless, causeless, chimerical,
empty, false, flimsy, foundationless, gratuitous,
idle, illogical, illusory, imaginary, unauthorized,
uncalled-for, unfounded, unjustified, unprovoked, unsupported, unwarranted; SEE CONCEPTS
267,552,582

grounds [*n1*] *estate, domain*
acreage, area, campus, country, district, environs, fields, gardens, habitat, holding, land, lot,
premises, property, real estate, realm, sphere,
spot, terrace, terrain, territory, tract, zone; SEE
CONCEPTS *508,516*

grounds [*n2*] *basis, premise*
account, antecedent, argument, base, bedrock*,
call, cause, chapter and verse*, demonstration,
determinant, dope*, evidence, excuse, factor,
footing, foundation, goods*, groundwork, inducement, info*, information*, infrastructure,
justification, motive, numbers, occasion, pretext,
proof, rationale, reason, root*, seat, straight
stuff*, substratum, test, testimony, trial, underpinning, wherefore, why, whyfor; SEE CONCEPTS
274,661

grounds [*n3*] *sediment*
deposit, dregs, grouts, leavings, lees, precipitate,
precipitation, residue, settlings; SEE CONCEPT
260

groundwork [*n*] *basis, fundamentals*
ABCs*, background, base, bedrock*, cornerstone*, footing, foundation, ground, infrastructure, origin, preliminaries, preparation, root,
substratum, underpinning, understructure; SEE
CONCEPTS *274,442,660,661*

group [*n*] *number of individuals collectively*
accumulation, aggregation, assemblage, assembly, association, assortment, band, batch, battery,
bevy, body, bunch, bundle, cartel, category,
chain, circle, class, clique, clot, club, clump,
cluster, clutch, collection, combination, combine, company, conglomerate, congregation, coterie, covey, crew, crowd, faction, formation,
gang, gathering, grade, league, lot, mess, organization, pack, parcel, party, passel, platoon, pool,
posse, set, shooting match, society, sort, suite,
syndicate, troop, trust; SEE CONCEPTS *391,432*

group [*v1*] *bring together*
arrange, assemble, associate, band together,
bracket, bunch, bunch up*, cluster, collect, congregate, consort, corral, crowd, gang around*,
gang up*, gather, get together, hang out*, harmonize, huddle, link, make the scene*, meet, organize, poke, punch*, round up*, scare up*,
systematize; SEE CONCEPTS *109,114*

group [*v2*] *classify, sort*
arrange, assemble, associate, assort, bracket, categorize, class, dispose, file, gather, marshal,
order, organize, pigeonhole*, put together,
range, rank; SEE CONCEPTS *18,84,158*

groupie [*n*] *devoted fan*
admirer, buff, devotee, follower, hanger-on, supporter; SEE CONCEPTS *352,366,423*

grove [*n*] *cluster of trees*
brake, coppice, copse, covert, forest, orchard,
plantation, spinney, stand, thicket, wood, woodland; SEE CONCEPTS *429,517*

grovel [*v*] *abase, demean oneself*
apple-polish*, beg, beg for mercy, beseech, blandish, bootlick*, bow and scrape*, brown-nose*,
butter up*, cater to, court, cower, crawl, creep,
cringe, crouch, eat crow*, eat dirt*, eat humble
pie*, fall all over*, fawn*, flatter, humble oneself, humor, implore, kiss one's feet*, kneel,
kowtow*, make much of*, make up to*, pamper,
play up to*, prostrate*, revere, snivel, soft-
soap*, stoop, suck up to*, truckle*, wheedle,
yes*; SEE CONCEPTS *384,633*

gr
gr

grow [v] *become larger, evolve*
abound, advance, age, amplify, arise, augment, become, branch out, breed, build, burgeon, burst forth, come, come to be, cultivate, develop, dilate, enlarge, expand, extend, fill out, flourish, gain, germinate, get bigger, get taller, heighten, increase, issue, luxuriate, maturate, mature, mount, multiply, originate, pop up*, produce, propagate, pullulate, raise, ripen, rise, shoot*, spread, spring up, sprout, stem, stretch, swell, thicken, thrive, turn, vegetate, wax*, widen; SEE CONCEPTS *427,469,704,775*

growl [n/v] *animal-like sound*
bark, bellow, gnarl, gnarr, grumble, grunt, howl, moan, roar, roll, rumble, snarl, thunder; SEE CONCEPTS *77,595*

grown-up [n] *adult*
gentleman, grown person, lady, mam, man, Miss, mister, Mr., Mrs., Ms., woman; SEE CONCEPT *424*

growth [n1] *development, progress*
advance, advancement, aggrandizement, augmentation, beefing up*, boost, buildup, crop, cultivation, enlargement, evolution, evolvement, expansion, extension, fleshing out*, flowering, gain, germination, heightening, hike, improvement, increase, maturation, maturing, multiplication, produce, production, proliferation, prosperity, rise, sprouting, stretching, success, surge, swell, thickening, unfolding, up, upping, vegetation, waxing*, widening; SEE CONCEPTS *427,469,703,704,775*

growth [n2] *tumor*
cancer, cancroid, excrescence, fibrousness, fibrous tissue, fungus, lump, mole, outgrowth, parasite, polyp, swelling, thickening, wen; SEE CONCEPT *306*

grub [n1] *larva*
caterpillar, entozoon, maggot, worm; SEE CONCEPT *398*

grub [n2] *food*
chow*, comestibles, eats*, edibles, feed, nosh*, nurture, provisions, rations, sustenance, viands, victuals, vittles*; SEE CONCEPTS *457,460*

grub [v1] *dig, uncover*
beat, break, burrow, clean, clear, comb, delve, excavate, ferret, fine-tooth-comb*, forage, hunt, poke, prepare, probe, pull up, rake, ransack, root, rummage, scour, search, shovel, spade, unearth, uproot; SEE CONCEPTS *178,216*

grub [v2] *work very hard*
drudge, grind, labor, moil, plod, slave, slog, sweat, toil; SEE CONCEPT *100*

grubby [adj] *dirty, disheveled*
besmeared, black, filthy, foul, frowzy*, grimy, grungy*, impure, messy, mucky*, nasty, scruffy, scuzzy*, seedy*, shabby, sloppy, slovenly, smutty*, soiled, sordid, squalid, unclean, uncleanly, unkempt, untidy, unwashed; SEE CONCEPTS *485,621*

grudge [n] *hard feelings*
animosity, animus, antipathy, aversion, bad blood*, bitterness, bone to pick*, dislike, enmity, grievance, hate, hatred, ill will, injury, injustice, malevolence, malice, maliciousness, malignancy, peeve, pet peeve*, pique, rancor, resentment, spite, spitefulness, spleen, venom; SEE CONCEPT *29*

grudge [v] *feel resentful; give unwillingly*
begrudge, be reluctant, be stingy*, complain,

covet, deny, envy, hold back, mind, pinch, refuse, resent, stint; SEE CONCEPT *21*

grueling [adj] *difficult, taxing*
arduous, backbreaking, brutal, chastening, crushing, demanding, excruciating, exhausting, fatiguing, fierce, grinding, hairy*, hard, harsh, heavy*, laborious, punishing, racking, severe, stiff, strenuous, tiring, torturous, trying; SEE CONCEPT *565*

gruesome [adj] *horrible, awful*
abominable, appalling, daunting, fearful, frightful, ghastly, grim, grisly, grody*, gross*, hideous, horrendous, horrid, horrific, horrifying, loathsome, lurid, macabre, monstrous, morbid, offensive, repugnant, repulsive, shocking, sick*, spine-tingling*, terrible, terrifying, ugly, weird*; SEE CONCEPTS *485,548*

gruff [adj1] *bad-tempered, rude*
abrupt, bearish, blunt, boisterous, boorish, brusque, churlish, crabbed*, crabby*, crude, crusty*, curt, discourteous, dour, fierce, grouchy*, grumpy*, ill-natured, impolite, morose, nasty, offhand, rough, saturnine, short, snappy*, snippy*, sour, sullen, surly, truculent, uncivil, ungracious, unmannerly; SEE CONCEPTS *267,401*

gruff [adj2] *rasping in sound*
cracked, croaking, croaky, grating, guttural, harsh, hoarse, husky, low, rough, throaty; SEE CONCEPT *594*

grumble [v1] *complain*
bellyache*, carp, find fault, fuss, gripe, groan, grouch*, grouse, kick, kvetch*, moan, protest, pule, repine, scold, snivel*, squawk*, whine; SEE CONCEPTS *44,52*

grumble [v2] *murmur, rumble*
bark, croak, gnarl, gnarr, growl, grunt, gurgle, mumble, mutter, roar, roll, snap, snarl, snuffle, splutter, whine; SEE CONCEPTS *65,77*

grump [n] *cranky person*
bear*, complainer, crab*, curmudgeon, grouch, malcontent, sorehead*, sourpuss*, whiner; SEE CONCEPTS *412,423*

grumpy [adj] *in a bad mood*
bad-tempered, cantankerous*, crabby*, cross, crotchety, disgruntled, dissatisfied, griping, grouchy*, grumbling, irritable, peevish, pettish, petulant, querulous, sulky, sullen, surly, testy, truculent; SEE CONCEPTS *401,403*

grungy [adj] *dirty and unkempt*
cruddy*, dilapidated, disgusting, disheveled, filthy, flimsy, foul, greasy, grimy, grubby, messy, nasty, offensive, repellent, revolting, rundown, scummy*, scuzzy*, shoddy, slimy, sloppy, trashy, unclean, unwashed, vile, wretched; SEE CONCEPTS *485,579*

guarantee [n] *pledge, promise*
agreement, assurance, attestation, bail, bargain, bond, certainty, certificate, certification, charter, collateral, contract, covenant, deposit, earnest, gage, guaranty, insurance, lock, oath, pawn, pipe, recognizance, security, sure thing*, surety, testament, token, undertaking, vow, warrant, warranty, word, word of honor; SEE CONCEPTS *71,271,685*

guarantee [v] *pledge, promise*
affirm, angel, answer for, assure, attest, aver, back, bankroll, be surety for, bind oneself, certify, confirm, cosign, endorse, ensure, evidence, evince, get behind*, give bond, grubstake, guaranty, insure, juice*, maintain, make bail*, make

certain, make sure, mortgage, pick up the check*, pick up the tab*, protect, prove, reassure, secure, sign for, stake, stand behind*, stand up for*, support, swear, testify, vouch for, wager, warrant, witness; SEE CONCEPTS *71,110*

guaranteed [*adj*] *made certain*
affirmed, approved, ascertained, assured, attested, bonded, certified, confirmed, endorsed, for a fact, for sure, have a lock on*, insured, on ice*, pledged, plighted, protected, sealed, secured, sure, sure enough*, sure-fire*, warranted; SEE CONCEPT *535*

guard [*n1*] *protector*
bouncer*, chaperone, chaperone, chaser*, convoyer, custodian, defender, escort, guardian, lookout, picket, sentinel, sentry, shepherd, shield, ward, warden, watch, watchperson; SEE CONCEPT *348*

guard [*n2*] *defense*
aegis, armament, armor, buffer, bulwark, pad, protection, rampart, safeguard, screen, security, shield, ward; SEE CONCEPT *712*

guard [*v*] *protect, watch*
attend, baby-sit, bulwark, chaperone, chaperone, conduct, convoy, cover, cover up, defend, escort, fend, keep, keep an eye on*, keep in view, keep under surveillance, look after, lookout, mind, observe, oversee, patrol, police*, preserve, ride shotgun for*, safeguard, save, screen, secure, see after, shelter, shepherd, shield, shotgun, stonewall*, superintend, supervise, tend; SEE CONCEPTS *96,134*

guarded [*adj*] *suspicious*
attentive, cagey, calculating, canny, careful, cautious, chary, circumspect, discreet, gingerly, leery, noncommittal, on the lookout*, overcautious, prudent, reserved, restrained, reticent, safe, vigilant, wary, watchful, with eyes peeled*; SEE CONCEPT *542*

guardian [*n*] *keeper, protector*
angel*, attendant, baby-sitter, bird dog*, cerberus, champion, chaperon, chaperone, conservator, cop*, curator, custodian, defender, escort, guard, keeper, nurse, overseer, paladin, patrol, preserver, safeguard, sentinel, shepherd, sitter, sponsor, superintendent, supervisor, trustee, vigilante, warden, watchdog*; SEE CONCEPTS *414, 423*

guerrilla [*n*] *bushfighter*
commando, freedom fighter, irregular, mercenary, professional soldier, resistance fighter, soldier of fortune, terrorist, underground fighter; SEE CONCEPT *358*

guess [*n*] *belief, speculation*
assumption, ballpark figure*, conclusion, conjecture, deduction, divination, estimate, fancy, feeling, guesstimate*, guesswork, hunch*, hypothesis, induction, inference, judgment, notion, opinion, postulate, postulation, prediction, presumption, presupposition, reckoning, shot*, shot in the dark*, sneaking suspicion*, stab*, supposal, supposition, surmisal, surmise, suspicion, theory, thesis, view; SEE CONCEPT *689*

guess [*v*] *try to figure out; imagine*
believe, calculate, chance, conjecture, dare say, deduce, deem, divine, estimate, fancy*, fathom, go out on a limb*, guesstimate*, happen upon*, hazard*, hypothesize, infer, judge, jump to a conclusion*, lump it*, opine, penetrate, pick, postulate, predicate, predict, presume, pretend,

reason, reckon, select, size up*, solve, speculate, suggest, suppose, surmise, survey, suspect, take a shot at*, take a stab at*, theorize, think, think likely, venture, work out*; SEE CONCEPT *28*

guest [*n*] *person accommodated, given hospitality*
bedfellow, boarder, caller, client, companion, company, customer, frequenter*, habitué, inmate, lodger, mate, out-of-towner*, partaker, patron, recipient, renter, roomer, sharer, sojourner, tenant, transient, vacationer, visitant, visitor; SEE CONCEPT *423*

guffaw [*n*] *burst of laughter*
belly laugh, deep laugh, howl, howling, laughter, loud laugh, roar, shout, shriek, snort; SEE CONCEPTS *77,185*

guidance [*n*] *counseling*
advice, auspices, conduct, conduction, control, conveyance, direction, government, help, instruction, intelligence, leadership, management, navigation, supervision, teaching; SEE CONCEPTS *75,274,278*

guide [*n1*] *something that or someone who leads*
adviser, attendant, captain, chaperon, cicerone, conductor, controller, convoy, counselor, criterion, design, director, docent, escort, example, exemplar, exhibitor, genie, genius, guiding spirit, guru, ideal, inspiration, lead, leader, lodestar, mentor, model, monitor, paradigm, pathfinder, pattern, pilot, pioneer, rudder, scout, standard, superintendent, teacher, usher, vanguard; SEE CONCEPTS *348,423,686*

guide [*n2*] *information, instructions*
ABCs*, beacon*, bellwether*, bible, catalog, chapter and verse*, clue, compendium, directory, enchiridion, guidebook, guiding light*, handbook, hot lead*, key, landmark, lodestar, manual, mark, marker, no-no's*, pointer, print, sign, signal, signpost, telltale, the book*, the numbers*, tip-off*, vade mecum; SEE CONCEPT *274*

guide [*v*] *direct, lead*
accompany, advise, attend, beacon*, chaperon, command, conduct, contrive, control, convoy, counsel, coxswain, educate, engineer, escort, govern, handle, have a handle on*, influence, instruct, manage, maneuver, marshal, navigate, oversee, pilot, quarterback*, regulate, route, rule, see, shepherd, show, show the way, spearhead*, steer, superintend, supervise, sway, teach, trailblaze*, train, usher; SEE CONCEPTS *75,110,117, 187*

guidebook [*n*] *handbook*
enchiridion, field guide, how-to book, instruction book, manual, map, reference book, road map, travel book, vade mecum; SEE CONCEPT *280*

guideline [*n*] *direction*
clue, code, ground rule, guidance, guide, instruction, key, mark, marker, precept, protocol, rule, signal, standard procedure; SEE CONCEPTS *271,274*

guild [*n*] *association, fellowship*
club, company, corporation, federation, group, interest group, league, lodge, order, organization, profession, society, sodality, trade, union; SEE CONCEPTS *381,387*

guile [*n*] *slyness, cleverness*
artfulness, artifice, chicanery, craft, craftiness, cunning, deceit, deception, dirty dealing*, dirty pool*, dirty trick*, dirty work*, dishonesty, dissemblance, dissimulation, double-cross*, duplic-

gr
gu

ity, foul play*, jive*, run-around*, ruse, sellout*, sharp practice*, stab in the back*, treachery, trickery, trickiness, wiliness; SEE CONCEPTS 645,657

guileless [adj] honest
aboveboard, artless, candid, frank, genuine, ingenuous, innocent, naive, natural, open, simple, simple-minded, sincere, straightforward, truthful, unaffected, undesigning, unsophisticated, unstudied; SEE CONCEPTS 267,542,545

guilt [n] blame; bad conscience over responsibility
answerability, blameworthiness, contrition, crime, criminality, culpability, delinquency, dereliction, disgrace, dishonor, error, failing, fault, indiscretion, infamy, iniquity, lapse, liability, malefaction, malfeasance, malpractice, misbehavior, misconduct, misstep, offense, onus, peccability, penitence, regret, remorse, responsibility, self-condemnation, self-reproach, shame, sin, sinfulness, slip, solecism, stigma, transgression, wickedness, wrong; SEE CONCEPTS 101,532, 645,690

guiltless [adj] blameless, not responsible
clean, clear, crimeless, exemplary, faultless, free, good, immaculate, impeccable, inculpable, innocent, irreproachable, pure, righteous, sinless, spotless, unimpeachable, unsullied, untainted, untarnished, virtuous; SEE CONCEPT 545

guilty [adj] blameworthy; found at fault
accusable, caught, censurable, censured, chargeable, condemned, conscience-stricken, contrite, convictable, convicted, criminal, culpable, damned, delinquent, depraved, doomed, erring, evil, felonious, hangdog*, impeached, incriminated, in error, iniquitous, in the wrong, judged, liable, licentious, offending, on one's head*, out of line*, proscribed, regretful, remorseful, reprehensible, responsible, rueful, sentenced, sheepish, sinful, sorry, wicked, wrong; SEE CONCEPT 545

guinea pig [n] test subject
examinee, experimental subject, lab animal, laboratory animal, test animal, testee, victim; SEE CONCEPTS 5,290

guise [n] appearance, pretense
air, aspect, behavior, cloak, color, cover, demeanor, disguise, disguisement, dress, facade, face, false front*, false show*, fashion, form, front, mask, mien, mode, pose, posture, role, seeming, semblance, shape, show, showing, simulacrum; SEE CONCEPTS 645,716

gulch [n] small ravine
arroyo, channel, cut, ditch, gap, gorge, gulley, trench, valley; SEE CONCEPTS 509,513

gulf [n1] sea inlet
basin, bay, bayou, bight, cove, firth, harbor, slough, sound, whirlpool; SEE CONCEPTS 509,514

gulf [n2] deep, gaping hole
abyss, breach, cave, cavity, chasm, cleft, crevasse, depth, depths, distance, expanse, gap, gulch, hiatus, hollow, opening, pit, ravine, rent, rift, separation, shaft, split, void, well, whirlpool; SEE CONCEPTS 509,513

gullible [adj] naive, trusting
being a sucker*, believing, biting, credulous, easily taken in*, easy mark*, falling hook line and sinker*, foolish, green*, innocent, kidding oneself*, mark*, silly, simple, sucker, susceptible, swallowing whole*, taken in*, taking the

bait*, trustful, tumbling for*, unskeptical, unsophisticated, unsuspecting, wide-eyed*; SEE CONCEPTS 402,542

gully [n] ravine, ditch
channel, chase, chasm, crevasse, culvert, gutter, notch, trench, watercourse; SEE CONCEPTS 509,513

gulp [n] swallow
choke, draught, gasp, mouthful, swig, swill; SEE CONCEPT 185

gulp [v] eat, drink fast
belt*, choke down*, chugalug*, consume, devour, dispatch, dispose, drop*, englut, gobble*, guzzle*, imbibe, ingurgitate, inhale*, pour, quaff, scarf down*, slop*, slosh*, stuff, swallow, swig, swill, take in, toss off*, wolf*, wolf down*; SEE CONCEPTS 169,185

gum [n] sticky substance
adhesive, amber, cement, cohesive substance, exudate, glue, mucilage, paste, pitch, plaster, resin, rosin, tar, wax; SEE CONCEPT 466

gumption [n] nerve, initiative
ability, acumen, astuteness, cleverness, commonsense, discernment, enterprise, get-up-and-go*, good sense, horse sense*, industry, judgment, perspicaciousness, perspicacity, resourcefulness, sagaciousness, sagacity, savvy, sense, shrewdness, spirit, wisdom, wit; SEE CONCEPT 411

gun [n] weapon that shoots
blaster*, cannon, difference*, equalizer*, flintlock, forty-five*, handgun, hardware*, howitzer, magnum, 9 mm.*, mortar, musket, ordnance, peashooter*, persuader*, piece*, pistol, revolver, rifle, rod*, Saturday-night special*, shotgun, thirty-eight*, Uzi*; SEE CONCEPT 500

gung ho [adj] extremely enthusiastic
anxious, ardent, dedicated, eager, enthused, excited, fanatical, fired up*, keyed up*, lively, passionate, spirited, zealous; SEE CONCEPTS 401,542

gurgle [n/v] burble, murmur
babble, bubble, crow, lap, plash, purl, ripple, slosh, splash, wash; SEE CONCEPTS 65,595

guru [n] mentor, guide
authority, guiding light*, leader, master, sage, teacher, tutor; SEE CONCEPT 350

guru [n2] technical expert
computer expert, computer geek, computer specialist, geek, techie; SEE CONCEPTS 348,350,416

gush [n] outpouring
burst, cascade, flood, flow, flush, issue, jet, run, rush, spate, spout, spring, spurt, stream, surge; SEE CONCEPTS 467,687

gush [v1] pour out
burst, cascade, emanate, emerge, flood, flow, flush, issue, jet, pour, roll, run, rush, sluice, spew, spout, spring, spurt, stream, surge, well; SEE CONCEPT 179

gush [v2] speak with overwhelming enthusiasm
babble*, blather, carry on about*, chatter, effervesce, effuse, enthuse, fall all over*, go on about*, jabber, make a to-do over*, overstate, prate, prattle, rave; SEE CONCEPT 49

gust [n] rush, eruption
access, blast, blow, breeze, burst, explosion, fit, flare-up, flurry, gale, outburst, paroxysm, passion, puff, sally, squall, storm, surge; SEE CONCEPTS 524,787

gusto [n] great enthusiasm
appetite, appreciation, ardor, brio, delectation,

delight, enjoyment, exhilaration, fervor, heart, liking, palate, passion, pleasure, relish, savor, taste, verve, zeal, zest; SEE CONCEPTS *411,657*

gusty [*adj*] *windy*
airy, blowy, blustering, blustery, breezy, hearty, robust, squally, stormy, tempestuous; SEE CONCEPT *525*

gut [*adj*] *intuitive*
basic, deep-seated, emotional, heartfelt, innate, inner, instinctive, interior, internal, intimate, involuntary, natural, spontaneous, unthinking, visceral, viscerous; SEE CONCEPT *403*

gut [*n*] *stomach and abdomen*
belly, bowels, duodenum, entrails, innards, intestines, paunch, tripes, tummy*, venter, viscera; SEE CONCEPT *393*

gut [*v*] *clean out, strip*
bowel, decimate, despoil, dilapidate, disembowel, draw, dress, empty, eviscerate, exenterate, loot, pillage, plunder, ransack, ravage, rifle, sack; SEE CONCEPTS *165,211*

gutless [*adj*] *timid*
abject, chicken*, chicken-hearted*, coward, cowardly, craven, faint-hearted*, feeble, irresolute, lily-livered*, pusillanimous, spineless*, submissive, weak, wimpy*, yellow*, yellow-bellied*; SEE CONCEPTS *404,542*

guts [*n*] *nerve, boldness*
audacity, backbone*, courage, daring, dauntlessness, effrontery, forcefulness, fortitude, grit*, hardihood, heart*, intestinal fortitude*, mettle, moxie*, pluck, resolution, sand*, spine*, spirit, spunk*, willpower; SEE CONCEPTS *411,657*

gutsy [*adj*] *bold, brave*
courageous, determined, gallant, game*, indomitable, intrepid, mettlesome, plucky, resolute, spirited, spunky*, staunch, unfearful, valiant; SEE CONCEPTS *404,542*

gutter [*n*] *ditch*
channel, conduit, culvert, dike, drain, duct, eaves, fosse, funnel, gully, moat, pipe, runnel, sewer, sluice, spout, sulcation, trench, trough, tube, watercourse; SEE CONCEPTS *440,513*

guttural [*adj*] *deep in sound*
glottal, grating, gravely, growling, gruff, harsh, hoarse, husky, inarticulate, low, rasping, rough, sepulchral, thick, throaty; SEE CONCEPT *594*

guy [*n*] *man*
bird*, bloke*, boy, brother, bud, buddy, cat*, chap, chum, dude*, feller*, fellow, gentleman, individual, male, person; SEE CONCEPTS *414,419*

guzzle [*v*] *drink down fast*
bolt*, booze*, carouse*, cram, devour, englut, gobble*, gorge, gormandize, imbibe, ingurgitate, knock back*, quaff, slop*, slosh*, soak, swig, swill, tipple; SEE CONCEPT *169*

gymnasium [*n*] *arena for sports, recreation*
alley, amphitheater, athletic club, center, circus, coliseum, course, exercise room, field house, floor, gym, health club, hippodrome, pit, recreation center, ring, rink, spa, stadium, sweatshop*, theater; SEE CONCEPTS *364,438,439*

gymnastics [*n*] *acrobatic exercise*
aerobatics, balance beam, bars, body-building, calisthenics, floor exercise, free exercise, gym, horse, rings, trampoline, trapeze, tumbling, vaulting, workout; SEE CONCEPT *363*

gyp [*v*] *rip-off*
bamboozle, bilk, cheat, deceive, defraud, dupe, fleece, flimflam*, gip, gull, hoodwink, hustle*, pull something*, rook, scam, stick*, swindle, take for a ride*, trick; SEE CONCEPT *59*

gyrate [*v*] *revolve*
circle, circulate, circumduct, gyre, pirouette, purl, roll, rotate, spin, spiral, turn, twirl, whirl, whirligig; SEE CONCEPTS *147,149*

H

habit [*n1*] *tendency, practice*
addiction, bent, bias, constitution, consuetude, convention, custom, dependence, disposition, fashion, fixation, fixed attitude, frame of mind*, gravitation, groove, habitude, hangup, impulsion, inclination, make-up*, manner, mannerism, mode, nature, obsession, pattern, penchant, persuasion, praxis, predisposition, proclivity, proneness, propensity, quirk, routine, rule, rut, second nature*, set, style, susceptibility, thing*, turn, usage, use, way, weakness, wont; SEE CONCEPT *644*

habit [*n2*] *dress, clothing, often for a particular purpose*
apparel, costume, garb, garment, habiliment, riding clothes, robe, vestment; SEE CONCEPT *451*

habitat/habitation [*n*] *place where someone resides*
abode, accommodations, address, apartment, berth, biosphere, cave, commorancy, condo, condominium, co-op, den, digs*, domicile, dwelling, element, environment, fireside, flat, haunt*, haven, hearth, hole*, home, home plate*, homestead, house, housing, locale, locality, lodging, neck of the woods*, nest, nook, occupancy, occupation, pad*, place, quarters, range, residence, residency, roof*, roost*, seat*, settlement, site, stamping ground*, stomping ground*, surroundings, terrain, territory, turf; SEE CONCEPT *515*

habitual [*adj*] *usual, established*
accepted, accustomed, addicted, addicting, automatic, chronic, common, confirmed, constant, continual, conventional, customary, cyclic, disciplined, familiar, fixed, frequent, hardened, ingrained, inveterate, iterated, iterative, mechanical, methodical, natural, normal, ordinary, perfunctory, permanent, perpetual, persistent, practiced, recurrent, regular, reiterative, repeated, repetitious, rooted, routine, seasoned, set, standard, steady, systematic, traditional, wonted; SEE CONCEPTS *530,547*

habituate [*v*] *prepare, accustom*
acclimate, acclimatize, addict, adjust, break in, condition, confirm, devote, discipline, endure, familiarize, harden, inure, make used to, school, season, take to, tolerate, train; SEE CONCEPTS *35,202*

hacienda [*n*] *large estate*
cattle ranch, farmhouse, large house, mansion, plantation, ranch; SEE CONCEPTS *439,516*

hack [*n1*] *person who does easy work for money*
drudge*, greasy grind*, grind*, hireling, lackey*, old pro*, plodder*, pro*, servant, slave, workhorse*; SEE CONCEPT *348*

gu
ha

hack [*n2*] *taxicab*
cab, carriage, coach, hackney, taxi, vehicle; SEE
CONCEPT *505*

hack [*n3/v*] *cut without care*
chop, clip, fell, gash, hackle, hew, lacerate, mangle, mutilate, notch, slash, whack; SEE CONCEPTS
137,176

hacker [*n*] *someone proficient at computers, especially a hobbyist*
application programmer, computer architect,
computer designer, computer jock, key puncher,
operator, programmer, systems analyst, systems
engineer, systems software specialist, systems
programmer, technician; SEE CONCEPTS *360,366*

hack it [*v*] *to succeed*
accomplish, avail, be successful, bring home the
bacon*, carry off*, come out on top*, come
through, cut it, cut the mustard*, deliver the
goods*, get to the top*, hit the mark*, make a go
of it*, make it*, make the cut*, make the grade*,
prevail, pull it off, score, win; SEE CONCEPTS
141,706

hackneyed [*adj*] *clichéd, tired*
antiquated, banal, common, commonplace, conventional, corny*, everyday, familiar tune*,
hokey*, moth-eaten*, obsolete, old, old-chest-
nut*, old-hat*, old-saw*, outdated, outmoded,
out-of-date, overworked, pedestrian*, played-
out*, quotidian, run-of-the-mill*, stale, stereotyped, stock, threadbare*, timeworn, tripe, trite,
unoriginal, well-worn, worn-out*; SEE CONCEPTS
267,530

haggard [*adj*] *worn, weakened*
ashen, careworn, drawn, emaciated, exhausted,
faded, fagged, fatigued, fretted, gaunt, ghastly,
lank, lean, pale, pallid, pinched, scraggy,
scrawny, shrunken, skinny, spare, starved, thin,
tired, wan, wasted, weak, wearied, worn-down,
wrinkled; SEE CONCEPTS *314,406,491*

haggle [*v*] *bicker, quarrel*
argue, bargain, barter, beat down*, cavil, chaffer,
deal, dicker*, dispute, hammer out a deal*,
horse-trade*, make a deal*, palter, quibble,
squabble, wrangle; SEE CONCEPT *46*

hail [*n*] *torrent*
barrage, bombardment, broadside, cannonade,
hailstorm, pelting, rain, salvo, shower, storm,
volley; SEE CONCEPTS *189,524*

hail [*v1*] *call to, yell for*
accost, address, flag, flag down*, greet, hello,
holler*, salute, shoulder, shout, signal, sing out*,
speak to, wave down, welcome, whistle down*,
whistle for*, yawp*, yoo-hoo*; SEE CONCEPTS
47,74,77

hail [*v2*] *honor, salute*
acclaim, acknowledge, applaud, cheer, commend, compliment, exalt, glorify, greet, hear it
for*, kudize, praise, recognize, recommend, root
for*, welcome; SEE CONCEPT *69*

hail [*v3*] *come from; originate*
be a native of, be born in, begin, claim as birthplace; SEE CONCEPT *648*

hail [*v4*] *rain down on*
barrage, batter, beat down upon, bombard, pelt,
shower, storm, volley; SEE CONCEPT *526*

hair [*n*] *threadlike growth on animate being*
beard, bristle, cilium, coiffure, cowlick, cut,
down, eyebrow, eyelash, feeler, fiber, filament,
fluff, fringe, frizzies*, fur, grass, haircut, hairstyle, lock, mane, mop*, moustache, quill, ruff,

shock, sideburn, split ends, strand, thatch, tress,
tuft, vibrissa, villus, whiskers, wig, wool; SEE
CONCEPT *392*

hairdresser [*n*] *hair stylist*
barber, beautician, coiffeur, coiffeuse, friseur;
SEE CONCEPT *348*

hairless [*adj*] *without growth on body part*
bald, baldheaded, beardless, clean-shaven, cue
ball*, depilated, egghead*, glabrate, glabrescent,
glabrous, shaved, shaven, shorn, skinhead*,
smooth, smooth-faced, tonsured, whiskerless;
SEE CONCEPT *406*

hair-raising [*adj*] *causing excitement*
bloodcurdling, breathtaking, chilling, cliff-hanging, electrifying, exciting, frightening, shocking,
spine-chilling, spine-tingling, suspenseful, terrifying; SEE CONCEPTS *529,542,548*

hairsplitting [*n*] *nitpicking*
bickering, carping, caviling, faultfinding, perfec-
tionism, pettiness, quibbling, sophistry; SEE CON-
CEPTS *671,706*

hairstyle [*n*] *cut, style of a head of hair*
afro*, beehive*, blow dry*, bob*, bouffant,
braid, brushcut, bubble*, bun, coiffure, crewcut,
cut, do*, dreadlocks, ducktail, fade, feather cut,
flattop*, flip, haircut, hairdo, headdress, horse
tail, mohawk, natural, pageboy, pigtails, pixie,
ponytail, razor cut; SEE CONCEPT *718*

hairy [*adj1*] *having much hair*
bearded, bewhiskered, bristly, bushy, downy,
fleecy, flocculent, fluffy, furry, fuzzy, hirsute,
lanate, pileous, piliferous, pilose, pubescent,
rough, shaggy, stubbly, tufted, unshaven, unshorn, villous, whiskered, woolly; SEE CONCEPT
406

hairy [*adj2*] *dangerous*
chancy, difficult, hazardous, jeopardous, perilous, risky, scary, treacherous, uncertain, unhealthy, unsound, wicked; SEE CONCEPT *548*

halcyon [*adj*] *calm, peaceful*
at peace, balmy, bucolic, gentle, golden, happy,
harmonious, palmy, pastoral, quiet, serene,
soothing, still, sunny, tranquil, untroubled; SEE
CONCEPTS *401,404,525,542,594*

hale [*adj*] *strong and healthy*
able-bodied, alive and kicking*, blooming, fit, fit
as a fiddle*, flourishing, healthy, hearty, husky,
in fine fettle*, in the pink*, right, robust, sane,
sound, stout, strapping, strong, trim, vigorous,
well, well-conditioned, wholesome; SEE CON-
CEPTS *314,489*

half [*adj*] *partial*
bisected, divided, even-steven*, fifty-fifty*, fractional, halved, incomplete, limited, moderate,
partly; SEE CONCEPT *785*

half [*n*] *one of two equal parts of a whole*
bisection, division, fifty percent, fraction, hemi-
sphere, moiety; SEE CONCEPT *835*

half-baked [*adj*] *stupid; not thought through*
backward, batty*, birdbrained*, blockheaded*,
boneheaded*, brainless, crazy, dumb, feeble-
minded, foolish, harebrained*, idiotic, ignorant,
ill-conceived, imbecilic, impractical, indiscreet,
moronic, poorly planned, retarded, senseless,
short-sighted, silly, slow, sophomoric, underdeveloped, unformed, witless; SEE CONCEPTS
403,529,548

half-breed [*n*] *mixed creation*
amalgam, blend, combination, conglomeration,
cross, cross-breed, hodgepodge*, hybrid, med-

ley, melange, miscegnation, mishmash*, mule, mutt*; SEE CONCEPTS *260,394*

halfhearted [*adj*] *without enthusiasm*
apathetic, cool, impassive, indifferent, irresolute, lackluster, listless, lukewarm, neutral, passive, perfunctory, spiritless, tame, tepid, unenthusiastic, uninterested; SEE CONCEPTS *401,542*

halfway [*adj*] *not complete; in the middle*
betwixt and between*, center, centermost, central, equidistant, imperfect, intermediate, medial, median, mid*, middlemost, midway, moderate, part, partial, part-way, smack dab*, smack in the middle*; SEE CONCEPTS *531,586*

halfway [*adv*] *not complete; in the middle*
comparatively, compromising, conciliatory, half the distance, imperfectly, incompletely, in part, insufficiently, medially, middling, midway, moderately, nearly, partially, partly, pretty*, rather, restrictedly, to a degree, to some extent, to the middle, unsatisfactorily; SEE CONCEPTS *531,586*

half-wit [*n*] *stupid person*
blockhead*, cretin, dimwit, dingbat*, dolt, dope*, dork*, dullard, dumbbell*, dummy*, dunce, dunderhead, fool, idiot, ignoramus, imbecile, lamebrain*, moron, nitwit, pea brain*, simpleton; SEE CONCEPTS *350,423*

hall [*n1*] *corridor*
anteroom, entrance, entranceway, entry, foyer, gallery, hallway, lobby, pass, passage, passageway, room, rotunda, vestibule; SEE CONCEPT *440*

hall [*n2*] *room for large affairs*
amphitheater, arena, armory, assembly room, auditorium, ballroom, casino, chamber, church, gallery, gym, gymnasium, lounge, lyceum, mart, meeting place, refectory, salon, stateroom, theater; SEE CONCEPTS *438,439,441,448*

hallmark [*n*] *symbol, authentication*
badge, certification, device, emblem, endorsement, indication, mark, ratification, seal, sign, signet, stamp, sure sign, telltale sign, trademark; SEE CONCEPTS *284,628*

hallowed [*adj*] *holy, revered*
anointed, beatified, blessed, consecrated, dedicated, divine, enshrined, holy, honored, inviolable, sacred, sacrosanct, sanctified, unprofane; SEE CONCEPT *568*

hallucinate [*v*] *imagine vividly*
blow one's mind*, daydream, envision, fantasize, freak out*, have visions, head trip*, hear voices*, trip*, visualize; SEE CONCEPT *34*

hallucination [*n*] *dream, delusion*
aberration, apparition, fantasy, figment of the imagination*, head trip*, illusion, mirage, phantasm, phantasmagoria, phantom, trip*, vision, wraith; SEE CONCEPTS *529,532,690*

halo [*n*] *ring of light*
aura, aureola, aureole, aurora, corona, crown of light, glory, halation, nimbus, radiance; SEE CONCEPTS *624,628*

halt [*n*] *end, stoppage*
arrest, break, break-off*, close, cutoff, freeze*, grinding halt, impasse, interruption, layoff, letup, pause, screaming halt*, screeching halt*, stand, standstill, stop, termination; SEE CONCEPT *119*

halt [*v1*] *stop, cause to stop*
adjourn, arrest, balk, bar, block, blow the whistle on*, break off*, bring to an end, bring to standstill, call it a day*, cease, cease fire, check, close down, come to an end, cool it*, curb*, cut short, desist, deter, draw up, drop anchor*, end, frus-

trate, hamper, hold at bay*, hold back, impede, intermit, interrupt, obstruct, pause, pull up*, punctuate, put a cork in*, rest, stall, stand still, stay, stem, stop, suspend, terminate, wait; SEE CONCEPTS *121,234*

halt [*v2*] *hesitate, stutter*
be defective, dither, falter, hobble, limp, pause, shilly-shally*, stagger, stammer, stumble, vacillate, waver, whiffle*, wiggle-waggle*; SEE CONCEPTS *234,721,804*

halting [*adj*] *hesitant*
awkward, bumbling, clumsy, doubtful, faltering, gauche, imperfect, indecisive, inept, irresolute, labored, limping, lumbering, maladroit, slow, stammering, stumbling, stuttering, tentative, uncertain, unhandy, vacillating, vacillatory, wavering, wooden*; SEE CONCEPTS *534,550*

halve [*v*] *cut in half*
bisect, divide equally, reduce by fifty percent, share equally, split in two; SEE CONCEPT *98*

hamburger [*n*] *ground beef sandwich*
beefburger, burger, cheeseburger, chopped beefsteak, ground chuck, ground round, ground sirloin, Salisbury steak; SEE CONCEPTS *457,460*

hamlet [*n*] *small village*
community, crossroads, district, small town, suburb; SEE CONCEPT *507*

hammer [*v*] *beat, hit*
bang, batter, bear down, clobber, defeat, drive, drub, fashion, forge, form, knock, make, pound, pummel, shape, strike, tap, thrash, trounce, wallop, whack, whomp; SEE CONCEPT *189*

hammer away/hammer into [*v*] *work hard at*
continue, drive home*, drub into*, drudge, drum into*, endeavor, grind*, grind into*, impress upon, instruct, keep on, peg away*, persevere, persist, plug away*, pound away*, repeat, stick to*, try hard, try repeatedly, work; SEE CONCEPTS *68,87,239*

hammer out [*v*] *bring to a conclusion*
accomplish, bring about, build, complete, construct, erect, establish, excogitate, fight through, finish, form, make, negotiate, produce, settle, set up, sort out, thrash out*, work out; SEE CONCEPTS *91,706*

hamper [*n*] *basket for storage*
bassinet, carton, crate, creel, laundry basket, pannier; SEE CONCEPT *494*

hamper [*v*] *impede, restrict*
baffle, balk, bar, bind, block, check, clog, cramp, cramp one's style*, cumber, curb, drag one's feet*, embarrass, encumber, entangle, fetter, foil, frustrate, get in the way*, hamstring*, handicap, hang up*, hinder, hobble, hog-tie*, hold up*, inconvenience, inhibit, interfere with, leash, obstruct, prevent, restrain, retard, shackle, slow down, stymie, thwart, tie, tie one's hands*, tie up, trammel; SEE CONCEPT *130*

hamstring [*v*] *disable*
cripple, debilitate, handicap, hinder, hobble, immobilize, impair, lame, maim, mangle, paralyze, weaken; SEE CONCEPTS *130,246*

hand [*n1*] *appendage at end of human arm, including fingers*
duke*, extremity, fin*, fist, grasp, grip, ham*, hold, hook, metacarpus, mitt*, palm, paw*, phalanges, shaker*; SEE CONCEPT *392*

hand [*n2*] *person who does labor*
aide, artificer, artisan, craftsperson, employee,

help, helper, hired person, laborer, operative, roustabout, worker; SEE CONCEPT *348*

hand [*n3*] *help, aid*
ability, agency, assistance, control, direction, guidance, influence, instruction, knack, lift, part, participation, relief, share, skill, succor, support; SEE CONCEPTS *110,630*

hand [*n4*] *handwriting*
calligraphy, chirography, longhand, script; SEE CONCEPT *79*

hand [*n5*] *round of applause*
clap, handclapping, ovation, thunderous reception; SEE CONCEPT *189*

handbag [*n*] *person's carryall*
backpack, bag, clutch, evening bag, grip, hide, knapsack, leather, pocketbook, portmanteau, purse, reticule; SEE CONCEPT *446*

handbook [*n*] *document giving instruction, information*
bible, compendium, directory, enchiridion, encyclopedia, fundamentals, guide, guidebook, instruction book, manual, text, textbook, vade mecum; SEE CONCEPT *280*

handful [*adj*] *a small quantity*
few, scattering, small number, smattering, some, spattering, sprinkling; SEE CONCEPT *789*

handicap [*n1*] *disadvantage*
affliction, baggage*, barrier, block, burden, detriment, disability, drawback, encumbrance, hangup*, hindrance, impairment, impediment, injury, limitation, load, millstone, obstacle, psychological baggage*, restriction, shortcoming, stumbling block*; SEE CONCEPTS *666,674*

handicap [*n2*] *advantage*
bulge, edge*, favor, head start*, odds, penalty, points*, start, upper hand*, vantage; SEE CONCEPT *693*

handicap [*v*] *give disadvantage*
burden, cripple, encumber, hamper, hamstring*, hinder, hog-tie*, hold back, impede, limit, put out of commission*, restrict, sideline*, take out*; SEE CONCEPTS *130,246*

handicraft [*n*] *artwork, skill*
achievement, art, artifact, artisanship, calling, craft, craftship, creation, design, handiwork, invention, métier, product, production, profession, result, trade, vocation; SEE CONCEPTS *259,630*

handle [*n1*] *something to grip*
arm, bail, crank, ear, grasp, haft, handgrip, helve, hilt, hold, holder, knob, shaft, stem, stock, tiller; SEE CONCEPTS *445,502,831*

handle [*n2*] *nickname*
appellation, byname, byword, cognomen, denomination, designation, moniker, name, nomen, sobriquet, style, title; SEE CONCEPT *683*

handle [*v1*] *touch*
check, examine, feel, finger*, fondle, grasp, hold, manipulate, maul, palpate, paw*, pick up, poke, test, thumb*, try; SEE CONCEPT *612*

handle [*v2*] *manage, take care of*
administer, advise, apply, behave toward, bestow, call the signals*, command, conduct, control, cope with, cut the mustard*, deal with, direct, discuss, dispense, dominate, employ, exercise, exploit, get a handle on*, govern, guide, hack it*, make out*, make the grade*, maneuver, manipulate, operate, play, ply, run things, serve, steer, supervise, swing, take, treat, use, utilize, wield, work; SEE CONCEPTS *91,117*

handle [*v3*] *carry as merchandise*
deal in, market, offer, retail, sell, stock, trade, traffic in; SEE CONCEPT *345*

handling [*n*] *management*
administration, approach, care, charge, conduct, direction, manipulation, running, styling, superintendence, supervision, treatment; SEE CONCEPT *117*

hand-me-down [*adj*] *secondhand*
not new, passed down, previously owned, used; SEE CONCEPTS *575,585*

hand out [*v*] *give to others*
bestow, deal out, deliver, devote, disburse, dish out, dispense, disseminate, distribute, donate, give away, give out, hand over, mete, present, provide; SEE CONCEPTS *108,140*

hand over [*v*] *give back; release*
abandon, cede, commend, commit, consign, deliver, dispense, donate, entrust, feed, find, fork out*, fork up*, give up, hand, leave, present, provide, relegate, relinquish, supply, surrender, transfer, turn over, waive, yield; SEE CONCEPTS *108,131*

handsome [*adj1*] *attractive*
admirable, aristocratic, athletic, august, beautiful, becoming, clean-cut, comely, dapper, elegant, fair, fashionable, fine, good-looking, graceful, impressive, lovely, majestic, noble, personable, pulchritudinous, robust, sharp, smart, smooth, spruce, stately, strong, stylish, suave, virile, well-dressed, well-proportioned; SEE CONCEPT *579*

handsome [*adj2*] *abundant*
ample, bounteous, bountiful, considerable, extensive, full, generous, gracious, large, lavish, liberal, magnanimous, munificent, openhanded, plentiful, princely, sizable, unsparing; SEE CONCEPT *781*

handsomely [*adv*] *abundantly*
amply, bountifully, generously, lavishly, liberally, magnanimously, munificently, nobly, plentifully, richly; SEE CONCEPT *781*

handwriting [*n*] *the way a person writes*
autography, calligraphy, chicken scratch*, chirography, ductus, griffonage, hand, hieroglyphics, longhand, manuscript, manuscription, mark, pencraft, penscript, scratching*, scrawl, scribble, script, scription, scrivenery, scrivening, style, writing; SEE CONCEPTS *284,625,628*

handy [*adj1*] *nearby*
accessible, adjacent, at hand, available, close, close-at-hand, close by, convenient, near, near-at-hand, on hand, ready, within reach; SEE CONCEPT *586*

handy [*adj2*] *easy to use*
adaptable, advantageous, available, beneficial, central, convenient, functional, gainful, helpful, manageable, neat, practicable, practical, profitable, ready, serviceable, useful, utile, wieldy; SEE CONCEPT *560*

handy [*adj3*] *adept physically*
able, adroit, clever, deft, dexterous, expert, fit, ingenious, nimble, proficient, ready, skilled, skillful; SEE CONCEPT *527*

hang [*v1*] *suspend or be suspended*
adhere, attach, beetle, be fastened, be in mid-air, be loose, bend, be pendent, be poised, bow, cling, cover, dangle, deck, decorate, depend, drape, drift, droop, drop, fasten, fix, flap, float, flop, furnish, hold, hover, impend, incline, lean,

loll, lop, lower, nail, overhang, pin, project, remain, rest, sag, stay up, stick, swing, tack, trail, wave; SEE CONCEPTS *144,201,746*

hang [*v2*] *kill by suspension from a rope*
execute, gibbet, hoist, lynch, noose, scrag, send to the gallows, stretch*, string up*, swing*; SEE CONCEPT *252*

hang [*v3*] *depend on future action*
await, be conditional upon, be contingent on, be dependent on, be determined by, be in limbo, be in suspense, cling, hinge, pend, rest, turn on; SEE CONCEPT *681*

hang about/hang around/hang out [*v*] *associate with; be residing in*
abide, affect, dally, frequent, get along with, haunt, have relations with, linger, live, loiter, reside, resort, roam, spend time, stand around, swell, tarry, waste time; SEE CONCEPTS *114,226*

hangdog [*adj*] *shamefaced*
ashamed, browbeaten, conscience-stricken, cowering, defeated, downcast, guilty, intimidated, sheepish, wretched; SEE CONCEPT *403*

hanger-on [*n*] *person who attends the powerful for status or benefit*
dependent, flunky*, follower, freeloader*, lackey*, leech*, nuisance, parasite, sponger*, sycophant, truckler*; SEE CONCEPT *423*

hang on [*v*] *continue, endure*
be tough, carry on, cling, clutch, go on, grasp, grip, hold fast, hold on, hold out, persevere, persist, remain; SEE CONCEPTS *23,239*

hangout [*n*] *place for socializing*
bar, den*, dive*, haunt*, home, honky-tonk*, joint*, purlieu, resort, stomping ground*, watering hole*; SEE CONCEPTS *439,447,449*

hangover [*n*] *result of heavy drinking*
aftereffect, big head*, delirium tremens, drunkenness, DTs*, headache, morning after*, shakes*, under the weather*, willies*, withdrawal; SEE CONCEPT *316*

hang tough [*v*] *endure*
bear, bear the brunt*, be patient with, brave, cope with, face, go through, grin and bear it*, gut it out*, hang in*, hang in there, keep up, live out, live through, meet with, never say die*, put up with, ride out*, sit through, stand, stick in there, stick it out*, stomach*, suffer, swallow*, take, take it*, tough it out*, weather, withstand; SEE CONCEPT *23*

hang-up [*n*] *preoccupation*
block, difficulty, dilemma, disturbance, impasse, inhibition, obsession, predicament, problem, reserve, restraint, thing; SEE CONCEPTS *532,674,690*

hanker after/hanker for [*v*] *desire strongly*
ache, covet, crave, hunger, itch, long, lust, partial to, pine, sigh, thirst, want, wish, yearn, yen; SEE CONCEPT *20*

hankering [*n*] *strong desire*
ache, craving, druthers*, fire in belly*, hunger, itch*, longing, munchies*, pining, thirst, urge, want, weakness, wish, yearning, yen; SEE CONCEPTS *20,709*

hanky-panky [*n*] *mischief*
chicane, chicanery, deception, devilry, double-dealing, fourberie, fraud, funny business*, knavery, machinations, monkey business*, sharp practice*, shenanigans*, skullduggery*, subterfuge, trickery; SEE CONCEPTS *59,384*

haphazard [*adj*] *without plan or organization*
accidental, aimless, all over the map*, any old way*, any which way*, arbitrary, careless, casual, chance, designless, desultory, devil-may-care*, disorderly, disorganized, erratic, fluke, helter-skelter*, hit-or-miss*, incidental, indiscriminate, irregular, loose, offhand, purposeless, random, reckless, slapdash, slipshod, spontaneous, sudden, unconcerned, unconscious, unconsidered, uncoordinated, unexpected, unmethodical, unorganized, unpremeditated, unsystematic, unthinking, willy-nilly*; SEE CONCEPTS *535,581*

hapless [*adj*] *unfortunate*
behind the eightball*, cursed, hexed, ill-fated, ill-starred, infelicitous, jinxed, jonah*, loser, luckless, miserable, poor fish*, sad sack*, snakebit*, star-crossed*, unhappy, unlucky, untoward, voodooed*, woeful, wretched; SEE CONCEPT *548*

happen [*v*] *come to pass; occur*
appear, arise, arrive, become a fact, become known, become of, befall, be found, betide, bump, chance, come about, come after, come into being, come into existence, come off, crop up*, develop, down, ensue, eventuate, fall, follow, go on, hit, issue, light, luck, materialize, meet, pass, present itself, proceed, recur, result, shake, smoke*, spring, stumble, stumble upon, supervene, take effect, take place, transpire, turn out, turn up, what goes*; SEE CONCEPT *4*

happening [*n*] *occurrence*
accident, adventure, affair, case, chance, circumstance, episode, event, experience, go*, incident, milestone, occasion, phenomenon, proceeding, scene, thing*; SEE CONCEPT *4*

happily [*adv1*] *with joy, pleasure*
agreeably, blissfully, blithely, brightly, buoyantly, cheerfully, contentedly, delightedly, delightfully, devotedly, elatedly, enthusiastically, exhilaratingly, exultantly, freely, gaily, gladly, gleefully, graciously, heartily, hilariously, jovially, joyfully, joyously, laughingly, light-heartedly, lightly, lovingly, merrily, optimistically, peacefully, playfully, sincerely, smilingly, sportively, vivaciously, willingly, with relish, with zeal, zestfully; SEE CONCEPTS *403,542*

happily [*adv2*] *successfully*
appropriately, aptly, auspiciously, favorably, felicitously, fortunately, gracefully, propitiously, prosperously, providentially, satisfyingly, seasonably, swimmingly, well; SEE CONCEPT *548*

happiness [*n*] *high spirits, satisfaction*
beatitude, blessedness, bliss, cheer, cheerfulness, cheeriness, content, contentment, delectation, delight, delirium, ecstasy, elation, enchantment, enjoyment, euphoria, exhilaration, exuberance, felicity, gaiety, geniality, gladness, glee, good cheer, good humor, good spirits, hilarity, hopefulness, joviality, joy, jubilation, laughter, light-heartedness, merriment, mirth, optimism, paradise, peace of mind, playfulness, pleasure, prosperity, rejoicing, sanctity, seventh heaven*, vivacity, well-being; SEE CONCEPT *410*

happy [*adj1*] *in high spirits; satisfied*
blessed, blest, blissful, blithe, can't complain*, captivated, cheerful, chipper, chirpy, content, contented, convivial, delighted, ecstatic, elated, exultant, flying high*, gay, glad, gleeful, gratified, intoxicated, jolly, joyful, joyous, jubilant,

laughing, light, lively, looking good*, merry, mirthful, on cloud nine*, overjoyed, peaceful, peppy, perky, playful, pleasant, pleased, sparkling, sunny, thrilled, tickled, tickled pink*, up, upbeat, walking on air*; SEE CONCEPT *403*

happy [*adj2*] *lucky*
accidental, advantageous, appropriate, apt, auspicious, befitting, casual, convenient, correct, effective, efficacious, enviable, favorable, felicitous, fitting, fortunate, incidental, just, meet, nice, opportune, promising, proper, propitious, providential, right, satisfactory, seasonable, successful, suitable, timely, well-timed; SEE CONCEPT *558*

happy-go-lucky [*adj*] *carefree and untroubled*
blithe, casual, cheerful, cool, devil-may-care*, easy, easygoing, feckless, free-minded, heedless, improvident, insouciant, irresponsible, lackadaisical*, lighthearted, nonchalant, reckless, unconcerned; SEE CONCEPTS *404,542*

hara-kiri [*n*] *ritual suicide*
belly cutting, ceremonious suicide, disembowelment, self-immolation, seppuku; SEE CONCEPTS *192,252*

harangue [*n*] *long lecture*
address, chewing out*, declamation, diatribe, discourse, exhortation, hassle, jeremiad, oration, philippic, reading out*, screed, sermon, speech, spiel*, spouting, tirade; SEE CONCEPTS *51,278*

harangue [*v*] *give a long lecture*
accost, address, apostrophize, buttonhole*, chew out*, declaim, exhort, get on a soapbox*, go on about*, hold forth, orate, perorate, rant, rave, soapbox*, spiel*, spout, stump, talk to, yell at; SEE CONCEPT *51*

harass [*v*] *badger*
annoy, attack, bait, bedevil, beleaguer, bother, bug*, burn*, despoil, devil*, distress, disturb, eat*, exasperate, exhaust, fatigue, foray, get to*, give a bad time*, give a hard time*, gnaw*, harry, hassle, heckle, hound*, intimidate, irk, irritate, jerk around*, macerate, maraud, noodge*, pain*, perplex, persecute, pester, plague, raid, rattle one's cage*, ride, strain, stress, tease, tire, torment, trouble, try, vex, weary, work on*, worry; SEE CONCEPTS *7,14,19*

harassment [*n*] *badgering*
aggravation, annoyance, bedevilment, bother, bothering, disturbance, exasperation, hassle, irking, irritation, molestation, nuisance, persecution, perturbation, pestering, provocation, provoking, torment, trouble, vexation, vexing; SEE CONCEPTS *14,313*

harbinger [*n*] *indication*
augury, forerunner, foretoken, herald, messenger, omen, portent, precursor, sign, signal; SEE CONCEPTS *74,284,529*

harbor [*n1*] *place for storing boats in the water*
anchorage, arm, bay, bight, breakwater, chuck, cove, dock, embankment, firth, gulf, haven, inlet, jetty, landing, mooring, pier, port, road, roadstead, wharf; SEE CONCEPTS *439,509,514*

harbor [*n2*] *place for seclusion*
asylum, cover, covert, harborage, haven, port, refuge, retreat, sanctuary, sanctum, security, shelter; SEE CONCEPT *515*

harbor [*v1*] *hide, protect*
accommodate, board, bunk, conceal, defend, domicile, entertain, guard, hold back, house, lodge, nurse, nurture, provide refuge, put up,

quarter, relieve, safeguard, screen, secrete, secure, shelter, shield, suppress, withhold; SEE CONCEPTS *134,188*

harbor [*v2*] *hold in imagination*
believe, brood over, cherish, cling to, consider, entertain, foster, hold, imagine, maintain, nurse, nurture, regard, retain; SEE CONCEPT *17*

hard [*adj1*] *rocklike*
adamantine, callous, compact, compacted, compressed, concentrated, consolidated, dense, firm, hardened, impenetrable, indurate, indurated, inflexible, iron*, packed, rigid, rocky, set, solid, stiff, stony, strong, thick, tough, unyielding; SEE CONCEPT *604*

hard [*adj2*] *difficult, exhausting*
arduous, backbreaking, bothersome, burdensome, complicated, demanding, difficile, distressing, effortful, exacting, fatiguing, formidable, grinding, hairy*, heavy*, Herculean*, intricate, involved, irksome, knotty*, labored, laborious, mean, merciless, murder, onerous, operose, rigorous, rough, rugged, scabrous, serious, severe, slavish, sticky, strenuous, terrible, tiring, toilful, toilsome, tough, troublesome, unsparing, uphill*, uphill battle*, wearing, wearisome, wearying; SEE CONCEPTS *529,538,565*

hard [*adj3*] *cruel, ruthless*
acrimonious, angry, antagonistic, austere, bitter, bleak, brutal, callous, cold, cold-blooded*, cold fish*, dark, disagreeable, distressing, dour, exacting, grievous, grim, hard as nails*, hard-boiled*, harsh, hostile, inclement, intemperate, intolerable, obdurate, painful, perverse, pitiless, rancorous, resentful, rigorous, rugged, severe, stern, strict, stringent, stubborn, thick-skinned*, tough, unfeeling, unjust, unkind, unpleasant, unrelenting, unsparing, unsympathetic, vengeful; SEE CONCEPTS *401,542*

hard [*adj4*] *true, indisputable*
absolute, actual, bare, cold, definite, down-to-earth, genuine, plain, positive, practical, pragmatic, realistic, sure, undeniable, unvarnished, verified; SEE CONCEPTS *535,582*

hard [*adv1*] *with great force*
actively, angrily, animatedly, boisterously, briskly, brutally, cruelly, earnestly, energetically, ferociously, fiercely, forcibly, frantically, furiously, heavily, intensely, keenly, like fury, madly, meanly, painfully, powerfully, relentlessly, rigorously, roughly, rowdily, savagely, seriously, severely, sharply, spiritedly, sprightly, stormily, strongly, tumultously/tumultuously, turbulently, uproariously, urgently, viciously, vigorously, violently, vivaciously, wildly, with all one's might; SEE CONCEPT *540*

hard [*adv2*] *with determination*
assiduously, closely, diligently, doggedly, earnestly, exhaustively, industriously, intensely, intensively, intently, painstakingly, persistently, searchingly, sharply, steadily, strenuously, thoroughly, unremittingly, untiringly; SEE CONCEPT *538*

hard [*adv3*] *with difficulty*
agonizingly, arduously, awkwardly, badly, burdensomely, carefully, cumbersomely, cumbrously, distressingly, exhaustingly, gruelingly, hardly, harshly, inconveniently, laboriously, painfully, ponderously, roughly, severely, stren-

uously, tiredly, toilsomely, unwieldily, vigorously, with great effort; SEE CONCEPT *565*

hard [*adv4*] *with resentment*
bitterly, hardly, keenly, rancorously, reluctantly, slowly, sorely; SEE CONCEPT *403*

hard [*adv5*] *in a fixed manner*
close, fast, firm, firmly, solidly, steadfastly, tight, tightly; SEE CONCEPTS *488,586*

hard-boiled [*adj*] *tough*
callous, firm, hard as nails*, hard-line*, hard-nosed*, hard-shelled*, headstrong, inflexible, obdurate, obstinate, rough, stern, strict, unbending, unfeeling; SEE CONCEPTS *403,542*

hard-core [*adj*] *dedicated*
determined, devoted, die-hard*, dyed-in-the-wool*, explicit, extreme, faithful, intransigent, obstinate, resolute, rigid, staunch, steadfast, stubborn, uncompromising, unwavering, unyielding; SEE CONCEPTS *535,542*

harden [*v1*] *make or become solid*
amalgamate, anneal, bake, brace, buttress, cake, calcify, callous, cement, close, clot, coagulate, compact, congeal, consolidate, contract, crystallize, curdle, densify, dry, firm, fix, fortify, fossilize, freeze, gird, indurate, jell, nerve, ossify, petrify, precipitate, press, reinforce, set, settle, solidify, starch, steel, stiffen, strengthen, temper, thicken, toughen, vitrify; SEE CONCEPTS *250,469*

harden [*v2*] *accustom*
acclimate, acclimatize, adapt, adjust, blunt,'brutalize, callous, callus, case-harden, climatize, coarsen, conform, deaden, develop, discipline, dull, embitter, habituate, indurate, inure, make callous, numb, paralyze, render insensitive, roughen, season, steel, stiffen, strengthen, stun, stupefy, teach, train; SEE CONCEPTS *35,235*

hardened [*adj*] *unfeeling*
accustomed, benumbed, callous, case-hardened, coldhearted*, contemptuous, cruel, disdainful, habituated, hard-as-nails*, hard-bitten*, hard-boiled*, hardhearted*, heartless, impenetrable, impious, inaccessible, indurated, inured, irreverent, obdurate, obtuse, prepared, resistant, seasoned, steeled, toughened, unashamed, unbending, uncaring, uncompassionate, unemotional, unrepenting, unsubmissive; SEE CONCEPTS *404,542*

hardhearted [*adj*] *cold, cruel*
brutish, callous, cold-blooded*, coldhearted*, hard, hard-boiled*, heartless, indifferent, inhuman, insensitive, intolerant, merciless, obdurate, pitiless, stony, uncaring, uncompassionate, unemotional, unfeeling, unkind, unsympathetic; SEE CONCEPTS *401,404*

hard-line [*adj*] *firm*
adamant, hard-boiled*, hard-core, hard-nosed*, inflexible, militant, stand pat*, staunch, steadfast, stern, stiff, strict, unbending, uncompromising, ungiving, unyielding; SEE CONCEPTS *267,403,542*

hardly [*adv*] *scarcely; with difficulty*
almost inconceivably, almost not, barely, by a hair, by no means, comparatively, detectably, faintly, gradually, imperceptibly, infrequently, just, little, no more than, not a bit, not at all, not by much, not likely, not markedly, not measurably, not much, not notably, not noticeably, not often, not quite, no way, once in a blue moon*, only, only just, perceptibly, practically, pretty near, rarely, scantly, seldom, simply, slightly,

somewhat, sparsely, sporadically, with trouble; SEE CONCEPTS *541,552,771*

hard-nosed/hardheaded [*adj*] *stubborn*
astute, bullheaded*, hard*, hard-boiled*, headstrong, intractable, levelheaded, locked in*, mulish, obstinate, pertinacious, perverse, pigheaded*, practical, pragmatic, rational, realistic, resolute, sensible, shrewd, sober, stand pat, tough, tough-nut*, unsentimental, unyielding, willful; SEE CONCEPTS *404,542*

hardship [*n*] *personal burden*
accident, adversity, affliction, asperity, austerity, calamity, case, catastrophe, curse, danger, destitution, difficulty, disaster, discomfort, distress, drudgery, fatigue, grief, grievance, hard knocks*, hazard, Herculean task*, injury, labor, mischance, misery, misfortune, need, oppression, peril, persecution, privation, rainy day*, rigor, rotten luck*, sorrow, suffering, toil, torment, tough break*, tough luck*, travail, trial, tribulation, trouble, uphill battle*, vicissitude, want, worry; SEE CONCEPTS *674,675*

hardware [*n*] *tools; fittings, especially made of metal*
accouterments, appliances, fasteners, fixtures, household furnishings, housewares, implements, ironware, kitchenware, metalware, plumbing, utensils; SEE CONCEPTS *338,499*

hardy [*adj*] *strong, tough*
able, able-bodied, acclimatized, brawny, burly, capable, enduring, firm, fit, fresh, hale, hardened, healthy, hearty, hefty, indefatigable, in fine fettle*, in good condition, in good shape, inured, lusty, mighty, muscular, physically fit, powerful, resistant, robust, rugged, seasoned, solid, sound, stalwart, staunch, stout, sturdy, substantial, tenacious, unflagging, vigorous, well; SEE CONCEPTS *314,485,489*

harebrained [*adj*] *stupid, unthinking*
absurd, asinine, barmy, bizarre, careless, changeable, crazy, dizzy*, empty-headed*, featherbrained*, flighty, foolish, frivolous, giddy, half-baked*, heedless, inane, irresponsible, loony*, mindless, preposterous, rash, rattlebrained, reckless, scatterbrained*, unstable, unsteady, wacky*, wild; SEE CONCEPTS *402,529*

harlot [*n*] *prostitute*
call girl, concubine, courtesan, fallen woman*, floozy*, hooker, hussy, lady of the evening, loose woman, nymphomaniac*, painted woman, slut, streetwalker, strumpet, tramp, whore; SEE CONCEPTS *348,412,415,419*

harm [*n*] *injury, evil*
abuse, banefulness, damage, deleteriousness, detriment, disservice, foul play*, hurt, ill, immorality, impairment, infliction, iniquity, loss, marring, mischance, mischief, misfortune, misuse, noxiousness, outrage, perniciousness, prejudice, ravage, ruin, ruination, sabotage, sin, sinfulness, vandalism, vice, violence, wear and tear*, wickedness, wrong; SEE CONCEPTS *309,674,728*

harm [*v*] *injure; cause evil*
abuse, blemish, bruise, cripple, crush, damage, dilapidate, discommode, disserve, do violence to, dump on*, get, hurt, ill-treat, impair, incommode, inconvenience, louse up*, maim, maltreat, mangle, mar, mess up*, misuse, molest, muck up*, mutilate, nick, outrage, prejudice, put down, ruin, sabotage, sap*, scathe, shatter, shock, spoil,

ha
ha

stab, tarnish, total, trample, traumatize, tweak*, undermine, vandalize, vitiate, wing*, wound, wreck, wrench, wrong, zing*; SEE CONCEPTS *7,19,246,313*

harmful [*adj*] *injurious, hurtful*
adverse, bad, baleful, baneful, calamitous, cataclysmic, catastrophic, consumptive, corroding, corrupting, crippling, damaging, deleterious, destructive, detrimental, dire, disadvantageous, disastrous, evil, harassing, incendiary, inimical, internecine, malefic, malicious, malignant, menacing, mischievous, murderous, nocuous, noxious, painful, pernicious, pestiferous, pestilential, risky, ruinous, sinful, sinister, subversive, toxic, undermining, unhealthy, unsafe, unwholesome, virulent; SEE CONCEPT *537*

harmless [*adj*] *not injurious or dangerous*
controllable, disarmed, gentle, guiltless, hurtless, innocent, innocuous, innoxious, inoffensive, inoperative, kind, manageable, naive, nonirritating, nontoxic, painless, paper-tiger*, powerless, pussycat*, reliable, safe, sanitary, simple, soft*, softie*, sound, sure, trustworthy, unobjectionable, unoffensive; SEE CONCEPT *537*

harmonious [*adj*] *agreeable, corresponding; friendly*
accordant, adapted, amicable, balanced, compatible, concordant, congenial, congruous, consonant, coordinated, cordial, dulcet, euphonious, harmonic, harmonizing, in accord, in chorus, in concert, in harmony, in step, in tune, in unison, like, matching, mellifluous, melodic, melodious, mix, musical, of one mind*, on same wavelength*, peaceful, rhythmical, silvery, similar, simpatico, sonorous, suitable, sweet-sounding, symmetrical, sympathetic, symphonic, symphonious, tuneful; SEE CONCEPT *563*

harmonize [*v*] *correspond, match*
accord, adapt, adjust, agree, arrange, attune, be in unison, be of one mind*, blend, carol, chime with, cohere, combine, compose, cooperate, coordinate, correlate, fit in with*, integrate, orchestrate, proportion, reconcile, reconciliate, relate, set, sing, suit, symphonize, synthesize, tune, unify, unite; SEE CONCEPTS *77,664*

harmony [*n1*] *social agreement*
accord, affinity, amicability, amity, compatibility, concord, conformity, consensus, consistency, cooperation, correspondence, empathy, friendship, good will, kinship, like-mindedness, meeting of minds*, peace, rapport, sympathy, tranquility, unanimity, understanding, unity; SEE CONCEPT *388*

harmony [*n2*] *correspondence, balance*
accord, agreement, articulation, chime, concord, concordance, conformance, conformity, congruity, consistency, consonance, fitness, form, integration, integrity, oneness, order, parallelism, proportion, regularity, suitability, symmetry, togetherness, tune, unity; SEE CONCEPT *664*

harmony [*n3*] *musical accordance*
arrangement, attunement, blend, blending, chime, chord, chorus, composition, concentus, concert, concinnity, concurrence, consonance, diapason, euphony, harmonics, mellifluousness, melodiousness, melody, organum, overtone, piece, polyphony, richness, symphony, triad, tune, tunefulness, unison, unity; SEE CONCEPTS *65,262,595*

harness [*n*] *gear for controlling an animal*
belt, equipment, strap, tack, tackle, trappings; SEE CONCEPT *496*

harness [*v*] *rein in; control*
accouter, apply, bind, bridle, channel, check, cinch, collar, constrain, couple, curb, domesticate, employ, equip, exploit, fasten, fetter, fit, furnish, gear, govern, hitch, hold, leash, limit, make productive, mobilize, muzzle, outfit, put in harness, render useful, rig, saddle, secure, strap, tackle, tame, tie, utilize, yoke; SEE CONCEPTS *94,130,191*

harried [*adj*] *pressured*
agitated, anxious, at wit's end*, beset, bothered, distressed, harassed, hard-pressed, stressed, troubled, worried; SEE CONCEPTS *403,690*

harrowing [*adj*] *dangerous, frightening*
agonizing, alarming, chilling, distressing, disturbing, excruciating, heartbreaking, heart-rending, nerve-racking, painful, racking, soaring, tearing, terrifying, tormenting, torturing, torturous, traumatic; SEE CONCEPTS *529,548*

harry [*v*] *pester, annoy*
attack, badger, bedevil, beleaguer, chivy, depredate, devastate, disturb, fret, gnaw, harass, hassle, irk, irritate, lay waste, molest, persecute, perturb, pillage, plague, plunder, ravage, sack, tease, torment, trouble, upset, vex, worry; SEE CONCEPTS *7,19*

harsh [*adj1*] *rough, crude (to the senses)*
acrid, asperous, astringent, bitter, bleak, cacophonous, caterwauling, clashing, coarse, cracked, craggy, creaking, croaking, disagreeing, discordant, dissonant, disturbing, earsplitting, flat, glaring, grating, grim, guttural, hard, hoarse, incompatible, jagged, jangling, jarring, noisy, not smooth, off-key*, out-of-key*, out-of-tune*, rasping, raucous, rigid, rugged, rusty, screeching, severe, sharp, sour, strident, stridulous, tuneless, uneven, unlevel, unmelodious, unmusical, unrelenting; SEE CONCEPTS *537,569*

harsh [*adj2*] *nasty, abusive*
austere, bitter, brutal, comfortless, cruel, cussed, discourteous, dour, grim, gruff, hairy*, hard, hard-boiled, hard-nosed*, hard-shell*, mean, pitiless, punitive, relentless, rude, ruthless, severe, sharp, stern, stringent, tough, uncivil, unfeeling, ungracious, unkind, unpleasant, unrelenting, wicked; SEE CONCEPTS *267,542*

harum-scarum [*adj*] *reckless*
carefree, careless, daring, disorderly, erratic, flighty, foolhardy, giddy, haphazard, hasty, imprudent, irresponsible, light-minded, negligent, rash, regardless, romping, scatty, thoughtless, wild; SEE CONCEPTS *401,542*

harvest [*n*] *crops; taking in of crops*
autumn, by-product, consequence, cropping, effect, fall, fruitage, fruition, garnering, gathering, harvesting, harvest-time, ingathering, intake, output, produce, reaping, repercussion, result, return, season, storing, summer, yield, yielding; SEE CONCEPTS *257,338,429*

harvest [*v*] *gathering of produce*
accumulate, acquire, amass, bin, cache, collect, crop, cull, cut, garner, gather, get, glean, harrow, hoard, mow, pick, pile up, plow, pluck, reap, squirrel*, stash, store, stow, strip, take in; SEE CONCEPTS *142,257*

hash [*n*] *mess, mix-up*
assortment, clutter, confusion, hodgepodge*,

hotchpotch*, jumble, litter, medley, melange, miscellany, mishmash*, muddle*, salmagundi*, shambles*, stew*; SEE CONCEPTS 260,432

hashish [n] *cannabis resin*
black hash*, black oil*, cannabis, dope, drug, ganja*, grass*, hash, hemp, marijuana, narcotic, pot*; SEE CONCEPT 307

hassle [n] *problem, fight*
altercation, argument, bickering, bother, clamor, commotion, difficulty, disagreement, dispute, inconvenience, quarrel, row, run-in*, squabble, struggle, trial, trouble, try, tumult, turmoil, tussle, uproar, upset, whirl, wrangle; SEE CONCEPTS 46,106,674

hassle [v] *bother, harass*
annoy, argue, argufy, badger, bedevil, beleaguer, bicker, dispute, dun, harry, hound, pester, plague, quibble, squabble, worry, wrangle; SEE CONCEPTS 14,16,46

haste [n] *extreme speed, hurry*
alacrity, briskness, bustle, carelessness, celerity, dash, dispatch, drive, expedition, expeditiousness, fleetness, flurry, foolhardiness, hastiness, heedlessness, hurly-burly*, hurriedness, hustle, hustling, impatience, impetuosity, incautiousness, nimbleness, pace, precipitancy, precipitateness, prematureness, press, promptitude, promptness, quickness, rapidity, rapidness, rashness, recklessness, rush, scamper, scramble, scurry, scuttle, swiftness, urgency, velocity; SEE CONCEPTS 755,818

hasten [v] *speed something; hurry*
accelerate, advance, bolt, bound, burn, bustle, clip*, cover ground*, dash, dispatch, expedite, express, flee, fly, gallop, get cracking*, get the lead out*, goad, haste, hie, hustle, leap, make haste, make tracks*, move quickly, not lose a minute*, pace, plunge, precipitate, press, push, quicken, race, run, rush, scamper, scoot, scurry, scuttle, shake a leg*, skip, sprint, spurt, step on it*, step up*, take wing*, tear, trot, urge, waste no time*, whip around*; SEE CONCEPTS 150,152

hastily [adv] *with great speed*
agilely, apace, carelessly, double-quick, expeditiously, fast, flat-out*, heedlessly, hurriedly, impetuously, impulsively, lickety-split*, nimbly, on spur of the moment*, posthaste, precipitately, prematurely, promptly, quickly, rapidly, rashly, recklessly, speedily, straightaway, subito, suddenly, swiftly, thoughtlessly, too quickly, unpremeditatedly; SEE CONCEPTS 544,588

hasty [adj] *speedy; without much thought*
abrupt, agile, brash, breakneck*, brief, brisk, careless, chop-chop*, cursory, eager, expeditious, fast, fiery, fleet, fleeting, foolhardy, harefooted*, headlong, heedless, hurried, ill-advised, impatient, impetuous, impulsive, incautious, inconsiderate, madcap*, on the double*, passing, PDQ*, perfunctory, precipitate, prompt, pronto*, quick, quickened, quickie, rapid, rash, reckless, rushed, short, slambang*, slapdash*, snappy*, sudden, superficial, swift, thoughtless, urgent; SEE CONCEPTS 542,588,799

hat [n] *covering for the head*
boater, bonnet, bowler, bucket, chapeau, fedora, headgear, headpiece, helmet, lid*, millinery, Panama, sailor*, skimmer, sombrero, Stetson, stove pipe*, straw*, tam, tam o'shanter*, tengallon*, topper*; SEE CONCEPT 451

hatch [v] *create, plan*
bear, brainstorm*, breed, bring forth, brood, cause, come up with, conceive, concoct, contrive, cook up*, design, devise, dream up*, engender, formulate, generate, get up, give birth, incubate, induce, invent, lay eggs, make, make up, occasion, originate, parent, plot, prepare, procreate, produce, project, provoke, scheme, set, sire, spawn, spitball*, think up*, throw together*, trump up*, whip up*, work up*; SEE CONCEPTS 36,173,251

hate [n] *extreme dislike*
abhorrence, abomination, anathema, animosity, animus, antagonism, antipathy, aversion, bête noire*, black beast*, bother, bugbear*, detestation, disgust, enmity, execration, frost*, grievance, gripe, hatred, horror, hostility, ill will, irritant, loathing, malevolence, malignity, mislike, nasty look, no love lost*, nuisance, objection, odium, pain, rancor, rankling, repugnance, repulsion, resentment, revenge, revulsion, scorn, spite, trouble, venom; SEE CONCEPT 29

hate [v] *dislike very strongly*
abhor, abominate, allergic to*, anathematize, bear a grudge against, be disgusted with, be hostile to, be loath, be reluctant, be repelled by, be sick of, be sorry, can't stand*, contemn, curse, deprecate, deride, despise, detest, disapprove, disdain, disfavor, disparage, down on*, execrate, feel malice to, have an aversion to*, have enough of*, have no use for*, loathe, look down on, nauseate*, not care for*, object to, recoil from, scorn, shudder at, shun, spit upon*, spurn; SEE CONCEPT 29

hateful [adj] *nasty, obnoxious*
abhorrent, abominable, accursed, awful, bitter, blasted, catty*, confounded, cursed, cussed, damnable, damned, despicable, despiteful, detestable, disgusting, evil, execrable, forbidding, foul, gross, heinous, horrid, infamous, invidious, loathsome, malevolent, malign, mean, odious, offensive, ornery*, pesky, pestiferous, repellent, repugnant, repulsive, resentful, revolting, shuddersome, spiteful, uncool*, undesirable, vicious, vile; SEE CONCEPTS 267,404

hatred [n] *severe dislike*
abhorrence, abomination, acrimony, alienation, allergy to*, animosity, animus, antagonism, antipathy, aversion, bitterness, coldness, contempt, detestation, disapproval, disfavor, disgust, displeasure, distaste, enmity, envy, execration, grudge, hard feelings*, hate, horror, hostility, ignominy, ill will, invidiousness, loathing, malevolence, malice, malignance, militancy, no use for*, odium, pique, prejudice, rancor, repugnance, repulsion, revenge, revulsion, scorn, spite, spleen, venom; SEE CONCEPT 29

haughtiness [n] *air of supremacy*
aloofness, arrogance, conceit, contempt, contemptuousness, disdain, disdainfulness, hauteur, insolence, loftiness, pomposity, pride, snobbishness, superbity, superciliousness; SEE CONCEPT 633

haughty [adj] *arrogant*
assuming, cavalier*, conceited, contemptuous, detached, disdainful, distant, egotistic, egotistical, high, high and mighty*, hoity-toity*, imperious, indifferent, lofty, on high horse*, overbearing, overweening, proud, reserved, scornful, sniffy*, snobbish, snooty*, snotty*,

ha
ha

stuck-up*, supercilious, superior, uppity*; SEE CONCEPT *401*

haul [*n*] *something obtained or moved*
booty, burden, cargo, catch, find, freight, gain, harvest, lading, load, loot*, payload*, spoils, takings*, yield; SEE CONCEPTS *337,338*

haul [*v*] *move, pull to another spot*
back, boost, bring, buck, carry, cart, convey, drag, draw, elevate, gun, heave, heel, hoist, hump, jag, lift, lug, pack, piggy back*, raise, rake, remove, ride, shift, shlep*, shoulder, tote, tow, trail, transport, trawl, truck, tug; SEE CONCEPTS *147,148*

haunt [*n*] *place for socializing*
abode, bar, clubhouse, cubbyhole*, den, dwelling, gathering place, habitat, hangout*, headquarters, home, lair, living quarters, locality, meeting place, niche, place, purlieu, range, rendezvous, resort, retreat, site, stomping ground*, trysting place, watering hole*; SEE CONCEPTS *435,516*

haunt [*v1*] *visit as a spirit*
agitate, agonize, annoy, appall, appear, bedevil, be ever present, beset, besiege, come back, disquiet, dwell, float, frighten, harass, harrow, hound*, hover, infest, inhabit, intrude, madden, manifest, materialize, molest, nettle, obsess, overrun, permeate, pervade, pester, plague, possess, prey on, rack*, reappear, recur, return, rise, spook*, stay with, tease, terrify, terrorize, torment, trouble, vex, voodoo*, walk, weigh on, worry; SEE CONCEPT *14*

haunt [*v2*] *spend a lot of time at*
affect, frequent, habituate, hang about*, hang around*, hang out*, infest, repair, resort, tarry at, visit; SEE CONCEPT *384*

haunting [*adj*] *unforgettable*
eerie, memorable, nagging, nostalgic, obsessive, ongoing, persistent, recurrent, repeated, spooky; SEE CONCEPTS *529,537*

hauteur [*n*] *arrogance*
airs, audacity, conceit, conceitedness, condescension, contempt, disdain, disdainfulness, egotism, gall, haughtiness, high-handedness, nerve, pomposity, pompousness, presumption, pride, self-importance, snobbishness, vanity; SEE CONCEPTS *411,633*

have [*v1*] *be in possession*
accept, acquire, admit, annex, bear, carry, chalk up, compass, corner, enjoy, gain, get, get hands on*, get hold of*, have in hand, hog*, hold, include, keep, land, latch on to*, lock up*, obtain, occupy, own, pick up, possess, procure, receive, retain, secure, sit on*, take, take in, teem with; SEE CONCEPTS *124,142,710*

have [*v2*] *endure, bear*
allow, become, be compelled to, be forced to, be one's duty to, be up to, consider, enjoy, entertain*, experience, fall on, feel, know, leave, let, meet with, must, need, ought, permit, put up with*, rest with, see, should, suffer, sustain, think about, tolerate, undergo; SEE CONCEPTS *23,83,646*

have [*v3*] *contain*
comprehend, comprise, embody, embrace, encompass, include, involve, subsume, take in; SEE CONCEPTS *642,742*

have [*v4*] *cheat, trick*
buy off*, deceive, dupe*, fix*, fool, outfox, outmaneuver, outsmart, outwit, overreach, swindle,

take in*, tamper with, undo*; SEE CONCEPTS *59,192*

have [*v5*] *bring into the world*
bear, beget, bring forth, deliver, give birth; SEE CONCEPT *374*

have a ball [*v*] *have fun*
beat the drum*, cut loose, enjoy, feast, get down*, get it on*, go to town*, jubilate, kick up one's heels*, let loose*, let off steam*, live it up*, make merry, paint the town red*, party, raise hell*, raise the roof*, rejoice, revel, revere; SEE CONCEPT *377*

haven [*n*] *refuge, port*
anchorage, asylum, cover, covert, harbor, harborage, retreat, roadstead, sanctuary, sanctum, shelter; SEE CONCEPTS *435,515*

have someone's number [*v*] *know someone's motives*
be onto someone, be wise to someone*, have someone pegged*, have someone sized up*, know what makes someone tick*, read someone; SEE CONCEPTS *15,18,37*

havoc [*n*] *chaotic situation*
calamity, cataclysm, catastrophe, chaos, confusion, damage, desolation, despoiling, destruction, devastation, dilapidation, disorder, disruption, loss, mayhem, plunder, rack and ruin*, ravages, ruination, shambles*, vandalism, waste, wreck, wreckage; SEE CONCEPT *674*

hawker [*n*] *peddler*
colporteur, costermonger, huckster, pitchperson, salesperson, seller, street seller, street vendor; SEE CONCEPTS *347,348*

hayseed [*n*] *bumpkin, yokel*
backwoodsman/woman, boor*, clodhopper*, country boy/girl, country bumpkin, country cousin*, hick*, hillbilly, rustic; SEE CONCEPT *413*

haywire [*adj*] *broken; crazy*
amiss, amok, batty, berserk, bonkers*, chaotic, confused, cracked, crazed, defective, disordered, disorganized, erratic, flipped, in a mess*, in pieces, insane, mad, messy, nuts, orderless, out of order, out of whack*, out to lunch*, psycho*, schizo*, screwball*, screwy*, touched*, unbalanced, unglued*, unhinged, wacky; SEE CONCEPTS *403,485*

hazard [*n1*] *danger*
double trouble*, dynamite, endangerment, hot potato*, imperilment, jeopardy, peril, risk, risky business*, thin ice*, threat; SEE CONCEPT *675*

hazard [*n2*] *luck, chance*
accident, adventure, coincidence, dynamite, fling*, fluke*, go*, hundred-to-one*, long shot, lucky break*, lucky hit*, misfortune, mishap, possibility, risk, risky business*, stroke of luck*, toss-up, venture, wager, way the ball bounces*, way the cookie crumbles*; SEE CONCEPT *693*

hazard [*v*] *take a chance; risk*
adventure, conjecture, dare, endanger, gamble, go for broke*, go out on limb*, guess, imperil, jeopardize, presume, proffer, skate on thin ice*, speculate, stake, submit, suppose, take a plunge*, throw out, try, venture, volunteer, wager; SEE CONCEPTS *28,87*

hazardous [*adj*] *dangerous, unpredictable*
chancy, dicey*, difficult, hairy*, haphazard, hot*, insecure, parlous, perilous, precarious, risky, touchy, uncertain, unhealthy, unsafe, unsound, venturesome, wicked; SEE CONCEPT *548*

haze [n] *cloudy air*
brume, cloud, dimness, film, fog, fumes, ground clouds, haziness, indistinctness, miasma, mist, murk, obscurity, smog, smokiness, smother, soup*, steam, vapor; SEE CONCEPT *524*

hazy [adj1] *cloudy*
bleared, bleary, blurred, blurry, clouded, crepuscular, dim, dull, dusky, faint, foggy, frosty, fuliginous, fumy, fuzzy, gauzy, indefinite, indistinct, misty, murky, mushy*, nebulous, obfuscated, obfuscous, obscure, opaque, overcast, rimy, screened, shadowy, smoggy, smoky, soupy*, steaming, thick, unclear, vague, vaporous, veiled; SEE CONCEPT *525*

hazy [adj2] *confused*
dazed, dizzy, dreamy, groggy, ill-defined, indefinite, indistinct, muddled, murky, nebulous, obscure, stuporous, tranced, uncertain, unclear, unintelligible, unsound, vague, whirling; SEE CONCEPTS *402,529*

head [adj] *most important; chief*
arch, champion, first, foremost, front, highest, leading, main, pioneer, preeminent, premier, prime, principal, stellar, supreme, topmost; SEE CONCEPTS *568,574*

head [n1] *top part of an animate body*
attic*, belfry*, brain, coconut*, cranium, crown, dome*, gray matter, noggin*, noodle*, pate, scalp, skull, thinker*, think tank*, top story*, upper story*, upstairs*; SEE CONCEPT *392*

head [n2] *leader*
boss, captain, chief, chieftain, commander, commanding officer, director, dominator, executive, honcho*, lead-off person*, manager, officer, president, principal, superintendent, supervisor, top dog*; SEE CONCEPT *347*

head [n3] *top part*
apex, banner, beak, bill, cap, cork, crest, crown, heading, headline, height, peak, pitch, point, promontory, streamer, summit, tip, vertex; SEE CONCEPT *836*

head [n4] *front, beginning*
commencement, first place, fore, forefront, fountainhead, origin, rise, source, start, van, vanguard; SEE CONCEPTS *648,727*

head [n5] *ability, intelligence*
aptitude, aptness, bent, brains, capacity, faculty, flair, genius, gift, intellect, knack, mentality, mind, talent, thought, turn, understanding; SEE CONCEPTS *409,630*

head [n6] *turning point*
acme, climax, conclusion, crisis, culmination, end; SEE CONCEPT *832*

head [v] *manage, oversee*
address, be first, be in charge, command, control, direct, dominate, go first, govern, guide, hold sway over*, lead, lead the way*, pioneer, precede, rule, run, supervise; SEE CONCEPT *117*

headache [n1] *difficulty, problem*
annoyance, bane, bother, dilemma, frustration, hassle, hindrance, inconvenience, nuisance, pain in the neck*, pest, predicament, quagmire, trouble, vexation, worry; SEE CONCEPTS *674,677*

headache [n2] *migraine*
cephalalgia, megrim, pounding head, splitting headache, throbbing head; SEE CONCEPTS *316,728*

headhunting [n] *recruiting*
executive recruiting, executive recruitment, recruitment, talent search; SEE CONCEPT *351*

heading [n1] *title*
caption, description, descriptor, headline, label, legend, lemma, rubric; SEE CONCEPT *283*

heading [n2] *course*
aim, angle, bearing, compass reading, direction, line, point, point of compass, route, track, trajectory, way; SEE CONCEPTS *501,514*

headlong [adj] *dangerous, reckless*
abrupt, brash, breakneck, daredevil, daring, foolhardy, hasty, hurried, impetuous, impulsive, inconsiderate, precipitant, precipitate, rash, rough, rushing, sudden, tempestuous, thoughtless; SEE CONCEPTS *542,588*

headquarters [n] *center of operations*
base, base of operations, central station, command post, company headquaters, high command, HQ, main office, nerve center; SEE CONCEPTS *312,439,441,448,449*

headstrong [adj] *stubborn*
bullheaded*, contrary, determined, foolhardy, froward, hard-core*, hard-nosed, hard-shell*, heedless, imprudent, impulsive, intractable, locked-in*, mule, mulish, murder, obstinate, perverse, pig-headed*, rash, reckless, refractory, self-willed, strong-minded, uncontrollable, ungovernable, unruly, unyielding, willful; SEE CONCEPTS *401,403*

headway [n] *progress*
advance, advancement, anabasis, ground, improvement, increase, march, proficiency, progression, promotion, way; SEE CONCEPTS *230,704*

heady [adj] *thrilling, intoxicating*
exciting, exhilarating, inebriating, overwhelming, potent, powerful, provocative, spirituous, stimulating, strong; SEE CONCEPT *529*

heal [v] *cure, recover*
alleviate, ameliorate, attend, bring around, compose, conciliate, convalesce, doctor, dress, fix, free, get well, harmonize, improve, knit, make healthy, make sound, make well, make whole, medicate, meliorate, mend, minister to, patch up, physic, put on feet again*, reanimate, rebuild, reconcile, regenerate, rehabilitate, rejuvenate, remedy, renew, renovate, repair, restore, resuscitate, revive, revivify, salve, set, settle, soothe, treat; SEE CONCEPTS *308,310*

healer [n] *faith healer*
curer, doctor, medicine man, mender, physician, shaman, therapist; SEE CONCEPT *357*

health [n] *physical, mental wellness*
bloom*, clean bill*, complexion, constitution, energy, euepsia, euphoria, fettle, fine feather*, fitness, form, good condition, haleness, hardihood, hardiness, healthfulness, healthiness, lustiness, pink*, prime*, robustness, salubriousness, salubrity, shape, soundness, stamina, state, strength, tone, tonicity, top form, verdure, vigor, well-being, wholeness; SEE CONCEPTS *316,410,720*

healthful/healthy [adj1] *good for one's wellness*
advantageous, aiding, aseptic, beneficial, benign, body-building, bracing, cathartic, clean, compensatory, conducive, corrective, desirable, disease-free, energy-giving, fresh, harmless, healing, health-giving, helpful, hygienic, innocuous, invigorating, mitigative, nourishing, nutritious, nutritive, profitable, pure, restorative, salubrious, salutary, sanatory, sanitary, stimulating, sustain-

ha
he

ing, tonic, unadulterated, unpolluted, untainted, useful, wholesome; SEE CONCEPT 537

healthy [adj2] *in good condition*
able-bodied, active, all right, athletic, blooming, bright-eyed*, bushy-tailed*, chipper*, firm, fit, flourishing, fresh, full of life*, hale, hardy, healthful, hearty, husky, in fine feather*, in fine fettle*, in good shape, in the pink*, lively, lusty, muscular, normal, physically fit, potent, restored, robust, rosy-cheeked*, safe and sound*, sound, stout, strong, sturdy, tough, trim, unimpaired, vigorous, virile, well, whole; SEE CONCEPTS 314,403

heap [n] *pile, accumulation*
abundance, agglomeration, aggregation, a lot*, amassment, assemblage, bank, batch, bulk, bunch, bundle, cargo, clump, cluster, collection, concentration, congeries, deposit, fullness, gathering, gobs*, great deal, harvest, haul, hill, hoard, jumble, load, lot, lots, lump, mass, million, mint, mound, mountain, much, ocean, oodles*, plenty, pot, profusion, quantity, scad*, stack, stock, stockpile, store, sum, thousand, ton, total, trillion, volume, whole; SEE CONCEPTS 432,787

heap [v] *amass, collect in pile*
accumulate, add, arrange, augment, bank, bunch, concentrate, deposit, dump, fill, fill up, gather, group, hoard, increase, load, lump, mass, mound, pack, stack, stockpile, store, swell; SEE CONCEPT 109

hear [v1] *detect by perceiving sound*
apprehend, attend, auscultate, be all ears*, become aware, catch, descry, devour, eavesdrop, get*, get an earful*, get wind of*, give an audience to*, give attention, give ears*, hark, hearken, heed, listen, make out*, overhear, pick up*, read, strain, take in*; SEE CONCEPTS 590,596

hear [v2] *become aware of information*
apperceive, ascertain, be advised, be informed, be led to believe, be told of, catch, catch on, descry, determine, discover, find out, gather, get the picture*, get wind of*, get wise to*, glean, have on good authority*, learn, pick up*, receive, see, tumble*, understand, unearth; SEE CONCEPTS 15,31

hearing [n1] *ability to perceive sound*
audition, auditory, auditory range, detecting, distinguishing, ear, earshot, effect, extent, faculty, hearing distance, listening, perception, range, reach, recording, sense; SEE CONCEPT 597

hearing [n2] *opportunity to present views, knowledge, or skill*
admittance, attendance, attention, audience, audit, audition, chance, conference, congress, consultation, council, discussion, inquiry, interview, investigation, meeting, negotiation, notice, parley, performance, presentation, reception, review, test, trial, tryout; SEE CONCEPTS 48,103,317,693

hearsay [n] *unsubstantiated information*
clothesline*, comment, cry, gossip, grapevine*, leak*, mere talk*, noise*, report, rumble*, rumor, scandal, scuttlebutt*, talk, talk of the town*, word of mouth*; SEE CONCEPTS 51,278

heart [n1] *person's emotions*
affection, benevolence, character, compassion, concern, disposition, feeling, gusto, humanity, inclination, love, nature, palate, pity, relish, response, sensitivity, sentiment, soul, sympathy, temperament, tenderness, understanding, zest; SEE CONCEPT 410

heart [n2] *courage*
boldness, bravery, dauntlessness, fortitude, gallantry, guts*, mettle, mind, moxie*, nerve, pluck, purpose, resolution, soul, spirit, spunk*, will; SEE CONCEPT 411

heart [n3] *essence, central part*
basic, bosom, bottom line*, center, coal and ice*, core, crux, focal point, focus, gist, hub, kernel, marrow, middle, nitty-gritty*, nub, nucleus, pith, polestar*, quick*, quintessence, root, seat, soul; SEE CONCEPT 826

heart [n4] *blood-pumping organ in an animate being*
cardiac organ, clock*, ticker*, vascular organ; SEE CONCEPTS 393,420

heartache [n] *anguish, sorrow*
affliction, agony, bitterness, broken heart, dejection, depression, despair, despondency, distress, dolor, grief, heartbreak, heavy heart, hurting, misery, pang, remorse, sadness, suffering, torment, torture; SEE CONCEPT 410

heart attack [n] *acute myocardial infarction*
angina pectoris, cardiac arrest, cardiovascular disease, coronary, coronary thrombosis; SEE CONCEPT 308

heartbreak [n] *mental or emotional misery*
affliction, agony, anguish, bale, bitterness, broken heart, care, desolation, despair, distress, grief, heartache, heartsickness, heavy heart*, pain, regret, remorse, rue, sorrow, suffering, torment, torture, woe; SEE CONCEPTS 410,728

heartbreaking [adj] *disappointing*
affecting, afflictive, agonizing, bitter, calamitous, cheerless, deplorable, dire, distressing, grievous, heart-rending, joyless, lamentable, moving, pitiful, poignant, regrettable, sad, touching, tragic, unfortunate; SEE CONCEPTS 529,537

hearten [v] *raise someone's spirits*
animate, arouse, assure, buck up, buoy, cheer, comfort, console, embolden, encourage, energize, enliven, incite, inspire, inspirit, rally, reassure, revivify, rouse, steel, stimulate, stir, strengthen; SEE CONCEPTS 7,22

heartfelt [adj] *genuine*
ardent, bona fide, cordial, deep, devout, earnest, fervent, heart-to-heart, hearty, honest, profound, sincere, true, unfeigned, warm, wholehearted; SEE CONCEPTS 267,582

heartless [adj] *without feeling; cold*
brutal, callous, cold-blooded*, cold fish*, cold-hearted*, cruel, hard, hard as nails*, hard-boiled*, hard-hearted*, harsh, inhuman, insensitive, merciless, obdurate, pitiless, ruthless, savage, thick-skinned*, uncaring, uncompassionate, unemotional, unfeeling, unkind, unsympathetic; SEE CONCEPTS 401,542

heartrending [adj] *arousing deep sympathy*
agonizing, distressing, doleful, excruciating, harrowing, heartbreaking, heartsickening, moving, piteous, pitiful, sad, tear-jerking, touching, tragic; SEE CONCEPTS 529,537

heartsick [adj] *despondent*
all torn up*, blue, bummed-out*, dejected, depressed, despairing, disappointed, disconsolate, disheartened, down, forlorn, grieving, heavy-hearted, inconsolable, low, melancholy, mournful, sad, unhappy, woebegone; SEE CONCEPT 403

heartwarming [*adj*] *pleasant*
cheering, encouraging, exhilarating, gladdening, heartening, heartfelt, inspiring, joyous, loving, stirring, sweet; SEE CONCEPTS *542,548,572*

hearty [*adj1*] *energetic, enthusiastic*
affable, animated, ardent, avid, back-slapping*, cheerful, cheery, cordial, deep, deepest, deep-felt, devout, eager, earnest, ebullient, effusive, exuberant, frank, friendly, gay, generous, genial, genuine, glad, gushing, heartfelt, honest, impassioned, intense, jolly, jovial, neighborly, passionate, profuse, real, responsive, sincere, true, unfeigned, unreserved, unrestrained, vivacious, warm, warmhearted, wholehearted, zealous; SEE CONCEPTS *401,542*

hearty [*adj2*] *healthy, full*
active, ample, energetic, filling, glowing, good, hale, hardy, nourishing, robust, sizable, solid, sound, square, strong, substantial, vigorous, well; SEE CONCEPTS *314,773*

heat [*n1*] *high temperature*
calefaction, calidity, dog days*, fever, fieriness, heatwave, hotness, hot spell, hot weather, incalescence, incandescence, sultriness, swelter, torridity, torridness, warmness, warmth; SEE CONCEPT *610*

heat [*n2*] *anger, passion*
agitation, ardor, desire, earnestness, excitement, ferocity, fervor, fever, fury, impetuosity, intensity, rage, vehemence, violence, warmth, zeal; SEE CONCEPTS *410,657*

heat [*v*] *make or become hot*
bake, bask, blaze, boil, broil, calorify, chafe, char, enflame, enkindle, fire, flame, flush, frizzle, fry, glow, grill, grow hot, grow warm, ignite, incandesce, incinerate, inflame, kindle, melt, oxidate, oxidize, perspire, raise the temperature, reheat, roast, scald, scorch, sear, seethe, set on fire, singe, smelt, steam, sun, swelter, tepefy, thaw, toast, warm, warm up; SEE CONCEPTS *255,469*

heated [*adj1*] *angry*
acrimonious, ardent, avid, bitter, excited, fervent, fervid, feverish, fierce, fiery, frenzied, furious, hectic, impassioned, indignant, intense, irate, ireful, mad, passionate, raging, stormy, tempestuous, vehement, violent, wrathful; SEE CONCEPT *267*

heated [*adj2*] *warmed*
baked, baking, boiling, broiled, broiling, burned, burning, burnt, cooked, fiery, fired, fried, hot, parched, scalding, scorched, scorching, sizzling, toasted; SEE CONCEPT *605*

heathen [*adj*] *not believing in Christian god*
agnostic, atheistic, barbarian, godless, idolatrous, infidel, irreligious, nonbeliever, pagan, profane, skeptic; SEE CONCEPT *545*

heave [*v1*] *lift, throw with effort*
boost, cast, chuck, drag, elevate, fling, haul, heft, hoist, hurl, launch, pitch, pull, raise, send, sling, toss, tug; SEE CONCEPTS *196,222*

heave [*v2*] *discharge with force; expel from digestive system by mouth*
billow, breathe, cast, dilate, disgorge, exhale, expand, gag, groan, huff, palpitate, pant, puff, puke*, retch, rise, sign, sob, spew, spit up, surge, suspire, swell, throb, throw up, upchuck*, vomit; SEE CONCEPTS *163,179*

heaven [*n*] *place where God lives; wonderful feeling*
afterworld, Arcadia, atmosphere, azure*, beyond, bliss, Canaan, dreamland, ecstasy, Elysium, empyrean, enchantment, eternal home, eternal rest, eternity, fairyland*, felicity, firmament, glory, great unknown*, happiness, happy hunting ground*, harmony, heights, hereafter, immortality, kingdom, kingdom come, life everlasting, life to come, next world, nirvana, paradise, pearly gates*, promised land*, rapture, Shangri-la*, sky*, the blue*, transport, upstairs*, Utopia, wonderland*, Zion; SEE CONCEPTS *370,410,435*

heavenly [*adj*] *very pleasant*
adorable, alluring, ambrosial, angelic, beatific, beautiful, blessed, blissful, celestial, cherubic, darling, delectable, delicious, delightful, divine, empyrean, enjoyable, entrancing, excellent, exquisite, extraterrestrial, glorious, godlike, holy, immortal, lovely, luscious, lush, paradisaical, rapturous, ravishing, scrumptious, seraphic, sublime, superhuman, supernal, supernatural, sweet, wonderful, yummy; SEE CONCEPTS *537,572*

heavy [*adj1*] *having great weight*
abundant, ample, awkward, beefy*, big, built, bulky, burdensome, chunky*, considerable, copious, corpulent, cumbersome, cumbrous, elephantine, enceinte, excessive, expectant, fat, fleshy, gravid, gross*, hefty, huge, laden, large, lead-footed*, loaded, lumbering, massive, obese, oppressed, overweight, parturient, ponderous, porcine, portly, pregnant, stout, substantial, top-heavy, two-ton*, unmanageable, unwieldy, weighted, weighty, zaftig*; SEE CONCEPT *491*

heavy [*adj2*] *difficult, severe*
abstruse, acroamatic, arduous, boisterous, burdensome, complex, complicated, confused, effortful, esoteric, formidable, grave, grievous, hard, harsh, intolerable, knotty*, labored, laborious, onerous, oppressive, profound, recondite, rough, serious, solemn, stormy, strenuous, tedious, tempestuous, toilsome, tough, troublesome, turbulent, vexatious, violent, wearisome, weighty, wild; SEE CONCEPTS *538,565,569*

heavy [*adj3*] *depressed, gloomy*
close, cloudy, crestfallen, damp, dark, dejected, despondent, disconsolate, dismal, downcast, dull, grieving, leaden, lowering, melancholy, oppressive, overcast, sad, sodden, soggy, sorrowful, stifling, wet; SEE CONCEPTS *403,525,548*

heavy [*adj4*] *listless, slow*
apathetic, comatose, dull, hebetudinous, indifferent, lethargic, sluggish, slumberous, torpid; SEE CONCEPT *584*

heckle [*v*] *jeer*
badger, bait, bother, bully, chivy, dis*, discomfit, disconcert, disrupt, disturb, embarrass, faze, gibe, hound*, interrupt, pester, plague, rattle, ride*, ridicule, shout at, taunt, tease, torment, worry; SEE CONCEPTS *44,47*

hectic [*adj*] *frantic, turbulent*
animated, boisterous, burning, chaotic, confused, disordered, excited, exciting, fervid, fevered, feverish, flurrying, flustering, frenetic, frenzied, furious, hassle, heated, hell broke loose*, jungle*, madhouse*, nutsy*, restless, riotous, riproaring, tumultuous, unsettled, wild, woolly*, zoolike*; SEE CONCEPT *548*

hedge [n] *boundary, obstacle, especially one made of plants*
barrier, bush, enclosure, fence, guard, hedgerow, hurdle, protection, quickset, screen, shrubbery, thicket, windbreak; SEE CONCEPTS *429,470*

hedge [v1] *avoid, dodge*
beat around the bush*, be noncommittal, blow hot and cold*, cop a plea*, cop out*, duck, equivocate, evade, flip-flop*, fudge*, give the run around*, hem and haw*, jive*, pass the buck*, prevaricate, pussyfoot*, quibble, run around, shilly-shally*, shuck*, shuffle, sidestep, sit on the fence*, stall, stonewall*, temporize, tergiversate, tergiverse, waffle*; SEE CONCEPTS *18,30*

hedge [v2] *enclose*
block, border, cage, confine, coop, corral, edge, fence, girdle, hem in, hinder, immure, obstruct, pen, restrict, ring, siege, surround; SEE CONCEPT *758*

hedonist [n] *person who seeks pleasure above other values*
bon vivant, debauchee, epicure, epicurean, glutton, gourmand, lecher, libertine, pleasuremonger, pleasureseeker, profligate, sensualist, sybarite, thrill-seeker, voluptuary; SEE CONCEPT *423*

heed [n] *care, thought*
application, attention, carefulness, caution, cognizance, concentration, concern, consideration, debate, deliberation, ear*, heedfulness, interest, listen up*, mark, mind*, note, notice, observance, observation, regard, remark, respect, spotlight*, study, tender loving care*, TLC*, watchfulness; SEE CONCEPTS *17,532*

heed [v] *give care, thought to*
attend, baby-sit, bear in mind, be aware, be guided by, catch, consider, dig*, do one's bidding*, follow, follow orders, get a load of*, give ear*, hark, hear, hearken, keep eye peeled*, keep tabs*, listen, mark, mind, mind the store*, note, obey, observe, pay attention, pick up, regard, ride herd on*, see, sit, spot, stay in line*, take notice of, take to heart*, toe the line*, watch, watch one's step*, watch out, watch over, watch the store*; SEE CONCEPTS *17,623*

heedless [adj] *careless*
asleep at the switch*, daydreaming, disregardful, fast and loose*, feckless, foolhardy, goofing off*, impetuous, imprudent, inadvertent, inattentive, incautious, inconsiderate, irreflective, neglectful, negligent, oblivious, out to lunch*, precipitate, rash, reckless, slapdash*, sloppy, thoughtless, uncaring, unmindful, unobservant, unthinking, unwary; SEE CONCEPT *401*

hefty [adj] *big, bulky*
ample, awkward, beefy*, brawny, burly, colossal, cumbersome, extensive, fat, forceful, heavy, hulking, husky, large, large-scale, major, massive, muscular, ponderous, powerful, robust, sizable, strapping*, strong, sturdy, substantial, thumping*, tremendous, unwieldy, vigorous, weighty; SEE CONCEPTS *491,773*

height [n1] *altitude, top part*
acme, apex, apogee, brow, ceiling, crest, crown, cusp, elevation, extent, highness, hill, loftiness, mountain, peak, pinnacle, pitch, prominence, rise, solstice, stature, summit, tallness, tip, tiptop, vertex, zenith; SEE CONCEPTS *741,743,791,836*

height [n2] *climax; importance*
acme, crest, crisis, crowning point, culmination,

dignity, eminence, end, exaltation, extremity, grandeur, heyday*, high point, limit, loftiness, maximum, ne plus ultra*, prominence, sublimity, top, ultimate, utmost degree, uttermost; SEE CONCEPTS *388,668,832*

heighten [v] *intensify*
add to, amplify, augment, boost, build up, elevate, enhance, enlarge, exalt, extend, improve, increase, lift, magnify, make higher, raise, send up, strengthen; SEE CONCEPTS *233,250*

heinous [adj] *horrifying, monstrous*
abhorrent, abominable, accursed, atrocious, awful, bad, beastly, crying, cursed, evil, execrable, flagitious, flagrant, frightful, godawful*, grave, gross*, hateful, hideous, horrendous, infamous, iniquitous, nefarious, odious, offensive, outrageous, raunchy, revolting, scandalous, shocking, stinking*, unspeakable, vicious, villainous; SEE CONCEPTS *529,548,570*

heir [n] *person who inherits possessions*
beneficiary, crown prince/princess, devisee, grantee, heritor, inheritor, next in line, scion, successor; SEE CONCEPTS *355,414*

heirloom [n] *something inherited, often antique*
antique, bequest, birthright, gift, heritage, inheritance, legacy, patrimony, reversion; SEE CONCEPT *337*

heist [n] *burglary, robbery*
break-in, breaking and entering, caper, crime, five-finger discount, holdup, larceny, pilferage, rip-off, stickup, sting, theft; SEE CONCEPT *139*

helicopter [n] *aircraft*
autogiro, chopper, copter, eggbeater*, whirlybird; SEE CONCEPT *504*

hell [n] *place of the condemned; bad situation*
Abaddon*, abyss, affliction, agony, anguish, blazes*, bottomless pit*, difficulty, everlasting fire*, fire and brimstone*, Gehenna*, grave, Hades, hell-fire, infernal regions, inferno, limbo, lower world, misery, nether world, nightmare, ordeal, pandemonium, perdition, pit, place of torment, purgatory, suffering, torment, trial, underworld, wretchedness; SEE CONCEPTS *370,435,674*

hell-bent [adj] *determined*
bent on, bound and determined, constant, decided, driven, firm, fixed, intent, obsessed, persevering, persistent, resolute, resolved, serious, set on, steadfast, strong-minded, strong-willed, stubborn, tenacious, unhesitating, unwavering; SEE CONCEPTS *404,542*

hellion [n] *troublemaker*
agent provocateur, agitator, demon, evildoer, firebrand*, heel*, incendiary, inciter, inflamer, instigator, loose cannon*, mischief-maker, punk*, rabblerouser*, rascal, recreant, rogue, rowdy*, smart aleck*, wise guy*; SEE CONCEPT *412*

hellish [adj] *fiendish; unpleasant*
abominable, accursed, atrocious, barbarous, cruel, damnable, damned, demonic, devilish, diabolical, horrible, infernal, monstrous, nefarious, satanic, terrible, vicious, wicked; SEE CONCEPTS *529,570*

helm [n] *wheel*
command, control, controls, driver's seat, leadership, reins, rudder, steering wheel, tiller; SEE CONCEPTS *436,464,502*

helmet [n] *headgear*
armor, busby, crash helmet, hard hat, hat, head

protector, kepi, safety helmet, shako; SEE CONCEPT *451*

help [*n1*] *assistance, relief*
advice, aid, assist, avail, balm*, benefit, comfort, cooperation, corrective, cure, guidance, hand, helping hand*, lift*, maintenance, nourishment, remedy, service, succor, support, sustenance, use, utility; SEE CONCEPTS *658,694*

help [*n2*] *employee*
abettor, adjutant, aide, ally, ancilla, assistant, attendant, auxiliary, collaborator, colleague, deputy, domestic, hand, helper, helpmate, mate, partner, representative, right-hand person*, servant, subsidiary, supporter, worker; SEE CONCEPT *348*

help [*v1*] *aid, assist*
abet, accommodate, advocate, back, ballyhoo*, befriend, benefit, be of use, bolster, boost, buck up*, cheer, cooperate, do a favor, do a service, do one's part*, encourage, endorse, further, go to bat for*, go with, hype*, intercede, lend a hand*, maintain, open doors*, patronize, plug*, promote, prop, puff*, push, relieve, root for*, sanction, save, second, serve, stand by, stick up for*, stimulate, stump for*, succor, support, sustain, take under one's wing*, uphold, work for; SEE CONCEPT *110*

help [*v2*] *improve*
alleviate, ameliorate, amend, attend, better, cure, doctor, ease, facilitate, heal, meliorate, mitigate, nourish, palliate, relieve, remedy, restore, revive, treat; SEE CONCEPT *244*

helper [*n*] *assistant*
abettor, accessory, accomplice, adherent, adjunct, aide, ally, appointee, apprentice, attendant, backer, backup*, coadjutant, coadjutor, collaborator, colleague, companion, deputy, fellow worker, follower, friend, gal Friday*, girl Friday*, gofer*, help, helpmate, henchman, man Friday*, paraprofessional, partner, right-hand man/woman, right-hand person, secretary, servant, subordinate, supporter, temp*, temporary worker; SEE CONCEPTS *348,423*

helpful [*adj*] *beneficial, beneficent*
accessible, accommodating, advantageous, applicable, benevolent, bettering, caring, conducive, considerate, constructive, contributive, convenient, cooperative, crucial, effectual, efficacious, essential, favorable, fortunate, friendly, good for, important, improving, instrumental, invaluable, kind, neighborly, operative, practical, pragmatic, productive, profitable, serendipitous, serviceable, significant, suitable, supportive, symbiotic, sympathetic, timely, usable, useful, utilitarian, valuable; SEE CONCEPTS *537,560*

helping [*n*] *portion of food*
allowance, course, dollop, meal, order, piece, plateful, ration, serving, share; SEE CONCEPT *457*

helpless [*adj*] *incapable, incompetent; vulnerable*
abandoned, basket-case*, debilitated, defenseless, dependent, destitute, disabled, exposed, feeble, forlorn, forsaken, friendless, handcuffed, impotent, inefficient, inexpert, infirm, invalid, over a barrel*, paralyzed, pinned*, powerless, prostrate, shiftless, tapped, tapped out*, unable, unfit, unprotected, up creek without paddle*, weak, with hands tied*; SEE CONCEPTS *401,542*

helter-skelter [*adv*] *carelessly, confused*
about, anyhow, any which way*, anywise, around, at random, cluttered, disorderly, haphazard, hastily, headlong, higgledy-piggledy*, hit-or-miss*, hotfoot*, hurriedly, impetuously, incautiously, in confusion, incontinently, irregular, jumbled, muddled, pell-mell*, random, randomly, rashly, recklessly, topsy-turvy*, tumultous/tumultuous, unmindfully, wildly; SEE CONCEPT *544*

hem [*n*] *border, edge*
brim, brink, define, edging, fringe, margin, perimeter, periphery, piping, rim, selvage, skirt, skirting, trimming, verge; SEE CONCEPTS *484,513*

he-man [*adj*] *masculine*
macho*, male, manful, manly, mannish, muscular, potent, virile; SEE CONCEPTS *371,408,648*

he-man [*n*] *masculine man*
caveman*, hunk*, macho man*, man's man, strong man, virile man; SEE CONCEPTS *414,419*

hem/hem in [*v*] *enclose, restrict*
begird, beset, border, bound, cage, circle, circumscribe, close in, confine, corral, define, edge, encircle, encompass, envelop, environ, fence, fringe, girdle, hedge in, immure, margin, pen, rim, ring, round, shut, shut in, skirt, surround, verge; SEE CONCEPTS *130,758*

hemorrhage [*v*] *bleed*
drain, extravasate, gush, lose blood, ooze, open vein, outflow, phlebotomize, seep, spill blood; SEE CONCEPT *185*

hence [*adv*] *for that reason; therefore*
accordingly, as a deduction, away, consequently, ergo, forward, from here, from now on, henceforth, henceforward, hereinafter, in the future, it follows that, on that account, onward, out, so, then, thence, thereupon, thus, wherefore; SEE CONCEPT *799*

henchman [*n*] *follower*
abettor, accessory, accomplice, adherent, adjunct, aide, ally, appointee, apprentice, assistant, attendant, backer, backup*, bodyguard, coadjutant, coadjutor, cohort, collaborator, colleague, companion, deputy, fellow worker, flunky, friend, gal Friday*, girl Friday*, gofer*, hanger-on, hatchet man/woman, help, helper, helpmate, lackey, man Friday*, partner, right-hand man/woman, right-hand person, secretary, servant, sidekick*, stooge*, subordinate, supporter, yes-person*; SEE CONCEPTS *348,423*

henpeck [*v*] *nag*
badger, berate, bother, bug*, bully, carp, fuss, give a hard time*, harass, hector, hound, intimidate, irritate, needle, pester, pick on*, ride, scold, torment; SEE CONCEPTS *7,19,52*

herald [*n*] *omen, messenger*
adviser, bearer, courier, crier, forerunner, harbinger, indication, outrider, precursor, prophet, reporter, runner, sign, signal, token; SEE CONCEPTS *274,284,423*

herald [*v*] *bring message*
advertise, announce, ballyhoo*, broadcast, declare, forerun, fozetoken, harbinger, indicate, pave the way*, portend, precede, preindicate, presage, proclaim, publicize, publish, pzomise, show, tout, trumpet*, usher in*; SEE CONCEPT *60*

herbicide [*n*] *poison*
DDT, defoliant, fungicide, insecticide, paraquat, pesticide, weedkiller; SEE CONCEPTS *307,475, 674,675*

Herculean [*adj*] *powerful, strong*
almighty, backbreaking, colossal, courageous, forceful, gargantuan, gigantic, hard, heroic,

he
he

huge, impressive, laborious, mighty, strenuous, tough, vigorous; SEE CONCEPTS *489,527,540,574*

herd [*n*] *large group*
assemblage, bevy, brood, clan, collection, covey, crowd, crush, drif , drove, flight, flock, gaggle, gathering, hoi polloi*, horde, lot, mass, mob, multitude, nest, (pack, people, populace, press, rabble, school, swarm, throng; SEE CONCEPTS *397,432*

herd [*v*] *gather; shepherd*
assemble, associate, collect, congregate, corral, drive, flock, force, goad, guide, huddle, lead, muster, poke, punch, rally, round up*, run, scare up*, spur; SEE CONCEPT *109*

here [*adv*] *in this place*
attendant, attending, available, hereabouts, hither, hitherto, in this direction, on board, on deck, on hand, on-the-spot, on this spot, present, within reach; SEE CONCEPT *583*

hereafter [*adv*] *from now on*
after this, eventually, hence, henceforth, henceforward, hereupon, in the course of time, in the future, ultimately; SEE CONCEPT *799*

hereafter [*n*] *life after death*
afterlife, aftertime, afterward, afterworld, by-and-by*, future, future existence, future life, heaven, hell, next world, offing, otherworld, the beyond*, to-be*, underworld, world to come*; SEE CONCEPT *370*

hereditary [*adj*] *inherited; transmitted at birth*
ancestral, bequeathed, $family, genealogical, genetic, handed down, heritable, inborn, inbred, inheritable, inherited, lineal, maternal, paternal, patrimonial, traditional, transmissible, transmitted, willed; SEE CONCEPT *549*

heredity [*n*] *transmission of traits from parents to offspring*
ancestry, congenital traits, constitution, eugenics, genesiology, genetic make-up, genetics, inborn character, inheritance; SEE CONCEPT *648*

heresy [*n*] *unorthodox opinion, especially in religious matters*
agnosticism, apostasy, atheism, blasphemy, defection, disbelief, dissent, dissidence, divergence, error, fallacy, heterodoxy, iconoclasm, impiety, infidelity, misbelief, nonconformism, nonconformity, paganism, revisionism, schism, sectarianism, secularism, sin; SEE CONCEPT *689*

heretical [*adj*] *unorthodox*
agnostic, apostate, atheistic, differing, disagreeing, dissenting, dissentive, dissident, freethinking, heterodox, iconoclastic, idolatrous, impious, infidel, misbelieving, miscreant, nonconformist, revisionist, schismatic, sectarian, skeptical, unbelieving; SEE CONCEPTS *529,545*

heritage [*n*] *person's background, tradition*
ancestry, bequest, birthright, convention, culture, custom, dowry, endowment, estate, fashion, heirship, heritance, inheritance, legacy, lot, patrimony, portion, right, share, tradition; SEE CONCEPTS *296,648,678*

hermeneutical [*adj*] *interpretive*
critical, demonstrative, explanatory, explicative, expository, illustrative, investigative, revealing; SEE CONCEPT *268*

hermeneutics [*n*] *the science of searching for hidden meaning in texts*
exegetics, exploration, interpretation, investigation, literary criticism, psychoanalytic criticism, revealing, unmasking; SEE CONCEPT *349*

hermit [*n*] *person who chose to live alone outside of human society*
anchoret, anchorite, ascetic, eremite, misanthrope, pillarist, recluse, skeptic, solitaire, solitarian, solitary, stylite; SEE CONCEPTS *361,423*

hero [*n*] *submarine sandwich*
grinder, hoagie, sub*, submarine*, torpedo; SEE CONCEPTS *457,460,461*

hero/heroine [*n*] *brave person; champion*
ace, adventurer, celebrity, combatant, conqueror, daredevil, demigod, diva, exemplar, gallant, god, goddess, great person, heavy, ideal, idol, lead, leading person*, lion, martyr, model, paladin, person of the hour*, popular figure, prima donna*, principal, protagonist, saint, star, superstar, tin god*, victor, worthy; SEE CONCEPTS *352,416*

heroic [*adj*] *brave, champion*
bigger than life*, bold, classic, courageous, daring, dauntless, doughty, elevated, epic, exaggerated, fearless, fire-eating*, gallant, grand, grandiose, gritty, gutsy*, gutty*, high-flown, impavid, inflated, intrepid, lion-hearted, mythological, noble, stand tall*, stouthearted, unafraid, undaunted, valiant, valorous; SEE CONCEPTS *401,404*

heroin [*n*] *smack*
big H*, candy*, crap*, diacetylmorphine, doojee*, dope, drug, flea powder*, H*, hard stuff*, horse*, junk*, mojo*, narcotic, opium, scag*, white stuff*; SEE CONCEPT *307*

heroism [*n*] *bravery*
boldness, courage, courageousness, daring, doughtiness, fearlessness, fortitude, gallantry, intrepidity, nobility, prowess, spirit, strength, valiance, valiancy, valor, valorousness; SEE CONCEPTS *411,633*

hesitant [*adj*] *uncertain, waiting*
afraid, averse, backward, dawdling, delaying, diffident, disinclined, doubtful, doubting, faltering, half-hearted, halting, hanging back, hesitating, indecisive, irresolute, lacking confidence, lazy, loath, reluctant, shy, skeptical, slow, tentative, timid, uneager, unpredictable, unsure, unwilling, vacillating, wavering; SEE CONCEPTS *534,535,542*

hesitate [*v*] *wait; be uncertain*
alternate, balance, balk, be irresolute, be reluctant, be unwilling, blow hot and cold*, dally, debate, defer, delay, demur, dillydally*, dither, doubt, equivocate, falter, flounder, fluctuate, fumble, hang*, hang back, hedge, hem and haw*, hold back, hold off, hover, linger, oscillate, pause, ponder, pull back, pussyfoot*, scruple, seesaw*, shift, shrink, shy away, sit on fence*, stammer, stop, straddle, stumble, stutter, swerve, tergiversate, think about, think twice*, vacillate, waffle*, waver, weigh; SEE CONCEPTS *21,121,681*

hesitation [*n*] *waiting; uncertainty*
averseness, dawdling, delay, delaying, demurral, doubt, dubiety, equivocation, faltering, fluctuation, fumbling, hemming and hawing*, hesitancy, indecision, indecisiveness, indisposition, irresolution, misgiving, mistrust, oscillation, pause, procrastination, qualm, reluctance, scruple, skepticism, stammering, stumbling, stuttering, unwillingness, vacillation, wavering; SEE CONCEPTS *21,121,410,681*

heterogeneous [*adj*] *assorted, miscellaneous*
amalgamate, composite, confused, conglomerate, contrary, contrasted, different, discordant, discrepant, disparate, dissimilar, divergent, diverse, diversified, incongruous, independent, inharmonious, jumbled, mingled, mixed, mongrel, mosaic, motley, multifarious, multiplex, odd, opposed, unallied, unlike, unrelated, variant, varied, variegated; SEE CONCEPT *564*

hex [*n*] *curse, spell*
abracadabra*, allure, bewitching, bewitchment, charm, conjuration, double whammy*, enchantment, evil eye, hexing, hocus-pocus*, jinx, magic, magic spell, mumbo-jumbo*, sorcery, voodoo*, whammy*; SEE CONCEPTS *370,673,689*

hiatus [*n*] *pause, interruption*
aperture, blank, breach, break, chasm, discontinuity, gap, interim, interval, lacuna, lapse, opening, rift, space; SEE CONCEPT *807*

hibernate [*v*] *lie dormant; sleep through cold weather*
hide, hole up, immure, lie torpid, sleep, vegetate, winter; SEE CONCEPT *315*

hick [*n*] *rustic*
backwoodsman/woman, boor, bumpkin, clodhopper, cornfed*, country boy/girl, country cousin*, countryman/woman, farmer, hayseed*, hillbilly, local yokel*, redneck*, rube, rural, yokel*; SEE CONCEPT *413*

hidden [*adj*] *unseen, secret*
abstruse, buried, clandestine, cloaked, close, clouded, concealed, covered, covert, cryptic, dark, disguised, eclipsed, esoteric, hermetic, hermetical, imperceivable, indiscernible, in the dark, invisible, latent, masked, mysterious, mystic, mystical, obscure, occult, out of view, private, QT*, recondite, screened, secluded, sequestered, shadowy, shrouded, surreptitious, ulterior, undercover, underground, undetected, undisclosed, unexposed, unknown, unrevealed, veiled, withheld; SEE CONCEPT *576*

hide [*v*] *conceal; remain unseen*
adumbrate, blot out, bury, cache, camouflage, cloak, cover, curtain*, disguise, dissemble, ditch, duck, eclipse, ensconce, go into hiding, go underground, harbor, hold back, hole up*, hush up, keep from, keep secret, lie low*, lock up, mask, not give away, not tell, obscure, plant, protect, put out of the way, reserve, salt away*, screen, secrete, shadow, shelter, shield, shroud, smuggle, squirrel*, stash, stifle, stow away, suppress, take cover, tuck away, veil, withhold; SEE CONCEPTS *17,188*

hideous [*adj*] *grotesque, horrible*
abominable, animal, appalling, awful, beast, bestial, detestable, disgusting, dreadful, frightful, ghastly, grim, grisly, gross*, gruesome, hateful, horrendous, horrid, loathsome, macabre, monstrous, morbid, nasty, odious, offensive, repellent, repugnant, repulsive, revolting, shocking, sick, sickening, terrible, terrifying, ugly, uncomely, unsightly, weird; SEE CONCEPTS *537,579*

hideout [*n*] *hiding place*
cover, den, hideaway, refuge, safe house, safe place, sanctuary, shelter; SEE CONCEPTS *198,515*

hierarchy [*n*] *order*
chain of command*, due order, echelons, grouping, pecking order, placing, position, pyramid, ranking, scale; SEE CONCEPT *727*

high [*adj 1*] *tall; at a great distance aloft*
aerial, alpine, altitudinous, big, colossal, elevated, eminent, flying, formidable, giant, gigantic, grand, great, high-reaching, high rise, hovering, huge, immense, large, lofty, long, sky-high, sky-scraping, soaring, steep, towering, tremendous, uplifted, upraised; SEE CONCEPTS *779,782*

high [*adj 2*] *extreme*
costly, dear, excessive, exorbitant, expensive, extraordinary, extravagant, grand, great, high-priced, intensified, lavish, luxurious, precious, rich, sharp, special, steep, stiff, strong, unusual; SEE CONCEPTS *334,569*

high [*adj 3*] *important*
arch, capital, chief, consequential, crucial, distinguished, eminent, essential, exalted, extreme, grave, influential, leading, necessary, noble, powerful, prominent, ruling, serious, significant, superior; SEE CONCEPT *567*

high [*adj 4*] *very happy*
boisterous, bouncy, cheerful, elated, excited, exhilarated, exuberant, joyful, lighthearted, merry, psyched*, pumped*; SEE CONCEPT *403*

high [*adj 5*] *intoxicated, drugged*
delirious, doped, drunk, euphoric, flying*, freaked out*, inebriated, on a trip*, potted*, spaced out*, stoned*, tanked*, tipsy; SEE CONCEPT *314*

high [*adj 6*] *shrill, strong (on the senses)*
acute, high-pitched, loud, malodorous, penetrating, piercing, piping, putrid, rancid, rank, reeking, sharp, smelly, soprano, strident, treble; SEE CONCEPTS *406,594,598*

high and mighty [*adj*] *haughty, overbearing*
arrogant, cavalier, cocky*, conceited, contemptuous, disdainful, egotistic, egotistical, highfalutin*, high-handed*, hoity-toity*, imperious, lofty, lordly, on high horse*, presumptuous, sniffy*, snobbish, snooty*, snotty, stuck-up*, stuffy, superior, uppity*; SEE CONCEPTS *401,404*

highbrow [*adj*] *intellectual*
bookish, brainy*, cerebral, cultivated, cultured, erudite, intellective, intelligent, learned, scholarly, studious, wise; SEE CONCEPT *402*

highbrow [*n*] *intellectual, very smart person*
academic, academician, bluestocking, brain*, egghead*, Einstein*, genius, illuminato, intelligentsia, literato, longhair, philosopher, sage, savant, scholar, thinker, whiz*; SEE CONCEPT *402*

high-class [*adj*] *first-class*
best, choice, classy, deluxe, elite, superior, supreme, upper-class, upper-crust*; SEE CONCEPTS *568,572*

highfalutin [*adj*] *pompous*
arrogant, boastful, conceited, flaunting, grandiose, high and mighty*, important, lofty, ostentatious, overbearing, presumptuous, pretentious, puffed up*, puffy, self-centered, stuck-up*, swanky, uppity*, vain; SEE CONCEPTS *267,401,542*

high-flown [*adj*] *exalted, lofty*
bombastic, elaborate, exaggerated, extravagant, grandiloquent, grandiose, inflated, showy, turgid; SEE CONCEPT *562*

high-handed [*adj*] *domineering*
authoritarian, autocratic, bossy, dictatorial, imperious, ironhanded, oppressive, overbearing, tyrannical; SEE CONCEPTS *319,401*

he
hi

highlight [n] *memorable part*
best part, climax, feature, focal point, focus, high point, high spot, main feature, peak; SEE CONCEPT *832*

highly [adv] *very, well*
awful, awfully, bloody*, but good*, decidedly, deeply, eminently, exceedingly, exceptionally, extraordinarily, extremely, greatly, hugely, immensely, jolly, mighty, mucho*, notably, parlous, plenty, powerful, profoundly, real, really, remarkably, right, so, so much*, strikingly, supremely, surpassingly, terribly, terrifically, too much*, tremendously, vastly, very much; SEE CONCEPTS *537,569*

high-minded [adj] *principled*
chivalrous, conscientious, ethical, honest, moral, noble, righteous, upright, virtuous; SEE CONCEPT *545*

high-powered [adj] *powerful*
authoritarian, authoritative, commanding, controlling, dominant, dynamic, effective, effectual, forceful, forcible, in control, influential, in the saddle*, mighty, potent, robust, ruling, strong, supreme, weighty; SEE CONCEPTS *489,527,540,574*

high society [n] *cultured class*
aristocracy, beau monde, beautiful people*, best people, cream of society, elite, fashionable society, high life, jet set*, polite society, privileged class, smart set, upper class; SEE CONCEPTS *387,388,417*

high-strung [adj] *nervous*
all shook up*, choked*, easily upset, edgy, excitable, fidgety, hyper*, impatient, irascible, irritable, jittery, jumpy, nervy, neurotic, on pins and needles*, on ragged edge, restless, sensitive, spooked*, stressed, taut, temperamental, tense, tight*, unrestful, uptight*, wired*, zonkers*; SEE CONCEPTS *401,404*

highway [n] *heavily traveled, capacious road*
artery, avenue, boulevard, drag*, four-lane*, freeway, interstate, parking lot*, parkway, path, pike*, roadway, skyway, street, superhighway, super slab*, thoroughfare, toll road, track, turnpike; SEE CONCEPT *501*

hijack [v] *seize control*
carjack, commandeer, kidnap, shanghai, skyjack, steal, take hostage; SEE CONCEPTS *90,139*

hijacker [n] *abductor*
carjacker, kidnapper, robber, skyjacker, terrorist, thief; SEE CONCEPTS *90,139*

hike [n] *journey by foot*
backpack, constitutional, excursion, exploration, march, ramble, tour, traipse, tramp, trek, trip, walk, walkabout; SEE CONCEPTS *149,224,363*

hike [v1] *walk for recreation*
backpack, explore, hit the road*, hoof*, leg it*, ramble, rove, stroll, stump, tour, tramp, travel, tromp; SEE CONCEPTS *149,224,363*

hike [v2] *raise, increase*
advance, boost, jack, jump, lift, pull up, put up, up*, upgrade; SEE CONCEPTS *236,245*

hilarious [adj] *very funny*
amusing, comical, convivial, entertaining, exhilarated, frolicsome, gay, gleeful, gut-busting*, happy, humorous, jocular, jolly, jovial, joyful, joyous, laughable, lively, merry, mirthful, noisy, priceless, riot, rollicking, scream, side-splitting*, uproarious, witty; SEE CONCEPT *529*

hill [n] *uprising of earth's surface; pile*
acclivity, ascent, bluff, butte, cliff, climb, down, drift, dune, elevation, eminence, esker, fell, gradient, headland, heap, height, highland, hillock, hilltop, hummock, inclination, incline, knoll, mesa, mound, mount, precipice, prominence, promontory, protuberance, range, ridge, rise, rising ground, shock, slope, stack, summit, talus, tor, upland; SEE CONCEPT *509*

hillbilly [n] *hayseed*
backwoodsman/woman, boor*, bumpkin, clodhopper*, country boy/girl, country bumpkin, country cousin*, hick*, rube, rustic, yokel; SEE CONCEPT *413*

hillock [n] *small hill*
acclivity, ascent, bluff, butte, cliff, drift, dune, elevation, esker, headland, heap, highland, hilltop, hummock, inclination, incline, knoll, mesa, mound, mount, precipice, prominence, promontory, ridge, rise, slope, summit; SEE CONCEPT *509*

hinder [v] *prevent, slow down*
arrest, balk, bar, block, bottleneck, box in, burden, check, choke, clog, contravene, counteract, crab, cramp, crimp, cripple, curb, debar, delay, deter, encumber, fetter, frustrate, get in the way*, hamper, hamstring*, handicap, hog-tie*, hold back, hold up, impede, inhibit, interfere, interrupt, louse up*, muzzle, neutralize, obstruct, offset, oppose, preclude, prohibit, resist, retard, shut out, snafu*, stay, stop, stymie*, terminate, thwart, trammel; SEE CONCEPTS *121,130*

hindrance [n] *obstruction, difficulty*
albatross*, baggage*, ball and chain*, bar, barrier, catch, Catch-22*, check, clog, crimp, cumbrance, deterrent, drag, drawback, encumbrance, excess baggage*, foot dragging*, glitch*, gridlock, handicap, hang-up*, hitch, impedance, impediment, interference, interruption, intervention, jam-up*, joker, limitation, lock, millstone*, monkey wrench*, obstacle, restraint, restriction, snag, stoppage, stumbling block*, trammel; SEE CONCEPTS *666,674*

hindsight [n] *retrospect*
experience, knowledge, looking back, Monday morning quarterbacking, recollection, remembering, 20/20 vision*, wisdom; SEE CONCEPTS *17,40,410*

hinge [n] *pivot, turning point*
articulation, axis, ball-and-socket, butt, elbow, hook, joint, juncture, knee, link, pin, spring, swivel; SEE CONCEPTS *471,498*

hinge [v] *be contingent on*
be subject to, be undecided, depend, hang, pend, pivot, rest, revolve around, stand on, turn, turn on; SEE CONCEPT *711*

hint [n] *indication; suggestion*
adumbration, advice, allusion, announcement, clue, communication, connotation, denotation, evidence, flea in ear*, glimmering, help, idea, implication, impression, inference, information, inkling, innuendo, insinuation, intimation, iota, lead, mention, notice, notion, observation, omen, pointer, print, reference, reminder, scent, sign, signification, smattering, suspicion, symptom, taste, telltale, tinge, tip, tip-off*, token, trace, warning, whiff*, whisper, wink*, word to wise*, wrinkle*; SEE CONCEPT *274*

hint [v] *suggest; indicate*
acquaint, adumbrate, advise, allude to, angle, apprise, bring up, broach, coax, connote, cue, drop,

expose, fish*, foreshadow, give an inkling*, impart, imply, infer, inform, insinuate, intimate, jog memory, leak*, let it be known, let out of bag*, make*, mention, point, prefigure, press, prompt, put flea in ear*, recall, refer to, remind, say in passing, shadow, signify, solicit, spring, tip off*, tip one's hand*, touch on*, whisper, wink*; SEE CONCEPTS 60,74,75

hinterland [n] *backcountry*
boondocks*, boonies*, borderland, brush, bush country, frontier, outback, sticks*, wasteland, wilderness, woods; SEE CONCEPTS 513,745

hip [adj] *fashionable, stylish*
all the rage*, chic, chichi*, contemporary, cool*, current, faddy*, hot*, in style, in-thing*, in vogue, latest*, latest thing*, mod*, modern, modish*, natty*, new, now, popular, smart, sophisticated, trendsetting, trendy, with it*; SEE CONCEPTS 579,580

hippie [n] *nonconformist*
beatnik, Bohemian, drop-out, flower child, freak, free spirit, freethinker, yippie; SEE CONCEPT 423

hire [v] *commission for responsibility, use*
add to payroll, appoint, authorize, book, bring in, bring on board, carry, charter, contract for, delegate, draft, employ, empower, engage, enlist, exploit, fill a position, find help, give a break*, give job to, give work, ink*, lease, let, make use of, obtain, occupy, pick, place, pledge, procure, promise, put on*, put to work, rent, retain, secure, select, sign on, sign up*, sublease, sublet, take on, truck with*, utilize; SEE CONCEPT 351

hiss [n] *buzzing sound; jeer*
boo, Bronx cheer*, buzz, catcall, contempt, derision, hoot, sibilance, sibilation; SEE CONCEPTS 278,595

hiss [v] *make buzzing sound; ridicule*
blow, boo, catcall, condemn, damn, decry, deride, disapprove, hoot, jeer, mock, rasp, revile, seethe, shout down, shrill, sibilate, siss, spit, wheeze, whirr, whisper, whistle, whiz; SEE CONCEPTS 52,77

historic [adj] *momentous, remarkable*
celebrated, consequential, extraordinary, famous, important, memorable, notable, outstanding, red-letter*, significant, well-known; SEE CONCEPTS 548,568

historical [adj] *recorded as actually having happened*
actual, ancient, archival, attested, authentic, chronicled, classical, commemorated, documented, factual, important, in truth, old, past, real, verifiable; SEE CONCEPTS 548,582,820

history [n1] *past events, experiences*
ancient times, antiquity, bygone times, days of old*, days of yore*, good old days*, old days*, olden days*, past, yesterday, yesteryear; SEE CONCEPTS 678,807

history [n2] *chronicle of events*
account, annals, autobiography, biography, diary, epic, journal, memoirs, narration, narrative, prehistory, recapitulation, recital, record, relation, report, saga, story, tale, version; SEE CONCEPTS 268,271

histrionic [adj] *overly dramatic*
melodramatic, overacting, overplayed, theatrical, thespian; SEE CONCEPTS 537,548

histrionics [n] *theatrics*
dramatics, dramatization, performance, performing; SEE CONCEPT 674

hit [n1] *strike, bump*
bang, bat, bell-ringer*, belt, blow, bonk, box*, buffet, butt, chop, clash, clip, clout, collision, cuff*, fisticuff, glance, impact, knock, lick*, one-two punch*, paste*, pat, plunk, punch, rap, roundhouse*, shock, shot, slap, slog, smack, smash, sock, spank, stroke, swat, swing, swipe, tap, uppercut, wallop, whammy*, whop, zap*, zinger*; SEE CONCEPTS 189,200

hit [n2] *entertainment success*
achievement, bang, click, favorite, knockout, masterstroke, sellout, sensation, smash, SRO*, triumph, winner, wow; SEE CONCEPT 706

hit [v1] *strike*
bang, bash, bat, batter, beat, belt, blast, blitz, box*, brain*, buffet, bump, clap, clip, clobber, clout, club, crack, cudgel, cuff*, dab, ding*, flail, flax, flog, give a black eye*, hammer*, hook, jab, kick, knock, knock around, knock out, KO*, lace, lambaste, larrup, lather, let fly*, let have it*, lob, nail*, pellet, pelt, percuss, pop, pound, punch, rap, ride roughshod*, slap, smack, sock, stone, swat, tap, thrash, thump, thwack, trash, uppercut, wallop, whack*, whang*; SEE CONCEPTS 189,200

hit [v2] *collide, bump into*
bang into, buffet, butt, carom, clash, crash, glance, jostle, knock, light, meet, meet head-on*, pat, rap, run into, scrape, sideswipe, smash, stumble, tap, thud, thump; SEE CONCEPTS 189,208

hit [v3] *accomplish*
achieve, affect, arrive at, attain, gain, influence, leave a mark, occur, overwhelm, reach, secure, strike, touch; SEE CONCEPTS 199,706

hitch [n] *problem, difficulty*
block, bug*, catch, check, delay, discontinuance, drawback, glitch*, hang-up, hindrance, hold-up, impediment, interruption, joker, mishap, snafu*, snag, stoppage, stumbling block, tangle, trouble; SEE CONCEPTS 666,674

hitch [v] *join, fasten*
attach, chain, connect, couple, harness, hook, lash, make fast, moor, strap, tether, tie, unite, yoke; SEE CONCEPTS 85,113,160

hit it off [v] *get along well*
be of one mind*, be on the same wavelength*, click, make friends, see eye to eye, take to; SEE CONCEPT 388

hit man [n] *professional killer*
assassin, contract killer, executioner, gunman, hatchet man, hired gun*, hired killer, murderer, triggerman; SEE CONCEPT 412

hit-or-miss [adj] *random*
accidental, aimless, arbitrary, casual, chance, contingent, fluky, fortuitous, haphazard, incidental, irregular, slipshod, trial-and error, unplanned, unpremeditated; SEE CONCEPTS 535,548,557

hoard [n] *stockpile*
abundance, accumulation, agglomeration, aggregation, amassment, backlog, cache, collection, conglomeration, cumulation, fund, garner, heap, inventory, mass, nest egg*, pile, reserve, reservoir, riches, stock, store, supply, treasure, treasure-trove*, trove, wealth; SEE CONCEPT 712

hoard [v] *put away, accumulate*
acquire, amass, buy up, cache, collect, deposit, garner, gather, hide, keep, lay away, lay up, pile up, put aside for rainy day*, put by, save, scrimp,

hi
ho

sock away*, squirrel*, stash, stockpile, store, stow away, treasure; SEE CONCEPTS *135,710*

hoarse [*adj*] *raspy in voice*
blatant, breathy, cracked, croaking, croaky, croupy, discordant, dry, grating, gravelly, growling, gruff, guttural, harsh, husky, indistinct, jarring, piercing, ragged, raucous, rough, scratching, squawking, stertorous, strident, stridulous, thick, throaty, uneven, whispering; SEE CONCEPT *594*

hoary [*adj1*] *ancient*
aged, age-old, antiquated, antique, elderly, lot of mileage*, old, older, old-fashioned, oldie*, out-of-date, relic, rusty, timeworn, venerable, very old; SEE CONCEPTS *578,797*

hoary [*adj2*] *gray or white*
frosty, gray-haired, graying, salt and pepper, silvery, snowy-haired, white-haired, whitish; SEE CONCEPT *618*

hoax [*n*] *trick*
cheat, cock-and-bull story*, con*, con game*, crock*, deceit, deception, dodge, fabrication, fake, falsification, fast one*, fast shuffle*, fib, flimflam*, fraud, gimmick, gyp*, hooey*, humbug*, hustle, imposture, joke, lie, practical joke, prank, put-on, racket, ruse, scam, sell, shift, snow job*, spoof, sting, swindle, whopper*; SEE CONCEPTS *59,63*

hoax [*v*] *trick*
bamboozle*, bluff, chicane, con, deceive, delude, dupe, fake out, fleece, flimflam*, fool, frame, gammon, gull, hoodwink*, Murphy*, play games with*, pull one's leg*, rook*, run a game on*, set up*, sting*, swindle, take for a ride*, take in*; SEE CONCEPT *59*

hobble [*v1*] *limp*
clump, dodder, falter, halt, hitch, scuff, shuffle, stagger, stumble, totter; SEE CONCEPT *151*

hobble [*v2*] *cripple, restrict*
clog, cramp, cramp one's style, crimp, curb, entrammel, fasten, fetter, gimp, hamper, hamstring*, hang up*, hinder, hog-tie*, leash, put a crimp in*, shackle, tie, trammel; SEE CONCEPT *130*

hobby [*n*] *pleasurable pastime*
amusement, art, avocation, bag*, craft, craze, distraction, diversion, divertissement, fad*, fancy, favorite occupation, fun, game, interest, kick*, labor of love*, leisure activity, leisure pursuit, obsession, occupation, pet topic, play, quest, relaxation, schtick*, shot, sideline, specialty, sport, thing*, vagary, weakness, whim, whimsy; SEE CONCEPTS *363,364*

hobgoblin [*n*] *mischievous goblin*
bogeyman, brownie, elf, fairy, fay, imp, leprechaun, pixie, puck, sprite; SEE CONCEPT *370*

hobo [*n*] *homeless person*
beggar, bum, derelict, drifter, migrant worker, street person, tramp, transient, vagabond, vagrant, wanderer, wino; SEE CONCEPTS *412,423*

hock [*v*] *pawn*
borrow, give security, pledge; SEE CONCEPTS *115,330*

hocus-pocus [*n*] *deception, magic*
abracadabra*, artifice, cant, chant, charm, cheating, chicanery, conjuring, deceit, delusion, flimflam*, fraud, gibberish, gobbledegook*, hoax, humbug, imposture, incantation, jargon, juggling, legerdemain, mumbo-jumbo*, mummery, nonsense, open-sesame*, rigmarole*, sleight of hand*, spell, swindle, trick, trickery; SEE CONCEPTS *59,278*

hodgepodge [*n*] *mixture, mess*
collection, combination, goulash*, hash, jumble, medley, mélange, miscellany, mishmash*, mixed bag, olio, patchwork, potpourri, salmagundi*; SEE CONCEPTS *260,432*

hog [*n1*] *pig*
boar, cob roller*, oinker*, piggy, piglet, porker*, razorback, shoat, sow, swine, warthog; SEE CONCEPTS *394,400*

hog [*n2*] *glutton*
cormorant, epicure, gorger*, gormandizer, gourmand, greedy eater, hefty eater, pig*, swine*; SEE CONCEPT *412*

hog [*v*] *be selfish*
be greedy, gobble up, grab all of, have all to oneself*, monopolize; SEE CONCEPTS *90,190*

hogwash [*n*] *nonsense*
absurdity, balderdash*, baloney*, BS*, bull*, bunk*, debris, drivel*, foolishness, hokum, hooey*, horsefeathers*, poppycock*, refuse, ridiculousness, rot, rubbish, trash, twaddle*; SEE CONCEPT *278*

hoi polloi [*n*] *the masses*
commonality, commoners, common people, rank and file, the herd, the multitude, the proletariat, the working class; SEE CONCEPTS *379,417*

hoist [*v*] *lift*
elevate, erect, heave, pick up, raise, rear, take up, uphold, uplift, upraise, uprear; SEE CONCEPT *196*

hokey [*adj*] *corny*
banal, commonplace, dull*, feeble, hackneyed, mawkish, old-fashioned, old hat*, sentimental, shopworn, stale, trite; SEE CONCEPT *550*

hold [*n*] *grasp, possession*
authority, clasp, clench, clinch, clout, clutch, control, dominance, dominion, grip, influence, occupancy, occupation, ownership, pull, purchase, retention, sway, tenacity, tenure; SEE CONCEPTS *190,343,710*

hold [*v1*] *have in one's hands, possession; grasp*
adhere, arrest, bind, bottle up, carry, catch, check, cherish, clasp, cleave, clench, clinch, cling, clutch, confine, contain, cork up*, cradle, detain, embrace, enclose, enjoy, fondle, freeze to*, grip, handle, hang on, have, hug, imprison, keep, keep close, keep out, lock up, maintain, not let go, nourish, occupy, own, palm, possess, press, put a lock on, restrain, retain, secure, seize, squeeze, stay put, stick, take, trammel, vise, wield, withhold, wring; SEE CONCEPTS *190,191,200,710*

hold [*v2*] *believe*
assume, aver, bet bottom dollar*, buy*, consider, credit, cross one's heart*, deem, entertain, esteem, feel, have hunch*, have sneaking suspicion*, judge, lap up, lay money on, maintain, okay, presume, reckon, regard, sense, set store by*, swear by, swear up and down*, take as gospel truth*, take stock in*, think, view; SEE CONCEPT *12*

hold [*v3*] *continue, endure*
apply, be in effect, be in force, be the case, be valid, exist, have bearing, hold good, hold true, last, operate, persevere, persist, remain, remain true, resist, stand up, stay, stay staunch, wear; SEE CONCEPT *239*

hold [*v4*] *support*
bear, bolster, brace, buttress, carry, lock, prop,

shore up, shoulder, stay, sustain, take, underpin, uphold; SEE CONCEPTS *110,190*

hold [*v5*] *have a capacity for*
accommodate, be equipped for, carry, comprise, contain, include, seat, take; SEE CONCEPTS *719,742*

hold [*v6*] *conduct meeting, function*
assemble, call, carry on, celebrate, convene, have, officiate, preside, run, solemnize; SEE CONCEPTS *324,384*

hold back/hold off [*v*] *repress*
bit, bridle, check, control, curb, defer, delay, deny, forbear, hold down, hold in, inhibit, keep, keep back, keep out, postpone, prevent, put off, refrain, refuse, restrain, stop, suppress, withhold; SEE CONCEPTS *121,130*

holdup [*n1*] *problem*
bottleneck*, delay, difficulty, gridlock*, hitch, obstruction, setback, snag, stoppage, traffic jam*, trouble, wait; SEE CONCEPTS *192,674*

holdup [*n2*] *take goods illegally by force*
burglary, crime, mugging, robbery, stickup, theft; SEE CONCEPT *192*

hold up [*v1*] *postpone*
delay, detain, hinder, hold off, impede, interfere, interrupt, pause, prorogue, retard, set back, slow down, stay, stop, suspend, waive; SEE CONCEPTS *121,130*

hold up [*v2*] *rob*
burglarize, mug, steal from, stick up, waylay; SEE CONCEPTS *139,192*

hole [*n1*] *opening in a solid object*
aperture, breach, break, burrow, cave, cavern, cavity, chamber, chasm, chink, cistern, cleft, covert, crack, cranny, crater, cut, den, dent, depression, dimple, dip, excavation, eyelet, fissure, foramen, fracture, gap, gash, gorge, hollow, hovel, keyhole, lacuna, lair, leak, mouth, nest, niche, nick, notch, orifice, outlet, passage, peephole, perforation, pit, pocket, pockmark, puncture, rent, retreat, scoop, shaft, shelter, space, split, tear, tunnel, vacuity, vent, void, window; SEE CONCEPT *513*

hole [*n2*] *predicament*
box*, corner*, difficulty, dilemma, emergency, fix, imbroglio, impasse, jam, mess, pickle*, plight, quandary, scrape, spot, tangle; SEE CONCEPT *674*

holiday [*n*] *celebratory day; time off*
anniversary, break, celebration, day of rest, feast, festival, festivity, fete, few days off*, fiesta, gala, gone fishing*, holy day, jubilee, layoff, leave, liberty, long weekend*, recess, red-letter day*, saint's day, vacation; SEE CONCEPTS *364,802*

holier-than-thou [*adj*] *self-righteously pious*
goody-goody, high-hat, judgmental, pietistic, sanctimonious, smug, snobbish, unctuous; SEE CONCEPT *401*

holiness [*n*] *religiousness*
asceticism, beatitude, blessedness, consecration, devotion, devoutness, divineness, divinity, faith, godliness, grace, humility, inviolability, piety, purity, religiosity, reverence, righteousness, sacredness, saintliness, sanctity, spirituality, unction, venerableness, virtuousness, worship; SEE CONCEPTS *368,645*

holistic [*adj*] *complete, whole*
aggregate, comprehensive, entire, full, integrated, total, universal; SEE CONCEPT *531*

holler [*v*] *shout, yell*
bawl, bellow, call, cheer, complain, cry, hoot, howl, roar, scream, screech, shriek, shrill, squawk, squeal, ululate, vociferate, wail, whoop, yap, yelp; SEE CONCEPTS *47,595*

hollow [*adj1*] *empty, hollowed out*
alveolate, arched, carved out, cavernous, cleft, concave, cupped, cup-shaped, curved, deep-set, depressed, dimpled, excavated, incurved, indented, infundibular, notched, not solid, pitted, striated, sunken, troughlike, unfilled, vacant, vaulted, void; SEE CONCEPTS *483,490*

hollow [*adj2*] *deep, resonant in sound*
cavernous, clangorous, dull, echoing, flat, ghostly, low, muffled, mute, muted, resounding, reverberant, ringing, roaring, rumbling, sepulchral, sounding, thunderous, toneless, vibrant, vibrating; SEE CONCEPT *594*

hollow [*adj3*] *meaningless*
empty, fruitless, futile, idle, nugatory, otiose, pointless, specious, unavailing, useless, vain, worthless; SEE CONCEPT *560*

hollow [*adj4*] *false, artificial*
cynical, deceitful, faithless, flimsy, hypocritical, insincere, treacherous, unsound, weak; SEE CONCEPT *267*

hollow [*n*] *empty or dented area*
basin, bottom, bowl, cave, cavern, cavity, chamber, channel, cleft, concavity, crater, cup, dale, den, depression, dimple, dip, dish, excavation, groove, gulf, hole, indentation, notch, pit, pocket, sag, scoop, sinkage, sinkhole, socket, trough, vacuity, valley, void; SEE CONCEPTS *740,754*

hollow [*v*] *empty out; make concave*
channel, chase, corrugate, dent, dig, dish, ditch, excavate, furrow, gorge, groove, indent, notch, pit, rabbet, remove, rut, scoop, shovel, trench; SEE CONCEPTS *178,211*

holocaust [*n*] *widespread destruction*
annihilation, carnage, catastrophe, devastation, extermination, extinction, genocide, immolation, inferno, massacre, mass murder, slaughter; SEE CONCEPT *252*

holy [*adj*] *religious, sacred*
angelic, believing, blessed, chaste, clean, consecrated, dedicated, devoted, devotional, devout, divine, faithful, faultless, glorified, god-fearing, godlike, godly, good, hallowed, humble, immaculate, innocent, just, moral, perfect, pietistic, pious, prayerful, pure, revered, reverent, righteous, sacrosanct, sainted, saintlike, saintly, sanctified, seraphic, spiritual, spotless, sublime, uncorrupt, undefiled, untainted, unworldly, upright, venerable, venerated, virtuous; SEE CONCEPTS *545,567,574*

homage [*n*] *devotion, admiration*
adoration, adulation, allegiance, awe, deference, duty, esteem, faithfulness, fealty, fidelity, genuflection, honor, kneeling, loyalty, obeisance, praise, respect, reverence, service, tribute, worship; SEE CONCEPTS *32,69*

home [*adj*] *domestic*
at ease, at rest, central, down home*, familiar, family, homely, homey, household, inland, in one's element*, internal, in the bosom*, local, national, native; SEE CONCEPT *536*

home [*n1*] *place where a human lives*
abode, address, apartment, asylum, boarding house, bungalow, cabin, castle, cave*, com-

ho
ho

morancy, condo, condominium, co-op, cottage, crash pad*, diggings*, digs*, domicile, dormitory, dump*, dwelling, farm, fireside*, flat, habitation, hangout*, haunt, hearth, hideout, hole in the wall*, home plate*, homestead, hospital, house, hut, joint*, living quarters, manor, mansion, nest*, orphanage, pad*, palace, parking place*, place, residence, resort, roof*, rooming house, roost*, shanty, shelter, trailer, turf, villa, where the hat is*; SEE CONCEPT 516

home [n2] *birthplace, environment*
abode, camping ground*, country, element, family, farm, fireside*, habitat, habitation, haunt, haven, hearth, hills, home ground, homeland, homestead, hometown, household, land, locality, neck of the woods*, neighborhood, range, roof, site, soil, stamping ground*, stomping ground*, territory; SEE CONCEPTS 510,515,648

homeboy [n] *friend*
bro*, brother*, buddy, fellow gang member, homie, neighbor; SEE CONCEPT 423

homegrown [adj] *grown at home*
domestic, homemade, native; SEE CONCEPT 536

homeless [adj] *displaced*
abandoned, banished, deported, derelict, desolate, destitute, disinherited, displaced, dispossessed, down-and-out*, estranged, exiled, forlorn, forsaken, friendless, houseless, itinerant, outcast, refugee, uncared-for, unhoused, unsettled, unwelcome, vagabond, vagrant, wandering, without a roof*; SEE CONCEPT 555

homely [adj1] *ordinary, comfortable*
comfy, cozy, domestic, everyday, familiar, friendly, homelike, homespun, homey, inelaborate, informal, modest, natural, plain, simple, snug, unaffected, unassuming, unostentatious, unpretentious, welcoming;   SEE   CONCEPTS 579,589

homely [adj2] *unattractive*
animal, disgusting, plain, ugly, unaesthetic, unalluring; SEE CONCEPT 579

homemade [adj] *made in the home*
do-it-yourself, handcrafted, handmade, homegrown, homespun, natural; SEE CONCEPT 536

homesick [adj] *nostalgic*
hankering, heartsick, lonely, longing for home, missing, wistful, yearning;   SEE   CONCEPTS 403,529

homespun [adj] *spun from home*
crude, handcrafted, handmade, homemade, ordinary, plain, rough, rustic, simple, unrefined, unsophisticated; SEE CONCEPT 536

homey [adj] *comfortable*
adequate, cared for, cheerful, comfy*, complacent, contented, cozy, delightful, easy, familiar, folksy, friendly, intimate, plain, pleasant, relaxed, rested, restful, simple, snug, snug as a bug in a rug*, soft, soothed, warm; SEE CONCEPT 572

homicidal [adj] *murderous*
bloodthirsty, deadly, lethal, maniacal, slaughterous, violent; SEE CONCEPTS 538,548,565

homicide [n] *killing*
assassination, big chill*, bloodshed, bump-off*, butchery, carnage, crime, death, erase*, foul play, hit, manslaughter, murder, offing, ride, rubout*, slaying; SEE CONCEPT 252

homogenous [adj] *similar, comparable*
akin, alike, analogous, cognate, consistent, homologous, identical, kindred, like, uniform, unvarying; SEE CONCEPTS 487,573

homosexual [adj] *sexually attracted to the same sex*
gay, homoerotic, homophile, lesbian; SEE CONCEPT 372

hone [v] *sharpen*
acuminate, edge, file, grind, make sharp, put an edge on, put a point on, whet; SEE CONCEPTS 137,250

honest [adj] *truthful, candid*
above-board, authentic, bona fide*, conscientious, decent, direct, equitable, ethical, fair, fair and square*, forthright, frank, genuine, highminded*, honorable, impartial, ingenuous, just, law-abiding*, lay it on the line*, like it is*, no lie*, on the level*, on the up and up*, open, outright, plain, proper, real, reliable, reputable, scrupulous, sincere, straight, straightforward, true, true blue*, trustworthy, trusty, undisguised, unfeigned, upfront*, upright, veracious, virtuous, what you see is what you get*; SEE CONCEPTS 267,545

honest-to-God [adj] *genuine*
absolute, accurate, actual, authentic, authenticated, bona fide, certain, certified, factual, for real*, for-sure, honest, honest-to-goodness*, kosher*, legit, legitimate, no buts about it*, official, on the level*, on the up-and-up, positive, real, really-truly*, real stuff*, straight, sure-enough, sure-thing, true, unquestionable, valid; SEE CONCEPT 582

honesty [n] *truthfulness, candidness*
bluntness, candor, confidence, conscientiousness, equity, evenhandedness, fairness, faithfulness, fidelity, frankness, genuineness, goodness, honor, impeccability, incorruptibility, integrity, justness, loyalty, morality, openness, outspokenness, plainness, principle, probity, rectitude, reputability, responsibility, right, scrupulousness, self-respect, sincerity, soundness, straightforwardness, straightness, trustiness, trustworthiness, uprightness, veracity, virtue; SEE CONCEPTS 633,645

honeyed [adj] *sweetened*
cajoling, candied, dulcet, flattering, ingratiating, sugarcoated, sugary; SEE CONCEPT 170

honk [v] *toot*
beep, blare, blast, blow, blow the horn, sound, sound one's horn, tootle; SEE CONCEPT 65

honor [n1] *respect*
account, adoration, adulation, aggrandizement, apotheosis, approbation, attention, canonization, celebration, confidence, consideration, credit, deference, deification, dignity, distinction, elevation, esteem, exaltation, faith, fame, fealty, glorification, glory, greatness, high standing, homage, immortalization, laud, laurel, lionization, notice, obeisance, popularity, praise, prestige, rank, recognition, renown, reputation, repute, reverence, tribute, trust, veneration, worship, wreath; SEE CONCEPTS 668,689

honor [n2] *integrity*
character, chastity, courage, decency, fairness, goodness, honestness, honesty, incorruption, incorruptness, innocence, modesty, morality, morals, principles, probity, purity, rectitude, righteousness, trustworthiness, truthfulness, uprightness, virtue; SEE CONCEPTS 411,645

honor [n3] *praise, award*
acclaim, accolade, adoration, badge, bays, com-

mendation, compliment, credit, decoration, deference, distinction, favor, homage, kudos, laurels, pleasure, privilege, recognition, regard, respect, reverence, source of pride, tribute, veneration; SEE CONCEPTS *278,337,689*

honor [*v*] *recognize, treat with respect*
acclaim, admire, adore, aggrandize, appreciate, be faithful, be true, celebrate, commemorate, commend, compliment, decorate, dignify, distinguish, ennoble, erect, esteem, exalt, give glad hand*, give key to city*, glorify, hallow, keep, laud, lionize, live up to, look up to, magnify, observe, praise, prize, revere, roll out red carpet*, sanctify, sublime, uprear, value, venerate, worship; SEE CONCEPTS *10,633*

honorable [*adj*] *reputable*
acclaimed, celebrated, chivalrous, conscientious, dependable, distinguished, eminent, esteemed, ethical, faithful, forthright, high-principled, honest, honored, illustrious, just, knightly, law-abiding, noble, notable, of good repute, on the up-and-up*, principled, reliable, respectable, righteous, sincere, sterling, straightforward, trustworthy, truthful, unstained, upright, virtuous; SEE CONCEPTS *545,567,574*

honorary [*adj*] *honorific*
celebratory, congratulatory, titular; SEE CONCEPTS *668,689*

hood/hoodlum [*n*] *gangster*
criminal, delinquent, gangster, goon*, hooligan, mobster, punk, rioter, rowdy, ruffian, thug, troublemaker; SEE CONCEPT *545*

hoodwink [*v*] *deceive*
bamboozle*, beat out of, bilk, bluff, buffalo*, burn, cheat, con, defraud, double-cross, dupe, fake, fleece, fool, gull, gyp*, hoax, hornswoggle, kid, mislead, pull a fast one*, pull the wool over one's eyes*, scam, screw, suck in*, swindle, take advantage of, take for a ride*, take to the cleaners*, trick, victimize; SEE CONCEPTS *7,19,59*

hook [*n*] *curved fastener*
angle, catch, clasp, crook, curve, grapnel, grapple, hasp, holder, link, lock, peg; SEE CONCEPTS *260,498*

hook [*v*] *grab, catch*
angle, bag, clasp, crook, curve, enmesh, ensnare, entrap, fasten, fix, hasp, lasso, net, pin, secure, snare, trap; SEE CONCEPT *190*

hooked [*adj*] *addicted*
absorbed, captivated, dependent, devoted, enamored, obsessed, prone, strung out*, under the influence; SEE CONCEPT *542*

hooker [*n*] *prostitute*
bawd, call girl, concubine, courtesan, fallen woman*, floozy*, harlot, hustler, lady of the evening, moll, nymphomaniac*, painted*, pro*, streetwalker, strumpet, whore, woman of the streets, working girl*; SEE CONCEPTS *348,412, 415,419*

hooligan [*n*] *hoodlum*
criminal, delinquent, gangster, goon*, hood, mobster, punk, rioter, rowdy, ruffian, thug, troublemaker; SEE CONCEPT *545*

hoopla [*n*] *excitement*
action, activity, brouhaha, bustle, buzz*, commotion, drama, elation, emotion, excitation, feeling, fever, fireworks*, flurry, frenzy, furor, fuss, heat*, hubbub*, hullabaloo*, hysteria, passion,

racket, rage, ruckus, rumpus, stir, thrill; SEE CONCEPTS *388,410,633*

hoot [*v*] *cry*
boo, catcall, heckle, hiss, howl, jeer, razz*, scoff at, scorn, scream, shout down, whistle; SEE CONCEPTS *44,47*

hop [*n/v*] *jump on one leg*
bounce, bound, caper, dance, hurdle, leap, lop, lope, skip, skitter, spring, step, trip, vault; SEE CONCEPT *194*

hope [*n*] *longing; dream*
achievement, ambition, anticipation, aspiration, assumption, belief, bright side*, buoyancy, castles in air*, concern, confidence, daydream, dependence, desire, endurance, expectancy, expectation, faith, fancy, fool's paradise*, fortune, gain, goal, greedy glutton*, hopefulness, light at end of tunnel*, optimism, pipe dream*, promise, promised land*, prospect, reliance, reverie, reward, rosiness, sanguineness, security, stock, thing with feathers*, Utopia, wish; SEE CONCEPTS *20,410,709*

hope [*v*] *long for, dream about*
anticipate, aspire, assume, await, believe, be sure of, cherish, contemplate, count on, deem likely, depend on, desire, expect, feel confident, foresee, hang in*, have faith, hold, keep fingers crossed*, knock on wood*, look at sunny side*, look forward to, pray, presume, promise oneself, rely, suppose, surmise, suspect, sweat*, sweat it*, sweat it out*, take heart*, think to, trust, watch for, wish; SEE CONCEPT *20*

hopeful [*adj1*] *optimistic, expectant*
anticipating, anticipative, assured, at ease, blithe, buoyant, calm, cheerful, comfortable, confident, content, eager, elated, emboldened, enthusiastic, expecting, faithful, forward-looking*, high, hoping, inspirited, keeping the faith*, lighthearted, looking forward to, reassured, rose-colored*, rosy*, sanguine, satisfied, serene, trustful, trusting, unflagging, upbeat; SEE CONCEPT *403*

hopeful [*adj2*] *promising, auspicious*
advantageous, arousing, beneficial, bright, cheerful, cheering, conducive, convenient, elating, encouraging, enlivening, exciting, expeditious, fair, favorable, fine, fit, flattering, fortifying, fortunate, golden, good, gracious, halcyon, heartening, helpful, inspiring, inspiriting, likely, lucky, opportune, pleasant, pleasing, probable, promiseful, propitious, providential, reasonable, reassuring, roseate, rosy*, rousing, stirring, suitable, sunny, timely, uplifting, well-timed; SEE CONCEPT *548*

hopeless [*adj*] *futile, pessimistic*
bad, beyond recall, cynical, dejected, demoralized, despairing, desperate, despondent, disconsolate, discouraging, downhearted, fatal, forlorn, gone*, goner*, helpless, ill-fated, impossible, impracticable, incurable, in despair, irredeemable, irreparable, irreversible, irrevocable, lost, menacing, no-win, past hope, pointless, sad, shot down*, sinister, sunk, threatening, tragic, unachievable, unavailing, unfortunate, unmitigable, up the creek*, useless, vain, woebegone, worsening; SEE CONCEPTS *529,548*

horde [*n*] *uncontrolled throng, pack*
band, crew, crowd, crush, drove, everybody, gang, gathering, host, jam, mob, multitude,

**ho
ho**

press, push, squash, swarm, troop, turnout, wall-to-wall*; SEE CONCEPTS 397,417

horizon [n] *skyline, extent*
border, boundary, compass, field of vision, ken, limit, perspective, prospect, purview, range, reach, realm, scope, sphere, stretch, vista; SEE CONCEPTS 484,509,529

horizontal [adj] *lying flat*
accumbent, aligned, even, flush, level, parallel, plane, recumbent, regular, smooth, straight, uniform; SEE CONCEPTS 581,583

horny [adj] *sexually aroused*
concupiscent, desiring, hard up, hot*, hot to trot*, lascivious, libidinous, lustful, oversexed, passionate, randy, turned on; SEE CONCEPT 372

horoscope [n] *astrological forecast*
astrology, crystal gazing, prediction; SEE CONCEPT 70

horrible/horrendous/horrid [adj] *repulsive, very unpleasant*
abhorrent, abominable, appalling, awful, beastly, cruel, detestable, disagreeable, disgusting, dreadful, eerie, execrable, fearful, frightful, ghastly, grim, grisly, gross*, gruesome, heinous, hideous, loathsome, lousy, lurid, mean, nasty, obnoxious, offensive, repellent, revolting, scandalous, scary, shameful, shocking, terrible, terrifying, ungodly, unholy, unkind; SEE CONCEPTS 529,537

horrify [v] *scare*
affright, alarm, appall, chill off*, consternate, daunt, disgust, dismay, frighten, intimidate, outrage, petrify, scare to death*, shake, shock, sicken, terrify, terrorize; SEE CONCEPTS 7,14,19

horror [n] *fear, revulsion*
abhorrence, abomination, alarm, antipathy, apprehension, aversion, awe, chiller, consternation, detestation, disgust, dislike, dismay, dread, fright, hate, hatred, loathing, monstrosity, panic, repugnance, terror, trepidation; SEE CONCEPTS 27,29,532,690

hors d'oeuvre [n] *appetizer*
antipasto, aperitif, canape, cocktail, dip, finger food, finger sandwich, munchies, sample, starter; SEE CONCEPTS 457,828

horse [n] *equine species*
bronco, colt, filly, foal, gelding, mare, mustang, nag, plug*, pony, stallion, steed; SEE CONCEPT 394

horse around [v] *fool around*
carry on, cavort, cut up, lark, monkey around*, play around; SEE CONCEPTS 114,384

horseplay [n] *rough play*
antics, buffoonery, capers, clowning, fooling around, fun and games, hijinks, misbehavior, pranks, rough-housing, rowdiness, shenanigans, tomfoolery; SEE CONCEPT 386

horticulture [n] *gardening*
agriculture, arboriculture, cultivation, farming, floriculture, groundskeeping, viniculture, viticulture; SEE CONCEPTS 205,257

hospitable [adj] *sociable, accommodating*
accessible, amenable, amicable, bountiful, charitable, companionable, convivial, cooperative, cordial, courteous, friendly, generous, genial, gracious, gregarious, kind, liberal, magnanimous, neighborly, obliging, open, open-minded, philanthropic, receptive, red-carpet treatment*, responsive, tolerant, welcoming; SEE CONCEPTS 542,555

hospital [n] *place where ill, injured are treated*
clinic, emergency room, health service, hospice, infirmary, institution, nursing home, rest home, sanatorium, sanitarium, sick bay*, surgery, ward; SEE CONCEPTS 312,439,449

hospitality [n] *neighborliness*
accommodation, affability, amiability, cheer, companionship, comradeship, consideration, conviviality, cordiality, entertainment, friendliness, generosity, geniality, good cheer, heartiness, hospitableness, obligingness, reception, sociability, warmth, welcome; SEE CONCEPTS 388,657

host [n1] *person who entertains, performs*
anchor, anchor person, emcee, entertainer, innkeeper, keeper, manager, moderator, owner, person of the house, presenter, proprietor; SEE CONCEPT 352

host [n2] *large group*
army, array, cloud, crowd, crush, drove, flock, gathering, horde, legion, multitude, myriad, rout, score, swarm, throng; SEE CONCEPTS 417,432

host [v] *entertain, accommodate*
do the honors*, introduce, pick up the check*, present, receive, spread oneself*, throw a party, treat, wine and dine*; SEE CONCEPTS 292,384

hostage [n] *person held captive until captor's demand is met*
captive, earnest, guaranty, pawn, pledge, prisoner, sacrificial lamb*, scapegoat*, security, surety, token, victim; SEE CONCEPTS 359,423

hostile [adj] *antagonistic, mean*
adverse, alien, allergic, anti*, argumentative, bellicose, belligerent, bitter, catty*, chill*, cold*, competitive, contentious, contrary, disapproving, dour, hateful, ill-disposed, inhospitable, inimical, malevolent, malicious, malignant, militant, nasty, opposed, opposite, oppugnant, ornery*, pugnacious, rancorous, scrappy*, sour*, spiteful, surly, unfavorable, unfriendly, unkind, unpropitious, unsociable, unsympathetic, unwelcoming, viperous, virulent, vitriolic, warlike; SEE CONCEPTS 401,542

hostility [n] *antagonism, meanness*
abhorrence, aggression, animosity, animus, antipathy, aversion, bad blood*, bellicosity, belligerence, bitterness, detestation, disaffection, enmity, estrangement, grudge, hatred, ill will, inimicality, malevolence, malice, opposition, rancor, resentment, spite, spleen, unfriendliness, venom, virulence, war, warpath; SEE CONCEPTS 633,657

hot [adj1] *very high in temperature*
baking, blazing, blistering, boiling, broiling, burning, calescent, close, decalescent, febrile, fevered, feverish, feverous, fiery, flaming, heated, humid, igneous, incandescent, like an oven*, on fire, ovenlike, parching, piping, recalescent, red*, roasting, scalding, scorching, searing, sizzling, smoking, steaming, stuffy, sultry, summery, sweltering, sweltry, thermogenic, torrid, tropic, tropical, very warm, warm, white*; SEE CONCEPT 605

hot [adj2] *spicy to taste*
acrid, biting, peppery, piquant, pungent, racy, sharp, spicy, zestful; SEE CONCEPT 613

hot [adj3] *passionate, vehement*
angry, animated, ardent, aroused, distracted, eager, enthusiastic, excited, fervent, fervid,

fierce, fiery, furious, ill-tempered, impassioned, impetuous, indignant, inflamed, intense, irascible, lustful, raging, stormy, temperamental, touchy, violent; SEE CONCEPTS *401,403*

hot [*adj4*] *new, in vogue*
approved, cool*, dandy, favored, fresh, glorious, groovy*, in demand, just out*, keen, latest*, marvelous, neat*, nifty*, peachy*, popular, recent, sought-after, super, trendy, up-to-the-minute*; SEE CONCEPT *589*

hot [*adj5*] *sexually excited*
aroused, carnal, concupiscent, erotic, lascivious, lewd, libidinous, lustful, passionate, prurient, salacious, sensual; SEE CONCEPTS *372,555*

hot dog [*n1*] *frankfurter*
foot long*, frank, pigs in a blanket, red-hot, weenie*, wiener; SEE CONCEPTS *399,457,460*

hot dog [*n2*] *showoff*
boaster, braggart, crowd-pleaser, granstander, showboat; SEE CONCEPT *412*

hotel [*n*] *place where one pays for accommodation*
auberge, boarding house, caravansary, dump*, fleabag*, flophouse*, hospice, hostel, hostelry, house, inn, lodging, motel, motor inn, public house, resort, roadhouse, rooming house, spa, tavern; SEE CONCEPTS *439,449,516*

hotheaded [*adj*] *quick-tempered*
easily provoked, excitable, explosive, hot-tempered, impetuous, passionate, rash, short-fused, touchy, volatile; SEE CONCEPTS *401,542,548*

hound [*n*] *dog*
afghan, airedale, akita, basset, beagle, bow-wow*, canine, dachshund, man's best friend*, mongrel, mutt, pointer, pooch, poodle, retriever; SEE CONCEPTS *394,400*

hound [*v*] *chase, badger*
annoy, bait, be at, beat the bushes*, be on one's back*, be on one's case*, be on one's tail*, bird-dog*, bother, bug, chivy, curdle, dog*, drive, give chase, goad, harass, harry, hassle, heckle, hector, hunt, hunt down, impel, leave no stone unturned*, persecute, pester, prod, provoke, pursue, rag*, rag on*, ride, scout, scratch, scratch around, search high heaven*, tail, take out after*, track down, turn inside out, turn upside down, yap at*; SEE CONCEPTS *7,19,207*

house [*n1*] *human habitat*
abode, apartment, box*, building, bullpen, castle, cave*, commorancy, condo, condominium, co-op, coop, crash pad*, crib*, cubbyhole*, den, diggings*, digs*, domicile, dump*, dwelling, edifice, flat, flophouse*, habitation, hole in the wall*, home, home plate*, homestead, joint, kennel, layout, lean-to*, mansion, pad, pied-à-terre, pigpen*, pigsty*, rack*, residence, residency, roof, roost*, setup, shack, shanty, turf*; SEE CONCEPTS *439,516*

house [*n2*] *family, ancestry*
clan, dynasty, family tree, folk, folks, household, kin, kindred, line, lineage, ménage, race, stock, tradition, tribe; SEE CONCEPT *296*

house [*n3*] *business establishment*
company, concern, corporation, firm, organization, outfit, partnership; SEE CONCEPT *325*

house [*n4*] *government body, sometimes elected, responsible for laws*
commons, congress, council, legislative body, legislature, parliament; SEE CONCEPT *299*

household [*adj*] *domestic*
domiciliary, everyday, family, home, homely, homey, ordinary, plain; SEE CONCEPT *536*

household [*n*] *domestic establishment*
family, family unit, folks, home, house, ménage; SEE CONCEPTS *296,516*

housekeeper [*n*] *domestic*
caretaker, chambermaid, house cleaner, housemaid, housewife, maid, servant; SEE CONCEPTS *348,415*

housework [*n*] *cleaning, maintaining a home*
administration, bed-making, cooking, domestic art, domestic science, dusting, home economics, homemaking, housecraft, housekeeping, ironing, laundering, management, mopping, sewing, stewardship, sweeping, washing; SEE CONCEPTS *165,170,202*

housing [*n*] *place of accommodation*
construction, digs*, dwelling, habitation, home, house, lodgment, quarter, quarterage, residence, roof, shelter, sheltering, stopping place; SEE CONCEPTS *388,516*

hovel [*n*] *tiny unkempt house*
burrow, cabin, cottage, den, dump*, hole*, hut, hutch, lean-to, pigpen*, pigsty*, rathole*, rattrap*, shack, shanty, shed, stall, sty*; SEE CONCEPT *516*

hover [*v*] *hang, float over*
be suspended, brood over, dance, drift, flicker, flit, flitter, flutter, fly, hang about, linger, poise, wait nearby, waver; SEE CONCEPT *154*

how [*adv*] *in what way or manner*
according to what, after what precedent, by means of, by virtue of what, by what means, by what method, by whose help, from what source, through what agency, through what medium, to what degree, whence, whereby, wherewith; SEE CONCEPT *544*

however [*adv*] *still, nevertheless*
after all, all the same, anyhow, be that as it may, but, despite, for all that, howbeit, in spite of, nonetheless, notwithstanding, on the other hand, per contra, though, withal, without regard to, yet; SEE CONCEPT *544*

howl [*n/v*] *long, painful cry*
bark, bawl, bay, bellow, blubber, clamor, groan, growl, hoot, keen, lament, moan, outcry, quest, roar, scream, shout, shriek, ululate, wail, weep, whimper, whine, yell, yelp, yip, yowl; SEE CONCEPTS *64,77,595*

hub [*n*] *center, focal point*
core, focus, heart, middle, nerve center*, pivot, polestar, seat; SEE CONCEPT *826*

hubbub [*n*] *commotion, disorder*
babel, bedlam, brouhaha*, clamor, confusion, din, disturbance, fuss, hassle, hell broke loose*, hue and cry*, hullabaloo*, hurly-burly*, jangle, noise, pandemonium, racket, riot, rowdydow*, ruckus, ruction, rumpus, to-do*, tumult, turmoil, uproar, whirl; SEE CONCEPTS *230,384,388*

hubris [*n*] *arrogance*
airs, audacity, brass*, cheek*, chutzpah*, cockiness, conceitedness, contemptuousness, disdain, insolence, loftiness, nerve, ostentation, overbearance, pomposity, pompousness, presumption, pretension, pretentiousness, self-importance, vanity; SEE CONCEPTS *411,633*

huckster [*n*] *peddler*
colporteur, costermonger, hawker, pitchperson,

salesperson, seller, street seller, street vendor; SEE CONCEPTS *347,348*

huddle [*n*] *assemblage, crowd, often disorganized*
bunch, chaos, cluster, clutter, confab*, conference, confusion, disarray, discussion, disorder, gathering, group, heap, jumble, mass, meeting, mess*, muddle; SEE CONCEPTS *230,260,417,432*

huddle [*v*] *meet, discuss*
bunch, cluster, confer, consult, converge, crouch, crowd, cuddle, curl up, draw together, flock, gather, herd, hug, hunch up*, mass, nestle, parley, powwow*, press, press close, snuggle, throng; SEE CONCEPTS *56,114,154*

hue [*n*] *color, shade*
aspect, cast, chroma, complexion, dye, tincture, tinge, tint, tone, value; SEE CONCEPT *622*

hue and cry [*n*] *public clamor*
brouhaha, bugle call, hullabaloo, outcry, protest, rallying cry, uproar; SEE CONCEPTS *46,65,106, 674*

huff [*n*] *bad mood*
anger, annoyance, dudgeon, miff, offense, passion, perturbation, pet*, pique, rage, snit*, stew*, temper, tiff, umbrage; SEE CONCEPT *410*

huff [*v*] *sigh, breathe out forcefully*
blow, expire, gasp, heave, pant, puff; SEE CONCEPT *163*

huffy [*adj*] *angry, in a bad mood*
angered, annoyed, crabbed, crabby, cross, crotchety, crusty, curt, disgruntled, exasperated, fractious, grumpy, huffish, hurt, insulted, irked, irritable, miffed, moody, moping, nettled, offended, peeved, peevish, pettish, petulant, piqued, provoked, put out*, querulous, resentful, riled, short, snappish, snappy, stewed, sulky, sullen, surly, testy, touchy, vexed, waspish; SEE CONCEPTS *401,403*

hug [*n*] *embrace*
affection, bear hug*, bunny hug*, caress, clasp, clinch, lock, squeeze, tight grip; SEE CONCEPTS *190,375*

hug [*v*] *hold close, cling to*
bear hug, be near to, cherish, clasp, clinch, cradle, cuddle, embrace, enbosom, enfold, envelop, fold in arms, follow closely, grasp, hold onto, keep close, lie close, lock, love, nestle, nurse, press, receive, retain, seize, squeeze, stay near, take in one's arms, welcome; SEE CONCEPTS *190,375*

huge [*adj*] *extremely large*
behemothic, bulky, colossal, cyclopean, elephantine, enormous, extensive, gargantuan, giant, gigantic, great, gross*, humongous, immeasurable, immense, jumbo, leviathan, lusty, magnificent, mammoth, massive, mighty, mondo*, monster*, monstrous*, monumental, mountainous, outsize, oversize, planetary, prodigious, stupendous, titanic*, towering, tremendous, vast, walloping, whopping*; SEE CONCEPTS *771,773*

hulk [*n*] *large piece, lump; remains*
blob, body, bulk, chunk, clod, clump, frame, hull, hunk, mass, ruins, shambles, shell, shipwreck, skeleton, wreck; SEE CONCEPT *829*

hulking [*adj*] *massive*
big, bulky, clumsy, colossal, cumbersome, elephantine, enormous, extensive, gargantuan, gigantic, grand, great, heavy, hefty, huge, immense, imposing, large, lumbering, mammoth, monumental, solid, titanic, towering,

tremendous, unwieldy, weighty; SEE CONCEPTS *773,781*

hull [*n*] *skeleton, body*
bark, case, casing, cast, covering, frame, framework, husk, mold, peel, peeling, pod, rind, shell, shuck, skin, structure; SEE CONCEPTS *484,829*

hullabaloo [*n*] *uproar*
bedlam, big scene*, brouhaha, chaos, clamor, commotion, confusion, free-for-all*, furor, fuss, hassle, hubbub, hue and cry, mayhem, melee, noise, pandemonium, racket*, riot, row, ruckus, to-do*; SEE CONCEPTS *46,65,106,230,384,388, 674*

hum [*v*] *buzz, vibrate*
bombilate, bombinate, bum, bumble, croon, drone, moan, mumble, murmur, purr, rustle, sing, sing low, sound, strum, throb, thrum, trill, warble, whir, whisper, zoom; SEE CONCEPTS *65,77*

human [*adj*] *characteristic of people*
animal, anthropoid, anthropological, anthropomorphic, biped, bipedal, civilized, creatural, ethnologic, ethological, fallible, fleshly, forgivable, hominal, homonid, homonine, humanistic, individual, mortal, personal, vulnerable; SEE CONCEPTS *406,549*

human [*n*] *person, homosapien*
being, biped, body, character, child, creature, homo sapien, individual, life, mortal, personage, soul, wight; SEE CONCEPT *417*

humane [*adj*] *kind, compassionate*
accommodating, altruistic, amiable, approachable, benevolent, benign, benignant, broadminded, charitable, clement, considerate, cordial, democratic, forbearing, forgiving, friendly, generous, genial, gentle, good, good-natured, gracious, helpful, human, humanitarian, indulgent, kindhearted, kindly, lenient, liberal, magnanimous, merciful, mild, natural, obliging, openminded, philanthropic, pitying, righteous, sympathetic, tender, tenderhearted, tolerant, understanding, unselfish, warmhearted; SEE CONCEPTS *401,542*

humanitarian [*adj*] *giving, compassionate*
altruistic, beneficent, benevolent, charitable, eleemosynary, generous, good, humane, idealistic, kindly, philanthropic, public-spirited; SEE CONCEPT *542*

humanitarian [*n*] *person who gives generously*
altruist, benefactor, bleeding heart*, do-gooder*, Good Samaritan*, good scout*, helper, patron, philanthropist; SEE CONCEPTS *416,423*

humanity [*n1*] *human race*
Homo sapiens, human beings, humankind, humanness, mankind, people, society; SEE CONCEPT *417*

humanity [*n2*] *benevolence*
altruism, amity, brotherly love, charity, compassion, empathy, feeling, friendship, generosity, goodness, goodwill, heart, kindheartedness, kindness, mercy, sympathy; SEE CONCEPT *410,633*

humankind [*n*] *the human race*
community, flesh, Homo sapiens, human beings, humanity, human species, mortality, mortals, people, populace, society; SEE CONCEPT *417*

humble [*adj1*] *meek, unassuming*
apprehensive, backward, bashful, biddable, blushing, content, courteous, deferential, demure, diffident, docile, fearful, gentle, hesitant,

lowly, manageable, mild, modest, obliging, obsequious, ordinary, polite, quiet, reserved, respectful, retiring, reverential, sedate, self-conscious, self-effacing, servile, sheepish, shy, simple, soft-spoken, standoffish, submissive, subservient, supplicatory, tentative, timid, timorous, tractable, unambitious, unobtrusive, unostentatious, unpretentious, withdrawn; SEE CONCEPTS *401,404*

humble [*adj2*] *poor, inferior*
base, beggarly, common, commonplace, contemptible, humdrum, ignoble, inglorious, insignificant, little, low, low-born, lowly, low-ranking, meager, mean, measly, menial, miserable, modest, obscure, ordinary, paltry, petty, pitiful, plebeian, proletarian, puny, rough, scrubby, seemly, servile, severe, shabby, simple, small, sordid, trivial, unassuming, uncouth, underprivileged, undistinguished, unfit, unimportant, unpretentious, unrefined, vulgar, wretched; SEE CONCEPTS *334,549,589*

humble [*v*] *shame, put down*
abase, abash, bemean, break, bring down*, cast down, chagrin, chasten, confound, confuse, crush*, cut to the quick*, debase, deflate, degrade, demean, demote, deny, discomfit, discredit, disgrace, embarrass, hide, humiliate, lower*, make eat dirt*, make one feel small*, mortify, overcome, pop one's balloon*, pull down*, put away*, put one away*, put to shame, reduce, silence, sink, snub, squash*, squelch, strike dumb, subdue, take down*, take down a peg*, upset; SEE CONCEPTS *14,16,44,52*

humbug [*n1*] *nonsense*
babble, balderdash*, baloney*, BS*, bull*, bunk*, drivel, empty talk, gibberish, hogwash*, hooey*, hot air*, poppycock*, pretense, rubbish, silliness, trash*; SEE CONCEPTS *230,388,633*

humbug [*n2*] *hoax*
con*, con game*, deceit, fast one*, flimflam*, fraud, gyp*, hustle, prank, put-on, scam, snow job*, spoof, sting, swindle; SEE CONCEPTS *59,63*

humdinger [*n*] *something extraordinary*
ace, beauty, champ, champion, crackerjack*, doozy, hit, hot stuff*, knockout, lulu, pip*, pistol*, smash hit, something, something else, whopper, winner; SEE CONCEPT *668*

humdrum [*adj*] *boring, uneventful*
arid, banausic, blah, bromidic, common, commonplace, dim, dime a dozen*, drab, dreary, dull, everyday, garden-variety*, insipid, lifeless, monotone, monotonous, mundane, ordinary, pedestrian, plodding, prosy, repetitious, routine, tedious, tiresome, toneless, treadmill, uninteresting, unvaried, vanilla*, wearisome, whitebread*; SEE CONCEPT *548*

humid [*adj*] *very damp, referring to weather*
boiling, clammy, close, dank, irriguous, moist, mucky, muggy, oppressive, sodden, soggy, steamy, sticky, stifling, stuffy, sultry, sweaty, sweltering, watery, wet; SEE CONCEPTS *525,603*

humidity [*n*] *very damp weather*
clamminess, dampness, dankness, dew, dewiness, evaporation, fogginess, heaviness, humectation, humidness, moistness, moisture, mugginess, oppressiveness, sogginess, steam, steaminess, stickiness, sultriness, sweatiness, swelter, thickness, vaporization, wet, wetness; SEE CONCEPTS *524,607*

humiliate [*v*] *embarrass, put down*
abase, abash, base, bemean, blister, break, bring down*, bring low*, cast down, chagrin, chasten, confound, confuse, conquer, crush*, cut down to size*, debase, degrade, demean, denigrate, deny, depress, discomfit, discountenance, disgrace, dishonor, downplay, humble, lower, make a fool of*, make ashamed, mortify, pan, play down, put out of countenance*, put to shame, rip*, run down*, shame, shoot down*, slam*, smear, snub, squash*, subdue, take down*, take down a peg*, tear down*, vanquish, wither; SEE CONCEPTS *14,44,52*

humiliation [*n*] *embarrassment*
abasement, affront, chagrin, comedown*, comeuppance, condescension, confusion, degradation, discomfiture, disgrace, dishonor, humbling, ignominy, indignity, loss of face*, mental pain, mortification, put-down, resignation, self-abasement, shame, submission, submissiveness, touché*; SEE CONCEPTS *388,410*

humility [*n*] *humbleness, modesty*
abasement, bashfulness, demureness, diffidence, docility, fawning, inferiority complex, lack of pride, lowliness, meekness, mortification, nonresistance, obedience, obsequiousness, passiveness, reserve, resignation, self-abasement, self-abnegation, servility, sheepishness, shyness, subjection, submissiveness, subservience, timidity, timorousness, unobtrusiveness, unpretentiousness; SEE CONCEPTS *633,657*

humor [*n1*] *comedy, funniness*
amusement, badinage, banter, buffoonery, clowning, comicality, comicalness, drollery, facetiousness, farce, flippancy, fun, gag, gaiety, happiness, high spirits, jest, jesting, jocoseness, jocularity, joke, joking, joyfulness, kidding, levity, lightness, playfulness, pleasantry, raillery, tomfoolery, whimsy, wisecrack, wit, witticism, wittiness; SEE CONCEPT *293*

humor [*n2*] *mood, temperament*
bee, bent, bias, caprice, character, complexion, conceit, disposition, fancy, frame of mind, individualism, individuality, makeup, mind, nature, notion, personality, propensity, quirk, spirits, strain, temper, tone, vagary, vein, whim; SEE CONCEPTS *9,410,411*

humorist [*n*] *comedian*
card*, clown, comedienne, comic, cutup, entertainer, jester, joker, jokesmith, jokester, satirist, stand-up comic, wisecracker, wit; SEE CONCEPTS *352,423*

humorous [*adj*] *funny, comical*
amusing, camp*, campy*, comic, droll, entertaining, facetious, farcical, hilarious, jocose, jocular, jokey, joshing, laughable, ludicrous, merry, playful, pleasant, priceless, ribald, screaming*, side-splitting*, too funny for words*, waggish, whimsical, witty; SEE CONCEPTS *267,529*

hump [*n*] *swelling, projection*
bulge, bump, convexedness, convexity, dune, elevation, eminence, excrescence, gibbosity, hill, hummock, hunch, knap, knob, knurl, kyphosis, mound, prominence, protrusion, protuberance, ridge, swell, tumescence; SEE CONCEPTS *471,513*

hunch [*n*] *feeling, idea*
anticipation, apprehension, auguration, augury, boding, clue, expectation, feeling in one's bones*, foreboding, forecast, foreknowledge, forewarning, forewisdom, funny feeling*, glim-

mer, hint, impression, inkling, instinct, intuition, misgiving, notion, omination, portent, preapprehension, precognition, preconceived notion, premonition, prenotation, prenotice, presage, presagement, prescience, presentiment, qualm, suspicion, thought; SEE CONCEPT *689*

hunch [*v*] *cower, crouch*
arch, bend, bow, curve, draw in, draw together, huddle, hump, lean, scrooch down, squat, stoop, tense; SEE CONCEPT *154*

hunger [*n*] *appetite for food, other desire*
ache, appetence, appetency, appetition, a stomach for*, big eyes*, bottomless pit*, craving, desire, emptiness, esurience, eyes for*, famine, famishment, gluttony, greed, greediness, hungriness, longing, lust, mania, munchies*, ravenousness, starvation, sweet tooth*, vacancy, void, voracity, want, yearning, yen; SEE CONCEPTS *20,709*

hungry [*adj*] *starving; desirous*
athirst, avid, carnivorous, could eat a horse*, covetous, craving, eager, edacious, empty, esurient, famished, famishing, flying light*, got the munchies*, greedy, hankering, hoggish, hollow, hungered, insatiate, keen, omnivorous, on empty stomach*, piggish*, rapacious, ravenous, starved, unfilled, unsatisfied, voracious, yearning; SEE CONCEPTS *20,406*

hunk [*n*] *chunk of solid material*
a lot*, batch, bit, block, bulk, bunch, clod, glob, gob*, large piece, loads*, loaf, lump, mass, morsel, nugget, piece, pile, portion, quantity, slab, slice, wad, wedge; SEE CONCEPTS *470,471*

hunt [*n*] *search, chase*
coursing, exploration, field sport, following, frisking, game, hounding, hunting, inquest, inquiry, inquisition, interrogation, investigation, look-see*, meddling, probe, prosecution, prying, pursuance, pursuing, pursuit, quest, race, raid, reconnaissance, research, rummage, scrutiny, seeking, sifting, snooping, sporting, steeplechase, study, tracing, trailing; SEE CONCEPTS *207,216*

hunt [*v1*] *chase for killing*
beat the bushes*, bird-dog*, capture, course, dog, drag, drive, fish, follow, give chase, grouse, gun*, gun for*, hawk, heel, hound, kill, look for, poach, press, pursue, ride, run, scent, scratch, scratch around, seek, shadow, shoot, snare, stalk, start, track, trail; SEE CONCEPTS *207,216,252,363*

hunt [*v2*] *look, search for*
be on the lookout*, cast about, delve, drag, examine, ferret out, fish for, forage, go after, grope, inquire, interrogate, investigate, look all over hell*, look high and low*, nose around*, probe, prowl, quest, question, ransack, rummage, run down, scour, scratch around*, search high heaven*, seek, sift, trace, trail, try to find, winnow; SEE CONCEPT *216*

hurdle [*n*] *barrier, obstacle*
bar, barricade, blockade, complication, difficulty, fence, hamper, handicap, hedge, hindrance, impediment, interference, mountain, obstruction, rub, snag, stumbling block, traverse, wall; SEE CONCEPTS *470,674*

hurdle [*v*] *jump over an obstacle*
bounce, bound, clear, conquer, down, hop, jump across, leap over, lick, lop, master, negotiate, over, overcome, saltate, scale, spring, surmount, vault; SEE CONCEPT *194*

hurl [*v*] *throw forcefully*
bung, cast, chuck, chunk, fire, fling, gun, heave, launch, let fly, lob, peg, pitch, project, propel, send, sling, toss; SEE CONCEPT *222*

hurricane [*n*] *violent windstorm*
blow, cyclone, gale, line storm, monsoon, storm, tempest, tornado, tropical cyclone, tropical storm, twister, typhoon, whirlwind; SEE CONCEPTS *524,526*

hurried [*adj*] *quick, rushed*
abrupt, breakneck, brief, cursory, fast, hasty, headlong, hectic, impetuous, perfunctory, precipitant, precipitate, precipitous, rushing, short, slapdash, speedy, subitaneous, sudden, superficial, swift; SEE CONCEPTS *548,588,799*

hurry [*n*] *speed in action, motion*
bustle, celerity, commotion, dash, dispatch, drive, expedition, expeditiousness, flurry, haste, precipitance, precipitateness, precipitation, promptitude, push, quickness, rush, rustle, scurry, speediness, swiftness, urgency; SEE CONCEPTS *657,748,755*

hurry [*v*] *act, move speedily*
accelerate, barrel, beeline*, be quick, bestir, breeze, bullet, burst, bustle, dash, dig in, drive, expedite, fleet, flit, fly, get a move on*, goad, go like lightning*, haste, hasten, hurry up, hustle, jog, lose no time, make haste, make short work of*, make time*, make tracks*, nip, push, quicken, race, rip, rocket, roll, run, rush, sally, scoot, scurry, shake a leg*, smoke, speed, speed up, spur, step on gas*, step on it*, turn on steam*, urge, whirl, whish, whisk, whiz, zip; SEE CONCEPTS *150,234*

hurt [*adj*] *physically or mentally injured*
aching, aggrieved, agonized, all torn up*, battered, bleeding, bruised, buffeted, burned, busted up*, contused, crushed, cut, damaged, disfigured, distressed, disturbed, grazed, harmed, hit, impaired, indignant, in pain, lacerated, marred, mauled, miffed, mutilated, nicked, offended, pained, piqued, put away, resentful, rueful, sad, scarred, scraped, scratched, shook, shot, sore, stricken, struck, suffering, tender, tortured, umbrageous, unhappy, warped, wounded; SEE CONCEPTS *314,403*

hurt [*n*] *injury; damage*
ache, black and blue*, blow, boo-boo*, bruise, chop, detriment, disadvantage, disaster, discomfort, disservice, distress, down, gash, harm, ill, ill-treatment, loss, mark, mischief, misfortune, nick, ouch, outrage, pain, pang, persecution, prejudice, ruin, scratch, sore, soreness, suffering, wound, wrong; SEE CONCEPTS *316,728*

hurt [*v1*] *cause physical pain; experience pain*
abuse, ache, afflict, ail, belt, be sore, be tender, bite, blemish, bruise, burn, cramp, cut, cut up, damage, disable, do violence, flail, flog, harm, impair, injure, kick, lacerate, lash, maltreat, mar, maul, mess up, nip, pierce, pinch, pommel, prick, pummel, punch, puncture, punish, rough up, shake up, slap, slug, smart, spank, spoil, squeeze, stab, sting, tear, throb, torment, torture, total, trouble, wax, whack, whip, wing, wound, wrack up, wring; SEE CONCEPTS *246,313*

hurt [*v2*] *cause mental pain*
abuse, afflict, aggrieve, annoy, burn, chafe, constrain, cut to the quick*, discomfit, discommode, displease, distress, excruciate, faze, give no quarter*, go for jugular*, grieve, hit where one

lives*, injure, lambaste, lay a bad trip on*, lean on*, martyr, martyrize, prejudice, punish, put down, put out, sadden, sting*, thumb nose at*, torment, torture, try, upset, vex, vitiate, work over*, wound, zing*; SEE CONCEPTS 7,14,19

hurtful [adj] *injurious, cruel*
aching, afflictive, bad, cutting, damaging, dangerous, deadly, deleterious, destructive, detrimental, disadvantageous, distressing, evil, harmful, hurting, malicious, mean, mischievous, nasty, nocuous, noxious, ominous, pernicious, poisonous, prejudicial, spiteful, unkind, upsetting, wounding; SEE CONCEPTS 537,542

hurtle [v] *plunge, charge*
bump, collide, fly, lunge, push, race, rush, rush headlong, scoot, scramble, shoot, speed, spurt, tear; SEE CONCEPT 150

husband [n] *married man*
bridegroom, companion, consort, groom, helpmate, hubby, mate, monogamist, monogynist, other half, partner, spouse; SEE CONCEPTS 414,419

hush [n] *quiet*
calm, lull, peace, peacefulness, quietude, silence, still, stillness, tranquility; SEE CONCEPT 65

hush [v] *attempt to make quiet*
burke, choke, gag, muffle, mute, muzzle, quiet, quieten, shush*, shut up, silence, stifle, still, stop, suppress; SEE CONCEPTS 65,87

hush-hush [adj] *secret*
clandestine, classified, closet, confidential, covert, dark, private, restricted, sub-rosa*, surreptitious, undercover, under-the-table*; SEE CONCEPT 576

hush up [v] *keep secret*
burke, conceal, cover, cover up, keep dark, sit on, smother, squash, stifle, suppress; SEE CONCEPT 266

husk [n] *covering, case*
aril, bark, case, chaff, glume, hull, outside, pod, rind, shell, shuck, skin; SEE CONCEPTS 428,484

husky [adj1] *deep, scratchy in sound*
croaking, croaky, growling, gruff, guttural, harsh, hoarse, loud, rasping, raucous, rough, throaty; SEE CONCEPT 594

husky [adj2] *big, burly*
brawny, gigantic, hefty, Herculean*, mighty, muscular, powerful, rugged, sinewy, stalwart, stocky, stout, strapping, strong, sturdy, thickset, well-built; SEE CONCEPT 773

hussy [n] *loose woman*
broad, floozy, jade, Jezebel, minx, slut, strumpet, tart*, tramp, trollop, vamp, wench, whore; SEE CONCEPTS 348,412,415,419

hustle [v] *hurry; work hurriedly*
apply oneself, be conscientious, bulldoze*, bustle, elbow, fly, force, haste, hasten, hotfoot*, impel, jog, press, push, race, rush, shove, speed, thrust, use elbow grease*; SEE CONCEPTS 91,150

hustler [n] *con artist; prostitute*
call girl, cheater, fast talker, floozy, grifter, hooker, rip-off artist*, scam artist, streetwalker, swindler, whore; SEE CONCEPTS 348,412,415,419

hut [n] *tiny, often roughly built, house*
box*, bungalow, cabana, cabin, camp, chalet, cot, cottage, crib*, den, dugout, dump*, hovel*, hutch, lean-to, lodge, log house, pigeonhole*, rathole*, refuge, shack, shanty, shed, shelter, summer house, tepee, wigwam; SEE CONCEPT 516

hybrid [n] *composite, mixture*
amalgam, bastard, combination, compound, cross, crossbreed, half-blood, half-breed, half-caste, incross, miscegenation, mongrel, mule, outcross; SEE CONCEPTS 260,394,414,429

hygiene [n] *cleanliness*
healthful living, hygienics, preventive medicine, public health, regimen, salutariness, sanitation, wholesomeness; SEE CONCEPTS 316,405

hygienic [adj] *clean*
aseptic, disinfected, germ-free, good, healthful, healthy, pure, salubrious, salutary, salutiferous, sanitary, sterile, uncontaminated, uninfected, wholesome; SEE CONCEPT 621

hymn [n] *religious song*
aria, canticle, carol, chant, choral, chorale, descant, ditty, evensong, hosanna, laud, lay, lied, littany, ode, oratorio, paean, psalm, shout, song of praise, worship song; SEE CONCEPTS 262,595

hype [n] *extensive publicity*
advertising, buildup*, plugging*, promotion; SEE CONCEPTS 292,324

hyperactive [adj] *excessively active*
excitable, high-strung, hyper*, overactive, overzealous, uncontrollable, wild; SEE CONCEPTS 401,404

hyperbole [n] *exaggeration*
amplification, big talk*, coloring*, distortion, embellishment, embroidering, enlargement, hype*, laying it on thick*, magnification, metaphor, mountain out of molehill*, overstatement, PR*, tall talk*; SEE CONCEPT 268

hypercritical [adj] *captious*
carping, caviling, censorious, critical, demanding, faultfinding, finicky, fussy, hair-splitting, hard to please, niggling, nit-picking, overcritical, persnickety; SEE CONCEPTS 267,404

hyperinflation [n] *extremely high, rising economic inflation*
devaluation, overextension, run-away inflation, wheelbarrow economics; SEE CONCEPT 335

hypermedia [n] *system giving access to multimedia information on a single subject*
data base, information bank, information retrieval; SEE CONCEPT 274

hypnotic [adj] *spellbinding, sleep-inducing*
anesthetic, anodyne, calmative, lenitive, mesmeric, mesmerizing, narcotic, opiate, sleepy, somniferous, somnolent, soothing, soporific, soporose, trance-inducing; SEE CONCEPTS 529,537

hypnotize [v] *put in trance; spellbind*
anesthetize, bring under control, captivate, charm, drug, dull the will, entrance, fascinate, hold under a spell, induce, lull to sleep, magnetize, make drowsy, make sleepy, mesmerize, narcotize, put to sleep, soothe, stupefy, subject to suggestion; SEE CONCEPT 250

hypocrisy [n] *deceitfulness, pretense*
affectation, bad faith*, bigotry, cant, casuistry, deceit, deception, dishonesty, display, dissembling, dissimulation, double-dealing, duplicity, false profession, falsity, fraud, glibness, imposture, insincerity, irreverence, lie, lip service*, mockery, pharisaicalness, pharisaism, phoniness, pietism, quackery, sanctimoniousness, sanctimony, speciousness, unctuousness; SEE CONCEPTS 63,633,657

hypocrite [n] *person who pretends, is deceitful*
actor, attitudinizer, backslider*, bigot, bluffer, casuist, charlatan, cheat, con artist, crook,

hu
hy

deceiver, decoy, dissembler, dissimulator, fake, faker, four-flusher*, fraud, hook*, humbug, impostor, informer, lip server*, malingerer, masquerader, mountebank, Pharisee, phony, playactor*, poser, pretender, quack*, smoothie*, sophist, swindler, trickster, two-face*, twotimer*, wolf in sheep's clothing*; SEE CONCEPT *412*

hypocritical [*adj*] *deceitful, pretending*
affected, artificial, assuming, bland, canting, captious, caviling, deceptive, deluding, dissembling, double, double-dealing, duplicitous, faithless, false, feigning, fishy*, fraudulent, glib, hollow, insincere, jivey, left-handed, lying, moralistic, oily, pharisaical, phony, pietistic, pious, sanctimonious, self-righteous, smooth, smooth-spoken, smooth-tongued*, snide, specious, spurious, two-faced*, unctuous, unnatural, unreliable; SEE CONCEPTS *267,401,542*

hypothesis [*n*] *theory*
antecedent, apriority, assignment, assumption, attribution, axiom, basis, belief, conclusion, condition, conjecture, data, deduction, demonstration, derivation, explanation, foundation, ground, guess, inference, interpretation, layout, lemma, philosophy, plan, position, postulate, premise, presupposition, principle, proposal, proposition, rationale, reason, scheme, shot in the dark*, speculation, starting point, suggestion, supposition, surmise, system, tentative law, term, theorem, thesis; SEE CONCEPTS *661,689*

hypothetical [*adj*] *guessed, assumed*
academic, assumptive, casual, concocted, conditional, conjecturable, conjectural, contestable, contingent, debatable, disputable, doubtful, equivocal, imaginary, imagined, indefinite, indeterminate, postulated, presumptive, presupposed, pretending, problematic, provisory, putative, questionable, refutable, speculative, stochastic, supposed, suppositional, suppositious, suspect, theoretic, theoretical, uncertain, unconfirmed, vague; SEE CONCEPTS *529,552,582*

hysteria [*n*] *state of extreme upset*
agitation, delirium, excitement, feverishness, frenzy, hysterics, madness, mirth, nervousness, panic, unreason; SEE CONCEPT *410*

hysterical [*adj*] *very upset, excited*
agitated, berserk, beside oneself, blazing, carried away*, convulsive, crazed, crazy, delirious, distracted, distraught, emotional, fiery, frantic, frenzied, fuming, furious, impassioned, impetuous, in a fit, incensed, irrepressible, mad, maddened, nervous, neurotic, overwrought, panic-stricken, passionate, possessed, rabid, raging, rampant, raving, seething, spasmodic, tempestuous, turbulent, uncontrollable, uncontrolled, unnerved, unrestrained, uproarious, vehement, violent, wild, worked up*; SEE CONCEPTS *403,542*

I

ice [*n*] *frozen water*
chunk, crystal, cube ice, diamonds*, dry ice, floe, glacier, glaze, hail, hailstone, iceberg, ice cube, icicle, permafrost, sleet; SEE CONCEPTS *470,514*

icky [*adj*] *not pleasant*
disgusting, horrible, loathsome, nasty, noisome, offensive, repellent, revolting, sickening, vile; SEE CONCEPT *570*

icon [*n*] *image*
figure, graphical user interface, graphic image, idol, ikon, likeness, painted image, picture, portrait, portrayal, representation, symbol; SEE CONCEPTS *259,667,716*

iconoclast [*n*] *detractor*
critic, cynic, denouncer, dissenter, dissident, heretic, image-breaker, nonbeliever, non-conformist, questioner, radical, rebel, revolutionist, ruiner, sceptic, unbeliever; SEE CONCEPTS *359,423*

icy [*adj1*] *frozen; slippery when frozen*
antarctic, arctic, biting, bitter, chill, chilled to the bone*, chilling, chilly, cold, freezing, frigid, frost-bound, frosty, frozen over, gelid, glacial, glaring, iced, polar, raw, refrigerated, rimy, shivering, shivery, sleeted, smooth as glass*; SEE CONCEPTS *605,606*

icy [*adj2*] *aloof*
chill, cold, distant, emotionless, forbidding, frigid, frosty, glacial, hostile, indifferent, steely, stony, unemotional, unfriendly, unwelcoming; SEE CONCEPTS *401,404*

idea [*n*] *something understood, planned, or believed*
abstraction, aim, approximation, belief, brainstorm*, clue, concept, conception, conclusion, conviction, design, doctrine, end, essence, estimate, fancy, feeling, flash*, form, guess, hint, hypothesis, import, impression, inkling, intention, interpretation, intimation, judgment, meaning, notion, object, objective, opinion, pattern, perception, plan, purpose, reason, scheme, sense, significance, solution, suggestion, suspicion, teaching, theory, thought, understanding, view, viewpoint; SEE CONCEPTS *529,660,661,689*

ideal [*adj1*] *model, perfect*
absolute, archetypal, classic, classical, complete, consummate, excellent, exemplary, fitting, flawless, have-it-all*, indefectible, optimal, paradigmatic, pie-in-the-sky*, prototypical, quintessential, representative, Shangri-la*, supreme; SEE CONCEPTS *533,574*

ideal [*adj2*] *conceptual; impractical*
abstract, chimerical, dreamlike, extravagant, fanciful, fictitious, high-flown, hypothetical, imaginary, intellectual, in the clouds*, ivory-tower*, mental, mercurial, notional, out-of-reach*, quixotic, theoretical, transcendent, transcendental, unattainable, unearthly, unreal, Utopian*, visionary; SEE CONCEPTS *529,552*

ideal [*n*] *model*
archetype, criterion, epitome, example, exemplar, goal, idol, jewel, last word*, mirror, nonesuch, nonpareil, paradigm, paragon, pattern, perfection, prototype, standard; SEE CONCEPTS *671,686*

idealist [*n*] *person who holds fancies in mind, who believes in perfection*
dreamer, enthusiast, escapist, optimist, Platonist, radical, romancer, romantic, romanticist, seer, stargazer, theorizer, transcendentalist, utopian, visionary; SEE CONCEPTS *359,416,423*

idealistic [*adj*] *visionary*
abstracted, chimerical, dreaming, idealized, impractical, optimistic, quixotic, radical, romantic,

starry-eyed, unrealistic, utopian; SEE CONCEPTS *529,560,582*

ideals [*n*] *moral beliefs*
ethics, goals, principles, standards, values; SEE CONCEPTS *645,689*

identical [*adj*] *alike, equal*
carbon copy*, corresponding, dead ringer*, ditto*, double, duplicate, equivalent, exact, identic, indistinguishable, interchangeable, like, like two peas in a pod*, look-alike, matching, same, same difference*, selfsame, spitting image*, tantamount, twin, very, very same, Xerox*; SEE CONCEPTS *487,566,573*

identification [*n*] *labeling; means of labeling*
apperception, assimilation, badge, bracelet, cataloging, classifying, credentials, description, dog tag, establishment, ID*, identity bracelet, letter of introduction, letter of recommendation, naming, papers, passport, recognition, tag, testimony; SEE CONCEPTS *268,271*

identify [*v*] *recognize; label*
analyze, button down*, card, catalog, classify, describe, determinate, determine, diagnose, diagnosticate, distinguish, establish, find, make out, name, peg*, pick out, pinpoint, place, put one's finger on*, select, separate, single out*, spot, tab*, tag*; SEE CONCEPTS *38,62*

identify with [*v*] *put oneself in the place of another*
ally, associate, empathize, feel for*, put in same category*, put oneself in another's shoes*, relate to, respond to, see through someone's eyes*, sympathize, think of in connection*, understand; SEE CONCEPTS *15,39*

identity [*n1*] *person's individuality*
character, circumstances, coherence, distinctiveness, existence, identification, integrity, ipseity, name, oneness, particularity, personality, self, selfdom, selfhood, selfness, singleness, singularity, status, uniqueness; SEE CONCEPT *411*

identity [*n2*] *similarity, correspondence*
accord, agreement, congruence, congruity, empathy, equality, equivalence, identicalness, likeness, oneness, rapport, resemblance, sameness, selfsameness, semblance, similitude, unanimity, uniformity, unity; SEE CONCEPTS *664,670*

ideology [*n*] *beliefs*
articles of faith*, credo, creed, culture, dogma, ideas, outlook, philosophy, principles, system, tenets, theory, view, Weltanschauung*; SEE CONCEPTS *688,689*

idiocy [*n*] *utter stupidity*
asininity, cretinism, derangement, fatuity, fatuousness, foolishness, imbecility, inanity, insanity, insipidity, lunacy, madness, senselessness, tomfoolery; SEE CONCEPTS *409,410*

idiom [*n*] *manner of speaking, turn of phrase*
argot, colloquialism, dialect, expression, idiosyncrasy, jargon, language, lingo*, localism, locution, parlance, patois, phrase, provincialism, set phrase, street talk*, style, talk, tongue, usage, vernacular, vernacularism, word; SEE CONCEPT *275*

idiosyncrasy [*n*] *oddity, quirk*
affectation, bit, characteristic, distinction, eccentricity, feature, habit, mannerism, peculiarity, singularity, trait, trick; SEE CONCEPTS *411,644*

idiot [*n*] *very stupid person*
blockhead, bonehead*, cretin, dimwit, dork, dumbbell, dunce, fool, ignoramus, imbecile, jerk, kook*, moron, nincompoop, ninny*, nitwit, out to lunch*, pinhead*, simpleton, stupid, tomfool, twit*; SEE CONCEPT *412*

idiotic [*adj*] *very stupid*
asinine, batty*, birdbrained*, crazy, daffy*, daft, dull, dumb, fatuous, foolhardy, foolish, harebrained*, imbecile, imbecilic, inane, insane, lunatic, moronic, senseless, silly, squirrelly*, thick-witted*, unintelligent; SEE CONCEPT *402*

idle [*adj1*] *not used; out of action*
abandoned, asleep, barren, closed down, dead, deserted, down, dusty, empty, gathering dust*, inactive, inert, jobless, laid-off, leisured, mothballed, motionless, on the bench*, on the shelf*, out of operation, out of work*, passive, quiet, redundant, resting, rusty, sleepy, stationary, still, uncultivated, unemployed, unoccupied, untouched, unused, vacant, void, waste, workless; SEE CONCEPTS *542,560*

idle [*adj2*] *lazy*
at rest, indolent, lackadaisical, resting, shiftless, slothful, sluggish, taking it easy*; SEE CONCEPTS *401,538*

idle [*adj3*] *worthless, ineffective*
abortive, bootless, empty, frivolous, fruitless, futile, groundless, hollow, insignificant, irrelevant, not serious, nugatory, of no avail*, otiose, pointless, rambling, superficial, trivial, unavailing, unhelpful, unnecessary, unproductive, unsuccessful, useless, vain; SEE CONCEPTS *267,560*

idleness [*n*] *laziness, inaction*
dawdling, dilly-dallying*, dormancy, droning, goof-off time*, hibernation, inactivity, indolence, inertia, joblessness, laze, lazing, leisure, lethargy, loafing, loitering, otiosity, own sweet time*, pottering, shiftlessness, sloth, slothfulness, slouch, slowness, sluggishness, stupor, time on one's hands*, time to burn*, time to kill*, time-wasting, torpidity, torpor, trifling, truancy, unemployment, vegetating; SEE CONCEPTS *657,677,681*

idol [*n*] *person greatly admired*
beloved, darling, dear, deity, desire, eidolon, false god, favorite, fetish, god, goddess, golden calf*, graven image, hero, icon, image, inamorata, pagan symbol, simulacrum, superstar; SEE CONCEPTS *352,423*

idolize [*v*] *think of very highly; worship*
admire, adore, apotheosize, bow down, canonize, deify, dote on, exalt, glorify, look up to*, love, put on a pedestal*, revere, reverence, venerate; SEE CONCEPTS *10,32*

idyllic [*adj*] *perfect; extremely pleasant*
arcadian, bucolic, charming, comfortable, halcyon, heavenly, ideal, idealized, out-of-this-world*, pastoral, peaceful, picturesque, pleasing, rustic, unspoiled; SEE CONCEPTS *529,572*

iffy [*adj*] *uncertain*
capricious, chancy, conditional, dicey, doubtful, erratic, fluctuant, incalculable, in lap of gods*, problematic, undecided, unpredictable, unsettled, up in the air*, whimsical; SEE CONCEPT *552*

ignite [*v*] *set on fire*
burn, burst into flames, catch fire, enkindle, fire, flare up, inflame, kindle, light, put match to*, set alight, set fire to, start up, take fire, touch off; SEE CONCEPT *249*

ignoble [*adj*] *lowly, unworthy*
abject, base, baseborn, coarse, common, con-

hy
ig

temptible, corrupt, craven, dastardly, degenerate, degraded, despicable, disgraceful, dishonorable, heinous, humble, infamous, inferior, lewd, low, mean, menial, modest, ordinary, peasant, petty, plain, plebeian, poor, rotten, scurvy, servile, shabby, shameful, simple, sordid, unwashed, vile, vulgar, wicked, wretched, wrong; SEE CONCEPTS *542,545,549*

ignorance [*n*] *unintelligence, inexperience*
benightedness, bewilderment, blindness, callowness, crudeness, darkness, denseness, disregard, dumbness, empty-headedness*, fog*, half-knowledge, illiteracy, incapacity, incomprehension, innocence, inscience, insensitivity, lack of education, mental incapacity, naiveté, nescience, oblivion, obtuseness, philistinism, rawness, sciolism, shallowness, simplicity, unawareness, unconsciousness, uncouthness, unenlightenment, unfamiliarity, unscholarliness, vagueness; SEE CONCEPTS *409,678*

ignorant [*adj*] *unaware, unknowing*
apprenticed, benighted, birdbrained*, blind to*, cretinous, dense, green*, illiterate, imbecilic, inexperienced, innocent, insensible, in the dark*, mindless, misinformed, moronic, naive, nescient, oblivious, obtuse, shallow, thick, unconscious, unconversant, uncultivated, uncultured, uneducated, unenlightened, uninformed, uninitiated, unintellectual, unknowledgeable, unlearned, unlettered, unmindful, unschooled, unsuspecting, untaught, untrained, unwitting, witless; SEE CONCEPTS *402,542*

ignore [*v*] *disregard on purpose*
avoid, be oblivious to, blink, brush off*, bury one's head in sand*, cold-shoulder*, discount, disdain, evade, fail, forget, let it go*, neglect, omit, overlook, overpass, pass over, pay no attention to, pay no mind*, pooh-pooh*, reject, scorn, shut eyes to*, slight, take no notice, tune out*, turn back on*, turn blind eye*, turn deaf ear; SEE CONCEPT *30*

ilk [*n*] *kind, type*
brand, class, classification, denomination, gender, kin, lot, order, persuasion, race, set, sort, species, variety; SEE CONCEPTS *378,411,673*

ill [*adj1*] *sick*
afflicted, ailing, a wreck*, below par*, bummed*, diseased, down, down with, feeling awful, feeling rotten, feeling terrible, got the bug*, indisposed, infirm, laid low*, off one's feet*, on sick list*, out of sorts*, peaked, poorly, queasy, rotten, run-down, running temperature, sick as a dog*, under the weather*, unhealthy, unwell, woozy*; SEE CONCEPT *314*

ill [*adj2*] *bad, evil*
acrimonious, adverse, antagonistic, cantankerous, cross, damaging, deleterious, detrimental, disrespectful, disturbing, foreboding, foul, harmful, harsh, hateful, hostile, hurtful, ill-mannered, impertinent, inauspicious, inimical, iniquitous, injurious, malevolent, malicious, nocent, nocuous, noxious, ominous, ruinous, sinister, sullen, surly, threatening, unfavorable, unfortunate, unfriendly, ungracious, unhealthy, unkind, unlucky, unpromising, unpropitious, unwholesome, vile, wicked, wrong; SEE CONCEPTS *537,545,570*

ill [*n*] *misfortune*
abuse, affection, affliction, ailment, badness, complaint, condition, cruelty, damage, depravity, destruction, disease, disorder, evil, harm, hurt, illness, indisposition, infirmity, injury, insult, malady, malaise, malice, mischief, misery, pain, sickness, suffering, syndrome, trial, tribulation, trouble, unpleasantness, wickedness, woe, wrong; SEE CONCEPTS *316,674,675*

ill-advised [*adj*] *unwise, not thought out*
brash, confused, foolhardy, foolish, half-baked*, hotheaded*, ill-considered, ill-judged, impolitic, imprudent, inappropriate, incautious, inconsiderate, indiscreet, inexpedient, injudicious, madcap*, misguided, off the top of one's head*, overhasty, rash, reckless, short-sighted*, thoughtless, unseemly, wrong; SEE CONCEPTS *544,548*

ill at ease [*adj*] *uncomfortable, nervous*
anxious, awkward, discomfited, disquieted, disturbed, doubtful, edgy, faltering, fidgety, hesitant, insecure, on edge*, on pins and needles*, on tenterhooks*, out of place*, restless, self-conscious, shy, suspicious, tense, uneasy, unrelaxed, unsettled, unsure; SEE CONCEPTS *401,403*

illegal [*adj*] *against the law*
actionable, banned, black-market*, bootleg*, contraband, criminal, crooked, extralegal, felonious, forbidden, heavy*, hot*, illegitimate, illicit, interdicted, irregular, lawless, not approved, not legal, outlawed, outside the law, prohibited, proscribed, prosecutable, racket, shady, smuggled, sub rosa, taboo, unauthorized, unconstitutional, under the table*, unlawful, unlicensed, unofficial, unwarrantable, unwarranted, verboten, violating, wildcat*, wrongful; SEE CONCEPTS *319,545*

illegible [*adj*] *unreadable*
cacographic, crabbed, cramped, difficult to read, faint, hard to make out*, hieroglyphic, indecipherable, indistinct, obscure, scrawled, unclear, undecipherable, unintelligible; SEE CONCEPTS *535,576*

illegitimate [*adj*] *not legal*
contraband, illegal, illicit, improper, invalid, misbegotten, spurious, supposititious, unauthorized, unconstitutional, unlawful, unsanctioned, wicked, wrong; SEE CONCEPTS *319,549*

ill-fated/ill-starred [*adj*] *doomed*
blighted, catastrophic, destroyed, disastrous, hapless, ill-omened, inauspicious, luckless, misfortunate, ruined, star-crossed*, unfortunate, unhappy, unlucky, untoward; SEE CONCEPTS *537,548*

illicit [*adj*] *not legal; forbidden*
adulterous, black-market*, bootleg*, clandestine, contraband, contrary to law, criminal, crooked, dirty*, felonious, furtive, guilty, heavy*, illegal, illegitimate, immoral, improper, in violation of law, lawless, out of line*, prohibited, racket, unauthorized, unlawful, unlicensed, wrong, wrongful; SEE CONCEPTS *319,545*

illiterate [*adj*] *unable to read well; lacking education*
benighted, catachrestic, ignorant, inerudite, solecistic, uneducated, unenlightened, ungrammatical, uninstructed, unlearned, unlettered, unread, unschooled, untaught, untutored; SEE CONCEPT *402*

ill-mannered [*adj*] *badly behaved*
bad-mannered, boorish, cheap, churlish, coarse, discourteous, disrespectful, ill-behaved, ill-bred, impertinent, impolite, insolent, loud, loudmouthed, loutish, raunchy*, raw, rough, rough-

neck*, rude, tacky*, uncivil, uncouth, ungracious, unmannerly, unrefined, vulgar; SEE CONCEPT *401*

ill-natured [*adj*] *bad-tempered*
catty, churlish, crabbed, crabby, cross, crotchety, cussed*, dirty*, disagreeable, disobliging, dyspeptic, hot-tempered, ill-humored, irritable, malevolent, malicious, mean, nasty, ornery*, perverse, petulant, spiteful, sulky, sullen, surly, temperamental, tempersome, touchy, unfriendly, unkind, unpleasant; SEE CONCEPTS *401,404*

illness [*n*] *disease; bad health*
affliction, ailing, ailment, attack, breakdown, bug*, collapse, complaint, confinement, convalescence, disability, diseasedness, disorder, disturbance, dose, failing health, fit, flu, ill health, indisposition, infirmity, malady, malaise, poor health, prostration, relapse, seizure, sickness, syndrome, unhealth, virus, what's going around*; SEE CONCEPT *306*

illogical [*adj*] *not making sense*
absurd, casuistic, cockeyed*, fallacious, false, fatuous, faulty, groundless, hollow, implausible, inconclusive, incongruous, inconsequent, inconsistent, incorrect, invalid, irrational, irrelevant, mad, meaningless, not following, nutty*, off the wall*, preposterous, screwy*, self-contradictory, senseless, sophistic, sophistical, specious, spurious, unconnected, unproved, unreasonable, unscientific, unsound, unsubstantial, untenable, wacky, without basis, without foundation; SEE CONCEPTS *267,529*

ill-suited [*adj*] *inappropriate*
bad form, ill-fitted, ill-matched, ill-timed, improper, inapt, incompatible, incorrect, irrelevant, malapropos, mismatched, out of character, out of its element, out of place, unbecoming, unfit, unfitting, unseemly, unsuitable, wrong; SEE CONCEPT *558*

ill-tempered [*adj*] *irritable*
annoyed, bad-tempered, bearish, cantankerous, choleric, crabby, cross, crotchety, grouchy, grumpy, irascible, moody, nasty, quick-tempered, sharp, snappy, sour, spiteful, surly, testy, touchy, vicious; SEE CONCEPTS *401,403*

ill-timed [*adj*] *not occurring at a suitable time*
awkward, badly timed, improper, inappropriate, inconvenient, inept, inopportune, malapropos, mistimed, unbecoming, unbefitting, unfavorable, unseasonable, unseemly, unsuitable, untimely, unwelcome; SEE CONCEPT *548*

illuminate [*v1*] *make light*
brighten, fire, flash, floodlight, highlight, hit with a light*, ignite, illume, illumine, irradiate, kindle, light, lighten, light up, limelight*, spot, spotlight; SEE CONCEPT *624*

illuminate [*v2*] *make clear; educate*
better, clarify, clear up, construe, define, dramatize, edify, elucidate, enlighten, explain, expound, express, finish, give insight, gloss, illustrate, improve, instruct, interpret, perfect, polish, shed light on*, uplight; SEE CONCEPTS *57,285*

illumination [*n1*] *light; making light*
beam, brightening, brightness, brilliance, flame, flash, gleam, lighting, lights, radiance, ray; SEE CONCEPTS *620,624*

illumination [*n2*] *clear understanding*
awareness, clarification, edification, education, enlightenment, information, insight, inspiration, instruction, perception, revelation, teaching; SEE CONCEPTS *274,409*

illusion [*n*] *false appearance; false belief*
apparition, bubble*, chimera, confusion, daydream, deception, déjà vu*, delusion, error, fallacy, false impression, fancy, fantasy, figment of imagination*, fool's paradise*, ghost, hallucination, head trip*, hocus-pocus*, idolism, ignus fatuus, image, invention, make-believe, mirage, misapprehension, misbelief, misconception, misimpression, mockery, myth, optical illusion, paramnesia, phantasm, pipe dream*, rainbow*, seeming, semblance, trip*, virtual reality; SEE CONCEPTS *689,716*

illusory/illusive [*adj*] *deceptive, false*
apparent, blue-sky*, chimerical, deceitful, delusive, delusory, fake, fallacious, fanciful, fantastic, fictional, fictitious, fictive, hallucinatory, ideal, imaginary, misleading, mistaken, ostensible, pseudo*, seeming, semblant, sham*, supposititious, unreal, untrue, visionary, whimsical; SEE CONCEPTS *529,552,582*

illustrate [*v1*] *demonstrate, exemplify*
allegorize, bring home**, clarify, clear, clear up, delineate, depict, disclose, draw a picture*, elucidate, emblematize, embody, emphasize, epitomize, evidence, evince, exhibit, explain, expose, expound, get across*, get over*, highlight, illuminate, imitate, instance, interpret, lay out*, limelight*, make clear, make plain, manifest, mark, mirror, ostend, personify, picture, point up*, portray, proclaim, represent, reveal, show, show and tell*, spotlight*, symbolize, typify, vivify; SEE CONCEPTS *57,97*

illustrate [*v2*] *explain by drawing, decorating*
adorn, delineate, depict, embellish, illuminate, limn, ornament, paint, picture, portray, represent, sketch; SEE CONCEPTS *57,174*

illustration [*n1*] *demonstration, exemplification*
analogy, case, case history, case in point, clarification, elucidation, example, explanation, for instance, instance, interpretation, model, representative, sample, sampling, specimen; SEE CONCEPTS *268,686*

illustration [*n2*] *drawing, artwork that assists explanation*
adornment, cartoon, decoration, depiction, design, engraving, etching, figure, frontispiece, halftone, image, line drawing, painting, photo, photograph, picture, plate, sketch, snapshot, tailpiece, vignette; SEE CONCEPT *259*

illustrative [*adj*] *explanatory*
allegorical, clarifying, comparative, corroborative, delineative, descriptive, diagrammatic, emblematic, exemplifying, explicatory, expository, figurative, graphic, iconographic, illuminative, illustrational, illustratory, imagistic, indicative, interpretive, metaphoric, pictorial, pictoric, representative, revealing, sample, specifying, symbolic, typical; SEE CONCEPT *267*

illustrious [*adj*] *famous, prominent*
big league*, brilliant, celeb*, celebrated, distinguished, eminent, esteemed, exalted, famed, glorious, great, heavy, lofty, monster*, name*, noble, notable, noted, outstanding, remarkable, renowned, resplendent, signal, splendid, star, sublime, superstar, well-known; SEE CONCEPT *568*

ill will [*n*] *hatred; hard feelings*
acrimony, animosity, animus, antagonism, an-

ig
il

tipathy, aversion, bad blood*, bad will, blame, despite, dislike, enmity, envy, feud, grudge, hate, hostility, malevolence, malice, maliciousness, no love lost*, objection, rancor, resentment, spite, spitefulness, spleen, unfriendliness, venom; SEE CONCEPT 29

image [n1] *representation; counterpart*
angel*, appearance, carbon*, carbon copy, carved figure, chip off old block*, copy, dead ringer*, double, drawing, effigy, equal, equivalent, facsimile, figure, form, icon, idol, illustration, likeness, match, model, photocopy, photograph, picture, portrait, reflection, replica, reproduction, similitude, simulacre, simulacrum, spitting image*, statue; SEE CONCEPTS *259,667,716*

image [n2] *concept*
apprehension, conceit, conception, construct, figure, idea, impression, intellection, mental picture, notion, perception, phantasm, thought, trope, vision; SEE CONCEPTS *529,689*

imaginable [adj] *believable, possible*
apprehensible, calculable, comprehensible, conceivable, conjectural, convincing, credible, likely, plausible, sensible, supposable, thinkable, under the sun*; SEE CONCEPTS *529,552*

imaginary [adj] *fictitious, invented*
abstract, apocryphal, apparitional, assumed, chimerical, deceptive, delusive, dreamed-up*, dreamlike, dreamy, fabulous, fancied, fanciful, fantastic, fictional, figmental, fool's paradise*, hallucinatory, hypothetical, ideal, illusive, illusory, imaginative, imagined, legendary, made-up, mythological, nonexistent, notional, phantasmal, phantasmic, quixotic, shadowy, spectral, supposed, suppositious, theoretical, trumped up*, unreal, unsubstantial, visionary, whimsical; SEE CONCEPTS *529,582*

imagination [n] *power to create in one's mind*
acuteness, artistry, awareness, chimera, cognition, conception, creation, creative thought, creativity, enterprise, fabrication, fancy, fantasy, flight of fancy*, idea, ideality, illusion, image, imagery, ingenuity, insight, inspiration, intelligence, invention, inventiveness, mental agility, notion, originality, perceptibility, realization, resourcefulness, sally, supposition, thought, thoughtfulness, unreality, verve, vision, visualization, wit, wittiness; SEE CONCEPTS *409,410*

imaginative [adj] *creative, inventive*
artistic, avant-garde, blue-sky*, brain wave, breaking ground, clever, dreamy, enterprising, extravagant, fanciful, fantastic, fertile, fictive, high-flown*, ingenious, inspired, offbeat, original, originative, pie-in-the-sky*, poetic, poetical, productive, quixotic, romantic, utopian, visionary, vivid, way out*, whimsical; SEE CONCEPTS *529,542*

imagine [v1] *dream up, conceive*
brainstorm, build castles in air*, conceptualize, conjure up, cook up*, create, depict, devise, envisage, envision, fabricate, fancy, fantasize, fantasy, feature, figure, form, frame, harbor, image, invent, make up, nurture, perceive, picture, plan, project, realize, scheme, see in one's mind*, spark, think of, think up, vision, visualize; SEE CONCEPT 43

imagine [v2] *assume, deduce*
apprehend, believe, conjecture, deem, expect, fancy, gather, guess, infer, presume, realize, reckon, suppose, surmise, suspect, take for granted, take it, think, understand; SEE CONCEPTS *12,26*

imbecile [adj] *stupid, foolish*
asinine, backward, deranged, dim-witted, dull, fatuous, feeble-minded, idiotic, imbecilic, inane, ludicrous, moronic, simple, simple-minded, slow, thick, witless; SEE CONCEPT 402

imbecile [n] *very stupid person*
birdbrain, dimwit, dolt, dummy, dunce, fool, idiot, jerk, lamebrain*, moron, pinhead*, simpleton; SEE CONCEPT 412

imbibe [v] *drink, often heavily*
absorb, assimilate, belt*, consume, down, gorge, guzzle*, ingest, ingurgitate, irrigate, partake, put away*, quaff, raise a few*, sip, swallow, swig*, swill*, toss*; SEE CONCEPT 169

imbroglio [n] *misunderstanding; fight*
altercation, argument, bickering, brawl, broil*, brouhaha*, complexity, complication, dispute, embarrassment, embroilment, entanglement, falling-out*, flack*, involvement, knock-down-drag-out*, miff*, quandary, quarrel, row, run-in*, soap opera*, spat, squabble; SEE CONCEPTS *46,106*

imbue [v] *infuse, saturate*
bathe, diffuse, impregnate, inculcate, infix, ingrain, inoculate, instill, invest, leaven, permeate, pervade, steep, suffuse; SEE CONCEPTS *209,236,245*

imitate [v] *pretend to be; do an impression of*
act like, affect, ape, assume, be like, borrow, burlesque, carbon*, caricature, clone, copy, counterfeit, ditto*, do like*, do likewise, duplicate, echo, emulate, falsify, feign, follow, follow in footsteps*, follow suit*, forge, impersonate, look like, match, mime, mimic, mirror, mock, model after, parallel, parody, pattern after, personate, play a part, pretend, put on*, reduplicate, reflect, repeat, replicate, reproduce, resemble, send up*, sham, simulate, spoof, take off*, travesty, Xerox*; SEE CONCEPTS *87,111,171*

imitation [n] *simulation, substitution*
apery, aping, carbon copy, clone, copy, counterfeit, counterfeiting, counterpart, ditto*, dupe*, duplicate, duplication, echoing, ersatz*, fake, forgery, image, impersonation, impression, likeness, match, matching, mime, mimicry, mirroring, mockery, parallel, paralleling, paraphrasing, parody, parroting, patterning, phony, picture, reflection, replica, representing, reproduction, resemblance, ringer, semblance, sham*, simulacrum, takeoff*, transcription, travesty, Xerox*; SEE CONCEPTS *171,260,716*

imitative [adj] *simulated, unoriginal*
artful, copied, copycat, copying, counterfeit, deceptive, derivative, echoic, emulative, emulous, following, forged, mimetic, mimic, mimicking, mock, onomatopoeic, parrot*, plagiarized, pseudo*, put-on*, reflecting, reflective, secondhand, sham*, simulant; SEE CONCEPT 582

immaculate [adj1] *very clean; unspoiled*
bright, clean, errorless, exquisite, faultless, flawless, impeccable, irreproachable, neat, pure, snowy*, spick-and-span*, spotless, spruce, stainless, taintless, trim, unexceptionable, unsoiled, unsullied; SEE CONCEPT 621

immaculate [adj2] *innocent, uncorrupted*
above reproach, chaste, clean, decent, faultless, flawless, guiltless, incorrupt, modest, perfect,

pure, sinless, spotless, stainless, unblemished, uncontaminated, undefiled, unpolluted, unsullied, untarnished, virtuous; SEE CONCEPTS *404,545*

immaterial [*adj1*] *irrelevant*
extraneous, foreign, impertinent, inapplicable, inapposite, inappropriate, inconsequential, inconsiderable, inconsiderate, inessential, insignificant, irrelative, matter of indifference, meaningless, no big deal*, no never mind*, of no account*, of no consequence*, of no importance*, trifling, trivial, unimportant, unnecessary; SEE CONCEPT *575*

immaterial [*adj2*] *not existing in physical form*
aerial, airy, apparitional, asomatous, bodiless, celestial, disbodied, discarnate, disembodied, dreamlike, dreamy, ethereal, ghostly, heavenly, impalpable, imponderable, incorporate, incorporeal, insensible, intangible, metaphysical, nonmaterial, nonphysical, psychic, shadowy, spectral, spiritlike, spiritual, subjective, supernatural, unearthly, unembodied, unfleshly, unsubstantial, unworldly, wraithlike; SEE CONCEPT *539*

immature [*adj*] *young, inexperienced*
adolescent, baby, babyish, callow, childish, crude, green*, half-grown, imperfect, infantile, infantine, jejune, juvenile, kid, kidstuff*, premature, puerile, raw, sophomoric, tender*, tenderfoot*, underdeveloped, undergrown, undeveloped, unfinished, unfledged, unformed, unripe, unseasonable, unseasoned, unsophisticated, untimely, wet behind ears*, youthful; SEE CONCEPTS *485,578,797*

immeasurable [*adj*] *infinite, incalculable*
alive with, bottomless, boundless, countless, crawling with, endless, extensive, illimitable, immense, indefinite, inestimable, inexhaustible, jillion*, large, limitless, measureless, no end of*, no end to*, umpteen*, unbounded, uncountable, unfathomable, unlimited, unmeasurable, unreckonable, vast, zillion*; SEE CONCEPTS *762,773,781*

immediate [*adj1*] *instantaneous; without delay*
actual, at once, at present time, at this moment, critical, current, existing, extant, first, hair-trigger*, instant, live, next, now, on hand*, paramount, present, pressing, prompt, up-to-date*, urgent; SEE CONCEPTS *567,585,812,820*

immediate [*adj2*] *near, next*
adjacent, close, contiguous, direct, firsthand, near-at-hand, nearby, nearest, nigh, primary, proximal, proximate, recent; SEE CONCEPTS *586,778*

immediately [*adv*] *at once, right away*
anon, at short notice, away, directly, double-time*, forthwith, hereupon, in a flash*, in a jiffy*, in a New York minute*, in nothing flat*, instantaneously, instanter, instantly, like now*, now, now or never*, on the dot*, on the double*, on the spot*, PDQ*, promptly, pronto*, rapidly, right now, shortly, soon, soon afterward, straight away*, straight off*, summarily, thereupon, this instant, this minute, tout de suite*, unhesitatingly, urgently, without delay, without hesitation; SEE CONCEPTS *544,820*

immemorial [*adj*] *ancient, old*
age-old, archaic, fixed, forever, long-standing, of yore, olden, prehistoric, primeval, rooted, time-honored, traditional; SEE CONCEPTS *578,797,799*

immense [*adj*] *extremely large*
barn door*, boundless, Brobdingnagian*, colossal, elephantine, endless, enormous, eternal, extensive, giant, gigantic, great, gross, huge, humongous, illimitable, immeasurable, infinite, interminable, jumbo*, limitless, mammoth, massive, measureless, mighty, monstrous, monumental, prodigious, stupendous, super, titanic*, tremendous, unbounded, vast; SEE CONCEPT *773*

immerse [*v1*] *submerge in liquid*
asperse, baptize, bathe, bury, christen, dip, douse, drench, drown, duck, dunk, merge, plunge, saturate, sink, slop, soak, souse, sprinkle, steep, submerse; SEE CONCEPT *256*

immerse [*v2*] *become deeply involved*
absorb, busy, engage, engross, interest, involve, occupy, soak, take up; SEE CONCEPTS *17,100*

immersed [*adj*] *deeply involved with*
absorbed, bound-up*, buried*, busy, consumed, deep, eat sleep and breathe*, engaged, engrossed, intent, into*, mesmerized, occupied, preoccupied, rapt, spellbound, taken up*, tied up*, turned on*, wrapped up*; SEE CONCEPT *542*

immigrant [*n*] *person from a foreign land*
adoptive citizen, alien, colonist, documented alien, foreigner, incomer, migrant, naturalized citizen, newcomer, outsider, pioneer, settler, undocumented alien; SEE CONCEPT *413*

immigrate [*v*] *enter a foreign area intending to live there*
arrive, colonize, come in, go in, migrate, settle; SEE CONCEPT *159*

imminent [*adj*] *at hand, on the way*
about to happen, approaching, brewing*, close, coming, expectant, fast-approaching, following, forthcoming, gathering, handwriting-on-the-wall*, immediate, impending, ineluctable, inescapable, inevasible, inevitable, in store*, in the air*, in the cards*, in the offing*, in the wind*, in view*, likely, looming, menacing, near, nearing, next, nigh, on its way, on the horizon, on the verge, overhanging, possible, probable, see it coming*, threatening, to come, unavoidable, unescapable; SEE CONCEPTS *548,820*

immobile [*adj*] *motionless, fixed*
anchored, at a standstill, at rest, frozen, immobilized, immotile, immovable, nailed, nailed down, pat, quiescent, rigid, riveted, rooted, stable, stagnant, static, stationary, steadfast, stiff, still, stock-still, stolid, unmovable, unmoving; SEE CONCEPTS *488,584*

immoderate [*adj*] *excessive, extreme*
dizzying, egregious, enormous, exaggerated, exorbitant, extravagant, inordinate, intemperate, overindulgent, profligate, steep, too much*, too-too*, towering, unbalanced, unbridled, uncalled-for*, unconscionable, uncontrolled, undue, unjustified, unmeasurable, unreasonable, unrestrained, unwarranted, wanton; SEE CONCEPTS *544,569*

immodest [*adj*] *shameless*
bawdy, bold, brazen, coarse, depraved, forward, indecent, lewd, obscene, revealing, risque, unashamed, unchaste, unseemly; SEE CONCEPTS *401,545*

immoral [*adj*] *evil, degenerate*
abandoned, bad, corrupt, debauched, depraved, dishonest, dissipated, dissolute, fast*, graceless, impure, indecent, iniquitous, lewd, licentious, loose*, nefarious, obscene, of easy virtue*, pornographic, profligate, rakish, reprobate, saturnalian, shameless, sinful, speedy, unchaste, un-

im
im

clean*, unethical, unprincipled, unscrupulous, vicious, vile, villainous, wicked, wrong, X-rated*; SEE CONCEPT *545*

immortal [*adj1*] *death-defying, imperishable*
abiding, amaranthine, ceaseless, constant, deathless, endless, enduring, eternal, evergreen, everlasting, incorruptible, indestructible, indissoluble, interminable, lasting, never-ceasing, never-ending, perdurable, perennial, permanent, perpetual, phoenixlike, sempiternal, timeless, undying, unfading; SEE CONCEPTS *539,798*

immortal [*adj2*] *famous*
celebrated, eminent, epic, genius, glorious, heroic, illustrious, laureate, paragon, storied; SEE CONCEPT *568*

immortality [*n1*] *endless life*
athanasia, deathlessness, endurance, eternal life, eternity, everlasting life, perpetuity, timelessness; SEE CONCEPTS *539,798*

immortality [*n2*] *enduring fame*
celebrity, fame, famousness, glorification, glory, greatness, lasting fame, renown; SEE CONCEPTS *388,668*

immovable [*adj*] *fixed, stubborn*
adamant, constant, dead set on*, dug in, fast, firm, hard-nosed, immobile, immotile, immutable, impassive, inflexible, intransigent, locked in*, motionless, obdurate, quiescent, resolute, rooted, secure, set, set in concrete*, set in stone*, solid, stable, stand pat*, stationary, steadfast, stick to guns*, stuck, tough nut*, unalterable, unchangeable, uncompromising, unmodifiable, unshakable, unwavering, unyielding; SEE CONCEPTS *404,488,534*

immune [*adj*] *invulnerable*
allowed, clear, exempt, favored, free, hardened to, insusceptible, irresponsible, licensed, not affected, not liable, not subject, privileged, protected, resistant, safe, unaffected, unanswerable, unliable, unsusceptible; SEE CONCEPTS *314,552*

immunity [*n*] *privilege, exemption*
amnesty, charter, exoneration, franchise, freedom, impunity, indemnity, invulnerability, liberty, license, prerogative, protection, release, resistance, right; SEE CONCEPTS *316,376,388*

immutable [*adj*] *unchangeable*
abiding, ageless, changeless, constant, enduring, fixed, immovable, inflexible, invariable, permanent, perpetual, sacrosanct, stable, steadfast, unalterable, unmodifiable; SEE CONCEPT *534*

imp [*n*] *mischievous child, small person*
brat, demon, devil, deviling, devilkin, elf, fiend, gamin, gnome, gremlin, hellion, minx, pixie, puck, rascal, rogue, scamp, sprite, troll, tyke, urchin, villain; SEE CONCEPT *412*

impact [*n1*] *collision, force*
appulse, bang, blow, bounce, brunt, buffet, bump, clash, concussion, contact, crash, crunch, crush, encounter, hit, impingement, jar, jolt, jounce, kick, knock, meeting, percussion, pound, punch, quake, quiver, ram, rap, rock, shake, shock, slap, smash, smashup, strike, stroke, thump, tremble, tremor, wallop; SEE CONCEPTS *189,641*

impact [*n2*] *effect*
brunt, burden, consequences, full force, impression, imprint, influence, mark, meaning, power, repercussion, significance, thrust, weight; SEE CONCEPT *230*

impact [*v*] *hit with force*
bang into, clash, collide, crack up, crash, crush, jolt, kick, register, smash, smash up, strike, wrack up*; SEE CONCEPT *189*

impair [*v*] *harm, hinder*
blemish, blunt, cheapen, damage, debase, debilitate, decrease, destroy, deteriorate, devaluate, devalue, diminish, ding*, disqualify, enervate, enfeeble, hurt, injure, invalidate, lessen, lose strength, make useless, mar, prejudice, queer, reduce, rough up*, spoil, tarnish, total, tweak, undermine, unfit, vitiate, weaken, worsen; SEE CONCEPTS *130,240,246*

impaired [*adj*] *injured, faulty*
broken, busted, damaged, debilitated, defective, down*, flawed, harmed, hurt, imperfect, kaput*, marred, on the blink*, on the fritz*, spoiled, unsound; SEE CONCEPTS *485,560*

impale [*v*] *stab*
lance, perforate, pierce, prick, punch, puncture, run through, skewer, skiver, spear, spike, stick, transfix; SEE CONCEPT *220*

impalpable [*adj*] *intangible, unsubstantial*
airy, delicate, disembodied, fine, imperceptible, imponderable, imprecise, inappreciable, incorporeal, indiscernible, indistinct, insensible, insubstantial, nebulous, shadowy, tenuous, thin, unapparent, unobservable, unperceivable, vague; SEE CONCEPTS *485,529,619*

impart [*v1*] *make known*
admit, announce, break, communicate, convey, disclose, discover, divulge, expose, inform, pass on, publish, relate, reveal, tell, transmit; SEE CONCEPT *60*

impart [*v2*] *give*
accord, afford, allow, bestow, cede, confer, contribute, grant, lead, offer, part with, present, relinquish, render, yield; SEE CONCEPT *108*

impartial [*adj*] *fair, unprejudiced*
candid, detached, disinterested, dispassionate, equal, equitable, evenhanded, fair-minded, impersonal, just, middle-of-the-road*, neutral, nondiscriminating, nondiscriminatory, nonpartisan, objective, on-the-fence, open-minded, unbiased, unbigoted, uncolored, unslanted, without favor; SEE CONCEPTS *403,542*

impasse [*n*] *stalemate*
box*, Catch-22*, cessation, corner*, cul-de-sac*, dead end, deadlock, dilemma, fix, gridlock, jam, mire*, morass*, pause, pickle*, plight, predicament, quandary, rest, scrape*, standoff, standstill; SEE CONCEPT *674*

impassioned [*adj*] *excited, vehement*
animated, ardent, blazing, burning, deep, fervent, fervid, fierce, fiery, fired up*, flaming, furious, glowing, heated*, hot-blooded*, inflamed, inspired, intense, melodramatic, moving, mushy, overemotional, passionate, perfervid, powerful, profound, red-hot*, romantic, rousing, sentimental, starry-eyed*, steamed up*, stirring, torrid, violent, vivid, warm, white-hot*, wild about, worked up*, zealous; SEE CONCEPT *403*

impassive [*adj*] *aloof, cool*
apathetic, callous, cold, cold-blooded*, collected, composed, dispassionate, dry, emotionless, hardened, heartless, imperturbable, indifferent, indurated, inexcitable, inexpressive, inscrutable, insensible, insusceptible, matter-of-fact, nonchalant, passionless, phlegmatic, placid, poker-faced*, reserved, reticent, sedate, self-con-

tained, serene, spiritless, stoic, stoical, stolid, taciturn, unconcerned, unemotional, unexcitable, unfeeling, unflappable, unimpressible, unmoved, unruffled, wooden; SEE CONCEPTS *404,542*

impatience [n] *inability, unwillingness to wait*
agitation, anger, annoyance, ants in pants*, anxiety, avidity, disquietude, eagerness, edginess, excitement, expectancy, fretfulness, haste, hastiness, heat*, impetuosity, intolerance, irritability, irritableness, nervousness, quick temper, rashness, restiveness, restlessness, shortness, snappiness, suspense, uneasiness, vehemence, violence; SEE CONCEPTS *633,657*

impatient [adj] *unable, unwilling to wait*
abrupt, agog, antsy, anxious, appetent, ardent, athirst, avid, breathless, brusque, chafing, choleric, curt, demanding, dying to*, eager, edgy, feverish, fretful, hasty, having short fuse*, headlong, hot-tempered, hot under collar*, impetuous, indignant, intolerant, irascible, irritable, itchy, keen, on pins and needles*, quick-tempered, racing one's motor*, restless, ripe*, snappy, straining, sudden, testy, thirsty, unforbearing, unindulgent, vehement, violent; SEE CONCEPTS *401,542*

impeach [v] *denounce, censure*
accuse, arraign, blame, bring charges against, call into question, call to account, cast aspersions on, cast doubt on, challenge, charge, criminate, criticize, discredit, disparage, hold at fault, impugn, incriminate, inculpate, indict, query, question, reprehend, reprimand, reprobate, tax, try; SEE CONCEPTS *44,52,317*

impeccable [adj] *above suspicion; flawless*
accurate, aces, A-okay*, apple-pie*, clean, correct, errorless, exact, exquisite, faultless, fleckless, immaculate, incorrupt, infallible, innocent, irreproachable, nice, note-perfect, on target*, perfect, precise, pure, right, sinless, stainless, ten*, unblemished, unerring, unflawed, unimpeachable; SEE CONCEPTS *535,574,621*

impecunious [adj] *poverty-stricken*
beggared, broke*, cleaned out*, destitute, dirt poor*, homeless, impoverished, indigent, insolvent, necessitous, needy, penniless, penurious, poor, strapped*, unprosperous; SEE CONCEPT *334*

impede [v] *obstruct, hinder*
bar, block, blow whistle on*, brake, check, clog, close off, cramp one's style*, curb, cut off, dam, delay, deter, discomfit, disconcert, disrupt, embarrass, faze, flag one*, freeze, hamper, hang up, hold up, interfere, oppose, rattle, restrain, retard, saddle with*, shut down, shut off, slow, slow down, stonewall*, stop, stymie, thwart; SEE CONCEPTS *121,130*

impediment [n] *obstruction, hindrance*
bar, barricade, barrier, block, blockage, bottleneck*, burden, catch*, Catch-22*, chain, check, clog, cramp, curb, dead weight*, defect, delay, deterrent, detriment, difficulty, disadvantage, drag*, drawback, encumbrance, fault, flaw, handicap, hazard, hitch, holdup, hurdle, inhibition, load, manacle, millstone*, obstacle, prohibition, red tape*, restraint, restriction, retardation, retardment, road block*, rub*, setback, shackle, snag, stoppage, stricture, stumbling block*, tie, trammel, wall; SEE CONCEPT *666*

impel [v] *prompt, incite*
actuate, boost, compel, constrain, drive, excite,

foment, force, goad, induce, influence, inspire, instigate, jog, lash, mobilize, motivate, move, oblige, poke, power, press, prod, propel, push, require, set in motion, shove, spur, start, stimulate, thrust, urge; SEE CONCEPTS *14,68,221,242*

impending [adj] *forthcoming*
approaching, at hand, brewing, coming, gathering, handwriting-on-the-wall*, hovering, imminent, in the cards*, in the offing*, in the wind*, looking to*, looming, menacing, near, nearing, ominous, on the horizon*, overhanging, portending, proximate, see it coming*, threatening, waiting to; SEE CONCEPTS *548,820*

impenetrable [adj1] *dense*
bulletproof, close, compact, firm, hard, hermetic, impassable, impermeable, impervious, inviolable, solid, substantial, thick, unpiercable; SEE CONCEPTS *483,604*

impenetrable [adj2] *incomprehensible*
arcane, baffling, cabalistic, dark, Delphic, enigmatic, enigmatical, hidden, incognizable, indiscernible, inexplicable, inscrutable, mysterious, mystic, obscure, sibylline, unaccountable, unfathomable, ungraspable, unintelligible, unknowable; SEE CONCEPTS *529,576*

imperative [adj1] *necessary*
acute, burning, clamant, clamorous, compulsory, critical, crucial, crying, essential, exigent, immediate, important, importunate, indispensable, inescapable, insistent, instant, no turning back*, obligatory, pressing, urgent, vital; SEE CONCEPT *546*

imperative [adj2] *authoritative*
aggressive, autocratic, bidding, bossy, commanding, dictatorial, dominant, domineering, harsh, high-handed, imperial, imperious, ordering, overbearing, peremptory, powerful, stern; SEE CONCEPTS *267,574*

imperceptible [adj] *hard to sense; faint*
ephemeral, evanescent, fine, gradual, impalpable, imponderable, inappreciable, inaudible, inconsiderable, inconspicuous, indiscernible, indistinct, indistinguishable, infinitesimal, insensible, insignificant, invisible, microscopic, minute, momentary, shadowy, slight, small, subtle, tiny, trivial, undetectable, unnoticeable, vague; SEE CONCEPTS *406,533*

imperfect [adj] *flawed*
amiss, below par, bottom-of-barrel*, broken, damaged, defective, deficient, disfigured, dud*, faulty, few bugs*, garbage*, immature, impaired, incomplete, inexact, injured, junk*, lemon*, limited, low, marred, minus, partial, patchy, rudimentary, schlocky*, sick, sketchy, two-bit*, undeveloped, unfinished, unsound, vicious, warped; SEE CONCEPTS *570,574,579*

imperfection [n] *flaw*
blemish, bug*, catch, defect, deficiency, deformity, demerit, disfigurement, failing, fallibility, fault, foible, frailty, glitch*, gremlin*, inadequacy, incompleteness, infirmity, insufficiency, peccadillo, problem, shortcoming, sin, stain, taint, weakness, weak point; SEE CONCEPTS *230,671,718*

imperil [v] *cause to be in danger*
chance it, compromise, endanger, expose, hazard, jeopard, jeopardize, jeopardy, menace, peril, risk; SEE CONCEPT *240*

imperious [adj] *bossy, overbearing*
arrogant, authoritative, autocratic, commanding,

im
im

compulsatory, compulsory, despotic, dictatorial, domineering, exacting, haughty, high-handed, imperative, imperial, mandatory, obligatory, oppressive, overweening, peremptory, required, tyrannical, tyrannous; SEE CONCEPTS 267,574

impermeable [adj] *impenetrable*
airtight, dense, hermetic, impassable, impervious, leak-proof, nonporous, sealed, waterproof, water-resistant, watertight; SEE CONCEPTS 483, 604

impersonal [adj] *cold, unfriendly*
abstract, bureaucratic, businesslike, candid, cold-blooded*, cold turkey*, colorless, cool, detached, disinterested, dispassionate, emotionless, equal, equitable, fair, formal, impartial, indifferent, inhuman, neutral, nondiscriminatory, objective, poker-faced*, remote, straight, strictly business*, unbiased, uncolored, unpassioned; SEE CONCEPTS 401,542,544

impersonate [v] *pretend to be another*
act, act a part, act like, act out, ape, assume character, ditto*, do, do an impression of, double as, dress as, enact, fake, imitate, make like*, masquerade as, mimic, mirror, pass oneself off as*, perform, personate, play, playact, play a role, portray, pose as, put on an act*, represent, take the part of; SEE CONCEPTS 59,292

impertinence [n] *boldness*
assurance, audacity, backchat, back talk*, brazenness, cheek*, chutzpah*, come-back*, crust*, disrespect, disrespectfulness, effrontery, forwardness, freshness, gall, guff, hardihood, impropriety, impudence, incivility, insolence, insolency, lip*, nerve, pertness, presumption, rudeness, sass*, smart mouth*, wisecrack*, wise guy*; SEE CONCEPT 633

impertinent [adj] *bold, disrespectful*
arrogant, brash, brassy*, brazen, contumelious, discourteous, disgracious, flip*, forward, fresh, ill-mannered, impolite, impudent, inappropriate, incongruous, inquisitive, insolent, interfering, intrusive, lippy*, meddlesome, meddling, nosy*, off base*, offensive, out of line*, pert, presumptuous, procacious, prying, rude, sassy*, smart, smart alecky*, uncalled-for*, uncivil, ungracious, unmannerly, unsuitable; SEE CONCEPT 401

imperturbable [adj] *calm, collected*
assured, complacent, composed, cool, cool as cucumber*, disimpassioned, equanimous, hard as nails*, immovable, nerveless, nonchalant, roll with punches*, sedate, self-possessed, self-satisfied, smug, stiff upper lip*, stoical, thick-skinned, tranquil, unaffected, undisturbed, unexcitable, unflappable, unmoved, unruffled, untouched; SEE CONCEPT 404

impervious [adj] *unable to be penetrated*
closed to, hermetic, immune, impassable, impassive, impenetrable, impermeable, imperviable, inaccessible, invulnerable, resistant, sealed, tight, unaffected, unapproachable, unmoved, unpierceable, unreceptive, watertight; SEE CONCEPTS 485,534,604

impetuous [adj] *acting without thinking*
abrupt, ardent, eager, fervid, fierce, furious, going off deep end*, hasty, headlong, hurried, impassioned, impulsive, passionate, precipitant, precipitate, precipitous, rash, restive, rushing, spontaneous, spur-of-the-moment, subitaneous, sudden, swift, unbridled, unexpected, unplanned, unpremeditated, unreflecting, unrestrained, un-

thinking, vehement, violent; SEE CONCEPTS 404,542

impetus [n] *stimulus, force*
catalyst, energy, goad, impulse, impulsion, incentive, incitation, incitement, momentum, motivation, power, pressure, push, spur, stimulant, urge; SEE CONCEPTS 641,661

impinge [v] *trespass*
affect, bear upon, disturb, encroach, influence, infringe, intrude, invade, make inroads, meddle, obtrude, pry, touch, violate; SEE CONCEPTS 14,156

impious [adj] *not religious*
agnostic, apostate, atheistic, blasphemous, canting, contrary, deceitful, defiling, desecrating, desecrative, diabolic, disobedient, disrespectful, godless, hardened, hypocritical, iconoclastic, immoral, iniquitous, irreligious, irreverent, perverted, pietistical, profane, recusant, reprobate, sacrilegious, sanctimonious, satanic, scandalous, sinful, unctuous, undutiful, unethical, unfaithful, ungodly, unhallowed, unholy, unregenerate, unrighteous, unsanctified, wayward, wicked; SEE CONCEPT 545

impish [adj] *mischievous*
casual, devilish, devil-may-care*, elfin, elvish, fiendish, flippant, free and easy*, fresh, frolicsome, giddy, jaunty, naughty, offhand, pert, pixieish, playful, prankish, puckish, rascally, saucy*, sportive, waggish; SEE CONCEPT 401

implacable [adj] *merciless, cruel*
grim, inexorable, inflexible, intractable, iron-fisted, mortal, pitiless, rancorous, relentless, remorseless, ruthless, unappeasable, unbending, uncompromising, unflinching, unforgiving, unrelenting, unyielding, vindictive; SEE CONCEPT 542

implausible [adj] *not likely*
doubtful, dubious, farfetched, far out*, fishy*, flimsy, for the birds*, full of holes*, impossible, improbable, inconceivable, incredible, obscure, problematic, puzzling, reachy, suspect, thin*, too much*, unbelievable, unconvincing, unreasonable, unsubstantial, weak, won't hold water*, won't wash*; SEE CONCEPT 552

implement [n] *agent, tool*
apparatus, appliance, contraption, contrivance, device, equipment, gadget, instrument, machine, utensil; SEE CONCEPT 499

implement [v] *start, put into action*
achieve, actualize, bring about, carry out, complete, effect, enable, enforce, execute, fulfill, invoke, make good*, make possible, materialize, perform, provide the means, put into effect, realize, resolve; SEE CONCEPTS 91,99,221

implicate [v] *imply, involve*
accuse, affect, associate, blame, charge, cite, compromise, concern, connect, embroil, entangle, frame, hint, impute, include, incriminate, inculpate, insinuate, lay at one's door*, link, mean, mire, name, pin on*, point finger at*, relate, stigmatize, suggest, tangle*; SEE CONCEPTS 44,112

implication [n] *association, suggestion*
assumption, conclusion, connection, connotation, entanglement, guess, hint, hypothesis, incrimination, indication, inference, innuendo, intimation, involvement, link, meaning, overtone, presumption, ramification, reference, significance, signification, undertone, union; SEE CONCEPTS 28,39,278

implicit [*adj*] *included without question, inherent, absolute*
accurate, certain, complete, constant, constructive, contained, definite, entire, firm, fixed, full, implicative, implied, inarticulate, inevitable, inferential, inferred, latent, practical, steadfast, tacit, taken for granted, total, undeclared, understood, unexpressed, unhesitating, unqualified, unquestioned, unreserved, unsaid, unshakable, unspoken, unuttered, virtual, wholehearted; SEE CONCEPTS *267,535,549*

implied [*adj*] *hinted at*
adumbrated, alluded to, allusive, connoted, constructive, figured, foreshadowed, hidden, implicit, indicated, indicative, indirect, inferential, inferred, inherent, insinuated, intended, involved, latent, lurking, meant, occult, parallel, perceptible, potential, significative, signified, suggested, symbolized, tacit, tacitly assumed, undeclared, understood, unexpressed, unsaid, unspoken, unuttered, wordless; SEE CONCEPTS *267,535*

implode [*v*] *collapse inward*
cave in, fall down, fall in, fold, fold up; SEE CONCEPTS *230,316,410,674*

implore [*v*] *beg*
appeal, beseech, conjure, crave, entreat, go on bended knee*, importune, plead, pray, solicit, supplicate, urge; SEE CONCEPT *48*

imply [*v*] *indicate, mean*
betoken, connote, denote, designate, entail, evidence, give a hint, hint, import, include, insinuate, intend, intimate, involve, mention, point to, presuppose, refer, signify, suggest; SEE CONCEPTS *75,97,682*

impolite [*adj*] *having bad manners*
bad-mannered, boorish, churlish, crude, discourteous, disgracious, disrespectful, ill-bred, ill-mannered, indecorous, indelicate, insolent, irritable, loutish, moody, oafish, rough, rude, sullen, uncivil, ungracious, unmannered, unmannerly, unrefined; SEE CONCEPT *401*

impolitic [*adj*] *unwise, careless*
brash, ill-advised, ill-judged, imprudent, inadvisable, inconsiderate, indiscreet, inexpedient, injudicious, maladroit, misguided, rash, stupid, tactless, undiplomatic, untimely; SEE CONCEPTS *401,544*

import [*n1*] *meaning*
acceptation, bearing, bottom line*, construction, drift*, gist*, heart*, implication, intendment, intention, interpretation, meat*, message, name of the game*, nature of beast*, nuts and bolts*, point, punch line*, purport, score*, sense, significance, significancy, signification, stuff*, thrust, understanding; SEE CONCEPT *682*

import [*n2*] *significance, weight*
consequence, design, emphasis, importance, intent, magnitude, moment, momentousness, object, objective, pith, purpose, signification, stress, substance, value, weightiness, worth; SEE CONCEPTS *346,668*

importance [*n1*] *significance, weight*
accent, attention, bearing, caliber, concern, concernment, consequence, denotation, distinction, drift*, effect, emphasis, force, gist*, gravity, import, influence, interest, materiality, moment, momentousness, notability, paramountcy, point, precedence, preponderance, preponderancy, priority, purport, relevance, sense, seriousness, signification, standing, stress, substance, tenor,

usefulness, value, weightiness; SEE CONCEPTS *346,668,682*

importance [*n2*] *prominence, standing*
consequence, conspicuousness, distinction, eminence, esteem, fame, greatness, influence, lionization, mark, notability, note, noteworthiness, rank, reputation, salience, status, usefulness, worth; SEE CONCEPTS *388,671*

important [*adj1*] *valuable, substantial*
big, big-league*, chief, considerable, conspicuous, critical, crucial, decisive, determining, earnest, essential, esteemed, exceptional, exigent, extensive, far-reaching, foremost, front-page*, grave, great, heavy, imperative, importunate, influential, large, marked, material, mattering much, meaningful, momentous, necessary, of moment, of note, of substance, paramount, ponderous, pressing, primary, principal, relevant, salient, serious, signal, significant, something, standout, urgent, vital, weighty; SEE CONCEPT *567*

important [*adj2*] *eminent, influential, outstanding*
aristocratic, big-time*, distinctive, distinguished, effective, esteemed, extraordinary, famous, first-class*, foremost, four-star*, front-page*, grand, heavy*, high-level, high profile, high-ranking, high-up, honored, illustrious, imposing, incomparable, leading, majestic, major-league*, noble, notable, noted, noteworthy, of note, page-one*, potent, powerful, preeminent, prominent, remarkable, seminal, signal, solid, superior, talented, top-drawer*, top-notch*, upper-class, VIP*, well-known; SEE CONCEPTS *555,574*

imported [*adj*] *brought in from another place*
alien, carried, choice, exotic, ferried, foreign, introduced, rare, sent, shipped, transported, trucked; SEE CONCEPT *549*

importunate [*adj*] *demanding, insistent*
burning, clamant, clamorous, crying, disturbing, dogged, earnest, exigent, harassing, imperative, instant, overly solicitous, persevering, persistent, pertinacious, pressing, solicitous, troublesome, urgent; SEE CONCEPTS *267,401*

importune [*v*] *demand, insist*
appeal, ask, badger, beg, beseech, beset, besiege, con*, crave, dun, egg on*, entreat, goose*, harass, hound*, implore, invoke, nag, persuade, pester, plague, plead, pray, press, sell, solicit, supplicate, urge, work on*; SEE CONCEPT *53*

impose [*v*] *set, dictate*
appoint, burden, charge, command, compel, constrain, decree, demand, encroach, enforce, enjoin, establish, exact, fix, foist, force, force upon, horn in, inflict, infringe, institute, introduce, intrude, lade, lay, lay down, lay down the law, levy, move in on, oblige, obtrude, ordain, order, place, prescribe, presume, promulgate, put, put foot down*, read riot act*, require, saddle*, take advantage, trespass, visit, wish, wreak, wreck; SEE CONCEPTS *18,53,133*

imposing [*adj*] *impressive*
august, big, commanding, dignified, effective, exciting, grand, grandiose, imperial, magnificent, majestic, massive, mega*, mind-blowing*, monumental, moving, noble, ominous, one for the book*, overblown, overwhelming, pretentious, regal, royal, something else*, something to write home about*, stately, stirring, striking, towering; SEE CONCEPTS *537,574,773*

im
im

imposition [*n1*] *deception*
artifice, cheating, con, craftiness, dissimulation, fraud, hoax, hocus-pocus*, hypocrisy, illusion, imposture, stratagem, trick, trickery; SEE CONCEPTS *59,645*

imposition [*n2*] *burden*
charge, command, constraint, demand, drag, duty, encroachment, encumbrance, intrusion, levy, pain, pain in the neck*, pressure, presumption, restraint, tax; SEE CONCEPTS *14,130*

impossible [*adj1*] *beyond the bounds of possibility*
absurd, beyond, contrary to reason, cureless, futile, hardly possible, hopeless, hundred-to-one*, impassable, impervious, impracticable, impractical, inaccessible, inconceivable, inexecutable, infeasible, insurmountable, irrealizable, irreparable, no-go*, not a prayer*, no-way*, no-win*, out of the question*, preposterous, too much, unachievable, unattainable, uncorrectable, unfeasible, unimaginable, unobtainable, unreasonable, unrecoverable, unthinkable, unworkable, useless, visionary, way out; SEE CONCEPT *552*

impossible [*adj2*] *intolerable, ungovernable*
absurd, egregious, hopeless, improper, incongruous, ludicrous, objectionable, offensive, outrageous, preposterous, unacceptable, unanswerable, undesirable, unreasonable, unsuitable; SEE CONCEPT *401*

impostor [*n*] *person pretending to be something else*
actor, beguiler, bluffer, charlatan, cheat, con artist, deceiver, empiric, fake, faker, four-flusher*, fraud, hypocrite, imitator, impersonator, masquerader, mimic, mocker, mountebank, pettifogger, phony, pretender, pseudo, quack, scorner, sham, sharper, shyster, trickster; SEE CONCEPT *412*

imposture [*n*] *fraud, trick*
artifice, cheat, con, copy, counterfeit, deceit, deception, fabrication, fake, feint, fiddle, flimflam*, forgery, gambit, hoax, hocus-pocus*, illusion, imitation, impersonation, imposition, make-believe, maneuver, masquerade, phony, ploy, pretense, pretension, put-on*, quackery, ruse, sell*, sham, sleight, spoof, stratagem, swindle, wile; SEE CONCEPTS *59,192,645,674*

impotent [*adj*] *disabled; unable to perform action*
barren, crippled, dud, effete, enervated, enfeebled, feeble, forceless, frail, gutless, helpless, inadequate, incapable, incapacitated, incompetent, ineffective, ineffectual, inept, infecund, infirm, nerveless, paper tiger*, paralyzed, powerless, prostrate, sterile, unfruitful, unproductive, weak; SEE CONCEPT *485*

impound [*v*] *confine*
cage, coop up, enclose, fence in, hold, imprison, keep, pen, seize, shut in, take; SEE CONCEPTS *121,130*

impoverished [*adj*] *poor, exhausted*
bankrupt, barren, beggared, broke, clean, depleted, destitute, distressed, drained, empty, flat*, flat broke*, have-not*, hurting, impecunious, indigent, insolvent, necessitous, needy, penurious, played out*, poverty-stricken, reduced, ruined, spent, sterile, strapped; SEE CONCEPTS *334,560*

impractical/impracticable [*adj*] *unrealistic*
abstract, absurd, chimerical, idealistic, illogical, impossible, impracticable, improbable, inapplicable, inefficacious, infeasible, inoperable, irrealizable, ivory-tower*, no-go*, nonfunctional, nonviable, not a prayer*, otherworldly, out of the question*, quixotic, romantic, speculative, starry-eyed*, theoretical, unattainable, unbusinesslike, unfeasible, unreal, unserviceable, unusable, unwise, unworkable, useless, visionary, wild, won't fly*; SEE CONCEPT *552*

impregnable [*adj*] *unyielding*
firm, fortified, impenetrable, indestructible, invincible, invulnerable, secure, solid, strong, unassailable; SEE CONCEPTS *489,540,551*

impregnate [*v*] *infuse, fill; make pregnant*
charge, conceive, drench, fecundate, fertilize, imbrue, implant, inoculate, inseminate, leaven, overflow, percolate, permeate, pervade, procreate, produce, reproduce, saturate, seethe, soak, sodden, souse, steep, suffuse, transfuse; SEE CONCEPTS *179,375*

impresario [*n*] *manager, producer*
director, showperson, sponsor, stage manager; SEE CONCEPT *347*

impress [*v1*] *influence*
affect, arouse, awe, be conspicuous, blow away*, buffalo*, bulldoze*, carry, electrify, enforce, enthuse, excite, faze, galvanize, get*, grab, grandstand*, inspire, kill*, knock out*, make a hit*, make an impression, make splash*, move, overawe, pique, provoke, push around*, register, score, show off, slay*, stimulate, stir, strike, sway, thrill, touch*; SEE CONCEPTS *7,19,22,261*

impress [*v2*] *press down to make design*
carve, dent, emboss, engrave, etch, imprint, indent, inscribe, mark, print, stamp; SEE CONCEPT *174*

impress [*v3*] *emphasize*
bring home*, drive home*, establish, fix, get into head*, inculcate, instill, press, set, stress; SEE CONCEPT *49*

impression [*n1*] *influence*
consequence, effect, feeling, impact, reaction, response, result, sway; SEE CONCEPT *230*

impression [*n2*] *feeling, idea*
apprehension, belief, conceit, concept, conception, conjecture, conviction, fancy, feel, hunch, image, inkling, intellection, memory, notion, opinion, perception, recollection, sensation, sense, supposition, suspicion, theory, thought, view; SEE CONCEPTS *529,689*

impression [*n3*] *design made by pressing*
brand, cast, dent, depression, dint, fingerprint, footprint, form, hollow, impress, imprint, indentation, mark, matrix, mold, outline, pattern, print, sign, spoor, stamp, stamping, trace, track, vestige; SEE CONCEPTS *284,625*

impression [*n4*] *pretending to be somebody*
imitation, impersonation, masquerade, parody, sendup, takeoff; SEE CONCEPT *263*

impressionable [*adj*] *easily taught; gullible*
affectable, affected, feeling, impressible, influenceable, ingenuous, open, perceptive, plastic*, receptive, responsive, sensible, sensile, sensitive, sentient, suggestible, susceptible, susceptive, vulnerable, wax-like; SEE CONCEPTS *402,403*

impressive [*adj*] *powerful, influential*
absorbing, affecting, arresting, august, awe-inspiring, consequential, cool*, deep*, dramatic,

effective, eloquent, excited, exciting, extraordinary, forcible, grand, impassioned, important, imposing, inspiring, intense, lavish, luxurious, majestic, massive, momentous, monumental, moving, noble, notable, penetrating, prime*, profound, remarkable, rousing, splendid, stately, stirring, striking, sumptuous, superb, thrilling, touching, towering, vital, well-done; SEE CONCEPTS *574,773*

imprint [*n*] *impression; symbol*
banner, dent, design, effect, emblem, heading, impress, indentation, influence, mark, name, print, sign, signature, stamp, trace, trademark; SEE CONCEPTS *284,625*

imprint [*v*] *stamp*
designate, engrave, establish, etch, fix, impress, inscribe, mark, offset, print; SEE CONCEPT *174*

imprison [*v*] *confine; put in jail*
apprehend, bastille, bottle up*, cage, check, circumscribe, closet, commit, constrain, curb, detain, fence in, hold, hold captive, hold hostage, hold in custody, ice*, immure, impound, incarcerate, intern, jail, keep, keep captive, keep in custody, limit, lock in, lock up, nab*, occlude, pen, put away, put behind bars, rail in, remand, restrain, send to prison, send up*, shut in, stockade, take prisoner, trammel; SEE CONCEPTS *90,191,317*

improbable [*adj*] *not likely*
doubtful, dubious, fanciful, far-fetched, flimsy*, hundred-to-one*, iffy*, implausible, inconceivable, not expected, outside chance*, questionable, rare, slim, slim and none*, unbelievable, uncertain, unconvincing, unheard of, unimaginable, unlikely, unsubstantial, weak; SEE CONCEPT *552*

impromptu [*adj/adv*] *unrehearsed, improvised*
ad-lib*, dashed off, extemporaneous, extempore, extemporized, fake, faked, improv*, improviso, offhand, off the cuff*, played by ear*, shot from the hip*, spontaneous, spur-of-the-moment, thrown off*, tossed off*, unpremeditated, unprepared, unscripted, unstudied, vamped, whipped up*, winged*; SEE CONCEPT *267*

improper [*adj1*] *not suitable*
abnormal, at odds, awkward, bad form, discordant, discrepant, erroneous, false, ill-advised, ill-timed, imprudent, inaccurate, inadmissible, inadvisable, inapplicable, inapposite, inappropriate, inapt, incongruous, incorrect, inexpedient, infelicitous, inharmonious, inopportune, irregular, ludicrous, malapropos, odd, off-base*, out-of-place*, out-of-season*, preposterous, unapt, unbefitting, uncalled-for*, uncomely, undue, unfit, unfitting, unseasonable, unsuitable, unsuited, untimely, unwarranted, wrong; SEE CONCEPT *558*

improper [*adj2*] *vulgar, immoral*
blue*, dirty, impolite, indecent, indecorous, indelicate, lewd, malodorous, naughty, risqué, rough, salacious, suggestive, unbecoming, unconventional, unequitable, unethical, ungodly, unjust, unrighteous, unrightful, unseemly, untoward, wrong, wrongful; SEE CONCEPTS *542,545*

impropriety [*n*] *bad taste, mistake*
barbarism, blunder, faux pas, gaffe, gaucherie, goof*, immodesty, impudence, incongruity, incorrectness, indecency, indecorum, inelegance, rudeness, slip*, solecism, unseemliness, unsuit-

ability, vulgarism, vulgarity; SEE CONCEPTS *101,278,674*

improve [*v*] *make or become better*
advance, ameliorate, amend, augment, better, boost, civilize, come around*, convalesce, correct, cultivate, develop, doctor up*, edit, elevate, emend, enhance, gain ground*, help, increase, lift, look up*, make strides, meliorate, mend, perk up*, pick up*, polish, progress, promote, purify, raise, rally, recover, rectify, recuperate, refine, reform, revamp, revise, rise, set right*, shape up*, sharpen, skyrocket*, straighten out*, take off*, touch up*, turn the corner*, update, upgrade; SEE CONCEPTS *244,700*

improvement [*n*] *bettering; something bettered*
advance, advancement, amelioration, amendment, augmentation, betterment, change, civilization, correction, cultivation, development, elevation, enhancement, enrichment, furtherance, gain, growth, increase, preferment, progress, progression, promotion, rally, reclamation, recovery, rectification, reformation, regeneration, renovation, revision, rise, upbeat, upgrade, upswing; SEE CONCEPTS *230,700*

improvident [*adj*] *careless, spendthrift*
extravagant, heedless, imprudent, inconsiderate, lavish, negligent, prodigal, profligate, profuse, reckless, shiftless, shortsighted, thoughtless, thriftless, uneconomical, unthrifty, wasteful; SEE CONCEPTS *334,542*

improvise [*v*] *make up*
ad-lib, brainstorm, coin, concoct, contrive, dash off*, devise, do offhand, do off top of head*, dream up, extemporize, fake, fake it, improv*, improvisate, invent, jam*, knock off*, make do*, slapdash*, spark, speak off the cuff*, throw together*, wing it*; SEE CONCEPTS *173,266*

improvised [*adj*] *made-up*
ad-lib, autoschediastic, Band-Aid*, extemporaneous, extempore, extemporized, fly-by-night*, hit-or-miss*, impromptu, improviso, makeshift, offhand, spontaneous, spur-of-the-moment*, unprepared, unrehearsed, unstudied; SEE CONCEPTS *267,589*

imprudent [*adj*] *without much thought*
brash, careless, foolhardy, foolish, heedless, ill-advised, ill-considered, ill-judged, impolitic, improvident, incautious, inconsiderate, indiscreet, inexpedient, injudicious, irresponsible, leaving self wide open*, off the deep end*, overhasty, playing with fire*, rash, reckless, temerarious, thoughtless, unadvisable, unthinking, unwise; SEE CONCEPTS *267,542*

impudent [*adj*] *bold, shameless*
arrant, audacious, barefaced, blatant, boldfaced, brassy, brazen, bumptious, cheeky*, cocky*, contumelious, cool*, flip*, forward, fresh, immodest, impertinent, insolent, nervy*, off-base*, overbold, pert, presumptuous, procacious, rude, sassy*, saucy*, smart*, smart-alecky*, unabashed, unblushing, wise*; SEE CONCEPT *401*

impugn [*v*] *criticize, challenge*
assail, attack, blast, break, call into question, cast aspersions upon, cast doubt upon, come down on*, contradict, contravene, cross, cut to shreds*, deny, disaffirm, dispute, gainsay, knock*, negate, negative, oppose, pin something on*, put down*, question, resist, run down, skin alive*, slam*, smear*, stick it to*, swipe at*, tar*, throw doubt on, throw the book at*, thumb nose at*,

traduce, trash, traverse, zap*, zing*; SEE CONCEPTS *52,58*

impulse [*n1*] *drive, resolve*
actuation, appeal, bent, caprice, catalyst, desire, disposition, excitant, extemporization, fancy, feeling, flash*, goad, hunch, impellent, impulsion, incitation, incitement, inclination, influence, inspiration, instinct, itch*, lash, lust, mind, motivation, motive, notion, passion, spontaneity, spur, thought, urge, vagary, whim, whimsy, wish, yen; SEE CONCEPTS *20,410*

impulse [*n2*] *throb, stimulus*
augmentation, beat, bump, catalyst, drive, force, impetus, impulsion, lash, momentum, movement, pressure, propulsion, pulsation, pulse, push, rush, shock, shove, stroke, surge, thrust, vibration; SEE CONCEPT *641*

impulsive [*adj*] *tending to act without thought*
abrupt, ad-lib*, automatic, careless, devil-may-care*, emotional, extemporaneous, flaky*, gone off deep end*, hasty, headlong, hot-and-cold*, impetuous, instinctive, intuitive, involuntary, jumping the gun*, mad, offhand, passionate, precipitate, quick, rash, spontaneous, sudden, swift, unconsidered, unexpected, unmeditated, unpredictable, unpremeditated, unprompted, up-and-down*, violent, winging it*; SEE CONCEPTS *401,542*

impunity [*n*] *freedom*
dispensation, exception, exemption, immunity, liberty, license, nonliability, permission, privilege, security; SEE CONCEPT *376*

impure [*adj*] *not clean mentally, physically; mixed*
admixed, adulterated, alloyed, carnal, coarse, common, contaminated, corrupt, debased, defiled, desecrated, diluted, dirty, doctored*, filthy, foul, gross*, grubby*, immodest, immoral, indecent, infected, lewd, nasty, not pure, obscene, polluted, profaned, smutty*, squalid, sullied, tainted, unchaste, unclean, unrefined, unwholesome, vile, vitiated, weighted, wicked; SEE CONCEPTS *545,621*

impurity [*n*] *contaminant*
adulteration, contamination, corruption, defilement, dirt, filth, foreign matter, grime, pestilence, poisoning, pollutant, pollution, scum, stain, taint, uncleanness; SEE CONCEPTS *230,306,674*

impute [*v*] *attribute*
accredit, accuse, adduce, ascribe, assign, blame, brand, censure, charge, credit, hang something on*, hint, indict, insinuate, intimate, lay, pin on*, refer, reference, stigmatize; SEE CONCEPTS *44,49*

inability [*n*] *disabling lack of talent, skill*
disqualification, failure, frailty, impotence, inadequacy, inaptitude, incapability, incapacitation, incapacity, incompetence, ineffectiveness, ineffectualness, inefficacy, inefficiency, ineptitude, ineptness, insufficiency, inutility, lack, necessity, powerlessness, shortcoming, unfitness, weakness; SEE CONCEPT *630*

inaccessible [*adj*] *out of reach*
aloof, away, beyond, distant, elusive, far, faraway, far-off, impassable, impervious, impracticable, insurmountable, not at hand*, out-of-the-way*, remote, unachievable, unapproachable, unattainable, unavailable, unfeasible, ungettable, unobtainable, unreachable, unrealizable, unworkable; SEE CONCEPT *576*

inaccuracy [*n*] *error, erroneousness*
blunder, corrigendum, deception, defect, erratum, exaggeration, fault, howler*, imprecision, incorrectness, inexactness, miscalculation, mistake, slip*, solecism, typo*, unfaithfulness, unreliability, wrong; SEE CONCEPTS *101,230*

inaccurate [*adj*] *erroneous*
all wet*, careless, counterfactual, defective, discrepant, doesn't wash*, fallacious, false, faulty, imprecise, incorrect, in error, inexact, mistaken, off, off base*, out*, specious, unfaithful, unreliable, unsound, untrue, way-off*, wide*, wild*, wrong; SEE CONCEPTS *565,582*

inactive [*adj*] *not engaged in action; inert, lazy*
abeyant, asleep, blah*, disengaged, do-nothing*, dormant, down, draggy, dull, idle, immobile, indolent, in holding pattern*, inoperative, jobless, latent, lax, lethargic, limp, low-key, mothballed*, motionless, on hold, ossified, out of action, out of commission*, out of service, out of work*, passive, quiescent, quiet, sedentary, slack, sleepy, slothful, slow, sluggish, somnolent, stable, static, still, torpid, unemployed, unoccupied, unused; SEE CONCEPTS *401,560,584*

inadequacy [*n*] *shortage, defect, inability*
blemish, dearth, defalcation, defectiveness, deficiency, deficit, drawback, failing, faultiness, flaw, imperfection, inadequateness, inaptness, incapacity, incompetence, incompetency, incompleteness, ineffectiveness, ineffectualness, inefficacy, inefficiency, ineptitude, insufficiency, lack, meagerness, paucity, poverty, scantiness, shortcoming, skimpiness, underage, unfitness, unsuitableness, weakness; SEE CONCEPTS *335,674,709*

inadequate [*adj*] *defective, insufficient, incompetent*
bare, barren, bush-league*, deficient, depleted, dry, failing, faulty, feeble, found wanting, glitch*, imperfect, impotent, inappreciable, inapt, incapable, incommensurate, incompetent, incomplete, inconsiderable, insubstantial, junk*, lacking, lame*, lemon*, lousy, low, meager, minus, miserly, niggardly, not enough, parsimonious, poor, scanty, scarce, short, shy*, sketchy*, skimpy*, small, spare, sparse, sterile, stinted, stunted*, thin*, too little, unequal, unproductive, unqualified, weak; SEE CONCEPTS *546,570,771*

inadmissible [*adj*] *not appropriate*
exceptionable, ill-favored, ill-timed, immaterial, improper, inappropriate, inapt, incompetent, inept, irrelevant, malapropos, objectionable, unacceptable, unallowable, unbecoming, undesirable, unfit, unqualified, unreasonable, unsatisfactory, unseemly, unsuited, unwanted, unwelcome; SEE CONCEPTS *319,558*

inadvertent [*adj*] *accidental*
careless, chance, feckless, heedless, irreflective, negligent, not on purpose, reckless, thoughtless, uncaring, unconcerned, undesigned, undevised, unheeding, unintended, unintentional, unmindful, unplanned, unpremeditated, unthinking, unthought, unwitting; SEE CONCEPTS *542,544*

inadvisable [*adj*] *not recommended*
careless, foolhardy, foolish, harebrained*, ill-advised, impolitic, improper, imprudent, inappropriate, incautious, inconvenient, indiscreet, inexpedient, injudicious, pointless, rash, undesirable, unsensible, unsuitable, unwise, wrong; SEE CONCEPTS *529,558*

inalienable [*adj*] *absolute, inherent*
basic, entailed, inbred, inviolable, natural, non-negotiable, nontransferable, sacrosanct, unassailable, untransferable; SEE CONCEPT 535

inane [*adj*] *stupid*
absurd, asinine, daft, empty, fatuous, flat, foolish, frivolous, futile, harebrained*, idiotic, illogical, imbecilic, innocuous, insipid, jejune, laughable, meaningless, mindless, pointless, puerile, ridiculous, sappy*, senseless, silly, trifling, unintelligent, vacant, vacuous, vain, vapid, weak, wishy-washy*, worthless; SEE CONCEPTS 542,548

inanimate [*adj*] *not alive, not organic*
azoic, cold, dead, defunct, dull, exanimate, extinct, idle, inactive, inert, inoperative, insensate, insentient, lifeless, mineral, motionless, nonanimal, nonvegetable, quiescent, soulless, spiritless; SEE CONCEPT 539

inapplicable [*adj*] *not relevant*
extraneous, foreign, garbage*, immaterial, impertinent, inapposite, inappropriate, inappurtenant, inapropos, inapt, inconsistent, irrelative, irrelevant, remote, unsuitable, unsuited; SEE CONCEPTS 546,558

inappropriate [*adj*] *not proper, suitable*
bad form, disproportionate, foot-in-mouth*, garbage*, ill-fitted, ill-suited, ill-timed, improper, inapplicable, inapropos, incongruous, inconsonant, incorrect, indecorous, inept, irrelevant, left-field*, malapropos, off*, out of line, out of place, tasteless, unbecoming, unbefitting, undue, unfit, unfitting, unmeet, unseasonable, unseemly, unsuitable, untimely, way off*, wrong, wrong-number*; SEE CONCEPT 558

inapt [*adj*] *incompetent; not suitable*
awkward, banal, clumsy, dull, flat, gauche, ill-adapted, ill-fitted, ill-suited, improper, inadept, inapposite, inappropriate, incongruous, inept, inexperienced, inexpert, infelicitous, insipid, jejune, maladroit, malapropos, slow, stupid, unable, undexterous, unfacile, unfit, unhandy, unmeet, unproficient, unskilled, unsuitable, unsuited, untimely; SEE CONCEPTS 527,558

inarticulate [*adj*] *unable to speak well*
blurred, dumb, faltering, halting, hesitant, hesitating, inaudible, incoherent, incomprehensible, indistinct, maundering, muffled, mumbled, mumbling, mute, obscure, reticent, silent, speechless, stammering, tongue-tied, unclear, unintelligible, unspoken, unuttered, unvocal, unvoiced, vague, voiceless, wordless; SEE CONCEPT 267

inattentive [*adj*] *negligent, not paying attention*
absent, absentminded, apathetic, blind, bored, careless, distracted, distrait, distraught, diverted, dreamy, faraway, heedless, inadvertent, indifferent, inobservant, listless, lost*, musing, neglectful, oblivious, off-guard*, out to lunch*, preoccupied, rapt, regardless, remiss, removed, scatterbrained*, thoughtless, unconscious, undiscerning, unheeding, unmindful, unnoticing, unobservant, unobserving, unperceiving, unthinking, unwatchful, vague; SEE CONCEPTS 403, 542

inaudible [*adj*] *silent*
closemouthed, faint, hushed, imperceptible, low, muffled, mum, mumbled, mute, muted, noiseless, nonvocal, not talkative, quiet, soundless, still, unclear, uncommunicative, unhearable, voiceless, wordless; SEE CONCEPT 594

inaugurate [*v*] *begin; install*
bow, break in, break the ice*, commence, commission, dedicate, get things rolling*, get under way*, induct, initiate, instate, institute, introduce, invest, jump, kick off*, launch, make up, open, ordain, originate, set in motion*, set up, start, usher in; SEE CONCEPT 221

inauguration [*n*] *installation of newcomers*
commencement, inaugural, induction, initiation, institution, investiture, launch, launching, opening, setting up; SEE CONCEPT 386

inauspicious [*adj*] *ominous, unpromising*
bad, baleful, baneful, black, dire, discouraging, evil, fateful, foreboding, ill-boding, ill-omened, impending, inopportune, sinister, threatening, unfavorable, unfortunate, unlucky, unpromising, unpropitious, untimely, untoward; SEE CONCEPTS 548,570

inborn/inbred [*adj*] *coming from birth; natural*
congenital, connate, connatural, constitutional, deep-seated, essential, hereditary, inbred, indigenous, indwelling, ingenerate, ingrained, inherent, inherited, innate, instinctive, intrinsic, intuitive, native, unacquired; SEE CONCEPTS 406,549

incalculable [*adj*] *countless, limitless*
boundless, capricious, chancy, enormous, erratic, fluctuant, iffy*, immense, incomputable, inestimable, infinite, innumerable, jillion*, measureless, no end of*, no end to*, numberless, uncertain, uncountable, unfixed, unforeseen, unpredictable, unreckonable, untold, vast, whimsical, without number, zillion*; SEE CONCEPTS 535,773,781

incandescent [*adj*] *glowing*
beaming, brilliant, effulgent, fulgent, intense, lambent, lucent, luminous, phosphorescent, radiant, red-hot*, refulgent, shining, white-hot*; SEE CONCEPT 617

incantation [*n*] *spell, magic*
abracadabra*, ala kazam*, bewitchment, black magic, chant, charm, conjuration, conjuring, enchantment, formula, hex, hocus-pocus*, hoodoo*, hymn, invocation, mumbo-jumbo*, necromancy, open sesame*, rune, sorcery, voodoo*, witchcraft, wizardry; SEE CONCEPTS 370,689

incapable [*adj*] *not adequate; helpless*
butterfingers*, disqualified, feeble, impotent, inadequate, incompetent, ineffective, ineligible, inept, inexperienced, inexpert, inproficient, insufficient, losing, naive, not equal to, not up to*, poor, powerless, unable, uncool*, unequipped, unfit, unqualified, unskilled, unskillful, unsuited, weak; SEE CONCEPT 527

incapacitate [*v*] *put out of action*
clip wings*, cripple, damage, disable, disarm, disenable, disqualify, hamstring*, hinder, hogtie*, hurt, immobilize, lame, lay up*, maim, paralyze, prostrate, put out of commission*, take out, undermine, weaken; SEE CONCEPTS 121,246

incapacitated [*adj*] *disabled*
bedridden, broken-down, confined, crippled, debilitated, handicapped, helpless, hurt, immobilized, impaired, impotent, incapable, infirm, laid-up, lame, maimed, out-of-action*, out of commission*, paralyzed, powerless, sidelined, weak, weakened, wornout; SEE CONCEPTS 314,527

im
in

incarcerate [v] *put in jail, confinement*
bastille, book*, cage*, commit, confine, constrain, coop up*, detain, hold, immure, impound, imprison, intern, jail, lock up, put away, put on ice*, put under lock and key*, railroad*, restrain, restrict, send up the river*, settle, slough, take away, throw book at*; SEE CONCEPTS *90,191,317*

incarnate [adj] *in bodily form*
embodied, exteriorized, externalized, human, in human form, in the flesh*, made flesh, manifested, materialized, personified, physical, real, substantiated, tangible, typified; SEE CONCEPTS *490,539*

incautious [adj] *not careful*
any old way*, bold, brash, careless, caught napping*, devil-may-care*, fast-and-loose*, foot-in-mouth*, hasty, heedless, hotheaded*, ill-advised, ill-judged, impetuous, improvident, imprudent, impulsive, inconsiderate, indiscreet, injudicious, madcap*, neglectful, negligent, off guard*, pay no mind*, playing with fire*, precipitate, rash, reckless, regardless, sticking one's neck out*, thoughtless, unalert, unguarded, unmindful, unthinking, unvigilant, unwatchful, wary, wide open*; SEE CONCEPTS *542,544*

incendiary [adj] *causing trouble, damage*
dangerous, demagogic, dissentious, inflammatory, malevolent, provocative, rabble-rousing*, seditious, subversive, treacherous, wicked; SEE CONCEPTS *537,570*

incendiary [n] *person who causes fire, trouble*
agitator, arsonist, criminal, demagogue, demonstrator, firebrand*, insurgent, pyromaniac, rabble-rouser*, rebel, revolutionary, rioter; SEE CONCEPT *412*

incense [n] *strongly fragrant smoke*
aroma, balm, bouquet, burnt offering, essence, flame, frankincense, fuel, myrrh, odor, perfume, punk, redolence, scent, spice; SEE CONCEPTS *599,600*

incense [v] *make very angry*
anger, ask for it*, bother, disgust, egg on*, enrage, exasperate, excite, fire up*, get a rise out of*, get under one's skin*, inflame, infuriate, ire, irritate, mad, madden, make blood boil*, make see red*, provoke, rile, umbrage; SEE CONCEPT *14*

incensed [adj] *very angry*
at end of one's rope*, buffaloed*, bugged*, bummed out*, burned up*, dogged, enraged, exasperated, fuming, furious, hacked, hot and bothered*, huffy*, indignant, infuriated, irate, ireful, mad, maddened, miffed, on the warpath*, peeved, riled, rousted, rubbed the wrong way*, steamed up*, up in arms*, uptight*, wrathful; SEE CONCEPT *403*

incentive [n] *lure, inducement*
allurement, bait, carrot*, catalyst, come-on*, consideration, determinant, drive, encouragement, enticement, excuse, exhortation, goad, ground, impetus, impulse, incitement, influence, insistence, inspiration, instigation, motivation, motive, persuasion, provocation, purpose, rationale, reason, reason why, spring, spur, stimulant, stimulation, stimulus, temptation, urge, whip; SEE CONCEPT *661*

inception [n] *beginning*
birth, commencement, dawn, derivation, fountain, inauguration, initiation, kickoff, origin, out-

set, provenance, provenience, rise, root, source, start, well, wellspring; SEE CONCEPTS *648,832*

incessant [adj] *never-ending, persistent*
ceaseless, constant, continual, continuous, day-and-night*, endless, eternal, everlasting, interminable, interminate, monotonous, nonstop, perpetual, relentless, round-the-clock*, timeless, unbroken, unceasing, unending, unrelenting, unremitting; SEE CONCEPTS *534,798*

inch [n] *one-twelfth of a foot/2.54 centimeters measured*
fingerbreadth, one thirty-sixth of a yard, square; SEE CONCEPTS *790,791*

inchoate [adj] *undeveloped, beginning*
amorphous, elementary, embryonic, formless, immature, imperfect, inceptive, incipient, just begun, nascent, preliminary, rudimentary, shapeless, unfinished, unformed, unshaped; SEE CONCEPTS *485,578,797*

incident [n] *occurrence*
adventure, circumstance, episode, event, fact, happening, matter, milestone, occasion, scene, trip; SEE CONCEPT *2*

incidental [adj] *related; minor*
accidental, accompanying, adventitious, ancillary, attendant, by-the-way*, casual, chance, circumstantial, coincidental, concomitant, concurrent, contingent, contributing, contributory, fluke*, fortuitous, irregular, nonessential, occasional, odd, random, secondary, subordinate, subsidiary; SEE CONCEPTS *547,548,577*

incidentally [adv] *by chance*
accidentally, as a by-product, as side effect, by the bye*, by the way, casually, fortuitously, in passing, in related manner, not by design, obiter, parenthetically, remotely, subordinately, unexpectedly; SEE CONCEPT *544*

incinerate [v] *reduce to ashes*
blaze, burn, combust, consume, cremate, flame, ignite, light, parch, scald, scorch, set a match to, torch; SEE CONCEPT *249*

incinerator [n] *furnace*
boiler, burner, cinerator, crematory, heater, heating system, oil burner; SEE CONCEPT *463*

incipient [adj] *developing*
basic, beginning, commencing, elementary, embryonic, fundamental, inceptive, inchoate, initial, initiative, initiatory, introductory, nascent, originating, start; SEE CONCEPT *585*

incision [n] *cut, slit*
carving, cleavage, cleft, dissection, gash, groove, laceration, mark, nick, nip, notch, opening, pierce, slash, stab, wound; SEE CONCEPT *309*

incisive [adj1] *intelligent*
acute, bright, clever, concise, keen, penetrating, perspicacious, piercing, profound, sharp, trenchant; SEE CONCEPT *402*

incisive [adj2] *sarcastic*
acerb, acerbic, acid, biting, caustic, clear-cut, concise, crisp, cutting, drilling, laconic, mordant, penetrating, sardonic, satirical, scathing, severe, sharp, slashing, succinct, tart, terse, trenchant; SEE CONCEPT *267*

incite [v] *encourage, provoke*
abet, activate, actuate, agitate, animate, arouse, coax, craze, drive, egg on*, encourage, excite, exhort, fan the fire*, foment, force, forward, further, get to*, goad, impel, induce, inflame, influence, inspire, inspirit, instigate, juice*, key up*, motivate, persuade, prick, promote, prompt, pro-

voke, psych*, push, put up to*, raise, rouse, set, set off*, solicit, spur, stimulate, stir up*, talk into, taunt, trigger, urge, whip up*, work up*; SEE CONCEPTS *14,221,242*

incivility [*n*] *discourtesy*
bad manners, coarseness, discourteousness, disrespect, impoliteness, rudeness, unmanderliness; SEE CONCEPTS *29,633*

inclement [*adj1*] *bitter, nasty (weather)*
brutal, cold, foul, hard, harsh, intemperate, raw, rigorous, rough, rugged, severe, stormy, tempestuous, violent, wintry; SEE CONCEPT *525*

inclement [*adj2*] *cruel, merciless*
callous, draconian, harsh, intemperate, pitiless, rigorous, ruthless, savage, severe, tyrannical, unfeeling, unkind, unmerciful; SEE CONCEPT *401*

inclination [*n1*] *tendency, bent*
affection, appetite, aptitude, aptness, attachment, attraction, bias, capability, capacity, cup of tea*, desire, disposition, drift, druthers*, fancy, fondness, groove*, idiosyncrasy, impulse, leaning, liking, mind, movement, partiality, penchant, persuasion, pleasure, predilection, predisposition, preference, prejudice, proclivity, proneness, propensity, slant*, soft spot*, stomach*, susceptibility, taste, temperament, thing*, trend, turn*, type, urge, velleity, weakness, whim, will, wish; SEE CONCEPTS *20,411,630*

inclination [*n2*] *slant, angle*
acclivity, bank, bend, bending, bevel, bow, bowing, cant, declivity, deviation, direction, downgrade, grade, gradient, hill, incline, lean, leaning, list, pitch, ramp, slope, tilt; SEE CONCEPT *738*

incline [*n*] *slope*
acclivity, approach, ascent, cant, declivity, descent, dip, grade, gradient, inclination, lean, leaning, plane, ramp, rise, slant, tilt; SEE CONCEPT *738*

incline [*v1*] *tend toward*
affect, be disposed, bend, be partial, be predisposed, be willing, bias, drive, favor, govern, gravitate toward, impel, induce, influence, lean to, look, make willing, move, not mind, persuade, predispose, prefer, prejudice, prompt, sway, turn, verge; SEE CONCEPT *657*

incline [*v2*] *bend, lean*
aim, bevel, bow, cant, cock, deviate, diverge, heel, lay, level, list, lower, nod, point, recline, skew, slant, slope, stoop, tend, tilt, tip, train, turn, veer, yaw; SEE CONCEPT *738*

inclined [*adj*] *having a preference*
apt, bent on, disposed, given, in the mood, likely, predisposed, prone, tending, willing; SEE CONCEPTS *542,552*

include [*v*] *contain, involve*
accommodate, add, admit, allow for, append, bear, be composed of, be made up of, build, build in, carry, combine, comprehend, comprise, consist of, constitute, count, cover, cut in on, embody, embrace, encircle, enclose, encompass, entail, enter, have, hold, implicate, incorporate, inject, insert, interject, interpolate, introduce, make allowance for, make room for, number, number among, receive, subsume, take in, take into account, teem with, work in; SEE CONCEPTS *112,532,643*

including [*adj*] *containing*
along with, among other things, as well as, containing, counting, in addition to, inclusive of, in conjunction with, made up of, not to mention, plus, together with, with; SEE CONCEPT *577*

inclusion [*n*] *addition*
admittance, composition, comprisal, embodiment, embracement, encompassment, formation, incorporation, insertion, involvement, subsumption; SEE CONCEPT *642*

inclusive [*adj*] *all-encompassing, all-embracing*
across-the-board*, all-around, all the options*, all together, ball-of-wax*, blanket*, broad, catchall*, comprehensive, encyclopedic, full, general, global, in toto*, overall, sweeping, umbrella*, wall-to-wall*, whole, without exception; SEE CONCEPT *772*

incognito [*adj*] *in disguise*
anonymous, bearded, camouflaged, concealed, disguised, hidden, incog*, isolated, masked, masquerading, obscure, under assumed name, unknown, unrecognized; SEE CONCEPTS *576,589*

incoherent [*adj*] *unintelligible*
breathless, confused, disconnected, discontinuous, discordant, disjointed, disordered, dumb, faltering, inarticulate, incohesive, incomprehensible, incongruous, inconsistent, indistinct, indistinguishable, irrational, jumbled, maundering, muddled, muffled, mumbling, mute, muttered, puzzling, rambling, stammering, stuttering, tongue-tied*, uncommunicative, unconnected, uncoordinated, uneven, unvocal, wandering, wild; SEE CONCEPT *267*

income [*n*] *money earned by work or investments*
assets, avails, benefits, bottom line*, cash, cash flow, commission, compensation, dividends, drawings, earnings, gains, gravy*, gross, harvest, honorarium, interest, in the black*, livelihood, means, net, pay, payoff, proceeds, profit, receipts, returns, revenue, royalty, salary, take home, wage; SEE CONCEPTS *340,344*

incomparable [*adj*] *superlative*
beyond compare, excellent, exceptional, ideal, inimitable, matchless, paramount, peerless, perfect, preeminent, second to none, sovereign, superior, supreme, surpassing, towering, transcendent, ultimate, unequalled, unmatchable, unmatched, unparalleled, unrivalled, unsurpassable; SEE CONCEPT *574*

incompatible [*adj*] *antagonistic, contradictory*
adverse, antipathetic, antipodal, antithetical, clashing, conflicting, contrary, counter, disagreeing, discordant, discrepant, disparate, factious, inadmissible, inappropriate, incoherent, inconformable, incongruous, inconsistent, inconsonant, inconstant, irreconcilable, jarring, marching to a different drummer*, mismatched, night and day*, offbeat*, opposed, opposite, poles apart*, unadapted, uncongenial, unsuitable, unsuited, warring, whale of difference*; SEE CONCEPT *564*

incompetent [*adj*] *unskillful, unable*
amateur, amateurish, awkward, bungling, bush-league*, clumsy, disqualified, floundering, helpless, inadequate, incapable, ineffectual, inefficient, ineligible, inept, inexperienced, inexpert, insufficient, maladroit, not cut out for*, not equal to, not have it*, out to lunch*, raw, unadapted, unequipped, unfit, unfitted, unhandy, uninitiated, unproficient, unqualified, unskilled, untrained, useless; SEE CONCEPT *527*

incomplete [*adj*] *unfinished, wanting*
abridged, broken, crude, defective, deficient, ex-

purgated, fractional, fragmentary, garbled, half-done, immature, imperfect, inadequate, incoherent, insufficient, lacking, meager, part, partial, rough, rude, rudimentary, short, sketchy, unaccomplished, unconsummated, under construction, undeveloped, undone, unexecuted, unpolished; SEE CONCEPT 531

incomprehensible [adj] *not understandable*
baffling, beats me*, beyond comprehension, beyond one's grasp*, clear as mud*, cryptic, Delphic*, enigmatic, fathomless, Greek*, impenetrable, incognizable, inconceivable, inscrutable, mysterious, mystifying, obscure, opaque, over one's head*, perplexing, puzzling, sibylline, unclear, unfathomable, ungraspable, unimaginable, unintelligible, unknowable; SEE CONCEPTS 402,529

inconceivable [adj] *beyond reason, belief*
extraordinary, fantastic, imcomprehensible, implausible, impossible, improbable, incogitable, incredible, insupposable, mind-boggling*, phony, rare, reachy, staggering, strange, thin*, unbelievable, unconvincing, unheard-of, unimaginable, unknowable, unlikely, unsubstantial, unthinkable, weak*, won't fly*, won't wash*; SEE CONCEPTS 529,552

inconclusive [adj] *up in the air*
ambiguous, deficient, incomplete, indecisive, indeterminate, lacking, open, uncertain, unconvincing, undecided, uneventful, unfateful, unfinished, unsatisfactory, unsettled, vague; SEE CONCEPTS 537,548

incongruous [adj] *out of place; absurd*
alien, bizarre, conflicting, contradictory, disconsonant, discordant, disparate, distorted, divergent, extraneous, fantastic, fitful, foreign, illogical, improper, inappropriate, inapropos, inapt, incoherent, incompatible, incongruent, inconsistent, irreconcilable, irregular, jumbled, lopsided, mismatched, out of keeping*, rambling, shifting, twisted, unavailing, unbalanced, unbecoming, unconnected, uncoordinated, uneven, unintelligible, unpredictable, unrelated, unsuitable, unsuited; SEE CONCEPTS 547,558

inconsequential/inconsiderable [adj] *of no significance*
casual, dinky*, entry-level*, exiguous, immaterial, inadequate, inappreciable, inconsequent, insignificant, insufficient, light, little, measly, minor, negligible, paltry, petty, picayune, puny, runt, scanty, shoestring*, skimpy, small, small potatoes*, small-time*, trifling, trivial, two-bit*, unconsidered, unimportant, wimpy*, worthless; SEE CONCEPT 575

inconsiderate [adj] *insensitive to others*
boorish, brash, careless, discourteous, hasty, impolite, incautious, indelicate, intolerant, reckless, rude, self-centered, selfish, sharp, short, tactless, thoughtless, unceremonious, uncharitable, ungracious, unkind, unthinking; SEE CONCEPT 401

inconsistent [adj] *contradictory, irregular*
at odds, at variance, capricious, changeable, conflicting, contrary, discordant, discrepant, dissonant, erratic, fickle, illogical, incoherent, incompatible, in conflict, incongruent, incongruous, inconstant, irreconcilable, lubricious, mercurial, out of step*, temperamental, uncertain, unpredictable, unstable, variable, warring; SEE CONCEPTS 534,564

inconsolable [adj] *brokenhearted*
comfortless, dejected, desolate, despairing, disconsolate, discouraged, distressed, forlorn, heartbroken, heartsick, sad, unconsolable; SEE CONCEPT 403

inconspicuous [adj] *hidden, unnoticeable*
camouflaged, concealed, dim, faint, hidden, indistinct, insignificant, low-key*, low-profile*, modest, muted, ordinary, plain, quiet, retiring, secretive, shy, soft-pedalled*, subtle, tenuous, unassuming, unemphatic, unobtrusive, unostentatious; SEE CONCEPTS 485,576

inconstant [adj] *changeable*
capricious, changeful, erratic, fickle, flickering, fluctuating, impulsive, inconsistent, intermittent, irregular, irresolute, mercurial, shifting, uncertain, undependable, unreliable, unsettled, unstable, vacillating, variable, varying, volatile, waffling, wavering; SEE CONCEPT 534

incontrovertible [adj] *beyond dispute*
accurate, authentic, certain, established, incontestable, indisputable, indubitable, irrefutable, nailed down*, no mistake*, no two ways about it*, positive, sure, surefire*, sure thing*, uncontestable, undeniable, unequivocable, unquestionable, unshakable; SEE CONCEPT 535

inconvenience [n] *bother, trouble*
aggravation, annoyance, awkwardness, bothersomeness, cumbersomeness, difficulty, disadvantage, disruption, disturbance, drawback, exasperation, fuss, hindrance, nuisance, pain*, stew*, trial, troublesomeness, uneasiness, unfitness, unhandiness, unsuitableness, untimeliness, unwieldiness, upset, vexation; SEE CONCEPT 674

inconvenience [v] *bother, trouble*
aggravate, discombobulate, discommode, discompose, disoblige, disrupt, disturb, exasperate, give a hard time*, give trouble*, hang up*, interfere, irk, make it tough*, meddle, put in a spot*, put on the spot*, put to trouble*, try, upset; SEE CONCEPTS 14,242

inconvenient [adj] *bothersome, troublesome*
annoying, awkward, cumbersome, detrimental, difficult, disadvantageous, discommoding, discommodious, disturbing, embarrassing, incommodious, inexpedient, inopportune, pestiferous, prejudicial, remote, tiresome, troublesome, unhandy, unmanageable, unseasonable, unsuitable, untimely, unwieldy, vexatious; SEE CONCEPTS 537,548

incorporate [v] *include, combine*
absorb, add to, amalgamate, assimilate, associate, blend, charter, coalesce, consolidate, cover, dub, embody, form, fuse, gang up*, hook in*, imbibe, integrate, join, link, merge, mix, organize, pool, put together, start, subsume, tie in*, unite; SEE CONCEPTS 112,113,324

incorrect [adj] *wrong*
counterfactual, erroneous, false, faulty, flawed, imprecise, improper, inaccurate, inappropriate, inexact, mistaken, not trustworthy, out*, specious, unfitting, unreliable, unseemly, unsound, unsuitable, untrue, way off*, wide of the mark*, wrong number*; SEE CONCEPTS 558,570

incorrigible [adj] *bad, hopeless*
abandoned, beastly, hardened, incurable, intractable, inveterate, irredeemable, irreparable, loser, recidivous, uncorrectable, unreformed, useless, wicked; SEE CONCEPT 570

incorruptible [*adj*] *honest, honorable*
above suspicion, imperishable, indestructible, inextinguishable, just, loyal, moral, perpetual, persistent, pure, reliable, straight, trustworthy, unbribable, undestroyable, untouchable, upright; SEE CONCEPTS *485,545*

increase [*n*] *addition, growth*
access, accession, accretion, accrual, accumulation, aggrandizement, augmentation, boost, breakthrough, burgeoning, cumulation, development, elaboration, enlargement, escalation, exaggeration, expansion, extension, gain, hike, incorporation, increment, inflation, intensification, maximization, merger, multiplication, optimization, raise, rise, spread, step-up, surge, swell, swelling, upgrade, upsurge, upturn, waxing; SEE CONCEPTS *763,780*

increase [*v*] *add or grow*
advance, aggrandize, aggravate, amplify, annex, augment, boost, broaden, build, build up, deepen, develop, dilate, distend, double, enhance, enlarge, escalate, exaggerate, expand, extend, further, heighten, inflate, intensify, lengthen, magnify, mark up, mount, multiply, pad*, progress, proliferate, prolong, protract, pullulate, raise, redouble, reinforce, rise, sharpen, slap on*, snowball*, spread, step up, strengthen, supplement, swarm, swell, tack on*, teem, thicken, triple, wax, widen; SEE CONCEPTS *236,245,780*

increasingly [*adv*] *to a greater extent*
more, more and more, progressively, with acceleration; SEE CONCEPT *772*

incredible [*adj1*] *beyond belief*
absurd, far-fetched, fishy*, flimsy*, implausible, impossible, improbable, incogitable, inconceivable, insupposable, outlandish, out of the question*, phony, preposterous, questionable, ridiculous, rings phony*, suspect, thin*, unbelievable, unconvincing, unimaginable, unsubstantial, untenable, unthinkable; SEE CONCEPT *552*

incredible [*adj2*] *marvellous*
ace*, amazing, astonishing, astounding, awe-inspiring, awesome, extraordinary, fabulous, glorious, great, prodigious, superhuman*, unreal*, wonderful; SEE CONCEPTS *529,572*

incredulous [*adj*] *unbelieving*
disbelieving, distrustful, doubtful, doubting, dubious, hesitant, mistrustful, questioning, quizzical, show-me*, skeptical, suspect, suspicious, uncertain, unconvinced, unsatisfied, wary; SEE CONCEPTS *403,529*

increment [*n*] *small step toward gain*
accession, accretion, accrual, accrument, addition, advancement, augmentation, enlargement, increase, profit, raise, rise, supplement; SEE CONCEPTS *763,780*

incriminate [*v*] *accuse*
allege, attack, attribute, blame, brand, bring charges, charge, cite, finger*, frame, hold accountable, implicate, inculpate, indict, involve, name, pin on*, point the finger at*, prosecute, serve summons; SEE CONCEPT *44*

incubus [*n*] *evil spirit*
demon, devil, fiend, goblin, hobgoblin, nightmare, succuba, succubus; SEE CONCEPTS *370,412*

inculcate [*v*] *implant, infuse information*
brainwash*, break down, communicate, drill, drum into*, educate, hammer into*, impart, impress, indoctrinate, inseminate, instill, instruct, plant, program, shape up, teach, work over*; SEE CONCEPTS *14,285*

incur [*v*] *bring upon oneself*
acquire, arouse, be subjected to, bring down on*, catch, contract, draw, earn, expose oneself to, gain, get, induce, meet with, obtain, provoke; SEE CONCEPT *93*

incurable [*adj*] *unfixable, unchangeable*
cureless, deadly, fatal, hopeless, immedicable, impossible, inoperable, irrecoverable, irremediable, irreparable, nowhere to go*, out of time*, remediless, serious, terminal, uncorrectable, unrecoverable; SEE CONCEPTS *485,548*

incursion [*n*] *invasion*
aggression, attack, foray, infiltration, inroad, intrusion, irruption, penetration, raid; SEE CONCEPTS *86,320*

indebted [*adj*] *under an obligation*
accountable, answerable for, appreciative, beholden, bound, bounden, chargeable, dutybound, grateful, honor-bound, hooked*, in debt, in hock*, liable, obligated, obliged, owed, owing, responsible, thankful; SEE CONCEPTS *334,546*

indecency [*n*] *obscenity, vulgarity*
bawdiness, coarseness, crudity, drunkenness, evil, foulness, grossness, immodesty, impropriety, impurity, incivility, indecorum, indelicacy, lewdness, licentiousness, offense, outrageousness, pornography, ribaldry, smuttiness, unseemliness, vileness; SEE CONCEPTS *633,645*

indecent [*adj*] *obscene, vulgar; offensive*
blue*, coarse, crude, dirty*, filthy, foul, foulmouthed, gross*, ill-bred, immodest, immoral, improper, impure, in bad taste, indecorous, indelicate, lewd, licentious, malodorous, offcolor*, outrageous, pornographic, raunchy*, raw, ridiculous, rough, salacious, scatological, shameless, shocking, smutty*, tasteless, unbecoming, undecorous, unseemly, untoward, vile, wicked, X-rated*; SEE CONCEPT *545*

indecisive [*adj*] *uncertain, indefinite*
astraddle, changeable, doubtful, faltering, halting, hemming and hawing*, hesitant, hesitating, hot and cold*, inconclusive, indeterminate, irresolute, of two minds*, on the fence*, tentative, unclear, undecided, undetermined, uneventful, unsettled, unstable, vacillating, waffling, wavering, weak-kneed*, wishy-washy*; SEE CONCEPTS *534,535*

indeed [*adv*] *actually*
absolutely, amen*, certainly, doubtlessly, easily, even, for real, in point of fact, in truth, much, naturally, of course, positively, really, strictly, surely, sure thing*, to be sure, truly, undeniably, undoubtedly, verily, veritably, very, very much, well; SEE CONCEPT *535*

indefatigable [*adj*] *untiring*
active, assiduous, bound and determined*, dead set on*, determined, diligent, dogged, energetic, hell-bent*, industrious, inexhaustible, ironclad, nose to grindstone*, painstaking, patient, persevering, persistent, pertinacious, relentless, sedulous, steadfast, stop at nothing*, strenuous, tireless, unfaltering, unflagging, unflinching, unremitting, unwavering, unwearied, unwearying, vigorous; SEE CONCEPT *542*

indefensible [*adj*] *inexcusable*
bad, faulty, inexpiable, insupportable, unforgiv-

in
in

able, unjustifiable, unpardonable, untenable, unwarrantable, wrong; SEE CONCEPTS *545,548*

indefinite [*adj*] *ambiguous, vague*
broad, confused, doubtful, dubious, equivocal, evasive, general, ill-defined, imprecise, indeterminable, indeterminate, indistinct, inexact, inexhaustible, infinite, innumerable, intangible, loose, obscure, shadowy, uncertain, unclear, undefined, undependable, undetermined, unfixed, unknown, unlimited, unsettled, unspecific, unsure, wide; SEE CONCEPT *535*

indefinitely [*adv*] *continually*
considerably, endlessly, forever, frequently, regularly, sine die, without end; SEE CONCEPT *798*

indelible [*adj*] *not able to be erased, indestructible*
enduring, ineffaceable, ineradicable, inerasable, inexpungible, inextirpable, ingrained, lasting, memorable, permanent, rememberable, stirring, unforgettable; SEE CONCEPTS *482,529*

indelicate [*adj*] *obscene, vulgar*
base, brash, brutish, callow, coarse, crude, earthy, embarrassing, immodest, improper, indecent, indecorous, lewd, low, lowbred, off-color*, offensive, outrageous, risqué, rude, suggestive, tasteless, unbecoming, unblushing, uncouth, unseemly, untactful, untoward; SEE CONCEPTS *544,545*

indent [*v*] *make a space; push in slightly*
bash, cave in, cut, dent, depress, dint, hollow, jag, mark, nick, notch, pink, pit, rabbet, rut, scallop, score, serrate; SEE CONCEPTS *158,201,208*

independence [*n*] *liberty, freedom*
ability, aptitude, autarchy, autonomy, home rule*, license, qualification, self-determination, self-government, self-reliance, self-rule, self-sufficiency, separation, sovereignty; SEE CONCEPTS *376,691*

independent [*adj*] *liberated, free*
absolute, autarchic, autarchical, autonomous, freewheeling, individualistic, nonaligned, nonpartisan, on one's own, self-contained, self-determining, self-governing, self-reliant, self-ruling, self-sufficient, self-supporting, separate, separated, sovereign, unaided, unallied, unconnected, unconstrained, uncontrolled, unregimented; SEE CONCEPT *554*

independently [*adv*] *alone*
all by one's self, apart, autonomously, by oneself, exclusive of, freely, individually, of one's own volition, one at a time, one by one, on one's own, separately, severally, singly, solo, unaided, unrestrictedly, unsupervised, without regard to, without support; SEE CONCEPT *554*

indescribable [*adj*] *beyond words*
impossible, incommunicable, indefinable, ineffable, inexpressible, nondescript, sublime, subtle, unspeakable, untellable, unutterable; SEE CONCEPT *267*

indestructible [*adj*] *lasting, unable to be destroyed*
abiding, deathless, durable, enduring, everlasting, immortal, immutable, imperishable, incorruptible, indelible, indissoluble, inexterminable, inextinguishable, inextirpable, irrefragable, irrefrangible, nonperishable, permanent, perpetual, unalterable, unbreakable, unchangeable, undestroyable, undying, unfading; SEE CONCEPTS *489,534*

indeterminate [*adj*] *uncertain, vague*
borderless, general, imprecise, inconclusive, indefinite, indistinct, inexact, undefined, undetermined, unfixed, unspecified, unstipulated; SEE CONCEPT *535*

index [*n*] *indication*
basis, clue, evidence, formula, guide, hand, indicant, indication, indicator, indicia, mark, model, needle, pointer, ratio, rule, sign, significant, symbol, symptom, token; SEE CONCEPTS *284,290*

index [*v*] *arrange, order*
alphabetize, catalogue, docket, file, list, record, tabulate; SEE CONCEPT *84*

indicate [*v*] *signify, display*
add up to, announce, argue, attest, augur, bespeak, be symptomatic, betoken, button down*, card, connote, demonstrate, denote, designate, evidence, evince, express, finger, hint, illustrate, imply, import, intimate, make, manifest, mark, mean, name, peg*, pin down*, pinpoint*, point out, point to, prove, read, record, register, reveal, show, sign, signal, slot, specify, suggest, symbolize, tab, tag, testify, witness; SEE CONCEPTS *74,118,266*

indication [*n*] *evidence, clue*
adumbration, attestation, augury, auspice, cue, earnest, explanation, expression, forewarning, gesture, hint, implication, index, indicia, inkling, intimation, manifestation, mark, nod, note, notion, omen, pledge, portent, preamble, prefiguration, prognostic, prolegomenon, proof, reminder, show, sign, signal, significant, signifier, suggestion, symptom, telltale, token, trace, vestige, warning, wind*, wink*; SEE CONCEPTS *74,278,284*

indicative [*adj*] *exhibitive*
apocalyptic, augural, auspicious, characteristic, connotative, demonstrative, denotative, denotive, designative, diagnostic, emblematic, evidential, evincive, expressive, inauspicious, indicatory, indicial, ominous, pointing to, prognostic, significant, significatory, suggestive, symbolic, symptomatic, testatory, testimonial; SEE CONCEPT *267*

indicator [*n*] *sign*
barometer, beacon, clue, dial, gauge, guide, hint, index, mark, meter, omen, pointer, signal, symbol, warning; SEE CONCEPTS *274,529,673,689*

indict [*v*] *accuse*
arraign, censure, charge, criminate, face with charges, finger*, frame*, impeach, incriminate, inculpate, prosecute, summon, tax; SEE CONCEPTS *44,317*

indictment [*n*] *accusation*
allegation, arraignment, bill, blame, censure, charge, citation, detention, findings, impeachment, incrimination, presentment, prosecution, statement, summons, warrant, writ; SEE CONCEPTS *44,317,318*

indifference [*n*] *absence of feeling, interest*
alienation, aloofness, apathy, callousness, carelessness, cold-bloodedness, coldness, cold shoulder*, coolness, detachment, disdain, disinterest, disinterestedness, dispassion, disregard, equity, heedlessness, immunity, impartiality, impassiveness, impassivity, inattention, inertia, insensitivity, insouciance, isolationism, lack, lethargy, listlessness, negligence, neutrality, nonchalance, noninterference, objectivity, stoicism, torpor, unconcern, unmindfulness; SEE CONCEPTS *410,657*

indifferent [*adj*] *unfeeling, uninterested*
aloof, apathetic, blasé, callous, cold, cool, detached, diffident, disinterested, dispassionate, distant, equitable, haughty, heartless, heedless, highbrow, impartial, impervious, inattentive, listless, neutral, nonchalant, nonpartisan, objective, passionless, phlegmatic, regardless, scornful, silent, stoical, supercilious, superior, unaroused, unbiased, uncaring, uncommunicative, unconcerned, unemotional, unimpressed, uninvolved, unmoved, unprejudiced, unresponsive, unsocial, unsympathetic; SEE CONCEPTS *403,542*

indigenous [*adj*] *native, inborn*
aboriginal, autochthonous, chthonic, congenital, connate, domestic, endemic, homegrown, inbred, inherent, inherited, innate, natural, original, primitive, unacquired; SEE CONCEPT *549*

indigent [*adj*] *poor*
beggared, busted, destitute, down and out*, flat broke*, hard up*, homeless, impecunious, impoverished, in want, necessitous, needy, penniless, penurious, poverty-stricken; SEE CONCEPT *334*

indigestion [*n*] *upset stomach*
acid indigestion, acidosis, digestive upset, dyspepsia, dyspepsy, flatulence, flu, gas, gaseous stomach, heartburn, nausea, pain; SEE CONCEPT *306*

indignant [*adj*] *angry*
acrimonious, annoyed, bent out of shape*, boiling*, bugged*, burned up*, disgruntled, displeased, exasperated, fuming, furious, heated, huffy*, in a huff*, incensed, irate, livid, mad, miffed, peeved, piqued, p.o.'d*, provoked, resentful, riled, scornful, seeing red*, up in arms*, upset, wrathful; SEE CONCEPTS *403,542*

indignation [*n*] *anger*
animus, boiling point*, danger, displeasure, exasperation, fury, huff*, ire, mad, miff*, pique, rage, resentment, rise, scorn, slow burn*, umbrage, wrath; SEE CONCEPTS *29,657*

indignity [*n*] *embarrassment, humiliation*
abuse, affront, backhanded compliment*, contumely, discourtesy, dishonor, disrespect, grievance, injury, injustice, insult, obloquy, opprobrium, outrage, put-down*, reproach, slap*, slight, slur, snub, take-down*, taunt; SEE CONCEPTS *278,410*

indirect [*adj*] *roundabout; unintended*
ambiguous, ancillary, circuitous, circular, circumlocutory, collateral, complicated, contingent, crooked, devious, discursive, duplicitous, erratic, eventual, implied, incidental, long, long-drawn-out*, long way home*, long-winded*, meandering, oblique, obscure, out-of-the-way, periphrastic, rambling, secondary, serpentine*, sidelong, sinister, sinuous, snaking*, sneaking, sneaky, subsidiary, tortuous, twisting, underhand, vagrant, wandering, winding, zigzag; SEE CONCEPTS *544,581*

indiscreet [*adj*] *injudicious*
careless, foolish, hasty, heedless, imprudent, inconsiderate, insensitive, rash, reckless, unthinking; SEE CONCEPT *542*

indiscretion [*n*] *mistake*
bumble, crudeness, dropping the ball*, dumb move*, error, excitability, faux pas, folly, foolishness, fool mistake*, foul-up, gaffe, gaucherie, goof*, hastiness, imprudence, indiscreetness, ingenuousness, lapse, miscue, misjudgment, miss-

peak, naíveté, rashness, recklessness, screw-up*, simple-mindedness, slip*, slip of the tongue*, slip-up*, stumble, stupidity, tactlessness, thoughtlessness, unseemliness; SEE CONCEPTS *101,633,674*

indiscriminate [*adj*] *random, chaotic*
aimless, assorted, broad, careless, confused, designless, desultory, extensive, general, haphazard, heterogeneous, hit-or-miss*, imperceptive, jumbled, mingled, miscellaneous, mixed, mongrel, motley*, multifarious, promiscuous, purposeless, shallow, spot, superficial, sweeping, unconsidered, uncritical, undiscriminating, unmethodical, unplanned, unselective, unsystematic, varied, variegated, wholesale*, wide; SEE CONCEPTS *403,542,585,772*

indispensable [*adj*] *necessary*
basal, basic, cardinal, crucial, essential, fundamental, imperative, key, necessitous, needed, needful, prerequisite, primary, required, requisite, vital; SEE CONCEPT *546*

indisposed [*adj1*] *not well*
ailing, below par, confined, down, down with*, feeling rotten*, got a bug*, ill, infirm, laid up*, on sick list*, out of action*, poorly, sick, sickly, under the weather*, unwell; SEE CONCEPT *314*

indisposed [*adj2*] *unwilling*
afraid, antagonistic, antipathetic, averse, backward, disinclined, hesitant, hostile, inimical, loath, reluctant, uncaring, uneager, uninclined; SEE CONCEPT *542*

indisputable [*adj*] *beyond doubt*
absolute, accurate, actual, certain, double-checked, evident, incontestable, incontrovertible, indubitable, irrefutable, no ifs ands or buts about it*, no mistake*, open and shut*, positive, real, sure, that's a fact*, true, unassailable, undeniable, undoubted, unfabled, unquestionable, veridical; SEE CONCEPTS *535,582*

indistinct [*adj*] *obscure, ambiguous*
bleared, bleary, blurred, confused, dark, dim, doubtful, faint, fuzzy, hazy, ill-defined, inaudible, inconspicuous, indefinite, indeterminate, indiscernible, indistinguishable, inexact, misty, muffled, murky, out of focus, shadowy, unclear, undefined, undetermined, unheard, unintelligible, vague, weak; SEE CONCEPTS *485,535*

indistinguishable [*adj*] *alike*
duplicate, equivalent, identic, identical, like, same, tantamount, twin; SEE CONCEPT *566*

individual [*adj*] *distinctive, exclusive*
alone, characteristic, definite, diacritic, diagnostic, different, discrete, distinct, especial, express, idiosyncratic, indivisible, lone, odd, only, original, own, particular, peculiar, personal, personalized, proper, reserved, respective, secluded, select, separate, several, single, singular, sole, solitary, special, specific, uncommon, unique, unitary, unusual; SEE CONCEPTS *404,564*

individual [*n*] *singular person, thing*
being, body, character, child, creature, dude*, entity, existence, human being, man, material, matter, mortal, number, party, person, personage, self, singleton, somebody, something, soul, stuff, substance, type, unit, woman; SEE CONCEPTS *389,433*

individuality [*n*] *personality*
air, character, complexion, difference, discreteness, disposition, dissimilarity, distinction, distinctiveness, eccentricity, habit, humor, identity,

idiosyncrasy, independence, individualism, ipseity, makeup, manner, nature, oddity, oneness, originality, particularity, peculiarity, rarity, seity, selfdom, selfhood, selfness, separateness, singleness, singularity, singularness, temper, temperament, uniqueness, unity, unlikeness, way; SEE CONCEPT *411*

individually [*adv*] *separately*
alone, apart, by oneself, distinctively, exclusively, independently, one at a time, one by one, personally, restrictedly, severally, singly, without help; SEE CONCEPT *544*

individual retirement account [*n*] *IRA*
Keogh plan, retirement plan, Roth IRA, self-funded retirement plan, tax-free savings account; SEE CONCEPTS *335,340,446,710*

indoctrinate [*v*] *brainwash*
break down, convince, drill, ground, imbue, implant, inculcate, influence, initiate, instill, instruct, plant, program, school, teach, train, work over; SEE CONCEPTS *14,285*

indolent [*adj*] *lazy*
drony, easygoing, fainéant, idle, inactive, inert, lackadaisical, languid, lax, lazy, lethargic, listless, resting, shiftless, slothful, slow, slow-going, sluggish, torpid; SEE CONCEPTS *538,542,584*

indomitable [*adj*] *steadfast, unyielding*
dogged, impassable, impregnable, insuperable, insurmountable, invincible, invulnerable, obstinate, pertinacious, resolute, ruthless, staunch, stubborn, unassailable, unbeatable, unconquerable, undefeatable, unflinching, willful; SEE CONCEPTS *404,489,534*

indubitably [*adv*] *unquestionably*
certainly, definitely, for sure, indeed, no question, of course, positively, surely, undoubtedly, without doubt; SEE CONCEPT *535*

induce [*v*] *cause to happen; encourage*
abet, activate, actuate, argue into, breed, bring about, bring around, bulldoze*, cajole, cause, coax, convince, draw, draw in, effect, engender, generate, get*, get up, give rise to, goose*, impel, incite, influence, instigate, lead to, make, motivate, move, occasion, persuade, press, prevail upon, procure, produce, promote, prompt, sell one on*, set in motion, soft-soap*, squeeze, steamroll*, suck in*, sway, sweet-talk*, talk into*, twist one's arm*, urge, wheedle, win over*; SEE CONCEPTS *14,68,242*

inducement [*n*] *incentive, motive*
attraction, bait, brainwash*, carrot*, cause, come-on*, con*, consideration, desire, encouragement, hard sell*, hook*, impulse, incitement, influence, leader, lure, reward, snow job*, soft soap*, spur, stimulus, sweet talk*, temptation, twist, urge; SEE CONCEPTS *68,661*

induct [*v*] *take into an organization*
conscript, draft, enlist, inaugurate, initiate, install, instate, introduce, invest, recruit, sign on, sign up, swear in; SEE CONCEPTS *50,88,320,384*

induction [*n1*] *taking in, initiation*
consecration, draft, entrance, greetings, inaugural, inauguration, installation, instatement, institution, introduction, investiture, ordination, selection; SEE CONCEPTS *320,384,685*

induction [*n2*] *inference*
conclusion, conjecture, deducement, generalization, judgment, logical reasoning, ratiocination, rationalization, reason; SEE CONCEPTS *37,689*

indulge [*v1*] *treat oneself or another to*
allow, baby, cater, coddle, cosset, delight, entertain, favor, foster, give in, give rein to*, go along, go easy on*, gratify, humor, mollycoddle*, nourish, oblige, pamper, pander, pet, please, regale, satiate, satisfy, spoil, spoil rotten*, take care of*, tickle, yield; SEE CONCEPT *110*

indulge [*v2*] *luxuriate in*
bask in, ego trip*, enjoy, go in for*, live it up*, look out for number one*, revel in, rollick*, take part, wallow in; SEE CONCEPT *20*

indulgence [*n*] *luxury; gratification*
allowance, appeasement, attention, babying*, coddling*, courtesy, endurance, excess, extravagance, favor, favoring, fondling, fondness, forbearance, fulfillment, goodwill, gratifying, hedonism, immoderation, intemperance, intemperateness, kindness, kowtowing*, lenience, leniency, pampering, partiality, patience, permissiveness, petting, placating, pleasing, privilege, profligacy, profligateness, satiation, satisfaction, service, spoiling, toadying*, tolerance, toleration, treating, understanding; SEE CONCEPTS *337,657,712*

indulgent [*adj*] *lenient, giving*
able to live with*, big*, charitable, clement, compassionate, complaisant, compliant, considerate, easy, easygoing, favorable, fond, forbearing, gentle, going along with*, going easy on*, gratifying, kind, kindly, liberal, merciful, mild, overpermissive, permissive, soft-shelled*, tender, tolerant, understanding; SEE CONCEPTS *404,542*

industrial [*adj*] *related to manufacturing*
automated, business, factory-made, industrialized, in industry, machine-made, manufactured, manufacturing, mechanical, mechanized, modern, smokestack, streamlined, technical; SEE CONCEPT *536*

industrious [*adj*] *hardworking*
active, assiduous, ball of fire*, burning, busy, conscientious, diligent, dynamic, eager, energetic, grind*, in full swing*, intent, involved, jumping, laborious, on the go*, operose, perky*, persevering, persistent, plugging, productive, psyched up on*, purposeful, sedulous, spirited, steady, tireless, zealous; SEE CONCEPT *538*

industry [*n1*] *manufacturing*
big business*, business, commerce, commercial enterprise, corporation, management, manufactory, megacorp*, mob, monopoly, multinational, outfit*, production, trade, traffic; SEE CONCEPTS *323,325*

industry [*n2*] *hard work*
activity, application, assiduity, attention, care, determination, diligence, dynamism, effort, energy, enterprise, intentness, inventiveness, labor, pains, patience, perseverance, persistence, tirelessness, toil, vigor, zeal; SEE CONCEPT *677*

inebriated [*adj*] *drunk*
blind drunk*, bombed, boozy, high*, inebriate, intoxicated, loaded*, plastered*, smashed*, tight*, tipsy, under the influence, wasted*; SEE CONCEPT *314*

ineffable [*adj*] *too great for words*
beyond words, celestial, divine, empyreal, empyrean, ethereal, heavenly, holy, ideal, impossible, incommunicable, incredible, indefinable, indescribable, inexpressible, nameless, sacred,

spiritual, too sacred for words*, transcendent, transcendental, unspeakable, untellable, unutterable; SEE CONCEPTS *267,574*

ineffective/ineffectual [*adj*] *weak, useless*
abortive, anticlimactic, barren, bootless, defeasible, feckless, feeble, forceless, fruitless, futile, idle, impotent, inadequate, incompetent, indecisive, inefficacious, inefficient, inept, inferior, innocuous, inoperative, invertebrate, lame, limited, neutralized, nugatory, null, null and void*, paltry, powerless, spineless, unable, unavailing, unfruitful, unproductive, unprofitable, unsuccessful, vain, void, withered, worthless; SEE CONCEPTS *537,560*

inefficient [*adj*] *not working well; wasteful*
can't hack it*, careless, disorganized, extravagant, faulty, feeble, half-baked*, improficient, improvident, incapable, incompetent, ineffective, ineffectual, inefficacious, inept, inexpert, not cut out for*, prodigal, shooting blanks*, slack, slipshod, sloppy, slovenly, unfit, unprepared, unqualified, unskilled, unskillful, untrained, weak; SEE CONCEPTS *402,527,560*

inelegant [*adj*] *clumsy, crude*
awkward, coarse, crass, gauche, graceless, gross, indelicate, labored, oafish, raw, rough, rude, stiff*, uncouth, uncultivated, uncultured, ungainly, ungraceful, unpolished, unrefined, vulgar, wooden*; SEE CONCEPTS *267,542,555*

ineligible [*adj*] *not qualified*
disqualified, inappropriate, incompetent, objectionable, ruled out, unacceptable, unavailable, undesirable, unequipped, unfit, unqualified, unsuitable; SEE CONCEPTS *402,558*

inept [*adj1*] *clumsy, unskilled; incompetent*
all thumbs*, artless, awkward, bumbling, bungling, butterfingers*, gauche, halting, inadept, incapable, incompetent, inefficient, inexpert, loser, maladroit, unapt, undexterous, unfacile, ungraceful, unhandy, unproficient, unskillful, wooden*; SEE CONCEPTS *402,527*

inept [*adj2*] *not suitable; improper*
absurd, ill-timed, inappropriate, inapt, infelicitous, malapropos, meaningless, not adapted, out of place*, pointless, ridiculous, undue, unfit, unseasonable, unseemly, unsuitable; SEE CONCEPT *558*

inequality [*n*] *prejudice; lack of balance*
asperity, bias, contrast, difference, discrimination, disparity, disproportion, dissimilarity, dissimilitude, diversity, imparity, incommensurateness, injustice, irregularity, one-sidedness, partisanship, preferentiality, roughness, unequivalence, unevenness, unfairness, unjustness, variation; SEE CONCEPT *665*

inequitable [*adj*] *unfair*
arbitrary, biased, discriminatory, one-sided, partial, partisan, prejudiced, unbalanced, unequal, unethical, uneven, unjust; SEE CONCEPTS *480,544,545,548*

inert [*adj*] *not moving; lifeless*
apathetic, asleep, dead, dormant, down, dull, idle, immobile, impassive, impotent, inactive, inanimate, indolent, languid, languorous, lazy, leaden, listless, motionless, numb, paralyzed, passive, phlegmatic, powerless, quiescent, quiet, slack, sleepy, slothful, sluggard, sluggish, slumberous, static, still, stolid, torpid, unmoving, unreactive, unresponsive; SEE CONCEPTS *542,584*

inertia [*n*] *disinclination to move; lifelessness*
apathy, deadness, drowsiness, dullness, idleness, immobility, immobilization, inactivity, indolence, languor, lassitude, laziness, lethargy, listlessness, oscitancy, paralysis, passivity, sloth, sluggishness, stillness, stupor, torpidity, torpor, unresponsiveness; SEE CONCEPTS *657,681*

inevitable [*adj*] *certain; cannot be avoided*
all locked up*, assured, binding, compulsory, decided, decreed, destined, determined, doomed, fated, fateful, fixed, for certain, foreordained, imminent, impending, ineluctable, ineludible, inescapable, inexorable, inflexible, in the bag*, irresistible, irrevocable, necessary, no ifs ands or buts*, obligatory, ordained, pat*, prescribed, settled, sure, unalterable, unavoidable, undeniable, unpreventable, without recourse; SEE CONCEPTS *535,552*

inexcusable [*adj*] *not forgivable*
blamable, blameworthy, censurable, criticizable, impermissible, indefensible, inexpiable, intolerable, outrageous, reprehensible, unallowable, unforgivable, unjustifiable, unpardonable, unpermissible, untenable, unwarrantable, wrong; SEE CONCEPTS *545,570*

inexhaustible [*adj1*] *unlimited*
bountiful, endless, infinite, limitless, never-ending, no end to*, numberless; SEE CONCEPT *772*

inexhaustible [*adj2*] *tireless*
enduring, indefatigable, unflagging, untiring, unwearying, vigorous; SEE CONCEPTS *538,542*

inexorable [*adj*] *cruel, pitiless*
adamant, adamantine, bound, bound and determined*, compulsory, dead set on*, dogged, hard, harsh, hell bent on*, immobile, immovable, implacable, ineluctable, inescapable, inflexible, ironclad, like death and taxes*, locked in*, mean business*, merciless, necessary, no going back*, obdurate, obstinate, relentless, remorseless, resolute, rigid, set in stone*, severe, single-minded, stubborn, unappeasable, unbending, uncompromising, unmovable, unrelenting, unyielding; SEE CONCEPTS *401,534*

inexpensive [*adj*] *not high priced*
bargain, budget, buy, cheap, cost next to nothing*, cut-rate, dime a dozen*, dirt-cheap*, economical, for a song*, half-price, low, low-cost, low-priced, marked down, modest, nominal, popular, popularly priced, real buy*, real steal*, reasonable, reduced, steal, thrifty; SEE CONCEPT *334*

inexperienced [*adj*] *unskilled, unfamiliar*
amateur, callow, fresh, green*, ignorant, immature, inept, inexpert, innocent, kid*, naive, new, prentice, raw*, rookie, rude, sophomoric, spring chicken*, tenderfoot*, unaccustomed, unacquainted, unconversant, undisciplined, unfamiliar with, unfledged, unpracticed, unschooled, unseasoned, unsophisticated, untrained, untried, unused, unversed, unworldly, verdant, wet behind ears*, young; SEE CONCEPTS *402,404,527*

inexplicable [*adj*] *beyond comprehension, explanation*
baffling, enigmatic, incomprehensible, indecipherable, indescribable, inexplainable, inscrutable, insoluble, mysterious, mystifying, obscure, odd, peculiar, puzzling, strange, unaccountable, undefinable, unexplainable, unfathomable, unintelligible, unsolvable; SEE CONCEPTS *267,529*

in
in

infallible [*adj*] *unerring, dependable*
acceptable, accurate, agreeable, apodictic, authoritative, certain, correct, effective, effectual, efficacious, efficient, exact, faultless, flawless, foolproof, handy, helpful, impeccable, incontrovertible, inerrable, inerrant, omniscient, perfect, positive, reliable, satisfactory, satisfying, sure, surefire, true, trustworthy, unbeatable, undeceivable, unfailing, unimpeachable, unquestionable, useful; SEE CONCEPTS *535,560,574*

infamous [*adj*] *shameful, bad in reputation*
abominable, atrocious, base, caitiff, contemptible, corrupt, degenerate, despicable, detestable, disgraceful, dishonorable, disreputable, egregious, evil, flagitious, foul, hateful, heinous, ignominious, ill-famed, iniquitous, loathsome, miscreant, monstrous, nefarious, notorious, odious, offensive, opprobrious, outrageous, perverse, questionable, rotten, scandalous, scurvy, shady, shocking, sorry, unhealthy, vicious, vile, villainous, wicked; SEE CONCEPTS *404,545,570*

infamy [*n*] *shameful, bad reputation*
abomination, atrocity, disapprobation, discredit, disesteem, disgrace, dishonor, disrepute, enormity, evil, ignominy, immorality, impropriety, notoriety, notoriousness, obloquy, odium, opprobrium, outrageousness, scandal, shame, stigma, villainy, wickedness; SEE CONCEPTS *411,645*

infant [*n*] *baby*
babe, bairn, bambino, bantling, bundle, child, kid, little one, neonate, newborn, small child, suckling, toddler, tot; SEE CONCEPTS *414,424*

infant/infantile [*adj*] *very young*
baby, babyish, callow, childish, childlike, dawning, developing, early, emergent, green*, growing, immature, infantine, initial, juvenile, kid, naive, nascent, newborn, puerile, tender, unfledged, unripe, weak, youthful; SEE CONCEPTS *542,578,797,820*

infatuated [*adj*] *in love with; obsessed*
beguiled, besotted, bewitched, captivated, carried away*, charmed, crazy about*, enamored, enraptured, far gone on*, fascinated, foolish, inflamed, intoxicated, possessed, seduced, silly*, smitten, spellbound, under a spell*; SEE CONCEPTS *32,403*

infect [*v*] *pollute, contaminate*
affect, blight, corrupt, defile, disease, influence, poison, spoil, spread among, spread to, taint, touch, vitiate; SEE CONCEPTS *143,246*

infection [*n*] *contamination*
bug*, communicability, contagion, contagiousness, corruption, defilement, disease, epidemic, flu, germs, impurity, insanitation, poison, pollution, septicity, virus, what's going around*; SEE CONCEPTS *230,306*

infectious [*adj*] *catching, spreading*
communicable, contagious, contaminating, corrupting, defiling, diseased, epidemic, infective, mephitic, miasmic, noxious, pestilent, pestiltial, poisoning, polluting, toxic, transferable, transmittable, virulent, vitiating; SEE CONCEPTS *314,559*

infer [*v*] *conclude*
arrive at, ascertain, assume, believe, collect, conjecture, construe, deduce, derive, draw, draw inference, figure, figure out, gather, glean, guess, induce, interpret, intuit, judge, presume, presuppose, reach conclusion, read between lines*, read into*, reason, reckon, speculate, suppose, surmise, think, understand; SEE CONCEPTS *12,15,37*

inference [*n*] *conclusion, deduction*
assumption, conjecture, corollary, guess, hint, interpretation, presumption, reading, reasoning, supposition; SEE CONCEPT *689*

inferior [*adj1*] *less in rank, importance*
back seat*, bottom, bottom-rung*, entry-level, junior, less, lesser, lower, menial, minor, minus, nether, peon, second, secondary, second-banana*, second-fiddle*, second-string*, smaller, subjacent, subordinate, subsidiary, under, underneath; SEE CONCEPT *567*

inferior [*adj2*] *poor, second-rate*
average, bad, base, common, déclassé, fair, good-for-nothing*, hack*, imperfect, indifferent, junk*, lemon*, lousy, low-grade, low-rent*, mean, mediocre, middling, ordinary, paltry, poorer, sad, second-class, sorry*, substandard, tawdry, two-bit*, worse, wretched; SEE CONCEPT *574*

inferior [*n*] *person of lesser rank, importance*
adherent, attendant, auxiliary, deputy, disciple, follower, hanger-on, hireling, junior, menial, minion, minor, peon, satellite, second banana*, subaltern, subject, subordinate, sycophant, underling; SEE CONCEPTS *348,423*

infernal [*adj*] *damned; underworld*
accursed, blamed, blasted, chthonian, confounded, cursed, cussed, damnable, demonic, devilish, diabolical, execrable, fiendish, hellish, lower, malevolent, malicious, monstrous, nether, satanic, subterranean, sulphurous, wicked; SEE CONCEPTS *536,545*

inferno [*n*] *hell*
blazes*, bottomless pit*, everlasting fire*, fire and brimstone*, Hades, hellfire, netherworld, purgatory, underworld; SEE CONCEPTS *370,435, 674*

infertile [*adj*] *not bearing fruit, young*
barren, depleted, drained, effete, exhausted, impotent, impoverished, infecund, nonproductive, sterile, unbearing, unfertile, unfruitful, unproductive; SEE CONCEPTS *406,560*

infest [*adj*] *flood, overrun*
abound, annoy, assail, beset, crawl, crowd, defile, fill, flock, harass, harry, infect, invade, overspread, overwhelm, pack, penetrate, pester, plague, pollute, press, ravage, swarm, teem, throng, worry; SEE CONCEPTS *14,86,179*

infidel [*n*] *nonbeliever*
agnostic, atheist, gentile, heathen, heretic, nonworshiper, pagan, unbeliever; SEE CONCEPT *689*

infidelity [*n*] *disloyalty to an obligation*
adultery, affair, bad faith, betrayal, cheating, duplicity, extramarital relations, faithlessness, falseness, falsity, inconstancy, lewdness, perfidiousness, perfidy, treacherousness, treachery, treason, two-timing*, unfaithfulness; SEE CONCEPTS *388,645*

infiltrate [*v*] *creep in*
access, crack*, edge in, filter through, foist, impregnate, insinuate, penetrate, percolate*, permeate, pervade, saturate, sneak in, tinge, work into, worm into*; SEE CONCEPTS *159,179*

infinite [*adj*] *limitless, without end*
absolute, all-embracing, bottomless, boundless, enduring, enormous, eternal, everlasting, illimitable, immeasurable, immense, incalculable, incessant, inestimable, inexhaustible, interminable,

measureless, million, never-ending, no end of, no end to, numberless, perdurable, perpetual, sempiternal, stupendous, supertemporal, supreme, total, unbounded, uncounted, unending, untold, vast, wide, without limit, without number; SEE CONCEPTS *762,781,798*

infinitesimal [*adj*] *small*
atomic, imperceptible, inappreciable, inconsiderable, insignificant, little, microscopic, miniature, minuscule, minute, negligible, teeny*, tiny, unnoticeable; SEE CONCEPTS *773,789*

infinity [*n*] *endlessness*
beyond, boundlessness, continuity, continuum, endless time, eternity, expanse, extent, immeasurability, immensity, infinitude, limitlessness, myriad, perpetuity, sempiternity, space, ubiquity, unlimited space, vastitude, vastness; SEE CONCEPTS *730,807*

infirm [*adj*] *sick, weak*
ailing, anemic, anile, debilitated, decrepit, delicate, enfeebled, failing, faint, faltering, feeble, flimsy, fragile, frail, halting, ill, insecure, irresolute, laid low*, lame, sensile, shaky, unsound, unstable, unsubstantial, vacillating, wavering, wobbly; SEE CONCEPTS *314,485,489*

infirmity [*n*] *weakness, sickness*
affliction, ailing, ailment, confinement, debilitation, debility, decay, decrepitude, defect, deficiency, disease, diseasedness, disorder, failing, fault, feebleness, flu, frailty, ill health, imperfection, indisposition, malady, malaise, shortcoming, sickliness, unhealth, unhealthiness, unwellness, vulnerability; SEE CONCEPTS *306, 674,732*

inflame [*v*] *anger, aggravate*
agitate, annoy, arouse, burn, disturb, embitter, enrage, exacerbate, exasperate, excite, fan, fire, fire up, foment, gall, get*, grate, heat, heat up, ignite, impassion, incense, increase, infuriate, intensify, intoxicate, irritate, kindle, light, madden, provoke, put out*, rile, roil, rouse, steam up, stimulate, vex, worsen; SEE CONCEPTS *7,14,19, 22,249*

inflammable [*adj*] *ready to burn*
burnable, combustible, dangerous, flammable, hazardous, ignitable, incendiary, risky, unsafe; SEE CONCEPT *485*

inflammation [*n*] *redness, swelling*
burning, infection, irritation, pain, rash, sore, tenderness; SEE CONCEPTS *306,309*

inflammatory [*adj*] *instigative, angering*
anarchic, demagogic, exciting, explosive, fiery, incendiary, incitive, inflaming, insurgent, intemperate, provocative, rabble-rousing*, rabid, rebellious, revolutionary, riotous, seditionary, seditious; SEE CONCEPTS *537,542*

inflate [*v*] *blow up, increase*
aerate, aggrandize, amplify, augment, balloon*, beef up*, bloat, boost, build up, cram*, dilate, distend, enlarge, escalate, exaggerate, exalt, expand, flesh out*, magnify, maximize, overestimate, pad*, puff up*, pump up*, pyramid, raise, spread, stretch, surcharge, swell up*, widen; SEE CONCEPTS *236,245,780*

inflated [*adj*] *exaggerated*
aggrandized, amplified, augmented, aureate, bloated, bombastic, diffuse, dilated, distended, dropsical, enlarged, euphuistic, extended, filled, flatulent, flowery, fustian, grandiloquent, grown, magnified, magniloquent, ostentatious,

overblown, overestimated, pompous, pretentious, prolix, puffed, pumped up, ranting, rhapsodical, rhetorical, showy, spread, stretched, surcharged, swollen, tumescent, tumid, turgid, verbose, windy, wordy; SEE CONCEPTS *267,773*

inflation [*n*] *increase, swelling*
aggrandizement, blowing up, boom, boost, buildup, distension, enhancement, enlargement, escalation, expansion, extension, hike, intensification, prosperity, puffiness, rise, spread, tumefaction; SEE CONCEPTS *335,763,780*

inflection [*n*] *accent, intonation*
articulation, change, emphasis, enunciation, modulation, pitch, pronunciation, sound, timbre, tonality, tone, tone of voice, variation; SEE CONCEPTS *65,595*

inflexible [*adj1*] *stubborn*
adamant, adamantine, determined, dogged, dyed-in-the-wool*, firm, fixed, hard, hard-and-fast*, immovable, immutable, implacable, indomitable, inexorable, intractable, iron, obdurate, obstinate, relentless, resolute, rigid, rigorous, set, set in one's ways*, single-minded, stand one's ground*, staunch, steadfast, steely, stiff, strict, stringent, unadaptable, unbending, unchangeable, uncompliant, uncompromising, unrelenting, unswayable, unyielding; SEE CONCEPT *404*

inflexible [*adj2*] *hardened, stiff*
hard, immalleable, impliable, inelastic, nonflexible, rigid, set, starched, taut, unbending; SEE CONCEPT *604*

inflict [*v*] *impose something*
administer, apply, bring upon, command, deal out, deliver, dispense, exact, expose, extort, force, force upon, give, give it to*, lay down the law*, levy, mete out, require, stick it to*, strike, subject, visit, wreak; SEE CONCEPTS *50,53,88,242*

influence [*n*] *power, authority*
access, agency, ascendancy, character, clout, command, connections, consequence, control, credit, direction, domination, dominion, drag, effect, esteem, fame, fix, force, grease*, guidance, hold, impact, importance, imprint, in, juice*, leadership, leverage, magnetism, mark, moment, money, monopoly, network, notoriety, predominance, prerogative, pressure, prestige, prominence, pull, repercussion, reputation, ropes*, rule, significance, spell, supremacy, sway, weight*; SEE CONCEPT *687*

influence [*v*] *lead to believe, do*
act upon, affect, alter, argue into, arouse, be recognized, bias, brainwash*, bribe, bring to bear, carry weight, change, channel, compel, control, count, determine, direct, dispose, form, get at*, guide, have a part in, impact on, impel, impress, incite, incline, induce, instigate, manipulate, modify, mold, move, persuade, predispose, prejudice, prevail, prompt, pull strings*, regulate, rouse, rule, seduce, sell, shape, snow*, sway, talk into, train, turn, urge, work upon; SEE CONCEPTS *18,68,242*

influential [*adj*] *effective, powerful*
affecting, authoritative, big-gun*, big-wheel*, controlling, dominant, efficacious, famous, forcible, governing, guiding, hot-dog*, important, impressive, inspiring, instrumental, leading, major-league*, meaningful, momentous, moving, name, persuasive, potent, prominent, significant, strong, substantial, telling, touching, weighty; SEE CONCEPTS *537,568*

in
in

influx [n] *flow, rush*
arrival, coming in, convergence, entrance, incursion, inflow, inpouring, inrush, introduction, inundation, invasion, penetration; SEE CONCEPTS *159,179,786*

infomercial [n] *full-length television program existing solely to market a product*
advertorial, commercial, demonstration, documentation, infotainment, paid announcement; SEE CONCEPT *277*

inform [v] *communicate knowledge, information*
acquaint, advise, apprise, betray, blab*, brief, caution, clue, edify, educate, endow, endue, enlighten, familiarize, fill in, forewarn, give a pointer, give a tip, give away, give two cents*, illuminate, inspire, instruct, invest, leak, let in on*, let know, level, make conversant with, notify, post, relate, send word, show the ropes*, snitch, squeal, tattle, teach, tell, tell on, tip, tout, update, warn, wise; SEE CONCEPT *60*

informal [adj] *casual, simple*
breezy, colloquial, congenial, cool*, democratic, down home*, easy, easygoing, everyday, extempore, familiar, folksy, frank, free, free-and-easy*, homey, improv*, inconspicuous, intimate, laid back*, loose, low-pressure, mellow, mixed, motley, natural, off-the-cuff*, open, ordinary, relaxed, spontaneous, sporty, straightforward, throwaway*, unceremonious, unconstrained, unconventional, unfussy, unofficial, unrestrained, urbane, without ceremony; SEE CONCEPTS *548,589*

informant/informer [n] *person who delivers news*
accuser, adviser, announcer, betrayer, blabbermouth*, canary*, crier, deep throat*, double-crosser, herald, interviewer, journalist, messenger, newscaster/newsperson, notifier, preacher, propagandist, rat*, reporter, sneak, source, stool pigeon*, tattler, tattletale; SEE CONCEPTS *348,354,423*

information [n] *facts, news*
advice, ammo*, break*, chapter and verse*, clue, confidence, counsel, cue, data, dirt*, dope*, dossier, earful*, enlightenment, erudition, illumination, info*, inside story*, instruction, intelligence, knowledge, leak, learning, lore, lowdown*, material, message, network, notice, notification, orientation, propaganda, report, science, scoop, score, tidings, tip, what's what*, whole story*, wisdom, word*; SEE CONCEPT *274*

informative [adj] *educational*
advisory, chatty, communicative, descriptive, edifying, educative, elucidative, enlightening, explanatory, forthcoming, gossipy, illuminating, informational, instructional, instructive, newsy, revealing, revelatory, significant; SEE CONCEPT *267*

informed [adj] *cognizant, conversant*
abreast, acquainted, apprized, au courant*, au fait*, briefed, enlightened, erudite, expert, familiar, in the know*, into*, knowledgeable, know the score*, know what's what*, learned, on top of*, posted*, primed*, reliable, savvy*, tuned in*, up*, up on*, up-to-date, versant, versed, well-read, wise to*; SEE CONCEPT *402*

infraction [n] *violation*
breach, breaking, contravention, crime, error, faux pas, infringement, lapse, offense, sin, slip*, transgression, trespass; SEE CONCEPTS *192,645*

infrastructure [n] *foundation*
base, footing, framework, groundwork, root, support, underpinning; SEE CONCEPTS *442,826*

infrequent [adj] *not happening regularly*
exceptional, few, few and far between*, isolated, limited, meager, occasional, odd, rare, scant, scanty, scarce, scattered, seldom, semioccasional, sparse, spasmodic, sporadic, stray, uncommon, unusual; SEE CONCEPT *530*

infringe [v] *violate*
borrow, breach, break, contravene, crash, disobey, encroach, entrench, impose, infract, intrude, invade, lift, meddle, obtrude, offend, pirate, presume, steal, transgress, trespass; SEE CONCEPTS *192,384*

infuriate [v] *make angry*
aggravate, anger, enrage, exasperate, incense, ire, irritate, madden, make blood boil*, provoke, rile, T-off*, umbrage; SEE CONCEPT *14*

infuse [v] *introduce; soak*
animate, breathe into, imbue, impart, implant, impregnate, inculcate, indoctrinate, ingrain, inoculate, inspire, instill, intersperse, invest, leaven, permeate, pervade, plant, saturate, steep, suffuse; SEE CONCEPTS *140,179,187*

ingenious [adj] *clever; brilliant*
able, adroit, artistic, bright, canny, crafty, creative, cunning, deviceful, dexterous, gifted, imaginative, innovational, innovative, innovatory, intelligent, inventive, original, ready, resourceful, shrewd, skillful, sly, subtle; SEE CONCEPT *402*

ingenuity [n] *cleverness*
ability, adroitness, astuteness, brains, brightness, brilliance, creativity, cunning, dexterity, flair, genius, gumption, intelligence, inventiveness, resourcefulness, shrewdness, skill, smartness, talent, wisdom, wit; SEE CONCEPT *409*

ingenuous [adj] *honest, trustful*
artless, candid, childlike, frank, green*, guileless, innocent, like a babe in the woods*, naive, natural, open, outspoken, plain, simple, sincere, square, straightforward, trusting, unaffected, unartful, unartificial, undisguised, unreserved, unschooled, unsophisticated, unstudied, up front*; SEE CONCEPTS *267,542,589*

ingest [v] *swallow*
absorb, consume, devour, digest, down, drink, eat, inhale; SEE CONCEPT *169*

inglorious [adj] *disgraceful*
blameworthy, contemptible, degrading, detestable, dishonorable, disreputable, ignoble, ignominious, offensive, reprehensible, shameful, unrespectable, unworthy; SEE CONCEPT *555*

ingrained [adj] *deep-rooted*
built-in, chronic, confirmed, congenital, constitutional, deep-seated, fixed, fundamental, hereditary, implanted, inborn, inbred, inbuilt, indelible, indwelling, ineradicable, inherent, innate, in the blood*, intrinsic, inveterate, rooted; SEE CONCEPTS *535,549*

ingratiate [v] *get on the good side of someone*
attract, blandish, brownnose*, captivate, charm, crawl, flatter, get in with*, grovel, hand a line*, insinuate oneself, kowtow*, play up to*, seek favor, truckle; SEE CONCEPTS *7,22,68*

ingratiating [adj] *fawning, servile*
charming, crawling, deferential, disarming, flattering, humble, insinuating, obsequious, saccha-

rine, serving, silken, smarmy, soft, sycophantic, toadying*, unctuous; SEE CONCEPT *401*

ingredient [n] *component of concoction*
additive, constituent, element, factor, fixing, fundamental, innards, integral, integrant, making, part, part and parcel*, piece; SEE CONCEPT *835*

inhabit [v] *take up residence in*
abide, crash, dwell, indwell, live, locate, lodge, make one's home, occupy, park, people, perch, populate, possess, reside, roost, settle, squat, stay, tenant; SEE CONCEPT *226*

inhabitant [n] *person who is resident of habitation*
aborigine, addressee, autochthon, boarder, citizen, colonist, denizen, dweller, householder, incumbent, indweller, inmate, lessee, lodger, native, neighbor, occupant, occupier, renter, resider, roomer, settler, squatter, suburbanite, tenant, urbanite; SEE CONCEPTS *354,413*

inhale [v] *breathe in*
drag, draw in, gasp, inspire, insufflate, puff, pull, respire, smell, sniff, snort, suck in; SEE CONCEPTS *163,601*

inherent [adj] *basic, hereditary*
built-in, characteristic, congenital, connate, constitutional, deep-rooted, deep-seated, distinctive, elementary, essential, fixed, fundamental, genetic, immanent, implicit, inborn, inbred, inbuilt, indigenous, indispensable, individual, indwelling, ingrained, inherited, innate, inner, instinctive, integral, integrated, internal, in the grain, intimate, intrinsic, inward, latent, native, natural, original, part and parcel*, resident, running in the family*, subjective, unalienable; SEE CONCEPTS *404,549*

inherit [v] *gain as possession from someone's death*
accede, acquire, be bequeathed, be granted, be left, come in for, come into, derive, fall heir, get, obtain, receive, succeed, take over; SEE CONCEPTS *124,317*

inheritance [n] *possession gained through someone's death*
bequest, birthright, devise, estate, gift, heirloom, heritage, heritance, legacy, primogeniture; SEE CONCEPT *337*

inherited [adj] *hereditary*
congenital, connate, genetic, handed down, inborn, inbred, innate, in the blood, in the genes, passed down, rooted; SEE CONCEPT *549*

inhibit [v] *restrict, prevent*
arrest, avert, bar, bit, bridle, check, constrain, cramp, curb, discourage, enjoin, faze, forbid, frustrate, hang up*, hinder, hog-tie*, hold back, hold down, hold in, impede, interdict, keep in, obstruct, outlaw, prohibit, put on brakes*, repress, restrain, sandbag*, stop, stymie, suppress, taboo*, ward, withhold; SEE CONCEPTS *121,130*

inhibited [adj] *shy*
bottled up*, cold, constrained, frustrated, guarded, hung up*, passionless, repressed, reserved, reticent, self-conscious, subdued, undemonstrative, unresponsive, uptight, withdrawn; SEE CONCEPTS *404,542*

inhibition [n] *restriction, hindrance*
bar, barrier, blockage, check, embargo, hangup, interdict, interference, obstacle, prevention, prohibition, reserve, restraint, reticence, self-consciousness, shyness, sublimation, suppression; SEE CONCEPTS *411,657*

inhospitable [adj] *unfriendly*
brusque, cold, cool, hostile, rude, short, uncongenial, unfavorable, ungenerous, unkind, unreceptive, unsociable, unwelcoming; SEE CONCEPT *401*

inhuman/inhumane [adj] *animal, savage*
barbaric, barbarous, bestial, brutal, cannibalistic, cold-blooded, cruel, devilish, diabolical, fell, ferocious, fiendish, fierce, grim, hateful, heartless, implacable, malicious, malign, malignant, mean, merciless, pitiless, relentless, remorseless, ruthless, truculent, uncompassionate, unfeeling, unkind, unrelenting, unsympathetic, vicious; SEE CONCEPTS *401,545*

inhumanity [n] *lack of compassion*
atrocity, barbarism, bloodthirstiness, brutality, brutishness, callousness, cold-bloodedness, cruelty, ferocity, heartlessness, maliciousness, ruthlessness, savagery, viciousness, violence; SEE CONCEPTS *29,645*

inimical [adj] *antagonistic, contrary*
adverse, antipathetic, destructive, disaffected, harmful, hostile, hurtful, ill, ill-disposed, inimicable, injurious, noxious, opposed, oppugnant, pernicious, repugnant, unfavorable, unfriendly, unwelcoming; SEE CONCEPTS *401,537*

inimitable [adj] *incomparable*
consummate, matchless, nonpareil, peerless, perfect, supreme, unequalled, unexampled, unique, unmatched, unparalleled, unrivalled, unsurpassable; SEE CONCEPT *574*

iniquity [n] *sin, evil*
abomination, baseness, crime, evildoing, heinousness, immorality, infamy, injustice, miscreancy, misdeed, offense, sinfulness, unfairness, unrighteousness, wickedness, wrong, wrongdoing; SEE CONCEPT *645*

initial [adj] *beginning, primary*
antecedent, basic, commencing, earliest, early, elementary, embryonic, first, foremost, fundamental, germinal, headmost, inaugural, inceptive, inchoate, incipient, infant, initiative, initiatory, introductory, leading, nascent, opening, original, pioneer, virgin; SEE CONCEPTS *585,799,828*

initiate [v1] *start, introduce*
admit, begin, break the ice*, come out with, come up with, commence, dream up, enter, get ball rolling*, get feet wet*, get under way, inaugurate, induct, install, instate, institute, intro*, invest, kick off*, launch, make up, open, originate, pioneer, set in motion, set up, take in, take up, trigger, usher in; SEE CONCEPT *221*

initiate [v2] *teach*
brief, coach, edify, enlighten, familiarize, indoctrinate, induct, inform, instate, instruct, introduce, invest, train; SEE CONCEPT *285*

initiation [n] *start, introduction*
admission, baptism, beginning, commencement, debut, enrollment, entrance, inaugural, inauguration, inception, indoctrination, induction, installation, instatement, investiture, preliminaries; SEE CONCEPTS *221,386*

initiative [n] *eagerness to do something*
action, ambition, drive, dynamism, energy, enterprise, enthusiasm, get-up-and-go*, gumption*, inventiveness, leadership, moxie*, originality, punch, push, resource, resourcefulness, spunk*, steam*, vigor; SEE CONCEPTS *411,657*

in
in

inject [*v1*] *put in, introduce*
add, drag in, force into, imbue, implant, impregnate, include, infuse, insert, instill, interjaculate, interject, place into, squeeze in, stick in, throw in; SEE CONCEPTS *187,208,209*

inject [*v2*] *introduce into bloodstream by use of a needle*
give a shot, inoculate, jab, mainline*, shoot, vaccinate; SEE CONCEPTS *179,310*

injection [*n*] *introduction into bloodstream*
booster, dose, dram, enema, inoculation, needle, vaccine; SEE CONCEPT *311*

injunction [*n*] *decree*
admonition, ban, bar, behest, bidding, charge, command, demand, dictate, embargo, enjoinder, exhortation, instruction, mandate, order, precept, prohibition, ruling, word, writ; SEE CONCEPTS *271,318*

injure [*v*] *hurt, harm*
abuse, aggrieve, batter, blemish, blight, break, contort, cripple, cut up, damage, deface, deform, disable, disfigure, distort, distress, do in*, draw blood*, foul, foul up, grieve, hack up, impair, maim, maltreat, mangle, mar, mutilate, pain, pique, prejudice, ruin, shake up, spoil, sting, tarnish, torment, torture, total, undermine, vitiate, wax, weaken, wound, wrong; SEE CONCEPT *246*

injurious [*adj*] *hurtful*
abusive, adverse, bad, baneful, corrupting, damaging, dangerous, deadly, deleterious, destructive, detrimental, disadvantageous, evil, harmful, iniquitous, insulting, libeling, mischievous, nocent, nocuous, noxious, opprobrious, pernicious, poisonous, prejudicial, ruinous, slanderous, unconducive, unhealthy, unjust, wrongful; SEE CONCEPTS *537,570*

injury [*n*] *hurt, harm*
abrasion, abuse, affliction, affront, agony, bad, bite, blemish, boo-boo*, bruise, burn, chop, cramp, cut, damage, deformation, detriment, discomfiture, disservice, distress, evil, fracture, gash, grievance, hemorrhage, ill, impairment, indignity, injustice, insult, laceration, lesion, libel, loss, mischief, misery, mutilation, nick, ouch*, outrage, pang, ruin, scar, scratch, shock, slander, sore, sprain, stab, sting, suffering, swelling, trauma, twinge, wound, wrong; SEE CONCEPTS *309,728*

injustice [*n*] *unfair treatment; bias*
abuse, breach, crime, crying shame*, damage, dirty deal*, discrimination, encroachment, favoritism, grievance, inequality, inequity, infraction, infringement, iniquity, malfeasance, malpractice, maltreatment, miscarriage, mischief, negligence, offense, onesidedness, oppression, outrage, partiality, partisanship, prejudice, railroad*, ruin, sellout*, transgression, trespass, unfairness, unjustness, unlawfulness, villainy, violation, wrong, wrongdoing; SEE CONCEPTS *192,645,674*

inkling [*n*] *idea, clue*
conception, cue, faintest idea*, foggiest idea*, glimmering, hint, hot lead*, hunch*, impression, indication, innuendo, intimation, lead, notion, sneaking suspicion*, suggestion, suspicion, tip, tipoff, whisper; SEE CONCEPT *689*

inlet [*n*] *arm of the sea*
basin, bay, bayou, bight, canal, channel, cove, creek, delta, entrance, estuary, firth, fjord, gulf,

harbor, ingress, loch, narrows, passage, slew, slough, sound, strait; SEE CONCEPTS *509,514*

inn [*n*] *accommodation for travellers*
auberge, hospice, hostel, hostelry, hotel, lodge, motel, public house, resort, roadhouse, saloon, tavern; SEE CONCEPTS *439,449,516*

innate [*adj*] *inherited, native*
congenital, connate, connatural, constitutional, deep-seated, elemental, essential, hereditary, inborn, inbred, indigenous, ingrained, inherent, instinctive, intrinsic, intuitive, natural, normal, regular, standard, typical, unacquired; SEE CONCEPTS *406,549*

inner [*adj1*] *central, middle physically*
close, constitutional, essential, familiar, focal, inherent, innermore, inside, interior, internal, intestinal, intimate, intrinsic, inward, nuclear; SEE CONCEPTS *826,830*

inner [*adj2*] *mental, private*
central, concealed, deep-rooted, deep-seated, emotional, esoteric, essential, focal, gut*, hidden, individual, inherent, innate, inside, interior, internal, intimate, intrinsic, intuitive, inward, personal, psychological, repressed, secret, spiritual, subconscious, unrevealed, visceral, viscerous; SEE CONCEPTS *529,576*

innocence [*n1*] *blamelessness*
chastity, clean hands*, clear conscience*, guiltlessness, immaculateness, impeccability, incorruptibility, incorruption, inculpability, probity, purity, righteousness, sinlessness, stainlessness, uprightness, virtue; SEE CONCEPT *645*

innocence [*n2*] *harmlessness, naïveté*
artlessness, candidness, credulousness, forthrightness, frankness, freshness, guilelessness, gullibility, ignorance, inexperience, ingenuousness, innocuousness, innoxiousness, inoffensiveness, lack, nescience, plainness, purity, simplicity, sincerity, unaffectedness, unawareness, unfamiliarity, unknowingness, unsophistication, unworldliness, virtue; SEE CONCEPTS *409,411*

innocent [*adj1*] *blameless*
above suspicion, angelic, chaste, clean, cleanhanded, clear, crimeless, exemplary, faultless, free of, good, guilt-free, guiltless, honest, immaculate, impeccable, impeccant, inculpable, in the clear*, irreproachable, lawful, legal, legitimate, licit, not guilty, pristine, pure, righteous, safe, sinless, spotless, stainless, unblemished, uncensurable, uncorrupt, unimpeachable, uninvolved, unoffending, unsullied, untainted, upright, virginal, virtuous; SEE CONCEPT *545*

innocent [*adj2*] *harmless, naive*
artless, childlike, credulous, frank, fresh, guileless, gullible, hurtless, ignorant, inexperienced, ingenuous, innocuous, innoxious, inobnoxious, inoffensive, offenseless, open, raw, safe, simple, soft, square, unacquainted, unartificial, uncool, unfamiliar, unhurtful, uninjurious, unmalicious, unobjectionable, unoffensive, unschooled, unsophisticated, unstudied, unsuspicious, unworldly, well-intentioned, wellmeant, wide-eyed, youthful; SEE CONCEPTS *404,542*

innocuous [*adj*] *harmless*
banal, bland, flat, innocent, innoxious, inobnoxious, inoffensive, insipid, jejune, kind, painless, safe, sapless, unobjectionable, unoffending, weak; SEE CONCEPTS *401,572*

innovation [n] *change, novelty*
addition, alteration, contraption, cutting edge*, departure, deviation, introduction, last word*, latest thing*, leading edge*, modernism, modernization, modification, mutation, newness, notion, permutation, shift, variation, vicissitude, wrinkle*; SEE CONCEPTS *260,529,660,665*

innovative [adj] *creative*
avant-garde, breaking new ground*, contemporary, cutting-edge*, deviceful, ingenious, innovational, innovatory, inventive, just out*, leading-edge*, new, newfangled*, original, originative, state-of-the-art; SEE CONCEPTS *529,578, 589,797*

innovator [n] *inventor*
avant-garde, creator, discoverer, groundbreaker, pioneer, trailblazer, trendsetter, vanguard; SEE CONCEPTS *348,413*

innuendo [n] *suggestion*
allusion, aside, aspersion, hint, implication, imputation, insinuation, intimation, overtone, reference, whisper; SEE CONCEPTS *75,278*

innumerable [adj] *many, infinite*
alive with*, beyond number, countless, frequent, incalculable, multitudinous, myriad, numberless, numerous, uncountable, unnumbered, untold; SEE CONCEPT *762*

inoculation [n] *immunization*
injection, prevention, shot, vaccination; SEE CONCEPT *310*

inoffensive [adj] *not obnoxious; harmless*
calm, clean, friendly, humble, innocent, innocuous, innoxious, mild, neutral, nonprovocative, peaceable, pleasant, quiet, retiring, safe, unobjectionable, unobtrusive, unoffending; SEE CONCEPTS *267,542*

inopportune [adj] *not appropriate or suitable*
contrary, disadvantageous, disturbing, ill-chosen, ill-timed, inappropriate, inauspicious, inconvenient, malapropos, mistimed, troublesome, unfavorable, unfortunate, unpropitious, unseasonable, unsuitable, untimely; SEE CONCEPT *558*

inordinate [adj] *excessive, extravagant*
disproportionate, dizzying, exorbitant, extortionate, extreme, gratuitous, immoderate, intemperate, irrational, outrageous, overindulgent, overmuch, preposterous, supererogatory, superfluous, surplus, too much, towering, uncalled-for, unconscionable, uncurbed, undue, unmeasurable, unreasonable, unrestrained, untempered, unwarranted, wanton, wasteful; SEE CONCEPTS *570,781*

inquest [n] *investigation*
delving, examination, hearing, inquiry, inquisition, probe, probing, quest, research, trial; SEE CONCEPTS *48,290,318*

inquire [v] *ask; look into*
analyze, catechize, examine, explore, feel out, go over, grill, hit, hit up, inspect, interrogate, investigate, knock, probe, prospect, pry, query, question, request information, roast, scrutinize, search, seek, seek information, sift, study, test the waters*; SEE CONCEPTS *24,48*

inquiring [adj] *wondering, curious*
analytical, catechistic, doubtful, examining, fact-finding, heuristic, inquisitive, interested, interrogative, investigative, investigatory, nosy, outward-looking, probing, prying, questioning,

quizzical, searching, Socratic, speculative, studious; SEE CONCEPTS *402,542*

inquiry [n] *asking; looking into*
analysis, audit, catechizing, check, cross-examination, delving, disquisition, examination, exploration, fishing expedition*, grilling, hearing, inquest, inquisition, inspection, interrogation, interrogatory, investigation, legwork*, poll, probe, probing, pursuit, Q and A*, query, quest, question, questioning, quizzing, request, research, scrutiny, search, study, survey, third degree*, trial balloon*; SEE CONCEPTS *24,48,290*

inquisitive [adj] *curious*
big-eyed*, challenging, forward, impertinent, inquiring, inquisitorial, interested, intrusive, investigative, meddlesome, meddling, nalytical, nosy, peering, personal, poking, presumptuous, probing, prying, questioning, scrutinizing, searching, sifting, snooping, speculative; SEE CONCEPT *402*

inroad [n] *advance, foray*
encroachment, impingement, incursion, intrusion, invasion, irruption, onslaught, raid, trespass; SEE CONCEPTS *86,704*

insane [adj] *mentally ill; foolish*
batty*, bizarre, cracked*, crazed, crazy, cuckoo*, daft, demented, derailed, deranged, fatuous, frenzied, idiotic, impractical, irrational, irresponsible, loony*, lunatic, mad, maniacal, mental, moonstruck*, nuts*, nutty*, off one's rocker*, of unsound mind, out of one's mind*, paranoid, preposterous, psychopathic, psychotic, rabid, raging, raving, schizophrenic, screwy, senseless, touched, unhinged, unsettled, wild; SEE CONCEPTS *314,403,548*

insanely [adv] *extremely*
crazily, ferociously, fiercely, furiously, idiotically, irrationally, stupidly, violently, wildly; SEE CONCEPT *569*

insanity [n] *mental illness; foolishness*
aberration, absurdity, alienation, craziness, delirium, delusion, dementia, derangement, distraction, dotage, folly, frenzy, hallucination, hysteria, illusion, inanity, irrationality, irresponsibility, lunacy, madness, mania, mental disorder, neurosis, phobia, preposterousness, psychopathy, psychosis, senselessness, unbalance, unreasonableness, witlessness; SEE CONCEPTS *316,410*

insatiable [adj] *voracious, wanting*
clamorous, crying, demanding, desiring, exigent, gluttonous, greedy, importunate, insatiate, insistent, intemperate, pressing, quenchless, rapacious, ravenous, unappeasable, unquenchable, unsatisfiable, unsatisfied, urgent, yearning; SEE CONCEPTS *20,403,546*

inscribe [v] *imprint, write*
book, carve, cut, engrave, engross, etch, impress, indite, list, record, register, scribe; SEE CONCEPT *79*

inscription [n] *message*
autograph, caption, dedication, engraving, epitaph, heading, imprint, label, legend, lettering, saying, signature, wording; SEE CONCEPT *283*

inscrutable [adj] *hidden, mysterious; blank*
ambiguous, arcane, cabalistic, deadpan*, difficult, enigmatic, impenetrable, incomprehensible, inexplicable, mysterial, mystic, poker-faced*, secret, sphinxlike, unaccountable, undiscoverable, unexplainable, unfathomable, unintelligible, unknowable, unreadable; SEE CONCEPTS *529,576*

in
in

insect [n] *bug*
ant, aphid, bedbug, bee, beetle, bumblebee, butterfly, cockroach, cootie, daddy longlegs, dragonfly, flea, fly, fruit fly, gnat, grasshopper, hornet, ladybug, louse, mite, mosquito, moth, pest, praying mantis, termite, tick, vermin, yellowjacket; SEE CONCEPT *398*

insecure [adj1] *uncertain, worried*
afraid, anxious, apprehensive, choked, Delphic, diffident, hanging by thread*, hesitant, jumpy, on thin ice*, questioning, shaky, touch and go*, touchy*, troubled, unassured, unconfident, unpoised, unsure, up in the air*, uptight*, vague; SEE CONCEPTS *403,542*

insecure [adj2] *dangerous, precarious*
defenseless, exposed, fluctuant, frail, hazardous, immature, insubstantial, loose, open to attack*, perilous, rickety, rocky, rootless, shaky, unguarded, unprotected, unreliable, unsafe, unshielded, unsound, unstable, unsteady, vacillating, vulnerable, wavering, weak, wobbly; SEE CONCEPTS *488,570*

insensitive [adj1] *indifferent, callous*
aloof, bloodless*, coldhearted*, crass, feelingless, hard, hard as nails*, hard-boiled*, hardened, hardhearted*, heartless, imperceptive, incurious, obtuse, stony, tactless, thick-skinned*, tough, uncaring, unconcerned, unfeeling, unkind, unresponsive, unsusceptible; SEE CONCEPT *401*

insensitive [adj2] *numb*
anesthetized, asleep, benumbed, dead, deadened, immune to, impervious to, insensible, nonreactive, senseless, unfeeling; SEE CONCEPT *406*

inseparable [adj] *unable to be divided*
as one, attached, conjoined, connected, entwined, inalienable, indissoluble, indivisible, inseverable, integral, integrated, intertwined, interwoven, molded, secure, tied up, unified, united, whole; SEE CONCEPT *531*

insert [v] *put, tuck in*
admit, drag in, embed, enter, fill in, imbed, implant, include, infix, infuse, inject, inlay, insinuate, instill, intercalate, interject, interlope, interpolate, interpose, introduce, intrude, lug in, obtrude, place, pop in*, root, set, shoehorn*, shove in, squeeze in, stick, work in; SEE CONCEPTS *201,209*

inside [adj1] *in the middle; interior*
central, indoors, inner, innermost, internal, intramural, inward, surrounded, under a roof; SEE CONCEPTS *583,830*

inside [adj2] *secret*
classified, closet, confidential, esoteric, exclusive, hushed, internal, limited, private, restricted; SEE CONCEPTS *529,576*

inside [adv] *within*
indoors, under a roof, under cover, within doors, within walls; SEE CONCEPT *583*

inside [n] *middle, lining*
belly, bowels, breast, center, contents, gut, heart, innards, inner portion, interior, recess, soul, stuffing, womb; SEE CONCEPT *830*

insidious [adj] *sneaky, tricky*
artful, astute, corrupt, crafty, crooked, cunning, dangerous, deceitful, deceptive, deep, designing, dishonest, disingenuous, duplicitous, ensnaring, false, foxy, guileful, intriguing, like a snake in the grass*, Machiavellian, perfidious, perilous, secret, slick, sly, smooth, snaky*, sneaking,

stealthy, subtle, surreptitious, treacherous, wily, wormlike*; SEE CONCEPTS *401,542,545*

insight [n] *intuitiveness, awareness*
acumen, click*, comprehension, discernment, divination, drift*, intuition, judgment, observation, penetration, perception, perceptivity, perspicacity, sagaciousness, sagacity, sageness, sapience, shrewdness, understanding, vision, wavelength*, wisdom; SEE CONCEPTS *409,410*

insightful [adj] *perceptive*
alert, astute, awake, aware, brainy, conscious, cute, discerning, ear to the ground*, intelligent, intuitive, keen, knowing, knowledgeable, knows what's what*, observant, penetrating, penetrative, quick, responsive, savvy, sensitive, sharp, shrewd, smart, tuned in*, understanding, wise; SEE CONCEPTS *402,542*

insignia [n] *emblem*
badge, coat of arms, crest, decoration, earmark, ensign, mark, paraphernalia, regalia, symbol; SEE CONCEPTS *259,284*

insignificant [adj] *not important; of no consequence*
casual, immaterial, inappreciable, inconsequential, inconsiderable, infinitesimal, irrelevant, lesser, light, lightweight*, little, meager, meaningless, minim, minimal, minor, minuscule, minute, negligible, nondescript, nonessential, not worth mentioning*, nugatory, paltry, petty, pointless, purportless, scanty, secondary, senseless, small, trifling, trivial, unimportant, unsubstantial; SEE CONCEPT *575*

insincere [adj] *dishonest, pretended*
ambidextrous, backhanded, deceitful, deceptive, devious, disingenuous, dissembling, dissimulating, double, double-dealing, duplicitous, evasive, faithless, fake, false, hollow, hypocritical, lying, mendacious, perfidious, phony, pretentious, put-on*, shifty, slick, sly, snide, two-faced*, unfaithful, untrue, untruthful; SEE CONCEPTS *267,542,545*

insinuate [v1] *hint, suggest*
allude, ascribe, connote, imply, impute, indicate, intimate, mention, propose, purport, refer, signify; SEE CONCEPTS *49,75*

insinuate [v2] *force one's way into*
curry favor*, edge in, fill in, foist, get in with*, horn in*, infiltrate, infuse, ingratiate, inject, insert, instill, intercalate, interject, interpose, introduce, muscle in*, slip in, wedge in, work in, worm in*; SEE CONCEPTS *159,208,384*

insipid [adj1] *dull, uninteresting*
anemic, arid, banal, beige, blah*, bland, characterless, colorless, commonplace, dead*, drab, driveling, dry, feeble, flat, ho-hum*, inane, innocuous, jejune, lifeless, limp, mild, mundane, nebbish, nothing, ordinary, plain, pointless, prosaic, prosy, slight, soft*, spiritless, stale, stupid, subdued, tame, tedious, tenuous, thin, tired, trite, unimaginative, vapid, watery, weak, weariful, wearisome, wishy-washy*; SEE CONCEPTS *402,404,537*

insipid [adj2] *tasteless*
bland, distasteful, flat, flavorless, jejune, mild, savorless, stale, unappetizing, unpalatable, unsavory, vapid, watered-down, watery; SEE CONCEPT *613*

insist [v] *order and expect; claim*
assert, asseverate, aver, be firm, contend, demand, hold, importune, lay down the law*,

maintain, persist, press, reiterate, repeat, request, require, stand firm, swear, take a stand*, urge, vow; SEE CONCEPTS *49,53*

insistent [*adj*] *demanding*
assertive, burning, clamant, clamorous, continuous, crying, dire, dogged, emphatic, exigent, forceful, imperative, imperious, importunate, incessant, obstinate, peremptory, perseverant, persevering, persistent, pressing, reiterative, resolute, resounding, unrelenting, urgent; SEE CONCEPTS *267,534,540*

insolence [*n*] *boldness, disrespect*
abuse, arrogance, audacity, back talk, brass*, brazenness, cheek*, chutzpah*, contempt, contemptuousness, contumely, effrontery, gall, guff*, hardihood, impertinence, impudence, incivility, insubordination, lip*, offensiveness, pertness, presumption, rudeness, sass*, sauce*, uncivility; SEE CONCEPT *633*

insolent [*adj*] *bold, disrespectful*
abusive, arrogant, barefaced, brassy*, brazen, breezy, contemptuous, contumelious, dictatorial, discourteous, disdainful, flip*, fresh, imperative, impertinent, impolite, impudent, insubordinate, insulting, magisterial, nervy, off-base*, offensive, out-of-line*, overbearing, peremptory, pert, procacious, put down, rude, sassy*, saucy*, smart, smart-alecky*, uncivil, ungracious; SEE CONCEPTS *267,401*

insoluble [*adj*] *mysterious, unable to be solved or answered*
baffling, difficult, impenetrable, indecipherable, inexplicable, inextricable, irresolvable, mystifying, obscure, unaccountable, unconcluded, unfathomable, unresolved, unsolvable, unsolved; SEE CONCEPTS *529,576*

insolvent [*adj*] *financially ruined*
bankrupt, broke*, broken, busted*, failed, foreclosed, in Chapter 11*, in Chapter 13*, indebted, in receivership, in the red*, lost, on the rocks*, out of money, strapped*, taken to the cleaners*, unbalanced, undone, wiped out*; SEE CONCEPT *334*

insomnia [*n*] *inability to sleep soundly*
indisposition, insomnolence, restlessness, sleeplessness, stress, tension, vigil, vigilance, wakefulness; SEE CONCEPT *315*

insouciant [*adj*] *easygoing, casual*
airy, breezy, buoyant, carefree, careless, free and easy*, gay, happy-go-lucky*, heedless, jaunty, lighthearted, nonchalant, sunny*, thoughtless, unconcerned, untroubled, unworried; SEE CONCEPTS *404,542*

inspect [*v*] *examine, check*
audit, canvass, case, catechize, check out, clock*, eye*, give the once-over*, go over, go through, inquire, interrogate, investigate, kick the tires*, look over, notice, observe, oversee, probe, question, review, scan, scope, scout, scrutinize, search, study, superintend, supervise, survey, vet, view, watch; SEE CONCEPTS *103,623*

inspection [*n*] *examination, check*
analysis, checkup, frisk, inquest, inquiry, inquisition, inventory, investigation, look-over, maneuvers, once-over*, pageant, parade, perlustration, probe, read, research, review, scan, scrutiny, search, superintendence, supervision, surveillance, survey, view; SEE CONCEPTS *103,290*

inspector [*n*] *examiner*
assessor, auditor, checker, controller, detective, investigator, monitor, overseer, police officer, private eye, reviewer, scrutinizer, sleuth, tester; SEE CONCEPT *348*

inspiration [*n*] *idea, stimulus*
afflatus, animus, approach, arousal, awakening, brainchild*, brainstorm*, creativity, deep think*, elevation, encouragement, enthusiasm, exaltation, fancy, flash*, genius, hunch*, illumination, impulse, incentive, inflatus, influence, insight, motivation, motive, muse, notion, revelation, rumble, spark, spur, stimulation, thought, vision, whim; SEE CONCEPTS *529,661*

inspire [*v*] *encourage, stimulate*
affect, animate, arouse, be responsible for, carry, cause, commove, elate, embolden, endue, enkindle, enliven, exalt, excite, exhilarate, fire up*, galvanize, get*, give impetus, give one an idea*, give rise to, hearten, imbue, impress, infect, inflame, influence, inform, infuse, inspirit, instill, invigorate, motivate, occasion, produce, provoke, quicken, reassure, set up, spark, spur, start off, stir, strike, sway, touch, trigger, urge, work up; SEE CONCEPTS *7,22,221,242*

instability [*n*] *imbalance, inconstancy*
alternation, anxiety, capriciousness, changeability, changeableness, disequilibrium, disquiet, fickleness, fitfulness, flightiness, fluctuation, fluidity, frailty, hesitation, immaturity, impermanence, inconsistency, inquietude, insecurity, irregularity, irresolution, mutability, oscillation, pliancy, precariousness, restlessness, shakiness, transience, uncertainty, unfixedness, unpredictability, unreliability, unsteadiness, vacillation, variability, volatility, vulnerability, wavering, weakness; SEE CONCEPTS *410,637,731*

install [*v*] *set up, establish*
build in, ensconce, fix, fix up, furnish, inaugurate, induct, instate, institute, introduce, invest, lay, line, lodge, place, plant, position, put in, settle, station; SEE CONCEPTS *201,221*

installation [*n1*] *establishment, inauguration*
accession, coronation, fitting, furnishing, inaugural, induction, installment, instatement, investiture, investment, launching, ordination, placing, positioning, setting up; SEE CONCEPTS *201,221,832*

installation [*n2*] *equipment*
base, establishment, fort, fortification, furnishings, lighting, machinery, plant, post, power, station, system, wiring; SEE CONCEPTS *439,463,496*

installment [*n*] *part, section*
chapter, division, earnest, episode, partial payment, payment, portion, repayment, token; SEE CONCEPTS *344,835*

instance [*n*] *case, situation*
case history, case in point, detail, example, exemplification, exponent, ground, illustration, item, occasion, occurrence, particular, precedent, proof, reason, representative, sample, sampling, specimen, time; SEE CONCEPTS *686,696,815*

instance [*v*] *name*
adduce, cite, exemplify, illustrate, mention, quote, refer, show, specify; SEE CONCEPT *73*

instant [*adj*] *immediate, urgent*
burning*, clamant, contemporary, crying*, current, dire, direct, exigent, existent, extant, fast, imperative, importunate, insistent, instantaneous, on-the-spot*, present, present-day, pressing, prompt, quick, split-second*; SEE CONCEPTS *544,588,799*

in
in

instant [n] *moment*
bat of the eye*, breath, crack, flash, jiffy*, juncture, minute, nothing flat*, occasion, point, sec*, second, shake*, short while, split second*, tick, time, trice, twinkling*, while, wink*; SEE CONCEPTS *802,808*

instantaneous [adj] *immediate*
direct, fast, hair-trigger*, in a flash*, instant, momentary, quick, rapid, spontaneous, transitory; SEE CONCEPT *820*

instantly [adv] *right now*
at once, away, directly, double-time*, first off*, forthwith, immediately, in a flash*, instantaneously, instanter, now, on a dime*, PDQ*, pronto*, right, right away, spontaneously, straight away*, there and then*, this minute, tout de suite*, without delay; SEE CONCEPTS *544,588,799*

instead [adv] *alternatively*
alternately, alternative, as a substitute, in lieu, in place of, in preference, on behalf of, on second thought, preferably, rather, rather than; SEE CONCEPT *560*

instigate [v] *influence, provoke*
abet, actuate, add fuel, bring about, egg on*, encourage, fire up*, foment, goad, hint, impel, incite, inflame, initiate, insinuate, kindle, make waves*, move, needle*, persuade, plan, plot, prompt, put up to, rabble-rouse*, raise, rouse, scheme, set on, spur, start, steam up, stimulate, stir up, suggest, turn on, urge, whip up*, work up; SEE CONCEPTS *7,19,22,221,242*

instigator [n] *troublemaker*
agent provocateur, agitator, firebrand, hellion, incendiary, inciter, inflamer, knave, meddler, mischief-maker, nuisance, provocateur*, punk*, rabble-rouser*, ringleader, sparkplug*, wise guy*; SEE CONCEPT *412*

instill [v] *implant, introduce*
brainwash*, catechize, diffuse, disseminate, engender, engraft, force in, imbue, impart, impregnate, impress, inculcate, indoctrinate, infiltrate, infix, infuse, inject, inoculate, inseminate, insert, insinuate, inspire, interject, intermix, program, propagandize, put in head*, suffuse, transfuse; SEE CONCEPTS *14,221,285*

instinct [n] *gut feeling, idea*
aptitude, faculty, feeling, funny feeling*, gift, gut reaction*, hunch, impulse, inclination, intuition, knack, know-how*, nose*, predisposition, proclivity, savvy*, sense, sentiment, sixth sense*, talent, tendency, urge; SEE CONCEPTS *529,689*

instinctive [adj] *reflex, automatic*
accustomed, by seat of one's pants*, congenital, habitual, impulsive, inborn, ingrained, inherent, innate, instinctual, intrinsic, intuitional, intuitive, involuntary, knee-jerk*, mechanical, native, natural, normal, regular, rooted, second-nature*, spontaneous, typical, unlearned, unmeditated, unpremeditated, unprompted, unthinking, visceral; SEE CONCEPT *544*

institute [n2] *law; custom*
convention, decree, decretum, doctrine, dogma, edict, establishment, fixture, habit, maxim, ordinance, practice, precedent, precept, prescript, principle, regulation, rite, ritual, rule, statute, tenet, tradition; SEE CONCEPTS *318,688*

institute [v] *begin; put into operation*
appoint, bow, break in, bring into being, come

out with, come up with, commence, constitute, create, enact, establish, fix, found, inaugurate, induct, initiate, install, introduce, invest, launch, make up, open, open up, ordain, organize, originate, pioneer, rev*, set in motion, settle, set up, start, usher in*; SEE CONCEPTS *173,221,242*

institute/institution [n1] *organization, usually educational*
academy, association, asylum, business, clinic, college, company, conservatory, establishment, fixture, foundation, guild, hospital, orphanage, school, seminar, seminary, society, system, think tank, university; SEE CONCEPTS *288,381,439*

instruct [v1] *inform, teach*
acquaint, advise, apprise, brainwash*, break in, break it to, brief, clue in, coach, counsel, discipline, disclose, drill, drum into*, educate, engineer, enlighten, give lessons, ground, guide, keep posted*, lead, lecture, level, notify, pilot, reveal, school, steer, tell, train, tutor, update, wise up*; SEE CONCEPTS *60,285*

instruct [v2] *order, command*
assign, bid, charge, define, direct, enjoin, prescribe, tell, warn; SEE CONCEPTS *53,61*

instruction [n1] *education*
apprenticeship, chalk talk*, coaching, direction, discipline, drilling, edification, enlightenment, grounding, guidance, information, lesson, preparation, schooling, teaching, training, tuition, tutelage; SEE CONCEPTS *274,285*

instruction [n2] *demand, command*
advice, briefing, direction, directive, information, injunction, mandate, order, plan, ruling; SEE CONCEPTS *274,278*

instructive [adj] *informative*
educational, educative, enlightening, explanatory, helpful, illuminating, informational, instructional, useful; SEE CONCEPT *267*

instructor [n] *person who educates*
adviser, coach, demonstrator, exponent, guide, lecturer, mentor, pedagogue, preceptor, professor, teacher, trainer, tutor; SEE CONCEPT *350*

instrument [n1] *tool, implement*
apparatus, appliance, contraption, contrivance, device, doodad*, equipment, gadget, gear, gizmo*, machine, machinery, mechanism, paraphernalia, tackle, utensil; SEE CONCEPTS *463,499*

instrument [n2] *means, agent*
agency, channel, factor, force, instrumentality, material, mechanism, medium, ministry, organ, vehicle, wherewithal; SEE CONCEPTS *6,687*

instrumental [adj] *influential, assisting*
active, auxiliary, conducive, contributory, helpful, helping, involved, of help, of service, partly responsible, serviceable, subsidiary, useful; SEE CONCEPT *560*

insubordinate [adj] *rebellious*
contrary, contumacious, defiant, disaffected, disobedient, disorderly, dissentious, factious, fractious, insurgent, intractable, mutinous, naughty, perverse, recalcitrant, refractory, riotous, seditious, treacherous, turbulent, uncompliant, uncomplying, undisciplined, ungovernable, unruly; SEE CONCEPT *401*

insubordination [n] *disobedience*
defiance, dereliction, disregard, dissension, indiscipline, infringement, insurrection, mutiny, noncompliance, noncooperation, nonobservance, rebellion, revolt, revolution, riot, sabotage; SEE CONCEPT *633*

insubstantial [adj] *weak, imaginary*
aerial, airy, chimerical, decrepit, ephemeral, false, fanciful, feeble, flimsy, fly-by-night*, fragile, frail, idle, illusory, immaterial, imponderable, incorporeal, infirm, intangible, metaphysical, petty, poor, puny, slender, slight, tenuous, thin, too little too late*, unreal, unsound, unsubstantial; SEE CONCEPT 485

insufferable [adj] *horrible, intolerable*
detestable, distressing, dreadful, impossible, insupportable, outrageous, painful, unacceptable, unbearable, unendurable, unspeakable; SEE CONCEPTS 529,537

insufficient [adj] *not enough; lacking*
bereft, defective, deficient, destitute, devoid, drained, dry, failing, faulty, imperfect, inadequate, incapable, incommensurate, incompetent, incomplete, infrequent, meager, minus, out of, poor, rare, scant, scarce, short, short of, shy, thin*, too little too late*, unample, unfinished, unfitted, unqualified, unsatisfactory, wanting; SEE CONCEPTS 546,771

insular [adj] *narrow-minded*
bigoted, circumscribed, closed, confined, contracted, cut off, detached, illiberal, inward-looking, isolated, limited, narrow, parochial, petty, prejudiced, provincial, restricted, secluded, separate, separated, sequestered; SEE CONCEPTS 403,583

insulate [v] *protect; close off*
coat, cocoon, cushion, cut off, inlay, island, isolate, keep apart, line, seclude, separate, sequester, set apart, shield, tape, treat, wrap; SEE CONCEPT 172

insult [n] *hateful communication*
abuse, affront, aspersion, black eye*, blasphemy, cheap shot*, contempt, contumely, derision, despite, discourtesy, disdainfulness, disgrace, disrespect, ignominy, impertinence, impudence, incivility, indignity, insolence, invective, libel, mockery, obloquy, offense, opprobrium, outrage, put-down, rudeness, scorn, scurrility, shame, slam, slanger, slap, slap in the face*, slight, snub, superciliousness, taunt, unpleasantry, vilification, vituperation; SEE CONCEPTS 52,54,278

insult [v] *abuse, offend*
abase, affront, aggravate, annoy, blister, curse, cut to the quick*, debase, degrade, deride, dishonor, disoblige, dump on*, flout, gird, humiliate, injure, irritate, jeer, libel, mock, outrage, pan*, provoke, put down*, revile, ridicule, roast*, scoff, slam*, slander, slight, sneer, snub, step on one's toes*, taunt, tease, underestimate, vex; SEE CONCEPTS 52,54

insulting [adj] *abusive*
biting, degrading, derogatory, discourteous, disparaging, disrespectful, hurtful, insolent, offensive, repulsive, ridiculing, rude, slighting, uncivil; SEE CONCEPTS 267,529,537

insurance [n] *protection, security*
allowance, assurance, backing, cover, coverage, guarantee, indemnification, indemnity, provision, safeguard, support, warrant, warranty; SEE CONCEPTS 318,332

insure [v] *protect, secure*
assure, cinch, cover, guarantee, guard, hedge, indemnify, register, safeguard, shield, underwrite, warrant; SEE CONCEPTS 317,330

insurgent [adj] *rebellious*
anarchical, contumacious, disobedient, factious, insubordinate, insurrectionary, mutinous, revolting, revolutionary, riotous, seditious; SEE CONCEPT 401

insurgent [n] *rebel*
agitator, anarch, anarchist, demonstrator, frondeur, insurrectionist, malcontent, mutineer, radical, resister, revolter, revolutionary, revolutionist, rioter; SEE CONCEPTS 359,412

insurmountable [adj] *impossible*
forget it, hopeless, impassable, impregnable, inaccessible, indomitable, ineluctable, insuperable, invincible, not a prayer*, no way*, no-win*, overwhelming, unbeatable, unconquerable, unmasterable; SEE CONCEPTS 552,565

insurrection [n] *rebellion*
coup, disorder, insurgence, insurgency, mutiny, revolt, revolution, riot, rising, sedition, uprising; SEE CONCEPTS 86,320

intact [adj] *undamaged; all in one piece*
complete, entire, flawless, imperforate, indiscrete, perfect, scatheless, sound, together, unblemished, unbroken, uncut, undefiled, unharmed, unhurt, unimpaired, uninjured, unmarred, unscathed, untouched, unviolated, whole; SEE CONCEPTS 485,531

intangible [adj] *indefinite, obscured*
abstract, abstruse, airy, dim, eluding, elusive, ethereal, evading, evanescent, evasive, hypothetical, impalpable, imperceptible, imponderable, inappreciable, incorporeal, indeterminate, insensible, invisible, rare, shadowy, slender, slight, unapparent, uncertain, unobservable, unreal, unsubstantial, unsure, vague; SEE CONCEPTS 535,582

integral [adj1] *necessary, basic*
component, constituent, elemental, essential, fundamental, indispensable, intrinsic, requisite; SEE CONCEPT 546

integral [adj2] *complete*
aggregate, choate, elemental, entire, full, indivisible, intact, part-and-parcel*, perfect, unbroken, undivided, whole; SEE CONCEPT 531

integrate [v] *mix, merge*
accommodate, amalgamate, arrange, articulate, assimilate, associate, attune, blend, coalesce, combine, come together, compact, concatenate, concentrate, conform, conjoin, consolidate, coordinate, desegregate, embody, fuse, get together, harmonize, incorporate, interface, intermix, join, knit, link, meld with, mesh, orchestrate, organize, proportion, reconcile, reconciliate, symphonize, synthesize, systematize, throw in together, tune, unify, unite, wed; SEE CONCEPTS 113,114

integrity [n1] *honor, uprightness*
candor, forthrightness, goodness, honestness, honesty, honorableness, incorruptibility, incorruption, principle, probity, purity, rectitude, righteousness, sincerity, straightforwardness, virtue; SEE CONCEPT 411

integrity [n2] *completeness*
absoluteness, coherence, cohesion, entireness, perfection, purity, simplicity, soundness, stability, totality, unity, wholeness; SEE CONCEPT 635

intellect [n] *capability of the mind; someone with capable mind*
ability, acumen, brains*, cerebration, comprehension, egghead*, genius, intellectual, intellectuality, intelligence, intuition, judgment, mentality, mind, psyche, pundit, reason, savvy,

in
in

sense, smarts, thinker, understanding, what it takes*, wits; SEE CONCEPTS *409,416*

intellectual [*adj*] *very smart*
bookish, brainy*, cerebral, creative, highbrow*, highbrowed*, intellective, intelligent, inventive, learned, mental, phrenic, psychological, rational, scholarly, studious, subjective, thoughtful; SEE CONCEPT *402*

intellectual [*n*] *very smart person*
academic, academician, avant-garde, brain*, braintruster*, doctor, egghead*, Einstein*, genius, highbrow*, intelligentsia, philosopher, pundit, sage, scholar, thinker, whiz*, wizard; SEE CONCEPTS *350,416*

intelligence [*n1*] *ability to perceive, understand*
acuity, acumen, agility, alertness, aptitude, brainpower, brains*, brightness, brilliance, capacity, cleverness, comprehension, coruscation, discernment, gray matter*, intellect, IQ*, judgment, luminosity, mentality, mind, penetration, perception, perspicacity, precocity, quickness, quotient, reason, sagacity, savvy, sense, skill, smarts, subtlety, the right stuff*, trenchancy, understanding, what it takes*, wit; SEE CONCEPT *409*

intelligence [*n2*] *secret information*
advice, clue, data, dirt, disclosure, facts, findings, hot tip*, info*, inside story*, knowledge, leak, lowdown*, news, notice, notification, picture, report, rumor, tidings, tip-off*, word*; SEE CONCEPT *274*

intelligent [*adj*] *very smart*
able, acute, alert, alive, all there*, apt, astute, brainy*, bright, brilliant, calculating, capable, clever, comprehending, creative, deep*, discerning, enlightened, exceptional, highbrow*, imaginative, ingenious, instructed, inventive, keen, knowing, knowledgeable, original, penetrating, perceptive, perspicacious, profound, quick, quick-witted, rational, ready, reasonable, resourceful, responsible, sage, sharp, smart, thinking, together*, understanding, well-informed, whiz*, wise, witty; SEE CONCEPT *402*

intelligible [*adj*] *understandable*
apprehensible, clear, comprehensible, distinct, fathomable, graspable, knowable, lucid, luminous, obvious, open, plain, unambiguous, unequivocal, unmistakable; SEE CONCEPT *529*

intend [*v*] *have in mind; determine*
add up, aim, appoint, aspire to, attempt, be determined, be resolved, connote, contemplate, decree, dedicate, denote, design, designate, destine, devote, endeavor, essay, expect, express, figure on, have in mind, hope to, import, indicate, look forward, mean, meditate, ordain, plan, plot, propose, purpose, reserve, resolve, scheme, set apart, set aside, signify, spell, strive, think, try; SEE CONCEPTS *18,36,73,129*

intended [*adj*] *engaged; destined*
accidentally on purpose*, advised, affianced, aforethought, asked for, betrothed, calculated, contemplated, contracted, designed, expected, future, intentional, meant, pinned, planned, plighted, prearranged, predestined, predetermined, promised, proposed, set, steady; SEE CONCEPT *552*

intense [*adj*] *forceful, severe; passionate*
acute, agonizing, all-consuming, ardent, biting, bitter, burning, close, concentrated, consuming, cutting, deep, diligent, eager, earnest, energetic,

exaggerated, exceptional, excessive, exquisite, extraordinary, extreme, fanatical, fervent, fervid, fierce, forcible, full, great, hard, harsh, heightened, impassioned, intensified, intensive, keen, marked, piercing, powerful, profound, protracted, pungent, sharp, shrill, stinging, strained, strong, supreme, undue, vehement, violent, vivid, zealous; SEE CONCEPT *569*

intensify [*v*] *make more forceful, severe*
accent, accentuate, add fuel*, add to, aggrandize, aggravate, augment, beef up*, boost, brighten, build up, concentrate, darken, deepen, emphasize, enhance, escalate, exacerbate, exalt, heat up*, heighten, increase, intensate, lighten, magnify, point, pour it on*, quicken, raise, redouble, reinforce, rise, rouse, set off, sharpen, spike*, step up, strengthen, stress, tone up, whet; SEE CONCEPTS *233,250*

intensity [*n*] *passion, force*
acuteness, anxiety, ardor, concentration, deepness, depth, earnestness, emotion, emphasis, energy, excess, excitement, extreme, extremity, fanaticism, ferment, ferociousness, ferocity, fervency, fervor, fierceness, fire, force, forcefulness, fury, high pitch*, intenseness, keenness, magnitude, might, nervousness, potency, power, severity, sharpness, strain, strength, tenseness, tension, vehemence, vigor, violence, volume, weightiness, wildness; SEE CONCEPTS *641,669*

intensive [*adj*] *exhaustive*
accelerated, all-out*, complete, comprehensive, concentrated, deep, demanding, fast, hard, in-depth, out-and-out*, profound, radical, severe, speeded-up*, thorough, thoroughgoing; SEE CONCEPT *531*

intent [*adj*] *determined, resolute*
absorbed, alert, attending, attentive, bent, bound, committed, concentrated, concentrating, decided, decisive, deep, eager, earnest, engaged, engrossed, enthusiastic, firm, fixed, hell-bent*, immersed, industrious, intense, minding, occupied, piercing, preoccupied, rapt, resolved, riveted*, set, settled, steadfast, steady, watchful, watching, wrapped up*; SEE CONCEPTS *403,542*

intent/intention [*n*] *aim, purpose*
acceptation, animus, bottom line*, conation, design, desire, drift, end, goal, heart, hope, idea, import, intendment, meaning, meat*, name of the game*, nature, notion, nub, nuts and bolts*, object, objective, plan, point, project, purport, scheme, score, sense, significance, significancy, signification, target, understanding, volition, will, wish; SEE CONCEPT *659*

intentional [*adj*] *deliberate*
advised, aforethought, calculated, considered, designed, designful, done on purpose, intended, meant, meditated, planned, prearranged, premeditated, proposed, purposed, studied, unforced, voluntary, willful, willing, witting; SEE CONCEPT *544*

intently [*adv*] *with concentration*
attentively, closely, fixedly, hard, keenly, searchingly, sharply, steadily, watchfully; SEE CONCEPTS *403,544*

inter [*v*] *bury*
cover up, entomb, inhume, inurn, lay to rest, plant, put away, sepulcher, sepulture, tomb; SEE CONCEPTS *172,178,367*

interact [*v*] *communicate*
collaborate, combine, connect, contact, cooper-

ate, get across*, get the message*, interface, interplay, interreact, join, keep in touch, merge, mesh, network, reach out, relate, touch, touch base*, unite; SEE CONCEPT 266

intercede [v] *mediate*
advocate, arbitrate, barge in, butt in*, intermediate, interpose, intervene, intrude, mix in, monkey with*, negotiate, plead, reconcile, speak, step in; SEE CONCEPTS 56,110

intercept [v] *head off; interrupt*
ambush, appropriate, arrest, block, catch, check, curb, cut in, cut off, deflect, head off at pass*, hijack, hinder, interlope, interpose, make off with, obstruct, prevent, seize, shortstop*, stop, take, take away; SEE CONCEPTS 121,164

interchange [n] *switch, exchange*
altering, alternation, barter, change, crossfire, give-and-take*, intersection, junction, mesh, networking, reciprocation, shift, trade, transposition, variation, varying; SEE CONCEPTS 104,697

interchange [v] *switch, exchange*
alternate, bandy, barter, commute, connect, contact, convert, interact, interface, mesh, network, reciprocate, relate, reverse, substitute, swap, trade, transpose; SEE CONCEPTS 56,104

interchangeable [adj] *identical, transposable*
changeable, commutable, compatible, converse, convertible, correspondent, equivalent, exchangeable, fungible, interconvertible, mutual, reciprocal, reciprocative, same, substitutable, synonymous, workalike; SEE CONCEPTS 487,573

intercourse [n1] *sexual act*
carnal knowledge, coition, coitus, copulation, fornication, intimacy, love-making, relations, sex, sexual relations; SEE CONCEPT 375

intercourse [n2] *communication; business exchange*
association, commerce, communion, connection, contact, converse, correspondence, dealings, give-and-take, interchange, intercommunication, mesh, networking, team play, teamwork, trade, traffic, transactions; SEE CONCEPTS 266,324

interest [n1] *attraction, curiosity*
absorption, activity, affection, attentiveness, care, case, concern, concernment, consequence, diversion, engrossment, enthusiasm, excitement, game, hobby, importance, interestedness, into, leisure activity, matter, moment, note, notice, passion, pastime, preoccupation, pursuit, racket, recreation, regard, relaxation, relevance, significance, sport, suspicion, sympathy, thing; SEE CONCEPTS 20,532,690

interest [n2] *advantage*
benefit, gain, good, profit, prosperity, welfare, well-being; SEE CONCEPT 693

interest [n3] *share, investment*
accrual, authority, bonus, claim, commitment, credit, discount, due, earnings, gain, influence, involvement, participation, percentage, piece, points, portion, premium, right, stake, title; SEE CONCEPTS 332,344,835

interest [v] *hold the attention of*
affect, amuse, appeal, appeal to, arouse, attract, be interesting to, concern, divert, engage, engross, entertain, enthrall, excite, fascinate, grab, hook, intrigue, involve, lure, move, perk up, pique, please, pull, sit up, snare, tantalize, tempt, titillate, touch, turn on; SEE CONCEPTS 7,11,22

interested [adj] *concerned, curious*
absorbed, affected, attentive, attracted, awakened,

biased, caught, drawn, eat sleep and breathe*, engrossed, enticed, excited, fascinated, fired*, gone*, hooked*, implicated, impressed, inspired, inspirited, intent, into*, involved, keen, lured, moved, obsessed, occupied, on the case*, open, partial, partisan, predisposed, prejudiced, responsive, roused, sold, stimulated, stirred, struck, sympathetic, taken, touched; SEE CONCEPT 403

interesting [adj] *appealing, entertaining*
absorbing, affecting, alluring, amusing, arresting, attractive, beautiful, captivating, charismatic, compelling, curious, delightful, elegant, enchanting, engaging, engrossing, enthralling, entrancing, exceptional, exotic, fascinating, fine, gracious, gripping, impressive, intriguing, inviting, lovely, magnetic, pleasing, pleasurable, prepossessing, provocative, readable, refreshing, riveting, stimulating, stirring, striking, suspicious, thought-provoking, unusual, winning; SEE CONCEPTS 529,572

interfere [v] *meddle, intervene*
baffle, balk, barge in, busybody*, butt in*, conflict, discommode, foil, fool with, frustrate, get in the way*, get involved, hamper, handicap, hang up*, hinder, hold up, horn in*, impede, incommode, inconvenience, inhibit, intercede, interlope, intermeddle, intermediate, intermit, interpose, intrude, jam, make*, mix in, obstruct, obtrude, oppose, poke nose in*, prevent, remit, step in, stop, suspend, tamper, thwart, trammel, trouble; SEE CONCEPTS 121,384

interference [n] *meddling, impedance*
arrest, background, backseat driving*, barging in*, barring, blocking, checking, choking, clashing, clogging, conflict, hampering, hindrance, intermeddling, interposition, intervention, intrusion, prying, resistance, retardation, tackling, tampering, trespassing; SEE CONCEPTS 121,384

interim [adj] *temporary*
acting, ad interim, caretaker*, improvised, intervening, makeshift, pro tem, pro tempore, provisional, stopgap, thrown-together*; SEE CONCEPT 560

interim [n] *interval*
breach, break, breather, breathing spell, coffee break, cutoff, downtime*, gap, hiatus, interlude, interregnum, interruption, lacuna, layoff, letup*, meantime, meanwhile, pause, take*, ten*, time*, time-out; SEE CONCEPTS 807,822

interior [adj] *inside, central*
autogenous, domestic, endogenous, gut, home, in-house, inland, inner, innermost, internal, intimate, inward, private, remote, secret, visceral, viscerous, within; SEE CONCEPTS 583,826,830

interior [n] *center, core*
belly, bosom, contents, heart, heartland, innards, inner parts, inside, internals, intrinsicality, lining, marrow, midst, pith, pulp, soul, substance, viscera, within; SEE CONCEPTS 742,826,830

interject [v] *throw in; interrupt*
add, fill in, force in, implant, import, include, infiltrate, infuse, ingrain, inject, insert, insinuate, intercalate, interpolate, interpose, intersperse, introduce, intrude, parenthesize, put in, splice, squeeze in; SEE CONCEPTS 14,51

interloper [n] *person who intrudes, meddles*
alien, busybody, intermeddler, intruder, meddler, obtruder, trespasser, uninvited guest, unwanted visitor; SEE CONCEPTS 412,423

in
in

interlude [n] *pause, break*
breathing space*, delay, episode, halt, hiatus, idyll, interim, intermission, interregnum, interruption, interval, lull, meantime, meanwhile, parenthesis, recess, respite, rest, spell, stop, stoppage, wait; SEE CONCEPT *807*

intermediary [n] *person who negotiates*
agent, broker, channel, connection, cutout, delegate, emissary, entrepreneur, fixer, go-between*, influence, instrument, interagent, interceder, intercessor, intermediate, mediator, medium, middle person, negotiator, organ, vehicle; SEE CONCEPTS *348,354*

intermediate [adj] *middle, in-between*
average, between, center, central, common, compromising, fair, halfway, indifferent, intermediary, interposed, intervening, mean, medial, median, mediocre, medium, mid, middling, midway, moderate, neutral, so-so*, standard, transitional; SEE CONCEPTS *585,830*

interment [n] *burial*
burying, entombment, funeral, inhumation, inurning, obsequy, sepulture; SEE CONCEPT *367*

interminable [adj] *infinite*
boring, boundless, ceaseless, constant, continuous, day-and-night*, dragged out*, dull, endless, eternal, everlasting, immeasurable, incessant, interminate, limitless, long, long-drawn-out*, long-winded, looped, never-ending, no end of*, no end to*, on a treadmill*, permanent, perpetual, protracted, spun out*, strung out*, timeless, unbound, unceasing, uninterrupted, unlimited, wearisome; SEE CONCEPT *798*

intermingle [v] *blend, mix*
amalgamate, associate, combine, come together, commingle, commix, fuse, immingle, interblend, interfuse, interlace, intermix, interweave, join, merge, mesh, network, pool, throw in with, throw together, wed; SEE CONCEPTS *113,114*

intermission [n] *break, recess*
abeyance, abeyancy, break-off, breather, breathing spell, cessation, doldrums, dormancy, downtime*, interim, interlude, interregnum, interruption, interval, latency, layoff, let-up*, lull, parenthesis, pause, quiescence, quiescency, respite, rest, spell, stop, stoppage, suspense, suspension, time, time-out, wait; SEE CONCEPT *807*

intermittent [adj] *irregular, sporadic*
alternate, arrested, broken, by bits and pieces*, checked, cyclic, cyclical, discontinuing, discontinuous, epochal, every other, fitful, here and there*, hit-or-miss*, infrequent, interrupted, isochronal, isochronous, iterant, iterative, metrical, now and then*, occasional, on and off*, periodic, periodical, punctuated, recurrent, recurring, rhythmic, rhythmical, seasonal, serial, shifting, spasmodic, stop-and-go*; SEE CONCEPTS *482,534,799*

internal [adj] *within*
centralized, circumscribed, civic, constitutional, domestic, enclosed, gut, home, indigenous, inherent, in-house, innate, inner, innermore, inside, interior, intestine, intimate, intramural, intrinsic, inward, municipal, national, native, private, subjective, visceral, viscerous; SEE CONCEPTS *536,585,826,830*

international [adj] *worldwide*
all-embracing, cosmopolitan, ecumenical, foreign, global, intercontinental, universal, world; SEE CONCEPTS *536,772*

Internet [n] *computer network*
ARPANET, computer network, cyberspace, hyperspace, infobahn, information highway, information superhighway, national information infrastructure, online network, the Net*, the Web*, W3, World Wide Web, WWW; SEE CONCEPTS *381,388,770*

interplay [n] *interaction*
coaction, exchange, give-and-take*, mesh, meshing, networking, reciprocation, reciprocity, team play*, teamwork, tit for tat*, transaction; SEE CONCEPT *266*

interpolate [v] *add*
admit, annex, append, enter, fill in, include, inject, insert, insinuate, intercalate, interjaculate, interject, interlope, interpose, introduce, intrude, throw in; SEE CONCEPTS *112,201,209*

interpret [v] *make sense of; define*
adapt, annotate, clarify, comment, commentate, construe, decipher, decode, delineate, depict, describe, elucidate, enact, exemplify, explain, explicate, expound, gather, gloss, illustrate, image, improvise, limn, make of, mimic, paraphrase, perform, picture, play, portray, read, reenact, render, represent, solve, spell out, take*, throw light on*, translate, understand, view; SEE CONCEPTS *57,292*

interpretation [n] *understanding*
analysis, apprehension, assimilation, awareness, clarification, comprehension, discernment, explanation, grasp, grip, insight, judgment, knowing, meaning, perception, reading, slant, translation; SEE CONCEPT *409*

interrogate [v] *ask pointed questions*
catechize, cross-examine, cross-question, examine, give the third degree*, go over*, grill, inquire, investigate, pump, put the screws to*, put through the wringer*, query, question, quiz, roast*, sweat out*, work over*; SEE CONCEPTS *48,53*

interrupt [v] *bother, interfere*
arrest, barge in, break, break in, break off, break train of thought*, bust in*, butt in*, check, chime in*, come between, crash, crowd in, cut, cut in on*, cut off*, cut short*, defer, delay, disconnect, discontinue, disjoin, disturb, disunite, divide, edge in, get in the way, halt, heckle, hinder, hold up, horn in, impede, in, infringe, inject, insinuate, intrude, lay aside, obstruct, prevent, punctuate, put in, separate, sever, shortstop*, stay, stop, suspend, work in; SEE CONCEPTS *51,121,384*

interruption [n] *break; interference*
abeyance, abeyancy, arrest, blackout, breach, break-off, cessation, check, cutoff, delay, disconnection, discontinuance, disruption, dissolution, disturbance, disuniting, division, doldrums, dormancy, gap, halt, hiatus, hindrance, hitch, impediment, interim, intermission, interval, intrusion, lacuna, latency, layoff, letup*, obstacle, obstruction, parenthesis, pause, quiescence, rift, rupture, separation, severance, split, stop, stoppage, suspension; SEE CONCEPTS *807,832*

intersect [v] *cut across; cross at a point*
bisect, break in two, change, converge, crisscross, cross, crosscut, cut, decussate, divide, intercross, join, meet, separate, touch, traverse; SEE CONCEPTS *113,738,749*

intersection [*n*] *crossroads*
circle, cloverleaf, crossing, crosswalk, crossway, interchange, junction, stop; SEE CONCEPT *501*

intersperse [*v*] *scatter*
bestrew, diffuse, distribute, infuse, interfuse, interlard, intermix, intersow, intersprinkle, pepper, sprinkle; SEE CONCEPTS *201,222*

interstice [*n*] *opening, crack*
aperture, chink, cleft, cranny, crevice, fissure, gap, hole, interval, slit, space; SEE CONCEPT *513*

intertwine/interweave [*v*] *twist around*
associate, braid, connect, convolute, crisscross, cross, entwine, interknit, interlace, intertwist, intervolve, interwind, interwreathe, link, mesh, network, relate, reticulate, tangle, tat, weave; SEE CONCEPTS *113,114*

interval [*n*] *break, pause*
breach, breathing space*, comma, delay, distance, downtime, five*, gap, hiatus, interim, interlude, intermission, interregnum, interruption, lacuna, layoff, letup, lull, meantime, opening, parenthesis, pausation, period, playtime, rest, season, space, spell, ten*, term, time, time-out, wait, while; SEE CONCEPTS *807,822*

intervene [*v1*] *mediate*
arbitrate, barge in, butt in*, come between, divide, horn in*, intercede, interfere, intermediate, interpose, interrupt, intrude, involve, meddle, mix in, muscle in*, negotiate, obtrude, part, put in two cents*, reconcile, separate, settle, sever, step in, take a hand*; SEE CONCEPTS *110,234,266*

intervene [*v2*] *happen*
bedevil, befall, come to pass, ensue, occur, succeed, supervene, take place; SEE CONCEPTS *4,242*

interview [*n*] *questioning and evaluation*
account, audience, call, call back, cattle call*, communication, conference, consultation, conversation, dialogue, examination, hearing, meeting, oral, parley, press conference, record, statement, talk; SEE CONCEPTS *48,351*

interview [*v*] *ask questions and evaluate*
consult, converse, examine, get for the record, get opinion, give oral examination, hold inquiry, interrogate, question, quiz, sound out, talk, talk to; SEE CONCEPTS *48,351*

interviewer [*n*] *questioner*
inquirer, inquistor, interrogator, reporter, talk-show host; SEE CONCEPTS *348,356*

intestinal/intestine [*adj*] *pertaining to digestive organs*
abdominal, alimentary, bowel, celiac, duodenal, gut, inner, inside, interior, internal, inward, rectal, stomachic, ventral, visceral; SEE CONCEPT *406*

in the bag [*adj*] *certain*
assured, bound, certified, cinched, concluded, decided, definite, ensured, fixed, guaranteed, insured, set, settled, sure; SEE CONCEPT *535*

intimacy [*n*] *closeness between people*
acquaintance, affection, affinity, close relationship, communion, confidence, confidentiality, experience, familiarity, friendship, inwardness, understanding; SEE CONCEPT *388*

intimate [*adj1*] *friendly, devoted*
affectionate, bosom, buddy-buddy*, cherished, chummy*, close, clubby*, comfy, confidential, cozy, dear, dearest, faithful, fast, fond, loving, mellow, mix, near, nearest, next, nice, regular, roommate, snug, warm; SEE CONCEPT *555*

intimate [*adj2*] *private, personal*
confidential, deep, deep-seated, detailed, elemental, essential, exhaustive, experienced, firsthand, guarded, gut*, immediate, inborn, inbred, in-depth, indwelling, ingrained, inherent, inmost, innate, innermost, interior, internal, intrinsic, penetrating, privy, profound, secret, special, thorough, trusted, uptight, visceral, viscerous; SEE CONCEPTS *529,549*

intimate [*n*] *a close friend; familiar person*
associate, bosom buddy*, chum, companion, comrade, confidant, confidante, crony, familiar, family, lover, mate, pal; SEE CONCEPTS *416,423*

intimate [*v*] *suggest; tip off*
affirm, air, allude, announce, assert, aver, avouch, communicate, connote, declare, drop a hint*, expose, express, hint, impart, imply, indicate, infer, insinuate, leak, let cat out of bag*, let it be known, make known, make noise*, profess, remind, spill the beans*, spring, state, utter, vent, voice, warn; SEE CONCEPTS *49,60,75*

intimation [*n*] *clue, hint*
allusion, announcement, breath, communication, cue, declaration, implication, indication, inkling, innuendo, insinuation, notice, notion, reminder, shade, shadow, strain, streak, suggestion, suspicion, telltale, tinge, tip, trace, warning, wind; SEE CONCEPTS *274,689*

intimidate [*v*] *frighten, threaten*
alarm, appall, awe, badger, bait, bludgeon, bluster, bowl over*, browbeat*, buffalo*, bulldoze*, bully, chill, coerce, compel, constrain, cow*, daunt, dishearten, dismay, dispirit, disquiet, dragoon, enforce, force, hound*, lean on*, oblige, overawe, push around*, ride*, ruffle, scare, showboat, spook, strong-arm, subdue, terrify, terrorize, twist someone's arm*; SEE CONCEPTS *7,14,19*

intimidating [*adj*] *threatening*
aggressive, bullying, frightening, pressuring, terrifying, terrorizing; SEE CONCEPTS *525,548,570*

intolerable [*adj*] *unacceptable; beyond bearing*
a bit much, enough already*, excruciating, extreme, impossible, insufferable, insupportable, last straw*, offensive, painful, unbearable, undesirable, unendurable; SEE CONCEPT *529*

intolerant [*adj*] *impatient, prejudiced*
antipathetic, averse, biased, bigoted, chauvinistic, communist, conservative, contemptuous, dictatorial, disdainful, dogmatic, fanatical, fractious, hateful, illiberal, indignant, individualistic, inflexible, irate, irritable, jaundiced, narrow, narrow-minded, obdurate, one-sided, outraged, racialist, racist, short-fuse*, small-minded*, snappy, stuffy, tilted, uncharitable, unfair, unforbearing, unindulgent, unsympathetic, unwilling, upset, waspish, worked-up*, xenophobic; SEE CONCEPTS *403,404,542*

intonation [*n*] *inflection*
accent, articulation, emphasis, enunciation, modulation, pitch, pronunciation, sound, tonality, tone, tone of voice; SEE CONCEPTS *65,595*

intoxicated [*adj1*] *drunk*
blind*, bombed*, boozed, buzzed*, drunken, high*, inebriated, loaded*, looped*, muddled, potted*, sloppy, smashed*, tanked*, three sheets to the wind*, tied one on*, tight*, tipsy, under the influence, unsober; SEE CONCEPT *406*

intoxicated [*adj2*] *extremely happy*
absorbed, affected, beside oneself, captivated,

in
in

concerned, delirious, dizzy, drunk, ecstatic, elated, enraptured, euphoric, excited, exhilarated, galvanized, high*, infatuated, interested, moved, piqued, quickened, sent*, stimulated, turned-on*; SEE CONCEPT *403*

intoxicating [*adj*] *causing great happiness*
exciting, exhilarant, exhilarating, exhilarative, eye-popping, heady, inspiring, provocative, rousing, stimulating, stirring, thrilling; SEE CONCEPT *537*

intractable /intransigent [*adj*] *difficult, stubborn*
awkward, bullheaded*, cantankerous, contrary, hang tough*, hard-line*, headstrong, immovable, incompliant, incurable, indocile, indomitable, insoluble, locked in*, mulish, obdurate, obstinate, pat, pertinacious, perverse, pigheaded*, recalcitrant, refractory, resolute, self-willed, set in stone, tenacious, tough, tough-nut*, unbending, uncompromising, uncooperative, undisciplined, ungovernable, unmanageable, unpliable, unruly, unyielding, wayward, wild, willful; SEE CONCEPTS *401,534,542*

intrepid [*adj*] *brave, nervy*
audacious, bodacious*, bold, courageous, daring, dauntless, doughty, fearless, gallant, game, gritty, gutsy*, heroic, impavid, lionhearted, nerveless, plucky, resolute, spunky*, stalwart, unafraid, undaunted, unflinching, valiant, valorous; SEE CONCEPT *401*

intricate [*adj*] *complicated, elaborate*
abstruse, baroque, Byzantine*, can of worms*, complex, convoluted, Daedal*, difficult, entangled, fancy, hard, high-tech*, involved, labyrinthine, obscure, perplexing, rococo, sophisticated, tangled, tortuous, tricky; SEE CONCEPT *562*

intrigue [*n1*] *scheme*
artifice, cabal, chicanery, collusion, complication, conspiracy, contrivance, deal, design, dodge, double-dealing*, fix, frame-up*, fraud, game, graft, hookup, little game*, machination, maneuver, manipulation, plan, plot, ruse, stratagem, trickery, wile; SEE CONCEPTS *192,660*

intrigue [*n2*] *love affair*
affair, amour, attachment, case, flirtation, infatuation, interlude, intimacy, liaison, romance; SEE CONCEPT *388*

intrigue [*v1*] *arouse curiosity*
appeal, attract, bait, captivate, charm, con, delight, draw, enchant, entertain, excite, fascinate, grab, hook, interest, lead on*, mousetrap*, pique, please, pull, rivet, tickle, titillate, tout; SEE CONCEPTS *7,11,22*

intrigue [*v2*] *plot*
angle, be in cahoots*, cogitate, collude, connive, conspire, contrive, cook up*, devise, finagle, frame up*, machinate, maneuver, operate, plan, promote, scheme, set up*, work hand in glove*; SEE CONCEPT *36*

intriguing [*adj*] *interesting*
absorbing, alluring, appealing, arousing, attractive, beguiling, captivating, compelling, curious, enchanting, enthralling, exciting, fascinating, gripping, provocative, puzzling, riveting, stimulating, stirring, thought-provoking; SEE CONCEPTS *529,572*

intrinsic [*adj*] *basic, inborn*
built-in, central, congenital, connate, constitutional, constitutive, deep-seated, elemental, essential, fundamental, genuine, hereditary, inbred, indwelling, inherent, inmost, innate, intimate, material, native, natural, particular, peculiar, real, true, underlying; SEE CONCEPTS *404,406,546*

introduce [*v1*] *make known; present*
acquaint, advance, air, announce, bring out, bring up, broach, come out with, do the honors*, familiarize, fix up, get things rolling*, get together, give introduction, harbinger*, herald, kick off, knock down, lead into, lead off, moot, offer, open, open up, originate, pave the way*, precede, preface, propose, put forward, recommend, set forth, spring with, start ball rolling*, submit, suggest, usher, ventilate; SEE CONCEPTS *60,384*

introduce [*v2*] *begin, institute*
admit, bring forward, bring in, commence, enter, establish, found, inaugurate, induct, initiate, innovate, install, invent, kick off*, launch, organize, pioneer, plan, preface, present, set up, start, unveil, usher in; SEE CONCEPT *221*

introduce [*v3*] *add, insert*
carry, enter, fill in, freight, import, include, infix, inject, inlay, inlet, inset, insinuate, instill, intercalate, interject, interpolate, interpose, put in, send, ship, throw in, transport, work in; SEE CONCEPTS *112,113,209*

introduction [*n*] *something new; something that begins*
addition, admittance, awakening, baptism, basic principles, basic text, beginning, commencement, debut, essentials, establishment, exordium, first acquaintance, first taste, foreword, inauguration, inception, induction, influx, ingress, initiation, insertion, installation, institution, interpolation, intro*, launch, lead, lead-in, opening, opening remarks, overture, pioneering, preamble, preface, preliminaries, prelude, presentation, primer, proem, prolegomenon, prologue, survey; SEE CONCEPTS *270,727,828*

introductory [*adj*] *preliminary, first*
anterior, basic, beginning, early, elementary, inaugural, incipient, inductive, initial, initiatory, opening, original, precursory, prefatory, prelusive, preparative, preparatory, primary, prior, proemial, provisional, rudimentary, starting; SEE CONCEPTS *546,585*

introspection [*n*] *self-analysis*
brooding, contemplation, deep thought, egoism, heart-searching, introversion, meditation, reflection, rumination, scrutiny, self-absorption, self-examination, self-observation, self-questioning, soul-searching; SEE CONCEPTS *24,410*

introvert [*n*] *person who retreats mentally*
autist, brooder, egoist, egotist, loner*, narcissist, self-observer, solitary, wallflower*; SEE CONCEPT *423*

introverted [*adj*] *reserved*
bashful, cautious, close-mouthed, cold*, collected, cool, demure, introspective, modest, offish, quiet, reclusive, restrained, secretive, shy, soft-spoken, solitary, standoffish, uncommunicative, withdrawn; SEE CONCEPTS *401,404*

intrude [*v*] *trespass, interrupt*
barge in, bother, butt in*, chisel in*, cut in, disturb, encroach, entrench, go beyond, hold up, horn in*, infringe, insinuate, intercalate, interfere, interject, interlope, intermeddle, interpolate, interpose, introduce, invade, meddle, obtrude,

overstep, pester, push in, thrust, violate; SEE CONCEPTS *14,159,208,266*

intruder [*n*] *person who trespasses*
burglar, criminal, gate-crasher*, infiltrator, interferer, interloper, interrupter, invader, meddler, nuisance, obtruder, prowler, raider, snooper, squatter, thief, trespasser; SEE CONCEPTS *412,423*

intrusive [*adj*] *obtrusive*
forward, interfering, invasive, meddlesome, meddling, nosy*, presumptuous, protruding, prying; SEE CONCEPTS *401,542*

intuition [*n*] *insight*
clairvoyance, discernment, divination, ESP*, feeling*, foreknowledge, gut reaction*, hunch*, innate knowledge, inspiration, instinct, intuitiveness, nose*, penetration, perception, perceptivity, premonition, presentiment, second sight*, sixth sense*; SEE CONCEPTS *409,689*

intuitive [*adj*] *instinctive*
automatic, direct, emotional, habitual, immediate, inherent, innate, instinctual, involuntary, natural, perceptive, spontaneous, understood, unreflecting, untaught, visceral; SEE CONCEPT *402*

inundate [*v*] *drown, overwhelm*
deluge, dunk, engulf, flood, glut, immerse, overflow, overrun, pour down on, snow*, submerge, swamp, whelm; SEE CONCEPTS *172,179*

inure [*v*] *accustom*
acclimate, familiarize, habituate, harden, make ready, season, toughen, train; SEE CONCEPTS *15,38*

invade [*v*] *attack and encroach*
access, assail, assault, breach, burglarize, burst in, crash, descend upon, entrench, fall on, foray, go in, infect, infest, infringe, inroad, interfere, loot, make inroads*, maraud, meddle, muscle in*, occupy, overrun, overspread, overswarm, penetrate, permeate, pervade, pillage, plunder, raid, ravage, storm, swarm over, trespass, violate; SEE CONCEPTS *86,159,320*

invalid [*adj1*] *worthless; unfounded*
bad, baseless, fallacious, false, ill-founded, illogical, inoperative, irrational, mad, not binding, not working, nugatory, null, null and void*, reasonless, sophistic, unreasonable, unreasoned, unscientific, unsound, untrue, void, wrong; SEE CONCEPTS *552,560*

invalid [*adj2*] *sickly*
ailing, bedridden, below par, debilitated, disabled, down, feeble, frail, ill, infirm, laid low*, on the sick list*, out of action*, peaked, poorly, run-down, sick, weak; SEE CONCEPT *314*

invalid [*n*] *sick person*
consumptive, convalescent, incurable, patient, shut-in, sufferer; SEE CONCEPT *424*

invalidate [*v*] *render null and void*
abate, abolish, abrogate, annihilate, annul, blow sky-high*, cancel, circumduct, counteract, counterbalance, disannul, discredit, disqualify, impair, negate, negative, neutralize, nix, nullify, offset, overrule, overthrow, quash, refute, revoke, shoot full of holes*, undermine, undo, unfit, weaken, X-out*; SEE CONCEPTS *121,234*

invaluable [*adj*] *priceless*
beyond price, costly, dear, expensive, helpful, inestimable, precious, serviceable, valuable; SEE CONCEPTS *334,568*

invariable [*adj*] *not changing*
changeless, consistent, constant, fixed, immov-

able, immutable, inalterable, inflexible, monotonous, perpetual, regular, rigid, same, set, static, unalterable, unchangeable, unchanging, undiversified, unfailing, uniform, unmodifiable, unrelieved, unvarying, unwavering; SEE CONCEPT *534*

invasion [*n*] *attack, encroachment*
aggression, assault, breach, entrenchment, foray, forced entrance, incursion, infiltration, infraction, infringement, inroad, intrusion, irruption, maraud, offense, offensive, onslaught, overstepping, raid, transgression, trespass, usurpation, violation; SEE CONCEPTS *86,159,320*

invective [*n*] *verbal abuse*
accusation, berating, billingsgate, blame, blasphemy, castigation, censure, condemnation, contumely, denunciation, diatribe, epithet, jeremiad, obloquy, philippic, reproach, revilement, sarcasm, scurrility, tirade, tongue-lashing*, vilification, vituperation; SEE CONCEPTS *44,52,54,278*

inveigh [*v*] *blame, denounce*
admonish, berate, blast, castigate, censure, condemn, crack down on*, except, expostulate, go after*, have at*, jump down one's throat*, kick, lambaste, lay into, lay out, let have it, object, protest, rail, read out*, recriminate, remonstrate, reproach, rip into, roast, scold, scorch, sound off, tongue-lash, trash*, upbraid, vituperate, work over*; SEE CONCEPTS *44,52,54*

inveigle [*v*] *entice, manipulate*
allure, bait, bamboozle, beguile, blandish, butter*, cajole, charm, coax, con*, decoy, egg on*, ensnare, entrap, get around*, honey*, hook, influence, jolly, lay it on thick*, lead on*, lure, maneuver, massage, oil*, overdo it, persuade, play up to, rope in*, seduce, snow*, soap*, soften up*, string along*, stroke*, sweet talk*, tempt, toll, urge, wheedle, work over*; SEE CONCEPTS *11,14,59*

invent [*v1*] *create, think up*
ad-lib, author, bear, bring into being, coin, come upon, come up with, compose, conceive, contrive, cook up*, design, devise, discover, dream up, envision, execute, fake, fashion, find, forge, form, formulate, frame, hatch, imagine, improve, improvise, inaugurate, initiate, jam*, knock off*, make, make up, mint, off-the-cuff*, originate, plan, produce, project, toss off*, turn out, wing*; SEE CONCEPTS *36,173,221*

invent [*v2*] *fabricate*
concoct, conjure up, create out of thin air*, equivocate, fake, falsify, feign, fib, forge, lie, make believe, make up, misrepresent, misstate, pretend, prevaricate, simulate, tell a white lie*, tell untruth, think up, trump up*, vamp; SEE CONCEPTS *59,63*

invention [*n1*] *creation, creativeness*
apparatus, black box*, brainchild*, coinage, concoction, contraption, contrivance, creativity, design, development, device, discovery, doodad*, gadget, genius, gimmick, gizmo*, imagination, ingenuity, innovation, inspiration, inventiveness, novelty, opus, original, originality, resourcefulness; SEE CONCEPTS *260,409,660*

invention [*n2*] *fabrication, lie*
deceit, fake, falsehood, fancy, fantasy, fib, fiction, figment, forgery, prevarication, sham*, story, tall story*, untruth, yarn*; SEE CONCEPTS *63,278*

inventive [*adj*] *creative*
adroit, artistic, avant-garde, breaking new

ground, causative, constructive, demiurgic, deviceful, fertile, forgetive, formative, fruitful, gifted, imaginative, ingenious, innovational, innovative, innovatory, inspired, original, originative, poetical, productive, resourceful, teeming; SEE CONCEPTS *402,542*

inventor [*n*] *discoverer*
architect, author, builder, coiner, creator, designer, experimenter, father, founder, innovator, maker, originator, pioneer; SEE CONCEPTS *348,352,361*

inventory [*n*] *list of stock; stock*
account, backlog, catalogue, file, fund, hoard, index, itemization, record, register, reserve, reservoir, roll, roster, schedule, stock book, stockpile, store, summary, supply, table, tabulation; SEE CONCEPTS *283,338*

inverse [*adj*] *opposite*
changed, contrary, converse, flipped, inverted, reverse, reversed, reverted, transposed, turned, turned over; SEE CONCEPT *564*

invert [*v*] *reverse; turn upside down*
alter, backtrack, capsize, change, convert, double back, evert, flip, flip-flop*, introvert, inverse, modify, overturn, renege, revert, tip, transplace, transpose, turn, turn down, turn inside out, turn over, turn the tables*, upend, upset, upturn; SEE CONCEPTS *213,232*

invest [*v1*] *contribute money to make money*
advance, back, bankroll, buy into, buy stock, devote, endow, endue, get into, go in for, imbue, infuse, intrust, lay out, lend, loan, pick up the tab*, plow back into*, plunge, provide, put in, put up dough*, salt away*, sink, spend, stake, supply; SEE CONCEPTS *115,330,341*

invest [*v2*] *give power or authority*
adopt, authorize, bequeath, charge, consecrate, empower, endow, endue, enthrone, establish, honor, inaugurate, induct, initiate, install, instate, license, ordain, sanction, vest; SEE CONCEPTS *50,88*

investigate [*v*] *check into thoroughly*
be all ears*, bug, case*, check out, check over, check up, consider, delve, dig, examine, explore, eyeball*, feel out, frisk, give the once over*, go into, inquire, inquisite, inspect, interrogate, listen in, look into, look over, look-see, make inquiry, muckrake, nose around*, poke, probe, prospect, pry, put to the test*, question, read, reconnoiter, research, review, run down, scout, scrutinize, search, sift, spy, stake out, study, tap, wiretap; SEE CONCEPTS *48,103,216*

investigation [*n*] *thorough check*
analysis, case, delving, examination, exploration, fact-finding, gander, hearing, hustle, inquest, inquiry, inquisition, inspection, legwork, observation, observing, pike, probe, probing, quest, quiz, research, review, scrutiny, search, sounding, study, survey, surveying; SEE CONCEPTS *48,103,216,290*

investigator [*n*] *person who checks thoroughly*
agent, analyst, attorney, auditor, detective, examiner, gumshoe*, hound*, inquirer, inspector, plainclothes officer, police, private detective, private eye, prosecutor, researcher, reviewer, Sherlock Holmes*, sleuth, snooper, spy, tester, undercover cop; SEE CONCEPTS *348,355*

investment [*n*] *something given, lent for a return*
advance, ante, asset, backing, bail, contribution, endowment, expenditure, expense, finance, financing, flutter, grant, hunch, inside, interests, investing, loan, money, piece, plunge, property, purchase, smart money*, spec*, speculation, stab*, stake, transaction, venture, vested interests; SEE CONCEPTS *330,332,340*

investor [*n*] *financier*
backer, banker, capitalist, lender, shareholder, stockholder, venture capitalist; SEE CONCEPTS *347,348,353*

inveterate [*adj*] *long-standing, established*
abiding, accustomed, addicted, chronic, confirmed, continuing, customary, deep-rooted, deep-seated, dyed-in-the-wool*, enduring, entrenched, fixed, habitual, habituated, hard-core*, hardened, inbred, incorrigible, incurable, indurated, ineradicable, ingrained, innate, lifelong, long-lasting, long-lived, obstinate, old, perennial, permanent, persistent, persisting, set, settled, stubborn, sworn, usual; SEE CONCEPTS *404,534,798*

invidious [*adj*] *hateful*
abominable, calumnious, defamatory, detestable, detracting, detractive, detractory, discriminatory, envious, envying, green-eyed*, jealous, libelous, maligning, obnoxious, odious, offensive, repugnant, scandalous, slanderous, slighting, undesirable, vilifying; SEE CONCEPTS *401,403*

invigorate [*v*] *stimulate*
activate, animate, brace, buck up, energize, enliven, excite, exhilarate, fortify, freshen, galvanize, harden, inspirit, liven up, nerve, pep up, perk up, pick up, quicken, rally, refresh, reinforce, rejuvenate, renew, restore, revitalize, rouse, snap up*, stir, strengthen, trigger, turn on*, vitalize, vivify, zap; SEE CONCEPTS *7,14,22,110*

invigorating [*adj*] *stimulating*
aesthetic, bracing, brisk, charged, energizing, exhilarating, exhilarative, fascinating, fresh, healthful, high*, hyper*, interesting, lively, quickening, refreshing, rejuvenating, rejuvenative, restorative, salubrious, tonic, uplifting, vitalizing; SEE CONCEPT *537*

invincible [*adj*] *indestructible*
bulletproof, impassable, impregnable, indomitable, insuperable, inviolable, invulnerable, irresistible, powerful, strong, unassailable, unattackable, unbeatable, unconquerable, undefeatable, unsurmountable, untouchable, unyielding; SEE CONCEPTS *489,540,551*

invisible [*adj*] *unable to be seen; hidden*
concealed, covert, deceptive, disguised, ethereal, gaseous, ghostly, ideal, impalpable, imperceptible, imponderable, inappreciable, inconspicuous, indiscernible, infinitesimal, insensible, intangible, masked, microscopic, not in sight, obliterated, obscured, occult, out of sight, perdu, screened, supernatural, ulterior, unapparent, undisclosed, ungraspable, unnoticeable, unobservable, unperceivable, unreal, unseeable, unseen, unviewable, vaporous, veiled, wraithlike; SEE CONCEPTS *485,582,619*

invitation [*n*] *proposal; asking*
allurement, appeal, attraction, begging, bid, bidding, call, challenge, compliments, coquetry, date, encouragement, enticement, feeler*, ground, hit, incitement, inducement, invite, lure, motive, offer, open door*, overture, paper, pass, petition, pressure, proffer, prompting, proposition, provocation, rain check*, reason, request,

solicitation, suggestion, summons, supplication, temptation, urge; SEE CONCEPTS *48,384*

invite [*v*] *ask to do something socially*
allure, appeal to, attract, beg, bid, bring on, call, command, countenance, court, draw, encourage, entice, entreat, give invitation, have in, have over, include as guest, insist, inveigle, invitation, issue, lead, lure, persuade, petition, ply, pray, press, prevail on, propose, provoke, request, send invitation, solicit, suggest, summon, supplicate, tempt, toll, urge, vamp, welcome, WOO; SEE CONCEPTS *48,68,384*

inviting [*adj*] *alluring, captivating*
agreeable, appealing, attractive, beguiling, bewitching, charming, cordial, delightful, encouraging, engaging, enticing, fascinating, intriguing, magnetic, mouthwatering, open, persuasive, pleasing, provocative, seductive, tempting, warm, welcoming, winning, winsome; SEE CONCEPTS *404,529,537*

in vitro [*adj*] *artificial*
artificial insemination, outside the womb, test-tube; SEE CONCEPTS *372,723*

invocation [*n*] *prayer*
abracadabra*, appeal, beseeching, calling, command, conjuration, entreaty, hocus-pocus*, hoodoo*, mumbo-jumbo*, petition, rune, summons, supplication, voodoo*; SEE CONCEPTS *48,278,368*

invoice [*n*] *itemized bill*
account, bill of sale, check, IOU, note, statement; SEE CONCEPTS *329,332*

invoke [*v1*] *call upon*
adjure, appeal to, beg, beseech, call forth, conjure, crave, entreat, implore, importune, petition, plead, pray, request, send for, solicit, summon, supplicate; SEE CONCEPT *48*

invoke [*v2*] *put into effect*
apply, call in, effect, enforce, have recourse to, implement, initiate, resort to, use; SEE CONCEPTS *50,88*

involuntary [*adj*] *automatic; not done willingly*
automatic, begrudging, blind, compulsory, conditioned, forced, grudging, habitual, impulsive, instinctive, instinctual, knee-jerk*, obligatory, reflex, reflexive, reluctant, spontaneous, uncalculated, unconscious, uncontrolled, unintended, unintentional, unmeditated, unpremeditated, unprompted, unthinking, unwilling, unwitting, will-less; SEE CONCEPT *544*

involve [*v*] *draw in; include*
absorb, affect, argue, associate, bind, catch, commit, complicate, comprehend, comprise, compromise, concern, connect, contain, cover, denote, embrace, embroil, engage, engross, enmesh, entail, entangle, grip, hold, hook, implicate, imply, incorporate, incriminate, inculpate, link, mean, mire, mix up*, necessitate, number, point to, preoccupy, presuppose, prove, relate, require, rivet, rope in, snarl up, suggest, take in, tangle, touch, wrap up in*; SEE CONCEPT *112*

involved [*adj1*] *complicated*
Byzantine*, complex, confusing, convoluted, difficult, elaborate, Ghordian*, high-tech*, intricate, knotty*, labyrinthine, mazy, muddled, ramified, sophisticated, tangled, tortuous, winding; SEE CONCEPT *562*

involved [*adj2*] *implicated in action*
affected, caught, concerned, eat sleep and breathe*, embarrassed, embroiled, enmeshed, entangled, hooked, immersed in, incriminated, interested, into, knee-deep in*, mixed up in*, mixed up with*, occupied, participating, taking part in, tangled, up to here in*, up to one's neck in*; SEE CONCEPTS *542,545*

invulnerable [*adj*] *invincible*
bulletproof, impassable, impenetrable, impregnable, indestructible, powerful, secure, strong, unbeatable, untouchable; SEE CONCEPTS *489,540,551*

inward [*adj1*] *ingoing*
entering, inbound, incoming, infiltrating, inflowing, inpouring, penetrating, through; SEE CONCEPT *581*

inward [*adj2*] *private*
confidential, hidden, inmost, inner, innermost, inside, intellectual, interior, internal, intimate, personal, privy, psychological, religious, secret, spiritual; SEE CONCEPT *529*

iota [*n*] *small bit*
atom, crumb, grain, hint, infinitesimal, jot, mite, molecule, nucleus, ounce, particle, ray, scintilla, scrap, smidgen, speck, trace, whit; SEE CONCEPT *831*

IRA [*n*] *individual retirement account*
Keogh plan, retirement plan, Roth IRA, self-funded retirement plan, tax-free savings account; SEE CONCEPTS *335,340,446,710*

irascible [*adj*] *crabby*
angry, bearish, bristly, cantankerous, choleric, crabbed, cranky, cross, feisty, fractious, grouchy, hasty, hot-tempered, huffy, ireful, irritable, ogre, passionate, peevish, petulant, querulous, quick-tempered, short-tempered, snappish, surly, testy, thin-skinned*, touchy, uptight; SEE CONCEPT *401*

irate [*adj*] *angry*
angered, annoyed, blown a gasket*, enraged, exasperated, fuming, furious, incensed, indignant, infuriated, irritated, livid, mad, piqued, provoked, riled, steamed*, ticked off*, up in arms*, worked up*, wrathful, wroth; SEE CONCEPTS *403,542*

ire [*n*] *anger*
annoyance, boiling point*, conniption, conniption fit*, displeasure, exasperation, fury, indignation, more heat than light*, passion, rage, slow burn*, wrath; SEE CONCEPT *410*

iridescent [*adj*] *rainbow-colored*
irised, lustrous, many-colored, nacreous, opalescent, opaline, pearly, polychromatic, prismatic, rainbowlike, shimmering; SEE CONCEPT *618*

irk [*v*] *aggravate; rub the wrong way*
abrade, annoy, bother, bug*, discommode, disturb, eat*, fret, gall, get on nerves*, get to*, give a hard time*, harass, incommode, inconvenience, irritate, make waves*, miff, nettle, peeve, provoke, put out*, rasp, rile, ruffle, trouble, vex; SEE CONCEPTS *7,19*

irksome [*adj*] *annoying*
aggravating, boring, bothersome, burdensome, irritating, tedious, tiresome, troublesome, troubling, vexing; SEE CONCEPT *529*

iron [*adj*] *hard, tough; inflexible*
adamant, adamantine, cruel, dense, ferric, ferrous, firm, heavy, immovable, implacable, indomitable, inexorable, insensible, obdurate, relentless, rigid, robust, steel, steely, strong, stubborn, thick, unbending, unyielding; SEE CONCEPTS *534,604*

in
ir

iron [*n1*] *hard, ferrous metal*
cast, coke, pig; SEE CONCEPT *476*
iron [*n2*] *restraint made of metal*
bond, chain, cuffs, fetter, handcuffs, leg irons,
manacles, shackles; SEE CONCEPT *476*
ironclad [*adj*] *fixed, rigid*
abiding, agreed, arranged, certain, changeless,
confirmed, definite, determinate, enduring, firm,
inflexible, in the bag*, planned, prearranged, settled, stated, stubborn, sure, unalterable, uncompromising, unwavering; SEE CONCEPTS *535,554*
ironic/ironical [*adj*] *sarcastic*
acrid, alert, arrogant, backbiting, biting, bitter,
burlesque, caustic, chaffing, clever, contemptuous, contradictory, critical, cutting, cynical, defiant, derisive, disparaging, double-edged,
exaggerated, implausible, incisive, incongruous,
jibing, keen, mocking, mordant, paradoxical,
pungent, quick-witted, ridiculous, sardonic,
satiric, satirical, scathing, scoffing, sharp, sneering, spicy, trenchant, twisted, uncomplimentary,
witty, wry; SEE CONCEPTS *267,548*
iron out [*v*] *reconcile a situation*
agree, arbitrate, clear up*, compromise, eliminate, eradicate, erase, expedite, get rid of*, harmonize, negotiate, put right*, reach agreement,
resolve, settle, settle differences, simplify,
smooth over*, sort out*, straighten out*, unravel;
SEE CONCEPT *126*
irony [*n*] *sarcasm*
banter, burlesque, contempt, contrariness, criticism, derision, humor, incongruity, jibe, mockery, mordancy, paradox, quip, raillery, repartee,
reproach, ridicule, sardonicism, satire, taunt,
twist, wit; SEE CONCEPTS *230,278*
irrational [*adj*] *illogical, senseless*
aberrant, absurd, brainless, cockamamie*, crazy,
delirious, demented, disconnected, disjointed,
distraught, fallacious, flaky*, foolish, freaky, incoherent, injudicious, insane, invalid, kooky*,
loony*, mad, mindless, nonsensical, nutty*, off-
the-wall*, preposterous, raving, reasonless,
ridiculous, silly, sophistic, specious, stupid, unreasonable, unreasoning, unsound, unstable, unthinking, unwise, wacky*, wild, wrong; SEE
CONCEPTS *402,403,529*
irreconcilable [*adj*] *hostile, conflicting*
clashing, diametrically opposed, discordant, discrepant, dissonant, hard-line, implacable, incompatible, incongruous, inconsistent, inexorable,
inflexible, inharmonious, intransigent, opposed,
reluctant, unappeasable, uncompromising, unfriendly; SEE CONCEPTS *401,564*
irrefutable [*adj*] *beyond question*
accurate, apodictic, can bet on it*, certain, double-checked, evident, final, inarguable, incontestable, incontrovertible, indisputable,
indubitable, invincible, ironclad, irrebuttable, irrefragable, irresistible, nof ifs ands or buts*, obvious, odds-on*, positive, proven, set, sure,
unanswerable, unassailable, undeniable, unimpeachable, unquestionable; SEE CONCEPTS
529,535,582
irregular [*adj1*] *random, variable*
aberrant, aimless, capricious, casual, changeable,
designless, desultory, disconnected, discontinuous, eccentric, erratic, faltering, fitful, fluctuating, fragmentary, haphazard, hit-or-miss*,
inconstant, indiscriminate, infrequent, intermittent, jerky, nonuniform, occasional, out of order,

patchy, purposeless, recurrent, shaky, shifting,
spasmodic, sporadic, uncertain, unconsidered,
uneven, unmethodical, unpunctual, unreliable,
unsettled, unsteady, unsystematic, up and
down*, weaving; SEE CONCEPTS *534,799*
irregular [*adj2*] *abnormal, peculiar*
aberrant, anomalous, atypical, capricious, deviant, different, disorderly, divergent, eccentric,
exceptional, extraordinary, immoderate, improper, inappropriate, inordinate, odd, off-key*,
queer, quirky, singular, strange, unconventional,
unique, unnatural, unofficial, unorthodox, unsuitable, unusual; SEE CONCEPT *547*
irregular [*adj3*] *bumpy, uneven*
aberrant, amorphous, asymmetrical, bent, broken, cockeyed*, craggy, crooked, devious, disproportionate, eccentric, elliptic, elliptical, hilly,
jagged, lopsided, lumpy, meandering, notched,
not uniform, off-balance, off-center, out of proportion, pitted, protuberant, rough, scarred, serrate, serrated, unaligned, unbalanced, unequal,
unsymmetrical, variable, wobbly, zigzagged; SEE
CONCEPTS *490,606*
irregularly [*adv*] *intermittently*
anyhow, any which way*, at intervals, by fits
and starts*, by turns, disconnectedly, eccentri-
cally, erratically, fitfully, haphazardly, helter-
skelter*, infrequently, in snatches*, jerkily, now
and again, occasionally, off and on*, out of sequence, periodically, slapdash, spasmodically,
sporadically, uncertainly, uncommonly, un-
evenly, unmethodically, unpunctually, willy-
nilly*; SEE CONCEPTS *544,548,799*
irrelevant [*adj*] *beside the point*
extraneous, foreign, garbage, immaterial, impertinent, inapplicable, inapposite, inappropriate, inappurtenant, inapropos, inapt, inconsequent,
inconsequential, insignificant, not connected
with, not germane, not pertaining to, off the
point, off the topic, out of order, out of place,
outside, pointless, remote, trivial, unapt, unconnected, unimportant, unnecessary, unrelated,
without reference; SEE CONCEPTS *560,575*
irreligious [*adj*] *ungodly*
agnostic, atheistic, blasphemous, faithless, freethinking, godless, heathen, iconoclastic, impious,
irreverent, pagan, sacrilegious, sinful, unbelieving, undevout, unholy; SEE CONCEPT *545*
irreparable [*adj*] *unable to be fixed*
beyond repair, broken, cureless, destroyed, hopeless, impossible, incorrigible, incurable, irrecoverable, irredeemable, irremediable, irremedial,
irreplaceable, irretrievable, irreversible, ruined,
uncorrectable, unrecoverable; SEE CONCEPTS
314,485
irrepressible [*adj*] *effervescent, vivacious*
boisterous, bubbling, buoyant, ebullient, enthusiastic, insuppressible, rebellious, rhapsodical,
tumultous/tumultuous, unconstrained, uncontainable, uncontrollable, unmanageable, unquenchable, unrestrainable, unrestrained, unruly,
unstoppable; SEE CONCEPT *401*
irreproachable [*adj*] *innocent*
beyond reproach, blameless, exemplary, faultless, good, guiltless, impeccable, inculpable, innocent, irreprehensible, irreprovable, perfect,
pure, reproachless, righteous, unblamable, unblemished, unimpeachable, virtuous; SEE CON-
CEPTS *545,574*

irresistible [*adj*] *compelling; inescapable*
alluring, beckoning, charming, enchanting, fascinating, glamorous, imperative, indomitable, ineluctable, inevitable, inexorable, invincible, lovable, overpowering, overwhelming, potent, powerful, ravishing, scrumptious, seductive, stunning, tempting, unavoidable, unconquerable, urgent; SEE CONCEPTS *529,574,579*

irresolute [*adj*] *indecisive*
changing, doubtful, doubting, faltering, fearful, fickle, fluctuating, halfhearted*, halting, hesitant, hesitating, hot-and-cold*, infirm, on-the-fence*, shaky, tentative, timid, uncertain, undecided, undetermined, unsettled, unstable, unsteady, vacillating, waffling*, wavering, weak, weak-kneed*, wimpy*, wishy-washy*, wobbly; SEE CONCEPTS *403,535*

irresponsible [*adj*] *careless, reckless*
capricious, carefree, devil-may-care*, feckless, fickle, flighty, fly-by-night*, giddy, harebrained, ill-considered, immature, immoral, incautious, lax, loose*, no-account*, rash, scatterbrained*, shiftless, thoughtless, unaccountable, unanswerable, uncareful, undependable, unpredictable, unreliable, unstable, untrustworthy, wild; SEE CONCEPTS *404,544*

irreverence [*n*] *disrespect*
blasphemy, cheek, derision, discourtesy, flippancy, heresy, impertinence, impiety, impudence, insult, mockery, profanity, ridicule, rudeness, sauciness*, sin, sinfulness; SEE CONCEPT *633*

irreverent [*adj*] *disrespectful*
aweless, cheeky*, cocky*, contemptuous, crusty*, derisive, flip*, flippant, fresh, iconoclastic, impertinent, impious, impudent, insolent, irreverential, mocking, out-of-line*, profane, rude, sacrilegious, sassy*, saucy*, tongue-in-cheek*, ungodly, unhallowed, unholy; SEE CONCEPT *401*

irrevocable [*adj*] *fixed, unchangeable*
certain, changeless, constant, doomed, established, fated, final, immutable, indelible, inevitable, invariable, irremediable, irretrievable, irreversible, lost, permanent, predestined, predetermined, settled, unalterable, unrepealable, unreversible; SEE CONCEPTS *534,551*

irritable [*adj*] *bad-tempered, crabby*
annoyed, bearish, brooding, cantankerous, carping, choleric, complaining, contentious, crabbed, cross, crotchety, disputatious, dissatisfied, dyspeptic, easily offended, exasperated, fiery, fractious, fretful, fretting, gloomy, grouchy, grumbling, hasty, hot, huffy, hypercritical, ill-humored, irascible, moody, morose, out of humor, oversensitive, peevish, petulant, plaintive, prickly, querulous, quick-tempered, resentful, sensitive, snappy, snarling, surly, tense, testy, touchy; SEE CONCEPTS *401,403*

irritate [*v1*] *upset, anger*
abrade, affront, aggravate, annoy, bother, bug*, burn*, chafe, confuse, distemper, disturb, drive up the wall*, enrage, exasperate, fret, gall, get, get on nerves*, get under skin*, grate, harass, incense, inflame, infuriate, irk, madden, needle*, nettle, offend, pain, peeve, pester, pique, provoke, put out, rankle, rasp, rattle, rile, roil, rub the wrong way*, ruffle, sour, try, vex; SEE CONCEPTS *7,19*

irritate [*v2*] *hurt, chafe*
aggravate, burn, erupt, fret, inflame, intensify,

itch, pain, redden, rub, sensitize, sharpen, sting, swell; SEE CONCEPT *246*

island [*n*] *land surrounded by body of water*
archipelago, atoll, bar, cay, enclave, haven, isle, islet, key, peninsula, reef, refuge, retreat, sanctuary, shelter; SEE CONCEPT *509*

isolate [*v*] *cut off, set apart*
abstract, block off, close off, confine, detach, disconnect, disengage, divide, divorce, insulate, island, keep apart, part, quarantine, remove, seclude, segregate, separate, sequester, sever, sunder; SEE CONCEPTS *188,201*

isolated [*adj*] *unique; private*
abandoned, abnormal, alone, anomalous, apart, backwoods*, confined, deserted, detached, exceptional, far-out, forsaken, hidden, incommunicado*, lonely, lonesome, off beaten track*, outlying, out-ofthe-way*, random, remote, retired, screened, secluded, segregated, sequestered, single, solitary, special, stranded, unaccompanied, unfrequented, unrelated, untypical, unusual, withdrawn; SEE CONCEPTS *577,583*

isolation [*n*] *seclusion*
aloneness, aloofness, beleaguerment, concealment, confinement, desolation, detachment, exile, hiding, monkhood, privacy, privateness, quarantine, reclusion, reclusiveness, remoteness, retreat, seclusiveness, segregation, sequestration, solitude, withdrawal; SEE CONCEPTS *135,188, 388,631*

issue [*n1*] *point in question*
affair, argument, concern, contention, controversy, matter, matter of contention, point, point of departure, problem, puzzle, question, subject, topic; SEE CONCEPTS *278,532*

issue [*n2*] *result*
causatum, conclusion, consequence, culmination, effect, end, end product, eventuality, finale, fruit, outcome, payoff, sequel, termination, upshot; SEE CONCEPT *230*

issue [*n3*] *edition of publication*
copy, impression, installment, number, printing; SEE CONCEPT *280*

issue [*n4*] *distribution*
circulation, delivery, dispersion, dissemination, granting, issuance, issuing, publication, sending out, supply, supplying; SEE CONCEPT *140*

issue [*n5*] *children*
brood, descendants, get, heirs, offspring, posterity, progeniture, progeny, scions, seed; SEE CONCEPTS *296,414*

issue [*v1*] *distribute*
air, allot, announce, assign, bring out, broadcast, circulate, consign, declare, deliver, dispatch, dispense, emit, get out, give out, promulgate, publish, put in circulation, put out, release, send, send out, transmit; SEE CONCEPTS *60,140,292*

issue [*v2*] *emit, emerge; come from*
appear, arise, be a consequence, birth, come forth, derive from, emanate, exude, flow, give off, give out, ooze, originate, proceed, release, rise, send forth, spring, spurt, stem, throw off, vent, well; SEE CONCEPTS *179,648*

itch [*n1*] *scratching; tingling*
crawling, creeping, irritation, itchiness, prickling, psoriasis, rawness, tickle; SEE CONCEPTS *608,728*

itch [*n2*] *strong desire*
aphrodisia, appetite, appetition, concupiscence, craving, eroticism, hankering, hunger, impulse,

ir
it

longing, lust, lustfulness, motive, passion, prurience, restlessness, urge, yearning, yen; SEE CONCEPTS *20,529*

itch [*v1*] *scratch; tingle*
crawl, creep, irritate, prick, prickle, sting, tickle, titillate; SEE CONCEPTS *185,313,612*

itch [*v2*] *desire strongly*
ache, be impatient, burn, chafe, crave, hanker, have a yen for, hunger, long, lust, pant, pine, sigh, thirst, want, yearn; SEE CONCEPT *20*

item [*n*] *part, article*
account, aspect, bit, blurb*, bulletin, column, component, consideration, conversation piece, detail, dispatch, element, entry, feature, incidental, information, matter, minor point, minutia, news, note, notice, novelty, paragraph, particular, piece, point, report, scoop*, scrap, specific, story, thing, write-up; SEE CONCEPTS *270,831, 835*

itemize [*v*] *keep detailed record*
catalog, circumstantiate, cite, count, detail, document, enumerate, individualize, instance, inventory, lay out, list, mention, number, particularize, quote, recite, record, recount, rehearse, relate, set out, specify, spell out, tally; SEE CONCEPTS *57,125*

itinerant [*adj*] *roaming*
afoot, ambulant, ambulatory, floating, gypsy, journeying, migratory, moving, nomadic, on foot, peripatetic, ranging, riding the rails*, roving, shifting, travelling, unsettled, vagabond, vagrant, wandering, wayfaring; SEE CONCEPTS *536,584*

itinerary [*n*] *plan of travel*
beat, circuit, course, guide, guidebook, journey, line, outline, path, program, route, run, schedule, tour, way; SEE CONCEPTS *281,660*

J

jab [*n/v*] *poke*
blow, buck, bump, bunt, dig, hit, jog, lunge, nudge, prod, punch, push, stab, tap, thrust; SEE CONCEPT *189*

jabber [*v*] *talk incessantly and trivially*
babble, blather*, chatter, drivel, gab, go on and on*, jaw, mumble, murmur, mutter, prate, ramble, run off at mouth*, shoot the breeze*, talk, tattle, utter, yak, yap; SEE CONCEPTS *51,56*

jacket [*n*] *covering*
case, casing, coat, envelope, folder, fur, hide, parka, pelt, sheath, skin, threads, tunic, wrapper, wrapping; SEE CONCEPTS *451,484*

jaded [*adj*] *exhausted, indifferent*
been around, blah*, blasé, bored, cool*, done it all*, dulled, fagged, fatigued, fed up*, had it*, mellow, sated, satiated, sick of*, spent, surfeited, tired, tired-out*, up to here*, wearied, weary, worn, worn-down, worn-out; SEE CONCEPTS *401,406*

jagged [*adj*] *ragged, notched*
asperous, barbed, broken, cleft, craggy, denticulate, harsh, indented, irregular, pointed, ridged, rough, rugged, scabrous, serrated, snaggy,

spiked, toothed, uneven, unlevel, unsmooth; SEE CONCEPTS *490,606*

jail [*n*] *place for incarceration*
bastille, black hole*, brig, bullpen*, can*, cell, clink*, cooler*, detention camp, dungeon, house of correction, inside*, jailhouse, joint*, lockup, pen, penal institution, penitentiary, pound, prison, rack*, reformatory, slammer*, solitary*, stir*, stockade, up the river*; SEE CONCEPTS *439,449,516*

jail [*v*] *incarcerate*
bastille, book, cage, can*, confine, constrain, detain, hold, immure, impound, imprison, lock up, prison, put away*, put behind bars*, put on ice*, railroad*, send up*, sentence, take away*, throw away the keys*, throw in dungeon, throw the book at*; SEE CONCEPT *317*

jailer [*n*] *prison warden*
correctional officer, corrections officer, guard, prison guard, turnkey; SEE CONCEPT *348*

jalopy [*n*] *old, dilapidated automobile*
bucket of bolts*, clunker, heap*, junker*, rattletrap*, tin lizzie*, wreck; SEE CONCEPTS *260,674*

jam [*n*] *troublesome situation*
bind, box, corner, difficulty, dilemma, fix, hole, hot water*, pickle*, plight, predicament, problem, quandary, scrape, spot, strait, trouble; SEE CONCEPT *674*

jam [*v*] *squeeze in; compress*
bear, bind, block, cease, clog, congest, cram, crowd, crush, elbow, force, halt, jam-pack, jostle, obstruct, pack, press, push, ram, squash, squish, stall, stick, stuff, tamp, throng, wad, wedge; SEE CONCEPTS *121,208*

jamboree [*n*] *noisy celebration*
bash*, blowout*, ceremony, convention, festival, gathering, hoopla, jubilee, party, rally, revelry, shindig, wingding*; SEE CONCEPT *377*

jangle [*n*] *cacophony of noises*
babel, clang, clangor, clash, din, dissonance, hubbub*, hullabaloo*, jar, pandemonium, racket, rattle, reverberation, roar, tumult, uproar; SEE CONCEPT *595*

jangle [*v*] *make clinking noises*
chime, clank, clash, clatter, conflict, disaccord, discord, disharmonize, hit a sour note*, jar, jingle, mismatch, rattle, vibrate; SEE CONCEPT *65*

janitor [*n*] *person who cleans and maintains*
attendant, caretaker, cleaning person, concierge, custodian, doorkeeper, doorperson, gatekeeper, house sitter, porter, sitter, super, superintendent, sweeper, watchperson; SEE CONCEPT *348*

jar [*n1*] *container*
basin, beaker, bottle, burette, can, chalice, crock, cruet, decanter, ewer, flagon, flask, jug, pitcher, pot, tun, urn, vase, vat, vessel; SEE CONCEPT *494*

jar [*n2*] *shocking hit*
bump, clash, collision, concussion, crash, impact, jolt, jounce, rock, smash, succussion, thud, thump; SEE CONCEPT *189*

jar [*v1*] *shock, jolt*
agitate, bang, bounce, bump, clash, convulse, crash, disturb, grate, grind, hit, irritate, jerk, jiggle, jounce, jump, offend, quake, rasp, rattle, rock, shake, slam, thump, tremor, vibrate, wiggle, wobble; SEE CONCEPTS *65,189*

jar [*v2*] *clash, disharmonize*
annoy, bicker, contend, disaccord, disagree, discompose, discord, grate, grind, interfere, irk, irri-

tate, jangle, mismatch, nettle, oppose, outrage, quarrel, shock, wrangle; SEE CONCEPTS *7,19*

jargon [*n*] *specialized language; dialect*
abracadabra*, argot, balderdash*, banality, bombast, bunk*, buzzwords*, cant, cliché, colloquialism, commonplace term, doublespeak, drivel, fustian, gibberish, hackneyed term, idiom, insipidity, lexicon, lingo*, mumbo jumbo*, neologism, newspeak, nonsense, overused term, palaver, parlance, patois, patter, rigmarole, shoptalk, slang, slanguage*, speech, stale language, street talk*, tongue, trite language, twaddle*, usage, vernacular, vocabulary; SEE CONCEPTS *275,276*

jaundiced [*adj*] *tainted, prejudiced*
biased, bigoted, bitter, colored, cynical, disapproving, distorted, envious, grudging, hostile, intolerant, jealous, one-sided, opprobrious, partial, partisan, preconceived, prepossessed, resentful, skeptical, spiteful, suspicious, tendentious, unfair, unfriendly, unindifferent, warped, yellow; SEE CONCEPTS *401,403,542*

jaunt [*n*] *expedition*
adventure, airing, amble, beat, canter, circuit, constitutional, course, cruise, drive, excursion, frolic, gallop, hike, jog, journey, junket, march, outing, patrol, peregrination, picnic, promenade, prowl, ramble, ride, round, roundabout, run, safari, sally, saunter, stroll, tour, tramp, travel, trek, trip, turn, voyage, walk; SEE CONCEPTS *159,195,224*

jaunty [*adj*] *lively*
airy, animated, bold, brash, breezy, buoyant, carefree, careless, cocky, dapper, dashing, debonair, devilish, devil-may-care*, easy, exhilarated, flip*, flippant, forward, free, fresh, frisky, frolicsome, gamesome, gay, high-spirited, hilarious, impetuous, impish, impudent, jocose, joking, jolly, jovial, light, natty, nervy, perky, playful, prankish, provocative, reckless, rollicking, self-confident, showy, smart, sportive, sporty, sprightly, spruce, swaggering, trim, venturesome, vivacious; SEE CONCEPTS *401,404*

jaw [*n*] *bones of chin*
bone, chops*, jowl, mandible, maxilla, mouth, muzzle*, orifice; SEE CONCEPT *392*

jaw [*v1*] *talk a lot*
babble, chat, chatter, gab*, gossip, jabber, lecture, orate, prate, prattle, yak; SEE CONCEPTS *51,56*

jaw [*v2*] *criticize*
abuse, baste, berate, blame, call on the carpet*, censure, rail, rate, revile, scold, tongue-lash*, upbraid, vituperate; SEE CONCEPT *52*

jazz [*n*] *style of music*
bebop*, blues, boogie*, boogie-woogie*, Dixieland, fusion jazz, hot jazz, improvisational music, jive*, ragtime, swing; SEE CONCEPT *595*

jazzed-up [*adj*] *souped up*
gassed-up, high geared, high performance, high speed, hopped-up*, pepped-up*, pumped-up*, revved-up*, speedy, supercharged; SEE CONCEPTS *401,404*

jazzy [*adj*] *fancy*
animated, exciting, flashy, gaudy, lively, salacious, sexy, smart, snazzy*, spirited, vivacious, wild, zestful, zippy*; SEE CONCEPTS *537,589*

jealous [*adj*] *desirous; wary*
anxious, apprehensive, attentive, begrudging, covetous, demanding, doubting, emulous, envi-

ous, envying, grabby, grasping, green-eyed, grudging, guarded, intolerant, invidious, jaundiced, mistrustful, monopolizing, possessive, possessory, protective, questioning, resentful, rival, skeptical, solicitous, suspicious, vigilant, watchful, zealous; SEE CONCEPTS *403,542*

jealousy [*n*] *envy*
backbiting, begrudging, covetousness, enviousness, evil eye*, green-eyed monster*, grudge, grudgingness, jaundiced eye*, resentfulness, resentment, spite; SEE CONCEPT *410*

jeans [*n*] *dungarees*
blue jeans, chaps, denims, Lees™, Levi's™, pants, trousers, Wranglers™; SEE CONCEPT *451*

jeer [*v*] *heckle*
banter, comeback, contemn, deride, dig*, fleer, flout, gibe, hector, hoot, jab, jest, laugh at, make a crack*, mock, poke fun, put down, put on, quip, ridicule, scoff, sneer, snipe, taunt; SEE CONCEPT *54*

jell [*v*] *coagulate*
clot, cohere, come together, condense, congeal, crystallize, finalize, form, freeze, gel, gelate, gelatinize, harden, jellify, jelly, materialize, set, solidify, stick, stiffen, take shape, thicken; SEE CONCEPTS *250,469*

jeopardize [*v*] *endanger*
be careless, chance, chance it*, gamble, hazard, imperil, lay on the line*, peril, put at risk, put in danger, put in jeopardy, risk, stake, subject to, tempt fate, threaten; SEE CONCEPTS *246,252,384*

jeopardy [*n*] *danger, trouble*
accident, chance, double-trouble*, endangerment, exposure, hazard, insecurity, liability, on the line*, on the spot*, out on a limb*, peril, precariousness, risk, venture, vulnerability; SEE CONCEPT *675*

jerk [*n1*] *a lurching move*
bounce, bump, flick, flop, jolt, pull, quake, quiver, shiver, snag, thrust, tug, tweak, twitch, wiggle, wrench, wriggle, yank; SEE CONCEPTS *80,149,150*

jerk [*n2*] *stupid, bumbling person*
brute, fool, idiot, nincompoop, ninny, oaf, rascal; SEE CONCEPT *423*

jerk [*v*] *move with lurch*
bounce, bump, dance, flick, fling, flip, flop, grab, hook, hurtle, jolt, lug, pluck, pull, quake, quiver, seize, shiver, shrug, sling, snag, snatch, throw, thrust, tug, tweak, twitch, vellicate, whisk, wiggle, wrench, wrest, wriggle, wring, yank; SEE CONCEPTS *150,152*

jerry-built [*adj*] *flimsy*
cheap, defective, insubstantial, jerry-rigged, junky, makeshift, ramshackle, rickety, shoddy, slipshod, unsound, unsubstantial; SEE CONCEPT *267*

jest [*n*] *joke*
banter, bon mot, crack, fun, funny, gag, game, hoax, jive, jolly, laugh, one-liner*, play, pleasantry, prank, quip, rib, rib-tickler*, ridicule, sally, spoof, sport, wisecrack, witticism; SEE CONCEPT *273*

jest [*v*] *joke*
banter, chaff, deride, flout, fool, fun*, gibe*, gird*, jeer, jive*, jolly*, josh*, kid, mock, needle*, put on, quip, rag*, razz*, rib*, roast*, scoff, sneer, spoof, tease; SEE CONCEPT *273*

jester [*n*] *person who jokes, plays jokes*
actor, antic, banterer, buffoon, card*, clown, co-

it
je

median, comic, cutup*, droll, fool, harlequin, humorist, japer, joker, jokester, larker, life of the party*, madcap*, pantaloon, practical joker, prankster, quipster, standup comic, trickster, wag*, wisecracker*, wit; SEE CONCEPT *423*

jet [*adj*] *black*
atramentous, coal-black, dark, ebon, ebony, inky, midnight, obsidian, pitch-black, pitch-dark, raven, sable; SEE CONCEPT *618*

jet [*n1*] *rush, gush of substance*
flow, fountain, spout, spray, spring, spritz, spurt, squirt, stream; SEE CONCEPTS *465,467*

jet [*n2*] *vehicle propelled by ejection of pressurized gas or liquid*
airbus, airplane, plane, supersonic, supersonic transport, turbo; SEE CONCEPTS *463,503*

jet [*v*] *spurt, gush*
flow, fly, issue, pour, roll, rush, shoot, soar, spew, spout, spritz, squirt, stream, surge, travel, zoom; SEE CONCEPT *179*

jet set [*n*] *high society*
beau monde, beautiful people, cream of society, elite, fashionable society, in-crowd, leisured class, moneyed class, polite society, smart set, the well-to-do, upper crust; SEE CONCEPTS *387,388,417*

jettison [*v*] *eject; throw overboard*
abandon, abdicate, cashier*, cast, cast off, deep-six*, discard, dump, expel, heave, hurl, junk*, maroon, reject, scrap*, shed, slough, throw away, unload*; SEE CONCEPTS *180,222*

jetty [*n*] *pier*
barrier, breakwater, dock, groin, landing, quay, seawall, slip, wharf; SEE CONCEPTS *439,443,479*

jewel [*n1*] *precious stone*
baguette, bauble, bead, bijou, birthstone, brilliant, gem, gemstone, glass, gullion, hardware*, ornament, rock*, sparkler*, stone, trinket; SEE CONCEPTS *446,474,478*

jewel [*n2*] *something, someone precious*
charm, find, gem, genius, ideal, masterpiece, nonesuch, nonpareil, paragon, pearl*, phenomenon, phoenix*, prize, prodigy, rarity, specialty, treasure, wonder; SEE CONCEPT *671*

jewelry [*n*] *precious stones, metals worn as decoration*
adornment, anklet, band, bangle, bauble, beads, bijou, bracelet, brass, brooch, cameo, chain, charm, choker, costume, cross, crown, diamonds, earring, finery, frippery, gem, glass*, gold, ice*, jewel, junk*, knickknack, lavaliere, locket, necklace, ornament, pendant, pin, regalia, ring, rock, rosary, silver, solitaire, sparkler, stickpin, stone, tiara, tie pin, treasure, trinket; SEE CONCEPT *446*

Jewish [*adj*] *Israelite*
Hasidic, Hebrew, Judaistic, Semitic; SEE CONCEPT *369*

Jezebel [*n*] *prostitute*
broad, fallen woman*, femme fatale, floozy*, harlot, hooker, hussy, jade, loose woman, scarlet, slut, strumpet, tart, trollop, vamp, whore; SEE CONCEPTS *348,412,415,419*

jibe [*v*] *agree*
accord, conform, correspond, dovetail, fit, fit in, go, harmonize, match, resemble, square, tally; SEE CONCEPT *664*

jiffy [*n*] *instant*
breath, crack, flash, jiff*, minute, moment, second, shake*, split second*, trice, twinkling*; SEE CONCEPT *808*

jiggle [*v*] *bounce up and down*
agitate, bob, fidget, jerk, jig, jigger, jog, joggle, shake, shimmer, shimmy, twitch, vellicate, wiggle; SEE CONCEPTS *150,152*

jilt [*v*] *abandon, betray*
break off*, coquette, deceive, desert, disappoint, discard, ditch*, drop*, dump*, forsake, get rid of, leave, leave at the altar*, leave flat*, reject, throw over*; SEE CONCEPTS *195,297,384*

jingle [*v*] *make metallic clinking noise*
chime, chink, chinkle, clamor, clang, clatter, clink, ding, jangle, rattle, reverberate, ring, sound, tingle, tinkle, tintannabulate; SEE CONCEPT *65*

jinx [*n*] *curse*
black magic, charm, enchantment, evil eye*, hex, hoodoo*, kiss of death*, nemesis, plague, spell, voodoo*; SEE CONCEPTS *230,679*

jinx [*v*] *curse*
bedevil, bewitch, cast a spell on, charm, condemn, damn*, enchant, give the evil eye*, hex; SEE CONCEPTS *14,192*

jitters [*n*] *nervousness*
anxiety, dither, fidgets, heebie-jeebies*, jumps, nerves, shakes, shivers, tenseness, willies*; SEE CONCEPTS *230,410,690*

jittery [*adj*] *nervous*
antsy*, anxious, apprehensive, edgy, excitable, fidgety, high-strung*, jumpy, on edge*, on pins and needles*, panicky, quivering, restless, shaky, skittish, spooked, tense, trembling, uneasy, uptight; SEE CONCEPTS *401,690*

job [*n1*] *employment*
activity, appointment, assignment, berth, billet, business, calling, capacity, career, chore, connection, craft, daily grind*, engagement, faculty, function, gig*, grind*, handicraft, line, livelihood, means, métier, niche, nine-to-five*, occupation, office, opening, operation, place, position, post, posting, profession, pursuit, racket*, rat race*, situation, spot, stint, swindle*, task, trade, vocation, work; SEE CONCEPTS *351,360*

job [*n2*] *task*
act, action, affair, assignment, burden, business, care, charge, chore, commission, concern, contribution, deed, devoir, duty, effort, enterprise, errand, function, matter, mission, obligation, office, operation, project, province, pursuit, responsibility, role, stint, task, taskwork, thing*, tour of duty, undertaking, venture, work; SEE CONCEPT *362*

jobless [*adj*] *unemployed*
between jobs*, collecting unemployment benefits, laid off, on the dole*, out of a job, out of work, without employment, without gainful employment, workless; SEE CONCEPT *538*

jock [*n*] *athlete*
competitor, letterman/woman, letterperson, player, sportsman/woman, sportsperson; SEE CONCEPT *366*

jockey [*v*] *maneuver*
direct, guide, handle, move, navigate, negotiate, pilot, position, ride, steer, turn, twist; SEE CONCEPTS *187,225*

jocular/jocose/jocund [*adj*] *funny, playful*
amusing, blithe, camp, cheerful, comic, comical, crazy, daffy, droll, facetious, flaky*, frolicsome, gay, gleeful, happy, humorous, jesting, jokey, joking, jolly, joshing, jovial, joyous, laughable,

lighthearted, lively, ludicrous, merry, mischievous, pleasant, roguish, sportive, teasing, wacky, waggish, whimsical, witty; SEE CONCEPTS *267,529*

jog [*v1*] *activate, push*
agitate, arouse, bounce, dig, hit, jab, jar, jerk, jiggle, joggle, jolt, jostle, jounce, nudge, press, prod, prompt, punch, remind, rock, shake, shove, stimulate, stir, suggest, whack; SEE CONCEPTS *14,208*

jog [*v2*] *run for recreation*
amble, canter, dash, dogtrot, lope, pace, sprint, trot; SEE CONCEPT *151*

John Hancock [*n*] *signature*
autograph, endorsement, inscription, mark, seal, undersignature; SEE CONCEPT *284*

join [*v1*] *unite*
accompany, add, adhere, affix, agglutinate, annex, append, assemble, associate, attach, blend, bracket, cement, clamp, clasp, clip, coadunate, coalesce, combine, compound, concrete, conjoin, conjugate, connect, copulate, couple, entwine, fasten, fuse, grapple, hitch on, incorporate, interlace, intermix, juxtapose, knit, leash, link, lock, lump together, marry, mate, melt, mix, pair, put together, slap on, span, splice, stick together, tack on, tag on, tie, tie up, touch, weave, wed, weld, yoke; SEE CONCEPT *113*

join [*v2*] *affiliate with organization*
align, associate with, be in, come aboard*, consort, cooperate, enlist, enroll, enter, fall in with*, follow, go to, mingle with, pair with, plug into*, side with, sign on, sign up, take part in, take up with, team up with, throw in with*, tie up with; SEE CONCEPT *114*

join [*v3*] *touch; border on*
abut, adjoin, be adjacent to, be at hand, be close to, be contiguous to, bound, butt, communicate, conjoin, extend, fringe, hem, lie beside, lie near, lie next to, line, march, meet, neighbor, open into, parallel, reach, rim, skirt, trench on, verge on; SEE CONCEPT *747*

joint [*adj*] *shared, combined*
collective, common, communal, concerted, conjoint, conjunct, consolidated, cooperative, hand in hand, intermutual, joined, mutual, public, united; SEE CONCEPTS *577,708*

joint [*n1*] *intersection, juncture*
abutment, articulation, bend, bond, bracket, bridge, concourse, confluence, conjuncture, connection, copula, coupling, crux, elbow, hinge, hyphen, impingement, interconnection, junction, knot, link, meeting, nexus, node, point, seam, splice, suture, swivel, tangency, tie, union, vinculum; SEE CONCEPTS *393,830,831*

joint [*n2*] *cheap hangout*
bar, club, dive*, hole in the wall*, honky-tonk*, juke joint*, roadhouse, tavern; SEE CONCEPTS *439,449*

jointly [*adv*] *as one*
accordingly, agreeably, alike, arm in arm*, coincidentally, collectively, combined, companionably, concomitantly, concurrently, conjointly, connectedly, cooperatively, en masse, hand in glove*, hand in hand*, harmoniously, in a group, in common, in company with, in concert, in conjunction, inextricably, in league, in partnership, inseparably, intimately, in unison, mutually, reciprocally, side by side*, similarly, simultane-

ously, synchronically, together, unitedly, with one another; SEE CONCEPT *577*

joke [*n1*] *fun, quip*
antic, bon mot, buffoonery, burlesque, caper, caprice, chestnut*, clowning, drollery, epigram, escapade, farce, frolic, gag, gambol, game, ha-ha*, hoodwinking*, horseplay*, humor, jape, jest, lark, laugh, mischief, monkeyshine*, mummery, one-liner*, parody, payoff, play, pleasantry, prank, pun, put-on, quirk, raillery, repartee, revel, rib, sally, saw, shaggy-dog story*, shenanigan*, snow job*, sport, spree, stunt, tomfoolery, trick, vagary, whimsy, wisecrack, witticism, yarn; SEE CONCEPT *273*

joke [*n2*] *person that is made fun of*
buffoon, butt, clown, derision, fool, goat, jackass, jestee, laughingstock, mockery, simpleton, sport, target; SEE CONCEPTS *412,423*

joke [*v*] *kid, tease*
banter, chaff, deceive, deride, fool, frolic, fun, gambol, horse around*, jape, jest, jive*, josh, josh, kid around, laugh, make merry, mock, needle, play, play the clown, play tricks, poke fun*, pull one's leg*, pun, put on, quip, rag, revel, rib, ridicule, roast*, spoof, sport, taunt, trick, wisecrack*; SEE CONCEPT *273*

joker [*n*] *person who kids, teases*
actor, banana*, buffoon, card*, clown, comedian, comic, cutup*, droll, farceur, fool, funster*, gagster*, humorist, jester, jokesmith, jokester, josher*, kidder, life of the party*, prankster*, punster*, quipster*, second banana*, stand-up comic, stooge, straight person, top banana*, trickster*, wag, wisecracker*, wit; SEE CONCEPTS *352,423*

jolly [*adj*] *laughing, joyful*
blithe, blithesome, bouncy, carefree, cheerful, chipper, chirpy, convivial, daffy, delightful, enjoyable, entertaining, festive, frolicsome, funny, gay, gladsome, gleeful, happy, hilarious, jocund, jokey, joshing, jovial, joyous, jubilant, larking, lighthearted, lots of laughs, merry, mirthful, playful, pleasant, sportive, sprightly, zippy*; SEE CONCEPTS *267,542,548*

jolt [*n*] *surprise; sudden push*
blow, bombshell*, bounce, bump, clash, collision, concussion, double whammy*, impact, jar, jerk, jog, jounce, jump, kick, lurch, percussion, punch, quiver, reversal, setback, shake, shock, shot, start, surprise, thunderbolt; SEE CONCEPTS *42,208*

jolt [*v*] *surprise; push suddenly*
astonish, bowl over*, bump, churn, convulse, discompose, disturb, floor, jar, jerk, jog, jostle, knock, knock over*, lay out*, perturb, rock, shake, shake up*, shock, shove, spring something on*, stagger, start, startle, stun, throw a curve*, upset; SEE CONCEPTS *42,208*

jostle [*v*] *bump, shake*
bang into, bulldoze*, bump heads*, butt*, crash, crowd, elbow, hustle, jab, jog, joggle, jolt, nudge, press, push, push around, push aside, rough and tumble*, scramble, shoulder, shove, squeeze, thrust; SEE CONCEPTS *152,189,208*

journal [*n*] *chronicle*
account, almanac, annals, annual, calendar, chronology, comic book, daily, daybook, diary, gazette, ledger, log, magazine, memento, memoir, minutes, monthly, newspaper, note, observation, organ, paper, periodical, publication, rag,

record, register, reminder, reminiscence, review, scandal sheet*, statement, tabloid, weekly; SEE CONCEPTS *271,280,801*

journalism [n] *reporting*
broadcast writing, news, newspaper writing, the fourth estate, the press, writing; SEE CONCEPTS *280,349,356*

journalist [n] *person who writes about factual events for a living*
announcer, broadcaster, columnist, commentator, contributor, correspondent, cub, editor, hack, media person, newspaper person, newsperson, pencil pusher*, press, publicist, reporter, scribe, scrivener, stringer*, television commentator, writer; SEE CONCEPTS *348,356*

journey [n] *excursion*
adventure, airing, beat, campaign, caravan, circuit, constitutional, course, crossing, drive, expedition, exploration, hike, itinerary, jaunt, junket, march, migration, odyssey, outing, passage, patrol, peregrination, pilgrimage, progress, promenade, quest, ramble, range, roaming, round, route, run, safari, sally, saunter, sojourn, stroll, survey, tour, tramp, transit, transmigration, travel, traveling, traverse, trek, trip, vagabondage, vagrancy, venture, visit, voyage, wandering, wayfaring; SEE CONCEPT *224*

journey [v] *travel*
circuit, cruise, fare, fly, globe trot*, go, go places, hie, hop, jaunt, jet, junket, knock about*, pass, peregrinate, proceed, process, push on, ramble, range, repair, roam, rove, safari, take a trip, tour, traverse, trek, voyage, wander, wend; SEE CONCEPT *224*

jovial [adj] *happy*
affable, airy, amiable, animated, bantering, blithe, blithesome, bouncy, buoyant, chaffing, cheery, chipper, chirpy, companionable, conversable, convivial, cordial, daffy*, delightful, dizzy*, enjoyable, facetious, festal, festive, gay, glad, gleeful, good-natured, hilarious, humorous, jocose, jocund, jokey, jolly, jollying, joshing, jubilant, larking, lighthearted, loony, lots of laughs*, merry, mirthful, nutty*, off-the-wall*, pleasant, sociable; SEE CONCEPTS *401,403*

joy [n] *great happiness, pleasure*
alleviation, amusement, animation, bliss, charm, cheer, comfort, delectation, delight, diversion, ecstasy, elation, exultation, exulting, felicity, festivity, frolic, fruition, gaiety, gem, gladness, glee, good humor, gratification, hilarity, humor, indulgence, jewel, jubilance, liveliness, luxury, merriment, mirth, pride, pride and joy, prize, rapture, ravishment, refreshment, regalement, rejoicing, revelry, satisfaction, solace, sport, transport, treasure, treat, wonder; SEE CONCEPTS *410,529*

joyful/joyous [adj] *happy*
blithesome, cheerful, cheery, delighted, ecstatic, effervescent, elated, enjoyable, enraptured, expansive, festive, flying*, gay, glad, gladsome, gratified, heartening, high*, high as a kite*, jubilant, lighthearted, merry, overjoyed, pleased, pleasurable, popping*, rapturous, satisfied, sunny*, sunny-side up*, transported, upbeat; SEE CONCEPTS *403,542,548*

joyless [adj] *unhappy*
black, bleak, blue, cheerless, dejected, depressant, depressed, depressing, dismal, dispirited, dispiriting, doleful, downcast, down in the mouth*, dragged, dreary, droopy, gloomy, have the blahs*, heavy*, low, melancholic, melancholy, miserable, mopey, mournful, sad, saddening, somber; SEE CONCEPTS *403,542,548*

jubilant [adj] *happy*
celebrating, doing handsprings*, elated, enraptured, euphoric, excited, exuberant, exultant, exulting, flipping, flying*, glad, gleeful, joyous, overjoyed, pleased, rejoicing, rhapsodic, thrilled, tickled*, triumphal, triumphant; SEE CONCEPTS *401,403*

Judas [n] *traitor*
backstabber, Benedict Arnold, betrayer, conspirator, deceiver, rat, turncoat, two-timer*, weasel; SEE CONCEPT *412*

judge [n] *person who arbitrates*
adjudicator, appraiser, arbiter, assessor, authority, bench, chancellor, conciliator, court, critic, evaluator, expert, honor, inspector, intercessor, intermediary, interpreter, judiciary, justice, justice of peace, legal official, magister, magistrate, marshal, moderator, negotiator, peacemaker, reconciler, referee, umpire, warden; SEE CONCEPT *355*

judge [v] *make decision from evidence; deduce*
act on, adjudge, adjudicate, appraise, appreciate, approximate, arbitrate, arrive, ascertain, assess, check, collect, conclude, condemn, consider, criticize, decide, decree, deduct, derive, determine, discern, distinguish, doom, draw, esteem, estimate, evaluate, examine, find, gather, give a hearing, make, make out, mediate, pass sentence, place, pronounce sentence, put, rate, reckon, referee, resolve, review, rule, sentence, settle, sit, size up, suppose, test, try, umpire, value; SEE CONCEPTS *18,317*

judgment [n1] *common sense*
acumen, acuteness, apprehension, astuteness, awareness, brains, capacity, comprehension, discernment, discrimination, experience, genius, grasp, incisiveness, ingenuity, intelligence, intuition, keenness, knowledge, mentality, penetration, perception, percipience, perspicacity, prudence, quickness, range, rationality, reach, readiness, reason, reasoning, sagacity, sanity, sapience, savvy, sense, sharpness, shrewdness, sophistication, soundness, taste, understanding, wisdom, wit; SEE CONCEPTS *37,409*

judgment [n2] *decision about blame*
analysis, appraisal, appreciation, arbitration, assaying, assessment, award, belief, close study, conclusion, contemplation, conviction, decree, deduction, determination, estimate, estimation, evaluation, examination, exploration, finding, idea, inference, inquest, inquiry, inquisition, inspection, observation, opinion, order, probing, pursuit, quest, reconnaissance, regard, report, research, resolution, result, review, ruling, scrutiny, search, sentence, sifting, summary, verdict, view, weigh-in; SEE CONCEPTS *103,689*

judgment [n3] *doom, fate*
affliction, castigation, chastisement, correction, damnation, infliction, manifestation, misfortune, mortification, punishment, retribution, visitation; SEE CONCEPT *679*

judicial [adj] *legal*
administrative, authoritative, constitutional, discriminating, distinguished, equitable, forensic, impartial, judgelike, judiciary, juridical, jurisdic-

tional, juristic, lawful, legalistic, magisterial, official, pontifical, principled, regular, statutory; SEE CONCEPT *319*

judicious [*adj*] *wise, thoughtful*
accurate, acute, astute, calculating, careful, cautious, circumspect, clear-sighted, considerate, considered, diplomatic, discerning, discreet, discriminating, efficacious, enlightened, expedient, far-sighted, informed, judicial, keen, perceptive, perspicacious, politic, profound, prudent, quick-witted, rational, reasonable, sagacious, sage, sane, sapient, seasonable, seemly, sensible, sharp, shrewd, skillful, sober, sophisticated, sound, thorough, wary, well-advised, well-judged, worldly-wise; SEE CONCEPTS *402,403, 542*

jug [*n*] *container for liquid*
amphora, beaker, bottle, bucket, canteen, carafe, crock, cruet, decanter, ewer, flagon, flask, growler, hooker, jar, pitcher, pot, tub, urn, vase, vessel; SEE CONCEPT *494*

juggle [*v*] *mislead, falsify; handle several things at once*
alter, beguile, betray, bluff, change, conjure, delude, disguise, doctor*, double-cross, fix, humbug*, illude, maneuver, manipulate, misrepresent, modify, perform magic, prestidigitate, shuffle, take in, tamper with, trim; SEE CONCEPTS *59,63*

juice [*n*] *liquid squeezed from fruit, plant*
abstract, alcohol, aqua vitae, distillation, drink, essence, extract, fluid, liquor, milk, nectar, oil, sap, sauce, secretion, serum, spirit, syrup, water; SEE CONCEPTS *428,467*

juicy [*adj1*] *moist*
dank, dewy, dripping, humid, liquid, luscious, lush, mellow, oily, oozy, pulpy, sappy, saturated, sauced, slippery, slushy, soaked, sodden, succulent, syrupy, viscid, watery, wet; SEE CONCEPT *603*

juicy [*adj2*] *exciting, interesting*
colorful, fascinating, intriguing, piquant, provocative, racy, risqué, sensational, spicy, suggestive, tantalizing, vivid; SEE CONCEPTS *537,548*

jumble [*n*] *hodgepodge*
assortment, chaos, clutter, confusion, derangement, disarrangement, disarray, disorder, farrago, gallimaufry, garbage, goulash, hash*, litter, medley, mélange, mess, miscellany, mishmash, mixture, muddle, olio, pastiche, patchwork, potpourri, salmagundi, scramble, shuffle, snarl, tangle, tumble; SEE CONCEPT *432*

jumble [*v*] *mix up, confuse*
clutter, confound, derange, disarrange, disarray, dishevel, disorder, disorganize, disturb, entangle, foul up, mess up, mistake, muddle, rummage, shuffle, snarl, tangle, tumble; SEE CONCEPTS *16,84*

jumbled [*adj*] *confused, mixed-up*
blurred, chaotic, cluttered, disarranged, disordered, disorderly, disorganized, in disarray, messy, misunderstood, out of order, scrambled, tangled, unsettled, unsorted, untidy; SEE CONCEPT *585*

jumbo [*adj*] *gigantic*
colossal, cyclopean, elephantine, giant, huge, immense, large, mammoth, mighty, oversized, prodigious; SEE CONCEPT *781*

jump [*n1*] *leap*
bob, bounce, bound, buck, canter, caper, capriole, dance, dive, drop, fall, gambade, gambol, hop, hopping, hurdle, jar, jerk, jolt, leapfrog, leapfrogging, leaping, lurch, nosedive, plummet, plunge, pounce, rise, saltation, shock, skip, skipping, spring, start, swerve, twitch, upspring, upsurge, vault, wrench; SEE CONCEPT *194*

jump [*n2*] *increase, advantage*
advance, ascent, augmentation, boost, handicap, head start, increment, inflation, rise, spurt, start, upper hand, upsurge, upturn; SEE CONCEPTS *704,763*

jump [*n3*] *obstacle*
bar, barricade, barrier, fence, hurdle, impediment, rail, stretch; SEE CONCEPTS *470,674*

jump [*v1*] *leap, spring*
bail out, barge, bob, bounce, bound, buck, canter, caper, clear, curvet, dive, drop, fall, gambol, hop, hurdle, hurtle, jerk, jiggle, jounce, lollop, lop, lunge, lurch, parachute, plummet, pop, quiver, rattle, ricochet, saltate, shake, skip, sky, somersault, surge, take, top, trip, vault, waver, wobble; SEE CONCEPT *194*

jump [*v2*] *recoil*
bob, bolt, bounce, carom, flinch, jerk, jounce, rebound, ricochet, spring, start, startle, wince; SEE CONCEPT *213*

jump [*v3*] *omit, avoid*
abandon, cancel, clear out, cover, cross out, digress, evade, leave, miss, nullify, overshoot, pass over, skip, switch; SEE CONCEPT *25*

jump [*v4*] *increase*
advance, ascend, boost, escalate, gain, hike, jack up, mount, put up, raise, rise, surge, up; SEE CONCEPTS *236,245,763*

jumpy [*adj*] *nervous*
agitated, antsy*, anxious, apprehensive, creepy*, excitable, excited, fidgety, frisky, high-strung*, jittery, on edge*, on pins and needles*, restless, sensitive, shaky, skittish, spooked, tense, timorous, unrestful; SEE CONCEPTS *401,690*

junction/juncture [*n1*] *link, connection*
alliance, annexation, articulation, assemblage, attachment, bond, coalition, coherence, collocation, combination, combine, concatenation, concourse, concursion, confluence, conjugation, consolidation, convergence, coupling, crossing, crossroads, dovetail, elbow, gathering, gore, hinge, hookup, interface, intersection, joining, joint, knee, linking, meeting, miter, mortise, node, pivot, plug-in, reunion, seam, splice, terminal, tie-in, tie-up, union, weld; SEE CONCEPTS *746,830*

juncture [*n2*] *turning point*
choice, circumstance, condition, contingency, crisis, crossroad, crux, emergency, exigency, instant, meeting point, moment, occasion, pass, pinch, plight, point, position, posture, predicament, quandary, state, status, strait, time, zero hour*; SEE CONCEPTS *388,693,815*

jungle [*n*] *wilderness full of plant and animal life*
boscage, bush, chaparral, forest, labyrinth, maze, morass, primeval forest, tangle, undergrowth, wasteland, web, wood, zoo; SEE CONCEPT *517*

junior [*adj*] *subordinate, younger*
inferior, lesser, lower, minor, second, secondary, second-string*; SEE CONCEPTS *574,578,797*

junk [*n*] *odds and ends; garbage*
clutter, collateral, debris, filth, hogwash*, litter,

jo
ju

miscellany, offal, refuse, rubbish, rubble, rummage, salvage, scrap, trash, waste; SEE CONCEPTS *260,432*

jurisdiction [*n*] *area of authority*
administration, arbitration, area, authority, bailiwick, bounds, circuit, command, commission, compass, confines, control, discretion, district, domination, dominion, empire, extent, field, hegemony, influence, inquisition, judicature, limits, magistracy, might, orbit, power, prerogative, province, purview, range, reach, reign, right, rule, say, scope, slot, sovereignty, sphere, stomping grounds*, supervision, sway, territory, turf*, zone; SEE CONCEPTS *198,376,651*

jurist [*n*] *jurisprudent*
attorney, barrister, counsel, counsellor, counselor, defender, judge, justice, lawyer, legal adviser, legal expert, legal scholar, magistrate; SEE CONCEPT *355*

jury [*n*] *panel that hears legal matter*
board, judges, peers, tribunal; SEE CONCEPTS *299,318*

just [*adj1*] *fair, impartial*
aloof, blameless, condign, conscientious, decent, dependable, dispassionate, due, equal, equitable, ethical, evenhanded, fair-minded, good, honest, honorable, lawful, nondiscriminatory, nonpartisan, objective, pure, reliable, right, righteous, rightful, rigid, scrupulous, strict, tried, true, trustworthy, unbiased, uncolored, upright, virtuous; SEE CONCEPTS *319,545*

just [*adj2*] *accurate, precise*
cogent, correct, exact, faithful, good, justified, normal, proper, regular, right, sound, strict, true, undistorted, veracious, veridical, well-founded, well-grounded; SEE CONCEPTS *535,582*

just [*adj3*] *suitable, appropriate*
apt, befitting, condign, deserved, due, felicitous, fit, fitting, happy, justified, legitimate, meet, merited, proper, reasonable, requisite, right, rightful, well-deserved; SEE CONCEPT *558*

just [*adv1*] *definitely*
absolutely, accurately, completely, directly, entirely, exactly, expressly, perfectly, precisely, right, sharp, smack-dab*, square, squarely, unmistakably; SEE CONCEPT *535*

just [*adv2*] *only now*
almost, a moment ago, approximately, at this moment, barely, by very little, hardly, just a while ago, just now, lately, nearly, now, presently, recently, right now, scarce, scarcely; SEE CONCEPTS *544,820*

just [*adv3*] *merely*
at most, but, no more than, nothing but, only, plainly, simply, solely; SEE CONCEPT *557*

just about [*adv*] *almost*
about, all but, approximately, around, as good as, close to, nearly, nigh, not quite, practically, well-nigh; SEE CONCEPTS *762,771,799*

justice [*n1*] *lawfulness, fairness*
amends, appeal, authority, authorization, charter, code, compensation, consideration, constitutionality, correction, credo, creed, decree, due process, equity, evenness, fair play, fair treatment, hearing, honesty, impartiality, integrity, judicatory, judicature, justness, law, legality, legalization, legal process, legitimacy, litigation, penalty, reasonableness, recompense, rectitude, redress, reparation, review, right, rule, sanction,

sentence, square deal*, truth; SEE CONCEPTS *376,645,691*

justice [*n2*] *person who oversees court of law*
chancellor, court, judge, magistrate, umpire*; SEE CONCEPT *354*

justifiable [*adj*] *reasonable, well-founded*
acceptable, admissible, allowable, condonable, defensible, excusable, fair, fit, forgivable, lawful, legit*, legitimate, licit, logical, pardonable, probable, proper, reasonable, remissible, right, rightful, sound, suitable, tenable, understandable, valid, vindicable, warrantable; SEE CONCEPTS *545,558*

justification [*n*] *reason, excuse*
absolution, account, acquittal, advocacy, answer, apologia, apology, approval, argument, basis, confirmation, defense, exculpation, exoneration, explanation, extenuation, grounds, idea, mitigation, palliation, palliative, plea, pretext, raison d'être, rationale, rationalization, rebuttal, redemption, reply, response, salvation, sanctification, song and dance*, story, support, validation, vindication, warrant, whatfor*, wherefore*, whitewashing*, whole idea*, why and wherefore*; SEE CONCEPT *661*

justify [*v*] *legitimize, substantiate*
absolve, acquit, advocate, alibi*, answer for, apologize for, approve, argue for, assert, be answerable for, bear out, brief, claim, clear, condone, confirm, contend, cop a plea*, countenance, crawl, defend, do justice to, establish, exculpate, excuse, exonerate, explain, favor, legalize, maintain, make allowances, make good*, palliate, pardon, plead, rationalize, rebut, show cause, speak in favor, square, stand up for, support, sustain, uphold, validate, verify, vindicate, warrant; SEE CONCEPTS *49,57*

justly [*adv*] *fairly*
accurately, befittingly, beneficently, benevolently, benignly, candidly, charitably, correctly, decently, decorously, duly, duteously, dutifully, equally, equitably, evenhandedly, fitly, fittingly, frankly, helpfully, honestly, honorably, impartially, lawfully, legally, legitimately, moderately, nicely, piously, properly, reasonably, respectably, righteously, rightfully, rightly, straightforwardly, temperately, tolerantly, unreservedly, uprightly, virtuously, well; SEE CONCEPTS *544,545*

jut [*v*] *extend*
beetle, bulge, elongate, impend, lengthen, overhang, poke, pop, pouch, project, protrude, protuberate, stand out, stick out; SEE CONCEPT *201*

juvenile [*adj*] *childish*
adolescent, babyish, beardless, blooming, boyish, budding, callow, childlike, developing, formative, fresh, girlish, green, growing, immature, inexperienced, infant, infantile, jejune, junior, kid stuff*, milk-fed*, naive, pubescent, puerile, teenage, tender, undeveloped, unfledged, unripe, unsophisticated, unweaned, vernal, young, younger, youthful; SEE CONCEPTS *401,578,797*

juvenile [*n*] *young person*
adolescent, boy, child, girl, infant, kid*, minor, youngster, youth; SEE CONCEPT *424*

juvenile delinquent [*n*] *hooligan, punk*
criminal, first offender, gangster, goon*, hood, hoodlum, punk, rowdy, ruffian, thug, troublemaker; SEE CONCEPT *412*

juxtapose [*v*] *place side by side*
appose, bring near, bring together, connect, pair, place in proximity, set side by side; SEE CONCEPTS *85,113,160*

K

kaput [*adj*] *ruined, wrecked*
all washed up*, belly-up*, burned out, cooked*, dead*, destroyed, done for, down and out, down for the count*, down the drain*, down the tubes*, finished, floored, had it, nonfunctioning, on the skids*, out of business, out of circulation, sunk, totaled, washed up, wiped out; SEE CONCEPT *252*

keel over [*v*] *fall, faint*
black out, capsize, collapse, drop, founder, go down, overturn, pass out, pitch, plunge, slump, swoon, topple, tumble, upset; SEE CONCEPTS *152,181*

keen [*adj1*] *enthusiastic*
agog, alert, animate, animated, anxious, appetent, ardent, athirst, avid, breathless, devoted, dying to*, eager, earnest, ebullient, fervent, fervid, fierce, fond of, gung ho*, impassioned, impatient, intense, intent, interested, lively, perfervid, spirited, sprightly, thirsty, vehement, vivacious, warm, zealous; SEE CONCEPTS *401,403*

keen [*adj2*] *sharp, piercing*
acid, acute, caustic, cutting, edged, extreme, fine, honed, incisive, intense, observant, penetrating, perceptive, pointed, quick-witted, razor-sharp*, sardonic, satirical, strong, tart, trenchant, unblunted; SEE CONCEPT *267*

keen [*adj3*] *intelligent*
astute, bright, brilliant, canny, clever, discerning, discriminating, Einstein*, nobody's fool*, perceptive, perspicacious, quick, sagacious, sapient, sensitive, sharp, sharp as a tack*, shrewd, whiz, wise; SEE CONCEPT *402*

keep [*v1*] *hold, maintain*
accumulate, amass, cache, care for, carry, conduct, conserve, control, deal in, deposit, detain, direct, enjoy, garner, grasp, grip, have, heap, hold back, manage, own, pile, place, possess, preserve, put, put up, reserve, retain, save, season, stack, stock, store, trade in, withhold; SEE CONCEPT *710*

keep [*v2*] *tend; provide for*
administer, attend, board, care for, carry on, command, conduct, continue, defend, direct, endure, feed, foster, guard, look after, maintain, manage, mind, minister to, nourish, nurture, operate, ordain, protect, provision, run, safeguard, shelter, shield, subsidize, support, sustain, victual, watch over; SEE CONCEPTS *110,140*

keep [*v3*] *prevent*
arrest, avert, block, check, constrain, control, curb, delay, detain, deter, hamper, hamstring, hinder, hold back, impede, inhibit, limit, obstruct, restrain, retard, shackle, stall, stop, withhold; SEE CONCEPT *121*

keep [*v4*] *commemorate; pay attention to*
adhere to, bless, celebrate, comply with, consecrate, fulfill, hold, honor, laud, obey, observe, perform, praise, regard, respect, ritualize, sanctify, solemnize; SEE CONCEPT *377*

keep at [*v*] *continue, endure*
be steadfast, carry on, complete, drudge, finish, grind, labor, last, maintain, persevere, persist, remain, slave, stay, stick, toil; SEE CONCEPTS *23,87*

keeper [*n*] *guardian*
archivist, attendant, caretaker, conservator, curator, custodian, defender, guard, jailer, lookout, overseer, protector, sentinel, sentry, steward, superintendent, supervisor, warden; SEE CONCEPTS *414,423*

keep one's cool [*v*] *remain calm*
control one's temper, go with the flow*, keep calm, keep cool*, keep one's shirt on*, restrain oneself; SEE CONCEPTS *121,130,191*

keepsake [*n*] *something precious*
emblem, favor, memento, memorial, relic, remembrance, reminder, souvenir, symbol, token, trophy; SEE CONCEPT *446*

keep up [*v*] *maintain, sustain*
balance, compete, contend, continue, emulate, go on, hold on, keep pace, keep step, match, pace, persevere, preserve, rival, run with, vie; SEE CONCEPTS *23,87,363*

keg [*n*] *barrel*
butt, cask, container, drum, firkin, hogshead, pipe, tub, tun, vat; SEE CONCEPT *494*

ken [*n*] *perception*
acumen, apprehending, apprehension, attention, attitude, awareness, cognizance, comprehension, concept, consciousness, grasp, idea, impression, insight, judgment, knowledge, light, notion, picture, realizing, recognition, sense, sight, understanding, vision; SEE CONCEPTS *409,410,689*

kernel [*n*] *seed, essence*
atom, bit, center, core, crux, fruit, germ, gist, grain, heart, hub, keynote, marrow, matter, meat, morsel, nub, nubbin, nut, part, piece, pith, root, substance, upshot; SEE CONCEPTS *668,826*

kettle [*n*] *metal pot*
boiler, cauldron, pot, steamer, teakettle, vat, vessel; SEE CONCEPT *494*

key [*adj*] *essential, important*
basic, chief, crucial, decisive, fundamental, indispensable, leading, main, major, material, pivotal, primary, principal, vital; SEE CONCEPT *568*

key [*n1*] *item that unlocks*
latchkey, opener, passkey, screw*, skeleton; SEE CONCEPT *499*

key [*n2*] *answer, solution*
blueprint, brand, cipher, clue, code, core, crux, cue, earmark, explanation, fulcrum, guide, hinge, index, indicator, interpretation, lead, lever, marker, means, nexus, nucleus, passport, password, pivot, pointer, root, sign, symptom, ticket, translation; SEE CONCEPTS *274,668*

keynote/keystone [*n*] *essence, theme*
basic idea, basis, center, core, cornerstone, criterion, crux, gist, heart, idea, kernel, linchpin, mainspring, marrow, measure, motive, nub, pith, principle, root, source, spring, standard, substance; SEE CONCEPTS *532,661,688*

kick [*n1*] *thrill, enjoyment*
bang*, buzz*, excitement, fun, gratification, hoot*, joy, pleasure, refreshment, sensation, stimulation, wallop*; SEE CONCEPTS *388,410*

kick [*n2*] *power, strength*
backlash, blow, boot*, force, intensity, jar, jolt,

pep, punch, pungency, snap, sparkle, tang, verve, vitality, zest, zing*; SEE CONCEPTS *641,732*

kick [*v1*] *hit with foot*
boot, calcitrate, dropkick, give the foot, jolt, punt; SEE CONCEPT *189*

kick [*v2*] *complain*
anathematize, carp, combat, condemn, criticize, curse, damn, except, execrate, expostulate, fight, fuss, gripe, grumble, inveigh, mumble, object, oppose, protest, rebel, remonstrate, repine, resist, spurn, wail, whine, withstand; SEE CONCEPT *52*

kick [*v3*] *quit a habit*
abandon, desist, give up, go cold turkey*, leave off, stop; SEE CONCEPT *234*

kickback [*n*] *bribe*
cut, gift, graft, money under the table*, oil*, payment, payoff, payola, percentage, recompense, reward, share; SEE CONCEPTS *192,344*

kick back [*v*] *relax*
breathe easy*, calm down*, catch one's breath, chill out*, collect oneself, compose oneself, cool off*, feel at home, hang loose*, lie down, loosen up, make oneself at home*, mellow out*, put one's feet up*, recline, rest, settle back, sit around, sit back, take a break*, take a breather*, take a load off*, take it easy*, take ten*, unwind, wind down; SEE CONCEPT *210*

kick in [*v*] *contribute*
ante up, chip in, commit, dish out*, dole out*, donate, fork over*, furnish, give, hand out, hand over, pitch in*, pony up*, provide; SEE CONCEPTS *108,140*

kick out [*v*] *get rid of*
ax, boot*, bounce*, can*, cashier*, chase, chuck, discharge, dismiss, drop, eject, evict, expel, extrude, fire, oust, out, reject, remove, sack*, throw out, toss out; SEE CONCEPTS *180,351,384*

kid [*n*] *young person*
baby, bairn, boy, child, daughter, girl, infant, juvenile, lad, lass, little one*, son, teenager, tot, youngster, youth; SEE CONCEPTS *414,424*

kid [*v*] *fool, ridicule*
bamboozle*, banter, beguile, bother, cozen, delude, dupe, flimflam*, fun*, gull, hoax, hoodwink, jape, jest, joke, jolly, josh, make fun of, make sport of, mock, pretend, rag*, razz, rib, roast, spoof, tease, trick; SEE CONCEPTS *59,273*

kid around [*v*] *tease*
annoy, badger, bait, banter, bother, chaff, disturb, dog*, fool around, give a hard time*, goad, harass, josh, lead on*, mock, needle*, nudge, pester, pick on*, rag*, razz*, rib*, ride, ridicule, roast*, taunt; SEE CONCEPTS *7,11,19,22*

kidnap [*v*] *abduct; hold for ransom*
bodysnatch*, bundle off, capture, carry away, carry off, coax, decoy, entice, grab, hijack, impress, inveigh, lay hands on, lure, make off with*, pirate, remove, run away with, seduce, seize, shanghai*, skyjack, snatch, spirit away*, steal, waylay; SEE CONCEPTS *90,139*

kill [*v1*] *deprive of existence; destroy*
annihilate, asphyxiate, assassinate, crucify, dispatch, do away with*, do in*, drown, dump, electrocute, eradicate, erase*, execute, exterminate, extirpate, finish, garrote, get*, guillotine, hang, hit*, immolate, liquidate, lynch, massacre, murder, neutralize, obliterate, off*, poison, polish off*, put away*, put to death, rub out*, sacrifice, slaughter, slay, smother, snuff, strangle,

suffocate, waste*, wipe out*, X-out*, zap*; SEE CONCEPT *252*

kill [*v2*] *turn off; cancel*
annul, cease, counteract, deaden, defeat, extinguish, forbid, halt, negative, neutralize, nix*, nullify, prohibit, quash, quell, recant, refuse, revoke, ruin, scotch*, shut off, smother, stifle, still, stop, suppress, turn out, veto; SEE CONCEPTS *121,239*

killer [*n*] *murderer*
assassin, butcher, cut-throat, executioner, exterminator, gunman/woman, gunperson, hitman/woman, hit person, hunter, slayer, soldier; SEE CONCEPT *412*

killing [*n*] *murder*
assassination, bloodshed, bumping off*, capital punishment, carnage, execution, extermination, homicide, manslaughter, massacre, slaughter, slaying; SEE CONCEPTS *192,252*

killjoy [*n*] *spoilsport*
complainer, dampener, doomsdayer, grinch*, grouch*, moaner, partypooper, pessimist, prophet of doom*, stick in the mud*, wet blanket*, whiner; SEE CONCEPTS *412,423*

kin [*n*] *blood relative*
affinity, blood, clan, connection, consanguinity, cousin, extraction, family, folk, house, kindred, kinsfolk, kinship, kinsperson, kith, lineage, member, people, race, relation, relationship, sibling, stock, tribe; SEE CONCEPTS *296,414,421*

kind [*adj*] *generous, good*
affectionate, all heart*, altruistic, amiable, amicable, beneficent, benevolent, benign, big, bleeding-heart*, bounteous, charitable, clement, compassionate, congenial, considerate, cordial, courteous, eleemosynary, friendly, gentle, goodhearted, gracious, heart in right place*, humane, humanitarian, indulgent, kindhearted, kindly, lenient, loving, mild, neighborly, obliging, philanthropic, propitious, softhearted, soft touch*, sympathetic, tenderhearted, thoughtful, tolerant, understanding; SEE CONCEPTS *401,404,542*

kind [*n1*] *class, species*
brand, breed, classification, family, genus, ilk, kin, order, race, set, sort, type, variety; SEE CONCEPT *378*

kind [*n2*] *type, character*
breed, complexion, connection, denomination, description, designation, essence, fiber, gender, habit, ilk, likes, lot, manner, mold, nature, number, persuasion, set, sort, stamp, stripe, style, temperament, tendency, tribe, variety, way; SEE CONCEPTS *411,673*

kindhearted [*adj*] *compassionate, helpful*
altruistic, amiable, amicable, considerate, generous, good, good-natured, gracious, humane, kind, merciful, responsive, softhearted, sympathetic, tender, tenderhearted, warm, warmhearted; SEE CONCEPTS *404,542*

kindle [*v1*] *start a fire*
blaze, burn, fire, flame, flare, glow, ignite, inflame, light, set alight, set fire; SEE CONCEPT *249*

kindle [*v2*] *excite, incite*
agitate, animate, arouse, awaken, bestir, burn up*, challenge, egg on*, enkindle, exasperate, fire up*, foment, get smoking*, induce, inflame, inspire, key up*, provoke, rally, rouse, sharpen, stimulate, stir, thrill, turn on*, wake, waken, whet, work up*; SEE CONCEPTS *7,14,22,221*

kindly [adj] compassionate, helpful
attentive, beneficial, benevolent, benign, benignant, cool, cordial, favorable, friendly, generous, genial, gentle, good, good-hearted, good-natured, gracious, hearty, humane, kind, kindhearted, mellow, merciful, mild, neighborly, pleasant, polite, sociable, sympathetic, thoughtful, warm; SEE CONCEPTS 404,542

kindly [adv] with compassion
affectionately, agreeably, benevolently, benignly, carefully, charitably, compassionately, considerately, cordially, courteously, delicately, generously, genially, good-naturedly, graciously, heedfully, helpfully, humanely, politely, solicitously, sympathetically, tenderly, thoughtfully, tolerantly, understandingly, well; SEE CONCEPTS 542,544

kindness [n1] compassion, generosity
affection, altruism, amiability, beneficence, benevolence, charity, clemency, consideration, cordiality, courtesy, decency, delicacy, fellow feeling, forbearance, gentleness, good intention, goodness, good will, grace, graciousness, heart, helpfulness, hospitality, humanity, indulgence, kindliness, magnanimity, mildness, patience, philanthropy, serviceability, solicitousness, solicitude, sweetness, sympathy, tact, tenderness, thoughtfulness, tolerance, understanding, unselfishness; SEE CONCEPTS 633,657

kindness [n2] helping act; service
accommodation, aid, alms, assistance, benediction, benefaction, benevolence, benison, blessing, boon, boost, bounty, charity, dispensation, favor, generosity, good deed, good turn, help, indulgence, lift, mercy, philanthropy, relief, succor; SEE CONCEPTS 110,657

kindred [adj] corresponding, matching
affiliated, agnate, akin, alike, allied, analogous, cognate, congeneric, congenial, connate, connatural, consanguine, germane, homogeneous, incident, kin, likable, parallel, related, similar; SEE CONCEPT 563

kindred [n] blood relative
affinity, blood, clan, connection, consanguinity, cousin, family, flesh, folk, homefolk, house, kin, kinsfolk, kinsperson, lineage, race, relation, relationship, stock, tribe; SEE CONCEPTS 296,414,421

kingdom [n] historically, an area ruled by a monarch
commonwealth, country, county, crown, division, domain, dominion, dynasty, empire, field, lands, monarchy, nation, possessions, principality, province, realm, reign, rule, scepter, sovereignty, sphere, state, suzerainty, sway, territory, throne, tract; SEE CONCEPTS 508,510

kink [n1] bend, twist
coil, corkscrew, crimp, crinkle, curl, curve, entanglement, frizz, knot, loop, tangle, wrinkle; SEE CONCEPT 436

kink [n2] spasm of muscular tissue
charley horse*, cramp, crick, knot, muscle spasm, pain, pang, pinch, stab, stitch, tweak, twinge; SEE CONCEPTS 185,728

kink [n3] complication
defect, difficulty, flaw, hitch, impediment, imperfection, knot, tangle; SEE CONCEPT 674

kink [n4] person's idiosyncrasy
eccentricity, fetish, foible, notion, peculiarity, quirk, singularity, vagary, whim; SEE CONCEPT 411

kinky [adj1] twisted
coiled, crimped, curled, curly, frizzled, frizzy, knotted, matted, matty, rolled, tangled; SEE CONCEPT 486

kinky [adj2] bizarre, perverted
degenerated, depraved, deviant, eccentric, far-out, licentious, odd, outlandish, outre, peculiar, queer, quirky, sick, strange, unconventional, unnatural, unusual, warped, weird; SEE CONCEPTS 372,542,589

kinship [n] family relationship
affinity, blood, clan, family, flesh, folk, kin, kindred, lineage, relations, tribe; SEE CONCEPTS 296,414,421

kiosk [n] gazebo
bandstand, booth, rotunda, stall, stand; SEE CONCEPTS 442,443

kismet [n] fate, fortune
chance, destination, destiny, divine will*, doom, handwriting on the wall*, horoscope, karma, Lady Luck*, lot, luck, portion, predestination, providence; SEE CONCEPT 679

kiss [n] touching lips to another
butterfly*, caress, embrace, endearment, osculation, peck, salutation, salute, smack*, smooch*; SEE CONCEPTS 185,375

kiss [v] touch one's lips to another's
blow, brush, butterfly*, French*, glance, graze, greet, lip*, make out*, mush*, neck*, osculate, peck, pucker up*, salute, smack*, smooch*; SEE CONCEPTS 185,375

kit [n] provisions, equipment
accoutrements, apparatus, assortment, bag, collection, container, effects, gear, impedimenta, implements, material, outfit, pack, paraphernalia, rig, satchel, selection, set, stock, stuff, suitcase, supplies, tackle, things, tools, trappings, utensils; SEE CONCEPTS 494,496

kitchen [n] room for cooking food
canteen, cookery, cookhouse, cook's room, cuisine, eat-in, gallery, galley, kitchenette, mess, scullery; SEE CONCEPT 448

kittenish [adj] frisky, playful
childish, coquettish, coy, elvish, flirtatious, frolicsome, fun-loving, impish, jaunty, mischievous, sportive; SEE CONCEPT 401

klutz [n] clumsy person
bungler, butterfingers*, dolt, dullard, lummox, oaf; SEE CONCEPT 412

knack [n] ability, talent
adroitness, aptitude, aptness, bent, capacity, command, dexterity, expertise, expertism, expertness, facility, faculty, flair, forte, genius, gift, handiness, hang of it*, head*, ingenuity, knowhow, mastership, nose*, propensity, quickness, readiness, savvy*, set, skill, skillfulness, trick, turn; SEE CONCEPTS 409,630

knead [v] mix by pressing
aerate, alter, blend, form, manipulate, massage, mold, ply, press, push, rub, shape, squeeze, stroke, twist, work; SEE CONCEPTS 170,208

kneel [v] get down on one's knees
bow, bow down, curtsey, do obeisance, genuflect, kowtow, prostrate oneself, stoop; SEE CONCEPT 154

knickknack [n] trinket; decorative piece
bagatelle, bauble, bibelot, bric-a-brac, conversation piece, curio, curiosity, device, embellishment, flummery, frill, furbelow, gadget*, miniature, notion, novelty, objet d'art, ornament,

ki
kn

plaything*, showpiece, souvenir, thingamajig*, toy, trapping, trifle, whatnot*, whimsy; SEE CONCEPTS *259,260,446*

knife [*n*] *cutting tool*
bayonet, blade, bolo, cutlass, cutter, cutting edge, dagger, edge, lance, lancet, machete, point, ripper, sabre, scalpel, scimitar, scythe, shank, shiv, sickle, skewer, skiver, steel, stiletto, switchblade, sword, tickler; SEE CONCEPTS *495,499*

knife [*v*] *stab with pointed tool*
brand, carve, chop down, clip, cut, hurt, impale, jag, kill, lacerate, lance, open up, pierce, shank, shiv, slash, slice, spit, stick, thrust, wound; SEE CONCEPTS *176,220,246*

knit [*v*] *intertwine*
affiliate, affix, ally, bind, cable, connect, contract, crochet, fasten, heal, interlace, intermingle, join, link, loop, mend, net, purl, repair, secure, sew, spin, tie, unite, weave, web; SEE CONCEPTS *113,202,218*

knob [*n*] *lump, handle*
bulge, bulk, bump, bunch, doorknob, hump, knot, knurl, latch, lever, nub, opener, projection, protrusion, protuberance, snag, stud, swell, swelling, trigger, tumor; SEE CONCEPTS *445,471*

knock [*n1*] *pushing, striking*
beating, blow, box, clip, conk, cuff, hammering, hit, injury, lick, rap, slap, smack, swat, swipe, thump, whack; SEE CONCEPT *189*

knock [*n2*] *strong criticism*
blame, censure, condemnation, defeat, failure, flak, pan, rap, rebuff, rejection, reversal, setback, stricture, swipe; SEE CONCEPTS *52,278*

knock [*v1*] *push over; strike*
abuse, bash, batter, beat, beat up, bob, bruise, buffet, clap, clout, cuff, damage, deck, drub*, fell, flatten, floor, hit, hurt, KO*, level, maltreat, manhandle, maul, mistreat, pound, punch, rap, roughhouse, slap, smack, tap, thrash, thump, thwack*, total, wallop, whack*, wound; SEE CONCEPT *189*

knock [*v2*] *criticize harshly*
abuse, alive*, belittle, blame, carp, cavil, censure, condemn, denounce, denunciate, deprecate, disparage, find fault, lambaste, reprehend, reprobate, run down*, skin*, slam; SEE CONCEPT *52*

knock about/knock around [*v*] *roam, wander*
drift, ramble, range, rove, traipse, travel, walk; SEE CONCEPTS *151,224*

knock off [*v1*] *kill*
assassinate, do away with*, do in*, dust*, eliminate, execute, finish, liquidate, murder, rub out*, shoot, slay, stab, waste; SEE CONCEPT *252*

knock off [*v2*] *steal*
filch, knock over, loot, pilfer, pinch, plunder, purloin, ransack, relieve, rifle, rip off*, rob, thieve; SEE CONCEPTS *139,192*

knock off [*v3*] *stop action; accomplish*
achieve, cease, complete, conclude, desist, discontinue, eliminate, finish, give over, halt, leave off, quit, stop work, succeed, surcease, terminate; SEE CONCEPTS *119,234*

knoll [*n*] *small hill*
acclivity, ascent, bluff, butte, cliff, drift, dune, elevation, esker, headland, heap, highland, hillock, hilltop, hummock, inclination, incline, knoll, mesa, mound, mount, precipice, prominence, promontory, ridge, rise, slope, summit; SEE CONCEPT *509*

knot [*n1*] *bow, loop*
bond, braid, bunch, coil, connection, contortion, entanglement, gnarl, helix, hitch, joint, kink, ligament, ligature, link, mat, nexus, perplexity, rosette, screw, snag, snarl, spiral, splice, tangle, tie, twirl, twist, vinculum, warp, whirl, whorl, yoke; SEE CONCEPTS *436,471*

knot [*n2*] *lump; crowd*
aggregation, assemblage, assortment, band, bunch, circle, clique, clump, cluster, collection, company, crew, gang, gathering, group, heap, mass, mob, pack, pile, set, squad, swarm, tuft; SEE CONCEPT *432*

knot [*v*] *weave, complicate*
bind, cord, entangle, knit, loop, secure, tat, tether, tie; SEE CONCEPTS *85,113,160*

knotty [*adj*] *troublesome*
baffling, complex, complicated, difficult, effortful, elaborate, formidable, Gordian*, hard, intricate, involved, labyrinthine, mazy, mystifying, perplexing, problematical, puzzling, ramified, reticular, rough, rugged, sophisticated, sticky*, terrible, thorny*, tough, tricky, uphill*; SEE CONCEPTS *529,565*

know [*v1*] *understand information*
apperceive, appreciate, apprehend, be acquainted, be cognizant, be conversant in, be informed, be learned, be master of, be read, be schooled, be versed, cognize, comprehend, differentiate, discern, discriminate, distinguish, experience, fathom, feel certain, get the idea*, grasp, have, have down pat*, have information, have knowledge of, keep up on, ken, learn, notice, on top of*, perceive, prize, realize, recognize, see, undergo; SEE CONCEPTS *15,38*

know [*v2*] *be familiar with*
associate, be acquainted with, be friends with, experience, feel, fraternize, get acquainted, have dealings with, identify, savor, see, sustain, taste, undergo; SEE CONCEPT *384*

know-how [*n*] *skill, talent*
ability, adroitness, aptitude, art, background, capability, command, craft, cunning, dexterity, experience, expertise, expertness, faculty, flair, ingenuity, knack, knowledge, proficiency, savoir-faire, wisdom; SEE CONCEPTS *409,630*

knowing [*adj*] *experienced, aware*
alive, apprehensive, astute, awake, brainy, bright, brilliant, canny, clever, cognizant, competent, conscious, conversant, cool*, crack*, deliberate, discerning, expert, insightful, intelligent, intended, intentional, judicious, knowledgeable, observant, perceptive, percipient, qualified, quick, quick-witted, sagacious, sage, sensible, sentient, sharp, skillful, slick*, smart, sophic, sophisticated, tuned-in, vigilant, watchful, well-informed, wise, with-it, witting, worldly, worldly-wise; SEE CONCEPT *402*

know-it-all [*n*] *intellectual, smart aleck*
braggart, brain*, smarty-pants*, walking encyclopedia, windbag, wiseacre, wise guy*; SEE CONCEPTS *412,423*

knowledge [*n*] *person's understanding; information*
ability, accomplishments, acquaintance, apprehension, attainments, awareness, cognition, comprehension, consciousness, dirt*, discernment, doctrine, dogma, dope*, education, enlightenment, erudition, expertise, facts, familiarity, goods*, grasp, inside story*, insight, instruction,

intelligence, judgment, know-how*, learning, light*, lore, observation, philosophy, picture, power*, principles, proficiency, recognition, scholarship, schooling, science, scoop*, substance, theory, tuition, wisdom; SEE CONCEPTS *274,409,529*

knowledgeable [*adj*] *aware, educated*
abreast, acquainted, alert, appreciative, apprised, au courant, au fait, brainy*, bright, brilliant, clever, cognizant, conscious, conversant, discerning, erudite, experienced, familiar, informed, insightful, intelligent, in the know, knowing, learned, lettered, omniscient, perceptive, plugged in*, posted, prescient, privy, quick-witted, sagacious, sage, savvy, scholarly, sensible, sharp, smart, sophic, sophisticated, tuned-in*, understanding, versed, well-informed, well-rounded, wise, with-it; SEE CONCEPT *402*

known [*adj*] *famous, popular*
accepted, acknowledged, admitted, avowed, celebrated, certified, common, confessed, conscious, down pat*, established, familiar, hackneyed, manifest, noted, notorious, obvious, patent, plain, proverbial, published, received, recognized, well-known; SEE CONCEPTS *529,567,576*

knurled [*adj*] *knotted*
bumpy, coarse, gnarled, knobby, knotty, rough; SEE CONCEPTS *485,606*

kook [*n*] *eccentric person*
crackpot, crank, crazy*, dingbat*, flake*, fruitcake*, lamebrain, lunatic, nut, screwball*, wacko*, weirdo; SEE CONCEPTS *412,423*

kosher [*adj1*] *ritually proper*
apropos, clean, decent, ritually pure, undefiled; SEE CONCEPTS *401,404*

kosher [*adj2*] *legitimate*
acceptable, according to law, authentic, genuine, legal, permissible, permitted, proper; SEE CONCEPTS *319,558,582*

kowtow [*v*] *grovel*
bow, brownnose*, cave in*, court, cower, cringe, fawn, flatter, fold, genuflect, give in, go along with, kneel, knuckle under, lie down and roll over*, pander, prostrate, say uncle*, stoop, toe the mark*; SEE CONCEPT *384*

kudos [*n*] *praise, acclaim*
applause, credit, distinction, eminence, esteem, fame, flattery, glory, honor, illustriousness, laudation, notability, pat on the back*, plaudits, plum*, PR*, preeminence, prestige, prominence, puff*, pumping up*, raves*, regard, renown, repute, strokes*; SEE CONCEPTS *69,268*

L

label [*n*] *marker, description; brand*
characterization, classification, company, design, epithet, hallmark, identification, insignia, logo, mark, number, price mark, stamp, sticker, tag, tally, ticket, trademark; SEE CONCEPTS *268,270,284*

label [*v*] *mark, describe; brand*
call, characterize, class, classify, define, designate, identify, name, specify, stamp, sticker, tag, tally; SEE CONCEPTS *62,79*

labor [*n1*] *work, undertaking*
activity, chore, daily grind, diligence, drudgery, effort, employment, endeavor, energy, exercise, exertion, grind*, gruntwork*, industry, job, moonlight*, operation, pains*, pull, push, strain, stress, struggle, sweat, toil, travail; SEE CONCEPTS *87,100,351,360,362*

labor [*n2*] *person(s) performing service*
apprentice, blue collar, breadwinner, employee, hack*, hand*, hard hat*, help, helper, hireling, instrument, laborer, learner, operative, prentice, proletariat, rank and file*, toiler, worker, work force, working people; SEE CONCEPTS *325,348*

labor [*n3*] *childbirth process*
birth, birth pangs, childbearing, contractions, delivery, giving birth, pains, parturition, throes, travail; SEE CONCEPT *374*

labor [*v*] *work very hard*
bear down, cultivate, drive, drudge, endeavor, exert oneself, grind, plod, plug away*, pour it on*, slave, strain, strive, struggle, sweat, tend, toil, travail, work oneself to the bone*; SEE CONCEPTS *87,100*

laboratory [*n*] *testing room*
chemistry laboratory, lab, research laboratory, workshop; SEE CONCEPTS *312,439,441,448,449*

labored [*adj*] *difficult to understand, unclear*
affected, arduous, awkward, clumsy, contrived, effortful, forced, hard, heavy, inept, maladroit, operose, overdone, overwrought, ponderous, stiff, strained, strenuous, studied, toilsome, unnatural, uphill*, weighty; SEE CONCEPT *538*

laborer [*n*] *worker*
blue-collar worker, drudge, farmhand, grunt, hand, hireling, manual worker, migrant worker, peon, unskilled worker, working man/woman, working stiff*; SEE CONCEPT *348*

laborious [*adj1*] *hard, difficult*
arduous, backbreaking, burdensome, effortful, fatiguing, forced, heavy, herculean*, labored, onerous, operose, ponderous, rough go*, stiff, strained, strenuous, tiresome, toilsome, tough, tough job*, wearing, wearisome, wicked*; SEE CONCEPTS *538,565*

laborious [*adj2*] *hardworking*
active, assiduous, diligent, indefatigable, industrious, operose, painstaking, persevering, sedulous, tireless, unflagging; SEE CONCEPTS *538,550*

labyrinth [*n*] *maze, complexity*
coil, complication, convolution, entanglement, intricacy, jungle, knot, mesh, morass, perplexity, problem, puzzle, riddle, skein, snarl, tangle, web; SEE CONCEPTS *436,663,666*

lace [*n1*] *netted material*
appliqué, banding, border, crochet, edging, filigree, mesh, net, netting, openwork, ornament, tatting, threadwork, tissue, trim, trimming; SEE CONCEPT *473*

lace [*n2*] *string used to connect*
band, cord, rope, shoelace, thong, thread, tie; SEE CONCEPT *475*

lace [*v*] *fasten, intertwine*
add, attach, bind, close, do up, fortify, interlace, interweave, mix, plat, spike, strap, thread, tie, twine; SEE CONCEPT *113*

lacerate [*v*] *tear, cut; wound*
claw, gash, harm, hurt, injure, jag, lance, maim, mangle, mutilate, puncture, rend, rip, score, serrate, slash, stab, torment, torture; SEE CONCEPTS *137,176,214,220,246*

kn
la

laceration [n] *cut, wound*
gash, injury, lesion, pierce, rip, slash, slice, slit, stab, tear; SEE CONCEPT *309*

lack [n] *deficiency, need*
abridgement, absence, curtailment, dearth, decrease, default, defect, deficit, depletion, deprivation, destitution, distress, exigency, exiguity, inadequacy, inferiority, insufficiency, insufficiency, loss, meagerness, miss, necessity, paucity, poverty, privation, reduction, retrenchment, scantiness, scarcity, shortage, shortcoming, shortfall, shortness, shrinkage, shrinking, slightness, stint, want; SEE CONCEPTS *707,709*

lack [v] *do not have*
be deficient in, be short of, be without, have need of, hurting for*, minus, miss, need, not got* out, require, too little too late*, want; SEE CONCEPTS *20,646*

lackadaisical [adj] *careless, indifferent*
abstracted, apathetic, daydreaming, disinterested, dreamy, dull, energyless, enervated, faineant, halfhearted, idle, inattentive, incurious, indolent, inert, laid-back, languid, languishing, languorous, lazy, lethargic, limp, listless, moony*, passive, romantic, sentimental, slothful, spiritless, spring fever*, unconcerned; SEE CONCEPTS *403,542,544*

lacking [adj] *wanting, deficient*
can't cut it*, coming up short*, defective, deprived of, flawed, impaired, inadequate, incomplete, minus, missing, needed, needing, not hacking it*, not making it*, sans, short, without; SEE CONCEPTS *546,771*

lackluster [adj] *dull, lifeless*
blah*, blind, boring, colorless, dark, dead, dim, drab, draggy*, dry, flat*, ho-hum*, laid-back*, leaden, lusterless, matte, muted, nothing*, obscure, pabulum*, prosaic, sombre, unimaginative, uninspired, vanilla*, vapid, zero*; SEE CONCEPTS *542,548,617*

laconic [adj] *short, to the point*
breviloquent, brief, brusque, compact, compendiary, compendious, concise, crisp, curt, pithy, sententious, short and sweet*, succinct, terse; SEE CONCEPTS *267,773,798*

lacquer [n] *coating*
covering, finish, glaze, lamination, layer, varnish, veneer; SEE CONCEPT *475*

lacy [adj] *delicate, netlike*
elegant, fancy, filigree, fine, frilly, gauzy, gossamer, lacelike, meshy, open, ornate, patterned, sheer, thin, transparent; SEE CONCEPT *606*

lad [n] *young man*
boy, buddy, child, fellow, guy, half-pint*, juvenile, kid*, runt*, schoolboy, son, stripling, youngster, youth; SEE CONCEPTS *419,424*

laden [adj] *loaded down*
burdened, charged, encumbered, fraught, full, hampered, oppressed, taxed, weighed down, weighted; SEE CONCEPTS *485,538*

lag [v] *move slowly; delay*
be behind, dally, dawdle, decrease, dillydally*, diminish, drag, drag one's feet*, ebb, fail, fall off, falter, flag, get no place fast*, hang back, hobble, idle, inch, inch along*, jelly, limp, linger, loiter, lose strength, lounge, plod, poke, procrastinate, put off, retard, saunter, shuffle, slacken, slouch, slow, slow up, stagger, stay, straggle, tail, tarry, tool, trail, trudge, wane; SEE CONCEPTS *151,153*

laggard [n] *straggler*
dawdler, idler, lingerer, loafer, lounger, slowpoke, slow starter; SEE CONCEPT *151*

lagoon [n] *shallow body of water*
bayou, gulf, marsh, pond, pool, shallows, shoal, tidal pond; SEE CONCEPT *514*

laid-back [adj] *relaxed*
easygoing, lax, low-pressure, mellow, undemanding, unhurried; SEE CONCEPT *404*

lair [n] *hideout, habitat*
burrow, cave, den, earth, form, hideaway, hole, nest, pen, refuge, resting place, retreat, sanctuary; SEE CONCEPT *515*

laissez-faire [n] *free enterprise, for the most part unrestrained by law*
free trade, indifference, individualism, live and let live*, neutrality, nonintervention; SEE CONCEPTS *388,691*

lake [n] *inland body of water*
basin, creek, inland sea, lagoon, lakelet, loch, mere, millpond, mouth, pond, pool, reservoir, sluice, spring, tarn; SEE CONCEPT *514*

lambaste [v] *punish, beat*
assail, attack, berate, blister, bludgeon, castigate, censure, criticize, cudgel, denounce, excoriate, flay, flog, hammer, hit, lash into*, pan, pelt, pound, pummel, rake over the coals*, read the riot act*, rebuke, reprimand, rip into, roast, scathe, scold, scorch, scourge, shellac, slam, slap, slash, smear, smother, strike, thrash, trim, upbraid, wallop, whip; SEE CONCEPTS *52,54,86*

lame [adj] *unable to walk properly*
bruised, deformed, disabled, game, gimp, gimpy, halt, handicapped, hobbling, limping, pained, raw, sidelined, sore, stiff; SEE CONCEPTS *314,489*

lame [adj2] *feeble, weak*
faltering, faulty, flabby, flimsy, inadequate, ineffective, inefficient, insufficient, poor, thin, unconvincing, unpersuasive, unpleasing, unsatisfactory, unsuitable; SEE CONCEPTS *558,570*

lament [v] *to mourn or grieve deeply*
bawl, beat one's breast*, bemoan, bewail, bleed, cry, deplore, eat one's heart out*, howl, hurt, kick self*, moan, rain, regret, repine, rue, sing, sob, sorrow, take it hard*, wail, weep; SEE CONCEPTS *52,54*

lamentable [adj] *upsetting, miserable*
afflictive, awful, bad, calamitous, deplorable, dire, dirty, distressing, doleful, dolorous, godawful, grievous, grim, heartbreaking, hurting, lousy, low, lugubrious, meager, mean, melancholy, mournful, pitiful, plaintive, poor, regretful, rotten, rueful, sad, sorrowful, stinking, tragic, unfavorable, unfortunate, unsatisfactory, woeful, wretched; SEE CONCEPTS *529,537*

lament/lamentation [n] *grief, complaint*
complaining, dirge, elegy, grieving, jeremiad, keen, keening, lament, moan, moaning, mourning, plaint, requiem, sob, sobbing, sorrow, tears, threnody, ululation, wail, wailing, weeping; SEE CONCEPTS *29,278,410*

laminate [v] *cover with veneer*
coat, exfoliate, face, flake, foil, foliate, layer, overlayer, plate, separate, split, stratify, veneer; SEE CONCEPT *172*

lamp [n] *lantern*
beacon, flashlight, gas lamp, gaslight, hurricane lamp, kerosene lamp, light, searchlight, torch; SEE CONCEPTS *620,624,628,810*

lampoon [*n*] *parody, satire*
burlesque, caricature, invective, pasquil, pasquinade, pastiche, ridicule, roast*, send-up*, skit, squib, takedown, takeoff*; SEE CONCEPTS *263,273*

lampoon [*v*] *ridicule, make fun of*
burlesque, caricature, jape, mock, parody, pasquinade, put on*, rail, roast*, satirize, send up*, squib, take off*, travesty; SEE CONCEPT *273*

lance [*v*] *pierce*
bore, cut, cut into, gash, gore, incise, penetrate, prick, puncture, slash, slice, slit, stab, stick into; SEE CONCEPTS *137,159,176,220*

land [*n*] *earth's surface; ownable property*
acreage, acres, area, beach, continent, country, countryside, dirt, district, earth, estate, expanse, extent, farming, farmland, field, ground, grounds, holding, home, homeland, loam, mainland, manor, nation, old sod, parcel, plot, province, purlieu, quarry, quinta, ranch, real estate, realty, region, shore, sod, soil, stretch, sweep, terra firma, terrain, territory, tillage, tract; SEE CONCEPTS *508,509,510,515*

land [*v1*] *arrive, come to rest on*
alight, berth, bring in, check in, come ashore, come down, come in, come to berth, debark, descend upon, disembark, ditch, dock, drop anchor, flatten out, get down, ground, level off, light on, make land, pilot, put down, put in, set down, set on deck, settle, sit down, splash down, steer, take down, thump, touch down; SEE CONCEPTS *159,181*

land [*v2*] *achieve, acquire*
annex, bring in, gain, get, have, obtain, pick up, procure, secure, win; SEE CONCEPTS *120,706*

landfill [*n*] *dump*
ash heap*, depot, disposal area, dumping ground, garbage lot, hazardous waste dump, junk pile*, junkyard, recycling station, refuse heap, rubbish pile, toxic waste site, transfer station; SEE CONCEPTS *438,449,680*

landlord [*n*] *owner of property leased*
freeholder, hotelier, hotelkeeper, innkeeper, lessor, property owner, proprietor, saw, squire; SEE CONCEPT *347*

landmark [*n1*] *historical or notable sight*
battleground, benchmark, bend, blaze, feature, fragment, guide, hill, mark, marker, memorial, milepost, milestone, monument, mountain, museum, promontory, remnant, ruins, souvenir, specimen, stone, survival, trace, tree, vantage point, vestige, waypost; SEE CONCEPTS *198,284,447*

landmark [*n2*] *turning point*
crisis, event, milepost, milestone, stage, watershed, waypost; SEE CONCEPTS *696,817*

landscape [*n*] *countryside; picture of countryside*
mural, outlook, painting, panorama, photograph, prospect, scene, scenery, sketch, view, vista; SEE CONCEPTS *259,509*

landslide [*n1*] *landslip*
avalanche, earthfall, mudslide, rockslide, snowslide; SEE CONCEPTS *509,524,786*

landslide [*n2*] *great victory*
advantage, clean sweep*, conquest, defeat, grand slam*, killing*, overthrow, superiority, sweep, triumph, win; SEE CONCEPTS *95,671,706,832*

lane [*n*] *road*
alley, artery, avenue, back street, boulevard, byway, drive, expressway, highway, parkway, passage, pathway, roadway, route, street, thoroughfare, throughway, thruway, turnpike; SEE CONCEPT *501*

language [*n*] *system of words for communication*
accent, argot, articulation, brogue, cant, communication, conversation, dialect, diction, dictionary, discourse, doublespeak*, expression, gibberish, idiom, interchange, jargon, lexicon, lingua franca, palaver, parlance, patois, phraseology, prose, signal, slang, sound, speech, style, talk, terminology, tongue, utterance, verbalization, vernacular, vocabulary, vocalization, voice, word, wording; SEE CONCEPT *276*

languid [*adj*] *drooping, dull, listless*
apathetic, blah*, blahs*, comatose, dopey, easy, energyless, enervated, faint, feeble, heavy, impassive, inactive, indifferent, inert, infirm, lackadaisical, laid-back, languishing, languorous, lazy, leaden, leisurely, lethargic, limp, moony*, nebbish, phlegmatic, pining, sickly, sleepyhead*, slow, sluggish, snoozy*, spiritless, supine, torpid, unconcerned, unenthusiastic, unhurried, uninterested, weak, weary, wimpy*; SEE CONCEPTS *403,542,584*

languish [*v*] *droop; become dull, listless*
be disregarded, be neglected, brood, conk out*, decline, desire, despond, deteriorate, die on vine*, dwindle, ebb, fade, fag, fag out, fail, faint, fizzle out, flag, go soft*, go to pieces*, grieve, hanker, hunger, knock out, long, pine, repine, rot, sicken, sigh, snivel, sorrow, suffer, tucker, waste, waste away, weaken, wilt, wither, yearn; SEE CONCEPTS *20,105,469*

languor [*n*] *lethargy*
apathy, dullness, fatigue, idleness, inaction, inactivity, laziness, listlessness, sluggishness, tiredness, torpor, weakness; SEE CONCEPTS *315,410,633,748*

lanky [*adj*] *tall and thin*
angular, attenuated, beanpole*, beanstalk*, bony, broomstick*, extenuated, gangling, gangly, gaunt, lean, meager, rangy, rawboned, scraggy, scrawny, slender, spare, spindling, spindly, stilt, stringy, twiggy*, weedy; SEE CONCEPTS *491,779*

lantern [*n*] *lamp*
beacon, flashlight, gas lamp, gaslight, hurricane lamp, kerosene lamp, light, searchlight, torch; SEE CONCEPTS *620,624,628,810*

lap [*n*] *orbit, circuit*
circle, course, distance, loop, round, tour; SEE CONCEPTS *364,436*

lap [*v1*] *slosh, wash against*
bathe, bubble, burble, drink, gurgle, lave, lick, lip, plash, purl, ripple, sip, slap, splash, sup, swish; SEE CONCEPT *144*

lap [*v2*] *overlap*
cover, enfold, envelop, fold, imbricate, overlie, override, ride, shingle, swaddle, swathe, turn, twist, wrap; SEE CONCEPTS *172,201*

lapse [*n1*] *mistake*
blunder, breach, bungle, crime, error, failing, failure, fault, flub, foible, frailty, gaff, goof, goof-up*, indiscretion, miscue, negligence, offense, omission, oversight, screw-up*, sin, slip, slip-up, transgression, trespass, trip*, vice, violation; SEE CONCEPTS *101,674*

lapse [*n2*] *break in action*
gap, intermission, interruption, interval, lacuna, lull, passage, pause; SEE CONCEPT *807*

la
la

lapse [*n3*] *backsliding*
decadence, declension, decline, degeneration, descent, deterioration, devolution, drop, fall, recession, regression, relapse, retrogradation, retrogression; SEE CONCEPTS *230,316,388*

lapse [*v*] *become void; fall back into previous pattern*
apostatize, backslide, become obsolete, cease, decline, degenerate, descend, deteriorate, die, elapse, end, expire, go by, pass, recede, recidivate, relapse, retrograde, return, revert, run out, slide, slip, subside, terminate, weaken; SEE CONCEPTS *119,698*

larceny [*n*] *theft*
burglary, crime, lift, misappropriation, pilfering, pinch, purloining, robbery, steal, stealing, thievery, thieving, touch*; SEE CONCEPTS *139,192*

larder [*n*] *provisions*
food supply, groceries, pantry, provender, stock, storage, supplies; SEE CONCEPTS *140,712*

large [*adj*] *big, abundant*
ample, barn door*, blimp*, booming, broad, bulky, capacious, colossal, comprehensive, considerable, copious, enormous, excessive, exorbitant, extensive, extravagant, full, generous, giant, gigantic, goodly, grand, grandiose, great, gross, hefty, huge, humongous*, immeasurable, immense, jumbo*, liberal, massive, monumental, mountainous, plentiful, populous, roomy, sizable, spacious, stupendous, substantial, super, sweeping, thumping, tidy, vast, voluminous, whopping*, wide; SEE CONCEPTS *773,781*

largely [*adv*] *to a great extent*
abundantly, as a rule, broadly, by and large, chiefly, commodiously, comprehensively, considerably, copiously, expansively, extensively, extravagantly, generally, generously, grandly, immoderately, imposingly, in a big way, in a grand manner, lavishly, liberally, magnificently, mainly, mostly, on a large scale, overall, predominantly, primarily, principally, prodigally, prodigiously, voluminously, widely; SEE CONCEPTS *544,772*

larger than life [*adj*] *legendary*
awesome, celebrated, extraordinary, famed, famous, immortal, imposing, impressive, mythical, renowned, towering; SEE CONCEPT *568*

largess [*adj*] *generosity*
aid, alms, altruistic, benefaction, benevolent, charitable, charity, donation, endowment, generous, gift, giving, philanthropy, thoughtful; SEE CONCEPTS *404,542*

lascivious [*adj*] *sexually aroused; displaying excessive interest in sex*
bawdy, blue, bodily, carnal, coarse, crude, evil-minded, fast*, fleshly, gross*, hard-core*, hot*, immoral, incontinent, indecent, lecherous, lewd, libertine, libidinous, licentious, low-down*, lubricious, lustful, nasty, obscene, off-color*, offensive, orgiastic, pornographic, prurient, randy, raunchy*, raw, ribald, rough, salacious, scurrilous, sensual, smutty*, soft-core*, steamy, suggestive, unchaste, voluptuous, vulgar, wanton, X-rated*; SEE CONCEPTS *372,403*

lash [*v1*] *beat, whip*
baste, batter, buffet, chastise, dash, drum, flagellate, flay, flog, hammer, hide, hit, horsewhip, knock, lam, lather, pound, pummel, scourge, smack, strap, strike, thrash, wear out, whale*; SEE CONCEPT *189*

lash [*v2*] *criticize harshly*
abuse, attack, baste, bawl out*, belabor, berate, blister, castigate, censure, chew out*, exprobate, flay, fulminate, jaw, lambaste, lampoon, ridicule, satirize, scold, tear into*, tell off*, tongue-lash*, upbraid; SEE CONCEPT *52*

lass [*n*] *young woman*
colleen, damsel, female, girl, lassie, maid, maiden, miss, missy; SEE CONCEPTS *548,585*

lassitude [*n*] *lethargy*
apathy, dullness, exhaustion, fatigue, idleness, inaction, inactivity, languor, laziness, listlessness, sleepiness, sluggishness, tiredness, torpor, weakness, weariness; SEE CONCEPTS *315,410, 633,748*

lasso [*n*] *lariat*
bola, halter, rope, snare; SEE CONCEPT *475*

last [*adj*] *final; newest*
aftermost, antipodal, at the end, bitter end, climactic, closing, concluding, conclusive, crowning, curtains*, definitive, determinate, determinative, end, ending, eventual, extreme, far, far-off, farthest, finishing, furthest, hindmost, lag, latest, least, lowest, meanest, most recent, once and for all*, outermost, rearmost, remotest, supreme, swan song*, terminal, ulterior, ultimate, utmost, uttermost; SEE CONCEPTS *585,778,799*

last [*n*] *end*
close, completion, conclusion, ending, finale, finis, finish, omega, termination; SEE CONCEPT *832*

lasting [*adj*] *enduring, unending*
abiding, constant, continual, continuing, deep-rooted, durable, endless, eternal, everlasting, forever, incessant, indelible, indissoluble, inexhaustible, inexpungible, in for the long haul*, lifelong, longstanding, long-term, old, perdurable, perennial, permanent, perpetual, persisting, stable, till the cows come home*, unceasing, undying, unremitting; SEE CONCEPTS *551,798*

lastly/last [*adv*] *in the end*
after, after all, all in all, at last, at the end, behind, bringing up rear*, finally, in conclusion, in the rear, to conclude, to sum up, ultimately; SEE CONCEPTS *585,799*

latch [*n*] *lock*
bar, bolt, catch, clamp, fastening, hasp, hook, padlock; SEE CONCEPTS *445,499*

latch [*v*] *fasten with lock*
bar, bolt, cinch, close, close up, lock, make fast, secure; SEE CONCEPTS *85,160*

late [*adj1*] *not on time*
backward, behind, behindhand, behind time, belated, blown*, delayed, dilatory, eleventh-hour*, gone, held up, hung up*, in a bind*, in the lurch*, jammed*, lagging, last-minute, missed the boat*, out of luck*, overdue, postponed, put off, remiss, slow, stayed, strapped*, tardy, too late, unpunctual; SEE CONCEPTS *548,799*

late [*adj2*] *new*
advanced, fresh, just out, modern, recent; SEE CONCEPTS *578,797*

late [*adj3*] *dead*
asleep, bygone, cold, deceased, defunct, departed, erstwhile, ex-*, exanimate, extinct, former, inanimate, lifeless, old, once, onetime, past, preceding, previous, quondam, sometime; SEE CONCEPT *539*

late [*adv*] *at the last minute*
backward, behind, behindhand, behind time, belatedly, dilatorily, slowly, tardily, unpunctual; SEE CONCEPT *799*

lately [*adv*] *new, recently*
afresh, anew, a short time ago, in recent times, just now, latterly, newly, not long ago, of late; SEE CONCEPT *820*

latent [*adj*] *dormant, hidden*
abeyant, between the lines, concealed, contained, covert, idle, immature, implied, in abeyance, inactive, inert, inferential, inferred, inherent, inoperative, intrinsic, invisible, involved, lurking, passive, possible, potential, quiescent, rudimentary, secret, sleeping, smoldering, suppressed, suspended, tacit, torpid, underdeveloped, underlying, undeveloped, unexposed, unexpressed, unrealized, unripe, unseen, veiled, vestigial; SEE CONCEPTS *404,576*

later [*adj*] *coming after*
downstream, ensuing, following, more recent, next, posterior, postliminary, proximate, subsequent, subsequential, succeeding, ulterior; SEE CONCEPT *799*

later [*adv*] *happening after*
after, afterward, again, at another time, behind, by and by*, come Sunday*, down the line*, down the road*, in a while, infra, in time, later on, latterly, more recent, next, subsequently, succeeding, thereafter; SEE CONCEPT *799*

lateral [*adj*] *sideways*
crabwise, edgeways, flanking, oblique, side, side-by-side, sidelong, sideward, sidewise, skirting; SEE CONCEPTS *581,583*

lather [*n1*] *bubbles*
cream, foam, froth, head, soap, soapsuds, spume, suds, yeast; SEE CONCEPTS *260,437*

lather [*n2*] *commotion, fuss*
agitation, bustle, clamor, confusion, dither, fever, flap*, fluster, hassle, hoopla*, hubbub*, hullabaloo*, state, stew*, storm*, sweat*, tizzy*, tumult, turbulence, turmoil, twitter*; SEE CONCEPTS *230,388*

lather [*v*] *cause to bubble*
beat, foam, froth, scrub, soap, wash, whip; SEE CONCEPT *165*

latitude [*n*] *freedom, room to move; scope*
breadth, compass, elbow room, extent, independence, indulgence, laxity, leeway, liberty, license, margin, play, range, reach, room, run, run of, space, span, spread, sweep, swing, unrestrictedness, width; SEE CONCEPTS *651,739,756,788*

latter [*adj*] *latest, concluding*
closing, eventual, final, following, hindmost, lag, last, last-mentioned, later, modern, rearmost, recent, second, terminal; SEE CONCEPTS *585,799*

lattice [*n*] *mesh, trellis*
filigree, frame, fretwork, grating, grid, grill, latticework, net, network, openwork, reticulation, screen, structure, tracery, web; SEE CONCEPT *259*

laud [*v*] *acclaim, praise*
admire, adore, approve, bless, boost, build up, celebrate, commend, compliment, cry up, eulogize, extol, flatter, glorify, hand it to*, honor, hymn, magnify, panegyrize, pat on the back*, revere, reverence, sing the praises of*, stroke, venerate, worship; SEE CONCEPT *69*

laudable [*adj*] *admirable*
commendable, creditable, deserving, estimable, excellent, mean, meritable, meritorious, of note,

praisable, praiseworthy, stellar, terrific, thankworthy, worthy; SEE CONCEPT *574*

laudatory [*adj*] *complimentary*
acclamatory, adulatory, approbative, approbatory, approving, commendatory, encomiastic, eulogistic, flattering, laudative, panegyrical, praiseful; SEE CONCEPT *267*

laugh [*v*] *expressing amusement, happiness with sound be*
be in stitches*, break up*, burst*, cachinnate, chortle, chuckle, convulsed*, crack up*, crow, die laughing*, fracture*, giggle, grin, guffaw, howl, roar, roll in the aisles*, scream, shriek, snicker, snort, split one's sides*, titter, whoop*; SEE CONCEPTS *77,185*

laughable [*adj*] *easily made fun of*
absurd, amusing, asinine, bizarre, camp, campy, comic, comical, derisive, derisory, diverting, droll, eccentric, entertaining, facetious, fantastic, farcical, funny, gelastic, har-har*, hilarious, humorous, inane, jocose, jocular, jokey, joshing, ludicrous, mirthful, mocking, nonsensical, preposterous, rich, ridiculous, riot, risible, scream, unusual, witty; SEE CONCEPTS *267,550*

laugh at [*v*] *ridicule*
belittle, deride, hoot, jeer, lampoon, make fun of, mock, scoff, taunt; SEE CONCEPT *54*

laugh/laughter [*n*] *audible expression of amusement*
amusement, cachinnation, cackle, chortle, chuckle, chuckling, crack-up*, crow, fit, gesture, giggle, giggling, glee, guffaw, hilarity, howling, merriment, mirth, peal, rejoicing, roar, shout, shriek, snicker, snigger, snort, sound, titter, yuck*; SEE CONCEPTS *77,185*

launch [*v1*] *send off*
barrage, bombard, bung, cast, catapult, discharge, dispatch, drive, eject, fire, fling, heave, hurl, lance, pitch, project, propel, send forth, set afloat, set in motion, shoot, sling, throw, toss; SEE CONCEPTS *179,222*

launch [*v2*] *begin, initiate*
bow, break the ice*, break the seal*, commence, embark upon, get show on road*, inaugurate, instigate, institute, introduce, jump, kick off*, open, originate, set going, start, start ball rolling*, usher in*; SEE CONCEPT *221*

launder [*v*] *wash*
clean, cleanse, do the laundry*, do the washing*, rinse; SEE CONCEPT *165*

laurels [*n*] *credit, praise*
acclaim, accolade, award, badge, bays, blue ribbon, commendation, crown, decoration, distinction, fame, feather in cap*, glory, gold, gold star*, kudos, prestige, recognition, renown, reward; SEE CONCEPTS *69,278,337*

lavatory [*n*] *bathroom*
latrine, powder room, restroom, shower, toilet, washroom, water closet, WC; SEE CONCEPT *448*

lavish [*adj*] *profuse; splendid*
abundant, bountiful, copious, effusive, exaggerated, excessive, extravagant, exuberant, first-class, free, generous, gorgeous, grand, immoderate, impressive, improvident, inordinate, intemperate, liberal, lush, luxuriant, luxurious, munificent, openhanded, opulent, plentiful, plush, posh, prodigal, profligate, profusive, prolific, riotous, ritzy, sumptuous, swanky, thriftless, unreasonable, unrestrained, unsparing,

la
la

unstinging, wasteful, wild; SEE CONCEPTS *334,589,781*

lavish [v] *pamper, shower*
be generous, be wasteful, deluge, dissipate, expend, fritter, give, go through, heap, pour, run through*, scatter, spend, spend money like water*, squander, thrust upon, waste; SEE CONCEPTS *110,327,341*

law [n1] *rules of a government, society*
act, assize, behest, bidding, bylaw, canon, case, caveat, charge, charter, code, command, commandment, constitution, covenant, decision, decree, decretum, demand, dictate, divestiture, due process, edict, enactment, equity, garnishment, injunction, institute, instruction, jurisprudence, legislation, mandate, measure, notice, order, ordinance, precedent, precept, prescript, prescription, reg, regulation, requirement, ruling, statute, subpoena, summons, warrant, writ; SEE CONCEPT *318*

law [n2] *standard, principle of behavior*
assumption, axiom, base, canon, cause, criterion, exigency, formula, foundation, fundamental, generalization, ground, guide, maxim, origin, postulate, precept, principium, proposal, proposition, reason, regulation, rule, source, theorem, truth, usage; SEE CONCEPT *688*

lawbreaker [n] *criminal*
blackmailer, black marketeer, con, convict, crook, culprit, delinquent, felon, fugitive, gangster, hood*, hoodlum, hooligan, jailbird, malefactor, mobster, offender, outlaw, racketeer, scofflaw; SEE CONCEPT *412*

lawful [adj] *allowable, legitimate*
authorized, bona fide, canonical, card-carrying*, commanded, condign, constitutional, decreed, due, enacted, enforced, enjoined, established, innocent, judged, judicial, jural, juridical, jurisprudent, just, justifiable, kosher*, legal, legalized, legislated, legit*, legitimatized, licit, mandated, official, of right, on the level*, on the up and up*, ordained, ordered, passed, permissible, proper, protected, rightful, ruled, statutory, valid, vested, warrantable, warranted; SEE CONCEPTS *319,545*

lawless [adj] *reckless, ungoverned*
anarchic, anarchical, anarchistic, bad, barbarous, chaotic, contumacious, criminal, despotic, disobedient, disordered, disorderly, evil, fierce, heterodox, infringing, insubordinate, insurgent, mutinous, nihilistic, noncompliant, nonconformist, piratical, rebellious, recusant, revolutionary, riotous, savage, seditious, tempestuous, terrorizing, traitorous, turbulent, tyrannous, uncivilized, uncultivated, unorthodox, unpeaceful, unrestrained, unruly, untamed, violent, warlike, wild; SEE CONCEPTS *319,545*

lawn [n] *cultivated area of green grass*
backyard, garden, grass, grassplot, green, park, plot, terrace, yard; SEE CONCEPTS *509,513,517*

lawsuit [n] *case brought to court*
accusation, action, argument, arraignment, assumpsit, bill, cause, claim, contest, dispute, impeachment, indictment, litigation, presentment, proceedings, prosecution, replevin, suit, trial; SEE CONCEPT *318*

lawyer [n] *person who is trained to counsel or argue in cases of law*
advocate, attorney, attorney-at-law, barrister, counsel, counsellor, counselor, defender, jurisprudent, jurist, legal adviser, legal eagle*, legist, member of the bar, mouthpiece*, pleader, practitioner, proctor, procurator, solicitor; SEE CONCEPT *355*

lax [adj] *slack, remiss*
any way*, asleep on job*, behindhand, broad, careless, casual, delinquent, derelict, devil-may-care*, disregardful, easygoing, flaccid, forgetful, general, imprecise, inaccurate, indefinite, indifferent, inexact, lenient, neglectful, negligent, nonspecific, oblivious, overindulgent, paying no mind*, regardless, shapeless, slipshod, sloppy, soft, unmindful, vague, yielding; SEE CONCEPTS *401,542,557*

laxative [n] *aperient*
cathartic, purgative; SEE CONCEPT *307*

lay [adj] *amateur, not trained in a religious or other profession*
inexpert, nonclerical, nonprofessional, nonspecialist, ordinary, secular, temporal, unsacred; SEE CONCEPT *530*

lay [v1] *put, place*
arrange, deposit, dispose, establish, fix, leave, locate, order, organize, plant, posit, position, repose, rest, set, set down, set out, settle, spread, stick, systematize; SEE CONCEPTS *158,201*

lay [v2] *produce, advance*
adduce, allege, bear, bring forth, bring forward, cite, deposit, generate, lodge, offer, present, put forward, submit, yield; SEE CONCEPTS *66,205*

lay [v3] *credit, allocate*
accredit, address, aim, allot, apply, ascribe, assess, assign, attribute, burden, cast, charge, direct, encumber, impose, impute, incline, level, point, refer, saddle, tax, train, turn, zero in*; SEE CONCEPTS *49,50,88,187*

lay [v4] *design, plan*
concoct, contrive, devise, hatch, plot, prepare, work out; SEE CONCEPT *36*

lay [v5] *make smooth*
allay, alleviate, appease, assuage, calm, even, flatten, flush, iron, level, plane, press, quiet, relieve, steam, still, suppress; SEE CONCEPTS *235,250*

lay [v6] *bet, wager*
gamble, game, give odds, hazard, play, risk, stake; SEE CONCEPT *363*

layer [n] *coating, tier*
band, bed, blanket, coat, coping, couch, course, cover, covering, film, flag, flap, floor, fold, girdle, lamina, lamination, lap, mantle, overlap, overlay, panel, ply, row, seam, sheet, slab, story, stratum, stripe, substratum, thickness, zone; SEE CONCEPTS *744,835*

lay into [v] *criticize, attack*
assail, battle, belabor, fire at*, invade, lambaste, let fly at*, set about; SEE CONCEPTS *52,86*

layoff [n] *dismissal from job or responsibility*
cutback, discharge, early retirement, respite, unemployment; SEE CONCEPT *351*

lay off [v1] *stop doing*
cease, desist, end, give a rest, give up, halt, leave alone, leave off, let up, lie by, quit, rest, spell; SEE CONCEPTS *119,234*

lay off [v2] *relieve of responsibility*
discharge, dismiss, drop, fire, let go, oust, pay off, retire early; SEE CONCEPT *351*

layout [n] *physical arrangement*
blueprint, chart, design, diagram, draft, forma-

tion, geography, map, organization, outline, plan, purpose; SEE CONCEPTS *625,660*

lay out [*v1*] *spend money*
disburse, expend, give, invest, lend, outlay, pay, put out, put up, shell out*; SEE CONCEPTS *327,341*

lay out [*v2*] *design, plan*
arrange, chart, diagram, display, exhibit, map, outline, set out, spread out; SEE CONCEPTS *36,158,174*

layperson [*n*] *amateur person, not trained in religious or other profession*
believer, dilettante, follower, laic, member, neophyte, nonprofessional, novice, outsider, parishioner, proselyte, recruit, secular; SEE CONCEPTS *361,423*

lay up [*v2*] *hurt, incapacitate*
beat up, confine, disable, harm, hospitalize, injure; SEE CONCEPT *246*

lay up/lay by [*v1*] *set aside, store*
accumulate, amass, build up, bury, conserve, cumulate, garner, hide, hoard, keep, lay in, preserve, put away, roll up, salt away, save, spare, store up, treasure; SEE CONCEPTS *120,134*

laziness [*n*] *unwillingness to work, be active*
apathy, dilatoriness, do-nothingness, dormancy, dreaminess, drowsiness, dullness, faineance, faineancy, heaviness, idleness, inactivity, indolence, inertia, inertness, lackadaisicalness, languidness, languorousness, laxness, leadenness, leisureliness, lethargy, listlessness, neglectfulness, negligence, otioseness, otiosity, passivity, remissness, slackness, sleepiness, sloth, slothfulness, slowness, sluggishness, stolidity, supineness, tardiness, torpescence, torpidness, weariness; SEE CONCEPTS *411,633*

lazy [*adj*] *inactive, sluggish*
apathetic, asleep on the job*, careless, comatose, dallying, dilatory, drowsy, dull, flagging, idle, inattentive, indifferent, indolent, inert, lackadaisical, laggard, lagging, languid, languorous, lethargic, lifeless, loafing, neglectful, out of it*, passive, procrastinating, remiss, shiftless, slack, sleepy, slothful, slow, slow-moving, snoozy*, somnolent, supine, tardy, tired, torpid, trifling, unconcerned, unenergetic, unindustrious, unpersevering, unready, weary; SEE CONCEPTS *401,404*

leach [*v*] *drain, empty*
extract, filter, filtrate, lixiviate, percolate, seep, strain, wash away; SEE CONCEPTS *142,211,225*

lead [*n1*] *first place, supremacy*
advance, advantage, ahead, bulge, cutting edge*, direction, edge, example, facade, front rank, guidance, head, heavy, leadership, margin, model, over, pilot, point, precedence, primacy, principal, priority, protagonist, spark, star, start, title role, top, top spot, vanguard; SEE CONCEPTS *668,693,828*

lead [*n2*] *clue*
evidence, guide, hint, indication, proof, sign, suggestion, tip, trace; SEE CONCEPTS *274,284*

lead [*v1*] *guide physically*
accompany, attend, be responsible for, chaperone, coerce, compel, conduct, convey, convoy, direct, drive, escort, find a way, force, get, go along with, guard, impel, induce, manage, pass along, persuade, pilot, point out, point the way, precede, prevail, protect, quarterback*, route, safeguard, see, shepherd, show, show around,

show in, show the way, span, squire, steer, traverse, usher, watch over; SEE CONCEPT *187*

lead [*v2*] *guide mentally; influence*
affect, bring, bring on, call the shots*, cause, command, conduce, contribute, convert, direct, dispose, draw, get the jump on*, go out in front*, govern, head, helm, incline, induce, introduce, manage, motivate, move, persuade, preside over, prevail, produce, prompt, quarterback*, result in, run things*, serve, shepherd, spearhead*, spur, supervise, tend, trail-blaze*; SEE CONCEPTS *68,117,221*

lead [*v3*] *surpass*
be ahead, blaze a trail*, come first*, exceed, excel, outdo, outstrip, precede, preface, transcend, usher; SEE CONCEPT *141*

lead (a life) [*v4*] *experience*
have, live, pass, spend, undergo; SEE CONCEPT *678*

leader [*n*] *person who guides*
boss, captain, chief, chieftain, commander, conductor, controller, counsellor, dean, dignitary, director, doyen, eminence, exec, forerunner, general, governor, guide, harbinger, head, herald, lead, lion*, luminary, manager, mistress, notability, notable, officer, pacesetter, pilot, pioneer, precursor, president, principal, rector, ringleader, ruler, shepherd, skipper, superintendent, superior; SEE CONCEPTS *347,354*

leadership [*n*] *guidance*
administration, authority, capacity, command, conduction, control, conveyance, direction, directorship, domination, foresight, hegemony, influence, initiative, management, pilotage, power, preeminence, primacy, skill, superintendency, superiority, supremacy, sway; SEE CONCEPTS *376,687*

leading [*adj*] *chief, superior*
arch, best, champion, dominant, dominating, famous, first, foremost, governing, greatest, headmost, highest, inaugural, initial, main, noted, notorious, number one*, outstanding, popular, preeminent, premier, primary, principal, prominent, ruling, stellar, top, well-known; SEE CONCEPTS *574,585*

leaf [*n1*] *green foliage of plant*
blade, bract, flag, foliole, frond, leaflet, needle, pad, petal, petiole, scale, stalk, stipule; SEE CONCEPT *428*

leaf [*n2*] *page of document*
folio, paper, sheet; SEE CONCEPT *270*

leaf [*v*] *flip through*
browse, dip into, glance, riff, riffle, run through, scan, skim, thumb; SEE CONCEPTS *72,623*

leafy [*adj*] *abundant in foliage*
abounding, abundant, covered, green, hidden, leafed, leaved, shaded, shady, umbrageous, verdant, wooded; SEE CONCEPTS *485,583*

league [*n1*] *association, federation*
alliance, band, bunch, circle, circuit, club, coalition, combination, combine, compact, company, confederacy, confederation, conference, consortium, crew, gang, group, guild, loop, mob, order, organization, outfit, partnership, pool, ring, society, sodality, union, unit; SEE CONCEPTS *365,381,387*

league [*n2*] *group of a certain ability*
category, circle, class, grade, grouping, level, pigeonhole*, rank, status, tier; SEE CONCEPTS *388,630*

la
le

league [v] *associate*
ally, amalgamate, band, coadjute, collaborate, combine, concur, confederate, conjoin, consolidate, cooperate, federate, join forces, unite; SEE CONCEPTS *8,10,114*

leak [n] *opening; seepage through opening*
aperture, chink, crack, crevice, decrease, destruction, detriment, drip, drop, escape, expenditure, exposure, fissure, flow, hole, leakage, leaking, loss, outgoing, percolation, pit, puncture, short circuit, slip; SEE CONCEPTS *116,513*

leak [v] *seep; make known*
break, come out, discharge, disclose, divulge, drip, drool, escape, exude, get out, give away, let slip*, make public, ooze, out, pass, pass on, percolate, reveal, slip, spill, spill the beans, tell, transpire, trickle; SEE CONCEPTS *60,116,179*

lean [adj] *bare, thin*
angular, anorexic, barren, beanpole*, bony, emaciated, gangling, gangly, gaunt, haggard, inadequate, infertile, lank, lanky, meager, no fat, pitiful, poor, rangy, rawboned, scanty, scraggy, scrawny, shadow*, sinewy, skinny, slender, slim, spare, sparse, stick, stilt, stringy, svelte, sylphlike, twiggy*, unfruitful, unproductive, wasted, wiry, wizened, worn; SEE CONCEPTS *485,491*

lean [v1] *bend, angle toward*
bear on, beetle, be off, be slanted, bow, cant, careen, cock, curve, decline, deflect, dip, divert, drift, droop, fasten on, hang on, heel, incline, jut, list, nod, overhang, pitch, place, prop, put weight on, recline, repose, rest, rest on, roll, sag, sheer, sink, slant, slope, tilt, tip, turn, twist, veer; SEE CONCEPTS *147,201,738*

lean [v2] *be disposed*
be prone, be willing, favor, gravitate toward, have propensity, incline, look, not mind, prefer, tend; SEE CONCEPT *20*

lean [v3] *count, depend on*
bank on*, believe in, bet bottom dollar*, bet on*, confide, gamble on*, have faith, hinge on*, lay money on*, put faith in, rely, trust; SEE CONCEPTS *12,26*

leaning [n] *tendency, bias*
aptitude, bent*, cup of tea*, disposition, drift, favor, favoritism, inclination, inclining, liking, mindset, partiality, penchant, predilection, predisposition, proclivity, proneness, propensity, sentiment, taste, thing, weakness; SEE CONCEPTS *20,32,689*

leap [n] *jump; increase*
bound, caper, escalation, frisk, hop, rise, skip, spring, surge, upsurge, upswing, vault; SEE CONCEPTS *194,780*

leap [v] *jump, jump over; increase*
advance, arise, ascend, bounce, bound, caper, cavort, clear, escalate, frisk, hop, hurdle, lop, mount, rise, rocket, saltate, skip, soar, spring, surge, vault; SEE CONCEPTS *194,780*

learn [v1] *acquire information*
apprentice, attain, become able, become versed, be taught, be trained, brush up on*, burn midnight oil*, commit to memory, con, crack the books*, cram*, determine, drink in*, enroll, gain, get, get down pat*, get the hang of*, get the knack of*, grasp, grind, imbibe, improve mind, lucubrate, major in, master, matriculate, memorize, minor in, peruse, pick up*, pore over, prepare, read, receive, review, soak up*, specialize

in, study, take course*, take in, train in, wade through*; SEE CONCEPTS *31,33*

learn [v2] *discover, find out*
ascertain, catch on, detect, determine, dig up*, discern, gain, gather, hear, see, smoke out*, stumble upon*, trip over, tumble, uncover, understand, unearth; SEE CONCEPTS *34,183*

learned [adj] *well-informed*
abstruse, academic, accomplished, bookish, brainy*, conversant, cultivated, cultured, deep*, educated, erudite, esoteric, experienced, expert, grave, grounded, highbrow*, intellectual, in the know*, judicious, lettered, literary, literate, omniscient, pansophic, pedantic, philosophic, philosophical, polymath, posted, professorial, recondite, sage, sapient, scholarly, scientific, sharp, skilled, solemn, solid, sound, studied, studious, versed, well-educated, well-grounded, well-read, well-rounded; SEE CONCEPT *402*

learner [n] *person who receives education*
abecedarian, apprentice, beginner, bookworm, catechumen, disciple, initiate, neophyte, novice, probationer, pupil, scholar, student, trainee; SEE CONCEPT *350*

learning [n] *education, knowledge*
acquirements, attainments, culture, erudition, information, letters, literature, lore, research, scholarship, schooling, science, study, training, tuition, wisdom; SEE CONCEPTS *274,409*

lease [v] *rent object, residence*
charter, hire, let, loan, rent out, sublease, sublet; SEE CONCEPTS *89,115*

leash [n] *rein*
bridle, chain, check, control, cord, curb, deterrent, hold, lead, restraint, rope, strap, tether; SEE CONCEPT *475*

leash [v] *rein, hold*
bridle, check, clog, control, curb, entrammel, fasten, fetter, hamper, hobble, hog-tie*, hold back, restrain, secure, shackle, suppress, tether, tie, tie up, trammel; SEE CONCEPT *191*

least [adj] *slightest, smallest*
atomic, bottom, entry-level, feeblest, fewest, finical, first, gutter, infinitesimal, last, lowest, meanest, microcosmic, microscopic, minimal, minimum, minute, minutest, molecular, most trivial, nadir, next to nothing*, niggling*, piddling*, poorest, second, short-end*, third*, tiniest, trivial, unimportant; SEE CONCEPTS *585,789*

leathery [adj] *hard, durable*
coriaceous, hardened, leatherlike, rough, rugged, strong, tough, wrinkled; SEE CONCEPTS *489,606*

leave [n1] *permission*
allowance, assent, authorization, concession, consent, dispensation, freedom, go-ahead*, green light*, liberty, okay, permit, sanction, sufferance, tolerance; SEE CONCEPTS *376,685*

leave [n2] *holiday, time off*
adieu, departure, farewell, furlough, goodbye, leave of absence, leave-taking, liberty, parting, retirement, sabbatical, vacation, withdrawal; SEE CONCEPTS *802,807*

leave [v1] *depart, abandon physically*
abscond, beat it*, break away, clear out*, come away, cut out, decamp, defect, desert, disappear, ditch*, elope, embark, emigrate, escape, exit, flee, flit, fly, forsake, give the slip*, go, go away, go forth, head out*, issue, migrate, move, move out, part, pull out*, push off*, quit, relinquish, remove oneself, retire, ride off*, run along*,

sally, say goodbye*, scram, set out, slip out, split*, start, step down, take a hike*, take leave, take off, vacate, vamoose*, vanish, walk out, withdraw; SEE CONCEPT 195

leave [v2] *abandon, renounce*
back out*, cease, cede, desert, desist, drop, drop out*, evacuate, forbear, forsake, give notice, give up*, hand over, knock off, maroon, quit, refrain, relinquish, resign, stop, surrender, terminate, waive, yield; SEE CONCEPT 234

leave [v3] *forget, neglect*
allow, drop, have, lay down, leave behind, let, let be, let continue, let go, let stay, mislay, omit, permit, suffer; SEE CONCEPTS 30,83

leave [v4] *give, especially after death*
allot, apportion, assign, bequeath, bequest, cede, commit, confide, consign, demise, devise, entrust, give over, hand down, leave behind, legate, refer, transmit, will; SEE CONCEPTS 108,317

leave off [v] *stop*
abstain, break off, cease, desist, discontinue, end, give over, give up, halt, knock off*, quit, refrain, surcease; SEE CONCEPT 234

lecherous [adj] *lustful, lewd*
carnal, concupiscent, corrupt, fast*, hot and heavy*, incontinent, lascivious, libertine, libidinous, licentious, low-down*, lubricious, prurient, raunchy*, salacious, satyric, sensual, unchaste, wanton; SEE CONCEPTS 372,401

lechery [n] *lewdness*
carnality, debauchery, lasciviousness, libertinism, licentiousness, lust, lustfulness, raunchiness, salaciousness, wantonness; SEE CONCEPTS 20,709

lectern [n] *reading desk*
ambo, platform, pulpit, reading stand, rostrum, stand, support; SEE CONCEPTS 440,443

lecture [n1] *lesson, speech*
address, allocution, chalk talk*, discourse, disquisition, harangue, instruction, oration, pep talk*, pitch*, soapbox*, spiel*, talk; SEE CONCEPTS 60,278

lecture [n2] *speech of criticism*
castigation, censure, chiding, dressing-down*, going-over*, harangue, moralism, preaching, preachment, rebuke, reprimand, reproof, scolding, sermon, talking-to*, telling off*; SEE CONCEPTS 52,54

lecture [v1] *give a lesson, speech*
address, declaim, deliver, discourse, expound, get on a soapbox*, give a talk, harangue, hold forth, orate, prelect, recite, speak, spiel*, spout, talk, teach; SEE CONCEPTS 60,266

lecture [v2] *criticize lengthily*
admonish, berate, chide, exprobate, flay, give going-over*, give piece of mind*, moralize, preach, rank on, rate, reprimand, reprove, scold, sermonize, tell off; SEE CONCEPT 52

ledge [n] *shelf*
bar, bench, berm, bracket, console, edge, jut, mantle, offset, path, projection, reef, ridge, rim, route, sill, step, strip, tier, track, trail, walk, way; SEE CONCEPTS 445,513

ledger [n] *account book*
books, daybook, journal, record book, register; SEE CONCEPTS 271,280,801

leech [n] *parasite*
barnacle, bloodsucker*, bum*, freeloader, scrounger, sponge*, sycophant; SEE CONCEPTS 394,412

leer [n/v] *look at longingly*
eye, eyeball*, gloat, goggle*, ogle, smirk, sneer, squint, stare, wink; SEE CONCEPT 623

leery [adj] *suspicious*
careful, cautious, chary, distrustful, doubting, dubious, on one's guard*, shy, skeptical, uncertain, unsure, wary; SEE CONCEPT 529

leeway [n] *room to move, grow*
elbow room*, extent, headway, latitude, margin, play, scope, space; SEE CONCEPT 739

left [adj1] *on west side when facing north*
hard to left, larboard, near, nigh side, port, portside, sinister, sinistral, south; SEE CONCEPTS 581,583

left [adj2] *politically radical*
leftist, left-wing, liberal, progressive, revolutionary, socialist; SEE CONCEPT 529

left [adj3] *abandoned*
continuing, departed, extra, forsaken, gone out, leftover, marooned, over, remaining, residual, split, staying; SEE CONCEPT 577

leftover [adj] *remaining, excess*
extra, residual, surplus, unconsumed, uneaten, untouched, unused, unwanted; SEE CONCEPTS 560,771

leftover [n] *remainder, remains*
debris, leavings, legacy, oddments, odds and ends*, orts, remnants, residue, scraps, surplus, survivor, trash; SEE CONCEPTS 260,457

left-wing [adj] *liberal*
communist, leftist, radical, socialist; SEE CONCEPTS 529,542

leg [n] *appendage used for support*
brace, column, lap, limb, member, part, pile, pole, portion, post, prop, section, segment, shank, stage, stake, stilt, stretch, stump, support, upright; SEE CONCEPTS 392,471,832

legacy [n] *inheritance, heritage*
bequest, birthright, devise, endowment, estate, gift, heirloom, throwback, tradition; SEE CONCEPTS 337,710

legal [adj] *allowable, permissible*
acknowledged, allowed, authorized, card-carrying*, chartered, clean*, condign, constitutional, contractual, decreed, due, enforced, enforcible, enjoined, fair, forensic, granted, innocent, judged, judicial, juridical, just, justifiable, justified, lawful, legalized, legit*, legitimate, licit, on the level*, on the up and up*, ordained, passed, precedented, prescribed, proper, protected, right, rightful, sanctioned, sound, statutory, straight, sure enough, valid, warranted, within the law; SEE CONCEPT 319

legalize [v] *allow, validate*
approve, authorize, clean up, codify, constitute, decree, decriminalize, enact, formulate, launder, legislate, legitimate, legitimatize, license, ordain, permit, regulate, sanction; SEE CONCEPTS 298,317

legend [n1] *story of the past, often fictitious*
fable, fiction, folklore, folk story, folk tale, lore, myth, mythology, mythos, narrative, saga, tale, tradition; SEE CONCEPT 282

legend [n2] *brief description in document*
cipher, code, device, epigraph, epitaph, head, heading, inscription, key, motto, rubric, table, underline; SEE CONCEPTS 268,270

legendary [adj1] *fictitious but well known*
allegorical, apocryphal, created, customary, doubtful, dubious, fabled, fabricated, fabulous,

le
le

fanciful, figmental, handed-down, imaginary, imaginative, improbable, invented, mythical, mythological, related, romantic, storied, told, traditional, unhistoric, unhistorical, unreal, unverifiable; SEE CONCEPTS *267,552*

legendary [*adj2*] *famous*
celebrated, famed, illustrious, immortal, renowned, well-known; SEE CONCEPT *568*

legerdemain [*n*] *sleight of hand*
artfulness, chicanery, conjuring, craftiness, cunning, deceit, deception, hocus-pocus, manipulation, trickery; SEE CONCEPTS *59,278*

legible [*adj*] *easy to read*
clear, coherent, decipherable, distinct, easily read, intelligible, lucid, neat, plain, readable, sharp, understandable; SEE CONCEPTS *267,535, 576*

legion [*adj*] *numerous*
countless, many, multifarious, multitudinal, multitudinous, myriad, numberless, populous, several, sundry, various, very many, voluminous; SEE CONCEPTS *762,781*

legion [*n*] *mass, force of people*
army, body, brigade, cloud, company, division, drove, flock, group, horde, host, multitude, myriad, number, phalanx, rout, scores, throng, troop; SEE CONCEPTS *322,387,417*

legislation [*n*] *law of a government*
act, bill, charter, codification, constitution, enactment, lawmaking, measure, prescription, regulation, ruling, statute; SEE CONCEPT *318*

legislative [*adj*] *lawmaking*
congressional, decreeing, enacting, jurisdictive, lawgiving, legislational, legislatorial, ordaining, parliamentarian, parliamentary, senatorial, statute-making, synodical; SEE CONCEPT *319*

legislator [*n*] *person in government who makes laws*
administrator, aldermember, assemblymember, council member, deputy, lawgiver, lawmaker, leader, member, member of Congress, parliamentarian, representative, senator; SEE CONCEPT *354*

legislature [*n*] *governmental body, most often elected, that makes laws*
assembly, body, chamber, congress, council, diet, house, house of representatives, lawmakers, parliament, plenum, senate, voice of the people; SEE CONCEPT *299*

legitimate [*adj*] *authentic, valid, legal*
accepted, accredited, acknowledged, admissible, appropriate, authorized, canonical, certain, cogent, consistent, correct, customary, fair, genuine, innocent, just, justifiable, lawful, licit, logical, natural, normal, official, on the level, on the up and up, orthodox, probable, proper, real, reasonable, received, recognized, regular, reliable, rightful, sanctioned, sensible, sound, statutory, sure, true, typical, usual, verifiable, warranted, well-founded; SEE CONCEPTS *319,558,582*

leisure [*n*] *free time and its activities*
chance, convenience, ease, freedom, holiday, idle hours, intermission, leave of absence, liberty, one's own sweet time*, opportunity, pause, quiet, range, recess, recreation, relaxation, repose, requiescence, respite, rest, retirement, sabbatical, scope, spare moments*, spare time, time, time off*, unemployment, vacant hour*, vacation; SEE CONCEPTS *363,681,807*

leisurely [*adj*] *casual, unhurried*
comfortable, delayed, deliberate, dilatory, easy, free, gentle, laggard, laid-back*, languid, lax, lazy, relaxed, restful, slack, slackened, slow, slow-moving, unhasty; SEE CONCEPTS *550,584, 799*

leisurely [*adv*] *casually, unhurriedly*
at one's convenience*, at one's leisure, calmly, comfortably, composedly, deliberately, dilatorily, easily, gradually, inactively, indolently, laggardly, langorously, languidly, lazily, lethargically, lingeringly, listlessly, slowly, sluggishly, taking one's time*, tardily, torpidly, with delay, without haste; SEE CONCEPTS *544,584,799*

lemon [*n*] *dud*
failure, flop, junk, piece of junk, reject; SEE CONCEPTS *412,423*

lend [*v*] *loan, accommodate*
add, advance, afford, allow, bestow, confer, contribute, entrust, extend, furnish, give, grant, impart, lay on one, lend-lease, let, loan shark*, oblige, permit, present, provide, shark, stake, supply, trust; SEE CONCEPTS *115,140*

length [*n*] *extent of object, distance, time*
breadth, compass, continuance, diameter, dimension, duration, elongation, endlessness, expanse, expansion, extensiveness, height, interval, lastingness, lengthiness, limit, linearity, loftiness, longitude, longness, magnitude, measure, mileage, orbit, panorama, period, piece, portion, protractedness, purview, quantity, radius, range, ranginess, reach, realm, remoteness, season, section, segment, space, spaciousness, span, stretch, stride, tallness, term, unit, width, year; SEE CONCEPTS *651,721,743,788,804*

lengthen [*v*] *extend*
amplify, augment, continue, dilate, distend, drag out, draw, draw out*, elongate, expand, increase, let out, make longer, pad, proceed, prolong, prolongate, protract, reach, spin out*, stretch, string out*; SEE CONCEPTS *236,239,245*

lengthy [*adj*] *extended*
diffuse, dragging, drawn-out, elongate, elongated, interminable, lengthened, long, longish, long-winded, overlong, padded, prolix, prolonged, protracted, tedious, tiresome, verbose, very long, wearisome, windy, wordy; SEE CONCEPTS *267,482,782*

lenient [*adj*] *permissive*
allowing, amiable, assuaging, assuasive, being big*, benign, benignant, charitable, clement, compassionate, complaisant, compliant, condoning, easy, easygoing, emollient, excusing, favoring, forbearing, forgiving, gentle, going easy on*, good-natured, humoring, indulgent, kind, kindly, letting, live with*, loving, merciful, mild, mollycoddling*, obliging, pampering, pardoning, permitting, soft, softhearted, soft-shell*, sparing, spoiling, sympathetic, tender, tolerant, yielding; SEE CONCEPTS *401,542*

leprechaun [*n*] *elf*
brownie, elfin, fairy, fay, gnome, nisse, pixie, sprite; SEE CONCEPT *370*

lesion [*n*] *injury, wound*
abrasion, bruise, contusion, cut, gash, laceration, scrape, scratch, sore; SEE CONCEPT *309*

less [*adj*] *smaller, inferior*
beneath, declined, deficient, depressed, diminished, excepting, fewer, lacking, lesser, limited, lower, minor, minus, negative, not as great, re-

duced, secondary, shortened, shorter, slighter, subordinate, subtracting, unsubstantial, without; SEE CONCEPTS *574,762,789*

less [*adv*] *little*
barely, in a lower degree, meagerly, to a smaller extent; SEE CONCEPTS *530,544*

lessen [*v*] *lower, reduce*
abate, abridge, amputate, attenuate, become smaller, clip, close, contract, crop, curtail, cut, cut back, decline, decrease, de-escalate, degrade, die down, dilute, diminish, downsize, drain, dwindle, ease, erode, grow less, impair, lighten, minify, minimize, mitigate, moderate, narrow, roll back, shrink, slacken, slack up, slow down, soft-pedal*, take the bite out*, take the edge off*, take the sting out*, taper, taper off, thin, truncate, weaken, wind down; SEE CONCEPTS *247,698,776*

lesser [*adj*] *inferior, secondary*
a notch under*, bottom, bush, bush-league*, dinky*, insignificant, less important, low, lower, minor, minor-league*, nether, second-fiddle*, second-string*, slighter, small, small-fry*, small-time*, subjacent, subordinate, third-string*, undersized; SEE CONCEPTS *575,793*

lesson [*n1*] *information taught*
assignment, chalk talk*, class, coaching, drill, education, exercise, homework, instruction, lecture, period, practice, quiz, reading, recitation, schooling, study, task, teaching, test, tutoring; SEE CONCEPTS *274,285,287*

lesson [*n2*] *helpful example, communication*
admonition, censure, chiding, deterrent, exemplar, helpful word, message, model, moral, noble action, notice, precept, punishment, rebuke, reprimand, reproof, scolding, warning; SEE CONCEPTS *123,661,686*

let [*v1*] *allow*
accredit, approve, authorize, be big*, cause, certify, commission, concede, enable, endorse, free up, give, give leave, give okay, give permission, grant, have, hear of, leave, license, live with, make, permit, sanction, sit still for*, suffer, tolerate, warrant; SEE CONCEPTS *50,83,88*

let [*v2*] *rent out object, property*
charter, hire, lease, sublease, sublet; SEE CONCEPTS *89,115*

letdown [*n*] *disappointment*
anticlimax, balk, bitter pill*, blow, chagrin, comedown, disgruntlement, disillusionment, frustration, setback, washout*; SEE CONCEPTS *410,728*

let down [*v*] *disappoint*
abandon, depress, disenchant, disillusion, dissatisfy, fail, fall short, leave in lurch*, leave stranded*, lower, pull down, take down; SEE CONCEPTS *7,19*

lethal [*adj*] *deadly*
baleful, dangerous, deathly, destructive, devastating, fatal, harmful, hurtful, malignant, mortal, mortiferous, mortuary, murderous, necrotic, noxious, pernicious, pestilent, pestilential, poisonous, virulent; SEE CONCEPT *537*

lethargic [*adj*] *lazy, sluggish*
apathetic, blah*, comatose, debilitated, dilatory, dopey, dormant, draggy*, drowsy, dull, enervated, having spring fever*, heavy, idle, impassive, inactive, indifferent, inert, lackadaisical, laggard, laid-back*, languid, languorous, listless, moony*, nebbish, out of it*, passive, phlegmatic,

sleepy, sleepyhead*, slothful, slow, slumberous, snoozy, somnolent, spiritless, stolid, stretchy, stupefied, supine, torpid, wimpy*; SEE CONCEPTS *401,403,584*

lethargy [*n*] *laziness, sluggishness*
apathy, coma, disinterest, disregard, drowsiness, dullness, hebetude, heedlessness, idleness, impassivity, inaction, inactivity, inanition, indifference, indolence, inertia, inertness, insouciance, languor, lassitude, listlessness, passiveness, phlegm, sleep, sleepiness, sloth, slowness, slumber, stupor, supineness, torpidity, torpidness, torpor, unconcern, unmindfulness; SEE CONCEPTS *315,410,633,748*

let off [*v*] *make not subject to punishment or action*
abandon, absolve, discharge, dispense, drop, excuse, exempt, exonerate, forgive, let go, pardon, privilege from, release, relieve, remove, spare; SEE CONCEPTS *50,83,88,317*

let on [*v*] *acknowledge, admit*
allow, avow, betray, concede, confess, disclose, divulge, give away, grant, hint, imply, indicate, let out, make known, mouth*, own, own up*, reveal, say, spill*, suggest, tell, uncover, unveil; SEE CONCEPTS *57,60*

letter [*n1*] *symbol of an alphabet*
ABCs*, alphabet, cap, capital, character, majuscule, minuscule, rune, sign, small letter, type, uncial; SEE CONCEPT *284*

letter [*n2*] *written communication*
acknowledgment, answer, billet, dispatch, epistle, junk mail*, kite, line, memo, memorandum, message, missive, note, postcard, reply, report, thank you; SEE CONCEPTS *271,278*

letup [*n*] *pause*
abatement, break, cessation, interval, lapse, lessening, lull, recess, remission, respite, slackening; SEE CONCEPT *807*

let up [*v*] *pause*
abate, cease, decrease, die down, die out, diminish, ease, ease off, ease up, ebb, fall, moderate, release, relent, slacken, slow down, stop, subside, wane; SEE CONCEPTS *240,698*

levee [*n*] *embankment*
bank, breakwater, dam, earthwork, mound; SEE CONCEPT *509*

level [*adj*] *smooth, balanced*
akin, aligned, alike, calm, commensurate, common, comparable, consistent, constant, continuous, equable, equivalent, even, exact, flat, flush, horizontal, identical, in line, leveled, like, lined up, matched, matching, of same height, on a line, on a par, on one plane, parallel, plain, planate, plane, planed, polished, precise, proportionate, regular, rolled, same, stable, steady, straight, trim, trimmed, unbroken, unfluctuating, uniform, uninterrupted; SEE CONCEPTS *401,490,566*

level [*n1*] *horizontal position or thing*
altitude, elevation, floor, height, layer, plain, plane, story, stratum, surface, zone; SEE CONCEPTS *738,744*

level [*n2*] *rank, position*
achievement, degree, grade, stage, standard, standing, status; SEE CONCEPTS *286,388*

level [*v1*] *make even*
equalize, equate, even, even off, even out, flatten, flush, grade, lay, make equal, make flat, mow, plane, press, roll, smooth, smoothen, straighten, surface; SEE CONCEPT *250*

le
le

level [v2] *destroy, demolish*
bring down, bulldoze*, devastate, down*, drop, equalize, fell, flatten, floor, ground, knock down, knock over, lay low, mow*, pull down, raze, ruin, smooth, tear down, waste*, wreck; SEE CONCEPTS *208,252*

level [v3] *be honest*
be above-board, be frank, be on the up and up*, be open, be straight, be straightforward, be upfront*, come clean*, come to terms*, keep nothing back*, talk straight*, tell the truth; SEE CONCEPT *49*

level [v4] *aim, direct*
address, beam, cast, focus, incline, lay, point, slant, train, turn, zero in on; SEE CONCEPT *187*

levelheaded [adj] *reasonable, calm*
all there*, balanced, collected, commonsensical, composed, cool, cool as cucumber*, coolheaded*, dependable, discreet, even-tempered, far-sighted, in one's right mind*, judicious, practical, prudent, rational, sane, self-possessed, sensible, steady, together, unflappable, wise, with all marbles*; SEE CONCEPTS *403,542*

leverage [n] *influence*
advantage, ascendancy, authority, bargaining chip*, break, clout, drag, edge, grease*, jump on*, power, pull, rank, ropes*, suction, weight; SEE CONCEPTS *687,693*

levity [n] *funniness, silliness*
absurdity, amusement, buoyancy, facetiousness, festivity, fickleness, flightiness, flippancy, folly, foolishness, frivolity, giddiness, happiness, high spirits, hilarity, jocularity, laughs, lightheartedness, mirth, picnic*, pleasantry, repartee, trifling, triviality, volatility, wit; SEE CONCEPTS *273,410*

levy [n] *assessment, tax*
burden, collection, custom, duty, exaction, excise, fee, gathering, imposition, impost, muster, tariff, toll; SEE CONCEPT *329*

levy [v] *assess, impose*
call, call up, charge, collect, demand, exact, extort, gather, lay on, place, put on, raise, set, summon, tax, wrest, wring; SEE CONCEPT *330*

lewd [adj] *vulgar, indecent*
bawdy, blue, coarse, erotic, fast*, filthy*, foulmouthed, gross*, hard-core*, immodest, immoral, improper, impure, in bad taste, incontinent, indelicate, lascivious, lecherous, libertine, libidinous, licentious, loose*, lustful, naughty, obscene, off-color*, pornographic, profligate, questionable, racy*, rakish, ribald, risqué, salacious, scandalous, scurrilous, shameless, smutty*, suggestive, taboo, unchaste, unclean, unconventional, unvirtuous, vile, wanton, wicked, X-rated*; SEE CONCEPTS *372,542,545*

lexicon [n] *collection of word meanings, usage*
dictionary, glossary, terminology, thesaurus, vocabulary, wordbook, wordlist, word stock; SEE CONCEPTS *276,280*

liability [n1] *answerability, responsibility*
accountability, accountableness, amenability, amenableness, arrearage, blame, burden, compulsion, culpability, debt, duty, indebtedness, obligation, onus, owing, subjection, susceptibility; SEE CONCEPT *645*

liability [n2] *burden, debt*
account, arrear, arrearage, bad news*, baggage*, balance, bite*, chance, chit*, contingency, contract, damage, debit, disadvantage, drag*, drawback, due*, encumbrance, handicap, hindrance, impediment, inconvenience, indebtedness, indebtment, involvement, IOU*, lease, loan, millstone*, minus, misfortune, mortgage, nuisance, obligation, onus, pledge, possibility, remainder, responsibility, tab; SEE CONCEPTS *332,674*

liability [n3] *chance, probability*
exposure, likelihood, openness, proneness, susceptibility, tendency, vulnerability, vulnerableness; SEE CONCEPTS *650,657*

liable [adj1] *answerable, responsible*
accountable, amenable, bound, chargeable, obligated, subject, tied; SEE CONCEPT *545*

liable [adj2] *open, likely*
apt, assailable, attackable, beatable, conquerable, disposed, exposed, given, inclined, in danger, penetrable, prone, sensitive, subject, susceptible, tending, verisimilar, vincible, vulnerable; SEE CONCEPTS *542,552*

liaison [n1] *person who acts as go-between*
communication, connection, contact, fixer, hookup, in, interchange, interface, intermediary, link; SEE CONCEPTS *348,354,423*

liaison [n2] *love affair*
amour, encounter, entanglement, fling, illicit romance, interlude, intrigue, romance; SEE CONCEPTS *32,388*

liar [n] *person who tells falsehood*
cheat, con artist, deceiver, deluder, dissimulator, equivocator, fabler, fabricator, fabulist, false witness, falsifier, fibber, maligner, misleader, perjurer, phony, prevaricator, promoter, storyteller, trickster*; SEE CONCEPT *412*

libel [n] *purposeful lie about someone, often malicious*
aspersion, calumny, defamation, denigration, lying, malicious, obloquy, smear, vituperation; SEE CONCEPTS *63,318*

libel [v] *purposefully lie about someone*
asperse, bad-mouth*, blister, burlesque, calumniate, caricature, crack, defame, denigrate, derogate, drag name through mud*, give a black eye*, knock, malign, mark*, mark wrong, revile, roast, scandalize, scorch, sizzle, slur, smear, tear down, traduce, travesty, vilify; SEE CONCEPTS *63,192*

libelous [adj] *derogatory*
aspersive, backbiting, calumniatory, calumnious, contumelious, debasing, defamatory, depreciative, detracting, detractory, disparaging, false, injurious, invidious, malevolent, malicious, maligning, opprobrious, pejorative, sarcastic, scurrilous, traducing, untrue, vilifying, vituperative; SEE CONCEPT *267*

liberal [adj1] *progressive*
advanced, avant-garde, broad, broad-minded, catholic, enlightened, flexible, free, general, high-minded, humanistic, humanitarian, indulgent, intelligent, interested, latitudinarian, left, lenient, libertarian, loose, magnanimous, permissive, radical, rational, reasonable, receiving, receptive, reformist, tolerant, unbiased, unbigoted, unconventional, understanding, unorthodox, unprejudiced; SEE CONCEPTS *529,542*

liberal [adj2] *giving, generous*
altruistic, beneficent, benevolent, bighearted*, bounteous, bountiful, casual, charitable, eleemosynary, exuberant, free, free-and-easy, handsome, kind, lavish, loose, munificent, openhanded, openhearted, philanthropic, princely,

prodigal, profuse, soft-touch, unselfish, unsparing, unstinging; SEE CONCEPTS *334,401,404*

liberal [*adj3*] *abundant, profuse*
ample, aplenty, bounteous, bountiful, copious, dime a dozen*, galore, generous, handsome, lavish, munificent, no end, plentiful, plenty, rich; SEE CONCEPT *771*

liberate [*v*] *give freedom*
bail one out*, deliver, detach, discharge, disembarrass, emancipate, free, free up*, get out from under*, let loose*, let out*, loose, loosen, manumit, redeem, release, rescue, save, save one's neck*, set free, unbind, unchain, unhook, unshackle; SEE CONCEPTS *83,110*

liberation [*n*] *freedom*
abolition, deliverance, democracy, emancipation, freeing, liberty, release, salvation, setting free, sovereignty, unchaining, unshackling; SEE CONCEPT *691*

liberty [*n*] *freedom*
autarchy, authorization, autonomy, birthright, carte blanche, choice, convenience, decision, deliverance, delivery, dispensation, emancipation, enfranchisement, enlightenment, exemption, franchise, free speech, immunity, independence, leave, leisure, liberation, license, opportunity, permission, power of choice, prerogative, privilege, relaxation, release, rest, right, sanction, self-determination, selfgovernment, sovereignty, suffrage, unconstraint; SEE CONCEPTS *388,691*

libidinous [*adj*] *lustful*
carnal, coarse, concupiscent, debauched, fast, hot*, impure, incontinent, lascivious, lecherous, libertine, loose*, obscene, passionate, prurient, salacious, satyric, sensual, unchaste, wanton, wicked; SEE CONCEPTS *372,545*

libido [*n*] *sex instinct*
eroticism, lust, passion, sex drive, sexual desire, sexuality, sexual urge, the hots*; SEE CONCEPTS *20,709*

library [*n*] *book repository*
athenaeum, atheneum, bibliotheca, book collection, book room, information center, media center, reference center, study; SEE CONCEPT *435*

license [*n1*] *authority, permission*
authorization, carte blanche*, certificate, charter, consent, dispensation, entitlement, exemption, freedom, go-ahead*, grant, green light*, immunity, independence, latitude, leave, liberty, okay*, permit, privilege, right, self-determination, ticket, unconstraint, warrant; SEE CONCEPT *685*

license [*n2*] *abandon, indulgence*
anarchy, animalism, arrogance, audacity, boldness, complacency, debauchery, disorder, effrontery, excess, forwardness, gluttony, immoderation, impropriety, irresponsibility, lawlessness, laxity, looseness, presumptuousness, prodigality, profligacy, refractoriness, relaxation, relaxedness, sauciness*, self-indulgence, sensuality, slackness, temerity, unrestraint, unruliness, wantonness, wildness; SEE CONCEPTS *633,645*

license [*v*] *authorize*
accredit, allow, certify, commission, empower, enable, let, permit, privilege, sanction, suffer, warrant; SEE CONCEPTS *50,83,88*

licentious [*adj*] *immoral, uncontrolled*
abandoned, amoral, animal, carnal, corrupt, debauched, depraved, desirous, disorderly, dissolute, fast, fast and loose*, fleshly, impure,

incontinent, in the fast lane*, lascivious, lax, lecherous, lewd, libertine, libidinous, lickerish, loose*, lubricious, lustful, oversexed, profligate, promiscuous, relaxed, reprobate, salacious, satyric, scabrous, sensual, swinging, unconstrained, uncontrollable, uncurbed, unmoral, unprincipled, unruly, wanton; SEE CONCEPTS *372,401,545*

lick [*n*] *light touch; little amount*
bit, brush, cast, dab, dash, hint, sample, smack, speck, stroke, suggestion, taste, tinge, trace, whiff; SEE CONCEPTS *612,831*

lick [*v1*] *touch with tongue*
brush, calm, caress, fondle, glance, gloss, graze, lap, lap against, move over, osculate, pass over, play, quiet, ripple, rub, soothe, stroke, sweep, taste, tongue, touch, wash; SEE CONCEPTS *185,612*

lick [*v2*] *play over with fire*
blaze, burn, dart, flick, flicker, fluctuate, flutter, ignite, kindle, leap, palpitate, quiver, ripple, run over, shoot, touch, tremble, vacillate, vibrate, waver; SEE CONCEPTS *249,612*

lick [*v3*] *defeat, sometimes by hitting*
beat, best, clobber, conquer, down, excel, flog, hit, hurdle, lambaste, master, outdo, outstrip, overcome, overwhelm, rout, slap, smear, smother, spank, strike, surmount, surpass, thrash, throw, top, trim, trounce, vanquish, wallop, whip; SEE CONCEPTS *95,141,189*

lid [*n*] *top covering*
cap, cover, hood, roof, top; SEE CONCEPT *836*

lie [*n*] *untruth*
aspersion, backbiting, calumniation, calumny, deceit, deception, defamation, detraction, dishonesty, disinformation, distortion, evasion, fable, fabrication, falsehood, falseness, falsification, falsity, fib, fiction, forgery, fraudulence, guile, hyperbole, inaccuracy, invention, libel, mendacity, misrepresentation, misstatement, myth, obloquy, perjury, prevarication, revilement, reviling, slander, subterfuge, tale, tall story*, vilification, white lie*, whopper; SEE CONCEPTS *63,278*

lie [*v1*] *tell an untruth*
bear false witness, beguile, be untruthful, break promise, BS*, bull*, con, concoct, deceive, delude, dissemble, dissimulate, distort, dupe*, equivocate, exaggerate, fabricate, fake, falsify, fib, forswear, frame, fudge, go back on*, invent, make believe, malign, misguide, misinform, misinstruct, mislead, misrepresent, misspeak, misstate, overdraw, palter, perjure, pervert, phony, plant*, prevaricate, promote, put on*, put up a front*, snow*, soft-soap*, string along*, victimize; SEE CONCEPT *63*

lie [*v2*] *be prostrate, flat*
be prone, be recumbent, be supine, couch, go to bed*, laze, lie down, loll, lounge, nap, recline, repose, rest, retire, siesta, sleep, sprawl, stretch out, turn in; SEE CONCEPTS *154,201*

lie [*v3*] *be situated*
be, be beside, be buried, be established, be even, be fixed, be found, be interred, be level, be located, belong, be on, be placed, be seated, beset, be smooth, exist, extend, have its seat in, occupy, prevail, reach, remain, spread, stretch; SEE CONCEPT *746*

life [*n1*] *animation, spirit*
activity, being, breath, brio, dash, élan*, élan

le
li

vital*, energy, enthusiasm, entity, esprit, essence, excitement, get-up-and-go*, go*, growth, heart, high spirits, impulse, lifeblood, liveliness, oomph*, sentience, soul, sparkle, verve, viability, vigor, vitality, vivacity, zest*, zing*; SEE CONCEPT *411*

life [*n2*] *existence, duration*
being, career, continuance, course, cycle, days, endurance, epoch, era, expectancy, extent, generation, history, length, life span, lifetime, longevity, orbit, period, pilgrimage, record, season, span, survival, time; SEE CONCEPTS *816,817*

life [*n3*] *being*
animal, animateness, animation, body, breath, consciousness, continuance, creature, endurance, entity, essence, existence, flesh, flesh and blood*, growth, human, human being, individual, living, living being, living thing, man, metabolism, mortal, mortal being, organism, person, personage, presence, soul, subsistence, substantiality, survival, symbiosis, viability, vitality, vital spark*, wildlife, woman; SEE CONCEPT *389*

life [*n4*] *history, biography*
autobiography, bio, career, confession, curriculum vitae, journal, life story, memoir, memorial, story; SEE CONCEPT *271*

life [*n5*] *person's experiences*
attainment, behavior, circumstances, conduct, development, enjoyment, enlightenment, growth, hand one is dealt*, happiness, human condition, journey, knowledge, lifestyle, participation, personality, realization, suffering, trials and tribulations*, vicissitudes, way of life*, world; SEE CONCEPT *678*

life-and-death [*adj*] *vitally important*
critical, crucial, determining, earth-shaking, essential, imperative, meaningful, paramount, pivotal, serious, significant, urgent, vital; SEE CONCEPT *567*

lifeless [*adj1*] *not living, not containing living things*
asleep, bare, barren, brute, cold, comatose, dead, deceased, defunct, departed, desert, empty, exanimate, extinct, faint, inanimate, inert, inorganic, insensate, insensible, late, out cold*, sterile, unconscious, uninhabited, waste; SEE CONCEPTS *485,539*

lifeless [*adj2*] *dull, spiritless*
blah*, cold, colorless, drab, draggy*, flat, hollow, insipid, lackluster, lethargic, listless, lusterless, nothing*, pabulum*, passive, prosaic, prosy, slothful, slow*, sluggish, spent, static, stiff*, torpid, wooden*, zero*; SEE CONCEPTS *401,542,584*

lifelike [*adj*] *realistic*
authentic, faithful, graphic, natural, original, real, representational, representative, true, true to life; SEE CONCEPT *582*

lifelong [*adj*] *lasting*
constant, continuing, deep-rooted, enduring, for life, inveterate, lifetime, livelong, long-lasting, long-lived, long-standing, old, perennial, permanent, persistent; SEE CONCEPT *798*

lifestyle [*n*] *way of life*
behavior, conduct, habits, style of living, way of acting; SEE CONCEPT *633*

lifetime [*n*] *span of animate being's existence*
all one's born days*, career, continuance, course, cradle to grave*, days, endurance, existence, life,

life span, natural life, period, time; SEE CONCEPT *817*

lifework [*n*] *person's calling*
business, career, interest, mission, occupation, profession, purpose, pursuit, vocation, work; SEE CONCEPTS *349,360*

lift [*n1*] *transportation*
car ride, drive, journey, passage, ride, run, transport; SEE CONCEPT *155*

lift [*n2*] *help, aid*
assist, assistance, boost, comfort, encouragement, hand, leg up*, pick-me-up*, reassurance, relief, secours, shot in the arm*, succor, support; SEE CONCEPTS *110,700*

lift [*v1*] *move upwards; ascend*
arise, aspire, bear aloft, boost, bring up, build up, buoy up, climb, come up, disappear, dissipate, draw up, elevate, erect, goose*, heft, hike, hike up, hoist, jack up, jump up, mount, move up, pick up, put up, raise, raise high, rear, rise, soar, take up, up, upheave, uphold, uplift, upraise, uprear, vanish; SEE CONCEPTS *196,200,236,245*

lift [*v2*] *repeal, revoke*
annul, cancel, countermand, dismantle, end, recall, relax, remove, rescind, reverse, stop, terminate; SEE CONCEPTS *234,317*

lift [*v3*] *steal*
abstract, appropriate, cop, copy, crib, filch, hook, nip, pilfer, pinch, pirate, plagiarize, pocket, purloin, snitch, swipe, take, thieve; SEE CONCEPTS *139,200*

lift [*v4*] *promote, improve*
advance, ameliorate, boost, build up, dignify, elevate, enhance, exalt, hike, jack up, raise, support, upgrade; SEE CONCEPTS *110,244*

liftoff [*n*] *rocket launch*
blast-off, rocket firing, rocket ignition, shot, take-off; SEE CONCEPTS *179,222*

ligature [*n*] *link*
band, bandage, binding, bond, connection, knot, ligament, nexus, rope, tie, yoke; SEE CONCEPTS *471,831*

light [*adj1*] *illuminated*
ablaze, aglow, bright, brilliant, burnished, clear, cloudless, flashing, fluorescent, glossy, glowing, lambent, lucent, luminous, lustrous, phosphorescent, polished, radiant, refulgent, resplendent, rich, scintillant, shining, shiny, sunny, unclouded, unobscured, vivid, well-lighted, well-lit; SEE CONCEPTS *617,618*

light [*adj2*] *blond, fair*
bleached, faded, fair-skinned, light-hued, light-skinned, light-toned, pale, pastel, tow-headed; SEE CONCEPTS *406,618*

light [*adj3*] *not heavy*
agile, airy, atmospheric, buoyant, crumbly, dainty, delicate, downy, easy, effervescent, ethereal, featherweight, feathery, filmy, flimsy, floatable, floating, fluffy, friable, frothy, gossamery, graceful, imponderous, inconsequential, insubstantial, light-footed, lightweight, lithe, little, loose, meager, nimble, petty, porous, portable, sandy, sheer, slender, slight, small, spongy, sprightly, sylphlike, thin, tissuelike, trifling, trivial, unheavy, unsubstantial, weightless; SEE CONCEPT *491*

light [*adj4*] *small in amount, content*
casual, digestible, faint, fractional, fragmentary, frivolous, frugal, gentle, hardly any, hardly

enough, inadequate, inconsequential, inconsiderable, indistinct, insignificant, insufficient, mild, minor, minuscule, minute, moderate, modest, not many, not much, not rich, puny, restricted, scanty, shoestring*, slight, soft, sparse, superficial, thin, tiny, trifling, trivial, unimportant, unsubstantial, weak, wee; SEE CONCEPTS *762,789*

light [*adj5*] *simple, easy*
effortless, facile, manageable, moderate, smooth, undemanding, unexacting, untaxing, untroublesome; SEE CONCEPT *538*

light [*adj6*] *funny, cheery*
airy, amusing, animated, blithe, carefree, cheerful, chipper*, chirpy, diverting, dizzy, entertaining, fickle, flighty, frivolous, gay, giddy, high, humorous, lighthearted, lively, merry, perky, pleasing, sunny, sunny-side up*, superficial, trifling, trivial, up, upbeat, witty; SEE CONCEPTS *401,542*

light [*n1*] *luminescence from sun or other source*
aurora, beacon, blaze, brightness, brilliance, brilliancy, bulb, candle, coruscation, dawn, daybreak, daylight, daytime, effulgence, emanation, flare, flash, fulgor, glare, gleam, glimmer, glint, glitter, glow, illumination, incandescence, irradiation, lambency, lamp, lantern, lighthouse, luminosity, luster, morn, morning, phosphorescence, radiance, radiation, ray, refulgence, scintillation, sheen, shine, sparkle, splendor, star, sun, sunbeam, sunrise, sunshine, taper, torch, window; SEE CONCEPTS *620,624,628,810*

light [*n2*] *context, point of view; understanding*
angle, approach, aspect, attitude, awareness, comprehension, condition, education, elucidation, enlightenment, example, exemplar, explanation, illustration, information, insight, interpretation, knowledge, model, paragon, slant, standing, vantage point, viewpoint; SEE CONCEPTS *274,409,682,686*

light [*v1*] *illuminate*
animate, brighten, cast, fire, flood, floodlight, furnish with light, highlight, ignite, illume, illumine, inflame, irradiate, kindle, lighten, light up, limelight, make bright, make visible, put on, shine, spot, spotlight, switch on, turn on; SEE CONCEPTS *250,624*

light [*v2*] *start on fire*
burn, enkindle, fire, flame, ignite, inflame, kindle, set fire to, set on fire, spark, strike a match; SEE CONCEPT *249*

light [*v3*] *step down; land*
alight, arrive, come down, deplane, detrain, disembark, drop, fly down, get down, perch, rest, roost, set down, settle, settle down, sit, sit down, stop, touch down; SEE CONCEPTS *159,181*

lighten [*v1*] *illuminate*
become light, brighten, flash, gleam, illume, irradiate, light, light up, make bright, shine; SEE CONCEPT *624*

lighten [*v2*] *reduce weight, load*
allay, alleviate, ameliorate, assuage, attenuate, buoy, change, comfort, cut down, decrease, dilute, disburden, disencumber, ease, empty, eradicate, extenuate, facilitate, free, jettison, lessen, levitate, make less, make lighter, mitigate, mollify, pour out, put off, reduce, relieve, remove, shift, take, take a load off*, thin, throw out, unburden, unload, uplight, upraise; SEE CONCEPTS *110,244,250*

lighten [*v3*] *cheer up; inspire*
brighten, buoy up, cheer, elate, encourage, gladden, hearten, lift, perk up, revive, take a load off; SEE CONCEPTS *7,22*

light-headed [*adj*] *silly; feeling faint*
changeable, delirious, dizzy, empty, featherbrained*, fickle, flighty, flippant, foolish, frivolous, gaga*, giddy, harebrained*, hazy, punchy*, reeling, rocky, scatterbrained*, shallow, superficial, swimming, swimmy, tired, trifling, vertiginous, whirling, woozy*; SEE CONCEPTS *314,401*

lighthearted [*adj*] *carefree, untroubled*
blithe, blithesome, bright, buoyant, cheerful, effervescent, expansive, feelgood*, frolicsome, gay, glad, gleeful, happy, happy-go-lucky*, high-spirited, insouciant, jocund, jolly, jovial, joyful, joyous, laid-back, lightsome, lively, merry, playful, resilient, spirited, sprightly, sunny, upbeat, vivacious, volatile; SEE CONCEPTS *404,542*

lightly [*adv*] *gently, effortlessly*
agilely, airily, breezily, carelessly, casually, daintily, delicately, easily, ethereally, faintly, flippantly, freely, frivolously, gingerly, heedlessly, indifferently, leniently, mildly, moderately, nimbly, peacefully, quietly, readily, simply, slightingly, slightly, smoothly, softly, sparingly, sparsely, subtly, tenderly, tenuously, thinly, thoughtlessly, timidly, unsubstantially, well; SEE CONCEPTS *538,544,584*

light out [*v*] *run away*
abscond, depart, escape, head, leave, make, make off, quit, set out, strike out, take a hike, take off; SEE CONCEPT *195*

lightweight [*adj*] *inconsequential*
failing, featherweight, foolish, imponderous, incompetent, insignificant, of no account, paltry, petty, slight, trifling, trivial, unimportant, weightless, worthless; SEE CONCEPTS *491,575*

likable [*adj*] *nice, pleasant*
agreeable, amiable, appealing, attractive, charismatic, charming, engaging, enjoyable, friendly, genial, good, good-natured, pleasing, preferable, relishable, sweet, sweet-natured, sympathetic, winning, winsome; SEE CONCEPT *404*

like [*adj*] *similar*
according to, agnate, akin, alike, allied, allying, analogous, approximating, approximative, close, coextensive, cognate, commensurate, comparable, compatible, conforming, congeneric, congenerous, consistent, consonant, corresponding, double, equal, equaling, equivalent, homologous, identical, in the manner of, jibing, matching, much the same, near, not far from, not unlike, on the order of, parallel, related, relating, resembling, same, selfsame, such, twin, undifferentiated, uniform; SEE CONCEPTS *487,573*

like [*v1*] *enjoy, be fond of*
admire, adore, appreciate, approve, be gratified by, be keen on, be partial to, be pleased by, be sweet on, care for, care to, cherish, delight in, derive pleasure from, dig*, dote on, esteem, exclaim, fancy, feast on, find appealing, get a kick out of*, go for*, hanker for, hold dear, indulge in, love, luxuriate in, prize, rejoice in, relish, revel in, savor, stuck on*, take an interest in, take delight in, take satisfaction in, take to; SEE CONCEPT *32*

like [*v2*] *choose, feel inclined*
care to, desire, elect, fancy, feel disposed, feel

li
li

like, have a preference for, incline toward, please, prefer, select, want, will, wish; SEE CONCEPTS *20,41*

likelihood [*n*] *chance of something happening*
coin flip*, direction, even break, fair shake, fifty-fifty*, fighting chance*, good chance*, liability, likeliness, long shot*, outside chance*, plausibility, possibility, presumption, probability, prospect, reasonableness, shot at*, strong possibility, tendency, toss-up*, trend; SEE CONCEPT *650*

likely [*adj*] *probable, apt, hopeful*
acceptable, achievable, anticipated, assuring, attainable, believeable, conceivable, conjecturable, credible, destined, disposed, expected, fair, favorite, feasible, given to, imaginable, inclined, in favor of, inferable, in the cards*, in the habit of*, liable, odds-on*, on the verge of, ostensible, plausible, possible, practicable, predisposed, presumable, promising, prone, rational, reasonable, seeming, subject to, supposable, tending, thinkable, true, up-and-coming*, verisimilar, workable; SEE CONCEPT *552*

likely [*adv*] *probably*
assumably, doubtless, doubtlessly, in all likelihood, in all probability, like as not, most likely, no doubt, presumably, presumptively, prima facie, seemingly, to all appearances; SEE CONCEPT *552*

like-minded [*adj*] *similar*
agreeing, compatible, harmonious, in accord, in agreement, in harmony, of one mind, unanimous; SEE CONCEPTS *487,573*

liken [*v*] *compare*
allegorize, approach, approximate to, assimilate, balance, bear comparison, be in the same class as*, be on a par with*, come up to, correlate, distinguish between, draw parallel, equal, equate, identify with, link, make like, match, notice similarities, parallel, put alongside, relate, resemble, show correspondence; SEE CONCEPT *39*

likeness [*n*] *correspondence in appearance; something that corresponds*
affinity, agreement, alikeness, analogousness, analogy, appearance, carbon, clone, comparableness, comparison, conformity, copy, counterpart, dead ringer*, delineation, depiction, ditto*, double, effigy, equality, equivalence, facsimile, form, guise, identicalness, identity, image, knock-off*, lookalike*, model, parallelism, photocopy, photograph, picture, portrait, replica, representation, reproduction, resemblance, sameness, semblance, similarity, simile, similitude, study, uniformity, Xerox*; SEE CONCEPTS *664,670,716*

likewise [*adj*] *also, similarly*
additionally, along, as well, besides, correspondingly, further, furthermore, in addition, in like manner, in the same way, more, moreover, so, too, withal; SEE CONCEPT *563*

liking [*n*] *fondness, taste*
affection, affinity, appetite, appreciation, attachment, attraction, bent, bias, desire, devotion, fancy, favoritism, inclination, love, mind, palate, partiality, passion, penchant, pleasure, predilection, preference, proneness, propensity, relish, soft spot*, stomach, sympathy, tendency, tooth, velleity, weakness, will; SEE CONCEPTS *20,32,529*

limb [*n*] *appendage*
arm, bough, branch, extension, extremity, fin, gam*, leg, lobe, member, offshoot, part, pin, pinion, process, projection, spray, sprig, spur, stem, switch, unit, wheel, wing; SEE CONCEPTS *392,428*

limber [*adj*] *flexible*
agile, deft, elastic, graceful, lissome, lithe, lithesome, loose, nimble, plastic, pliable, pliant, resilient, springy, spry, supple; SEE CONCEPTS *406,488*

limbo [*n*] *state of uncertainty*
demilitarized zone, left field*, nothingness, nowhere, oblivion, out there*, Siberia*; SEE CONCEPTS *679,705*

limit [*n1*] *greatest extent*
absolute, bitter end*, border, bottom line*, bound, bourne, breaking point*, brim, brink, cap, ceiling, check, circumscription, conclusion, confinement, confines, curb, cutoff point*, deadline, destination, edge, end, end point, extremity, far out, farthest point, farthest reach, fence, finality, goal, limitation, margin, maximum, obstruction, restraint, restriction, rim, termination, the max*, the most*, tops*, ultimate, utmost, verge; SEE CONCEPTS *529,548,832*

limit [*n2*] *physical boundary*
border, borderland, compass, confines, edge, end, extent, extreme, extremity, frontier, perimeter, periphery, precinct, purlieu; SEE CONCEPTS *513,745*

limit [*v*] *confine, restrict*
appoint, assign, bar, bottle up, bound, cap, check, circumscribe, constrict, contract, cork, cramp, curb, define, delimit, delimitate, demarcate, draw the line, fix, hem in, hinder, inhibit, keep the lid on*, lessen, narrow, prescribe, ration, reduce, restrain, set, specify; SEE CONCEPTS *5,130*

limitation [*n*] *restraint, disadvantage*
bar, block, check, circumspection, condition, constraint, control, cramp, curb, definition, drawback, impediment, inhibition, injunction, modification, obstruction, qualification, reservation, restriction, snag, stint, stricture, taboo; SEE CONCEPTS *666,674*

limited [*adj1*] *restricted, definite*
bound, bounded, checked, circumscribed, confined, constrained, controlled, curbed, defined, delimited, determinate, finite, fixed, hampered, hemmed in, local, modified, narrow, particular, precise, qualified, reserved, restrained, sectional, topical; SEE CONCEPTS *554,557*

limited [*adj2*] *inadequate, short*
cramped, diminished, faulty, ineffectual, insufficient, little, mean, minimal, narrow, paltry, poor, reduced, restricted, set, small, unsatisfactory; SEE CONCEPT *771*

limitless [*adj*] *never-ending, infinite*
bottomless, boundless, countless, endless, illimitable, immeasurable, immense, incomprehensible, indefinite, inexhaustible, innumerable, measureless, no end of*, no end to*, no holds barred*, no strings*, numberless, unbounded, uncalculable, undefined, unending, unfathomable, unlimited, untold, vast, wide-open; SEE CONCEPTS *762,771,798*

limp [*adj*] *not stiff; weak*
bending, debilitated, drooping, droopy, ductile, enervated, exhausted, feeble, flabby, flaccid, flexible, flexuous, flimsy, floppy, impressible, infirm, languid, languishing, lax, lethargic, limber,

listless, loose, plastic, pliable, pliant, relaxed, slack, soft, spent, spiritless, supple, tired, unsubstantial, weakened, wearied, worn out, yielding; SEE CONCEPTS *490,604*

limp [*n*] *faltering walk*
bad wheel, falter, flat wheel, floppy, gimp, halt, hitch, hobble, lameness; SEE CONCEPT *151*

limp [*v*] *walk with faltering step*
clump, dodder, falter, flag, gimp, halt, hitch, hobble, hop, lag, scuff, shamble, shuffle, stagger, stumble, teeter, totter, waddle, walk lamely; SEE CONCEPT *151*

limpid [*adj*] *clear, comprehensible*
bright, comprehensible, crystal-clear, crystalline, definite, distinct, filmy, intelligible, lucid, luculent, obvious, pellucid, perspicuous, pure, see-through, thin, translucent, transparent, transpicuous, unambiguous; SEE CONCEPT *535*

line [*n1*] *mark, stroke; border*
band, bar, borderline, boundary, channel, configuration, contour, crease, dash, delineation, demarcation, edge, figuration, figure, frontier, furrow, groove, limit, lineament, lineation, outline, profile, rule, score, scratch, silhouette, streak, stripe, tracing, underline, wrinkle; SEE CONCEPTS *284,436*

line [*n2*] *row, succession; course*
arrangement, array, axis, band, block, border, catalogue, channel, column, concatenation, crack, direction, division, drain, echelon, file, fissure, formation, furrow, groove, group, lane, length, list, magazine, mark, order, path, progression, queue, rank, ridge, road, route, row, scar, seam, sequence, series, street, string, thread, tier, track, train, trajectory, trench, way; SEE CONCEPTS *501,727,738,744*

line [*n3*] *cord, rope*
cable, filament, strand, string, thread, wire; SEE CONCEPT *475*

line [*n4*] *belief, policy*
approach, avenue, course, course of action, ideology, method, polity, position, practice, principle, procedure, program, route, scheme, system; SEE CONCEPTS *688,689*

line [*n5*] *person's calling, interest*
activity, area, business, department, employment, field, forte, job, occupation, profession, province, pursuit, racket*, specialization, trade, vocation, work; SEE CONCEPTS *349,360*

line [*n6*] *ancestry*
breed, descent, family, heredity, lineage, pedigree, race, stock, strain, succession; SEE CONCEPT *296*

line [*n7*] *written communication*
card, letter, message, note, postcard, report, word; SEE CONCEPT *271*

line [*n8*] *hint; influential communication*
clue, indication, information, lead, patter, persuasion, pitch, prepared speech, song and dance*, spiel*; SEE CONCEPT *278*

line [*n9*] *merchandise carried by store*
commodity, goods, involvement, materials, produce, trade, vendibles, wares; SEE CONCEPT *338*

line [*v1*] *border, mark*
abut, adjoin, align, allineate, array, bound, butt against, communicate, crease, cut, delineate, draw, edge, fix, follow, fringe, furrow, group, inscribe, join, line up, march, marshal, neighbor, order, ordinate, outline, place, queue, range,

rank, rim, rule, score, skirt, touch, trace, underline, verge; SEE CONCEPTS *79,84,753*

line [*v2*] *put covering inside object*
bush, ceil, cover, encrust, face, fill, incrust, interline, overlay, panel, quilt, reinforce, sheath, stuff, wad, wainscot; SEE CONCEPTS *172,218*

lineage [*n*] *ancestry*
birth, blood, breed, clan, descendants, descent, extraction, family, folk, forbears, genealogy, heredity, house, kin, kindred, line, offspring, origin, pedigree, progenitors, progeny, race, stirps, stock, succession, tribe; SEE CONCEPT *296*

linger [*v1*] *loiter, delay*
amble, be dilatory, be long, be tardy, crawl, dally, dawdle, dillydally*, drift, falter, fool around*, fritter away*, goof off*, hang around*, hang out*, hesitate, hobble, idle, lag, loll, lumber, mope, mosey, plod, poke, procrastinate, put off, putter, remain, saunter, shuffle, sit around, slouch*, stagger, stay, stick around, stop, stroll, take one's time*, tarry, tool, totter, trail, traipse, trifle, trudge, vacillate, wait, wait around; SEE CONCEPTS *151,681*

linger [*v2*] *continue, endure*
abide, bide, cling, hang on, last, persist, remain, stand, stay, stick around, survive, wait; SEE CONCEPTS *23,239*

lingo [*n*] *dialect spoken by a group*
argot, cant, idiom, jargon, language, patois, patter, slang, speech, talk, tongue, vernacular, vocabulary; SEE CONCEPT *276*

liniment [*n*] *ointment*
balm, cream, dressing, embrocation, emollient, lenitive, lotion, medicine, salve, unguent; SEE CONCEPTS *311,466*

link [*n*] *component, connection*
articulation, association, attachment, bond, channel, connective, constituent, contact, copula, coupler, coupling, division, element, fastening, hitch, hookup, in, interconnection, interface, intersection, joining, joint, junction, knot, ligament, ligation, ligature, loop, member, network, nexus, part, piece, relationship, ring, seam, section, splice, tie, tie-up, vinculum, weld, yoke; SEE CONCEPTS *471,835*

link [*v*] *connect*
associate, attach, bind, bracket, combine, conjoin, conjugate, couple, fasten, group, hitch on, hook up, identify, incorporate, interface, join, meld with, network, plug into, relate, slap on, tack on, tag along, tag on, team up with, throw in with*, tie, tie in with, unite, yoke; SEE CONCEPTS *113,114,193*

lionize [*v*] *celebrate*
acclaim, adulate, aggrandize, eulogize, exalt, glorify, hero-worship, honor, idolize, immortalize, praise, roll out the red carpet*, show respect, worship; SEE CONCEPT *69*

lip [*n1*] *edge, brink*
border, brim, chops, flange, flare, labium, labrum, margin, nozzle, overlap, portal, projection, rim, spout; SEE CONCEPTS *392,484,513*

lip [*n2*] *insolence*
back talk, cheek*, effrontery, guff*, impertinence, jaw*, mouth*, rudeness, sass*, sauce*, sauciness*; SEE CONCEPTS *54,278*

lip service [*n*] *empty talk*
duplicity, hollow words, insincerity, token agreement, tongue in cheek, unctuousness; SEE CONCEPTS *267,542,545*

li
li

liquefy [v] *melt*
deliquesce, dissolve, thaw; SEE CONCEPTS *250, 255*

liqueur [n] *liquor*
alcohol, alcoholic beverage, aperitif, booze*, brandy, cognac, cordial, flavored drink, intoxicant, port, spirits; SEE CONCEPT *455*

liquid [adj1] *fluid, flowing, melting*
aqueous, damp, deliquescent, dissolvable, dissolved, dulcet, fluent, fluidic, fusible, ichorous, juicy, liquefied, liquescent, liquiform, luscious, mellifluent, mellifluous, mellow, meltable, melted, moist, molten, moving, pulpy, running, runny, sappy, serous, smooth, soft, solvent, splashing, succulent, thawed, thin, uncongealed, viscous, watery, wet; SEE CONCEPTS *485,584,603*

liquid [adj2] *readily available*
convertible, fluid, free, marketable, negotiable, quick, ready, realizable, usable; SEE CONCEPT *334*

liquid [n] *fluid*
aqua, aqueous material, broth, elixir, extract, flow, flux, goo*, goop*, juice, liquor, melted material, nectar, sap, secretion, slop*, solution, swill*; SEE CONCEPT *467*

liquidate [v1] *pay; change into cash*
cash, cash in, cash out, clear, convert, discharge, exchange, honor, pay off, quit, realize, reimburse, repay, satisfy, sell off, sell up, settle, square; SEE CONCEPT *330*

liquidate [v2] *destroy, dissolve*
abolish, annihilate, annul, cancel, dispatch, do away with*, do in*, eliminate, exterminate, finish off*, get rid of*, kill, murder, purge, remove, rub out*, silence, terminate, vaporize, wipe out*; SEE CONCEPT *252*

liquor [n] *drink; alcoholic beverage*
alcohol, aqua vitae, booze*, broth, decoction, drinkable, elixir, extract, firewater*, fluid, hard stuff*, inebriant, infusion, intoxicant, liquid, moonshine*, poison*, potable, sauce*, solvent, spirits, stock, the bottle*, whiskey; SEE CONCEPT *455*

lissom [adj] *supple*
adaptable, agile, bendable, bending, elastic, flexible, graceful, limber, lithe, lithesome, loose, malleable, moldable, pliable, pliant, resilient, rubber, springy, stretchy, wiry; SEE CONCEPTS *488,604*

list [n] *record, tabulation*
account, agenda, archive, arrangement, ballot, bill, brief, bulletin, calendar, canon, catalog, catalogue, census, checklist, contents, dictionary, directory, docket, draft, enumeration, file, gazette, index, inventory, invoice, lexicon, lineup, listing, loop, manifest, memorandum, menu, outline, panel, poll, program, prospectus, register, roll, roll call, row, schedule, screed, scroll, series, slate, statistics, syllabus, table, tally, thesaurus, ticket, timetable, vocabulary; SEE CONCEPT *281*

list [v1] *keep a record; tabulate*
arrange, bill, book, button down, calender, catalogue, census, chart, chronicle, classify, detail, docket, enroll, enter, enumerate, file, index, inscribe, insert, inventory, invoice, itemize, keep count, manifest, note, numerate, particularize, peg, place, poll, post, put down as, put down for, record, register, run down, schedule, set down,

specialize, specify, spell out, tab, tally, tick off, write down; SEE CONCEPTS *79,125*

list [v2] *lean, slant*
cant, careen, heel, incline, pitch, recline, slope, tilt, tip; SEE CONCEPTS *154,201,738*

listen [v] *hear and pay attention*
accept, admit, adopt, attend, audit, auscult, auscultate, be all ears*, be attentive, catch, concentrate, eavesdrop, entertain, get, get a load of*, give an audience to, give attention, give heed to, hang on words*, hark, harken, hearken, hear out, hear tell, lend an ear*, mind, monitor, obey, observe, overhear, pick up on*, prick up ears*, receive, take advice*, take into consideration*, take notice, take under advisement*, tune in, tune in on*, welcome; SEE CONCEPT *596*

listless [adj] *spiritless, without energy*
absent, abstracted, apathetic, blah*, bored, careless, dormant, dreamy, drowsy, dull, easygoing, energyless, enervated, faint, heavy, heedless, impassive, inanimate, inattentive, indifferent, indolent, inert, insouciant, lackadaisical, lagging, laid-back*, languid, languishing, languorous, leaden, lethargic, lifeless, limp, lukewarm, lymphatic, mopish, neutral, out of it*, passive, phlegmatic, slack, sleepy, slow, sluggish, stupid, supine, thoughtless, torpid, uninterested, vacant; SEE CONCEPTS *401,584*

litany [n] *recital of items, often part of religious services*
account, catalogue, enumeration, invocation, list, petition, prayer, recitation, refrain, repetition, supplication, tale; SEE CONCEPTS *278,368*

literacy [n] *ability to read*
articulacy, articulateness, background, cultivation, education, knowledge, learning, proficiency, refinement, scholarship; SEE CONCEPTS *409,630*

literal [adj] *word for word; exact, real*
accurate, actual, apparent, authentic, bona fide, close, critical, faithful, genuine, gospel, methodical, natural, not figurative, ordinary, plain, scrupulous, simple, strict, to the letter*, true, undeviating, unerring, unexaggerated, unvarnished, usual, veracious, verbal, verbatim, veritable, written; SEE CONCEPTS *267,557*

literally [adv] *word for word; exactly*
actually, completely, correctly, direct, directly, faithfully, indisputably, letter by letter*, literatim, not figuratively, plainly, precisely, really, rightly, rigorously, sic*, simply, straight, strictly, to the letter*, truly, undeviatingly, undisputably, unerringly, unmistakably, verbatim, veritably; SEE CONCEPTS *267,557*

literary [adj] *concerning books*
belletristic, bookish, classical, erudite, formal, learned, lettered, literate, scholarly, well-read; SEE CONCEPTS *267,536*

literate [adj] *able to read and write*
cultivated, cultured, educated, instructed, knowledgeable, learned, lettered, scholarly, schooled; SEE CONCEPT *402*

literature [n] *written matter, both fictional and nonfictional*
abstract, article, belles-lettres, biography, books, brochure, classics, comment, composition, critique, discourse, discussion, disquisition, dissertation, drama, essay, exposition, findings, history, humanities, information, leaflet, letters, lit*, literary works, lore, novel, observation,

pamphlet, paper, poetry, precis, prose, report, research, story, summary, theme, thesis, tract, treatise, treatment, writings, written work; SEE CONCEPT 280

lithe [adj] *flexible, graceful and slender*
agile, lean, lightsome, limber, lissome, loose, nimble, pliable, pliant, slight, slim, spare, supple, thin; SEE CONCEPTS 488,491,584

litigate [v] *bring matter before court of law*
appeal, contest, dispute, drag into court*, file suit, go to court, go to law, institute legal proceedings, press charges, prosecute, see one in court*, sue, take the law on*; SEE CONCEPT 317

litigation [n] *matter coming before court of law*
action, case, cause, contention, dispute, lawsuit, process, prosecution, suit, trial; SEE CONCEPT 318

litigious [adj] *quarrelsome*
argumentative, belligerent, combative, contentious, disputable; SEE CONCEPTS 401,542

litter [n1] *mess, debris*
clutter, collateral, confusion, detritus, disarray, disorder, garbage, hash, hodgepodge, jumble, jungle, junk, mishmash, muck, muddle, offal, rash, refuse, rubbish, rummage, scattering, scramble, shuffle, trash, untidiness, waste; SEE CONCEPTS 260,432

litter [n2] *animal offspring*
brood, cubs, family, kittens, piglets, progeny, puppies, school, young; SEE CONCEPTS 394,397

litter [v] *make a mess*
clutter, confuse, derange, dirty, disarrange, disarray, disorder, jumble, mess up, scatter, strew; SEE CONCEPT 254

little [adj1] *small in size, amount*
babyish, bantam, brief, cramped, diminutive, dinky, elfin, embryonic, fleeting, hardly any, hasty, immature, imperceptible, inappreciable, inconsiderable, infant, infinitesimal, insufficient, junior, light, Lilliputian*, limited, meager, microscopic, mini, miniature, minute, not big, not large, peanut*, petite, scant, short, short-lived, shrimpy*, shriveled, skimpy, slight, snub, sparse, stubby, stunted, teeny, tiny, toy, truncated, undersized, undeveloped, wee, wizened, young; SEE CONCEPTS 773,789

little [adj2] *not important*
casual, inconsiderable, insignificant, light, minor, minute, negligible, paltry, petty, shoestring*, small, trifling, trivial, unimportant; SEE CONCEPT 575

little [adj3] *narrow-minded*
base, bigoted, cheap, contemptible, hidebound, illiberal, ineffectual, limited, mean, narrow, paltry, petty, provincial, self-centered, selfish, set, small, small-minded, vulgar, wicked; SEE CONCEPT 404

little [adv] *infrequently, not much*
a little, barely, hardly, hardly ever, not many, not often, not quite, only just, rarely, scarcely, seldom, somewhat; SEE CONCEPTS 530,544

little [n] *small amount of something*
bit, dab, dash, fragment, hint, modicum, particle, pinch, snippet, soupçon, speck, spot, taste, touch, trace, trifle, whit; SEE CONCEPT 835

liturgy [n] *worship, ceremony*
celebration, ceremonial, form, formality, formula, observance, rite, ritual, sacrament, service, services; SEE CONCEPT 368

livable [adj] *adequate, acceptable*
bearable, comfortable, cozy, endurable, fit, habitable, homey, inhabitable, lodgeable, passable, satisfactory, snug, sufferable, supportable, sustainable, tenantable, tolerable, worthwhile; SEE CONCEPTS 485,558

live [adj1] *existent*
alive, animate, aware, breathing, conscious, living, vital; SEE CONCEPT 539

live [adj2] *energetic, vigorous*
active, alert, brisk, burning, controversial, current, dynamic, earnest, effective, effectual, efficacious, efficient, functioning, hot*, lively, operative, pertinent, pressing, prevalent, running, topical, unsettled, vital, vivid, working; SEE CONCEPTS 542,560

live [v1] *exist*
abide, be, be alive, breathe, continue, draw breath, endure, get along, get by, have life, last, lead, maintain, make it, move, pass, persist, prevail, remain, remain alive, subsist, survive; SEE CONCEPT 407

live [v2] *inhabit a dwelling*
abide, bide, bunk*, crash*, dwell, hang one's hat*, hang out*, locate, lodge, nest, occupy, perch, reside, roost, settle; SEE CONCEPT 226

live [v3] *enjoy being alive*
be happy, delight, experience, flourish, love, luxuriate, make the most of, prosper, relish, savor, take pleasure, thrive; SEE CONCEPT 678

live [v4] *make money to support living*
acquire a livelihood, earn a living, earn money, fare, feed, get along*, get by*, maintain, make ends meet*, make it, profit, subsist, support; SEE CONCEPT 351

livelihood [n] *occupation*
alimentation, art, bread and butter*, business, circumstances, craft, employment, game*, grind*, income, job, keep*, living, maintenance, means, nine-to-five*, profession, racket*, rat race*, resources, slot, source of income, subsistence, support, sustenance, thing*, trade, vocation, what one is into*, work; SEE CONCEPTS 349,351,360

lively [adj] *energetic, active, busy*
agile, alert, animate, animated, astir, blithe, blithesome, bouncy, bright, brisk, buoyant, bustling, buzzing, cheerful, chipper*, chirpy*, complex, dashing, driving, effervescent, enjoyable, enterprising, entertaining, festive, frisky, frolicsome, full of pep*, gay, go-go*, happy, hyper*, industrious, involved, jocund, jumping, keen, merry, nimble, peppy*, perky, pert, provocative, quick, refreshing, rousing, snappy, sparkling, spirited, sprightly, spry, stimulating, stirring, vigorous, vivacious, zippy*; SEE CONCEPTS 401,542,548

livid [adj1] *pale, ashen*
ashy, blanched, bloodless, colorless, discolored, dusky, gloomy, greyish, grisly, leaden, lurid, murky, pallid, pasty, wan, waxen; SEE CONCEPT 618

livid [adj2] *bruised*
black-and-blue, contused, purple; SEE CONCEPT 618

livid [adj3] *extremely angry*
beside oneself, black*, boiling, enraged, exasperated, flaming, fuming, furious, hot*, incensed, indignant, infuriated, mad, offended, outraged; SEE CONCEPTS 403,542

living [adj] *existing, active*
alert, alive, animated, around, awake, breathing,

li
li

brisk, contemporary, continuing, current, developing, dynamic, existent, extant, in use, live, lively, ongoing, operative, persisting, strong, subsisting, ticking, vigorous, vital, warm; SEE CONCEPTS *539,560*

living [n] *lifestyle; source of income*
alimentation, bread and butter*, existence, income, job, keep*, livelihood, maintenance, means, mode, occupation, salt*, subsistence, support, sustainment, sustenance, sustentation, way, work; SEE CONCEPTS *335,351*

load [n1] *cargo, freight*
amount, bale, bundle, capacity, charge, consignment, contents, encumbrance, goods, haul, heft, hindrance, lading, mass, pack, parcel, part, payload, shipment, shot, weight; SEE CONCEPTS *338,432*

load [n2] *burden, pressure*
affliction, albatross, care, charge, cumber, deadweight*, drag, drain, duty, encumbrance, excess baggage*, incubus, liability, millstone*, obligation, onus, oppression, responsibility, task, tax, trouble, trust, weight, worry; SEE CONCEPT *674*

load [v1] *burden, saddle*
arrange, ballast, bear, carry, charge, chock, choke, containerize, cram, fill, flood, freight, glut, gorge, heap, heap up, jam*, lade, lumber, mass, oversupply, pack, pile, pile it on, pile up, place, pour in, put aboard, ram in, stack, store, stow, stuff, surfeit, swamp, top, top off, weigh, weigh down, weight; SEE CONCEPT *209*

load [v2] *overburden, pressure*
burden, charge, encumber, hamper, lade, oppress, saddle, task, tax, trouble, weigh down, weight, worry; SEE CONCEPT *14*

loaf [n] *block of something*
bun, cake, cube, dough, lump, mass, pastry, roll, slab, twist; SEE CONCEPTS *436,457,460,461*

loaf [v] *be idle, lazy*
be inactive, be indolent, be slothful, be unoccupied, bum*, bum around*, dally, dillydally*, dream, drift, evade, fool around*, fritter away*, goldbrick, hang out*, idle, kill time*, knock around*, laze, let down, lie, loiter, loll, lounge, lounge around, malinger, not lift a finger*, pass time, piddle, relax, saunter, shirk, sit around, slack, slow down, stall, stand around, stroll, take it easy, trifle, twiddle thumbs*, vegetate, waste time, while away hours*; SEE CONCEPTS *210,681*

loafer [n] *person who is idle, lazy*
beachcomber, deadbeat, do-nothing, good-for-nothing*, goof-off*, idler, lazybones*, lounger, malingerer, ne'er-do-well*, shirker, slacker, slouch, sluggard, sponger, wanderer, waster, wastrel; SEE CONCEPT *412*

loan [n] *money given temporarily*
accommodation, advance, allowance, credit, extension, floater, investment, mortgage, time payment, trust; SEE CONCEPT *332*

loan [v] *give money, possession temporarily*
accommodate, advance, allow, credit, lay on one, lend, let out, provide, score, scratch, stake, touch; SEE CONCEPT *115*

loath [adj] *against, averse*
afraid, counter, disinclined, hesitant, indisposed, opposed, reluctant, remiss, resisting, uneager, unwilling; SEE CONCEPTS *29,542*

loathe [v] *dislike strongly*
abhor, abominate, be allergic to*, be down on, decline, despise, detest, execrate, feel repug-

nance, find disgusting, hate, have aversion to, have no use for*, refuse, reject, repudiate, revolt, spurn; SEE CONCEPT *29*

loathing [n] *abhorrence*
contempt, detestation, disgust, dislike, enmity, hatred, repugnance, revulsion; SEE CONCEPT *29*

loathsome [adj] *hateful*
abhorrent, abominable, beastly, bitchy*, creepy, deplorable, detestable, disgusting, execrable, gross, hideous, horrible, invidious, lousy, nasty, nauseating, obnoxious, odious, offensive, pesky, pestiferous, repellent, repugnant, repulsive, revolting, sleazy*, slimy*, uncool*, vile; SEE CONCEPTS *485,529,570*

lob [v] *toss*
chuck, flip, hurl, launch, loft, pitch, project, propel; SEE CONCEPT *222*

lobby [n] *entrance hall*
antechamber, corridor, doorway, foyer, gateway, hall, hallway, passage, passageway, porch, vestibule, waiting room; SEE CONCEPTS *441,448*

lobby [v] *press for political action*
advance, affect, alter, bill, billboard*, boost, bring pressure to bear*, build up, campaign for, change, drum, exert influence, further, hard sell*, high pressure, hype*, induce, influence, make a pitch for*, modify, persuade, pitch, plug, politick, press, pressure, procure, promote, pull strings*, push, put pressure on, request, sell, sell on*, soft-sell*, soft-soap*, solicit, solicit votes, splash, spot, sway, sweet-talk*, thump, urge; SEE CONCEPTS *68,300*

lobbyist [n] *special interest representative*
activist, influence peddler, mover and shaker, person of influence, powerbroker, pressure group; SEE CONCEPTS *348,354*

local [adj] *of a community, restricted to immediate area*
bounded, civic, confined, district, divisional, geographical, insular, legendary, limited, narrow, neighborhood, parish, parochial, provincial, regional, sectarian, sectional, small-town, territorial, town, vernacular; SEE CONCEPT *536*

local [n] *person deeply rooted in community*
character, inhabitant, native, resident; SEE CONCEPTS *413,423*

locale/locality [n] *physical setting*
area, bailiwick, belt, district, domain, haunt, hole, home, location, locus, neck of the woods*, neighborhood, place, position, region, scene, sector, site, sphere, spot, stage, stomping ground*, territory, theater, tract, turf, venue, vicinity, zone; SEE CONCEPT *198*

localize [v] *confine*
center, contain, limit, narrow, pinpoint, restrain, restrict, stop from spreading; SEE CONCEPTS *121,130*

locate [v1] *find*
come across, come upon, detect, determine, discover, establish, ferret out*, get at, happen upon, hit upon, hook*, lay one's hands on*, light upon*, meet with, pick up on, pin down, pinpoint, place, position, read, search out, smell out, smoke out*, spot, station, strike, stumble on, track down, trip over*, uncover, unearth, zero in on*; SEE CONCEPT *183*

locate [v2] *settle*
dig in, dispose, dwell, establish, fix, hang one's hat*, inhabit, park, place, put, reside, seat, set, situate, squat, stand; SEE CONCEPT *226*

located [*adj*] *situated*
based, occupying, placed, positioned, posted, stationed; SEE CONCEPTS *158,201*
location [*n*] *place of residence or activity*
area, bearings, district, fix*, hole, locale, locality, locus, neck of the woods*, neighborhood, part, point, position, post, region, scene, section, site, situation, spot, station, tract, turf, venue, whereabouts; SEE CONCEPT *198*
lock [*n*] *device that fastens and bars free passage*
bar, bolt, bond, catch, clamp, clasp, clinch, connection, fastening, fixture, grapple, grip, hasp, hook, junction, latch, link, padlock; SEE CONCEPT *499*
lock [*v*] *fasten, clasp*
bar, bolt, button, button up, clench, close, clutch, embrace, encircle, enclose, engage, entwine, grapple, grasp, hug, join, latch, link, mesh, press, seal, secure, shut, turn the key, unite; SEE CONCEPTS *85,160*
locker [*n*] *compartment*
cabinet, chest, closet, trunk; SEE CONCEPT *440*
locomotion [*n*] *movement*
action, mobileness, mobility, motion, moving, progression, travel, travelling; SEE CONCEPTS *2,145,697*
locution [*n*] *phrasing*
accent, articulation, dialect, diction, expression, inflection, language, phraseology; SEE CONCEPT *77*
lodge [*n*] *cabin; vacation residence*
abode, auberge, burrow, camp, chalet, cottage, couch, country house, den, dormitory, dwelling, gatehouse, haunt, home, hospice, hostel, hostelry, hotel, house, hut, inn, motel, public house, retreat, roadhouse, shack, shanty, shelter, stopover, tavern, villa; SEE CONCEPT *516*
lodge [*v1*] *become fixed or wedged*
abide, catch, come to rest, embed, entrench, fix, imbed, implant, infix, ingrain, install, plant, remain, root, stay, stick; SEE CONCEPT *201*
lodge [*v2*] *stay at temporary residence*
abide, accommodate, bestow, board, bunk, canton, crash, domicile, dwell, entertain, harbor, hole up*, hostel, house, locate, nest, park*, perch*, put up, quarter, rent, reside, room, roost*, shelter, sojourn, squat, station, stay, stay over, stop; SEE CONCEPT *226*
lodging [*n*] *accommodation for rent*
abode, address, apartment, bed and breakfast, boarding house, camp, castle, chambers, cover, domicile, dorm, dwelling, habitation, harbor, home, hostel, hotel, inn, lodge, lodgment, motel, palace, pied-à-terre, place, port, protection, quarters, residence, resort, roof, room, room and board, rooming house, shelter; SEE CONCEPT *516*
loft [*n*] *room on upper floor*
apartment, attic, dormer, garret, storage, studio; SEE CONCEPT *448*
lofty [*adj1*] *high, elevated*
aerial, airy, high-rise, lifted, raised, sky-high, skyscraping, skyward, soaring, spiring, tall, towering; SEE CONCEPT *779*
lofty [*adj2*] *grand, stately*
arresting, benevolent, big, chivalrous, commanding, considerate, dignified, distinguished, elevated, exalted, generous, great, illustrious, imposing, magnanimous, majestic, noble, renowned, striking, sublime, superb, superior, utopian, visionary; SEE CONCEPT *574*

lofty [*adj3*] *arrogant, high and mighty*
ambitious, cavalier, condescending, disdainful, grandiose, haughty, high-minded, immodest, insolent, overbearing, patronizing, pretentious, proud, snooty, supercilious; SEE CONCEPT *401*
log [*n1*] *stump of tree*
block, bole, chunk, length, piece, stick, timber, trunk, wood; SEE CONCEPTS *428,479*
log [*n2*] *record*
account, book, chart, daybook, diary, journal, listing, logbook, register, tally; SEE CONCEPT *271*
logic [*n*] *science of reasoning*
antithesis and synthesis, argumentation, coherence, connection, course of thought, deduction, dialectic, good sense, induction, inference, linkage, philosophy, ratiocination, rationale, relationship, sanity, sense, sound judgment, syllogism, syllogistics, thesis, train of thought; SEE CONCEPTS *37,349,689*
logical [*adj1*] *probable, reasonable*
analytic, analytical, clear, cogent, coherent, commonsensical, compelling, congruent, consequent, consistent, convincing, deducible, discerning, discriminating, extensional, fair, germane, holding together, holding water*, inferential, intelligent, judicious, juridicious, justifiable, kosher*, legit*, legitimate, lucid, most likely, necessary, obvious, perceptive, perspicuous, pertinent, plausible, rational, relevant, sensible, sound, subtle, telling, valid, well-organized, wise; SEE CONCEPTS *402,529,552*
logistics [*n*] *management*
coordination, engineering, masterminding, organization, planning, plans, strategy, systematization; SEE CONCEPT *660*
logo [*n*] *trademark*
brand, brand name, emblem, identification, imprint, label, logotype, symbol, tag; SEE CONCEPTS *259,284*
loiter [*v*] *hang around; stroll*
amble, dabble, dally*, dawdle, delay, diddle, drag, flag, fritter away, get no place fast*, halt, hover, idle, lag, linger, loaf, loll, lounge, pass time, pause, poke, procrastinate, put off, ramble, saunter, shamble, shuffle, slacken, slough, tarry, trail, traipse, wait, waste time; SEE CONCEPTS *151,210,681*
loll [*v*] *lay sprawled*
bum, dangle, dawdle, droop, drop, flap, flop, goof off, hang, hang loose, idle, laze, lean, loaf, loiter, lounge, recline, relax, rest, sag, slouch, slump, sprawl; SEE CONCEPTS *154,210*
lone [*adj*] *by oneself; only*
abandoned, alone, deserted, forsaken, isolated, lonely, lonesome, one, onliest, particular, secluded, separate, separated, single, singular, sole, solitary, solo, stag, unaccompanied, unique; SEE CONCEPT *577*
loneliness [*n*] *isolation*
alienation, aloneness, desolation, forlornness, friendlessness, heartache, lonesomeness, remoteness, seclusion, solitariness, solitude, withdrawal; SEE CONCEPTS *135,188,388,631*
lonely [*adj1*] *feeling friendless, forlorn*
abandoned, alone, apart, by oneself, comfortless, companionless, deserted, desolate, destitute, disconsolate, down, empty, estranged, forsaken, godforsaken, homeless, isolated, left, lone, lonesome, outcast, reclusive, rejected, renounced, secluded, single, solitary, troglodytic, unattended,

li
lo

unbefriended, uncherished, unsocial, withdrawn; SEE CONCEPTS *403,555*

lonely [*adj2*] *out-of-the-way*
alone, deserted, desolate, godforsaken, isolated, obscure, off the beaten track*, private, quiet, remote, removed, retired, secluded, secret, sequestered, solitary, unfrequented, uninhabited; SEE CONCEPT *583*

loner [*n*] *recluse*
anomic, hermit, introvert, lone wolf*, outsider, solitary; SEE CONCEPTS *361,423*

lonesome [*adj*] *forlorn, friendless*
alone, cheerless, companionless, deserted, desolate, dreary, gloomy, homesick, isolated, lone, lonely, solitary; SEE CONCEPTS *403,555*

long [*adj1*] *extended in space or time*
continued, deep, distant, drawn out, elongate, elongated, enduring, enlarged, expanded, extensive, faraway, far-off, far-reaching, gangling, great, high, lanky, lasting, lengthened, lengthy, lingering, lofty, longish, outstretched, prolonged, protracted, rangy, remote, running, spread out, spun out, stretch, stretched, stretching, stringy, sustained, tall, towering; SEE CONCEPTS *482,779,798*

long [*adj2*] *interminable, excessive in length*
boundless, delayed, diffuse, diffusive, dilatory, dragging, drawn-out, for ages*, forever and a day*, late, lengthy, limitless, lingering, long-drawn-out*, long-winded*, overlong, prolix, prolonged, protracted, slow, sustained, tardy, unending, verbose, without end, wordy; SEE CONCEPTS *544,798*

long [*v*] *desire, crave*
ache, aim, aspire, covet, dream of, hanker, have a yen for, hunger, itch, lust, miss, pine, sigh, spoil for, suspire, thirst, want, wish, yearn; SEE CONCEPT *20*

longevity [*n*] *long life*
durability, endurance, lastingness, old age; SEE CONCEPTS *411,633*

longing [*adj*] *desirous*
anxious, ardent, avid, craving, eager, hungry, languishing, pining, ravenous, wishful, wistful, yearning; SEE CONCEPT *403*

longing [*n*] *strong desire*
ambition, aspiration, coveting, craving, fire in the belly*, hankering, hunger, hungering, itch, pining, thirst, urge, wish, yearning, yen; SEE CONCEPTS *20,709*

long shot [*n*] *outside chance*
fluke, hundred-to-one shot, little chance, lucky shot, no chance, off-chance, one in a million*, slim chance, small chance; SEE CONCEPT *679*

long-standing [*adj*] *existing for some time*
abiding, durable, enduring, established, fixed, lasting, long-established, long-lasting, long-lived, traditional; SEE CONCEPTS *551,798*

long-winded [*adj*] *wordy*
bombastic, chatty*, gabby*, garrulous, loquacious, palaverous, prolix, rambling, talkative, verbose, voluble; SEE CONCEPT *267*

look [*n1*] *visual examination*
attention, beholding, case, cast, contemplation, evil eye*, eye*, flash, gander, gaze, glance, glimpse, gun, inspection, introspection, keeping watch, leer, look-see*, marking, noticing, observation, once-over, peek, reconnaissance, regard, regarding, review, scrutiny, sight, slant, specula-

tion, squint, stare, surveillance, survey, swivel, view, viewing; SEE CONCEPT *623*

look [*n2*] *characteristic, stylish appearance*
air, aspect, bearing, cast, complexion, countenance, demeanor, effect, expression, face, fashion, guise, manner, mien, mug*, physiognomy, presence, seeming, semblance, visage; SEE CONCEPTS *655,673,716*

look [*v1*] *examine visually*
admire, attend, behold, beware, consider, contemplate, eye, feast one's eyes*, flash, focus, gape, gawk, gaze, get a load of, glance, glower, goggle, heed, inspect, mark, mind, note, notice, observe, ogle, peep, peer, pore over, read, regard, rubberneck*, scan, scout, scrutinize, see, spot, spy, stare, study, survey, take a gander*, take in the sights*, tend, view, watch; SEE CONCEPT *623*

look [*v2*] *appear, seem to be*
display, evidence, exhibit, express, indicate, look like, make clear, manifest, present, resemble, show, sound, strike as; SEE CONCEPTS *261,716*

look [*v3*] *expect, anticipate*
await, count on, divine, forecast, foretell, hope, hunt, reckon on, search, seek; SEE CONCEPT *26*

look [*v4*] *face*
front, front on, give onto, overlook; SEE CONCEPT *746*

look-alike [*n*] *double*
carbon copy, clone, copy, dead ringer*, duplicate, impersonator, match, replica, ringer*, spitting image*, stand-in*, twin; SEE CONCEPTS *664,716*

look down on [*v*] *hold in contempt*
abhor, contemn, despise, disdain, scorn, scout, sneer, spurn, turn nose up at*; SEE CONCEPT *29*

look into [*v*] *check, research*
audit, check out, delve into, dig, examine, explore, follow up, go into, inquire, inspect, investigate, look over, make inquiry, probe, prospect, scrutinize, sift, study; SEE CONCEPT *103*

lookout [*n*] *guard; place from which to guard*
anchor, beacon, belvedere, case, catbird seat*, citadel, crow's nest*, cupola, eagle eye*, hawk, observance, observation, observatory, outlook, overlook, panorama, patrol, post, scene, scout, sentinel, sentry, spotter, station, surveillance, tip, tower, view, vigil, vigilance, ward, watch, watcher, watch person watchtower*, weather eye*; SEE CONCEPTS *198,358,623*

look out [*v*] *be wary*
be alert, be careful, be on guard, beware, check out, have a care, heads up*, hearken, keep an eye out*, keep tabs*, listen, mind, notice, pay attention, peg*, pick up on*, scope, shotgun*, size up, spot, spy, watch out; SEE CONCEPTS *35,623*

look up [*v1*] *research*
come upon, confirm, discover, find, hunt for, peruse, scan, search for, seek, seek out, track down; SEE CONCEPTS *72,216*

look up [*v2*] *improve*
advance, ameliorate, come along, convalesce, gain, get better, mend, perk up, pick up, progress, recuperate, shape up, show improvement; SEE CONCEPTS *303,700*

loom [*v*] *appear, often imposingly*
approach, await, be at hand*, become visible, be coming, be forthcoming, be imminent, be in the cards*, be in the wind*, be near, break through, brew, bulk, come forth, come into view, come on, come on the scene*, dawn, dominate, em-

anate, emerge, figure, gather, hang over, hover, impend, impress, issue, lower, make up, menace, mount, near, overhang, overshadow, overtop, portend, rear, rise, seem huge, seem large, show, soar, stand out, take shape, threaten, top, tower; SEE CONCEPTS *118,159,261*

loony [*adj*] *crazy*
ape, barmy, batty, berserk, bonkers*, cracked, crazed, cuckoo, daffy*, daft, delirious, demented, deranged, flaky, flipped out*, insane, kooky, lunatic, mad, maniacal, mental*, nuts, nutty, out of one's mind*, out to lunch*, psycho*, screwball*, screwy*, silly, touched*, unbalanced, wacky; SEE CONCEPT *403*

loony bin [*n*] *mental health facility*
bughouse*, funny farm*, insane asylum, madhouse*, mental hospital, mental institution, nut house*, psychiatric hospital, psychiatric ward, sanatorium; SEE CONCEPTS *312,439,516*

loop [*n*] *circle, spiral*
bend, circuit, circumference, coil, convolution, curl, curve, eyelet, hoop, kink, knot, loophole, noose, ring, twirl, twist, whorl, wreath; SEE CONCEPT *436*

loop [*v*] *circle, spiral*
arc, arch, begird, bend, bow, braid, coil, compass, connect, crook, curl, curve, curve around, encircle, encompass, fold, gird, girdle, join, knot, ring, roll, surround, tie together, turn, twist, wind around; SEE CONCEPTS *147,201,754*

loophole [*n*] *escape*
alternative, escape clause, means of escape, outlet, technicality, way out; SEE CONCEPT *102*

loose [*adj1*] *not tight; unconstrained*
apart, asunder, at large, baggy, clear, detached, disconnected, easy, escaped, flabby, flaccid, floating, free, hanging, insecure, lax, liberated, limp, loosened, movable, not fitting, relaxed, released, separate, slack, slackened, sloppy, unattached, unbolted, unbound, unbuttoned, uncaged, unclasped, unconfined, unconnected, undone, unfastened, unfettered, unhinged, unhooked, unlatched, unlocked, unpinned, unrestrained, unrestricted, unsecured, unshackled, untied, wobbly; SEE CONCEPT *485*

loose [*adj2*] *indefinite, vague*
detached, diffuse, disconnected, disordered, ill-defined, imprecise, inaccurate, indistinct, negligent, obscure, rambling, random, remiss; SEE CONCEPTS *267,529*

loose [*adj3*] *promiscuous*
abandoned, capricious, careless, corrupt, debauched, disreputable, dissipated, dissolute, easy, fast, heedless, high living*, immoral, imprudent, inconstant, lax, lewd, libertine, licentious, light, negligent, out of control*, playing, profligate, rash, reckless, speeding, swinging, thoughtless, unchaste, unmindful, unrestrained, wanton; SEE CONCEPTS *372,401,545*

loose/loosen [*v*] *set free; unbind*
alleviate, become unfastened, break up, deliver, detach, discharge, disconnect, disengage, disenthrall, disjoin, ease, ease off, emancipate, extricate, free, let go, let out, liberate, manumit, mitigate, relax, release, separate, slacken, unbar, unbolt, unbuckle, unbutton, unchain, unclasp, undo, unfasten, unfix, unhitch, unhook, unlace, unlash, unlatch, unleash, unlock, unloose, unpin, unscrew, unsnap, unstick, unstrap, untie,

untighten, work free, work loose; SEE CONCEPTS *127,250*

loot [*n*] *stolen goods*
booty, dough*, graft, haul, hot goods*, lift*, make*, money, pickings*, pillage, plunder, plunderage, prize, seizure, spoils, squeeze, take*; SEE CONCEPTS *337,340*

loot [*v*] *steal goods*
appropriate, boost, burglarize, despoil, grab, gut, liberate, lift, loft, make, moonlight requisition*, pillage, plunder, raid, ransack, ravage, relieve, requisition, rifle, rip off*, rob, sack, salvage, smash and grab*, snatch, snitch*, stick up, swipe, take, thieve, tip over; SEE CONCEPTS *139,192*

looter [*n*] *thief*
criminal, marauder, pilferer, pillager, plunderer, raider, ransacker, ravager, spoiler; SEE CONCEPT *412*

lop [*v*] *trim*
chop, clip, crop, cut, cut back, cut down, mow, pare, pare down, prune, shear, snip, truncate; SEE CONCEPTS *176,236,247*

lope [*v*] *stride*
bound, canter, gallop, run, trot; SEE CONCEPT *149*

lopsided [*adj*] *leaning, falling to one side; larger on one side*
askew, asymmetrical, awry, cockeyed, crooked, disproportional, disproportionate, inclinatory, irregular, nonsymmetrical, off-balance, one-sided, out of shape, overbalanced, squint, tilting, top-heavy, unbalanced, unequal, uneven, unsteady, warped; SEE CONCEPT *480*

loquacious [*adj*] *talkative*
babbling, chattering, chatty, fluent, gabby*, garrulous, gossipy, jabbering, long-winded*, loose-lipped*, motormouth*, multiloquent, prolix, verbose, voluble, wordy, yacking*; SEE CONCEPTS *267,401*

lore [*n*] *myths, traditional wisdom*
adage, belief, custom, doctrine, enlightenment, erudition, experience, fable, folklore, information, knowledge, learning, legend, letters, mythology, mythos, saga, saw, saying, scholarship, science, superstition, tale, teaching, tradition; SEE CONCEPTS *274,282,287*

lose [*v1*] *be deprived of; mislay*
be careless, become poorer, be impoverished, bereave, be reduced, capitulate, consume, default, deplete, disinherit, displace, dispossess, dissipate, divest, drain, drop, exhaust, expend, fail, fail to keep, fall short, forfeit, forget, give up, lavish, misplace, miss, misspend, oust, pass up, relinquish, rob, sacrifice, squander, suffer, suffer loss, surrender, use up, waste, yield; SEE CONCEPTS *116,156*

lose [*v2*] *be defeated*
be humbled, be outdistanced, be sunk, be taken to cleaners*, be the loser, be worsted*, come up short, decline, drop, drop a bundle*, fall, kiss goodbye*, lose out, miss, succumb, suffer defeat, take a beating*, take the count*, take the heat*, yield; SEE CONCEPTS *384,674*

lose [*v3*] *escape, avoid*
clear, dodge, duck, elude, evade, give the slip*, leave behind, outrun, rid, shake, shake off*, slip away, stray, throw off*, unburden, wander from; SEE CONCEPTS *30,102*

loser [*n*] *person, thing that fails*
also-ran*, deadbeat*, defeated, disadvantaged,

lo
lo

down-and-outer*, dud*, failure, flop*, flunkee*, has-been, underdog, underprivileged; SEE CONCEPTS *412,423,433*

loss [n] *misfortune, deficit; something misplaced or lost*
accident, bad luck, bereavement, calamity, casualty, cataclysm, catastrophe, cost, damage, death, debit, debt, defeat, deficiency, depletion, deprivation, destitution, destruction, detriment, disadvantage, disappearance, disaster, dispossession, failure, fall, fatality, forfeiture, harm, hurt, impairment, injury, losing, misadventure, mishap, mislaying, misplacing, need, perdition, privation, retardation, ruin, sacrifice, shrinkage, squandering, trial, trouble, undoing, want, waste, wreckage; SEE CONCEPTS *407,674,707*

lost [adj1] *missing, off-track*
absent, adrift, astray, at sea, cast away, disappeared, disoriented, down the drain*, fallen between cracks*, forfeit, forfeited, gone, gone astray, hidden, invisible, irrecoverable, irretrievable, irrevocable, kiss goodbye*, lacking, minus, mislaid, misplaced, missed, nowhere to be found*, obscured, off-course, out the window*, strayed, unredeemed, vanished, wandering, wayward, without; SEE CONCEPT *576*

lost [adj2] *extinct, destroyed*
abolished, annihilated, bygone, consumed, dead, demolished, devastated, dissipated, eradicated, exterminated, forgotten, frittered, gone, lapsed, misspent, misused, obliterated, obsolete, out-of-date, past, perished, ruined, squandered, unremembered, wasted, wiped out*, wrecked; SEE CONCEPTS *539,560*

lost [adj3] *distracted, dreaming*
absent, absentminded, absorbed, abstracted, bemused, bewildered, distrait, dreamy, engrossed, entranced, faraway, feeble, going in circles*, ignorant, inconscient, musing, perplexed, preoccupied, rapt, spellbound, taken in*, taken up*, unconscious, wasted; SEE CONCEPT *403*

lot [n1] *piece of property*
acreage, allotment, apportionment, area, block, clearing, division, field, frontage, parcel, part, patch, percentage, piece, plat, plot, plottage, portion, property, real estate, tract; SEE CONCEPTS *509,710*

lot [n2] *quantity, often large*
abundance, aggregate, aggregation, amplitude, assortment, barrel, batch, body, bunch, bundle, circle, clump, cluster, clutch, collection, conglomerate, conglomeration, consignment, crowd, great deal, group, heap, load, mass, mess*, much, multiplicity, number, ocean, oodles, order, pack, pile, plenitude, plenty, push, reams, requisition, scores, set, stack, stacks; SEE CONCEPTS *432,787*

lot [n3] *portion, share*
allotment, allowance, bite, cut, parcel, part, percentage, piece, quota, ration, slice, take; SEE CONCEPTS *710,835*

lot [n4] *fate, destiny*
accident, break, breaks, chance, circumstance, decree, doom, foreordination, fortune, hand one is dealt*, hazard, karma, kismet, Moirai, plight, portion, predestination, run of luck*, way cookie crumbles*, wheel of fortune*; SEE CONCEPT *679*

lothario [n] *womanizer*
Casanova, Don Juan, gigolo, ladies' man, ladykiller, lecher, libertine, lover, philanderer, rake,

Romeo, seducer, skirt chaser, stud*, wolf*; SEE CONCEPTS *372,401*

lotion [n] *creamy solution*
balm, cosmetic, cream, demulcent, embrocation, lenitive, liniment, medicine, ointment, palliative, preparation, salve, unguent, wash; SEE CONCEPTS *311,446,466*

lottery [n] *drawing*
chance, door prize, gambling, game of chance, Lotto, luck of the draw, numbers game, raffle, sweepstake; SEE CONCEPTS *28,363*

loud [adj1] *blaring, noisy*
big, blatant, blustering, boisterous, booming, cacophonous, clamorous, crashing, deafening, deep, ear-piercing, ear-splitting, emphatic, forte, full, full-mouthed, fulminating, heavy, high-sounding, intense, loud-voiced, lusty, obstreperous, pealing, piercing, powerful, rambunctious, raucous, resonant, resounding, ringing, roaring, rowdy, sonorous, stentorian, strident, strong, thundering, tumultuous, turbulent, turned up, uproarious, vehement, vociferous, wakes the dead*; SEE CONCEPTS *592,594*

loud [adj2] *offensive, gaudy*
brash, brassy, brazen, chintzy, coarse, crass, crude, flamboyant, flashy, garish, glaring, gross, lurid, meretricious, obnoxious, obtrusive, ostentatious, raucous, rude, showy, tasteless, tawdry, vulgar; SEE CONCEPTS *401,542,589*

loudmouthed [adj] *loud-voiced*
bellowing, bigmouthed, big-voiced, blustering, boisterous, full-throated, obnoxious, vociferous; SEE CONCEPT *401*

lounge [n] *club, socializing place*
bar, barroom, club room, cocktail lounge, dive*, drinkery, hideaway, lobby, mezzanine, parlor, pub, reception, saloon, spot, tap, taproom, watering hole*; SEE CONCEPTS *293,449*

lounge [v] *lie about, waste time*
bum*, dawdle, fritter away, goldbrick*, goof off*, idle, kill time*, laze, loaf, loiter, loll*, pass time, recline, relax, repose, saunter, sprawl, take it easy*; SEE CONCEPTS *154,210,681*

lousy [adj] *very bad*
awful, base, contemptible, despicable, dirty, disliked, execrable, faulty, harmful, hateful, horrible, inferior, low, mean, miserable, no good*, outrageous, poor, rotten, second-rate*, shoddy, slovenly, terrible, unpopular, unwelcome, vicious, vile; SEE CONCEPT *571*

lout [n] *boor*
barbarian, bear, boob*, brute, buffoon, bumpkin, cad, churl, clod, clodhopper, dolt, dork*, goon*, lummox, oaf, philistine, rube, slob*, vulgarian; SEE CONCEPT *423*

loutish [adj] *boorish*
bad-mannered, barbaric, bearish, bungling, cantankerous, churlish, cloddish, clodhopping*, clownish, clumsy, coarse, dense, doltish, gross*, gruff, ill-bred, ill-mannered, impolite, loud, oafish, ornery, rough, rude, rustic, swinish, uncivilized, uncouth, uncultured, uneducated, unmannerly, unpolished, unrefined, vulgar; SEE CONCEPT *404*

lovable [adj] *very likable; endearing*
adorable, agreeable, alluring, amiable, angelic, appealing, attractive, bewitching, captivating, charming, cuddly, delightful, desirable, enchanting, engaging, enthralling, entrancing, fascinating, fetching, friendly, genial, lovely, lovesome,

pleasing, ravishing, seductive, sweet, winning, winsome; SEE CONCEPT *404*

love [*n1*] *adoration; very strong liking*
adulation, affection, affiliation, allegiance, amity, amorousness, amour, appreciation, ardency, ardor, attachment, case*, cherishing, crush, delight, devotedness, devotion, emotion, enchantment, enjoyment, fervor, fidelity, flame, fondness, friendship, hankering, idolatry, inclination, infatuation, involvement, like, lust, mad for, partiality, passion, piety, rapture, regard, relish, respect, sentiment, soft spot*, taste, tenderness, weakness, worship, yearning, zeal; SEE CONCEPT *32*

love [*n2*] *person who is loved by another*
admirer, angel, beau, beloved, boyfriend, courter, darling, dear, dearest, dear one, flame, girlfriend, honey, inamorata, inamorato, Juliet*, loved one, lover, paramour, passion, Romeo*, spark, suitor, swain, sweet, sweetheart, truelove, valentine; SEE CONCEPT *423*

love [*v1*] *adore, like very much*
admire, adulate, be attached to, be captivated by, be crazy about, be enamored of, be enchanted by, be fascinated with, be fond of, be in love with, canonize, care for, cherish, choose, deify, delight in, dote on, esteem, exalt, fall for, fancy, glorify, go for*, gone on*, have affection for, have it bad*, hold dear, hold high, idolize, long for, lose one's heart to*, prefer, prize, put on pedestal*, think the world of*, thrive with, treasure, venerate, wild for*, worship; SEE CONCEPT *32*

love [*v2*] *have sexual relations*
caress, clasp, cling, cosset, court, cuddle, draw close, embrace, feel, fondle, hold, hug, kiss, lick, look tenderly, make love, neck*, pet*, press, shine, soothe, stroke, take into one's arms, tryst, woo; SEE CONCEPTS *375,384*

love affair [*n*] *sexual relationship outside of marriage*
adultery, affair, amour, devotion, extracurricular activity*, flirtation, intrigue, liaison, love, menage à trois, passion, romance, thing, triangle; SEE CONCEPTS *375,388*

love handles [*n*] *bulging waistline*
fat, flab, hate handles*, keg*, middle age spread*, spare tire*; SEE CONCEPTS *723,734*

lovelorn [*n*] *unloved*
bereft, crossed in love, dejected, forsaken, jilted, loveless, lovesick, rejected, spurned; SEE CONCEPTS *21,30,384*

lovely [*adj*] *beautiful, charming; agreeable*
admirable, adorable, alluring, amiable, attractive, beauteous, bewitching, captivating, comely, dainty, delectable, delicate, delicious, delightful, enchanting, engaging, enjoyable, exquisite, fair, good-looking, gorgeous, graceful, gratifying, handsome, knockout, lovesome, nice, picture, pleasant, pleasing, pretty, pulchritudinous, rare, scrumptious, splendid, stunning, sweet, winning; SEE CONCEPTS *537,579,589*

lovemaking [*n*] *sexual activity*
carnal knowledge, coition, coitus, copulation, coquetting, courting, courtship, cuddling, dalliance, fondling, fooling around, foreplay, hugging, intercourse, intimacy, kissing, mating, screwing, sexual intercourse, sexual relations, smooching*, snuggling, sucking face*; SEE CONCEPT *375*

lover [*n*] *person having sexual relationship*
admirer, beau, beloved, boyfriend, companion,

courter, darling, dear, dearest, escort, fiancé, fiancée, flame, girlfriend, idolizer, inamorata, inamorato, infatuate, Juliet*, paramour, petitioner, Romeo*, significant other, solicitor, steady, suitor, suppliant, swain, sweetheart, truelove, valentine, wooer; SEE CONCEPT *423*

lovesick [*adj*] *longing*
desiring, infatuated, languishing, lovelorn, pining, yearning; SEE CONCEPTS *21,30,384*

loving [*adj*] *expressing adoration*
admiring, affectionate, amatory, amiable, amorous, anxious, appreciative, ardent, attached, attentive, benevolent, bound up, caring, concerned, considerate, cordial, dear, demonstrative, devoted, doting, earnest, enamored, erotic, expressive, faithful, fervent, fond, friendly, generous, idolatrous, impassioned, infatuated, kind, liking, loyal, passionate, respecting, reverent, reverential, romantic, sentimental, solicitous, tender, thoughtful, valuing, warm, warm-hearted, worshipful, zealous; SEE CONCEPTS *372,401,542*

low [*adj1*] *close to the ground; short*
below, beneath, bottom, bottommost, crouched, decumbent, deep, depressed, flat, ground-level, inferior, junior, lesser, level, little, lowering, low-hanging, low-lying, low-set, minor, nether, not high, profound, prostrate, rock-bottom, shallow, small, squat, squatty, stunted, subjacent, subsided, sunken, under, unelevated; SEE CONCEPTS *583,779,782,793*

low [*adj2*] *reduced; mediocre*
cheap, cut, cut-rate*, deficient, depleted, economical, inadequate, inexpensive, inferior, insignificant, little, low-grade, marked down, meager, moderate, modest, nominal, paltry, poor, puny, reasonable, scant, second-rate*, shoddy, slashed, small, sparse, substandard, trifling, uncostly, worthless; SEE CONCEPTS *334,574,789*

low [*adj3*] *crude, vulgar*
abject, base, blue, coarse, common, contemptible, crass, crumby, dastardly, degraded, depraved, despicable, disgraceful, dishonorable, disreputable, gross*, ignoble, ill-bred, inelegant, mean, menial, miserable, nasty, obscene, off-color*, offensive, raw, rough, rude, scrubby, scruffy*, scurvy, servile, sordid, unbecoming, uncouth, undignified, unrefined, unworthy, vile, woebegone, woeful, wretched; SEE CONCEPTS *404,542*

low [*adj4*] *living in, coming from poor circumstances*
base, baseborn, humble, ignoble, lowborn, lowly, mean, meek, obscure, plain, plebeian, poor, rude, simple, unpretentious, unwashed; SEE CONCEPT *549*

low [*adj5*] *depressed*
bad, blue*, crestfallen, dejected, despondent, disheartened, down, down and out*, downcast, downhearted, down in the dumps*, down in the mouth*, dragged, fed up, forlorn, gloomy, glum, in the pits*, low-down*, miserable, moody, morose, sad, singing the blues*, spiritless, unhappy; SEE CONCEPT *403*

low [*adj6*] *not feeling well*
ailing, debilitated, dizzy, dying, exhausted, faint, feeble, frail, ill, indisposed, poorly, prostrate, reduced, sick, sickly, sinking, stricken, unwell, weak; SEE CONCEPT *314*

lo
lo

low [*adj7*] *not loud*
faint, gentle, hushed, muffled, muted, quiet, soft, subdued, whispered; SEE CONCEPT *594*

lowbrowed [*adj*] *uncultivated, vulgar*
ignorant, illiterate, uneducated, unlearned, unlettered, unread, unrefined, unschooled, unsophisticated, untaught, untutored; SEE CONCEPT *402*

lower [*adj*] *under, inferior*
bush-league*, curtailed, decreased, diminished, junior, lessened, lesser, low, lower rung, minor, nether, pared down, reduced, secondary, second-class, second-fiddle*, second-string*, smaller, subjacent, subordinate, under; SEE CONCEPTS *586,772*

lower [*v1*] *let down; fall*
bring low, cast down, couch, demit, depress, descend, detrude, droop, drop, ground, let down, make lower, push down, reduce, set down, sink, submerge, take down; SEE CONCEPT *181*

lower [*v2*] *reduce, minimize*
abate, clip, curtail, cut, cut back, cut down, decrease, decry, de-escalate, deflate, demote, depreciate, devaluate, devalue, diminish, downgrade, downsize, lessen, mark down, moderate, pare, prune, roll back, scale down, shave, slash, soften, tone down, undervalue, write off; SEE CONCEPTS *236,240,247*

lower [*v3*] *belittle, disgrace*
abase, bemean, cast down, condescend, debase, degrade, deign, demean, depress, devalue, downgrade, humble, humiliate, stoop; SEE CONCEPTS *7,19*

low-key [*adj*] *subdued*
easygoing, laid-back*, loose, low-pitched, muffled, muted, played down, quiet, relaxed, restrained, sober, softened, soft-sell*, subtle, toned down, understated; SEE CONCEPTS *542,544,548*

lowly [*adj*] *inferior, plain*
average, base, baseborn, cast down, common, commonplace, docile, dutiful, everyday, gentle, humble, ignoble, low, lowborn, mean, meek, menial, mild, modest, mundane, obscure, obsequious, ordinary, plebeian, poor, proletarian, prosaic, retiring, reverential, servile, simple, submissive, subordinate, unassuming, unpretentious, withdrawing; SEE CONCEPTS *404,547,549*

loyal [*adj*] *faithful, dependable*
allegiant, ardent, attached, behind one, believing, coming through, constant, devoted, dutiful, dyed-in-the-wool*, firm, on one's side*, patriotic, resolute, staunch, steadfast, steady, tried-and-true*, true, true-blue*, trustworthy, trusty, unfailing, unswerving, unwavering; SEE CONCEPTS *404,545*

loyalty [*n*] *faithfulness, dependability*
adherence, allegiance, ardor, attachment, bond, conscientiousness, constancy, devotedness, devotion, duty, earnestness, faith, fealty, fidelity, homage, honesty, honor, incorruptibility, integrity, inviolability, obedience, patriotism, probity, reliability, resolution, scrupulousness, sincerity, single-mindedness, singleness, staunchness, steadfastness, subjection, submission, support, tie, troth, trueheartedness, trueness, trustiness, trustworthiness, truth, truthfulness, uprightness, zeal; SEE CONCEPTS *411,645*

LSD [*n*] *lysergic acid diethylamide*
acid, blotter acid*, blue heaven*, California sunshine*, cubes*, dots*, drug, electric Kool-aid*, hallucinogen, instant Zen*, Lucy in the sky with diamonds*, mellow yellows*, microdots*, Owsley, Owsley's acid, purple haze, strawberry fields*, sunshine, tabs*, yellow sunshine*; SEE CONCEPT *307*

lubricant [*n*] *lubricator*
coating, grease, oil, silicone, wax, WD40™; SEE CONCEPT *606*

lubricate [*v*] *make slippery*
anoint, cream, grease, lard, lube, make, oil, oil the wheels*, slick, smear, smooth, tallow, wax; SEE CONCEPT *202*

lucid [*adj1*] *evident, obvious*
apprehensible, clear, clear-cut, comprehendible, comprehensible, crystal clear, distinct, explicit, fathomable, graspable, intelligible, knowable, limpid, luminous, pellucid, plain, translucent, transparent, transpicuous, unambiguous, unblurred, understandable; SEE CONCEPT *529*

lucid [*adj2*] *brilliant, shining*
beaming, bright, effulgent, gleaming, incandescent, lambent, luminous, lustrous, radiant, refulgent, resplendent; SEE CONCEPT *617*

lucid [*adj3*] *clear, transparent*
clear, crystalline, diaphanous, gauzy, glassy, limpid, obvious, pellucid, pure, sheer, translucent, transpicuous, unblurred; SEE CONCEPTS *606,619*

lucid [*adj4*] *clearheaded, sensible*
all there, compos mentis, cool, got head together*, in right mind, normal, rational, reasonable, right, sane, sober, sound, together; SEE CONCEPTS *402,403*

Lucifer [*n*] *Satan*
archangel, beast, Beelzebub, devil, diablo, evil one, fallen angel, Mephistopheles, Prince of Darkness; SEE CONCEPTS *370,412*

luck [*n1*] *good fortune*
advantage, big break*, blessing, break*, fluke*, fortunateness, godsend*, good luck, happiness, health, in the cards*, karma*, kismet*, luckiness, lucky break*, occasion, opportunity, profit, prosperity, run of luck*, serendipity, smile*, streak of luck, stroke, success, triumph, victory, weal, wealth, win, windfall; SEE CONCEPT *693*

luck [*n2*] *chance*
accident, break, destiny, fate, fifty-fifty*, fortuity, fortune, hap*, happenstance, hazard, occasion, occurrence, toss-up*, unforeseen event; SEE CONCEPT *679*

luckily [*adv*] *happily*
by chance, favorably, fortuitously, fortunately, opportunely, propitiously, providentially; SEE CONCEPTS *544,572*

lucky [*adj*] *fortunate, opportune*
advantageous, adventitious, all systems go*, auspicious, beneficial, benign, blessed, charmed, coming up roses*, everything going*, favored, felicitous, fortuitous, getting a break*, golden, happy, hit it big*, holding aces*, hopeful, hot*, in the groove*, into something, on a roll*, on a streak, promising, propitious, prosperous, providential, serendipitous, striking it rich*, successful, timely, well; SEE CONCEPTS *537,572*

lucrative [*adj*] *productive, well-paid*
advantageous, cost effective, fatness, fruitful, gainful, good, high-income*, in the black*, money-making, paying, profitable, remunerative, sweet, worthwhile; SEE CONCEPT *334*

lucre [n] *money, profits*
capital, cash, earnings, funds, gain, gate*, gravy*, income, proceeds, receipts, resources, revenue, riches, take*, wealth; SEE CONCEPTS *332,340,344,693*

ludicrous [adj] *absurd, ridiculous*
antic, bizarre, burlesque, comic, comical, crazy, droll, fantastic, farcical, foolish, funny, gelastic, grotesque, incongruous, laughable, nonsensical, odd, outlandish, preposterous, risible, silly, zany; SEE CONCEPT *548*

lug [v] *drag something around*
bear, buck, carry, convey, draw, ferry, haul, heave, hump, jerk, lift, lurch, pack, pull, rake, schlepp*, snap, tote, tow, transport, trawl, tug, vellicate, yank; SEE CONCEPT *206*

luggage [n] *bag, suitcase*
baggage, carry-on, case, fortnighter, gear, impedimenta, paraphernalia, suit bag, things*, tote bag, trunk, valise; SEE CONCEPTS *446,494*

lukewarm [adj1] *slightly heated*
blood-warm, milk-warm, tepid, warm, warmish; SEE CONCEPT *605*

lukewarm [adj2] *indifferent, unenthusiastic*
apathetic, chilly, cold, cool, halfhearted, hesitant, indecisive, irresolute, phlegmatic, tepid, uncertain, uncommitted, unconcerned, undecided, uninterested, unresolved, unresponsive, wishy-washy*; SEE CONCEPTS *403,542*

lull [n] *pause, calm*
abeyance, break, breather, breathing spell, calmness, coffee break, comma*, downtime*, hiatus, hush, layoff, letup, pausation, quiescence, quiet, respite, silence, stillness, stop, time-out*, tranquility; SEE CONCEPT *807*

lull [v] *calm, ease off*
abate, allay, balm, becalm, cease, chill out*, compose, cool*, cool off*, decrease, die down, diminish, dwindle, ebb, fall, hush, lay back, let up, lullaby, moderate, pacify, put a lid on*, qualify, quell, quiet, quiet down, settle, slacken, soft-pedal*, soothe, still, stroke, subdue, subside, take it easy*, take the edge*, take the sting out*, temper, tranquilize, wane; SEE CONCEPTS *7,22,210,698*

lumber [v1] *walk heavily, clumsily*
barge, clump, galumph, lump, plod, shamble, shuffle, slog, stump, trudge, trundle, waddle; SEE CONCEPT *151*

lumber [v2] *burden*
charge, cumber, encumber, impose upon, lade, land, load, saddle, tax, weigh; SEE CONCEPT *14*

lumbering [adj] *clumsy, awkward*
blundering, bovine, bumbling, clodhopping*, clunking, elephantine, gauche, gawky, halting, heavy, heavy-footed, hulking, inept, klutzy*, lead-footed*, lumpish, maladroit, overgrown, ponderous, splay, two left feet*, ungainly, unhandy, unwieldy, wooden; SEE CONCEPTS *406,584*

luminary [n] *very important person*
big name*, celeb*, celebrity, dignitary, eminence, leader, lion*, name, notability, notable, personage, personality, somebody*, star, superstar, VIP*, worthy; SEE CONCEPTS *352,423*

luminescent [adj] *glowing, shining*
bright, effulgent, fluorescent, luminous, phosphorescent, radiant; SEE CONCEPT *617*

luminous [adj1] *bright, glowing*
beaming, brilliant, clear, crystal, effulgent, fulgent, illuminated, incandescent, lambent, lighted, lit, lucent, lucid, luminescent, lustrous, radiant, refulgent, resplendent, shining, translucent, transparent, vivid; SEE CONCEPT *617*

luminous [adj2] *obvious, understandable*
apprehensible, bright, brilliant, clear, comprehendible, comprehensible, evident, fathomable, graspable, intelligible, knowable, lucid, perspicacious, perspicuous; SEE CONCEPT *529*

lummox [n] *oaf*
beast, blunderer, boor, bruiser, brute, bumpkin, chump*, clod, clodhopper, clown, dolt, dumb ox*, dunce, fool, goon*, half-wit*, hayseed, idiot, imbecile, klutz*, loser, lout*, lunkhead, moron, nincompoop*, ox*, sap*, simpleton*, yokel; SEE CONCEPT *412*

lump [n] *clump, mass*
agglomeration, ball, bit, block, bulge, bulk, bump, bunch, cake, chip, chunk, cluster, crumb, dab, gob, group, growth, handful, hunk, knot, knurl, lot, morsel, mountain, much, nugget, part, peck, piece, pile, portion, protrusion, protuberance, scrap, section, solid, spot, swelling, tumescence, tumor, wad, wedge; SEE CONCEPTS *432,470,471*

lump [v] *tolerate, withstand*
abide, bear, brook, digest, endure, put up with, stand, stomach, suffer, swallow, take; SEE CONCEPT *23*

lunacy [n] *craziness, madness*
aberration, absurdity, alienation, asininity, dementia, derangement, distraction, fatuity, folly, foolhardiness, foolishness, idiocy, imbalance, imbecility, inanity, ineptitude, insanity, mania, psychopathy, psychosis, senselessness, silliness, stupidity; SEE CONCEPTS *410,633*

lunatic [adj] *crazy, mad*
absurd, baked*, balmy*, bananas*, bonkers*, cracked, crazed, daft, demented, deranged, dippy*, flaky*, flipped out*, foolish, freaked out*, fried*, idiotic, insane, irrational, kooky*, loco, maniac, maniacal, nonsensical, nutty*, preposterous, psyched out*, psychotic, schizoid*, screwy*, stupid, unsound, whacko*, zany; SEE CONCEPTS *401,403*

lunatic [n] *person who is crazy, mad*
crackpot*, crank, cuckoo*, demoniac, flake*, fruitcake*, kook*, lamebrain*, loon*, maniac, neurotic, nut*, paranoid, psycho*, psychopath, psychotic, scatterbrain, schizophrenic, sociopathic; SEE CONCEPTS *412,809*

lunge [n] *pounce*
charge, cut, jab, jump, pass, spring, stab, swing, swipe, thrust; SEE CONCEPTS *159,194*

lunge [v] *pounce, dive for*
bound, burst, charge, cut, dash, drive, fall upon, hit, jab, jump, leap, lurch, pitch, plunge, poke, push, set upon, stab, strike, surge, thrust; SEE CONCEPTS *159,194*

lurch [v] *move toward with jerk*
blunder, bumble, careen, dodge, duck, falter, flounder, heave, jerk, lean, list, move to the side, pitch, reel, rock, roll, seesaw, slide, slip, stagger, stumble, sway, swing, teeter, tilt, toss, totter, wallow, weave, wobble, yaw; SEE CONCEPTS *80,150,152,194*

lure [n] *bait*
allurement, ambush, appeal, attraction, bribe, call, camouflage, carrot*, come-on*, con game*, decoy, delusion, draw, enticement, fake, gim-

lo
lu

mick, hook, illusion, incentive, inducement, inveiglement, invitation, magnet*, mousetrap*, pull, seducement, seduction, siren song*, sitting duck*, snare, sweetener*, temptation, tout, trap, trick; SEE CONCEPTS *32,529*

lure [v] *attract, seduce*
allure, bag, bait, beckon, beguile, bewitch, cajole, captivate, capture, catch, charm, come on*, decoy, drag, draw, enchant, ensnare, entice, fascinate, grab, haul, hit on*, hook, inveigle, invite, lead on, pull, rope, steer, suck in*, sweep off one's feet*, tempt, train, turn on; SEE CONCEPT *11*

lurid [adj] *shocking, gruesome*
ashen, bloody, deep, disgusting, distinct, exaggerated, extreme, fiery, ghastly, gory*, graphic, grim, grisly, hideous, horrible, horrid, horrifying, livid, low-down, macabre, melodramatic, obscene, off-color*, offensive, purple*, racy, raunchy, revolting, rough, salty, sanguine*, savage, sensational, sinister, startling, terrible, terrifying, violent, vivid, yellow*; SEE CONCEPTS *267,537*

lurk [v] *hide; move stealthily*
conceal oneself, creep, crouch, go furtively, gumshoe, lie in wait, prowl, skulk, slide, slink, slip, snake, sneak, snoop, stay hidden, steal, wait; SEE CONCEPTS *151,188*

luscious [adj] *delicious, delectable*
adorable, ambrosial, appetizing, choice, darling, delish, deluxe, distinctive, divine, exquisite, flamboyant, flavorsome, heavenly, honeyed, juicy, lush, luxurious, mellow, mouth-watering, nectarious, opulent, ornate, palatable, palatial, piquant, rare, rich, savory, scrumptious, succulent, sumptuous, sweet, toothsome, voluptuous, yummy*; SEE CONCEPTS *574,613*

lush [adj] *profuse and delightful*
abundant, ambrosial, delectable, delicious, deluxe, dense, elaborate, extensive, extravagant, exuberant, flourishing, fresh, grand, green, heavenly, juicy, lavish, luscious, luxuriant, luxurious, opulent, ornate, overgrown, palatial, plush, prodigal, prolific, rank, rich, riotous, ripe, ritzy, scrumptious, sensuous, succulent, sumptuous, teeming, tender, verdant, voluptuous; SEE CONCEPTS *574,589,771*

lust [n] *appetite, passion*
animalism, aphrodisia, appetence, appetition, avidity, carnality, concupiscence, covetousness, craving, cupidity, desire, eroticism, excitement, fervor, greed, hunger, itch, lasciviousness, lechery, lewdness, libido, licentiousness, longing, prurience, pruriency, salaciousness, salacity, sensualism, sensuality, thirst, urge, wantonness, weakness, yen; SEE CONCEPTS *20,709*

lust [v] *desire strongly*
ache, be consumed with desire, be hot for*, covet, crave, hanker, hunger for, itch, long, need, pine, thirst, want, wish, yearn, yen; SEE CONCEPT *20*

luster [n] *gloss, shine*
afterglow, brightness, brilliance, brilliancy, burnish, candescence, dazzle, effulgence, glaze, gleam, glint, glitter, glow, incandescence, iridescence, lambency, luminousness, opalescence, polish, radiance, refulgence, resplendence, sheen, shimmer, sparkle; SEE CONCEPT *620*

lustrous [adj] *glossy, shining*
bright, burnished, dazzling, effulgent, fulgent,

glacé, gleaming, glinting, glistening, glorious, glowing, incandescent, lambent, lucent, luminous, polished, radiant, refulgent, shimmering, shiny, sparkling, splendid, waxy; SEE CONCEPT *617*

lusty [adj] *energetic, healthy*
brawny, dynamic, hale, hearty, potent, powerful, red-blooded, robust, rugged, stalwart, stout, strapping, strenuous, strong, sturdy, tough, vigorous, vital; SEE CONCEPTS *314,485,489*

luxuriant [adj] *profuse, plush*
abundant, ample, copious, deluxe, dense, elaborate, excessive, extravagant, exuberant, fancy, fecund, fertile, flamboyant, flourishing, fruitful, lavish, luscious, lush, opulent, overflowing, palatial, plenteous, plentiful, prodigal, productive, profusive, prolific, rampant, rank, rich, riotous, sumptuous, superabundant, teeming, thriving; SEE CONCEPTS *574,771*

luxuriate [adj] *indulge, prosper*
abound, bask, be in clover*, bloom, burgeon, delight, eat up*, enjoy, feast, flourish, grow, increase, live extravagantly, live high on hog*, live in luxury*, live it up*, love, overdo, relish, revel, riot, roll, rollick, take it easy*, thrive, wallow, wanton; SEE CONCEPTS *539,544,589*

luxurious [adj] *affluent, indulgent*
comfortable, costly, deluxe, easy, elaborate, epicurean, expensive, extravagant, fancy, fit for a king/queen*, gorgeous, grand, grandiose, gratifying, hedonistic, immoderate, imposing, impressive, in the lap of luxury, lavish, luscious, lush, magnificent, majestic, opulent, ostentatious, palatial, pampered, pleasurable, pleasure-loving, plush, plushy, posh, pretentious, rich, ritzy*, self-indulgent, sensual, sensuous, splendid, stately, sumptuous, sybaritic, upscale, voluptuous, well-appointed; SEE CONCEPTS *544,574,589*

luxury [n] *great pleasure, indulgence*
affluence, bliss, comfort, delight, enjoyment, exorbitance, extravagance, frill, gratification, hedonism, high living, immoderation, intemperance, leisure, luxuriousness, opulence, rarity, richness, satisfaction, splendor, sumptuousness, treat, well-being; SEE CONCEPTS *337,388,712*

lying [adj] *dishonest*
committing perjury, deceitful, deceptive, delusive, delusory, dissembling, dissimulating, double-crossing*, double-dealing*, equivocating, false, falsifying, fibbing, guileful, inventing, mendacious, misleading, misrepresenting, misstating, perfidious, prevaricating, shifty, treacherous, tricky, two-faced*, two-timing*, unreliable, untruthful, wrong; SEE CONCEPT *267*

lynching [n] *hanging*
capital punishment, execution, mob justice*, stringing up*, the gallows*, vigilante justice; SEE CONCEPT *252*

lyric [adj] *musical*
choral, coloratura, mellifluous, melodic, melodious, poetic, songful, songlike, tuneful; SEE CONCEPT *594*

lyrical [adj] *musical*
agreeable, blending, chiming, choral, dulcet, emotional, euphonious, expressive, harmonious, lilting, melodic, melodious, operatic, orchestral, passionate, pleasing, poetic, rhapsodic, rhythmic, songful, songlike, soulful, sweet-sounding, symphonic, symphonious, tuneful; SEE CONCEPT *594*

lyricist [n] *songwriter*
composer, lyrist, musician, music writer, poet, songsmith, songwriter; SEE CONCEPT *352*

M

macabre [adj] *eerie; deathlike*
cadaverous, deathly, dreadful, frightening, frightful, ghastly, ghostly, ghoulish, grim, grisly, gruesome, hideous, horrible, horrid, lurid, morbid, offensive, scary, spookish, spooky, terrible, unearthly, weird; SEE CONCEPTS *537,547*

macaroni [n] *pasta*
noodles, penne, shells, spaghetti, tortellini; SEE CONCEPTS *457,460,461*

Machiavellian [adj] *scheming*
artful, astute, calculating, conniving, contriving, crafty, cunning, deceitful, devious, expedient, opportunist, plotting, shrewd, sly, underhanded, unscrupulous, wily; SEE CONCEPTS *401,545*

machinate [v] *maneuver, plot*
cogitate, collude, come up with, connive, conspire, contrive, design, devise, engineer, finagle, hatch, intrigue, invent, plan, play games*, promote, pull strings*, scheme, trump up*, wangle; SEE CONCEPT *36*

machination [n] *maneuver, plot*
artifice, cabal, conspiracy, design, device, dirty work*, dodge*, intrigue, monkey business*, on the make*, ploy, practice, ruse, scheme, sellout, skullduggery*, song and dance*, stratagem, trick; SEE CONCEPT *660*

machine [n1] *device that performs a task*
apparatus, appliance, automaton, automobile, computer, contraption, contrivance, engine, gadget, implement, instrument, mechanism, motor, robot, thingamabob*, tool, vehicle, widget*; SEE CONCEPT *463*

machine [n2] *well-run political organization*
agency, lineup, machinery, movement, party, ring, setup, structure, system; SEE CONCEPT *301*

machine [n3] *person who acts automatically*
agent, automaton, clone, drudge, grind, laborer, mechanical, puppet, robot, zombie*; SEE CONCEPTS *348,423*

machinery [n] *devices performing work*
accouterment, agency, agent, apparatus, appliance, channel, contraption, contrivance, engine, equipment, gadget, gear, habiliments, implement, instrument, materiel, means, mechanism, medium, method, motor, organ, outfit, paraphernalia, shifts, structure, system, tackle, tool, utensil, vehicle, works; SEE CONCEPTS *463,770*

machismo [n] *masculinity*
macho*, male, manful, manliness, mannish, masculine, muscular, virile; SEE CONCEPTS *371,408,648*

macho [adj] *masculine*
aggressive, cocky, courageous, manful, manly, potent, ultramasculine, virile; SEE CONCEPTS *371,408,648*

mad [adj1] *crazy, insane*
aberrant, absurd, bananas*, batty, crazed, cuckoo*, daft, delirious, demented, deranged, distracted, fantastic, foolhardy, foolish, frantic, frenetic, frenzied, illogical, imprudent, invalid, irrational, kooky*, loony*, ludicrous, lunatic, mental, non compos mentis, nonsensical, nutty*, off one's rocker*, of unsound mind, out of one's mind*, preposterous, psychotic, rabid, raving, senseless, unbalanced, unhinged, unreasonable, unsafe, unsound, unstable, wacky*; SEE CONCEPTS *403,529*

mad [adj2] *angry*
abandoned, agitated, berserk, distracted, distraught, enraged, exasperated, excited, frantic, frenetic, fuming, furious, incensed, infuriated, irritated, livid, provoked, raging, resentful, seeing red*, uncontrolled, very upset, wild, wrathful; SEE CONCEPT *403*

mad [adj3] *enthusiastic; in love*
ardent, avid, crazy, daft, devoted, enamoured, enthused, fanatical, fond, hooked*, impassioned, infatuated, keen, nuts*, wild, zealous; SEE CONCEPTS *32,403*

madcap [adj] *crazy, impulsive*
brash, foolhardy, foolish, frivolous, harebrained*, heedless, hotheaded, ill-advised, imprudent, incautious, inconsiderate, lively, rash, reckless, stupid, thoughtless, wild; SEE CONCEPT *548*

madden [v] *make angry*
anger, annoy, bother, craze, derange, distract, drive crazy, drive insane, drive out of mind*, drive to distraction*, enrage, exasperate, frenzy, incense, inflame, infuriate, ire, irritate, make see red*, pester, possess, provoke, shatter, steam up*, umbrage, unbalance, unhinge*, upset, vex; SEE CONCEPTS *7,19*

maddening [adj] *irritating*
aggravating, annoying, exasperating, frustrating, infuriating, provoking, riling, troubling, trying, vexatious; SEE CONCEPTS *529,565*

made-up [adj] *invented mentally*
fabricated, false, fictional, imaginary, make-believe, mythical, prepared, specious, trumped-up, unreal, untrue; SEE CONCEPT *582*

madhouse [n] *place where mentally ill live; place full of commotion*
asylum, bedlam, chaos, insane asylum, loony bin*, mental hospital, mental institution, pandemonium, psychiatric hospital, sanitarium, turmoil, uproar; SEE CONCEPTS *312,449,516,674*

madly [adj] *wildly, fiercely*
absurdly, crazily, deliriously, dementedly, desperately, devotedly, distractedly, energetically, exceedingly, excessively, excitedly, extremely, foolishly, frantically, frenziedly, furiously, hard, hastily, hurriedly, hysterically, insanely, intensely, irrationally, like mad, ludicrously, nonsensically, passionately, psychotically, quickly, rabidly, rapidly, rashly, recklessly, senselessly, something fierce, speedily, stormily, to distraction, tumultously/tumultuously, turbulently, unreasonably, violently; SEE CONCEPTS *537,540,544*

madness [n] *insanity*
aberration, absurdity, craziness, delirium, delusion, dementia, derangement, fanaticism, foolishness, hysteria, irrationality, lunacy, madness, mania, mental disorder, mental illness, neurosis, phobia, psychopathy, psychosis, stupidity, unbalance; SEE CONCEPTS *316,410*

lu
ma

mad person [*n*] *person who is considered mentally ill*
bedlamite, crazy person, demented, deranged, idiot, imbecile, loon, lunatic, maniac, mental case*, patient, psycho*, psychopath, psychotic, raver*, schizophrenic, sociopath; SEE CONCEPTS *412,423*

maelstrom [*n1*] *agitation*
bedlam, chaos, confusion, disorder, flap*, fuss, pandemonium, turbulence, turmoil, uproar; SEE CONCEPTS *230,674*

maelstrom [*n2*] *whirlpool*
eddy, stir, swirl, undercurrent, undertow, vortex, whirl; SEE CONCEPT *514*

magazine [*n1*] *periodic publication*
annual, bimonthly, biweekly, booklet, broadside, brochure, circular, daily, digest, gazette, glossy, joint, journal, manual, monthly, newsletter, newspaper, organ, pamphlet, paper, periodical, pulp*, quarterly, rag*, review, semiweekly, sheet*, slick, throwaway*, weekly; SEE CONCEPT *280*

magazine [*n2*] *arsenal of weapons*
ammunition dump, armory, cache, depository, depot, munitions dump, repertory, repository, store, storehouse, warehouse; SEE CONCEPTS *321,500*

magic [*n*] *supernatural power; appearance of impossible feats by tricks*
abracadabra*, alchemy, allurement, astrology, augury, bewitchment, black art, conjuring, conjury, devilry, diabolism, divination, enchantment, exorcism, fascination, foreboding, fortune-telling, hocuspocus*, horoscopy, illusion, incantation, legerdemain, magnetism, necromancy, occultism, power, prediction, presage, prestidigitation, prophecy, rune, sleight of hand, soothsaying, sorcery, sortilege, spell, superstition, taboo, thaumaturgy, trickery, voodoo, voodooism, witchcraft, wizardry; SEE CONCEPTS *370,689*

magician [*n*] *person who performs supernatural feats or tricks*
archimage, charmer, conjurer, diabolist, diviner, enchanter, enchantress, exorciser, exorcist, fortune-teller, genie, genius, illusionist, marvel, medicine person, medium, miracle worker, necromancer, prophet, satanist, seer, shaman, siren, soothsayer, sorcerer, spellbinder, thaumaturge, theurgist, trickster, virtuoso, voodoo, warlock, witch, witch doctor, wizard; SEE CONCEPTS *352,361*

magic/magical [*adj*] *bewitching, charming*
bewitched, charismatic, clairvoyant, conjuring, demoniac, diabolic, eerie, enchanted, enchanting, ensorcelled, entranced, entrancing, extraordinary, fascinating, fiendish, ghostly, haunted, imaginary, magnetic, marvelous, miraculous, mysterious, mystic, mythical, necromantic, occult, otherworldly, parapsychological, runic, sorcerous, spectral, spellbinding, spellbound, spiritualistic, spooky, telekinetic, thaumaturgic, tranced, uncanny, unusual, weird, witching, witchlike, wizardly, wonderful; SEE CONCEPTS *537,548,582*

magistrate [*n*] *civil officer*
bailiff, JP, judge, justice, justice of the peace; SEE CONCEPT *354*

magnanimous [*adj*] *giving and kind*
all heart, altruistic, beneficent, benevolent, big,

bighearted, bountiful, charitable, considerate, forgiving, free, generous, great, greathearted, handsome, has heart in right place*, highminded, kindly, knightly, liberal, lofty, loose, munificent, noble, openhanded, Santa Claus*, selfless, soft*, soft-touch*, ungrudging, unselfish, unstinting; SEE CONCEPTS *404,542*

magnate [*n*] *important person, usually in business*
aristocrat, bigwig*, businessperson, capitalist, captain of industry, chief, figure, financier, industrialist, leader, lion*, merchant, mogul, name, noble, notable, peer, personage, plutocrat, tycoon, VIP*; SEE CONCEPT *347*

magnetic [*adj*] *drawing, attractive*
alluring, appealing, arresting, bewitching, captivating, charismatic, charming, enchanting, entrancing, fascinating, hypnotic, inviting, irresistible, mesmerizing, pulling, seductive; SEE CONCEPTS *404,537*

magnetism [*n*] *charm, attractiveness*
allure, appeal, attraction, captivatingness, charisma, draw, drawing power, enchantment, fascination, glamour, hypnotism, influence, lure, magic, mesmerism, power, pull, seductiveness, spell, witchcraft, witchery; SEE CONCEPTS *411,676*

magnificent [*adj*] *glorious, wonderful*
arresting, august, brilliant, chivalric, commanding, elegant, elevated, exalted, excellent, fine, glittering, gorgeous, grand, grandiose, highminded, imperial, imposing, impressive, lavish, lofty, luxurious, magnanimous, magnific, majestic, noble, opulent, outstanding, palatial, plush, pompous, posh, proud, radiant, regal, resplendent, rich, royal, smashing, splendid, standout, stately, striking, sublime, sumptuous, superb, superior, superlative, swanky, towering, transcendent; SEE CONCEPTS *485,572*

magnify [*v1*] *enlarge, intensify*
aggrandize, aggravate, amplify, augment, bless, blow up, boost, build up, deepen, dignify, dilate, distend, enhance, ennoble, eulogize, exalt, expand, extend, glorify, heighten, hike, hike up, increase, inflate, intensate, jack up, jump up, mount, multiply, pad, pyramid, redouble, rise, rouse, run up, step up, sweeten, swell; SEE CONCEPTS *236,244,245*

magnify [*v2*] *exaggerate, blow out of proportion*
aggravate, blow up*, boost, color, dramatize, embellish, embroider, enhance, fudge*, inflate, make mountain of molehill*, overcharge, overdo, overdraw, overemphasize, overestimate, overplay, overrate, overstate, overstress, pad*, puff up*, pyramid; SEE CONCEPTS *49,69,266*

magnitude [*n1*] *importance*
consequence, degree, eminence, grandeur, greatness, import, mark, moment, momentousness, note, pith, significance, signification, weight, weightiness; SEE CONCEPT *668*

magnitude [*n2*] *size*
admeasurement, amount, amplitude, bigness, breadth, bulk, capacity, compass, dimension, dimensions, enormity, enormousness, expanse, extent, greatness, hugeness, immensity, intensity, largeness, mass, measure, measurement, proportion, proportions, quantity, range, reach, sizableness, space, strength, tremendousness, vastness, volume; SEE CONCEPT *730*

maharishi [*n*] *spiritual leader*
guru, master, mentor, mystic, spiritual guide, swami, teacher; SEE CONCEPT *350*

maiden [*adj*] *earliest*
beginning, first, fresh, inaugural, initial, initiatory, intact, introductory, new, original, pioneer, primary, prime, unbroached, untapped, untried, unused; SEE CONCEPTS *548,585*

mail [*n*] *written correspondence; system for sending correspondence*
air mail, communication, junk mail, letter, package, parcel, post, postal service, postcard, post office; SEE CONCEPTS *271,770*

mail [*v*] *send through the postal system*
dispatch, drop, express, forward, post, send by mail, transmit; SEE CONCEPT *217*

maim [*v*] *cripple, put out of action*
batter, blemish, break, castrate, crush, damage, deface, disable, disfigure, dismember, disqualify, gimp*, hack, hamstring*, harm, hog-tie*, hurt, impair, incapacitate, injure, lame, mangle, mar, massacre, maul, mayhem, mutilate, spoil, truncate, warp, wound; SEE CONCEPT *246*

main [*adj1*] *principal, predominant*
capital, cardinal, central, chief, controlling, critical, crucial, essential, foremost, fundamental, head, leading, major, necessary, outstanding, paramount, particular, preeminent, premier, prevailing, primary, prime, special, star, stellar, supreme, vital; SEE CONCEPTS *546,567,829*

main [*adj2*] *absolute, utter*
brute, direct, downright, entire, mere, only, pure, sheer, simple, undisguised, utmost; SEE CONCEPT *535*

main [*n*] *pipe for system*
cable, channel, conduit, duct, line, trough, trunk; SEE CONCEPT *494*

mainly [*adv*] *for the most part*
above all, chiefly, essentially, first and foremost, generally, in general, in the main, largely, mostly, most of all, on the whole, overall, predominantly, primarily, principally, substantially, to the greatest extent, usually; SEE CONCEPTS *530,544,772*

mainstay [*n*] *chief support*
anchor, backbone, brace, bulwark, buttress, crutch*, good right arm*, linchpin*, maintainer, pillar, prop, right-hand person*, sinew, staff, standby, stay, strength, supporter, sustainer, upholder; SEE CONCEPTS *646,712*

mainstream [*adj*] *prevailing*
accepted, average, common, conventional, current, dominant, established, general, normal, popular, predominant, primary, regular, standard, typical, widespread; SEE CONCEPT *530*

maintain [*v1*] *care for, keep up*
advance, carry on, conserve, continue, control, cultivate, finance, go on with, guard, keep, keep going, look after, manage, nurture, perpetuate, persevere, preserve, prolong, protect, provide, renew, repair, retain, save, supply, support, sustain, take care of, uphold; SEE CONCEPTS *134,140*

maintain [*v2*] *assert, claim; argue for*
advocate, affirm, allege, asseverate, attest, aver, avow, back, champion, contend, correct, declare, defend, emphasize, fight for, hold, insist, justify, persist, plead for, profess, protest, rectify, report, right, say, stand by, state, stress, uphold, vindicate; SEE CONCEPTS *46,49,68*

maintenance [*n*] *perpetuation, support; sustenance*
aliment, alimentation, alimony, allowance, bacon*, bread, bread and butter*, care, carrying, conservation, continuance, continuation, food, keep, keeping, livelihood, living, nurture, preservation, prolongation, provision, repairs, resources, retainment, salt*, subsistence, supply, sustaining, sustainment, sustention, upkeep, wherewithal; SEE CONCEPTS *134,340,457,712*

majestic [*adj*] *impressive, splendid*
august, awesome, ceremonious, cool, courtly, dignified, elevated, exalted, fab*, grand, grandiose, imperial, imposing, lofty, magnific, magnificent, marvelous, mind-blowing*, monumental, noble, out of this world*, pompous, regal, royal, smashing, sovereign, stately, stunning, sublime, sumptuous, superb; SEE CONCEPTS *567,572,574*

major [*adj1*] *bigger*
above, better, big, chief, considerable, dominant, elder, exceeding, extensive, extreme, greater, hefty, higher, large, larger, large-scale, leading, main, most, oversized, primary, senior, sizable, superior, supreme, ultra, upper, uppermost; SEE CONCEPTS *574,773*

major [*adj2*] *important*
big, chief, critical, crucial, dangerous, grave, great, grievous, heavyweight, influential, life and death*, main, major-league, meaningful, notable, outstanding, overshadowing, preeminent, principal, radical, serious, significant, star, stellar, top, vital, weighty; SEE CONCEPT *568*

majority [*n1*] *plurality, most*
best part*, bulk, greater number, greater part, larger part, lion's share*, mass, max*, more, more than half*, preponderance, superiority; SEE CONCEPTS *766,829,835*

majority [*n2*] *adulthood*
age of consent, drinking age, estate, full age, legal maturity, manhood, maturity, prime, prime of life*, ripe age*, seniority, voting age, womanhood; SEE CONCEPTS *715,817*

make [*v1*] *create, build*
accomplish, adjust, arrange, assemble, beget, brew, bring about, cause, compose, conceive, constitute, construct, cook, cook up*, dash off*, draw on, dream up, effect, engender, fabricate, fashion, forge, form, frame, generate, get ready, give rise to, hatch, initiate, invent, knock off*, lead to, manufacture, mold, occasion, originate, parent, prepare, procreate, produce, put together, secure, shape, spawn, synthesize, tear off, throw together*, whip, whip out*; SEE CONCEPTS *168,173,205,221*

make [*v2*] *induce, compel*
bring about, cause, coerce, concuss, constrain, dragoon, drive, effect, force, horn in*, impel, impress, initiate, interfere, meddle, oblige, press, pressurize, prevail upon, require, secure, shotgun, start, tamper; SEE CONCEPTS *14,221*

make [*v3*] *designate, appoint*
advance, assign, constitute, create, delegate, elect, finger, install, invest, name, nominate, ordain, proffer, select, tap, tender; SEE CONCEPTS *50,88*

make [*v4*] *enact, execute*
act, carry on, carry out, carry through, conduct, declare, decree, do, draft, draw up, effect, engage in, establish, fix, form, formulate, frame, legis-

late, pass, perform, practice, prepare, prosecute, wage; SEE CONCEPTS *91,100,242*

make [*v5*] *add up to; constitute*
amount to, come to, compose, compound, comprise, construct, embody, equal, fabricate, form, make up, mix, organize, put together, represent, structure, synthesize, texture; SEE CONCEPTS *664,667*

make [*v6*] *estimate, infer*
calculate, collect, conclude, deduce, deduct, derive, dope out, draw, figure, gather, gauge, judge, reckon, suppose, think; SEE CONCEPTS *15,37*

make [*v7*] *earn, acquire*
bring home bacon*, bring in, clean up*, clear, gain, get, harvest, hustle, net, obtain, pull, pull down*, rate, realize, reap, receive, secure, sock*, take in; SEE CONCEPTS *120,124,351*

make [*v8*] *arrive, aim at*
advance, arrive at, arrive in time, attain, bear, break for, catch, get to, go, head, light out, meet, move, proceed, progress, reach, set out, strike out, take off; SEE CONCEPTS *159,224*

make-believe [*adj*] *imagined, unreal*
acted, dream, false, fantasized, fantasy, fictional, fraudulent, imaginary, made-up, mock, pretend, pretended, sham, simulated; SEE CONCEPTS *529,582*

make-believe [*n*] *unreality*
charade, disguise, dissimulation, dream, fairy tale, fakery, fantasy, imagination, pageant, playacting, pretense, pretension, pretentiousness, sham; SEE CONCEPTS *689,725*

make believe [*v*] *pretend, dream*
act as if, act as though, counterfeit, enact, fantasize, feign, fool, imagine, play, playact*, simulate; SEE CONCEPTS *12,59*

make off [*v*] *flee, run away*
abscond, bolt*, clear, cut and run, decamp, depart, escape, fly*, go, leave, make away, quit, retire, run, run for it, run off, scamper, scoot, skedaddle*, skip*, withdraw; SEE CONCEPTS *102,150,195*

make out [*v1*] *see, recognize*
detect, discern, discover, distinguish, espy, notice, observe, perceive, remark; SEE CONCEPT *626*

make out [*v2*] *understand*
accept, catch, collect, compass, comprehend, conclude, decipher, deduce, deduct, derive, dig, fathom, follow, gather, grasp, infer, judge, perceive, realize, recognize, see, take in, work out; SEE CONCEPTS *15,18*

make out [*v3*] *get by, succeed*
accomplish, achieve, do, do well enough, do with, endure, fare, flourish, get along, get on, manage, muddle through, prosper, score, thrive; SEE CONCEPTS *23,91,140*

makeshift [*adj*] *temporary*
alternative, Band-Aid*, expedient, hit-or-miss*, make-do*, provisional, quick-and-dirty*, slapdash*, stopgap, substitute, temp, throwaway*; SEE CONCEPTS *551,560*

makeshift [*n*] *temporary help*
expediency, expedient, last resort, pis aller, recourse, refuge, replacement, resort, resource, shift, stopgap, substitute; SEE CONCEPTS *658,712*

makeup [*n1*] *cosmetics*
blush, face*, foundation, greasepaint, lipstick, maquillage, paint, pancake, powder*; SEE CONCEPT *446*

makeup [*n2*] *structure, composition*
architecture, arrangement, assembly, configuration, constitution, construction, content, contents, design, form, format, formation, layout, order, ordering, organization, plan, scheme, setup, shape, spread, style; SEE CONCEPT *757*

makeup [*n3*] *person's character*
build, cast, complexion, constitution, disposition, fiber, figure, frame of mind, grain, humor, individualism, individuality, make, mold, nature, personality, stamp, stripe, temper, temperament, vein; SEE CONCEPT *411*

make up [*v1*] *create*
ad-lib*, blend, coin, combine, compose, compound, concoct, construct, contrive, cook up*, devise, dream up, fabricate, fake it, fashion, fix, formulate, frame, fuse, hatch, improv*, improvise, invent, join, knock off, make, meld, merge, mingle, mix, originate, play by ear*, prepare, pretend, put together, ready, trump up, whip up*, wing it*, write; SEE CONCEPTS *173,202*

make up [*v2*] *comprise, constitute*
complete, compose, consist, fill, form, furnish, include, make, meet, provide, supply; SEE CONCEPT *643*

make up [*v3*] *compensate, reconcile*
accommodate, atone, balance, bury the hatchet*, come to terms, compose, conciliate, counterbalance, counterpoise, countervail, forgive and forget, make amends, make peace, mend, offset, outweigh, pacify, recompense, redeem, redress, requite, set off, settle, shake hands; SEE CONCEPTS *126,384*

maladjusted [*adj*] *maladapted*
abnormal, disturbed*, messed up*, muddled, neurotic, unfit, unstable; SEE CONCEPT *547*

maladroit [*adj1*] *awkward, clumsy*
all thumbs*, blundering, bumbling, bungling, clunky, floundering, gauche, halting, heavy-handed, inept, inexpert, klutzy*, lumbering, stumbling, two left feet*, ungraceful, unhandy, unskillful; SEE CONCEPTS *401,584*

maladroit [*adj2*] *tactless*
brash, gauche, impolitic, inconsiderate, inelegant, insensitive, thoughtless, undiplomatic, untactful, untoward; SEE CONCEPT *401*

malady [*n*] *disease*
ache, affection, affliction, ailment, attack, blight, bug*, cancer, complaint, condition, contagion, debility, disability, disorder, distemper, epidemic, fever, flu, ill health, illness, infection, infirmity, inflammation, plague, sickness, syndrome, virus; SEE CONCEPT *306*

malaise [*n*] *depression, sickness*
angst, anxiety, debility, decrepitude, despair, discomfort, disquiet, distress, doldrums, enervation, feebleness, illness, infirmity, infirmness, lassitude, melancholy, pain, sickliness, unease, uneasiness, unhealthiness, weakness; SEE CONCEPTS *316,410*

malarky [*n*] *nonsense*
absurdity, babble, balderdash*, baloney*, bombast, bull*, bunk*, drivel, foolishness, gibberish, giddiness, hogwash*, hot air*, jive*, poppycock*, prattle, rubbish, silliness, trash*; SEE CONCEPTS *230,388,633*

malcontent [*adj*] *dissatisfied*
belly-aching, complaining, discontented, disgruntled, unhappy, unsatisfied; SEE CONCEPT *403*

male [*adj*] *masculine*
macho*, manful, manlike, manly, paternal, potent, virile; SEE CONCEPTS *371,408*

male [*n*] *man*
boy, brother, father, fellow, gent*, gentleman, grandfather, guy, he, husband, Mr., sir, son; SEE CONCEPT *419*

malediction [*n*] *curse*
anathema, commination, curse word, cuss, cuss word, damn, damnation, damning, darn, denunciation, dirty name*, dirty word*, execration, expletive, four-letter word*, imprecation, jinx, no-no*, oath, swear word, whammy*; SEE CONCEPT *278*

malevolent [*adj*] *hateful*
bad-natured, baleful, catty*, despiteful, dirty, evil, evil-minded, hellish, hostile, lousy, malicious, malign, malignant, murder, murderous, pernicious, poison, rancorous, rough, sinister, spiteful, tough, vengeful, vicious, vindictive, waspish, wicked; SEE CONCEPTS *401,542*

malformation [*n*] *deformity*
abberation, abnormality, defect, disfigurement, impairment, injury, malconformation, misshape, monstrosity, mutation; SEE CONCEPT *580*

malformed [*adj*] *distorted*
abnormal, contorted, crooked, deformed, grotesque, irregular, misshapen, twisted, warped; SEE CONCEPT *486*

malfunction [*n*] *breakdown, failure*
bug*, defect, fault, flaw, glitch*, gremlin*, impairment, slip; SEE CONCEPTS *658,674*

malice [*n*] *hate, vengefulness*
acerbity, animosity, animus, antipathy, bad blood, bane, bile, bitterness, despite, despitefulness, dirt, dislike, down, enmity, evil, grudge, hatefulness, hatred, hostility, ill will, implacability, malevolence, maliciousness, malignance, malignity, meanness, mordacity, poison, rancor, repugnance, resentment, spite, spitefulness, spleen, umbrage, venom, viciousness, vindictiveness; SEE CONCEPT *29*

malicious [*adj*] *hateful*
awful, bad-natured, baleful, beastly, bitter, catty*, cussed, deleterious, despiteful, detrimental, envious, evil, evil-minded, green*, green-eyed*, gross*, ill-disposed, injurious, jealous, low, malevolent, malign, malignant, mean, mischievous, nasty, noxious, ornery, pernicious, petty, poisonous, rancorous, resentful, spiteful, uncool*, vengeful, venomous, vicious, virulent, wicked; SEE CONCEPTS *267,401,542*

malign [*adj*] *hurtful, injurious*
antagonistic, antipathetic, bad, baleful, baneful, deleterious, despiteful, destructive, detrimental, evil, harmful, hateful, hostile, inimical, malefic, maleficent, malevolent, malignant, noxious, pernicious, rancorous, sinister, spiteful, vicious, wicked; SEE CONCEPTS *267,537,542*

malign [*v*] *slander, defame*
abuse, accuse, asperse, backbite*, bad-mouth*, befoul, besmirch, bespatter, blacken, calumniate, cast aspersion, curse, decry, defile, denigrate, depreciate, derogate, detract, dirty*, disparage, harm, injure, insult, misrepresent, mudsling, opprobriate, pollute, rap, revile, roast*, run down*, scandalize, slur, smear, soil, spatter*, speak ill of, stain, sully, taint, take a swipe at*, tarnish, tear down, traduce, vilify, villainize, vituperate; SEE CONCEPTS *44,52,54,63*

malignant [*adj*] *diseased*
cancerous, deadly, destructive, fatal, internecine, lethal, mortal, pestilential, poisonous; SEE CONCEPT *314*

malingerer [*n*] *slacker*
dodger, goof-off, idler, loafer, shirker; SEE CONCEPT *412*

mall [*n*] *commercial complex with many individual retail stores*
commercial center, market, mart, mini-mart, plaza, shopping center, shopping mall; SEE CONCEPTS *325,439,449*

mall [*n1*] *shopping center*
marketplace, shopping complex, shopping mall, shopping plaza; SEE CONCEPTS *323,333,449*

mall [*n2*] *promenade*
alameda, boardwalk, boulevard, esplanade, parade, public walk, walk; SEE CONCEPT *501*

malleable [*adj*] *pliable*
adaptable, compliant, ductile, flexible, governable, go-with-the-flow*, impressionable, manageable, moldable, plastic, pliant, putty in hands*, rolls with punches*, soft, submissive, supple, tractable, tractile, transformable, workable, yielding; SEE CONCEPTS *403,485*

malnutrition [*n*] *poor nutrition*
anorexia nervosa, bulimia, dietary deficiency, hunger, malnourishment, starvation, undernourishment; SEE CONCEPTS *20,709*

malodorous [*adj*] *foul-smelling*
bad, decayed, decomposed, fetid, foul, frowzy, funky*, fusty, gamy*, high*, infested, lousy, mephitic, musty, nasty, nauseating, noisome, noxious, off*, offensive, pestilential, poisonous, polluted, putrid, rancid, rank, reeking, rotten, smelly, stale, stenchful, stinking, strong, tainted, vile; SEE CONCEPT *598*

malpractice [*n*] *abuse, misconduct*
carelessness, dereliction, malefaction, misbehavior, misdeed, mismanagement, negligence, offense, transgression, violation; SEE CONCEPTS *101,156,310,324*

mammoth [*adj*] *huge*
behemothic, colossal, elephantine, enormous, gargantuan, giant, gigantic, high, immense, jumbo, large, leviathan, long, massive, mighty, monstrous, monumental, mountainous, prodigious, stupendous, titanic, vast; SEE CONCEPT *773*

man [*n2*] *male human*
beau, boyfriend, brother, father, fellow, gentleman, grandfather, guy, he, husband, Mr., nephew, papa, sir, son, spouse, swain*, uncle; SEE CONCEPT *419*

manacle [*n*] *handcuff*
bond, bracelet, chain, fetter, iron, pinion, shackle; SEE CONCEPT *497*

manage [*v1*] *be in charge, control*
administer, advocate, boss, call the shots*, call upon, captain, care for, carry on, command, concert, conduct, counsel, designate, direct, disburse, dominate, engage in, engineer, execute, govern, guide, handle, head, hold down*, influence, instruct, maintain, manipulate, minister, officiate, operate, oversee, pilot, ply, preside, regulate, request, rule, run, run the show, steer, superintend, supervise, take care of, take over, take the helm*, train, use, watch, watch over, wield; SEE CONCEPTS *94,117*

manage [*v2*] *accomplish*
achieve, arrange, bring about, bring off, carry out, con*, contrive, cook*, cope with, deal with, doctor*, effect, engineer, execute, finagle, fix, jockey*, plant*, play games*, pull strings*, push around, put one over*, rig*, scam*, succeed, swing, upstage, wangle*, work; SEE CONCEPTS *91,706*

manage [*v3*] *survive, get by*
bear up, carry on, cope, endure, fare, get along*, get on*, make do*, make out*, muddle, scrape by*, shift, stagger; SEE CONCEPTS *23,407*

manageable [*adj*] *controllable*
amendable, convenient, docile, easy, feasible, governable, obedient, submissive, tamable, tractable, trained, workable; SEE CONCEPTS *401,404*

management [*n1*] *persons running an organization*
administration, authority, board, bosses, brass, directorate, directors, employers, execs*, executive, executives, executive suite, front office*, head, mainframe*, management, micro management*, person upstairs*, top brass*, upstairs*; SEE CONCEPT *325*

management [*n2*] *running an organization*
administration, care, charge, command, conduct, control, direction, governance, government, guidance, handling, intendance, manipulation, operation, oversight, rule, superintendence, superintendency, supervision; SEE CONCEPTS *117,324*

manager [*n*] *person who runs organization*
administrator, boss, comptroller, conductor, controller, director, exec*, executive, governor, handler, head, head person, officer, official, organizer, overseer, producer, proprietor, slavedriver*, straw boss*, superintendent, supervisor, zookeeper*; SEE CONCEPT *347*

mandate [*n*] *authority, order*
authorization, behest, bidding, blank check*, carte blanche*, charge, command, commission, decree, dictate, directive, edict, fiat, go-ahead*, green light*, imperative, injunction, instruction, okay*, precept, sanction, warrant, word*; SEE CONCEPTS *318,685*

mandatory [*adj*] *required, necessary*
binding, commanding, compelling, compulsatory, compulsory, de rigueur, essential, forced, imperative, imperious, indispensable, involuntary, irremissible, needful, obligatory, requisite; SEE CONCEPT *546*

maneuver [*n1*] *move, tactic*
action, angle, artifice, contrivance, curveball, demarche, device, dodge, fancy footwork*, feint, finesse, gambit, game, gimmick, intrigue, jig*, machination, manipulation, measure, movement, plan, play, plot, ploy, procedure, proceeding, ruse, scheme, shenanigans*, shuffle*, step, stratagem, stunt, subterfuge, trick; SEE CONCEPTS *6,660*

maneuver [*n2*] *military practice, operation*
battle, deployment, drill, evolution, exercise, measure, movement, parade, plan, procedure, proceeding, stratagem, tactics, war games; SEE CONCEPT *320*

maneuver [*v1*] *plan, scheme*
angle, beguile, cheat, come up with, con*, conspire, contrive, cook, design, devise, doctor, engineer, exploit, fence, finagle, finesse, go around,

intrigue, jockey, leave holding the bag*, machinate, manage, manipulate, move, navigate, operate, play, play games*, plot, proceed, pull strings*, push around, put one over*, rig, scam, sham, shift, trick, upstage, wangle, work; SEE CONCEPTS *36,59*

maneuver [*v2*] *direct physically*
deploy, dispense, drive, exercise, guide, handle, manipulate, move, navigate, negotiate, pilot, ply, steer, swing, wield; SEE CONCEPTS *187,225*

mangle [*v*] *mutilate, deform*
batter, break, bruise, butcher, carve, contort, crush, cut, damage, deface, destroy, disfigure, distort, flay, hack, hash, impair, injure, lacerate, maim, mar, maul, rend, ruin, separate, slash, slay, slice, slit, spoil, tear, wound, wreck; SEE CONCEPTS *176,246,252*

mangy [*adj*] *scruffy*
decrepit, dirty, impoverished, indigent, mean, moth-eaten*, poor, ragtag*, shabby, shoddy, sick, sleazy*, squalid, tattered; SEE CONCEPTS *485,621*

manhood/womanhood [*n*] *physical maturity and strength of adult male or female*
adulthood, coming of age*, fecundity, femininity, fertility, manfulness, manliness, masculinity, mettle, potency, virility, womanliness, womanness; SEE CONCEPTS *633,715*

mania [*n*] *fixation, madness*
aberration, ax to grind*, bee*, bee in bonnet*, bug*, bug in ear*, compulsion, craving, craze, craziness, delirium, dementia, derangement, desire, disorder, enthusiasm, fad, fancy, fascination, fetish, fixed idea, frenzy, furor, grabber*, hang-up*, idée fixe, infatuation, insanity, lunacy, monomania, obsession, on the brain*, partiality, passion, preoccupation, rage, thing, tiger*, tiger by the tail*; SEE CONCEPTS *20,32,410,529*

maniac [*n*] *person who is crazy, overenthusiastic*
bedlamite, bigot, crackpot*, enthusiast, fan, fanatic, fiend, flake*, freak, fruitcake*, kook*, loon, loony*, lunatic, madperson, nut*, nutcase*, psycho*, psychopath, schizoid*, screwball*, Section 8*, zealot; SEE CONCEPT *412*

manic/maniacal [*adj*] *overexcited, crazy*
berserk, crazed, demented, deranged, excited, flipped*, flipped out*, freaked out*, freaky*, frenzied, high*, insane, lunatic, mad, nutty*, psychotic, rabid, raving, turned-out, unbalanced, up*, wild; SEE CONCEPT *403*

manifest [*adj*] *clear, obvious*
apparent, big as life*, bold, clear-cut*, conspicuous, crystal clear*, disclosed, distinct, divulged, evidenced, evident, evinced, glaring, noticeable, open, palpable, patent, plain, prominent, revealed, shown, straightforward, told, unambiguous, unmistakable, visible; SEE CONCEPTS *529,576*

manifest [*v*] *exhibit, make plain*
confirm, declare, demonstrate, display, embody, establish, evidence, evince, expose, express, exteriorize, externalize, flash, illustrate, incarnate, let it all hang out*, mark, materialize, objectify, ostend, parade, personalize, personify, personize, proclaim, prove, reveal, set forth, show, show and tell*, showcase, signify, sport, strut, substantiate, suggest, utter, vent, voice, wave around*; SEE CONCEPTS *118,261*

manifestation [*n*] *exhibition, proof*
appearance, demonstration, disclosure, display,

explanation, exposure, expression, indication, instance, mark, materialization, meaning, phenomenon, revelation, show, sign, symptom, token; SEE CONCEPTS *642,672*

manifesto [*n*] *public declaration*
announcement, notice, platform, policy, proclamation, promulgation, public notice, statement of belief; SEE CONCEPTS *271,274,278*

manifold [*adj*] *abundant, many*
assorted, complex, copious, different, diverse, diversified, diversiform, multifarious, multifold, multiform, multiple, multiplied, multitudinous, multivarious, numerous, sundry, varied, various; SEE CONCEPTS *564,762,781*

manipulate [*v1*] *maneuver, handle physically*
employ, feel, finger*, form, manage, mold, operate, ply, shape, swing, thumb*, use, wield, work; SEE CONCEPTS *225,612*

manipulate [*v2*] *change to suit one's desire*
beguile, conduct, control, direct, engineer, exploit, finagle, finesse, guide, handle, influence, jockey, machinate, maneuver, massage, mold, negotiate, play, play games*, pull strings*, pull wires*, push around, shape, steer, upstage, use; SEE CONCEPTS *14,234*

manner [*n1*] *person's behavior, conduct*
address, affectation, affectedness, air, appearance, aspect, bearing, comportment, demeanor, deportment, idiosyncrasy, look, mannerism, mien, peculiarity, presence, style, tone, turn, way; SEE CONCEPTS *411,633,644*

manner [*n2*] *method, approach*
consuetude, custom, fashion, form, genre, habit, habitude, line, means, mode, modus, practice, procedure, process, routine, style, system, tack, technique, tenor, tone, trick, usage, use, vein, way, wise, wont; SEE CONCEPTS *6,660*

manner [*n3*] *class, category*
brand, breed, form, kind, nature, sort, type, variety; SEE CONCEPT *378*

mannered [*adj*] *affected, put-on*
airish*, apish*, artificial, artsy, campy*, chichi*, conscious, gone Hollywood*, highfaluting*, posed, pretentious, self-conscious, stilted, stuck up*, unnatural; SEE CONCEPT *401*

mannerism [*n*] *peculiarity of how someone behaves, acts*
affectation, air, characteristic, eccentricity, foible, habit, idiosyncrasy, oddness, pose, pretension, queerness, quirk, singularity, trait, trick; SEE CONCEPT *644*

mannerly [*adj*] *polite, well-behaved*
charming, civil, civilized, considerate, courteous, decorous, genteel, gracious, polished, refined, respectful, well-bred, well-mannered; SEE CONCEPT *401*

manners [*n*] *polite, refined social behavior*
amenities, bearing, behavior, breeding, carriage, ceremony, civilities, comportment, conduct, courtesy, culture, decorum, demeanor, deportment, dignity, elegance, etiquette, formalities, good breeding, good form, mien, mores, polish, politeness, politesse, propriety, protocol, p's and q's*, refinement, social graces, sophistication, taste, urbanity; SEE CONCEPT *633*

mansion [*n*] *very large house*
abode, building, castle, chateau, dwelling, estate, habitation, hall, home, manor, palace, residence, seat, villa; SEE CONCEPTS *439,516*

manslaughter [*n*] *killing without malicious forethought*
crime, foul play*, hit*, homicide, killing, murder; SEE CONCEPT *252*

manual [*adj*] *done by hand*
chiral, hand-operated, human, not automatic, physical, standard; SEE CONCEPT *544*

manual [*n*] *book giving instruction*
bible, compendium, cookbook, enchiridion, guide, guidebook, handbook, primer, reference book, schoolbook, text, textbook, workbook; SEE CONCEPT *280*

manufacture [*v1*] *build, produce*
accomplish, assemble, carve, cast, cobble*, complete, compose, construct, create, execute, fabricate, fashion, forge, form, frame, fudge together*, machine, make, make up, mass-produce, mill, mold, prefab, process, put together, shape, synthesize, throw together, tool, turn out; SEE CONCEPT *205*

manufacture [*v2*] *concoct, invent*
contrive, cook up*, create, devise, fabricate, hatch, make up, produce, think up, trump up*; SEE CONCEPTS *35,36*

manufacture/manufacturing [*n*] *production of processed goods*
accomplishment, assembling, assembly, casting, completion, composing, composition, construction, creation, doing, erection, fabrication, finishing, forging, formation, making, mass-production, preparing, produce, tooling; SEE CONCEPT *324*

manure [*n*] *fertilizer*
buffalo chips*, compost, cow chips*, cowplop*, droppings, dung, excrement, guano, maul*, meadow muffins*, mulch; SEE CONCEPTS *260,399,429*

manuscript [*n*] *book, script*
article, composition, document, hard copy, palimpsest, text; SEE CONCEPTS *263,271*

many [*adj*] *profuse, abundant*
abounding, alive with, bounteous, bountiful, copious, countless, crowded, divers, frequent, innumerable, legion, lousy with*, manifold, multifarious, multifold, multiplied, multitudinous, myriad, no end of*, numberless, numerous, plentiful, populous, prevalent, rife, several, sundry, teeming, umpteen, uncounted, varied, various; SEE CONCEPTS *762,771*

many [*n*] *abundance; a lot*
gobs*, heaps*, horde, jillion*, large numbers, mass, multitude, oodles*, piles*, plenty, scads*, scores, thousands, throng, tons, umpteen*, whole slew*; SEE CONCEPTS *432,787*

map [*n*] *chart of geographic area*
atlas, delineation, design, diagram, draft, drawing, elevation, globe, graph, ground plan, outline, picture, plan, plat, portrayal, print, projection, sketch, topographical depiction, tracing; SEE CONCEPT *625*

mapmaker [*n*] *cartographer*
mapper, surveyor, topographer; SEE CONCEPTS *37,103,291*

mar [*v*] *hurt, damage*
bend, blemish, blight, blot, break, bruise, deface, deform, detract, ding*, disfigure, foul up, harm, impair, injure, louse up, maim, mangle, mess up*, mutilate, queer*, rough up, ruin, scar, scratch, shake up, spoil, stain, sully, taint, tar-

ma
ma

nish, tweak, vitiate, warp, wreck; SEE CONCEPT
246

marathon [*n*] *long-distance race*
cross-country race, endurance run, test of endurance; SEE CONCEPT *363*

maraud [*v*] *pillage and plunder*
despoil, forage, foray, harass, harry, loot, raid,
ransack, ravage, sack; SEE CONCEPTS *86,139*

marauder [*n*] *pillager, raider*
bandit, buccaneer, corsair, freebooter, looter,
outlaw, pirate, plunderer, ravager, robber, thief;
SEE CONCEPT *412*

march [*v*] *walk with deliberation*
advance, boot, debouch, drill, file, forge ahead,
go on, hoof it*, journey, mount, move, move out,
pace, parade, patrol, pound, pound the pavement*, proceed, progress, promenade, range,
space, stalk, step, step out, stomp, stride, strut,
traipse, tramp, tread; SEE CONCEPT *150*

margin [*n*] *border; room around something*
allowance, bound, boundary, brim, brink, compass, confine, edge, elbowroom*, extra, field,
frame, hem, latitude, leeway, limit, lip, perimeter, periphery, play, rim, scope, selvage, shore,
side, skirt, space, surplus, trimming, verge; SEE
CONCEPTS *270,484,513*

marginal [*adj*] *borderline; slight*
bordering, insignificant, low, minimal, minor,
negligible, on the edge, peripheral, rimming,
small, verging; SEE CONCEPTS *513,789*

marijuana [*n*] *grass, pot*
Acapulco gold*, bhang*, cannabis, Columbian*,
doobie*, dope*, ganja*, hash, hashish, hemp,
herb*, Jamaican*, joint, loco weed*, maryjane*,
Maui wowie*, Mexican*, Panama red*, reefer,
roach, sinsemilla, tea*, weed*; SEE CONCEPT *307*

marina [*n*] *dock*
berth, boat basin, boatyard, harbor, landing,
moorings, pier, port, quay, slip, wharf; SEE CON-
CEPT *439*

marinate [*v*] *soak*
bathe, brine, immerse, marinade, pickle, season,
souse, steep; SEE CONCEPT *256*

marine/maritime [*adj*] *concerning the sea*
abyssal, aquatic, coastal, deep-sea, hydrographic,
littoral, maritime, natatorial, nautical, naval, navigational, Neptunian, oceangoing, oceanic,
oceanographic, of the sea, pelagic, saltwater, sea,
seafaring, seagoing, seashore, seaside, shore; SEE
CONCEPT *536*

mariner [*n*] *person who makes living on the sea*
bluejacket*, captain, crew, mate, navigator,
sailor, salt*, sea dog*, seafarer, shipmate, swab*,
yachtie*; SEE CONCEPTS *348,366*

marionette [*n*] *puppet*
doll, dummy, fantoccini, figurine, manikin, moppet; SEE CONCEPTS *423,446*

marital [*adj*] *concerning marriage*
conjugal, connubial, married, matrimonial, nuptial, spousal, wedded; SEE CONCEPT *555*

maritime [*adj*] *nautical*
aquatic, deep-sea, marine, naval, oceangoing,
oceanic, pelagic, seafaring, seagoing; SEE CON-
CEPT *536*

mark [*n1*] *blemish; character*
autograph, blaze, blot, blotch, brand, brand
name, bruise, check, cross, dent, dot, impression,
imprint, ink, John Hancock*, John Henry*, label,
line, logo, nick, pock, point, record, register, representation, scar, score, scratch, sign, signature,

smudge, splotch, spot, stain, stamp, streak,
stroke, symbol, tag, ticket, trace, trademark, underlining, X*; SEE CONCEPTS *79,284*

mark [*n2*] *characteristic, symptom*
affection, attribute, badge, blaze, brand, character, device, distinction, earmark, emblem, evidence, feature, hallmark, idiosyncrasy, image,
impression, incision, index, indication, indicia,
label, marking, note, particularity, peculiarity,
print, proof, property, quality, seal, sign, significant, stamp, symbol, token, trait, type, virtue;
SEE CONCEPTS *411,644,716*

mark [*n3*] *criterion, standard*
gauge, level, measure, norm, yardstick; SEE CON-
CEPTS *561,783*

mark [*n4*] *goal, target*
aim, ambition, bull's eye*, duty, end, function,
object, objective, prey, purpose, use; SEE CON-
CEPT *659*

mark [*n5*] *importance*
consequence, dignity, distinction, effect, eminence, fame, influence, manifestation, notability,
note, notice, prestige, quality, regard, result,
standing, value; SEE CONCEPTS *346,668*

mark [*v1*] *blemish, stain*
autograph, blaze, blot, blotch, brand, bruise,
chalk, check, dent, dot, impress, imprint, initial,
ink, inscribe, label, letter, nick, pinpoint, point,
print, scar, score, scratch, seal, sign, smudge,
splotch, stamp, streak, stroke, trace, underline,
write, X*; SEE CONCEPTS *79,250*

mark [*v2*] *characterize*
bespeak, betoken, brand, check off, demonstrate,
denote, designate, distinguish, earmark, evidence, evince, exemplify, exhibit, feature, identify, illustrate, indicate, individualize,
individuate, label, manifest, mark off, ostend,
point out, point up*, proclaim, qualify, remark,
set apart, show, show up, signalize, signify, singularize, stake out*, stamp; SEE CONCEPT *261*

mark [*v3*] *see, notice*
attend, behold, chronicle, discern, distinguish,
eye, hearken, mind, note, observe, pay attention,
pay heed, perceive, regard, register, remark, take
notice of, view, watch, write down; SEE CON-
CEPTS *38,626*

marked [*adj*] *apparent, obvious*
arresting, clear, considerable, conspicuous, decided, distinct, evident, manifest, notable, noted,
noticeable, outstanding, patent, pointed, prominent, pronounced, remarkable, salient, signal,
striking; SEE CONCEPTS *485,535,589*

markedly [*adv*] *distinctly*
clearly, considerably, conspicuously, decidedly,
especially, evidently, greatly, manifestly, notably, noticeably, obviously, outstandingly, particularly, patently, remarkably, signally,
strikingly, to a great extent; SEE CONCEPTS
535,544

market [*v*] *package and sell goods*
advertise, barter, display, exchange, merchandise, offer for sale, retail, vend, wholesale; SEE
CONCEPTS *324,345*

marketable [*adj*] *easily sold; in demand*
bankable, commercial, fit, for sale, good, hot*,
merchandisable, merchantable, profitable, sal-
able, sellable, selling, sought after, sound, traffi-
cable, vendible, wanted; SEE CONCEPTS *334,546*

market/mart [*n*] *place, venue for selling goods*
bazaar, bodega, booth, business, chain store, co-

op, corner store, deli, delicatessen, department store, dimestore, drugstore, emporium, exchange, fair, general store, grocery store, mall, mart, outlet, shop, shopping mall, showroom, souk, square, stall, stock exchange, store, supermarket, trading post, truck, variety store, warehouse; SEE CONCEPTS *323,333,449*

maroon [v] *abandon*
beach, cast ashore, cast away, desert, forsake, isolate, leave, leave high and dry*, strand; SEE CONCEPTS *195,384*

marriage [n] *legal joining of two people; a union*
alliance, amalgamation, association, confederation, conjugality, connubiality, consortium, coupling, espousal, holy matrimony, link, match, mating, matrimony, merger, monogamy, nuptials, pledging, sacrament, spousal, tie, tie that binds*, wedded bliss*, wedded state, wedding, wedding bells*, wedding ceremony, wedlock; SEE CONCEPTS *297,388*

marrow [n] *heart, essence*
bottom, core, cream, essentiality, gist, kernel, meat, pith, quick, quintessence, quintessential, soul, spirit, stuff, substance, virtuality; SEE CONCEPT *826*

marry [v] *become husband and wife in legal ceremony*
ally, associate, become one, bond, catch*, combine, conjoin, conjugate, contract, couple, drop anchor*, espouse, get hitched*, get married, join, knit, land*, lead to altar, link, match, mate, merge, one, pledge, plight one's troth, promise, relate, settle down*, take vows, tie, tie the knot*, unify, unite, walk down aisle*, wed, yoke; SEE CONCEPT *297*

marsh [n] *swamp*
bog, estuary, everglade, fen, mire, morass, moss, quag, quagmire, slough, swampland, wetland; SEE CONCEPT *509*

marshal [v] *organize, guide*
align, arrange, array, assemble, collect, conduct, deploy, direct, dispose, distribute, draw up, escort, gather, group, lead, line up, methodize, mobilize, muster, order, rally, rank, shepherd, space, systematize, usher; SEE CONCEPTS *84,117,187*

marshy [adj] *swampy*
boggy, fenny, miry, moory, mucky, paludal, quaggy, soggy; SEE CONCEPT *509*

martial [adj] *having to do with armed hostilities*
aggressive, bellicose, belligerent, combative, hostile, military, pugnacious, soldierly, warlike; SEE CONCEPT *401*

martinet [n] *disciplinarian*
authoritarian, bully, despot, drillmaster, drill sergeant, enforcer, hard master, slavedriver, stickler, taskmaster, tyrant; SEE CONCEPTS *350,354,423*

martyrdom [n] *suffering endured for sake of a cause*
affliction, agonizing, agony, anguish, crucifixion, devotion, distress, mortification, ordeal, pain, persecution, sacrifice, self-immolation, self-sacrifice, torment, torture, unselfishness; SEE CONCEPTS *410,411*

marvel [n] *wonder*
curiosity, genius, miracle, one for the books*, phenomenon, portent, prodigy, sensation, something else*, stunner, whiz; SEE CONCEPTS *529,671*

marvel [v] *be amazed*
be awed, be surprised, feel surprise, gape, gaze, goggle, stand in awe, stare, wonder; SEE CONCEPT *17*

marvelous [adj1] *hard to believe; amazing*
astonishing, astounding, awe-inspiring, awesome, awful, bewildering, breathtaking, confounding, difficult to believe, extraordinary, fabulous, fantastic, implausible, improbable, incomprehensible, inconceivable, incredible, miraculous, phenomenal, prodigious, remarkable, singular, spectacular, staggering, strange, striking, stunning, stupendous, supernatural, surprising, unbelievable, unimaginable, unlikely, unusual, wonderful, wondrous; SEE CONCEPTS *529,552*

marvelous [adj2] *superb, great*
agreeable, astonishing, bad*, boss*, colossal, cool*, divine, dreamy*, enjoyable, excellent, fab*, fabulous, fantastic, glorious, greatest, groovy*, hot*, keen, magnificent, neat*, out of this world*, outrageous, peachy, pleasant, pleasurable, prime*, rewarding, satisfying, sensational, smashing, solid*, solid gold*, spectacular, splendid, stupendous, super, supreme, swell, terrific, wonderful; SEE CONCEPT *574*

masculinity/masculine [n/adj] *manly*
andric, gender, macho*, male, manful, mannish, potent, virile; SEE CONCEPTS *371,372,408,648*

mash [v] *smash, squash*
brew, bruise, chew, crush, decoct, grind, hash, infuse, macerate, masticate, mush up, pound, press, pulp, pulverize, push, reduce, scrunch, squeeze, squish, steep, triturate; SEE CONCEPTS *170,186,208*

mask [n] *false face, cover*
affectation, air*, appearance, aspect, beard*, blind, camouflage, cloak*, concealment, cover-up, disguise, disguisement, dissembling, dissimulation, domino*, facade, fig leaf*, front, guise, hood, masquerade, pose, posture, pretense, pretext, put-on*, screen, semblance, show*, simulation, veil*, veneer, visage, visor, window dressing*; SEE CONCEPTS *450,716*

mask [v] *disguise*
beard, camouflage, cloak, conceal, cover, cover up, defend, dissemble, dissimulate, dress up, front, guard, hide, obscure, protect, safeguard, screen, secrete, shield, veil; SEE CONCEPTS *172,188,384*

masquerade [n] *disguise; social occasion for disguises*
carnival, circus, cloak, color, costume, costume ball, cover, cover-up, deception, dissimulation, domino*, facade, festivity, front, guise, impersonation, imposture, Mardi Gras*, mask, masked ball, masking, mummery, personation, pose, pretense, put-on, revel, screen, show, subterfuge, veil; SEE CONCEPTS *172,188,383,451*

masquerade [v] *disguise*
attitudinize, dissemble, dissimulate, frolic, impersonate, mask, pass as, pass for, pass off, pose, posture, pretend, revel; SEE CONCEPT *59*

mass [n1] *body of matter; considerable portion*
accumulation, aggregate, assemblage, band, batch, block, bulk, bunch, chunk, clot, coagulation, collection, combination, concretion, conglomeration, core, corpus, crowd, entirety, gob, great deal, greater part, group, heap, horde, host, hunk, knot, lion's share*, load, lot, lump, major-

ity, mob, mound, mountain, much, number, object, peck, piece, pile, plurality, preponderance, pyramid, quantity, shock, stack, staple, stockpile, sum, sum total, throng, totality, troop, volume, wad, whole; SEE CONCEPTS *432,787,835*

mass [*n2*] *bulk, measurement*
dimension, extent, greatness, magnitude, size, span, volume; SEE CONCEPT *792*

massacre [*n*] *killing of many*
annihilation, assassination, bloodbath, bloodshed, butchery, carnage, decimation, extermination, genocide, internecion, murder, slaughter, slaying; SEE CONCEPT *252*

massacre [*v*] *kill, often in great numbers*
annihilate, butcher, decimate, depopulate, exterminate, mass murder, murder, slaughter, slay; SEE CONCEPT *252*

massage [*n*] *kneading of body parts*
back rub, beating, chirapsia, manipulation, rolfing*, rubbing, rubbing-down, stroking; SEE CONCEPTS *308,310*

massage [*v*] *knead body parts*
caress, manipulate, pat, press, push, rolf*, rub, rub down, stimulate, stroke; SEE CONCEPTS *208,308,310*

masses [*n*] *public, crowd*
commonalty, common people, great unwashed*, hoi polloi*, lower class, mob, multitude, proletariat, rabble, rank and file*, riffraff*; SEE CONCEPT *417*

massive [*adj*] *large*
big, bulky, colossal, cracking, cumbersome, cumbrous, elephantine, enormous, extensive, gargantuan, gigantic, grand, great, gross, heavy, hefty, huge, hulking, immense, imposing, impressive, mammoth, mighty, monster, monumental, mountainous, ponderous, prodigious, solid, stately, substantial, titanic, towering, tremendous, unwieldy, vast, walloping, weighty, whopping*; SEE CONCEPTS *773,781*

master [*adj1*] *expert*
ace*, adept, crack*, crackerjack*, experienced, masterly, proficient, skilled, skillful; SEE CONCEPT *527*

master [*adj2*] *main*
ascendant, chief, controlling, foremost, grand, great, leading, major, original, overbearing, paramount, predominant, predominate, preponderant, prevalent, prime, principal, regnant, sovereign, supreme; SEE CONCEPT *568*

master [*n1*] *person in charge, female or male*
administrator, boss, captain, chief, chieftain, commandant, commander, commanding officer, conqueror, controller, director, employer, general, governor, guide, guru, head, head person, instructor, judge, lord, manager, matriarch, overlord, overseer, owner, patriarch, pedagogue, preceptor, principal, pro, ruler, schoolmaster/mistress, skipper, slave driver*, spiritual leader, superintendent, supervisor, swami*, taskmaster, teacher, top dog*, tutor, wheel*; SEE CONCEPTS *347,350,354*

master [*n2*] *expert, skilled person, female or male*
ace*, adept, artist, artiste, authority, buff*, champion, connoisseur, conqueror, doctor, doyen, doyenne, genius, guru, maestro, maven, old hand*, old pro*, past master, prima donna*, pro, professional, proficient, pundit, real pro*, sage,

savant, scientist, shark*, victor, virtuoso, whiz*, whiz-bang*, winner, wizard; SEE CONCEPTS *350,366,423*

master [*v1*] *learn; become proficient*
acquire, beat the game*, beat the system*, bone up*, bury yourself in*, comprehend, cram, excel in, gain mastery, get down cold*, get down pat*, get hold of*, get the hang of*, get the knack of*, grasp, grind, hit the books*, learn the ropes*, megastudy*, pick up, study, swamp*, understand; SEE CONCEPTS *31,630*

masterful [*adj*] *expert, skilled*
adept, adroit, clever, consummate, crack, crackerjack*, deft, dexterous, excellent, exquisite, fine, finished, first-rate, master, masterly, preeminent, proficient, skillful, superior, superlative, supreme, transcendent; SEE CONCEPT *527*

masterpiece [*n*] *respected work of art*
chef d'oeuvre, classic, cream*, cream of the crop*, flower, gem*, jewel*, magnum opus, masterstroke, master work, model, monument, perfection, pièce de résistance*, prize, showpiece, standard, tour de force*, treasure; SEE CONCEPT *259*

mastery [*n1*] *command, expertise*
ability, acquirement, adeptness, adroitness, attainment, capacity, cleverness, comprehension, cunning, deftness, dexterity, expertism, expertness, familiarity, finesse, genius, grasp, grip, ken, knack, know-how, knowledge, mastership, power, proficiency, prowess, skill, understanding, virtuosity, wizardry; SEE CONCEPT *630*

match [*n1*] *competition*
bout, contest, engagement, event, game, meet, race, rivalry, sport, test, trial; SEE CONCEPT *363*

match [*n2*] *counterpart, equal*
adversary, analogue, antagonist, approximation, companion, competitor, complement, copy, correlate, countertype, dead ringer*, double, duplicate, equivalent, like, lookalike, mate, opponent, parallel, peer, replica, ringer*, rival, spitting image*, twin; SEE CONCEPTS *664,667,716*

match [*n3*] *couple*
affiliation, alliance, combination, duet, espousal, marriage, mating, pair, pairing, partnership, union; SEE CONCEPTS *297,388*

matching [*adj*] *corresponding, equal*
analogous, comparable, coordinating, double, duplicate, equivalent, identical, like, paired, parallel, same, twin; SEE CONCEPT *566*

matchless [*adj*] *unequalled, unique*
alone, consummate, excellent, exquisite, incomparable, inimitable, nonpareil, only, peerless, perfect, superior, superlative, supreme, unapproached, unmatched, unparalleled, unrivaled; SEE CONCEPT *574*

mate [*n*] *one of a pair; partner*
acquaintance, alter ego, analog, assistant, associate, bedmate, bride, buddy*, chum*, classmate, cohort, colleague, companion, compeer, complement, comrade, concomitant, consort, coordinate, counterpart, coworker, crony, double, duplicate, familiar, friend, groom, helper, helpmate, intimate, match, pal*, peer, playmate, reciprocal, roommate, schoolmate, sidekick*, spouse, twin; SEE CONCEPTS *296,423,664*

mate [*v*] *marry and breed*
cohabit, copulate, couple, crossbreed, generate, join, land*, match, merge, pair, procreate, serve,

ma
ma

tie, tie the knot*, wed, yoke; SEE CONCEPTS 297,375

material [*adj1*] *bodily, tangible*
actual, animal, appreciable, carnal, concrete, corporeal, earthly, fleshly, incarnate, nonspiritual, objective, palpable, perceptible, phenomenal, physical, real, sensible, sensual, substantial, true, worldly; SEE CONCEPT 485

material [*adj2*] *important, relevant*
ad rem, applicable, applicative, apposite, apropos, big, cardinal, consequential, considerable, essential, fundamental, germane, grave, indispensable, intrinsic, key, meaningful, momentous, pertinent, pointful, primary, serious, significant, substantial, vital, weighty; SEE CONCEPT 567

material [*n1*] *matter, fabric*
being, body, bolt, cloth, component, constituent, crop, element, entity, equipment, gear, goods, habiliments, individual, ingredient, machinery, materiel, object, outfit, paraphernalia, staple, stock, stuff, substance, supply, tackle, textile, thing; SEE CONCEPTS 475,523

material [*n2*] *written matter*
data, evidence, facts, information, notes, reading, text, work; SEE CONCEPTS 271,274

materialistic [*adj*] *thinking mainly about physical things*
acquisitive, banausic, carnal, earthly-minded, earthy, greedy, material, mundane, object-oriented, possessive, profane, secular, sensual, temporal, terrestrial, unspiritual; SEE CONCEPT 542

materialize [*v*] *come into being*
actualize, appear, become concrete, become real, become visual, be incarnate, be realized, coalesce, come about, come to pass, corporealize, develop, embody, emerge, entify, evolve, exteriorize, externalize, happen, hypostatize, make real, manifest, metamorphose, objectify, occur, personalize, personify, personize, pragmatize, realize, reify, substantialize, substantiate, symbolize, take form, take place, take shape, turn up, typify, unfold, visualize; SEE CONCEPTS 105,173,184,231,251

maternity [*n*] *period of being pregnant with child*
gestation, maternology, motherhood, parenthood; SEE CONCEPTS 316,817

mathematical [*adj*] *concerning manipulation of numbers*
algebraic, algorithmic, analytical, arithmetical, computative, geometrical, math, measurable, numerical, scientific, trigonometric; SEE CONCEPT 762

mathematics [*n*] *arithmetic*
addition, algebra, calculation, calculus, division, figures, geometry, math, multiplication, numbers, subtraction, trigonometry; SEE CONCEPTS 349,764

matriculate [*v*] *begin, enroll*
enter, join, register, sign up for; SEE CONCEPTS 114,119

matrimonial [*adj*] *married*
betrothed, conjugal, connubial, engaged, epithalamic, espoused, marital, nuptial, spousal, wedded, wedding; SEE CONCEPT 555

matrimony [*n*] *being joined in marriage*
alliance, bells*, conjugality, connubiality, marital rites, marriage, match, nuptials, shotgun wedding*, union, wedding, wedding bells*, wedding ceremony, wedlock; SEE CONCEPT 297

matrix [*n*] *something from which another originates*
cast, forge, form, grid, model, mold, origin, pattern, source, womb; SEE CONCEPT 648

matronly [*adj*] *womanly*
dignified, female, honorable, ladylike, mature, motherly, respected, stately; SEE CONCEPTS 404,555,574

matted [*adj*] *tangled*
disordered, kinky, knotted, rumpled, snarled, tousled, twisted, uncombed; SEE CONCEPT 606

matter [*n1*] *substance*
amount, being, body, constituents, corporeality, corporeity, element, entity, individual, material, materialness, object, phenomenon, physical world, protoplasm, quantity, stuff, substantiality, sum, thing; SEE CONCEPTS 407,433,470

matter [*n2*] *concern, issue*
affair, bag, business, circumstance, episode, event, goings-on*, incident, job, lookout, nub, occurrence, proceeding, question, shooting match*, situation, subject, thing, topic, transaction, undertaking; SEE CONCEPTS 532,696

matter [*n3*] *subject, thesis*
argument, context, focus, head, interest, motif, motive, point, purport, resolution, sense, subject matter, substance, text, theme, topic; SEE CONCEPTS 349,529

matter [*n4*] *significance, meaning*
amount, body, burden, consequence, content, core, extent, gist*, import, importance, magnitude, meat, moment, neighborhood, note, order, pith, range, sense, substance, text, tune, upshot, vicinity, weight; SEE CONCEPTS 651,668

matter [*n5*] *difficulty, problem*
circumstance, complication, distress, grievance, perplexity, predicament, to-do*, trouble, upset, worry; SEE CONCEPTS 666,674

matter [*n6*] *secretion of a sore*
discharge, infection, maturation, purulence, pus, suppuration, ulceration; SEE CONCEPTS 311,467

matter [*v*] *be of consequence, importance*
affect, be important, be of value, be substantive, carry weight, count, cut ice*, express, have influence, imply, import, involve, make a difference, mean, mean something, signify, value, weigh; SEE CONCEPTS 7,19,22,130,682

matter-of-fact [*adj*] *realistic, unembellished*
apathetic, calm, cold, cold-blooded*, deadpan, down-to-earth*, dry, dull, earthy, emotionless, factual, feasible, flat, hard-boiled*, impassive, impersonal, lifeless, mundane, naked*, objective, phlegmatic, plain, practical, pragmatic, prosaic, prosy, serious, sober, stoic, stolid, unaffected, unidealistic, unimaginative, unimpassioned, unsentimental, unvarnished; SEE CONCEPTS 267,582

mature [*adj*] *adult, grown-up*
complete, cultivated, cultured, developed, fit, full-blown, full-fledged, full-grown, fully grown, grown, in full bloom, in one's prime, matured, mellow, mellowed, of age, perfected, prepared, prime, ready, ripe, ripened, seasoned, settled, sophisticated; SEE CONCEPTS 485,578,797

mature [*v*] *become adult, fully grown*
advance, age, arrive, attain majority, become experienced, become wise, bloom, blossom, come of age, culminate, develop, evolve, fill out, flower*, grow, grow up, maturate, mellow*, mushroom*, perfect, prime, progress, reach

adulthood, reach majority, ripen, round, season, settle down*, shoot up*; SEE CONCEPT *704*

maturity [n] *adulthood, full growth*
ability, advancement, capability, civilization, completion, cultivation, development, experience, fitness, full bloom, fullness, majority, manhood, maturation, matureness, maturescence, mellowness, mentality, perfection, postpubescence, prime, prime of life, readiness, ripeness, sophistication, wisdom, womanhood; SEE CONCEPTS *678,715,720*

maudlin [adj] *teary, overemotional*
bathetic, befuddled, confused, cornball*, drippy*, gushing, insipid, lachrymose, mawkish, mushy*, romantic, schmaltzy*, sentimental, slush*, soap*, soapy*, soppy*, syrupy*, tearful, tear-jerking*, weak, weepy; SEE CONCEPTS *529,542*

maul [v] *mangle, abuse*
bang, bash, batter, beat, beat up, bludgeon, break face, buffet, claw, clean, drub, flagellate, flail, handle roughly, hit, hurt, ill-treat, knock about*, knock around*, lacerate, lash, lean on*, let have it*, maltreat, molest, mug, muscle, paste*, paw, pelt, pound, pummel, put in the hospital*, rough up, skin, take care of*, thrash, trample, wax, whip, work over*; SEE CONCEPTS *189,246*

mausoleum [n] *tomb*
burial, burial chamber, burial place, catacomb, cemetery, charnel house, coffin, crypt, grave, monument, sepulcher, vault; SEE CONCEPT *305*

mauve [adj] *purplish color*
lavender, lilac, plum, violaceous, violet; SEE CONCEPT *618*

maverick [n] *person who takes chances, departs from accepted course*
bohemian, dissenter, extremist, malcontent, nonconformist, radical; SEE CONCEPTS *348,423*

mawkish [adj] *sentimental, emotional*
bathetic, cloying, feeble, gooey*, gushing, gushy*, lovey-dovey*, maudlin, mushy*, nauseating, romantic, sappy*, schmaltzy*, sickening, sloppy, tear-jerking*, teary; SEE CONCEPTS *401,542*

maxim [n] *saying*
adage, aphorism, apophthegm, axiom, belief, brocard, byword, canon, commonplace, device, dictum, epithet, formula, law, moral, motto, platitude, precept, prescript, proverb, rule, saw, tenet, theorem, truism; SEE CONCEPTS *278,689*

maximum [adj] *highest, utmost*
best, biggest, greatest, largest, maximal, most, mostest, outside, paramount, superlative, supreme, top, topmost, ultimate; SEE CONCEPTS *574,762,781*

maximum [n] *upper limit, greatest amount*
apex, apogee, ceiling, climax, crest, culmination, extremity, height, max*, maxi*, most, nonpareil, peak, pinnacle, preeminence, record, summit, supremacy, the end*, top, utmost, uttermost, zenith; SEE CONCEPTS *706,766,836*

maybe [adv] *possibly*
as it may be, can be, conceivable, conceivably, could be, credible, feasible, imaginably, it could be, might be, obtainable, perchance, perhaps, weather permitting; SEE CONCEPT *552*

mayhem [n] *chaos, confusion*
anarchy, commotion, destruction, disorder, fracas, havoc, pandemonium, trouble, violence; SEE CONCEPTS *106,675*

maze [n] *labyrinth; confusion*
bewilderment, convolution, entanglement, hodgepodge, imbroglio, intricacy, jungle, knot, meander, meandering, mesh, miscellany, morass, muddle, network, perplexity, puzzle, quandary, skein, snarl, tangle, torsion, twist, uncertainty, web, winding; SEE CONCEPTS *436,529,674*

meadow [n] *grassy field*
bottoms*, carpet*, grassland, heath, lea, mead, pasturage, pasture, plain, prairie, rug*, steppe, veldt; SEE CONCEPT *509*

meager [adj1] *small, inadequate; poor*
bare, barren, deficient, exiguous, flimsy, inappreciable, inconsiderable, infertile, insubstantial, insufficient, little, mere, minimum, miserable, paltry, puny, scant, scanty, scrimp, scrimpy, shabby, short, skimp, skimpy, slender, slight, spare, sparse, subtle, tenuous, too little too late*, unfinished, unfruitful, unproductive, wanting, weak; SEE CONCEPTS *546,789*

meager [adj2] *very thin*
angular, bare, beanpole*, beanstalk*, bony, broomstick*, emaciated, gangling, gangly, gaunt, hungry, lacking, lank, lanky, lean, lithe, little, narrow, rattleboned, rawboned, scraggy, scrawny, skin and bones*, skinny, slender, slim, spare, starved, stinted, stunted, tenuous, underfed, wanting, willowy, withered; SEE CONCEPT *491*

meal [n] *food, often taken by several individuals together*
banquet, blue plate*, board, breakfast, brunch, carryout, chow*, chow time*, collation, cookout, dessert, din-din*, dinner, eats*, fare, feast, feed, grub*, lunch, luncheon, mess, munchies*, picnic, potluck, refection, refreshment, regalement, repast, snack, special*, spread, square meal*, supper, table, tea; SEE CONCEPT *459*

mean [adj1] *ungenerous*
close, greedy, mercenary, mingy, miserly, niggard, parsimonious, penny-pinching*, penurious, rapacious, scrimpy, selfish, stingy, tight, tightfisted*; SEE CONCEPT *334*

mean [adj2] *hostile, rude*
bad-tempered, callous, cantankerous, churlish, contemptible, dangerous, despicable, difficult, dirty*, disagreeable, dishonorable, down*, evil, formidable, hard, hard-nosed*, ignoble, ill-tempered, infamous, knavish, liverish, lousy*, lowdown and dirty*, malicious, malign, nasty, perfidious, pesky, rotten, rough, rugged, scurrilous, shameless, sinking, snide, sour, the lowest*, touch, treacherous, troublesome, ugly, unfriendly, unpleasant, unscrupulous, vexatious, vicious, vile; SEE CONCEPTS *267,401,542*

mean [adj3] *poor; of or in inferior circumstances*
base, beggarly, common, contemptible, déclassé, down-at-heel*, hack, humble, ignoble, ineffectual, inferior, insignificant, limited, low, lowborn, lowly, mediocre, menial, miserable, modest, narrow, obscure, ordinary, paltry, petty, pitiful, plebeian, proletarian, run-down*, scruffy*, second-class*, second-rate, seedy*, servile, shabby*, sordid, squalid, tawdry, undistinguished, unwashed, vulgar, wretched; SEE CONCEPTS *334,485,589*

mean [adj4] *average*
common, conventional, halfway, intermediate, medial, median, mediocre, medium, middle,

middling, normal, popular, standard, traditional; SEE CONCEPTS *547,585*

mean [*n*] *average*
balance, center, compromise, happy medium, median, middle, middle course, midpoint, norm, par; SEE CONCEPTS *727,830*

mean [*v1*] *signify, convey*
add up, adumbrate, allude, allude to, argue, attest, augur, betoken, connote, denote, designate, determine, drive at*, express, foreshadow, foretell, herald, hint at, imply, import, indicate, intimate, involve, name, point to, portend, presage, promise, purport, represent, say, speak of, spell, stand for, suggest, symbolize, tell the meaning of, touch on; SEE CONCEPTS *55,73,682*

mean [*v2*] *have in mind; intend*
aim, anticipate, aspire, contemplate, design, desire, destine, direct, expect, fate, fit, make, match, plan, predestine, preordain, propose, purpose, resolve, set out, suit, want, wish; SEE CONCEPTS *26,36*

meander [*v*] *wander, zigzag*
be all over the map*, change, drift, extravagate, gallivant, get sidetracked, peregrinate, ramble, range, recoil, roam, rove, snake, stray, stroll, traipse, turn, twine, twist, vagabond, wind; SEE CONCEPTS *151,738*

meaning [*n1*] *message, signification*
acceptation, allusion, bearing, bottom line*, connotation, content, context, definition, denotation, drift, effect, essence, explanation, force, gist, heart*, hint, implication, import, interpretation, intimation, meat, name of the game*, nature of beast*, nitty-gritty*, nuance, nuts and bolts*, pith, point, purport, sense, significance, spirit, stuff, subject, subject matter, substance, suggestion, symbolization, tenor, thrust, understanding, upshot, use, value, worth; SEE CONCEPTS *278,661,682*

meaning [*n2*] *intention, aim*
animus, design, end, goal, idea, intent, interest, object, plan, point, purpose, trend; SEE CONCEPT *659*

meaningful [*adj*] *significant*
allusive, big, clear, concise, consequential, considerable, deep, eloquent, essential, exact, explicit, expressive, heavy, important, indicative, intelligible, material, momentous, pointed, pregnant, purposeful, relevant, sententious, serious, substantial, succinct, suggestive, useful, valid, weighty, worthwhile; SEE CONCEPTS *267,567*

meaningless [*adj*] *without use, value, worth*
absurd, aimless, blank, doesn't cut it*, doublespeak*, double-talk*, empty, feckless, fustian, futile, good-for-nothing, hollow, hot air*, inane, inconsequential, insignificant, insubstantial, nonsensical, nothing, nugatory, pointless, purportless, purposeless, senseless, trifling, trivial, unimportant, unmeaning, unpurposed, useless, vacant, vague, vain, valueless, vapid, worthless; SEE CONCEPT *575*

means [*n1*] *way, method*
agency, agent, aid, apparatus, auspices, avenue, channel, course, dodge*, equipment, expedient, factor, fashion, gimmick*, instrument, instrumentality, instrumentation, intermediary, machinery, manner, measure, mechanism, medium, ministry, mode, modus operandi, organ, organization, paraphernalia, path, power, process, road, route, step, stepping-stone, system, tactic, technique, trick, vehicle, ways and means*; SEE CONCEPT *6*

means [*n2*] *wealth, resources*
ace in the hole*, affluence, assets, backing, bankroll, budget, bundle, capital, dough*, estate, finances, fortune, funds, holdings, income, intangibles, kitty*, money, nest egg*, nut*, pocket, possessions, property, purse, rainy day*, reserves, revenue, riches, savings, securities, sock*, stake, stuff, substance, ways and means*, wherewithal; SEE CONCEPTS *332,340*

meantime [*n/adv*] *in the intervening time*
at the same time, concurrently, for now, for the duration, for the moment, for then, interim, interregnum, interruption, interval, in the interim, in the interval, in the meanwhile, meanwhile, recess, simultaneously, while; SEE CONCEPTS *799,807*

meanwhile [*adv*] *at the same time*
ad interim, concurrently, during the interval, for now, for the duration, for the moment, for then, for the time being, in the interim, in the interval, in the intervening time, in the meantime, meantime, simultaneously, till, until, up to, when; SEE CONCEPT *799*

measly [*adj*] *skimpy*
beggarly, contemptible, insignificant, meager, mean, miserable, miserly, niggling*, paltry, pathetic, petty, picayune, piddling*, pitiful, poor, puny, scanty, stingy, trifling, trivial, ungenerous, unimportant, valueless, worthless; SEE CONCEPT *789*

measurable [*adj*] *determinable*
assessable, calculable, commensurate, computable, fathomable, gaugeable, material, mensurable, perceptible, quantifiable, quantitative, significant, surveyable, weighable; SEE CONCEPT *529*

measure [*n1*] *portion, scope*
admeasurement, admensuration, allotment, allowance, amount, amplification, amplitude, area, bang, breadth, bulk, capacity, degree, depth, dimension, distance, duration, extent, fix, frequency, height, hit, magnitude, mass, meed, mensuration, nip, part, pitch, proportion, quantity, quantum, quota, range, ratio, ration, reach, share, shot, size, slug, span, strength, sum, volume, weight; SEE CONCEPTS *787,792,835*

measure [*n2*] *standard, rule*
benchmark*, canon, criterion, example, gauge, meter, method, model, norm, pattern, scale, system, test, touchstone*, trial, type, yardstick; SEE CONCEPTS *686,688*

measure [*n3*] *preventive or institutive action*
act, action, agency, bounds, control, course, deed, device, effort, expedient, limit, limitation, makeshift, maneuver, means, moderation, move, procedure, proceeding, project, proposal, proposition, resort, resource, restraint, shift, step, stopgap*, strategem; SEE CONCEPT *5*

measure [*n4*] *bill, law*
act, enactment, project, proposal, proposition, resolution, statute; SEE CONCEPT *318*

measure [*n5*] *beat, rhythm*
accent, cadence, cadency, division, melody, meter, rhyme, step, stress, stroke, swing, tempo, throb, time, tune, verse, vibration; SEE CONCEPTS *65,262*

measure [*v*] *calculate, judge*
adapt, adjust, align, appraise, assess, average,

beat, blend, bound, calibrate, caliper, check, check out, choose, compute, delimit, demarcate, determine, dope out*, estimate, evaluate, even, eye*, figure, fit, gauge, gradate, grade, graduate, level, limit, line, look over, mark, mark out, mete, pace off, peg*, plumb, portion, quantify, rank, rate, read, reckon, regulate, rhyme, rule, scale, shade, size, size up, sound, square, stroke, survey, tailor, take account, time, value, weigh; SEE CONCEPTS *103,197,764*

measurement [*n*] *calculation*
altitude, amount, amplitude, analysis, appraisal, area, assessment, calibration, capacity, computation, degree, density, depth, determination, dimension, distance, estimation, evaluation, extent, frequency, height, judgment, length, magnitude, mass, measure, mensuration, metage, pitch, quantification, quantity, range, reach, scope, size, survey, thickness, time, valuation, volume, weight, width; SEE CONCEPTS *730,792*

meat [*n1*] *flesh of animal consumed as food*
aliment, brawn, chow, comestible, eats*, edible, fare, food, foodstuff, grub*, muscle, nourishment, nutriment, provision, ration, subsistence, sustenance, victual; SEE CONCEPTS *399,457,460*

meat [*n2*] *core, gist*
burden, essence, heart, kernel, marrow, matter, nub, nucleus, pith, point, sense, short, substance, thrust, upshot; SEE CONCEPTS *682,826*

meat-eating [*adj*] *carnivorous*
cannibalistic, flesh-eating, omophagous, predacious; SEE CONCEPT *401*

meaty [*adj*] *significant*
compact, epigrammatic, factual, full of content, interesting, meaningful, pithy, pointed, profound, rich, substantial, weighty; SEE CONCEPT *267*

mecca [*n*] *center, goal*
aim, capital, destination, focal point, focus, heart, hub, nerve center, objective, purpose; SEE CONCEPTS *435,438,507,659*

mechanical [*adj*] *done by machine; machinelike*
automated, automatic, cold, cursory, emotionless, fixed, habitual, impersonal, instinctive, involuntary, laborsaving, lifeless, machine-driven, matter-of-fact, monotonous, perfunctory, programmed, routine, spiritless, standardized, stereotyped, unchanging, unconscious, unfeeling, unthinking, useful; SEE CONCEPT *544*

mechanism [*n1*] *machine, device*
apparatus, appliance, black box*, components, contrivance, doohickey*, gadget, gears, gimmick, innards, instrument, machinery, motor, structure, system, tool, workings, works; SEE CONCEPT *463*

mechanism [*n2*] *means, method*
agency, execution, functioning, medium, operation, performance, procedure, process, system, technique, workings; SEE CONCEPT *6*

mechanize [*v*] *automate*
equip, industrialize, motorize, rig; SEE CONCEPTS *538,549*

medal [*n*] *decoration of honor*
badge, commemoration, gold, hardware*, laurel, medallion, reward, ribbon, wreath; SEE CONCEPTS *337,476*

meddle [*v*] *intervene, interfere*
abuse rights, advance, barge in, break in on, busybody*, butt in*, chime in, come uninvited, crash the gates*, dabble in, encroach, encumber,

fool with, hinder, horn in*, impede, impose, infringe, inquire, interlope, intermeddle, interpose, intrude, invade, kibitz*, mess around*, mix in, molest, obtrude, pry, push in, put two cents in*, sidewalk-superintend*, snoop*, stick nose in*, tamper, trespass, worm in*; SEE CONCEPTS *14,384*

meddlesome [*adj*] *interfereing*
busy, busybody*, chiseling*, curious, encumbering, hindering, impeding, impertinent, intermeddling, interposing, interrupting, intruding, intrusive, kibitzing*, meddling, mischievous, nosy, obstructive, officious, prying, pushy, snooping*, snoopy*, tampering, troublesome; SEE CONCEPT *555*

media [*n*] *communication by publication or broadcast*
announcement, announcing, cable, communications, correspondence, disclosure, expression, intelligence, news, publishing, radio, television; SEE CONCEPT *279*

median [*n/adj*] *middle*
average, center, centermost, central, equidistant, halfway, intermediary, intermediate, mean, medial, mid, middlemost, midmost, midpoint, midway, par; SEE CONCEPTS *585,727,746,830*

mediate [*v*] *try to bring to an agreement*
act as middle*, arbitrate, bring to terms, conciliate, deal, go fifty-fifty*, intercede, interfere, intermediate, interpose, intervene, make a deal, make peace, meet halfway*, moderate, negotiate, propitiate, reconcile, referee, resolve, restore harmony, settle, step in, strike happy medium*, trade off, umpire; SEE CONCEPTS *126,324,384*

mediation [*n*] *attempt to bring to agreement*
arbitration, conciliation, intercession, interposition, intervention, negotiation, reconciliation; SEE CONCEPTS *126,324,384*

mediator [*n*] *person who negotiates agreement*
advocate, arbiter, arbitrator, broker, conciliator, fixer, go-between*, interagent, interceder, intermediary, intermediator, judge, medium, middle person, moderator, negotiator, peacemaker, ref*, referee, rent-a-judge*, troubleshooter*, umpire; SEE CONCEPTS *348,423*

medicine/medication [*n*] *substance that helps cure, alleviate, or prevent illness*
anesthetic, antibiotic, antidote, antiseptic, antitoxin, balm, biologic, capsule, cure, dose, drug, elixir, injection, inoculation, liniment, lotion, medicament, ointment, pharmaceutical, pharmacon, physic, pill, potion, prescription, remedy, salve, sedative, serum, tablet, tincture, tonic, vaccination, vaccine; SEE CONCEPT *307*

medieval [*adj*] *having to do with the Middle Ages; old*
antediluvian, antiquated, antique, archaic, feudal, Gothic, old, old-fashioned, primitive, unenlightened; SEE CONCEPTS *549,578,797*

mediocre [*adj*] *average, commonplace*
characterless, colorless, common, conventional, decent, dull, fair, fairish, fair to middling*, humdrum*, indifferent, inferior, insignificant, intermediate, mainstream, mean, medium, middling, moderate, no great shakes*, of poor quality, ordinary, passable, pedestrian, run-of-the-mill*, second-rate, so-so*, standard, tolerable, undistinguished, unexceptional, uninspired, vanilla*; SEE CONCEPTS *533,547*

meditate [*v*] *think deeply about*
brood over, cogitate, consider, contemplate, deliberate, design, devise, dream, entertain idea*, figure, have in mind*, intend, moon*, mull over, muse, plan, ponder, purpose, put on thinking cap*, puzzle over, reflect, revolve, roll, ruminate, say to oneself, scheme, speculate, study, think, think over, track, view, weigh; SEE CONCEPT *17*

meditation [*n*] *deep thought*
concentration, contemplation, introspection, pondering, quiet time, reflection, rumination, self-examination; SEE CONCEPTS *17,24*

medium [*adj*] *midway, average*
common, commonplace, fair, fairish, intermediate, mean, medial, median, mediocre, middle, middling, moderate, neutral, normal, ordinary, par, passable, popular, run-of-the-mill*, so-so*, standard, tolerable; SEE CONCEPTS *533,547*

medium [*n1*] *means, mode*
agency, agent, avenue, channel, clairvoyant, factor, form, instrument, instrumentality, intermediate, measure, mechanism, ministry, organ, psychic, seer, tool, vehicle, way; SEE CONCEPTS *658,712*

medium [*n2*] *atmosphere, setting*
ambience, ambient, climate, conditions, element, habitat, influences, milieu, surroundings; SEE CONCEPTS *673,696*

medium [*n3*] *area of artistic expression*
art, drama, interpretation, manifestation, mark, music, painting, revelation, sculpture, speech, writing; SEE CONCEPTS *259,263,293*

medley [*n*] *miscellany*
assortment, brew, collection, combo, composition, confusion, conglomeration, farrago, hodgepodge, jumble, mélange, melee, mingling, mishmash, mixture, pasticcio, pastiche, patchwork, potpourri, salmagundi, variety; SEE CONCEPTS *262,432*

meek [*adj*] *shy; compliant*
acquiescent, deferential, docile, forbearing, gentle, humble, lenient, longanimous, long-suffering, lowly, manageable, mild, milquetoast*, modest, nothing, orderly, pabulum*, passive, patient, peaceful, plain, resigned, serene, soft, spineless, spiritless, subdued, submissive, tame, timid, tolerant, unassuming, unpretentious, unresisting, weak, weak-kneed*, wishy-washy*, yielding, zero*; SEE CONCEPT *401*

meet [*adj*] *fitting*
accommodated, applicable, appropriate, apt, conformed, equitable, expedient, fair, felicitous, fit, good, happy, just, proper, reconciled, right, suitable, timely; SEE CONCEPT *558*

meet [*n*] *sporting event involving several participants*
athletic event, competition, conflict, contest, event, match, meeting, tournament, tourney; SEE CONCEPT *363*

meet [*v1*] *happen on*
accost, affront, brush against, bump into, chance on, clash, collide, come across, come up against, confront, contact, cross, dig up*, encounter, engage, experience, face, fall in with*, find, front, get together, grapple, greet, hit, light, luck*, make a meet, meet face to face, rendezvous with, rub eyeballs*, run across, run into, run up against, salute, see, strike, stumble, touch shoulders*, tumble, tussle, wrestle; SEE CONCEPTS *183,384,626*

meet [*v2*] *connect, join*
abut, adhere, adjoin, border, coincide, connect, converge, cross, intersect, link, link up, reach, touch, unite; SEE CONCEPTS *612,759*

meet [*v3*] *perform, carry out*
answer, approach, come up to, comply, cope with, discharge, equal, execute, fit, fulfill, gratify, handle, match, measure up, rival, satisfy, suffice, tie, touch; SEE CONCEPT *91*

meet [*v4*] *come together, convene*
appear, assemble, be introduced, be present, be presented, collect, congregate, converge, enter in, flock, foregather, gather, get together, get to know, join, make acquaintance, muster, open, rally, rendezvous, show, sit; SEE CONCEPTS *114,324*

meeting [*n1*] *gathering, conference*
affair, assemblage, assembly, assignation, audience, bunch, call, cattle call*, company, competition, conclave, concourse, concursion, confab*, conflict, confrontation, congregation, congress, contest, convention, convocation, date, encounter, engagement, gang, get-together, huddle, introduction, meet, one on one*, parley, powwow*, rally, rendezvous, reunion, session, showdown, talk, tryst, turnout*; SEE CONCEPTS *324,363,384*

meeting [*n2*] *convergence, intersection*
abutment, agreement, apposition, concourse, confluence, conjunction, connection, contact, crossing, joining, junction, juxtaposition, unification, union; SEE CONCEPTS *113,684*

melancholy [*adj*] *depressed, sad*
blue*, dejected, despondent, destroyed, disconsolate, dismal, dispirited, doleful, dolorous, down*, down and out*, downbeat, downcast, downhearted, down in the dumps*, down in the mouth*, dragged, droopy, funereal, gloomy, glum, grim, heavyhearted, in blue funk*, joyless, lachrymose, low, low-spirited, lugubrious, mirthless, miserable, moody, moony*, mournful, pensive, saddened, saddening, somber, sorrowful, sorry*, torn up, trite, unhappy, wet blanket*, wistful, woebegone, woeful; SEE CONCEPT *403*

melancholy [*n*] *depression, sadness*
blahs*, blue devils*, blue funk*, blues*, boredom, bummer*, dejection, despair, desperation, despondency, dismals, dolefuls, dolor, downer*, down trip*, dumps, ennui, funk, gloom, gloominess, grief, letdown, low spirits, miserableness, misery, mopes*, mournfulness, pensiveness, sorrow, tedium, unhappiness, wistfulness, woe, wretchedness; SEE CONCEPT *410*

mélange [*n*] *mixture*
assortment, combo, confusion, farrago, gallimaufry, hodgepodge, jumble, medley, miscellany, mishmash, mix, mixed bag, pasticcio, pastiche, patchwork, potpourri, salmagundi, soup, stew; SEE CONCEPT *432*

meld [*v*] *blend, bring together*
amalgamate, associate, compound, dissolve, feather in, fuse, interblend, interface, interfuse, intermingle, marry, merge, mingle, mix, unite; SEE CONCEPTS *113,193*

melee [*n*] *battle, fight*
affray, battle royal*, brawl, broil, brouhaha*, brush, clash, donnybrook*, fracas, fray, free-for-all*, knock-down-drag-out*, row, ruckus, ruction, rumpus, scrimmage, scuffle, set-to*,

skirmish, to-do*, tussle, words; SEE CONCEPT
106
mellifluous [*adj*] *smooth and sweet sounding*
  agreeable, dulcet, euphonic, fluid, harmonic,
  honeyed, mellow, pleasing, resonant, songful,
  soothing, symphonious, tuned, tuneful; SEE CON-
  CEPT *594*
mellow [*adj*] *ripe, mature; softened*
  aged, cultured, cured, delicate, developed, dulcet, flavorful, full, full-flavored, fully developed,
  juicy, matured, mellifluent, mellifluous, melodious, perfect, perfected, rich, ripened, rounded,
  sapid, savory, seasoned, smooth, soft, soothing,
  sweet, tuneful; SEE CONCEPTS *462,578,594,797*
mellow [*v*] *ripen, mature*
  age, arrive, develop, grow, grow up, improve,
  maturate, milden, mollify, perfect, ripe, season,
  settle down, soften, sweeten; SEE CONCEPTS
  678,704
melodious/melodic [*adj*] *harmonious, musical*
  accordant, agreeable, assonant, canorous, clear,
  concordant, dulcet, euphonic, euphonious, harmonic, in tune, mellifluous, mellow, pleasing,
  resonant, silvery, soft, songful, sweet, sweet-
  sounding, symphonic, symphonious, tuned, tuneful, well-tuned; SEE CONCEPT *594*
melodramatic [*adj*] *extravagant in speech, behavior*
  artificial, blood-and-thunder*, cliff-hanging*,
  cloak-and-dagger*, exaggerated, ham*,
  hammy*, histrionic, hokey*, overdramatic, overemotional, sensational, spectacular, stagy, theatrical; SEE CONCEPT *542*
melody [*n*] *harmony, tune*
  air, aria, assonance, carillon, chant, chime, concord, consonance, descant, diapason, euphony,
  inflection, lay, lyric, measure, melodiousness,
  music, musicality, refrain, resonance, run, song,
  strain, theme, tunefulness, unison; SEE CONCEPTS
  262,595
melt [*v1*] *liquefy; dissolve*
  cook, deliquesce, diffuse, disappear, disintegrate,
  disperse, evanesce, evaporate, fade, flow, flux,
  fuse, go, heat, merge, pass away, render, run,
  smelt, soften, thaw, vanish, warm, waste away;
  SEE CONCEPTS *250,255*
melt [*v2*] *give in, yield*
  become lenient, disarm, forgive, mollify, relax,
  relent, show mercy, soften, touch; SEE CONCEPT
  35
member [*n1*] *part of a group*
  affiliate, associate, branch, chapter, component,
  comrade, constituent, cut, division, joiner, offshoot, parcel, piece, portion, post, representative,
  section, segment, unit; SEE CONCEPTS
  417,834,835
member [*n2*] *appendage*
  arm, component, constituent, element, extremity,
  feature, fragment, leg, limb, organ, part, portion,
  segment; SEE CONCEPT *392*
membership [*n*] *belonging to organization;
  those belonging to a group*
  associates, association, body, club, company, enrollment, fellows, group, members, participation,
  society; SEE CONCEPTS *381,417*
membrane [*n*] *covering layer*
  film, lamina, leaf, mucosa, sheath, sheet; SEE
  CONCEPT *484*
memento [*n*] *souvenir*
  keepsake, memorial, relic, remembrance, re-

membrancer, reminder, token, trace, trophy, vestige; SEE CONCEPTS *337,446*
memoir [*n*] *record of experiences*
  account, anecdote, annal, autobiography, bio*,
  biography, chronicle, confessions, diary, discourse, dissertation, essay, journal, life, life
  story, memory, monograph, narrative, note, recollection, register, reminiscence, thesis, tractate,
  transactions, treatise, vita; SEE CONCEPTS
  271,280,282
memorabilia [*n*] *mementos*
  annals, archives, collectibles, keepsakes, relics,
  remembrances, reminders, souvenirs, tokens, tro-
  phies; SEE CONCEPTS *337,446*
memorable [*adj*] *noteworthy, significant*
  A-1*, big-league*, bodacious, catchy, celebrated, critical, crucial, decisive, distinguished,
  doozie*, enduring, eventful, extraordinary, famous, great, heavy*, heavyweight*, historic,
  hot*, illustrious, important, impressive, indelible, interesting, lasting, major-league, meaningful, mind-blowing*, momentous, monumental,
  notable, observable, red-letter*, remarkable, rememberable, rubric, serious, signal, something,
  standout, striking, super, surpassing, terrible, terrific, top-drawer, unforgettable; SEE CONCEPTS
  529,548
memorandum/memo [*n*] *written note*
  announcement, chit, diary, directive, dispatch,
  epistle, jotting, letter, message, minute, missive,
  notation, notice, record, reminder, tickler; SEE
  CONCEPTS *271,277,278*
memorial [*adj*] *commemorative*
  canonizing, celebrative, commemoratory, conse-
  crating, consecrative, dedicatory, deifying, en-
  shrining, in tribute, memorializing, monumental,
  remembering; SEE CONCEPT *537*
memorial [*n*] *monument, testimonial in honor,
  praise*
  cairn, ceremony, column, headstone, inscription,
  keepsake, mausoleum, memento, monolith,
  obelisk, pillar, plaque, record, relic, remembrance, reminder, shaft, slab, souvenir, statue,
  stele, tablet, token, tombstone, trophy; SEE CON-
  CEPTS *337,386*
memorize [*v*] *remember*
  commit to memory, cram, fix in the mind, keep
  forever, know, know by heart, learn, learn by
  heart, master, nail down, recall, recollect, remind, retain, store; SEE CONCEPT *40*
memory [*n1*] *ability to hold in the mind*
  anamnesis, awareness, camera-eye*, cognizance,
  consciousness, dead-eye*, flashback, memoriza-
  tion, mind, mindfulness, mind's eye*, recall, recapture, recognition, recollection, reflection,
  remembrance, reminiscence, retention, retentive-
  ness, retrospection, subconsciousness, thought;
  SEE CONCEPT *409*
memory [*n2*] *specific thing remembered*
  concept, cue, fantasy, hint, image, jog, memo,
  memoir, mnemonic, picture, prod, prompt, reminder, representation, suggestion, thought, vision; SEE CONCEPTS *529,678*
menace [*n*] *danger; pest*
  annoyance, caution, commination, hazard, intimidation, jeopardy, nuisance, peril, plague, risk,
  scare, threat, thunder, trouble, troublemaker,
  warning; SEE CONCEPTS *412,675*
menace [*v*] *bother, frighten*
  alarm, bad-eye*, browbeat, bully, chill, compro-

mise, endanger, hazard, impend, imperil, intimidate, jeopardize, lean on, loom, lower, overhang, peril, portend, push around, put heat on*, risk, scare, scare hell out of*, spook, terrorize, threaten, torment, whip around*; SEE CONCEPTS *7,19*

menacing [*adj*] *intimidating, ominous*
alarming, approaching, dangerous, frightening, imminent, impending, intimidatory, looming, louring, lowering, minacious, minatory, overhanging, threatening; SEE CONCEPTS *401,537,548*

menagerie [*adj*] *zoo*
aquarium, collection, exhibition, safari park, wildlife park, zoological garden; SEE CONCEPTS *509,513*

mend [*v*] *correct, improve, fix*
aid, ameliorate, amend, better, condition, convalesce, cure, darn, doctor, emend, fiddle with, gain, get better, get well, heal, knit, look up, overhaul, patch, perk up, ready, rebuild, recondition, reconstruct, recover, rectify, recuperate, redress, refit, reform, refurbish, rejuvenate, remedy, renew, renovate, repair, restore, retouch, revamp, revise, right, service, sew; SEE CONCEPTS *126,244,303,700*

mendacious [*adj*] *dishonest*
deceitful, deceptive, duplicitous, equivocating, erroneous, fallacious, false, fibbing, fraudulent, insincere, lying, paltering, perfidious, perjured, prevaricating, shifty, spurious, untrue, untruthful, wrong; SEE CONCEPT *267*

menial [*adj*] *lowly, low-status*
abject, base, baseborn, boring, common, degrading, demeaning, dull, fawning, grovelling, humble, humdrum, ignoble, ignominious, low, mean, obeisant, obsequious, routine, servile, slavish, sorry, subservient, sycophantic, unskilled, vile; SEE CONCEPTS *574,575*

men's movement [*n*] *men's attempt to redefine gender roles*
gender revisionism, male reform, men's liberation, men's studies; SEE CONCEPT *388*

mental [*adj1*] *concerning the mind*
brainy*, cerebral, clairvoyant, deep, heavy, ideological, imaginative, immaterial, inner, intellective, intellectual, mysterious, phrenic, psychic, psychical, psychological, rational, reasoning, spiritual, subconscious, subjective, subliminal, telepathic, thinking, thoughtful, unreal; SEE CONCEPTS *402,403*

mental [*adj2*] *insane*
deranged, disturbed, fruity, loco*, lunatic, mad, maniac, mentally ill, mindless, non compos mentis, nuts*, nutsy*, psychiatric, psychotic, unbalanced, unstable; SEE CONCEPTS *314,403*

mental hospital [*n*] *psychiatric hospital*
bughouse*, funny farm*, insane asylum, loony bin*, madhouse*, mental health facility, mental institution, nuthouse*, psychiatric ward, sanatorium; SEE CONCEPTS *312,439,516*

mental illness [*n*] *mental disorder*
depression, emotional disorder, emotional instability, insanity, maladjustment, mania, mental sickness, nervous breakdown, neurosis, neurotic disorder, personality disorder, phobia, psychosis, schizophrenia; SEE CONCEPTS *316,410*

mentality [*n*] *state of mind; intelligence*
attitude, brainpower, brains, cast, character, comprehension, disposition, frame of mind*, headset*, intellect, intelligence quotient, IQ,

makeup, mental age, mind, mindset*, outlook, personality, psychology, rationality, reasoning, routine, sense, turn of mind*, understanding, way of thinking*, wit; SEE CONCEPTS *409,411*

mention [*n*] *referral, observation*
acknowledgment, allusion, citation, comment, footnote, indication, naming, note, notice, notification, recognition, reference, remark, specifying, tribute, utterance; SEE CONCEPTS *73,278*

mention [*v*] *refer to*
acknowledge, acquaint, adduce, advert, allude to, bring up, broach, call attention to, cite, communicate, declare, designate, detail, disclose, discuss, divulge, enumerate, hint at, impart, infer, instance, intimate, introduce, make known, name, notice, notify, observe, point out, point to, quote, recount, remark, report, reveal, speak about, speak of, specify, state, suggest, tell, throw out, touch on; SEE CONCEPT *73*

mentor [*n*] *person who advises*
adviser, coach, counsellor, guide, instructor, teacher, trainer, tutor; SEE CONCEPT *350*

menu [*n*] *list from which to choose, often to choose food*
bill of fare, card, carte, carte du jour, cuisine, food, spread, table; SEE CONCEPT *283*

mercenary [*adj*] *greedy for money*
acquisitive, avaricious, bribable, corrupt, covetous, grabby, grasping, miserly, money-grubbing, selfish, sordid, stingy, unethical, unprincipled, unscrupulous, venal; SEE CONCEPT *401*

mercenary [*n*] *person who fights, kills for money*
hireling, legionnaire, merc, professional soldier, slave, soldier of fortune, warrior; SEE CONCEPTS *358,412*

merchandise [*n*] *goods for sale*
commodity, effects, job lot, line, material, number, produce, product, seconds, staple, stock, stuff, truck, vendible, wares; SEE CONCEPT *338*

merchandise [*v*] *sell goods*
advertise, buy and sell, deal in, distribute, do business in, market, promote, publicize, retail, trade, traffic in, vend, wholesale; SEE CONCEPT *345*

merchant [*n*] *person who sells goods*
broker, businessperson, consigner, dealer, exporter, handler, jobber, marketer, operator, retailer, salesperson, seller, sender, shipper, shopkeeper, storekeeper, trader, tradesperson, trafficker, tycoon, vendor, wholesaler; SEE CONCEPT *347*

merciful [*adj*] *kind, sparing*
all heart*, beneficent, benign, benignant, bleeding heart*, charitable, clement, compassionate, condoning, easygoing, feeling, forbearing, forgiving, generous, gentle, gracious, heart in right place*, humane, humanitarian, indulgent, kindly, lenient, liberal, mild, pardoning, pitiful, pitying, soft*, softhearted*, sympathetic, tender, tenderhearted, tolerant; SEE CONCEPTS *401,542*

merciless [*adj*] *mean, heartless*
barbarous, callous, compassionless, cruel, cutthroat, dog-eat-dog*, fierce, gratuitous, grim, hard, hardhearted, harsh, hatchet job*, having a killer instinct*, implacable, inexorable, inhumane, iron-fisted, mean machine*, mortal, pitiless, relentless, ruthless, severe, unappeasable, uncalled-for, unfeeling, unflinching, unforgiving, unmerciful, unpitying, unrelenting, unsparing,

me
me

unsympathetic, unyielding, wanton; SEE CON-CEPTS *401,542*

mercurial [*adj*] *flighty, temperamental*
blowing hot and cold*, bubbleheaded*, buoyant, capricious, changeable, effervescent, elastic, erratic, expansive, fickle, flaky, flip*, fluctuating, gaga*, gay, impulsive, inconstant, irregular, irrepressible, lighthearted, lively, lubricious, mad, mobile, movable, quicksilver, resilient, short-fuse*, spirited, sprightly, ticklish, unpredictable, unstable, up-and-down*, variable, volatile, yo-yo*; SEE CONCEPTS *401,404*

mercy [*n*] *kindness, compassion*
benevolence, benignancy, blessing, boon, charity, clemency, commiseration, favor, forbearance, forgiveness, generosity, gentleness, godsend, goodwill, grace, humanity, kindliness, lenience, leniency, lenity, lifesaver, luck, mildness, pity, quarter, relief, ruth, softheartedness, sympathy, tenderness, tolerance; SEE CONCEPTS *32,633*

mere [*adj*] *nothing more; absolute*
bald, bare, blunt, common, complete, entire, insignificant, little, minor, plain, poor, pure, pure and simple, sheer, simple, small, stark, unadorned, unadulterated, unmitigated, unmixed, utter, very; SEE CONCEPTS *535,589*

meretricious [*adj*] *gaudy, flashy*
blatant, bogus, brazen, chintzy, counterfeit, garish, glaring, insincere, loud, misleading, ornate, phony, plastic*, put-on*, sham, showy, spurious, superficial, tawdry, tinsel, trashy; SEE CONCEPTS *542,589*

merge [*v*] *bring or come together*
absorb, amalgamate, assimilate, become lost in, become partners, be swallowed up*, blend, cement, centralize, coalesce, combine, come aboard*, compound, conglomerate, consolidate, converge, deal one in, fuse, hitch on*, hook up*, immerge, incorporate, interface, intermingle, intermix, join, join up, line up, marry, meet, meld, melt into, mingle, mix, network, plug into, pool, slap on, submerge, synthesize, tack on*, tag, team up*, throw in together*, tie in, unite; SEE CONCEPTS *113,193,324*

merger [*n*] *consolidation*
alliance, amalgamation, cahoots*, coadunation, coalition, combination, fusion, hookup, incorporation, lineup, melding, mergence, merging, organization, pool, takeover, tie-in, tie-up, unification, union; SEE CONCEPTS *323,324,703*

meridian [*n*] *summit, climax*
acme, apex, apogee, crest, culmination, extremity, high noon, high-water mark, peak, pinnacle, zenith; SEE CONCEPTS *832,836*

merit [*n*] *advantage*
arete, asset, benefit, caliber, credit, desert, dignity, excellence, excellency, good, goodness, honor, integrity, perfection, quality, stature, strong point, talent, value, virtue, worth, worthiness; SEE CONCEPT *693*

merit [*v*] *be entitled to*
be in line for, be worthy, deserve, earn, get one's comeuppance*, get one's due*, get one's just desserts*, get what is coming*, have a claim, have a right, have coming, incur, justify, rate, warrant; SEE CONCEPT *129*

meritorious [*adj*] *honorable, commendable*
admirable, boss*, choice, creditable, deserving, estimable, excellent, exemplary, golden, good,

laudable, meritable, noble, praisable, praiseworthy, right, righteous, thankworthy, top drawer*, virtuous, winner, world-beating*, worthy; SEE CONCEPTS *404,548,572*

merriment/merrymaking [*n*] *enjoyment, amusement*
brawl, buffoonery, cheerfulness, conviviality, festivity, frolic, fun, fun and games*, gaiety, glee, happiness, hilarity, hoopla*, indulgence, jocularity, jocundity, jollity, joviality, joy, laughs, laughter, levity, liveliness, mirth, picnic, recreation, revel, revelry, self-indulgence, shindig, sport, whoopee*, wingding*; SEE CONCEPTS *386,410*

merry [*adj*] *very happy; festive*
amusing, blithe, blithesome, boisterous, boon, carefree, cheerful, comic, comical, convivial, enjoyable, entertaining, facetious, frolicsome, fun-loving, funny, gay, glad, gleeful, grooving*, hilarious, humorous, jocund, jolly, joyful, joyous, jumping, larking, lighthearted, lively, mad, mirthful, perky, pleasant, riotous, rip-roaring*, rocking, rollicking, saturnalian, sportive, sunny, unconstrained, uproarious, vivacious, wild, winsome, zappy*, zingy*, zippy*; SEE CONCEPTS *403,548,572*

mesa [*n*] *plateau*
butte, elevation, highland, plain, tableland, upland; SEE CONCEPTS *509,744*

mesh [*n*] *netting, entanglement*
cobweb, jungle, knot, labyrinth, maze, morass, net, network, plexus, reticulation, screen, skein, snare, snarl, tangle, toils, tracery, trap, web; SEE CONCEPTS *473,770,733*

mesh [*v*] *entangle, connect*
agree, catch, coincide, combine, come together, coordinate, dovetail, engage, enmesh, ensnare, fit, fit together, harmonize, interlock, knit, net, snare, tangle, trap; SEE CONCEPTS *113,193*

mesmerize [*v*] *captivate*
catch up, control, deaden, drug, ensorcell, enthrall, entrance, fascinate, grip, hold spellbound, hypnotize, magnetize, numb, render unconscious, spellbind, stupefy; SEE CONCEPTS *11,14*

mess [*n1*] *disorder, litter*
botch, chaos, clutter, combination, compound, confusion, debris, dirtiness, disarray, discombobulation*, disorganization, every which way*, eyesore, fright, hash, hodgepodge, jumble, mayhem, mishmash, monstrosity, salmagundi, shambles, sight, turmoil, untidiness, wreck, wreckage; SEE CONCEPTS *230,260*

mess [*n2*] *difficulty, predicament*
dilemma, fix, imbroglio, jam, mix-up, muddle, perplexity, pickle*, plight, stew; SEE CONCEPT *674*

message [*n1*] *communication, often written*
bulletin, cannonball, communiqué, directive, dispatch, dope, earful, epistle, information, intelligence, intimation, letter, memo, memorandum, missive, news, note, notice, paper, report, tidings, wire, word; SEE CONCEPTS *271,274*

message [*n2*] *meaning, idea*
acceptation, import, intendment, moral, point, purport, sense, significance, significancy, signification, theme, understanding; SEE CONCEPTS *661,682*

mess around [*v*] *fiddle; goof off*
amuse oneself, dabble, dawdle, doodle, fool around, loiter, muck around*, play, play around,

play the fool*, potter, puddle, putter, tinker, trifle; SEE CONCEPTS *87,363*

messenger [*n*] *person carrying information to another*
agent, ambassador, bearer, carrier, commissionaire, courier, crier, delegate, delivery person, detachment, detail, dispatcher, emissary, envoy, errand person*, flag-bearer, forerunner, go-between*, gofer*, harbinger, herald, intermediary, mediator, minister, post, precursor, prophet, runner, schlepper*; SEE CONCEPT *348*

mess up [*v*] *disorder, dirty*
befoul, besmirch, bobble, bollix*, botch, bungle, clutter, confuse, damage, derange, destroy, disarrange, discompose, dishevel, disorganize, disturb, foul, goof up*, gum up*, jumble, litter, louse up, muddle, pollute, ruin, rummage, scramble, screw up*, smear, soil, spoil, unsettle, upset; SEE CONCEPTS *158,252,254*

messy [*adj*] *cluttered, dirty*
blotchy*, careless, chaotic, confused, disheveled, disordered, disorganized, grimy, grubby*, littered, muddled, raunchy*, rumpled, slapdash*, slipshod*, sloppy, slovenly, unfastidious, unkempt, untidy; SEE CONCEPTS *485,621*

metal [*n*] *lustrous chemical element*
alloy, casting, deposit, foil, hardware, ingot, leaf, load, mail, mineral, native rock, ore, plate, solder, vein; SEE CONCEPT *476*

metamorphose [*v*] *convert, transform*
age, alter, be reborn, change, commute, develop, diverge, mature, mutate, remake, remodel, reshape, ripen, transfigure, translate, transmogrify, transmute, transubstantiate, vary; SEE CONCEPTS *469,697,701*

metamorphosis [*n*] *conversion, transformation*
alteration, change, changeover, evolution, mutation, rebirth, transfiguration, transfigurement, translation, transmogrification, transmutation, transubstantiation; SEE CONCEPTS *469,697,701*

metaphor [*n*] *figure of speech, implied comparison*
allegory, analogy, emblem, hope, image, metonymy, personification, similitude, symbol, trope; SEE CONCEPT *275*

metaphorical [*adj*] *figurative*
allegorical, denotative, descriptive, emblematic, illustrative, metaphoric, representative, symbolic, tropological; SEE CONCEPTS *267,582*

metaphysical [*adj*] *not physical; without physical presence*
abstract, abstruse, bodiless, deep, difficult, discarnate, esoteric, eternal, fundamental, highflown, ideal, immaterial, impalpable, incorporeal, insubstantial, intangible, intellectual, jesuitic, mystical, nonmaterial, nonphysical, numinous, oversubtle, philosophical, preternatural, profound, recondite, spiritual, superhuman, superior, supermundane, supernatural, suprahuman, supramundane, supranatural, theoretical, transcendental, unearthly, unfleshly, universal, unphysical, unreal, unsubstantial; SEE CONCEPTS *529,582*

mete [*v*] *administer, distribute*
admeasure, allocate, allot, allow, apportion, assign, deal, dispense, divide, dole, give, lot, measure, parcel, portion, ration, share; SEE CONCEPTS *98,108*

meteoric [*adj*] *brief, sudden*
dazzling, ephemeral, flashing, fleeting, momen-

tary, overnight, rapid, spectacular, speedy, swift, transient; SEE CONCEPTS *548,798,799*

meteorology [*n*] *weather science*
aerology, climatology, weather forecasting; SEE CONCEPTS *522,524*

meter [*n*] *rhythm, beat*
cadence, cadency, feet, lilt, measure, mora, music, pattern, poetry, rhyme, structure, swing; SEE CONCEPTS *65,262*

method [*n1*] *means, procedure*
adjustment, approach, arrangement, channels, course, custom, design, disposal, disposition, fashion, form, formula, habit, line, manner, mechanism, method, mode, modus, modus operandi, nuts and bolts*, plan, practice, proceeding, process, program, receipt, recipe, red tape*, ritual, rote, routine, rubric, rule, rut, schema, scheme, shortcut, style, system, tack, tactics, technic, technique, tenor, the book*, usage, way, ways and means*, wise, wrinkle*; SEE CONCEPTS *6,660*

method [*n2*] *order, pattern*
arrangement, classification, design, form, orderliness, organization, plan, planning, purpose, regularity, structure, system; SEE CONCEPTS *727,770*

methodical/methodic [*adj*] *organized, precise*
all together, analytical, businesslike, by the book*, by the numbers, careful, cut-and-dried*, deliberate, disciplined, efficient, exact, fixed, framed, in a groove*, logical, methodized, meticulous, neat, ordered, orderly, painstaking, planned, regular, scrupulous, set-up*, structured, systematic, tidy, together, well-regulated; SEE CONCEPTS *326,542,544,585*

methodology [*n*] *methods*
approach, channels, design, manner, mode, plan, practice, procedure, process, program, style, technique, way; SEE CONCEPTS *6,644*

meticulous [*adj*] *detailed, perfectionist*
accurate, cautious, conscientious, conscionable, crossing the t's*, dotting the i's*, exact, fastidious, fussy, heedful, microscopic, nitpicking*, painstaking, particular, persnickety*, picky, precise, punctilious, punctual, scrupulous, stickling, strict, thorough; SEE CONCEPTS *542,544,557*

metier [*n*] *occupation*
calling, chosen work, craft, day gig*, employment, field, forte, job, line of work, one's specialty, profession, pursuit, racket*, thing*, trade, vocation, walk of life*, work; SEE CONCEPTS *349,351,360*

metropolis [*n*] *major city*
capital, downtown, megalopolis, metropolitan area, municipality; SEE CONCEPT *507*

metropolitan [*adj*] *concerning a city*
city, cosmopolitan, modern, municipal, urban, urbane; SEE CONCEPT *536*

mettle [*n*] *boldness, strength of character*
animation, ardor, backbone, bravery, caliber, courage, daring, dauntlessness, disposition, energy, fire, force, fortitude, gallantry, gameness, grit*, guts*, hardihood, heart*, indomitability, kidney*, life*, makeup, moxie, nature, nerve, pluck, quality, resolution, resolve, spirit, spunk, stamina, stamp*, starch, temper, temperament, valor, vigor, vitality; SEE CONCEPT *411*

miasma [*n*] *effluvium*
fetor, foul air, fumes, gas, mephitis, odor, pollu-

tion, reek, smell, smog, stench, stink, vapor; SEE
CONCEPT *465*

microbe [*n*] *bacteria*
bacillus, bacterium, bug*, crud, germ, microorganism, pathogen, plague, virus; SEE CONCEPT *306*

microorganism [*n*] *germ*
bacterium, bug*, disease, disease-causing agent, microbe, parasite, pathogen, plague, virus; SEE CONCEPTS *306,392*

microscopic [*adj*] *tiny, almost undetectable*
atomic, diminutive, imperceptible, infinitesimal, invisible, little, minuscule, minute, negligible, teeny*, wee*; SEE CONCEPTS *773,789*

microwave [*v*] *cook*
bake, heat, melt, nuke*, warm up, zap*; SEE CONCEPT *170*

middle [*adj*] *central*
average, between, betwixt and between*, center, centermost, equidistant, halfway, inner, inside, intermediate, intervening, mainstream, mean, medial, median, medium, mezzo*, middlemost, middle of the road*, midmost, smack in the middle, straddling the fence*; SEE CONCEPTS *547,583,830*

middle [*n*] *center*
core, deep, focus, halfway, halfway point, heart, inside, marrow, mean, media, midpoint, midriff, midsection, midst, thick, waist; SEE CONCEPTS *746,761,830,833*

middle-of-the-road [*adj*] *moderate*
balanced, cautious, compromising, conservative, controlled, disciplined, even, impartial, indifferent, inexpensive, midway, mild, modest, neutral, noncommittal, nonpartisan, not excessive, on the fence*, reasonable, straight; SEE CONCEPTS *533,575*

middle person [*n*] *person who acts as intermediary*
agent, broker, connection, distributor, entrepreneur, fixer, go-between*, influence, interagent, interceder, intercessor, intermediate, intermediator, jobber*, mediator, representative, salesperson, wholesaler; SEE CONCEPT *348*

middling [*adj*] *adequate, okay*
all right, average, common, conventional, decent, fair, fairish, good, indifferent, intermediate, mean, mediocre, medium, moderate, modest, okay, ordinary, passable, run-of-the-mill*, so-so*, tolerable, traditional, unexceptional, unremarkable; SEE CONCEPT *547*

midget [*adj*] *short, small*
baby, diminutive, knee-high*, Lilliputian, miniature, minikin, pocket, teensy*, teeny*, tiny; SEE CONCEPTS *773,779*

midget [*n*] *small person*
bantam, gnome, homuncule, homunculus, Lilliputian*, little person, manikin, midge, runt*; SEE CONCEPT *424*

midnight [*n*] *middle of the night*
bewitching hour*, dead of night*, 12 o'clock at night, small hours*, twelve o'clock at night, witching hour*; SEE CONCEPTS *801,802,806*

midst [*n*] *middle, core*
betwixt and between*, bosom, center, deep, depths, halfway, heart, hub, interior, mean, medium, midpoint, nucleus, thick; SEE CONCEPT *830*

mien [*n*] *person's presence, manner*
act, address, air, appearance, aspect, aura, bearing, carriage, countenance, demeanor, deportment, expression, front, image, look, mannerism, port, set, style; SEE CONCEPTS *411,644*

miff [*v*] *annoy*
aggrieve, bother, displease, hurt, irk, irritate, nettle, offend, pester, pique, provoke, put out, resent, upset, vex; SEE CONCEPTS *7,19*

might [*n*] *ability, power*
adequacy, arm, authority, capability, capacity, clout, command, competence, control, domination, efficacy, efficiency, energy, force, forcefulness, forcibleness, get-up-and-go*, jurisdiction, lustiness, mastery, moxie*, muscle*, potency, powerfulness, prowess, puissance, punch, qualification, qualifiedness, sinew*, steam, strength, strenuousness, strong arm*, sway, valor, vigor, vigorousness; SEE CONCEPTS *411,641,732*

mightily [*adv1*] *very much, extremely*
decidedly, exceedingly, greatly, highly, hugely, intensely, mighty, notably, surpassingly, very; SEE CONCEPT *569*

mightily [*adv2*] *forcefully*
arduously, energetically, forcibly, hard, hardly, laboriously, lustily, might and main*, powerfully, strenuously, strongly, vigorously, with all one's strength; SEE CONCEPTS *540,544*

mighty [*adj1*] *forceful, powerful*
boss*, doughty, hardy, indomitable, lusty, muscular, omnipotent, potent, powerhouse, puissant, robust, stalwart, steamroller*, stout, strapping, strengthy, strong, strong as ox*, sturdy, vigorous, wieldy; SEE CONCEPTS *489,540*

mighty [*adj2*] *gigantic, monumental*
august, bulky, colossal, considerable, dynamic, eminent, enormous, extensive, extraordinary, grand, great, heroic, high, huge, illustrious, immense, imposing, impressive, intense, irresistible, large, magnificent, majestic, massive, moving, notable, prodigious, renowned, stupendous, titanic, towering, tremendous, vast; SEE CONCEPTS *537,773,781*

migrant [*n*] *person who moves to a foreign place*
departer, drifter, emigrant, evacuee, expatriate, gypsy, immigrant, itinerant, migrator, mover, nomad, rover, tinker, transient, traveler, vagrant, wanderer; SEE CONCEPT *413*

migrant/migratory [*adj*] *moving, traveling*
casual, changing, drifting, emigrating, errant, gypsy, immigrant, immigrating, impermanent, itinerant, migrative, migratorial, mobile, nomad, nomadic, on the move, passing over, passing through, peripatetic, ranging, roving, seasonal, shifting, temporary, tramp, transient, transmigratory, unsettled, vagabond, vagrant, wandering; SEE CONCEPT *584*

migrate [*v*] *move, travel to another place*
drift, emigrate, immigrate, journey, leave, nomadize, range, roam, rove, shift, transmigrate, trek, voyage, wander; SEE CONCEPTS *198,224*

mild [*adj1*] *gentle, temperate, nonirritating*
balmy, benign, benignant, blah*, bland, breezy, calm, choice, clear, clement, cool, dainty, delicate, demulcent, easy, emollient, exquisite, faint, fine, flat, genial, ho-hum*, lenient, lenitive, light, lukewarm, medium, mellow, moderate, mollifying, nothing, nothing much*, pabulum, pacific, peaceful, placid, smooth, soft, soothing, sunny, tempered, tepid, untroubled, vanilla*, warm, weak, wimpy*; SEE CONCEPTS *485,525,537*

mild [*adj2*] *easygoing, pleasant in personality*
amiable, balmy, bland, calm, clement, compassionate, complaisant, deferential, docile, dull, easy, equable, feeble, flat, forbearant, forbearing, forgiving, gentle, good-humored, good-natured, good-tempered, humane, indulgent, insipid, jejune, kind, lenient, meek, mellow, merciful, mild-mannered, moderate, obeisant, obliging, pacific, patient, peaceable, placid, · serene, smooth, soft, spiritless, subdued, submissive, subservient, tame, temperate, tender, tranquil, unassuming, vapid, warm; SEE CONCEPTS *401,404*

mile [*n*] *5, 280 feet/1.609 kilometers measured*
nautical, square, statute; SEE CONCEPTS *790,791*

milestone [*n*] *achievement*
anniversary, breakthrough, discovery, event, landmark, milepost, occasion, turning point, waypost; SEE CONCEPTS *2,706*

milieu [*n*] *environment, atmosphere*
ambience, ambient, background, bag, climate, element, locale, location, medium, mise-en-scène, nabe, neighborhood, place, scene, setting, space, sphere, surroundings, turf; SEE CONCEPT *673*

militant [*adj*] *aggressive, combative*
active, assertive, assertory, bellicose, belligerent, combating, contending, contentious, embattled, fighting, gladiatorial, in arms, martial, militaristic, military, offensive, pugnacious, pushy, quarrelsome, scrappy, self-assertive, truculent, up in arms, vigorous, warlike, warring; SEE CONCEPT *401*

militant [*n*] *person who fights, is aggressive*
activist, belligerent, combatant, demonstrator, fighter, objector, partisan, protester, rioter, warrior; SEE CONCEPTS *358,359*

military [*adj*] *soldierlike; concerning the armed forces*
aggressive, armed, army, combatant, combative, fighting, martial, militant, militaristic, noncivil, soldierly, warlike, warmongering; SEE CONCEPT *536*

military [*n*] *armed force*
air force, army, force, marines, navy, service, servicepeople, soldiery, troop; SEE CONCEPT *322*

milk [*n*] *liquid produced by mammals*
buttermilk, chalk*, condensed, cream, evaporated, formula, goat, half-and-half, homogenized, laiche, low fat, moo juice*, pasteurized, powdered, raw, skim, two-percent, whole; SEE CONCEPT *467*

milk [*v*] *tap; exploit*
bleed, drain, draw off, elicit, empty, evince, evoke, exhaust, express, extort, extract, fleece, impose on, let out, press, pump, siphon, suck, take advantage, take out, use, wring; SEE CONCEPTS *139,142,156,225*

milksop [*n*] *coward*
baby*, caitiff, chicken*, chicken heart*, chicken liver*, cry-baby, deserter, fraidy-cat*, jellyfish*, lily liver, momma's boy*, namby-pamby, pansy, pantywaist, quitter, scaredy cat*, sissy*, weakling, wimp, wuss*, wussy*, yellow, yellow belly*; SEE CONCEPT *423*

milky [*adj*] *white, cloudy*
alabaster, clouded, frosted, lacteal, lacteous, lactescent, milk-white, opalescent, opaline, opaque, pearly, whitish; SEE CONCEPT *618*

mill [*n*] *factory*
foundry, manufactory, plant, shop, sweatshop, works; SEE CONCEPTS *439,449*

mill [*v*] *grind*
comminute, crush, granulate, grate, pound, powder, press, pulverize; SEE CONCEPT *186*

millenium [*n*] *one thousand years*
one-thousandth anniversary, turn of the century; SEE CONCEPTS *807,816*

millstone [*n*] *burden*
accountability, affliction, albatross*, anxiety, ball and chain*, blame, charge, concern, cross, deadweight, difficulty, encumbrance, grievance, hardship, hindrance, load, mental weight, misfortune, onus, punishment, responsibility, strain, stress, task, thorn in one's side*, trial, trouble, worry; SEE CONCEPTS *532,690*

mimic [*n*] *person who imitates*
actor, caricaturist, comedian, copycat, imitator, impersonator, impressionist, mime, mummer, parodist, parrot, performer, playactor, player, thespian, trouper; SEE CONCEPT *352*

mimic [*v*] *imitate, mock*
act, ape, burlesque, caricature, copy, copycat, ditto*, do, do like*, echo, enact, fake, go like*, impersonate, look like*, make believe, make fun of, make like*, mime, mirror, pantomime, parody, parrot, perform, personate, play, resemble, ridicule, sham, simulate, take off*, travesty; SEE CONCEPTS *54,59,111,171*

mince [*v1*] *chop up*
chip, crumble, cut, dice, divide, grind, hack, hash, whack; SEE CONCEPT *176*

mince [*v2*] *pose, put on airs*
attitudinize, flounce, posture, prance, sashay, strut; SEE CONCEPT *59*

mince [*v3*] *euphemize, hold back in communication*
alleviate, decrease, diminish, extenuate, lessen, minimize, moderate, palliate, soften, spare, tone down, weaken; SEE CONCEPT *266*

mincing [*adj*] *affected, pretentious*
artificial, dainty, delicate, effeminate, fastidious, finical, finicky, fussy, genteel, insincere, la-di-da*, nice, particular, persnickety, precious, sissy, squeamish, stilted, too-too*, unnatural; SEE CONCEPTS *401,404*

mind [*n1*] *intelligence*
apperception, attention, brain*, brainpower, brains*, capacity, cognizance, conception, consciousness, creativity, faculty, function, genius, head, imagination, ingenuity, instinct, intellect, intellectual, intellectuality, intuition, judgment, lucidity, marbles*, mentality, observation, perception, percipience, power, psyche, ratiocination, reason, reasoning, regard, sanity, sense, soul, soundness, spirit, talent, thinker, thought, understanding, wisdom, wits; SEE CONCEPTS *393,409*

mind [*n2*] *memory*
attention, cognizance, concentration, head, mark, note, notice, observance, observation, recollection, regard, remark, remembrance, subconscious, thinking, thoughts; SEE CONCEPTS *409,630*

mind [*n3*] *inclination, tendency; belief*
attitude, bent, conviction, desire, determination, disposition, eye, fancy, feeling, humor, impulse, intention, judgment, leaning, liking, mood, notion, opinion, outlook, persuasion, pleasure,

mi
mi

point of view, purpose, sentiment, strain, temper, temperament, thoughts, tone, urge, vein, view, way of thinking, will, wish; SEE CONCEPTS *20,657,689*

mind [*v1*] *be bothered; care*
be affronted, be opposed, complain, deplore, disapprove, dislike, look askance at, object, resent, take offense; SEE CONCEPTS *21,29*

mind [*v2*] *comply, obey*
adhere to, attend, behave, do as told, follow, follow orders, heed, keep, listen, mark, note, notice, observe, pay attention, pay heed, regard, respect, take heed, watch; SEE CONCEPTS *23,91*

mind [*v3*] *attend, tend*
baby-sit, be attentive, behold, care for, discern, discipline, ensure, give heed to, govern, guard, have charge of, keep an eye on*, listen up, look, make certain, mark, mind the store*, note, notice, observe, oversee, perceive, regard, ride herd on*, see, sit, superintend, supervise, watch; SEE CONCEPTS *110,295,596,623*

mind [*v4*] *be careful*
be cautious, be concerned, be on guard, be solicitous, be wary, have a care, mind one's p's and q's*, take care, tend, toe the line*, trouble, watch, watch one's step*, watch out*; SEE CONCEPT *34*

mind [*v5*] *remember*
bethink, bring to mind, cite, recall, recollect, remind, reminisce, retain; SEE CONCEPT *40*

mind-blowing [*adj*] *amazing, intense*
astonishing, eye-opening, hallucinatory, mind-altering, mind-boggling, overwhelming, psychedelic, staggering, stunning, wonderful; SEE CONCEPTS *547,572*

mind-boggling [*adj*] *overwhelming*
amazing, astonishing, breathtaking, eye-opening, mind-blowing, spectacular, staggering, startling, stunning, stupendous, surprising, wonderful; SEE CONCEPTS *547,572*

mindful [*adj*] *attentive, aware*
alert, alive to, apprehensive, au courant, be up on*, cagey, careful, cautious, chary, cognizant, conscientious, conscious, conversant, heedful, in the know, know all the answers*, knowing, know ins and outs*, knowledgeable, observant, observative, observing, on one's toes*, on the ball*, on the job*, on to*, plugged in*, regardful, respectful, sensible, solicitous, thoughtful, tuned in*, vigilant, wary, watchful, with eyes peeled*; SEE CONCEPTS *402,403,542*

mindless [*adj*] *oblivious, stupid; automatic*
asinine, brutish, careless, daydreaming, foolish, forgetful, gratuitous, heedless, idiotic, imbecilic, inattentive, mooning, moony, moronic, neglectful, negligent, nitwitted, obtuse, out, out of it*, rash, senseless, silly, simple, spaced-out*, thoughtless, unaware, unintelligent, unmindful, unthinking, witless; SEE CONCEPTS *403,538*

mind reader [*n*] *psychic*
augur, channeller, clairvoyant, diviner, fortuneteller, haruspex, horoscopist, medium, mentalist, oracle, palm reader, prophet, seer, soothsayer, telepathis; SEE CONCEPT *423*

mind-set [*n*] *mental attitude*
air, approach, belief, character, demeanor, disposition, frame of mind, headset, inclination, mental outlook, mental state, mood, opinion, perspective, philosophy, point of view, position, sentiment, stance, stand, standing, standpoint,

temperament, view, way of thinking; SEE CONCEPTS *410,689*

mine [*n*] *deposit, supply*
abundance, bed, bonanza, ditch, excavation, field, fount, fountain, fund, gold mine, hoard, lode, pit, quarry, reserve, shaft, source, spring, stock, store, treasure trove, treasury, trench, vein, wealth, well, wellspring; SEE CONCEPTS *449,509,712*

mine [*v*] *dig up*
burrow, delve, dig for, drill, excavate, extract, hew, pan, quarry, sap, scoop, shovel, unearth, work; SEE CONCEPT *178*

mingle [*v1*] *physically join*
admix, alloy, blend, coalesce, commingle, compound, intermingle, intermix, interweave, make up, marry, meld, merge, mix, unite, wed; SEE CONCEPT *193*

mingle [*v2*] *socialize*
associate, circulate, consort, fraternize, gang up*, hang out*, hobnob, mix, network, pool, rub shoulders*, tie in, work the room*; SEE CONCEPT *384*

miniature [*adj*] *tiny*
baby, diminutive, itsy-bitsy*, itty-bitty*, Lilliputian*, little, midget, mini, minikin, minuscule, minute, mite, model, petite, pint-sized, pocket, reduced, scaled-down, small, small-scale, teensy*, teeny*, toy, wee; SEE CONCEPTS *773,789*

miniature [*n*] *tiny thing*
baby, insignificancy, midget, model, pocket edition, toy; SEE CONCEPT *730*

minimal [*adj*] *littlest, slightest*
basal, basic, essential, fundamental, least, least possible, lowest, minimum, nominal, smallest, token; SEE CONCEPTS *762,773,789*

minimize [*v*] *make smaller; underrate*
abbreviate, attenuate, belittle, cheapen, curtail, cut down to size, cut rate, decrease, decry, deprecate, depreciate, derogate, detract, diminish, discount, disparage, downplay*, dwarf*, knock*, knock down*, lessen, make light of*, make little of, miniaturize, pan, play down, pooh-pooh*, poor-mouth*, prune, put down, reduce, run down, shrink, underestimate, underplay; SEE CONCEPTS *54,240,247*

minimum [*adj*] *least, lowest*
least possible, littlest, merest, minimal, slightest, smallest, tiniest; SEE CONCEPTS *762,789*

minimum [*n*] *lowest amount*
atom, bottom, dab, depth, dot, gleam, grain, hair, iota, jot, least, lowest, margin, modicum, molecule, nadir, narrowest, particle, pittance, point, scintilla, scruple, shadow, slightest, smallest, smidgen, soupçon, spark, speck, trifle, whit; SEE CONCEPTS *787,831*

minion [*n*] *sycophant*
backscratcher*, backslapper*, bootlicker*, brownnoser*, dependent, doormat, fan, fawner, flatterer, flunky*, follower, groupie, hanger-on*, lackey, parasite, puppet, slave, stooge*, subordinate, toady, yes-man/woman, yes-person; SEE CONCEPTS *352,366,423*

miniscule/minuscule [*adj*] *tiny, very small*
diminutive, dwarf, infinitesimal, itsy-bitsy, Lilliputian, little, meager, microscopic, mini*, miniature, minute, pint-sized*, puny*, short, slight, small-scale, stunted, teensy*, teeny, trivial, undersized, wee*; SEE CONCEPTS *773,789*

minister [*n1*] *person in charge of church*
abbot, archbishop, archdeacon, bishop, chaplain, clergy, clergyperson, cleric, clerical, clerk, confessor, curate, deacon, dean, diocesan, divine, ecclesiastic, lecturer, missionary, monk, parson, pastor, preacher, prelate, priest, pulpiteer, rector, reverend, shepherd, vicar; SEE CONCEPT *361*

minister [*n2*] *person high in government*
administrator, agent, aide, ambassador, assistant, cabinet member, consul, delegate, diplomat, envoy, executive, legate, liaison, lieutenant, officeholder, official, plenipotentiary, premier, prime minister, secretary; SEE CONCEPT *354*

minister [*v*] *help, serve*
accommodate, administer, aid, answer, attend, be solicitous of, cater to, cure, doctor, do for, foster, heal, nurse, pander, pander to, remedy, succor, take care of, tend, treat, wait on, watch over; SEE CONCEPT *110*

minor [*adj*] *insignificant, small*
accessory, below the mark, bush-league*, casual, dependent, dinky*, inconsequential, inconsiderable, inferior, junior, lesser, light, low, minus, negligible, paltry, petty, piddling, secondary, second-string*, slight, smaller, small-fry*, small-time, subordinate, subsidiary, tacky, trifling, trivial, two-bit*, unimportant, younger; SEE CONCEPTS *575,773,789*

minor [*n*] *person under legal age of maturity*
adolescent, baby, boy, child, girl, infant, junior, juvenile, lad, little one, schoolboy, schoolgirl, teenager, underage, youngster, youth; SEE CONCEPT *424*

mint [*adj*] *brand-new*
excellent, first-class, fresh, intact, original, perfect, spanking-new*, spick-and-span*, unblemished, undamaged, unmarred, untarnished, virgin; SEE CONCEPTS *574,578,797*

mint [*n*] *a lot of money*
boodle, bundle, fortune, heap, million, packet, pile, pot, roll, wad; SEE CONCEPTS *340,787*

mint [*v*] *create, coin*
cast, construct, devise, fabricate, fashion, forge, invent, issue, make, make up, mold, monetize, produce, provide, punch, stamp, strike, think up; SEE CONCEPTS *43,173,205,251*

minute [*adj1*] *very small*
atomic, diminutive, exact, exiguous, fine, inconsiderable, infinitesimal, insignificant, invisible, little, microbic, microscopic, miniature, minim, minimal, minuscule, molecular, peewee*, piddling, precise, puny, slender, teeny-weeny*, tiny, wee; SEE CONCEPTS *773,789*

minute [*adj2*] *unimportant*
immaterial, inconsiderable, insignificant, light, little, minor, negligible, nonessential, paltry, petty, picayune, piddling, puny, slight, small, trifling, trivial; SEE CONCEPT *575*

minute [*adj3*] *exact, precise*
blow-by-blow*, careful, circumstantial, clock-like, close, critical, detailed, elaborate, exhaustive, full, itemized, meticulous, painstaking, particular, particularized, punctilious, scrupulous, specialized, thorough; SEE CONCEPT *557*

minute [*n*] *brief time period*
bat of an eye*, breath, breathing, crack, flash, instant, jiffy*, min*, mo*, moment, nothing flat*, sec*, second, shake, short time*, sixtieth of hour, sixty seconds, split second, twinkling*; SEE CONCEPTS *803,807,821*

minutiae [*n*] *trivial detail*
incidental, minor detail, small detail, trifle, trivia, triviality, trivial matter, unimportant detail, useless information; SEE CONCEPTS *274,543*

miracle [*n*] *wonderful, surprising event or thing*
marvel, phenomenon, portent, prodigy, rarity, revelation, sensation, stunner, supernatural occurrence, surprise, thaumaturgy, unusualness, wonder; SEE CONCEPTS *671,689,693*

miraculous [*adj*] *surprisingly wonderful*
amazing, anomalous, astonishing, astounding, awesome, extraordinary, fabulous, freakish, heavy, incredible, inexplicable, magical, marvelous, monstrous, numinous, phenomenal, preternatural, prodigious, spectacular, staggering, strange, stupefying, stupendous, superhuman, superior, supermundane, supernatural, supranatural, thaumaturgic, the utmost, unaccountable, unbelievable, unearthly, unimaginable, unreal, wonderworking, wondrous; SEE CONCEPTS *529,548,572*

mirage [*n*] *imaginary vision*
delusion, fantasy, hallucination, ignis fatuus, illusion, optical illusion, phantasm; SEE CONCEPTS *529,628*

mire [*n*] *muck, morass*
bog, dirt, fen, glop*, goo*, gunk*, marsh, moss, mud, ooze*, quagmire, quicksand, slime*, swamp; SEE CONCEPTS *509,674*

mire [*v*] *delay, catch up in*
bog down, cling, decelerate, detain, dirty, embroil, enmesh, ensnare, entangle, entrap, flounder, hang up, implicate, involve, retard, set back, sink, slow down, slow up, snare, soil, stick, tangle, trap; SEE CONCEPTS *112,121*

mirror [*n*] *glass that reflects image*
cheval glass, gaper, hand glass, imager, looking glass, pier glass, polished metal, reflector, seeing glass, speculum; SEE CONCEPTS *443,470*

mirror [*v*] *copy, reflect*
act like, depict, double, echo, embody, emulate, epitomize, exemplify, follow, glass, illustrate, image, imitate, make like*, mimic, personify, represent, show, simulate, symbolize, take off*, typify; SEE CONCEPTS *111,118,171*

mirth [*n*] *great joy*
amusement, cheer, cheerfulness, convulsions, entertainment, festivity, frivolity, frolic, fun, gaiety, gladness, glee, happiness, hilarity, hysteria, hysterics, jocularity, jocundity, jollity, joviality, joyousness, kicks*, laughs, laughter, levity, lightheartedness, merriment, merrymaking, pleasure, rejoicing, revelry, sport, whoopee*; SEE CONCEPTS *388,410*

mirthful [*adj*] *merry*
amusing, blithe, blithesome, carefree, cheerful, cheery, convivial, enjoyable, entertaining, festive, frolicsome, fun-loving, funny, gay, glad, gleeful, happy, jocund, jolly, joyful, joyous, larking, lighthearted, lively, perky, playful, sunny, vivacious; SEE CONCEPTS *403,548,572*

misadventure [*n*] *bad luck, mishap*
accident, adversity, bad break*, blunder, calamity, casualty, cataclysm, catastrophe, debacle, disaster, error, failure, faux pas, ill fortune, lapse, mischance, misfortune, reverse, setback, slip, tragedy, woe; SEE CONCEPT *674*

misanthrope [*n*] *person who hates others*
cynic, doubter, egoist, egotist, hater, isolate,

loner, misanthropist, recluse, skeptic; SEE CONCEPT *412*

misanthropic [*adj*] *unsociable, cynical*
antisocial, egoistic, egotistical, eremitic, hating, inhumane, malevolent, misanthropical, reclusive, reserved, sarcastic, selfish, solitary, standoffish, unfriendly; SEE CONCEPT *404*

misapprehend [*v*] *get the wrong idea, impression*
blunder, confuse, err, misconceive, misconstrue, misinterpret, misread, miss, mistake, misunderstand; SEE CONCEPT *15*

misappropriate [*v*] *use wrongly; steal*
abuse, appropriate, defalcate, embezzle, misapply, misspend, misuse, peculate, plunder, pocket, rob, swindle; SEE CONCEPTS *139,156,341*

misbegotten [*adj*] *illegitimate, illicit*
baseborn, bastard, dishonest, disreputable, illegal, natural, poor, shady, spurious, stolen, supposititious, unlawful, unrespectable; SEE CONCEPTS *319,549*

misbehave [*v*] *act in inappropriate manner*
act up, be at fault, be bad, be dissolute, be guilty, be immoral, be indecorous, be insubordinate, be mischievous, bend the law*, be out of line*, be out of order*, be reprehensible, carry on, cut up, deviate, do evil, do wrong, fail, fool around*, get into mischief, go astray, go wrong, make trouble, misconduct, offend, roughhouse*, sin, sow wild oats*, take a wrong turn*, transgress, trespass; SEE CONCEPTS *633,645*

misbehavior [*n*] *naughty act, conduct*
acting up*, fault, immorality, impropriety, incivility, indiscipline, insubordination, mischief, misconduct, misdeed, misdemeanor, misdoing, monkey business*, naughtiness, rudeness, shenanigans*, transgression, wrongdoing; SEE CONCEPTS *633,645*

miscalculate [*v*] *make a mistake*
blow*, blunder, discount, disregard, drop the ball*, err, get signals crossed*, get wrong, go wrong, mess up*, misconstrue, miscount, misinterpret, misjudge, misread, misreckon, miss by a mile*, misunderstand, mix up, overestimate, overlook, overrate, overvalue, slip up, stumble, underestimate, underrate, undervalue; SEE CONCEPT *101*

miscarriage [*n*] *failure*
abortion, botch, breakdown, defeat, error, interruption, malfunction, misadventure, mischance, misfire, mishap, miss, mistake, nonsuccess, perversion, undoing; SEE CONCEPTS *230,699*

miscellaneous [*adj*] *diversified, various*
assorted, confused, conglomerate, different, disordered, disparate, divergent, divers, diverse, heterogeneous, indiscriminate, jumbled, many, mingled, mixed, motley, muddled, multifarious, multiform, odd, promiscuous, scattered, scrambled, sundry, unmatched, unsorted, varied, variegated; SEE CONCEPT *564*

miscellany [*n*] *varied collection*
accumulation, aggregation, anthology, assortment, brew, collectanea, combination, combo, compilation, conglomeration, cumulation, diversity, farrago, gallimaufry, garbage*, hash, hodgepodge, jumble, medley, mélange, melee, mess, mishmash, mix, mixed bag, mixture, muddle, odds and ends*, olio, pasticcio, pastiche, patchwork, potpourri, salad, salmagundi, smorgasbord, stew, variety; SEE CONCEPTS *432,665*

mischief [*n*] *trouble, damage*
atrocity, catastrophe, devilment, devilry, dirty trick*, evil, fault, friskiness, frolicsomeness, funny business*, gag, harm, high jinks*, hurt, ill, impishness, injury, misbehavior, mischievousness, misconduct, misdoing, misfortune, monkey business*, naughtiness, outrage, playfulness, prank, rascality, roguery, roguishness, sabotage, shenanigans, sportiveness, transgression, vandalism, waggery, waggishness, waywardness, wrong, wrongdoing; SEE CONCEPTS *192,633,645*

mischievous [*adj*] *devilish, wicked*
arch, artful, bad, bothersome, damaging, dangerous, deleterious, destructive, detrimental, dickens*, evil, exasperating, foxy*, frolicsome, harmful, hazardous, holy terror*, hurtful, ill, ill-behaved, impish, injurious, insidious, irksome, malicious, malignant, misbehaving, naughty, nocuous, perilous, pernicious, playful, precarious, puckish, rascal, rascally, risky, rude, sinful, sly, spiteful, sportive, teasing, tricky, troublesome, vexatious, vexing, vicious, wayward; SEE CONCEPTS *401,545*

misconception [*n*] *wrong idea, impression*
delusion, error, fallacy, fault, misapprehension, misconstruction, misinterpretation, mistake, mistaken belief, misunderstanding; SEE CONCEPTS *409,689*

misconduct [*n*] *bad or unethical behavior*
delinquency, dereliction, evil, immorality, impropriety, malfeasance, malpractice, malversation, misbehavior, mischief, misdemeanor, misdoing, mismanagement, naughtiness, offense, rudeness, transgression, wrongdoing; SEE CONCEPTS *192,633,645*

misconstrue [*v*] *get a wrong or false impression*
distort, exaggerate, misapprehend, misconceive, misinterpret, misjudge, misread, mistake, mistranslate, misunderstand, pervert, take the wrong way; SEE CONCEPT *15*

miscreant [*adj*] *evil, immoral*
corrupt, criminal, degenerate, depraved, flagitious, infamous, iniquitous, nefarious, perverse, rascally, reprehensible, reprobate, unhealthy, unprincipled, vicious, villainous, wicked; SEE CONCEPTS *401,545*

miscreant [*n*] *person who is very bad, immoral*
blackguard, black sheep*, bootlegger, bully, cad, caitiff, convict, criminal, culprit, delinquent, drunkard, evildoer, felon, fink*, heel*, hoodlum, jailbird, loafer, louse*, lowlife*, malefactor, outcast, outlaw, pickpocket, racketeer, rapscallion, rascal, rat*, reprobate, rowdy, ruffian, scalawag, scamp, scoundrel, scum*, sinner, sneak, vagabond, villain, wretch, wrongdoer; SEE CONCEPT *412*

misdeed/misdemeanor [*n*] *sin, crime*
breach of law, criminality, dirt*, dirty deed*, dirty pool*, fault, infringement, malefaction, misbehavior, misconduct, miscue, offense, peccadillo, slipup, transgression, trespass, villainy, violation, wrong, wrongdoing; SEE CONCEPTS *192,633,645*

miser [*n*] *person who hoards money, possessions*
cheapskate*, churl, harpy*, hoarder, moneygrubber*, penny-pincher*, pinchfist*, pinchpenny*, Scrooge*, stiff*, tightwad*; SEE CONCEPTS *348,412,423*

miserable [*adj*] *unhappy, depressed*
afflicted, agonized, ailing, anguished, broken-

hearted, crestfallen, dejected, desolate, despairing, despondent, destroyed, disconsolate, discontented, distressed, doleful, dolorous, down, downcast, down in the mouth*, forlorn, gloomy, heartbroken, hopeless, hurt, hurting, ill, injured, in pain, melancholy, mournful, on a downer*, pained, pathetic, pitiable, racked, rueful, ruthful, sad, sick, sickly, sorrowful, strained, suffering, tormented, tortured, tragic, troubled, woebegone, wounded, wretched; SEE CONCEPT *403*

miserable [*adj2*] *destitute, shabby*
abject, bad, contemptible, deplorable, despicable, detestable, disgraceful, godforsaken, impoverished, indigent, inferior, lamentable, low, meager, mean, needy, paltry, pathetic, penniless, piteous, pitiable, poor, poverty-stricken, sad, scanty, scurvy, shameful, sordid, sorry, squalid, tragic, vile, worthless, wretched; SEE CONCEPTS *485,570*

miserly [*adj*] *greedy, stingy*
abject, avaricious, beggarly, cheapskate*, churlish, close, close-fisted, covetous, grasping, ignoble, illiberal, mean, parsimonious, penny-pinching*, penurious, skinflint*, sordid, tightfisted*, ungenerous; SEE CONCEPTS *326,334,401,404*

misery [*n1*] *pain, mental or physical*
ache, agony, anguish, anvil chorus, bad news*, blues*, depression, desolation, despair, despondency, discomfort, distress, dolor, gloom, grief, hardship, headache, heartache, hurting, melancholy, pang, passion, sadness, sorrow, squalor, stitch, suffering, throe, torment, torture, twinge, unhappiness, woe, worriment, worry, wretchedness; SEE CONCEPT *728*

misery [*n2*] *trouble, disaster*
adversity, affliction, anxiety, bitter pill*, burden, calamity, catastrophe, curse, destitution, difficulty, grief, indigence, load, misfortune, need, ordeal, penury, poverty, privation, problem, sordidness, sorrow, squalor, trial, tribulation, want, woe; SEE CONCEPTS *335,666,674*

misfire [*v*] *fail*
abort, backfire, blunder, break down, come to nothing, explode, fall flat*, fall short*, fizzle, fizzle out, fizz out, flop, flounder, go up in smoke*, go wrong, miscarry, miss, peter out, poop out, slip; SEE CONCEPT *699*

misfit [*n*] *nonconformist*
beatnik*, bohemian*, different breed*, dissenter, dissident, dropout, eccentric, fish out of water*, freak*, individualist, lone wolf, loser, oddball, odd man out, offbeat, outsider, weirdo*; SEE CONCEPTS *359,423*

misfortune/mishap [*n*] *bad luck; disaster*
accident, adversity, affliction, annoyance, anxiety, bad break*, bad news*, blow*, burden, calamity, casuality, cataclysm, catastrophe, contretemps, cross, crunch, debacle, disadvantage, disappointment, discomfort, dole, failure, hard luck*, hardship, harm, inconvenience, infelicity, loss, misadventure, mischance, misery, nuisance, reverse, rotten luck, setback, stroke of bad luck*, tough luck*, tragedy, trial, tribulation, trouble, unpleasantness, visitation, worry; SEE CONCEPTS *674,679*

misgiving [*n*] *uncertainty*
anxiety, apprehension, apprehensiveness, distrust, doubt, fear, foreboding, hesitation, mis-

trust, premonition, prenotion, presage, presentiment, qualm, reservation, scruple, suspicion, unbelief, unease, worry; SEE CONCEPTS *21,689,690*

misguided [*adj*] *ill-advised, deluded*
bearded, bum-steer*, confused, deceived, disinformed, erroneous, faked-out*, foolish, imprudent, indiscreet, inexpedient, injudicious, led up the garden path*, misled, misplaced, mistaken, stonewalled*, uncalled for, unreasonable, unwarranted, unwise, wrong; SEE CONCEPTS *544,548,570*

mishandle/mismanage [*v*] *mess up*
abuse, be incompetent, be inefficient, blow, blunder, botch*, bungle, confound, err, flub*, foul up, fumble, goof*, goof up*, gum up*, harm, make a hash of*, make a mess of*, maladminister, misapply, misconduct, misdirect, misemploy, misgovern, mistreat, misuse, muff*, overlook, pervert, prostitute, put foot in*, screw up*, shoot oneself in foot*; SEE CONCEPTS *101,156,384*

mishap [*n*] *accident*
blow, blunder, calamity, collision, crack-up*, disaster, fender-bender*, fluke*, hazard, ill-fortune, misadventure, misfortune, mistake, pileup*, rear-ender*, setback, smash*, smashup*, stack-up*, total*, wrack-up*; SEE CONCEPT *674*

mishmash [*n*] *hodgepodge*
collection, combination, goulash*, hash, jumble, medley, melange, mess, miscellany, mixed bag, mixture, olio, patchwork, potpourri, salmagundi*; SEE CONCEPTS *260,432*

misinform [*v*] *give wrong information intentionally*
bait and switch*, cover up, deceive, disinform, doublespeak*, double-talk*, lead astray, lie, misdirect, misguide, mislead, misstate, mousetrap*, pervert, prevaricate, put on*, put on an act*, put on false front*, put up smoke screen*, signify, string along*, wrong steer*; SEE CONCEPT *63*

misjudge [*v*] *get the wrong idea*
bark up wrong tree*, be misled, be overcritical, be partial, be unfair, be wrong, come to hasty conclusion, dogmatize, drop the ball*, err, misapprehend, miscalculate, miscomprehend, misconceive, misconjecture, misconstrue, misdeem, misreckon, miss by a mile*, mistake, misthink, misunderstand, overestimate, overrate, prejudge, presume, presuppose, put foot in*, stumble, suppose, underestimate, underrate; SEE CONCEPTS *12,18,101*

mislead [*v*] *give someone the wrong idea, information*
bait, beguile, betray, bilk, bluff, bunk, cheat, cozen, deceive, defraud, delude, double-cross*, dupe, enmesh, ensnare, entangle, entice, fool, fudge*, gull, hoax, hoodwink*, hose*, illude, inveigle, juggle, lead astray, lead on*, lie, lure, misdirect, misguide, misinform, misrepresent, outwit, overreach, pervert, pull wool over eyes*, put on*, rip off*, rook, rope in*, scam, seduce, shaft, snow*, take in, tempt, trick, victimize; SEE CONCEPTS *59,63*

misleading [*adj*] *deceptive, confusing*
ambiguous, beguiling, bewildering, casuistical, catchy, confounding, deceitful, deceiving, deluding, delusive, delusory, demagogic, disingenuous, distracting, evasive, fallacious, false,

inaccurate, perplexing, puzzling, sophistical, specious, spurious, tricky, wrong; SEE CONCEPTS *267,548*

mismatch [*n*] *disparity*
discrepancy, disproportion, dissemblance, dissimilarity, divergence, divergency, diverseness, imbalance, imparity, incongruity, inequality, unevenness; SEE CONCEPT *665*

misogynist [*n*] *woman-hater*
anti-feminist, male chauvinist, misanthrope, sexist; SEE CONCEPT *689*

misplace [*v*] *lose; be unable to find*
be unable to lay hands on*, confuse, disarrange, dishevel, disorder, disorganize, displace, disturb, forget whereabouts of, lose track of, misfile, mislay, miss, mix, muss, place unwisely, place wrongly, put in wrong place, remove, scatter, unsettle; SEE CONCEPTS *116,201*

misrepresentation [*n*] *falsehood*
adulteration, coloring, distortion, exaggeration, fabrication, false light, falsification, lie, misstatement, mutilation, not a true picture*, slant, story*, stretch, tall story*, twist, untruth; SEE CONCEPTS *63,580*

misrepresent/misquote [*v*] *lie, distort*
adulterate, angle, beard*, belie, build up, cloak, color, con, confuse, cover up, disguise, distort, dress, embellish, embroider, equivocate, exaggerate, falsify, garble, give snow job*, mangle, mask, miscolor, misinterpret, misreport, misstate, overdraw, overstate, palter, pervert, phony up*, pirate*, prevaricate, promote, puff*, skew, slant, snow*, spread it on*, stretch, take out of context*, throw a curve*, trump up*, twist, warp; SEE CONCEPT *63*

miss [*n1*] *failure*
absence, blunder, default, defect, error, fault, loss, mishap, mistake, omission, oversight, slip, want; SEE CONCEPTS *101,699*

miss [*v1*] *fail, make a mistake*
be late for, blow, blunder, botch, disregard, drop, drop the ball*, err, fall flat on face*, fall short, flub*, forget, fumble, ignore, juggle, let go, let slip, lose, miscarry, misfire, mislay, misplace, muff*, neglect, omit, overlook, overshoot, pass over, pass up, skip, slight, slip, trip, trip up, undershoot; SEE CONCEPTS *101,699*

miss [*v2*] *want; feel a loss*
crave, desire, long, need, pine, wish, yearn; SEE CONCEPT *20*

misshapen [*adj*] *deformed*
askew, awry, bent, blemished, bowed, buckled, contorted, crooked, curved, damaged, disfigured, disjointed, distorted, grotesque, ill-made, irregular, malformed, mangled, marred, out of shape, twisted, ugly, unshapely, warped; SEE CONCEPTS *485,486*

missile [*n*] *projectile weapon*
ammunition, arrow, bat, bird*, bolt, bomb, bullet, cartridge, dart, MX*, pellet, projectile, rocket, shot, stealth, trajectile; SEE CONCEPT *500*

missing [*adj*] *gone, absent*
astray, away, AWOL*, disappeared, lacking, left behind, left out, lost, mislaid, misplaced, not present, nowhere to be found*, omitted, removed, short, unaccounted for, wanting; SEE CONCEPTS *539,576*

mission [*n*] *person's task, responsibility*
aim, assignment, business, calling, charge, commission, duty, end, errand, goal, job, lifework, object, objective, office, operation, profession, purpose, pursuit, quest, sortie, trade, trust, undertaking, vocation, work; SEE CONCEPTS *360,362,659*

missionary [*n*] *person who aids, does religious work*
apostle, clergy, clergyperson, converter, evangelist, herald, messenger, minister, missioner, pastor, preacher, promoter, propagandist, proselytizer, revivalist, teacher; SEE CONCEPTS *361,416*

missive [*n*] *written communication*
dispatch, epistle, letter, line, memo, memorandum, message, note, report, word; SEE CONCEPTS *271,278*

misspent [*adj*] *wasted*
blown*, dissipated, down the drain*, idle, imprudent, misapplied, prodigal, profitless, squandered, thrown away; SEE CONCEPTS *544,560,570*

misstatement [*n*] *misrepresentation*
adulteration, coloring, distortion, exaggeration, fabrication, falsehood, false light, falsification, inaccuracy, lie, misstatement, mutilation, not a true picture*, slant, story*, stretch, tall story*, twist, untruth; SEE CONCEPTS *63,580*

misstep [*n*] *mistake, wrong move*
bad move*, blunder, bungle, error, failure, false step, faux pas, fluff*, gaffe, indiscretion, lapse, miscue, miss, slip, slipup*, stumble, trip; SEE CONCEPTS *101,674,699*

mist [*n*] *film, vapor*
brume, cloud, condensation, dew, drizzle, fog, ground clouds, haze, moisture, rain, smog, soup*, spray, steam, visibility zero*; SEE CONCEPT *524*

mist [*v*] *cloud, steam up*
becloud, befog, blur, dim, drizzle, film, fog, haze, mizzle, murk, obscure, overcast, overcloud, rain, shower, sprinkle, steam; SEE CONCEPT *526*

mistake [*n*] *error, misunderstanding*
aberration, blooper*, blunder, boo-boo*, bungle, confusion, delusion, erratum, false move, false step, fault, faux pas, flub*, fluff*, gaffe, illusion, inaccuracy, inadvertence, lapse, misapplication, misapprehension, miscalculation, misconception, misinterpretation, misjudgment, misprint, misstatement, misstep, muddle, neglect, omission, overestimation, oversight, slight, slip, slip of tongue*, slipup*, snafu*, solecism, trip*, typographical error, underestimation; SEE CONCEPTS *101,230,410*

mistake [*v*] *mix up, misunderstand*
addle, be off the mark*, be wrong, blunder, botch*, bungle, confound, confuse, deceive oneself, err, fail, get wrong, goof*, have wrong impression, jumble, lapse, make a mess*, misapprehend, miscalculate, misconceive, misconstrue, miscount, misdeem, misinterpret, misjudge, misknow, misread, miss, miss the boat*, not know, omit, overestimate, overlook, put foot in*, slip*, slip up*, snarl, take for*, tangle, underestimate; SEE CONCEPTS *15,101*

mistaken [*adj*] *wrong, incorrect*
all wet*, at fault, barking up wrong tree*, confounded, confused, confused with, deceived, deluded, duped, erroneous, fallacious, false, faulty, fooled, ill-advised, illogical, inaccurate, inappropriate, misconstrued, misguided, misinformed, misinterpreting, misjudging, misled, misunder-

standing, off base*, off track*, tricked, unadvised, under wrong impression, unfounded, unreal, unsound, untrue, warranted, way off*, wide of mark*, wrongly identified, wrong number*; SEE CONCEPTS 402,529

mistreat [v] *treat badly or wrongly*
abuse, backbite, bash, brutalize, bung up*, chop, do wrong, dump on*, give black eye*, handle roughly, harm, injure, kick around, knock around, maltreat, maul, mess up, misuse, molest, outrage, push around, rip, roughhouse*, rough up, shake up, total*, trash*, wax*, wound, wrong; SEE CONCEPTS 14,156,246

mistrust [n] *doubtfulness*
apprehension, chariness, concern, distrust, doubt, dubiety, dubiosity, fear, foreboding, incertitude, misgiving, presentiment, scruple, skepticism, suspicion, uncertainty, wariness, wonder; SEE CONCEPTS 21,27,690

mistrust [v] *doubt*
apprehend, beware, be wary, challenge, disbelieve, dispute, distrust, fear, have doubts, question, scruple, suspect, suspicion; SEE CONCEPT 21

misty [adj] *filmy, obscure*
bleary, blurred, closed in, clouded, cloudy, dark, dewy, dim, enveloped, foggy, fuzzy, hazy, indistinct, murky, mushy, nebulous, opaque, overcast, shrouded, socked in, soupy*, unclear, vague, vaporous; SEE CONCEPTS 525,603,617

misunderstand [v] *get the wrong idea*
be at cross purposes*, be bewildered, be confused, be perplexed, confound, confuse, fail, get signals crossed*, get signals mixed*, get wrong, get wrong impression*, misapply, misapprehend, miscalculate, miscomprehend, misconceive, misconstrue, misinterpret, misjudge, misknow, misread, misreckon, miss*, miss the point*, mistake, not register*, take amiss, take wrongly; SEE CONCEPT 15

misunderstanding [n1] *instance of having the wrong idea*
confounding, confusion, delusion, error, false impression, misapprehension, misconception, misconstruction, misinterpretation, misjudgment, misreckoning, mistake, mix-up; SEE CONCEPT 409

misunderstanding [n2] *argument, fight*
bad vibes*, blowup*, breach, break, clash, conflict, crossed wires*, debate, difference, difficulty, disagreement, discord, dissension, falling-out*, feud, fuss, quarrel, rift, row, run-in*, rupture, set-to, sour note*, spat, squabble, tiff*, variance, words*; SEE CONCEPTS 46,106

misuse [n] *abuse; wrong application*
abusage, barbarism, catachresis, corruption, cruel treatment, desecration, dissipation, exploitation, harm, ill-treatment, injury, malapropism, maltreatment, misapplication, misemployment, mistreatment, misusage, perversion, profanation, prostitution, rough handling, solecism, squandering, waste; SEE CONCEPT 156

misuse [v] *abuse; apply wrongly*
blow*, brutalize, corrupt, cut up, desecrate, dissipate, exploit, go through, handle roughly, illtreat, maltreat, maul, mess up*, misapply, misemploy, mistreat, molest, outrage, pervert, profane, prostitute, run through*, shake up, squander, waste, wrong; SEE CONCEPT 156

mitigate [v] *check, diminish, lighten*
abate, allay, alleviate, appease, assuage, blunt, calm, come together, cool*, dull, ease, extenuate, lessen, meet halfway*, moderate, modify, mollify, pacify, palliate, placate, quiet, reduce, relieve, remit, soften, soothe, subdue, take the edge off*, temper, tone down, tranquilize, weaken; SEE CONCEPTS 233,240

mix [v1] *combine, join*
admix, adulterate, alloy, amalgamate, associate, blend, braid, coalesce, commingle, commix, compound, conjoin, cross, embody, fuse, hybridize, incorporate, infiltrate, infuse, instill, interbreed, intermingle, interweave, jumble, knead, link, lump, make up, merge, mingle, mix up, put together, saturate, stir, suffuse, synthesize, tangle, transfuse, unite, weave, work in; SEE CONCEPTS 113,193

mix [v2] *socialize*
associate, come together, consort, get along, hang out, hobnob, join, mingle; SEE CONCEPT 114

mixed [adj] *assorted, combined*
alloyed, amalgamated, assimilated, assorted, blended, brewed, composite, compound, conglomerate, crossbred, crossed, different, disordered, diverse, diversified, embodied, fused, heterogeneous, hybrid, hybridized, incorporated, infused, interbred, interdenominational, joint, kneaded, married, merged, mingled, miscellaneous, mongrel, motley, multifarious, tied, transfused, united, varied, woven; SEE CONCEPTS 485,564,772

mixed bag [n] *assortment*
all shapes and sizes, array, choice, collection, combination, combo*, diversity, hodgepodge, jumble, medley, melange, miscellany, mishmash, mixture, potpourri; SEE CONCEPTS 432,665

mixed-up [adj] *confused*
baffled, befuddled, bewildered, come apart*, confounded, dazed, discombobulated*, disconcerted, disorganized, disoriented, flummoxed, flustered, lost, muddled, out to lunch*, perplexed, puzzled, stumped, thrown off balance*; SEE CONCEPT 403

mix/mixture [n] *assortment, combination*
admixture, adulteration, alloy, amalgam, amalgamation, assimilation, association, batter, blend, brew, combine, combo, commixture, composite, compound, concoction, confection, conglomeration, cross, crossing, dough, fusion, goulash, grab bag*, hodgepodge, hybrid, hybridization, incorporation, infiltration, interfusion, jumble, mash, medley, melange, merger, mingling, miscellany, mishmash, mixed bag, mosaic, package, patchwork, potpourri, salmagundi, saturation, soup*, stew*, transfusion, union, variety; SEE CONCEPTS 260,432

mix-up [n] *confusion, misunderstanding*
botch*, chaos, commotion, disorder, jumble, mess, mistake, muddle, shambles*, tangle, turmoil; SEE CONCEPTS 230,674

mix up [v] *confuse*
addle, befuddle, bewilder, confound, derange, disorder, disorganize, disrupt, distract, disturb, dizzy, fluster, foul up*, jumble, mess up*, mistake, muddle, perplex, puzzle, snafu*, upset; SEE CONCEPTS 16,158

moan [n] *groan, complaint*
beef, cry, gripe, grouse, grumble, lament, lamen-

tation, plaint, sigh, sob, wail, whine; SEE CON-
CEPTS *52,77*

moan [*v*] *groan, complain*
bemoan, bewail, carp, deplore, grieve, gripe,
grouse, grumble, keen, lament, mourn, sigh, sob,
wail, whine; SEE CONCEPTS *52,77*

moat [*n*] *ditch*
canal, channel, fosse, gully, trench; SEE CON-
CEPTS *509,513*

mob [*n*] *large group of people*
assemblage, body, cabal, camp, canaille, cattle,
circle, clan, class, clique, collection, commonality, company, coterie, crew, crowd, crush, drove,
flock, gang, gathering, herd, horde, host, jam, lot,
mass, masses, multitude, pack, populace, posse,
press, proletariat, rabble, riffraff*, ring, riot,
scum, set, swarm, throng, troop; SEE CONCEPTS
378,417,432

mob [*v*] *come upon by pushing; surround*
attack, cram, crowd, fill, hustle, jam, jostle, overrun, pack, riot, set upon, swarm, throng; SEE
CONCEPTS *208,758*

mobile [*adj*] *movable, travelling*
adaptable, ambulatory, changeable, fluid, free,
itinerant, liquid, locomotive, loose, migrant, migratory, motile, motorized, moving, mutable, nomadic, peripatetic, portable, roaming, roving,
unsettled, unstable, unstationary, unsteadfast, unsteady, versatile, wandering; SEE CONCEPTS
576,584

mobilize [*v*] *ready for action, movement*
activate, actuate, animate, assemble, call to arms,
call up, catalyze, circulate, drive, gather, get
ready, impel, make ready, marshal, muster, organize, prepare, propel, put in motion, rally, ready,
set in motion, set off; SEE CONCEPTS
148,187,221,320

mobster [*n*] *gangster*
criminal, crook, godfather, goon, gunman/
woman, hit man/woman, hood, hoodlum, hooligan*, Mafioso*, member of the family*, outlaw,
racketeer, soldier*, thug, wiseguy*; SEE CON-
CEPT *412*

mock [*adj*] *artificial, fake*
apish*, bogus*, counterfeit, dummy, ersatz*,
faked, false, feigned, forged, fraudulent, hokey*,
imitation, imitative, make-believe, mimic,
phony, pretended, pseudo*, put-on*, quasi*,
sham*, simulated, so-called*, spurious, substitute, unreal; SEE CONCEPTS *566,582*

mock [*v1*] *ridicule*
buffoon, burlesque, caricature, chaff, deride,
flout, hoot, insult, jape, jeer, kid, laugh at, make
fun of, needle, parody, poke fun at*, rally, rib*,
scoff, scorn, show contempt, sneer, taunt, tease,
thumb nose at*, travesty; SEE CONCEPTS *7,19,49*

mock [*v2*] *mimic*
affect, ape, assume, burlesque, caricature, counterfeit, ditto*, do, fake, feign, hoke, imitate, lampoon, mime, mirror, parody, satirize, send up*,
simulate, take off*, travesty; SEE CONCEPT *111*

mock [*v3*] *deceive*
beguile, belie, betray, challenge, cheat, defeat,
defy, delude, disappoint, double-cross*, dupe,
elude, foil, fool, frustrate, juggle, let down*, mislead, sell out*, thwart; SEE CONCEPTS *59,63*

mockery [*n1*] *joke, parody*
burlesque, butt*, caricature, deception, farce, imitation, jest, lampoon, laughingstock, mimicry,

mock, pretense, send-up*, sham*, spoof, sport*,
take-off*, travesty; SEE CONCEPTS *111,278*

mockery [*n2*] *insult, disrespect*
contempt, contumely, derision, disdain, disparagement, gibe, jeer, ridicule, scoffing, scorn,
sport; SEE CONCEPTS *49,278*

mode [*n1*] *manner, way*
approach, book, channels, condition, course, custom, fashion, form, mechanism, method, modus,
nuts and bolts*, plan, posture, practice, procedure, process, quality, rule, situation, state, status, style, system, technique, tone, vein, wise;
SEE CONCEPTS *6,644*

mode [*n2*] *trend, fad*
chic, convention, craze, cry, dernier cri*, fashion, furor, last word*, latest thing*, latest wrinkle*, look, mainstream, now*, rage*, style,
thing*, vogue; SEE CONCEPTS *529,655*

model [*adj*] *typical, ideal*
archetypal, classic, classical, commendable,
copy, dummy, exemplary, facsimile, flawless, illustrative, imitation, miniature, paradigmatic,
perfect, prototypical, quintessential, representative, standard, typical, very; SEE CONCEPTS
566,574

model [*n1*] *imitation, replica*
cartoon, clone, copy, copycat, dead ringer*,
ditto*, dummy, duplicate, effigy, engraving, facsimile, figure, figurine, game plan, illustration,
image, knock-off, layout, look-alike, miniature,
mock-up, painting, paste-up, photograph, picture, pocket, portrait, print, relief, representation,
ringer*, setup, sketch, spitting image*, statue,
statuette, tracing, visual; SEE CONCEPTS
259,625,628,667

model [*n2*] *example, standard*
apotheosis, archetype, beau ideal, criterion, design, emblem, embodiment, epitome, exemplar,
gauge, hero, ideal, lodestar, mirror, mold, nonesuch, nonpareil, original, paradigm, paragon,
pattern, prototype, quintessence, role model,
saint, symbol, touchstone, type; SEE CONCEPTS
686,688

model [*n3*] *person, thing that poses*
dummy, manikin, mannequin, nude, sitter, subject; SEE CONCEPT *348*

model [*n4*] *type, version*
configuration, design, form, kind, mark, mode,
style, variety; SEE CONCEPTS *378,463,505,654*

model [*v1*] *form, shape*
base, carve, cast, create, design, fashion, mold,
pattern, plan, sculpt; SEE CONCEPT *184*

model [*v2*] *display, pose*
parade, represent, set example, show off, sit,
sport, wear; SEE CONCEPT *138*

moderate [*adj1*] *calm, temperate*
abstinent, balanced, bearable, careful, cautious,
compromising, conservative, considerate, considered, controlled, cool, deliberate, disciplined,
dispassionate, equable, even, gentle, impartial,
inconsiderable, inexpensive, judicious, limited,
low-key, measured, middle-of-the-road*, midway, mild, modest, monotonous, neutral, nonpartisan, not excessive, pacific, peaceable, pleasant,
reasonable, reserved, restrained, sober, soft,
steady, straight, tame, tolerable, tolerant, tranquil, untroubled; SEE CONCEPTS *533,563*

moderate [*adj2*] *fair, average, so-so*
bland, fairish*, fair to middling*, inconsequential, inconsiderable, indifferent, intermediate,

mean, mediocre, medium, middling*, ordinary, paltry, passable, piddling*, trifling, trivial, unexceptional; SEE CONCEPTS *547,575*

moderate [v1] *restrain, control*
abate, allay, alleviate, appease, assuage, calm, chasten, check, constrain, cool*, cool out*, curb, decline, decrease, die down, diminish, ease off, fall, lessen, let up, meet halfway, mitigate, modify, modulate, mollify, pacify, play down, qualify, quiet, reduce, regulate, relent, relieve, repress, slacken, slow, soften, soft-pedal, subdue, subside, tame, temper, tone down, wane; SEE CONCEPTS *94,130,240*

moderate [v2] *mediate, arbitrate*
chair, judge, make peace*, negotiate, preside, referee, take the chair*, umpire; SEE CONCEPTS *18,317*

moderately [adv] *to a degree, to some extent*
a little, averagely, enough, fairly, gently, in moderation, in reason, kind of, more or less*, more than not*, not exactly, passably, pretty, quite, quite a bit, rather, reasonably, slightly, some, something, somewhat, sort of, so-so*, temperately, tolerable, tolerably, tolerantly, within limits*, within reason*; SEE CONCEPTS *544,772*

moderation [n] *temperance*
balance, calmness, composure, constraint, coolness, dispassionateness, equanimity, fairness, forbearance, golden mean, judiciousness, justice, justness, lenity, measure, mildness, moderateness, patience, poise, quiet, reasonableness, restraint, sedateness, sedation, sobriety, steadiness, toleration; SEE CONCEPTS *633,657*

moderator [n] *mitigator*
alleviator, mediator, pacifier, peacemaker, referee, soother, stabilizer; SEE CONCEPTS *348,366*

modern [adj] *new, up-to-date*
avant-garde, coincident, concomitant, concurrent, contempo, contemporary, current, cutting-edge*, fresh, last word*, late, latest, latter-day*, leading-edge*, modernistic, modernized, modish, neoteric, newfangled*, new-fashioned, novel, now, present, present-day, prevailing, prevalent, recent, state-of-the-art*, stylish, today, twenty-first century*, up-to-the-minute, with-it*; SEE CONCEPTS *578,589,797*

modernize [v] *bring up to date; remodel*
improve, refresh, regenerate, rejuvenate, remake, renew, renovate, restore, revamp, revive, update; SEE CONCEPTS *168,177,202*

modest [adj1] *shy*
bashful, blushing, chaste, coy, demure, diffident, discreet, humble, lowly, meek, moderate, nice, proper, prudent, quiet, reserved, resigned, reticent, retiring, seemly, self-conscious, self-effacing, sheepish, silent, simple, temperate, timid, unassertive, unassuming, unassured, unboastful, unobtrusive, unpresuming, unpretending, unpretentious, withdrawing; SEE CONCEPTS *401,404*

modest [adj2] *limited, ordinary*
average, cheap, discreet, dry, economical, fair, humble, inelaborate, inexpensive, middling, moderate, natural, plain, reasonable, simple, small, unadorned, unaffected, unembellished, unembroidered, unexceptional, unexcessive, unextravagant, unextreme, unobtrusive, unornamented, unostentatious, unpretentious, unradical, unstudied; SEE CONCEPTS *334,547,562*

modesty [n] *shyness*
bashfulness, celibacy, chastity, constraint, coy-

ness, decency, delicacy, demureness, diffidence, discreetness, humbleness, humility, inhibition, innocence, lack of pretension, meekness, propriety, prudery, purity, quietness, reserve, reticence, self-effacement, simplicity, timidity, unobtrusiveness, unostentatiousness, unpretentiousness, virtue; SEE CONCEPT *633*

modicum [n] *bit, small amount*
atom, crumb, dash, drop, fraction, fragment, grain, inch, iota, jot, little, minim, mite, molecule, ounce, particle, pinch, scrap, shred, smidge, speck, tinge, touch, trifle, whit; SEE CONCEPT *831*

modify [v1] *alter, change*
adapt, adjust, become, convert, correct, customize, doctor, mutate, recast, redo, reform, remodel, reorganize, repair, reshape, revise, rework, shift gears*, switch over, transfigure, transform, transmogrify, transmute, turn, turn one around*, turn over new leaf*, turn the corner*, turn the tables*, tweak*, vary; SEE CONCEPT *232*

modify [v2] *lessen, reduce*
abate, curb, decrease, limit, lower, mitigate, moderate, modulate, qualify, relax, remit, restrain, restrict, slacken, soften, temper, tone down; SEE CONCEPTS *236,240,247*

modish [adj] *fashionable*
a la mode*, all the rage*, chic, contemporary, current, dashing, exclusive, faddy, fresh, happening, hip*, in*, in-thing*, last-word, latest, mod*, now*, smart, stylish, swank, swish*, trendy, up-to-date, up-to-the-minute, vogue, voguish, with-it*; SEE CONCEPTS *578,589,797*

modulate [v] *adjust, harmonize*
attune, balance, fine-tune, inflect, regulate, restrain, revamp, switch, temper, tone, transmogrify, tune, tweak, vary; SEE CONCEPT *202*

modus operandi [n] *mode of operation*
manner, method, method of operation, M.O., procedure, process, rule of thumb, technique, way, way of doing things, workings; SEE CONCEPTS *6,630*

mogul [n] *person who has great power, many possessions*
executive, key player*, king, magnate, notable, personage, potentate, prince, princess queen, royalty, top brass*, tycoon, VIP*; SEE CONCEPTS *347,354*

moist [adj] *wet, wettish*
clammy, damp, dampish, dank, dewy, dripping, drippy, drizzly, humid, irriguous, muggy, not dry, oozy*, rainy, soggy, teary, watery; SEE CONCEPT *603*

moisten [v] *make wet, damp*
bathe, bedew, dampen, dip, drench, humidify, lick, mist, moisturize, rain on, rinse, saturate, shower, soak, sog, sop, splash, splatter, spray, sprinkle, squirt, steam, steep, wash, water, water down, waterlog, wet; SEE CONCEPT *256*

moisture [n] *dampness; liquid*
damp, dankness, dew, drizzle, fog, humidity, mist, perspiration, precipitation, rain, sweat, water, wateriness, wet, wetness; SEE CONCEPTS *467,524*

moisturizer [n] *lotion*
balm, cream, demulcent, emollient, liniment, oil, ointment, salve, unction, unguent; SEE CONCEPTS *311,446,466,467,468*

mold [n] *form, pattern*
cast, cavity, character, class, depression, descrip-

tion, design, die, frame, image, impression, kind, lot, matrix, model, nature, shape, sort, stamp, type, womb; SEE CONCEPTS *378,411,436*

mold [*v*] *form, give shape*
build, construct, devise, erect, fashion, forge, form, frame, make, pat, plan, plant, plot, put together, round, scheme, sculpt, whittle; SEE CONCEPTS *173,175,184,251*

moldy [*adj*] *musty*
airless, dirty, funky, mildewed, mildewy, putrid, rotten, rotting, smelly, stale, stuffy; SEE CONCEPTS *578,598,603,797*

mole [*n1*] *blemish*
beauty mark, beauty spot, birthmark, blot, freckle, nevus, strawberry mark; SEE CONCEPT *580*

mole [*n2*] *spy*
agent, double agent, infiltrator, informer, inside man/woman, secret agent; SEE CONCEPTS *348,412*

molecule [*n*] *smallest part*
bit, fragment, iota, jot, minim, mite, modicum, mote, ounce, particle, ray, speck, unit; SEE CONCEPTS *393,831*

molest [*v1*] *physically abuse*
accost, assail, attack, disorganize, displace, disturb, encroach, fondle, harm, hinder, hurt, illtreat, injure, interfere, intrude, maltreat, meddle, misuse, rape; SEE CONCEPTS *246,375*

molest [*v2*] *bother, annoy*
abuse, afflict, badger, bait, bedevil, beset, break in, bug*, confuse, discommode, discompose, disquiet, disturb, encroach, frighten, harass, harry, heckle, hector, interrupt, intrude, irk, irritate, obtrude, persecute, perturb, pester, plague, pother, pursue, scare, tease, terrify, torment, trouble, upset, vex, worry; SEE CONCEPTS *7,14,19*

mollify [*v*] *pacify, soothe*
abate, allay, alleviate, ameliorate, appease, assuage, blunt, calm, compose, conciliate, cool, cushion, decrease, diminish, dulcify, ease, fix up, lessen, lighten, lull, mellow, mitigate, moderate, modify, pacify, patch things up*, placate, propitiate, quell, quiet, reduce, relieve, soften, sweeten, take sting out*, temper, tranquilize; SEE CONCEPTS *7,22,244,698*

mollycoddle [*v*] *pamper*
baby, caress, cater to, coddle, cosset, dandle*, fondle, indulge, overindulge, overprotect, pet, spoil, wait on; SEE CONCEPTS *136,295*

molt [*v*] *shed*
cast off, decorticate, doff, exuviate, peel, pull off, slough, take off; SEE CONCEPTS *142,176,179,180,181,211*

molten [*adj*] *melted*
fused, glowing, igneous, liquefied, smelted; SEE CONCEPTS *250,255*

mom [*n*] *mother*
child-bearer, grandmother, ma*, mama*, matriarch, matron, mommy*, mum*, mumsy*, parent; SEE CONCEPTS *394,400,414*

moment [*n1*] *brief time period*
bit, breathing, crack, date, flash, hour, instant, jiff*, jiffy*, juncture, minute, nothing flat*, no time*, occasion, point, point in time, sec*, second, shake, split second*, stage, three winks*, tick*, time, trice*, twinkle*, twinkling*, while, wink*; SEE CONCEPTS *807,808*

moment [*n2*] *importance*
advantage, avail, concern, consequence, gravity, import, magnitude, momentousness, note, pith, profit, seriousness, significance, signification, substance, use, value, weight, weightiness, worth; SEE CONCEPT *668*

momentarily [*adv*] *for a short time*
briefly, for a little while, for a minute, for a moment, for an instant, for a second, for a short time, for a short while, immediately, instantly, now, right now, temporarily; SEE CONCEPT *820*

momentary [*adj*] *brief, fleeting*
cursory, dreamlike, ephemeral, evanescent, flashing, flitting*, flying, fugacious, fugitive, gone in flash*, hasty, impermanent, impulsive, instantaneous, in wink of an eye*, like lightning, passing, quick, shifting, short, short-lived, spasmodic, summary, temporary, transient, transitory, vanishing, volatile; SEE CONCEPT *798*

momentous [*adj*] *important; serious*
big, chips are down*, consequential, considerable, critical, crucial, decisive, earth-shaking, earth-shattering, epochal, eventful, far-reaching, fateful, grave, heavy, heavy number, historic, material, meaningful, memorable, notable, of moment, outstanding, pivotal, significant, substantial, vital, weighty; SEE CONCEPT *568*

momentum [*n*] *impetus, push*
drive, energy, force, impulse, power, propulsion, strength, thrust; SEE CONCEPTS *641,712*

monarch [*n*] *ruler*
autocrat, crowned head, despot, emperor, empress, king, majesty, potentate, prince, princess, queen, sovereign; SEE CONCEPTS *354,422*

monastery [*n*] *place where monks live*
abbey, cloister, friary, house, lamasery, priory, religious community; SEE CONCEPTS *368,439,516*

monetary [*adj*] *concerning money, finances*
budgetary, capital, cash, commercial, financial, fiscal, pecuniary, pocket; SEE CONCEPT *339*

money [*n*] *currency accepted as exchange for goods, services*
almighty dollar*, banknote, bankroll, bill, bread*, bucks*, capital, cash, check, chips, coin, coinage, dough*, finances, fund, funds, gold, gravy*, greenback*, hard cash*, legal tender, loot*, medium of exchange, pay, payment, pesos*, property, resources, riches, roll, salary, silver, specie, treasure, wad*, wage, wealth, wherewithal*; SEE CONCEPT *340*

moneyed [*adj*] *rich*
affluent, fat-cat*, flush*, leisure-class*, loaded*, opulent, prosperous, upper-class, upscale, uptown, wealthy, well-heeled*, well-off*, well-to-do*; SEE CONCEPT *334*

moneymaking [*adj*] *producing profit*
advantageous, gainful, going, good, lucrative, paying, profitable, remunerative, successful, thriving, well-paying; SEE CONCEPT *334*

mongrel [*n*] *animal of mixed background*
bastard, cross, crossbreed, cur, half-blood, halfbreed, hybrid, mixed breed, mixture, mule, mutt; SEE CONCEPT *394*

moniker [*n*] *nickname*
appellation, byname, denomination, handle*, label, pet name*, sobriquet, tag*; SEE CONCEPTS *268,683*

monitor [*n*] *person who watches, oversees*
adviser, auditor, counselor, director, eavesdropper, guide, informant, invigilator, listener, overseer, supervisor, watchdog; SEE CONCEPTS *348,350*

monitor [v] *listen, watch carefully*
advise, audit, check, control, counsel, follow, keep an eye on*, keep track of*, observe, oversee, record, scan, supervise, survey, track; SEE CONCEPTS *117,596,623*

monk [n] *man who devotes life to contemplation of god*
abbot, anchorite, ascetic, brother, cenobite, eremite, friar, hermit, monastic, priest, recluse, religious, solitary; SEE CONCEPT *361*

monkey [n] *primate*
anthropoid, ape, baboon, chimpanzee, gorilla, imp, lemur, monk, orangutan, rascal, scamp, simian; SEE CONCEPT *394*

monkey [v] *fiddle, tamper with*
busybody, butt in*, fool, fool around*, fool with*, horn in*, interfere, interlope, intermeddle, make*, meddle, mess, play, pry, tinker, trifle; SEE CONCEPTS *87,612*

monkey business [n] *foolishness*
absurdity, absurdness, antics, carrying-on*, craziness, disobedience, foolery, high jinks, horse feathers*, horseplay, inanity, insanity, irresponsibility, ludicrousness, lunacy, misbehavior, mischief-making, nonsense, poppycock*, silliness, stupidity, tommyrot*; SEE CONCEPT *633*

monolithic [adj] *massive*
big, bulky, colossal, consistent, elephantine, enormous, gargantuan, giant, gigantic, grand, great, huge, hulking, immense, immovable, imposing, mammoth, permanent, solid, titanic, towering, uniform, vast, whopping*; SEE CONCEPTS *773,781*

monologue [n] *speech by one person*
address, descant, discourse, disquisition, harangue, lecture, sermon, soliloquy, speech, stand-up bit*, talk; SEE CONCEPTS *266,278*

monopolize [v] *dominate, control*
absorb, acquire, bogart, consume, copyright, corner, corner the market*, devour, employ, engross, exclude, exercise control, have, hog*, hold, keep to oneself, lock up*, manage, own, own exclusively, patent, possess, restrain, sew up*, sit on*, syndicate, take over, take up, use, utilize; SEE CONCEPTS *94,324,710*

monopoly [n] *something held, owned exclusively*
cartel, consortium, copyright, corner, holding, oligopoly, ownership, patent, pool, possessorship, proprietorship, syndicate, trust; SEE CONCEPT *710*

monotonous [adj] *all the same, remaining the same*
banausic, blah*, boring, colorless, dreary, droning, dull, dull as dishwater*, flat, flat as pancake*, ho-hum*, humdrum*, monotone, nothing, pedestrian, plodding, prosaic, puts one to sleep*, recurrent, reiterated, repetitious, repetitive, samely, sing-song*, soporific, tedious, tiresome, toneless, treadmill, unchanged, unchanging, uniform, uninflected, uninteresting, unrelieved, unvaried, unvarying, wearisome, wearying; SEE CONCEPTS *529,534,544*

monotony [n] *boredom; sameness*
colorlessness, continuance, continuity, dreariness, dryness, dullness, ennui, equability, evenness, flatness, humdrum*, identicalness, invariability, levelness, likeness, monotone, monotonousness, oneness, repetitiousness, repetitiveness, routine, same old thing*, similarity, tediousness, tedium, tiresomeness, unchange-

ableness, uniformity, wearisomeness; SEE CONCEPTS *410,637,673*

monster [n] *giant animal; supernatural being*
abnormality, barbarian, beast, behemoth, brute, centaur, colossus, demon, devil, dragon, fiend, Frankenstein, freak, giant, hellion, horror, leviathan, lusus naturae, mammoth, miscreation, monstrosity, mutant, ogre, phoenix, savage, titan, villain, werewolf, whale; SEE CONCEPTS *370,394,412*

monstrosity [n] *freak*
abnormality, atrocity, deformity, dreadfulness, enormity, eyesore, freakishness, frightfulness, grotesqueness, heinousness, hideousness, horror, monster, mutant, mutation; SEE CONCEPTS *411,657*

monstrous [adj1] *unnatural, shocking*
aberrant, abnormal, atrocious, cruel, desperate, devilish, diabolical, disgraceful, dreadful, egregious, evil, fiendish, flagitious, foul, freakish, frightful, grotesque, gruesome, heinous, hellish, hideous, horrendous, horrible, horrifying, infamous, inhuman, intolerable, loathsome, macabre, miscreated, morbid, obscene, odious, ominous, outrageous, preposterous, rank, satanic, scandalous, teratoid, terrible, uncanny, unusual, vicious, villainous; SEE CONCEPTS *537,564,582*

monstrous [adj2] *very large*
colossal, cracking, elephantine, enormous, fantastic, gargantuan, giant, gigantic, grandiose, great, huge, immense, impressive, magnificent, mammoth, massive, monumental, prodigious, stupendous, titanic, towering, tremendous, vast, whopping; SEE CONCEPTS *773,781*

monument [n] *memorial, remembrance*
cairn, cenotaph, column, commemoration, erection, footstone, gravestone, headstone, ledger, magnum opus, marker, masterpiece, mausoleum, memento, monolith, obelisk, pile, pillar, record, reminder, shrine, slab, statue, stele, stone, tablet, testament, token, tomb, tombstone, tower, tribute, witness; SEE CONCEPTS *259,271,305,470*

monumental [adj] *impressive, overwhelming*
awe-inspiring, awesome, classic, enduring, enormous, fantastic, gigantic, grand, great, historic, huge, immense, immortal, important, lasting, lofty, majestic, mammoth, massive, memorable, mighty, mortal, mountainous, outstanding, prodigious, significant, stupendous, towering, tremendous, unforgettable, vast; SEE CONCEPTS *568,773*

mooch [v] *cadge*
beg, borrow, bum*, bum off*, freeload, leach off*, scrounge, sponge; SEE CONCEPT *89*

mood [n] *state of mind*
affection, air, atmosphere, attitude, aura, bent*, blues*, caprice, character, color*, condition, crotchet, cue, depression, desire, disposition, doldrums, dumps*, emotion, fancy, feel*, feeling, frame of mind*, high spirits, humor, inclination, individuality, low spirits, melancholy, mind, personality, pleasure, propensity, response, scene, semblance, soul, spirit, strain, temper, temperament, tendency, tenor, timbre, vagary, vein, whim, wish; SEE CONCEPTS *410,411,673*

moody [adj] *crabby, temperamental*
angry, cantankerous, capricious, changeable, crabbed*, crestfallen, cross, dismal, doleful, dour, downcast, down in the dumps*, down in the mouth*, erratic, fickle, fitful, flighty, frown-

mo
mo

ing, gloomy, glum, huffy, ill-humored, ill-tempered, impulsive, in a huff*, in the doldrums, introspective, irascible, irritable, lugubrious, melancholy, mercurial, miserable, moping, morose, offended, out of sorts*, pensive, petulant, piqued, sad, saturnine, short-tempered, splenetic, sulky, sullen, testy, touchy; SEE CONCEPT *403*

moon [*n*] *Earth's satellite*
celestial body, crescent, full moon, half-moon, heavenly body, new moon, old moon, orb of night*, planetoid, pumpkin*, quarter-moon, satellite; SEE CONCEPTS *511,809*

moon [*v*] *dream about; desire*
daydream, idle, languish, mope, pine, waste time, yearn; SEE CONCEPT *20*

moonshine [*n*] *illegally distilled alcohol*
bathtub gin*, bootleg, firewater*, home brew, hooch*, mountain dew*, rotgut*, white lightning; SEE CONCEPTS *454,467*

moor [*v*] *anchor, fasten securely*
berth, catch, chain, dock, fix, lash, make fast, picket, secure, tether, tie, tie up; SEE CONCEPTS *85,160*

mooring [*n*] *landing*
anchorage, berth, dock, harbor, marina, pier, port, station, wharf; SEE CONCEPTS *439*

moot [*adj*] *doubtful, arguable*
at issue, contestable, controversial, debatable, disputable, dubious, open, open to debate, problematic, questionable, suspect, uncertain, undecided, unresolved, unsettled; SEE CONCEPT *535*

mop [*n1*] *tangle of material, often used to absorb liquid*
duster, sponge, squeegee, swab, sweeper, towel; SEE CONCEPTS *392,499*

mop [*n2*] *thick mass of hair*
mane, shock, tangle, thatch, tresses; SEE CONCEPT *399*

mop [*v*] *clean by using water and cloth*
dab, dust, pat, polish, rub, soak up, sponge, squeegee, swab, towel off, wash, wipe; SEE CONCEPT *165*

mope [*v*] *pout, be dejected*
ache, be apathetic, be down in the mouth*, be gloomy, be in a funk*, bleed*, brood, chafe, despair, despond, droop, eat one's heart out, fret, grieve, grumble, grump, idle, lament, languish, lose heart, moon, pine, pine away*, regret, repine, sink, stew over*, sulk, sweat over*, waste time*, wear a long face*, yearn; SEE CONCEPTS *20,410*

moral [*adj*] *ethical, honest*
aboveboard, blameless, chaste, conscientious, correct, courteous, decent, decorous, dutiful, elevated, exemplary, good, high-minded, honorable, immaculate, incorruptible, innocent, just, kindly, kosher*, laudable, meet, meritorious, modest, moralistic, noble, praiseworthy, principled, proper, pure, respectable, right, righteous, saintly, salt of the earth*, scrupulous, seemly, square, straight, true-blue*, trustworthy, truthful, upright, upstanding, virtuous, worthy; SEE CONCEPT *545*

moral [*n*] *lesson, proverb*
adage, aphorism, apophthegm, axiom, dictum, epigram, gnome, maxim, meaning, message, moralism, motto, point, precept, rule, saw, saying, sermon, significance, truism; SEE CONCEPTS *278,283*

morale [*n*] *confidence, self-esteem*
assurance, attitude, disposition, drive, esprit, esprit de corps, heart, humor, mettle, mood, outlook, resolve, self-confidence, self-possession, spirit, temper, temperament, turn, vigor; SEE CONCEPTS *410,411*

morality [*n*] *ethics, honesty*
chastity, conduct, decency, ethicality, ethicalness, gentleness, godliness, good habits, goodness, honor, ideals, incorruptibility, incorruption, integrity, justice, manners, moral code, morals, mores, philosophy, principle, principles, probity, purity, rectitude, righteousness, rightness, saintliness, standards, uprightness, virtue, worthiness; SEE CONCEPT *645*

moralize [*v*] *preach*
admonish, edify, lecture, pass judgment, pontificate, pontify, preachify, sermonize, teach; SEE CONCEPTS *51,75*

morals [*n*] *personal principles, standards*
behavior, beliefs, conduct, customs, dogmas, ethic, ethics, habits, ideals, integrity, manners, morality, mores, policies, scruples; SEE CONCEPTS *411,645,688*

morass [*n*] *bog; mess*
chaos, confusion, fen, jam, jungle, knot, labyrinth, marsh, maze, mesh, mix-up, muddle, quagmire, skein, snarl, swamp, tangle, web; SEE CONCEPTS *230,509*

moratorium [*n*] *suspension*
abeyance, abeyancy, adjournment, ban, break, breather*, breathing spell*, deferment, delay, downtime*, five*, freeze, grace period, halt, pause, postponement, reprieve, respite, stay, truce; SEE CONCEPTS *119,807,832*

morbid [*adj*] *gloomy, nasty, sickly*
aberrant, abnormal, ailing, brooding, dark, deadly, depressed, despondent, diseased, dreadful, frightful, ghastly, ghoulish, grim, grisly, gruesome, hideous, horrid, infected, irascible, macabre, malignant, melancholy, monstrous, moody, pessimistic, saturnine, sick, somber, sullen, unhealthy, unnatural, unsound, unusual, unwholesome; SEE CONCEPTS *314,403,537*

mordant [*adj*] *sarcastic*
acerb, acerbic, acid, biting, bitter, caustic, cutting, cynical, disparaging, disrespectful, mean, poignant, pointed, sardonic, scathing, sharp; SEE CONCEPT *267*

more [*adj*] *additional, greater*
added, aggrandized, also, amassed, and, another, augmented, besides, bounteous, deeper, else, enhanced, exceeding, expanded, extended, extra, farther, fresh, further, heavier, higher, in addition, increased, innumerable, larger, likewise, major, massed, more than that, new, numerous, other, over and above, spare, supplementary, too many, wider; SEE CONCEPTS *762,771*

more [*adv*] *to a greater extent*
additionally, along with, also, as well, besides, better, beyond, further, furthermore, in addition, likewise, longer, moreover, over, too, withal; SEE CONCEPTS *544,772*

more or less [*adv*] *approximately*
about, almost, around, ballpark figure*, bordering on, circa, close to, in the ballpark*, in the neighborhood of, in the vicinity of, just about, not far from, not quite, on average, relatively, roughly, thereabouts, very close; SEE CONCEPT *566*

moreover [*adv*] *additionally*
also, as well, besides, by the same token*, further, furthermore, in addition, likewise, more, to boot*, too, what is more*, withal, yet; SEE CONCEPTS *544,772*

mores [*n*] *traditional customs*
attitude, codes, established ways, etiquette, formalities, manners, morals, policies, practices, principles, protocol, rites, rituals, routines, rules, social conduct, standards, way of life; SEE CONCEPTS *644,687*

morgue [*n*] *mortuary*
charnel house, crematory, funeral home, funeral parlor; SEE CONCEPTS *172,386*

moribund [*adj*] *dying*
at death's door*, at the end of the rope*, declining, done for*, doomed, expiring, fading, fated, going, mortal, mortally ill, one foot in the grave*, on one's deathbed, on one's last leg*, passing, perishing; SEE CONCEPT *539*

morning [*n*] *first part of the day*
after midnight, AM, ante meridiem, aurora, before lunch, before noon, breakfast time*, break of day, cockcrow*, crack of dawn*, dawn, daybreak, daylight, dayspring, early bright*, first blush*, foreday, forenoon, morn*, morningtide, morrow, prime*, sunrise, sunup, wee hours*; SEE CONCEPTS *801,802,806,810*

moron [*n*] *stupid person*
addlepate, blockhead*, boob*, dimwit, dingbat*, dolt, dope*, dork*, dumbbell*, dummy*, dunce, fool, halfwit, idiot, ignoramus, imbecile, lamebrain*, loony*, loser*, mental defective*, nerd*, simpleton; SEE CONCEPT *423*

moronic [*adj*] *stupid*
asinine, brainless, dense, dimwitted, doltish, dopey*, dumb, foolish, half-baked*, idiotic, ill-advised, imbecilic, inane, irresponsible, ludicrous, mindless, nonsensical, pointless, senseless, unintelligent, unthinking; SEE CONCEPTS *402,548*

morose [*adj*] *depressed, pessimistic*
acrimonious, blue*, brusque, cantankerous, choleric, churlish, crabbed*, crabby*, cranky*, cross, dolorous, dour, down, down in the dumps*, down in the mouth*, frowning, gloomy, glum, grouchy, gruff, harsh, having blue devils*, having the blahs*, ill-humored, ill-tempered, in a bad mood*, in a blue funk*, irritable, low, melancholy, moody, moping, mournful, perverse, perversely, sad, saturnine, singing the blues*, snappish, sour, splenetic, sulky, sullen, surly, taciturn, testy, troubled, ugly; SEE CONCEPT *403*

morsel [*n*] *tiny piece*
bait, bit, bite, chunk, crumb, cut, delicacy, drop, fraction, fragment, grain, hunk, lump, mouthful, nibble, nosh, part, sample, scrap, segment, slice, snack, soupcon, taste, tidbit, treat; SEE CONCEPTS *457,458,831,835*

mortal [*adj1*] *deadly*
bitter, death-dealing, deathly, destructive, dire, ending, extreme, fatal, grave, great, grievous, grim, intense, killing, last, lethal, malignant, merciless, monstrous, mortiferous, murderous, noxious, pestilent, pestilential, poisonous, relentless, remorseless, ruthless, severe, terminal, terrible, unrelenting; SEE CONCEPT *537*

mortal [*adj2*] *human*
animate, bipedal, corporeal, creatural, earthly,

ecce homo, ephemeral, evanescent, fading, finite, frail, fugacious, impermanent, momentary, passing, perishable, precarious, sublunary, temporal, transient, weak, worldly; SEE CONCEPT *549*

mortal [*n*] *human being*
animal, being, body, character, creature, earthling, human, individual, living soul, man, naked ape, party, person, personage, soul, woman; SEE CONCEPT *417*

mortality [*n1*] *death*
bloodshed, carnage, deadliness, destruction, dying, extinction, fatality, killing, lethality, loss of life; SEE CONCEPT *407*

mortality [*n2*] *humanness*
being, ephemerality, flesh, Homo sapiens, humanity, humankind, human race, impermanence, temporality, transience; SEE CONCEPTS *417,648*

mortally [*adv*] *fatally*
badly, critically, gravely, painfully, seriously; SEE CONCEPTS *544,565,568*

mortgage [*n*] *loan agreement*
contract, debt, deed, homeowner's loan, pledge, title; SEE CONCEPT *332*

mortician [*n*] *undertaker*
embalmer, funeral director; SEE CONCEPT *304*

mortification [*n*] *humiliation*
abasement, affront, bring down, chagrin, condescension, degradation, disgrace, dishonor, embarrassment, humbling, ignominy, loss of face*, put-down, resignation, shame; SEE CONCEPTS *388,410*

mortify [*v*] *embarrass*
abase, abash, affront, annoy, belittle, chagrin, chasten, confound, control, crush, deflate, deny, disappoint, discipline, discomfit, disgrace, displease, get one's comeuppance*, harass, humble, humiliate, put to shame, ridicule, shame, subdue, take down a peg*, take the wind out*, vex, worry; SEE CONCEPTS *7,19,52,54*

mortuary [*n*] *funeral home*
charnel house, crematory, funeral parlor, morgue; SEE CONCEPT *304*

mosaic [*n*] *collage*
checker, montage, motley, patchwork, plaid, tessellation, variegation; SEE CONCEPTS *259,625*

mosey [*v*] *saunter*
amble, dally, dilly-dally, drift, linger, loiter, meander, mope*, move slowly, ramble, stroll along, take a stroll, take it easy, traipse, walk slowly; SEE CONCEPT *151*

mosque [*n*] *temple*
cathedral, chapel, church, holy place, house of God, house of worship, masjid, place of worship, sanctuary, shrine, synagogue, tabernacle; SEE CONCEPTS *368,439*

mossback [*n*] *old-fashioned person*
conservative, fuddy-duddy*, geezer*, old fogy*, old geezer*, square*; SEE CONCEPT *424*

most [*adj*] *best, greatest*
better, biggest, greater, highest, largest, lion's share*, max*, maximum, ultimate, utmost, uttermost; SEE CONCEPTS *771,772*

most [*adv*] *nearly all; extremely*
about, all but, almost, approximately, close, eminently, exceedingly, in the majority, mightily, much, nearly, nigh, practically, remarkably, super, surpassingly, too, very, well-nigh; SEE CONCEPTS *544,569,771*

mostly [*adv*] *generally, mainly*
above all, almost entirely, as a rule*, chiefly,

customarily, essentially, for the most part*, frequently, in many instances*, largely, many times, most often, often, on the whole*, overall, particularly, predominantly, primarily, principally, regularly, usually; SEE CONCEPTS *544,548,772*

mote [*n*] *speck* ‑
atom, bit, crumb, dot, fleck, fragment, grain, iota, particle, small thing, smidgen, speckle, tiny bit, trace; SEE CONCEPT *831*

motel [*n*] *temporary, short-term residence, often for travelers*
cabin, court, hotel, inn, lodge, motor court, resort, roadhouse; SEE CONCEPTS *439,449,516*

moth-eaten [*adj*] *shabby; stale*
ancient, antiquated, archaic, dated, decayed, decrepit, dilapidated, moribund, old-fashioned, outdated, ragged, tattered, threadbare, worn-out; SEE CONCEPT *485*

mother [*n*] *female person who has borne children*
ancestor, child-bearer, creator, forebearer, mom*, mommy*, origin, parent, predecessor, procreator, progenitor, source; SEE CONCEPTS *394,400,414,415,423*

motif [*n*] *central theme*
concept, design, idea, logo, notion, pattern, structure, subject; SEE CONCEPTS *278,682,689*

motion [*n1*] *movement, action*
act, advance, agitation, ambulation, body English*, change, changing, direction, drift, dynamics, flow, fluctuation, flux, full swing*, gesticulation, gesture, high sign*, inclination, kinetics, locomotion, mobility, motility, move, oscillation, passage, passing, progress, sign, signal, stir, stirring, stream, sway, sweep, swing, tendency, travel, wave, wavering; SEE CONCEPT *145*

motion [*n2*] *formal suggestion in a meeting*
plan, proposal, proposition, recommendation, submission; SEE CONCEPTS *75,278*

motion [*v*] *gesture, direct*
beckon, flag, gesticulate, guide, invite, move, nod, sign, signal, signalize, wave; SEE CONCEPT *149*

motionless [*adj*] *calm, not moving*
apoplectic, at a standstill, at rest, becalmed, dead, deadlocked, deathly, firm, fixed, frozen, halted, immobile, immotile, inanimate, inert, lifeless, numb, palsied, paralyzed, petrified, quiescent, quiet, spellbound, stable, stagnant, stalled, standing, static, stationary, steadfast, still, stock-still, torpid, transfixed, unmovable, unmoved, unmoving; SEE CONCEPTS *488,584*

motion picture [*n*] *movie*
cine, cinema, cinematics, cinematograph, feature film, film, flick*, moving picture, picture show, silver screen*, talkie*, talking picture, videotape; SEE CONCEPTS *263,293*

motivate [*v*] *stimulate, instigate*
actuate, arouse, bring, cause, dispose, draw, drive, egg on*, excite, fire, galvanize, give incentive, goad, goose*, impel, incite, incline, induce, innervate, innerve, inspire, inspirit, lead, move, persuade, pique, predetermine, predispose, prevail upon, prompt, propel, provoke, quicken, rouse, set afoot, set astir, sound, spark, spur, suggest, sway, touch off, trigger, whet; SEE CONCEPTS *14,68,242*

motivation [*n*] *ambition, inspiration*
action, actuation, angle, catalyst, desire, disposition, drive, encouragement, fire, get up and go*, gimmick, goose*, hunger, impetus, impulse, impulsion, incentive, incitation, incitement, inclination, inducement, instigation, interest, kick*, motive, persuasion, predetermination, predisposition, provocation, push, reason, right stuff*, spur, stimulus, suggestion, wish; SEE CONCEPTS *20,411,689*

motive [*n*] *reason, purpose*
aim, antecedent, basis, cause, consideration, design, determinant, drive, emotion, end, feeling, grounds, idea, impulse, incentive, incitement, inducement, influence, inspiration, intent, intention, mainspring, motivation, object, occasion, passion, rationale, root, spring, spur, stimulus, thinking; SEE CONCEPTS *20,661,689*

motley [*adj*] *mixed, varied*
assorted, conglomerate, dappled, discrepant, disparate, dissimilar, diversified, heterogeneous, indiscriminate, kaleidoscopic, mingled, miscellaneous, mixed, mottled, multicolor, multicolored, multiform, multihued, polychromatic, prismatic, rainbow, unlike, varicolored, variegated, various, versicolor; SEE CONCEPTS *564,618,772*

motor [*n*] *engine*
cylinder, diesel, generator, mechanism, piston, power train, transformer, turbine, what's under the hood*; SEE CONCEPTS *463,464*

motorcade [*n*] *procession of motor vehicles*
caravan, convoy, parade; SEE CONCEPTS *432,503*

motorcycle [*n*] *motorbike*
chopper*, dirt bike, enduro, hog*, minibike, moped, scooter; SEE CONCEPTS *364,505*

motor home [*n*] *recreational vehicle*
camper, mobile home, RV; SEE CONCEPT *505*

motorized [*adj*] *power-driven*
mechanical, mechanized, powered; SEE CONCEPT *544*

mottled [*adj*] *speckled*
blotchy, checkered, dappled, flecked, freckled, maculate, marbled, motley, piebald, pied, skewbald, spotted, streaked, tabby, variegated; SEE CONCEPTS *606,618*

motto [*n*] *saying, slogan*
adage, aphorism, apothegm, battle cry, byword, catchphrase, cry, epigram, formula, maxim, precept, proverb, rallying cry, rule, saw, sentiment, shibboleth, war cry, watchword, word; SEE CONCEPT *278*

mound [*n*] *heap, hill*
anthill, bank, drift, dune, embankment, hillock, knoll, mass, molehill, mountain, pile, rise, shock, stack, tumulus; SEE CONCEPTS *432,509*

mount [*v1*] *climb*
arise, ascend, back, bestride, clamber up, climb onto, climb up on, escalade, escalate, get astride, get up on, go up, jump on, lift, rise, scale, soar, tower, up, vault; SEE CONCEPTS *149,154,166*

mount [*v2*] *increase, grow*
accumulate, aggravate, augment, build, deepen, enhance, enlarge, escalate, expand, heighten, intensate, intensify, multiply, pile up, redouble, rise, rouse, swell, upsurge, wax; SEE CONCEPTS *704,780*

mount [*v3*] *affix, frame*
emplace, exhibit, fit, install, place, position, prepare, produce, put in place, put on, set up, show, stage; SEE CONCEPTS *174,261*

mountain [n] *very large hill*
abundance, alp, bank, bluff, butte, cliff, crag, dome, drift, elevation, eminence, glob, heap, height, hump, mass, mesa, mound, mount, palisade, peak, pike, pile, precipice, pyramid, range, ridge, shock, sierra, stack, ton, tor, volcano; SEE CONCEPTS *432,509*

mountaineer [n] *mountain climber*
alpinist, backpacker, climber, cragsman, cragswoman, hiker, rock climber; SEE CONCEPTS *149,224,363*

mountaineering [n] *mountain climbing*
alpinism, backpacking, hiking, hill-climbing, rock-climbing; SEE CONCEPTS *149,224,363*

mountainous [adj] *hilly; large*
alpine, big, colossal, gigantic, highland, huge, mammoth, tall, towering; SEE CONCEPT *509*

mountebank [n] *charlatan*
cheat, con man/woman*, grifter, imposter, rip-off artist*, swindler; SEE CONCEPT *412*

mourn [v] *be sad over loss*
ache, agonize, anguish, be brokenhearted*, bemoan, be sad, bewail, bleed, blubber, carry on, complain, cry, deplore, fret, grieve, hurt, keen, lament, languish, long for, miss, moan, pine, regret, repine, rue, sigh, sob, sorrow, suffer, take it hard*, wail, wear black*, weep, wring hands*, yearn; SEE CONCEPTS *23,410*

mournful [adj] *sorrowful*
anguished, bereft, cheerless, depressed, disconsolate, distressing, doleful, dolent, forlorn, full of sorrow, grief-stricken, grieving, grievous, heartbroken, in mourning, in pain, in sorrow, lamentable, pitiful, sad, sombre, woeful; SEE CONCEPT *403*

mourning [n] *sadness, time of sadness*
aching, bereavement, blackness, crying, darkness, grief, grieving, keening, lamentation, lamenting, languishing, moaning, pining, repining, sorrowing, wailing, weeping, woe; SEE CONCEPTS *388,410*

mousy [adj] *drab; quiet*
bashful, colorless, diffident, dull, indeterminate, ineffectual, pale, plain, self-effacing, shy, timid, timorous, unassertive, unassuming; SEE CONCEPTS *401,618*

mouth [n1] *opening*
aperture, beak, box, cavity, chops*, clam, crevice, delta, door, embouchement, entrance, estuary, firth, fly trap, funnel, gate, gills, gob, harbor, inlet, jaws, kisser*, lips, mush*, orifice, portal, rim, trap*, yap*; SEE CONCEPTS *392,513*

mouth [n2] *backtalk*
boasting, braggadocio, bragging, cheek, empty talk*, freshness, gas*, guff*, hot air*, idle talk, impudence, insolence, lip*, rudeness, sass*, sauce*; SEE CONCEPTS *54,278*

mouth off [v] *talk back*
answer back, come back at, sass, sass back, wise off; SEE CONCEPTS *44,52*

mouthpiece [n] *spokesperson*
agent, delegate, PR person, representative, speaker, spokesman, spokeswoman; SEE CONCEPTS *348,354,359*

mouth-watering [adj] *appetizing*
aperitive, appealing, delectable, delicious, divine*, flavorsome, full of flavor, heavenly*, luscious, palatable, piquant, saporous, savory, scrumptious, succulent, tasty, tempting, yummy*; SEE CONCEPT *613*

mouthy [adj] *talkative*
big-mouthed*, chattering, chatty*, full of hot air*, gabby, garrulous, gossipy, long-winded*, loose-lipped*, loudmouthed*, ranting, talky, vociferous, windy*; SEE CONCEPT *267*

movable [adj] *transportable*
adaptable, adjustable, ambulatory, conveyable, deployable, detachable, in parts, liftable, loose, mobile, motile, moving, not fastened, not fixed, on wheels, portable, portative, removable, separable, shiftable, transferable, turnable, unattached, unfastened, unstationary, unsteady; SEE CONCEPTS *488,584*

move [n] *progress, deed*
act, action, alteration, change, maneuver, measure, modification, motion, movement, ploy, procedure, proceeding, shift, step, stir, stirring, stratagem, stroke, turn, variation; SEE CONCEPTS *2,660*

move [v1] *be in motion, put in motion*
actuate, advance, blow, budge, bustle, carry, change, climb, crawl, cross, depart, dislocate, disturb, drift, drive, exit, flow, fly, get away, get going, get off, glide, go, go away, head for, hurry, impel, jump, leap, leave, locomote, march, migrate, off-load, position, proceed, progress, propel, pull out, push, quit, relocate, remove, roll, run, scram, shift, ship, shove, skip out, split, stir, switch, take off, transfer, transport, transpose, travel, traverse, walk, withdraw; SEE CONCEPTS *147,149,198*

move [v2] *motivate, influence*
activate, actuate, advocate, affect, agitate, bring, bring up, budge, carry, cause, convert, draw up, drive, excite, get going, give rise to, impel, impress, incite, induce, inspire, inspirit, instigate, introduce, lead, operate, persuade, play on, prevail upon, prompt, propel, propose, push, put forward, quicken, recommend, rouse, shift, shove, start, stimulate, stir, strike, submit, suggest, sway, touch, tug, at, turn, urge, work on; SEE CONCEPTS *7,19,22,75,242*

movement [n1] *motion, activity*
act, action, advance, agitation, alteration, change, changing, deed, development, displacement, dynamism, evolution, evolving, exercise, flight, flow, flux, gesture, journey, journeying, locomotion, maneuver, migration, mobility, motility, movableness, move, moving, operation, operativeness, passage, progress, progression, regression, roaming, shift, shifting, steps, stir, stirring, transferal, transit, translating, transplanting, undertaking, velocity, voyaging, wandering; SEE CONCEPTS *2,145,697*

movement [n2] *drive, campaign*
change, crusade, current, demonstration, displacement, drift, evolution, faction, flight, flow, front, group, grouping, march, mobilization, organization, party, patrol, shift, sweep, swing, tendency, transfer, transition, trend, unrest, withdrawal; SEE CONCEPTS *381,697*

mover and shaker [n] *doer*
achiever, catalyst, enterprising person, entrepreneur, generator, go-getter*, mover, player*, producer, spark plug*, upstart, wheeler and dealer*; SEE CONCEPT *347*

movie [n] *presentation of action on continuous film*
cine, cinema, cinematics, cinematograph, feature, film, flick*, motion picture, moving picture,

mo
mo

photoplay, picture, screenplay, show, silent*, silver screen*, talkie*, talking picture, videotape; SEE CONCEPTS 263,293

moving [*adj1*] *affecting, exciting*
affective, arousing, awakening, breathless, dynamic, eloquent, emotional, emotive, expressive, facund, far-out*, felt in gut*, grabbed by*, gripping, hairy*, heartbreaking, heartrending, impelling, impressive, inspirational, inspiring, meaningful, mind-bending*, mind-blowing*, motivating, persuasive, poignant, propelling, provoking, quickening, rallying, rousing, sententious, significant, something*, stimulating, stimulative, stirring, stunning, touching, turned on by*; SEE CONCEPTS 529,537

moving [*adj2*] *mobile*
advancing, changing, climbing, evolving, flying, going, jumping, motile, movable, nomadic, portable, progressing, roaming, roving, running, shifting, traversing, unfixed, unstable, unsteadfast, unsteady, walking; SEE CONCEPTS 488,584

mow [*v*] *cut*
clip, crop, scythe, shear, sickle, trim; SEE CONCEPTS 137,176,236,247

moxie [*n*] *courage*
adventuresomeness, adventurousness, audacity, backbone, boldness, braveness, bravery, daring, dash, dauntlessness, determination, fearlessness, fortitude, gameness, grit, guts, hardihood, mettle, nerve, pluck, prowess, spirit, spunk, stamina, tenacity, toughness, valor; SEE CONCEPTS 411,633

much [*adj*] *plenty*
abundant, adequate, a lot of*, ample, complete, considerable, copious, countless, endless, enough, everywhere, extravagant, full, galore, generous, great, heaps*, immeasurable, jampacked*, lavish, loads*, lotsa*, many, mega*, mucho*, no end*, plenteous, plentiful, profuse, satisfying, scads*, sizable, substantial, sufficient, very many, voluminous; SEE CONCEPTS 772,781

much [*adv*] *greatly, a lot*
again and again, a great deal*, considerably, decidedly, eminently, exceedingly, exceptionally, extremely, frequently, highly, hugely, indeed, notably, oft, often, over and over*, regularly, repeatedly, surpassingly, time and time again*, very; SEE CONCEPTS 530,544,548

much [*n*] *a great deal*
abundance, all kinds of*, a lot*, amplitude, appreciable amount, barrel, breadth, completeness, copiousness, excess, exuberance, fullness, gobs*, great quantity, heaps*, loads*, lots*, lump, mass, mess*, mountain, multiplicity, oodles*, overage, oversupply, pack, peck, pile, plentifulness, plenty, plethora, profuseness, riches, scads*, sufficiency, superabundance, superfluity, thousands, tons*, very much, volume, wealth; SEE CONCEPT 771

mud [*n*] *wet dirt*
clay, mire, muck, ooze, silt, slab, sludge, slush; SEE CONCEPT 509

muddle [*n*] *confused state*
ataxia, awkwardness, botch, chaos, clutter, complexity, complication, confusion, daze, difficulty, dilemma, disarrangement, disarray, disorder, disorganization, emergency, encumbrance, fog, foul-up*, hash, haze, intricacy, involvement, jumble, mess, mess and a half*, mix-up*, muss*, perplexity, plight, predicament, quandary, rat's

nest*, screw-up*, shambles*, snarl, struggle, tangle, trouble; SEE CONCEPTS 230,410,666

muddle [*v*] *confuse, disorganize*
addle, befuddle, bewilder, blunder, botch, bungle, clutter, complicate, confound, daze, derange, disarrange, discombobulate*, disorder, disorient, disturb, entangle, fluster, foul, foul up*, jumble, louse up, make a mess of*, mess, misarrange, mix, mix up*, muck, mumble, murmur, nonplus, perplex, perturb, psych out*, rattle, ravel, ruffle, scramble, shuffle, snafu*, snarl, spoil, stir up, stumble, stupefy, tangle, throw, throw off, tumble; SEE CONCEPTS 16,84,242

muddled [*adj*] *confused*
addled, befuddled, bewildered, blurred, chaotic, convoluted, dazed, disarranged, disarrayed, disordered, disorderly, disorganized, in disarray, jumbled, messy, mixed up, scrambled, topsyturvy, untidy; SEE CONCEPT 585

muddy [*adj*] *dark and cloudy*
addled, bemired, bespattered, black, blurred, boggy*, caked, confused, dingy, dirty, dull, filthy, flat, foul, fuzzy, gloomy, greasy, grimy, grubby*, gummy*, gunky*, hazy, impure, indistinct, marshy, miry, mucky*, obscure, opaque, roily, sloppy, slushy, smoky, sodden, soggy, soiled, subfuse, swampy, turbid, unclean, unclear; SEE CONCEPTS 485,606,618

mudslinging [*n*] *smear campaign*
character assassination, defamation, dirty politics, dragging one's name through the mud, negative campaign, slander; SEE CONCEPT 54

muff [*v*] *bungle*
blunder, boggle, botch, choke*, drop the ball*, err, flub, foul up, fumble, goof up*, make a mess of, mess up, miscalculate, mishandle, mismanage, screw up*, slip; SEE CONCEPT 101

muffle [*v*] *suppress, make quiet*
conceal, cover, cushion, dampen, deaden, decrease, drown, dull, envelop, gag, hide, hush, mellow, mute, muzzle, put the lid on*, quieten, shut down, silence, sit down on*, smother, soften, soft-pedal*, squelch, stifle, subdue, tone down*, wrap*; SEE CONCEPTS 65,121,240

muffled [*adj*] *quietened*
deadened, dim, dull, faint, flat, indistinct, mute, muted, obscure, silenced, stifled, strangled, subdued, suppressed; SEE CONCEPT 594

mug [*n1*] *drinking cup*
coffee cup, demitasse, flagon, jug, stoup, tankard, toby; SEE CONCEPT 494

mug [*n2*] *face*
countenance, frown, grimace, kisser*, mask, profile, puss*; SEE CONCEPTS 484,716,836

mug [*v*] *hold up*
assault, hold up*, purse-snatch, rob, steal, stick up*; SEE CONCEPTS 52,86

muggy [*adj*] *humid*
clammy*, close, damp, dampish, dank, moist, mucky*, oppressive, soggy, sticky, stuffy, sultry; SEE CONCEPTS 525,603

mulish [*adj*] *obstinate*
adamant, bullheaded, dead set on*, dogged, firm, hardheaded, headstrong, immovable, inflexible, intractable, obdurate, opinionated, persistent, pigheaded*, recalcitrant, relentless, singleminded, steadfast, strong-minded, stubborn, tenacious; SEE CONCEPTS 401,404,542

mull [*v*] *think about seriously*
brood over, chaw, consider, contemplate, delay,

deliberate, examine, figure, hammer away at*, linger, meditate, moon*, muse on, ponder, pore over, procrastinate, rack one's brains*, reflect, review, revolve, ruminate, stew over*, study, sweat over*, think over, turn over, weigh, woolgather*; SEE CONCEPT *17*

multicolored [*adj*] *having various hues*
checkered, dappled, flecked, kaleidoscopic, marbled, motley, mottled, multicolor, particolored, piebald, pied, polychrome, prismatic, speckled, spotted, streaked, varicolored, veined, versicolor; SEE CONCEPT *618*

multiculturalism [*n*] *doctrine acknowledging contributions and interests of many cultures*
cross-culturalism, cultural diversity, diversity, ethnic inclusiveness, ethnic mosaic, multiracialism, pluralism; SEE CONCEPTS *665,689*

multimedia [*n*] *combined use of several media*
interactive media, intermedia, mixed media; SEE CONCEPT *274*

multinational [*adj*] *international*
continental, global, intercontinental, multicultural, universal, worldwide; SEE CONCEPTS *536,772*

multiple/multifarious [*adj*] *diversified, miscellaneous*
assorted, collective, conglomerate, different, diverse, diversiform, heterogeneous, indiscriminate, legion, manifold, many, mixed, motley, multiform, multiplex, multitudinal, multitudinous, numerous, populous, several, sundry, varied, variegated, various, voluminous; SEE CONCEPTS *564,762,772*

multiply [*v*] *increase; reproduce*
accumulate, add, aggrandize, aggregate, augment, boost, breed, build up, compound, cube, double, enlarge, expand, extend, generate, heighten, magnify, manifold, mount, populate, procreate, produce, proliferate, propagate, raise, repeat, rise, spread, square; SEE CONCEPTS *171,374*

multitude [*n*] *large group*
aggregation, army, assemblage, assembly, collection, commonalty, concourse, congregation, crowd, crush, drove, great number, heap, herd, horde, host, infinitude, infinity, jam*, legion, loads, lot, lots*, majority, mass, mob, much, myriad, number, numbers, ocean*, oodles*, people, plenitude, plurality, populace, proletariat, public, push*, quantity, scores*, sea, slew*, swarm, throng, turnout; SEE CONCEPTS *417,432*

multitudinous [*adj*] *many, considerable*
abounding, abundant, copious, countless, great, heaps*, infinite, innumerable, innumerous, legion, manifold, multifarious, myriad, numberless, numerous, populous, profuse, several, sundry, teeming, uncountable, uncounted, unnumbered, untold, various, voluminous; SEE CONCEPTS *762,781*

mum [*adj*] *silent*
bashful, buttoned up*, clammed up*, closemouthed, hushed, mute, muted, nonvocal, not forthcoming, not talkative, quiet, reserved, secretive, shy, soundless, speechless, still, tightlipped, tongue-tied, uncommunicative, unsociable, unspeaking, voiceless, wordless, zipped*; SEE CONCEPT *594*

mumble [*v*] *say low and inarticulately*
grumble, maunder, murmur, mutter, ramble, rumble, say to oneself, speak, stammer, stutter,

swallow, talk, utter, verbalize, vocalize, voice, whimper, whine, whisper; SEE CONCEPTS *47,77*

munch [*v*] *chew, eat*
bite, break up, champ, chomp, crunch, crush, grind, mash, masticate, press, reduce, ruminate, scrunch, smash, soften; SEE CONCEPTS *169,185*

mundane [*adj*] *ordinary*
banal, commonplace, day-to-day, earthly, everyday, humdrum*, lowly, normal, prosaic, routine, workaday*, workday, worldly; SEE CONCEPT *547*

municipal [*adj*] *concerning cities*
borough, burghal, city, civic, civil, community, corporate, domestic, home, incorporated, internal, local, metropolitan, native, public, town, urban; SEE CONCEPT *536*

municipality [*n*] *city*
borough, community, district, metropolis, precinct, town, township, village; SEE CONCEPT *507*

munificent [*adj*] *giving, generous*
beneficent, benevolent, big, big-hearted, bounteous, bountiful, charitable, free, handsome, kind, lavish, liberal, loose, magnanimous, openhanded, philanthropic, rich, unsparing, unstinting; SEE CONCEPTS *334,401*

munitions [*n*] *ammunition*
ammo*, armament, arsenal, bombs, bullets, explosives, grenades, gunpowder, missiles, shells, torpedos, weapons; SEE CONCEPTS *498,500*

murder [*n*] *killing*
annihilation, assassination, blood, bloodshed, butchery, carnage, crime, death, destruction, dispatching, felony, foul play*, hit*, homicide, knifing, liquidation, lynching, manslaughter, massacre, off*, offing*, one-way ticket*, rub out*, shooting, slaying, taking out*, terrorism, the business*, the works*; SEE CONCEPTS *192,252*

murder [*v*] *kill*
abolish, asphyxiate, assassinate, behead, blot out*, bump off*, butcher, chill*, cool*, decapitate, defeat, destroy, dispatch, do in*, drub*, dust off*, electrocute, eliminate, eradicate, execute, exterminate, extinguish, finish, garotte, guillotine, hang, hit*, knife, knock off*, liquidate, lynch, mangle, mar, massacre, misuse, off*, put away*, rub out*, ruin, shoot, slaughter, slay, smother, snuff, spoil, strangle, take a life, take for a ride*, take out*, thrash*, waste*; SEE CONCEPTS *192,252*

murderer [*n*] *person who kills*
assassin, butcher, criminal, cutthroat, enforcer, executioner, hit-and-run*, hit person*, homicide, killer, manslaughterer, perpetrator, slaughterer, slayer, soldier, trigger person*; SEE CONCEPT *412*

murderous [*adj*] *difficult*
arduous, brutal, criminal, cruel, dangerous, deadly, destroying, destructive, devastating, exhausting, fell, ferocious, harrowing, hellish, killing, lethal, ruinous, sapping, savage, strenuous, unpleasant; SEE CONCEPTS *538,548,565*

murk [*n*] *darkness*
dimness, dusk, gloom, murkiness; SEE CONCEPT *620*

murky [*adj*] *gloomy, obscure*
black, caliginous, cheerless, cloudy, dark, darkened, dim, dingy, dirty, dismal, drab, dreary, dull, dun*, dusk, dusky, filthy, foggy, foul, fuzzy, glowering, gray, grubby*, impenetrable, lowering, misty, mucky, muddy, nasty, nebulous,

nubilous, overcast, roily, sad, smoky, somber, squalid, stormy, tenebrous, turbid, unclean; SEE CONCEPTS *617,618*

murmur [*n*] *low, continuous sound*
babble, buzz, buzzing, drone, grumble, hum, humming, mumble, murmuration, mutter, muttering, purr, rumble, rumor, undertone, whisper, whispering; SEE CONCEPTS *65,595*

murmur [*v*] *make low, continuous sound*
babble, burble, buzz, drip, drone, flow, growl, gurgle, hum, meander, moan, mumble, mutter, purl, purr, ripple, rumble, stage-whisper, stammer, stutter, susurrate, tinkle, trickle, utter, verbalize, vocalize, voice, whisper; SEE CONCEPTS *65,77*

muscle [*n1*] *large fibers of animal body*
beef, brawn, flesh, meat, might, sinew, tendon, thew, tissue; SEE CONCEPTS *393,420*

muscle [*n2*] *power, influence*
brawn, clout, energy, force, forcefulness, might, potency, sinew, stamina, strength, strong arm*, sturdiness, weight; SEE CONCEPTS *641,687*

muscular [*adj*] *powerfully built*
able-bodied, athletic, brawny, bruising, burly, fibrous, hefty, Herculean*, hulky, husky, lusty, mighty, muscled, powerful, powerhouse*, pumped up*, ripped*, robust, ropy, sinewy, stalwart, stout, strapping, stringy, strong, sturdy, tiger*, tough, vigorous, well-built, wiry; SEE CONCEPTS *485,489*

muse [*v*] *think about, dream*
be lost in thought*, brood, build castles in air*, chew over*, cogitate, consider, contemplate, deliberate, feel, meditate, moon*, mull over, percolate, ponder, puzzle over, reflect, revolve, roll, ruminate, speculate, think, think over, turn over, weigh; SEE CONCEPT *17*

museum [*n*] *place for viewing artifacts or exhibits*
archive, building, depository, exhibition, foundation, gallery, hall, institution, library, menagerie, repository, salon, storehouse, treasury, vault; SEE CONCEPTS *439,449*

mushroom [*v*] *sprout; grow quickly*
augment, blow up, boom, burgeon, burst, detonate, expand, explode, flourish, go off, grow, grow rapidly, increase, luxuriate, proliferate, shoot up, spread, spring up; SEE CONCEPTS *179,704*

mushy [*adj1*] *doughy, soft*
gelatinous, jelled, mashy*, muddy, pap*, pastelike, pulpous, pulpy, quaggy, semiliquid, semisolid, slushy, spongy, squashy*, squishy*; SEE CONCEPTS *604,606*

mushy [*adj2*] *romantic, corny*
bathetic, effusive, emotional, lovey-dovey*, maudlin, mawkish, saccharine, schmaltzy*, sentimental, sloppy*, slushy*, soppy*, sugary, syrupy, tear-jerking, weepy, wet; SEE CONCEPTS *267,542*

music [*n*] *sounds that are pleasant, harmonized*
a cappella, acoustic, air, bebop, bop, chamber, classical, folk, fusion, hard rock, harmony, heavy metal, hymn, instrumental, jazz, measure, melody, modern, opera, piece, plainsong, popular, ragtime, rap, refrain, rock, rock and roll, singing, song, soul, strain, swing, tune; SEE CONCEPTS *263,595*

musical [*adj*] *harmonic, lyrical*
agreeable, blending, chiming, choral, consonant, dulcet, euphonious, harmonious, lilting, mellow, melodic, melodious, operatic, orchestral, pleasing, rhythmic, silvery, songful, sweet, sweetsounding, symphonic, symphonious, tuned, tuneful, vocal; SEE CONCEPT *594*

music hall [*n*] *concert hall*
amphitheater, auditorium, opera house, theater; SEE CONCEPTS *263,293,439,448*

musician [*n*] *person who performs music*
artist, artiste, composer, conductor, diva, entertainer, instrumentalist, performer, player, session player, soloist, virtuoso, vocalist; SEE CONCEPT *352*

muss [*n*] *disorder*
chaos, confusion, disarrangement, hash, mess, mess-up, mix-up*, muddle, shambles, turmoil; SEE CONCEPTS *230,674*

muss [*v*] *dishevel, disorder*
clutter, crumple, disarrange, disarray, disorganize, disrupt, disturb, jumble, mess up, mix up*, muddle, ruffle, rummage, rumple, tangle, tousle, upset, wrinkle; SEE CONCEPT *158*

must [*n*] *necessity, essential*
charge, commitment, committal, condition, devoir, duty, fundamental, imperative, necessary, need, obligation, ought, precondition, prerequisite, requirement, requisite, right, sine qua non; SEE CONCEPTS *646,709*

must [*v*] *ought, should*
be compelled, be destined, be directed, be doomed*, be driven*, be made, be necessitated, be obliged, be one's fate, be ordered, be required, got to, have, have got to*, have no choice, have to, must needs*, need, pushed to the wall*; SEE CONCEPT *650*

muster [*n*] *gathering*
aggregation, assemblage, assembly, call-up*, collection, company, congeries, convocation, crowd, draft, group, head count*, meeting, mobilization, nose count*, rally, roll, roll call*, roster, roundup*; SEE CONCEPTS *417,432*

muster [*v*] *gather, come together*
assemble, call together, call up, collect, congregate, congress, convene, convoke, enroll, enter, group, join up, marshal, meet, mobilize, organize, raise, rally, rendezvous, round up, sign on, sign up, summon; SEE CONCEPT *109*

musty [*adj1*] *stuffy, aged*
airless, ancient, antediluvian, antique, crumbling, dank, decayed, decrepit, dirty, dried-out*, dry, fetid, filthy, frowzy*, malodorous, mildewed, mildewy, moldy, moth-eaten*, noisome, old, putrid, rotten, smelly, spoiled, squalid, stale, stuffy; SEE CONCEPTS *578,598,603,797*

musty [*adj2*] *worn-out, clichéd*
ancient, antiquated, banal, common, commonplace, dull, hackneyed, hoary, obsolete, old-fashioned, old hat*, shopworn*, stale, stereotypical, threadbare, timeworn*, tired, trite, warmedover*, worn; SEE CONCEPTS *267,530,578,797*

mutant [*n*] *mutation*
abnormality, deformity, deviation, freak, freak of nature, monster; SEE CONCEPTS *424,580*

mutation [*n*] *metamorphosis*
alteration, anomaly, change, deviant, deviation, evolution, innovation, modification, mutant, novelty, permutation, transfiguration, transformation, variation, vicissitude; SEE CONCEPTS *665,697*

mute [*adj*] *unable to speak*
aphasiac, aphasic, aphonic, muffled, mum, quiet, silenced, silent, speechless, tongueless, tongue-tied, unexpressed, unpronounced, unsounded, unspeaking, unspoken, voiceless, wordless; SEE CONCEPT *593*

mute [*v*] *muffle, tone down sound*
benumb, bottle up*, cork up*, dampen, deaden, decrease the volume, drown, gag, hush, keep it down*, lower, moderate, muzzle, pipe down*, put damper on*, put the lid on*, reduce, silence, soften, soft-pedal*, subdue, turn down; SEE CONCEPTS *65,240*

mutilate [*v*] *maim, damage*
adulterate, amputate, batter, bowdlerize, butcher, cripple, crush, cut to pieces, cut up, deface, disable, disfigure, dismember, distort, expurgate, hack*, hash up*, hurt, injure, lacerate, lame, mangle, mar, mess up*, ravage, scratch, spoil, weaken; SEE CONCEPTS *176,246*

mutilated [*adj*] *dismembered*
amputated, disfigured, maimed, mangled, marred; SEE CONCEPTS *137,246,250*

mutinous [*adj*] *rebellious*
anarchistic, contumacious, defiant, disloyal, disobediant, disorderly, dissident, factious, iconoclastic, insubordinate, insurgent, insurrectionary, radical, rebel, revolutionary, rioting, riotous, subversive, traitorous, treasonable, ungovernable, unmanageable; SEE CONCEPTS *401,529,542*

mutiny [*n*] *defiance, resistance*
disobedience, insubordination, insurrection, refusal to obey, revolt, revolution, riot, rising, strike, uprising; SEE CONCEPTS *300,388,633*

mutiny [*v*] *defy, revolt*
be insubordinate, disobey, insurrect, kick over, rebel, refuse to obey, resist, rise against, rise up, strike; SEE CONCEPTS *300,384*

mutter [*v*] *grumble, mumble*
complain, croak, groan, grouch*, grouse, growl, grunt, moan, muddle, murmur, rumble, snarl, sputter, swallow, whisper; SEE CONCEPTS *52,77*

mutual [*adj*] *shared, common*
associated, bilateral, collective, communal, conjoint, conjunct, connected, convertible, correlative, dependent, give-and-take*, given and taken*, interactive, interchangeable, interchanged, interdependent, intermutual, joint, partaken, participated, public, reciprocal, reciprocated, related, requited, respective, returned, two-sided*, united; SEE CONCEPTS *563,708*

mutual fund [*n*] *stock fund*
bond fund, hedge fund, individual retirement account, investment fund, IRA, 401(k) fund, money market funds, retirement plan; SEE CONCEPTS *330,332,340*

mutually [*adv*] *together*
all at once, as a group, by agreement, by contract, commonly, conjointly, cooperatively, en masse, in collaboration, in combination, in conjunction, jointly, reciprocally, respectively; SEE CONCEPTS *544,577*

muzzle [*n*] *covering for control*
cage, cover, envelope, gag, guard, sheath, wrap; SEE CONCEPT *172*

muzzle [*v*] *gag, quiet*
bottle up*, censor, check, choke, clamp down on*, cork, crack down on*, curb, dry up*, dummy up*, hush, ice*, muffle, prevent, quieten,

repress, restrain, restrict, shush, shut down, silence, squash, squelch, stifle, still, stop, suppress, tongue-tie*, trammel; SEE CONCEPTS *121,250*

myopic [*adj*] *able only to see things near at hand*
astigmatic, biased, blind, halfsighted, nearsighted, presbyopic, shortsighted; SEE CONCEPT *619*

myriad [*adj*] *innumerable*
countless, endless, gobs*, heaping, immeasurable, incalculable, infinite, multiple, multitudinous, no end of*, numberless, thousand-and-one*, uncounted, untold, variable; SEE CONCEPTS *762,781*

myriad [*n*] *a lot*
army, flood, heap, horde, host, loads*, mint, mountain*, multitude, oodles*, scores, slew, stacks*, swarm, thousands*; SEE CONCEPT *787*

mysterious [*adj*] *secret, concealed*
abstruse, alchemistic, arcane, astrological, baffling, cabalistic, covert, cryptic, curious, dark, difficult, enigmatic, enigmatical, equivocal, esoteric, furtive, hidden, impenetrable, incomprehensible, inexplicable, inscrutable, insoluble, magical, mystical, mystifying, necromantic, obscure, occult, oracular, perplexing, puzzling, recondite, secretive, sphinxlike, spiritual, strange, subjective, symbolic, transcendental, uncanny, unfathomable, unknowable, unknown, unnatural, veiled, weird; SEE CONCEPTS *529,576*

mystery [*n*] *puzzle, secret*
abstruseness, brainteaser*, braintwister*, charade, chiller, cliffhanger*, closed book*, conundrum, crux, cryptogram, difficulty, enigma, grabber, inscrutability, inscrutableness, mind-boggler*, mystification, occult, oracle, perplexity, poser, problem, puzzlement, question, rebus, riddle, rune, secrecy, sixty-four-thousand-dollar question*, sphinx, stickler, stumper, subtlety, teaser, thriller, tough nut to crack*, twister, whodunit*, why*; SEE CONCEPTS *282,532,696*

mystic/mystical [*adj*] *secret, esoteric*
abstruse, anagogic, arcane, cabalistic, cryptic, enigmatical, hidden, imaginary, impenetrable, inscrutable, magic, magical, metaphysical, mysterial, mysterious, necromantic, nonrational, numinous, occult, otherworldly, paranormal, preternatural, quixotic, sorcerous, spiritual, supernatural, telestic, thaumaturgic, transcendental, unaccountable, unknowable, visionary, wizardly; SEE CONCEPTS *529,549,582*

mystify [*v*] *bewilder, confuse*
baffle, bamboozle*, beat*, befog*, buffalo*, confound, deceive, elude, escape, floor*, fog in*, hoodwink*, lick*, lie, perplex, puzzle, stump*, throw*, trick; SEE CONCEPT *16*

mystique [*n*] *person's strong impression*
attitude, awe, character, charisma, charm, complex, fascination, glamour, magic, nature, spell, temperament; SEE CONCEPT *411*

myth [*n*] *fictitious story, often ancient*
allegory, apologue, creation, delusion, fable, fabrication, fairy story, fancy, fantasy, fiction, figment, folk ballad, folk tale, illusion, imagination, invention, legend, lore, mythos, parable, saga, superstition, tale, tall story*, tradition; SEE CONCEPT *282*

mythical/mythological [*adj*] *make-believe, fairytale*
allegorical, chimerical, created, fabled, fabricated, fabulous, false, fanciful, fantasy, fictitious,

fictive, folkloric, imaginary, invented, legendary, made-up, mythic, nonexistent, pretended, storied, supposititious, traditional, unreal, untrue, visionary, whimsical; SEE CONCEPTS *267,582*

mythology [*n*] *folklore*
belief, conviction, folk tales, legend, lore, mythicism, mythos, myths, stories, tradition; SEE CONCEPT *282*

N

nab [*v*] *seize*
apprehend, arrest, capture, catch, clutch, cop*, detain, grab, nail*, pick up*, run in*, snatch*, take*, take into custody; SEE CONCEPTS *90,317*

nadir [*n*] *lowest point*
all-time low, base, bottom, floor, low point, record low, rock bottom, zero level; SEE CONCEPT *442*

nag [*v*] *harass, bother*
annoy, badger, bait, berate, bug*, carp at, dog*, eat*, egg*, find fault, fuss, give a hard time*, goad, harry, heckle, hector, hound, importune, irk, irritate, needle, nudge*, pester, pick at, plague, prod, provoke, ride, scold, take it out on*, tease, torment, upbraid, urge, vex, work on*, worry; SEE CONCEPTS *7,19,52*

nail [*v1*] *fasten, fix with pointed object*
attach, beat, bind, drive, hammer, hit, hold, join, pin, pound, secure, sock*, spike, strike, tack, whack*; SEE CONCEPTS *85,160,189*

nail [*v2*] *capture, arrest*
apprehend, bag, catch, collar*, detain, get*, hook*, nab, pinch*, prehend, secure, seize, take*; SEE CONCEPTS *90,317*

naive [*adj*] *childlike, trusting*
aboveboard, artless, callow, candid, confiding, countrified, credulous, forthright, frank, fresh, green*, guileless, gullible, harmless, ignorant, impulsive, ingenuous, innocent, innocuous, instinctive, jejune, lamb*, like a babe in the woods*, natural, open, original, patsy*, plain, simple, simple-minded, sincere, spontaneous, square, sucker*, unaffected, unjaded, unpretentious, unschooled, unsophisticated, unsuspecting, unsuspicious, untaught, unworldly, virgin, wide-eyed*; SEE CONCEPTS *401,542,678*

naïveté [*n*] *innocence, gullibility*
artlessness, callowness, candor, childishness, credulity, frankness, guilelessness, inexperience, ingenuousness, naturalness, openness, simplicity; SEE CONCEPTS *633,657,678*

naked [*adj1*] *without covering*
au naturel, bald, bare, bared, bare-skinned, barren, defenseless, denuded, disrobed, divested, exposed, helpless, in birthday suit*, in dishabille*, in the altogether*, in the buff*, in the raw*, leafless, natural, nude, open, peeled*, raw, stark-naked*, stripped, threadbare, unclad, unclothed, unconcealed, uncovered, undraped, undressed, unprotected, unveiled, vulnerable, without a stitch*; SEE CONCEPTS *485,589*

naked [*adj2*] *manifest, evident*
artless, blatant, disclosed, discovered, dry, matter-of-fact, obvious, open, overt, palpable,

patent, plain, pure, revealed, sheer, simple, stark, unadorned, undisguised, unexaggerated, unmistakable, unqualified, unvarnished; SEE CONCEPTS *267,529*

namby-pamby [*n*] *pansy*
baby*, caitiff, chicken*, chicken heart*, chicken liver*, coward, cry-baby, fraidy-cat*, jellyfish*, lily liver, milksop, momma's boy*, pantywaist, quitter, scaredy cat*, sissy*, weakling, wimp, wuss*, wussy*, yellow, yellow belly*; SEE CONCEPT *423*

name [*n1*] *title given to something, someone*
agname, agnomen, alias, appellation, autograph, autonym, brand, cognomen, compellation, denomination, designation, epithet, eponym, flag*, handle*, head, heading, label, matronymic, moniker, monogram, nickname, nom de guerre, nom de plume, nomen, patronymic, pen name, pet name, place name, prenomen, proper name, pseudonym, rubric, sign, signature, sobriquet, stage name, style, surname, tag, term, trade name; SEE CONCEPTS *268,683*

name [*n2*] *fame, distinction*
character, credit, eminence, esteem, honor, note, praise, renown, rep*, report, reputation, repute; SEE CONCEPTS *388,668*

name [*n3*] *celebrity*
big name*, celeb*, entertainer, headliner, hero, lion*, luminary, notability, notable, personality, somebody*, star, superstar; SEE CONCEPTS *352,366*

name [*v1*] *give a title*
baptize, call, characterize, christen, classify, cognominate, define, denominate, designate, dub, entitle, give a handle*, identify, label, nickname, nomenclature, put tag on, style, tag, term, ticket, title; SEE CONCEPT *62*

name [*v2*] *choose, designate*
announce, appoint, cite, classify, commission, connote, declare, delegate, denote, elect, identify, index, instance, list, make, mark, mention, nominate, peg*, pin down*, point to, put down for, put finger on*, recognize, refer to, remark, select, signify, single out, slot, specify, suggest, tab, tag, tap; SEE CONCEPTS *41,50,88*

name-dropper [*n*] *snob*
social climber, status seeker; SEE CONCEPT *423*

nameless [*adj*] *unknown, anonymous*
incognito, inconspicuous, innominate, obscure, pseudonymous, unacknowledged, uncelebrated, undesignated, undistinguished, unfamed, unheard-of, unnamed, unnoted, unsung, untitled, whatchamacallit*, X*; SEE CONCEPTS *267,576*

namely [*adv*] *that is to say*
by way of explanation, especially, expressly, id est*, i.e., in other words, in plain English*, particularly, scilicet, specially, specifically, strictly speaking, that is, to wit, videlicet, viz.; SEE CONCEPT *557*

nanny [*n*] *children's nurse*
au pair, baby-sitter, governess, nursemaid, wet nurse; SEE CONCEPT *295*

nap [*n1*] *short, light sleep*
break, catnap, doze, few z's*, forty winks*, interlude, intermission, microsleep*, nod, pause, respite, rest, shuteye*, siesta, snooze*, spot; SEE CONCEPT *315*

nap [*n2*] *grain of material*
down, feel, fiber, grit, outside, pile, roughness,

shag, smoothness, surface, tooth, wale, warp, weave, weft, woof; SEE CONCEPTS *473,611*

nap [*v*] *take a short, light sleep*
catch forty winks*, catnap, doze, drop off*, drowse, get some shut-eye*, grab some z's*, nod, nod off, rack*, relax, rest, sleep, snooze, take a siesta*, take a snooze*; SEE CONCEPTS *210,315*

napkin [*n*] *linen*
cloth, doily, moist towelette, serviette, towel, wipe; SEE CONCEPT *473*

nappy [*adj*] *fuzzy*
downy, frizzy, furry, hairy, kinky, napped, velutinous, woolly; SEE CONCEPT *606*

narcissistic [*adj*] *concerned only with oneself*
conceited, egotistic, egotistical, self-centered, self-involved, self-loving, stuck-up*, vain, vainglorious; SEE CONCEPTS *401,404*

narcotic [*adj*] *dulling, painkilling*
analgesic, anesthetic, calming, deadening, hypnotic, numbing, opiate, sedative, somnifacient, somnific, somnolent, somnorific, soporiferous, soporific, stupefactive, stupefying; SEE CONCEPT *537*

narcotic [*n*] *powerful drug inducing anesthesia or sleep*
analgesic, anesthetic, anodyne, dope*, downer*, fix*, hard drug, hard stuff*, heroin, hypnotic, junk*, laudanum, lenitive, merchandise*, nepenthe, opiate, opium, painkiller, sedative, somnifacient, soporific, stuff*, stupefacient, tranquilizer; SEE CONCEPT *307*

narrate [*v*] *describe, detail*
characterize, chronicle, delineate, depict, descant, disclose, discourse, enumerate, expatiate, give an account of, hold forth, make known, paint, picture, portray, proclaim, recite, recount, rehearse, relate, repeat, report, reveal, set forth, spin, state, tell, tell a story, unfold; SEE CONCEPTS *55,72*

narration [*n*] *description, reading*
account, anecdote, explanation, narrative, recital, recounting, recounting, rehearsal, relation, report, story, storytelling, tale, telling, voice-over*, yarn*; SEE CONCEPTS *55,72,282*

narrative [*adj*] *storylike, chronological*
anecdotal, fictional, fictive, historical, narrated, recounted, reported, retold, sequential; SEE CONCEPT *267*

narrative [*n*] *story, tale*
account, anecdote, book, chronicle, chronology, description, detail, fiction, history, line, long and short of it*, narration, plot, potboiler*, recount, report, statement, version, yarn*; SEE CONCEPTS *271,282*

narrator [*n*] *storyteller*
author, chronicler, describer, novelist, raconteur, reporter, teller of tales, writer, yarn spinner; SEE CONCEPTS *348,356*

narrow [*adj1*] *confined, restricted*
attenuated, circumscribed, close, compressed, confining, constricted, contracted, cramped, definite, determinate, exclusive, exiguous, fine, fixed, incapacious, limited, linear, meager, near, paltry, pent, pinched, precarious, precise, scant, scanty, select, set, shrunken, slender, slim, small, spare, strait, taper, tapered, tapering, thin, threadlike, tight; SEE CONCEPTS *554,773*

narrow [*adj2*] *intolerant, small-minded*
biased, bigoted, conservative, conventional, dog-

matic, hidebound, illiberal, inexorable, inflexible, narrow-minded, obdurate, parochial, partial, prejudiced, reactionary; SEE CONCEPTS *403,542*

narrow [*adj3*] *cheap, stingy*
avaricious, close, mean, mercenary, scrimpy*, tight*, ungenerous; SEE CONCEPT *334*

narrow [*v*] *reduce, simplify*
circumscribe, constrict, contract, diminish, limit, taper, tighten; SEE CONCEPTS *130,236,247*

narrowly [*adv*] *just, closely*
almost, barely, by a hair*, by a whisker*, by narrow margin, carefully, close, nearly, only just, painstakingly, scarcely, scrutinizingly; SEE CONCEPTS *544,799*

narrow-minded [*adj*] *biased, intolerant*
bigoted, conservative, conventional, hidebound, illiberal, insular, narrow, opinionated, parochial, petty, prejudiced, provincial, reactionary, shortsighted, small-minded, strait-laced, unenlarged; SEE CONCEPTS *403,542*

nasty [*adj1*] *disgusting, offensive*
awful, beastly, bum*, dirty, disagreeable, fierce, filthy, foul, gross, grubby, hellish, horrible, horrid, icky*, impure, loathsome, lousy, malodorous, mephitic, murderous*, nauseating, noisome, noxious, objectionable, obnoxious, obscene, odious, ornery, outrageous, poison, polluted, raunchy*, repellent, repugnant, repulsive, revolting, rough, sickening, soiled, squalid, stinking, tough, unappetizing, unclean, uncleanly, ungodly, unholy, unpleasant, vile, vulgar, yucky*; SEE CONCEPTS *485,548,571*

nasty [*adj2*] *indecent, smutty*
blue*, coarse, dirty, filthy, foul, gross, immodest, immoral, improper, impure, indecorous, indelicate, lascivious, lewd, licentious, obscene, pornographic, raunchy*, ribald, scatological, shameful, unseemly, vulgar, wicked, X-rated*; SEE CONCEPTS *372,545*

nasty [*adj3*] *bad-tempered, mean*
abusive, annoying, beastly, critical, cruel, despicable, disagreeable, distasteful, evil, fierce, hateful, malevolent, malicious, malign, malignant, ornery, ruthless, sarcastic, sordid, spiteful, squalid, unkind, unpleasant, vicious, vile, wicked; SEE CONCEPT *401*

nasty [*adj4*] *injurious, dangerous*
bad, critical, damaging, harmful, noxious, painful, poisonous, serious, severe, ugly; SEE CONCEPT *537*

nation [*n*] *country with its own government*
body politic, commonwealth, community, democracy, domain, dominion, empire, land, monarchy, people, populace, population, principality, public, race, realm, republic, society, sovereignty, state, tribe, union; SEE CONCEPT *510*

national [*adj*] *concerning a country with a government*
civic, civil, communal, countrywide, domestic, ethnic, federal, general, governmental, home, imperial, inland, internal, interstate, nationwide, native, politic, political, public, royal, social, societal, sovereign, state, sweeping, vernacular, widespread; SEE CONCEPT *536*

nationality [*n*] *place of birth*
allegiance, body politic, citizenship, community, country, ethnic group, nation, native land, origin, political home, race, society; SEE CONCEPTS *380,510*

my
na

native [*adj1*] *innate, inherent*
built-in, congenital, connate, connatural, constitutional, endemic, essential, fundamental, genuine, hereditary, implanted, inborn, inbred, indigenous, ingrained, inherited, instinctive, intrinsic, inveterate, inwrought, natal, natural, original, real, unacquired, wild; SEE CONCEPTS *404,549*

native [*adj2*] *domestic, home*
aboriginal, autochthonous, belonging, endemic, from, homegrown, homemade, indigenous, inland, internal, local, municipal, national, original, primary, primeval, primitive, regional, related, vernacular; SEE CONCEPT *536*

native [*n*] *person born in the country in which he/she dwells*
aboriginal, aborigine, ancient, autochthon, citizen, dweller, home towner, indigene, inhabitant, local, national; SEE CONCEPT *413*

native land [*n*] *homeland*
fatherland, God's country, home, mother country, motherland, native soil, the old country*; SEE CONCEPTS *510,515,648*

natty [*adj*] *dapper*
chic, chichi, classy, clean, dainty, dashing, dressed to kill*, dressed to the nines*, elegant, fashionable, neat, prim, sharp, slick, smart, snazzy*, spiffy*, spruce, spruced up, stylish, swanky, trim, well-groomed; SEE CONCEPT *579*

natural [*adj1*] *normal, everyday*
accustomed, anticipated, characteristic, common, commonplace, congenital, connatural, consistent, constant, counted on, customary, essential, familiar, general, habitual, inborn, indigenous, ingenerate, inherent, innate, instinctive, intuitive, involuntary, legitimate, logical, looked for, matter-of-course, natal, native, ordinary, prevailing, prevalent, probable, reasonable, regular, relied on, spontaneous, typic, typical, unacquired, uncontrolled, uniform, universal, usual; SEE CONCEPTS *530,547*

natural [*adj2*] *open, unaffected*
artless, being oneself, candid, childlike, credulous, direct, easy, folksy, forthright, frank, genuine, homey*, ignorant, impulsive, inartificial, ingenuous, innocent, instinctive, laid-back*, naive, plain, primitive, provincial, real, rustic, simple, simplehearted, sincere, spontaneous, straightforward, trusting, unassumed, uncontrived, undesigning, unembarrassed, unfeigned, unforced, unlabored, unpolished, unpretentious, unschooled, unsophisticated, unstudied, unworldly, up-front*; SEE CONCEPTS *267,401,404*

natural [*adj3*] *organic, unrefined*
agrarian, agrestal, crude, native, plain, pure, raw, unbleached, uncultivated, undomesticated, unmixed, unpolished, unprocessed, whole, wild; SEE CONCEPTS *462,485*

naturally [*adv*] *as anticipated*
artlessly, but of course*, by birth, by nature, candidly, casually, characteristically, commonly, consistently, customarily, easily, freely, generally, genuinely, habitually, impulsively, informally, innocently, instinctively, normally, openly, ordinarily, readily, simply, spontaneously, typically, unaffectedly, uniformly, unpretentiously, usually; SEE CONCEPT *544*

natural selection [*n*] *Darwinism*
Darwinian theory, evolution, evolutionism, social Darwinism, survival of the fittest; SEE CONCEPT *704*

nature [*n1*] *character, disposition*
attributes, being, bottom line*, complexion, constitution, description, drift, essence, essentiality, features, heart*, humor, individualism, individuality, like, makeup, meat*, mood, name of game*, name of tune*, nature of beast*, outlook, personality, point, quality, score, stuff, temper, temperament, texture, traits, type; SEE CONCEPTS *411,682*

nature [*n2*] *type, kind*
anatomy, brand, cast, category, character, color, conformation, description, figure, framework, ilk, shape, sort, species, stripe*, structure, style, variety, way; SEE CONCEPT *378*

nature [*n3*] *earth, creation*
cosmos, country, countryside, environment, forest, generation, landscape, macrocosm, megacosm, natural history, outdoors, scenery, seascape, setting, universe, view, world; SEE CONCEPTS *407,429,509,511*

naughty [*adj1*] *bad, misbehaved*
annoying, badly behaved*, contrary, disobedient, disorderly, evil, exasperating, fiendish, fractious, froward, headstrong, impish, indecorous, insubordinate, intractable, mischievous, obstreperous, perverse, playful, rascally, raunchy, recalcitrant, refractory, rough, rowdy, sinful, teasing, tough, ungovernable, unmanageable, unruly, wanton, wayward, wicked, willful, worthless, wrong; SEE CONCEPT *401*

naughty [*adj2*] *obscene, vulgar*
adult, bawdy, blue*, dirty*, hot*, improper, lascivious, lewd, loose*, off-color*, pornographic, purple*, ribald, risqué, steamy*; SEE CONCEPTS *372,545*

nausea [*n*] *sickness in stomach; revulsion*
abhorrence, aversion, biliousness, disgust, hatred, loathing, offense, qualm, qualms, queasiness, regurgitation, rejection, repugnance, retching, squeamishness, vomiting; SEE CONCEPTS *316,410*

nauseate [*v*] *make sick; disgust*
bother, disturb, horrify, offend, reluct, repel, repulse, revolt, sicken; SEE CONCEPTS *14,308*

nauseating [*adj*] *nauseous*
abhorrent, detestable, disgusting, distasteful, fulsome, loathsome, offensive, repugnant, repulsive, revolting, sickening; SEE CONCEPTS *314,529*

nauseous [*adj*] *disgusting*
abhorrent, brackish, detestable, distasteful, ill, loathsome, nauseated, nauseating, offensive, queasy, repugnant, repulsive, revolting, rocky*, seasick, sick, sick as dog*, sickening, squeamish; SEE CONCEPTS *314,529*

nautical/naval [*adj*] *concerning ships, sea*
abyssal, aquatic, boating, cruising, deep-sea, marine, maritime, navigating, navigational, oceangoing, oceanic, oceanographic, pelagic, rowing, sailing, sailorly, salty, seafaring, seagoing, sea-loving, thalassic, yachting; SEE CONCEPT *536*

navigate [*v*] *guide along route, often over water*
captain*, cross, cruise, direct, drive, handle, head out for*, helm, journey, lay the course*, maneuver, operate, pilot, plan, plot, ride out, sail, skipper*, steer, voyage; SEE CONCEPTS *148,187,224*

navigation [*n*] *traveling, guiding along route, often over water*
aeronautics, boating, cruising, exploration, fly-

ing, helmsmanship, nautics, navigating, ocean travel, pilotage, piloting, plotting a course, sailing, seafaring, seamanship, shipping, steerage, steering, voyage, voyaging, yachting; SEE CONCEPTS *155,187,224*

navigator [*n*] *course plotter*
helmsman, pilot, steersman, wheelman; SEE CONCEPT *348*

navy [*n*] *fleet*
argosy, armada, flotilla, marine defense, merchant marine, naval force, sea force, sea power, vessels, warships; SEE CONCEPTS *322,432,506*

naysayer [*n*] *pessimist*
complainer, cynic, defeatist, downer, gloomy, killjoy*, misanthrope, party pooper*, prophet of doom*, sourpuss*, wet blanket*; SEE CONCEPTS *412,423*

near [*adj1*] *close by physically*
abreast, abutting, adjacent, adjoining, alongside, along toward, approximal, around, at close quarters, available, beside, bordering, burning, close, close-at-hand, close-by, close shave*, conterminous, contiguous, convenient, hair's breadth*, handy, immediate, in close proximity*, near-at-hand*, nearby, neighboring, next door*, nigh*, not remote, practically, proximal, proximate, ready, side-by-side, touching, vincinal, warm*, within stone's throw*; SEE CONCEPTS *586,778*

near [*adj2*] *close in time; forthcoming*
approaching, approximate, at hand, coming, comparative, expected, imminent, impending, in the offing*, looming, near-at-hand*, next, relative; SEE CONCEPTS *812,820*

near [*adj3*] *familiar*
affecting, akin*, allied, attached, close, connected, dear, friendly, intimate, related, touching; SEE CONCEPT *555*

nearby [*adj*] *adjoining*
adjacent, close, close-at-hand, close-by, contiguous, convenient, handy, immediate, neighboring, proximate, ready; SEE CONCEPTS *586,778*

nearby [*adv*] *within reach*
about, at close quarters, close, close at hand, hard, near, near-at-hand*, nigh*, not far away; SEE CONCEPTS *586,778*

nearing [*adj*] *approaching*
advancing, approximating, coming, forthcoming, imminent, impending, oncoming, threatening, upcoming; SEE CONCEPTS *548,820*

nearly [*adv*] *almost*
about, all but*, approaching, approximately, as good as*, circa*, close but no cigar*, closely, give or take a little*, in effect, in essence, in substance, in the ballpark*, in the neighborhood*, just about, more or less, most, much, nearabout, not quite, practically, pretty near, roughly, round, roundly, some, somewhere, upwards of*, virtually, well-nigh*, within a little*; SEE CONCEPT *566*

near miss [*n*] *close call*
close shave, narrow escape, near hit; SEE CONCEPT *747*

nearsighted [*adj*] *myopic*
blind as a bat*, purblind, shortsighted; SEE CONCEPT *619*

neat [*adj1*] *arranged well, uncluttered*
accurate, apple-pie order*, chic*, correct, dainty, dapper, elegant, exact, fastidious, finical, finicky, immaculate, in good order, in good shape, methodical, natty, neat as a pin*, nice, orderly, precise, prim, proper, regular, shipshape*, sleek, slick, smart, spick-and-span*, spotless, spruce, systematic, tidy, trim, well-groomed, well-kept; SEE CONCEPTS *485,589,621*

neat [*adj2*] *clever, practiced*
able, adept, adroit, agile, apt, artful, deft, dexterous, efficient, effortless, elegant, expert, finished, graceful, handy, nimble, precise, proficient, quick, ready, skillful, speedy, stylish, well-judged; SEE CONCEPTS *527,542*

neaten [*v*] *tidy*
arrange, clean, clear the decks*, fix up, groom, order, put in good shape, put in order, shape up, spruce up*, straighten up, whip into shape*; SEE CONCEPT *250*

neatly [*adv*] *tidily*
accurately, adeptly, adroitly, aptly, cleanly, efficiently, expertly, fastidiously, handily, methodically, nicely, orderly, precisely, skillfully, sprucely; SEE CONCEPTS *326,485,585,589*

nebulous [*adj*] *confused, obscure*
ambiguous, amorphous, cloudy, dark, dim, hazy, imprecise, indefinite, indeterminate, indistinct, misty, murky, shadowy, shapeless, uncertain, unclear, unformed, vague; SEE CONCEPTS *535,617*

necessarily [*adv*] *inevitably, certainly*
accordingly, as a matter of course*, automatically, axiomatically, beyond one's control*, by definition, by its own nature*, cardinally, come what may*, compulsorily, consequently, exigently, from within*, fundamentally, incontrovertibly, indubitably, ineluctably, inescapably, inexorably, irresistibly, naturally, no doubt, of course, of necessity, perforce, positively, pressingly, significantly, undoubtedly, unpreventably, unquestionably, vitally, willy-nilly*, without fail*; SEE CONCEPTS *535,544*

necessary [*adj1*] *essential*
all-important, basic, binding, bottom-line*, cardinal, chief, compelling, compulsory, crucial, decisive, de rigueur*, elementary, exigent, expedient, fundamental, imperative, incumbent on, indispensable, mandatory, momentous, name of game*, needed, needful, obligatory, paramount, prerequisite, pressing, prime, principal, quintessential, required, requisite, significant, specified, unavoidable, urgent, vital, wanted; SEE CONCEPTS *546,568*

necessary [*adj2*] *inevitable*
assured, certain, fated, imminent, ineluctable, ineludible, inerrant, inescapable, inevasible, inexorable, infallible, returnless, unavoidable, undeniable, unescapable; SEE CONCEPTS *535,548*

necessitate [*v*] *call for, make necessary*
ask, behoove, cause, coerce, command, compel, constrain, crave, demand, drive, entail, force, impel, make, oblige, postulate, require, take; SEE CONCEPTS *53,242,646*

necessity [*n*] *need, essentiality*
call, cause, claim, compulsion, demand, desideratum, duress, essence, essential, exaction, exigency, fundamental, godsend*, imperative, indispensability, inevitability, inexorableness, life or death*, must, necessary, needfulness, no alternative, no choice, obligation, pinch, precondition, prerequisite, privation, requirement, requisite, sine qua non, stress, undeniability, urgency, vital part, vitals, want; SEE CONCEPTS *646,709*

na
ne

necking [n] *kissing*
canoodling, caressing, cuddling, embracing, fondling, lovemaking, making love*, making out*, parking*, petting, smooching, sucking face*; SEE CONCEPTS *185,375*

necklace [n] *chain*
beads, carcanet, choker, jewelry, lavalliere, locket, pearls, pendant, riviere, strand, string; SEE CONCEPT *446*

necromancy [n] *sorcery*
abracadabra*, alchemy, bewitchment, black art, black magic, charm, conjuring, devilry, divination, enchantment, evil eye, hocus-pocus*, incantation, jinx, magic, mumbo-jumbo*, mysticism, occultism, spell, thaumaturgy, voodoo, witchcraft, witchery, witching, wizardry; SEE CONCEPTS *370,689*

necropolis [n] *cemetery*
boot hill*, catacomb, charnel, charnel house, churchyard, city of the dead*, crypt, funerary grounds, God's acre*, graveyard, potter's field, sepulcher, tomb, vault; SEE CONCEPTS *305,368*

need [n1] *want, requirement*
charge, commitment, committal, compulsion, demand, desideratum, devoir, duty, essential, exigency, extremity, longing, must, obligation, occasion, ought, requisite, right, the urge, urgency, use, weakness, wish; SEE CONCEPTS *20,709*

need [n2] *poverty*
deprivation, destitution, distress, extremity, impecuniousness, impoverishment, inadequacy, indigence, insufficiency, lack, neediness, paucity, pennilessness, penury, poorness, privation, shortage, want; SEE CONCEPTS *335,709*

need [n3] *emergency; pressing lack*
deficiency, exigency, inadequacy, insufficiency, necessity, obligation, shortage, urgency, want; SEE CONCEPTS *646,709*

need [v] *want something*
be deficient, be deprived, be down and out*, be hard up*, be inadequate, be in need of, be in want, be needy, be poor, be short, be without, call for, claim, covet, crave, demand, desire, die for*, do without, drive for*, exact, feel a dearth of*, feel the necessity for, feel the pinch*, go hungry*, hanker, have occasion for, have occasion to, have use for*, hunger, hurt for, lack, long, lust, miss, necessitate, pine, require, suffer privation, thirst, wish, yearn for; SEE CONCEPTS *20,646*

needle [v] *tease, annoy*
aggravate, badger, bait, bedevil, bother, examine, gnaw, goad, harass, hector, irk, irritate, nag, nettle, pester, plague, prick, prod, provoke, question, quiz, ride*, rile, ruffle, spur, sting, taunt, tweak*, worry; SEE CONCEPTS *7,19,54*

needless [adj] *unnecessary, groundless*
causeless, dispensable, excessive, expendable, gratuitous, inessential, nonessential, pointless, redundant, superfluous, uncalled-for, undesired, unrequired, unwanted, useless; SEE CONCEPTS *546,575*

needlework [n] *needlepoint*
crocheting, darning, embroidery, knitting, lace, quilting, sewing, stitchery, stitching, tatting; SEE CONCEPT *128*

needy [adj] *deprived, impoverished*
beggared, dead broke*, destitute, dirt poor*, disadvantaged, down-and-out*, down at heel*,

down to last cent*, flat*, impecunious, indigent, necessitous, penniless, penurious, poor, poverty-stricken, underprivileged, unprosperous; SEE CONCEPT *334*

ne'-er-do-well [n] *irresponsible person*
bum*, good-for-nothing, idler, lazybones*, loafer, sloucher, wastrel; SEE CONCEPT *412*

nefarious [adj] *bad, sinful*
abominable, atrocious, base, corrupt, criminal, degenerate, depraved, detestable, dreadful, evil, execrable, flagitious, flagrant, foul, glaring, gross, heinous, horrible, infamous, infernal, iniquitous, miscreant, monstrous, odious, opprobrious, outrageous, perverse, putrid, rank, rotten, shameful, treacherous, vicious, vile, villainous, wicked; SEE CONCEPTS *401,545,548*

negate [v] *contradict, countermand*
abate, abolish, abrogate, annihilate, annul, belie, blackball*, break with*, cancel, cancel out, controvert, countercheck, cross*, deny, ding*, disaffirm, disallow, disprove, dump*, fly in the face of*, frustrate, gainsay, impugn, invalidate, kill, negative, neutralize, nullify, oppose, put down, quash*, rebut, redress, refute, repeal, rescind, retract, reverse, revoke, stonewall*, traverse, turn down, turn thumbs down*, undo, vitiate, void; SEE CONCEPTS *46,50,88,121*

negation [n] *contradiction, denial*
antithesis, antonym, blank, cancellation, contrary, converse, counterpart, disavowal, disclaimer, forget it*, gainsaying, inverse, negatory, neutralization, no, nonexistence, nothingness, nullification, nullity, opposite, opposition, proscription, refusal, rejection, renunciation, repudiation, reverse, vacuity, veto, void; SEE CONCEPTS *121,278,685*

negative [adj] *bad, contradictory*
abrogating, adverse, against, annulling, antagonistic, anti, balky, colorless, con, contrary, contravening, counteractive, cynical, denying, detrimental, disallowing, disavowing, dissentient, dissenting, gainsaying, gloomy, impugning, invalidating, jaundiced, naysaying, neutralizing, nugatory, nullifying, opposing, pessimistic, privative, recusant, refusing, rejecting, removed, repugnant, resisting, resistive, unaffirmative, unenthusiastic, unfavorable, uninterested, unwilling, weak; SEE CONCEPTS *267,403,570*

negative [n] *contradiction*
denial, disavowal, nay, refusal, refutation; SEE CONCEPT *278*

negative attitude [n] *pessimism*
chip on one's shoulder*, cynicism, dim view*, expectation of the worst, gloomy outlook, hopelessness, lack of confidence, low spirits, negativism; SEE CONCEPTS *410,689*

neglect [n1] *disregard*
carelessness, coolness, delinquency, disdain, disregardance, disrespect, heedlessness, inadvertence, inattention, inconsideration, indifference, laxity, laxness, oversight, scorn, slight, thoughtlessness, unconcern; SEE CONCEPTS *410,657*

neglect [n2] *failure, default*
carelessness, chaos, delay, delinquency, dereliction, dilapidation, forgetfulness, lapse, laxity, laxness, limbo, neglectfulness, negligence, omission, oversight, pretermission, remissness, slackness, slovenliness; SEE CONCEPTS *674,699*

neglect [*v1*] *be indifferent, leave alone*
affront, brush aside, brush off, condemn, depreciate, despise, detest, discount, disdain, dismiss, disregard, have nothing to do with*, ignore, keep at arm's length*, keep one's distance*, laugh off*, let go*, live with*, make light of*, not care for*, overlook, pass by, pass over, pass up, pay no attention to, pay no mind*, preterit, rebuff, reject, scant, scorn, shrug off*, slight, slur, spurn, tune out*, underestimate; SEE CONCEPTS *30,681*

neglect [*v2*] *fail to do; forget*
be careless, be derelict, be irresponsible, be negligent, be remiss, bypass, defer, discard, dismiss, disregard, elide, evade, gloss over*, let pass*, let slide*, look the other way*, lose sight of*, miss, not trouble oneself*, omit, overleap, overlook, overpass, pass over, postpone, procrastinate, shirk, skimp, skip, suspend, think little of*, trifle; SEE CONCEPTS *101,699*

neglectful [*adj*] *careless, failing*
behindhand, delinquent, derelict, disregardful, heedless, inattentive, indifferent, lax, lazy, negligent, regardless, remiss, slack, thoughtless, uncaring, unmindful; SEE CONCEPTS *401,542*

negligee [*n*] *nightgown*
camisole, dishabille, nightdress, nightie, peignoir, robe, teddy, wrap, wrapper; SEE CONCEPT *451*

negligence [*n*] *carelessness*
disregard, failure, forgetfulness, heedlessness, inattention, inattentiveness, laxity, laxness, neglect, neglectfulness, oversight, thoughtlessness, unpreparedness; SEE CONCEPTS *30,633*

negligent [*adj*] *careless, indifferent*
asleep at switch*, behindhand, cursory, delinquent, derelict, discinct, disregardful, forgetful, heedless, inadvertent, inattentive, inconsiderate, incurious, lax, neglectful, nonchalant, offhand, regardless, remiss, slack, slapdash*, slipshod*, sloppy*, slovenly, thoughtless, unconcerned, unheedful, unmindful, unthinking; SEE CONCEPTS *401,542*

negligible [*adj*] *insignificant*
imperceptible, inconsequential, minor, minute, off*, outside, petty, remote, slender, slight, slim, small, trifling, trivial, unimportant; SEE CONCEPTS *552,575,789*

negotiate [*v1*] *bargain, discuss*
accommodate, adjudicate, adjust, agree, arbitrate, arrange, bring to terms*, bury the hatchet*, come across with*, compose, concert, conciliate, confer, connect, consult, contract, covenant, cut a deal*, deal, debate, dicker*, haggle, hammer out a deal*, handle, horse trade*, intercede, make a deal, make peace*, make terms*, manage, mediate, moderate, network, parley*, referee, settle, step in*, stipulate, swap, transact, treat, umpire*, work out*, work out a deal; SEE CONCEPTS *8,56,68*

negotiate [*v2*] *traverse, cross*
clear, get around, get over, get past, hurdle, leap over, overleap, pass, pass through, surmount, vault; SEE CONCEPTS *149,224*

negotiation [*n*] *bargaining*
agreement, arbitration, colloquy, compromise, conference, consultation, debate, diplomacy, discussion, intervention, mediation, meeting, transaction; SEE CONCEPTS *56,68,684*

negotiator [*n*] *person who bargains, controls discussion*
adjudicator, ambassador, arbitrator, broker, delegate, diplomat, fixer*, go-between*, interagent, intermediary, intermedium, judge, mediator, middleperson, moderator; SEE CONCEPTS *348,354,423*

neighbor [*n*] *person who lives close by*
acquaintance, bystander, friend, homebody*, nearby resident, next-door neighbor; SEE CONCEPT *423*

neighbor [*v*] *be next to*
abut, adjoin, be adjacent, be contiguous, be near, be nearby, border, butt against, communicate, connect, join, line, march, surround, touch, verge; SEE CONCEPT *759*

neighborhood [*n*] *community, surroundings*
adjacency, area, block, closeness, confines, contiguity, district, environs, ghetto, hood, jungle*, locale, locality, nearness, neck of the woods*, parish, part, precinct, propinquity, proximity, purlieus, quarter, region, section, slum, stomping ground*, street, suburb, territory, tract, turf, vicinage, vicinity, ward, zone, zoo*; SEE CONCEPTS *198,379,516*

neighborly [*adj*] *friendly*
amiable, civil, companionable, considerate, cooperative, cordial, genial, gracious, gregarious, harmonious, helpful, hospitable, kind, obliging, sociable, social, well-disposed; SEE CONCEPT *401*

neither here nor there [*adj*] *irrelevant*
beside the point, extraneous, immaterial, impertinent, inconsequential, not connected with, not germane, not pertaining to, off the point, off the topic, pointless, trivial, unconnected, unimportant; SEE CONCEPTS *560,575*

nemesis [*n*] *bane*
adversary, affliction, bête noire, curse, infliction, opponent, plague, rival, ruination, scourge, torment; SEE CONCEPTS *529,674*

neologism [*n*] *new word*
buzz word*, coinage, neology, new phrase, slang, synthetic word*, vogue word*; SEE CONCEPT *275*

neophyte [*n*] *beginner*
abecedarian, amateur, apprentice, colt*, fledgling, freshman, greenhorn, new boy/girl, newcomer, new kid on the block*, novice, recruit, rookie*, tenderfoot*, trainee, tyro*; SEE CONCEPTS *423,424*

nepotism [*n*] *favoritism*
bias, discrimination, inequity, one-sidedness, partiality, partisanship, preference, preferential treatment; SEE CONCEPTS *41,388,645*

nerd [*n*] *geek*
dolt, dork*, dweeb*, fool, goober*, goofball*, jerk*, oaf, techie*, trekkie*, weirdo; SEE CONCEPTS *564,570*

nerve [*n*] *daring, boldness*
assumption, assurance, audacity, backbone, brass*, bravery, brazenness, cheek*, chutzpah*, confidence, coolness, courage, crust*, determination, effrontery, endurance, energy, face*, fearlessness, firmness, force, fortitude, gall*, gameness, grit*, guts*, hardihood, hardiness, heart*, impertinence, impudence, insolence, intestinal fortitude, intrepidity, mettle, might, moxie*, pluck*, presumption, resolution, sauce*, spirit, spunk*, starch*, steadfastness, stomach*, temerity, vigor, will; SEE CONCEPT *411*

nerve [v] *strengthen, hearten*
animate, brace, cheer, embolden, encourage, enhearten, fortify, inspirit, invigorate, steel; SEE CONCEPTS 7,14,22

nerve center [n] *control center*
command post, core, focal point, focus, headquarters, heart, HQ, hub; SEE CONCEPTS 532,826,829

nerveless [adj1] *calm, cool*
collected, composed, controlled, impassive, imperturbable, intrepid, patient, self-possessed, tranquil, unemotional; SEE CONCEPT 542

nerveless [adj2] *scared to death*
afraid, cowardly, debilitated, enervated, fearful, feeble, nervous, petrified, spineless*, timid, weak, yellow-bellied*; SEE CONCEPTS 401,403

nerve-racking [adj] *distressing*
aggravating, annoying, disquieting, disturbing, exasperating, irksome, irritating, maddening, stressful, taxing, tense, trying, upsetting; SEE CONCEPTS 548,565

nerves [n] *extreme anxiety*
fretfulness, hysteria, imbalance, irritation, nervousness, neurasthenia, sleeplessness, strain, stress, tenseness, tension; SEE CONCEPT 410

nervous [adj] *anxious, fearful*
afraid, agitated, annoyed, apprehensive, basket case*, bothered, concerned, distressed, disturbed, edgy, excitable, fidgety, fitful, flustered, fussy*, hesitant, high-strung*, hysterical, irritable, jittery*, jumpy*, nervy*, neurotic, on edge*, overwrought, querulous, restive, ruffled, sensitive, shaky*, shrinking, shy, skittish, snappish, solicitous, spooked*, taut, tense, timid, timorous, troubled, twitchy*, uneasy, unrestful, unstrung*, upset, uptight, volatile, weak, wired*, worried; SEE CONCEPTS 403,542

nervous breakdown [n] *mental collapse*
burnout*, crackup*, depression, emotional collapse, nervous exhaustion, nervous prostration, shattered nerves; SEE CONCEPT 410

nervousness [n] *anxious state*
agitation, all-overs*, anger, animation, butterflies*, cold sweat*, creeps*, delirium, discomfiture, disquiet, disquietude, dithers*, excitability, feverishness, fidgets*, flap*, fluster*, fuss*, impatience, jitters*, jumps*, moodiness, neurasthenia, neuroticism, perturbation, quivers, sensitivity, shakes, stage fright, stimulation, stress, tension, timidity, tizzy*, to-do*, touchiness, trembles*, tremulousness, turbulence, uneasiness, willies*, worry; SEE CONCEPTS 410,657

nervy [adj] *bold, pushy*
cheeky*, crass, crude, forward, fresh*, impudent, inconsiderate, pert, plucky*, rude, sassy*, smart, smart-alecky*, wise; SEE CONCEPT 401

nest [n] *home*
aerie, breeding ground, burrow, den, haunt, hideaway, lair, refuge, roost; SEE CONCEPTS 198,515

nest egg [n] *savings*
backup, cache, funds, investment, life savings, mad money*, means, money in the bank, piggy bank, provisions, rainy day fund*, reserves, resources, savings account, stash*, stockpile; SEE CONCEPTS 335,340,446,710

nestle [v] *curl up*
bundle, burrow, cuddle, huddle, lie against, lie close, make snug*, move close, nuzzle, settle down, snug*, snuggle, take shelter; SEE CONCEPTS 154,612

net [adj] *profiting*
after deductions, after taxes, clear, excluding, exclusive, final, irreducible, pure, remaining, take-home, undeductible; SEE CONCEPT 334

net [n] *mesh, web*
cloth, fabric, lace, lacework, lattice, netting, network, openwork, reticulum, screen, tracery; SEE CONCEPTS 473,770

net [v1] *capture*
bag*, catch, enmesh, ensnare, entangle, hook*, lasso*, nab*, trap; SEE CONCEPT 90

net [v2] *gain after expenses*
accumulate, bring in, clean up, clear, earn, make, profit, realize, reap; SEE CONCEPT 330

nettle [v] *provoke, upset*
annoy, chafe, disgust, disturb, exasperate, fret, get*, goad, harass, huff, incense, insult, irritate, miff, peeve*, pester, pet, pique, put out*, rile, roil, ruffle, snit*, stew*, sting*, tease, tiff*, vex; SEE CONCEPTS 7,14,19

nettlesome [adj] *irritating*
aggravating, annoying, bothersome, burdensome, distressing, disturbing, exasperating, irksome, nagging, troublesome, trying, vexatious, vexing; SEE CONCEPTS 529,537

network [n] *system of connections*
arrangement, artery, chain, checkerboard*, circuitry, complex, convolution, crisscross*, fabric, fiber, grid, grill*, grillwork, hookup, interconnections, jungle, labyrinth, maze, mesh, net, netting, nexus, organization, patchwork*, plexus, reticulation, reticule, screening, structure, system, tessellation, tracks, wattle, weave, web, wiring; SEE CONCEPTS 381,388,770

network [v] *to socialize for professional or personal gain*
associate, circulate, hobnob, make contacts, meet, meet and greet*, mingle, rub elbows*, schmooze*; SEE CONCEPT 384

neurosis [n] *mental disturbance, disorder*
aberration, abnormality, affliction, breakdown, compulsion, crack-up*, derangement, deviation, hysteria, inhibition, insanity, instability, madness, maladjustment, mental illness, neurasthenia, obsession, personality disorder, phobia, psychological disorder, psychopathy; SEE CONCEPTS 316,410

neurotic [adj] *mentally maladjusted*
aberrant, abnormal, anxious, basket case*, bundle of nerves*, choked*, clutched*, compulsive, deviant, disordered, disoriented, distraught, disturbed, erratic, hung up*, hysteric, inhibited, manic, nervous, nervous wreck*, obsessive, overwrought, psychoneurotic, unhealthy, unstable, upset, uptight, wired*; SEE CONCEPTS 314,403

neuter [v] *remove sex organs*
alter, castrate, change, desexualize, doctor, dress, fix, geld, make barren, make impotent, make infertile, make sexless, mutilate, spay, sterilize, unsex; SEE CONCEPTS 157,250

neutral [adj] *impartial, noncommittal*
aloof, bystanding, calm, clinical, collected, cool, detached, disengaged, disinterested, dispassionate, easy, evenhanded, fair-minded, impersonal, inactive, indifferent, inert, middle-of-road*, nonaligned, nonbelligerent, nonchalant, noncombatant, nonparticipating, nonpartisan, on sidelines*, on the fence*, pacifistic, poker-faced*, relaxed, unaligned, unbiased, uncommitted, unconcerned,

undecided, uninvolved, unprejudiced; SEE CONCEPTS *403,542*

neutral [*adj2*] *flat, dull to senses*
abstract, achromatic, colorless, drab, expressionless, indeterminate, indistinct, indistinguishable, intermediate, toneless, undefined, vague, vanilla; SEE CONCEPTS *485,537,618*

neutralize [*v*] *counteract*
abrogate, annul, balance, cancel, compensate for, conquer, counterbalance, countercheck, counterpoise, countervail, defeat, frustrate, invalidate, negate, negative, nullify, offset, overcome, override, overrule, redress, subdue, undo; SEE CONCEPTS *121,232*

never [*adv*] *not at any time*
at no time, don't hold your breath*, forget it, nevermore, not at all, not ever, not in any way, not in the least, not on your life*, not under any condition, no way*; SEE CONCEPT *799*

never-ending [*adj*] *continual, unceasing*
amaranthine, boundless, ceaseless, constant, continuous, endless, eternal, everlasting, immortal, incessant, interminable, nonstop, perpetual, persistent, relentless, timeless, unbroken, unchanging, uninterrupted, unremitting; SEE CONCEPTS *482,798*

nevertheless [*adv*] *however*
after all, although, but, even so, even though, howbeit, nonetheless, not the less, notwithstanding, regardless, still, still and all, though, withal, yet; SEE CONCEPT *544*

new [*adj1*] *recent, fresh*
advanced, au courant, brand-new, contemporary, current, cutting-edge*, dewy, different, dissimilar, distinct, fashionable, inexperienced, just out*, late, latest, modern, modernistic, modish*, neoteric, newfangled*, novel, now*, original, recent, spick-and-span*, state-of-the-art, strange, topical, ultramodern, unaccustomed, uncontaminated, unfamiliar, unique, unknown, unlike, unseasoned, unskilled, unspoiled, untouched, untrained, untried, untrodden, unused, unusual, up-to-date, virgin, youthful; SEE CONCEPTS *564,578,797*

new [*adj2*] *additional*
added, another, else, extra, farther, fresh, further, increased, more, other, supplementary; SEE CONCEPTS *771,824*

new [*adj3*] *modernized, restored*
altered, changed, improved, redesigned, refreshed, regenerated, renewed, revived; SEE CONCEPT *589*

new [*adv*] *recently*
afresh, anew, freshly, lately, newly, of late; SEE CONCEPT *820*

new age [*adj*] *of a broad-ranging consciousness-raising movement*
Age of Aquarius*, alternative, astrological, balanced, crystal healing, holistic, mystic, occult, planetary, spiritual, supernaturalist; SEE CONCEPTS *403,529*

newborn [*n*] *infant*
babe, baby, bairn, bambino, bantling, bundle, child, kid, little one, neonate, nursling, small child, suckling, tot; SEE CONCEPTS *414,424*

newcomer [*n*] *person who has just arrived in area*
alien, arrival, beginner, blow-in*, colt*, foreigner, greenhorn*, immigrant, incomer, Johnny-come-lately*, late arrival, latecomer, maverick,

neophyte, new kid on the block*, novice, novitiate, outsider, rookie, settler, stranger, tenderfoot*; SEE CONCEPTS *413,423*

newfangled [*adj*] *quite recent*
contemporary, fashionable, fresh, gimmicky*, in vogue, modern, modernistic, neoteric, new, new-fashioned, novel, popular, unique; SEE CONCEPTS *578,589,797*

newly [*adv*] *recently*
anew, freshly, just, lately, latterly, of late; SEE CONCEPT *820*

news [*n*] *information, revelation*
account, advice, announcement, broadcast, bulletin, cable, cognizance, communication, communiqué, copy, data, description, disclosure, discovery, dispatch, enlightenment, exposé, eye-opener*, front-page news*, headlines, hearsay, intelligence, itemization, knowledge, leak, low-down, message, narration, news flash, particularization, recital, recognition, release, report, rumor, scandal, scoop*, specification, statement, story, telecast, telegram, telling, the goods*, tidings*, word*; SEE CONCEPTS *268,274,293*

newscaster [*n*] *broadcaster*
anchor, anchor man/woman, anchor person, announcer, commentator, news anchor, news commentator, reporter; SEE CONCEPTS *60,292*

newsletter [*n*] *special interest publication*
bulletin, journal, magazine, pamphlet, report; SEE CONCEPTS *279,280*

newsman/newswoman [*n*] *reporter*
anchor, anchor man/woman, anchor person, announcer, columnist, copy editor, correspondent, cub*, editor, foreign correspondent, ink slinger*, interviewer, investigative reporter, journalist, legman/woman*, newscaster, newshound, newspaperman/woman, newswriter, pressman/woman, stringer, war correspondent, writer; SEE CONCEPTS *348,356*

newspaper [*n*] *regular, continuous publication containing information*
biweekly, bulldog*, community, daily, extra, gazette, journal, magazine, metropolitan, organ, paper, periodical, press, rag*, record, review, scandal sheet*, sheet, tabloid, trade, weekly; SEE CONCEPTS *279,280*

newsworthy [*adj*] *important*
consequential, critical, crucial, essential, far-reaching, front-page*, great, influential, material, meaningful, momentous, of note, of substance, paramount, relevant, serious, significant, urgent, vital; SEE CONCEPT *567*

next [*adj*] *coming immediately after in space, time, order*
abutting, adjacent, adjoining, after, alongside, attached, back-to-back, beside, close, closest, coming, consequent, co-terminous, ensuing, following, hard by*, later, meeting, nearest, neighboring, on the side, proximate, side-by-side, subsequent, succeeding, touching; SEE CONCEPTS *585,586,799*

next [*adv*] *immediately after in time, space, order*
after, afterward, afterwhile, behind, by and by, closely, coming up, following, later, latterly, next off, subsequently, thereafter; SEE CONCEPTS *585,586,799*

nibble [*n*] *morsel, bite*
crumb, peck, snack, soupçon, taste, tidbit; SEE CONCEPTS *458,831*

nibble [v] *bite, pick at*
crop, eat, eat like a bird*, gnaw, munch, nip*,
nosh on*, peck*, snack; SEE CONCEPT *169*

nice [*adj1*] *likable, agreeable*
admirable, amiable, approved, attractive, becoming, charming, commendable, considerate, copacetic, cordial, courteous, decorous, delightful,
ducky, fair, favorable, fine and dandy*, friendly,
genial, gentle, good, gracious, helpful, ingratiating, inviting, kind, kindly, lovely, nifty*, obliging, okay*, peachy*, pleasant, pleasurable,
polite, prepossessing, seemly, simpatico, superior, swell, unpresumptuous, welcome, well-
mannered, winning, winsome; SEE CONCEPTS
404,548,572

nice [*adj2*] *precise, neat, refined*
accurate, becoming, befitting, careful, choosy,
conforming, correct, critical, cultured, dainty,
decent, delicate, discerning, discriminating, distinguishing, exact, exacting, fastidious, fine, fine-
spun, finical, finicking, finicky*, fussy*, genteel,
hairsplitting*, meticulous, minute, particular,
persnickety*, picky*, proper, respectable, right,
rigorous, scrupulous, seemly, squeamish, strict,
subtle, tidy, trim, trivial*, virtuous, well-bred;
SEE CONCEPTS *542,557,558*

niche [*n*] *place all one's own*
alcove, byplace, calling, compartment, corner,
cranny*, cubbyhole*, hole, hollow, indentation,
nook, opening, pigeonhole*, position, recess,
slot, vocation; SEE CONCEPTS *440,513,630*

nick [*n/v*] *chip, scratch*
cut, damage, dent, dint, indent, jag, knock, mark,
mill, notch, scar, score, slit; SEE CONCEPTS
137,176,208

nickname [*n*] *informal title*
appellation, byname, byword, denomination,
diminutive, epithet, familiar name, handle*,
label, moniker, pet name*, sobriquet, style, tag*;
SEE CONCEPTS *268,683*

nifty [*adj*] *marvelous*
chic, clever, cool*, dandy, enjoyable, excellent,
groovy*, keen, neat, peachy*, pleasing, quick,
sharp, smart, spruce, stylish, super, swell, terrific; SEE CONCEPT *572*

night [*n*] *part of day after sundown and before
sunrise*
after dark, after hours*, bedtime, before dawn,
black*, blackness, dark, dark hours, darkness,
dead of night*, dim, duskiness, dusk to dawn,
evening, eventide, gloom, midnight, nightfall,
nighttide, nighttime, obscurity*, pitch dark, twilight, witching hour*; SEE CONCEPTS
620,801,806,810

nightclub [*n*] *place for evening entertainment*
bar, bistro, cabaret, café, casino, disco*, discotheque, dive*, hideaway*, honky-tonk*,
joint*, nightery, night spot, nitery, restaurant,
roadhouse, saloon, speakeasy*, spot, supper
club, tavern, theatre, watering hole*; SEE CON-
CEPTS *293,439,449*

nightfall [*n*] *beginning of darkness*
black*, crepuscule, dim, dusk, eve, eventide,
sundown, sunset, twilight, vespers; SEE CONCEPT
810

nightgown [*n*] *dress in which to sleep*
bedgown, lingerie, negligee, nightdress,
nightie*, nightrobe, nightshirt, pajamas, PJs*,
sleeper*; SEE CONCEPT *451*

nightly [*adj/adv*] *each evening; after dark*
at night, by night, every night, in the night, night
after night, nights, nighttime, nocturnal, noctur-
nally; SEE CONCEPTS *541,799,801*

nightmare [*n*] *bad dream or experience*
dream, fancy, fantasy, hallucination, horror, illusion, incubus, ordeal, phantasm, succubus, torment, trial, tribulation, vision; SEE CONCEPTS
315,674

nightmarish [*adj*] *frightening*
alarming, awful, chilling, creepy, dire, direful,
disquieting, dreadful, eerie, fearful, fearsome,
ghastly, ghoulish, grim, grisly, hair-raising, hellish, horrible, horrid, horrifying, macabre, morbid, ominous, petrifying, scary, spooky, terrible,
terrifying, traumatic, unnerving; SEE CONCEPTS
529,537

night stick [*n*] *billy club*
billy*, blackjack, cudgel, police officer's club,
shillelagh; SEE CONCEPTS *470,499*

nihilism [*n*] *refusal to believe*
abnegation, agnosticism, anarchy, atheism, denial, disbelief, disorder, lawlessness, mob rule*,
nonbelief, rejection, renunciation, repudiation,
skepticism, terrorism; SEE CONCEPT *689*

nil [*adj*] *nonexistent*
naught, nihil, nix*, none, nothing, nought, zero;
SEE CONCEPTS *539,762,771*

nimble [*adj*] *dexterous, smart*
active, adept, adroit, agile, alert, bright, brisk,
clever, deft, handy, light, lissome, lithe, lively,
proficient, prompt, quick, quick-witted, ready,
skillful, sprightly, spry, swift, vigilant, wide-
awake; SEE CONCEPTS *402,527,584*

nip [*n*] *swallow, taste*
bite, catch, dram, drop, finger, jolt, morsel,
mouthful, nibble, pinch, portion, shot*, sip,
slug*, snifter, soupçon, toothful; SEE CONCEPTS
458,831

nip [*v1*] *bite; take small part*
catch, clip, compress, grip, munch, nab at*, nibble, pinch, sink teeth into*, snag, snap*, snip*,
squeeze*, take a chunk out of*, tweak, twinge,
twitch; SEE CONCEPTS *142,169,190*

nip [*v2*] *stop, thwart*
arrest, balk, blight, check, dash, end, frustrate;
SEE CONCEPTS *121,234*

nirvana [*n*] *enlightenment*
awakening, bliss, cloud nine*, ecstasy, happiness, heaven, joy, paradise, peace, serenity, tranquillity; SEE CONCEPT *409*

nitty-gritty [*n*] *heart of the matter*
basics, bottom line*, chief part, chief thing, core,
essential part, focus, fundamentals, gist, important matter, nuts and bolts*, root, the facts*; SEE
CONCEPTS *442,668,826*

nitwit [*n*] *idiot*
blockhead, bonehead*, cretin, dimwit, dork,
dumbbell, dummy, dunce, fool, halfwit, ignoramus, imbecile, jerk, moron, nincompoop,
ninny*, numbskull, pinhead*, simpleton, stupid
person; SEE CONCEPT *412*

nobility [*n*] *aristocracy; eminence*
dignity, elevation, elite, ennoblement, exaltation,
excellence, generosity, gentry, glorification,
grandeur, greatness, high society, honor, illustriousness, incorruptibility, integrity, loftiness,
magnanimity, magnificence, majesty, nobleness,
patricians, peerage, royalty, ruling class, society,
stateliness, sublimity, superiority, upper class,

uprightness, virtue, worthiness; SEE CONCEPTS *378,388,668*

noble [*adj1*] *aristocratic*
gentle, highborn, imperial, kingly, nobiliary, patrician, queenly, titled, wellborn; SEE CONCEPTS *549,555*

noble [*adj2*] *dignified, excellent*
august, beneficent, benevolent, benign, big, bounteous, brilliant, charitable, courtly, cultivated, dignified, distinguished, elevated, eminent, extraordinary, first-rate, generous, gracious, grand, great, great-hearted, high-minded, honorable, humane, imposing, impressive, liberal, lofty, magnanimous, magnificent, meritorious, preeminent, refined, remarkable, reputable, splendid, stately, sublime, supreme, sympathetic, tolerant, upright, virtuous, worthy; SEE CONCEPTS *401,404,572*

noble [*n*] *member of royal or important family*
archduchess, archduke, aristocrat, blue blood*, count, countess, duchess, duke, emperor, empress, gentleman, gentlewoman, lady, lord, patrician, peer, prince, princess, royalty, silk stocking*; SEE CONCEPTS *422,423*

nobody/nonentity [*n*] *person of little importance*
cipher, insignificancy, lightweight*, menial, nix*, nothing, parvenu*, small potato*, squirt*, upstart, wimp*, zero*, zip; SEE CONCEPT *423*

nocturnal [*adj*] *happening at night*
after dark, late, night, night-loving, nightly, nighttime; SEE CONCEPTS *799,801*

nod [*n*] *gesture of the head*
acceptance, acknowledgment, affirmative, beckon, bow, dip, greeting, inclination, indication, permission, salute, sign, signal, yes; SEE CONCEPTS *74,185,685*

nod [*v1*] *gesture with head*
acknowledge, acquiesce, agree, approve, assent, beckon, bend, bow, concur, consent, curtsy, dip, duck, greet, indicate, recognize, respond, salute, say yes, sign, signal; SEE CONCEPTS *10,50,74,88,185*

nod [*v2*] *fall asleep*
become inattentive, be sleepy, doze, drift, drift off, droop, drowse, nap, sleep, slump; SEE CONCEPTS *210,315,681*

node/nodule [*n*] *knot, growth*
bud, bulge, bump, burl, clot, knob, lump, protuberance, swelling, tumor; SEE CONCEPTS *471,831*

noise [*n*] *sound that is loud or not harmonious*
babble, babel, bang, bedlam, bellow, bewailing, blare, blast, boisterousness, boom, buzz, cacophony, caterwauling, clamor, clang, clatter, commotion, crash, cry, detonation, din, discord, disquiet, disquietude, drumming, eruption, explosion, fanfare, fireworks, fracas*, fuss*, hoohah*, hubbub*, hullabaloo*, jangle, lamentation, outcry, pandemonium, peal, racket, ring, roar, row, shot, shouting, sonance, squawk, stridency, talk, thud, tumult, turbulence, uproar, uproariousness, yelling, yelp; SEE CONCEPTS *521,595*

noiseless [*adj*] *quiet*
hushed, hushful, inaudible, mute, muted, silent, soundless, speechless, still, voiceless, wordless; SEE CONCEPT *594*

noiseproof [*adj*] *soundproof*
insulated, nonresonant, silent; SEE CONCEPT *594*

noisome [*adj*] *immoral, bad, offensive*
baneful, dangerous, deadly, deleterious, disgusting, fetid, foul, harmful, horrid, hurtful, injurious, insalubrious, insalutary, loathsome, malodorous, mephitic, mischievous, nauseating, noxious, pernicious, pestiferous, pestilential, poisonous, putrid, rank, reeking, repulsive, sickening, sickly, smelly, stinking, unhealthful, unhealthy, unwholesome, vile, yucky*; SEE CONCEPTS *537,571,598*

noisy [*adj*] *very loud and unharmonious in sound*
blatant, blusterous, boisterous, booming, cacophonous, chattering, clamorous, clangorous, clattery, deafening, disorderly, ear-popping*, ear-splitting*, jumping, loudmouth, obstreperous, piercing, rackety, raising Cain*, raising the roof*, rambunctious, raspy, riotous, rowdy, screaming, strepitous, strident, tumultous/tumultuous, turbulent, turned up, uproarious, vociferous; SEE CONCEPTS *592,594*

nomad [*n*] *person who wanders from place to place*
hobo, itinerant, migrant, pilgrim, rambler, roamer, rover, vagabond, wanderer, wayfarer; SEE CONCEPT *413*

nomadic [*adj*] *itinerant*
drifting, gypsy, itinerate, migrant, migratory, pastoral, perambulant, perambulatory, peripatetic, roaming, roving, traveling, vagabond, vagrant, wandering, wayfaring; SEE CONCEPTS *401,536,584*

nom de plume [*n*] *pen name*
AKA*, alias, anonym, assumed name, nickname, nom de guerre, professional name, pseudonym; SEE CONCEPTS *268,683*

nomenclature [*n*] *vocabulary*
classification, codification, glossary, locution, phraseology, taxonomy, terminology; SEE CONCEPTS *275,276,683*

nominal [*adj1*] *supposed, theoretical*
alleged, apparent, as advertised, formal, given, honorary, in effect only, in name only, mentioned, named, ostensible, pretended, professed, puppet, purported, seeming, self-styled, simple, so-called, stated, suggested, titular; SEE CONCEPT *582*

nominal [*adj2*] *insignificant*
cheap, inconsiderable, inexpensive, low, low-priced, meaningless, minimal, small, symbolic, token, trifling, trivial, unnecessary; SEE CONCEPTS *334,575,789*

nominate [*v*] *designate, select*
appoint, assign, call, choose, cognominate, commission, decide, denominate, draft, elect, elevate, empower, intend, make, mean, name, offer, present, proffer, propose, purpose, put down for, put up, recommend, slate, slot, specify, submit, suggest, tab, tap, tender, term; SEE CONCEPTS *41,50,75,88,300*

nomination [*n*] *appointment for responsibility*
choice, designation, election, naming, proposal, recommendation, selection, suggestion; SEE CONCEPTS *41,50,75,88,300*

nominee [*n*] *candidate*
applicant, appointee, aspirant, contender, contestant, entrant, hopeful*, office-seeker, runner, seeker; SEE CONCEPT *359*

nonagression [*n*] *pacifism*
nonviolence, passivity, peaceableness; SEE CONCEPTS *7,22,250*

nonchalant [*adj*] *easygoing, laid back*
airy, aloof, apathetic, blasé, calm, careless, casual, cold, collected, composed, cool, detached,

ni
no

disimpassioned, disinterested, dispassionate, easy, effortless, happy, impassive, imperturbable, incurious, indifferent, insouciant, lackadaisical, light, listless, loose, lukewarm, mellow, neglectful, negligent, neutral, offhand, placid, serene, smooth, trifling, uncaring, unconcerned, unemotional, unexcited, unfeeling, unflappable, unimpressible, unperturbed, unruffled, untroubled; SEE CONCEPTS 401,404,542

noncommittal [adj] *unwilling to decide*
ambiguous, buttoned up*, careful, cautious, circumspect, clammed up*, constrained, discreet, equivocal, evasive, even-steven*, guarded, hushhush*, incommunicable, indefinite, judicious, middle-ground*, middle-of-the-road*, neutral, on-the-fence*, politic, reserved, restrained, tactful, temporizing, tentative, unrevealing, vague, wary, zipped*; SEE CONCEPTS 267,403,542

noncompliant [adj] *unwilling to go along with something*
belligerent, contumacious, declinatory, declining, divergent, impatient, irregular, negative, objecting, rebellious, recalcitrant, refractory, refusing, restive, truculent; SEE CONCEPTS 401,542

nonconforming [adj] *nonobservant*
independent, individualistic, marching to the beat of a different drummer*, nonadhering, noncompliant, one's own sweet way*, radical, unorthodox; SEE CONCEPT 554

nonconformist [adj] *unwilling to behave, believe as most do*
beatnik*, bohemian*, dissident, freak*, heretical, heterodox, hippie*, iconoclastic, maverick, oddball, offbeat, original, rebel, schismatic*, sectarian, swinger, unorthodox, weird*; SEE CONCEPTS 401,542

nonconformist [n] *person who goes against normal behavior, beliefs*
beatnik*, bohemian*, demonstrator, different breed*, dissenter, dissentient, dissident, dropout, eccentric, fish out of water*, freak*, heretic, iconoclast, individualist, liberal, malcontent, maverick, misbeliever, night person, oddball, offbeat, original, protester, radical, rebel, sectary, separatist, swinger, weirdo*; SEE CONCEPTS 359,423

nonconformity [n] *belief, behavior different from most*
bohemianism, breach, contumaciousness, denial, disaffection, disagreement, disapprobation, disapproval, discordance, disobedience, dissent, eccentricity, exception, heresy, heterodoxy, iconoclasm, insubordination, lawlessness, mutinousness, negation, nonacceptance, nonagreement, noncompliance, nonconsent, objection, opposition, originality, recalcitrance, recusance, recusancy, rejection, strangeness, transgressiveness, unconventionality, uniqueness, unorthodoxy, unruliness, veto, violation; SEE CONCEPTS 633,657,689

nondescript [adj] *undistinguished, commonplace*
characterless, colorless, common, dull, empty, featureless, garden*, indescribable, indeterminate, mousy*, ordinary, unclassifiable, unclassified, unexceptional, uninspiring, uninteresting, unmemorable, unremarkable, vague; SEE CONCEPTS 529,537,547

none [prep] *not one thing*
nil, nobody, no one, no one at all, no part, not a bit, not any, not anyone, not anything, not a soul, not a thing, nothing, not one, zero, zilch*; SEE CONCEPT 407

nonessential [adj] *not needed or important*
deadwood*, dispensable, excess baggage*, excessive, expendable, extraneous, inessential, insignificant, peripheral, petty, superfluous, trivial, unimportant, unnecessary; SEE CONCEPTS 546,575

nonexistent [adj] *fictional, not real*
absent, airy, baseless, blank, chimerical, dead, defunct, departed, dreamlike, dreamy, empty, ethereal, extinct, extinguished, fancied, flimsy, gone, gossamery, groundless, hallucinatory, hypothetical, illusory, imaginary, imagined, immaterial, imponderable, insubstantial, legendary, lost, missing, mythical, negative, null, null and void*, passed away, passed on, perished, shadowy, tenuous, ungrounded, unreal, unsubstantial, vacant, vague, vaporous, void, without foundation; SEE CONCEPTS 539,582

nonpartisan [adj] *impartial; not political*
detached, equitable, fair, free-wheeling*, independent, indifferent, just, middle-of-the-road*, neutral, nonaligned, nondiscriminatory, objective, on one's own*, on-the-fence*, playing it cool*, unaffected, unaffiliated, unbiased, unbigoted, uncolored, unimplicated, uninfluenced, uninvolved, unprejudiced; SEE CONCEPT 542

nonplus [v] *confuse, perplex*
astonish, astound, baffle, balk, beat, bewilder, boggle, buffalo*, confound, daze, discomfit, disconcert, discountenance, dismay, dumbfound, embarrass, faze, floor*, flurry, fluster, frustrate, get*, mess with one's head*, muddle, mystify, overcome, paralyze, puzzle, rattle, rattle one's cage*, stagger, stick, stump, stun, stymie*, take aback, throw*, throw into tizzy*, thwart; SEE CONCEPTS 14,16

nonsense [n] *craziness, ridiculousness*
absurdity, babble, balderdash*, baloney*, bananas*, bombast, bull*, bunk*, claptrap*, drivel, fatuity, flightiness, folly, foolishness, fun, gibberish, giddiness, hogwash*, hooey*, hot air*, imprudence, inanity, irrationality, jazz, jest, jive*, joke, ludicrousness, madness, mumbo jumbo*, palaver, poppycock*, prattle, pretense, ranting, rashness, rot, rubbish, scrawl, scribble, senselessness, silliness, soft soap*, stupidity, thoughtlessness, trash*, tripe*; SEE CONCEPTS 230,388,633

nonstop [adj] *continuous, direct*
ceaseless, constant, endless, incessant, interminable, relentless, round-the-clock*, steady, unbroken, unending, unfaltering, uninterrupted, unremitting; SEE CONCEPTS 482,584,798

nonviolence [n] *abstention from violence*
nonaggression, pacification, pacifism, passiveness, passivity, peaceableness; SEE CONCEPTS 388,691

nonviolent [adj] *peaceful*
irenic, nonbelligerent, pacifist, passive, peaceable, quiet, resistant, without violence; SEE CONCEPT 401

nook [n] *corner, cubbyhole*
alcove, byplace, cavity, compartment, cranny, crevice, den, hideout, hole, inglenook, niche, opening, quoin, recess, retreat; SEE CONCEPTS 440,513

noon [n] *the middle of a day*
apex, high noon, meridian, midday, noonday, noontide, noontime, twelve noon, twelve o'clock; SEE CONCEPTS *801,802,806*

norm [n] *average, standard*
barometer, benchmark*, criterion, gauge, mean, measure, median, medium, model, par, pattern, rule, scale, touchstone*, type, yardstick; SEE CONCEPTS *647,686,688*

normal [adj1] *common, usual*
accustomed, acknowledged, average, commonplace, conventional, customary, general, habitual, mean, median, methodical, natural, orderly, ordinary, popular, prevalent, regular, routine, run-of-the-mill*, standard, traditional, typic, typical, unexceptional; SEE CONCEPT *547*

normal [adj2] *sane, rational*
all there*, compos mentis*, cool*, healthy, in good health, in one's right mind*, lucid, reasonable, right, right-minded, sound, together, well-adjusted, whole, wholesome; SEE CONCEPTS *314,403*

normally [adv] *usually*
as a rule, commonly, habitually, in accordance with, ordinarily, regularly, typically; SEE CONCEPT *547*

north [adj/adv] *toward the top pole of the earth*
arctic, boreal, cold, frozen, hyperborean, northbound, northerly, northern, northmost, northward, polar, septentrional, toward North Pole, tundra; SEE CONCEPTS *581,583*

nose [n] *smelling organ of animate being*
adenoids, beak*, bill*, horn*, muzzle*, nares, nostrils, olfactory nerves, proboscis, schnoz*, smeller*, sneezer*, sniffer*, snoot*, snout*, snuffer*, whiffer*; SEE CONCEPTS *392,601*

nose [v] *detect, search*
busybody*, examine, inspect, meddle, mouse*, pry, scent, smell, sniff, snoop*; SEE CONCEPTS *103,216*

nosh [n] *snack*
bite, bite to eat*, break, goodies*, grub, light meal, midnight snack, pickings, refreshment, tidbit, tiny meal; SEE CONCEPTS *457,459*

nosh [v] *snack*
eat between meals, munch, nibble, pick at, taste; SEE CONCEPT *169*

nostalgia [n] *pleasant remembrances*
fond memories*, hearts and flowers*, homesickness, longing, pining, reminiscence, remorse, schmaltz*, sentimentality, tear-jerker*, wistfulness, yearning; SEE CONCEPTS *20,410*

nostalgic [adj] *longingly remembering*
cornball*, down memory lane*, drippy*, homesick, like yesterday*, lonesome, longing, mushy*, regretful, sappy*, sentimental, sloppy, syrupy*, wistful, yearning; SEE CONCEPTS *403,529*

nostrum [n] *cure-all, often ineffective*
catholicon, cure, drug, elixir, fix, formula, home remedy, medicine, panacea, patent medicine, potion, quack medicine*, quick fix*, remedy, treatment; SEE CONCEPTS *307,311*

nosy [adj] *curious; prying*
eavesdropping, inquisitive, inquisitorial, inquisitory, interested, interfering, intermeddling, intrusive, meddlesome, personal, searching, snooping, snoopy; SEE CONCEPT *401*

notable [adj] *important; famous*
big-league*, bodacious*, celebrated, celebrious, conspicuous, distingué, distinguished, eminent, eventful, evident, extraordinary, famed, great, heavy*, high-profile*, illustrious, major-league*, manifest, marked, memorable, momentous, nameable, noteworthy, noticeable, notorious, observable, outstanding, preeminent, prominent, pronounced, rare, red-letter*, remarkable, renowned, rubric, serious, something else*, striking, top-drawer*, uncommon, unusual, well-known; SEE CONCEPT *568*

notable [n] *person who is famous, important*
big name*, big shot*, big-time operator*, big wheel*, celebrity, chief, dignitary, eminence, executive, figure*, heavyweight*, high-up, hot-dog*, leader, lion*, luminary, magnate, mogul, name, notability, personage, personality, poohbah*, power, somebody*, star, superstar, VIP*, worthy; SEE CONCEPTS *347,352,423*

notably [adv] *especially*
conspicuously, distinctly, exceedingly, exceptionally, extremely, greatly, highly, hugely, markedly, noticeably, outstandingly, particularly, prominently, remarkably, reputably, signally, strikingly, uncommonly, very; SEE CONCEPT *569*

notarize [v] *certify*
attest, authenticate, document, endorse, register, sign and seal, swear, validate, verify, witness; SEE CONCEPTS *50,88*

notary [n] *notary public*
certifier, commissioner for oaths, court clerk, endorser, public official, recorder, registrar, scrivener, signatory, witness; SEE CONCEPTS *355,423*

notation [n] *written remarks*
characters, chit, code, documentation, figures, jotting, memo, memorandum, note, noting, record, representation, script, signs, symbols, system; SEE CONCEPTS *268,284*

not born yesterday [adj] *experienced*
battle-scarred, been around, canny, cunning, on the ball*, savvy, seasoned, trained, unbelieving, wise, worldly; SEE CONCEPTS *402,527*

notch [n1] *indentation*
cleft, cut, gap, gash, groove, incision, indent, indenture, mark, mill, nick, nock, rabbet, rut, score, scratch; SEE CONCEPT *513*

notch [n2] *level within classification*
cut, degree, grade, rung, stage, step; SEE CONCEPTS *388,744*

notch [v] *indent*
chisel, cleave, crenelate, crimp, cut, dent, gash, incise, jag, mark, mill, nick, scallop, score, scratch; SEE CONCEPTS *137,176,208*

note [n2] *symbol, often used in reference to music*
character, degree, figure, flat, indication, interval, key, lick*, mark, natural, pitch, representation, scale, sharp, sign, step, token, tone; SEE CONCEPTS *262,284*

note [n3] *attention, heed*
cognizance, mark, mind, notice, observance, observation, regard, remark; SEE CONCEPT *529*

note [v] *observe, perceive*
catch, clock, denote, descry, designate, dig, discern, discover, distinguish, document, enter, get a load of*, get an eyeful*, heed, indicate, jot down, mark, mention, notice, pick up on*, put down, record, register, remark, see, set down,

no
no

spot, take in*, transcribe, view, write, write down; SEE CONCEPTS *34,626*

notebook [*n*] *writing tablet*
binder, blotter, daybook, diary, exercise book, journal, log, loose-leaf notebook, memo book, pad, scratch pad, spiral notebook, workbook; SEE CONCEPT *271*

noted [*adj*] *famous, eminent*
acclaimed, celeb, celebrated, conspicuous, distinguished, esteemed, illustrious, leading, name, notable, notorious, of note, popular, prominent, recognized, redoubted, renowned, somebody, star, well-known; SEE CONCEPT *568*

note/notes [*n1*] *written communication*
agenda, annotation, calendar, comment, commentary, datum, definition, diary, dispatch, entry, epistle, gloss, inscription, jotting, journal, letter, line, marginalia, mark, memo, memorandum, message, minute, missive, obiter dictum, observation, record, remark, reminder, scratch, scrawl, scribble, summary, thank-you, word; SEE CONCEPT *271*

notes [*n*] *outline*
annotation, draft, impressions, jottings, marginalia, record, report, rough draft, summary, synopsis; SEE CONCEPT *268*

noteworthy [*adj*] *important*
boss*, conspicuous, cool*, evident, exceptional, extraordinary, heavy*, high-profile*, hot*, major-league*, manifest, meaningful, memorable, mind-blowing*, murder, nameable, notable, noticeable, observable, outstanding, patent, prominent, red-letter*, remarkable, serious, significant, something else*, splash*, stand-out*, super, terrific, the end*, underlined*, unique, unusual, utmost; SEE CONCEPTS *567,568*

nothingness [*n2*] *insignificance*
pettiness, smallness, unimportance, worthlessness; SEE CONCEPT *668*

nothing/nothingness [*n*] *emptiness, nonexistence*
annihilation, aught, blank, cipher, extinction, fly speck*, insignificancy, naught, nihility, nobody, nonbeing, nonentity, not anything, nought, nullity, obliteration, oblivion, shutout*, trifle, void, wind*, zero*, zilch*, zip; SEE CONCEPTS *407,707*

nothing to it [*adj*] *effortless*
a breeze*, child's play*, duck soup*, easy, easy as ABC*, easy as pie*, no problem*, no sweat*, painless, piece of cake*, simple, snap*, uncomplicated; SEE CONCEPT *565*

notice [*n1*] *observation*
apprehension, attention, care, cognizance, concern, consideration, ear, grasp, heed, mark, mind, note, observance, regard, remark, respect, thought, understanding; SEE CONCEPTS *34,532*

notice [*n2*] *announcement, information*
admonition, advertisement, advice, caution, caveat, circular, clue, comment, comments, communication, criticism, critique, cue, declaration, directive, enlightenment, goods*, handbill, info*, instruction, intelligence, intimation, know*, lowdown*, manifesto, memo, memorandum, news, note, notification, order, picture, poster, proclamation, remark, review, score, sign, squib*, story, tip, warning, whole story*, write-up; SEE CONCEPTS *271,274,278*

notice [*v*] *observe, perceive*
acknowledge, advert, allude, catch, clock, descry, detect, dig*, discern, distinguish, espy, flash on*, get a load of*, heed, look at, make

out*, mark, mind, note, pick up on, recognize, refer, regard, remark, see, spot, take in; SEE CONCEPTS *34,626*

noticeable [*adj*] *conspicuous, evident*
apparent, appreciable, arresting, arrestive, big as life*, can't miss it*, clear, distinct, eye-catching, manifest, marked, notable, noteworthy, observable, obvious, open and shut*, outstanding, palpable, patent, perceptible, plain, pointed, prominent, remarkable, salient, sensational, signal, spectacular, striking, under one's nose*, unmistakable; SEE CONCEPTS *529,537,567*

notification [*n*] *announcement*
advertisement, advisory, alert, bulletin, communication, communique, declaration, information, message, news, notice, proclamation, release, report, statement, warning; SEE CONCEPTS *49,274*

notify [*v*] *inform*
acquaint, advise, air, alert, announce, apprise, assert, blazon, brief, broadcast, cable, caution, circulate, clue in, convey, cue, debrief, declare, disclose, disseminate, divulge, enlighten, express, fill in, give, herald, hint, let in on, let know, make known, mention, pass out, post, proclaim, promulgate, publish, radio, report, reveal, send word, speak, spread, state, suggest, talk, teach, telephone, tell, tip off, vent, warn, wire, wise up*, write; SEE CONCEPTS *60,79*

notion [*n1*] *belief, idea*
angle, apprehension, approach, assumption, awareness, clue, comprehension, conceit, concept, conception, consciousness, consideration, cue, discernment, flash, hint, image, imagination, impression, inclination, indication, inkling, insight, intellection, intimation, intuition, judgment, knowledge, opinion, penetration, perception, sentiment, slant, spark, suggestion, telltale, thought, twist, understanding, view, wind, wrinkle; SEE CONCEPTS *529,532,689*

notion [*n2*] *whim, desire*
caprice, conceit, fancy, humor, imagination, impulse, inclination, wish; SEE CONCEPT *20*

notoriety [*n*] *reputation*
ballyhoo*, celebrity, center stage*, dishonor, disrepute, éclat*, fame, flak*, infamy, ink*, name*, obloquy, opprobrium, renown, rep*, scandal, splash*, spotlight*, wise*; SEE CONCEPTS *388,411*

notorious [*adj*] *known for a trait, often an unadmirable one*
belled, blatant, crying, dishonorable, disreputable, flagrant, glaring, ill-famed, infamous, leading, noted, obvious, open, opprobrious, overt, patent, popular, prominent, questionable, scandalous, shady, shameful, undisputed, wanted, well-known, wicked; SEE CONCEPT *404*

notwithstanding [*adv/prep*] *although, however*
after all, against, at any rate, but, despite, for all that, howbeit, in any case, in any event, in spite of, nevertheless, nonetheless, on the other hand, regardless of, though, to the contrary, withal, yet; SEE CONCEPT *544*

nourish [*v*] *feed, care for*
attend, cherish, comfort, cultivate, encourage, foster, furnish, maintain, nurse, nurture, promote, provide, supply, support, sustain, tend; SEE CONCEPTS *140,295*

nourishing [*adj*] *healthful*
alimentative, beneficial, health-giving, healthy,

nutrient, nutrimental, nutritious, nutritive, wholesome; SEE CONCEPTS *462,537*

nourishment [*n*] *food*
aliment, diet, feed, foodstuff, home cooking*,
maintenance, nutriment, nutrition, pabulum,
pap*, provender, support, sustenance, viands,
victuals, vittles*; SEE CONCEPT *457*

nouveau riche [*n*] *new rich*
DINK*, parvenu, social climber, upstart, vulgarian, yuppie*; SEE CONCEPT *423*

novel [*adj*] *new, original*
at cutting edge*, atypical, avant-garde, breaking
new ground*, contemporary, different, far cry*,
fresh, funky*, innovative, just out*, modernistic,
neoteric, newfangled, new-fashioned, now*, odd,
offbeat, peculiar, rare, recent, singular, strange,
uncommon, unfamiliar, unique, unusual; SEE
CONCEPTS *564,578,797*

novel [*n*] *fictional book*
best-seller, cliff-hanger, fiction, narrative, novel-
ette, novella, paperback, potboiler*, prose, romance, story, tale, yarn*; SEE CONCEPT *280*

novelty [*n1*] *newness, originality*
change, crazy*, creation, dernier cri*, freshness,
innovation, last word*, modernity, mutation,
newfangled contraption, oddball, oddity, original, origination, permutation, recentness, sport*,
strangeness, surprise, unfamiliarity, uniqueness,
vicissitude, weird*; SEE CONCEPTS *665,697,715*

novelty [*n2*] *trinket, gadget*
bagatelle*, bauble, bibelot*, conversation piece,
curio, curiosity, gewgaw*, gimcrack*, gimmick,
item, knick-knack, memento, objet d'art*, oddity, souvenir, trifle, whatnot*; SEE CONCEPTS
260,446

novice [*n*] *person just learning something*
amateur, apprentice, beginner, colt*, convert*,
cub*, first of May*, fledgling, greenhorn, gremlin, know from nothing*, learner, mark*, neophyte, newcomer, new kid on the block*,
novitiate, plebe, postulant, prentice, probationer,
proselyte, punk*, pupil, recruit, rookie, starter,
student, tenderfoot*, trainee; SEE CONCEPTS
348,350,423

now [*adv*] *presently*
any more, at once, at the moment, at this moment, at this time, away, directly, first off, forthwith, here and now, immediately, in a minute, in
a moment, in nothing flat, instanter, instantly,
just now, like now*, momentarily, nowadays, on
the double*, PDQ*, promptly, pronto*, right
away, right now, soon, straightaway, these days,
this day, today; SEE CONCEPTS *812,820*

now and then [*adv*] *once in a while*
at intervals, at times, every now and then, every
once in a while, every so often, from time to
time, hardly, infrequently, intermittently, irregularly, now and again, occasionally, off and on,
once in a blue moon*, on occasion, periodically,
sometimes, sporadically; SEE CONCEPTS *530,541*

noxious [*adj*] *deadly, injurious*
baneful, corrupting, dangerous, deleterious, destructive, detrimental, fetid, foul, harmful, hurtful, insalubrious, insalutary, noisome,
pernicious, pestiferous, pestilent, pestilential,
poisonous, putrid, sickly, spoiled, stinking, toxic,
unhealthful, unhealthy, unwholesome, venomous, virulent; SEE CONCEPTS *485,537*

nozzle [*n*] *spout*
cock, faucet, spigot, tap; SEE CONCEPTS
445,464,499

nuance [*n*] *slight difference; shading*
dash, degree, distinction, gradation, hint, implication, nicety, refinement, shade, shadow,
soupçon, subtlety, suggestion, suspicion, tinge,
touch, trace; SEE CONCEPT *665*

nub [*n1*] *core, gist*
basic, bottom line*, crux, essence, heart*, kernel,
meat*, meat and potatoes*, nitty-gritty*, nubbin,
nucleus, pith, point, short, substance, upshot; SEE
CONCEPTS *661,682,826*

nub [*n2*] *bump, knot*
bulge, knob, lump, node, protuberance, swelling;
SEE CONCEPT *471*

nuclear energy [*n*] *nuclear power*
atomic energy, atomic power, nuclear fission
power, nuclear fusion power, thermonuclear
power; SEE CONCEPT *520*

nuclear reactor [*n*] *atomic reactor*
atomic pile, atomic power plant, breeder reactor,
core reactor, nuclear power plant, thermonuclear
reactor; SEE CONCEPT *520*

nuclear weapon [*n*] *explosive driven by nuclear
energy*
A-bomb, atomic bomb, atomic weapon, doomsday machine*, H-bomb, hydrogen bomb, min-
inuke*, mirv*, MX*, neutron bomb, nuke*; SEE
CONCEPT *500*

nucleus [*n*] *core; basis for something's beginning*
bud, center, crux, embryo, focus, foundation,
germ, heart, hub, kernel, matter, nub, pivot,
premise, principle, seed, spark; SEE CONCEPTS
393,826,828

nude [*adj*] *without clothes, covering*
au naturel*, bald, bare, bare-skinned, buck
naked*, dishabille*, disrobed, exposed, garment-
less, in birthday suit, in one's skin*, in the altogether*, naked, peeled*, raw, skin, stark,
stark-naked*, stripped, unattired, unclad, unclothed, uncovered, undraped, undressed, wearing only a smile*, without a stitch*; SEE
CONCEPT *485*

nudge [*n/v*] *bump, elbow*
dig, jab, jog, poke, prod, punch, push, shove, tap,
touch; SEE CONCEPTS *208,612*

nudity [*n*] *nakedness*
bareness, birthday suit*, natural state, naturism,
nudism, the buff*, the nude, the raw*, undress;
SEE CONCEPT *453*

nugget [*n*] *lump, solid piece; often of metal ore*
asset, bullion, chunk, clod, clump, gold, hunk,
ingot, mass, plum, rock, treasure, wad*; SEE
CONCEPT *471*

nuisance [*n*] *annoyance; annoying person*
besetment, blister, bore, bother, botheration,
botherment, bum*, creep, drag*, drip*, exasperation, frump, gadfly, headache*, inconvenience,
infliction, insect*, irritant, irritation, louse, nag*,
nudge*, offense, pain, pain in the neck*, pest,
pester, pesterer, pill*, plague, poor excuse*,
problem, terror, trouble, vexation; SEE CONCEPTS
412,674

nuke [*n*] *nuclear weapon*
A-bomb, atomic bomb, atomic weapon, doomsday machine*, H-bomb, hydrogen bomb, neutron bomb; SEE CONCEPT *500*

no
nu

nuke [*v1*] *attack with nuclear weapons*
annihilate, bomb, destroy, eliminate, incinerate, kill, obliterate, wipe out; SEE CONCEPTS *86,252*
nuke [*v2*] *cook*
bake, brown, heat, microwave, warm up, zap; SEE CONCEPT *170*
null [*adj*] *ineffectual, valueless*
absent, bad, barren, characterless, imaginary, ineffective, inefficacious, inoperative, invalid, negative, nonexistent, nothing, null and void*, powerless, unavailing, unreal, unsanctioned, useless, vain, void, worthless; SEE CONCEPTS *560,570*
nullify [*v*] *cancel, revoke*
abate, abolish, abrogate, annihilate, annul, ax, blue pencil*, bring to naught*, call all bets off*, compensate, confine, counteract, counterbalance, countervail, disannul, forget it*, invalidate, kill*, limit, negate, neutralize, nig*, offset, quash*, render null and void*, renege, renig*, repeal, rescind, restrict, scratch*, scrub*, squash*, stamp out*, take out*, torpedo*, trash*, undo, veto, vitiate, void, wash out*, wipe out*, zap*; SEE CONCEPTS *50,88,121,234*
numb [*adj*] *deadened, insensitive*
aloof, anesthetized, apathetic, asleep, benumbed, callous, casual, comatose, dazed, dead, detached, disinterested, frozen, immobilized, incurious, indifferent, insensate, insensible, insentient, lethargic, listless, numbed, paralyzed, phlegmatic, remote, senseless, stupefied, stuporous, torpid, unconcerned, unconscious, uncurious, unfeeling, uninterested; SEE CONCEPTS *403,609*
numb [*v*] *deaden*
anesthetize, benumb, blunt, chill, desensitize, dull, freeze, frost, immobilize, obtund, paralyze, stun, stupefy; SEE CONCEPTS *250,255*
number [*n1*] *unit of the mathematical system*
cardinal, character, chiffer, cipher, count, decimal, denominator, digit, emblem, figure, folio, fraction, googol, integer, numeral, numerator, ordinal, prime, representation, sign, statistic, sum, symbol, total, whole number; SEE CONCEPTS *765,784*
number [*n2*] *aggregate, bunch*
abundance, amount, caboodle*, collection, company, conglomeration, crowd, estimate, flock, horde, jillion*, lot, manifoldness, many, multitude, plenitude, plenty, product, quantity, slew*, sum, throng, total, totality, umpteen*, volume, whole, zillion*; SEE CONCEPTS *432,787*
number [*v*] *count, calculate*
account, add, add up, aggregate, amount, come, computer, count heads*, count noses*, count off, enumerate, estimate, figure in, figure out, include, keep tabs, numerate, reckon, run, run down, run into, run to, sum, take account of, tale, tally, tell, tick off*, total, tote*, tote up*; SEE CONCEPT *764*
numbered [*adj*] *limited in number*
categorized, checked, contained, counted, designated, doomed, enumerated, fated, fixed, included, indicated, marked, specified, told, totalled; SEE CONCEPT *554*
numberless [*adj*] *infinite*
countless, endless, heaps*, incalculable, innumerable, jillion, many, multitudinous, myriad, no end of*, no end to*, numerous, umpteen*, uncountable, uncounted, unnumbered, untold, zillion*; SEE CONCEPTS *482,762,781*

numbskull [*n*] *idiot*
blockhead, bonehead*, buffoon, cretin, dimwit, dolt, dork, dumbbell, dummy, dunce, fathead*, fool, halfwit, ignoramus, imbecile, jerk, moron, nincompoop, ninny*, nitwit, pinhead*, simpleton, stupid person; SEE CONCEPT *412*
numeral [*n*] *symbol of mathematical system*
character, chiffer, cipher, digit, figure, integer, number; SEE CONCEPTS *284,784*
numeric/numerical [*adj*] *concerning mathematics*
algebraic, algorithmic, arithmetic, arithmetical, binary, differential, digital, exponent, exponential, fraction, fractional, integral, logarithm, logarithmic, mathematical, numeral, numerary, statistical; SEE CONCEPT *762*
numerous [*adj*] *many, abundant*
big, copious, diverse, great, infinite, large, legion, lousy with*, multifarious, multitudinal, multitudinous, plentiful, populous, profuse, rife, scads*, several, sundry, thick, umpteen*, various, voluminous, zillion*; SEE CONCEPTS *762,781*
nun [*n*] *woman in religious order*
abbess, anchorite, canoness, mother superior, postulant, prioress, religious woman, sister, vestal; SEE CONCEPT *361*
nunnery [*n*] *convent*
abbey, cloister, monastery, priory, religious community, retreat; SEE CONCEPTS *368,516*
nuptial [*adj*] *concerning marriage*
bridal, conjugal, connubial, espousal, marital, married, matrimonial, spousal, wedded, wedding; SEE CONCEPT *555*
nuptials [*n*] *marriage ceremony*
bridal, espousal, marriage, matrimony, spousal, wedding; SEE CONCEPT *297*
nurse [*n*] *person who tends to sick, cares for someone*
assistant, attendant, baby sitter, caretaker, foster parent, medic, minder, nurse practitioner, practical nurse, registered nurse, RN, sitter, therapist, wet nurse; SEE CONCEPTS *357,414*
nurse [*v1*] *care for, tend*
advance, aid, attend, baby-sit, cherish, cradle, cultivate, encourage, father, feed, forward, foster, further, harbor, humor, immunize, indulge, inoculate, irradiate, keep alive, keep an eye on*, keep tabs on*, look after, medicate, minister to, mother, nourish, nurture, pamper, preserve, promote, see to, serve, sit, succor, support, take care of, take charge of, treat, vaccinate, wait on, watch out for, watch over; SEE CONCEPTS *110,140*
nurse [*v2*] *give milk, usually from breast*
bottle-feed, breast-feed, cradle, dry-nurse, feed, give suck, lactate, nourish, nurture, suck, suckle, wet-nurse; SEE CONCEPTS *140,295*
nursemaid [*n*] *nanny*
au pair, baby-sitter, governess, nurserymaid, wet nurse; SEE CONCEPT *295*
nursing home [*n*] *convalescent home*
convalescent hospital, old folks home*, old people's home, rest home, retirement home; SEE CONCEPTS *312,439,449*
nurture [*n*] *development, nourishment*
breeding, care, diet, discipline, edibles, education, feed, food, instruction, nutriment, provender, provisions, rearing, subsistence, sustenance,

training, upbringing, viands, victuals; SEE CONCEPTS *457,712*

nurture [v] *feed, care for*
back, bolster, bring up, cherish, cultivate, develop, discipline, educate, foster, instruct, nourish, nurse, nursle, provide, raise, rear, school, support, sustain, tend, train, uphold; SEE CONCEPTS *110,140,295*

nut [n1] *seed of fruit, vegetable*
achene, caryopsis, kernel, stone, utricle; SEE CONCEPT *428*

nut [n2] *crazy, overenthusiastic person*
bedlamite, bigot, crackpot, crank, dement, eccentric, fanatic, fiend, freak, harebrain*, loony*, lunatic, maniac, non compos mentis, screwball*, zealot; SEE CONCEPTS *412,423*

nut house [n] *mental health facility*
bughouse*, funny farm*, insane asylum, loony bin, madhouse*, mental hospital, mental institution, psychiatric hospital, psychiatric ward, sanatorium; SEE CONCEPTS *312,439,516*

nutrient [n] *source of nourishment*
fiber, food, health food, mineral, nutriment, supplements, vitamin; SEE CONCEPT *457*

nutrition [n] *food*
diet, menu, nourishment, nutriment, subsistence, sustenance, victuals; SEE CONCEPT *457*

nutritious [adj] *healthy*
alimental, alimentative, balanced, beneficial, good, healthful, health-giving, invigorating, nourishing, nutrient, nutrimental, nutritive, salubrious, salutary, strengthening, wholesome; SEE CONCEPT *462*

nuts/nutty [adj] *mentally deranged*
absurd, batty*, bedlamite, cracked*, crazy, daffy, daft, demented, eccentric, enthusiastic, foolish, gung ho*, harebrained*, insane, irrational, keen, kooky, loony, lunatic, mad, out of one's mind*, ridiculous, touched, unusual, wacky*, warm, zealous; SEE CONCEPT *403*

nuzzle [v] *cuddle*
bundle, burrow, caress, fondle, nestle, nudge, pet, snug, snuggle; SEE CONCEPTS *190,612*

nylons [n] *stockings*
hose, hosiery, panty hose, tights; SEE CONCEPT *451*

nymph [n] *female nature spirit*
dryad, fairy, goddess, mermaid, naiad, nymphet, spirit, sprite, sylph; SEE CONCEPTS *415,424*

O

oaf [n] *person who is clumsy, stupid*
beast, blunderer, bruiser, brute, chump*, clod, clown, dolt, dumb ox*, dunce, fool, goon*, idiot, imbecile, klutz*, loser, lout*, moron, nincompoop*, ox*, sap*, simpleton; SEE CONCEPT *412*

oafish [adj] *clumsy, stupid*
all thumbs*, blundering, blunderous, bumbling, bungling, butterfingered*, dumb, gawkish, gawky, graceless, half-witted*, heavy-handed, idiotic, ignorant, inelegant, inept, klutzy*, lubberly, lumbering, lumpish, moronic, simple, simpleminded, slow, stumbling, uncoordinated,

undexterous, ungainly, unintelligent; SEE CONCEPTS *401,402,548,584*

oasis [n1] *spring*
fountain, watering hole, well, wellspring; SEE CONCEPT *514*

oasis [n2] *refuge*
asylum, cover, escape, harbor, haven, hideaway, resting place, retreat, safe place, sanctuary, sanctum, shelter; SEE CONCEPTS *198,515*

oath [n1] *promise*
adjuration, affidavit, affirmation, avowal, bond, contract, deposition, pledge, profession, sworn declaration, sworn statement, testimony, vow, word, word of honor; SEE CONCEPTS *71,278*

oath [n2] *curse*
blasphemy, cuss*, cuss word*, dirty name*, dirty word*, expletive, four-letter word*, imprecation, malediction, no-no*, profanity, strong language, swearword; SEE CONCEPTS *54,278*

obdurate [adj] *pigheaded, stubborn*
adamant, bullhead*, callous, cold fish*, dogged, firm, fixed, hanging tough*, hard, hard-boiled*, hard-hearted*, hard-nosed*, harsh, heartless, immovable, implacable, indurate, inexorable, inflexible, iron*, mean, mulish*, obstinate, perverse, relentless, rigid, set in stone*, stiff-necked*, thick-skinned*, tough, tough nut to crack*, unbending, uncompassionate, uncompromising, uncooperative, unemotional, unfeeling, unimpressible, unrelenting, unshakable, unsympathetic, unyielding; SEE CONCEPTS *401,542*

obedience [n] *good behavior; submissiveness*
accordance, acquiescence, agreement, compliance, conformability, conformity, deference, docility, duteousness, dutifulness, duty, manageability, meekness, observance, orderliness, quietness, respect, reverence, servility, submission, subservience, tameness, tractability, willingness; SEE CONCEPTS *411,633*

obedient [adj] *well-behaved; submissive*
acquiescent, amenable, at one's beck and call*, attentive, biddable, complaisant, compliant, controllable, deferential, devoted, docile, docious, duteous, dutiful, faithful, governable, honoring, in one's clutches*, in one's pocket*, in one's power*, law-abiding, loyal, obeisant, obliging, observant, on a string*, pliant, regardful, resigned, respectful, reverential, sheeplike*, subservient, tame, tractable, under control, venerating, well-trained, willing, wrapped around finger*, yielding; SEE CONCEPTS *401,404*

obeisance [n] *salutation*
allegiance, bending of the knee*, bow, curtsy, deference, fealty, genuflection, homage, honor, kowtow*, loyalty, praise, respect, reverence, salaam*; SEE CONCEPTS *154,384*

obeisant [adj] *showing respect*
courtly, deferential, dutiful, regarding, respectful, respecting, reverent, reverential, servile, standing; SEE CONCEPT *401*

obese [adj] *very overweight*
adipose, avoirdupois, corpulent, fat, fleshy*, gross*, heavy, outsize, paunchy, plump, porcine, portly, pudgy, rotund, stout; SEE CONCEPT *491*

obesity [n] *corpulence*
bulk, chubbiness, chunkiness, fatness, overweight, paunchiness, plumpness, portliness, rotundness, stoutness; SEE CONCEPT *734*

nu
ob

obey [v] *conform, give in*
abide by, accede, accept, accord, acquiesce, act upon, adhere to, agree, answer, assent, be loyal to, be ruled by, bow to*, carry out, comply, concur, discharge, do as one says, do one's bidding, do one's duty, do what is expected, do what one is told, embrace, execute, follow, fulfill, get in line*, give way*, heed, hold fast*, keep, knuckle under*, live by, mind, observe, perform, play second fiddle*, respond, serve, submit, surrender, take orders, toe the line*; SEE CONCEPTS *91,136*

obfuscate [v] *confuse*
baffle, becloud, befuddle, bewilder, cloud, complicate, conceal, confound, darken, fog, fuddle, muddle, obscure, perplex, puzzle, rattle; SEE CONCEPT *16*

obituary [n] *notice of person's death*
announcement, death notice, eulogy, mortuary tribute, necrology, obit, register; SEE CONCEPTS *268,270*

object [n1] *thing able to be seen/felt/perceived*
article, body, bulk, commodity, doodad*, doohickey*, entity, fact, gadget, gizmo*, item, mass, matter, phenomenon, reality, something, substance, thingamajig*, volume, whatchamacallit*, widget*; SEE CONCEPT *433*

object [n2] *purpose, use*
aim, design, duty, end, end in view, end purpose, function, goal, idea, intent, intention, mark, mission, motive, objective, point, reason, target, view, wish; SEE CONCEPT *659*

object [n3] *aim, recipient*
butt*, focus, ground zero*, receiver, target, victim, zero*; SEE CONCEPTS *124,532*

object [v] *disagree, argue against*
balk, be displeased, challenge, complain, crab*, criticize, cross, demur, deprecate, disapprove, disavow, discommend, discountenance, disesteem, dispute, dissent, except, expostulate, frown, go-one-on-one*, gripe, grouse, inveigh, kick*, make a stink*, mix it up with*, oppose, protest, rail, raise objection, rant, rave, remonstrate, sound off*, spurn, squawk*, storm, take exception, take on, tangle*; SEE CONCEPTS *12,21,46*

objection [n] *argument, disagreement*
cavil, censure, challenge, counter-argument, criticism, declination, demur, demurral, demurring, difficulty, disapprobation, disapproval, discontent, disesteem, disinclination, dislike, displeasure, dissatisfaction, doubt, exception, grievance, gripe, hesitation, kick, niggle*, odium, opposition, protest, protestation, question, rejection, reluctance, remonstrance, remonstration, repugnancy, revilement, scruple, shrinking, squawk*, stink*, unwillingness; SEE CONCEPTS *21,46,410,689*

objectionable [adj] *not nice; unpleasant*
abhorrent, censurable, deplorable, disagreeable, dislikable, displeasing, distasteful, exceptionable, ill-favored, inadmissible, indecorous, inexpedient, insufferable, intolerable, invidious, loathsome, lousy, murder, noxious, obnoxious, offensive, opprobrious, poison, regrettable, repellent, reprehensible, repugnant, repulsive, revolting, unacceptable, undesirable, unfit, unpalatable, unsatisfactory, unseemly, unsuit-

able, unwanted, unwelcome; SEE CONCEPTS *548,558,570*

objective [adj] *fair, impartial*
cold, cool, detached, disinterested, dispassionate, equitable, evenhanded, impersonal, judicial, just, like it is*, nondiscriminatory, nonpartisan, open-minded*, straight, strictly business*, unbiased, uncolored, unemotional, uninvolved, unprejudiced, unprepossessed; SEE CONCEPTS *403,542*

objective [n] *aim, goal*
ambition, aspiration, design, end, end in view*, ground zero*, intention, mark, mission, object, purpose, target, zero*; SEE CONCEPT *659*

objectively [adv] *impartially*
considerately, detachedly, disinterestedly, dispassionately, equitably, evenhandedly, indifferently, justly, neutrally, on the up and up*, open-mindedly*, soberly, squarely, with an open mind*, with impartiality, with objectivity, without favor, without prejudice; SEE CONCEPTS *542,544*

objectivity [n] *impartiality*
detachment, disinterest, disinterestedness, dispassion, equality, equitableness, indifference, neutrality, open-mindedness; SEE CONCEPTS *403,542*

objet d'art [n] *work of art*
bibelot, bric-a-brac, collector's item, collector's piece, curio, knickknack; SEE CONCEPT *446*

objurgate [v] *berate*
bawl out, castigate, censure, chastise, chew out*, chide, give one hell*, jump all over*, rake over the coals*, rebuke, reprimand, reproach, scold, upbraid; SEE CONCEPT *52*

obligate [v] *require*
astrict, bind, constrain, force, indebt, make indebted, oblige, restrain, restrict; SEE CONCEPTS *53,130,646*

obligated [adj] *bound*
bounden, called by duty, committed, compelled, contracted, duty-bound, enslaved, forced, indebted, indentured, obliged, pledged, required, tied, under obligation, urged; SEE CONCEPT *554*

obligation [n] *responsibility*
accountability, accountableness, agreement, bond, burden, business, call, cause, charge, chit*, commitment, committal, compulsion, conscience, constraint, contract, debit, debt, devoir, due bill, dues, duty, engagement, IOU*, liability, must, necessity, need, occasion, onus, ought, part, place, promise, requirement, restraint, right, trust, understanding; SEE CONCEPTS *329,335,388,645*

obligatory [adj] *essential, required*
binding, coercive, compulsatory, compulsory, de rigueur, enforced, imperative, imperious, mandatory, necessary, requisite, unavoidable; SEE CONCEPT *546*

oblige [v1] *require*
bind, coerce, command, compel, constrain, force, impel, make, necessitate, obligate, shotgun*; SEE CONCEPTS *14,242,646*

oblige [v2] *do a favor or kindness*
accommodate, aid, assist, avail, bend over backward*, benefit, come around, contribute, convenience, don't make waves*, favor, fill the bill*, fit in, go fifty-fifty*, gratify, grin and bear it*, help, indulge, make a deal*, make room*, meet halfway*, please, profit, put oneself out*, roll

with it*, serve, swim with the tide*, take it*, toe the mark*; SEE CONCEPTS *110,136,384*

obliged [*adj*] *bound*
bounden, called by duty, committed, compelled, contracted, duty-bound, enslaved, forced, indebted, indentured, obligated, pledged, required, tied, under obligation, urged; SEE CONCEPT *554*

obliging [*adj*] *friendly, helpful*
accommodating, agreeable, amiable, cheerful, civil, complaisant, considerate, cooperative, courteous, eager to please, easy, easygoing, good-humored, good-natured, hospitable, kind, lenient, mild, polite, willing; SEE CONCEPTS *401,404*

oblique [*adj1*] *slanting; at an angle*
angled, askance, askew, aslant, asymmetrical, awry, bent, cater-cornered, crooked, diagonal, distorted, diverging, inclined, inclining, leaning, on the bias, pitched, pitching, sideways, skew, slanted, sloped, sloping, strained, tilted, tilting, tipped, tipping, turned, twisted; SEE CONCEPTS *485,490*

oblique [*adj2*] *indirect, evasive*
backhanded, circuitous, circular, circumlocutory, collateral, devious, implied, obliquitous, obscure, roundabout, sidelong, vague; SEE CONCEPT *267*

obliterate [*v*] *destroy*
annihilate, ax*, black out*, blot out*, blue pencil*, bog, cancel, cover, cut, defeat, delete, do in*, efface, eliminate, eradicate, erase, expunge, exterminate, extirpate, finish, finish off*, kill, knock off*, knock out*, KO*, level*, liquidate, mark out, nix*, obscure, off, ravage, root out*, rub off*, rub out*, scratch, scrub, shoot down, sink, smash, squash, take apart, take out*, torpedo*, total*, trash*, wash out*, waste, wipe off face of earth*, wipe out*, X-out*, zap*; SEE CONCEPT *252*

oblivion [*n1*] *mental blankness*
abeyance, amnesia, carelessness, disregard, forgetfulness, inadvertence, indifference, insensibility, insensibleness, Lethe*, neglect, nirvana*, obliviousness, unawareness, unconcern, unconsciousness, unmindfulness; SEE CONCEPTS *410,633*

oblivion [*n2*] *nothingness, obscurity*
blackness, darkness, eclipse, emptiness, extinction, limbo, nihility, nirvana*, nonexistence, nothing, nowhere*, nullity, out there*, void; SEE CONCEPTS *407,672,679*

oblivious [*adj*] *unaware, ignorant*
absent, absentminded, absorbed, abstracted, amnesic, blind*, blundering, careless, deaf*, disregardful, distracted, dreamy, forgetful, forgetting, gone, heedless, inattentive, incognizant, inconversant, insensible, neglectful, negligent, not all there*, out to lunch*, overlooking, preoccupied, regardless, spacey*, strung out*, unacquainted, unconcerned, unconscious, undiscerning, unfamiliar, uninformed, uninstructed, unknowing, unmindful, unnoticing, unobservant, unrecognizing, unwitting, zonked*; SEE CONCEPTS *402,403,542*

oblong [*adj*] *elongated and rounded*
egg-shaped, ellipsoidal, elliptical, elongate, long, oval, ovaliform, ovaloid, ovate, ovated, ovoid, rectangular; SEE CONCEPT *486*

obloquy [*n*] *calumny*
abuse, animadversion, aspersion, bad press, cen-

sure, criticism, defamation, disgrace, humiliation, ignominy, insult, invective, reproach, slander, vituperation; SEE CONCEPTS *271,277,278*

obnoxious [*adj*] *offensive, repulsive*
abhorrent, abominable, annoying, awful, beastly*, big mouth*, detestable, disagreeable, disgusting, dislikable, displeasing, foul, gross*, hateable, hateful, heel, horrid, insufferable, invidious, loathsome, mean, nasty, nauseating, objectionable, odious, off-color*, ornery, pain in the neck*, pesky*, pestiferous, pill*, repellent, reprehensible, repugnant, revolting, rotten, sickening, stinking, unpleasant; SEE CONCEPTS *267,401,542*

obscene [*adj*] *indecent, offensive, immoral*
atrocious, barnyard*, bawdy, blue*, coarse, crude, dirty*, disgusting, evil, filthy, foul, gross, heinous, hideous, horrible, immodest, improper, impure, lascivious, lewd, licentious, loathsome, loose*, lustful, nasty, noisome, outrageous, porno*, pornographic, profane, prurient, rank*, raunchy*, raw, repellent, repugnant, ribald, salacious, scabrous, scatological, scurrilous, shameless, shocking, sickening, smutty*, suggestive, unchaste, unclean, unwholesome, vile, wanton, wicked, X-rated*; SEE CONCEPTS *267,372,545*

obscenity [*n*] *indecency, immorality; vulgarism*
abomination, affront, atrocity, bawdiness, blight, blueness*, coarseness, curse, dirtiness, dirty name*, dirty word*, evil, filthiness, foulness, four-letter word*, immodesty, impropriety, impurity, indecency, indelicacy, lewdness, licentiousness, lubricity, offense, outrage, porn*, pornography, profanity, prurience, salacity, scatology, scurrility, sleaze*, smut*, smuttiness, suggestiveness, swearword, vileness, vulgarity, wrong, X-rating*; SEE CONCEPTS *278,645*

obscure [*adj1*] *not easily understood*
abstruse, ambiguous, arcane, clear as mud*, complicated, concealed, confusing, cryptic, dark, deep, dim, doubtful, enigmatic, enigmatical, esoteric, far-out, hazy, hidden, illegible, illogical, impenetrable, incomprehensible, inconceivable, incredible, indecisive, indefinite, indeterminate, indistinct, inexplicable, inscrutable, insoluble, intricate, involved, mysterious, occult, opaque, recondite, unaccountable, unbelievable, unclear, undefined, unfathomable, unintelligible, vague; SEE CONCEPT *529*

obscure [*adj2*] *cloudy, shadowy*
blurred, caliginous, clouded, dark, dense, dim, dusk, dusky, faint, fuliginous, gloomy, indistinct, lightless, murky, obfuscated, shady, somber, tenebrous, umbrageous, unilluminated, unlit, veiled; SEE CONCEPT *617*

obscure [*adj3*] *out-of-the-way, little-known*
abstruse, arcane, blind, cabalistic, close, covered, cryptic, dark, deep, devious, distant, enigmatic, esoteric, far, far-off, hidden, humble, inaccessible, inconspicuous, inglorious, invisible, irrelevant, lonesome, lowly, minor, mysterious, nameless, odd, oracular, orphic, rare, recondite, remote, removed, reticent, retired, secluded, secret, secretive, seldom seen, sequestered, solitary, undisclosed, undistinguished, unheard-of, unhonored, unimportant, unknown, unnoted, unseen, unsung; SEE CONCEPT *576*

obscure [*v*] *conceal, hide*
adumbrate, becloud, bedim, befog, belie, blear, blind, block, block out, blur, camouflage, cloak,

cloud, cloud the issue*, con, confuse, cover, cover up, darken, dim, disguise, double-talk*, eclipse, equivocate, falsify, fog, fuzz, gloom, gray, haze, mask, misrepresent, mist, muddy, muddy the waters*, murk, obfuscate, overcast, overcloud, overshadow, pettifog*, screen, shade, shadow, shroud, stonewall*, throw up smoke screen*, veil, wrap; SEE CONCEPTS *16,63,172,188*

obsequious [*adj*] *groveling, submissive*
abject, beggarly, brownnosing*, complacent, compliable, compliant, cringing, crouching, deferential, enslaved, fawning, flattering, ingratiating, kowtowing*, menial, obeisant, oily*, parasitic, parasitical, prostrate, respectful, servile, slavish, sneaking, sniveling, spineless*, stipendiary, subject, submissive, subordinate, subservient, sycophantic, toadying*, unctuous; SEE CONCEPTS *401,404*

obsequy [*n*] *funeral ceremony*
eulogy, funeral rite, funeral service; SEE CONCEPTS *69,278*

observable [*adj*] *apparent*
appreciable, clear, detectable, discernible, discoverable, evident, noticeable, obvious, open, palpable, patent, perceivable, perceptible, recognizable, sensible, tangible, visible; SEE CONCEPTS *529,576*

observance [*n1*] *attention to, knowledge of something*
acknowledgment, acquittal, acquittance, adherence, awareness, carrying out, celebration, cognizance, compliance, discharge, fidelity, fulfillment, heed, heeding, honoring, keeping, mark, mind, note, notice, obedience, observation, performance, regard, remark, satisfaction; SEE CONCEPTS *409,410,633*

observance [*n2*] *ceremony, rite*
celebration, ceremonial, custom, fashion, form, formality, liturgy, performance, practice, ritual, rule, service, tradition; SEE CONCEPTS *377,384,688*

observant [*adj*] *alert, watchful*
advertent, alive, attentive, bright, clear-sighted*, comprehending, considering, contemplating, correct, deducing, detecting, discerning, discovering, discriminating, eager, eagle-eyed*, heedful, intelligent, intentive, interested, keen, mindful, not missing a trick*, obedient, observative, on one's toes*, on the ball*, penetrating, perceptive, questioning, quick, regardful, searching, sensitive, sharp, sharp-eyed*, surveying, understanding, vigilant, wide-awake*; SEE CONCEPTS *402,403*

observation [*n1*] *attention, scrutiny*
ascertainment, check, cognition, cognizance, conclusion, consideration, detection, estimation, examination, experience, heedfulness, information, inspection, investigation, knowledge, mark, measurement, mind, monitoring, note, notice, noticing, once-over*, overlook, perception, probe, recognizing, regard, remark, research, review, search, study, supervision, surveillance, view, watching; SEE CONCEPTS *409,410*

observation [*n2*] *comment on something scrutinized*
annotation, catch phrase, comeback, commentary, crack*, finding, mention, mouthful*, note, obiter dictum, opinion, pronouncement, reflection, remark, saying, say so*, thought, utterance, wisecrack; SEE CONCEPTS *51,278*

observe [*v1*] *see, notice*
beam, behold, catch, contemplate, detect, dig, discern, discover, distinguish, eagle-eye*, espy, examine, eyeball*, flash*, get a load of*, get an eyeful of*, inspect, keep one's eye on*, lamp*, look at, make out*, mark, mind, monitor, note, pay attention to, perceive, pick up on*, read, recognize, regard, scrutinize, spot, spy, study, survey, take in*, view, watch, witness; SEE CONCEPTS *24,34,103,265,626*

observe [*v2*] *comment, remark*
animadvert, commentate, declare, mention, mouth off*, note, opine, say, state, wisecrack; SEE CONCEPT *51*

observe [*v3*] *celebrate, commemorate*
dedicate, hold, honor, keep, remember, respect, revere, reverence, solemnize, venerate; SEE CONCEPT *377*

observe [*v4*] *abide by, obey*
adhere, adopt, comply, comply with, conform, follow, fulfill, heed, honor, keep, mind, perform, respect; SEE CONCEPTS *91,384*

observer [*n*] *spectator*
beholder, bystander, eyewitness, gaper, gazer, looker, looker-on, onlooker, viewer, watcher, witness; SEE CONCEPTS *366,423*

obsess [*v*] *preoccupy*
beset, consume, dominate, engross, grip, harass, haunt, hold, infatuate, possess, torment; SEE CONCEPT *403*

obsessed [*adj*] *consumed, driven about belief, desire*
bedeviled, beset, bewitched, captivated, controlled, dogged*, dominated, eat sleep and breathe*, engrossed, fiendish, fixated, gripped, harassed, haunted, have on the brain*, held, hooked, hung up on*, immersed in, infatuated, into*, overpowered, plagued*, possessed, preoccupied, prepossessed, really into*, seized, taken over, tied up*, tormented, troubled, turned on, up to here in*, wound up with*, wrapped up in*; SEE CONCEPTS *403,404*

obsession [*n*] *fixation; consumption with belief, desire*
attraction, ax to grind*, bug in ear*, case*, complex, compulsion, concrete idea, craze*, crush, delusion, enthusiasm, fancy, fascination, fetish, hang-up*, idée fixe, infatuation, mania, monkey*, must, neurosis, one-track mind*, passion, phantom, phobia, preoccupation, something on the brain*, thing*, tiger by the tail*; SEE CONCEPTS *20,410,529,689,690*

obsolete [*adj*] *no longer in use, in vogue*
anachronistic, ancient, antediluvian, antiquated, antique, archaic, bygone, dated, dead, dead and gone*, dinosaur*, discarded, disused, done for*, dusty, extinct, fossil, gone, had it*, has-been*, horse and buggy*, kaput*, moldy*, moth-eaten*, old, old-fashioned, old-hat, old-school, out*, outmoded, out-of-date, out-of-fashion, outworn, passé, stale, superannuated, superseded, timeworn, unfashionable; SEE CONCEPTS *539,560,589*

obstacle [*n*] *impediment, barrier*
bar, block, booby trap*, bump*, catch, Catch-22*, check, clog*, crimp*, difficulty, disincentive, encumbrance, hamper, handicap, hang-up*, hardship, hindrance, hitch*, hurdle, interference, interruption, joker*, monkey wrench*, mountain, obstruction, restriction, rub*, snag, stumbling

block*, traverse, vicissitude; SEE CONCEPTS *470,532,666,674*

obstinate [*adj*] *stubborn, determined*
adamant, cantankerous, contradictory, contrary, contumacious, convinced, dead set on*, dogged, dogmatic, firm, hard, hardened, headstrong, heady, immovable, indomitable, inflexible, intractable, intransigent, locked in*, mulish*, obdurate, opinionated, opinionative, persistent, pertinacious, perverse, pigheaded*, recalcitrant, refractory, relentless, resolved, restive, self-willed, steadfast, strong-minded, tenacious, unalterable, unflinching, unmanageable, unyielding, willful; SEE CONCEPTS *401,542*

obstreperous [*adj*] *noisy*
blusterous, boisterous, booming, clamorous, disorderly, loud, out of hand, piercing, raising Cain*, raising the roof*, rambunctious, riotous, rowdy, screaming, strepitous, tumultous, unmanageable, unruly, uproarious, vociferous, wild; SEE CONCEPTS *592,594*

obstruct [*v*] *prevent, restrict*
arrest, bar, barricade, block, check, choke, clog, close, congest, crab, curb, cut off, drag one's feet*, fill, foul up, frustrate, get in the way*, hamper, hamstring*, hang up*, hide, hinder, hold up, impede, inhibit, interfere, interrupt, mask, monkey with*, obscure, occlude, plug, restrain, retard, sandbag*, shield, shut off, slow down, stall, stonewall*, stop, stopper, stymie*, terminate, throttle, thwart, trammel, weigh down; SEE CONCEPTS *5,121,130*

obstruction [*n*] *obstacle, impediment*
bar, barricade, barrier, block, blockage, blocking, booby trap*, check, checkmate*, circumvention, difficulty, gridlock*, hamper, hindrance, hurdle, interference, jam*, lock, monkey wrench*, mountain*, restraint, roadblock*, snag, stop, stoppage, stumbling block*, trammel, trouble, wall; SEE CONCEPTS *470,532,666,674*

obtain [*v*] *get, acquire*
access, accomplish, achieve, annex, attain, beg borrow or steal*, capture, chalk up*, collect, come by, compass, cop*, corral, drum up*, earn, effect, fetch, gain, gather, get at, get hold of*, get one's hands on*, glean, gobble up*, grab, have, hoard, inherit, invade, lay up, make use of, nab*, occupy, pick up, pocket*, procure, purchase, reach, realize, reap, receive, recover, retrieve, salvage, save, score, scrape together, scrape up, secure, seize, snag, take, wangle, win; SEE CONCEPT *120*

obtainable [*adj*] *achievable, available*
at hand*, attainable, derivable, duck soup*, gettable, in stock, no problem*, no sweat*, on deck*, on offer*, on tap*, piece of cake*, procurable, purchasable, pushover, ready, realizable, securable, there for the taking*, to be had*; SEE CONCEPTS *528,576*

obtrusive [*adj*] *pushy, obvious*
bulging, busy, forward, impertinent, importunate, interfering, intrusive, jutting, meddlesome, meddling, nosy, noticeable, officious, presumptuous, projecting, prominent, protruding, protuberant, prying, sticking out; SEE CONCEPTS *401,542*

obtuse [*adj1*] *slow to understand*
dense, dopey*, dull*, dumb, imperceptive, insensitive, opaque, slow on uptake*, stolid, thick, uncomprehending, unintelligent; SEE CONCEPT *402*

obtuse [*adj2*] *blunt, not sharp*
round, rounded; SEE CONCEPTS *485,486*

obviate [*v*] *make unnecessary*
anticipate, avert, block, counter, counteract, deter, do away with, forestall, forfend, hinder, interfere, interpose, intervene, preclude, prevent, remove, restrain, rule out, stave off, ward; SEE CONCEPT *121*

obvious [*adj*] *apparent, understandable*
accessible, barefaced, bright, clear, clear as a bell*, conclusive, conspicuous, discernible, distinct, distinguishable, evident, explicit, exposed, glaring, indisputable, in evidence, lucid, manifest, noticeable, observable, open, overt, palpable, patent, perceivable, perceptible, plain, precise, prominent, pronounced, public, recognizable, self-evident, self-explanatory, standing out, straightforward, transparent, unconcealed, undeniable, undisguised, unmistakable, unsubtle, visible; SEE CONCEPTS *485,529*

obviously [*adv*] *unmistakably*
apparently, certainly, clearly, definitely, distinctly, evidently, incontestably, noticeably, of course, openly, plainly, seemingly, surely, undeniably, undoubtedly, unquestionably, visibly, without doubt; SEE CONCEPTS *535,552*

occasion [*n1*] *chance*
break*, convenience, demand, excuse, incident, instant, moment, need, occurrence, opening, opportunity, possibility, season, shot*, show, time, use; SEE CONCEPT *693*

occasion [*n2*] *reason, cause*
antecedent, basis, call, circumstance, determinant, excuse, foundation, ground, grounds, incident, inducement, influence, justification, motivation, motive, necessity, obligation, prompting, provocation, purpose, right, warrant; SEE CONCEPT *661*

occasion [*n3*] *event, happening*
affair, celebration, circumstance, episode, experience, go*, goings-on*, happening, incident, instant, milepost*, milestone, moment, occurrence, scene, thing*, time, while; SEE CONCEPTS *2,386*

occasion [*v*] *make happen, bring about*
breed, cause, create, do, effect, elicit, engender, evoke, generate, give rise to, hatch, induce, influence, inspire, lead to, move, muster, originate, persuade, produce, prompt, provoke, work up; SEE CONCEPTS *68,242*

occasional [*adj*] *irregular, sporadic*
casual, desultory, especial, exceptional, exclusive, few, incidental, infrequent, intermittent, not habitual, odd, off and on*, particular, random, rare, scarce, seldom, semioccasional, special, specific, uncommon, unfrequent, unusual; SEE CONCEPTS *530,541*

occasionally [*adv*] *every now and then*
at intervals, at random, at times, every so often, from time to time, hardly, infrequently, irregularly, now and again, once in a blue moon*, once in a while, once or twice*, on occasion, periodically, seldom, sometimes, sporadically, uncommonly; SEE CONCEPTS *530,541*

occlude [*v*] *block, prevent*
choke, clog, close, close out, congest, curb, fill, hinder, impede, leave out, lock out, obstruct, plug, seal, shut, stopper, stop up, throttle; SEE CONCEPTS *121,201*

occlusion [*n*] *obstruction*
barricade, barrier, block, blockage, blocking,

closure, stoppage; SEE CONCEPTS *470,532,666, 674*

occult [*adj*] *mysterious, secret; supernatural*
abstruse, acroamatic, arcane, cabalistic, concealed, deep, eerie, esoteric, hermetic, hidden, invisible, magic, magical, mystic, mystical, obscure, orphic, preternatural, profound, psychic, recondite, transmundane, unearthly, unknown, unrevealed, veiled, weird; SEE CONCEPTS *576,582*

occupancy [*n*] *residence of place*
control, deed, habitation, holding, inhabitance, inhabitancy, occupation, ownership, possession, retention, settlement, tenancy, tenure, term, title, use; SEE CONCEPTS *518,710*

occupant [*n*] *person who resides in a place*
addressee, denizen, dweller, holder, householder, incumbent, indweller, inhabitant, lessee, occupier, possessor, renter, resident, resider, tenant, user; SEE CONCEPT *414*

occupation [*n1*] *profession, business*
activity, affair, calling, chosen work, craft, daily grind*, day gig*, do, dodge*, employment, game*, grindstone*, hang*, job, lick*, line, line of work, métier, moonlight*, nine-to-five*, play*, post, pursuit, racket*, rat race*, slot*, thing*, trade, vocation, walk of life*, what one is into*, work; SEE CONCEPTS *349,351,360*

occupation [*n2*] *control, possession*
habitation, holding, inhabitancy, inhabitation, occupancy, ownership, residence, settlement, tenancy, tenure, title, use; SEE CONCEPTS *518,710*

occupation [*n3*] *seizure, takeover*
attack, capture, conquest, entering, foreign rule, invasion, subjugation; SEE CONCEPTS *86,90,320*

occupied [*adj1*] *busy*
active, clocked up*, employed, engaged, engrossed, head over heels*, tied up*, too much on plate*, working; SEE CONCEPT *542*

occupied [*adj2*] *inhabited; in use*
busy, engaged, full, leased, lived-in*, peopled*, populated, populous, rented, settled, taken, unavailable, utilized; SEE CONCEPT *560*

occupy [*v1*] *be busy with*
absorb, amuse, attend, be active with, be concerned with, busy, divert, employ, engage, engross, entertain, fill, hold attention, immerse, interest, involve, keep busy, monopolize, preoccupy, soak, take up, tie up, utilize; SEE CONCEPTS *7,17,19,22*

occupy [*v2*] *reside; use*
be established, be in command, be in residence, cover, dwell, ensconce, establish, fill, hold, inhabit, involve, keep, live in, maintain, own, people, permeate, pervade, populate, possess, remain, sit, stay, take up, tenant, utilize; SEE CONCEPTS *225,226*

occupy [*v3*] *seize, take over*
capture, conquer, garrison, hold, invade, keep, obtain, overrun, take possession; SEE CONCEPTS *86,90,320*

occur [*v1*] *take place, happen*
action, appear, arise, befall, be found, be present, betide, chance, come about, come off*, come to pass, cook*, crop up, develop, ensue, eventualize, eventuate, exist, follow, go, jell*, manifest, materialize, obtain, present itself, result, shake*, show, smoke*, take place, transpire, turn out, turn up; SEE CONCEPTS *4,242*

occur [*v2*] *come to mind*
come to one*, cross one's mind*, dawn on*, expose, flash*, go through one's head*, hit, offer itself, present itself, reveal, spring to mind*, strike, suggest itself; SEE CONCEPTS *34,43*

occurrence [*n*] *happening, development*
accident, adventure, affair, appearance, circumstance, condition, contingency, emergency, episode, event, exigency, existence, incidence, incident, instance, juncture, manifestation, materialization, occasion, pass, piece, proceeding, routine, scene, situation, state, thing*, transaction, transpiration; SEE CONCEPTS *3,4,230,696*

ocean [*n*] *very large body of water*
blue*, bounding main*, brine, briny*, briny deep*, Davy Jones's locker*, deep, drink*, high seas*, main, pond, puddle, salt water, sea, seaway, Seven Seas, sink, tide; SEE CONCEPT *514*

oceanic [*adj*] *marine*
aquatic, coastal, maritime, nautical, naval, oceangoing, oceanographic, of the sea, pelagic, seafaring, seagoing; SEE CONCEPT *536*

odd/oddball [*adj1*] *unusual, abnormal*
atypical, avant-garde, bizarre, character, crazy, curious, deviant, different, eccentric, erratic, exceptional, extraordinary, fantastic, flaky*, freak*, freakish*, freaky*, funny, idiosyncratic, irregular, kinky*, kooky*, offbeat, off-the-wall*, outlandish, out of the ordinary, peculiar, quaint, queer, rare, remarkable, singular, spacey*, strange, uncanny, uncommon, unconventional, unique, way out*, weird, weirdo*, whimsical; SEE CONCEPTS *404,542,564*

odd [*adj2*] *miscellaneous, various*
accidental, casual, chance, contingent, different, fluky*, fortuitous, fragmentary, incidental, irregular, occasional, odd-lot*, periodic, random, seasonal, sundry, varied; SEE CONCEPT *552*

odd [*adj3*] *single, unmatched; uneven*
additional, alone, exceeding, individual, irregular, left, leftover, lone, lonely, over, over and above, remaining, singular, sole, solitary, spare, surplus, unconsumed, unitary, unpaired; SEE CONCEPTS *480,577*

oddity [*n1*] *abnormality*
anomaly, bizarreness, characteristic, conversation piece, curiosity, eccentricity, extraordinariness, freak, freakishness, idiosyncrasy, incongruity, irregularity, kink, oddness, outlandishness, peculiarity, phenomenon, queerness, quirk, rarity, singularity, strangeness, unconventionality, unnaturalness; SEE CONCEPTS *260,411,665*

oddity/oddball [*n2*] *person who is very different*
case*, character, duck*, eccentric, fish out of water*, maverick, misfit, odd bird*, original*, rara avis, screwball*, weirdo*; SEE CONCEPT *423*

odds [*n1*] *advantage*
allowance, benefit, bulge, difference, disparity, dissimilarity, distinction, draw, edge, handicap, head start, lead, overlay, start, superiority, vantage; SEE CONCEPT *693*

odds [*n2*] *probability*
balance, chances, favor, likelihood, superiority, toss-up; SEE CONCEPT *650*

odds and ends [*n*] *miscellaneous paraphernalia*
assortment, bits, bits and pieces*, debris, etcetera*, hodgepodge, jumble, leavings, litter, medley, mélange, melee, miscellany, motley, oddments, olio, particles, potpourri, remnants,

rest, rubbish, rummage, scraps, sundry items, this and that*; SEE CONCEPTS *260,432,446*

odds-on-favorite [*n*] *front-runner*
best bet, contender, favorite, first choice, top seed; SEE CONCEPTS *423,446*

ode [*n*] *poem*
ballad, composition, epode, limerick, lyric, poesy, rhyme, song, sonnet, verse; SEE CONCEPTS *268,282*

odious [*adj*] *hateful, horrible*
abhorrent, abominable, creepy*, detestable, disgusting, execrable, foul, hateable, horrid, loathsome, mean, obnoxious, offensive, ornery, pain in the neck*, repellent, repugnant, repulsive, revolting, unpleasant, vile; SEE CONCEPTS *401,404*

odium [*n*] *shame, dishonor*
abhorrence, antipathy, aversion, bar sinister*, black eye*, blame, blot, blur, brand, censure, condemnation, detestation, disapproval, discredit, disesteem, disfavor, disgrace, dislike, dispprobation, disrepute, enmity, execration, hate, hatred, ignominy, infamy, malice, obloquy, onus, opprobrium, rebuke, reprobation, resentment, slur, spot, stain, stigma; SEE CONCEPTS *29,388*

odor [*n*] *scent*
air, aroma, bouquet, effluvium, efflux, emanation, essence, exhalation, flavor, fragrance, musk, perfume, pungence, pungency, redolence, smell, snuff, stench, stink, tang, tincture, trail, whiff; SEE CONCEPT *599*

odorless [*adj*] *without fragrance*
deodorant, deodorizing, flat, inodorous, odorfree, unaromatic, unfragrant, unperfumed, unscented, unsmelling; SEE CONCEPT *598*

odorous [*adj*] *having fragrance*
aromatic, balmy, dank, effluvious, fetid, flavorsome, flowery, foul, fragrant, heady, honeyed, loud, malodorous, mephitic, miasmic, moldy, musty, nauseous, odoriferant, odoriferous, offensive, olfactive, olfactory, perfumatory, perfumed, perfumy, pungent, putrid, redolent, reeking, rotten, savorous, savory, scented, scentful, scent-laden, skunky*, smelly, spicy, stagnant, stale, stinking, strong, sweet, sweet-scented, sweet-smelling, tumaceous, unsavory, whiffy*; SEE CONCEPT *598*

odyssey [*n*] *journey*
adventure, excursion, expedition, exploration, pilgrimage, quest, sojourn, tour, travels, trek, trip, voyage, wanderings; SEE CONCEPT *224*

of course [*adv*] *as expected*
by all means, certainly, definitely, indeed, indubitably, naturally, obviously, surely, undoubtedly, without a doubt; SEE CONCEPT *544*

off [*adj1*] *gone; remote*
absent, canceled, finished, inoperative, negligible, not employed, not on duty, on vacation, outside, postponed, slender, slight, slim, small, unavailable; SEE CONCEPT *552*

off [*adj2*] *inferior; spoiled*
bad, decomposed, disappointing, disheartening, displeasing, low-quality, mortifying, not up to par*, not up to snuff*, poor, putrid, quiet, rancid, rotten, slack, sour, substandard, turned, unrewarding, unsatisfactory; SEE CONCEPT *570*

off [*adv*] *apart, away*
above, absent, afar, ahead, aside, away from, behind, below, beneath, beside, disappearing, divergent, elsewhere, far, farther away, gone away,

in the distance, not here, out, over, removed, to one side, turning aside, up front, vanishing; SEE CONCEPTS *583,778*

off and on [*adv*] *intermittently*
alternately, at intervals, at times, every once in a while, every so often, fluctuating, from time to time, irregularly, now and then, occasionally, once in a while, on occasion, sometimes, sporadically, vacillating, variably; SEE CONCEPTS *530,541*

offbeat [*adj*] *strange, very different*
bizarre, bohemian*, eccentric, far-out, freaky, fresh, idiosyncratic, novel, oddball, outré, uncommon, unconventional, unique, unorthodox, unusual, way-out*, weird; SEE CONCEPT *564*

off-center [*adj*] *wide*
adrift, askew, astray, far-off, inaccurate, off-course, off-target, off the mark, stray; SEE CONCEPTS *581,583*

off-color [*adj*] *risqué*
blue*, indelicate, purple*, racy*, salty*, shady, suggestive, vulgar, wicked; SEE CONCEPT *545*

off-course [*adj*] *strayed*
astray, confused, disoriented, lost, lost one's bearing, off-track, roaming, roving; SEE CONCEPTS *576,583*

offend [*v*] *displease, insult*
affront, aggrieve, anger, annoy, antagonize, be disagreeable, disgruntle, disgust, disoblige, distress, disturb, exasperate, fret, gall, horrify, hurt, irritate, jar, miff, nauseate, nettle, outrage, pain, pique, provoke, repel, repulse, rile, shock, sicken, sin, slight, slur, snub, sting, transgress, trespass, turn one off*, upset, vex, wound, zing*; SEE CONCEPTS *7,14,19*

offender [*n*] *perpetrator*
con*, convict, criminal, crook, culprit, delinquent, felon, guilty party, guilty person, jailbird*, lawbreaker, malefactor, sinner, suspect, transgressor, wrongdoer; SEE CONCEPT *91*

offense [*n1*] *violation, trespass*
breach, crime, delinquency, fault, infraction, lapse, malfeasance, misdeed, misdemeanor, peccadillo, sin, transgression, wrong, wrongdoing; SEE CONCEPTS *192,691*

offense [*n2*] *insult, displeasure*
affront, aggression, assailment, assault, attack, battery, black eye*, blitz*, blitzkrieg*, dig*, dirty dig*, harm, hit*, hurt, indignation, indignity, injury, injustice, left-handed compliment*, mugging, offensive, onset, onslaught, outrage, push*, put-down*, slam*, slap in the face*, slight, snub, zinger*; SEE CONCEPTS *52,278*

offense [*n3*] *anger, hard feelings*
annoyance, conniption*, displeasure, explosion, fit, flare-up*, huff, indignation, ire, miff, needle*, outburst, pique, resentment, scene, tantrum, tizzy*, umbrage, wounded feelings, wrath; SEE CONCEPT *410*

offensive [*adj1*] *disrespectful, insulting; displeasing*
abhorrent, abusive, annoying, biting, cutting, detestable, disagreeable, discourteous, distasteful, dreadful, embarrassing, evil, foul, ghastly, grisly, gross, hideous, horrible, horrid, impertinent, insolent, invidious, irritating, nauseating, objectionable, obnoxious, odious, off-color*, offending, opprobrious, outrageous, repellent, reprehensible, repugnant, repulsive, revolting,

rotten, rude, shocking, stinking*, terrible, uncivil, unmannerly; SEE CONCEPTS *267,529,537*

offensive [*adj2*] *attacking*
aggressive, assailing, assaulting, belligerent, invading; SEE CONCEPT *548*

offensive [*n*] *attack*
aggression, assailment, assault, drive, invasion,
onset, onslaught, push; SEE CONCEPTS *86,320*

offer [*n*] *proposal, suggestion*
action, attempt, bid, endeavor, essay, feeler*,
hit*, overture, pass*, pitch*, presentation, proposition, propoundment, rendition, submission, tender; SEE CONCEPTS *66,67,278*

offer [*v1*] *present, propose for acceptance*
accord, advance, afford, allow, award, be at service, bid, come forward, display, donate, exhibit,
extend, furnish, give, grant, hold out, lay at one's
feet*, make available, move, place at disposal*,
ply, pose, press, proffer, propound, provide, put
forth, put forward, put on the market, put up, put
up for sale, sacrifice, show, submit, suggest, tender, volunteer; SEE CONCEPT *67*

offer [*v2*] *propose*
adduce, advance, advise, allege, cite, make a motion, make a pitch*, present, proposition, submit,
suggest; SEE CONCEPT *66*

offer [*v3*] *try*
assay, attempt, endeavor, essay, seek, strive,
struggle, undertake; SEE CONCEPT *87*

offering [*n*] *donation*
alms, atonement, benefaction, beneficence, charity, contribution, expiation, gift, oblation, present, sacrifice, subscription; SEE CONCEPTS
337,340

off-guard [*adj*] *unprepared*
asleep, asleep on the job*, daydreaming, flat-
footed*, inattentive, napping, spaced out*,
unalert, unready, unsuspecting, unvigilant, unwatchful, zoned out*; SEE CONCEPTS *403,542*

offhand [*adj1*] *abrupt, careless*
aloof, breezy, brusque, casual, cavalier, cool*,
curt, easygoing, folksy, glib, informal, laid-back,
mellow, perfunctory, unceremonious, unconcerned, uninterested; SEE CONCEPTS *267,401,542*

offhand [*adj2/adv*] *ad-lib, extemporaneous*
extemporary, extempore, impromptu, improvised, informal, off the cuff*, off the hip*, off
the top of head*, spontaneous, spur-of-the-moment*, throwaway*, unpremeditated, unprepared, unrehearsed, unstudied, without
preparation; SEE CONCEPT *267*

office [*n1*] *business, responsibility*
appointment, berth, billet, capacity, charge, commission, connection, duty, employment, function, job, obligation, occupation, performance,
place, post, province, responsibility, role, service, situation, spot, station, trust, work; SEE
CONCEPTS *351,362,376*

office [*n2*] *place of business*
agency, building, bureau, cave*, center, department, facility, factory, foundry, room, salt
mines*, setup, shop, store, suite, warehouse,
workstation; SEE CONCEPTS *312,439,441,448,449*

officer [*n1*] *person who has high position in organization*
administrator, agent, appointee, bureaucrat,
chief, civil servant, deputy, dignitary, director,
executive, functionary, head, leader, magistrate,
manager, officeholder, official, president, public
servant, representative; SEE CONCEPT *347*

officer [*n2*] *person in law enforcement*
arm*, badge*, black and white*, captain, cop*,
deputy, detective, flatfoot*, mounty, police, police officer, sergeant, sheriff; SEE CONCEPTS
354,355,358

official [*adj*] *authorized, legitimate*
accredited, approved, authentic, authenticated,
authoritative, bona fide, canonical, cathedral,
ceremonious, certified, cleared, conclusive, correct, customary, decided, decisive, definite, endorsed, established, ex cathedra, ex officio,
fitting, formal, legitimate, licensed, okay*, ordered, orthodox, positive, precise, proper, real,
recognized, rightful, sanctioned, suitable, true,
valid; SEE CONCEPT *535*

official [*n*] *person representing organization*
administrator, agent, big shot*, boss, brains*,
brass*, bureaucrat, CEO*, chancellor, civil servant, commissioner, comptroller, dignitary, director, exec*, executive, front office*,
functionary, governor, head person, higher-up*,
incumbent, leader, magistrate, manager, marshal,
mayor, minister, officeholder, officer, panjan-
drum, premier, president, representative, secretary, top*, top brass*, top dog*, top drawer*,
treasurer; SEE CONCEPTS *347,354*

officiate [*v*] *oversee, manage*
act, boss, chair, command, conduct, direct, do
the honors*, emcee, function, govern, handle,
preside, run, serve, superintend, umpire; SEE
CONCEPT *117*

officious [*adj*] *self-important, dictatorial*
busy, forward, impertinent, inquisitive, interfering, intrusive, meddlesome, meddling, obtrusive,
opinionated, overzealous, pragmatic, pushy,
rude; SEE CONCEPT *404*

off-key [*adj*] *not harmonious*
abnormal, anomalous, clinker*, deviant, discordant, dissonant, divergent, inharmonious, irregular, jarring, out of keeping*, out of tune*, sour*,
sour note*, unnatural; SEE CONCEPT *594*

off-limits [*adj*] *prohibited*
against the law, banned, barred, forbidden, illegal, illicit, no-no*, not allowed, outlawed, out of
bounds*, restricted, taboo, unlawful, verboten;
SEE CONCEPTS *554,576*

offset [*v*] *counterbalance, compensate*
account, allow for, atone for, balance, be equivalent, cancel out, charge, counteract, counterpoise, counterpose, countervail, equal, equalize,
equipoise, make amends, make up for, negate,
neutralize, outweigh, recompense, redeem, requite, set off; SEE CONCEPTS *126,232*

offshoot [*n*] *development, product*
adjunct, appendage, branch, by-product, derivative, descendant, limb, outgrowth, spin-off,
sprout; SEE CONCEPTS *260,824*

offspring [*n*] *child, children*
baby, bambino*, brood, chip off old block*, cub,
descendant, family, generation, heir, heredity,
issue, kid*, lineage, offshoot, posterity, produce,
progeniture, progeny, pup*, scion, seed, spawn,
succession, successor, young; SEE CONCEPTS
296,414

off the cuff [*adj*] *impromptu*
ad-lib, extemporaneous, improv*, improvised,
improviso, off-hand, played by ear*, shot from
the hip*, spontaneous, spur-of-the-moment, unpremeditated, unprepared, unrehearsed, un-

scripted, whipped up*, winged*; SEE CONCEPT *267*

off the record [*adj*] *confidential*
arcane, backdoor, classified, hushed, hush-hush*, in private, inside, not for publication, not public, on the QT, private, privy, secret, unofficial; SEE CONCEPTS *267,576*

often [*adv*] *frequently*
again and again, a number of times, generally, many a time, much, oftentimes, ofttimes, over and over, recurrently, regularly, repeatedly, time after time, time and again, usually; SEE CONCEPT *541*

ogle [*v*] *stare*
eagle eye*, eye, eyeball*, fix, focus, gape at, gawk, gaze, glare, goggle*, lay eyes on*, leer, look, look fixedly, make eyes at, peer, rivet, rubberneck*, watch; SEE CONCEPT *623*

ogre [*n*] *nasty person*
demon, devil, fiend, giant, monster, monstrosity, specter, troll; SEE CONCEPT *412*

oil [*v*] *lubricate*
anoint, coat, grease, lard, lube, pomade, slick, smear; SEE CONCEPTS *172,256*

oily [*adj1*] *fatty, greasy*
adipose, buttery, creamy, lardy, lubricant, lubricative, lubricous, lustrous, oiled, oil-soaked, oleaginous, polished, rich, saponaceous, sleek, slippery, smeary, smooth, soapy, soothing, swimming, unctuous, waxy; SEE CONCEPTS *603,606*

oily [*adj2*] *flattering*
bland*, cajoling, coaxing, compliant, fulsome, glib, gushing*, hypocritical, ingratiating, insinuating, obsequious, plausible, servile, slick, smarmy*, smooth, smooth-tongued*, suave, supple, unctuous; SEE CONCEPTS *267,401*

ointment [*n*] *cream for treatment*
balm, cerate, demulcent, dressing, embrocation, emollient, lenitive, liniment, lotion, medicine, salve, unguent; SEE CONCEPTS *311,466*

okay [*adj*] *acceptable, satisfactory*
accurate, adequate, all right, approved, convenient, correct, fair, fine, good, in order, middling, not bad, passable, permitted, so-so*, surely, tolerable; SEE CONCEPT *558*

okay [*n*] *agreement*
acceptance, affirmation, approbation, approval, assent, authorization, benediction, blessing, consent, endorsement, favor, go-ahead*, green light*, permission, sanction, say-so*, seal of approval*, yes; SEE CONCEPT *684*

okay [*v*] *agree to*
accept, accredit, approve, authorize, certify, condone, confirm, consent to, endorse, give one's consent, give the go-ahead*, give the green light*, notarize, pass, rubber-stamp*, sanction, say yes to; SEE CONCEPTS *10,50,88*

old [*adj1*] *advanced in age*
aged, along in years*, ancient, broken down*, debilitated, decrepit, elderly, enfeebled, exhausted, experienced, fossil*, geriatric, getting on*, gray, gray-haired*, grizzled*, hoary*, impaired, inactive, infirm, mature, matured, not young, olden, oldish, over the hill*, past one's prime*, seasoned, senile, senior, skilled, superannuated, tired, venerable, versed, veteran, wasted*; SEE CONCEPTS *578,797*

old [*adj2*] *obsolete, outdated*
aboriginal, age-old, antediluvian, antiquated, antique, archaic, bygone, cast-off, crumbling, dated, decayed, demode, done, early, erstwhile, former, hackneyed*, immemorial, late, motheaten*, of old, of yore, olden, oldfangled, old-fashioned, old-time, once, onetime, original, outmoded, out-of-date, passé, past, primeval, primitive, primordial, pristine, quondam, relic, remote, rusty, sometime, stale, superannuated, time-worn, traditional, unfashionable, unoriginal, venerable, worn-out; SEE CONCEPTS *558,560,799*

old [*adj3*] *traditional, long-established*
age-old, constant, continuing, enduring, established, experienced, familiar, firm, hardened, inveterate, lifelong, long-lasting, long-lived, of long standing, perennial, perpetual, practiced, skilled, solid, staying, steady, time-honored, versed, veteran, vintage; SEE CONCEPTS *482,530,798*

old age [*n*] *latter part of animate life*
advancing years*, age, agedness, autumn of life*, caducity, debility, declining years*, decrepitude, dotage, elderliness, evening of life*, feebleness, golden age*, golden years*, infirmity, second childhood*, senectitude, senescence, senility, years; SEE CONCEPTS *715,817*

old country [*n*] *native land*
fatherland, homeland, mother country, motherland, the old country*; SEE CONCEPT *516*

older [*adj*] *most senior*
earlier, elder, eldest, first, first-born, former, lower, of a former period, of an earlier time, preceding, prior, senior; SEE CONCEPTS *578,585,797*

old-fashioned [*adj*] *outmoded, obsolete*
ancient, antiquated, antique, archaic, behind the times*, bygone, corny*, dated, dead*, demode, demoded, disapproved, dowdy*, extinct, grown old, moldy*, musty, neglected, not current, not modern, not with it*, obsolescent, odd*, of old, of olden days*, of the old school*, olden, oldfangled*, old-hat*, old-time, out*, outdated, out-of-date, out of it*, out-of-style, outworn, passé*, past, primitive, rococo*, superannuated, unfashionable, unstylish, vintage; SEE CONCEPTS *578,589,797,799*

old hand [*n*] *person experienced in something*
expert, longtimer, old guard*, old school*, old-timer*, pro*, vet*, veteran; SEE CONCEPT *423*

old school [*adj*] *traditional*
acceptable, accustomed, classic, classical, conservative, conventional, customary, habitual, long-established, old, old line, popular, regular, rooted, time-honored; SEE CONCEPTS *530,533*

old-timer [*n*] *elderly person*
fossil*, geezer*, golden-ager, gramps*, mossback, old dog*, old hand, old soldier, senior, veteran, war-horse; SEE CONCEPT *424*

old wives' tale [*n*] *superstition*
fairy story, fallacy, false belief, folklore, folk tale, legend, lore, myth, notion, tall story, tall tale; SEE CONCEPTS *282,689*

oligarchic [*adj*] *governed by small group*
cabalistic, cliquey*, elite, exclusive, select; SEE CONCEPTS *554,568*

omen [*n*] *sign of something to come*
augury, auspice, bodement, boding, foreboding, foretoken, harbinger, indication, portent, premonition, presage, prognostic, prognostication, prophecy, straw, warning, writing on the wall*; SEE CONCEPTS *74,278,689*

of
om

ominous [*adj*] *menacing, foreboding*
apocalyptic, augural, baleful, baneful, clouded, dangerous, dark, dire, direful, dismal, doomed, doomful, fateful, fearful, forbidding, gloomy, grim, haunting, hostile, ill-boding, ill-fated, impending, inauspicious, inhospitable, lowering, malefic, malificent, malign, minatory, perilous, portentous, precursive, premonitory, presaging, prescient, prophetic, sinister, suggestive, threatening, unfriendly, unlucky, unpromising, unpropitious; SEE CONCEPT *548*

omission [*n*] *something forgotten or excluded*
blank, breach, break, cancellation, carelessness, chasm, cutting out, default, disregard, disregardance, elimination, elision, excluding, exclusion, failing, failure, forgetfulness, gap, hiatus, ignoring, inadvertence, inadvertency, lack, lacuna, lapse, leaving out, missing, neglect, noninclusion, overlook, overlooking, oversight, passing over, preclusion, preterition, pretermission, prohibition, repudiation, skip, slighting, slip, withholding; SEE CONCEPTS *25,116,699*

omit [*v*] *exclude, forget*
bar, blink at*, bypass, cancel, cast aside, count out, cut, cut out, delete, discard, dismiss, disregard, drop, edit, eliminate, evade, except, fail, ignore, knock off, leave out, leave undone, let go, let slide*, miss, miss out, neglect, overlook, overpass, pass by, pass over, preclude, prohibit, reject, repudiate, skip, slight, snip, trim, void, withhold, X-out*; SEE CONCEPTS *25,121,211*

omitted [*adj*] *excluded*
absent, deleted, erased, expunged, forgotten, left out, missing, neglected, overlooked, precluded; SEE CONCEPTS *121,211*

omnipotent [*adj*] *all-powerful*
almighty, divine, godlike, mighty, supreme, unlimited, unrestricted; SEE CONCEPT *574*

omnipresent [*adj*] *all-present*
everywhere, infinite, pervading, pervasive, ubiquitary, ubiquitous, universal; SEE CONCEPT *583*

omniscient [*adj*] *all-knowing*
all-seeing, almighty, infinite, knowledgeable, pansophical, preeminent, wise; SEE CONCEPT *402*

on [*adv*] *in contact; ahead of*
about, above, adjacent, against, approaching, at, beside, close to, covering, forth, forward, held, leaning on, near, next, on top of, onward, over, resting on, situated on, supported, touching, toward, upon, with; SEE CONCEPTS *585,586,750*

on and off [*adv*] *intermittently*
at intervals, at times, discontinuously, every now and then, every once in a while, every so often, from time to time, hardly, infrequently, intermittently, irregularly, now and again, now and then, occasionally, off and on, once in a blue moon*, once in a while, on occasion, periodically, sometimes, sporadically; SEE CONCEPTS *530,541*

on and on [*adv*] *continuously*
ad nauseam, constantly, forever, never-ending, perpetually, relentlessly, repeatedly, steadily, unceasingly, unremittingly; SEE CONCEPTS *534,798*

on call [*adj*] *standing by*
accessible, at hand, at one's fingertip, night call, on alert, on the spot, prepared, within reach; SEE CONCEPT *576*

once [*adj/adv*] *in the past; occurred one time only*
already, a single time, at one time, away back, back, back when, before, but once, bygone, earlier, erstwhile, formerly, heretofore, in the old days, in the olden days, in times gone by, in times past, late, long ago, old, once only, once upon a time, one, one time before, one time previously, only one time, on one occasion, previously, quondam, sometime, this time, time was, whilom; SEE CONCEPTS *799,820*

once and for all [*adv*] *finally*
after all, at last, at long last*, at the end, conclusively, in conclusion, in the end, it's about time*, sooner or later*; SEE CONCEPT *799*

once in a while [*adv*] *occasionally*
at intervals, at times, every now and then, every so often, from time to time, hardly, infrequently, irregularly, now and again, once in a blue moon*, on occasion, periodically, rarely, seldom, sometimes, sporadically; SEE CONCEPTS *530,541*

oncoming [*adj*] *impending*
advancing, approaching, coming, expected, forthcoming, imminent, looming, nearing, onrushing, upcoming; SEE CONCEPTS *548,799*

on duty [*adj*] *working*
busy, clocked in*, engaged, in a job, in gear, laboring, obliged, on the job, punched in*; SEE CONCEPTS *538,560*

one [*adj*] *individual*
alone, definite, different, lone, odd, one and only, only, particular, peculiar, precise, separate, single, singular, sole, solitary, special, specific, uncommon, unique; SEE CONCEPTS *577,762,789*

one by one [*adv*] *in succession*
gradually, individually, little by little, one at a time, singly, step by step; SEE CONCEPTS *544,588,799*

on edge [*adj*] *tense*
agitated, anxious, apprehensive, beside oneself*, bundle of nerves*, edgy, excited, fidgety, highstrung*, hyper*, impatient, in a tizzy*, jittery, jumpy, keyed up*, nerve-racking, nervous, nervous wreck*, overanxious, restless, stressful, unnerved, uptight, wired*, worried, wound up*; SEE CONCEPTS *401,403,548*

onerous [*adj*] *difficult; requiring hard labor*
arduous, austere, backbreaking, burdensome, crushing, cumbersome, demanding, difficult, distressing, embittering, exacting, excessive, exhausting, exigent, fatiguing, formidable, galling, grave, grinding, grueling, hard*, harsh, headache, heavy*, intolerable, irksome, laborious, merciless, oppressive, overpowering, overtaxing, painful, plodding, ponderous, pressing, responsible, rigorous, serious, severe, strenuous, taxing, tiresome, tiring, toilsome, troublesome, vexatious, weighty; SEE CONCEPTS *538,565*

one-sided [*adj*] *biased*
colored, discriminatory, favorably, inclined, influenced, partisan, predisposed, prejudiced, unequal, unfair, unjust; SEE CONCEPTS *403,542*

one-track mind [*n*] *obsession*
attraction, compulsion, fascination, fixation, hang-up*, infatuation, passion, preoccupation, tunnel vision; SEE CONCEPTS *20,410,529,689,690*

ongoing [*adj*] *continuous*
advancing, continuing, current, developing, evolving, extant, growing, heading, in process, in progress, marching, open-ended, progressing, successful, unfinished, unfolding; SEE CONCEPTS *482,798*

on guard [*adj*] *defensive*
alert, averting, cautious, checking, defending, expectant, guarding, preservative, preventive, protecting, safeguarding, vigilant, warding off, watchful, withstanding; SEE CONCEPTS *401,550*

on-line [*adj*] *electronically connected*
accessible by computer, installed, linked, networked, on stream*, operative, plugged in, ready for use, wired; SEE CONCEPT *274*

onlooker [*n*] *person observing an event*
beholder, bystander, eyewitness, looker-on, observer, sightseer, spectator, viewer, watcher, witness; SEE CONCEPT *423*

only [*adj*] *singular*
alone, apart, by oneself, exclusive, individual, isolated, lone, matchless, once in a lifetime, one, one and only, one shot, onliest, particular, peerless, single, sole, solitary, solo, unaccompanied, unequaled, unique, unparalleled, unrivaled; SEE CONCEPT *577*

only [*adv*] *barely; exclusively*
alone, at most, but, entirely, hardly, just, merely, nothing but, particularly, plainly, purely, simply, solely, totally, uniquely, utterly, wholly; SEE CONCEPTS *535,772*

on paper [*adv*] *in theory*
abstractly, conceivably, hypothetically, theoretically; SEE CONCEPT *529*

on purpose [*adv*] *deliberately*
after consideration, by design, calculatingly, consciously, designed, freely, in cold blood, intentionally, knowingly, premeditatively, purposely, purposively, voluntarily, willfully, with eyes wide open*, wittingly; SEE CONCEPTS *401,542*

onrush [*n*] *rush*
attack, avalanche, blitz, charge, dash, deluge, flood, flow, flux, haste, hastiness, hurriedness, hurry, onslaught, push, race, scramble, stampede, storm, stream, surge, swiftness; SEE CONCEPTS *145,748,818*

onset [*n*] *beginning; attack*
access, aggression, assailment, assault, birth, charge, commencement, dawn, dawning, encounter, inception, incipience, kickoff*, offense, offensive, onfall, onrush, onslaught, opening, origin, outbreak, outset, outstart, rush, seizure, start; SEE CONCEPTS *86,221,832*

onslaught [*n*] *attack*
aggression, assailment, assault, blitz, charge, incursion, invasion, offense, offensive, onfall, onrush, onset; SEE CONCEPT *86*

on the ball [*adj*] *alert*
active, all ears*, attentive, bright, cagey*, careful, clever, good hands*, heads up*, intelligent, lively, observant, on guard*, on one's toes*, on the job*, on the lookout*, on the stick*, perceptive, quick, ready, sharp, spirited, vigilant, watchful, wise, with it*; SEE CONCEPTS *402,403*

on the blink [*adj*] *broken*
busted, defective, disabled, down, fallen apart, faulty, gone to pieces*, haywire, in disrepair, in need of repair, inoperable, in the shop*, kaput*, not functioning, not working, on the fritz*, on the shelf*, out, out of commission*, out of kilter*, out of order, out of whack*, run-down, shot, spent, wrecked; SEE CONCEPTS *485,560*

on the double [*adv*] *quickly*
chop-chop*, expeditiously, fast, flat-out*, fleetly, full tilt*, hastily, hurriedly, in a flash*, in haste, lickety-split*, like a shot*, like greased lightning*, like wildfire*, promptly, pronto, quick, rapidly, swift, swiftly; SEE CONCEPTS *588,799*

on the fence [*adj*] *undecided*
ambivalent, betwixt and between*, blowing hot and cold*, borderline, debatable, divided, hemming and hawing*, hesitant, iffy*, impartial, indecisive, in the middle*, irresolute, neutral, not definite, not sure, of two minds*, open, running hot and cold*, tentative, torn, uncertain, unclear, uncommitted, undetermined, unsure, up in the air*, waffling, wavering, wishy-washy*; SEE CONCEPTS *403,529*

on the house [*adj*] *free*
chargeless, complimentary, compliments of the house, costless, for nothing, for the asking, freebie*, free of cost, free ride*, gratis, gratuitous, no charge, on the cuff*; SEE CONCEPT *334*

on the level [*adj*] *legitimate*
aboveboard, accepted, accredited, authentic, authorized, for real*, honest, lawful, official, on the up and up, proper, sanctioned, straight, true, valid, verifiable; SEE CONCEPTS *319,558,582*

on the wagon [*adj*] *sober*
abstaining, abstemious, abstinent, cold sober*, dry, drying out, nonindulgent, not drinking, not drunk, not partaking of alcohol, restrained, took the pledge*; SEE CONCEPT *401*

onus [*n*] *burden*
bar sinister*, black eye*, blame, blot, blur, brand, charge, culpability, deadweight*, duty, encumbrance, fault, guilt, incubus, liability, load, millstone*, obligation, odium, oppression, responsibility, slur, spot, stain, stigma, task, tax, weight; SEE CONCEPTS *388,674*

onward/onwards [*adv*] *ahead, beyond*
alee, along, forth, forward, in front, in front of, moving, on, on ahead; SEE CONCEPTS *585,778*

oodles [*n*] *a lot*
abundance, billions, gobs*, heaps*, large number, loads, lots, many, masses, millions, piles*, plenty, scads*, thousands, tons, zillions; SEE CONCEPTS *432,786*

oomph [*n*] *energy*
animation, ardor, birr, dash, drive, effectiveness, endurance, exertion, fire, force, forcefulness, fortitude, get-up-and-go*, go, hardihood, initiative, intensity, juice, life, liveliness, might, moxie*, muscle, pep, pizzazz, pluck, potency, power, punch, spirit, stamina, steam, strength, vigor, vim, virility, vitality, zeal, zest, zing, zip; SEE CONCEPT *411*

ooze [*n*] *liquid emitted*
alluvium, fluid, glop*, goo*, gook*, gunk*, mire, muck*, mud, silt, slime*, sludge; SEE CONCEPTS *466,467*

ooze [*v*] *emit liquid*
bleed, discharge, drain, dribble, drip, drop, escape, exude, filter, flow, issue, leach, leak, overflow, percolate, perspire, seep, spurt, strain, sweat, swelter, trickle, weep, well; SEE CONCEPT *179*

opaque [*adj1*] *clouded, muddy*
blurred, cloudy, dark, darkened, dim, dirty, dull, dusky, filmy, foggy, frosty, fuliginous, gloomy, hazy, impenetrable, lusterless, misty, muddied, murky, nontranslucent, nontransparent, nubilous, obfuscated, shady, smoky, sooty, thick, turbid; SEE CONCEPTS *606,617,618*

om
op

opaque [*adj2*] *hard to understand*
abstruse, amphibological, arcane, baffling, concealed, cryptic, difficult, enigmatic, equivocal, imperceptive, incomprehensible, nubilous, obscure, obtuse, perplexing, purblind, tenebrous, uncertain, unclear, unfathomable, unintelligible, vague; SEE CONCEPT *529*

open [*adj1*] *unfastened, unclosed*
accessible, agape, airy, ajar, bare, clear, cleared, dehiscent, disclosed, emptied, expanded, expansive, exposed, extended, extensive, free, gaping, made passable, naked, navigable, passable, patent, patulous, peeled, removed, rent, revealed, ringent, rolling, spacious, spread out, stripped, susceptible, unbarred, unblocked, unbolted, unburdened, uncluttered, uncovered, unfolded, unfurled, unimpeded, unlocked, unobstructed, unplugged, unsealed, unshut, unstopped, vacated, wide, yawning; SEE CONCEPTS *485,576*

open [*adj2*] *accessible; not forbidden*
admissible, agreeable, allowable, approachable, appropriate, attainable, available, employable, fit, free, general, getable*, nondiscriminatory, not posted, obtainable, on deck*, on tap*, open-door*, operative, permitted, practicable, proper, public, reachable, securable, suitable, to be had*, unconditional, unoccupied, unqualified, unrestricted, usable, vacant, welcoming, within reach; SEE CONCEPTS *560,576*

open [*adj3*] *clear, obvious*
apparent, avowed, barefaced, blatant, conspicuous, downright, evident, flagrant, frank, manifest, noticeable, overt, plain, unconcealed, undisguised, visible, well-known; SEE CONCEPTS *267,535*

open [*adj4*] *undecided*
ambiguous, arguable, controversial, debatable, doubtful, dubious, dubitable, equivocal, indecisive, in question, moot, problematic, questionable, uncertain, unresolved, unsettled, up for discussion*, up in the air*, yet to be decided*; SEE CONCEPTS *267,529*

open [*adj5*] *honest, objective*
artless, candid, disinterested, fair, frank, free, guileless, impartial, ingenuous, innocent, lay it on the line*, mellow, natural, objective, on the level*, open-and-shut*, openhearted*, plain, receptive, sincere, straightforward, talking turkey*, transparent, unbiased, uncommitted, unconcealed, undisguised, undissembled, unprejudiced, unreserved, up-front*; SEE CONCEPTS *267,542*

open [*v1*] *begin*
begin business, bow, commence, convene, embark, get things rolling*, inaugurate, initiate, jump, kick off, launch, meet, raise the curtain*, ring in*, set in motion, set up shop*, sit, start, start the ball rolling*; SEE CONCEPT *221*

open [*v2*] *clear, expose; spread*
bare, break in, break out, broach, burst, bust in, come apart, crack, disclose, display, disrupt, expand, fissure, free, gap, gape, hole, jimmy, kick in, lacerate, lance, penetrate, perforate, pierce, pop, puncture, release, reveal, rupture, separate, sever, slit, slot, split, tap, throw wide, unbar, unblock, unbolt, unclose, unclothe, uncork, uncover, undo, unfasten, unfold, unfurl, unlatch, unlock, unroll, unseal, unshut, unstop, untie, unwrap, vent, ventilate, yawn, yawp; SEE CONCEPTS *135,250,469*

open-and-shut [*adj*] *obvious*
apparent, cinched, clear, clear as a bell*, conclusive, cut and dried, distinguishable, easy, evident, explicit, glaring, indisputable, ordinary, plain, routine, self-evident, self-explanatory, simple, straightforward, undeniable, undisguised, unmistakable; SEE CONCEPTS *485,529*

openhanded [*adj*] *generous*
altruistic, benevolent, big, big-hearted, bountiful, charitable, considerate, giving, helpful, hospitable, kind, kindhearted, kindly, liberal, magnanimous, philanthropic, thoughtful, unselfish; SEE CONCEPTS *404,542*

openhearted [*adj1*] *frank*
aboveboard, bare-faced*, blunt, candid, direct, downright, forthright, from the hip*, honest, lay it on the line*, like it is*, matter-of-fact, open, plain, plainspoken, saying what one thinks*, sincere, straight, straightforward, truthful, up front*; SEE CONCEPTS *267,582*

openhearted [*adj2*] *kindly*
benevolent, compassionate, friendly, generous, good, good-hearted, gracious, humane, kind, kindhearted, neighborly, sympathetic, thoughtful; SEE CONCEPTS *404,542*

opening [*n1*] *gap, hole*
aperture, breach, break, cavity, chink, cleft, crack, cranny, crevice, cut, discontinuity, door, fissure, hatch, interstice, mouth, orifice, outlet, perforation, recess, rent, rift, rupture, scuttle, slit, slot, space, split, spout, tear, vent, window; SEE CONCEPT *513*

opening [*n2*] *chance*
availability, big break*, connection, cut*, fling*, go*, go-at*, in the running*, iron in the fire*, look-in*, occasion, opportunity, place, possibility, run, scope, shot*, show, squeak*, time, vacancy, whack*; SEE CONCEPT *693*

opening [*n3*] *beginning*
birth, coming out, commencement, curtain-raiser*, dawn, inauguration, inception, initiation, kickoff, launch, launching, onset, opener, outset, start; SEE CONCEPT *832*

openly [*adv*] *honestly*
aboveboard, artlessly, blatantly, brazenly, candidly, face to face, flagrantly, forthrightly, frankly, fully, honestly, in broad daylight, in full view, ingenuously, in public, in the open, naively, naturally, plainly, publicly, readily, shamelessly, simply, straight, unabashedly, unashamedly, under one's nose*, unhesitatingly, unreservedly, wantonly, warts and all*, willingly, without pretense, without reserve; SEE CONCEPTS *267,544*

open-minded [*adj*] *receptive*
acceptant, acceptive, approachable, broad-minded, impartial, interested, observant, open to suggestions, perceptive, persuadable, swayable, tolerant, unbiased, understanding; SEE CONCEPT *404*

operable [*adj*] *possible*
achievable, conceivable, doable, feasible, obtainable, practicable, realizable, serviceable, viable, workable; SEE CONCEPTS *528,552,576*

operate [*v1*] *perform, function*
accomplish, achieve, act, act on, advance, behave, be in action, bend, benefit, bring about, burn, carry on, click*, compel, complete, concern, conduct, contact, contrive, convey, cook*, determine, direct, do, enforce, engage, exert, fin-

ish, fulfill, get results, go, hit*, hum, influence, keep, lift, move, ordain, percolate, proceed, produce, produce a result, progress, promote, react, revolve, roll, run, serve, spin, take, tick, transport, turn, work; SEE CONCEPTS *91,680,706*

operate [*v2*] *manage, use*
administer, be in charge, be in driver's seat*, be in saddle*, call the play*, call the shots*, call the signals*, carry on, command, conduct, drive, handle, hold the reins*, keep, make go*, maneuver, manipulate, ordain, pilot, play, ply, pull the strings*, pull the wires*, run, run the show*, run things*, sit on top of*, steer, wield, work; SEE CONCEPTS *94,117,148*

operate [*v3*] *perform surgery*
amputate, carve up, cut, excise, explore, open up, remove, set, transplant, treat; SEE CONCEPT *310*

operation [*n1*] *movement, working*
act, action, activity, affair, agency, application, ballgame*, bit, carrying on, conveyance, course, deal, deed, doing, effect, effort, employment, engagement, enterprise, exercise, exercising, exertion, exploitation, force, handiwork, happening, influence, instrumentality, labor, manipulation, motion, movement, performance, play, procedure, proceeding, process, progress, progression, scene, service, transaction, transference, trip, undertaking, use, work, workmanship; SEE CONCEPTS *658,680*

operation [*n2*] *business concern*
affair, deal, enterprise, proceeding, transaction, undertaking; SEE CONCEPTS *324,325*

operation [*n3*] *surgical procedure*
biopsy, excision, surgery; SEE CONCEPT *310*

operational [*adj*] *functional*
fit, in service, in working order, operative, practicable, practical, prepared, ready, serviceable, usable, useful, viable, workable, working; SEE CONCEPT *560*

operative [*adj*] *active, functioning; influential*
accessible, alive, crucial, current, dynamic, effective, efficient, employable, functional, important, indicative, in force, in operation, key, live, open, operational, practicable, relevant, running, serviceable, significant, standing, usable, workable, working; SEE CONCEPTS *560,567*

opine [*v*] *think*
believe, conceive, conclude, declare, express an opinion, feel, guess, imagine, judge, presume, say, suggest, suppose, surmise, venture; SEE CONCEPTS *12,26*

opinion [*n*] *belief*
assessment, assumption, attitude, conception, conclusion, conjecture, estimate, estimation, eye*, fancy, feeling, guess, hypothesis, idea, imagining, impression, inclination, inference, judgment, mind, notion, persuasion, point of view, postulate, presumption, presupposition, reaction, say-so*, sentiment, slant, speculation, supposition, surmise, suspicion, take*, theorem, theory, thesis, think*, thought, view, viewpoint; SEE CONCEPT *689*

opinionated [*adj*] *believing very strongly and conveying it*
adamant, arbitrary, assertive, biased, bigoted, bossy, bullheaded*, cocksure*, cocky*, conceited, dictatorial, doctrinaire, dogmatic, hardline*, high-handed, inflexible, intransigent, locked in*, obdurate, obstinate, one-sided, oracular, overbearing, pigheaded*, positive, prag-

matic, pragmatical, prejudiced, self-assertive, set in stone*, set-on, single-minded, stubborn, tilted, uncompromising, unyielding, weighted; SEE CONCEPTS *267,404*

opium [*n*] *narcotic*
brown stuff*, codeine, dope, drug, heroin, hypnotic, morphine, opiate, papaverine, poppy, sleep-inducer, soporific, tar; SEE CONCEPT *307*

opponent [*n*] *person with whom one competes*
adversary, antagonist, anti*, aspirant, assailant, bandit*, bidder, candidate, challenger, competitor, con, contestant, counteragent, dark horse*, disputant, dissentient, enemy, entrant, foe, litigant, match, opposer, opposition, oppugnant, player, rival; SEE CONCEPT *366*

opportune [*adj*] *advantageous, lucky*
appropriate, apt, auspicious, convenient, favorable, felicitous, fit, fitting, fortuitous, fortunate, happy, helpful, pat, proper, propitious, seasonable, suitable, timely, timeous, well-timed; SEE CONCEPTS *548,572*

opportunity [*n*] *lucky chance; favorable circumstances*
befalling, break*, connection, contingency, convenience, cut*, event, excuse, fair shake*, fighting chance*, fitness, fling*, fortuity, freedom, go*, good fortune, good luck, happening, hope, hour, iron in the fire*, juncture, leisure, liberty, moment, occasion, one's move*, one's say*, one's turn*, opening, pass, prayer*, probability, relief, room, run, scope, shot*, show, space, spell, squeak, stab, the hunt*, the running*, time, turn, whack*; SEE CONCEPT *693*

oppose [*v1*] *fight, obstruct*
argue, assail, assault, attack, bar, battle, bombard, call in question, check, combat, confront, contradict, controvert, counter, counterattack, cross, debate, defy, deny, disagree, disapprove, dispute, encounter, expose, face, face down*, fight, fly in the face of*, frown at, gainsay, hinder, neutralize, not countenance, prevent, protest, resist, reverse, run counter to, search out, speak against, stand up to, take a stand, take issue, take on, taunt, thwart, turn the tables*, withstand; SEE CONCEPTS *21,54,106*

oppose [*v2*] *compare, play off*
array, confront, contrast, counter, counterbalance, face, match, pit, set against, vie; SEE CONCEPTS *73,363*

opposed/opposing [*adj*] *antagonistic, against*
against the grain*, allergic*, anti*, antipathetic, antithetical, antonymous, at cross-purposes, at odds, averse, battling, clashing, combating, conflicting, confronting, contrary, controverting, counter, crossing, defending, defensive, denying, disagreeing, disputed, disputing, dissentient, enemy, exposing, facing, gainsaying, hostile, incompatible, inimical, in opposition, irreconcilable, objecting, obstructive, opposite, protesting, repelling, restrictive, rival, up against, warring; SEE CONCEPTS *403,542,564*

opposite [*adj*] *unlike, conflicting; completely different*
adverse, antagonistic, antipodal, antipodean, antithetical, contradictory, contrapositive, contrary, contrasted, corresponding, counter, crosswise, diametric, diametrically opposed, different, differing, dissimilar, diverse, facing, flip-side*, fronting, hostile, inconsistent, independent, inimical, inverse, irreconcilable, obverse, opposed,

op
op

ornery*, paradoxical, polar, repugnant, retrograde, reverse, reversed, separate, unalike, unconnected, unrelated, unsimilar, violative, vis-à-vis; SEE CONCEPT *564*

opposite [*n*] *something completely unlike another*
adverse, antilogy, antipode, antipole, antithesis, antonym, contra*, contradiction, contrary, contrast, converse, counterpart, foil, inverse, obverse, opposition, other extreme*, other side*, other side of coin*, paradox, reverse, vice versa; SEE CONCEPT *665*

opposition [*n1*] *obstruction, antagonism*
action, antinomy, antithesis, aversion, brush, civil disobedience, clash, combat, competition, con, conflict, confronting, contention, contest, contradistinction, contraposition, contrariety, counteraction, counterattack, defense, defiance, disapproval, duel, encounter, engagement, fray, grapple, hostility, negativism, obstructiveness, opposure, oppugnancy, prevention, repugnance, repulsion, resistance, rivalry, skirmish, strife, struggle, unfriendliness, violation, war, warfare; SEE CONCEPTS *29,92,106,665*

opposition [*n2*] *person, people competing*
adversary, antagonist, disputant, enemy, foe, iconoclast, opponent, other side, rebel, rival; SEE CONCEPTS *348,366*

oppress [*v*] *depress, subdue*
abuse, afflict, aggrieve, annoy, beat down*, burden, crush, despotize, dishearten, dispirit, distress, encumber, force, handicap, harass, harry, hound*, keep down, maltreat, outrage, overcome, overload, overpower, overthrow, overwhelm, persecute, pick on, plague, press, prey on, put down, put screws to*, put the squeeze on*, put upon, ride, rule, sadden, saddle*, smother, strain, subjugate, suppress, tax, torment, torture, trample, trouble, tyrannize, vex, weigh heavy upon, worry, wrong; SEE CONCEPTS *7,14,19,133*

oppressed [*adj*] *downtrodden*
abject, abused, a slave to*, at one's feet*, at one's mercy*, burdened, destitute, distressed, enslaved, exploited, have-not, helpless, maltreated, mistreated, persecuted, subservient, suppressed, tormented, tyrannized, underfoot*, under one's thumb*; SEE CONCEPT *542*

oppression [*n*] *misery, hardship*
abuse, abusiveness, autocracy, brutality, calamity, coercion, compulsion, conquering, control, cruelty, despotism, dictatorship, domination, fascism, force, forcibleness, hardness, harshness, injury, injustice, iron hand*, maltreatment, martial law, overthrowing, persecution, severity, subduing, subjection, suffering, torment, tyrany; SEE CONCEPTS *14,320,674*

oppressive [*adj1*] *overwhelming, repressive*
backbreaking*, bleak, brutal, burdensome, confining, cruel, demanding, depressing, depressive, despotic, dictatorial, discouraging, disheartening, dismal, dispiriting, exacting, exigent, gloomy, grievous, grinding, harsh, headache*, heavy, heavy-handed*, hefty, inhuman, ironhanded*, mean, onerous, overbearing, rough going*, severe, somber, superincumbent, taxing, tough, troublesome, tyrannical, unjust, weighty; SEE CONCEPTS *537,548*

oppressive [*adj2*] *hot and humid*
airless, close, heavy, muggy, overpowering, steam bath*, steamy, sticky, stifling, stuffy, suffocating, sultry, sweat box*, torrid; SEE CONCEPT *525*

oppressor [*n*] *tyrant*
absolute ruler, authoritarian, autocrat, bully, despot, dictator, martinet, persecutor, slave driver, taskmaster; SEE CONCEPTS *354,412*

opprobrious [*adj*] *abusive, hateful*
abasing, calumniatory, contemptuous, contumelious, damaging, debasing, defamatory, defaming, denigrating, depreciative, derogative, despicable, despiteful, detractive, disgracing, dishonoring, disparaging, humiliating, hurting, injuring, injurious, insolent, insulting, invective, libeling, malevolent, malign, malignant, maligning, notorious, offending, offensive, pejorative, reproaching, reviling, scandalous, scurrilous, shaming, spiteful, truculent, vile, vitriolic, vituperative, vulgar; SEE CONCEPTS *267,404,542*

opprobrium [*n*] *disgrace*
black eye*, blemish, debasement, debasing, degradation, discredit, dishonor, disrepute, disrespect, humiliation, ignominy, ill repute, infamy, loss of honor, obloquy, shame, stain, stigma, tarnish; SEE CONCEPT *388*

oppugn [*v*] *oppose*
argue, attack, call into question, contradict, controvert, criticize, debate, shoot down, take issue; SEE CONCEPTS *21,54,106*

opt [*v*] *choose*
cull, decide, elect, exercise choice, go for*, make a selection, mark, pick, prefer, select, single out*, take; SEE CONCEPT *41*

optimal [*adj*] *optimum*
A1*, ace, best, capital, 24-carat*, choice, choicest, excellent, flawless, gilt-edge*, greatest, highest, ideal, matchless, maximum, most advantageous, most favorable, peak, peerless, perfect, select, solid gold*, superlative, top, world class*; SEE CONCEPT *574*

optimism [*n*] *state of having positive beliefs*
anticipation, assurance, brightness, buoyancy, calmness, certainty, cheer, cheerfulness, confidence, easiness, elation, encouragement, enthusiasm, exhilaration, expectation, good cheer, happiness, hopefulness, idealism, looking on bright side*, positivism, rose-colored glasses*, sanguineness, sureness, trust; SEE CONCEPTS *410,689*

optimist [*n*] *positive thinker*
dreamer, hoper, idealist, Pollyanna; SEE CONCEPT *529*

optimistic [*adj*] *believing positively*
assured, bright, buoyant, cheerful, cheering, confident, encouraged, expectant, happy, high, hopeful, hoping, idealistic, keeping the faith, merry, on cloud nine*, on top of world*, positive, promising, ray of sunshine*, rose-colored*, rosy, sanguine, sunny*, trusting, upbeat, Utopian; SEE CONCEPTS *404,542*

optimum [*adj*] *best*
A1*, ace, capital, -carat*, choice, choicest, excellent, flawless, gilt-edge*, greatest, highest, ideal, matchless, maximum, most advantageous, most favorable, optimal, peak, peerless, perfect, select, solid gold*, superlative, world class*; SEE CONCEPT *574*

option [*n*] *alternative*
advantage, benefit, choice, claim, dibs*, dilemma, discretion, druthers, election, flipside*, franchise, free will*, grant, license, opportunity,

other side of coin*, pickup, preference, prerogative, privilege, right, selection, take it or leave it*; SEE CONCEPTS *376,712*

optional [*adj*] *possible; available as choice*
alternative, arbitrary, discretional, discretionary, elective, extra, facultative, free, noncompulsory, nonobligatory, no strings attached*, not required, open, unforced, unrestricted, up to the individual, volitional, voluntary; SEE CONCEPTS *552,576*

opulence [*n*] *wealth*
abundance, affluence, belongings, excess, fortune, goods, lap of luxury, lavishness, luxury, means, money, plenitude, possessions, property, prosperity, prosperousness, riches, stocks and bonds, substance, substantiality; SEE CONCEPTS *340,710*

opulent [*adj*] *rich, luxurious, profuse*
abundant, affluent, copious, deluxe, extravagant, exuberant, frilly*, lavish, luscious, luxuriant, moneyed, ostentatious, palatial, plentiful, plush, pretentious, prodigal, profusive, prolific, prosperous, rich, riotous, showy, sumptuous, swank, upholstered*, velvet*, wealthy, well-heeled*, well-off*, well-to-do*; SEE CONCEPTS *334,589,781*

opus [*n*] *great work of writing or music*
composition, creation, magnum opus, music, oeuvre, piece, product, production; SEE CONCEPTS *263,271*

oracle [*n*] *prophecy*
answer, apocalypse, augury, canon, commandment, divination, edict, fortune, law, prediction, prognostication, revelation, vision; SEE CONCEPTS *70,278,689*

oracular [*adj*] *prophetic*
ambiguous, anticipating, apocalyptic, arcane, auguring, auspicious, authoritative, cabalistic, clairvoyant, cryptic, Delphian, discovering, divining, divulging, dogmatic, fatidic, foreboding, forecasting, foretelling, imperious, interpretive, mantic, mysterious, mystical, obscure, occult, ominous, peremptory, portending, portentous, positive, predicting, presaging, prescient, proclaiming, prognosticating, prophesying, sage, secret, sibylline, significant, soothsaying, vague, vatic, venerable, wise; SEE CONCEPT *267*

oral [*adj*] *spoken*
articulate, ejaculatory, lingual, narrated, phonated, phonetic, phonic, recounted, related, said, sonant, sounded, told, unwritten, uttered, verbal, viva voce, vocal, voiced, word-of-mouth; SEE CONCEPT *267*

orange [*n/adj*] *combination of red and yellow*
apricot, bittersweet, cantaloupe, carrot, coral, peach, red-yellow, salmon, tangerine, titian; SEE CONCEPTS *618,622*

orate [*v*] *speak*
address, expound, grandstand, lecture, moralize, pontificate, preach, sermonize, talk, vociferate; SEE CONCEPTS *60,285*

oration [*n*] *speech*
address, chalk talk*, declamation, discourse, harangue, homily, lecture, pep talk*, pitch*, sermon, soapbox*, spiel*; SEE CONCEPTS *266,278*

orator [*n*] *speaker*
declaimer, lector, lecturer, pontificator, preacher, public speaker, reciter, rhetorician, sermonizer; SEE CONCEPTS *60,285*

oratory [*n*] *public speaking*
articulation, declamation, diction, elocution, elo-

quence, grandiloquence, rhetoric, speaking, speech, speechifying, speechmaking; SEE CONCEPTS *60,285*

orb [*n*] *globe*
ball, circle, eye*, lamp, ring, rondure, round, sphere; SEE CONCEPT *436*

orbit [*n1*] *circuit, revolution*
apogee, circle, circumgyration, course, curve, cycle, ellipse, lap, locus, path, pattern, perigee, rotation, round, track, trajectory; SEE CONCEPTS *436,738*

orbit [*n2*] *influence, domain*
ambit, area, arena, boundary, bounds, career, circle, circumference, compass, course, department, dominion, extension, extent, field, jurisdiction, limit, pilgrimage, precinct, province, purview, radius, range, reach, realm, scope, sphere, sweep; SEE CONCEPTS *349,673,687*

orchard [*n*] *fruit farm*
fruit garden, garden, grove, plantation, vineyard; SEE CONCEPTS *449,509,517*

orchestra [*n*] *symphony*
band, ensemble, group, sinfonietta; SEE CONCEPT *294*

orchestrate [*v*] *organize; cause to happen*
arrange, blend, compose, concert, coordinate, harmonize, integrate, manage, present, put together, score, set up, symphonize, synthesize, unify; SEE CONCEPTS *117,242*

ordain [*v*] *establish, install*
anoint, appoint, bless, call, commission, consecrate, constitute, deal, deal with, decree, delegate, destine, dictate, elect, enact, enjoin, fix, frock, impose, institute, invest, lay down the law*, legislate, nominate, order, prescribe, pronounce, put foot down*, rule, set, walk heavy*, will; SEE CONCEPTS *18,50,88,317*

ordeal [*n*] *trouble, suffering*
affliction, agony, anguish, calamity, calvary, cross, crucible, difficulty, distress, nightmare, test, torment, torture, trial, tribulation, visitation; SEE CONCEPTS *674,728*

order [*n1*] *arrangement, organization*
adjustment, aligning, array, assortment, cast, categorization, classification, codification, composition, computation, disposal, disposition, distribution, establishment, form, grouping, harmony, layout, line, lineup, management, method, neatness, ordering, orderliness, pattern, placement, plan, procedure, procession, progression, propriety, regularity, regulation, rule, scale, scheme, sequence, series, setup, standardization, structure, succession, symmetry, system, tidiness, uniformity; SEE CONCEPT *727*

order [*n2*] *lawfulness*
calm, control, decorousness, decorum, discipline, goodness, integrity, law, law and order, niceness, orderliness, peace, peacefulness, probity, properness, propriety, quiet, rectitude, rightness, seemliness, suitability, tranquility, uprightness; SEE CONCEPTS *633,691*

order [*n3*] *class, status*
bracket, branch, breed, cast, caste, degree, description, estate, family, feather, genre, genus, grade, hierarchy, ilk, kidney, kind, line, nature, pecking order*, pigeonhole*, place, position, rank, set, slot, sort, species, station, stripe, subclass, taxonomic group, type; SEE CONCEPT *378*

order [*n4*] *command*
authorization, behest, bidding, charge, com-

op
or

mandment, decree, dictate, direction, directive, injunction, instruction, law, mandate, ordinance, permission, precept, regulation, rule, say-so*, stipulation, ukase, word*; SEE CONCEPTS *53,278,685*

order [*n5*] *request; purchase agreement*
amount, application, booking, bulk, commission, engagement, goods, materials, purchase, quantity, requisition, reservation, reserve, shipment, stipulation; SEE CONCEPTS *332,338,684*

order [*n6*] *organization*
association, brotherhood, club, community, company, fraternity, guild, league, lodge, sect, sisterhood, society, sodality, sorority, union; SEE CONCEPT *387*

order [*v1*] *command, authorize*
adjure, apply for, bid, book, buy, call for, call the shots*, call the signals*, charge, contract for, decree, dictate, direct, enact, engage, enjoin, hire, instruct, obtain, ordain, prescribe, pull strings*, request, require, reserve, rule the roost*, secure, send away for, tell, warn; SEE CONCEPTS *50,53,88,327*

order [*v2*] *arrange, organize*
adapt, adjust, align, alphabetize, array, assign, catalogue, class, classify, codify, conduct, control, dispose, distribute, establish, file, fix, formalize, furnish, group, index, lay out, line, line up, locate, manage, marshal, methodize, neaten, normalize, pattern, place, plan, put away, put to rights*, range, regiment, regularize, regulate, right, routine, set guidelines, set in order, settle, sort out, space, standardize, streamline, systematize, tabulate, tidy; SEE CONCEPTS *84,158*

order about [*v*] *dominate*
boss, bully, call the shots*, command, control, dictate, direct, influence, keep under one's thumb*, manage, master, run the show*; SEE CONCEPTS *94,117,298*

ordered [*adj*] *orderly*
all together, arranged, businesslike, controlled, disciplined, in good shape, in order, law-abiding, methodical, neat, organized, peaceable, precise, shipshape*, systematic, systematized, tidy, well-behaved, well-organized; SEE CONCEPTS *326,485,585,589*

orderly [*adj1*] *methodical, organized*
alike, all together, arranged, businesslike, careful, clean, conventional, correct, exact, fixed, formal, framed, in apple-pie order*, in good shape, in order, in shape, methodic, neat, neat as button*, neat as pin*, precise, regular, regulated, scientific, set-up, shipshape*, slick, spick-and-span*, systematic, systematized, thorough, tidy, together, to rights*, trim, uncluttered, uniform; SEE CONCEPTS *326,485,585,589*

orderly [*adj2*] *well-behaved*
at peace, calm, controlled, decorous, disciplined, docile, law-abiding, manageable, nonviolent, obedient, peaceable, quiet, restrained, submissive, tranquil, well-mannered; SEE CONCEPT *401*

ordinance [*n*] *law, rule*
authorization, canon, code, command, decree, dictum, direction, edict, enactment, fiat, mandate, order, precept, prescript, reg, regulation, ruling, statute, ukase; SEE CONCEPT *318*

ordinarily [*adv*] *usually*
as a rule, commonly, customarily, frequently, generally, habitually, in general, normally, regularly; SEE CONCEPT *530*

ordinary [*adj1*] *common, regular*
accustomed, customary, established, everyday, familiar, frequent, general, habitual, humdrum*, natural, normal, popular, prevailing, public, quotidian, routine, run-of-the-mill*, settled, standard, stock, traditional, typical, usual, wonted; SEE CONCEPTS *533,547*

ordinary [*adj2*] *average; not distinctive*
characterless, common, commonplace, conventional, dull, fair, familiar, garden*, garden variety*, generic, habitual, homespun, household, humble, indifferent, inferior, mean, mediocre, modest, no great shakes*, normal, pedestrian, plain, plastic, prosaic, quotidian, routine, runof-the-mill*, second-rate, simple, so-so*, stereotyped, undistinguished, uneventful, unexceptional, uninspired, unmemorable, unnoteworthy, unpretentious, unremarkable, usual, vanilla*, white-bread*, workaday; SEE CONCEPTS *530,575*

ordnance [*n*] *artillery*
arms, big guns*, bombs, heavy stuff*, missiles, munitions, weapons; SEE CONCEPTS *322,500*

organ [*n*] *means, tool*
agency, agent, channel, device, element, forum, implement, instrument, journal, magazine, medium, member, ministry, mouthpiece, newspaper, paper, part, periodical, process, publication, review, structure, unit, vehicle, voice, way; SEE CONCEPTS *280,499,712*

organic [*adj*] *basic, natural*
amoebic, anatomical, animate, basal, biological, biotic, cellular, constitutional, elemental, essential, fundamental, inherent, innate, integral, live, living, necessary, nuclear, original, plasmic, primary, prime, primitive, principal, structural, vital; SEE CONCEPT *549*

organism [*n*] *living thing*
animal, being, body, creature, entity, morphon, person, plant, structure; SEE CONCEPTS *389,429*

organization [*n1*] *arrangement, arranging*
alignment, assembling, assembly, chemistry, composition, configuration, conformation, constitution, construction, coordination, design, disposal, format, formation, forming, formulation, framework, grouping, harmony, institution, make-up, making, management, method, methodology, organism, organizing, pattern, plan, planning, regulation, running, situation, standard, standardization, structure, structuring, symmetry, system, unity, whole; SEE CONCEPTS *84,117,727*

organization [*n2*] *group bound by interest/work/goal*
affiliation, aggregation, alliance, association, band, body, business, cartel, circle, clique, club, coalition, combination, combine, company, concern, concord, confederation, consortium, cooperative, corporation, coterie, crew, establishment, federation, fraternity, guild, house, industry, institute, institution, league, lodge, machine, monopoly, order, outfit, party, profession, set, society, sodality, sorority, squad, syndicate, team, trade, troupe, trust, union; SEE CONCEPT *381*

organize [*v*] *arrange, systematize*
adapt, adjust, be responsible for, catalogue, classify, codify, combine, compose, constitute, construct, coordinate, correlate, create, dispose, establish, fashion, fit, form, formulate, frame, get

going*, get together, group, harmonize, lick into shape*, line up, look after, marshal, methodize, mold, pigeonhole*, put in order, put together, range, regulate, run, see to, settle, set up, shape, standardize, straighten, straighten out, tabulate, tailor, take care of, whip into shape*; SEE CONCEPTS *36,84,158*

organized [*adj*] *arranged, systematized*
catalogued, classified, coordinated, correlated, formed, formulated, grouped, methodized, standardized, straightened out, tabulated; SEE CONCEPTS *84,94*

organized crime [*n*] *the underworld*
Cosa Nostra, gangland, Mafia, mob, organized crime family, the syndicate; SEE CONCEPTS *412,645*

organizer [*n*] *planner*
arranger, coordinator, designer, developer, facilitator, promoter; SEE CONCEPT *347*

orgasm [*n*] *climax*
ejaculation, frenzy, peak, spasm; SEE CONCEPTS *706,836*

orgy [*n*] *celebration devoted to sensual enjoyment*
bacchanal, bacchanalia, bender*, binge*, blowout*, bout*, carousal, circus*, debauch, dissipation, excess, feast, fling*, indulgence, jag*, merrymaking, overindulgence, party, rampage*, revel, revelry, saturnalia, splurge, spree, surfeit, tear*; SEE CONCEPTS *377,383*

orient [*v*] *familiarize*
acclimatize, adapt, adjust, align, conform, determine, direct, get one's bearings*, locate, orientate, turn; SEE CONCEPTS *35,202*

orientation [*n*] *introduction, adjustment*
acclimatization, adaptation, assimilation, bearings, breaking in*, coordination, direction, familiarization, fix*, lay of the land*, location, position, sense of direction, settling in*; SEE CONCEPTS *31,832*

orifice [*n*] *opening*
aperture, cavity, crack, hole, mouth, outlet, slit, spout, vent, window; SEE CONCEPT *513*

origin [*n1*] *cause, basis*
agent, ancestor, ancestry, antecedent, author, base, causality, causation, connection, creator, derivation, determinant, egg*, element, embryo, fountain, generator, germ, horse's mouth*, impulse, inception, inducement, influence, inspiration, mainspring, motive, nucleus, occasion, parent, parentage, principle, producer, progenitor, provenance, provenience, root, roots, seed, source, spring, stock, well, wellspring; SEE CONCEPTS *229,648,661*

origin [*n2*] *beginning, inception*
alpha, birth, blast off, commencement, creation, dawn, dawning, day one*, early stage, embarkation, emergence, entrance, entry, forging, foundation, genesis, git go*, inauguration, ingress, initiation, introduction, launch, nativity, opener, origination, outbreak, outset, rise, square one*, start, starting point*; SEE CONCEPT *832*

origin [*n3*] *family, heritage*
ancestry, beginnings, birth, blood, descent, extraction, lineage, maternity, parentage, paternity, pedigree, stock; SEE CONCEPT *296*

original [*adj1*] *earliest*
aboriginal, archetypal, authentic, autochthonous, beginning, commencing, early, elementary, embryonic, first, first-hand, genuine, inceptive, infant, initial, introductory, opening, pioneer, primary, prime, primeval, primitive, primordial, pristine, prototypal, rudimental, rudimentary, starting, underivative, underived; SEE CONCEPTS *549,585*

original [*adj2*] *fresh, new*
avant garde, breaking new ground*, causal, causative, conceiving, creative, demiurgic, devising, envisioning, fertile, formative, generative, imaginative, ingenious, innovational, innovative, innovatory, inspiring, inventive, novel, originative, productive, quick, ready, resourceful, seminal, sensitive, unconventional, unprecedented, untried, unusual; SEE CONCEPTS *578,589,797*

original [*n1*] *standard, prototype*
archetype, coinage, creation, exemplar, forerunner, invention, model, novelty, paradigm, pattern, precedent, precursor, type; SEE CONCEPTS *260,686*

original [*n2*] *person who is eccentric*
anomaly, card*, case*, character, eccentric, nonconformist, oddball, oddity, queer, weirdo*; SEE CONCEPT *423*

originality [*n*] *creativeness*
boldness, brilliance, cleverness, creative spirit, creativity, daring, freshness, imagination, imaginativeness, individuality, ingeniousness, ingenuity, innovation, innovativeness, invention, inventiveness, modernity, new idea, newness, nonconformity, novelty, resourcefulness, spirit, unconventionality, unorthodoxy; SEE CONCEPTS *409,410*

originally [*adv*] *initially*
at first, at the outset, at the start, basically, by birth, by origin, first, formerly, incipiently, in the beginning, in the first place, primarily, primitively, to begin with; SEE CONCEPTS *578,585,797,799*

originate [*v1*] *begin; spring*
arise, be born, birth, come, come from, come into existence, commence, dawn, derive, emanate, emerge, flow, hail from, issue, proceed, result, rise, start, stem; SEE CONCEPTS *105,221*

originate [*v2*] *create, introduce*
break the ice*, bring about, cause, coin, come up with, compose, conceive, develop, discover, evolve, form, formulate, found, generate, give birth to, hatch, inaugurate, initiate, innovate, institute, invent, launch, make, open up, parent, pioneer, procreate, produce, set in motion, set up, spark, spawn, start, think up, usher in; SEE CONCEPTS *43,173,251*

origination [*n*] *origin*
beginning, birth, commencement, conception, creation, dawn, dawning, discovery, genesis, innovation, introduction, launch, source, start, starting point*; SEE CONCEPT *832*

originator [*n*] *creator*
architect, author, begetter, designer, discoverer, father, founder, initiator, innovator, inventor, maker, mastermind, mother, pioneer, producer; SEE CONCEPTS *348,352,361*

ornament [*n*] *decoration*
accessory, adornment, art, bauble, beautification, design, doodad*, embellishment, embroidery, flower, frill, frou frou*, garnish, gewgaw*, gimcrack*, gingerbread*, honor, jewel, knickknack*, pride, treasure, trimming, trinket; SEE CONCEPTS *259,476*

or
or

ornament [v] *decorate*
adorn, array, beautify, bedeck, bedizen, brighten, deck, dress, dress up*, embellish, embroider, enrich, festoon, fix up*, garnish, gild, grace, ornamentalize, polish, prank, prettify, primp, prink, smarten*, spruce up*, trim; SEE CONCEPTS *162,167,177*

ornamental [adj] *decorative*
accessory, adorning, attractive, beautiful, beautifying, decking, decorating, delicate, dressy, elaborate, embellishing, enhancing, exquisite, fancy, festooned, florid, for show*, furbishing, garnishing, heightening, luxurious, ornate, setting off*, showy; SEE CONCEPTS *579,589*

ornate [adj] *fancily decorated*
adorned, aureate, baroque, beautiful, bedecked, bright, brilliant, busy, colored, convoluted, dazzling, elaborate, elegant, embroidered, fancy, fine, flamboyant, flashy, flaunting, florid, flowery, fussy, gaudy, gilded, glamorous, glitzy, glossy, high-wrought, jeweled, lavish, luscious, magnificent, meretricious, opulent, ornamented, ostentatious, overdone, overelaborate, pretentious, resplendent, rich, rococo, showy, sparkling, splashy, sumptuous, superficial, tawdry, variegated; SEE CONCEPTS *579,589*

ornery [adj] *mean*
cantankerous, contemptible, crabby, cranky, crusty*, difficult, disagreeable, grouchy*, grumpy*, hard-nosed*, ignoble, ill-tempered, irritable, nasty, obstinate, quarrelsome, rotten, sour, surly, testy, unfriendly, vicious; SEE CONCEPTS *267,401,542*

orphan [n] *child without parents*
foundling, ragamuffin*, stray, waif; SEE CONCEPT *414*

orthodox [adj] *accepted, traditional*
according to the book*, acknowledged, admitted, approved, authoritative, buttoned-down*, by the numbers*, canonical, conformist, conservative, conventional, correct, customary, devout, diehard, doctrinal, established, in line*, legitimate, official, old-line*, pious, proper, punctilious, reactionary, received, recognized, religious, right, rightful, sanctioned, sound, square, standard, straight, straight arrow, traditional, traditionalistic, true, well-established; SEE CONCEPTS *533,558*

oscillate [v] *change back and forth*
be unsteady, dangle, fishtail, flicker, fluctuate, librate, lurch, palpitate, pendulate, pitch, pivot, reel, ripple, rock, roll, seesaw, stagger, sway, swing, switch, swivel, teeter, teeter-totter*, thrash, toss, totter, undulate, vacillate, vary, vibrate, waddle, wag, waggle, waltz, wave, waver, whirl, wiggle, wobble; SEE CONCEPTS *13,147,697*

ossified [adj] *bony*
fossilized, hard, hardened, petrified, rigid; SEE CONCEPTS *404,542*

ossify [v] *become hard from aging*
congeal, fossilize, freeze, harden, indurate, petrify, solidify, stiffen, thicken, turn to bone; SEE CONCEPT *469*

ossuary [n] *urn*
container, receptacle, vault, vessel; SEE CONCEPT *494*

ostensible [adj] *alleged, supposed*
apparent, avowed, colorable, demonstrative, exhibited, illusive, illusory, likely, manifest, notable, outward, plausible, pretended, professed, purported, quasi, seeming, semblant, so-called*, specious, superficial; SEE CONCEPTS *552,582*

ostensibly [adv] *apparently*
at first blush*, evidently, externally, for all intents and purposes*, for show*, officially, on the face*, on the surface*, outwardly, professedly, seemingly, sensibly, superficially, supposedly, to the eye*; SEE CONCEPT *582*

ostentation [n] *exhibitionism, flashiness*
affectation, array, boast, boasting, brag, braggadocio*, bragging, bravado, demonstration, display, exhibition, false front*, flamboyance, flash*, flaunting, flourish, fuss, garishness, grandstand play*, magnificence, pageant, pageantry, parade, parading, pomp, pomposity, pompousness, pretending, pretension, pretentiousness, put-on, shine*, show, showiness, showing off*, showoff*, spectacle, splendor, splurge, swagger*, swaggering, swank*, vainglory, vaunt*, vaunting*, window-dressing; SEE CONCEPTS *633,655*

ostentatious [adj] *flashy, showy*
boastful, chichi*, classy, conspicuous, crass*, dashing, egotistic, exhibitionistic, extravagant, flamboyant, flatulent, flaunted, fussy, garish, gaudy, gay, glittery, grandiose, highfaluting*, jaunty, loud, obtrusive, peacocky, pompous, pretentious, spectacular, splashy, splurgy, sporty, swank, swanky*, theatrical, tinsel*, tony*, uptown*, vain, vulgar; SEE CONCEPTS *401,589*

ostracism [n] *banishment*
avoidance, blackballing, boycott, cold-shouldering, exclusion, excommunication, exile, expulsion, isolation, rejection, shunning; SEE CONCEPTS *25,130*

ostracize [v] *exile, banish*
avoid, blackball*, blacklist*, boycott, cast out, cold-shoulder*, cut, deport, displace, drop, exclude, excommunicate, expatriate, expel, expulse, leave in the cold, oust, reject, shun, shut out, snub, throw out; SEE CONCEPTS *25,384*

other [adj1] *additional, added*
alternative, another, auxiliary, else, extra, farther, fresh, further, more, new, spare, supplementary; SEE CONCEPT *771*

other [adj2] *different*
contrasting, disparate, dissimilar, distant, distinct, divergent, diverse, opposite, otherwise, remaining, separate, unalike, unequal, unlike, unrelated, variant; SEE CONCEPT *564*

otherwise [adv] *in another way; alternatively*
any other way, contrarily, differently, diversely, elseways, if not, in different circumstances, on the other hand, or else, or then, under other conditions, variously; SEE CONCEPT *544*

otherworldly [adj] *extraterrestrial; psychic*
alien, ethereal, heavenly, magical, mystical, out of this world, spiritual, supernatural, transcendental, uncanny, unearthly, unworldly, visionary; SEE CONCEPTS *529,549,582*

ounce [n] *one-sixteenth of a pound/28.35 grams of weight*
avoirdupois, troy, uncia; SEE CONCEPT *795*

oust [v] *expel, get rid of*
banish, bereave, boot out*, bounce*, bundle off*, cast out, chase, depose, deprive, dethrone, discharge, disinherit, dislodge, displace, dispossess, divest, drive out, eject, evict, expulse, fire, force out, give the 1-2-3*, kick out, lay off, let go, lose, ostracize, pack off, pink slip*, relegate,

remove, rob, sack, send packing*, show the door*, throw out, topple, transport, turn out, unseat; SEE CONCEPTS *25,211,351*

ouster [*n*] *ejection*
banishment, disbarment, discharge, dismissal, eviction, expulsion, loss of right, overthrow, removal, sack, the heave-ho*; SEE CONCEPTS *179,222*

out [*adj*] *not possible; gone*
absent, antiquated, at an end, away, behind the times*, cold, dated, dead, demode, doused, ended, exhausted, expired, extinguished, finished, impossible, not allowed, not on, old-fashioned, old-hat*, outmoded, outside, passé, ruled out, unacceptable, unfashionable, used up; SEE CONCEPTS *539,552,576*

out [*adv*] *outside, outdoors*
out of doors, outward, without; SEE CONCEPT *583*

out-and-out [*adj*] *complete*
absolute, arrant, consummate, downright, full, outright, perfect, thorough, thoroughgoing, through-and-through, total, uncompromising, undiminished, unmitigated, unqualified, utter, whole; SEE CONCEPT *531*

outbreak [*n*] *sudden happening*
beginning, blowup, brawl, break, breaking, burst, bursting, commencement, commotion, convulsion, crack, crash, dawn, detonation, discharge, disorder, disruption, ebullition, effervescence, epidemic, eruption, explosion, fit, flare-up, flash, fury, gush, gushing, insurrection, irruption, mutiny, onset, outburst, outpouring, paroxysm, plague, rebellion, rending, revolution, roar, sally, sortie, spasm, spurt, storm, sundering, surge, thunder, tumult, uprising, volley; SEE CONCEPTS *2,86,179,832*

outburst [*n*] *fit of temper*
access, attack, blow, burst, conniption*, discharge, eruption, explosion, flare, flare-up, frenzy, gush, gust, outbreak, outpouring, paroxysm, rapture, scene, spasm, storm, surge, tantrum, transport, upheaval; SEE CONCEPT *633*

outcast [*n*] *person who is unwanted, not accepted*
bum*, castaway, deportee, derelict, displaced person, exile, expatriate, fugitive, gypsy, hobo*, persona non grata*, rascal, refugee, reprobate, tramp, untouchable, vagabond, vagrant, wretch; SEE CONCEPT *423*

outclass [*v*] *surpass*
beat, best, better, cap, dominate, eclipse, exceed, excel, go beyond, go one better*, improve upon, outdistance, outdo, outhussle, outmatch, outpace, outperform, outplay, outrank, outrival, outrun, outshine, outstrip, pass, put to shame*, rise above, surmount, top, tower, win the race; SEE CONCEPT *141*

out cold [*adj*] *unconscious*
benumbed, blacked out*, comatose, dead to the world*, down for the count*, drowsy, feeling no pain*, flattened*, in a trance, numb, on the canvas*, out, out like a light*, passed out*, put away*, senseless, zonked*; SEE CONCEPTS *314,539*

outcome [*n*] *consequence, effect*
aftereffect, aftermath, blowoff, causatum, chain reaction*, conclusion, end, end result*, event, fallout, issue, payback*, payoff*, reaction, result, score, sequel, upshot*; SEE CONCEPT *230*

outcry [*n*] *scream, exclamation*
clamor, commotion, complaint, convulsion, cry,

ferment, flak*, hoo-ha*, howl, hubba-hubba*, hullabaloo*, noise, objection, outburst, protest, screech, tumult, uproar, upturn, yell; SEE CONCEPTS *77,278*

outdated/out-of-date [*adj*] *old-fashioned*
anachronous, antiquated, antique, archaic, back number*, behind the times*, dated, démodé, dusty, has-been*, moth-eaten*, musty, not with it*, obsolete, old, old-hat*, out, outmoded, out-of-style*, passé, square, tired, unfashionable, vintage; SEE CONCEPTS *578,589,797*

outdistance [*v*] *outrun*
beat, best, better, exceed, go beyond, go one better*, leave behind, outclass, outdo, outhussle, outpace, outperform, outplay, overtake, pass, surpass, top, win the race; SEE CONCEPT *141*

outdo [*v*] *better, overcome*
beat, best, blow out of water*, bulldoze*, bury*, cook*, cream*, defeat, do in*, down*, eclipse, exceed, excel, fake out*, go one better*, leave behind*, lick*, outclass, outdistance, outfox, outgun, outjockey, outmaneuver, outrival, outshine, outsmart, outstrip, pull a fast one*, shake off*, shoot ahead*, snow*, surpass, top, transcend, trash*; SEE CONCEPTS *95,141*

outdoor [*adj/adv*] *in the open air*
alfresco, casual, free, garden, healthful, hilltop, informal, in the open, invigorating, mountain, natural, nature-loving, out-of-doors, out of the house, outside, patio, picnic, rustic, unrestricted, woods, yard; SEE CONCEPT *583*

outdoors [*n*] *open air; nature*
bucolic surroundings, country, countryside, environment, fresh air, garden, green earth*, hill, mountain, open, out-of-doors, patio, without, woods, yard; SEE CONCEPT *198*

outer [*adj*] *external, exposed*
alien, beyond, exoteric, exterior, extraneous, extrinsic, outermost, outlying, outmost, outside, outward, over, peripheral, remote, superficial, surface, without; SEE CONCEPTS *484,583*

outermost [*adj*] *outer*
beyond, distant, fringe, furthermost, outlying, outmost, outward, peripheral, remote; SEE CONCEPTS *484,583*

outfit [*n1*] *set of clothes or equipment*
accoutrements, apparatus, appliances, clothing, costume, ensemble, garb, gear, get-up*, guise, kit, machinery, materiel, outlay, paraphernalia, provisions, rig, rigging, suit, supplies, tackle, togs, trappings*, wardrobe; SEE CONCEPTS *451,496*

outfit [*n2*] *large group; business*
band, clique, company, concern, corps, coterie, crew, enterprise, establishment, firm, house, organization, party, set, squad, team, troop, troupe, unit; SEE CONCEPTS *325,417*

outfit [*v*] *clothe, equip*
accoutre, appoint, arm, deck out*, drape, fit out*, furnish, gear, prepare, provide, provision, rig up*, stock, suit, supply, tog*, turn out*; SEE CONCEPTS *167,182*

outflank [*v*] *outmaneuver*
beat, best, better, defeat, excel, outclass, outdo, outfox, outperform, outplay, outshine, outsmart, outwit, surpass, top; SEE CONCEPT *141*

outflow [*n*] *efflux*
discharge, drainage, effluence, effluent, effluvium, effusion, emergence, gush, gushing out-

pouring, rush, spout, stream, streaming; SEE CONCEPTS *179,748*

outfox [*v*] *outsmart*
best, defeat, excel, outclass, outdo, outperform, outplay, outwit, surpass, top; SEE CONCEPT *141*

outgoing [*adj1*] *demonstrative, extroverted*
approachable, civil, communicative, cordial, easy, expansive, extrovert, friendly, genial, gregarious, informal, kind, open, sociable, sympathetic, unconstrained, unreserved, unrestrained, warm; SEE CONCEPT *404*

outgoing [*adj2*] *leaving*
departing, ex-*, former, last, migratory, outbound, outward-bound, past, retiring, withdrawing; SEE CONCEPTS *581,584*

outgrowth [*n1*] *projection*
bulge, enlargement, excrescence, jut, node, offshoot, outcrop, process, prolongation, prominence, protuberance, shoot, sprout, swelling; SEE CONCEPTS *471,824*

outgrowth [*n2*] *product, consequence*
aftereffect, branch, by-product*, derivative, descendant, development, effect, emergence, end, end result*, issue, member, offshoot, offspring, outcome, result, spin-off*, yield; SEE CONCEPTS *230,260*

outhouse [*n*] *toilet*
bathroom, latrine, lavatory, outbuilding, privy, washroom, water closet, WC; SEE CONCEPT *448*

outing [*n*] *short trip*
airing, drive, excursion, expedition, jaunt, junket, long weekend, picnic, pleasure trip, roundabout, spin*, vacation, weekend; SEE CONCEPTS *224,386*

outing [*n2*] *politically motivated exposure of another's secrets*
announcement, declaration, demystification, disclosure, proclamation, revealing, tossing, uncloseting, unmasking; SEE CONCEPT *60*

outlandish [*adj*] *bizarre, strange*
alien, awkward, barbaric, barbarous, boorish, clumsy, curious, droll, eccentric, erratic, exotic, extravagant, fantastic, far-out*, foreign, freakish, gauche, graceless, grotesque, kinky*, odd, outrageous, outré, peculiar, preposterous, quaint, queer, ridiculous, rude, singular, tasteless, ultra, unconventional, uncouth, unheard-of*, unorthodox, unusual, weird, whimsical, wild; SEE CONCEPTS *401,548*

outlast [*v*] *endure beyond another*
hang on, outlive, outstay, outwear, remain, survive; SEE CONCEPT *407*

outlaw [*n*] *person who is running from the law*
bandit, brigand, con, criminal, crook, desperado, drifter, ex-con, fugitive, gangster, gunslinger*, hood*, hoodlum, hooligan*, jailbird, marauder, mobster, mug*, outcast, pariah, racketeer, robber, wrong number*; SEE CONCEPT *412*

outlaw [*v*] *prohibit; make illegal*
ban, banish, bar, condemn, damn, disallow, embargo, enjoin, exclude, forbid, illegalize, inhibit, interdict, prevent, proscribe, stop, taboo; SEE CONCEPTS *121,317*

outlay [*n*] *expenses*
bite*, bottom line*, charge, cost, damage, disbursement, expenditure, expense, highway robbery*, investment, price tag, score*, setback*, spending, tab*, throw*, tune*; SEE CONCEPT *344*

outlet [*n1*] *place or means of escape, release*
aperture, avenue, break, channel, crack, duct, egress, escape, exit, hole, nozzle, opening, orifice, porthole, release, safety valve, spout, tear, vent, way out; SEE CONCEPTS *513,693*

outlet [*n2*] *store that sells discounted items*
factory store, market, mill store, seconds store, shop, showroom; SEE CONCEPTS *439,448,449*

outline [*n1*] *plan, sketch*
bare facts*, blueprint, diagram, draft, drawing, floor plan, frame, framework, ground plan, layout, main features, recapitulation, résumé, rough draft, rough idea, rundown, skeleton, summary, synopsis, thumbnail sketch*, tracing; SEE CONCEPT *268*

outline [*n2*] *form, tracing of an object*
configuration, conformation, contour, delineation, figuration, figure, profile, shape, silhouette; SEE CONCEPTS *436,625*

outline [*v*] *sketch out; plan*
adumbrate, block out, characterize, chart, delineate, describe, draft, lay out, paint, plot, recapitulate, rough out, skeleton, skeletonize, summarize, tell about, trace; SEE CONCEPTS *36,55,174*

outlive [*v*] *outlast*
continue, endure, hang on, outstay, prevail, remain, survive; SEE CONCEPT *407*

outlook [*n1*] *point of view*
angle*, attitude, direction, frame of mind*, headset*, mind-set*, perspective, routine, scope, side, size of it*, slant*, standpoint, viewpoint, views, vision; SEE CONCEPTS *410,689*

outlook [*n2*] *probable future*
appearances, chance, expectation, forecast, law of averages*, likelihood, normal course, opening, opportunity, possibility, probability, prospect, prospects, risk; SEE CONCEPT *679*

outlook [*n3*] *scene, view*
aspect, lookout, panorama, perspective, prospect, scape, sight, vista; SEE CONCEPTS *509,628*

outlying [*adj*] *in rural area; remote*
afar, backwoods, distant, external, faraway, farflung*, far-off, off-lying, outer, out-of-the-way*, peripheral, provincial, removed; SEE CONCEPT *583*

outmoded [*adj*] *obsolete, old-fashioned*
anachronistic, antediluvian, antiquated, antique, archaic, behind the times*, bent, bygone, dated, dead, démodé, dinosaur*, disused, extinct, fossilized, has-been*, horse and buggy*, moldy*, moth-eaten*, musty*, obsolescent, obsolete, olden, old-hat*, old-time, out, out-of-date, out-of-style, outworn, passé*, superannuated, superseded, tired, unfashionable, unstylish, unusable, vintage; SEE CONCEPTS *560,578,589,797*

out of the closet [*adj*] *open*
brought to light, candid, disclosed, divulged, exposed, open and aboveboard, open to view, out in the open, revealed, unveiled; SEE CONCEPT *60*

output [*n*] *something produced*
achievement, amount, crop, gain, harvest, making, manufacture, manufacturing, producing, product, production, productivity, profit, take, turnout, yield; SEE CONCEPTS *205,260*

outrage [*n1*] *atrocity, evil*
abuse, affront, barbarism, damage, desecration, enormity, evildoing, harm, hurt, indignity, inhumanity, injury, insult, mischief, misdoing, offense, profanation, rape, rapine, ravishing, ruin, shock, violation, violence, wrongdoing; SEE CONCEPTS *192,645,674*

outrage [n2] *anger*
blowup, flare-up*, fury, huff*, hurt, indignation, resentment, ruckus*, shock*, stew*, storm*, wrath; SEE CONCEPT **29**

outrage [v] *wrong, offend, abuse*
affront, aggrieve, boil over*, burn up*, defile, deflower, desecrate, do violence to, fire up*, force, ill-treat, incense, infuriate, injure, insult, jar*, kick up a row*, madden, make hit the ceiling*, maltreat, mistreat, misuse, oppress, persecute, raise Cain*, rape, ravage, ravish, reach boiling point*, scandalize, shock, spoil, violate, whip up*; SEE CONCEPTS **7,19,29,246**

outrageous [adj1] *very bad*
abominable, atrocious, barbaric, beastly, brazen, contemptible, contumelious, corrupt, criminal, debasing, debauching, degenerate, depraving, disgraceful, disgracing, egregious, flagitious, flagrant, gross, heinous, horrendous, horrible, ignoble, infamous, inhuman, iniquitous, malevolent, monstrous, nefarious, notorious, odious, opprobrious, scandalous, scurrilous, shameless, shaming, shocking, sinful, unbearable, ungodly, unspeakable, villainous, violent, wanton, wicked; SEE CONCEPT **571**

outrageous [adj2] *beyond reasonable limits*
barbarous, crazy*, excessive, exorbitant, extortionate, extravagant, immoderate, inordinate, last straw*, offensive, out of bounds*, preposterous, scandalous, shocking, steep*, too much*, uncivilized, unconscionable, unreasonable; SEE CONCEPTS **569,771**

outright [adj] *complete, unconditional*
absolute, all, arrant, consummate, definite, direct, downright, entire, flat, gross, out-and-out*, perfect, positive, pure, straightforward, thorough, thoroughgoing, total, undeniable, unequivocal, unmitigated, unqualified, utter, whole, wholesale; SEE CONCEPTS **531,535**

outside [adj1] *external*
alfresco, alien, apart from, away from, exterior, extramural, extraneous, extreme, farther, farthest, foreign, furthest, open-air, out, outdoor, outer, outermost, outward, over, surface; SEE CONCEPTS **484,583**

outside [adj2] *slight, slim*
distant, faint, far, marginal, negligible, off, remote, slender, small, unlikely; SEE CONCEPTS **552,789**

outside [n] *exterior; out-of-doors*
appearance, covering, facade, face, front, integument, open, open air, outdoors, seeming, sheath, skin, surface, topside, without; SEE CONCEPTS **198,484**

outsider [n] *person who is foreign to something*
alien, floater*, foreigner, incomer*, interloper, intruder, newcomer, odd one out*, outlander, refugee, stranger; SEE CONCEPTS **413,423**

outskirts [n] *edge of a geographic area*
bedroom community*, border, boundary, edge, environs, limit, outpost, periphery, purlieu, purlieus, sticks*, suburb, suburbia, vicinity; SEE CONCEPTS **508,513**

outspoken [adj] *explicit, unreserved*
abrupt, artless, blunt, calling a spade a spade*, candid, direct, forthright, frank, free, laying it on the line*, open, plain, plain-spoken, point-blank*, round, square, straightforward, strident, talking turkey*, unceremonious, unequivocal,

unreticent, up front*, vocal; SEE CONCEPTS **267,404**

outstanding [adj1] *superior, excellent*
A-1*, ace*, A-number-1*, bad*, boss*, capital*, celebrated, chief, cool*, crack*, distinguished, dominant, eminent, eventful, exceptional, famous, far-out*, great, greatest, hundred-proof*, important, impressive, magnificent, main, major, meritorious, momentous, mostest, number one*, out-of-sight*, out-of-this-world*, phenomenal, predominant, preeminent, primo*, principal, special, standout, star, steller, super, superior, superlative, tops*, well-known, world-class; SEE CONCEPTS **568,574**

outstanding [adj2] *noticeable, striking*
arresting, arrestive, conspicuous, distinguished, eye-catching, important, leading, marked, memorable, notable, noteworthy, prominent, pronounced, remarkable, salient, signal; SEE CONCEPTS **485,537**

outstanding [adj3] *referring to an unpaid debt*
due, mature, ongoing, open, overdue, owing, payable, pending, remaining, uncollected, unresolved, unsettled; SEE CONCEPT **334**

outward [adj] *visible; for appearances*
apparent, evident, exterior, external, from within, noticeable, observable, obvious, on the surface, open, ostensible, out, outer, outside, over, perceptible, superficial, surface, to the eye, toward the edge; SEE CONCEPTS **576,581,583**

outwardly [adv] *to all appearances*
apparently, as far as one can see, evidently, externally, for all intents and purposes*, in appearance, officially, on the face of it, on the surface, ostensibly, professedly, seemingly, superficially, to the eye; SEE CONCEPTS **544,576**

outweigh [v] *override, dominate*
atone for, balance, cancel out, compensate, counterbalance, counterpoise, countervail, eclipse, exceed, excel, make up for, offset, outbalance, outrival, outrun, overcome, overshadow, predominate, preponderate, prevail, set off, surpass, take precedence, tip the scales; SEE CONCEPT **141**

outwit/outsmart [v] *get the better of; figure out before another*
baffle, bamboozle*, beat*, bewilder, cap, cheat, circumvent, con*, confuse, deceive, defeat, defraud, dupe, end-run*, fake out*, finagle*, fox*, goose*, gull*, have*, hoax, hoodwink, lead astray*, make a fool of*, make a monkey of*, mislead, outdo, outfox, outgeneral, outguess, outjockey, outmaneuver, outthink, overreach, pull a fast one on*, put one over on*, run circles around*, swindle, take in*, top*, trick, worst*; SEE CONCEPTS **15,59**

oval [adj] *long and rounded in shape*
egg-shaped, ellipsoidal, elliptic, elliptical, oblong, ooid, ovaloid, ovate, oviform, ovoid; SEE CONCEPT **486**

ovation [n] *clapping and cheers*
acclaim, acclamation, applause, big hand*, bravos, cheering, hand, laudation, plaudits, praise, salvo, testimonial, tribute; SEE CONCEPTS **69,264**

over [adj1] *accomplished*
ancient history, at an end, by, bygone, closed, completed, concluded, done, done with, ended, finished, gone, past, settled, up; SEE CONCEPTS **531,548**

OU
OV

over [*adj2/adv1*] *in addition*
additionally, beyond, ever, excessively, extra, extremely, immensely, in excess, inordinately, left over, more, over and above, overly, overmuch, remaining, superfluous, surplus, too, unduly, unused; SEE CONCEPTS *544,771*

over [*adv2*] *above*
aloft, beyond, covering, farther up, higher than, in heaven, in the sky, off, on high, on top of, overhead, overtop, straight up, traversely, upstairs; SEE CONCEPTS *583,793*

overabundance [*n*] *excess*
embarrassment of riches*, glut, nimiety, overflow, overkill, overmuch, oversupply, plethora, profusion, superabundance, superfluity, surfeit, surplus, surplusage, too much*; SEE CONCEPTS *767,787*

overall [*adj*] *complete, general*
all-embracing, blanket, comprehensive, global, inclusive, long-range, long-term, sweeping, thorough, total, umbrella; SEE CONCEPT *772*

overall [*adv*] *in general*
all over, chiefly, everyplace, everywhere, generally speaking, in the long run, largely, mainly, mostly, on the whole, predominantly, primarily, principally, throughout; SEE CONCEPTS *548,772*

overbearing [*adj*] *arrogant, domineering*
ascendant, autocratic, bossy, cavalier, cocky*, despotic, dictatorial, disdainful, dogmatic, egotistic, haughty, high-and-mighty*, high-handed*, imperative, imperial, imperious, insolent, magisterial, officious, oppressive, overweening, paramount, peremptory, predominant, preponderant, prevalent, proud, regnant, sniffy*, snotty*, sovereign, stuffy, supercilious, superior, tyrannical, uppity*; SEE CONCEPTS *401,404*

overblown [*adj*] *excessive, too much*
aureate, bombastic, disproportionate, euphuistic, flowery, fulsome, grandiloquent, hyped up*, immoderate, inflated, magniloquent, oratorical, overdone, pompous, pretentious, profuse, rhetorical, sonorous, superfluous, turgid, undue, verbose, windy; SEE CONCEPTS *267,548*

overcast [*adj*] *cloudy, darkened*
clouded, clouded over, dark, dismal, dreary, dull, gray, hazy, leaden, lowering, murky, nebulous, not clear, not fair, oppressive, somber, sunless, threatening; SEE CONCEPT *525*

overcome [*adj*] *overwhelmed; visibly moved*
affected, at a loss for words, beaten, blown-away*, bowled over*, buried*, conquered, defeated, overthrown, run-over*, speechless, swamped, swept off one's feet*, taken*, unable to continue; SEE CONCEPT *403*

overcome [*v*] *beat, defeat*
best*, be victorious, come out on top*, conquer, crush, down*, drown, get around*, get the better of*, hurdle, knock over*, knock socks off*, lick*, master, outlive, overpower, overthrow, overwhelm, prevail, prostrate, reduce, render, rise above*, shock, stun, subdue, subjugate, surmount, survive, throw*, triumph over, vanquish, weather*, whelm*, win, worst*; SEE CONCEPT *95*

overconfident [*adj*] *overly sure of oneself*
brash, careless, cocksure*, cocky*, foolhardy, heading for a fall*, heedless, hubristic, impudent, overweening, presuming, presumptuous, pushy*, rash, reckless, self-assertive; SEE CONCEPTS *401,542*

overdo [*v*] *go to extremes; carry too far*
amplify, be intemperate, belabor, bite off too much*, do to death, drive oneself, exaggerate, fatigue, go overboard*, go too far*, hype, lay it on*, magnify, make federal case*, not know when to stop*, overburden, overestimate, overindulge, overload, overplay, overrate, overreach, overstate, overtax, overtire, overuse, overvalue, overwork, pile on*, pressure, puff*, run into the ground*, run riot*, strain oneself, stretch, talk big*, wear down*, wear oneself out*; SEE CONCEPTS *87,112,156*

overdue [*adj*] *late, behind schedule*
behindhand, behind time, belated, delinquent, due, held up*, hung up*, jammed*, long delayed, mature, not punctual, outstanding, owing, payable, tardy, unpaid, unpunctual, unsettled; SEE CONCEPTS *334,548,799*

overflow [*n*] *flood, inundation*
advance, cataclysm, cataract, congestion, deluge, discharge, encroachment, enforcement, engorgement, excess, exuberance, flash flood, flooding, infringement, niagara, overabundance, overcrowding, overkill, overmuch, overproduction, plethora, pour, propulsion, push, redundancy, spate, spill, spillover, submergence, submersion, superfluity, surfeit, surplus, torrent; SEE CONCEPT *740*

overflow [*v*] *pour out, flood*
brim, bubble over, cascade, cover, deluge, discharge, drain, drown, engulf, fall over, gush, inundate, irrupt, issue, jet, leak, overbrim, overrun, overtop, pour, run over, rush, shed, shower, slop, slosh, soak, spill, spill over, spout, spray, spurt, squirt, submerge, surge, swamp, water, wave, well, well over, wet, whelm; SEE CONCEPTS *179,256,740*

overhang [*v*] *bulge, hang over*
beetle, be imminent, be suspended, cast a shadow, command, dangle over, droop over, endanger, extend, flap over, impend, jut, loom, menace, overtop, poke, portend, pouch, project, protrude, rise above, stand out, stick out, swing over, threaten, tower above; SEE CONCEPT *752*

overhaul [*v*] *redo, restore*
check, debug, doctor*, do up*, examine, fiddle with*, fix, give facelift*, improve, inspect, mend, modernize, patch, rebuild, recondition, reconstruct, reexamine, renew, repair, retread, revamp, service, survey; SEE CONCEPTS *126,202,212*

overhead [*adj/adv*] *up above*
above, aerial, aloft, atop, hanging, in the sky, on high, over, overhanging, roof, skyward, upper, upward; SEE CONCEPT *586*

overhead [*n*] *general, continuing costs of operation*
budget, burden, cost, depreciation, expense, expenses, insurance, outlay, rent, upkeep, utilities; SEE CONCEPTS *329,332*

overjoyed [*adj*] *extremely happy*
charmed, delighted, deliriously happy, elated, euphoric, happy as a clam*, happy as a lark*, joyful, jubilant, on cloud nine*, only too happy*, over the moon*, rapturous, ravished, thrilled, tickled pink*, transported; SEE CONCEPT *403*

overlap [*v*] *lie over something else*
extend along, flap, fold over, go beyond, imbricate, lap over, overhang, overlay, overlie, overrun, project, protrude, ride, run over, shingle; SEE CONCEPT *759*

overlook [*v1*] *disregard, neglect*
discount, disdain, fail to notice, forget, ignore, leave out, leave undone, let fall between the cracks*, let go, let slide*, make light of*, miss, omit, overpass, pass, pass by, pay no attention, slight, slip up*; SEE CONCEPTS *30,101,699*

overlook [*v2*] *make allowances for*
bear with*, blink at*, condone, disregard, excuse, forgive, go along with, grin and bear it*, handle, ignore, let bygones be bygones*, let go, let pass*, live with*, look the other way, pay no mind*, play past*, put up with*, roll with punches*, stand for, stomach, swim with the tide*, take, tune out*, turn blind eye to*, whitewash*, wink at*, wipe slate clean*; SEE CONCEPTS *10,83*

overlook [*v3*] *have a view of something*
afford a view, command, command a view, dominate, front on, give on, give upon, have a prospect of, inspect, look down, look out, look out on, look over, mount, oversee, overtop, soar above, surmount, survey, top, tower over, view, watch over; SEE CONCEPT *752*

overlook [*v4*] *supervise*
boss, chaperon, control, oversee, quarterback*, superintend, survey; SEE CONCEPTS *94,117*

overly [*adv*] *excessively*
ever, exceedingly, extremely, immensely, immoderately, inordinately, over, overfull, overmuch, too, too much, too-too*, unduly, very much; SEE CONCEPT *544*

overplay [*v*] *be dramatic*
accent, accentuate, blow out of proportion*, dramatize, exaggerate, get carried away*, ham it up*, hyperbolize, labor at, lay it on thick*, magnify, maximize, mug*, overact, overdo, overdraw, overemphasize, overstate, overstress, overuse, overwork, point up*, show off*, stretch; SEE CONCEPTS *59,87,292*

overpower [*v*] *beat; get the upper hand*
bear down, beat down, blank, blow away*, bulldoze*, bury, clobber, conquer, cream*, crush, defeat, drown, drub*, immobilize, knock out*, lay one out*, murder*, overcome, overthrow, overwhelm, prostrate, put away*, quell, reduce, roll over*, rout, shellack*, shut off*, smash*, subdue, subjugate, swamp*, take care of*, take out*, torpedo*, total*, trash*, trounce, vanquish, waste*, wax*, whelm*; SEE CONCEPTS *95,191*

overrate [*v*] *assign too much value, importance*
assess too highly, build up, exaggerate, exceed, expect too much of, magnify, make too much of*, overassess, overesteem, overestimate, overpraise, overprize, overreckon, oversell, overvalue, rate too highly, think too highly of*, think too much of*; SEE CONCEPTS *12,49*

overrated [*adj*] *overvalued*
exaggerated, hyped-up, overestimated, overpaid, overpriced, overpromoted, puffed up, pumped up*; SEE CONCEPTS *267,542,562*

override/overrule [*v*] *cancel, reverse a decision*
alter, annul, bend to one's will*, control, countermand, direct, disallow, disregard, dominate, govern, ignore, influence, invalidate, make null and void*, make void, not heed, nullify, outvote, outweigh, overturn, prevail over, quash, recall, repeal, rescind, revoke, ride roughshod*, rule against, set aside, supersede, sway, take no account of, thwart, trample, upset, vanquish, veto; SEE CONCEPTS *50,88,121,298,317*

overriding [*adj*] *central, most important*
cardinal, compelling, determining, dominant, final, main, major, number one*, overruling, paramount, pivotal, predominant, prevailing, primary, prime, principal, ruling, supreme, ultimate; SEE CONCEPT *568*

overrule [*v*] *repeal*
abrogate, annul, cancel, disallow, invalidate, negate, nullify, override, overturn, quash, rescind, reverse, revoke, strike down, veto, void; SEE CONCEPTS *50,88,121,234*

overrun [*v1*] *defeat, invade*
beat, clobber, drub*, foray, inroad, lambaste, lick*, massacre, occupy, overwhelm, put to flight, raid, rout, swamp*, thrash, trim, whip; SEE CONCEPTS *86,95*

overrun [*v2*] *infest, spread over; exceed*
beset, choke, deluge, go beyond, inundate, invade, overflow, overgrow, overshoot, overspread, overstep, overwhelm, permeate, ravage, run on, run over, spill, spread like wildfire*, surge, surpass, swarm, well over; SEE CONCEPTS *172,179,651*

overseas [*adj*] *across an ocean*
abroad, across, away, foreign, in foreign land, transatlantic, transoceanic, transpacific; SEE CONCEPT *583*

oversee [*v*] *manage, supervise*
baby-sit*, be in driver's seat*, boss, call the shots*, captain, chaperon, command, eye*, herd, inspect, keep one's eye on*, look after, overlook, quarterback*, ride herd on*, run the show*, shepherd, sit on top of*, skipper, superintend, survey, watch; SEE CONCEPT *117*

overseer [*n*] *person who supervises others' work*
executive, head, head honcho*, manager, pit boss*, straw boss*, superintendent, supervisor; SEE CONCEPT *347*

overshadow [*v*] *make obscure, dim, vague*
adumbrate, becloud, bedim, cloud, command, darken, dim, dominate, dwarf, eclipse, excel, govern, haze, leave in the shade*, obfuscate, outshine, outweigh, overcast, overcloud, overweigh, preponderate, rise above*, rule, shadow, steal spotlight*, surpass, take precedence, tower above*, veil; SEE CONCEPTS *620,668*

oversight [*n1*] *failure, omission*
blank*, blunder, carelessness, chasm, default, delinquency, dereliction, disregard, error, fault, inattention, lapse, laxity, miscue, mistake, neglect, overlook, overlooking, preterition, pretermission, skip, slip, slipup*; SEE CONCEPT *101*

oversight [*n2*] *care, supervision*
administration, aegis, charge, check, control, custody, direction, guard, guardianship, handling, inspection, intendance, keep, keeping, maintenance, management, superintendence, surveillance, tutelage; SEE CONCEPT *117*

overstate [*v*] *exaggerate*
amplify, blow out of proportion*, boast, boost, brag, build up, embellish, embroider, emphasize, enlarge, exalt, expand, fabricate, fudge*, heighten, hike, inflate, lay it on thick*, lie, magnify, misquote, misreport, misrepresent, overdo, overemphasize, overestimate, pad*, play up, puff; SEE CONCEPT *63*

overt [*adj*] *obvious, unconcealed*
apparent, clear, definite, manifest, observable, open, patent, plain, public, undisguised, visible; SEE CONCEPT *535*

OV
OV

overtake [v] *catch; pass*
beat, befall, better, catch up with, come upon, engulf, gain on, get past, get to, happen, hit, leave behind, outdistance, outdo, outstrip, overhaul, overwhelm, reach, strike, take by surprise; SEE CONCEPTS *95,141*

overthrow [v] *defeat, destroy*
abolish, beat, bring down, bring to ruin, conquer, crush, demolish, depose, dethrone, do away with, eradicate, exterminate, knock down, knock over, level, liquidate, oust, overcome, overpower, overrun, overturn, overwhelm, purge, put an end to, raze, ruin, subdue, subjugate, subvert, terminate, tip, topple, tumble, unseat, upend, upset, vanquish; SEE CONCEPTS *95,252,320*

overtone [n] *implication, hint*
association, connotation, flavor, inference, innuendo, intimation, meaning, nuance, sense, suggestion, tone, undercurrent, undertone; SEE CONCEPT *278*

overture [n] *introduction, approach*
advance, bid, conciliatory move, exordium, foreword, invitation, offer, opening, preamble, preface, prelude, prelusion, presentation, proem, prologue, proposal, proposition, signal, suggestion, tender; SEE CONCEPTS *278,384,828,832*

overturn [v] *flip over*
annul, bring down, capsize, countermand, down, invalidate, invert, keel over, knock down, knock over, nullify, overbalance, prostrate, repeal, rescind, reverse, roll, set aside, spill, tip over, topple, tumble, turn over, turn upside down, upend, upset, upturn, void; SEE CONCEPTS *147,232*

overview [n] *survey*
analysis, apercu, audit, capsulization, critique, examination, inquiry, inspection, outline, pandect, precis, review, scrutiny, sketch, study, syllabus, synopsis, thumbnail, view; SEE CONCEPTS *37,103,197,271,291*

overweight [adj] *heavier than average*
ample, bulky, corpulent, fat, fleshy, gross, heavy, hefty, huge, massive, obese, outsize, overfed, overstuffed, plump, portly, pudgy, rotund, stout, upholstered*, weighty; SEE CONCEPT *491*

overwhelm [v1] *flood, beat physically*
bury, conquer, crush, defeat, deluge, destroy, drown, drub*, engulf, inundate, massacre, overcome, overflow, overpower, overrun, overthrow, rout, smother, submerge, swamp, thrash, total*, whip*, win*; SEE CONCEPTS *86,95*

overwhelm [v2] *astonish, devastate*
bewilder, blow out of the water*, bowl over*, confound, confuse, demoralize, destroy, disturb, do in*, downgrade*, drown, dumbfound, floor*, kill*, overcome, overpower, prostrate, puzzle, render speechless*, run circles around, shatter, shock, stagger, steamroller*, stun, subordinate, surprise, swamp, upset, wreck; SEE CONCEPTS *16,42*

overwhelming [adj] *overpowering*
amazing, astounding, breathtaking, crushing, devastating, exciting, eye-opening, mind-boggling, overcoming, paralyzing, shattering, staggering, stunning, vast; SEE CONCEPT *42*

overwrought [adj] *exhausted and excited*
affected, agitated, all shook up*, beside oneself*, crazy, distracted, emotional, excitable, fired-up*, flipped out*, frantic, freaked-out*, high*, hot-and-bothered*, hot under collar*, hyper*, in a state*, keyed-up*, nervous, neurotic, on edge*,

overexcited, overstrung, overworked, spent, steamed up*, stirred*, strung-out*, tense, tired, uneasy, unstrung*, uptight*, weary, wired, worked-up, worn, wound-up; SEE CONCEPTS *401,403,542*

owe [v] *have an obligation*
be beholden, be bound, be contracted, behind, be in arrears, be in debt, be indebted, be into one for, be obligated, be under obligation, feel bound, get on credit, have borrowed, incur, in hock*, lost, on the tab*, ought to, run up a bill*; SEE CONCEPT *335*

owing [adj] *unpaid*
attributable, comeuppance, due, in debt, mature, matured, outstanding, overdue, owed, payable, unsettled; SEE CONCEPT *334*

own [adj] *belonging to individual*
endemic, hers, his, individual, inherent, intrinsic, its, mine, owned, particular, peculiar, personal, private, resident, theirs, very own, yours; SEE CONCEPT *710*

own [v1] *possess; be responsible for*
be in possession of, be possessed of, boast, control, dominate, enjoy, fall heir to, have, have in hand, have rights, have title, hold, inherit, keep, occupy, reserve, retain; SEE CONCEPT *710*

own [v2] *acknowledge, admit*
allow, assent to, avow, come clean*, concede, confess, declare, disclose, grant, let on*, make clean breast of*, own up, recognize, tell the truth; SEE CONCEPT *57*

owner [n] *person who has possession of something*
buyer, governor, heir, heir-apparent, heiress, heritor, holder, keeper, landowner, legatee, partner, possessor, proprietor, purchaser, sharer, squire, titleholder; SEE CONCEPTS *343,347,414*

ownership [n] *possession of property*
buying, claim, control, cut, deed, dominion, end, hand, having, holding, occupancy, partnership, piece, possessorship, property, proprietary rights, proprietorship, purchase, purchasing, residence, slice, takeover, tenancy, tenure, title, use; SEE CONCEPT *710*

P

pace [n1] *steps in walking*
clip, footstep, gait, getalong, lick*, measure, step, stride, tread, walk; SEE CONCEPT *149*

pace [n2] *speed, tempo of motion*
beat, bounce, celerity, clip, downbeat, lick*, momentum, motion, movement, progress, quickness, rapidity, rapidness, rate, swiftness, time, velocity; SEE CONCEPTS *755,818*

pace [v1] *walk back and forth*
ambulate, canter, foot it*, gallop, hoof*, march, patrol, pound*, step, stride, traipse, tread, troop, trot, walk up and down; SEE CONCEPT *149*

pace [v2] *measure by footsteps*
count, determine, mark out, step, step off*; SEE CONCEPTS *291,764*

pacesetter [n] *pacemaker*
bellwether, forerunner, leader, pacer, pioneer; SEE CONCEPTS *347,354*

pacific [*adj*] *appeasing, peaceful*
amicable, at peace, calm, conciliatory, diplomatic, friendly, gentle, neutral, peaceable, peace-loving, peacemaking, placatory, placid, quiet, serene, tranquil, untroubled; SEE CONCEPTS *485,542*

pacifist [*n*] *peace-lover*
antiwar demonstrator, conscientious objector, dove, passive resister, peacemaker, peacemonger, peacenik; SEE CONCEPTS *354,416*

pacify [*v*] *make peaceful; appease*
allay, ameliorate, assuage, bury the hatchet*, butter up*, calm, chasten, compose, con, conciliate, cool, dulcify, fix up, grease*, kiss and make up*, lay back, lull, make peace, mitigate, moderate, mollify, pacificate, placate, propitiate, put the lid on*, qualify, quell, quiet, relieve, repress, silence, smooth over, soften, soft-pedal*, soothe, square, still, stroke, subdue, sweeten*, take the edge off*, tame, temper, tranquilize; SEE CONCEPTS *7,22,250*

pack [*n1*] *kit, package*
backpack, baggage, bale, bundle, burden, equipment, haversack, knapsack, load, luggage, outfit, parcel, rucksack, truss; SEE CONCEPTS *260,446,496*

pack [*n2*] *group, bunch*
assemblage, band, barrel, bundle, circle, collection, company, crew, crowd, deck, drove, flock, gang, great deal, heap, herd, horde, lot, lump, mess, mob, much, multiplicity, number, peck, pile, press, set, swarm, throng, troop; SEE CONCEPTS *397,417,432*

pack [*v1*] *make ready for transport*
batch, bind, brace, bunch, bundle, burden, collect, dispose, fasten, gather, get ready, load, package, put in order, store, stow, tie, warehouse; SEE CONCEPT *202*

pack [*v2*] *fill, compact*
arrange, bind, charge, chock, choke, compress, condense, contract, cram, crowd, drive in, heap, insert, jam, jam-pack*, lade, load, mob, pile, press, push, put away, ram, ram in*, sardine*, squeeze, stuff, tamp, throng, thrust in, top off, wedge; SEE CONCEPT *209*

pack [*v3*] *transport, carry*
bear, buck, convey, ferry, freight, gun, haul, heel, hump, jag, journey, lug, piggyback*, ride, shlep*, shoulder, tote, trek, truck; SEE CONCEPTS *148,217*

package [*n*] *bundle; whole*
amalgamation, assortment, bag, baggage, bale, batch, biddle, bottle, box, bunch, burden, can, carton, combination, container, crate, entity, kit, load, lot, luggage, pack, packet, parcel, pile, sack, sheaf, stack, suitcase, tin, trunk, unit; SEE CONCEPTS *432,494*

packed [*adj*] *full*
arranged, awash, brimful, brimming, bundled, chock, chock-full*, compact, compressed, congested, consigned, crammed, crowded, filled, full to the gills*, jammed, jam-packed*, loaded, mobbed, overflowing, overloaded, packed like sardines*, seething, serried, stuffed, swarming, to the roof*, tumid, up to the hilt*, up to the rafters*, wall-to-wall*, wrapped; SEE CONCEPTS *481,483,740,774*

packet [*n*] *small, often flat, bundle*
bag, carton, container, envelope, file, folder,

package, parcel, wrapper, wrapping; SEE CONCEPT *494*

pact [*n*] *agreement*
alliance, arrangement, bargain, bond, compact, concord, concordat, contract, convention, covenant, deal, league, paper, piece of paper, protocol, settlement, transaction, treaty, understanding; SEE CONCEPTS *271,684*

pad/padding [*n1*] *protection*
buffer, cushion, filling, packing, stuffing, wad, wadding, waste; SEE CONCEPTS *473,475*

pad [*n2*] *tablet of paper*
block, jotter, memorandum, notebook, notepad, paper, parchment, quire, ream, scratch, scratch pad, slips; SEE CONCEPTS *260,475*

pad [*n3*] *dwelling, room*
abode, coop*, crib*, digs*, hangout*, hideout*, hive*, house, layout*, lodging, quarters, residence, residency, setup*; SEE CONCEPT *516*

pad [*v1*] *protect with cushioning*
cushion, fill, fill out, line, pack, protect, shape, stuff; SEE CONCEPTS *134,202*

pad [*v2*] *elaborate, amplify*
augment, bulk, embellish, embroider, enlarge, exaggerate, expand, fill out, flesh out*, fudge*, increase, inflate, lengthen, magnify, overdraw, overstate, protract, spin, stretch; SEE CONCEPTS *63,244*

pad [*v3*] *walk quietly; walk ploddingly*
creep, go barefoot, hike, march, patter*, pitter-patter*, plod, pussyfoot*, sneak, steal, traipse, tramp, trek, trudge; SEE CONCEPT *149*

paddle [*n*] *item used for propelling object*
oar, paddlewheel, pole, propeller, pull, scull, sweep; SEE CONCEPTS *479,499*

paddle [*v*] *propel with arms or tool*
boat, cruise, cut water*, drift, drive, navigate, oar, pull, row, run rapids*, scull, sky an oar*, slop, splash, stir, sweep, thrash, wade; SEE CONCEPT *147*

pagan [*adj*] *irreligious*
agnostic, atheistic, heathen, idolatrous, impious, infidel, polytheistic, profane; SEE CONCEPT *542*

pagan [*n*] *person who does not believe in an orthodox religion*
agnostic, atheist, doubter, freethinker, heathen, heretic, iconoclast, idolater, idolist, infidel, paganist, pantheist, polytheist, scoffer, skeptic, unbeliever; SEE CONCEPTS *361,423*

page [*n1*] *sheet of paper*
folio, leaf, recto, side, signature, surface, verso; SEE CONCEPT *475*

page [*n2*] *person who serves others*
attendant, bellhop, equerry, errand runner, servant, youth; SEE CONCEPTS *348,354*

page [*v1*] *call for over communications system*
announce, beep, call, call out, call the name of, hunt for, preconize, seek, send for, summon; SEE CONCEPTS *74,78*

page [*v2*] *mark sheets of document*
check, count, foliate, number, paginate; SEE CONCEPTS *79,764*

pageant [*n*] *spectacle or contest*
celebration, charade, display, exhibition, exposition, extravaganza, fair, make-believe, motorcade, parade, pomp, procession, ritual, show, tableau; SEE CONCEPTS *292,377*

pageantry [*n*] *flashy display*
affectation, array, ceremonial, ceremony, extravagance, fanfare, flourish, formality, glitter,

ov
pa

grandeur, grandiosity, magnificence, ostentation, pageant, panoply, parade, pomp, pomposity, show, spectacle, splash, splendor; SEE CONCEPTS 335,377,655

pain [n] *physical suffering*
ache, affliction, agony, burn, catch, convulsion, cramp, crick, discomfort, distress, fever, gripe, hurt, illness, injury, irritation, laceration, malady, misery, pang, paroxysm, prick, sickness, smarting, soreness, spasm, sting, stitch, strain, tenderness, throb, throe, tingle, torment, torture, trouble, twinge, wound; SEE CONCEPTS 316,728

pain [n2] *mental suffering*
affliction, agony, anguish, anxiety, bitterness, despondency, distress, grief, heartache, hurt, malaise, martyrdom, misery, rack, sadness, shock, suffering, torment, torture, travail, tribulation, woe, worry, wretchedness; SEE CONCEPTS 410,728

pain [n3] *problem*
aggravation, annoyance, bore, bother, drag, effort, exertion, irritation, nuisance, pest, trouble, vexation; SEE CONCEPT 532

pain [v] *bother, trouble*
ache, afflict, aggrieve, agonize, ail, anguish, annoy, bite, chafe, chasten, constrain, convulse, cut to the quick*, discomfort, disquiet, distress, exasperate, excruciate, gall, grieve, gripe, harass, harm, harrow, hit where one lives*, hurt, inflame, injure, irk, irritate, nick, prick, punish, rack, rile, sadden, smart, sting, strain, stress, suffer, throb, tingle, torment, torture, upset, vex, worry, wound; SEE CONCEPTS 7,19,246

painful [adj] *physically or mentally agonizing*
aching, afflictive, agonizing, arduous, awful, biting, burning, caustic, difficult, dire, disagreeable, distasteful, distressing, dreadful, excruciating, extreme, extremely bad, grievous, hard, harrowing, hurtful, hurting, inflamed, irritated, laborious, piercing, raw, saddening, sensitive, severe, sharp, smarting, sore, stinging, tedious, tender, terrible, throbbing, tormenting, troublesome, trying, uncomfortable, unpleasant, vexatious; SEE CONCEPTS 529,537

painkiller [n] *anesthetic*
alleviative, analgesic, anodyne, aspirin, dope*, drug, medicine, morphine, ointment, opiate, pain reliever, sedative, tranquilizer; SEE CONCEPT 307

painstaking [adj] *meticulous, thorough*
assiduous, by the book*, by the numbers*, careful, conscientious, conscionable, diligent, earnest, exact, exacting, finicky, fussbudget*, fussy, hard-working, heedful, industrious, particular, persevering, persnickety*, picky, punctilious, punctual, scrupulous, sedulous, stickler*, strenuous, thoroughgoing; SEE CONCEPTS 326,538

paint [n] *tinted covering*
acrylic, chroma, color, coloring, cosmetic, dye, emulsion, enamel, flat, gloss, greasepaint, latex, makeup, oil, overlay, pigment, rouge, stain, tempera, varnish, veneer, wax; SEE CONCEPTS 467,475

paint [v] *apply colored tint, often to make design*
brush, catch a likeness, coat, color, compose, cover, cover up, daub, decorate, delineate, depict, design, draft, draw, dye, figure, fresco, gloss over, limn, ornament, outline, picture, portray, put on coats*, represent, shade, sketch, slap on*,

slather, stipple, swab, tint, touch up, wash; SEE CONCEPTS 172,174

pair [n] *two of something*
brace, combination, combine, combo, couple, deuce, doublet, duality, duo, dyad, match, mates, span, team, twins, two, two of a kind, twosome, yoke; SEE CONCEPTS 432,784

pair [v] *make, become a twosome*
balance, bracket, combine, couple, join, marry, match, match up, mate, pair off, put together, team, twin, unite, wed, yoke; SEE CONCEPT 113

pajamas [n] *sleeping clothes*
jamas*, jammies*, jams*, loungewear, lounging robe, nightdress, nightie*, nightshirt, nightwear, PJ's*, sleeper, sleeping suit; SEE CONCEPT 451

pal [n] *person's friend*
amiga, amigo, associate, boon companion*, bosom buddy*, bro*, brother, buddy, chum, companion, comrade, connate, crony, cuz, good buddy*, homeboy, homegirl, mate, sidekick, sis*, sister; SEE CONCEPT 423

palace [n] *royal or enormous home*
alcazar, castle, chateau, dwelling, hall, manor, mansion, official residence, royal residence; SEE CONCEPT 516

palatable [adj] *delicious, agreeable*
acceptable, A-OK*, aperitive, appetizing, attractive, cool, copacetic, delectable, delightful, divine, enjoyable, fair, flavorsome, good-tasting, heavenly, home-cooking*, luscious, mellow, mouthwatering, peachy, pleasant, relishing, sapid, saporific, saporous, satisfactory, savory, scrumptious, sugar-coated*, sweetened, tasteful, tasty, tempting, toothsome, toothy*, yummy*; SEE CONCEPTS 529,613

palatial [adj] *grand, opulent*
deluxe, grandiose, illustrious, imposing, impressive, lush, luxuriant, luxurious, magnificent, majestic, monumental, noble, plush, regal, rich, silken, spacious, splendid, stately, sumptuous, upholstered; SEE CONCEPTS 334,485,589

pale [adj] *light in color or effect*
anemic, ashen, ashy, blanched, bleached, bloodless, cadaverous, colorless, deathlike, dim, doughy, dull, faded, faint, feeble, ghastly, gray, haggard, inadequate, ineffective, ineffectual, insubstantial, livid, lurid, pallid, pasty, poor, sallow, sick, sickly, spectral, thin, unsubstantial, wan, washed-out, waxen, waxlike, weak, white, whitish; SEE CONCEPTS 537,618

pale [v] *become, make lighter or weakened*
blanch, decrease, dim, diminish, dull, fade, faint, go white, grow dull, lessen, lose color, lose luster, muddy, tarnish, whiten; SEE CONCEPTS 240,250

pall [n] *cloud, gloom*
cloak, cloth, covering, damp, damper, dismay, mantle, melancholy, shadow, shroud, veil; SEE CONCEPTS 620,674

pall [v] *bore, tire*
become dull, become tedious, cloy, disgust, fill, glut, gorge, jade, sate, satiate, sicken, surfeit, weary; SEE CONCEPTS 7,19

palliate [v] *gloss over; cover up*
abate, allay, alleviate, apologize for, assuage, camouflage, cloak, conceal, condone, cover, diminish, disguise, dissemble, ease, exculpate, excuse, extenuate, gloze, hide, hush up*, justify, lessen, lighten, make light of*, mask, minimize, mitigate, moderate, mollify, prettify, put on a

Band-Aid*, qualify, quick fix*, relieve, screen, soften, soothe, sugarcoat*, temper, varnish, veil, veneer, vindicate, white, whiten, whitewash*; SEE CONCEPTS *57,59,172,188*

pallid [*adj*] *pale*
anemic, ashen, ashy, blanched, bloodless, colorless, dull, faded, feeble, ghastly, gray, lackluster, lifeless, pasty, sallow, sickly, spiritless, uninspired, wan, weak, whitish; SEE CONCEPTS *537,618*

pallor [*n*] *paleness*
achromatic, bloodlessness, cadaverousness, colorlessness, etiolation, pallidity, pastiness, sallowness, wanness, whiteness; SEE CONCEPTS *537,618*

palpable [*adj1*] *clear, obvious*
apparent, appreciable, arresting, believable, blatant, certain, colorable, conspicuous, credible, detectable, discernible, distinct, evident, manifest, noticeable, observable, open, ostensible, patent, perceivable, perceptible, plain, plausible, positive, remarkable, seeming, sensible, straightforward, striking, sure, tangible, unequivocal, unmistakable, visible; SEE CONCEPTS *529,535*

palpable [*adj2*] *concrete, real*
material, sensible, solid, substantial, tactile, tangible, touchable; SEE CONCEPTS *485,582*

palpitate [*v*] *beat at a rapid pace, like a heart*
flutter, pitpat*, pitter-patter*, pound, pulsate, pulse, quiver, shiver, throb, tremble, vibrate; SEE CONCEPTS *152,308*

palsied [*adj*] *crippled*
arthritic, atonic, debilitated, disabled, diseased, helpless, neurasthenic, paralytic, paralyzed, rheumatic, sclerotic, shaking, shaky, sick, spastic, trembling, tremorous, weak; SEE CONCEPTS *314,485*

palsy-walsy [*adj*] *very friendly*
affectionate, buddy-buddy*, chummy*, close, clubby, confiding, fond, intimate, kissy-huggy*, lovey-dovey*, neighborly, pally, thick; SEE CONCEPT *555*

paltry [*adj*] *poor; worthless*
base, beggarly, cheap, common, contemptible, derisory, despicable, inconsiderable, ineffectual, insignificant, limited, low, low-down*, meager, mean, measly, minor, miserable, narrow, petty, picayune, piddling, pitiful, puny, set, shabby, shoddy, sleazy*, slight, small, sorry*, trashy, trifling, trivial, unconsequential, unimportant, vile, wretched; SEE CONCEPTS *334,485*

pamper [*v*] *serve one's every need, whim*
baby, caress, cater to, coddle, cosset, dandle*, fondle, gratify, humor, indulge, mollycoddle*, overindulge, pet, please, regale, satisfy, spare the rod*, spoil, spoil rotten*, tickle, yield; SEE CONCEPTS *136,295*

pamphlet [*n*] *booklet*
announcement, broadside, brochure, bulletin, circular, compilation, flyer*, folder, handout, leaflet, throwaway*, tract, tractate; SEE CONCEPTS *271,280*

pan [*n*] *container for cooking food*
bucket, casserole, double boiler, frying pan, kettle, pail, pannikin, pot, roaster, saucepan, sheet, skillet, vessel; SEE CONCEPTS *493,494*

pan [*v1*] *look, search for over a wide area*
follow, move, scan, separate, sift, sweep, swing, track, traverse, wash; SEE CONCEPT *216*

pan [*v2*] *criticize strongly*
blame, censure, condemn, cut up, denounce, de-

nunciate, disparage, flay, hammer, jeer at, knock, rap, reprehend, review unfavorably, roast, slam; SEE CONCEPT *52*

panacea [*n*] *cure-all*
catholicon, cure, elixir, nostrum, patent medicine, relief, remedy; SEE CONCEPTS *307,311*

panache [*n*] *person's flamboyant spirit*
brio, charisma, dash, élan, flair, flamboyance, flourish, style, swagger, verve, vigor; SEE CONCEPT *411*

pancake [*n*] *flat, round breakfast cake*
batter cake, blanket*, cake, crepe, flapjack, griddlecake, hot cake, johnnycake, jonnycake, sourdough, waffle, wheat*, wheat cake; SEE CONCEPTS *457,461*

pandemonium [*n*] *craziness, commotion*
anarchy, babel, bedlam, bluster, brouhaha*, chaos, clamor, clatter, confusion, din, hassle, hubbub*, hue and cry*, hullabaloo*, jangle, noise, racket, riot, ruckus*, rumpus, tumult, turbulence, turmoil, uproar; SEE CONCEPTS *388,674*

pander [*v*] *cater to, indulge*
brownnose*, cajole, fall all over*, gratify, lay it on*, massage, play the game*, play up to*, please, politic, satisfy, snow*, soap*, soften up, stroke, suck up to*; SEE CONCEPTS *59,136,384*

panel [*n*] *committee*
board, bureau, cabinet, commission, consultants, council, forum, group, jury, representatives, task force, tribunal; SEE CONCEPT *381*

pang [*n*] *ache, twinge*
agony, anguish, bite, discomfort, distress, gripe, misery, pain, prick, spasm, stab, sting, stitch, throb, throe, wrench; SEE CONCEPT *728*

panhandle [*v*] *beg*
ask alms, bum*, cadge*, freeload*, hit up*, hold out one's hand*, hustle, live hand to mouth*, mooch*, pass the hat*, scrounge, solicit charity, sponge*; SEE CONCEPT *53*

panic [*n1*] *extreme fright*
agitation, alarm, cold feet*, confusion, consternation, crush, dismay, dread, fear, frenzy, horror, hysteria, jam, rush, scare, stampede, terror, trepidation; SEE CONCEPTS *27,410,690*

panic [*n2*] *sudden drop in value in financial markets*
Black Monday*, bust, crash, depression, rainy day*, slump; SEE CONCEPT *335*

panic [*v*] *become, make afraid or distressed*
alarm, become hysterical, be terror-stricken, chicken out*, clutch, come apart, freeze up*, go to pieces*, have a fit*, lose it*, lose nerve*, overreact, push panic button*, run scared*, scare, shake in boots*, stampede, startle, terrify, unnerve; SEE CONCEPTS *14,27*

panorama [*n*] *scene, horizon*
bird's-eye view*, compass, dimension, diorama, extent, orbit, overview, perspective, picture, prospect, purview, radius, range, reach, scenery, scenic view, scope, spectacle, survey, sweep, view, vista; SEE CONCEPTS *529,628,651*

panoramic [*adj*] *sweeping*
all-around, all-embracing, all-encompassing, all-inclusive, bird's-eye*, blanket, broad, complete, comprehensive, far-reaching, full, panned, scenic, wide-ranging; SEE CONCEPTS *531,772*

pan out [*v*] *come to pass; succeed*
click*, come out*, culminate, eventuate, go, go over*, happen, net*, prove out, result, turn out, work out, yield; SEE CONCEPT *706*

pa
pa

pant [*v1*] *gasp for air*
be out of breath, blow, breathe, chuff, gulp, heave, huff, palpitate, puff, snort, throb, wheeze, whiff, wind; SEE CONCEPT *163*

pant [*v2*] *long for*
ache, aim, aspire, covet, crave, desire, hunger, lust, pine, sigh, thirst, want, wish, yearn; SEE CONCEPT *20*

panties [*n*] *women's underwear*
bikini, briefs, intimate things, lingerie, underclothes, undergarment, underpants, undies; SEE CONCEPT *451*

pantry [*n*] *kitchen storage room*
buttery, cellar, chamber, closet, cupboard, larder, store room; SEE CONCEPT *448*

pants [*n*] *clothing for legs, lower half of body*
Bermudas*, bloomers, blue jeans, boxer shorts, breeches, briefs, britches*, chaps*, chinos, clam diggers*, cords*, corduroys, denims, drawers, dungarees, jeans, jodhpurs, knickers, overalls, pantaloons*, panties*, pedal pushers*, shorts, slacks, trousers, underpants; SEE CONCEPT *451*

pantywaist [*n*] *sissy*
baby*, chicken*, coward, cry-baby, fraidy-cat*, milksop, momma's boy*, namby-pamby, pansy, scaredy cat*, weakling, wimp*, wuss*, wussy*; SEE CONCEPT *423*

paparazzi [*n*] *photographers*
cameraperson, celebrity photographer, freelance photographer, paparazzo, shutterbug; SEE CONCEPT *352*

paper [*adj*] *thin, flimsy*
cardboard, disposable, insubstantial, paper-thin, papery, wafer-thin; SEE CONCEPT *606*

paper [*n2*] *newspaper*
daily, gazette, journal, news, organ, rag*, weekly; SEE CONCEPT *280*

paper [*n3*] *thesis, article*
analysis, assignment, composition, critique, dissertation, essay, examination, monograph, report, script, study, theme, treatise; SEE CONCEPTS *271,280*

paper [*n4*] *material upon which one writes*
card, filing card, letterhead, newsprint, note, note card, note pad, onion skin, pad, papyrus, parchment, poster, rag, sheet, stationery, tissue, vellum; SEE CONCEPTS *260,475*

paper [*v*] *line with material*
cover, hang, paste up, plaster, wallpaper; SEE CONCEPTS *172,177*

paper/papers [*n1*] *legal document*
affidavit, archive, bill, certificate, certification, citation, contract, credentials, data, deed, diaries, diploma, documentation, dossier, file, grant, ID*, identification papers, indictment, instrument, letter, letters, order, passport, plea, record, subpoena, summons, testimony, token, visa, voucher, warrant, will, writ, writings; SEE CONCEPTS *271,318*

par [*n*] *average, equilibrium*
adequation, balance, coequality, criterion, equal footing, equality, equatability, equivalence, equivalency, level, mean, median, model, norm, parity, sameness, standard, usual; SEE CONCEPTS *636,667*

parable [*n*] *moral story*
allegory, fable, legend, lesson, tale, teaching; SEE CONCEPT *282*

parade [*n*] *pageant, display*
array, autocade, cavalcade, ceremony, column, demonstration, exhibition, fanfare, flaunting, line, march, ostentation, panoply, pomp, procession, review, ritual, shine, show, spectacle, train, vaunting; SEE CONCEPTS *377,386*

parade [*v*] *show off; march*
advertise, air, boast, brag, brandish, declare, demonstrate, disclose, display, disport, divulge, exhibit, expose, flash, flaunt, march in review, prance, proclaim, publish, reveal, sport, strut, swagger, trot out*, vaunt; SEE CONCEPT *261*

paradigm [*n*] *example*
archetype, beau ideal*, chart, criterion, ensample, exemplar, ideal, mirror, model, original, pattern, prototype, sample, standard; SEE CONCEPT *686*

paradise [*n*] *land, feeling of great pleasure; absence of evil*
Arcadia*, ballpark, bliss, cloud nine*, delight, divine abode*, Eden*, felicity, happy hunting ground*, heaven, heavenly kingdom, kingdom come*, next world*, pearly gates*, promised land, Shangri-la*, Utopia*, wonderland, Zion*; SEE CONCEPTS *370,410,515*

paradox [*n*] *contradiction, puzzle*
absurdity, ambiguity, anomaly, catch, Catch-22*, enigma, error, inconsistency, mistake, mystery, nonsense, oddity, opposite, reverse; SEE CONCEPT *532*

paragon [*n*] *outstanding example*
apotheosis, archetype, beau ideal*, beauty, best, champ, champion, crackerjack*, cream*, criterion, cynosure, epitome, essence, exemplar, gem, ideal, jewel*, love, lovely, model, nonesuch, nonpareil, original, paradigm, pattern, peach*, perfection, pick, prototype, quintessence, standard, sublimation, tops*, trump*, ultimate; SEE CONCEPTS *671,686*

parallel [*adj1*] *aligned, side-by-side*
alongside, coextending, coextensive, coordinate, equidistant, extending equally, in the same direction, lateral, laterally, never meeting, running alongside; SEE CONCEPTS *581,586*

parallel [*adj2*] *akin, similar*
agnate, alike, analogous, comparable, complementary, conforming, consonant, correspondent, corresponding, equal, identical, like, matching, resembling, uniform; SEE CONCEPTS *487,573*

parallel [*n*] *complement, correlation*
analogue, analogy, comparison, corollary, correlate, correspondence, correspondent, counterpart, countertype, double, duplicate, duplication, equal, equivalent, homologue, kin*, likeness, match, parallelism, resemblance, similarity, twin; SEE CONCEPTS *667,670*

parallel [*v*] *be alike*
agree, assimilate, collimate, collocate, compare, complement, conform, copy, correlate, correspond, equal, equate, imitate, keep pace, liken, match, paragon, parallelize; SEE CONCEPTS *111,171,667*

paralytic [*adj*] *impaired in movement*
diplegic, disabled, immobile, immobilized, inactive, incapacitated, insensible, lame, numb, palsied, palsified, paralyzed, paraplegic, powerless, quadriplegic; SEE CONCEPTS *314,485*

paralyze [*v*] *immobilize*
anesthetize, appall, arrest, astound, bemuse, benumb, bring to grinding halt*, close, daunt, daze, deaden, debilitate, demolish, destroy, disable, disarm, enfeeble, freeze, halt, incapacitate,

knock out, lame, make inert, make nerveless, nonplus, numb, palsy, petrify, prostrate, shut down*, stop dead*, stun, stupefy, transfix, weaken; SEE CONCEPTS *14,121,246,252*

paramedic [*n*] *emergency medical technician*
ambulance attendant, EMT, medical assistant, nurse; SEE CONCEPTS *357,414*

parameter [*n*] *limit*
constant, criterion, framework, guideline, limitation, restriction, specification; SEE CONCEPT *688*

paramount [*adj*] *principal, superior*
ascendant, capital, cardinal, chief, commanding, controlling, crowning, dominant, eminent, first, foremost, headmost, leading, main, outstanding, overbearing, predominant, predominate, preeminent, premier, preponderant, prevalent, primary, prime, regnant, sovereign, supreme; SEE CONCEPTS *568,574*

paramour [*n*] *lover*
admirer, beau, boyfriend, concubine, courter, courtesan, doxy, escort, fiancé, fiancée, girlfriend, inamorata, inamorato, kept woman, mistress, steady, sweetheart; SEE CONCEPTS *415,423*

paranormal [*adj*] *supernatural*
abnormal, celestial, ghostly, metaphysical, mysterious, mystic, occult, phenomenal, preternatural, psychic, spectral, transcendental, uncomprehensible, unearthly; SEE CONCEPT *582*

parapet [*n*] *bulwark*
barricade, barrier, bastion, buffet, buttress, defense, embankment, fortification, partition, protection, protective wall, rampart, safeguard; SEE CONCEPTS *96,729*

paraphernalia [*n*] *equipment, belongings*
accoutrements, apparatus, appurtenances, baggage, effects, equipage, gear, habiliments, impedimenta, impediments, machinery, material, materiel, outfit, regalia, stuff, tackle, things, trappings; SEE CONCEPTS *446,496*

paraphrase [*n*] *translation, interpretation*
digest, explanation, rehash, rendering, rendition, rephrasing, restatement, rewording, summary, version; SEE CONCEPTS *55,57,268*

paraphrase [*v*] *interpret, translate*
express in other words, express in own words, recapitulate, rehash, render, rephrase, restate, reword, summarize, transcribe; SEE CONCEPTS *55,57*

parasite [*n*] *something that exists by taking from or depending on another*
barnacle, bloodsucker*, bootlicker*, deadbeat*, dependent, flunky, freeloader*, groupie*, hanger-on*, idler, leech, scrounger, sponge*, stooge*, sucker*, sycophant, taker*; SEE CONCEPTS *394,412*

parcel [*n1*] *container prepared to be sent*
bindle, bundle, carton, load, pack, package, packet; SEE CONCEPT *494*

parcel [*n2*] *group, bunch*
array, band, batch, body, clot, clump, cluster, clutch, collection, company, crew, crowd, gang, lot, pack; SEE CONCEPT *432*

parcel [*n3*] *piece of land*
acreage, plat, plot, property, tract; SEE CONCEPTS *509,513*

parcel [*n4*] *part, piece*
bite, chunk, cut, division, lion's share*, member, moiety, piece of the action*, portion, rake-off*, section, segment, slice; SEE CONCEPTS *829,835*

parch [*v*] *dry, burn*
blister, brown, dehydrate, desiccate, dry up, evaporate, exsiccate, make thirsty, scorch, sear, shrivel, stale, wither; SEE CONCEPTS *249,255*

parched [*adj*] *dry*
arid, burned, cotton-mouth*, dehydrated, dried out, dried up*, dry as dust*, scorched, shriveled, thirsty, waterless, withered; SEE CONCEPT *603*

pardon [*n*] *forgiveness*
absolution, acquittal, allowance, amnesty, anchor, clemency, commute, conciliation, condonation, discharge, exculpation, excuse, exoneration, forbearance, freeing, grace, indemnification, indemnity, indulgence, justification, kindness, lifeboat*, lifesaver*, mercy, release, remission, reprieve, vindication; SEE CONCEPTS *10,318,685*

pardon [*v*] *forgive*
absolve, accept, acquit, amnesty, blink at*, bury the hatchet*, clear, condone, discharge, exculpate, excuse, exonerate, free, give absolution, grant amnesty, justify, let off*, let off easy*, liberate, lifeboat*, overlook, release, remit, reprieve, rescue, spring*, suspend charges, tolerate, wink at*, wipe slate clean*, write off*; SEE CONCEPTS *10,50,88,317*

pare [*v*] *peel, trim*
carve, clip, crop, cut, cut back, cut down, decorticate, decrease, dock, flay, knock off, lop, lower, mark down, prune, reduce, scalp, scrape, shave, shear, skin, skive, slash, strip, thin, uncover; SEE CONCEPTS *176,202,236,247*

parent [*n*] *person, source of product*
ancestor, architect, author, begetter, cause, center, creator, father, folks, forerunner, fountainhead, guardian, mother, origin, originator, procreator, progenitor, prototype, root, source, wellspring; SEE CONCEPTS *414,648*

parental [*adj*] *having the quality or nature of a parent*
affectionate, benevolent, benign, caring, comforting, devoted, fatherly, fond, forbearing, gentle, indulgent, kind, loving, maternal, matriarchal, motherly, paternal, patriarchal, protective, sheltering, supportive, tender, warm, watchful; SEE CONCEPTS *401,542*

parenthetical [*adj*] *incidental*
bracketed, by the way, episodic, explanatory, extraneous, extrinsic, incidental, in parenthesis, inserted, intermediate, interposed, qualifying, related, subordinate; SEE CONCEPTS *544,577*

pariah [*n*] *social outcast*
bum*, castaway, deportee, derelict, displaced person, exile, expatriate, fugitive, hobo*, leper, outsider, persona non grata*, rascal, refugee, tramp, undesirable, vagabond, vagrant, waif; SEE CONCEPT *423*

parish [*n*] *congregation of a church*
archdiocese, bethel, church, churchgoers, community, flock*, fold*, parishioners, territory; SEE CONCEPT *369*

parity [*n*] *equality, balance*
adequation, affinity, agreement, analogy, approximation, closeness, coequality, conformity, congruity, consistency, correspondence, equal terms, equivalence, equivalency, likeness, nearness, par, parallelism, paraphernalia, resemblance, sameness, similarity, similitude, uniformity, unity; SEE CONCEPTS *667,670*

pa
pa

park [n] *land that is reserved for pleasure, recreation*
esplanade, estate, forest, garden, grass, green, grounds, lawn, lot, meadow, parkland, place, playground, plaza, pleasure garden, recreation area, square, tract, village green, woodland; SEE CONCEPTS *509,513*

park [v] *place vehicle in a position*
deposit, leave, line up, maneuver, order, position, put, seat, stand, station, store; SEE CONCEPTS *148,201*

parlance [n] *idiom*
argot, colloquialism, dialect, diction, expression, idiosyncrasy, jargon, language, lingo*, localism, locution, patois, phrase, provincialism, set phrase, speech, street talk*, talk, tongue, vernacular; SEE CONCEPT 275

parlay [v] *bet; maneuver*
engineer, gamble, jockey, lay down, manage, move, plan, play, risk, speculate, venture, wager; SEE CONCEPTS *36,59,292,330*

parlor [n] *sitting room*
drawing room, front room, guest room, living room, lounge, reception, salon, waiting room; SEE CONCEPT *448*

parochial [adj] *narrow-minded, restricted*
biased, bigoted, conservative, conventional, insular, inward-looking, limited, local, narrow, petty, prejudiced, provincial, regional, sectarian, sectional, shallow, small-minded, small-town; SEE CONCEPT *542*

parody [n] *imitation, spoof*
apology, burlesque, caricature, cartoon, copy, derision, farce, irony, jest, joke, lampoon, mime, mimicry, misrepresentation, mockery, mock-heroic*, pastiche, play-on*, raillery, rib*, ridicule, roast*, satire, send-up*, skit, takeoff*, travesty; SEE CONCEPTS *59,273,292*

parody [v] *imitate, spoof*
ape, burlesque, caricature, copy, deride, disparage, distort, do a takeoff of*, exaggerate, impersonate, jeer, jest, joke, lampoon, laugh at, mime, mimic, mock, poke fun at, put on*, ridicule, roast, satirize, send up, sheik*, take off*, travesty; SEE CONCEPTS *59,111,273*

paroxysm [n] *seizure, spasm*
agitation, anger, attack, convulsion, eruption, excitement, explosion, fit, flare-up*, frenzy, frothing, fuming, furor, fury, hysterics, outbreak, outburst, passion, rage, violence; SEE CONCEPTS *308,316,410*

parrot [v] *repeat*
ape, chant, copy, copycat, echo, imitate, mime, mimic, quote, recite, reiterate; SEE CONCEPTS *47,77,171*

parry [v] *ward off, circumvent*
anticipate, avoid, block, bypass, deflect, dodge, duck*, elude, evade, fence*, fend off, forestall, hold at bay*, preclude, prevent, rebuff, rebuke, repel, repulse, resist, shirk, shun, sidestep, stave off; SEE CONCEPTS *25,30,121*

parsimonious [adj] *penny-pinching*
avaricious, chintzy*, close, frugal, greedy, illiberal, mean, miserly, penurious, prudent, saving, scrimpy, selfish, skinflint*, sparing, stingy*, tight*, tightfisted*, tightwad*; SEE CONCEPTS *334,401*

parson [n] *cleric*
chaplain, churchman/woman, clergyman/woman,

ecclesiastic, minister, padre, pastor, preacher, priest, rector, reverend, vicar; SEE CONCEPT *361*

part [n1] *piece, portion of something*
allotment, any, apportionment, articulation, atom, bit, bite, branch, chip, chunk, component, constituent, cut, department, detail, division, element, extra, factor, fraction, fragment, helping, hunk, ingredient, installment, item, limb, lot, lump, measure, meed, member, module, moiety, molecule, organ, parcel, particle, partition, piece, quantum, quota, ration, scrap, section, sector, segment, share, side, slab, slice, sliver, splinter, subdivision, unit; SEE CONCEPT *834*

part [n2] *person or group's interest, concern*
behalf, bit, business, capacity, cause, charge, duty, faction, function, involvement, office, party, place, responsibility, role, say, share, side, task, work; SEE CONCEPTS *362,532*

part [n3] *theatrical role*
antagonist, bit, bit part, cameo, character, dialogue, hero, lead, leading role, lines, minor role, piece, principal character, protagonist, romantic lead, silent bit, stock character, straight part, supporting role, title role, villain, walk-on; SEE CONCEPT *263*

part [v1] *break, disconnect*
articulate, break up, cleave, come apart, detach, dichotomize, disjoin, dismantle, dissever, disunite, divide, factor, itemize, particularize, partition, portion, rend, section, segment, separate, sever, slice, split, strip, subdivide, sunder, tear; SEE CONCEPTS *98,135*

part [v2] *leave, go away from someone*
break, break off, break up, clear out*, cut and run*, dedomicile, depart, ease out, go, go separate ways*, hit the road*, leave flat*, part company, pull out*, push off, quit, quit the scene*, say goodbye, separate, ship out*, shove off*, split, split up*, take a hike*, take leave, take off, walk out on, withdraw; SEE CONCEPTS *195,297,384*

partake [v] *eat, share*
be a party to, be in on, be into, consume, devour, divide, engage, enter into, feed, get in the act, have a finger in, ingest, participate, receive, sample, savor, sip, sit in, sit in on, take, take part, tune in; SEE CONCEPTS *169,225*

partial [adj1] *incomplete*
fractional, fragmentary, half done, halfway, imperfect, limited, part, sectional, uncompleted, unfinished, unperformed; SEE CONCEPT *531*

partial [adj2] *biased, prejudiced*
colored, discriminatory, disposed, favorably inclined, influenced, interested, jaundiced, minded, one-sided, partisan, predisposed, prepossessed, tendentious, unfair, unindifferent, unjust, warped; SEE CONCEPTS *403,542*

partiality [n] *favoritism, fondness*
affinity, bias, cup of tea*, dish, druthers*, flash, inclination, inclining, leaning, liking, love, partisanship, penchant, predilection, predisposition, preference, prejudice, proclivity, propensity, taste, tendency, thing*, type, weakness; SEE CONCEPTS *32,709*

partially [adv] *incompletely*
by degrees, by installments, fractionally, halfway, in part, in some measure, little by little, moderately, not wholly, partly, piece by piece, piecemeal, somewhat, to a certain degree, to a certain extent; SEE CONCEPTS *531,544*

participant [*n*] *person who takes part in activity*
actor, aide, a party to, assistant, associate, attendant, colleague, contributor, helper, in, member, partaker, participator, partner, party, player, shareholder, sharer; SEE CONCEPTS *352,366,423*

participate [*v*] *take part in activity*
aid, associate with, be a participant, be a party to, be into*, chip in*, come in, compete, concur, cooperate, engage, engage in, enter into, get in on*, get in on the act*, go into, have a hand in*, have to do with, join in, latch on*, lend a hand, partake, perform, play, share, sit in*, sit in on*, strive, take an interest in, tune in*; SEE CONCEPT *100*

particle [*n*] *atom, piece*
bit, crumb, dot, dribble, drop, fleck, fragment, grain, hoot*, iota, jot, minim, mite, modicum, molecule, morsel, mote, ounce, ray, scrap, scruple, seed, shred, smidgen, smithereen, speck, spot, stitch, whit; SEE CONCEPT *831*

particular [*adj 1*] *exact, specific*
accurate, appropriate, blow-by-blow*, circumstantial, clocklike, detailed, distinct, especial, express, full, individual, intrinsic, itemized, limited, local, meticulous, minute, painstaking, particularized, peculiar, precise, scrupulous, selective, singular, special, thorough, topical; SEE CONCEPT *557*

particular [*adj 2*] *notable, uncommon*
especial, exceptional, exclusive, lone, marked, noteworthy, odd, one, only, peculiar, personal, remarkable, respective, separate, single, singular, sole, solitary, unique, unusual; SEE CONCEPT *564*

particular [*adj 3*] *finicky, demanding*
careful, choicy, choosy, critical, dainty, discriminating, exacting, fastidious, finical, fussbudget*, fussy, hard to please, meticulous, nice, nit-picking*, persnickety*, picky*, rough, stickler*, tough; SEE CONCEPTS *404,542*

particular [*n*] *detail*
ABC's*, article, bottom line*, brass tacks*, case, chapter and verse*, circumstance, clue, cue, element, fact, facts of life, feature, gospel, item, know*, lowdown*, nitty-gritty*, nuts and bolts*, picture, point, rundown*, scoop*, score*, speciality, specific, specification, story, thing*, what's what*, whole story*; SEE CONCEPTS *274,532,832*

particularly [*adv*] *specifically*
decidedly, distinctly, especially, exceptionally, explicitly, expressly, individually, in particular, markedly, notably, outstandingly, peculiarly, principally, singularly, specially, surprisingly, uncommonly, unusually; SEE CONCEPT *557*

parting [*adj*] *farewell*
departing, final, goodbye, last, valedictory; SEE CONCEPT *267*

parting [*n*] *goodbye, separation*
adieu, bisection, break, breaking, breakup, crossroads*, departure, detachment, divergence, division, farewell, going, leave-taking, on the rocks*, partition, rift, rupture, severance, split, split-up, valediction; SEE CONCEPTS *195,297,384*

partisan [*adj*] *interested, factional*
accessory, adhering, biased, bigoted, blind, cliquish, colored, conspiratorial, denominational, devoted, diehard*, exclusive, fanatic, jaundiced, one-sided, overzealous, partial, prejudiced, prepossessed, sectarian, sympathetic, tendentious,

unjust, unreasoning, warped, zealous; SEE CONCEPTS *401,542,548*

partisan [*n*] *person devoted to another or cause*
accessory, adherent, backer, champion, cohort, defender, devotee, disciple, follower, satellite, stalwart, supporter, sycophant, sympathizer, upholder, votary, zealot; SEE CONCEPTS *359,423*

partition [*n*] *divider, division*
allotment, apportionment, barrier, detachment, disconnection, dissolution, distribution, disunion, dividing, hindrance, obstruction, parting, portion, rationing, rupture, screen, segregation, separation, severance, share, splitting, wall; SEE CONCEPTS *98,440,443,470*

partition [*v*] *divide, separate*
apportion, cut, cut in, cut into, cut up, deal, disburse, dispense, disperse, distribute, divvy up*, dole out*, fence off*, measure out, parcel out, portion, screen, section, segment, separate, share, size into, slice, split, split up, subdivide, wall off*; SEE CONCEPTS *98,135*

partly [*adv*] *not completely*
at best, at least, at most, at worst, bit by bit, by degrees, carelessly, halfway, inadequately, in a general way, in bits and pieces*, incompletely, in part, in some measure, in some ways, insufficiently, little by little, measurably, notably, not entirely, not fully, noticeably, not strictly speaking, not wholly, partially, piece by piece, piecemeal, relatively, slightly, so far as possible, somewhat, to a certain degree, to a certain extent, up to a certain point, within limits*; SEE CONCEPT *531*

partner [*n*] *person who takes part with another*
accomplice, ally, assistant, associate, buddy, chum*, cohort, collaborator, colleague, companion, comrade, confederate, consort, coworker, crony*, date, friend, helper, helpmate, husband, mate, pal*, participant, playmate, sidekick*, spouse, teammate, wife; SEE CONCEPTS *348,414,423*

partnership [*n*] *alliance; participation*
affiliation, assistance, association, band, body, brotherhood, business, cahoots*, cartel, chumminess, clique, club, combination, combine, community, companionship, company, conglomerate, conjunction, connection, consociation, cooperation, cooperative, corporation, coterie, crew, faction, firm, fraternity, friendship, gang, help, hookup, house, interest, joining, lodge, mob, organization, ownership, party, ring, sharing, sisterhood, society, sorority, tie-up, togetherness, union; SEE CONCEPTS *325,381,388*

party [*n 1*] *social gathering*
affair, amusement, at-home*, ball, banquet, barbecue, bash*, blowout*, carousal, carousing*, celebration, cocktails, coffee klatch, coming-out, dinner, diversion*, do*, entertainment, feast, festive occasion, festivity, fete, fun, function, gala, get-together, luncheon, movable feast*, orgy*, prom, reception, riot, shindig*, social, soiree, splurge, spree*, tea; SEE CONCEPT *383*

party [*n 2*] *gang, group*
assembly, band, bevy, body, bunch, cluster, company, corps, covey, crew, crowd, detachment, force, gathering, mob, multitude, outfit, squad, team, troop, troupe, unit; SEE CONCEPTS *417,432*

party [*n 3*] *group supporting certain beliefs*
alliance, association, bloc, body, cabal, clique,

pa
pa

coalition, combination, combine, confederacy, coterie, electorate, faction, grouping, junta, league, ring, sect, set, side, union; SEE CONCEPTS *301,381*

party [*n4*] *individual*
being, body, character, creature, human, man, mortal, part, person, personage, somebody, someone, woman; SEE CONCEPT *417*

party [*n5*] *person(s) involved in legal action*
actor, agent, cojuror, compurgator, confederate, contractor, defendant, litigant, partaker, participant, participator, plaintiff, plotter, sharer; SEE CONCEPT *355*

pass [*n1*] *opening through solid*
canyon, cut, gap, gorge, passage, passageway, path, ravine; SEE CONCEPTS *509,513*

pass [*n2*] *authorization, permission*
admission, chit*, comp, free ride*, furlough, identification, license, order, paper, passport, permit, safe-conduct*, ticket, visa, warrant; SEE CONCEPTS *271,685*

pass [*n3*] *sexual proposition*
advance, approach, overture, play, suggestion; SEE CONCEPTS *375,384*

pass [*n4*] *predicament*
condition, contingency, crisis, crossroads*, emergency, exigency, juncture, pinch, plight, situation, stage, state, strait, turning point*, zero hour*; SEE CONCEPT *674*

pass [*v1*] *go by, elapse; move onward*
befall, blow past, catch, come off, come to pass, come up, crawl, cross, cruise, depart, develop, drag, fall out, fare, flow, fly, fly by, get ahead, give, glide, glide by, go, go past, happen, hie, journey, lapse, leave, linger, move, occur, pass away, pass by, proceed, progress, push on, reach, repair, rise, roll, run, run by, run out, slip away, take place, transpire, travel, wend; SEE CONCEPTS *2,149,242*

pass [*v2*] *surpass, beat*
exceed, excel, go beyond, go by, leave behind, outdistance, outdo, outgo, outrace, outshine, outstrip, shoot ahead of, surmount, top, transcend; SEE CONCEPT *141*

pass [*v3*] *succeed, graduate*
answer, do, get through, matriculate, pass muster, qualify, suffice, suit; SEE CONCEPT *706*

pass [*v4*] *give, transfer*
buck, convey, deliver, exchange, hand, hand over, kick, let have, reach, relinquish, send, shoot, throw, transmit; SEE CONCEPTS *108,217*

pass [*v5*] *cease*
blow over*, cash in*, close, decease, demise, depart, die, disappear, discontinue, dissolve, drop, dwindle, ebb, end, evaporate, expire, fade, go, melt away, pass away, perish, peter out*, stop, succumb, terminate, vanish, wane; SEE CONCEPTS *105,119*

pass [*v6*] *enact, legislate*
accept, adopt, approve, authorize, become law, become ratified, become valid, be established, be ordained, be sanctioned, carry, decree, engage, establish, ordain, pledge, promise, ratify, sanction, undertake, validate, vote in; SEE CONCEPTS *298,317*

pass [*v7*] *express formally*
claim, declare, deliver, pronounce, state, utter; SEE CONCEPTS *49,60*

pass [*v8*] *decide not to do*
decline, discount, disregard, fail, forget, ignore,

miss, neglect, not heed, omit, overlook, pass on, pass up, refuse, skip, slight; SEE CONCEPTS *25,30*

pass [*v9*] *rid of waste*
defecate, discharge, eliminate, emit, empty, evacuate, excrete, expel, exude, give off, send forth, void; SEE CONCEPT *179*

passable [*adj1*] *acceptable, admissible*
adequate, allowable, all right, average, common, fair, fair enough, mediocre, middling, moderate, not too bad*, ordinary, presentable, respectable, so-so*, tolerable, unexceptional; SEE CONCEPT *558*

passable [*adj2*] *clear and able to be traveled*
accessible, attainable, beaten, broad, crossable, easy, fair, graded, motorable, navigable, open, penetrable, reachable, travelable, traveled, traversable, unblocked, unobstructed; SEE CONCEPTS *559,576*

passage/passageway [*n1*] *path for travel*
access, alley, alleyway, avenue, channel, corridor, course, doorway, entrance, entrance hall, exit, gap, hall, hallway, lane, line, lobby, opening, pathway, road, route, shaft, subway, thoroughfare, tunnel, vestibule, way; SEE CONCEPTS *440,501*

passage [*n2*] *excerpt from document*
clause, extract, paragraph, piece, portion, quotation, reading, section, sentence, text, transition, verse; SEE CONCEPT *270*

passage [*n3*] *travel*
advance, change, conversion, crossing, flow, journey, motion, movement, passing, progress, progression, tour, traject, transfer, transference, transit, transition, transmission, transmittal, transmittance, traverse, traversing, trek, trip, voyage; SEE CONCEPTS *145,217,224,704*

passage [*n4*] *authorization; enactment*
acceptance, allowance, establishment, freedom, legalization, legislation, passing, passport, permission, ratification, right, safe-conduct, visa, warrant; SEE CONCEPTS *318,685*

passageway [*n*] *corridor*
aisle, alley, couloir, entrance hall, entranceway, hall, hallway, ingress, lobby, passage, path, walkway; SEE CONCEPT *440*

pass away [*v*] *die*
decease, demise, depart, drop, expire, pass on, perish, succumb; SEE CONCEPT *304*

pass by [*v*] *neglect, forget*
abandon, disregard, fail, ignore, leave, miss, not choose, omit, overlook, overpass, pass over; SEE CONCEPTS *25,30*

passé [*adj*] *old-fashioned*
antiquated, belated, dated, dead, démodé, disused, extinct, has-been*, obsolete, outdated, outmoded, out-of-date, outworn, superseded, unfashionable, yesterday; SEE CONCEPTS *578,589,797*

passenger [*n*] *person who rides in vehicle conducted by another*
commuter, customer, excursionist, fare*, hitchhiker, patron, pilgrim, rider, tourist, traveler, voyager, wanderer, wayfarer; SEE CONCEPT *423*

passing [*adj1*] *brief, casual*
cursory, ephemeral, evanescent, fleeting, fugacious, fugitive, glancing, hasty, impermanent, momentary, quick, shallow, short, short-lived, slight, superficial, temporary, transient, transitory; SEE CONCEPTS *551,798*

passing [n] *death*
decease, defunction, demise, dissolution, end, finish, loss, silence, sleep, termination; SEE CONCEPT *304*

passion [n1] *strong emotion*
affection, affectivity, agony, anger, animation, ardor, dedication, devotion, distress, dolor, eagerness, ecstasy, excitement, feeling, fervor, fire, fit, flare-up, frenzy, fury, heat, hurrah, indignation, intensity, ire, joy, misery, outbreak, outburst, paroxysm, rage, rapture, resentment, sentiment, spirit, storm, suffering, temper, transport, vehemence, warmth, wrath, zeal, zest; SEE CONCEPT *410*

passion [n2] *adoration, love*
affection, amorousness, amour, appetite, ardor, attachment, concupiscence, craving, crush*, desire, emoting, eroticism, excitement, fondness, infatuation, keenness, lust, prurience, urge, weakness, yen; SEE CONCEPTS *32,372*

passion [n3] *strong interest*
craving, craze, drive, enthusiasm, fad*, fancy, fascination, idol, infatuation, jazz*, mania, obsession; SEE CONCEPTS *349,532,690*

passionate [adj1] *sensual, desirous*
amorous, ardent, aroused, concupiscent, desirous, erotic, heavy*, hot*, lascivious, libidinous, loving, lustful, prurient, romantic, sexy, steamy*, stimulated, sultry, turned-on*, wanton, wistful; SEE CONCEPT *372*

passionate [adj2] *excited; enthusiastic*
affecting, animated, ardent, blazing, burning, deep, dramatic, eager, eloquent, emotional, expressive, fervent, fervid, fierce, fiery, flaming, forceful, frenzied, glowing, headlong, heartfelt, heated, high-powered, high-pressure, hot*, hot-blooded*, impassioned, impetuous, impulsive, inspiring, intense, melodramatic, moving, poignant, precipitate, quickened, spirited, steamed up*, stimulated, stirring, strong, thrilling, vehement, violent, warm, wild, zealous; SEE CONCEPTS *401,542*

passionate [adj3] *angry*
all shook up*, choleric, enraged, fiery, frantic, furious, hotheaded*, hottempered*, inflamed, irascible, irritable, mean, peppery, quick-tempered, shaken, steamed-up*, stormy, tempestuous, testy, touchy*, vehement, violent; SEE CONCEPTS *401,542*

passive [adj] *lifeless, inactive*
acquiescent, apathetic, asleep, bearing, compliant, cool, docile, enduring, flat, forbearing, going through motions*, hands off*, idle, indifferent, inert, laid-back*, latent, long-suffering, moony, motionless, nonresistant, nonviolent, patient, phlegmatic, poker-faced*, quiescent, quiet, receptive, resigned, sleepy, static, stolid, submissive, tractable, unassertive, unflappable, uninvolved, unresisting, walking through it*, yielding; SEE CONCEPTS *542,584*

pass off [v] *give because one does not want it*
eject, foist, make a pretense of*, palm, palm off*, send forth, work off; SEE CONCEPT *108*

pass out [v] *become unconscious, usually from abusing a substance*
black out*, drop, faint, keel over*, lose consciousness, swoon; SEE CONCEPT *308*

pass over [v] *ignore, disregard*
dismiss, fail, forget, miss, neglect, not dwell on, omit, overlook, overpass, pass, pass by, skip, take no notice of*; SEE CONCEPTS *25,30*

passport [n] *identification of origin, country*
authorization, credentials, key, license, pass, permit, safe-conduct*, ticket, travel permit, visa, warrant; SEE CONCEPTS *271,685*

password [n] *secret word given for entry*
countersign, identification, key, key word, open sesame*, parole, phrase, signal, ticket, watchword, word; SEE CONCEPT *278*

past [adj1] *preceding, done*
accomplished, ago, antecedent, anterior, completed, elapsed, ended, extinct, finished, foregoing, forgotten, former, gone, gone by, over, over and done, precedent, previous, prior, spent; SEE CONCEPTS *531,585*

past [adj2] *olden, former*
ages ago*, ancient, ancient history*, back when*, behind one*, bygone, bypast, down memory lane*, earlier, early, erstwhile, ex-*, foregoing, gone-by*, good old days*, late, latter, latter-day, long-ago, old, olden days*, once, onetime, over, preceding, previous, prior, quondam, recent, retired, sometime, time was*, way back*, way back when*; SEE CONCEPT *820*

past [n1] *time gone by*
antiquity, days gone by*, former times, good old days*, history, long ago, olden days*, old lang syne, old times*, time immemorial*, times past*, years ago*, yesterday, yesteryear, yore; SEE CONCEPTS *807,811,816,818*

paste [n/v] *glue, adhesive*
cement, fasten, fix, gum, mucilage, patch, plaster, spit, stick, stickum*; SEE CONCEPTS *85,160,466*

pastel [adj] *muted in color*
delicate, light, pale, soft-hued, toned; SEE CONCEPT *618*

pastiche [n] *work of art formed from disparate sources*
assortment, collage, collection, compilation, copy, hodgepodge, imitation, mishmosh*, paste-up, patchwork, potpourri, reappropriation, reproduction, synthesis; SEE CONCEPT *260*

pastime [n] *leisure activity*
amusement, distraction, diversion, entertainment, fun, fun and games*, game, hobby, play, recreation, relaxation, sport; SEE CONCEPT *363*

pastor [n] *person who conducts church services*
cleric, divine, ecclesiastic, minister, parson, preacher, priest, rector, reverend, shepherd, vicar; SEE CONCEPT *361*

pastoral [adj] *peaceful, especially referring to the countryside*
agrarian, agrestic, Arcadian, bucolic, countrified, country, idyllic, outland, provincial, rural, rustic, simple, sylvan; SEE CONCEPT *583*

pastry [n] *baked product made with flour*
bread, cake, croissant, dainty, Danish, delicacy, doughnut, éclair, panettone, patisserie, phyllo, pie, strudel, sweet roll, tart, turnover; SEE CONCEPTS *457,461*

pasty [adj1] *sticky*
adhesive, doughy, gelatinous, gluelike, gluey, glutinous, gooey, mucilaginous, starchy; SEE CONCEPT *606*

pasty [adj2] *pale*
anemic, ashen, bloodless, dull, pallid, sallow, sickly, unhealthy, wan, waxen; SEE CONCEPT *618*

pa
pa

pat [*adj*] *relevant, suitable*
apposite, apropos, apt, auspicious, felicitous, fitting, happy, neat, opportune, pertinent, propitious, rehearsed, timely, to the point; SEE CONCEPT *558*

pat [*adv*] *exactly, fittingly*
aptly, faultlessly, flawlessly, just right, opportunely, perfectly, plumb, precisely, relevantly, seasonably; SEE CONCEPTS *535,557*

pat [*n1/v*] *tap, touch*
beat, caress, dab, fondle, form, hit, massage, mold, pet, punch, rub, slap, stroke, tip, whittle; SEE CONCEPTS *184,189,612*

pat [*n2*] *small slice or slab*
cake, dab, lump, piece, portion; SEE CONCEPTS *458,835*

patch [*n1*] *piece, spot, area*
bit, blob, chunk, fix, ground, hunk, land, lot, plat, plot, scrap, shred, stretch, strip, tract; SEE CONCEPTS *452,471,513*

patch [*n2*] *piece applied to cover a gap or lack*
application, appliqué, Band-Aid*, mend, reinforcement; SEE CONCEPTS *452,831*

patch [*v*] *fix, mend*
cobble, cover, darn, do up, fiddle with, overhaul, rebuild, recondition, reconstruct, reinforce, repair, retread, revamp, sew; SEE CONCEPTS *212,218*

patch up [*v*] *settle differences*
adjust, appease, bury the hatchet*, compensate, conciliate, make friends*, mediate, negotiate, placate, restore, settle*, smooth; SEE CONCEPT *384*

patchwork [*n*] *mixture, hodgepodge*
check, confusion, disorder, hash*, jumble, medley, miscellany, mishmash, muddle, olio, pastiche, plaid, salad*, salmagundi, stew*, tartan; SEE CONCEPTS *260,432,475*

patchy [*adj*] *spotty, not consistent*
erratic, fitful, irregular, random, sketchy, uneven, variable, varying; SEE CONCEPT *482*

patent [*adj*] *unconcealed, conspicuous*
apparent, barefaced*, blatant, clear, clear-cut, controlled, crystal clear*, distinct, downright, evident, exclusive, flagrant, glaring, gross*, indisputable, limited, manifest, obvious, open, open and shut*, palpable, plain, prominent, rank, straightforward, transparent, unequivocal, unmistakable; SEE CONCEPT *576*

patent [*n*] *copyright on an invention*
charter, concession, control, franchise, license, limitation, privilege, protection; SEE CONCEPTS *271,318,685*

path [*n*] *course, way*
aisle, artery, avenue, beat, beaten path, boulevard, byway, crosscut, direction, drag, footpath, groove, highway, lane, line, pass, passage, pathway, procedure, rail, road, roadway, route, rut, shortcut, street, stroll, terrace, thoroughfare, track, trail, walk, walkway; SEE CONCEPTS *6,501*

pathetic [*adj*] *sad, affecting*
commiserable, deplorable, distressing, feeble, heartbreaking, heartrending*, inadequate, lamentable, meager, melting, miserable, moving, paltry, petty, piteous, pitiable, pitiful, plaintive, poignant, poor, puny, rueful, sorry*, tender, touching, useless, woeful, worthless, wretched; SEE CONCEPTS *485,529*

pathos [*n*] *deep sadness*
desolation, emotion, feeling, passion, pitiable-
ness, pitifulness, plaintiveness, poignance, poignancy, sentiment; SEE CONCEPT *410*

patience [*n*] *capacity, willingness to endure*
backbone*, bearing, calmness, composure, constancy, cool*, diligence, endurance, equanimity, even temper, forbearance, fortitude, grit*, guts*, gutsiness, heart, humility, imperturbability, intestinal fortitude*, legs*, leniency, longanimity, long-suffering, moderation, moxie*, nonresistance, passiveness, passivity, perseverance, persistence, poise, resignation, restraint, self-control, serenity, starch*, staying power*, stoicism, submission, sufferance, tolerance, toleration, yielding; SEE CONCEPTS *411,657*

patient [*adj*] *capable, willing to endure*
accommodating, calm, composed, easy-going, enduring, even-tempered, forbearing, forgiving, gentle, imperturbable, indulgent, lenient, long-suffering, meek, mild, mild-tempered, persevering, persistent, philosophic, philosophical, quiet, resigned, self-possessed, serene, stoical, submissive, tolerant, tranquil, uncomplaining, understanding, unruffled, untiring; SEE CONCEPTS *404,542*

patient [*n*] *person being treated for medical problem*
case, convalescent, emergency, inmate, invalid, outpatient, shut-in, sick person, subject, sufferer, victim; SEE CONCEPT *357*

patio [*n*] *porch*
balcony, courtyard, deck, veranda; SEE CONCEPTS *509,513*

patrician [*adj*] *upper-class*
aristocratic, blue-blooded*, gentle, grand, highborn, high-class, noble, royal, well-born; SEE CONCEPTS *334,549*

patrician [*n*] *person born to upper-class*
aristocrat, blue blood*, gentleperson, noble, nobleperson, peer, silk stocking*, upper cruster*; SEE CONCEPT *423*

patriot [*n*] *person who loves his or her country*
flag-waver*, good citizen, jingoist*, loyalist, nationalist, partisan, patrioteer, statesperson, ultranationalist, volunteer; SEE CONCEPT *413*

patriotism [*n*] *love of one's country*
allegiance, chauvinism, flag-waving, loyalty, nationalism, public spirit; SEE CONCEPT *689*

patrol [*n*] *guarding; guard*
convoying, defending, escorting, garrison, lookout, patroler, policing, protecting, protection, rounds, safeguarding, scouting, sentinel, spy, vigilance, watch, watching, watchperson; SEE CONCEPTS *134,354,358*

patrol [*v*] *guard, protect*
cruise, inspect, keep guard, keep watch, make the rounds*, mount, police, pound, range, ride shotgun, safeguard, shotgun, walk the beat*, watch; SEE CONCEPTS *134,623*

patron [*n1*] *person who supports a cause*
advocate, angel*, backer, benefactor, booster, champion, defender, encourager, fairy godparent*, fan, financer, friend, front*, guarantor, guardian, guide, head, helper, leader, partisan, patron saint*, philanthropist, protector, sponsor, supporter, surety, sympathizer, well-wisher; SEE CONCEPTS *348,359,423*

patron [*n2*] *person who does business at establishment*
buyer, client, customer, frequenter, habitué, purchaser, shopper; SEE CONCEPT *348*

patronage [*n1*] *support of a cause*
advocacy, aegis, aid, assistance, auspices, backing, benefaction, championship, encouragement, financing, grant, guardianship, help, promotion, protection, recommendation, sponsorship, subsidy, support; SEE CONCEPTS *110,332,341*

patronage [*n2*] *business done at an establishment*
buying, clientage, clientele, commerce, custom, shopping, trade, trading, traffic; SEE CONCEPTS *323,324*

patronage [*n3*] *condescension*
civility, cronyism, deference, deigning, disdain, insolence, patronization, patronizing, stooping, sufferance, toleration; SEE CONCEPTS *83,300*

patronize [*v1*] *condescend*
be gracious to, be lofty, be overbearing, deign, favor, indulge, look down on*, pat on the back*, snub, stoop, talk down to*, toss a few crumbs*, treat as inferior, treat badly, treat like a child*; SEE CONCEPT *384*

patronize [*v2*] *support a cause*
assist, back, befriend, foster, fund, help, maintain, promote, sponsor, subscribe to; SEE CONCEPTS *110,341*

patronize [*v3*] *do business at an establishment*
be a client, be a customer, buy, buy from, deal with, frequent, give business to, habituate, purchase from, shop at, shop with, trade with; SEE CONCEPTS *324,327*

patsy [*n*] *fall guy*
boob*, chump, doormat*, dupe, easy mark*, fool, goat*, gull*, pigeon*, pushover*, sap*, scapegoat, schmuck*, sitting duck*, stooge, sucker, victim, weakling; SEE CONCEPT *412*

patter [*n1/v1*] *light walk; soft beat*
chatter, pad, pat, pelt, pitapat*, pitter-patter*, rat-a-tat*, rattle, scurry, scuttle, skip, tap, tiptoe, trip; SEE CONCEPTS *65,149*

patter [*n2*] *casual talk*
argot, cant, chatter, dialect, jabber*, jargon, jive*, line*, lingo, monologue, patois, pitch*, prattle*, slant*, spiel*, vernacular; SEE CONCEPTS *276,278*

patter [*v2*] *gab, chatter*
babble, blab*, clack*, hold forth*, jabber, jaw*, prate, prattle, rattle, spiel*, spout, tattle, yak*, yakety-yak*; SEE CONCEPT *266*

pattern [*n1*] *design, motif*
arrangement, decoration, device, diagram, figure, guide, impression, instruction, markings, mold, motive, original, ornament, patterning, plan, stencil, template, trim; SEE CONCEPTS *259,625*

pattern [*n2*] *arrangement, order*
constellation, kind, method, orderliness, plan, sequence, shape, sort, style, system, type, variety; SEE CONCEPTS *6,727,770*

pattern [*n3*] *model, example*
archetype, beau ideal*, copy, criterion, cynosure, ensample, exemplar, guide, mirror, norm, original, paradigm, paragon, prototype, sample, specimen, standard; SEE CONCEPT *686*

pattern [*v*] *copy, imitate; decorate*
design, emulate, follow, form, model, mold, order, shape, style, trim; SEE CONCEPTS *111,171*

paucity [*n*] *lack, scarcity*
absence, dearth, deficiency, famine, fewness, insufficiency, insufficiency, meagerness, paltriness, poverty, rarity, scantiness, scarceness,

shortage, slenderness, slightness, smallness, sparseness, sparsity; SEE CONCEPTS *335,646,767*

paunch [*n*] *large stomach*
abdomen, belly, bulge, epigastrium, fat, gut, potbelly*, spare tire*, tummy*; SEE CONCEPT *399*

pauper [*n*] *person who is poor*
almsperson, bankrupt, beggar, bum, dependent, destitute, down-and-out*, have-not*, homeless person, indigent, insolvent, in the gutter*, lazarus*, mendicant, poor person, supplicant; SEE CONCEPT *423*

pause [*n*] *wait, delay*
abeyance, break, break-off*, breathing space*, breathing spell*, caesura, cessation, coffee break*, comma*, cutoff, deadlock, discontinuance, downtime*, freeze*, gap, gridlock*, halt, happy hour*, hesitancy, hesitation, hiatus, hitch*, hush*, interim, interlude, intermission, interregnum, interruption, interval, lacuna, lapse, layoff, letup*, lull, pausation, recess, respite, rest, rest period, stand, standstill, stay, stillness, stopover, stoppage, suspension, time out*; SEE CONCEPT *807*

pause [*v*] *wait, delay*
break it up*, call time*, catch one's breath*, cease, come to standstill*, deliberate, desist, discontinue, drop, halt, hesitate, hold back, interrupt, put on hold, reflect, rest, shake, sideline, stop briefly, suspend, take a break*, take a breather*, take five*, take ten*, think twice*, waver; SEE CONCEPTS *119,121,234*

pave [*v*] *cover with asphalt, concrete*
brick, cobblestone, flagstone, gravel, lay asphalt, lay concrete, macadamize, surface, tar, tile; SEE CONCEPTS *168,172*

pavement [*n*] *blacktop*
asphalt, concrete, flagstone, road, sidewalk, tar; SEE CONCEPT *604*

pavilion [*n*] *domed building or tent*
awning, canopy, cover, covering, dome, structure; SEE CONCEPT *439*

paw [*v*] *touch roughly*
clap, claw, clutch, dig, feel, finger, fondle, grab, grate, grope, handle, hit, maul, molest, palpate, pat, rake, rasp, rub, scratch, search, slap, smite, stroke; SEE CONCEPTS *375,612*

pawn [*n1*] *security for a loan*
assurance, bond, collateral, earnest, forfeit, gage, gambit, guarantee, guaranty, pledge, security, token, warrant; SEE CONCEPT *332*

pawn [*n2*] *person who is a fool*
creature, dupe*, instrument, mark*, patsy*, pigeon*, puppet, stooge*, sucker*, tool, toy, victim; SEE CONCEPT *412*

pawn [*v*] *give as security for a loan*
deposit, give in earnest, hazard, hock*, hook*, mortgage, pledge; SEE CONCEPTS *115,330*

pay [*n*] *earnings from employment*
allowance, bacon*, bread*, commission, compensation, consideration, defrayment, emoluments, fee, hire*, honorarium, income, indemnity, meed, payment, perquisite, pittance, proceeds, profit, reckoning, recompensation, recompense, redress, reimbursement, remuneration, reparation, requital, return, reward, salary, satisfaction, scale, settlement, stipend, stipendium, take-home*, takings*, wage, wages; SEE CONCEPTS *329,332,340,344*

pay [*v1*] *give money for goods, services*
adjust, bear the cost, bear the expense, bequeath,

pa
pa

bestow, chip in*, clear, come through, compensate, confer, cough up*, defray, dig up*, disburse, discharge, extend, foot*, foot the bill*, grant, handle, hand over*, honor, kick in*, liquidate, make payment, meet, offer, plunk down*, prepay, present, proffer, put up*, recompense, recoup, refund, reimburse, remit, remunerate, render, repay, requite, reward, satisfy, settle, stake, take care of*; SEE CONCEPTS *327,341,351*

pay [v2] *be advantageous*
benefit, be worthwhile, repay, serve; SEE CONCEPT *700*

pay [v3] *make amends*
answer, atone, be punished, compensate, get just desserts*, suffer, suffer consequences; SEE CONCEPT *23*

pay [v4] *profit, yield*
be profitable, be remunerative, bring in, kick back*, make a return, make money, pay dividends, pay off*, pay out*, produce, provide a living, return, show gain, show profit, sweeten*, yield profit; SEE CONCEPT *330*

pay [v5] *get revenge*
avenge oneself, get even, make up for, pay back*, pay one's dues*, punish, reciprocate, recompense, repay, requite, retaliate, settle a score*, square, square things*; SEE CONCEPT *122*

payable [adj] *to be paid*
due, mature, maturing, obligatory, outstanding, overdue, owed, owing, receivable, unpaid, unsettled; SEE CONCEPT *334*

payback [n] *return*
accrual, accruement, compensation, gain, gate, income, interest, proceeds, profit, reciprocation, recompense, reimbursement, reparation, repayment, reward, take, yield; SEE CONCEPTS *340,710*

pay dirt [n] *profit*
accumulation, benefit, bottom line*, cleanup, earnings, gate*, goods*, gravy*, harvest, killing*, net, payoff, proceeds, receipts, return, revenue, score*, split*, surplus, take*, winnings; SEE CONCEPTS *332,344,693*

payment [n] *fee; installment of fee*
acquittal, advance, alimony, amends, amortization, amount, annuity, award, bounty, cash, defrayal, defrayment, deposit, disbursement, discharge, down, fee, hire, indemnification, outlay, part, paying, pay-off, pension, portion, premium, quittance, reckoning, recompense, redress, refund, reimbursement, remittance, remuneration, reparation, repayment, requital, restitution, retaliation, return, reward, salary, settlement, subsidy, sum, support, wage; SEE CONCEPT *344*

payoff [n] *conclusion, climax*
adjustment, clincher*, consequence, culmination, day of reckoning*, finale, final reckoning*, judgment, moment of truth*, outcome, pay, payment, punch line*, result, retribution, reward, settlement, upshot*; SEE CONCEPTS *230,679*

peace [n1] *harmony, agreement*
accord, amity, armistice, cessation, conciliation, concord, friendship, love, neutrality, order, pacification, pacifism, reconciliation, treaty, truce, unanimity, union, unity; SEE CONCEPTS *388,691*

peace [n2] *calm, serenity*
amity, calmness, composure, concord, congeniality, contentment, equanimity, harmony, hush, lull, peacefulness, placidity, quiet, quietude, relaxation, repose, reserve, rest, silence, stillness,

sympathy, tranquility; SEE CONCEPTS *410,705, 720*

peaceable [adj] *friendly, serene*
amiable, amicable, calm, complacent, conciliatory, gentle, irenic, mild, neighborly, nonviolent, pacific, pacificatory, pacifist, peaceful, peaceloving, placid, quiet, restful, still, tranquil; SEE CONCEPT *548*

peaceful [adj] *friendly, serene*
all quiet, amicable, at peace, bloodless, calm, collected, composed, constant, easeful, equable, free from strife*, gentle, halcyon, harmonious, irenic, level, mellow, neutral, neutralist, nonbelligerent, nonviolent, on friendly terms*, on good terms*, pacifistic, peaceable, peace-loving, placatory, placid, quiet, restful, smooth, sociable, steady, still, tranquil, undisturbed, unruffled, untroubled, without hostility; SEE CONCEPTS *485,542*

peacemaker [n] *person who settles problem*
appeaser, arbitrator, conciliator, diplomat, makepeace, mediator, negotiator, pacificator, pacifier, pacifist, peacekeeper, peacemonger*, placater, statesperson; SEE CONCEPTS *354,416*

peak [n1] *top of something*
aiguille, alp, apex, brow, bump, cope, crest, crown, hill, mount, mountain, pinnacle, point, roof, spike, summit, tip, vertex; SEE CONCEPTS *509,836*

peak [n2] *maximum, zenith*
acme, apex, apogee, capstone, climax, crown, culmination, greatest, height, high point, meridian, ne plus ultra, pinnacle, summit, tip, top; SEE CONCEPTS *668,766,767,832*

peak [v] *reach highest point*
be at height, climax, come to a head*, crest, culminate, reach the top, reach the zenith, top out*; SEE CONCEPTS *763,780*

peaked [adj] *pale, sick*
ailing, bilious, emaciated, ill, in bad shape*, peaky, poorly, sickly, under the weather*, wan; SEE CONCEPTS *314,618*

peal [n] *chime, clang*
blast, carillon, clamor, clap, crash, resounding, reverberation, ring, ringing, roar, rumble, sound, thunder, tintinnabulation*; SEE CONCEPT *595*

peal [v] *chime, clang*
bell, bong, crack, crash, knell, resonate, resound, reverberate, ring, ring out, roar, roll, rumble, sound, strike, thunder, tintinnabulate*, toll; SEE CONCEPT *65*

pearly [adj] *opalescent*
fair, frosted, iridescent, ivory, milky, nacreous, off-white, opaline, pearl, silver; SEE CONCEPT *618*

peasant [n] *farmer*
boor, bumpkin, countryman/woman, cropper, farmhand, hayseed*, hick*, hired hand, laborer, peon, planter, provincial, rube, rustic, serf, sharecropper, villein; SEE CONCEPTS *347,348,423*

peccadillo [n] *small fault*
bad habit, faux pas, impropriety, indiscretion, minor fault, minor infraction, minor sin, misdemeanor, petty offense, slight transgression, small infraction, small sin, venial sin, vice; SEE CONCEPTS *372,645*

peck [n/v] *bite*
beak, dig, hit, jab, kiss, mark, nibble, pick, pinch, poke, prick, rap, strike, tap; SEE CONCEPTS *169,189*

pecking order [*n*] *hierarchy*
chain of command*, corporate ladder, due order, echelons, grouping, order, placing, position, ranking, scale; SEE CONCEPT *727*

peculiar [*adj1*] *characteristic, distinguishing*
appropriate, diacritic, diagnostic, distinct, distinctive, endemic, exclusive, idiosyncratic, individual, intrinsic, local, particular, personal, private, proper, restricted, special, specific, typical, unique; SEE CONCEPTS *404,557*

peculiar [*adj2*] *bizarre, odd*
abnormal, bent*, creepy*, curious, eccentric, exceptional, extraordinary, flaky*, freakish, freaky, funny, idiosyncratic, kinky*, kooky*, oddball, offbeat, off-the-wall*, outlandish, quaint, queer, singular, strange, uncommon, unconventional, uncustomary, unusual, wacky*, way-out*, weird, wonderful; SEE CONCEPTS *404,564*

peculiarity [*n*] *characteristic; oddity*
abnormality, affectation, attribute, bizarreness, character, distinctiveness, eccentricity, feature, foible, freakishness, gimmick, idiosyncrasy, kink*, mannerism, mark, odd trait, particularity, property, quality, queerness, quirk, savor, schtick*, singularity, slant*, specialty, trait, twist*, unusualness; SEE CONCEPTS *411,665*

pecuniary [*adj*] *financial*
banking, budgeting, business, economic, fiscal, monetary; SEE CONCEPT *334*

pedagogic [*adj*] *educational*
academic, dogmatic, instructive, learned, professorial, profound, scholastic, teaching; SEE CONCEPTS *529,536*

pedantic [*adj*] *bookish, precise*
abstruse, academic, arid, didactic, doctrinaire, donnish, dry, dull, egotistic, erudite, formal, fussy, hairsplitting*, learned, nit-picking, ostentatious, overnice, particular, pedagogic, pompous, priggish*, punctilious, scholastic, schoolish, sententious, stilted; SEE CONCEPTS *401,529*

peddle [*v*] *sell door to door*
canvas*, hawk*, huckster*, market, monger*, push, shove, solicit, trade, vend; SEE CONCEPT *345*

peddler [*n*] *hawker*
huckster, salesperson, street vendor, vendor; SEE CONCEPT *348*

pedestrian [*adj*] *everyday, dull*
banal, banausic, blah*, boring, commonplace, dim, dreary, flat, humdrum*, inane, jejune, mediocre, monotone, monotonous, mundane, ordinary, platitudinous, plodding, prosaic, run-of-the-mill*, stodgy, truistic, unimaginative, uninspired, uninteresting, wishy-washy*; SEE CONCEPTS *530,547*

pedestrian [*n*] *person traveling on foot*
ambler, hiker, jaywalker*, passerby, stroller, walker; SEE CONCEPT *366*

pedigree [*adj*] *purebred*
full-blooded, pedigreed, pure-blood, thoroughbred; SEE CONCEPT *549*

pedigree [*n*] *ancestry, heritage*
blood, breed, clan, derivation, descent, extraction, family, family tree, genealogy, heredity, line, lineage, origin, race, stirps, stock; SEE CONCEPT *296*

peek/peep [*n*] *sneaked look*
blink, gander*, glance, glimpse, look-see, sight; SEE CONCEPT *623*

peek/peep [*v*] *sneak a look*
blink, glance, glimpse, have a gander*, look, peer, snatch, snoop, spy, squint, stare, take a look; SEE CONCEPT *623*

peel [*n*] *skin, covering*
bark, cover, epicarp, exocarp, husk, peeling, pellicle, rind, shell, shuck; SEE CONCEPTS *428,484*

peel [*v*] *take off outer covering*
decorticate, delaminate, desquamate, excorticate, exfoliate, flake, flay, pare, pull off, scale, shave, skin, strip, tear off, uncover; SEE CONCEPTS *142,176,211*

peep [*n1/v1*] *chirp*
chatter, cheep, chirrup, chuck, churr, coo, cry, hoot, pipe, squeak, tweet, twitter; SEE CONCEPT *64*

peep/peer [*v2*] *appear briefly*
become visible, crop up, emerge, open to view, peep out, peer out, show partially; SEE CONCEPT *261*

peer [*n*] *person who is another's equal*
associate, coequal, companion, compeer, like, match, rival; SEE CONCEPT *423*

peer [*v1*] *scan, scrutinize*
bore, eagle eye*, eye*, eyeball*, focus, gape, gawk, gaze, get a load of, glare, glim, gloat, inspect, look, peep, pin*, pry, rubberneck*, snoop, spy, squint, stare; SEE CONCEPTS *103,623*

peerless [*adj*] *having no equal; superior*
aces*, all-time, alone, best, beyond compare, champion, excellent, faultless, gilt-edge*, greatest, incomparable, matchless, most, nonpareil*, only, outstanding, perfect, second to none*, solid-gold*, super, superlative, supreme, tops*, unequaled, unexampled, unique, unmatched, unparagoned, unparalleled, unrivaled, unsurpassed, world class*; SEE CONCEPT *574*

peeve [*n*] *something strongly disliked*
annoyance, bother, gripe, nuisance, pest, sore point*, vexation; SEE CONCEPTS *532,690*

peeve [*v*] *bother, annoy*
aggravate, anger, bug*, bum*, burn*, disturb, drive up the wall*, exasperate, gall, get, get one's goat*, hack*, irk, irritate, miff*, nettle, pique, provoke, put out, rile, roil, rub the wrong way*, steam*, T-off*, vex; SEE CONCEPTS *7,19*

peevish [*adj*] *irritable, testy*
acrimonious, angry, bad-tempered, cantankerous, captious, carping, caviling, childish, churlish, complaining, crabbed*, cranky, critical, cross, crotchety*, crusty*, cussed, fault-finding, fractious, fretful, fretting, grouchy, grousing, growling, grumpy, huffy, ill-natured, mean, morose, obstinate, ogre, ornery, out-of-sorts*, pertinacious, petulant, querulous, short-tempered, snappy, splenetic, sulky, sullen, surly, tetchy, touchy, ugly, waspish, waspy, whining; SEE CONCEPTS *401,542*

peg [*v*] *attach*
clinch, fasten, fix, join, make fast, pin, secure, tighten; SEE CONCEPTS *85,160*

pejorative [*adj*] *negative, belittling*
debasing, deprecatory, depreciatory, derisive, derogatory, detracting, detractive, detractory, disadvantageous, disparaging, irreverent, rude, slighting, uncomplimentary, unpleasant; SEE CONCEPT *267*

pell-mell [*adj*] *disordered*
chaotic, confused, disarrayed, disorganized, hap-

pa
pe

hazard, muddled, tumultous/tumultuous; SEE CONCEPTS *562,585*

pell-mell [*adv*] *hurriedly and carelessly*
foolishly, full tilt*, hastily, headlong, heedlessly, helter-skelter, impetuously, incontinently, indiscreetly, posthaste, precipitiously, rashly, recklessly, thoughtlessly; SEE CONCEPTS *544,799*

pell-mell [*n*] *disorder*
anarchy, ataxia, chaos, clutter, confusion, disarray, ferment, helter-skelter, huddle, muddle, pandemonium, snarl, tumult, turmoil, upheaval; SEE CONCEPT *674*

pelt [*n*] *animal fur*
coat, epidermis, fell, hair, hide, jacket, skin, slough, wool; SEE CONCEPT *399*

pelt [*v*] *beat; throw hard*
assail, batter, belabor, belt, bombard, career, cast, charge, dash, hammer, hurl, knock, lapidate, pepper, pound, pour, pummel, rain, rush, shoot, shower, sling, speed, stone, strike, swat, tear, thrash, wallop; SEE CONCEPTS *189,222*

pen [*n1*] *enclosure*
cage, coop, corral, fence, fold, hedge, hutch, jail, penitentiary, prison, sty, wall*; SEE CONCEPTS *439,443*

pen [*n2*] *writing instrument*
ball point, felt-tip, fountain pen, marker, nib, quill, reed, stick, stylograph; SEE CONCEPTS *277,499*

pen [*v1*] *enclose*
box, cage, case, close in, confine, coop, corral, fence in, hedge, hem in, mew*, shut in; SEE CONCEPTS *191,758*

pen [*v2*] *write*
autograph, commit to paper, compose, draft, draw up, engross, indict, jot down; SEE CONCEPT *79*

penal [*adj*] *disciplinary*
chastening, corrective, penalizing, punishing, punitive, punitory, reformatory, retributive; SEE CONCEPTS *548,583*

penalize [*v*] *punish*
amerce, castigate, chasten, chastise, condemn, correct, discipline, dock*, fine, handicap, hit with*, impose penalty, inflict handicap, judge, mulct, put at disadvantage, scold, slap with*, throw the book at*; SEE CONCEPT *122*

penalty [*n*] *punishment*
amends, amercement, cost, damages, disadvantage, discipline, dues, fall, fine, forfeit, forfeiture, handicap, mortification, mulct, price, rap*, retribution; SEE CONCEPTS *344,679*

penance [*n*] *reparation for wrong*
absolution, atonement, attrition, compensation, compunction, confession, contrition, expiation, forgiveness, hair shirt*, mortification, penalty, penitence, punishment, purgation, remorse, remorsefulness, repentance, retribution, rue, ruth, sackcloth and ashes*, self-flagellation*, shrift, sorrow, suffering; SEE CONCEPTS *126,367,384,410*

penchant [*n*] *fondness, inclination*
affection, affinity, attachment, bias, disposition, druthers*, inclining, itch*, leaning, liking, partiality, predilection, predisposition, proclivity, proneness, propensity, taste, tendency, tilt*, turn*, weakness, yen; SEE CONCEPTS *20,32,411,709*

pending [*adj*] *about to happen*
awaiting, continuing, dependent, forthcoming, hanging, imminent, impending, indeterminate, in line*, in the balance*, in the offing*, in the works*, ominous, on board*, on line*, pensile, undecided, undetermined, unsettled, up in the air*; SEE CONCEPT *548*

pendulous/pendent [*adj*] *hanging*
dangling, dependent, drooping, pending, pendulant, pensile, suspended, swinging; SEE CONCEPTS *485,584*

penetrate [*v1*] *pierce; get through physically*
access, barge in, bayonet, blow in, bore, break in, breeze in, bust in, charge, come, crack, diffuse, drill, drive, eat through, encroach, enter, filter in, force, get in, gore, go through, impale, infiltrate, ingress, insert, insinuate, introduce, invade, jab, knife, make a hole, make an entrance, pass through, percolate, perforate, permeate, pervade, pop in, prick, probe, puncture, ream, run into, saturate, seep, sink into, spear, stab, stick into, suffuse, thrust, trespass; SEE CONCEPTS *159,179,220*

penetrate [*v2*] *understand or be understood*
affect, become clear, come across*, comprehend, decipher, discern, fathom, figure out, get across*, get over*, get through*, get to the bottom*, grasp, impress, perceive, put over*, see through*, sink in*, soak in*, touch, unravel, work out; SEE CONCEPT *15*

penetrating [*adj1*] *stinging, harsh*
biting, carrying, clear-cut, crisp, cutting, edged, entering, forcing, going through, infiltrating, ingoing, intrusive, passing through, penetrant, permeating, pervasive, piercing, pointed, puncturing, pungent, sharp, shrill, strong, trenchant; SEE CONCEPTS *267,537*

penetrating [*adj2*] *intelligent*
acute, astute, critical, discerning, discriminating, incisive, keen, penetrative, perceptive, perspicacious, profound, quick, quick-witted, sagacious, searching, sharp, sharp-witted, shrewd; SEE CONCEPT *402*

penitence [*n*] *shame, sorrow*
anguish, attrition, compunction, contriteness, contrition, debasement, degradation, distress, grief, humbling, humiliation, penance, qualm, regret, remorse, remorsefulness, repentance, rue, ruefulness, ruth, sadness, scruple, self-castigation, self-condemnation, self-flagellation, self-punishment, self-reproach; SEE CONCEPT *410*

penitent [*adj*] *shamed, sorrowful*
abject, apologetic, atoning, attritional, compunctious, conscience-stricken, contrite, penitential, regretful, remorseful, repentant, rueful, sorry; SEE CONCEPTS *403,542*

penitentiary [*n*] *jail*
big house*, campus, can*, college, cooler*, correctional institution, inside*, joint*, lockup*, pen*, penal institution, prison, reformatory, slammer*, stockade; SEE CONCEPTS *439,449,516*

pen name [*n*] *pseudonym*
AKA*, alias, anonym, assumed name, nickname, nom de guerre, nom de plume, professional name, pseudonym; SEE CONCEPTS *268,683*

pennant [*n*] *flag, banner*
banderole, bunting, burgee, color, decoration, emblem, ensign, jack, pennon, screamer, standard, streamer; SEE CONCEPTS *260,473*

penniless [*adj*] *without any money*
bankrupt, broke*, clean*, cleaned out*, dead broke*, destitute, dirt poor*, down to last

penny*, flat*, flat broke*, impecunious, impoverished, indigent, in the gutter*, lacking, moneyless, necessitous, needy, on last leg*, over a barrel*, penurious, poor, poverty-stricken, ruined, strapped*, tapped out*, without a dime*; SEE CONCEPT 334

pension [n] benefits paid after retirement
allowance, annuity, gift, grant, IRA*, payment, premium, retirement account, reward, social security, subsidy, subvention, superannuation, support; SEE CONCEPTS 332,344

pensive [adj] meditative, solemn
absorbed, abstracted, attentive, cogitative, contemplative, dreamy, grave, musing, pondering, preoccupied, reflecting, reflective, ruminating, ruminative, serious, sober, speculative, thinking, thoughtful, wistful, withdrawn; SEE CONCEPT 403

pent-up [adj] held within
bottled-up, bridled, checked, constrained, curbed, held-back, held in check, inhibited, repressed, restrained, restricted, smothered, stifled, suppressed; SEE CONCEPTS 401,403

penurious [adj] stingy
avaricious, cheap, chintzy*, close-fisted, costive, curmudgeonly, economical, frugal, greedy, hoarding, miserly, parsimonious, penny-pinching, pennywise*, pinchpenny*, saving, scrimping, sparing, thrifty, tightfisted, uncharitable, ungenerous, ungiving; SEE CONCEPTS 326,334,401

peon [n] menial worker
drudge, farmhand, farm worker, gopher, laborer, peasant, serf, servant, slave, unskilled laborer; SEE CONCEPT 348

people [n] human beings
bodies, body politic*, bourgeois, cats*, citizens, clan, commonality, common people, community, crowd, family, folk, folks, general public, heads*, herd, hoi polloi*, horde, humanity, humankind, human race, humans, inhabitants, John/Jane Q. Public*, kin, masses, mob, mortals, multitude, nation, nationality, person in the street*, persons, plebeians, populace, population, proletariat, public, rabble, race, rank and file*, riffraff*, society, tribe; SEE CONCEPTS 296,379,380,417

pep [n] vim, vigor
animation, bang, birr, energy, get-up-and-go*, go, gusto, hardihood, high spirits, life, liveliness, moxie*, potency, punch*, push, snap*, spirit, starch*, tuck*, verve, vitality, vivacity, zip*; SEE CONCEPTS 411,633

peppery [adj1] highly seasoned
fiery, hot, piquant, poignant, pungent, racy, snappy, spicy, zestful, zesty; SEE CONCEPT 613

peppery [adj2] irritable; sarcastic
acute, angry, astringent, biting, caustic, choleric, cranky, cross, fiery, hot-tempered, incisive, irascible, keen, lively, passionate, quick-tempered, sharp, sharp-tempered, snappish, spirited, spunky, stinging, testy, touchy, trenchant, waspish; SEE CONCEPTS 267,401,542

peppy [adj] lively, vigorous
active, alert, animate, animated, bright, gay, keen, perky, sparkling, spirited, sprightly, vivacious; SEE CONCEPTS 401,404

pep up [v] invigorate, inspire
animate, enliven, exhilarate, jazz up*, quicken, stimulate, vitalize, vivify; SEE CONCEPTS 7,22

perceive [v1] notice, see
apperceive, apprehend, be aware of, behold, descry, discern, discover, distinguish, divine, espy, feel, grasp, identify, look, make out, mark, mind, note, observe, realize, recognize, regard, remark, seize, sense, spot, spy, take; SEE CONCEPTS 38,626

perceive [v2] understand
appreciate, apprehend, comprehend, conclude, copy, deduce, distinguish, feature, feel, flash*, gather, get, get the message*, get the picture*, grasp, know, learn, pin*, read, realize, recognize, see, sense, track; SEE CONCEPT 15

percentage [n] portion, allotment
allowance, bite, bonus, chunk, commission, corner*, cut, discount, division, duty, fee, holdout, interest, juice*, payoff, percent, piece, piece of the action*, points*, proportion, quota, rate, ratio, section, slice*, split*, taste*, winnings; SEE CONCEPTS 766,784,835

perceptible [adj] noticeable, obvious
apparent, appreciable, audible, clear, cognizable, conspicuous, detectable, discernible, distinct, distinguishable, evident, lucid, observable, palpable, perceivable, perspicuous, recognizable, sensible, signal, tangible, understandable, visible; SEE CONCEPTS 529,576

perception [n] understanding, idea
acumen, apprehending, apprehension, approach, attention, attitude, awareness, big idea*, brainchild*, brain wave*, conceit, concept, conception, consciousness, discernment, feeling, flash, grasp, image, impression, insight, intellection, judgment, knowledge, light, notion, observation, opinion, perspicacity, picture, plan, realizing, recognition, sagacity, sensation, sense, study, taste, thought, viewpoint; SEE CONCEPTS 409,410,689

perceptive [adj] alert, sensitive
acute, astute, awake, aware, brainy*, conscious, discerning, discreet, ear to the ground*, gnostic, incisive, insighted, insightful, intuitive, judicious, keen, knowing, knowledgeable, knows what's what*, observant, penetrating, penetrative, percipient, perspicacious, quick, rational, responsive, sagacious, sage, savvy*, sharp, sophic, tuned in*, wise, wise to*; SEE CONCEPTS 402,542

perch [n] object placed high for sitting on
branch, landing place, lounge, pole, post, resting place, roost, seat; SEE CONCEPTS 443,479

perch [v] sit atop of
alight, balance, land, light, rest, roost, set down, settle, sit on, squat, touch down; SEE CONCEPT 154

percolate [v] seep, drip (liquid)
bleed, bubble, charge, drain, exude, filter, filtrate, impregnate, leach, ooze, pass through, penetrate, perk, permeate, pervade, saturate, strain, sweat, transfuse, transude, weep; SEE CONCEPTS 179,181

perdition [n] hell
Abaddon*, abyss, affliction, bottomless pit*, condemnation, damnation, everlasting fire*, fire and brimstone*, Gehenna*, Hades, infernal regions, inferno, loss of the soul, lower world, nether world, pit, place of torment, punishment, purgatory, ruin, suffering, underworld; SEE CONCEPTS 370,435,674

pe
pe

peremptory [*adj*] *overbearing, authoritative*
absolute, arbitrary, assertive, autocratic, binding, bossy, categorical, certain, commanding, compelling, decided, decisive, dictatorial, dogmatic, domineering, final, finished, firm, fixed, high-handed, imperative, imperial, imperious, incontrovertible, intolerant, irrefutable, magisterial, obligatory, obstinate, positive, rigorous, severe, stringent, tyrannical, uncompromising, undeniable; SEE CONCEPTS *535,537,542*

perennial [*adj*] *enduring, perpetual*
abiding, annual, ceaseless, chronic, constant, continual, continuing, deathless, durable, eternal, everlasting, immortal, imperishable, incessant, inveterate, lasting, lifelong, long-lasting, long-lived, longstanding, never-ending, old, perdurable, permanent, persistent, recurrent, seasonal, sustained, unceasing, unchanging, undying, unfailing, uninterrupted, yearlong, yearly; SEE CONCEPTS *539,798*

perfect [*adj1*] *flawless, superlative*
absolute, accomplished, aces*, adept, A-OK*, beyond compare, blameless, classical, consummate, crowning, culminating, defectless, excellent, excelling, experienced, expert, faultless, finished, foolproof, ideal, immaculate, impeccable, indefectible, matchless, out-of-this-world*, paradisiac, paradisiacal, peerless, pure, skilled, skillful, sound, splendid, spotless, stainless, sublime, superb, supreme, ten*, unblemished, unequaled, unmarred, untainted, untarnished, utopian; SEE CONCEPT *574*

perfect [*adj2*] *whole, intact*
absolute, choate, complete, completed, consummate, downright, entire, finished, flawless, full, gross, integral, out-and-out*, outright, positive, rank, sheer, simple, sound, unadulterated, unalloyed, unblemished, unbroken, undamaged, unimpaired, unmitigated, unmixed, unqualified, utter; SEE CONCEPTS *482,485*

perfect [*adj3*] *accurate, correct*
appropriate, bull's-eye*, certain, close, dead-on*, definite, distinct, exact, express, faithful, fit, ideal, model, needed, on target*, on the button*, on the money*, precise, proper, required, requisite, right, sharp, strict, suitable, textbook, to a T*, to a turn*, true, unerring, very; SEE CONCEPTS *535,557,558*

perfect [*v*] *polish; achieve*
accomplish, ameliorate, carry out, complete, consummate, crown, cultivate, develop, effect, elaborate, finish, fulfill, hone, idealize, improve, perform, put finishing touch on, realize, refine, round, slick, smooth; SEE CONCEPTS *91,244,706*

perfection [*n*] *achievement, completeness*
accomplishment, achieving, acme, arete, completion, consummation, crown, ending, entireness, evolution, exactness, excellence, excellency, exquisiteness, faultlessness, finish, finishing, fulfillment, ideal, idealism, impeccability, integrity, maturity, merit, paragon, perfectness, phoenix, precision, purity, quality, realization, ripeness, sublimity, superiority, supremacy, transcendence, virtue, wholeness; SEE CONCEPTS *671,706*

perfectionist [*n*] *stickler*
formalist, fussbudget, fusspot, idealist, nitpicker, purist, quibbler; SEE CONCEPTS *359,416,423*

perfectly [*adv1*] *absolutely*
altogether, completely, consummately, entirely, fully, quite, thoroughly, totally, utterly, well, wholly; SEE CONCEPTS *531,544*

perfectly [*adv2*] *without flaw*
admirably, correctly, excellently, exquisitely, faultlessly, fitly, flawlessly, ideally, impeccably, superbly, superlatively, supremely, to perfection, wonderfully; SEE CONCEPT *574*

perfidious [*adj*] *treacherous*
betraying, deceitful, deceptive, double-crossing*, double-dealing*, faithless, false, insidious, misleading, recreant, shifty*, slick*, snake in the grass*, traitorous, two-faced*, two-timing*, undependable, unfaithful, unloyal, unreliable, untrustworthy; SEE CONCEPTS *401,404*

perforate [*v*] *make a hole in*
bore, drill, drive, hole, honeycomb*, penetrate, permeate, pierce, pit, poke full of holes*, probe, punch, puncture, shoot full of holes*, slit, stab; SEE CONCEPT *220*

perform [*v1*] *carry out, accomplish*
achieve, act, be engaged in, behave, bring about, bring off, carry through, carry to completion, complete, comply, deliver the goods*, discharge, dispose of, do, do justice to*, do to a turn*, effect, end, enforce, execute, finish, fulfill, function, go that route*, implement, meet, move, observe, operate, percolate, perk, pull off*, put through, react, realize, run with the ball*, satisfy, take, take care of business*, tick, transact, wind up, work; SEE CONCEPTS *91,199*

perform [*v2*] *act, depict as entertainment*
act out, appear as, be on, bring down the house*, discourse, display, do a number*, do a turn*, dramatize, emote, enact, execute, exhibit, give, go on, ham*, ham it up*, impersonate, offer, personate, play, playact, present, produce, put on, render, represent, show, stage, tread the boards*; SEE CONCEPT *292*

performance [*n1*] *accomplishment*
achievement, act, administration, attainment, carrying out, completion, conduct, consummation, discharge, doing, enforcement, execution, exploit, feat, fruition, fulfillment, pursuance, realization, work; SEE CONCEPT *706*

performance [*n2*] *acting, depiction*
act, appearance, ballet, behavior, burlesque, business, ceremony, concert, custom, dance, display, drama, exhibition, gig*, interpretation, matinee, offering, opera, pageant, play, portrayal, presentation, production, recital, rehearsal, representation, review, revue, rigmarole, rite, set, show, special, spectacle, stage show, stunt, to-do*; SEE CONCEPT *263*

performance [*n3*] *efficiency*
action, conduct, effectiveness, efficacy, exercise, functioning, operation, practice, pursuit, running, working; SEE CONCEPT *630*

perfume [*n*] *scent, often manufactured and packaged for personal use*
aroma, attar, balm, balminess, bouquet, cologne, eau de cologne, essence, fragrance, incense, odor, oil, redolence, sachet, smell, spice, sweetness; SEE CONCEPTS *599,600*

perfunctory [*adj*] *automatic, unthinking*
apathetic, careless, cool, cursory, disinterested, going through the motions*, heedless, impersonal, inattentive, indifferent, involuntary, lackadaisical, laid-back*, mechanical, negligent,

offhand, phoning it in*, routine, sketchy, slip-shod*, slovenly, standard, stereotyped, stock, su-perficial, unaware, unconcerned, uninterested, usual, walking through it*, wooden*; SEE CON-CEPTS *542,544*

perhaps [*adv*] *possibly*
as it may be, as the case may be, conceivably, feasibly, for all one knows, imaginably, it may be, maybe, perchance, reasonably; SEE CONCEPT *552*

peril [*n*] *danger, risk*
cause for alarm*, double trouble*, endanger-ment, exposure, hazard, insecurity, jeopardy, lia-bility, menace, openness, pitfall, risky business*, uncertainty, vulnerability; SEE CONCEPT *675*

perilous [*adj*] *dangerous*
chancy, delicate, dicey*, dynamite, exposed, hairy*, hazardous, insecure, loaded*, on thin ice*, playing with fire*, precarious, risky, rugged, Russian roulette*, shaky, threatening, ticklish, touch and go*, touchy, treacherous, un-certain, unhealthy, unsafe, unsound, unstable, unsteady, unsure, vulnerable, wicked*; SEE CON-CEPTS *548,587*

perimeter [*n*] *circumference, border*
ambit, borderline, boundary, bounds, brim, brink, circuit, compass, confines, edge, fringe, hem, limit, margin, outline, periphery, skirt, verge; SEE CONCEPTS *484,745,792*

period [*n1*] *extent of time*
aeon, age, course, cycle, date, days, duration, epoch, era, generation, interval, measure, season, space, span, spell, stage, stretch, term, time, while, years; SEE CONCEPTS *807,822*

period [*n2*] *ending*
cessation, close, closing, closure, conclusion, discontinuance, end, limit, stop, termination; SEE CONCEPT *832*

periodic [*adj*] *at fixed intervals*
alternate, annual, at various times, centennial, cyclic, cyclical, daily, epochal, every once in a while, every so often, fluctuating, hourly, infre-quent, intermittent, isochronal, isochronous, monthly, occasional, on-again-off-again*, on certain occasions, orbital, perennial, periodical, recurrent, recurring, regular, repeated, rhythmic, routine, seasonal, serial, spasmodic, sporadic, weekly, yearly; SEE CONCEPTS *541,799*

periodical [*n*] *regular publication*
journal, mag*, magazine, monthly, newspaper, number, paper, quarterly, rag*, review, serial, sheet*, slick*, throwaway*, weekly; SEE CON-CEPT *280*

peripatetic [*adj*] *constantly traveling*
ambulant, itinerant, itinerate, migrant, mobile, nomadic, perambulant, roaming, roving, vagabond, vagrant, wandering, wayfaring; SEE CONCEPTS *401,584*

peripheral [*adj*] *minor, outside*
beside the point, borderline, exterior, external, incidental, inessential, irrelevant, minor, outer, outermost, perimetric, secondary, superficial, surface, tangential, unimportant; SEE CONCEPTS *575,583,831*

periphery [*n*] *outskirts, outer edge*
ambit, border, boundary, brim, brink, circuit, cir-cumference, compass, covering, edge, fringe, hem, margin, outside, perimeter, rim, skirt, verge; SEE CONCEPTS *484,745*

perish [*v*] *die, decline, decay*
be destroyed, be killed, be lost, bite the dust*, break down, buy the farm*, cease, check out*, collapse, corrupt, croak, crumble, decease, de-compose, demise, depart, disappear, disintegrate, end, expire, fall, give up the ghost*, go, go under, kick the bucket*, lose life, OD*, pass, pass away, pass on, rot, succumb, vanish, waste*, wither; SEE CONCEPTS *13,105,304*

perishable [*adj*] *liable to spoil, rot*
decaying, decomposable, destructible, easily spoiled, short-lived, unstable; SEE CONCEPTS *462,485*

perjure [*v*] *give false testimony*
bear false witness*, commit perjury, deceive, de-lude, equivocate, falsify, forswear, lie, lie under oath, mislead, prevaricate, swear falsely, trick; SEE CONCEPTS *63,317*

perjury [*n*] *lying while under oath*
deceitfulness, deception, dishonesty, falsehood, false oath, false swearing, false testimony, falsi-fication, untruth, untruthfulness; SEE CONCEPTS *63,278*

perk [*n*] *benefit*
advantage, bonus, dividend, extra, fringe benefit, gratuity, gravy*, lagniappe, largess, perquisite, plus, tip; SEE CONCEPT *344*

perk up [*v*] *cheer*
ameliorate, be refreshed, brighten, buck up*, cheer up, convalesce, gain, improve, invigorate, liven up, look up, mend, pep up, rally, recover, recuperate, refresh, renew, revive, shake, take heart*; SEE CONCEPTS *7,22,244,308*

perky [*adj*] *animated, happy*
active, alert, aware, bouncy, bright, bright-eyed and bushy-tailed*, brisk, bubbly, buoyant, cheer-ful, cheery, gay, in fine fettle*, jaunty, lively, spirited, sprightly, sunny, vivacious; SEE CON-CEPTS *401,404*

permanent [*adj*] *constant, lasting*
abiding, changeless, continual, diurnal, durable, enduring, everlasting, fixed, forever, forever and a day*, for keeps*, immutable, imperishable, in-destructible, in for the long haul*, invariable, long-lasting, perdurable, perduring, perennial, perpetual, persistent, set, set in concrete*, set in stone*, stable, steadfast, unchanging, unfading; SEE CONCEPTS *551,649,798*

permeable [*adj*] *absorbent, penetrable*
absorptive, accessible, enterable, passable, pervi-ous, porose, porous, spongelike, spongy; SEE CONCEPTS *576,604,606*

permeate [*v*] *filter, spread throughout*
charge, diffuse, drench, fill, go through, imbue, impregnate, infiltrate, infuse, ingrain, interfuse, invade, pass through, penetrate, percolate, per-vade, pierce, saturate, seep, soak, stab, stalk, steep, suffuse, transfuse; SEE CONCEPTS *159,179,256*

permissible [*adj*] *allowable, legal*
acceptable, admissible, all right, approved, au-thorized, bearable, endorsed, kosher*, lawful, le-galized, legit*, legitimate, licit, okay*, on the up and up*, permitted, proper, sanctioned, tolerable, tolerated, unforbidden, unprohibited; SEE CON-CEPTS *319,548,554*

permission [*n*] *authorization, consent*
acceptance, acknowledgment, acquiescence, ad-mission, agreement, allowance, approbation, ap-proval, assent, avowal, canonization, carte

pe
pe

blanche*, concession, concurrence, condonance, condonation, dispensation, empowerment, endorsement, freedom, imprimatur, indulgence, leave, letting, liberty, license, okay, permit, privilege, promise, recognition, rubber stamp*, sanctification, sanction, stamp of approval*, sufferance, tolerance, toleration, verification, warrant; SEE CONCEPTS *50,83,88,376,685*

permissive [*adj*] *lenient*
acquiescent, agreeable, allowing, approving, easy-going, forbearing, free, indulgent, latitudinarian, lax, liberal, open-minded, permitting, susceptible, tolerant; SEE CONCEPT *401*

permit [*n*] *authorization*
admittance, allowance, charter, concession, consent, empowering, favor, franchise, go-ahead*, grant, green light*, indulgence, leave, legalization, liberty, license, pass, passport, patent, permission, privilege, safe-conduct, sanction, sufferance, toleration, visa, warrant; SEE CONCEPTS *271,376,685*

permit [*v*] *allow participation*
abet, accede, accept, acquiesce, admit, agree, authorize, bless, blink at*, boost, buy, charter, concede, concur, condone, consent, empower, enable, endorse, endure, franchise, give leave, give permission, go for, grant, have, humor, indulge, leave, let, let pass, license, okay, pass, privilege, sanctify, sanction, say yes, shake on*, sign, sign off on*, suffer, take kindly to*, thumbs up*, tolerate, warrant, wink at*; SEE CONCEPTS *50,83,88*

pernicious [*adj*] *bad, hurtful*
baleful, damaging, dangerous, deadly, deleterious, destructive, detrimental, devastating, evil, fatal, harmful, iniquitous, injurious, killing, lethal, maleficent, malevolent, malicious, malign, malignant, miasmatic, miasmic, mortal, nefarious, noisome, noxious, offensive, pestiferous, pestilent, pestilential, poisonous, prejudicial, ruinous, sinister, toxic, venomous, virulent, wicked; SEE CONCEPTS *537,548,571*

perpendicular [*adj*] *at right angles to*
erect, horizontal, on end, plumb, sheer, standing, stand-up, steep, straight, straight-up, upright, vertical; SEE CONCEPTS *581,583*

perpetrate [*v*] *be responsible for*
act, bring about, carry out, commit, do, effect, enact, execute, inflict, perform, pull, up and do*, wreak; SEE CONCEPT *91*

perpetual [*adj*] *continual, lasting*
abiding, ceaseless, constant, continued, continuous, endless, enduring, eternal, everlasting, going on, immortal, imperishable, incessant, infinite, interminable, intermittent, never-ceasing, never-ending, perdurable, perennial, permanent, persistent, recurrent, recurring, reoccurring, repeated, repeating, repetitious, returning, sempiternal, unceasing, unchanging, undying, unending, unfailing, uninterrupted, unremitting, without end; SEE CONCEPTS *551,649,798,799*

perpetuate [*v*] *keep going*
bolster, conserve, continue, eternalize, eternize, immortalize, keep, keep alive, keep in existence, keep up, maintain, preserve, secure, support, sustain; SEE CONCEPT *239*

perplex [*v*] *confuse, mix up*
astonish, astound, baffle, balk, befuddle, beset, bewilder, buffalo*, complicate, confound, discombobulate*, discompose, dumbfound, encum-

ber, entangle, fog, get to*, involve, jumble, muck, muddle, muddy the waters*, mystify, nonplus, perturb, pose, puzzle, rattle, ravel, snarl up, stumble, stump, surprise, tangle, thicken, thwart; SEE CONCEPTS *16,84*

perquisite [*n*] *fringe benefit*
advantage, bonus, dividend, extra, gratuity, gravy*, lagniappe, largess, perk*, plus, reward, tip; SEE CONCEPT *344*

per se [*adv*] *essentially*
alone, as such, by and of itself, by definition, by itself, by its very nature, fundamentally, independently, in essence, in itself, intrinsically, of itself, singularly, solely, virtually; SEE CONCEPTS *544,577*

persecute [*v*] *wrong, torment*
afflict, aggrieve, annoy, badger, bait, beat, be on one's case*, bother, crucify, distress, dog*, dragoon, drive up the wall*, exile, expel, harass, hector, hound*, hunt, ill-treat, injure, maltreat, martyr, molest, oppress, outrage, pester, pick on, plague, pursue, tease, torture, tyrannize, vex, victimize, worry; SEE CONCEPTS *7,19,44,246*

perseverance [*n*] *diligence, hard work*
backbone*, constancy, continuance, cool, dedication, determination, doggedness, drive, endurance, grit*, guts*, immovability, indefatigability, moxie*, persistence, pertinacity, pluck*, prolonging, purposefulness, pursuance, resolution, sedulity, spunk, stamina, steadfastness, stick-to-itiveness*, tenacity; SEE CONCEPTS *411,633*

persevere [*v*] *keep at; work hard*
be determined, be resolved, be stubborn, carry on, continue, endure, go for broke*, go for it*, go on, hang in*, hang tough*, hold fast*, hold on, keep driving*, keep going, keep on, leave no stone unturned*, maintain, persist, plug away*, press on, proceed, pursue, remain, see it through*, stand firm*, stay the course*, stick with it*; SEE CONCEPTS *87,239*

persist [*v*] *carry on, carry through*
abide, be resolute, be stubborn, continue, endure, follow through*, follow up*, go all the way*, go on, go the limit*, grind, hold on, insist, keep up*, last, leave no stone unturned*, linger, obtain, perdure, perseverate, persevere, prevail, pursue, recur, remain, repeat, see through, stick it out*, stick to guns*, strive, tough it out*; SEE CONCEPTS *23,87,91,239*

persistent [*adj*] *determined; continuous*
assiduous, bound, bound and determined*, bulldogged*, constant, continual, dogged, endless, enduring, firm, fixed, immovable, incessant, indefatigable, in for long haul*, insistent, interminable, like bad penny*, never-ending, obdurate, obstinate, perpetual, perseverant, persevering, persisting, pertinacious, relentless, repeated, resolute, steadfast, steady, sticky*, stubborn, tenacious, tireless, unflagging, unrelenting, unremitting, unshakable; SEE CONCEPTS *326,401,404,538*

persnickety [*adj*] *fussy, particular*
careful, choosy, fastidious, finicky, nice, picky; SEE CONCEPT *404*

person [*n*] *human being*
being, body, character, creature, customer, gal, guy, human, identity, individual, individuality, joker*, life, living soul, man, mortal, party, per-

sonage, personality, self, somebody, soul, specimen, spirit, unit*, woman; SEE CONCEPT *417*

personable [*adj*] *friendly, sociable*
aces*, affable, agreeable, all heart*, all right*, amiable, attractive, charming, easygoing, good egg*, gregarious, likable, nice, okay, pleasant, pleasing, presentable, sweetheart*, white-hat*, winning; SEE CONCEPT *404*

personage/personality [*n/n2*] *celebrity, notable*
big shot*, bigwig*, brass*, celeb*, chief, cynosure, dignitary, distinguished person, eminence, face*, hot shot*, individual, luminary, monster*, name*, public figure, somebody, star, superstar, top dog*, VIP*, worthy; SEE CONCEPTS *352,354,423*

personal [*adj*] *private, individual*
claimed, exclusive, intimate, own, particular, peculiar, privy, retired, secluded, secret, special; SEE CONCEPT *536*

personal computer [*n*] *computer*
clone, desktop computer, home computer, IBM PC, laptop*, MAC, Macintosh, microcomputer, minicomputer, PC; SEE CONCEPTS *269,463*

personality [*n1*] *person's character, traits*
charisma, charm, complexion, disposition, dynamism, emotions, identity, individuality, likableness, magnetism, makeup, nature, psyche, self, selfdom, selfhood, singularity, temper, temperament; SEE CONCEPT *411*

personally [*adv*] *independently*
alone, by oneself, directly, for oneself, for one's part, individualistically, individually, in one's own view, in person, in the flesh, narrowly, on one's own, privately, solely, specially, subjectively; SEE CONCEPTS *544,577*

personify [*v*] *represent some other being, character*
act out, body forth, contain, copy, emblematize, embody, epitomize, exemplify, express, exteriorize, externalize, hominify, humanize, illustrate, image, imitate, impersonate, incarnate, live as, make human, manifest, materialize, mirror, objectify, personize, substantiate, symbolize, typify; SEE CONCEPTS *261,716*

personnel [*n*] *employees of business or other enterprise*
cadre, corps, crew, faculty, group, helpers, human resources, members, men and women, office, organization, people, shop, staff, troop, troops, workers, work force; SEE CONCEPTS *325,417*

perspective [*n*] *view, outlook*
angle, aspect, attitude, broad view, context, frame of reference*, headset*, landscape, mindset*, objectivity, overview, panorama, proportion, prospect, relation, relative importance, relativity, scene, size of it*, viewpoint, vista, way of looking; SEE CONCEPTS *410,629,689*

perspicacious [*adj*] *observant, perceptive*
acute, alert, astute, aware, clear-sighted, clever, discerning, heady*, judicious, keen, penetrating, percipient, sagacious, savvy*, sharp, sharp-witted, shrewd; SEE CONCEPT *402*

perspicuous [*adj*] *clear, obvious*
apparent, clear-cut, comprehensible, crystal*, crystal-clear*, distinct, easily understood, explicit, intelligible, limpid, lucent, lucid, luminous, pellucid, plain, self-evident, straightforward, transparent, unambiguous, unblurred, understandable; SEE CONCEPT *529*

perspire [*v*] *become wet with sweat*
be damp, be wet, break a sweat*, drip, exude, get in a lather*, glow, lather, pour, secrete, swelter; SEE CONCEPTS *185,469*

persuade [*v*] *cause to believe; convince to do*
actuate, advise, affect, allure, argue into, assure, blandish, brainwash*, bring around, bring to senses, cajole, coax, convert, counsel, draw, enlist, entice, exhort, gain confidence of, get, impel, impress, incite, incline, induce, influence, inveigle, lead, lead to believe, lead to do, move, prevail upon, prompt, propagandize, proselyte, proselytize, reason, satisfy, seduce, sell, stroke, sway, talk into, touch, turn on to, urge, wear down*, wheedle, win argument, win over, woo, work over; SEE CONCEPT *68*

persuasion [*n1*] *influencing to do, believe*
alignment, alluring, arm-twist*, blandishment, brainwashing*, cajolery, cogency, con*, conversion, enticement, exhortation, force, goose*, hard sell*, hook*, inducement, inveiglement, persuasiveness, potency, power, promote, pull*, seduction, sell*, snow job*, soft soap*, squeeze*, sweet talk*, wheedling, winning over, working over; SEE CONCEPTS *68,687*

persuasion [*n2*] *belief, religion*
bias, camp, certitude, church, communion, connection, conviction, credo, creed, cult, denomination, eye, faction, faith, feeling, mind*, opinion, partiality, party, predilection, prejudice, school, school of thought*, sect, sentiment, side, tenet, view; SEE CONCEPT *689*

persuasive [*adj*] *effective, influential*
actuating, alluring, cogent, compelling, conclusive, convictive, convincing, credible, effectual, efficacious, efficient, eloquent, energetic, enticing, forceful, forcible, impelling, impressive, inducing, inspiring, inveigling, logical, luring, moving, plausible, pointed, potent, powerful, seductive, slick, smooth, sound, stimulating, stringent, strong, swaying, telling, touching, unctuous, valid, weighty, wheedling, winning; SEE CONCEPTS *267,537,542*

pert [*adj*] *lively, bold*
animated, audacious, brash, brazen, breezy, bright, brisk, cheeky*, dapper, daring, dashing, disrespectful, flip*, flippant, forward, fresh, gay, impertinent, impudent, insolent, jaunty, keen, nervy, perky, presumptuous, sassy*, saucy*, smart, smart-alecky*, spirited, sprightly, vivacious, wise; SEE CONCEPTS *401,404*

pertain [*v*] *be relevant to*
affect, appertain, apply, associate, be appropriate, bear on, befit, belong, be part of, be pertinent, combine, concern, connect, inhere with, join, refer, regard, relate, touch, vest; SEE CONCEPT *532*

pertinent [*adj*] *relevant, suitable*
admissible, ad rem, applicable, apposite, appropriate, apropos, apt, connected, fit, fitting, germane, kosher*, legit*, material, on target*, on the button*, on the nose*, opportune, pat*, pertaining, proper, related, right on, to the point, to the purpose; SEE CONCEPT *558*

perturb [*v*] *upset, unsettle*
agitate, alarm, annoy, bewilder, bother, bug*, confound, confuse, disarrange, discompose, disconcert, discountenance, dismay, disorder, disquiet, disturb, flurry, fluster, irritate, make a scene*, make waves*, muddle, needle, perplex,

pe
pe

pester, ruffle, stir up*, trouble, vex, worry; SEE CONCEPTS *7,16,19*

peruse [*v*] *check out; examine*
analyze, browse, glance over, inspect, look through, pore over, read, scan, scrutinize, skim, study; SEE CONCEPTS *72,103*

pervade [*v*] *affect strongly; spread through*
charge, diffuse, extend, fill, imbue, impregnate, infuse, overspread, penetrate, percolate, permeate, suffuse, transfuse; SEE CONCEPTS *172,179*

pervasive [*adj*] *extensive*
all over the place*, can't get away from*, common, general, inescapable, omnipresent, permeating, pervading, prevalent, rife, ubiquitous, universal, wall-to-wall*, widespread; SEE CONCEPT *772*

perverse [*adj*] *mean, ornery; troublesome*
abnormal, bad-tempered, cantankerous, capricious, contradictory, contrary, contumacious, corrupt, crabby*, cross, degenerate, delinquent, depraved, deviant, disobedient, dogged*, erring, fractious, hard-nosed*, headstrong, intractable, intransigent, irritable, miscreant, mulish*, nefarious, obdurate, obstinate, petulant, pigheaded*, rebellious, refractory, rotten*, self-willed, spiteful, stubborn, unhealthy, unmanageable, unreasonable, unyielding, villainous, wayward, wicked, willful; SEE CONCEPTS *401,542,571*

perversion [*n*] *sexual abnormality*
aberration, anomaly, corruption, debauchery, deviance, fetish, immorality, kink*, kinkiness, sexual deviation; SEE CONCEPT *545*

pervert [*n*] *person who lacks morals*
debauchee, degenerate, deviant, deviate, freak, weirdo*; SEE CONCEPT *412*

pervert [*v*] *twist, turn away from what is acceptable or correct*
abuse, adulterate, alloy, animalize, brainwash, color, corrupt, cut*, debase, debauch, demoralize, deprave, desecrate, distort, divert, doctor, doctor up*, fake, falsify, fudge*, garble, misconstrue, misinterpret, misrepresent, misstate, mistreat, misuse, outrage, phony up*, prostitute, ruin, salt*, seduce, spike, vitiate, warp, water*; SEE CONCEPTS *14,63,156,252*

perverted [*adj*] *immoral, evil*
abandoned, aberrant, abnormal, abused, contorted, corrupt, corrupted, debased, debauched, defiled, depraved, deviant, deviating, distorted, foreign, grotesque, impaired, kinky*, misguided, misused, monstrous, outraged, polluted, queer, sick, tainted, twisted, unhealthy, unnatural, vicious, vitiate, vitiated, warped, wicked; SEE CONCEPTS *485,545*

pesky [*adj*] *bothersome*
annoying, disturbing, irksome, mean, nettlesome, peeving, provoking, troublesome, ugly, vexatious, vexing, wicked; SEE CONCEPTS *529,537*

pessimism [*n*] *belief in bad outcome*
cynicism, dark side*, dejection, depression, despair, despondency, dim view*, distrust, dyspepsia, expectation of worst, gloom, gloominess, gloomy outlook, glumness, grief, hopelessness, low spirits, melancholy, sadness, unhappiness; SEE CONCEPTS *410,689*

pessimist [*n*] *person who expects bad outcome*
complainer, crepehanger*, cynic, defeatist, depreciator, downer, gloomy, killjoy*, misanthrope, party pooper*, prophet of doom*,

sourpuss*, wet blanket*, worrier, worrywart*; SEE CONCEPTS *412,423*

pessimistic [*adj*] *expecting bad outcome*
bleak, cynical, dark, dejected, depressed, despairing, despondent, discouraged, distrustful, downhearted, fatalistic, foreboding, gloomy, glum, hopeless, melancholy, misanthropic, morbid, morose, resigned, sad, sullen, troubled, worried; SEE CONCEPTS *403,548*

pest [*n*] *person or thing that presents problem*
annoyance, badgerer, bane, besetment, blight, blister, bore, bother, botheration, bug*, contagion, crashing bore*, creep, curse, drag, drip, epidemic, exasperation, headache*, infection, irritant, irritation, nag, nudge, nuisance, pain*, pain in the neck*, pesterer, pestilence, pill*, plague*, scourge*, tease*, thorn in side*, tormentor, trial*, trouble, vexation, virus*; SEE CONCEPTS *306,398,412,674*

pester [*v*] *bother, harass*
annoy, badger, be at, bedevil, beleaguer, bug*, disturb, dog*, drive crazy, drive up the wall*, fret, get at*, get in one's hair*, get on one's nerves*, get to*, harry, hassle, hector, hound, importune, insist, irk, mess with*, nag, nudge, pick at*, plague, provoke, remind, ride*, tantalize, tease, torment, work on*, worry; SEE CONCEPTS *7,19,48*

pestilence [*n*] *epidemic*
contagion, disease, endemic, infection, outbreak, plague, rash, scourge, sickness, virus; SEE CONCEPTS *306,316*

pestilent/pestilential [*adj*] *dangerous, harmful*
baneful, contagious, contaminating, corrupting, deadly, deleterious, destructive, detrimental, diseased, evil, fatal, infectious, injurious, lethal, mortal, noxious, pernicious, pestiferous, ruinous, tainting, troublesome, vicious; SEE CONCEPTS *314,537*

pet [*adj*] *favorite*
affectionate, cherished, darling, dear, dearest, endearing, favored, loved, precious, preferred, special; SEE CONCEPTS *568,574*

pet [*n*] *favorite thing, person*
apple of eye*, beloved, cat, darling, dear, dog, evergreen*, idol, jewel*, love, lover, persona grata*, treasure*; SEE CONCEPTS *394,416*

pet [*v*] *stroke, kiss*
baby, caress, coddle, cosset, cuddle, dandle, embrace, fondle, grab, hug, love, make love, neck*, pamper, pat, smooch*, spoil, spoon*, touch; SEE CONCEPTS *375,612*

peter out [*v*] *dwindle, decrease*
abate, come to nothing*, die out*, diminish, drain, ebb, evaporate, fade, fail, give out, lessen, pall, rebate, recede, run dry, run out, stop, taper off, wane; SEE CONCEPTS *105,698*

petite [*adj*] *small*
baby, bantam, dainty, delicate, diminutive, elfin, little, miniature, minikin*, slight, smallish, tiny, wee*; SEE CONCEPTS *773,779,789*

petition [*n*] *appeal, plea*
address, application, entreaty, imploration, imprecation, invocation, memorial, prayer, request, round robin, solicitation, suit, supplication; SEE CONCEPTS *271,662*

petition [*v*] *plead, appeal for*
adjure, ask, beg, beseech, call upon, entreat, impetrate, implore, pray, press, put in for, request,

seek, solicit, sue, supplicate, urge; SEE CONCEPTS *48,53*

petrified [*adj1*] *hardened*
calcified, fossilized, frozen, ossified, solidified; SEE CONCEPTS *483,604*

petrified [*adj2*] *terrified*
afraid, alarmed, anxious, dazed, fearful, frightened, frozen, have cold feet*, immobilized, in a cold sweat*, in a panic*, numb, panicky, pushing the panic button*, scared, scared stiff*, shocked, speechless, spooked, startled, stunned, terrorized, terror-stricken, unnerved; SEE CONCEPTS *403,690*

petrify [*v1*] *make hard*
calcify, clarify, fossilize, harden, lapidify, mineralize, set, solidify, turn to stone; SEE CONCEPT *250*

petrify [*v2*] *frighten*
alarm, amaze, appall, astonish, astound, benumb, chill, confound, daze, dismay, dumbfound, horrify, immobilize, numb, paralyze, put chill on*, scare, scare silly*, scare stiff*, spook*, startle, stun, stupefy, terrify, transfix; SEE CONCEPTS *7,14,19,42*

petroleum [*n*] *oil*
crude oil, fossil fuel, fuel, gas, gasoline, kerosene, naphtha, natural gas, petrol; SEE CONCEPTS *467,520,523,661*

petty [*adj*] *trivial, insignificant*
base, casual, cheap, contemptible, frivolous, inconsequent, inconsiderable, inessential, inferior, irrelevant, junior, lesser, light, little, lower, measly, minor, narrow-minded, negligible, nickel-and-dime*, niggling*, paltry, peanut*, penny-ante*, pettifogging*, picayune, piddling*, scratch, secondary, shabby, shallow, shoestring*, slight, small, small-minded, subordinate, trifling, two-bit*, unimportant; SEE CONCEPTS *403,575*

petulant [*adj*] *crabby, moody*
bad-tempered, captious, caviling, complaining, cranky*, cross, crybaby*, displeased, fault-finding, fractious, fretful, grouchy, grumbling, huffy, ill-humored, impatient, irritable, mean, peevish, perverse, pouting, querulous, snappish, sour, sulky, sullen, testy, touchy, ungracious, uptight*, waspish, whining, whiny; SEE CONCEPTS *401,542*

phantom [*n*] *ghost; figment of the imagination*
apparition, chimera, daydream, delusion, dream, eidolon, figment, hallucination, haunt, ignis fatuus, illusion, mirage, nightmare, phantasm, revenant, shade, shadow, specter, spirit, spook, vision, wraith; SEE CONCEPTS *370,529*

pharmacist [*n*] *druggist*
apothecary, pharmacologist; SEE CONCEPT *357*

phase [*n*] *period in life of something*
appearance, aspect, chapter, condition, development, facet, juncture, point, position, posture, stage, state, step, time; SEE CONCEPTS *816,834*

phenomenal [*adj*] *astounding, exceptional*
extraordinary, fantastic, marvelous, miraculous, outstanding, preternatural, prodigious, rare, remarkable, sensational, singular, substantial, uncommon, unique, unparalleled, unusual, unwonted, wondrous; SEE CONCEPTS *564,574*

phenomenology [*n*] *study of subject and objects of a person's experience*
intentionality, life-world, lived experience, meaning-making; SEE CONCEPTS *282,349*

phenomenon [*n*] *rare occurrence; wonder*
abnormality, actuality, anomaly, appearance, aspect, circumstance, curiosity, episode, event, exception, experience, fact, happening, incident, marvel, miracle, nonpareil, one for the books*, paradox, peculiarity, portent, prodigy, rara avis*, rarity, reality, sensation, sight, something else*, spectacle, stunner*, uniqueness; SEE CONCEPTS *230,529,678*

philanderer [*n*] *person who has many love affairs*
adulterer, chaser, cruiser, dallier, debaucher, flirt, gallant, lover, operator*, swinger; SEE CONCEPT *423*

philanthropic [*adj*] *charitable, giving*
altruistic, beneficent, benevolent, benignant, big-hearted, bountiful, contributing, donating, eleemosynary, generous, good, gracious, helpful, humane, humanitarian, kind, kindhearted, liberal, magnanimous, munificent, openhanded, patriotic, public-spirited; SEE CONCEPTS *404,542*

philanthropist [*n*] *humanitarian*
altruist, benefactor, bleeding heart*, contributor, do-gooder*, donor, Good Samaritan*, good scout*, helper, patron; SEE CONCEPTS *416,423*

philanthropy [*n*] *humanitarianism*
alms, alms-giving, altruism, assistance, benefaction, beneficence, charity, contribution, dole, donation, endowment, fund, generosity, gifting, good works, helping hand*, relief; SEE CONCEPTS *337,657*

philosopher [*n*] *deep thinker*
logician, sage, savant, sophist, theorist, wise person; SEE CONCEPTS *349,687,689*

philosophical/philosophic [*adj1*] *thinking deeply, rationally*
abstract, cogitative, deep, erudite, judicious, learned, logical, pensive, profound, rational, reflective, sagacious, sapient, theoretical, thoughtful, wise; SEE CONCEPT *402*

philosophical/philosophic [*adj2*] *calm, serene*
collected, commonsensical, composed, cool*, cool as cucumber*, enduring, impassive, imperturbable, patient, resigned, stoical, tranquil, unagitated, unflappable, unmoved, unruffled; SEE CONCEPT *401*

philosophy [*n*] *principles, knowledge*
aesthetics, attitude, axiom, beliefs, conception, convictions, doctrine, idea, ideology, logic, metaphysics, ontology, outlook, rationalism, reason, reasoning, system, tenet, theory, thinking, thought, truth, values, view, viewpoint, wisdom; SEE CONCEPTS *349,688,689*

phlegmatic [*adj*] *unemotional*
along for the ride*, apathetic, blah*, cold, cool, deadpan, desensitized, disinterested, dispassionate, dull, emotionless, flat, frigid, groggy, indifferent, lethargic, lifeless, listless, passionless, passive, sluggish, uncompassionate, undemonstrative, unexcitable, unfeeling, uninvolved, unresponsive; SEE CONCEPTS *401,403*

phobia [*n*] *fear*
anxiety, aversion, avoidance, awe, detestation, disgust, dislike, distaste, dread, fear, hang-up*, hatred, horror, irrationality, loathing, neurosis, obsession, repulsion, resentment, revulsion, terror, thing*, thing about*; SEE CONCEPTS *27,29,529*

phobic [*adj*] *fearful*
afraid, anxious, apprehensive, discomposed, disquieted, disturbed, frightened, have cold feet*, irrational, jittery, jumpy, nervous, neurotic, pan-

pe
ph

icky, scared, shy, skittish, tense, worried; SEE
CONCEPT *401*

phony [*adj*] *fake, false*
affected, artificial, assumed, bogus, counterfeit,
forged, imitation, pseudo, put-on*, sham*, spurious, trick; SEE CONCEPT *582*

photocopy [*n/v*] *mechanical image produced
from a copier; making the image*
copy, duplicate, reproduce, stat, velox, Xerox;
SEE CONCEPT *269*

photograph [*n*] *a still picture taken with a camera*
blowup, close-up, image, Kodachrome*,
Kodak*, likeness, microfilm, mug*, negative,
photo, photostat, pic*, picture, pinup*, pix*, Polaroid*, portrait, positive, print, shot*, slide,
snap, snapshot, transparency; SEE CONCEPT *265*

photograph [*v*] *take a picture with a camera*
capture*, capture on film*, cinematize, close-
up*, copy, film, get, get a likeness*, get a shot*,
illustrate, lens*, make a picture*, microfilm,
mug*, photo, photoengrave, photostat, picture,
print, record, reproduce, roll, shoot, snap*, snapshot, take*, turn*, X-ray*; SEE CONCEPT *174*

photographer [*n*] *cameraperson*
freelance photographer, paparazzo, photojour-
nalist, shutterbug; SEE CONCEPT *352*

photographic [*adj*] *exact, retentive in detail*
accurate, cinematic, detailed, faithful, filmic,
graphic, lifelike, minute, natural, pictorial, picturesque, precise, realistic, true-to-life*, visual,
vivid; SEE CONCEPT *557*

phrase [,*n*] *group of words; way of speaking*
byword, catchphrase, catchword, diction, expression, idiom, locution, maxim, motto, parlance,
phraseology, phrasing, remark, saying, shibboleth, slogan, styling, tag, terminology, utterance,
verbalism, verbiage, watchword, wordage, wording; SEE CONCEPTS *275,278*

phrase [*v*] *express in words carefully*
couch, formulate, frame, present, put, put into
words, say, term, utter, voice, word; SEE CON-
CEPT *55*

physical [*adj1*] *tangible, material*
concrete, corporeal, environmental, gross, materialistic, natural, objective, palpable, phenomenal, ponderable, real, sensible, solid, somatic,
substantial, visible; SEE CONCEPT *582*

physical [*adj2*] *concerning the body*
bodily, brute, carnal, corporal, corporeal, earthly,
fleshly, incarnate, mortal, personal, somatic, unspiritual, visceral; SEE CONCEPT *485*

physician [*n*] *person trained in medical science*
bones*, doc*, doctor, general practitioner,
healer, intern, MD*, medic, medical practitioner,
quack*, sawbones*, specialist, surgeon; SEE
CONCEPT *357*

physique [*n*] *build of human body*
anatomy, body, built, character, configuration,
constitution, corpus, figure, form, frame, habit,
habitus, makeup, muscles, nature, shape, structure, type; SEE CONCEPTS *405,757*

picayune [*adj*] *trivial*
diminutive, everyday, frivolous, immaterial, incidental, inconsequential, inconsiderable, insignificant, irrelevant, little, meager, mean,
meaningless, minor, minute, negligible,
nonessential, of no account*, paltry, petty, piddling*, puny, slight, small, superficial, trifling,
trite, unimportant; SEE CONCEPT *575*

pick [*n*] *a chosen option, usually the choicest*
aces, bag, best, choice, choosing, cream*, crème
de la crème*, cup of tea*, decision, druthers*,
elect, elite, flower*, preference, pride, prime,
prize, select, selection, top, tops; SEE CONCEPTS
529,671

pick [*v1*] *choose, select*
cull, decide upon, elect, finger*, fix upon, go
down the line*, hand-pick, mark, name, optate,
opt for, pick and choose, pick out, prefer, say so,
separate, settle on, sift out*, single out, slot, sort
out, tab, tag, take, take it or leave it*, tap, winnow; SEE CONCEPT *41*

pick [*v2*] *gather, harvest*
accumulate, choose, collect, cull, cut, draw,
pluck, pull; SEE CONCEPTS *41,109,206*

pick [*v3*] *break into something closed, locked*
break open, crack, dent, force, hit, indent, jimmy,
open, pry, strike; SEE CONCEPT *192*

pick at/pick on [*v*] *nag, provoke*
badger, bait, blame, bully, carp, cavil, criticize,
find fault, foment, get at*, get to*, goad, hector,
incite, instigate, quibble, start, tease, torment;
SEE CONCEPTS *7,19,52*

picket [*n1*] *post of structure*
pale, paling, palisade, panel, peg, pillar, rail,
stake, stanchion, upright; SEE CONCEPTS *445,479*

picket [*n2*] *person who demonstrates for cause*
demonstrator, picketer, protester, striker; SEE
CONCEPTS *348,359*

picket [*n3*] *person acting as guard*
guard, lookout, patrol, scout, sentinel, sentry,
spotter, vedette, ward, watch, watchperson; SEE
CONCEPT *348*

picket [*v*] *protest against, for cause*
blockade, boycott, demonstrate, hit the bricks*,
strike, walk out; SEE CONCEPTS *300,351*

pickle [*n*] *sticky situation*
bind, box*, corner*, difficulty, dilemma, disorder, fix, hole*, hot water*, jam*, predicament,
quandary, scrape, spot*, tight spot*; SEE CON-
CEPT *674*

pickle [*v*] *preserve fruit or vegetable*
can, cure, keep, marinade, salt, souse, steep; SEE
CONCEPT *170*

pick-me-up [*n*] *stimulant*
analeptic, catalyst, drug, energizer, incentive,
motivation, motive, restorative, reviver, shot in
the arm*, spark pulg*, spur, stimulus, tonic,
upper; SEE CONCEPTS *240,307,661*

pick up [*v1*] *lift, raise*
elevate, gather, grasp, hoist, rear, take up, uphold, uplift, upraise, uprear; SEE CONCEPT *196*

pick up [*v2*] *obtain, find*
acquire, annex, buy, chalk up*, come across,
compass, cull, extract, gain, garner, gather, get,
get the hang of*, glean, happen upon*, have,
learn, procure, purchase, score, secure, take; SEE
CONCEPTS *31,120,183*

pick up [*v3*] *improve*
continue, gain, gain ground*, get better, get well,
increase, make a comeback*, mend, perk up*,
rally, recommence, recover, renew, reopen,
restart, resume, swell, take up; SEE CONCEPTS
234,700

pick up [*v4*] *call for socially*
accompany, collect, drop in for*, get*, give a
lift*, go for*, go to get*, invite, offer, proposition, stop for*; SEE CONCEPTS *224,384*

pick up [*v5*] *arrest for crime*
apprehend, book*, bust*, collar*, detain, nab, pinch*, pull in*, run in*, take into custody; SEE CONCEPT *317*

picky [*adj*] *choosy, finicky*
captious, critical, dainty, fastidious, fault-finding, fussy, nice, particular, persnickety; SEE CONCEPT *404*

picnic [*n1*] *outdoor meal*
barbecue, clambake, cookout, dining alfresco, excursion, fish fry, outing, weiner roast; SEE CONCEPTS *386,459*

picnic [*n2*] *easy undertaking*
breeze*, child's play*, cinch, duck soup*, kid stuff*, lark*, light work, no trouble, piece of cake*, pushover*, setup*, smooth sailing*, snap, sure thing, walkover*; SEE CONCEPTS *362,693*

picture [*n1*] *illustration, likeness of something*
account, art, blueprint, canvas, cartoon, copy, delineation, depiction, description, doodle, double, draft, drawing, duplicate, effigy, engraving, figure, icon, image, impression, lookalike, outline, painting, panorama, photo, photograph, piece, portrait, portrayal, presentment, print, re-creation, replica, report, representation, ringer*, similitude, simulacrum, sketch, spectacle, spitting image*, statue, tableau, twin; SEE CONCEPTS *259,625*

picture [*n2*] *perfect example*
archetype, embodiment, epitome, essence, idea, personification; SEE CONCEPT *686*

picture [*n3*] *entertainment film*
cartoon, cinema, flick*, motion picture, movie, moving picture, photoplay, picture show, show; SEE CONCEPT *293*

picture [*v1*] *depict, describe*
delineate, draw, illustrate, image, interpret, limn, paint, photograph, portray, render, represent, show, sketch; SEE CONCEPTS *79,174*

picture [*v2*] *form vision in one's mind*
conceive of, create, daydream, dream, envision, fancy, fantasize, imagine, portray, see, see in the mind's eye*, visualize; SEE CONCEPTS *17,43*

picturesque [*adj*] *attractive, referring to scenery*
arresting, artistic, beautiful, charming, colorful, graphic, photographic, pictorial, pleasant, pretty, quaint, scenic, striking, vivid; SEE CONCEPTS *579,589*

piddling [*adj*] *insignificant*
derisory, little, measly*, niggling*, paltry, peanut*, pettifogging*, petty, picayune, puny, trifling, trivial, unimportant, useless, worthless; SEE CONCEPTS *575,789*

piddly [*adj*] *meager, trivial*
barren, deficient, diddly*, flimsy, inconsiderable, insubstantial, insufficient, little, measly*, mere, microscopic, minute, negligible, paltry, petty, puny, rinky-dink*, scant, scrimpy, short, skimpy, slight, small, sparse, superficial, too little too late*, two-bit*, unproductive, worthless; SEE CONCEPTS *546,789*

piece [*n1*] *part*
allotment, bit, bite, chunk, cut, division, dole, end, example, fraction, fragment, gob, half, hunk, instance, interest, iota, item, length, lot, lump, member, moiety, morsel, parcel, percentage, portion, quantity, quota, sample, scrap, section, segment, share, shred, slice, smithereen*, specimen; SEE CONCEPTS *834,835*

piece [*n2*] *work of art, music, writing*
arrangement, article, bit, composition, creation, discourse, dissertation, engraving, exposition, icon, item, lines, painting, paper, part, photograph, print, production, sketch, song, statue, study, theme, thesis, treatise, treatment, vignette, work; SEE CONCEPTS *259,262,263,271*

piece [*v*] *put together*
assemble, combine, compose, create, fix, join, make, mend, patch, repair, restore, unite; SEE CONCEPTS *113,173,193,251*

piece de resistance [*n1*] *outstanding accomplishment*
achievement, chef d'oeuvre, feat, great performance, jewel, magnum opus, masterpiece, master work, prize, showpiece, tour de force*; SEE CONCEPT *259*

piecemeal [*adj/adv*] *bit by bit*
at intervals, by degrees, by fits and starts*, fitfully, fragmentary, gradual, gradually, intermittent, intermittently, interrupted, little by little*, partial, partially, patchy, spotty, step by step*; SEE CONCEPTS *531,544*

pier [*n*] *support; place for boats*
berth, buttress, column, dam, dock, jetty, landing, levee, mole, pierage, pilaster, pile, piling, pillar, post, promenade, quay, slip, upright, wharf; SEE CONCEPTS *439,443,479*

pierce [*v*] *cut, penetrate*
bore, break, break in, break through, cleave, crack, crack open, drill, enter, gash, incise, intrude, pass through, perforate, plow, prick, probe, puncture, run through, slash, slice, slit, spike, stab, stick into, transfix; SEE CONCEPTS *137,159,176,220*

piercing [*adj*] *intense to the senses*
acute, agonizing, arctic, biting, bitter, blaring, cold, deafening, earsplitting, excruciating, exquisite, fierce, freezing, frosty, high, high-pitched, keen, knifelike, loud, numbing, painful, penetrating, powerful, racking, raw, roaring, severe, sharp, shattering, shooting, shrill, stabbing, stentorian, stentorious, thin, treble, wintry; SEE CONCEPTS *406,537,592,594*

piety [*n*] *devotion, religiousness*
allegiance, application, ardor, belief, devoutness, docility, dutifulness, duty, faith, fealty, fervor, fidelity, godliness, grace, holiness, loyalty, obedience, passion, religion, religiosity, reverence, sanctity, veneration, zeal; SEE CONCEPTS *633,689*

piffle [*n*] *nonsense*
balderdash*, baloney*, bull*, bunk*, drivel, empty talk, foolishness, futile talk, gibberish, hogwash*, hooey*, hot air*, jive*, palaver, poppycock*, prattle, rubbish, silliness, trash*, useless words; SEE CONCEPTS *230,388,633*

pig [*n*] *animal of swine family*
boar, cob roller*, hog, piggy*, piglet, porker*, porky, shoat, sow, swine; SEE CONCEPTS *394,400*

pigeonhole [*n*] *compartment*
box, carrel, chamber, corner, cranny, cubbyhole, cubicle, hole, niche, nook, place, pocket, recess, section, slot, stall; SEE CONCEPT *434*

pigeonhole [*v*] *categorize; shelve*
assort, class, classify, defer, delay, dismiss, file, group, hold, hold off, hold up, label, lay aside, peg*, postpone, put aside, put down as, put off, put on hold, put on ice*, put on the bank burner*, rank, sideline, sort, tab, table, type cast; SEE CONCEPTS *39,121*

ph
pi

pigheaded [*adj*] *stubborn*
bullheaded, contrary, dense*, forward, headstrong, inflexible, insistent, intractable, mulish*, obstinate, perverse, recalcitrant, self-willed, stiffnecked, stupid*, unyielding, willful; SEE CONCEPTS *404,542*

pigment [*n*] *color, shade*
colorant, coloring, coloring matter, dye, dyestuff, oil, paint, stain, tincture, tint; SEE CONCEPTS *259,622*

pig out [*v*] *overeat*
binge, blimp out*, devour, dive in*, eat like a horse*, eat to excess, feed, gluttonize, gobble, gorge, gormandize, gulp, guzzle, hoover*, overindulge, pork out*, scarf out*, shovel it in*, stuff oneself, wolf*; SEE CONCEPT *169*

pile [*n1*] *heap, collection*
accumulation, aggregate, aggregation, amassment, assemblage, assortment, bank, barrel, buildup, chunk, conglomeration, drift, gob, great deal, hill, hoard, hunk, jumble, lump, mass, mound, mountain, much, ocean, oodles*, pack, peck, pyramid, quantity, shock, stack, stockpile; SEE CONCEPTS *432,787*

pile [*n2*] *wealth*
affluence, boodle*, bundle*, dough*, fortune, mint*, money, pot*, riches, wad*; SEE CONCEPTS *335,340*

pile [*v*] *gather, pack; put on top of another*
accumulate, amass, assemble, bank, bunch, collect, crowd, crush, fill, flock, heap, hill, hoard, jam, load, mass, mound, rush, stack, store; SEE CONCEPTS *84,109,201,750*

pilfer [*v*] *steal, embezzle*
annex, appropriate, borrow, cop*, crib*, filch*, liberate*, lift*, moonlight*, palm*, pinch*, pluck*, purloin, requisition, rip off*, rob, scrounge, snare, snatch, swipe, take, thieve, walk off with*; SEE CONCEPTS *139,142,192*

pilgrimage [*n*] *long journey*
crusade, excursion, expedition, mission, tour, travel, trip, wayfaring; SEE CONCEPT *224*

pill [*n1*] *capsule of medicine*
bolus, dose, lozenge, medicine, pellet, pilule, tablet, troche; SEE CONCEPTS *307,470*

pill [*n2*] *person who is annoying*
bore, drag*, nuisance, pain*, pain in the neck*, pest, trial*; SEE CONCEPTS *412,423*

pillage [*v*] *plunder, destroy*
appropriate, arrogate, confiscate, depredate, desecrate, desolate, despoil, devastate, devour, gut, invade, lay waste*, lift*, loot, maraud, nab*, pilfer, pinch*, purloin, raid, ransack, ravage, rifle*, rob, ruin, sack, spoil, spoliate, steal, strip, thieve, trespass, waste; SEE CONCEPTS *86,139,252*

pillar [*n1*] *column of building, or freestanding column*
colonnade, mast, obelisk, pedestal, pier, pilaster, piling, post, prop, shaft, stanchion, support, tower, upright; SEE CONCEPT *440*

pillar [*n2*] *mainstay; source of strength*
backbone*, guider, leader, light*, rock*, sinew, supporter, tower of strength*, upholder, worthy; SEE CONCEPTS *423,712*

pilot [*n*] *person who guides aircraft, ship, or other vehicle*
ace*, aerialist, aeronaut, aviator, bellwether*, captain, conductor, coxswain, dean, director, doyen/doyenne, eagle*, flier*, flyer, guide, helmsperson, jockey*, lead, leader, navigator,

one at the controls, one at the wheel, scout*, steerer, steersperson, wheelperson; SEE CONCEPT *348*

pimple [*n*] *small swelling on the skin*
abscess, acne, beauty spot, blackhead, blemish, blister, boil, bump, carbuncle, caruncle, excrescence, furuncle, hickey*, inflammation, lump, papula, papule, pustule, spot, whitehead, zit*; SEE CONCEPT *306*

pin [*v*] *attach, hold in place*
affix, bind, clasp, close, fasten, fix, hold down, hold fast, immobilize, join, pinion, press, restrain, secure; SEE CONCEPTS *85,160,190*

pinch [*n1*] *tight pressing*
compression, confinement, contraction, cramp, grasp, grasping, hurt, limitation, nip, nipping, pressure, squeeze, torment, tweak, twinge; SEE CONCEPT *728*

pinch [*n2*] *small amount*
bit, dash, drop, jot, mite, small quantity, soupçon, speck, splash, splatter, taste; SEE CONCEPT *831*

pinch [*n3*] *predicament*
box*, clutch, contingency, crisis, crunch*, difficulty, emergency, exigency, hardship, juncture, necessity, oppression, pass, plight, pressure, strait, stress, tight spot*, tight squeeze*, turning point*, zero hour*; SEE CONCEPT *674*

pinch [*v1*] *press tightly*
chafe, compress, confine, cramp, crush, grasp, hurt, nip, pain, squeeze, tweak, twinge, wrench, wrest, wring; SEE CONCEPTS *219,313*

pinch [*v2*] *be stingy*
afflict, distress, economize, oppress, pinch pennies*, press, scrape, scrimp, skimp, spare, stint; SEE CONCEPT *330*

pinch [*v3*] *steal*
cop*, crib*, filch*, knock off*, lift*, nab*, pilfer, purloin, rob, snatch, swipe, take; SEE CONCEPT *139*

pinch [*v4*] *arrest*
apprehend, bust*, collar*, detain, hold, nab*, pick up*, pull in*, run in*, take into custody; SEE CONCEPTS *90,317*

pine [*v*] *long for*
ache, agonize, brood, carry a torch*, covet, crave, desire, dream, fret, grieve, hanker, languish for, lust after, mope*, mourn, sigh, spoil for*, thirst for, want, wish, yearn, yen for; SEE CONCEPT *20*

pink [*n1/adj*] *rose color*
blush, coral, flush, fuchsia, rose, roseate, salmon; SEE CONCEPT *622*

pink [*n2*] *best condition*
acme*, best, bloom*, fitness, good health, height*, peak, perfection, prime, summit, trim*, verdure; SEE CONCEPTS *316,388*

pink [*v*] *cut in zigzag*
incise, notch, perforate, prick, punch, scallop, score; SEE CONCEPT *176*

pinnacle [*n*] *top, crest*
acme, apex, apogee, climax, cone, crown, culmination, greatest, height, max*, most*, needle*, obelisk, peak, pyramid, spire, steeple, summit, tops, tower, vertex, zenith; SEE CONCEPTS *706,836*

pinpoint [*v*] *define, locate*
determinate, diagnose, distinguish, finger*, get a fix on*, home in on*, identify, place, recognize, spot; SEE CONCEPTS *38,183*

pioneer [*adj*] *early, first*
avant-garde, brave, experimental, head, inaugural, initial, lead, original, primary, prime; SEE CONCEPT *585*

pioneer [*n*] *person who finds a new place, founds something*
colonist, colonizer, developer, explorer, founder, frontier settler, guide, homesteader, immigrant, innovator, leader, pathfinder, pilgrim, scout, settler, squatter, trailblazer; SEE CONCEPTS *348,413*

pioneer [*v*] *invent; lay the groundwork*
begin, colonize, create, develop, discover, establish, explore, found, go out in front*, initiate, instigate, institute, launch, map out, open up, originate, prepare, show the way, spearhead*, start, take the lead, trailblaze*; SEE CONCEPTS *173,221,324*

pious [*adj*] *dedicated, religious*
born-again*, clerical, devoted, devout, divine, ecclesiastical, godly, goody-goody*, orthodox, prayerful, priestly, reverent, righteous, sacred, saintly, sanctimonious, spiritual; SEE CONCEPT *401*

pipe [*n*] *passage, tube*
aqueduct, canal, channel, conduit, conveyer, duct, hose, line, main, pipeline, sewer, spout, trough, vent, vessel; SEE CONCEPTS *475,499*

pipe [*v1*] *conduct through tube, passage*
bring in, carry, channel, convey, funnel, siphon, supply, traject, transmit; SEE CONCEPT *217*

pipe [*v2*] *make a sound; peep*
blubber*, boohoo*, cheep*, cry, play, say, shout, sing, sob, sound, speak, talk, toot*, trill, tweet, twitter, wail, warble, weep, whistle; SEE CONCEPTS *47,65,77*

pipe dream [*n*] *fantasy*
air castle, airy hope, castle in the sky*, chimera, daydream, fantastic notion, fool's paradise*, unreal hope, wishful thinking; SEE CONCEPTS *20,529,689*

pipsqueak [*n*] *nonentity*
nobody, runt, shrimp, squirt, twerp, whippersnapper; SEE CONCEPT *424*

piquant [*adj*] *flavorful, biting*
highly-seasoned, interesting, lively, peppery, poignant, provocative, pungent, racy, savory, sharp, snappy, sparkling, spicy, spirited, stimulating, stinging, tangy, tart, well-flavored, with a kick*, zestful, zesty; SEE CONCEPTS *529,613*

pique [*n*] *anger, irritation*
annoyance, blowup*, conniption*, dander*, displeasure, flare-up, grudge, huff, hurt, irk, miff*, offense, peeve, pet*, provocation, resentment, rise, ruckus*, slow burn*, snit, sore*, stew*, storm*, tiff*, umbrage, vexation; SEE CONCEPTS *29,410*

pique [*v*] *offend, provoke*
absorb, affront, annoy, arouse, bother, bug*, displease, egg on*, exasperate, excite, fire up*, gall, galvanize, get*, get a rise out of*, get under skin*, give a hard time*, give the business*, goad, goose*, grab, ignite, incense, irk, irritate, kindle, make waves*, miff*, mortify, motivate, move, nettle, offend, peeve, prick, put out*, quicken, rile, rouse, spur, stimulate, sting*, stir, vex, whet, work up*, wound; SEE CONCEPTS *7,14,19,22*

piracy [*n*] *robbery*
bootlegging, buccaneering, commandeering, copying, freebooting, hijacking, infringement, marauding, pirating, plagiarism, rapine, stealing, swashbuckling, theft; SEE CONCEPTS *139,192*

pirate [*n*] *buccaneer*
corsair, filibuster, freebooter, marauder, picaroon, privateer, raider, rover, sea rover; SEE CONCEPT *412*

pissed off [*adj*] *angry*
affronted, annoyed, bent out of shape*, boiling*, cross, displeased, enraged, fighting mad*, fit to be tied*, fuming, furious, hopping mad*, hot, huffy*, in a tizzy*, incensed, inflamed, infuriated, irate, irritated, livid, mad, maddened, offended, outraged, peed*, peeved off*, provoked, raging, riled, sore, steamed, steamed up, steaming, storming, t'd off*, tee'd off*, ticked off*; SEE CONCEPT *403*

pistol [*n*] *revolver*
firearm, forty-five*, gun, handgun, piece*, rod*, Saturday night special*, six-shooter, thirty-eight*; SEE CONCEPT *500*

pit [*n*] *hole, cavity*
abyss, chasm, crater, dent, depression, dimple, excavation, grave, gulf, hell, hollow, indentation, mine, perforation, pockmark, pothole, puncture, shaft, tomb, trench, well; SEE CONCEPTS *509,513*

pit [*v*] *oppose, play off*
contend, counter, match, put in opposition, set against, vie; SEE CONCEPTS *92,363*

pitch [*n1*] *tilt*
angle, cant, degree, dip, gradient, height, incline, level, point, slant, slope, steepness; SEE CONCEPTS *692,738*

pitch [*n2*] *tone of sound*
frequency, harmonic, modulation, rate, sound, timbre; SEE CONCEPT *65*

pitch [*n3*] *talk to convince*
patter*, persuasion, sales talk, song and dance*, spiel*; SEE CONCEPTS *68,278*

pitch [*v1*] *throw, hurl*
bung, cast, chuck*, fire, fling, gun, heave, launch, lob, peg, sling, toss, unseat; SEE CONCEPT *222*

pitch [*v2*] *put up, erect*
fix, locate, place, plant, raise, settle, set up, station; SEE CONCEPT *168*

pitch [*v3*] *dive, roll*
ascend, bend, bicker, careen, descend, dip, drive, drop, fall, flounder, go down, heave, lean, lunge, lurch, plunge, rise, rock, seesaw, slope, slump, stagger, tilt, topple, toss, tumble, vault, wallow, welter, yaw; SEE CONCEPTS *147,181,201*

pitcher [*n1*] *jug*
amphora, bottle, canteen, carafe, container, crock, cruet, decanter, ewer, flagon, flask, jar, vase, vessel; SEE CONCEPT *494*

pitcher [*n2*] *baseball pitcher*
ace*, baseball player, closer, hurler, knuckleballer, middle reliever, reliever; SEE CONCEPT *366*

pitch in [*v*] *help; get busy*
aid, attack, begin, buckle down*, chip in*, come through, commence, contribute, cooperate, do, do one's bit*, fall to*, get cracking*, get going, go to it*, hop to it*, join in, jump in*, launch, lend a hand*, participate, plunge into*, set about, set to, subscribe, tackle, tee off*, volunteer, wade in; SEE CONCEPTS *100,110*

piteous [*adj*] *miserable, pathetic*
beseeching, commiserable, deplorable, distressing, doleful, dolorous, entreating, grievous,

heartbreaking, heart-rending, imploring, lamentable, melancholy, mournful, moving, pitiable, pitiful, plaintive, poignant, poor, rueful, ruined, sad, sorrowful, supplicating, woeful, wretched; SEE CONCEPTS *485,529*

pitfall [*n*] *hazard, trap*
booby trap*, catch*, danger, deadfall*, difficulty, downfall, drawback, entanglement, hook*, mesh*, mousetrap*, peril, pit*, quicksand*, risk, setup*, snag*, snare, swindle*, toil, web; SEE CONCEPTS *674,679*

pithy [*adj*] *brief, to the point*
cogent, compact, concise, crisp, curt, down to brass tacks*, effective, epigrammatic, expressive, honed, laconic, meaningful, meaty*, pointed, short, short-and-sweet*, significant, succinct, terse, trenchant; SEE CONCEPT *267*

pitiful [*adj*] *in bad shape; poor*
abject, affecting, afflicted, arousing, base, beggarly, cheap, cheerless, comfortless, commiserative, compassionate, contemptible, deplorable, despicable, dismal, distressed, distressing, grievous, heartbreaking, heartrending, inadequate, insignificant, joyless, lamentable, low, mean, miserable, mournful, moving, paltry, pathetic, piteous, pitiable, sad, scurvy, shabby, sorrowful, sorry, stirring, suffering, tearful, touching, vile, woeful, worthless, wretched; SEE CONCEPTS *485,529*

pitiless [*adj*] *without mercy or care*
austere, barbarous, brutal, callous, cold*, cold-blooded*, coldhearted*, cruel, cutthroat*, dog-eat-dog*, frigid, hardhearted*, harsh, hatchetjob*, heartless, implacable, indifferent, inexorable, inhuman, inhumane, insensible, killer instinct*, mean, merciless, obdurate, relentless, remorseless, ruthless, satanic, savage, soulless*; SEE CONCEPT *401*

pittance [*n*] *small amount*
allowance, bit, chicken feed*, dribble*, drop*, drop in the bucket*, inadequacy, insufficiency, mite, modicum, peanuts*, pension, portion, ration, scrap*, slave wages*, smidgen, trace, trifle; SEE CONCEPTS *344,787*

pity [*n1*] *feeling of mercy toward another*
benevolence, charity, clemency, comfort, commiseration, compassion, compunction, condolement, condolence, dejection, distress, empathy, favor, forbearance, goodness, grace, humanity, kindliness, kindness, lenity, melancholy, mercy, philanthropy, quarter, rue, ruth, sadness, solace, sorrow, sympathy, tenderness, understanding, warmth; SEE CONCEPTS *410,657*

pity [*n2*] *sad situation*
bad luck, catastrophe, crime, crisis, crying shame*, disaster, mischance, misfortune, mishap, regret, shame, sin; SEE CONCEPT *674*

pity [*v*] *feel sorry for; spare*
ache*, be sorry for, be sympathetic, bleed for*, comfort, commiserate, condole, console, feel for, feel with, forgive, give quarter*, grant amnesty, grieve with, have compassion, have mercy on, identify with, lament with, pardon, put out of one's misery*, relent, reprieve, show forgiveness*, show sympathy*, solace, soothe, sympathize, take pity on*, understand, weep for*; SEE CONCEPTS *10,34,83*

pivot [*n*] *center point about which something revolves*
axis, axle, center, focal point, fulcrum, heart,

hinge, hub, kingpin, shaft, spindle, swivel, turning point; SEE CONCEPTS *445,464,498,830*

pivot [*v*] *revolve around center point*
be contingent, depend, hang, hinge, rely, rotate, sheer, spin, swivel, turn, twirl, veer, volte-face, wheel, whip, whirl; SEE CONCEPTS *147,532*

pivotal [*adj*] *important*
cardinal, central, climactic, critical, crucial, decisive, determining, essential, focal, middle, momentous, overriding, overruling, principal, ruling, vital; SEE CONCEPT *568*

pixie [*n*] *fairy*
bogie, brownie, elf, fay, gnome, goblin, gremlin, hob, imp, leprechaun, nisse, puck, spirit, sprite; SEE CONCEPT *370*

pizzazz [*n*] *energy; flamboyance*
ability, animation, aptitude, bounce, dash, drive, effectiveness, elan, fire, force, forcefulness, get-up-and-go*, gift, hustle, intensity, juice, knack, life, liveliness, moxie*, muscle, oomph*, panache, pep, pluck, potency, power, presence, punch, push, shine*, spirit, splash*, spunk, stamina, vim, virility, vitality, vivacity, zeal, zest, zing, zip*; SEE CONCEPTS *411,630,706*

placard [*n*] *sign, notice*
advertisement, announcement, banner, bill, billboard, handbill, marquee, poster, public notice, signboard; SEE CONCEPTS *271,284*

placate [*v*] *soothe, pacify*
appease, assuage, calm, cheer, comfort, conciliate, humor, make peace*, make up*, mollify, pacify, play up to*, pour oil on*, propitiate, reconcile, satisfy, soft-pedal*, soothe, stroke*, sweeten, tranquilize, win over*; SEE CONCEPTS *7,22,126*

place [*n1*] *location with purpose, function*
abode, accommodation, apartment, area, berth, city, community, compass, corner, country, distance, district, domicile, dwelling, field, habitat, hamlet, hangout, hole*, home, house, joint, latitude, lay, locale, locality, locus, longitude, neighborhood, niche, nook, pad*, part, plant, point, position, property, quarter, region, reservation, residence, room, seat, section, site, situation, spot, station, stead, suburb, town, venue, vicinity, village, volume, whereabouts, zone; SEE CONCEPTS *435,515*

place [*n2*] *position, rank*
capacity, character, footing, grade, pecking order*, slot, standing, state, station, status; SEE CONCEPT *388*

place [*n3*] *job, employment*
appointment, berth, connection, occupation, office, position, post, profession, situation, spot, trade; SEE CONCEPT *360*

place [*n4*] *duty, role*
affair, charge, concern, function, prerogative, responsibility, right; SEE CONCEPT *532*

place [*v1*] *locate, situate*
allocate, allot, assign, deposit, distribute, establish, finger, fix, install, lay, lodge, nail, park, peg, plant, position, put, quarter, repose, rest, set, settle, spot, stand, station, stick, store, stow; SEE CONCEPT *201*

place [*v2*] *order, sort*
allocate, appoint, approximate, arrange, assign, call, charge, class, classify, commission, constitute, delegate, deputize, designate, entrust, estimate, fix, give, grade, group, judge, name,

nominate, ordain, put, rank, reckon; SEE CONCEPTS *50,84,88,98*

place [*v3*] *identify, recognize*
associate, determinate, determine, diagnose, distinguish, figure out*, finger*, indicate, know, nail*, peg*, pinpoint, put one's finger on*, remember, set in context, spot, tell; SEE CONCEPT *38*

placebo [*n*] *fake pill*
inactive drug, inactive medicine, inactive substance, sugar pill, test substance; SEE CONCEPTS *260,412*

placid [*adj*] *calm, mild*
collected, composed, cool*, cool as a cucumber*, detached, easygoing, equable, even, even-tempered, gentle, halcyon, hushed, imperturbable, irenic, peaceful, poised, quiet, restful, self-possessed, serene, still, tranquil; SEE CONCEPTS *401,485*

plagiarism [*n*] *copying of another's written work*
appropriation, borrowing, counterfeiting, cribbing, falsification, fraud, infringement, lifting, literary theft, piracy, stealing, theft; SEE CONCEPTS *139,192*

plague [*n1*] *disease that is widespread*
affliction, contagion, curse, epidemic, hydra, infection, infestation, influenza, invasion, outbreak, pandemic, pestilence, rash, ravage, scourge; SEE CONCEPT *306*

plague [*n2*] *annoyance, curse*
affliction, aggravation, bane, besetment, blast, blight, bother, botheration, calamity, cancer, evil, exasperation, hydra, irritant, nuisance, pain, pest, problem, scourge, thorn in side, torment, trial, vexation; SEE CONCEPTS *674,679*

plague [*v*] *annoy, disturb*
afflict, badger, bedevil, beleaguer, bother, chafe, fret, gall, gnaw, harass, harry, hassle, haunt, hector, hound, infest, irk, molest, pain, persecute, pester, pursue, ride, tease, torment, torture, trouble, vex, worry; SEE CONCEPTS *7,14,19*

plaid [*adj*] *checkered*
checked, tartan, variegated; SEE CONCEPTS *259,625*

plain [*adj1*] *clear, obvious*
apparent, audible, big as life*, broad, comprehensible, definite, distinct, evident, legible, lucid, manifest, open, open-and-shut*, palpable, patent, talking turkey*, transparent, understandable, visible; SEE CONCEPTS *529,535,576*

plain [*adj2*] *straightforward in speech*
abrupt, artless, blunt, candid, direct, forthright, frank, guileless, honest, impolite, ingenuous, open, outspoken, rude, sincere; SEE CONCEPT *267*

plain [*adj3*] *normal, everyday*
average, common, commonplace, conventional, dull, homely, lowly, modest, ordinary, quotidian, routine, simple, traditional, usual, vanilla*, white-bread*, workaday; SEE CONCEPT *547*

plain [*adj4*] *unembellished, basic*
austere, bare, bare bones*, clean, discreet, dry, modest, muted, pure, restrained, severe, simple, spartan, stark, stripped down, unvarnished, vanilla*; SEE CONCEPTS *485,589*

plain [*adj5*] *ugly*
deformed, hard on the eyes*, homely, not beautiful, ordinary, plain-featured; SEE CONCEPT *579*

plain [*n*] *level land*
champaign, expanse, field, flat, flatland, grassland, heath, level, meadow, moor, moorland,

open country, plateau, prairie, steppe, tundra; SEE CONCEPT *509*

plaintive [*adj*] *pathetic, woebegone*
beefing*, bellyaching*, cantankerous, crabby*, cranky*, disconsolate, doleful, grief-stricken, grievous, grousing, grumpy*, heartrending, lamenting, lugubrious, melancholy, mournful, out of sorts*, pathetic, piteous, pitiful, rueful, sad, saddening, sorrowful, wailing, wistful, woeful; SEE CONCEPTS *401,529*

plan [*n1*] *scheme, design, way of doing things*
aim, angle, animus, arrangement, big picture*, contrivance, course of action, deal, device, disposition, expedient, game plan, gimmick, ground plan, idea, intent, intention, layout, machination, meaning, means, method, orderliness, outline, pattern, picture, platform, plot, policy, procedure, program, project, projection, proposal, proposition, purpose, scenario, stratagem, strategy, suggestion, system, tactics, treatment, trick, undertaking; SEE CONCEPT *660*

plan [*n2*] *written description; diagram*
agenda, agendum, blueprint, chart, delineation, draft, drawing, form, illustration, layout, map, projection, prospectus, representation, road map, rough draft, scale drawing, sketch, time line, view; SEE CONCEPTS *268,271,625*

plan [*v1*] *think out; prepare in advance*
arrange, bargain for, block out, blueprint, brainstorm*, calculate, concoct, conspire, contemplate, contrive, cook up*, craft, design, devise, draft, engineer, figure on, figure out, fix to, form, formulate, frame, hatch*, intrigue, invent, lay in provisions, line up*, make arrangements, map, meditate, organize, outline, plot, project, quarterback*, ready, reckon on, represent, rough in*, scheme, set out, shape, sketch, steer, trace, work out; SEE CONCEPT *36*

plan [*v2*] *intend, mean*
aim, bargain for*, contemplate, count on, design, envisage, foresee, have every intention*, mind, propose, purpose, reckon on*; SEE CONCEPTS *26,35*

plane [*adj*] *level, horizontal*
even, flat, flush, plain, planate, regular, smooth, uniform; SEE CONCEPTS *490,581*

plane [*n1*] *flat surface; level*
condition, degree, extension, face, facet, footing, grade, horizontal, obverse, position, sphere, stratum; SEE CONCEPTS *744,757*

plane [*n2*] *aircraft*
airbus, airplane, airship, bird*, craft, crate, jet, ship, twin-engine; SEE CONCEPT *504*

planet [*n*] *celestial body orbiting a star*
apple*, asteroid, earth, globe, heavenly body, luminous body, marble, orb*, planetoid, sphere, terrene, wandering star*, world; SEE CONCEPT *511*

plant [*n1*] *organism belonging to the vegetable kingdom*
annual, biennial, bush, creeper*, cutting*, flower, grass, greenery, herb, perennial, seedling, shoot, shrub, slip, sprout, tree, vine, weed; SEE CONCEPT *429*

plant [*n2*] *factory and its buildings, equipment*
apparatus, forge, foundry, gear, machinery, manufactory, mill, shop, works, yard; SEE CONCEPTS *439,449,463,496*

plant [*v1*] *put in the ground for growing*
bury, cover, farm, grow, implant, pitch, pot,

pi
pl

raise, scatter, seed, seed down, set out, sow, start, stock, transplant; SEE CONCEPTS *178,253*

plant [*v2*] *establish, set*
deposit, fix, found, imbed, insert, install, institute, lodge, park, plank, plank down, plop, plunk, root, settle, station; SEE CONCEPTS *18,201,221*

plantation [*n*] *large farm*
estate, farmstead, hacienda, homestead, orchard, ranch, vineyard; SEE CONCEPTS *258,449,509,517*

plaster [*n*] *thick, gooey material that hardens*
adhesive, binding, cement, coat, dressing, glue, gum, gypsum, lime, mortar, mucilage, paste, plaster of Paris, stucco; SEE CONCEPTS *466,475*

plaster [*v*] *spread, smear*
adhere, bedaub, besmear, bind, cement, coat, cover, daub, glue, gum, overlay, paste, smudge; SEE CONCEPT *202*

plastered [*adj*] *drunk*
bashed, blitzed*, bombed*, boozed up*, buzzed*, crocked*, dead drunk*, dead to the world*, drinking, drunk as a skunk*, drunken, feeling good*, feeling no pain*, flushed*, flying*, fried*, gone*, groggy, half-crocked*, half in the bag*, high*, hooched up*, inebriated, juiced*, liquored up*, lit*, loaded*, pissed*, polluted*, potted*, sauced*, schnockered*, seeing double*, sloshed*, stewed*, stoned*, tanked*, three sheets to the wind*, tipsy, totaled*, under the influence, under the table*, wasted*, woozy*, zonked*; SEE CONCEPTS *314,545*

plastic [*adj1*] *flexible, soft; made of manufactured, treated compounds*
bending, ductile, elastic, fictile, formable, moldable, molded, pliable, pliant, resilient, shapeable, supple, workable; SEE CONCEPT *604*

plastic [*adj2*] *easily influenced*
amenable, bending, compliant, docile, ductile, flexible, giving, impressionable, influenceable, malleable, manageable, moldable, pliable, pliant, receptive, responsive, suggestible, supple, susceptible, tractable, yielding; SEE CONCEPT *542*

plastic [*adj3*] *artificial; made of manufactured compounds*
cast, chemical, ersatz, false, manufactured, phony, pseudo*, substitute, synthetic, unnatural; SEE CONCEPT *582*

plastic surgery [*n*] *cosmetic surgery*
blepharoplasty, breast implant, breast reduction, collagen injections, dermabrasion, dermatoplasty, eyelift, face-lift, face-lifting, liposuction, mammaplasty, mammoplasty, nose job, reconstructive surgery, rhinoplasty, skin grafting, suction lipectomy, tummy tuck; SEE CONCEPT *310*

plate [*n1*] *dish or meal served*
bowl, casserole, course, helping, platter, portion, service, serving, trencher; SEE CONCEPTS *459,493*

plate [*n2*] *sheet, panel*
coat, disc, flake, foil, lamella, lamina, layer, leaf, plane, print, scale, slab, slice, spangle, stratum; SEE CONCEPT *475*

plate [*v*] *coat with metallic material*
anodize, bronze, chrome, cover, electroplate, enamel, encrust, face, flake, foil, gild, laminate, layer, nickel, overlay, platinize, scale, silver, stratify; SEE CONCEPTS *172,202*

plateau [*n*] *level; flat, often high, land*
elevation, highland, mesa, plain, stage, table, tableland, upland; SEE CONCEPTS *509,744*

platform [*n1*] *stand or stage*
belvedere, dais, floor, podium, pulpit, rostrum,

scaffold, scaffolding, staging, terrace; SEE CONCEPTS *440,443*

platform [*n2*] *political stance, promises*
manifesto, objectives, party line*, plank, policy, principle, program, soapbox*, stump*, tenets; SEE CONCEPTS *278,689*

platitude [*n*] *dull, overused saying*
banality, boiler plate*, bromide*, buzzword, chestnut*, cliché, commonplace, corn*, evenness, familiar tune*, flatness, hackneyed saying, high camp*, hokum*, inanity, insipidity, monotony, motto, old chestnut*, old story*, potboiler*, prosaicism, proverb, saw*, shibboleth, stereotype, tag*, triteness, trite remark, triviality, truism, vapidity, verbiage; SEE CONCEPTS *278,388*

platonic [*adj*] *expressing nonphysical love*
ideal, idealistic, intellectual, quixotic, spiritual, transcendent, Utopian, visionary; SEE CONCEPTS *403,555*

platoon [*n*] *group of military people*
army, array, batch, battery, bunch, clump, cluster, company, detachment, lot, outfit, parcel, patrol, set, squad, squadron, team, troop, unit; SEE CONCEPTS *322,417*

plaudits [*n*] *applause*
acclaim, acclamation, accolade, big hand, cheering, cheers, clapping, commendation, hand, hurrahs, kudos, laudation, ovation, praise, raves, rooting, stamping, standing ovation; SEE CONCEPTS *69,189*

plausible [*adj*] *reasonable, believable*
conceivable, credible, creditable, like enough*, likely, logical, persuasive, possible, presumable, probable, smooth, sound, supposable, tenable, valid, very likely; SEE CONCEPT *552*

play [*n1*] *theater piece*
comedy, curtain-raiser*, drama, entertainment, farce, flop*, hit*, mask*, musical, one-act*, opera, performance, potboiler*, show, smash*, smash hit*, stage show, theatrical, tragedy, turkey*; SEE CONCEPT *263*

play [*n2*] *amusement, entertainment*
caper, dalliance, delight, disport, diversion, foolery, frisk, frolic, fun, gambol, game, gaming, happiness, humor, jest, joking, lark, match, pastime, pleasure, prank, recreation, relaxation, romp, sport, sportiveness, teasing; SEE CONCEPTS *292,363*

play [*n3*] *latitude, range*
action, activity, elbowroom*, exercise, give, leeway, margin, motion, movement, operation, room, scope, space, sweep, swing, working*; SEE CONCEPTS *651,745*

play [*v1*] *have fun*
amuse oneself, be life of party*, caper, carouse, carry on, cavort, clown, cut capers, cut up*, dally, dance, disport, divert, entertain oneself, fool around, frisk, frolic, gambol, go on a spree*, horse around*, idle away, joke, jump, kibitz*, kick up heels*, let go*, let loose*, let one's hair down*, make merry, mess around*, rejoice, revel, romp, show off, skip, sport, toy, trifle; SEE CONCEPTS *292,384*

play [*v2*] *compete in sport*
be on a team, challenge, contend, contest, disport, engage in, participate, recreate, rival, sport, take on, take part, vie; SEE CONCEPTS *92,363*

play [*v3*] *act; take the part of*
act the part of, discourse, do*, enact, execute,

ham*, ham it up*, impersonate, lay an egg*, perform, personate, playact, play a gig*, portray, present, read a part, represent, take the role of, tread the boards*; SEE CONCEPT *292*

play [*v4*] *gamble, risk*
bet, chance, exploit, finesse, game, hazard, jockey*, lay money on*, maneuver, manipulate, put, set, speculate, stake, take, wager; SEE CONCEPTS *341,363*

play [*v5*] *produce music*
blow, bow, drum, execute, fiddle, fidget, finger, operate, pedal, perform, render, tickle, work; SEE CONCEPT *65*

play ball [*v*] *cooperate*
agree, be in cahoots, collaborate, comply with, conspire, go along with, join forces, join in, participate, play the game*, pull together, stick together, work together; SEE CONCEPTS *110,112*

play dirty [*v*] *cheat*
bamboozle*, beguile, bend the rules*, bilk, burn, caboodle, chisel, con, deceive, defraud, do a number on*, double-cross, double-deal, dupe, finagle, fleece, flimflam, fudge*, hit below the belt*, hoodwink, hose, mislead, pull something funny*, rip off*, rook*, sandbag, scam, screw, shaft, stack the cards*, stretch the rules*, sucker, swindle, trick, victimize; SEE CONCEPTS *59,139,192*

play down [*v*] *pretend as if something were unimportant*
belittle, deemphasize, gloss over*, hold back*, make light of*, make little of*, minimize, mute, restrain, soften, soft-pedal*, underplay, underrate; SEE CONCEPTS *49,59,63*

player [*n1*] *person participating in sport*
amateur, athlete, champ, competitor, contestant, jock*, member, opponent, participant, pro, professional, rookie, sportsperson, superjock*, sweat*, team player; SEE CONCEPT *366*

player [*n2*] *person who acts in performance*
actor, bit player, entertainer, extra, ham*, hambone*, impersonator, lead, mime, mimic, performer, playactor, scene stealer*, stand-in, star, thespian, trouper, understudy, walk-on; SEE CONCEPT *352*

player [*n3*] *person who produces music*
artist, instrumentalist, musician, music maker, performer, rocker, soloist, virtuoso; SEE CONCEPT *352*

playful [*adj*] *funny, fun-loving*
antic, blithe, cheerful, coltish*, comical, elvish*, feeling one's oats*, flirtatious, frisky, frolicsome, full of pep*, gamesome, gay, good-natured, impish, jaunty, jesting, jocund, joking, joyous, lighthearted, lively, merry, mirthful, mischievous, prankish, puckish, rollicking, snappy, spirited, sportive, sprightly, teasing, tongue-in-cheek*, vivacious, waggish, whimsical, zippy*; SEE CONCEPTS *401,542*

playground [*n*] *recreation area*
jungle gym, park, playing field; SEE CONCEPTS *509,513*

play it safe [*v*] *be cautious*
avoid risk, be on the safe side, hedge one's bets*, take no chances, take precautions; SEE CONCEPTS *401,403*

plaything [*n*] *toy*
amusement, bauble, doll, gadget, game, gimcrack, pastime, trifle, trinket; SEE CONCEPT *446*

play up [*v*] *emphasize*
accentuate, bring to the fore*, call attention to, feature, highlight, italicize*, magnify, make a production of*, point up, stress, turn spotlight on*, underline, underscore; SEE CONCEPT *49*

playwright [*n*] *person who writes for the theater*
author, dramatist, dramaturge, dramaturgist, librettist, scenarist, scripter, tragedian, writer; SEE CONCEPT *348*

plaza [*n*] *central location, spot*
common, court, green, park, square, village green; SEE CONCEPTS *509,513*

plea [*n1*] *begging request*
appeal, application, entreaty, imploration, imprecation, intercession, orison, overture, petition, prayer, round robin*, solicitation, suit, supplication; SEE CONCEPT *662*

plea [*n2*] *excuse, defense*
action, alibi, allegation, apology, argument, cause, claim, cop-out*, explanation, extenuation, fish tale*, justification, mitigation, out, palliation, pleading, pretext, rationalization, right, song and dance*, story, vindication, whitewash*; SEE CONCEPTS *57,278,318*

plead [*v1*] *beg, request*
appeal, ask, beseech, cop a plea*, crave, crawl, entreat, entreaty, implore, importune, make up for, petition, pray, solicit, square things*, supplicate; SEE CONCEPT *48*

plead [*v2*] *present a defense*
adduce, advocate, allege, answer charges, argue, assert, avouch, cite, cop a plea*, declare, give evidence, maintain, plea bargain, present, put forward, respond, use as excuse, vouch; SEE CONCEPTS *49,317*

pleasant [*adj*] *acceptable; friendly*
affable, agreeable, amiable, amusing, bland, charming, cheerful, civil, civilized, congenial, convivial, cool*, copacetic, cordial, delectable, delightful, diplomatic, enchanting, engaging, enjoyable, fine, fine and dandy*, fun, genial, good-humored, gracious, gratifying, homey, jolly, jovial, kindly, likable, lovely, mild, mild-mannered, nice, obliging, pleasing, pleasurable, polite, refreshing, satisfying, social, soft, sweet, sympathetic, urbane, welcome; SEE CONCEPTS *542,548,572*

pleasantry [*n*] *nice remark*
badinage, banter, bon mot*, humor, jest, joke, joking, levity, merriment, quip, quirk, repartee, sally*, squib*, wit, witticism; SEE CONCEPTS *273,278*

please [*v1*] *delight, make happy*
amuse, charm, cheer, content, enchant, entertain, fill the bill*, gladden, go over big*, grab, gratify, hit the spot*, humor, indulge, kill*, make the grade*, overjoy, satisfy, score, suit, sweep off feet*, tickle*, tickle pink*, titillate, turn on*, wow*; SEE CONCEPTS *7,22*

please [*v2*] *will, elect to do*
be inclined, choose, command, demand, desire, like, opt, prefer, see fit, want, wish; SEE CONCEPT *20*

pleasing/pleasurable [*adj*] *welcome, nice*
agreeable, amiable, amusing, charming, congenial, delightful, enchanting, engaging, enjoyable, entertaining, favorable, good, grateful, gratifying, likable, luscious, musical, palatable, pleasant, polite, satisfactory, satisfying, savory, suitable, sweet, winning; SEE CONCEPTS *537,572*

pl
pl

pleasure [n1] *delight, happiness*
amusement, bliss, buzz*, comfort, contentment, delectation, diversion, ease, enjoyment, entertainment, felicity, flash*, fruition, game, gladness, gluttony, gratification, gusto, hobby, indulgence, joie de vivre, joy, joyride*, kick*, kicks*, luxury, primrose path*, recreation, relish, revelry, satisfaction, seasoning, self-indulgence, solace, spice, thrill, titillation, turn-on*, velvet*, zest; SEE CONCEPTS *388,410*

pleasure [n2] *will, inclination*
choice, command, desire, fancy, liking, mind, option, preference, purpose, velleity, want, wish; SEE CONCEPTS *20,659*

plebeian [adj] *base, lower-class*
banal, coarse, common, conventional, humble, ignoble, low, lowborn, lowly, mean, ordinary, pedestrian, popular, proletarian, traditional, uncultivated, unrefined, unsophisticated, unwashed*, vulgar, working-class; SEE CONCEPT *549*

plebeian [n] *person of lower class*
commonalty, commoner, common people, peasant, person in the street*, pleb*, plebe*, proletarian, rank and file*; SEE CONCEPTS *413,423*

pledge [n1] *word of honor*
agreement, assurance, covenant, guarantee, health, oath, promise, toast, undertaking, vow, warrant, word; SEE CONCEPTS *71,278*

pledge [n2] *sign of good faith*
bail, bond, collateral, deposit, earnest, gage, guarantee, guaranty, pawn, security, surety, token, warrant, warranty; SEE CONCEPTS *318,332,446*

pledge [v] *guarantee; give word of honor*
contract, covenant, engage, give word*, hock*, hook*, mortgage, pawn, plight, promise, sign for, soak*, swear, undertake, vouch, vow; SEE CONCEPT *71*

plenary [adj] *entire, whole*
absolute, complete, full, general, inclusive, open, sweeping, thorough; SEE CONCEPT *531*

plentiful/plenty [adj] *abundant, productive*
abounding, ample, bounteous, bountiful, bumper*, chock-full*, complete, copious, enough, excessive, extravagant, exuberant, fertile, flowing, flush*, fruitful, full, fulsome, generous, improvident, infinite, large, lavish, liberal, lousy with*, lush, luxuriant, overflowing, plenteous, prodigal, profuse, prolific, replete, rife, sufficient, superabundant, superfluous, swarming, swimming, teeming; SEE CONCEPTS *762,781*

plenty [n] *much, abundance*
affluence, avalanche*, capacity, copiousness, cornucopia, deluge*, enough, flood*, fruitfulness, full house*, fund, good deal*, great deal*, heaps*, loads*, lots, luxury, mass, masses*, mine*, mountains*, oodles*, opulence, peck*, piles*, plethora, profusion, prosperity, quantity, stacks*, store, sufficiency, torrent*, volume, wealth; SEE CONCEPTS *767,787*

plethora [n] *excess*
deluge, flood, glut, many, much, overabundance, overflow, overkill, overmuch, plenty, profusion, superabundance, superfluity, surfeit, surplus; SEE CONCEPTS *767,787*

pliable [adj] *bendable, adaptable*
compliant, docile, ductile, easily led, easy, flexible, impressionable, limber, lithe, malleable, manageable, manipulable, moldable, obedient, plastic, pliant, putty*, receptive, responsive, rolling with the punches*, spongy, submissive, supple, susceptible, tractable, yielding; SEE CONCEPTS *404,488*

plight [n] *dilemma, difficulty; situation*
bad news*, circumstances, condition, corner*, double trouble*, extremity, fix*, hole*, impasse, jam, perplexity, pickle*, pinch*, predicament, quandary, scrape*, spot*, state*, straits, tight situation, trouble; SEE CONCEPTS *666,674*

plod [v1] *walk heavily*
clump*, drag, flounder, hike, lumber*, plug, schlepp*, slog*, stamp, stomp, toil, tramp, trample, tread, tromp, trudge, wallow; SEE CONCEPT *151*

plod [v2] *work slowly and under duress*
bear down*, buckle down*, drudge, grind, knuckle down*, labor, persevere, plough through*, plug away*, scratch*, slave, sweat*, toil; SEE CONCEPTS *87,677*

plot [n1] *plan, scheme*
artifice, booby trap*, cabal, collusion, complicity, connivance, conniving, conspiracy, contrivance, covin, design, device, fix, frame, frame-up*, game, intrigue, little game*, machination, maneuver, practice, ruse, scam, setup, stratagem, trick; SEE CONCEPT *660*

plot [n2] *story line*
action, design, development, enactment, events, incidents, movement, narrative, outline, picture, progress, scenario, scene, scheme, story, structure, subject, suspense, theme, thread, unfolding; SEE CONCEPTS *264,282*

plot [n3] *tract of land*
acreage, allotment, area, division, ground, land, lot, parcel, patch, piece, plat, spread; SEE CONCEPTS *509,513*

plot [v1] *plan, scheme*
angle, brew*, cabal, cogitate, collude, conceive, concoct, connive, conspire, contrive, cook up*, design, devise, draft, finagle, frame, hatch*, imagine, intrigue, lay*, machinate, maneuver, operate, outline, project, promote, rough out*, set up, sketch, wangle; SEE CONCEPT *36*

plot [v2] *map out; draw*
calculate, chart, compute, draft, lay out, locate, mark, outline, put forward; SEE CONCEPTS *36,79,174*

plow [v] *dig up ground for cultivation*
break, break ground, bulldoze, cultivate, farm, furrow, harrow, harvest, list, push, rake, reap, ridge, rush, shove, smash, till, trench, turn, turn over; SEE CONCEPT *178*

ploy [n] *game, trick*
artifice, contrivance, device, dodge, feint, gambit, maneuver, move, play, ruse, scheme, stratagem, subterfuge, tactic, wile; SEE CONCEPT *59*

pluck [n] *person's resolution, courage*
backbone*, boldness, bravery, dauntlessness, determination, grit, guts*, hardihood, heart*, intestinal fortitude*, intrepidity, mettle, moxie*, nerve, resolution, spirit, spunk; SEE CONCEPT *411*

pluck [v] *grab, pull out; pick at*
catch, clutch, collect, cull, draw, finger, gather, harvest, jerk, plunk, pull at, snatch, strum, tug, tweak, yank; SEE CONCEPT *206*

plucky [adj] *brave*
adventurous, bold, confident, courageous, daring, determined, fearless, game, gritty, gutsy, heroic, lionhearted, nervy, persevering, spirited,

sporting, spunky, stalwart, tenacious, unafraid, undaunted, unfearful, valiant; SEE CONCEPT *401*

plug [*n1*] *stopper*
bung, connection, cork, filling, fitting, occlusion, river, spigot, stopple, tampon, wedge; SEE CONCEPTS *471,836*

plug [*n2*] *publicity*
advertisement, blurb*, good word*, hype*, mention, push*, write-up; SEE CONCEPT *274*

plug [*v1*] *stop up*
block, bung, choke, clog, close, congest, cork, cover, drive in, fill, obstruct, occlude, pack, ram, seal, secure, stop, stopper, stopple, stuff; SEE CONCEPT *209*

plug [*v2*] *publicize*
advertise, boost*, build up*, hype*, mention, promote, push*, write up; SEE CONCEPTS *49,60*

plum [*n*] *reward, prize*
asset, bonus, carrot*, catch*, cream*, dividend, find, meed, nugget*, pick, premium, treasure; SEE CONCEPTS *337,712*

plumb [*adj*] *vertical*
erect, perpendicular, sheer, straight, straight up, up and down, upright; SEE CONCEPT *581*

plumb [*v*] *probe, go into*
delve, explore, fathom, gauge, get to the bottom of*, measure, penetrate, search, sound, take soundings, unravel; SEE CONCEPTS *181,216,291*

plummet [*v*] *fall hard and fast*
collapse, crash, decline, decrease, descend, dip, dive, downturn, drop, drop down, dump, fall, nose-dive, plunge, precipitate, sink, skid, stoop, swoop, tumble; SEE CONCEPTS *181,698,763*

plump [*adj*] *chubby, fat*
beefy*, burly, buxom, chunky*, corpulent, filled, fleshy, full, obese, portly, pudgy*, rotund, round, stout, tubby*; SEE CONCEPT *491*

plunder [*n*] *something stolen*
booty, goods*, graft, hot goods*, loot, make*, pickings*, pillage, plunderage, prey, prize, quarry, rapine, raven, spoil, stuff*, take*, trappings*, winnings*; SEE CONCEPT *710*

plunder [*v*] *ravage, steal*
appropriate, burn, depredate, despoil, devastate, fleece, forage, foray, grab, gut, kip, knock off*, knock over*, lay waste, liberate, lift, loft, loot, maraud, moonlight requisition*, pillage, prey, prowl, raid, ransack, relieve, requisition, rifle, rip off*, rob, sack, salvage, smash and grab*, snatch, spoil, stick up*, strip; SEE CONCEPTS *86,139,252*

plunge [*n*] *quick drop; enthusiastic attempt*
belly flop*, descent, dive, duck, dunk, fall, high dive, immersion, investment, jump, nose-dive, spree, submergence, submersion, swoop, venture; SEE CONCEPTS *100,150,152,181,194*

plunge [*v*] *dive or fall fast*
belly-flop*, career, cast, charge, dash, descend, dip, drive, drop, duck, fling, go down, go the limit, go whole hog*, hurtle, immerge, immerse, jump, keel, lunge, lurch, nose-dive, pitch, plummet, plunk, propel, rush, shoot the works*, sink, sound, submerge, submerse, swoop, take a flyer*, take a header*, tear, throw, throw oneself, thrust, topple, tumble; SEE CONCEPTS *100,150,152,181,194*

plunk [*v*] *throw down*
drop, dump, plonk, plop, plump, unload; SEE CONCEPTS *181,200*

plural [*adj*] *more than one*
dual, many, multiple, not alone, not singular, numerous; SEE CONCEPTS *564,762,772*

plurality [*n*] *large part of a group*
advantage, bulk, greater part, lead, majority, mass, most, multiplicity, nearly all, numerousness, preponderance, profusion, variety; SEE CONCEPTS *382,829*

plus [*adj*] *added, extra*
additional, augmented, boosted, enlarged, expanded, increased, positive, supplementary, surplus; SEE CONCEPTS *762,771*

plus [*n*] *asset; something added*
advantage, benefit, bonus, extra, gain, good point, overage, overstock, oversupply, perk, surplus; SEE CONCEPT *693*

plush [*adj*] *luxurious, rich*
costly, deluxe, elegant, lavish, luscious, lush, luxury, opulent, palatial, ritzy, silken, sumptuous; SEE CONCEPTS *334,589*

ply [*v*] *use, work at*
carry on, dispense, employ, exercise, exert, follow, function, handle, maneuver, manipulate, practice, pursue, put out, swing, throw, utilize, wield; SEE CONCEPTS *100,225*

poach [*v*] *infringe upon; trespass*
appropriate, encroach, filch, fish illegally, hunt illegally, intrude, pilfer, plunder, rob, smuggle, steal; SEE CONCEPTS *139,192*

pocket [*adj*] *small, portable*
abridged, canned, capsule, compact, concise, condensed, diminutive, epitomized, itsy-bitsy*, little, midget, miniature, minute, peewee*, pint-sized*, potted, tiny, wee; SEE CONCEPT *773*

pocket [*n*] *cavity, pouch*
bag, chamber, compartment, hole, hollow, opening, receptacle, sack, socket; SEE CONCEPTS *452,513*

pocket [*v*] *help oneself to something*
abstract, appropriate, conceal, enclose, filch, hide, lift, nab, pilfer, pinch, purloin, shoplift, steal, swipe, take; SEE CONCEPTS *139,142*

pocketbook [*n*] *accessory for carrying personal items*
bag, clutch, frame, handbag, hide, leather, pouch, purse, reticule, suitcase, wallet; SEE CONCEPTS *446,450*

pockmark [*n*] *pitlike scare*
blemish, cavity, crater, dent, dimple, pimple, welt, zit; SEE CONCEPT *580*

pod [*n/v*] *encasement of vegetable seeds*
capsule, case, covering, hull, husk, sheath, sheathing, shell, shuck, skin, vessel; SEE CONCEPTS *428,484*

podium [*n*] *structure from which speakers orate*
dais, platform, pulpit, rostrum, soapbox*, stage, stump*; SEE CONCEPT *443*

poem [*n*] *highly expressive, rhythmical literary piece*
ballad, beat, blank verse, composition, creation, epic, free verse, haiku, limerick, lines, lyric, ode, poesy, poetry, quatrain, rhyme, rime, rune, sestina, song, sonnet, verse, villanelle, words, writing; SEE CONCEPTS *268,282*

poet [*n*] *person who writes expressive, rhythmic verse*
artist, author, balladist, bard, dilettante, dramatist, librettist, lyricist, lyrist, maker, metrist, odist, parodist, poetaster, rhapsodist, rhymer,

pl
po

rimer, sonnetist, versifier, writer; SEE CONCEPTS *348,423*

poetic [*adj*] *with rhythm and beauty; related to poetic composition*
anapestic, dactylic, dramatic, elegiac, epic, epical, epodic, iambic, idyllic, imaginative, lyric, lyrical, melodious, metrical, odic, rhythmical, romantic, songlike, tuneful; SEE CONCEPT *267*

poetry [*n*] *expressive, rhythmic literary work*
balladry, doggerel, metrical composition, paean, poems, poesy, rhyme, rhyming, rime, rune, song, stanza, verse, versification; SEE CONCEPTS *268,282,349*

poignant [*adj1*] *affecting, painful*
agitating, agonizing, bitter, distressing, disturbing, emotional, heartbreaking, heartrending, impressive, intense, moving, passionate, pathetic, perturbing, piteous, pitiful, sad, sentimental, sorrowful, touching, upsetting; SEE CONCEPTS *529,548*

poignant [*adj2*] *sharp, bitter*
acrid, acute, biting, caustic, keen, penetrating, peppery, piercing, piquant, pointed, pungent, racy, sarcastic, severe, snappy, spicy, stinging, tangy, zesty; SEE CONCEPTS *267,613*

point [*n1*] *speck*
bit, count, dot, fleck, flyspeck, full stop, iota, mark, minim, mite, mote, notch, particle, period, scrap, stop, tittle, trace; SEE CONCEPTS *79,831*

point [*n2*] *specific location*
locality, locus, place, position, site, situation, spot, stage, station, where; SEE CONCEPT *198*

point [*n3*] *sharp end, top, end of extension*
apex, awn, barb, beak, bill, cape, claw, cusp, dagger, foreland, head, headland, jag, nib, pin point, prick, prickler, promontory, prong, snag, spike, spine, spire, spur, sticker, stiletto, summit, sword, thorn, tine, tip, tooth; SEE CONCEPTS *827,836*

point [*n4*] *circumstance, stage; limited time*
brink, condition, date, degree, duration, edge, extent, instant, juncture, limit, moment, period, point in time, position, threshold, time, verge, very minute; SEE CONCEPTS *696,815*

point [*n5*] *goal, aim*
appeal, attraction, bottom line*, charm, cogency, design, effectiveness, end, fascination, intent, intention, interest, motive, name of the game*, nitty-gritty*, nub, nuts and bolts*, object, objective, punch*, purpose, reason, significance, use, usefulness, utility, validity, validness; SEE CONCEPT *659*

point [*n6*] *meaning, essence*
argument, bottom line*, burden, core, crux, drift, force, gist, head, heart, idea, import, kicker*, main idea, marrow, matter, meat*, motif, motive, name of the game*, nitty-gritty*, nub, nuts and bolts*, pith, pointer, proposition, punch line*, question, score, stuff, subject, subject matter, text, theme, thrust, tip, tip-off*, topic; SEE CONCEPTS *274,682*

point [*n7*] *aspect, characteristic*
attribute, case, circumstance, circumstantial, constituent, detail, element, facet, feature, instance, item, material, nicety, part, particular, peculiarity, property, quality, respect, side, thing*, trait; SEE CONCEPTS *274,411,654*

point [*n8*] *scoring unit of sport competition*
count, mark, notch, score, tally; SEE CONCEPTS *364,784*

point [*v1*] *show as probable; call attention*
bespeak, button down*, denote, designate, direct, finger*, hint, imply, indicate, lead, make*, name, offer, peg*, pin down*, put down for*, put finger on*, signify, suggest, tab*, tag*; SEE CONCEPTS *118,138*

point [*v2*] *direct, lead*
aim, beam*, bring to bear, cast, face, guide, head, influence, lay, level, look, slant, steer, tend, train, turn, zero in*; SEE CONCEPTS *187,201,623*

pointed [*adj1*] *having a sharp end or part*
acicular, aciculate, acuminate, acuminous, acute, barbed, cornered, cuspidate, edged, fine, keen, mucronate, peaked, piked, pointy, pronged, sharp, sharp-cornered, spiked; SEE CONCEPTS *490,606*

pointed [*adj2*] *penetrating, biting*
accurate, acid, acute, barbed, boiled down, calling a spade a spade*, cutting, in a nutshell*, incisive, insinuating, keen, laid on the line*, legit, meaty*, on the button*, on the nose*, pertinent, pregnant, right-on*, right to it*, sarcastic, sharp, short-and-sweet*, tart, telling, trenchant; SEE CONCEPT *267*

pointer [*n1*] *indicator*
arrow, dial, director, gauge, guide, hand, index, mark, needle, register, rod, signal; SEE CONCEPTS *464,498*

pointer [*n2*] *hint, suggestion*
advice, caution, clue, information, recommendation, steer, tip, tip-off, warning; SEE CONCEPTS *75,274*

pointless [*adj*] *ridiculous, senseless*
absurd, aimless, around in circles*, fruitless, futile, going nowhere*, impotent, inane, inconsequential, ineffective, ineffectual, insignificant, in vicious circle*, irrelevant, meaningless, needle in haystack*, nongermane, nonsensical, not pertinent, on treadmill*, powerless, purportless, remote, silly, stupid, trivial, unavailing, uninteresting, unnecessary, unproductive, unprofitable, useless, vague, vain, worthless; SEE CONCEPTS *529,548*

point out [*v*] *call attention to*
advert, allude, bring up, denote, designate, identify, indicate, mention, refer, remind, reveal, show, specify; SEE CONCEPTS *49,73,261*

poise [*n*] *self-composure, dignity*
address, aplomb, assurance, balance, bearing, calmness, confidence, cool, coolness, delicatesse, diplomacy, elegance, equability, equanimity, equilibrium, grace, gravity, polish, presence, presence of mind, sangfroid, savoir-faire, self-assurance, self-possession, serenity, stasis, tact, tactfulness, tranquility; SEE CONCEPTS *633,717*

poise [*v*] *balance, suspend*
ballast, be ready, brood, float, hang, hold, hover, position, stabilize, stand, steady, support, wait; SEE CONCEPT *154*

poison [*n*] *substance that causes harm, death*
adulteration, bacteria, bane, blight, cancer, contagion, contamination, corruption, germ, infection, malignancy, miasma, toxicant, toxin, toxoid, venin, venom, virus; SEE CONCEPTS *307,475,674,675*

poison [*v*] *contaminate, pollute*
adulterate, corrupt, debase, defile, deprave, destroy, envenom, fester, harm, infect, injure, kill, make ill, murder, pervert, stain, subvert, taint,

undermine, vitiate, warp; SEE CONCEPTS *14,246,252*

poison/poisonous [*adj*] *harmful*
bad, baleful, baneful, corrupt, corruptive, dangerous, deadly, deleterious, destructive, detrimental, evil, fatal, hurtful, infective, lethal, malicious, malignant, mephitic, miasmatic, morbid, mortal, nocuous, noisome, noxious, peccant, pernicious, pestiferous, pestilential, septic, toxic, toxicant, toxiferous, venomous, vicious, viperous, virulent; SEE CONCEPT *537*

poke [*n*] *push, thrust*
blow, boost, bunt, butt, dig, hit, jab, nudge, prod, punch, shove, stab; SEE CONCEPTS *189,208*

poke [*v1*] *push at; thrust*
arouse, awaken, bulge, butt*, crowd, dig, elbow*, goose*, hit, jab, jostle, jut, nudge*, overhang, prod, project, protrude, provoke, punch, ram, rouse, shoulder*, shove, stab, stand out, stick, stick out, stimulate, stir; SEE CONCEPTS *189,208,723*

poke [*v2*] *interfere, snoop*
busybody*, butt in*, intrude, meddle, nose*, peek, pry, tamper; SEE CONCEPT *384*

poke [*v3*] *move along slowly*
dally, dawdle, delay, drag, get no place fast*, idle, lag, loiter, mosey*, procrastinate, put off*, shlep along*, tarry, toddle*, trail; SEE CONCEPT *151*

poker [*n*] *card game*
blind poker, draw poker, five-card stud poker, seven-card stud poker, straight poker, strip poker, stud poker; SEE CONCEPTS *260,271*

polar [*adj1*] *cold*
arctic, extreme, farthest, freezing, frigid, frozen, glacial, icy, north, south, terminal; SEE CONCEPTS *583,605*

polar [*adj2*] *opposite, opposed*
antagonistic, antipodal, antipodean, antithetical, contradictory, contrary, converse, counter, diametric, reverse; SEE CONCEPT *564*

pole [*n*] *bar, post*
beam, extremity, flagpole, flagstaff, leg, mast, pile, plank, rod, shaft, spar, staff, stake, standard, stave, stick, stilt, stud, terminus; SEE CONCEPTS *440,470,475,479*

police/police officer [*n*] *person, people hired to uphold the laws*
arm of the law*, badge*, bear*, beat cop, black and white*, blue*, bluecoat*, bobby, constable, constabulary, cop*, copper*, corps*, detective, fed*, flatfoot*, force, gendarme, heat*, law, law enforcement, narc*, patrol; SEE CONCEPTS *299,354*

policy [*n*] *procedure, tactics*
action, administration, approach, arrangement, behavior, channels, code, course, custom, design, guideline, line, management, method, order, organization, plan, polity, practice, program, protocol, red tape*, rule, scheme, stratagem, strategy, tenet, the book*, the numbers*, theory; SEE CONCEPTS *6,271,660,688*

polish [*n1*] *shine, brightness*
brilliance, burnish, finish, glaze, glint, gloss, luster, sheen, smoothness, sparkle, varnish, veneer, wax; SEE CONCEPTS *492,611,620*

polish [*n2*] *cultivated look, performance*
breeding, class, cultivation, culture, elegance, finesse, finish, grace, politesse, refinement, style, suavity, urbanity; SEE CONCEPTS *388,633,655*

polish [*v1*] *shine, buff*
brighten, burnish, clean, finish, furbish, glaze, gloss, rub, scour, scrub, sleek, slick, smooth, wax; SEE CONCEPTS *202,215*

polish [*v2*] *improve performance, look*
amend, better, brush up, correct, cultivate, emend, enhance, finish, furbish, make improvement, mature, mend, perfect, refine, round, sleek, slick, smooth, touch up; SEE CONCEPT *244*

polish off [*v*] *finish using*
consume, devour, dispatch, dispose of, do away with*, down*, eat, eat up, eliminate, get rid of*, liquidate, put away*, swill*, use up, wolf*; SEE CONCEPTS *169,225*

polite [*adj*] *mannerly, civilized*
affable, amenable, amiable, attentive, bland, civil, complaisant, concerned, conciliatory, condescending, considerate, cordial, courteous, courtly, cultured, deferential, diplomatic, elegant, friendly, genteel, gentle, good-natured, gracious, mild, neighborly, nice, obliging, obsequious, pleasant, polished, politic, punctilious, refined, respectful, smooth, sociable, solicitous, sympathetic, thoughtful, urbane, well-behaved, well-bred, well-mannered; SEE CONCEPT *401*

politic [*adj*] *wise, tactful*
adroit, advisable, canny*, cool, delicate, diplomatic, discreet, expedient, in one's best interests*, judicious, on the lookout*, perspicacious, prudent, sagacious, sensible, sharp, shrewd, smooth, tactical, tuned in*, urbane; SEE CONCEPT *401*

political [*adj*] *governmental*
bureaucratic, civic, constitutional, economical, legislative, official; SEE CONCEPT *535*

politically correct [*adj*] *sensitive to other political views*
bias-free, considerate, diplomatic, gender-free, inclusive, inoffensive, liberal, multicultural, nondiscriminatory, nonracist, nonsexist, PC*, respectful, sensitive; SEE CONCEPTS *529,542*

politician [*n*] *person pursuing or occupying elective office*
baby-kisser*, boss, chieftain, congressperson, democrat, grandstander*, handshaker*, lawmaker, leader, legislator, member of Congress, member of parliament, officeholder, office seeker, orator, partisan, party member, president, public servant, republican, senator, speaker, statesperson, whistle-stopper*; SEE CONCEPT *359*

politics [*n*] *art and science of administration of government*
affairs of state, backroom*, campaigning, civics, domestic affairs, electioneering, foreign affairs, government, government policy, hat in the ring*, internal affairs, jungle*, legislature, matters of state, political science, polity, smoke-filled room*, statecraft, stateship, zoo*; SEE CONCEPTS *300,301*

poll [*n*] *census; tally of answers to questions of opinion*
ballot, canvass, count, figures, opinion, returns, sampling, survey, vote, voting; SEE CONCEPTS *48,300*

poll [*v*] *take census; question*
ballot, canvass, enroll, examine, interview, list, register, sample, send up a balloon*, survey, tally, test the waters*, vote; SEE CONCEPTS *48,300*

po
po

pollster [*n*] *polltaker.*
canvasser, market researcher, public opinion gatherer, sampler, survey taker; SEE CONCEPTS *37,103,197,291*

pollutant [*n*] *contaminant*
hazardous waste, poison, pollution, toxic waste, toxin; SEE CONCEPT *720*

pollute [*v*] *make dirty; corrupt*
adulterate, alloy, befoul, besmirch, contaminate, debase, debauch, defile, deprave, desecrate, dirty, dishonor, foul, infect, make filthy, mar, poison, profane, soil, spoil, stain, sully, taint, violate; SEE CONCEPTS *246,254*

pollution [*n*] *dirtiness, contamination*
abuse, adulteration, besmearing, besmirching, blight, corruption, decomposition, defilement, desecration, deterioration, dirtying, fouling, foulness, impairment, impurity, infection, misuse, polluting, profanation, rottenness, soiling, spoliation, taint, tainting, uncleanness, vitiation; SEE CONCEPT *720*

Pollyanna [*n*] *optimist*
dreamer, hoper, idealist, positive thinker; SEE CONCEPTS *410,689*

poltergeist [*n*] *ghost*
apparition, appearance, banshee, demon, doppelganger, haunter, kelpie, phantasm, phantom, revenant, specter, spirit, spook, vision, visitor; SEE CONCEPT *370*

polygamy [*n*] *plural marriage*
bigamy, polyandry, polygyny; SEE CONCEPTS *297,388*

pomp [*n*] *pageantry, display*
affectation, array, ceremonial, ceremony, fanfare, flourish, formality, grandeur, grandiosity, magnificence, ostentation, pageant, panoply, parade, pomposity, ritual, shine, show, solemnity, splendor, state, vainglory; SEE CONCEPTS *335,377,655*

pompous [*adj*] *arrogant, egotistic*
affected, bloated, boastful, bombastic, conceited, flatulent, flaunting, flowery, fustian, grandiloquent, grandiose, high and mighty*, highfaluting*, high-flown*, imperious, important, inflated, magisterial, magniloquent, narcissistic, orotund, ostentatious, overbearing, overblown, pontifical, portentous, presumptuous, pretentious, puffed up*, puffy*, rhetorical, self-centered, self-important, selfish, showy, sonorous, stuck-up*, supercilious, turgid, uppity*, vain, vainglorious, windy*; SEE CONCEPTS *267,401,542*

poncho [*n*] *cloak*
cape, capote, coat, manteau, mantle, raincoat, shawl, wrap; SEE CONCEPTS *451,475,680*

pond [*n*] *small body of water*
basin, dew, duck pond, lagoon, lily pond, millpond, pool, puddle, small lake, splash; SEE CONCEPT *514*

ponder [*v*] *think about seriously*
appraise, brood, build castles in air*, cerebrate, cogitate, consider, contemplate, daydream, debate, deliberate, dwell, evaluate, examine, excogitate, figure, give thought to, meditate, mind, moon*, mull, mull over, muse, noodle around*, perpend, pipe dream*, put on thinking cap*, puzzle over, reason, reflect, revolve, roll, ruminate, speculate, study, think out, think over, turn over, weigh, woolgather*; SEE CONCEPTS *17,24*

ponderous [*adj1*] *heavy, cumbersome*
awkward, bulky, burdensome, clumsy, cum-

brous, dull, elephantine, graceless, hefty, huge, laborious, lifeless, lumbering, massive, onerous, oppressive, substantial, troublesome, unhandy, unwieldy, weighty; SEE CONCEPTS *491,565*

ponderous [*adj2*] *dreary, tedious*
arid, barren, cardboard*, dry, dull, heavy, humdrum*, labored, lifeless, long-winded*, monotonous, pedantic, pedestrian, plodding, prolix, stiff*, stilted, stodgy, stuffy*, vapid, verbose, wooden*; SEE CONCEPTS *267,529,542*

pontificate [*v*] *sermonize*
address, admonish, dogmatize, evangelize, get on a soapbox*, give sermon, harangue, lecture, minister, moralize, preach, pulpiteer, teach; SEE CONCEPTS *51,75,285,367*

pool [*n1*] *collection of liquid*
basin, bath, lagoon, lake, mere, millpond, mud puddle, natatorium, pond, puddle, splash, swimming pool, tank, tarn; SEE CONCEPTS *364,514*

pool [*n2*] *supply of money, goods*
bank, combine, conglomerate, equipment, funds, group, jackpot, kitty*, pot, provisions, stakes; SEE CONCEPTS *340,432*

pool [*v*] *combine*
amalgamate, blend, join forces, league, merge, put together, share; SEE CONCEPTS *113,193*

pooped [*adj*] *tired*
beat*, burned out*, bushed*, collapsing, dead on one's feet*, dog-tired*, done for*, done in*, drained, drooping, drowsy, enervated, exhausted, fatigued, fried*, out of gas*, overworked, played out*, run-down, run ragged, shot*, sleepy, spent, tuckered out, wasted, weary, worn out; SEE CONCEPTS *314,403,406*

poor [*adj1*] *lacking sufficient money*
bad off*, bankrupt, beggared, beggarly, behind eight ball*, broke*, destitute, dirt poor*, down-and-out*, empty-handed*, flat*, flat broke*, fortuneless, hard up*, impecunious, impoverished, indigent, in need, insolvent, in want, low, meager, moneyless, necessitous, needy, pauperized, penniless, penurious, pinched*, poverty-stricken, reduced*, scanty*, stone broke*, strapped*, suffering, truly needy, underprivileged, unprosperous; SEE CONCEPT *334*

poor [*adj2*] *deficient, inadequate*
base, below par, common, contemptible, crude, diminutive, dwarfed, exiguous, faulty, feeble, humble, imperfect, incomplete, inferior, insignificant, insufficient, lacking, low-grade, lowly, meager, mean, mediocre, miserable, modest, niggardly*, ordinary, paltry, pitiable, pitiful, plain, reduced, rotten, scanty, second-rate*, shabby, shoddy, skimpy, slight, sorry*, sparse, subnormal, subpar, substandard, trifling, trivial, unsatisfactory, valueless, weak, worthless; SEE CONCEPTS *570,574*

poor [*adj3*] *weak, unfertile*
bare, barren, depleted, exhausted, feeble, fruitless, impaired, imperfect, impoverished, indisposed, infertile, infirm, puny, sick, sterile, unfruitful, unproductive, worthless; SEE CONCEPT *314*

poor [*adj4*] *unfortunate, unhappy*
commiserable, hapless, ill-fated, luckless, miserable, pathetic, piteous, pitiable, pitiful, rueful, unlucky, wretched; SEE CONCEPTS *542,548*

poorly [*adj*] *not well*
ailing, below par, failing, ill, indisposed, low,

mean, out of sorts*, rotten*, sick, sickly, under the weather*, unwell; SEE CONCEPT *314*

poorly [*adv*] *unsatisfactorily*
badly, crudely, defectively, inadequately, incompetently, inexpertly, inferiorly, insufficiently, meanly, shabbily, unsuccessfully; SEE CONCEPTS *544,571,574*

pop [*n*] *bang*
burst, crack, explosion, jump, leap, report, snap, strike, thrust, whack; SEE CONCEPT *595*

pop [*v*] *jump, burst*
appear, bang, blow, crack, dart, explode, go, go off, hit, insert, leap, protrude, push, put, report, rise, shove, snap, sock, stick, strike, thrust, whack; SEE CONCEPT *145*

poppycock [*n*] *nonsense*
babble, balderdash*, baloney*, bull*, bunk*, drivel, empty talk, foolery, foolishness, gibberish, hogwash*, hooey*, hot air*, jive*, malarkey, mumbo jumbo*, palaver, prattle, rubbish, silliness, trash*; SEE CONCEPTS *230,388,633*

popular [*adj1*] *well-known, favorite*
accepted, approved, attractive, beloved, caught on*, celebrated, crowd-pleasing*, faddish*, famous, fashionable, favored, in*, in demand, in favor, in the mainstream*, in vogue, leading, likable, liked, lovable, noted, notorious, now*, okay*, pleasing, praised, preferred, prevailing, prominent, promoted, right stuff*, run-after*, selling, social, societal, sought, sought-after, stylish, suitable, the rage*, thing*, trendy, well-liked, well-received; SEE CONCEPTS *555,589*

popular [*adj2*] *common, standard*
accepted, accessible, adopted, approved, conventional, current, demanded, embraced, familiar, general, in demand, in use, ordinary, prevailing, prevalent, proletarian, public, rampant, regnant, rife, ruling, stock, ubiquitous, universal, widespread; SEE CONCEPT *530*

popularity [*n*] *recognition, celebrity*
acceptance, acclaim, adoration, approval, currency, demand, esteem, fame, fashion, fashionableness, favor, following, heyday, idolization, lionization, prevalence, regard, renown, reputation, repute, universality, vogue; SEE CONCEPTS *388,655*

popularize [*v*] *make widely popular, accessible*
catch on, disseminate, familiarize, generalize, give currency, make available, promote, restore, resurrect, revive, simplify, spread, universalize; SEE CONCEPTS *324,384*

population [*n*] *inhabitants of a place*
citizenry, community, culture, denizens, dwellers, folk, natives, people, populace, public, residents, society, state; SEE CONCEPT *379*

populous [*adj*] *packed with inhabitants*
crawling, crowded, dense, heavily populated, jammed, legion, many, multifarious, multitudinal, multitudinous, numerous, occupied, overpopulated, peopled, populated, settled, several, swarming, teeming, thick, thronged, various, voluminous; SEE CONCEPT *583*

porch [*n*] *patio*
balcony, deck, portico, steps, stoop, veranda; SEE CONCEPTS *509,513*

pore [*n*] *small aperture in skin*
foramen, opening, orifice, outlet, stoma, sweat gland, vesicle; SEE CONCEPT *418*

pore [*v*] *go over carefully*
brood, contemplate, dwell on, examine, look over, muse, peruse, ponder, read, regard, scan, scrutinize, study; SEE CONCEPTS *24,72,103*

pornographic [*adj*] *obscene*
adult, immoral, indecent, lewd, off-color, offensive, porn*, porno*, prurient, purple*, raunchy*, rough, salacious, sexy, smutty*, steamy*, X-rated*; SEE CONCEPTS *267,372,545*

pornography [*n*] *obscenity*
adult material, adult movie, bawdiness, dirt, dirty movie, erotica, filth, girlie magazine, hard-core pornography, indecency, obscene materials, porn, porno, porno film, sexploitation, sexually explicit material, skin flick, smut, soft-core pornography, stag film, X-rated material, X-rated movie; SEE CONCEPTS *372,545*

porous [*adj*] *having holes; absorbent*
absorptive, penetrable, permeable, pervious, spongelike, spongy; SEE CONCEPT *606*

port [*n*] *place for boat docking, traffic, and storage*
anchorage, boatyard, dockage, docks, dockyard, gate, harbor, harborage, haven, landing, piers, refuge, retreat, roads, roadstead, sanctuary, seaport, shelter, wharf; SEE CONCEPTS *449,509*

portable [*adj*] *easily transported*
carriageable, cartable, compact, convenient, conveyable, easily carried, handy, haulable, light, lightweight, manageable, movable, portative, transportable, wieldy; SEE CONCEPTS *491,584, 773*

portal [*n*] *hole or door in vessel*
doorway, entrance, entry, entryway, gate, gateway, ingress, opening, way in; SEE CONCEPT *502*

portend [*v*] *foreshadow, indicate*
adumbrate, augur, be in the cards*, bespeak, betoken, bode, call*, crystal-ball*, forebode, forecast, foreshow, foretell, foretoken, forewarn, harbinger, have a hunch, herald, hint, omen, point to, predict, premonish, presage, prognosticate, promise, prophesy, read, see coming*, threaten, warn of; SEE CONCEPTS *71,78,261*

portent [*n1*] *indication, forewarning*
augury, bodement, boding, caution, clue, foreboding, foreshadowing, foretoken, funny feeling*, handwriting on the wall*, harbinger, hunch, omen, premonition, presage, presentiment, prognostic, prognostication, sign, sinking feeling*, threat, vibes*, warning; SEE CONCEPT *278*

portent [*n2*] *miracle*
marvel, phenomenon, prodigy, sensation, stunner, wonder; SEE CONCEPTS *230,529*

portentous [*adj*] *exciting; foreboding*
alarming, amazing, apocalyptic, astounding, augural, destined, doomed, exhilarating, extraordinary, fated, fateful, haunting, ill-boding, ill-fated, impending, important, inauspicious, inspiring, intriguing, ominous, phenomenal, premonitory, prophetic, remarkable, suggestive, threatening, thrilling; SEE CONCEPTS *529,542,548*

porter [*n*] *person who serves as attendant, caretaker*
baggage carrier, bearer, bellhop, carrier, concierge, doorkeeper, doorperson, gatekeeper, janitor, red cap*, sky cap*, transporter; SEE CONCEPT *348*

portfolio [*n*] *flat case for transporting papers*
attaché case, bag, brief bag, briefcase, case, container, envelope, folder, notebook, valise; SEE CONCEPT *494*

po
po

portion [*n1*] *share, cut, ration*
allocation, allotment, allowance, apportionment, bang, bit, chunk, division, divvy*, drag*, dram, excerpt, extract, fix, fraction, fragment, gob, helping, hit, hunk, lagniappe, lion's share*, lot, lump, measure, meed, member, moiety, morsel, parcel, part, piece, piece of action*, plum, quantity, quantum, quota, scrap, section, segment, serving, shot*, slug*, smithereen*, taste; SEE CONCEPT *835*

portion [*n2*] *fate, destiny*
circumstance, cup*, doom, fortune, kismet*, lot*, luck; SEE CONCEPT *679*

portion [*v*] *divide into pieces*
administer, allocate, allot, apportion, assign, deal, dispense, distribute, divvy up*, dole out*, mete out*, parcel, part, partition, piece, prorate, quota, ration, section, share, shift; SEE CONCEPTS *98,140*

portly [*adv*] *bulky, fat*
ample, avoirdupois, beefy*, broad, burly, corpulent, fleshy, heavy, hefty, husky, large, obese, overweight, plump, rotund, stout; SEE CONCEPT *491*

portrait [*n*] *drawn representation; description*
account, characterization, depiction, figure, image, likeness, model, painting, photograph, picture, portraiture, portrayal, profile, silhouette, simulacrum, sketch, snapshot, spitting image*, vignette; SEE CONCEPTS *259,268,625*

portray [*v*] *represent, imitate*
act like, characterize, copy, delineate, depict, describe, draw, duplicate, figure, illustrate, image, impersonate, interpret, limn, mimic, paint, parody, photograph, picture, render, reproduce, simulate, sketch; SEE CONCEPTS *55,174,265*

pose [*n*] *artificial position*
act, affectation, air, attitude, attitudinizing, bearing, carriage, facade, fake, false show, front, guise, mannerism, masquerade, mien, posture, posturing, pretense, pretension, role, stance, stand; SEE CONCEPTS *633,716*

pose [*v1*] *sit, stand in place*
arrange, model, peacock, poise, position, posture, sit for, strike a pose, strut; SEE CONCEPTS *154,174*

pose [*v2*] *pretend, fake*
act, affect, attitudinize, feign, grandstand*, impersonate, make believe, make out like*, masquerade, pass off*, peacock*, playact, posture, profess, purport, put on airs*, put up a front*, sham*, show off*, strike an attitude*, take off as*; SEE CONCEPTS *59,63,633*

pose [*v3*] *offer, put forward idea*
advance, ask, extend, give, hold out, posit, prefer, present, proffer, propose, proposition, propound, put, query, question, set, submit, suggest, tender; SEE CONCEPTS *66,67,75*

posh [*adj*] *luxurious, upper-class*
chic, classy, deluxe, elegant, exclusive, fashionable, grand, high-class, la-di-da*, luxury, modish*, opulent, rich, ritzy*, smart, swank, swanky*, swish*, trendy; SEE CONCEPTS *334,589*

position [*n1*] *physical place*
area, bearings, district, environment, fix, geography, ground, locale, locality, location, locus, point, post, reference, region, scene, seat, setting, site, situation, space, spot, stand, station, surroundings, topography, tract, whereabouts*; SEE CONCEPT *198*

position [*n2*] *posture, stance*
arrangement, attitude, ballgame*, bearing, carriage, circumstances, condition, deportment, disposition, form, habit, how things stack up*, like it is*, manner, mien, pass, plight, port, pose, predicament, situation, spot, stand, state, status, strait, the size of it*; SEE CONCEPT *696*

position [*n3*] *belief, point of view*
angle, attitude, color, judgment, opinion, outlook, slant, stance, stand, standpoint, view, viewpoint; SEE CONCEPT *689*

position [*n4*] *class, stature*
cachet, capacity, caste, character, consequence, dignity, footing, importance, place, prestige, rank, reputation, situation, sphere, standing, station, status; SEE CONCEPTS *378,388*

position [*n5*] *responsibility in business or other enterprise*
berth, billet, capacity, connection, do*, duty, employment, function, job, nine-to-five*, occupation, office, place, post, profession, role, situation, slot*, spot*, trade; SEE CONCEPTS *324,349,360*

position [*v*] *place physically in location*
arrange, array, dispose, fix, lay out, locate, put, set, settle, stand, stick; SEE CONCEPTS *158,201*

positive [*adj1*] *definite, certain*
absolute, actual, affirmative, assured, categorical, clear, clear-cut, cocksure*, cold*, complete, conclusive, concrete, confident, consummate, convinced, decided, decisive, direct, downright, explicit, express, factual, firm, forceful, forcible, genuine, hard, inarguable, incontestable, incontrovertible, indisputable, indubitable, irrefutable, out-and-out*, outright, perfect, rank, real, specific, sure, thorough, thoroughgoing, unambiguous, undeniable, unequivocal, unmistakable, unmitigated; SEE CONCEPTS *535,582*

positive [*adj2*] *beneficial, helpful*
affirmative, constructive, effective, efficacious, forward-looking, good, practical, productive, progressive, reasonable, sound, useful; SEE CONCEPT *572*

positively [*adv*] *absolutely, definitely*
amen*, assuredly, categorically, certainly, doubtless, doubtlessly, easily, emphatically, firmly, flat*, flat out*, for a fact*, indubitably, no catch*, no holds barred*, no ifs ands or buts*, no kicker*, no strings attached*, on the money*, on the nose*, really truly*, right on*, sure, surely, the ticket*, to a tee*, undeniably, undoubtedly, unequivocally, unmistakably, unquestionably, with certainty, without qualification; SEE CONCEPTS *535,544,582*

possess [*v*] *have or obtain*
acquire, bear, be blessed with, be born with, be endowed with, carry, control, corner*, corner the market*, dominate, enjoy, get hands on*, get hold of*, grab, have to name*, hog*, hold, latch on to, lock up, maintain, occupy, own, retain, seize, sit on, take over, take possession; SEE CONCEPTS *120,710*

possessed [*adj*] *bewitched; under a spell*
bedeviled, berserk*, consumed, crazed*, cursed, demented, enchanted, enthralled, fiendish, frenetic, frenzied, gone*, haunted, hooked*, insane, into*, mad*, obsessed, raving*, taken over*, violent; SEE CONCEPT *401*

possession [*n1*] *control, ownership*
custody, dominion, hold, occupancy, occupation,

possessorship, proprietary, proprietary rights, proprietorship, retention, tenancy, tenure, title; SEE CONCEPTS *343,710*

possession [*n2*] *something owned; property*
accessories, appointments, appurtenances, assets, baggage, belongings, chattels, effects, equipment, estate, fixtures, furnishings, furniture, goods, impedimenta, paraphernalia, province, real estate, settlement, tangibles, territory, things, trappings, tricks, wealth; SEE CONCEPTS *446,710*

possessive [*adj*] *greedy*
acquisitive, avaricious, controlling, craving, desirous, dominating, grabby, grasping, hoggish*, selfish; SEE CONCEPTS *326,403,542*

possibilities [*n*] *potential*
capabilities, potentiality, promise, prospects, talent; SEE CONCEPTS *411,650*

possibility [*n*] *feasibility, likelihood; chance*
achievability, action, attainableness, break, circumstance, contingency, fair shake*, fifty-fifty*, fling*, fluke*, fortuity, happening, hazard, hope, incident, instance, liability, likeliness, occasion, occurrence, odds*, opportunity, outside chance*, plausibility, play*, potentiality, practicability, prayer*, probability, prospect, risk*, shot*, stab*, toss-up*, workableness; SEE CONCEPTS *650,693*

possible [*adj*] *likely, attainable*
accessible, achievable, adventitious, advisable, available, breeze*, can do*, cinch, conceivable, credible, dependent, desirable, doable, dormant, duck soup*, easy as pie*, expedient, feasible, fortuitous, hopeful, hypothetical, imaginable, indeterminate, latent, no sweat*, obtainable, piece of cake*, potential, practicable, probable, promising, pushover*, realizable, setup, simple as ABC*, snap, thinkable, uncertain, viable, welcome, within reach, workable; SEE CONCEPTS *528,552,576*

possibly [*adv*] *by chance; in some way*
at all, by any chance, by any means, conceivably, could be, God willing*, if possible, in any way, likely, maybe, not impossibly, peradventure, perchance, perhaps, probably, within realm of possibility; SEE CONCEPTS *544,552*

post [*n1*] *upright support*
column, doorpost, leg, mast, newel, pale, palisade, panel, pedestal, picket, pile, pillar, pole, prop, rail, shaft, stake, standard, stilt, stock, stud; SEE CONCEPTS *440,445,470,479*

post [*n2*] *job, employment*
appointment, assignment, berth, billet, office, place, position, situation; SEE CONCEPTS *351,362*

post [*n3*] *lookout, station*
beat, locus, place, position, whereabouts; SEE CONCEPTS *198,321,439*

post [*n4*] *mail service*
collection, delivery, mail, PO*, postal service, post office; SEE CONCEPTS *299,770*

post [*v1*] *situate, position*
assign, establish, locate, place, put, set, station; SEE CONCEPT *201*

post [*v2*] *advise, inform*
acquaint, apprive, brief, clue, fill in, notify, put wise to, report, tell, warn, wise up; SEE CONCEPT *60*

poster [*n*] *large paper advertisement*
affiche, announcement, banner, bill, billboard, broadside, handbill, notice, placard, public no-tice, sheet, sign, signboard, sticker; SEE CONCEPT *271*

posterior [*adj1*] *rear*
after, back, behind, dorsal, hind, hinder, hindmost, in back of, last, retral; SEE CONCEPTS *583,827*

posterior [*adj2*] *subsequent*
after, coming after, ensuing, following, later, latter, next, postliminary, subsequential, succeeding; SEE CONCEPTS *585,799*

posterior [*n*] *behind of animate being*
back, backside, bottom, butt*, buttocks, can*, cheeks*, derriere, duff*, fanny*, hind part, keester*, moon*, rear, rear end, rump, seat, tail, tail end, tuchis*, tush*; SEE CONCEPT *392*

posterity [*n*] *future generations*
breed, brood, children, descendants, family, heirs, issue, lineage, next generation, offspring, progeniture, progeny, scions, seed, stock, succeeding generations, successors, unborn; SEE CONCEPT *296*

posthaste [*adj/adv*] *fast*
at once, breakneck*, directly, double-quick*, expeditious, flat-out*, fleet, fleetly, full tilt*, hastily, hasty, headlong, lickety-split*, pell-mell*, promptly, pronto, quick, quickly, rapid, rapidly, speedily, speedy, straightaway, swift, swiftly; SEE CONCEPTS *544,588,799*

postmortem [*adj*] *following death*
future, later, posthumous, postmundane, postobit, post-obituary; SEE CONCEPT *799*

postmortem [*n*] *analysis after death*
autopsy, coroner's report, dissection, examination, necropsy, post*; SEE CONCEPTS *103,310*

postpone [*v*] *put off till later time*
adjourn, cool it*, defer, delay, give a rain check*, hang fire*, hold off, hold over, hold up, lay over, pigeonhole*, prorogue, put back, put on back burner*, put on hold, shelve, suspend, table; SEE CONCEPT *130*

postulate [*v*] *suppose, figure*
advance, affirm, assert, assume, aver, estimate, guess, hypothesize, posit, predicate, premise, presuppose, propose, put forward, speculate, suppose, take for granted, theorize; SEE CONCEPTS *12,26*

posture [*n1*] *stance, circumstance*
aspect, attitude, bearing, brace, carriage, condition, demeanor, deportment, disposition, mien, mode, phase, port, pose, position, positure, presence, set, situation, state; SEE CONCEPTS *657,723*

posture [*n2*] *beliefs*
attitude, disposition, feeling, frame of mind, inclination, mood, outlook, point of view, sentiment, stance, standpoint; SEE CONCEPT *410*

posture [*v*] *display an attitude*
affect, attitudinize, display, do a bit*, do for effect*, fake, fake it, make a show*, masquerade, pass for, pass off, playact, pose, put on airs*, put up a front*, show off*; SEE CONCEPTS *59,261*

pot [*n1*] *container, cauldron*
basin, bowl, bucket, can, canister, crock, crucible, cup, jar, jug, kettle, mug, pan, pitcher, receptacle, saucepan, tankard, urn, vessel; SEE CONCEPT *494*

pot [*n2*] *marijuana*
cannabis, grass*, hashish, maryjane*, weed*; SEE CONCEPT *307*

potable [*adj*] *drinkable*
edible, palatable, safe to drink; SEE CONCEPT *169*

po
po

potable [n] *beverage*
alcoholic beverage, cooler, draft, drink, libation, liquor; SEE CONCEPT *454*

potency [n] *effectiveness*
authority, birr, capability, capacity, command, control, dominion, efficacy, efficiency, energy, force, go*, hardihood, influence, juice*, kick*, might, moxie*, muscle*, pep, potential, power, puissance, punch, sinew*, snap, sock*, steam*, strength, sway, vigor, virtue, what it takes*, zap*, zing*, zip*; SEE CONCEPTS *411,676,732*

potent [adj] *effective, powerful, forceful*
almighty, authoritative, ball of fire*, cogent, commanding, compelling, convincing, dynamic, efficacious, forcible, full-bodied, go-getter*, great, gutsy*, impressive, influential, lusty, mighty, persuasive, powerhouse, puissant, punchy, robust, spanking, stiff, strong, sturdy, telling, trenchant, useful, vigorous; SEE CONCEPTS *372,489,540*

potentate [n] *monarch*
autocrat, chief, chieftain, crowned head, despot, dictator, emperor, empress, head of state, king, leader, majesty, prince, princess, queen, royalty, ruler, sovereign; SEE CONCEPTS *354,422*

potential [adj] *promising*
abeyant, budding, conceivable, dormant, embryonic, future, hidden, imaginable, implied, inherent, latent, likely, lurking, plausible, possible, prepatent, probable, quiescent, thinkable, undeveloped, unrealized, within realm of possibility; SEE CONCEPTS *528,552*

potential [n] *possibility for achievement*
ability, aptitude, capability, capacity, potentiality, power, the makings*, what it takes*, wherewithal; SEE CONCEPTS *650,706*

pothole [n] *chuckhole*
cavity, crater, depression, dip, fracture, gap, hole, pit, pocket, rut, split; SEE CONCEPT *513*

potion [n] *concoction prepared for mental or physical effect*
aromatic, brew, cordial, cup, dose, draft, dram, draught, drink, elixir, libation, liquid, liquor, medicine, mixture, nip, philter, remedy, restorative, spirits, stimulant, tonic; SEE CONCEPTS *307,467*

potpourri [n] *miscellany*
assortment, blend, collection, combination, combo, gallimaufry, goulash, hash, hodgepodge, medley, mélange, mishmash, mixed bag, mixture, motley, olio*, pastiche*, patchwork, salmagundi*, soup, stew; SEE CONCEPTS *260,432*

pottery [n] *containers made from clay; clay art*
ceramics, crockery, earthenware, firing, glazing, porcelain, porcelainware, stoneware, terra cotta; SEE CONCEPTS *174,259,494*

pouch [n] *soft container, often made of cloth or skin*
bag, pocket, poke, purse, receptacle, sac, sack; SEE CONCEPTS *446,450,494*

pounce [n/v] *leap at; take by surprise*
ambush, attack, bound, dart, dash, dive, drop, fall upon, jump, snatch, spring, strike, surge, swoop, take unawares; SEE CONCEPTS *86,159,194*

pound [n] *sixteen ounces/.454 kilograms of weight*
avoirdupois, pint, troy; SEE CONCEPT *795*

pound [v1] *crush; beat rhythmically*
batter, belabor, bruise, buffet, clobber, comminute, drub, hammer, hit, malleate, palpitate, pelt, pestle, powder, pulsate, pulse, pulverize, pummel, stomp, strike, thrash, throb, thump, tramp, triturate, wallop; SEE CONCEPTS *150,186,189*

pound [v2] *impress; make someone listen*
din, drive, drub, drum, grave, hammer, stamp; SEE CONCEPTS *14,49*

pour [v] *be or make flowing*
cascade, cataract, course, crowd, decant, deluge, discharge, drain, drench, emit, flood, flow, give off, gush, inundate, issue, jet, let flow, proceed, rain, rill, roll, run, rush, sheet, shower, sluice, spew, spill, splash, spout, spring, stream, surge, swarm, teem, throng; SEE CONCEPTS *146,179,209*

pout [n] *sad face*
frown, glower, long face, moue, sullen look; SEE CONCEPT *716*

pout [v] *make a sad face; be sad*
be cross, be in bad mood*, be moody, be petulant, be sullen, frown, grouch, grump*, make a long face*, make a moue, mope, stick one's lip out*, sulk; SEE CONCEPTS *261,410*

poverty [n] *want; extreme need, often financial*
abjection, aridity, bankruptcy, barrenness, beggary, dearth, debt, deficiency, deficit, depletion, destitution, difficulty, distress, emptiness, exiguity, famine, hardship, impecuniousness, impoverishment, inadequacy, indigence, insolvency, insufficiency, lack, meagerness, necessitousness, necessity, pass, paucity, pauperism, pennilessness, penury, pinch, poorness, privation, reduction, scarcity, shortage, starvation, straits, underdevelopment, vacancy; SEE CONCEPTS *335,709*

poverty-stricken [adj] *in great need; financially poor*
bad off*, bankrupt, beggared, beggarly, broke*, destitute, dirt poor*, distressed, down-and-out*, hard up*, impecunious, impoverished, indigent, in dire circumstances, in want, moneyless, necessitous, needful, needy, penniless, penurious, short*, stone broke*, stranded*, strapped*, unmoneyed, wanting; SEE CONCEPT *334*

powder [n] *fine, loose grains made by crushing a solid*
crumb, dust, film, grain, grit, meal, particle, pounce, pulverulence, seed, talc; SEE CONCEPTS *471,831*

powder [v] *crush into fine grains; sprinkle fine grains*
abrade, bray, comminute, cover, crumble, crunch, dredge, dust, file, flour, granulate, grate, grind, pestle, pound, pulverize, rasp, reduce, scatter, scrape, smash, strew, triturate; SEE CONCEPTS *186,222*

powdery [adj] *consisting of fine, loose grains*
arenaceous, arenose, branny, chalky, crumbling, crumbly, dry, dusty, fine, floury, friable, grainy, granular, gravelly, gritty, impalpable, loose, mealy, pulverized, pulverulent, sandy; SEE CONCEPT *606*

power [n1] *ability, competence*
aptitude, bent, capability, capacity, competency, dynamism, effectiveness, efficacy, endowment, faculty, function, gift, influence, potential, potentiality, qualification, skill, talent, turn, virtue; SEE CONCEPT *630*

power [n2] *physical ability, capacity*
applied force, arm*, brawn, dynamism, energy, force, forcefulness, horsepower, intensity, me-

chanical energy, might, muscle*, omnipotence, potency, potential, puissance, sinew*, strength, vigor, vim, virtue, voltage, weight; SEE CONCEPTS *520,641,732*

power [*n3*] *control, dominance*
ascendancy, authority, authorization, birthright, clout, command, connection, diadem, direction, domination, dominion, hegemony, imperium, influence, inside track*, jurisdiction, law, leadership, license, management, might, moxie*, omnipotence, paramountcy, predominance, prerogative, prestige, privilege, regency, right, rule, say-so*, sovereignty, steam, strength, strings*, superiority, supremacy, sway, warrant, weight*, wire*; SEE CONCEPTS *376,671*

powerful [*adj*] *strong, effective*
able, all-powerful, almighty, authoritarian, authoritative, capable, cogent, commanding, compelling, competent, controlling, convincing, dominant, dynamic, effectual, efficacious, energetic, forceful, forcible, impressive, in control, influential, in the saddle*, mighty, omnipotent, overruling, paramount, persuasive, potent, preeminent, prevailing, puissant, robust, ruling, sovereign, stalwart, strapping*, strengthy, sturdy, supreme, telling, upper hand*, vigorous, weighty, wicked*, wieldy; SEE CONCEPTS *489,527,540,574*

powerfully [*adv*] *with energy, authority*
effectively, energetically, forcefully, forcibly, hard, intensely, mightily, severely, strongly, vigorously, with might and main; SEE CONCEPTS *540,544,569*

powerless [*adj*] *weak; unable*
blank, chicken*, debilitated, defenseless, dependent, disabled, disenfranchised, etiolated, feeble, frail, gutless, helpless, impotent, incapable, incapacitated, ineffective, ineffectual, inert, infirm, out of gas*, paralyzed, passive, prostrate, subject, supine, tied, unarmed, unfit, vulnerable, wimp*, wishy-washy*; SEE CONCEPTS *489,527*

powwow [*n*] *discussion*
confab*, confabulation, conference, consultation, council, get-together, huddle, meeting, palaver, parley, talk; SEE CONCEPTS *56,324,384*

powwow [*v*] *discuss*
advise, confab*, confabulate, confer, consult, get together, go into a huddle*, huddle, meet, palaver, parley, talk, treat; SEE CONCEPT *56*

practicable [*adj*] *within the realm of possibility*
accessible, achievable, applicable, attainable, doable, employable, feasible, functional, handy, open, operative, performable, possible, practical, serviceable, usable, useful, utile, utilizable, viable, workable; SEE CONCEPT *560*

practical [*adj1*] *realistic, useful*
applied, both feet on the ground*, businesslike, commonsensical, constructive, doable, down-to-earth, efficient, empirical, experimental, factual, feasible, functional, handy, hard-boiled*, implicit, in action, in operation, matter-of-fact*, nuts and bolts*, operative, orderly, possible, practicable, pragmatic, rational, reasonable, sane, sensible, serviceable, sober, solid, sound, systematic, unidealistic, unromantic, usable, utile, utilitarian, virtual, workable, workaday, working; SEE CONCEPTS *533,542,560*

practical [*adj2*] *experienced, proficient*
accomplished, cosmopolitan, effective, efficient, qualified, seasoned, skilled, sophisticated,

trained, versed, vet*, veteran, working, worldly, worldly-wise; SEE CONCEPTS *326,527,528,678*

practically [*adj*] *almost; nearly*
about, all but, approximately, as good as, as much as, basically, close to, essentially, for all intents and purposes*, fundamentally, in effect, in essence, morally, most, much, nearly, nigh, virtually, well-nigh; SEE CONCEPTS *531,772*

practice [*n1*] *routine, usual procedure*
convenance, convention, custom, fashion, form, habit, habitude, manner, method, mode, praxis, proceeding, process, rule, system, tradition, trick, usage, use, usefulness, utility, way, wont; SEE CONCEPT *688*

practice [*n2*] *exercise, application*
action, assignment, background, discipline, drill, drilling, effect, experience, homework, iteration, operation, preparation, prepping, recitation, recounting, rehearsal, relating, repetition, seasoning, study, training, tune-up, use, work-out; SEE CONCEPTS *87,100,658*

practice [*n3*] *business; clientele of business*
career, clients, patients, profession, vocation, work; SEE CONCEPTS *325,417*

practice [*v1*] *repeat action to improve*
become seasoned, build up, discipline, do again, dress, dress rehearse*, drill, dry run*, exercise, go over, habituate, hone, iterate, polish, prepare, recite, rehearse, run through, shake-down*, sharpen, study, train, try out, tune up, walk through, warm up, work, work out; SEE CONCEPTS *87,100*

practice [*v2*] *carry out; undertake*
apply, carry on, do, engage in, execute, follow, fulfill, function, live up to, observe, perform, ply, pursue, put into effect, specialize in, work at; SEE CONCEPTS *91,310,317,324*

practitioner [*n*] *expert*
doctor, master, pro, professional, specialist; SEE CONCEPTS *348,350,416*

pragmatic [*adj*] *sensible*
businesslike, commonsensical, down-to-earth, efficient, hard, hard-boiled*, hardheaded*, logical, matter-of-fact, practical, realistic, sober, unidealistic, utilitarian; SEE CONCEPTS *401,542*

prairie [*n*] *grassland*
grassy field, meadow, pasturage, pasture, plain, savanna, steppe, veldt; SEE CONCEPT *509*

praise [*n*] *congratulations; adoration*
acclaim, acclamation, accolade, applause, appreciation, approbation, approval, big hand*, boost, bravo, celebration, cheer, cheering, citation, commendation, compliment, cry, devotion, encomium, esteem, eulogy, exaltation, extolment, flattery, glorification, glory, good word*, homage, hurrah, hymn, kudos*, laudation, obeisance, ovation, panegyric, pat on the back*, plaudit, puff*, rave, recognition, recommendation, regard, sycophancy, thanks, tribute, worship; SEE CONCEPTS *69,278*

praise [*v*] *congratulate; adore*
acclaim, admire, adulate, advocate, aggrandize, applaud, appreciate, approve, bless, boost, bow down*, build up*, cajole, celebrate, cheer, cite, clap, commend, compliment, cry up*, dignify, distinguish, elevate, endorse, ennoble, eulogize, exalt, extol, flatter, give thanks, glorify, hail, honor, laud, make much of*, panegyrize, pay homage, pay tribute, proclaim, puff*, rave over, recommend, resound, reverence, root*, sanction,

po
pr

sing the praises*, smile on*, stroke*, tout, worship; SEE CONCEPT 69

praiseworthy [adj] deserving congratulations, adoration
admirable, commendable, creditable, estimable, excellent, exemplary, fine, gnarly, gone, honorable, keen, laudable, meritable, meritorious, pillar, salt of earth*, select, slick, stellar, swell, thankworthy, tough, worthy; SEE CONCEPTS 568,574

prance [v] cavort; show off
bound, caper, dance, flounce, foot it*, frisk, gambol, hoof it*, jump, leap, mince, parade, romp, sashay, skip, spring, stalk, step, strut, swagger, sweep, tread; SEE CONCEPTS 150,292,384

prank [n] practical joke; frivolity
antic, caper, caprice, escapade, fancy, fooling, frolic, gag, gambol, high jinks*, horseplay*, hotfoot*, lark, levity, lightness, monkeyshines*, play, put-on, rib*, rollick, roughhouse*, roughhousing*, rowdiness, shenanigans, shine*, skylarking*, spoof, sport, tomfoolery, trick, whim; SEE CONCEPTS 59,384

prattle [n] babble
blubbering, burble, chatter, chit-chat, drivel, gab, gabble, gibberish, gossip, hot air*, idle talk, jabber, jabbering, jargon, murmur, ranting, small talk, tattling, trivial talk, twaddle; SEE CONCEPTS 266,278

pray [v] plead; call upon for help, answer
adjure, appeal, ask, beseech, brace, commune with, crave, cry for, entreat, implore, importune, invocate, invoke, petition, recite, request, say, solicit, sue, supplicate, urge; SEE CONCEPTS 48,367

prayer [n] pleading, especially with a deity; request for help, answer
adoration, appeal, application, begging, benediction, beseeching, communion, devotion, entreaty, grace, imploration, imploring, imprecation, invocation, litany, orison, petition, plea, pleading, request, rogation, service, suit, supplication, worship; SEE CONCEPTS 48,367,662

preach [v1] speak publicly about beliefs
address, deliver, deliver sermon, evangelize, exhort, give sermon, homilize, inform, minister, mission, missionary, orate, prophesy, pulpiteer, sermonize, talk, teach; SEE CONCEPTS 51,285,367

preach [v2] lecture, moralize
admonish, advocate, blow, exhort, get on a soapbox*, harangue, pile it on*, preachify, sermonize, talk big*, urge; SEE CONCEPTS 51,75

preacher [n] person who gives religious instruction
clergy, cleric, clerical, divine, ecclesiastic, evangelist, evangelizer, minister, missionary, parson, pulpiter, reverend, revivalist, sermonizer; SEE CONCEPT 361

precarious [adj] tricky, doubtful
ambiguous, borderline, chancy, contingent, dangerous, delicate, dicey*, dubious, dynamite, equivocal, hairy*, hanging by a thread*, hazardous, iffy*, impugnable, indecisive, insecure, loaded, on thin ice*, open, out on a limb*, perilous, problematic, risky, rocky, rugged*, sensitive, shaky, slippery, ticklish, touch and go*, touchy, uncertain, unhealthy, unreliable, unsafe, unsettled, unstable, unsteady, unsure; SEE CONCEPTS 535,587

precaution [n] carefulness; preventative measure
anticipation, canniness, care, caution, circumspection, discreetness, discretion, foresight, forethought, insurance, protection, providence, provision, prudence, regard, safeguard, safety measure, wariness; SEE CONCEPTS 410,633,729

precede [v] go ahead of
antecede, antedate, anticipate, be ahead of, come first, forerun, foreshadow, go before, go in advance, guide, harbinger, have a head start*, head, head up, herald, in space, introduce, lead, light the way*, order announce, outrank, pace, pave the way*, pioneer, predate, pre-exist, preface, presage, rank, ring in*, run ahead, scout, take precedence, time, usher; SEE CONCEPTS 727,747,813,818

precedence [n] highest in rank; first in order
antecedence, anteposition, earliness, lead, precedency, precession, preeminence, preexistence, preference, prevenience, previousness, primary, priority, rank, seniority, superiority, supremacy; SEE CONCEPTS 671,727,747,818

precedent [n] authoritative example
antecedent, authority, criterion, exemplar, instance, model, paradigm; SEE CONCEPT 686

preceding [adj] earlier, above
above-mentioned, above-named, aforeknown, aforementioned, aforesaid, ahead of, antecedent, anterior, before, erstwhile, foregoing, forerunning, former, forward, front, head, heretofore, introductory, lead, leading, one time, other, past, pioneer, pioneering, precedent, precursive, precursory, preexistent, prefatory, preliminary, preparatory, prevenient, previous, prior, supra; SEE CONCEPTS 585,586,799,811,818

precept [n] law, rule of behavior, action
axiom, behest, bidding, byword, canon, command, commandment, decree, decretum, direction, doctrine, dogma, edict, formula, fundamental, guideline, injunction, instruction, law, mandate, maxim, motto, order, ordinance, prescript, principle, regulation, rule, saying, statute, tenet; SEE CONCEPTS 318,688

precinct [n] subdivision
area, community, department, development, district, division, neighborhood, provence, quarter, section, tract, ward, zone; SEE CONCEPTS 513,835

precious [adj1] favorite, valued
adored, beloved, cherished, darling, dear, dearest, idolized, inestimable, loved, pet, prized, treasured; SEE CONCEPTS 529,567

precious [adj2] expensive; rare
choice, costly, dear, exquisite, fine, high-priced, inestimable, invaluable, priceless, prizable, prized, recherché, rich, treasurable, valuable, worth a king's ransom*, worth eyeteeth*, worth one's weight in gold*; SEE CONCEPT 334

precious [adj3] extremely sophisticated and picky
affected, alembicated, artful, artificial, chichi*, choosy, dainty, delicate, fastidious, finicky, fragile, fussy, la-di-da*, nice, ostentatious, overnice, overrefined, particular, persnickety*, precieux, pretentious, refined, showy, stagy, studied; SEE CONCEPT 401

precipice [n] face or brink of a rock, mountain
bluff, cliff, crag, height, sheer drop, steep; SEE CONCEPTS 509,513

precipitate [v] *hurry, speed*
accelerate, advance, bring on, cast, discharge, dispatch, expedite, fling, further, hasten, hurl, launch, let fly, press, push forward, quicken, send forth, speed up, throw, trigger; SEE CONCEPTS *152,242,704*

precipitation [n] *moisture in air or falling from sky*
cloudburst, condensation, drizzle, hail, hailstorm, heavy dew, precip*, rain, rainfall, rainstorm, sleet, snow, storm, wetness; SEE CONCEPTS *467,524,526*

precipitous [adj2] *steep, falling sharply*
abrupt, arduous, craggy, dizzy, dizzying, high, perpendicular, precipitate, sharp, sheer; SEE CONCEPTS *490,583,779*

precipitous/precipitate [adj1] *fast, sudden; impulsive; initial*
abrupt, breakneck*, brief, frantic, gone off half-cocked*, harum-scarum*, hasty, headlong, heedless, hurried, ill-advised, impatient, impetuous, indiscreet, jump the gun*, madcap, off the hip*, off the top of head*, plunging, precipitant, quick, rapid, rash, reckless, refractory, rushing, subitaneous, swift, unanticipated, uncontrolled, unexpected, unforeseen, violent, willful, without warning; SEE CONCEPTS *229,401,542,588,799*

precis [n] *abridgment*
abstract, aperçu, compendium, condensation, digest, outline, pandect, résumé, rundown, sketch, summary, survey, syllabus, synopsis; SEE CONCEPT *283*

precise [adj1] *exact, accurate*
absolute, actual, categorical, circumscribed, clear-cut, correct, decisive, definite, determinate, explicit, express, fixed, individual, limited, literal, narrow, nice, on the button*, on the money*, on the nose*, particular, proper, restricted, right, rigid, rigorous, specific, strict, stringent, unequivocal, very, well-defined; SEE CONCEPTS *535,557,653*

precise [adj2] *meticulous, fastidious*
careful, ceremonious, choosy, exact, finicky, formal, fussy, genteel, inflexible, nice, particular, persnickety*, picky, priggish, prim, prissy, punctilious, rigid, scrupulous, stickling, stiff*, strict, stuffy, uncompromising; SEE CONCEPTS *401,542*

precisely [adv] *exactly, just*
absolutely, accurately, as well, correctly, definitely, even, expressly, for a fact, for sure, just so, literally, no ifs ands or buts*, no mistake*, on the button*, on the money*, on the nose*, plumb, right, sharp, smack*, smack-dab*, specifically, square, squarely, strictly, sure, sure thing*, the ticket*, the very thing*, to a tee*, yes; SEE CONCEPTS *535,557*

precision [n] *accuracy*
attention, care, carefulness, correctness, definiteness, definitiveness, definitude, exactitude, exactness, fidelity, heed, meticulousness, nicety, particularity, preciseness, rigor, sureness; SEE CONCEPTS *638,654*

preclude [v] *inhibit; make impossible*
avert, cease, check, debar, deter, discontinue, exclude, forestall, forfend, hinder, impede, interrupt, make impracticable, obviate, prevent, prohibit, put a stop to, quit, restrain, rule out, stave off, stop, ward; SEE CONCEPTS *121,234*

precocious [adj] *exceptionally smart, ahead of age in understanding*
advanced, aggressive, ahead of time*, beforehand, bold, brassy*, bright, cheeky*, cocky*, developed, early, flip*, flippant, forward, fresh, intelligent, mature, nervy, premature, presumptuous, pushy, quick, sassy*, smart-alecky*; SEE CONCEPT *402*

precognition [n] *clairvoyance*
acumen, discernment, ESP, extra sensory perception, feeling, foreknowledge, foresight, fortunetelling, insight, intuition, omen, penetration, perception, prediction, premonition, prophecy, psyche, second sight, sixth sense*, telepathy; SEE CONCEPTS *409,410*

preconception [n] *idea formed before event occurs or facts are received*
assumption, bias, delusion, illusion, inclination, notion, preconceived idea, predisposition, prejudgment, prejudice, prepossession, presumption, presupposition; SEE CONCEPT *689*

precursor [n1] *something that indicates outcome or event beforehand*
forerunner, harbinger, herald, messenger, outrider, usher, vanguard; SEE CONCEPTS *70,278*

precursor [n2] *something that precedes another*
ancestor, antecedent, antecessor, forebear, foregoer, forerunner, original, originator, parent, pioneer, predecessor, prototype; SEE CONCEPTS *648,727,828*

predator [n] *hunter, killer*
animal of prey, beast of prey, carnivore, meat-eater; SEE CONCEPT *252*

predatory [adj] *eating, destroying for sustenance or without conscience*
bloodthirsty, carnivorous, depredatory, despoiling, greedy, hungry, hunting, marauding, pillaging, plundering, predacious, predative, preying, rapacious, raptorial, ravaging, ravening, thieving, voracious, vulturine, vulturous, wolfish; SEE CONCEPTS *401,406*

predecessor [n] *something, someone that comes before*
ancestor, antecedent, antecessor, forebear, foregoer, forerunner, former, precursor, previous, prior, prototype; SEE CONCEPTS *414,828*

predestination [n] *destiny*
course of events, divine decree, fate, foreordination, fortune, God's will, inevitability, karma, kismet*, ordinance, portion, predetermination, way the ball bounces*, way the cookie crumbles*, what is written*; SEE CONCEPT *679*

predetermined [adj] *decided in advance*
agreed, arranged, calculated, cut and dried*, deliberate, destined, determined, doomed, fated, fixed, foredestined, foreordained, forethought, planned, prearranged, precogitated, predestined, premeditated, preordained, preplanned, proposed, set, settled, set up; SEE CONCEPT *548*

predicament [n] *difficult situation*
asperity, bad news*, bind*, Catch-22*, circumstance, clutch, condition, corner*, crisis, deadlock, deep water*, dilemma, drag*, emergency, exigency, fix*, hang-up*, hardship, hole, hot water*, imbroglio, impasse, jam*, juncture, large order*, lot, mess*, muddle, pass, perplexity, pickle*, pinch, plight, position, posture, puzzle, quagmire, quandary, rigor, rough go*, scrape*, soup*, spot*, state*, strait, tall order* ticklish

spot* tight situation* trouble, vicissitude; SEE CONCEPTS *388,674*

predict [v] *express an outcome in advance*
adumbrate, anticipate, augur, be afraid, call, call it, conclude, conjecture, croak, crystal-ball* divine, envision, figure, figure out, forebode, forecast, foresee, forespeak, foretell, gather, guess, have a hunch*, hazard a guess*, infer, judge, make book*, omen, portend, presage, presume, prognosticate, prophesy, psych out*, read, see coming*, see handwriting on wall*, size up*, soothsay, suppose, surmise, telegraph*, think, vaticinate; SEE CONCEPT *70*

predictable [adj] *easy to foretell*
anticipated, calculable, certain, expected, foreseeable, foreseen, likely, prepared, sure, surefire*; SEE CONCEPTS *404,542,548*

prediction [n] *declaration made in advance of event*
anticipation, augury, cast, conjecture, crystal gazing*, divination, dope, forecast, forecasting, foresight, foretelling, fortune-telling, guess, horoscope, hunch*, indicator, omen, palmistry, presage, prevision, prognosis, prognostication, prophecy, soothsaying, surmising, tip, vaticination, zodiac; SEE CONCEPTS *70,278,689*

predilection [n] *inclination, preference toward something*
bent*, bias, cup of tea*, dish*, druthers*, fancy, flash, fondness, groove, inclining, leaning, liking, love, mindset*, partiality, penchant, predisposition, proclivity, proneness, propensity, taste*, tendency, thing*, type, weakness; SEE CONCEPTS *20,32,709*

predispose [v] *influence to believe something*
activate, affect, animate, bend*, bias, cultivate, dispose, govern, impress, incline, indoctrinate, induce, inspire, lead, make expectant, make of a mind to*, prejudice, prepare, prime, prompt, stimulate, strike, sway, teach, urge; SEE CONCEPTS *12,14,26,68*

predisposed [adj] *willing, inclined*
agreeable, amenable, biased, eager, enthusiastic, fain, given to, liable, likely, minded, partial, prone, ready, subject, susceptible; SEE CONCEPT *403*

predisposition [n] *willingness, inclination*
bent*, bias, choice, cup of tea*, dish*, disposition, druthers*, flash, groove, leaning, likelihood, liking, option, partiality, penchant, potentiality, predilection, preference, proclivity, proneness, propensity, susceptibility, tendency, thing*, type, weakness; SEE CONCEPTS *20,32,410,709*

predominant [adj] *ruling; most important*
absolute, all-powerful, almighty, arbitrary, ascendant, authoritative, capital, chief, controlling, directing, dominant, dominating, effective, efficacious, governing, holding the reins*, imperious, influential, leading, main, mighty, official, omnipotent, overbearing, overpowering, paramount, potent, predominate, preponderant, prevailing, prevalent, primary, prime, principal, prominent, reigning, sovereign, superior, superlative, supervisory, supreme, surpassing, transcendent, weighty; SEE CONCEPTS *568,574*

predominate [v] *be the most important, noticeable*
carry weight*, command, dominate, domineer, get the upper hand*, govern, hold sway*, manage, outweigh, overrule, overshadow, preponder-ate, prevail, reign, rule, tell; SEE CONCEPTS *94,117,141*

preeminent [adj] *most important; superior*
capital, chief, consummate, distinguished, dominant, excellent, foremost, incomparable, main, major, matchless, number one*, outstanding, paramount, peerless, predominant, principal, renowned, stellar, supreme, surpassing, towering, transcendent, ultimate, unequalled, unmatchable, unrivalled, unsurpassable, unsurpassed; SEE CONCEPTS *568,574*

preempt [v] *take over in place of another*
accroach, acquire, annex, anticipate, appropriate, arrogate, assume, bump, commandeer, confiscate, expropriate, obtain, seize, sequester, take, usurp; SEE CONCEPTS *121,142,234*

preface [n] *introduction*
beginning, exordium, explanation, foreword, overture, preamble, preliminary, prelude, prelusion, proem, prolegomenon, prologue; SEE CONCEPT *270*

preface [v] *introduce*
begin, commence, launch, lead, lead up to, open, precede, prefix, usher; SEE CONCEPTS *57,221*

prefer [v] *favor; single out*
adopt, advance, aggrandize, be partial to, be turned on to, choose, cull, desire, elect, elevate, fancy, finger, fix upon, go for, incline, like better, mark, optate, opt for, pick, place, pose, present, promote, propone, proposition, propound, put, put forward, raise, select, suggest, tag, take, tap, upgrade, wish, would rather*, would sooner*; SEE CONCEPTS *20,41*

preference [n1] *first choice*
alternative, choice, cup of tea*, desire, druthers*, election, favorite, flash*, groove, inclination, option, partiality, pick, predilection, prepossession, propensity, say, say so*, selection, top, weakness; SEE CONCEPTS *20,529,709*

preference [n2] *favorable treatment*
advancement, advantage, elevation, favoritism, first place, precedence, preferment, prelation, pride of place, priority, promotion, upgrading; SEE CONCEPT *693*

preferred [adj] *favorite, chosen*
adopted, approved, culled, decided upon, elected, endorsed, fancied, favored, handpicked, liked, named, picked, popular, sanctioned, selected, set apart, settled upon, singled out, taken, well-liked; SEE CONCEPTS *555,574*

pregnancy [n] *gestation*
child-bearing, fertilization, germination, gravidity, gravidness, impregnation, parturiency, propagation; SEE CONCEPT *427*

pregnant [adj1] *carrying developing offspring within the body*
abundant, anticipating, carrying a child, enceinte, expectant, expecting*, fecund, fertile, fraught, fruitful, gestating, gravid, heavy, hopeful, in family way*, parous, parturient, preggers*, productive, prolific, replete, teeming, with child*; SEE CONCEPTS *406,485*

pregnant [adj2] *significant, meaningful*
charged, cogent, consequential, creative, eloquent, expressive, fecund, imaginative, important, inventive, loaded, momentous, original, pointed, redolent, rich, seminal, sententious, suggestive, telling, weighty; SEE CONCEPTS *267,567*

prehistoric [adj] *before recorded history*
ancient, antediluvian, antiquated, archaic, earli-

est, early, old, olden, primeval, primitive, primordial; SEE CONCEPTS *558,560,799*

prejudice [*n*] *belief without basis, information; intolerance*
ageism, animosity, antipathy, apartheid, aversion, bad opinion, bias, bigotry, chauvinism, contemptuousness, detriment, discrimination, disgust, dislike, displeasure, disrelish, enmity, foregone conclusion, illiberality, injustice, jaundiced eye, mindset*, misjudgment, narrow-mindedness, one-sidedness, partiality, pique, preconceived notion, preconception, prejudgment, prepossession, racism, repugnance, revulsion, sexism, slant, spleen, tilt, twist, umbrage, unfairness, warp, xenophobia; SEE CONCEPT *689*

prejudice [*v*] *influence another's beliefs without basis, information*
angle*, bend*, bias, blemish*, color*, damage, dispose, distort, harm, hinder, hurt, impair, incline, indoctrinate, injure, jaundice, mar, poison*, predispose, prejudge, prepossess, skew*, slant*, spoil, sway*, twist*, undermine, vitiate, warp*; SEE CONCEPTS *7,14,19*

prejudicial [*adj*] *harmful, undermining*
bad, biased, bigoted, counterproductive, damaging, deleterious, detrimental, differential, disadvantageous, discriminatory, evil, hurtful, inimical, injurious, mischievous, nocuous, unfavorable, unjust; SEE CONCEPTS *537,545,570*

preliminary [*adj*] *introductory, initial*
basic, elemental, elementary, exploratory, first, fundamental, inductive, initiatory, opening, pilot, preceding, precursory, prefatory, preparatory, preparing, primal, primary, prior, qualifying, readying, test, trial; SEE CONCEPTS *549,585,799*

preliminary [*n*] *introductory event; beginning*
first round, foundation, groundwork, initiation, introduction, opening, preamble, preface, prelims*, prelude, preparation, start; SEE CONCEPTS *828,832*

prelude [*n*] *beginning of event*
commencement, curtain-raiser*, exordium, foreword, intro*, introduction, overture, preamble, preface, preliminary, prelusion, preparation, proem, prolegomenon, prologue, start; SEE CONCEPTS *264,832*

premature [*adj1*] *earlier in occurrence than anticipated*
a bit previous, abortive, early on, embryonic, forward, green*, immature, incomplete, inopportune, overearly, oversoon, precipitate, predeveloped, previous, raw*, soon, unanticipated, undeveloped, unfledged, unripe, untimely; SEE CONCEPTS *485,549*

premature [*adj2*] *rash, impulsive*
half-baked*, half-cocked*, hasty, ill-considered, inopportune, jumping the gun*, overhasty, precipitate, previous, too soon, untimely; SEE CONCEPTS *401,542*

premeditated [*adj*] *planned, intended*
advised, aforethought, calculated, conscious, considered, contrived, deliberate, designed, fixed, framed up, intentional, laid-out*, prepense, purposed, rigged*, set-up*, sewn-up*, stacked deck*, studied, thought-out, willful; SEE CONCEPTS *542,548*

premier [*adj*] *leading; original*
arch, beginning, champion, chief, earliest, first, foremost, head, highest, inaugural, initial, main,

opening, primary, prime, principal; SEE CONCEPTS *568,585*

premiere [*n*] *original production*
beginning, debut, first night, first performance, first showing, opening, opening night; SEE CONCEPTS *263,832*

premise [*n*] *hypothesis, argument*
apriorism, assertion, assumption, basis, evidence, ground, posit, postulate, postulation, presumption, presupposition, proof, proposition, supposition, thesis; SEE CONCEPTS *529,689*

premise [*v*] *hypothesize*
announce, assume, begin, commence, introduce, posit, postulate, predicate, presume, presuppose, start, state, suppose; SEE CONCEPTS *18,37*

premises [*n*] *grounds and buildings*
bounds, campus, digs, establishment, fix, flat, hangout*, home, house, joint*, land, lay, layout, limits, neck of the woods*, office, pad, place, plant, property, real estate*, roof, scene, site, spot, terrace, turf, zone; SEE CONCEPTS *198,515*

premium [*adj*] *excellent*
choice, exceptional, prime, select, selected, superior; SEE CONCEPT *574*

premium [*n*] *bonus, prize*
appreciation, boon, bounty, carrot*, dividend, extra, fee*, gravy*, guerdon, meed, percentage, perk*, perquisite, plum*, recompense, regard, remuneration, reward, spiff*, stock, store, value; SEE CONCEPTS *337,344*

premonition [*n*] *feeling that an event is about to occur*
apprehension, apprehensiveness, feeling, feeling in bones*, foreboding, forewarning, funny feeling, handwriting on wall*, hunch, idea, intuition, misgiving, omen, portent, prenotion, presage, presentiment, sign, sinking feeling, suspicion, vibes, vibrations, warning, wind change*, winds*, winds of change*, worriment; SEE CONCEPTS *410,529,689,690*

preoccupied [*adj*] *busy; mentally caught up in something*
absent, absent-minded, absorbed, abstracted, airheaded*, asleep*, bemused, bugged*, daydreaming, deep*, distracted, distrait, engaged, engrossed, faraway, fascinated, forgetful, have on the brain*, heedless, hung up*, immersed, inconscient, intent, lost, lost in thought*, mooning*, moony*, oblivious, obsessed, rapt, removed, spellbound, spread out*, taken up, unaware, woolgathering*, wrapped-up*; SEE CONCEPT *403*

preparation [*n1*] *development, readiness*
alertness, anticipation, arrangement, background, base, basis, build-up*, construction, dry run*, education, establishment, evolution, expectation, fitting, foresight, formation, foundation, gestation, getting ready, groundwork, homework, incubation, lead time*, making ready, manufacture, measure, plan, precaution, preparedness, preparing, provision, putting in order, qualification, readying, rehearsal, rundown, safeguard, schoolwork, study, substructure, training, tryout, workout; SEE CONCEPTS *35,202,285*

preparation [*n2*] *something concocted, put together*
arrangement, blend, brew, composition, compound, concoction, confection, decoction, medicine, mixture, product, tincture; SEE CONCEPT *260*

pr
pr

preparatory [*adj*] *introductory, basic*
before, elementary, in advance of, in anticipation of, inductive, opening, precautionary, prefatory, preliminary, prelusive, prep*, preparative, previous, primary, prior to; SEE CONCEPTS *546,585*

prepare [*v*] *make or get ready*
adapt, adjust, anticipate, appoint, arrange, assemble, brace, build up, coach, concoct, construct, contrive, cook, develop, dispose, draw up, endow, equip, fabricate, fashion, fill in, fit, fit out, fix, form, formulate, fortify, furnish, gird, groom, lay the groundwork, make, make provision, make up, outfit, perfect, plan, practice, prime, produce, provide, put in order, put together, qualify, ready, settle, smooth the way*, steel*, strengthen, supply, train, turn out, warm up; SEE CONCEPTS *35,202*

prepared [*adj*] *ready in body or mind*
able, adapted, adjusted, all bases covered*, all set*, all systems go*, arranged, available, disposed, fit, fixed, framed, gaffed, groomed, handy, inclined, in order, in readiness, minded, of a mind, on guard*, planned, predisposed, prepped, primed, processed, psyched-up*, put up, qualified, rehearsed, rigged*, set, set-up, sewed-up, stacked, up*, up on*, willing, wired*; SEE CONCEPTS *403,485,560*

preponderance [*n*] *great numbers; supremacy*
advantage, ascendancy, bigger half*, bulk, command, dominance, domination, dominion, extensiveness, greater part, lion's share*, mass, max*, mostest, power, predominance, prevalence, superiority, sway, weight; SEE CONCEPTS *671,687,767*

prepossessed [*adj*] *made partial by initial impression*
biased, colored, inclined, jaundiced, one-sided, opinionated, partisan, predisposed, prejudiced, tendentious, unindifferent, warped; SEE CONCEPTS *403,542*

prepossessing [*adj*] *attractive, handsome*
alluring, amiable, appealing, attracting, beautiful, bewitching, captivating, charming, drawing, enchanting, engaging, fair, fascinating, fetching, good-looking, inviting, likable, lovable, magnetic, pleasant, pleasing, striking, taking, winning; SEE CONCEPTS *404,537*

preposterous [*adj*] *ridiculous, bizarre*
absurd, asinine, crazy, excessive, exorbitant, extravagant, extreme, fantastic, far-out*, foolish, harebrained*, impossible, incredible, insane, irrational, laughable, ludicrous, monstrous, nonsensical, out of the question*, outrageous, senseless, shocking, silly, stupid, taking the cake*, thick*, too much*, unbelievable, unreasonable, unthinkable, unusual, wacky*, wild; SEE CONCEPTS *529,548,552*

prerequisite [*adj*] *necessary*
called for, essential, expedient, imperative, important, indispensable, mandatory, necessitous, needful, obligatory, of the essence, required, requisite, vital; SEE CONCEPT *546*

prerequisite [*n*] *condition, necessity*
essential, imperative, must, need, postulate, precondition, qualification, requirement, requisite, sine qua non; SEE CONCEPTS *646,709*

prerogative [*n*] *right, privilege*
advantage, appanage, authority, birthright, choice, claim, droit, due, exemption, immunity, liberty, perquisite, sanction, title; SEE CONCEPT *376*

presage [*n*] *prediction, indication*
apprehension, apprehensiveness, augury, auspice, bodement, boding, forecast, foretoken, forewarning, harbinger, intimation, misgiving, omen, portent, premonition, prenotion, presentiment, prognostic, prognostication, prophecy, sign, warning; SEE CONCEPTS *410,529,689*

presage [*v*] *predict or have a feeling*
adumbrate, announce, augur, betoken, bode, divine, feel, forebode, forecast, forerun, foresee, foreshadow, foreshow, foretell, foretoken, forewarn, harbinger, herald, intuit, omen, point to, portend, preindicate, prognosticate, promise, prophesy, sense, signify, soothsay, vaticinate, warn; SEE CONCEPTS *34,70,118*

preschool [*n*] *nursery school*
day care center, kindergarten, playgroup, pre-K; SEE CONCEPTS *287,289*

prescribe [*v*] *stipulate action to be taken*
appoint, assign, choose, command, decide, decree, define, designate, determine, dictate, direct, enjoin, establish, fix, guide, impose, lay down, ordain, order, pick out, require, rule, select, set, settle, specify, write prescription; SEE CONCEPTS *50,60,61,88*

prescription [*n*] *formula, medicine*
decree, direction, drug, edict, instruction, law, mixture, ordinance, preparation, prescript, recipe, regulation, remedy, rule; SEE CONCEPTS *274,307,311,318*

presence [*n1*] *occupancy, attendance*
being, companionship, company, existence, habitation, inhabitance, latency, occupation, omnipresence, potentiality, residence, subsistence, ubiety, ubiquity, whereabouts; SEE CONCEPTS *407,518,710*

presence [*n2*] *appearance, demeanor*
address, air, aspect, aura, bearing, behavior, carriage, comportment, deportment, ease, look, mien, personality, poise, port, seeming, self-assurance, set; SEE CONCEPTS *411,673,716*

presence [*n3*] *closeness, vicinity*
immediate circle, nearness, neighborhood, propinquity, proximity; SEE CONCEPT *747*

presence [*n4*] *ghost*
apparition, manifestation, shade, specter, spirit, supernatural being, wraith; SEE CONCEPT *370*

presence [*n5*] *composure of mind*
acumen, alertness, aplomb, calmness, cool, coolness, imperturbability, levelheadedness, quickness, sangfroid, self-assurance, self-command, self-composure, self-possession, sensibility, sobriety, watchfulness, wits; SEE CONCEPTS *410,657*

presence of mind [*n*] *coolheadedness*
calm, clearheadedness, coolness, patience; SEE CONCEPTS *388,411,720*

present [*adj1*] *existing; at this time*
ad hoc, already, at this moment, begun, being, coeval, commenced, contemporaneous, contemporary, current, even now, existent, extant, for the time being, going on, immediate, in duration, in process, instant, just now, modern, nowadays, present-day, prompt, started, today, topical, under consideration, up-to-date; SEE CONCEPT *820*

present [*adj2*] *nearby, here*
accounted for, at hand, attendant, available, existent, in attendance, in view, made the scene*, near, on board, on deck, on hand, on-the-spot,

ready, show up, there, there with bells on*, within reach; SEE CONCEPTS *539,583*

present [*n1*] *existing time*
here and now, instant, nonce, now, present moment, the time being, this day, this time, today; SEE CONCEPTS *802,807,815*

present [*n2*] *gift*
benefaction, benevolence, boon, bounty, compliment, donation, endowment, favor, gifting, giveaway, goodie*, grant, gratuity, handout, largess, lump, offering, stake, write-off; SEE CONCEPT *337*

present [*v1*] *introduce; demonstrate*
acquaint, adduce, advance, allege, cite, declare, display, do, do the honors, exhibit, expose, expound, extend, fix up, get together, give, give an introduction, hold out, imply, infer, intimate, lay, make a pitch*, make known, manifest, mount, offer, open to view, perform, pitch, pose, produce, proffer, proposition, put forward, put on, raise, recount, relate, roll out, show, stage, state, submit, suggest, tender, trot out; SEE CONCEPTS *66,261*

present [*v2*] *give, hand over*
award, bestow, come up with, confer, devote, donate, entrust, furnish, gift, give away, grant, hand out, kick in*, lay on*, offer, proffer, put at disposal, put forth; SEE CONCEPTS *67,108*

presentable [*adj*] *respectable; fit to be seen*
acceptable, attractive, becoming, decent, fit, good enough*, not bad*, okay*, passable, prepared, proper, satisfactory, suitable, tolerable; SEE CONCEPTS *558,579*

presentation [*n*] *performance; something given, displayed*
act, appearance, arrangement, award, bestowal, coming out, conferral, debut, delivering, delivery, demonstration, display, dog and pony show*, donation, exhibition, exposition, giving, introduction, investiture, knockdown*, launch, launching, offering, overture, pitch, present, production, proposal, proposition, reception, remembrance, rendition, representation, sales pitch*, show, staging, submission; SEE CONCEPTS *261,263,337*

presentiment [*n*] *anticipation, expectation*
apprehension, apprehensiveness, discomposure, disquietude, disturbance, fear, feeling, feeling in bones*, foreboding, forecast, forethought, funny feeling*, handwriting on wall*, hunch, intuition, misgiving, perturbation, premonition, prenotion, presage, sinking feeling, vibes*, worriment; SEE CONCEPTS *410,532,689*

presently [*adv*] *in a short while*
anon, before long, before you know it, by and by, directly, down the line*, down the pike*, down the road*, immediately, in a minute, in a moment, in a short time, now, nowadays, pretty soon, shortly, soon, today, without delay; SEE CONCEPT *820*

preservation [*n*] *maintenance, protection*
canning, care, conservancy, conservation, curing, defense, evaporation, freezing, guard, guardianship, keeping, perpetuation, pickling, preserval, refrigeration, safeguard, safeguarding, safekeeping, safety, salvation, saving, security, shield, storage, support, sustentation, tanning, upholding, ward; SEE CONCEPTS *134,170,202,257*

preserve [*v*] *care for, maintain; continue*
bottle, can, conserve, cure, defend, evaporate,

freeze, guard, keep, keep up, mothball*, mummify, perpetuate, pickle, process, protect, put up, refrigerate, retain, safeguard, save, season, secure, shelter, shield, store, sustain, uphold; SEE CONCEPTS *134,170,202*

preserves [*n*] *thickened fruit prepared for storage and use as a condiment*
confection, confiture, conserve, extract, gelatin, jam, jell, jelly, marmalade, pectin, spread, sweet; SEE CONCEPTS *457,461*

preside [*v*] *be in authority*
administer, advise, be at the head of*, be in driver's seat*, call the signals*, carry on, chair, conduct, control, direct, do the honors, govern, handle, head, head up, keep, lead, manage, officiate, operate, ordain, oversee, pull the strings*, run, run the show*, sit on top of*, supervise; SEE CONCEPTS *94,117*

president [*n*] *chief executive*
boss, CEO, chief executive officer, chief of state, commander-in-chief, head of state, leader, person in charge, premier, prime minister; SEE CONCEPT *347*

press [*n1*] *people or person working in communications*
columnist, correspondent, editor, fourth estate*, interviewer, journalism, journalist, magazine, media, newspaper, newsperson, paper, periodical, photographer, publicist, publisher, reporter, writer; SEE CONCEPTS *280,349,356*

press [*n2*] *horde, large group*
bunch, crowd, crush, drove, flock, herd, host, mob, multitude, pack, push, swarm, throng; SEE CONCEPT *432*

press [*n3*] *strain, pressure*
bustle, confusion, demand, hassle, haste, hurry, rush, stress, urgency; SEE CONCEPTS *230,674*

press [*v1*] *push on with force*
bear down, bear heavily, bulldoze*, clasp, compress, condense, constrain, crowd, crush, cumber, depress, embrace, enfold, express, finish, flatten, force down, hold, hug, impel, iron, jam, level, mangle, mash, mass, move, pack, pile, pin down, ram, reduce, scrunch, shove, smooth, squash, squeeze, squish, steam, stuff, thrust, unwrinkle, weigh; SEE CONCEPTS *191,208*

press [*v2*] *pressure, trouble*
afflict, assail, beg, beset, besiege, buttonhole*, come at, compel, constrain, demand, depress, disquiet, enjoin, entreat, exhort, force, harass, implore, importune, insist on, lean on, oppress, petition, plague, plead, pressurize, push, railroad*, sadden, sell, squeeze, sue, supplicate, torment, urge, vex, weigh down, work on, worry; SEE CONCEPT *14*

pressing [*adj*] *important; urgent*
acute, burning, claiming, clamant, clamorous, compelling, constraining, critical, crucial, crying, demanding, dire, distressing, exacting, exigent, forcing, heat-on*, high-priority, hurry-up*, immediate, imperative, importunate, insistent, instant, life-and-death*, obliging, requiring, serious, vital; SEE CONCEPTS *548,568*

pressure [*n1*] *physical force, weight*
burden, compressing, compression, crushing, encumbrance, heaviness, load, mass, shear, squeeze, squeezing, strain, strength, stress, tension, thrust; SEE CONCEPTS *641,734*

pressure [*n2*] *demand, difficulty*
adversity, affliction, albatross*, burden, choke,

clout, coercion, compulsion, confinement, constraint, crunch, discipline, distress, drag, duress, exigency, force, full court press*, hardship, hassle, heat, hurry, influence, inside track*, load, misfortune, necessity, obligation, persuasion, power, press, pressure cooker*, pull, requirement, strain, stress, sway, tension, trouble, unnaturalness, urgency, weight; SEE CONCEPTS *14,666,674,687*

pressure [*v*] *bother, urge*
come at, compel, constrain, drive, impel, insist, lean on*, politick, press, push, push around*, rush, sell, squeeze, twist arm*, work over*; SEE CONCEPTS *7,14,19,22*

prestige [*n*] *fame, influence*
authority, cachet, celebrity, consequence, control, credit, dignity, distinction, éclat*, eminence, esteem, fame, illustriousness, importance, kudos*, position, power, preeminence, prominence, prominency, rank, regard, renown, reputation, repute, standing, state, stature, status, sway, weight; SEE CONCEPTS *388,668*

prestigious [*adj*] *famous, influential*
celebrated, distinguished, eminent, esteemed, exalted, famed, great, illustrious, important, imposing, impressive, notable, prominent, renowned, reputable, respected; SEE CONCEPTS *555,568*

presumably [*adv*] *likely, reasonably*
apparently, assumably, credible, doubtless, doubtlessly, hypothetically, in all likelihood, in all probability, indubitably, it would seem, most likely, on the face of it, presumptively, probably, seemingly, supposedly, surely, theoretically, unquestionably; SEE CONCEPTS *544,552*

presume [*v1*] *make assumption; believe*
assume, bank on*, believe, conclude, conjecture, consider, count on, depend, figure, gather, guess, infer, jump the gun*, posit, postulate, predicate, premise, presuppose, pretend, rely, speculate, suppose, surmise, take for granted, take it, think, trust; SEE CONCEPTS *12,26,28*

presume [*v2*] *dare; take the liberty*
go so far, have the audacity, impose, infringe, intrude, make bold, undertake, venture; SEE CONCEPT *87*

presumption [*n1*] *belief, hypothesis*
anticipation, apriorism, assumption, basis, chance, conjecture, grounds, guess, likelihood, opinion, plausibility, posit, postulate, postulation, premise, presupposition, probability, reason, shot, shot in the dark*, sneaking suspicion*, stab, supposition, surmise, suspicion, thesis; SEE CONCEPT *689*

presumption [*n2*] *forwardness, daring*
arrogance, assurance, audacity, boldness, brashness, brass, cheek*, chutzpah*, confidence, contumely, effrontery, gall, impudence, insolence, nerve, presumptuousness, rudeness, temerity; SEE CONCEPT *633*

presumptuous [*adj*] *self-confident*
arrogant, audacious, bold, cheeky*, conceited, confident, contumelious, egotistic, foolhardy, forward, fresh, insolent, overconfident, overfamiliar, overweening, pompous, presuming, pretentious, pushy, rash, rude, self-assertive, self-assured, self-satisfied, smug, supercilious, uppity*; SEE CONCEPTS *401,542*

pretend [*v1*] *fake, falsify*
act, affect, allege, assume, be deceitful, beguile, be hypocritical, bluff, cheat, claim, claim falsely,

counterfeit, cozen, deceive, delude, dissemble, dissimulate, dupe, fake out*, feign, fish*, fool, fudge*, hoodwink*, impersonate, jazz*, jive*, lay claim*, let on*, make out*, malinger, masquerade, mislead, pass off*, pass oneself off as*, profess, purport, put on*, put up a front*, sham*, shuck and jive*, simulate, stonewall*, sucker*, whitewash*; SEE CONCEPTS *59,63*

pretend [*v2*] *play the part of*
act, assume the role, imagine, imitate, impersonate, make as if, make believe, make out like, make up, masquerade, mimic, play, playact, portray, pose, purport, put on a front*, put on airs*, put on an act*, represent, reproduce, suppose; SEE CONCEPTS *111,171,292,384*

pretended [*adj*] *alleged; imaginary*
affected, artificial, assumed, avowed, bluffing, bogus, charlatan, cheating, concealed, counterfeit, covered, dissimulated, factitious, fake, false, falsified, feigned, fictitious, impostrous, imposturous, lying, make-believe, masked, mock, ostensible, phony, pretend, professed, pseudo*, purported, put-on*, quack*, sham*, shammed*, simulated, so-called, spurious, supposed; SEE CONCEPTS *545,582*

pretense [*n*] *falsehood, affected show; cover*
act, acting, affectation, appearance, artifice, charade, claim, cloak, deceit, deception, display, dissimulation, double-dealing*, dumb act*, evasion, excuse, fabrication, facade, fakery, faking, falsification, feigning, gag, guise, insincerity, invention, make-believe, mask, masquerade, misrepresentation, misstatement, ostentation, posing, posturing, pretentiousness, pretext, routine, ruse, schtick*, semblance, sham*, shuffling, simulation, stall, stunt, subterfuge, trickery, veil, veneer, wile; SEE CONCEPTS *59,63,633,716*

pretension [*n1*] *airs, snobbishness*
affectation, big talk*, charade, conceit, disguise, fake*, false front*, front, hypocrisy, ostentation, phony, pomposity, pretentiousness, put-on*, self-importance, show, showboat*, showiness, showoff, snobbery, splash*, vainglory, vanity; SEE CONCEPT *633*

pretension [*n2*] *false claim, assertion of importance*
allegation, ambition, ambitiousness, aspiration, assumption, charade, declaration, demand, disguise, maintenance, make-believe, pageant, pretense, pretext, profession, title; SEE CONCEPTS *278,657*

pretentious [*adj*] *snobbish, conceited*
affected, arty, assuming, aureate, big*, bombastic, chichi*, conspicuous, euphuistic, exaggerated, extravagant, feigned, flamboyant, flashy, flaunting, flowery, gaudy, grandiloquent, grandiose, highfaluting*, high-flown*, high-sounding*, hollow, imposing, inflated, jazzy*, la-di-da*, lofty, magniloquent, mincing, ornate, ostentatious, overambitious, overblown, pompous, puffed up*, put-on*, rhetorical, showy, specious, splashy, stilted, swank, too-too*, tumid, turgid, utopian, vainglorious; SEE CONCEPTS *401,542,589*

preternatural [*adj*] *unusual, abnormal*
aberrant, anomalous, atypical, deviant, deviative, extraordinary, ghostly, inexplicable, irregular, marvelous, miraculous, mysterious, odd, peculiar, strange, superhuman, superior, supermundane, supernatural, unaccountable, unearthly,

unnatural, unrepresentative, untypical; SEE CONCEPT *564*

pretext [*n*] *disguise; alleged reason*
affectation, alibi, appearance, bluff, cleanup, cloak, color*, coloring*, copout*, cover, cover story*, cover-up*, device, excuse, face, feint, fig leaf*, front, guise, mask, masquerade, plea, ploy, pretense, red herring*, routine, ruse, semblance, show, simulation, song and dance*, stall, stratagem, subterfuge, veil*; SEE CONCEPTS *59,661,716*

pretty [*adj*] *attractive*
appealing, beauteous, beautiful, boss*, charming, cheerful, cher*, comely, cute, dainty, darling, delicate, delightful, dishy*, dreamboat*, elegant, eyeful*, fair, fine, foxy*, good-looking, graceful, handsome, looker, lovely, neat, nice, picture, pleasant, pleasing, pulchritudinous, tasteful; SEE CONCEPT *579*

pretty [*adv*] *considerable; somewhat*
a little, ample, fairly, kind of, large, moderately, more or less, much, notable, pretty much, quite, rather, reasonably, sizable, some, something, sort of, tolerably; SEE CONCEPTS *531,569*

prevail [*v*] *dominate, control*
abound, beat, be common, be current, be prevalent, best, be usual, be victorious, be widespread, carry, come out on top*, command, conquer, domineer, exist generally, gain, get there, go great guns*, go places*, hit pay dirt*, luck out*, make it, make out, master, move out, obtain, overcome, overrule, predominate, preponderate, prove, reign, succeed, take off, triumph, win; SEE CONCEPTS *94,95,141*

prevailing [*adj*] *general, dominant*
all-embracing, by the numbers*, catholic, common, comprehensive, current, customary, ecumenical, established, familiar, fashionable, influential, in style, in vogue, main, operative, ordinary, popular, predominant, predominating, preponderating, prevalent, principal, rampant, regnant, regular, rife, ruling, set, steady, sweeping, universal, usual, widespread, worldwide; SEE CONCEPT *530*

prevail upon/prevail on [*v*] *persuade, influence*
affect, argue into, bring around, convince, crack, dispose, draw, get, get around, impress, incline, induce, promote, prompt, put across, ram down throat*, sell*, suck in*, sway, talk into, win over; SEE CONCEPT *68*

prevalent [*adj1*] *accepted, widespread*
accustomed, common, commonplace, current, customary, established, everyday, extensive, faddy, frequent, general, habitual, in use, latest*, latest word*, leading edge*, natural, new, normal, now*, ongoing, popular, prevailing, rampant, regnant, regular, rife, run-of-the-mill*, state-of-the-art*, stylish, swinging, trendy, typic, typical, ubiquitous, universal, up-to-date, usual, with it*, wonted; SEE CONCEPTS *530,547,589*

prevalent [*adj2*] *governing, superior*
ascendant, compelling, dominant, overbearing, paramount, powerful, predominant, predominate, preponderant, prevailing, regnant, ruling, sovereign, successful; SEE CONCEPTS *536,574*

prevaricate [*v*] *deceive; stretch the truth*
beat around the bush*, beg the question*, belie, cavil, con, distort, dodge, equivocate, evade, exaggerate, fabricate, falsify, fib, garble, hedge, invent, jive*, lie*, misrepresent, misspeak, palter,

phony up*, put on*, quibble, shift, shuffle, tergiversate; SEE CONCEPT *63*

prevent [*v*] *keep from happening or continuing*
anticipate, arrest, avert, avoid, baffle, balk, bar, block, check, chill*, cool, cork, counter, counteract, dam, debar, defend against, foil, forbid, forestall, forfend, frustrate, halt, hamper, head off, hinder, hold back, hold off, impede, inhibit, intercept, interdict, interrupt, keep lid on*, limit, nip in the bud*, obstruct, obviate, preclude, prohibit, put an end to, put a stop to, repress, restrain, restrict, retard, rule out, shut out, stave off, stop, thwart, turn aside, ward off; SEE CONCEPT *121*

prevention [*n*] *stop*
avoidance, blockage, deterence, determent, forestalling, halt, hindrance, impediment, inhibitor, interception, interruption, obstacle, obstruction, prohibition, stoppage, thwarting; SEE CONCEPTS *240,832*

preview [*n*] *preliminary showing*
examination, preliminary study, research, show, sneak, sneak peek*, survey, viewing; SEE CONCEPTS *263,292,832*

previous [*adj1*] *former, prior*
antecedent, anterior, earlier, erstwhile, ex, foregoing, one-time, past, precedent, preceding, quondam, sometime; SEE CONCEPTS *585,811,818,820*

previous [*adj2*] *premature*
ahead of, early, inopportune, overearly, oversoon, precipitate, soon, too early, too soon, unfounded, untimely, unwarranted; SEE CONCEPTS *558,799*

previously [*adv*] *earlier*
ahead, already, ante, antecedently, at one time, away back, a while ago, back, back when, before, beforehand, erstwhile, fore, formerly, forward, heretofore, hitherto, in advance, in anticipation, in days gone by, in the past, long ago, once, one-shot, precedently, then, time was, until now; SEE CONCEPT *820*

prey [*n*] *target of attack*
casualty, chased*, dupe*, game, kill, loot, mark, martyr, mug*, pillage, quarry, quest, raven, spoil, sufferer, underdog, victim; SEE CONCEPTS *394,423*

prey on [*v*] *attack, terrorize*
blackmail, bleed, bully, burden, consume, depredate, devour, distress, eat, exploit, feed on, fleece, haunt, hunt, intimidate, live off, load, oppress, plunder, raid, seize, take advantage of, tax, trouble, victimize, weigh, worry; SEE CONCEPTS *14,86,169*

price [*n1*] *financial value*
amount, appraisal, appraisement, asking price, assessment, barter, bill, bounty, ceiling, charge, compensation, consideration, cost, damage, demand, disbursement, discount, dues, estimate, exaction, expenditure, expense, face value, fare, fee, figure, hire, outlay, output, pay, payment, premium, prize, quotation, ransom, rate, reckoning, retail, return, reward, score, sticker*, tab, tariff, ticket, toll, tune*, valuation, wages, wholesale, worth; SEE CONCEPT *329*

price [*n2*] *consequences of action*
cost, expense, penalty, sacrifice, toll; SEE CONCEPT *230*

price [*v*] *assess financial value*
appraise, cost, estimate, evaluate, fix, mark

down, mark up, put a price on, rate, reduce, sticker, value; SEE CONCEPT *330*

priceless [*adj1*] *precious, irreplaceable*
beyond price, cherished, collectible, costly, dear, expensive, incalculable, incomparable, inestimable, invaluable, out-of-bounds*, out-of-sight*, prized, rare, rich, treasured, valuable, valued, without price, worth a king's ransom*, worth its weight in gold*; SEE CONCEPTS *334,568*

priceless [*adj2*] *extremely funny*
absurd, amusing, comic, droll, hilarious, humorous, killing, rib-tickling*, ridiculous, riotous, scream, sidesplitting; SEE CONCEPT *267*

prick [*n*] *small hole made by stab*
cut, gash, jab, jag, perforation, pinhole, prickle, puncture, stab, wound; SEE CONCEPT *309*

prick [*v*] *stab, perforate*
bore, cut, drill, enter, hurt, jab, lance, pierce, pink, punch, puncture, slash, slit, smart, spur, sting; SEE CONCEPT *220*

prickly [*adj1*] *thorny or difficult*
annoying, barbed, bothersome, brambly, briery, bristly, complicated, echinated, intricate, involved, knotty, nettlesome, pointed, sharp, spiny, stimulating, ticklish, tricky, troublesome, trying; SEE CONCEPTS *485,565*

prickly [*adj2*] *irritable, bad-tempered*
cantankerous, edgy, fractious, fretful, grumpy, irritable, peevish, petulant, snappish, touchy, waspish; SEE CONCEPT *401*

pride [*n1*] *self-esteem*
amour-propre, delight, dignity, ego, egoism, egotism, ego trip, face, gratification, happiness, honor, joy, pleasure, pridefulness, repletion, satisfaction, self-admiration, self-confidence, self-glorification, self-love, self-regard, self-respect, self-satisfaction, self-sufficiency, self-trust, self-worth, sufficiency; SEE CONCEPT *411*

pride [*n2*] *arrogance, self-importance*
airs, assumption, big-headedness*, cockiness*, conceit, condescension, contumely, disdain, disdainfulness, egoism, egotism, haughtiness, hauteur, hubris, huff, immodesty, insolence, loftiness, narcissism, overconfidence, patronage, pragmatism, presumption, pretension, pretentiousness, proud flesh*, self-exaltation, self-love, smugness, snobbery, superbity, superciliousness, swagger, swelled head*, vainglory, vanity; SEE CONCEPT *633*

pride [*n3*] *treasure; best*
boast, choice, cream, elite, fat, flower*, gem*, glory, jewel*, pick, pride and joy*, prime, prize, top*; SEE CONCEPTS *446,668,689*

pride [*v*] *take pleasure in accomplishment*
be proud, boast, brag, congratulate, crow, exult, felicitate, flatter oneself, gasconade, glory in, hold head high, overbear, pique*, plume*, prance, preen, presume, puff up*, revel in, strut, swagger, swell, vaunt; SEE CONCEPTS *10,633*

priest [*n*] *man who is minister in Roman or Orthodox Catholic church*
clergyperson, cleric, curate, divine, ecclesiastic, elder, father, father confessor, friar, holy man, lama, man of God, man of the cloth*, monk, padre, pontiff, preacher, rector, vicar; SEE CONCEPT *361*

priesthood [*n*] *clergy*
canonicate, canonry, cardinalate, deaconry, diaconate, ecclesiastics, ministry, pastorate, rabbinate, the cloth, the pulpit; SEE CONCEPT *369*

prim [*adj*] *particular, fussy*
blue-nose*, ceremonial, ceremonious, choosy, cleanly, conventional, correct, dapper*, decorous, demure, fastidious, formal, genteel, good, goody-goody*, nice, nit-picking*, orderly, overmodest, polite, precise, priggish, prissy, proper, prudish, puritanical, rigid, shipshape*, spic-and-span*, spruce, stickling, stiff, straight, strait-laced, stuffy*, tidy, uncluttered, upright, Victorian, well-groomed, wooden*; SEE CONCEPTS *401,404*

prima donna [*n1*] *star*
diva, first lady, headliner, leading lady, lead vocalist, opera singer, singer, soloist, superstar, topliner*; SEE CONCEPTS *352,366*

prima donna [*n2*] *temperamental person*
conceited person, crybaby, egotist, narcissist, princess, self-centered person, spoiled brat, vain person; SEE CONCEPT *411*

primal [*adj*] *primeval; primary*
aboriginal, ancient, central, chief, earliest, early, first, fundamental, highest, old, original, paramount, past, prehistoric, primitive, primordial, principal, pristine; SEE CONCEPT *799*

primarily [*adv1*] *generally; for the most part*
above all, basically, chiefly, especially, essentially, fundamentally, generally, largely, mainly, mostly, on the whole, overall, predominantly, principally; SEE CONCEPTS *531,544,772*

primarily [*adv2*] *in the beginning*
at first, at the start, first and foremost, from the start, initially, in the first place, originally, primitively; SEE CONCEPTS *548,799*

primary/prime [*adj1*] *best, principal*
capital, cardinal, chief, crackerjack*, dominant, excellent, fab*, first, first-class*, greatest, heavy, highest, hot*, leading, main, number one*, paramount, primo*, state-of-the-art*, stellar, top, top-of-the-line*, tough*, world-class*; SEE CONCEPTS *567,574*

primary/prime [*adj2*] *earliest*
aboriginal, beginning, direct, first, firsthand, immediate, initial, original, pioneer, primal, primeval, primitive, primordial, pristine; SEE CONCEPTS *585,799*

primary/prime [*adj3*] *basic, fundamental*
basal, beginning, bottom, central, elemental, elementary, essential, first, foundational, introductory, meat-and-potatoes*, original, primitive, principal, radical, rudimentary, simple, three R's*, ultimate, underivative, underived, underlying; SEE CONCEPTS *549,585*

prime [*n1*] *best part of existence*
best, best days*, bloom, choice, cream*, elite, fat*, flower*, flowering*, height, heyday, maturity, peak, perfection, pink*, prize, spring, springtime, top, verdure, vitality, zenith; SEE CONCEPT *816*

prime [*n2*] *beginning; spring*
adolescence, aurora, dawn, daybreak, dew, greenness*, juvenility, morn*, morning, opening, puberty, pubescence, springtime, start, sunrise, sunup, tender years*, vitality, youth, youthfulness; SEE CONCEPTS *817,832*

prime [*v*] *get ready; prepare*
break in, brief, clue*, coach, cram, excite, fill in, fit, galvanize, groom, inform, innervate, make ready, motivate, move, notify, prep*, provoke, rehearse, stimulate, tell, train; SEE CONCEPTS *7,19,22,35,202*

prime minister [*n*] *premier*
chancellor, chief executive, chief of state, commander-in-chief, head of state, leader, person in charge, president; SEE CONCEPTS *347,354*

primeval [*adj*] *ancient*
earliest, early, first, old, original, prehistoric, primal, primary, primitive, primordial, pristine; SEE CONCEPT *799*

primitive [*adj1*] *ancient, original*
archaic, basic, earliest, early, elementary, essential, first, fundamental, old, primal, primary, primeval, primordial, pristine, substratal, underivative, underived, underlying, undeveloped, unevolved; SEE CONCEPT *799*

primitive [*adj2*] *barbaric, crude*
animal, atavistic, austere, barbarian, barbarous, brutish, childlike, fierce, ignorant, naive, natural, nonliterate, preliterate, raw, rough, rude, rudimentary, savage, simple, uncivilized, uncultivated, uncultured, underdeveloped, undeveloped, undomesticated, unlearned, unrefined, unsophisticated, untamed, untaught, untrained, untutored, vestigial, wild; SEE CONCEPTS *406,485*

primordial [*adj*] *earliest*
basic, early, elemental, first, fundamental, original, prehistoric, primal, primary, prime, primeval, primitive, pristine, radical; SEE CONCEPT *799*

primp [*v*] *beautify and dress nicely*
deck out*, dress up, fix up, get dressed up, groom, gussy up*, preen, prepare, slick*, smarten, spiff, spruce, titivate; SEE CONCEPTS *162,167,202*

principal [*adj*] *most important*
arch, capital, cardinal, champion, chief, controlling, crowning, dominant, essential, first, foremost, greatest, head, highest, incomparable, key, leading, main, mainline, major, matchless, maximum, outstanding, paramount, peerless, predominant, preeminent, premier, prevailing, primary, prime, prominent, second-to-none, sovereign, star, stellar, strongest, supereminent, superior, supreme, transcendent, unapproachable, unequaled, unparalleled, unrivaled; SEE CONCEPTS *568,574*

principal [*n1*] *person in charge of organization, often an educational one*
administrator, boss, chief, dean, director, exec*, head, key player*, lead, leader, preceptor, protagonist, rector, ruler, star, superintendent; SEE CONCEPTS *347,350*

principal [*n2*] *original amount of property either owned or owed*
assets, capital, capital funds, money; SEE CONCEPT *332*

principally [*adv*] *mainly*
above all, basically, before anything else, cardinally, chiefly, dominantly, eminently, especially, essentially, first and foremost, first of all, for the most part, fundamentally, generally, importantly, in the first place, in the main, largely, materially, mostly, notably, particularly, peculiarly, predominantly, preeminently, prevailingly, prevalently, primarily, substantially, superlatively, supremely, to a great degree, universally, vitally; SEE CONCEPTS *531,544,772*

principle [*n1*] *law, standard*
assumption, axiom, basis, canon, convention, criterion, dictum, doctrine, dogma, ethic, form, formula, foundation, fundamental, golden rule*,

ground, maxim, origin, postulate, precept, prescript, principium, proposition, regulation, rule, source, theorem, truth, usage, verity; SEE CONCEPTS *318,688*

principle/principles [*n2*] *belief, morality; morals*
attitude, character, code, conduct, conscience, credo, ethic, ethics, faith, ideals, integrity, opinion, policy, probity, rectitude, scruples, sense of duty, sense of honor, system, teaching, tenet, uprightness; SEE CONCEPTS *645,689*

print [*n*] *publication; something impressed*
black-and-white*, book, characters, composition, copy, edition, engraving, face, font, impress, impression, imprint, indentation, issue, lettering, letters, lithograph, magazine, newspaper, newsprint, periodical, photograph, printed matter, stamp, type, typeface, typescript, typesetting, writing; SEE CONCEPTS *259,265,280*

print [*v*] *produce writing, impression; reproduce publication*
calligraph, compose, disseminate, engrave, go to press, impress, imprint, issue, let roll, letter, mark, offset, publish, put to bed*, reissue, reprint, run off, set, set type, stamp, strike off; SEE CONCEPTS *174,203,205*

printer [*n1*] *typesetter*
compositor, pressperson, publisher, typographer; SEE CONCEPTS *174,203,205*

printer [*n2*] *computer peripheral device*
ball printer, character printer, color printer, daisy-wheel printer, dot-matrix printer, graphics printer, ink-jet printer, laser printer, LCD printer, LED printer, line printer, thermal printer; SEE CONCEPT *463*

prior [*adj*] *earlier*
above-mentioned, aforementioned, ahead, antecedent, anterior, before, foregoing, former, forward, past, precedent, preceding, preexistent, preexisting, previous; SEE CONCEPTS *811,812,818,820*

priority [*n*] *first concern*
antecedence, arrangement, crash project*, greatest importance, lead, order, precedence, preeminence, preference, prerogative, previousness, rank, right of way*, seniority, superiority, supremacy, transcendence; SEE CONCEPTS *532,668,727*

prison [*n*] *residence for incarcerating criminals*
bastille, can*, clink*, confinement, cooler*, dungeon, G*, guardhouse, jail, keep, lockup, pen*, penal institution, penitentiary, reformatory, slammer*, statesville*, stockade, up the river*; SEE CONCEPTS *439,449,516*

prisoner [*n*] *person jailed for crime; person kept against their will*
captive, chain gang member, con, convict, culprit, detainee, hostage, internee, jailbird*, lag*, lifer*, loser*, tough*, yardbird*; SEE CONCEPT *412*

prissy [*adj*] *particular and fussy*
epicene, fastidious, finicky, genteel, goody-goody*, goody-two-shoes*, overnice, pansified, persnickety, picky, precious, prim, prim and proper*, prudish, puritanical, sissified, sissy, squeamish, stickling, strait-laced, stuffy*, tight-laced*, Victorian; SEE CONCEPTS *401,404*

pristine [*adj*] *clean, pure; primeval*
earliest, early, first, immaculate, intact, natural, original, primal, purified, refined, sanitary, snowy, spotless, stainless, sterile, sterilized,

pr
pr

taintless, unadulterated, uncorrupted, undebased, unpolluted, unsoiled, unspotted, unstained, unsullied, untainted, untarnished, untouched, virginal, wholesome; SEE CONCEPTS *621,799*

privacy [*n*] *solitude, secrecy*
aloofness, clandestineness, concealment, confidentiality, isolation, one's space, penetralia, privateness, quiet, retirement, retreat, seclusion, separateness, separation, sequestration, solitude; SEE CONCEPTS *388,631,714*

private [*adj1*] *personal, intimate*
behind the scenes*, clandestine, closet*, close to one's chest*, confidential, discreet, exclusive, hushed, hush-hush*, independent, individual, inside, nonpublic, not open, off the record*, own, particular, privy*, reserved, secret, separate, special, under one's hat*, unofficial; SEE CONCEPTS *267,406*

private [*adj2*] *hidden, isolated*
concealed, discreet, quiet, removed, retired, secluded, secret, separate, sequestered, solitary, withdrawn; SEE CONCEPTS *576,583*

private [*n*] *lowest rank of person enlisted in armed service*
enlisted person, first-class*, GI, infantry, private soldier, sailor, second-class*, soldier; SEE CONCEPT *358*

private eye [*n*] *private detective*
agent, bird dog*, bloodhound*, cop, dick*, peeper*, P.I.*, private investigator, sleuth, snoop*, tail*; SEE CONCEPT *348*

privation [*n*] *deprivation*
destitution, disadvantage, hardship, indigence, lack, necessity, need, neediness, poverty, want; SEE CONCEPTS *121,142,709*

privilege [*n*] *right, due*
advantage, allowance, appanage, appurtenance, authority, authorization, benefit, birthright, boon, chance, charter, claim, concession, entitlement, event, exemption, favor, franchise, freedom, grant, immunity, liberty, license, opportunity, perquisite, prerogative, right, sanction; SEE CONCEPT *376*

privileged [*adj1*] *favored, elite*
advantaged, entitled, honored, indulged, powerful, ruling, special; SEE CONCEPTS *334,574*

privileged [*adj2*] *allowed, exempt*
authorized, chartered, eligible, empowered, entitled, excused, franchised, free, furnished, granted, immune, kosher*, legit*, licensed, okay*, okayed*, palatine, qualified, sanctioned, special, vested; SEE CONCEPT *548*

privileged [*adj3*] *confidential, secret*
exceptional, for eyes only*, inside, not for publication, off the record*, on the QT*, privy, special, top secret, under one's hat*; SEE CONCEPT *267*

privy [*adj1*] *secret*
buried, concealed, confidential, covert, hidden, hush-hush*, obscured, off the record*, personal, private, separate, shrouded, ulterior; SEE CONCEPTS *267,576*

privy [*adj2*] *aware*
acquainted, apprised, cognizant, conscious, informed, in on*, in the know*, private, privileged, wise; SEE CONCEPT *402*

prize [*adj*] *best*
award-winning, champion, choice, cream*, elite, fat*, first-class*, first-rate*, outstanding, pick, prime, top, topnotch, winning; SEE CONCEPT *574*

prize [*n1*] *award, winnings*
accolade, acquirement, acquisition, advantage, blue ribbon*, bonus, bounty, cake*, capture, carrot*, championship, citation, crown, decoration, dividend, feather in cap*, first place*, gold*, gold star*, gravy*, guerdon, haul, honor, inducement, jackpot, laurel, loot*, medal, meed, payoff, pickings*, pillage, plum*, plunder*, possession, premium, privilege, purse, recompense, requital, reward, scholarship, spoil, spoils, stakes, strokes*, swag*, title, trophy, windfall; SEE CONCEPTS *337,344,693,710*

prize [*n2*] *goal; best*
aim, ambition, choice, conquest, cream*, desire, elite, fat, flower*, gain, gold*, hope, pick, pride, prime, top*; SEE CONCEPTS *659,709*

prize [*v*] *value highly*
appreciate, apprize, cherish, count, enshrine, esteem, guard, hold dear, rate, regard highly, set store by*, treasure; SEE CONCEPTS *10,32*

probability [*n*] *likelihood of something happening*
anticipation, chance, chances, conceivability, contingency, credibility, expectation, feasibility, hazard, liability, likeliness, odds, outside chance*, plausibility, possibility, practicability, prayer, presumption, promise, prospect, reasonableness, shot, snowball's chance*, toss-up*; SEE CONCEPT *650*

probable [*adj*] *likely to happen*
apparent, believable, credible, earthly, feasible, illusory, in the cards*, mortal, most likely, odds-on*, ostensible, plausible, possible, presumable, presumed, rational, reasonable, seeming; SEE CONCEPT *552*

probably [*adv*] *likely to happen*
apparently, as likely as not, assumably, as the case may be, believably, dollars to doughnuts*, doubtless, expediently, feasibly, imaginably, in all likelihood, in all probability, like enough, maybe, most likely, no doubt, one can assume, perchance, perhaps, plausibly, possibly, practicably, presumably, presumptively, reasonably, seemingly, to all appearances; SEE CONCEPT *552*

probation [*n*] *trial period*
apprenticeship, noviciate, test period, trial; SEE CONCEPTS *87,290,291*

probe [*n*] *investigation*
delving, detection, examination, exploration, fishing expedition*, inquest, inquiry, inquisition, legwork*, probing, quest, research, scrutiny, study, third degree*; SEE CONCEPTS *31,103,216,290*

probe [*v*] *explore, investigate*
ask, catechize, check, check out, check over, check up, delve into, dig, examine, eye, feel around, feel out, go into, inquire, interrogate, look into, look-see, penetrate, pierce, prod, prospect, put out a feeler*, query, quiz, scrutinize, search, sift, sound, sound out, study, test, test the waters*, verify; SEE CONCEPTS *31,103,216*

probity [*n*] *fairness, honesty*
equity, fidelity, goodness, honor, integrity, justice, morality, rectitude, righteousness, rightness, sincerity, trustworthiness, truthfulness, uprightness, virtue, worth; SEE CONCEPTS *411,645*

problem [*n1*] *difficulty; bad situation*
botheration, box*, can of worms*, complication, count*, crunch*, dilemma, disagreement, dispute, disputed point, doubt, headache*, hitch*,

hot water*, issue, mess*, obstacle, pickle*, point at issue*, predicament, quandary, question, scrape*, squeeze*, trouble, worriment; SEE CONCEPTS *666,674*

problem [*n2*] *puzzle, question*
brainteaser*, bugaboo*, cliff-hanger*, conundrum, enigma, example, grabber*, illustration, intricacy, mind-boggler*, mystery, poser*, puzzler, query, riddle, sixty-four thousand dollar question*, stickler, stumper, teaser, twister; SEE CONCEPTS *529,532*

problematic [*adj*] *open to doubt*
ambiguous, arguable, chancy, debatable, disputable, doubtful, dubious, dubitable, enigmatic, iffy*, indecisive, moot, open, precarious, problematical, puzzling, questionable, suspect, tricky, uncertain, unsettled, up for grabs*; SEE CONCEPT *529*

procedure [*n*] *process, system for accomplishing something*
action, agenda, agendum, channels, conduct, course, custom, daily grind*, fashion, form, formula, game plan*, gimmick, grind, idea, layout, line, maneuver, measure, method, mode, modus operandi, move, nuts and bolts*, operation, performance, plan, policy, polity, practice, proceeding, program, red tape*, routine, scheme, setup, step, strategy, style, the book*, the numbers*, transaction; SEE CONCEPT *6*

proceed [*v1*] *physically or mentally carry on, carry out*
advance, continue, fare, get, get going, get on with, get under way*, go ahead, go on, hie, journey, make a start, march, move on, move out, pass, press on, progress, push on, repair, set in motion, travel, wend; SEE CONCEPTS *43,91*

proceed [*v2*] *flow from; originate*
arise, come, derive, emanate, ensue, extend, follow, head, issue, pass, result, rise, spring, stem; SEE CONCEPTS *179,230,676*

proceeding [*n*] *undertaking, course of action*
act, action, adventure, casualty, circumstance, come off, deed, exercise, experiment, go-down*, goings-on*, happening, incident, maneuver, measure, move, movement, occurrence, operation, performance, procedure, process, step, transaction, venture; SEE CONCEPTS *2,3*

proceedings [*n*] *account, report of event*
affairs, annals, archives, business, dealings, documents, doings*, matters, minutes, records, transactions; SEE CONCEPT *271*

proceeds [*n*] *earnings from business*
gain, gate, handle, income, interest, lucre, produce, product, profit, receipts, result, returns, revenue, reward, split, take, takings, till, yield; SEE CONCEPT *344*

process [*n*] *method; series of actions to achieve result*
action, advance, case, channels*, course, course of action*, development, evolution, fashion, formation, growth, manner, means, measure, mechanism, mode, modus operandi, movement, operation, outgrowth, performance, practice, procedure, proceeding, progress, progression, red tape*, routine, rule, stage, step, suit, system, technique, transaction, trial, unfolding, way, wise, working; SEE CONCEPT *6*

process [*v*] *subject to series of actions to achieve result*
alter, concoct, convert, deal with, dispose of, ful-

fill, handle, make ready, prepare, refine, take care of, transform, treat; SEE CONCEPT *204*

procession [*n*] *parade, sequence*
advance, autocade, cavalcade, column, consecution, cortege, course, cycle, file, march, motorcade, movement, order, process, run, series, string, succession, train; SEE CONCEPTS *155,727*

proclaim [*v*] *advertise, make known*
affirm, announce, annunciate, blast, blaze, blazon, broadcast, call, circulate, declare, demonstrate, disseminate, enunciate, evidence, evince, exhibit, expound, get on a soapbox*, give out, herald, illustrate, indicate, manifest, mark, ostend, pass the word*, profess, promulgate, publish, shoot off mouth*, shout out, show, sound off, spiel*, spout, spread it around*, stump*, trumpet*, utter, vent, ventilate, voice; SEE CONCEPTS *49,60*

proclamation [*n*] *advertisement, announcement*
broadcast, declaration, decree, edict, manifesto, notice, notification, promulgation, pronouncement, pronunciamento*, publication; SEE CONCEPTS *271,278*

proclivity [*n*] *inclination, tendency*
bent*, bias, cup of tea*, disposition, druthers, facility, flash*, groove*, inclining, leaning, liableness, penchant, predilection, predisposition, proneness, propensity, thing for*, type, weakness; SEE CONCEPTS *20,32,411*

procrastinate [*v*] *delay, put off doing*
adjourn, be dilatory, cool*, dally, dawdle, defer, drag, drag one's feet*, give the run around*, goldbrick*, hang fire*, hesitate, hold off, lag*, let slide, linger, loiter, pause, play a waiting game*, play for time*, poke*, postpone, prolong, protract, retard, shilly-shally*, stall, stay, suspend, tarry, temporize, wait; SEE CONCEPTS *121,237,681*

procreate [*v*] *reproduce*
beget, breed, conceive, create, engender, father, generate, get, give birth to, hatch, impregnate, make, mother, multiply, originate, parent, produce, progenerate, proliferate, propagate, sire, spawn; SEE CONCEPTS *173,251,374*

procure [*v*] *acquire, obtain*
annex, appropriate, bring around, buy, buy out, buy up, come by, compass, cop*, corral, draw, earn, effect, find, gain, get, get hold of, grab, have, induce, land*, latch on to, lay hands on, make a haul*, manage to get*, persuade, pick up, prevail upon, promote, purchase, score, secure, solicit, wangle, win; SEE CONCEPTS *68,120,327*

prod [*v1*] *poke at*
crowd, dig, drive, elbow, goose, jab, jog, nudge, press, prick, punch, push, shove; SEE CONCEPT *208*

prod [*v2*] *urge, incite*
crowd*, egg on*, excite, exhort, goad, goose*, impel, instigate, jog memory, motivate, move, pique, prick, prompt, propel, provoke, push, remind, rouse, sic*, sound, spark, spur, stimulate, stir up, trigger, turn on; SEE CONCEPTS *7,19,22,242*

prodigal [*adj1*] *wasteful*
dissipated, excessive, extravagant, immoderate, improvident, intemperate, lavish, profligate, reckless, spendthrift, squandering, wanton; SEE CONCEPTS *401,560*

prodigal [*adj2*] *luxurious, profuse*
abundant, bounteous, bountiful, copious, exuber-

pr
pr

ant, lavish, lush, luxuriant, moneyed, munificent, opulent, riotous, sumptuous, superabundant, teeming; SEE CONCEPTS *334,781*

prodigal [*n*] *person who spends a lot*
big spender*, compulsive shopper*, deep pockets*, dissipator, high roller*, profligate, spender, spendthrift, sport, squanderer, waster, wastrel; SEE CONCEPTS *348,412*

prodigious [*adj1*] *huge, enormous*
big, colossal*, fantastic, giant, gigantic, gross, Herculean*, immeasurable, immense, inordinate, jumbo*, king-size*, large, mammoth, massive, mighty, monstrous, monumental, mortal, stupendous, towering, tremendous, vast; SEE CONCEPTS *773,781*

prodigious [*adj2*] *extraordinary, fabulous*
abnormal, amazing, astonishing, astounding, bad, exceptional, fab*, fantastic, heavy, impressive, marvelous, miraculous, out-of-this-world*, phenomenal, preternatural, remarkable, spectacular, staggering, startling, state-of-the-art*, striking, stupendous, surprising, unreal, unusual, utmost, wonderful; SEE CONCEPTS *567,572,574*

prodigy [*n*] *person or thing that is extraordinary*
brain*, child genius, curiosity, enormity, freak*, genius, intellect, marvel, mastermind, miracle, monster, natural, one in a million*, phenomenon, portent, rare bird*, rarity, sensation, spectacle, stunner, talent, whiz*, whiz kid*, wizard, wonder, wonder child, wunderkind; SEE CONCEPTS *416,671,706*

produce [*n*] *fruit and vegetables*
crop, fruitage, goods, greengrocery, harvest, outcome, outgrowth, outturn, production, yield; SEE CONCEPTS *426,429,431,457,461*

produce [*v1*] *generate, create*
afford, assemble, author, bear, beget, blossom, breed, bring forth, bring out, build, come through, compose, conceive, construct, contribute, cultivate, deliver, design, develop, devise, effectuate, engender, erect, fabricate, fetch, flower, form, frame, furnish, give, give birth, give forth, imagine, invent, make, manufacture, multiply, offer, originate, parent, present, procreate, propagate, provide, put together, render, reproduce, return, show fruit, supply, turn out, write, yield; SEE CONCEPTS *173,205,251,374*

produce [*v2*] *cause, effect*
beget, breed, bring about, draw on, engender, generate, get up, give rise to, hatch, induce, make, make for*, muster, occasion, provoke, result in, secure, set off, work up; SEE CONCEPT *242*

produce [*v3*] *demonstrate, show*
advance, bring forward, bring to light, display, exhibit, offer, present, put forward, set forth, unfold; SEE CONCEPT *261*

produce [*v4*] *put on a public performance*
act, come through, direct, do, exhibit, make, mount, percolate, perform, perk, play, present, pull off*, show, stage; SEE CONCEPTS *292,324*

product [*n*] *result or goods created*
aftermath, amount, artifact, blend, brand, brew, by-product, commodity, compound, concoction, confection, consequence, contrivance, creation, crop, decoction, device, effect, emolument, fabrication, fruit, gain, handiwork, invention, issue, legacy, line, manufacture, merchandise, offshoot, outcome, outgrowth, output, preparation, produce, production, profit, realization, result, re-

turns, spinoff, stock, synthetic, upshot, work, yield; SEE CONCEPTS *230,338*

production [*n*] *creating of goods, result*
assembly, authoring, bearing, blossoming, construction, creation, direction, elongation, engendering, extention, fabrication, formulation, fructification, generation, giving, lengthening, making, management, manufacture, manufacturing, origination, preparation, presentation, producing, prolongation, protraction, provision, rendering, reproduction, return, staging, yielding; SEE CONCEPT *205*

productive [*adj*] *fruitful, creative*
advantageous, beneficial, constructive, dynamic, effective, energetic, fecund, fertile, gainful, generative, gratifying, inventive, plentiful, producing, profitable, prolific, rewarding, rich, teeming, useful, valuable, vigorous, worthwhile; SEE CONCEPTS *537,542,560*

productivity [*n*] *output, work rate*
abundance, capacity, fecundity, fertility, mass production, potency, production, productiveness, richness, yield; SEE CONCEPT *630*

profane [*adj*] *immoral, crude, disrespectful of religion*
abusive, atheistic, blasphemous, coarse, dirty*, filthy*, foul, godless, heathen, idolatrous, impious, impure, indecent, infidel, irreligious, irreverent, irreverential, mundane, nasty, obscene, pagan, profanatory, raunchy, sacrilegious, sinful, smutty*, temporal, transient, transitory, unconsecrated, ungodly, unhallowed, unholy, unsanctified, vulgar, wicked, worldly; SEE CONCEPTS *267,401,545*

profane [*v*] *defile, desecrate*
abuse, be evil, befoul, blaspheme, commit sacrilege, commit sin, contaminate, curse, cuss, damn, darn, debase, despoil, do wrong, flame, hoodoo*, misuse, mock, mudsling*, pervert, pollute, prostitute, put double whammy on*, revile, scorn, swear, talk dirty*, tar, trash, vice, violate, vitiate, voodoo*; SEE CONCEPTS *44,52,58,63*

profanity [*n*] *foul language*
abuse, blasphemy, curse, cursing, cuss, cuss word, dirty language*, dirty name*, dirty word*, execration, four-letter word*, impiety, imprecation, irreverence, malediction, no-no*, obscenity, profaneness, sacrilege, swearing, swearword, taboo; SEE CONCEPTS *278,645*

profess [*v*] *declare, assert*
acknowledge, act as if, admit, affirm, allege, announce, asseverate, aver, avouch, avow, blow hot air*, certify, claim, come out*, confess, confirm, constate, croon, cross heart*, depose, dissemble, fake, feign, get off chest*, get on soapbox*, maintain, make out, open up*, own, own up*, predicate, pretend, proclaim, purport, say so*, sing*, soapbox*, spiel*, spout*, state, stump*, swear on bible*, swear up and down*, talk big*, vouch; SEE CONCEPTS *49,63*

profession [*n1*] *line of work requiring academic or practical preparation*
art, avocation, berth, billet, biz*, business, calling, career, chosen work, concern, craft, dodge*, employment, engagement, field, game*, handicraft, lifework, line*, line of work*, métier, occupation, office, position, post, pursuit, rat race*, role, service, situation, slot*, specialty, sphere, thing*, trade, undertaking, vocation, walk of life*; SEE CONCEPT *360*

profession [n2] *declaration*
acknowledgment, affirmation, assertion, attestation, avowal, claim, confession, pretense, statement, testimony, vow; SEE CONCEPT *278*

professional [adj] *skilled, trained*
able, ace, acknowledged, adept, competent, crackerjack*, efficient, experienced, expert, finished, knowing one's stuff*, known, learned, licensed, on the ball*, polished, practiced, proficient, qualified, sharp, skillful, slick*, there*, up to speed*, well-qualified; SEE CONCEPTS *326,402,527,528*

professional [n] *person prepared for work by extended study or practice*
adept, artist, artiste, authority, brain*, egghead*, expert, hotshot*, old hand*, old pro*, old warhorse*, phenom, powerhouse, pro, proficient, pundit, shark, specialist, star, superstar, virtuoso, whiz*, whiz kid*, wizard; SEE CONCEPTS *347,348*

professor [n] *person who teaches college courses*
assistant, brain*, educator, egghead*, faculty member, fellow, instructor, lecturer, pedagogue, principal, prof*, pundit, quant*, rocket scientist*, sage, savant, teacher, tutor; SEE CONCEPT *350*

proffer [v] *suggest, offer*
extend, gift, give, hand, hit on, hold out, make a pitch*, pose, present, propose, proposition, propound, submit, tender, volunteer; SEE CONCEPTS *66,67,75*

proficiency [n] *ability, skillfulness*
accomplishment, advance, advancement, aptitude, chops, competence, dexterity, efficiency, expertise, expertness, facility, formula, green thumb*, headway*, knack*, know-how*, knowledge, learning, makings, mastery, moxie*, oil*, progress, right stuff*, savvy*, skill, stuff, talent, what it takes*; SEE CONCEPTS *409,630,706*

proficient [adj] *able, skilled*
accomplished, adept, apt, capable, clever, competent, consummate, conversant, crack*, crackerjack*, drilled, effective, effectual, efficient, exercised, experienced, expert, finished, gifted, on the beam*, phenom, pro, qualified, savvy*, sharp, skillful, slick*, talented, trained, up to speed*, versed, whiz*, with it*; SEE CONCEPTS *402,527,528*

profile [n1] *drawing of outline*
contour, delineation, figuration, figure, form, likeness, line, lineament, lineation, portrait, shadow, shape, side view, silhouette, sketch; SEE CONCEPTS *259,625*

profile [n2] *description, characterization*
analysis, biography, character sketch, chart, diagram, review, sketch, study, survey, thumbnail sketch, vignette, vita; SEE CONCEPTS *268,283*

profit [n] *gain*
accumulation, acquisition, advancement, advantage, aggrandizement, augmentation, avail, benefit, bottom line*, cleanup, earnings, emoluments, gate*, goods*, gravy*, gross, harvest, income, interest, killing, lucre, net, output, outturn, percentage, proceeds, product, production, receipt, receipts, remuneration, return, revenue, saving, skim*, split*, surplus, take*, takings*, turnout, use, value, velvet*, winnings, yield; SEE CONCEPTS *332,344,693*

profit [v] *gain; get or give an advantage*
aid, avail, benefit, be of advantage, better, capitalize on, cash in on, clean up, clear, contribute, earn, exploit, help, improve, learn from, make a haul*, make a killing*, make capital, make good use of*, make it big*, make money, make the most of*, pay, pay off, promote, prosper, put to good use*, realize, reap the benefit*, recover, score, serve*, stand in good stead*, take advantage of, thrive, turn to advantage, use, utilize, work for; SEE CONCEPTS *110,124,330,693*

profitable [adj] *advantageous; money-making*
assisting, beneficial, commercial, conducive, contributive, cost-effective, effective, effectual, favorable, fruitful, gainful, going*, good, instrumental, in the black*, lucrative, paid off, paying, paying well, practical, pragmatic, productive, remunerative, rewarding, self-sustaining, serviceable, successful, sustaining, sweet*, useful, valuable, well-paying, worthwhile; SEE CONCEPTS *334,537,572*

profligate [adj1] *immoral, corrupt*
abandoned, debauched, degenerate, depraved, dissipated, dissolute, iniquitous, lax, lewd, libertine, licentious, loose, promiscuous, reprobate, shameless, unprincipled, vicious, vitiated, wanton, wicked, wild; SEE CONCEPT *545*

profligate [adj2] *wasteful*
extravagant, immoderate, improvident, lavish, prodigal, reckless, spendthrift, squandering; SEE CONCEPTS *334,401*

profligate [n] *person who is immoral*
debauchee, degenerate, dissipater, good-for-nothing*, lecher, libertine, nighthawk*, no-good*, old goat*, operator*, prodigal, rake, reprobate, roué, swinger, waster, wastrel; SEE CONCEPT *412*

profound [adj1] *intellectual, thoughtful*
abstruse, acroamatic, deep, difficult, discerning, enlightened, erudite, esoteric, heavy*, hermetic, informed, intellectual, intelligent, knowing, knowledgeable, learned, mysterious, occult, Orphic, penetrating, philosophical, recondite, reflective, sagacious, sage, scholarly, secret, serious, shrewd, skilled, subtle, thorough, weighty, wise; SEE CONCEPTS *402,529*

profound [adj2] *bottomless*
abysmal, buried, cavernous, deep, fathomless, subterranean, yawning; SEE CONCEPT *777*

profound [adj3] *intense; emotional*
abject, absolute, acute, consummate, deep, deeply felt, deep-seated, exhaustive, extensive, extreme, far-reaching, great, hard, heartfelt, heartrending, hearty, keen, out-and-out*, pronounced, sincere, thorough, total, utter; SEE CONCEPTS *403,531,569*

profuse [adj] *abundant, excessive*
abounding, alive with*, ample, aplenty, bounteous, bountiful, copious, crawling with*, dime a dozen*, extravagant, extreme, exuberant, fulsome, galore, generous, immoderate, lavish, liberal, lush, luxuriant, no end*, openhanded, opulent, overflowing, plentiful, plenty, prodigal, profusive, prolific, riotous, sumptuous, superfluous, swarming, teeming, thick with*, unstinting; SEE CONCEPTS *762,781*

profusion [n] *abundance*
ampleness, copiousness, excess, extravagance, flood, glut, great quantity, opulence, outpouring, overflow, plenitude, plenty, prosperity, prosperousness, surplus, wealth; SEE CONCEPTS *710,767*

pr
pr

progeny [*n*] *offspring*
begats, breed, children, descendants, family, get*, issue, kids*, lineage, posterity, progeniture, race, scions, seed, stock, young; SEE CONCEPTS *296,414*

prognosis [*n*] *forecast*
cast, diagnosis, expectation, foretelling, guess, prediction, prevision, prognostication, projection, prophecy, speculation, surmise; SEE CONCEPTS *274,689*

prognosticate [*v*] *predict, foretell*
adumbrate, augur, betoken, call it*, crystal-ball*, divine, forebode, forecast, foreshadow, harbinger, have a hunch*, herald, make book*, point to, portend, presage, prophesy, read, see coming*, soothsay, vaticinate; SEE CONCEPT *70*

prognosticator [*n*] *forecaster*
augur, channeller, diviner, fortune-teller, medium, oracle, prophet, seer, soothsayer, telepathist, visionary; SEE CONCEPT *423*

program [*n1*] *agenda, list*
affairs, appointments, arrangements, bill, bulletin, business, calendar, card, catalog, chores, curriculum, details, docket, happenings, index, lineup, listing, meetings, memoranda, necessary acts*, order of business*, order of events*, order of the day*, plan, plans, preparations, record, schedule, series of events, slate, syllabus, things to do*, timetable; SEE CONCEPTS *281,283*

program [*n2*] *scheme, plan*
course, design, instructions, line, order, plan of action, policy, polity, procedure, project, sequence; SEE CONCEPTS *274,660*

program [*n3*] *performance in medium*
broadcast, presentation, production, show; SEE CONCEPT *263*

program [*v*] *plan out; supply instructions*
arrange, bill, book, budget, calculate, compile, compute, design, draft, edit, engage, enter, estimate, feed, figure, formulate, get on line*, itemize, lay on, lay out, line up, list, map out, pencil in*, poll, prearrange, prioritize, process, register, schedule, set, set up, slate, work out; SEE CONCEPTS *36,60,84,384*

progress [*n*] *advancement, gain*
advance, amelioration, anabasis, betterment, boost, break, breakthrough, buildup, course, dash, development, evolution, evolvement, expedition, flowering, growth, headway, hike, impetus, improvement, increase, journey, lunge, march, momentum, motion, movement, ongoing, pace, passage, process, procession, proficiency, progression, promotion, rate, rise, step forward, stride, tour, unfolding, voyage, way; SEE CONCEPTS *704,706*

progress [*v1*] *move forward*
advance, continue, cover ground*, dash, edge, forge ahead, gain ground, get along, get on, go forward, keep going, lunge, make headway*, make strides*, move on, proceed, shoot, speed, travel; SEE CONCEPTS *149,159*

progress [*v2*] *improve, advance*
ameliorate, become better, better, blossom, boost, develop, gain, grow, increase, make first rate, mature, shape up, straighten up, truck, turn over new leaf*, upgrade; SEE CONCEPT *700*

progression [*n*] *progress*
advance, advancement, amelioration, betterment, boost, break, breakthrough, development, evolution, evolvement, forward march, furtherance,

getting ahead, giant strides, going forward, growth, headway, improvement, promotion, step forward; SEE CONCEPTS *704,706*

progressive [*adj*] *liberal; growing*
accelerating, advanced, advancing, avant-garde*, bleeding-heart*, broad, broad-minded, continuing, continuous, developing, dynamic, enlightened, enterprising, escalating, forward-looking, go-ahead*, gradual, graduated, increasing, intensifying, left*, left of center*, lenient, modern, ongoing, onward, open-minded, radical, reformist, revolutionary, tolerant, up-and-coming*, up-to-date, wide; SEE CONCEPTS *542,544*

prohibit [*v*] *make impossible; stop*
ban, block, bottle up*, box in*, bring to screeching halt*, constrain, cool*, cork*, debar, disallow, enjoin, forbid, forfend, freeze*, gridlock, halt, hamper, hang up*, hinder, hold up, impede, inhibit, interdict, jam up*, keep lid on*, kill, lock up, nix, obstruct, outlaw, pass on*, preclude, prevent, proscribe, put a lock on*, put a stopper in*, put chill on*, put down, put half nelson on*, restrain, restrict, rule out, shut out, spike*, stymie*, taboo*, throw cold water on*, tie up*, veto, zing*; SEE CONCEPTS *50,88,121,130,317*

prohibited [*adj*] *forbidden*
banned, barred, closed down, contraband, crooked*, illegal, illicit, no-no*, not allowed, not approved, off limits*, out of bounds*, out of line*, proscribed, refused, restricted, shady*, taboo, verboten, vetoed, wildcat*; SEE CONCEPTS *554,576*

prohibition [*n*] *ban, forbiddance*
bar, constraint, disallowance, don't*, embargo, exclusion, injunction, interdict, interdiction, negation, no-no*, obstruction, off limits*, out of bounds*, prevention, proscription, refusal, repudiation, restriction, taboo, temperance, veto; SEE CONCEPTS *121,130,652,691*

prohibitive [*adj*] *restrictive; beyond one's financial means*
conditional, excessive, exorbitant, expensive, extortionate, forbidding, high-priced, limiting, preposterous, preventing, prohibiting, proscriptive, repressive, restraining, sky-high*, steep*, suppressive; SEE CONCEPTS *334,554*

project [*n*] *undertaking, work*
activity, adventure, affair, aim, assignment, baby*, blueprint*, business, concern, deal, design, enterprise, exploit, feat, game plan, intention, job, matter, occupation, outline, pet*, plan, program, proposal, proposition, scheme, setup, strategy, task, thing*, venture; SEE CONCEPTS *324,349,362*

project [*v1*] *plan*
arrange, blueprint, calculate, cast, chart, conceive, contemplate, contrive, delineate, design, devise, diagram, draft, envisage, envision, estimate, extrapolate, feature, forecast, frame, gauge, image, imagine, intend, map out, outline, predetermine, predict, propose, purpose, reckon, scheme, see, think, vision, visualize; SEE CONCEPTS *28,36,37,70*

project [*v2*] *bulge, hang out*
be conspicuous, beetle, be prominent, extend, hang over, jut, lengthen, overhang, poke, pop out, pout, prolong, protrude, protuberate, push out, stand out, stick out, stretch out, thrust out; SEE CONCEPT *747*

project [*v3*] *throw, discharge*
cast, fling, heave, hurl, launch, pitch, propel, shoot, transmit; SEE CONCEPTS *179,222*

projection [*n1*] *bulge, overhang*
bump, bunch, eaves, extension, hook, jut, knob, ledge, outthrust, point, prolongation, prominence, protrusion, protuberance, ridge, rim, shelf, sill, spine, spur, step, swelling; SEE CONCEPTS *471,509,513*

projection [*n2*] *prediction*
calculation, computation, estimate, estimation, extrapolation, forecast, guess, prognostication, reckoning; SEE CONCEPTS *28,278*

proletariat [*n*] *working class*
blue-collar workers, bourgeoisie, commoners, common people, hoi polloi, lower class, peasant, plebeians, proletarian, rank and file, working stiff; SEE CONCEPTS *413,423*

proliferate [*v*] *increase quickly*
breed, burgeon, engender, escalate, expand, generate, grow rapidly, multiply, mushroom*, procreate, propagate, reproduce, run riot*, snowball*; SEE CONCEPT *780*

prolific [*adj*] *fruitful, productive*
abounding, abundant, bountiful, breeding, copious, creative, fecund, fertile, generating, generative, luxuriant, profuse, proliferant, rank, reproducing, reproductive, rich, spawning, swarming, teeming, yielding; SEE CONCEPTS *485,542*

prologue [*n*] *preface*
beginning, exordium, explanation, foreword, introduction, opening, overture, preamble, prelude, proem, prolegomenon; SEE CONCEPT *270*

prolong [*v*] *extend, draw out*
carry on, continue, delay, drag one's feet*, drag out*, hold, hold up, increase, lengthen, let it ride*, make longer, pad*, perpetuate, protract, spin out*, stall, stretch, stretch out; SEE CONCEPTS *239,250*

prominence [*n1*] *something that sticks out*
bulge, bump, cliff, conspicuousness, crag, crest, elevation, eminence, headland, height, high point, jutting, markedness, mound, pinnacle, projection, promontory, protrusion, protuberance, rise, spur, swelling, tor; SEE CONCEPTS *513,836*

prominence [*n2*] *distinction, outstandingness*
celebrity, eminence, fame, greatness, illustriousness, importance, influence, kudos*, name, notability, precedence, preeminence, prestige, rank, renown, reputation, salience, specialness, standing, top billing*, weight; SEE CONCEPT *668*

prominent [*adj1*] *sticking out; conspicuous*
arresting, beetling, bulging, easily seen, embossed, extended, extrusive, eye-catching, flashy, hanging out, hilly, in the foreground, jutting, marked, noticeable, obtrusive, obvious, outstanding, projecting, pronounced, protruding, protrusive, protuberant, raised, relieved, remarkable, rough, rugged, salient, shooting out, signal, standing out, striking, to the fore, unmistakable; SEE CONCEPTS *485,583,619*

prominent [*adj2*] *important; famous*
big-league*, big-name*, big-shot*, celebrated, chief, distinguished, eminent, famed, foremost, great, high-profile*, leading, main, notable, noted, notorious, outstanding, popular, preeminent, renowned, respected, top, underlined, VIP*, well-known, well-thought-of, world-class*; SEE CONCEPT *568*

promiscuous [*adj*] *indiscriminately sexually active*
abandoned, debauched, dissipated, dissolute, easy*, fast*, immoral, indiscriminate, lax, libertine, licentious, loose*, of easy virtue, oversexed, profligate, pushover, unbridled, unchaste, undiscriminating, unrestricted, wanton, wild; SEE CONCEPTS *372,545*

promise [*n1*] *one's word that something will be done*
affiance, affirmation, agreement, asseveration, assurance, avowal, betrothal, bond, commitment, compact, consent, contract, covenant, earnest, engagement, espousal, guarantee, insurance, marriage, oath, obligation, pact, parole, pawn, pledge, plight, profession, promissory note, sacred word, security, stipulation, swear, swearing, token, troth, undertaking, vow, warrant, warranty, word, word of honor; SEE CONCEPTS *71,278*

promise [*n2*] *hope, possibility*
ability, aptitude, capability, capacity, encouragement, flair, good omen, outlook, potential, talent; SEE CONCEPTS *630,650*

promise [*v1*] *give word that something will be done*
accede, affiance, affirm, agree, answer for, assent, asseverate, assure, bargain, betroth, bind, commit, compact, consent, contract, covenant, cross heart*, declare, engage, ensure, espouse, guarantee, hock*, insure, live up to*, mortgage, obligate, pass, pawn*, pledge, plight, profess, say so*, secure, stipulate, string along*, subscribe, swear, swear on bible*, swear up and down*, take an oath, undertake, underwrite, vouch, vow, warrant; SEE CONCEPT *71*

promise [*v2*] *bring hope, possibility*
augur, bespeak, betoken, bode, denote, encourage, forebode, foreshadow, foretoken, give hope, hint, hold out hope*, hold probability, indicate, lead to expect, like, look, omen, portend, presage, seem likely, show signs of*, suggest; SEE CONCEPTS *118,650*

promising [*adj*] *hopeful*
able, assuring, auspicious, bright, encouraging, favorable, gifted, happy, likely, lucky, propitious, reassuring, rising, roseate, rosy, talented, up-and-coming; SEE CONCEPTS *406,548*

promontory [*n*] *headland*
bluff, cape, cheronese, foreland, jetty, jutty, peninsula, point, ridge; SEE CONCEPTS *509,514*

promote [*v1*] *help, advance*
advertise, advocate, aid, assist, avail, back, befriend, benefit, bolster, boost, build up*, call attention to, champion, contribute, cooperate, cry*, develop, encourage, endorse, espouse, forward, foster, further, get behind, hype*, improve, nourish, nurture, patronize, plug*, popularize, propagandize, publicize, puff*, push, push for, recommend, sell, serve, speak for, speed, sponsor, stimulate, subsidize, succor, support, uphold, urge, work for; SEE CONCEPTS *49,110,324*

promote [*v2*] *give a higher position in organization*
advance, aggrandize, ascend, better, dignify, elevate, ennoble, exalt, favor, graduate, honor, increase, kick upstairs*, magnify, move up, prefer, raise, skip, up*, upgrade; SEE CONCEPT *351*

promoter [*n*] *supporter*
advertiser, advocate, ally, backer, booster, en-

pr
pr

dorser, follower, organizer, publicist, sponsor; SEE CONCEPT *423*

promotion [*n1*] *higher position in organization*
advance, advancement, advocacy, aggrandizement, backing, betterment, boost, break, breakthrough, buildup, bump, elevation, encouragement, ennoblement, exaltation, favoring, furtherance, go-ahead*, hike, honor, improvement, jump, jump up, lift, move up, preference, preferment, prelation, progress, raise, rise, step up, support, upgrade, upgrading; SEE CONCEPT *351*

promotion [*n2*] *publicity*
advertising, advertising campaign, ballyhoo*, blurb*, buildup*, hard sell*, hoopla*, hype*, notice, pitch, pizzazz*, plug*, PR*, press*, pressagentry, promo*, propaganda, publicity, public relations, puff*, puffery*, pushing, squib*; SEE CONCEPTS *49,110,271,324*

prompt [*adj*] *early, responsive*
alert, apt, brisk, eager, efficient, expeditious, immediate, instant, instantaneous, on the ball*, on the button*, on the dot*, on the nose*, on time, precise, punctual, quick, rapid, ready, smart, speedy, swift, timely, unhesitating, vigilant, watchful, wide-awake, willing; SEE CONCEPTS *401,799*

prompt [*n*] *hint*
cue, help, jog, jolt, mnemonic, prod, reminder, spur, stimulus, twit; SEE CONCEPT *274*

prompt [*v*] *incite, cue*
advise, aid, arouse, assist, bring up, call forth, cause, convince, draw, egg on*, elicit, evoke, exhort, get, give rise to, goad, help, help out, hint, impel, imply, indicate, induce, inspire, instigate, jog, mention, motivate, move, occasion, persuade, prick*, prod, propel, propose, provoke, refresh, remind, sic*, spur, stimulate, suggest, talk into, urge, win over; SEE CONCEPTS *68,242*

promptly [*adv*] *immediately*
at once, directly, expeditiously, fast, flat-out*, fleetly, hastily, in nothing flat*, instantly, lickety-split*, like a shot*, now, on the dot*, on the double*, on time, PDQ*, posthaste, pronto, punctually, quickly, rapidly, right away, sharp, speedily, straightaway, swiftly, unhesitatingly; SEE CONCEPTS *544,799*

promulgate [*v*] *make known*
advertise, announce, annunciate, broadcast, call, circulate, communicate, declare, decree, disseminate, drum, issue, make public, notify, pass the word*, proclaim, promote, publish, sound, spread, toot, trumpet; SEE CONCEPT *60*

prone [*adj1*] *lying down*
decumbent, face down, flat, horizontal, level, procumbent, prostrate, reclining, recumbent, resupine, supine; SEE CONCEPT *583*

prone [*adj2*] *liable, likely*
apt, bent, devoted, disposed, exposed, fain, given, inclined, minded, open, predisposed, ready, sensitive, subject, susceptible, tending, willing; SEE CONCEPTS *542,552*

pronounce [*v1*] *produce words vocally*
accent, articulate, enunciate, phonate, say, sound, speak, stress, utter, verbalize, vocalize, voice; SEE CONCEPT *47*

pronounce [*v2*] *announce, declare*
affirm, assert, blast, call, decree, deliver, drum, judge, mouth, proclaim, say, sound off, spread around, trumpet, verbalize; SEE CONCEPT *49*

pronounced [*adj*] *distinct, evident*
arresting, assured, broad, clear, clear-cut, conspicuous, decided, definite, marked, notable, noticeable, obvious, outstanding, striking, strong, unmistakable; SEE CONCEPTS *535,576,619*

pronouncement [*n*] *declaration, statement*
advertisement, announcement, broadcast, decree, dictum, edict, judgment, manifesto, notification, proclamation, promulgation, pronunciamento*, publication, report, ukase; SEE CONCEPTS *271,274,278*

proof [*n1*] *evidence, authentication*
affidavit, argument, attestation, averment, case, certification, chapter and verse*, clincher*, clue, confirmation, corroboration, credentials, criterion, cue*, data, demonstration, deposition, documents, establishment, exhibit, facts, goods*, grabber*, grounds, information, lowdown*, nitty-gritty*, paper trail*, picture, reason, reasons, record, scoop*, score*, skinny*, smoking gun*, straight stuff*, substantiation, testament, testimony, trace, validation, verification, warrant, wherefore*, why*, whyfor*, witness; SEE CONCEPT *274*

proof [*n2*] *photographic print*
galley, galley proof, impression, page proof, pass, pull, repro, revise, slip, stereo, trial, trial print, trial proof; SEE CONCEPT *265*

proofread [*v*] *copyedit*
analyze, blue-pencil*, check, correct, cut, delete, edit, go over, rearrange, refine, remove errors, rephrase, revise, strike out; SEE CONCEPTS *79,126,203*

prop [*n*] *support*
aid, assistance, brace, buttress, column, mainstay, post, shore, stanchion, stay, strengthener, strut, truss, underpinning; SEE CONCEPTS *440,470*

prop [*v*] *hold up or lean against*
bear up, bolster, brace, buoy, buttress, carry, maintain, rest, set, shore, stand, stay, strengthen, support, sustain, truss, underprop, uphold; SEE CONCEPTS *190,201*

propaganda [*n*] *information that is designed to mislead or persuade*
advertising, agitprop, announcement, brainwashing*, disinformation, doctrine, evangelism, handout, hogwash*, hype*, implantation, inculcation, indoctrination, newspeak, promotion, promulgation, proselytism, publication, publicity; SEE CONCEPT *278*

propagate [*v1*] *breed, reproduce*
bear, beget, engender, father, fecundate, fertilize, generate, grow, impregnate, increase, inseminate, make pregnant, mother, multiply, originate, procreate, produce, proliferate, raise, sire; SEE CONCEPT *374*

propagate [*v2*] *spread, make known*
broadcast, circulate, develop, diffuse, disperse, disseminate, distribute, proclaim, promulgate, publicize, publish, radiate, scatter, strew, transmit; SEE CONCEPTS *60,222*

propel [*v*] *throw; release into air*
actuate, drive, force, impel, launch, mobilize, move, press, push, send, set going, set in motion, shoot, shove, start, thrust; SEE CONCEPTS *208,221,222*

propensity [*n*] *inclination, weakness*
ability, aptness, bent*, bias, capacity, competence, disposition, flash, inclining, leaning, liability, partiality, penchant, predilection, pre-

disposition, proclivity, proneness, susceptibility, sweet tooth*, talent, tendency, thing*, tilt*, yen; SEE CONCEPTS *20,411,630,709*

proper [*adj1*] *suitable*
able, applicable, appropriate, apt, au fait, becoming, befitting, capable, competent, convenient, decent, desired, felicitous, fit, fitting, good, happy, just, legitimate, meet, qualified, right, suited, true, useful; SEE CONCEPT *558*

proper [*adj2*] *mannerly, decent*
becoming, befitting, by the book*, by the numbers*, comely, comme il faut*, conforming, correct, decorous, demure, de rigueur*, genteel, in line, kosher*, moral, nice, polite, precise, priggish, prim, prissy, prudish, punctilious, puritanical, refined, respectable, right, seemly, solid, square*, stone, straight*, strait-laced*, stuffy*; SEE CONCEPTS *401,404*

proper [*adj3*] *conventional, correct*
absolute, accepted, accurate, arrant, complete, consummate, customary, decorous, established, exact, formal, free of error, on target*, on the button*, on the nose*, on the right track*, orthodox, out-and-out*, precise, right, unmistaken, usual, utter; SEE CONCEPTS *326,533*

proper [*adj4*] *individual, personal*
characteristic, distinctive, idiosyncratic, own, particular, peculiar, private, respective, special, specific; SEE CONCEPTS *549,557*

property [*n1*] *possessions, real estate*
acreage, acres, assets, belongings, buildings, capital, chattels, claim, dominion, effects, equity, estate, farm, freehold, goods, holdings, home, house, inheritance, land, means, ownership, plot, possessorship, premises, proprietary, proprietorship, realty, resources, riches, substance, title, tract, wealth, worth; SEE CONCEPTS *446,509,515,710*

property [*n2*] *characteristic, feature*
ability, affection, attribute, character, hallmark, idiosyncrasy, mark, peculiarity, quality, trait, virtue; SEE CONCEPTS *411,654*

prophecy [*n*] *prediction*
apocalypse, augury, cast, divination, forecast, foretelling, oracle, presage, prevision, prognosis, prognostication, revelation, second sight, soothsaying, vision; SEE CONCEPTS *70,278,689*

prophesy [*v*] *predict, warn*
adumbrate, augur, call*, call the turn*, crystalball*, divine, forecast, foresee, foretell, forewarn, have a hunch*, make book*, portend, predict, presage, prognosticate, psych it out*, see coming*, soothsay, vaticinate; SEE CONCEPT *70*

prophet [*n*] *person, thing that predicts future*
astrologer, augur, auspex, bard, clairvoyant, diviner, druid, evocator, forecaster, fortuneteller, haruspex, horoscopist, magus, medium, meteorologist, oracle, ovate, palmist, predictor, prognosticator, prophesier, reader, seer, seeress, sibyl, soothsayer, sorcerer, tea-leaf reader, witch, wizard; SEE CONCEPTS *361,423*

prophetic [*adj*] *telling of the future*
apocalyptic, augural, Delphian*, divinatory, fatidic, foreshadowing, mantic, occult, oracular, predictive, presaging, prescient, prognostic, prophetical, pythonic, sibylline, vaticinal, veiled; SEE CONCEPT *267*

propitious [*adj1*] *full of promise; good, favorable*
advantageous, auspicious, beneficial, benign, brave, bright, dexter, encouraging, favoring, fortunate, happy, hopeful, lucky, opportune, pat*, promising, prosperous, rosy, seasonable, timely, toward, useful, well-timed; SEE CONCEPTS *548,560,572*

propitious [*adj2*] *friendly*
benevolent, benign, favorably inclined, gracious, kind, nice, well-disposed; SEE CONCEPT *401*

proponent [*n*] *person who advocates, supports cause*
advocate, backer, champion, defender, enthusiast, exponent, expounder, friend, partisan, patron, protector, second, seconder, spokesperson, subscriber, supporter, upholder, vindicator; SEE CONCEPTS *355,359,423*

proportion [*n1*] *relative amount, size of part to whole*
admeasurement, amplitude, apportionment, breadth, bulk, capacity, cut, degree, dimension, distribution, division, equation, expanse, extent, fraction, magnitude, measure, measurement, part, percentage, portion, quota, rate, ratio, relationship, scale, scope, segment, share, volume; SEE CONCEPTS *730,783*

proportion [*n2*] *balance between parts of whole*
agreement, congruity, correspondence, harmony, symmetry; SEE CONCEPTS *664,717*

proportionate/proportional [*adj*] *balanced, corresponding*
commensurable, commensurate, comparable, comparative, compatible, consistent, contingent, correlative, correspondent, corresponding, dependent, equal, equitable, equivalent, even, in proportion, just, reciprocal, relative, symmetrical, uniform; SEE CONCEPTS *480,563*

proportions [*n*] *measurements*
amount, area, breadth, compass, depth, diameter, dimensions, expanse, extent, height, length, magnitude, range, scope, size, volume, width; SEE CONCEPTS *730,792*

proposal [*n*] *suggestion, presentation for action*
angle, bid, big idea*, brain child*, design, feeler*, game plan*, idea, layout, motion, offer, outline, overture, pass, picture, pitch, plan, proffer, program, project, proposition, recommendation, scenario, scheme, setup, tender, terms; SEE CONCEPTS *271,324,662*

propose [*v1*] *suggest, present for action*
adduce, advance, advise, affirm, ask, assert, broach, come up with*, contend, counsel, hit on*, hold out, introduce, invite, kibitz*, lay before*, lay on the line*, make a motion, make a pitch*, move for, name, nominate, offer, pose, prefer, press, proffer, propone, proposition, propound, put forward, put to, put up, recommend, request, set forth, solicit, speak one's piece*, spitball*, state, submit, tender, urge, volunteer; SEE CONCEPTS *66,75*

propose [*v2*] *intend; have in mind*
aim, contemplate, design, have every intention, mean, mind, plan, purpose, scheme; SEE CONCEPTS *26,36*

propose [*v3*] *ask for hand in marriage*
ask in marriage, fire the question*, get down on one knee*, make a proposal, offer marriage, pop the question*, press one's suit*; SEE CONCEPTS *48,297*

proposition [*n*] *suggestion; scheme*
hypothesis, invitation, motion, overture, plan, premise, presentation, proffer, program, project,

pr
pr

proposal, recommendation; SEE CONCEPTS *384,662*

proposition [*v*] *make suggestion, often improper*
accost, approach, ask, pose, prefer, propose, propound, put, solicit, suggest; SEE CONCEPTS *48,375*

proprietor [*n*] *person who owns something*
freeholder*, front office, holder, land owner, meal ticket*, owner, possessor, proprietary, titleholder; SEE CONCEPTS *343,347*

propriety [*n1*] *suitableness, appropriateness*
accordance, advisability, agreeableness, appositeness, aptness, becomingness, compatibility, concord, congruity, consonance, convenience, correctness, correspondence, decorum, ethicality, expedience, fitness, harmony, justice, legitimacy, meetness, morality, order, pleasantness, properness, recommendability, rectitude, respectability, rightness, seemliness, suitability; SEE CONCEPT *656*

propriety [*n2*] *good manners*
accepted conduct, amenities, breeding, civilities, correctness, courtesy, decency, decorum, delicacy, dignity, etiquette, good behavior, good form, modesty, mores*, niceties, politeness, politesse, protocol, punctilio, rectitude, refinement, respectability, rules of conduct, seemliness, social conventions, social grace, the done thing*; SEE CONCEPTS *633,644*

propulsion [*n*] *force*
drive, effort, energy, full head of steam*, horsepower, impulse, momentum, muscle, power, pressure, punch, push, speed, steam, strength, stress, tension, thrust, velocity; SEE CONCEPTS *641,724*

pro rata [*adv*] *in proportion*
correlatively, proportionately, respectively; SEE CONCEPTS *480,563*

prosaic [*adj*] *unimaginative*
actual, banal, blah*, boring, clean, colorless, common, commonplace, dead*, diddly*, drab, dry, dull, everyday, factual, flat*, garden-variety*, hackneyed, ho-hum*, humdrum*, irksome, lackluster, lifeless, literal, lowly, lusterless, matter-of-fact, monotonous, mundane, nothing, nowhere, ordinary, pabulum*, pedestrian, platitudinous, plebeian, practicable, practical, prose, prosy, routine, square, stale, tame, tedious, trite, uneventful, unexceptional, uninspiring, vanilla*, vapid, workaday, yawn*, zero*; SEE CONCEPTS *267,537,547*

proscribe [*v*] *condemn, exclude*
ban, banish, blackball*, boycott, censure, damn, denounce, deport, doom*, embargo, excommunicate, exile, expatriate, expel, forbid, interdict, ostracize, outlaw, prohibit, reject, sentence; SEE CONCEPTS *25,121,317*

prose [*n*] *written, nonrhythmic literature*
book, composition, essay, exposition, fiction, nonfiction, speech, story, talk, text, tongue*, writing; SEE CONCEPTS *268,271*

prosecute [*v1*] *bring action against in court*
arraign, bring suit, bring to trial, contest, do, haul into court*, indict, involve in litigation, law, litigate, prefer charges, pull up, put away*, put on docket, put on trial, see in court*, seek redress, sue, summon, take to court, try, turn on the heat*; SEE CONCEPT *317*

prosecute [*v2*] *follow through, persevere*
carry on, carry through, conduct, continue, direct, discharge, engage in, execute, follow up, manage, perform, persist, practice, pursue, put through, see through, wage, work at; SEE CONCEPT *91*

proselytize [*v*] *convert, espouse*
accept, adopt, advocate, alter conviction, approve, be born again*, cause to adopt, change belief, convince, defend, embrace, get into*, persuade, stand behind*, sway, uphold; SEE CONCEPTS *10,12,14,35*

prospect [*n1*] *outlook for future*
anticipation, calculation, chance, contemplation, expectancy, expectation, forecast, future, hope, in the cards*, irons in the fire*, likelihood, odds, opening, plan, possibility, presumption, probability, promise, proposal, thought; SEE CONCEPTS *689,693*

prospect [*n2*] *landscape, vista*
aspect, lookout, outlook, overlook, panorama, perspective, scape, scene, sight, spectacle, view, vision; SEE CONCEPTS *509,628*

prospect [*v*] *look for; seek*
delve, dig, explore, go after, go into, inquire, investigate, look, look into, probe, search, sift, survey; SEE CONCEPT *216*

prospective [*adj*] *anticipated, potential*
about to be, approaching, awaited, coming, considered, destined, eventual, expected, forthcoming, future, hoped-for, imminent, impending, intended, likely, looked-for, planned, possible, promised, proposed, soon-to-be, to be*, to come; SEE CONCEPTS *548,552*

prospectus [*n*] *details, outline of event*
announcement, catalogue, conspectus, design, list, plan, program, scheme, syllabus, synopsis; SEE CONCEPT *283*

prosper [*v*] *be fortunate; succeed*
advance, arrive, augment, batten, bear, bear fruit, become rich, become wealthy, be enriched, benefit, bloom, blossom, catch on*, do well, do wonders*, fare well, fatten*, feather nest*, flourish, flower, gain, get on*, get there*, go places*, go to town*, grow rich, hit it big, hit the jackpot*, increase, make a killing*, make good*, make it*, make mark*, make money, make out*, multiply, produce, progress, rise, score*, strike it rich*, thrive, turn out well, yield; SEE CONCEPT *706*

prosperity [*n*] *affluence, good fortune*
abundance, accomplishment, advantage, arrival, bed of roses*, benefit, boom, clover, do, ease*, easy street*, exorbitance, expansion, flying colors*, fortune, good, good times, gravy train*, growth, high on the hog*, increase, inflation, interest, life of luxury*, luxury, opulence, plenteousness, plenty, prosperousness, riches, success, successfulness, the good life*, thriving, velvet, victory, wealth, welfare, well-being; SEE CONCEPTS *335,706*

prosperous [*adj1*] *successful, thriving*
affluent, blooming, booming, comfortable, doing well, easy, flourishing, fortunate, halcyon, in clover*, in the money*, lousy rich, lucky, mainline*, moneyed, money to burn*, on top of heap*, opulent, palmy, prospering, rich, roaring, robust, sitting pretty*, snug, substantial, upperclass*, uptown, wealthy, well, well-heeled*, well-off, well-to-do; SEE CONCEPTS *334,528*

prosperous [*adj2*] *promising, advantageous*
appropriate, auspicious, bright, convenient, de-

sirable, favorable, felicitous, fortunate, good, happy, lucky, opportune, profitable, propitious, seasonable, timely, well-timed; SEE CONCEPTS *548,572*

prostitute [*n*] *person who sells own abilities, talent, or name for inferior purpose*
betrayer, cheater, deceiver, gigolo, hustler, seducer; SEE CONCEPT *412*

prostitute [*v*] *to put one's talent to an unworthy use*
abuse, cheapen, corrupt, debase, debauch, degrade, demean, deprave, devalue, misapply, misemploy, misuse, pervert, profane, vitiate; SEE CONCEPTS *156,645*

prostrate [*adj1*] *flat, horizontal*
abject, bowed low, procumbent, prone, reclining, recumbent, supine; SEE CONCEPT *583*

prostrate [*adj2*] *helpless*
beaten, defenseless, disarmed, impotent, open, overcome, overpowered, overwhelmed, paralyzed, powerless, reduced, weak; SEE CONCEPT *542*

prostrate [*adj3*] *tired, worn*
crippled, dejected, depressed, disarmed, drained, drowned, exhausted, fagged*, fallen, frazzled*, immobilized, incapacitated, inconsolable, knocked over*, obedient, overcome, paralyzed, pooped*, spent*, submissive, subservient, tuckered*, wearied, worn out; SEE CONCEPTS *406,485*

prostrate [*v1*] *fall on knees; submit*
abase, bow, bow down, cast before, cringe, fall at feet, give in, grovel, kneel, kowtow*, obey, surrender; SEE CONCEPT *384*

prostrate [*v2*] *overwhelm; wear out*
bring low, cripple, debilitate, defeat, destroy, disable, disarm, drain, drown, exhaust, fatigue, fell, floor, frazzle*, immobilize, impair, incapacitate, knock over, level, mow*, overcome, overpower, overthrow, overtire, overturn, paralyze, reduce, ruin, sap, tire, tucker out*, weary, whelm, wreck; SEE CONCEPTS *95,250,252*

protagonist [*n*] *person who takes the lead; central figure of narrative*
advocate, central character, champion, combatant, exemplar, exponent, hero, idol, lead, lead character, leader, mainstay, prime mover, principal, standard-bearer, warrior; SEE CONCEPTS *352,359,423*

protect [*v*] *take care of; guard from harm*
assure, bulwark, care for, champion, chaperon, conserve, cover, cover all bases*, cover up, cushion, defend, fend, foster, give refuge, give sanctuary*, go to bat for*, harbor, hedge, insulate, keep, keep safe, look after, preserve, ride shotgun for*, safeguard, save, screen, secure, sentinel, shade, shelter, shield, shotgun*, stand guard, stonewall*, support, take under wing*, watch, watch over; SEE CONCEPTS *96,134*

protection [*n*] *care, guardianship*
aegis, armament, armor, assurance, barrier, buffer, bulwark, camouflage, certainty, charge, conservation, cover, custody, defense, fix, guard, guarding, insurance, invulnerability, preservation, protecting, reassurance, refuge, safeguard, safekeeping, safety, salvation, screen, security, self-defense, shelter, shield, stability, strength, surety, tutelage, umbrella*, ward, wardship; SEE CONCEPTS *712,729*

protective [*adj*] *guarding, securing*
careful, conservational, conservative, covering,

custodial, defensive, emergency, guardian, insulating, jealous, possessive, preservative, protecting, safeguarding, sheltering, shielding, vigilant, warm, watchful; SEE CONCEPTS *542,550*

protégé [*n*] *dependant, pupil*
apprentice, charge, discovery, star student, student, ward; SEE CONCEPTS *348,423*

protest [*n*] *complaint, disapproval*
bellyache*, big stink*, blackball*, challenge, clamor, declaration, demonstration, demur, demurral, difficulty, dissent, flak*, formal complaint, grievance, gripe, grouse*, holler*, howl, kick*, knock*, march, moratorium, nix, objection, outcry, protestation, question, rally, remonstrance, remonstration, revolt, riot, stink*, tumult, turmoil; SEE CONCEPTS *52,54,300*

protest [*v*] *complain, disapprove; argue against*
affirm, assert, asseverate, attest, avouch, avow, back-talk*, be against, be displeased by, blast*, buck, combat, constate, contend, cry out, declare, demonstrate, demur, disagree, except, expostulate, fight, holler, howl, insist, inveigh against, kick*, maintain, make a stink*, object, oppose, predicate, profess, put up a fight*, rebel, remonstrate, resist, revolt, say no*, sound off*, squawk*, take exception*, testify, thumbs down*; SEE CONCEPTS *46,52,54,300*

protocol [*n*] *rules of conduct, behavior in certain situation*
agreement, code, compact, concordat, contract, conventions, courtesy, covenant, custom, decorum, etiquette, formalities, good form, manners, obligation, order, pact, politesse, propriety, p's and q's*, treaty; SEE CONCEPTS *684,688*

prototype [*n*] *original, example*
ancestor, antecedent, antecessor, archetype, criterion, first, forerunner, ideal, mock-up*, model, norm, paradigm, pattern, precedent, precursor, predecessor, standard, type; SEE CONCEPT *686*

protract [*v*] *extend, draw out*
continue, cool*, defer, delay, drag on*, drag out*, draw, elongate, hold off, hold up, keep going, lengthen, pad*, postpone, procrastinate, prolong, prolongate, put off, put on hold, spin out*, stall, stretch, stretch out; SEE CONCEPTS *237,239,250*

protrude [*v*] *stick out*
beetle, bulge, butt out, come through, distend, extend, extrude, jut, jut out, obtrude, overhang, point, poke, pop, pouch, pout, project, shoot out, stand out, start, stick up, swell; SEE CONCEPTS *208,746*

protuberance [*n*] *lump, outgrowth*
bulge, bump, excrescence, jut, jutting, knob, outthrust, process, projection, prominence, protrusion, swelling, tumor; SEE CONCEPTS *471,824*

proud [*adj1*] *pleased, pleasing*
appreciative, august, content, contented, dignified, eminent, fiery, fine, glad, glorious, gorgeous, grand, gratified, gratifying, great, great-hearted, honored, illustrious, imposing, impressive, magnificent, majestic, memorable, noble, red-letter*, rewarding, satisfied, satisfying, self-respecting, spirited, splendid, stately, sublime, superb, valiant, vigorous, well-pleased; SEE CONCEPTS *403,572,574*

proud [*adj2*] *arrogant, self-important*
bloated, boastful, cavalier, cocky*, conceited, contemptuous, cool*, disdainful, dismissive, domineering, egotistic, egotistical, haughty,

pr
pr

high-and-mighty*, high-handed*, huffy*, imperious, insolent, lofty, narcissistic, ostentatious, overbearing, pompous, presumptuous, pretentious, puffed up*, scornful, self-satisfied, sniffy*, snobbish, snooty*, stuck-up*, supercilious, superior, vain, vainglorious; SEE CONCEPTS *401,542*
prove [v] *establish facts; put to a test*
add up, affirm, analyze, ascertain, assay, attest, authenticate, back, bear out, certify, check, confirm, convince, corroborate, declare, demonstrate, determine, document, end up, evidence, evince, examine, experiment, explain, find, fix, have a case*, justify, make evident, manifest, pan out*, result, settle, show, show clearly, show once and for all*, substantiate, sustain, test, testify, trial, try, turn out, uphold, validate, verify, warrant, witness; SEE CONCEPTS *57,118,138*
proverb [n] *saying referring to common fact, knowledge*
adage, aphorism, apophthegm, axiom, byword, catch phrase, daffodil*, dictum, epigram, folk wisdom, gnome, maxim, moral, motto, platitude, precept, repartee, saw*, text, truism, witticism, word; SEE CONCEPTS *275,278*
proverbial [adj] *conventional, traditional*
accepted, acknowledged, archetypal, axiomatic, current, customary, famed, familiar, famous, general, legendary, notorious, self-evident, time-honored, typical, unquestioned, well-known; SEE CONCEPT *530*
provide [v1] *supply, support*
accommodate, add, administer, afford, arrange, bestow, bring, care, cater, contribute, dispense, equip, favor, feather*, feed, fit, fit out, fix up, fix up with, furnish, give, grant, hand over, heel*, impart, implement, indulge, keep, lend, line, look after, maintain, minister, outfit, prepare, present, procure, produce, proffer, provision, ration, ready, render, replenish, serve, stake, stock, stock up*, store, sustain, take care of, transfer, turn out, yield; SEE CONCEPTS *108,110,136,140*
provide [v2] *determine, specify*
condition, lay down, postulate, require, state, stipulate; SEE CONCEPTS *18,646*
provident [adj] *careful, frugal*
canny, cautious, discreet, economical, expedient, far-sighted, foresighted, judicious, penny-pinching*, politic, prepared, prudent, sagacious, saving, shrewd, sparing, thrifty, tight, unwasteful, vigilant, well-prepared, wise; SEE CONCEPTS *334,401*
providing/provided [conj] *as long as; with the understanding*
contingent upon, given, if, if and only if, in case, in the case that, in the event, on condition, on the assumption, on these terms, subject to, supposing, with the proviso; SEE CONCEPTS *544,546*
province [n] *area of rule, responsibility*
arena, bailiwick, business, calling, canton, capacity, champaign, charge, colony, concern, county, demesne, department, dependency, district, division, domain, dominion, duty, employment, field, function, jurisdiction, line, office, orbit, part, post, pursuit, realm, region, role, section, shire, sphere, terrain, territory, tract, walk, work, zone; SEE CONCEPTS *198,349,362,508,532*
provincial [adj] *countrified; limited*
bigoted, bucolic, country, hidebound, homegrown, homespun, insular, inward-looking, local, narrow, narrow-minded, parochial, pas-

toral, petty, rude, rural, rustic, sectarian, small-minded, small-town, uninformed, unpolished, unsophisticated; SEE CONCEPTS *403,549,589*
provision [n1] *supplies, supplying*
accouterment, arrangement, catering, emergency, equipping, fitting out, foundation, furnishing, groundwork, outline, plan, prearrangement, precaution, preparation, procurement, providing, stock, store, supplying; SEE CONCEPTS *140,712*
provisional [adj] *contingent, tentative*
conditional, dependent, ephemeral, experimental, interim, limited, makeshift, passing, pro tem, provisionary, provisory, qualified, rough-and-ready*, stopgap*, temporary, test, transient, transitional; SEE CONCEPTS *546,554,711*
provision/proviso [n2] *stipulation, condition of agreement*
agreement, catch*, Catch-22*, clause, demand, fine print*, joker*, kicker*, limitation, prerequisite, qualification, requirement, reservation, restriction, rider, small print*, specification, stipulation, strings*, term, terms; SEE CONCEPTS *270,684,711*
provocation [n] *incitement, stimulus*
affront, annoyance, bothering, brickbat*, casus belli, cause, challenge, dare, defy, grabber*, grievance, grounds, harassment, incentive, indignity, inducement, injury, instigation, insult, irking, justification, motivation, offense, provoking, reason, taunt, vexation, vexing; SEE CONCEPTS *14,240,532*
provocative [adj1] *aggravating*
annoying, challenging, disturbing, exciting, galling, goading, heady, incensing, inciting, influential, inspirational, insulting, intoxicating, offensive, outrageous, provoking, pushing, spurring, stimulant, stimulating; SEE CONCEPT *529*
provocative [adj2] *sexually stimulating*
alluring, arousing, enchanting, erotic, exciting, heady, interesting, intoxicating, intriguing, inviting, seductive, sexy, stimulating, suggestive, tantalizing, tempting; SEE CONCEPTS *372,537*
provoke [v1] *make angry*
abet, abrade, affront, aggravate, anger, annoy, bother, bug*, chafe, enrage, exasperate, exercise, foment, fret, gall*, get*, get on one's nerves*, get under one's skin*, grate, hit where one lives*, incense, incite, inflame, infuriate, insult, irk, irritate, madden, make blood boil*, make waves*, nag, offend, perturb, pique, put out, raise, rile, roil, ruffle, set*, set on*, try one's patience*, upset, vex, whip up*, work into lather*, work up*; SEE CONCEPTS *7,19*
provoke [v2] *start, evoke; stimulate*
animate, arouse, awaken, begin, bestir, bring about, bring down, bring on, bring to one's feet*, build up, call forth, cause, challenge, draw forth, electrify, elicit, enthuse, excite, fire, fire up*, galvanize, generate, give rise to, incite, induce, inflame, innervate, innerve, inspire, instigate, kindle, lead to, make, motivate, move, occasion, pique, precipitate, prime, produce, promote, prompt, quicken, rally, rouse, roust, stir, suscitate, thrill, titillate, titivate, waken, whet; SEE CONCEPTS *7,19,22,221,242*
prowess [n1] *ability, skill*
accomplishment, address, adeptness, adroitness, aptitude, attainment, command, deftness, dexter-

ity, excellence, expertise, expertness, facility, genius, mastery, readiness, sleight, talent; SEE CONCEPT *630*

prowess [*n2*] *bravery*
backbone*, boldness, courage, daring, dauntlessness, fearlessness, gallantry, grit*, guts*, heart*, heroism, intrepidity, mettle, moxie*, nerve, pluck, right stuff*, spunk, starch*, stomach*, stuff*, true grit*, valiance, valiancy, valor, valorousness, what it takes*; SEE CONCEPTS *411,633*

prowl [*v*] *move stealthily*
cruise, hunt, lurk, nose around*, patrol, range, roam, rove, scavenge, skulk, slink, snake, sneak, stalk, steal, stroll, tramp; SEE CONCEPT *151*

prowler [*n*] *thief*
burglar, crook, housebreaker, lurker, pilferer*, robber, sneakthief*; SEE CONCEPT *412*

proximity [*n*] *nearness to something*
adjacency, appropinquity, closeness, concurrence, contiguity, contiguousness, immediacy, juxtaposition, propinquity, togetherness; SEE CONCEPT *747*

proxy [*n*] *agent*
alternate, ambassador, assignee, attorney, backup, broker, delegate, deputy, emissary, envoy, executor, intermediary, lawyer, mediary, negotiator, representative, stand-in, substitute, surrogate; SEE CONCEPT *348*

prude [*n*] *prig*
goody-goody, goody two-shoes*, Mrs. Grundy, old maid, puritan, Victorian; SEE CONCEPT *416*

prudent [*adj*] *wise, sensible in action and thought*
advisable, canny, careful, cautious, circumspect, discerning, discreet, economical, far-sighted, frugal, hedging one's bets*, judgmatic, judicious, leery, playing safe*, politic, provident, reasonable, sagacious, sage, sane, sapient, shrewd, sound, sparing, tactical, thinking twice*, thrifty, vigilant, wary; SEE CONCEPTS *401,542*

prudish [*adj*] *shy and strict in behavior*
affected, artificial, austere, bigoted, conventional, demure, fastidious, finicky*, genteel, illiberal, mincing, narrow, narrow-minded, offish, overexact, overmodest, overnice, precise, pretentious, priggish*, prim, prissy*, proper, puritanical, rigid, rigorous, scrupulous, severe, simpering, square, squeamish*, starchy*, stern, stiff*, stilted, strait-laced, stuffy, uptight*, Victorian*; SEE CONCEPT *401*

prune [*v*] *trim; cut short*
clip, cut back, dock, eliminate, exclude, gut, knock off, lop, pare down, reduce, shape, shave, shear, shorten, skive, snip, thin; SEE CONCEPTS *137,176,236,247*

prurient [*adj*] *lascivious*
bawdy, carnal, crude, desirous, erotic, fleshly, horny, hot*, lecherous, lewd, libertine, libidinous, licentious, lustful, obscene, offensive, orgiastic, pornographic, raunchy*, salacious, sensual, sexual, smutty*, suggestive, unchaste, vulgar; SEE CONCEPTS *372,403*

pry [*v1*] *interfere in someone else's business*
be a busybody*, be all ears*, be curious, be inquisitive, be nosy, bug*, ferret out, gape, gaze, hunt, inquire, intrude, investigate, listen in, meddle, nose, peek, peep, peer, poke, poke nose into*, ransack, reconnoiter, rubberneck*, search, snoop, spy, stare, tap, tune in on*, wiretap; SEE CONCEPTS *216,384,623*

pry [*v2*] *force or break open*
disengage, disjoin, divide, elevate, elicit, extort, extract, heave, hoist, jimmy, lever, lift, move, pick up, press, prize, pull, push, raise, rear, separate, take up, tear, tilt, turn, turn out, twist, uplift, upraise, uprear, wrest, wring; SEE CONCEPTS *196,206,211*

psalm [*n*] *song of praise*
canticle, celebration, chant, chorale, eulogy, hymn, paean, shout, verse; SEE CONCEPT *595*

pseudo [*adj*] *artificial, fake*
bogus, counterfeit, ersatz, false, imitation, mock, not genuine, not kosher*, not legit*, not real, phony, pirate, pretend, pretended, quasi*, sham*, simulated, spurious, wrong; SEE CONCEPT *582*

pseudonym [*n*] *false name*
AKA*, alias, ananym, anonym, assumed name, handle*, incognito*, nickname, nom de guerre, nom de plume, pen name, professional name, stage name, summer name*; SEE CONCEPTS *268,683*

psyche [*n*] *innermost self; personality*
anima, animus, character, ego, élan vital, essential nature, individuality, inner child, inner self, mind, pneuma, self, soul, spirit, spirituality, subconscious, true being; SEE CONCEPTS *410,411*

psyched [*adj*] *excited*
animated, aroused, awakened, beside oneself*, charged, delighted, eager, enthusiastic, feverish, fired up*, high*, inspired, juiced up*, keyed up*, moved, on fire*, passionate, pumped, stimulated, stirred, thrilled, wild, worked up; SEE CONCEPTS *401,403*

psychedelic [*adj*] *affecting the mind so as to produce vivid visions*
consciousness-expanding, crazy*, experimental, freaky*, hallucinatory, hallucinogenic, kaleidoscopic, mind-bending*, mind-blowing*, mind-changing, mind-expanding*, multicolored*, psychoactive, psychotomimetic, psychotropic, trip*; SEE CONCEPTS *529,537*

psychiatrist [*n*] *person who treats mental disorders*
analyst, clinician, doctor, psychoanalyst, psychologist, psychotherapist, shrink*, therapist; SEE CONCEPT *357*

psychic [*adj*] *extrasensory in perception*
analytic, cerebral, clairvoyant, immaterial, impressible, impressionable, intellective, intellectual, mental, metaphysical, mystic, occult, preternatural, psychal, psychical, psychogenic, psychological, responsive, sensible, sensile, sensitive, sentient, spiritual, supernatural, supersensible, supersensitive, supersensory, supersensual, susceptible, susceptive, telekinetic, telepathic, transmundane, unworldly; SEE CONCEPTS *402,403*

psychobabble [*n*] *rhetoric using psychological-terms*
argot, buzzword, jargon, patter, pop psych*, psychospeak, self-help; SEE CONCEPT *275*

psychological [*adj*] *concerning the mind*
cerebral, cognitive, emotional, experimental, imaginary, intellective, intellectual, in the mind, mental, psychical, subconscious, subjective, unconscious; SEE CONCEPTS *403,536*

psychology [*n*] *study of the mind; emotional and mental constitution*
attitude, behaviorism, medicine, mental make-up, mental processes, personality study, psych*,

pr
ps

science of the mind, therapy, way of thinking*, where head is at*; SEE CONCEPTS *349,360,410*

psychopath [*n*] *person who is mentally deranged, often prone to hurt others*
antisocial personality, insane person, lunatic, mad person, maniac, mental case*, nutcase*, psycho*, psychotic, schizoid*, sociopath, unstable personality; SEE CONCEPT *412*

psychotic [*adj*] *mentally deranged*
certifiable*, crazy, demented, distracted, flipped-out*, insane, lunatic, mad, manic-depressive, mental, non compos mentis, nuts*, off one's rocker*, over the edge*, psycho*, psychopathic, schizophrenic, sick, unbalanced, unhinged*; SEE CONCEPT *403*

pub [*n*] *business where liquor and food are served*
after-hours joint*, ale house*, bar, barroom, beer joint*, drinkery, drinking establishment, gin mill*, inn, joint*, lounge, public house, roadhouse, saloon, taproom, tavern; SEE CONCEPTS *439,448,449*

puberty [*n*] *young adulthood*
adolescence, awkward stage*, boyhood, girlhood, greenness*, high-school years, juvenescence, juvenility, potency, preadolescence, pubescence, spring*, springtide*, springtime*, teenage years, teens, youth, youthfulness; SEE CONCEPT *817*

public [*adj1*] *community, general*
accessible, city, civic, civil, common, communal, conjoint, conjunct, country, federal, free, free to all, government, governmental, intermutual, metropolitan, municipal, mutual, national, not private, open, open-door, popular, social, state, universal, unrestricted, urban, widespread, without charge; SEE CONCEPTS *536,576*

public [*adj2*] *known, acknowledged*
exposed, general, in circulation, notorious, obvious, open, overt, patent, plain, popular, prevalent, published, recognized, social, societal, usual, vulgar, widespread; SEE CONCEPTS *267,530*

public [*n*] *people of community; people interested in something*
audience, bodies*, buyers, citizens, clientele, commonalty, community, country, electorate, everyone, followers, following, heads, masses, men and women, mob, multitude, nation, patrons, people, populace, population, society, suite, supporters, voters; SEE CONCEPTS *379,417*

publication [*n1*] *printing of written or visual material*
advertisement, airing, announcement, appearance, broadcast, broadcasting, communication, declaration, disclosure, discovery, dissemination, divulgation, issuance, issuing, notification, proclamation, promulgation, pronunciamento, publicity, public relations, publishing, reporting, revelation, statement, ventilation, writing; SEE CONCEPTS *60,274,292*

publication [*n2*] *something printed for reading*
annual, book, booklet, brochure, handbill, information, issue, leaflet, magazine, news, newsletter, newspaper, pamphlet, periodical; SEE CONCEPT *280*

publicity [*n*] *promotion of something, someone*
advertising, announcement, announcing, attention, ballyhoo*, big noise*, billing, blurb*, boost*, broadcasting, build-up*, clout*, commercial, currency, distribution, fame, handout, hoopla*, hype*, ink*, limelight*, noise*, notoriety, pitch, plug*, PR*, press, press-agentry, promo*, promulgation, propaganda, public notice, public relations, puff*, puffery*, pushing, réclame, release, report, scratch*, spotlight*, spread, write-up; SEE CONCEPTS *274,280,293*

publicize [*v*] *make widely known; promote*
advance, advertise, announce, bill, billboard, boost*, broadcast, build up*, cry, drum*, extol, hard sell*, headline, hype*, immortalize, make a pitch for, pitch, play up*, plug*, press-agent, promulgate, propagandize, puff*, push, put on the map*, skywrite*, soft-sell*, splash, spot*, spotlight*, spread, tout, trumpet*, write up; SEE CONCEPTS *60,292,324*

publish [*v*] *have printed, issue*
announce, bring out, broadcast, circulate, communicate, declare, disclose, distribute, divulge, let it be known*, print, proclaim, produce, promulgate, publicize, put in print, put out, report, spotlight; SEE CONCEPTS *60,140,292*

pucker [*n*] *wrinkle*
crease, crinkle, crumple, fold, furrow, plait, ruck, ruckle; SEE CONCEPT *754*

pucker [*v*] *draw together; wrinkle*
cockle, compress, condense, contract, crease, crinkle, crumple, fold, furrow, gather, knit, purse, ruckle, ruck up, ruffle, screw up, squeeze, tighten; SEE CONCEPTS *185,219*

pudgy [*adj*] *slightly fat*
chubby*, hefty, plump, plumpish, rotund, round, stout, thick-bodied, tubby*; SEE CONCEPTS *491,773*

puerile [*adj*] *childish*
babyish, babylike, callow, foolish, green*, immature, inane, inexperienced, infantile, irresponsible, jejune, juvenile, naive, petty, ridiculous, silly, trivial, unfledged, ungrown, weak, young; SEE CONCEPTS *401,578,797*

puff [*n1*] *blast of air*
breath, draft, drag, draught, draw, emanation, flatus, flurry, gust, pull, smoke, waft, whiff, wind, wisp; SEE CONCEPTS *437,524*

puff [*n2*] *advertisement*
advertising, blurb*, boost*, buildup*, commendation, favorable mention, good word, hype*, laudation, plug*, praise, press-agentry, promo*, promotion, publicity, puffery*, push*, sales talk, write-up; SEE CONCEPTS *69,278,324*

puff [*v1*] *inhale or exhale air*
blow, breathe, distend, drag, draw, enlarge, fill, gasp, gulp, heave, huff, huff and puff*, inflate, pant, pull at, pull on, smoke, suck, swell, wheeze, whiff; SEE CONCEPTS *163,185,526*

puff [*v2*] *publicize*
admire, advertise, ballyhoo*, blow up*, build, commend, congratulate, cry*, flatter, hype*, overpraise, plug*, praise, press-agent*, promote, push; SEE CONCEPTS *49,69*

puffy [*adj*] *swollen*
billowy, bloated, blown, bulgy, distended, distent, enlarged, expanded, full, increased, inflamed, inflated, puffed up; SEE CONCEPT *485*

pugnacious [*adj*] *belligerent*
aggressive, antagonistic, argumentative, bellicose, brawling, cantankerous, chip on shoulder*, choleric, combative, contentious, defiant, disputatious, have a bone to pick*, hot-tempered, irascible, irritable, itching to fight*, militant,

petulant, pushing, pushy*, quarrelsome, ready to fight, rebellious, salty*, scrappy*, self-assertive, truculent, warlike; SEE CONCEPTS *401,542*

pulchritude [*n*] *beauty*
adorableness, allure, allurement, attraction, elegance, exquisiteness, glamor, good looks, handsomeness, loveliness, physical attractiveness, prettiness, shapeliness; SEE CONCEPT *718*

pull [*v1*] *drawing something with force*
cull, dislocate, drag, evolve, extract, gather, haul, heave, jerk, lug, paddle, pick, pluck, remove, rend, rip, row, schlepp*, sprain, strain, stretch, take out, tear, tow, trail, truck, tug, twitch, uproot, weed*, wrench, yank; SEE CONCEPT *206*

pull [*v2*] *attract*
draw, entice, get, lure, magnetize, obtain, pick up, secure, win; SEE CONCEPT *11*

pull down [*v*] *destroy; knock over*
annihilate, bulldoze, decimate, demolish, destruct, dismantle, let down, lower, raze, remove, ruin, take down, tear down, wreck; SEE CONCEPT *252*

pull in [*v1*] *arrest*
apprehend, bust, collar, detain, nab, nail, pick up, pinch, run in, take into custody; SEE CONCEPTS *90,317*

pull in [*v2*] *attract, obtain*
absorb, bring in, clear, draw, draw in, earn, gain, gross, make, net, pocket, suck, take home*; SEE CONCEPT *120*

pull off [*v*] *accomplish*
achieve, bring off, carry out, manage, score, score a success, secure, succeed, win; SEE CONCEPTS *91,706*

pull out [*v*] *quit*
abandon, depart, evacuate, exit, get off, go, leave, retire, retreat, shove off, stop, stop participating, take off, withdraw; SEE CONCEPTS *119,121,195*

pull through [*v*] *recover*
come through, get better, get over, improve, rally, ride out*, survive, triumph, weather*; SEE CONCEPTS *303,700,706*

pull up [*v*] *stop, halt*
arrive, brake, bring up, come to a halt, come to a stop, draw up, fetch up, get there, haul up, pause, reach a standstill; SEE CONCEPTS *119,121,159*

pulp [*adj*] *cheap, vulgar, especially regarding reading material*
lurid, mushy, rubbish, sensational, trash, trashy; SEE CONCEPT *267*

pulp [*n*] *flesh of plant, animal*
batter, curd, dough, grume, jam, marrow, mash, mush, pap, paste, pomace, poultice, sarcocarp, semisolid, soft part, sponge, triturate; SEE CONCEPTS *399,428*

pulp [*v*] *mash, pulverize*
bruise, coagulate, crush, gelatinate, macerate, squash, triturate; SEE CONCEPTS *208,219*

pulpit [*n*] *structure from which sermon is given*
desk, lectern, platform, podium, rostrum, soapbox*, stage, stump*; SEE CONCEPTS *368,443*

pulsate/pulse [*v*] *quiver, beat*
drum, fluctuate, hammer, oscillate, palpitate, pound, pump, roar, throb, thrum, thud, thump, tick, vibrate; SEE CONCEPTS *147,185*

pulse [*n*] *rhythm, beat*
beating, oscillation, pulsation, stroke, throb, throbbing, vibration; SEE CONCEPTS *147,185*

pulverize [*v1*] *smash by beating, crushing*
abrade, atomize, beat, bray, break up, buck, comminute, contriturate, crumble, crunch, crush, flour, fragment, fragmentalize, fragmentize, granulate, grate, grind, levigate, micronize, mill, mull, pestle, pound, powder, shatter, splinter, triturate; SEE CONCEPTS *186,219*

pulverize [*v2*] *destroy*
annihilate, crush, decimate, defeat, demolish, destruct, dynamite, flatten, rub out*, ruin, shatter, smash, tear down*, vanquish, vaporize, wax, wreck; SEE CONCEPT *252*

pummel [*v*] *beat, pommel*
bash, batter, belt, clout, club, crush, cudgel, flog, hammer, hit, knock, lash, let one have it*, lick, mash, maul, pelt, pound, punch, ram, slug, smack, strike, swat, thrash, trounce, wallop, whale, wham, whip; SEE CONCEPTS *189,246*

pump [*v1*] *draw or push out*
bail out, blow up, dilate, distend, draft, drain, draw, draw off, drive, drive out, elevate, empty, force, force out, inflate, inject, pour, push, send, siphon, supply, swell, tap; SEE CONCEPTS *142,206,208*

pump [*v2*] *question relentlessly*
cross-examine, draw out, give the third degree*, grill, interrogate, probe, query, question, quiz, worm out of*; SEE CONCEPTS *48,53*

pumped [*adj*] *excited*
animated, aroused, awakened, beside oneself*, charged, cranked up, delighted, eager, enthusiastic, feverish, fired up*, geared up, high*, inspired, juiced up*, keyed up*, moved, on fire*, passionate, psyched, rarin' to go*, stimulated, stirred, thrilled, wild, worked up; SEE CONCEPTS *401,403*

pun [*n*] *play on words*
ambiguity, calembour, conceit, double entendre, double meaning, equivoque, joke, paronomasia, quibble, quip, witticism; SEE CONCEPTS *273,278*

punch [*n1/v1*] *hit*
bash, belt, biff, blow, bop, box, buffet, clip, clout, cuff, dig, jab, jog, knock, lollop, nudge, one-two*, plug, plunk*, poke, prod, pummel, rap, shot, slam, slap, slug, smack, smash, sock, strike, stroke, thrust, thump, wallop; SEE CONCEPT *189*

punch [*n2*] *energy, vigor*
bite, cogency, drive, effectiveness, force, forcefulness, impact, point, validity, validness, verve; SEE CONCEPTS *676,682*

punch [*v2*] *perforate, prick*
bore, cut, drill, jab, pierce, poke, puncture, stab, stamp; SEE CONCEPT *220*

punch-drunk [*adj*] *dazed*
agog, baffled, befuddled, confused, dazzled, dizzy, dumbfounded, dumbstruck, flustered, lost, muddled, perplexed, punchy*, puzzled, rattled, slap-happy, staggered; SEE CONCEPTS *402,403*

punctilio [*n*] *etiquette*
ceremony, civility, code, convention, courtesy, customs, decorum, dignity, form, formalities, formality, mores, nicety, politesse, proper behavior, protocol, p's and q's*, refinement, rules, social graces; SEE CONCEPT *633*

punctilious [*adj*] *careful, finicky*
ceremonious, conscientious, conscionable, conventional, exact, formal, formalistic, fussy, good eye*, heedful, meticulous, nice, observant, overconscientious, overscrupulous, painstaking, par-

ps
pu

ticular, persnickety, precise, proper, punctual, right on*, scrupulous, strict; SEE CONCEPTS *401,542,557*

punctual [*adj*] *on time*
accurate, careful, conscientious, conscionable, constant, cyclic, dependable, early, exact, expeditious, fussy, heedful, in good time*, meticulous, on schedule, on the button*, on the dot*, on the nose*, painstaking, particular, periodic, precise, prompt, punctilious, quick, ready, recurrent, regular, reliable, scrupulous, seasonable, steady, strict, timely, under the wire*; SEE CONCEPTS *544,550,799*

punctuate [*v*] *lay stress on*
accent, accentuate, break, divide, emphasize, interject, interrupt, intersect, intersperse, mark, pepper*, point, point up*, separate, sprinkle, stress, underline; SEE CONCEPTS *49,79,98,266*

puncture [*n*] *hole, rupture*
break, cut, damage, flat, flat tire*, jab, leak, nick, opening, perforation, prick, slit, stab; SEE CONCEPTS *309,513,674*

puncture [*v1*] *poke hole in*
bore, cut, cut through, deflate, drill, go down, go flat, knife, lacerate, lance, nick, open, penetrate, perforate, pierce, prick, punch, riddle, rupture; SEE CONCEPTS *137,220*

puncture [*v2*] *deflate someone's idea, feelings*
blow sky high*, discourage, discredit, disillusion, disprove, explode, flatten*, humble, knock bottom out*, knock props from under*, poke full of holes*, shoot full of holes*, take down a peg*, take wind out of sails*; SEE CONCEPTS *7,19,54*

pundit [*n*] *person who is authority*
auger, bookworm, brain*, buff, cereb*, cognoscenti, egghead*, expert, intellectual, learned one, philosopher, professor, savant, scholar, solon, teacher, thinker; SEE CONCEPTS *416,423*

pungent [*adj1*] *highly flavored*
acid, acrid, aromatic, bitter, effluvious, hot, nosey*, odoriferous, peppery, piquant, poignant, racy, rich, salty, seasoned, sharp, snappy, sour, spicy, stinging, stinking*, strong, tangy, tart, whiffy*, zesty; SEE CONCEPT *613*

pungent [*adj2*] *sharp, stinging in speech*
acrimonious, acute, barbed, biting, bitter, caustic, cutting, exciting, hot, incisive, keen, mordant, penetrating, peppery, piercing, poignant, pointed, provocative, racy, salt, salty, sarcastic, scathing, snappy, spicy, stimulating, stringent, telling, trenchant, zesty; SEE CONCEPT *267*

punish [*v*] *penalize for wrongdoing*
abuse, attend to, batter, beat, beat up, blacklist, castigate, chasten, chastise, correct, crack down on*, cuff, debar, defrock, discipline, dismiss, do in, execute, exile, expel, fine, flog, give a going over*, give the works*, harm, hurt, immure, incarcerate, injure, knock about, lash, lecture, maltreat, misuse, oppress, paddle, rap knuckles*, reprove, rough up, scourge, sentence, slap wrist, spank, switch, teach a lesson, throw the book at*, train, whip; SEE CONCEPT *122*

punishment [*n*] *penalty*
abuse, amercement, beating, castigation, chastening, chastisement, comeuppance, confiscation, correction, deprivation, disciplinary action, discipline, forfeit, forfeiture, gallows, hard work, infliction, just desserts*, lumps, maltreatment, mortification, mulct, ostracism, pain, penance,

proof, punitive measures, purgatory, reparation, retribution, rod, rough treatment, sanction, sequestration, short shrift*, slave labor*, suffering, torture, trial, unhappiness, victimization, what for*; SEE CONCEPT *123*

punitive [*adj*] *concerning punishment*
castigating, correctional, disciplinary, in reprisal, in retaliation, penal, punishing, punitory, retaliative, retaliatory, revengeful, vindictive; SEE CONCEPT *319*

punk [*n*] *hoodlum*
bully, criminal, delinquent, gangster, goon*, hood, hooligan, mobster, rioter, rowdy, ruffian, thug, troublemaker; SEE CONCEPT *412*

puny [*adj*] *small, insignificant*
diminutive, feeble, fragile, frail, half-pint*, inconsequential, inferior, infirm, little, measly*, minor, niggling*, nothing, paltry, peanut*, peewee*, petty, picayune, piddling*, pint-sized*, runt, shrimp*, small-fry*, small time*, stunted, tiny, trifling, trivial, two-bit*, unconsequential, underfed, undersized, undeveloped, unsound, unsubstantial, weak, weakly, wee*, worthless, zero*, zilch*; SEE CONCEPTS *489,575,773*

pupil [*n*] *person who is learning something*
adherent, attendant, beginner, bookworm*, brain*, catechumen, disciple, first-year student, follower, graduate student, junior, learner, neophyte, novice, satellite, scholar, schoolboy/girl, senior, sophomore, student, tenderfoot*, undergraduate; SEE CONCEPT *350*

puppet [*n*] *person or toy manipulated by another*
creature, doll, dupe*, figurehead, figurine, instrument, jerk*, manikin, marionette, moppet, mouthpiece*, patsy*, pawn, pushover, schlemiel*, servant, soft touch*, stooge*, tool*, victim; SEE CONCEPTS *423,446*

purchase [*n*] *possession obtained with money*
acquirement, acquisition, asset, bargain, booty*, buy, gain, investment, property, steal; SEE CONCEPTS *446,710*

purchase [*v*] *buy, obtain*
achieve, acquire, attain, come by, cop*, deal in, earn, gain, get hold of, go shopping, invest, make a buy, make a purchase, market, patronize, pay for, pick up, procure, realize, redeem, secure, shop, shop for, take, take up, truck*, win; SEE CONCEPT *327*

pure [*adj1*] *unmixed, genuine*
authentic, bright, classic, clear, complete, fair, flawless, kosher*, limpid, lucid, natural, neat, out-and-out*, pellucid, perfect, plain, plenary, pure and simple, real, simple, straight, total, transparent, true, twenty-four carat*, unadulterated, unalloyed, unclouded, undiluted, unmingled; SEE CONCEPT *485*

pure [*adj2*] *clean, uncontaminated*
disinfected, germ-free, immaculate, intemerate, pasteurized, pristine, purified, refined, sanitary, snowy, spotless, stainless, sterile, sterilized, taintless, unadulterated, unblemished, undebased, unpolluted, unsoiled, unspotted, unstained, unsullied, untainted, untarnished, wholesome; SEE CONCEPT *621*

pure [*adj3*] *virginal, chaste*
babe in woods*, blameless, celibate, clean, continent, decent, exemplary, fresh, good, guileless, honest, immaculate, inculpable, innocent, inviolate, irreproachable, kid, lily white*, maidenly, modest, pure as driven snow*, righteous, sinless,

spotless, stainless, true, unblemished, unblighted, uncorrupted, undefiled, unprofaned, unspotted, unstained, unsullied, upright, virgin, virtuous, wet behind ears*, wide-eyed; SEE CONCEPT *372*

pure [*adj4*] *absolute, utter*
blasted*, blessed*, complete, confounded, infernal*, mere, out-and-out, sheer, thorough, unmitigated, unqualified; SEE CONCEPTS *531,535*

pure [*adj5*] *theoretical*
abstract, academic, philosophical, speculative, tentative, unproved; SEE CONCEPT *529*

purely [*adv*] *simply, absolutely*
all, all in all, altogether, barely, completely, entirely, essentially, exactly, exclusively, in toto*, just, merely, only, plainly, quite, solely, totally, utterly, wholly; SEE CONCEPTS *531,544*

purgatory [*n*] *hell*
Abaddon*, abyss, bottomless pit*, everlasting fire*, fire and brimstone*, Gehenna, Hades, infernal regions, limbo, lower world, nether world, perdition, pit, place of torment, suffering, underworld; SEE CONCEPTS *370,435,674*

purge [*n*] *elimination, removal*
abolition, abstersion, catharsis, clarification, cleaning, cleanup, coup, crushing, disposal, disposition, ejection, eradication, evacuation, excretion, expulsion, expurgation, extermination, extirpation, liquidation, murder, purification, reign of terror*, suppression, witch hunt; SEE CONCEPTS *165,211,252*

purge [*v*] *rid of; clean out*
abolish, absolve, clarify, cleanse, clear, depurate, disabuse, dismiss, dispose of, do away with*, eject, eradicate, erase, excrete, exonerate, expel, expiate, expunge, exterminate, forgive, kill, liquidate, oust, pardon, prevent, purify, remove, rout out, shake out*, sweep out, unload, wash, wipe off map*, wipe out; SEE CONCEPTS *165,211,252*

purification [*n*] *freeing, cleansing*
ablution, absolution, atonement, baptism, bathing, catharsis, depuration, disinfection, distillation, expiation, expurgation, forgiveness, grace, lavation, laving, lustration, purgation, purge, purifying, rarefaction, rebirth, redemption, refinement, regeneration, salvation, sanctification, washing; SEE CONCEPTS *165,367*

purify [*v*] *free; make clean*
absolve, aerate, aerify, atone, chasten, clarify, clean, cleanse, clear, decontaminate, deodorize, depurate, deterge, disinfect, edulcorate, elutriate, exculpate, exonerate, expiate, filter, fumigate, lustrate, oxygenate, purge, rarify, redeem, refine, remit, sanctify, sanitize, shrive, sublimate, wash; SEE CONCEPTS *165,367*

puritanical [*adj*] *proper, straitlaced*
abstinent, austere, conforming, moral, priggish, prim, prissy, prudish, rigid, stern, strict, stuffy; SEE CONCEPTS *401,404*

purloin [*v*] *steal*
appropriate, burglarize, cheat, defraud, embezzle, filch, heist, lift*, make off with*, misappropriate, pilfer, pillage, pinch*, plunder, poach, rip off*, shoplift, snitch, swindle, take, thieve; SEE CONCEPT *139*

purple [*n/adj*] *blue and red colors mixed together*
amaranthine, amethyst, bluish red, color, heliotrope, lavender, lilac, magenta, mauve, mul-

berry, orchid, perse, plum, pomegranate, reddish blue, violaceous, violet, wine; SEE CONCEPTS *618,622*

purport [*n*] *meaning, implication*
acceptation, aim, bearing, burden, connotation, core, design, drift, gist, heart, idea, import, intendment, intent, intention, matter, meat, message, nub, object, objective, pith, plan, point, purpose, score, sense, significance, significancy, signification, spirit, stuff, substance, tendency, tenor, thrust, understanding, upshot; SEE CONCEPTS *20,659,660,689*

purport [*v*] *assert, mean*
allege, betoken, claim, convey, declare, denote, express, imply, import, indicate, intend, maintain, point to, pose as, pretend, proclaim, profess, signify, suggest; SEE CONCEPTS *49,682*

purpose [*n1*] *intention, meaning, aim*
ambition, animus, aspiration, big idea*, bourn, calculation, design, desire, destination, determination, direction, dream, drift, end, expectation, function, goal, hope, idea, intendment, intent, mecca, mission, object, objective, plan, point, premeditation, principle, project, proposal, proposition, prospect, reason, resolve, scheme, scope, target, ulterior motive, view, whatfor*, where one's headed*, whole idea*, why and wherefore*, whyfor*, will, wish; SEE CONCEPTS *20,659,660,689*

purpose [*n2*] *persistence, resolve*
confidence, constancy, determination, faith, firmness, resolution, single-mindedness, steadfastness, tenacity, will; SEE CONCEPTS *633,644*

purpose [*n3*] *use*
advantage, avail, benefit, duty, effect, function, gain, goal, good, mark, mission, object, objective, outcome, profit, result, return, target, utility; SEE CONCEPTS *658,694*

purpose [*v*] *intend, set sights on*
aim, aspire, bid for, commit, conclude, consider, contemplate, decide, design, determine, have a mind to*, have in view, intend, make up one's mind*, mean, meditate, mind, plan, ponder, propose, pursue, resolve, think to, work for, work toward; SEE CONCEPTS *18,36,87*

purposeful [*adj*] *resolved to do something*
bent, be out for blood*, bound, calculated, dead set on*, decided, deliberate, determined, firm, fixed, intense, intent, mean business*, obstinate, persistent, playing hard ball*, positive, purposive, resolute, settled, single-minded, stalwart, staunch, steadfast, steady, strong-willed, stubborn, telelogical, tenacious, undeviating, unfaltering, unwavering; SEE CONCEPTS *326,403,542*

purposeless [*adj*] *useless, insignificant*
aimless, designless, desultory, drifting, empty, feckless, floundering, fustian, goalless, good-for-nothing*, haphazard, hit-or-miss*, indiscriminate, irregular, meaningless, motiveless, needless, nonsensical, pointless, purportless, random, senseless, uncalled for, undirected, unhelpful, unnecessary, unplanned, unprofitable, unpurposed, vacuous, wanton, worthless; SEE CONCEPTS *544,560*

purposely [*adv*] *intentionally*
advisedly, by design, calculatedly, consciously, deliberately, designedly, explicitly, expressly, knowingly, on purpose, prepensely, purposely, willfully, with intent; SEE CONCEPTS *529,544*

pu
pu

purse [*n1*] *tote for carrying personal items*
bag, billfold, bursa, carryall, clutch, frame, handbag, hide, leather, lizard, moneybag, pocket, pocketbook, poke, pouch, receptacle, reticule, sack, wallet; SEE CONCEPTS *339,446,450,494*

purse [*n2*] *award; winnings*
coffers, exchequer, funds, gift, means, money, present, prize, resources, reward, stake, treasury, wealth, wherewithal; SEE CONCEPTS *337,344*

purse [*v*] *press together*
close, cockle, contract, crease, knit, pucker, ruffle, tighten, wrinkle; SEE CONCEPTS *185,208*

pursue [*v1*] *chase, follow*
accompany, attend, badger, bait, bird-dog*, bug, camp on the doorstep of*, chivy, dog*, fish*, give chase, go after, harass, harry, haunt, hound, hunt, hunt down, move behind, nose around*, oppress, persevere, persist, plague, play catch up*, poke around, prowl after, ride, run after, run down, scout out, search for, search high heaven*, search out, seek, shadow, stalk, tag, tail*, take out after*, trace, track, track down, trail; SEE CONCEPT *207*

pursue [*v2*] *have as one's goal*
aim for, aspire to, attempt, desire, go in for, go out for, have a go at, purpose, seek, strive for, try for, work for, work toward; SEE CONCEPTS *20,36*

pursue [*v3*] *persist, persevere*
adhere, apply oneself, carry on, conduct, continue, cultivate, engage in, hold to, keep on, maintain, perform, ply, practice, proceed, prosecute, see through, tackle, wage, work at; SEE CONCEPTS *87,100,239*

pursue [*v4*] *seek social alliance with*
address, call, chase, chase after, court, date, go after, go for, pay attention, pay court*, play up to, rush*, spark, sue, sweetheart*, woo; SEE CONCEPT *384*

pursuit [*n1*] *chase, search*
following, going all out, hunt, hunting, inquiry, pursual, pursuance, pursuing, quest, reaching, seeking, stalk, tracking, trail, trailing; SEE CONCEPT *207*

pursuit [*n2*] *occupation, interest of person*
accomplishing, accomplishment, activity, biz*, business, calling, career, do*, employment, game*, go*, hang*, hobby, job, line*, occupation, pastime, pleasure, racket, thing*, undertaking, venture, vocation, work; SEE CONCEPT *349*

push [*n1*] *physical force*
advance, assault, attack, bearing, blow, butt, charge, drive, driving, effort, energy, exerting, exertion, forcing, impact, jolt, lean, mass, nudge, offensive, onset, poke, prod, propulsion, shove, shoving, straining, thrust, thrusting, weight; SEE CONCEPTS *200,208,641,724*

push [*n2*] *mental determination*
ambition, drive, dynamism, energy, enterprise, get-up-and-go*, go*, gumption*, guts*, initiative, pep, punch, snap, spunk, starch, vigor, vitality; SEE CONCEPTS *410,411*

push [*v1*] *thrust, press with force*
accelerate, bear down, budge, bulldoze*, bump, butt, crowd, crush against, depress, dig, drive, elbow, exert, force, gore, high pressure*, hustle, impel, jam, jostle, launch, lie on, make one's way*, move, muscle, nudge, poke, pour it on*, pressure, propel, put the arm on*, railroad*, ram*, rest on, shift, shoulder, shove, squash,

squeeze, squish, steamroll*, stir, strain, strong-arm*; SEE CONCEPTS *200,208,243*

push [*v2*] *incite, urge*
bear down, browbeat, bulldoze*, coerce, constrain, dragoon, egg on*, encourage, exert influence, expedite, fire up*, goad, goose*, go to town on*, hurry, impel, influence, inspire, jolly, key up*, kid, lean on*, motivate, oblige, overpress, persuade, pour it on*, press, pressure, prod, push around, put the screws to*, put up to*, railroad*, sell on*, speed, speed up, spur, squeeze, steamroll*, strong-arm*, turn on*; SEE CONCEPTS *14,68,243*

push [*v3*] *advertise, promote*
advance, boost, cry up*, hype*, make known, plug*, propagandize, publicize, puff*; SEE CONCEPTS *49,324*

push off/push on [*v*] *leave; go to another place*
beat it*, continue, depart, exit, fare, get away, get lost*, go, go away, hie, hit the road*, journey, keep going, launch, light out, make oneself scarce*, make progress, pass, proceed, process, pull out, quit, repair, shove off, start, take off, travel, wend, withdraw; SEE CONCEPTS *195,704*

pushover [*n*] *something or someone easily influenced*
breeze, child's play*, chump*, cinch, duck soup*, easy game*, easy mark*, easy pickings*, fool, kid stuff*, picnic*, piece of cake*, setup, snap, soft touch*, stooge*, sucker, victim, walkover; SEE CONCEPTS *423,693*

pushy [*adj*] *aggressive, offensive*
ambitious, assertive, bold, brash, bumptious, forceful, loud, militant, obnoxious, obtrusive, officious, presumptuous, pushful, pushing, self-assertive; SEE CONCEPTS *401,404*

pussyfoot [*v*] *be cautious*
avoid, beat around the bush*, be noncommittal, creep, dodge, duck the issues, equivocate, evade, glide, hedge, hem and haw*, lurk, play it close to the vest*, prevaricate, prowl, shuffle, sidestep, sit on the fence*, skirt*, skulk, slide, slink, slip, sneak, steal, tergiversate, tergiverse, tiptoe, tread warily, watch one's step*, weasel*; SEE CONCEPTS *151,410*

put [*v1*] *position*
bring, concenter, concentrate, deposit, embed, establish, fasten, fix, fixate, focus, insert, install, invest, lay, nail, park, peg, place, plank, plank down, plant, plop, plunk, plunk down, quarter, repose, rest, rivet, seat, set, settle, situate, stick; SEE CONCEPT *201*

put [*v2*] *propose; express in words*
advance, air, bring forward, couch, express, formulate, forward, give, offer, phrase, pose, posit, prefer, present, propone, proposition, propound, render, set, set before, state, submit, suggest, tender, translate, transpose, turn, utter, vent, ventilate, word; SEE CONCEPTS *47,66,67*

put [*v3*] *commit, assign*
condemn, consign, constrain, doom, employ, enjoin, force, impose, induce, inflict, levy, make, oblige, require, set, subject, subject to; SEE CONCEPTS *14,242*

putative [*adj*] *commonly believed*
accepted, alleged, assumed, conjectural, hypothetical, imputed, presumed, presumptive, reported, reputed, supposed, suppositional, supposititious; SEE CONCEPT *529*

put away [*v2*] *incarcerate*
certify, commit, confine, institutionalize, jail, lock up; SEE CONCEPT *317*

put away [*v3*] *consume*
devour, eat up, gobble*, gulp down, polish off*, punish, put down, shift, swill, wolf down*; SEE CONCEPT *169*

put away [*v4*] *kill*
assassinate, bury, cool*, cut off, destroy, dispatch, do away with, do in*, dust off*, execute, finish, inter, knock off*, liquidate, murder, plant, put down*, put out of its misery*, put to sleep*, slay, tomb; SEE CONCEPT *252*

put away/put aside/put by [*v1/v*] *keep in reserve*
cache, deposit, keep, lay aside, lay away, lay by, lay in, put by, put out of the way, salt away*, save, set aside, squirrel away*, stockpile, store, store away*, stow away*; SEE CONCEPTS *129,134*

put-down [*n*] *nasty commentary*
cut*, dig*, disparagement, gibe*, humiliation, indignity, insult, jibe*, knock*, pan*, rebuff, sarcasm, slight, sneer*, snub, suppression; SEE CONCEPTS *54,278*

put down [*v1*] *write into record*
enter, inscribe, jot down, log, record, set down, take down, transcribe, write down; SEE CONCEPT *79*

put down [*v2*] *subdue*
annihilate, crush, defeat, dismiss, extinguish, quash*, quell, reject, repress, silence, squash*, stamp out*, suppress; SEE CONCEPTS *95,252*

put down [*v3*] *comment negatively*
belittle, condemn, crush, decry, deflate, derogate, discount, dismiss, disparage, downcry, humiliate, minimize, mortify, opprobriate, reject, run down, shame, slight, snub, write off; SEE CONCEPT *54*

put off [*v*] *defer, delay*
adjourn, dally, dawdle, dillydally*, drag one's feet*, hold off, hold over, lag*, lay over, linger, loiter, poke*, postpone, prorogue, put back, reschedule, retard, shelve, stay, suspend, tarry, trail; SEE CONCEPTS *121,234*

put on [*v1*] *pretend*
act, affect, assume, bluff, confound, confuse, counterfeit, deceive, don, fake, feign, make believe, masquerade, playact, pose, pull, put on a front, put on an act, sham, simulate, strike, take on, trick; SEE CONCEPT *59*

put on [*v2*] *stage a performance*
do, mount, present, produce, show; SEE CONCEPT *292*

put out [*v1*] *upset, irritate; inconvenience*
aggravate, anger, annoy, bother, burn, confound, discomfit, discommode, discompose, disconcert, discountenance, disoblige, displease, dissatisfy, disturb, embarrass, exasperate, gall, get*, grate, harass, impose upon, incommode, inflame, irk, nettle, perturb, provoke, put on the spot*, rile, roil, trouble, vex; SEE CONCEPTS *7,14,19*

put out [*v2*] *extinguish fire*
blow out, douse, out, quench, smother, snuff out, stamp out; SEE CONCEPT *252*

putrefy [*v*] *rot*
break down, corrupt, crumble, decay, decompose, deteriorate, disintegrate, go bad*, molder, putresce, spoil, stink, taint, turn; SEE CONCEPT *469*

putrid [*adj*] *rotten, stinking*
bad, contaminated, corrupt, decayed, decom-

posed, fetid, foul, high, malodorous, moldered, nidorous, noisome, off, putrefied, rancid, rank, reeking, rotting, smelly, spoiled, strong, tainted, whiffy*; SEE CONCEPTS *485,598*

putter [*v*] *dawdle*
doodle, fiddle, fritter, goof around*, loiter, mess, mess around*, niggle, poke*, potter*, puddle*, shuffle around, tinker*; SEE CONCEPTS *87,210*

put up [*v1*] *accommodate guest*
bestow, billet, board, bunk, domicile, entertain, give lodging, harbor, house, lodge, make welcome, provide, quarter, take in; SEE CONCEPTS *324,384*

put up [*v2*] *build, erect*
construct, fabricate, forge, make, put together, raise, rear, shape, uprear; SEE CONCEPT *168*

puzzle [*v1*] *baffle, confuse*
addle, amaze, bamboozle*, beat, befog, befuddle, bemuse, bewilder, buffalo*, complicate, confound, discombobulate*, disconcert, distract, disturb, dumbfound, flabbergast, floor*, flummox, foil, frustrate, get to*, mystify, nonplus, obscure, perplex, pose, profundicate, psych out*, put off, rattle, snow*, stir, stumble, stump, throw; SEE CONCEPT *16*

puzzle [*v2*] *wonder about*
ask oneself, brood, cudgel, marvel, mull over, muse, ponder, rack one's brains*, study, think about, think hard; SEE CONCEPT *17*

puzzled [*adj*] *confused*
at a loss*, at sea*, baffled, bewildered, bollixed, clueless, come apart, come unzipped*, discombobulated*, dopey*, doubtful, floored*, foggy, fouled up*, hung up*, in a fog*, lost, loused up*, messed up*, mind-blown*, mixed up*, mucked up*, mystified, nonplussed, perplexed, rattled, screwed up*, shook, shook up, spaced out*, stuck, stumped, thrown, unglued*, without a clue; SEE CONCEPTS *403,690*

puzzling [*adj*] *confusing*
abstruse, ambiguous, baffling, bewildering, beyond one, difficult, enigmatic, hard, incomprehensible, inexplicable, involved, knotty, labyrinthine, misleading, mystifying, obscure, perplexing, surprising, unaccountable, unclear, unfathomable; SEE CONCEPT *529*

pyramid [*n*] *monument*
cairn, cenotaph, edifice, mastaba, memorial, monolith, obelisk, shrine, tomb, tribute; SEE CONCEPTS *259,271,305,470*

Q

quack [*adj*] *counterfeit*
bum*, dishonest, dissembling, fake, false, fraudulent, phony, pretended, pretentious, pseudo*, sham*, simulated, unprincipled; SEE CONCEPT *582*

quack [*n*] *person who pretends to be an expert*
actor, bum*, bunco artist, charlatan, cheat, con artist, counterfeiter, counterfeiter, fake, faker, flimflammer*, four-flusher*, fraud, hoser*, humbug, impostor, mountebank, phony, playactor, pretender, pseudo*, put-on*, quacksalver*, sham,

shammer*, shark*, sharp*, simulator, slicker*, whip*; SEE CONCEPT *412*

quaff [*v*] *drink down*
down, gulp, guzzle, imbibe, ingurgitate, partake, sip, sup, swallow, swig, swill, toss; SEE CONCEPT *169*

quagmire [*n1*] *bad situation*
box*, corner*, difficulty, dilemma, entanglement, fix, hole*, imbroglio, impasse, involvement, jam, mire, morass, muddle, pass, perplexity, pickle*, pinch*, plight, predicament, quandary, scrape, trouble; SEE CONCEPTS *666,674*

quagmire [*n2*] *bog*
fen, marsh, marshland, mire, morass, moss, quag, quicksand, slough, swamp; SEE CONCEPT *509*

quail [*v*] *cower, shrink*
blanch, blench, cringe, droop, faint, falter, flinch, have cold feet*, quake, recoil, shake, shudder, start, tremble, wince; SEE CONCEPTS *35,149,195*

quaint [*adj1*] *strange, odd*
bizarre, curious, droll, eccentric, erratic, fanciful, fantastic, freakish, freaky*, funny, idiosyncratic, laughable, oddball, offbeat, off the beaten track*, original, outlandish, peculiar, queer, singular, special, unusual, weird*, whimsical; SEE CONCEPTS *564,589*

quaint [*adj2*] *old-fashioned; nostalgically attractive*
affected, ancient, antiquated, antique, archaic, artful, baroque, captivating, charming, colonial, curious, cute, enchanting, fanciful, Gothic*, ingenious, old-world, picturesque, pleasing, Victorian*, whimsical; SEE CONCEPTS *578,589,797*

quake [*n*] *earthquake*
aftershock, convulsion, quaker, seism, shake, shock, temblor, tremblor, tremor; SEE CONCEPT *526*

quake [*v*] *shake, vibrate*
convulse, cower, fluctuate, jar, jitter, move, pulsate, quail, quiver, rock, shiver, shrink, shudder, throb, totter, tremble, tremor, twitter, waver, wobble; SEE CONCEPT *152*

qualification [*n1*] *ability, aptitude*
accomplishment, adequacy, attainment, attribute, capability, capacity, competence, eligibility, endowment, experience, fitness, goods, makings, might, qualifiedness, quality, skill, stuff, suitability, suitableness, what it takes*; SEE CONCEPT *630*

qualification [*n2*] *requirement, restriction*
allowance, caveat, condition, contingency, criterion, essential, exception, exemption, limitation, modification, need, objection, postulate, prerequisite, provision, proviso, requisite, reservation, stipulation; SEE CONCEPTS *646,652*

qualified [*adj1*] *able, skillful*
accomplished, adept, adequate, all around, au fait, capable, catechized, certified, competent, disciplined, efficient, equipped, examined, experienced, expert, fit, fitted, good, instructed, knowledgeable, licensed, practiced, pro*, proficient, proper, proved, quizzed, talented, tested, trained, tried, up to snuff*, up to speed*, vet*, veteran, war-horse*, wicked; SEE CONCEPT *527*

qualified [*adj2*] *limited, restricted*
bounded, circumscribed, conditional, confined, contingent, definite, determined, equivocal,

fixed, guarded, modified, partial, provisional, reserved; SEE CONCEPT *554*

qualify [*v1*] *make or become ready, prepared*
authorize, capacitate, certify, check out, come up to snuff*, commission, condition, cut it*, earn one's wings*, empower, enable, endow, entitle, equip, fill the bill*, fit, get by*, ground, hack it*, make it*, make the cut*, make the grade*, measure up, meet, pass, pass muster*, permit, ready, sanction, score, suffice, suit, train; SEE CONCEPTS *99,630*

qualify [*v2*] *lessen, restrict*
abate, adapt, alter, assuage, change, circumscribe, diminish, ease, limit, mitigate, moderate, modify, modulate, reduce, regulate, restrain, soften, temper, vary, weaken; SEE CONCEPTS *240,698*

qualify [*v3*] *characterize, distinguish*
ascribe, assign, attribute, describe, designate, impute, individualize, individuate, mark, name, predicate, signalize, singularize; SEE CONCEPT *411*

quality [*n1*] *characteristic, feature*
affection, affirmation, aspect, attribute, character, condition, constitution, description, element, endowment, essence, factor, genius, individuality, kind, make, mark, name of tune*, nature, nature of beast*, parameter, peculiarity, predication, property, savor, sort, trait, virtue, way of it*; SEE CONCEPT *543*

quality [*n2*] *value, status*
arete, caliber, capacity, character, class, condition, distinction, excellence, excellency, footing, grade, group, kind, merit, perfection, place, position, preeminence, rank, repute, standing, state, station, stature, step, superbness, superiority, variety, virtue, worth; SEE CONCEPTS *346,378,668*

qualm [*n*] *nagging doubt*
agitation, anxiety, apprehension, compunction, conscience, demur, disquiet, foreboding, hesitation, indecision, insecurity, misdoubt, misgiving, mistrust, nervousness, objection, pang, perturbation, presentiment, regret, reluctance, remonstrance, remorse, scruple, suspicion, twinge, uncertainty, unease, uneasiness; SEE CONCEPTS *410,532*

quandary [*n*] *delicate situation*
bewilderment, bind, Catch-22*, clutch, corner*, difficulty, dilemma, double trouble*, doubt, embarrassment, hang-up*, impasse, mire, perplexity, pickle*, plight, predicament, puzzle, spot*, strait, uncertainty, up a tree*; SEE CONCEPTS *532,674,690*

quantify [*v*] *measure*
appraise, assess, calibrate, check, compute, count, determine, estimate, evaluate, figure, gauge, look over, rank, rate, size, specify, value, weigh; SEE CONCEPTS *103,197,764*

quantity [*n*] *number or amount*
abundance, aggregate, allotment, amplitude, batch, body, budget, bulk, capacity, deal, expanse, extent, figure, greatness, length, load, lot, magnitude, mass, measure, multitude, part, pile, portion, profusion, quota, size, sum, total, variety, volume; SEE CONCEPT *787*

quantum leap [*n*] *abrupt change*
advance, breakthrough, giant strides, jump, leaps and bounds, radical change; SEE CONCEPTS *230,260,701*

quarantine [*n*] *isolation*
detention, lazaretto, seclusion, segregation, separation, sequestration; SEE CONCEPTS *135,188, 388,631*

quarantine [*v*] *isolate*
block off, close off, confine, cordon, detach, insulate, keep apart, remove, restrict, seal off, seclude, segregate, separate, sequester; SEE CONCEPTS *188,201*

quarrel [*n*] *disagreement*
affray, altercation, argument, battle royal*, beef*, bickering*, brannigan*, brawl, breach, broil*, catfight*, combat, commotion, complaint, contention, controversy, difference, difference of opinion, difficulty, disapproval, discord, disputation, dispute, dissension, dissidence, disturbance, dust*, falling-out*, feud, fight, fisticuffs*, fracas, fray, fuss, hassle, misunderstanding, objection, rhubarb*, row, ruckus*, run-in, scrap, set-to*, spat, squabble, strife, struggle, tiff, tumult, vendetta, wrangle; SEE CONCEPTS *46,106*

quarrel [*v*] *disagree*
altercate, argue, battle, be at loggerheads*, bicker, brawl, break with, bump, carp, caterwaul, cavil, charge, clash, collide, complain, contend, contest, cross swords*, differ, disapprove, dispute, dissent, divide, embroil, fall out*, feud, fight, find fault, get tough with*, hassle, have it out*, have words*, lock horns*, mix it up*, object to, row, scrap, set to, spar, spat, squabble, strive, struggle, take exception, take on, tangle, vary, war, wrangle; SEE CONCEPTS *46,106*

quarrelsome [*adj*] *being disagreeable*
argumentative, bad-tempered, bellicose, belligerent, brawling, cantankerous, cat-and-dog*, choleric, churlish, combative, contentious, crabby*, cross, disputatious, dissentious, excitable, fiery, fractious, gladiatorial, hasty, have chip on shoulder*, hotheaded*, huffy, impassioned, irascible, irritable, litigious, ornery, passionate, peevish, pettish, petulant, pugnacious, querulous, ructious, snappy, tempestuous, thin-skinned*, touchy, truculent, turbulent, unruly, violent, war; SEE CONCEPTS *401,542*

quarry [*n*] *goal*
aim, chase, game, objective, prey, prize, quest, raven, victim; SEE CONCEPT *659*

quarter [*n1*] *one of four equal parts*
division, farthing, fourth, one-fourth, part, portion, quad, quadrant, quartern, section, semester, span, term, two bits*; SEE CONCEPT *835*

quarter [*n2*] *area, neighborhood*
barrio, bearing, direction, district, division, domain, ghetto, inner city, locality, location, neck of the woods*, old town, part, place, point, position, precinct, province, region, section, sector, side, skid row, slum, spot, station, stomping ground*, territory, turf, zone, zoo*; SEE CONCEPTS *508,512*

quarter [*n3*] *forgiveness*
clemency, compassion, favor, grace, leniency, lenity, mercy, pity; SEE CONCEPTS *410,633*

quarter [*v1*] *divide into four equal parts*
cleave, cut, cut up, dismember, fourth; SEE CONCEPT *98*

quarter [*v2*] *provide lodging*
accommodate, billet, board, bunk, canton, domicile, domiciliate, entertain, establish, harbor, house, install, lodge, place, post, put up, settle, shelter, station; SEE CONCEPT *140*

quarters [*n*] *place to live or sleep*
abode, accommodation, apartment, barracks, billet, cabin, cantonment, chambers, condo, cottage, digs*, domicile, dorm, dwelling, flat, fraternity, habitat, habitation, home, house, lodge, lodging, place, post, ranch, residence, room, roost*, shelter, sorority, station, tent; SEE CONCEPT *516*

quash [*v1*] *destroy, defeat*
annihilate, beat, crush, extinguish, extirpate, overcome, overthrow, put down, quell, quench, repress, scrunch*, snow under*, squash*, squish*, subdue, suppress, trash; SEE CONCEPTS *95,252*

quash [*v2*] *nullify, cancel*
abrogate, annul, black out*, bottle up*, clamp down on, cork up*, crack down on*, declare null and void*, discharge, dissolve, hush up*, invalidate, kill, negate, overrule, overthrow, put damper on*, put the lid on*, repeal, rescind, reverse, revoke, set aside, shut down, squelch, undo, vacate, veto, vitiate, void, watergate*; SEE CONCEPTS *121,234,266*

quasi [*adj*] *almost; to a certain extent*
apparent, apparently, fake, mock, near, nominal, partly, pretended, pseudo-*, seeming, seemingly, semi-, sham*, so-called, supposedly, synthetic, virtual, would-be*; SEE CONCEPT *582*

queasy [*adj*] *not feeling well; not comfortable*
anxious, bilious, concerned, fidgety, green around gills*, groggy, ill, ill at ease, indisposed, nauseated, pukish, qualmish, queer, restless, rocky*, sick, sick as a dog*, sickly, squeamish, troubled, uncertain, uncomfortable, under the weather*, uneasy, unwell, upset, worried; SEE CONCEPTS *314,403*

queer [*adj1*] *odd; abnormal*
anomalous, atypical, bizarre, crazy, curious, demented, disquieting, doubtful, droll, dubious, eccentric, eerie, erratic, extraordinary, fishy*, flaky*, fly ball*, freaky*, funny, idiosyncratic, irrational, irregular, kinky*, kooky*, mad, mysterious, oddball, off the wall*, outlandish, outré, peculiar, puzzling, quaint, questionable, remarkable, shady, singular, strange, suspicious, touched, unbalanced, uncanny, uncommon, unconventional, unhinged, unnatural, unorthodox, unusual, wacky*, weird; SEE CONCEPTS *404,548,564*

queer [*adj2*] *not feeling well*
dizzy, faint, giddy, green*, ill, lightheaded, pukish*, qualmish, qualmy*, queasy*, reeling, sick, squeamish*, uneasy; SEE CONCEPT *314*

quell [*v1*] *defeat, suppress*
annihilate, conquer, crush, extinguish, hush up*, kill, overcome, overpower, put down, put the lid on*, queer, quench, shut down, silence, sit on, stamp out*, stifle, stop, subdue, subjugate, vanquish; SEE CONCEPTS *95,121,234*

quell [*v2*] *alleviate, calm*
allay, appease, assuage, check, compose, deaden, dull, ease, mitigate, moderate, mollify, pacify, quiet, reduce, silence, soothe, still; SEE CONCEPTS *7,22,110*

quench [*v1*] *destroy, extinguish*
annihilate, check, choke, crush, dampen, decimate, demolish, destruct, dismantle, douse, end, kill, knock down, moisten, put down, put out, quash*, quell, raze, ruin, shatter, smother, snuff out*, stifle, suppress, wreck; SEE CONCEPTS *234,252*

qu
qu

quench [v2] *satisfy, especially thirst*
allay, alleviate, appease, assuage, content, cool*, glut, gorge, gratify, lighten, mitigate, moisten, relieve, sate, satiate, slake; SEE CONCEPTS *136,244*

querulous [adj] *grouchy, hard to please*
bearish, bemoaning, cantankerous, captious, carping, censorious, complaining, critical, cross, crying, deploring, discontented, dissatisfied, edgy, fault-finding, fretful, grousing, grumbling, grumbly, huffy* irascible, irritable, lamenting, out of sorts* peevish, petulant, plaintive, scrappy, snappy, sour, testy, thin-skinned* touchy, uptight, wailing, waspish, waspy, whimpering, whining, whiny; SEE CONCEPTS *401,542*

query [n] *demand for answers*
concern, doubt, dubiety, inquiry, interrogation, interrogatory, mistrust, objection, problem, question, questioning, reservation, skepticism, suspicion, uncertainty; SEE CONCEPTS *21,48,53,662*

query [v] *ask*
catechize, challenge, disbelieve, dispute, distrust, doubt, enquire, examine, hit up, impeach, impugn, inquire, interrogate, knock, mistrust, put out a feeler* question, quiz, suspect, test the waters*; SEE CONCEPTS *21,48,53*

quest [n] *search, exploration*
adventure, chase, crusade, delving, enterprise, examination, expedition, hunt, inquest, inquiry, inquisition, investigation, journey, mission, pilgrimmage, prey, probe, probing, pursual, pursuit, quarry, research, seeking, voyage; SEE CONCEPTS *48,103,216*

question [n1] *asking for answer*
catechism, examination, inquest, inquiring, inquiry, inquisition, interrogation, interrogatory, investigation, poll, Q and A*, query, questioning, third degree*, wringer*; SEE CONCEPTS *48,53*

question [n2] *controversy, doubt*
argument, challenge, confusion, contention, debate, demur, demurral, difficulty, dispute, dubiety, enigma, misgiving, mystery, objection, problem, protest, puzzle, query, remonstrance, remonstration, uncertainty; SEE CONCEPTS *666,674*

question [n3] *issue, point at issue*
discussion, motion, point, problem, proposal, proposition, subject, theme, topic; SEE CONCEPTS *532,690*

question [v1] *ask for answer*
ask about, catechize, challenge, cross-examine, enquire, examine, give the third degree*, go over, grill, hit*, hit up*, hold out for, inquire, interrogate, interview, investigate, knock*, make inquiry, petition, pick one's brains*, probe, pry, pump, put through the wringer*, put to the question*, query, quest, quiz, raise question, roast*, search, seek, show curiosity, solicit, sound out*, sweat it out of*, work over*; SEE CONCEPTS *48,53*

question [v2] *doubt*
call into question, cast doubt upon, challenge, controvert, disbelieve, dispute, distrust, hesitate, impeach, impugn, mistrust, oppose, puzzle over, query, suspect, suspicion, wonder about; SEE CONCEPT *21*

questionable [adj] *doubtful, uncertain*
ambiguous, apocryphal, arguable, contingent, controversial, controvertible, cryptic, debatable, disputable, dubious, dubitable, enigmatic, equivocal, fishy*, hard to believe, hypothetical, iffy*, indecisive, indefinite, indeterminate, moot, mysterious, obscure, occult, open to doubt, open to question, oracular, paradoxical, problematic, problematical, provisional, shady, suspect, suspicious, unconfirmed, undefined, under advisement, under examination, unproven, unreliable, unsettled, vague; SEE CONCEPTS *529,535*

queue [n] *sequence*
chain, concatenation, echelon, file, line, order, progression, rank, row, series, string, succession, tail, tier, train; SEE CONCEPTS *432,727*

quibble [n] *objection, complaint*
artifice, cavil, criticism, dodge, duplicity, equivocation, evasion, hair-splitter*, nicety, niggle*, nit-picker*, pretense, prevarication, protest, quiddity, quirk, shift, sophism, subterfuge, subtlety; SEE CONCEPTS *46,52*

quibble [v] *disagree over minor issues*
altercate, argue over, argufy, avoid, bicker, blow hot and cold*, carp, catch at straws*, cavil, chicane, criticize, dispute, equivocate, evade, fence*, flip-flop*, hassle, have at it*, hem and haw*, hypercriticize*, make a big thing about*, nit-pick*, paralogize, pettifog*, pretend, prevaricate, put up an argument, set to, shift, spar, split hairs*, squabble, talk back, waffle, wrangle; SEE CONCEPTS *46,52*

quick [adj1] *fast, speedy*
abrupt, accelerated, active, agile, alert, a move on*, animated, ASAP*, breakneck*, brief, brisk, cursory, curt, double time*, energetic, expeditious, expeditive, express, fleet, flying, going, harefooted*, hasty, headlong, hurried, immediate, impatient, impetuous, instantaneous, keen, lively, mercurial, move it, nimble, on the double*, perfunctory, posthaste, prompt, pronto*, rapid, snappy, spirited, sprightly, spry, sudden, swift, the lead out*, winged*; SEE CONCEPTS *544,588*

quick [adj2] *smart*
able, active, acute, adept, adroit, all there, apt, astute, bright, canny, capable, clever, competent, deft, dexterous, discerning, effective, effectual, intelligent, keen, knowing, nimble-witted, on the ball*, perceptive, perspicacious, prompt, quick on the draw, quick on the trigger*, quick on the uptake*, quick-witted, ready, receptive, savvy*, sharp, sharp as a tack*, shrewd, skillful, slick, smart as a whip*, vigorous, whiz*, wired*, wise; SEE CONCEPT *402*

quicken [v] *make faster; invigorate*
accelerate, activate, actuate, animate, arouse, awaken, dispatch, energize, excite, expedite, galvanize, goad, grow, hasten, hurry, impel, incite, increase, innervate, innerve, inspire, kindle, liven, make haste, motivate, move, pique, precipitate, promote, refresh, revitalize, revive, rouse, shake up, speed, spring, spur, step up, stimulate, stir, strengthen, urge, vitalize, vivificate, vivify; SEE CONCEPTS *7,19,22,250*

quickly [adv] *fast*
apace, briskly, chop-chop*, expeditiously, flatout*, fleetly, full tilt*, hastily, hurriedly, immediately, in a flash*, in haste, in nothing flat*, in short order*, instantaneously, instantly, lickety-split*, like a bat out of hell*, like a flash*, like a

shot*, promptly, pronto, quick, rapidly, speedily, swift, swiftly; SEE CONCEPTS *588,799*

quick-tempered [*adj*] *easily upset, angered*
choleric, cranky, cross, excitable, fiery, hot-tempered, impatient, impulsive, inflammable, irascible, irritable, passionate, peppery, petulant, quarrelsome, ratty, sensitive, short-tempered, shrewish, splenetic, temperamental, testy, waspish; SEE CONCEPTS *401,404*

quick-witted [*adj*] *smart*
acute, agile, alert, apt, astute, brainy, bright, brilliant, canny, clever, facetious, humorous, intelligent, keen, knowing, nimble-witted, on the ball*, penetrating, penetrative, perceptive, prompt, quick, quick on the draw*, quick on the uptake*, ready, savvy*, sharp, sharp as a tack*, sharp-sighted, sharp-witted, shrewd, slick*, whiz*, wired*, wise, witty; SEE CONCEPTS *267,402*

quiet [*adj1*] *without or with little sound*
buttoned up*, clammed up*, close, close-mouthed, could hear a pin drop*, dumb, hushed, hushful, inaudible, low, low-pitched, muffled, mute, muted, noiseless, not saying boo*, peaceful, quiescent, quieted, reserved, reticent, secretive, silent, soft, soundless, speechless, still, stilled, taciturn, tight-lipped*, uncommunicative, unexpressed, unspeaking, unuttered, whist; SEE CONCEPTS *592,594*

quiet [*adj2*] *calm, peaceful*
collected, contented, docile, fixed, gentle, halcyon, hushed, inactive, isolated, level, meek, mild, motionless, pacific, placid, private, remote, reserved, restful, retired, secluded, secret, sedate, sequestered, serene, shy, smooth, stable, stagnant, still, tranquil, unanxious, undisturbed, unexcited, unfrequented, unruffled, untroubled; SEE CONCEPTS *401,583,584,705*

quiet [*adj3*] *simple, unobtrusive*
conservative, homely, inobtrusive, modest, plain, restrained, sober, subdued, tasteful, unassuming, unpretentious; SEE CONCEPT *589*

quiet [*n*] *calmness, silence*
calm, cessation, dead air*, ease, hush, lull, noiselessness, peace, quietness, quietude, relaxation, repose, rest, serenity, soundlessness, speechlessness, still, stillness, stop, termination, tranquillity; SEE CONCEPTS *65,315,592,673,705*

quiet [*v*] *make silent, calm*
allay, ameliorate, appease, assuage, becalm, button one's lip*, calm down, can it, choke, clam up*, compose, console, cool it*, cool out*, dummy up*, fix up, gag, gratify, hold it down, hush, ice*, inactivate, lull, moderate, mollify, muffle, muzzle, pacify, palliate, patch things up*, please, quieten, reconcile, relax, satisfy, settle, shush, shut up, silence, slack, smooth, soften, soft-pedal*, soothe, square, squash, squelch, still, stroke, subdue, take the bite out of*, tranquilize; SEE CONCEPTS *126,244,266*

quilt [*n*] *thick bedcovering made of patches*
batt, bedspread, blanket, comforter, counterpane, cover, coverlet, down, duvet, eiderdown, pad, patchwork, pouf, puff; SEE CONCEPTS *445,451,473*

quintessence [*n*] *essence, core*
apotheosis, bottom, distillation, epitome, essentiality, extract, gist, heart, kernel, last word, lifeblood, marrow, pith, quiddity, soul, spirit, stuff, substance, ultimate, virtuality; SEE CONCEPTS *682,826*

quip [*n*] *witty communication, often verbal*
badinage, banter, bon mot, crack, drollery, gag, gibe, insult, jeer, jest, joke, mockery, offense, pleasantry, pun, repartee, retort, riposte, sally, satire, spoof, wisecrack, witticism; SEE CONCEPTS *273,278*

quirk [*n*] *oddity of personality, way of doing something*
aberration, caprice, characteristic, conceit, crotchet, eccentricity, equivocation, fancy, fetish, foible, habit, humor, idée fixe, idiosyncrasy, irregularity, kink, knack, mannerism, peculiarity, quibble, singularity, subterfuge, trait, turn, twist, vagary, whim, whimsy; SEE CONCEPTS *411,644*

quit [*v1*] *abandon, leave*
abdicate, blow*, book*, bow out, check out, cut out*, decamp, depart, desert, drop, drop out, evacuate, exit, forsake, get off, give up, go, go away from, hang it up*, leave flat*, leave hanging*, pull out, push off*, relinquish, renounce, resign, retire, run out on, surrender, take a walk*, take off, throw over*, vacate, walk out on, withdraw, yield; SEE CONCEPT *195*

quit [*v2*] *stop doing something*
abandon, break off, call it a day*, call it quits*, cease, conclude, cut it out*, desist, discontinue, drop, end, get on the wagon*, give notice, give over*, give up, halt, hang it up*, kick over*, kick the habit*, knock off*, leave, leave off*, pack in*, quit cold, resign, retire, secede, sew up*, surcease, suspend, take the cure*, terminate, wind up*, withdraw, wrap up*; SEE CONCEPTS *119,234*

quite [*adv1*] *completely*
absolutely, actually, all, all in all, all told, altogether, considerably, entirely, fully, in all respects, in fact, in reality, in toto, in truth, just, largely, perfectly, positively, precisely, purely, really, thoroughly, totally, truly, utterly, well, wholly, without reservation; SEE CONCEPTS *531,582*

quite [*adv2*] *to a certain extent*
considerably, fairly, far, moderately, more or less, pretty, rather, reasonably, relatively, significantly, somewhat, to some degree, very; SEE CONCEPTS *569,772*

quiver [*n*] *shaking, vibration*
convulsion, flash, glimmer, glitter, oscillation, palpitation, pulsation, shake, shimmer, shiver, shudder, sparkle, spasm, throb, tic, tremble, tremor, twinkle; SEE CONCEPT *152*

quiver [*v*] *shake, vibrate*
agitate, beat, convulse, dither, jitter, oscillate, palpitate, pulsate, pulse, quake, quaver, shiver, shudder, thrill, throb, tremble, tremor, twitter; SEE CONCEPT *152*

quixotic [*adj*] *idealistic*
chimerical, chivalrous, dreaming, dreamy, foolish, impetuous, impractical, impulsive, romantic, starry-eyed, unrealistic, utopian, visionary; SEE CONCEPTS *529,560,582*

quiz [*n*] *questioning, often in an organized academic setting*
blue book*, check, exam, examination, investigation, query, shotgun*, test; SEE CONCEPT *290*

quiz [*v*] *question*
ask, catechize, check, cross-examine, examine, give the third degree*, grill*, inquire, interrogate, investigate, pick one's brains*, pump*, query, test; SEE CONCEPT *48*

quizzical [*adj*] *appearing confused or curious*
amusing, aporetic, arch, bantering, derisive, disbelieving, eccentric, incredulous, inquiring, inquisitive, mocking, odd, probing, quaint, queer, questioning, sardonic, searching, show-me*, skeptical, supercilious, suspicious, teasing, unbelieving, unusual; SEE CONCEPTS 267,485

quota [*n*] *portion allotted to something*
allocation, allotment, allowance, apportionment, assignment, bite, chunk, cut, division, divvy*, end, lot, measure, meed, part, partage, percentage, piece, piece of action*, proportion, quantum, ration, share, slice, split; SEE CONCEPTS 768,835

quotation/quote [*n1*] *repetition of something spoken or written by someone*
citation, citing, cutting, excerpt, passage, quote, recitation, reference, saying, selection; SEE CONCEPTS 274,278

quotation/quote [*n2*] *financial estimate*
bid, bid price, charge, cost, current price, figure, market price, price, price named, published price, quote, rate, stated price, tender; SEE CONCEPTS 274,332,784

quote [*v*] *repeat something spoken, written by another*
adduce, attest, cite, detail, excerpt, extract, instance, name, paraphrase, parrot, proclaim, recall, recite, recollect, reference, refer to, retell; SEE CONCEPTS 79,171

R

rabble [*n*] *mob*
commonality, commoners, crowd, drove, flock, gang, gathering, herd, hoi polloi, horde, lower class, mass, masses, multitude, pack, proletariat, rank and file, riffraff, ring, riot, scum, throng; SEE CONCEPTS 378,417,432

rabid [*adj*] *very angry; maniacal*
berserk, bigoted, bitten, corybantic, crazed*, crazy, delirious, deranged, enthusiastic, extreme, extremist, fanatical, fervent, flipped*, foaming at the mouth*, frantic, freaked out*, frenetic, frenzied, furious, hot*, infuriated, insane, intemperate, intolerant, irrational, keen, mad, mad-dog*, narrow-minded, nutty*, obsessed, overboard, poisoned, radical, raging, revolutionary, sick*, sizzling, smoking*, steamed up*, ultra, ultraist, violent, virulent, wild, zealous; SEE CONCEPT 403

race [*n1*] *pursuit; running, speeding*
chase, clash, clip, competition, contention, contest, course, dash, engagement, event, go, marathon, match, meet, relay, rivalry, run, rush, scurry, sprint, spurt; SEE CONCEPT 363

race [*n2*] *ethnic group*
blood, breed, clan, color, cultural group, culture, family, folk, house, issue, kin, kind, kindred, line, lineage, nation, nationality, offspring, people, progeny, seed, species, stock, strain, tribe, type, variety; SEE CONCEPT 380

race [*n3*] *stream, river*
branch, brook, creek, duct, gill, raceway, rill, rindle, rivulet, run, runnel, sluice, tide; SEE CONCEPT 514

race [*v*] *run, speed in competition*
boil, bolt, bustle, career, chase, compete, contest, course, dart, dash, fling, fly, gallop, haste, hasten, hie, hurry, hustle, lash, outstrip, plunge ahead, post, pursue, rush, scamper, scramble, scud, scuttle, shoot, skim, sprint, spurt, swoop, tear, whisk, wing; SEE CONCEPTS 150,363

racial [*adj*] *ethnic*
ancestral, ethnological, folk, genealogical, genetic, hereditary, lineal, national, phyletic, phylogenetic, tribal; SEE CONCEPT 549

racism [*n*] *prejudice against an ethnic group*
apartheid, bias, bigotry, discrimination, illiberality, one-sidedness, partiality, racialism, sectarianism, segregation, unfairness; SEE CONCEPT 689

racist [*adj*] *bigoted*
anti-Semitic, biased, illiberal, intolerant, narrow-minded, opinionated, partial, prejudiced, sectarian, small-minded, xenophobic; SEE CONCEPTS 403,555

racist [*n*] *bigot*
anti-Semite, black supremacist, chauvinist, diehard, doctrinaire, fanatic, klansperson, opinionated person, prejudiced person, sectarian, segregationist, sexist person, white supremacist, xenophobe; SEE CONCEPTS 359,423

rack [*n*] *frame, framework*
arbor, bed, box, bracket, counter, furniture, holder, ledge, perch, receptacle, shelf, stand, structure, trestle; SEE CONCEPTS 443,479

rack [*v*] *torture; strain*
afflict, agonize, crucify, distress, excruciate, force, harass, harrow, martyr, oppress, pain, persecute, pull, shake, stress, stretch, tear, torment, try, wrench, wring; SEE CONCEPTS 7,19,246

racket [*n1*] *commotion; fight*
agitation, babel, battle, blare, brawl, clamor, clangor, clash, clatter, din, disturbance, fracas, free-for-all*, fuss, hoo-ha*, hubbub*, jangle, noise, outcry, pandemonium, riot, roar, row, ruction, rumpus*, shouting, shuffle, squabble, squall, stir, to-do*, tumult, turbulence, turmoil, uproar, vociferation, wrangle; SEE CONCEPTS 65,106,230

racket [*n2*] *criminal activity*
cheating, confidence game, con game, conspiracy, corruption, crime, dirty pool*, dishonesty, dodge, extortion, fraud, game, graft, illegality, illicit scheme, intrigue, lawlessness, lay, plot, push, scheme, shakedown, squeeze*, swindle, swindling, theft, trick, underworld; SEE CONCEPT 192

rack up [*v*] *achieve, gain*
accomplish, acquire, actualize, attain, carry out, do, earn, get done, obtain, produce, reach, realize, score, wind up; SEE CONCEPT 706

racy [*adj1*] *energetic, zestful*
animated, bright, buoyant, clever, distinctive, entertaining, exciting, exhilarating, fiery, forceful, forcible, gingery, heady, keen, lively, mettlesome, peppery, piquant, playful, poignant, pungent, rich, salty, saucy*, sharp, snappy, sparkling, spicy, spirited, sportive, sprightly, stimulating, strong, tangy, tart, tasty, vigorous, vivacious, witty, zesty; SEE CONCEPTS 401,613

racy [*adj2*] *risqué, vulgar*
bawdy, blue*, broad, erotic, immodest, indecent, indelicate, lewd, lurid, naughty, off-color*, purple*, shady*, smutty*, spicy*, suggestive, wicked; SEE CONCEPTS 267,545

radar [*n*] *radio detecting and ranging*
direction finding, scanning system, sonar, tracking system; SEE CONCEPT *279*

radiance [*n1*] *brightness, luminescence*
brilliance, effulgence, glare, gleam, glitter, glow, incandescence, light, luminosity, luster, resplendence, shine; SEE CONCEPT *620*

radiance [*n2*] *happiness*
delight, gaiety, joy, pleasure, rapture, warmth; SEE CONCEPT *633*

radiant [*adj1*] *bright, luminous*
beaming, brilliant, effulgent, gleaming, glittering, glorious, glowing, incandescent, lambent, lucent, lustrous, radiating, refulgent, resplendent, shining, sparkling, sunny; SEE CONCEPT *617*

radiant [*adj2*] *happy in appearance*
beaming, beatific, blissful, bright, cheerful, cheery, delighted, ecstatic, gay, glad, glowing, joyful, joyous, rapturous; SEE CONCEPT *401*

radiate [*v*] *give off; scatter*
afford, beam, branch out, broadcast, circulate, diffuse, disseminate, distribute, diverge, emanate, emit, expand, give out, gleam, glitter, illumine, irradiate, issue, light up, pour, proliferate, propagate, ramble, ramify, send out, shed, shine, shoot out, spread, spread out, sprinkle, strew, throw out, transmit, yield; SEE CONCEPTS *118,217,620,716*

radical [*adj1*] *fundamental, basic*
basal, bottom, cardinal, constitutional, deep-seated, essential, foundational, inherent, innate, intrinsic, meat-and-potatoes*, native, natural, organic, original, primal, primary, primitive, profound, thoroughgoing, underlying, vital; SEE CONCEPTS *546,549*

radical [*adj2*] *deviating by extremes*
advanced, anarchistic, complete, entire, excessive, extremist, fanatical, far-out*, freethinking, iconoclastic, immoderate, insubordinate, insurgent, insurrectionary, intransigent, lawless, leftist, militant, mutinous, nihilistic, progressive, rabid, rebellious, recalcitrant, recusant, refractory, restive, revolutionary, riotous, seditious, severe, sweeping, thorough, ultra, ultraist, uncompromising, violent, way out*; SEE CONCEPTS *403,529,542*

radical [*n*] *person who advocates significant, often extreme change*
agitator, anarchist, avant-garde, extremist, fanatic, firebrand, freethinker, iconoclast, insurgent, insurrectionist, leftist, left-winger, militant, mutineer, nihilist, nonconformist, objector, pacifist, progressive, rebel, reformer, renegade, revolter, revolutionary, rioter, secessionist, subversive, ultraist; SEE CONCEPT *359*

radio [*n*] *communication by electronic air waves*
AM-FM, CB, Marconi, radionics, radiotelegraph, radiotelegraphy, radiotelephone, radiotelephonics, receiver, shortwave, telegraphy, telephony, transmission, Walkman, wireless; SEE CONCEPT *279*

radius [*n*] *range, sweep*
ambit, boundary, compass, expanse, extension, extent, interval, limit, orbit, purview, reach, semidiameter, space, span, spoke; SEE CONCEPT *651*

raffish [*adj*] *unmindful of social conventions*
bohemian*, careless, casual, coarse, dashing, devil-may-care*, disreputable, fast*, gay, jaunty, rakish, sporty, tasteless, tawdry, unconventional, uncouth, vulgar, wild; SEE CONCEPT *401*

raffle [*n*] *lottery for a prize*
bet, betting, disposition, draw, drawing, flier*, gambling, game of chance, gaming, long odds*, lots*, numbers*, numbers game*, pool, random shot, speculation, stake, sweep, sweepstake, tossup*, wager, wagering; SEE CONCEPTS *363,364*

ragamuffin [*n*] *person who is poor, tattered*
beggar, bum*, gamin, guttersnipe*, hobo, loafer, orphan, scarecrow, street person, tatterdemalion*, tramp, urchin, vagabond, vagrant, waif, wastrel; SEE CONCEPTS *412,423*

rage [*n1*] *extreme anger*
acerbity, acrimony, agitation, animosity, apoplexy, asperity, bitterness, blowup*, bluster, choler, convulsion, dander, eruption, exasperation, excitement, explosion, ferment, ferocity, fireworks, frenzy, furor, fury, gall, heat*, hemorrhage, huff*, hysterics, indignation, ire, irritation, madness, mania, obsession, outburst, paroxysm, passion, rampage, raving, resentment, spasm, spleen, squall, storm, tantrum, temper, umbrage, uproar, upset, vehemence, violence, winging*, wrath; SEE CONCEPTS *410,657*

rage [*n2*] *something in vogue; popular notion*
caprice, chic, conceit, craze, crotchet, cry, dernier cri, enthusiasm, fad, fancy, fashion, freak, furor, happening, hot spot*, in*, in-spot*, in-thing*, last word*, latest*, latest thing*, latest wrinkle*, mania, mode, newest wrinkle*, now*, passion, style, thing*, up to the minute*, vagary, whim; SEE CONCEPTS *388,655*

rage [*v*] *be angry*
be beside oneself*, be furious, be uncontrollable, blow a fuse*, blow one's top*, blow up*, boil over*, bristle, chafe, champ at bit*, erupt, fly off the handle*, foam at the mouth*, fret, fulminate, fume, go berserk, have a fit, have a tantrum, let off steam*, look daggers*, make a fuss over, overflow, rail at, rampage, rant, rant and rave*, rave, roar, scold, scream, seethe, snap at, splutter, steam, storm, surge, tear, throw a fit*, work oneself into sweat*, yell; SEE CONCEPTS *29,410*

ragged [*adj*] *worn-out; in shreds*
badly dressed, badly worn, battered, broken, contemptible, crude, desultory, dilapidated, dingy, disorganized, down at the heel*, fragmented, frayed, frazzled, full of holes*, in holes*, in rags, in tatters*, irregular, jagged, mean, moth-eaten, notched, patched, poor, poorly made, rent, rough, rugged, scraggy, seedy, serrated, shabby, shaggy, shoddy, shredded, tacky*, tattered, tatty*, threadbare, torn, uneven, unfinished, unkempt, unpressed, worse for wear*; SEE CONCEPT *485*

raging [*adj*] *violent; mad*
angry, at boiling point*, bent*, bent out of shape*, beside oneself*, blowing a gasket*, blowing one's top*, blustering, blustery, boiling mad*, boiling over*, enraged, fit to be tied*, frenzied, fuming, furious, going ape*, incensed, infuriated, irate, mad as a hornet*, on the warpath*, rabid*, ranting and raving*, raving, raving mad*, rough, seeing red*, seething, stormy, tempestuous, throwing a fit, turbulent, wild; SEE CONCEPTS *403,542*

raid [*n*] *attack, seizure*
arrest, assault, break-in, bust, capture, descent,

qu
ra

foray, forced entrance, hit-and-run*, incursion, inroad, invasion, irruption, onset, onslaught, pull, reconnaissance, roundup, sally*, shootup*, sortie*, surprise attack, sweep, tipover*; SEE CONCEPTS *86,317*

raid [*v*] *attack, pillage*
assail, assault, blockade, bomb, bombard, breach, break in, charge, descend on, despoil, devastate, fall upon, fire on, forage, foray, harass, harry, heat, inroad, invade, knock off*, knock over*, lean against, lean on, loot, maraud, march on, overrun, pirate, plunder, rake, ransack, rifle, rob, sack, sally, sally forth, shell, slough, spoliate, storm, strafe, strike, sweep, swoop, tip over*, torpedo, waste; SEE CONCEPT *86*

rail [*v*] *criticize harshly*
abuse, attack, bawl out*, berate, blast, castigate, censure, chew out*, complain, fulminate, fume, inveigh, jaw, objurgate, rant, rate, revile, scold, thunder, tongue-lash*, upbraid, vituperate, vociferate, whip; SEE CONCEPT *52*

rail/railing [*n*] *post, pole along an edge*
balustrade, banister, bar, barrier, fence, paling, rails, rest, siding; SEE CONCEPTS *443,479*

railroad [*n*] *train line*
elevated railway, line, metro, monorail, rail line, railway, streetcar line, subway, tracks, trolley line, tube, underground railway; SEE CONCEPTS *155,503*

rain [*n*] *downpour of water or other substance*
cat-and-dog weather*, cloudburst, condensation, deluge, drencher, drizzle, fall, flood, flurry, hail, heavy dew, liquid sunshine*, mist, monsoon, pour, pouring, precip*, precipitation, raindrops, rainfall, rainstorm, sheets, shower, showers, sleet, spate, spit, sprinkle, sprinkling, stream, sun shower*, torrent, volley*, wet stuff*, window washer*; SEE CONCEPT *526*

rain [*v*] *drop water or other substance*
bestow, bucket, come down in buckets*, deposit, drizzle, fall, hail, lavish, mist, patter, pour, shower, sleet, sprinkle, storm; SEE CONCEPT *526*

rainbow [*n*] *color spectrum*
arc, band of color, bow, crescent, curve, prism, variegation; SEE CONCEPT *436*

raise [*n*] *increase in salary or position*
accession, accretion, addition, advance, augmentation, boost, bump, hike, hold-up*, increment, jump, jump-up*, leg*, leg-up*, move-up*, promotion, raising, rise, step-up*; SEE CONCEPTS *344,351,763*

raise [*v1*] *lift; build from the ground*
boost, bring up, construct, elevate, erect, establish, exalt, heave, hoist, hold up, lever, lift, lift up, mount, move up, place up, promote, pry, pull up, put on its end, put up, rear, run up, set up, set upright, shove, stand up, take up, throw up, upcast, upheave, uplift, upraise, uprear; SEE CONCEPTS *168,196*

raise [*v2*] *increase, augment*
advance, aggravate, amplify, assemble, boost, build up, collect, congregate, congress, dignify, enhance, enlarge, escalate, exaggerate, exalt, fetch up, forgather, form, gather, get, goose*, goose up*, heighten, hike, hike up*, honor, inflate, intensify, jack up, jump, jump up, levy, look up, magnify, mass, mobilize, mushroom*, muster, obtain, perk up, pick up, promote, put up, pyramid, rally, recruit, reinforce, rendezvous,

run up*, send through the roof*, shoot up, snowball*, strengthen, up; SEE CONCEPTS *236,244,245*

raise [*v3*] *start up, motivate; introduce*
abet, activate, advance, arouse, awaken, bring up, broach, cause, evoke, excite, foment, foster, incite, instigate, kindle, moot, motivate, provoke, put forward, resurrect, set, set on, stir up, suggest, whip up; SEE CONCEPTS *75,221*

raise [*v4*] *nurture, care for*
breed, bring up, cultivate, develop, drag up, fetch up, foster, group, grow, nourish, nurse, plant, produce, propagate, provide, rear, sow, suckle, support, train, wean; SEE CONCEPTS *253,257,295*

raison d'etre [*n*] *reason for being*
basis, justification for existing, rationale, reason for existing, reason why; SEE CONCEPT *661*

rake [*v*] *scrape up, hoe*
break up, clean up, clear, clear up, collect, comb, enfilade, examine, finecomb, fine-tooth-comb*, gather, grade, graze, grub, harrow, hunt, ransack, rasp, remove, rummage, scan, scour, scrape, scratch, scrutinize, search, smooth, sweep, weed; SEE CONCEPTS *109,165,178,216*

rakish [*adj*] *charming and immoral*
abandoned, chic, dashing, debauched, depraved, devil-may-care*, dissipated, dissolute, fashionable, fast*, flashy, gay, jaunty, lecherous, licentious, loose*, natty, prodigal, profligate, raffish, saucy, sinful, smart, sporty, wanton, wild; SEE CONCEPTS *401,545*

rally [*n1*] *celebratory meeting*
assemblage, assembly, celebration, clambake*, convention, convocation, get-together, mass meeting, meet, pep rally, pow-wow*, session; SEE CONCEPTS *377,386*

rally [*n2*] *turn for the better*
comeback, improvement, recovery, recuperation, renewal, resurgence, revival, turning point; SEE CONCEPT *700*

rally [*v1*] *reorganize, unite*
arouse, assemble, awaken, bestir, bond together, bring together, bring to order, call to arms*, challenge, charge, collect, come about, come together, come to order, convene, counterattack, encourage, fire, gather, get together, inspirit, kindle, marshal, mobilize, muster, organize, reassemble, redouble, reform, refresh, regroup, rejuvenate, renew, restore, resurrect, resuscitate, revive, round up, rouse, summon, surge, urge, wake, waken, whet, wreak havoc*; SEE CONCEPTS *7,22,117,320*

rally [*v2*] *revive; take a turn for the better*
bounce back, brace up, come along, come around, come from behind, enliven, get act together*, get back in shape*, get better, get second wind*, grow stronger, improve, invigorate, make a comeback, perk up, pick up, pull through, recover, recuperate, refresh, regain strength, shape up, snap out of it, surge, turn around, turn things around*; SEE CONCEPT *700*

ram [*v*] *bang into; pack forcibly*
beat, butt, collide with, cram, crash, crowd, dash, dig, drive, drum, force, hammer, hit, hook, impact, jack, jam-pack, pack, plunge, poke, pound, run, run into, sink, slam, smash, stab, stick, strike, strike head-on, stuff, tamp, thrust, wedge; SEE CONCEPTS *189,208,209*

ramble [*n*] *aimless walk*
constitutional, excursion, hike, perambulation,

peregrination, roaming, roving, saunter, stroll, tour, traipse, trip, turn; SEE CONCEPTS *151,224*

ramble [*v1*] *wander about; travel aimlessly*
amble, bat around*, be all over the map*, branch off, clamber, climb, cruise, depart, digress, divagate, diverge, drift, excurse, extend, fork, gad, gallivant, get sidetracked*, knock about*, knock around*, meander, perambulate, percolate, peregrinate, promenade, range, roam, rove, saunter, scramble, snake, sprangle, sprawl, spread, spread-eagle, straddle, straggle, stray, stroll, trail, traipse, turn, twist, walk, wind, zigzag; SEE CONCEPTS *151,154,581,692*

ramble [*v2*] *talk aimlessly, endlessly*
amplify, babble, beat around bush*, be diffuse, blather, chatter, depart, descant, digress, divagate, diverge, drift, drivel, dwell on, enlarge, excurse, expatiate, get off the subject*, go astray, go off on tangent*, go on and on*, gossip, harp on, lose the thread*, maunder, meander, prose, protract, rant and rave*, rattle on*, stray, talk nonsense, talk off top of head*, talk randomly, wander; SEE CONCEPT *51*

rambling [*adj1*] *disconnected, wordy*
circuitous, confused, desultory, diffuse, digressive, discursive, disjointed, incoherent, incongruous, irregular, long-winded, periphrastic, prolix; SEE CONCEPT *267*

rambling [*adj2*] *sprawling, spread out*
at length, covering, gangling, here and there, irregular, random, scattered, spreading, straggling, strewn, trailing, unplanned; SEE CONCEPTS *485,772*

rambunctious [*adj*] *loud, energetic*
boisterous, noisy, raucous, rough, rowdy, rude, termagant, tumultous/tumultuous, turbulent, unruly; SEE CONCEPT *542*

ramification [*n*] *consequence, development*
bifurcation, branch, branching, breaking, complication, consequence, divarication, division, excrescence, extension, forking, offshoot, outgrowth, partition, radiation, result, sequel, subdividing, subdivision, upshot; SEE CONCEPTS *98,230,824*

ramp [*n*] *incline*
access, adit, grade, gradient, hill, inclination, inclined plane, rise, slope; SEE CONCEPTS *443,757*

rampage [*n*] *storm, violence*
binge, blowup, boiling point*, destruction, disturbance, ferment, fling, frenzy, fury, mad*, more heat than light*, orgy, rage, ruckus, splurge, spree, tear, tempest, tumult, turmoil, uproar, wingding; SEE CONCEPT *86*

rampage [*v*] *go crazy; storm*
go berserk, rage, run amuck, run riot, run wild, tear; SEE CONCEPTS *86,384*

rampant [*adj*] *uncontrolled, out of hand*
aggressive, blustering, boisterous, clamorous, dominant, epidemic, exceeding bounds, excessive, extravagant, exuberant, fanatical, flagrant, furious, growing, impetuous, impulsive, luxuriant, on the rampage, out of control, outrageous, pandemic, predominant, prevalent, profuse, raging, rampaging, rank, rife, riotous, spreading, tumultous/tumultuous, turbulent, unbridled, unchecked, uncontrollable, ungovernable, unrestrained, unruly, vehement, violent, wanton, widespread, wild; SEE CONCEPTS *544,554,772*

rampart [*n*] *fortification, stronghold*
barricade, barrier, bastion, breastwork, bulwark, defense, earthwork, elevation, embankment, fence, fort, guard, hill, mound, parapet, protection, ridge, security, support, vallation, wall; SEE CONCEPTS *321,439,509*

ramshackle [*adj*] *falling apart; in poor condition*
broken-down, crumbling, decrepit, derelict, dilapidated, flimsy, jerry-built*, rickety, shabby, shaky, tottering, tumble-down, unfirm, unsafe, unsteady; SEE CONCEPTS *485,488*

ranch [*n*] *farm*
acreage, cattle farm, dairy farm, estate, farmstead, hacienda, homestead, land, plantation; SEE CONCEPTS *258,449,517*

rancid [*adj*] *rotten, strong-smelling*
bad, carious, contaminated, curdled, decomposing, disagreeable, disgusting, evil-smelling, feculent, fetid, foul, frowzy, fusty, gamy, high, impure, loathsome, malodorous, moldy, musty, nasty, nidorous, noisome, noxious, off, offensive, olid, polluted, putrefactive, putrefied, putrescent, putrid, rank, reeky, repulsive, sharp, smelly, sour, soured, stale, stinking, strong, tainted, turned, unhealthy, whiffy; SEE CONCEPTS *462,570,598,613*

rancor [*n*] *bitterness, hatefulness*
acerbity, acrimony, animosity, animus, antagonism, antipathy, aversion, bad blood*, bile*, dudgeon, enmity, grudge, hardness of heart*, harshness, hate, hatred, hostility, ill feeling, ill will, malevolence, malice, malignity, mordacity, pique, resentfulness, resentment, retaliation, revengefulness, ruthlessness, spite, spitefulness, spleen, umbrage, uncharitableness, unfriendliness, variance, vengeance, vengefulness, venom, vindictiveness, virulence; SEE CONCEPTS *29,410,633*

random [*adj*] *haphazard, chance*
accidental, adventitious, aimless, arbitrary, casual, contingent, designless, desultory, driftless, fluky, fortuitous, hit-or-miss*, incidental, indiscriminate, irregular, objectless, odd, promiscuous, purposeless, slapdash*, spot, stray, unaimed, unconsidered, unplanned, unpremeditated; SEE CONCEPTS *535,548,557*

range [*n1*] *sphere, distance, extent*
ambit, amplitude, area, bounds, circle, compass, confines, diapason, dimension, dimensions, domain, earshot*, elbowroom*, expanse, extension, extensity, field, gamut, hearing, ken, latitude, leeway, length, limits, magnitude, matter, neighborhood, orbit, order, panorama, parameters, play, province, purview, radius, reach, realm, run, run of, scope, space, span, spectrum, sphere, spread, stretch, sweep, swing, territory, tune, vicinity, width; SEE CONCEPTS *651,743,745,756,761,788*

range [*n2*] *order, series*
assortment, chain, class, collection, file, gamut, kind, line, lot, rank, row, selection, sequence, sort, string, tier, variety; SEE CONCEPTS *727,769*

range [*v1*] *order, categorize*
align, allineate, arrange, array, assort, bias, bracket, catalogue, categorize, class, classify, dispose, draw up, file, grade, group, incline, line, line up, pigeonhole*, predispose, rank; SEE CONCEPTS *84,158*

range [*v2*] *wander, roam*
circumambulate, cover, cross, cruise, drift, encompass, explore, float, follow one's nose*, gallivant, globe-trot*, hit the road*, hit the trail*,

ra
ra

make circuit, meander, pass over, ply, prowl, ramble, reach, reconnoiter, rove, scour, search, spread, straggle, stray, stroll, sweep, traipse, tramp, travel, traverse, trek; SEE CONCEPTS *151,224*

range [*v3*] *extend; change within limits*
differ, diverge from, fluctuate, go, reach, run, stretch, vary, vary between; SEE CONCEPT *697*

rangy [*adj*] *long and lean*
gangling, gangly, lanky, leggy, long-legged, long-limbed, reedy, skinny, spindling, spindly, thin, weedy; SEE CONCEPTS *491,779*

rank [*adj1*] *stinking, foul*
bad, dank, disagreeable, disgusting, evil-smelling, feculent, fetid, funky*, fusty*, gamy*, graveolent, gross*, high, humid, loathsome, mephitic, moldy, musty, nasty, nauseating, noisome, noxious, obnoxious, off, offensive, olid, pungent, putrescent, putrid, rancid, reeking, repulsive, revolting, smelly, sour, stale, strong, strong-smelling, tainted, turned; SEE CONCEPT *598*

rank [*adj2*] *abundant, luxurious*
coarse, dense, excessive, extreme, exuberant, fertile, flourishing, fructiferous, grown, high-growing, junglelike, lavish, lush, luxuriant, over-abundant, overgrown, productive, profuse, prolific, rampant, rich, semitropical, tropical, vigorous, wild; SEE CONCEPT *485*

rank [*adj3*] *utter, absolute*
arrant, blatant, capital, complete, conspicuous, consummate, downright, egregious, excessive, extravagant, flagrant, glaring, gross, noticeable, outright, outstanding, perfect, positive, rampant, sheer, thorough, total, undisguised, unmitigated; SEE CONCEPTS *531,535*

rank [*adj4*] *obscene, vulgar*
abusive, atrocious, coarse, crass, dirty, filthy, foul, gross, indecent, nasty, outrageous, raunchy, scurrilous, shocking, smutty, wicked; SEE CONCEPT *545*

rank [*n1*] *standing in a system, often a social one*
ancestry, authority, birth, blood, cachet, capacity, caste, circumstance, class, classification, condition, consequence, degree, dignity, distinction, division, echelon, estate, esteem, family, footing, grade, hierarchy, level, nobility, note, order, paramountcy, parentage, pecking order, pedigree, place, position, primacy, privilege, quality, reputation, seniority, situation, slot, sort, sovereignty, sphere, state, station, stature, status, stock, stratum, supremacy, type; SEE CONCEPTS *296,378,388,744*

rank [*n2*] *column, tier of individuals*
echelon, file, formation, group, hierarchy, line, queue, range, row, series, string; SEE CONCEPT *727*

rank [*v1*] *line up; classify in system*
align, arrange, array, assign, assort, button down*, class, dispose, establish, estimate, evaluate, fix*, give precedence, grade, include, judge, list, locate, marshal, order, peg, pigeonhole*, place, place in formation, position, put, put away, put down as, put down for, put in line, range, rate, regard, settle, size up, sort, tab, typecast, valuate, value; SEE CONCEPTS *37,84,158*

rank [*v2*] *be worthwhile; have supremacy*
antecede, be classed, belong, be worth, come first, count among, forerun, go ahead of, go before, have the advantage, outrank, precede, stand, take the lead; SEE CONCEPTS *388,671*

rankle [*v*] *annoy, irritate*
aggravate, anger, bother, chafe, embitter, exasperate, fester, fret, gall, get one's goat*, harass, hurt, inflame, irk, irritate, mortify, nettle, obsess, pain, pester, plague, rile, torment, vex; SEE CONCEPTS *7,14,19*

ransack [*v*] *turn inside out in search; ravage*
appropriate, comb, despoil, explore, ferret, filch, go over with a fine-tooth comb*, go through, gut*, hunt, investigate, lay waste, leave no stone unturned*, lift, look all over for*, look high and low*, look into, loot, make off with*, maraud, overhaul, peer, pilfer, pillage, pinch, plunder, poach, probe, pry, purloin, raid, rake, rape, ravish, rifle, rob, rummage, rustle, sack, scan, scour, scrutinize, search, seek, seize, shake down*, sound, spoil, spy, steal, strip, take away, thieve; SEE CONCEPTS *103,139,142,216*

ransom [*n*] *blackmail money paid for return of possession or person*
bribe, compensation, deliverance, expiation, liberation money, payment, payoff, price, redemption, release, rescue; SEE CONCEPT *344*

ransom [*v*] *pay blackmail money for return of possession or person*
buy freedom of, buy out, deliver, emancipate, extricate, free, liberate, manumit, obtain release of, pay for release of, recover, redeem, regain, release, reprise, repurchase, rescue, save, set free, unchain, unfetter; SEE CONCEPTS *127,131,341*

rant [*n*] *yelling, raving*
bluster, bombast, diatribe, fustian, harangue, oration, philippic, rhapsody, rhetoric, rodomontade, tirade, vociferation; SEE CONCEPTS *44,49,52*

rant [*v*] *yell, rave*
bellow, bloviate, blow one's top*, bluster, carry on, clamor, cry, declaim, fume, harangue, mouth, objurgate, orate, perorate, rage, rail, roar, scold, shout, sizzle*, soapbox*, sound off*, spiel*, spout*, storm*, stump*, take on*, vociferate; SEE CONCEPTS *44,49,52*

rap [*n1/v1*] *hit quickly and lightly*
beat, blow, conk, crack, knock, lick, pat, strike, swat, swipe, tap, whack; SEE CONCEPT *189*

rap [*n2*] *conversation*
causerie, chat, chin*, colloquy, confabulation, conference, deliberation, dialogue, discourse, discussion, prose, talk, ventilation, yarn; SEE CONCEPTS *56,266*

rap [*n3*] *blame; criticism*
admonishment, admonition, censure, chiding, flak, knock, pan*, punishment, rebuke, reprimand, reproach, reproof, responsibility, sentence, swipe; SEE CONCEPTS *52,123,317*

rap [*v2*] *talk casually; speak abruptly*
babble, bark, chat, chatter, chitchat, confabulate, converse, discourse, jabber, palaver, run off at the mouth*, spit, talk; SEE CONCEPTS *56,266*

rap [*v3*] *criticize*
blame, castigate, censure, condemn, denounce, denunciate, knock*, pan*, reprehend, reprimand, reprobate, scold, skin, tick off*; SEE CONCEPT *52*

rapacious [*adj*] *plundering*
avaricious, ferocious, furious, greedy, marauding, murderous, predatory, preying, ravening, ravenous, savage, voracious; SEE CONCEPTS *326,403,406,542*

rape [n] *defilement; a forced sexual assault*
abduction, abuse, criminal attack, depredation, despoilment, despoliation, forcible violation, maltreatment, molestation, pillage, plunder, plundering, rapine, spoliation, statutory offense, violation; SEE CONCEPTS *192,375*

rape [v] *sexual assault by force; act of plunder*
abuse, attack, betray, compromise, corrupt, deceive, despoil, force, loot, molest, pillage, plunder, ransack, ruin, sack, seize, spoliate, violate; SEE CONCEPTS *192,375*

rapid [adj] *very quick*
accelerated, active, agile, breakneck, brisk, double time, expeditious, expeditive, express, fast, fleet, fleet of foot*, flying, hasty, hurried, in nothing flat*, light-footed*, like a house on fire*, lively, mercurial, nimble, on the double*, precipitate, prompt, quick as a wink*, quickened, ready, really rolling*, screaming*, speedy, spry, swift, winged; SEE CONCEPTS *541,588,799*

rapidity [n] *quickness*
acceleration, alacrity, bat, briskness, celerity, dispatch, expedition, fleetness, gait, haste, hurry, pace, precipitateness, promptitude, promptness, rapidness, rush, speed, speediness, swiftness, velocity; SEE CONCEPTS *755,805*

rapidly [adv] *very quickly*
at speed, briskly, expeditiously, fast, flat out*, full tilt*, hastily, hurriedly, immediately, in a hurry, in a rush, in haste, lickety-split*, like a shot*, posthaste, precipitately, promptly, speedily, swiftly, with dispatch; SEE CONCEPTS *544,588,799*

rapport [n] *understanding between people*
affinity, agreement, bond, compatibility, concord, cotton, empathy, good vibes*, good vibrations, groove, harmony, hitting it off*, interrelationship, link, relationship, same wavelength*, simpatico*, soul, sympathy, the groove*, togetherness, unity; SEE CONCEPT *388*

rapprochement [n] *restoration of harmony*
agreement, cordiality, detente, friendliness, friendship, harmonization, harmony, reconcilement, reconciliation, reunion, softening; SEE CONCEPTS *384,388*

rapt [adj] *absorbed, fascinated*
absent, absent-minded, abstracted, beguiled, bewitched, blissful, busy, captivated, carried away*, caught up in*, charmed, daydreaming, deep*, delighted, dreaming, ecstatic, employed, enamored, engaged, engrossed, enraptured, enthralled, entranced, gripped, happy, held, hung up*, hypnotized, immersed, inattentive, intent, involved, lost, oblivious, occupied, overwhelmed, preoccupied, rapturous, ravished, spellbound, taken*, transported, unconscious, wrapped*, wrapped up*; SEE CONCEPT *403*

rapture [n] *extreme happiness and delight in something*
at-oneness*, beatitude, bliss, buoyancy, cheer, cloud nine*, communion, contentment, cool*, delectation, ecstasy, elation, elysium, enchantment, enjoyment, enthusiasm, euphoria, exaltation, exhilaration, felicity, gaiety, gladness, glory, good spirits, gratification, heaven, inspiration, joy, jubilation, nirvana, paradise, passion, pleasure, ravishment, rhapsody, satisfaction, seventh heaven*, spell, transport, well-being; SEE CONCEPTS *32,410*

rare [adj1] *exceptional, infrequent*
attenuate, attenuated, deficient, extraordinary, few, few and far between*, flimsy, inconceivable, isolated, light, limited, occasional, out of the ordinary, rarefied, recherché, scanty, scarce, scattered, seldom, semioccasional, short, singular, sparse, sporadic, strange, subtile, subtle, tenuous, thin, uncommon, unfrequent, unheard of, unimaginable, unique, unlikely, unthinkable, unusual, unwonted; SEE CONCEPTS *530,576*

rare [adj2] *precious, excellent*
admirable, choice, dainty, delicate, elegant, exquisite, extreme, fine, great, incomparable, invaluable, matchless, peerless, priceless, recherché, rich, select, superb, superlative, unique; SEE CONCEPT *574*

rare [adj3] *not fully cooked*
bloody, half-cooked, half-raw, moderately done, nearly raw, not done, rarely done, red, undercooked, underdone; SEE CONCEPT *462*

rarely [adv] *not often; exceptionally*
almost never, barely, extra, extraordinarily, extremely, finely, hardly, hardly ever, infrequently, little, notably, now and then, once in a while, once in blue moon*, on rare occasions, remarkably, scarcely ever, seldom, singularly, uncommon, uncommonly, unfrequently, unoften, unusually; SEE CONCEPTS *530,541*

rascal [n] *person who is unprincipled, does not work hard*
beggar, blackguard, black sheep*, bully, bum, cad, cardsharp*, charlatan, cheat, delinquent, devil, disgrace, felon, fraud, good-for-nothing*, grafter, hooligan*, hypocrite, idler, imp, liar, loafer, mischief-maker, miscreant, opportunist, pretender, prodigal, profligate, recreant, reprobate, robber, rowdy, ruffian, scamp, scoundrel, sinner, skunk*, sneak*, swindler, tough*, tramp, trickster, varmint*, villain, wastrel, wretch; SEE CONCEPT *412*

rash [adj] *careless, impulsive*
adventurous, audacious, bold, brash, daring, determined, devil-may-care*, fiery, foolhardy, frenzied, furious, harebrained, hasty, headlong, headstrong, heedless, hotheaded, ill-advised, ill-considered, impetuous, imprudent, incautious, indiscreet, injudicious, insuppressible, irrational, jumping to conclusions*, madcap, overhasty, passionate, precipitant, precipitate, premature, reckless, thoughtless, unguarded, unthinking, unwary, venturesome, venturous, wild; SEE CONCEPT *401*

rash [n] *outbreak of disease or condition*
breakout, epidemic, eruption, flood, hives, pandemic, plague, series, spate, succession, wave; SEE CONCEPTS *230,306*

rasp [v] *grind, rub*
abrade, bray, excoriate, file, grate, irk, irritate, jar, pound, raze, rub, sand, scour, scrape, scratch, vex, wear; SEE CONCEPTS *7,19,186,215*

raspy [adj] *rough*
cracked, croaky, dry, grating, gravelly, gruff, harsh, hoarse, husky, scratchy, thick, throaty; SEE CONCEPT *594*

rat [n] *informer*
backstabber, betrayer, blabbermouth*, canary*, deep throat*, double-crosser, fink, informant, sneak, snitch, source, squealer, stoolie, stool pigeon*, tattler, tattletale, turncoat, whistleblower; SEE CONCEPTS *348,354,423*

ra
ra

rate [*n1*] *ratio, proportion*
amount, comparison, degree, estimate, percentage, progression, quota, relation, relationship, relative, scale, standard, weight; SEE CONCEPT *768*

rate [*n2*] *fee charged for service, privilege, goods*
allowance, charge, cost, dues, duty, estimate, figure, hire, price, price tag, quotation, tab, tariff, tax, toll, valuation; SEE CONCEPTS *329,766*

rate [*n3*] *speed, pace*
clip, dash, flow, gait, gallop, hop, measure, motion, movement, pace, spurt, tempo, time, tread, velocity; SEE CONCEPT *755*

rate [*v1*] *judge, classify*
adjudge, admire, appraise, apprise, assay, assess, button down*, calculate, class, consider, count, deem, determine, esteem, estimate, evaluate, fix, grade, guess at, measure, peg, pigeonhole*, price, put away, put down as*, put down for*, rank, reckon, redline*, regard, relate to standard, respect, score, set at, size up*, stand in with, survey, tab*, tag, take one's measure, think highly of, typecast*, valuate, value, weigh; SEE CONCEPTS *12,37*

rate [*v2*] *be entitled to*
be accepted, be favorite, be welcome, be worthy, deserve, earn, merit, prosper, succeed, triumph; SEE CONCEPTS *129,376,388*

rather [*adv1*] *moderately*
a bit, a little, averagely, comparatively, enough, fairly, in a certain degree, kind of, more or less, passably, pretty, quite, ratherish, reasonably, relatively, slightly, some, something, somewhat, sort of, so-so*, tolerably, to some degree, to some extent; SEE CONCEPTS *544,548*

rather [*adv2*] *significantly*
a good bit, considerably, noticeably, quite, somewhat, very, well; SEE CONCEPTS *544,772*

rather [*adv3*] *preferably; instead*
alternately, alternatively, as a matter of choice, by choice, by preference, first, in lieu of, in preference, just as soon, more readily, more willingly, much sooner, sooner, willingly; SEE CONCEPT *529*

ratify [*v*] *affirm, authorize*
accredit, approve, authenticate, bear out, bind, bless, certify, commission, confirm, consent, corroborate, endorse, establish, give stamp of approval*, go for*, license, okay*, rubber stamp*, sanction, sign, substantiate, uphold, validate; SEE CONCEPTS *50,88*

rating [*n*] *grade*
appraisal, assessment, category, class, classification, degree, judgment, level, mark, order, rank, score, standard, tier, valuation; SEE CONCEPTS *286,378,665,727,744*

ratio [*n*] *percentage, relation of part to whole*
arrangement, correlation, correspondence, equation, fraction, proportion, proportionality, quota, quotient, rate, relationship, scale; SEE CONCEPT *768*

ration [*n*] *allotment of limited supply*
allowance, apportionment, assignment, bit, consignment, cut, distribution, division, dole, drag, food, helping, measure, meed, part, piece of action*, portion, provender, provision, quantum, quota, share, store, supply; SEE CONCEPTS *457,835*

ration [*v*] *divide something into portions*
allocate, allot, apportion, assign, budget, conserve, control, deal, distribute, divvy*, divvy up*, dole, give out, issue, limit, measure out, mete, mete out, parcel, parcel out, proportion, prorate, quota, restrict, save, share; SEE CONCEPTS *98,140*

rational [*adj*] *realistic; of sound mind*
all there*, analytical, balanced, calm, cerebral, circumspect, cognitive, collected, cool*, deductive, deliberate, discerning, discriminating, enlightened, far-sighted, impartial, intellectual, intelligent, judicious, knowing, levelheaded, logical, lucid, normal, objective, perspicacious, philosophic, prudent, ratiocinative, reasonable, reasoning, reflective, sagacious, sane, sensible, sober, sound, stable, synthetic, thinking, thoughtful, together, well-advised, wise; SEE CONCEPT *402*

rationale [*n*] *logic for belief, action*
account, excuse, explanation, exposition, grounds, hypothesis, justification, motivation, motive, philosophy, principle, raison d'être, rationalization, reason, reasons, song and dance*, sour grapes*, story*, the big idea*, theory, the whole idea*, whatfor*, why and wherefore*, whyfor*; SEE CONCEPT *661*

rationalize [*v*] *make excuse; justify*
account for, apply logic, cop a plea*, cop out*, deliberate, elucidate, excise, excuse, explain away, extenuate, give alibi*, intellectualize, justify, make allowance, reason, reason out, reconcile, resolve, think, think through, vindicate; SEE CONCEPT *57*

rattle [*v1*] *bang, jiggle*
bicker, bounce, clack, clatter, drum, jangle, jar, jolt, jounce, knock, shake, shatter, sound, vibrate; SEE CONCEPTS *65,152*

rattle [*v2*] *talk aimlessly, endlessly*
babble, cackle, chat, chatter, clack, gab, gabble, gush, jabber, jaw, list, prate, prattle, reel off, run on, run through, yak; SEE CONCEPT *51*

rattle [*v3*] *disconcert, upset someone*
abash, addle, bewilder, bother, confound, confuse, discombobulate, discomfit, discompose, discountenance, distract, disturb, embarrass, faze, flummox, frighten, get to*, muddle, nonplus, perplex, perturb, psych out*, put off, put out, put out of countenance, rattle one's cage*, scare, shake, throw, unnerve; SEE CONCEPT *16*

raucous [*adj1*] *noisy, rough*
absonant, acute, atonal, blaring, blatant, braying, brusque, cacophonous, discordant, dissonant, dry, ear-piercing, grating, grinding, gruff, harsh, hoarse, husky, inharmonious, jarring, loud, piercing, rasping, sharp, squawking, stertorous, strident, thick, unharmonious, unmusical; SEE CONCEPTS *592,594*

raucous [*adj2*] *rowdy*
boisterous, disorderly, intemperate, rambunctious, tumultous/tumultuous, turbulent, unruly; SEE CONCEPT *401*

raunchy [*adj*] *lewd, obscene*
bawdy, dirty, erotic, filthy*, foul-mouthed, gross*, hard-core*, improper, in bad taste, lascivious, lecherous, lustful, naughty, off-color*, pornographic, racy*, risqué, sexually explicit, smutty, suggestive, taboo, vulgar, wicked, X-rated*; SEE CONCEPTS *372,542,545*

ravage [v] *destroy, ransack*
annihilate, break up, capture, consume, cream*, crush, damage, demolish, desecrate, desolate, despoil, devastate, dismantle, disorganize, disrupt, exterminate, extinguish, forage, foray, gut, harry, impair, lay waste, leave in ruins, loot, overrun, overthrow, overwhelm, pillage, pirate, plunder, prey, prostrate, pull down, raid, rape, raze, rob, ruin, sack, seize, shatter, sink, smash, spoil, spoliate, stamp out, strip, sweep away, total*, trample, trash, waste, wreak havoc, wreck, wrest; SEE CONCEPTS *86,252*

rave [v1] *talk endlessly*
babble, be delirious, bloviate, blow one's top*, carry on*, come unglued*, declaim, flip one's lid*, freak out*, fume, gabble, go ape*, go bananas*, go crazy, go mad, harangue, jabber, make a to-do*, mouth, orate, perorate, prate, prattle, rage, rail, rant, rattle on, roar, run amuck*, splutter, storm, talk wildly, thunder, wander; SEE CONCEPTS *51,54*

rave [v2] *be very enthusiastic*
be delighted, be excited, be mad about, be wild about, bubble*, carry on about*, cry up*, effervesce, enthuse, fall all over*, go on about*, gush, make a to-do*, praise, rhapsodize; SEE CONCEPTS *49,410*

ravel [v] *come apart; unwind*
disentangle, free, loosen, make plain, smooth out, unbraid, unravel, unsnarl, untangle, untwine, untwist, unweave, unwind, weave out; SEE CONCEPTS *250,469*

ravenous [adj] *very hungry; desirous*
avaricious, could eat a horse*, covetous, devouring, edacious, empty, famished, ferocious, gluttonous, grasping, greedy, insatiable, insatiate, omnivorous, predatory, rapacious, ravening, starved, starved to death*, starving, voracious, wolfish; SEE CONCEPT *406*

ravine [n] *gap in earth's surface*
abyss, arroyo, break, canyon, chasm, clove, coulee, crevasse, crevice, cut, defile, ditch, fissure, flume, gorge, gulch, gulf, gully, notch, pass, valley, wash; SEE CONCEPTS *509,513*

ravish [v1] *enchant*
allure, attract, bewitch, captivate, charm, delight, draw, enrapture, enthrall, entrance, fascinate, hold, hypnotize, magnetize, mesmerize, overjoy, please, spellbind, trance, transport; SEE CONCEPT *11*

ravish [v2] *sexually assault*
abduct, abuse, force, rape, violate; SEE CONCEPTS *192,375*

ravishing [adj] *attractive*
adorable, alluring, appealing, beautiful, bewitching, captivating, charming, dazzling, enchanting, enticing, glamorous, good-looking, gorgeous, handsome, inviting, lovely, luring, pleasing, pretty, radiant, seductive, stunning, tantalizing; SEE CONCEPTS *529,579*

raw [adj1] *not cooked, prepared*
basic, bloody, callow, coarse, crude, fibrous, fresh, green, hard, immature, impure, native, natural, organic, rough, roughhewn, rude, unbaked, uncooked, undercooked, underdone, undressed, unfashioned, unformed, unfried, ungraded, unpasteurized, unprepared, unprocessed, unrefined, unripe, unsorted, unstained, untreated; SEE CONCEPTS *462,485*

raw [adj2] *exposed, tender, referring to skin*
abraded, au naturel, blistered, bruised, chafed, cut, dressed, galled, grazed, naked, nude, open, pared, peeled, scraped, scratched, sensitive, skinned, sore, unclad, unclothed, uncovered, wounded; SEE CONCEPTS *406,485*

raw [adj3] *inexperienced*
callow, fresh, green, ignorant, immature, inexperienced, new, unconversant, undisciplined, unpracticed, unseasoned, unskilled, untaught, untrained, untried, unversed, young; SEE CONCEPT *527*

raw [adj4] *vulgar, nasty*
coarse, crass, crude, dirty, filthy, foul, gross, indecent, inelegant, low, mean, obscene, pornographic, rank, rough, rude, smutty, uncouth, unrefined, unscrupulous; SEE CONCEPTS *372,545*

raw [adj5] *harsh, unpleasant, referring to weather*
biting, bitter, bleak, breezy, chill, chilly, cold, damp, freezing, piercing, wet, wind-swept, windy; SEE CONCEPT *525*

ray [n] *beam; indication*
bar, blaze, blink, emanation, flash, flicker, gleam, glimmer, glint, glitter, hint, incandescence, irradiation, light, moonbeam, patch, pencil, radiance, radiation, scintilla, shaft, shine, spark, sparkle, streak, stream, sunbeam, trace, wave; SEE CONCEPTS *624,628*

raze [v] *flatten, knock down; wipe out*
batter, blow down, bomb, break down, bulldoze, capsize, cast down, crash, decimate, delete, demolish, destroy, dynamite, efface, erase, expunge, extinguish, extirpate, fell, level, mow down, obliterate, overthrow, overturn, pull down, reduce, remove, rub out*, ruin, scatter, scratch out, smash, spill, strike out, subvert, tear down, tear up, throw down, topple, total, unbuild, undo, unmake, upset, wipe out, wrack, wreck, zap*; SEE CONCEPT *252*

reach [n] *extent, range; stretch*
ability, ambit, capacity, command, compass, distance, extension, gamut, grasp, horizon, influence, jurisdiction, ken, latitude, magnitude, mastery, orbit, play, power, purview, radius, scope, spread, sweep, swing; SEE CONCEPTS *651,756*

reach [v1] *arrive at*
arrive, attain, catch up to, check in, clock in*, come, come to, enter, gain on*, get as far as, get in, get to, hit, hit town*, land, make, make it, make the scene*, overtake, ring in*, roll in, show, show up, sign in, turn up, wind up at; SEE CONCEPT *159*

reach [v2] *stretch to; touch*
approach, attain, buck, carry to, come at, come up to, contact, continue to, encompass, end, equal, extend to, feel for, get a hold of, get hold of, get to, go, go as far as, go on, go to, grasp, hand, hold out, join, lead, lunge, make, make contact with, overtake, pass, pass along, put out, roll on, seize, shake hands, shoot, span, spread, stand, strain, strike; SEE CONCEPTS *108,612,756*

reach [v3] *attain; rise*
accomplish, achieve, amount to, arrive at, climb to, come to, drop, fall, gain, move, rack up*, realize, score, sink, win; SEE CONCEPTS *706,763,780*

reach [v4] *communicate with*
affect, approach, contact, get, get in touch, get

ra
re

through, get to, influence, keep in contact, keep in touch, maintain, move, sway, touch; SEE CONCEPTS *7,19,22,266*

react [*v*] *respond; conduct oneself*
acknowledge, act, answer, answer back, backfire, be affected, behave, boomerang*, bounce back*, counter, echo, feel, function, get back at, give a snappy comeback*, give back, have a funny feeling*, have vibes*, operate, perform, proceed, rebound, reciprocate, recoil, recur, reply, return, revert, take, talk back, turn back, work; SEE CONCEPTS *45,633*

reaction [*n1*] *response*
acknowledgment, answer, attitude, backfire, backlash, back talk*, boomerang*, comeback, compensation, counteraction, counterbalance, counterpoise, double-take*, echo, feedback, feeling, hit, kick, kickback, knee-jerk*, lip*, opinion, reagency, rebound, reception, receptivity, reciprocation, recoil, reflection, reflex, rejoinder, repercussion, reply, retort, return, reverberation, revulsion, sass*, snappy comeback*, take*, vibes*, wisecrack; SEE CONCEPTS *45,633*

reaction [*n2*] *political conservativism*
backlash, backsliding, counterrevolution, obscurantism, regression, relapse, retreat, retrenchment, retrogression, right, right wing, status quo, Toryism, withdrawal; SEE CONCEPTS *300,689*

reactionary [*adj*] *conservative*
counterrevolutionary, die-hard*, obscurantist, old-line*, orthodox, regressive, retrogressive, right, rightist*, rigid, standpat*, tory*, traditional, traditionalistic; SEE CONCEPTS *529,542*

reactionary [*n*] *person who is politically conservative*
bitter-ender*, counterrevolutionary, diehard*, hard hat*, intransigent, obscurantist, reactionist, rightist*, right-winger, royalist, standpatter*, Tory*, traditionalist, ultraconservative; SEE CONCEPT *359*

read [*v1*] *look at and understand written word*
apprehend, bury oneself in*, comprehend, construe, decipher, dip into*, discover, flip through*, gather, glance, go over, go through, interpret, know, leaf through*, learn, make out*, perceive, peruse, pore over*, refer to, scan, scratch the surface*, see, skim, study, translate, unravel, view; SEE CONCEPT *72*

read [*v2*] *express, state*
affirm, announce, assert, declaim, deliver, display, explain, expound, hold, indicate, mark, paraphrase, pronounce, recite, record, register, render, restate, say, show, speak, utter; SEE CONCEPT *266*

readable [*adj1*] *understandable, legible*
clear, coherent, comprehensible, decipherable, distinct, explicit, flowing, fluent, graphic, intelligible, lucid, orderly, plain, precise, regular, simple, smooth, straightforward, tidy, unequivocal, unmistakable; SEE CONCEPTS *272,529*

readable [*adj2*] *pleasurable to peruse*
absorbing, amusing, appealing, brilliant, clever, easy, eloquent, engaging, engrossing, enjoyable, entertaining, enthralling, exciting, fascinating, gratifying, gripping, ingenious, interesting, inviting, pleasant, pleasing, relaxing, rewarding, satisfying, smooth, stimulating, well-written, worthwhile; SEE CONCEPT *272*

readily [*adv*] *quickly; effortlessly*
at once, at the drop of a hat*, cheerfully, eagerly,

easily, facilely, freely, gladly, hands down*, immediately, in a jiffy*, in no time*, lightly, no sweat*, nothing to it*, piece of cake*, promptly, quick as a wink*, right away, slick as whistle*, smoothly, speedily, straight away, swimmingly, unhesitatingly, well, willingly, without delay, without demur, without difficulty, without hesitation; SEE CONCEPTS *544,820*

readiness [*n*] *skill; eagerness*
address, adroitness, alacrity, aptness, deftness, dexterity, dispatch, ease, eloquence, expedience, expedition, facility, fitness, fluency, good will, handiness, inclination, keenness, maturity, preparation, preparedness, promptitude, promptness, prowess, quickness, rapidity, ripeness, sleight, volubility, willingness; SEE CONCEPTS *630,633,678*

reading [*n*] *interpretation of written word*
account, book-learning, commentary, conception, construction, edification, education, erudition, examination, grasp, impression, inspection, knowledge, learning, lesson, paraphrase, perusal, rendering, rendition, review, scholarship, scrutiny, study, translation, treatment, understanding, version; SEE CONCEPTS *72,271,274*

ready [*adj1*] *prepared; available*
accessible, adjusted, all set, all systems go*, anticipating, apt, arranged, at beck and call*, at fingertips*, at hand, at the ready, champing a bit*, close to hand, completed, convenient, covered, equal to, equipped, expectant, fit, fixed for, handy, in line, in order, in place, in position, in readiness, in the saddle*, near, on call, on hand, on tap*, on the brink*, open to, organized, primed, qualified, ripe, set, waiting, wired*; SEE CONCEPTS *560,576,799*

ready [*adj2*] *willing, inclined*
agreeable, apt, ardent, disposed, eager, enthusiastic, fain, game, game for, glad, happy, keen, minded, predisposed, prompt, prone, psyched up*, wired*, zealous; SEE CONCEPTS *401,542*

ready [*adj3*] *skillful, intelligent*
active, acute, adept, adroit, alert, apt, astute, bright, brilliant, clever, deft, dexterous, dynamic, expert, handy, keen, live, masterly, perceptive, proficient, prompt, quick, quick-witted, rapid, resourceful, sharp, skilled, smart; SEE CONCEPTS *402,527*

ready [*v*] *prepare*
arrange, brace, brief, clear the decks*, equip, fill in, fit, fit out, fix, fortify, gear up*, get, get ready, get set, gird, keep posted*, let in on*, make, make ready, make up, order, organize, pave the way*, post, prep, provide, psych up*, put on to*, set, strengthen, warm up, wise up*; SEE CONCEPTS *35,60,202*

real [*adj*] *genuine in existence*
absolute, actual, authentic, bodily, bona fide, certain, concrete, corporal, corporeal, de facto, embodied, essential, evident, existent, existing, factual, firm, heartfelt, honest, incarnate, indubitable, in the flesh*, intrinsic, irrefutable, legitimate, live, material, original, palpable, perceptible, physical, positive, present, right, rightful, sensible, sincere, solid, sound, stable, substantial, substantive, tangible, true, unaffected, undeniable, undoubted, unfeigned, valid, veritable; SEE CONCEPT *582*

realistic [*adj1*] *sensible, matter-of-fact*
astute, businesslike, commonsense, down-to-

earth, earthy, hard, hard-boiled*, levelheaded, practical, pragmatic, pragmatical, prudent, rational, real, reasonable, sane, sensible, shrewd, sober, sound, unfantastic, unidealistic, unromantic, unsentimental, utilitarian; SEE CONCEPTS *403,542,548*

realistic [*adj2*] *genuine*
authentic, faithful, graphic, lifelike, natural, original, representational, representative, true, true to life, truthful; SEE CONCEPT *582*

reality [*n*] *facts of existence*
absoluteness, actuality, authenticity, being, bottom line*, brass tacks*, certainty, concreteness, corporeality, deed, entity, existence, genuineness, how things are*, like it is*, materiality, matter, name of the game*, nuts and bolts*, object, palpability, perceptibility, phenomenon, presence, realism, realness, real world*, sensibility, solidity, substance, substantiality, substantive, tangibility, truth, validity, verisimilitude, verity, way of it*, what's what*; SEE CONCEPTS *689,725*

realize [*v1*] *appreciate, become aware of*
apprehend, be cognizant of, become conscious of, catch, catch on*, comprehend, conceive, discern, envisage, envision, fancy*, feature*, get, get it*, get the idea*, get the picture*, get through one's head*, grasp, image, imagine, know, pick up*, recognize, see daylight*, take in*, think, understand, vision, visualize; SEE CONCEPT *15*

realize [*v2*] *accomplish*
actualize, bring about, bring off*, bring to fruition, carry out, carry through, complete, consummate, corporealize, do, effect, effectuate, fulfill, make concrete, make good*, make happen, materialize, perfect, perform, reify; SEE CONCEPT *91*

realize [*v3*] *gain, earn*
accomplish, achieve, acquire, attain, bring in, clear, get, go for*, make, make a profit, net, obtain, produce, rack up*, reach, receive, score*, sell for, take in, win; SEE CONCEPTS *120,124,330*

really [*adv*] *without a doubt*
absolutely, actually, admittedly, as a matter of fact, assuredly, authentically, beyond doubt, categorically, certainly, de facto, easily, for real*, genuinely, honestly, in actuality, indeed, indubitably, in effect, in fact, in point of fact, in reality, legitimately, literally, no ifs ands or buts*, nothing else but, of course, positively, precisely, surely, truly, undoubtedly, unmistakably, unquestionably, verily, well; SEE CONCEPTS *535,582*

realm [*n*] *area of responsibility or rule*
branch, compass, country, department, dimension, domain, dominion, empire, expanse, extent, field, ground, kingdom, land, monarchy, neck of the woods*, neighborhood, orbit, place, principality, province, purview, radius, range, reach, region, scope, sphere, state, stomping grounds*, sweep, territory, turf*, world, zone; SEE CONCEPTS *349,362,512,651*

reap [*v*] *collect, harvest*
acquire, bring in, come to have, crop, cull, cut, derive, draw, gain, garner, gather, get, get as a result, glean, ingather, mow, obtain, pick, pick up, pluck, procure, produce, profit, realize, receive, recover, retrieve, secure, strip, take in, win; SEE CONCEPTS *109,120,124,257*

rear [*adj*] *back, end*
aft, after, astern, backward, behind, dorsal, following, hind, hinder, hindermost, hindmost, last, mizzen, posterior, postern, rearmost, rearward, retral, reverse, stern, tail; SEE CONCEPT *583*

rear [*n*] *back or end part*
afterpart, back, back door*, back end, back seat*, backside, behind, bottom, butt, buttocks, end, heel, hind, hind part, hindquarters, posterior, postern, rear end, rear guard, rearward, reverse, rump, seat, stern, tail, tail end, tailpiece, tush*; SEE CONCEPTS *825,827*

rear [*v1*] *raise young*
breed, bring up, care for, cultivate, educate, foster, grow, nurse, nurture, propagate, train; SEE CONCEPT *295*

rear [*v2*] *lift, rise*
bring up, elevate, hoist, hold up, jump, leap, loom, pick up, raise, set upright, soar, spring up, support, take up, tower, turn up, uphold, uplift, upraise; SEE CONCEPTS *194,196,741*

rear [*v3*] *build*
construct, erect, fabricate, put up, raise, set up, unrear; SEE CONCEPT *168*

reason [*n1*] *mental analysis*
acumen, apprehension, argumentation, bounds, brain*, brains*, comprehension, deduction, dialectics, discernment, generalization, induction, inference, intellect, intellection, judgment, limits, logic, lucidity, marbles*, mentality, mind, moderation, propriety, ratiocination, rationalism, rationality, rationalization, reasonableness, reasoning, saneness, sanity, sense, senses*, sensibleness, sound mind, soundness, speculation, understanding, wisdom, wit; SEE CONCEPTS *37,409*

reason [*n2*] *intention, aim*
antecedent, argument, basis, cause, consideration, design, determinant, end, goal, grounds, idea, impetus, incentive, inducement, motivation, motive, object, occasion, proof, purpose, rationale, root, spring, target, ulterior motive, warrant, wherefore*, why, why and wherefore*, whyfor*; SEE CONCEPT *659*

reason [*n3*] *explanation for an action*
account, apologia, apology, argument, case, cover, defense, excuse, exposition, ground, idea, justification, notion, proof, rationale, rationalization, song and dance*, sour grapes*, the whole idea*, vindication, whatfor*, wherefore*, why*, why and wherefore*, whyfor*; SEE CONCEPT *661*

reason [*v1*] *mentally analyze*
adduce, cerebrate, cogitate, conclude, contemplate, decide, deduce, deduct, deliberate, draw conclusion, draw from, examine, figure out, gather, generalize, infer, make out, philosophize, ratiocinate, rationalize, reflect, resolve, solve, speculate, study, suppose, syllogize, think, think through, thresh out, work out; SEE CONCEPT *37*

reason [*v2*] *argue, persuade*
bring around, contend, debate, demonstrate, discourse, discuss, dispute, dissuade, establish, expostulate, justify, move, point out, prevail upon, prove, remonstrate, show error of ways*, talk into, talk out of, urge, win over; SEE CONCEPTS *46,56,68*

reasonable [*adj1*] *moderate, tolerable*
acceptable, analytical, average, cheap, circumspect, conservative, controlled, discreet, equitable, fair, feasible, fit, honest, humane,

re
re

impartial, inexpensive, judicious, just, justifiable, knowing, legit, legitimate, low-cost, low-priced, making sense, modest, objective, okay, plausible, politic, proper, prudent, rational, reflective, restrained, right, sane, sapient, sensible, sound, standing to reason*, temperate, understandable, unexcessive, unextreme, valid, within reason; SEE CONCEPTS 547,558

reasonable [adj2] *intelligent, practical*
advisable, all there*, arguable, believeable, cerebral, clear-cut, cognitive, commonsensical, conscious, consequent, consistent, cool*, credible, in one's right mind*, judicious, justifiable, level-headed, logical, perceiving, percipient, plausible, ratiocinative, rational, reasoned, reasoning, reflective, sane, sensible, sober, sound, tenable, thoughtful, thought-out, tolerant, unbiased, unprejudiced, well-advised, wise; SEE CONCEPT 402

reasoning [n] *logic, interpretation*
acumen, analysis, apriority, argument, case, cogitation, concluding, corollary, deduction, dialectics, exposition, generalization, hypothesis, illation, induction, inference, interpretation, logistics, premise, proof, proposition, ratiocination, rationale, rationalizing, reason, syllogism, syllogization, thinking, thought, train of thought; SEE CONCEPTS 37,529

reassure [v] *restore confidence to*
assure, bolster, brace, buoy, cheer, comfort, console, convince, encourage, give a lift*, give confidence, guarantee, hearten, inspire, inspirit, perk up, pick up*, put one's mind to rest*, relieve, snap one out of it*; SEE CONCEPTS 7,22

rebate [n] *refund given to purchaser*
abatement, allowance, bonus, deduction, discount, kickback, payback, reduction, reimbursement, remission, repayment, subtraction; SEE CONCEPT 344

rebel [adj] *not obeying*
insubordinate, insurgent, insurrectionary, mutinous, rebellious, revolutionary; SEE CONCEPT 401

rebel [n] *person who does not obey*
agitator, anarchist, antagonist, apostate, demagogue, deserter, disectarian, dissenter, experientialist, experimenter, frondeur, guerrilla, heretic, iconoclast, independent, individualist, innovator, insurgent, insurrectionary, malcontent, mutineer, nihilist, nonconformist, opponent, overthrower, recreant, renegade, resistance, revolter, revolutionary, revolutionist, rioter, schismatic, secessionist, seditionist, separatist, subverter, traitor, turncoat; SEE CONCEPTS 359,412,423

rebel [v] *refuse to obey*
be insubordinate, boycott, break with*, censure, combat, come out against*, criticize, defy, denounce, disobey, dissent, drop out*, fight, get out of line*, insurrect, make waves*, mutiny, oppose, opt out*, overthrow, overturn, remonstrate, renounce, resist, revolt, riot, rise up*, rock the boat*, run amok*, secede, strike, take up arms, turn against, upset; SEE CONCEPTS 106,633

rebellion [n] *disobedience; revolt*
apostasy, defiance, disobedience, dissent, heresy, insubordination, insurgence, insurgency, insurrection, nonconformity, revolution, rising, schism, uprising; SEE CONCEPTS 106,300,320,633

rebellious [adj] *disobedient, unmanageable*
alienated, anarchistic, attacking, bellicose, contumacious, defiant, difficult, disaffected, disloyal, disobedient, disorderly, dissident, factious, fractious, iconoclastic, incorrigible, individualistic, insurgent, insurrectionary, intractable, mutinous, obstinate, pugnacious, quarrelsome, radical, rebel, recalcitrant, refractory, resistant, restless, revolutionary, rioting, riotous, sabotaging, seditious, threatening, treasonable, turbulent, ungovernable, unruly, warring; SEE CONCEPTS 401,529,542

rebound [v] *bounce back; ricochet*
backfire, boomerang, convalesce, get back on one's feet*, get better, get in shape, get well, heal, kick back, make a comeback*, mend, overcome, pick up, pull through, rally, recoil, recuperate, regain one's health, rejuvenate, return, return to form, revive, snap back*, spring back, start anew; SEE CONCEPTS 150,194,195,303,700

rebuff [n] *turning away; ignoring*
brushoff*, check, cold shoulder*, cut, defeat, denial, discouragement, go-by*, hard time*, insult, kick in the teeth*, nix*, nothing doing*, opposition, rebuke, refusal, rejection, reprimand, repulse, slight, snub, thumbs down*, turndown; SEE CONCEPTS 30,278

rebuff [v] *turn away; give the cold shoulder**
beat off, brush off, check, chide, cross, cut, decline, deny, disallow, discourage, dismiss, disregard, fend off, hold off, ignore, keep at a distance*, keep at arm's length*, keep at bay, lash out at, neglect, not hear of, oppose, pass up, push back, put in one's place*, put off, rebuke, refuse, reject, repel, reprove, repudiate, repulse, resist, send away, slight, snub, spurn, stave off, tell off*, turn down, ward off; SEE CONCEPTS 30,54

rebuke [n] *reprimand; harsh criticism*
admonishment, admonition, affliction, bawling-out*, berating, blame, castigation, censure, chewing-out*, chiding, comeuppance, condemnation, correction, disapproval, dressing-down*, earful*, expostulation, going-over*, hard time*, kick in the teeth*, lecture, lesson, objurgation, ostracism, punishment, put-down, rap*, rating, rebuff, refusal, remonstrance, reprehension, reproach, reproof, reproval, repulse, row, scolding, slap in the face*, snub, talking-to*, telling-off*, tongue-lashing*, upbraiding; SEE CONCEPTS 44,52,278

rebuke [v] *reprimand; criticize harshly*
admonish, bawl out*, berate, blame, call on the carpet*, carp on, castigate, censure, chew out*, chide, climb all over*, dress down*, fry*, go after*, jawbone*, jump down one's throat*, jump on*, lay into*, lean on*, lecture, lesson, monish, oppose, pay, rake, read*, reprehend, reprimand, reproach, reprove, rip*, scold, sit on*, sound off*, take to task*, tear apart*, tell off*, tick off*, upbraid, zap*; SEE CONCEPTS 44,52

rebut [v] *argue against; prove wrong*
break, come back at, confound, confute, controvert, cross, defeat, deny, disconfirm, disprove, evert, fend off, get back at, hold off, invalidate, keep off, negate, negative, overturn, prove false, quash, refute, repel, repulse, stave off, take on, top, ward off; SEE CONCEPTS 46,54

rebuttal [n] *counterstatement*
answer, confutation, counteraccusation, counterargument, countercharge, counterclaim, defense, rejoinder, reply; SEE CONCEPTS 274,278

recalcitrant [*adj*] *disobedient, uncontrollable*
contrary, contumacious, defiant, fractious, indomitable, insubmissive, insubordinate, intractable, obstinate, opposing, radical, rebellious, refractory, resistant, resisting, stubborn, undisciplinable, undisciplined, ungovernable, unmanageable, unruly, untoward, unwilling, wayward, wild, willful, withstanding; SEE CONCEPT *401*

recall [*n1*] *remembrance*
anamnesis, memory, recollection, reminiscence; SEE CONCEPT *529*

recall [*n2*] *request for return*
annulment, cancellation, nullification, recision, repeal, rescindment, rescission, retraction, revocation, withdrawal; SEE CONCEPTS *662,685*

recall [*v1*] *remember*
arouse, awaken, bethink, bring to mind, call to mind, call up, cite, come to one, educe, elicit, evoke, extract, flash, flash on*, look back, mind, nail it down*, recollect, reestablish, reinstate, reintroduce, remind, reminisce, renew, retain, retrospect, revive, ring a bell*, rouse, stir, strike a note*, summon, think back*, think of, waken; SEE CONCEPT *40*

recall [*v2*] *ask for return of offending thing*
abjure, annul, call back, call in, cancel, countermand, discharge, dismantle, dismiss, disqualify, forswear, lift, nullify, palinode, recant, repeal, rescind, retract, reverse, revoke, suspend, take back, unsay, withdraw; SEE CONCEPTS *50,88,131,143*

recant [*v*] *take back something said*
abjure, abnegate, abrogate, annul, apostatize, back down, back off, back out, backtrack*, call back, cancel, contradict, countermand, deny, dial back*, disavow, disclaim, disown, eat one's words*, forswear, go back on one's word*, nullify, recall, renege, renounce, repeal, repudiate, rescind, retract, revoke, take back, unsay, void, weasel out*, welsh*, withdraw, worm out of*; SEE CONCEPTS *25,266*

recapitulate [*v*] *go over something again*
epitomize, go over same ground*, go the same round*, outline, paraphrase, recap*, recount, rehash, reiterate, repeat, rephrase, replay, restate, review, reword, run over*, run through again*, summarize, sum up; SEE CONCEPT *266*

recede [*v*] *withdraw; diminish*
abate, back, close, decline, decrease, depart, die off, diminish, drain away, draw back, drop, dwindle, ebb, fade, fall back, flow back, go away, go back, lessen, reduce, regress, retire, retract, retreat, retrocede, retrograde, retrogress, return, shrink, sink, subside, taper, wane; SEE CONCEPTS *195,698,776*

receipt [*n1*] *acknowledgment of delivery*
cancellation, certificate, chit, counterfoil, declaration, discharge, letter, notice, proof of purchase, quittance, release, sales slip, slip, stub, voucher; SEE CONCEPTS *271,332*

receipt [*n2*] *delivery of goods*
acceptance, accession, acquiring, acquisition, admission, admitting, arrival, getting, intaking, receiving, reception, recipience, taking; SEE CONCEPT *124*

receipts [*n*] *money earned in business venture*
bottom line*, cash flow, comings in*, earnings, gain, gate, get*, gross, handle*, income, net, proceeds, profit, return, revenue, revenue stream,

royalty, take*, take-in*, taking*; SEE CONCEPT *344*

receive [*v1*] *accept delivery of something*
accept, acquire, admit, apprehend, appropriate, arrogate, assume, be given, be informed, be in receipt of, be told, catch, collect, come by, come into, cop*, corral*, derive, draw, earn, gain, gather, get, get from, get hands on*, get hold of*, grab, hear, hold, inherit, latch on to*, make, obtain, perceive, pick up, pocket*, procure, pull, pull down*, reap, redeem, secure, seize, snag*, take, take in, take possession, win; SEE CONCEPT *124*

receive [*v2*] *endure, sustain*
bear, be subjected to, encounter, experience, go through, meet with, suffer, undergo; SEE CONCEPT *23*

receive [*v3*] *take in guest or member*
accept, accommodate, admit, allow entrance, bring in, entertain, greet, host, induct, initiate, install, introduce, invite, let in, let through, make comfortable, make welcome, meet, permit, roll out red carpet*, shake hands*, show in, take in, usher in, welcome; SEE CONCEPTS *50,83,88,140*

recent [*adj*] *current*
contempo*, contemporary, fresh, hot off the fire*, hot off the press*, just out*, late, latter, latter-day, modern, modernistic, neoteric, new, newborn, newfangled, novel, present-day, the latest*, today, up-to-date, young; SEE CONCEPTS *578,797,820*

recently [*adv*] *currently*
afresh, anew, freshly, in recent past, in recent times, just a while ago, just now, lately, latterly, new, newly, not long ago, of late, short while ago, the other day; SEE CONCEPT *820*

receptacle [*n*] *container for disposal, storage*
bowl, box, holder, hopper, repository, vessel, wastebasket; SEE CONCEPT *494*

reception [*n1*] *acceptance; acknowledgment*
accession, acquisition, admission, disposition, encounter, gathering, greeting, induction, introduction, meeting, reaction, receipt, receiving, recipience, recognition, response, salutation, treatment, welcome; SEE CONCEPTS *83,124,384*

reception [*n2*] *celebratory party*
buffet, dinner, do*, entertainment, function, gathering, levee, matinee, soiree, supper, tea; SEE CONCEPT *383*

receptive [*adj*] *open to new ideas*
acceptant, acceptive, accessible, alert, amenable, approachable, bright, favorable, friendly, hospitable, influenceable, interested, observant, open, open-minded, open to suggestions, perceptive, persuadable, pushover*, quick on the uptake*, ready, recipient, responsive, sensitive, suggestible, susceptible, swayable, sympathetic, welcoming, well-disposed; SEE CONCEPT *404*

recess [*n1*] *niche, corner*
alcove, ambush, angle, apse, bay, break, carrel, cavity, cell, closet, cove, cranny, crutch, crypt, cubicle, dent, depression, depths, embrasure, fork, heart, hiding place, hole, hollow, indentation, mouth, nook, opening, oriel, penetralia, reaches, retreat, secret place, slot, socket; SEE CONCEPTS *440,513*

recess [*n2*] *break, interval in action*
break-off, breather*, breathing spell*, cessation, closure, coffee break*, cutoff, downtime*, halt,

re
re

happy hour*, hiatus, holiday, interlude, intermission, interregnum, layoff, letup, lull, pause, respite, rest, stop, suspension, ten*, time-out, vacation; SEE CONCEPT *807*

recess [*v*] *stop action*
adjourn, break off*, break up*, call time*, dissolve, drop, drop it, pigeonhole*, prorogate, prorogue, put on hold, rise, shake, sideline*, take a break, take a breather*, take five*, take ten*, terminate; SEE CONCEPTS *119,121*

recession [*n*] *reversal of action; reduction of business activity*
bad times*, bankruptcy, big trouble*, bottom-out*, bust, collapse, decline, deflation, depression, downturn, hard times*, inflation, rainy days*, shakeout*, slide, slump, stagnation, unemployment; SEE CONCEPT *335*

recharge [*v*] *revitalize*
bounce back*, breathe new life into*, bring back to life*, come to life, energize, invigorate, reenergize, refresh, regenerate, rejuvenate, renew, restore, resuscitate, revitalize, revive; SEE CONCEPTS *13,221,469,697*

recipe [*n*] *directions, formula*
compound, ingredients, instructions, method, modus operandi, prescription, procedure, process, program, receipt, technique; SEE CONCEPT *274*

reciprocal [*adj*] *exchanged, alternate*
changeable, companion, complementary, convertible, coordinate, correlative, corresponding, dependent, double, duplicate, equivalent, exchangeable, fellow, give-and-take*, interchangeable, interdependent, matching, mutual, reciprocative, reciprocatory, twin; SEE CONCEPTS *566,577*

reciprocate [*v*] *exchange, alternate; equal*
barter, be equivalent, correspond, equal, feel in return, interchange, make up for*, match, pay one's dues*, recompense, render, repay, reply, requite, respond, retaliate, retort, return, return the compliment*, scratch one's back*, serve out, share, square, swap, swing, tit for tat*, trade, vacillate; SEE CONCEPTS *45,104,384*

recital [*n*] *narrative, rendering*
account, concert, description, detailing, enumeration, fable, musical, musicale, narration, narrative, performance, portrayal, presentation, reading, recapitulation, recitation, recountal, recounting, rehearsal, relation, repetition, report, statement, story, tale, telling; SEE CONCEPTS *263,264*

recitation [*n*] *reading to audience*
address, appeal, declaiming, delivery, discourse, discoursing, discussion, exercise, holding forth, lecture, monologue, narrating, narration, oration, passage, performance, piece, playing, proclamation, recital, recounting, rehearsal, rendering, report, selection, soliloquizing, speaking, talk, telling; SEE CONCEPTS *72,263,266*

recite [*v*] *read out loud; narrate*
account for, address, answer, chant, communicate, convey, declaim, delineate, deliver, describe, detail, discourse, dramatize, enact, enlarge, enumerate, expatiate, explain, give an account, give a report, give verbal account, hold forth, impart, interpret, itemize, mention, narrate, parrot*, perform, picture, portray, quote, recapitulate, recount, reel off*, rehearse, relate, render,

repeat, reply, report, retell, soliloquize, speak, state, tell, utter; SEE CONCEPTS *55,57,72,266*

reckless [*adj*] *irresponsible in thought, deed*
adventuresome, adventurous, any which way*, audacious, brash, breakneck, carefree, careless, daredevil, daring, desperate, devil-may-care*, fast and loose*, feckless, foolhardy, harebrained, hasty, headlong, heedless, helter-skelter, hopeless, hotheaded*, ill-advised, imprudent, inattentive, incautious, inconsiderate, indiscreet, kooky*, madcap, mindless, negligent, overventuresome, playing with fire*, precipitate, rash, regardless, temerarious, thoughtless, uncareful, venturesome, venturous, wild; SEE CONCEPTS *401,542*

reckon [*v1*] *add up; evaluate*
account, appraise, approximate, calculate, call, cast, cipher, compute, conjecture, consider, count, count heads*, count noses*, deem, enumerate, esteem, estimate, figure, figure out, foot, gauge, guess, hold, judge, keep tabs*, look upon, number, place, put, rate, regard, run down, square, sum, surmise, take account of, tally, think of, tick off*, tot, total, tote*, tote up*, tot up, view; SEE CONCEPTS *37,764*

reckon [*v2*] *suppose, imagine*
assume, bank on, bargain for, believe, be of the opinion, build on, conjecture, count on, depend on, expect, fancy, gather, guess, plan on, rely on, surmise, suspect, take, think, trust in, understand; SEE CONCEPTS *12,26*

reckoning [*n*] *computation, account*
adding, addition, arithmetic, bad news*, bill, calculation, charge, check, ciphering, cost, count, counting, debt, due, estimate, estimation, fee, figuring, grunt*, invoice, IOU*, score, settlement, statement, summation, tab, working; SEE CONCEPT *331*

recline [*v*] *lie down*
be recumbent, cant, heel, lay down, lean, lie, list, loll, lounge, repose, rest, slant, slope, sprawl, stretch, stretch out, tilt, tip; SEE CONCEPTS *154,201*

recluse [*n*] *person who does not want social contact*
anchorite, ascetic, cenobite, eremite, hermit, monk, nun, solitaire, solitary, troglodyte; SEE CONCEPT *423*

recluse/reclusive [*adj*] *hermitlike, unsociable*
antisocial, ascetic, cloistered, eremetic, hermetic, isolated, misanthropic, monastic, reserved, retiring, secluded, secluse, seclusive, sequestered, solitary, standoffish, withdrawn; SEE CONCEPTS *404,555*

recognition [*n1*] *identification, acknowledgment*
acceptance, acknowledging, admission, allowance, apperception, appreciation, apprehending, assimilation, avowal, awareness, cognizance, concession, confession, consciousness, detection, discovery, double take*, high sign*, identifying, memory, notice, noticing, perceiving, perception, realization, recall, recalling, recognizance, recollection, recurrence, remembering, remembrance, respect, salute, sensibility, tumble*, understanding, verifying; SEE CONCEPT *38*

recognition [*n2*] *appreciation given*
acceptance, acknowledgment, approval, attention, credit, esteem, gratitude, greeting, honor, notice, pat on back*, pat on head*, plum*, puff*,

puffing up*, pumping up*, rave, regard, renown, salute, strokes*; SEE CONCEPTS *10,337,689*

recognize [*v1*] *identify*
admit, be familiar, button down*, descry, determinate, diagnose, diagnosticate, distinguish, espy, finger*, flash on*, know, know again, make*, make out, nail*, note, notice, observe, peg*, perceive, pinpoint, place, recall, recollect, remark, remember, ring a bell*, see, sight, spot, tab, tag, verify; SEE CONCEPT *38*

recognize [*v2*] *acknowledge, understand; approve*
accept, admit, agree, allow, appreciate, assent, avow, be aware of, comprehend, concede, confess, grant, greet, honor, make, own, perceive, realize, respect, salute, sanction, see; SEE CONCEPT *15*

recoil [*v*] *shrink away*
backfire, balk, blanch, blench, blink, carom, cringe, demur, dodge, draw back, duck, falter, flinch, hesitate, jerk, kick, pull back, quail, quake, react, rebound, reel, resile, shake, shirk, shrink, shudder, shy away, spring, start, step back, stick, stickle, swerve, tremble, turn away, waver, wince, withdraw; SEE CONCEPTS *150,194,195*

recollect [*v*] *remember*
arouse, awaken, bethink, bring to mind, call to mind, cite, come to one, flash, flash on*, look back on, mind, place, recall, recognize, remind, reminisce, retain, retrospect, revive, rouse, stir, summon, waken; SEE CONCEPT *40*

recommend [*v*] *advise, approve*
acclaim, advance, advocate, applaud, back, be all for*, be satisfied with, celebrate, commend, compliment, confirm, counsel, endorse, enjoin, esteem, eulogize, exalt, exhort, extol, favor, front for*, glorify, go on record for*, hold up, justify, laud, magnify, plug*, praise, prescribe, prize, propose, put forward, put in a good word*, put on to*, sanction, second, speak highly of, speak well of, stand by, steer, suggest, think highly of, uphold, urge, value, vouch for; SEE CONCEPTS *10,75*

recommendation [*n*] *advice, approval*
advocacy, approbation, blessing, certificate, character reference, charge, commendation, counsel, direction, endorsement, esteem, eulogy, favorable mention, good word*, guidance, injunction, instruction, judgment, letter of support, order, pass, plug*, praise, proposal, proposition, reference, sanction, steer*, suggestion, support, testimonial, tip, tribute, two cents' worth*, urging; SEE CONCEPTS *274,278*

recompense [*n*] *something returned, paid back*
amends, atonement, bus fare*, compensation, cue, damages, emolument, expiation, gravy*, indemnification, indemnity, overcompensation, pay, payment, propitiation, quittance, recoupment, recovery, redemption, redress, remuneration, reparation, repayment, requital, restitution, retrieval, retrievement, return, reward, salvo, satisfaction, solatium, sweetener*, tip, wages; SEE CONCEPTS *340,344*

recompense [*v*] *pay back, make restitution*
ante up*, atone, atone for, balance, comp*, compensate, cough up*, counterbalance, counterpoise, countervail, do business*, equalize, expiate, fix, give satisfaction, grease*, indemnify, make amends, make good*, make up for,

offset, overcompensate, pay, pay for, propitiate, put out*, reciprocate, recoup, recover, redress, reimburse, remunerate, repay, requite, retaliate, retrieve, return, reward, satisfy, spring for, square*, sweeten the pot*, swing for*, take care of; SEE CONCEPTS *126,341*

reconcile [*v1*] *make peace; adjust*
accommodate, accord, accustom, appease, arbitrate, arrange, assuage, attune, bring together, bring to terms, bury the hatchet*, come together, compose, conciliate, conform, cool*, coordinate, fit, fix up, get together on, harmonize, integrate, intercede, kiss and make up*, make matters up, make up, mediate, mitigate, pacify, patch things up*, patch up*, placate, propitiate, proportion, reconciliate, rectify, re-establish, regulate, resolve, restore harmony, reunite, settle, suit, tune, win over; SEE CONCEPTS *384,697*

reconcile [*v2*] *resign oneself to something*
accept, accommodate, get used to*, make the best of*, put up with*, resign, submit, yield; SEE CONCEPT *23*

recondite [*adj*] *mysterious, obscure*
abstruse, academic, acroamatic, arcane, cabalistic, concealed, cryptic, dark, deep, difficult, esoteric, hard, heavy*, hermetic, hidden, involved, little-known, mystic, mystical, occult, orphic, pedantic, profound, scholarly, secret; SEE CONCEPTS *529,576*

reconnaissance [*n*] *inspection*
exploration, investigation, maneuvers, probe, recon, reconnoiter, review, scan, scrutiny, search, surveillance, survey; SEE CONCEPTS *103,290*

reconsider [*v*] *think about again*
amend, change one's mind, consider again, correct, emend, go over, have second thoughts*, polish, rearrange, reassess, recheck, reevaluate, reexamine, rehash, replan, rethink, retrace, review, revise, reweigh, rework, run through, see in a new light*, sleep on, take another look, think better of*, think over, think twice*, work over; SEE CONCEPT *17*

reconstruct [*v*] *reorganize, build up*
copy, deduce, doctor*, do up*, fix, fix up, make over, modernize, overhaul, patch, piece together, reassemble, rebuild, recast, recondition, reconstitute, recreate, reestablish, refashion, reform, regenerate, rehabilitate, rejuvenate, remake, remodel, remold, renovate, reorient, repair, replace, reproduce, reshuffle, restore, retool, revamp, rework; SEE CONCEPTS *84,168,171*

record [*n1*] *account of event or proceedings*
almanac, annals, archive, archives, chronicle, comic book*, diary, directory, document, documentation, entry, evidence, file, history, inscription, jacket, journal, legend, log, manuscript, memo, memoir, memorandum, memorial, minutes, monument, note, paper trail*, register, registry, remembrance, report, script, scroll, story, swindle sheet*, testimony, trace, track record*, transcript, transcription, witness, writing, written material; SEE CONCEPTS *271,281*

record [*n2*] *background, experience*
accomplishment, administration, career, case history, conduct, curriculum vitae, history, past behavior, performance, reign, studies, track record*, way of life*, work; SEE CONCEPT *678*

record [*n3*] *achievement*
ceiling, maximum; SEE CONCEPT *706*

re
re

record [v1] *write down; store information*
book, can*, catalog, chalk up*, chronicle, copy, cut, cut a track*, document, dub*, enroll, enter, enumerate, file, indite, inscribe, insert, jot down, keep account, lay down, list, log, make a recording, mark, mark down, matriculate, note, post, preserve, put down, put in writing, put on file*, put on paper*, put on tape*, register, report, set down, tabulate, take down, tape, tape-record, transcribe, video*, videotape, wax*, write in; SEE CONCEPT *125*

record [v2] *give evidence of*
contain, designate, explain, indicate, mark, point out, point to, read, register, say, show; SEE CONCEPT *261*

recount [v] *tell a story*
break a story*, convey, delineate, depict, describe, detail, echo, enumerate, give an account of, itemize, narrate, picture, play back, portray, recap*, recapitulate, recite, rehash, rehearse, relate, repeat, report, run by again*, run down*, run through*, say again, state, tell, track, unload, verbalize; SEE CONCEPTS *55,266*

recoup [v] *recover, make up for*
compensate, get back, get out from under*, get well, make good, make redress for, make well, redeem, refund, regain, reimburse, remunerate, repay, repossess, requite, retrieve, satisfy, win back; SEE CONCEPTS *124,126,342,700*

recourse [n] *alternative*
aid, appeal, choice, expediency, expedient, help, makeshift, option, refuge, remedy, resort, resource, shift, stand-by, stopgap, substitute, support, way out; SEE CONCEPTS *693,712*

recover [v1] *find again*
balance, bring back, catch up, compensate, get back, make good, obtain again, offset, reacquire, recapture, reclaim, recoup, recruit, redeem, rediscover, regain, reoccupy, repair, replevin, replevy, repossess, rescue, restore, resume, retake, retrieve, salvage, take back, win back; SEE CONCEPTS *120,183*

recover [v2] *improve in health*
be out of woods*, better, bounce back*, come around, convalesce, feel oneself again*, forge ahead, gain, get back on feet*, get better, get in shape, get out from under*, get over, get well, grow, heal, increase, make a comeback*, mend, overcome, perk up*, pick up, pull through, rally, rebound, recuperate, refresh, regain one's health, regain one's strength, rejuvenate, renew, restore, return to form, revive, snap back*, sober up*, start anew, take turn for better; SEE CONCEPTS *303,700*

recreation [n] *sports, games, special interests*
amusement, avocation, ball*, disport, dissipation, distraction, diversion, divertissement, ease, enjoyment, entertainment, exercise, festivity, field day*, frolic, fun, fun and games*, game, hilarity, hobby, holiday, jollity, laughs*, leisure activity, mirth, pastime, picnic, play, playtime, pleasure, R and R*, rec, refreshment, relaxation, relief, repose, rollick, sport, vacation; SEE CONCEPTS *363,364*

recruit [n] *person beginning service*
apprentice, beginner, convert, draftee, enlisted person, fledgling, GI*, greenhorn*, helper, initiate, learner, neophyte, newcomer, new person, novice, novitiate, plebe*, proselyte, rookie,

sailor, selectee, serviceperson, soldier, tenderfoot*, trainee, volunteer; SEE CONCEPTS *348,358*

recruit [v] *gather resources*
augment, better, build up, call to arms, call up, deliver, draft, engage, enlist, enroll, fill up, find human resources, gain, impress, improve, induct, levy, mobilize, muster, obtain, procure, proselytize, raise, reanimate, recoup, recover, recuperate, refresh, regain, reinforce, renew, repair, replenish, repossess, restore, retrieve, revive, round up, select, sign on, sign up, store up, strengthen, supply, take in, take on, win over; SEE CONCEPTS *41,109,120,320*

rectify [v] *correct a situation; make something right*
adjust, amend, clean up, clean up act*, debug, dial back*, doctor, emend, fix, fix up, go over, improve, launder, make good*, make up for*, mend, pay one's dues*, pick up, put right, recalibrate, redress, reform, remedy, repair, revise, right, scrub, shape up, square, straighten out, straighten up, turn things around*; SEE CONCEPT *126*

recumbent [adj] *lying down*
decumbent, flat, horizontal, level, procumbent, prostrate, reclining, resupine, sprawling, supine; SEE CONCEPT *583*

recuperate [v] *improve in health*
ameliorate, be on the mend*, be out of the woods*, bounce back*, convalesce, gain, get back on one's feet*, get better, get well, heal, look up, make a comeback*, mend, perk up*, pick up, pull out of it*, pull through, rally, recover, regain health, snap out of it*, turn the corner*; SEE CONCEPTS *303,700*

recur [v] *happen again; repeat in one's mind*
be remembered, be repeated, come again, come and go, come back, crop up again*, haunt thoughts*, iterate, persist, reappear, recrudesce, reiterate, repeat, return, return to mind, revert, run through one's mind*, turn back; SEE CONCEPTS *3,242*

recurrent [adj] *repeating*
alternate, chain, continued, cyclical, frequent, habitual, intermittent, isochronal, isochronous, periodic, periodical, recurring, regular, reoccurring, repeated, repetitive, rolling; SEE CONCEPTS *541,544*

red [n/adj] *color of blood; shade resembling such a color*
bittersweet, bloodshot, blooming, blush, brick, burgundy, cardinal, carmine, cerise, cherry, chestnut, claret, copper, coral, crimson, dahlia, flaming, florid, flushed, fuchsia, garnet, geranium, glowing, healthy, inflamed, infrared, magenta, maroon, pink, puce, rose, roseate, rosy, rubicund, ruby, ruddy, rufescent, russet, rust, salmon, sanguine, scarlet, titian, vermilion, wine; SEE CONCEPTS *618,622*

redden [v] *blush, make rosy*
bloody, color, crimson, dye, encarmine, encarnadine, flush, glow, go red, mantle, paint, pink, pinken, rose, rouge, rubify, rubric, rubricate, ruby, ruddle, ruddy, rust, suffuse, tint, turn red; SEE CONCEPTS *250,469*

redeem [v1] *recover possession*
buy back, buy off, call in, cash, cash in, change, cover, defray, discharge, exchange, get back, make good, pay off, purchase, ransom, recapture, reclaim, recoup, regain, reinstate, repay, re-

plevin, replevy, repossess, repurchase, restore, retrieve, settle, take in, trade in, win back; SEE CONCEPTS *104,131,327*

redeem [*v2*] *free; buy the freedom of*
deliver, disenthrall, disimprison, emancipate, extricate, liberate, loose, manumit, pay ransom, ransom, release, rescue, save, set free, unbind, unchain, unfetter; SEE CONCEPTS *127,327*

redeem [*v3*] *atone for; compensate*
abide by, absolve, acquit, adhere to, balance, carry out, compensate, counterbalance, counterpoise, countervail, defray, discharge, fulfill, hold to, keep, keep the faith*, make amends, make good, make up for, meet, offset, outweigh, perform, redress, rehabilitate, reinstate, restore, satisfy, save, set off; SEE CONCEPTS *91,126*

red herring [*n*] *distraction*
attention-grabber, bait, commotion, deviation, disturbance, diversion, gimmick, interruption, maneuver, ploy, smoke screen, wild-goose chase*; SEE CONCEPTS *293,410,532,690*

redneck [*n*] *hick*
backwoodsman/woman, boor, bumpkin, clodhopper, cornfed*, country boy/girl, country cousin*, countryman/woman, farmer, good old boy*, hayseed*, hillbilly, local yokel*, rube, rural, rustic, yokel*; SEE CONCEPT *413*

redolent [*adj*] *aromatic; suggestive*
ambrosial, balmy, evocative, fragrant, odoriferous, perfumed, pungent, remindful, reminiscent, scented, sweet-smelling; SEE CONCEPTS *267,529, 598*

redress [*n*] *help, compensation*
aid, amendment, amends, assistance, atonement, balancing, change, conciliation, correction, cure, ease, indemnity, justice, offsetting, payment, quittance, recompense, rectification, reestablishment, reformation, rehabilitation, relief, remedy, remission, remodeling, renewal, repair, reparation, reprisal, requital, restitution, retribution, return, revision, reward, reworking, satisfaction, vengeance; SEE CONCEPTS *344,712*

redress [*v*] *change, rectify*
adjust, amend, annul, balance, cancel, compensate, correct, counteract, countercheck, dial back*, ease, even out, frustrate, make amends, make reparation, make restitution, make up for, mend, negate, negative, neutralize, pay for, pay one's dues*, put right*, recalibrate, recompense, reform, regulate, relieve, remedy, repair, restore, revise, square, turn around, turn over new leaf*, turn things around*, vindicate; SEE CONCEPTS *126,697*

red tape [*n*] *bureaucracy*
authority, city hall*, government, management, officialdom, officialism, powers that be*, proper channels, regulatory commission, the Establishment*, the system*; SEE CONCEPTS *325,770*

reduce [*v1*] *make less; decrease*
abate, abridge, bankrupt, bant, break, cheapen, chop, clip, contract, curtail, cut, cut back, cut down, debase, deflate, depreciate, depress, diet, dilute, diminish, discount, drain, dwindle, go on a diet*, impair, impoverish, lessen, lose weight, lower, mark down, moderate, nutshell, pare, pauperize, rebate, recede, roll back, ruin, scale down, shave, shorten, slash, slim, slow down, step down, take off weight, taper, taper off, tone down, trim, truncate, turn down, weaken, wind down; SEE CONCEPTS *137,236,240,247,698*

reduce [*v2*] *defeat*
bear down, beat down, break, bring, conquer, cripple, crush, disable, drive, enfeeble, force, master, overcome, overpower, ruin, subdue, subjugate, undermine, vanquish, weaken; SEE CONCEPT *95*

reduce [*v3*] *humble, humiliate*
abase, break, bring low, bump*, bust*, declass, degrade, demerit, demote, disgrade, disrate, downgrade, lower, take down a peg*; SEE CONCEPTS *7,19,384*

redundant [*adj*] *excessive; repetitious*
bombastic, de trop*, diffuse, extra, extravagant, inessential, inordinate, iterating, long-winded*, loquacious, oratorical, padded*, palaverous, periphrastic, pleonastic, prolix, reiterating, spare, supererogatory, superfluous, supernumerary, surplus, tautological, unnecessary, unwanted, verbose, wordy; SEE CONCEPTS *553,781*

reef [*n*] *underwater or partially submerged ledge*
atoll, bank, bar, beach, cay, coral reef, ridge, rock, rock barrier, sand bar, shoal, skerry; SEE CONCEPT *509*

reek [*n*] *strong odor*
effluvium, fetor, mephitis, smell, stench, stink; SEE CONCEPT *600*

reek [*v*] *smell of; be characterized by*
be permeated by, be redolent of, emit, fume, give off odor, have an odor, smell, smoke, steam, stench, stink; SEE CONCEPT *600*

reel [*v*] *wobble; spin around*
bob, careen, falter, feel giddy, go around, lurch, pitch, revolve, rock, roll, shake, stagger, stumble, sway, swim, swing, swirl, teeter, titubate, totter, turn, twirl, waver, weave, wheel, whirl; SEE CONCEPTS *151,153*

refer [*v1*] *mention*
accredit, adduce, advert, allude, ascribe, assign, associate, attribute, bring up, charge, cite, credit, designate, direct attention, excerpt, exemplify, extract, give as example, glance, hint, impute, indicate, insert, instance, interpolate, introduce, invoke, lay, make allusion, make mention of, make reference, name, notice, point, point out, put down to, quote, speak about, speak of, specify, touch on; SEE CONCEPT *73*

refer [*v2*] *direct, guide*
commit, consign, deliver, hand in, hand over, introduce, pass on, point, put in touch, recommend, relegate, send, submit, transfer, turn over; SEE CONCEPTS *143,187*

refer [*v3*] *concern, apply*
answer, appertain, be about, be a matter of, bear upon, be directed to, belong, be relevant, connect, correspond with, cover, deal with, encompass, have a bearing on, have reference, have relation, have to do with, hold, include, incorporate, involve, pertain, point, regard, relate, take in, touch; SEE CONCEPT *532*

refer [*v4*] *seek information*
advise, apply, commune, confer, consult, go, have recourse, look up, recur, repair, resort, run, turn, turn to; SEE CONCEPTS *72,216*

referee [*n*] *person who mediates, judges*
adjudicator, arbiter, arbitrator, conciliator, judge, ref*, umpire; SEE CONCEPTS *348,366*

referee [*v*] *judge, mediate*
adjudge, adjudicate, arbitrate, umpire; SEE CONCEPT *18*

re
re

reference [*n1*] *remark, citation*
advertence, allusion, associating, attributing, bringing up, connecting, hint, implication, indicating, innuendo, insinuation, mention, mentioning, note, plug*, pointing out, quotation, relating, resource, source, stating; SEE CONCEPT *278*

reference [*n2*] *testimonial of good character*
certificate, certification, character, credentials, endorsement, good word, recommendation, tribute; SEE CONCEPTS *69,274*

reference [*n3*] *printed matter with information*
archives, cyclopedia, dictionary, encyclopedia, evidence, source, thesaurus, writing; SEE CONCEPTS *271,280*

refine [*v1*] *purify*
clarify, cleanse, distill, filter, process, rarefy, strain; SEE CONCEPT *165*

refine [*v2*] *perfect, polish*
better, civilize, clarify, cultivate, elevate, explain, hone, improve, make clear, round, sleek, slick, smooth, temper; SEE CONCEPT *244*

refined [*adj1*] *cultured, civilized*
aesthetic, civil, classy*, courteous, courtly, cultivated, delicate, discerning, discriminating, elegant, enlightened, exact, fastidious, fine, finespun, genteel, gracious, high-brow*, highminded, nice, plush, polished, polite, posh, precise, punctilious, restrained, ritzy*, sensitive, snazzy*, sophisticated, spiffy*, suave, sublime, subtle, swanky*, tasteful, urbane, well-bred, well-mannered; SEE CONCEPTS *401,555,589*

refined [*adj2*] *cleaned of impurities*
aerated, boiled down, clarified, clean, cleansed, distilled, drained, expurgated, filtered, processed, pure, purified, rarefied, strained, washed; SEE CONCEPT *621*

refinement [*n1*] *cleansing*
clarification, cleaning, depuration, detersion, distillation, draining, filtering, processing, purification, rarefaction, rectification; SEE CONCEPT *165*

refinement [*n2*] *cultivation, civilization*
affability, civility, courtesy, courtliness, delicacy, dignity, discrimination, elegance, enlightenment, erudition, fastidiousness, fineness, fine point*, finesse, fine tuning*, finish, gentility, gentleness, good breeding, good manners, grace, graciousness, knowledge, lore, nicety, nuance, polish, politeness, politesse, precision, sophistication, style, suavity, subtlety, tact, taste, urbanity; SEE CONCEPTS *388,633,655*

reflect [*v1*] *give back*
cast, catch, copy, echo, emulate, flash, follow, give forth, imitate, match, mirror, rebound, repeat, repercuss, reply, reproduce, resonate, resound, return, reverberate, reverse, revert, shine, take after, throw back; SEE CONCEPTS *65,171,624*

reflect [*v2*] *think about*
cerebrate, chew*, cogitate, consider, contemplate, deliberate, meditate, mull over, muse, ponder, reason, ruminate, speculate, stew*, study, think, weigh, wonder; SEE CONCEPTS *17,24*

reflect [*v3*] *demonstrate, indicate*
bear out, bespeak, communicate, display, evince, exhibit, express, indicate, manifest, reveal, show; SEE CONCEPT *261*

reflection [*n1*] *thought, thinking*
absorption, brainwork, cerebration, cogitation, consideration, contemplation, deliberation, idea, imagination, impression, meditation, musing, observation, opinion, pensiveness, pondering, rumination, speculation, study, view; SEE CONCEPTS *17,24*

reflection [*n2*] *mirror image*
appearance, counterpart, duplicate, echo, idea, image, impression, light, likeness, picture, representation, reproduction, shadow; SEE CONCEPT *628*

reflection [*n3*] *criticism*
animadversion, aspersion, blame, censure, derogation, discredit, disesteem, imputation, obloquy, reproach, slam, slur, stricture; SEE CONCEPT *52*

reflective [*adj*] *thoughtful*
cogitating, contemplative, deliberate, meditative, pensive, pondering, reasoning, ruminative, speculative, studious; SEE CONCEPT *403*

reform [*v*] *correct, rectify*
ameliorate, amend, better, bring up to code*, change one's ways*, clean up, clean up one's act*, convert, correct, cure, emend, go straight*, improve, make amends, make over, mend, rearrange, rebuild, reclaim, reconstitute, reconstruct, redeem, refashion, regenerate, rehabilitate, remake, remedy, remodel, renew, renovate, reorganize, repair, resolve, restore, revise, revolutionize, rework, shape up, standardize, swear off, transform, turn over a new leaf*, uplift; SEE CONCEPTS *35,110,126,202*

reformatory [*n*] *reform school*
boot camp*, cooler*, correctional facility, correctional institution, jail, penal institution, penitentiary, prison, training school; SEE CONCEPTS *439,449,516*

refrain [*n*] *chorus of musical piece*
burden, melody, music, song, strain, theme, tune, undersong; SEE CONCEPTS *264,595*

refrain [*v*] *do without; keep from doing*
abstain, arrest, avoid, be temperate, cease, check, curb, desist, eschew, forbear, forgo, give up, go on the wagon*, halt, inhibit, interrupt, keep, leave off, not do, pass, pass up, quit, renounce, resist, restrain, sit out*, stop, take the cure*, take the pledge*, withhold; SEE CONCEPTS *121,681*

refresh [*v*] *make like new; give new life*
brace, breathe new life into, bring around, brush up, cheer, cool, enliven, exhilarate, freshen, inspirit, jog, modernize, prod, prompt, quicken, reanimate, recreate, regain, reinvigorate, rejuvenate, renovate, repair, replenish, restore, resuscitate, revitalize, revive, revivify, stimulate, update, vivify; SEE CONCEPTS *35,202,697*

refreshing [*adj*] *new; rejuvenating*
bracing, cooling, different, energizing, exhilarating, fresh, invigorating, novel, original, rejuvenating, restorative, restoring, revitalizing, revivifying, stimulating, thirst-quenching, unique; SEE CONCEPTS *564,578,797*

refreshment [*n*] *small amount of food or drink*
bite, pick-me-up*, snack, spread, tidbit; SEE CONCEPT *457*

refrigerate [*v*] *chill, usually in storage*
air-condition, air-cool, cool, freeze, ice, keep cold, make cold; SEE CONCEPTS *202,255*

refuge [*n*] *place to hide, have privacy*
ambush, anchorage, asylum, cover, covert, den, escape, exit, expedient, fortress, harbor, harborage, haven, hideaway, hideout, hiding place, hole, home, immunity, ivory tower*, makeshift, opening, outlet, port, preserve, protection, recourse, resort, resource, retreat, safe place, sanc-

tuary, security, shelter, shield, stopgap*, stronghold, way out*; SEE CONCEPTS *198,515*

refugee [*n*] *person running from something, often oppression*
alien, boat person*, castaway, defector, derelict, deserter, displaced person, DP*, emigrant, émigré, escapee, evacuee, exile, expatriate, expellee, foreigner, foundling, fugitive, homeless person, leper, maroon, outcast, outlaw, prodigal, renegade, runaway, stateless person; SEE CONCEPTS *359,413*

refund [*n*] *returned money*
acquittance, allowance, compensation, consolation, discharge, discount, give-back*, give-up*, kickback, money back, payment, rebate, reimbursement, remuneration, repayment, restitution, retribution, return, satisfaction, settlement; SEE CONCEPTS *340,344*

refund [*v*] *return money; rebate*
adjust, balance, compensate, give back, honor a claim, indemnify, make amends, make good*, make repayment, make up for, pay back, recompense, recoup, redeem, redress, reimburse, relinquish, remit, remunerate, repay, restore, reward, settle; SEE CONCEPT *341*

refurbish [*v*] *spruce up*
clean up, do up*, fix up, gussy up*, mend, modernize, overhaul, recondition, redo, reequip, refit, refresh, rehab, rehabilitate, rejuvenate, remodel, renew, renovate, repair, restore, retread, revamp, set to rights, spruce, update; SEE CONCEPTS *177,202*

refusal [*n*] *denial of responsibility; unwillingness*
abnegation, ban, choice, cold shoulder*, declension, declination, defiance, disallowance, disapproval, disavowal, disclaimer, discountenancing, disfavor, dissent, enjoinment, exclusion, forbidding, interdiction, knockback*, negation, nix*, no, nonacceptance, noncompliance, nonconsent, option, pass*, prohibition, proscription, rebuff, refutation, regrets, rejection, renouncement, renunciation, repudiation, repulse, repulsion, reversal, thumbs down*, turndown, veto, withholding, writ; SEE CONCEPTS *278,633*

refuse [*n*] *garbage*
debris, dregs, dross, dump, dust, hogwash*, junk, leavings, litter, muck, offal, rejectamenta*, remains, residue, rubbish, scraps, scum*, sediment, slop*, sweepings, swill, trash, waste, waste matter; SEE CONCEPT *260*

refuse [*v*] *deny; say no*
beg off, brush off*, decline, demur, desist, disaccord, disallow, disapprove, dispense with, dissent, dodge, evade, give thumbs down to*, hold back, hold off, hold out, ignore, make excuses, nix*, not budge, not budget, not buy*, not care to*, pass up, protest, rebuff, refuse to receive, regret, reject, repel, reprobate, repudiate, send off*, send regrets*, set aside*, shun, spurn, turn away, turn deaf ear to*, turn down, turn from, turn one's back on*, withdraw, withhold; SEE CONCEPTS *30,49,266*

refute [*v*] *prove false; discredit*
abnegate, argue against, blow sky high*, break, burn, burn down, cancel, cancel out, confute, contend, contradict, contravene, convict, counter, crush, debate, demolish, disclaim, disconfirm, dispose of, disprove, dispute, evert, explode, expose, gainsay, give the lie to*, give thumbs down to*, invalidate, negate, oppose, overthrow, parry,

quash, rebut, reply to, repudiate, shoot down, shoot full of holes*, show up, silence, squelch, take a stand against, tear down*, top*; SEE CONCEPT *54*

regain [*v*] *get back, get back to*
achieve, attain, compass, gain, get out from under, get well, make well, reach, reach again, reacquire, reattain, recapture, reclaim, recoup, recover, recruit, redeem, repossess, retake, retrieve, return to, save, take back, win back; SEE CONCEPTS *120,124,131*

regal [*adj*] *fit for royalty*
august, glorious, imposing, kingly, magnificent, majestic, monarchial, monarchical, noble, proud, queenly, resplendent, royal, sovereign, splendid, stately, sublime; SEE CONCEPT *589*

regale [*v*] *throw a party; have fun*
amuse, delight, divert, entertain, feast, fracture, give a party, grab, gratify, have a get-together, laugh it up, nurture, party, please, ply, refresh, satisfy, serve, toss a party; SEE CONCEPTS *292,384*

regard [*n1*] *attention, look*
care, carefulness, cognizance, concern, consciousness, curiosity, gaze, glance, heed, interest, interestedness, mark, mind, note, notice, observance, observation, once-over*, remark, scrutiny, stare, view; SEE CONCEPTS *596,623,626, 690*

regard [*n2*] *affection, good opinion*
account, appreciation, approbation, approval, attachment, care, cherishing, concern, consideration, curiosity, deference, devotion, esteem, estimation, favor, fondness, homage, honor, interest, interestedness, liking, love, note, opinion, prizing, reputation, repute, respect, reverence, satisfaction, store, sympathy, thought, value, valuing, veneration, worship; SEE CONCEPTS *10,532,689*

regard [*n3*] *feature, detail*
aspect, bearing, concern, connection, item, matter, particular, point, reference, relation, relevance, respect; SEE CONCEPTS *532,644*

regard [*v1*] *look at; listen to*
advertise, attend, beam, behold, contemplate, eye, eyeball*, flash, gaze, get a load of*, give attention, heed, look on, mark, mind, note, notice, observe, overlook, pay attention, pipe*, pore over*, read, remark, respect, scan, scrutinize, see, spy, stare at, take into consideration, take notice of, view, watch, witness; SEE CONCEPTS *596,623,626*

regard [*v2*] *believe, judge*
account, adjudge, admire, assay, assess, consider, deem, esteem, estimate, look upon, rate, reckon, respect, revere, see, suppose, surmise, think, treat, value, view; SEE CONCEPTS *10,12*

regard [*v3*] *have something to do with*
apply to, bear upon, be relevant to, concern, have a bearing on, have to do with*, interest, pertain to, refer to, relate to; SEE CONCEPT *532*

regardful [*adj*] *attentive, observant*
advertent, arrect, aware, careful, considerate, deferential, duteous, dutiful, heedful, intentive, mindful, observative, observing, respectful, thoughtful, watchful; SEE CONCEPT *401*

regardless [*adj*] *indifferent, unconcerned*
behindhand, blind, careless, coarse, crude, deaf, delinquent, derelict, disregarding, heedless, inadvertent, inattentive, inconsiderate, insensitive,

re
re

lax, listless, mindless, neglectful, negligent, nonobservant, rash, reckless, remiss, rude, slack, unfeeling, unheeding, uninterested, unmindful; SEE CONCEPT *401*

regardless [*adv*] *despite everything*
against, although, anyway, aside from, at any cost, but, come what may, despite, distinct from, for all that, in any case, in spite of everything, leaving aside, nevertheless, no matter what, nonetheless, notwithstanding, without considering, without regard to; SEE CONCEPTS *544,548*

regards [*n*] *best wishes*
commendations, compliments, deference, devoirs, good wishes, greeting, love, love and kisses*, remembrances, respects, salutation, salutations; SEE CONCEPT *278*

regenerate [*v*] *breathe new life into*
change, exhilarate, inspirit, invigorate, produce, raise from the dead*, reanimate, reawaken, reconstruct, recreate, reestablish, refresh, reinvigorate, rejuvenate, renew, renovate, reproduce, restore, revive, revivify, uplift; SEE CONCEPTS *7,22,173,202,251*

regime [*n*] *leadership of organization*
administration, dynasty, establishment, government, incumbency, management, pecking order*, reign, rule, system, tenure; SEE CONCEPTS *299,325*

region [*n*] *area, domain; scope*
arena, bailiwick, belt, block, clearing, country, demesne, district, division, domain, dominion, environs, expanse, field, ghetto, ground, inner city, jungle, land, locale, locality, neck of woods*, neighborhood, part, place, precinct, province, quarter, range, realm, scene, section, sector, shire, sphere, stomping ground*, suburb, terrain, territory, tract, turf*, vicinity, walk, ward, world, zone; SEE CONCEPTS *198,508,512*

register [*n*] *list, record*
annals, archives, book, catalog, catalogue, chronicle, diary, entry, file, ledger, log, memorandum, registry, roll, roll call, roster, schedule, scroll; SEE CONCEPT *281*

register [*v1*] *enter in list, record*
catalogue, check in, chronicle, enlist, enroll, file, inscribe, join, list, note, record, schedule, set down, sign on, sign up, sign up for, subscribe, take down, weigh in; SEE CONCEPTS *79,114,125*

register [*v2*] *indicate, reveal*
be shown, bespeak, betray, disclose, display, exhibit, express, manifest, mark, point out, point to, read, record, reflect, say, show; SEE CONCEPT *261*

register [*v3*] *make an impression*
come home to, dawn on, get through to, have an effect on, impress, sink in, tell; SEE CONCEPTS *7,19,22*

regress [*v*] *return to earlier way of doing things*
backslide, degenerate, deteriorate, ebb, fall away, fall back, fall off, go back, lapse, lose ground, recede, relapse, retreat, retrogress, revert, roll back, sink, throw back, turn back; SEE CONCEPTS *633,698*

regret [*n*] *upset over past action*
affliction, anguish, annoyance, apologies, apology, bitterness, care, compunction, concern, conscience, contrition, demur, disappointment, discomfort, dissatisfaction, dole, grief, heartache, heartbreak, lamentation, misgiving, nostalgia, pang, penitence, qualm, regretfulness, remorse, repentance, ruefulness, scruple, self-accusation, self-condemnation, self-disgust, self-reproach, sorrow, uneasiness, woe, worry; SEE CONCEPTS *21,410*

regret [*v*] *be upset about*
apologize, be disturbed, bemoan, be sorry for, bewail, cry over*, cry over spilled milk*, deplore, deprecate, disapprove, feel remorse, feel sorry, feel uneasy, grieve, have compunctions*, have qualms*, kick oneself*, lament, look back, miss, moan, mourn, repent, repine, rue, weep, weep over; SEE CONCEPTS *21,410*

regretful [*adj*] *sad, sorry*
apologetic, ashamed, attritional, compunctious, contrite, disappointed, mournful, penitent, remorseful, repentant, rueful, sorrowful; SEE CONCEPT *403*

regrettable [*adj*] *unfortunate, wrong*
afflictive, calamitous, deplorable, dire, disappointing, distressing, dreadful, grievous, heartbreaking, ill-advised, lamentable, pitiable, pitiful, sad, shameful, unfavorable, unhappy, woeful; SEE CONCEPTS *548,571*

regular [*adj1*] *normal, common*
approved, bona fide, classic, commonplace, correct, customary, daily, established, everyday, formal, general, habitual, lawful, legitimate, natural, normal, official, ordinary, orthodox, prevailing, prevalent, proper, routine, run-of-the-mill*, sanctioned, standard, time-honored, traditional, typic, typical, unexceptional, unvarying, usual; SEE CONCEPTS *530,533,547*

regular [*adj2*] *orderly, consistent, balanced*
accordant, alternating, arranged, automatic, classified, congruous, consonant, constant, cyclic, dependable, efficient, established, even, exact, expected, fixed, flat, formal, harmonious, in order, invariable, level, measured, mechanical, methodical, momentary, ordered, organized, patterned, periodic, precise, probable, punctual, rational, recurrent, regulated, rhythmic, routine, serial, set, smooth, standardized, stated, steady, straight, successive, symmetrical, systematic, uniform; SEE CONCEPTS *326,544,566,585*

regulate [*v*] *manage, organize*
adapt, adjust, administer, allocate, arrange, balance, classify, conduct, control, coordinate, correct, determine, direct, dispose, fit, fix, govern, guide, handle, improve, legislate, measure, methodize, moderate, modulate, monitor, order, oversee, pull things together*, put in order, readjust, reconcile, rectify, rule, run, set, settle, shape up*, square, standardize, straighten up, superintend, supervise, systematize, temper, time, true, tune, tune up*; SEE CONCEPTS *94,117*

regulation [*n1*] *managing, organizing*
adjustment, administration, arrangement, classification, codification, control, coordination, direction, governance, governing, government, guidance, handling, management, moderation, modulation, reconciliation, regimentation, reorganization, settlement, standardization, superintendence, supervision, systematization, tuning; SEE CONCEPTS *94,117*

regulation [*n2*] *rule, requirement*
bible, book, canon, chapter and verse*, code, commandment, decree, decretum, dictate, direction, edict, law, no-nos*, numbers, order, ordinance, precept, prescript, principle, procedure, reg*, standing order, statute; SEE CONCEPTS *318,688*

regurgitate [v] *vomit*
be seasick*, be sick, boff*, drive the bus*, dry heave*, eject, emit, expel, gag*, heave*, hurl*, lose one's lunch*, pray to the porcelain god*, puke*, ralph*, retch, spew, spit up, throw up, toss one's cookies*, upchuck*, urp*; SEE CONCEPTS *179,185,308*

rehabilitate [v] *renovate, adjust*
change, clear, convert, fix up, furbish, improve, make good*, mend, rebuild, reclaim, recondition, reconstitute, reconstruct, recover, redeem, reestablish, reform, refurbish, rehab*, reinstate, reintegrate, reinvigorate, rejuvenate, renew, restitute, restore, save; SEE CONCEPTS *35,126,134,202*

rehash [v] *talk over again*
change, discuss, reiterate, repeat, rephrase, restate, reuse, rework, rewrite, say again, state differently; SEE CONCEPT *56*

rehearsal [n] *preparation for performance*
call, description, drill, dry run*, experiment, going-over, practice, practice session, prep*, reading, readying, recital, recitation, recounting, rehearsing, relation, retelling, run-through, shakedown*, test flight*, trial balloon*, trial performance, tryout, workout; SEE CONCEPTS *264,292,363*

rehearse [v] *prepare for performance*
act, depict, describe, do over, drill, dry run*, experiment, go over, go through, hold a reading*, hone, iterate, learn one's part, narrate, practice, ready, recapitulate, recite, recount, reenact, reiterate, relate, repeat, review, run lines, run through, study, take from the top*, tell, test, train, try out, tune up, walk through*, warm up, work out; SEE CONCEPTS *266,292,363*

reign [n] *rule, dominion*
administration, ascendancy, command, control, dynasty, empire, hegemony, incumbency, influence, monarchy, power, regime, sovereignty, supremacy, sway, tenure; SEE CONCEPTS *198,376*

reign [v] *have power over; prevail*
administer, be in power, be in the driver's seat*, be supreme, boss, command, dominate, domineer, govern, head up, helm, hold power, hold sway*, influence, manage, obtain, occupy, overrule, predominate, preponderate, rule, rule the roost*, run the show*, run things*, sit, superabound, wear the crown*; SEE CONCEPTS *117,298*

reimburse [v] *pay back something owed*
balance, compensate, indemnify, make reparations, make up for, offset, pay, recompense, recover, refund, remunerate, repay, requite, restore, return, square, square up; SEE CONCEPT *341*

rein [n] *restraint, control*
bit, brake, bridle, check, curb, deterrent, governor, halter, harness, hold, line, restriction, strap; SEE CONCEPT *499*

rein [v] *restrain, control*
bridle, check, collect, compose, cool, curb, halt, hold, hold back, limit, repress, restrict, simmer down, slow down, smother, suppress; SEE CONCEPT *130*

reinforce [v] *strengthen, augment*
add fuel to fire*, add to, back up, beef up*, bolster, boost, build up, buttress, carry, emphasize, energize, enlarge, fortify, harden, heat up, hype, increase, lend a hand, multiply, pick up, pillar,

prop, prop up, punch up, shore up, soup up*, stand up for, stiffen, stress, stroke, supplement, support, sustain, toughen, underline; SEE CONCEPTS *5,236,245,250*

reinstate [v] *give back responsibility*
bring back, put back, put in power again, recall, redeem, reelect, reestablish, rehabilitate, rehire, reintroduce, reinvest, renew, replace, restore, return, revive; SEE CONCEPTS *351,384*

reiterate [v] *say or do again*
come again, ditto*, double-check, echo, go over again, ingeminate, iterate, play back, recap*, recapitulate, recheck, rehash, renew, repeat, reprise, resay, restate, retell, rewarn, say again; SEE CONCEPTS *100,171,266*

reject [v] *say no to*
burn*, cashier*, cast aside, cast off, cast out, chuck, decline, deny, despise, disallow, disbelieve, discard, discount, discredit, disdain, dismiss, eliminate, exclude*, give thumbs down to*, jettison, jilt, kill*, nix*, not buy*, pass by, pass on, pass up, put down, rebuff, refuse, renounce, repel, reprobate, repudiate, repulse, scoff, scorn, scout, scrap, second, shed, shoot down*, shun, slough, spurn, throw away, throw out, turn down, veto; SEE CONCEPTS *21,30,180*

rejection [n] *denial, refusal*
bounce, brushoff*, cold shoulder*, disallowance, dismissal, elimination, exclusion, hard time*, kick in teeth*, nix*, no dice*, no go*, nothing doing*, no way*, pass*, rebuff, renunciation, repudiation, slap in the face*, thumbs down*, turndown, veto; SEE CONCEPTS *21,30,180*

rejoice [v] *be very happy about something*
be glad, be overjoyed, celebrate, delight, enjoy, exult, feel happy, glory, joy, jump for joy, make merry, revel, triumph; SEE CONCEPT *410*

rejoinder [n] *answer, reply*
comeback, confutation, counteraccusation, counterargument, countercharge, counterclaim, counterstatement, defense, rebuttal, repartee, response, retort, return, wisecrack; SEE CONCEPTS *274,278*

rejuvenate [v] *make new again*
breathe new life into*, do, do up*, exhilarate, give face lift to*, give new life to, make young again, modernize, reanimate, reclaim, recondition, reconstruct, recover, refresh, refurbish, regenerate, rehab, reinvigorate, renew, renovate, restitute, restore, retread, revitalize, revivify, spruce, spruce up*, update; SEE CONCEPTS *35,202*

relapse [n] *deterioration, weakening*
backsliding, fall, fall from grace*, lapse, loss, recidivism, recurrence, regression, repetition, retrogression, return, reversion, setback, turn for the worse*, worsening; SEE CONCEPT *698*

relapse [v] *deteriorate, weaken*
backslide, be overcome, be overtaken, degenerate, fade, fail, fall, fall back, lapse, recidivate, regress, retrogress, revert, sicken, sink, slide back, slip back, suffer, turn back, worsen; SEE CONCEPT *698*

relate [v1] *give an account of*
break a story*, chronicle, clue one in*, depict, describe, detail, disclose, divulge, express, get off one's chest*, give the word*, impart, itemize, lay it on the line*, let one's hair down*, narrate, particularize, picture, present, recite, recount, rehearse, report, retell, reveal, run down, run

re
re

through, set forth, shoot the breeze*, sling*, spill, spill the beans*, spin a yarn*, state, tell, track, verbalize; SEE CONCEPT 55

relate [v2] *correlate, pertain*
affect, ally, appertain, apply, ascribe, assign, associate, bear upon, be joined with, be relevant to, bracket, combine, compare, concern, conjoin, connect, consociate, coordinate, correspond to, couple, credit, have reference to, have to do with, identify with, impute, interconnect, interdepend, interrelate, join, link, orient, orientate, pertain, refer, tie in with, touch, unite, yoke; SEE CONCEPT 532

related [adj] *connected, accompanying*
affiliated, agnate, akin, alike, allied, analogous, associated, cognate, complementary, concomitant, connate, connatural, consanguine, convertible, correlated, correspondent, dependent, enmeshed, fraternal, germane, incident, interchangeable, interconnected, interdependent, interrelated, intertwined, interwoven, in the same category, in touch with, joint, knit together*, like, linked, mutual, of that ilk, parallel, pertinent, reciprocal, relevant, similar, tied up; SEE CONCEPTS 487,573,577

relation [n] *connection, family connection*
affiliation, affinity, alliance, association, consanguinity, kin, kindred, kinship, kinsperson, liaison, propinquity, relationship, relative, sibling, similarity; SEE CONCEPTS 296,414,421,714

relationship [n] *connection; friendship*
accord, affair, affiliation, affinity, alliance, analogy, appositeness, association, bond, communication, conjunction, consanguinity, consociation, contact, contingency, correlation, dependence, dependency, exchange, homogeneity, hookup, interconnection, interrelation, interrelationship, kinship, liaison, likeness, link, marriage, nearness, network, parallel, pertinence, pertinency, proportion, rapport, ratio, relation, relativity, relevance, similarity, tie, tie-in, tie-up; SEE CONCEPTS 388,714

relative [adj1] *comparative, respective*
about, allied, analogous, approximate, associated, concerning, conditional, connected, contingent, corresponding, dependent, in regard to, near, parallel, proportionate, reciprocal, referring, related, relating to, reliant, with respect to; SEE CONCEPT 563

relative [adj2] *pertinent, applicable*
apposite, appropriate, appurtenant, apropos, contingent, dependent, germane, pertaining, referring, related, relevant; SEE CONCEPT 558

relative [n] *member of a family*
agnate, aunt, blood, brother-in-law, clansperson, cognate, connection, cousin, father, father-in-law, folk, folks, grandparents, great-grandparents, in-laws, kinsperson, mother, mother-in-law, nephew, niece, relation, sib*, sibling, sister-in-law, stepbrother, stepparent, stepsister, uncle; SEE CONCEPT 414

relatively [adv] *in or by comparison*
almost, approximately, comparably, comparatively, nearly, proportionately, rather, somewhat, to some extent; SEE CONCEPTS 544,772

relax [v1] *be or feel at ease*
breathe easy*, calm, calm down*, collect oneself, compose oneself, cool off*, ease off, feel at home, hang loose*, knock off*, laze, let oneself go*, lie down, loosen up, make oneself at home*, put one's feet up*, recline, repose, rest, settle back, simmer down*, sit around, sit back, soften, stop work, take a break*, take a breather*, take it easy*, take one's time*, take ten*, take time out*, tranquilize, unbend, unlax*, unwind; SEE CONCEPT 210

relax [v2] *diminish, lessen*
abate, ease, ease off, ebb, lax, let up, loose, loosen, lose speed, lower, mitigate, moderate, modify, modulate, reduce, relieve, remit, slack, slacken, slow, slow down, untighten, weaken; SEE CONCEPTS 240,698

relaxation [n] *entertainment; resting or recovering*
alleviation, amusement, assuagement, diversion, enjoyment, fun, leisure, loosening, mitigation, pleasure, reclining, recreation, refreshment, relief, repose, requiescence, rest; SEE CONCEPTS 210,292,363

relay [v] *pass on, transmit*
broadcast, carry, communicate, deliver, hand down, hand on, hand over, send, send forth, spread, transfer, turn over; SEE CONCEPT 143

release [n1] *delivery; dispensation*
absolution, acquittal, acquittance, charge, clemency, commute, deliverance, discharge, dispensation, emancipation, exemption, exoneration, floater, freedom, freeing, let-off*, liberation, liberty, lifeboat, lifesaver, manumission, relief, spring, turnout, walkout; SEE CONCEPTS 127,685

release [n2] *publication*
announcement, flash*, handout, issue, leak, news, notice, offering, proclamation, propaganda, publicity, story; SEE CONCEPTS 271,280

release [v] *let go, let out*
absolve, acquit, bail out, cast loose, clear, commute, deliver, discharge, disengage, dispense, drop, emancipate, exculpate, excuse, exempt, exonerate, extricate, free, give off, give out, go easy on, issue, leak, let off, let off steam*, let up on*, liberate, loose, loosen, manumit, open up, set at large, set free, set loose, spring, surrender, take out, turn loose, turn out, unbind, unchain, undo, unfasten, unfetter, unleash, unloose, unshackle, untie, vent, wipe slate clean*, yield; SEE CONCEPTS 50,60,88,127,143

relegate [v1] *assign, transfer*
accredit, charge, commend, commit, confide, consign, credit, delegate, entrust, hand over, pass on, refer, turn over; SEE CONCEPTS 41,143

relegate [v2] *banish, downgrade*
demote, deport, dismiss, displace, eject, exile, expatriate, expel, expulse, lag, ostracize, remove, throw out, transport; SEE CONCEPTS 30,121,211

relent [v] *die down; let up*
acquiesce, be merciful, capitulate, cave in*, change one's mind, come around, comply, cool it*, cry uncle*, die away, drop, ease, ease off, ease up on*, ebb, fall, fold, forbear, give in, give quarter*, give some slack*, give up, give way, go along with, go easy on*, have mercy, have pity, lay back, let go, let it happen*, lighten up*, mellow out*, melt, moderate, quit, relax, say uncle*, show mercy, slacken, slow, soften, subside, wane, weaken, yield; SEE CONCEPTS 35,698,776

relentless [adj1] *cruel, merciless*
adamant, bound, bound and determined, dead set on*, determined, dogged, ferocious, fierce, go

for broke*, grim, hang in*, hang-tough*, hard, harsh, implacable, inexorable, inflexible, inhuman, mortal, obdurate, pitiless, remorseless, rigid, rigorous, ruthless, single-minded, stiff, stop at nothing, strict, stringent, unappeasable, unbending, uncompromising, undeviating, unflinching, unforgiving, unrelenting, unstoppable, unyielding, vindictive; SEE CONCEPT *401*

relentless [adj2] *continuous, neverending*
incessant, nonstop, persistent, pertinacious, punishing, sustained, tenacious, unabated, unbroken, unfaltering, unflagging, unrelenting, unrelieved, unremitting, unstoppable; SEE CONCEPTS *326, 534,798*

relevant [adj] *appropriate; to the purpose*
accordant, admissible, ad rem, allowable, applicable, applicatory, apposite, appurtenant, apt, becoming, cognate, compatible, concerning, conformant, conforming, congruent, congruous, consistent, consonant, correlated, correspondent, fit, fitting, germane, harmonious, having direct bearing on, having to do with, important, material, on the button*, on the nose*, pat*, pertaining to, pertinent, pointful, proper, referring, related, relative, significant, suitable, suited, to the point, weighty; SEE CONCEPT *558*

reliable [adj] *trustworthy*
candid, careful, certain, conscientious, constant, decent, decisive, definite, dependable, determined, devoted, faithful, firm, good, high-principled, honest, honorable, impeccable, incorrupt, loyal, okay, positive, predictable, proved, reputable, respectable, responsible, righteous, safe, sincere, solid, sound, stable, staunch, steadfast, steady, sterling, strong, sure, there, tried, tried-and-true*, true, true-blue*, true-hearted, trusty, unequivocal, unfailing, unimpeachable, upright, veracious; SEE CONCEPTS *535,542,544*

reliance [n] *confidence*
assurance, belief, credence, credit, dependence, faith, hope, interdependence, interdependency, stock, trust; SEE CONCEPT *689*

relic [n] *something saved from the past*
antique, antiquity, archaism, artifact, curio, curiosity, evidence, fragment, heirloom, keepsake, memento, memorial, monument, remains, remembrance, remembrancer, reminder, remnant, residue, ruins, scrap, souvenir, survival, testimonial, token, trace, trophy, vestige; SEE CONCEPT *446*

relief [n] *remedy, aid; relaxation*
abatement, allayment, alleviation, amelioration, appeasement, assistance, assuagement, balm, break, breather, cheer, comfort, comforting, consolation, contentment, cure, deliverance, diversion, ease, easement, extrication, fix, hand, happiness, help, let-up, lift, lightening, load off one's mind*, maintenance, mitigation, mollification, palliative, quick fix*, refreshment, release, remedy, remission, reprieve, respite, rest, restfulness, satisfaction, softening, solace, succor, support, sustenance; SEE CONCEPTS *681,712*

relieve [v1] *make less painful; let up on*
abate, allay, alleviate, appease, assuage, break, brighten, calm, comfort, console, cure, decrease, diminish, divert, dull, ease, free, interrupt, lighten, mitigate, moderate, mollify, palliate, qualify, quiet, relax, salve, slacken, soften, solace, soothe, subdue, take load off one's chest*,

take load off one's mind*, temper, vary; SEE CONCEPTS *244,700*

relieve [v2] *help; give assistance*
aid, assist, bring aid, give a break*, give a hand*, give a rest, spell, stand in for, substitute for, succor, support, sustain, take over from, take the place of; SEE CONCEPT *110*

relieve [v3] *remove blame, responsibility*
absolve, deliver, discharge, disembarrass, disencumber, dismiss, dispense, excuse, exempt, force to resign, free, let off, privilege, pull, release, spare, throw out, unburden, yank*; SEE CONCEPTS *50,88,351*

religion [n] *belief in divinity; system of beliefs*
church, communion, creed, cult, denomination, devotion, doctrine, higher power, morality, myth, mythology, observance, orthodoxy, pietism, piety, prayer, preference, religiosity, rites, ritual, sacrifice, sanctification, sect, spirituality, spiritual-mindedness, standards, superstition, theology, veneration; SEE CONCEPTS *368,689*

religious [adj1] *concerning belief in divinity*
believing, born-again*, canonical, churchgoing, churchly, clerical, deistic, devotional, devout, divine, doctrinal, ecclesiastical, god-fearing, godly, holy, ministerial, moral, orthodox, pietistic, pious, pontifical, prayerful, priestly, pure, reverent, righteous, sacerdotal, sacred, sacrosanct, saintlike, saintly, scriptural, sectarian, spiritual, supernatural, theistic, theological; SEE CONCEPTS *536,545*

religious [adj2] *conscientious, scrupulous*
exact, faithful, fastidious, meticulous, punctilious, rigid, rigorous, steadfast, unerring, unswerving; SEE CONCEPT *538*

relinquish [v] *give up, let go*
abandon, abdicate, abnegate, back down, cast, cast off, cede, cut loose*, desert, discard, ditch*, drop, drop like hot potato*, drop out, dump*, forbear, forgo, forsake, forswear, hand over, kick, kiss good-bye*, lay aside, leave, opt out, quit, quit cold turkey*, release, renounce, repudiate, resign, retire from, sacrifice, shed, stand down, surrender, swear off*, take the oath*, take the pledge*, vacate, waive, withdraw, yield; SEE CONCEPTS *119,127,234*

relish [n] *great appreciation of something*
appetite, bias, delectation, diversion, enjoying, enjoyment, fancy, flair, flavor, fondness, gusto, heart, leaning, liking, love, loving, palate, partiality, penchant, pleasure, predilection, prejudice, propensity, sapidity, sapor, savor, smack, stomach, tang, taste, zest; SEE CONCEPTS *20,32*

relish [v] *look forward to; appreciate*
admire, be fond of, cherish, delight in, dig*, enjoy, fancy, go, go for*, like, luxuriate in, mind, prefer, revel in, savor, taste; SEE CONCEPT *32*

reluctant [adj] *unenthusiastic, unwilling*
afraid, averse, backward, calculating, cautious, chary, circumspect, demurring, diffident, discouraged, disheartened, disinclined, grudging, hanging back, hesitant, hesitating, indisposed, involuntary, laggard, loath, opposed, queasy, recalcitrant, remiss, shy, slack, slow, squeamish, tardy, uncertain, uneager, wary; SEE CONCEPT *401*

rely [v] *have confidence in*
await, bank, be confident of, believe in, be sure of, bet, bet bottom dollar on*, build, calculate,

re
re

commit, confide, count, depend, entrust, expect, gamble on, have faith in, hope, lay money on*, lean, look, reckon, ride on coattails*, swear by*, trust; SEE CONCEPTS *12,26*

remain [v] *stay, wait*
abide, be left, bide, bivouac, bunk*, cling, continue, delay, dwell, endure, freeze, go on, halt, hang, hang out, hold over, hold the fort*, hover, inhabit, keep on, last, linger, live, lodge, make camp, nest, outlast, outlive, pause, perch, persist, prevail, put on hold, remain standing, reside, rest, roost, sit out, sit through, sit tight*, sojourn, squat, stand, stay behind, stay in, stay over, stay put, stick around, stop, survive, tarry, visit, wait; SEE CONCEPTS *23,239,681,804*

remainder [n] *balance, residue*
bottom of barrel*, butt, carry-over, detritus, dregs, excess, fragment, garbage, hangover*, heel, junk, leavings, leftover, obverse, oddment, odds and ends*, overplus, refuse, relic, remains, remnant, residuum, rest, ruins, salvage, scrap, stump, surplus, trace, vestige, waste, wreck, wreckage; SEE CONCEPTS *260,835*

remark [n] *comment, observation*
acknowledgment, annotation, assertion, attention, back talk, bon mot*, cognizance, comeback, commentary, conclusion, consideration, crack*, declaration, elucidation, exegesis, explanation, explication, exposition, expression, gloss, heed, illustration, interpretation, mention, mind, note, notice, obiter dictum, observance, observation, opinion, point, recognition, reflection, regard, saying, statement, talk, thought, two cents' worth*, utterance, wisecrack, witticism, word; SEE CONCEPTS *51,278*

remark [v] *notice and comment*
animadvert, behold, catch, commentate, crack*, declare, descry, espy, heed, make out, mark, mention, mouth off*, note, observe, pass comment, perceive, pick up on, reflect, regard, say, see, speak, spot, state, take note, take notice, utter, wisecrack; SEE CONCEPTS *38,51,626*

remarkable [adj] *extraordinary, unusual*
arresting, arrestive, conspicuous, curious, distinguished, exceptional, famous, gilt-edged*, greatest, important, impressive, marked, miraculous, momentous, notable, noteworthy, noticeable, odd, outstanding, peculiar, phenomenal, preeminent, primo*, prominent, rare, salient, signal, significant, singular, smashing, solid, splashy*, strange, striking, super, surprising, uncommon, uncustomary, unique, unordinary, unwonted, weighty, wicked*, wonderful, world class*, zero cool*; SEE CONCEPT *574*

remedial [adj] *healing, restorative*
alleviative, antidotal, antiseptic, corrective, curative, curing, healthful, health-giving, invigorating, medicating, medicinal, purifying, recuperative, reformative, remedying, repairing, restitutive, restorative, sanative, sanatory, solving, soothing, therapeutic, tonic, treating, vulnerary, wholesome; SEE CONCEPT *537*

remedy [n] *cure, solution*
antidote, assistance, biologic, corrective, counteractant, counteraction, counteractive, counteragent, countermeasure, counterstep, cure-all*, drug, elixir, fix, improvement, medicament, medicant, medicine, panacea, pharmaceutical, pharmacon, physic, pill, quick fix*, redress, re-

lief, restorative, support, therapy, treatment; SEE CONCEPTS *307,311,693,712*

remedy [v] *fix, cure*
aid, alleviate, ameliorate, amend, assuage, attend, change, clean up, clean up one's act*, control, correct, debug*, doctor, ease, fiddle with, fix up, go over, heal, help, launder, make up for, mitigate, palliate, pick up, put right, recalibrate, rectify, redress, reform, relieve, renew, repair, restore, revise, right, scrub, set right, set to rights*, shape up, solve, soothe, square*, square up*, straighten out, treat, upgrade; SEE CONCEPTS *126,212,310*

remember [v] *keep in mind; summon into mind*
bear in mind, bethink, brood over, call to mind, call up, cite, commemorate, conjure up, dig into the past*, dwell upon, educe, elicit, enshrine, extract, fix in the mind, flash on*, get, go back, have memories, hold dear*, keep forever, know by heart*, learn, look back, memorialize, memorize, mind, nail down*, recall, recognize, recollect, refresh memory, relive, remind, reminisce, retain, retrospect, revive, revoke, ring a bell*, strike a note*, summon up, think back, treasure; SEE CONCEPT *40*

remembrance [n1] *memory, recollection*
afterthought, anamnesis, flash*, flashback*, hindsight*, mental image, mind, recall, recognition, reconstruction, regard, reminiscence, retrospect, thought; SEE CONCEPTS *40,529*

remembrance [n2] *gift, testimonial*
commemoration, favor, keepsake, memento, memorial, monument, present, relic, remembrancer, reminder, reward, souvenir, token, trophy; SEE CONCEPT *337*

remind [v] *awaken memories of something*
admonish, advise, bethink, bring back to, bring to mind, call attention, call to mind, call up, caution, cite, emphasize, give a cue*, hint, imply, intimate, jog one's memory*, make one remember, make one think, mention, note, point out, prod, prompt, put in mind, recall, recollect, refresh memory, remember, reminisce, retain, retrospect, revive, stir up, stress, suggest, warn; SEE CONCEPTS *7,19,22,40,78*

reminder [n] *warning, notice; keepsake*
admonition, expression, gesture, hint, indication, intimation, memento, memo, memorandum, memorial, note, notice, relic, remembrance, remembrancer, sign, souvenir, suggestion, token, trinket, trophy; SEE CONCEPTS *271,278,529*

reminisce [v] *go over in one's memory*
bethink, call up, cite, hark back, live in the past, look back, mind, muse over, recall, recollect, remember, remind, retain, retrospect, review, revive, think back; SEE CONCEPTS *17,40*

reminiscent [adj] *suggestive of something in the past*
bringing to mind, evocative, implicative, mnemonic, nostalgic, recollective, redolent, remindful, similar; SEE CONCEPT *529*

remiss [adj] *careless, thoughtless*
any old way*, any which way*, asleep at switch*, asleep on job*, behindhand, culpable, daydreaming, defaultant, delinquent, derelict, dilatory, disregardful, fainéant, forgetful, heedless, inattentive, indifferent, indolent, lackadaisical, lax, lazy, neglectful, negligent, regardless, slack, slapdash, slipshod, sloppy, slothful, slow,

tardy, uninterested, unmindful, woolgathering*; SEE CONCEPT *401*

remission [*n1*] *acquittal, pardon*
absolution, amnesty, discharge, excuse, exemption, exoneration, forgiveness, indulgence, mercy, pardon, release, reprieve; SEE CONCEPT *685*

remission [*n2*] *pause; lessening*
abatement, abeyance, alleviation, amelioration, break, decrease, delay, diminution, ebb, interruption, let-up, lull, moderation, reduction, relaxation, release, respite, suspension; SEE CONCEPTS *303,698,807*

remit [*v1*] *send, transfer*
address, consign, dispatch, forward, mail, make payment, pay, post, route, settle, ship, square, transmit; SEE CONCEPTS *217,341*

remit [*v2*] *stop, postpone*
abate, absolve, alleviate, amnesty, cancel, condone, decrease, defer, delay, desist, diminish, dwindle, ease up, excuse, exonerate, fall away, forbear, forgive, halt, hold off, hold up, intermit, mitigate, moderate, modify, modulate, pardon, prorogue, put off, reduce, relax, release, repeal, reprieve, rescind, respite, shelve, sink, slack, slacken, soften, stay, suspend, wane, weaken; SEE CONCEPTS *234,698*

remnant [*n*] *leftover part*
balance, bit, dregs, dross, end, end piece, excess, fragment, hangover*, heel, leavings, lees, leftovers, odds and ends*, orts, part, particle, piece, portion, remainder, remains, residual, residue, residuum, rest, rump, scrap, shred, strip, surplus, survival, vestige; SEE CONCEPTS *260,835*

remodel [*v*] *reconstruct*
do up*, fix, fix up, make over, modernize, overhaul, reassemble, rebuild, recast, recondition, recreate, redesign, refurbish, rehabilitate, rejuvenate, remake, renovate, repair, restore, revamp, upgrade; SEE CONCEPTS *84,168,171*

remonstrate [*v*] *argue against anim*
advert, blame, censure, challenge, combat, complain, criticize, decry, demur, deprecate, disapprove, disparage, dispute, dissent, except, expostulate, fight, find fault, frown upon, inveigh, kick*, nag, object, oppose, pick at, protest, rain, recriminate, resist, scold, sound off*, take exception, take issue, withstand; SEE CONCEPTS *46,52,54*

remorse [*n*] *guilty or bad conscience*
anguish, attrition, compassion, compunction, contriteness, contrition, grief, guilt, pangs of conscience*, penance, penitence, penitency, pity, regret, remorsefulness, repentance, rue, ruefulness, self-reproach, shame, sorrow; SEE CONCEPTS *410,728*

remorseful [*adj*] *guilty, ashamed*
apologetic, attritional, chastened, compunctious, conscience-stricken, contrite, guilt-ridden, mournful, penitent, penitential, regretful, repentant, rueful, sad, self-reproachful, sorrowful, sorry; SEE CONCEPT *401*

remorseless [*adj*] *without guilt in spite of wrongdoing*
avaricious, barbarous, bloody, callous, cruel, fierce, forbidding, greedy, grim, hard, hard-bitten, hardened, hard-hearted, harsh, impenitent, implacable, inexorable, inhuman, inhumane, insensitive, intolerant, merciless, murderous, obdurate, pitiless, relentless, rigorous, ruthless,

sanguinary, savage, shameless, sour, tough, tyrannical, uncompassionate, uncontrite, unforgiving, unmerciful, unregenerate, unrelenting, unremitting, unrepenting, unyielding, vindictive; SEE CONCEPT *401*

remote [*adj1*] *out-of-the-way; in the distance*
alien, back, backwoods, beyond, boondocks*, devious, distant, far, faraway, far-flung, far-off, foreign, frontier, godforsaken*, god-knows-where*, in a backwater*, inaccessible, isolated, lonely, lonesome, middle of nowhere*, obscure, off-lying, off the beaten path*, outlandish, outlying, private, removed, retired, secluded, secret, undiscovered, unknown, unsettled, wild; SEE CONCEPT *583*

remote [*adj2*] *irrelevant, unrelated*
abstracted, alien, alone, apart, detached, exclusive, extraneous, extrinsic, farfetched, foreign, immaterial, inappropriate, indirect, nongermane, obscure, outside, pointless, removed, strange, unconnected; SEE CONCEPTS *564,575*

remote [*adj3*] *unlikely, improbable*
doubtful, dubious, faint, implausible, inconsiderable, meager, negligible, off, outside, poor, slender, slight, slim, small; SEE CONCEPT *552*

remote [*adj4*] *cold, detached; unapproachable*
abstracted, aloof, casual, cool*, disinterested, distant, faraway, icy, incurious, indifferent, introspective, introverted, laid-back*, offish, putting on airs, removed, reserved, standoffish, stuck up, uncommunicative, unconcerned, uninterested, uninvolved, uppity, withdrawn; SEE CONCEPTS *401,404*

remove [*v1*] *lift or move object; take off, away*
abolish, abstract, amputate, carry away, carry off, cart away, clear away, cut out, delete, depose, detach, dethrone, dig out, discard, discharge, dislodge, dismiss, displace, disturb, do away with, doff, efface, eject, eliminate, erase, evacuate, expel, expunge, extract, get rid of, junk*, oust, pull out, purge, raise, relegate, rip out, separate, shed, ship, skim, strike out, take down, take out, tear out, throw out, transfer, transport, unload, unseat, uproot, wipe out*, withdraw; SEE CONCEPT *211*

remove [*v2*] *do away with; kill*
assassinate, blot out*, clear away, dispose of, do away with, do in*, drag, drag down, efface, eliminate, eradicate, erase, exclude, execute, expunge, exterminate, extirpate, get rid of, liquidate, murder, obliterate, purge, scratch, sterilize, take down, take out, waste*, wipe out*; SEE CONCEPTS *121,252*

remunerate [*v*] *compensate, reward*
accord, ante up*, award, dish out*, do business*, grant, guerdon, indemnify, pay, pay off, pay up, post, recompense, redress, reimburse, repay, requite, shell out*, spring for*, vouchsafe; SEE CONCEPT *341*

renaissance [*n*] *rebirth*
awakening, invigoration, new dawn, reawakening, regeneration, rejuvenation, renascence, renewal, resurgence, revitalization, revival; SEE CONCEPTS *119,221*

render [*v1*] *contribute*
cede, deliver, distribute, exchange, furnish, give, give back, give up, hand over, impart, make available, make restitution, minister, part with, pay, pay back, present, provide, relinquish, repay, restore, return, show, submit, supply, sur-

render, swap, tender, trade, turn over, yield; SEE
CONCEPTS *108,140*
render [*v2*] *show; execute*
act, administer, administrate, carry out, delineate, depict, display, do, evince, exhibit, give,
govern, image, interpret, limn, manifest, perform, picture, play, portray, present, represent;
SEE CONCEPTS *91,261*
render [*v3*] *translate, explain*
construe, deliver, interpret, paraphrase, pass, put,
reproduce, restate, reword, state, transcribe,
transliterate, transpose, turn; SEE CONCEPTS
57,266
rendezvous [*n1*] *get-together*
affair, appointment, assignation, blind date, date,
double date, engagement, heavy date*, matinee,
meet, meeting, one night stand*, tête-à-tête,
tryst; SEE CONCEPT *384*
rendezvous [*n2*] *place for get-together*
gathering point, hangout*, haunt, love nest*,
meeting place, purlieu, resort, spot, stomping
ground*, venue, watering hole*; SEE CONCEPT
198
rendezvous [*v*] *meet, often secretly*
assemble, be closeted, be reunited, collect, come
together, congregate, congress, converge, forgather, gather, get together, join up, meet behind
closed doors*, meet privately, muster, raise,
rally; SEE CONCEPT *384*
rendition [*n*] *explanation; interpretation*
arrangement, construction, delivery, depiction,
execution, interpretation, performance, portrayal,
presentation, reading, rendering, transcription,
translation, version; SEE CONCEPTS *263,278*
renegade [*adj*] *rebellious*
apostate, backsliding, disloyal, dissident, heterodox, mutinous, outlaw, radical, reactionary,
rebel, recreant, revolutionary, runaway, schismatic, traitorous, unfaithful, untraditional; SEE
CONCEPTS *401,542*
renegade [*n*] *person who is rebellious*
abandoner, apostate, backslider, betrayer, defector, deserter, dissident, double-crosser*, escapee,
exile, forsaker, fugitive, heretic, iconoclast, insurgent, mutineer, outlaw, rebel, recreant,
refugee, runaway, schismatic, snake*, snake in
the grass*, tergiversator, traitor, turnabout, turncoat; SEE CONCEPTS *359,412*
renege [*v*] *go back on one's word*
break one's promise, cop out*, default, reverse,
weasel out*, welsh; SEE CONCEPTS *59,63,330*
renew [*v*] *start over; refurbish*
begin again, brace, breathe new life into*, bring
up to date*, continue, exhilarate, extend, fix up,
freshen, gentrify, go over, mend, modernize,
overhaul, prolong, reaffirm, reawaken, recommence, recondition, recreate, reestablish, refit,
refresh, regenerate, rehabilitate, reinvigorate, rejuvenate, remodel, renovate, reopen, repair, repeat, replace, replenish, restate, restock, restore,
resume, resuscitate, reveal, revitalize, revive,
spruce, stimulate, transform; SEE CONCEPTS
35,202,221
renounce [*v*] *abandon, reject*
abdicate, abjure, abnegate, abstain from, aposta-
cize, arrogate, cast off, decline, defect, demit,
deny, desert, disavow, discard, disclaim, disown,
divorce oneself from*, drop out, dump*, eschew,
forgo, forsake, forswear, give up, leave flat*,
leave off, opt out, quit, rat*, recant, reject, relin-

quish, repudiate, resign, sell out*, spurn, swear
off, take the pledge*, tergiversate, tergiverse,
throw off, throw over, toss over, turn, waive,
walk out on, wash hands of*; SEE CONCEPTS
30,54,195
renovate [*v*] *fix up, modernize*
clean, cleanse, do*, do up*, face-lift*, gussy up*,
make over, overhaul, reactivate, recondition, reconstitute, recreate, refit, reform, refresh, refurbish, rehabilitate, rekindle, remake, remodel,
renew, repair, restore, resurrect, resuscitate, retread, retrieve, revamp, revitalize, revive, revivify, spruce, spruce up*, update; SEE CONCEPTS
168,177,202
renown [*adj*] *fame*
acclaim, celebrity, distinction, éclat, eminence,
glory, honor, illustriousness, kudos, luster, mark,
note, notoriety, preeminence, prestige, prominence, prominency, rep*, reputation, repute, stardom; SEE CONCEPT *668*
renowned [*adj*] *famous*
acclaimed, celebrated, celebrious, distinguished,
eminent, esteemed, extolled, famed, great, illustrious, in the limelight*, lauded, monster*,
name*, notable, noted, of note, outstanding,
praised, prominent, redoubted, signal, splashy,
star, superstar, well-known; SEE CONCEPTS
568,574
rent [*n1*] *fee paid for use, service, or privilege*
hire, lease, payment, rental, tariff; SEE CONCEPT
329
rent [*n2*] *opening, split*
breach, break, chink, cleavage, crack, discord,
dissension, division, faction, fissure, flaw, fracture, gash, hole, perforation, rift, rip, rupture,
schism, slash, slit, tatter, tear; SEE CONCEPTS
513,665
rent [*v*] *pay or charge fee for use, service, or
privilege*
allow the use of, borrow, charter, contract, engage, hire, lease, lend, let, loan, make available,
put on loan, sublet, take it; SEE CONCEPTS *89,115*
renunciation [*n*] *abandonment, rejection*
abdication, abjuration, abnegation, abstention,
cancellation, denial, disavowal, disclaimer, eschewal, eschewing, forbearing, forswearing, giving up, rebuff, refusal, relinquishment,
remission, renouncement, repeal, repudiation,
resignation, sacrifice, self-abnegation, self-denial, self-sacrifice, spurning, surrender, veto,
waiver, yielding; SEE CONCEPTS *30,54,195*
repair [*n*] *restoration, fixing*
adjustment, darn, improvement, mend, new part,
overhaul, patch, reconstruction, reformation, rehabilitation, replacement, substitution; SEE CON-
CEPTS *513,700,824*
repair [*v1*] *fix, restore*
compensate for, correct, darn, debug*, doctor*,
do up*, emend, fiddle with, give a face-lift*,
heal, improve, make good, make up for, mend,
overhaul, patch, patch up, put back together, put
in order, put right, rebuild, recondition, recover,
rectify, redress, reform, refresh, refurbish, rejuvenate, remedy, renew, renovate, restore, retread,
retrieve, revamp, revive, right, settle, sew,
square*, touch up; SEE CONCEPT *212*
repair [*v2*] *leave; retire*
apply, betake oneself, fare, go, head for, hie,
journey, move, pass, proceed, process, push on,

recur, refer, remove, resort, run, set off for, travel, turn, wend, withdraw; SEE CONCEPT *195*

reparation [*n*] *compensation, amends*
adjustment, apology, atonement, damages, dues, emolument, expiation, indemnification, indemnity, making good, payment, penance, propitiation, quittance, recompense, redemption, redress, remuneration, renewal, repair, repayment, reprisal, requital, restitution, retribution, reward, satisfaction, settlement, squaring things*; SEE CONCEPTS *337,344,712*

repartee [*n*] *pleasant conversation*
answer, badinage, banter, bon mot*, comeback, humor, irony, persiflage, pleasantry, quip, raillery, rejoinder, reply, response, retort, riposte, sally, sarcasm, satire, wit, witticism, wittiness, wordplay; SEE CONCEPTS *45,56,266*

repast [*n*] *meal*
banquet, chow*, eats*, fare, feast, feed, food, grub*, mess, refection, refreshment, snack, spread, victuals; SEE CONCEPT *459*

repay [*v1*] *give back money or possession*
accord, award, balance, compensate, indemnify, make amends, make restitution, make up for, offset, pay back, pay dues, rebate, recompense, refund, reimburse, remunerate, requite, restore, return, reward, settle up, square*; SEE CONCEPTS *131,341*

repay [*v2*] *get even; obtain restitution for past injustice*
avenge, even the score, get back at, get revenge, make reprisal, pay back, reciprocate, requite, retaliate, return, return the compliment*, revenge, settle the score*, square accounts*; SEE CONCEPTS *7,19,246,384*

repeal [*n*] *cancellation*
abolition, abrogation, annulment, invalidation, nullification, rescinding, rescindment, rescission, revocation, withdrawal; SEE CONCEPTS *121,318,685*

repeal [*v*] *declare null and void*
abolish, abrogate, annul, back out, backpedal*, blow, call off*, cancel, countermand, dismantle, invalidate, kill*, KO*, lift, nix*, nullify, opt out, recall, renig, rescind, reverse, revoke, scrub, set aside, shoot down, stand down, throw over, vacate, void, wash out, weasel out*, wipe out, withdraw, worm out*, X-out*, zap*; SEE CONCEPTS *50,88,121,317*

repeat [*n*] *something done over; duplicate*
echo, recapitulation, reiteration, repetition, replay, reproduction, rerun, reshowing; SEE CONCEPT *695*

repeat [*v*] *duplicate, do again*
chime, come again, din, ditto*, drum into*, duplicate, echo, go over again, hold over, imitate, ingeminate, iterate, make like*, occur again, play back, play over, quote, read back, reappear, recapitulate, recast, reciprocate, recite, reconstruct, recrudesce, recur, redo, refashion, reform, rehash*, rehearse, reissue, reiterate, relate, remake, renew, reoccur, replay, reprise, reproduce, rerun, resay, reshow, restate, retell, return, revert, revolve, rework*, run over, sing same old song*; SEE CONCEPTS *91,111,171*

repeatedly [*adv*] *over and over again*
again, again and again, frequently, many a time, many times, much, oft, often, oftentimes, ofttimes, regularly, time after time, time and again; SEE CONCEPT *553*

repel [*v1*] *push away; repulse*
beat back, beat off, brush off, buck, cast aside, chase away, check, confront, cool*, cut, decline, dismiss, disown, dispute, drive away, drive back, drive off, duel, fend off, fight, force back, force off, give cold shoulder to*, hold back, hold off, keep at arm's length*, keep at bay*, keep off, kick, knock down, oppose, parry, push back, put down, put to flight, rebuff, rebut, refuse, reject, resist, stand up against, stave off, traverse, turn down, ward off, withstand; SEE CONCEPTS *30,208*

repel [*v2*] *induce aversion*
disgust, give a pain in neck*, make sick*, offend, put off*, reluct, repulse, revolt, sicken, turn off*, turn one's stomach*; SEE CONCEPTS *7,19,303*

repent [*v*] *ask forgiveness*
apologize, atone, be ashamed, be contrite, be sorry, bewail, deplore, feel remorse, have qualms, lament, reform, regret, relent, reproach oneself, rue, see error of ways*, show penitence, sorrow; SEE CONCEPTS *48,410*

repentance [*n*] *feeling bad for past action*
attrition, compunction, conscience, contriteness, contrition, grief, guilt, penitence, penitency, regret, remorse, rue, ruth, self-reproach, sorriness, sorrow; SEE CONCEPTS *410,728*

repercussion [*n*] *consequence*
backlash, chain reaction, echo, effect, fallout, feedback, flak*, follow-through*, follow-up, impact, imprint, influence, kickback*, mark, reaction, rebound, recoil, re-echo, result, reverberation, side effect, spinoff*, waves*; SEE CONCEPT *230*

repertory [*n*] *collection*
bit, cache, depot, list, range, rep*, repertoire, repository, routine, schtick*, stock, stockroom, store, storehouse, stunt*, supply; SEE CONCEPTS *263,432,712*

repetition [*n*] *duplication; doing again*
alliteration, broken record*, chant, chorus, copy, echo, encore, ingemination, iteracy, iterance, iteration, litany, paraphrase, periodicity, perseveration, practice, reappearance, recapitulation, recital, recurrence, redundancy, rehearsal, reiteration, relation, renewal, reoccurrence, repeat, repetitiousness, replication, report, reproduction, restatement, return, rhythm, rote, tautology; SEE CONCEPT *695*

repetitious [*adj*] *wordy, tedious*
alliterative, boring, dull, echoic, iterant, iterative, long-winded, plangent, pleonastic, prolix, recapitulatory, redundant, reiterative, repeating, repetitive, resonant, tautological, verbose, windy; SEE CONCEPT *553*

replace [*v*] *take the place of; put in place of*
alter, back up, change, compensate, displace, fill in, follow, front for*, give back, mend, oust, outplace, patch, pinch hit for*, put back, reconstitute, recoup, recover, redeem, redress, reestablish, refund, regain, reimburse, reinstate, repay, restitute, restore, retrieve, ring, ring in, shift, sit in, stand in, stand in lieu of, step into shoes of*, sub*, substitute, succeed, supersede, supplant, supply, swap places, take out, take over, take over from; SEE CONCEPTS *104,128,211,697*

replenish [*v*] *fill, stock*
furnish, make up, provide, provision, refill, refresh, reload, renew, replace, restock, restore, stock, top; SEE CONCEPTS *140,209*

replete [*adj*] *full, well-stocked*
abounding, abundant, alive, awash, brimful, brimming, charged, chock-full*, complete, crammed, crowded, filled, full up*, glutted, gorged, jammed, jam-packed, lavish, loaded, luxurious, overfed, overflowing, packed, plenteous, rife, sated, satiated, stuffed, swarming, teeming, thronged, well-provided; SEE CONCEPTS *483,740*

replica [*n*] *duplicate*
carbon, carbon copy, chip off old block*, clone, copy, ditto*, dupe*, facsimile, flimsy*, imitation, likeness, lookalike, mimeo, mimic, miniature, model, photocopy, reduplication, repeat, replication, repro, reproduction, stat, Xerox*; SEE CONCEPTS *260,670,686*

reply [*n*] *answer*
acknowledgment, antiphon, back talk*, comeback, counter, echo, feedback, knee-jerk reaction*, lip*, reaction, reciprocation, rejoinder, respond, response, retaliation, retort, return, riposte, sass*, snappy comeback*, vibes*, wisecrack; SEE CONCEPT *278*

reply [*v*] *answer*
acknowledge, be in touch*, come back*, counter, echo, feedback, field the question*, get back to, react, reciprocate, rejoin, respond, retaliate, retort, return, riposte, shoot back*, squelch*, top*, write back; SEE CONCEPT *45*

report [*n1*] *account, story*
address, announcement, article, blow by blow*, brief, broadcast, cable, chronicle, communication, communique, declaration, description, detail, digest, dispatch, handout, history, hot wire*, information, message, narration, narrative, news, note, opinion, outline, paper, picture, piece, precis, proclamation, pronouncement, recital, record, relation, release, résumé, rundown, scoop*, statement, summary, tale, telegram, tidings, version, wire, word*, write-up; SEE CONCEPTS *274,282,283*

report [*n2*] *gossip, talk*
advice, blow by blow*, buzz*, canard, chat, chatter, chitchat, comment, conversation, cry*, dirt*, earful, grapevine*, hash*, hearsay, intelligence, murmur, news, prating, rumble*, rumor, scandal, scuttlebutt*, small talk*, speech, tattle, the latest*, tidings, whispering, word*; SEE CONCEPTS *51,278*

report [*n3*] *loud noise*
bang, blast, boom, crack, crash, detonation, discharge, explosion, reverberation, sound; SEE CONCEPT *595*

report [*n4*] *reputation*
character, esteem, fame, name, regard, rep*, repute; SEE CONCEPT *388*

report [*v1*] *communicate information, knowledge*
account for, advise, air, announce, bring word, broadcast, cable, circulate, cover, declare, describe, detail, disclose, document, enunciate, give an account of, give the facts, impart, inform, inscribe, itemize, list, make known, make public, mention, narrate, note, notify, pass on, present, proclaim, promulgate, provide details, publish, recite, record, recount, rehearse, relate, relay, retail, reveal, set forth, spread, state, summarize, telephone, tell, trumpet, wire, write up; SEE CONCEPT *60*

report [*v2*] *present oneself*
appear, arrive, be at hand, be present, clock in*,

come, get to, reach, show, show up, turn up*; SEE CONCEPT *159*

reporter [*n*] *person who informs*
anchor, anchorperson, announcer, columnist, correspondent, cub*, editor, ink slinger*, interviewer, journalist, legperson*, newscaster, newshound*, newsperson, newswriter, press person, scribe, scrivener, stringer, writer; SEE CONCEPTS *348,356*

repose [*n*] *restfulness; calm*
ease, inaction, inactivity, leisure, peace, quiet, quietness, quietude, refreshment, relaxation, relaxing, renewal, requiescence, respite, rest, restoration, sleep, slumber, stillness, tranquillity; SEE CONCEPTS *410,681,720*

repose [*v*] *relax; recline*
deposit, lay down, lie, lie down, loaf, loll, lounge, place, rest, settle, settle down, slant, sleep, slumber, stretch, stretch out, take it easy, tilt; SEE CONCEPTS *154,210*

repository [*n*] *warehouse*
archive, depository, depot, magazine, safe, stockroom, storage place, storehouse, store room, vault; SEE CONCEPTS *435,439,449*

repossess [*v*] *take back*
get back, obtain again, reacquire, recapture, reclaim, recover, retake, retrieve; SEE CONCEPTS *120,183*

reprehensible [*adj*] *very bad; shameful*
amiss, blamable, blameworthy, censurable, condemnable, culpable, delinquent, demeritorious, discreditable, disgraceful, errant, erring, guilty, ignoble, objectionable, opprobrious, remiss, sinful, unholy, unworthy, wicked; SEE CONCEPT *571*

represent [*v1*] *present image of; symbolize*
act as, act as broker, act for, act in place of, appear as, assume the role of, be, be agent for, be attorney for, be proxy for, betoken, body, buy for, copy, correspond to, do business for, emblematize, embody, enact, epitomize, equal, equate, exemplify, exhibit, express, factor, hold office, imitate, impersonate, mean, perform, personify, play the part, produce, put on, reproduce, sell for, serve, serve as, show, speak for, stage, stand for, steward, substitute, symbolize, typify; SEE CONCEPTS *87,317,682,716*

represent [*v2*] *depict, show*
body forth, delineate, denote, describe, design, designate, display, draft, enact, evoke, exhibit, express, hint, illustrate, interpret, limn, mirror, narrate, outline, picture, portray, realize, relate, render, reproduce, run down, run through, sketch, suggest, track; SEE CONCEPTS *138,261*

representative [*adj*] *characteristic, typical*
adumbrative, archetypal, classic, classical, delineative, depictive, emblematic, evocative, exemplary, ideal, illustrative, model, presentational, prototypal, prototypical, quintessential, rep*, symbolic, symbolical; SEE CONCEPTS *487,573*

representative [*n1*] *person who acts in the stead of another*
agent, assemblyperson, attorney, commissioner, congressperson, councilor, councilperson, counselor, delegate, deputy, lawyer, legislator, member, messenger, proxy, rep*, salesperson, senator, spokesperson; SEE CONCEPTS *348,354*

representative [*n2*] *typical example*
archetype, case, case history, embodiment, epitome, exemplar, illustration, instance, personifi-

cation, sample, sampling, specimen, type; SEE CONCEPT *686*

repress [*v*] *keep back, hold in*
black out*, bottle, chasten, check, collect, compose, control, cool*, cork*, crush, curb, gridlock*, hinder, hold back, inhibit, jam up, keep in, keep in check, keep under wraps*, kill*, lock, master, muffle, overcome, overpower, quash, quelch, quell, rein, restrain, shush, silence, simmer down*, smother, squelch, stifle, subdue, subjugate, suppress, swallow, throw cold water on*, tie up*; SEE CONCEPTS *121,130*

reprieve [*n*] *relief of blame, responsibility*
abatement, abeyance, absolution, acquittal, alleviation, amnesty, anchor*, clearance, clemency, commute, deferment, freeing, let-up*, lifeboat*, lifesaver*, mitigation, palliation, pardon, postponement, release, remission, respite, spring*, stay, suspension, truce; SEE CONCEPTS *318,685*

reprieve [*v*] *relieve of blame, responsibility*
abate, absolve, allay, alleviate, amnesty, excuse, forgive, grant a stay, let go, let off, let off the hook*, let off this time*, let up on*, mitigate, palliate, pardon, postpone, remit, respite; SEE CONCEPTS *50,88,317*

reprimand [*n*] *oral punishment*
admonishment, admonition, bawling out*, blame, calling down*, castigation, censure, chiding, comeuppance, dressing-down*, going over*, grooming, hard time*, lecture, piece of one's mind*, ragging*, rap*, rebuke, reprehension, reproof, scolding, slap on wrist*, talking-to, telling-off, tongue-lashing, what for*; SEE CONCEPTS *123,278*

reprimand [*v*] *blame, scold*
admonish, call on the carpet*, castigate, censure, check, chew out*, chide, come down on*, criticize, denounce, dress down*, give piece of one's mind*, give the dickens*, lecture, lesson, light into*, lower the boom*, monish, rap, rebuke, reprehend, reproach, reprove, take to task*, tell off, tick off*, upbraid; SEE CONCEPTS *44,52*

reprisal [*n*] *revenge*
avengement, avenging, counterblow, counterstroke, eye for an eye*, paying back, requital, retaliation, retribution, vengeance; SEE CONCEPT *384*

reproach [*n*] *strong criticism; dishonor*
abuse, admonishment, admonition, blame, blemish, censure, chiding, condemnation, contempt, disapproval, discredit, disgrace, disrepute, ignominy, indignity, obloquy, odium, opprobrium, rap*, rebuke, reprehension, reprimand, reproof, scorn, shame, slight, slur, stain, stigma; SEE CONCEPTS *44,52,123,388*

reproach [*v*] *find fault with*
abuse, admonish, blame, call down, call to task*, cavil, censure, chide, condemn, criticize, defame, discredit, disparage, give comeuppance*, give the devil*, jawbone*, lay on*, lesson, rake, ream, rebuke, reprehend, reprimand, reprove, scold, sit on*, take to task, trim, upbraid; SEE CONCEPTS *44,52*

reprobate [*adj*] *shameless*
bad, corrupt, degenerate, foul, immoral, improper, incorrigible, lewd, rude, sinful, unprincipled, vile, wanton, wicked; SEE CONCEPTS *401,545*

reproduce [*v1*] *make more copies of*
carbon*, clone, copy, do again, dupe*, duplicate, echo, emulate, engross, follow, imitate, knock off, manifold, match, mimeo*, mimeograph, mirror, parallel, photocopy, photograph, photostat, pirate, portray, print, reawaken, recount, recreate, redo, reduplicate, reenact, reflect, relive, remake, repeat, replicate, represent, reprint, restamp, revive, stereotype, transcribe, type, Xerox*; SEE CONCEPTS *111,171*

reproduce [*v2*] *make something new; give birth*
bear, beget, breed, engender, father, fecundate, generate, hatch, impregnate, mother, multiply, procreate, produce young, progenerate, proliferate, propagate, repopulate, sire, spawn; SEE CONCEPTS *173,251,374*

reproduction [*n*] *something duplicated; duplication*
breeding, carbon*, carbon copy, chip off old block*, clone, copy, ditto*, dupe*, facsimile, fake, flimsy, generation, imitation, increase, look-alike, mimeo*, mimeograph, mirror image*, multiplication, offprint, photocopy, photograph, Photostat, pic*, picture, portrayal, print, procreation, proliferation, propagation, recreation, reduplication, reenactment, renewal, replica, replication, reprinting, repro*, revival, stat, transcription, twin, Xerox*, X-ray*; SEE CONCEPTS *173,625,670,716*

reprove [*v*] *rebuke*
admonish, bawl out*, berate, castigate, censure, chew out*, chide, condemn, jump down one's throat*, lambaste, lay into*, lecture, read the riot act*, reprimand, reproach, scold, take to task*, upbraid; SEE CONCEPTS *44,52*

repudiate [*v*] *reject; turn one's back on*
abandon, abjure, apostatize, banish, be against, break with, cast, cast off, cut off, decline, default, defect, demur, deny, desert, disacknowledge, disapprove, disavow, discard, disclaim, dishonor, disinherit, dismiss, disown, dump, flush*, fly in the face of*, forsake, nix*, oust, rat*, recant, refuse, renounce, repeal, reprobate, rescind, retract, reverse, revoke, spurn, tergiversate, tergiverse, turn, turn down, wash one's hands of*; SEE CONCEPTS *13,21,30*

repugnant [*adj*] *bad, obnoxious; hostile*
abhorrent, abominable, adverse, against, alien, antagonistic, antipathetic, averse, conflicting, contradictory, counter, creepy*, different, disagreeable, disgusting, distasteful, extraneous, extrinsic, foreign, foul, hateful, horrid, incompatible, inconsistent, inconsonant, inimical, in opposition, invidious, loathsome, nasty, nauseating, noisome, objectionable, odious, offensive, opposed, opposite, repellent, revolting, revulsive, sickening, unconformable, unfitted, unfriendly, vile; SEE CONCEPTS *401,564,571*

repulse [*n*] *snub; rejection*
brush-off*, check, cold shoulder*, defeat, disappointment, failure, nix*, nothing doing*, rebuff, refusal, reverse, slap in the face*, spurning, thumbs down*, turndown; SEE CONCEPTS *388,674*

repulse [*v1*] *push away*
beat off, brush off*, check, defeat, drive back, fend off, fight off, heave-ho*, hold off, keep off, kick in the teeth*, nix*, overthrow, push back, put down, rebuff, rebut, reject, repel, resist, set back, stave off, throw back, ward off; SEE CONCEPTS *96,208*

re
re

repulse [v2] *make sick*
disdain, disgust, disregard, give a pain*, rebuff, refuse, reject, reluct, repel, revolt, sicken, snub, spurn, turn down, turn off; SEE CONCEPTS *21,410*

repulsion [n] *hatred, disgust*
abhorrence, abomination, antipathy, aversion, denial, detestation, disrelish, distaste, hate, horror, loathing, malice, rebuff, refusal, repugnance, repugnancy, resentment, revolt, revulsion, snub; SEE CONCEPT *29*

repulsive [adj] *very disgusting, offensive*
abhorrent, abominable, animal*, creepy*, disagreeable, distasteful, forbidding, foul, gross, hateful, hideous, horrid, loathsome, nasty, nauseating, noisome, objectionable, obnoxious, odious, off-putting, pugnacious, repellent, revolting, sickening, sleazy*, ugly, undesirable, unpleasant, unsightly, vile; SEE CONCEPTS *529,571,579*

reputable [adj] *worthy of respect*
acclaimed, celebrated, conscientious, constant, creditable, dependable, distinguished, eminent, esteemed, estimable, excellent, fair, faithful, famed, famous, favored, good, high-principled, high-ranking, honest, honorable, honored, illustrious, in high favor, just, legitimate, notable, of good repute, popular, prominent, redoubted, reliable, renowned, respectable, righteous, salt of the earth*, sincere, straightforward, trustworthy, truthful, upright, well-known, well-thought-of; SEE CONCEPTS *545,567,574*

reputation [n] *commonly held opinion of person's character*
acceptability, account, approval, authority, character, credit, dependability, distinction, éclat, eminence, esteem, estimation, fame, favor, honor, influence, mark*, name*, notoriety, opinion, position, prestige, privilege, prominence, rank, regard, reliability, renown, rep*, report, repute, respectability, standing, stature, trustworthiness, weight; SEE CONCEPTS *388,411,689*

reputed [adj] *believed*
accounted, alleged, assumed, conjectural, considered, deemed, estimated, gossiped, held, hypothetical, ostensible, putative, reckoned, regarded, reported, rumored, said, seeming, supposed, suppositional, supposititious, supposititious, suppositive, suppository, thought; SEE CONCEPT *529*

request [n] *question or petition*
appeal, application, asking, begging, call, commercial, demand, desire, entreaty, inquiry, invitation, offer, prayer, recourse, requisition, solicitation, suit, supplication; SEE CONCEPT *662*

request [v] *ask for*
appeal, apply, beg, beseech, bespeak, call for, demand, desire, entreat, hit, hit up for*, hold out for*, hustle*, inquire, petition, pray, promote, put in for*, requisition, seek, solicit, sponge*, sue, supplicate, touch; SEE CONCEPT *53*

requiem [n] *hymn, mass*
canticle, ceremony, chant, death song, dirge, elegy, eulogy, funeral hymn, liturgy, memorial service, monody, psalm, religious song, ritual, sermon, threnody, worship; SEE CONCEPTS *262,368,595*

require [v1] *need, want*
crave, depend upon, desire, feel necessity for, have need, hurting for, lack, miss, stand in need, wish; SEE CONCEPTS *20,646*

require [v2] *ask, demand; necessitate*
assert oneself, beg, beseech, bid, call for, call upon, cause, challenge, claim, command, compel, constrain, crave, demand, direct, enjoin, entail, exact, expect, insist upon, instruct, involve, look for, obligate, oblige, order, postulate, push for, request, requisition, solicit, take; SEE CONCEPTS *53,646*

required/requisite [adj] *necessary*
appropriate, called for, compulsatory, compulsory, condign, demanded, deserved, due, enforced, essential, imperative, imperious, indispensable, just, mandatory, needed, needful, obligatory, prerequisite, prescribed, recommended, right, rightful, set, suitable, unavoidable, vital; SEE CONCEPT *546*

requirement/requisite [n] *necessity, want*
claim, compulsion, concern, condition, demand, desideratum, element, engrossment, essential, exaction, exigency, extremity, fulfillment, fundamental, imperative, lack, must, need, obligation, obsession, pinch, precondition, preliminary, preoccupation, prepossession, prerequisite, prescription, provision, proviso, qualification, sine qua non, specification, stipulation, terms, urgency, vital part; SEE CONCEPTS *646,709*

requisition [n] *demand; application for need*
appropriation, call, commandeering, demand, occupation, request, seizure, summons, takeover; SEE CONCEPT *662*

requisition [v] *ask for; apply for something needed*
buy, call for, challenge, claim, demand, exact, order, postulate, put dibs on*, put in for, request, require, solicit; SEE CONCEPTS *48,53*

requite [v] *compensate, give in return*
indemnify, make, make amends, make good, pay, pay off, quit, reciprocate, recompense, redeem, redress, reimburse, remunerate, repay, respond, restitution, retaliate, return, revenge, reward, satisfy, settle; SEE CONCEPTS *126,131,341,384*

rescind [v] *declare null and void*
abolish, abrogate, annul, back out of, backpedal*, backwater*, call off, cancel, countermand, crawl out of*, dismantle, forget, invalidate, lift, nix*, overturn, pull the plug*, quash, recall, remove, renege, repeal, retract, reverse, revoke, scrub*, set aside, void, wangle out*, weasel out*, X-out*; SEE CONCEPTS *121,234,317*

rescue [n] *saving from danger*
deliverance, delivery, disembarrassment, disentanglement, emancipation, exploit, extrication, feat, heroics, heroism, liberation, performance, ransom, reclaiming, reclamation, recovering, recovery, redemption, release, relief, salvage, salvation, saving; SEE CONCEPT *134*

rescue [v] *save from danger*
bail one out*, conserve, deliver, disembarrass, disentangle, emancipate, extricate, free, get off the hook*, get out, get out of hock*, give a break, hold over, keep, liberate, manumit, preserve, protect, pull out of the fire*, ransom, recapture, recover, redeem, regain, release, retain, retrieve, safeguard, salvage, save life of, set free, spring*, unleash, unloose; SEE CONCEPT *134*

research [n] *examination, study*
analysis, delving, experimentation, exploration, fact-finding, fishing expedition*, groundwork, inquest, inquiry, inquisition, investigation, leg-

work*, probe, probing, quest, R and D*, scrutiny; SEE CONCEPTS *349,362*

research [v] *examine, study*
analyze, consult, do tests, experiment, explore, inquire, investigate, look into, look up, play around with*, probe, read up on, scrutinize; SEE CONCEPTS *31,103*

researcher [n] *research worker*
analyst, analyzer, clinician, experimenter, investigator, scientist, tester; SEE CONCEPTS *348,357*

resemblance [n] *correspondence, similarity*
affinity, alikeness, analogy, birds of a feather*, carbon*, carbon copy, clone, closeness, coincidence, comparability, comparison, conformity, counterpart, double, facsimile, image, kinship, likeness, like of, look-alike, parallel, parity, peas in a pod*, ringer*, sameness, semblance, simile, similitude, spitting image*, two of a kind*, Xerox*; SEE CONCEPTS *664,670,716*

resemble [v] *look or be like*
appear like, approximate, bear resemblance to, be similar to, be the very picture of*, bring to mind, coincide, come close to, come near, correspond to, double, duplicate, echo, favor, feature, follow, have earmarks of*, have signs of, match, mirror, parallel, pass for, relate, remind one of, seem like, simulate, smack of*, sound like, take after; SEE CONCEPTS *664,670,716*

resent [v] *be angry about*
bear a grudge, begrudge, be in a huff*, be insulted, be offended by, be put off by*, be rubbed wrong way*, be vexed, dislike, feel bitter, feel sore*, frown at, get nose out of joint*, grudge, harbor a grudge*, have hard feelings*, object to, take amiss, take as an insult, take exception, take offense, take umbrage; SEE CONCEPTS *29,410*

resentment [n] *hate, anger*
acerbity, acrimony, animosity, animus, annoyance, antagonism, bad feeling, bitterness, choler, cynicism, displeasure, dudgeon, exacerbation, exasperation, fog, fury, grudge, huff, hurt, ill feeling, ill will, indignation, ire, irritation, malice, malignity, miff, offense, outrage, passion, perturbation, pique, rage, rancor, rise, spite, umbrage, vehemence, vexation, wrath; SEE CONCEPTS *29,410*

reservation [n1] *condition, stipulation*
catch, circumscription, demur, doubt, fine print*, grain of salt*, hesitancy, kicker*, provision, proviso, qualification, restriction, scruple, skepticism, string*, strings*, terms; SEE CONCEPTS *646,711*

reservation [n2] *the act of holding something, or thing held for future use*
bespeaking, booking, exclusive possession, place, restriction, retaining, retainment, setting aside, withholding; SEE CONCEPT *710*

reservation [n3] *habitat for large group*
enclave, homeland, preserve, reserve, sanctuary, territory, tract; SEE CONCEPTS *512,516*

reserve [n1] *supply*
ace in hole*, assets, backlog, cache, capital, drop, emergency fund*, fund, hoard, insurance, inventory, nest egg*, plant, provisions, rainy day fund*, reservoir, resources, savings, stash*, stock, stockpile, store, wealth; SEE CONCEPTS *340,710,712*

reserve [n2] *coolness of manner*
aloofness, backwardness, calmness, caution, coldness, constraint, coyness, demureness, diffidence, formality, inhibition, modesty, quietness, reluctance, repression, reservation, restraint, reticence, secretiveness, self-restraint, shyness, silence, suppression, taciturnity, uncommunicativeness, unresponsiveness; SEE CONCEPT *633*

reserve [v1] *keep, hold back*
conserve, defer, delay, duck*, have, hoard, hold, keep back, keep out, lay up, maintain, plant, possess, postpone, preserve, put away, put by, put off, retain, save, set aside, squirrel*, squirrel away*, stash, stockpile, store, store up, stow away, withhold; SEE CONCEPT *129*

reserve [v2] *hold for future use*
bespeak, book, contract, engage, prearrange, preengage, retain, schedule, secure; SEE CONCEPT *53*

reserved [adj1] *silent, unsociable; constrained*
aloof, backward, bashful, cautious, ceremonious, close, close-mouthed, cold*, collected, composed, conventional, cool, demure, diffident, distant, eremitic, formal, frigid, gentle, icy*, mild, misanthropic, modest, noncommittal, offish, peaceful, placid, prim, quiet, reclusive, restrained, reticent, retiring, secretive, sedate, self-contained, serene, shy, soft-spoken, solitary, standoffish, taciturn, unapproachable, uncommunicative, uncompanionable, undemonstrative, unresponsive, withdrawn; SEE CONCEPTS *401,404*

reserved [adj2] *held for future use*
appropriated, arrogated, booked, claimed, engaged, kept, laid away, limited, preempted, private, qualified, restricted, retained, roped off, set apart, set aside, spoken for, taken; SEE CONCEPTS *576,710*

reservoir [n] *accumulation, repository*
backlog, basin, cistern, container, fund, holder, lake, nest egg*, pond, pool, receptacle, reserve, source, spring, stock, stockpile, storage, store, supply, tank, tarn; SEE CONCEPTS *514,712*

reside [v] *live or exist in*
abide, be intrinsic to, be vested, bide, consist, continue, crash*, dig*, dwell, endure, hang one's hat*, inhabit, inhere, lie, locate, lodge, nest, occupy, park*, people, perch, populate, remain, rest with, roost, settle, sojourn, squat, stay, take up residence, tenant; SEE CONCEPTS *226,407*

residence [n] *place for living*
abode, address, apartment, condo, co-op, domicile, dwelling, habitation, hall, headquarters, hole, home, homeplate*, house, household, inhabitancy, inhabitation, living quarters, lodging, manor, mansion, occupancy, occupation, palace, rack*, roof*, roost*, seat, settlement, villa; SEE CONCEPT *516*

resident [n] *person living in a particular place*
citizen, denizen, dweller, habitant, householder, indweller, inhabitant, inmate, liver, local, lodger, native, occupant, resider, squatter, suburbanite, tenant, urbanite; SEE CONCEPT *413*

residual [adj] *leftover*
balance, continuing, enduring, extra, lingering, net, remaining, surplus, unconsumed, unused, vestigal; SEE CONCEPTS *560,771*

residue [n] *leftover part*
balance, debris, dregs, dross, excess, extra, garbage, heel, junk, leavings, leftovers, orts, parings, remainder, remains, remnant, residual, residuum, rest, scourings, scraps, scum, sewage,

re
re

shavings, silt, slag, surplus, trash; SEE CONCEPTS *260,432*

resign [*v*] *give up responsibility*
abandon, abdicate, bail out, bow out, capitulate, cease work, cede, demit, divorce oneself from, drop, drop out, end service, fold, forgo, forsake, give notice, give up the ship*, hand in resignation, hand over, hang it up*, leave, quit, relinquish, renounce, retire, secede, separate oneself from, sign off, stand aside, stand down, step down, surrender, terminate, throw in the towel*, turn over, vacate, waive, walk out, wash hands of*, yield; SEE CONCEPTS *119,195,351*

resignation [*n1*] *relinquishment of responsibility*
abandonment, abdication, departure, giving up, leaving, notice, quitting, renunciation, retirement, surrender, tendering, termination, vacating, withdrawal; SEE CONCEPTS *119,195,351*

resignation [*n2*] *endurance, passivity*
acceptance, acquiescence, compliance, conformity, deference, docility, forbearing, fortitude, humbleness, humility, longanimity, lowliness, meekness, modesty, nonresistance, patience, patientness, resignedness, submission, submissiveness, sufferance; SEE CONCEPTS *410,657*

resigned [*adj*] *enduring, passive*
accommodated, acquiescent, adapted, adjusted, agreeable, amenable, biddable, calm, compliant, cordial, deferential, docile, genial, gentle, long-suffering, manageable, nonresisting, obedient, patient, peaceable, philosophical, pliant, quiescent, quiet, ready, reconciled, relinquishing, renouncing, satisfied, stoical, subdued, submissive, subservient, tame, tolerant, tractable, unassertive, unprotesting, unresisting, well-disposed, willing, yielding; SEE CONCEPTS *401,542*

resilient [*adj*] *bouncy, flexible*
airy, buoyant, effervescent, elastic, expansive, hardy, irrepressible, plastic, pliable, quick to recover, rebounding, rolling with punches*, rubbery, snapping back, springy, stretchy, strong, supple, tough, volatile; SEE CONCEPTS *488,489*

resist [*v*] *withstand, oppose*
abide, abstain from, antagonize, assail, assault, battle, bear, brook, buck, check, combat, confront, contend, continue, counteract, countervail, curb, defy, die hard, dispute, duel, endure, fight back, forbear, forgo, hinder, hold, hold off, hold out against, keep from, leave alone, maintain, persevere, persist, prevent, put up a fight, refrain, refuse, remain, remain firm, repel, stand up to, stay, stonewall*, struggle against, suffer, thwart, traverse, turn down, weather, withstand; SEE CONCEPTS *23,35,96,106*

resistance [*n*] *fighting, opposition*
battle, blocking, check, combat, contention, counteraction, cover, defiance, detention, fight, friction, halting, hindrance, holding, impedance, impediment, impeding, intransigence, obstruction, parrying, protecting, protection, rebuff, refusal, retardation, safeguard, screen, shield, stand, striking back, struggle, support, warding off, watch, withstanding; SEE CONCEPTS *23,96,106,410*

resolute [*adj*] *determined, strong-willed*
adamant, bold, constant, courageous, dead set on*, decided, dogged, faithful, firm, fixed, immutable, inflexible, intent upon, intrepid, loyal, meaning business*, obstinate, persevering, persistent, persisting, purposeful, relentless, re-solved, serious, set, settled, staunch, steadfast, steady, strong, stubborn, tenacious, true, unbending, unchanging, uncompromising, undaunted, unfaltering, unflagging, unflinching, unshakable, unshaken, unwavering, unyielding, valiant; SEE CONCEPTS *403,542*

resolution [*n1*] *determination, strong will*
aim, boldness, constancy, courage, dauntlessness, decidedness, decision, declaration, dedication, determination, doggedness, earnestness, energy, firmness, fixed purpose, fortitude, guts*, heart*, immovability, intent, intention, judgment, mettle, moxie*, obstinacy, perseverance, pluck, purpose, purposefulness, purposiveness, relentlessness, resoluteness, resolve, settlement, sincerity, spirit, spunk, staunchness, staying power, steadfastness, stubbornness, tenacity, verdict, willpower; SEE CONCEPTS *410,657*

resolution [*n2*] *answer, judgment*
analysis, assertion, breakdown, call, conclusion, decision, declaration, determination, dissection, elucidation, end, exposition, finding, interpretation, motion, nod, outcome, pay dirt*, presentation, proposal, proposition, quick fix*, recitation, recommendation, resolve, settlement, solution, solving, sorting out, ticket*, unravelling, upshot, verdict, working out; SEE CONCEPTS *18,230,274*

resolve [*n*] *decision, determination*
boldness, conclusion, courage, decidedness, design, earnestness, firmness, fixed purpose, intention, objective, project, purpose, purposefulness, purposiveness, resoluteness, resolution, steadfastness, undertaking, will, willpower; SEE CONCEPTS *410,659,689*

resolve [*v*] *make up one's mind; find solution*
agree, analyze, anatomize, answer, break, break down, choose, clear up, clinch*, conclude, deal with, decide, decipher, decree, design, determine, dissect, dissolve, elect, elucidate, fathom, figure, fix, intend, iron out*, lick, make a point of, pan out*, pass upon, propose, purpose, puzzle out, remain firm, rule, settle, solve, take a stand, undertake, unfold, unravel, untangle, unzip*, will, work, work out, work through; SEE CONCEPTS *15,18,24*

resonant [*adj*] *vibrant in sound*
beating, booming, clangorous, consonant, deep, deep-toned, earsplitting, echoing, electrifying, enhanced, full, heightened, intensified, loud, mellow, noisy, orotund, plangent, powerful, profound, pulsating, pulsing, resounding, reverberant, reverberating, rich, ringing, roaring, round, sonorant, sonorous, stentorian, strident, thrilling, throbbing, thundering, thunderous; SEE CONCEPT *594*

resonate [*v*] *resound*
echo, oscillate, reproduce, reverberate, ring, sound, vibrate; SEE CONCEPT *65,91,171*

resort [*n1*] *vacation place*
camp, fat farm*, hangout, harbor, haunt, haven, hideaway, hideout, holiday spot, hotel, hot spring*, inn, lodge, mineral spring, motel, nest, park, purlieu, refuge, rendezvous, retreat, spa, spot, spring, stomping ground*, tourist center, tourist trap*; SEE CONCEPTS *198,516*

resort [*n2*] *alternative, recourse*
chance, course, device, expediency, expedient, hope, makeshift, opportunity, possibility, reference, refuge, relief, resource, shift, stopgap, substitute, surrogate; SEE CONCEPTS *693,712*

resort [v] *have recourse to; make use of*
address, affect, apply, avail oneself of, benefit by, bring into play, devote, direct, employ, exercise, fall back on, frequent, go, go to, haunt, head for, look to, make use of, put to use, recur, recur to, refer to, repair, run, take up, try, turn, turn to, use, utilize, visit; SEE CONCEPT *225*

resound [v] *resonate*
boom, bounce back, echo, reproduce, reverberate, ring, sound, vibrate; SEE CONCEPTS *65,91,171*

resource [n] *supply drawn upon, either material or nonmaterial*
ability, appliance, artifice, assets, capability, capital, cleverness, contraption, contrivance, course, creation, device, expedient, fortune, hoard, ingenuity, initiative, inventiveness, makeshift, means, measure, method, mode, nest egg*, property, quick-wittedness, recourse, refuge, relief, reserve, resourcefulness, riches, shift, source, step, stock, stockpile, store, stratagem, substance, substitute, support, surrogate, system, talent, way, wealth, worth; SEE CONCEPTS *340,523,658,710,712*

resourceful [adj] *imaginative*
able, active, adventurous, aggressive, bright, capable, clever, creative, enterprising, ingenious, intelligent, inventive, original, quick-witted, sharp, talented, venturesome; SEE CONCEPT *402*

resources [n] *money, possessions, natural resources*
ace in hole*, assets, backing, bankroll, basics, belongings, budget, capital, collateral, effects, funds, holdings, income, kitty*, material goods, means, nest egg*, nut*, property, reserves, revenue, riches, savings, sock*, stuff, supplies, the goods*, ways and means*, wealth, wherewithal*; SEE CONCEPTS *340,446,523,710,712*

respect [n1] *admiration given by others*
account, adoration, appreciation, approbation, awe, consideration, courtesy, deference, dignity, esteem, estimation, favor, fear, homage, honor, obeisance, ovation, recognition, regard, repute, reverence, testimonial, tribute, veneration, worship; SEE CONCEPT *689*

respect [n2] *way, sense*
aspect, bearing, character, connection, detail, facet, feature, matter, particular, point, reference, regard, relation; SEE CONCEPT *682*

respect [v] *admire; obey*
abide by, adhere to, adore, appreciate, attend, be awed by, be kind to, comply with, defer to, esteem, follow, have good opinion of, have high opinion, heed, honor, look up to, note, notice, observe of, pay attention, recognize, regard, revere, reverence, set store by, show consideration, show courtesy, spare, take into account, think highly of, uphold, value, venerate; SEE CONCEPTS *10,32*

respectable [adj1] *good, honest*
admirable, appropriate, august, becoming, befitting, comely, conforming, correct, creditable, decent, decorous, dignified, done, estimable, fair, honorable, mediocre, moderate, modest, nice, ordinary, passable, presentable, proper, redoubtable, redoubted, reputable, reputed, respected, satisfactory, seemly, sublime, suitable, tolerable, upright, venerable, virtuous, well-thought-of, worthy; SEE CONCEPT *572*

respectable [adj2] *substantial, ample*
appreciable, considerable, decent, fair, fairly good, good, goodly, presentable, reasonable, sensible, sizable, tidy, tolerable; SEE CONCEPT *771*

respectful [adj] *courteous, mannerly*
admiring, appreciative, civil, considerate, courtly, deferential, duteous, dutiful, gracious, humble, obedient, obeisant, polite, recognizing, regardful, regarding, reverent, reverential, self-effacing, solicitous, submissive, upholding, venerating, well-mannered; SEE CONCEPT *401*

respective [adj] *particular, specific*
corresponding, each, individual, own, personal, relevant, separate, several, singular, various; SEE CONCEPT *556*

respects [n] *good wishes*
best wishes, compliments, courtesies, deference, devoirs, greetings, kind wishes, regards, salaam*, salutations; SEE CONCEPT *278*

respite [n] *pause, suspension in activity*
acquittal, adjournment, break, breath*, breather*, breathing space*, cessation, coffee break*, deadlock, deferment, delay, deliverance, discharge, downtime*, ease, exculpation, five*, forgiveness, halt, hiatus, immunity, intermission, interregnum, interruption, interval, layoff, leisure, letup*, lull, moratorium, pardon, postponement, protraction, recess, relaxation, release, relief, reprieve, rest, stay, stop, ten*, time, time out*, truce; SEE CONCEPTS *121,681,807*

resplendent [adj] *bright, radiant*
beaming, blazing, brilliant, dazzling, effulgent, flaming, gleaming, glittering, glorious, glossy, glowing, gorgeous, irradiant, luminous, lustrous, magnificent, proud, refulgent, shining, shiny, splendid, splendiferous, splendorous, sublime, superb; SEE CONCEPTS *579,589,617*

respond [v] *act in answer to something*
acknowledge, act in response, answer, answer back, behave, be in touch with, come back, come back at, come in, counter, feedback, feel for, field the question*, get back to*, get in touch, react, reciprocate, rejoin, reply, retort, return, talk back; SEE CONCEPTS *45,384*

response [n] *answer, reaction*
acknowledgment, antiphon, back talk*, comeback, counter, double-take*, echo, feedback, hit, kickback*, knee-jerk reaction*, lip*, rejoinder, reply, respond, retort, return, reverberation, riposte, sass*, snappy comeback*, vibes*, wisecrack; SEE CONCEPT *278*

responsibility [n1] *accountability, blame*
albatross*, amenability, answerability, authority, boundness, burden, care, charge, constraint, contract, culpability, duty, encumbrance, engagement, fault, guilt, holding the bag*, importance, incubus, incumbency, liability, obligation, obligatoriness, onus, pledge, power, rap, restraint, subjection, trust; SEE CONCEPT *645*

responsibility [n2] *maturity, trustworthiness*
ability, capableness, capacity, competency, conscientiousness, dependability, dependableness, efficiency, faithfulness, firmness, honesty, level-headedness, loyalty, rationality, reliability, sensibleness, soberness, stability, steadfastness, trustiness, uprightness; SEE CONCEPTS *411,633*

responsible [adj1] *accountable, in charge*
answerable, at fault, at the helm, authoritative, bonded, bound, bound to, carrying the load, cen-

re
re

surable, chargeable, compelled, constrained, contracted, culpable, decision-making, devolving on, duty-bound, engaged, executive, exposed, fettered, guilty, hampered, held, high, important, in authority, in control, incumbent, liable, minding the store*, obligated, obliged, on the hook*, open, pledged, subject, susceptive, sworn to, tied, to blame, under contract, under obligation; SEE CONCEPT 545

responsible [*adj2*] *trustworthy, mature*
able, adult, capable, competent, conscientious, dependable, dutiful, effective, efficient, faithful, firm, levelheaded, loyal, qualified, rational, reliable, self-reliant, sensible, sober, sound, stable, steadfast, steady, tried, trusty, upright; SEE CONCEPTS *401,404*

responsive [*adj*] *quick to react*
acknowledging, active, alive, answering, awake, aware, compassionate, conscious, forthcoming, impressionable, influenceable, kindhearted, open, passionate, perceptive, persuadable, reactive, receptive, replying, respondent, sensible, sensile, sensitive, sentient, sharp, softhearted, susceptible, susceptive, sympathetic, tender, warm, warmhearted; SEE CONCEPTS *401,542*

rest [*n1*] *inactivity*
break, breather*, breathing space*, calm, calmness, cessation, coffee break*, comfort, composure, cutoff, downtime*, doze, dreaminess, ease, forty winks*, halt, holiday, hush, idleness, interlude, intermission, interval, leisure, letup*, lull, motionlessness, nap, pause, peace, quiescence, quiet, quietude, recess, recreation, refreshment, relaxation, relief, repose, respite, siesta, silence, sleep, slumber, somnolence, standstill, stay, stillness, stop, time off, tranquillity, vacation; SEE CONCEPTS *315,681,807*

rest [*n2*] *remainder of something*
balance, bottom of barrel*, dregs, dross, excess, heel, leavings, leftovers, odds and ends*, orts, others, overplus, remains, remnant, residual, residue, residum, rump, superfluity, surplus; SEE CONCEPTS *260,835*

rest [*n3*] *base, foundation*
basis, bed, bottom, footing, ground, groundwork, holder, pedestal, pediment, pillar, prop, seat, seating, shelf, stand, stay, support, trestle; SEE CONCEPTS *442,825*

rest [*v1*] *be calm; sleep*
be at ease, be comfortable, breathe, compose oneself, doze, dream, drowse, ease off, ease up, idle, laze, lean, let down, let up, lie by, lie down, lie still, loaf, loll, lounge, nap, nod, put feet up*, recline, refresh oneself, relax, repose, sit down, slack, slacken, slack off, sleep, slumber, snooze, spell, stretch out, take a break, take a nap, take five*, take it easy*, take life easy*, take ten*, take time out, unbend, unlax*, unwind, wind down; SEE CONCEPTS *210,315,681*

rest [*v2*] *lie, recline*
be quiet, be supported, lay, lean, lie still, loll, lounge, pause, prop, repose, roost, settle, sit, stand, stand still, stretch out; SEE CONCEPTS *154,681*

rest [*v3*] *depend, hinge*
base, be based, be contingent, be dependent, be founded, be seated on, be supported, be upheld, bottom, count, establish, found, ground, hang, lie, predicate, rely, reside, stay, turn; SEE CONCEPT *711*

restaurant [*n*] *business establishment serving food and drink*
bar, café, cafeteria, canteen, chophouse*, coffee shop, diner, dining room, dive*, doughnut shop, drive-in, eatery, eating house, eating place, fastfood place, greasy spoon*, grill, hamburger stand, hashery*, hideaway*, hotdog stand, inn, joint*, luncheonette, lunchroom, night club, outlet*, pizzeria, saloon, soda fountain, watering hole*; SEE CONCEPTS *439,448,449*

restful [*adj*] *quiet*
calm, comfortable, contented, hushed, inactive, motionless, pacific, peaceful, placid, relaxed, relaxing, retired, sedate, serene, soothing, still, tranquil, unanxious, unexcited, untroubled; SEE CONCEPTS *401,583,705*

restitution [*n*] *compensation, repayment*
amends, dues, indemnification, indemnity, payment, quittance, rebate, recompense, redress, refund, reimbursement, remuneration, reparation, reprisal, requital, restoration, return, satisfaction, squaring things*; SEE CONCEPT *344*

restive [*adj*] *impatient, nervous*
agitated, balky, contrary, edgy, fidgety, fractious, fretful, froward, ill at ease, jittery, jumpy, nervy, obstinate, on edge, ornery*, perverse, recalcitrant, refractory, restless, stubborn, tense, uneasy, unruly, unyielding, uptight; SEE CONCEPTS *401,542*

restless [*adj*] *not content; moving about*
active, agitated, antsy*, anxious, bundle of nerves*, bustling, changeable, disturbed, edgy, fidgeting, fidgety, fitful, footloose*, fretful, hurried, ill at ease, inconstant, intermittent, irresolute, itchy*, jumpy, nervous, nomadic, on edge, perturbed, restive, roving, sleepless, spasmodic, strung out*, tossing and turning*, transient, troubled, turbulent, uneasy, unpeaceful, unquiet, unrestful, unruly, unsettled, unstable, unsteady, wandering, worried; SEE CONCEPTS *403,542,584*

restlessness [*n*] *constant motion; discontent*
activity, agitation, ailment, ants*, antsiness*, anxiety, bustle, disquiet, disquietude, disturbance, edginess, excitability, ferment, fitfulness, fretfulness, hurry, inconstancy, inquietude, insomnia, instability, jitters, jumpiness, movement, nervousness, restiveness, transience, turbulence, turmoil, uneasiness, unrest, unsettledness, worriedness; SEE CONCEPTS *410,657,748*

restore [*v1*] *fix, make new*
bring back, build up, cure, heal, improve, make healthy, make restitution, mend, modernize, reanimate, rebuild, recall, recondition, reconstitute, reconstruct, recover, redeem, reenforce, reerect, re-establish, refresh, refurbish, rehabilitate, reimpose, reinstate, reintroduce, rejuvenate, renew, renovate, repair, replace, rescue, retouch, revitalize, revive, revivify, set to rights, strengthen, touch up, update, win back; SEE CONCEPTS *126,212,244*

restore [*v2*] *give back*
hand back, put back, replace, return, send back; SEE CONCEPTS *131,232*

restrain [*v*] *keep under control; hold back*
arrest, bind, bottle up, box up, bridle, chain, check, choke back, circumscribe, confine, constrain, contain, control, cool*, cork*, crack down*, curb, curtail, debar, delimit, detain, deter, direct, fetter, gag, govern, guide, hamper, handicap, harness, hem in, hinder, hogtie*, hold,

impound, imprison, inhibit, jail, keep, keep down, keep in line*, kill*, limit, lock up, manacle, muzzle, pinion, prevent, proscribe, pull back, repress, restrict, sit on, stay, subdue, suppress, tie down, tie up; SEE CONCEPTS *121,130,191*

restrained [*adj*] *calm, quiet*
bottled up, calm and collected, chilled, conservative, controlled, cool, corked up, discreet, in charge, in check, inobtrusive, laid-back*, mild, moderate, muted, on a leash*, plain, reasonable, reticent, retiring, self-controlled, shrinking, soft, steady, subdued, tasteful, temperate, unaffable, undemonstrative, under control, under wraps*, unexcessive, unexpansive, unextreme, unobtrusive, uptight, withdrawn; SEE CONCEPTS *401,542*

restraint [*n1*] *self-control*
abstemiousness, abstinence, caution, coercion, command, compulsion, confines, constraint, control, coolness, curtailment, economy, forbearance, grip, hindrance, hold, inhibition, limitation, moderation, prevention, repression, reserve, restriction, secretiveness, self-denial, self-discipline, self-government, self-possession, self-restraint, silence, suppression, unnaturalness, withholding; SEE CONCEPT *633*

restraint [*n2*] *limitation; something that holds*
abridgment, arrest, ban, bar, barrier, bondage, bridle, captivity, chains, check, command, confinement, constraint, cramp, curb, decrease, deprivation, detention, determent, deterrence, embargo, fetters, hindrance, impediment, imprisonment, instruction, interdict, limit, manacles, obstacle, obstruction, order, pinions, prohibition, reduction, rein, repression, restriction, rope, stop, stoppage, straitjacket, string*, taboo, weight; SEE CONCEPTS *5,666,674*

restrict [*v*] *confine, limit situation or ability to participate*
bind, bottle up, bound, chain, check, circumscribe, come down on, constrict, contain, contract, cool down, cramp, curb, decrease, define, delimit, delimitate, demarcate, demark, diminish, encircle, enclose, hamper, handicap, hang up, hem in, hold back, hold down, impede, inclose, inhibit, keep within bounds, keep within limits, moderate, modify, narrow, pin down, prelimit, put away, put on ice*, qualify, reduce, regulate, restrain, send up, shorten, shrink, shut in, surround, temper, tether, tie; SEE CONCEPT *130*

restriction [*n*] *limit*
ball and chain*, bounds, brake, catch, check, circumscription, condition, confinement, constraint, containment, contraction, control, cramp, curb, custody, demarcation, excess baggage*, fine print*, glitch*, grain of salt*, handicap, hangup*, inhibition, limitation, limits, lock*, no-no*, qualification, regulation, reservation, restraint, rule, small difficulty, stint, stipulation, stricture, string*, stumbling block*; SEE CONCEPTS *666,674*

result [*n*] *effect brought about by something*
aftereffect, aftermath, arrangement, backwash*, by-product, close, completion, conclusion, consequence, consummation, corollary, creature, crop, decision, denouement, determination, development, emanation, end, ensual, event, eventuality, execution, finish, fruit*, fruition, harvest, issue, offshoot*, outcome, outcropping, outgrowth, payoff, proceeds, product, production,

reaction, repercussion, returns, sequel, sequence, settlement, termination, upshot; SEE CONCEPT *230*

result [*v*] *happen, develop*
accrue, appear, arise, attend, become of, be due to, come about, come forth, come from, come of, come out, conclude, culminate, derive, effect, emanate, emerge, end, ensue, eventualize, eventuate, finish, flow, follow, fruit, germinate, grow, happen, issue, occur, originate, pan out, proceed, produce, rise, spring, stem, terminate, turn out, wind up, work out; SEE CONCEPTS *4,119,242*

résumé [*n*] *outline of experience*
abstract, bio*, biography, curriculum vitae, CV*, digest, epitome, precis, recapitulation, review, rundown, sum, summary, summation, summing-up, synopsis, vita, work history; SEE CONCEPTS *271,283*

resume [*v*] *begin again*
assume again, carry on, come back, continue, go on, go on with, keep on, keep up, occupy again, pick up, proceed, reassume, recapitulate, recommence, recoup, regain, reinstitute, reoccupy, reopen, repossess, restart, retake, return to, take back, take up; SEE CONCEPTS *221,239*

resurgence [*n*] *revival*
comeback, reawakening, rebirth, rebound, recovery, rejuvenation, renaissance, renascence, renewal, restoration, resurrection, return, revitalization, triumph; SEE CONCEPTS *119,221,706*

resurrection [*n*] *awakening from the dead*
reappearance, reawakening, rebirth, restoration, resurgence, return to life, revival; SEE CONCEPTS *119,221*

resuscitate [*v*] *revive*
arouse, awaken, breathe new life into*, bring back to life, bring to*, come to life, energize, enkindle, enliven, give mouth-to-mouth resuscitation, invigorate, perform CPR, rejuvenate, renovate, restore, resurrect, revitalize, save, wake up; SEE CONCEPTS *13,221,469,697*

retain [*v1*] *hold on to physically or mentally*
absorb, bear in mind, cling to, clutch, contain, detain, enjoy, grasp, hand onto, have, hold, hold fast, husband, keep, keep in mind, keep possession, maintain, memorize, mind, own, possess, preserve, put away, recall, recognize, recollect, remember, reminisce, reserve, restrain, retrospect, save, withhold; SEE CONCEPTS *40,190,710*

retain [*v2*] *hire*
commission, contract, employ, engage, maintain, pay, reserve; SEE CONCEPT *351*

retaliate [*v*] *get even with someone*
even the score*, exact retribution, get, get back at, give and take*, make reprisal, pay, pay back, reciprocate, recompense, repay, requite, retrospect, return, return the compliment, revenge, revive, settle, square accounts*, strike back, take an eye for an eye*, take revenge, turn the tables on*, turn upon, wreak vengeance; SEE CONCEPTS *126,384*

retard [*v*] *hinder, obstruct*
arrest, back off, baffle, balk, bog, bog down, brake, bring to screeching halt*, check, choke, choke off, clog, close off, crimp, dawdle, decelerate, decrease, defer, delay, detain, down, encumber, falter, fetter, flag, hamper, handicap, hang up, hesitate, hold back, hold up, impede, lessen, let up, loaf, loiter, mire, poke, postpone,

re
re

reduce, retardate, set back, shut down, shut off, slacken, slow down, slow up, stall, take down; SEE CONCEPTS *121,130,190,240*

reticent [*adj*] *secretive, quiet*
bashful, clammed up*, close, close-mouthed, dried up*, dummied up*, hesitant, mum, reserved, restrained, shy, silent, taciturn, tight-lipped, uncommunicative, unforthcoming, unspeaking, uptight*; SEE CONCEPTS *267,401*

retire [*v*] *leave a place or responsibility*
absent oneself, decamp, deny oneself, depart, draw back, ebb, exit, fall back, get away, get off, give ground, give up work, give way, go, go away, go to bed, go to one's room*, go to sleep, hand over, hit the sack*, leave service, make vacant, part, pull back, pull out, recede, regress, relinquish, remove, repeal, rescind, resign, retreat, revoke, run along, rusticate, secede, seclude oneself, separate, sever connections, stop working, surrender, take off, turn in, withdraw, yield; SEE CONCEPTS *195,234,351*

retiring [*adj*] *shy, undemonstrative*
backward, bashful, coy, demure, diffident, humble, meek, modest, nongregarious, not forward, quiet, rabbity, recessive, reclusive, reserved, restrained, reticent, self-effacing, shrinking, timid, timorous, unaffable, unassertive, unassuming, unexpansive, unsociable, withdrawing, withdrawn; SEE CONCEPT *401*

retort [*n*] *snappy answer*
antiphon, back answer, back talk, comeback, cooler, counter, crack*, gag*, jape, jest, joke, lip*, parting shot*, quip, rejoinder, repartee, reply, reprisal, respond, response, retaliation, return, revenge, riposte, sally, snappy comeback*, topper*, wisecrack, witticism; SEE CONCEPT *278*

retort [*v*] *answer*
answer back, come back at*, counter, crack*, rebut, rejoin, repay, reply, requite, respond, retaliate, return, riposte, sass*, shoot back*, snap back*, squelch*, talk back, top*; SEE CONCEPT *45*

retract [*v*] *take back; renege on*
abjure, back, back down, back off, back out of, call off, cancel, change one's mind, countermand, deny, disavow, disclaim, disown, draw in, eat one's words*, eliminate, exclude, fall back, forget it, forswear, go back on, have change of heart*, nig*, pull back, pull in, recall, recant, recede, reel in*, renege, renounce, repeal, repudiate, rescind, retreat, retrocede, retrograde, reverse, revoke, rule out, sheathe, suspend, take back, take in, unsay, welsh*, withdraw; SEE CONCEPTS *25,49,119,697*

retreat [*n1*] *departure*
ebb, evacuation, flight, retirement, withdrawal; SEE CONCEPTS *30,195*

retreat [*n2*] *place one goes for peace*
adytum, ark, asylum, cell, cloister, convent, cover, covert, defense, den, habitat, harbor, haunt, haven, hermitage, hideaway, hiding place, ivory tower*, port, privacy, refuge, resort, retirement, safe house, safe place, sanctuary, seclusion, security, shelter, solitude; SEE CONCEPT *516*

retreat [*v*] *pull back, go away*
abandon, avoid, back, back away, back down, back off, back out, backtrack, beat it, cave in, decamp, depart, disengage, draw back, ebb, elude, escape, evacuate, evade, fall back, fold, give ground, go, go along with, go back, hand over,

hide, keep aloof, keep apart, lay down, leave, move back, opt out*, pull out, quail, quit, recede, recoil, reel, regress, relinquish, resign, retire, retrocede, retrograde, reverse, run, seclude oneself, sequester, shrink, start back, turn tail*, vacate, withdraw; SEE CONCEPTS *30,195*

retribution [*n*] *payback for another's action*
avengement, avenging, comeuppance, compensation, counterblow, eye for an eye*, just desserts*, justice, punishment, reckoning, recompense, redress, repayment, reprisal, requital, retaliation, revanche, revenge, reward, satisfaction, vengeance, what for*; SEE CONCEPTS *123,126,384*

retrieve [*v*] *get back*
bring back, fetch, get back, reacquire, recall, recapture, reclaim, recoup, recover, recruit, redeem, regain, repair, repossess, rescue, restore, salvage, save, win back; SEE CONCEPTS *120,124,131*

retrospect [*n*] *afterthought*
hindsight, recollection, reconsideration, reexamination, remembering, remembrance, reminiscence, retrospection, review, revision, survey; SEE CONCEPTS *17,40,410*

return [*n1*] *coming again*
acknowledgment, answer, appearance, arrival, coming, entrance, entry, homecoming, occurrence, reaction, reappearance, rebound, recoil, recoiling, recompense, recompensing, recovery, recrudescence, recurrence, reestablishment, reinstatement, rejoinder, reoccurrence, replacement, repossession, restitution, restoration, restoring, retreat, reversion, revisitation; SEE CONCEPTS *4,695*

return [*n2*] *earnings, benefit*
accrual, accruement, advantage, avail, compensation, gain, gate, income, interest, lucre, proceeds, profit, reciprocation, recompense, reimbursement, reparation, repayment, requital, results, retaliation, revenue, reward, take*, takings, yield; SEE CONCEPTS *340,710*

return [*n3*] *answer*
antiphon, comeback, rejoinder, reply, respond, response, retort, riposte; SEE CONCEPT *278*

return [*n4*] *summary*
account, form, list, record, report, statement, tabulation; SEE CONCEPTS *283,331*

return [*v1*] *go back, turn back*
back up, bounce back, circle back, come again, come back, double back, go again, hark back to, move back, react, reappear, rebound, recoil, reconsider, recrudesce, recur, reel back, reenter, reexamine, reoccur, repair, repeat, retire, retrace steps, retreat, revert, revisit, revolve, rotate, turn, turn back; SEE CONCEPTS *159,242*

return [*v2*] *give back, send back*
bestow, carry back, convey, give, hand back, make restitution, pay back, put back, react, rebate, reciprocate, recompense, reestablish, refund, reimburse, reinsert, reinstate, remit, render, repay, replace, requite, reseat, restitute, restore, retaliate, roll back, send, take back, thrust back, toss back, transmit; SEE CONCEPTS *108,131,217*

return [*v3*] *earn*
bring in, cash in on*, clean up*, clear*, make, make a killing*, net, pay, pay dividend, pay off, repay, score, show profit, yield; SEE CONCEPT *330*

return [*v4*] *answer*
announce, arrive at, bring in, come back, come in, come to, communicate, declare, deliver, pass, rejoin, render, reply, report, respond, retort, state, submit; SEE CONCEPT *45*

reunion [*n*] *social gathering*
assembly, get-together, homecoming, making up*, reconciliation, reuniting; SEE CONCEPTS *109,113*

revamp [*v*] *renovate*
clean, do up*, face-lift*, make over, overhaul, recondition, refresh, refurbish, rehabilitate, remake, remodel, renew, repair, restore, resurrect, retread, revitalize, revive, spruce up*, update; SEE CONCEPTS *168,177,202*

reveal [*v1*] *disclose, tell*
acknowledge, admit, affirm, announce, avow, betray, break the news*, bring out into open*, bring to light*, broadcast, come out with, communicate, concede, confess, declare, divulge, explain, expose, get out of system*, give away, give out, give the low-down*, impart, inform, leak, let cat out of the bag*, let fall, let on, let out, let slip*, make known, make plain, make public, notify, proclaim, publish, put cards on table*, report, talk, tell, unfold, utter; SEE CONCEPT *60*

reveal [*v2*] *show, uncover*
bare, disclose, display, exhibit, expose, flash, lay bare, manifest, open, unclothe, unearth, unmask, unveil; SEE CONCEPT *138*

revel [*n*] *celebration, merrymaking*
bacchanal, carousal, carouse, debauch, festivity, frolic, gaiety, gala, high jinks*, jollification, jollity, merriment, party, reveling, revelment, saturnalia, skylarking*, spree, wassail, whoopee*; SEE CONCEPTS *292,377*

revel [*v*] *take pleasure; celebrate*
bask, blow off steam*, carouse, carry on, crow, cut loose*, delight, enjoy, fool around*, frolic, gloat, go on a spree*, indulge, kick up heels*, kid around*, lap up*, lark, let go*, let loose*, live it up*, luxuriate, make merry, paint the town*, rejoice, relish, riot, roister, roll, rollick, run around, savor, step out, thrive, wallow, whoop it up*; SEE CONCEPTS *292,377,384*

revelation [*n*] *disclosure, telling*
adumbration, announcement, apocalypse, betrayal, blow by blow*, break, broadcasting, clue, communication, cue, discovery, display, divination, divulgement, earful, exhibition, expose, exposition, exposure, eye-opener*, flash, foreshadowing, inspiration, leak, lightning bolt*, manifestation, news, oracle, proclamation, prophecy, publication, scoop*, showing, sign, the latest*, tip, uncovering, unearthing, unveiling, vision; SEE CONCEPTS *60,274*

revelry [*n*] *merrymaking*
carousal, carouse, celebration, debauch, debauchery, entertainment, festival, festivity, fun, gaiety, high jinks*, jollification, jollity, party, reveling, revelment, saturnalia, spree, whoop-de-do*, whoopla*; SEE CONCEPTS *377,384*

revenge [*n*] *retaliation for wrong, grievance*
animus, attack, avenging, avengment, counterblow, counterinsurgency, counterplay, eye for an eye*, fight, getting even*, ill will, implacability, malevolence, measure for measure, rancor, repayment, reprisal, requital, retribution, return, ruthlessness, satisfaction, sortie, spitefulness, tit for tat*, vengeance, vengefulness, vindictiveness; SEE CONCEPTS *86,122,384*

revenge [*v*] *retaliate for wrong, grievance*
avenge, be out for blood*, defend, even the score*, fight back, fix, fix one's wagon*, get, get back at, get even, give comeuppance, give just desserts*, hit back, justify, kick back, make reprisal, match, pay back, pay back in spades*, pay off, punish, reciprocate, redress, repay, requite, retort, return, return the compliment*, score, settle up, settle with, square, stick it to, take an eye for an eye*, turn the tables on*, venge, vindicate; SEE CONCEPTS *86,122,384*

revenue [*n*] *income, profit*
acquirement, annuity, bottom line*, cash flow, credit, dividend, earnings, emolument, fruits*, fund, gain, gate*, get*, gravy*, handle*, interest, means, net, pay, payoff, perquisite, proceeds, receipt, resources, return, reward, salary, split*, stock, strength, take*, takings*, wages, wealth, yield; SEE CONCEPTS *329,332,344*

reverberate [*v*] *vibrate in sound*
echo, react, rebound, recoil, redound, re-echo, resound, ring; SEE CONCEPT *65*

reverence [*n*] *high opinion of something*
admiration, adoration, apotheosis, approbation, approval, awe, bow, deference, deification, devotion, devoutness, esteem, fealty, fear, genuflection, high esteem, homage, honor, love, loyalty, obeisance, obsequiousness, piety, praise, prostration, religiousness, respect, veneration, worship; SEE CONCEPTS *10,32*

reverent [*adj*] *respectful*
admiring, appreciative, deferential, devout, dutiful, gracious, humble, obedient, obeisant, pious, polite, regardful, reverential, solemn, upholding, worshipping; SEE CONCEPT *401*

revere/reverence [*v*] *have a high opinion of*
admire, adore, apotheosize, appreciate, be in awe of, cherish, defer to, deify, enjoy, esteem, exalt, hold in awe, honor, look up to*, love, magnify, pay homage, prize, put on pedestal*, regard, respect, think highly of, treasure, value, venerate, worship; SEE CONCEPTS *10,32*

reverie [*n*] *daydream*
absent-mindedness, absorption, abstraction, castle-building*, castles in the air*, contemplation, detachment, dreaminess, dreaming, fantasy, fool's paradise*, head trip*, inattention, meditation, mind trip*, muse, musing, pensiveness, phantasy, pipe dream*, preoccupation, study, thought, trance, trip*, woolgathering*; SEE CONCEPTS *529,532*

reversal [*n*] *about-face*
annulment, backpedaling, cancellation, change in direction, doubleback, repeal, rescinding, retraction, switch, turnabout, turnaround, U-turn, volte-face; SEE CONCEPT *697*

reverse [*n1*] *opposite*
about-face, antipode, antipole, antithesis, back, bottom, change of mind, contra, contradiction, contradictory, contrary, converse, counter, counterpole, flip-flop*, flip side*, inverse, other side, overturning, rear, regression, retrogression, retroversion, reversal, reversement, reversion, switch, turn, turnabout, turn around, turning, underside, verso, volte-face, wrong side; SEE CONCEPTS *665,697,738*

reverse [*n2*] *bad luck; failure*
adversity, affliction, bath, blow, catastrophe,

check, conquering, defeat, disappointment, hardship, misadventure, misfortune, mishap, repulse, reversal, setback, trial, turnabout, vanquishment, vicissitude; SEE CONCEPTS *674,679*

reverse [*v1*] *turn upside down or backwards*
about-face*, back, backpedal*, backtrack, back up, capsize, double back*, evaginate, evert, exchange, flip-flop*, go back, go backwards, interchange, inverse, invert, move backwards, overturn, rearrange, retreat, revert, shift, switch, transfer, transplace, transpose, turn around, turn back, turn over, upend, upset; SEE CONCEPTS *158,213,697*

reverse [*v2*] *cancel, change*
alter, annul, backpedal*, backtrack, convert, countermand, declare null and void*, dismantle, double back*, flip-flop*, invalidate, lift, modify, negate, nullify, overrule, overset, overthrow, overturn, quash, recall, renege, repeal, rescind, retract, revoke, set aside, turn around, turn the tables*, undo, upset; SEE CONCEPTS *13,234,697*

revert [*v*] *return to an earlier, less-developed condition*
about-face*, backslide, change, come back, decline, degenerate, deteriorate, fall off the wagon*, flip-flop*, go back, hark back, inverse, invert, lapse, react, recrudesce, recur, regress, relapse, resume, retrograde, retrogress, return, take up where left off*, throw back, transpose, turn, turn back; SEE CONCEPTS *13,385,698*

review [*n1*] *examination, study*
analysis, another look*, audit, check, checkup, drill, file, fresh look*, inspection, march past*, once-over*, parade, procession, reassessment, recapitulation, reconsideration, reflection, report, rethink, retrospect, revision, scan, scrutiny, second look, second thought, survey, view; SEE CONCEPTS *24,103*

review [*n2*] *critique; summary*
abstract, analysis, appraisal, article, assessment, blurb, book review, canvass, column, comment, commentary, criticism, discourse, discussion, dissertation, essay, evaluation, exposition, inspection, investigation, journal, judgment, magazine, mention, monograph, notice, organ, outline, pan*, periodical, recapitulation, redraft, reviewal, revision, study, synopsis, theme, thesis, treatise, write-up; SEE CONCEPTS *280,283*

review [*v1*] *go over again*
analyze, brush up*, call to mind, check out, check thoroughly, debrief, go over, hash over*, look at again, look back on, polish up, reassess, recall, recap*, recapitulate, recollect, reconsider, reevaluate, reexamine, reflect on, rehash*, remember, rethink, revise, revisit, run over, run through, run up flagpole*, summon up, take another look, think over; SEE CONCEPT *103*

review [*v2*] *criticize, scrutinize*
assess, bad-mouth*, correct, discuss, evaluate, examine, give one's opinion, inspect, judge, knock*, pan*, put down*, rave, read through, reedit, revise, rip, skin alive*, slam*, study, swipe at*, take down*, trash*, weigh, write a critique, zap*; SEE CONCEPTS *49,52*

reviewer [*n*] *critic*
analyst, appraiser, commentator, connoisseur, evaluator, expert, interpreter, judge, reporter; SEE CONCEPT *348*

revile [*v*] *scold*
abuse, admonish, berate, blame, castigate, censure, chide, criticize, denigrate, denounce, disparage, give a talking to*, lambaste, lay down the law*, lecture, rake over the coals*, ream, reprimand, reproach, reprobate, reprove, scorn, tongue-lash, vilify, vituperate; SEE CONCEPTS *44,52,54*

revise [*v*] *correct, edit*
alter, amend, blue pencil*, change, clean up, compare, cut, debug, develop, emend, go over, improve, launder, look over, modify, overhaul, perfect, polish, recalibrate, recast, reconsider, redo, redraft, redraw, reexamine, rehash, reorganize, restyle, revamp, review, rework, rewrite, run through, scan, scrub, scrutinize, study, tighten, update, upgrade; SEE CONCEPTS *79,126,244*

revision [*n*] *change; rewriting*
afterlight, alteration, amendment, correction, editing, emendation, homework, improvement, modification, overhauling, polish, recension, reconsideration, rectification, rectifying, redaction, redraft, reediting, reexamination, rescript, restyling, retrospect, retrospection, review, revisal, revise, updating; SEE CONCEPTS *79,126,244,700*

revival [*n*] *rebirth, reawakening*
awakening, cheering, consolation, enkindling, freshening, invigoration, quickening, reanimation, recovery, recrudescence, regeneration, rejuvenation, renaissance, renascence, renewal, restoration, resurgence, resurrection, resuscitation, revitalization, revivification, risorgimento; SEE CONCEPTS *119,221*

revive [*v*] *start again; bring back to life*
animate, arouse, awaken, bounce back*, breathe new life into*, brighten, bring around*, bring to*, cheer, come around*, come to life, comfort, console, encourage, energize, enkindle, enliven, exhilarate, gladden, inspirit, invigorate, make whole*, overcome, please, quicken, rally, reanimate, recondition, recover, refresh, rejuvenate, rekindle, relieve, renew, renovate, repair, restore, resurrect, resuscitate, revitalize, rouse, snap out of it*, solace, spring up*, strengthen, touch up*, wake up; SEE CONCEPTS *13,221,469,697*

revoke [*v*] *take back; cancel*
abjure, abolish, abrogate, annul, back out of, backpedal*, call back, call off, countermand, counterorder, declare null and void*, deny, disclaim, dismantle, dismiss, disown, erase, expunge, forswear, invalidate, lift, negate, nix*, nullify, obliterate, quash*, recall, recant, remove, renounce, repeal, repudiate, rescind, retract, reverse, rub out*, scrub*, set aside, vacate, void, wipe out*, withdraw; SEE CONCEPTS *50,88,121,234*

revolt [*n*] *uprising*
defection, displeasure, insurgency, insurrection, mutiny, rebellion, revolution, rising, sedition; SEE CONCEPTS *106,300,320*

revolt [*v1*] *rebel, rise up against*
arise, boycott, break, defect, defy, drop out, get out of line*, insurrect, make waves*, mutiny, oppose, opt out, overthrow, overturn, rebel, renounce, resist, riot, rock the boat*, strike, take up arms, turn against; SEE CONCEPTS *106,300,320*

revolt [*v2*] *disgust, nauseate*
crawl*, gross out*, make flesh crawl*, make sick, offend, pain, reluct, repel, repulse, shock,

sicken, turn off*, turn stomach*; SEE CONCEPTS
7,19

revolting [*adj*] *disgusting, nauseating*
abhorrent, abominable, appalling, awful, distasteful, foul, gross, horrible, horrid, loathsome, nasty, nauseous, noisome, obnoxious, obscene, offensive, repellent, repugnant, repulsive, rotten, shocking, sickening, sleazy*, vile; SEE CONCEPT
529

revolution [*n1*] *drastic action or change, often in politics*
anarchy, bloodshed, cabal, coup, coup d'état, crime, debacle, destruction, disorder, foment, golpe, guerrilla activity, innovation, insubordination, insurgency, metamorphosis, mutiny, outbreak, overthrow, overturn, plot, radical change, rebellion, reformation, reversal, revolt, rising, row, shake-up, shift, strife, strike, subversion, transformation, tumult, turbulence, turmoil, turnover, underground activity, unrest, upheaval, uprising, uproar, upset, violence; SEE CONCEPTS
106,300,320,697

revolution [*n2*] *circuit around something*
circle, circumvolution, cycle, gyration, gyre, lap, orbit, pirouette, reel, revolve, revolving, roll, rotation, round, spin, swirl, turn, turning, twirl, wheel, whirl; SEE CONCEPTS *436,484,738,792*

revolutionary [*adj1*] *rebellious*
anarchistic, defiant, disobedient, disorderly, factious, insubordinate, insurgent, mutinous, radical, rebel, rioting, riotous, subversive, warring; SEE CONCEPTS *401,529,542*

revolutionary [*adj2*] *new, progressive*
advanced, advancing, avant-garde*, contemporary, cutting edge*, developing, forward-looking, innovative, just out*, latest, left, modern, novel, open-minded, radical, state-of-the-art*, up-and-coming*; SEE CONCEPTS *542,544,564, 578,797*

revolve [*v1*] *turn, circle*
circumduct, go around, gyrate, gyre, orbit, roll, rotate, spin, turn around, twist, wheel, whirl; SEE CONCEPTS *147,738*

revolve [*v2*] *think about*
consider, deliberate, meditate, mull over, muse, ponder, reflect, roll, ruminate, study, think over, turn over in mind; SEE CONCEPT *17*

revulsion [*n*] *disgust, hatred*
abhorrence, abomination, aversion, detestation, dislike, distaste, hate, horror, loathing, recoil, repugnance, repulsion; SEE CONCEPT *29*

reward [*n*] *payment, prize*
accolade, award, benefit, bonus, bounty, carrot*, comeuppance, compensation, crown*, cue, dividend, feather in cap*, fringe benefit, gain, garland, goodies*, gravy*, grease*, guerdon, honor, just deserts*, meed, merit, perks*, plum*, premium, profit, punishment, recompense, remuneration, repayment, requital, retribution, return, salve, strokes*, sweetener*, tip, wages; SEE CONCEPTS *337,344*

reward [*v*] *pay; give prize*
compensate, honor, recompense, remunerate, repay, requite, stroke*, sugarcoat*, take care of*, tip; SEE CONCEPTS *108,132,341*

rewarding [*adj*] *beneficial, pleasing*
advantageous, edifying, fruitful, fulfilling, gainful, gratifying, productive, profitable, remunerative, satisfying, valuable, worthwhile; SEE CONCEPTS *548,572*

rhetoric [*n*] *wordiness; long speech*
address, balderdash*, big talk*, bombast, composition, discourse, elocution, eloquence, flowery language, fustian, grandiloquence, hot air*, hyperbole, magniloquence, oration, oratory, pomposity, rant, verbosity; SEE CONCEPTS *51,277,278*

rhetorical [*adj*] *wordy; flowery in speech*
articulate, aureate, bombastic, declamatory, eloquent, embellished, euphuistic, exaggerated, flamboyant, flashy*, florid, fluent, glib*, grand, grandiloquent, grandiose, high-flown, hyperbolic, imposing, inflated, magniloquent, mouthy, oratorical, ornate, ostentatious, overblown, overdone, overwrought, pompous, pretentious, showy, silver-tongued, sonorous, stilted, swollen, tumescent, tumid, turgid, verbose, vocal, voluble, windy*; SEE CONCEPT *267*

rhyme [*n*] *poetry in which lines end with like sounds*
alliteration, beat, cadence, couplet, doggerel, half-rhyme, harmony, iambic pentameter, measure, meter, nursery rhyme, ode, poem, poesy, poetry, rhythm, rune, slant rhyme, song, tune, verse, vowel-chime; SEE CONCEPTS *278,595*

rhythm [*n*] *beat, accent of sound, music*
bounce, cadence, cadency, downbeat, flow, lilt, measure, meter, metre, movement, pattern, periodicity, pulse, regularity, rhyme, rise and fall, swing, tempo, time, uniformity; SEE CONCEPT *595*

ribald [*adj*] *vulgar, obscene*
base, bawdy, blue*, coarse, devilish, earthy, fast*, filthy*, foul-mouthed, gross*, indecent, indecorous, juicy, lascivious, lewd, licentious, low-down and dirty, naughty, off-color, out of line*, purple*, racy, rascally, raunchy, raw*, risqué*, rogue, rough, rude, salacious, salty, scabrous, scurrilous, sly, smutty, spicy*, unbecoming; SEE CONCEPTS *267,401*

rich [*adj1*] *having a lot of money*
affluent, bloated, comfortable, easy, fat, filthy rich*, flush, gilded, in clover*, independent, in the money*, loaded*, made of money*, moneyed, opulent, plush, propertied, prosperous, rolling in it*, swimming, upscale, uptown, wealthy, well-heeled*, well-off*, well provided for*, well-to-do*, worth a million*; SEE CONCEPT *334*

rich [*adj2*] *abundant, well-supplied*
abounding, ample, chic, classy, copious, costly, deluxe, elaborate, elegant, embellished, expensive, exquisite, extravagant, exuberant, fancy, fecund, fertile, fine, fruitful, full, gorgeous, grand, high-class, lavish, lush, luxurious, magnificent, ornate, palatial, plenteous, plentiful, plush, posh, precious, priceless, productive, prolific, resplendent, ritzy*, smart, snazzy*, spiffy, splendid, stylish, sumptuous, superb, swank*, swanky*, swell*, valuable, well-endowed; SEE CONCEPTS *334,589,771*

rich [*adj3*] *flavorful*
creamy, delicious, fatty, full-bodied, heavy, highly flavored, juicy, luscious, nourishing, nutritious, oily, satisfying, savory, spicy, succulent, sustaining, sweet, tasty; SEE CONCEPT *613*

rich [*adj4*] *full in color or sound*
bright, canorous, deep, dulcet, eloquent, expressive, intense, mellifluous, mellow, resonant, ro-

re
ri

tund, significant, silvery, sonorous, strong, vibrant, vivid, warm; SEE CONCEPTS *406,594,618*

rich [*adj5*] *very funny*
absurd, amusing, comical, diverting, droll, entertaining, farcical, foolish, hilarious, humorous, incongruous, laughable, ludicrous, odd, preposterous, queer, ridiculous, risible, side-splitting*, slaying*, splitting*, strange; SEE CONCEPTS *267,529*

rich [*n*] *wealthy people or institutions*
bountiful, haves*, landed, monied, nouveau riche, old money, upper class, upper crust*, well-to-do*; SEE CONCEPT *423*

riches [*n*] *money and possessions*
abundance, affluence, assets, clover, fortune, gold, lap of luxury*, means, opulence, plenty, property, resources, richness, substance, treasure, wealth, worth; SEE CONCEPTS *335,340,446,710*

rickety [*adj*] *unsound, broken-down*
broken, decrepit, derelict, dilapidated, feeble, flimsy, fragile, frail, imperfect, infirm, insecure, jerry-built*, precarious, ramshackle, rattletrap*, rocky, shaky, tottering, tottery*, tumble-down, unsteady, wavering, weak, wobbly; SEE CONCEPT *488*

ricochet [*v*] *rebound*
backfire, boomerang, bounce back, deflect, kick back, recoil, return, snap back*, spring back; SEE CONCEPTS *150,194,195,303,700*

rid [*v*] *do away with; free*
abolish, clear, deliver, disabuse, disburden, disembarrass, disencumber, dump*, eject, eliminate, eradicate, expel, exterminate, extinguish, extirpate, fire, give the brush*, heave-ho*, junk*, kiss goodbye*, liberate, make free, purge, release, relieve, remove, roust, scrap, send packing*, shake off, shed, throw away, throw out, toss out, unburden, unload, uproot; SEE CONCEPTS *180,211*

riddle [*n*] *brain-teaser*
bewilderment, brain-twister*, charade, closed book*, complexity, complication, confusion, conundrum, cryptogram, dilemma, distraction, doubt, embarrassment, enigma, entanglement, intricacy, knotty question*, labyrinth, maze, mind-boggler*, mystery, mystification, perplexity, plight, poser, predicament, problem, puzzle, puzzlement, quandary, question, rebus, sixty-four dollar question*, stickler*, strait, stumper*, teaser, tough nut to crack*, tough proposition, twister*; SEE CONCEPT *532*

riddle [*v*] *perforate, permeate*
bore, corrupt, damage, honeycomb*, impair, infest, mar, pepper, pervade, pierce, pit, puncture, spoil; SEE CONCEPTS *156,220*

ride [*n*] *journey, trip in vehicle*
airing, commute, drive, excursion, expedition, hitch, jaunt, joyride*, lift, outing, pick up*, run, spin, Sunday drive, tour, transportation, turn, whirl; SEE CONCEPT *224*

ride [*v1*] *carry or be carried*
be supported, control, cruise, curb, direct, drift, drive, float, go, go with, guide, handle, hitch a ride*, hitchhike, journey, manage, motor, move, post, progress, restrain, roll, sit, sit on, thumb a ride*, tool around*, tour, travel; SEE CONCEPTS *94,148,224*

ride [*v2*] *dominate, oppress*
afflict, annoy, badger, bait, be arbitrary, be autocratic, berate, disparage, domineer, enslave, grip,

harass, harry, haunt, hector, hound, override, persecute, rate, reproach, revile, scold, torment, torture, tyrannize, upbraid; SEE CONCEPTS *7,14,19*

rider [*n1*] *equestrian; commuter*
cowboy, driver, gaucho, horseback rider, horseman/woman, passenger, straphanger*, suburbanite, traveler; SEE CONCEPT *348*

rider [*n2*] *amendment, clause*
addendum, addition, adjunct, alteration, attachment, clarification, codicil, measure, modification, revision, supplement; SEE CONCEPT *270*

ridge [*n*] *raised part of solid*
backbone, chine, corrugation, crease, crinkle, elevation, esker, fold, furrow, hill, hogback, moraine, parapet, plica, pole, range, rib, rim, rimple, rivel, ruck, seam, spine, upland, wrinkle; SEE CONCEPTS *471,509,513*

ridicule [*n*] *contemptuous laughter at someone or something*
badinage, banter, buffoonery, burlesque, caricature, chaff, comeback, contempt, derision, dig*, disdain, disparagement, farce, foolery, gibe, irony, jab*, jeer, laughter, leer, mockery, mordancy, needling, parody, parting shot*, persiflage, putdown*, put-on*, raillery, rally, razz*, rib*, roast*, sarcasm, sardonicism, satire, scorn, slam*, sneer*, swipe*, taunt, taunting, travesty; SEE CONCEPTS *54,59*

ridicule [*v*] *make contemptuous fun of something or someone*
banter, caricature, cartoon, chaff, deflate, deride, expose, fleer, gibe, haze, humiliate, jape, jeer, jive, jolly, josh*, kid, lampoon, laugh at, make a fool of*, make a game of*, make a laughingstock*, make fun of, mimic, mock, needle, pan*, parody, poke fun at*, pooh-pooh*, pull one's leg*, put down*, quiz, rag, rail at, rally, raz*, rib*, ride*, roast*, run down*, satirize, scoff, scorn, send up*, show up, sneer, takeoff, taunt, travesty, twit, unmask; SEE CONCEPTS *54,59*

ridiculous [*adj*] *stupid, funny*
absurd, antic, bizarre, comic, comical, contemptible, daffy*, derisory, droll, fantastic, farcical, foolheaded*, foolish, gelastic, goofy*, grotesque, harebrained*, hilarious, impossible, incredible, jerky*, laughable, ludicrous, nonsensical, nutty*, outrageous, preposterous, risible, sappy*, silly, slaphappy*, unbelievable, wacky*; SEE CONCEPTS *529,548,552*

rife [*adj*] *overflowing*
abounding, abundant, alive, common, current, epidemic, extensive, frequent, general, many, multitudinous, numerous, pandemic, plentiful, popular, prevailing, prevalent, profuse, raging, rampant, regnant, replete, ruling, swarming, teeming, thronged, ubiquitous, universal, widespread; SEE CONCEPTS *771,772*

riffraff [*n*] *rabble*
commonality, commoners, dregs of society*, gang, gathering, hoi polloi, lower class, mob, one-percenters, outcast, rank and file, ring, scum, trash, undesirables, vermin; SEE CONCEPTS *378,417,432*

rifle [*v*] *ransack*
burglarize, burgle, despoil, go through, grab, gut, loot, pillage, plunder, rip, rip off*, rob, rummage, sack, smash and grab*, strip, take, tip over*, trash*, waste*; SEE CONCEPT *139*

rift [*n1*] *break, crack*
breach, chink, cleavage, cleft, cranny, crevice, fault, fissure, flaw, fracture, gap, hiatus, interruption, interval, opening, parting, rent, rima, rime, space, split; SEE CONCEPT *513*

rift [*n2*] *difference of opinion*
alienation, breach, break, clash, disagreement, division, estrangement, falling out*, misunderstanding, quarrel, rupture, schism, separation, split; SEE CONCEPTS *46,106,388*

rig [*n*] *equipment*
accouterments, apparatus, equipage, fittings, fixtures, gear, machinery, outfit, paraphernalia, tackle; SEE CONCEPT *496*

rig [*v1*] *outfit, supply*
accouter, appoint, arm, array, attire, clothe, costume, dress, equip, fit out, furnish, gear, kit, provision, set up, turn out; SEE CONCEPTS *140,167, 182*

rig [*v2*] *arrange for certain outcome*
doctor, engineer, fake, falsify, fiddle with*, fix, gerrymander*, juggle, manipulate, tamper with, trump up*; SEE CONCEPTS *202,697*

right [*adj1*] *fair, just*
appropriate, condign, conscientious, deserved, due, equitable, ethical, fitting, good, honest, honorable, justifiable, lawful, legal, legitimate, merited, moral, proper, requisite, righteous, rightful, scrupulous, stand-up*, suitable, true, upright, virtuous; SEE CONCEPT *545*

right [*adj2*] *accurate, precise*
absolute, admissible, amen, authentic, bona fide, complete, correct, exact, factual, faithful, free of error, genuine, immaculate, indubitable, inerrant, infallible, just, nice, on the money*, on the nose*, out-and-out*, perfect, proper, punctilious, real, right as rain*, righteous, right on*, rigorous, satisfactory, solemn, sound, strict, sure, thoroughgoing, true, undistorted, undoubted, unerring, unmistaken, utter, valid, veracious, veridical, veritable, watertight*; SEE CONCEPTS *535,557,582*

right [*adj3*] *appropriate, fitting*
acceptable, adequate, advantageous, all right, becoming, befitting, comely, comme il faut, common, condign, convenient, correct, decent, decorous, deserved, desirable, done*, due, favorable, felicitous, fit, good, happy, ideal, merited, nice, opportune, proper, propitious, requisite, rightful, satisfactory, seemly, sufficient, suitable, tolerable; SEE CONCEPTS *558,572*

right [*adj4*] *sane, healthy*
all there, balanced, circumspect, compos mentis, discerning, discreet, enlightened, far-sighted, fine, fit, hale, in good health*, in the pink*, judicious, lucid, normal, penetrating, rational, reasonable, sound, unimpaired, up to par*, well, wise; SEE CONCEPTS *314,403*

right [*adj5*] *conservative politically*
die-hard*, old-line*, orthodox, reactionary, right wing, traditionalistic; SEE CONCEPTS *529,689*

right [*adj6*] *opposite of left*
clockwise, dexter, dextral, right-handed; SEE CONCEPT *581*

right [*adv1*] *accurately, precisely*
absolutely, all the way, altogether, bang*, clear, completely, correctly, entirely, exactly, factually, fully, genuinely, just, perfectly, precisely, quite, sharp, slap, smack-dab*, square, squarely, thoroughly, totally, truly, utterly, well, wholly; SEE CONCEPTS *531,557,582*

right [*adv2*] *appropriately, suitably*
acceptably, adequately, amply, aptly, becomingly, befittingly, fittingly, properly, satisfactorily, well; SEE CONCEPTS *558,572*

right [*adv3*] *fairly, justly*
conscientiously, decently, dispassionately, equitably, ethically, evenly, honestly, honorably, impartially, lawfully, legitimately, morally, objectively, properly, reliably, righteously, sincerely, squarely, virtuously, without bias, without prejudice; SEE CONCEPT *545*

right [*adv4*] *beneficially*
advantageous, exceedingly, extremely, favorably, for the better, fortunately, highly, notably, perfectly, remarkably, to advantage, very, well; SEE CONCEPTS *537,572*

right [*adv5*] *directly, without delay*
at once, away, direct, due, first off, forthwith, immediately, instanter, instantly, now, promptly, quickly, right away, straight, straight away, straightly, undeviatingly; SEE CONCEPT *799*

right [*n1*] *privilege*
advantage, appanage, authority, benefit, birthright, business, claim, comeuppance, desert, deserving, due, exemption, favor, franchise, freedom, immunity, interest, liberty, license, merit, permission, perquisite, power, preference, prerogative, priority, title; SEE CONCEPT *376*

right [*n2*] *justice, morality*
correctness, emancipation, enfranchisement, equity, freedom, good, goodness, honor, independence, integrity, lawfulness, legality, liberty, morality, properness, propriety, reason, rectitude, righteousness, rightness, straight, truth, uprightness, virtue; SEE CONCEPT *645*

right [*v*] *fix, correct*
adjust, amend, balance, clean up, compensate for, debug*, dial back*, doctor*, do justice, emend, fiddle with*, fix up, go straight, launder, make up for, mend, overhaul, patch, pick up, put in place, put right, recalibrate, recompense, recondition, reconstruct, rectify, redress, repair, restore, reward, scrub, set straight, settle, set upright, shape up, sort out, square, straighten, straighten out, turn around, vindicate; SEE CONCEPTS *126,212*

righteous [*adj*] *good, honest*
angelic, blameless, charitable, commendable, conscientious, creditable, deserving, devoted, devout, dutiful, equitable, ethical, exemplary, fair, faithful, godlike, guiltless, holy, honorable, impartial, innocent, irreproachable, just, laudable, law-abiding, matchless, meritorious, moral, noble, peerless, philanthropic, philanthropical, praiseworthy, punctilious, pure, reverent, right-minded, saintly, scrupulous, sinless, spiritual, sterling, trustworthy, upright, virtuous, worthy; SEE CONCEPT *545*

rightful [*adj*] *legitimate*
applicable, appropriate, apt, authorized, befitting, bona fide, canonical, card-carrying*, condign, deserved, due, ethical, fair, fit, fitting, holding water, honest, just, kosher*, lawful, legal, legit*, merited, moral, moralistic, noble, official, on the level*, on the up and up*, orthodox, permitted, principled, proper, real, requisite, right, right-minded, suitable, true, twenty-four carat*, valid, virtuous; SEE CONCEPTS *545,558*

ri
ri

right stuff [*n*] *essential qualities*
abilities, bravery, courage, credentials, dependability, drive, experience, guts, knowledge, power, self-confidence, skills, talent, what it takes; SEE CONCEPT *630*

rigid [*adj*] *stiff, strict, severe*
adamant, adamantine, austere, bullheaded, changeless, chiseled*, dead set*, definite, determined, exact, firm, fixed, hard, hard-line*, harsh, incompliant, inelastic, inexorable, inflexible, intransigent, invariable, locked in*, obdurate, rigorous, set, set in stone*, single-minded, solid, static, stern, strait-laced*, stringent, tough nut to crack*, unalterable, unbending, unbreakable, unchanging, uncompromising, undeviating, unmoving, unpermissive, unrelenting, unyielding; SEE CONCEPTS *403,534,535*

rigmarole [*n*] *nonsense*
babble, balderdash*, baloney, blather, bull, bunk*, drivel, foolishness, gibberish, gobbledygook*, hogwash*, hot air*, jargon, jive*, madness, mumbo jumbo*, palaver, poppycock*, prattle, rubbish, senselessness, silliness, trash*; SEE CONCEPTS *230,388,633*

rigor [*n*] *strictness, exactness*
accuracy, affliction, asperity, austerity, conscientiousness, conventionalism, difficulty, exactitude, firmness, hardness, hardship, harshness, inclemency, inflexibility, intolerance, meticulousness, obduracy, ordeal, preciseness, precision, privation, punctiliousness, rigidity, roughness, severity, sternness, stiffness, stringency, suffering, tenacity, thoroughness, traditionalism, trial, tribulation, vicissitude, visitation; SEE CONCEPTS *638,654,666*

rigorous [*adj*] *severe; exact*
accurate, ascetic, austere, bitter, brutal, burdensome, correct, definite, dogmatic, exact, exacting, hard, harsh, inclement, inflexible, intemperate, ironhanded, meticulous, nice, onerous, oppressive, precise, proper, punctilious, right, rigid, rugged, scrupulous, stern, stiff, strict, stringent, uncompromising, unpermissive; SEE CONCEPTS *535,557,565*

rile [*v*] *anger, upset*
acerbate, aggravate, annoy, bother, bug*, disturb, exasperate, gall, get one's goat*, get under skin*, grate, inflame, irk, irritate, nettle, peeve, pique, provoke, put out*, roil, rub one the wrong way*, try one's patience*, vex; SEE CONCEPTS *7,19*

rim [*n*] *border; top edge*
band, brim, brink, brow, circumference, confine, curb, end, fringe, hem, ledge, limit, line, lip, margin, outline, perimeter, periphery, ring, skirt, strip, terminus, top, verge; SEE CONCEPTS *484,836*

ring [*n1*] *circle; circular object*
arena, band, brim, circlet, circuit, circus, enclosure, eye, girdle, halo, hoop, loop, ringlet, rink, round; SEE CONCEPTS *436,446*

ring [*n2*] *group participating together*
association, band, bloc, bunch, cabal, camp, cartel, cell, circle, clan, clique, coalition, combination, combine, corner, coterie, crew, crowd, faction, gang, in-group, junta, junto, knot, Mafia, mob, monopoly, organization, outfit, party, pool, push, racket, syndicate, troop, troupe, trust; SEE CONCEPTS *325,381*

ring [*n3*] *chime, bell-like noise*
buzz, call, clangor, clank, jangle, jingle, knell,

peal, reverberation, tinkle, toll, vibration; SEE CONCEPT *595*

ring [*v1*] *encircle*
begird, belt, circle, circumscribe, compass, confine, enclose, encompass, gird, girdle, hem in, inclose, loop, move around, rim, round, seal off, surround; SEE CONCEPT *758*

ring [*v2*] *chime; make bell-like noise*
bang, beat, bong, buzz, clang, clap, jangle, jingle, knell, peal, play, pull, punch, resonate, resound, reverberate, sound, strike, tinkle, tintinnabulate, toll, vibrate; SEE CONCEPT *65*

ringleader [*n*] *leader*
agitator, boss, brains*, captain, chief, chieftain, commander, general, head, head honcho*, inciter, instigator, mastermind, orchestrator, president, ruler, skipper, spokesperson, troublemaker; SEE CONCEPTS *347,354*

rinse [*v*] *wash off, out*
bathe, clean, cleanse, dip, flush, soak, splash, wash, water, wet; SEE CONCEPTS *165,256*

riot [*n1*] *uprising, disorder*
anarchism, anarchy, branigan*, brawl, burst, commotion, confusion, distemper, disturbance, flap, fray, free-for-all*, fuss, hassle, lawlessness, misrule, mix-up, mob violence, protest, quarrel, racket, row, ruckus, ruction, rumble, rumpus, run-in, scene, shivaree, shower, snarl, stir, storm, street fighting, strife, to-do*, trouble, tumult, turbulence, turmoil, uproar, wingding*; SEE CONCEPTS *106,300*

riot [*n2*] *very funny happening*
boisterousness, carousal, confusion, excess, extravaganza, festivity, flourish, frolic, high jinks*, howl*, jollification, lark, merrymaking, panic*, revelry, romp, scream*, sensation, show, sidesplitter*, skylark*, smash*, splash*, tumult, uproar, wow*; SEE CONCEPTS *384,386*

riot [*v*] *protest; cause an uproar*
arise, debauch, dissipate, fight, go on rampage, racket, rampage, rebel, revolt, rise, run riot*, stir up trouble*, take to the streets*; SEE CONCEPTS *106,300*

riotous [*adj*] *chaotic, wild*
anarchic, deranged, disordered, disorderly, disorganized, helter-skelter*, insurrectionary, lawless, mutinous, out of control, rampageous, rebellious, rowdy, tumultuous, turbid, turbulent, uncontrolled, unruly, violent; SEE CONCEPT *548*

rip [*n*] *tear, cut*
cleavage, gash, hole, laceration, rent, slash, slit, split; SEE CONCEPTS *309,513*

rip [*v*] *tear, cut*
burst, claw, cleave, fray, frazzle, gash, hack, lacerate, rend, rive, score, shred, slash, slit, split; SEE CONCEPT *214*

ripe [*adj1*] *fully developed; experienced*
accomplished, adult, aged, completed, conditioned, consummate, enlightened, enriched, filled out, finished, fit, full, full-blown, full-fledged, fully grown, grown, grown-up, increased, informed, in readiness, judicious, learned, mature, matured, mellow, overdue, perfected, plump, prepared, prime, ready, ripened, sagacious, seasoned, skilled, skillful, sound, timely, usable, versed, well-timed, wise; SEE CONCEPTS *462,560,578,797*

ripe [*adj2*] *favorable, ideal*
auspicious, opportune, right, suitable, timely; SEE CONCEPT *558*

rip-off [*n*] *trick; robbery*
cheat, con*, exploitation, fraud, gyp*, larceny, lift*, pinch*, purloining, racket*, steal, stealing, swindle, theft, thievery, thieving; SEE CONCEPTS *139,192*

rip off [*v*] *rob; trick*
abuse, appropriate, bleed*, cheat, con*, cop*, defraud, dupe, exploit, filch*, fleece*, heist, impose on*, lift*, nab*, pilfer, pinch, plunder, ransack, relieve, rifle, skin*, soak*, stick*, swindle, swipe, thieve, use; SEE CONCEPTS *139,192*

ripple [*n*] *wave; wrinkle*
billow, breaker, crest, curl, fold, furrow, line, rippling, rush, surge, swell, tide, undulation, whitecap; SEE CONCEPTS *147,436,514*

ripple [*v*] *wave*
coil, curl, flow, fluctuate, flutter, motion, oscillate, palpitate, pulsate, quiver, splash, stir, surge, sway, swell, swish, undulate, vacillate, vibrate; SEE CONCEPTS *74,147,149*

rise [*n1*] *increase, improvement*
acceleration, accession, accretion, addition, advance, advancement, aggrandizement, ascent, augmentation, boost, breakthrough, climb, distention, doubling, enlargement, growth, heightening, hike, increment, inflation, intensification, intensifying, multiplication, piling up, progress, promotion, raise, stacking up, step-up, surge, swell, upgrade, upsurge, upswing, upturn, waxing; SEE CONCEPTS *700,780*

rise [*n2*] *movement upward; upward slope*
acclivity, ascension, ascent, climb, elevation, eminence, highland, hillock, incline, lift, mount, rising, rising ground, soaring, surge, towering, upland, upsurge; SEE CONCEPTS *166,738,752*

rise [*v1*] *get up; ascend*
arise, arouse, aspire, awake, be erect, be located, be situated, blast off*, bob up*, climb, come up, get out of bed, get steeper, get to one's feet*, go uphill, grow, have foundation, levitate, lift, mount, move up, pile out*, push up, reach up, rise and shine*, rise up, rocket, roll out*, rouse, scale, sit up, slope upwards, soar, sprout, stand up, straighten up, surface, surge, surmount, sweep upward, tower, turn out, up*, upspring; SEE CONCEPTS *154,166,738*

rise [*v2*] *increase, grow*
accelerate, add to, advance, aggravate, arise, ascend, augment, billow, build, bulge, climb, deepen, distend, double, enhance, enlarge, expand, go through the roof*, go up, heighten, improve, inflate, intensate, intensify, levitate, lift, magnify, mount, move up, multiply, perk up, pick up, pile up, raise, redouble, rouse, soar, speed up, spread, stack up, swell, take off, upsurge, wax; SEE CONCEPTS *700,780*

rise [*v3*] *progress in business*
advance, be elevated, be promoted, better oneself, climb the ladder*, flourish, get on, get somewhere*, go places*, progress, prosper, succeed, thrive, work one's way up*; SEE CONCEPTS *351,704*

rise [*v4*] *become apparent*
appear, arise, befall, begin, betide, chance, come, crop up, dawn, derive, develop, emanate, emerge, eventuate, fall out*, flare up, flow, go, happen, head, issue, loom, occur, originate, proceed, spring, stem, surface, transpire, turn up*; SEE CONCEPTS *4,716*

rise [*v5*] *rebel*
insurrect, mount, mutiny, resist, revolt, riot, take up arms*; SEE CONCEPT *106*

risk [*n*] *chance taken*
accident, contingency, danger, exposedness, exposure, flyer*, fortuity, fortune, gamble, hazard, header, jeopardy, liability, liableness, luck, openness, opportunity, peril, plunge, possibility, prospect, shot in the dark*, speculation, stab*, uncertainty, venture, wager; SEE CONCEPTS *675,693*

risk [*v*] *take a chance*
adventure, beard, be caught short*, brave, chance, compromise, confront, dare, defy, defy danger, encounter, endanger, expose to danger, face, gamble, go out of one's depth*, hang by a thread*, hazard, imperil, jeopardize, jeopardy, leap before looking*, leave to luck*, meet, menace, peril, play with fire*, plunge, put in jeopardy, run the chance, run the risk, skate on thin ice*, speculate, tackle, take a flyer*, take a header*, take a plunge*, take on*, take the liberty*, venture, wager; SEE CONCEPTS *87,100*

risky [*adj*] *dangerous*
chancy, delicate, dicey*, endangered, fraught with danger*, going for broke*, hairy*, hanging by a thread*, hazardous, iffy*, insecure, jeopardous, long shot*, not a prayer*, off the deep end*, on slippery ground*, on the spot*, on thin ice*, out on a limb*, perilous, playing with fire*, precarious, rocky*, sensitive, speculative, ticklish, touch-and-go*, touchy, treacherous, tricky, uncertain, unhealthy, unsafe, unsound, venturesome, wicked, wide-open; SEE CONCEPT *548*

risqué [*adj*] *improper, referring to sex*
amoral, bawdy*, blue*, breezy, crude, daring, dirty, earthy, erotic, filthy*, foul, gross*, hot*, immodest, immoral, indecent, indecorous, indelicate, indiscreet, inelegant, lewd, lurid, naughty, obscene, off-base*, off-color, offensive, out-of-line, provocative, purple*, racy, raw, ribald, salacious, salty, shady, sizzling, smart, smutty, spicy*, suggestive, unrefined, vulgar, wanton, warm, wicked, X-rated*; SEE CONCEPTS *267,545,548*

rite [*n*] *ceremony, tradition*
act, celebration, ceremonial, communion, custom, form, formality, liturgy, observance, occasion, ordinance, practice, procedure, ritual, sacrament, service, solemnity; SEE CONCEPTS *377,386*

ritual [*n*] *ceremony, tradition*
act, ceremonial, communion, convention, custom, form, formality, habit, liturgy, observance, ordinance, practice, prescription, procedure, protocol, red tape*, rite, routine, sacrament, service, solemnity, stereotype, usage; SEE CONCEPTS *386,634,688*

ritzy [*adj*] *elegant, luxurious*
aristocratic, chic, choice, classy, cultivated, dignified, elaborate, expensive, exquisite, fancy, fine, grand, grandiose, handsome, lavish, lush, opulent, ornamented, ornate, ostentatious, overdone, plush, posh, refined, rich, snazzy, stately, stuffy, sumptuous, swank; SEE CONCEPTS *544,574,579,589*

rival [*adj*] *opposing*
battling, combatant, combating, competing, competitive, conflicting, contending, contesting, cut-

ri
ri

throat, disputing, emulating, emulous, equal, opposed, striving, vying; SEE CONCEPTS *542,564*

rival [*n*] *person who opposes in competition*
adversary, antagonist, bandit, buddy, challenger, competition, competitor, contender, contestant, emulator, entrant, equal, equivalent, match, opponent, opposite number, peer; SEE CONCEPTS *348,366,423*

rival [*v*] *oppose; be a match for*
amount, approach, approximate, bear comparison with*, come near to*, come up to*, compare with, compete, contend, contest, correspond, emulate, equal, go after, go for, jockey for position*, match, measure up to, meet, near, partake, resemble, rivalize, scramble for, seek to displace, tie, touch, vie with; SEE CONCEPTS *92,667*

rivalry [*n*] *competition*
antagonism, athletic event, bout, candidacy, clash, conflict, contest, duel, emulation, encounter, engagement, event, fight, game, jealousy, match, matchup, one on one*, opposition, race, sport, strife, struggle, tournament, tug-of-war; SEE CONCEPTS *92,363*

river [*n*] *waterway*
beck, branch, brook, course, creek, estuary, rill, rivulet, run, runnel, stream, tributary, watercourse; SEE CONCEPT *514*

riveting [*adj*] *fascinating, gripping*
absorbing, alluring, appealing, bewitching, captivating, compelling, enchanting, engaging, engrossing, enthralling, enticing, hypnotic, intriguing, irresistible, magnetic, mesmerizing, seducing, seductive, spellbinding; SEE CONCEPT *529*

road [*n*] *path upon which travel occurs*
alley, artery, asphalt, avenue, back street, boulevard, byway, cobblestone, concrete, course, crossroad, direction, drag*, dragway, drive, expressway, highway, lane, line, main drag*, parking lot*, parkway, passage, pathway, pavement, pike, roadway, route, street, subway, terrace, thoroughfare, throughway, thruway, track, trail, turnpike, viaduct, way; SEE CONCEPT *501*

roam [*v*] *wander about*
bum*, bum around*, drift, gad, gallivant, hike, hit the road*, knock around*, meander, peregrinate, prowl, ramble, range, rove, saunter, straggle, stray, stroll, struggle along, traipse, tramp, travel, traverse, trek, vagabond, walk; SEE CONCEPTS *151,224*

roar [*n1*] *growl, howl*
barrage, bawl, bay, bellow, blast, bluster, boom, clamor, clash, crash, cry, detonation, din, drum, explosion, holler, outcry, reverberation, rumble, shout, thunder, uproar, yell; SEE CONCEPTS *77,595*

roar [*n2/v2*] *laugh loudly*
belly laugh, guffaw, hoot, howl, scream; SEE CONCEPT *77*

roar [*v1*] *growl, howl*
bark, bawl, bay, bellow, blast, bluster, boom, brawl, bray, clamor, crash, cry, detonate, din, drum, explode, holler, rebound, reecho, repercuss, resound, reverberate, roll, rout, rumble, shout, sound, thunder, trumpet, vociferate, yell; SEE CONCEPTS *64,77*

rob [*v*] *steal, deprive*
abscond, appropriate, bereave, break into, burglarize, burgle, cheat, con, cop*, defalcate, defraud, despoil, disinherit, dispossess, divest, do

out of*, embezzle, filch*, heist, hijack, hold up*, hustle, liberate, lift*, loot, lose, mug, oust, peculate, pilfer, pillage, pinch, plunder, promote, purloin, raid, ransack, relieve, requisition, rifle, rip off*, roll*, sack*, scrounge, snitch*, stick up, strip, strong-arm*, swindle, swipe, take, thieve, withhold; SEE CONCEPTS *139,142,192*

robber [*n*] *person who steals*
bandit, brigand, buccaneer, burglar, cardsharper*, cat burglar, cattle thief*, cheat*, chiseler*, con artist, corsair, crook, desperado, despoiler, fence, forager, fraud, grafter, hijacker, holdup artist*, housebreaker, looter, marauder, mugger, operator, pickpocket, pilferer, pillager, pirate, plunderer, prowler, punk*, raider, rustler, safe-cracker, sandbagger*, second-story operator*, shoplifter, stealer, stickup, swindler, thief, thug; SEE CONCEPT *412*

robbery [*n*] *stealing*
break-in, burglary, caper, embezzlement, felony, heist*, hit, holdup*, job, larceny, looting, mortal sin, mugging, purse-snatching, stickup*, theft, thievery, unlawful act, wrongdoing; SEE CONCEPT *192*

robe [*n*] *gown, often for wearing at home*
bathrobe, cape, costume, covering, dress, dressing gown, frock, garment, habit, housecoat, kimono, mantle, muumuu, negligee, outfit, peignoir, vestment, wrapper; SEE CONCEPT *451*

robot [*n*] *android, machine*
automation, bionic person, cyborg, mechanical person; SEE CONCEPT *463*

robust [*adj*] *healthy, strong*
able-bodied, athletic, boisterous, booming, brawny, built, concentrated, fit, fit as fiddle*, flourishing, full-bodied, hale, hardy, hearty, hefty, husky, in fine fettle*, in good health, in good shape, in the pink*, live, lusty, muscular, peppy, potent, powerful, powerhouse, prospering, prosperous, roaring, rough, rugged, sinewy, snappy, sound, stout, strapping, sturdy, thriving, tiger*, tough, vigorous, well, wicked*, zappy*, zippy*; SEE CONCEPTS *314,489,613*

rock [*n1*] *stone*
bedrock, boulder, cobblestone, crag, crust, earth, gravel, lava, lodge, mass, metal, mineral, ore, pebble, promontory, quarry, reef, rubble, shelf, slab, slag; SEE CONCEPTS *470,474,477,478,509,523*

rock [*n2*] *foundation*
anchor, bulwark, cornerstone, defense, mainstay, protection, Rock of Gibraltar*, strength, support; SEE CONCEPTS *442,712*

rock [*v*] *move back and forth*
agitate, billow, careen, concuss, convulse, falter, heave, jiggle, jog, jolt, jounce, lurch, move, oscillate, pitch, push and pull, quake, quaver, quiver, reel, roll, roll about, shake, shock, stagger, sway, swing, toss, totter, tremble, undulate, vibrate, wobble; SEE CONCEPTS *147,149*

rocket [*n*] *projectile*
booster, firework, guided missile, ICBM, intercontinental ballistic missile, missile, spacecraft, spaceship, torpedo, weapon; SEE CONCEPT *500*

rocket [*v*] *shoot up*
ascend, climb, escalate, go through the ceiling, grow, lift, rise, sail, skyrocket, soar, take off*, tower, zoom; SEE CONCEPTS *148,150*

rock the boat [*v*] *cause trouble*
complain, disagree, disturb, make a stink*, make

waves*, not conform*, object, protest, stir things up*, upset the apple cart*; SEE CONCEPTS *46,52,54,300*

rocky [*adj1*] *rugged, stony*
bouldered, craggy, flinty, hard, inflexible, jagged, lapidarian, lithic, pebbly, petrified, petrous, rockbound, rock-ribbed, rough, solid, stonelike; SEE CONCEPTS *485,604*

rocky [*adj2*] *unyielding, inflexible*
adamant, bloodless, firm, flinty, hard, impassible, insensate, insensible, insensitive, obdurate, pitiless, rocklike, rough, rugged, solid, steady, tough; SEE CONCEPT *401*

rocky [*adj3*] *doubtful, undependable*
dizzy, ill, rickety, shaky, sick, sickly, staggering, ticklish, tottering, tricky, uncertain, unreliable, unstable, unsteady, unwell, weak, wobbly; SEE CONCEPTS *314,488,489*

rod [*n*] *bar, pole*
baton, billet, birch, cane, cylinder, dowel, ingot, mace, pin, rodule, scepter, sceptre, shaft, slab, spike, staff, stave, stick, strip, switch, wand; SEE CONCEPTS *436,470,479*

rogue [*n*] *person who deceives, swindles*
bad egg*, bad news*, blackguard*, black sheep*, charlatan, cheat, cheater, con artist, criminal, crook, defrauder, devil, fraud, heel*, hooligan*, lowlife*, mischief, miscreant, monstrosity, ne'er-do-well*, outlaw, problem*, rapscallion, rascal, reprobate, scalawag, scamp, scoundrel, swindler, trickster, villain; SEE CONCEPT *412*

roguish [*adj*] *deceitful; mischievous*
beguiling, crafty, crooked, cunning, deceiving, deceptive, devilish, dishonest, fraudulent, impish, knavish, lying, naughty, playful, puckish, rascally, shifty, slick, sly, sneaky, tricky, underhand, underhanded, unprincipled, untruthful; SEE CONCEPTS *401,545*

role [*n1*] *impersonation of a character*
act, acting, appearance, aspect, bit, character, clothing, execution, extra, guise, hero, ingenue, lead, look, part, performance, personification, piece, player, portrayal, presentation, representation, seeming, semblance, show, star, stint, super, title, walk-on; SEE CONCEPTS *263,716*

role [*n2*] *duty, function*
act, bit, business, capacity, execution, game*, guise, job, office, part, piece, pose, position, post, posture, province, stint, task, what one is into*; SEE CONCEPTS *362,694*

roll [*n1*] *revolving, turning*
cycle, gyration, reel, revolution, rotation, run, spin, trundling, turn, twirl, undulation, whirl; SEE CONCEPTS *147,201*

roll [*n2*] *cylindrical object*
ball, barrel, bobbin, cartouche, coil, cone, convolution, cornucopia, cylinder, fold, reel, rundle, scroll, shell, spiral, spool, trundle, volute, wheel, whorl; SEE CONCEPT *436*

roll [*n3*] *list, roster*
annals, catalog, census, chronicle, directory, head count, index, muster, nose count*, register, roll call, schedule, scroll, table; SEE CONCEPT *281*

roll [*n4*] *growl, reverberation*
barrage, boom, booming, clangor, drone, drumbeat, drumming, echoing, grumble, quaver, racket, rat-a-tat*, resonance, roar, rumble, rumbling, thunder; SEE CONCEPT *595*

roll [*v1*] *revolve, turn; proceed smoothly*
alternate, be in sequence, bowl, circle, circumduct, coil, curve, drape, drive, eddy, elapse, enfold, entwine, envelop, flow, fold, follow, furl, go around, go past, gyrate, gyre, impel, pass, pirouette, pivot, propel, reel, rock, rotate, run, spin, spiral, succeed, swaddle, swathe, swing around, swirl, swivel, trundle, twirl, twist, undulate, wheel, whirl, wind, wrap; SEE CONCEPTS *147,201*

roll [*v2*] *spread out*
even, flatten, grind, level, press, pulverize, smooth; SEE CONCEPTS *137,208,250*

roll [*v3*] *thunder, reverberate*
bombinate, boom, cannonade, drum, echo, growl, grumble, hum, pattern, quaver, rattle, re-echo, resound, roar, ruffle, rumble, rustle, sound, trill, whirr; SEE CONCEPT *65*

roll [*v4*] *rock, sway*
billow, drift, flow, glide, heave, incline, jibe, lean, lumber, lurch, pitch, ramble, range, reel, roam, rove, run, stagger, stray, surge, swagger, swing, toss, tumble, undulate, waddle, wallow, wave, welter, yaw; SEE CONCEPTS *147,149*

rollicking [*adj*] *fun-loving, lively*
antic, boisterous, carefree, cavorting, cheerful, devil-may-care*, exuberant, frisky, frolicsome, glad, happy, hearty, jaunty, jovial, joyful, joyous, lighthearted, merry, playful, rip-roaring*, romping, spirited, sportive, sprightly; SEE CONCEPTS *401,548*

roly-poly [*adj*] *pudgy*
buxom, chubby*, dumpy, fat, hefty, obese, overweight, plump, plumpish, rotund, round, stout, thick-bodied, tubby*; SEE CONCEPTS *491,773*

romance [*n1*] *love affair*
affair, affair of the heart*, amour, attachment, courtship, enchantment, fascination, fling, flirtation, intrigue, liaison, love, love story, passion, relationship; SEE CONCEPTS *375,384*

romance [*n2*] *fanciful story or narrative*
ballad, fairy tale, fantasy, fiction, idealization, idyll, legend, love story, lyric, melodrama, novel, story, tale, tear-jerker*; SEE CONCEPT *280*

romance [*n3*] *adventure, flight of fancy*
charm, color, excitement, exoticness, fairy tale, fancy, fantasy, fascination, glamour, hazard, idealization, idyll, mystery, nostalgia, risk, sentiment, venture; SEE CONCEPT *673*

romantic [*adj*] *sentimental, idealistic*
adventurous, amorous, bathetic, charming, chimerical, chivalrous, colorful, corny*, daring, dreamy, enchanting, erotic, exciting, exotic, extravagant, fairy-tale, fanciful, fantastic, fascinating, fond, glamorous, idyllic, impractical, lovey-dovey*, loving, maudlin, mushy*, mysterious, nostalgic, passionate, picturesque, poetic, quixotic, sloppy*, soppy*, starry-eyed, syrupy, tear-jerking*, tender, unrealistic, utopian, visionary, whimsical, wild; SEE CONCEPTS *403,542,548*

romp [*n*] *fun; caper*
antic, cakewalk*, cavort, dance, escapade, frisk, frolic, gambol, hop, lark, leap, play, rollick, rout, skip, sport; SEE CONCEPTS *292,384*

romp [*v*] *have fun, enjoy oneself*
caper, cavort, celebrate, cut capers*, cut up*, fool around*, frisk, frolic, gambol, go on the town*, kid around*, lark, let loose*, make merry,

ri
ro

play, prance, revel, roister, rollic, skip, skylark, sport, whoop it up*; SEE CONCEPTS *292,384*

rookie [*n*] *novice*
amateur, apprentice, beginner, colt*, cub*, fledgling, freshman/woman, greenhorn, neophyte, newcomer, new kid on the block*, tenderfoot*, trainee; SEE CONCEPTS *348,350,423*

room [*n1*] *space, range*
allowance, area, capacity, chance, clearance, compass, elbowroom, expanse, extent, latitude, leeway, license, margin, occasion, opening, opportunity, place, play, range, reach, rein, rope, scope, sway, sweep, territory, vastness, volume; SEE CONCEPTS *651,756*

room [*n2*] *enclosed section of building designed for specific purpose*
accommodation, alcove, apartment, cabin, cave*, chamber, cubbyhole, cubicle, den, flat, flop*, joint*, lodging, niche, office, setup*, suite, turf, vault; SEE CONCEPT *448*

roomy [*adj*] *having ample space*
ample, broad, capacious, commodious, extensive, generous, large, sizable, spacious, wide; SEE CONCEPT *583*

root [*n*] *base, core*
basis, bedrock, beginnings, bottom, cause, center, crux, derivation, essence, essentiality, footing, foundation, fountain, fountainhead, fundamental, germ, ground, groundwork, heart, inception, infrastructure, mainspring, marrow, motive, nub, nucleus, occasion, origin, pith, provenance, provenience, quick, quintessence, radicle, radix, reason, rhizome, rock bottom*, seat, seed, soul, source, starting point, stem, stuff, substance, substratum, tuber, underpinning, well; SEE CONCEPTS *442,648,661,826,829*

root [*v*] *dig and search*
burrow, delve, embed, ferret, forage, grub, grub up, hunt, ingrain, lodge, nose, place, poke, pry, rummage; SEE CONCEPT *178*

rootin'-tootin [*adj*] *rowdy*
boisterous, disorderly, loud, loudmouthed, mischievous, noisy, rambunctious, raucous, unruly, uproarious, vigorous, wild; SEE CONCEPT *401*

roots [*n*] *ancestry*
background, birthplace, blood, breed, descent, family history, family tree, genealogy, heritage, kindred, line, lineage, origin, parentage, pedigree, race; SEE CONCEPTS *414,648*

rope [*n*] *cord, line*
braiding, cable, cordage, hawser, lace, lanyard, lariat, lasso, strand, string, tape, thread, twine; SEE CONCEPT *475*

roster [*n*] *list of items, names*
agenda, catalog, head count, index, inventory, listing, muster, nose count*, program, record, register, roll, roll call, rota, schedule, scroll, table; SEE CONCEPTS *281,283*

rosy [*adj1*] *pink, reddish in color*
aflush, blooming, blushing, colored, coral, deep pink, fresh, glowing, healthy-looking, high-colored, incarnadine, pale red, peach, red, red-complexioned, red-faced, roseate, rose-colored, rubicund, ruddy; SEE CONCEPT *618*

rosy [*adj2*] *cheerful, hopeful*
alluring, auspicious, bright, encouraging, favorable, glowing, likely, optimistic, pleasing, promising, reassuring, roseate, rose-colored, sunny; SEE CONCEPTS *529,548*

rot [*n1*] *corrosion, disintegration*
blight, canker, corrosion, decay, decomposition, deterioration, mold, putrefaction, putrescence; SEE CONCEPTS *469,698*

rot [*n2*] *garbage, nonsense*
balderdash, bilge, bunk, claptrap, drivel, foolishness, guff, hogwash, hooey*, moonshine*, poppycock, rubbish, silliness, stuff and nonsense*, tommyrot; SEE CONCEPTS *278,529*

rot [*v*] *corrode, deteriorate*
break down, corrupt, crumble, debase, debauch, decay, decline, decompose, degenerate, demoralize, deprave, descend, disimprove, disintegrate, fester, go bad*, go downhill*, go to pot*, languish, molder, perish, pervert, putrefy, retrograde, sink, spoil, stain, taint, turn, warp, waste away, wither, worsen; SEE CONCEPTS *240,469,698*

rotary [*adj*] *turning*
encircling, gyral, gyratory, revolving, rotating, rotational, rotatory, spinning, vertiginous, vorticular, whirligig, whirling; SEE CONCEPTS *581,584*

rotate [*v1*] *go around in circle*
circle, circumduct, circumvolve, gyrate, gyre, move, pirouette, pivot, reel, revolve, roll, spin, swivel, troll, trundle, turn, twirl, twist, waltz, wheel, whirl, whirligig, whirr; SEE CONCEPTS *147,738*

rotate [*v2*] *alternate*
bandy, ensue, exchange, follow, follow in sequence, interchange, relieve, spell, succeed, switch, take turns; SEE CONCEPTS *104,697*

rotten [*adj1*] *decayed, decaying*
bad, bad-smelling, corroded, corrupt, crumbled, crumbling, decomposed, decomposing, disgusting, disintegrated, disintegrating, fecal, feculent, festering, fetid, foul, gross, infected, loathsome, loud, mephitic, moldering, moldy, noisome, noxious, offensive, overripe, perished, polluted, purulent, pustular, putrescent, putrid, putrified, rancid, rank, rotting, smelling, sour, spoiled, stale, stinking, strong, tainted, touched, unsound; SEE CONCEPTS *462,485*

rotten [*adj2*] *dishonest, immoral*
bent, bribable, contaminated, corrupt, crooked, debauched, deceitful, defiled, degenerate, depraved, dirtied, dishonorable, disloyal, faithless, filthy, flagitious, impure, mercenary, nefarious, perfidious, perverse, polluted, soiled, sullied, tainted, treacherous, unclean, untrustworthy, venal, vicious, villainous, vitiated; SEE CONCEPTS *404,545*

rotten [*adj3*] *despicable, inferior, bad*
amiss, base, below par*, bruised, bum*, contemptible, crummy*, defective, deplorable, dirty, disagreeable, disappointing, diseased, displeasing, dissatisfactory, filthy, impaired, inadequate, injured, lousy*, low-grade, mean, nasty, poor, punk*, regrettable, rough, scurrilous, shaky, sorry, sour, substandard, unacceptable, unfortunate, unhappy, unlucky, unpleasant, unsatisfactory, unsound, vile, wasted, wicked, withering, wrong; SEE CONCEPTS *570,571,574*

rotund [*adj1*] *fat*
beefy*, big, broad, burly, chunky*, dumpy, elephantine, fleshy, heavy, heavyset, hefty, husky, obese, overweight, plump, plumpish, portly, pudgy*, roly-poly*, round, solid, stout, tubby*, weighty; SEE CONCEPT *491*

rotund [*adj2*] *sonorous*
booming, loud, resonant, resounding; SEE CON-
CEPTS *592,594*

rough [*adj1*] *uneven, irregular*
asperous, bearded, brambly, bristly, broken,
bumpy, bushy, chapped, choppy, coarse,
cragged, craggy, cross-grained, disheveled,
fuzzy, hairy, harsh, jagged, knobby, knotty,
nappy, nodular, not smooth, ridged, rocky, ruffled, rugged, scabrous, scraggy, shaggy, sharp,
stony, tangled, tousled, tufted, unequal, uneven,
unfinished, unlevel, unshaven, unshorn, woolly,
wrinkled, wrinkly; SEE CONCEPTS *485,606*

rough [*adj2*] *stormy; not quiet*
agitated, blustering, blustery, boisterous, buffeting, cacophonous, choppy, coarse, discordant,
dry, furious, grating, gruff, harsh, hoarse, husky,
inclement, inharmonious, jarring, raging, rasping, raucous, rugged, squally, stridulent, tempestuous, tumultous/tumultuous, turbulent,
unmusical, wild; SEE CONCEPTS *525,592,594*

rough [*adj3*] *rude, impolite*
bearish, bluff, blunt, boisterous, boorish, brief,
brusque, churlish, coarse, crass, crude, cruel,
crusty, curt, discourteous, drastic, extreme,
gross*, hairy*, hard, harsh, ill-mannered, improper, inconsiderate, indecorous, indelicate, inelegant, loud, loutish, mean, nasty, raw, rowdy,
severe, sharp, short, tough, unceremonious, uncivil, uncouth, uncultivated, uncultured, unfeeling, ungracious, unjust, unmannerly, unpleasant,
unpolished, unrefined, untutored, violent, vulgar;
SEE CONCEPTS *267,401*

rough [*adj4*] *basic, incomplete*
austere, crude, cursory, formless, hard, imperfect, raw, rough-and-ready*, roughhewn,
rudimentary, shapeless, sketchy, spartan, uncompleted, uncut, undressed, unfashioned,
unfinished, unformed, unhewn, unpolished, unprocessed, unrefined, unwrought; SEE CONCEPT
531

rough [*adj5*] *approximate*
amorphous, estimated, foggy, general, hazy, imprecise, inexact, proximate, rude, sketchy, uncertain, unprecise, vague; SEE CONCEPT *557*

roughly [*adv*] *about*
approximately, around, in the ball park*, in the
neighborhood, more or less, practically, pretty
near, somewhere around; SEE CONCEPT *583*

rough out [*v*] *do preliminary design*
adumbrate, block out, chalk, characterize, delineate, draft, outline, plan, skeleton, sketch, suggest; SEE CONCEPTS *36,79,174*

rough up [*v*] *beat up*
bash, batter, hit, knock about, knock around,
maltreat, mishandle, mistreat, roughhouse, slap
around, thrash; SEE CONCEPTS *189,246*

round [*adj1*] *ball-shaped; semicircular area*
annular, arced, arched, arciform, bent, bowed,
bulbous, circular, coiled, curled, curved, curvilinear, cylindrical, discoid, disk-shaped, domical,
egg-shaped, elliptical, globose, globular, looped,
orbed, orbicular, orbiculate, oval, ringed, rotund,
rounded, spherical, spheroid, spiral; SEE CON-
CEPT *486*

round [*adj2*] *complete*
accomplished, done, entire, finished, full,
rounded, solid, unbroken, undivided, whole; SEE
CONCEPT *531*

round [*adj3*] *full-bodied, ample in size*
chubby, expansive, fleshy, generous, large,
plump, plumpish, pudgy*, roly-poly*, rotund,
rounded, tubby; SEE CONCEPTS *491,773*

round [*adj4*] *resonant, rich in sound*
consonant, full, mellifluous, orotund, plangent,
resounding, ringing, rotund, sonorous, vibrant;
SEE CONCEPT *594*

round [*adj5*] *honest, direct*
blunt, candid, frank, free, outspoken, plain,
straightforward, unmodified, vocal; SEE CONCEPT
267

round [*adv*] *approximate*
about, all but, almost, around, as good as, close
to, in the neighborhood of, just about, most, near,
nearly, practically, roughly; SEE CONCEPT *762*

round [*n1*] *globe, ball; semicircular area*
arc, arch, band, bend, bow, circle, circlet, curvation, curvature, curve, disc, disk, equator, eye,
gyre, hoop, loop, orb, orbit, ring, ringlet, sphere,
wheel; SEE CONCEPT *436*

round [*n2*] *cycle, stage*
ambit, beat, bout, circuit, circulation, circumvolution, compass, course, division, gyration, lap,
level, performance, period, revolution, rotation,
round trip, routine, schedule, sequence, series,
session, succession, tour, turn, wheel, whirl; SEE
CONCEPTS *364,727,807*

round [*n3*] *unit of ammunition*
bullet, cartridge, charge, discharge, load, shell,
shot; SEE CONCEPTS *498,500*

round [*v1*] *turn; encircle*
begird, bypass, circle, circulate, circumnavigate,
compass, encompass, flank, gird, girdle, go
around, gyrate, hem, pivot, revolve, ring, roll, rotate, skirt, spin, surround, wheel, whirl; SEE CON-
CEPTS *147,149,187*

round [*v2*] *make curved; remove angles*
arch, bend, bow, coil, convolute, crook, curl,
curve, form, loop, mold, perfect, polish, recurve,
refine, shape, sleek, slick, smooth, whorl; SEE
CONCEPTS *184,202*

roundabout [*adj*] *indirect*
ambiguous, circuitous, circular, circumlocutory,
collateral, deviating, devious, discursive, evasive, meandering, oblique, obliquitous, periphrastic, taking the long way*, tortuous; SEE
CONCEPTS *559,581,584*

round off [*v*] *finish*
bring to a close, cap, climax, close, complete,
conclude, crown, culminate, finish off, settle, top
off; SEE CONCEPT *234*

roundup [*n*] *collection, collation*
assembly, branding, gathering, herding, mar-
shalling, muster, rally, summary, survey; SEE
CONCEPTS *257,397*

round up [*v*] *collect, gather*
assemble, bring in, bring together, cluster, drive,
group, herd, marshal, muster, rally; SEE CON-
CEPTS *109,257*

rouse [*v1*] *wake*
arouse, awake, awaken, call, get up, raise, rise,
stir, wake up; SEE CONCEPT *250*

rouse [*v2*] *stimulate, excite*
aggravate, agitate, anger, animate, arouse, ask
for it*, awaken, bestir, bug*, challenge, craze,
deepen, disturb, enhance, enliven, exhilarate, fire
up*, foment, galvanize, get going, heighten, incite, inflame, innervate, innerve, instigate, intensate, intensify, key up*, kindle, magnify, make

ro
ro

waves*, mount, move, needle, pep up*, pique, provoke, quicken, rally, redouble, rile, rise, startle, steam up*, stir, trigger, urge, vivify, wake, waken, wake up, whet, whip up*, work up; SEE CONCEPTS *7,22,244*

rousing [*adj*] *stirring*
active, alert, animated, astir, bouncy, bright, brisk, buoyant, bustling, busy, buzzing, chirpy, dashing, energetic, enthusiastic, frisky, full of pep*, hyper*, industrious, jumping, lively, peppy*, perky, refreshing, snappy, spirited, spry, stimulating, vigorous, zippy*; SEE CONCEPTS *401,542,548*

rout [*n*] *overwhelming defeat*
beating, clobbering*, comedown, confusion, debacle, disaster, drubbing*, embarrassment, flight, hiding, overthrow, retreat, romp, ruin, shambles, shutout, thrashing, trashing*, upset, vanquishment, walkover*, washout*, waxing*, whipping; SEE CONCEPTS *95,119,363*

rout [*v*] *defeat overwhelmingly*
bash, beat, blow out of water*, bulldoze*, bury*, chase, clean up on*, clobber, conquer, cream*, crush, cut to pieces*, destroy, discomfit, dispel, drive off, expel, finish*, hunt, kill*, lambaste*, larrup*, murder*, outmaneuver, overpower, overthrow, put to flight*, repulse, scatter, scuttle, shut out*, skunk*, subdue, subjugate, swamp*, torpedo*, total*, trounce, vanquish, wallop, wax*, whip, wipe off map*, wipe out*, worst, zap*; SEE CONCEPT *95*

route [*n*] *path over which someone or something travels*
avenue, beat, beeline, byway, circuit, course, detour, digression, direction, divergence, itinerary, journey, line, meandering, passage, pavement, pike, plot, program, rambling, range, road, round, rounds, run, short cut, tack, track, trail, wandering, way; SEE CONCEPTS *501,660*

route [*v*] *send along a path*
address, conduct, consign, convey, direct, dispatch, escort, forward, guide, lead, pilot, remit, see, shepherd, ship, show, steer, transmit; SEE CONCEPTS *187,217*

routine [*adj*] *habitual*
accepted, accustomed, chronic, conventional, customary, everyday, familiar, general, methodical, normal, ordinary, periodic, plain, quotidian, regular, seasonal, standard, typical, unremarkable, usual, wonted, workaday; SEE CONCEPTS *530,547,548*

routine [*n*] *habitual activity*
act, beaten path*, bit, channels, custom, cycle, daily grind*, drill, formula, grind*, groove*, habit, line, method, order, pace, pattern, piece, practice, procedure, program, rat race*, rote, round, rut, schtick*, spiel*, system, tack, technique, treadmill, usage, way, wont; SEE CONCEPTS *6,362,770*

row [*n1*] *sequence, series*
bank, chain, column, consecution, echelon, file, line, order, progression, queue, range, rank, string, succession, tier, train; SEE CONCEPTS *432,727,744*

row [*n2*] *fight, ruckus*
affray, altercation, bickering, brawl, castigation, commotion, controversy, dispute, disturbance, falling-out*, fracas, fray, fuss, knock-down-drag-out*, lecture, melee, noise, quarrel, racket, reprimand, reproof, riot, rumpus, run-in*, scrap*, set-to*, shouting match*, squabble, talking-to*, telling-off*, tiff, tongue-lashing*, trouble, tumult, uproar, words*, wrangle; SEE CONCEPTS *46,52,106*

row [*v1*] *move boat with paddle*
drag, oar, paddle, pull, punt, sail, scud, scull, sky an oar, swim*; SEE CONCEPT *187*

row [*v2*] *argue, fight*
bawl out, berate, bicker, brawl, call on the carpet*, dispute, jaw, quarrel, ream, scold, scrap, spat, squabble, tiff, tongue-lash*, wrangle; SEE CONCEPTS *46,106*

rowdy [*adj*] *boisterous, noisy*
disorderly, lawless, loud, loudmouthed, loutish, mischievous, obstreperous, rambunctious, raucous, rebellious, rough, roughhouse, rude, turbulent, unruly, uproarious, wild; SEE CONCEPT *401*

rowdy [*n*] *person who is boisterous, noisy*
brawler, bully, hellion, hooligan, lout, punk, roughneck, ruffian, terror*, troublemaker; SEE CONCEPT *412*

royal [*adj*] *monarchical, grand*
aristocratic, august, authoritative, baronial, commanding, dignified, elevated, eminent, grandiose, high, high-born, honorable, illustrious, imperial, imposing, impressive, kingly, lofty, magnificent, majestic, noble, queenly, regal, regnant, reigning, renowned, resplendent, ruling, sovereign, splendid, stately, superb, superior, supreme, worthy; SEE CONCEPTS *549,574*

rub [*n1*] *stroke, massage*
abrasion, attrition, brushing, caress, friction, grinding, kneading, pat, polish, rasping, scouring, scraping, shine, smear, smoothing, stroking, swab, swipe, wear, wipe; SEE CONCEPT *215*

rub [*n2*] *difficulty, problem*
bar, catch, crimp, dilemma, drawback, hamper, hindrance, hitch, hurdle, impediment, obstacle, predicament, snag, stumbling block*, traverse, trouble; SEE CONCEPTS *666,674*

rub [*v*] *stroke, massage*
abrade, anoint, apply, bark, brush, buff, burnish, caress, chafe, clean, coat, cover, curry, daub, erase, erode, excoriate, file, fray, fret, furbish, glance, glaze, gloss, grate, graze, grind, knead, mop, paint, pat, plaster, polish, put, rasp, scour, scrape, scrub, shine, slather, smear, smooth, spread, swab, triturate, wear, wear down, wipe; SEE CONCEPT *215*

rubberneck [*v*] *stare*
eagle eye*, eye, eyeball*, focus, gawk, gaze, glare, goggle*, lay eyes on*, look, ogle, peer, rivet; SEE CONCEPT *623*

rubbish [*n1*] *garbage*
debris, dregs, dross, junk, litter, lumber, offal, refuse, rubble, rummage, scrap, sweepings, trash, waste; SEE CONCEPT *260*

rubbish [*n2*] *nonsense*
balderdash, bilge*, bunkum, drivel, gibberish, hogwash, hooey*, poppycock, rot*, stuff and nonsense*, tommyrot; SEE CONCEPTS *230,278*

rubdown [*n*] *massage*
back rub, chirapsia, kneading, manipulation, stroking; SEE CONCEPTS *308,310*

rub the wrong way [*v*] *irritate*
aggravate, anger, annoy, bother, bug*, disturb, drive up the wall*, enrage, get on one's nerves*, get to, get under one's skin*, infuriate, irk, needle*, pester, rattle, ruffle one's feathers; SEE CONCEPTS *7,19*

ruckus [n] *disturbance*
big scene*, big stink*, bother, brawl, brouhaha*, commotion, disorder, disruption, distraction, explosion, fisticuffs, fracas, fray, fuss, hubbub*, hullabaloo*, interruption, quarrel, racket, rampage, riot, rumble, rumpus, stink*, stir, turmoil, upheaval, uprising, uproar; SEE CONCEPTS *388,410,674,720*

ruddy [adj] *pinkish, blushing*
blooming, blowsy, bronzed, crimson, florid, flush, flushed, fresh, full-blooded, glowing, healthy, pink, red, red-complexioned, reddish, roseate, rosy, rubicund, ruby, sanguine, scarlet; SEE CONCEPT *618*

rude [adj1] *disrespectful, rough*
abrupt, abusive, bad-mannered, barbarian, barbaric, barbarous, blunt, boorish, brusque, brutish, cheeky, churlish, coarse, crabbed, crude, curt, discourteous, graceless, gross, gruff, ignorant, illiterate, impertinent, impolite, impudent, inconsiderate, insolent, insulting, intrusive, loutish, low, obscene, offhand, peremptory, raw, savage, scurrilous, short, surly, uncivil, uncivilized, uncouth, uncultured, uneducated, ungracious, unmannerly, unpolished, unrefined, vulgar, wild; SEE CONCEPTS *267,401*

rude [adj2] *crude, primitive*
angular, artless, barbarous, callow, coarse, formless, fresh, green, ignorant, inartistic, inelegant, inexperienced, inexpert, makeshift, primal, raw, rough, roughhewn, roughly made, rudimental, rudimentary, shapeless, simple, uncivilized, unconversant, uncultivated, unfashioned, unfinished, unformed, unhewn, unpolished, unprocessed, unrefined, wild; SEE CONCEPTS *490, 531*

rude [adj3] *sudden; approximate*
abrupt, guessed, harsh, imperfect, imprecise, inexact, in the ballpark*, proximate, rough, sharp, startling, stormy, surmised, turbulent, unpleasant, unprecise, violent; SEE CONCEPTS *557,799*

rudimentary [adj] *basic, fundamental*
abecedarian, basal, beginning, early, elemental, elementary, embryonic, immature, initial, introductory, larval, nuts-and-bolts*, primary, primitive, simple, simplest, uncompleted, undeveloped, vestigial; SEE CONCEPTS *546,549*

rudiments [n] *fundamentals*
ABCs*, basics, beginnings, elements, essentials, first principles, foundation, guts*, heart, nittygritty, principles; SEE CONCEPTS *668,687,826, 829*

rue [v] *regret*
apologize, be sorry for, cry over*, deplore, feel remorse, feel sorry, grieve, kick oneself*, lament, mourn, weep over*; SEE CONCEPTS *21,410*

rueful [adj] *regretful*
apologetic, ashamed, deplorable, lamentable, mournful, remorseful, repentant, sad, sorrowful, sorry; SEE CONCEPT *403*

ruffian [n] *hoodlum*
brute, bully, criminal, delinquent, gangster, goon*, hood, hooligan, mobster, punk, rioter, rowdy, thug, tough guy*, troublemaker; SEE CONCEPT *412*

ruffle [v1] *mess up*
cockle, confuse, crease, crinkle, crumple, crush, derange, disarrange, discompose, dishevel, disorder, pucker, purse, rifle, rumple, tangle, tousle, wrinkle; SEE CONCEPT *158*

ruffle [v2] *upset, irritate*
abrade, agitate, anger, annoy, bluster, bother, browbeat, bully, chafe, confuse, cow*, disconcert, disquiet, disturb, excite, floor*, flummox, flurry, fluster, fret, fuddle, gall, get to*, harass, intimidate, irk, nettle, peeve, perturb, provoke, put off, put out, rattle, rattle one's cage*, shake up*, stir, stump, throw into tizzy*, torment, trouble, unsettle, vex, wear, worry; SEE CONCEPTS *7,14,19*

rug [n1] *carpet*
carpeting, floor covering, mat, matting, runner, shag*, tapestry, throw rug, wall-to-wall carpeting; SEE CONCEPT *473*

rug [n2] *hairpiece*
false hair, hair extension, hair implant, hair weaving, toupee, wig; SEE CONCEPT *392*

rugged [adj1] *bumpy, weathered*
asperous, broken, coarse, craggy, difficult, furrowed, harsh, hilly, irregular, jagged, leathery, lumpy, mountainous, ragged, rocky, rough, roughhewn, scabrous, scraggy, stark, uneven, unlevel, unpolished, unrefined, unsmooth, weather-beaten, worn, wrinkled; SEE CONCEPTS *490,606*

rugged [adj2] *severe, violent*
bitter, brutal, difficult, hard, harsh, inclement, intemperate, rigorous, rough, stormy, tempestuous, turbulent; SEE CONCEPTS *525,537*

rugged [adj3] *uncouth, crude*
barbarous, blunt, boorish, churlish, graceless, illbred, loutish, rude, uncultured, unpolished, unrefined; SEE CONCEPT *401*

rugged [adj4] *difficult, rigorous*
arduous, demanding, exacting, formidable, hairy*, hard, harsh, heavy*, heavy sledding*, knotty*, laborious, large order*, mean, murder*, no picnic*, operose, rough, stern, strenuous, taxing, tough, trying, uncompromising, uphill*; SEE CONCEPTS *538,565*

rugged [adj5] *big, strong*
able-bodied, athletic, brawny, energetic, forceful, hale, hardy, healthy, husky, indefatigable, lusty, muscular, robust, sturdy, tough, unflagging, vigorous, well-built; SEE CONCEPTS *314,489*

ruin [n] *situation of devastation*
atrophy, bane, bankruptcy, bath, breakdown, collapse, confusion, crackup, crash, crumbling, damage, decay, defeat, degeneracy, degeneration, demolition, destitution, destruction, deterioration, dilapidation, disintegration, disrepair, dissolution, downfall, downgrade, extinction, failure, fall, havoc, insolvency, loss, nemesis, overthrow, ruination, skids*, subversion, the end*, undoing, waste, waterloo, wreck, wreckage; SEE CONCEPT *674*

ruin [v] *devastate, destroy*
bankrupt, beggar, botch, break, bring down, bring to ruin, bust, clean out, crush, decimate, deface, defeat, defile, demolish, deplete, deplore, depredate, desecrate, despoil, devour, dilapidate, disfigure, do in*, drain, exhaust, fleece, impoverish, injure, lay waste, maim, make a mess of, mangle, mar, mutilate, overthrow, overturn, overwhelm, pauperize, pillage, rape, ravish, raze, reduce, sack, shatter, smash, spoil, spoilate, total, use up, wipe out*, wrack, wreak havoc on, wreck; SEE CONCEPTS *234,246,252*

ro
ru

ruinous [*adj*] *disastrous, devastating*
annihilative, baleful, baneful, calamitous, cataclysmic, catastrophic, crippling, damaging, deadly, deleterious, depleting, dire, disastrous, draining, exhausting, extravagant, fatal, fateful, harmful, hurtful, immoderate, impoverishing, injurious, murderous, noxious, pernicious, shattering, suicidal, unfortunate, wasteful, withering, wrackful; SEE CONCEPTS *537,548,570*

ruins [*n*] *buildings that are dilapidated*
ashes, debris, destruction, detritus, foundation, relics, remains, remnants, residue, rubble, traces, vestiges, wreck, wreckage; SEE CONCEPTS *439,733*

rule [*n1*] *standard, principle of behavior*
aphorism, apothegm, assize, axiom, basis, brocard, canon, chapter and verse*, command, commandment, criterion, decorum, decree, decretion, dictum, direction, edict, etiquette, formula, fundamental, gnome, guide, guideline, keynote, keystone, law, maxim, model, moral, no-no's*, order, ordinance, precedent, precept, prescription, propriety, regimen, regulation, ruling, statute, tenet, test, the book*, the numbers*, truism; SEE CONCEPT *688*

rule [*n2*] *leadership of organization*
administration, ascendancy, authority, command, control, direction, domination, dominion, empire, government, influence, jurisdiction, power, regime, regnancy, reign, sovereignty, supremacy, sway; SEE CONCEPTS *299,376*

rule [*n3*] *method, way*
course, custom, formula, habit, normalcy, normality, order of things, policy, practice, procedure, routine; SEE CONCEPTS *6,647*

rule [*v1*] *govern, manage*
administer, be in authority, be in driver's seat*, be in power, bridle, command, conduct, control, crack the whip*, curb, decree, dictate, direct, dominate, domineer, guide, hold sway*, hold the reins*, keep under one's thumb*, lay down the law*, lead, order, overrule, predominate, preponderate, preside, prevail, regulate, reign, restrain, rule the roost*, run, run the show*, sit on top of*, sway, take over; SEE CONCEPTS *117,133,298*

rule [*v2*] *judge, decide*
adjudge, adjudicate, conclude, decree, deduce, determine, establish, figure, find, fix, gather, hold, infer, lay down, pass upon, postulate, prescribe, pronounce, resolve, settle, theorize; SEE CONCEPTS *18,81*

rule out [*v*] *exclude, reject*
abolish, avert, ban, bate, cancel, count out, debar, deter, dismiss, eliminate, except, forbid, forestall, forfend, leave out, not consider, obviate, preclude, prevent, prohibit, proscribe, recant, revoke, stave off, suspend, ward off; SEE CONCEPTS *25,121*

ruler [*n*] *historically, person who ruled an area*
baron, baroness, caesar, caliph, contessa, count, countess, crowned head, czar, czarina, dame, duchess, duke, dynast, emperor, empress, gerent, imperator, kaiser, khan, king, lady, lord, magnate, maharajah, maharani, majesty, mikado, · mogul, monarch, oligarch, overlord, pasha, potentate, prince, princess, queen, rajah, rani, rex, royal, shah, sovereign, sultan, sultana, tycoon; SEE CONCEPT *422*

ruler [*n2*] *tool for measuring or calculating length*
folding rule, measure, measuring stick, rule, slide rule, straightedge, T-square, yardstick; SEE CONCEPT *499*

ruling [*adj1*] *dominant, governing*
cardinal, central, commanding, controlling, leading, overriding, overruling, pivotal, regnant, reigning, sovereign, supreme, upper; SEE CONCEPT *574*

ruling [*adj2*] *prevailing, main*
chief, current, dominant, pivotal, popular, predominant, preeminent, preponderant, prevalent, principal, rampant, rife, widespread; SEE CONCEPT *568*

ruling [*n*] *judgment, decree*
adjudication, decision, directive, edict, finding, judgment, law, order, precept, pronouncement, resolution, rule, ukase, verdict; SEE CONCEPT *318*

rumble [*v*] *growl, thunder*
boom, grumble, resound, roar, roll; SEE CONCEPT *65*

ruminate [*v*] *think about seriously*
brainstorm*, brood, chew over, cogitate, consider, contemplate, deliberate, excogitate, figure, meditate, mull over, muse, ponder, rack one's brains*, reflect, revolve, stew about*, think, turn over, use one's head*, weigh; SEE CONCEPT *24*

rummage [*v*] *ransack, search*
beat the bushes*, comb, delve, dig out, disarrange, disarray, disorder, disorganize, disrupt, disturb, examine, explore, ferret out, fish, forage, grub, hunt, jumble, leave no stone unturned*, look high and low*, mess up, mix up, poke, rake, root, scour, search high heaven*, seek, shake, shake down, spy, toss, turn inside out*, turn upside down*; SEE CONCEPTS *158,216*

rumor [*n*] *talk about supposed truth*
back-fence talk*, breeze*, bruit, canard, comment, cry, dispatch, earful*, fabrication, falsehood, fame, fiction, gossip, grapevine*, hearsay, hoax, innuendo, intelligence, invention, lie, news, notoriety, report, repute, rumble, scandal, scuttlebutt*, story, suggestion, supposition, tale, tattle, tidings, whisper, wire*, word; SEE CONCEPTS *274,277,278*

rumor [*v*] *tell a supposed truth*
bruit, buzz*, circulate, gossip, noise about*, pass around, publish, report, say, talk, tattle, whisper; SEE CONCEPTS *49,54*

rump [*n*] *bottom, posterior of animal or human*
back, backside, beam, behind, breech, bum*, butt, butt end, buttocks, can*, croup, derrière, duff*, fanny*, haunches, hind end, hindquarters, keister*, moon*, prat, rear, rear end, sacrum, seat, tail*, tail end, tush*; SEE CONCEPTS *392,825*

rumple [*v*] *crush, wrinkle*
bedraggle, cockle, crease, crimp, crinkle, crumple, derange, dishevel, disorder, fold, mess up, muss up, pucker, ruck up, ruffle, screw up, scrunch, seam, tousle, wreathe; SEE CONCEPTS *137,219,250*

rumpus [*n*] *clamor*
brouhaha*, commotion, discord, disturbance, donnybrook, fracas, fuss, hassle, hubba-hubba*, hubbub, hullabaloo*, noise, outcry, pandemonium, racket, rhubarb, ruckus, tumult, turmoil, upheaval, uproar; SEE CONCEPTS *386,595,674*

run [*n1*] *fast moving on foot*
amble, bound, break, canter, dart, dash, drop, es-

cape, fall, flight, gallop, jog, lope, pace, race, rush, scamper, scuttle, spring, sprint, spurt, tear, trot, whisk; SEE CONCEPTS *150,195*

run [*n2*] *journey*
drive, excursion, jaunt, joy ride*, lift, outing, ride, round, spin, tour, travel, trip; SEE CONCEPT *224*

run [*n3*] *sequence, course*
bearing, chain, continuance, continuation, continuity, current, cycle, drift, duration, endurance, field, flow, line, motion, movement, passage, path, period, persistence, progress, prolongation, round, route, season, series, spell, streak, stream, stretch, string, succession, swing, tendency, tenor, tide, trend, way; SEE CONCEPTS *721,727,738*

run [*v1*] *move fast on foot*
abscond, amble, barrel, beat it*, bolt, bound, bustle, canter, career, clear out, course, cut and run*, dart, dash, decamp, depart, dog it*, escape, flee, flit, fly, gallop, go like lightning*, hasten, hie, hotfoot*, hurry, hustle, jog, leg it*, light out*, lope, make a break*, make off, make tracks*, pace, race, rush, scamper, scoot, scorch, scramble, scud, scurry, shag, shoot, skedaddle*, skip, skitter, smoke*, speed, spring, sprint, spurt, take flight, take off, tear, tear out, travel, trot, whisk; SEE CONCEPTS *150,195*

run [*v2*] *move rapidly, flowingly*
bleed, cascade, course, deliquesce, diffuse, discharge, dissolve, drop, fall, flow, flux, fuse, glide, go, go soft, gush, issue, leak, leap, liquefy, melt, pass, pour, proceed, roll, sail, scud, skim, slide, spill, spin, spout, spread, stream, thaw, tumble, turn to liquid, whirl, whiz; SEE CONCEPT *146*

run [*v3*] *operate, drive*
act, bear, carry, command, control, convey, go, govern, handle, manage, maneuver, move, perform, ply, propel, tick, transport, use, work; SEE CONCEPTS *225,680*

run [*v4*] *manage, supervise*
administer, be in charge, be in driver's seat*, be in saddle*, boss, carry on, conduct, control, coordinate, direct, head, head up*, helm*, keep, lead, look after, operate, ordain, oversee, own, pull the strings*, regulate, ride herd on*, superintend, take care of*; SEE CONCEPT *117*

run [*v5*] *continue, range*
be current, circulate, cover, encompass, extend, go, go around, go on, last, lie, move past, persevere, proceed, reach, spread, stretch, trail, vary; SEE CONCEPTS *651,721*

run [*v6*] *attempt to be elected to public office*
be a candidate, challenge, compete, contend, contest, hit the campaign trail*, kiss babies*, oppose, politick, race, ring doorbells*, shake hands*, stand, stump, whistlestop*; SEE CONCEPT *300*

run-around [*n*] *avoidance*
come-off, delay, detour, difficulty, diversion, elusion, escape, escaping, eschewal, evasion, inertia, postponement, roundabout, shunning; SEE CONCEPTS *30,121*

runaway [*adj*] *out of control*
delinquent, disorderly, escaped, fleeing, fugitive, loose, out of hand*, running, uncontrolled, wild; SEE CONCEPT *401*

runaway [*n*] *person who is trying to escape*
absconder, delinquent, deserter, escapee, es-

caper, fugitive, lawbreaker, maroon, offender, truant, wanted person; SEE CONCEPT *412*

run-down [*adj*] *shabby, in bad shape*
abandoned, beat-up, below par, broken-down, crumbling, debilitated, decrepit, derelict, deserted, desolate, dilapidated, dingy, dog-eared*, down-at-the-heel*, drained, enervated, exhausted, fatigued, forsaken, frowzy*, in a bad way*, neglected, old, out of condition, peaked, ramshackle, ratty*, rickety, seedy, shabby, tacky, tattered, tired, tumble-down, uncared-for, under the weather*, unhealthy, untended, used up, weak, weary, worn-out; SEE CONCEPTS *314,485,570*

rundown [*n*] *summary*
briefing, outline, precis, recap*, recapitulation, report, résumé, review, run-through, sketch, synopsis; SEE CONCEPT *283*

run down [*v*] *ridicule*
belittle, criticize, decry, defame, denigrate, depreciate, derogate, detract, diminish, disparage, dispraise, downcry, knock*, make fun of, opprobriate, revile, speak ill of, vilify; SEE CONCEPTS *52,54*

rung [*n*] *notch, step*
bar, board, crossbar, crosspiece, degree, grade, level, rod, round, rundle, stage, tread; SEE CONCEPTS *471,744*

run-in [*n*] *argument*
altercation, bickering, brush, confrontation, contretemps, dispute, encounter, falling-out*, fight, hassle, quarrel, row, set-to*, skirmish, tussle; SEE CONCEPTS *46,106*

run in [*v*] *arrest*
apprehend, bust, collar, cop*, detain, handcuff, jail, nab, pick up, pinch*, pull in, put the cuffs on*, take into custody, throw in jail*; SEE CONCEPTS *298,317*

running [*adj*] *continuous, flowing, operating*
active, alive, constant, cursive, dynamic, easy, effortless, executing, fluent, functioning, going, in action, incessant, in operation, in succession, live, moving, operative, perpetual, proceeding, producing, smooth, together, unbroken, unceasing, uninterrupted, working; SEE CONCEPTS *538,560,584*

running [*adv*] *continually*
consecutively, continuously, night and day*, successively, together, unintermittently, uninterruptedly; SEE CONCEPTS *482,798*

running [*n*] *management of organization*
administration, care, charge, conduct, control, coordination, direction, functioning, handling, intendance, leadership, maintenance, operation, organization, oversight, performance, regulation, superintendency, supervision, working; SEE CONCEPT *117*

run-of-the-mill [*adj*] *average*
common, commonplace, customary, dime a dozen, everyday, fair, fair to middling*, garden-variety*, humdrum, intermediate, mainstream, mediocre, medium, middle of the road*, middling, ordinary, regular, routine, so-so*, undistinguished, unexceptional, usual; SEE CONCEPT *547*

run out [*v*] *fail, be exhausted*
be cleaned out*, be out of, cease, close, come to a close, depart, dissipate, dry up, end, exhaust, expire, finish, give out, go, have no more, have none left, lose, peter out*, stop, terminate, tire,

ru
ru

waste, waste away, weaken, wear out; SEE CON-CEPTS *105,699*

runt [*n*] *very small person*
half-pint*, homunculus, Lilliputian, midget, pee-wee*, punk*, shrimp*; SEE CONCEPT *424*

run through [*v*] *use up; waste*
blow, consume, dissipate, exhaust, expend, fin-ish, fritter away, lose, spend, squander, throw away, wash up; SEE CONCEPT *156*

rupture [*n1*] *break, split*
breach, burst, cleavage, cleft, crack, division, fis-sure, fracture, hernia, herniation, parting, rent, schism, tear; SEE CONCEPTS *309,513*

rupture [*n2*] *disagreement, dissolution*
altercation, breach, break, break-up, bustup*, clash, contention, detachment, disruption, disunion, division, divorce, divorcement, es-trangement, falling-out, feud, hostility, misun-derstanding, parting, partition, quarrel, rift, schism, separation, split, split-up*; SEE CON-CEPTS *46,388*

rupture [*v1*] *break open*
breach, burst, cleave, crack, disrupt, divide, erupt, fracture, hold, open, part, puncture, rend, rive, separate, sever, shatter, split, sunder, tear; SEE CONCEPTS *98,246,308*

rupture [*v2*] *disagree; dissolve union*
break off, break up, come between, disjoin, dis-rupt, dissect, dissever, disunite, divide, divorce, part, separate, split, split up, sunder; SEE CON-CEPTS *297,384*

rural [*adj*] *country, not urban*
agrarian, agricultural, agronomic, Arcadian, backwoods, bucolic, countrified, farm, georgic, idyllic, natural, outland, pastoral, provincial, ranch, rustic, rustical, simple, sylvan, unsophisti-cated; SEE CONCEPT *583*

ruse [*n*] *trick, deception*
angle, artifice, blind, booby trap*, curveball*, deceit, device, dodge, feint, gambit, game, game plan*, gimmick, hoax, imposture, jig*, maneu-ver, ploy, scenario, sham, shenanigans*, shift, stratagem, stunt, subterfuge, switch*, twist*, wile; SEE CONCEPTS *59,674*

rush [*n1*] *hurry, speed*
blitz, charge, dash, dispatch, expedition, flood, flow, flux, haste, hastiness, hurriedness, precipi-tance, precipitancy, precipitation, race, scramble, stream, surge, swiftness, urgency; SEE CONCEPTS *145,748,818*

rush [*n2*] *attack*
assault, blitz, charge, onslaught, push, storm, surge, violence; SEE CONCEPT *86*

rush [*v1*] *hurry, speed*
accelerate, barrel, bolt, break, career, charge, chase, course, dart, dash, dispatch, expedite, fire up*, fleet, fling, flit, fly, get cracking*, get the lead out*, go like lightning*, haste, hasten, hot-foot*, hurry up, hustle, lose no time*, make haste, make short work of*, press, push, quicken, race, roll, run, scramble, scud, scurry, shake a leg*, shoot, speed up, sprint, step on gas*, streak, surge, tear, whiz*, zip*, zoom*; SEE CONCEPTS *91,150,152*

rush [*v2*] *charge, attack*
capture, overcome, storm, surge, take by storm*; SEE CONCEPT *86*

rust [*n*] *corrosion*
blight, corruption, decay, decomposition, dilapi-

dation, mold, oxidation, rot, wear; SEE CONCEPTS *309,720*

rust [*v*] *corrode*
decay, decline, degenerate, deteriorate, oxidize, stale, tarnish, wither; SEE CONCEPT *469*

rustic [*adj1*] *country, rural*
agrarian, agricultural, Arcadian, artless, austere, bucolic, countrified, homely, homespun, homey, honest, natural, outland, pastoral, picturesque, plain, primitive, provincial, simple, sylvan, unaf-fected, unpolished, unrefined, unsophisticated, verdant; SEE CONCEPTS *583,589*

rustic [*adj2*] *crude, uncouth*
awkward, boorish, churlish, clodhopping, clown-ish, coarse, countrified, dull, foolish, graceless, ignorant, inelegant, loutish, maladroit, rough, rude, stupid, uncultured, uneducated, ungainly, unmannerly, unpolished, unsophisticated; SEE CONCEPT *401*

rustic [*n*] *person from the country, with little ex-perience*
backwoodsperson, boor, country cousin*, coun-tryperson, farmer, hayseed*, hick*, hillbilly, mountaineer, peasant, provincial, redneck*, rural, yokel*; SEE CONCEPT *413*

rustle [*n*] *whisper, swish*
crackle, crepitation, crinkling, friction, noise, patter, ripple, rustling, sound, stir; SEE CONCEPT *595*

rustle [*v*] *swish, whisper*
crackle, crepitate, crinkle, hum, murmur, patter, sigh, stir, tap, whir, whish, whoosh; SEE CONCEPT *65*

rustle up [*v*] *provide*
accommodate, arrange, assemble, bring, cater, cook, furnish, get ready, give, hand over, in-dulge, make, prepare, present, produce, put to-gether, ready, render, scrape up, serve, supply, take care of, turn out; SEE CONCEPTS *35,108,110, 136,140,202*

rusty [*adj1*] *corroded*
decayed, oxidized, rust-covered, rusted; SEE CONCEPT *485*

rusty [*adj2*] *out of practice; inexperienced*
deficient, impaired, neglected, not what it was*, sluggish, soft, stale, unpracticed, unqualified, weak; SEE CONCEPT *527*

rut [*n1*] *groove, indentation*
furrow, gouge, hollow, pothole, rabbet, score, track, trench, trough; SEE CONCEPT *513*

rut [*n2*] *routine of daily life*
circle, circuit, course, custom, daily grind*, dead end*, grind*, groove, habit, humdrum*, pace, pattern, performance, practice, procedure, rote, round, system, treadmill, usage, wont; SEE CON-CEPTS *6,647*

ruthless [*adj*] *mean, heartless*
adamant, barbarous, brutal, callous, cold, cold-blooded, cruel, cutthroat, dog-eat-dog*, feral, fe-rocious, fierce, grim, hard, hard-hearted, harsh, implacable, inexorable, inhuman, ironfisted, killer, malevolent, merciless, mortal, obdurate, pitiless, rancorous, relentless, remorseless, re-vengeful, sadistic, savage, severe, stern, stony, surly, unappeasable, unfeeling, unforgiving, un-merciful, unrelenting, unsympathetic, unyield-ing, vicious, vindictive, without pity; SEE CONCEPTS *401,404*

S

sabbatical [n] *leave*
break, furlough, holiday, leave of absence, liberty, recess, time off, vacation; SEE CONCEPTS 802,807

sable [adj] *very dark in color*
black, dark, dusky, dusty, ebon, ebony, gloomy, inky, jet, jetty, murky, pitch-black, pitch-dark, raven, somber; SEE CONCEPT 618

sabotage [n] *damage*
demolition, destruction, disruption, impairment, injury, mischief, overthrow, subversion, subversiveness, treachery, treason, undermining, vandalism, wreckage, wrecking; SEE CONCEPTS 86,246,252

sabotage [v] *incapacitate, damage*
attack, block, bollix, break up, cripple, deep six*, destroy, disable, disrupt, do*, do in*, foul up*, frustrate, hamper, hinder, louse up*, mess up*, obstruct, put out of action, put out of commission*, screw up*, subvert, take out*, throw a monkey wrench into*, torpedo*, undermine, vandalize, wreck; SEE CONCEPTS 86,246,252

sack [v1] *remove from position of responsibility*
ax*, bounce*, can*, cashier, discharge, dismiss, drop, expel, fire, give a pink slip*, give marching orders*, give the boot*, kick out, send packing*, ship, terminate; SEE CONCEPT 351

sack [v2] *raid, plunder*
demolish, depredate, desecrate, desolate, despoil, destroy, devastate, devour, fleece, gut, lay waste, loot, maraud, pillage, ravage, rifle, rob, ruin, spoil, spoliate, strip, waste; SEE CONCEPTS 139,252

sacrament [n] *rite*
baptism, celebration, ceremony, communion, confession, confirmation, custom, holy orders, liturgy, marriage, matrimony, oath, observance, practice, ritual, service, vow; SEE CONCEPTS 377,386

sacred [adj1] *holy, blessed*
angelic, cherished, consecrated, divine, enshrined, godly, hallowed, numinous, pious, pure, religious, revered, sacramental, saintly, sanctified, solemn, spiritual, unprofane, venerable; SEE CONCEPT 574

sacred [adj2] *protected*
dedicated, defended, guarded, immune, inviolable, inviolate, invulnerable, sacrosanct, secure, shielded, untouchable; SEE CONCEPT 587

sacrifice [v] *give up, let go*
cede, drop, endure, eschew, forfeit, forgo, immolate, kiss goodbye*, lose, offer, offer up, part with, renounce, resign oneself to, spare, suffer, surrender, waive, yield; SEE CONCEPTS 108,116

sacrilege [n] *irreverence*
blasphemy, crime, curse, desecration, heresy, impiety, mockery, offense, profanation, profaneness, profanity, sin, violation; SEE CONCEPT 645

sacrilegious [adj] *profane*
atheistic, blasphemous, desecrating, dirty*, filthy*, foul, godless, heathen, impious, indecent, infidel, irreligious, irreverent, irreverential, obscene, pagan, sinful, ungodly, unhallowed, unholy, violating; SEE CONCEPTS 267,401,545

sacrosanct [adj] *sacred*
blessed, consecrated, divine, godly, hallowed,

holy, pious, pure, religious, revered, sacramental, saintly, sanctified, spiritual, unprofane, venerated; SEE CONCEPT 574

sad [adj1] *unhappy, depressed*
bereaved, bitter, blue*, cheerless, dejected, despairing, despondent, disconsolate, dismal, distressed, doleful, down, downcast, down in dumps*, down in mouth*, forlorn, gloomy, glum, grief-stricken, grieved, heartbroken, heartsick, heavyhearted, hurting, in doldrums*, in grief, in the dumps*, languishing, low, low-spirited, lugubrious, melancholy, morbid, morose, mournful, out of sorts*, pensive, pessimistic, sick at heart*, somber, sorrowful, sorry, troubled, weeping, wistful, woebegone; SEE CONCEPT 403

sad [adj2] *unfortunate, distressing*
bad, calamitous, dark, dejecting, deplorable, depressing, disastrous, discomposing, discouraging, disheartening, dismal, dispiriting, dreary, funereal, grave, grievous, hapless, heart-rending, joyless, lachrymose, lamentable, lugubrious, melancholic, miserable, moving, oppressive, pathetic, pitiable, pitiful, poignant, regrettable, saddening, serious, shabby, sorry, tearful, tear-jerking*, tragic, unhappy, unsatisfactory, upsetting, wretched; SEE CONCEPTS 529,548

sadden [v] *upset, depress*
break one's heart*, bring one down*, bum out*, cast down, dampen spirits, dash, deject, deplore, desolate, discourage, dishearten, dispirit, distress, down, drag down*, grieve, make blue*, oppress, press, put a damper on*, put into a funk*, throw cold water on*, turn one off*, weigh down*; SEE CONCEPTS 7,19

sadistic [adj] *cruel, perverted*
barbarous, brutal, fiendish, perverse, ruthless, vicious; SEE CONCEPTS 542,545

sadness [n] *unhappiness, depression*
anguish, blahs*, bleakness, blue devils*, blue funk*, broken heart*, bummer, cheerlessness, dejection, despondency, disconsolateness, dismals*, dispiritedness, distress, dolefulness, dolor, downcastness, downer*, dysphoria, forlornness, funk, gloominess, grief, grieving, heartache, heartbreak, heavy heart*, hopelessness, letdown, listlessness, melancholy, misery, moodiness, mopes*, mournfulness, mourning, poignancy, sorrow, sorrowfulness, the blues*, the dumps*, tribulation, woe; SEE CONCEPT 410

safari [n] *hunting expedition*
hunt, journey, quest, trek, trip; SEE CONCEPT 224

safe [adj1] *free from harm*
buttoned up*, cherished, free from danger, guarded, home-free*, impervious, impregnable, in safety, intact, inviolable, invulnerable, maintained, okay*, out of danger, out of harm's way*, preserved, protected, safe and sound*, safeguarded, secure, sheltered, shielded, sitting pretty*, snug, tended, unassailable, undamaged, under lock and key*, under one's wing*, unharmed, unhurt, uninjured, unmolested, unscathed, unthreatened, vindicated, watched; SEE CONCEPT 587

safe [adj2] *not dangerous*
certain, checked, clear, competent, decontaminated, dependable, harmless, healthy, innocent, innocuous, innoxious, inoffensive, neutralized, nonpoisonous, nontoxic, pure, reliable, risk-free, riskless, secure, sound, tame, trustworthy, unin-

**ru
sa**

jurious, unpolluted, wholesome; SEE CONCEPTS *314,537,548*

safe [*adj3*] *cautious, conservative*
calculating, careful, chary, circumspect, competent, considerate, dependable, discreet, gingerly, guarded, on safe side*, prudent, realistic, reliable, sure, tried and true*, trustworthy, unadventurous, wary; SEE CONCEPTS *401,542*

safeguard [*n*] *protection*
aegis, armament, armor, buffer, bulwark, convoy, defense, escort, guard, screen, security, shield, surety, ward; SEE CONCEPT *712*

safeguard [*v*] *protect*
assure, bulwark, conserve, cover, defend, ensure, fend, guard, insure, look after, preserve, ride shotgun*, save, screen, secure, shield, watch over; SEE CONCEPT *96*

safekeeping [*n*] *protection*
aegis, assurance, care, certainty, cover, custody, guardianship, guarding, insurance, preservation, protecting, reassurance, refuge, safeguard, security, shelter, supervision, trust; SEE CONCEPTS *712,729*

safety [*n*] *protection from harm*
assurance, asylum, cover, defense, freedom, immunity, impregnability, inviolability, invulnerability, refuge, safeness, sanctuary, security, shelter; SEE CONCEPT *729*

safety net [*n*] *level of economic security guaranteed by government*
benefits, buffer, government aid, insurance, precaution, protective umbrella, safeguard, subsidy; SEE CONCEPT *344*

sag [*n*] *drop, decline*
basin, cant, concavity, depression, dip, distortion, downslide*, downswing*, downtrend, downturn, droop, fall, fall-off, hollow, list, settling, sink, sinkage, sinkhole, sinking, slant, slip, slump, tilt; SEE CONCEPTS *181,698,776*

sag [*v*] *droop*
bag, bend, bow, bulge, cave in, curve, dangle, decline, dip, drop, drop off, fail, fall, fall away, fall off, flag, flap, flop, give way, hang, hang down, languish, lean, settle, sink, slide, slip, slump, swag, wilt; SEE CONCEPTS *181,698,776*

saga [*n*] *story, often long*
adventure, chronicle, epic, legend, narrative, soap opera*, tale, yarn; SEE CONCEPT *282*

sagacious [*adj*] *smart, judicious*
acute, apt, astucious, astute, cagey, canny, clear-sighted, clever, cool*, discerning, discriminating, far-sighted, foxy*, gnostic, heady, hip*, insightful, intelligent, keen, knowing, knowledgeable, perceptive, perspicacious, prudent, rational, sage, sapient, savvy*, sensible, sharp, shrewd, smooth, sophic, wise, witty; SEE CONCEPT *402*

sagacity [*n*] *wisdom*
acumen, astuteness, brains*, clear thinking, common sense, comprehension, discernment, discrimination, enlightenment, experience, foresight, good judgment, insight, intelligence, judgment, knowledge, level-headedness, perceptiveness, perspicacity, practicality, prudence, sageness, sapience, sense, shrewdness, understanding; SEE CONCEPT *409*

sage [*adj*] *wise*
astute, aware, careful, clever, contemplative, cunning, discerning, educated, enlightened, experienced, foresighted, informed, insightful, intelligent, intuitive, judicious, knowing, knowledgeable, learned, perceptive, reflective, sagacious, sapient, scholarly, sensible, sharp, shrewd, smart, sound, thoughtful, understanding; SEE CONCEPT *402*

sage [*n*] *wise person*
guide, guru, intellect, intellectual, learned person, mahatma, master, mentor, philosopher, pundit, savant, teacher, thinker, wise man/woman; SEE CONCEPTS *350,409,416*

sail [*v*] *travel through water, air; glide*
boat, captain, cast anchor, cast off, cross, cruise, dart, drift, embark, flit, float, fly, get under way*, leave, make headway, motor, move, navigate, pilot, put to sea*, reach, run, scud, set sail, shoot, skim, skipper, skirr, soar, steer, sweep, tack, voyage, weigh anchor, wing; SEE CONCEPT *224*

sailboat [*n*] *a boat propelled with wind by sailcloth*
bark, brig, brigantine, catamaran, clipper, craft, cutter, dory, gaff-rigged sailboat, galleon, galley, jack, ketch, pinnace, ragboat*, schooner, ship, skiff, sloop, Sunfish, tall ship, vessel, windjammer, wooden boat, yacht, yawl; SEE CONCEPT *506*

sailor [*n*] *person who travels by sea*
able-bodied sailor, bluejacket*, boater, cadet, circumnavigator, deck hand, diver, hearty*, jack*, lascar*, marine, mariner, mate, middy, midshipman/woman, navigator, old salt*, pilot, pirate, salt*, sea dog*, seafarer, sea person, shellback*, shipmate, swab, swabber*, swabbie*, tar*, tarpaulin*, water dog*, windjammer*, yachter; SEE CONCEPTS *348,358,366*

saint [*n*] *holy person*
angel, glorified soul, good person, holy being, loved one, martyr, pietist; SEE CONCEPTS *361,370*

saintly [*adj*] *good, righteous*
angelic, beatific, blameless, blessed, devout, divine, god-fearing, godly, holy, pious, pure, religious, sainted, saintlike, seraph, sinless, upright, upstanding, virtuous, worthy; SEE CONCEPT *404*

sake [*n1*] *benefit, gain*
account, advantage, behalf, consideration, good, interest, profit, regard, respect, welfare, well-being; SEE CONCEPT *693*

sake [*n2*] *reason, objective*
aim, cause, consequence, end, final cause, motive, principle, purpose, score; SEE CONCEPTS *659,661*

salacious [*adj*] *lascivious*
bawdy, carnal, erotic, fast*, horny, hot*, indecent, lecherous, lewd, libertine, libidinous, licentious, lubricious, lustful, nasty, obscene, orgiastic, prurient, raunchy, sensual, smutty*, steamy, suggestive, voluptuous, wanton; SEE CONCEPTS *372,403*

salad [*n*] *dish of vegetables*
coleslaw, fruit salad, greens, mixed greens, potato salad, tossed salad, Waldorf salad; SEE CONCEPT *431*

salary [*n*] *money paid for work done*
bacon*, bread*, earnings, emolument, fee, hire, income, pay, payroll, recompense, remuneration, scale, stipend, take, take-home*, wage, wages; SEE CONCEPT *344*

sale [*n*] *exchange of object for money*
auction, barter, business, buying, clearance, closeout, commerce, consuming, deal, demand, disposal, dumping, enterprise, marketing, negoti-

ation, purchase, purchasing, reduction, selling, trade, transaction, unloading, vending, vendition; SEE CONCEPTS *324,345*

salesperson [*n*] *salesman/woman*
businessperson, clerk, dealer, peddler, rep, sales assistant, salesclerk, salesgirl, saleslady, sales rep, sales representative, seller, store clerk, traveling salesperson, vendor; SEE CONCEPT *348*

salient [*adj*] *noticeable, important*
arresting, arrestive, conspicuous, famous, impressive, intrusive, jutting, marked, moving, notable, obtrusive, obvious, outstanding, pertinent, projecting, prominent, pronounced, protruding, remarkable, signal, significant, striking, weighty; SEE CONCEPT *567*

saliva [*n*] *spit*
dribble, drool, froth, slaver, slobber, spittle, sputum; SEE CONCEPT *467*

sallow [*adj*] *pale, unhealthy*
anemic, ashen, ashy, bilious, colorless, dull, greenish-yellow, jaundiced, muddy, pallid, pasty, wan, waxy, yellowish; SEE CONCEPT *618*

saloon [*n*] *business establishment that primarily serves liquor*
alehouse, bar, barroom, beer joint*, cocktail lounge, dive*, drinkery, gin mill*, hangout*, joint*, night club, pub, public house, speakeasy, taproom, tavern, watering hole*; SEE CONCEPTS *439,448,449*

salt away [*v*] *save, store up*
accumulate, amass, bank, cache, hide, hoard, invest, lay aside, lay away, put away, put by, put in the bank, save, save for rainy day*, set aside, spare, stash, stockpile; SEE CONCEPT *330*

salty [*adj1*] *flavored with sodium chloride*
acrid, alkaline, brackish, briny, highly flavored, oversalted, pungent, saliferous, saline, salt, salted, saltish, sour; SEE CONCEPTS *462,613*

salty [*adj2*] *spicy, colorful*
humorous, lively, piquant, pungent, racy, sharp, snappy, tangy, tart, witty, zestful; SEE CONCEPTS *401,589*

salubrious [*adj*] *health-giving*
beneficial, good, healthful, healthy, hygienic, invigorating, salutary, sanitary, wholesome; SEE CONCEPTS *560,572*

salutary [*adj*] *healthy*
aiding, beneficial, fit, good, healing, healthful, nourishing, nutritious, restorative, salubrious, sound, tonic, well, wholesome; SEE CONCEPTS *314,462,537545*

salute [*v*] *greet; honor*
accost, acknowledge, address, bow, call to, congratulate, hail, pay homage, pay respects, pay tribute, present arms, receive, recognize, snap to attention*, speak, take hat off to*; welcome; SEE CONCEPTS *38,69,320*

salute/salutation [*n*] *greeting, recognition*
address, bow, howdy*, kiss, obeisance, tribute, welcome; SEE CONCEPT *38*

salvage [*v*] *save, rescue*
deliver, get back, glean, ransom, reclaim, recover, redeem, regain, restore, retrieve, salve; SEE CONCEPT *134*

salvation [*n*] *rescue, saving*
conservancy, conservation, deliverance, emancipation, escape, exemption, extrication, keeping, liberation, lifeline, pardon, preserval, preservation, redemption, release, reprieve, restoration, safekeeping, sustentation; SEE CONCEPT *134*

salve [*n*] *ointment for relief of pain or illness*
aid, balm, cerate, counterirritant, cream, cure, dressing, emolient, help, liniment, lotion, lubricant, medication, medicine, remedy, unction, unguent; SEE CONCEPTS *311,466*

salve [*v*] *soothe*
alleviate, ally, assuage, balm, becalm, calm, calm down, cool off*, ease, heal, mollify, pacify, pour oil on*, quiet, relieve, settle, smooth down, soften, still, take the edge off*, take the sting out of*, unburden, untrouble; SEE CONCEPTS *7,22,110,384*

same [*adj1*] *alike, identical*
aforementioned, aforesaid, carbon*, carbon-copy*, clone, coequal, comparable, compatible, corresponding, ditto*, double, dupe*, duplicate, equal, equivalent, indistinguishable, interchangeable, in the same manner, like, likewise, look-alike, related, same difference, selfsame, similar, similarly, synonymous, tantamount, twin, very, Xerox*; SEE CONCEPTS *487,566,573*

same [*adj2*] *unchanging*
changeless, consistent, constant, invariable, perpetual, unaltered, unchanged, unfailing, uniform, unvarying; SEE CONCEPT *534*

sameness [*n*] *likeness, similarity*
adequation, alikeness, analogy, equality, equivalency, identicalness, identity, indistinguishability, monotony, no difference, oneness, par, parity, predictability, repetition, resemblance, selfsameness, standardization, tedium, uniformity, unison, unity, unvariedness; SEE CONCEPTS *667,670*

sample [*n*] *example, model*
bit, bite, case, case history, constituent, cross section, element, exemplification, fragment, illustration, indication, individual, instance, morsel, part, pattern, piece, portion, representative, sampling, segment, sign, specimen, typification, unit; SEE CONCEPTS *686,835*

sample [*v*] *taste, try*
examine, experience, experiment, inspect, partake, savor, sip, test; SEE CONCEPTS *103,616*

sanctify [*v*] *hold in highest esteem*
absolve, anoint, bless, cleanse, consecrate, dedicate, deify, enshrine, glorify, hallow, purify, set apart, worship; SEE CONCEPTS *10,12*

sanctimonious [*adj*] *self-righteous*
bigoted, canting, deceiving, false, goody-goody*, holier-than-thou*, hypocritical, insincere, pharisaical, pietistic, pious, preachy, self-satisfied, smug, stuffy, unctuous; SEE CONCEPTS *401,404*

sanction [*n1*] *authorization*
acquiescence, allowance, approbation, approval, assent, authority, backing, confirmation, consent, countenance, encouragement, endorsement, fiat, go-ahead*, green light*, leave, nod, okay*, permission, permit, ratification, recommendation, seal of approval*, stamp of approval*, sufferance, support, word; SEE CONCEPT *685*

sanction [*n2*] *embargo, punishment*
ban, boycott, coercive measure, command, decree, injunction, penalty, punitive measure, sentence, writ; SEE CONCEPT *123*

sanction [*v*] *authorize, confirm*
accredit, allow, approve, back, bless, certify, commission, countenance, empower, endorse, get behind*, give the go-ahead*, give the green light*, give the nod*, go for*, license, okay*,

sa
sa

permit, ratify, support, vouch for, warrant; SEE CONCEPTS *50,88*

sanctioned [*adj*] *authorized*
accepted, accredited, allowed, approved, confirmed, empowered, licensed, okayed, permitted, warranted; SEE CONCEPTS *542,798*

sanctity [*n*] *holiness*
asceticism, blessedness, consecration, devotion, devoutness, divineness, divinity, faith, godliness, goodness, grace, hallowedness, inviolability, mercy, piety, purity, religiousness, reverence, righteousness, sacredness, saintliness, solemnity, spirituality, venerableness; SEE CONCEPTS *368,645*

sanctuary [*n1*] *church; holiest room or area in religious building*
altar, chancel, holy place, sanctorium, sanctum, shrine, temple; SEE CONCEPTS *368,439,448*

sanctuary [*n2*] *place to hide, be safe*
asylum, church, convent, cover, covert, defense, den, harbor, harborage, haven, hideaway, hideout, hole, hole-up*, ivory tower*, oasis, port, protection, refuge, resort, retreat, safe house, screen, shelter, shield; SEE CONCEPTS *515,516*

sanctuary [*n3*] *safe place for wildlife*
asylum, conservation area, game refuge, harborage, national park, nature preserve, park, preserve, refuge, reserve, retreat, shelter; SEE CONCEPT *517*

sandwich [*n*] *grinder*
BLT, club sandwich, Dagwood*, hero*, hoagie, open-faced sandwich, Reuben, sub, submarine sandwich; SEE CONCEPTS *457,460,461*

sane [*adj*] *mentally sound; reasonable*
all there*, balanced, both oars in water*, commonsensical, compos mentis, discerning, fair-minded, fit, having all marbles*, healthy, in one's right mind*, intelligent, judicious, level-headed, logical, lucid, moderate, normal, of sound mind, oriented, playing with full deck*, prudent, rational, right, right-minded, sagacious, sage, sapient, self-possessed, sensible, sober, sound, steady, together*, well, wise; SEE CONCEPTS *314,402,403*

sanguine [*adj1*] *happy; optimistic*
animated, assured, buoyant, cheerful, confident, enthusiastic, expectant, hopeful, lively, positive, secure, self-assured, self-confident, spirited, undoubtful, upbeat; SEE CONCEPTS *403,542*

sanguine [*adj2*] *reddish; flushed*
bloody, florid, flush, glowing, red, rubicund, ruddy, scarlet; SEE CONCEPT *618*

sanitary [*adj*] *clean, germ-free*
healthful, healthy, hygienic, prophylactic, purified, salubrious, sanative, sterile, uncontaminated, uninfected, unpolluted, unsullied, wholesome; SEE CONCEPT *621*

sanitize [*v*] *sterilize*
antisepticize, asceptize, aseptify, clean, decontaminate, disinfect, freshen, fumigate, make sanitary, purify; SEE CONCEPTS *231,250*

sanity [*n*] *mental health; soundness of judgment*
acumen, balance, clear mind, common sense, comprehension, good judgment, healthy mind, intelligence, judiciousness, levelheadedness, lucidity, lucidness, marbles*, normality, prudence, rationality, reason, reasonableness, right mind*, sagacity, saneness, sense, sound mind, soundness, stability, understanding, wit; SEE CONCEPTS *409,410*

sap [*n*] *stupid person*
chump, dolt, dupe, fool, idiot, jerk, nitwit, patsy*, pigeon*, simpleton, sucker*, weakling; SEE CONCEPT *412*

sap [*v*] *squeeze out; weaken*
attenuate, bleed, blunt, cripple, debilitate, deplete, destroy, devitalize, disable, drain, enervate, enfeeble, erode, exhaust, impair, prostrate, rob, ruin, subvert, undermine, vitiate, wear down, wreck; SEE CONCEPTS *142,156,240,246*

sapient [*adj*] *sagacious*
acute, astucious, astute, cagey*, canny, clear-sighted, clever, contemplative, discerning, discriminating, educated, enlightened, experienced, far-sighted, foxy*, informed, insightful, intelligent, judicious, keen, knowing, knowledgeable, perceptive, reflective, sage, scholarly, sensible, sharp, shrewd, smart, thoughtful, wise; SEE CONCEPT *402*

sappy [*adj*] *foolish, sentimental*
absurd, balmy, bathetic, crazy*, drippy*, idiotic, illogical, insane, loony*, maudlin, mushy*, preposterous, silly, slushy*, soppy*, sticky*, stupid; SEE CONCEPTS *403,542*

sarcasm [*n*] *mocking remark*
acrimony, aspersion, banter, bitterness, burlesque, causticness, censure, comeback, contempt, corrosiveness, criticism, cut*, cynicism, derision, dig*, disparagement, flouting, invective, irony, lampooning, mockery, mordancy, put-down*, raillery, rancor, ridicule, satire, scoffing, scorn, sharpness, sneering, superciliousness, wisecrack; SEE CONCEPTS *52,54,277,278*

sarcastic [*adj*] *nasty, mocking in speech*
acerb, acerbic, acid, acrimonious, arrogant, austere, backhanded, biting, bitter, brusque, captious, carping, caustic, chaffing, contemptuous, contumelious, corrosive, cussed*, cutting, cynical, derisive, disillusioned, disparaging, disrespectful, evil, hostile, irascible, ironical, mean, mordant, needling, offensive, ornery*, salty*, sardonic, satirical, saucy*, scorching, scornful, scurrilous, severe, sharp, smart-alecky*, snarling, sneering, taunting, trenchant, twitting, weisenheiming*; SEE CONCEPT *267*

sardonic [*adj*] *sarcastic*
acerbic, arrogant, biting, bitter, carping, caustic, cynical, derisive, disrespectful, evil, irascible, mean, mocking, mordant, nasty, offensive, salty*, satirical, scorching, scornful, sharp, smart-alecky*, sneering, taunting, wise*; SEE CONCEPT *267*

sass [*n*] *back talk*
answer, cheek, guff, lip, mouth, nasty reply, retort, sauce; SEE CONCEPTS *46,278*

sass [*v*] *talk back*
answer back, give lip*, mouth off*, wise off*; SEE CONCEPT *401*

sassy [*adj*] *impudent*
arrant, audacious, bold, brassy, brazen, cheeky*, discourteous, disrespectful, flip*, flippant, fresh, insolent, mouthy*, overbold, rude, saucy*, smart-alecky*, smart-mouthed, wise; SEE CONCEPT *401*

Satan [*n*] *the Devil*
Angel of Darkness, Antichrist, Apollyon, archfiend, Beelzebub, demon, Diabolus, King of Hell, Lucifer, Mephistopheles, Prince of Darkness, the Evil Spirit; SEE CONCEPTS *370,412*

satanic [*adj*] *demonic*
crazed, cruel, devilish, diabolic, diabolical, evil, fiendish, frenetic, hellish, infernal, mad, maniacal, possessed, unhallowed, vicious, wicked; SEE CONCEPTS *404,545*

satchel [*n*] *small bag*
attache, backpack, briefcase, carryall, carry-on, duffel bag, garment bag, handbag, haversack, knapsack, overnight bag, pack, pouch, rucksack, saddlebag, suitcase, tote, travel bag; SEE CONCEPTS *339,450,494*

satiate [*v*] *stuff, satisfy completely or excessively*
cloy, content, feed to gills*, fill, glut, gorge, gratify, indulge, jade, nauseate, overdose, overfill, pall, sate, saturate, slake, surfeit; SEE CONCEPTS *169,740*

satire [*n*] *ridicule intended to expose truth*
banter, burlesque, caricature, causticity, chaffing, irony, lampoon, lampoonery, mockery, parody, pasquinade, persiflage, play-on, put-on*, raillery, sarcasm, send-up*, skit, spoof, squib*, takeoff*, travesty, wit, witticism; SEE CONCEPTS *263,271,280*

satirical/satiric [*adj*] *mocking*
abusive, bantering, biting, bitter, burlesque, caustic, censorious, chaffing, cutting, cynical, farcical, incisive, ironical, lampooning, mordant, paradoxical, parodying, pungent, ridiculing, sarcastic, sardonic, spoofing, taunting; SEE CONCEPT *267*

satirize [*v*] *ridicule*
banter, burlesque, caricature, caricaturize, cartoon, deride, haze, humiliate, jape, jeer, jive, josh, kid, lampoon, laugh at, make a fool of*, make fun of, mimic, mock, needle, pan*, parody, poke fun at*, pull one's leg, raz*, rib*, ride*, roast*, spoof; SEE CONCEPTS *54,59*

satisfaction [*n*] *giving or enjoying a state of comfort, content*
achievement, amends, amusement, atonement, bliss, cheerfulness, comfort, compensation, complacency, conciliation, contentedness, contentment, delight, ease, enjoyment, fulfillment, gladness, good fortune, gratification, happiness, indemnification, indulgence, joy, justice, peace of mind, pleasure, pride, propitiation, recompense, redress, refreshment, reimbursement, relief, reparation, repletion, resolution, reward, satiety, serenity, settlement, vindication, wellbeing; SEE CONCEPTS *344,410,720*

satisfactory [*adj*] *acceptable, sufficient*
adequate, all right, ample, A-OK*, appeasing, assuaging, assuasive, average, cogent, comfortable, competent, cool*, decent, delighting, enough, fair, fulfilling, good, good enough, gratifying, groovy*, passable, peachy*, pleasing, satisfying, solid, sound, sufficing, suitable, tolerable, unexceptional, up to snuff*, valid; SEE CONCEPTS *529,558,560*

satisfy [*v1*] *please, content*
amuse, animate, appease, assuage, befriend, brighten up, captivate, capture, cheer, cloy, comfort, conciliate, content, delight, do the trick*, elate, enliven, entertain, enthrall, exhilarate, fascinate, fill, fill the bill*, flatter, get by, gladden, glut, gorge, gratify, hit the spot*, humor, indulge, make merry, make the grade*, mollify, pacify, placate, propitiate, quench, rejoice, sate, satiate, score, sell, sell on, slake, suit, surfeit; SEE CONCEPTS *7,22*

satisfy [*v2*] *answer, persuade*
accomplish, appease, assuage, assure, avail, be adequate, be enough, be sufficient, come up to, complete, comply with, conform to, convince, dispel doubt, do, equip, fill, fulfill, furnish, get by, induce, inveigle, keep promise, make good, make the grade*, meet, observe, pass muster*, perform, provide, put mind at ease*, qualify, quiet, reassure, score, sell, serve, serve the purpose*, suffice, tide over*, win over; SEE CONCEPTS *108,140,656*

satisfy [*v3*] *pay, compensate*
answer, atone, clear up, disburse, discharge, indemnify, liquidate, make good*, make reparation, meet, pay off, quit, recompense, remunerate, repay, requite, reward, settle, square*; SEE CONCEPTS *126,341*

satisfying [*adj*] *fulfilling*
delightful, enjoyable, favorable, gratifying, hitting the spot, pleasant, pleasing, pleasurable, refreshing, rewarding, satiating, satisfactory, savory, sweet; SEE CONCEPTS *537,572*

saturate [*v*] *drench, wet through*
bathe, douche, douse, imbue, immerse, impregnate, infuse, overfill, penetrate, percolate, permeate, pervade, sate, satiate, soak, sop, souse, steep, suffuse, surfeit, transfuse, wash, waterlog; SEE CONCEPT *256*

saturnine [*adj*] *gloomy*
blue*, cheerless, dejected, depressed, desolate, despondent, dispirited, dour, down, down in the dumps*, forlorn, glum, grave, hopeless, in low spirits*, in the dumps*, low, melancholy, miserable, moping, morose, sad, solemn, sorrowful, sulky, sullen, unhappy, woebegone, woeful; SEE CONCEPT *403*

saucy [*adj*] *disrespectful*
arch, audacious, bold, brash, brazen, cheeky*, combative, contumelious, flip*, flippant, forward, fresh, impertinent, impudent, insolent, intrusive, meddlesome, nervy, obtrusive, pert, presumptuous, rude, sassy, smart, smart-alecky*, smug, snippy*, volatile, weisenheiming*, wise; SEE CONCEPTS *267,401*

saunter [*n*] *stroll*
airing, amble, constitutional, promenade, ramble, turn, walk; SEE CONCEPT *151*

saunter [*v*] *stroll along*
amble, ankle, dally, drift, linger, loiter, meander, mope*, mosey*, ooze*, percolate, promenade, ramble, roam, rove, sashay, stump, tarry, toddle, traipse, trill, wander; SEE CONCEPT *151*

savage [*adj1*] *wild, untamed*
aboriginal, ancient, archaic, barbarian, barbaric, bestial, brutal, brute, crude, earliest, feral, ferocious, fierce, first, fundamental, harsh, in a state of nature, lupine, native, natural, nonliterate, original, primary, primeval, primitive, primordial, pristine, rough, rude, rugged, rustic, simple, turbulent, unbroken, uncivilized, uncultivated, uncultured, undomesticated, unmodified, unrestrained, unspoiled, vicious; SEE CONCEPTS *401,485*

savage [*adj2*] *cruel, vicious*
atrocious, barbarous, beastly, bestial, bloodthirsty, bloody, brutal, brutish, cold-blooded, crazed, demoniac, destructive, devilish, diabolical, fell, feral, ferine, ferocious, fierce, frantic, furious, grim, harsh, heartless, hellish, infernal, inhuman, inhumane, malevolent, malicious, mer-

ciless, murderous, pitiless, rabid, raging, rapacious, ravening, relentless, remorseless, ruthless, sadistic, truculent, unrelenting, violent, wolfish; SEE CONCEPTS *401,540,542*

savanna/savannah [*n*] *grassland*
grassy field, llano, meadow, pasturage, pasture, plain, prairie, steppe, veldt; SEE CONCEPT *509*

savant [*n*] *scholar*
academic, bookworm, brain*, egghead*, expert, intellect, intellectual, learned person, learner, master, philosopher, pundit, sage, wise person; SEE CONCEPT *350*

save [*v1*] *rescue*
bail out, come to rescue, defend, deliver, emancipate, extricate, free, get off the hook*, get out of hock*, give a break, liberate, pull out of fire*, ransom, recover, redeem, salvage, save one's neck*, set free, spring, unchain, unshackle; SEE CONCEPTS *127,134*

save [*v2*] *economize; set money aside for later use*
amass, be frugal, be thrifty, cache, collect, conserve, cut corners*, deposit, economize, feather nest*, gather, hide away, hoard, hold, keep, lay aside, lay away, maintain, make ends meet*, manage, pile up, pinch pennies*, put by, reserve, retrench, roll back*, salt away*, save for rainy day*, scrimp, skimp, sock away*, spare, squirrel*, stash, stockpile, store, stow away, tighten belt*, treasure; SEE CONCEPTS *120,129,330*

save [*v3*] *guard, protect*
conserve, defend, keep safe, keep up, look after, maintain, preserve, safeguard, screen, shield, sustain, take care of; SEE CONCEPTS *96,117*

savings [*n*] *provision for future*
accumulation, ace in hole*, cache, fund, funds, gleanings, harvest, hoard, investment, kitty*, mattress full*, means, money in the bank, nest egg*, property, provision, provisions, rainy day fund*, reserve, reserves, resources, riches, sock, stake, stockpile, store; SEE CONCEPTS *335,340, 446,710*

savior [*n*] *person who redeems, aids in time of difficulty*
conservator, defender, deliverer, friend in need*, Good Samaritan*, guardian, guardian angel, hero, liberator, preserver, protector, rescuer, salvager, salvation; SEE CONCEPTS *370,416*

savor [*n1*] *taste, flavor*
odor, piquancy, relish, salt, sapidity, sapor, scent, smack, smell, spice, tang, tinge, zest; SEE CONCEPT *614*

savor [*n2*] *distinctive quality*
affection, attribute, character, characteristic, excitement, feature, flavor, interest, mark, property, salt, spice, trait, virtue, zest; SEE CONCEPTS *411,543*

savor [*v*] *delight in, enjoy*
appreciate, experience, feel, gloat, know, like, luxuriate in, partake, relish, revel in, sample, sip, smack, smell, taste; SEE CONCEPTS *32,616*

savory [*adj*] *pleasing, delicious in flavor*
agreeable, ambrosial, aperitive, appetizing, aromatic, dainty, decent, delectable, exquisite, fragrant, full-flavored, good, luscious, mellow, mouthwatering, palatable, perfumed, piquant, pungent, redolent, relishing, respectable, rich, sapid, savorous, scrumptious, spicy, sweet, tangy, tasty, tempting, toothsome, wholesome; SEE CONCEPT *613*

savvy [*adj*] *shrewd*
acute, astute, brainy*, cagey*, calculating, canny, clever, crafty, cunning, discerning, experienced, far-sighted, foxy*, heady*, ingenious, intelligent, in the know*, judicious, keen, knowing, on the ball*, perceptive, sagacious, sensible, sharp, slick*, sly, smart, smooth, streetwise, wise; SEE CONCEPTS *401,402*

savvy [*n*] *shrewdness*
acumen, awareness, comprehension, discernment, experience, grasp, grip, insight, intellect, intelligence, judgment, know-how, knowing, knowledge, mastery, perception, perceptiveness, sense, sharpness, smarts*, understanding; SEE CONCEPT *409*

say [*v*] *make declaration*
add, affirm, allege, announce, answer, assert, break silence*, claim, come out with, communicate, conjecture, convey, declare, deliver, disclose, divulge, do, estimate, express, flap*, gab*, give voice*, guess, imagine, imply, jaw, judge, lip*, maintain, make known, mention, opine, orate, perform, pronounce, put forth, put into words, rap*, read, recite, rehearse, relate, remark, render, repeat, reply, report, respond, reveal, rumor, speak, spiel*, state, suggest, tell, utter, verbalize, voice, yak*; SEE CONCEPTS *51,266*

saying [*n*] *maxim, proverb*
adage, aphorism, apophthegm, axiom, byword, dictum, epigram, motto, precept, saw, statement, truism; SEE CONCEPT *278*

scads [*n*] *large quantity,*
bags*, barrels*, bunches, bundles*, gobs*, heaps*, jillion*, large number, loads, lots, many and then some*, oodles*, piles, plenty, scores, stacks, tons, zillions; SEE CONCEPTS *432,787*

scale [*n1*] *graduated system*
calibration, computation, degrees, extent, gamut, gradation, hierarchy, ladder, order, pecking order*, progression, proportion, range, ranking, rate, ratio, reach, register, rule, scope, sequence, series, spectrum, spread, steps, system, way; SEE CONCEPTS *651,744,770,788*

scale [*n2*] *thin covering, skin*
film, flake, incrustation, lamina, layer, plate, scurf; SEE CONCEPTS *399,484*

scale [*v1*] *ascend, climb*
clamber, escalade, escalate, go up, mount, surmount; SEE CONCEPT *166*

scale [*v2*] *measure*
adjust, balance, calibrate, compare, compute, estimate, gauge, graduate, proportion, prorate, regulate, size; SEE CONCEPT *764*

scam [*n*] *swindle*
blackmail, cheating, con, con game, crooked deal*, deceit, deception, dirty pool*, double-cross*, double-dealing*, extortion, fast one*, flimflam*, fraud, hoax, hosing*, hustle, racket*, rip-off*, shady deal*, shakedown, sham, shell game*, snow job*, sting, sucker game*; SEE CONCEPTS *59,139,192*

scamp [*n*] *rascal*
cheat, cheater, delinquent, fraud, hooligan*, liar, mischief-maker, prankster, rapscallion, reprobate, rogue, rowdy, ruffian, scalawag, scallywag, scoundrel, shyster, sneak, swindler, trickster, troublemaker, villain, whippersnapper; SEE CONCEPT *412*

scamper [v] *run, dash*
bolt, dart, flee, fly, hasten, hie, hurry, light out, make off, race, romp, rush off, scoot, scurry, scuttle, shoot, skedaddle*, skip, speed, speed away, sprint, tear, trot, whip, zip*; SEE CONCEPT *150*

scan [v] *look over, scrutinize lightly*
browse, check, consider, contemplate, dip into*, examine, flash*, flip through, give the once-over*, glance at, glance over, have a look-see*, inquire, investigate, leaf through*, look, look through, look up and down*, overlook, regard, riff, riffle, rumble, run over, run through, scour, search, size up, skim, study, survey, sweep, take a gander*, take stock of*, thumb through*; SEE CONCEPTS *103,623*

scandal [n] *public embarrassment*
aspersion, backbiting, backstabbing, belittlement, calumny, crime, defamation, depreciation, detraction, dirty linen*, discredit, disgrace, dishonor, disparagement, disrepute, dynamite, eavesdropping, gossip, hearsay, idle rumor, ignominy, infamy, mud, obloquy, opprobrium, reproach, rumor, scorcher, shame, sin, skeleton in closet*, slander, tale, talk, turpitude, wrongdoing; SEE CONCEPTS *278,645,674*

scandalous [adj] *disreputable*
atrocious, backbiting, calumnious, crying, defamatory, desperate, detracting, detractive, disgraceful, gossiping, heinous, ignominious, infamous, libelous, maligning, monstrous, odious, opprobrious, outrageous, red hot*, scurrilous, shameful, shocking, slanderous, traducing, unseemly, untrue, vilifying; SEE CONCEPT *545*

scant/scanty [adj] *inadequate*
bare, barely sufficient, close, deficient, exiguous, failing, insufficient, limited, little, meager, minimal, narrow, poor, rare, restricted, scrimpy, short, shy, skimpy, slender, spare, sparing, sparse, stingy, thin, tight, wanting; SEE CONCEPTS *766,767,789*

scapegoat [n] *person who takes blame for another's action*
boob*, chump, doormat*, dupe, easy mark*, fall guy*, fool, goat*, gull*, mark*, patsy, pigeon*, pushover*, sacrifice, sap*, schmuck*, sitting duck*, stooge, sucker, victim, weakling; SEE CONCEPT *412*

scar [n] *blemish from previous injury or illness*
blister, cacatrice, cicatrix, crater, defect, discoloration, disfigurement, flaw, hurt, mark, pockmark, scab, track, wound; SEE CONCEPT *580*

scar [v] *mark, hurt*
beat, blemish, brand, cut, damage, deface, disfigure, flaw, injure, maim, mar, pinch, score, scratch, slash, stab, traumatize; SEE CONCEPTS *7,19,137,176,246*

scarce [adj] *insufficient, infrequent*
at a premium, deficient, failing, few, few and far between*, in short supply, limited, occasional, rare, scant, scanty, seldom, seldom met with, semioccasional, short, shortened, shy, sparse, sporadic, truncated, uncommon, unusual, wanting; SEE CONCEPTS *541,789*

scarcely [adv] *barely*
hardly, imperceptibly, infrequently, just, just barely, only just, rarely, scantily, seldom, slightly; SEE CONCEPTS *541,789*

scare [n] *frightened state*
alarm, alert, fright, panic, shock, start, terror; SEE CONCEPTS *230,410*

scare [v] *frighten someone*
affright, alarm, awe, chill, daunt, dismay, freeze, give a fright, give a turn*, intimidate, panic, paralyze, petrify, scare silly*, scare stiff*, scare the pants off*, shake up*, shock, spook, startle, strike terror in, terrify, terrorize; SEE CONCEPTS *7,19,42*

scared [adj] *frightened*
afraid, aghast, anxious, fearful, having cold feet*, panicked, panicky, panic-stricken, petrified, shaken, startled, terrified, terror-stricken; SEE CONCEPT *403*

scarf [n] *muffler*
ascot, bandanna, boa, kerchief, neckwear, shawl, stole, wrapping; SEE CONCEPT *451*

scary [adj] *frightening, terrifying*
alarming, bloodcurdling, chilling, creepy, eerie, hair-raising, hairy*, horrendous, horrifying, intimidating, shocking, spine-chilling, spooky, unnerving; SEE CONCEPTS *529,548*

scathing [adj] *nasty, critical in remarks*
belittling, biting, brutal, burning, caustic, cruel, cutting, harsh, mordacious, mordant, salty, sarcastic, scorching, scornful, searing, severe, sulphurous, trenchant, withering; SEE CONCEPT *267*

scatter [v] *strew, disperse*
besprinkle, broadcast, cast, derange, diffuse, disband, discard, disject, dispel, disseminate, dissipate, distribute, disunite, diverge, divide, expend, fling, intersperse, litter, migrate, part, pour, put to flight*, run away, scramble, separate, set, set asunder, sever, shatter, shed, shower, sow, spend, split up, spray, spread, sprinkle, sunder, take off in all directions*, throw around, throw out; SEE CONCEPTS *179,217,222*

scatterbrained [adj] *not thinking clearly*
birdbrained*, careless, dizzy, empty-headed*, featherbrained*, flighty, forgetful, frivolous, giddy, harebrained*, illogical, inattentive, irrational, irresponsible, madcap, silly, slaphappy*, stupid, thoughtless; SEE CONCEPT *402*

scenario [n] *master plan; sequence of events*
book, outline, pages, plot, résumé, rundown, scheme, sides, sketch, story line, summary, synopsis; SEE CONCEPTS *282,283,660*

scene [n1] *setting of a performance or event*
arena, backdrop, background, blackout, display, exhibition, flat, flats, landscape, locale, locality, location, mise en scène, outlook, pageant, picture, place, representation, scenery, seascape, set, setting, show, sight, site, spectacle, spot, stage, tableau, theater, view; SEE CONCEPTS *263,625, 628*

scene [n2] *part of a dramatic performance*
act, bit, episode, incident, part, piece, routine, schtick, spot; SEE CONCEPT *264*

scene [n3] *display of emotion*
carrying-on*, commotion, confrontation, exhibition, fit, fuss, performance, row, tantrum, temper tantrum, to-do*, upset; SEE CONCEPT *633*

scene [n4] *field of interest*
arena, business, compass, culture, environment, field, milieu, setting, sphere, world; SEE CONCEPT *349*

scenery [n] *surroundings*
backdrop, decor, flat, flats, furnishings, furniture, landscape, mise en scène, neighborhood, proper-

sa
sc

ties, props, prospect, set, setting, spectacle, sphere, stage set, stage setting, terrain, view, vista; SEE CONCEPTS *263,628*

scenic [*adj*] *beautiful, picturesque*
breathtaking, dramatic, grand, impressive, panoramic, spectacular, striking; SEE CONCEPTS *485,579*

scent [*n*] *smell, aroma*
aura, balm, bouquet, essence, fragrance, incense, odor, perfume, redolence, spice, tang, track, trail, whiff; SEE CONCEPT *599*

scent [*v*] *detect, smell*
be on the track of*, be on the trail of*, discern, get wind of*, nose, nose out*, recognize, sense, sniff; SEE CONCEPTS *601,602*

scented [*adj*] *fragrant*
ambrosial, aromal, aromatic, balmy, delectable, odoriferous, odorous, perfumed, perfumy, redolent, smelling, spicy, sweet-smelling; SEE CONCEPT *598*

schedule [*n*] *plan for one's time*
agenda, appointments, calendar, catalog, chart, diagram, docket, inventory, itinerary, lineup*, list, order of business, program, record, registry, roll, roster, sked*, table, timetable; SEE CONCEPTS *271,283,660*

schedule [*v*] *plan one's time*
appoint, arrange, be due, book, card, catalog, engage, get on line*, line up*, list, note, organize, pencil in*, program, record, register, reserve, set, set up, sew up*, slate, time, write in one's book*; SEE CONCEPTS *36,125*

scheme [*n1*] *course of action*
arrangement, blueprint, chart, codification, contrivance, design, device, diagram, disposition, draft, expedient, game plan, layout, order, ordering, outline, pattern, plan, presentation, program, project, proposal, proposition, purpose, schedule, schema, strategy, suggestion, system, tactics, theory; SEE CONCEPTS *271,625,660*

scheme [*n2*] *plot, maneuver to get result*
action, angle*, brainchild*, cabal, conspiracy, covin, dodge*, frame-up*, game, game plan*, gimmick, hookup*, hustle, hype*, intrigue, layout, machination, picture*, pitch, ploy, practice, proposition, put-up job*, ruse, scenario, scene, setup*, shift*, story, stratagem, subterfuge, tactics, trick*, twist*; SEE CONCEPTS *59,645,660*

scheming [*adj*] *deceitful, sly*
artful, calculating, conniving, crafty, cunning, designing, duplicitous, foxy, slippery, tricky, underhand, wily; SEE CONCEPT *542*

schism [*n*] *separation*
alienation, break, breakup, difference, disagreement, discord, dissension, disunion, division, divorce, faction, fissure, fracture, gap, parting, rift, rupture, secession, splinter group, split; SEE CONCEPTS *135,195,297,388*

schlemiel [*n*] *dolt*
blockhead*, boob*, bungler, dimwit*, dope, dork*, dumbbell*, dunce, fool, goof*, goon*, idiot, ignoramus, jerk, lunkhead*, meathead*, nincompoop*, ninny*, nitwit*, sap*, schmuck, simpleton, stooge*, stupid; SEE CONCEPTS *412,423*

schlep [*v*] *lug*
carry, drag, haul, heave, lift, lurch, pull, tote, tow, tug, yank; SEE CONCEPT *206*

scholar [*n*] *person who is very involved in education and learning*
academic, augur, bookish person, bookworm*, brain*, critic, disciple, doctor, egghead*, gnome*, grind*, intellectual, learned person, learner, litterateur, person of letters, philosopher, professor, pupil, sage, savant, schoolchild, scientist, student, teacher, tool, wise person; SEE CONCEPT *350*

scholarly [*adj*] *academic*
bookish, cultured, educated, erudite, intellectual, learned, lettered, literate, longhair*, scholastic, schooled, studious, taught, trained, well-read; SEE CONCEPT *402*

scholarship [*n1*] *knowledge*
ability, awareness, cognition, comprehension, discernment, education, erudition, expertise, grasp, insight, instruction, intelligence, know-how*, learnedness, learning, lore, philosophy, schooling, wisdom; SEE CONCEPTS *274,409,529*

scholarship [*n2*] *grant*
assistance, award, bursary, charity, donation, fellowship, financial aid, reward; SEE CONCEPTS *337,344*

school [*n1*] *place, system for educating*
academy, alma mater, blackboard*, college, department, discipline, establishment, faculty, hall, halls of ivy*, institute, institution, jail*, schoolhouse, seminary, university; SEE CONCEPTS *287,289*

school [*n2*] *persons receiving education*
academy, adherents, circle, class, clique, denomination, devotees, disciples, faction, followers, following, group, party, pupils, sect, set; SEE CONCEPTS *288,350*

school [*n3*] *body of philosophy on subject*
belief, creed, faith, outlook, persuasion, school of thought, stamp*, way, way of life; SEE CONCEPTS *349,689*

school [*v*] *teach*
advance, coach, control, cultivate, direct, discipline, drill, educate, guide, indoctrinate, inform, instruct, lead, manage, prepare, prime, show, train, tutor, verse; SEE CONCEPT *285*

science [*n*] *methodical study of part of material world*
art, body of knowledge, branch, discipline, education, erudition, information, learning, lore, scholarship, skill, system, technique, wisdom; SEE CONCEPTS *274,349,360*

scientific [*adj*] *systematic; discovered through experimentation*
accurate, clear, controlled, deductive, exact, experimental, logical, mathematical, methodical, objective, precise, sound; SEE CONCEPT *535*

scientist [*n*] *researcher*
analyst, chemist, examiner, expert, lab technician, physicist, prober, tester; SEE CONCEPTS *349,362*

scintilla [*n*] *small bit, trace*
atom, crumb, dab, dash, drop, flash, hint, iota, particle, pinch, ray, shade, shred, small quantity, smidgen, soupcon, sparkle, speck, spot, whiff, whisper; SEE CONCEPTS *529,831*

scintillating [*adj*] *bright, stimulating*
animated, brilliant, clever, dazzling, ebullient, exciting, flashing, gleaming, glimmering, glinting, glittering, lively, shining, smart, sparkling, sprightly, twinkling, witty; SEE CONCEPTS *401,529,617*

scion [n] *offshoot, descendant*
begotten, branch, brood, child, chip off old block*, graft, heir, heiress, issue, junior, offspring, progeny, seed, shoot, slip, sprout, successor, twig; SEE CONCEPTS *414,428*

scoff [v] *make fun of; despise*
belittle, boo*, contemn, deride, dig at*, disbelieve, discount, discredit, disdain, flout, gibe, jeer, knock*, laugh at, make light of*, mock, pan*, poke fun at, pooh-pooh*, rag*, rally, reject, revile, ride, ridicule, scorn, show contempt, sneer, tease; SEE CONCEPT *54*

scold [v] *find fault with*
abuse, admonish, asperse, berate, blame, castigate, cavil, censure, chasten, chide, criticize, denounce, disparage, dress down*, expostulate, give a talking-to*, jump on*, keep aft*, lay down the law*, lecture, light into*, nag, objurate, preach, put down, rail, rake over the coals*, rate, ream, rebuke, recriminate, reprimand, reproach, reprobate, reprove, revail, take to task*, taunt, tell off*, upbraid, vilify, vituperate; SEE CONCEPTS *44,52,54*

scoop [n1] *utensil, tool for shovelling*
bail, dipper, ladle, shovel, spade, spoon, trowel; SEE CONCEPTS *493,499*

scoop [n2] *previously secret information that is suddenly public*
beat, exclusive, exposé, inside story*, news, revelation, sensation; SEE CONCEPT *274*

scoop [v] *dig up; shovel*
bail, clear away, dig, dig out, dip, empty, excavate, gather, gouge, grub, hollow, lade, ladle, lift, pick up, remove, scrape, spade, sweep away, sweep up, take up; SEE CONCEPT *178*

scoot [v] *hurry*
accelerate, beeline*, be quick, bolt, clear out, dart, dash, expedite, fly, get a move on*, go like lightning, hasten, hurry up, hustle, make haste, make time*, make tracks*, move, move fast, race, run, rush, scamper, scurry, shake a leg*, skedaddle, speed, split, spur, step on it*, vamoose, whiz, zip; SEE CONCEPTS *150,234*

scope [n] *extent or range of something*
ambit, amplitude, area, breadth, capacity, compass, comprehensiveness, confines, elbow room*, extension, field, field of reference, freedom, fullness, latitude, leeway, liberty, margin, opportunity, orbit, outlook, play, purview, radius, reach, room, run, space, span, sphere, wideness; SEE CONCEPTS *651,739,788*

scorch [v] *burn*
bake, blacken, blister, broil, char, cook, melt, parch, roast, scald, sear, seethe, shrivel, simmer, singe, stale, stew, swelter, wither; SEE CONCEPTS *249,255*

score [n1] *total, points*
account, addition, aggregate, amount, average, count, final count, grade, mark, number, outcome, rate, reckoning, record, result, stock, sum, summary, summation, tab, tally; SEE CONCEPTS *364,784*

score/scores [n2] *large group; a great number*
army, cloud, crowd, drove, flock, host, hundred, legion, lot, mass, million, multitude, myriad, rout, swarm, throng, very many; SEE CONCEPT *432*

score [n3] *musical arrangement*
charts, composition, music, orchestration, transcript; SEE CONCEPT *262*

score [n4] *obligation; account payable*
account, amount due, bill, charge, debt, grievance, grudge, injury, injustice, invoice, reckoning, statement, tab, tally, total; SEE CONCEPTS *332,645*

score [v1] *keep count*
add, calculate, chalk up, count, enumerate, keep tally, rack up*, reckon, record, register, tally, total; SEE CONCEPTS *125,764*

score [v2] *achieve, succeed*
accomplish, amass, arrive, attain, chalk up*, connect, flourish, gain, gain advantage, get*, hit pay dirt*, impress, luck out*, make a killing*, make an impression*, make the grade*, notch, procure, prosper, pull off*, put over*, rack up*, reach, realize, secure, take the cake*, thrive, triumph, win; SEE CONCEPTS *704,706*

score [v3] *cut, nick*
cleave, crosshatch, deface, furrow, gash, gouge, graze, groove, indent, line, mark, mill, notch, scrape, scratch, serrate, slash, slit; SEE CONCEPTS *137,176*

score [v4] *write a musical arrangement*
adapt, arrange, compose, orchestrate, set; SEE CONCEPTS *79,292*

scorn [n] *contempt toward something*
contemptuousness, contumely, derision, despisal, despisement, despite, disdain, disparagement, disregard, jeering, mockery, ridicule, sarcasm, scoffing, scornfulness, slight, sneer, sport, taunting, teasing; SEE CONCEPTS *29,54*

scorn [v] *hold in contempt; look down on*
abhor, avoid, be above, confute, consider beneath one*, contemn, defy, deride, despise, disdain, disregard, flout, gibe, hate, ignore, make fun of, mock, put down, refuse, refute, reject, renounce, repudiate, ridicule, run down*, scoff at, shun, slight, sneer, spurn, taunt, trash*, turn back on*, turn nose up at*; SEE CONCEPTS *21,30,52,54*

scoundrel [n] *person who is deceptive and uncaring of others*
bad egg*, bad news*, blackguard*, black sheep*, caitiff, cheat, creep, crook, dastard, good-for-nothing*, heel, imp, incorrigible, lowlife*, maggot*, mischiefmaker, miscreant, ne'er-do-well*, rascal, reprobate, scalawag, scamp, thief, vagabond, villain, wretch; SEE CONCEPT *412*

scour [v1] *clean, polish thoroughly*
abrade, brush, buff, burnish, cleanse, flush, furbish, mop, pumice, purge, rub, sand, scrub, wash, whiten; SEE CONCEPT *165*

scour [v2] *search thoroughly*
beat, comb, ferret out, find, forage, go over with a fine-tooth comb*, grub, hunt, inquire, leave no stone unturned*, look for, look high and low*, look up and down*, rake, ransack, rout, rummage, seek, track down, turn inside out*, turn upside-down*; SEE CONCEPT *216*

scourge [n] *plague, torment*
affliction, bane, correction, curse, infliction, misfortune, penalty, pest, pestilence, punishment, terror, visitation; SEE CONCEPTS *674,675*

scourge [v] *beat, punish, often physically*
afflict, belt, cane*, castigate, chastise, curse, discipline, excoriate, flail, flog, harass, hit, horsewhip*, lambaste*, lash, penalize, plague, scathe, scorch*, tan*, terrorize, thrash, torment, trounce, wallop*, whale*, whip; SEE CONCEPTS *14,52, 122,189*

SC
SC

scout [n] *person who is searching, investigating*
advance, adventurer, detective, escort, explorer, guard, lookout, outpost, outrider, patrol, picket, pioneer, precursor, reconnoiterer, recruiter, runner, sleuth, spotter, spy, vanguard; SEE CONCEPTS *348,358*

scout [v] *investigate, check out*
case, examine, explore, ferret, have a look-see*, hunt, inspect, look for, observe, probe, reconnoiter, run reconnaissance, rustle up*, search, seek, set eyes on*, spot, spy, stake out, survey, take in, track down, watch; SEE CONCEPTS *103,216,623*

scowl [n] *frown*
black look*, dirty look*, evil eye*, glower, grimace; SEE CONCEPTS *185,716*

scowl [v] *frown*
disapprove, glare, gloom, glower, grimace, look daggers at*, lour, lower, make a face*; SEE CONCEPT *185*

scraggly [adj] *ragged*
badly dressed, badly worn, bedraggled, dilapidated, dingy, dirty, disheveled, frayed, frazzled, full of holes*, grubby*, grungy*, in tatters*, messy, moth-eaten, scruffy, shabby, sloppy, tacky*, tattered, threadbare, torn, unclean, uncombed, ungroomed, unkempt, worse for wear*; SEE CONCEPTS *485,621*

scram [v] *leave quickly*
beat it*, clear out*, decamp, depart, disappear, get lost*, go away, hightail*, make oneself scarce*, make tracks*, scoot*, skedaddle*, take off, vamoose*; SEE CONCEPT *195*

scramble [n] *mix-up, confusion*
clutter, commotion, competition, conglomeration, free-for-all*, hash*, hassle, hustle, jumble, jungle, litter, melee, mishmash, muddle, race, rat race*, rush, shuffle, struggle, tumble, tussle; SEE CONCEPTS *230,388,432*

scramble [v] *race; get into position clumsily*
clamber, climb, contend, crawl, hasten, jockey for position*, jostle, look alive*, make haste, move, push, run, rush, scrabble, scurry, scuttle, strive, struggle, swarm, trek, vie; SEE CONCEPTS *87,150*

scrap [n1] *tiny bit of something*
atom, bite, bits and pieces*, butt, castoff, chip, chunk, crumb, cutting, discard, end, fragment, glob, gob, grain, hunk, iota, jot, junk, leaving, leftover*, lump, mite, modicum, morsel, mouthful, odds and ends*, orts, part, particle, piece, portion, remains, shred, slice, sliver, smithereen*, snatch, snippet, speck, stump, trace, waste; SEE CONCEPTS *831,835*

scrap [n2] *argument, fight*
affray, battle, brawl, broil*, disagreement, dispute, fracas, fray, quarrel, row, scuffle, set-to*, squabble, tiff*, wrangle; SEE CONCEPTS *46,106*

scrap [v1] *abandon; throw away*
abandon, break up, cast, chuck, consign to scrap heap*, demolish, discard, dismiss, dispense with, ditch, do away with*, drop, forsake, get rid of, jettison, junk, put out to pasture*, reject, retire, shed, slough, throw out, toss out, write off; SEE CONCEPTS *121,180*

scrap [v2] *fight, argue*
battle, bicker, caterwaul, come to blows*, fall out, have shouting match*, have words*, quarrel, row, spat, squabble, tiff, wrangle; SEE CONCEPTS *46,106*

scrape [n] *bad or embarrassing situation*
awkward situation, corner*, difficulty, dilemma, discomfiture, distress, embarrassment, fix*, hole*, jam*, mess*, pickle*, plight, predicament, tight spot*, trouble; SEE CONCEPT *674*

scrape [v1] *scratch, remove outer layer*
abrade, bark, bray, chafe, clean, erase, file, grate, graze, grind, irritate, pare, peel, rasp, rub, scour, scuff, shave, skin, squeak, thin, triturate; SEE CONCEPTS *165,186,215*

scrape [v2] *be very frugal*
cut it close*, get along, get by, pinch, save, scrimp, shave, skimp, stint, struggle; SEE CONCEPT *330*

scratch [n] *small cut or mark*
blemish, claw mark, gash, graze, hurt, laceration, score, scrape; SEE CONCEPTS *309,513*

scratch [v1] *cut; make a mark on*
claw, damage, etch, grate, graze, incise, lacerate, mark, prick, rasp, rub, scarify, score, scrape, scrawl, scribble; SEE CONCEPTS *79,176*

scratch [v2] *cancel*
annul, delete, eliminate, erase, pull, pull out, strike, withdraw; SEE CONCEPT *121*

scrawl [v] *write erratically*
doodle, inscribe, scrabble, scratch, scribble, squiggle; SEE CONCEPT *79*

scrawny [adj] *unhealthily thin*
angular, bony, gaunt, lank, lanky, lean, rawboned, scraggy, skeletal, skin-and-bones*, skinny, spare, undernourished, underweight; SEE CONCEPTS *490,491,773*

scream [n1] *outcry*
cry, high-pitched shout, holler*, howl, screech, shriek, wail, yell, yelp; SEE CONCEPT *595*

scream [n2] *person or thing that is very funny*
card*, character*, comedian, comedienne, comic, entertainer, guffaw*, hoot*, howl*, joker, laugh, panic*, riot, sensation, sidesplitter*, wit; SEE CONCEPTS *423,529*

scream [v] *cry out*
bawl, bellow, blare, caterwaul, holler*, howl, jar, roar, screak, screech, shout, shriek, shrill, sing out, squeal, voice, wail, yell, yip, yowl; SEE CONCEPT *77*

screen [n] *protection used in or as furniture, motion picture display*
awning, canopy, cloak, concealment, cover, covering, curtain, divider, envelope, guard, hedge, mantle, mask, net, partition, security, shade, shelter, shield, shroud, veil; SEE CONCEPTS *277,440,443,445,473*

screen [v1] *hide, protect*
adumbrate, blind, block out, bulwark, bury, cache, camouflage, cloak, close, conceal, cover, cover up, defend, disguise, ensconce, fend, guard, mask, obscure, obstruct, safeguard, seclude, secrete, secure, separate, shade, shadow, shelter, shield, shroud, shut off, shut out, shutter, stash, umbrage, veil, wall off; SEE CONCEPTS *96,188*

screen [v2] *examine and choose*
cull, eliminate, evaluate, extract, filter, gauge, grade, pick out, process, riddle, scan, select, separate, sieve, sift, sort, winnow; SEE CONCEPT *41*

screw [v1] *twist in*
spiral, tighten, turn, twine, wind, work; SEE CONCEPTS *85,160*

screw [v2] *twist, contort*
contract, crimp, crinkle, crumple, distort, pucker,

rimple, ruck up, rumple, scrunch, wrinkle; SEE CONCEPT *219*

screw [*v3*] *pressure*
bilk, bleed, cheat, chisel, coerce, constrain, defraud, do*, exact, extort, extract, force, hold a knife to*, oppress, pinch*, pressurize, put screws to*, ream*, shake down*, squeeze, wrench, wrest, wring; SEE CONCEPTS *14,192*

screw up [*v*] *make a mess of*
blow, bobble, bollix*, botch, bungle, confuse, flub*, foul up, goof*, goof up*, louse, make hash of*, mess, mess up, mishandle, mismanage, muck up*, muddle, muff, queer, snafu*, spoil; SEE CONCEPT *101*

screwy [*adj*] *eccentric*
abnormal, batty, bizarre, crazy, daft, dotty, far out*, flaky, funky*, irregular, kooky, mad, nutty, odd, oddball, offbeat, off-center, off the wall*, out in left field*, outlandish, peculiar, queer, quirky, strange, uncommon, unconventional, weird; SEE CONCEPTS *547,564*

scribble [*v*] *write illegibly*
doodle, jot, scratch, scrawl, squiggle, write badly, write erratically; SEE CONCEPT *79*

scrimp [*v*] *economize*
be cheap, be economical, be frugal, be prudent, be sparing, conserve, curtail, cut back, cut corners*, make ends meet*, pinch pennies*, run a tight ship*, save, skimp, stretch a dollar*, tighten one's belt*; SEE CONCEPT *330*

script [*n1*] *handwriting*
calligraphy, characters, chirography, fist, hand, letters, longhand, penmanship, writing; SEE CONCEPTS *79,284*

script [*n2*] *story for a performance*
article, book, copy, dialogue, libretto, lines, manuscript, playbook, scenario, text, typescript, words; SEE CONCEPTS *263,271*

Scrooge [*n*] *skinflint*
cheapskate, meanie, misanthrope, misanthropist, miser, moneygrubber, niggard, penny-pincher, tightwad; SEE CONCEPT *412*

scrounge [*v*] *beg, forage for*
bum, freeload, hunt, sponge, wheedle; SEE CONCEPTS *48,216*

scrub [*v1*] *clean with force*
abrade, brush, buff, cleanse, mop, polish, rub, scour, wash; SEE CONCEPT *165*

scrub [*v2*] *cancel*
abandon, abolish, abort, call off, delete, discontinue, do away with, drop, forget about, give up; SEE CONCEPTS *121,234*

scruffy [*adj*] *rough, bedraggled*
badly groomed, frowzy*, mangy*, messy, ragged, run-down, seedy, shabby, slovenly, tacky*, tattered, threadbare, ungroomed, unkempt, untidy; SEE CONCEPTS *485,589*

scrumptious [*adj*] *delicious*
ambrosial, appetizing, delectable, delightful, exquisite, heavenly, inviting, luscious, lush, magnificent, mouthwatering, rich, succulent, tasty, yummy; SEE CONCEPTS *529,613*

scruple [*n*] *misgiving, doubt*
anxiety, caution, censor, compunction, conscience, demur, difficulty, faltering, hesitancy, hesitation, pause, perplexity, qualm, reconsideration, reluctance, reluctancy, second thought*, squeamishness, superego, twinge, uneasiness; SEE CONCEPTS *532,690*

scruple [*v*] *balk, have misgivings*
be loath, be reluctant, be unwilling, boggle, demur, doubt, falter, fret, gag, have qualms, hesitate, question, shy, stick, stickle, stumble, think twice about*, vacillate, waver, worry; SEE CONCEPT *21*

scrupulous [*adj*] *extremely careful*
conscientious, conscionable, critical, exact, fastidious, fussy, heedful, honest, honorable, just, meticulous, minute, moral, nice, painstaking, particular, precise, principled, punctilious, punctual, right, rigorous, strict, thinking twice*, true, upright; SEE CONCEPTS *401,538,542*

scrutinize [*v*] *examine closely*
analyze, burn up, candle, canvass, case, check, check out, check over, comb*, consider, contemplate, dig, dissect, explore, eyeball*, get a load of*, go over with a fine-tooth comb*, inquire into, inspect, investigate, look over, overlook, peg*, penetrate, perlustrate, peruse, pierce, pore over, probe, put under a microscope*, scan, scope, scrutinate, search, sift, smoke*, stare, study, survey, take the measure of, view, watch, weigh; SEE CONCEPTS *24,103,623*

scrutiny [*n*] *close examination*
analysis, audit, close-up, eagle eye*, exploration, inquiry, inspection, investigation, long hard look*, perlustration, perusal, review, scan, search, sifting, study, surveillance, survey, tab*, the eye*, view; SEE CONCEPTS *24,103,623*

scuffle [*n*] *fight*
affray, brawl, broil, commotion, disturbance, fracas, fray, fuss*, go*, jump, mix-up, row, ruckus, ruction, rumpus, scrap, set-to*, shuffle, strife, tussle, wrangle; SEE CONCEPT *106*

scuffle [*v*] *fight*
clash, come to blows, contend, cuff, grapple, jostle, skirmish, struggle, tussle, wrestle; SEE CONCEPT *106*

sculpture [*v*] *form a three-dimensional art object*
carve, cast, chisel, cut, engrave, fashion, hew, model, mold, sculp, sculpt, shape; SEE CONCEPTS *137,174,184*

scum [*n1*] *superficial impurities, dirt*
algae, crust, dross, film, froth, residue, scruff, spume, waste; SEE CONCEPT *260*

scum [*n2*] *people who are bad, despicable*
curs*, dregs, lowest, mass, mob, proletariat, rabble, riffraff, rubbish*, scum of the earth*, trash*, unwashed, vermin; SEE CONCEPT *412*

scurrilous [*adj*] *foul-mouthed, vulgar*
abusive, coarse, contumelious, defamatory, dirty, filthy, foul, gross, indecent, infamous, insulting, invective, lewd, low, nasty, obscene, offending, offensive, opprobrious, outrageous, raunchy, ribald, salacious, scabrous, scandalous, shameless, slanderous, smutty*, truculent, vituperative, vituperatory, vituperous; SEE CONCEPTS *267,542,545*

scurry [*v*] *move along swiftly*
barrel, bustle, dart, dash, dust, fly, hasten, hop along, hurry, race, rip, run, rush, scamper, scoot, scud, scutter, scuttle, shoot, skim, sprint, step along, tear, whirl, whisk, zip*; SEE CONCEPT *150*

scuttlebutt [*n*] *gossip*
babble, back-fence talk*, blather, chatter, chitchat, dirty laundry*, grapevine*, hearsay, meddling, prattle, rumor, talk; SEE CONCEPTS *274,278*

sea [*n*] *large body of water; large mass*
abundance, blue*, bounding main*, brine,

sc
se

briny*, briny deep*, Davy Jones's locker*, deep, drink*, expanse, lake, main, multitude, number, ocean, plethora, pond, profusion, sheet, splash*, surf, swell, waves; SEE CONCEPT *514*

seafarer [*n*] *sailor*
bluejacket, boater, boatman/woman, deck hand, mariner, mate, middy, midshipman/woman, old salt*, pirate, sailorman/woman, sea dog*, seaman/woman, swabbie*, yachtsman/woman; SEE CONCEPTS *348,358,366*

seal [*n*] *authentication; stamp*
allowance, assurance, attestation, authorization, cachet, confirmation, imprimatur, insignia, notification, permission, permit, ratification, signet, sticker, tape, tie; SEE CONCEPTS *284,685*

seal [*v1*] *make airtight*
close, cork, enclose, fasten, gum, isolate, paste, plaster, plug, quarantine, secure, segregate, shut, stop, stopper, stop up, waterproof; SEE CONCEPTS *85,160*

seal [*v2*] *ensure, finalize*
assure, attest, authenticate, clinch, conclude, confirm, consummate, establish, ratify, settle, shake hands on*, stamp, validate; SEE CONCEPTS *234,324*

seam [*n*] *line where two objects are connected*
bond, closure, connection, coupling, gore, gusset, hem, joint, junction, juncture, pleat, stitching, suture, tuck, union; SEE CONCEPTS *452,471*

seaman/woman [*n*] *sailor*
bluejacket, boater, boatman/woman, deck hand, mariner, mate, middy, midshipman/woman, old salt*, pirate, sailorman/woman, sea dog*, seafarer, swabbie*, yachtsman/woman; SEE CONCEPTS *348,358,366*

seamy [*adj*] *corrupt, unwholesome*
bad, dark, degraded, disagreeable, disappointing, disreputable, disturbing, low, nasty, rough, sordid, squalid, unpleasant; SEE CONCEPT *545*

sear [*v*] *dry, burn*
blight, brand, brown, burn up, cauterize, cook, dehydrate, desiccate, dry out, dry up, exsiccate, harden, parch, scorch, seal, shrivel, sizzle, tan, toast, wilt, wither; SEE CONCEPTS *170,249*

search [*n*] *seeking to find something*
chase, examination, exploration, fishing expedition*, frisking*, going-over*, hunt, inquest, inquiry, inspection, investigation, legwork*, perquisition, pursual, pursuance, pursuing, pursuit, quest, research, rummage, scrutiny, shakedown*, wild-goose chase*, witch hunt*; SEE CONCEPT *216*

search [*v*] *seek to find something*
beat, beat about, cast about, chase after, check, comb, examine, explore, ferret, forage, frisk, go in quest of, go over with a fine-tooth comb*, go through, grope, grub, gun for*, hunt, hunt for, inquire, inspect, investigate, leave no stone unturned*, look, look for, look high and low*, look over, poke into, probe, prospect, pry, quest, rake, ransack, rifle through, root, rummage, run down, scan, scour, scout, scrutinize, seek, shake down, sift, smell around, study, track down, turn inside out*, turn upside down*; SEE CONCEPT *216*

searching [*adj*] *probing*
curious, experimental, exploratory, fact-finding, inquiring, inquisitive, penetrating, seeking, sharp, studious; SEE CONCEPT *402*

seashore [*n*] *beach*
bank, coast, littoral, oceanfront, seaboard,

seafront, seaside, shingle, shore, strand, waterfront; SEE CONCEPTS *509,514*

season [*n*] *time of year governed by annual equinoxes*
autumn, division, fall, interval, juncture, occasion, opportunity, period, spell, spring, summer, term, time, while, winter; SEE CONCEPT *814*

season [*v1*] *flavor food*
color, enliven, lace, leaven, pep, pepper, salt, spice; SEE CONCEPT *170*

season [*v2*] *acclimatize, prepare*
acclimate, accustom, anneal, climatize, discipline, fit, habituate, harden, inure, mature, qualify, school, steel, temper, toughen, train; SEE CONCEPTS *35,202*

seasonable [*adj*] *timely, appropriate*
apropos, apt, auspicious, convenient, favorable, fit, opportune, pertinent, propitious, prosperous, providential, relevant, seasonal, suitable, timeous, towardly, welcome, well-timed; SEE CONCEPT *558*

seasoned [*adj*] *experienced*
accomplished, adept, battle-scarred, been around*, been there*, competent, expert, familiar, hardened, instructed, knowledgeable, matured, old hand*, practiced, prepared, pro, professional, qualified, skillful, tested, toughened, trained, tried, vet, veteran, weathered, wise, worldly, worldly wise*; SEE CONCEPTS *402,527*

seasoning [*n*] *flavoring for food*
condiment, dressing, gravy, herb, pepper, pungency, relish, salt, sauce, spice, zest; SEE CONCEPTS *457,461*

seat [*n1*] *furniture for sitting, reclining*
bench, chair, chaise lounge, chesterfield, couch, davenport, lounge, loveseat, pew, recliner, settee, settle, stall, stool, wing chair; SEE CONCEPT *443*

seat [*n2*] *central location of organization*
abode, axis, capital, center, cradle, focal point, fulcrum, headquarters, heart, house, hub, location, mansion, nerve center, place, polestar, post, residence, site, situation, source, spot, station; SEE CONCEPT *198*

seat [*n3*] *base, foundation*
basement, basis, bed, bottom, cause, fitting, footing, ground, groundwork, rest, seating, support; SEE CONCEPT *442*

seat [*n4*] *rear end of animate being*
backside, behind, bottom, breech, derrière, duff*, fanny*, fundament*, keister*, posterior, rear, rear end, rump, tush*; SEE CONCEPTS *392,825, 827*

seat [*v*] *place in furniture, position*
accommodate, deposit, establish, fix, hold, install, locate, lounge, nestle, perch, plant, put, roost, set, settle, sit, squat, take; SEE CONCEPTS *154,201,384*

secede [*v*] *pull away; split from*
abdicate, apostatize, break with, disaffiliate, leave, quit, resign, retire, retract, retreat, separate, withdraw; SEE CONCEPTS *119,298,384*

secession [*n*] *withdrawal*
breakaway, breakup, defection, disaffiliation, dissension, disunion, division, exiting, parting, rift, rupture, schism, separation, splinter group, split; SEE CONCEPTS *135,195,211,297,388,685*

seclude [*v*] *isolate, hide*
blockade, boycott, cloister, closet, conceal, confine, cover, embargo, enclose, evict, immure, os-

tracize, quarantine, retire, screen, segregate, separate, sequester, shut off, withdraw; SEE CONCEPTS *121,135,188*

secluded [*adj*] *isolated, sheltered*
abandoned, alone, aloof, beleaguered, blockaded, cloistered, close, closet, confidential, covert, cut off, deserted, hermetic, hidden, incommunicado, insular, isolate, lonely, lonesome, off the beaten track*, out-of-the-way*, personal, private, quarantined, quiet, reclusive, remote, removed, reserved, retired, screened, secluse, seclusive, secret, segregated, sequestered, shut off, shy, singular, solitary, tucked away*, unapproachable, unfrequented, uninhabited, unsociable, withdrawn; SEE CONCEPTS *401,576,583*

seclusion [*n*] *isolation*
aloneness, aloofness, beleaguerment, blockade, concealment, desolation, detachment, hiding, privacy, privateness, quarantine, reclusion, reclusiveness, remoteness, retirement, retreat, seclusiveness, separateness, separation, sequestration, shelter, solitude, withdrawal; SEE CONCEPTS *135,188,388,631*

second [*adj*] *next; subordinate*
additional, alternative, another, double, duplicate, extra, following, further, inferior, lesser, lower, next, next in order, other, place, repeated, reproduction, runner-up, secondary, subsequent, succeeding, supporting, twin, unimportant; SEE CONCEPTS *575,585*

second [*n1*] *shortest interval of time*
bat of an eye*, flash, instant, jiffy*, moment, nothing flat*, sec*, shake*, split second, twinkling*, wink; SEE CONCEPTS *803,821*

second [*n2*] *support; duplicate*
assistant, backer, double, exponent, helper, placer, proponent, reproduction, runner-up, supporter, twin; SEE CONCEPTS *423,670*

second [*v*] *support, advance a suggestion*
aid, approve, assist, back, back up, encourage, endorse, forward, further, give moral support, go along with, promote, stand by, uphold; SEE CONCEPTS *298,324,384*

secondary [*adj1*] *subordinate; less important*
accessory, alternate, auxiliary, backup, bush-league*, collateral, consequential, contingent, dependent, dinky*, extra, inconsiderable, inferior, insignificant, lesser, lower, minor, minor-league*, petty, relief, reserve, second, second-rate, small, small-fry*, small-time*, subject, subservient, subsidiary, substract, supporting, tributary, trivial, under, unimportant; SEE CONCEPTS *574,575*

secondary [*adj2*] *derivative*
auxiliary, borrowed, consequent, dependent, derivate, derivational, derived, developed, eventual, indirect, proximate, resultant, resulting, second-hand, subordinate, subsequent, subsidiary, vicarious; SEE CONCEPT *549*

secondhand [*adj*] *used*
handed down, hand-me-down, not new, old, preowned, previously owned, unnew; SEE CONCEPTS *578,797*

second-rate/second-class [*adj*] *inferior, cheap*
cheap and dirty*, common, commonplace, déclassé, hack*, low-grade, low-quality, mean, mediocre, poor, shoddy*, substandard, tacky*, tawdry; SEE CONCEPTS *334,567,574*

secrecy [*n*] *concealment*
clandestineness, confidence, confidentiality, covertness, dark, darkness, furtiveness, hiding, hush, isolation, mystery, privacy, reticence, retirement, seclusion, secretiveness, secretness, silence, solitude, stealth, suppression, surreptitiousness; SEE CONCEPT *631*

secret [*adj1*] *hidden, unrevealed*
abstruse, ambiguous, arcane, backdoor, camouflaged, classified, cloak-and-dagger*, close, closet, clouded, conspiratorial, covered, covert, cryptic, dark, deep, disguised, enigmatical, esoteric, furtive, hush-hush*, mysterious, mystic, mystical, obscure, occult, on the QT*, out-of-the-way*, private, recondite, reticent, retired, secluded, shrouded, strange, undercover, underground, under wraps*, undisclosed, unenlightened, unfrequented, unintelligible, unknown, unpublished, unseen, veiled; SEE CONCEPTS *529,576*

secret [*adj2*] *underhand, clandestine*
backdoor, backstairs, camouflaged, classified, close, confidential, covert, cryptic, discreet, disguised, dissembled, dissimulated, furtive, hush-hush*, in ambush, incognito, inside, restricted, secretive, sly, sneak, sneaky, stealthy, sub-rosa, surreptitious, top secret, unacknowledged, under false pretense*, underhanded, under-the-table*; SEE CONCEPTS *545,576*

secret [*n*] *something kept hidden, unrevealed*
cipher, classified information, code, confidence, confidential information, enigma, formula, key, magic number*, mystery, occult, oracle, password, privileged information, puzzle, skeleton in cupboard*, unknown; SEE CONCEPTS *274,631*

secretary [*n1*] *office worker*
assistant, clerk, executive secretary, receptionist, typist, word processor; SEE CONCEPT *348*

secretary [*n2*] *desk*
bureau, davenport, escritoire, secretaire, writing desk, writing table; SEE CONCEPT *443*

secrete [*v1*] *hide*
bury, cache, conceal, cover, cover up, deposit, disguise, ditch, ensconce, finesse, harbor, hide out, keep quiet, keep secret, keep to oneself, keep under wraps*, palm*, paper, plant, screen, seclude, secure, shroud, squirrel*, stash, stash away, stonewall*, stow, sweep under rug*, veil, whitewash*, withhold; SEE CONCEPTS *188,266*

secrete [*v2*] *give off, emit*
discharge, emanate, excrete, extravasate, extrude, exude, perspire, produce, sweat; SEE CONCEPTS *146,179*

secretive [*adj*] *uncommunicative*
backstairs*, buttoned up*, cagey, clammed up*, close, close-mouthed*, covert, cryptic, enigmatic, feline, furtive, hushed, in chambers*, in privacy*, in private, in the background*, in the dark*, on the QT*, reserved, reticent, silent, taciturn, tight-lipped*, undercover, unforthcoming, withdrawn, zipped*; SEE CONCEPTS *267,548*

secretly [*adv*] *in hidden manner*
behind closed doors*, behind someone's back*, by stealth, clandestinely, confidentially, covertly, furtively, hush-hush*, in camera*, in confidence, in holes and corners*, in secret, insidiously, in strict confidence*, intimately, obscurely, on the QT*, on the quiet*, on the sly*, personally, privately, privily, quietly, slyly, stealthily, sub rosa, surreptitiously, underhandedly, under the table*, unobserved; SEE CONCEPTS *267,548*

se
se

sect [n] *school of thought*
camp, church, communion, connection, creed, crew, cult, denomination, division, faction, faith, following, group, order, party, persuasion, religion, school, splinter group, team, wing; SEE CONCEPTS *381,382*

sectarian [adj] *narrow-minded, exclusive*
bigoted, clannish, cliquish, dissident, doctrinaire, dogmatic, factional, fanatic, fanatical, hidebound, insular, limited, local, nonconforming, nonconformist, parochial, partisan, provincial, rigid, schismatic, skeptical, small-town*, splinter; SEE CONCEPT *403*

sectarian [n] *person who is narrow-minded*
adherent, bigot, cohort, disciple, dissenter, dissident, dogmatist, extremist, fanatic, heretic, maverick, misbeliever, nonconformist, partisan, radical, rebel, revolutionary, satellite, schismatic, separatist, supporter, true believer, zealot; SEE CONCEPTS *359,423*

section [n] *division, portion*
area, belt, bite, branch, category, chunk, classification, component, cross section, cut, department, district, drag, end, field, fraction, fragment, hunk, installment, locality, lump, member, moiety, parcel, part, passage, piece, precinct, quarter, region, sample, sector, segment, share, slice, slot, sphere, split, subdivision, territory, tier, tract, vicinity, zone; SEE CONCEPT *835*

sectional [adj] *localized, divided*
exclusive, factional, local, narrow, partial, regional, selfish, separate, separatist; SEE CONCEPTS *557,785*

sector [n] *area, subdivision*
category, district, division, part, precinct, quarter, region, stratum, zone; SEE CONCEPTS *508,835*

secular [adj] *not spiritual or religious*
civil, earthly, laic, laical, lay, material, materialistic, nonclerical, nonreligious, of this world*, profane, temporal, unsacred, worldly; SEE CONCEPTS *529,549*

secure [adj1] *safe*
defended, guarded, immune, impregnable, out of harm's way, protected, riskless, safe, sheltered, shielded, unassailable, undamaged, unharmed; SEE CONCEPT *587*

secure [adj2] *fastened, stable*
adjusted, anchored, bound, buttoned down*, fast, firm, fixed, fortified, immovable, iron, locked, nailed, safe and sound*, set, solid, solid as a rock*, sound, staunch, steady, strong, sure, tenacious, tight; SEE CONCEPT *488*

secure [adj3] *certain, definite*
able, absolute, assured, at ease, balanced, carefree, cinch, conclusive, confident, determined, easy, established, firm, hopeful, in the bag*, locked on*, nailed down*, on ice*, reassured, reliable, resolute, sanguine, self-assured, self-confident, settled, shoo-in*, solid, sound, stable, steadfast, steady, strong, sure, sure thing*, tried and true*, unanxious, undoubtful, well-founded; SEE CONCEPTS *403,535*

secure [v1] *obtain*
access, achieve, acquire, annex, assure, bag*, buy, capture, catch, chalk up*, cinch, come by, ensure, gain, get, get hold of, grasp, guarantee, have, hook, insure, land, lock, lock up, make sure, pick up, procure, rack up*, take, win; SEE CONCEPT *120*

secure [v2] *attach, tie up*
adjust, anchor, batten down, bind, bolt, button, button down, catch, cement, chain, clamp, clinch, close, fasten, fix, hitch, hook on, lash, lock, lock up, make fast, moor, nail, padlock, pinion, rivet, settle, tack, tie, tie down, tighten; SEE CONCEPTS *85,160*

secure [v3] *protect, make safe*
assure, bulwark, cover, defend, ensure, fend, guarantee, guard, insure, safeguard, screen, shield; SEE CONCEPT *96*

security [n1] *safety, protection*
aegis, agreement, armament, armor, asylum, bail, bond, care, collateral, compact, contract, covenant, cover, custody, defense, earnest, freedom, guarantee, guard, immunity, insurance, pact, pawn, pledge, precaution, preservation, promise, protection, redemption, refuge, retreat, safeguard, safekeeping, safeness, safety measure, salvation, sanctuary, shelter, shield, surety, surveillance, token, ward, warrant; SEE CONCEPTS *712,729*

security [n2] *peace of mind*
assurance, calm, certainty, confidence, conviction, ease, freedom, positiveness, reliance, soundness, sureness, surety; SEE CONCEPT *410*

sedate [adj] *calm, collected*
cold sober*, composed, cool, cool as cucumber*, decorous, deliberate, demure, dignified, dispassionate, earnest, grave, imperturbable, laidback*, no-nonsense, placid, proper, quiet, seemly, serene, serious, sober, solemn, somber, staid, steady, tranquil, unflappable, unruffled; SEE CONCEPTS *404,542*

sedative [adj] *soothing*
allaying, anodyne, calmative, calming, lenitive, relaxing, sleep-inducing, soporific, tranquillizing; SEE CONCEPT *537*

sedative [n] *soothing agent, medicine*
analgesic, anodyne, barbiturate, calmant, calmative, depressant, dope*, downer, drug, hypnotic, knockout pill, medication, narcotic, nerve medicine, opiate, pacifier, pain-killer, pain pill*, quietive, sleeping pill, tranquillizer; SEE CONCEPT *307*

sedentary [adj] *motionless, lazy*
desk, desk-bound, idle, inactive, seated, settled, sitting, sluggish, stationary, torpid; SEE CONCEPTS *542,584*

sediment [n] *solid residue from liquid solution*
debris, deposit, dregs, dross, gook*, grounds, gunk*, lees, matter, powder, precipitate, precipitation, residuum, settling, silt, slag, solids, trash, waste; SEE CONCEPT *260*

sedition [n] *rebellion*
agitation, defiance, disobedience, dissent, insubordination, insurgence, insurgency, insurrection, mutiny, revolt, revolution, treason, uprising; SEE CONCEPTS *106,300,320,633*

seditious [adj] *rebellious*
anarchistic, bellicose, defiant, disloyal, disobedient, disorderly, dissident, factious, iconoclastic, insurgent, insurrectionary, mutinous, radical, rebel, resistant, revolutionary, riotous, subversive, treasonable, warring; SEE CONCEPTS *401,529,542*

seduce [v1] *tempt, ensnare*
bait, beguile, betray, bribe, coax, deceive, decoy, delude, draw, entice, entrap, hook, induce, inveigle, invite, lead astray*, lead on*, lure, mislead,

mousetrap*, persuade, pull, rope in, steer, string along*, sucker*, wheedle; SEE CONCEPT *11*

seduce [*v2*] *entice sexually*
allure, attract, beguile, captivate, charm, come on to*, enamour, entrance, sweep off one's feet*, tempt; SEE CONCEPT *375*

seduction [*n*] *enticement*
allurement, attraction, cajolery, come-on*, inducement, lure, persuasion, tantalizing, temptation; SEE CONCEPTS *7,19,22,68*

seductive [*adj*] *alluring, sexy*
attracting, attractive, beguiling, bewitching, captivating, charming, come-hither*, desirable, drawing, enchanting, enticing, fascinating, flirtatious, inviting, irresistible, magnetic, provocative, ravishing, siren, specious, tempting; SEE CONCEPTS *372,579*

sedulous [*adj*] *assiduous*
active, busy, determined, diligent, hard-working, industrious, laborious, persevering, plugging, tireless; SEE CONCEPTS *538,542*

see [*v1*] *perceive with eyes*
beam, be apprised of, behold, catch a glimpse of, catch sight of, clock*, contemplate, descry, detect, discern, distinguish, espy, examine, eye, flash, gape, gawk, gaze, get a load of*, glare, glimpse, heed, identify, inspect, lay eyes on*, look, look at, make out, mark, mind, note, notice, observe, pay attention to, peek, peep, peer, peg*, penetrate, pierce, recognize, regard, remark, scan, scope, scrutinize, sight, spot, spy, stare, survey, take notice, view, watch, witness; SEE CONCEPTS *590,626*

see [*v2*] *appreciate, comprehend*
appraise, ascertain, behold, catch, catch on, conceive, descry, determine, discern, discover, distinguish, envisage, envision, espy, experience, fancy, fathom, feature, feel, find out, follow, get, get the drift*, get the hang of*, grasp, have, hear, imagine, investigate, know, learn, make out, mark, mind, note, notice, observe, perceive, ponder, realize, recognize, remark, study, suffer, sustain, take in, think, tumble, undergo, understand, unearth, view, visualize, weigh; SEE CONCEPTS *15,31,43*

see [*v3*] *accompany, guide*
associate with, attend, bear company, call, come by, come over, conduct, consort with, date, direct, drop by, drop in, encounter, escort, go out with, go with, keep company with, lead, look up, meet, pilot, pop in, receive, route, run into, shepherd, show, speak to, steer, stop by, stop in, take out, usher, visit, walk; SEE CONCEPTS *187,227,384*

see [*v4*] *visualize*
anticipate, conceive, divine, envisage, envision, fancy, feature, foresee, foretell, imagine, picture, realize, think, vision; SEE CONCEPT *12*

seed [*n1*] *beginning, source*
berry, bud, cell, conceit, concept, conception, core, corn, ear, egg, embryo, germ, grain, image, impression, inkling, kernel, notion, nucleus, nut, ovule, ovum, particle, rudiment, semen, spark, sperm, spore, start, suspicion; SEE CONCEPTS *393,428,648*

seed [*n2*] *children*
brood, descendants, heirs, issue, offspring, posterity, progeniture, progeny, race, scions, spawn, successors; SEE CONCEPT *414*

seedy [*adj*] *run-down, dilapidated*
ailing, beat up, bedraggled, crummy*, decaying, decrepit, dingy, dog-eared*, down-at-the-heel*, drooping, droopy, faded, flagging, frowzy, gone to seed*, grubby, in a bad way*, mangy, messy, neglected, old, overgrown, poor, poorly, ragged, ratty, sagging, scruffy, shabby, sickly, sleazy*, slovenly, squalid, tacky, tattered, threadbare, tired, torn, unkempt, untidy, unwell, used up, wilted, wilting, worn; SEE CONCEPTS *485,570*

seek [*v1*] *look for*
be after, beat the bushes*, bird-dog*, bob for, cast about, chase, comb, delve, delve for, dig for, dragnet, explore, fan, ferret out, fish, fish for*, follow, go after, gun for*, hunt, inquire, investigate, leave no stone unturned*, look about, look around, look high and low*, mouse*, nose*, prowl, pursue, quest, ransack, root, run after, scout, scratch, search for, search out, sniff out*, track down; SEE CONCEPT *216*

seek [*v2*] *try, attempt*
aim, aspire to, assay, endeavor, essay, have a go at*, offer, pursue, strive, struggle, undertake; SEE CONCEPT *87*

seek [*v3*] *ask, inquire*
beg, entreat, find out, invite, petition, query, request, solicit; SEE CONCEPT *48*

seem [*v*] *appear; give the impression*
assume, be suggestive of, convey the impression, create the impression, give the feeling of*, give the idea of*, have the appearance of, have the aspects of, have the earmarks of*, have the features of, have the qualities of, hint, imply, insinuate, intimate, look, look as if, look like, look to be, make a show of, pretend, resemble, show, show every sign of, sound, sound like, strike one as being, suggest; SEE CONCEPT *543*

seeming [*adj*] *apparent*
appearing, illusive, illusory, ostensible, outward, professed, quasi-, semblant, specious, surface; SEE CONCEPTS *487,573*

seemly [*adj*] *appropriate, suitable*
becoming, befitting, comme il faut, compatible, conforming, congenial, congruous, consistent, consonant, correct, decent, decorous, fit, fitting, in good taste, meet, nice, pleasing, proper, suited, timely; SEE CONCEPT *558*

seep [*v*] *leak*
bleed, drain, drip, exude, flow, ooze, percolate, permeate, soak, sweat, transude, trickle, weep, well; SEE CONCEPTS *146,179*

seer [*n*] *clairvoyant*
augur, channeller, crystal ball gazer, diviner, forecaster, fortune-teller, medium, oracle, palm reader, prophet, psychic, soothsayer; SEE CONCEPT *423*

seethe [*v*] *be very angry*
be furious, be incensed, be livid, be mad, be on the warpath*, blow one's stack*, blow up*, boil, breathe fire*, bristle, burn, ferment, flare, flip, foam, foam at mouth*, froth, fume, hit the ceiling*, rage, see red*, simmer, smolder, spark, stew*, storm; SEE CONCEPTS *29,34*

segment [*n*] *part of something*
articulation, bit, compartment, cut, division, member, moiety, parcel, piece, portion, section, sector, slice, subdivision, wedge; SEE CONCEPT *835*

segregate [*v*] *discriminate and separate*
choose, close off, cut off, disconnect, dissociate,

divide, insulate, island, isolate, quarantine, select, sequester, set apart, sever, single out, split
up; SEE CONCEPTS *21,135,645*

segregation [*n*] *separation*
apartheid, discrimination, dissociation, disunion,
division, exlusion, isolation, partition, seclusion,
splitting up; SEE CONCEPTS *135,195,297,388*

seize [*v1*] *grab, take*
appropriate, catch, catch hold of, clasp, clench,
clinch, clutch, compass, embrace, enclose, enfold, envelope, fasten, grapple, grasp, grip, hang
onto, hold fast, lay hands on*, lay hold of*,
pinch, pluck, snag, snatch, squeeze, take hold of;
SEE CONCEPTS *142,164,190*

seize [*v2*] *abduct; take by force*
ambush, annex, apprehend, appropriate, arrest,
arrogate, bag, bust, capture, carry off, catch,
claw, clutch, commandeer, confiscate, conquer,
exact, force, gain, get, grab, grasp, hijack, hook,
impound, incorporate, kidnap, lift, nab, nail*, occupy, overcome, overpower, overrun, overwhelm, pick up, pounce, secure, snag, snare,
spirit away*, subdue, take, take by storm*, take
captive, take over, take possession of, throttle,
trap, usurp, wrench; SEE CONCEPT *90*

seizure [*n1*] *convulsive attack*
access, breakdown, convulsion, fit, illness,
paroxysm, spasm, spell, stroke, throe, turn; SEE
CONCEPT *308*

seizure [*n2*] *capture, taking*
abduction, annexation, apprehension, arrest,
bust*, collar*, commandeering, confiscation,
drop, grab, grabbing, hook*, pinch*, seizing,
snatch; SEE CONCEPT *90*

seldom [*adv*] *infrequently*
a few times, every now and then, from time to
time, hardly, hardly ever, in a few cases, inhabit-
ually, irregularly, little, not often, not very often,
occasionally, on and off, once in a blue moon*,
once in a while, rarely, scarcely, scarcely ever,
semioccasionally, sometimes, sporadically, uncommonly, unoften, unusually, whimsically; SEE
CONCEPT *541*

select [*adj*] *excellent, elite, preferable*
best, blue-chip*, boss*, choice, chosen, cool*,
cream*, culled, delicate, discriminating, eclectic,
elect, elegant, exclusive, exquisite, favored, first-
class*, first-rate*, handpicked, limited, number
one*, pick, picked, posh, preferred, prime, privileged, rare, recherché, screened, selected, selective, special, superior, top, topnotch, tops*,
weeded*, winner, winnowed, world-class*; SEE
CONCEPTS *574,653*

select [*v*] *pick out, prefer from among choices*
choose, cull, decide, elect, make, make a choice,
make a selection, mark, name, opt, optate, opt
for, peg*, pick, pin down, say so*, single out,
slot*, sort out, tab*, tag*, take, tap*, winnow;
SEE CONCEPT *41*

selection [*n*] *preference from among choices*
alternative, choice, choosing, collection, culling,
draft, druthers*, election, excerpt, option, pick,
picking; SEE CONCEPT *529*

selective [*adj*] *discriminating*
careful, choicy, choosy, discerning, discriminatory, eclectic, fussy, judicious, particular, persnickety*, picky, scrupulous, select; SEE
CONCEPTS *404,542*

self-assured [*adj*] *confident*
assured, believing, bold, brave, cocksure*,

cocky, courageous, expectant, expecting, fearless, overconfident, positive, puffed up*, secure,
sure, unafraid; SEE CONCEPTS *403,404*

self-centered [*adj*] *absorbed with oneself*
egocentric, egoistic, egomaniacal, egotistic, egotistical, grandstanding, having a swelled head*,
independent, inward-looking, know-it-all*, narcissistic, on an ego trip*, self-absorbed, self-indulgent, self-interested, self-involved, selfish,
self-seeking, self-serving, self-sufficient, stuck
on oneself*, wrapped up with oneself*; SEE CON-
CEPT *404*

self-confident [*adj*] *secure with oneself*
assured, fearless, hotdog*, hotshot*, know-it-
all*, poised, sanguine, self-assured, self-reliant,
sure of oneself, undoubtful; SEE CONCEPT *404*

self-conscious [*adj*] *insecure with oneself*
affected, anxious, artificial, awkward, bashful,
diffident, discomfited, embarrassed, ill-at-ease,
mannered, nervous, out of countenance, shamefaced, sheepish, shy, stiff, stilted, uncertain, uncomfortable, uneasy, unsure; SEE CONCEPTS
401,404

self-control [*n*] *willpower over one's actions*
abstemiousness, aplomb, balance, constraint,
dignity, discipline, discretion, poise, repression,
reserve, restraint, reticence, self-constraint, self-
discipline, self-government, sobriety, stability,
stoicism, strength of character; SEE CONCEPT *633*

self-evident/self-explanatory [*adj*] *obvious*
apparent, axiomatic, clear, comprehensible, incontrovertible, inescapable, manifest, patently
true, plain, prima facie, undeniable, understandable, unmistakable, unquestionable, visible; SEE
CONCEPTS *529,548*

self-important [*adj*] *conceited*
arrogant, bigheaded*, cocky, egotistical, full of
hot air*, immodest, know-it-all, overbearing,
pompous, puffed up*, smug, stuck up*, swollen-
headed*, vain, vainglorious; SEE CONCEPT *404*

selfish [*adj*] *thinking only of oneself*
egocentric, egoistic, egoistical, egomaniacal,
egotistic, egotistical, greedy*, hoggish*, mean,
mercenary, miserly, narcissistic, narrow, narrow-
minded, out for number one*, parsimonious,
prejudiced, self-centered, self-indulgent, self-interested, self-seeking, stingy, ungenerous,
wrapped up in oneself*; SEE CONCEPTS *404,542*

self-reliant [*adj*] *independent*
autonomous, on one's own, self-contained, self-
governing, self-sufficient, self-supporting, self-
sustaining, unaided, unallied; SEE CONCEPT *554*

self-respect/self-esteem [*n*] *pride in oneself*
amour-propre, conceit, confidence, dignity,
egotism, faith in oneself, morale, narcissism,
self-assurance, self-content, self-regard, self-
satisfaction, vanity, worth; SEE CONCEPTS *411,
689*

self-righteous [*adj*] *smug*
affected, canting, complacent, egotistical, goody-
goody*, holier-than-thou*, hypocritical, noble,
pharisaic, pietistic, pious, preachy, sanctimonious, self-satisfied, superior; SEE CONCEPTS
401,542

self-satisfaction [*n*] *pride, contentment*
complacency, conceit, glow, peace of mind, self-
approbation, self-approval, self-pleasure, smugness; SEE CONCEPTS *410,689*

self-satisfied [*adj*] *proud, content*
complacent, conceited, egotistic, flushed,

pleased, puffed up*, self-congratulatory, smug, vain; SEE CONCEPTS *404,542*

self-sufficient [*adj*] *able to take care of oneself*
arrogant, closed, competent, conceited, confident, doing one's own thing*, efficient, egotistic, haughty, independent, individual, on one's own, out for number one*, self-confident, self-dependent, self-sufficing, self-supported, self-supporting, self-sustained, self-sustaining, smug, unit; SEE CONCEPTS *334,404*

sell [*v1*] *exchange an object for money*
advertise, auction, bargain, barter, be in business*, boost, clinch the deal, close, close the deal, contract, deal in, dispose, drum, dump, exchange, handle, hawk, hustle, market, merchandise, move, peddle, persuade, pitch, plug, puff*, push, put across, put up for sale, retail, retain, snow, soft sell*, soft soap*, spiel*, stock, sweet talk*, trade, traffic, unload, vend, wholesale; SEE CONCEPT *345*

seller [*n*] *person who gives object in exchange for money*
agent, auctioneer, businessperson, dealer, marketer, merchant, peddler, representative, retailer, sales help, salesperson, shopkeeper, storekeeper, trader, tradesperson, vendor; SEE CONCEPTS *347,348*

sell/sell out [*v2*] *betray*
beguile, break faith, bunk, cross, deceive, deliver up, delude, disappoint, double-cross*, fail, four-flush*, give away, give up, mislead, play false, rat on*, sell down the river*, stab in the back*, surrender, take in, violate; SEE CONCEPTS *14,63*

semblance [*n*] *aura, appearance*
affinity, air, alikeness, analogy, aspect, bearing, comparison, facade, face, false front*, feel, feeling, figure, form, front, guise, image, likeness, mask, mien, mood, pose, pretense, resemblance, seeming, show, showing, similarity, simile, similitude, simulacrum, veil, veneer; SEE CONCEPTS *673,716*

semester [*n*] *term*
course, period, quarter, session; SEE CONCEPTS *807,822*

seminar [*n*] *conference*
convention, discussion, forum, group discussion, meeting, open discussion, palaver, powwow*, rap session, round table, symposium, workshop; SEE CONCEPTS *56,324,386*

semiotics [*n*] *study of signs as elements of communication*
langue, parole, pragamatics, semantics, sign systems, symbolism, syntactics; SEE CONCEPT *349*

send [*v1*] *transmit, transfer through a system*
accelerate, address, advance, assign, broadcast, cast, circulate, commission, commit, communicate, consign, convey, delegate, deliver, detail, direct, dispatch, drop, emit, expedite, express, fire, fling, forward, freight, get under way, give off, grant, hasten, hurl, hurry off, impart, issue, let fly, mail, post, propel, put out, radiate, relay, remit, route, rush off, ship, shoot, televise, troll, wire; SEE CONCEPTS *217,223*

send [*v2*] *please*
charm, delight, electrify, enrapture, enthrall, enthuse, excite, intoxicate, move, please, ravish, stir, thrill, titillate, turn on; SEE CONCEPTS *7,11,22*

senile [*adj*] *failing in physical and mental capabilities due to old age*
aged, ancient, anile, decrepit, doddering, doting, enfeebled, feeble, imbecile, infirm, in second childhood*, old, senescent, shattered, sick, weak; SEE CONCEPTS *314,402,403*

senior [*adj*] *older or of higher rank*
chief, elder, higher, leading, major, more advanced, next higher, superior; SEE CONCEPTS *574,578,585,797*

senior [*n*] *older person*
ancient, doyen, doyenne, elder, elderly person, first-born, golden-ager*, grandfather, grandmother, head, matriarch, old folk*, oldster*, old-timer*, patriarch, pensioner, retired person, senior citizen; SEE CONCEPTS *414,424*

seniority [*n*] *rank in organization due to length of service*
advantage, antiquity, eldership, precedence, preference, priority, rank, ranking, standing, station, superiority; SEE CONCEPTS *671,727*

sensation [*n1*] *feeling, perception*
awareness, consciousness, emotion, gut reaction*, impression, passion, response, sense, sensibility, sensitiveness, sensitivity, sentiment, susceptibility, thought, tingle, vibes*; SEE CONCEPTS *34,410,529*

sensation [*n2*] *something wonderful or awe-inspiring*
agitation, bomb*, bombshell*, commotion, excitement, flash, furor, hit, marvel, miracle, phenomenon, portent, prodigy, scandal, stir, stunner, surprise, thrill, wonder, wow*; SEE CONCEPTS *293,529*

sensational [*adj1*] *startling, exaggerated*
amazing, arresting, astounding, breathtaking, coarse, colored, conspicuous, dramatic, electrifying, emotional, excessive, exciting, extravagant, hair-raising, horrifying, juicy*, livid, lurid, marked, melodramatic, noticeable, outstanding, piquant, pointed, prominent, pungent, remarkable, revealing, rough, salient, scandalous, sensationalistic, shocking, signal, spectacular, staggering, stimulating, sultry, tabloid*, thrilling, vulgar, X-rated*; SEE CONCEPTS *267,537,545*

sensational [*adj2*] *excellent, superb*
agitating, astonishing, breathtaking, cool*, dandy*, divine, dramatic, eloquent, exceptional, exciting, fabulous, first-class*, glorious, impressive, incredible, keen, marvelous, mind-blowing, most*, moving, out of this world*, smashing, spectacular, stirring, surprising, thrilling, zero cool*; SEE CONCEPT *574*

sensationalism [*n*] *exaggeration*
aggrandizement, boasting, excess, fabrication, fish story*, hype, hyperbole, overemphasis, puffery, tabloid journalism, tall story*, whopper*, yellow journalism*; SEE CONCEPTS *63,278,663*

sense [*n1*] *feeling of animate being*
faculty, feel, function, hearing, impression, kinesthesia, sensation, sensibility, sensitivity, sight, smell, taste, touch; SEE CONCEPT *405*

sense [*n2*] *awareness, perception*
ability, appreciation, atmosphere, aura, brains, capacity, clear-headedness, cleverness, cognizance, common sense, consciousness, discernment, discrimination, feel, feeling, gumption*, imagination, impression, insight, intellect, intelligence, intuition, judgment, knowledge, mental-

se
se

ity, mind, premonition, presentiment, prudence, quickness, reason, reasoning, recognition, sagacity, sanity, sentiment, sharpness, smarts*, soul, spirit, tact, thought, understanding, wisdom, wit; SEE CONCEPTS 33,409

sense [n3] *point, meaning*
acceptation, advantage, bottom line*, burden, core, definition, denotatiton, drift, gist, good, heart, implication, import, intendment, interpretation, logic, matter, meat*, meat and potatoes*, message, name of the game*, nature of the beast*, nitty-gritty*, nuance, nub, nuts and bolts*, punch line*, purport, purpose, reason, short, significance, significancy, signification, stuff, substance, thrust, understanding, upshot, use, value, worth; SEE CONCEPTS 668,682

sense [v] *become aware of*
anticipate, apperceive, appreciate, apprehend, believe, be with it, catch, catch on, catch the drift*, consider, credit, deem, dig*, discern, divine, feel, feel in bones*, feel in gut*, get the drift*, get the idea*, get the impression*, get the picture*, get vibes*, grasp, have a feeling*, have a hunch*, hold, know, notice, observe, perceive, pick up, read, realize, savvy*, suspect, take in, think, understand; SEE CONCEPT 34

senseless [adj] *silly, meaningless*
absurd, asinine, batty, crazy, daft, doublespeak*, double talk*, fatuous, flaky, foolish, idiotic, illogical, imbecilic, inane, incongruous, inconsistent, insignificant, irrational, ludicrous, mad, mindless, moronic, nonsensical, nutty, pointless, purportless, purposeless, ridiculous, simple, stupid, trivial, unimportant, unintelligent, unmeaning, unreasonable, unsound, unwise, wacky*, without rhyme or reason*; SEE CONCEPTS 548,558

sensibility [n] *responsiveness; ability to feel*
affection, appreciation, awareness, discernment, emotion, feeling, gut reaction*, heart*, insight, intuition, judgment, keenness, perceptiveness, rationale, sensation, sense, sensitiveness, sensitivity, sentiment, susceptibility, taste, vibes*; SEE CONCEPTS 409,410

sensible [adj] *realistic, reasonable*
all there*, astute, attentive, au courant, aware, canny, cognizant, commonsensical, conscious, consequent, conversant, cool*, discerning, discreet, discriminating, down-to-earth, far-sighted, having all one's marbles*, informed, in right mind, intelligent, judicious, knowing, logical, matter-of-fact, practical, prudent, rational, sagacious, sage, sane, sentient, shrewd, sober, sound, together, well-reasoned, well-thought-out, wise, witting; SEE CONCEPTS 402,542

sensitive [adj1] *impressionable*
acute, cognizant, conscious, delicate, easily affected, emotionable, emotional, feeling, fine, high-strung, hung up*, hypersensitive, impressible, irritable, keen, knowing, nervous, oversensitive, perceiving, perceptive, precarious, precise, psychic, reactive, receptive, responsive, seeing, sensatory, sensile, sensorial, sensory, sentient, supersensitive, susceptible, tense, ticklish, touchy, touchy feely*, tricky, tuned in*, turned on to*, umbrageous, understanding, unstable, wired*; SEE CONCEPT 403

sensitive [adj2] *easily hurt*
delicate, easily harmed, painful, sore, tender; SEE CONCEPT 406

sensitivity [n] *responsiveness to stimuli*
acuteness, affectibility, awareness, consciousness, delicacy, feeling, impressionability, nervousness, reactiveness, reactivity, receptiveness, sensation, sense, sensitiveness, subtlety, susceptibility, sympathy; SEE CONCEPTS 405,410

sensory [adj] *affecting animate nerve organs*
acoustic, afferent, audible, audiovisual, auditory, aural, auricular, clear, discernible, distinct, gustative, gustatory, hearable, lingual, neural, neurological, ocular, olfactive, olfactory, ophthalmic, optic, perceptible, phonic, plain, receptive, sensational, sensatory, sensible, sensual, sonic, tactile, visual; SEE CONCEPT 406

sensual [adj] *physical, erotic*
animal, animalistic, arousing, bodily, carnal, debauched, delightful, epicurean, exciting, fleshly, heavy*, hedonic, hot*, lascivious, lecherous, lewd, libidinous, licentious, lustful, moving, pleasing, rough, sensuous, sexual, sexy, sharpened, steamy, stimulating, stirring, tactile, unchaste, unspiritual, voluptuous, X-rated*; SEE CONCEPTS 372,401

sensuous [adj] *gratifying to senses*
carnal, epicurean, exciting, fleshly, fleshy, hedonistic, luscious, lush, luxurious, passionate, physical, pleasurable, pleasure-loving, pleasure-seeking, primrose, rich, self-indulgent, sensory, sensual, sensualistic, sumptuous, sybaritic, voluptuous; SEE CONCEPTS 372,537

sentence [n] *punishing decree*
book, censure, clock, condemnation, considered opinion, decision, determination, dictum, doom, edict, fall, getup*, hitch, jolt, judgment, knock, order, penalty, pronouncement, punishment, rap*, ruling, sending up the river*, sleep, stretch, term, time, trick, vacation, verdict; SEE CONCEPT 318

sentence [v] *decide punishment*
adjudge, adjudicate, blame, condemn, confine, convict, damn, denounce, devote, doom, impound, imprison, incarcerate, jail, judge, mete out, ordain, pass judgment, penalize, proscribe, punish, put away*, put on ice*, railroad*, rule, send to prison, send up the river*, settle, take the fall*, throw the book at*; SEE CONCEPTS 122,317

sentient [adj] *conscious*
able to recognize, alert, apperceptive, attentive, awake, aware, cognizant, feeling, informed, in on*, in the right mind, knowing, noticing, observing, perceiving, receptive, recognizing, responsive, seeing, sensitive to, understanding, watchful; SEE CONCEPTS 402,539

sentiment [n] *emotion, belief*
affect, affectivity, attitude, bias, conception, conviction, disposition, emotionalism, eye, feeling, hearts and flowers*, idea, inclination, inclining, judgment, leaning, mind, opinion, overemotionalism, partiality, passion, penchant, persuasion, position, posture, predilection, propensity, romanticism, sensibility, sentimentality, slant, softheartedness, tendency, tender feeling, tenderness, thought, view, way of thinking; SEE CONCEPTS 32,410,689

sentimental [adj] *emotional, romantic*
affected, affectionate, corny*, demonstrative, dewy-eyed, dreamy, effusive, gushing, gushy, idealistic, impressionable, inane, insipid, jejune, languishing, lovey-dovey*, loving, maudlin, moonstruck*, mushy*, nostalgic, overacted,

overemotional, passionate, pathetic, rosewater*, saccharine*, sappy*, schmaltzy*, silly, simpering, sloppy*, slushy*, soapy*, soft, softhearted*, sugary*, sweet, syrupy*, tearful, tear-jerking*, tender, touching, vapid, visionary, weepy; SEE CONCEPTS *267,401,542*

sentinel [n] *sentry*
guard, keeper, lookout, picket, protector, watchman/woman, watchperson; SEE CONCEPT *348*

separate [adj1] *disconnected*
abstracted, apart, apportioned, asunder, cut apart, cut in two, detached, disassociated, discrete, disembodied, disjointed, distant, distributed, disunited, divergent, divided, divorced, far between, free, independent, in halves, isolated, loose, marked, parted, partitioned, put asunder, removed, scattered, set apart, set asunder, severed, sovereign, sundered, unattached, unconnected; SEE CONCEPT *577*

separate [adj2] *alone, individual*
apart, autonomous, detached, different, discrete, distinct, distinctive, diverse, free, independent, lone, one, only, particular, peculiar, several, single, sole, solitary, unique, various; SEE CONCEPTS *557,564*

separate [v1] *remove something from group; keep or set apart*
break, break off, cleave, come apart, come away, come between, detach, dichotomize, disconnect, disentangle, disjoin, disjoint, dissect, dissever, distribute, divide, divorce, intersect, part, rupture, sever, split, split up, sunder, uncombine, uncouple, undo; SEE CONCEPT *135*

separate [v2] *isolate, segregate*
assign, break up, classify, close off, comb, compartment, compartmentalize, cut off, discriminate, distribute, draw apart, group, insulate, interval, intervene, island, order, put on one side, rope off, seclude, sequester, sift, single out, sort, space, split up, stand between, winnow; SEE CONCEPTS *158,201*

separate [v3] *part company in a romantic relationship or marriage*
alienate, bifurcate, break it off*, break off, break up, dedomicile, depart, discontinue, disunify, disunite, diverge, divorce, drop, estrange, go away, go different ways*, go separate ways*, leave, part, pull out, split up, take leave, uncouple, unlink, untie the knot*; SEE CONCEPTS *297,384*

separately [adv] *alone, individually*
apart, clearly, definitely, disjointly, distinctly, independently, one at a time, one by one, personally, severally, singly, solely; SEE CONCEPTS *544,577*

separation [n] *being apart; break-up*
break, break-up, dedomiciling, departure, detachment, disconnection, disengagement, disjunction, disrelation, dissociation, dissolution, disunion, division, divorce, divorcement, embarkation, estrangement, farewell, leave-taking*, parting, parting of the ways*, partition, pffft*, rift, rupture, segregation, severance, split, split-up*; SEE CONCEPTS *135,195,297,388*

sepulchral [adj] *gloomy*
black, bleak, cheerless, dark, deathly, dismal, dreary, forlorn, funereal, grave, hollow, morbid, mournful, obscure, somber; SEE CONCEPTS *525,617,618*

sequel [n] *follow-up*
aftereffect, aftermath, alternation, causatum, chain, close, closing, conclusion, consecution, consequence, continuation, development, effect, end, ending, epilogue, eventuality, finish, finishing, issue, order, outcome, part two*, payoff, progression, result, row, sequence, sequent, series, spin-off*, termination, train, upshot; SEE CONCEPTS *271,293,824,832*

sequence [n] *series, order*
arrangement, array, catenation, chain, classification, concatenation, consecution, consecutiveness, continuance, continuity, continuousness, course, cycle, disposition, distribution, flow, graduation, grouping, ordering, pecking order*, perpetuity, placement, procession, progression, row, run, sequel, skein, streak, string, subsequence, succession, successiveness, track, train; SEE CONCEPTS *721,727*

sequential [adj] *occurring in an order*
consecutive, constant, continuous, following, incessant, later, next, persistent, regular, sequent, serial, steady, subsequent, subsequential, succedent, succeeding, successive; SEE CONCEPTS *482,548,585*

sequester [v] *isolate, seclude*
cloister, close off, cut off, draw back, enisle, hide, insulate, island, secrete, segregate, separate, set apart, set off, withdraw; SEE CONCEPTS *90,188*

serendipity [n] *accidental discovery*
blessing, break*, dumb luck*, fluke*, good luck, happenstance, happy chance, luck, lucky break*, stumbling upon, tripping over; SEE CONCEPT *693*

serene [adj] *calm, undisturbed*
at peace, clear, collected, comfortable, composed, content, cool*, cool as a cucumber*, dispassionate, easy, easygoing, fair, halcyon, imperturbable, laid-back*, limpid, patient, peaceful, pellucid, phlegmatic, placid, poised, quiescent, quiet, reconciled, resting, satisfied, sedate, self-possessed, smooth, still, stoical, tranquil, undisturbed, unflappable, unruffled, untroubled; SEE CONCEPTS *401,485*

serenity [n] *calm, peacefulness*
calmness, composure, cool, patience, peace, peace of mind, placidity, quietness, quietude, stillness, tranquillity; SEE CONCEPTS *633,673*

serf [n] *slave*
bondservant, bondsman/woman, chattel, laborer, peon, servant, vassal, villain, villein; SEE CONCEPT *348*

serial [adj] *in continuing order*
consecutive, continual, continued, continuing, ensuing, following, going on, sequent, sequential, succedent, succeeding, successional, successive; SEE CONCEPTS *482,585*

series [n] *order, succession*
alternation, arrangement, array, category, chain, classification, column, consecution, continuity, course, file, gradation, group, line, list, procession, progression, range, row, run, scale, sequel, sequence, set, skein, streak, string, suit, suite, tier, train; SEE CONCEPTS *721,727,769*

serious [adj] *somber, humorless*
austere, bound, bound and determined*, businesslike, cold sober*, contemplative, deadpan*, deliberate, determined, downbeat*, earnest, funereal, genuine, go for broke*, grave, grim, honest, intent, long-faced*, meditative,

se
se

no-nonsense*, pensive, pokerfaced*, reflective, resolute, resolved, sedate, set, severe, sincere, sober, solemn, staid, steady, stern, thoughtful, unhumorous, unsmiling, weighty; SEE CONCEPTS *403,542*

serious [*adj2*] *crucial, weighty*
arduous, dangerous, deep, difficult, far-reaching, fateful, fell, formidable, grave, grievous, grim, hard, heavy, important, laborious, major, meaning business*, meaningful, menacing, momentous, no joke*, no laughing matter*, of consequence, operose, out for blood*, playing hard ball*, pressing, severe, significant, smoking*, sobering, strenuous, strictly business*, threatening, tough, ugly, unamusing, unhumorous, urgent, worrying; SEE CONCEPTS *538,565, 568*

seriously [*adv1*] *not humorously*
actively, all joking aside*, cool it*, cut the comedy*, determinedly, down, earnestly, fervently, for real*, gravely, in all conscience, in all seriousness, in earnest, intently, passionately, purposefully, resolutely, sedately, simmer down*, sincerely, soberly, solemnly, sternly, straighten out, thoughtfully, vigorously, with a straight face*, with forethought, with sobriety, zealously; SEE CONCEPTS *535,542,544*

seriously [*adv2*] *dangerously, critically*
acutely, badly, decidedly, deplorably, distressingly, gravely, grievously, harmfully, intensely, menacingly, perilously, precariously, quite, regrettably, severely, sorely, threateningly, very; SEE CONCEPTS *544,565,568*

seriousness [*n1*] *humorlessness*
calmness, coolness, earnest, earnestness, gravity, intentness, sedateness, serious-mindedness, sincerity, sober-mindedness, sobriety, solemnity, staidness, sternness, thoughtfulness; SEE CONCEPTS *410,657*

seriousness [*n2*] *danger; criticalness*
enormity, gravity, importance, moment, significance, urgency, weight; SEE CONCEPTS *668,675*

sermon [*n*] *instructive speech with a moral*
address, advice, discourse, doctrine, exhortation, harangue, homily, lecture, lesson, moralism, pastoral, preach, preaching, preachment, tirade; SEE CONCEPTS *278,368*

serpentine [*adj*] *winding; sly*
anfractuous, artful, cagey, circuitous, clever, coiling, convoluted, crafty, cunning, curved, curvy, foxy, indirect, mazy, meandering, meandrous, shrewd, sinuous, slick, slinky, snakelike, snaky*, subtle, supple, twisting, twisting and turning*, wily; SEE CONCEPTS *401,542,581*

serrated [*adj*] *jagged*
denticulate, indented, notched, ragged, sawlike, sawtooth, saw-toothed, scored, serrate, serried, serriform, serrulate, toothed; SEE CONCEPT *486*

servant [*n*] *person who waits on another*
assistant, attendant, cleaning person, dependent, domestic, drudge, help, helper, hireling, live-in, menial, minion, retainer, serf, server, slave; SEE CONCEPT *348*

serve [*v1*] *aid, help; supply*
arrange, assist, attend to, be of assistance, be of use, care for, deal, deliver, dish up*, distribute, do for, give, handle, hit, minister to, nurse, oblige, play, present, provide, provision, set out, succor, wait on, work for; SEE CONCEPTS *110,136,140*

serve [*v2*] *act, do*
accept, agree, attend, be employed by, carry on, complete, discharge, follow, fulfill, function, go through, hearken, labor, obey, observe, officiate, pass, perform, subserve, toil, work; SEE CONCEPT *91*

serve [*v3*] *suffice; do the work of*
advantage, answer, answer the purpose, apply, avail, be acceptable, be adequate, be good enough, benefit, be of use, be useful, content, do, do duty as, fill the bill*, fit, function, make, profit, satisfy, service, suit, work, work for; SEE CONCEPTS *656,658*

service [*n1*] *aid, help*
account, advantage, applicability, appropriateness, assistance, avail, benefit, business, check, courtesy, dispensation, duty, employ, employment, favor, fitness, indulgence, kindness, labor, maintenance, ministration, office, overhaul, relevance, serviceability, servicing, supply, use, usefulness, utility, value, work; SEE CONCEPTS *110,324,658*

service [*n2*] *rite of a church*
ceremonial, ceremony, formality, function, liturgy, observance, ritual, sermon, worship; SEE CONCEPT *368*

service [*n3*] *time in military operation*
action, active duty, combat, duty, fighting, sting; SEE CONCEPTS *320,321*

serviceable [*adj*] *useful, functional*
advantageous, aiding, assistive, beneficial, convenient, dependable, durable, efficient, handy, hard-wearing, helpful, invaluable, operative, practical, profitable, usable, utile, utilitarian, valuable; SEE CONCEPT *560*

servile [*adj*] *grovelling, subservient*
abject, base, beggarly, bootlicking, craven, cringing, despicable, eating crow*, eating humble pie*, fawning, humble, ignoble, low, mean, obedient, obeisant, obsequious, passive, slavish, submissive, sycophantic, toadying, unctuous, unresisting; SEE CONCEPTS *401,404*

servitude [*n*] *slavery*
bondage, bonds, chains, confinement, enslavement, obedience, peonage, serfdom, serfhood, subjection, subjugation, thrall, thralldom, vassalage, yoke; SEE CONCEPTS *388,410*

session [*n*] *meeting, gathering*
affair, assembly, concourse, conference, discussion, get-together, hearing, huddle, jam session*, meet, period, showdown, sitting, term; SEE CONCEPTS *114,324*

set [*adj1*] *decided*
agreed, appointed, arranged, bent, certain, concluded, confirmed, customary, dead set on*, decisive, definite, determined, entrenched, established, firm, fixed, hanging tough*, immovable, intent, inveterate, ironclad, locked in*, obstinate, pat, pigheaded*, prearranged, predetermined, prescribed, regular, resolute, resolved, rigid, rooted, scheduled, set in stone*, settled, solid as a rock*, specified, stated, steadfast, stiff-necked, stipulated, stubborn, unflappable, usual, well-set; SEE CONCEPTS *535,542*

set [*adj2*] *firm, hardened; inflexible*
entrenched, fixed, hard and fast, hidebound, immovable, jelled, located, placed, positioned, rigid, settled, sited, situate, situated, solid, stable, stiff, strict, stubborn, unyielding; SEE CONCEPT *488*

set [*n1*] *physical bearing*
address, air, attitude, carriage, comportment, demeanor, deportment, fit, hang, inclination, mien, port, position, posture, presence, turn; SEE CONCEPT 757

set [*n2*] *stage setting*
flats, mise en scène, scene, scenery, setting, stage set; SEE CONCEPT 263

set [*n3*] *group, assortment*
array, assemblage, band, batch, body, bunch, bundle, camp, circle, clan, class, clique, clump, cluster, clutch, collection, company, compendium, coterie, crew, crowd, faction, gaggle, gang, kit, lot, mob, organization, outfit, pack, push, rat pack*, sect, series; SEE CONCEPTS 417,432,769

set [*v1*] *position, place*
affix, aim, anchor, apply, arrange, bestow, cast, deposit, direct, embed, ensconce, establish, fasten, fix, head, insert, install, introduce, lay, level, locate, lock, lodge, make fast, make ready, mount, park, plank, plant, plop, plunk, point, post, prepare, put, rest, seat, settle, situate, spread, station, stick, train, turn, wedge, zero in*; SEE CONCEPTS 201,202

set [*v2*] *decide upon*
agree upon, allocate, allot, appoint, arrange, assign, conclude, decree, designate, determine, dictate, direct, establish, estimate, fix, fix price, impose, instruct, lay down, make, name, ordain, prescribe, price, rate, regulate, resolve, schedule, settle, specify, stipulate, value; SEE CONCEPT 18

set [*v3*] *harden*
become firm, cake, clot, coagulate, condense, congeal, crystallize, fix, gel, gelate, gelatinize, jell, jellify, jelly, solidify, stiffen, thicken; SEE CONCEPT 250

set [*v4*] *decline*
descend, dip, disappear, drop, go down, sink, subside, vanish; SEE CONCEPT 181

set [*v5*] *start, incite*
abet, begin, commence, foment, initiate, instigate, provoke, put in motion, raise, set on*, stir up*, whip up*; SEE CONCEPT 221

setback [*n*] *disappointment*
about-face*, backset, bath*, blow, bottom, check, comedown, defeat, delay, difficulty, drawing board*, flip-flop*, hindrance, hitch*, hold-up, impediment, misfortune, obstacle, rebuff, regress, regression, reversal, reversal of fortune, reverse, slowdown, stumbling block*, trouble, upset, whole new ballgame*; SEE CONCEPTS 388,674,679

set back [*v*] *delay, hinder*
bog down*, decelerate, defeat, detain, embog, hang up*, hold up, impede, mire, retard, reverse, slow, slow down, slow up; SEE CONCEPT 130

setting [*n*] *scene, background*
ambience, backdrop, context, distance, environment, frame, framework, horizon, jungle, locale, location, mise en scène, mounting, perspective, set, shade, shadow, site, stage set, stage setting, surroundings; SEE CONCEPTS 198,263

settle [*v1*] *straighten out, resolve*
achieve, adjudicate, adjust, appoint, arrange, call the shots*, choose, cinch, clean up, clear, clear up, clinch, come to a conclusion, come to a decision, come to an agreement, complete, concert, conclude, confirm, decide, determine, discharge, dispose, end, establish, figure, fix, form judg-

ment, judge, make a decision, make certain, mediate, nail down*, negotiate, order, pay, put an end to, put into order, reconcile, regulate, rule, satisfy, seal, set to rights, square, verify, work out; SEE CONCEPTS 18,126,341

settle [*v2*] *calm, relieve*
allay, assure, becalm, compose, lull, pacify, quell, quiet, quieten, reassure, relax, sedate, soothe, still, tranquilize; SEE CONCEPTS 7,22,469

settle [*v3*] *come to rest; fall*
alight, bed down, decline, descend, flop, immerse, land, lay, light, lodge, perch, place, plop, plunge, put, repose, roost, seat, set down, settle down, sink, sit, submerge, submerse, subside, touch down; SEE CONCEPT 181

settle [*v4*] *make one's home*
abide, colonize, dwell, establish, hang up one's hat*, inhabit, keep house, live, locate, lodge, move to, park, put down roots*, reside, set up home, squat, take root*, take up residence; SEE CONCEPT 226

settlement [*n1*] *decision, conclusion*
adjustment, agreement, arrangement, clearance, compact, compensation, completion, conclusion, confirmation, contract, covenant, deal, defrayal, determination, discharge, disposition, establishment, happy medium*, liquidation, pay, payment, payoff, quietus, reimbursement, remuneration, resolution, satisfaction, showdown, termination, trade-off, working out; SEE CONCEPTS 230,684

settlement [*n2*] *community*
colonization, colony, encampment, establishment, foundation, habitation, hamlet, inhabitancy, occupancy, occupation, outpost, plantation, principality, residence; SEE CONCEPTS 512,515

set up [*v*] *start*
arrange, assemble, back, begin, build, build up, compose, constitute, construct, create, elevate, erect, establish, excite, exhilarate, found, inaugurate, initiate, inspire, install, institute, introduce, launch, make provision for, open, organize, originate, prearrange, prepare, put together, put up, raise, rear, stimulate, strengthen, subsidize, usher in; SEE CONCEPT 221

sever [*v1*] *cut apart*
bisect, carve, cleave, cut, cut in two, detach, disconnect, disjoin, dissect, dissever, dissociate, disunite, divide, part, rend, rive, separate, slice, split, sunder; SEE CONCEPTS 98,176

sever [*v2*] *dissociate*
abandon, break off, disjoint, dissolve, divide, divorce, put an end to, separate, terminate; SEE CONCEPTS 297,384

several [*adj*] *assorted, various*
a few, a lot, any, certain, considerable, definite, different, disparate, distinct, divers, diverse, handful, hardly any, indefinite, individual, infrequent, manifold, many, not many, numerous, only a few, particular, personal, plural, proportionate, quite a few, rare, respective, scant, scanty, scarce, scarcely any, separate, single, small number, some, sparse, special, specific, sundry; SEE CONCEPTS 564,762

severe [*adj1*] *uncompromising, stern*
astringent, austere, biting, caustic, close, cold, cruel, cutting, disapproving, dour, earnest, firm, flinty, forbidding, grave, grim, hard, hardnosed*, harsh, inconsiderate, inexorable, inflexi-

se
se

ble, iron-handed, obdurate, oppressive, peremptory, pitiless, relentless, resolute, resolved, rigid, satirical, scathing, serious, sober, stern, stiff*, strait-laced*, strict, tight-lipped*, unalterable, unbending, unchanging, unfeeling, unrelenting, unsmiling, unsparing; SEE CONCEPTS 401,534,542

severe [adj2] *difficult, harsh*
acute, arduous, ascetic, austere, bitter, bleak, consequential, critical, dangerous, dear, demanding, despotic, distressing, domineering, drastic, effortful, exacting, extreme, fierce, forbidding, grave, grim, grinding, hard, heavy, hefty, implacable, inclement, intemperate, intense, mordant, oppressive, overbearing, pitiless, punishing, rigorous, rugged, serious, sharp, sore, strenuous, stringent, taxing, toilsome, tough, tyrannical, unpleasant, unrelenting, violent, weighty, wicked; SEE CONCEPTS 565,569

severely [adv] *harshly*
acutely, badly, critically, dangerously, extremely, firmly, gravely, hard, hardly, intensely, markedly, painfully, rigorously, roughly, seriously, sharply, sorely, sternly, strictly, with an iron hand; SEE CONCEPT 569

sew [v] *prepare fabric for clothing, covering*
baste, bind, embroider, fasten, piece, seam, stitch, tack, tailor, work; SEE CONCEPT 218

sewage [n] *waste*
discharge, excess, excrement, garbage, junk, leavings, rubbish, runoff, slop, trash; SEE CONCEPT 260

sex [n1] *male or female gender*
femininity, manhood, manliness, masculinity, sexuality, womanhood, womanliness; SEE CONCEPT 648

sex [n2] *intercourse between animate beings*
birds and the bees*, coition, coitus, copulation, facts of life*, fornication, generation, intimacy, lovemaking, magnetism, procreation, relations, reproduction, sensuality, sexuality; SEE CONCEPT 375

sex appeal [n] *magnetism*
allure, appeal, attraction, attractiveness, charisma, charm, drawing power, enchantment, glamour, it*, lure, pull, seductiveness; SEE CONCEPTS 411,676

sexism [n] *sex discrimination*
bias, bigotry, chauvinism, inequality, inequity, partiality, prejudice; SEE CONCEPTS 29,689

sexual [adj] *concerning reproduction, intercourse*
animal, animalistic, bestial, carnal, erotic, fleshly, generative, genital, genitive, intimate, loving, passionate, procreative, reproductive, sensual, sharing, venereal, voluptuous, wanton; SEE CONCEPT 372

sexual assault [n] *violation*
date rape, grope, molestation, rape, ravishment, sex crime, sexual abuse; SEE CONCEPTS 192,375

sexual harassment [n] *unwanted sexual advances*
inappropriate behavior, sexual abuse, sexual pressure, suggestive comments, unprofessional behavior, victimization; SEE CONCEPT 246

sexually transmitted disease [n] *STD*
acquired immune deficiency syndrome, AIDS, chancroid, chlamydia, crab louse, crabs, genital herpes, genital warts, gonorrhea, herpes, herpes simplex, HIV, scabies, SIDA, social disease,

syphilis, tabes dorsalis, VD, venereal disease; SEE CONCEPT 306

sexy [adj] *being erotically attractive to another*
arousing, come-hither*, cuddly, flirtatious, hot*, inviting, kissable, libidinous, mature, provocative, provoking, racy, risqué, seductive, sensual, sensuous, slinky*, spicy*, steamy*, suggestive, titillating, voluptuous; SEE CONCEPT 372

shabby [adj1] *broken-down; in poor shape*
bare, bedraggled, crummy, decayed, decaying, decrepit, degenerated, desolate, deteriorated, deteriorating, dilapidated, dingy, disfigured, disreputable, dog-eared*, faded, frayed, gone to seed*, mangy, meager, mean, miserable, moth-eaten, neglected, pitiful, poor, poverty-stricken, ragged, ramshackle, ratty, rickety, ruined, ruinous, rundown, scrubby, scruffy, seedy, shoddy, sleazy, slipshod, squalid, tacky, tattered, threadbare, tired, worn, worn-out, worse for wear*, wretched; SEE CONCEPT 485

shabby [adj2] *despicable*
beggarly, cheap, contemptible, despisable, dirty, disgraceful, dishonorable, disreputable, ignoble, ignominious, inconsiderate, inglorious, low, low-down, mean, mercenary, miserly, rotten, scummy, selfish, shady, shameful, shoddy, sordid, sorry, stingy, thoughtless, unkind, unworthy; SEE CONCEPTS 401,404

shack [n] *shanty*
cabin, camp, cottage, hut, lean-to, shed, shelter, small house, tiny house; SEE CONCEPT 516

shackle [n] *restraint*
bracelet, chain, cuff, electronic ankle bracelet, fetter, handcuff, irons, leg-iron, manacle, rope, trammel; SEE CONCEPTS 130,191,500

shackle [v] *restrain*
bind, chain, confine, cuff, fetter, handcuff, hogtie*, hold, hold captive, manacle, put a straitjacket on*, secure, tie up, trammel; SEE CONCEPTS 130,191

shade [n1] *dimness*
adumbration, blackness, coolness, cover, darkness, dusk, gloominess, obscuration, obscurity, penumbra, screen, semidarkness, shadiness, shadow, shadows, umbra, umbrage; SEE CONCEPT 620

shade [n2] *blind, shield*
awning, canopy, cover, covering, curtain, screen, veil; SEE CONCEPT 445

shade [n3] *color, hue*
brilliance, cast, saturation, stain, tinge, tint, tone; SEE CONCEPTS 620,622

shade [n4] *slight difference*
amount, cast, dash, degree, distinction, gradation, hint, nuance, proposal, semblance, soupçon, spice, streak, suggestion, suspicion, tincture, tinge, trace, variation, variety; SEE CONCEPT 665

shade [n5] *ghost*
apparition, bogey, haunt, manes, phantasm, phantom, revenant, shadow, specter, spirit, umbra, wraith; SEE CONCEPT 370

shade [v] *shut out the light*
adumbrate, be overcast, blacken, cast a shadow, cloud, cloud over, cloud up, conceal, cover, darken, deepen, dim, eclipse, gray, hide, inumbrate, mute, obscure, overshadow, protect, screen, shadow, shelter, shield, shutter, tone down, umbrage, veil; SEE CONCEPTS 250,526

shadow [n1] *darkness*
adumbration, cover, dark, dimness, dusk, gloom,

obscuration, obscurity, penumbra, protection, shade, shelter, umbra, umbrage; SEE CONCEPTS *620,622*

shadow [*n2*] *hint, suggestion*
breath, intimation, memento, relic, smack, suspicion, tincture, tinge, touch, trace, vestige; SEE CONCEPT *278*

shadow [*v1*] *make dark*
adumbrate, becloud, bedim, cast a shadow, cloud, darken, dim, gray, haze, inumbrate, obscure, overcast, overcloud, overhang, overshadow, screen, shade, shelter, shield, umbrage, veil; SEE CONCEPT *250*

shadow [*v2*] *follow secretly*
dog, keep in sight, pursue, spy on, stalk, tag, tail, trail, watch; SEE CONCEPT *207*

shady [*adj1*] *dark, covered*
adumbral, bosky, cloudy, cool, dim, dusky, indistinct, leafy, out of the sun*, screened, shaded, shadowed, shadowy, sheltered, umbrageous, umbrous, under a cloud, vague; SEE CONCEPTS *485,617*

shady [*adj2*] *disreputable, suspicious*
crooked, disgraceful, dishonest, dishonorable, dubious, fishy, ignominious, infamous, inglorious, notorious, questionable, scandalous, shabby, shameful, shifty, shoddy, slippery, suspect, suspicious, underhanded, unethical, unrespectable, unscrupulous, untrustworthy; SEE CONCEPT *545*

shaggy [*adj*] *hairy, unkempt*
furry, hirsute, long-haired, ragged, rough, ruffled, rugged, uncombed, unshorn; SEE CONCEPT *485*

shake [*v1*] *quiver, tremble*
agitate, brandish, bump, chatter, churn, commove, concuss, convulse, discompose, disquiet, disturb, dither, dodder, flap, flicker, flit, flitter, flourish, fluctuate, flutter, jar, jerk, jig, joggle, jolt, jounce, move, oscillate, palpitate, perturb, quail, quake, quaver, rattle, reel, rock, roil, ruffle, set in motion, shimmer, shimmy, shiver, shudder, stagger, stir up, succuss, sway, swing, totter, tremble, tremor, twitter, upset, vibrate, waggle, water, wave, whip, wobble; SEE CONCEPTS *150,152*

shake [*v2*] *upset deeply*
appall, bother, consternate, daunt, discompose, dismay, distress, disturb, frighten, horrify, impair, intimidate, jar, knock props out*, make waves*, move, rattle, throw, throw a curve*, undermine, unnerve, unsettle, unstring, upset, weaken, worry; SEE CONCEPTS *7,19*

shake off [*v*] *lose by getting away*
clear, dislodge, drop, elude, get away from, get rid of, give the slip*, leave behind, remove, rid oneself of, throw off, unburden; SEE CONCEPTS *102,195*

shake up [*v*] *upset, unsettle*
agitate, break with past*, cause revolution*, churn up*, clean out, clean up, clear out, disturb, liquidate, make a clean sweep*, mix, overturn, purge, remove, reorganize, rid, shock, stir up, turn upside down*; SEE CONCEPTS *14,324*

shaky [*adj1*] *trembling*
all aquiver*, aquake, aquiver, ashake, faltering, fluctuant, infirm, insecure, jellylike, jerry-built*, jittery, nervous, not set, precarious, quaking, quivery, rattletrap, rickety, rocky, rootless, shaking, tottering, tottery, trembling, tremorous, tremulous, tumbledown, unfirm, unsettled, un-

sound, unstable, unsteady, unsure, vacillating, wavering, weak, wobbly, yielding; SEE CONCEPT *488*

shaky [*adj2*] *doubtful*
dubious, indecisive, not dependable, not reliable, precarious, problematic, questionable, suspect, uncertain, unclear, undependable, unreliable, unsettled, unsound, unsteady, unsupported, unsure; SEE CONCEPT *535*

shallow [*adj1*] *not deep*
cursory, depthless, empty, flat, hollow, inconsiderable, sand bar, shelf, shoal, slight, superficial, surface, trifling, trivial, unsound; SEE CONCEPTS *737,777*

shallow [*adj2*] *unintelligent, ignorant*
cursory, empty, empty-headed, farcical, featherbrained, flighty, flimsy, foolish, frivolous, frothy, half-baked*, hollow, idle, inane, lightweight, meaningless, paltry, petty, piddling, puerile, simple, sketchy, skin-deep*, slight, superficial, surface, trifling, trivial, uncritical, unthinking, vain, wishy-washy*; SEE CONCEPT *402*

sham [*adj*] *artificial, counterfeit*
adulterated, affected, assumed, bogus*, dummy, ersatz*, fake, false, feigned, fictitious, forged, fraudulent, imitation, lying, make-believe, misleading, mock, phony, plaster*, pretend, pretended, pseudo*, simulated, so-called, spurious, substitute, synthetic, untrue; SEE CONCEPT *582*

sham [*n*] *hoax, trick*
burlesque, cant, caricature, cheat, counterfeit, cover-up, deceit, deception, facade, fake, fakery, false front, farce, feint, flimflam*, forgery, fraud, hypocrisy, hypocriticalness, imitation, impostor, imposture, jive*, mock, mockery, pharisaism, phoniness, pretend, pretense, pretext, pseudo*, put-on, sell, smoke*, snow job*, spoof, travesty, whitewash; SEE CONCEPTS *59,192*

sham [*v*] *trick; pull a hoax*
act, affect, ape, assume, bluff, copy, counterfeit, create, do a number*, fake, fake it, feign, imitate, invent, lie, make like, mislead, mock, play possum*, pretend, put on, put up a front*, shuck and jive*, simulate, sucker*; SEE CONCEPTS *59,111,171*

shaman [*n*] *religious specialist*
healer, medicine man, priest, sorcerer, witch doctor; SEE CONCEPT *361*

shambles [*n*] *a mess*
anarchy, babel, bedlam, botch, chaos, confusion, disarray, disorder, disorganization, hash, havoc, hodge-podge, madhouse, maelstrom, mess-up, mix-up, muddle; SEE CONCEPTS *230,674*

shame [*n*] *disgrace, embarrassment*
abashment, bad conscience*, blot, chagrin, compunction, confusion, contempt, contrition, degradation, derision, discomposure, discredit, disesteem, dishonor, disrepute, guilt, humiliation, ignominy, ill repute, infamy, irritation, loss of face*, mortification, obloquy, odium, opprobrium, pang, pudency, remorse, reproach, scandal, self-disgust, self-reproach, self-reproof, shamefacedness, skeleton in the cupboard*, smear, stigma, stupefaction, treachery; SEE CONCEPTS *388,410*

shame [*v*] *disgrace, embarrass*
abash, blot, confound, cut down to size*, debase, defile, degrade, disconcert, discredit, dishonor, give a black eye*, humble, humiliate, mortify, reproach, ridicule, shoot down*, smear, stain,

se
sh

take down*, take down a peg*; SEE CONCEPTS
7,14,19

shamefaced [*adj*] *embarrassed*
abashed, chagrined, disgraced, guilty, humble,
humbled, humiliated, mortified, regretful,
shamed, sorry; SEE CONCEPT *550*

shameful [*adj*] *atrocious; disreputable*
base, carnal, contemptible, corrupt, dastardly,
debauched, degrading, diabolical, disgraceful,
dishonorable, drunken, embarrassing, flagrant,
heinous, humiliating, ignominious, immodest,
immoral, impure, indecent, infamous, intemperate, lewd, low, mean, mortifying, notorious, obscene, opprobrious, outrageous, profligate,
reprehensible, reprobate, ribald, scandalous,
shaming, shocking, sinful, unbecoming, unclean,
unworthy, vile, villainous, vulgar, wicked; SEE
CONCEPTS *401,545,571*

shameless [*adj*] *corrupt, indecent*
abandoned, arrant, audacious, barefaced, bold,
brash, brassy, brazen, cheeky*, depraved, dissolute, flagrant, forward, hardened, high-
handed*, immodest, immoral, improper,
impudent, incorrigible, insolent, lewd, outrageous, overbold, presumptuous, profligate,
reprobate, rude, unabashed, unashamed, unblushing, unchaste, unprincipled, wanton; SEE
CONCEPTS *401,545*

shanghai [*v*] *kidnap*
abduct, capture, carry away, carry off, grab, hijack, hold for ransom, pirate, run away with,
seize, skyjack, snatch; SEE CONCEPTS *90,139*

Shangri-la [*n*] *utopia*
Arcadia, bliss, Eden, Elysian Fields*, Erehwon*,
Garden of Eden, heaven, paradise, promised
land*, seventh heaven, Xanadu; SEE CONCEPTS
370,689

shanty [*n*] *shack*
cabin, camp, cottage, hut, lean-to, shed, shelter,
small house, tiny house; SEE CONCEPT *516*

shape [*n1*] *form, structure*
appearance, architecture, aspect, body, build,
cast, chassis, circumscription, configuration,
conformation, constitution, construction, contour, cut, embodiment, figure, format, frame,
guise, likeness, lineation, lines, look, make,
metamorphosis, model, mold, outline, pattern,
profile, semblance, shadow, silhouette, simulacrum, stamp, symmetry; SEE CONCEPTS
436,754,757

shape [*n2*] *condition, health*
case, estate, fettle, fitness, kilter, order, repair,
state, trim, whack*; SEE CONCEPTS *316,720*

shape [*v1*] *form, create*
assemble, block out, bring together, build, carve,
cast, chisel, construct, crystallize, cut, embody,
fabricate, fashion, forge, frame, hew, knead,
make, mint, model, mold, pat, pattern, produce,
roughhew, sculpture, sketch, stamp, streamline,
throw together*, trim, whittle; SEE CONCEPTS
137,184

shape [*v2*] *devise, plan*
accommodate, adapt, become, define, develop,
form, frame, grow, guide, modify, prepare, regulate, remodel, tailor, take form, work up; SEE
CONCEPT *36*

shapeless [*adj*] *formless*
abnormal, amorphic, amorphous, anomalous,
assymetrical, baggy, deformed, disfigured, embryonic, ill-formed, inchoate, indefinite, indeterminate, indistinct, invisible, irregular, malformed, misshapen, mutilated, nebulous, undeveloped, unformed, ungraceful, unmade,
unshapely, unstructured, unsymmetrical, vague,
without character, without form; SEE CONCEPTS
486,589

shapely [*adj*] *well-proportioned*
balanced, beautiful, built, comely, curvaceous,
elegant, full-figured, graceful, neat, pleasing,
proportioned, regular, rounded, sightly, statuesque, sylphlike, symmetrical, trim, well-
formed, well-turned; SEE CONCEPTS *406,490*

share [*n*] *portion, allotment*
allowance, apportionment, bite, chunk, claim,
commission, contribution, cut, cut in, cut up, divide, dividend, division, divvy*, dose, drag*,
due, end, fifty-fifty*, fraction, fragment, halver,
helping, heritage, interest, lagniappe, lot, measure, meed, parcel, part, partage, percentage,
piece, pittance, plum, points, proportion, quantum, quota, quotient, quotum, rake-off*, ration,
segment, serving, slice, split, stake, taste,
whack*; SEE CONCEPTS *710,835*

share [*v*] *use in common with others*
accord, administer, allot, apportion, assign, be a
party to, bestow, cut the pie*, deal, dispense, distribute, divide, divide with, divvy*, divvy up*,
dole out, experience, give and take, give out, go
Dutch*, go fifty-fifty*, go halves*, go in with,
have a hand in, have a portion of, mete out, parcel out, part, partake, participate, partition, pay
half, piece up, prorate, quota, ration, receive,
shift, slice, slice up, split, split up, take a part of,
yield; SEE CONCEPTS *98,100,384*

sharp [*adj1*] *knifelike, cutting*
aciculate, acuate, acuminate, acuminous, acute,
apical, barbed, briery, cuspate, cuspidate, edged,
fine, ground fine, honed, horned, jagged, keen,
keen-edged, knife-edged, needlelike, needle-
pointed, peaked, pointed, pointy, prickly,
pronged, razor-sharp, salient, serrated, sharp-
edged, sharpened, spiked, spiky, spiny, splintery,
stinging, tapered, tapering, thorny, tined, tipped,
unblunted, whetted; SEE CONCEPT *486*

sharp [*adj2*] *sudden*
abrupt, distinct, extreme, intense, marked; SEE
CONCEPTS *581,799*

sharp [*adj3*] *perceptive, quick-witted*
acute, adroit, alert, apt, astute, brainy, bright,
brilliant, canny, clever, critical, cute, discerning,
discriminating, fast, foxy*, having smarts*, ingenious, intelligent, keen, knowing, nimble, nobody's fool*, not born yesterday*, observant, on
the ball*, original, penetrating, penetrative,
quick, quick on the trigger*, quick on the uptake*, ready, resourceful, savvy*, sensitive,
slick, smart, smart as a tack*, subtle, wise; SEE
CONCEPT *402*

sharp [*adj4*] *dishonest, deceitful*
artful, bent, crafty, cunning, designing, ornery,
salty, shady, shrewd, slick, slippery, sly, smart,
snaky, two-faced*, underhand, unethical, unscrupulous, wily; SEE CONCEPT *545*

sharp [*adj5*] *severe, intense*
acute, agonizing, biting, cutting, distinct, distressing, drilling, excruciating, fierce, keen,
knifelike, painful, paralyzing, penetrating, piercing, shooting, smart, sore, stabbing, stinging, violent; SEE CONCEPTS *537,569*

sharp [adj6] *distinct, well-defined*
audible, clear, clear-cut, crisp, definite, explicit, obvious, visible; SEE CONCEPT *535*

sharp [adj7] *stylish*
chic, classy, dashing, distinctive, dressy, excellent, fashionable, fine, first-class*, fly*, in style, smart, snappy*, swank*, tony*, trendy; SEE CONCEPT *589*

sharp [adj8] *hurtful, bitter in speech*
acrimonious, angry, barbed, biting, caustic, cutting, double-edged, harsh, incisive, inconsiderate, penetrating, peppery, piercing, pointed, pungent, sarcastic, sardonic, scathing, severe, short, stabbing, stinging, tart, thoughtless, trenchant, unceremonious, ungracious, virulent, vitriolic; SEE CONCEPT *267*

sharp [adj9] *having strong affect on animate senses*
acerbic, acid, acrid, active, astringent, austere, bitter, brisk, burning, harsh, hot, lively, odorous, piquant, pungent, sour, strong-smelling, suffocating, tart, vigorous, vinegary; SEE CONCEPTS *537,598,613*

sharp [adv] *on time*
abruptly, accurately, bang, exactly, just, on the button*, on the dot*, precisely, promptly, punctually, right, smack-dab*, square, squarely, suddenly; SEE CONCEPT *799*

sharpen [v] *make knifelike*
acuminate, dress, edge, file, grind, hone, make acute, make sharp, put an edge on, put a point on, sharp, stroke, strop, taper, whet; SEE CONCEPTS *137,250*

sharp-tongued [adj] *critical*
belittling, biting, carping, censuring, condemning, cursing, cutting, cynical, demeaning, derogatory, harsh, hypercritical, mean, nasty, sarcastic, satirical; SEE CONCEPT *267*

shatter [v1] *break into small pieces*
blast, blight, burst, crack, crash, crunch, crush, dash, demolish, destroy, disable, exhaust, explode, fracture, fragment, fragmentalize, fragmentize, impair, implode, overturn, pulverize, rend, rive, ruin, scrunch, shiver, smash, smash to smithereens*, smatter, snap, splinter, splinterize*, split, torpedo*, total*, wrack up*, wreck; SEE CONCEPTS *246,252*

shatter [v2] *hurt someone badly*
break a heart*, crush, destroy, devastate, dumbfound, rattle, ruin, upset; SEE CONCEPTS *7,19*

shave [v] *cut outer covering off*
barber, brush, clip, crop, cut, cut back, cut down, decorticate, graze, kiss, make bare, pare, peel, plane, prune, shear, shingle, shred, skim, skin, slash, slice thin, sliver, strip, touch, trim; SEE CONCEPTS *137,162,176,202*

shear [v] *clip, cut*
crop, cut back, fleece, groom, mow, pare, prune, shave, shorten, snip, trim; SEE CONCEPTS *137,176*

shed [v] *cast off*
afford, beam, cashier, cast, diffuse, disburden, discard, doff, drop, emit, exude, exuviate, give, give forth, jettison, junk, let fall, molt, pour forth, radiate, reject, scatter, scrap, send forth, shower, slip, slough, spill, sprinkle, take off, throw, throw away, throw out, yield; SEE CONCEPTS *179,180,181,211*

sheen [n] *brightness, shine*
burnish, finish, glaze, gleam, glint, gloss, luster, patina, polish, shimmer, shininess, wax; SEE CONCEPT *620*

sheepish [adj] *shy, embarrassed*
abashed, ashamed, chagrined, diffident, docile, foolish, guilty, mortified, retiring, self-conscious, shamefaced, silly, tame, timid, timorous, uncomfortable; SEE CONCEPT *401*

sheer [adj1] *abrupt, steep*
arduous, erect, headlong, perpendicular, precipitate, precipitous, sideling, upright; SEE CONCEPTS *490,581*

sheer [adj2] *utter, absolute*
altogether, arrant, blasted, blessed, complete, confounded, downright, gross, infernal, out-and-out*, outright, perfect, pure, quite, rank, simple, single, thoroughgoing, total, unadulterated, unalloyed, undiluted, unmitigated, unmixed, unqualified; SEE CONCEPTS *531,535,544*

sheer [adj3] *see-through, thin*
airy, chiffon, clear, cobwebby, delicate, diaphanous, filmy, fine, flimsy, fragile, gauzy, gossamer, lacy, limpid, lucid, pellucid, pure, slight, smooth, soft, tiffany, translucent, transparent; SEE CONCEPT *606*

sheet [n] *coating, covering; page*
area, blanket, coat, expanse, film, foil, folio, lamina, layer, leaf, membrane, overlay, pane, panel, piece, plate, ply, slab, stratum, stretch, surface, sweep, veneer; SEE CONCEPTS *172,270,475,484*

shelf [n] *jutting, flat area or piece*
bank, bracket, console, counter, cupboard, ledge, mantelpiece, mantle, rack, reef, ridge, rock, shallow, shoal; SEE CONCEPTS *445,509,513*

shell [n] *structure; covering*
carapace, case, chassis, crust, frame, framework, hull, husk, integument, nut, pericarp, plastron, pod, scale, shard, shuck, skeleton, skin; SEE CONCEPTS *399,428,484*

shell out [v] *give*
ante up, disburse, expend, fork over*, hand over, lay out, outlay, pay, pay for, pay out, spend; SEE CONCEPT *341*

shelter [n] *protection, habitat*
apartment, asylum, cave, condo, co-op, cover, covert, crib*, defense, den, digs*, dwelling, guard, guardian, harbor, harborage, haven, hermitage, hide, hideaway, hideout, hole in the wall*, home, homeplate*, house, housing, hut, joint*, lodging, pad*, pen, port, preserve, protector, quarterage, rack, refuge, retirement, retreat, roof, roof over head*, roost*, safety, sanctuary, screen, security, shack, shade, shadow, shed, shield, tent, tower, turf, umbrella; SEE CONCEPTS *515,712*

shelter [v] *provide safety, cover*
chamber, conceal, cover, cover up, defend, enclose, guard, harbor, haven, hide, house, lodge, preserve, protect, roof, safeguard, screen, secure, shield, surround, take care of, take in, ward, watch over; SEE CONCEPTS *134,188*

shelve [v] *defer, postpone*
delay, dismiss, drop, freeze*, give up, hang up, hold, hold off, hold over, hold up, lay aside, mothball*, pigeonhole*, prolong, prorogue, put aside, put off, put on back burner*, put on hold, put on ice*, scrub*, sideline, slow up, stay, suspend, table, tie up, waive; SEE CONCEPT *121*

shenanigans [n] *mischief*
antics, capers, dirty trick*, fooling around, frolicsomeness, funny business*, gag, hanky-

sh
sh

panky*, high jinks*, horseplay, horsing around, misbehavior, mischievousness, monkey business*, naughtiness, nonsense, prank, trouble, vandalism; SEE CONCEPTS *192,633,645*

shield [*n*] *protection*
absorber, aegis, armament, armor, buckler, buffer, bulwark, bumper, cover, defense, escutcheon, guard, mail, rampart, safeguard, screen, security, shelter, ward; SEE CONCEPTS *712,729*

shield [*v*] *protect*
bulwark, chamber, conceal, cover, cover all bases*, cover up, defend, fend, give cover, give shelter, go to bat for*, guard, harbor, haven, house, ride shotgun*, roof, safeguard, screen, secure, shelter, shotgun*, stonewall*, take under one's wing*, ward off; SEE CONCEPTS *96,134*

shift [*n1*] *switch, fluctuation*
about-face*, alteration, bend, change, changeover, conversion, deflection, deviation, displacement, double, fault, modification, move, passage, permutation, rearrangement, removal, shifting, substitution, switch, tack, transfer, transference, transformation, transit, translocation, turn, variation, veering, yaw; SEE CONCEPTS *213,697*

shift [*n2*] *trick, stratagem*
artifice, contrivance, craft, device, dodge, equivocation, evasion, expediency, expedient, gambit, hoax, makeshift, maneuver, move, ploy, recourse, refuge, resort, resource, ruse, stopgap*, strategy, substitute, subterfuge, wile; SEE CONCEPTS *59,660*

shift [*n3*] *time served doing work*
bout, go, period, spell, stint, time, tour, trick, turn, working time; SEE CONCEPT *802*

shift [*v*] *switch, fluctuate*
about-face*, alter, blow hot and cold*, bottom out*, budge, change, change gears, cook*, deviate, dial back*, dislocate, displace, disturb, do up*, drift, exchange, fault, flip-flop*, hem and haw*, move, move around, move over, rearrange, recalibrate, relocate, remove, replace, reposition, ship, shuffle, slip, stir, substitute, swap places, swerve, switch over, tack, transfer, transmogrify, transpose, turn, turn around, turn the corner*, turn the tables*, vacillate, vary, veer, waffle, yo-yo*; SEE CONCEPTS *213,232,697*

shiftless [*adj*] *lazy*
apathetic, dallying, directionless, good-for-nothing, idle, inattentive, incompetent, indolent, lackadaisical, laggard, lagging, lethargic, lifeless, loafing, procrastinating, slack, slothful, unambitious, unenergetic, unindustrious, unmotivated; SEE CONCEPTS *401,404*

shifty [*adj*] *deceitful, untrustworthy*
cagey, collusive, conniving, contriving, crafty, crooked, cunning, devious, dishonest, dodging, duplicitous, elusive, equivocating, evasive, fly-by-night*, foxy, fraudulent, furtive, insidious, lying, mendacious, prevaricative, prevaricatory, roguish, scheming, shady, shrewd, shuffling, slick, slimy*, slippery, sly, sneaky, treacherous, tricky, underhand, unhonest, unprincipled, untruthful, wily; SEE CONCEPTS *401,404*

shimmer [*n*] *gleam*
blinking, coruscation, diffused light, flash, glimmer, glint, glisten, glitter, gloss, glow, incandescence, iridescence, luster, phosphorescence,

scintillation, sheen, spangle, spark, sparkle, twinkle; SEE CONCEPTS *620,624*

shimmer [*v*] *glisten*
blaze, coruscate, dance, flare, flash, gleam, glint, glow, jiggle, phosphoresce, scintillate, shimmy, shine, sparkle, twinkle; SEE CONCEPT *624*

shindig [*n*] *party*
affair, ball, banquet, barbecue, bash*, blowout*, celebration, dance, dinner, feast, festivity, function, gala, get-together, reception, shindy, social gathering; SEE CONCEPT *383*

shine [*n*] *brightness; polish*
flash, glare, glaze, gleam, glint, glitz, gloss, lambency, light, luminosity, luster, patina, polish, radiance, rub, sheen, shimmer, show, sparkle; SEE CONCEPT *620*

shine [*v1*] *give off or reflect light*
beam, bedazzle, blaze, blink, burn, dazzle, deflect, emit light, flare, flash, flicker, give light, glare, gleam, glimmer, glisten, glitter, glow, illuminate, illumine, incandesce, irradiate, luminesce, mirror, radiate, scintillate, shimmer, sparkle, twinkle; SEE CONCEPT *624*

shine [*v2*] *polish, burnish*
brush, buff, buff up, finish, furbish, give a sheen, glance, glaze, gloss, make brilliant, put a finish on, put a gloss on, rub, scour, sleek, wax; SEE CONCEPT *202*

shiny [*adj*] *bright, glistening*
agleam, burnished, clear, gleaming, glossy, lustrous, polished, satiny, sheeny, slick, sparkling, sunny; SEE CONCEPT *617*

ship [*v*] *send, transport*
address, consign, direct, dispatch, drop, embark, export, forward, freight, go aboard, haul, move, put on board, remit, route, shift, ship out, smuggle, transfer, transmit; SEE CONCEPTS *148,217*

shipshape [*adj*] *tidy*
businesslike, chipper, clean, in good shape, in tip-top condition, neat, ordered, orderly, spick-and-span*, trim, uncluttered, well-groomed, well-kept; SEE CONCEPTS *485,585,621*

shirk [*v*] *avoid, get out of responsibility*
bypass, cheat, creep, dodge, dog*, duck, elude, eschew, evade, fence, get around, goldbrick*, lie down on job*, lurk, malinger, parry, pussyfoot*, quit, shuffle off, shun, sidestep, skulk, slack, slink, slip, slough off, snake, sneak, steal; SEE CONCEPTS *30,59,681*

shirker [*n*] *slacker*
avoider, bum, deadbeat*, goldbrick, good-for-nothing, goof-off*, idler, loafer, quitter, slouch; SEE CONCEPTS *412,423*

shiver [*v1*] *shake, tremble*
be cold, dither, flutter, freeze, have the quivers, have the shakes, palpitate, quake, quaver, quiver, shudder, tremor, twitter, vibrate, wave; SEE CONCEPTS *152,185*

shiver [*v2*] *shatter; break into small pieces*
burst, crack, fragment, fragmentalize, pash, rive, smash, smash to smithereens*, smatter, splinter, splinterize*; SEE CONCEPTS *246,252*

shock [*n*] *complete surprise; blow*
awe, bombshell*, breakdown, bump, clash, collapse, collision, concussion, confusion, consternation, crash, distress, disturbance, double whammy*, earthquake, encounter, excitement, eye-opener*, hysteria, impact, injury, jarring, jolt, percussion, prostration, ram, scare, start, stroke, stupefaction, stupor, trauma, traumatism,

turn, upset, whammy*, wreck; SEE CONCEPTS *33,309,529*

shock [*v*] *completely surprise*
abash, agitate, anger, antagonize, appall, astound, awe, bowl over*, daze, disgust, dismay, displease, disquiet, disturb, electrify, flabbergast, flood, floor*, give a turn*, hit like ton of bricks*, horrify, insult, jar, jolt, knock out*, nauseate, numb, offend, outrage, overcome, overwhelm, paralyze, revolt, rock, scandalize, shake, shake up, sicken, stagger, startle, stun, stupefy, throw a curve*, traumatize, unsettle; SEE CONCEPT *42*

shocking [*adj*] *outrageous; very surprising*
abominable, appalling, atrocious, awful, burning, crying, desperate, detestable, direful, disgraceful, disgusting, disquieting, distressing, dreadful, fearful, formidable, foul, frightful, ghastly, glaring, hateful, heinous, hideous, horrible, horrific, horrifying, loathsome, monstrous, nauseating, odious, offensive, repulsive, revolting, scandalous, shameful, sickening, stupefying, terrible, ugly, unspeakable; SEE CONCEPTS *548,571*

shoddy [*adj*] *in bad shape*
base, broken-down, cheap, cheesy*, common, dilapidated, dingy, discreditable, disgraceful, dishonorable, disreputable, gaudy, ignominious, inferior, inglorious, junky, makeshift, mean, not up to snuff*, paltry, plastic, poor, pretentious, run-down, scruffy*, second-rate*, seedy, shabby, shady, shameful, sleazy*, slipshod, tacky*, tawdry, trashy, unrespectable; SEE CONCEPTS *485,571*

shoe [*n*] *footwear*
basketball shoe, boat shoe, boot, cleat, clog, cowboy boot, flip-flops*, footgear, golf shoe, high heels, hightops*, loafer, moccasin, penny loafer, platform shoe, pump, running shoe, sandals, slipper, sneaker, tennis shoe, wing-tip, work shoe; SEE CONCEPT *451*

shoot [*v1*] *discharge a projectile, often to injure or kill*
bag*, barrage, blast, bombard, bring down, catapult, dispatch, drop the hammer*, emit, execute, expel, explode, fire, fling, gun, hit, hurl, ignite, kill, launch, let fly, let go with, loose, murder, open fire*, open up*, pick off*, plug, pop*, project, propel, pull the trigger, pump*, set off, throw lead*, torpedo, trigger, zap*; SEE CONCEPTS *179,246,252*

shoot [*v2*] *dash*
boil, bolt, charge, chase, dart, flash, fling, fly, gallop, hotfoot*, hurry, hurtle, lash, pass, race, reach, run, rush, scoot, skirr, speed, spring, spurt, streak, tear, whisk, whiz; SEE CONCEPTS *150,152*

shoot the breeze [*v*] *chat, converse*
BS*, chatter, chew the fat*, gab*, palaver, prate, prattle*, run off at the mouth*, schmooze*, shoot the bull*, yack*, yap*; SEE CONCEPT *266*

shop [*n*] *place of retail business*
boutique, chain, deli, department store, emporium, five-and-dime, market, mill, outlet, showroom, stand, store, supermarket; SEE CONCEPTS *439,441,448,449*

shop [*v*] *look for merchandise to buy*
buy, go shopping, hunt for, look for, market, purchase, try to buy; SEE CONCEPTS *327,330*

shopkeeper [*n*] *merchant*
businessperson, dealer, entrepreneur, proprietor, retailer, salesperson, seller, storekeeper, store owner, vendor, wholesaler; SEE CONCEPT *347*

shoplift [*v*] *steal*
burglarize, carry off, defraud, embezzle, heist, hold up, lift*, loot, make off with*, pilfer, pillage, pinch*, rip off*, run off with*, snatch*, stick up*, swipe, take, walk off with*; SEE CONCEPT *139*

shopper [*n*] *customer*
browser, buyer, client, clientele, consumer, patron, prospect, purchaser, window-shopper; SEE CONCEPT *348*

shopping [*n*] *buying*
browsing, e-commerce, electronic commerce, purchasing, spending; SEE CONCEPT *327*

shore [*n*] *waterside*
bank, beach, border, brim, brink, coast, coastland, embankment, lakeshore, lakeside, littoral, margin, river bank, riverside, sand, sands, seaboard, seacoast, seashore, shingle, strand, waterfront; SEE CONCEPT *509*

shore [*v*] *reinforce*
bear up, bolster, brace, bulwark, buttress, carry, hold, prop, strengthen, support, sustain, underpin, upbear, uphold; SEE CONCEPTS *110,190*

short [*adj1*] *abridged*
abbreviate, abbreviated, aphoristic, bare, boiled down, breviloquent, brief, compendiary, compendious, compressed, concise, condensed, curtailed, curtate, cut short, cut to the bone*, decreased, decurtate, diminished, epigrammatic, fleeting, in a nutshell*, laconic, lessened, little, momentary, not protracted, pithy, pointed, precise, sententious, short and sweet*, shortened, short-lived, short-term, succinct, summarized, summary, terse, undersized, unprolonged, unsustained; SEE CONCEPTS *267,272,798*

short [*adj2*] *not tall*
abbreviated, chunky, close to the ground, compact, diminutive, little, low, not long, petite, pint-sized*, pocket, pocket-sized*, runty, sawed-off*, skimpy, slight, small, squat, squatty, stocky, stubby, stunted, thick, thickset, tiny, undersized, wee; SEE CONCEPTS *773,779,782*

short [*adj3*] *insufficient*
deficient, exiguous, failing, inadequate, lacking, limited, low on, meager, needing, niggardly, poor, scant, scanty, scarce, short-handed*, shy, skimpy, slender, slim, sparse, tight, wanting; SEE CONCEPTS *527,560,762*

short [*adj4*] *abrupt, discourteous*
bad-tempered, blunt, breviloquent, brief, brusque, curt, direct, gruff, impolite, inconsiderate, irascible, offhand, rude, sharp, short-spoken, short-tempered, snappy*, snippety*, snippy*, straight, terse, testy, thoughtless, unceremonious, uncivil, ungracious; SEE CONCEPTS *267,401*

short [*adj5*] *crumbly*
brittle, crisp, crunchy, delicate, fragile, friable; SEE CONCEPT *462*

short [*adv*] *abruptly*
aback, by surprise, forthwith, sudden, suddenly, unanticipatedly, unaware, unawares, unexpectedly, without delay, without hesitation, without warning; SEE CONCEPT *799*

shortage [*n*] *deficiency*
curtailment, dearth, defalcation, deficit, failure, inadequacy, insufficiency, lack, lapse, leanness, paucity, pinch, poverty, scantiness, scarcity, shortfall, tightness, underage, want, weakness; SEE CONCEPTS *646,709,767*

sh
sh

shortchange [*v*] *cheat*
bamboozle*, bilk, deceive, defraud, double-deal, dupe, finagle, fleece, flimflam, gyp*, hose, mislead, rip off*, rook*, sandbag, scam, screw, shaft, stiff, swindle, take, trick; SEE CONCEPTS *59,139,192*

shortcoming [*n*] *weak point*
bug*, catch*, defect, deficiency, demerit, drawback, failing, fault, flaw, frailty, imperfection, infirmity, lack, lapse, sin, weakness; SEE CONCEPTS *411,666,674,679*

shorten [*v*] *diminish, decrease*
abbreviate, abridge, blue pencil*, bob, boil down*, chop, clip, compress, condense, contract, curtail, cut, cut back, cut down, cut to the bone*, dock, edit, elide, excerpt, lessen, lop, make a long story short*, minimize, put in a nutshell*, reduce, retrench, shrink, slash, snip, trim; SEE CONCEPTS *137,236,240,247*

shortfall [*n*] *deficit; imperfection*
arrears, default, defectiveness, deficiency, flaw, inadequacy, incompleteness, insufficiency, insufficiency, in the hole*, in the red, lack, loss, red ink*, shortage, shortcoming, underage; SEE CONCEPTS *230,335,646,671,718*

short-lived [*adj*] *temporary*
brief, ephemeral, evanescent, fleeting, fugacious, fugitive, impermanent, momentary, passing, short, short-haul*, short-run, short-term, transient, transitory; SEE CONCEPT *798*

shortly [*adv*] *right away*
anon, any minute now, before long, by and by, in a little while, presently, proximately, quickly, soon; SEE CONCEPT *820*

short-sighted [*adj*] *unmindful of future consequences*
astigmatic, blind, careless, foolish, headlong, ill-advised, ill-considered, imperceptive, impolitic, impractical, improvident, imprudent, injudicious, myopic, near-sighted, rash, stupid, unsagacious, unwary; SEE CONCEPTS *401,542*

shot [*n1*] *try, chance*
attempt, break, conjecture, effort, endeavor, fling*, go*, guess, occasion, opening, opportunity, pop*, show, slap*, stab*, surmise, time, turn, whack*, whirl*; SEE CONCEPT *693*

shot [*n2*] *discharge; ammunition*
ball, buckshot, bullet, dart, lead, lob, missile, pellet, projectile, slug, throw; SEE CONCEPT *498*

shoulder [*v1*] *be responsible for*
accept, assume, bear, carry, take on, take upon oneself; SEE CONCEPT *23*

shoulder [*v2*] *push, jostle*
bulldoze*, elbow, hustle, nudge, press, push aside, shove, thrust; SEE CONCEPT *208*

shout [*n*] *loud outcry*
bark, bawl, bellow, call, cheer, clamor, cry, howl, hue, roar, salvo, scream, screech, shriek, squall, squawk, tumult, vociferation, whoop*, yammer*, yap*, yawp*, yell; SEE CONCEPTS *77,595*

shout [*v*] *cry out loudly*
bawl, bay, bellow, call out, cheer, clamor, exclaim, holler*, raise voice, roar, scream, screech, shriek, squall, squawk, vociferate, whoop*, yammer*, yap*, yawp*, yell; SEE CONCEPT *77*

shove [*v*] *push without gentleness*
boost, buck, bulldoze*, cram, crowd, dig, drive, elbow, hustle, impel, jab, jam, jostle, nudge,

poke, press, prod, propel, shoulder, thrust; SEE CONCEPT *208*

shove off [*v*] *leave quickly*
blow, clear out, depart, exit, get off, go, go away, pull out, push off, quit, run along, start out, take off, vamoose*; SEE CONCEPT *195*

show [*n1*] *demonstration, exhibition*
appearance, array, display, expo*, exposition, fair, fanfare, fireworks, grandstand, manifestation, occurrence, pageant, pageantry, panoply, parade, pomp, presentation, program, representation, shine*, showboat*, showing, sight, spectacle, splash*, view; SEE CONCEPT *261*

show [*n2*] *entertainment event*
act, appearance, burlesque, carnival, cinema, comedy, drama, entertainment, film, flick*, motion picture, movie, pageant, picture, play, presentation, production, showing, spectacle; SEE CONCEPTS *263,293*

show [*n3*] *false front; appearance given*
affectation, air, display, effect, face*, front, grandstand play*, guise, illusion, impression, likeness, make-believe*, ostentation, parade, pose, pretense, pretext, profession, seeming, semblance, sham, shine*, showboat*, showing, simulacrum, splash*; SEE CONCEPTS *633,716*

show [*v1*] *actively exhibit something*
afford, air, arrive, attend, bare, blazon, brandish, deal in, demonstrate, display, disport, exhibit, expose, flash, flaunt, flourish, lay bare, lay out, mount, offer, parade, present, produce, proffer, put on, reveal, sell, set out, showcase, show off, sport, spread, stage, streak, submit, supply, trot out, unfold, unfurl, unveil, vaunt, wave; SEE CONCEPT *138*

show [*v2*] *passively exhibit something*
appear, arrive, assert, be visible, blow in, clarify, come, demonstrate, determine, disclose, discover, display, divulge, elucidate, emerge, establish, evidence, evince, explain, get, get in, illustrate, indicate, instruct, lay out, loom, make known, make out, make the scene*, manifest, mark, materialize, note, ostend, point, present, proclaim, project, prove, put in appearance, reach, register, reveal, show one's face*, show up, teach, testify to, turn up, unveil; SEE CONCEPT *261*

show [*v3*] *grant*
accord, act with, bestow, confer, dispense, give; SEE CONCEPT *108*

show [*v4*] *accompany*
attend, conduct, direct, escort, guide, lead, pilot, route, see, shepherd, steer; SEE CONCEPTS *187,384*

show business [*n*] *entertainment industry*
Broadway, Hollywood, motion picture industry, movie industry, show biz, the stage, the theater; SEE CONCEPTS *383,384,386,388*

showdown [*n*] *confrontation*
breaking point, clash, climax, crisis, culmination, exposé, moment of truth, unfolding; SEE CONCEPTS *388,674*

shower [*n*] *precipitation*
cloudburst, deluge, downpour, drizzle, flood, hail, rain, rainstorm, sleet, storm, thunderstorm; SEE CONCEPTS *467,524,526*

shower [*v1*] *rain*
come down in buckets*, downpour, drench, drizzle, fall, hail, mist, patter, pour, sleet, spray, sprinkle, storm; SEE CONCEPT *526*

shower [v2] *lavish*
be generous, deluge, give, pamper; SEE CONCEPTS *110,327,341*

showoff [n] *person who brags about him-or herself*
boaster, braggadocio, braggart, egotist, exhibitionist, swaggerer, vulgarian; SEE CONCEPT *412*

show off [v] *flaunt; brag*
advertise, boast, brandish, demonstrate, display, disport, exhibit, expose, flash*, hand a line*, make a spectacle of, parade, spread out, swagger, trot out*; SEE CONCEPTS *49,261*

showpiece [n] *exhibit*
display, masterpiece, model, work of art; SEE CONCEPTS *259,261*

show up [v1] *arrive, attend*
appear, be conspicuous, be visible, blow in*, come, get, get in, make an appearance, put in appearance, reach, show, stand out, turn up; SEE CONCEPT *159*

show up [v2] *expose, embarrass*
belittle, convict, debunk, defeat, discover, discredit, highlight, invalidate, lay bare, let down, mortify, pinpoint, put spotlight on*, put to shame*, reveal, shame, show in bad light*, uncloak, undress, unmask, unshroud, worst; SEE CONCEPTS *54,60*

showy [adj] *flamboyant, flashy*
classy, dashing, flash, garish, gaudy, glaring, histrionic, jazzy*, loud, luxurious, meretricious, opulent, ornate, ostentatious, overdone, overwrought, peacocky, pompous, pretentious, resplendent, screaming, sensational, snazzy*, splashy, splendiferous, sumptuous, swank*, tawdry, tinsel*, tony*; SEE CONCEPT *589*

shred [n] *tiny piece*
atom, bit, cantlet, crumb, fragment, grain, iota, jot, modicum, ounce, part, particle, rag, ray, ribbon, scintilla, scrap, shadow, sliver, smidgen, snippet, speck, stitch, tatter, trace, whit; SEE CONCEPT *831*

shred [v] *cut into ribbons*
cut, fray, frazzle, make ragged, reduce, shave, sliver, strip, tatter, tear; SEE CONCEPT *176*

shrewd [adj] *clever, intelligent*
acute, argute, artful, astucious, astute, brainy*, cagey, calculating, canny, crafty, cunning, cutting*, deep*, discerning, discriminating, farsighted, foxy*, heady*, ingenious, inside, in the know*, judicious, keen, knowing, on the inside*, on top of*, penetrating, perceptive, perspicacious, piercing, probing, profound, prudent, quick-witted, sagacious, savvy*, sensible, shark, sharp, slick*, slippery*, sly, smart, smooth, streetwise, tricky, underhand, up on*, wily, wise, wised up*; SEE CONCEPTS *401,402*

shriek [n/v] *high-pitched scream*
blare, cry, howl, screech, shout, shrill, squawk, squeal, wail, whoop, yell; SEE CONCEPTS *77,595*

shrill [adj] *high-pitched, harsh in sound*
acute, argute, blaring, blatant, cacophonous, clanging, clangorous, deafening, discordant, earpiercing, ear-splitting, high, metallic, noisy, penetrating, piercing, piping, raucous, screeching, sharp, strident, thin, treble; SEE CONCEPTS *592,594*

shrine [n] *tribute to a god, idol, or spirit*
altar, chapel, church, enshrinement, grave, hallowed place, holy place, mausoleum, reliquary, sacred place, sanctorium, sanctuary, sanctum, sepulcher, temple; SEE CONCEPTS *368,439,448*

shrink [v1] *become smaller*
compress, concentrate, condense, constrict, contract, decrease, deflate, diminish, drop off, dwindle, fail, fall off, fall short, grow smaller, lessen, narrow, reduce, shorten, shrivel, wane, waste, waste away, weaken, wither, wrinkle; SEE CONCEPTS *137,698,776*

shrink [v2] *recoil, shy away*
blench, boggle, contract, cower, cringe, crouch, demur, draw back, flinch, hang back, huddle, quail, recede, refuse, retire, retreat, scruple, shudder, slink, wince, withdraw; SEE CONCEPTS *188,195*

shrivel [v] *dehydrate, dry up*
burn, contract, desiccate, dwindle, fossilize, mummify, mummy, parch, scorch, sear, shrink, stale, welter, wilt, wither, wizen, wrinkle; SEE CONCEPTS *137,250,255*

shudder [v] *shake, quiver*
convulse, dither, gyrate, jitter, quake, shimmy, shiver, tremble, tremor, twitter, wave; SEE CONCEPTS *34,150,152*

shuffle [v1] *move along lazily*
drag, limp, muddle, pad, scrape, scuff, scuffle, shamble, straggle, stumble, trail; SEE CONCEPT *151*

shuffle [v2] *rearrange, mix up*
break the deck*, change, change the order, confuse, disarrange, disarray, discompose, dislocate, disorder, disorganize, disrupt, disturb, intermix, jumble, mess up*, shift; SEE CONCEPTS *158,363*

shun [v] *avoid, ignore*
bilk, cold-shoulder*, cut, decline, despise, disdain, ditch*, dodge, double, duck, elude, escape, eschew, evade, get around, give a wide berth*, give the runaround*, have no part of*, have nothing to do with*, hide out, keep away from, keep clear of, neglect, palm off*, pass up, refuse, reject, scorn, shake, shake off, shy, snub, stall, stand aloof from, stay shy of, steer clear of*, turn back on*; SEE CONCEPTS *30,384*

shut [v] *close*
bar, batten down*, cage, close down, close up, confine, draw, drop the curtain*, enclose, exclude, fasten, fold, fold up, imprison, lock, push, put to, seal, secure, shut down, slam, wall off; SEE CONCEPTS *85,121,160,206,208,324*

shut off/shut out [v] *exclude; screen*
bar, beleaguer, blockade, block out, close, conceal, cover, debar, discontinue, evict, fence off, hide, keep out, lock out, mask, obstruct, ostracize, refuse, seclude, shroud, veil; SEE CONCEPTS *25,121,188*

shuttle [n] *space shuttle*
airplane, plane, shuttle bus, spacecraft, spaceport, train, transporter; SEE CONCEPT *504*

shuttle [v] *travel back and forth*
commute, drive back and forth, go back and forth, transport to and fro, travel; SEE CONCEPT *224*

shut up [v] *be or make quiet*
bottle up*, choke, dry up*, dummy up*, fall silent, gag, hold tongue*, hush, keep trap shut*, muzzle, pipe down*, quiet, quieten, quit chattering, shush*, silence, soft-pedal*, still, stop talking; SEE CONCEPT *77*

shy [adj1] *quiet and self-conscious*
afraid, apprehensive, averse, backward, bashful,

cautious, chary, circumspect, conscious, coy, demure, diffident, disinclined, distrustful, fearful, hesitant, humble, introvert, introverted, loath, loner, modest, nervous, recessive, reluctant, reserved, reticent, retiring, self-effacing, shamefaced, sheepish, shrinking, skittish, suspicious, timid, unassertive, unassured, uneager, uneffusive, unresponsive, unsocial, unwilling, wary; SEE CONCEPTS *401,404*

shy [*adj2*] *lacking, failing*
deficient, inadequate, insufficient, scant, scanty, scarce, short, unsufficient, wanting; SEE CONCEPTS *546,762,789*

shyster [*n*] *unscrupulous lawyer; swindler*
ambulance chaser, cheater, chiseler, crooked lawyer, mouthpiece*, pettifogger, scammer, trickster, unethical lawyer; SEE CONCEPT *412*

sick [*adj1*] *not healthy, not feeling well*
ailing, bedridden, broken down, confined, debilitated, declining, defective, delicate, diseased, disordered, down, feeble, feverish, frail, funny*, green*, hospitalized, ill, impaired, imperfect, in a bad way*, incurable, indisposed, infected, infirm, in poor health, invalid, laid-up, lousy, mean, nauseated, not so hot*, peaked, poorly, qualmish, queasy, rickety, rocky, rotten, run down, sick as a dog*, suffering, tottering, under medication, under the weather*, unhealthy, unwell, weak, wobbly; SEE CONCEPT *314*

sick [*adj2*] *morbid, gross*
black, ghoulish, macabre, morose, sadistic, sickly; SEE CONCEPTS *537,571*

sick [*adj3*] *fed up, displeased*
blasé, bored, disgusted, jaded, revolted, satiated, tired, up to here with*, weary; SEE CONCEPT *403*

sicken [*v*] *revolt, make ill*
affect, afflict, derange, disgust, disorder, gross out*, nauseate, offend, reluct, repel, repulse, turn, turn one's stomach*, unhinge, unsettle, upset; SEE CONCEPTS *14,246*

sickening [*adj*] *disgusting, awful*
diseased, distasteful, foul, gross*, icky*, loathsome, nasty, nauseating, nauseous, noisome, offensive, putrid, repugnant, repulsive, revolting, rotten, stinking, stomach-turning, tainted; SEE CONCEPTS *529,571*

sickly [*adj1*] *not healthy*
ailing, below par, bilious, cranky, delicate, diseased, down, dragging, faint, feeble, indisposed, infirm, in poor health, lackluster, laid-low, languid, low, mean, off-color*, out of action*, out of shape*, pallid, peaked, peaky, pining, poorly, rocky, run-down, seedy, sickish, unhealthy, wan, weak; SEE CONCEPT *314*

sickly [*adj2*] *revolting*
bilious, cloying, insalubrious, mawkish, morbid, morose, nauseating, noisome, noxious, sick, unwholesome; SEE CONCEPTS *537,571*

sickness [*n*] *ill or abnormal condition*
affection, affliction, ailment, bug*, complaint, condition, disease, diseasedness, disorder, ill, ill health, illness, indisposition, infirmity, malady, nausea, queasiness, syndrome, unhealth, unhealthfulness, unwellness; SEE CONCEPT *306*

side [*adj*] *minor; flanking*
ancillary, incidental, indirect, lateral, lesser, marginal, not the main, oblique, off-center, postern, roundabout, secondary, sidelong, sideward, sideways, sidewise, skirting, subordinate, subsidiary, superficial; SEE CONCEPT *575*

side [*n1*] *edge, exteriority of object*
aspect, attitude, border, bottom, boundary, direction, disposition, division, elevation, face, facet, flank, front, hand, haunch, jamb, lee, limit, loin, margin, part, perimeter, periphery, posture, quarter, rear, rim, sector, stance, stand, surface, top, verge, view, wing; SEE CONCEPTS *513,835*

side [*n2*] *point of view*
angle, appearance, aspect, belief, direction, facet, hand, light, opinion, outlook, phase, position, slant, stand, standpoint, viewpoint; SEE CONCEPT *689*

side [*n3*] *opposing person or view*
behalf, belligerent, camp, cause, combatant, competition, contestant, crew, enemy, faction, foe, interest, part, party, rival, sect, team; SEE CONCEPTS *301,365*

sidekick [*n*] *companion*
accompaniment, accomplice, aide, ally, amigo, assistant, associate, buddy, chum, cohort, colleague, comrade, consort, coworker, crony, friend, pal, partner, playmate; SEE CONCEPT *423*

sidesplitting [*adj*] *extremely funny*
amusing, entertaining, farcical, good-humored, hilarious, hysterical, joking, knee-slapper*, silly, slapstick, uproarious, witty; SEE CONCEPTS *267,529,537*

sidestep [*v*] *dodge*
avoid, bypass, dance around*, ditch, duck, elude, escape, evade, fudge*, get around, get out of, give the slip*, go around, juke, pussyfoot*, put the move on*, shake, shake off*, shirk, skip out on*, skirt, weasel*; SEE CONCEPTS *59,102*

sidetrack [*v*] *divert*
alter, avert, change, deflect, digress, redirect, swerve, switch, veer; SEE CONCEPTS *187,213*

sideways [*adv*] *to the edge, exteriority*
alongside, aside, aslant, aslope, athwart, broadside, crabwise, edgeways, indirectly, laterally, obliquely, side by side, sidelong, sidewards, slanting, slantingly, slantwise, sloping, to the side; SEE CONCEPTS *581,583*

sift [*v*] *take out residue; remove impurities*
analyze, clean, colander, comb, delve into, dig into, drain, evaluate, examine, explore, fathom, filter, go into, go through, grade, inquire, investigate, look into, pan, part, pore over, probe, prospect, purify, riddle, screen, scrutinize, search, separate, sieve, size, sort, strain, winnow; SEE CONCEPTS *103,165*

sigh [*v1*] *breathe out heavily*
blow, complain, cry, exhale, gasp, grieve, groan, howl, lament, moan, murmur, pant, respire, roar, sob, sorrow, sough, suspire, wheeze, whine, whisper, whistle; SEE CONCEPT *163*

sigh [*v2*] *long for*
ache, crave, dream, hanker, hunger, languish, lust, mourn, pine, suspire, thirst, yearn; SEE CONCEPT *20*

sight [*n1*] *ability to perceive with eyes*
afterimage, appearance, apperception, apprehension, eye, eyes, eyeshot, eyesight, field of vision, ken, perception, range of vision, seeing, view, viewing, visibility, vision; SEE CONCEPT *629*

sight [*n2*] *spectacle*
display, exhibit, exhibition, outlook, pageant, parade, point of interest, scene, show, view, vista; SEE CONCEPTS *261,293*

sight [*n3*] *horrifying person or thing*
blot, eyesore, fright, mess, monstrosity, ogre,

ogress, scarecrow, slob, spectacle, tramp; SEE CONCEPTS *412,513*

sight [*v*] *see*
behold, discern, distinguish, eyeball*, make out*, observe, perceive, spot, view, witness; SEE CONCEPT *626*

sign [*n1*] *indication, evidence*
assurance, augury, auspice, badge, beacon, bell, caution, clue, divination, flag, flash, foreboding, foreknowledge, foreshadowing, foretoken, forewarning, gesture, giveaway, handwriting on wall*, harbinger, herald, high sign*, hint, light, manifestation, mark, nod, note, omen, portent, precursor, prediction, premonition, presage, presentiment, prognostic, proof, signal, suggestion, symbol, symptom, token, trace, vestige, warning, wave, whistle, wink; SEE CONCEPTS *274,529,673,689*

sign [*n2*] *document with information; symbol*
badge, board, character, cipher, crest, device, emblem, ensign, guidepost, insignia, logo, mark, notice, placard, proof, representation, signboard, signpost, symbolization, token, type, warning; SEE CONCEPTS *271,284*

sign [*v1*] *write name*
acknowledge, authorize, autograph, confirm, endorse, initial, ink, inscribe, put John Hancock on*, put John Henry on*, rubber-stamp*, set one's hand to*, signature, subscribe, witness; SEE CONCEPT *79*

sign [*v2*] *motion to another*
beckon, express, flag, gesticulate, gesture, indicate, motion, signal, signalize, signify, use sign language, wave; SEE CONCEPT *74*

signal [*adj*] *extraordinary, outstanding*
arresting, arrestive, characteristic, conspicuous, distinctive, distinguished, eminent, exceptional, eye-catching, famous, illustrious, individual, marked, memorable, momentous, notable, noteworthy, noticeable, peculiar, prominent, pronounced, remarkable, renowned, salient, significant, striking; SEE CONCEPTS *568,574*

signal [*n*] *indication; authorization*
alarm, alert, beacon, bleep, blinker, cue, flag, flare, gesture, go-ahead*, green light*, high sign*, indicator, mark, Mayday*, movement, nod, okay*, omen, sign, SOS*, tocsin, token, wink; SEE CONCEPTS *74,284,529,685*

signal [*v*] *indicate; give a sign to*
beckon, communicate, flag, flash, gesticulate, gesture, motion, nod, semaphore, sign, signalize, warn, wave, wink; SEE CONCEPT *74*

significance [*n1*] *meaning*
acceptation, bottom line*, connotation, drift, force, heart, implication, import, intendment, kicker*, meat*, message, name of the game*, nature of the beast*, nitty-gritty*, nub, nuts and bolts*, point, punch line*, purport, score, sense, significancy, signification, stuff, understanding; SEE CONCEPT *682*

significance [*n2*] *importance*
authority, consequence, consideration, credit, excellence, gravity, import, impressiveness, influence, magnitude, matter, merit, moment, momentousness, perfection, pith, prestige, relevance, signification, virtue, weight, weightiness; SEE CONCEPT *668*

significant [*adj1*] *telling, meaningful*
cogent, compelling, convincing, denoting, eloquent, expressing, expressive, facund, forceful,

heavy, important, indicative, knowing, meaning, momentous, powerful, pregnant, representative, rich, sententious, serious, sound, suggestive, symbolic, valid, weighty; SEE CONCEPTS *267,567*

significant [*adj2*] *important, critical*
big, carrying a lot of weight*, consequential, considerable, heavy, material, meaningful, momentous, notable, noteworthy, serious, substantial, vital, weighty; SEE CONCEPT *568*

signify [*v1*] *mean, indicate*
add up to, announce, bear, be a sign of, bespeak, betoken, carry, communicate, connote, convey, denote, disclose, evidence, evince, exhibit, express, flash, imply, import, insinuate, intend, intimate, manifest, matter, portend, proclaim, purport, represent, show, sign, spell, stand for, suggest, symbolize, talk, tell, wink; SEE CONCEPTS *55,266,682*

signify [*v2*] *be of importance*
be of consequence, be of significance, carry weight, count, import, matter, mean, weigh; SEE CONCEPT *668*

silence [*n*] *absence of sound, speech*
blackout, calm, censorship, dead air, death, dumbness, hush, hush-hush*, inarticulateness, iron curtain*, laconism, lull, muteness, noiselessness, peace, quiescence, quiet, quietness, quietude, quietus, reserve, reticence, saturninity, secrecy, sleep, speechlessness, still, stillness, sulk, sullenness, taciturnity, uncommunicativeness; SEE CONCEPT *65*

silence [*v*] *make or be quiet*
choke off*, clam, clam up*, close up, cool it*, cut off, cut short, dampen, deaden, decrease the volume, dry up*, dull, dumb, dummy up*, extinguish, gag, hold one's tongue*, hush, hush-hush*, hush one's mouth*, keep it down*, lull, muffle, mute, muzzle, overawe, pipe down*, quash, quell, quiet, quiet down, quieten, say nothing, shush*, shut up, sit on*, soft-pedal*, squelch, stifle, still, strike dumb*, subdue, suppress, tongue-tie*; SEE CONCEPT *266*

silent [*adj1*] *quiet; speechless*
bashful, buttoned up*, checked, clammed up*, close, closed up, closemouthed, curbed, dumb, dummied up*, faint, hush, hushed, iced*, inarticulate, incoherent, inconversable, indistinct, inhibited, laconic, mousy, mum, mute, muted, noiseless, nonvocal, not talkative, reserved, restrained, reticent, shy, silentious, soundless, still, struck dumb, taciturn, tongue-tied, unclear, uncommunicative, unheard, unsociable, unspeaking, voiceless, wordless, zipped*; SEE CONCEPT *594*

silent [*adj2*] *understood, implied*
aphonic, implicit, indescribable, inexpressible, nameless, tacit, unexpressed, unpronounced, unspoken, unuttered, unvoiced, wordless; SEE CONCEPT *267*

silhouette [*n*] *outline*
contour, delineation, etching, figuration, form, likeness, line, lineament, lineation, portrait, profile, shade, shadow, shape; SEE CONCEPTS *259,625*

silky [*adj*] *very smooth; like satin*
cottony, delicate, glossy, like silk, luxurious, plush, satiny, silk, silken, sleek, soft, tender, velvety; SEE CONCEPT *606*

silly [*adj*] *absurd, giddy, foolish*
asinine, balmy, brainless, childish, crazy, dippy*,

sh
si

dizzy*, empty, empty-headed*, fatuous, feather-brained*, flighty, foolhardy, frivolous, hare-brained*, idiotic, ignorant, illogical, immature, imprudent, inane, inappropriate, inconsistent, ir-rational, irresponsible, ludicrous, meaningless, muddle-headed*, nitwitted, nonsensical, point-less, preposterous, puerile, ridiculous, senseless, sheepheaded*, simple, simpleminded, stupid, un-intelligent, unreasonable, unwise, vacuous, wit-less; SEE CONCEPTS *401,403,542*

silver [*adj*] *shiny gray in color*
argent, argentate, bright, lustrous, pale, pearly, plated, resplendent, silvered, silvery, sterling, white; SEE CONCEPT *618*

similar [*adj*] *very much alike*
agnate, akin, allied, analogous, coincident, coin-cidental, coinciding, collateral, companion, com-parable, complementary, congruent, congruous, consonant, consubstantial, correlative, corre-sponding, homogeneous, identical, in agreement, kin, kindred, like, matching, much the same, par-allel, reciprocal, related, resembling, same, twin, uniform; SEE CONCEPTS *487,573*

similarity [*n*] *likeness, correspondence*
affinity, agreement, alikeness, analogy, approxi-mation, association, closeness, coincidence, col-lation, community, comparability, comparison, concordance, concurrence, conformity, congru-ence, congruity, connection, correlation, dead ringer*, harmony, homogeneity, identity, interre-lation, kinship, likes of, look-alike, parallel, par-allelism, parity, peas in a pod*, proportion, reciprocity, relation, relationship, resemblance, sameness, semblance, simile, similitude, syn-onymity, two of a kind*; SEE CONCEPT *670*

simmer [*v*] *boil, smolder*
be agitated, be angry, be tense, be uptight*, bub-ble, burn, churn, cook, effervesce, ferment, fizz, fret, fricassee, fume, parboil, rage, seethe, smart, sparkle, stew, stir, warm; SEE CONCEPTS *35,170,410*

simple [*adj1*] *clear, understandable; easy*
child's play*, cinch*, clean, easy as pie*, effort-less, elementary, facile, incomplex, intelligible, light, lucid, manageable, mild, no problem*, no sweat*, not difficult, picnic*, piece of cake*, plain, quiet, self-explanatory, simple as ABC*, smooth, snap*, straightforward, transparent, un-complicated, uninvolved, unmistakable, untrou-blesome, walkover*; SEE CONCEPTS *529,538*

simple [*adj2*] *uncluttered, natural*
absolute, austere, classic, clean, discreet, ele-mentary, folksy, homely, homey, humble, in-elaborate, lowly, mere, modest, not complex, open and shut*, plain, pure, pure and simple*, rustic, sheer, single, Spartan, unadorned, unadul-terated, unaffected, unalloyed, unblended, un-combined, uncomplicated, uncompounded, undecorated, unelaborate, unembellished, un-fussy, unmitigated, unmixed, unornamented, un-ostentatious, unpretentious, unqualified, vanilla*; SEE CONCEPTS *562,589*

simple [*adj3*] *childlike, innocent*
amateur, artless, bald, basic, childish, direct, frank, green, guileless, honest, ingenuous, naive, naked, natural, plain, sincere, square, stark, trusting, unaffected, unartificial, undeniable, unexperienced, unpretentious, unschooled, unso-phisticated, unstudied, unvarnished; SEE CON-CEPTS *267,401,542*

simple [*adj4*] *feeble-minded; not intelligent*
amateur, asinine, backward, brainless, credulous, dense, dimwitted, dull, dumb, fat, feeble, foolish, green*, gullible, half-witted, idiotic, ignorant, il-literate, imbecile, inane, inexperienced, inexpert, insensate, mindless, moronic, nitwitted, obtuse, senseless, shallow, silly, simple-minded, slow, soft, soft-headed*, stupid, thick, uneducated, un-intelligent, witless; SEE CONCEPT *402*

simpleminded [*adj*] *unsophisticated*
brainless, childlike, clueless, crude, dumb, fee-ble-minded, idiotic, ignorant, moronic, naïve, slow, stupid, uncomplicated, unschooled, un-studied, untutored, unworldly; SEE CONCEPTS *401,548,562*

simpleton [*n*] *fool*
birdbrain*, blockhead*, bonehead*, boob*, buf-foon, clod*, clown, dimwit*, dolt*, dope*, dunce, dunderhead*, fathead*, idiot, ignoramus, imbecile, jerk*, lamebrain*, lunkhead*, moron, nitwit, numskull*, oaf, stooge*; SEE CONCEPTS *412,423*

simplicity [*n*] *absence of complication, sophisti-cation*
artlessness, candor, chastity, clarity, classicality, clean lines, clearness, directness, ease, easiness, elementariness, guilelessness, homogeneity, in-genuousness, innocence, integrity, lack of adorn-ment, modesty, monotony, naïveté, naivety, naturalness, obviousness, openness, plainness, primitiveness, purity, restraint, severity, single-ness, straightforwardness, uniformity, unity; SEE CONCEPTS *633,655,663*

simplify [*v*] *make easy, intelligible*
abridge, analyze, boil down, break down, break it down, chasten, clarify, clean it up*, clean up, clear up, cut down, cut the frills*, decipher, dis-entangle, disinvolve, draw a picture*, elucidate, explain, facilitate, get down to basics*, get to the meat*, hit the high spots*, interpret, lay out, let daylight in*, let sunlight in*, make clear, make perfectly clear, make plain, order, put in a nut-shell*, put one straight*, reduce, shorten, spell out, streamline, unscramble; SEE CONCEPTS *57,110,261*

simply [*adv1*] *plainly, clearly*
artlessly, candidly, commonly, directly, easily, frankly, guilelessly, honestly, ingenuously, intel-ligibly, matter-of-factly, modestly, naturally, openly, ordinarily, quietly, sincerely, straightfor-wardly, unaffectedly, unpretentiously, without any elaboration; SEE CONCEPTS *544,562*

simply [*adv2*] *merely*
barely, but, just, only, purely, solely, utterly; SEE CONCEPTS *544,557*

simply [*adv3*] *absolutely, completely*
in fact, ltogether, really, totally, unreservedly, ut-terly, wholly; SEE CONCEPTS *531,535*

simulate [*v*] *pretend, imitate*
act, act like, affect, ape, assume, bluff, borrow, cheat, concoct, copy, counterfeit, crib*, deceive, disguise, dissemble, do, do a take-off*, do like*, equivocate, exaggerate, fabricate, fake, favor, feature, feign, fence, gloss over, invent, knock off*, lie, lift, make believe, mimic, mirror, mis-represent, phony, pirate, play, playact, pose, pre-varicate, put on*, put on an act*, replicate, reproduce, resemble, steal; SEE CONCEPTS *59,63,111,171*

simulation [n] *imitation*
carbon copy, clone, copy, counterfeit, duplicate, duplication, facsimile, fake, image, likeness, match, mirroring, paralleling, reflection, replica, reproduction, sham; SEE CONCEPTS *171,260,716*

simultaneous [adj] *happening at about the same time*
accompanying, agreeing, at the same time, coetaneous, coeval, coexistent, coexisting, coincident, coinciding, concurrent, concurring, contemporaneous, contemporary, dead heat*, in sync*, synchronal, synchronic, synchronous, with the beat*; SEE CONCEPTS *548,799*

sin [n] *illegal or immoral action*
anger, covetousness, crime, damnation, debt, deficiency, demerit, disobedience, envy, error, evil, evil-doing, fault, gluttony, guilt, immorality, imperfection, iniquity, lust, misdeed, offense, peccability, peccadillo, peccancy, pride, shortcoming, sinfulness, sloth, tort, transgression, trespass, ungodliness, unrighteousness, veniality, vice, violation, wickedness, wrong, wrongdoing, wrongness; SEE CONCEPTS *101,645*

sin [v] *commit illegal or immoral action*
backslide*, break commandment, break law, cheat, commit crime, deviate, do wrong, err, fall, fall from grace*, lapse, live in sin, misbehave, misconduct, offend, sow wild oats*, stray, take the primrose path*, transgress, trespass, wallow in the mire*, wander; SEE CONCEPTS *101,375,645*

sincere [adj] *straightforward, honest*
aboveboard, actual, artless, bona fide, candid, dead-level*, dear, devout, earnest, faithful, forthright, frank, genuine, guileless, heartfelt, honest to God*, like it is*, meant, natural, no fooling*, no-nonsense*, on the level*, on the line*, on up and up*, open, outspoken, plain, pretensionless, real, regular, righteous, saintly, serious, square*, sure enough, true, true-blue*, trustworthy, twenty-four carat*, unaffected, undesigning, undissembled, unfeigned, unpretentious, upfront*, wholehearted; SEE CONCEPTS *267,401,542*

sincerely [adv] *seriously, honestly*
aboveboard, candidly, deeply, earnestly, frankly, from bottom of heart, genuinely, in all conscience, in all sincerity, ingenuously, in good faith, naturally, profoundly, really, truly, truthfully, wholeheartedly, without equivocation; SEE CONCEPTS *267,582*

sincerity [n] *straightforwardness, honesty*
artlessness, bona fides, candor, earnestness, frankness, genuineness, good faith, goodwill, guilelessness, heart, honor, impartiality, innocence, justice, openness, probity, reliability, seriousness, sincereness, singleness, trustworthiness, truth, truthfulness, veracity, wholeheartedness; SEE CONCEPTS *633,657*

sinewy [adj] *stringy, tough*
athletic, brawny, fibrous, firm, hard, leathery, muscular, powerful, strong, sturdy, vigorous; SEE CONCEPTS *314,485,489,490*

sinful [adj] *immoral, criminal*
amiss, bad, base, blamable, blameful, blameworthy, censurable, corrupt, culpable, damnable, demeritorious, depraved, disgraceful, erring, evil, guilty, iniquitous, irreligious, low, morally wrong, reprehensible, reprobate, shameful, ungodly, unholy, unregenerate, unrighteous, vicious, vile, wicked, wrong; SEE CONCEPTS *545,548*

sing [v1] *carry a tune with one's voice*
belt out*, burst into song*, buzz*, canary*, cantillate, carol, chant, chirp, choir, croon, descant, duet, groan*, harmonize, hum, hymn, intone, lift up a voice*, line out*, lullaby, make melody*, mouth, pipe, purr*, resound, roar, serenade, shout, singsong, solo, trill, troll, tune, vocalize, wait, warble, whine, whistle, yodel; SEE CONCEPTS *47,77,292*

sing [v2] *tattle on someone*
betray, blow the whistle*, fink*, inform, peach*, rat*, snitch*, spill the beans*, talk, turn in; SEE CONCEPTS *60,317*

singe [v] *burn*
blacken, blaze, brand, brown, cauterize, char, cook, flame, ignite, incinerate, parch, scald, scorch, sear, toast, torch; SEE CONCEPT *249*

singer [n] *person who can carry a tune*
accompanist, artist, artiste, chanter, chanteuse, choralist, chorister, crooner, diva, intoner, melodist, minstrel, musician, nightingale, serenader, soloist, songbird, songster, troubadour, vocalist, voice, warbler, yodeler; SEE CONCEPT *352*

single [adj1] *alone, distinct*
distinct, distinguished, especial, exceptional, exclusive, individual, indivisible, isolated, lone, loner, not general, not public, odd, one, only, original, particular, peerless, personal, private, rare, restricted, secluded, separate, separated, simple, singled-out, singular, sole, solitary, special, specific, strange, unalloyed, unblended, uncommon, uncompounded, undivided, unique, unitary, unmixed, unrivaled, unshared, unusual, without equal; SEE CONCEPTS *564,577,762*

single [adj2] *not married*
bachelor, companionless, divorced, eligible, free, living alone, loner, separated, sole, solo, spouseless, unattached, unfettered, unmarried, unwed; SEE CONCEPT *555*

single-handed [adj] *unassisted*
alone, by oneself, independent, on one's own, solitary, solo, unaided; SEE CONCEPTS *577,583*

singles bar [n] *dating bar*
bar, club, cocktail lounge, lounge, meat market*, nightclub, pickup joint*, pub; SEE CONCEPTS *325,439*

singly [adv] *individually*
apart, independently, one at a time, one by one, particularly, respectively, separately, severally; SEE CONCEPT *577*

singular [adj1] *unique, odd*
atypical, avant-garde, bizarre, breaking new ground*, conspicuous, cool*, curious, eccentric, eminent, exceptional, extraordinary, loner, noteworthy, original, outlandish, out-of-the-way, outstanding, peculiar, prodigious, puzzling, queer, rare, remarkable, special, strange, uncommon, unimaginable, unordinary, unparalleled, unprecedented, unthinkable, unusual, unwonted, weird; SEE CONCEPT *577*

singular [adj2] *alone, separate*
certain, definite, discrete, exclusive, individual, one, only, particular, respective, single, sole, solitary, solo, unique, unrepeatable; SEE CONCEPT *577*

sinister [adj] *nasty, menacing*
adverse, apocalyptic, bad, baleful, baneful,

si
si

blackhearted, corrupt, deleterious, dire, disastrous, dishonest, disquieting, doomful, evil, foreboding, harmful, hurtful, ill-boding, inauspicious, injurious, lowering, malefic, malevolent, malign, malignant, menacing, mischievous, obnoxious, ominous, pernicious, perverse, poisonous, portentous, threatening, unfavorable, unfortunate, unlucky, unpropitious, woeful; SEE CONCEPTS *401,548,571*

sink [*v1*] *fall in, go under*
bore, bring down, capsize, cast down, cave in, couch, decline, demit, depress, descend, dig, dip, disappear, drill, drive, droop, drop, drown, ebb, engulf, excavate, fall, flounder, force down, founder, go down, go to the bottom, immerse, lay, let down, lower, overturn, overwhelm, plummet, plunge, put down, ram, regress, run, sag, scuttle, set, settle, shipwreck, slope, slump, stab, stick, stoop, submerge, subside, swamp, thrust, tip over, touch bottom, wreck; SEE CONCEPTS *181,213*

sink [*v2*] *fall, decrease*
abate, collapse, diminish, drop, lapse, lessen, relapse, retrogress, slip, slump, subside, wane; SEE CONCEPTS *698,776*

sink [*v3*] *deteriorate*
decay, decline, decrease, degenerate, depreciate, descend, deteriorate, die, diminish, disimprove, disintegrate, dwindle, fade, fail, flag, go downhill*, lessen, retrograde, rot, spoil, waste, weaken, worsen; SEE CONCEPTS *469,698*

sink [*v4*] *be humble or humbled*
abase, bemean, be reduced to, cast down, debase, degrade, demean, humiliate, lower, stoop, succumb; SEE CONCEPTS *7,19,35*

sinuous [*adj*] *winding, twisting*
anfractuous, circuitous, coiling, convoluted, crooked, curved, curvy, deviative, devious, flexuous, indirect, meandering, meandrous, serpentine, snaky*, supple, tortuous, twisting and turning*, undulating, vagrant; SEE CONCEPT *581*

sip [*v*] *drink slowly*
drink in, extract, imbibe, partake, quaff, sample, savor, sup, swallow, taste, toss; SEE CONCEPT *169*

sissy [*n*] *weakling*
baby, chicken*, coward, cream puff*, crybaby, daisy*, jellyfish*, milksop, momma's boy*, namby-pamby, pansy, pantywaist*, pushover, wimp*, wuss*, yellow belly*; SEE CONCEPTS *412,423*

sister [*n*] *female sibling*
blood sister, kin, kinsperson, relation, relative, twin; SEE CONCEPTS *414,415*

sit [*v1*] *rest on one's behind*
bear on, be seated, cover, ensconce, give feet a rest*, grab a chair*, have a place, have a seat, hunker*, install, lie, park*, perch*, plop down*, pose, posture, put it there*, relax, remain, rest, seat, seat oneself, settle, squat, take a load off*, take a place, take a seat; SEE CONCEPTS *154,201*

sit [*v2*] *hold a meeting*
assemble, be in session, come together, convene, deliberate, hold an assembly, meet, officiate, open, preside; SEE CONCEPTS *324,384*

site [*n*] *place of activity*
fix, ground, habitat, hangout, haunt, home, lay, layout, locale, locality, location, locus, mise en scène, plot, point, position, post, range, scene,

section, situation, slot, spot, station, wherever, X marks the spot*; SEE CONCEPT *198*

sit-in [*n*] *protest*
complaint, demonstration, fast, grievance, love-in*, march, peace march, rally, revolt, riot, strike, walkout; SEE CONCEPTS *52,54,261,300*

sit tight [*v*] *be patient, wait*
anticipate, bide one's time*, cool it*, fill time, hang around*, hang out, hold on, hold the phone*, keep your shirt on*, lie in wait*, lie low*, linger, mark time*, put on hold*, stall, stand by, stay put*, stick around*; SEE CONCEPTS *210,681*

situate [*v*] *locate*
establish, fix, park, place, position, put, put in place, set, settle, stand; SEE CONCEPT *226*

situated [*adj*] *located*
established, fixed, occupying, parked, placed, planted, positioned, set, settled, stationed; SEE CONCEPT *488*

situation [*n1*] *place of activity*
bearings, direction, footing, latitude, locale, locality, location, locus, longitude, position, post, seat, setting, site, spot, stage, station, where, whereabouts; SEE CONCEPT *198*

situation [*n2*] *circumstances, status*
ballgame*, bargain, capacity, case, character, condition, footing*, how things stack up*, like it is*, mode, picture, place, plight, position, posture, rank, scene, size of it*, sphere, stage, standing, standpoint, state, state of affairs, station, status quo*; SEE CONCEPTS *388,696*

situation [*n3*] *employment status*
appointment, berth, billet, capacity, connection, employment, engagement, hire, job, office, place, placement, position, post, profession, spot, trade; SEE CONCEPTS *351,360,668*

sixth sense [*n*] *intuition*
clairvoyance, divination, ESP*, extrasensory perception, feeling, foreknowledge, gut feeling*, instinct, perception, premonition, second sight*, vibes; SEE CONCEPTS *409,689*

sizable [*adj*] *considerable, large*
ample, big, burly, capacious, comprehensive, decent, decent-sized, extensive, good, goodly, great, gross, hefty, husky, jumbo*, largish, major, massive, ponderous, respectable, sensible, spacious, strapping, substantial, tidy, voluminous, whopping*; SEE CONCEPT *781*

size [*n*] *extent or bulk of some dimension*
admeasurement, amount, amplitude, area, bigness, body, breadth, caliber, capaciousness, capacity, content, diameter, dimensions, enormity, extension, extent, greatness, height, highness, hugeness, immensity, intensity, largeness, length, magnitude, mass, measurement, proportion, proportions, range, scope, spread, stature, stretch, substance, substantiality, tonnage, vastness, volume, voluminosity, width; SEE CONCEPTS *730,792*

sizzle [*v*] *hiss, fry*
broil, brown, buzz, cook, crackle, fizz, fizzle, frizzle, grill, roast, sear, sibilate, spit, sputter, swish, wheeze, whisper, whiz; SEE CONCEPTS *65,170*

skate [*v*] *slide*
coast, flow, glide, glissade, ice skate, roller skate, sail along, skim; SEE CONCEPTS *150,152*

skedaddle [*v*] *flee*
blow*, bolt, clear out, dart, dash, decamp, expe-

dite, fly, fly the coop*, get a move on*, go like lightning, hasten, hightail it*, hurry, hurry up, hustle, leave, make haste, make oneself scarce*, make time*, make tracks*, move, move fast, race, run, rush, scamper, scat, scoot, scurry, shake a leg*, speed, split, spur, step on it*, take off, vamoose, whiz, zip; SEE CONCEPTS *102,150,195,234*

skeleton [n] *structure of bones in animate being or supports in an object*
bones, bony structure, cage, design, draft, frame, framework, osteology, outline, scaffolding, sketch, support; SEE CONCEPTS *393,733*

skeptic [n] *person who is leery, unbelieving*
agnostic, apostate, atheist, cynic, disbeliever, dissenter, doubter, doubting Thomas*, freethinker, heathen, heretic, infidel, materialist, misanthrope, misbeliever, nihilist, pagan, pessimist, profaner, questioner, rationalist, scoffer, unbeliever; SEE CONCEPTS *361,423*

skeptical [adj] *disbelieving, leery*
agnostic, aporetic, cynical, dissenting, doubtful, doubting, dubious, freethinking, hesitating, incredulous, mistrustful, questioning, quizzical, scoffing, show-me*, suspicious, unbelieving, unconvinced; SEE CONCEPT *403*

skepticism [n] *doubt*
agnosticism, apprehension, disbelief, distrust, dubiety, dubiousness, faithlessness, hesitation, indecision, lack of confidence, leeriness, questioning, reluctance, suspicion, uncertainty; SEE CONCEPTS *21,410,689,690*

sketch [n] *drawing, outline*
account, adumbration, aperçu, blueprint, cartoon, chart, compendium, configuration, copy, delineation, depiction, description, design, diagram, digest, doodle, draft, figuration, figure, form, illustration, likeness, monograph, painting, picture, piece, plan, portrayal, precis, report, representation, rough, shape, skeleton, summary, survey, syllabus, version, vignette; SEE CONCEPTS *268,283,625*

sketch [v] *draw, outline*
adumbrate, block out*, blueprint*, chalk, characterize, chart, delineate, depict, describe, design, detail, develop, diagram, doodle, draft, lay out*, line, map out, paint, plan, plot, portray, represent, rough out*, skeleton, skeletonize, trace; SEE CONCEPTS *36,174*

sketchy [adj] *rough, incomplete*
coarse, crude, cursory, defective, depthless, faulty, imperfect, inadequate, insufficient, introductory, outline, perfunctory, preliminary, rough, scrappy, shallow, skimpy, slight, superficial, uncritical, unfinished, vague; SEE CONCEPT *531*

skew [v] *distort*
alter, bend, bias, change, color, contort, curve, doctor*, fake, falsify, fudge*, misrepresent, misshape, slant, throw off balance, twist, warp; SEE CONCEPTS *63,137,232,250*

skid [v] *slide against will*
drift, glide, go into skid, move, sheer, skew, slip, slue, swerve, veer; SEE CONCEPT *152*

skill [n] *ability, talent to do something*
accomplishment, address, adroitness, aptitude, art, artistry, cleverness, clout, command, competence, craft, cunning, deftness, dexterity, dodge*, ease, experience, expertise, expertism, expertness, facility, finesse, goods*, handiness, ingenuity, intelligence, job, knack*, know-how*, line,

makings, moxie*, one's thing*, profession, proficiency, prowess, quickness, readiness, right stuff*, savvy*, skillfulness, sleight, smarts*, stuff*, technique, trade, what it takes*; SEE CONCEPTS *409,630*

skillful [adj] *able, talented*
accomplished, adept, adroit, a hand at*, apt, brainy, clever, competent, cool*, crack*, crackerjack*, dexterous, experienced, expert, good, handy, into*, learned, old*, on the ball*, practical, practiced, prepared, pretty, primed, pro*, professional, proficient, quick, ready, really into*, savvy*, seasoned, sharp, skilled, smart, smooth, there*, trained, tuned in*, versant, versed, vet*, veteran, well-versed, whiz, wicked*, wised up*; SEE CONCEPTS *402,527*

skim [v1] *remove the top part*
brush, cream, dip, get the cream, glance, graze, ladle, ream, scoop, separate, shave, top; SEE CONCEPT *211*

skim [v2] *glide over quickly, lightly*
brush, carom, coast, dart, float, fly, graze, kiss, ricochet, sail, scud, shoot, skate, skip, skirr, skitter, smooth along, soar, trip; SEE CONCEPTS *150,152*

skim [v3] *look through cursorily*
browse, brush over, dip, examine, flip through, get the cream*, give the once-over*, glance, glance over, go once over lightly*, hit the high spots*, leaf through*, read, read swiftly, riff, riffle, run eye over*, scan, skip, thumb through*, turn the pages*; SEE CONCEPTS *72,103,623*

skimp [v] *be cheap or frugal about*
be mean with, be sparing, cut corners*, make ends meet*, pinch, pinch pennies*, roll back, save, scamp, scant, scrape, screw, scrimp, slight, spare, stint, tighten one's belt*, withhold; SEE CONCEPT *330*

skimpy [adj] *sparse, inadequate*
deficient, exiguous, failing, insufficient, meager, miserly, niggardly, poor, scant, scanty, scrimp, scrimpy, short, shy, sparse, stingy, thin, tight, unsufficient, wanting; SEE CONCEPTS *334,762,789*

skin [n] *outer covering, especially of animate being*
bark, carapace, case, casing, coating, crust, cutis, derma, dermis, epidermis, fell, film, fur, hide, hull, husk, integument, jacket, membrane, outside, parchment, peel, pelt, rind, sheath, sheathing, shell, shuck, slough, surface, tegument, vellum; SEE CONCEPTS *392,428,484*

skin [v] *remove outer covering*
abrade, bare, bark, cast, cut off, decorticate, excoriate, exuviate, flay, gall, graze, hull, husk, lay bare, pare, peel, pull off, remove, rind, scale, scalp, scrape, shave, shed, shuck, slough, strip, trim; SEE CONCEPTS *176,211*

skin-deep [adj] *superficial*
apparent, casual, cursory, empty, flimsy, meaningless, one-dimensional, on the surface, shallow, trivial; SEE CONCEPTS *557,777*

skinflint [n] *cheapskate*
hoarder, miser, moneygrubber*, penny-pincher*, pinchfist*, pinchpenny*, Scrooge*, tightwad; SEE CONCEPTS *348,412,423*

skinny [adj] *very thin*
angular, bony, emaciated, gaunt, lank, lanky, lean, like a rail*, malnourished, rawboned, scraggy, scrawny, skeletal, skin-and-bone*, slen-

der, spare, twiggy, undernourished, underweight; SEE CONCEPTS *490,491*

skip [*v1*] *bounce or jump over*
bob, bolt, bound, buck, canter, caper, carom, cavort, dance, flee, flit, fly, frisk, gambol, glance, graze, hippety-hop*, hop, leap, lope, make off, prance, ricochet, run, scamper, scoot, skedaddle*, skim, skirr, skitter, spring, step, tiptoe, trip; SEE CONCEPTS *150,194*

skip [*v2*] *avoid, miss*
cut, desert, disregard, escape, eschew, flee, leave out, miss out, neglect, omit, pass over, pass up, play hooky*, run away, skim over, split; SEE CONCEPTS *30,681*

skirmish [*n*] *fight*
altercation, argument, battle, bout, brawl, brush, clash, combat, conflict, confrontation, disagreement, dispute, encounter, engagement, feud, fisticuffs*, fracas, fray, melee, quarrel, row, ruckus, rumble, run-in*, scrap*, scuffle, strife, tiff, tussle, war; SEE CONCEPT *106*

skirmish [*v*] *fight*
altercate, argue, battle, bicker, brawl, clash, combat, conflict, cross swords, dispute, do battle, engage, feud, go to war, grapple, mix it up*, quarrel, scrap, scuffle, spar, struggle, tussle, wage war, war, wrangle, wrestle; SEE CONCEPT *106*

skirt [*n1*] *border, edge*
brim, brink, fringe, hem, margin, outskirts, perimeter, periphery, purlieus, rim, skirting, verge; SEE CONCEPTS *484,825*

skirt [*n2*] *ladies' garment that hangs from waist*
culottes, dirndl, dress, hoop, kilt, midi, mini, pannier, petticoat, sarong, tutu; SEE CONCEPT *451*

skirt [*v1*] *border; be on the edge*
bound, define, edge, flank, fringe, hem, lie along, lie alongside, margin, rim, surround, verge; SEE CONCEPT *751*

skirt [*v2*] *avoid; get around*
burke, bypass, circumnavigate, circumvent, detour, dodge, duck, elude, equivocate, escape, evade, hedge, ignore, sidestep, skip, steer clear of; SEE CONCEPTS *30,102,147*

skit [*n*] *sketch*
act, parody, performance, play, satire, spoof, takeoff; SEE CONCEPT *263*

skittish [*adj*] *very nervous*
agitable, alarmable, capricious, changeable, combustible, dizzy*, edgy, excitable, excited, fearful, fickle, fidgety, flighty, frivolous, giddy, harebrained, high-strung*, irresponsible, jumpy, lightheaded, lively, peppy, playful, restive, scatterbrained*, sensitive, spirited, undependable, unreliable, volative, whimsical, zippy*; SEE CONCEPT *401*

skulk [*v*] *lurk; shirk*
avoid, bypass, conceal oneself, creep, crouch, dodge, elude, evade, hide, lie in wait, prowl, pussyfoot*, sidestep, slack, slink, snake, sneak, snoop, steal; SEE CONCEPTS *30,59,151,188,681*

sky [*n*] *Earth's atmosphere*
azure, celestial sphere, empyrean, firmament, heavens, lid*, the blue*, upper atmosphere, vault, vault of heaven*, welkin, wild blue yonder*; SEE CONCEPT *437*

skyrocket [*v*] *soar*
arise, ascend, catapult, escalate, go through the ceiling*, go through the roof*, lift, rise, rocket,

shoot, shoot up, take off, tower, vault up, zoom; SEE CONCEPTS *148,150*

skyscraper [*n*] *tall building*
high-rise, high-rise building, superstructure, tower; SEE CONCEPTS *439,441*

slab [*n*] *chunk of solid object*
bar, billet, bit, board, boulder, chip, cut, cutting, hunk, ingot, lump, muck, piece, plate, portion, rod, slice, stave, stick, stone, strip, wedge; SEE CONCEPTS *471,835*

slack [*adj1*] *loose, baggy; inactive*
dull, easy, feeble, flabby, flaccid, flexible, flimsy, inert, infirm, laggard, lax, leisurely, limp, not taut, passive, quaggy, quiet, relaxed, sloppy, slow, slow-moving, sluggish, soft, supine, unsteady, weak; SEE CONCEPTS *485,584,589*

slack [*adj2*] *lazy, negligent*
asleep on the job*, behindhand, careless, delinquent, derelict, dilatory, disregardful, dormant, dull, easy-going, faineant, idle, inactive, inattentive, indolent, inert, lackadaisical, lax, lethargic, neglectful, not busy, permissive, quiescent, quiet, regardless, remiss, slothful, slow, slow-moving, sluggish, stagnant, tardy; SEE CONCEPT *538*

slack [*n*] *looseness, excess*
give, leeway, play, room, slackening, slowdown, slow-up; SEE CONCEPTS *513,807*

slacker [*n*] *shirker*
avoider, bum, deadbeat*, goldbrick, good-for-nothing, goof-off*, idler, loafer, quitter, slouch; SEE CONCEPTS *412,423*

slack/slacken [*v*] *do little or nothing; loosen*
abate, decrease, diminish, dodge, drop off, dwindle, ease, ease off, featherbed*, flag, goldbrick*, goof off*, idle, lax, lay back, lessen, let up, lie down on job*, loose, moderate, neglect, relax, relax, release, shirk, slack off, slow down, taper, tire, untighten, wane; SEE CONCEPTS *210,681,698*

slam [*n1*] *loud noise from impact*
bang, bash, blast, blow, boom, burst, clap, crack, crash, ding, pound, smack, smash, whack, wham; SEE CONCEPTS *189,595*

slam [*n2*] *harsh criticism*
animadversion, aspersion, jab, obloquy, potshot*, slap*, slur*, stricture, swipe*; SEE CONCEPTS *52,278*

slam [*v1*] *throw or push very hard*
bang, bat, batter, beat, belt, blast, clobber, close, crash, cudgel, dash, fling, hammer, hit, hurl, knock, pound, shut, slap, slug, smash, strike, swat, thump, thwack, wallop; SEE CONCEPTS *189,208,222*

slam [*v2*] *criticize very harshly*
attack, castigate, damn, excoriate, flay, lambaste*, lash into*, pan, scathe, scourge, shoot down, slap, slash, vilify; SEE CONCEPTS *52,54*

slander [*n*] *scandalous remark*
aspersion, backbiting*, backstabbing*, belittlement, black eye*, calumny, defamation, depreciation, detraction, dirt*, dirty linen*, disparagement, hit*, libel, lie, misrepresentation, muckraking, mud*, mud-slinging*, obloquy, rap*, scandal, slam*, slime*, smear*, tale; SEE CONCEPTS *54,192,278*

slander [*v*] *make a scandalous remark*
asperse, assail, attack, backbite*, bad-mouth*, belie, belittle, besmirch, blacken name*, blaspheme, blister, blot, calumniate, cast a slur on, curse, damage, decry, defame, defile, denigrate,

depreciate, derogate, detract, dishonor, disparage, give a bad name*, hit*, hurt, injure, libel, malign, muckrake, pan*, plaster, revile, roast*, run smear campaign*, scandalize, scorch, slam*, sling mud*, slur, smear, smirch, sneer, strumpet, sully, tarnish, tear down, traduce, vilify; SEE CONCEPTS *54,192*

slang [*n*] *casual dialect*
argot, cant, colloquialism, informal speech, jargon, lingo, neologism, patois, patter, pidgin, shoptalk, slanguage* street talk, vernacular, vulgarism, vulgarity; SEE CONCEPT *276*

slant [*n1*] *angle, slope*
camber, cant, declination, diagonal, grade, gradient, inclination, incline, lean, leaning, pitch, rake, ramp, tilt; SEE CONCEPT *738*

slant [*n2*] *particular opinion*
angle, attitude, bias, direction, emphasis, judgment, leaning, one-sidedness, outlook, point of view, predilection, predisposition, prejudice, prepossession, sentiment, side, standpoint, view, viewpoint; SEE CONCEPT *689*

slant [*v1*] *angle off, slope*
aim, bank, beam, bend, bevel, cant, decline, descend, deviate, direct, diverge, grade, heel, incline, lean, level, lie obliquely, list, point, skew, splay, swerve, tilt, tip, train, veer; SEE CONCEPTS *201,738*

slant [*v2*] *change to suit; distort*
aim, angle, bias, color, concentrate, direct, focus, influence, orient, point, prejudice, train, twist, warp, weight; SEE CONCEPTS *63,266*

slap [*n/v*] *hard hit, often with hand*
bang, bash, blip, blow, box, buffet, bust, chop, clap, clout, crack, cuff, pat, percuss, poke, potch, punch, slam, smack, sock, spank, strike, swat, wallop, whack, wham; SEE CONCEPT *189*

slapdash [*adj*] *careless*
clumsy, haphazard, hasty, heedless, improvident, irresponsible, lackadaisical, lax, messy, negligent, nonchalant, reckless, slipshod, sloppy; SEE CONCEPT *542*

slaphappy [*adj*] *dazed*
befuddled, bewildered, dazzled, gaga*, giddy, groggy*, hazy, punch-drunk*, punchy*, puzzled, senile, silly, staggered, staggering, tipsy, unsteady, weak in the knees*, weak-kneed*, wobbly, woozy; SEE CONCEPTS *314,480*

slash [*v1*] *cut*
carve, chop, gash, hack, incise, injure, lacerate, open up, pierce, rend, rip, score, sever, slice, slit, wound; SEE CONCEPTS *137,176*

slash [*v2*] *reduce greatly*
abbreviate, abridge, clip, curtail, cut, cut back, cut down, drop, hack, lower, mark down, pare, retrench, shave, shorten; SEE CONCEPTS *236,240,247*

slaughter [*n*] *killing*
annihilation, bloodbath, bloodshed, butchery, carnage, destruction, extermination, liquidation, massacre, murder, slaying; SEE CONCEPT *252*

slaughter [*v*] *kill*
butcher, crush, decimate, defeat, destroy, do in* exterminate, finish, liquidate, maim, mangle, massacre, murder, mutilate, overwhelm, rout, slay, stick, thrash, torture, total* trounce, vanquish, waste, wipe out*; SEE CONCEPT *252*

slave [*n*] *person who serves, often under duress*
bondservant, captive, chattel, drudge, help, laborer, menial, peon, retainer, serf, servant, skivvy, subservient, thrall, toiler, vassal, victim, worker, workhorse; SEE CONCEPT *348*

slave [*v*] *work very hard*
be servile, drudge, grind, grovel, grub, muck, plod, skivvy, slog, toil, work fingers to bone*; SEE CONCEPT *87*

slavery [*n*] *state of working under duress or without freedom*
bondage, bullwork, captivity, chains* constraint, drudge, drudgery, enslavement, enthrallment, feudalism, grind, helotry, indenture, labor, menial labor, moil, peonage, restraint, serfdom, serfhood, servitude, subjection, subjugation, thrall, thralldom, toil, vassalage, work; SEE CONCEPTS *324,388*

slay [*v*] *kill*
annihilate, assassinate, butcher, cut off, destroy, dispatch, do*, do away with, do in*, down*, eliminate, erase, execute, exterminate, finish, hit, knock off*, liquidate, massacre, murder, neutralize, put away*, rub out*, slaughter, snuff*, waste*; SEE CONCEPT *252*

sleazebag [*n*] *creep*
crud*, degenerate, deviant, dip*, dirtbag*, dirtball*, pervert, pig*, scum*, scumbag*, scuzzbag*, sleaze*, sleazeball*, slimebag*, slimeball*, slimebucket*, slob*, weirdo*; SEE CONCEPT *412*

sleazy [*adj*] *disreputable*
base, broken-down, cheap, common, dilapidated, flimsy, limp, low, mean, paltry, poor, run-down, seedy, shabby, shoddy, sordid, squalid, tacky*, trashy, unsubstantial; SEE CONCEPTS *334,485,589*

sled [*n*] *sleigh*
bobsled, dog sled, horse sleigh, luge, sledge, toboggan; SEE CONCEPTS *187,217*

sleek [*adj*] *smooth, glossy*
glassy, glistening, lustrous, polished, satin, shiny, silken, silky; SEE CONCEPT *606*

sleep [*n*] *suspension of consciousness*
bedtime, catnap, coma, dormancy, doze, dream, dullness, few z's*, forty winks*, hibernation, lethargy, nap, nod, repose, rest, sack time*, sandman*, shuteye*, siesta, slumber, slumberland*, snooze, torpidity, torpor, trance; SEE CONCEPT *315*

sleep [*v*] *suspend consciousness*
bed down*, bunk*, catch a wink*, catch forty winks*, catnap, conk out*, cop some z's*, crash*, doze, dream, drop off*, drowse, fall asleep, fall out*, flop*, hibernate, hit the hay*, hit the sack*, languish, nap, nod, nod off, oversleep, relax, repose, rest, retire, sack out*, saw wood*, slumber, snooze, snore, take a nap, turn in*, yawn, zonk out*, zzz*; SEE CONCEPT *315*

sleepless [*adj*] *insomniac, restless*
active, alert, antsy*, anxious, bustling, edgy, fidgeting, fidgety, jumpy, nervous, on edge, strung out*, tossing and turning*, troubled, unsettled, wakeful, wide-awake, wired*, worried; SEE CONCEPTS *403,542,584*

sleepy [*adj*] *tired, dull*
asleep, blah*, comatose, dopey*, dozy, draggy, drowsy, heavy, hypnotic, inactive, lethargic, listless, out*, out of it*, quiet, sleeping, sleepyhead*, slow, sluggish, slumberous, slumbersome, snoozy*, somnolent, soporific, torpid, yawning; SEE CONCEPTS *315,539*

sk
sl

sleigh [n] *sled*
bobsled, dog sled, horse sleigh, luge, sledge, toboggan; SEE CONCEPTS *187,217*

slender/slim [adj1] *thin, not heavy*
attenuate, beanpole*, beanstalk*, fine, insubstantial, lean, lithe, narrow, reedy, skeleton, skinny, slight, spare, stalky, stick, svelte, sylphlike, tenuous, threadlike, trim, twiggy, willowy; SEE CONCEPTS *490,491*

slender/slim [adj2] *inadequate, flimsy*
bare, deficient, faint, feeble, fragile, inconsiderable, insufficient, little, meager, poor, remote, scant, scanty, scarce, short, shy, slight, small, spare, tenuous, thin, wanting, weak; SEE CONCEPTS *552,771*

sleuth [n] *detective*
agent, bloodhound*, cop, dick*, eavesdropper, flatfoot*, gumshoe*, investigator, P.I.*, police officer, private detective, private eye, private investigator, sleuthhound, spy, tail*, tracker; SEE CONCEPT *348*

slice [n] *piece; share*
allotment, allowance, bite, chop, cut, helping, lot, part, piece of pie*, portion, quota, segment, sliver, thin piece, triangle, wedge; SEE CONCEPT *835*

slice [v] *cut into portions, shares*
carve, chiv, cleave, dissect, dissever, divide, gash, hack, incise, pierce, segment, sever, shave, shred, slash, slit, split, strip, subdivide, sunder; SEE CONCEPTS *98,137,176*

slick [adj1] *smooth, polished*
glossy, greasy, icy, lubricious, oily, oleaginous, shiny, sleek, sleeky, slippery, slithery, soapy; SEE CONCEPT *606*

slick [adj2] *smart, clever*
adroit, cagey, canny, deft, dextrous, foxy, glib, knowing, meretricious, plausible, professional, quick, sharp, shrewd, skillful, sly, smooth, smooth-spoken, sophisticated, specious, streetwise*, unctuous, urbane, wise; SEE CONCEPTS *401,402*

slide [v] *move smoothly; move down*
accelerate, coast, drift, drive, drop, fall, fall off, flow, glide, glissade, launch, move, move along, move over, propel, sag, scooch*, shift, shove, skate, skid, skim, slip, slither, slump, smooth along, spill, stream, thrust, toboggan, tumble, veer; SEE CONCEPTS *150,152*

slight [adj1] *insignificant, small*
fat, feeble, inconsiderable, insubstantial, meager, minor, modest, negligible, off, outside, paltry, petty, piddling, remote, scanty, slender, slim, sparse, superficial, trifling, trivial, unessential, unimportant, weak; SEE CONCEPTS *575,762,789*

slight [adj2] *thin, small in build*
attenuate, broomstick*, dainty, delicate, feeble, flimsy, fragile, frail, light, reedy, shadow, skeleton, skinny, slender, slim, spare, stick, twiggy; SEE CONCEPTS *490,491*

slight [n] *insult, disrespect*
affront, brush-off, call-down, cold shoulder*, contempt, cut, discourtesy, disdain, disregard, inattention, indifference, kick, neglect, putdown*, rebuff, rejection, slap in the face*, snub; SEE CONCEPTS *30,384,529*

slight [v] *offend, insult*
affront, blink at, brush off, chill, contemn, cool*, cut*, despise, discount, disdain, disparage, disregard, fail, flout, forget, give the brush*, give the

cold shoulder to*, ignore, make light of, neglect, not give time of day*, omit, overlook, poohpooh*, reject, scoff, scorn, show disrespect, shrug off, skip, slur, sneeze at*, snub, treat with contempt, turn deaf ear to*, upstage; SEE CONCEPTS *7,19,30,384*

slightly [adv] *a little*
hardly, hardly at all, hardly noticeable, imperceptibly, inappreciably, inconsiderably, insignificantly, kind of, lightly, marginally, more or less, on a small scale, pretty, scarcely any, somewhat, to some degree, to some extent; SEE CONCEPTS *544,772*

slim [v] *lose weight*
diet, reduce, slenderize; SEE CONCEPT *202*

slime [n] *muck, gelled waste*
fungus, glop*, goo*, gunk*, mire, mucus, mud, ooze, scum, sludge; SEE CONCEPT *260*

slimy [adj] *oozy, gooey*
clammy, glutinous, miry, mucky, mucous, muculent, muddy, scummy, viscous, yukky*; SEE CONCEPTS *485,621*

sling [v] *throw or hang over*
bung, cast, catapult, chuck, dangle, fire, fling, heave, hoist, hurl, launch, lob, peg, pitch, raise, send, shoot, suspend, swing, toss, weight; SEE CONCEPTS *181,222*

slink/slither [v] *creep by*
coast, cower, glide, glissade, go stealthily, gumshoe*, lurk, meander, pass quietly, prowl, pussyfoot*, shirk, sidle, skitter, skulk, slick, slide, slip, snake, sneak, steal, undulate; SEE CONCEPT *151*

slip [n1] *error, goof*
blooper*, blunder, bungle, failure, fault, flub*, fluff*, foul-up*, gaff, howler*, imprudence, indiscretion, lapse, misdeed, misstep, mistake, muff*, omission, oversight, screw-up*, slip of the tongue*, slip-up*, trip; SEE CONCEPT *101*

slip [n2] *piece of paper*
label, leaf, page, sheet, sliver, strip, tag, ticket; SEE CONCEPTS *270,475*

slip [v1] *fall; glide*
drop, glissade, lose balance, lose footing, lurch, move, shift, skate, skid, slick, slide, slither, smooth along, totter, trip; SEE CONCEPTS *150,152*

slip [v2] *err*
blunder, drop the ball*, flub*, fluff*, goof*, go wrong, make a mistake, miscalculate, misjudge, mistake, muff*, put foot in mouth*, slip up, stumble, trip; SEE CONCEPT *101*

slippery [adj1] *smooth, slick*
glace, glassy, glazed, glistening, greasy, icy, like a skating rink*, lubricious, lustrous, perilous, polished, satiny, silky, sleek, slimy, soapy, unctuous, unsafe, unstable, unsteady, waxy, wet; SEE CONCEPT *606*

slippery [adj2] *uncertain, unreliable*
cagey, changeable, crafty, cunning, devious, dishonest, duplicitous, elusive, evasive, false, flyby-night*, foxy, inconstant, insecure, mutable, shifty, slick, slithery, smooth, sneaky, treacherous, tricky, two-faced*, unpredictable, unsafe, unstable, unsteady, untrustworthy, variable; SEE CONCEPTS *401,534,535*

slipshod [adj] *careless; not well done*
bedraggled, botched*, disheveled, faulty, fly-bynight*, fouled-up*, haphazard, imperfect, inaccurate, inexact, junky*, loose, messed-up, messy, neglected, negligent, raunchy, screwed-up*,

scrubby*, scruffy*, shabby*, shoddy*, slap-dash*, sloppy, slovenly, tacky*, tattered, thread-bare, unkempt, unmeticulous, unsystematic, unthorough, untidy; SEE CONCEPTS *485,570,589*

slipup [*n*] *error*
blooper, blunder, boner*, boo-boo*, bungle, faux pas, flaw, glitch, goof*, lapse, miscalculation, miscue, misjudgment, misstep, mistake, misun-derstanding, oversight, screwup, slight, stumble, transgression; SEE CONCEPTS *101,230,674,699*

slit [*n*] *small opening, cut*
aperture, breach, cleavage, cleft, crack, crevice, fissure, gash, hole, incision, rent, split, tear; SEE CONCEPT *513*

slit [*v*] *cut open*
gash, incise, knife, lance, pierce, rip, sever, slash, slice, slot, split open, tear; SEE CONCEPT *176*

slither [*v*] *slide*
coast, crawl, glide, glissade, move, skate, skid, slink, slip, snake*, sneak, wriggle; SEE CONCEPTS *150,152*

sliver [*n*] *tiny piece, usually of wood or metal*
bit, flake, fragment, paring, shaving, shred, slice, slip, snip, snippet, splinter, thorn; SEE CONCEPTS *471,831*

slobber [*v*] *drool*
dribble, drip, drivel, froth, salivate, slabber, slaver, water at the mouth; SEE CONCEPT *185*

slog [*v*] *plod*
bear down*, buckle down*, drag, drudge, floun-der, grind, labor, lumber*, plough through*, plug, schlepp*, slave, stomp, sweat*, toil, tramp, trample, trudge; SEE CONCEPTS *87,151,677*

slogan [*n*] *motto*
byword, catchphrase, catchword, expression, idiom, jingle, phrase, proverb, rallying cry*, say-ing, shibboleth*, trademark*, war cry*, watch-word; SEE CONCEPT *278*

slop [*v*] *splash; make a mess*
dash, drip, flounder, let run out, let run over, overflow, slosh, smear, smudge, spatter, spill, splatter, spray, wallow; SEE CONCEPT *250*

slope [*n*] *slant, tilt*
abruptness, bank, bend, bevel, bias, cant, decli-nation, declivity, deflection, descent, deviation, diagonal, downgrade, gradient, hill, inclination, incline, lean, leaning, obliqueness, obliquity, pitch, ramp, rise, rising ground, shelf, skew, steepness, swag, sway, tip; SEE CONCEPTS *738,757*

slope [*v*] *slant, tilt*
angle, ascend, bank, bevel, cant, descend, dip, drop, drop away, fall, heel, incline, lean, list, pitch, rake, recline, rise, shelve, skew, splay, tip; SEE CONCEPTS *201,738*

sloppy [*adj*] *messy*
awkward, bedraggled, botched, careless, clumsy, dingy, dirty, disheveled, inattentive, mediocre, muddy, not clean, poor, slapdash, slipshod, slovenly, sludgy*, slushy*, splashy*, tacky*, un-kempt, unthorough, untidy, watery, wet; SEE CONCEPTS *531,603,621*

slot [*n*] *opening, place*
aperture, channel, cut, groove, hole, niche, posi-tion, recess, slit, socket, space, time, vacancy; SEE CONCEPT *513*

sloth [*n*] *laziness*
do-nothingness, idleness, inactivity, indolence, inertia, lackadaisicalness, languidness, laxness, lethargy, listlessness, slackness, slothfulness,

slowness, sluggishness, supineness; SEE CON-CEPTS *411,633*

slothful [*adj*] *lazy*
comatose, dallying, dull, idle, inactive, inatten-tive, indolent, inert, lackadaisical, laggard, lag-ging, languid, lethargic, lifeless, listless, loafing, passive, procrastinating, slack, slow, sluggish, snoozy*, supine, tired, unenergetic; SEE CON-CEPTS *401,404*

slouch [*v*] *slump over*
be lazy, bend, bow, crouch, droop, lean, loaf, loll, lounge, sag, stoop, wilt; SEE CONCEPTS *154,201*

slovenly [*adj*] *dirty, disordered*
bedraggled, botched, careless, dingy, disheveled, disorderly, dowdy, down-at-the-heel*, frowzy*, frumpy*, grody*, grubby, grungy*, heedless, icky*, loose, messed up*, messy, mussy, negli-gent, pigpen*, raunchy, seedy, slack, slapdash, sleazy*, slipshod, sloppy, tacky, topsy-turvy, un-fastidious, unkempt, unthorough, untidy; SEE CONCEPTS *485,621*

slow [*adj1*] *unhurried, lazy*
apathetic, crawling, creeping, dawdling, delay-ing, deliberate, dilatory, disinclined, dreamy, drowsy, easy, gradual, heavy, idle, impercepti-ble, inactive, indolent, inert, lackadaisical, lag-gard, lagging, leaden, leisurely, lethargic, listless, loitering, measured, moderate, negligent, passive, phlegmatic, plodding, ponderous, post-poning, procrastinating, quiet, reluctant, remiss, slack, sleepy, slothful, slow-moving, sluggish, snaillike, stagnant, supine, tardy, torpid, tortoise-like; SEE CONCEPTS *538,584,588*

slow [*adj2*] *behind, late*
backward, behindhand, belated, conservative, dead, delayed, detained, dilatory, down, draggy*, dull, gradual, hindered, impeded, inactive, lin-gering, long-delayed, long-drawn-out*, low, moderate, off, overdue, prolonged, protracted, reduced, slack, sleepy, sluggish, stagnant, stiff, tame, tardy, tedious, time-consuming, unevent-ful, unproductive, unprogressive, unpunctual; SEE CONCEPTS *529,537,548*

slow [*adj3*] *unintelligent*
backward, dense, dim, dimwitted, dull, dumb, dunce, imbecile, limited, moronic, obtuse, sim-ple, slow on the uptake*, stupid, thick, unrespon-sive; SEE CONCEPT *402*

slow [*v*] *delay, restrict*
abate, anchor it, back-water*, bog down, brake, check, choke, curb, curtail, cut back, cut down, decelerate, decrease, detain, diminish, ease off, ease up, embog, handicap, hinder, hit the brakes*, hold back, hold up, impede, keep wait-ing, lag, lessen, let down flaps*, loiter, lose speed, lose steam*, mire, moderate, postpone, procrastinate, qualify, quiet, reduce, reduce speed, reef, regulate, rein in, relax, retard, retar-date, set back, slacken, stall, stunt, temper, wind down; SEE CONCEPTS *130,234,250*

slowdown [*n*] *slacking off; gradual decrease*
arrest, deceleration, decline, delay, downtrend, downturn, drop, drop-off, falloff, freeze, inactiv-ity, retardation, slack, slackening, slow-up, stag-nation, stoppage, strike; SEE CONCEPTS *121,130*

slowpoke [*n*] *laggard*
dawdler, dilly-dallyer, idler, plodder, procrasti-nator, slug, sluggard, snail, straggler; SEE CON-CEPTS *121,237,681*

sludge [*n*] *mud*

glop*, goo*, goop*, grease, gunk*, mire, muck, oil, ooze, scum, sediment, silt, slime, slop; SEE CONCEPT *260*

slug [*v*] *hit*

bang, bash, bat, batter, beat, belt, box*, bump, clobber, clock*, clout, club, crack, flail, flog, hammer*, jab, knock, KO*, lambaste, let have it*, nail*, pelt, pop, pound, punch, slam, slap, smack, sock, swat, thrash, thwack, wallop, whack*, whale; SEE CONCEPTS *189,200*

slugfest [*n*] *fight*

altercation, argument, battle, battle royal*, bout, brawl, clash, conflict, dispute, dogfight, donny-brook, engagement, feud, fisticuffs*, fracas, fray, free-for-all*, melee, riot, ruckus, rumble, struggle, tussle, war; SEE CONCEPT *106*

sluggish [*adj*] *dull, slow-moving*

apathetic, blah*, comatose, dopey*, down, dragging, draggy*, drippy*, heavy, hebetudinous, inactive, indolent, inert, laid-back*, languid, languorous, leaden, lethargic, lifeless, listless, lumpish, mooney*, off, phlegmatic, pokey*, slack, sleepyheaded*, slothful, slow, sluggard, slumberous, stagnant, stiff, sullen, torpid, unresponsive; SEE CONCEPTS *401,584*

slum [*n*] *ghetto*

blighted area, public squalor, run-down neighborhood, shanty town, skid row, tenement housing; SEE CONCEPTS *335,709*

slumber [*n*] *sleep*

coma, dormancy, doze, drowse, forty winks*, inactivity, languor, lethargy, nap, repose, rest, sack time*, shut-eye*, snooze, stupor, torpor; SEE CONCEPT *315*

slump [*n*] *decline, failure*

bad period, bad times, blight, blue devils*, blue funk*, bottom, bust, collapse, crash, depreciation, depression, descent, dip, downer*, downslide*, downswing*, downtrend, downturn, drop, dumps*, fall, falling-off*, funk, hard times*, letdown*, low, rainy days*, recession, reverse, rut, sag, slide, slip, stagnation, the skids*, trough; SEE CONCEPTS *335,410,674*

slump [*v*] *decline, sink*

bend, blight, cave in, collapse, crash, decay, deteriorate, droop, drop, fall, fall off*, go down, go downhill*, go to ruin*, hunch, keel over, loll, pitch, plummet, plunge, reach new low*, sag, slide, slip, slouch, topple, tumble; SEE CONCEPTS *181,698,699,763*

slur [*n*] *insult*

accusation, affront, animadversion, aspersion, bar sinister*, black eye*, blemish, blot, blur, brand, brickbat*, calumny, dirty dig*, discredit, disgrace, dump, expose, hit, innuendo, insinuation, knock, obloquy, odium, onus, put-down*, rap*, reflection, reproach, slam, smear, stain, stigma, stricture, zinger*; SEE CONCEPTS *44,54,278*

slur [*v1*] *insult*

blacken, blemish, blister, blot, blow off*, brand, calumniate, cap, chop*, cut to the quick*, cut up*, defame, denigrate, detract, discredit, disgrace, dump on*, give a black eye*, hit where one lives*, insinuate, kick in the teeth*, libel, malign, miff, offend, push, put down*, reproach, roast*, scorch*, skin alive*, slander, slap in the face*, slight, smear*, snub, spatter, stain, tear

down, traduce, vilify, zing*; SEE CONCEPTS *7,19,44,54*

slur [*v2*] *mumble words*

garble, mispronounce, miss, skip, stutter; SEE CONCEPT *47*

sly [*adj*] *clever, devious*

arch, artful, astute, bluffing, cagey, calculating, canny, captious, conniving, covert, crafty, crooked, cunning, deceitful, deceptive, delusive, designing, dishonest, dishonorable, dissembling, double-dealing, elusive, foxy, furtive, guileful, illusory, impish, ingenious, insidious, intriguing, mean, mischievous, plotting, roguish, scheming, secret, sharp, shifty, shrewd, slick, smart, smooth, sneaking, stealthy, subtle, traitorous, treacherous, tricky, underhand, unscrupulous, wily; SEE CONCEPTS *401,542*

smack [*adv*] *directly, exactly*

accurately, bang*, clearly, just, plumb, point-blank*, precisely, right, sharp, square, squarely, straight; SEE CONCEPT *557*

smack [*n/v*] *strike, often with hand*

bang, blip, blow, box, buffet, chop, clap, clout, crack, cuff, hit, pat, punch, slap, snap, sock, spank, tap; SEE CONCEPT *189*

small [*adj1*] *tiny in size, quantity*

baby, bantam, bitty*, cramped, diminutive, humble, immature, inadequate, inconsequential, inconsiderable, insufficient, limited, little, meager, microscopic, mini*, miniature, minuscule, minute, modest, narrow, paltry, petite, petty, picayune, piddling*, pint-sized*, pitiful, pocket-sized*, poor, puny*, runty*, scanty, scrubby, short, shrimp*, slight, small-scale, stunted, teensy*, teeny, toy, trifling, trivial, undersized, unpretentious, wee*, young; SEE CONCEPTS *773,789*

small [*adj2*] *unimportant*

bush-league*, inadequate, inconsiderable, ineffectual, inferior, insignificant, lesser, light, limited, lower, mean, minor, minor-league*, minute, narrow, negligible, paltry, petty, secondary, set, small-fry*, small-time*, trifling, trivial, unessential; SEE CONCEPT *575*

small [*adj3*] *narrow-minded, nasty*

base, grudging, ignoble, illiberal, limited, little, mean, narrow, petty, selfish, set, vulgar; SEE CONCEPT *401*

small-minded [*adj*] *narrow-minded*

biased, bigoted, conservative, illiberal, intolerant, opinionated, petty, prejudiced, selfish, short-sighted; SEE CONCEPTS *403,542*

small talk [*n*] *casual conversation*

babble, blab*, blather, chatter, chitchat*, gossip, idle chatter, idle talk, jabber*, prattle, yakking*; SEE CONCEPTS *274,278*

small-time [*adj*] *minor*

bush-league*, dinky*, inconsequential, inconsiderable, insignificant, low, petty, piddling, secondary, second-string*, trivial, two-bit*, unimportant; SEE CONCEPTS *575,773,789*

smart [*adj1*] *intelligent*

acute, adept, agile, alert, apt, astute, bold, brainy*, bright, brilliant, brisk, canny, clever, crafty, effective, eggheaded*, fresh, genius, good, impertinent, ingenious, keen, knowing, long-haired*, nervy, nimble, on the ball*, pert, pointed, quick, quick-witted, ready, resourceful, sassy, sharp, shrewd, skull, slick*, whiz*, wise; SEE CONCEPT *402*

smart [*adj2*] *stylish, fashionable*
chic, dapper, dashing, dressed to kill*, elegant, exclusive, fine, fly*, in fashion, last word*, latest thing*, modish, natty, neat, snappy, spruce, swank, trendy, trim, well turned-out, with it*; SEE CONCEPT *589*

smart [*adj3*] *brisk, lively*
active, bold, brazen, cracking, energetic, forward, good, jaunty, nervy, pert, quick, saucy, scintillating, spanking, spirited, sprightly, vigorous; SEE CONCEPTS *401,542*

smart [*v*] *hurt, pain*
ache, be painful, bite, burn, prick, prickle, sting, suffer, throb, tingle; SEE CONCEPTS *246,728*

smart-aleck [*n*] *wise guy*
bigmouth*, know-it-all*, smart ass*, smartypants*, wiseacre, wiseass, wisenheimer; SEE CONCEPT *412*

smarts [*n*] *intelligence*
acuity, acumen, alertness, aptitude, brainpower, brains*, brightness, brilliance, cleverness, competence, comprehension, gray matter*, intellect, IQ*, judgment, know-how, mind, perception, perspicacity, precocity, reason, savvy, sense, the right stuff*, understanding, what it takes*; SEE CONCEPT *409*

smash [*n1*] *collision; defeat*
accident, bang, bash, blast, blow, boom, breakdown, breaking, breakup, burst, clap, collapse, crack, crack-up, crash, debacle, destruction, disaster, downfall, failure, pile-up, ruin, shattering, slam, smash-up, sock, wallop, welt, whack, wham, wreck; SEE CONCEPTS *674,675*

smash [*n2*] *great success*
hit, knockout, sensation, wow*; SEE CONCEPT *706*

smash [*v1*] *break into pieces*
bang, belt, blast, break to smithereens*, burst, clobber, collide, crack, crash, crush, demolish, disintegrate, fracture, fragment, hit, make mincemeat of*, pound, powder, pulverize, rive, scrunch, shatter, shiver, slam, slug, splinter, squash, squish, trash, wallop; SEE CONCEPTS *246,252*

smash [*v2*] *defeat, destroy*
annihilate, break up, decimate, demolish, destruct, disrupt, lay in ruins*, lay waste*, overthrow, overturn, put out of action*, put out of commission*, raze, ruin, shatter, tear down, topple, trash, tumble, wreck; SEE CONCEPTS *95,252*

smashup [*n*] *wreck*
accident, collision, crack-up*, crash, fender bender, impact, jolt, mess, pile-up*, rear-ender*, sideswipe, total, wreckage; SEE CONCEPTS *189,260,674*

smear [*v1*] *rub on, spread over*
apply, bedaub, besmirch, blur, coat, cover, dab, daub, defile, dirty, discolor, overlay, overspread, patch, plaster, slop, smudge, soil, spatter, spray, sprinkle, stain, sully, taint, tar, tarnish; SEE CONCEPTS *172,202,215*

smear [*v2*] *tarnish a reputation*
asperse, bad-mouth*, befoul, besmirch, blacken, blackguard*, blister, calumniate, defame, defile, denigrate, discolor, drag through mud*, give a black eye*, hit*, libel, malign, pan*, poormouth*, rap*, rip up*, scorch*, slam*, slander, sling mud*, slur, sully, taint, traduce, vilify; SEE CONCEPTS *54,63*

smear campaign [*n*] *mudslinging*
character assassination, defamation of character, dragging one's name through the mud*, slander, whispering campaign; SEE CONCEPTS *54,192,278*

smell [*n*] *odor*
aroma, bouquet, emanation, essence, flavor, fragrance, incense, perfume, redolence, savor, scent, spice, stench, stink, tang, trace, trail, whiff; SEE CONCEPTS *590,599*

smell [*v1*] *perceive with the nose*
breathe, detect, discover, find, get a whiff*, identify, inhale, nose, scent, sniff, snuff; SEE CONCEPTS *590,601,602*

smell [*v2*] *have an odor*
be malodorous, funk*, reek, smell to high heaven*, stench, stink, whiff; SEE CONCEPT *600*

smelly [*adj*] *having a bad odor*
evil-smelling, fetid, foul, foul-smelling, funky*, high, malodorous, mephitic, noisome, olid, putrid, rancid, rank, reeking, stinking, strong, strong-smelling, whiffy*; SEE CONCEPT *598*

smidgen [*n*] *tiny amount*
atom, chicken feed*, crumb, dab, dash, drop, fraction, fragment, grain, iota, little bit, mite, morsel, particle, pinch, scintilla, scrap, shard, shaving, shred, sliver, small amount, small bit, small quantity, speck, tad, taste, trace, wee bit*, whiff, whisper; SEE CONCEPTS *529,831,835*

smile [*v*] *put on a happy expression*
beam, be gracious, express friendliness, express tenderness, grin, laugh, look amused, look delighted, look happy, look pleased, simper, smirk; SEE CONCEPT *185*

smirk [*n*] *sly smile*
beam, grin, leer, simper, smug look, sneer; SEE CONCEPT *185*

smog [*n*] *air pollution*
acid rain, carbon dioxide, fog, haze, smoke, soot; SEE CONCEPT *720*

smoke [*n*] *fume; cigarette*
butt*, cig*, exhaust, fog, gas, mist, pollution, smog, soot, vapor; SEE CONCEPT *720*

smoke detector [*n*] *smoke alarm*
danger signal, emergency alarm, fire alarm, fire bell, heat sensor, siren; SEE CONCEPTS *269,463*

smoky [*adj*] *hazy, sooty*
begrimed, black, burning, caliginous, dingy, fumy, gray, grimy, messy, murky, reeking, silvery, smoke-colored, smoldering, thick, vaporous; SEE CONCEPTS *485,618*

smolder [*v*] *burn, simmer*
boil, bubble, churn, consume, erupt, explode, ferment, fester, fulminate, fume, seethe, smoke, steam, stir; SEE CONCEPTS *35,249*

smooch [*v*] *kiss*
butterfly*, French*, greet, lip*, make out*, mush*, neck*, park*, peck, pucker up*, smack; SEE CONCEPTS *185,375*

smooth [*adj1*] *level, unwrinkled; flowing*
bland, continuous, creamy, easy, effortless, equable, even, flat, fluent, fluid, flush, frictionless, gentle, glassy, glossy, hairless, horizontal, invariable, lustrous, mild, mirrorlike, monotonous, peaceful, plain, planate, plane, polished, quiet, regular, rhythmic, rippleless, serene, shaven, shiny, silky, sleek, soft, soothing, stable, steady, still, tranquil, unbroken, undeviating, undisturbed, uneventful, uniform, uninterrupted, unruffled, untroubled, unvarying, velvety; SEE CONCEPTS *406,480,606*

sl
sm

smooth [*adj2*] *suave in behavior*
agreeable, bland, civilized, courteous, courtly, facile, genial, glib, ingratiating, mellow, mild, persuasive, pleasant, polite, slick, smarmy*, unctuous, urbane; SEE CONCEPT *401*

smooth [*v1*] *make level*
burnish, clear, even, flatten, flush, glaze, gloss, grade, iron, lay, level, make uniform, perfect, plane, polish, press, refine, round, sand, sleek, slick, varnish; SEE CONCEPTS *137,250*

smooth [*v2*] *make peace*
allay, alleviate, appease, assuage, calm, comfort, cool*, ease, extenuate, facilitate, iron out, mellow, mitigate, mollify, palliate, pat, pave the way*, soften, stroke, take the edge off*, take the sting out*; SEE CONCEPTS *7,22*

smother [*v*] *extinguish; cover, hide*
asphyxiate, choke, collect, compose, conceal, control, cool, cork, douse, envelop, heap, hush up*, inundate, keep back, kill, muffle, overwhelm, quash, quell, quench, rein, repress, restrain, shower, shroud, simmer down, snuff, squelch, stamp out, stifle, strangle, suffocate, suppress, surround, throttle; SEE CONCEPTS *130,172,188,234*

smudge [*n*] *dirt smear*
blemish, blot, blur, macule, smut, smutch, soiled spot, spot; SEE CONCEPT *723*

smudge [*v*] *smear, dirty*
begrime, blacken, blotch, blur, daub, defile, foul, grime, mark, plaster, slop, smirch, soil, spatter, sully, taint, tarnish; SEE CONCEPT *254*

smug [*adj*] *pleased with oneself*
complacent, conceited, egoistic, egotistical, holier-than-thou*, hotshot*, pompous, priggish, puffed-up*, self-contented, self-righteous, self-satisfied, snobbish, stuck on oneself*, stuck-up*, stuffy, superior, vainglorious; SEE CONCEPTS *404,542*

smuggle [*v*] *transfer illegal goods*
bootleg, deal, export, hide, moonshine*, pirate, push, run, run contraband*, run rum*, snake in*; SEE CONCEPT *192*

smut [*n*] *pornography*
adult material, adult movie, bawdiness, dirt, dirty movie, erotica, filth, girlie magazine, hard-core pornography, indecency, indecent material, obscene materials, obscenity, porn, porno, porno film, sexploitation, sexually explicit material, skin flick, smut, soft-core pornography, stag film, X-rated material, X-rated movie; SEE CONCEPTS *267,372,545*

smutty [*adj*] *obscene, vulgar*
bawdy, blue*, coarse, crude, dirty, filthy, foul, immoral, improper, indecent, indelicate, lewd, nasty, off-color, pornographic, prurient, racy, raunchy, raw, risqué, rough, salacious, salty, scatological, suggestive, X-rated*; SEE CONCEPTS *267,372,545*

snack [*n*] *tiny meal*
bite, bite to eat*, break, eats*, goodies*, grub*, light meal, lunch, luncheon, midnight snack, morsel, munch*, nibble, nosh*, pickings, piece, refreshment, tea, tidbit; SEE CONCEPTS *457,459*

snafu [*n*] *mistake*
blooper*, blunder, bungle, confusion, error, false step, faux pas, flub*, foul-up, goof-up, mess, miscalculation, misjudgment, misunderstanding, mix-up, oversight, screw-up*, slip, slipup*; SEE CONCEPTS *101,230,410*

snag [*n*] *complication in situation*
bar, barrier, blockade, brake, bug*, catch, Catch-22, clog, crimp, cropper, crunch, curb, difficulty, disadvantage, drag*, drawback, fix*, glitch, hamper, hitch, hold-up*, hole*, hurdle, impediment, inconvenience, knot, obstacle, obstruction, pickle*, problem, puzzler, scrape, spot, stumbling block, the rub*, tight spot*; SEE CONCEPTS *666,674*

snag [*v*] *catch on something*
hole, nail, rip, run into, tear; SEE CONCEPT *214*

snaky [*adj1*] *winding*
anfractuous, convoluted, entwined, flexuous, indirect, meandering, meandrous, serpentine, sinuous, tortuous, twisted, twisting, writhing, zigzag; SEE CONCEPT *581*

snaky [*adj2*] *devious, sly*
crafty, insidious, lurking, perfidious, slinking, sneaky, subtle, treacherous, venomous, vipery, virulent; SEE CONCEPT *401*

snap [*n*] *easy thing to accomplish*
breeze*, child's play*, cinch, duck soup*, ease, easy as pie*, kid stuff*, no problem, picnic*, pie*, smooth sailing*, soft touch*, walkover*; SEE CONCEPT *693*

snap [*v1*] *separate, break*
click, come apart, crack, crackle, fracture, give way, pop; SEE CONCEPTS *98,246*

snap [*v2*] *bite, seize*
bite at, catch, clutch, grab, grasp, grip, jerk, lurch, nip, snatch, twitch, yank; SEE CONCEPTS *90,191*

snap [*v3*] *speak sharply*
bark, flare, flash, fly off the handle*, get angry, growl, grumble, grunt, jump down throat*, lash out, retort, roar, snarl, snort, take it out on*, vent, yell; SEE CONCEPTS *54,77*

snappy [*adj1*] *nasty, irritable*
cross, disagreeable, edgy, fractious, hasty, huffy, petulant, quick-tempered, snappish, tart, testy, touchy, waspish; SEE CONCEPTS *267,401*

snappy [*adj2*] *fashionable*
chic, classy, dapper, dashing, fly*, in good taste, modish, natty, sharp, smart, stylish, swank*, tony*, trendy, up-to-the-minute, with style; SEE CONCEPT *589*

snappy [*adj3*] *fast*
abrupt, breakneck, expeditious, fleet, harefooted, hasty, immediate, instant, on-the-spot, quick, rapid, speedy, sudden, swift, unpremeditated; SEE CONCEPTS *588,799*

snare [*n*] *trap*
allurement, bait, booby trap*, catch, come-on*, deception, decoy, enticement, entrapment, inveiglement, lure, net, noose, pitfall, quicksand, seducement, temptation, trick, wire*; SEE CONCEPTS *529,674*

snare [*v*] *catch, trap*
arrest, bag*, corral*, decoy, enmesh, entangle, entrap, get hands on*, involve, land, lure, net, pull in, round up, seduce, seize, tempt, wire*; SEE CONCEPTS *11,90*

snarl [*n*] *complication, mess*
chaos, clutter, complexity, confusion, disarray, disorder, entanglement, intricacy, intricateness, jam, jungle, knot, labyrinth, maze, mishmash, morass, muddle, muss, skein, swarm, tangle, web; SEE CONCEPTS *663,666,674*

snarl [*v1*] *grumble*
abuse, bark, bluster, bully, complain, fulminate,

gnarl, gnash teeth, growl, mumble, murmur, mutter, quarrel, show teeth, snap, threaten, thunder, yelp; SEE CONCEPT 77

snarl [v2] *complicate, mess up*
confuse, embroil, enmesh, ensnarl, entangle, entwine, involve, muck, muddle, perplex, ravel, tangle; SEE CONCEPTS 16,158

snatch [n] *small part*
bit, fragment, piece, smattering, snippet, spell; SEE CONCEPTS 264,832

snatch [v] *grab away*
abduct, catch, clap hands on, clutch, collar*, gain, get fingers on*, grapple, grasp, grip, jerk, jump, kidnap, make off with, nab, nail*, pluck, pull, rescue, seize, snag, spirit away, steal, take, win, wrench, wrest, yank; SEE CONCEPTS 90,191

snazzy [adj] *stylish*
attractive, beautiful, chic, chichi*, classy, dapper, dashing, dressed to kill*, dressy, fashionable, flashy, in vogue, jazzy, nifty, now*, ritzy, sharp, slick*, smart, snappy, sophisticated, swank*, trendy, upscale, uptown, voguish; SEE CONCEPTS 579,589

sneak [n] *person who is very dishonest*
cheater, con artist, coward, cur, dastard, heel*, informer, louse, rascal, reptile, scoundrel, skunk*, slink*, snake*, snake in grass*, toad*, weasel*, wretch; SEE CONCEPT 412

sneak [v] *move stealthily*
ambush, case, cheat, cower, crawl, creep, deceive, delude, evade, glide, gumshoe*, hide, lurk, mooch, move secretly, ooze, pad, pass, prowl, pussyfoot*, secrete, shirk, sidle, skulk, slide, slink, slip, slither, sly, smuggle, snake, snook, spirit, steal, worm; SEE CONCEPTS 151,188

sneaker [n] *running shoe*
basketball shoe, cleat, footgear, footwear, gym shoe, hightop*, rubber-soled shoe, shoe, sneak, tennis shoe; SEE CONCEPT 451

sneaky [adj] *underhanded, dishonest*
base, contemptible, cowardly, deceitful, devious, disingenuous, double-dealing*, duplicitous, furtive, guileful, indirect, low, malicious, mean, nasty, recreant, secretive, shifty, slippery, sly, sneaking, snide, stealthy, surreptitious, tricky, underhand, unreliable, unscrupulous, untrustworthy, yellow*; SEE CONCEPTS 267,401,542

sneer [v] *mock, condemn*
affront, belittle, burlesque, caricature, crack, curl one's lip at*, decry, deride, detract, disdain, disparage, dump, fleer, flout, gibe, gird, give Bronx cheer, grin, hold in contempt*, hold up to ridicule*, insult, jeer, jest, lampoon, laugh at, leer, look down on, put down, quip at, rally, rank out, ridicule, satirize, scoff, scorn, slam, slight, smile, sneeze at*, sniff at*, snigger, swipe, taunt, travesty, turn up one's nose*, twit, underrate; SEE CONCEPTS 30,52,54

sneeze at [v] *disregard*
blink at*, brush aside, brush away, brush off, discount, have no use for*, laugh off*, let pass*, look the other way*, overlook, pass over, pay no attention to, pay no heed to, pay no mind*, shut eyes to*, slight, snub, take lightly, take no notice of, turn a blind eye*, turn a deaf ear*; SEE CONCEPT 30

snicker/snigger/sniggle [v] *laugh at mockingly*
chortle, chuckle, giggle, guffaw, hee-haw, smirk, sneer, teehee, titter; SEE CONCEPT 77

snide [adj] *hateful, nasty*
base, cynical, disparaging, hurtful, insinuating, malicious, mean, sarcastic, scornful, sneering, spiteful, unkind; SEE CONCEPT 401

sniff [v] *breathe in*
detect, inhale, inspire, nose, scent, smell, snift, snuff, snuffle; SEE CONCEPTS 601,602

snippy [adj] *curt*
abrupt, blunt, brief, brusque, churlish, gruff, impertinent, rude, sharp, sharp-tongued, snappish, snippety; SEE CONCEPT 267

snitch [n] *informer*
betrayer, blabbermouth*, canary*, deep throat*, double-crosser, fink*, informant, narc*, nark*, rat*, sneak, snitcher, source, squealer*, stoolie*, stool pigeon*, tattler, tattletale, tipster*, turncoat, weasel*,   whistle-blower;   SEE   CONCEPTS 348,354,423

snitch [v1] *steal*
burglarize, carry off, defraud, embezzle, heist, hold up, keep, lift*, loot, make off with*, pickpocket, pilfer, pillage, pinch*, plunder, poach, remove, rip off*, shoplift, swipe, take, walk off with*; SEE CONCEPT 139

snitch [v2] *inform*
betray, blab*, confess, give away, leak, rat on*, squeal, tattle, tell, tell on, tip, turn in; SEE CONCEPT 60

snob [n] *person who looks down on others*
braggart, highbrow, name-dropper, parvenu, pretender, smarty pants*, stiff neck*, upstart; SEE CONCEPT 423

snobbish [adj] *stuck-up, conceited*
aloof, arrogant, condescending, egotistic, haughty, high-and-mighty*, high-flown*, high-hat*, ostentatious, overbearing, patronizing, persnickety*, pompous, pretentious, putting on airs*, remote, sniffy*, snippy*, snooty*, snotty*, supercilious, superior, swanky, tony*, uppish, uppity*; SEE CONCEPT 401

snoop [n] *person who noses around*
busybody, butt-in*, detective, eavesdropper, ferret, gumshoe*, meddler, peeping Tom*, pragmatist, pry, pryer, quidnunc, rubberneck*, scout, sleuth, snooper; SEE CONCEPTS 348,423

snoop [v] *nose around*
busybody*, interfere, intrude, meddle, mess with, mouse*, nose, peek, peep, peer, poke, poke nose in*, pry, snook, spy, stare; SEE CONCEPTS 216,384,623

snooty [adj] *haughty*
arrogant, cavalier*, conceited, condescending, egotistic, egotistical, high and mighty*, hoitytoity, la-di-da*, lofty, on a high horse*, pompous, pretentious, snobbish, snotty*, stuckup*, superior, uppity*; SEE CONCEPT 401

snooze [n] *light sleep*
catnap, doze, forty winks*, nap, siesta, slumber; SEE CONCEPT 315

snooze [v] *sleep lightly*
catnap, doze, drop off, drowse, nap, nod off*, siesta, slumber, take forty winks*; SEE CONCEPTS 210,315

snore [v] *make sounds when sleeping*
breathe heavily, saw logs*, saw wood*, sleep, snort, snuffle, wheeze; SEE CONCEPTS 77,315

snotty [adj] *arrogant*
cheeky, cocky, conceited, fresh, haughty, high and mighty*, highfalutin'*, impertinent, know-it-all*, la-di-da*, pompous, pretentious, puffed

sm
sn

up*, sassy, self-important, smart-alecky, smug, snippy*, snobby, snooty, stuck-up*, uppity; SEE CONCEPTS *401,404*

snub [*v*] *give someone the cold shoulder*

act cool*, boycott, brush off*, burr, censure, chill, cool, cut, cut dead*, disdain, disregard, duck, give the brush*, humble, humiliate, ice*, ice out*, ignore, look coldly upon, look right through*, mortify, neglect, not give time of day*, offend, ostracize, pass up, put down, put the chill on*, rebuff, scold, scorn, shame, shun, slight, slur, snob, swank, upstage; SEE CONCEPTS *30,54,384*

snug [*adj*] *cozy, warm*

close, comfortable, comfy, compact, convenient, cushy, easeful, easy, homelike, homely, intimate, neat, restful, sheltered, snug as a bug in a rug*, soft, substantial, tight, trim, well-off; SEE CONCEPT *485*

snuggle [*v*] *cuddle*

bundle, burrow, curl up, grasp, huddle, hug, nestle, nuzzle, snug, spoon; SEE CONCEPTS *190,201*

soak [*v*] *drench, wet*

absorb, assimilate, bathe, damp, dip, drink, drown, dunk, flood, imbrue, immerge, immerse, impregnate, infiltrate, infuse, macerate, marinate, merge, moisten, penetrate, percolate, permeate, pour into, pour on, saturate, seethe, soften, sop, souse, steep, submerge, take in, wash, water, waterlog; SEE CONCEPT *256*

soaked [*adj*] *saturated*

dank, drenched, dripping, drowned, soaking, sodden, soggy, sopping, soppy, soused, waterlogged, wet, wringing-wet; SEE CONCEPT *603*

soar [*v*] *climb, fly*

arise, ascend, aspire, escalate, glide, lift, mount, rise, rocket, sail, shoot, shoot up, skyrocket, top, tower, up, uprear, wing; SEE CONCEPTS *148,150*

soaring [*adj*] *high*

aerial, ascending, climbing, elevated, flying, going through the ceiling*, going through the roof*, high-reaching, lofty, sky-high, steep, towering; SEE CONCEPTS *779,782*

sob [*v*] *cry hard*

bawl, blub, blubber, boohoo*, break down, cry a river*, cry convulsively, cry eyes out*, howl, lament, shed tears, snivel, turn on waterworks*, wail, weep, whimper; SEE CONCEPTS *185,410*

sober [*adj1*] *not partaking of alcohol*

abstaining, abstemious, abstinent, ascetic, calm, clear-headed, cold sober*, continent, controlled, dry, moderate, nonindulgent, not drunk, on the wagon*, restrained, sedate, self-possessed, serious, steady, temperate, took the pledge*; SEE CONCEPT *401*

sober [*adj2*] *calm, peaceful; dull*

abnegating, abstaining, calm, clear-headed, cold, collected, composed, constrained, cool, dark, disciplined, dispassionate, down-to-earth*, drab, earnest, eschewing, forgoing, grave, hard-boiled*, imperturbable, inhibited, levelheaded, low-key, lucid, no-nonsense, pacific, peaceful, plain, practical, quiet, rational, realistic, reasonable, reserved, restrained, sedate, serene, serious, severe, soft, solemn, somber, sound, staid, steady, subdued, toned down, unexcited, unimpassioned, unruffled; SEE CONCEPTS *401,542*

sobriety [*n*] *abstinence*

abstaining, abstemiousness, continence, moderation, refraining, self-restraint, soberness, teetotalism, temperance; SEE CONCEPT *633*

sobriquet [*n*] *nickname*

AKA*, alias, anonym, appellation, assumed name, byname, handle*, label, moniker, nom de guerre, nom de plume, nomenclature, pen name, pet name*, professional name, pseudonym, tag*; SEE CONCEPTS *268,683*

so-called [*adj*] *supposed*

alleged, allegedly, commonly named, formal, nominal, ostensible, pretended, professed, purported, self-named, self-styled, soi-disant, supposed, titular, wrongly named; SEE CONCEPT *552*

sociable [*adj*] *friendly, outgoing*

accessible, affable, approachable, close, clubby*, companionable, conversable, convivial, cordial, familiar, genial, good-natured, gregarious, intimate, neighborly, regular, social, warm; SEE CONCEPTS *401,555*

social [*adj*] *public, friendly*

amusing, civil, collective, common, communal, communicative, community, companionable, convivial, cordial, diverting, entertaining, familiar, general, gracious, gregarious, group, hospitable, informative, mannerly, neighborly, nice, organized, pleasant, pleasurable, polished, polite, popular, public, sociable, societal; SEE CONCEPTS *536,555*

socialism [*n*] *socialist government*

Bolshevism, collective ownership, collectivism, communism, Fabianism, Leninism, Maoism, Marxism, state ownerhsip; SEE CONCEPT *301*

socialite [*n*] *aristocrat*

blueblood, Brahmin, deb*, debutante, gentleperson, lace curtain*, member of the upper class, noble, patrician, silk stocking, upper cruster; SEE CONCEPT *423*

socialize [*v*] *be friendly at gatherings*

associate, chum with*, club*, consort, entertain, fraternize, get about, get around, get together, go out, hang around with*, hang out, hobnob, join, keep company, league, make advances, make the rounds*, mingle, mix, pal around*, run with*, tie up with*; SEE CONCEPT *384*

society [*n1*] *humankind, people*

association, camaraderie, civilization, commonality, commonwealth, community, companionship, company, comradeship, culture, friendship, general public, humanity, jungle*, nation, population, public, rat race*, social order, world, zoo*; SEE CONCEPTS *379,417*

society [*n2*] *organization, institution*

alliance, association, circle, clan, clique, club, companionship, comradeship, corporation, coterie, gang, group, guild, hookup, institute, league, network, order, outfit, ring, sodality, syndicate, tie-in*, tie-up*, union; SEE CONCEPTS *381,387*

society [*n3*] *upper class of people*

aristocracy, beau monde*, beautiful people*, country set*, elite, flower*, gentry, glitterati*, haut monde, high society, jet set*, main line, patriciate, polite society, quality, smart set*, top drawer*, upper crust*, who's who*; SEE CONCEPTS *387,388,417*

sociopath [*n*] *psychopath*

antisocial personality, crazy person, deranged person, insane person, lunatic, mad person, maniac, psycho*, psychotic, schizoid*; SEE CONCEPT *412*

sock [n/v] *hit hard*
beat, belt, bop, buffet, chop, clout, cuff, ding, nail, paste, punch, slap, smack, smash, soak, whack; SEE CONCEPT *189*

sofa [n] *couch*
chaise longue, chesterfield, convertible couch, davenport, daybed, divan, futon, love seat, ottoman, settee, sofa bed, window seat; SEE CONCEPT *443*

soft [adj1] *cushioned, squishy*
bendable, comfortable, comfy, cottony, cozy, creamy, cushiony, cushy, delicate, doughy, downy, ductile, easeful, easy, elastic, feathery, fine, flabby, fleecy, fleshy, flexible, flimsy, flocculent, flowing, fluffy, fluid, formless, furry, gelatinous, impressible, limp, malleable, moldable, mushy, pappy, pithy, plastic, pliable, pulpy, quaggy, rounded, satiny, silken, silky, smooth, snug, spongy, squashy, supple, thin, velvety, yielding; SEE CONCEPTS *488,606*

soft [adj2] *faint, temperate*
ashen, balmy, bland, caressing, comfortable, cool, cushy, delicate, diffuse, dim, dimmed, dulcet, dull, dusky, faint, gentle, hazy, lenient, light, low, low-key, mellifluous, mellow, melodious, mild, misty, murmured, muted, pale, pallid, pastel, pleasing, quiet, restful, shaded, smooth, sober, soothing, subdued, sweet, tinted, toned down, twilight, understated, wan, whispered; SEE CONCEPTS *525,537,592,618*

soft [adj3] *compassionate*
affectionate, amiable, benign, courteous, easy, easy-going, effortless, gentle, gracious, indulgent, kind, kindly, lax, lenient, liberal, manageable, overindulgent, permissive, pitying, sensitive, sentimental, simple, spineless, sympathetic, tender, tender-hearted, undemanding, weak; SEE CONCEPT *401*

soft [adj4] *out of condition*
doughy, fat, flabby, flaccid, fleshy, formless, gone to seed*, limp, out of shape*, overindulged, pampered, untrained, weak; SEE CONCEPTS *314,485*

soft [adj5] *stupid*
daft, fatuous, feeble-minded, foolish, silly, simple, witless; SEE CONCEPT *402*

soften [v] *calm, soothe*
abate, allay, alleviate, appease, assuage, become tender, bend, cushion, diminish, disintegrate, dissolve, ease, enfeeble, give, knead, lessen, lighten, lower, mash, mellow, melt, mitigate, moderate, modify, moisten, mollify, palliate, qualify, quell, relax, relent, still, subdue, temper, tenderize, thaw, tone down, turn down, weaken, yield; SEE CONCEPT *250*

softhearted [adj] *tender*
all heart*, benevolent, big-hearted, bleeding-heart*, caring, charitable, compassionate, considerate, emotional, forgiving, generous, gentle, kind, lenient, merciful, moving, sensitive, sentimental, soft, sympathetic, tenderhearted, warm, warmhearted; SEE CONCEPTS *401,542*

softly [adv] *lightly*
agilely, airily, breezily, carelessly, daintily, delicately, faintly, gently, gingerly, gradually, nimbly, quietly, smoothly, tenderly; SEE CONCEPTS *538,544,584*

soft-spoken [adj] *quiet*
close-mouthed, gentle, hushed, hushful, low,

low-keyed, low-pitched, mild, muffled, peaceful, reserved, silent, soft, still; SEE CONCEPTS *592,594*

software [n] *computer program*
application software, bundled software, courseware, file management system, freeware, groupware, operating system, presentation software, productivity software, program, shareware, spreadsheet, systems software, vaporware; SEE CONCEPTS *269,463*

soggy [adj] *damp or soaking*
clammy, dank, dripping, heavy, humid, moist, mucky, muggy, mushy, pasty, pulpy, saturated, soaked, sodden, soft, sopping, spongy, sticky, sultry, waterlogged; SEE CONCEPT *603*

soil [n1] *earth, dirt*
clay, dry land, dust, grime, ground, land, loam, soot, terra firma; SEE CONCEPT *509*

soil [n2] *land where one lives*
country, home, homeland, homestead, region, spread, terra firma; SEE CONCEPTS *198,510,511*

soil [v] *make dirty*
bedraggle, befoul, begrime, besmirch, contaminate, crumb, debase, defile, degrade, dirty, discolor, disgrace, foul, grime, maculate, mess, mess up, muck*, muck up*, muddy, muss*, muss up*, pollute, shame, smear, smudge, spatter, spoil, spot, stain, sully, taint, tar, tarnish; SEE CONCEPT *254*

sojourn [n] *brief travel; visit*
layover, residence, rest, stay, stop, stopover, tarriance, vacation; SEE CONCEPTS *224,226,227*

sojourn [v] *travel briefly; visit*
abide, dwell, inhabit, linger, lodge, nest, perch, reside, rest, roost, squat, stay, stay over, stop, tarry, vacation; SEE CONCEPTS *224,226,227*

solace [n] *comfort, peace*
alleviation, assuagement, condolement, condolence, consolation, pity, relief; SEE CONCEPTS *7,22,410*

solace [v] *give comfort, peace*
allay, alleviate, buck up, cheer, comfort, condole with, console, mitigate, soften, soothe, upraise; SEE CONCEPTS *7,22*

soldier [n] *person serving in military*
airforce member, cadet, cavalryperson, commando, conscript, draftee, enlisted person, fighter, GI*, Green Beret, guard, guerrilla, gunner, infantry, infantryperson, marine, mercenary, military person, musketeer, officer, paratrooper, pilot, private, rank, recruit, scout, selectee, serviceperson, soldier, soldier-at-arms, trooper, veteran, volunteer, warmonger, warrior; SEE CONCEPT *358*

sole [adj] *alone, singular*
ace, exclusive, individual, lone, one, one and only, onliest, only, only one, particular, remaining, separate, single, solitary, solo, unique, unshared; SEE CONCEPTS *555,564,577*

solely [adv] *only, alone*
barely, but, completely, entirely, exclusively, individually, merely, onliest, purely, simply, single-handedly, singly, singularly, totally, undividedly, wholly; SEE CONCEPTS *544,577*

solemn [adj1] *quiet, serious*
austere, brooding, cold sober*, deliberate, dignified, downbeat, earnest, funereal, glum, grave, heavy, intense, matter of life and death*, moody, no fooling*, no-nonsense*, pensive, portentous, reflective, sedate, sober, somber, staid, stern, thoughtful, weighty; SEE CONCEPTS *403,542*

sn
so

solemn [*adj2*] *impressive, sacred*
august, awe-inspiring, ceremonial, ceremonious, conventional, devotional, dignified, divine, formal, full, grand, grave, hallowed, holy, imposing, impressive, magnificent, majestic, momentous, ostentatious, overwhelming, plenary, religious, reverential, ritual, sanctified, stately, venerable; SEE CONCEPT *574*

solicit [*v*] *plead for; try to sell*
accost, apply, approach, ask, beg, beseech, bespeak, bum, cadge, call, canvass, challenge, claim, come on to*, crave, demand, desire, drum*, drum up*, entreat, exact, go, hawk, hit on*, hit up*, hustle, implore, importune, inquire, mooch, panhandle, pass the hat*, peddle, petition, postulate, pray, promote, proposition, query, question, refer, request, require, requisition, resort, seduce, seek, sponge, steer, sue for, supplicate, touch, tout, turn, whistle for*; SEE CONCEPTS *53,345*

solicitous [*adj*] *worried*
anxious, appetent, apprehensive, ardent, athirst, attentive, avid, beside oneself, careful, caring, concerned, devoted, eager, earnest, heedful, impatient, keen, loving, mindful, raring, regardful, tender, thirsty, troubled, uneasy, worried sick*, worried stiff*, zealous; SEE CONCEPT *403*

solicitude [*n*] *worry, anxiety*
attention, attentiveness, care, compunction, concern, concernment, considerateness, consideration, disquiet, disquietude, heed, presentiment, qualm, regard, scruple, tender loving care*, TLC*, unease, uneasiness, watchfulness; SEE CONCEPT *410*

solid [*adj1*] *hard, dimensional*
brick wall*, close, compact, compacted, concentrated, concrete, consolidated, dense, firm, fixed, heavy, hefty, hulk, hunk, husky, massed, material, physical, rock, rocklike, rooted, secure, set, sound, stable, strong, sturdy, substantial, thick, tight, unshakable; SEE CONCEPTS *483,604*

solid [*adj2*] *continuous, complete*
agreed, brick wall*, consecutive, consentient, continued, firm, like a rock, regular, set in stone*, stable, steady, unalloyed, unanimous, unbroken, undivided, uninterrupted, united, unmixed; SEE CONCEPTS *482,488,531*

solid [*adj3*] *dependable, reliable*
cogent, constant, decent, estimable, genuine, good, law-abiding, levelheaded, pure, real, satisfactory, satisfying, sensible, serious, sober, sound, stalwart, steadfast, trustworthy, trusty, upright, upstanding, valid, worthy; SEE CONCEPTS *401,534*

solidarity [*n*] *unity*
accord, agreement, alliance, comradeship, confederation, consensus, federation, fellowship, harmony, indivisibility, oneness, sameness, support, teamwork, unanimity, undividedness, unification, uniformity, union; SEE CONCEPTS *664, 714,837*

solidify [*v*] *harden*
amalgamate, anneal, bake, cake, cement, clot, coagulate, cohere, congeal, crystallize, densify, dry, firm, freeze, jell, petrify, set, stiffen, strengthen, thicken; SEE CONCEPTS *250,469*

solitary [*adj*] *alone, single; unsociable*
aloof, antisocial, cloistered, companionless, deserted, desolate, distant, eremetic, forsaken, friendless, hermitical, hidden, individual, introverted, isolated, lone, lonely, lonesome, lorn, misanthropic, offish, only, out-of-the-way*, particular, reclusive, remote, reserved, retired, secluded, separate, sequestered, singular, sole, solo, stag, standoffish, unaccompanied, unapproachable, unattended, uncompanionable, unfrequented, unique, unsocial, withdrawn; SEE CONCEPTS *555,577,583*

solitude [*n*] *aloneness*
confinement, desert, detachment, emptiness, isolation, loneliness, loneness, lonesomeness, peace and quiet*, privacy, quarantine, reclusiveness, retirement, seclusion, separateness, silence, solitariness, waste, wasteland, wilderness, withdrawal; SEE CONCEPTS *388,673,714*

solo [*adj*] *alone*
by oneself, companionless, friendless, individual, in solitary*, me and my shadow*, me myself and I*, on one's own, single, solitary, stag, unaccompanied, unaided, unassisted, unescorted, unmarried; SEE CONCEPTS *577,583*

solution [*n1*] *answer, resolution*
Band-Aid*, clarification, elucidation, explanation, explication, key, pay dirt*, quick fix*, result, solving, the ticket*, unfolding, unraveling, unravelment; SEE CONCEPTS *230,661,712*

solution [*n2*] *mixture of liquid and another substance*
blend, compound, dissolvent, elixir, emulsion, extract, fluid, juice, mix, sap, solvent, suspension; SEE CONCEPTS *260,467*

solve [*v*] *answer, resolve*
break*, clarify, clear up, construe, crack*, deal with, decide, decipher, decode, determine, disentangle, divine, do, elucidate, enlighten, explain, expound, fathom, figure out, find out, fix, get, get right, get to the bottom*, have, hit, hit upon*, illuminate, interpret, iron out*, lick*, make a dent*, make out*, pan out*, put two and two together*, puzzle, reason, settle, think out, unfold, unlock, unravel, unriddle, untangle, work, work out; SEE CONCEPTS *15,18,37*

solvent [*adj*] *financially sound*
able to pay, financially stable, firm, fit, in the pink*, out of the red*, solid, stable; SEE CONCEPTS *314,488*

somber [*adj*] *sad, depressing*
black, bleak, blue*, caliginous, cloudy, dark, depressive, dim, dingy, dire, dismal, dispiriting, doleful, down, drab, dragged, dreary, dull, dusky, earnest, funereal, gloomy, grave, grim, hurting, joyless, lugubrious, melancholy, mournful, murky, no-nonsense, obscure, sad, sedate, sepulchral, serious, shadowy, shady, sober, solemn, sourpuss, staid, tenebrous, weighty; SEE CONCEPTS *403,485,529*

somebody [*n*] *person of fame, importance*
celebrity, dignitary, heavyweight*, household name*, luminary, name*, notable, one, personage, person of note, public figure, so-and-so*, someone*, some person*, star, superstar, VIP*, whoever*; SEE CONCEPT *423*

someday [*adv*] *eventually*
after a while, anytime, at a future time, finally, in a time to come, on a day, one day, one fine day*, one of these days, one time, one time or another, sometime, sooner or later, subsequently, ultimately, yet; SEE CONCEPTS *548,820*

somehow [*adv*] *by some means*
after a fashion, anyhow, anyway, anywise, by

hook or crook*, come what may*, in one way or another, in some such way, in some way, one way or another, somehow or another, somehow or other; SEE CONCEPT *544*

something [*n*] *entity*
article, being, commodity, existence, existent, individual, object, substance, thing; SEE CONCEPT *433*

sometimes [*adv*] *every now and then*
at intervals, at times, consistently, constantly, ever and again, every so often, frequently, from time to time, here and there, intermittently, now and again, now and then, occasionally, off and on, once in a blue moon*, once in a while, on occasion, periodically, recurrently; SEE CONCEPT *805*

somewhat [*adv*] *to some extent*
adequately, a little, bearably, considerably, fairly, far, incompletely, in part, insignificantly, kind of, moderately, more or less, not much, partially, pretty, quite, rather, ratherish, significantly, slightly, some, something, sort of, to a degree, tolerably, well; SEE CONCEPTS *548,569,772*

somewhere [*adv*] *in, or at some place*
about, any old place, around, around somewhere, elsewhere, here and there, in one place or another, kicking around*, parts unknown*, scattered, someplace, someplace or another, someplace or other, somewheres; SEE CONCEPT *583*

somnolent [*adj*] *sleepy*
asleep, dozy, drowsy, listless, nodding off, out of it*, sleeping, snoozy*, soporific, tired; SEE CONCEPTS *315,539*

song [*n*] *melody sung or played with musical instrument*
air, anthem, aria, ballad, canticle, carol, chant, chorale, chorus, ditty, expression, golden oldie*, hymn, lay, lullaby, lyric, melody, number, oldie*, opera, piece, poem, psalm, refrain, rock, rock and roll, round, shanty, strain, tune, verse, vocal; SEE CONCEPTS *262,293,595*

sonorous [*adj*] *resonant*
booming, full-voiced, loud, loud-voiced, powerful, resounding, reverberating, rich, ringing, rotund, thundering; SEE CONCEPTS *592,594*

soon [*adv*] *in the near future*
anon, any minute now, before long, betimes, by and by, coming down the pike*, directly, early, ere long, expeditiously, fast, fleetly, forthwith, hastily, in a little while, in a minute, in a second, in a short time, in due time, in short order, instantly, in time, lickety-split*, on time, posthaste, presently, promptly, pronto, quick, quickly, rapidly, short, shortly, speedily; SEE CONCEPTS *548,798,820*

soothe [*v*] *calm, ease*
allay, alleviate, appease, assuage, balm, becalm, butter up*, calm down, cheer, compose, console, cool, cool off*, dulcify, help, hush, lighten, lull, make nice*, make up, mitigate, mollify, pacify, patch things up*, play up to*, pour oil on*, quiet, quieten, relieve, settle, smooth down, soften, square, still, stroke, subdue, take the edge off*, take the sting out*, tranquilize, unburden, untrouble; SEE CONCEPTS *7,22,110,384*

soothing [*adj*] *comforting*
alleviating, calming, consolatory, consoling, easing, mollifying, pacifying, palliative, reassuring,

relaxing, relieving, remedying, softening, tranquilizing, warming; SEE CONCEPT *529*

soothsayer [*n*] *seer*
augur, channeller, clairvoyant, crystal ball gazer, diviner, forecaster, fortune-teller, medium, oracle, palm reader, prophet, psychic, soothsayer; SEE CONCEPT *423*

sophisticated [*adj1*] *cosmopolitan, cultured*
adult, artificial, been around, blasé, bored, citified, cool*, couth, cultivated, cynical, disenchanted, disillusioned, experienced, in, in the know*, into*, jaded, jet-set*, knowing, laid-back*, mature, mondaine, on to*, practical, practiced, refined, schooled, seasoned, sharp, skeptical, smooth, stagy*, streetwise, studied, suave, svelte, switched on*, uptown*, urbane, well-bred, wised up*, wise to*, with it*, worldly, worldly wise, world-weary; SEE CONCEPTS *401,404,589*

sophisticated [*adj2*] *complex, advanced*
complicated, delicate, elaborate, highly developed, intricate, involved, knotty, labyrinthine, modern, multifaceted, refined, subtle; SEE CONCEPT *562*

sophistication [*n*] *culture, style*
composure, elegance, finesse, poise, refinement, savoir faire, savoir vivre, social grace, tact, urbanity, worldliness, worldly wisdom; SEE CONCEPTS *388,633,655*

sophomoric [*adj*] *inexperienced*
brash, foolish, naive, reckless, young; SEE CONCEPT *401*

soporific [*adj*] *sleepy; sleep-inducing*
anesthetic, balmy, calming, deadening, dozy*, drowsy, dull, hypnotic, mesmerizing, narcotic, nodding, numbing, opiate, quietening, sedative, slumberous, snoozy*, somniferous, somnolent, soothing, tranquilizing; SEE CONCEPTS *537,539*

sopping [*adj*] *wet*
dank, drenched, dripping, drowned, saturated, soaked, soaking, sodden, soggy, soppy, soused, water-logged, wringing-wet; SEE CONCEPT *603*

sorcerer [*n*] *wizard*
alchemist, augurer, charmer, clairvoyant, conjurer, diviner, enchanter, fortune-teller, magician, medium, necromancer, occultist, seer, shaman, soothsayer, sorceress, thaumaturge, warlock, witch; SEE CONCEPT *361*

sorcery [*n*] *black magic, witchcraft*
abracadabra*, alchemy, bewitchment, black art, charm, conjuring, devilry, divination, enchantment, evil eye, hocus-pocus*, hoodoo*, incantation, jinx, magic, mumbo-jumbo*, necromancy, spell, thaumaturgy, voodoo, witchery, witching, wizardry; SEE CONCEPTS *370,689*

sordid [*adj*] *dirty, bad, low*
abject, avaricious, base, black, calculated, corrupt, covetous, debauched, degenerate, degraded, despicable, disreputable, dowdy, filthy, foul, grasping, grubby, ignoble, impure, low-down, mean, mercenary, miserable, miserly, nasty, poor, scurvy, seedy, selfish, self-seeking, servile, shabby, shameful, sleazy, slovenly, slum, slummy, small, small-minded, squalid, unclean, uncleanly, ungenerous, venal, vicious, vile, wretched; SEE CONCEPTS *334,545,571*

sore [*adj1*] *hurt physically*
abscessed, aching, acute, afflicted, annoying, bruised, burned, burning, chafed, critical, distressing, extreme, hurtful, hurting, inflamed, irri-

tated, pained, painful, raw, reddened, sensitive, severe, sharp, smarting, tender, ulcerated, uncomfortable, unpleasant, vexatious; SEE CONCEPT *314*

sore [*adj2*] *angry; hurt mentally*
afflicted, aggrieved, annoyed, annoying, critical, distressing, grieved, grieving, indignant, irked, irritated, pained, peeved, pressing, resentful, sensitive, smarting, stung, troubled, upset, urgent, vexed, weighty; SEE CONCEPT *403*

sorrow [*n*] *extreme upset, grief*
affliction, agony, anguish, bad news*, big trouble*, blow, blues*, care, catastrophe, dejection, depression, distress, dolor, grieving, hardship, heartache, heartbreak, lamenting, melancholy, misery, misfortune, mourning, pain, rain*, regret, remorse, repentence, rue, sadness, suffering, trial, tribulation, trouble, unhappiness, weeping, woe, worry, wretchedness; SEE CONCEPT *410*

sorrow [*v*] *be very upset, grieved*
agonize, bemoan, be sad, bewail, carry on, cry a river*, deplore, eat heart out*, grieve, groan, hang crepe*, lament, moan, mourn, regret, sing the blues*, sob, take on*, weep; SEE CONCEPTS *34,410*

sorrowful [*adj*] *very upset; grieving*
affecting, afflicted, dejected, depressed, disconsolate, distressing, doleful, dolent, full of sorrow, grievous, heartbroken, heartrending, heavyhearted, hurting, in mourning, in pain, in sorrow, lamentable, lugubrious, melancholy, miserable, mournful, painful, piteous, plaintive, rueful, ruthful, sad, sick at heart*, singing the blues*, sorry, tearful, tear-jerking*, unhappy, woebegone, woeful, wretched; SEE CONCEPT *403*

sorry [*adj1*] *remorseful, regretful*
apologetic, attritional, compunctious, conscience-stricken, contrite, guilt-ridden, melted, penitent, penitential, repentant, self-accusing, self-condemnatory, self-reproachful, shamefaced, softened, touched; SEE CONCEPTS *403,545*

sorry [*adj2*] *sad, heartbroken*
bad, disconsolate, distressed, grieved, heavyhearted, melancholy, mournful, pitiful, rueful, saddened, sorrowful, unhappy; SEE CONCEPT *403*

sorry [*adj3*] *despicable, pathetic*
abject, base, beggarly, cheap, contemptible, deplorable, despisable, disgraceful, dismal, distressing, inadequate, insignificant, mean, miserable, paltry, piteous, pitiable, pitiful, poor, sad, scruffy*, scummy*, scurvy, shabby, shoddy, small, trifling, trivial, unimportant, vile, worthless, wretched; SEE CONCEPTS *485,529*

sort [*n*] *type, variety*
array, batch, battery, body, brand, breed, category, character, class, clutch, denomination, description, family, genus, group, ilk, kind, likes, likes of*, lot, make, nature, number, order, parcel, quality, race, set, species, stamp, stripe, style, suite; SEE CONCEPT *378*

sort [*v*] *place in order*
arrange, assort, button down*, catalogue, categorize, choose, class, classify, comb, cull, distribute, divide, file, grade, group, order, peg, pick, pigeonhole*, put down as, put down for, put in order, put in shape, put to rights*, rank, riddle, screen, select, separate, sift, size up, systematize, tab, typecast, winnow; SEE CONCEPTS *84,158*

sortie [*n*] *armed attack*
assault, charge, invasion, mission, offense, raid, rush, sally*, strike; SEE CONCEPTS *86,317*

so-so [*adj*] *adequate, passable*
average, enough, fair, fairish, fair to middling*, indifferent, mediocre, medium, middling*, moderate, not bad*, okay*, ordinary, respectable, run-of-the-mill*, tolerable, undistinguished; SEE CONCEPTS *533,575*

soul [*n1*] *psyche, inspiration, energy*
anima, animating principle, animation, animus, ardor, bosom, bottom, breast, breath of life, cause, conscience, courage, disposition, ego, elan vital, essence, feeling, fervor, force, genius, heart, individuality, intellect, intelligence, life, marrow, mind, nobility, noumenon, personality, pith, pneuma, principle, quintessence, reason, recesses of heart*, secret self*, spirit, spiritual being, stuff, substance, thought, vital force, vitality, vivacity; SEE CONCEPTS *409,410,411*

soul [*n2*] *being*
body, character, creature, ghost, human being, individual, living soul*, man, mortal, person, personage, phantom, shadow, spirit, umbra, woman; SEE CONCEPT *389*

soulful [*adj*] *emotional*
ardent, deep, expressive, feeling, fervent, fervid, fiery, impassioned, meaningful, moving, passionate, stirred, stirring, tender, touching; SEE CONCEPTS *403,542*

soul-searching [*n*] *introspection*
contemplation, deep thought, heart-searching, meditation, reflection, rumination, self-analysis, self-examination, self-questioning; SEE CONCEPTS *24,410*

sound [*adj1*] *complete, healthy*
alive and kicking*, effectual, entire, firm, fit, flawless, hale, hearty, intact, in the pink*, perfect, right, right as rain*, robust, safe, sane, solid, stable, sturdy, substantial, thorough, total, unblemished, undamaged, undecayed, unhurt, unimpaired, uninjured, up to snuff*, vibrant, vigorous, vital, well, well-constructed, whole, wholesome, wrapped tight*; SEE CONCEPTS *314,488*

sound [*adj2*] *logical, reasonable*
accurate, advisable, all there*, cogent, commonsensical, consequent, convincing, cool*, correct, deep, exact, fair, faultless, flawless, got it together*, impeccable, intellectual, judicious, just, levelheaded, orthodox, precise, profound, proper, prudent, rational, reliable, responsible, right, right-minded, right-thinking, satisfactory, satisfying, sensible, sober, solid, telling, thoughtful, together*, true, trustworthy, valid, well-advised, well-founded, well-grounded, wise; SEE CONCEPTS *403,529,558*

sound [*adj3*] *accepted, established*
all there*, authoritative, canonical, dependable, fair, faithful, fly*, go*, hanging together*, holding together*, holding up*, holding up in wash*, holding water*, kosher*, legal, legit*, loyal, orthodox, proper, proven, received, recognized, reliable, reputable, safe, sanctioned, secure, significant, solid, solvent, stable, standing up*, tried-and-true*, true, valid, washing; SEE CONCEPTS *535,552,582*

sound [*n*] *something heard or audible*
accent, din, harmony, intonation, loudness, melody, modulation, music, noise, note, pitch,

racket, report, resonance, reverberation, ringing, softness, sonance, sonancy, sonority, sonorousness, static, tenor, tonality, tone, vibration, voice; SEE CONCEPT *595*

sound [*v1*] *produce noise*
babble, bang, bark, blare, blow, boom, burst, buzz, cackle, chatter, clack, clang, clank, clap, clatter, clink, crash, creak, detonate, echo, emit, explode, hum, jabber, jangle, jar, moan, murmur, patter, play, rattle, reflect, resonate, resound, reverberate, ring, roar, rumble, shout, shriek, shrill, sing, slam, smash, snort, squawk, thud, thump, thunder, toot, trumpet, vibrate, whine, whisper; SEE CONCEPT *65*

sound [*v2*] *give the impression*
appear, appear to be, look, seem, strike as being; SEE CONCEPTS *316,716*

sound bite [*n*] *very brief broadcast statement*
blurb*, buzzword, clip, excerpt, fifteen minutes of fame*, newsbreak, news item, notation, note, one-liner, outtake, passage, photo opportunity, piece, quotation, quote, saying, selection, slogan, snippet, spot news; SEE CONCEPT *277*

soundproof [*adj*] *silent*
hushed, insulated, noiseless, quiet, soundless; SEE CONCEPT *594*

soupçon [*n*] *small amount*
atom, crumb, dab, dash, drop, flash, hint, iota, particle, pinch, ray, scintilla, shade, shred, small bit, small quantity, smidgen, sparkle, speck, spot, suggestion, tinge, trace, whiff, whisper; SEE CONCEPTS *529,831*

sour [*adj1*] *bad-tasting; gone bad*
acerb, acetic, acetose, acetous, acid, acidic, acidulated, acrid, astringent, bad, biting, bitter, briny, caustic, curdled, cutting, dry, fermented, green, keen, musty, peppery, piquant, pungent, rancid, salty, sharp, soured, sourish, stinging, tart, turned, unpleasant, unripe, unsavory, unwholesome, vinegary, with a kick*; SEE CONCEPTS *462,613*

sour [*adj2*] *in a bad mood*
acid, acrid, acrimonious, bitter, churlish, crabby, cynical, disagreeable, discontented, displeasing, embittered, grouchy, grudging, ill-natured, ill-tempered, irritable, jaundiced, on edge*, peevish, rotten, tart, ungenerous, unhappy, unpleasant, waspish; SEE CONCEPTS *403,542*

sour [*v*] *alienate*
acidify, curdle, disenchant, embitter, envenom, exacerbate, exasperate, make sour, spoil, turn, turn off; SEE CONCEPTS *14,250*

source [*n*] *beginning; point of supply*
antecedent, author, authority, authorship, begetter, birthplace, cause, commencement, connection, dawn, dawning, derivation, determinant, expert, father, fount, fountain, fountainhead, horse's mouth*, inception, informant, maternity, mother, onset, opening, origin, origination, originator, parent, paternity, provenance, provenience, rise, rising, root, specialist, spring, start, starting point, wellspring; SEE CONCEPT *648*

sourpuss [*n*] *grouch*
bellyacher*, crab, crank, crosspatch, curmudgeon, faultfinder, griper, growler, grumbler, grump*, killjoy, moaner, sorehead*, sulker, whiner; SEE CONCEPTS *412,423*

souse [*v*] *make very wet*
brine, deluge, dip, douse, drench, drown, duck, dunk, immerse, impregnate, marinate, pickle,

preserve, seethe, soak, sop, steep, submerge, submerse, waterlog, wet; SEE CONCEPT *256*

soused [*adj*] *drunk*
bashed, boozed up*, buzzed*, crocked*, feeling no pain*, flushed*, flying*, groggy, high*, inebriated, intoxicated, juiced*, laced*, liquored up*, lit*, plastered*, potted*, seeing double*, sloshed*, smashed*, stewed*, stoned*, tanked*, three sheets to the wind*, tipsy, totaled*, under the influence, under the table*, wasted*; SEE CONCEPTS *314,545*

souvenir [*n*] *keepsake from event*
gift, memento, memorial, relic, remembrance, remembrancer, reminder, token, trophy; SEE CONCEPTS *337,446*

sovereign [*adj*] *dominant, effective*
absolute, ascendant, autonomous, chief, commanding, directing, effectual, efficacious, excellent, guiding, highest, imperial, independent, lofty, majestic, monarchal, monarchial, overbearing, paramount, predominant, predominate, preponderant, prevalent, principal, regal, regnant, reigning, royal, ruling, self-governed, supreme, unlimited; SEE CONCEPTS *536,568*

sovereign [*n*] *supreme ruler*
autocrat, chief, czar, emperor, empress, king, leader, majesty, monarch, potentate, prince, princess, queen, ruler; SEE CONCEPT *354*

sovereignty [*n*] *domination*
ascendancy, ascendant, dominance, dominion, jurisdiction, preeminence, prepotence, prepotency, primacy, supremacy, supreme power, sway; SEE CONCEPT *299*

sow [*v*] *plant*
broadcast, disject, disseminate, drill, fling, grow, implant, inseminate, lodge, pitch, propagate, put in, raise, scatter, seed, strew, toss; SEE CONCEPTS *253,257*

spa [*n*] *resort*
day spa, fat farm*, health club, health facility, holiday spot, hotel, hot spring*, lodge, mineral spring resort, sanitarium, sauna, whirlpool; SEE CONCEPTS *198,516*

space [*n1*] *room, scope*
amplitude, area, arena, blank, breadth, capacity, compass, distance, elbowroom, expanse, expansion, extension, extent, field, gap, headroom, headway, infinity, interval, lacuna, leeway, location, margin, omission, play, range, reach, slot, spaciousness, sphere, spot, spread, stretch, territory, tract, turf, volume, zone; SEE CONCEPTS *739,746,756*

space [*n2*] *time interval*
bit, duration, period, season, span, spell, stretch, term, time, while; SEE CONCEPT *807*

spacecraft [*n*] *spaceship*
flying saucer, rocket, rocket ship, satellite, shuttle, space capsule, space probe, space shuttle, UFO, unidentified flying object; SEE CONCEPT *504*

spacey/spacy [*adj*] *eccentric*
beat*, bizarre, crazy, dizzy, erratic, far out*, flaky, flighty, freakish, kooky, nutty, odd, oddball, offbeat, off-center, off the wall*, out in left field, out to lunch*, peculiar, quirky, spaced out*, strange, way out*, weird; SEE CONCEPTS *547,564*

spacious [*adj*] *extensive, expansive*
ample, big, boundless, broad, capacious, cavernous, comfortable, commodious, endless, enor-

mous, extended, generous, great, huge, immense, infinite, large, limitless, roomy, sizable, uncrowded, vast, voluminous, wide, widespread; SEE CONCEPTS *481,482,774*

span [*n*] *distance, duration*
amount, compass, extent, interval, length, measure, period, reach, space, spell, spread, stretch, term, time; SEE CONCEPTS *756,807,822*

span [*v*] *stretch over*
arch, bridge, connect, cover, cross, extend, ford, go across, link, pass over, range, reach, traverse, vault; SEE CONCEPT *756*

spank [*v*] *slap, usually on bottom*
belt, blip, box, buffet, cane, chastise, clobber, clout, cuff, flax, flog, hide, larrup*, lash, lather*, leather*, lick, paddle, punch, punish, put over one's knee*, smack, sock, tan*, tan one's hide*, thrash, trim, wallop, welt, whip, whup*; SEE CONCEPT *189*

spare [*adj1*] *extra, reserve*
additional, backup, de trop, emergency, free, in excess, in reserve, in store, lagniappe, leftover, more than enough*, odd, option, over, supererogatory, superfluous, supernumerary, surplus, unoccupied, unused, unwanted; SEE CONCEPTS *771,824*

spare [*adj2*] *thin; sparse*
angular, bony, economical, exiguous, frugal, gaunt, lank, lanky, lean, meager, modest, poor, rangy, rawboned, scant, scanty, scraggy, scrawny, shadow, skimpy, skinny, slender, slight, slim, sparing, sparse, stick, stilt, stingy, wiry; SEE CONCEPTS *490,491,771*

spare [*v1*] *do or manage without*
afford, allow, bestow, dispense with, give, grant, part with, pinch, provide, put by, relinquish, salt away*, save, scrape, scrimp, short, skimp, stint, supply; SEE CONCEPT *129*

spare [*v2*] *forgive; have mercy upon*
absolve, bail out, be lenient, be merciful, discharge, dispense, excuse, exempt, forbear, get off the hook*, get out of hock*, give a break*, give quarter to, go easy on*, leave, let go, let off*, pardon, pity, privilege from, pull out of the fire*, refrain from, release, relent, relieve from, save bacon*, save from, save neck*, spring; SEE CONCEPTS *50,88,134*

sparing [*adj*] *careful, economical*
avaricious, canny, chary, close, cost-conscious, frugal, humane, mean, money-conscious, parsimonious, provident, prudent, saving, stewardly, stingy, thrifty, tight, tight-fisted, tolerant, ungiving, unwasteful, wary; SEE CONCEPTS *334,401*

spark [*n*] *flash, trace*
atom, beam, fire, flare, flicker, gleam, glint, glitter, glow, hint, jot, nucleus, ray, scintilla, scintillation, scrap, sparkle, spit, vestige; SEE CONCEPTS *519,624,828,831*

spark [*v*] *start, inspire*
animate, excite, kindle, precipitate, provoke, set in motion, set off, stimulate, stir, touch off, trigger; SEE CONCEPT *221*

sparkle [*n*] *glitter, shine*
animation, brilliance, coruscation, dash, dazzle, élan, flash, flicker, gaiety, gleam, glimmer, glint, glitz, glow, life, panache, radiance, scintillation, shimmer, show, spark, spirit, twinkle, vim, vitality, vivacity, zap*, zip*; SEE CONCEPTS *411,624,628*

sparkle [*v*] *glitter, shine*
beam, bubble, coruscate, dance, effervesce, fizz, fizzle, flash, flicker, gleam, glimmer, glint, glisten, glow, scintillate, shimmer, spark, twinkle, wink; SEE CONCEPT *624*

sparse [*adj*] *very few and scattered*
dispersed, exiguous, few and far between, inadequate, infrequent, meager, occasional, poor, rare, scant, scanty, scarce, scrimpy, skimpy, spare, sporadic, thin, uncommon; SEE CONCEPTS *762,789*

spasm [*n*] *twitch, fit*
access, attack, burst, contraction, convulsion, eruption, frenzy, jerk, outburst, pain, paroxysm, seizure, throe, yank; SEE CONCEPTS *185,728*

spasmodic [*adj*] *twitching, erratic*
bits and pieces*, changeable, choppy, convulsive, desultory, fitful, fits and starts*, intermittent, irregular, jerky, on-again-off-again*, periodic, shaky, spastic, sporadic, spotty, spurtive, uncertain; SEE CONCEPTS *482,530,541*

spat [*n*] *dispute, quarrel*
altercation, argument, beef*, bickering, brouhaha, conflict, difference of opinion, disagreement, discord, dissension, embroilment, falling-out, feud, flare-up, fracas, friction, fuss, hubbub, miff*, misunderstanding, row, rumpus*, run-in*, squabble, strife, tiff, words; SEE CONCEPTS *46,106,278*

spatter [*v*] *splash, sprinkle*
bespatter, bestrew, broadcast, dash, daub, dirty, discharge, disperse, dot, douse, dribble, mottle, polka-dot, scatter, shower, slop, smudge, soil, spangle, speck, speckle, splutter, spot, spray, sputter, stipple, strew, swash, wet; SEE CONCEPTS *172,179,256*

spawn [*v*] *produce*
bring forth, create, father, generate, give rise to, hatch, issue, make, mother, originate, parent, procreate, reproduce, sire; SEE CONCEPTS *173,251,374*

speak [*v1*] *talk*
allege, articulate, assert, aver, blab*, break silence, chat, chew*, communicate, converse, convey, declare, deliver, descant, discourse, drawl, enunciate, expatiate, express, gab*, gas*, go*, jaw*, lip*, make known, make public, modulate, mouth, mumble, murmur, mutter, open one's mouth, perorate, pop off*, pronounce, put into words, rap*, say, shout, sound, speak one's piece*, spiel*, spill, state, tell, utter, verbalize, vocalize, voice, whisper, yak*, yakkety-yak*, yammer; SEE CONCEPTS *47,266*

speak [*v2*] *address; give a lecture*
argue, declaim, descant, discourse, get across, harangue, hold forth, orate, pitch, plead, prelect, recite, sermonize, spiel*, spout*, stump, talk; SEE CONCEPTS *60,285*

speaker [*n*] *talker*
after-dinner speaker, announcer, elocutionist, keynoter, lecturer, mouthpiece, orator, public speaker, rhetorician, speechmaker, spokesperson; SEE CONCEPT *348*

speak out/speak up [*v*] *make one's position known*
assert, come out with, declare, have one's say*, insist, let voice be heard*, make oneself heard, make plain, say loud and clear*, sound off*, speak loudly, speak one's mind*, stand up for; SEE CONCEPTS *49,57*

spearhead [v] *lead, start*
bring, bring on, cause, direct, get the jump on*, go out in front*, guide, head, helm, influence, initiate, introduce, launch, motivate, move, originate, persuade, pioneer, produce, prompt, quarterback*, run things*, shepherd, spur, trailblaze*; SEE CONCEPTS *68,117,221*

special [adj] *distinguished, distinctive; important in own way*
appropriate, best, certain, characteristic, chief, choice, defined, definite, designated, determinate, different, earmarked, especial, exceptional, exclusive, express, extraordinary, festive, first, gala, individual, limited, main, major, marked, memorable, momentous, out of the ordinary, particular, peculiar, personal, primary, proper, rare, red-letter*, reserved, restricted, select, set, significant, smashing*, sole, specialized, specific, uncommon, unique, unreal*, unusual; SEE CONCEPTS *557,564,567*

specialist [n] *person who is an expert in a field*
ace, adept, authority, connoisseur, consultant, devotee, doctor, guru*, old hand*, old pro*, pro*, professional, pundit, sage, savant, scholar, technician, veteran, virtuoso*; SEE CONCEPTS *347,357*

specialize [v] *concentrate on specific area*
be into, develop oneself in, do one's thing*, go in for, have a weakness for*, limit oneself to, practice, practice exclusively, pursue, study intensively, train, work in; SEE CONCEPTS *91,324*

specially [adv] *particularly*
distinctively, especially, expressly, in specie, specifically, uniquely; SEE CONCEPT *557*

specialty [n] *distinctive feature; concentration*
career, claim to fame, cup of tea*, distinguishing feature, field of concentration, forte, game*, hobby, job, long suit*, magnum opus*, major, masterpiece, minor, number, object of attention, object of study, occupation, pièce de résistance*, practice, profession, pursuit, racket*, special, speciality, special project, thing*, vocation, weakness, work; SEE CONCEPT *349*

species [n] *class, variety*
breed, category, collection, description, division, group, kind, likes*, lot, nature, number, order, sort, stripe*, type; SEE CONCEPT *378*

specific [adj] *particular, distinguishing*
bull's eye*, categorical, characteristic, clean-cut, clear-cut, cut fine*, dead on*, definite, definitive, different, distinct, downright, drawn fine, especial, exact, explicit, express, flat out*, hit nail on head*, individual, limited, on target, outright, peculiar, precise, reserved, restricted, right on, set, sole, special, specialized, straight-out, unambiguous, unequivocal, unique; SEE CONCEPTS *535,557,564*

specifically [adv] *expressly, particularly*
accurately, categorically, characteristically, clearly, concretely, correctly, definitely, distinctively, especially, exactly, explicitly, in detail, indicatively, individually, in specie, minutely, peculiarly, pointedly, precisely, respectively, specially; SEE CONCEPTS *557,564*

specification [n] *requirement, qualification*
blueprint, condition, designation, detail, item, particular, particularization, spec*, stipulation, term; SEE CONCEPTS *270,646*

specify [v] *designate; decide definitely*
be specific, blueprint*, button down*, cite, come to the point, condition, define, detail, determine, draw a picture*, enumerate, establish, finger*, fix, get down to brass tacks*, get to the point*, go into detail, indicate, individualize, instance, inventory, itemize, lay out, limit, list, make, mention, name, particularize, peg, pin down, point out, precise, put down, put finger on*, set, settle, show clearly, slot, specialize, specificate, specificize, spell out, stipulate, tab, tag, tick off; SEE CONCEPTS *18,57*

specimen [n] *example, sample*
case, case history, copy, cross section, embodiment, exemplar, exemplification, exhibit, illustration, individual, instance, model, part, pattern, proof, representation, representative, sampling, sort, species, type, unit, variety; SEE CONCEPTS *686,831*

specious [adj] *misleading*
apparent, apparently right, beguiling, captious, casuistic, colorable, credible, deceptive, delusive, empty, erroneous, fallacious, false, flattering, hollow, idle, illogical, inaccurate, incorrect, likely, nugatory, ostensible, ostentatious, plausible, presumable, presumptive, pretentious, probable, seeming, sophistic, sophisticated, spurious, unsound, untrue, vain, wrong; SEE CONCEPTS *552,582*

speck [n] *tiny bit*
atom, blemish, blot, crumb, defect, dot, fault, flaw, fleck, flyspeck, grain, iota, jot, mark, mite, modicum, molecule, mote, particle, point, shred, smidgen, speckle, splotch, spot, stain, trace, whit; SEE CONCEPT *831*

speckled [adj] *dotted*
brindled, dappled, flaked, flecked, freckled, mosaic, motley, mottled, particolored, patchy, peppered, punctate, spotted, spotty, sprinkled, stippled, studded, variegated; SEE CONCEPTS *485,618*

spectacle [n] *something showy; exhibition*
comedy, curiosity, demonstration, display, drama, event, exposition, extravaganza, marvel, movie, pageant, parade, performance, phenomenon, play, production, representation, scene, show, sight, spectacular, tableau, view, wonder; SEE CONCEPTS *261,529*

spectacles [n] *eyeglasses*
bifocals, blinkers*, contact lenses, contacts, glasses, goggles, lorgnette, monocle, pair of glasses, pince-nez, reading glasses, shades*, specs*, sunglasses, trifocals; SEE CONCEPT *446*

spectacular [adj] *wonderful, impressive*
amazing, astonishing, astounding, breathtaking, daring, dazzling, dramatic, eye-catching, fabulous, fantastic, grand, histrionic, magnificent, marked, marvelous, miraculous, prodigious, razzle-dazzle*, remarkable, sensational, splendid, staggering, striking, stunning, stupendous, theatrical, thrilling, wondrous; SEE CONCEPTS *529,537,574*

spectator [n] *person who watches event*
beholder, bystander, clapper, eyewitness, fan, gaper*, gazer, kibitzer*, looker, looker-on, moviegoer, observer, onlooker, perceiver, playgoer, seer, showgoer, sports fan, standee, stander-by, theatergoer, viewer, watcher, witness; SEE CONCEPTS *366,423*

specter [n] *ghost*
apparition, appearance, demon, doppelganger,

sp
sp

phantasm, phantom, poltergeist, presence, shadow, spirit, spook, vision; SEE CONCEPT *370*

spectral [*adj*] *ghostly*
apparitional, eerie, haunted, illusory, phantasmal, phantom, scary, shadowy, spiritual, spooky, supernatural; SEE CONCEPTS *485,537*

speculate [*v1*] *think about deeply and theorize*
beat one's brains*, brainstorm*, build castles in air*, call it, call the turn, cerebrate, chew over*, cogitate, conjecture, consider, contemplate, deliberate, dope*, dope out*, excogitate, figure, figure out*, guess, guesstimate*, have a hunch*, hazard a guess, head trip*, hypothesize, kick around*, meditate, muse, pipe-dream*, psych out*, read, read between lines*, reason, reflect, review, ruminate, run it up flagpole*, scheme, size up, study, suppose, surmise, suspect, weigh, wonder; SEE CONCEPTS *17,24,28,37*

speculate [*v2*] *gamble, risk*
dare, hazard, make book*, margin up*, play, play the market*, plunge, pour money into*, spec*, stick neck out*, take a chance, take a flier*, take a fling*, venture, wildcat; SEE CONCEPTS *28,330,363*

speculation [*n1*] *theory, guess*
belief, brainwork*, cerebration, cogitation, conjecture, consideration, contemplation, deliberation, excogitation, guesstimate*, guesswork, hunch, hypothesis, meditation, opinion, reflection, review, shot, shot in the dark*, sneaking suspicion*, stab, stab in the dark*, studying, supposition, surmise, thinking, thought, weighing; SEE CONCEPTS *24,28,529,689*

speculation [*n2*] *risk, gamble*
backing, flier*, flutter, gambling, hazard, hunch, piece, plunge, right money*, risky business*, risky venture, shot, shot in the dark*, smart money*, spec*, speculative enterprise, stab*, venture, wager; SEE CONCEPTS *192,330,363*

speculative [*adj*] *theoretical*
abstract, analytical, assumed, conceptive, dangerous, dicey, experimental, formularized, hairy, hazardous, hypothetical, ideal, idealized, ideological, iffy, intellectual, in theory, logical, notional, philosophical, presumed, risky, uncertain, unproved, unproven, unsubstantiated; SEE CONCEPT *529*

speech [*n1*] *talk*
accent, articulation, communication, conversation, dialect, dialogue, diction, discussion, doublespeak*, double talk*, elocution, enunciation, expressing, expression, idiom, intercourse, jargon, language, lingo, locution, mother tongue, native tongue, oral communication, palaver, parlance, prattle, pronunciation, prose, speaking, spiel, tone, tongue, utterance, verbalization, vernacular, vocal expression, vocalization, vocalizing, voice, voicing; SEE CONCEPTS *47,266,276*

speech [*n2*] *formal talk to audience*
address, allocution, appeal, bombast, chalk talk*, commentary, debate, declamation, diatribe, discourse, disquisition, dissertation, eulogy, exhortation, harangue, homily, invocation, keynote, lecture, opus, oration, oratory, panegyric, paper, parlance, parley, pep talk*, pitch, prelection, recitation, rhetoric, salutation, sermon, spiel*, stump*, tirade, valedictory; SEE CONCEPTS *60,285*

speechless [*adj*] *without ability to talk*
aghast, amazed, aphonic, astounded, buttoned up*, clammed up*, close-mouthed, cool*, cool as cucumber*, dazed, dumb, dumbfounded, dumbstruck, inarticulate, mum, mute, not saying boo*, reserved, shocked, silent, taciturn, thunderstruck*, tight-lipped*, tongue-tied*, uncommunicative, unflappable, voiceless, wordless; SEE CONCEPT *267*

speed [*n*] *rate of motion, often a high rate*
acceleration, activity, agility, alacrity, breeze, briskness, celerity, clip, dispatch, eagerness, expedition, fleetness, gait, haste, headway, hurry, hustle, legerity, lick, liveliness, momentum, pace, precipitancy, precipitation, promptitude, promptness, quickness, rapidity, rapidness, readiness, rush, rustle, snap, steam, swiftness, urgency, velocity; SEE CONCEPT *755*

speed [*v*] *move along quickly*
advance, aid, assist, barrel, belt, bomb, boost, bowl over, career, cover ground*, cut along, dispatch, expedite, facilitate, flash, fly, further, gallop, gather momentum, gear up*, get a move on*, get moving, get under way, go all out*, go fast, go like the wind*, hasten, help, hightail*, hurry, impel, lose no time*, make haste, open up throttle*, press on, promote, quicken, race, ride, run, rush, sail, spring, step on it*, tear, urge, whiz, zoom; SEE CONCEPTS *110,150,152*

speedy [*adj*] *fast, quick*
accelerated, agile, alacritous, breakneck, brisk, expeditious, express, fleet, harefooted, hasty, headlong, hurried, immediate, lissome, lively, nimble, precipitate, prompt, quick-fire, rapid, rapid-fire, ready, snappy, summary, supersonic, swift, ultrasonic, winged; SEE CONCEPTS *548,584,588*

spell [*n1*] *interval, period*
bit, bout, course, go, hitch, interlude, intermission, patch, relay, season, shift, space, stint, streak, stretch, term, time, tour, tour of duty, trick, turn, while; SEE CONCEPTS *807,817,822*

spell [*n2*] *magical aura over an entity*
abracadabra*, allure, amulet, bewitching, bewitchment, charm, conjuration, enchanting, enchantment, exorcism, fascination, glamour, hex, hexing, hocus-pocus*, incantation, jinx, magic, mumbo-jumbo*, rune, sorcery, talisman, trance, voodoo*, whack*, whammy*, witchery; SEE CONCEPTS *370,673,689*

spell [*n3*] *seizure*
access, attack, fit, illness, jag, paroxysm, spasm, stroke, throe, turn; SEE CONCEPTS *306,308*

spell [*v1*] *mean, imply*
add up to, amount to, augur, connote, denote, express, herald, import, indicate, intend, point to, portend, presage, promise, signify, suggest; SEE CONCEPTS *55,74,75*

spell [*v2*] *give rest, relief*
allow, breathe, free, lay off, lie by, release, relieve, stand in for, take over, take the place of; SEE CONCEPTS *83,110*

spellbound [*adj*] *enchanted, fascinated*
agape, amazed, bemused, bewildered, bewitched, breathless, captivated, caught up, charmed, enthralled, gripped, held, hooked, mesmerized, open-mouthed, petrified, possessed, rapt, transfixed, transported, under a spell; SEE CONCEPT *403*

spell out [*v*] *clarify, explain*
break down, brief, clear up, clue in, decipher, decode, define, describe, diagram, draw a map*,

expound, fill someone in*, get across*, go into detail, illustrate, interpret, justify, make plain*, point out, put across, put in plain English*, teach, tell, throw light upon*, translate, unfold, unravel, untangle; SEE CONCEPT 57

spend [v1] *give, pay out*
absorb, allocate, ante up*, apply, bestow, blow*, cast away, come across, come through, concentrate, confer, consume, contribute, cough up*, defray, deplete, disburse, dispense, dissipate, donate, drain, drop, employ, empty, evote, exhaust, expend, foot the bill*, fritter, give, hand out, invest, lavish, lay out, liquidate, misspend, outlay, pay down, pay up, put in, run through, settle, shell out*, spring for*, squander, throw away, use, use up, waste; SEE CONCEPTS 156,169,225, 341

spend [v2] *use time; occupy*
consume, devote, drift, employ, fill, fool around*, fritter, go, idle, kill, laze, let pass, misuse, pass, put in, squander, waste, while away*; SEE CONCEPT 100

spendthrift [n] *person careless with money*
big spender*, dissipater, high-roller*, improvident, imprudent, prodigal, profligate, spender, sport, squanderer, waster, wastrel; SEE CONCEPTS 348,353,423

spent [adj] *used up, gone; tired out*
all in*, bleary, blown, burnt-out*, bushed, consumed, dead*, debilitated, depleted, disbursed, dissipated, dog-tired*, done-in*, down the drain*, drained, effete, enervated, exhausted, expended, fagged, far-gone*, finished, had it*, limp, lost, played-out*, prostrate, ready to drop*, shattered, shot, thrown away, used, washed-up*, wasted, weakened, wearied, weary, worn out; SEE CONCEPTS 314,560,771

spew [v] *spit out*
belch, bring up, cascade, disgorge, eject, eruct, erupt, expel, flood, gush, heave, irrupt, puke*, regurgitate, scatter, spit, spit up, spread, spritz, throw up, urp*, vomit; SEE CONCEPTS 179,308

sphere [n1] *globular object*
apple*, ball, big blue marble*, circle, Earth, globe, globule, orb, pellet, pill, planet, rondure, round; SEE CONCEPTS 436,511

sphere [n2] *domain of influence*
bailiwick, capacity, champaign, circle, class, compass, demesne, department, dominion, employment, field, function, ground, jungle, jurisdiction, level, neck of the woods*, orbit, pale, position, precinct, province, range, rank, realm, scope, station, stomping ground*, stratum, terrain, territory, turf*, walk of life, zone; SEE CONCEPTS 349,388,687

spice [n] *flavor, zest*
aroma, color, excitement, fragrance, gusto, guts*, kick, pep, piquancy, pungency, relish, salt, savor, scent, seasoning, tang, zap*, zip*; SEE CONCEPTS 614,673

spick-and-span [adj] *spotless*
clean, fresh, gleaming, hygienic, immaculate, neat, polished, pure, sanitary, shining, shipshape, tidy, unsoiled, unstained, untarnished, very clean; SEE CONCEPTS 404,621

spicy [adj1] *pungent, flavorful*
ambrosial, appetizing, aromal, aromatic, distinctive, fiery, flavorsome, fragrant, fresh, herbaceous, highly seasoned, hot, keen, odoriferous, peppery, perfumed, piquant, poignant, racy,

redolent, savory, scented, seasoned, snappy, spirited, sweet, tangy, tasty, zesty, zippy*; SEE CONCEPT 613

spicy [adj2] *off-color, vulgar*
breezy, broad, erotic, hot*, indelicate, racy, red hot*, ribald, risqué, salty*, scandalous, sensational, sophisticated, suggestive, titillating, unseemly, wicked, X-rated*; SEE CONCEPTS 267,372,545

spiel [n] *patter, sales pitch*
chatter, empty talk, jabber*, jive*, line*, pitch*, sales talk, song and dance*; SEE CONCEPTS 276,278

spiffy [adj] *stylish*
a la mode*, beautiful, chic, chichi*, classy, dandy, dapper, dashing, dressed to kill*, fashionable, high-class*, in fashion, in vogue, jazzy*, mod*, now*, ritzy, sharp, showy, sleek, slick*, smart, snappy*, snazzy*, stunning, swank*, upscale, uptown, voguish; SEE CONCEPTS 579,589

spike [v] *pierce*
fasten, impale, lance, make fast, nail, pin, prick, skewer, spear, spit, stick, transfix; SEE CONCEPT 220

spill [v1] *slop, drop*
discharge, disgorge, dribble, drip, empty, flow, lose, overfill, overflow, overrun, overturn, pour, run, run out, run over, scatter, shed, spill over, splash, splatter, spray, sprinkle, spurt, squirt, stream, throw off, upset, well over; SEE CONCEPTS 179,181

spill [v2] *reveal*
betray, blab, blow, disclose, divulge, give away, inform, let the cat out of the bag*, mouth, squeal, tattle, tell; SEE CONCEPT 60

spin [n] *circular motion*
circuit, gyration, revolution, roll, rotation, spiral, turn, twist, whirl; SEE CONCEPT 748

spin [v] *go around, make go around*
gyrate, gyre, oscillate, pendulate, pirouette, purl, reel, revolve, rotate, spiral, swim, turn, twirl, twist, wheel, whirl; SEE CONCEPTS 150,152,218

spine [n] *backbone*
back, bone, chine, rachis, ridge, spinal column, vertebrae, vertebral column; SEE CONCEPTS 393,420

spineless [adj] *cowardly*
amoebalike*, faint-hearted, fearful, feeble, forceless, frightened, gutless*, impotent, inadequate, ineffective, ineffectual, invertebrate, irresolute, lily-livered*, nerveless, pithless, soft, spiritless, squeamish, submissive, timid, vacillating, weak, weak-kneed, weak-willed, yellow*, yellow-bellied*; SEE CONCEPTS 401,542

spin-off [n] *offshoot*
adjunct, branch, by-product, derivative, descendant, division, offspring, outgrowth, sequel; SEE CONCEPTS 260,824

spiral [adj] *curling, winding*
circling, circular, circumvoluted, cochlear, coiled, corkscrew, curled, helical, helicoid, radial, rolled, screw-shaped, scrolled, tendrillar, tortile, voluted, whorled, wound; SEE CONCEPT 486

spiral [n] *curled shape*
coil, corkscrew, curlicue, flourish, gyration, gyre, helix, quirk, screw, volute, whorl; SEE CONCEPT 436

spirit [n1] *soul, attitude*
air, animation, ardor, backbone*, boldness,

breath, character, complexion, courage, dauntlessness, disposition, earnestness, energy, enterprise, enthusiasm, essence, fire, force, frame of mind, gameness, grit*, guts*, heart, humor, jazz*, life, life force, liveliness, mettle, mood, morale, motivation, nerve, oomph*, outlook, psyche, quality, resolution, resolve, sparkle, spunk*, stoutheartedness, substance, temper, temperament, tenor, vigor, vitality, vital spark, warmth, will, willpower, zest; SEE CONCEPTS 407,411

spirit [n2] *atmosphere, essence*
feeling, genius, gist, humor, intent, intention, meaning, purport, purpose, quality, sense, substance, temper, tenor, timbre; tone; SEE CONCEPTS 673,682

spirit [n3] *ghost*
apparition, eidolon, phantasm, phantom, poltergeist, shade, shadow, soul, specter, spook, sprite, supernatural being, umbra, vision, wraith; SEE CONCEPT 370

spirited [adj] *lively, vivacious*
active, alert, animate, animated, ardent, audacious, avid, bold, bouncy, brave, bright, burning, chirpy, courageous, dauntless, eager, effervescent, energetic, enthusiastic, fearless, fiery, full of life, game, gingery*, gritty, gutsy*, high-spirited, hot, hyper*, intrepid, jumping, keen, mettlesome, nervy, passionate, peppery, peppy, plucky, resolute, rocking, sharp, snappy, sparkling, sprightly, spunky, vigorous, zappy*, zealous, zesty, zingy*, zippy*; SEE CONCEPTS 404,542

spiritless [adj] *depressed*
apathetic, blah*, blue*, broken, cast down, dejected, despondent, disconsolate, dispirited, dopey*, down, downcast, downhearted, down in the dumps*, down in the mouth*, draggy, drippy, droopy, dull, enervated, flat*, flat tire*, inanimate, indifferent, lackadaisical, lackluster, languid, languishing, languorous, lifeless, limp, listless, low, melancholic, melancholy, mopy, slothful, subdued, submissive, tame, torpid, unconcerned, unenthusiastic, unmoved, zero*; SEE CONCEPTS 403,542

spiritual [adj] *religious, otherworldly*
airy, asomatous, devotional, discarnate, disembodied, divine, ethereal, extramundane, ghostly, holy, immaterial, incorporeal, intangible, metaphysical, nonmaterial, nonphysical, platonic, pure, rarefied, refined, sacred, supernal, unfleshly, unphysical; SEE CONCEPTS 536,582

spit [n] *saliva*
discharge, dribble, drool, slaver, spittle, sputum, water; SEE CONCEPT 467

spit [v] *eject saliva or substance*
discharge, drool, expectorate, hawk, hiss, sibilate, sizz, slobber, spatter, spew, splutter, spritz, sputter, throw out; SEE CONCEPTS 179,185

spite [n] *hateful feeling*
animosity, antipathy, bad blood*, contempt, despite, enmity, gall, grudge, harsh feeling, hate, hatred, ill will, malevolence, malice, maliciousness, malignity, peeve, pique, rancor, resentment, revenge, spitefulness, spleen, umbrage, vengeance, vengefulness, venom, vindictiveness; SEE CONCEPT 29

spite [v] *offend, hurt*
annoy, begrudge, beset, crab*, cramp style*, discomfit, gall, get even*, grudge, hang up*, harass, harm, injure, louse up*, needle, nettle, persecute, pique, provoke, put out*, upset the apple cart*, vex; SEE CONCEPTS 7,19,121

spiteful [adj] *hurtful, nasty*
accidentally on purpose*, angry, barbed, catty*, cruel, cussed*, despiteful, dirty, evil, hateful, ill-disposed, ill-natured, malevolent, malicious, malign, malignant, mean, ornery*, rancorous, snide, spleenful, splenetic, venomous, vicious, vindictive, waspish, wicked; SEE CONCEPTS 401,542

spitting image [n] *look-alike*
carbon copy, clone, double, duplicate, exact likeness, likeness, match, replica, ringer*, twin, very image; SEE CONCEPTS 414,664,670

splash [n] *spattering, impact*
burst, dash, display, effect, patch, sensation, splurge, stir, touch; SEE CONCEPT 676

splash [v] *throw liquid*
bathe, bespatter, broadcast, dabble, dash, douse, drench, drown, get wet, moisten, paddle, plash, plunge, shower, slop, slosh, soak, sop, spatter, splatter, spray, spread, sprinkle, squirt, strew, throw, wade, wallow, wet; SEE CONCEPTS 222,256

splatter [v] *splash*
bespatter, douse, drench, drown, get wet, moisten, plunge, shower, slosh, soak, sop, spatter, spray, sprinkle, squirt, wet; SEE CONCEPTS 222,256

splendid [adj1] *luxurious, expensive*
baroque, beaming, beautiful, bright, brilliant, costly, dazzling, elegant, fab*, fat*, flamboyant, glittering, glowing, gorgeous, grand, grandiose, imposing, impressive, lavish, lustrous, mad*, magnificent, magnifico, marvelous, ornate, plush, posh, radiant, refulgent, resplendent, rich, solid gold*, splashy, splendiferous, splendrous, sumptuous, superb, swanky*; SEE CONCEPTS 334,485,589

splendid [adj2] *excellent, illustrious*
admirable, brilliant, celebrated, distinguished, divine, eminent, exceptional, exquisite, fantastic, fine, first-class, glorious, gorgeous, grand, great, heroic, impressive, magnificent, marvelous, matchless, outstanding, peerless, premium, proud, rare, remarkable, renowned, resplendent, royal, splendiferous, splendorous, sterling, sublime, superb, superlative, supreme, transcendent, unparalleled, unsurpassed, very good, wonderful; SEE CONCEPTS 568,574

splendor [n] *radiance, glory*
brightness, brilliance, ceremony, dazzle, display, effulgence, gorgeousness, grandeur, luster, magnificence, majesty, pageant, pomp, refulgence, renown, resplendence, richness, show, solemnity, spectacle, stateliness, sumptuousness; SEE CONCEPTS 620,655,673

splice [v] *join, interweave*
braid, entwine, graft, hitch, interlace, intertwine, intertwist, knit, marry, mate, mesh, plait, tie, unite, weave, wed, yoke; SEE CONCEPT 193

splinter [n] *thin piece of solid*
bit, chip, flake, fragment, needle, paring, shaving, sliver, wood; SEE CONCEPTS 471,479,831

splinter [v] *break into thin, small pieces*
break to smithereens*, burst, disintegrate, fracture, fragment, pash, rive, shatter, shiver, smash, split; SEE CONCEPT 246

split [n1] *opening*
breach, chasm, chink, cleavage, cleft, crack, damage, division, fissure, gap, rent, rift, rima, ri-

mation, rime, rip, rupture, separation, slash, slit, tear; SEE CONCEPT *513*

split [*n2*] *difference, disunion*
alienation, breach, break, break-up, discord, disruption, dissension, divergence, division, estrangement, fissure, fracture, partition, rent, rift, rupture, schism; SEE CONCEPTS *297,388*

split [*v1*] *break up, pull apart*
bifurcate, branch, break, burst, cleave, come apart, come undone, crack, dichotomize, disband, disjoin, dissever, disunite, diverge, divide, divorce, fork, gape, give way, go separate ways, hack, isolate, open, part, part company, put asunder, rend, rip, rive, separate, sever, slash, slit, snap, splinter, sunder, tear, whack; SEE CONCEPTS *135,176,297*

split [*v2*] *divide into parts*
allocate, allot, apportion, carve up, distribute, divide, divvy*, divvy up*, dole, go even-steven*, go fifty-fifty*, halve, mete out, parcel out, partition, share, slice, slice the pie*, slice up; SEE CONCEPT *98*

split up [*v*] *keep apart; segregate; separate*
break off, break up, come apart, detach, disband, disconnect, divide, divorce, go separate ways, group, part, part company, rope off, seclude, sever, sort, stand between, undo; SEE CONCEPTS *135,158,201,297,384*

splurge [*v*] *spend lavishly*
be extravagant, binge, celebrate, fling, give a party*, rampage, spread; SEE CONCEPTS *327,377*

spoil [*v1*] *ruin, hurt*
blemish, damage, debase, deface, defile, demolish, depredate, desecrate, desolate, despoil, destroy, devastate, disfigure, disgrace, harm, impair, injure, make useless, mar, mess up*, muck up*, pillage, plunder, prejudice, ravage, sack, smash, spoliate, squash, take apart, tarnish, trash*, undo, upset, vitiate, waste, wreck; SEE CONCEPTS *246,252*

spoil [*v2*] *baby, indulge*
accommodate, cater to, coddle, cosset, favor, humor, kill with kindness*, mollycoddle*, oblige, overindulge, pamper, spoon-feed*; SEE CONCEPTS *14,136*

spoil [*v3*] *decay, turn bad*
addle, become tainted, become useless, break down, crumble, curdle, decompose, deteriorate, disintegrate, go bad, go off, mildew, molder, putrefy, rot, taint, turn; SEE CONCEPTS *456,469*

spoils [*n*] *possessions stolen or gained*
booty*, cut*, gain, goods, graft, hot goods*, loot, make*, pickings, pillage, plunder, prey, prize, squeeze, swag, take; SEE CONCEPTS *337,710*

spoken [*adj*] *by word of mouth*
announced, articulate, communicated, expressed, lingual, mentioned, oral, phonetic, phonic, put into words, said, sonant, told, traditional, unwritten, uttered, verbal, viva voce, voiced; SEE CONCEPT *267*

spokesperson [*n*] *person who communicates for another*
agent, champion, delegate, deputy, mediator, mouth, mouthpiece*, prolocutor, prophet, protagonist, representative, speaker, stand-in, substitute, talker; SEE CONCEPTS *348,354,359*

sponge [*n*] *moocher*
bum*, cadger, deadbeat*, freeloader*, hanger-on, leech*, panhandler, parasite, scrounger; SEE CONCEPTS *412,423*

sponge [*v*] *mooch*
beg, bum*, cadge, chisel*, freeload*, hit up*, hustle, live off of, panhandle, scrounge; SEE CONCEPT *53*

spongy [*adj*] *cushioned, absorbent*
absorptive, cushiony, elastic, light, mushy, pappy, porous, pulpous, pulpy, resilient, rubbery, soft, springy, squishy, yielding; SEE CONCEPT *606*

sponsor [*n*] *person who helps, promotes another*
adherent, advocate, angel*, backer, benefactor, godparent, grubstaker, guarantor, mainstay, patron, promoter, supporter, surety, sustainer, underwriter; SEE CONCEPTS *348,423*

sponsor [*v*] *help, promote*
answer for, back, bankroll, be responsible for, finance, fund, grubstake, guarantee, patronize, put up money, stake, subsidize, vouch for; SEE CONCEPTS *110,341*

spontaneous [*adj*] *impulsive, willing*
ad-lib*, automatic, break loose, casual, down, extemporaneous, extempore, free, free spirited, from the hip*, impetuous, impromptu, improvised, inevitable, instinctive, involuntary, irresistible, natural, offhand, off the cuff*, off top of head*, simple, unartful, unavoidable, unbidden, uncompelled, unconscious, unconstrained, uncontrived, uncontrolled, unforced, unintentional, unplanned, unpremeditated, unprompted, unsophisticated, unstudied, up front, voluntary; SEE CONCEPTS *401,542,548*

spoof [*n*] *trick, mockery*
bluff, bon mot, burlesque, caricature, cheat, deceit, deception, fake, flim-flam*, game, hoax, imposture, jest, joke, lampoon, parody, phony, prank, put-on, quip, satire, sell, send-up*, sham, take-off, travesty, trickery, wisecrack; SEE CONCEPTS *59,273*

spook [*v*] *frighten, scare*
alarm, curdle the blood*, discomfort, horrify, make one's blood run cold*, make one's teeth chatter*, panic, petrify, scare away, scare stiff*, scare the pants off of*, scare to death*, startle, strike terror into*, terrify, unnerve; SEE CONCEPTS *7,14,19,42*

spooky [*adj*] *frightening*
chilling, creepy, eerie, ghostly, mysterious, ominous, scary, spine-chilling, supernatural, uncanny, unearthly, weird; SEE CONCEPTS *529,537*

spoon-feed [*v*] *pamper*
baby, cater to, coddle, give in, indulge, mollycoddle*, overindulge, spoil, spoil rotten*; SEE CONCEPTS *136,295*

sporadic [*adj*] *on and off*
bits and pieces*, desultory, few, fitful, fits and starts*, hit-or-miss*, infrequent, intermittent, irregular, isolated, occasional, on-again-off-again*, random, rare, scarce, scattered, seldom, semioccasional, spasmodic, spotty, uncommon, unfrequent; SEE CONCEPT *541*

sport [*n1*] *recreational activity; entertainment*
action, amusement, athletics, ball, disport, diversion, exercise, frolic, fun, fun and games*, gaiety, game, games, pastime, physical activity, picnic, play, pleasure, recreation; SEE CONCEPT *363*

sport [*n2*] *fun, joking*
badinage, banter, derision, drollery, escapade, frolic, horseplay, jest, jesting, joke, jollification,

jollity, kidding, laughter, merriment, mirth, mockery, mummery, nonsense, pleasantry, practical joke, raillery, scorn, teasing, tomfoolery, trifling; SEE CONCEPTS *59,273*

sport [*n3*] *person who takes kidding*
buffoon, butt, jestee, joke, laughingstock, mock, mockery, object of derision, object of ridicule, plaything, target; SEE CONCEPT *423*

sport [*v*] *display, wear*
be dressed in, don, exhibit, have on, model, show off; SEE CONCEPTS *167,261*

sporting/sportive [*adj*] *playful and fair*
antic, coltish, considerate, devil-may-care*, frisky, frolicsome, full of fun*, game, gamesome, gay, generous, impish, jaunty, joyous, larkish, lively, merry, mischievous, reasonable, roguish, rollicking, sportspersonlike, sprightly, square, wild; SEE CONCEPT *401*

sportsmanship [*n*] *integrity*
fairness, forthrightness, gamemanship, goodness, honesty, honor, honorableness, principle, righteousness, sincerity, virtue; SEE CONCEPT *411*

sporty [*adj*] *casual; flashy*
brazen, flamboyant, flaunting, gaudy, glittering, glittery, glitzy, informal, jazzy*, loud, natty, ornate, showy, snazzy; SEE CONCEPTS *401,542,589*

spot [*n1*] *mark, stain*
atom, blemish, blot, blotch, daub, discoloration, dollop, dram, drop, flaw, iota, jot, little bit, mite, molecule, mote, nip, particle, pimple, pinch, shot, smidgen, smudge, snort, speck, taint, whit; SEE CONCEPTS *284,831*

spot [*n2*] *location*
hangout*, hole*, joint*, layout, locality, locus, office, pad, place, plant, point, position, post, roof, scene, seat, section, sector, site, situation, slot, station, wherever*, X*, X marks the spot*; SEE CONCEPT *198*

spot [*n3*] *bad situation*
box*, corner*, difficulty, dilemma, fix, hole*, jam, mess, pickle*, plight, predicament, quandary, scrape, trouble; SEE CONCEPTS *666,674*

spot [*n4*] *position in organization*
appointment, berth, billet, connection, job, office, place, post, responsibility, situation, station, work; SEE CONCEPTS *351,362*

spot [*v1*] *mark, stain*
besmirch, bespatter, blot, blotch, dapple, dirty, dot, fleck, maculate, marble, mottle, pepper, pimple, soil, spatter, speck, speckle, splash, splotch, stipple, streak, stripe, stud, sully, taint, tarnish; SEE CONCEPTS *79,179*

spot [*v2*] *see, recognize*
catch, catch sight of, descry, detect, determinate, diagnose, discern, discover, distinguish, encounter, espy, ferret out, find, identify, locate, make out, meet with, observe, pick out, pinpoint, place, point out, sight, trace, track, turn up; SEE CONCEPTS *38,183,626*

spotless [*adj*] *very clean; innocent*
above reproach, blameless, chaste, clean, decent, faultless, flawless, gleaming, hygienic, immaculate, irreproachable, modest, pure, sanitary, shining, snowy, stainless, unblemished, undefiled, unimpeachable, unsoiled, unstained, unsullied, untarnished; SEE CONCEPTS *404,621*

spotlight [*n*] *attention; bright beam of light*
center stage, fame, flashlight, floodlight, interest,

light, limelight, notoriety, public attention, public eye, publicity; SEE CONCEPTS *388,624,668*

spotlight [*v*] *focus attention on*
accentuate, draw attention, feature, floodlight*, give prominence, highlight, illuminate, limelight*, point up, publicize, put on center stage*; SEE CONCEPTS *261,292*

spotted [*adj*] *speckled*
blotched, dappled, dotted, flaked, flecked, freckled, mosaic, motley, patchy, pied, spotty, sprinkled; SEE CONCEPTS *485,618*

spotty [*adj*] *blotchy, irregular*
desultory, erratic, flickering, fluctuating, not uniform, on-again-off-again*, patchy, pimply, spasmodic, sporadic, unequal, uneven; SEE CONCEPT *534*

spouse [*n*] *one of a married couple*
better half*, bride, companion, groom, helpmate, husband, man, mate, partner, roommate, wife, woman; SEE CONCEPT *414*

spout [*v1*] *spurt, emit*
cascade, discharge, eject, erupt, expel, exude, gush, jet, pour, roll, shoot, spill, spray, squirt, stream, surge; SEE CONCEPT *179*

spout [*v2*] *talk forcefully*
boast, brag, chatter, declaim, expatiate, go on, gush, harangue, hold forth, orate, pontificate, ramble, rant, sermonize, shoot off one's mouth*, speechify, spellbind, spiel, vapor, yell; SEE CONCEPTS *49,51*

sprawl [*v*] *sit or lie spread out*
drape, extend, flop, lie, lie spread-eagle*, loll, lounge, ramble, recline, sit, slouch, slump, spread, straddle, straggle, stretch, trail; SEE CONCEPT *201*

spray [*n*] *fine mist*
aerosol, atomizer, drizzle, droplets, duster, fog, froth, moisture, spindrift, splash, sprayer, sprinkler, vaporizer; SEE CONCEPTS *514,680*

spray [*v*] *sprinkle, diffuse*
atomize, drizzle, dust, scatter, shoot, shower, smear, spatter, splash, spritz, squirt, throw around; SEE CONCEPTS *179,256*

spread [*n1*] *expansion, development; extent*
advance, advancement, compass, diffusion, dispersion, dissemination, enlargement, escalation, expanse, extension, increase, period, profusion, proliferation, radiation, ramification, range, reach, scope, span, spreading, stretch, suffusion, sweep, term, transfusion, transmission; SEE CONCEPTS *651,704,721,788*

spread [*n2*] *outlay of food, meal*
array, banquet, blowout, dinner, feast, lunch, regale, repast; SEE CONCEPT *459*

spread [*v1*] *open or fan out*
arrange, array, be displayed, be distributed, bloat, branch off, broaden, cast, circulate, coat, cover, daub, develop, diffuse, dilate, disperse, diverge, enlarge, escalate, even out, expand, extend, flatten, flow, gloss, increase, lay, lengthen, level, lie, multiply, mushroom, open, outstretch, overlay, paint, pervade, prepare, proliferate, radiate, reach, roll out, set, settle, smear, sprawl, spray, stretch, strew, suffuse, swell, uncoil, unfold, unfurl, unroll, untwist, unwind, widen; SEE CONCEPTS *158,172,201*

spread [*v2*] *publicize*
advertise, blazon, broadcast, cast, circulate, declare, diffuse, disseminate, distribute, make known, make public, proclaim, promulgate,

propagate, publish, radiate, scatter, shed, sow, strew, transmit; SEE CONCEPT *60*

spree [*n*] *wild activity*
bacchanalia, ball, bash, binge, caper, carousal, carouse, carousing, celebration, field day*, fling, frolic, high jinks*, high time*, jag, jamboree, junket, lark, merry-go-round*, orgy, party, rampage, revel, rip*, spending expedition, splurge, tear*; SEE CONCEPTS *327,377,384*

sprightly [*adj*] *fun, vivacious*
active, agile, airy, alert, animate, animated, blithe, bouncy, breezy, bright, brisk, cheerful, cheery, chipper, chirpy, clever, dapper, dashing, energetic, fairylike, frolicsome, gay, good, grooving, hyper, jaunty, jolly, joyous, jumping, keen, keen-witted, light, lively, nimble, peppy, perky, playful, quick, quick-witted, saucy, scintillating, smart, snappy, spirited, sportive, spry, swinging, zappy*, zingy*, zippy*; SEE CONCEPTS *401,404,542*

spring [*n1*] *jump, skip*
bounce, bounciness, bound, buck, buoyancy, elasticity, flexibility, give, hop, leap, recoil, resilience, saltation, springiness, vault; SEE CONCEPTS *194,731*

spring [*n2*] *season following winter*
blackberry winter*, budding, budtime, flowering, prime, seedtime, springtide, springtime, vernal equinox, vernal season; SEE CONCEPT *814*

spring [*n3*] *origin*
beginning, cause, consideration, fount, fountain, fountainhead, impetus, motive, root, source, stimulus, well, wellspring, whence; SEE CONCEPTS *648,661*

spring [*n4*] *body of rushing waters*
artesian well, baths, fountain, geyser, hot spring, hydrolysate, spa, thermal spring, watering place, wells; SEE CONCEPT *514*

spring [*v1*] *jump, skip*
bolt, bounce, bound, hippety hop*, hop, hurdle, leap, lop, lope, rebound, recoil, skitter, start, startle, trip, vault; SEE CONCEPT *194*

spring [*v2*] *originate, emerge*
appear, arise, arrive, be derived, be descended, begin, birth, burgeon, come, come into being, come into existence, come out, commence, derive, descend, develop, emanate, flow, grow, hatch, head, issue, loom, mushroom, proceed, rise, shoot up, start, stem, upspring; SEE CONCEPTS *105,302,373*

springy [*adj*] *elastic*
adaptable, bouncy, flexible, limber, malleable, pliable, pliant, resilient, rubberlike, rubbery, stretchable, stretchy; SEE CONCEPTS *490,606*

sprinkle [*v*] *scatter, disseminate*
baptize, christen, dampen, dot, dredge, dust, freckle, mist, moisten, pepper, powder, rain, shake, shower, smear, speck, speckle, spit, spot, spray, spritz, squirt, strew, stud; SEE CONCEPTS *179,222,256*

sprinkling [*n*] *hint, dash*
admixture, dust, dusting, few, handful, lick, mixture, powdering, scattering, several, smattering, sprinkle, strain, taste, tinge, touch, trace; SEE CONCEPT *831*

sprint [*v*] *run very fast*
dart, dash, go at top speed, hotfoot*, race, rush, scamper, scoot, scurry, shoot, tear, whiz; SEE CONCEPT *150*

sprout [*v*] *develop*
bud, burgeon, germinate, grow, push, shoot, shoot up, spring, take root, vegetate; SEE CONCEPT *257*

spruce [*adj*] *stylish, neat*
classy, clean, dainty, dapper, elegant, prim, smart, tidy, trim, well-groomed; SEE CONCEPT *589*

spruce up [*v*] *make neat, well-groomed*
brush, deck out*, dress up, fix up, groom, prim, primp, sleek, slick, smarten, tidy, titivate, wash; SEE CONCEPTS *162,167,202*

spry [*adj*] *active, vivacious*
agile, alert, brisk, energetic, fleet, full of pep, healthy, in full swing*, lithe, nimble, on the go*, prompt, quick, quick on the draw*, ready, robust, rocking, sound, spirited, sprightly, supple, vigorous; SEE CONCEPT *401*

spunk [*n*] *courage, nerve*
backbone, determination, doggedness, fortitude, gameness, grit*, gumption*, guts*, intestinal fortitude*, mettle, moxie*, pluck, resolution, spirit, toughness, true grit*; SEE CONCEPTS *411,633*

spunky [*adj*] *spirited*
active, alert, animated, bold, bouncy, brave, chirpy, courageous, eager, energetic, enthusiastic, fearless, fiery, full of life, full of spirit, game, gritty, gutsy*, high-spirited, peppy, plucky, snappy, sprightly, tough, vigorous, zesty, zippy*; SEE CONCEPTS *404,542*

spur [*n*] *incitement, stimulus*
activation, actuation, catalyst, excitant, goad, goose*, impetus, impulse, incentive, incitation, inducement, motivation, motive, needle*, prick, stimulant, trigger, turn-on*, urge; SEE CONCEPT *661*

spur [*v*] *incite, prompt*
animate, arouse, awaken, countenance, drive, egg on*, exhort, favor, fire up*, goad, goose*, impel, instigate, key up, press, prick, prod, propel, push, put up to, rally, rouse, sic*, spark, stimulate, stir, trigger, turn on, urge, work up; SEE CONCEPTS *14,65*

spurious [*adj*] *counterfeit, fake*
affected, apocryphal, artificial, assumed, bastard*, bent, bogus, bum, contrived, deceitful, deceptive, dummy*, ersatz, faked, false, feigned, forged, framed, illegitimate, imitation, make-believe, mock, phony, pirate, pretend, pretended, pseudo*, put-on*, sham*, simulated, specious, substitute, unauthentic, ungenuine, unreal; SEE CONCEPT *582*

spurn [*v*] *turn away; ignore*
air, contemn, cut, decline, despise, disapprove, disdain, dismiss, disregard, drop, dump, flout, flush*, give the cold shoulder*, hold in contempt, look down on*, nix*, not hear of*, pass by, rebuff, refuse, reject, reprobate, repudiate, repulse, scoff, scorn, slight, sneer, sneeze at*, snub, steer clear*, turn down, turn nose up at*; SEE CONCEPTS *21,30,384*

spurt [*n*] *burst of activity*
access, commotion, discharge, eruption, explosion, fit, jet, outburst, rush, spate, spritz, squirt, stream, surge; SEE CONCEPTS *1,119,179*

spurt [*v*] *erupt*
burst, emerge, flow, flow out, gush, issue, jet, ooze, pour out, shoot, spew, spout, spritz, squirt, stream, surge, well; SEE CONCEPT *179*

sp
sp

spy [*n*] *person who secretly finds out about another's business*
agent, detective, double agent, emissary, espionage agent, foreign agent, informer, inside agent, intelligencer, investigator, lookout, mole*, observer, operative, patrol, picket, plant*, scout, secret agent, secret service, sleeper, sleuth, snoop, spook, spotter, undercover agent, watcher; SEE CONCEPTS *348,412*

spy [*v*] *secretly follow, watch another's actions*
case, catch sight of, discover, examine, eyeball*, fish out*, get a load of*, glimpse, keep under surveillance, look for, meddle, notice, observe, peep, pry, recon*, reconnoiter, scout, scrutinize, search, set eyes on, shadow, sleuth, snoop, spot, stag, stake out, tail, take in, take note, trail, view, watch; SEE CONCEPTS *103,623*

squabble [*n*] *argument*
altercation, bickering, controversy, difference, difference of opinion, disagreement, dispute, feud, fight, flap*, fuss*, hassle, quarrel, row*, scene*, scrap*, set-to*, spat*, tiff*, words*, wrangle; SEE CONCEPT *46*

squabble [*v*] *argue*
argufy, bicker, brawl, clash, disagree, dispute, encounter, fall out*, fight, hassle, have words*, quarrel, quibble, row, scrap, spat, tiff*, wrangle; SEE CONCEPT *46*

squad [*n*] *team, crew*
band, battalion, company, division, force, gang, group, regiment, squadron, troop; SEE CONCEPTS *322,365,417*

squalid [*adj*] *poor, run-down*
abominable, base, broken-down, decayed, despicable, dingy, dirty, disgusting, disheveled, fetid, filthy, foul, grimy, gruesome, horrible, horrid, ignoble, impure, low, mean, miry, moldy, muddy, musty, nasty, odorous, offensive, poverty-stricken, ramshackle, reeking, repellent, repulsive, scurvy, seedy, shabby, shoddy, sloppy, slovenly, soiled, sordid, ugly, unclean, unkempt, vile, wretched; SEE CONCEPTS *334,485,570*

squalor [*n*] *filth, poverty*
decay, destitution, dirtiness, foulness, grunginess, impoverishment, indigence, poorness, seediness, starvation, wretchedness; SEE CONCEPTS *335,709*

squander [*v*] *fritter away, use up*
be prodigal with, be wasteful, blow*, cash out*, consume, dissipate, expend, frivol, frivol away, go through, lavish, misspend, misuse, prodigalize, put out*, run through, scatter, spend, spend like water*, spring for*, throw away, throw money around*, trifle, waste; SEE CONCEPTS *156,225,327*

square [*adj1*] *honest, genuine*
aboveboard, decent, equal, equitable, ethical, even, fair, fair-and-square, impartial, impersonal, just, nonpartisan, objective, on-the-level, sporting, sportspersonlike, straight, straightforward, unbiased, unprejudiced, upright; SEE CONCEPTS *267,542*

square [*adj2*] *four-sided*
boxlike, boxy, equal-sided, equilateral, foursquare, orthogonal, quadrate, quadratic, quadratical, rectangular, rectilinear, right-angled, squared, squarish; SEE CONCEPT *486*

square [*adj3*] *old-fashioned, conventional*
behind the times, bourgeois, button-down*, con-

servative, dated, orthodox, out-of-date, straight*, strait-laced*, stuffy*; SEE CONCEPTS *401,404*

square [*n1*] *person who is old-fashioned, conventional*
antediluvian, conservative, diehard*, fuddy-duddy*, reactionary, stick-in-the-mud*, traditionalist; SEE CONCEPT *423*

square [*n2*] *municipal park*
area, center, circle, common, green, plaza, space, village green; SEE CONCEPT *509*

square [*v1*] *correspond, agree*
accord, balance, check out, coincide, conform, dovetail*, fit, fit in, gee, harmonize, jibe, match, reconcile, tally; SEE CONCEPT *664*

square [*v2*] *pay off, satisfy*
balance, bribe, buy, buy off, clear, clear off, clear up, corrupt, discharge, fix, have, liquidate, make even, pay, pay up, quit, rig, settle, tamper with; SEE CONCEPT *341*

square [*v3*] *adapt, regulate*
accommodate, adjust, align, conform, even up, fit, level, quadrate, reconcile, suit, tailor, tailor-make*, true; SEE CONCEPTS *126,202*

squash [*v*] *compress*
annihilate, bear, bruise, crowd, crush, distort, extinguish, flatten, jam, kill, macerate, mash, pound, press, pulp, push, put down, quash, quell, scrunch, shut down, sit on, smash, squeeze, squish, stamp on, suppress, trample, triturate; SEE CONCEPTS *121,208,219*

squat [*adj*] *short and stocky*
broad, chunky, dumpy*, fat, heavy, heavyset, splay, thick, thick-bodied, thickset; SEE CONCEPTS *491,773,779*

squat [*v*] *lower body by bending knees*
bow, cower, crouch, hunch, hunker down, perch, roost, settle, sit, stoop; SEE CONCEPT *201*

squawk [*v1*] *make high-pitched, animal-like sound*
cackle, caw, crow, cry, hoot, screech, yap, yawp, yelp; SEE CONCEPTS *64,77*

squawk [*v2*] *gripe*
bellyache*, complain, kick up a fuss*, protest, raise Cain*, squeal, yammer; SEE CONCEPTS *52,54*

squeak [*v*] *make sharp, high-pitched sound*
cheep, creak, cry, grate, peep, pipe, scream, screech, scritch, shrill, sing, sound, squeal, talk, whine, yelp; SEE CONCEPTS *64,65*

squeal [*n/v1*] *yell in a loud and high-pitched manner*
bleat, cheep, creak, grate, howl, peep, rasp, scream, scream bloody murder*, screech, shout, shriek, shrill, squawk, wail, yelp, yip, yowl; SEE CONCEPTS *64,77*

squeal [*v2*] *inform on*
betray, blab*, complain, protest, rat on*, sell down the river*, sing*, snitch*, squawk*, talk, tattle, tattletale*, tell; SEE CONCEPTS *54,60*

squeamish [*adj*] *nauseated; finicky*
annoyed, captious, delicate, disgusted, dizzy, exacting, fastidious, fussy, hypercritical, mincing, particular, prim, prudish, puritanical, qualmish, queasy, queer, scrupulous, shaky, sick, sickly, sick to one's stomach*, strait-laced, unsettled, upset, vertiginous; SEE CONCEPTS *314,401,404*

squeeze [*n*] *pressure, crushing*
clasp, clutch, congestion, crowd, crunch, crush, embrace, force, handclasp, hold, hug, influence,

jam, press, restraint, squash; SEE CONCEPTS *219,674,687*

squeeze [*v1*] *exert pressure on sides, parts of something*
bear, choke, clasp, clip, clutch, compress, contract, cram, crowd, crush, cuddle, embrace, enfold, force, grip, hold tight, hug, jam, jostle, nip, pack, pinch, press, quash, ram, scrunch, squash, squish, strangle, stuff, throttle, thrust, wedge, wring; SEE CONCEPT *219*

squeeze [*v2*] *try to get money out of*
bleed*, bring pressure to bear, eke out, extort, extract, lean on*, milk*, oppress, pinch*, pressure, pressurize*, put screws to*, shake down*, wrench, wring; SEE CONCEPTS *53,192,342*

squelch [*v*] *suppress, restrain*
black out, censure, crush, extinguish, kill, muffle, oppress, quelch, quench, repress, settle, shush, sit on, smother, squash, stifle, strangle, thwart; SEE CONCEPT *130*

squint [*v*] *scrunch up eyes when viewing*
cock the eye, look, look askance, look crosseyed, peek, peep, screw up eyes, squinch*; SEE CONCEPTS *185,623*

squire [*v*] *accompany*
assist, attend, chaperon, companion, date, escort, serve; SEE CONCEPTS *384,714*

squirm [*v*] *wiggle, fidget*
agonize, flounder, shift, skew, squiggle, toss, twist, wind, worm, wriggle, writhe; SEE CONCEPT *213*

squirt [*v*] *squeeze out liquid*
eject, emit, flow, jet, pour, spatter, spit, splash, splur, spray, sprinkle, spritz, spurt, stream, surge; SEE CONCEPTS *179,256*

squish [*v*] *squash*
crush, flatten, jam, mash, pound, press, scrunch, sit on, smash, squeeze, stamp on, trample; SEE CONCEPTS *121,208,219*

stab [*n1*] *piercing cut*
ache, blow, gash, hurt, incision, jab, jag, pang, piercing, prick, puncture, rent, stick, thrust, transfixion, twinge, wound; SEE CONCEPT *309*

stab [*n2*] *attempt*
attempt, crack*, endeavor, essay, fling*, go*, one's best*, shot*, try, venture, whack*, whirl*; SEE CONCEPT *87*

stab [*v*] *puncture, pierce with sharp, pointed object*
bayonet, brand, carve, chop, cleave, clip, cut, drive, gore, hit, hurt, injure, jab, jag, knife, open up, penetrate, pierce, plow, plunge, prick, prong, punch, ram, run through, saber, shank, sink, slice, spear, stick, thrust, transfix, wound; SEE CONCEPT *220*

stability [*n*] *resistance of some degree*
adherence, aplomb, assurance, backbone, balance, cohesion, constancy, dependability, determination, durability, endurance, establishment, firmness, immobility, immovability, maturity, permanence, perseverance, resoluteness, security, solidity, solidness, soundness, stableness, steadfastness, steadiness, strength, substantiality, support, toughness; SEE CONCEPTS *411,731*

stabilize [*v*] *make or keep in steady state; make resistant to change*
balance, ballast, bolt, brace, buttress, counterbalance, counterpoise, equalize, fasten, firm, firm up*, fix, freeze*, maintain, ossify, poise, preserve, prop, secure, set, settle, stabilitate, steady,

stiffen, support, sustain, uphold; SEE CONCEPTS *110,250*

stab in the back [*v*] *betray*
abandon, be disloyal, be unfaithful, break promise, commit treason, cross, deceive, doublecross, finger*, go back on, inform on, play Judas*, sell down the river*, sell out, trick, turn in, turn informer, turn traitor; SEE CONCEPT *384*

stable [*adj*] *constant, fixed; resistant*
abiding, anchored, balanced, brick-wall*, calm, deep-rooted, durable, enduring, equable, established, even, fast, firm, immutable, invariable, lasting, nailed, perdurable, permanent, poised, reliable, resolute, safe, secure, set, set in stone*, solid, solid as a rock*, sound, stabile, stalwart, stationary, staunch, staying put, steadfast, steady, stout, strong, sturdy, substantial, sure, together, tough, unalterable, unchangeable, unfluctuating, uniform, unvarying, unwavering, well-built, well-founded; SEE CONCEPTS *404,488*

stack [*n*] *pile*
assemblage, bank, bundle, cock, drift, heap, hill, hoard, load, mass, mound, mountain, pack, pyramid, sheaf; SEE CONCEPTS *432,440,509*

stack [*v*] *pile up*
accumulate, amass, bank up, cock, drift, heap, hill, load, mound, pile, rick, stockpile; SEE CONCEPTS *109,158*

stadium [*n*] *arena for recreation or spectating*
amphitheater, athletic field, bowl, coliseum, diamond, field, garden, gridiron, gymnasium, pit, ring, stade, strand; SEE CONCEPT *438*

staff [*n1*] *employees of organization*
agents, assistants, cadre, cast, crew, deputies, faculty, force, help, officers, operatives, organization, personnel, servants, shop, teachers, team, workers, work force; SEE CONCEPT *325*

staff [*n2*] *stick, usually for walking*
cane, club, pikestaff, pole, prop, rod, stave, walking stick, wand; SEE CONCEPTS *311,479*

stage [*n1*] *level, period within structure or system*
date, degree, division, footing, grade, juncture, lap, leg, length, moment, node, notch, phase, plane, point, point in time, rung, standing, status, step; SEE CONCEPTS *727,744,816*

stage [*n2*] *theater platform; theater life*
arena, boards*, Broadway, dais, drama, footlights, frame, legit*, limelight*, mise-en-scène, off-Broadway, play, scaffold, scaffolding, scene, scenery, set, setting, show biz*, show business, spotlight, stage set, staging, theater; SEE CONCEPTS *263,349,438,439,448*

stage [*v*] *arrange, produce*
bring out, do, engineer, execute, give, mount, open, orchestrate, organize, perform, play, present, put on, show; SEE CONCEPTS *94,292*

stagger [*v1*] *walk falteringly*
alternate, careen, dither, falter, halt, hesitate, lurch, overlap, pitch, reel, shake, stammer, step, sway, swing, teeter, titubate, topple, totter, vacillate, waver, wheel, whiffle, wobble, zigzag; SEE CONCEPT *151*

stagger [*v2*] *astound, shock*
amaze, astonish, boggle, bowl over*, confound, consternate, devastate, dumbfound, flabbergast, floor*, give a shock, nonplus, overpower, overwhelm, paralyze, perplex, puzzle, shake, shatter, startle, strike dumb*, stump, stun, stupefy, surprise, take aback, take breath away*, throw off balance*; SEE CONCEPTS *7,19,42*

sp
st

staggering [*adj*] *overwhelming*
amazing, astonishing, astounding, distressing, mind-blowing, mind-boggling, shocking, stunning; SEE CONCEPTS *548,571*

stagnant [*adj*] *motionless, dirty*
brackish, dead, dormant, filthy, foul, idle, immobile, inactive, inert, lifeless, listless, passive, putrid, quiet, sluggish, stale, standing, static, stationary, still, unmoving; SEE CONCEPTS *584,621*

stagnate [*v*] *deteriorate by lack of action*
constipate, decay, decline, fester, go to seed*, hibernate, idle, languish, lie fallow, not move, putrefy, rot, rust, stall, stand, stand still, stifle, stultify, trammel, vegetate; SEE CONCEPTS *698,748*

staid [*adj*] *restrained, set*
calm, cold sober*, collected, composed, cool, decorous, demure, dignified, earnest, formal, grave, no-nonsense*, quiet, sedate, self-restrained, serious, settled, sober, solemn, somber, starchy, steady, stuffy, weighty; SEE CONCEPTS *401,404*

stain [*n*] *spot of dirt, blot bar*
black eye*, blemish, blot, blotch, blur, brand, color, discoloration, disgrace, dishonor, drip, dye, infamy, ink spot, mottle, odium, onus, reproach, shame, sinister*, slur, smirch, smudge, spatter, speck, splotch, spot, stigma, tint; SEE CONCEPTS *230,622*

stain [*v*] *dirty, taint*
animalize, bastardize, besmirch, bestialize, blacken, blemish, blot, brutalize, color, contaminate, corrupt, daub, debase, debauch, defile, demoralize, deprave, discolor, disgrace, drag through the mud*, dye, mark, pervert, smear, smudge, soil, spot, sully, tar, tarnish, tinge, tint; SEE CONCEPTS *54,250,254*

stake [*n1*] *pole*
pale, paling, picket, post, rod, spike, stave, stick; SEE CONCEPTS *471,479*

stake [*n2*] *bet, wager*
ante, chance, hazard, peril, pledge, pot, risk, venture; SEE CONCEPTS *329,363*

stake [*n3*] *share, investment*
award, claim, concern, interest, involvement, prize, purse; SEE CONCEPTS *344,710,835*

stake [*v*] *bet, wager*
back, bankroll*, capitalize, chance, finance, gamble, game, grubstake*, hazard, imperil, jeopardize, lay, play, pledge, put, put on, risk, set, stake down, venture; SEE CONCEPTS *330,363*

stale [*adj1*] *old, decayed*
dried, dry, faded, fetid, flat, fusty, hard, insipid, malodorous, musty, noisome, parched, rank, reeking, smelly, sour, spoiled, stagnant, stenchy, stinking, tasteless, watery, weak, zestless; SEE CONCEPTS *462,485,598*

stale [*adj2*] *overused, out-of-date*
antiquated, banal, bent, cliché, clichéd, cliché-ridden, common, commonplace, corny*, dead, drab, dull, dusty, effete, flat, fusty, hackneyed, insipid, like a dinosaur*, mawkish, moth-eaten*, out*, passé, past, platitudinous, repetitious, shopworn, stereotyped, threadbare, timeworn, tired, trite, unoriginal, well-worn, worn-out, yesterday's*, zestless; SEE CONCEPTS *267,578,589,797*

stalemate [*n*] *deadlock*
arrest, Catch-22*, check, delay, draw, gridlock, impasse, pause, standoff, standstill, tie; SEE CONCEPTS *230,807,832*

stalk [*n*] *stem of plant*
axis, bent, helm, pedicel, pedicle, reed, shaft, spike, spire, support, trunk, twig, upright; SEE CONCEPT *428*

stalk [*v*] *follow, creep up on*
ambush, approach, chase, drive, flush out, haunt, hunt, pace, pursue, shadow, striddle, stride, tail, track, trail, walk up to; SEE CONCEPTS *149,159,749*

stall [*v*] *delay for own purposes*
arrest, avoid the issue*, beat around the bush*, brake, check, die, drag one's feet*, equivocate, fence, filibuster, halt, hamper, hedge, hinder, hold off, interrupt, not move, play for time*, postpone, prevaricate, put off, quibble, shut down, slow, slow down, stand, stand off, stand still, stay, still, stonewall*, stop, suspend, take one's time*, tarry, temporize; SEE CONCEPTS *121,234*

stalwart [*adj*] *strong, valiant*
athletic, bold, bound, bound and determined*, brave, brawny, brick-wall*, courageous, daring, dauntless, dead set on*, dependable, fearless, forceful, gutsy*, hanging tough*, hefty, husky, indomitable, intrepid, lusty, muscular, nervy*, powerhouse*, redoubtable, robust, rugged, sinewy, solid, spunky*, staunch, steamroller*, stout, stouthearted, strapping, sturdy, substantial, tenacious, tough, unafraid, undaunted, valorous, vigorous; SEE CONCEPTS *404,489*

stamina [*n*] *strength, vigor*
backbone*, endurance, energy, force, fortitude, grit*, guts*, gutsiness, heart, indefatigability, intestinal fortitude*, legs*, lustiness, moxie*, power, power of endurance, resilience, resistance, starch*, staying power, tolerance, toleration, vim, vitality, zip*; SEE CONCEPTS *411,732*

stammer [*v*] *stutter in speech*
falter, halt, hammer, hem and haw*, hesitate, jabber, lurch, pause, repeat, splutter, sputter, stop, stumble, wobble; SEE CONCEPTS *47,266*

stamp [*n1*] *impression, symbol, seal*
brand, cast, earmark, emblem, hallmark, impress, imprint, indentation, mark, mold, print, signature, sticker; SEE CONCEPTS *259,284*

stamp [*n2*] *character*
breed, cast, cut, description, fashion, form, ilk, kind, lot, mold, sort, stripe, type; SEE CONCEPT *411*

stamp [*v1*] *step on hard*
beat, clomp, clump, crush, stomp, stump, tramp, trample, tromp; SEE CONCEPT *149*

stamp [*v2*] *imprint; press mark on*
brand, cast, drive, engrave, etch, fix, grave, hammer, impress, infix, inscribe, letter, mark, mold, offset, pound, print; SEE CONCEPTS *79,174*

stampede [*n*] *rush of animals*
charge, chase, crash, dash, flight, fling, hurry, panic, rout, run, scattering, shoot, smash, tear; SEE CONCEPT *152*

stamp out [*v*] *extinguish*
abolish, blot out*, crush, destroy, eliminate, end, eradicate, expunge, exterminate, kill, put down, quell, snuff out, suppress, wipe out*; SEE CONCEPTS *95,252*

stance [*n*] *position, posture*
attitude, bearing, carriage, color, deportment,

posture, say-so*, slant, stand, standpoint, viewpoint; SEE CONCEPTS *689,757*

stand [*n1*] *position, opinion*
angle, attitude, belief, carriage, determination, notion, poise, pose, sentiment, slant, sound, stance, standpoint, twist, two cents' worth*, view; SEE CONCEPT *689*

stand [*n2*] *base, stage*
board, booth, bracket, counter, dais, frame, gantry, grandstand, place, platform, rack, rank, staging, stall, station, support, table; SEE CONCEPTS *442,443*

stand [*v1*] *be or get upright*
be erect, be on feet, be vertical, cock, dispose, erect, jump up, locate, mount, place, poise, position, put, rank, rise, set, settle; SEE CONCEPT *201*

stand [*v3*] *be in force, exist*
be located, belong, be situated, be valid, continue, endure, fill, halt, hold, last, obtain, occupy, pause, prevail, remain, rest, stay, stop, take up; SEE CONCEPT *407*

standard [*adj*] *regular, approved*
accepted, authoritative, average, basic, boilerplate*, canonical, classic, common, customary, definitive, established, everyday, garden variety*, general, normal, official, orthodox, popular, prevailing, recognized, regulation, run-of-the-mill*, set, staple, stock, typical, usual, vanilla*; SEE CONCEPT *533*

standard [*n1*] *guideline, principle*
archetype, average, axiom, barometer, beau ideal, belief, benchmark, canon, code, criterion, ethics, example, exemplar, fundamental, gauge, grade, guide, guideline, ideal, ideals, law, mean, measure, median, mirror, model, morals, norm, par, paradigm, pattern, principle, requirement, rule, rule of thumb*, sample, specification, test, touchstone, type, yardstick; SEE CONCEPT *688*

standard [*n2*] *flag*
banderole, banner, bannerol, color, colors, emblem, ensign, figure, insignia, jack, pennant, streamer, symbol; SEE CONCEPT *475*

standardize [*v*] *make regular, similar*
assimilate, bring into line, homogenize, institute, institutionalize, mass produce, normalize, order, regiment, stereotype, systematize; SEE CONCEPT *126*

standby [*n*] *substitute*
assistant, backup, deputy, double, fill-in, pinch-hitter*, relief, replacement, reserve, stalwart, stand-in, sub*, successor, temp*, temporary, understudy; SEE CONCEPTS *423,712*

stand for [*v*] *signify, mean*
answer for, appear for, betoken, denote, exemplify, imply, indicate, represent, signify, suggest, symbol, symbolize; SEE CONCEPT *682*

standing [*adj*] *permanent*
continuing, existing, fixed, perpetual, regular, repeated; SEE CONCEPT *551*

standing [*n*] *position, rank*
cachet, capacity, character, condition, consequence, credit, dignity, eminence, estimation, footing, place, prestige, reputation, repute, scene, situation, slot, state, station, stature, status, term; SEE CONCEPTS *388,727*

standoff [*n*] *draw, tie*
dead heat*, deadlock, drawn battle*, even game, impasse, level, Mexican standoff*, stalemate, toss-up, wash; SEE CONCEPTS *364,667*

standoffish [*adj*] *cold, distant*
aloof, antisocial, cool, distant, eremitic, haughty, indifferent, misanthropic, reclusive, remote, reserved, solitary, unapproachable, uncompanionable, unsociable, withdrawn; SEE CONCEPTS *401,404*

stand out [*v*] *be conspicuous, prominent*
attract attention, be distinct, beetle, be highlighted, be striking, bulge, bulk, catch the eye, emerge, jut, loom, overhang, poke, pouch, project, protrude, stick out; SEE CONCEPT *716*

standpoint [*n*] *belief, position*
angle, attitude, judgment, opinion, outlook, point of view, stance, stand, view, viewpoint; SEE CONCEPT *689*

stand/stand for [*v2*] *endure, bear*
abide, allow, bear with, brook, cope, countenance, experience, handle, hang on, hold, last, live with, put up with, resign oneself to, stay the course*, stomach*, submit, suffer, support, sustain, swallow, take, tolerate, undergo, wear, weather, withstand; SEE CONCEPT *23*

standstill [*n*] *stop*
arrest, cessation, check, checkmate, corner*, dead end*, deadlock, dead stop*, delay, gridlock, halt, hole, impasse, inaction, pause, stalemate, standoff, wait; SEE CONCEPTS *119,832*

staple [*adj*] *necessary, basic*
chief, essential, fundamental, important, in demand, key, main, popular, predominant, primary, principal, standard; SEE CONCEPT *546*

star [*adj*] *famous, illustrious*
brilliant, capital, celebrated, chief, dominant, leading, main, major, outstanding, paramount, predominant, preeminent, principal, prominent, talented, well-known; SEE CONCEPT *568*

star [*n*] *person who is famous*
celebrity, draw*, favorite, headliner, hero, idol, lead, leading role, luminary, name, starlet, superstar, topliner*; SEE CONCEPTS *352,366*

starchy [*adj*] *formal, stiff*
ceremonious, conventional, inflexible, mannered, prim, reserved, rigid, starched*, stilted, strait-laced, strict, stuffy*; SEE CONCEPT *401*

star-crossed [*adj*] *doomed*
catastrophic, cursed, damned, disastrous, ill-fated, ill-omened, ill-starred, jinxed, luckless, misfortunate, unfortunate, unlucky; SEE CONCEPTS *537,548*

stardom [*n*] *fame*
acclaim, celebrity, distinction, éclat, eminence, esteem, glory, greatness, honor, illustriousness, immortality, nobility, notoriety, popularity, preeminence, prestige, prominence, public esteem, recognition, renown, standing; SEE CONCEPTS *388,668*

stare [*v*] *gape, watch*
beam*, bore*, eagle eye*, eye, eyeball*, fix, focus, gawk, gaze, glare, glim*, goggle*, lay eyes on*, look, look fixedly, ogle, peer, rivet, rubberneck*, take in; SEE CONCEPT *623*

stark [*adj1*] *utter, absolute*
abrupt, arrant, bald, bare, blasted, blessed, blunt, complete, confounded, consummate, downright, entire, firm, flagrant, gross, infernal, out-and-out*, outright, palpable, patent, pure, rank, severe, sheer, simple, stiff, unalloyed, unmitigated; SEE CONCEPTS *531,569*

stark [*adj2*] *bare, unadorned*
au naturel, austere, bald, barren, bleak, chaste,

st
st

clear, cold, depressing, desolate, dreary, empty, forsaken, grim, harsh, naked, nude, plain, raw, severe, solitary, stripped, unclad, unclothed, uncovered, undraped, vacant, vacuous, void; SEE CONCEPT 485

starry-eyed [adj] *unrealistic*
dreaming, half-baked*, hoping, impossible, improbable, ivory-tower*, nonrealistic, not sensible, on cloud nine*, optimistic, romantic, silly; SEE CONCEPTS 552,560

start [n1] *beginning*
alpha*, birth, bow, commencement, countdown, dawn, dawning, day one*, derivation, embarkation, exit, first step, flying start*, foundation, inauguration, inception, initiation, jump-off, kickoff*, leaving, onset, opening, origin, outset, running start, setting out, source, spring, square one*, start-off, takeoff; SEE CONCEPTS 648,832

start [n2] *advantage*
allowance, backing, break, bulge, chance, draw, edge, handicap, head start, helping hand, introduction, lead, odds, opening, opportunity, sponsorship, vantage; SEE CONCEPT 693

start [n3] *flinch*
convulsion, jar, jump, scare, shock, spasm, turn, twitch; SEE CONCEPTS 150,194

start [v1] *begin; come into existence*
activate, appear, arise, arouse, come into being, commence, create, depart, embark, engender, enter upon, establish, found, get going, get under way*, go ahead, hit the road*, inaugurate, incite, initiate, instigate, institute, introduce, issue, launch, lay foundation, leave, light, make a beginning, open, originate, pioneer, rise, rouse, sally forth, see light, set in motion, set out, set up, spring, take first step*, take the plunge*, turn on; SEE CONCEPTS 221,241

start [v2] *flinch*
blanch, blench, bolt, bounce, bound, buck, dart, draw back, jerk, jump, jump the gun*, leap, quail, recoil, shrink, shy, spring, squinch, startle, twitch, wince; SEE CONCEPTS 150,194

startle [v] *frighten, surprise*
affright, agitate, alarm, amaze, astonish, astound, awe, bolt, consternate, floor, fright, give a turn*, jump, make jump, rock, scare, scare to death*, shake up, shock, spook, spring, spring something on*, stagger, start, stun, take aback, terrify, terrorize; SEE CONCEPTS 7,19,42

starving/starved [adj] *deprived of food*
could eat a horse*, craving, dehydrated, drawn, dying, emaciated, empty, faint, famished, haggard, hungering, hungry, malnourished, peaked, peckish, perishing, pinched, ravenous, skinny, thin, underfed, undernourished, weakened; SEE CONCEPTS 406,546

state [n1] *condition or mode of being*
accompaniment, attitude, capacity, case, category, chances, character, circumstance, circumstances, contingency, element, environment, essential, estate, event, eventuality, fix, footing, form, frame of mind, humor, imperative, juncture, limitation, mood, nature, occasion, occurrence, outlook, pass, phase, plight, position, posture, predicament, prerequisite, proviso, reputation, requirement, shape, situation, spirits, stand, standing, state of affairs, station, status, stipulation, time, welfare; SEE CONCEPTS 410,639,696,701,720

state [n2] *dignity, grandeur*
cachet, ceremony, consequence, display, glory, majesty, pomp, position, prestige, rank, splendor, standing, stature, status, style; SEE CONCEPT 388

state [n3] *government, country*
body politic, commonwealth, community, federation, land, nation, republic, sovereignty, territory, union; SEE CONCEPTS 508,510

state [v] *declare, assert*
affirm, air, articulate, asseverate, aver, bring out, chime in*, come out with, deliver, describe, elucidate, enounce, enumerate, enunciate, explain, expound, express, give, give blow-by-blow*, give rundown*, interpret, narrate, pitch, present, pronounce, propound, put, recite, recount, rehearse, relate, report, say, set forth, speak, specify, spiel*, tell, throw out*, utter, vent, ventilate, voice; SEE CONCEPTS 49,51,55

stately [adj] *dignified, impressive*
august, ceremonial, ceremonious, conventional, courtly, deliberate, elegant, elevated, formal, gallant, gracious, grand, grandiose, haughty, high, highfaluting*, high-minded*, imperial, imperious, imposing, kingly, large, lofty, luxurious, magnificent, majestic, massive, measured, monumental, noble, opulent, palatial, pompous, portly, proud, queenly, regal, royal, solemn, stiff, sumptuous, superb, towering; SEE CONCEPTS 401,574,589

statement [n1] *declaration, assertion*
ABCs*, account, acknowledgment, affidavit, affirmation, allegation, announcement, articulation, aside, asseveration, assurance, averment, avowal, blow-by-blow*, charge, comment, communication, communiqué, description, dictum, ejaculation, explanation, make*, manifesto, mention, narrative, observation, picture, presentation, presentment, proclamation, profession, protestation, recital, recitation, relation, remark, report, rundown, testimony, utterance, ventilation, verbalization, vocalization, voice, word; SEE CONCEPTS 271,274,278

statement [n2] *account of finances*
affidavit, audit, bill, budget, charge, invoice, reckoning, record, report, score, tab; SEE CONCEPT 331

state-of-the-art [adj] *up-to-date*
advanced, all the rage*, au courant, avant-garde, brand-new, contemporary, cutting edge*, fashionable, in, in-thing*, leading edge, modernistic, new, newest, newfangled, red-hot*, stylish, trendsetting, trendy, ultramodern, up-to-the-minute; SEE CONCEPTS 578,589,797,799

static [adj] *motionless, changeless*
at a standstill, constant, deadlocked, fixed, format, gridlocked, immobile, immovable, inactive, inert, latent, passive, rigid, stabile, stable, stagnant, stalled, standing still, stationary, sticky, still, stopped, stuck, unchanging, unfluctuating, unmoving, unvarying; SEE CONCEPTS 534,584

station [n1] *headquarters, base*
base of operations, depot, home office, house, location, locus, main office, place, position, post, seat, site, situation, spot, stop, terminal, whereabouts; SEE CONCEPT 198

station [n2] *social or occupational status*
appointment, business, calling, capacity, caste, character, class, duty, employment, estate, footing, grade, level, occupation, order, place, position, post, rank, service, situation, sphere,

standing, state, stratum; SEE CONCEPTS *349,376,388*

station [*v*] *place at a location*
allot, appoint, assign, base, commission, establish, fix, garrison, install, lodge, park, plant, post, put, set; SEE CONCEPTS *50,88,201,320,351*

stationary [*adj*] *not moving; fixed*
anchored, at a standstill, immobile, inert, moored, motionless, nailed*, nailed down*, parked*, pat*, permanent, stable, stagnant, standing, static, stock-still, unmoving; SEE CONCEPTS *488,551*

stationery [*n*] *writing materials*
envelopes, letterhead, office supplies, pen and paper, writing paper; SEE CONCEPTS *260,475*

statue [*n*] *trophy or memorial*
bronze, bust, cast, effigy, figure, icon, image, ivory, likeness, marble, piece, representation, sculpture, simulacrum, statuary, statuette, torso; SEE CONCEPT *259*

statuesque [*adj*] *tall and dignifed*
beautiful, graceful, grand, imposing, majestic, regal, shapely, stately, trim, well-proportioned; SEE CONCEPTS *579,589,779*

stature [*n*] *importance*
ability, cachet, caliber, capacity, competence, consequence, development, dignity, elevation, eminence, growth, merit, position, prestige, prominence, qualification, quality, rank, size, standing, state, station, status, tallness, value, virtue, worth; SEE CONCEPTS *668,741*

status [*n*] *rank*
cachet, caliber, capacity, character, condition, consequence, degree, dignity, distinction, eminence, footing, grade, merit, mode, place, position, prestige, prominence, quality, rating, renown, situation, stage, standing, state, station, stature, worth; SEE CONCEPTS *388,668*

status quo [*n*] *existing conditions*
circumstances, how things stand, no change, state, state of affairs; SEE CONCEPTS *410,639,696, 701,720*

statute [*n*] *rule, law*
act, assize, bill, canon, decree, decretum, edict, enactment, measure, ordinance, precept, regulation; SEE CONCEPT *318*

staunch [*adj*] *resolute, dependable*
allegiant, ardent, constant, faithful, fast, firm, inflexible, liege, loyal, reliable, secure, sound, stable, stalwart, steadfast, stiff, stout, strong, sure, tough, tried-and-true, true, true-blue, trustworthy, trusty; SEE CONCEPTS *401,534,542*

stay [*n1*] *visit*
break, halt, holiday, sojourn, stop, stopover, vacation; SEE CONCEPT *227*

stay [*n2*] *hold, delay*
deferment, halt, pause, postponement, remission, reprieve, standstill, stop, stopping, suspension; SEE CONCEPTS *121,832*

stay [*n3*] *support, underpinning*
brace, buttress, column, hold, prop, reinforcement, shore, shoring, stanchion, truss, underpropping; SEE CONCEPTS *440,445*

stay [*v1*] *wait*
abide, bide, bunk, continue, dally, delay, endure, establish oneself, halt, hang, hang about, hang around, hang in, hang out, hold the fort*, hover, lag, last, linger, loiter, nest, outstay, pause, perch, procrastinate, put down roots*, remain, reprieve, reside, respite, roost*, settle, sit tight*,

sojourn, squat, stand, stay out, stay put, stick around*, stop, sweat*, sweat it out*, tarry; SEE CONCEPTS *210,681*

stay [*v2*] *visit*
be accommodated, bide, dwell, live, lodge, put up, sojourn, stop, stop over, tarry; SEE CONCEPTS *226,227*

stay [*v3*] *hold in abeyance*
adjourn, arrest, check, curb, defer, delay, detain, discontinue, halt, hinder, hold, hold over, impede, intermit, interrupt, obstruct, postpone, prevent, prorogue, put off, shelve, stall, stop, suspend, ward off; SEE CONCEPT *121*

staying power [*n*] *stamina*
backbone*, endurance, fortitude, grit*, guts*, gutsiness, heart, intestinal fortitude*, legs*, power of endurance, resilience, tolerance, vitality; SEE CONCEPTS *411,732*

steadfast [*adj*] *loyal, steady*
abiding, adamant, allegiant, ardent, bound, changeless, constant, dedicated, dependable, enduring, established, faithful, fast, firm, fixed, immobile, immovable, inexorable, inflexible, intense, intent, liege, never-failing, obdurate, persevering, relentless, reliable, resolute, rigid, single-minded, stable, staunch, stubborn, sure, tried-and-true, true, true-blue*, unbending, unfaltering, unflinching, unmovable, unqualified, unquestioning, unswerving, unwavering, unyielding, wholehearted; SEE CONCEPTS *401,534, 542*

steady [*adj1*] *stable, fixed*
abiding, brick-wall*, certain, changeless, constant, durable, enduring, equable, even, firm, immovable, never-failing, patterned, regular, reliable, safe, set, set in stone*, solid, solid as a rock*, stable, steadfast, steady-going, substantial, sure, unchangeable, unchanging, unfaltering, unfluctuating, uniform, unqualified, unquestioning, unshaken, unvarying, unwavering; SEE CONCEPTS *488,534*

steady [*adj2*] *continuing*
ceaseless, confirmed, consistent, constant, continuous, equable, eternal, even, faithful, habitual, incessant, never-ending, nonstop, persistent, regular, rhythmic, stabile, stable, steady-going, unbroken, unfaltering, unfluctuating, uniform, uninterrupted, unremitting, unvarying, unwavering; SEE CONCEPT *798*

steady [*adj3*] *balanced, faithful in mind*
allegiant, ardent, calm, constant, cool, dependable, equable, fast, imperturbable, intense, levelheaded, liege, loyal, poised, reliable, reserved, resolute, sedate, self-possessed, sensible, serene, serious-minded, settled, single-minded, sober, staid, staunch, steadfast, unswerving, unwavering, wholehearted; SEE CONCEPTS *403,542*

steal [*v1*] *take something without permission*
abduct, appropriate, blackmail, burglarize, carry off, cheat, cozen, defraud, despoil, divert, embezzle, heist, hold for ransom, hold up, housebreak*, keep, kidnap, lift*, loot, make off with*, misappropriate, peculate, pilfer, pillage, pinch*, pirate, plagiarize, plunder, poach, purloin, ransack, remove, rifle, rip off*, run off with*, sack*, shoplift, snitch*, spirit away*, stick up*, strip, swindle, swipe, take, take possession of, thieve, walk off with*, withdraw; SEE CONCEPT *139*

steal [*v2*] *sneak around*
creep, flit, glide, go stealthily, insinuate, lurk,

st
st

pass quietly, skulk, slide, slink, slip, snake, tiptoe; SEE CONCEPTS *151,207*

stealthy [*adj*] *quiet and secretive*
catlike, catty*, clandestine, covert, crafty, cunning, enigmatic, feline, furtive, hush-hush*, noiseless, private, secret, shifty, silent, skulking, slinking, sly, sneak, sneaking, sneaky, sub-rosa*, surreptitious, undercover, underhand, under wraps*, wily; SEE CONCEPTS *401,576*

steam [*n*] *energy*
beef, force, might, muscle, potency, power, puissance, sinew, strength, vigor, vim; SEE CONCEPT *633*

steel [*v*] *prepare oneself*
animate, brace, buck up*, cheer, embolden, encourage, fortify, gird, grit teeth*, harden, hearten, inspirit, make up one's mind*, prepare, rally, ready, reinforce, strengthen; SEE CONCEPT *35*

steep [*adj1*] *extreme in direction, course*
abrupt, arduous, breakneck, declivitous, elevated, erect, headlong, high, hilly, lifted, lofty, perpendicular, precipitate, precipitous, prerupt, raised, sharp, sheer, straight-up; SEE CONCEPT *581*

steep [*adj2*] *very expensive*
dizzying, excessive, exorbitant, extortionate, extreme, high, immoderate, inordinate, overpriced, stiff, towering, uncalled-for, undue, unmeasurable, unreasonable; SEE CONCEPTS *334,762*

steep [*v*] *let soak*
bathe, damp, drench, fill, imbue, immerse, impregnate, infuse, ingrain, invest, macerate, marinate, moisten, permeate, pervade, saturate, soak, sodden, sop, souse, submerge, suffuse, waterlog; SEE CONCEPT *256*

steer [*v*] *guide, direct on a course*
beacon, be in the driver's seat*, captain, conduct, control, drive, escort, govern, head for, helm, herd, lead, pilot, point, route, run, run things, see, shepherd, show, skipper*, take over, take the helm, take the reins; SEE CONCEPTS *94,187*

stem [*n*] *stalk of plant*
axis, branch, pedicel, pedicle, peduncle, petiole, shoot, stock, trunk; SEE CONCEPT *428*

stem [*v1*] *come from*
arise, be bred, be brought about, be caused, be generated, derive, develop, emanate, flow, head, issue, originate, proceed, rise, spring; SEE CONCEPT *648*

stem [*v2*] *prevent, stop*
arrest, bring to a standstill, check, contain, control, curb, dam, hinder, hold back, oppose, resist, restrain, stay, withstand; SEE CONCEPT *121*

stench [*n*] *foul odor*
fetor, funk*, malodor, mephitis, noisomeness, redolence, smell, stink*; SEE CONCEPTS *599,600*

step [*n1*] *pace of feet in walking*
footfall, footprint, footstep, gait, impression, mark, print, spoor, stride, trace, track, trail, tread, vestige, walk; SEE CONCEPT *149*

step [*n2*] *action, move*
act, advance, advancement, deed, degree, expedient, gradation, grade, level, maneuver, means, measure, motion, notch, phase, point, procedure, proceeding, process, progression, rank, remove, rung, stage, start; SEE CONCEPTS *1,832*

step [*n3*] *one level of stairs*
doorstep, gradation, notch, rest, round, run, rung, stair, tread; SEE CONCEPTS *440,445*

step [*v*] *move foot to walk*
advance, ambulate, ascend, dance, descend, go backward, go down, go forward, go up, hoof, mince, move backward, move forward, pace, prance, skip, stride, tiptoe, traipse, tread, trip, troop, walk; SEE CONCEPT *149*

step down [*v*] *resign*
abandon, abdicate, bow out, cease work, drop out, give notice, hand in resignation, hang it up*, leave, quit, retire, sign off, terminate, throw in the towel*, walk out; SEE CONCEPTS *119,195,351*

step in [*v*] *become involved*
arrive, be invited, chip in*, come, enter, intercede, interfere, intermediate, interpose, intervene, lend a hand*, mediate, negotiate, take action; SEE CONCEPTS *100,324,384*

step up [*v*] *accelerate*
augment, boost, escalate, hasten, hurry, improve, increase, intensify, lift, quicken, raise, shake up, speed, speed up, up; SEE CONCEPTS *236,244,245*

stereotype [*n*] *idea held as standard, example*
average, boilerplate*, convention, custom, fashion, formula, institution, mold, pattern, received idea; SEE CONCEPT *686*

stereotype [*v*] *categorize as being example, standard*
catalogue, conventionalize, define, dub, institutionalize, methodize, normalize, pigeonhole*, regulate, standardize, systematize, take to be, typecast*; SEE CONCEPTS *38,49*

stereotyped [*adj*] *standard, conventional*
banal, clichéd, cliché-ridden, commonplace, corny*, dull, hackneyed, mass-produced, ordinary, overused, platitudinous, played out*, stale, standardized, stock, threadbare*, tired*, trite, unoriginal, well-worn, worn-out, worn thin; SEE CONCEPT *530*

sterile [*adj*] *unproductive, clean*
antiseptic, arid, aseptic, bare, barren, bleak, dead, decontaminated, desert, desolate, disinfected, dry, effete, empty, fallow, fruitless, futile, gaunt, germ-free, hygienic, impotent, infecund, infertile, pasteurized, sanitary, septic, sterilized, unfruitful, uninfected, unprofitable, unprolific, vain, waste, without issue; SEE CONCEPTS *485,621*

sterilize [*v*] *make clean or unproductive*
alter, antisepticize, asceptize, aseptify, autoclave, castrate, change, clean, decontaminate, desexualize, disinfect, emasculate, fix, fumigate, incapacitate, make sterile, neuter, pasteurize, purify, sanitize, spay; SEE CONCEPTS *231,250*

sterling [*adj*] *high-quality*
admirable, choice, excellent, exquisite, fine, first-rate, grand, magnificent, marvelous, outstanding, pure, splendid, stunning, superior, the best, very best; SEE CONCEPT *574*

stern [*adj*] *serious, authoritarian*
ascetic, astringent, austere, bitter, bullheaded, by the book*, cruel, disciplinary, dyed-in-the-wool*, flinty, forbidding, frowning, grim, hangtough*, hard, hard-boiled*, hard-core*, hardheaded*, hard-line*, hard-nosed*, hardshell*, harsh, implacable, inexorable, inflexible, mortified, mulish, relentless, rigid, rigorous, rough, severe, steely, stiff-necked*, strict, stubborn, tough, unrelenting, unsparing, unyielding; SEE CONCEPTS *401,542*

stew [*n1*] *mixture, miscellany*
brew, goulash*, hash, jumble, medley, mélange,

mishmash, mulligan*, olio*, pasticcio*, pie*, potpourri, salmagundi*, soup; SEE CONCEPTS *432,457,460,461*

stew [*n2*] *commotion; mental upset*
agitation, confusion, dither, flap, fretting, fuming, fuss, lather, pother, snit, sweat, tizzy, tumult, turbulence, turmoil, worry; SEE CONCEPT *410*

stew [*v*] *worry; steam*
boil, chafe, cook, fret, fume, fuss, pother, seethe, simmer; SEE CONCEPT *35*

stick [*n*] *pole, often wooden*
bar, bat, baton, billet, birch, bludgeon, board, branch, cane, club, cudgel, drumstick, ferrule, ingot, mast, rod, rule, ruler, shoot, slab, slat, staff, stake, stalk, stave, stem, strip, switch, timber, twig, wand, wedge; SEE CONCEPTS *470,479*

stick [*v1*] *adhere, affix*
attach, be bogged down, become embedded, become immobilized, bind, bond, braze, catch, cement, clasp, cleave, cling, cling like ivy*, clog, cohere, fasten, fix, freeze to, fuse, glue, hold, hold fast, hold on, hug, jam, join, linger, lodge, paste, persist, remain, snag, solder, stay, stay put, stick like barnacle*, stick together, unite, weld; SEE CONCEPTS *85,160*

stick [*v2*] *poke with pointed object*
dig, drive, gore, impale, insert, jab, penetrate, pierce, pin, plunge, prod, puncture, ram, run, sink, spear, stab, thrust, transfix; SEE CONCEPT *220*

stick [*v3*] *position, lay*
deposit, drop, establish, fix, install, place, plant, plonk, plunk, put, set, settle, store, stuff; SEE CONCEPT *201*

stick [*v4*] *endure*
abide, bear, bear up under, brook, get on with, go, grin and bear it*, last, persist, put up with, see through, stand, stay, stomach*, suffer, support, take, take it, tolerate, weather; SEE CONCEPT *23*

stick-in-the-mud [*n*] *person set in ways*
antediluvian, conservative, diehard*, fossil*, mossback*, old fogy*, reactionary; SEE CONCEPT *423*

stick out [*v*] *bulge*
beetle, come through, extend, extrude, jut, obtrude, outthrust, overhang, poke, pouch, pout, project, pretend, protrude, push, show, stand out; SEE CONCEPT *751*

stickup [*n*] *holdup*
armed robbery, burglary, crime, mugging, robbery, stealing, theft; SEE CONCEPT *192*

sticky [*adj1*] *gummy, adhesive*
agglutinative, clinging, gluey, glutinous, ropy, syrupy, tacky, tenacious, viscid, viscous; SEE CONCEPT *606*

sticky [*adj2*] *humid and hot*
clammy, close, dank, mucky, muggy, oppressive, soggy, sultry, sweltering; SEE CONCEPT *525*

sticky [*adj3*] *difficult, embarrassing*
awkward, delicate, discomforting, formidable, hairy*, hard, heavy*, knotty, laborious, nasty, operose, painful, rough, rugged, strenuous, thorny, tricky, unpleasant; SEE CONCEPT *565*

stiff [*adj1*] *hard, inflexible*
annealed, arthritic, benumbed, brittle, buckram, cemented, chilled, congealed, contracted, creaky, firm, fixed, frozen, graceless, hardened, immalleable, impliable, incompliant, indurate, inelastic, jelled, mechanical, numbed, ossified,

petrified, refractory, resistant, rheumatic, rigid, set, solid, solidified, starched, starchy, stark, steely, stiff as a board*, stony, taut, tense, thick, thickened, tight, unbending, unflexible, ungraceful, unsupple, unyielding, wooden; SEE CONCEPT *604*

stiff [*adj2*] *formal, standoffish*
angular, artificial, austere, ceremonious, cold, constrained, forced, hardheaded, headstrong, inflexible, intractable, labored, mannered, obstinate, pertinacious, pompous, priggish, prim, punctilious, relentless, starchy, stilted, strong, stubborn, uneasy, ungainly, ungraceful, unnatural, unrelaxed, unrelenting, wooden; SEE CONCEPT *401*

stiff [*adj3*] *difficult*
arduous, exacting, fatiguing, formidable, hard, laborious, tough, trying, uphill; SEE CONCEPT *565*

stiff [*adj4*] *extreme, severe*
austere, brisk, cruel, drastic, exact, excessive, exorbitant, extravagant, great, hard, harsh, heavy, immoderate, inexorable, inordinate, oppressive, pitiless, potent, powerful, rigorous, sharp, steep, strict, stringent, strong, towering, unconscionable, undue, vigorous; SEE CONCEPTS *540,569*

stiffen [*v*] *make or become harder*
anneal, benumb, brace, cake, candy, cement, chill, clot, coagulate, condense, congeal, crystallize, curdle, firm, fix, freeze, gel, harden, inflate, inspissate, jell, jelly, ossify, petrify, precipitate, prop, reinforce, set, solidify, stabilize, starch, steady, strengthen, tauten, tense, thicken; SEE CONCEPTS *137,250,469*

stifle [*v*] *prevent, restrain*
asphyxiate, black out, bring to screeching halt*, burke, check, choke, choke back, clamp down*, clam up*, constipate, cork, cover up, crack down*, curb, dry up*, extinguish, gag, hold it down, hush, hush up, kill*, muffle, muzzle, prevent, put the lid on*, repress, restrain, shut up, silence, sit on*, smother, spike, squash, squelch, stagnate, stop, strangle, stultify, suffocate, suppress, torpedo*, trammel; SEE CONCEPTS *121,130,191*

stigma [*n*] *shame*
bar sinister*, besmirchment, black mark*, blame, blemish, blot, brand, disfigurement, disgrace, dishonor, imputation, lost face*, mark, odium, onus, reproach, scar, slur, spot, stain, taint; SEE CONCEPTS *230,388,689*

stigmatize [*v*] *brand, label*
characterize, class, classify, defame, denounce, designate, disgrace, mark, stamp, tag; SEE CONCEPTS *62,79*

still [*adj*] *calm, motionless, quiet*
at rest, buttoned up*, clammed up*, closed, close-mouthed, deathlike, deathly, deathly quiet, deathly still, fixed, halcyon, hushed, hushful, inert, lifeless, noiseless, pacific, peaceful, placid, restful, sealed, serene, silent, smooth, soundless, stable, stagnant, static, stationary, stock-still, tranquil, undisturbed, unruffled, unstirring, untroubled, whist; SEE CONCEPTS *584,594*

still [*conj*] *however*
after all, besides, but, even, for all that, furthermore, howbeit, nevertheless, nonetheless, notwithstanding, still and all, though, withal, yet; SEE CONCEPT *544*

st
st

still [n] *quiet*
hush, noiselessness, peace, quietness, quietude, silence, soundlessness, still, stillness, tranquillity; SEE CONCEPTS *65,748*

still [v] *make quiet, motionless, calm*
allay, alleviate, appease, arrest, balm, becalm, calm, choke, compose, decrease volume, fix, gag, hush, lull, muffle, muzzle, pacify, quiet, quieten, settle, shush*, shut down, shut up, silence, slack, smooth, smooth over, soothe, squash, squelch, stall, stop, subdue, tranquilize; SEE CONCEPTS *7,22,65,121*

stillness [n] *silence*
calm, calmness, hush, inaction, inactivity, lull, noiselessness, peace, placidity, quiet, quietness, quietude, serenity, still, tranquility; SEE CONCEPTS *65,388,411,720*

stilted [adj] *artificial, pretentious*
affected, angular, aureate, bombastic, constrained, decorous, egotistic, euphuistic, flowery, forced, formal, genteel, grandiloquent, high-flown, high-sounding, inflated, labored, magniloquent, mincing, overblown, pedantic, pompous, prim, rhetorical, sonorous, stiff, unnatural, wooden; SEE CONCEPTS *267,401*

stimulant [n] *substance that invigorates*
analeptic, bracer, catalyst, drug, energizer, excitant, goad, impetus, impulse, incentive, incitation, incitement, motivation, motive, pick-me-up*, restorative, reviver, shot in the arm*, spark plug*, spur, stimulus, tonic, upper; SEE CONCEPTS *240,307,661*

stimulate [v] *excite, provoke*
activate, animate, arouse, build a fire under*, commove, dynamize, elate, encourage, energize, enliven, exhilarate, fan, fire, fire up*, foment, foster, galvanize, get one going*, get one started*, goad, grab, hook, impel, incite, inflame, innervate, innerve, inspire, instigate, jazz*, juice*, key up*, motivate, move, perk, pique, prod, prompt, quicken, rouse, send, set up, spark, spirit, spur, steam up*, stir up*, support, trigger, turn on*, urge, vitalize, vivify, wake up*, whet, work up*; SEE CONCEPTS *14,242*

stimulating [adj] *exciting*
adrenalizing, appealing, arousing, bracing, breathtaking, challenging, electrifying, energizing, exhilarating, gripping, hair-raising*, hectic, inspiring, interesting, invigorating, lively, moving, provocative, rousing, spine-tingling*, stirring, thought-provoking, thrilling, titillating; SEE CONCEPTS *529,542,548*

stimulus [n] *provocation*
bang*, boost, catalyst, cause, charge, encouragement, eye-opener*, fillip, fireworks*, flash*, goad, impetus, impulse, incentive, incitation, incitement, inducement, instigation, invitation, kick*, motivation, motive, piquing, propellant, provocation, push, shot in the arm*, spur, stimulant, stimulation, sting*, turn-on*, urging; SEE CONCEPTS *240,307,661*

sting [v] *prick, pain*
bite, burn, electrify, hurt, injure, inspire, needle, pique, poke, prickle, smart, tingle, wound; SEE CONCEPTS *220,246,313,728*

stingy [adj] *penny-pinching, averse to spending money*
acquisitive, avaricious, chary, cheap, chintzy*, churlish, close, close-fisted, costive, covetous, curmudgeonly, economical, extortionate, frugal, grasping, greedy, grudging, ignoble, illiberal, ironfisted, mean, miserly, narrow, near, parsimonious, pennywise*, penurious, petty, pinch-penny*, rapacious, saving, scrimping, scurvy, selfish, skimping, sordid, sparing, thrifty, tightfisted, uncharitable, ungenerous, ungiving; SEE CONCEPTS *326,334,401*

stink [n] *bad smell*
fetor, foulness, foul odor, malodor, noisomeness, offensive smell, stench; SEE CONCEPTS *599,600*

stink [v1] *smell badly*
be offensive, be rotten, funk*, have an odor, offend, reek*, smell up, stink to high heaven*; SEE CONCEPT *600*

stink [v2] *be lousy, bad*
be abhorrent, be detestable, be held in disrepute, be no good, be offensive, be rotten, have a bad name*, smell; SEE CONCEPTS *230,388*

stinking [adj] *smelly*
fetid, foul, foul-smelling, funky*, malodorous, mephitic, noisome, odiferous, offensive, putrid, rancid, rank, reeking, stenchy, stinking, strong-smelling; SEE CONCEPT *598*

stint [n] *period of responsibility*
assignment, bit, chore, consignment, duty, job, participation, quota, share, shift, spell, stretch, task, term, time, tour, turn, work; SEE CONCEPTS *362,807,822*

stint [v] *economize; hold back*
be frugal, begrudge, be parsimonious, be sparing, be stingy, confine, cut corners*, define, go easy on, grudge, limit, make ends meet*, penny-pinch*, pinch, restrain, roll back*, save, save for rainy day*, scrape, scrimp, skimp on*, sock away*, spare, squirrel*, stash, tighten belt*, withhold; SEE CONCEPT *330*

stipend [n] *payment for services*
allowance, award, consideration, emolument, fee, gratuity, hire, pay, pension, salary, take, wage; SEE CONCEPT *344*

stipulate [v] *decide on conditions*
agree, arrange, bargain, condition, contract, covenant, designate, detail, engage, guarantee, impose, insist upon, lay down, lay finger on, make, make a point, name, particularize, pin down, pledge, postulate, promise, provide, put down for, require, settle, slot, specificate, specificize, specify, spell out, state; SEE CONCEPTS *8,18,60*

stipulation [n] *condition of agreement*
agreement, arrangement, circumscription, clause, contract, designation, engagement, fine print*, limit, obligation, precondition, prerequisite, provision, proviso, qualification, requirement, reservation, restriction, settlement, sine qua non, small print*, specification, string attached*, term, terms; SEE CONCEPTS *270,318,684*

stir [n] *commotion, excitement*
activity, ado, agitation, backwash*, bustle, din, disorder, disquiet, disturbance, ferment, flap*, flurry, furor, fuss, movement, pandemonium, pother, racket, row, scene, to-do*, tumult, turmoil, uproar, whirl, whirlwind; SEE CONCEPTS *230,388*

stir [v1] *mix up, agitate*
beat, blend, disturb, flutter, mix, move, move about, quiver, rustle, shake, toss, tremble, whip, whisk; SEE CONCEPTS *158,170*

stir [v2] *incite, stimulate*
abet, actuate, add fuel to fire*, adjy*, affect, agi-

tate, animate, arouse, awaken, bestir, challenge, craze, drive, electrify, energize, excite, feed the fire*, foment, galvanize, impel, inflame, inspire, kindle, make waves*, motivate, move, prompt, provoke, psych*, quicken, raise, rally, rile, rouse, roust, rout, set, spark, spook*, spur, stimulate, stir embers*, stir up, switch on, thrill, touch, trigger, urge, vitalize, wake, waken, whet, whip up*, work up*; SEE CONCEPTS *14,221*

stir [*v3*] *get up and going*
awake, awaken, bestir, be up and about, budge, exert, get a move on*, get moving, hasten, look alive, make an effort, mill about, move, rouse, shake a leg*, wake, waken; SEE CONCEPT *149*

stirring [*adj*] *moving, rousing*
arousing, awakening, dynamic, electrifying, emotional, exhilarating, gripping, heartbreaking, heartrending, inspirational, inspiring, motivating, provoking, stimulating, touching; SEE CONCEPTS *529,537*

stock [*adj*] *commonplace*
banal, basic, common, conventional, customary, dull, established, formal, hackneyed, normal, ordinary, overused, regular, routine, run-of-the-mill*, set, standard, staple, stereotyped, traditional, trite, typical, usual, worn-out; SEE CONCEPTS *530,547*

stock [*n1*] *merchandise*
accumulation, array, articles, assets, assortment, backlog, cache, choice, commodities, fund, goods, hoard, inventory, nest egg*, produce, range, reserve, reservoir, selection, stockpile, store, supply, variety, wares; SEE CONCEPT *338*

stock [*n2*] *animals raised on a farm*
animals, beasts, cattle, cows, domestic, farm animals, flock, fowl, herd, hogs, horses, livestock, pigs, sheep, swine; SEE CONCEPTS *394,397*

stock [*n3*] *ancestry*
background, breed, clan, descent, extraction, family, folk, forebears, house, kin, kindred, line, lineage, line of descent, parentage, pedigree, race, species, strain, tribe, type, variety; SEE CONCEPTS *296,378*

stock [*n4*] *investment in company*
assets, blue chips, bonds, capital, convertible, funds, over-the-counter*, paper, property, share; SEE CONCEPT *332*

stock [*n5*] *estimation, faith*
appraisal, appraisement, assessment, confidence, count, dependence, estimate, evaluation, figure, hope, inventory, judgment, reliance, review, trust; SEE CONCEPTS *37,689,764*

stock [*v*] *supply with merchandise*
accumulate, amass, carry, deal in, equip, fill, furnish, gather, handle, have, hoard, keep, keep on hand, lay in, provide, provision, put away, reserve, save, sell, stockpile, store, stow away, trade in; SEE CONCEPTS *140,182,324*

stockade [*n*] *enclosure; jail*
barrier, cage, camp, can*, cell, clink*, cooler*, coop, corral, detention camp, dungeon, fence, jailhouse, joint*, pen, penal institution, penitentiary, pound, prison, protection, slammer*, sty; SEE CONCEPTS *439,448,449,513,516*

stock market [*n*] *stock exchange*
American Stock Exchange, AMEX, Big Board, Chicago Board of Trade, commodities exchange, Dow Jones, futures exchange, NASDAQ, National Association of Securities Dealers Auto-

mated Quotations, New York Stock Exchange, Wall Street; SEE CONCEPTS *323,333,449*

stockpile [*n*] *supply*
accumulation, buildup, cache, hoard, inventory, nest egg, reserve, source, stash, stock, store, surplus; SEE CONCEPT *712*

stockpile [*v*] *stock*
accumulate, amass, build up, gather, hoard, keep on hand, put away, reserve, save, squirrel away, stash, stock up, store, stow away; SEE CONCEPTS *140,182,324*

stocky [*adj*] *short and overweight; short and muscular*
chunky, corpulent, fat, heavyset, plump, solid, squat, stout, stubby, sturdy, thick, thickset; SEE CONCEPTS *491,773*

stodgy [*adj*] *dull, stuffy*
banausic, boring, dim, dreary, formal, heavy, labored, monotonous, pedantic, pedestrian, plodding, ponderous, staid, tedious, turgid, unexciting, unimaginative, uninspired, uninteresting, weighty; SEE CONCEPTS *401,404*

stoic/stoical [*adj*] *philosophic, calm*
aloof, apathetic, cool, cool as cucumber*, detached, dispassionate, dry, enduring, impassive, imperturbable, indifferent, indomitable, long-suffering, matter-of-fact, patient, phlegmatic, resigned, rolling with punches*, self-controlled, sober, stolid, unconcerned, unemotional, unflappable, unmoved; SEE CONCEPTS *401,404*

stolid [*adj*] *apathetic, stupid*
blunt, bovine, dense, doltish, dry, dull, dumb, heavy, impassive, inactive, indifferent, inert, lumpish, matter-of-fact, obtuse, passive, phlegmatic, slow, stoic, supine, unemotional, unexcitable, wooden; SEE CONCEPTS *401,402*

stomach [*n1*] *digestive organ of animate being; exterior*
abdominal region abdomen, belly, below the belt*, breadbasket*, gut, inside, insides, maw*, paunch, pot*, potbelly*, solar plexus, spare tire*, tummy*; SEE CONCEPTS *393,420*

stomach [*n2*] *appetite*
appetence, desire, inclination, mind, relish, taste, tooth; SEE CONCEPT *20*

stomach [*v*] *endure, tolerate*
abide, bear, bear with, bite the bullet*, brook, digest, grin and bear it*, live with*, put up with, reconcile oneself, resign oneself, stand, submit to, suffer, swallow, sweat, take, tolerate; SEE CONCEPT *23*

stone [*n*] *hard piece of earth's surface*
boulder, crag, crystal, gem, grain, gravel, jewel, metal, mineral, ore, pebble, rock; SEE CONCEPTS *474,477*

stoned [*adj*] *high on alcohol or drugs*
baked*, bombed*, boozed up*, buzzed*, doped, drugged, drunk, feeling no pain*, flying*, fried, inebriated, intoxicated, loaded, on a trip*, plastered, ripped*, sloshed*, smashed*, spaced out*, stewed*, strung out*, tanked*, tipsy, totaled*, tripping*, wasted*; SEE CONCEPT *314*

stony [*adj*] *hard, icy in appearance, response*
adamant, blank, callous, chilly, cold, cold-blooded, coldhearted, cruel, expressionless, firm, frigid, hard-boiled*, hardened, heartless, hostile, indifferent, inexorable, inflexible, merciless, obdurate, pitiless, rough, tough, uncompassionate, unfeeling, unforgiving, unrelenting, unresponsive, unsympathetic; SEE CONCEPTS *401,485*

st
st

stooge [n] *dupe*
chump*, easy mark*, fall guy, flunky, fool, lackey, patsy*, pawn, pigeon*, puppet, pushover*, sap*, sucker, victim; SEE CONCEPT *423*

stool pigeon [n] *informer*
betrayer, blabbermouth*, canary*, decoy, deep throat*, double-crosser, fink*, informant, narc*, nark*, rat*, sneak, snitch, snitcher, source, squealer*, stoolie*, tattler, tattletale, tipster*, turncoat, weasel*, whistle-blower; SEE CONCEPTS *348,354,423*

stoop [n] *slouched posture*
droop, round shoulders, sag, slouch, slump; SEE CONCEPT *757*

stoop [v1] *bow down*
be bowed, bend, be servile, bow, cringe, crouch, descend, dip, duck, hunch, incline, kneel, lean, relax, sink, slant, squat; SEE CONCEPTS *181,201*

stoop [v2] *condescend; lower oneself to another*
accommodate, act beneath oneself, concede, debase oneself, deign, demean oneself, descend, favor, oblige, patronize, relax, resort, sink, thaw, unbend, vouchsafe; SEE CONCEPTS *35,384*

stop [n1] *end, halt; impediment*
bar, barricade, blank wall*, block, blockade, break, break off, brick wall*, cease, cessation, check, close, closing, conclusion, control, cutoff, desistance, discontinuation, ending, fence, finish, freeze*, grinding halt*, hindrance, layoff, letup, lull, pause, plug, roadblock*, screeching halt*, standstill, stay, stoppage, termination, wall; SEE CONCEPTS *240,832*

stop [n2] *visit; place of rest*
break, depot, destination, halt, rest, sojourn, stage, station, stay, stopover, termination, terminus; SEE CONCEPTS *198,227*

stop [v1] *bring or come to a halt or end*
be over, blow off*, break, break off, call it a day*, cease, close, cold turkey*, come to a standstill*, conclude, cool it*, cut out*, cut short, desist, discontinue, draw up, drop, end, finish, halt, hang it up*, hold, kill, pause, pull up, put an end to, quit, quit cold*, refrain, run its course*, scrub*, shut down, sign off*, stall, stand, stay, tarry, terminate, wind up*, wrap up*; SEE CONCEPTS *119,234,237*

stop [v2] *prevent, hold back*
arrest, avoid, bar, block, bottle, break, check, choke, choke off, clog, close, congest, cut off, disrupt, fill, fix, forestall, frustrate, gag, hinder, hush, impede, intercept, interrupt, muzzle, obstruct, occlude, plug, put a stop to, rein in, repress, restrain, seal, shut down, shut off, shut out, silence, stall, staunch, stay, stem, still, stopper, suspend, throw over, turn off, ward off; SEE CONCEPT *121*

stopgap [adj] *temporarily helping*
Band-Aid*, emergency, expedient, impromptu, improvised, makeshift, practical, provisional, rough-and-ready*, rough-and-tumble*, substitute, temp, temporary, throwaway*; SEE CONCEPTS *551,560*

stopgap [n] *temporary help*
Band-Aid*, expediency, expedient, improvisation, makeshift, pis aller*, recourse, refuge, resort, resource, shift, substitute, temporary expedient; SEE CONCEPT *712*

stoppage [n] *halt, curtailment*
abeyance, arrest, blockage, check, close, closure, cutoff, deduction, discontinuance, down, downtime*, hindrance, interruption, layoff, lockout, obstruction, occlusion, shutdown, sit-down, standstill, stopping, walkout; SEE CONCEPT *832*

store [n1] *collection, supply*
abundance, accumulation, backlog, cache, fount, fountain, fund, hoard, inventory, lode, lot, mine, nest egg*, plenty, plethora, provision, quantity, reserve, reservoir, savings, spring, stock, stockpile, treasure, wares, wealth, well; SEE CONCEPTS *432,710*

store [n2] *place for keeping supply*
arsenal, bank, barn, box, cache, conservatory, depository, depot, magazine, pantry, repository, reservoir, stable, storehouse, storeroom, tank, treasury, vault, warehouse; SEE CONCEPTS *439,441,448,494*

store [n3] *business establishment that sells goods*
boutique, chain store, convenience store, deli, department store, discount house, discount store, drugstore, emporium, five-and-dime*, five-and-ten*, grocery store, market, mart, outlet, repository, shop, shopping center, showroom, specialty shop, stand, storehouse, super*, superette*, supermarket; SEE CONCEPTS *325,439,448,449*

store [v] *collect and put aside*
accumulate, amass, bank, bin, bottle, bury, cache, can, cumulate, deposit, freeze, garner, hide, hive, hoard, hutch, keep, keep in reserve, lay away, lay up*, lock away, lock up, mothball*, pack, pack away, park, plant, put, put away, put by, put in storage, reserve, roll up, salt away*, save, save for rainy day*, sock away*, squirrel*, stash, stock, stockpile, treasure, victual, warehouse; SEE CONCEPTS *109,129*

storekeeper [n] *shopkeeper*
businessperson, dealer, entrepreneur, grocer, merchant, proprietor, retailer, salesperson, seller, storekeeper, store owner, vendor, wholesaler; SEE CONCEPT *347*

storeroom [n] *repository*
archive, arsenal, cellar, depository, depot, granary, magazine, safe, silo, stockroom, storage place, storehouse, vault, warehouse; SEE CONCEPTS *435,439,449*

storm [n1] *strong weather*
blast, blizzard, blow, cloudburst, cyclone, disturbance, downpour, gale, gust, hurricane, monsoon, precip*, precipitation, raining cats and dogs*, snowstorm, squall, tempest, tornado, twister, whirlwind, windstorm; SEE CONCEPT *526*

storm [n2] *commotion, turmoil*
agitation, anger, annoyance, assault, attack, barrage, blitz, blitzkrieg, bluster, bomb, bombardment, broadside, burst, bustle, cannonade, clamor, clatter, convulsion, disturbance, drumfire, furor, fury, fusillade, hail, hassle, hysteria, offensive, onset, onslaught, outbreak, outburst, outcry, passion, perturbation, pother, rabidity, racket, rage, rampancy, roar, row, ruction, rumpus, rush, salvo, squall, stir, strife, temper, tumult, upheaval, violence, volley; SEE CONCEPTS *86,230,674*

storm [v] *attack, rush*
aggress, assail, assault, beset, blow violently, bluster, breathe fire*, burn up*, carry on*, charge, come at*, complain, drizzle, drop, fly, fume, go on, howl, pour, rage, rain, rant, rave, rip, roar, scold, set in, sizzle, sound off, spit, squall, stalk,

steam up*, stomp, strike, take by storm*, take on*, tear, thunder*; SEE CONCEPTS 52,86,150,526

stormy [*adj*] *rough (referring to weather)*
bitter, blowy, blustering, blustery, boisterous, cold, coming down*, damp, dirty, foul, frigid, furious, gusty, howling, menacing, murky, pouring, raging, raining cats and dogs*, rainy, riproaring*, roaring, savage, squally, stormful, storming, tempestuous, threatening, torrid, turbulent, violent, wet, wild, windy; SEE CONCEPT 525

story [*n1*] *account, news*
adventure, allegory, anecdote, apologue, article, autobiography, beat, biography, book, chronicle, cliffhanger*, comedy, conte, description, drama, epic, fable, fairy tale, fantasy, feature, fiction, folktale, gag, history, information, legend, long and short of it*, memoir, myth, narration, narrative, news item, nonfiction, novel, old saw*, parable, potboiler*, recital, record, relation, report, romance, saga, scoop*, sequel, serial, spiel*, tale, tragedy, version, yarn*; SEE CONCEPTS 270,274,282

story [*n2*] *lie*
canard, cock-and-bull story*, fabrication, falsehood, falsity, fib, fiction, misrepresentation, prevarication, tale, untruism, untruth, white lie*; SEE CONCEPTS 278,282

stout [*adj1*] *overweight*
big, bulky, burly, corpulent, fat, fleshy, heavy, obese, plenitudinous, plump, porcine, portly, rotund, substantial, thick-bodied, tubby, upholstered, weighty, zaftig*; SEE CONCEPTS 491,773

stout [*adj2*] *strong, brawny*
able-bodied, athletic, hard, hardy, hulking, husky, indomitable, invincible, lusty, muscular, robust, stable, stalwart, staunch, strapping, sturdy, substantial, tenacious, tough, vigorous; SEE CONCEPTS 489,490

stout [*adj3*] *courageous*
bold, brave, dauntless, fearless, gallant, heroic, intrepid, lionhearted, plucky, resolute, stalwart, undaunted, valiant, valorous; SEE CONCEPTS 403,542

stouthearted [*adj*] *brave, courageous*
adventurous, bold, daring, dashing, fearless, gallant, game, gritty, gutsy, hardy, heroic, lionhearted, plucky, spunky, stalwart, unafraid, undaunted, unfearful, valiant; SEE CONCEPT 401

stove [*n*] *range; furnace*
boiler, convection oven, cooker, electric stove, heater, kiln, microwave, oven, toaster oven, warmer, wood stove; SEE CONCEPT 463

stow [*v*] *reserve, store*
bundle, deposit, load, pack, pack like sardines*, put away, secrete, stash, stuff, top off, tuck, warehouse*; SEE CONCEPT 209

straggle [*v*] *wander, stray*
be late, dawdle, drift, lag, loiter, maunder, meander, poke, poke around, ramble, range, roam, rove, scramble, spread, straddle, string out, tail, trail; SEE CONCEPT 151

straight [*adj1*] *aligned; not curved*
beeline*, collinear, consecutive, continuous, direct, erect, even, horizontal, in a line, in a row, inflexible, in line, invariable, level, like an arrow*, lineal, linear, near, nonstop, perpendicular, plumb, precipitous, rectilineal, rectilinear, right, running, sheer, short, smooth, solid, square, straightforward, successive, through, true, unbent, unbroken, uncurled, undeviating,

undistorted, uninterrupted, unrelieved, unswerving, upright, vertical; SEE CONCEPTS 482,486,581

straight [*adj2*] *honest, fair*
aboveboard, accurate, authentic, bald, blunt, candid, categorical, decent, equitable, fair and square*, forthright, frank, good, honorable, just, law-abiding, moral, outright, plain, point-blank*, reliable, respectable, straightforward, summary, trustworthy, unqualified, upright; SEE CONCEPTS 267,542

straight [*adj3*] *orderly*
arranged, correct, exact, in order, neat, organized, put to rights, right, shipshape*, sorted, tidy; SEE CONCEPTS 535,585

straight [*adj4*] *unmixed*
concentrated, neat, out-and-out*, plain, pure, strong, thoroughgoing, unadulterated, undiluted, unmodified, unqualified; SEE CONCEPTS 462,621

straight [*adj5*] *conventional, square*
bourgeois, buttoned-down*, conservative, orthodox, traditional; SEE CONCEPT 404

straight [*adv1*] *immediately, directly*
as the crow flies*, at once, away, dead*, direct, due, exactly, first off, forthwith, in direct line, instanter, instantly, lineally, now, point-blank*, right, right away, straightaway, straightforwardly, straightly, undeviatingly; SEE CONCEPTS 581,820

straight [*adv2*] *honestly*
candidly, frankly, in plain English*, no holds barred*, no punches*, point-blank*; SEE CONCEPTS 267,544

straighten [*v*] *put in neat or aligned order*
align, arrange, compose, correct, even, level, make plumb, make straight, neaten, order, put in order, put perpendicular, put straight, put to rights, put upright, put vertical, rectify, set to rights, smarten up*, spruce up*, tidy, unbend, uncoil, uncurl, unfold, unravel, unsnarl, untwist; SEE CONCEPTS 158,202,231

straightforward [*adj1*] *honest*
aboveboard, barefaced*, candid, direct, forthright, frank, genuine, guileless, honorable, just, laid on the line*, level, like it is*, mellow*, open, outspoken, plain, plain-dealing*, pretenseless, right-on*, sincere, square-shooting*, straight, straight-arrow*, talking turkey*, truthful, unconcealed, undisguised, undissembled, undissembling, unequivocal, unvarnished, up front*, upright, upstanding, veracious; SEE CONCEPT 267

straightforward [*adj2*] *simple, easy*
apparent, clear, clear-cut, direct, distinct, elementary, evident, manifest, palpable, patent, plain, routine, straight, through, unambiguous, uncomplicated, undemanding, unequivocal, uninterrupted; SEE CONCEPTS 535,538

strain [*n1*] *pain, due to exertion*
ache, anxiety, bruise, brunt, burden, constriction, effort, endeavor, exertion, force, injury, jerk, pressure, pull, sprain, stress, stretch, struggle, tautness, tension, tensity, twist, wrench; SEE CONCEPT 728

strain [*n2*] *ancestry*
blood, breed, descent, extraction, family, lineage, pedigree, race, species, stock; SEE CONCEPTS 296,380

strain [*n3*] *suggestion, hint*
humor, manner, mind, shade, soupçon, spirit, streak, style, suspicion, temper, tendency, tinge,

st
st

tone, touch, trace, trait, vein, way; SEE CONCEPTS *410,529,682*

strain [*n4*] *melody*
air, descant, diapason, lay, measure, song, tune, warble; SEE CONCEPTS *262,595*

strain [*v1*] *stretch, often to limit*
constrict, distend, distort, draw tight, drive, exert, extend, fatigue, injure, overexert, overtax, overwork, pull, push, push to the limit, rack, sprain, task, tauten, tax, tear, tighten, tire, twist, weaken, wrench; SEE CONCEPTS *156,206,208,313*

strain [*v2*] *work very hard*
bear down, endeavor, exert, go all out*, go for broke*, grind, hammer, hustle, labor, moil, peg away*, plug, push, strive, struggle, sweat, toil, try; SEE CONCEPT *87*

strain [*v3*] *filter*
exude, percolate, purify, refine, riddle, screen, seep, separate, sieve, sift; SEE CONCEPTS *135,202*

strain [*v4*] *cause mental stress*
distress, harass, hassle, irk, pain, pick at, push, stress, trouble, try; SEE CONCEPTS *7,19*

strained [*adj*] *forced, pretended*
artificial, at end of rope*, awkward, choked, constrained, difficult, embarrassed, false, farfetched, hard put*, in a state*, labored, nervous wreck*, put, self-conscious, stiff, strung out*, taut, tense, tight, uncomfortable, uneasy, unglued, unnatural, unrelaxed, uptight, wired*, wreck*; SEE CONCEPTS *267,401*

strait [*n1*] *crisis, difficulty*
bewilderment, bind, bottleneck*, choke point*, contingency, crossroad, dilemma, distress, embarrassment, emergency, exigency, extremity, hardship, hole*, mess*, mystification, pass, perplexity, pinch*, plight, predicament, rigor, squeeze*, turning point*, vicissitude, zero hour*; SEE CONCEPT *674*

strait [*n2*] *water channel*
inlet, narrows, sound; SEE CONCEPT *514*

strait-laced [*adj*] *prudish*
old-maidish, priggish*, prim, prissy*, proper, puritanical, rigid, square, starchy, stiff*, strict, stuffy, uptight*, Victorian*; SEE CONCEPT *401*

strand [*n*] *fine thread*
fiber, filament, length, lock, rope, string, tress; SEE CONCEPTS *392,452,475*

stranded [*adj*] *marooned, abandoned*
aground, ashore, beached, cast away, godforsaken*, grounded, helpless, high and dry*, homeless, left at the altar*, left in the lurch*, on the rocks*, out in left field*, passed up, penniless, run aground, shipwrecked, sidelined, sidetracked*, wrecked; SEE CONCEPT *577*

strange [*adj1*] *deviating, unfamiliar*
aberrant, abnormal, astonishing, astounding, atypical, bizarre, curious, different, eccentric, erratic, exceptional, extraordinary, fantastic, far-out*, funny, idiosyncratic, ignorant, inexperienced, irregular, marvelous, mystifying, new, newfangled*, odd, oddball*, off, offbeat*, outlandish, out-of-the-way*, peculiar, perplexing, quaint, queer, rare, remarkable, singular, unaccountable, unaccustomed, uncanny, uncommon, unheard of, unseasoned, unusual, weird, wonderful; SEE CONCEPT *564*

strange [*adj2*] *exotic, foreign*
alien, apart, awkward, detached, external, faraway, irrelevant, isolated, lost, new, novel, out of place, outside, remote, romanesque, romantic,

unexplored, unfamiliar, unknown, unrelated, untried; SEE CONCEPTS *549,576*

stranger [*n*] *person who is unfamiliar*
alien, drifter, foreign body, foreigner, guest, immigrant, incomer, interloper, intruder, itinerant person, migrant, migratory worker, new arrival, newcomer, outcomer, outlander, out-of-stater*, outsider, party crasher*, perfect stranger*, squatter*, transient, uninvited person, unknown, unknown person, visitor, wanderer; SEE CONCEPTS *413,423*

strangle [*v*] *choke, stifle*
asphyxiate, gag, garrote/garrotte, inhibit, kill, muffle, quelch, repress, restrain, shush, smother, squelch, strangulate, subdue, suffocate, suppress, throttle; SEE CONCEPTS *130,191,252*

strap [*n*] *long piece of material*
band, belt, harness, leash, strop, switch, thong, tie, whip; SEE CONCEPTS *471,475*

strapped [*adj*] *destitute*
beggared, broke*, dirt poor*, flat*, fortuneless, impoverished, out of money, penniless, penurious, poor, stone-broke*; SEE CONCEPT *334*

strapping [*adj*] *big and strong*
brawny, burly, hefty, hulk, hulking, hunk, husky, ox, powerful, powerhouse, robust, stalwart, stout, sturdy, tall, vigorous, well-built; SEE CONCEPTS *489,773*

stratagem [*n*] *trick*
action, angle, artifice, bit*, booby trap*, brainchild*, con, deception, device, dodge, feint, gambit, game, game plan*, gimmick, grift, intrigue, layout, maneuver, method, pitch, plan, play, plot, ploy, pretext, proposition, racket, ruse, scenario, scene, scheme, setup, shift, slant, stall, story, subterfuge, switch, twist, wile; SEE CONCEPTS *59,660*

strategic [*adj1*] *crucial*
cardinal, critical, decisive, imperative, important, key, necessary, vital; SEE CONCEPTS *546,567*

strategic [*adj2*] *clever, calculated*
cunning, deliberate, diplomatic, dishonest, planned, politic, tricky; SEE CONCEPT *544*

strategy [*n*] *plan of action*
action, angle, approach, artifice, blueprint*, brainchild*, craft, cunning, design, game, game plan*, gimmick, grand design, layout, maneuvering, method, plan, planning, policy, procedure, program, project, proposition, racket*, scenario, scene, scheme, setup, slant, story, subtlety, system, tactics; SEE CONCEPT *660*

stray [*adj*] *abandoned, wandering*
devious, erratic, homeless, lost, roaming, roving, vagrant; SEE CONCEPT *583*

stray [*v1*] *deviate, err*
circumlocute, depart, digress, divagate, diverge, do wrong, excurse, get off the subject*, get off the track*, get sidetracked*, go off on a tangent*, ramble, sin, wander; SEE CONCEPTS *101,266*

stray [*v2*] *wander; get lost*
be abandoned, be lost, deviate, drift, err, gad*, gallivant, go all over the map*, go amiss, go astray, lose one's way, meander, ramble, range, roam, rove, straggle, swerve, traipse, turn, wander away, wander off; SEE CONCEPT *149*

streak [*n*] *vein, line; small part*
band, bar, beam, dash, element, hint, intimation, layer, ray, ridge, rule, shade, slash, smear, strain, stream, strip, stripe, stroke, suggestion, suspi-

cion, touch, trace; SEE CONCEPTS *436,628,657,727*

streak [*v*] *make a line on*
band, dapple, daub, fleck, marble, slash, smear, spot, strake, striate, stripe, variegate, vein; SEE CONCEPT *250*

stream [*n*] *small river*
beck, branch, brook, burn, course, creek, current, drift, flood, flow, freshet, race, rill, rindle, rivulet, run, runnel, rush, spate, spritz, surge, tide, torrent, tributary, watercourse; SEE CONCEPT *514*

stream [*v*] *flow from*
cascade, continue, course, emerge, emit, flood, glide, gush, issue, move past, pour, roll, run, shed, sluice, spill, spout, spritz, spurt, surge; SEE CONCEPTS *146,179*

street [*n*] *path upon which travel occurs*
artery, avenue, back alley*, boulevard, byway, court, dead end*, drag*, drive, highway, lane, parkway, passage, pavement, place, road, roadway, route, row, stroll, terrace, thoroughfare, track, trail, turf*, way; SEE CONCEPT *501*

street person [*n*] *homeless person*
bag lady, beggar, bum, derelict, drifter, hobo, vagabond, vagrant, wino; SEE CONCEPT *539*

street smart [*adj*] *shrewd*
artful, astute, cagey, calculating, canny, clever, crafty, cunning, experienced, foxy*, ingenious, intelligent, perceptive, quick-witted, savvy*, seasoned, sharp, slick*, sly, smart, smooth, streetwise, wily, wise; SEE CONCEPTS *401,402*

strength [*n1*] *stamina, mental or physical*
backbone, body, brawn, brawniness, brute force*, clout, courage, durability, energy, firmness, force, fortitude, hardiness, health, healthiness, lustiness, might, muscle, nerve, physique, pith, potency, pow*, power, powerhouse*, robustness, security, sinew, sock*, soundness, stability, stableness, stalwartness, steadiness, steamroller, stoutness, strong arm*, sturdiness, substance, tenacity, toughness, verdure, vigor, vim, vitality, zip*; SEE CONCEPTS *410,732*

strength [*n2*] *intensity*
clout, cogency, concentration, depth, effectiveness, efficacy, energy, extremity, fervor, force, juice*, kick*, potency, power, resolution, spirit, vehemence, vigor, virtue; SEE CONCEPT *669*

strength [*n3*] *advantage, substance*
anchor, asset, body, burden, connection, core, gist, guts, in, intestinal fortitude, license, mainstay, meat, pith, purport, security, sense, strong point, succor, upper hand, weight, wire; SEE CONCEPTS *682,693*

strengthen [*v1*] *make more forceful, powerful*
add, add fuel to fire*, anneal, ascend, bolster, brace, build up, buttress, confirm, corroborate, empower, enhance, enlarge, establish, extend, fortify, harden, heighten, increase, intensify, invigorate, justify, make firm, mount, multiply, regenerate, reinforce, rejuvenate, renew, restore, rise, set up, sinew*, steel, step up, substantiate, support, sustain, temper, tone, tone up, toughen, wax*; SEE CONCEPTS *244,250*

strengthen [*v2*] *encourage, hearten*
animate, back, back up, bear out, bloom, brace, brace up, burgeon, carry weight, cheer, consolidate, embolden, enhearten, enliven, flourish, flower, fortify, gather resources, gird, give weight, harden, inspirit, invigorate, nerve, nour-

ish, prepare, prosper, rally, ready, refresh, rejuvenate, restore, steel, substantiate, temper, thrive, toughen, uphold; SEE CONCEPTS *7,22,35*

strenuous [*adj1*] *difficult; requiring hard work*
arduous, demanding, effortful, energy-consuming, exhausting, hard, Herculean, laborious, mean, operose, taxing, toilful, toilsome, tough, tough going*, uphill*, wicked; SEE CONCEPT *538*

strenuous [*adj2*] *energetic, zealous*
active, aggressive, ardent, bold, determined, dynamic, eager, earnest, lusty, persistent, redblooded, resolute, spirited, strong, tireless, vigorous, vital; SEE CONCEPTS *401,542*

stress [*n1*] *emphasis*
accent, accentuation, beat, force, import, importance, significance, urgency, weight; SEE CONCEPTS *65,668*

stress [*n2*] *physical or mental pressure*
affliction, agony, alarm, albatross*, anxiety, apprehensiveness, burden, clutch, crunch, disquiet, disquietude, distention, draw, dread, expectancy, extension, fear, fearfulness, ferment, flutter, force, hardship, hassle, heat, impatience, intensity, misgiving, mistrust, nervousness, nervous tension, oppression, overextension, passion, protraction, pull, restlessness, spring, strain, stretch, tautness, tenseness, tension, tensity, tightness, traction, trauma, trepidation, trial, urgency, worry; SEE CONCEPTS *410,720,728*

stress [*v1*] *accentuate, emphasize*
accent, belabor, dwell on, feature, harp on*, headline*, italicize*, lay emphasis on, make emphatic, play up, point up, repeat, rub in*, spot, spotlight*, underline*, underscore*; SEE CONCEPTS *49,68*

stress [*v2*] *put under physical or mental pressure*
afflict, burden, crunch, distend, force, fret, hassle, overdo, overextend, pull, put in traction*, put on trial*, spring, strain, stretch, tense, tense up*, traumatize, worry; SEE CONCEPTS *7,19,246,313*

stretch [*n1*] *expanse*
amplitude, area, branch, breadth, bridge, compass, dimension, distance, expansion, extension, extent, gamut, length, orbit, proliferation, purview, radius, range, reach, region, scope, space, span, spread, sweep, tract, wing; SEE CONCEPTS *651,721,746*

stretch [*n2*] *period of time*
bit, continuance, duration, extent, length, run, space, span, spell, stint, term, time, while; SEE CONCEPTS *807,822*

stretch [*v*] *extend, elongate*
amplify, branch out, bridge, burst forth, cover, crane, develop, distend, drag out, draw, draw out, expand, fill, go, grow, inflate, lengthen, lie out, magnify, make, make taut, make tense, open, overlap, pad, prolong, prolongate, protract, pull, pull out, pyramid, rack, range, reach, recline, repose, run, shoot up, span, spin out, spread, spread out, spring up, strain, string out, swell, tauten, tighten, unfold, unroll, widen; SEE CONCEPTS *137,250*

strict [*adj1*] *authoritarian*
austere, dead set*, disciplinary, dour, draconian*, exacting, firm, forbidding, grim, hard, hard-boiled*, harsh, iron-fisted*, no-nonsense*, oppressive, picky, prudish, punctilious, puritanical, rigid, rigorous, scrupulous, set, severe, square, stern, stickling, straight, strait-laced*,

st
st

stringent, stuffy*, tough, unpermissive, unsparing, uptight*; SEE CONCEPTS *401,542*

strict [*adj2*] *accurate, absolute*
close, complete, exact, faithful, just, meticulous, particular, perfect, precise, religious, right, scrupulous, total, true, undistorted, utter, veracious, veridical; SEE CONCEPTS *535,557*

stride [*v*] *walk purposefully*
clump, drill, march, pace, parade, pound, stalk, stamp, stomp, striddle, stump, traipse, tramp, tromp; SEE CONCEPT *149*

strident [*adj*] *harsh, shrill*
blatant, boisterous, clamorous, clashing, discordant, grating, hoarse, jangling, jarring, loud, noisy, obstreperous, rasping, raucous, screeching, squawky, squeaky, stentorian, stertorous, stridulant, stridulous, unmusical, vociferant, vociferous; SEE CONCEPTS *592,594*

strife [*n*] *struggle, battle*
affray, altercation, animosity, argument, bickering, blowup, brawl, clash, combat, competition, conflict, contention, contest, controversy, difference, disagreement, discord, dispute, dissension, dissent, dissidence, disunity, emulation, faction, factionalism, fighting, friction, fuss, hassle, quarrel, rivalry, spat, squabble, squabbling, static, striving, tug of war*, variance, warfare, words*, wrangle, wrangling; SEE CONCEPTS *46,106,674*

strike [*v1*] *hit hard*
bang, bash, beat, boff, bonk, box, buffet, bump into, chastise, clash, clobber, clout, collide, conk*, crash, cuff*, drive, force, hammer, impel, knock, percuss, plant*, pop*, pound, pummel, punch, punish, run into, slap, slug, smack, smash into, sock, swat, thrust, thump, touch, wallop, whop*; SEE CONCEPT *189*

strike [*v2*] *make an impact*
affect, be plausible, carry, come to mind*, dawn on*, get*, have semblance, hit*, impress, influence, inspire, look, move, occur to, reach, register*, seem, sway, touch; SEE CONCEPTS *7,19,22,716*

strike [*v3*] *find, discover*
achieve, arrive at, attain, catch, chance upon*, come across, come upon, dig up*, effect, encounter, happen upon*, hit upon*, lay bare*, light upon, open up, reach, seize, stumble across*, take, turn up*, uncover, unearth; SEE CONCEPTS *120,183*

strike [*v4*] *devastate, affect*
afflict, aggress, assail, assault, attack, beset, deal a blow, excruciate, fall upon, harrow, hit, invade, martyr, rack, set upon, smite, storm, torment, torture, try, wring; SEE CONCEPTS *7,19*

strike [*v5*] *walk out of job in protest*
arbitrate, be on strike, boycott, go on strike, hit the bricks*, hold out, mediate, mutiny, negotiate, picket, quit, refuse to work, resist, revolt, sit down*, sit in*, slow down, stick out, stop, tie up; SEE CONCEPT *351*

strike out [*v*] *leave to begin new venture*
bear, begin, get under way*, head, initiate, light out*, make, set out, start, start out, take off*; SEE CONCEPT *195*

striking [*adj*] *extraordinary; beautiful*
arresting, arrestive, astonishing, attractive, bizarre, charming, cogent, commanding, compelling, confounding, conspicuous, dazzling, distinguished, dynamite, electrifying, eye-catching, fascinating, forceful, forcible, handsome, impressive, jazzy*, lofty, marked, memorable, noteworthy, noticeable, out of the ordinary*, outstanding, powerful, prominent, remarkable, salient, showy, signal, singular, staggering, startling, stunning, surprising, telling, unusual, wonderful, wondrous; SEE CONCEPTS *574,579*

string [*n1*] *long fiber*
cord, rope, strand, twine, twist; SEE CONCEPT *475*

string [*n2*] *succession, series*
chain, consecution, echelon, file, line, order, procession, queue, rank, row, sequel, sequence, strand, tier, train; SEE CONCEPTS *727,769*

string along [*v*] *play with; keep dangling*
bluff, coquet, dally, deceive, dupe, flirt, fool, hoax, lead on*, put one over on*, take for a ride*, toy, trifle, wanton; SEE CONCEPT *59*

stringent [*adj*] *rigid, tight*
acrimonious, binding, brick-wall*, by the book*, by the numbers*, compelling, confining, convincing, dead set on*, demanding, draconian, drawing, dyed-in-the-wool*, exacting, forceful, hard, hard-nosed*, harsh, inflexible, ironclad, iron-fisted, picky, poignant, powerful, rigorous, rough, set, severe, stiff, strict, tough, unpermissive, valid; SEE CONCEPTS *401,535,569*

stringy [*adj*] *long, thin*
fibrous, gangling, gristly, lank, lanky, muscular, reedy, ropy, sinewy, spindling, spindly, threadlike, tough, wiry; SEE CONCEPT *490*

strip [*n*] *thin piece of material*
band, banding, bar, belt,. billet, bit, fillet, ingot, layer, ribbon, rod, section, segment, shred, slab, slip, stick, stripe, swathe, tape, tongue; SEE CONCEPTS *471,834*

strip [*v*] *bare, uncover*
decorticate, denude, deprive, despoil, dismantle, displace, disrobe, divest, empty, excorticate, expose, gut, hull, husk, lay bare, lift, peel, pillage, plunder, ransack, ravage, remove, rob, scale, shave, shed, shuck, skin, slip out of, spoil, take off, tear, unclothe, undress, withdraw; SEE CONCEPT *211*

stripe [*n*] *line, strip*
band, banding, bar, border, decoration, division, fillet, layer, ribbon, rule, streak, striation, stroke; SEE CONCEPTS *284,622*

strive [*v*] *try for, exert oneself*
aim, assay, attempt, bear down, bend over backward*, break one's neck*, compete, contend, do one's best*, do one's utmost*, drive, endeavor, essay, fight, go after, go all out*, go for broke*, go for the jugular*, go the limit*, hassle, jockey*, knock oneself out*, labor, leave no stone unturned*, make every effort, moil, offer, push, scramble, seek, shoot for*, strain, struggle, sweat, tackle, take on, toil, try hard, tug*, work; SEE CONCEPT *87*

stroke [*n1*] *accomplishment*
achievement, blow*, feat, flourish, hit*, move, movement; SEE CONCEPT *706*

stroke [*n2*] *seizure*
apoplexy, attack, collapse, convulsion, fit, shock; SEE CONCEPTS *33,308*

stroke [*v*] *pat lengthwise*
brush, caress, chuck, comfort, fondle, pet, rub, smooth, soothe, tickle; SEE CONCEPT *612*

stroll [*n*] *lazy walk*
airing, breath of fresh air*, constitutional, cruise, excursion, promenade, ramble, saunter, turn; SEE CONCEPT *151*

stroll [v] *walk along lazily*
amble, cruise, drift, gallivant, linger, make one's way*, mope*, mosey*, promenade, ramble, roam, rove, sashay*, saunter, toddle, traipse, tramp, wander; SEE CONCEPT *151*

strong [adj1] *healthy, powerful*
able, able-bodied, active, athletic, big, capable, durable, enduring, energetic, firm, fixed, forceful, forcible, hale, hard as nails*, hardy, hearty, heavy, heavy-duty*, in fine feather*, mighty, muscular, reinforced, robust, rugged, secure, sinewy, solid, sound, stable, stalwart, stark, staunch, steady, stout, strapping, sturdy, substantial, tenacious, tough, unyielding, vigorous, well-built, well-founded, well-made; SEE CONCEPTS *314,489,540*

strong [adj2] *determined, resolute*
aggressive, brave, clear, cogent, courageous, dedicated, deep, eager, fervent, fervid, fierce, firm, forceful, gutsy*, handful*, hard-nosed*, independent, intelligent, intense, iron-willed, keen, mean, perceptive, plucky, potent, pushy, resilient, resourceful, sagacious, self-assertive, severe, staunch, steadfast, take charge*, tenacious, tough, unbending, uncompromising, unyielding, vehement, violent, wicked*, zealous; SEE CONCEPTS *403,542*

strong [adj3] *distinct, unmistakable*
clear, clear-cut, cogent, compelling, convincing, effective, fast, firm, forceful, formidable, great, hard, influential, marked, mighty, overpowering, persuasive, potent, powerful, redoubtable, secure, sharp, sound, stiff, stimulating, telling, trenchant, urgent, weighty, well-established, well-founded; SEE CONCEPTS *535,537*

strong [adj4] *extreme*
acute, draconian, drastic, forceful, intense, keen, severe, sharp, strict; SEE CONCEPT *569*

strong [adj5] *forceful on the senses*
biting, bold, bright, brilliant, concentrated, dazzling, effective, fetid, full-bodied, glaring, hard, heady, high, highly flavored, highly seasoned, hot, inebriating, intoxicating, loud, malodorous, noisome, piquant, potent, powerful, pungent, pure, rancid, rank, rich, robust, sharp, spicy, stark, stimulating, stinking, straight, strong-flavored, undiluted, unmixed; SEE CONCEPTS *462,598,618*

stronghold [n] *refuge*
bastion, bulwark, castle, citadel, fastness, fort, fortification, fortress, garrison, keep, presidio, redoubt; SEE CONCEPTS *439,712*

structure [n1] *makeup, form*
anatomy, architecture, arrangement, build, complex, configuration, conformation, construction, design, fabric, fabrication, format, formation, frame, framework, interrelation, make, morphology, network, order, organization, skeleton, system, texture; SEE CONCEPT *733*

structure [n2] *building*
cage, construction, edifice, erection, fabric, house, pile, pile of bricks*, rockpile, skyscraper; SEE CONCEPT *439*

struggle [n] *hard try; fight to win*
attempt, battle, brush, clash, combat, conflict, contest, effort, encounter, endeavor, essay, exertion, free-for-all*, grind, hassle, jam, jump, labor, long haul*, pains*, roughhouse*, row, scramble, set-to*, skirmish, strife, striving, toil, trial, tussle, undertaking, work, wrangle; SEE CONCEPTS *87,106,674*

struggle [v1] *labor, work*
assay, attempt, bend over backwards*, break one's back*, break one's neck*, cope, dig, endeavor, exert oneself, give it one's best shot*, give the old college try*, go all out*, grind, hassle, have one's nose to grindstone*, hustle, make every effort*, offer, plug, plug away*, scratch, seek, slave, strain, strive, sweat, tackle, take a crack*, take a stab*, take on, toil, try, try one's hardest*, undertake, work like a dog*; SEE CONCEPT *87*

struggle [v2] *fight, wrestle*
battle, brawl, buck, bump heads*, compete, contend, contest, cross swords*, go up against*, grapple, hassle, lock horns*, put up a fight*, romp, rough-house*, row, scrap, scuffle, shuffle, slug, smack, tangle; SEE CONCEPT *106*

strumpet [n] *prostitute*
call girl*, harlot, hooker, hussy, lady of the evening*, slut, streetwalker, whore, woman of the street*; SEE CONCEPT *412*

strut [v] *walk pompously*
flaunt, flounce, grandstand*, mince, parade, peacock*, play to audience, prance, put on airs*, sashay*, show off, stalk, stride, swagger, swank, sweep; SEE CONCEPTS *149,261*

stub [n] *stumpy end*
butt, counterfoil, dock, remainder, remnant, root, short end*, snag, stump, tag, tail, tail end*; SEE CONCEPTS *825,827*

stubborn [adj] *obstinate, unyielding*
adamant, balky, bullheaded, cantankerous, contumacious, cussed*, determined, dogged, firm, fixed, hardheaded, headstrong, inexorable, inflexible, insubordinate, intractable, mulish, obdurate, opinionated, ornery*, persevering, persistent, pertinacious, perverse, pigheaded*, rebellious, recalcitrant, refractory, relentless, rigid, self-willed, set in one's ways*, single-minded, steadfast, stiff-necked*, tenacious, tough, unbending, unmanageable, unreasonable, unshakable, untoward, willful; SEE CONCEPTS *401,404*

stubby [adj] *short and thick*
fat, heavyset, squat, stocky, stout, stumpy, thick-bodied, thickset; SEE CONCEPTS *491,773,779*

stuck-up [adj] *snobbish*
arrogant, big-headed, cocky, conceited, condescending, egotistic, haughty, high-and-mighty*, hoity-toity, nose in the air*, ostentatious, patronizing, pompous, pretentious, puffed up, snippy*, snooty*, snotty*, too big for one's britches*, uppity*, vain; SEE CONCEPT *401*

student [n] *person actively learning*
apprentice, disciple, docent, first-year student, grad, graduate, junior, learner, novice, observer, pupil, registrant, scholar, schoolchild, skill, sophomore, undergrad*, undergraduate; SEE CONCEPT *350*

studied [adj] *intentional*
advised, affected, aforethought, calculated, conscious, considered, deliberate, designed, examined, gone into, investigated, planned, plotted, premeditated, prepared, prepense, purposeful, reviewed, studious, thought-about, thoughtful, thought-out, thought-through, voluntary, well-considered, willful, willing; SEE CONCEPTS *538,548*

st
st

studious [*adj*] *scholarly, attentive*
academic, assiduous, bookish*, bookworm*, busy, careful, contemplative, diligent, eager, earnest, grubbing, hard-working, industrious, intellectual, learned, lettered, meditative, reflective, sedulous, serious, thoughtful, well-informed, well-read; SEE CONCEPTS *402,538*

study [*n*] *learning, analysis*
abstraction, academic work, analyzing, application, attention, class, cogitation, comparison, concentration, consideration, contemplation, course, cramming, debate, deliberation, examination, exercise, inquiry, inspection, investigation, lesson, meditation, memorizing, muse, musing, pondering, questioning, reading, reasoning, reflection, research, reverie, review, rumination, schoolwork, scrutiny, subject, survey, thought, trance, weighing; SEE CONCEPTS *31,103*

study [*v1*] *contemplate, learn*
apply oneself, bone up*, brood over, burn midnight oil*, bury oneself in*, coach, cogitate, consider, crack the books*, cram, dig*, dive into*, examine, excogitate, go into, go over, grind*, hit the books*, inquire, learn, learn the ropes*, lucubrate, meditate, mind, mull over, perpend, peruse, plug*, plunge, polish up*, ponder, pore over*, read, read up, refresh, think, think out, think over, tutor, weigh; SEE CONCEPT *31*

study [*v2*] *examine, analyze*
brainstorm*, canvass, case, check out, check over, check up, compare, deliberate, do research, figure, give the eagle eye*, inspect, investigate, keep tabs*, look into, peruse, read, research, scope, scrutinize, sort out, survey, view; SEE CONCEPT *103*

stuff [*n1*] *personal belongings*
being, effects, equipment, gear, goods, impedimenta, individual, junk*, kit, luggage, objects, paraphernalia, possessions, substance, tackle, things, trappings; SEE CONCEPTS *432,446*

stuff [*n2*] *essence, substance*
bottom, bottom line*, essentiality, heart, marrow*, matter, meat*, nitty-gritty*, nuts and bolts*, pith, principle, quintessence, soul, staple, virtuality; SEE CONCEPTS *668,682*

stuff [*n3*] *fabric*
cloth, material, raw material, textile, woven material; SEE CONCEPT *167*

stuff [*v*] *load with*
choke up, clog up, compress, congest, cram, crowd, fill, fill to overflowing, fill to the brim, force, glut, gobble, gorge, gormandize, guzzle, jam, jam-pack*, overfill, overindulge, overstuff, pack, pad, push, ram, sate, satiate, shove, squeeze, stow, wad, wedge; SEE CONCEPTS *169,209*

stuffed [*adj*] *crammed*
bursting, crowded, filled, full, glutted, gorged, jammed, jam-packed*, loaded, overflowing, packed, packed like sardines*, running over, satisfied, saturated, tight; SEE CONCEPTS *481,483,773,774,786*

stuffy [*adj1*] *close, oppressive*
airless, breathless, confined, fetid, heavy, humid, muggy, stagnant, stale, stifling, suffocating, sultry, thick, unventilated; SEE CONCEPT *525*

stuffy [*adj2*] *old-fashioned, prim*
arrogant, bloated, conventional, dreary, dull, fusty, genteel, humorless, important, magisterial, musty, narrow-minded, pompous, priggish, prim

and proper*, prissy, prudish, puffy, puritanical, self-important, staid, stilted, stodgy, straitlaced*, uninteresting, Victorian*; SEE CONCEPTS *401,404*

stumble [*v1*] *slip, stagger*
blunder, bumble, careen, err, fall, fall down, falter, flounder, hesitate, limp, lose balance, lumber, lurch, muddle, pitch, reel, shuffle, stammer, swing, tilt, topple, totter, trip, wallow, waver, wobble; SEE CONCEPTS *101,181*

stumble [*v2*] *happen upon*
blunder upon*, bump, chance, chance upon*, come across, come up against, discover, encounter, fall upon, find, happen upon*, hit, light, light upon*, luck*, meet, run across, stub toe on*, tumble, turn up; SEE CONCEPTS *183,693*

stumbling block [*n*] *impediment*
barricade, barrier, blockage, catch*, Catch-22*, clog, delay, difficulty, drag*, drawback, handicap, hindrance, holdup, hurdle, obstacle, obstruction, road block*, setback, snag; SEE CONCEPT *666*

stump [*n*] *end piece*
butt, end, projection, stub, tail end, tip; SEE CONCEPTS *825,827*

stump [*v1*] *confuse, bewilder*
baffle, bring up short, confound, dumbfound, foil, mystify, nonplus, outwit, perplex, puzzle, stagger, stick, stop, stymie; SEE CONCEPT *16*

stump [*v2*] *walk with deliberation*
barge, clomp, clump, galumph, lumber, plod, stamp, stomp, stumble, trudge; SEE CONCEPT *149*

stunned [*adj*] *dazed*
aghast, amazed, astonished, astounded, bewildered, blown away*, bowled over*, breathless, confounded, confused, dismayed, dumbfounded, flabbergasted, floored, frozen, numb, overcome, overwhelmed, shocked, speechless, startled, stumped, stupefied, surprised, taken aback; SEE CONCEPT *403*

stunning [*adj*] *beautiful, marvelous*
beauteous, bonny, brilliant, comely, dazzling, devastating, excellent, fair, famous, fine, first-class*, first-rate*, gorgeous, great, handsome, heavenly, impressive, lovely, number one*, out of this world*, pretty, ravishing, remarkable, royal, sensational, smashing, spectacular, striking, superior, top, wonderful; SEE CONCEPTS *574,579*

stun/stupefy [*v*] *amaze, shock*
astonish, astound, bemuse, bewilder, blow away*, bowl over*, confound, confuse, daze, dumbfound, flabbergast, floor*, fog*, give a turn*, hit like ton of bricks*, knock out*, knock over*, knock unconscious, muddle, overcome, overpower, overwhelm, paralyze, petrify, rock*, shake up*, stagger, strike dumb*, surprise, take breath away*, throw a curve*; SEE CONCEPT *42*

stunt [*n*] *deed, trick*
achievement, act, antic, caper, exploit, feat, feature, performance, sketch, skit, tour de force; SEE CONCEPTS *264,384*

stunted [*adj*] *kept from growing*
bantam, diminutive, dwarf, dwarfed, dwarfish, half-pint*, little, measly, mite, peanut*, pee-wee*, pint-sized*, runted, runtish, runty, scrub, short, shot, shrimp*, small, small fry*, tiny, undergrown, undersized, wee*, yea big*, yea high*; SEE CONCEPTS *773,779*

stupefied [*adj*] *dazed*
amazed, astonished, astounded, bewildered,

blown away*, bowled over*, breathless, confounded, confused, dismayed, dumbfounded, flabbergasted, floored, frozen, numb, overcome, overwhelmed, puzzled, shocked, speechless, startled, stumped, stunned, surprised, taken aback; SEE CONCEPT *403*

stupendous [*adj*] *wonderful, amazing*
astonishing, astounding, breathtaking, colossal, dynamite, enormous, fab*, fabulous, fantastic, fat*, gigantic, great, huge, marvelous, mind-blowing*, mind-boggling*, miraculous, monster, monumental, overwhelming, phenomenal, prodigious, radical*, smashing, spectacular, staggering, stunning, super, superb, surprising, terrific, titantic, too much*, tremendous, unreal*, utmost*, vast, wonderful, wondrous; SEE CONCEPTS *574,781*

stupid [*adj*] *not intelligent; irresponsible*
brainless, dazed, deficient, dense, dim, doltish, dopey*, dull, dumb, dummy*, foolish, futile, gullible, half-baked*, half-witted*, idiotic, ill-advised, imbecilic, inane, indiscreet, insensate, irrelevant, irresponsible, laughable, loser*, ludicrous, meaningless, mindless, moronic, naive, nonsensical, obtuse, out to lunch*, pointless, puerile, rash, senseless, shortsighted, simple, simpleminded, slow, sluggish, stolid, stupefied, thick, thick-headed*, trivial, unintelligent, unthinking, witless; SEE CONCEPTS *402,548*

stupor [*n*] *daze, unconsciousness*
amazement, anaesthesia, apathy, asphyxia, bewilderment, coma, dullness, fainting, hebetude, hypnosis, inertia, inertness, insensibility, languor, lassitude, lethargy, narcosis, numbness, petrifaction, sleep, slumber, somnolence, sopor, stupefaction, suspended animation, swoon, swooning, torpor, trance; SEE CONCEPTS *315,316*

sturdy [*adj*] *solid, durable*
athletic, built to last*, bulky, determined, durable, firm, flourishing, hardy, hearty, hefty, hulking, husky, lusty, muscular, powerful, powerhouse*, resolute, robust, rugged, secure, solid, sound, stalwart, staunch, steadfast, stiff, stout, stouthearted, strapping, strong, strong-arm*, substantial, tenacious, tough, unyielding, vigorous, well-built, well-made; SEE CONCEPTS *314,488, 489*

stutter [*v*] *speak haltingly*
dribble, falter, hesitate, splutter, sputter, stammer, stumble; SEE CONCEPT *77*

style [*n1*] *fashion, manner*
appearance, approach, bearing, behavior, carriage, characteristic, cup of tea*, custom, cut*, description, design, druthers*, flash*, form, genre, groove*, habit, hand, idiosyncrasy, kind, method, mode, number, pattern, peculiarity, rage*, sort, spirit, strain, technique, tenor, thing*, tone, trait, trend, type, variety, vein, vogue, way; SEE CONCEPTS *411,655*

style [*n2*] *fashionableness*
chichi*, comfort, cosmopolitanism, craze, dash, delicacy, dernier cri, dressiness, ease, élan, elegance, fad, flair, grace, grandeur, luxury, mode, panache, polish, rage, refinement, savoir-faire, smartness, sophistication, stylishness, taste, thing*, urbanity, vogue; SEE CONCEPTS *655,668*

style [*n3*] *way of speaking, writing, expressing oneself*
diction, expression, mode of expression, phrase-

ology, phrasing, treatment, turn of phrase*, vein, wording; SEE CONCEPT *276*

style [*v*] *name, title*
address, baptize, call, christen, denominate, designate, dub, entitle, label, name, term; SEE CONCEPT *62*

stylish [*adj*] *fashionable*
à la mode*, beautiful, chic, chichi*, classy, dap, dapper, dashing, dressed to kill*, dressed to the teeth*, dressy, fly*, groovy*, high-class*, in, in fashion, in the mainstream*, in vogue, jazzy*, latest, mod*, modernistic, new, nifty, now*, ostentatious, polished, pretentious, rakish, ritzy, sassy*, sharp, showy, sleek, slick*, smart, snappy*, snazzy*, swank*, swell, tony*, trendy, upscale, up-to-date, uptown, urbane, voguish; SEE CONCEPTS *579,589*

stymie [*v*] *frustrate, hinder*
balk, block, choke off, confound, corner, crab*, cramp, cramp one's style*, crimp, cut off, dead-end*, defeat, foil, give the run around*, hang fire*, hang up*, hold off, hold up, impede, mystify, nonplus, obstruct, pigeonhole*, prevent, put on back burner*, put on hold, puzzle, shelve, snooker*, stall, stonewall*, stump, throw a monkey wrench into*, thwart; SEE CONCEPTS *121,130*

suave [*adj*] *charming, smooth*
affable, agreeable, bland, civilized, cordial, courteous, courtly, cultivated, cultured, diplomatic, distingué, fulsome, genial, glib, gracious, ingratiating, obliging, oily*, pleasant, pleasing, polished, polite, politic, refined, smooth-tongued*, sociable, soft*, soft-spoken, sophisticated, unctuous, urbane, well-bred, worldly; SEE CONCEPTS *401,404*

subconscious [*adj*] *innermost in thought*
hidden, inmost, inner, intuitive, latent, mental, repressed, subliminal, suppressed, unconscious; SEE CONCEPT *529*

subconscious [*n*] *inner thoughts*
essence, mind, psyche, soul, subconsciousness, subliminal, subliminal self, submerged mind, underconsciousness, undersense; SEE CONCEPT *410*

subdivision [*n*] *smaller entity of whole*
class, community, development, group, lower group, minor group, subclass, subsidiary, tract; SEE CONCEPTS *513,835*

subdue [*v*] *keep under control; moderate*
bear down, beat down, break, break in, check, conquer, control, crush, defeat, discipline, dominate, drop, extinguish, gentle, get the better of*, get the upper hand*, get under control, humble, mellow, overcome, overpower, overrun, put down, quash, quell, quench, quiet, quieten, reduce, repress, restrain, shut down, soften, squelch, subjugate, suppress, tame, temper, tone down, trample, triumph over, vanquish; SEE CONCEPTS *121,130,252*

subdued [*adj*] *quiet, controlled*
chastened, crestfallen, dejected, dim, domestic, domesticated, downcast, down in the mouth*, grave, hushed, inobtrusive, low-key*, mellow*, moderated, muted, neutral, out of spirits*, repentant, repressed, restrained, sad, serious, shaded, sober, soft, softened, solemn, submissive, subtle, tasteful, tempered, toned down, unobtrusive; SEE CONCEPTS *401,403,594*

subject [*adj*] *at the mercy of; answerable*
accountable, apt, at one's feet*, bound by, captive, collateral, conditional, contingent, con-

st
su

trolled, dependent, directed, disposed, enslaved, exposed, governed, in danger of, inferior, liable, likely, obedient, open, prone, provisional, ruled, satellite, secondary, sensitive, servile, slavish, sub*, subaltern, subjugated, submissive, subordinate, subservient, substract, susceptible, tentative, tributary, under, vulnerable; SEE CONCEPTS *552,575*

subject [*n1*] *issue, matter*
affair, argument, business, case, chapter, class, core, course, discussion, field of reference, gist, head, idea, item, material, matter at hand, meat*, motif, motion, motive, object, point, principal object, problem, proposal, question, resolution, study, subject matter, substance, text, theme, theorem, thesis, thought, topic; SEE CONCEPTS *529,532,689*

subject [*n2*] *one under authority of another*
case, client, customer, dependent, guinea pig*, liege, national, patient, serf, subordinate, vassal; SEE CONCEPTS *413,423*

subjective [*adj*] *emotional; based on inner experience rather than fact*
abstract, biased, fanciful, idiosyncratic, illusory, individual, instinctive, introspective, introverted, intuitive, nonobjective, nonrepresentative, personal, prejudiced, unobjective; SEE CONCEPTS *529,542*

subjugate [*v*] *overpower, defeat*
bear down, beat down, bring to heel*, bring to knees*, coerce, compel, conquer, crush, enslave, enthrall, force, hold sway, keep under thumb*, kick around*, overcome, overthrow, put down, quell, reduce, reel back in*, rule, rule over, subdue, suppress, tame, triumph, vanquish; SEE CONCEPTS *95,117,133*

sublime [*adj*] *great, magnificent*
abstract, august, divine, dynamite, elevated, eminent, exalted, glorious, gorgeous, grand, heavenly, high, holy, ideal, imposing, lofty, majestic, noble, outrageous, proud, resplendent, sacred, spiritual, splendiferous, splendorous, stately, super, superb, the most*, too much*, transcendent, transcendental; SEE CONCEPT *574*

submarine [*n1*] *sub*
nuclear submarine, submersible, U-boat, underwater craft, underwater robot; SEE CONCEPT *506*

submarine [*n2*] *sandwich*
grinder, hero, hoagie, sub*, torpedo; SEE CONCEPTS *457,460,461*

submerge [*v*] *dunk in liquid*
deluge, descend, dip, douse, drench, drown, duck, engulf, flood, go down, go under, immerse, impregnate, inundate, overflow, overwhelm, plunge, sink, sound, souse, submerse, subside, swamp, whelm; SEE CONCEPTS *181,256*

submission [*n*] *compliance*
acquiescence, appeasement, assent, backing down, bowing, capitulation, cringing, defeatism, deference, docility, giving in, humbleness, humility, malleability, meekness, nonresistance, obedience, passivism, passivity, pliabilty, prostration, recreancy, resignation, servility, subjection, submissiveness, submitting, surrender, tractability, unassertiveness, yielding; SEE CONCEPT *633*

submissive [*adj*] *compliant*
abject, accommodating, acquiescent, amenable, bowing down, comformable, complying, deferential, docile, domesticated, dutiful, giving-in*,

humble, ingratiating, lowly, malleable, meek, menial, nonresistant, nonresisting, obedient, obeisant, obeying, obsequious, passive, patient, pliable, pliant, resigned, servile, slavish, subdued, tame, tractable, uncomplaining, unresisting, yes*, yielding; SEE CONCEPT *401*

submit [*v1*] *comply, endure*
abide, accede, acknowledge, acquiesce, agree, appease, bend, be submissive, bow, buckle, capitulate, cave, cede, concede, defer, eat crow*, fold, give away, give ground, give in, give way, go with the flow*, grin and bear it*, humor, indulge, knuckle, knuckle under*, kowtow*, lay down arms, obey, put up with, quit, relent, relinquish, resign oneself, say uncle*, stoop, succumb, surrender, throw in the towel*, toe the line*, tolerate, truckle, withstand, yield; SEE CONCEPT *23*

submit [*v2*] *present, offer; argue for*
advance, advise, affirm, argue, assert, claim, commit, contend, hand in, make a pitch*, move, proffer, propose, proposition, propound, put, put forward, refer, state, suggest, table, tender, theorize, urge, volunteer; SEE CONCEPT *66*

subordinate [*adj*] *lesser, supplementary*
accessory, adjuvant, ancillary, auxiliary, baser, below par, collateral, contributory, dependent, inferior, insignificant, junior, low, lower, minor, paltry, satellite, secondary, second-fiddle*, second-string*, smaller, sub, subaltern, subalternate, subject, submissive, subnormal, subservient, subsidiary, substract, tributary, under, underaverage, unequal; SEE CONCEPT *575*

subordinate [*n*] *person that serves another*
aide, assistant, attendant, dependent, deputy, flunky*, gofer*, helper, inferior, junior, peon, poor relation*, scrub*, second, second fiddle*, second string*, serf, servant, slave, subaltern, third string*, underling; SEE CONCEPTS *348,423*

subpoena [*n*] *writ*
command, court order, decree, mandate, summons, warrant, written order; SEE CONCEPT *318*

subpoena [*v*] *issue a writ*
cite, order to testify, serve a court order, serve notice, summon; SEE CONCEPT *318*

subscribe [*v1*] *pay for use; contribute*
advocate, ante up*, buy, chip in*, come through*, consent, donate, do one's part*, endorse, enroll, give, grant, ink*, make a deal*, offer, pitch in*, pledge, promise, put up*, register, second, set, sign, signature, sign up*, support; SEE CONCEPTS *129,341*

subscribe [*v2*] *agree*
accede, acquiesce, advocate, approve, assent, autograph*, back, bless, boost, consent, cosign, countenance, ditto*, endorse, favor, get behind*, give stamp of approval* give the go-ahead*, go along with*, hold with*, ink*, obey, okay*, put John Hancock on*, rubber-stamp*, sanction, sign, signature, support, take, undersign, underwrite, yes*; SEE CONCEPTS *10,50,88*

subsequent [*adj*] *after*
consecutive, consequent, consequential, ensuing, following, later, next, posterior, postliminary, proximate, resultant, resulting, sequent, sequential, serial, subsequential, succeeding, successional, successive; SEE CONCEPTS *585,820*

subsequently [*adv*] *afterward*
after, afterwards, afterwhile, at a later date, behind, by and by, consequently, finally, infra, in

the aftermath, in the end, later, latterly, next; SEE CONCEPTS *585,820*

subservient [*adj1*] *extremely compliant*
abject, acquiescent, a slave to*, at one's beck and call*, at one's mercy*, bootlicking, cowering, cringing, dancing, deferential, docile, fawning, ignoble, inferior, in one's clutches*, in one's pocket*, in one's power*, mean, menial, obeisant, obsequious, resigned, servile, slavish, subject, submissive, sycophantic, under one's thumb*; SEE CONCEPTS *401,404*

subservient [*adj2*] *secondary, useful*
accessory, adjuvant, ancillary, appurtenant, auxiliary, bush-league*, collateral, conducive, contributory, flunky, helpful, inferior, instrumental, minor, serviceable, subordinate, subsidiary, supplemental, supplementary; SEE CONCEPTS *560,575*

subside [*v*] *die down; decrease*
abate, cave in, collapse, decline, de-escalate, descend, die away, diminish, drop, dwindle, ease, ease off, ebb, fall, let up, level off, lower, lull, melt, moderate, peter out*, quieten, recede, settle, sink, slacken, taper, wane; SEE CONCEPTS *181,698,776*

subsidiary [*adj*] *secondary, helpful*
accessory, adjuvant, aiding, ancillary, appurtenant, assistant, assisting, auxiliary, backup, branch, collateral, contributory, cooperative, lesser, minor, serviceable, subject, subordinate, subservient, supplemental, supplementary, tributory, useful; SEE CONCEPTS *560,575*

subsidize [*v*] *give money to get started*
angel*, back, bankroll*, contribute, endow, finance, fund, grubstake*, help, juice*, pick up the check*, pick up the tab*, prime the pump*, promote, put up the money for, sponsor, stake, support, underwrite; SEE CONCEPTS *110,341*

subsidy [*n*] *money given to help another*
aid, alimony, allowance, appropriation, assistance, bequest, bonus, bounty, contribution, endowment, fellowship, financial aid, gift, grant, gratuity, help, honorarium, indemnity, payment, pension, premium, reward, scholarship, subsidization, subvention, support, tribute; SEE CONCEPTS *337,344*

subsist [*v*] *keep going, living*
barely exist*, be, breathe, continue, eke out a living*, eke out an existence*, endure, exist, get along*, get by*, hang in*, hang on*, hang tough*, just make it*, last, live, make ends meet*, make it*, manage, move, remain, remain alive, ride out*, scrape by*, stay alive, stick it out*, stick with it*, survive, sustain; SEE CONCEPTS *23,330,407*

subsistence [*n*] *provisions for survival*
affluence, aliment, alimentation, bread*, bread and butter*, capital, circumstances, competence, earnings, existence, food, fortune, gratuity, income, independence, keep, legacy, livelihood, living, maintenance, means, money, necessities, nurture, pension, property, provision, ration, resources, riches, salary, salt*, substance, support, sustenance, upkeep, victuals, wages, wealth, wherewithal; SEE CONCEPTS *446,457,646,710*

substance [*n1*] *entity, element*
actuality, animal, being, body, bulk, concreteness, core, corpus, fabric, force, hunk, individual, item, mass, material, matter, object, person, phenomenon, reality, something, staple, stuff, texture, thing; SEE CONCEPTS *433,478,523*

substance [*n2*] *essence, meaning*
ABCs*, amount, basis, body, bottom, bottom line*, brass tacks*, burden, center, core, corpus, crux, drift, effect, essentiality, focus, general meaning, gist, gravamen, guts*, heart, import, innards, kernel, marrow, mass, matter, meat*, name of the game*, nitty-gritty*, nub, nuts and bolts*, pith, point, purport, quintessence, sense, significance, soul, staple, strength, stuff, subject, sum total*, tenor, theme, thrust, upshot, virtuality, way of it*; SEE CONCEPTS *682,689*

substance [*n3*] *wealth*
affluence, assets, estate, fortune, means, property, resources, riches, worth; SEE CONCEPT *335*

substance abuse [*n*] *chemical abuse*
addiction, alcoholic addiction, alcoholism, drug abuse, drug dependence, habit; SEE CONCEPTS *20,316,709*

substandard [*adj*] *inferior*
bad, base, below average, below par, below standard, cheap, inadequate, junk*, lemon*, lousy, low-grade, poor, second-rate, shoddy, subpar, unacceptable; SEE CONCEPT *574*

substantial [*adj1*] *important, ample*
abundant, big, big-deal*, bulky, consequential, considerable, durable, extraordinary, firm, generous, goodly, heavy, heavyweight, hefty, key, large, major-league*, massive, material, meaningful, momentous, plentiful, principal, serious, significant, sizable, solid, sound, stable, steady, stout, strong, sturdy, superabundant, tidy, valuable, vast, weighty, well-built, worthwhile; SEE CONCEPTS *568,773,781*

substantial [*adj2*] *material, real*
actual, card-carrying*, concrete, corporeal, existent, for real*, honest-to-god*, legit*, objective, phenomenal, physical, positive, righteous, sensible, solid, sure enough*, tangible, true, twenty-four-carat*, valid, visible, weighty; SEE CONCEPT *582*

substantial [*adj3*] *rich*
affluent, comfortable, easy, opulent, prosperous, snug, solid, solvent, wealthy, well, well-heeled, well-off, well-to-do; SEE CONCEPT *334*

substantially [*adv*] *to a large extent*
considerably, essentially, extensively, heavily, in essence, in fact, in reality, in substance, in the main, largely, mainly, materially, much, really; SEE CONCEPTS *569,772*

substantiate [*v*] *back up a statement, idea*
actualize, affirm, approve, attest to, authenticate, bear out, check out, check up, complete, confirm, corroborate, debunk, demonstrate, establish, incarnate, justify, manifest, materialize, objectify, personify, prove, ratify, realize, reify, support, test, try, try on, try out, validate, verify; SEE CONCEPTS *49,138,317*

substitute [*adj*] *alternative*
acting, additional, alternate, another, artificial, backup, counterfeit, dummy, ersatz*, experimental, false, imitation, makeshift, mock, near, other, provisional, proxy, pseudo*, replacement, representative, reserve, second, sham, simulated, spurious, stopgap*, substitutive, supplemental, supplementary, supposititious, surrogate, symbolic, temporary, tentative, vicarial, vicarious; SEE CONCEPTS *560,575*

su
su

substitute [*n*] *someone or something that takes the place of another*

agent, alternate, assistant, auxiliary, backup, changeling, delegate, deputy, dernier ressort*, double, dummy, equivalent, expediency, expedient, fill-in, ghost, ghost writer, locum, locum tenens, makeshift, pinch-hitter*, procurator, proxy, recourse, refuge, relay, relief, replacement, representative, reserve, resort, resource, stand-by, stand-in, stopgap*, sub*, succedaneum, successor, supplanter, supply, surrogate, symbol, temp*, temporary, temporary expedient, understudy, vicar; SEE CONCEPTS *423,712*

substitute [*v*] *interchange, exchange*

act for, alternate, answer for, back up, be in place of, change, commute, cover for, deputize, displace, do the work of, double for, fill in for, fill one's position, go as, proxy, relieve, replace, serve in one's stead, spell, stand for, stand in for, sub*, supersede, supplant, swap, swap places with*, switch, take another's place, take over; SEE CONCEPTS *87,104*

subterranean [*adj*] *hidden, underground*

below ground, buried, covered, covert, hush-hush*, on the QT*, private, secret, subterrestrial, subversive, sunken, underfoot, under wraps*; SEE CONCEPT *583*

subtle [*adj1*] *nice, quiet, delicate*

attenuate, attenuated, deep, discriminating, ethereal, exquisite, faint, fine, finespun, hairline, hairsplitting, illusive, implied, inconspicuous, indirect, indistinct, inferred, ingenious, insinuated, mental, penetrating, profound, refined, slight, sophisticated, suggestive, tenuous, thin, understated; SEE CONCEPTS *537,544*

subtle [*adj2*] *clever, cunning*

analytic, analytical, artful, astute, complex, crafty, deep, designing, detailed, devious, dexterous, exacting, foxy, guileful, insidious, intriguing, keen, penetrating, perceptive, precise, ratiocinative, scheming, shrewd, skillful, sly, wily; SEE CONCEPT *402*

subtract [*v*] *take away*

decrease, deduct, detract, diminish, discount, draw back, knock off, remove, take, take from, take off, take out, withdraw, withhold; SEE CONCEPTS *211,764*

suburb [*n*] *neighborhood outside of but reliant on nearby large city*

bedroom community*, burb*, country, countryside, environs, fringe, hamlet, hinterland, outlying area, outpost, outskirts, precinct, purlieu, residential area, slub, suburbia, village; SEE CONCEPTS *508,512*

subversive [*adj*] *rebellious, destructive*

incendiary, inflammatory, insurgent, insurrectionary, overthrowing, perversive, riotous, ruinous, seditious, treasonous, underground, undermining; SEE CONCEPT *401*

subvert [*v*] *rebel, destroy*

capsize, contaminate, corrupt, debase, defeat, demolish, deprave, depress, extinguish, invalidate, invert, level, overthrow, overturn, pervert, poison, pull down, raze, reverse, ruin, sabotage, supersede, supplant, suppress, topple, tumble, undermine, upset, vitiate, wreck; SEE CONCEPTS *86,95,252*

succeed [*v1*] *attain good outcome*

accomplish, achieve, acquire, arrive, avail, benefit, be successful, carry off*, come off*, conquer, distance, do all right*, do the trick*, earn, flourish, fulfill, gain, get, get to the top*, grow famous, hit*, make a fortune*, make good*, make it*, make out*, obtain, outdistance, outwit, overcome, possess, prevail, profit, prosper, pull off*, realize, reap, receive, recover, retrieve, score, secure, surmount, thrive, triumph, turn out*, vanquish, win, work, worst; SEE CONCEPTS *141,706*

succeed [*v2*] *come after; take the place of*

accede, assume, be subsequent, come into, come into possession, come next, displace, ensue, enter upon, follow, follow after, follow in order, go next, inherit, postdate, replace, result, supersede, supervene, supplant, take over; SEE CONCEPTS *727,749,813*

succeeding/successive [*adj*] *following*

alternating, consecutive, ensuing, following after, in a row, in line, next, next in line for, next in order, next off, next up, rotating, sequent, sequential, serial, seriate, subsequent, subsequential, succedent, successional; SEE CONCEPTS *585,811,812,818,820*

success [*n*] *favorable outcome*

accomplishment, achievement, advance, arrival, ascendancy, attainment, bed of roses*, benefit, big hit*, boom*, clover*, consummation, do well, Easy Street*, éclat, eminence, fame, flying colors*, fortune, fruition, gain, good luck*, good times*, grand slam*, gravy train*, happiness, happy days*, hit, killing, lap of luxury*, laugher*, maturation, profit, progress, prosperity, realization, reward, savvy, sensation, snap, strike, successfulness, triumph, victory, walkaway*, walkover*, win; SEE CONCEPTS *693,706*

successful [*adj*] *favorable, profitable*

acknowledged, advantageous, ahead of the game*, at the top*, at top of ladder*, auspicious, bestselling, blooming, blossoming, booming, champion, crowned, efficacious, extraordinary, flourishing, fortuitous, fortunate, fruitful, happy, lucky, lucrative, moneymaking, notable, noteworthy, on track*, out in front*, outstanding, paying, prosperous, rewarding, rolling, strong, thriving, top, triumphant, unbeaten, undefeated, victorious, wealthy; SEE CONCEPT *528*

successor [*n*] *heir*

beneficiary, descendant, follower, heritor, inheritor, next in line, replacement, scion; SEE CONCEPTS *355,414*

succinct [*adj*] *brief, to the point*

blunt, boiled down*, breviloquent, brusque, compact, compendiary, compendious, concise, condensed, curt, cut to the bone*, in a nutshell*, in few words*, laconic, pithy, short, summary, terse; SEE CONCEPT *267*

succulent [*adj*] *juicy, delicious*

divine, heavenly, luscious, lush, mellow, moist, mouthwatering, pulpy, rich, sappy, tasty, yummy*; SEE CONCEPTS *462,613*

succumb [*v*] *die or surrender*

accede, bow, break down, buckle, capitulate, cave, cave in*, cease, collapse, croak, decease, defer, demise, depart, drop, eat crow*, expire, fall, fall victim to, flake out*, fold, give in, give into, give out, give up the ghost*, give way, go, go down, go under, knuckle, knuckle under*, meet waterloo*, pack it in*, pass, pass away, perish, quit, show white flag*, submit, take the

count*, throw in the towel*, wilt, yield; SEE CON-
CEPTS *35,105,385*

such [*adj/conj*] *aforementioned, specific*
aforesaid, akin, alike, analogous, comparable,
corresponding, equivalent, like, parallel, said,
similar, such a one, such a person, such a thing,
suchlike, that, the, this; SEE CONCEPT *557*

sudden [*adj*] *unexpected; happening quickly*
abrupt, accelerated, acute, expeditious, fast,
flash, fleet, hasty, headlong, hurried, immediate,
impetuous, impromptu, impulsive, out of the
blue*, precipitant, precipitate, precipitous, quick,
quickened, rapid, rash, rushing, spasmodic,
speeded, subito, swift, unforeseen, unusual; SEE
CONCEPT *799*

suddenly [*adv*] *unexpectedly*
aback, abruptly, all at once, all of a sudden, asud-
den, forthwith, on spur of moment*, quickly,
short, sudden, swiftly, unanticipatedly, unaware,
unawares, without warning; SEE CONCEPT *799*

sue [*v*] *bring legal charges against*
accuse, appeal, beg, beseech, bring an action,
charge, claim, claim damages, contest, demand,
drag into court, enter a plea, entreat, file, file a
claim, file suit, follow up, haul into court, have
the law on, have up, indict, institute legal proceedings, litigate, petition, plead, prefer charges
against, prosecute, pull up, put away, see in
court, solicit, summon, supplicate, take out after,
take to court; SEE CONCEPT *317*

suffer [*v1*] *be in pain*
ache, agonize, ail, be affected, be at disadvantage, be convulsed, be handicapped, be impaired,
be racked, be wounded, brave, complain of, deteriorate, droop, endure, experience, fall off, feel
wretched, flag, get, go through, grieve, have a
bad time*, hurt, languish, pain, sicken, smart,
undergo, writhe; SEE CONCEPTS *308,313*

suffer [*v2*] *endure, permit*
abide, accept, acquiesce, admit, allow, bear, bear
with, bleed, bow, brave, brook, carry the torch*,
concede, countenance, encounter, experience,
feel, go through, have, hurt, indulge, know, let,
license, live with, put up with, receive, sanction,
see, sit and take it, stand, stomach*, submit, support, sustain, swallow*, sweat*, take*, take it*,
tolerate, undergo, wait out, yield; SEE CONCEPTS
23,83

suffering [*n*] *pain, agony*
adversity, affliction, anguish, difficulty, discomfort, distress, dolor, hardship, martyrdom, misery, misfortune, ordeal, passion, torment, torture;
SEE CONCEPT *728*

suffice [*v*] *be adequate, enough*
answer, avail, be good enough, be sufficient, be
the ticket*, content, do, do the trick*, fill the
bill*, get by, go over big*, hack it*, hit the spot*,
make a hit*, make the grade*, meet, meet requirement, satisfy, serve, suit; SEE CONCEPT *713*

sufficient [*adj*] *enough, adequate*
acceptable, agreeable, all right*, ample, aplenty,
appreciate, comfortable, commensurable, commensurate, common, competent, copious, decent, due, galore, pleasing, plenteous, plentiful,
plenty, proportionate, satisfactory, sufficing, tolerable, unexceptionable, unexceptional, unobjectionable; SEE CONCEPTS *558,560,771*

suffocate [*v*] *choke*
asphyxiate, drown, smother, stifle, strangle; SEE
CONCEPTS *163,246*

sugarcoat [*v*] *sweeten*
add sugar, add sweetening, alleviate, candy-coat,
make more appealing, make sweet, mollify,
pacify, soften up, soothe; SEE CONCEPTS *7,22,170*

suggest [*v1*] *convey advice, plan, desire*
advance, advise, advocate, broach, commend,
conjecture, exhort, give a tip*, move, offer,
plug*, pose, prefer, propone, propose, proposition, propound, put, put forward, put in two
cents*, put on to something*, recommend, steer,
submit, theorize, tip, tip off*, tout; SEE CONCEPT
75

suggest [*v2*] *imply; bring to mind*
adumbrate, advert, allude, be a sign of, connote,
cross the mind, denote, evoke, hint, indicate,
infer, insinuate, intimate, lead to believe, occur,
point, point in direction of, promise, put in mind
of, refer, represent, shadow, signify, symbolize,
typify; SEE CONCEPTS *74,682*

suggestion [*n1*] *advice, plan*
advancement, angle, approach, bid, big idea*,
bit*, brainchild*, charge, commendation, exhortation, game plan*, gimmick, hot lead*, idea, injunction, instruction, invitation, lead, motion,
opinion, outline, pitch, presentation, proffer, proposal, proposition, recommendation, reminder,
resolution, scheme, setup, sneaking suspicion*,
steer*, submission, telltale, tender, testimonial,
thesis, tip, tip-off*; SEE CONCEPTS *278,689*

suggestion [*n2*] *hint, implication*
allusion, association, autosuggestion, breath,
clue, connotation, cue, indication, inkling, innuendo, insinuation, intimation, notion, overtone,
reminder, self-suggestion, shade, signification,
smack, soupçon, strain, suspicion, symbol, symbolism, symbolization, symbology, telltale,
thought, tinge, trace, undertone, vein, whisper,
wind; SEE CONCEPT *529*

suggestive [*adj1*] *signifying*
evocative, evocatory, expressive, giving an
inkling*, indicative, intriguing, pregnant, redolent, remindful, reminiscent, significative, symbolic, symptomatic; SEE CONCEPTS *267,529*

suggestive [*adj2*] *dirty, vulgar*
bawdy, blue*, broad, erotic, immodest, improper, indecent, indelicate, obscene, off-color*,
provocative, prurient, racy, ribald, risqué, rude,
seductive, sexy, shady, tempting, titillating, unseemly, wicked; SEE CONCEPTS *372,545*

suit [*n1*] *matching top and bottom clothing*
clothing, costume, dress, ensemble, getup*, gray
flannel*, habit, livery, outfit, threads*, tuxedo,
uniform, wardrobe; SEE CONCEPT *451*

suit [*n2*] *legal action*
case, cause, lawsuit, litigation, proceeding, prosecution, trial; SEE CONCEPT *318*

suit [*n3*] *appeal, request*
address, application, asking, attention, court,
courtship, entreaty, imploration, imprecation, invocation, petition, plea, prayer, requesting, solicitation, soliciting, supplication, wooing; SEE
CONCEPT *662*

suit [*v1*] *be acceptable, appropriate*
accord, agree, answer, answer a need, become,
befit, benefit, be proper for, beseem, be seemly,
check, check out, conform, correspond, cut the
mustard*, do, enhance, fill the bill*, fit, fit in,
flatter, fulfill, get by, go, go together, go with,
gratify, harmonize, make the grade*, match, pass

su
su

muster*, please, satisfy, serve, square, suffice, tally; SEE CONCEPT *656*

suit [*v2*] *adapt, tailor*
accommodate, adjust, amuse, change, conform, entertain, fashion, fill, fit, fit in, gratify, modify, please, proportion, quadrate, readjust, reconcile, revise, satisfy, tailor-make*, toe the mark*; SEE CONCEPTS *126,697*

suitable [*adj*] *appropriate, acceptable*
advisable, applicable, apposite, apt, becoming, befitting, commodious, condign, convenient, co-pacetic, correct, cut out for*, deserved, due, ex-pedient, felicitous, fit, fitting, good, good enough*, handy, happy, in character, in keeping*, just, kosher*, legit*, meet, merited, nice, okay*, opportune, peachy, pertinent, politic, pre-sentable, proper, reasonable, relevant, requisite, right, righteous, rightful, satisfactory, seemly, sufficient, suited, swell, up to snuff*, useful, user friendly; SEE CONCEPT *558*

suite [*n1*] *set of rooms or furniture*
apartment, array, batch, body, chambers, collec-tion, flat, group, lodging, lot, parcel, rental, se-ries, set, tenement; SEE CONCEPTS *441,516*

suite [*n2*] *entourage of people*
array, attendants, batch, body, clutch, cortege, court, escort, faculty, followers, group, lot, re-tainers, retinue, servants, set, staff, train; SEE CONCEPT *417*

suite [*n3*] *series*
chain, concatenation, consecution, line, order, progression, row, scale, sequel, sequence, string, succession, train; SEE CONCEPT *727*

suitor [*n*] *person who desires another*
admirer, beau, boyfriend, cavalier*, courter, date, follower, girlfriend, lover, man, paramour, supplicant, swain, woman, wooer; SEE CONCEPT *423*

sulk [*v*] *pout*
be down in the mouth*, be in a huff*, be morose, be out of sorts*, be silent, brood, frown, gloom, glower, gripe, grouse, grump*, look sullen, lower, moon*, mope*, scowl, take on; SEE CON-CEPTS *35,52*

sulky [*adj*] *sullen*
brooding, cheerless, crabby*, depressed, dismal, dour, fretful, frowning, gloomy, glum, gruff, grumpy*, ill-humored, irritable, mean, moody, moping, morose, obstinate, ornery*, pouting, pouty, sour, sourpussed*, sulking, withdrawn; SEE CONCEPT *403*

sullen [*adj*] *brooding, upset*
bad-tempered, cheerless, churlish, crabbed*, crabby*, cross, cynical, dismal, dour, dull, fret-ful, frowning, gloomy, glowering, glum, gruff, grumpy*, heavy, hostile, ill-humored, inert, irri-table, malevolent, malicious, malign, mean, moody, morose, obstinate, ornery*, out of sorts*, peevish, perverse, pessimistic, petulant, pouting, pouty, querulous, saturnine, silent, somber, sour, sourpussed*, stubborn, sulking, sulky, surly, tenebrific, tenebrous, ugly, unsociable, uptight*; SEE CONCEPT *403*

sully [*v*] *soil, stain*
besmirch, blacken, blot, contaminate, corrupt, debase, debauch, defile, dirty, discolor, disgrace, dishonor, drag through the mud*, make unclean, mark, smear, smudge, spot, taint, tar, tarnish; SEE CONCEPTS *54,250,254*

sultry [*adj1*] *hot and humid*
baking, broiling, burning, close, hot, mucky, muggy, oppressive, red-hot*, scorching, sizzling, smothering, soggy, sticky, stifling, stuffy, suffo-cating, sweltering, sweltry, torrid, wet; SEE CON-CEPTS *525,605*

sultry [*adj2*] *sensuous*
desirable, erotic, heavy*, hot*, lurid, passionate, provocative, seductive, sexy, steamy*, volup-tuous, X-rated*; SEE CONCEPT *372*

sum [*n*] *total*
aggregate, all, amount, body, bulk, entirety, en-tity, epitome, gross, integral, mass, quantity, reckoning, résumé, score, structure, summary, summation, sum total*, synopsis, system, tally, totality, value, whole, works*, worth; SEE CON-CEPTS *432,784,787*

summarily [*adv*] *without delay*
arbitrarily, at short notice, expeditiously, forth-with, immediately, on the spot, peremptorily, promptly, readily, speedily, swiftly, without waste; SEE CONCEPTS *544,799*

summarize [*v*] *give a rundown*
abridge, abstract, boil down*, cipher, compile, condense, cut, cut back, cut down, digest, encap-sulate, epitomize, get to meat*, give main points, inventory, outline, pare, precis, prune*, put in a nutshell*, recap*, recapitulate, rehash*, retro-grade, review, run down*, run through*, shorten, skim, snip, sum, summate, sum up, synopsize, trim; SEE CONCEPTS *55,236,247*

summary [*adj*] *concise, to the point*
arbitrary, boiled down*, breviloquent, brief, compact, compacted, compendiary, compen-dious, condensed, cursory, curt, hasty, in a nut-shell*, laconic, perfunctory, pithy*, recapped, rehashed, run-down, run-through, short, short and sweet*, succinct, terse; SEE CONCEPTS *267,272*

summary [*n*] *short statement of main points*
abbreviation, abridgment, abstract, analysis, apercu, brief, capitulation, case, compendium, condensation, conspectus, core, digest, epitome, essence, extract, inventory, long and short of it*, nutshell*, outline, pandect, precis, prospectus, recap*, recapitulation, reduction, rehash*, report, résumé, review, roundup, rundown, run-through, sense, skeleton*, sketch, sum and substance*, summing-up*, survey, syllabus, synopsis, ver-sion, wrap-up*; SEE CONCEPT *283*

summer [*n*] *hot season of the year*
daylight savings time*, dog days*, heat, mid-summer, picnic days*, riot time*, summer sol-stice, summertide, summertime, sunny season, vacation; SEE CONCEPT *814*

summit [*n*] *top, crowning point*
acme, apex, apogee, capstone, climax, crest, crown, culmination, head, height, max, meridian, most, peak, pinnacle, roof, vertex, zenith; SEE CONCEPT *836*

summon [*v*] *call to a place*
arouse, ask, assemble, beckon, beep, bid, call, call back, call for, call forth, call in, call into ac-tion, call together, call upon, charge, cite, com-mand, conjure, convene, convoke, direct, draft, draw on, enjoin, gather, hail, invite, invoke, mo-bilize, motion, muster, order, petition, rally, re-call, request, ring, rouse, send for, sign, signal, subpoena, toll; SEE CONCEPT *53*

sumptuous [*adj*] *luxurious, splendid*
awe-inspiring, beautiful, costly, dear, deluxe, elegant, expensive, extravagant, gorgeous, grand, grandiose, imposing, impressive, lavish, luscious, luxuriant, magnificent, opulent, out of this world, palatial, plush, pompous, posh, prodigal, profuse, rich, ritzy*, splendiferous, superb, swank*, ultra*, upholstered; SEE CONCEPTS *334,485,574*

sum up [*v*] *form an opinion of; summarize*
close, conclude, condense, digest, epitomize, estimate, examine, get the measure of, inventory, put in a nutshell*, recapitulate, review, size up, sum, synopsize, total; SEE CONCEPT *55*

sunder [*v*] *separate, sever*
break, break apart, break off, come apart, cut in two, detach, disconnect, disjoin, divide, part, rend, slice, split, split up, uncouple, undo, wedge apart; SEE CONCEPT *135*

sundry [*adj*] *miscellaneous*
assorted, different, divers, manifold, many, quite a few, several, some, varied, various; SEE CONCEPTS *564,772*

sunken [*adj*] *depressed, hollowed; submerged*
buried, caved-in, concave, fallen-in, immersed, indented, recessed; SEE CONCEPT *490*

sunny [*adj1*] *bright, clear (referring to weather)*
brilliant, clarion, cloudless, fine, light, luminous, pleasant, radiant, rainless, shining, shiny, summery, sunlit, sunshiny, unclouded, undarkened; SEE CONCEPTS *525,617*

sunny [*adj2*] *happy*
beaming, blithe, buoyant, cheerful, cheery, chirpy, genial, joyful, lighthearted, lightsome, optimistic, pleasant, smiling, sunbeamy; SEE CONCEPTS *401,542*

sunrise [*n*] *rise of sun above horizon*
aurora, break of day*, bright, cockcrow*, dawn, dawning, daybreak, daylight, early bright*, light, morn, morning, sunup; SEE CONCEPT *810*

sunscreen [*n*] *sunblock*
skin protection, sunblocker, sun cream, suntan lotion; SEE CONCEPTS *466,467,468*

sunset [*n*] *fall of sun below horizon*
close of day, crepuscular light, dusk, eve, evening, eventide, gloaming, nightfall, sundown, twilight; SEE CONCEPT *810*

super [*adj*] *excellent*
cool*, divine, glorious, great, groovy*, hot*, incomparable, keen, magnificent, marvelous, matchless, neat, outstanding, peerless, sensational, smashing*, superb, terrific, topnotch, wonderful; SEE CONCEPT *574*

superabundance [*n*] *overabundance*
excess, glut, great quantity, more than enough, overflow, overmuch, oversupply, plenty, plethora, superfluity, surfeit, surplus, too much*; SEE CONCEPTS *767,787*

superb [*adj*] *excellent, first-rate*
admirable, august, best, breathtaking, choice, elegant, elevated, exalted, exquisite, fine, glorious, gorgeous, grand, great, lofty, magnificent, majestic, marvelous, matchless, noble, optimal, optimum, outstanding, peerless, prime, proud, resplendent, solid, splendid, splendiferous, splendorous, standout, state-of-the-art*, stunning, sublime, super, superior, superlative, unrivaled, very best; SEE CONCEPT *574*

supercilious [*adj*] *arrogant, stuck-up*
bossy, cavalier, cocky*, condescending, con-

temptuous, disdainful, egotistic, haughty, high-and-mighty*, imperious, insolent, lofty, nervy*, overbearing, patronizing, proud, putting on airs*, scornful, snobby, superior, uppity*, vainglorious; SEE CONCEPT *401*

superficial [*adj*] *without depth, detail*
apparent, casual, cosmetic, cursory, depthless, desultory, empty, evident, exterior, external, flash, flimsy, frivolous, general, glib, half-baked*, hasty, hurried, ignorant, inattentive, lightweight, nodding, one-dimensional*, on the surface*, ostensible, outward, partial, passing, perfunctory, peripheral, quick-fix*, seeming, shallow, shoal, silly, sketchy, skin-deep*, slapdash*, slight, smattery, summary, surface, tip of the iceberg*, trivial, uncritical, warped; SEE CONCEPTS *557,777*

superficially [*adv*] *lightly; without care*
apparently, at first glance, carelessly, casually, externally, extraneously, flimsily, frivolously, hastily, ignorantly, not profoundly, not thoroughly, once over lightly*, on the surface*, ostensibly, outwardly, partially, skim, to the casual eye*; SEE CONCEPTS *531,544*

superfluous [*adj*] *extra, unnecessary*
abounding, de trop, dispensable, excess, excessive, exorbitant, expendable, extravagant, extreme, gratuitous, inessential, in excess, inordinate, lavish, leftover, needless, nonessential, overflowing, overmuch, pleonastic, profuse, redundant, remaining, residuary, spare, superabundant, supererogatory, superfluent, supernumerary, surplus, unasked, uncalled-for, unneeded, unrequired, unwanted, useless; SEE CONCEPTS *546,560,824*

superintendent [*n*] *person who oversees organization*
administrator, boss, caretaker, chief, conductor, controller, curator, custodian, director, foreperson, governor, head, head person, inspector, manager, overseer, sitter, slave driver*, straw boss*, super*, supervisor, zookeeper*; SEE CONCEPT *347*

superior [*adj1*] *better, greater, higher; excellent*
above, a cut above*, admirable, capital, choice, dandy, deluxe, distinguished, exceeding, excellent, exceptional, exclusive, expert, famous, fine, finer, first-class, first-rate, first-string*, five-star*, good, good quality, grander, high-caliber, high-class, major, more advanced, more skillful, noteworthy, of higher rank, over, overlying, paramount, predominant, preferable, preferred, premium, prevailing, primary, remarkable, senior, superhuman, superincumbent, surpassing, unrivalled; SEE CONCEPT *574*

superior [*adj2*] *arrogant, haughty*
airy, bossy, cavalier, cocky*, condescending, cool, disdainful, high-and-mighty*, high-hat*, insolent, lofty, overbearing, patronizing, pretentious, proud, snobbish, stuck-up*, supercilious, uppity*, upstage*, wiseguy*; SEE CONCEPT *401*

superior [*n*] *person higher or highest in rank*
boss, brass*, CEO*, chief, chieftain, director, elder, exec*, executive, head, head honcho*, heavyweight*, higher-up*, key player*, leader, manager, principal, ruler, senior, supervisor, VIP*; SEE CONCEPT *347*

superiority [*n*] *advantage, predominance*
ahead, ascendancy, authority, better, bulge, dominance, edge, eminence, excellence, influence,

su
su

lead, meliority, nobility, perfection, position, power, predomination, preeminence, preponderance, prestige, prevalence, pull, rank, spark, supremacy, top, transcendence, upper hand*, vantage, victory, whip hand*; SEE CONCEPT 671

superlative [*adj*] *excellent, first-class*
A-1*, accomplished, all-time*, best, capital, consummate, crack, effusive, exaggerated, excessive, extreme, finished, gilt-edge*, greatest, highest, hundred-proof*, inflated, magnificent, matchless, of highest order*, optimum, outstanding, peerless, standout*, superb, supreme, surpassing, tops*, transcendent, unexcelled, unparalleled, unrivaled, unsurpassed, winning, world-class*; SEE CONCEPT 574

supernal [*adj*] *celestial*
angelic, astral, elevated, empyreal, empyrean, ethereal, heavenly, lofty, otherworldly, seraphic, uplifted; SEE CONCEPTS 536,673

supernatural [*adj*] *mysterious, not of this world*
abnormal, celestial, concealed, dark, fabulous, fairy, ghostly, heavenly, hidden, impenetrable, invisible, legendary, metaphysical, miraculous, mystic, mythical, mythological, numinous, obscure, occult, paranormal, phantom, phenomenal, preternatural, psychic, rare, secret, spectral, superhuman, superior, supermundane, superordinary, supranatural, transcendental, uncanny, uncomprehensible, unearthly, unfathomable, unintelligible, unknowable, unknown, unnatural, unrevealed, unusual; SEE CONCEPT 582

supersede [*v*] *take the place of; override*
abandon, annul, desert, discard, displace, forsake, oust, outmode, outplace, overrule, reject, remove, replace, repudiate, set aside, succeed, supplant, supplement, suspend, take over, usurp; SEE CONCEPTS 128,141

superstition [*n*] *belief in sign of things to come*
false belief, fear, irrationality, notion, shibboleth*, unfounded fear; SEE CONCEPT 689

supervise [*v*] *manage people, project*
administer, be in charge*, be in driver's seat*, be in the saddle, be on duty, be responsible for, boss, call the play*, call the shots*, chaperon, conduct, control, crack the whip*, deal with, direct, handle, inspect, keep an eye on*, look after, overlook, oversee, preside over, quarterback*, ride herd on*, run, run the show*, run things*, sit on top of*, superintend, survey, take care of; SEE CONCEPT 117

supervision [*n*] *management of people, project*
administration, auspices, care, charge, conduct, control, direction, guidance, handling, instruction, intendance, oversight, running, superintendence, superintendency, surveillance; SEE CONCEPT 117

supervisor [*n*] *person who manages people, project*
administrator, boss, brass hat*, caretaker, chief, curator, custodian, director, executive, foreperson, head, inspector, manager, overseer, slave driver*, straw boss*, super*, superintendent, zookeeper*; SEE CONCEPT 347

supine [*adj1*] *lying down*
decumbent, flat, flat on one's back, horizontal, level, procumbent, prone, prostrate, reclining, recumbent, stretched out; SEE CONCEPT 583

supine [*adj2*] *inactive*
do-nothing*, dormant, dull, idle, indolent, inert, lackadaisical, lax, lazy, lethargic, listless, motionless, passive, quiet, sedentary, slack, sleepy, slothful, sluggish, unoccupied, unresponsive; SEE CONCEPTS 401,560,584

supplant [*v*] *displace, replace*
back up, bounce, cast out, crowd, cut out, eject, expel, fill in, force, force out, front for, oust, outplace, overthrow, remove, ring, ring in, sit in, stand in, substitute, succeed, supersede, swap places with, take out, take over, take the place of, transfer, undermine, unseat, usurp; SEE CONCEPT 128

supple [*adj*] *bendable*
adaptable, agile, bending, ductile, elastic, flexible, graceful, limber, lissome, lithe, lithesome, malleable, moldable, plastic, pliable, pliant, resilient, rubber, springy, stretch, stretchy, svelte, willowy, wiry, yielding; SEE CONCEPTS 488,604

supplement [*n*] *something added*
added feature*, addendum, addition, additive, appendix, bell*, bells and whistles*, codicil, complement, continuation, extra, insert, option, postscript, pullout, rider, sequel, spin-off*, subsidiary; SEE CONCEPTS 270,824

supplement [*v*] *add to*
add fuel to fire*, augment, beef up*, build up, buttress, complement, complete, enhance, enrich, extend, fill out, fill up, fortify, heat up*, improve, increase, jazz up*, pad*, punch up*, reinforce, step up, strengthen, subsidize, supply, top; SEE CONCEPTS 236,244,245

supplementary [*adj*] *additional*
accompanying, added, ancillary, appended, augmenting, auxiliary, extra, increased, more; SEE CONCEPT 771

supplicate [*v*] *ask for, pray for*
appeal, beg, beseech, desire, petition, pray, put in for*, seek, solicit; SEE CONCEPT 53

supplies [*n*] *equipment, provisions*
food, foodstuffs, items, material, materials, necessities, provender, rations, raw materials, replenishments, stock, store, stores; SEE CONCEPTS 446,451,457

supply [*n*] *reserve of goods*
accumulation, amount, backlog, cache, fund, hoard, inventory, number, quantity, reservoir, source, stock, stockpile, store, surplus; SEE CONCEPT 712

supply [*v*] *furnish, provide, give a resource*
afford, cater, cater to, come across with*, come through*, come up with, contribute, deliver, dispense, drop, endow, equip, feed, fill, find, fix up, fulfill, give with, grant, hand, hand over, heel*, kick in*, minister, outfit, pony up*, produce, provide, provision, purvey, put out, put up, replenish, satisfy, stake, stock, store, transfer, turn over, victual, yield; SEE CONCEPTS 107,140

support [*n1*] *something that holds up structure*
abutment, agency, back, backing, base, bed, bedding, block, brace, buttress, collar, column, cornerstone, device, flotation, foothold, footing, foundation, fulcrum, groundwork, guide, hold, lining, means, medium, pillar, platform, pole, post, prop, rampart, reinforcement, rest, rib, rod, shore, stake, stanchion, stave, stay, stiffener, stilt, substratum, substructure, sustentation, timber, underpinning; SEE CONCEPTS 440,442,445, 471

support [*n2*] *help, approval*
aid, assist, assistance, backing, blessing, championship, comfort, encouragement, friendship, fur-

therance, hand, lift, loyalty, moral support, patronage, protection, relief, succor, sustenance; SEE CONCEPTS *10,110,388,712*

support [*n3*] *food, money, possessions for staying alive*
alimentation, alimony, allowance, care, keep, livelihood, living, maintenance, necessities, nutriment, payment, provision, relief, responsibility, stock, stores, subsidy, subsistence, sustenance, upkeep, victuals; SEE CONCEPTS *340,446,457,712*

support/supporter [*n4*] *person who helps another*
adherent, advocate, ally, angel*, apologist, backbone, backer, benefactor, champion, cohort, comforter, confederate, coworker, defender, disciple, endorser, espouser, exponent, expounder, fan, follower, friend, helper, mainstay, maintainer, partisan, patron, pillar, preserver, prop, proponent, satellite*, second, sponsor, stalwart, stay, subscriber, supporter, sustainer, tower of strength*, upholder, well-wisher*; SEE CONCEPT *423*

support [*v1*] *hold up*
base, be a foundation for, bear, bed, bolster, bottom, brace, buttress, carry, cradle, crutch, embed, found, ground, hold, keep from falling, keep up, mainstay, poise, prop, reinforce, shore, shore up, shoulder, stand, stay, strut, sustain, undergird, upbear, uphold; SEE CONCEPT *190*

support [*v2*] *take care of, provide for*
angel*, attend to, back, bankroll*, be a source of strength*, bring up, buoy up, care for, chaperon, cherish, earn one's keep, encourage, feed, finance, fortify, foster, fund, give a leg up*, guard, keep, keep an eye on*, look after, maintain, make a living, nourish, nurse, pay expenses of, pay for, pick up the check*, prop, put up money for*, raise, set up, sponsor, stake, stiffen, strengthen, stroke, subsidize, succor, sustain, underwrite, uphold; SEE CONCEPTS *7,19,22,140, 295,341*

support [*v3*] *defend, advocate belief*
abet, advance, agree with, aid, approve, assist, back, bear out, bolster, boost, boost morale, carry, champion, cheer, comfort, countenance, endorse, establish, forward, foster, get behind*, go along with, go to bat for*, help, hold, justify, keep up, maintain, plead for, promote, pull for, put forward, rally round, second, side with, stand behind, stand up for, stay, stick by*, stick up for*, substantiate, sustain, take one's side*, take the part of*, throw in one's lot with*, throw in with*, uphold, verify; SEE CONCEPTS *10,49,110*

support [*v4*] *endure*
abide, bear, bear with, brook, carry on, continue, countenance, go, go through, handle, keep up, live with*, maintain, put up with*, stand, stand for*, stay the course*, stick it out*, stomach*, submit, suffer, swallow*, sweat out*, take, tolerate, undergo, wait out; SEE CONCEPT *23*

suppose [*v1*] *assume, guess*
accept, admit, brainstorm, calculate, conjecture, cook up*, dare-say*, deem, divine, dream, estimate, expect, figure, go out on a limb*, grant, guess, guesstimate*, hazard a guess*, hypothesize, imagine, infer, judge, opine, posit, predicate, presume, presuppose, pretend, spark, speculate, surmise, suspect, take, take for

granted, theorize, think, understand; SEE CONCEPT *28*

suppose [*v2*] *believe*
assume, be afraid, conceive, conclude, conjecture, consider, deem, dream, expect, fancy, feel, gather, have a hunch*, have sneaking suspicion*, hypothesize, imagine, judge, postulate, pretend, reckon, regard, suspect, swear by, take, take as gospel truth*, take stock in*, think, understand, view; SEE CONCEPT *12*

supposition [*n*] *guess, belief*
apriorism, assumption, condition, conjecture, doubt, guessing, guesstimate*, guesswork, hunch, hypothesis, idea, likelihood, notion, opinion, posit, postulate, postulation, premise, presumption, presupposition, rough guess*, shot in the dark*, sneaking suspicion*, speculation, stab in the dark*, suppose, surmise, suspicion, theory, thesis, view; SEE CONCEPT *689*

suppress [*v*] *restrain, hold in check*
abolish, annihilate, beat down, bottle, bring to naught, burke, censor, check, clamp, conceal, conquer, contain, cover up, crack down on, crush, curb, cut off, extinguish, hold back, hold down, hold in, interrupt, keep in, keep secret, muffle, muzzle, overcome, overpower, overthrow, put an end to, put down, put kibosh on*, put lid on*, quash, quell, quench, repress, shush*, silence, sit on*, smother, snuff out*, spike, squash*, stamp out*, stifle, stop, subdue, trample, withhold; SEE CONCEPTS *121,130,252*

supremacy [*n*] *total domination*
absolute rule, ascendancy, authority, command, control, dominance, dominion, driver's seat*, paramountcy, power, predominance, preeminence, preponderance, prepotence, primacy, principality, sovereignty, superiority, supreme authority, sway, transcendence; SEE CONCEPTS *133,376*

supreme [*adj*] *greatest, principal*
absolute, best, cardinal, chief, closing, crowning, culminating, excellent, extreme, final, first, foremost, head, highest, incomparable, last, leading, marvelous, matchless, maximum, paramount, peerless, perfect, predominant, preeminent, prevailing, prime, sovereign, superb, superlative, surpassing, terminal, top, top-drawer*, towering, transcendent, ultimate, unequaled, unmatched, unparalleled, unsurpassable, unsurpassed, utmost; SEE CONCEPTS *568,574*

surcharge [*n*] *fee*
additional charge, cost, expense, extra, overcharge, overload, payment, price, surtax, tax; SEE CONCEPTS *329,344*

sure [*adj1*] *certain, definite*
abiding, assured, changeless, clear, confident, constant, convinced, convincing, decided, doubtless, enduring, firm, fixed, for a fact, free from doubt*, genuine, incontestable, incontrovertible, indisputable, indubitable, never-failing, persuaded, positive, real, satisfied, set, steadfast, steady, telling, unchangeable, unchanging, uncompromising, undeniable, unequivocal, unfailing, unfaltering, unqualified, unquestionable, unquestioning, unshakable, unshaken, unvarying, unwavering, valid; SEE CONCEPT *535*

sure [*adj2*] *physically stable*
fast, firm, fixed, safe, secure, solid, staunch, steady, strong; SEE CONCEPT *488*

sure [*adj3*] *inevitable*
assured, bound, certain, guaranteed, indisputable, ineluctable, inerrant, inescapable, infallible, irrevocable, surefire, unavoidable, unerring, unfailing; SEE CONCEPT *548*

sure [*adj4*] *self-confident*
arrogant, assured, certain, composed, confident, decided, decisive, positive, self-assured, self-possessed; SEE CONCEPT *401*

surely [*adv*] *without doubt*
absolutely, admittedly, assuredly, beyond doubt, beyond shadow of doubt*, certainly, clearly, come what may*, conclusively, decidedly, definitely, distinctly, doubtlessly, evidently, explicitly, fixedly, for certain, for real, indeed, indubitably, inevitably, inexorably, infallibly, irrefutably, manifestly, nothing else but, plainly, positively, rain or shine*, to be sure, undoubtedly, unequivocally, unerringly, unfailingly, unmistakably, unquestionably, unshakably, with certainty, without fail; SEE CONCEPT *535*

sure thing [*n*] *certainty*
all sewn up*, belief, cinch, definiteness, foregone conclusion, lock*, open and shut case*, positiveness, rain or shine*, safe bet, shoo-in*, small risk, sure bet*, surefire*, surety; SEE CONCEPTS *638,725*

surface [*adj*] *external*
apparent, covering, depthless, exterior, facial, outer, outside, outward, shallow, shoal, superficial, top; SEE CONCEPTS *485,583*

surface [*n*] *external part of something*
area, cover, covering, expanse, exterior, exteriority, externality, facade, face, facet, level, obverse, outside, peel, periphery, plane, rind, side, skin, stretch, superficiality, superficies, top, veneer; SEE CONCEPT *484*

surface [*v*] *come to the top of*
appear, arise, come to light, come up, crop up, emerge, flare up, materialize, rise, transpire; SEE CONCEPTS *166,716*

surfeit [*n*] *excess*
bellyful*, excess, glut*, overabundance, overflow, overfullness, overindulgence, overkill, overmuch, overplus, plenitude, plethora, profusion, remainder, repletion, satiety, satisfaction, saturation, superabundance, superfluity, surplus, up to here*; SEE CONCEPT *740*

surfeit [*v*] *overfill*
cloy, cram, eat, fill, glut, gorge, jade, overfeed, overindulge, pall, sate, satiate, satisfy, stuff; SEE CONCEPTS *209,740*

surge [*n*] *rush, usually of liquid*
billow, breaker, deluge, efflux, flood, flow, growth, gush, intensification, outpouring, rise, roll, surf, swell, upsurge, wave; SEE CONCEPTS *432,467,787*

surge [*v*] *rush, usually in liquid form*
arise, billow, climb, deluge, eddy, flow, grow, gush, heave, mount, pour, ripple, rise, roll, sluice, stream, swell, swirl, tower, undulate, well forth; SEE CONCEPTS *146,179*

surly [*adj*] *gruff, bearish*
boorish, brusque, churlish, cross, crusty, curmudgeonly, discourteous, dour, fractious, glum, grouchy, ill-mannered, ill-natured, irritable, morose, perverse, rude, saturnine, sulky, sullen, testy, ugly, uncivil, ungracious; SEE CONCEPT *401*

surmise [*n*] *guess, conclusion*
assumption, attempt, conjecture, deduction, guesstimate*, guesswork, hunch, hypothesis, idea, inference, notion, opinion, possibility, presumption, sneaking suspicion*, speculation, supposition, suspicion, theory, thought; SEE CONCEPTS *529,689*

surmise [*v*] *come to a conclusion*
assume, conclude, conjecture, consider, deduce, fancy, guess, guesstimate*, hazard a guess*, hypothesize, imagine, infer, opine, presume, pretend, regard, risk assuming, speculate, suppose, suspect, take a shot*, take a stab*, theorize, think, venture a guess; SEE CONCEPTS *18,28*

surmount [*v*] *overcome, triumph over*
best, better, cap, clear, conquer, crest, crown, defeat, down, exceed, hurdle, leap, lick*, negotiate, outdo, outstrip, over, overpower, overtop, pass, prevail over, rise above, subdue, surpass, throw*, top*, vanquish, vault; SEE CONCEPTS *95,141*

surname [*n*] *family name*
cognomen, last name, matronymic, metronymic, patronymic; SEE CONCEPTS *268,683*

surpass [*v*] *outdo something or someone*
beat, best, better, cap, eclipse, exceed, excel, go beyond, go one better*, improve upon, outdistance, outgo, outmatch, outpace, outperform, outrank, outrival, outrun, outshine, outstep, outstrip, outweigh, override, overshadow, overstep, pass, put to shame*, rank*, surmount, top, tower, tower above*, transcend, trump*; SEE CONCEPT *141*

surplus [*adj*] *extra*
de trop, excess, in excess, leftover, odd*, over, remaining, spare, superfluent, superfluous, supernumerary, too much, unused; SEE CONCEPTS *560,781,824*

surplus [*n*] *extra material*
balance, excess, overage, overflow, overkill, overmuch, overrun, overstock, oversupply, plethora, plus, remainder, residue, something extra, superabundance, superfluity, surfeit, surplusage, the limit, too much; SEE CONCEPTS *260,658,824*

surprise [*n*] *something amazing; state of amazement*
abruptness, amazement, astonishment, astoundment, attack, awe, bewilderment, bombshell*, consternation, curiosity, curveball*, disappointment, disillusion, eye-opener*, fortune, godsend*, incredulity, jolt*, kick*, marvel, miracle, miscalculation, phenomenon, portent, precipitance, precipitation, precipitousness, prodigy, rarity, revelation, shock, start, stupefaction, suddenness, thunderbolt*, unexpected, unforeseen, whammy*, wonder, wonderment; SEE CONCEPTS *410,529*

surprise [*v1*] *astonish; cause amazement*
amaze, astound, awe, bewilder, blow away*, bowl over*, cause wonder, confound, confuse, consternate, daze, dazzle, discomfit, disconcert, dismay, dumbfound, electrify, flabbergast, floor, jar, jolt, leave aghast, leave open-mouthed, nonplus, overwhelm, perplex, petrify, rattle, rock, shake up, shock, spring something on, stagger, startle, strike dumb*, strike with awe, stun, stupefy, take aback, take one's breath away*, throw a curve*, unsettle; SEE CONCEPT *42*

surprise [*v2*] *sneak up on; catch*
ambush, burst in on, bushwhack*, capture, catch

in the act*, catch off-balance*, catch off-guard*, catch red-handed*, catch unawares*, come down on, discover, drop in on, grab, grasp, lay for, lie in wait*, nab, seize, spring on, startle, take, take by surprise, waylay; SEE CONCEPTS *42,86*

surprising [*adj*] *unexpected*
accidental, amazing, astonishing, chance, electrifying, extraordinary, fortuitous, from left field*, impulsive, out of the blue*, remarkable, shocking, startling, stunning, sudden, unanticipated, unforeseen, unpredictable, unpredicted, without warning, wonderful; SEE CONCEPTS *544,548*

surrender [*n*] *giving up; resignation*
abandonment, abdication, acquiescence, appeasement, capitulation, cessation, dedition, delivery, giving way, relenting, relinquishment, renunciation, submission, succumbing, white flag*, yielding; SEE CONCEPTS *67,108,119,320*

surrender [*v*] *give up; resign*
abandon, buckle under*, capitulate, cave in*, cede, commit, concede, consign, cry uncle*, deliver up, eat crow*, eat humble pie*, entrust, fall, fold, forego, give in, go along with, go down, go under, hand over, knuckle, knuckle under*, leave, let go, pack it in*, part with, play dead*, put up white flag*, quit, relinquish, renounce, roll over*, submit, succumb, throw in the towel*, toss it in*, waive, yield; SEE CONCEPTS *67,108,119,320*

surreptitious [*adj*] *sneaky, secret*
clandestine, covert, fraudulent, furtive, hidden, hole-and-corner*, hush-hush*, on the QT*, on the sly*, private, skulking, slinking, sly, sneaking, stealthy, sub-rosa, unauthorized, undercover, underhand, under-the-table*, under wraps*, veiled; SEE CONCEPT *548*

surrogate [*n*] *person or thing that acts as substitute*
agent, alternate, backup, delegate, deputy, expediency, expedient, fill-in, makeshift, pinch hitter*, proxy, recourse, refuge, replacement, representative, resort, resource, stand-in, stopgap*, sub*; SEE CONCEPTS *348,414,423*

surround [*v*] *enclose, encircle something*
beleaguer, beset, besiege, blockade, border, bound, box in, circle, circumscribe, circumvent, close around, close in, close in on, compass, confine, edge, enclave, encompass, envelop, environ, fence in, fringe, gird, girdle, go around, hem in, inundate, invest, lay siege to, limit, loop, margin, outline, rim, ring, round, shut in, skirt, verge; SEE CONCEPT *758*

surroundings [*n*] *environment*
ambience, atmosphere, background, climate, community, environs, home, location, medium, milieu, neighborhood, setting, vicinity; SEE CONCEPTS *198,673*

surveillance [*n*] *close observation, following*
body mike*, bug*, bugging*, care, control, direction, eagle eye*, examination, eye, inspection, lookout, peeled eye*, scrutiny, spying, stakeout, superintendence, supervision, surveyance, tab*, tail*, tap*, track*, vigil, vigilance, watch, wiretap; SEE CONCEPTS *103,298,749*

survey [*n*] *scrutiny, examination*
analysis, aperçu, audit, check, compendium, critique, digest, inquiry, inspection, outline, overview, pandect, perlustration, perusal, precis, review, sample, scan, sketch, study, syllabus, view; SEE CONCEPTS *37,103,197,271,291*

survey [*v*] *scrutinize, take stock of*
appraise, assay, assess, canvass, case, check, check out, check over, check up, contemplate, estimate, evaluate, examine, give the once over*, inspect, look over, look upon, measure, observe, overlook, oversee, plan, plot, prospect, rate, read, reconnoiter, research, review, scan, scope, scrutinize, set at, size, size up, stake out, study, summarize, superintend, supervise, take stock of*, test the waters*, valuate, value, view; SEE CONCEPTS *37,48,103,197,291*

survive [*v*] *continue to live*
bear, be extant, be left, carry on, carry through, come through, cut it, endure, exist, get on, get through, go all the way*, go the limit*, handle, hold out, keep, keep afloat, last, live, live down, live on, live out, live through, make a comeback*, make the cut*, outlast, outlive, outwear, persevere, persist, pull out of it*, pull through, recover, remain, remain alive, revive, ride out*, see through, stand up, subsist, suffer, sustain, tough it out*, weather, withstand; SEE CONCEPTS *23,239,407*

susceptible [*adj*] *exposed, naive*
affected, aroused, be taken in, disposed, easily moved, easy, fall for, given, gullible, impressed, impressible, impressionable, inclined, influenced, liable, mark, movable, nonresistant, obnoxious, open, out on a limb*, persuadable, predisposed, prone, pushover, ready, receptive, responsive, roused, sensible, sensile, sensitive, sentient, sitting duck*, soft, stirred, subject, sucker*, suggestible, susceptive, swallow, swayed, tender, touched, tumble for*, vulnerable, wide open; SEE CONCEPTS *403,542*

suspect [*adj*] *doubtful*
doubtable, dubious, fishy*, incredible, open, problematic, pseudo*, questionable, ridiculous, shaky*, suspected, suspicious, thick*, thin*, unbelievable, uncertain, unclear, unlikely, unsure; SEE CONCEPTS *529,582*

suspect [*v*] *distrust; guess*
assume, be afraid, believe, conceive, conclude, conjecture, consider, disbelieve, doubt, expect, feel, gather, harbor suspicion*, have a hunch*, have doubt, have sneaking suspicion*, hazard a guess*, hold, imagine, mistrust, presume, reckon, smell a rat*, speculate, suppose, surmise, think, think probable, understand, wonder; SEE CONCEPTS *21,28*

suspend [*v1*] *hang from above*
append, attach, be pendent, dangle, depend, hang down, hang up, hook up, sling, swing, wave; SEE CONCEPTS *181,190*

suspend [*v2*] *delay, hold off*
adjourn, arrest, bar, break up, can, cease, check, count out, cut short, debar, defer, discontinue, eject, eliminate, exclude, file, halt, hang, hang fire*, hang up, hold up, inactivate, intermit, interrupt, lay aside, lay off, lay on the table*, lay over, omit, pigeonhole*, pink-slip*, postpone, procrastinate, prorogue, protract, put an end to, put a stop to, put off, put on back burner*, put on hold, put on ice*, put on the shelf*, reject, retard, rule out, shelve, stave off, stay, waive, withhold; SEE CONCEPTS *119,121,130,351*

suspense [*n*] *anticipation*
anxiety, apprehension, chiller*, cliff-hanger*, cloak and dagger*, confusion, dilemma, doubt, eagerness, expectancy, expectation, grabber*,

hesitancy, hesitation, impatience, indecision, indecisiveness, insecurity, irresolution, page-turner*, perplexity, potboiler*, tension, thriller*, uncertainty, wavering; SEE CONCEPTS *410,679*

suspension [*n*] *delay*
abeyance, abeyancy, adjournment, break, breather*, breathing spell*, cessation, coffee break*, concluding, conclusion, cutoff, deferment, disbarment, discontinuation, discontinuing, doldrums, dormancy, downtime*, end, ending, finish, five*, freeze, halt, heave-ho*, intermission, interruption, latency, layoff, letup, moratorium, pause, period, postponement, quiescence, quiescency, remission, respite, stay, stoppage, suspense, ten*, termination, time-out; SEE CONCEPTS *119,807,832*

suspicion [*n1*] *doubt*
bad vibes*, chariness, conjecture, cynicism, distrust, dubiety, dubiosity, funny feeling*, guess, guesswork, gut feeling*, hunch, idea, impression, incertitude, incredulity, jealousy, lack of confidence, misgiving, mistrust, nonbelief, notion, qualm, skepticism, sneaking suspicion*, supposition, surmise, uncertainty, wariness, wonder; SEE CONCEPTS *532,689,690*

suspicion [*n2*] *hint, trace*
cast, glimmer, intimation, shade, shadow, smell, soupçon, strain, streak, suggestion, tinge, touch, whiff; SEE CONCEPTS *529,831*

suspicious [*adj1*] *distrustful*
apprehensive, cagey, careful, cautious, doubtful, green-eyed*, incredulous, in doubt, jealous, leery, mistrustful, not born yesterday* on the lookout*, questioning, quizzical, skeptical, suspect, suspecting, unbelieving, uptight*, wary, watchful, without belief, without faith, wondering; SEE CONCEPTS *403,542*

suspicious [*adj2*] *doubtful, fishy*
borderline, debatable, different, disputable, doubtable, dubious, equivocal, farfetched, funny*, irregular, not kosher*, open, open to doubt, open to question, out of line*, overt, peculiar, phony, problematic, queer, questionable, reaching, rings untrue*, shady, shaky*, suspect, too much*, uncertain, uncommon, unsure, unusual, won't wash*; SEE CONCEPTS *529,564*

sustain [*v1*] *keep up, maintain*
aid, approve, assist, back, bankroll, bear, befriend, bolster, brace, buoy, buttress, carry, comfort, confirm, continue, convey, defend, endorse, favor, feed, foster, go for, help, keep alive, keep from falling, keep going, lend a hand*, lug, nourish, nurse, nurture, pack, preserve, prolong, prop, protract, provide for, ratify, relieve, save, shore up, stand by, stick up for, supply, support, tote, transfer, transport, uphold, validate, verify; SEE CONCEPTS *110,140,190*

sustain [*v2*] *endure, experience*
abide, bear, bear up under, bear with, brook, digest, encounter, feel, go, hang in, have, know, live with*, put up with*, see, stand*, stand up to, stomach*, suffer, take it, tolerate, undergo, withstand; SEE CONCEPTS *23,678*

sustenance [*n*] *necessities for existence*
aid, aliment, bacon*, bread*, bread and butter*, comestible, daily bread*, eatables, edibles, food, keep, livelihood, maintenance, nourishment, nutrition, pap*, provender, provision, ration, refreshment, salt*, subsistence, support, victual, wherewithal; SEE CONCEPTS *340,446,457,709*

svelte [*adj*] *thin and well-built*
graceful, lean, lissom, lithe, slender, slinky, smooth, sylphlike, willowy; SEE CONCEPTS *490,491*

swagger [*v*] *show off; walk pompously*
bluster, boast, brag, brandish, bully, cock, flourish, gasconade, gloat, grandstand*, hector, look big*, lord, parade, parade one's wares*, peacock*, play to the crowd*, pontificate, prance, put on, put on airs*, sashay*, saunter, strut, swank*, swashbuckle*, sway, sweep, swell; SEE CONCEPTS *49,149,716*

swallow [*v1*] *consume*
absorb, belt*, bolt*, chugalug*, devour, dispatch, dispose, down, drink, drop, eat, gobble, gulp, imbibe, ingest, ingurgitate, inhale, put away, quaff, sip, slurp, swig, swill, take, toss, wash down*, wolf; SEE CONCEPT *169*

swallow [*v2*] *believe without much thought*
accept, be naive, buy, fall for; SEE CONCEPT *12*

swami [*n*] *religious teacher*
guiding light*, guru, master, mentor, mystic, sage, teacher, yogi; SEE CONCEPT *350*

swamp [*n*] *wet land covered with vegetation*
bog, bottoms, everglade, fen, glade, holm, marsh, marshland, mire, moor, morass, mud, muskeg, peat bog, polder, quag, quagmire, slough, swale, swampland; SEE CONCEPT *509*

swamp [*v*] *overwhelm, flood*
beset, besiege, crowd, drench, drown, engulf, inundate, overcrowd, overflow, overload, satiate, saturate, sink, snow*, submerge, submerse, surfeit, swallow up, upset, wash, waterlog, whelm; SEE CONCEPTS *146,179,641*

swank/swanky [*adj*] *plush, stylish*
chichi*, classy, deluxe, exclusive, expensive, fancy, fashionable, flamboyant, flashy, glamorous, grand, lavish, luxurious, ostentatious, peacocky, plushy*, posh, pretentious, rich, ritzy*, sharp, showy, smart, snappy, splashy, sumptuous, tony*, trendy, with-it*; SEE CONCEPT *589*

swan song [*n*] *final appearance or performance*
adieu, climax, closer*, conclusion, crowning achievement, crowning glory*, culmination, end piece, finis, goodbye, last act, last hurrah, peroration, windup*; SEE CONCEPT *832*

swap/swop [*v*] *exchange*
bandy, bargain, barter, change, interchange, substitute, switch, trade, traffic, truck; SEE CONCEPT *104*

swarm [*n*] *large, moving group*
army, bevy, blowout, concourse, covey, crowd, crush, drove, flock, herd, horde, host, jam, mass, mob, multitude, myriad, pack, press, push, school, shoal, throng, troop, turnout; SEE CONCEPTS *397,417,432*

swarm [*v*] *move forward as a group*
abound, be alive, be numerous, cluster, congregate, crawl, crowd, flock, flow, gather, gather like bees*, jam, mass, mob, move in a crowd, overrun, pullulate, rush together, stream, teem, throng; SEE CONCEPTS *113,114,159*

swarthy [*adj*] *dark-complexioned*
black, brown, brunet, dark, dark-hued, darkish, dark-skinned, dusky, swart, tan, tawny; SEE CONCEPT *618*

swat [*v*] *hit*
beat, belt, biff, box, buffet, clobber, clout, cuff,

ding, knock, slap, slug, smack, smash, sock, strike, wallop, whack; SEE CONCEPT *189*

sway [*n*] *strong influence*
amplitude, authority, clout, command, control, dominion, empire, expanse, government, jurisdiction, mastery, might, power, predominance, range, reach, regime, reign, rule, run, scope, sovereignty, spread, stretch, sweep; SEE CONCEPTS *376,687*

sway [*v1*] *move back and forth*
bend, blow hot and cold*, careen, fluctuate, hem and haw*, incline, lean, lurch, oscillate, pendulate, pulsate, rock, roll, stagger, swagger, swing, undulate, vibrate, wave, waver, weave, wobble, yo-yo*; SEE CONCEPTS *13,145,151*

sway [*v2*] *influence, affect*
bias, brainwash, carry, conduct, control, crack*, direct, dispose, dominate, get*, govern, guide, hold sway over, hook, impact on, impress, incline, induce, inspire, lead by the nose*, manage, move, overrule, persuade, predispose, prevail on, put across, reign, rule, rule over, sell*, soften up*, strike, suck in*, touch, turn one's head*, twist one's arm*, whitewash*, win over, work on; SEE CONCEPTS *14,68,117*

swear [*v1*] *declare under oath*
affirm, assert, attest, avow, covenant, cross one's heart*, depend on, depose, give one's word*, give witness, have confidence in, maintain, make an affidavit, pledge oneself, plight, promise, rely on, say so*, state, state under oath, swear by, swear to God*, swear up and down*, take an oath, testify, trust, vouch, vow, warrant; SEE CONCEPT *49*

swear [*v2*] *speak profanely; be vulgar*
bedamn, be foul-mouthed, blaspheme, curse, cuss*, execrate, flame*, imprecate, take name in vain*, talk dirty*, use bad language*, utter profanity; SEE CONCEPTS *52,54*

swear by [*v*] *be certain, recommend*
advocate, back, bank on, believe in, be satisfied with, compliment, depend on it, endorse, go on the record for*, have faith in, plug*, praise, put in a good word*, speak highly of, speak well of, stand by, suggest, think highly of, vouch for; SEE CONCEPTS *10,75*

swearing [*n*] *foul language*
bad language*, blasphemy, cursing, cuss*, cussing*, dirty language*, dirty name*, dirty talk*, dirty word*, execration, expletives, four-letter word*, imprecation, malediction, no-no*, profanity, swearword; SEE CONCEPTS *54,276,278*

sweat [*n1*] *body's perspiring*
diaphoresis, excretion, exudation, perspiration, steam, transudation; SEE CONCEPTS *185,467*

sweat [*n2*] *hard work*
backbreaker*, chore, drudgery, effort, grind, labor, moil, slavery, task, toil, travail, work; SEE CONCEPTS *362,677*

sweat [*v1*] *perspire*
break out in a sweat, drip, eject, exude, glow, ooze, secrete, seep, spout, swelter, transude, wilt; SEE CONCEPT *185*

sweat [*v2*] *worry about; bear*
abide, agonize, be on pins and needles*, be on tenterhooks*, brook, chafe, endure, exert, fret, go, labor, lose sleep over*, stand, stay the course*, stick it out*, stomach*, suffer, take, toil, tolerate, torture, work hard; SEE CONCEPTS *23,35*

sweaty [*adj*] *damp with perspiration*
bathed, clammy, covered with sweat, drenched, dripping, drippy, glowing, hot, moist, perspiring, perspiry, soaked, sticky, stinky, sweating, wet; SEE CONCEPT *406*

sweep [*n1*] *range, extent*
ambit, breadth, compass, extension, latitude, length, orbit, purview, radius, reach, region, scope, span, stretch, vista; SEE CONCEPTS *651,756,788*

sweep [*n2*] *movement*
arc, bend, course, curve, gesture, move, play, progress, stroke, swing; SEE CONCEPTS *145,748*

sweep [*v1*] *brush off, away*
broom, brush, brush up, clean, clear, clear up, mop, ready, remove, scrub, tidy, vacuum; SEE CONCEPT *165*

sweep [*v2*] *fly, glide*
career, fleet, flit, flounce, glance, hurtle, pass, sail, scud, skim, tear, wing, zoom; SEE CONCEPTS *150,152*

sweeping [*adj*] *wide-ranging*
across-the-board, all-around, all-embracing, all-encompassing, all-inclusive, all-out, bird's-eye*, blanket, broad, complete, comprehensive, exaggerated, exhaustive, extensive, full, general, global, inclusive, indiscriminate, out-and-out*, overall, overdrawn, overstated, radical, thorough, thorough-going, unqualified, vast, wall-to-wall*, whole-hog*, wholesale*, wide; SEE CONCEPTS *531,772*

sweet [*adj1*] *sugary*
candied, candy-coated, cloying, delicious, honeyed, like candy, like honey, luscious, nectarous, saccharine, sugar-coated, sugared, sweetened, syrupy, toothsome; SEE CONCEPTS *462,613*

sweet [*adj2*] *friendly, kind*
affectionate, agreeable, amiable, angelic, appealing, attractive, beautiful, beloved, charming, cherished, companionable, considerate, darling, dear, dearest, delectable, delicious, delightful, dulcet, engaging, fair, generous, gentle, good-humored, good-natured, heavenly, lovable, loving, luscious, mild, mushy, patient, pet, pleasant, pleasing, precious, reasonable, saccharine, sweet-tempered, sympathetic, taking, tender, thoughtful, treasured, unselfish, winning, winsome; SEE CONCEPTS *401,404,542*

sweet [*adj3*] *nice-smelling*
ambrosial, aromal, aromatic, balmy, clean, fragrant, fresh, new, perfumed, perfumy, pure, redolent, savory, scented, spicy, sweet-smelling, wholesome; SEE CONCEPT *598*

sweet [*adj4*] *nice-sounding*
dulcet, euphonic, euphonious, harmonious, mellifluous, mellow, melodic, melodious, musical, orotund, rich, rotund, silver-tongued, silvery, smooth, soft, sonorous, soothing, sweet-sounding, tuneful; SEE CONCEPT *594*

sweet [*n*] *sugary food*
bonbon, candy, chocolate, confection, confectionery, confiture, delight, dessert, enjoyment, final course, gratification, joy, pleasure, pudding, snack, sugarplum, sweetmeat; SEE CONCEPTS *457,461*

sweeten [*v1*] *add sugar*
add sweetening, candy, candy-coat, honey, make sweet, make toothsome, mull, sugar, sugar-coat; SEE CONCEPT *170*

SU
SW

sweeten [v2] *make happy; appease*
alleviate, assuage, conciliate, mollify, pacify, placate, propitiate, soften up, soothe; SEE CONCEPTS *7,22*

sweetheart [n] *person whom another loves*
admirer, beau, beloved, boyfriend, companion, darling, dear, dear one, flame, girlfriend, heartthrob, honey*, inamorata, inamorato, love, lovebird*, lover, one and only*, paramour, pet, significant other, steady*, suitor, swain, sweet, treasure*, truelove, valentine; SEE CONCEPTS *414,423*

swell [adj] *wonderful*
awesome, cool*, dandy*, deluxe, desirable, excellent, exclusive, fashionable, fine, fly*, grand, groovy*, keen, marvelous, neat, nifty, plush, posh, ritzy*, smart, stylish, super, terrific; SEE CONCEPTS *548,574*

swell [n] *large increase, flow*
billow, crescendo, growth, ripple, rise, seat, surf, surge, undulation, uprise, wave; SEE CONCEPT *780*

swell [v] *become larger*
accumulate, add to, aggravate, amplify, augment, balloon, become bloated, become distended, become swollen, be inflated, belly, billow, blister, bloat, bulge, dilate, distend, enhance, enlarge, expand, extend, fatten, fill out, grow, grow larger, heighten, increase, intensity, mount, plump, pouch, pout, protrude, puff, puff up, rise, round out, surge, tumefy, uprise, well up; SEE CONCEPTS *236,245,780*

swelling [n] *physical growth; lump*
abscess, blister, boil, bruise, bulge, bump, bunion, carbuncle, contusion, corn, dilation, distention, enlargement, hump, increase, inflammation, injury, knob, knurl, node, nodule, pimple, pock, protuberance, puff, puffiness, pustule, ridge, sore, tumescence, tumor, wale, wart, weal, welt; SEE CONCEPTS *306,309*

sweltering [adj] *very hot*
airless, baking, broiling, burning, close, fiery, humid, oppressive, perspiring, scorching, sizzling, stewing, sticky, stifling, stuffy, sultry, sweaty, sweltry, torrid; SEE CONCEPT *605*

swerve [v] *turn aside, often to avoid collision*
bend, deflect, depart, depart from, deviate, dip, diverge, err, get off course, go off course, incline, lurch, move, sheer, sheer off, shift, sideslip, sidestep, skew, skid, slue, stray, swing, tack, train off, turn, veer, wander, waver, wind; SEE CONCEPTS *150,195,201*

swift [adj] *very fast*
abrupt, alacritous, barrelling, breakneck, cracking*, double-quick*, expeditious, express, fleet, fleet-footed*, flying, hasty, headlong, hurried, in nothing flat*, like crazy*, like mad*, nimble, on the double*, precipitate, prompt, pronto, quick, rapid, ready, screaming, shaking a leg*, short, short-lived, snappy*, spanking*, speedball*, speedy, sudden, supersonic, unexpected, winged*; SEE CONCEPTS *588,799*

swiftly/swift [adv] *very fast*
apace, double-quick*, expeditiously, flat-out*, fleetly, full tilt*, hastily, hurriedly, in no time*, posthaste, promptly, quick, quickly, rapidly, speedily, without losing time*, without warning*; SEE CONCEPTS *588,799*

swim [v] *make way through water using arms, legs*
bathe, breast-stroke, crawl, dive, dog paddle, float, freestyle, glide, go for a swim, go swimming, go wading, high-dive, move, paddle, practice, race, skinny-dip*, slip, stroke, submerge, take a dip, wade; SEE CONCEPT *363*

swimmingly [adv] *very well*
as planned, cosily, easily, effectively, effortlessly, favorably, fortunately, happily, like a dream*, like clockwork*, prosperously, quickly, satisfyingly, smoothly, successfully, well, with flying colors*, with no trouble, without a hitch*; SEE CONCEPTS *528,544*

swimsuit [n] *bathing suit*
bathing costume, beach costume, beachwear, bikini, jams, maillot, one-piece, swimwear, thong, trunks, two-piece; SEE CONCEPT *451*

swindle [n] *cheating, stealing*
blackmail, cheat, con, crooked deal*, deceit, deception, dirty pool*, double-cross*, double-dealing*, extortion, fake, fast one*, fast shuffle*, frame-up, fraud, hoax, hustle, imposture, knavery, racket*, rip-off*, scam, sell, shady deal*, shakedown, sham, sharp practice*, shell game*, sting, trick, trickery; SEE CONCEPTS *59,139,192*

swindle [v] *cheat, steal*
bamboozle, beat*, bilk, clip*, con*, cozen, deceive, defraud, diddle*, do*, dupe, extort, fleece*, flimflam*, fool, frame*, fudge*, gouge*, gull*, hoodwink, overcharge, pluck, pull a fast one*, put one over on*, rip off*, rook, run a game on*, sandbag, scam, sell a bill of goods*, set up, shaft, stiff*, sting*, sucker, take for a ride*, take to the cleaners*, trick, trim*, victimize; SEE CONCEPTS *59,139,192*

swindler [n] *person who cheats another*
absconder, charlatan, cheat, cheater, chiseler, clip, con artist, confidence artist, counterfeiter, crook, deceiver, defrauder, dodger, double-dealer, falsifier, forger, four-flusher*, fraud, gouger, grifter, impostor, mechanic, mountebank, operator, rascal, rook, scammer, scoundrel, shark, sharp, sharper, slicker, thief, trickster; SEE CONCEPT *412*

swing [n] *moving back and forth*
beat, cadence, cadency, fluctuation, lilt, measure, meter, motion, oscillation, rhythm, stroke, sway, swaying, tempo, undulation, vibration; SEE CONCEPTS *65,748*

swing [v] *move back and forth; be suspended*
avert, away, be pendent, curve, dangle, deflect, divert, flap, fluctuate, hang, lurch, oscillate, palpitate, pendulate, pitch, pivot, reel, revolve, rock, roll, rotate, sheer, shunt, suspend, sway, swerve, swivel, turn, turn about, turn on an axis, twirl, undulate, vary, veer, vibrate, volte-face, wag, waggle, wave, wheel, whirl, wiggle, wobble; SEE CONCEPT *145*

swipe [n/v1] *hit*
bash, blow, clip, clout, clump, cuff, knock, lash out, lick, rap, slap, smack, sock, strike, swat, wallop, wipe; SEE CONCEPT *189*

swipe [v2] *steal*
appropriate, cop, filch, heist, hook, lift, make off with, nab, nick, pilfer, pinch, purloin, sneak, snitch; SEE CONCEPT *139*

swirl [v] *spin around*
agitate, boil, churn, coil, crimp, crisp, curl, eddy,

purl, roil, roll, snake, surge, swoosh*, twirl, whirl, whirlpool, whorl, wriggle; SEE CONCEPTS *145,738*

swish [*adj*] *fashionable, elegant*
classy, deluxe, exclusive, grand, in, plush, posh, ritzy*, smart, stylish, sumptuous, swank, swell, tony*, trendy, with-it*; SEE CONCEPT *589*

switch [*n*] *change, exchange*
about-face, alteration, change of direction, reversal, shift, substitution, swap, transformation; SEE CONCEPT *697*

switch [*v*] *change, exchange*
change course, convert, deflect, deviate, divert, interchange, rearrange, replace, shift, shunt, sidetrack, substitute, swap, trade, turn, turnabout, turn aside, veer; SEE CONCEPTS *104,232,697*

swivel [*v*] *spin around axis*
hinge, pirouette, pivot, revolve, rotate, swing around, turn, whirl; SEE CONCEPT *145*

swollen [*adj*] *enlarged*
bloated, bulgy, distended, distent, inflamed, inflated, puffed, puffy, tumescent, tumid; SEE CONCEPT *485*

swoon [*v*] *faint*
become unconscious, be overcome, black out, collapse, drop, feel giddy, feel lightheaded, go out like a light*, keel over, lose consciousness, pass out, weaken; SEE CONCEPTS *303,308*

swoop [*v*] *descend quickly*
dive, fall, plummet, plunge, pounce, rush, slide, stoop, sweep; SEE CONCEPTS *150,181*

sycophant [*n*] *person who caters to another*
adulator, backscratcher*, backslapper*, bootlicker*, brownnoser*, doormat*, fan, fawner, flatterer, flunky*, groupie*, groveler, handshaker*, hanger-on*, lackey, minion, parasite, politician, puppet, slave; SEE CONCEPT *423*

syllabus [*n*] *summary*
apercu, capitulation, conspectus, curriculum, outline, program, review, rundown, schedule, sketch, synopsis; SEE CONCEPT *283*

symbol [*n*] *letter, character, sign of written communication*
attribute, badge, denotation, design, device, emblem, figure, image, indication, logo, mark, motif, note, numeral, pattern, regalia, representation, stamp, token, type; SEE CONCEPT *284*

symbolic [*adj*] *representative*
allegorical, characteristic, denotative, emblematic, figurative, indicative, indicatory, significant, suggestive, symptomatic, token, typical; SEE CONCEPT *267*

symbolize [*v*] *represent; stand for*
betoken, body forth, connote, denote, emblematize, embody, epitomize, exemplify, express, illustrate, indicate, mean, mirror, personify, show, signify, suggest, symbol, typify; SEE CONCEPTS *74,138,682*

symmetrical [*adj*] *well-proportioned*
balanced, commensurable, commensurate, equal, in proportion, proportional, regular, shapely, well-formed; SEE CONCEPTS *480,485,579*

symmetry [*n*] *proportion*
agreement, arrangement, balance, centrality, conformity, correspondence, equality, equilibrium, equipoise, equivalence, evenness, finish, form, harmony, order, proportionality, regularity, rhythm, shapeliness, similarity; SEE CONCEPTS *716,717*

sympathetic [*adj1*] *concerned, feeling*
affectionate, all heart*, appreciating, benign, benignant, caring, commiserating, compassionate, comprehending, condoling, considerate, having heart in right place*, interested, kind, kindhearted, kindly, loving, pitying, responsive, sensitive, soft, softhearted, supportive, sympathizing, tender, thoughtful, understanding, vicarious, warm, warmhearted; SEE CONCEPT *542*

sympathetic [*adj2*] *agreeable, friendly*
amenable, appreciative, approving, companionable, compatible, congenial, congruous, consistent, consonant, cool, down, encouraging, favorably disposed, having a heart*, in sympathy with, like-minded, on same wavelength*, open, open-minded, pro*, receptive, responsive, simpatico, tuned in*, vicarious, well-disposed, well-intentioned; SEE CONCEPTS *401,542,563*

sympathize [*v*] *feel for, be compassionate*
ache, agree, appreciate, be in accord, be in sympathy, be kind to, be there for*, be understanding, bleed for*, comfort, commiserate, compassionate, comprehend, condole, emphathize, feel heart go out to*, go along with, grieve with, have compassion, identify with, love, offer consolation, pick up on, pity, relate to*, share another's sorrow, show kindliness, show mercy, show tenderness, side with*, tune in*, understand; SEE CONCEPTS *34,110*

sympathy [*n1*] *shared feeling*
accord, affinity, agreement, alliance, attraction, benignancy, close relation, commiseration, compassion, concord, congeniality, connection, correspondence, empathy, feelings, fellow feeling, harmony, heart, kindliness, kindness, mutual attraction, mutual fondness, rapport, responsiveness, sensitivity, tenderness, understanding, union, unity, warmheartedness, warmth; SEE CONCEPTS *388,410,664*

sympathy [*n2*] *pity*
aid, cheer, comfort, commiseration, compassion, condolence, consolation, empathy, encouragement, reassurance, rue, ruth, solace, tenderness, thoughtfulness, understanding; SEE CONCEPTS *410,633*

symposium [*n*] *conference*
colloquium, convention, discussion, discussion group, forum, gabfest*, huddle, meeting, panel discussion, parley, powwow, rap session, round table, seminar, talk; SEE CONCEPTS *56,324,386*

symptom [*n*] *sign of illness or problem*
evidence, expression, index, indication, indicia, manifestation, mark, note, significant, syndrome, token, warning; SEE CONCEPTS *306,316*

symptomatic [*adj*] *indicative*
associated, characteristic, demonstrative, denotative, denotive, designative, emblematic, evidential, indicating, pointing to, significant, suggestive, symbolic; SEE CONCEPT *267*

synagogue [*n*] *church*
abbey, cathedral, chapel, house of God, house of prayer, house of worship, mosque, parish, shrine, shul, tabernacle, temple; SEE CONCEPTS *368,449*

synchronize [*v*] *coordinate*
adjust, agree, atune, harmonize, integrate, keep time with, match, mesh, organize, pool proportion, pull together, put in sync*, set; SEE CONCEPTS *36,84,158*

SW
SY

syndicate [n] *group of business entities*
association, board, bunch, cabinet, cartel, chain, chamber, combine, committee, company, conglomerate, council, crew, gang, group, megacorp*, mob, multinational*, organization, outfit, partnership, pool, ring, trust, union; SEE CONCEPTS *323,325*

syndrome [n] *disease, condition*
affection, ailment, complaint, complex, diagnostics, disorder, infirmity, malady, problem, prognostics, sickness, sign, symptoms; SEE CONCEPTS *306,316,674*

synergy [n] *collaboration, cooperation*
alliance, coaction, combined effort, harmony, symbiosis, synergism, team effort, teaming, teamwork, union, unity, working together; SEE CONCEPTS *110,112,388,677*

synonymous [adj] *equivalent*
alike, apposite, coincident, compatible, convertible, correspondent, corresponding, equal, identical, identified, interchangeable, like, one and the same, same, similar, synonymic, tantamount; SEE CONCEPTS *487,573*

synopsis [n] *digest, summary*
abridgment, abstract, aperçu, breviary, brief, capsule, compendium, condensation, conspectus, epitome, outline, précis, recap*, résumé, review, rundown, run-through, sketch; SEE CONCEPT *283*

synthesis [n] *combining; combination*
amalgam, amalgamation, blend, building a whole, coalescence, composite, compound, constructing, construction, entirety, forming, fusion, integrating, integration, making one, organism, organization, structure, unification, union, unit, welding, whole; SEE CONCEPTS *113,837*

synthesize [v] *combine; make whole*
amalgamate, arrange, blend, harmonize, incorporate, integrate, manufacture, orchestrate, symphonize, unify; SEE CONCEPTS *113,205*

synthetic [adj] *artificial*
constructed, counterfeit, ersatz*, fabricated, factitious, fake, false, hokey*, made, makeshift, manufactured, mock, phony, plastic, unnatural; SEE CONCEPTS *485,582*

system [n1] *order, whole*
arrangement, classification, combination, complex, conformity, coordination, entity, fixed order, frame of reference, ideology, integral, integrate, logical order, orderliness, organization, philosophy, red tape*, regularity, rule, scheme, setup, structure, sum, theory, totality; SEE CONCEPTS *770,837*

system [n2] *method, plan*
arrangement, artifice, course of action, custom, definite plan, fashion, logical process, manner, methodicalness, methodology, mode, modus, modus operandi, operation, orderliness, orderly process, pattern, policy, practice, procedure, proceeding, process, regularity, routine, scheme, strategy, structure, systematic process, systematization, tactics, technique, theory, usage, way, wise; SEE CONCEPT *6*

systematic [adj] *orderly*
analytical, arranged, businesslike, complete, efficient, logical, methodic, methodical, ordered, organized, out-and-out*, precise, regular, standardized, systematized, thoroughgoing, well-ordered; SEE CONCEPTS *557,585*

systematize [v] *put in order*
arrange, array, contrive, design, devise, dispose, establish, frame, get act together, institute, make uniform, marshal, methodize, order, organize, plan, project, pull together, rationalize, regulate, schematize, shape up, standardize, straighten up, systemize, tighten up; SEE CONCEPTS *84,94*

T

tab [n1] *ticket, label*
bookmark, clip, flag, flap, holder, logo, loop, marker, slip, sticker, stop, strip, tag; SEE CONCEPTS *270,475*

tab [n2] *bill for service*
account, charge, check, cost, invoice, price, price tag, rate, reckoning, score, statement, tariff; SEE CONCEPT *329*

table [n1] *furniture upon which to work, eat*
bar, bench, board, buffet, bureau, console, counter, desk, dining table, dinner table, dresser, lectern, pulpit, sideboard, sink, slab, stand, wagon; SEE CONCEPT *443*

table [n2] *meal*
bill of fare, board, cuisine, diet, fare, food, meat and drink, menu, spread, victuals; SEE CONCEPT *459*

table [n3] *flatland*
flat, mesa, plain, plateau, tableland, upland; SEE CONCEPT *509*

table [n4] *diagram with columns of information*
agenda, appendix, canon, catalogue, chart, compendium, digest, graph, illustration, index, inventory, list, plan, record, register, roll, schedule, statistics, summary, synopsis, table of contents, tabulation; SEE CONCEPTS *283,625*

table [v] *postpone a proposition*
cool*, defer, delay, enter, hang*, hold off, hold up, move, pigeonhole*, propose, put aside, put forward, put off, put on back burner*, put on hold*, put on ice*, put on the shelf*, shelve, submit, suggest; SEE CONCEPTS *121,324*

tableau [n] *scene, often painted*
illustration, picture, representation, spectacle, view; SEE CONCEPTS *625,716*

tablet [n1] *sheaf of papers that are connected*
book, folder, memo pad, notebook, pad, quire, ream, scratch, scratch pad, sheets; SEE CONCEPT *475*

tablet [n2] *encapsulated medicine*
cake, capsule, dose, lozenge, medicine, pellet, pill, square, troche; SEE CONCEPT *307*

tableware [n] *flatware*
dishes, forks, glasses, glassware, knives, silverware, spoons, utensils; SEE CONCEPTS *433,499*

tabloid [n] *newspaper*
paper, rag*, scandal sheet*, sheet; SEE CONCEPTS *279,280*

taboo [adj] *not allowed, permitted*
anathema, banned, beyond the pale*, disapproved, forbidden, frowned on*, illegal, off limits*, outlawed, out of bounds*, prohibited, proscribed, reserved, restricted, ruled out, unacceptable, unmentionable, unthinkable; SEE CONCEPT *548*

taboo [n] *something not allowed, permitted*
anathema, ban, disapproval, don't*, forbiddance,

inhibition, interdict, law, limitation, no-no*, prohibition, proscription, regulation, religious convention, reservation, restraint, restriction, sanction, social convention, stricture, superstition, thou-shalt-not*; SEE CONCEPTS *532,688*

tabulate [*v*] *figure, classify*
alphabetize, arrange, catalogue, categorize, chart, codify, digest, enumerate, formulate, grade, index, list, methodize, order, range, register, systematize, tabularize; SEE CONCEPTS *84,764*

tacit [*adj*] *taken for granted; not said aloud*
alluded to, allusive, assumed, hinted at, implicit, implied, inarticulate, indirect, inferred, intimated, silent, suggested, undeclared, understood, unexpressed, unsaid, unspoken, unstated, unvoiced, wordless; SEE CONCEPTS *529,548*

taciturn [*adj*] *uncommunicative*
aloof, antisocial, brooding, clammed up*, close, close-mouthed*, cold, curt, distant, dour, dried-up*, dumb, laconic, mum, mute, quiet, reserved, reticent, sententious, silent, sparing, speechless, tight-lipped*, unexpressive, unforthcoming, withdrawn; SEE CONCEPTS *267,401*

tack [*n1*] *course of movement*
aim, alteration, approach, bearing, bend, deflection, deviation, digression, direction, double, echelon, heading, line, method, oblique course, path, plan, point of sail, procedure, set, shift, siding, sidling, sweep, swerve, switch, tactic, tangent, turn, variation, way, yaw, zigzag; SEE CONCEPTS *692,738*

tack [*n2*] *short pin for attaching*
brad, nail, point, pushpin, staple, thumbtack; SEE CONCEPT *475*

tack [*v*] *attach*
add, affix, annex, append, baste, fasten, fix, hem, mount, nail, paste, pin, sew, staple, stitch, tag, tie; SEE CONCEPTS *85,160,218*

tackle [*n*] *equipment for activity*
accouterment, apparatus, appliance, gear, goods, habiliments, hook, impedimenta, implements, line, machinery, materiel, outfit, paraphernalia, rig, rigging, tools, trappings; SEE CONCEPT *496*

tackle [*v1*] *make an effort*
accept, apply oneself, attack, attempt, bang away at*, begin, come to grips with*, deal with, devote oneself to, embark upon, engage in, essay, give a try*, give a whirl*, go for it*, launch, make a run at*, pitch into, set about, square off*, start the ball rolling*, take a shot at*, take in hand*, take on, take up, try, try on for size*, turn one's hand to*, turn to, undertake, work on; SEE CONCEPTS *87,100*

tackle [*v2*] *jump on and grab*
attack, block, bring down, bring to the ground*, catch, challenge, clutch, confront, down, grapple, grasp, halt, intercept, nail, put the freeze on*, sack, seize, smear, stop, take, take hold of, throw, throw down, upset; SEE CONCEPTS *90,164,191*

tacky [*adj*] *cheap, tasteless*
broken-down, crude, dilapidated, dingy, dowdy, down-at-heel*, faded, frumpy*, gaudy, inelegant, mangy*, messy, nasty*, outmoded, out-of-date, poky*, ratty, run-down, seedy, shabby, shoddy, sleazy*, sloppy*, slovenly, stodgy, threadbare, unbecoming, unkempt, unstylish, unsuitable, untidy, vulgar; SEE CONCEPTS *485,589*

tact [*n*] *finesse, thoughtfulness*
acumen, acuteness, address, adroitness, amenity, aptness, care, common sense, consideration, control, courtesy, delicacy, delicatesse, diplomacy, discernment, discretion, discrimination, gallantry, good taste, head, horse sense*, intelligence, judgment, penetration, perception, perspicacity, poise, policy, politicness, presence, prudence, refinement, repose, savoir-faire, sensitivity, skill, smoothness, suavity, subtlety, tactfulness, understanding, urbanity; SEE CONCEPT *633*

tactful [*adj*] *thoughtful, careful*
adroit, aware, cautious, civil, considerate, courteous, deft, delicate, diplomatic, discreet, gentle, judicious, observant, perceptive, poised, polished, polite, politic, prudent, sensitive, skilled, skillful, suave, subtle, sympathetic, tactical, understanding, urbane, wise; SEE CONCEPT *401*

tactical [*adj*] *strategic*
calculated, clever, cunning, deliberate, diplomatic, planned, politic, prudent, skillful, smart, well-planned; SEE CONCEPT *544*

tactics [*n*] *strategy*
approach, campaign, channels, course, defense, device, disposition, generalship, line, maneuver, maneuvering, means, method, move, plan, plan of attack, ploy, policy, procedure, red tape*, scheme, stratagem, system, tack, technique, trick, way; SEE CONCEPT *660*

tactile [*adj*] *touchable*
material, palpable, physical, solid, tactual, tangible; SEE CONCEPTS *529,582*

tactless [*adj*] *unthinking, careless*
awkward, blundering, boorish, brash, bungling, clumsy, crude, discourteous, gauche, gruff, harsh, hasty, impolite, impolitic, imprudent, inconsiderate, indelicate, indiscreet, inept, injudicious, insensitive, maladroit, misunderstanding, rash, rough, rude, sharp, stupid, thoughtless, uncivil, unconsiderate, undiplomatic, unfeeling, unkind, unperceptive, unpolished, unsubtle, unsympathetic, untactful, vulgar; SEE CONCEPT *401*

tag [*n*] *label, ticket*
badge, button, card, check, chip, docket, emblem, flap, ID*, identification, inscription, insignia, logo, mark, marker, motto, note, pin, slip, stamp, sticker, stub, tab, tally, trademark, voucher; SEE CONCEPTS *270,284,475*

tag [*v1*] *label; attach label*
add, adjoin, affix, annex, append, call, check, christen, designate, docket, dub, earmark, fasten, hold, identify, mark, name, nickname, style, tack, tally, tap, term, ticket, title, touch; SEE CONCEPTS *62,85,160*

tag [*v2*] *follow*
accompany, attend, bedog, chase, dog, heel, hunt, pursue, shadow, tail, trace, track, track down, trail; SEE CONCEPT *207*

tail [*n*] *end piece, part*
appendage, behind, butt*, buttocks, caudal appendage, conclusion, empennage, end, extremity, fag end, hind end, hindmost part, hind part, last part, posterior, rear, rear end, reverse, rudder, rump*, stub, tag, tag end, tailpiece, train, tush*, wagger*; SEE CONCEPTS *392,825,827*

tail [*v*] *follow*
bedog, dog, eye*, hound, keep an eye on, pursue, shadow, stalk, tag, track, trail; SEE CONCEPT *207*

tailor [*n*] *person who sews clothing*
clothier, costumier, couturier, dressmaker, gar-

ment maker, needle worker*, outfitter, suit maker; SEE CONCEPT *348*

tailor [*v*] *make to fit; adjust*
accommodate, adapt, alter, conform, convert, custom-make, cut, cut to fit, dovetail*, fashion, fit, make to order, modify, mold, quadrate, reconcile, shape, shape up, square, style, suit, tailor-make*; SEE CONCEPTS *126,202,218*

tailor-made [*adj*] *custom-made*
comfortable, custom-built, custom-fit, fitted, made-to-measure, made to order, perfect, snug, suitable, suited, tailored; SEE CONCEPT *558*

taint [*n*] *contamination, corruption*
black mark, blemish, blot, contagion, defect, disgrace, dishonor, fault, flaw, infection, pollution, shame, smear, spot, stain, stigma; SEE CONCEPTS *230,388*

taint [*v*] *dirty, contaminate; ruin*
adulterate, besmirch, blacken, blemish, blight, blot, blur, brand, break down, cast a slur, cloud, cook, corrupt, crud up*, crumble, cut, damage, debase, decay, decompose, defile, deprave, discolor, discredit, disgrace, dishonor, disintegrate, doctor, foul, give a bad name*, harm, hurt, infect, muddy, poison, pollute, putrefy, rot, shame, smear, soil, spike, spoil, stain, stigmatize, sully, tar, tarnish, trash*, turn, water, water down; SEE CONCEPTS *246,254,384*

take [*n*] *profit*
booty*, catch, catching, cut, gate, haul*, holding, part, proceeds, receipts, return, returns, revenue, share, takings, yield; SEE CONCEPT *344*

take [*v1*] *get; help oneself to*
abduct, accept, acquire, arrest, attain, capture, carry off, carve out, catch, clasp, clutch, collar*, collect, earn, ensnare, entrap, gain possession, gather up, get hold of, grab, grasp, grip, handle, haul in, have, hold, lay hold of, obtain, overtake, pick up, prehend, pull in, reach, reap, receive, secure, seize, snag, snatch, strike, take hold of, take in, win; SEE CONCEPTS *120,142*

take [*v2*] *steal*
abduct, abstract, accroach, annex, appropriate, arrogate, borrow, carry off, commandeer, confiscate, expropriate, filch*, haul in, liberate, lift*, misappropriate, nab*, nail*, nip*, pick up, pinch*, pluck, pocket*, preempt, pull in, purloin, rip off*, run off with*, salvage, seize, sequester, snag, snare, snatch*, snitch*, swipe*, take in; SEE CONCEPT *139*

take [*v3*] *buy; reserve*
book, borrow, charter, choose, cull, decide on, derive, draw, elect, engage, gain, get, hire, lease, mark, obtain, optate, opt for, pay for, pick, prefer, procure, purchase, rent, select, single out; SEE CONCEPTS *41,327*

take [*v4*] *endure*
abide, accept, accommodate, bear, bear with, brave, brook, contain, give access, go, go through, grin and bear it*, hack*, hang in*, hang on*, hang tough*, hold, let in, live with, put up with, receive, ride out*, stand, stand for, stick it out*, stomach, submit to, suffer, swallow, take it, take it lying down*, take it on the chin*, tolerate, undergo, weather, welcome, withstand; SEE CONCEPT *23*

take [*v5*] *consume*
devour, down, drink, eat, feed, feed on, imbibe,

ingest, inhale, meal, partake of, swallow; SEE CONCEPT *169*

take [*v6*] *accept, adopt; use*
accommodate, admit, appropriate, assume, be aware of, behave, bring, deal with, delight in, do, effect, enjoy, enter upon, execute, exercise, exert, experience, function, give access, have, include, let in, like, luxuriate in, make, observe, operate, perform, play, practice, put in practice, react, receive, relish, sense, serve, take in, treat, undertake, utilize, welcome, work; SEE CONCEPTS *100,124,225*

take [*v7*] *understand*
accept, apprehend, assume, be aware of, believe, catch, compass, comprehend, consider, deem, expect, experience, feel, follow, gather, grasp, hold, imagine, interpret as, know, look upon, observe, perceive, presume, receive, reckon*, regard, see, see as, sense, suppose, suspect, take in, think, think of as; SEE CONCEPT *15*

take [*v8*] *win; be successful*
beat, be efficacious, do the trick, have effect, operate, prevail, succeed, triumph, work; SEE CONCEPT *706*

take [*v9*] *carry, transport; accompany*
attend, back, bear, bring, buck, cart, conduct, convey, convoy, drive, escort, ferry, fetch, go with, guide, gun, haul, heel, jag, journey, lead, lug, move, pack, piggyback*, pilot, ride, schlepp*, shoulder, steer, tote, tour, trek, truck, usher; SEE CONCEPTS *114,187,217*

take [*v10*] *captivate, enchant*
allure, attract, become popular, bewitch, charm, delight, draw, entertain, fascinate, magnetize, overwhelm, please, wile, win favor; SEE CONCEPT *11*

take [*v11*] *require*
ask, call for, crave, demand, necessitate, need; SEE CONCEPT *646*

take [*v12*] *subtract*
deduct, discount, draw back, eliminate, knock off, remove, subtract, take away, take off, take out; SEE CONCEPTS *211,236,247*

take [*v13*] *cheat, deceive*
bamboozle*, beat*, bilk, con, cozen, defraud, do*, dupe, fiddle, flimflam*, gull, hoodwink, pull a fast one*, swindle, take for a ride*, trick; SEE CONCEPTS *59,192*

take [*v14*] *contract, catch*
be seized, come down with*, derive, draw, get, sicken with, take sick with; SEE CONCEPT *308*

take a crack at [*v*] *try*
attempt, do one's best*, drive for, give a go*, give a whirl*, go after, go all out*, go for, have a crack*, have a go*, have a rip*, have a shot*, have a stab*, have a whack*, make an attempt, make an effort, make a pass at*, make a stab*, risk, shoot for*, tackle, undertake, vie for; SEE CONCEPT *87*

take after [*v*] *emulate*
act like, be like, copy, ditto*, do like*, follow, follow in the footsteps of*, follow suit*, follow the example of*, imitate, inherit, look like, make like*, mimic, mirror, pattern after*, rival; SEE CONCEPTS *87,171*

take back [*v*] *retract*
abjure, back down, backpedal, call off, cancel, change one's mind, eat one's words*, forget it, go back on, have change of heart*, recall, recant,

reclaim, renege, repeal, repossess, repudiate, rescind, revoke, withdraw; SEE CONCEPTS *25,49,119,697*

take down [*v1*] *write down*
inscribe, jot down, make a note of, minute, note, note down, put on record, record, set down, transcribe; SEE CONCEPT *125*

take down [*v2*] *humble*
deflate, humiliate, let down, lower, mortify, pull down, put down, take apart; SEE CONCEPTS *7,19,52*

take in [*v1*] *deceive, fool*
beguile, betray, bilk, bluff, cheat, con, defraud, delude, do*, double-cross*, dupe, flimflam*, four-flush*, gull, hoodwink, lie, mislead, pull wool over eyes*, swindle, trick; SEE CONCEPT *59*

take in [*v2*] *understand*
absorb, assimilate, comprehend, digest, get, grasp, perceive, receive, savvy, see, soak up, take; SEE CONCEPT *15*

take it [*v*] *accept, endure*
acknowledge, agree, bear with, bite the bullet, capitulate, don't make waves*, don't rock the boat*, face the music*, go along with, grin and bear it*, hang tough, live with, play the game*, put up with, sit still for*, stand for, stick it out, stomach, submit to, suffer, swallow, take, take one's lumps*, take one's medicine*, tolerate; SEE CONCEPT *23*

takeoff [*n1*] *leaving*
ascent, climb, departure, hop, jump, launch, liftoff, rise, upward flight; SEE CONCEPTS *148,195,224*

takeoff [*n2*] *mockery, satire*
burlesque, caricature, cartoon, comedy, imitation, lampoon, mocking, parody, ridicule, send-up, spoof, travesty; SEE CONCEPTS *111,263,292*

take off [*v1*] *leave; leave the ground*
ascend, bear, beat it, become airborne, begone, blast off, blow*, clear out*, decamp, depart, disappear, exit, get off, get out, go, go away, head, hightail*, hit the road*, hit the trail*, lift off, light out*, make*, pull out, quit, scram*, set out*, shove off*, soar, split, take to the air*, vamoose*, withdraw; SEE CONCEPTS *148,195,224*

take off [*v2*] *mock, satirize*
ape, burlesque, caricature, imitate, lampoon, mimic, parody, ridicule, send up, spoof, travesty; SEE CONCEPTS *111,273,292*

take on [*v1*] *assume, accept*
acquire, add, address oneself to, adopt, agree to do, annex, append, attempt, become, begin, come to have, commence, develop, embrace, employ, endeavor, engage, enlist, enroll, espouse, handle, have a go at*, hire, launch, put on, retain, set about, tackle, take in hand*, take up, take upon oneself*, try, turn, undertake, venture; SEE CONCEPTS *87,221*

take on [*v2*] *compete*
attack, battle, contend, contest, encounter, engage, face, fight, match, meet, oppose, pit, vie; SEE CONCEPT *92*

take on [*v3*] *challenge, oppose*
brave, buck*, call out, confront, dare, defy, denounce, dispute, face off, go eyeball to eyeball with*, go one on one with*, go toe to toe with*, go up against, hang in*, insist upon, investigate, invite competition, make a stand, object to, question, stand up to, throw down the gauntlet*; SEE CONCEPT *53*

take up [*v*] *begin or start again*
adopt, assume, become involved in, carry on, commence, continue, embrace, engage in, enter, espouse, follow through, get off, go on, initiate, kick off, open, pick up, proceed, recommence, renew, reopen, restart, resume, set to, start, tackle, take on, tee off, undertake; SEE CONCEPTS *221,239*

tale [*n1*] *story*
account, anecdote, fable, fairy tale, fiction, folk tale, legend, myth, narration, narrative, novel, relation, report, romance, saga, short story, yarn; SEE CONCEPT *282*

tale [*n2*] *made-up story*
canard, chestnut*, clothesline*, cock-and-bull story*, defamation, detraction, exaggeration, fabrication, falsehood, falsity, fib, fiction, lie, misrepresentation, prevarication, rigmarole*, rumor, scandal, slander, spiel*, tall story*, untruism, untruth, yarn*; SEE CONCEPTS *278,282*

talent [*n*] *ability*
aptitude, aptness, art, a way with*, bent*, capability, capacity, craft, endowment, expertise, facility, faculty, flair, forte, genius, gift, green thumb*, head*, inventiveness, knack*, know-how*, nose*, power, savvy*, set, skill, smarts*, the formula*, the goods*, the right stuff*, thing*, turn*, what it takes*; SEE CONCEPT *630*

talented [*adj*] *gifted*
able, accomplished, adept, adroit, artistic, brilliant, capable, clever, cut out for, endowed, expert, having a knack*, ingenious, intelligent, masterly, proficient, shining at*, skilled, smart; SEE CONCEPTS *402,527,528*

talisman [*n*] *charm*
fetish, good-luck piece, juju, lucky piece, phylactery, rabbit's foot; SEE CONCEPTS *260,284,446*

talk [*n1*] *speech, address to group*
allocution, chalk talk*, declamation, descant, discourse, disquisition, dissertation, epilogue, exhortation, expatiation, harangue, homily, lecture, monologue, oration, peroration, prelection, recitation, screed, sermon, spiel*; SEE CONCEPTS *60,285*

talk [*n2*] *gossip*
allusion, badinage, banter, blather*, bombast, bunk*, buzz*, cant, chat, chatter, chitchat, conversation, cry, gab, grapevine*, hearsay, hint, hot air*, idle talk, innuendo, insinuation, jaw*, jive*, lip*, noise, nonsense*, palaver, persiflage, prose, racket*, raillery, report, rot*, rubbish*, rumble*, rumor, scuttlebutt*, small talk, tête-à-tête, trash*, yarn*; SEE CONCEPTS *51,278*

talk [*n3*] *discussion*
argument, colloquy, conclave, confabulation, conference, consultation, conversation, deliberation, dialogue, earful, encounter, eyeball-to-eyeball*, huddle*, interlocution, interview, meeting, negotiation, palaver, parlance, parley, powwow*, seminar, spiel*, straight talk, symposium, ventilation, visit; SEE CONCEPT *56*

talk [*n4*] *communication with language*
argot, chatter, dialect, discourse, jargon, lingo, locution, parlance, patois, slang, speaking, speech, utterance, verbalization, vocalization, words; SEE CONCEPTS *47,65*

talk [*v1*] *produce words; inform*
articulate, babble, broach, chant, chat, chatter, comment on, communicate, confess, converse, describe, divulge, drawl, drone, express, flap

one's tongue*, gab, gabble*, give voice to, gossip, influence, intone, notify, palaver, parley, patter, persuade, prate, prattle, pronounce, reveal, rhapsodize, run on*, say, sing*, soliloquize, speak, spill the beans*, spout, squeak*, squeal*, talk one's leg off*, tell, tell all*, use, utter, ventriloquize, verbalize, voice, yak*; SEE CONCEPTS *60,266*

talk [v2] *discuss with another*
argue, be in contact, canvass, carry on conversation, chew*, collogue, commune, confabulate, confer, confide, consult, contact, deliberate, dialogue, engage in conversation, exchange, go into a huddle*, groupthink*, have a meet*, hold discussion, huddle*, interact, interface, interview, join in conversation, keep in touch*, negotiate, network*, palaver, parley, reach out, reason, relate, thrash out*, touch*, touch base*, vent, visit; SEE CONCEPT *56*

talk [v3] *address group*
accost, deliver a speech, discourse, give a talk, give speech, harangue, hold forth, induce, influence, lecture, orate, persuade, pitch, prelect, sermonize, speak, spiel*, spout*, stump*, sway*; SEE CONCEPTS *60,285*

talkative [adj] *excessively communicative*
articulate, big-mouthed*, chattering, chatty*, effusive, eloquent, flaky, full of hot air*, gabby*, garrulous, glib, gossipy, long-winded*, loose-lipped*, loquacious, loudmouthed*, mouthy*, multiloquent, prolix, rattling, slick*, smooth*, talky, verbal, verbose, vocal, voluble, windy*, wordy; SEE CONCEPT *267*

tall [adj1] *high in stature, length*
alpine, altitudinous, beanstalk*, big, elevated, giant, great, high-reaching, lank, lanky, lofty, rangy, sizable, sky-high, skyscraping, soaring, statuesque, towering; SEE CONCEPTS *779,782*

tall [adj2] *exaggerated, unreasonable*
absurd, demanding, difficult, embellished, exorbitant, farfetched, hard, implausible, impossible, outlandish, overblown, preposterous, steep, unbelievable; SEE CONCEPTS *529,565*

tally [n] *count, record*
account, mark, poll, reckoning, running total, score, summation, tab, total; SEE CONCEPTS *283,787*

tally [v] *add up; count, record*
catalog, compute, enumerate, inventory, itemize, keep score, mark, mark down, number, numerate, reckon, register, sum, tale, tell, total, write down; SEE CONCEPTS *125,764*

tame [adj1] *domesticated, compliant*
acclimatized, amenable, biddable, bridled, broken, busted, civilized, cultivated, disciplined, docile, domestic, fearless, gentle, gentle as a lamb*, habituated, harmless, harnessed, housebroken, kindly, manageable, meek, mild, muzzled, obedient, overcome, pliable, pliant, subdued, submissive, tractable, trained, unafraid, unresisting, yoked*; SEE CONCEPT *401*

tame [adj2] *dull, uninteresting*
bland, bloodless, boiled down*, boring, conventional, diluted, feeble, flat*, halfhearted, humdrum*, insipid, lifeless, limp, mild, monotonous, prosaic, routine, spiritless, tedious, unexciting, uninspiring, vapid, weak, wearisome, whitebread*, without punch*; SEE CONCEPTS *529,542,548*

tame [v] *domesticate, make compliant*
break, break in, break the spirit*, bridle, bring to heel*, bust, check, conquer, curb, discipline, domesticize, domiciliate, enslave, gentle, housebreak, house-train, humble, mitigate, mute, pacify, repress, restrain, soften, subdue, subjugate, suppress, temper, tone down, train, vanquish, water down*; SEE CONCEPTS *14,250*

tamper [v1] *interfere, alter*
busybody*, butt in*, change, cook, cut, damage, destroy, diversify, doctor, fiddle with*, fool, horn in*, interfere, interlope, interpose, intrude, irrigate, manipulate, meddle, mess around with*, monkey around*, muck about*, phony up*, plant*, poke nose into*, spike*, tinker, vary, water*; SEE CONCEPT *232*

tamper [v2] *bribe*
buy, buy off, corrupt, fix, get to, have, influence, lubricate, manipulate, reach, rig, square*; SEE CONCEPT *192*

tan [n/adj] *light brown*
beige, biscuit, bronze, brown, brownish, buff, cream, drab, ecru, gold, khaki, leather-colored, natural, olive, olive-brown, saddle, sand, suntan, tawny, umber, yellowish; SEE CONCEPTS *618,622*

tan [v] *flog, whip*
baste, beat, belt, cane, dust someone's britches*, flay, hide, hit, lambaste, lash, leather, paddle, paddlewhack, punish, spank, strap, strike, switch, tan one's hide*, thrash, warm someone's seat*, wax, whack, whale*, whomp*; SEE CONCEPT *189*

tang [n] *biting taste or odor*
aroma, bite, flavor, guts*, kick*, nip, piquancy, pungency, reek, relish, sapidity, sapor, savor, scent, smack*, smell, spiciness, tanginess, thrill, twang, zest, zip*; SEE CONCEPTS *599,600,614*

tangible [adj] *real, concrete*
actual, appreciable, corporeal, definite, detectable, discernible, distinct, embodied, evident, factual, gross, incarnated, manifest, material, objective, observable, obvious, palpable, patent, perceivable, perceptible, phenomenal, physical, plain, positive, sensible, solid, stable, substantial, tactile, touchable, verifiable, visible, well-grounded; SEE CONCEPTS *529,582*

tangle [n] *knot, confusion*
coil, complication, entanglement, jam, jungle, labyrinth, mass, mat, maze, mesh, mess, mix-up, morass, muddle, rummage, skein, snag, snarl, twist, web; SEE CONCEPTS *230,674,720*

tangle [v] *knot, complicate*
catch, coil, confuse, derange, discompose, disorganize, drag into, embroil, enmesh, ensnare, entangle, entrap, foul up*, hamper, implicate, interlace, interlock, intertwist, interweave, involve, jam, kink, make a party to*, mat, mesh, mess up*, mix up*, muck up*, obstruct, perplex, ravel, snarl, tie up, trap, twist, unbalance, upset; SEE CONCEPTS *112,190*

tangy [adj] *sharp, spicy*
appetizing, aromatic, biting, bitter, fiery, flavorful, flavorsome, harsh, highly seasoned, hot, peppery, piquant, pungent, salty, seasoned, sweet, tart, tasty, vinegary, zesty, zippy*; SEE CONCEPTS *537,598,613*

tantalize [v] *provoke, tease*
annoy, badger, baffle, bait, bedevil, beleaguer, charm, entice, fascinate, frustrate, gnaw, harass,

harry, keep hanging*, lead on, make mouth water*, pester, plague, taunt, thwart, titillate, torment, torture, worry; SEE CONCEPTS *7,11,19,22*

tantamount [*adj*] *same*
alike, as good as, commensurate, duplicate, equal, equivalent, identical, indistinguishable, like, parallel, same as, selfsame, synonymous, uniform, very; SEE CONCEPTS *487,573*

tantrum [*n*] *fit*
anger, animosity, conniption, dander*, flare-up, hemorrhage*, huff*, hysterics, outburst, storm*, temper, temper tantrum, wax; SEE CONCEPTS *306,384*

tap [*n*] *faucet*
bibcock, cock, egress, hydrant, nozzle, petcock, spigot, spout, stopcock, valve; SEE CONCEPTS *445,464*

tap [*v1*] *hit lightly*
beat, bob, dab, drum, knock, palpate, pat, percuss, rap, strike, tag, thud, thump, tip, touch; SEE CONCEPT *189*

tap [*v2*] *pierce to drain*
bleed, bore, broach, draft, drain, draw, draw forth, draw off, draw out, drill, empty, lance, milk, mine, open, penetrate, perforate, pump, riddle, siphon, spear, spike, stab, unplug, unstopper, use, utilize; SEE CONCEPTS *142,220*

tape [*n*] *ribbon of material*
band, braid, edging, line, rope, strip; SEE CONCEPT *475*

tape [*v1*] *stick together with material*
bandage, bind, bond, fasten, hold together, rope, seal, secure, support, swathe, tie, tie up, truss, wire, wrap; SEE CONCEPTS *85,160*

tape [*v2*] *record sounds, sights*
audiotape, make a tape, register, tape-record, video, videotape; SEE CONCEPTS *125,292*

taper/taper off [*v*] *decrease to a point*
abate, bate, close, come to a point, die away, die out, diminish, drain, dwindle, fade, lessen, narrow, recede, reduce, rescind, subside, thin, thin out, wane, weaken, wind down; SEE CONCEPTS *137,698,776*

tardy [*adj*] *late*
backward, behindhand, belated, dawdling, delayed, delinquent, detained, dilatory, held up, hung up*, in a bind, jammed, laggard, loitering, not arrived, not done, overdue, procrastinating, retarded, slack, slow, sluggish, strapped for time*, too late, unpunctual; SEE CONCEPTS *542,548,799*

target [*n1*] *aim, goal*
ambition, bull's-eye*, destination, duty, end, function, ground zero*, intention, mark, object, objective, point, purpose, spot, use; SEE CONCEPT *659*

target [*n2*] *person as object of ridicule*
butt*, byword, game, mark*, pigeon*, prey, quarry, scapegoat*, scorn, sitting duck*, sport, victim; SEE CONCEPT *423*

tariff [*n*] *tax or fee*
assessment, charge, cost, duty, excise, impost, levy, price, price tag, rate, tab, tax, toll; SEE CONCEPT *329*

tarnish [*v*] *dirty, corrupt*
befoul, begrime, blacken, blemish, blot, contaminate, damage, darken, defame, defile, dim, discolor, disgrace, dull, embarrass, grime, harm, hurt, impair, injure, lose luster, lose shine, mar, muddy, pale, pollute, rust, slander, smear,

smudge, soil, spoil, spot, stain, sully, taint, tar, vitiate; SEE CONCEPTS *246,254,469*

tarry [*v*] *dawdle, delay*
abide, bide, dally, drag, drag one's feet*, dwell, filibuster, get no place fast*, goof around*, hang around*, hold the phone*, lag, linger, lodge, loiter, lose time, pause, poke, procrastinate, put off, remain, rest, sojourn, stall, stay, stick around, stop, stop over, tail, take one's time*, temporize, tool*, trail, visit, wait, warm a chair*; SEE CONCEPTS *35,151,210*

tart [*adj*] *bitter, sour in taste or effect*
acerb, acerbic, acetose, acid, acidulous, acrimonious, astringent, barbed, biting, caustic, cutting, dry, harsh, nasty, piquant, pungent, scathing, sharp, short, snappish, snappy, snippy, tangy, testy, trenchant, vinegary, wounding; SEE CONCEPTS *267,613*

tart [*n*] *pastry*
bun, Danish, eclair, fruit tart, pie, popover, roll, turnover; SEE CONCEPT *457*

task [*n*] *job or chore, often assigned*
assignment, bother, burden, business, calling, charge, daily grind*, deadweight*, duty, effort, employment, enterprise, errand, exercise, fun and games*, function, gig*, grind*, grindstone*, headache*, job, labor, load, long row to hoe*, millstone*, mission, nuisance, occupation, office, onus, pain, project, province, responsibility, stint, strain, tax, toil, trouble, undertaking, vocation, work; SEE CONCEPTS *362,666*

task [*v*] *assign, burden*
charge, encumber, entrust, exhaust, lade, load, oppress, overload, push, saddle, strain, tax, test, weary, weigh, weight; SEE CONCEPTS *14,112,666*

taskmaster [*n*] *slave driver*
boss, director, disciplinarian, dominator, employer, foreperson, head honcho*, manager, overseer, owner, person in charge, supervisor, taskperson, tyrant; SEE CONCEPT *347*

taste [*n1*] *flavor of some quality*
aftertaste, aroma, bang*, bitter, drive, ginger, jolt, kick*, oomph*, palatableness, piquancy, punch*, relish, salt, sapidity, sapor, savor, savoriness, smack, sour, sting*, suggestion, sweet, tang*, wallop, zest, zing*, zip*; SEE CONCEPT *614*

taste [*n2*] *tiny sample*
appetizer, bit, bite, canapé, chaw, dash, delicacy, drop, fragment, hint, hors d'oeuvre, morsel, mouthful, nip, sampling, sip, soupçon, spoonful, sprinkling, suggestion, swallow, tidbit, tincture, tinge, titbit, touch, trifle, whiff*, wink*; SEE CONCEPTS *458,835*

taste [*n3*] *inclination, preference*
affection, appetence, appetite, attachment, bent*, comprehension, cup of tea*, desire, disposition, druthers*, fancy, fondness, gusto, heart, leaning, liking, palate, partiality, penchant, predilection, predisposition, prepossession, relish, soft spot*, stomach*, tendency, thing*, type, understanding, weakness, zest; SEE CONCEPTS *20,32,529,659*

taste [*n4*] *capacity to sense flavor*
appetence, appetite, gout, gustation, palate, stomach, taste buds, tongue; SEE CONCEPTS *590,615*

taste [*n5*] *judgment, propriety*
acumen, acuteness, aestheticism, appreciation, correctness, cultivation, culture, decorum, delicacy, discernment, discretion, discrimination,

ta
ta

distinction, elegance, feeling, finesse, good taste, grace, nicety, penetration, perception, polish, politeness, refinement, restraint, style, susceptibility, tact, tactfulness, tastefulness; SEE CONCEPTS *388,411,655,689*

taste [*v1*] *judge, try*
assay, bite, chew, criticize, differentiate, discern, distinguish, eat, enjoy, lick, nibble, partake, perceive, relish, sample, savor, sense, sip, test, touch, try, try the flavor of; SEE CONCEPTS *169,616*

taste [*v2*] *experience*
appreciate, be exposed to, come up against, encounter, feel, have knowledge of, know, meet with, partake of, perceive, run up against, savor, undergo; SEE CONCEPT *678*

tasteful [*adj*] *nice, refined*
aesthetically pleasing, artistic, beautiful, charming, chaste, classical, classy, cultivated, cultured, delectable, delicate, discriminating, elegant, esthetic, exquisite, fastidious, fine, graceful, gratifying, handsome, harmonious, in good taste, pleasing, plush, polished, posh, precise, pure, quiet, restrained, rich, savory, smart, snazzy*, spiffy*, splendiferous, stylish, subdued, swank*, tasty, unaffected, unobtrusive, uptown*; SEE CONCEPTS *529,574,589*

tasteless [*adj1*] *without flavor*
big zero*, blah*, bland, boring, distasteful, dull, flat, flavorless, insipid, mild, nowhere*, pabulum*, plain, plain vanilla*, savorless, stale, tame, thin, unappetizing, uninspired, uninteresting, unpalatable, unpleasurable, unsavory, unseasoned, vanilla*, vapid, watered-down, watery, weak, without spice, zero*; SEE CONCEPT *613*

tasteless [*adj2*] *cheap, vulgar*
artificial, barbaric, barbarous, coarse, crass, crude, flashy, foolish, garish, gaudy, graceless, hideous, impolite, improper, indecorous, indelicate, indiscreet, inelegant, loud, low, low-down, low-down-and-dirty*, makeshift*, off-color*, ornate, ostentatious, outlandish, pretentious, raunchy*, rough, rude, showy, stupid, tacky, tactless, tawdry, trivial, uncouth, unlovely, unpolished, unrefined, unseemly, unsightly, useless, wild; SEE CONCEPTS *401,570,589*

tasty [*adj*] *delicious*
appetizing, delectable, delish*, divine, flavorful, flavorsome, flavory, full-flavored, good-tasting, heavenly, luscious, mellow, palatable, piquant, pungent, sapid, savory, scrumptious, spicy, sugar-coated, sweetened, tasteful, toothsome, toothy, yummy, zestful; SEE CONCEPT *613*

tattered [*adj*] *shredded*
badly dressed, badly worn, battered, broken, dilapidated, frayed, frazzled, full of holes*, in rags, in shreds, in tatters*, moth-eaten, poorly made, ripped, rugged, scraggy, seedy, shabby, shaggy, shoddy, threadbare, torn, torn to pieces, unkempt; SEE CONCEPT *485*

tattle [*v*] *gossip; tell rumor*
babble, blab*, chat, chatter, give away, give the show away*, gossip, have a big mouth*, jabber, leak, noise, prate, prattle*, rumor, snitch, spill, spill the beans*, spread rumor*, squeal, talk, talk idly, tell on, tell tale*, yak*; SEE CONCEPTS *54,60*

tattletale/tattler [*n*] *person who gossips, tells rumors*
bigmouth*, blabberer, blabbermouth*, busybody, canary*, fat mouth*, fink*, gossip, informer, rat*, rumormonger, scandalmonger, snitch*, squealer*, stool pigeon*, talebearer, taleteller, telltale*, tipster, troublemaker, whistleblower, windbag*; SEE CONCEPTS *412,423*

taunt [*n*] *provocation; teasing*
backhanded compliment*, barb, brickbat*, censure, comeback, crack, cut, derision, dig, dirty dig*, dump, gibe, insult, jab, jeer, mockery, outrage, parting shot*, put-down*, reproach, ridicule, sarcasm, slam*, slap*, snappy comeback*, swipe*; SEE CONCEPTS *7,19,266*

taunt [*v*] *provoke, reproach; tease*
affront, bother, deride, dig*, disdain, dump on*, flout, insult, jab*, jeer, lout, mock, offend, outrage, put down, quiz, rally, revile, ridicule, scoff at, scorn, scout, slam*, slap*, sneer, swipe at, tantalize, torment, twitter, upbraid; SEE CONCEPTS *7,19,54*

taut [*adj*] *rigid, tight*
close, firm, flexed, snug, stiff, strained, stressed, stretched, tense, tightly drawn, trim, unyielding; SEE CONCEPTS *488,604*

tavern [*n*] *business establishment for serving drink, food*
alehouse, bar, barroom, beer joint*, dive*, drinkery, gin mill*, grog shop*, honky tonk*, hostelry, hotel, inn, joint*, lodge, lounge, night spot, nineteenth hole*, pub, public house, roadhouse, saloon, speakeasy*, suds*, taphouse*, taproom, watering hole*; SEE CONCEPTS *439,448,449*

tawdry [*adj*] *cheap, tasteless*
blatant, brazen, chintzy*, common, crude, dirty, flaring, flashy, flaunting, garish, gaudy, gimcrack, glaring, glittering, glitzy, jazzy, junky*, loud, meretricious, obtrusive, offensive, plastic, poor, raffish, screaming, showy, sleazy*, sporty, tacky*, tinsel, vulgar; SEE CONCEPTS *334,589*

tax [*n1*] *charge levied by government on property, income*
assessment, bite*, brokerage, capitation, contribution, cost, custom, dues, duty, excise, expense, fine, giveaway*, imposition, impost, levy, obligation, pork barrel*, price, rate, salvage, tariff, tithe, toll, towage, tribute; SEE CONCEPT *329*

tax [*n2*] *burden*
albatross*, charge, deadweight*, demand, difficulty, drain, duty, imposition, load, millstone*, onus, pressure, strain, task, weight; SEE CONCEPTS *362,666*

tax [*v1*] *levy charge on property, income*
assess, charge, charge duty, demand, demand toll, enact, exact, exact tribute, extract, impose, lay an impost, rate, require contribution, tithe; SEE CONCEPT *298*

tax [*v2*] *burden*
charge, cumber, drain, encumber, enervate, exhaust, lade, load, make demands on, oppress, overburden, overtax, overuse, overwork, press hard on, pressure, prey on, push, put pressure on, saddle, sap, strain, stress, stretch, task, tire, try, weaken, wear out, weary, weigh, weigh down, weigh heavily on, weight; SEE CONCEPTS *14,208,240*

tax [*v3*] *accuse*
arraign, blame, censure, charge, criminate, impeach, impugn, impute, incriminate, inculpate, indict, reproach, reprove; SEE CONCEPT *44*

taxing [*adj*] *burdensome*
demanding, difficult, disturbing, enervating, exacting, exigent, grievous, heavy, onerous, oppressive, punishing, sapping, stressful, tedious, tiring, tough, troublesome, trying, wearing, wearisome, weighty; SEE CONCEPT 565

teach [*v*] *educate; instill knowledge*
advise, brainwash*, break in*, brief, catechize, coach, communicate, cram, demonstrate, develop, direct, discipline, drill, edify, enlighten, exercise, explain, expound, fit, form, give instruction, give lessons, give the facts, ground, guide, illustrate, imbue, impart, implant, improve mind, inculcate, indoctrinate, inform, initiate, instruct, interpret, lecture, nurture, open eyes*, polish up*, pound into*, prepare, profess, rear, school, sharpen, show, show the ropes*, train, tutor; SEE CONCEPT 285

teacher [*n*] *person who educates*
abecedary, adviser, assistant, coach, disciplinarian, educator, faculty member, guide, instructor, lecturer, mentor, pedagogue, preceptor, professor, pundit, scholar, schoolteacher, supervisor, teach*, trainer, tutor; SEE CONCEPT 350

teaching [*n*] *education*
apprenticeship, book learning*, coaching, cultivation, culture, discipline, drilling, enlightenment, guidance, instruction, learning, reading, schooling, training, tutelage, tutoring; SEE CONCEPTS 285,287,409

team [*n*] *group, crew*
aggregation, band, body, bunch, club, company, contingent, duo, faction, foursome, gang, lineup, organization, outfit, pair, partners, party, rig, sect, set, side, span, squad, stable, string, tandem, trio, troop, troupe, unit, workers, yoke; SEE CONCEPTS 365,397,417

teamwork [*n*] *collaboration, cooperation*
alliance, assistance, coalition, combined effort, confederacy, confederation, doing business with, esprit de corps, federation, harmony, help, joint effort, partisanship, partnership, pulling together, symbiosis, synergism, synergy, team effort, teaming, union, unity, working together; SEE CONCEPTS 110,112,388,677

tear [*n1*] *rip, cut*
breach, break, crack, damage, fissure, gash, hole, imperfection, laceration, mutilation, rent, run, rupture, scratch, split, tatter; SEE CONCEPT 513

tear/tears [*n2*] *droplets from eyes, often caused by emotion*
blubbering*, crying, discharge, distress, drops, grieving, lachryma, lamentation, lamenting, moisture, mourning, pain, regret, sadness, sob, sob act*, sobbing, sorrow, teardrop, wailing, water, waterworks*, weep, weeping, weeps*, whimpering, woe; SEE CONCEPTS 185,467

tear [*n3*] *wild action*
bender, binge, bust, carousal, carouse, drunk, spree, wassail; SEE CONCEPTS 383,384

tear [*v1*] *cut, rip an object*
break, claw, cleave, crack, damage, divide, evulse, extract, fray, frazzle, gash, grab, impair, incise, injure, lacerate, mangle, mutilate, pluck, pull, pull apart, rend, ribbon, rift, rive, run, rupture, scratch, seize, separate, sever, shred, slash, slit, snatch, split, sunder, wrench, wrest, yank; SEE CONCEPTS 206,214

tear [*v2*] *move very fast*
boil, bolt, career, charge, chase, course, dart,

dash, fling, fly, gallop, hurry, lash, race, run, rush, shoot, speed, spring, zoom; SEE CONCEPTS 150,152

tear down [*v*] *demolish, raze*
annihilate, bulldoze, crush, decimate, devastate, devour, dilapidate, disassemble, dismantle, flatten, knock down, level, obliterate, pulverize, ruin, smash, take apart, total*, trash*, wipe off the map*, wreck; SEE CONCEPTS 169,252

tearful [*adj*] *crying, very upset*
bawling*, blubbering*, blubbery*, distressed, dolorous, in tears, lachrymose, lamentable, lamenting, moist, mournful, pathetic, pitiable, pitiful, poignant, sad, sniveling*, sobbing, sorrowful, teary, watery, weeping, wet, whimpering, woeful; SEE CONCEPTS 401,403

tease [*v*] *aggravate, provoke*
annoy, badger, bait, banter, be at, bedevil, beleaguer, bother, chaff, devil, disturb, dog*, gibe, give a hard time*, gnaw, goad, harass, harry, hector, importune, jive*, josh, lead on*, mock, needle*, nudge, pester, pick on*, plague, put down*, rag*, rally, razz*, rib*, ride, ridicule, roast*, send up*, slam, snap, sound, spoof, swipe at, tantalize, taunt, torment, vex, worry; SEE CONCEPTS 7,11,19,22

technical [*adj*] *concerning details, mechanics*
abstruse, high-tech*, industrial, mechanical, methodological, occupational, professional, restricted, scholarly, scientific, special, specialized, technological, vocational; SEE CONCEPT 536

technicality [*n*] *loophole; minor detail*
escape clause, formality, minor point, nothing to speak of, nothing to write home about; SEE CONCEPT 633

technique [*n*] *method*
address, approach, art, artistry, capability, capacity, course, craft, delivery, execution, facility, fashion, knack*, know-how*, manner, means, mode, modus, modus operandi, performance, procedure, proficiency, routine, skill, style, system, tactics, technic, touch, usage, way, wise; SEE CONCEPTS 6,630

technology [*n*] *electronics, science*
applied science, automation, computers, electronic components, high tech*, hi tech*, industrial science, machinery, mechanics, mechanization, robotics, scientific know-how, scientific knowledge, technical knowledge, telecommunications; SEE CONCEPTS 463,499

tedious [*adj*] *dull, monotonous*
annoying, arid, banal, boring, bromidic, drab, dragging, draggy*, dreary, drudging, dry, dull as dishwater*, dusty*, endless, enervating, exhausting, fatiguing, ho-hum*, humdrum, insipid, irksome, laborious, lifeless, long-drawn-out*, mortal, pabulum*, poky*, prosaic, prosy, slow, snooze*, soporific, tiresome, tiring, unexciting, uninteresting, vapid, weariful, wearisome; SEE CONCEPTS 529,548

tedium [*n*] *dullness, monotony*
banality, boredom, deadness*, doldrums, drabness, dreariness, ennui, irksomeness, lack of interest, lifelessness, routine, sameness, tediousness, tiresomeness, wearisomeness, yawn*; SEE CONCEPTS 388,410,668

teem [*v*] *be abundant, full*
abound, bear, be crawling with, be full of, be numerous, be plentiful, be prolific, brim, bristle,

ta
te

burst, burst at seams*, bustle, crawl, crowd, flow, grow, jam, overflow, overrun, pack, pour, pour out, produce, prosper, pullulate, rain, roll in, shower, superabound, swarm, swell, swim in, wallow in; SEE CONCEPTS *146,179,740*

teeming [*adj*] *abundant, full*
alive, brimful, brimming, bristling, bursting, chock-full, crammed, crawling, filled, fruitful, multitudinous, numerous, overflowing, packed, plentiful, populous, pregnant, replete, rife, swarming, thick, thronged; SEE CONCEPTS *481,483,774*

teenager [*n*] *adolescent*
juvenile, minor, stripling, sweet sixteen*, teen, teenybopper*, youngster, youth; SEE CONCEPT *424*

teeny/teensy [*adj*] *very small*
diminutive, Lilliputian, microscopic, miniature, minuscule, minute, teensy-weensy*, teeny-weeny*, tiny, wee, weeny*; SEE CONCEPTS *773,789*

teeter [*v*] *wobble back and forth*
balance, dangle, falter, flutter, lurch, pivot, quiver, reel, rock, seesaw, stagger, stammer, stumble, sway, teeter-totter*, topple, totter, tremble, tremble precariously, waver, weave, wiggle; SEE CONCEPT *145*

telecast [*n*] *broadcast*
air time, newscast, program, show, simulcast, transmission; SEE CONCEPTS *274,293*

telegram [*n*] *message sent by coded radio signals*
buzzer, cable, cablegram, call, coded message, flash, radiogram, report, signal, summons, telegraph, telegraphic message, teletype, telex, wire; SEE CONCEPTS *269,271*

telepathy [*n*] *ability to know another's thoughts*
clairvoyance, ESP*, extrasensory perception, insight, mind-reading, parapsychology, premonition, presentiment, second sight*, sixth sense*, spiritualism, telepathic transmission, telesthesia, thought transference; SEE CONCEPTS *410,630*

telephone [*v*] *communicate through telephone system*
buzz*, call, call up, contact, dial, get back to*, get on the horn*, get on the line*, give a call, give a jingle*, give a ring*, make a call, phone, pick up*, put a call through*, ring, ring up, touch base with*; SEE CONCEPTS *225,266,269*

televise [*v*] *broadcast*
air, announce, beam, be on the air, communicate, go on the air, go on the airwaves, put on television, put on the air, show, simulcast, transmit; SEE CONCEPTS *60,292*

television [*n*] *visual and audio entertainment transmitted via radio waves*
audio, baby-sitter*, boob tube*, box*, eye*, idiot box*, receiver, small screen, station, telly*, tube, TV, TV set, vid*, video; SEE CONCEPTS *277,279,293,463*

tell [*v1*] *communicate*
acquaint, advise, announce, apprise, authorize, bid, break the news*, call upon, clue in*, command, confess, declare, direct, disclose, divulge, enjoin, explain, express, fill in*, give facts, give out, impart, inform, instruct, keep posted*, lay open*, leak, leave word, let in on*, let know, let slip*, level, make known, mention, notify, open up, order, proclaim, put before, recite, reel off*,

report, represent, require, reveal, say, speak, spit it out*, state, summon, utter; SEE CONCEPT *266*

tell [*v2*] *narrate, describe*
chronicle, depict, express, give an account of, portray, recount, rehearse, relate, report, set forth, speak, state; SEE CONCEPT *55*

tell [*v3*] *understand, discern*
ascertain, be sure, clinch, comprehend, deduce, determine, differentiate, discover, discriminate, distinguish, divine, find out, identify, know, know for certain, learn, make out, perceive, recognize, see; SEE CONCEPT *15*

tell [*v4*] *carry weight*
count, have effect, have force, make presence felt, make presence known, militate, register, take effect, take its toll*, weigh; SEE CONCEPT *676*

tell [*v5*] *calculate*
compute, count, count one by one, enumerate, number, numerate, reckon, tale, tally; SEE CONCEPT *764*

telling [*adj*] *effective, significant*
cogent, considerable, conspicuous, convincing, crucial, decisive, devastating, effectual, forceful, forcible, important, impressive, influential, marked, operative, potent, powerful, satisfactory, satisfying, solid, sound, striking, trenchant, valid, weighty; SEE CONCEPTS *537,567*

tell off [*v*] *reprimand; criticize harshly*
berate, censure, chide, give piece of one's mind*, give tongue-lashing*, lecture, rail, rake over the coals*, rebuke, reproach, reprove, revile, scold, take to task*, tick off*, upbraid, vituperate; SEE CONCEPTS *44,52*

telltale [*adj*] *revealing*
disclosing, evidential, giveaway, indicatory, informative, meaningful, pointing to, prognostic, significant, significatory, suggestive; SEE CONCEPT *267*

temerity [*n*] *nerve, audacity*
assurance, boldness, brass*, carelessness, daring, effrontery, foolhardiness, forwardness, gall, hardihood, hastiness, heedlessness, impertinence, impetuosity, imprudence, impudence, impulsiveness, indiscretion, intrepidity, intrusiveness, nerve, overconfidence, pluck, precipitancy, precipitateness, precipitation, presumption, rashness, recklessness, rudeness, thoughtlessness, venturesomeness; SEE CONCEPTS *411,633*

temper [*n1*] *state of mind*
atmosphere, attitude, attribute, aura, character, climate, complexion, condition, constitution, disposition, drift, frame of mind, humor, individualism, individuality, leaning, makeup, mind, mood, nature, orientation, outlook, peculiarity, personality, posture, property, quality, scene, soul, spirit, state, strain, style, temperament, tendency, tenor, thing*, timbre, tone, trend, type, vein, way; SEE CONCEPTS *410,411*

temper [*n2*] *angriness; bad mood*
acerbity, anger, annoyance, bad-humor, cantankerousness, crossness, dander*, excitability, fit, fretfulness, furor, fury, grouchiness, heat*, hotheadedness, huffiness, ill-humor, impatience, irascibility, ire, irritability, irritation, miff, outburst, passion, peevishness, petulance, pugnacity, rage, resentment, sensitivity, short fuse*, slow burn*, snit, sourness, stew*, sullenness,

surliness, tantrum, tartness, tear*, tiff, tizzy*, touchiness, wax; SEE CONCEPTS *29,410*

temper [*n3*] *calmness*
calm, composure, cool, coolness, equanimity, good humor, moderation, poise, self-control, tranquility; SEE CONCEPTS *32,410*

temper [*v1*] *calm, moderate*
abate, adjust, admix, allay, alleviate, assuage, chill out*, cool, cool out*, curb, dilute, ease, fine tune, lessen, make reasonable, mitigate, modulate, mollify, monkey around with*, pacify, palliate, relieve, restrain, revamp, soften, soft-pedal*, soothe, switch, take the bite out of*, take the edge off*, take the sting out of*, tone down, transmogrify, weaken; SEE CONCEPTS *7,22,110,126*

temper [*v2*] *harden*
anneal, bake, braze, cement, chill, congeal, dry, indurate, mold, petrify, set, solidify, starch, steel, stiffen, strengthen, toughen, toughen up; SEE CONCEPTS *250,726*

temperament [*n*] *disposition, personality*
attitude, bent, capacity, cast, character, complexion, constitution, distinctiveness, ego, emotions, frame of mind, humor, idiosyncrasy, inclination, individualism, individuality, inner nature, intellect, kind, makeup, mentality, mettle, mood, nature, outlook, peculiarity, quality, soul, spirit, stamp, structure, susceptibility, temperament, tendency, turn, type, way; SEE CONCEPTS *410,411*

temperamental [*adj*] *angry most of the time; moody*
capricious, changeable, cussed*, easily upset, emotional, erratic, excitable, explosive, fickle, fiery, froward, headstrong, high-strung*, hotheaded*, hyper*, hypersensitive, impatient, in bad mood, inconsistent, irritable, mean, mercurial, neurotic, ornery, passionate, petulant, sensitive, thin-skinned*, ticklish, touchy, uncertain, undependable, unpredictable, unreliable, unstable, variable, volatile, willful; SEE CONCEPT *403*

temperance [*n*] *self-restraint; abstinence*
abnegation, abstemiousness, asceticism, astringency, austerity, conservatism, constraint, continence, control, discretion, eschewal, forbearance, forgoing, frugality, golden mean*, happy medium*, measure, moderateness, moderation, moderatism, mortification, prohibition, prudence, reasonableness, refrainment, restraint, sacrifice, self-control, self-denial, self-deprivation, self-discipline, soberness, sobriety, stoicism, teetotalism, uninebriation, unintoxication; SEE CONCEPTS *410,633*

temperate [*adj1*] *calm, moderate*
agreeable, balmy, checked, clement, collected, composed, conservative, constant, cool, curbed, discreet, dispassionate, equable, even, even-tempered, fair, gentle, levelheaded, medium, mild, modest, pleasant, reasonable, regulated, restrained, self-controlled, self-restrained, sensible, sober, soft, stable, steady, unexcessive, unextreme, unimpassioned, warm; SEE CONCEPTS *525,542,547*

temperate [*adj2*] *controlled, sober*
abstemious, abstentious, abstinent, continent, moderate, restrained, self-restraining; SEE CONCEPT *401*

temperature [*n*] *hotness, coldness of some degree*
body heat, calefaction, climate, cold, condition, degrees, febricity, feverishness, heat, incalescence, pyrexia, thermal reading, warmth; SEE CONCEPT *610*

tempest [*n*] *wild storm; commotion*
blizzard, bluster, chaos, convulsion, cyclone, disturbance, ferment, furor, gale, hurricane, squall, tornado, tumult, typhoon, upheaval, uproar, wildness, windstorm; SEE CONCEPTS *230,526*

tempestuous [*adj*] *wild, stormy*
agitated, blustering, blustery, boisterous, breezy, coarse, emotional, excited, feverish, furious, gusty, heated, hysterical, impassioned, intense, passionate, raging, rough, rugged, squally, storming, tumultous/tumultuous, turbulent, unbridled, uncontrolled, unrestrained, violent, windy; SEE CONCEPTS *401,525,542*

temple [*n*] *house of worship*
cathedral, chapel, church, holy place, house, house of God*, house of prayer*, mosque, pagoda, pantheon, place of worship, sanctuary, shrine, synagogue, tabernacle; SEE CONCEPTS *368,439*

tempo [*n*] *beat, rhythm*
bounce, cadence, downbeat, measure, meter, momentum, pace, pulse, rate, speed, time, velocity; SEE CONCEPT *65*

temporal [*adj1*] *material, worldly*
banausic, carnal, civil, earthly, earthy, fleshly, lay, materialistic, mortal, mundane, nonsacred, nonspiritual, physical, profane, secular, sensual, subcelestial, sublunary, terrestrial, unhallowed, unsacred, unsanctified, unspiritual; SEE CONCEPT *582*

temporal [*adj2*] *momentary*
chronological, ephemeral, evanescent, fleeting, fugacious, fugitive, impermanent, momentary, of time, passing, short-lived, temporary, transient, transitory; SEE CONCEPT *799*

temporary [*adj*] *lasting only a short while*
acting, ad hoc, ad interim, alternate, Band-Aid*, brief, changeable, ephemeral, evanescent, fleeting, for the time being*, fugacious, fugitive, impermanent, interim, limited, make-do*, makeshift*, momentary, mortal, overnight, passing, perishable, pro tem, pro tempore, provisional, provisory, shifting, short, short-lived, slapdash*, stopgap*, substitute, summary, supply, temp*, transient, transitory, unfixed, unstable, volatile; SEE CONCEPTS *551,798*

tempt [*v*] *lure, entice*
allure, appeal to, attract, bait, butter up*, captivate, charm, coax, court, dare, decoy, draw, draw out, entrap, fascinate, honey*, hook*, incite, induce, influence, instigate, intrigue, inveigle, invite, lead on, make mouth water*, motivate, mousetrap*, move, oil, persuade, play up to, promote, provoke, risk, rouse, seduce, solicit, stimulate, tantalize, test, train, try, turn one's head*, wheedle, whet, woo*; SEE CONCEPTS *11,68*

temptation [*n*] *lure, attraction*
allurement, appeal, attractiveness, bait, blandishment, coaxing, come-on*, decoy, draw, enticement, fancy, fascination, hankering, inducement, inveiglement, invitation, provocation, pull, seducement, seduction, snare, tantalization, trap*, yen; SEE CONCEPTS *20,529,532,690,709*

te
te

tempting [*adj*] *alluring, inviting*
appetizing, attractive, charming, divine, enticing, fascinating, fetching, heavenly, intriguing, luring, magnetic, mouth-watering*, provoking, rousing, scrumptious, seductive, tantalizing, yummy*; SEE CONCEPTS *462,529*

tenable [*adj*] *reasonable*
arguable, believable, condonable, credible, defendable, defensible, excusable, impregnable, justifiable, maintainable, plausible, rational, reliable, secure, sound, strong, trustworthy, viable, vindicable, warrantable; SEE CONCEPTS *552,558*

tenacious [*adj1*] *strong, unyielding*
adamant, bound, clinging, coherent, cohesive, determined, dogged, fast, firm, forceful, inflexible, intransigent, iron, meaning business*, mulish, obdurate, obstinate, persevering, persistent, persisting, pertinacious, possessive, purposeful, relentless, resolute, retentive, set, solid, spunky, stalwart, staunch, steadfast, stout, strong-willed, stubborn, sturdy, sure, tight, tough, true, unforgetful, unshakable, unswerving; SEE CONCEPTS *326,401,489,542*

tenacious [*adj2*] *sticky*
adhesive, clinging, clingy, fast, firm, fixed, glutinous, gummy, inseparable, mucilaginous, resisting, retentive, secure, set, tacky, tight, viscid, viscose, viscous, waxy; SEE CONCEPTS *488,606*

tenacity [*n*] *diligence, stubbornness*
application, backbone, chutzpah*, clock*, courage, determination, doggedness, firmness, grit, guts*, gutsiness*, guttiness*, heart*, inflexibility, intestinal fortitude*, intransigence, moxie*, nerve, obduracy, obstinacy, perseverance, persistence, pertinacity, resoluteness, resolution, resolve, spunk, starch*, staunchness, steadfastness, stick-to-itiveness*, stomach*, strength of purpose, true grit*, what it takes*, willfulness; SEE CONCEPTS *411,657*

tenant [*n*] *person who leases a place*
addressee, boarder, dweller, holder, householder, indweller, inhabitant, leaseholder, lessee, lodger, occupant, occupier, possessor, renter, rent payer, resident, roomer; SEE CONCEPTS *348,423*

tend [*v1*] *be apt, likely*
aim, bear, be biased, be conducive, be disposed, be inclined, be in the habit of, be liable, bend, be predisposed, be prejudiced, conduce, contribute, dispose, drift, favor, go, gravitate, have an inclination, have a tendency, head, impel, incline, influence, lead, lean, look, make for, move, move toward, point, redound, result in, serve to, trend, turn, verge on; SEE CONCEPTS *411,650*

tend [*v2*] *care for*
accomplish, administer, attend, baby-sit, cater to, cherish, control, corral, cultivate, defend, direct, do, do for, feed, foster, guard, handle, keep, keep an eye on*, keep tabs on*, look after, maintain, manage, mind, minister to, nurse, nurture, oversee, perform, protect, ride herd on*, safeguard, see after, see to, serve, shepherd, shield, sit, superintend, supervise, take care of, take under wing*, wait on, watch, watch out for, watch over; SEE CONCEPTS *136,257,295*

tendency [*n1*] *inclination to think or do in a certain way*
addiction, affection, bent*, bias, current, custom, disposition, drift, habit, impulse, inclining, leaning, liability, mind, mindset*, partiality, penchant, predilection, predisposition, proclivity, proneness, propensity, readiness, run, set, shift, slant, susceptibility, temperament, thing*, trend, turn, type, usage, way*, weakness; SEE CONCEPT *657*

tendency [*n2*] *direction of movement*
aim, bearing, bent, bias, course, current, curve, drift, drive, heading, inclination, leaning, movement, purport, run, shift, tenor, trend, turn, turning, way; SEE CONCEPTS *692,738*

tender [*adj1*] *fragile, soft*
breakable, dainty, delicate, effete, feeble, frail, supple, weak; SEE CONCEPTS *604,606*

tender [*adj2*] *young, inexperienced*
callow, childish, childlike, green*, immature, impressionable, new, raw*, rookie*, sensitive, unripe, vernal, vulnerable, wet behind the ears*, youthful; SEE CONCEPTS *578,797*

tender [*adj3*] *affectionate, loving*
all heart*, amorous, benevolent, bleeding-heart*, caring, charitable, commiserative, compassionate, considerate, demonstrative, emotional, evocative, fond, forgiving, gentle, humane, kind, lenient, lovey-dovey*, merciful, mild, moving, mushy*, poignant, responsive, romantic, sensitive, sentimental, soft, softhearted, solicitous, sympathetic, tenderhearted, thoughtful, ticklish, tolerant, touching, touchy, warm, warmhearted, yielding; SEE CONCEPTS *401,542*

tender [*adj4*] *painful, sore*
aching, acute, bruised, delicate, hypersensitive, inflamed, irritated, oversensitive, raw, sensitive, smarting, thin-skinned, ticklish, touchy; SEE CONCEPTS *314,403,548*

tenderfoot [*n*] *newcomer*
amateur, beginner, colt*, greenhorn*, Johnny-come-lately*, neophyte, new kid on the block*, novice, novitiate, rookie, tyro; SEE CONCEPTS *413,423*

tenderhearted [*adj*] *tender*
affectionate, all heart*, benevolent, bleeding heart*, caring, charitable, compassionate, considerate, emotional, forgiving, gentle, humane, kind, kindhearted, lenient, loving, merciful, mushy*, sensitive, sentimental, soft, softhearted, sweet, sympathetic, thoughtful, understanding, warm, warmhearted; SEE CONCEPTS *401,542*

tenebrous [*adj*] *dark, ominous*
ambiguous, amphibological, caliginous, dim, dingy, dusk, dusky, equivocal, gloomy, lightless, murky, obscure, shadowy, shady, somber, sunless, uncertain, unclear, unexplicit, unilluminated, unintelligible, unlit, vague; SEE CONCEPTS *535,617*

tenement [*n*] *apartment house*
apartment complex, boarding house, coop, cooperative, den*, digs*, dump*, flat, high-rise, high-rise apartment building, living quarters, pad*, project housing, rental, slum; SEE CONCEPTS *448,516*

tenet [*n*] *belief, principle*
article of faith, assumption, canon, conception, conviction, credo, creed, doctrine, dogma, faith, impression, maxim, opinion, persuasion, position, precept, presumption, profession, rule, self-conviction, system, teaching, thesis, trust, view; SEE CONCEPTS *688,689*

tenor [*n1*] *meaning, intent*
aim, body, burden, core, course, course of thought, current, direction, drift, evolution, gist, inclination, meat, mood, path, pith, purport, pur-

pose, run, sense, stuff, substance, tendency, theme, tone, trend, way; SEE CONCEPTS *529,682*

tenor [*n2*] *high male voice*
alto, countertenor, falsetto; SEE CONCEPT *65*

tense [*adj1*] *tight, stretched*
close, firm, rigid, stiff, strained, taut; SEE CONCEPTS *485,604*

tense [*adj2*] *under stress, pressure*
agitated, anxious, apprehensive, beside oneself*, bundle of nerves*, choked, clutched, concerned, edgy, excited, fidgety, fluttery, high-strung*, hung up*, hyper*, in a tizzy*, jittery, jumpy, keyed up*, moved, moving, nerve-racking, nervous, nervous wreck*, on edge, overanxious, overwrought, queasy, restive, restless, shaky, shot*, shot to pieces*, strained, stressful, strung out*, uneasy, unnerved, unquiet, up the wall*, uptight*, white knuckled*, wired*, worried, worrying, wound up*, wreck*; SEE CONCEPTS *401,403,548*

tension [*n1*] *tightness*
astriction, balance, constriction, force, pressure, rigidity, stiffness, strain, straining, stress, stretching, tautness, tenseness, tensity; SEE CONCEPTS *723,726*

tension [*n2*] *mental stress*
agitation, antsiness*, ants in pants*, anxiety, apprehension, bad feeling*, brunt, concern, discomfort, disquiet, edginess, hostility, jitters*, jumps*, nail-biting*, nerves, nervousness, pins and needles*, pressure, restlessness, shakes*, strain, suspense, unease, uneasiness, worriment, worry; SEE CONCEPT *410*

tent [*n*] *portable canvas shelter*
big top*, canvas, pavilion, tabernacle, tepee, tupik, wigwam, yurt; SEE CONCEPTS *515,712*

tentative [*adj1*] *conditional, experimental*
acting, ad interim, conjectural, contingent, dependent, iffy*, indefinite, makeshift, not final, not settled, on trial, open for consideration, probationary, provisional, provisionary, provisory, speculative, subject to change, temporary, test, trial, unconfirmed, undecided, unsettled; SEE CONCEPTS *551,552*

tentative [*adj2*] *indefinite, uncertain*
backward, cautious, diffident, disinclined, doubtful, faltering, halting, hesitant, irresolute, reluctant, timid, undecided, unsure, vacillating, vacillatory, wobbly; SEE CONCEPTS *534,535,542*

tenuous [*adj*] *weak, thin*
aerial, airy, attenuate, attenuated, delicate, doubtful, dubious, ethereal, fine, flimsy, gossamer, insignificant, insubstantial, light, narrow, nebulous, questionable, rare, rarefied, reedy, shaky, sketchy, slender, slight, slim, subtle, twiggy; SEE CONCEPTS *489,491,575*

tenure [*n*] *time in position of responsibility*
administration, clamp, clasp, clench, clinch, clutch, dynasty, grasp, grip, hold, holding, incumbency, occupancy, occupation, ownership, possession, proprietorship, regime, reign, residence, security, tenancy, term; SEE CONCEPTS *287,816*

tepid [*adj*] *lukewarm*
apathetic, cool, disinterested, dull, halfhearted, indifferent, languid, lifeless, mild, milk-warm, moderate, slightly warm, spiritless, temperate, unenthusiastic, unlively, warm, warmish; SEE CONCEPTS *542,605*

term [*n1*] *description of a concept*
appellation, article, caption, denomination, designation, expression, head, indication, language, locution, moniker*, name, nomenclature, phrase, style, terminology, title, vocable, word; SEE CONCEPTS *275,683*

term [*n2*] *time period*
course, cycle, duration, go*, hitch*, interval, phase, quarter, season, semester, session, space, span, spell, standing, stretch, time, tour, turn, while; SEE CONCEPTS *807,822*

term [*n3*] *limit*
bound, boundary, close, conclusion, confine, confines, culmination, end, finish, fruition, limitation, terminus; SEE CONCEPTS *745,832*

term [*v*] *name something*
baptize, call, christen, denominate, describe, designate, dub, entitle, label, style, subtitle, tag, title; SEE CONCEPT *62*

terminal [*adj*] *final, deadly*
bounding, check out*, closing, concluding, eventual, extreme, fatal, hindmost, incurable, killing, lag, last, latest, latter, lethal, limiting, mortal, on way out*, period, ultimate, utmost; SEE CONCEPTS *314,548*

terminal [*n1*] *end of road; limit*
boundary, depot, end, end of the line, extremity, station, termination, terminus; SEE CONCEPTS *198,745*

terminal [*n2*] *computer screen, computer input/output device*
cathode ray tube, CRT*, display, input device, monitor, screen, VDT*, video display; SEE CONCEPT *463*

terminate [*v*] *stop, finish*
abolish, abort, achieve, adjourn, annul, bounce, bound, bring to an end, cancel, cease, close, come to an end, complete, conclude, confine, cut off, define, desist, determine, discharge, discontinue, dismiss, dissolve, drop, eliminate, end, expire, extinguish, fire, halt, issue, lapse, limit, perfect, prorogate, prorogue, put an end to, recess, restrict, result, run out, sack, scratch, scrub*, tether, ultimate, wind down, wind up*, wrap*, wrap up*; SEE CONCEPTS *119,121,234*

termination [*n*] *end*
abortion, ballgame*, cease, cessation, close, completion, conclusion, consequence, curtains*, cut-off*, desistance, discontinuation, effect, ending, end of the line*, expiry, finale, finis, finish, issue, kiss-off*, outcome, payoff*, period, result, stop, terminus, windup*, wrap-up*; SEE CONCEPTS *119,832*

terminology [*n*] *wording*
choice of words, diction, jargon, language, lingo, locution, nomenclature, onomastics, phraseology, phrasing, turn of phrase, vocabulary, wordage, words; SEE CONCEPTS *278,682*

terms [*n1*] *conditions, agreement*
charge, circumstances, conclusion, condition, details, fee, fine print*, items, nitty-gritty*, particulars, payment, points, premise, premises, price, provision, provisions, proviso, provisos, qualifications, rate, reservation, size of it*, small print*, specifications, stipulation, stipulations, strings*, treaty, understanding, what it is*; SEE CONCEPTS *270,318,684*

terms [*n2*] *status of relationship*
balance, equality, equivalence, footing, par, par-

te
te

ity, position, relations, relationship, standing; SEE CONCEPT *388*

terrain [*n*] *landscape*
area, bailiwick, contour, country, domain, dominion, field, form, ground, land, profile, province, region, shape, soil, sphere, territory, topography, turf; SEE CONCEPTS *508,509*

terrestrial [*adj*] *earthly*
earthbound, earthlike, earthy, global, mundane, physical, profane, prosaic, secular, sublunary, subsolar, telluric, temporal, terrene, uncelestial, unspiritual, worldly; SEE CONCEPT *536*

terrible [*adj*] *bad, horrible*
abhorrent, appalling, atrocious, awe-inspiring, awesome, awful, beastly, dangerous, desperate, dire, disastrous, disturbing, dread, dreaded, dreadful, extreme, fearful, frightful, ghastly, gruesome, harrowing, hateful, hideous, horrendous, horrible, horrid, horrifying, inconvenient, loathsome, monstrous, obnoxious, odious, offensive, petrifying, poor, repulsive, revolting, rotten, serious, severe, shocking, unfortunate, unnerving, unpleasant, unwelcome, vile; SEE CONCEPT *571*

terribly [*adv*] *very*
awfully, badly, decidedly, desperately, discouragingly, disturbingly, drastically, dreadfully, exceedingly, extremely, fearfully, frightfully, gravely, greatly, highly, horribly, intensely, markedly, mightily, much, notoriously, remarkably, seriously, staggeringly, thoroughly, unbelievably, unfortunately, unhappily; SEE CONCEPTS *569,570*

terrific [*adj1*] *intense*
agitating, appalling, awesome, awful, deafening, disquieting, dreadful, enormous, excessive, extreme, fearful, fierce, formidable, frightful, gigantic, great, harsh, horrible, horrific, huge, immense, large, monstrous, severe, shocking, terrible, terrorizing, thunderous, tremendous, upsetting; SEE CONCEPT *569*

terrific [*adj2*] *wonderful*
ace*, amazing, breathtaking, divine, excellent, fabulous, fantastic, fine, glorious, great, groovy*, hot*, keen*, magnificent, marvelous, outstanding, sensational, smashing*, stupendous, super, superb, swell, very good; SEE CONCEPT *572*

terrify [*v*] *scare*
alarm, appall, awe, chill, dismay, freeze, fright, frighten, horrify, intimidate, paralyze, petrify, scare stiff*, scare the pants off of*, scare to death*, shock, spook, startle, strike fear into*, stun, stupefy, terrorize; SEE CONCEPTS *7,19,42*

territory [*n*] *domain, region*
area, belt, block, boundary, colony, commonwealth, country, district, dominion, empire, enclave, exclave, expanse, extent, field, land, mandate, nation, neck of the woods*, neighborhood, province, quarter, section, sector, sphere, state, stomping grounds*, street, terrain, terrene, township, tract, turf*, walk, zone; SEE CONCEPTS *198,349,508*

terror [*n*] *intense fear*
alarm, anxiety, awe, consternation, dismay, dread, fearfulness, fright, horror, intimidation, panic, shock, trepidation, trepidity; SEE CONCEPTS *27,690*

terrorize [*v*] *upset, threaten*
alarm, appall, awe, bludgeon, browbeat, bulldoze*, bully, coerce, cow, dismay, dragoon,

fright, frighten, hector, horrify, intimidate, menace, oppress, petrify, scare, scare to death*, shock, spook, startle, strike terror into*, strongarm*, terrify; SEE CONCEPTS *7,14,19*

terse [*adj*] *brief, short*
abrupt, aphoristic, boiled down*, breviloquent, brusque, clear-cut, clipped, close, compact, compendiary, compendious, concise, condensed, crisp, cryptic, curt, cut to the bone*, elliptical, epigrammatic, exact, gnomic, in a nutshell*, incisive, laconic, lean, neat, pithy, pointed, precise, sententious, short and sweet*, snappy, succinct, summary, taut, to the point, trenchant; SEE CONCEPTS *267,272*

test [*n*] *examination, quiz*
analysis, approval, assessment, attempt, blue book*, catechism, check, comp*, confirmation, corroboration, countdown, criterion, dry run*, elimination, essay, evaluation, exam, experiment, final, fling*, go*, inquest, inquiry, inspection, investigation, lick*, oral*, ordeal, pop quiz, preliminary, probation, probing, proof, questionnaire, scrutiny, search, shibboleth, standard, substantiation, touchstone*, trial, trial and error*, trial run, try, tryout, verification, yardstick*; SEE CONCEPTS *5,290*

test [*v*] *examine, quiz*
analyze, assay, assess, check, confirm, demonstrate, experiment, experimentalize, give a tryout, inquire, investigate, look into, make a trial run, match up, prove, prove out, put to the test*, question, run idea by someone*, run it up a flagpole*, see how it flies*, see how wind blows*, send up a balloon*, shake down*, stack up, substantiate, try, try on, try on for size*, try out, validate, verify; SEE CONCEPTS *5,103,291*

testament [*n*] *tribute; last wishes*
attestation, colloquy, confirmation, covenant, demonstration, earnest, evidence, exemplification, instrument, proof, testimonial, testimony, will, witness; SEE CONCEPT *318*

tested [*adj*] *proven*
approved, certified, creditworthy, dependable, loyal, proved, reliable, safe, tried-and-true*, trustworthy, trusty; SEE CONCEPT *535*

testify [*v*] *vouch for; give testimony*
affirm, announce, argue, assert, attest, bear witness, bespeak, betoken, certify, corroborate, cross one's heart*, declare, demonstrate, depone, depose, evince, give evidence, give facts, give one's word*, indicate, make evident, mount, point to, prove, say so*, show, sing*, stand up for, state, swear, swear to, swear up and down*, token, warrant, witness; SEE CONCEPTS *49,317*

testimonial [*n*] *tribute*
affidavit, appreciation, attestation, certificate, character, commemoration, commendation, confirmation, credential, degree, endorsement, evidence, homage, honor, indication, manifestation, memorial, memorialization, monument, ovation, plug*, proof, recommendation, reference, remembrance, salute, salvo, say-so*, show, sign, symbol, testament, testimony, token, voucher, witness; SEE CONCEPTS *49,278,318*

testimony [*n*] *declaration about truth; proof*
affidavit, affirmation, attestation, avowal, confirmation, corroboration, data, demonstration, deposition, documentation, evidence, facts, grounds, illustration, indication, information, manifestation, profession, statement, submission,

substantiation, support, testament, verification, witness; SEE CONCEPTS 49,278,318

testy [adj] irritable, touchy
annoyed, bad-tempered, cantankerous, captious, choleric, crabbed, cranky*, cross, crotchety, edgy, exasperated, fretful, grouchy, grumpy*, impatient, irascible, mean, ornery*, out of sorts, peevish, peppery, petulant, quarrelsome, quick-tempered, short-tempered, snappy*, splenetic, sullen, thin-skinned*, uptight*, waspish; SEE CONCEPTS 401,403,542

tete-a-tete [n] conversation
chat, colloquy, confabulation, confidential discussion, consultation, cozy chat, dialogue, discussion, exchange, face-to-face talk, fireside chat, friendly chat, heart-to-heart talk, intimate discussion, one-on-one talk, pillow talk*, pow-wow*, talk; SEE CONCEPT 266

tether [n] fastening
binding, bond, chain, cord, fetter, halter, harness, lead, leash, picket, restraint, rope, shackle; SEE CONCEPT 475

tether [v] fasten
batten, bind, chain, fetter, leash, manacle, moor, picket, restrain, rope, secure, shackle, tie; SEE CONCEPTS 85,160

text [n1] subject matter of document
argument, body, consideration, content, contents, context, document, extract, fundamentals, head, idea, issue, line, lines, main body, matter, motify, motive, paragraph, passage, point, quotation, sentence, stanza, subject, theme, thesis, topic, verse, vocabulary, wording, words; SEE CONCEPTS 270,682

text [n2] book used in education
assignment, class book, course book, handbook, manual, reader, reference, reference book, required reading, schoolbook, source, syllabus, textbook, workbook; SEE CONCEPTS 280,287

textbook [n] text
assigned book, class book, course book, primer, reader, required reading, schoolbook, workbook; SEE CONCEPTS 280,287

texture [n] characteristics of a surface
arrangement, balance, being, character, coarseness, composition, consistency, constitution, disposition, essence, essentiality, fabric, feel, feeling, fiber, fineness, flexibility, form, framework, grain, intermixture, make, makeup, nap, nature, organization, pattern, quality, roughness, scheme, sense, smoothness, stiffness, strategy, structure, surface, taste, tissue, touch, warp, weave, web, woof; SEE CONCEPTS 611,673,682

thank [v] express gratitude
acknowledge, be grateful, be indebted, be obligated, be obliged, bless, bow down*, give thanks, kiss*, praise, say thank you, show appreciation, show courtesy, show gratitude, smile on*; SEE CONCEPTS 60,69,76

thankful [adj] appreciative
beholden, content, contented, grateful, gratified, indebted, much obliged, obliged, overwhelmed, pleased, relieved, satisfied; SEE CONCEPTS 401,403

thankless [adj1] unappreciated
barren, disagreeable, distasteful, fruitless, futile, miserable, not worth it*, ungrateful, unpleasant, unprofitable, unrecognized, unrequited, unreturned, unrewarding, useless, vain, wretched; SEE CONCEPTS 538,548

thankless [adj2] unappreciative, inconsiderate (in behavior)
careless, cruel, heedless, inappreciative, rude, self-centered, thoughtless, ungracious, ungrateful, unmindful, unthankful; SEE CONCEPT 401

thanks [n] spoken or written appreciation
acknowledgment, benediction, blessing, credit, grace, gramercy, gratefulness, gratitude, praise, recognition, thankfulness, thanksgiving, thank you note; SEE CONCEPTS 60,69,278

thaw [v] unfreeze, warm
become liquid, become soft, defrost, deliquesce, dissolve, flow, flux, fuse, liquefy, loosen, melt, mollify, open up, relax, relent, run, soften, unbend, warm up; SEE CONCEPTS 13,255,469

theater/theatre [n] stage, building for performance
amphitheater, arena, assembly hall, auditorium, barn, boards*, cinema, coliseum, concert hall, deck, drama, drive-in, footlights, hall, hippodrome, house, locale, movie, movie house, oak*, odeum, opera house, playhouse, room, scene, show hall, site; SEE CONCEPTS 263,293,439,448

theatrical [adj] dramatic
affected, amateur, artificial, campy*, ceremonious, comic, dramaturgic, exaggerated, ham*, hammy*, histrionic, legitimate, mannered, melodramatic, meretricious, operatic, ostentatious, pompous, schmaltzy*, show, showy, staged, stilted, superficial, theatric, thespian, tragic, unnatural, unreal, vaudeville; SEE CONCEPTS 401,536

theft [n] stealing
annexation, appropriation, break-in, burglary, caper, cheating, crime, defrauding, deprivation, embezzlement, extortion, filch, fleece*, fraud, grab*, heist, holdup, hustle*, job*, larceny, lift*, looting, mugging, peculation, pilferage, pilfering, pillage, pinch*, piracy, plunder, purloining, racket*, rapacity, rip-off*, robbery, robbing, score*, shoplifting, snatch*, snitch*, steal, stickup, swindle, swindling, swiping*, thievery, thieving, touch*, vandalism; SEE CONCEPTS 139,192

theme [n1] idea, subject matter
affair, argument, burden, business, case, head, keynote, leitmotif, line, matter, matter in hand, motif, motive, point, point at issue, problem, proposition, question, stuff, subject, text, thesis, thought, topic; SEE CONCEPTS 278,682,689

theme [n2] written composition
article, description, dissertation, essay, exercise, exposition, manuscript, paper, report, statement, thesis; SEE CONCEPT 271

then [adv1] before; at another time
again, all at once, anon, at that instant, at that moment, at that point, at that time, before long, formerly, later, next, on that occasion, soon after, suddenly, thereupon, when, years ago; SEE CONCEPT 799

then [adv2] therefore
accordingly, consequently, ergo, from that time, from then on, from there on, hence, so, thence, thenceforth, thereupon, thus, whence; SEE CONCEPT 548

theological [adj] religious, concerning a god-centered philosophy
apostolic, canonical, churchly, deistic, divine, doctrinal, ecclesiastical, metaphysical, scriptural, theistic; SEE CONCEPT 536

te
th

theorem [n] *explanation based on hypothesis and experiments*
assumption, axiom, belief, deduction, dictum, doctrine, formula, fundamental, law, postulate, principium, principle, proposition, rule, statement, theory, thesis; SEE CONCEPTS *529,688,689*

theoretical [adj] *hypothetical*
abstract, academic, analytical, as a premise, assumed, codified, conjectural, contingent, formalistic, formularized, general, ideal, idealized, ideational, ideological, imaginative, impractical, instanced, intellectual, in the abstract, in theory, logical, metaphysical, notional, on paper*, pedantic, philosophical, postulated, presumed, problematical, pure, quixotic, speculative, suppositional, tentative, transcendent, transcendental, unearthly, unproved, unsubstantiated, vague; SEE CONCEPT *529*

theorize [v] *hypothesize*
conjecture, formulate, guess, project, propound, speculate, submit, suggest, suppose, think; SEE CONCEPT *43*

theory [n] *hypothesis, belief*
approach, argument, assumption, base, basis, belief, code, codification, concept, conditions, conjecture, doctrine, dogma, feeling, formularization, foundation, grounds, guess, guesswork, hunch, idea, ideology, impression, method, outlook, philosophy, plan, position, postulate, premise, presentiment, presumption, proposal, provision, rationale, scheme, shot*, speculation, stab*, supposal, suppose, supposition, surmise, suspicion, system, systemization, theorem, thesis, understanding; SEE CONCEPTS *529,689*

therapeutic [adj] *healing*
ameliorative, analeptic, beneficial, corrective, curative, good, remedial, restorative, salubrious, salutary, sanative; SEE CONCEPT *537*

therapist [n] *counselor*
adviser, analyst, clinician, doctor, physician, psychiatrist, psychoanalyst, psychologist, psychotherapist, shrink*; SEE CONCEPT *357*

therapy [n] *healing treatment*
analysis, cure, healing, medicine, remedial treatment, remedy, therapeutics; SEE CONCEPT *310*

thereabout [adv] *about there*
almost, approximately, around, close at hand, in the neighborhood, in the vicinity, just about, near, nearby, nearly, roughly; SEE CONCEPTS *581,586*

thereafter [adv] *from that time forward*
after that, consequently, following, forever after, from that day forward, from that day on, from there on, hereafter, thenceforth, thenceforward; SEE CONCEPT *799*

therefore [adv] *as a result; for that reason*
accordingly, and so, consequently, ergo, for, forasmuch as, for this reason, hence, inasmuch as, in consequence, in that event, on account of, on the grounds, since, so, then, thence, therefrom, thereupon, thus, to that end, whence, wherefore; SEE CONCEPTS *230,676*

thermal [adj] *warm*
heated, hot, lukewarm, melting, roasting, scorching, sizzling, snug, summery, sweltering, thermic, toasty; SEE CONCEPT *605*

thesaurus [n] *dictionary of synonyms and antonyms*
glossary, language reference book, lexicon, ono-

masticon, reference book, sourcebook, storehouse of words, terminology, treasury of words, vocabulary, word list; SEE CONCEPT *280*

thesis [n1] *belief, assumption to be tested*
apriorism, contention, contestation, hypothesis, idea, line, opinion, point, posit, position, postulate, postulation, premise, presumption, presupposition, principle, proposal, proposition, sentiment, statement, supposition, surmise, theory, view; SEE CONCEPTS *529,689*

thesis [n2] *written dissertation*
argument, argumentation, composition, discourse, disquisition, essay, exposition, memoir, monograph, monography, paper, research, theme, tractate, treatise; SEE CONCEPTS *271,287*

thespian [n] *actor, actress*
artist, bit player, character, entertainer, extra, ham*, headliner, idol, lead, performer, play-actor, player, star, straight person, thesp*, understudy; SEE CONCEPT *352*

thick [adj1] *deep, bulky*
blubbery, broad, bulky, burly, chunky, compact, concrete, consolidated, fat, firm, hard, heavy, high, husky, massive, obese, pudgy, solid, squat, stocky, stubby, stumpy, substantial, thickset, wide; SEE CONCEPTS *491,773*

thick [adj2] *concentrated, dense*
caked, clabbered, close, clotted, coagulated, compact, compressed, concrete, condensed, congealed, consolidated, crowded, curdled, deep, firm, fixed, gelatinous, gloppy*, gooey, gummous, gummy, gunky*, heavy, impenetrable, impervious, jelled, jellied, opaque, ossified, ropy, set, sloppy, solid, solidified, stiff, syrupy, thickened, turbid, viscid, viscous, vitrified; SEE CONCEPTS *483,606*

thick [adj3] *crowded, packed*
abundant, brimming, bristling, bursting, chock-full*, close, compact, compressed, concentrated, condensed, considerable, covered, crammed, crawling with*, dense, frequent, full, great, heaped, impenetrable, impervious, inspissated, like sardines*, localized, multitudinous, numerous, populated, populous, profuse, rank, replete, several, solid, swarming, teeming, tight; SEE CONCEPT *771*

thick [adj4] *stupid*
blockheaded, boneheaded, brainless, dense, dim-witted, doltish, dopey*, dull, dumb, ignorant, insensitive, moronic, numbskulled, obtuse, slow, slow-witted, thickheaded; SEE CONCEPT *402*

thick [adj5] *dense (referring to weather)*
cloudy, dull, foggy, heavy, impenetrable, indistinct, muddy, obscure, soupy*, turbid; SEE CONCEPT *525*

thick [adj6] *friendly*
chummy*, close, confidential, cordial, devoted, familiar, hand in glove*, inseparable, intimate, on good terms; SEE CONCEPT *555*

thick [adj7] *unreasonable*
excessive, flimsy*, implausible, improbable, inconceivable, incredible, thin*, too much*, unbelievable, unconvincing, unfair, unjust, unsubstantial; SEE CONCEPTS *529,548*

thicken [v] *set; make more dense*
add, buttress, cake, clabber, clot, coagulate, condense, congeal, curdle, deepen, enlarge, expand, freeze, gel, grow thick, harden, inspissate, jell, jelly, ossify, petrify, reinforce, solidify, stiffen, swell, widen; SEE CONCEPTS *137,250,469*

thick-skinned [*adj*] *hardened*
benumbed, callous, coldhearted*, hard-as-nails*, hardhearted*, insensitive, seasoned, tough, toughened, unbending, unfeeling; SEE CONCEPTS *404,542*

thief [*n*] *person who steals*
bandit, burglar, cat burglar, cheat, clip*, criminal, crook, defalcator, embezzler, heister*, highway robber, hijacker, holdup artist, housebreaker, kleptomaniac, larcener, larcenist, lifter*, moonlighter*, mugger, owl*, pickpocket, pilferer, pirate, plunderer, porch climber*, prowler, punk*, purloiner, robber, scrounger, shoplifter, sniper, spider*, stealer, stickup artist*, swindler; SEE CONCEPT *412*

thieving/thievish [*adj*] *criminal*
crooked, cunning, dishonest, fraudulent, furtive, kleptomaniacal*, larcenous, light-fingered*, pilfering, piratic*, plunderous, predatory, rapacious, secretive, sly, spoliative, stealthy, sticky-fingered*; SEE CONCEPT *401*

thin [*adj1*] *fine, light, slender*
attenuate, attenuated, beanpole*, beanstalk*, bony*, cadaverous, delicate, emaciated, ethereal, featherweight, fragile, gangling, gangly, gaunt, haggard, lank, lanky, lean, lightweight, meager, narrow, peaked, pinched, pole*, puny*, rangy, rarefied, rawboned, reedy, rickety, scraggy*, scrawny, shadow, shriveled, skeletal, skinny, slight, slim, slinky, small, spare, spindly, stalky*, starved, stick*, stilt*, subtle, threadlike, twiggy*, twiglike, undernourished, underweight, wan, wasted, wizened; SEE CONCEPTS *491,773*

thin [*adj2*] *transparent, fine*
attenuate, attenuated, delicate, diaphanous, filmy, flimsy, gossamer, paper-thin, permeable, rare, rarefied, refined, see-through, sheer, slight, slim, subtile, subtle, tenuous, translucent, unsubstantial, wafer-thin, wispy; SEE CONCEPT *606*

thin [*adj3*] *deficient, weak*
diluted, feeble*, flat*, flimsy*, implausible, improbable, inadequate, inconceivable, incredible, insubstantial, insufficient, lame, meager, poor, questionable, scant, scanty, scarce, scattered, shallow, sketchy, skimpy*, slight, sparse, stretched, superficial, thick*, transparent, unbelievable, unconvincing, unpersuasive, unsubstantial, untenable, vapid, weak-kneed*; SEE CONCEPT *771*

thin [*adj4*] *diluted*
diffuse, dilute, dispersed, fine, light, rarefied, refined, runny, subtle, watery, weak, wishy-washy*; SEE CONCEPT *485*

thin [*v*] *make diluted or less dense*
attenuate, cook, cut, cut back, decrease, delete, diminish, disperse, doctor, edit, emaciate, expand, extenuate, irrigate, lace*, needle*, prune, rarefy, reduce, refine, shave, spike, trim, water, water down, weaken, weed out; SEE CONCEPTS *137,250*

thing [*n1*] *something felt, seen, perceived*
affair, anything, apparatus, article, being, body, business, circumstance, commodity, concept, concern, configuration, contrivance, corporeality, creature, device, element, entity, everything, existence, existent, fact, figure, form, gadget, goods, implement, individual, information, instrument, item, machine, material, materiality, matter, means, mechanism, object, part, person, phenomenon, piece, point, portion, shape, situa-

tion, stuff, subject, substance, tool, word; SEE CONCEPT *433*

thing [*n2*] *act*
accomplishment, action, circumstance, deed, doing, duty, episode, event, eventuality, exploit, feat, happening, incident, job, movement, obligation, occasion, occurrence, phenomenon, proceeding, stunt, task, work; SEE CONCEPT *3*

thing [*n3*] *aspect, characteristic*
article, attribute, detail, element, facet, factor, feature, item, particular, point, property, quality, statement, thought, trait; SEE CONCEPTS *411,657,834*

thing [*n5*] *idea, obsession*
attitude, bee in bonnet*, craze, fad, fetish, fixation, hang-up*, idée fixe, impression, mania, notion, opinion, phobia, preoccupation, quirk, style, thought; SEE CONCEPT *529*

thing/things [*n4*] *personal possessions*
apparel, attire, baggage, belongings, chattels, clothes, clothing, duds*, effects, equipment, gear, goods, habiliments, impedimenta, luggage, odds and ends*, paraphernalia, personal effects, personals*, property, raiment, stuff, trappings, tricks; SEE CONCEPTS *446,451*

think [*v1*] *believe; anticipate*
assume, be convinced, comprehend, conceive, conclude, consider, credit, deem, determine, envisage, envision, esteem, estimate, expect, fancy, feature, feel, foresee, gather, guess, hold, image, imagine, judge, plan for, presume, project, realize, reckon, regard, see, sense, suppose, surmise, suspect, take, understand, vision, visualize; SEE CONCEPTS *12,26*

think [*v2*] *contemplate*
analyze, appraise, appreciate, brood, cerebrate, cogitate, comprehend, conceive, consider, deduce, deliberate, estimate, evaluate, examine, figure out, have in mind, ideate, imagine, infer, intellectualize, judge, logicalize, meditate, mull, mull over, muse, ponder, rack one's brains*, rationalize, reason, reflect, resolve, revolve, ruminate, sort out, speculate, stew*, stop to consider, study, take under consideration, turn over, use one's head*, weigh; SEE CONCEPTS *17,33,43*

think [*v3*] *remember*
call to mind, recall, recollect, reminisce; SEE CONCEPT *40*

thinkable [*adj*] *believable, feasible*
cogitable, comprehendible, comprehensible, conceivable, convincing, imaginable, likely, possible, practicable, practical, presumable, reasonable, supposable, within realm of possibility*, within the limits; SEE CONCEPT *529*

thin-skinned [*adj*] *sensitive*
delicate, easily hurt, hypersensitive, oversensitive, soft, touchy, vulnerable; SEE CONCEPT *406*

third world [*n*] *underdeveloped countries*
developing countries, developing nations, economically developing countries, economically developing nations, emergent nations, underdeveloped nations; SEE CONCEPTS *378,391*

thirst [*n*] *craving (especially for liquid)*
appetite, aridity, desire, drought, dryness, eagerness, hankering, hunger, keenness, longing, lust, passion, thirstiness, yearning, yen; SEE CONCEPTS *20,709*

thirsty [*adj*] *dry, desirous (especially for liquid)*
agog*, anxious, appetent, ardent, arid, athirst, avid, bone-dry*, breathless, burning, cotton-

th
th

mouthed*, craving, crazy for*, dehydrated, droughty, dry as dust*, dying for*, eager, greedy, hankering, hungry, impatient, inclined, itching for*, juiceless, keen, longing, lusting, parched, partial to, sapless, thirsting, waterless, wild for*, yearning; SEE CONCEPTS *403,603*

thorny [*adj1*] *sharp, pointed*
barbed, briery, bristling, bristly, prickly, spiked, spiky, spinous, spiny, stinging, thistly; SEE CONCEPT *485*

thorny [*adj2*] *difficult, problematic*
awkward, baffling, bothersome, formidable, harassing, hard, irksome, nettlesome, perplexing, prickly, severe, sticky, ticklish, tough, tricky, troublesome, trying, unpleasant, upsetting, vexatious, worrying; SEE CONCEPT *565*

thoroughbred [*adj*] *pure, unmixed*
blood, full-blooded, graded, papered, pedigree, pedigreed, pure-blooded, purebred; SEE CONCEPT *549*

thoroughly [*adv1*] *exhaustively*
all, assiduously, carefully, completely, comprehensively, conscientiously, earnestly, efficiently, exceedingly, exceptionally, extremely, flat out*, from A to Z*, from top to bottom*, fully, hard, highly, hugely, in and out*, in detail, inside out*, intensely, intensively, meticulously, notably, painstakingly, remarkably, scrupulously, strikingly, sweepingly, through and through*, throughout, unremittingly, up and down*, very, whole hog*, wholly; SEE CONCEPTS *531,538*

thoroughly [*adv2*] *utterly*
absolutely, altogether, completely, downright, entirely, fully, perfectly, plumb, quite, totally, to the full, well, wholly, without reservation; SEE CONCEPTS *531,535,557*

thorough/thoroughgoing [*adj1*] *exhaustive*
absolute, all-embracing, all-inclusive, all-out*, all the way*, assiduous, blow-by-blow*, careful, circumstantial, clocklike, complete, comprehensive, conscientious, detailed, efficient, exact, from A to Z*, full, full-dress*, in-depth, intensive, itemized, meticulous, minute, painstaking, particular, particularized, plenty, royal, scrupulous, slam bang*, soup to nuts*, sweeping, tough, whole-hog*; SEE CONCEPTS *531,538*

thorough/thoroughgoing [*adj2*] *absolute, utter*
arrant, complete, consummate, downright, entire, out-and-out*, outright, perfect, pure, rank, sheer, straight-out*, total, unmitigated, unqualified; SEE CONCEPTS *531,535,557*

though [*adv*] *however*
after all, all the same, for all that, howbeit, nevertheless, nonetheless, notwithstanding, still, still and all, withal, yet; SEE CONCEPT *544*

though [*conj*] *while*
albeit, allowing, although, but, despite, despite the fact, even if, even supposing, even though, granted, howbeit, if, much as, notwithstanding, when, whereas; SEE CONCEPT *544*

thought [*n1*] *formation of mental objects*
anticipation, apprehending, attention, brainwork, cerebration, cogitation, cognition, concluding, consideration, considering, contemplation, deducing, deduction, deliberation, deriving, discerning, heed, hope, ideation, inducing, inferring, introspection, intuition, judging, knowing, logic, meditation, musing, perceiving, rationalization, rationalizing, realizing, reasoning, reflection, regard, rumination, scrutiny, seeing,

speculation, study, theorization, thinking, understanding; SEE CONCEPTS *17,43,409,410*

thought [*n2*] *idea, concept*
aim, anxiety, appreciation, aspiration, assessment, assumption, attentiveness, belief, brainchild*, brainstorm*, caring, compassion, conception, concern, conclusion, conjecture, conviction, design, dream, drift, estimation, expectation, fancy, feeling, guess, hope, hypothesis, image, inference, intention, intuition, judgment, kindness, knowledge, notion, object, opinion, plan, premise, prospect, purpose, regard, reverie, solicitude, supposition, sympathy, theory, thinking, understanding, view, worry; SEE CONCEPT *529*

thoughtful [*adj1*] *caring, mindful*
anxious, astute, attentive, aware, benign, canny, careful, cautious, charitable, chivalrous, circumspect, civil, concerned, considerate, cooperative, courteous, deliberate, diplomatic, discreet, friendly, gallant, gracious, heedful, helpful, indulgent, kind, kindly, mindful, neighborly, obliging, observant, observative, observing, polite, prudent, regardful, responsive, sensitive, social, solicitous, tactful, unselfish, wary, well-bred, well thought-out; SEE CONCEPTS *401,555*

thoughtful [*adj2*] *contemplative, introspective*
absorbed, analytical, attentive, brainy*, calculating, cerebral, cogitative, deep, deliberative, discerning, earnest, engrossed, farsighted, grave, intellectual, intent, keen, levelheaded, logical, lost in thought*, meditative, melancholy, museful, musing, pensive, philosophic, pondering, preoccupied, rapt, rational, reasonable, reasoning, reflecting, reflective, retrospective, ruminative, serious, sober, studious, subjective, thinking, wise, wistful; SEE CONCEPTS *402,403, 542*

thoughtless [*adj1*] *inconsiderate*
antisocial, apathetic, asocial, blind, boorish, brash, deaf, discourteous, egocentric, hasty, heedless, hot-headed, impolite, inattentive, incautious, indelicate, indifferent, indiscreet, insensitive, listless, madcap, neglectful, negligent, primitive, rash, reckless, rude, self-centered, selfish, sharp, short, tactless, uncaring, unceremonious, unconcerned, undiplomatic, ungracious, unheeding, unkind, unmindful, unrefined; SEE CONCEPTS *401,555*

thoughtless [*adj2*] *absent-minded, unobservant*
bovine, careless, confused, doltish, dull, empty-headed, flighty, foolish, heedless, ill-advised, ill-considered, imprudent, inadvertent, inane, inattentive, incomprehensible, inept, injudicious, irrational, irreflective, lamebrained*, loony*, mindless, neglectful, negligent, obtuse, puerile, rash, reckless, regardless, remiss, senseless, silly, stupid, undiscerning, unheeding, unmindful, unreasonable, unreasoning, unreflective, unthinking, vacuous, witless; SEE CONCEPTS *402,403,542*

thought-provoking [*adj*] *stimulating*
absorbing, captivating, exciting, fascinating, gripping, inspirational, interesting, intriguing, inviting, provocative, refreshing, riveting, stirring; SEE CONCEPTS *372,529,537,572*

thrash [*v*] *flail about; beat*
batter, beat up, belabor, belt, birch, buffet, bury, cane, chasten, chastise, clobber, crush, defeat, flagellate, flog, jerk, kill, lambaste*, lick, maul, murder, overwhelm, paste, pelt, pitch, pound,

pummel, punish, rout, rush, scourge, seesaw, slaughter, spank, stir, strike, surge, tan, tan one's hide*, thresh, toss, toss and turn*, trash, trim, trounce, wallop, wax*, whip, work over*, writhe; SEE CONCEPTS *95,189*

threadbare [*adj1*] *worn, frayed*
beat up*, damaged, dilapidated, dingy, dog-eared, down-at-the-heel*, faded, frowzy*, impaired, injured, old, ragged, ratty*, run-down, scruffy, seedy, shabby, shopworn, tacky, tattered, timeworn, used, used-up, worn-out, worse for wear*; SEE CONCEPTS *485,606*

threadbare [*adj2*] *trite, corny*
banal, bathetic, cliché, clichéd, cliché-ridden, common, commonplace, conventional, dull, everyday, familiar, hackneyed, imitative, moth-eaten*, musty, overused, poor, set, stale, stereotyped, stock, tedious, tired, uncreative, well-worn, worn-out; SEE CONCEPT *267*

threads [*n*] *clothes, clothing*
accouterment, apparel, attire, civvies*, costume, dress, duds*, finery, garb, garments, gear, habiliment, outfit, personal attire, rags*, raiment, Sunday best*, wardrobe, weeds*; SEE CONCEPT *451*

threat [*n*] *warning; danger*
blackmail, bluff, commination, fix, foreboding, foreshadowing, fulmination, hazard, impendence, intimidation, menace, omen, peril, portent, presage, risk, thunder, writing on the wall*; SEE CONCEPTS *278,675*

threaten [*v1*] *warn, pressure*
abuse, admonish, augur, blackmail, bluster, browbeat, bully, caution, comminate, cow, enforce, flex muscles*, forebode, forewarn, fulminate, growl, intimidate, look daggers*, make threat, menace, portend, presage, pressurize, push around*, scare, scowl, shake fist at*, snarl, spook, terrorize, torment, walk heavy*; SEE CONCEPTS *7,19,78*

threaten [*v2*] *endanger*
advance, approach, be dangerous, be gathering, be imminent, be in the air*, be in the offing*, be on the horizon*, brewing, come on, forebode, foreshadow, frighten, hang over*, impend, imperil, jeopardize, loom, overhang, portend, presage, put at risk, put in jeopardy, warn; SEE CONCEPTS *231,407*

threatening [*adj*] *menacing, ominous*
aggressive, alarming, apocalyptic, at hand, baleful, baneful, black, bullying, cautionary, close, comminatory, dangerous, dire, fateful, forthcoming, grim, ill-boding, imminent, impendent, impending, inauspicious, intimidatory, looming, loury, lowering, lowery, minacious, minatory, near, overhanging, portending, portentous, scowling, sinister, terrorizing, ugly, unlucky, unpropitious, unsafe, upcoming, warning; SEE CONCEPTS *525,548,570*

threshold [*n*] *opening; beginning*
brink, dawn, door, doorstep, doorway, edge, entrance, gate, inception, origin, outset, point, point of departure, sill, start, starting point, verge, vestibule; SEE CONCEPTS *440,513,648,832*

thrift [*n*] *economy*
austerity, carefulness, economizing, frugality, parsimony, providence, prudence, saving, stinginess, thriftiness; SEE CONCEPT *335*

thrifty [*adj*] *economical*
canny, careful, chary, cheap, chintzy*, close*, close-fisted, conserving, frugal, mean, parsimo-nious, penny-pinching, preserving, provident, prudent, saving, scrimpy*, sparing, steal, stingy*, tight*, unwasteful; SEE CONCEPTS *334,401*

thrill [*n*] *sudden excitement*
adventure, bang*, blast, charge*, circus, fireworks, flash*, flush*, fun, good feeling, inspiration, kicks*, lift*, pleasure, refreshment, response, sensation, stimulation, tingle*, titillation, turn-on*, twitter*, upper*, wallop*; SEE CONCEPTS *32,529*

thrill [*v*] *excite, stimulate*
animate, arouse, blow away*, delight, electrify, enchant, enthuse, fire up*, flush, flutter, galvanize, glow, go over big*, grab*, inspire, juice*, key up*, knock one's socks off*, move, palpitate, quicken, quiver, race one's motor*, rally, rouse, score, send, stir, stir up, tickle*, tingle*, titillate, tremble, turn on*, wow*; SEE CONCEPTS *7,22*

thrilling [*adj*] *exciting*
blood-tingling*, boss*, breathtaking, electrifying, enchanting, exquisite, fab*, fabulous, frantic, gripping, hair-raising*, large, mad, magnificent, mind-bending*, mind-blowing*, miraculous, overwhelming, rip-roaring*, riveting, rousing, sensational, shivering, stimulating, stirring, swinging, trembling, wild, wondrous, zero cool*; SEE CONCEPTS *548,572*

thrive [*v*] *do well*
advance, arrive, batten, bear fruit, bloom, blossom, boom, burgeon, develop, flourish, get ahead*, get fat*, get on*, get places*, get there*, grow, grow rich, increase, make a go*, mushroom*, progress, prosper, radiate, rise, score*, shine, shoot up, succeed, turn out well, wax; SEE CONCEPTS *704,706*

thriving [*adj*] *successful*
advancing, arrived, blooming, booming, burgeoning, cooking*, developing, doing well, flourishing, going strong*, growing, have it made*, have the wherewithal*, healthy, home free*, on top of heap*, progressing, prolific, prospering, prosperous, rich, roaring, robust, rolling*, sitting pretty*, wealthy; SEE CONCEPTS *334,528*

throb [*v*] *pulsate, beat*
flutter, palpitate, pitpat, pound, pulse, resonate, thrill, thump, tingle, tremble, twitter, vibrate; SEE CONCEPTS *152,185*

throng [*n*] *large crowd*
assemblage, assembly, bunch, collection, concourse, congregation, crush, drove, everybody, flock, gathering, horde, host, jam, mass, mob, multitude, pack, press, push, sellout, swarm; SEE CONCEPTS *417,432*

throttle [*v*] *choke*
burke, control, gag, inhibit, silence, smother, stifle, strangle, strangulate, suppress; SEE CONCEPT *191*

through [*adj1*] *done*
buttoned up*, complete, completed, concluded, ended, finis*, finished, in the bag*, over, terminated, wound up*, wrapped up*; SEE CONCEPTS *531,548*

through [*adj2*] *direct*
constant, free, nonstop, one-way, opened, rapid, regular, straight, straightforward, unbroken, unhindered, uninterrupted; SEE CONCEPTS *482,581*

th
th

through [*prep1*] *by way of*
as a consequence, as a result, at the hand of, because of, by, by dint of, by means of, by reason, by the agency of, by virtue of, for, in consequence of, in virtue of, per, through the medium of, using, via, with, with the help of; SEE CONCEPT *544*

through [*prep2*] *between, during*
about, by, clear, for the period, from beginning to end, in, in and out, in the middle, into, past, round, straight, throughout, within; SEE CONCEPTS *583,798*

throughout [*adj*] *during the whole of*
all over, all the time, all through, around, at full length, completely, during, every bit, everyplace, everywhere, far and near, far and wide, for the duration, from beginning to end, from end to end, from one end to the other, from start to finish, from the start, from the word go*, high and low, in all respects, in every place, in everything, inside and out, on all accounts*, over, overall, right through, round, the whole time, through the whole of, to the end, up and down; SEE CONCEPTS *482,531,798*

throw [*v1*] *propel something through the air*
bandy, barrage, bombard, buck, bunt, butt, cant, cast, catapult, chuck, dash, deliver, discharge, dislodge, drive, fell, fire, flick, fling, fling off, flip, floor, force, heave, hurl, impel, lapidate, launch, let fly*, let go, lift, lob, overturn, overwhelm, peg, pellet, pelt, pepper, pitch, precipitate, project, push, put, scatter, send, shove, shower, shy, sling, splatter, spray, sprinkle, start, stone, strew, thrust, toss, tumble, unhorse, unseat, upset, volley, waft; SEE CONCEPT *222*

throw [*v2*] *confuse*
addle, astonish, baffle, befuddle, bewilder, confound, disconcert, distract, disturb, dizzy, dumbfound, fluster, mix up*, throw off*, unsettle, upset; SEE CONCEPT *16*

throw away [*v1*] *dispose of*
abandon, cast, cast off, chase, clear, discard, dismiss, dispense with, ditch*, drop*, dump*, eject, eliminate, evict, extrude, free oneself of, get rid of, jettison, junk*, lose, refuse, reject, rid oneself of, scrap*, shake off*, shed, shuck, slip, throw off, throw out, turn down, unburden; SEE CONCEPT *180*

throw away [*v2*] *waste*
be wasteful, blow, consume, dissipate, fail to exploit, fritter, lose, refuse, reject, squander, trifle, turn down; SEE CONCEPT *156*

throw off [*v*] *elude, escape*
abuse, deceive, evade, get away from, give the slip*, leave behind, lose, outdistance, outrun, shake off, trick; SEE CONCEPT *102*

throw out [*v*] *comment*
bring forward, bring to light*, bring up, chime in*, come out with, declare, deliver, produce, reveal, say, state, suggest, tell, utter; SEE CONCEPT *51*

throw over [*v*] *abandon, leave*
break up with, break with, desert, discard, drop, eighty-six*, finish with, forsake, jilt*, quit, renounce, split up with, walk out on*; SEE CONCEPTS *195,384*

throw up [*v1*] *vomit, be nauseous*
be sick, bring up, disgorge, heave, puke*, regurgitate, retch, spew, spit up, upchuck*; SEE CONCEPTS *179,308*

throw up [*v2*] *build quickly*
build overnight*, jerrybuild*, knock together*, patch, put together, roughcast, roughhew, run up*, slap together*, throw together; SEE CONCEPT *168*

thrust [*n1*] *point of communication*
burden, core, effect, gist, meaning, meat*, pith*, purport, sense, short, substance, upshot; SEE CONCEPT *682*

thrust [*n2*] *forward movement*
advance, blitz, boost, drive, impetus, impulsion, jump, lunge, momentum, onset, onslaught, poke, pressure, prod, propulsion, punch, push, shove, stab, whack, wham; SEE CONCEPTS *208,222*

thrust [*v*] *push hard*
advance, assail, assault, attack, bear down, boost, buck, butt, chuck, chunk, clip, clout, crowd, cut, dig, drive, elbow*, embed, fire, force, heave, hump, impale, impel, interject, jab, jam, jostle, lob, lunge, nick, nudge, peg, pierce, pitch, plunge, poke, pour it on*, press, prod, propel, punch, push forward, put, railroad*, ram, run, shove, sink, sling, smack, stab*, stick, toss, transfix, urge, wham*; SEE CONCEPTS *208,222*

thud/thump [*n/v*] *dull crash; dull sound*
bang, beat, blow, clonk, clout, clump, clunk, fall, flutter, hammer, hit, knock, plop, poke, pound, pounding, pulse, rap, slap, smack, strike, throb, thunk*, thwack*, wallop*, whack*; SEE CONCEPTS *65,181,189*

thug [*n*] *hoodlum*
assassin, bandit, bully, criminal, delinquent, gang member, gangster, goon*, gorilla*, gunman, hired killer, hood, hooligan, killer, mobster, murderer, professional killer, punk, rioter, rowdy, ruffian, troublemaker; SEE CONCEPT *412*

thunder [*n*] *crashing sound*
barrage, blast, boom, booming, cannonade, clap, cracking, crash, crashing, detonation, discharge, drumfire, explosion, fulmination, outburst, peal, pealing, roar, rumble, rumbling, thunderbolt, thundercrack, uproar; SEE CONCEPTS *524,595*

thunder [*v1*] *boom, crash*
blast, clamor, clap, crack, deafen, detonate, drum, explode, peal, resound, reverberate, roar, rumble, storm; SEE CONCEPTS *65,521,526*

thunder [*v2*] *yell at*
bark, bellow, curse, declaim, denounce, fulminate, gnarl, growl, rail, roar, shout, snarl, threaten, utter threat; SEE CONCEPTS *52,54*

thunderstruck [*adj*] *amazed, astonished*
agape, aghast, astounded, awestruck, bowled over*, confounded, dazed, dismayed, dumbfounded, flabbergasted, floored, overwhelmed, petrified, shocked, staggered, startled, stunned; SEE CONCEPTS *403,690*

thus [*adv1*] *in this manner*
along these lines, as follows, hence, in kind, in such a way, in this fashion, in this way, just like that, like so, like this, so, thus and so, thus and thus, thusly, to such a degree; SEE CONCEPT *544*

thus [*adv2*] *accordingly*
consequently, ergo, for this reason, hence, on that account, so, then, therefore, thereupon; SEE CONCEPT *544*

thwart [*v*] *stop, hinder*
baffle, balk, beat, bilk, check, circumvent, confuse, counter, crab*, cramp, crimp, cross, curb, dash, defeat, disappoint, ditch, dodge, double-cross*, duck, foil, foul up*, frustrate, give the

slip*, hold up, impede, louse up*, match, obstruct, oppose, outwit, pit, play off, prevent, queer*, restrain, ruin, scotch*, skin, snafu*, stymie, take down, take wind out of*, trammel, upset, upset one's apple cart*; SEE CONCEPTS *121,130*

tiara [*n*] *crown*
chaplet, circlet, coronal, coronet, crown jewels, diadem, garland, headband, headdress, miter, royal crown, wreath; SEE CONCEPT *452*

tic [*n*] *spasm*
contraction, fit, jerk, twitch; SEE CONCEPT *308*

tick [*n1*] *clicking sound; one beat*
beat, blow, clack, click, clicking, flash, instant, metallic sound, minute, moment, pulsation, pulse, rap, second, shake, tap, tapping, throb, ticktock, twinkling, wink; SEE CONCEPTS *595,808,810*

tick [*n2*] *checkmark*
check, cross, dash, flick, indication, line, mark, stroke, X*; SEE CONCEPT *284*

tick [*v*] *click*
beat, clack, pulsate, tap, thump, ticktock; SEE CONCEPTS *65,189*

ticket [*n*] *authorization on paper*
admission, badge, board, card, certificate, check, chit, coupon, credential, docket, document, invite, key, label, license, marker, note, notice, open sesame, paper, pass, passage, passport, password, permit, raincheck, receipt, record, slip, sticker, stub, tab, tag, token, voucher; SEE CONCEPTS *271,685*

tickle [*v*] *make laugh*
amuse, brush, caress, convulse, delight, divert, enchant, entertain, excite, gratify, itch, pat, pet, please, stimulate, stroke, thrill, tingle, titillate, touch, vellicate; SEE CONCEPTS *7,22,612*

ticklish [*adj*] *difficult, tricky*
awkward, capricious, chancy, changeable, critical, dangerous, delicate, fickle, inconstant, mercurial, nice, precarious, risky, rocky, sensitive, temperamental, thorny, touchy, trying, uncertain, unstable, unsteady, variable, volatile; SEE CONCEPTS *548,565*

tidbit [*n*] *tiny portion*
bit, bite, delicacy, goody*, morsel, mouthful, snack, soupçon, titbit, treat; SEE CONCEPTS *458,835*

tide [*n*] *flow, current*
course, direction, drag, drift, ebb, eddy, flood, flow, flux, movement, race, run, rush, sluice, spate, stream, tendency, torrent, trend, undercurrent, undertow, vortex, wave, whirlpool; SEE CONCEPT *514*

tide over [*v*] *help along*
aid, assist, bridge the gap*, keep head above water*, keep one going, see through; SEE CONCEPT *110*

tidings [*n*] *greetings, news*
advice, bulletin, communication, dirt, information, intelligence, message, report, word; SEE CONCEPT *274*

tidy [*adj1*] *clean, neat*
apple-pie order*, businesslike, chipper*, cleanly, in good shape, methodical, neat as a pin*, ordered, orderly, shipshape*, sleek, snug, spick-and-span*, spruce, systematic, to rights*, trim, uncluttered, well-groomed, well-kept, well-ordered; SEE CONCEPTS *485,585,621*

tidy [*adj2*] *considerable*
ample, fair, generous, good, goodly, handsome, healthy, large, largish, respectable, sizable, substantial, vast; SEE CONCEPTS *762,781*

tidy [*v*] *make neat and orderly*
clean, clear the decks*, fix up, frame*, get act together*, groom, neaten, order, police, pull together, put in good shape, put in order, put in shape, put to rights*, shape up, spruce, spruce up*, straighten, straighten up, tauten, whip into shape*; SEE CONCEPT *250*

tie [*n1*] *fastening*
attachment, band, bandage, bond, brace, connection, cord, fastener, fetter, gag, hookup, joint, knot, ligament, ligature, link, network, nexus, outfit, rope, strap, string, tackle, tie-in, tie-up, yoke, zipper; SEE CONCEPT *680*

tie [*n2*] *deadlock*
dead heat*, draw, drawn battle*, equivalence, even game, level, photo finish*, push, stalemate, standoff; SEE CONCEPTS *364,667*

tie [*n3*] *relationship*
affiliation, allegiance, association, bond, commitment, connection, duty, hookup, kinship, liaison, network, obligation, outfit, tie-in; SEE CONCEPT *388*

tie [*v1*] *connect, interlace*
anchor, attach, band, bind, cinch, clinch, do up, fasten, gird, join, knot, lash, link, make a bow, make a hitch, make a knot, make fast, marry, moor, rivet, rope, secure, splice, tether, tie up, tighten, truss, unite, wed; SEE CONCEPTS *85,160,193*

tie [*v3*] *equal*
balance, be even, be neck and neck*, be on a par, break even*, deadlock*, draw, even up, keep up with, match, measure up, meet, parallel, rival, touch; SEE CONCEPTS *92,667*

tier [*n*] *level*
bank, category, class, course, echelon, file, grade, group, grouping, layer, league, line, order, pigeonhole*, queue, range, rank, row, series, story, stratum, string; SEE CONCEPTS *378,727,744*

tie/tie up [*v2*] *hamper, hinder*
bind, clog, confine, curb, delay, entrammel, fetter, hog-tie*, hold, leash, limit, lock up, obstruct, restrain, restrict, shackle, stop, tie one's hands*, trammel; SEE CONCEPT *130*

tiff [*n*] *argument*
altercation, bad mood, bickering, difference, disagreement, dispute, falling-out*, fit, huff*, miff*, pet, quarrel, row*, run-in*, scrap, spat, squabble, sulk, tantrum, temper, words*, wrangle; SEE CONCEPTS *46,674*

tight [*adj1*] *close, snug*
bound, clasped, close-fitting, compact, constricted, contracted, cramped, crowded, dense, drawn, enduring, established, fast, firm, fixed, hidebound, inflexible, invulnerable, narrow, quick, rigid, secure, set, skintight, solid, stable, steady, stiff, strained, stretched, strong, sturdy, taut, tenacious, tense, thick, tightened, unbending, unyielding; SEE CONCEPTS *483,485*

tight [*adj2*] *sealed*
airtight, blind, blocked, bolted, choking, clumped, cramping, crushing, cutting, fast, fastened, firm, fixed, hermetic, hermetically sealed, impenetrable, impermeable, impervious, locked, nailed, obstructed, padlocked, pinching, plugged, proof, sealed, secure, short, shrunken, shut,

skintight, slammed, smothering, snapped, sound, stopped up, tied, tied up, uncomfortable, watertight; SEE CONCEPTS *489,576*

tight [*adj3*] *stingy*
cheap, close, grasping, mean, miserly, parsimonious, penny-pinching*, penurious, sparing, tightfisted; SEE CONCEPTS *334,401*

tight [*adj4*] *difficult, troublesome*
arduous, close, critical, dangerous, distressing, disturbing, exacting, hazardous, near, perilous, precarious, punishing, rough, sticky, tense, ticklish, tough, tricky, trying, upsetting, worrisome; SEE CONCEPTS *548,565*

tight [*adj5*] *intoxicated*
boozy*, buzzed*, drunk, drunken, high*, inebriated, loaded*, pickled*, plastered*, smashed*, stewed*, stoned*, tipsy, under the influence; SEE CONCEPTS *401,406*

tighten [*v*] *constrict*
bind, clench, close, compress, condense, congeal, contract, cramp, crush, fasten, fix, grip, harden, narrow, pinch, pressure, rigidify, screw, secure, squeeze, stiffen, strain, strangle, stretch, tauten, tense, toughen; SEE CONCEPTS *250,469,697*

tightfisted [*adj*] *cheap*
chintzy*, close-fisted, economical, frugal, greedy, mean, mingy, miserly, money-conscious, parsimonious, penny-pinching, pennywise*, penurious, pinchpenny*, saving, scrimping, stingy, thrifty, tight*, tight-wad*, ungenerous; SEE CONCEPTS *326,332,334,401*

tight-lipped [*adj*] *silent*
buttoned up*, clammed up*, closemouthed, dumb, hushed, mum, mute, muted, not talkative, quiet, reserved, restrained, reticent, secretive, taciturn, tongue-tied, zipped; SEE CONCEPT *594*

tightwad [*n*] *miser*
cheapskate*, churl, hoarder, moneygrubber*, penny-pincher*, pinchfist*, pinchpenny*, Scrooge*, skinflint, stiff; SEE CONCEPTS *348,412, 423*

till [*n*] *cash box*
box, cash drawer, cash register, kitty*, money box, safe, tray, treasury, vault; SEE CONCEPT *339*

till [*v*] *cultivate land*
dig, dress, farm, grow, harrow, hoe, labor, mulch, plant, plough, plow, prepare, raise crops, sow, tend, turn, turn over, work; SEE CONCEPTS *253,257*

tilt [*n1*] *lean, slope*
angle, cant, dip, drop, fall, grade, gradient, inclination, incline, leaning, list, pitch, rake, slant, slide; SEE CONCEPT *738*

tilt [*n2*] *fight*
attack, bout, clash, collision, combat, conflict, contest, duel, encounter, fracas, joust, meet, scrimmage, scuffle, set-to, skirmish, struggle, tournament, tourney, tussle; SEE CONCEPT *106*

tilt [*v1*] *lean, slant*
bend, cant, careen, dip, heel, incline, list, lurch, pitch, rake, recline, seesaw, set at an angle, shift, slope, slouch, swag, sway, tip, turn, yaw; SEE CONCEPTS *147,149*

tilt [*v2*] *attack, fight*
break, charge, clash, combat, contend, cross swords*, duel, encounter, joust, overthrow, spar, thrust; SEE CONCEPT *106*

timber [*n*] *trees, wood*
balk, beam, board, boom, club, forest, frame, girder, grove, hardwood, log, mast, plank, pole, rafter, rib, stake, timberland, weald, woodland, wood lot, woods; SEE CONCEPTS *430,479*

time [*n1*] *temporal length of event or entity's existence, period*
age, allotment, bit, bout, chronology, clock, continuance, date, day, duration, epoch, era, eternity, extent, future, generation, go*, hour, infinity, instance, instant, interval, juncture, lastingness, life, life span, lifetime, many a moon*, moment, month, occasion, pace, past, point, present, season, second, shift, space, span, spell, stage, stint, stretch, tempo, term, tide, tour, turn, week, while, year; SEE CONCEPTS *801,806,809,819,823*

time [*n2*] *opportunity*
break, chance, heyday, look-in*, occasion, opening, peak, shot, show, squeak*; SEE CONCEPT *693*

time-honored [*adj*] *traditional*
accustomed, ancestral, classic, classical, conventional, customary, fixed, folk, historic, long-established, old, popular, regular, rooted, standard, taken for granted, universal, usual, vintage, widespread; SEE CONCEPTS *530,533,547*

timeless [*adj*] *eternal*
abiding, ageless, always, amaranthine, constant, continual, continued, dateless, deathless, endless, enduring, everlasting, forever, illimitable, immemorial, immortal, indefinite, infinite, lasting, never-ending, perennial, permanent, perpetual, persistent, undying, unending, without end; SEE CONCEPTS *482,798*

timely [*adj*] *at the right time*
appropriate, auspicious, convenient, favorable, fit, fitting, in good time*, in the nick of time*, judicious, likely, meet, modern, now, opportune, pat, promising, prompt, proper, propitious, prosperous, punctual, seasonable, suitable, timeous, towardly, up-to-date, up-to-the-minute, well-timed, with it*; SEE CONCEPTS *558,799*

timetable [*n*] *schedule*
agenda, appointments, calendar, chart, chronology, docket, itinerary, list, order of business, plan, program, record; SEE CONCEPTS *271,283, 660*

timid [*adj*] *shy*
afraid, ambivalent, apprehensive, badgered, bashful, browbeaten, bullied, capricious, cowardly, cowed, cowering, coy, daunted, demure, diffident, fainthearted, fearful, feeble, frightened, gentle, having cold feet*, humble, intimidated, irresolute, milquetoast, modest, mousy, nervous, pusillanimous, retiring, shaky, shrinking, shy, soft, spineless, spiritless, submissive, timid, timorous, trembling, unassertive, unassured, unnerved, vacillating, wavering, weak, yellow*; SEE CONCEPT *401*

tinge [*n1*] *color*
cast, colorant, coloration, coloring, dye, dyestuff, hue, nib, pigment, shade, stain, tincture, tint, tone, wash; SEE CONCEPT *622*

tinge [*n2*] *hint*
bit, dash, drop, intimation, nib, pinch, shade, smack, smattering, soupçon, sprinkling, strain, streak, suggestion, tincture, touch, trace; SEE CONCEPTS *529,831*

tinge [*v*] *color*
complexion, dye, imbue, impregnate, infiltrate, saturate, shade, stain, streak, suffuse, tincture, tint; SEE CONCEPT *250*

tingle [*v*] *feel tickled, itchy*
creep, get excited, have goose bumps*, itch, prickle, shiver, sting, thrill, throb, tickle, twitter; SEE CONCEPT *612*

tinker [*v*] *fiddle with*
dabble, doodle*, fix, mess*, mess with*, monkey*, muck about*, niggle*, play, play with, puddle, putter, repair, take apart, toy, trifle with; SEE CONCEPTS *87,212*

tinkle [*v*] *jingle, ring*
chime, chink, chinkle, clink, ding, jangle, make bell sound, plink, sound, ting, tingle, tintinnabulate; SEE CONCEPT *65*

tint [*n*] *shade of color*
cast, chroma, color, coloration, complexion, dash, dye, flush, glow, hint, hue, luminosity, pigmentation, rinse, stain, suggestion, taint, tinct, tincture, tinge, tone, touch, trace, wash; SEE CONCEPT *622*

tint [*v*] *color with a certain shade*
affect, complexion, dye, influence, rinse, shade, stain, taint, tincture, tinge, touch, wash; SEE CONCEPT *250*

tiny [*adj*] *very small*
bitsy*, bitty, diminutive, infinitesimal, insignificant, itsy-bitsy*, itty-bitty*, Lilliputian, little, microscopic, midget, mini*, miniature, minikin, minimum, minuscular, minuscule, minute, negligible, pee-wee*, petite, pint-sized*, pocket, pocket-size*, puny, slight, teensy*, teensy-weensy*, teeny*, trifling, wee, yea big*; SEE CONCEPTS *762,773,789*

tip/tipoff [*n1*] *inside information*
bang*, bug*, buzz*, clue, cue, dope*, forecast, hint, in*, information, inkling, inside wire, knowledge, news, point, pointer, prediction, prompt, secret information, steer*, suggestion, two cents' worth*, warning, whisper, word, word of advice, word to the wise*; SEE CONCEPT *274*

tip [*n2*] *very top*
apex, cap, crown, cusp, edge, end, extremity, head, nip, peak, point, stub, summit, tiptop, vertex; SEE CONCEPT *836*

tip [*n3*] *gratuity paid*
compensation, cue, fee, gift, handout, lagniappe, money, one-way*, perk, perquisite, pourboire, reward, small change, something*, sweetener; SEE CONCEPT *344*

tip [*v1*] *knock over; cause to lean*
bend, cant, capsize, careen, dump, empty, heel, incline, lean, list, overset, overturn, pour, recline, shift, slant, slope, spill, tilt, topple, topple over, turn over, unload, upend, upset, upturn; SEE CONCEPTS *189,201,208*

tip [*v2*] *give inside information*
advise, caution, clue, cue, forewarn, give a clue, give a hint, give the low-down*, hint, prompt, steer, suggest, tip off, warn; SEE CONCEPT *60*

tipsy [*adj*] *inebriated*
addled, dazed, drunk, drunken, fuddled, happy, high*, intoxicated, irrigated*, lit*, loaded*, mellow, merry, stewed*, tight, unsteady, woozy; SEE CONCEPTS *401,406*

tirade [*n*] *abuse, outburst*
anger, berating, censure, condemnation, denunciation, diatribe, dispute, fulmination, harangue, invective, jeremiad*, lecture, malediction, philippic*, ranting, revilement, screed, sermon,

tongue-lashing*, vituperation; SEE CONCEPTS *44,54,278*

tire [*v*] *exhaust, weary*
annoy, bore, burn out*, bush*, collapse, crawl, debilitate, deject, depress, disgust, dishearten, dispirit, displease, distress, drain, droop, drop, enervate, ennui, exasperate, fag, fail, faint, fatigue, flag, fold, give out, go stale, grow weary, harass, irk, irritate, jade, nauseate, overburden, overstrain, overtax, overwork, pain, pall, peter out*, poop out*, prostrate, put to sleep, sap, sicken, sink, strain, tax, vex, weaken, wear, wear down, wear out, weary, wilt, worry, yawn*; SEE CONCEPTS *13,14,469*

tired [*adj*] *exhausted, weary*
all in*, annoyed, asleep, beat*, bored, broken-down, burned out*, collapsing, consumed, dead on one's feet*, distressed, dog-tired*, done for*, done in*, drained, drooping, droopy, drowsy, empty, enervated, exasperated, fagged, faint, fatigued, fed up*, finished, flagging, haggard, irked, irritated, jaded, narcoleptic, overtaxed, overworked, petered out*, played out*, pooped*, prostrated, run-down, sick of, sleepy, spent, stale, tuckered out*, wasted, weary, worn, worn out; SEE CONCEPTS *314,403,406*

tireless [*adj*] *determined*
active, ball of fire*, eager, energetic, enthusiastic, grind, hard-working*, hyper*, incessant, indefatigable, industrious, jumping, on the go*, perky, persevering, resolute, steadfast, strenuous, unflagging, untiring, unwearied, unwearying, vigorous; SEE CONCEPTS *538,542*

tiresome [*adj*] *irritating, exasperating*
a bit much*, annoying, arduous, boresome, boring, burdensome, demanding, difficult, drag, dragging, drudging, dull, enervative, exacting, exhausting, fatiguing, flat, hard, heavy, hefty, ho-hum*, humdrum, irksome, jading, laborious, monotonous, nowhere, onerous, oppressive, strenuous, tedious, tired, tiring, too much*, tough, trying, uncool*, uninteresting, unrelieved, vexatious, wearing, wearisome, wearying, yawn*; SEE CONCEPTS *529,537,538*

titanic [*adj*] *gigantic, very large*
Brobdingnagian*, colossal, elephantine, enormous, epic, gargantuan, giant, Herculean*, huge, immense, jumbo*, larger-than-life, mammoth, massive, monstrous, monumental, titan, towering, tremendous, vast; SEE CONCEPTS *491,773, 779,781*

titillate [*v*] *excite, stimulate*
amuse, arouse, entertain, grab, grapple, hook, interest, palpate, provoke, switch on, tantalize, tease, thrill, tickle, tickle pink*, turn on; SEE CONCEPTS *7,11,22*

title [*n1*] *heading, label*
appellation, banner, caption, close, description, head, headline, inscription, legend, name, rubric, salutation, sign, streamer, style, subtitle; SEE CONCEPT *283*

title [*n2*] *name*
appellation, appellative, brand, cognomen, denomination, designation, epithet, handle*, honorific, label, moniker*, nom de plume, nomen, pseudonym, sobriquet, style, tab*, tag*, term; SEE CONCEPT *683*

title [*n3*] *possession, laurel*
authority, championship, claim, commission, crest, crown, decoration, deed, degree, desert,

dibs*, due, entitlement, holding, justification, license, medal, merit, ownership, power, prerogative, pretense, pretension, privilege, proof, ribbon, right; SEE CONCEPTS *376,710*

title [*v*] *name*
baptize, call, christen, denominate, designate, dub, entitle, label, style, term; SEE CONCEPT *62*

toady [*n*] *sycophant*
adulator, apple polisher, ass-kisser*, back-scratcher*, backslapper*, bootlicker*, brown-noser*, doormat, doter, fan, fawner, flatterer, flunky, groupie*, hanger-on*, kiss-up*, lackey, minion, teacher's pet, yes-person*; SEE CONCEPT *423*

toady [*v*] *fawn*
apple-polish*, be servile, bootlick*, brownnose*, butter up*, cajole, fall all over, kiss one's knees*, flatter, honey up*, kiss one's feet*, kiss-up*, kowtow*, lay it on*, lick boots*, massage*, oil*, pay court*, play up to*, scratch one's back*, stroke*, suck up to*, truckle, woo*; SEE CONCEPTS *110,384*

toast [*n*] *salutation when drinking alcohol*
acknowledgment, celebration, ceremony, commemoration, compliment, down, drink, health, honor, pledge, proposal, salute, sentiment, shingle, thanksgiving, tribute; SEE CONCEPT *278*

toast [*v*] *brown with heat*
cook, crisp, dry, grill, heat, parch, roast, warm; SEE CONCEPT *170*

toddler [*n*] *baby*
child, infant, kid, little one*, preschooler, rug rat*, tot, youngster; SEE CONCEPTS *414,424*

to-do [*n*] *commotion, excitement*
agitation, bother, brouhaha*, bustle, clamor, disorder, disturbance, flap*, furor, fuss, hassle, hoo-ha*, hoopla*, hubbub*, hurly-burly*, hurrah, performance, pother, quarrel, racket, ruction, rumpus, stir, tumult, turmoil, unrest, uproar, whirl; SEE CONCEPTS *230,674*

together [*adj*] *composed*
calm, cool*, in sync*, stable, well-adjusted, well-balanced, well-organized; SEE CONCEPT *542*

together [*adv1*] *as a group; all at once*
all together, as one, at one fell swoop*, closely, coincidentally, collectively, combined, commonly, concertedly, concomitantly, concurrently, conjointly, contemporaneously, en masse, hand in glove*, hand in hand*, in a body, in concert, in cooperation, in one breath*, in sync*, in unison, jointly, mutually, on the beat*, side by side, simultaneously, synchronically, unanimously, unitedly, with one accord, with one voice, with the beat; SEE CONCEPTS *538,544,548*

together [*adv2*] *in a row*
consecutively, continually, continuously, in succession, night and day, one after the other, on end, running, successively, unintermittedly, without a break, without interruption; SEE CONCEPTS *482,585*

toil [*n*] *hard work*
application, drudgery, effort, exertion, industry, labor, moil, nine-to-five*, occupation, pains*, sweat, travail; SEE CONCEPTS *100,362,677*

toil [*v*] *work hard*
drive, drudge, grind, knock oneself out*, labor, moil, peg away*, plod, plug, push oneself, slave, strain, strive, struggle, sweat, tug, work, work like a dog*; SEE CONCEPTS *100,677*

toilsome [*adj*] *laborious*
arduous, backbreaking, burdensome, demanding, difficult, exhausting, hard, labored, onerous, operose, rough, strenuous, taxing, tiresome, uphill*; SEE CONCEPT *538*

token [*n*] *indication, remembrance*
badge, clue, demonstration, earnest, evidence, expression, favor, gift, index, indicia, keepsake, manifestation, mark, memento, memorial, note, omen, pawn, pledge, presage, proof, relic, reminder, representation, sample, security, sign, significant, souvenir, symbol, symptom, trophy, warning, warrant; SEE CONCEPTS *284,337,529*

tolerable [*adj*] *acceptable, good enough*
adequate, allowable, all right, average, bearable, better than nothing*, common, decent, endurable, fair, fairly good, fair to middling*, goodish*, indifferent, livable, mediocre, middling*, not bad*, okay*, ordinary, passable, presentable, respectable, run-of-the-mill*, satisfactory, so-so*, sufferable, sufficient, supportable, sustainable, tidy, unexceptionable, unexceptional, unimpeachable; SEE CONCEPTS *529,548*

tolerance [*n1*] *open-mindedness*
altruism, benevolence, broad-mindedness, charity, clemency, compassion, concession, endurance, forbearance, freedom, good will, grace, humanity, indulgence, kindness, lenience, leniency, lenity, liberalism, liberality, liberalness, license, magnanimity, mercifulness, mercy, patience, permission, permissiveness, sensitivity, sufferance, sympathy, toleration, understanding; SEE CONCEPTS *410,657*

tolerance [*n2*] *fortitude, grit*
endurance, guts*, hardiness, hardness, opposition, patience, resilience, resistance, stamina, staying power*, steadfastness, steadiness, strength, sufferance, toughness, vigor; SEE CONCEPT *732*

tolerant [*adj*] *open-minded, easygoing*
advanced, benevolent, big, broad, broad-minded, catholic, charitable, clement, complaisant, condoning, easy on, easy with, excusing, fair, forbearing, forgiving, free and easy*, humane, indulgent, kindhearted*, lax, lenient, liberal, long-suffering*, magnanimous, merciful, patient, permissive, progressive, radical, receptive, soft, sophisticated, sympathetic, understanding, unprejudiced, wide; SEE CONCEPTS *403,542*

tolerate [*v*] *allow, indulge*
abide, accept, admit, authorize, bear, bear with, blink at*, brook, condone, consent to, countenance, endure, go, go along with, have, hear, humor, live with, permit, pocket, put up with, receive, sanction, sit and take it*, sit still for*, stand, stand for, stay the course*, stomach*, string along, submit to, suffer, sustain, swallow*, take, tough out*, undergo, wink at*; SEE CONCEPTS *23,83*

toll [*n1*] *fee*
assessment, charge, cost, customs, demand, duty, exaction, expense, impost, levy, payment, price, rate, tariff, tax, tribute; SEE CONCEPT *329*

toll [*n2*] *damage, deaths*
casualties, cost, expense, inroad, loss, losses, penalty, price; SEE CONCEPT *230*

toll [*v*] *ring out*
announce, bell, bong, call, chime, clang, knell, peal, signal, sound, strike, summon, warn; SEE CONCEPT *65*

tomb [*n*] *burial place*
box, burial, burial chamber, catacomb, coffin, crypt, grave, mausoleum, monument, pit, sepulcher, trough, vault; SEE CONCEPT *305*

tome [*n*] *large, scholarly book*
classic, great work, magnum opus, novel, opus, publication, reference book, schoolbook, textbook, title, tradebook, volume, work, writing; SEE CONCEPT *280*

tomfoolery [*n*] *nonsense*
absurdity, antics, bunk, carrying-on*, clowning, craziness, folly, foolery, fooling around, foolishness, fun, funny business, giddiness, high jinks, horseplay, insanity, irresponsibility, joking, kidding around, ludicrousness, lunacy, madness, ridiculousness, senselessness, shenanigans*, silliness; SEE CONCEPTS *230,388,633*

tone [*n1*] *pitch, volume*
accent, emphasis, force, inflection, intonation, modulation, resonance, strength, stress, timbre, tonality; SEE CONCEPT *65*

tone [*n2*] *attitude, spirit*
air, approach, aspect, character, condition, current, drift, effect, expression, fashion, feel, frame, grain, habit, humor, manner, mind, mode, mood, movement, nature, note, quality, state of things, strain, style, temper, tenor, trend, vein; SEE CONCEPTS *655,673,682*

tone [*n3*] *color*
blend, cast, coloration, hue, shade, tinge, tint, value; SEE CONCEPT *622*

tone [*n4*] *condition of the body*
elasticity, health, healthiness, resiliency, strength, tonicity, tonus, vigor; SEE CONCEPT *316*

tone down [*v*] *moderate*
chill out*, cloud, dampen, darken, deepen, dim, mitigate, modulate, play down, reduce, restrain, shade, sober, soften, soft-pedal*, subdue, temper; SEE CONCEPT *240*

tongue [*n*] *language*
argot, articulation, dialect, discourse, expression, idiom, language, lingo, parlance, patois, speech, talk, utterance, vernacular, voice; SEE CONCEPT *276*

tongue-in-cheek [*adj*] *facetious*
amusing, blithe, clever, comic, comical, dry, farcical, flip*, flippant, funny, humorous, in fun, in jest, ironic, ironical, irreverent, jesting, jocular, joking, joshing, laughable, not serious, playful, pulling one's leg*, putting one on*, sarcastic, satirical, smart, whimsical, wisecracking, witty; SEE CONCEPT *267*

tongue-tied [*adj*] *speechless*
aghast, amazed, astounded, at a loss for words, bashful, choked up, dazed, dumbfounded, dumbstruck, inarticulate, mum, mute, shocked, shy, silent, stammering, uncommunicative, voiceless; SEE CONCEPT *267*

tonic [*n*] *restorative drink, medicine*
analeptic, boost, bracer, conditioner, cordial, drug, fillip, invigorator, livener, pick-me-up*, pickup, refresher, restorative, roborant, shot in the arm*, stimulant, strengthener; SEE CONCEPT *307*

too [*adv1*] *also*
additionally, along, as well, besides, further, furthermore, in addition, into the bargain, likewise, more, moreover, to boot, withal; SEE CONCEPTS *544,771*

too [*adv2*] *excessively*
awfully, beyond, ever, exceptionally, exorbitantly, extremely, greatly, highly, immensely, immoderately, in excess, inordinately, notably, over, over and above, overly, overmuch, remarkably, strikingly, unconscionably, unduly, unreasonably, very; SEE CONCEPTS *569,772*

tool [*n1*] *instrument used to shape, form, finish*
apparatus, appliance, contraption, contrivance, device, engine, gadget, gizmo*, implement, job, machine, means, mechanism, utensil, weapon, whatchamacallit*; SEE CONCEPT *499*

tool [*n2*] *person who allows himself to be used*
accessory, accomplice, agent, auxiliary, chump*, creature, dupe, easy mark*, figurehead, flunky*, go-between, greenhorn*, hireling, idiot, intermediary, jackal, lackey, mark*, medium, messenger, minion, patsy*, pawn, peon, puppet, stooge, stool pigeon*, sucker*; SEE CONCEPTS *348,412,423*

toothsome [*adj*] *delicious*
adorable, ambrosial, appetizing, delectable, delightful, divine, flavorful, good, heavenly, luscious, lush, mouthwatering, nectarous, nice, palatable, pleasant, pleasing, rich, savory, scrumptious, sweet, tasteful, tasty, titillating, yummy*; SEE CONCEPTS *572,613*

top [*adj*] *best, most important; highest*
apical, capital, chief, crack, crowning, culminating, dominant, elite, excellent, fine, finest, first, first-class, first-rate, five-star*, foremost, greatest, head, lead, leading, loftiest, maximal, maximum, outside, paramount, preeminent, primary, prime, principal, ruling, sovereign, superior, supreme, tiptop*, top-drawer*, topmost, topnotch, upper, uppermost; SEE CONCEPTS *567,574,583*

top [*n1*] *highest point*
acme, apex, apogee, cap, capital, ceiling, climax, cork, cover, crest, crown, culmination, cusp, face, fastigium, finial, head, height, high point, lid, limit, maximum, meridian, peak, pinnacle, point, roof, spire, stopper, summit, superficies, surface, tip, utmost, vertex, zenith; SEE CONCEPT *836*

top [*n2*] *highest rank*
best, captain, chief, choice, cream, elite, first place, flower, head, lead, leader, pick, pride, prime, prize, utmost; SEE CONCEPT *668*

top [*v1*] *place on or reach highest part*
ascend, cap, climb, cloak, clothe, cover, crest, crown, face, finish, garnish, piggyback*, protect, reinforce, roof, scale, spread over, superimpose, surmount, tip; SEE CONCEPTS *172,201,750*

top [*v2*] *surpass*
bash, beat, be first, best, better, blow away*, clobber*, eclipse, exceed, excel, fake out*, finagle*, fox*, go beyond, goose*, outdo, outfox, outshine, outstrip, overrun, run circles around*, shut out*, total*, transcend; SEE CONCEPTS *95,141*

top [*v3*] *remove the upper part*
amputate, cream, crop, curtail, cut off, decapitate, detruncate, dock, file off, lop off, pare, pollard, prune, ream, scrape off, shave off, shear, shorten, skim, trim, truncate; SEE CONCEPT *211*

topic [*n*] *subject matter*
affair, argument, business, case, division, field, head, issue, material, matter, matter in hand, moot point, motif, motion, motive, point, point in

ti
to

question, problem, proposition, question, resolution, subject, text, theme, theorem, thesis; SEE CONCEPT *532*

topical [*adj1*] *current*
contemporary, modern, newsworthy, nominal, popular, subjective, thematic, up-to-date; SEE CONCEPT *820*

topical [*adj2*] *restricted, local*
confined, insular, limited, parochial, particular, regional, sectional; SEE CONCEPTS *557,583*

top-level [*adj*] *high-ranking, important*
aristocratic, distinguished, esteemed, famous, first-class*, foremost, four-star*, front-page*, grand, high-level, high-profile, high-up, honored, illustrious, leading, majestic, major-league*, noble, notable, noted, noteworthy, powerful, preeminent, prominent, top-drawer*, top-notch*, upper-class, VIP*, well-known; SEE CONCEPTS *555,574*

top-notch [*adj*] *first-rate*
A-1, ace, blue-chip*, choice, excellent, fine, first-class, first-string*, five-star, highest quality, in a class all by itself*, prime*, sound, superior, supreme, tiptop*, top-level, uppermost, very best, very good; SEE CONCEPT *574*

topple [*v*] *fall or knock over; overthrow*
bring down, capsize, collapse, do a pratfall*, fall, falter, founder, go belly up*, go down, hit the dirt*, keel over, knock down, land, lose it*, lurch, nose-dive, oust, overbalance, overturn, pitch, plunge, slump, stagger, stumble, take a header*, teeter, tip over, totter, tumble, turn over, unhorse, unseat, upset; SEE CONCEPTS *95,147,181,208*

topsy-turvy [*adj*] *mixed-up*
chaotic, cluttered, cockeyed, confused, disarranged, disheveled, disjointed, dislocated, disordered, disorderly, disorganized, downside-up*, inside-out, inverted, jumbled, littered, messy, muddled, overturned, pell-mell*, riotous, tangled, tumultous/tumultuous, unhinged, untidy, upended, upside-down, upturned; SEE CONCEPTS *485,548,585*

torment [*n*] *severe mental distress*
affliction, agony, anguish, annoyance, bane, bother, excruciation, harassment, hell, irritation, misery, nag, nagging, nuisance, pain, pain in the neck*, persecution, pest, plague, provocation, rack, scourge, suffering, torture, trouble, vexation, worry; SEE CONCEPTS *410,728*

torment [*v*] *be or make very upset*
abuse, afflict, agonize, annoy, bait, bedevil, bone, bother, break, crucify, devil, distress, drive bananas*, drive up the wall*, excruciate, give a hard time*, harass, harrow, harry, heckle, hound, hurt, irritate, mistreat, molest, nag, pain, persecute, pester, plague, play cat and mouse*, provoke, punish, put through wringer*, rack, rub salt in wound*, smite, tease, torture, trouble, try, vex, worry, wring; SEE CONCEPTS *7,19,313*

torn [*adj1*] *cut open*
broken, burst, cleaved, cracked, damaged, divided, fractured, gashed, impaired, lacerated, mangled, ragged, rent, ripped, ruptured, severed, shabby, slashed, sliced, slit, snapped, split, wrenched; SEE CONCEPT *485*

torn [*adj2*] *undecided*
divided, irresolute, of two minds*, split, uncertain, unsure, vacillating, wavering; SEE CONCEPTS *403,542*

torpid [*adj*] *lazy, slow*
apathetic, benumbed, comatose, dopey*, dormant, drowsy, dull, faineant, heavy, hebetudinous, idle, inactive, indifferent, indolent, inert, lackadaisical, languid, languorous, latent, leaden, lethargic, listless, lymphatic, motionless, numb, paralyzed, passive, slothful, slow-moving, sluggish, slumberous, sodden, somnolent, stagnant, static, stupid, stuporous; SEE CONCEPTS *401,538*

torpor [*n*] *lethargy*
apathy, disinterest, dormancy, drowsiness, dullness, idleness, impassivity, inaction, inactivity, languor, laziness, lifelessness, listlessness, passiveness, sleepiness, sloth, slowness, sluggishness, slumber, stupor, torpidity, torpidness; SEE CONCEPTS *315,410,633,748*

torrent [*n*] *heavy flow*
cascade, cataclysm, cataract, cloudburst, deluge, downpour, effusion, flood, flooding, flux, gush, inundation, niagara, outburst, overflow, pour, rush, shower, spate, stream, tide, waterfall; SEE CONCEPTS *146,179,526*

torrid [*adj1*] *very hot*
arid, austral, blazing, blistering, boiling, broiling, burning, dried, dry, fiery, heated, parched, parching, red-hot*, scalding, scorched, scorching, sizzling, stifling, sultry, sweltering, tropic, tropical; SEE CONCEPT *605*

torrid [*adj2*] *sensuous*
ardent, blazing, burning, erotic, fervent, flaming, hot*, hot-blooded*, impassioned, intense, passionate, red-hot*, sexy, steamy*, sultry, whitehot*; SEE CONCEPT *372*

tortuous [*adj1*] *very twisted*
anfractuous, bent, circuitous, convoluted, crooked, curved, flexuous, indirect, involute, labyrinthine, mazy, meandering, meandrous, roundabout, serpentine, sinuous, snaky, twisting, vermiculate, winding, zigzag; SEE CONCEPT *581*

tortuous [*adj2*] *complicated*
ambiguous, convoluted, cunning, deceptive, devious, indirect, involute, involved, misleading, perverse, roundabout, tricky; SEE CONCEPT *562*

torture [*n*] *severe mental or physical pain*
ache, affliction, agony, anguish, cruciation, crucifixion, distress, dolor, excruciation, impalement, laceration, martyrdom, misery, pang, persecution, rack, suffering, third degree*, torment, tribulation, twinge; SEE CONCEPTS *410,728*

torture [*v*] *upset or hurt severely*
abuse, afflict, agonize, annoy, beat, bother, crucify, distress, disturb, excruciate, grill, harrow, impale, injure, irritate, lacerate, maim, mangle, martyr, martyrize, mistreat, mutilate, oppress, pain, persecute, rack, smite, torment, try, whip, wound, wring, wrong; SEE CONCEPTS *7,19,246,313*

toss [*n/v1*] *throw*
bung, cast, chuck, chunk, fire, fling, flip, heave, hurl, launch, lob, peg, pitch, project, propel, sling, twirl, wing; SEE CONCEPT *222*

toss [*v2*] *move back and forth*
agitate, agonize, bob, buffet, disturb, flounder, heave, jiggle, joggle, jolt, labor, lurch, move restlessly, oscillate, pitch, rise and fall, rock, roll, seesaw, shake, squirm, stir, sway, swing, thrash, tumble, undulate, wallow, wave, wobble, wriggle, writhe; SEE CONCEPT *147*

total [*adj*] *complete, thorough*
absolute, all-out, comprehensive, consummate,

downright, entire, every, full, full-blown, full-scale, gross, inclusive, integral, out-and-out, out-right, overall, perfect, plenary, positive, sheer, sweeping, thoroughgoing, totalitarian, uncondi-tional, undisputed, undivided, unlimited, unmiti-gated, unqualified, unreserved, unrestricted, utter, whole; SEE CONCEPTS *531,762*

total [*n*] *whole*
aggregate, all, amount, body, budget, bulk, en-tirety, flat out*, full amount, gross, jackpot*, mass, quantity, quantum, result, sum, sum total*, tale, the works*, totality; SEE CONCEPTS *787,837*

total [*v*] *add up*
add, aggregate, amount to, calculate, cast, come, come to, comprise, consist of, equal, figure, foot, mount up to, number, pile up, reach, reckon, re-sult in, ring up*, run into, run to, stack up, sum-mate, sum up, totalize, tote*, yield; SEE CONCEPT *764*

totalitarian [*adj*] *dictatorial*
absolute, authoritarian, autocratic, communist*, despotic, fascistic, monolithic, Nazi*, one-party, oppressive, total, totalistic, tyrannical, undemoc-ratic; SEE CONCEPT *536*

totally [*adv*] *completely*
absolutely, all, all in all, altogether, comprehen-sively, consummately, entirely, exactly, exclu-sively, flat out*, full blast*, fully, in toto*, just, perfectly, quite, thoroughly, top to bottom*, un-conditionally, unmitigatedly, utterly, wholeheart-edly, wholly; SEE CONCEPT *531*

totter [*v*] *move falteringly*
blunder, careen, dodder, falter, flounder, hesitate, lurch, quake, quiver, reel, rock, roll, seesaw, shake, shimmy, slide, slip, stagger, stammer, stumble, sway, teeter, topple, tremble, trip, walk unsteadily, waver, weave, wheel, wobble, zigzag; SEE CONCEPT *151*

touch [*n1*] *physical contact*
blow, brush, caress, collision, communication, contact, contingence, crash, cuddling, embrace, feel, feeling, fondling, graze, grope, handling, hit, hug, impact, junction, kiss, lick, manipula-tion, nudge, palpation, pat, peck, perception, per-cussion, petting, push, rub, rubbing, scratch, shock, stroke, stroking, tactility, taction, tap, taste, touching; SEE CONCEPTS *590,608,612*

touch [*n2*] *tiny amount*
bit, dash, detail, drop, hint, inkling, intimation, jot, pinch, scent, shade, smack, small amount, smattering, soupçon, speck, spot, streak, sugges-tion, suspicion, taste, tincture, tinge, trace, whiff; SEE CONCEPTS *529,831,832*

touch [*n3*] *manner, method*
ability, acquaintance, adeptness, adroitness, ap-proach, art, artistry, awareness, characteristic, command, communication, contact, deftness, di-rection, effect, facility, faculty, familiarity, fin-ish, flair, hand, handiwork, influence, knack, mastery, skill, style, talent, technique, trademark, understanding, virtuosity, way; SEE CONCEPTS *6,630,655*

touch [*v1*] *make physical contact*
abut, adjoin, be in contact, border, brush, butt on, caress, come together, communicate, contact, converge, dab, examine, feel, feel up*, finger, fondle, frisk, glance, graze, grope, handle, hit, impinge upon, inspect, join, kiss, lay a finger on*, lick, line, manipulate, march, massage, meet, neighbor, osculate, palm, palpate, partake,

pat, paw, percuss, pet, probe, push, reach, rub, scrutinize, sip, smooth, strike, stroke, suck, sweep, tag, tap, taste, thumb, tickle, tip, toy, verge; SEE CONCEPT *612*

touch [*v2*] *have an effect on*
affect, arouse, carry, disturb, excite, feel out, get through to*, get to*, grab, impress, influence, in-spire, make an impression*, mark, melt, move, quicken, soften, stimulate, stir, strike, strike a chord*, stroke, sway, tug at the heart*, upset; SEE CONCEPTS *7,19,22*

touch [*v3*] *have to do with; regard*
affect, be a party to, bear on, bear upon, be asso-ciated with, belong to, center upon, concern, concern oneself with, consume, deal with, drink, eat, get involved in, handle, have to do with, in-terest, involve, partake of, pertain to, refer to, use, utilize; SEE CONCEPT *532*

touch [*v4*] *make mention*
allude to, bring in, cover, deal with, discuss, go over, mention, note, refer to, speak of, treat; SEE CONCEPT *51*

touch [*v5*] *compare with; correspond to*
amount, approach, be a match for*, be in the same league*, be on a par*, come near, come to, come up to, equal, hold a candle to*, match, measure up, meet, parallel, partake of, rival, tie, verge on; SEE CONCEPT *561*

touched [*adj1*] *deeply moved emotionally*
affected, disturbed, grabbed*, impressed, melted*, softened, stirred, swayed, turned on by*, turned on to*, upset; SEE CONCEPTS *403,542*

touched [*adj2*] *crazy*
batty*, bizarre, bonkers*, cuckoo*, daft, eccen-tric, fanatic, flighty, insane, neurotic, not all there*, not right*, nuts*, nutty*, obsessed, out of one's mind*, peculiar, pixilated, queer, un-hinged; SEE CONCEPTS *402,403*

touching [*adj1*] *affecting, moving emotionally*
compassionate, emotive, heartbreaking, heart-rending, impressive, melting, mind-blowing*, pathetic, piteous, pitiable, pitiful, poignant, re-sponsive, sad, stirring, stunning, sympathetic, tear-jerking, tender, wistful; SEE CONCEPTS *529,537*

touch up [*v*] *fix up; improve*
amend, brush up, do up, enhance, finish off, give a face-lift*, gloss, make improvements, modify, patch up, perfect, polish, put finishing touches on*, remodel, renew, renovate, repair, retouch, revamp, rework, round off, tease*; SEE CONCEPTS *212,244*

touchy [*adj*] *easily offended*
bad-tempered, bundle of nerves*, cantankerous, captious, choleric, crabbed, cranky, cross, deli-cate, dicey*, grouchy, grumpy, hazardous, hy-persensitive, irascible, irritable, jumpy*, mean, ornery*, oversensitive, peevish, perturbable, pet-tish, petulant, precarious, querulous, quick-tempered, risky, sensitive, splenetic, surly, temperamental, testy, thin-skinned*, ticklish*, tricky, unpredictable, unsafe, uptight*, volatile, wired up*, wound up*; SEE CONCEPTS *401,542,548*

tough [*adj1*] *sturdy, strong*
brawny, cohesive, conditioned, dense, durable, fibrous, firm, fit, flinty, hard, hard as nails*, hard-bitten*, hardened, hardy, healthy, indigestible, inflexible, leathery, lusty, mighty, molded, re-silient, resistant, rigid, robust, rugged, seasoned,

to
to

sinewy, solid, stalwart, steeled, stiff, stout, strapping, tenacious, tight, tough as nails*, unbreakable, unyielding, vigorous, withstanding; SEE CONCEPTS *314,489*

tough [*adj2*] *obstinate, rough*
adamant, arbitrary, callous, confirmed, cruel, desperate, drastic, exacting, ferocious, fierce, firm, fixed, hard, hard-bitten*, hard-boiled*, hard-line*, hard-nosed*, hard-shelled*, harsh, headstrong, immutable, inflexible, intractable, merciless, narrow, obdurate, pugnacious, refractory, resolute, ruffianly, ruthless, savage, severe, stern, stiff, strict, stubborn, taut, terrible, unalterable, unbending, uncompromising, uncontrollable, unforgiving, unmanageable, unyielding, vicious, violent; SEE CONCEPTS *403,542*

tough [*adj3*] *difficult, laborious*
arduous, backbreaking*, baffling, burdensome, demanding, effortful, exacting, exhausting, exigent, grievous, hairy*, handful*, hard, heavy, intractable, intricate, irksome, knotty*, labored, mean, no piece of cake*, onerous, oppressive, perplexing, puzzling, resisting, severe, stiff, strenuous, taxing, thorny, toilsome, troublesome, trying, unyielding, uphill*, weighty*, wicked; SEE CONCEPTS *538,565*

tough [*n*] *person who is rowdy, mean*
bruiser, brute, bully, criminal, gangster, goon*, hood*, hoodlum, hooligan, punk*, rough*, roughneck, rowdy, ruffian, thug, villain; SEE CONCEPT *412*

toughen [*v*] *harden*
acclimate, acclimatize, anneal, brutalize, climatize, develop, inure, make difficult, season, strengthen, temper; SEE CONCEPTS *202,250*

toupee [*n*] *wig*
false hair, hair extension, hair implant, hairpiece, hair weaving, periwig, peruke, postiche, rug*; SEE CONCEPT *392*

tour [*n*] *journey; stint*
bout*, circle tour*, circuit, course, cruise, excursion, expedition, getaway*, go*, hitch*, hop*, jaunt*, junket, outing, overnight*, peregrination, progress, road, round*, roundabout*, round trip, run, shift, spell, stretch, stump*, swing*, time, travel, trek, trick*, trip, turn, voyage, weekend, whistle-stop*; SEE CONCEPTS *81,224,807*

tour [*v*] *visit, journey*
barnstorm*, cruise, explore, globe-trot*, go on the road*, holiday*, hop*, jaunt, jet, junket, peregrinate, sightsee, stump*, swing*, take a trip, travel, vacation, voyage; SEE CONCEPTS *224,227*

tour de force [*n*] *great achievement*
accomplishment, attainment, conquest, deed, exploit, masterpiece, performance, stroke of genius, success, triumph, victory; SEE CONCEPTS *1,706*

tourist [*n*] *person who visits a place*
day-tripper, excursionist, globetrotter, jet-setter, journeyer, rubberneck*, sightseer, stranger, traveler, tripper*, vacationist, visitor, voyager, wayfarer; SEE CONCEPT *423*

tournament [*n*] *sporting competition*
clash, contest, duel, event, fight, games, joust, match, meet, meeting, series, sport, test, tilt, tourney; SEE CONCEPT *363*

tousled [*adj*] *disarrayed*
beat-up*, dirty, disarranged, disheveled, disordered, grubby*, messed-up*, messy, mussed-

up*, ruffled, rumpled, sloppy, tangled, uncombed, unkempt; SEE CONCEPTS *485,589*

tout [*v*] *brag about, show off*
acclaim, ballyhoo*, boost, give a boost*, herald, laud, plug*, praise, proclaim, promote, publicize, push, steer, tip, tip off*, trumpet; SEE CONCEPTS *69,138*

tow [*v*] *pull along*
drag, draw, ferry, haul, lug, propel, push, trail, trawl, tug, yank; SEE CONCEPT *206*

toward/towards [*prep1*] *on the way to; near*
against, almost, approaching, close to, coming up, contra, en route, facing, for, fronting, headed for, in relation to, in the direction of, in the vicinity, just before, moving, nearing, nearly, not quite, on the road to, over against, pointing to, proceeding, shortly before, to, via, vis-a'-vis; SEE CONCEPT *586*

toward/towards [*prep2*] *concerning*
about, against, anent, apropos, as for, as to, for, in re, re, regarding, with regard to, with respect to; SEE CONCEPT *532*

tower [*n*] *very high building or building part*
belfry, castle, citadel, cloud buster*, column, fort, fortification, fortress, high rise*, keep, lookout, mast, minaret, monolith, obelisk, pillar, refuge, skyscraper, spire, steeple, stronghold, turret; SEE CONCEPTS *439,440*

tower [*v*] *rise above*
ascend, be above, dominate, exceed, extend above, look down, look over, loom, mount, overlook, overtop, rear, soar, surmount, surpass, top, transcend; SEE CONCEPTS *141,752*

towering [*adj*] *huge, excessive*
aerial, airy, colossal, elevated, extraordinary, extravagant, extreme, fantastic, gigantic, great, high, immoderate, imperial, imposing, impressive, inordinate, intense, lofty, magnificent, massive, mighty, monumental, outstanding, paramount, preeminent, prodigious, skyscraping, soaring, spiring, stately, stupendous, sublime, superior, supreme, surpassing, tall, towery, transcendent, tremendous, ultimate, undue, unmatchable, unmeasurable; SEE CONCEPTS *567,779*

town [*n*] *incorporated community*
apple*, boondocks, borough, burg*, city, hamlet, metropolis, municipality, seat, sticks*, township, whistle-stop*; SEE CONCEPTS *507,508*

toxic [*adj*] *poisonous*
baneful, deadly, harmful, lethal, mephitic, noxious, pernicious, pestilential, poison, septic, toxicant, venomous, virulent; SEE CONCEPT *537*

toxin [*n*] *poison*
blight, cancer, contagion, contamination, germ, infection, noxious substance, poisonous substance, toxicant, toxoid, venom, virus; SEE CONCEPTS *307,475,674,675*

toy [*n*] *entertainment article*
bauble, curio, doll, game, knickknack, novelty, plaything, trifle, trinket; SEE CONCEPT *446*

toy [*v*] *play with*
amuse oneself, coquet, cosset, dally, dandle, fiddle, flirt, fool, fool around*, jest, lead on, mess around*, pet, play, play around, play games, sport, string along*, tease, trifle, wanton; SEE CONCEPT *384*

trace [*n*] *evidence; small bit*
breath, crumb, dab, dash, drop, element, footmark, footprint, fragment, hint, indication, inti-

mation, iota, jot, mark, memento, minimum, nib, nuance, particle, pinch, proof, record, relic, remains, remnant, scintilla, shade, shadow, shred, sign, slot, smell, smidgen, snippet, soupçon, speck, spoor, spot, sprinkling, strain, streak, suggestion, survival, suspicion, taste, tincture, tinge, tittle, token, touch, track, trail, tread, trifle, vestige, whiff, whisper; SEE CONCEPTS *529,831*

trace [*v1*] *seek, follow*
ascertain, detect, determine, discern, discover, ferret out, find, hunt, perceive, pursue, run down, search for, shadow, smell out, spoor, spot, stalk, track, trail, unearth; SEE CONCEPTS *207,216*

trace [*v2*] *draw around*
chart, copy, delineate, depict, duplicate, map, mark out, outline, record, reproduce, show, sketch; SEE CONCEPTS *79,174*

track [*n1*] *mark, print made by something*
clue, footmark, footprint, footstep, groove, impress, impression, imprint, indication, memorial, monument, path, print, record, remains, remnant, rut, scent, sign, slot, spoor, step, symbol, token, trace, tract, trail, tread, vestige, wake; SEE CONCEPTS *513,628*

track [*n2*] *path, way*
alley, artery, avenue, beaten path*, boulevard, clearing, course, cut*, drag*, footpath, highway, lane, line, orbit, passage, pathway, rail, rails, road, roadway, route, street, thoroughfare, track, trackway, trail, trajectory, walk; SEE CONCEPT *501*

track/track down [*v*] *follow, pursue*
apprehend, beat the bushes*, be hot on the trail*, bird-dog*, bring to light*, capture, catch, chase, cover, dig up, discover, do, dog*, dog footsteps of*, draw an inference, expose, ferret out, find, go after, hunt, piece together, put together, run down, scout, shadow, smell out*, sniff out*, stalk, stick to, tail, trace, trail, travel, traverse, unearth; SEE CONCEPTS *183,207,216*

tract [*n*] *area, lot*
amplitude, belt, district, estate, expanse, extent, field, parcel, part, piece, plat, plot, portion, quarter, region, section, sector, spread, stretch, zone; SEE CONCEPTS *508,513*

tractable [*adj*] *manageable*
acquiescent, amenable, biddable, complaisant, compliant, controllable, docile, ductile, facile, flexible, game, going along with*, governable, hanging loose*, malleable, meek, obedient, persuadable, plastic, pliable, pliant, putty in hands*, rolling with punches*, subdued, submissive, tame, tractile, willing, workable, yielding; SEE CONCEPTS *401,488,542*

traction [*n*] *physical resistance, friction*
absorption, adherence, adhesion, constriction, contraction, drag, draught, drawing, grip, haulage, pull, pulling, purchase, resorption, strain, stress, stretch, suck, suction, towage; SEE CONCEPTS *731,748*

trade [*n1*] *buying and selling*
barter, business, clientele, commerce, contract, custom, customers, deal, dealing, enterprise, exchange, industry, interchange, market, merchantry, patronage, public, sales, swap, traffic, transaction, truck; SEE CONCEPTS *324,327,330, 345*

trade [*n2*] *profession, work*
art, avocation, business, calling, craft, employment, game, handicraft, job, line, line of work,

métier, nine-to-five*, occupation, position, pursuit, skill, thing*, vocation; SEE CONCEPTS *349,360*

trademark [*n*] *logo, symbol*
brand, brand name, identification, initials, label, logo, logotype, mark, stamp, tag; SEE CONCEPTS *259,284*

tradition [*n*] *established practice*
attitude, belief, birthright, conclusion, convention, culture, custom, customs, ethic, ethics, fable, folklore, form, habit, heritage, idea, inheritance, institution, law, legend, lore, mores, myth, mythology, mythos, opinion, practice, praxis, ritual, unwritten law, usage, wisdom; SEE CONCEPT *688*

traditional [*adj*] *usual, established*
acceptable, accustomed, acknowledged, ancestral, classic, classical, common, conventional, customary, doctrinal, fixed, folk, habitual, historic, immemorial, long-established, old, oral, popular, prescribed, regular, rooted, sanctioned, taken for granted, time-honored, transmitted, universal, unwritten, widely used, widespread; SEE CONCEPTS *530,533*

traffic [*n1*] *coming and going*
cartage, flux, freight, gridlock, influx, jam, movement, parking lot*, passage, passengers, rush hour, service, shipment, transfer, transit, transport, transportation, travel, truckage, vehicles; SEE CONCEPTS *224,505,770*

traffic [*n2*] *buying and selling*
barter, business, closeness, commerce, communication, communion, connection, custom, dealing, dealings*, doings*, exchange, familiarity, industry, interchange, intercourse, intimacy, merchantry, patronage, peddling, relations, relationship, soliciting, trade, transactions, truck*; SEE CONCEPTS *330,335*

traffic [*v*] *buy and sell; do business*
bargain, barter, black-market*, bootleg*, connect with, contact, deal, deal in*, dicker, exchange, fence, handle, have dealings, have transaction, horse trade*, interact, interface, make a deal, market, moonshine*, negotiate, network, peddle, push, reach out, relate, shove, swap, touch, touch base*, trade, truck*, work out; SEE CONCEPTS *324,327,330,345*

tragedy [*n*] *disaster*
adversity, affliction, bad fortune, bad luck, blight, blow, calamity, cataclysm, catastrophe, contretemps, curse, curtains*, dole, dolor, doom, downer*, failure, hard knocks*, hardship, humiliation, lot, misadventure, mischance, misfortune, mishap, reverse, shock, struggle, the worst*, unluckiness, waterloo*, woe, wreck; SEE CONCEPTS *674,675*

tragic [*adj*] *catastrophic, very bad*
adverse, anguished, appalling, awful, calamitous, cataclysmic, crushing, deadly, deathly, deplorable, desolate, destructive, dire, disastrous, doleful, dreadful, fatal, fateful, forlorn, grievous, grim, hapless, harrowing, heartbreaking, heartrending, ill-fated, ill-starred, lamentable, miserable, mournful, painful, pathetic, pitiable, pitiful, ruinous, sad, shocking, sorrowful, terrible, unfortunate, unhappy, woeful, wretched; SEE CONCEPTS *548,571*

trail [*n*] *path, track*
aisle, beaten track*, byway, footpath, footprints, footsteps, groove*, mark, marks, pathway, road,

to
tr

route, rut, scent, spoor, stream, stroll, tail, trace, train, wake, way; SEE CONCEPT *501*

trail [*v*] *lag behind, follow*
bedog, bring up the rear*, chase, dally, dangle, dawdle, delay, dog*, drag, draggle, draw, droop, drop back, extend, fall back, fall behind, falter, flag, follow a scent*, halt, hang, hang back, hang down, haul, hunt, lag, linger, loiter, nose out*, plod, poke, poke along*, procrastinate, pull, pursue, shadow, shag, spook*, spoor, stalk, straggle, stream, string along*, tag along*, tail, take out after, tarry, tow, trace, track, traipse, trudge; SEE CONCEPTS *207,727,753*

train [*n*] *series*
alternation, appendage, caravan, chain, column, concatenation, consecution, convoy, cortege, course, court, entourage, file, following, gradation, line, order, procession, progression, retinue, row, run, scale, sequel, sequence, set, string, succession, suite, tail, thread, tier, track, trail, wake; SEE CONCEPTS *432,727*

train [*v1*] *prepare*
accustom, brainwash*, break in, care for, coach, cultivate, develop, discipline, drill, drum into, dry run*, educate, enlighten, equip, exercise, get a workout, get in shape, ground, grow strong, guide, habituate, harden, hone, improve, instruct, inure, make ready, mold, prime, qualify, rear, rehearse, run through, school, season, shape, sharpen, show the ropes*, study, tame, teach, tutor, update, warm up*, whip into shape*, wise up*, work out; SEE CONCEPTS *35,202,285*

train [*v2*] *aim at*
beam, bring to bear, cast, cock, direct, draw a bead*, focus, get in one's sights*, head, incline, lay, level, line up, point, slant, turn, zero in*; SEE CONCEPT *201*

trainee [*n*] *beginner*
abecedarian, amateur, apprentice, buckwheater*, cadet, colt*, greenhorn, learner, neophyte, newcomer, new kid on the block*, novice, novitiate, pupil, recruit, rookie, starter, student, tenderfoot*, tyro; SEE CONCEPTS *423,424*

trainer [*n*] *instructor, teacher*
adviser, breeder, coach, demonstrator, drill sergeant, guide, handler, lecturer, mentor, professor, tutor; SEE CONCEPT *350*

training [*n*] *preparation*
background, basics, buildup, chalk talk*, coaching, cultivation, discipline, domestication, drill, education, exercise, foundation, grounding, groundwork, guidance, indoctrination, instruction, practice, preliminaries, preparation, principles, readying, schooling, seasoning, sharpening, teaching, tuition, tune-up*, tutelage, upbringing, warm-up*, workout*; SEE CONCEPTS *202,285, 678*

traipse [*v*] *walk*
amble, ambulate, gad, go on foot*, hike, knock about*, lumber, march, meander, pace, parade, plod, prance, promenade, roam, rove, shuffle, step, stride, stroll, strut, take a walk, tour, travel on foot, traverse, trek, troop, trudge, wander; SEE CONCEPT *149*

trait [*n*] *characteristic*
affection, attribute, birthmark, cast, character, custom, denominator, feature, habit, idiosyncrasy, lineament, manner, mannerism, mark, nature of the beast*, oddity, peculiarity, point,

property, quality, quirk, savor, thing*, trick, virtue; SEE CONCEPTS *411,644,834*

traitor [*n*] *person who is disloyal*
apostate, backslider*, back-stabber*, Benedict Arnold*, betrayer, conspirator, deceiver, defector, deserter, double-crosser*, fink*, hypocrite, impostor, informer, intriguer, Judas*, miscreant, quisling, rebel, renegade, snake*, sneak*, snitch*, snitcher*, spy, squealer*, stool pigeon*, tattletale, traducer, treasonist, turncoat, two-timer*, whistle-blower*, wolf*; SEE CONCEPT *412*

traitorous [*adj*] *disloyal*
apostate, betraying, double-crossing, faithless, perfidious, recreant, subversive, treacherous, treasonable, treasonous, two-faced*, two-timing, undutiful, unfaithful, unpatriotic, untrue, wormlike; SEE CONCEPT *401*

trajectory [*n*] *course*
curve, direction, flight, flow, line, movement, orbit, path, range, route, track, trail; SEE CONCEPTS *501,514*

tramp [*n1*] *person who is poor, desperate*
beggar, bum, derelict, down-and-out*, drifter, floater, hitchhiker, hobo, homeless person, loafer, outcast, panhandler, vagabond, vagrant, wanderer; SEE CONCEPT *412*

tramp [*n2*] *heavy walk*
cruise, excursion, expedition, footfall, footstep, hike, jaunt, march, ramble, saunter, slog, stomp, stroll, tour, traipse, tread, trek, turn, walking trip; SEE CONCEPTS *151,224*

tramp [*v*] *walk heavily*
crush, footslog, gallop, hike, hop, march, navigate, plod, pound, ramble, range, roam, rove, slog, stamp, stodge, stomp, stump, thud, toil, tour, traipse, trample, tread, trek, trip, tromp, trudge, walk over; SEE CONCEPTS *151,224*

trample [*v*] *walk forcibly over*
bruise, crush, encroach, flatten, grind, hurt, infringe, injure, override, overwhelm, pound, ride roughshod over*, run over, squash, stamp, step on, stomp, tramp, tread, tromp, violate; SEE CONCEPTS *137,208,246*

trance [*n*] *hypnotic state*
abstraction, coma, daze, dream, ecstasy, glaze, insensibility, muse, petrifaction, rapture, reverie, spell, study, stupor, transfixion, transfixture, unconsciousness; SEE CONCEPT *410*

tranquil [*adj*] *quiet, peaceful*
agreeable, amicable, at ease, at peace, balmy, calm, collected, comforting, composed, cool, easy, easygoing, even, even-tempered, gentle, halcyon, hushed, lenient, low, measured, mild, moderate, murmuring, pacific, paradisiacal, pastoral, patient, placid, pleasing, poised, possessed, quiet, reasonable, restful, sedate, sedative, serene, smooth, sober, soft, soothing, stable, still, tame, temperate, undisturbed, unexcitable, unexcited, unperturbed, unruffled, untroubled, whispering; SEE CONCEPTS *525,542,594*

tranquility [*n*] *peace, quiet*
ataraxia, calm, calmness, composure, coolness, equanimity, hush, imperturbability, imperturbation, law and order, order, peacefulness, placidity, quietness, quietude, repose, rest, restfulness, sedateness, serenity, stillness; SEE CONCEPTS *65,673*

tranquilize [*v*] *make calm, quiet*
balm, calm, calm down, compose, hush, lull,

pacify, put at rest, quell, quiet, quieten, relax, sedate, settle one's nerves*, soothe, still, subdue, unruffle; SEE CONCEPTS *7,22,310*

transact [v] *do business, carry out*
accomplish, button down*, button up*, buy, carry on, clinch, close, conclude, conduct, discharge, do*, effectuate, enact, execute, finish, handle, jell, manage, move, negotiate, operate, perform, prosecute, pull off, run with the ball*, see to, sell, settle, sew up*, take care of, TCB*, work out a deal*, wrap up*; SEE CONCEPTS *91,223,324,330,706*

transaction [n] *business dealing; undertaking*
act, action, activity, affair, agreement, bargain, bond, business, buying, compact, contract, convention, coup, covenant, deal, deed, disposal, doings*, enterprise, event, execution, goings-on*, happening, intercourse, matter, negotiation, occurrence, pact, performance, play, proceeding, purchase, purchasing, sale, selling, step; SEE CONCEPTS *223,324,330,684*

transcend [v] *go beyond; surpass*
beat, best, be superior, better, eclipse, exceed, excel, go above, leave behind, leave in the dust*, outdo, outrival, outshine, outstrip, outvie, overstep, overtop, rise above, top, transform; SEE CONCEPT *141*

transcendent/transcendental [adj] *extraordinary, superior*
absolute, abstract, accomplished, beyond grasp, boundless, consummate, entire, eternal, exceeding, fantastic, finished, hypothetical, ideal, incomparable, infinite, innate, intact, intellectual, intuitive, matchless, obscure, original, otherworldly, peerless, perfect, preeminent, primordial, second to none*, sublime, supernatural, supreme, surpassing, theoretical, towering, transcending, transmundane, ultimate, unequalable, unequalled, unique, unparalleled, unrivalled, whole; SEE CONCEPT *574*

transcribe [v] *transfer to another medium*
copy out, decipher, duplicate, engross, interpret, note, record, render, reprint, reproduce, rewrite, set out, take down, tape, tape-record, transfer, translate, transliterate, write out; SEE CONCEPTS *79,125,171*

transcript [n] *copy*
carbon copy*, ditto*, duplicate, facsimile, hard copy, imprint, manuscript, mimeograph, minutes, notes, print, record, recorded material, recording, reprint, reproduction, transcription, translation; SEE CONCEPTS *269,667,716*

transfer [n] *change of possession*
alteration, assignment, conduction, convection, deportation, displacement, move, relegation, relocation, removal, shift, substitution, transference, translation, transmission, transmittal, transposition, variation; SEE CONCEPTS *108,143,217,223*

transfer [v] *pass possession to*
assign, bear, bring, carry, cart, cede, change, consign, convert, convey, deed, delegate, deliver, dislocate, dispatch, dispense, displace, disturb, express, feed, ferry, find, forward, give, hand, hand over, haul, lug, mail, make over, metamorphose, move, pass on, pass the buck*, post, provide, relegate, relocate, remove, sell, send, shift, ship, shoulder, sign over, supply, taxi, tote, transfigure, translate, transmit, transmogrify, trans-

mute, transplant, transport, transpose, turn over; SEE CONCEPTS *108,143,217,223,243*

transfix [v1] *hold one's attention*
bewitch, captivate, enchant, engross, fascinate, hold, hypnotize, mesmerize, palsy, paralyze, petrify, rivet, root, spellbind, stop in one's tracks*, stop one dead*, stun; SEE CONCEPTS *11,14*

transfix [v2] *pierce*
fix, impale, lance, nail down, penetrate, pin down, puncture, run through, skewer, skiver, spear, spike, spit, stick, transpierce; SEE CONCEPT *220*

transform [v] *change completely*
alter, commute, convert, cook, denature, doctor, make over, metamorphose, mold, mutate, reconstruct, remodel, renew, revamp, revolutionize, shift gears*, sing different tune*, switch, switch over, transfer, transfigure, translate, transmogrify, transmute, transpose, turn around, turn over new leaf*, turn the corner*, turn the tables*; SEE CONCEPTS *232,697*

transformation [n] *complete change*
about-face*, alteration, changeover, conversion, flip-flop*, metamorphosis, radical change, renewal, revolution, shift, switch, transfiguration, transmogrification, transmutation; SEE CONCEPT *697*

transgression [n] *violation, misbehavior*
breach, breaking of the law, contravention, crime, defiance, disobedience, encroachment, erring, error, fault, infraction, infringement, iniquity, lapse, misdeed, misdemeanor, offense, overstepping, sin, slip, trespass, vice, wrong, wrongdoing; SEE CONCEPTS *101,192,645*

transient/transitory [adj] *temporary, brief*
changeable, deciduous, emigrating, ephemeral, evanescent, flash, fleeting, flitting, fly-by-night*, flying, fugacious, fugitive, going by, impermanent, insubstantial, migrating, momentary, moving, passing, provisional, short, short-lived, short-term, temporal, transmigratory, unstable, vacating, volatile; SEE CONCEPT *798*

transit [n] *transportation*
alteration, carriage, carrying, conveyance, crossing, infiltration, motion, movement, osmosis, passage, penetration, permeation, portage, shift, shipment, transfer, transference, transport, transporting, travel, traverse; SEE CONCEPTS *155,224*

transition [n] *change, often major*
alteration, changeover, conversion, development, evolution, flux, growth, metamorphosis, metastasis, passage, passing, progress, progression, realignment, shift, transformation, transit, transmutation, turn, turning point, upheaval; SEE CONCEPT *697*

translate [v1] *interpret, explain*
construe, convert, decipher, decode, do into, elucidate, explicate, gloss, make clear, metaphrase, paraphrase, put, render, reword, simplify, spell out, transcribe, transliterate, transpose, turn; SEE CONCEPTS *55,57*

translate [v2] *change*
alter, commute, convert, metamorphose, transfigure, transform, transmogrify, transmute, transpose, turn; SEE CONCEPT *232*

translation [n] *rewording; interpretation*
adaptation, construction, crib*, decoding, elucidation, explanation, gloss, key, metaphrase, paraphrase, reading, rendering, rendition,

rephrasing, restatement, simplification, transcription, transliteration, version; SEE CONCEPTS 268,277,278

translator [n] *interpreter*
adapter, cryptographer, cryptologist, decoder, dragoman, explainer, glossator, linguist, polyglot; SEE CONCEPTS 57,292

translucent [adj] *clear*
clear-cut, crystal, crystalline, diaphanous, glassy, limpid, lucent, lucid, luminous, pellucid, see-through, semiopaque, semitransparent, translucid, unblurred; SEE CONCEPT 618

transmit [v] *communicate, send*
address, bear, bequeath, break, broadcast, carry, channel, conduct, consign, convey, diffuse, dispatch, disseminate, drop a line*, drop a note*, forward, funnel, give a call*, give a ring*, hand down, hand on, impart, instill, issue, mail, pass on, pipe, put on the air*, radio, relay, remit, route, send, send out, ship, siphon, spread, take, traject, transfer, transfuse, translate, transport; SEE CONCEPTS 217,266,292

transparent [adj1] *see-through*
cellophane, clear, crystal-clear, crystalline, diaphanous, filmy, gauzy, glassy, gossamer, hyaline, limpid, lucent, lucid, pellucid, permeable, plain, sheer, thin, tiffany, translucent, transpicuous, vitreous; SEE CONCEPTS 606,618

transparent [adj2] *obvious, understandable*
apparent, articulate, artless, candid, clear-cut, direct, distinct, distinguishable, easily seen, easy, evident, explicit, forthright, frank, guileless, honest, ingenuous, manifest, open, patent, perspicuous, plain, plain-spoken, recognizable, self-explanatory, sincere, straight, straightforward, unambiguous, undisguised, unequivocal, unmistakable, unsophisticated, visible; SEE CONCEPT 267

transpire [v1] *occur, happen*
arise, befall, betide, chance, come about, come to pass, develop, ensue, eventuate, fall out*, gel, go, occur, result, shake, take place, turn up; SEE CONCEPT 3

transpire [v2] *become known*
be disclosed, be discovered, be made public, break, come out, come to light, emerge, get out, leak; SEE CONCEPTS 261,266

transplant [v] *relocate*
displace, emigrate, graft, immigrate, move, readapt, recondition, remove, reorient, reset, resettle, revamp, shift, transfer, transpose, uproot; SEE CONCEPTS 213,310

transport [n1] *move, transfer*
carriage, carrier, carrying, carting, conveyance, conveying, conveyor, freightage, hauling, lift, movement, mover, moving, passage, removal, shipment, shipping, transference, transferring, transit, transportation, transporting, transshipment, truckage, vehicle; SEE CONCEPTS 155,503

transport [n2] *delight*
ardor, bliss, cloud nine*, ecstasy, enchantment, enthusiasm, euphoria, fervor, happiness, heaven, passion, rapture, ravishment, rhapsody, seventh heaven*; SEE CONCEPTS 32,410

transport [v1] *move, transfer*
back, bear, bring, carry, conduct, convey, ferry, fetch, haul, heel*, jag, lug, pack, piggyback*, remove, ride, run, schlepp*, ship, shoulder, take, tote, truck; SEE CONCEPTS 147,187,217

transport [v2] *exile*
banish, cast out, deport, displace, expel, expulse, oust, relegate, sentence; SEE CONCEPTS 211,317

transport [v3] *captivate, delight*
agitate, carry away, electrify, elevate, enchant, enrapture, entrance, excite, inflame, move, provoke, quicken, ravish, send, slay, spellbind, stimulate, stir, thrill, trance, uplight, wow; SEE CONCEPTS 7,22

transpose [v] *swap, switch*
alter, backtrack*, change, commute, convert, double back, exchange, flip-flop*, interchange, inverse, invert, metamorphose, move, put, rearrange, relocate, render, reorder, reverse, revert, shift, substitute, transfer, transfigure, transform, translate, transmogrify, transmute, turn, turn the tables*; SEE CONCEPTS 104,232,697

trap [n] *snare, trick*
allurement, ambuscade, ambush, artifice, bait, booby trap*, come-on*, conspiracy, deception, decoy, device, dragnet, enticement, feint, gambit, hook*, intrigue, inveiglement, lasso*, lure, machination, maneuver, net, noose, pitfall, plot, ploy, prank, quagmire, quicksand, ruse, seducement, snag*, stratagem, subterfuge, temptation, wile; SEE CONCEPT 674

trap [v] *catch, snare; trick*
ambuscade, ambush, beguile, box in*, circumvent, collar*, corner*, corral*, deceive, decoy, dupe, enmesh, ensnare, entangle, entrap, fool, grab, hook, inveigle, land*, mousetrap*, nab, nail*, net, overtake, rope in*, seduce, snag, suck in*, surprise, take, tangle, trammel, trip up*; SEE CONCEPTS 59,90

trappings [n] *paraphernalia, equipment*
accouterment, adornment, apparel, appointment, decoration, dress, embellishment, finery, fitting, fixture, furnishing, gear, livery, ornament, panoply, personal effects, raiment, rigging, things, trimming; SEE CONCEPTS 446,451,496

trash [n1] *garbage*
debris, dregs, droppings, dross, excess, filth, fragments, junk, leavings, litter, oddments, odds and ends*, offal, pieces, refuse, residue, rubbish, rubble, rummage, scourings, scrap, scraps, scum*, sediment, shavings, sweepings, waste; SEE CONCEPTS 260,834

trash [n3] *ridiculous communication*
balderdash, bilge*, drivel, foolish talk, hogwash, inanity, malarkey*, nonsense, rot, rubbish, tripe, twaddle; SEE CONCEPT 278

trashy [adj] *worthless*
abandoned, barren, bogus, cheap, cheesy, crappy*, cruddy*, crummy*, despicable, empty, flimsy, garbage, good-for-nothing*, grungy, inferior, junky, lousy, low in quality, no-good*, ratty, raunchy, shabby, shoddy, sleazy, tawdry, useless, valueless; SEE CONCEPTS 560,570,575, 589

trauma [n] *severe mental or physical pain*
agony, anguish, blow, collapse, confusion, damage, derangement, disturbance, hurt, injury, jolt, ordeal, outburst, shock, strain, stress, suffering, torture, traumatization, upheaval, upset, wound; SEE CONCEPT 728

travel [n] *journey*
biking, commutation, cruising, drive, driving, excursion, expedition, flying, globe-trotting*, hop*, junket, movement, navigation, overnight, passage, peregrination, ramble, ride, riding, sail-

ing, seafaring, sightseeing, swing, tour, touring, transit, trek, trekking, trip, voyage, voyaging, walk, wandering, wanderlust, wayfaring, weekend; SEE CONCEPT *224*

travel [*v*] *journey on a trip or tour*
adventure, carry, cover, cover ground, cross, cruise, drive, explore, fly, get through, go, go abroad, go camping, go into orbit*, go riding, hop*, jaunt, jet*, junket*, knock around, make a journey, make one's way, migrate, motor, move, overnight*, proceed, progress, ramble, roam, rove, sail, scour, set forth, set out, sightsee, take a boat, take a plane, take a train, take a trip, tour, transmit, traverse, trek, vacation, visit, voyage, walk, wander, weekend*, wend; SEE CONCEPT *224*

traveler [*n*] *person who journeys*
adventurer, barnstormer*, bum*, commuter, displaced person, drifter, excursionist, expeditionist, explorer, floater, gadabout*, globetrotter, gypsy, haj, hiker, hobo, itinerant, jet-setter, journeyer, junketer, migrant, navigator, nomad, passenger, peddler, pilgrim, rambler, roamer, rover, sailor, seafarer, sightseer, tourist, tramp, transmigrant, trekker, tripper, trouper, truant, vagabond, vagrant, voyager, wanderer, wayfarer; SEE CONCEPTS *348,423*

traverse [*v1*] *cross over; travel*
bisect, bridge, cover, crisscross, cross, cut across, decussate, do, go across, go over, intersect, move over, negotiate, pace, pass over, pass through, perambulate, peregrinate, ply, quarter, range, roam, span, track, transverse, travel over, tread, walk, wander; SEE CONCEPTS *147,201,692,750*

traverse [*v2*] *resist, contradict*
balk, buck, check, combat, contest, contravene, counter, counteract, cross, deny, disaffirm, dispute, duel, fight, frustrate, gainsay, go against, hinder, impede, impugn, negate, negative, obstruct, oppose, repel, thwart, withstand; SEE CONCEPTS *54,121*

travesty [*n*] *spoof, ridicule*
burlesque, caricature, distortion, exaggeration, farce, lampoon, lampoonery, mimicry, mock, mockery, parody, perversion, play, put-on*, roast*, satire, send-up*, sham*, takeoff*; SEE CONCEPTS *273,292*

travesty [*v*] *ridicule, spoof*
ape, burlesque, caricature, deride, distort, imitate, lampoon, make a mockery of, make fun of, mimic, mock, parody, pervert, play on*, put on*, satirize, send up*, sham*, take off*; SEE CONCEPTS *273,292*

treacherous [*adj1*] *dishonest, disloyal*
betraying, catchy, deceitful, deceptive, double-crossing*, double-dealing*, duplicitous, faithless, false, false-hearted, fly-by-night*, insidious, misleading, perfidious, recreant, shifty*, slick*, slippery*, snake in the grass*, traitorous, treasonable, tricky, two-faced*, two-timing*, undependable, unfaithful, unloyal, unreliable, untrue, untrustworthy; SEE CONCEPTS *401,404*

treacherous [*adj2*] *dangerous*
alarming, chancy, deceptive, difficult, dissembled, faulty, hairy*, hazardous, icy*, insecure, jeopardous, menacing, misleading, ominous, perilous, precarious, risky, shaky, slippery, ticklish, tricky, undependable, unhealthy, unreliable, un-

safe, unsound, unstable, wicked; SEE CONCEPTS *565,587*

treachery [*n*] *disloyalty, dishonesty*
betrayal, bunco, corruption, dirty dealing*, dirty pool*, dirty trick*, dirty work*, disaffection, dodge, double-cross*, double-dealing*, duplicity, faithlessness, fake, falseness, fast shuffle*, flimflam*, grift, gyp*, infidelity, perfidiousness, perfidy, put-on*, racket*, recreancy, scam*, sellout, shell game*, skin game*, spoof, stab in the back*, sweet talk*, treacherousness, treason, two-timing*, whitewash*; SEE CONCEPTS *633,645*

tread [*n*] *walk*
footstep, footsteps, gait, march, pace, step, stride, trace, track, tramp; SEE CONCEPTS *149,284*

tread [*v*] *walk; bear down*
ambulate, crush, foot, hike, hoof, march, oppress, pace, plod, quell, repress, squash, stamp, stamp on, step, step on, stride, subdue, subjugate, suppress, traipse, tramp, trample, troop, trudge; SEE CONCEPT *149*

treason [*n*] *disloyalty*
breach of faith, crime, deceit, deceitfulness, deception, disaffection, dishonesty, duplicity, faithlessness, le 'se majesté, mutiny, perfidy, revolt, revolutionary, sedition, seditious act, seditiousness, subversion, traitorousness, treachery; SEE CONCEPTS *192,645*

treasonous [*adj*] *disloyal*
apostate, betraying, double-crossing, faithless, insubordinate, mutinous, perfidious, recreant, subversive, traitorous, treacherous, treasonable, two-faced*, two-timing, undutiful, unfaithful, unpatriotic, untrue, wormlike; SEE CONCEPT *401*

treasure [*n*] *prized possession or entity*
abundance, apple of one's eye*, cache, capital, cash, catch*, darling, find, fortune, funds, gem, gold, hoard, jewel, money, nest egg*, nonpareil, paragon, pearl*, pile*, plum*, pride and joy*, prize, reserve, riches, richness, store, treasure trove, valuable, wealth; SEE CONCEPTS *332,337,446,710*

treasure [*v*] *hold dear*
adore, appreciate, apprize, cherish, conserve, dote on, esteem, guard, idolize, love, preserve, prize, revere, reverence, save, value, venerate, worship; SEE CONCEPT *32*

treasury [*n*] *place where money, valuables are kept*
archive, bank, bursar, bursary, cache, chest, coffer, damper, depository, exchange, exchequer, Fort Knox*, gallery, hoard, museum, register, repository, safe, storage, store, storehouse, strongbox, treasure house, vault; SEE CONCEPTS *339,439,449*

treat [*n*] *pleasing entity or occurrence*
amusement, banquet, celebration, dainty, delicacy, delight, enjoyment, entertainment, feast, fun, gift, goody*, gratification, joy, party, pleasure, refreshment, satisfaction, surprise, sweet, thrill, tidbit; SEE CONCEPTS *457,529,693*

treat [*v1*] *act, behave towards*
account, act with regard to, appraise, conduct, conduct oneself toward, consider, deal with*, employ, estimate, evaluate, handle, have business with*, have recourse to*, have to do with*, hold, look upon, manage, negotiate, play, rate, react toward, regard, respect, serve, take, use, value, wield; SEE CONCEPT *633*

tr
tr

treat [*v2*] *doctor, medicate*
administer, apply treatment, attend, care for, cure, dose, dress, heal, medicament, minister to, nurse, operate, prescribe; SEE CONCEPT *310*

treat [*v3*] *pay the bill for someone else*
amuse, blow, buy for, divert, entertain, escort, feast, foot the bill*, give, indulge, pay for, pick up the check*, pick up the tab*, play host*, provide, regale, satisfy, set up, spring for*, stake, stand*, take out, wine and dine*; SEE CONCEPTS *327,384*

treat [*v4*] *be concerned with; discuss*
advise, approach, arrange, comment, confabulate, confer, consider, consult, contain, criticize, deal with, deliberate, discourse on, discuss, enlarge upon, explain, go into, interpret, manipulate, reason, review, speak about, study, tackle, talk about, think, touch upon, weigh, write about; SEE CONCEPTS *17,56*

treatise [*n*] *written study of a subject*
argument, book, commentary, composition, discourse, discussion, disquisition, dissertation, essay, exposition, memoir, monograph, pamphlet, paper, review, script, thesis, tract, tractate, work, writing; SEE CONCEPTS *271,280*

treatment [*n1*] *medical care*
analysis, cure, diet, doctoring, healing, hospitalization, medication, medicine, operation, prescription, regimen, remedy, surgery, therapeutics, therapy; SEE CONCEPT *310*

treatment [*n2*] *handling of entity, situation*
action towards, angle, approach, behavior towards, conduct, custom, dealing, employment, execution, habit, line, management, manipulation, manner, method, mode, modus operandi, practice, procedure, proceeding, processing, reception, strategy, usage, way; SEE CONCEPTS *117,633*

treaty [*n*] *agreement, contract*
accord, alliance, arrangement, bargain, bond, cartel, charter, compact, concord, concordat, convention, covenant, deal, entente, league, negotiation, pact, reconciliation, sanction, settlement, understanding; SEE CONCEPTS *684,685*

tree [*n*] *large plant enclosed in bark and shedding leaves*
forest, hardwood, pulp, sapling, seedling, shrub, softwood, stock, timber, wood, woods; SEE CONCEPT *430*

trek [*n*] *long journey*
expedition, footslog, hegira, hike, long haul, march, odyssey, peregrination, slog, tramp, travel, trip; SEE CONCEPT *224*

trek [*v*] *journey*
be on the move*, be on the trail*, foot, hike, hit the road*, march, migrate, plod, range, roam, rove, slog, traipse, tramp, travel, trudge, walk; SEE CONCEPT *224*

tremble [*v*] *shake, vibrate*
flutter, have the shakes*, jar, jitter, oscillate, palpitate, quake, quaver, quiver, rock, shiver, shudder, teeter, throb, totter, tremor, wobble; SEE CONCEPT *152*

tremendous [*adj*] *huge, overwhelming*
amazing, appalling, astounding, awesome, awful, blimp, colossal, cracking, deafening, dreadful, enormous, excellent, exceptional, extraordinary, fabulous, fantastic, fearful, formidable, frightful, gargantuan, gigantic, great, great big*, huge, humongous, immense, incredible,

jumbo*, large, mammoth, marvelous, massive, mondo*, monstrous, monumental, prodigious, stupendous, super, terrible, terrific, titanic, towering, vast, whale*, whopper, whopping, wonderful; SEE CONCEPTS *574,773,781*

tremor [*n*] *shaking, shock*
agitation, earthquake, flutter, quake, quaking, quaver, quiver, quivering, ripple, shake, shiver, shivering, tremble, trembling, trepidation, upheaval, vibration, wobble; SEE CONCEPTS *145,526*

trench [*n*] *ditch, channel dug in earth*
arroyo, canal, cut, depression, dike, drain, drill, dugout, earthwork, entrenchment, excavation, fosse, foxhole, furrow, gorge, gulch, gully, gutter, hollow, main, moat, pit, rut, sink, trough, tube, waterway; SEE CONCEPTS *509,513*

trenchant [*adj*] *sarcastic, scathing*
acerbic, acid, acidulous, acute, astringent, biting, caustic, clear, clear-cut, crisp, critical, crushing, cutting, distinct, driving, dynamic, effective, effectual, emphatic, energetic, explicit, forceful, forcible, graphic, hurtful, impressive, incisive, intense, keen, mordant, penetrating, piquant, pointed, potent, powerful, pungent, razor-sharp*, salient, salty*, sardonic, sententious, severe, sharp, significant, strong, tart, to the point, unequivocal, unsparing, vigorous, weighty, well-defined; SEE CONCEPTS *267,537*

trend [*n1*] *flow, current*
aim, bearing, bent, bias, course, direction, drift, inclination, leaning, movement, orientation, progression, run, swing, tendency, tenor, wind; SEE CONCEPTS *230,657,738*

trend [*n2*] *style, fashion that is in favor*
craze, cry, fad, furor, in-thing*, latest thing*, look, mode, newest wrinkle*, rage, thing*, vogue; SEE CONCEPT *655*

trendy [*adj*] *in fashion, style*
a' la mode*, contemporary, fashionable, fly*, in, in vogue, latest, modish*, now*, popular, stylish, swank*, tony*, up-to-the-minute, voguish, with-it*; SEE CONCEPT *589*

trepidation [*n*] *anxiety, worry*
agitation, alarm, apprehension, blue funk*, butterflies*, cold feet*, cold sweat*, consternation, creeps*, dismay, disquiet, disturbance, dread, emotion, excitement, fear, fright, goose bumps*, horror, jitters, nervousness, palpitation, panic, perturbation, shock, terror, trepidity, uneasiness, worriment; SEE CONCEPT *27*

trespass [*n*] *invasion, offense*
breach, contravention, crime, delinquency, encroachment, entrenchment, error, evildoing, fault, infraction, infringement, iniquity, injury, intrusion, misbehavior, misconduct, misdeed, misdemeanor, obtrusion, poaching, sin, transgression, unlawful entry, violation, wrongdoing, wrongful entry; SEE CONCEPTS *101,192,645,691*

trespass [*v*] *infringe, offend*
butt in*, chisel in*, crash, crash the gates*, deviate, displease, do wrong by, encroach, entrench, err, horn in*, interlope, intrude, invade, kibitz*, lapse, meddle, misbehave, mix in, muscle in*, nose in*, obtrude, overstep, penetrate, poach, poke, sin, stick nose in*, transgress, violate, wrong; SEE CONCEPTS *101,159,192,384*

trial [*adj*] *experimental*
balloon, exploratory, pilot, preliminary, proba-

tionary, provisional, tentative, test, testing; SEE CONCEPTS *548,560*

trial [*n1*] *test*
analysis, assay, attempt, audition, check, crack*, dry run*, effort, endeavor, essay, examination, experience, experiment, experimentation, fling*, go*, hassle*, investigation, lick*, probation, proof, R and D*, research and development, shakedown*, shot*, showcase*, stab*, striving, struggle, testing, test run, trial and error*, trial run, try, try on*, tryout, undertaking, venture, whack*, workout; SEE CONCEPTS *87,290,291*

trial [*n2*] *legal proceeding*
action, arraignment, case, citation, claim, contest, counterclaim, court action, court martial, cross-examination, habeas corpus, hearing, impeachment, indictment, lawsuit, litigation, prosecution, rap*, seizure, suit, tribunal; SEE CONCEPTS *317,691*

trial [*n3*] *trouble, big problem*
adversity, affliction, albatross*, anguish, annoyance, bane, blow, bother, burden, calvary, care, complication, cross to bear*, crucible*, difficulty, distress, drag*, grief, hardship, hard time*, hassle*, heartbreak, inconvenience, irritation, load, misery, misfortune, nightmare, nuisance, ordeal, pain, pain in the neck*, pest, plague, rigor, severe test, sorrow, suffering, thorn, tribulation, trying time*, unhappiness, vexation, vicissitude, visitation, woe, wretchedness; SEE CONCEPTS *674,728*

tribe [*n*] *ethnic group; family*
association, blood, caste, clan, class, division, dynasty, horde, house, ilk, kin, kind, kindred, lineage, people, race, seed, society, sort, stock, type; SEE CONCEPTS *296,380,421*

tribulation [*n*] *pain, unhappiness*
adversity, affliction, albatross*, bad luck*, blow*, bummer*, burden, care, cross to bear*, crucible*, curse, difficulty, distress, double whammy*, downer*, drag*, grief, hard knock*, hard time*, headache*, heartache*, misery, misfortune, oppression, ordeal, persecution, rainy day*, reverse, sorrow, suffering, trial, trouble, vexation, visitation, woe, worry, wretchedness, wronging; SEE CONCEPTS *666,728*

tribunal [*n*] *court*
bar, bench, board, committee, council, court of justice, forum, judge, judiciary, justice, law court, magistrate, seat of judgment; SEE CONCEPTS *299,318*

tributary [*adj*] *secondary; branch*
accessory, dependent, feeding, minor, satellite, shoot, side, sub, subject, subordinate, under; SEE CONCEPT *560*

tribute [*n*] *testimonial, praise*
accolade, acknowledgment, applause, appreciation, citation, commendation, compliment, encomium, esteem, eulogy, gift, gratitude, honor, laudation, memorial, offering, panegyric, recognition, recommendation, respect, salutation, salvo; SEE CONCEPTS *69,278*

trick [*n1*] *deceit*
ambush, artifice, blind, bluff, casuistry, cheat, chicanery, circumvention, con*, concealment, conspiracy, conundrum, cover, deception, decoy, delusion, device, disguise, distortion, dodge*, double-dealing, duplicity, equivocation, evasion, fabrication, fake, falsehood, feint, forgery, fraud, game, gimmick, hoax, illusion, imposition, im-

posture, intrigue, invention, machination, maneuver, perjury, plot, ploy, pretense, ruse, snare, stratagem, subterfuge, swindle, trap, treachery, wile; SEE CONCEPTS *59,645*

trick [*n2*] *prank, joke*
accomplishment, antic, caper, catch, device, escapade, feat, frolic, funny business, gag*, gambol, jape, jest, lark, monkeyshine*, practical joke, put-on*, shenanigan*, sleight of hand, sport, stunt, tomfoolery; SEE CONCEPTS *59,273,384*

trick [*n3*] *expertise, know-how*
ability, art, command, craft, device, facility, gift, hang, knack, method, secret, skill, swing, technique; SEE CONCEPT *630*

trick [*n4*] *characteristic, habit*
crotchet, custom, foible, habitude, idiosyncrasy, manner, mannerism, peculiarity, practice, praxis, quirk, trait, usage, use, way, wont; SEE CONCEPTS *411,657*

trick [*n5*] *time working at something*
bout, go*, hitch, shift, spell, stint, tour, turn; SEE CONCEPT *807*

trick [*v*] *fool; play joke on*
bamboozle, catch*, cheat, con, deceive, defraud, delude, disinform, double deal*, dupe, fake, flimflam*, fool, gull, hoax, hocus-pocus*, hoodwink, impose upon, jive*, mislead, outwit, play for a fool*, pull wool over*, put one over on*, rook*, screw*, set up*, swindle, take for a ride*, take in*, throw, trap, victimize; SEE CONCEPT *59*

trickery [*n*] *deception, joke*
bait and switch*, cheat, cheating, chicane, chicanery, con, deceit, dishonesty, dodge, double-cross*, double-dealing*, dupery, fast shuffle*, flimflam*, fourberie, fraud, funny business*, guile, hoax, imposture, pretense, quackery, razzle-dazzle*, scam, sharp practice, shell game*, shenanigans*, snow job*, sting*, stunt, swindling, underhandedness; SEE CONCEPTS *59,645*

trickle [*v*] *run out*
crawl, creep, distill, dribble, drip, drop, exude, flow, issue, leak, ooze, percolate, seep, stream, trill, weep; SEE CONCEPTS *146,179*

tricky [*adj1*] *complicated, difficult*
catchy, complex, critical, delicate, intricate, involved, knotty*, perplexing, precarious, problematic, quirky, risky, rocky, sensitive, sticky, thorny, ticklish, touch-and-go*, touchy, undependable, unstable; SEE CONCEPT *562*

tricky [*adj2*] *deceptive, sly*
artful, astute, cagey, catchy, clever, crafty, cunning, deceitful, deep, delusive, delusory, devious, dishonest, foxy, greasy*, guileful, insidious, intelligent, keen, misleading, scheming, shady, sharp, shifty, shrewd, slick*, slippery*, smooth, streetwise*, subtle, treacherous, wily, witted, wry; SEE CONCEPT *401*

tried [*adj*] *reliable*
approved, certified, constant, demonstrated, dependable, faithful, proved, secure, staunch, steadfast, tested, tried-and-true*, true-blue*, trustworthy, trusty, used; SEE CONCEPT *535*

tried-and-true [*adj*] *tested*
approved, certified, creditworthy, dependable, loyal, proved, proven, reliable, safe, tried, trustworthy, trusty; SEE CONCEPT *535*

trifle [*n1*] *novelty item*
bagatelle, bauble, bibelot, curio, gewgaw*, knickknack, nothing*, novelty, objet d'art, play-

thing, toy, trinket, triviality, whatnot*; SEE CONCEPT **446**

trifle [n2] *very small amout*
bit, dash, diddly*, drop, eyelash*, fly speck*, fraction, hint, jot, little, no big deal*, particle, picayune*, piece, pinch, shade, smack, soupçon, speck, spice, spot, squat, suggestion, suspicion, touch, trace; SEE CONCEPTS **668,831**

trifle [v] *toy with; mess around*
amuse oneself, be insincere, coquet, dabble, dally, dawdle, dilly-dally*, doodle, fidget, flirt, fool, fool around*, fool with*, fribble*, fritter, futz around*, horse around*, idle, indulge in, lead on, loiter, lollygag*, lounge, mess with*, misuse, monkey, monkey with*, palter, philander, play, play games with*, play with, potter, putter, squander, string along*, toy, twiddle, use up, wanton, waste, waste time, wink at*; SEE CONCEPTS **210,292,363**

trifling [adj] *insignificant, worthless*
banal, dinky*, empty, forget it*, frivolous, hollow, idle, idling, inane, inconsequential, inconsiderable, insipid, jejune, loitering, measly, minuscule, negligible, niggling*, no big deal*, no big thing*, nugatory, paltry, petty, picayune, piddling, puny, shallow, silly, slight, small, tiny, trivial, unimportant, vain, valueless, vapid; SEE CONCEPTS **575,789**

trigger [v] *cause to happen*
activate, bring about, cause, elicit, generate, give rise to, produce, prompt, provoke, set in motion, set off, spark, start; SEE CONCEPT **242**

trim [adj1] *neat, orderly*
apple-pie order*, clean, clean-cut, compact, dapper, fit, in good shape, neat as a pin*, nice, shipshape*, slick, smart, snug, spick-and-span*, spruce, streamlined, symmetrical, tidy, to rights*, uncluttered, well-groomed; SEE CONCEPTS **485,621**

trim [adj2] *shapely*
beautiful, clean, comely, fit, graceful, in fine fettle*, in good shape, sleek, slender, slick, slim, statuesque, streamlined, svelte, well-balanced, well-proportioned, willowy; SEE CONCEPTS **314,490,491**

trim [n1] *decoration*
adornment, border, edging, embellishment, frill, fringe, garnish, gingerbread*, ornamentation, piping, trimming; SEE CONCEPTS **475,824**

trim [n2] *condition, health*
commission, fettle*, fitness, form, kilter*, order, repair, shape, situation, state, whack*; SEE CONCEPT **316**

trim [v1] *cut shorter*
abbreviate, barber, blue pencil*, bob, boil down*, clip, crop, curtail, cut, cut back, cut down, dock, edit, even up, lop, mow, pare, pare down, plane, prune, put in a nutshell*, shave, shear, shorten, slice off, snip, tidy, truncate, whittle down*; SEE CONCEPTS **176,236,247**

trim [v2] *decorate*
adorn, array, beautify, bedeck, beribbon, deck, dress, dress up, embellish, emblazon, embroider, garnish, ornament, prank, pretty up*, prink*, spangle, spruce up*; SEE CONCEPTS **162,177**

trim [v3] *beat, defeat*
clobber, drub, lambaste, lick, smother, thrash, trounce, wax*, whip; SEE CONCEPT **95**

trimmings [n] *accessories, extras*
accent, accompaniments, additions, clippings, decorations, fixings, frills, garnish, ornaments, supplements, trappings; SEE CONCEPT **834**

trinket [n] *knickknack*
bagatelle, bauble, bead, bibelot, curio, doodad*, gadget, gewgaw*, gimcrack*, glass*, hardware, jewel, jewelry, junk, nothing*, novelty, objet d'art, ornament, plaything, rock*, sparkler*, stone, toy, trifle, whatnot*; SEE CONCEPT **446**

trio/triple [n] *three of something*
leash, set of three, ternion, threesome, trey, triad, triangle, trilogy, trine, trinity, triplet, triplicate, triptych, triumvirate, triune, troika; SEE CONCEPTS **784,787**

trip [n1] *journey, excursion*
cruise, errand, expedition, foray, hop*, jaunt, junket, outing, overnight, peregrination, ramble*, run, swing*, tour, travel, trek, voyage, weekend; SEE CONCEPT **224**

trip [n2] *error, blunder*
bungle, fall, false move, false step, faux pas*, indiscretion, lapse, misstep, mistake, slip, stumble; SEE CONCEPTS **101,230**

trip [v] *fall, err*
buck, canter, confuse, disconcert, fall, fall over, founder, frolic, go headlong*, go wrong, hop, lapse, lope, lose balance, lose footing, lurch, make a faux pas*, miscalculate, misstep, pitch, play, plunge, skip, slide, slip, slip on, slip up, sprawl, spring, stumble, throw off, topple, tumble, unsettle; SEE CONCEPTS **101,149**

tripe [n] *nonsense, rubbish*
balderdash, baloney*, bilge, bosh, BS*, bull*, bunk*, drivel, garbage, gibberish, hogwash, hooey*, hot air*, poppycock, trash; SEE CONCEPTS **230,278**

trite [adj] *silly, commonplace*
banal, bathetic, bromidic, chain, cliché, clichéd, common, cornball*, corny*, drained, dull, exhausted, familiar tune*, flat, hackneyed, hokey*, jejune, mildewed*, moth-eaten*, musty*, old hat*, ordinary, pedestrian, platitudinous, prosaic, ready-made, routine, run-of-the-mill*, set, shopworn, stale, stereotyped, stock, threadbare, timeworn, tired, uninspired, unoriginal, used-up, vapid, warmed-over*, well-worn, worn, wornout; SEE CONCEPTS **267,530**

triumph [n1] *extreme happiness*
celebration, elation, exultance, exultation, festivity, joy, jubilance, jubilation, jubilee, merriment, pride, rejoicing, reveling; SEE CONCEPT **410**

triumph [n2] *victory, achievement*
accomplishment, ascendancy, attainment, big hit*, big win*, cinch, clean sweep*, conquest, coup, feat, feather in cap*, gain, grand slam*, hit, hole in one*, homer*, pushover*, riot, score, sell, sensation, shoo-in*, smash-hit*, splash, success, sure bet*, sure thing*, surmounting, takeover, the gold*, tour de force*, vanquishing, vanquishment, walkover*, win; SEE CONCEPT **706**

triumph [v1] *be very happy*
celebrate, crow, delight, exult, gloat, glory, jubilate, rejoice, revel, swagger; SEE CONCEPT **32**

triumph [v2] *achieve, succeed*
beat the game*, beat the system*, best, blow away*, carry the day*, come out on top*, conquer, dominate, flourish, get last laugh*, overcome, overwhelm, prevail, prosper, sink, strike it big*, subdue, sweep, take it all*, take the cake*,

thrive, trounce, vanquish, win, win hands down*, win out*; SEE CONCEPTS *95,141,706*

triumphant [*adj*] *successful*
boastful, celebratory, champion, conquering, dominant, elated, exultant, glorious, happy, in the lead*, jubilant, looking good, lucky, on top, out front*, prizewinning, proud, rejoicing, swaggering, triumphal, unbeaten, undefeated, victorious, winning; SEE CONCEPT *528*

trivia [*n*] *details*
fine points, memorabilia, minutiae, trifles, trivialities; SEE CONCEPTS *274,543*

trivial [*adj*] *not important*
atomic, beside the point*, commonplace, diminutive, evanescent, everyday, flimsy, frivolous, immaterial, inappreciable, incidental, inconsequential, inconsiderable, insignificant, irrelevant, little, meager, mean, meaningless, microscopic, minor, minute, momentary, negligible, nonessential, nugatory, of no account, paltry, petty, piddling*, puny, scanty, skin-deep*, slight, small, superficial, trifling, trite, unimportant, valueless, vanishing, worthless; SEE CONCEPT *575*

troll [*n*] *elf*
demon, dwarf, giant, gnome, goblin, hobgoblin, kobold, leprechaun, monster, mythical creature, ogre; SEE CONCEPT *412*

troop/troops [*n*] *group, often military*
armed forces, army, assemblage, assembly, band, body, bunch, collection, combatants, company, contingent, corps, crew, crowd, delegation, drove, fighting forces, flock, forces, gang, gathering, herd, horde, host, legion, military, multitude, number, outfit, pack, party, personnel, service personnel, soldiers, soldiery, squad, swarm, team, throng, troopers, troupe, unit; SEE CONCEPTS *322,417*

trophy [*n*] *physical award*
blue ribbon*, booty, citation, crown, cup, decoration, gold*, gold star*, guerdon, keepsake, laurels, medal, memento, memorial, palm, prize, reminder, ribbon, souvenir, spoils*, token; SEE CONCEPT *337*

tropical [*adj*] *warm and humid*
close, equatorial, hot, lush, steamy, sticky, stifling, sultry, sweaty, sweltering, torrid, tropic; SEE CONCEPTS *525,605*

trot [*v*] *move along briskly*
amble, canter, go, hurry, jog, lope, pad, rack, ride, run, scamper, step lively; SEE CONCEPT *150*

trot out [*v*] *bring forward*
brandish, bring up, come out with, display, disport, drag up, exhibit, expose, flash, flaunt, parade, recite, rehearse, reiterate, relate, repeat, represent, show, show off; SEE CONCEPT *138*

troubadour [*n*] *singer*
accompanist, artist, balladeer, bard, crooner, jongleur, minnesinger, minstrel, musician, poet, serenader, songster, songwriter, trouveur, vocalist; SEE CONCEPT *352*

trouble [*n1*] *annoyance, worry*
agitation, anxiety, bad news*, bind, bother, commotion, concern, danger, difficulty, dilemma, dire straits, discontent, discord, disorder, disquiet, dissatisfaction, distress, disturbance, grief, hang-up*, heartache, hindrance, hot water*, inconvenience, irritation, mess, misfortune, nuisance, pain, pest, pickle*, predicament, problem, puzzle, row, scrape, sorrow, spot, strain, stress, strife, struggle, suffering, task, torment, tribula-

tion, tumult, unrest, vexation, woe; SEE CONCEPTS *532,674,675,690,728*

trouble [*n2*] *something requiring great effort*
ado, attention, bother, bustle, care, concern, difficulty, effort, exertion, flurry, fuss, hardship, inconvenience, labor, pains, pother, rigor, strain, stress, struggle, thought, trial, while, work, worry; SEE CONCEPTS *666,677*

trouble [*n3*] *bad health*
affliction, ailment, complaint, curse, defect, disability, disease, disorder, failure, illness, malady, malfunction, upset; SEE CONCEPT *316*

trouble [*v1*] *bother, worry*
afflict, agitate, ail, annoy, bug*, burden, burn up*, concern, discommode, discompose, disconcert, disoblige, disquiet, distress, disturb, drive up the wall*, flip out*, fret, get to, give a bad time*, give a hard time*, grieve, harass, harry, impose on, inconvenience, irk, irritate, make a fuss*, make a scene*, make waves*, pain, perplex, perturb, pester, plague, psych*, put out*, sadden, spook*, stir up, strain, stress, torment, try, upset, vex; SEE CONCEPTS *7,19*

trouble [*v2*] *make an effort*
be concerned with, exert, go to the effort of, take pains*, take the time*; SEE CONCEPT *100*

troublemaker [*n*] *person who causes a problem*
agent provocateur, agitator, bad actor*, firebrand*, gremlin*, heel*, hellion, incendiary, inciter, inflamer, instigator, loose cannon*, meddler, mischief-maker, nuisance, phony*, punk*, rabble-rouser*, rascal, recreant, smart aleck*, snake*, stormy petrel*, weasel*; SEE CONCEPT *412*

troubleshooter [*n*] *fixer, repair person*
maintenance person, mender, Mr. Fixit*, service person, technician; SEE CONCEPTS *126,212*

troublesome [*adj*] *bothersome, worrisome*
alarming, annoying, arduous, burdensome, damaging, dangerous, demanding, difficult, disquieting, harassing, hard, heavy, importunate, inconvenient, infestive, intractable, irksome, irritating, laborious, mean, messy, murder, oppressive, painful, pesky, pestiferous, pestilential, problematic, refractory, repressive, rough, taxing, tiresome, tough, tricky, troublous, trying, ugly, ungovernable, unruly, uphill, upsetting, vexatious, vexing, wearisome, wicked, worrying; SEE CONCEPTS *529,565*

trough [*n*] *gutter, depression*
canal, channel, crib, cup, dike, dip, ditch, duct, flume, furrow, gully, hollow, manger, moat, trench, watercourse; SEE CONCEPTS *509,513*

trounce [*v*] *defeat overwhelmingly*
bash, beat, blank, bury, bust*, cap, clobber, conquer, cook one's goose*, crush, drub, dust*, fix one's wagon*, flog, hammer*, lambaste*, lather*, lick*, make mincemeat of*, murder, overcome, overwhelm, paste*, pommel*, put away*, rout, swamp, thrash*, total*, trash*, walk over*, wallop*, waste*, wax*, whip, win, wipe off the mat*; SEE CONCEPT *95*

troupe [*n*] *company*
acting company, actors, association, band, cast, crew, ensemble, gang*, group, party, performers, repertory company, stock company, team, troop; SEE CONCEPT *417*

trousers [*n*] *pants*
bloomers, blue jeans, breeches, britches*, chaps*, chinos, cords*, corduroys, denims, dun-

garees, jeans, knickers, overalls, pantaloons, rompers, slacks; SEE CONCEPT *451*

truant [*adj*] *absent*
absent without leave, astray, away, AWOL*, cutting class*, gone, hooky*, missing, no-show*, not present, playing hooky*, skipping school*; SEE CONCEPT *583*

truant [*n*] *absentee*
delinquent, deserter, draft dodger, hooky player, malingerer, no-show*, runaway, shirker; SEE CONCEPTS *358,412,423*

truce [*n*] *peaceful solution*
accord, agreement, amnesty, armistice, break, breather*, cease-fire, cessation, de-escalation, detente, halt, intermission, interval, letup, lull, moratorium, olive branch*, pause, peace, reconciliation, reprieve, respite, rest, stay, suspension, temporary peace, terms, treaty, white flag*, wind-down*; SEE CONCEPTS *230,298,684*

truck [*n1*] *commerce, merchandise*
barter, business, buying and selling, commercial goods, commodities, communication, communion, connection, contact, dealings, exchange, goods*, intercourse, relations, stock, stuff*, trade, traffic, wares*; SEE CONCEPTS *324,330,338*

truck [*n2*] *wheeled vehicle for hauling*
buggy*, car, carryall, crate*, dump, eighteen-wheeler*, four by eight*, four by four*, four-wheel drive*, freighter, jeep, lorry, pickup, rig*, semi*, van, wagon, wheels*; SEE CONCEPT *505*

truck [*v*] *buy and sell*
bargain, barter, deal, deal in*, do business, exchange, handle, have dealings, negotiate, peddle, retail, swap, trade, traffic, transact, wholesale*; SEE CONCEPTS *324,327,345*

truckle [*v*] *fawn*
apple-polish*, be servile, bootlick*, brownnose*, butter up*, cajole, fall all over, fall on one's knees*, flatter, grovel, honey up*, kiss one's feet*, kiss-up*, kowtow*, lay it on*, lick boots*, massage*, oil*, pay court*, play up to*, scratch one's back*, stroke*, suck up to*, toady, truckle, woo*; SEE CONCEPTS *110,384*

truculent [*adj*] *belligerent, hateful*
abusive, aggressive, antagonistic, bad-tempered, barbarous, bellicose, browbeating, brutal, bullying, caustic, combative, contentious, contumelious, cowing, cross, defiant, ferocious, fierce, frightening, harsh, hostile, inhuman, inhumane, intimidating, invective, mean, militant, mordacious, mordant, obstreperous, opprobrious, ornery*, pugnacious, quarrelsome, rude, savage, scathing, scrappy, scurrilous, sharp, sullen, terrifying, terrorizing, trenchant, violent, vituperative, vituperous; SEE CONCEPTS *267,401*

trudge [*v*] *walk heavily*
clump, drag oneself*, footslog, hike, lumber, march, plod, plug along*, schlepp*, slog, step, stumble, stump, traipse, tramp, tread, trek, wade; SEE CONCEPT *151*

true [*adj1*] *real, valid; concordant with facts*
accurate, actual, appropriate, authentic, authoritative, bona fide, correct, dependable, direct, exact, factual, fitting, genuine, honest, indubitable, kosher*, lawful, legal, legitimate, natural, normal, on target*, perfect, precise, proper, pure, regular, right, rightful, sincere, straight, sure-enough*, trustworthy, truthful, typical, undeniable, undesigning, undoubted, unerring, unfaked, unfeigned, unquestionable, veracious,

veridical, veritable, very, wash*; SEE CONCEPTS *267,535,582*

true [*adj2*] *loyal*
allegiant, ardent, confirmed, conscientious, constant, creditable, dedicated, dependable, devoted, dutiful, estimable, faithful, fast, firm, high-principled, honest, honorable, just, liege, no lie*, on the up and up*, pure, reliable, resolute, right, right-minded, scrupulous, sincere, square, staunch, steadfast, steady, straight, strict, sure, true-blue*, truehearted, trustworthy, trusty, unaffected, undistorted, unfeigned, unswerving, up front*, upright, veracious, veridical, wholehearted, worthy; SEE CONCEPTS *267,401,542*

true [*adv*] *honestly, accurately*
correctly, on target, perfectly, precisely, properly, rightly, truthfully, unerringly, veraciously, veritably; SEE CONCEPTS *267,535,544*

true-blue [*adj*] *faithful, loyal*
allegiant, ardent, behind one, dedicated, dependable, devoted, die-hard, dutiful, firm, genuine, hard-core*, honorable, patriotic, staunch, steadfast, sure, tried, tried-and-true*, trustworthy, truthful, upright; SEE CONCEPTS *401,545*

truly [*adv*] *really, doubtlessly*
absolutely, accurately, actually, authentically, beyond doubt, beyond question, confirmedly, constantly, correctly, de facto, definitely, devotedly, exactly, factually, faithfully, firmly, genuinely, honestly, honorably, in actuality, in fact, in reality, in truth, legitimately, loyally, positively, precisely, reliably, righteously, rightly, sincerely, staunchly, steadily, surely, truthfully, unequivocally, veraciously, veritably, very, with all one's heart*, with devotion, without a doubt; SEE CONCEPTS *267,535,582*

trumped up [*adj*] *false*
bogus, concocted, cooked-up*, deceitful, dishonest, fabricated, fake, falsified, fictitious, fishy, framed, fraudulent, imaginary, incorrect, invalid, invented, lying, made up, misleading, phony, sham, unfounded, unsound, untrue; SEE CONCEPTS *267,570,582*

truncate [*v*] *shorten*
abbreviate, abridge, clip, crop, curtail, cut, cut off, cut short, lop, pare, prune, shear, top, trim; SEE CONCEPTS *137,236,247*

trunk [*n1*] *body, core*
block, bole, butt, column, log, soma, stalk, stem, stock, thorax, torso; SEE CONCEPTS *392,428,826*

trunk [*n2*] *long nose of animal*
beak, proboscis, prow, snoot*, snout; SEE CONCEPT *399*

trunk [*n3*] *container, box*
bag, baggage, bin, case, chest, coffer, coffin, crate, foot locker, locker, luggage, portmanteau, suitcase, wardrobe; SEE CONCEPTS *494,502*

trust [*n1*] *belief in something as true, trustworthy*
assurance, certainty, certitude, confidence, conviction, credence, credit, dependence, entrustment, expectation, faith, gospel truth*, hope, positiveness, reliance, stock, store, sureness; SEE CONCEPT *689*

trust [*n2*] *responsibility, custody*
account, care, charge, duty, guard, guardianship, keeping, liability, moment, obligation, protection, safekeeping, trusteeship, ward; SEE CONCEPTS *376,645*

trust [*n3*] *large company*
bunch, business, cartel, chain, combine, con-

glomerate, corporation, crew, crowd, gang, group, institution, megacorp*, mob, monopoly, multinational organization, outfit, pool, ring, syndicate; SEE CONCEPTS *323,325*

trust [*v1*] *believe, place confidence in*
accredit, assume, bank on, be convinced, bet bottom dollar on*, bet on, build on, calculate on, confide in, count on, depend on, expect, gamble on, have faith in, hope, imagine, lay money on*, lean on, look to, place confidence in, place trust in, presume, reckon on, rely upon, suppose, surmise, swear by, take, take at face value*, think likely; SEE CONCEPT *12*

trust [*v2*] *give to for safekeeping*
advance, aid, assign, command, commission, commit, confer, confide, consign, delegate, entrust, give over, grant, lend, let, let out, loan, make trustee, patronize, put into hands of, sign over, store, transfer, turn over; SEE CONCEPT *115*

trustee [*n*] *administrator*
agent, custodian, executor, executrix, fiduciary, guardian, keeper, warden; SEE CONCEPTS *414,423*

trusting [*adj*] *trustful*
believing, confiding, credulous, gullible, innocent, naïve, undoubting, unquestioning, unsuspecting, unsuspicious; SEE CONCEPTS *401,542, 678*

trustworthy/trusty [*adj*] *reliable, believable*
accurate, always there*, authentic, authoritative, convincing, credible, dependable, ethical, exact, honest, honorable, kosher*, levelheaded, mature, on the level*, on up and up*, open, plausible, principled, realistic, responsible, righteous, rock solid*, saintly, secure, sensible, solid, square, steadfast, straight, there*, to be trusted, tried, tried-and-true*, true, true-blue*, trustable, truthful, unfailing, up-front*, upright, valid, veracious; SEE CONCEPTS *267,404,535*

truth [*n1*] *reality, validity*
accuracy, actuality, authenticity, axiom, case, certainty, correctness, dope*, exactitude, exactness, fact, facts, factualism, factuality, factualness, genuineness, gospel*, gospel truth*, honest truth*, infallibility, inside track*, legitimacy, maxim, naked truth*, nitty-gritty*, perfection, picture, plain talk, precision, principle, rectitude, rightness, scoop, score, trueness, truism, truthfulness, unvarnished truth, veracity, verisimilitude, verity, whole story*; SEE CONCEPTS *278,638,725*

truth [*n2*] *honesty, loyalty*
authenticity, candor, constancy, dedication, devotion, dutifulness, faith, faithfulness, fidelity, frankness, integrity, openness, realism, revelation, sincerity, uprightness, veridicality, verity; SEE CONCEPT *657*

truthful [*adj*] *accurate, honest*
believable, candid, correct, exact, factual, faithful, forthright, frank, guileless, ingenuous, just, kosher*, legit*, like it is*, literal, on the level*, on the up and up*, open, outspoken, plainspoken, precise, real, realistic, reliable, righteous, scrupulous, sincere, square, straight, straightforward, true, true-blue*, trustworthy, truth-telling, unfeigned, unreserved, veracious, veritable; SEE CONCEPTS *267,542*

try [*n*] *attempt*
all one's got*, best shot*, bid, crack*, dab, effort, endeavor, essay, fling*, go*, jab*, pop*,

shot*, slap*, stab*, striving, struggle, trial, undertaking, whack*, whirl*; SEE CONCEPTS *87,677*

try [*v1*] *attempt*
aim, aspire, attack, bear down, chip away at*, compete, contend, contest, do one's best*, drive for, endeavor, essay, exert oneself, go after, go all out*, go for, have a crack*, have a go*, have a shot*, have a stab*, have a whack*, knock oneself out*, labor, lift a finger*, make a bid, make an attempt, make an effort, make a pass at*, propose, put oneself out*, risk, seek, shoot for*, speculate, strive, struggle, tackle, undertake, venture, vie for, work, wrangle; SEE CONCEPT *87*

try [*v2*] *experiment, test*
appraise, assay, check, check out, evaluate, examine, inspect, investigate, judge, prove, put to the proof*, put to the test*, sample, scrutinize, taste, try out, weigh; SEE CONCEPTS *103,291*

try [*v3*] *bother, afflict*
agonize, annoy, crucify, distress, excruciate, harass, inconvenience, irk, irritate, martyr, pain, plague, rack, strain, stress, tax, tire, torment, torture, trouble, upset, vex, weary, wring; SEE CONCEPTS *7,19*

try [*v4*] *bring before a judge*
adjudge, adjudicate, arbitrate, decide, examine, give a hearing, hear, judge, referee, sit in judgment; SEE CONCEPT *317*

trying [*adj*] *difficult, bothersome*
aggravating, annoying, arduous, demanding, exacting, exasperating, exigent, fatiguing, hard, irksome, irritating, onerous, oppressive, pestilent, provocative, rough, severe, sticky, strenuous, stressful, taxing, tight, tiresome, tough, tricky, troublesome, upsetting, vexing, wearisome, weighty; SEE CONCEPTS *548,565*

try on/try out [*v*] *evaluate, test*
appraise, audition, check out, demonstrate, experiment, fit, give a try, have a dry run*, have a fitting*, inspect, practice, probe, prove, put into practice, put to the test, sample, scrutinize, taste, try for size, wear; SEE CONCEPTS *103,167,291, 453*

tryst [*n*] *meeting during a love affair*
appointment, assignation, date, engagement, meet, meeting, rendezvous, union; SEE CONCEPTS *375,384*

tubby [*adj*] *fat*
beefy*, big, brawny, broad, bulging, bulky, burly, chubby*, chunky*, dumpy, elephantine, fleshy, gargantuan, gross, heavy, heavyset*, hefty, husky, large, obese, oversize, overweight, plump, portly, potbellied, pudgy*, roly-poly*, stout, weighty; SEE CONCEPT *491*

tuck [*v*] *fold together*
constrict, contract, draw together, enfold, gather, hem, insert, make snug, pinch, plait, pleat, push, put in, seam, squeeze in, swaddle, wrap; SEE CONCEPTS *193,218*

tuckered out [*adj*] *tired*
asleep, beat*, burned out*, collapsing, dead on one's feet*, dog-tired*, done for*, done in*, drained, drooping, droopy, drowsy, enervated, exasperated, exhausted, fatigued, finished, overworked, played out*, pooped*, run-down, sleepy, spent, wasted, weary, worn out; SEE CONCEPTS *314,403,406*

tuft [*n*] *clump of strands of something*
bunch, cluster, collection, cowlick, feathers,

tr
tu

group, knot, plumage, ruff, shock, topknot, tussock; SEE CONCEPTS *392,432,471*

tug [*n/v*] *quick pull*
drag, draw, haul, heave, jerk, lug, strain, toil, tow, traction, wrench, yank; SEE CONCEPT *206*

tuition [*n*] *education; education costs*
charge, expenditure, fee, instruction, lessons, price, schooling, teaching, training, tutelage, tutoring; SEE CONCEPT *287*

tumble [*v*] *fall or make fall awkwardly*
bowl down, bring down, descend, dip, disarrange, disarray, disorder, disturb, do a pratfall, down, drop, fall headlong*, flatten, floor, flop, go belly up*, go down, hit the dirt*, jumble, keel, keel over, knock down, knock over, level, lose footing, lose it*, mess up, nose-dive, pitch, plummet, plunge, roll, sag, skid, slip, slump, spill, stumble, take a header*, tip over, topple, toss, trip, unsettle, upset; SEE CONCEPTS *147,149,181*

tumescent [*adj*] *swollen*
bloated, bulging, bulgy, bursting, distended, distent, enlarged, expanding, inflated, puffed, puffy, tumid; SEE CONCEPT *485*

tummy [*n*] *stomach*
abdomen, belly, below the belt*, breadbasket*, gut, insides, paunch, pot*, solar plexus, spare tire*; SEE CONCEPTS *393,420*

tumor [*n*] *abnormal growth in animate being*
bump, cancer, carcinoma, cyst, lump, neoplasm, sarcoma, swelling, tumefaction; SEE CONCEPT *316*

tumult [*n*] *uproar, confusion*
ado, affray, agitation, altercation, babel, bedlam, brawl, clamor, commotion, convulsion, din, disorder, disturbance, dither, excitement, ferment, fight, fracas, fuss, hassle*, jangle, lather*, maelstrom, noise, outbreak, outcry, pandemonium, paroxysm, pother, quarrel, racket, riot, row, ruction, seething, stir, strife, turbulence, turmoil, unrest, unsettlement, upheaval, upturn, wildness; SEE CONCEPTS *230,674*

tumultous/tumultuous [*adj*] *confused; in an uproar*
agitated, boisterous, clamorous, disorderly, disturbed, excited, fierce, hectic, irregular, lawless, noisy, obstreperous, passionate, raging, rambunctious, raucous, restless, riotous, rowdy, rowdydowdy, rumbunctious, stormy, termagant, turbulent, unrestrained, unruly, uproarious, violent, vociferous, wild; SEE CONCEPT *548*

tundra [*n*] *plain*
expanse, field, flat, flatland, open country, plateau, prairie, steppe, wasteland; SEE CONCEPT *509*

tune [*n1*] *melody, harmony*
air, aria, carol, chorus, composition, concert, consonance, descant, diapason, ditty*, harmony, jingle, lay, measure, melodia, motif, number, piece, song, strain, theme, warble; SEE CONCEPTS *264,595*

tune [*n2*] *agreement*
accord, chime, chorus, concert, concord, concordance, consonance, euphony, harmony, pitch, sympathy, unison; SEE CONCEPTS *670,714*

tuneful [*adj*] *melodic, melodious*
canorous, catchy*, dulcet, euphonic, euphonious, harmonic, harmonious, in tune, musical, pleasing, pleasing to the ear, resonant, songful,

sonorous, sweet-sounding, symphonic, symphonious, tuned, well-tuned; SEE CONCEPT *594*

tune/tune up [*v*] *bring into harmony*
accommodate, adapt, adjust, attune, conform, coordinate, dial, fix, harmonize, integrate, modulate, pitch, proportion, reconcile, regulate, set, string, tighten; SEE CONCEPTS *65,126*

tunnel [*n*] *covered passageway*
adit, burrow, channel, crawl space, crawlway, crosscut, drift, hole, hole in the wall*, mine, passage, pit, shaft, subway, tube, underpass; SEE CONCEPTS *509,513*

tunnel [*v*] *dig a passage through*
burrow, excavate, mine, penetrate, sap, scoop out, undermine; SEE CONCEPT *178*

turbulent [*adj1*] *unsettled, raging (referring to weather)*
agitated, bitter, blustering, blustery, boiling, bumpy, choppy, coarse, confused, destructive, disordered, disturbed, fierce, foaming, furious, howling, inclement, moiling, noisy, restless, riotous, roaring, rough, ruffled, rugged, stirred up, stormful, storming, stormy, swirling, tempestuous, thunderous, tremulous, tumultous/tumultuous, unstable, violent, wild; SEE CONCEPT *525*

turbulent [*adj2*] *rebellious, unmanageable*
agitated, anarchic, angry, bitter, boisterous, chaotic, demonstrative, destructive, disorderly, excited, fierce, fiery, foaming, insubordinate, lawless, mutinous, obstreperous, passionate, perturbed, quarrelsome, rabid, rambunctious, rampant, raucous, refractory, riotous, rough, roughhouse*, rowdy, rude, seditious, shaking, stern, storming, termagant, tumultous/tumultuous, unbridled, uncontrolled, undisciplined, ungovernable, unruly, untamed, uproarious, vehement, violent, vociferous, wild; SEE CONCEPT *401*

turmoil [*n*] *chaos*
agitation, ailment, anxiety, anxiousness, bedlam, bustle, commotion, confusion, disorder, disquiet, disquietude, distress, disturbance, dither, ferment, flap*, flurry, free-for-all*, fuss, hassle*, hectic, hubbub*, lather*, mix-up, noise, pandemonium, pother, restiveness, restlessness, riot, row, ruckus, stir, strife, to-do*, topsy-turvy, trouble, tumult, turbulence, unrest, uproar, violence, whirl; SEE CONCEPTS *230,674*

turn [*n1*] *revolution, curving*
about-face, angle, bend, bias, bow, branch, change, changeabout, circle, circuit, circulation, circumvolution, corner, curve, cycle, departure, detour, deviation, direction, drift, flection, flexure, fork, gyration, gyre, heading, hook, pirouette, pivot, quirk, retroversion, reversal, reverse, reversion, right-about, roll, rotation, round, shift, spin, spiral, swing, tack, tendency, trend, turnabout, turning, twist, twisting, wheel, whirl, wind, winding, yaw; SEE CONCEPTS *198,738,754*

turn [*n2*] *sudden change*
alteration, bend, branch, crotch, deflection, departure, detour, deviation, digression, distortion, divarication, double, fork, modification, mutation, shift, tack, twist, variation, warp, yaw; SEE CONCEPT *697*

turn [*n3*] *chance, opportunity*
accomplishment, act, action, bit, bout, crack*, deed, favor, fling*, gesture, go*, go around*, move, period, round, routine, say*, service, shift,

shot*, spell, stint, succession, time, tour, trick, try; SEE CONCEPT *693*

turn [*n4*] *walk, outing*
airing, circuit, constitutional, drive, excursion, jaunt, promenade, ramble, ride, saunter, spin, stroll; SEE CONCEPTS *147,224,363*

turn [*n5*] *aptitude, knack*
affinity, aptness, bent, bias, bump, disposition, faculty, flair, genius, gift, head, inclination, leaning, predisposition, propensity, talent; SEE CONCEPTS *411,630*

turn [*n6*] *scare*
attack, blow, fit, fright, jolt, seizure, shock, spell, start, surprise; SEE CONCEPTS *230,410*

turn [*v1*] *revolve, curve*
arc, bend, circle, circulate, circumduct, come around, corner, cut, eddy, go around, go round, ground, gyrate, gyre, hang a left*, hang a right*, incline, loop, make a left, make a right, move in a circle, negotiate, orbit, oscillate, pass, pass around, pirouette, pivot, revolve, roll, rotate, round, spin, sway, swing, swivel, take a bend*, twirl, twist, vibrate, weave, wheel, whirl, wind, yaw; SEE CONCEPTS *147,201,738,748*

turn [*v2*] *reverse; change course*
about-face, aim, alter, alternate, backslide, call off, capsize, change, change position, convert, curve, depart, detour, detract, deviate, digress, direct, diverge, double back, face about, go back, incline, inverse, invert, loop, move, pivot, rechannel, recoil, redirect, regress, relapse, retrace, return, revert, sheer, shift, shunt, shy away, sidetrack, subvert, sway, swerve, swing, swirl, switch, tack, transform, twist, upset, vary, veer, volte-face, wheel, whip, whirl, zigzag; SEE CONCEPTS *195,198,213*

turn [*v3*] *adapt, fit*
alter, become, change, change into, come, convert, divert, fashion, form, get, go, grow into, metamorphose, modify, mold, mutate, pass into, put, refashion, remake, remodel, render, run, shape, transfigure, transform, translate, transmute, transpose, vary, wax; SEE CONCEPTS *232,697*

turn [*v4*] *become sour or tainted*
acidify, become rancid, break down, crumble, curdle, decay, decompose, disintegrate, dull, ferment, go bad, molder, putrefy, rot, sour, spoil, taint; SEE CONCEPTS *456,469*

turn [*v5*] *use; resort to*
address, appeal, apply, approach, bend, be predisposed to, devote, direct, employ, favor, give, go, have recourse, incline, lend, look, prefer, recur, repair, run, tend, throw, turn one's energies to*, turn one's hand to*, undertake, utilize; SEE CONCEPTS *100,225*

turn [*v6*] *sicken*
derange, discompose, disgust, disorder, make one sick*, nauseate, revolt, unbalance, undo, unhinge*, unsettle, upset; SEE CONCEPTS *7,19,250*

turn [*v7*] *change one's mind; defect*
apostatize, bring round, change sides, desert, go over, influence, persuade, prejudice, prevail upon, rat*, renege, renounce, repudiate, retract, talk into, tergiversate, tergiverse; SEE CONCEPTS *21,41,54*

turn [*v8*] *twist a body part*
bruise, crick, dislocate, hurt, sprain, strain, wrench; SEE CONCEPT *246*

turnabout [*n*] *about-face*
changeabout, change of direction, doubleback, flip-flop, reversal, reverse, shift, turnaround, U-turn, volte-face; SEE CONCEPT *697*

turncoat [*n*] *traitor*
apostate, back-stabber*, Benedict Arnold*, betrayer, conspirator, deceiver, defector, deserter, double-crosser*, fink*, informer, Judas*, quisling, rat*, rebel, renegade, snake*, sneak*, snitch*, spy, squealer*, stool pigeon*, tattletale, tergiversator, treasonist, two-timer*, whistle-blower*; SEE CONCEPT *412*

turn down [*v*] *reject*
decline, disapprove, dismiss, rebuff, refuse, reprobate, repudiate, say no, scorn, spurn, throw out; SEE CONCEPTS *18,54*

turn in [*v*] *go to bed*
bed, catch some z's*, flop*, go to sleep, hit the hay*, hit the sack*, lie down, nap, pile in, rest, retire, roll in; SEE CONCEPT *210*

turning point [*n*] *crucial occurrence*
axis, change, climacteric, climax, contingency, crisis, critical moment, critical period, crossing, crossroads, crux, culmination, decisive moment, development, emergency, exigency, hinge, juncture, moment of truth*, pass, peak, pinch, pivot, shift, strait, transition, twist, zero hour*; SEE CONCEPTS *679,832*

turn off [*v1*] *disgust*
alienate, bore, disenchant, disinterest, displease, irritate, lose one's interest, make one sick*, nauseate, offend, put off, repel, sicken; SEE CONCEPTS *7,19*

turn off [*v2*] *stop from operating*
close, cut, cut out, douse, extinguish, halt, hit the switch*, kill*, log off, put out, shut, shut down, shut off, switch off, turn out, unplug; SEE CONCEPTS *121,234*

turn on [*v1*] *excite, please*
arouse, attract, captivate, enchant, get started, initiate, introduce, show, stimulate, stir up, thrill, titillate, work up; SEE CONCEPT *11*

turn on [*v2*] *start the operation of*
activate, begin, energize, get started, ignite, initiate, introduce, log on, put in gear, put on, set in motion, start up, switch on; SEE CONCEPT *221*

turnout [*n1*] *group assembling for event*
assemblage, assembly, attendance, audience, congregation, crowd, gate, gathering, number, throng; SEE CONCEPT *417*

turnout [*n2*] *amount produced*
aggregate, output, outturn, product, production, productivity, quota, turnover, volume, yield; SEE CONCEPTS *338,787*

turn out [*v1*] *equip; produce*
accouter, appoint, arm, bear, bring out, build, clothe, dress, fabricate, finish, fit, fit out*, furnish, make, manufacture, outfit, process, put out, rig*, rig out*, yield; SEE CONCEPTS *167,205,234*

turn out [*v2*] *get out of bed*
appear, arise, come, emerge, get up, pile out*, rise, rise and shine*, roll out*, show up, uprise, wake, wake up; SEE CONCEPT *159*

turn over [*v1*] *give, transfer*
assign, come across with, commend, commit, confer, confide, consign, convey, delegate, deliver, entrust, feed, find, furnish, give over, give up, hand, hand over, pass on, provide, relegate, relinquish, render, supply, surrender, yield; SEE CONCEPTS *108,143*

tu
tu

turn over [v2] *think about seriously*
consider, contemplate, deliberate, give thought to, meditate, mull over, muse, ponder, reflect on, revolve, roll, ruminate, think over, wonder about; SEE CONCEPTS *17,24*

turnpike [n] *highway*
expressway, four-lane*, freeway, interstate, parkway, pike*, roadway, state highway, superhighway, toll road; SEE CONCEPT *501*

turn up [v1] *come, arrive*
appear, attend, blow in*, come, come in, enter, get, get in, make an appearance*, materialize, pop in*, punch in*, put in an appearance*, reach, roll in*, show, show up*, weigh in*; SEE CONCEPT *159*

turn up [v2] *discover or be discovered*
become known, be found, bring to light*, catch, come across, come to light*, come to pass, crop up, descry, detect, dig up*, disclose, encounter, espy, expose, find, hit upon*, learn, meet, meet with*, pop up*, reveal, see, spot, track, track down*, transpire, uncover, unearth; SEE CONCEPTS *31,183*

turpitude [n] *depravity*
baseness, corruption, criminality, debasement, debauchery, degradation, evil, immorality, improbity, lewdness, licentiousness, perversion, sinfulness, vice, viciousness, vileness, wickedness; SEE CONCEPT *645*

tussle [n] *struggle*
battle, brawl, brush, clash, combat, conflict, contest, donnybrook, encounter, fight, fray, free-for-all*, grind, hassle, jam, roughhouse, row, rumble*, scramble, scrap*, scuffle, skirmish, strife, undertaking; SEE CONCEPTS *87,106,674*

tussle [v] *struggle*
battle, box, brawl, bump heads*, conflict, contest, fight, go up against*, grapple, hassle, lock horns*, put up a fight*, romp, rough-house*, row, scrap, scuffle, tangle, wrestle; SEE CONCEPT *106*

tutelage [n] *guardianship; teaching*
apprenticeship, care, coaching, custody, drilling, education, guidance, instruction, lesson, preparation, protection, schooling, supervision, training, tutoring; SEE CONCEPTS *274,285*

tutor [n] *person who teaches another privately*
coach, educator, governor, grind, guardian, guide, instructor, lecturer, mentor, preceptor, private teacher, prof*, teach*, teacher; SEE CONCEPT *350*

tutor [v] *teach someone privately*
clue, coach, direct, discipline, drill, drum into*, edify, educate, guide, instruct, lay it out for*, lecture, let in on*, ready, school, train, update; SEE CONCEPT *285*

twaddle [n] *nonsense*
babble, balderdash*, baloney*, BS*, bull, bunk*, chatter, crap*, drivel, foolishness, gibberish, hogwash*, hooey*, hot air*, idle talk, jive*, mumbo jumbo*, palaver, poppycock*, prattle, rubbish, silliness, trash*, tripe; SEE CONCEPTS *230,388,633*

twilight [n] *onset of darkness at end of day*
afterglow, afterlight, crepuscular light, decline, dimness, dusk, early evening, ebb, end, evening, eventide, gloaming, half-light, last phase*, late-afternoon, night, nightfall, sundown, sunset; SEE CONCEPTS *810,832*

twin [adj] *duplicate, similar*
accompanying, bifold, binary, copied, corresponding, coupled, double, dual, duplicating, geminate, identical, joint, like, matched, matching, paired, parallel, same, second, selfsame, twofold, very same; SEE CONCEPTS *487,563,573*

twin [n] *something exactly like another*
clone, companion, coordinate, corollary, counterpart, doppelgänger, double, duplicate, fraternal twin, identical twin, likeness, lookalike, match, mate, reciprocal, ringer*, Siamese twin; SEE CONCEPTS *414,664,670*

twine [n] *rope, cord*
braid, coil, convolution, cordage, knot, snarl, string, tangle, thread, twist, whorl, yarn; SEE CONCEPT *475*

twine [v] *coil, twist together*
bend, braid, corkscrew, curl, encircle, enmesh, entangle, entwine, interlace, interweave, knit, loop, meander, plait, spiral, splice, surround, tangle, twist, undulate, weave, wind, wrap, wreathe; SEE CONCEPTS *147,201,742*

twinge [n] *sharp pain*
ache, bite, gripe, lancination, misery, pang, pinch, prick, shiver, smart, spasm, stab, stitch, throb, throe, tic, tweak, twist, twitch; SEE CONCEPT *728*

twinkle [v] *glimmer, shine*
blink, coruscate, flash, flicker, gleam, glint, glisten, glitter, glow, illuminate, light, light up, scintillate, shimmer, sparkle, wink; SEE CONCEPT *624*

twirl [v] *turn around circularly*
gyrate, gyre, pirouette, pivot, purl, revolve, rotate, spin, turn, twist, wheel, whirl, whirligig, wind; SEE CONCEPTS *150,152*

twist [n1] *curl, spin*
arc, bend, braid, coil, convolution, curlicue, curve, flourish, hank, helix, jerk, meander, plug, ply, pull, roll, spiral, swivel, torsion, turn, twine, undulation, warp, wind, wrench, yank, zigzag; SEE CONCEPTS *738,754*

twist [n2] *sudden development; oddity*
aberration, bent, change, characteristic, confusion, crotchet, eccentricity, entanglement, foible, idiosyncrasy, kink, knot, mess, mix-up, peculiarity, proclivity, quirk, revelation, screw up*, slant, snarl, surprise, tangle, trait, turn, variation; SEE CONCEPTS *411,832*

twist [v1] *curl, spin*
coil, contort, corkscrew, encircle, entwine, intertwine, rick, screw, spiral, sprain, squirm, swivel, turn, turn around, twine, twirl, warp, weave, wiggle, wind, wrap, wrap around, wreathe, wrench, wriggle, wring, writhe, zigzag; SEE CONCEPTS *80,147,184,201,206,738*

twist [v2] *misrepresent*
alter, belie, change, color, contort, distort, falsify, garble, misquote, misstate, pervert, warp; SEE CONCEPT *63*

twitch [v] *have a spasm*
beat, blink, clasp, clutch, flutter, grab, grasp, grip, jerk, jiggle, jump, kick, lug, lurch, nip, pain, palpitate, pluck, pull, seize, shiver, shudder, snap, snatch, squirm, tic, tremble, tug, twinge, vellicate, yank; SEE CONCEPTS *185,206*

two-bit [adj] *cheap, worth very little*
base, catchpenny, cheesy, crappy*, cruddy*, garbage, gaudy, inferior, junky*, lousy, no good, piddling, poor, ratty, rinky-dink*, second-rate,

shoddy, sleazy, small-time*, tatty, trashy, value-less, worthless; SEE CONCEPT *589*

two-faced [*adj*] *deceitful*
artful, backstabbing, beguiling, crafty, cunning, deceiving, deceptive, dishonest, double-dealing, foxy, fraudulent, guileful, hypocritical, insincere, knavish, lying, misleading, shifty, sly, sneaky, tricky, underhanded, untruthful; SEE CONCEPT *401*

two-time [*v*] *deceive*
backstab, be dishonest, be disloyal, betray, be unfaithful, burn, cheat, con, defraud, double-cross, dupe, mislead, take advantage of, trick, victimize; SEE CONCEPTS *7,19,59*

tycoon [*n*] *person who has a lot of money, power*
administrator, big shot*, boss, business person, capitalist, captain of industry*, director, entre-preneur, executive, fat cat*, financier, industrial-ist, investor, magnate, mogul, wealthy person; SEE CONCEPT *347*

type [*n1*] *class, kind*
blazon, brand, breed, cast, category, character, classification, cut, description, feather, form, genre, group, ilk, likes, lot, mold, nature, num-ber, order, persuasion, rubric, sample, sort, species, specimen, stamp, standard, strain, subdi-vision, variety, way; SEE CONCEPTS *378,411*

type [*n2*] *example, model*
archetype, epitome, essence, exemplar, original, paradigm, pattern, personification, prototype, quintessence, representative, sample, specimen, standard; SEE CONCEPT *686*

type [*n3*] *printed characters*
case, emblem, face, figure, font, point size, print, printing, sign, symbol; SEE CONCEPTS *79,284*

type [*v1*] *classify*
arrange, button down*, categorize, class, peg, pi-geonhole*, put away, put down as, sort, stan-dardize, stereotype, tab*, typecast; SEE CONCEPTS *18,84*

type [*v2*] *hit keys on machine to print document*
copy, dash off*, enter data, hunt-and-peck*, tele-type, touch, touch-type, transcribe, typewrite, write; SEE CONCEPTS *79,199,203*

typical [*adj*] *usual, conventional*
archetypal, archetypical, average, characteristic, classic, classical, common, commonplace, em-blematic, essential, everyday, exemplary, ex-pected, general, habitual, ideal, illustrative, in character*, indicative, in keeping, matter-of-course*, model, natural, normal, old hat*, ordi-nary, orthodox, paradigmatic, patterned, prevalent, prototypal, prototypical, quintessen-tial, regular, representative, standard, standard-ized, stock, suggestive, symbolic, typic, unexceptional; SEE CONCEPTS *530,533,547*

typify [*v*] *represent, characterize*
body forth, characterize, describe, emblematize, embody, epitomize, exemplify, feature, illustrate, incarnate, mean, mirror, model, personify, stand for, sum up, symbolize; SEE CONCEPTS *55,261,682*

tyrannical [*adj*] *despotic, oppressive*
authoritarian, autocratic, brutal, cruel, demand-ing, dictatorial, domineering, harsh, heavy-handed*, ironhanded*, mean, overbearing, repressive, ruthless, totalitarian, tough, unjust; SEE CONCEPTS *537,548*

tyranny [*n*] *dictatorship*
absolutism, authoritarianism, autocracy, coer-cion, cruelty, despotism, domination, fascism, high-handedness, imperiousness, monocracy, oligarchy, oppression, peremptoriness, reign of terror*, severity, terrorism, totalitarianism, total-ity, unreasonableness; SEE CONCEPTS *299,301*

tyrant [*n*] *person who dictates, oppresses*
absolute ruler, absolutist, authoritarian, autocrat, bully, despot, dictator, Hitler*, inquisitor, mar-tinet, oppressor, slave driver*, Stalin*; SEE CON-CEPTS *354,412*

tyro [*n*] *beginner*
abecedarian, amateur, apprentice, buckwheater*, cadet, colt*, greenhorn, learner, neophyte, new-comer, new kid on the block*, novice, novitiate, pupil, recruit, rookie, starter, student, tender-foot*, trainee; SEE CONCEPTS *423,424*

U

ubiquitous [*adj*] *ever-present*
all-over, everywhere, omnipresent, pervasive, ubiquitary, universal, wall-to-wall*; SEE CON-CEPT *530*

UFO [*n*] *unidentified flying object*
extraterrestrial spacecraft, flying saucer, rocket, rocketship, spaceship; SEE CONCEPT *504*

ugly [*adj1*] *unattractive*
animal, appalling, awful, bad-looking, beastly, deformed, disfigured, foul, frightful, grisly, gross, grotesque, hard-featured, hideous, homely, horrid, ill-favored, loathsome, misshapen, mon-strous, not much to look at*, plain, repelling, re-pugnant, repulsive, revolting, unbeautiful, uncomely, uninviting, unlovely, unprepossess-ing, unseemly, unsightly; SEE CONCEPT *579*

ugly [*adj2*] *unpleasant, disagreeable*
base, despicable, dirty, disgusting, distasteful, filthy, foul, frightful, hideous, horrid, ignoble, low, low-down, mean, messy, monstrous, nasty, nauseous, noisome, objectionable, odious, offen-sive, pesky, repellent, repugnant, repulsive, re-volting, scandalous, servile, shocking, sickening, sordid, sorry, terrible, troublesome, troublous, vexatious, vile, wicked, wretched; SEE CONCEPTS *403,571*

ugly [*adj3*] *dangerous, threatening*
angry, bellicose, black, cantankerous, crabbed, crabby, dark, disagreeable, dour, evil, fell, for-bidding, formidable, gloomy, glum, grave, griev-ous, major, malevolent, menacing, morose, nasty, obnoxious, ominous, pugnacious, quarrel-some, rough, saturnine, scowling, serious, sinis-ter, spiteful, sullen, surly, treacherous, truculent, vicious, violent, wicked; SEE CONCEPTS *401,548*

ulterior [*adj*] *secret; pertaining to a hidden goal*
ambiguous, buried, concealed, covert, cryptic, dark, enigmatic, equivocal, guarded, hidden, im-plied, obscure, obscured, personal, privy, remote, secondary, selfish, shrouded, under cover, under wraps*, undisclosed, undivulged, unexpressed, unsaid; SEE CONCEPTS *544,576*

ultimate [*adj1*] *last, final*
capping, chips down*, closing, concluding, con-clusive, decisive, end, eventual, extreme, far out*, farthermost, farthest, final curtain*, further-

most, furthest, hindmost, latest, latter, lattermost, most distant, terminal; SEE CONCEPTS *799,820*

ultimate [*adj2*] *best, greatest*
extreme, highest, incomparable, max*, maxi*, maximum, most, paramount, preeminent, significant, superlative, supreme, surpassing, the most, topmost, towering, transcendent, unequalable, unmatchable, unsurpassable, utmost; SEE CONCEPTS *568,574*

ultimate [*adj3*] *fundamental*
absolute, basic, categorical, elemental, empyreal, empyrean, primary, radical, sublime, transcendental; SEE CONCEPTS *535,546*

ultimately [*adv*] *eventually*
after all, after a while, as a conclusion, at last, at long last, at the close, basically, by and by, climactically, conclusively, finally, fundamentally, hereafter, in conclusion, in consummation, in due time, in future, in the end, in the sequel, presently, sequentially, someday, sometime, somewhere, sooner or later, yet; SEE CONCEPT *820*

ultimatum [*n*] *final offer*
conditions, demand, final notice, final proposal, final terms, final warning, final word, last chance, last offer, last word, sticking point, warning; SEE CONCEPT *662*

ultra [*adj*] *extreme*
all out*, drastic, excessive, extremist, fanatical, far-out*, gone*, immoderate, outlandish, out of bounds*, outré, rabid*, radical, revolutionary, too much*; SEE CONCEPTS *562,569*

ultramodern [*adj*] *up-to-date*
advanced, ahead of its time, avant-garde, contemporary, current, cutting-edge*, fresh, futuristic, latest, leading-edge*, modernistic, modish, new, new-fashioned, nontraditional, now, present-day, revolutionary, state-of-the-art*, stylish, today, twenty-first century*, up-to-the-minute; SEE CONCEPTS *168,177,202*

umbrage [*n*] *personal displeasure*
anger, annoyance, chagrin, exasperation, fury, grudge, high dudgeon*, huff, indignation, injury, ire, irking, irritation, miff*, nettling*, offense, pique, provoking, rage, resentment, sense of injury, vexation, wrath; SEE CONCEPTS *29,410*

umpire [*n*] *person who settles dispute*
adjudicator, arbiter, arbitrator, assessor, compromiser, inspector, judge, justice, mediator, moderator, negotiator, peacemaker, proprietor, ref*, referee, settler, ump*; SEE CONCEPTS *348,366,423*

unable [*adj*] *not having talent, skill*
can't cut it*, can't hack it*, can't make the grade*, clumsy, helpless, hog-tied*, impotent, impuissant, inadequate, incapable, incapacitated, incompetent, ineffectual, inefficacious, inefficient, inept, inoperative, no can do*, no good*, not able, not cut out for*, not equal to*, not up to*, out of commission*, powerless, sidelined*, unfit, unfitted, unqualified, unskilled, weak; SEE CONCEPT *527*

unabridged [*adj*] *not shortened*
complete, entire, full-length, intact, total, unabbreviated, uncondensed, uncut, unexpurgated, unshortened, whole; SEE CONCEPTS *267,531*

unacceptable [*adj*] *not suitable or satisfactory*
below par*, damaged, disagreeable, displeasing, distasteful, exceptionable, half-baked*, ill-favored, improper, inadmissible, insupportable,

lousy*, not up to snuff*, objectionable, obnoxious, offensive, reject, repugnant, unappealing, undesirable, uninviting, unpleasant, unsatisfactory, unwanted, unwelcome, won't do*; SEE CONCEPTS *529,558*

unaccompanied [*adj*] *alone*
abandoned, a cappella*, apart, by oneself, deserted, detached, hermit, individual, isolate, isolated, lone, loner, odd, on one's own, removed, single, solitary, solo, stag, traveling light*, unattended, unescorted; SEE CONCEPTS *555,577*

unaccountable [*adj*] *not explainable; mysterious*
arcane, astonishing, baffling, extraordinary, impenetrable, incomprehensible, inexplicable, inscrutable, mystic, odd, peculiar, puzzling, strange, uncommon, unexplainable, unfathomable, unheard-of, unintelligible, unknowable, unusual, unwonted; SEE CONCEPTS *529,564*

unaccustomed [*adj1*] *not prepared, ready; new*
ignorant, incompetent, inexperienced, newcome, not given to*, not used to, novice, to green*, unacquainted, unfamiliar with, uninformed, uninstructed, unpracticed, unseasoned, unskilled, untaught, untrained, unused to, unversed in; SEE CONCEPTS *527,678*

unaccustomed [*adj2*] *new, strange*
alien, altered, bizarre, different, eccentric, exceptional, exotic, foreign, imported, novel, outlandish, out of the ordinary, quaint, remarkable, singular, special, surprising, uncommon, unconventional, uncustomary, unexpected, unfamiliar, unknown, unorthodox, unprecedented, unusual, unwonted, variant; SEE CONCEPTS *547,564*

unadorned [*adj*] *plain, simple*
austere, bare, basic, modest, stark, stripped down, undecorated, unembellished; SEE CONCEPTS *485,589*

unadulterated [*adj*] *clean, pure; unmixed*
immaculate, purified, refined, sanitary, spotless, stainless, sterile, sterilized, unblemished, uncontaminated, uncorrupted, undebased, undefiled, undiluted, unpolluted, unsoiled, unstained, unsullied, untainted, untarnished, untouched, wholesome; SEE CONCEPT *621*

unadvised [*adj*] *not smart; careless*
brash, hasty, heedless, hot-headed, ignorant, ill-advised, imprudent, inadvisable, incautious, inconsiderate, indiscreet, injudicious, in the dark*, rash, reckless, thoughtless, unaware, unconsidered, uninformed, unknowing, unsuspecting, unwarned, unwary, unwise; SEE CONCEPTS *403,548*

unaffected [*adj1*] *honest, unsophisticated*
artless, candid, direct, folksy*, forthright, frank, genuine, guileless, homey*, ingenuous, modest, naive, natural, plain, simple, sincere, single, spontaneous, straightforward, true, unartificial, unassuming, unpretentious, unschooled, unspoilt, unstudied, up front*; SEE CONCEPTS *401,404*

unaffected [*adj2*] *unchanged, unmoved*
aloof, callous, calm, casual, cold fish*, cool, easy-going, hard-boiled*, hard-hearted*, impassive, impervious, laid-back*, not influenced, proof, steady, thick-skinned*, unaltered, unconcerned, unexcited, unimpressed, uninfluenced, unresponsive, unruffled, unstirred, untouched; SEE CONCEPTS *542,548*

unafraid [*adj*] *fearless*
assured, ballsy*, bold, brassy, brave, cheeky, cocky, confident, courageous, daring, dashing,

dauntless, gallant, game, gritty, gutsy, having nerves of steel*, heroic, nervy, plucky, spunky, sure, undaunted, unfearing, unfrightened, unscared, unshakable, valiant; SEE CONCEPT *401*

unanimous [*adj*] *in agreement; uncontested*
accepted, accordant, agreed, agreeing, as one, assenting, collective, combined, common, communal, concerted, concordant, concurrent, consensual, consentient, consistent, consonant, harmonious, homogeneous, in complete accord, like-minded, of one mind, popular, public, shared, single, solid, undisputed, undivided, unified, united, universal, unquestioned, with one voice*; SEE CONCEPTS *8,267,563*

unappetizing [*adj*] *distasteful*
flat, flavorless, grody*, gross, icky*, insipid, savorless, stinky, tasteless, unappealing, unattractive, uninteresting, uninviting, unpalatable, unpleasant, unsavory, vapid, yucky*; SEE CONCEPTS *462,529*

unapproachable [*adj1*] *unfriendly*
aloof, chilly*, cold, cool, distant, frigid, hesitant, inaccessible, remote, reserved, standoffish, uncommunicative, unsociable, withdrawn; SEE CONCEPTS *404,555*

unapproachable [*adj2*] *difficult to get to*
inaccessible, out of reach, out-of-the-way, remote, unattainable, unobtainable, unreachable; SEE CONCEPT *576*

unarmed [*adj*] *disarmed*
exposed, hands tied*, helpless, indefensible, like a sitting duck*, naked*, open, powerless, unguarded, unprotected, unshielded, vulnerable, weaponless, wide open*; SEE CONCEPTS *555,576*

unasked [*adj*] *voluntary*
arrogant, gratuitous, impudent, not asked, of one's own accord, overbearing, presumptuous, spontaneous, supererogatory, unbidden, uncalled-for, undemanded, undesired, uninvited, unprompted, unrequested, unsought, unwanted, unwelcome, voluntarily, willing, without prompting; SEE CONCEPTS *401,558*

unassuming [*adj*] *shy*
backward, bashful, diffident, humble, lowly, meek, modest, mousy*, plain, prim, quiet, reserved, retiring, self-effacing, simple, unambitious, unassertive, unobtrusive, unostentatious, unpretending, unpretentious; SEE CONCEPTS *401,404*

unattached [*adj*] *disconnected, free*
apart, at liberty, autonomous, available, detached, fancy-free*, footloose*, independent, off the hook*, on one's own*, separate, single, unaffiliated, uncommited, unconnected, uninvolved, unmarried; SEE CONCEPTS *267,401,482,542*

unattractive [*adj*] *ugly*
bad-looking, beastly, deformed, disfigured, disgusting, frightful, gross, grotesque, hideous, homely, horrid, monstrous, not much to look at*, plain, repelling, repugnant, repulsive, revolting, unalluring, unappealing, unsightly; SEE CONCEPT *579*

unauthorized [*adj*] *not sanctioned, permitted*
crooked*, dirty*, illegal, illegitimate, no-no*, off base*, out of bounds*, out of line*, over the line*, pirated, shady*, unapproved, unconstitutional, under the table*, unjustified, unlawful, unofficial, unsanctioned, unwarranted, wildcat*, wrongful; SEE CONCEPTS *319,548*

unavailing [*adj*] *futile*
barren, empty, exhausted, fruitless, idle, impractical, ineffective, ineffectual, in vain, on a treadmill*, save one's breath*, to no avail*, to no effect*, to no purpose*, trifling, trivial, unavailing, unproductive, unprofitable, unsuccessful, useless, vain, valueless, worthless; SEE CONCEPTS *528,543,560*

unavoidable [*adj*] *bound to happen*
certain, compulsory, fated, impending, ineluctable, ineludible, inescapable, inevasible, inevitable, inexorable, locked up*, necessary, obligatory, open and shut*, set, sure, unescapable; SEE CONCEPT *535*

unaware [*adj*] *ignorant*
blind, careless, caught napping*, daydreaming, deaf, deaf to*, doped*, forgetful, heedless, ignorant, in a daze*, inattentive, incognizant, inconversant, insensible, mooning, negligent, nescient, not all there*, not cognizant, oblivious, out cold*, out of it*, out to lunch*, spacey*, unacquainted, unconcerned, unconscious, unenlightened, unfamiliar, uninformed, uninstructed, unknowing, unmindful, unsuspecting, unwitting; SEE CONCEPT *402*

unawares [*adv*] *without warning; suddenly*
aback, abruptly, accidentally, by accident, by mistake, by surprise, carelessly, ignorantly, inadvertently, mistakenly, off guard, short, sudden, surprisingly, unconsciously, unexpectedly, unintentionally, unknowingly, unprepared, unready, unwittingly, without warning; SEE CONCEPTS *544,548,799*

unbalanced [*adj1*] *not even, stable*
asymmetric, asymmetrical, disproportionate, irregular, lopsided, not balanced, off-balance, shaky, top-heavy, treacherous, unequal, uneven, unstable, unsteady, unsymmetrical, wobbly; SEE CONCEPT *480*

unbalanced [*adj2*] *crazy; mentally disturbed*
batty*, daft, demented, deranged, eccentric, erratic, flaky*, freaky*, insane, irrational, kinky*, kooky*, lunatic, mad, nobody home*, non compos mentis*, not all there*, nutty*, out to lunch*, psychotic, touched, troubled, unglued*, unhinged*, unscrewed*, unsound, unstable; SEE CONCEPT *403*

unbearable [*adj*] *very bad; too much*
a bit much*, enough, heavy-handed*, inadmissible, insufferable, insupportable, intolerable, last straw*, oppressive, unacceptable, unendurable, unsurpassable; SEE CONCEPTS *537,571*

unbecoming [*adj*] *improper, unsuitable*
awkward, clumsy, discreditable, gauche, illsuited, inappropriate, inapt, incongruous, indecent, indecorous, indelicate, inept, maladroit, malapropos, offensive, rough, salacious, tacky*, tasteless, unattractive, unbefitting, uncomely, undue, unfair, unfit, unfitting, unflattering, ungodly, unhandsome, unlovely, unseasonable, unseemly, unsightly, unsuited, untimely, untoward, unworthy; SEE CONCEPTS *558,579,589*

unbelievable [*adj*] *beyond the imagination*
astonishing, beyond belief, cockamamie*, cockeyed*, doubtful, dubious, far-fetched, fishy*, flaky*, flimsy*, for the birds*, full of holes*, harebrained*, implausible, impossible, improbable, incogitable, inconceivable, incredible, kooky*, lamebrained*, open to doubt, outlandish, past belief, phony, preposterous, ques-

ul
un

tionable, reaching, scatterbrained*, screwy*, staggering, suspect, thick*, thin*, too much*, unconvincing, unimaginable, unsubstantial, unthinkable, weak, won't hold water*, won't wash*; SEE CONCEPTS *529,548*

unbelieving [*adj*] *skeptical*
agnostic, cynical, disbelieving, distrustful, doubtful, doubting, dubious, freethinking, leery, mistrustful, nonbelieving, not born yesterday*, questioning, show-me*, suspicious, unconvinced; SEE CONCEPT *403*

unbending [*adj*] *rigid, tough*
aloof, crisp, distant, do or die*, dug in*, firm, formal, hard as nails*, hard-line*, hold one's ground*, hold the fort*, hold the line*, incompliant, inelastic, inexorable, inflexible, intractable, locked in*, obdurate, obstinate, relentless, reserved, resolute, set in stone*, severe, singleminded, standing one's ground*, standing pat*, sticking to one's guns*, stiff, strict, stubborn, uncompromising, unflexible, unrelenting, unswayable, unyielding, uptight; SEE CONCEPTS *401,534,604*

unbiased [*adj*] *not prejudiced*
aloof, cold, disinterested, dispassionate, equal, equitable, even-handed, fair, honest, impartial, just, neutral, nondiscriminatory, nonpartisan, objective, on the fence*, open-minded, straight, unbigoted, uncolored, uninterested, unprejudiced; SEE CONCEPT *542*

unblemished [*adj*] *not flawed*
chaste, clean, decent, faultless, flawless, immaculate, intact, modest, perfect, pure, sound, spotless, stainless, undamaged, undefiled, unflawed, unhurt, unimpaired, uninjured, unmarked, unmarred, unspotted, unstained, unsullied, untarnished, whole; SEE CONCEPTS *485,621*

unbreakable [*adj*] *strong, tough*
adamantine, armored, brass-bound, durable, everlasting, firm, incorruptible, indestructible, infrangible, invulnerable, lasting, nonbreakable, perdurable, resistant, rugged, shatterproof, solid, tight, toughened, unshakable, unyielding; SEE CONCEPTS *488,489,798*

unbridled [*adj*] *unrestrained*
berserk, chaotic, crazed, crazy, enthusiastic, hysterical, madcap, noisy, rabid, riotous, turbulent, unchecked, unconstrained, uncontrolled, uncurbed, undisciplined, ungovernable, unmanageable, violent, wild; SEE CONCEPT *401*

unbroken [*v*] *continuous, whole*
ceaseless, constant, deep, endless, entire, even, fast, incessant, intact, perfect, perpetual, profound, progressive, regular, solid, sound, successive, total, undisturbed, unimpaired, uninterrupted, unremitting, unruffled, untroubled; SEE CONCEPTS *482,485,798*

unburden [*adj*] *get rid of*
clear, confess, confide, disburden, discharge, disclose, disencumber, dispose of, divulge, dump, ease, empty, get off one's chest*, lay bare*, let hair down*, lighten, lose, lose out with it*, own, relieve, relinquish, reveal, shake, shake off*, tell all*, throw off, unbosom, unload; SEE CONCEPTS *60,211,244*

uncalled-for [*adj*] *unnecessary*
accidental, avoidable, fortuitous, futile, inappropriate, inessential, needless, nonessential, not required, optional, unessential, uninvited, unneeded, unrequired, unwanted, unwarranted, unwelcome, useless; SEE CONCEPT *546*

uncanny [*adj*] *very strange, unusual*
astonishing, astounding, creepy, devilish, eerie, exceptional, extraordinary, fantastic, ghostly, ghoulish, incredible, inexplainable, inspired, magical, miraculous, mysterious, mystifying, preternatural, prodigious, queer, remarkable, scary, secret, singular, spooky, superhuman, supernatural, supernormal, supranormal, unearthly, unheard-of, unnatural, weird; SEE CONCEPTS *537,564*

uncaring [*adj*] *indifferent*
aloof, blasé, callous, cold, cool, detached, disinterested, dispassionate, heartless, impervious, listless, nonchalant, passionless, unaroused, unconcerned, unemotional, uninvolved, unmoved, unsympathetic; SEE CONCEPTS *403,542*

unceasing [*adj*] *incessant*
ceaseless, constant, continual, continuous, day-and-night*, endless, eternal, everlasting, lasting, never-ending, nonstop, permanent, perpetual, persistent, relentless, round-the-clock*, steady, unending, uninterrupted, unyielding; SEE CONCEPTS *534,798*

uncertain [*adj*] *doubtful, changeable*
ambiguous, ambivalent, chancy, conjectural, dubious, erratic, fitful, hanging by a thread*, hazy, hesitant, iffy*, incalculable, inconstant, indefinite, indeterminate, indistinct, insecure, irregular, irresolute, on thin ice*, precarious, questionable, risky, speculative, touch and go*, unclear, unconfirmed, undecided, undetermined, unfixed, unforeseeable, unpredictable, unreliable, unresolved, unsettled, unsure, up for grabs*, up in the air*, vacillating, vague, variable, wavering; SEE CONCEPTS *529,534,535*

uncertainty [*n*] *doubt, changeableness*
ambiguity, ambivalence, anxiety, bewilderment, concern, confusion, conjecture, contingency, dilemma, disquiet, distrust, doubtfulness, dubiety, guesswork, hesitancy, hesitation, incertitude, inconclusiveness, indecision, irresolution, lack of confidence, misgiving, mistrust, mystification, oscillation, perplexity, puzzle, puzzlement, qualm, quandary, query, questionableness, reserve, scruple, skepticism, suspicion, trouble, uneasiness, unpredictability, vagueness, wonder, worry; SEE CONCEPTS *388,410,696*

unchangeable [*adj*] *constant, steadfast*
changeless, continuing, firm, fixed, immovable, immutable, inalterable, inevitable, inflexible, invariable, irreversible, permanent, resolute, stable, strong, unalterable, unmodifiable, unmovable; SEE CONCEPT *534*

unchanging [*adj*] *constant, permanent*
abiding, changeless, consistent, continuing, enduring, equable, eternal, even, fixed, immutable, imperishable, invariable, lasting, perpetual, rigid, same, stabile, static, unchanged, unfading, unfailing, unfluctuating, uniform, unvarying; SEE CONCEPTS *534,551,649*

uncharted [*adj*] *unknown*
alien, concealed, distant, exotic, faraway, far-off, foreign, hidden, little known, remote, undiscovered, unexplored, unheard-of, unidentified, unmapped, unnamed; SEE CONCEPT *576*

uncivil [*adj*] *rude*
abrupt, bad-mannered, barbaric, blunt, boorish, coarse, curt, discourteous, gross, gruff, ill-man-

nered, impolite, inconsiderate, insulting, mannerless, uncivilized, uncouth, uncultured, unfriendly, ungentlemanly, unmannerly, unpolished, unrefined, vulgar; SEE CONCEPTS *267,401*

uncivilized [*adj*] *wild, uncultured*
barbarian, barbaric, barbarous, boorish, brutish, churlish, coarse, crass, crude, discourteous, disrespectful, gross, ill-bred, impertinent, impolite, loutish, mannerless, outrageous, philistine, primitive, rude, rugged, savage, unconscionable, uncontrolled, uncouth, uncultivated, uneducated, ungodly, unholy, unmannered, unpolished, unrefined, unsophisticated, vulgar, wicked; SEE CONCEPT *401*

unclean [*adj*] *dirty*
bedraggled, befouled, besmirched, black, blurred, common, contaminated, corrupt, decayed, defiled, desecrated, dusty, evil, feculent, fetid, filthy, foul, grimy, impure, messy, muddy, nasty, polluted, profaned, putrescent, putrid, rancid, rank, rotten, sloppy, slovenly, smeared, smudged, soiled, sooty, sordid, spotted, squalid, stable, stained, stall, stinking, sullied, tainted, tarnished, unhealthful, vile; SEE CONCEPT *621*

uncomfortable [*adj1*] *painful, rough*
afflictive, agonizing, annoying, awkward, bitter, cramped, difficult, disagreeable, distressing, dolorous, excruciating, galling, grievous, hard, harsh, ill-fitting, incommodious, irritating, thorny, torturing, troublesome, vexatious, wearisome; SEE CONCEPTS *529,537,583*

uncomfortable [*adj2*] *distressed, upset*
aching, angry, anguished, annoyed, awkward, chafed, cheerless, comfortless, confused, discomfited, discomposed, disquieted, disturbed, embarrassed, exhausted, fatigued, galled, harsh, hurt, ill at ease, in pain, miserable, nervous, pained, restless, self-conscious, smarting, sore, stiff, strained, suffering, tired, troubled, uneasy, vexed, weary, worn, wracked, wretched; SEE CONCEPTS *403,485*

uncommitted [*adj*] *free; not involved*
cut loose*, don't care*, fence-sitting*, floating, free-spirited, laid-back*, middle ground*, middle of the road*, neutral, nonaligned, nonpartisan, on the fence*, restrained, unaffiliated, unattached, uninvolved, unpledged; SEE CONCEPTS *403,542*

uncommon [*adj1*] *very different*
aberrant, abnormal, anomalous, arcane, bizarre, curious, eccentric, egregious, exceptional, exotic, extraordinary, extreme, fantastic, few, freakish, infrequent, irregular, nondescript, noteworthy, novel, odd, original, out of the ordinary, out of the way*, outré, peculiar, prodigious, queer, rare, remarkable, scarce, seldom, singular, sporadic, startling, strange, surprising, unaccustomed, unconventional, uncustomary, unfamiliar, unheard of, unique, unorthodox, unusual, weird; SEE CONCEPT *564*

uncommon [*adj2*] *wonderful, exceptional*
distinctive, extraordinary, incomparable, inimitable, notable, noteworthy, outstanding, rare, remarkable, singular, special, superior, unimaginable, unique, unparalleled, unprecedented, unthinkable, unwonted; SEE CONCEPT *574*

uncommonly [*adv*] *infrequently*
exceptionally, extra, extremely, hardly ever, in few instances, irregularly, not often, now and then, occasionally, oddly, on occasion, particu-

larly, peculiarly, rarely, remarkably, scarcely ever, seldom, sporadically, strangely, unusually, very; SEE CONCEPT *541*

uncommunicative [*adj*] *shy, silent*
aloof, buttoned up*, clammed up*, close, close-mouthed*, curt, distant, dried up*, evasive, guarded, hush-hush*, offish*, on the QT*, quiet, reserved, reticent, retiring, secretive, short, standoffish, taciturn, tight-lipped*, unapproachable, unresponsive, unsociable; SEE CONCEPT *267*

uncomplicated [*adj*] *easy*
apparent, basic, child's play*, cinch, clear, easily done, effortless, elementary, evident, manageable, no bother*, no problem*, no sweat*, not burdensome, not difficult, nothing to it*, no trouble, obvious, painless, piece of cake*, simple, simple as ABC*, snap, straightforward, uninvolved; SEE CONCEPT *565*

uncompromising [*adj*] *stubborn*
brick-wall*, decided, determined, firm, hardcore*, hard-line*, inexorable, inflexible, intransigent, locked, obdurate, obstinate, pigheaded*, relentless, resolute, rigid, set in stone*, single-minded, steadfast, stiff-necked*, strict, strong, tough, unbending; SEE CONCEPTS *401,542*

unconcerned [*adj*] *carefree; apathetic*
aloof, blind, blithe, callous, careless, cold, cool, deaf, detached, dispassionate, distant, easy, feckless, forgetful, hardened, hard-hearted, heedless, impassive, inattentive, incurious, indifferent, insensible, insensitive, insouciant, lackadaisical, lukewarm, negligent, neutral, nonchalant, oblivious, phlegmatic, relaxed, reserved, self-centered, serene, stony, supine, unbothered, uninterested, uninvolved, unmoved, unperturbed, unruffled, unsympathetic, untroubled, unworried; SEE CONCEPTS *403,542*

unconditional [*adj*] *absolute, total*
actual, all out, assured, categorical, certain, clear, complete, decisive, definite, determinate, downright, entire, explicit, final, flat out, full, genuine, indubitable, no catch*, no fine print*, no holds barred*, no ifs ands or buts*, no kicker*, no strings*, open, out-and-out*, outright, plenary, positive, straight out, thorough, thoroughgoing, unconstrained, unequivocal, unlimited, unmistakable, unmitigated, unqualified, unquestionable, unreserved, unrestricted, utter, whole, wide; SEE CONCEPTS *531,535,544*

unconscionable [*adj*] *immoral, immoderate*
amoral, barbarous, conscienceless, criminal, dishonest, excessive, exorbitant, extravagant, extreme, inordinate, knavish, outrageous, preposterous, sneaky, too much*, uncivilized, undue, unethical, unfair, ungodly, unholy, unjust, unprincipled, unreasonable, unscrupulous, wanton, wicked; SEE CONCEPTS *545,569*

unconscious [*adj1*] *not awake; out cold*
benumbed, blacked out*, bombed*, cold*, comatose, dead to the world*, drowsy, entranced, feeling no pain*, flattened*, inanimate, in a trance, inert, insensate, insensible, knocked*, lethargic, numb, on the canvas*, out, out like a light*, palsied, paralyzed, passed out*, put away*, raving, senseless, stunned, stupefied, swooning, torpid, tranced, zonked*; SEE CONCEPTS *314,539*

unconscious [*adj2*] *ignorant; automatic*
accidental, gut*, ignorant, inadvertent, inattentive, inherent, innate, instinctive, involuntary, la-

tent, lost, reflex, repressed, subconscious, subliminal, suppressed, unaware, uncalculated, undeliberate, unheeding, unintended, unintentional, unmindful, unpremeditated, unrealized, unwitting; SEE CONCEPTS *542,544*

unconstitutional [*adj*] *illegal*
against the law, banned, criminal, felonious, forbidden, illegitimate, illicit, lawless, not legal, outlawed, prohibited, prosecutable, unauthorized, unlawful, violating, wrongful; SEE CONCEPTS *319,545*

uncontrollable [*adj*] *wild; carried away*
beside oneself, disorderly, excited, fractious, frantic, freaked, furious, headstrong, indocile, indomitable, insuppressible, insurgent, intractable, irrepressible, irresistible, lawless, like a loose cannon*, mad, obdurate, obstinate, recalcitrant, strong, stubborn, uncontainable, undisciplinable, undisciplined, ungovernable, unmanageable, unrestrainable, unruly, violent; SEE CONCEPT *401*

unconventional [*adj*] *very different; odd*
anarchistic, atypical, avant-garde, beat, bizarre, crazy, eccentric, far-out*, freakish, freaky, free and easy*, idiosyncratic, informal, irregular, kinky*, kooky*, nonconformist, oddball*, offbeat, off the beaten track*, off the wall*, original, out in left field*, out of the ordinary, unceremonious, uncommon, uncustomary, unique, unorthodox, unusual, way-out*, weirdo*; SEE CONCEPT *564*

uncoordinated [*adj*] *awkward, clumsy*
all thumbs*, bumbling, bungling, butterfingered*, gawkish, gawky, graceless, heavy-handed, klutzy*, like a bull in a china shop*, lumbering, not agile, stumbling, unadept, ungainly, ungraceful, unhandy, unskillful; SEE CONCEPTS *401,402,584*

uncouth [*adj*] *clumsy, uncultivated*
awkward, barbaric, boorish, cheap, clownish, clumsy, coarse, crass, crude, discourteous, disgracious, gawky, graceless, gross, heavy-handed, ill-bred, ill-mannered, impertinent, impolite, inelegant, loud, loud-mouthed, loutish, oafish, raunchy, raw, rough, rude, rustic, strange, tacky*, uncalled-for*, uncivil, uncivilized, uncultivated, ungainly, ungenteel, ungentlemanly, unpolished, unrefined, unseemly, vulgar; SEE CONCEPT *401*

uncover [*v*] *reveal, disclose*
bare, betray, break, bring to light*, crack, denude, dig up*, disclose, discover, display, divulge, expose, give away, hit upon, lay bare, lay open, leak, make known, open, open up, reveal, show, strike, strip, stumble on, subject, tap, tell, tip one's hand*, unclothe, unearth, unmask, unveil, unwrap; SEE CONCEPTS *60,183,261*

uncovered [*adj*] *exposed*
bare, brought to light*, caught, disclosed, discovered, divulged, dug up*, found out, laid bare*, made public, naked, nude, on display, on view, revealed, shown, solved, stripped, unconcealed, unmasked, unprotected, unveiled, visible, vulnerable, weakened; SEE CONCEPT *576*

uncritical [*adj*] *casual, unfussy*
careless, cursory, easily pleased, imperceptive, imprecise, imprudent, inaccurate, indiscriminate, offhand, perfunctory, shallow, slipshod, superficial, undiscerning, undiscriminating, unexacting, uninformed, unperceptive, unselective, unthinking; SEE CONCEPT *542*

undaunted [*adj*] *brave, bold*
audacious, coming on strong*, courageous, dauntless, fearless, fire-eating*, gallant, icy*, indomitable, intrepid, not discouraged, not put off*, resolute, spunky, steadfast, unafraid, unalarmed, unapprehensive, undeterred, undiscouraged, undismayed, unfaltering, unflinching, unshrinking, valiant, valorous; SEE CONCEPT *401*

undecided [*adj*] *not sure, not definite*
ambivalent, betwixt and between*, blowing hot and cold*, borderline, debatable, dithering*, doubtful, dubious, equivocal, hemming and hawing*, hesitant, iffy*, indecisive, indefinite, in the middle*, irresolute, moot, of two minds*, on the fence*, open, pendent, pending, running hot and cold*, tentative, torn, uncertain, unclear, uncommitted, undetermined, unfinished, unsettled, unsure, up in the air*, vague, waffling, wavering, wishy-washy*; SEE CONCEPTS *403,529*

undeniable [*adj*] *definite, proven*
actual, beyond doubt, beyond question, binding, certain, clear, compulsory, evident, for sure*, inarguable, incontestable, incontrovertible, indisputable, indubitable, irrefutable, manifest, necessary, no ifs and or buts*, obligatory, obvious, open and shut*, patent, positive, real, sound, sure, sure thing*, true, unanswerable, unassailable, undoubted, unquestionable; SEE CONCEPT *535*

undependable [*adj*] *irresponsible*
bum, capricious, careless, changeable, dubious, erratic, fickle, fly-by-night*, inconsistent, inconstant, indefinite, indeterminate, loose*, no bargain*, no-good*, treacherous, trick, tricky, trustless, unassured, uncertain, unpredictable, unreliable, unsafe, unsound, unstable, unsure, untrustworthy, variable; SEE CONCEPTS *401,535*

under [*adv1/prep1*] *below*
beneath, bottom, concealed by, covered by, down, downward, held down, inferior, lower, nether, on the bottom, on the nether side, on the underside, pinned, pressed down, supporting, to the bottom, underneath; SEE CONCEPTS *586,735,793*

under [*adv2/prep2*] *secondary*
amenable, belonging, collateral, consequent, corollary, dependent, directed, following, governed, included, inferior, in the power of, junior, lesser, low, lower, obedient, obeying, reporting, sub, subject, subjugated, subordinate, subsequent, subservient, subsidiary, substract, subsumed; SEE CONCEPTS *560,575,577*

undercover [*adj*] *secret, spy*
clandestine, concealed, confidential, covert, creep, furtive, hidden, hole-and-corner*, hush-hush*, incognito*, intelligence, on the QT*, private, stealth, stealthy, sub-rosa*, surreptitious, underground, underhand, underneath, under wraps*; SEE CONCEPTS *544,576*

undercurrent [*n*] *drift, pull*
atmosphere, aura, crosscurrent, direction, eddy, feeling, flavor, hint, inclination, indication, insinuation, intimation, murmur, overtone, propensity, riptide, sense, suggestion, tendency, tenor, tinge, trace, trend, underflow, undertone, undertow, vibes*, vibrations; SEE CONCEPTS *673,738*

underdog [*n*] *unlikely winner in a contest or struggle*
bottom dog, dark horse, longshot, out-of-towner; SEE CONCEPTS *366,423*

underestimate [v] *minimize; rate too low*
belittle, deprecate, depreciate, disesteem, disparage, make light of*, miscalculate, miscarry, not do justice*, put down*, sell short*, slight, think too little of*, underrate, undervalue; SEE CONCEPTS *12,54,764*

undergo [v] *be subjected to*
abide, bear, bear up, bow, defer, encounter, endure, experience, feel, go through, have, know, meet with, put up with, see, share, stand, submit to, suffer, support, sustain, tolerate, weather, withstand, yield; SEE CONCEPT *23*

underground [adj1] *below the surface*
below ground, buried, covered, in the recesses, subterranean, subterrestrial, sunken, underfoot; SEE CONCEPT *583*

underground [adj2] *secret, subversive*
alternative, avant-garde, clandestine, concealed, covert, experimental, hidden, hush-hush*, on the QT*, on the sly*, private, radical, resistant, resistive, revolutionary, surreptitious, unbowed, unconventional, undercover, under wraps*, unusual; SEE CONCEPTS *564,576*

underhand [adj] *deceitful*
clandestine, concealed, crafty, crooked, cunning, deceptive, devious, dirty-dealing*, dishonest, dishonorable, double-crossing*, duplicitous, fraudulent, furtive, guileful, hush-hush*, indirect, insidious, oblique, on the QT*, on the quiet*, secret, secretive, shady, shifty, slippery*, sly*, sneaking, sneaky, stealthy, sub-rosa, surreptitious, treacherous, tricky, two-faced*, two-timing*, undercover, underhanded, under wraps*, unethical, unfair, unjust, unscrupulous, wily; SEE CONCEPTS *401,544*

underline [v] *emphasize; mark*
accentuate, bracket, call attention to, caption, check off, draw attention to, feature, give emphasis, highlight, indicate, interlineate, italicize, play up, point to, point up, rule, stress, underscore; SEE CONCEPTS *49,79*

underling [n] *subordinate*
aide, assistant, attendant, deputy, flunky*, gofer*, helper, inferior, lackey*, minion, peon, scrub*, second, second fiddle*, second stringer*, serf, servant, slave; SEE CONCEPTS *348,423*

underlying [adj] *fundamental*
basal, basic, bottom, bottom-line*, cardinal, concealed, critical, crucial, elemental, elementary, essential, hidden, indispensable, intrinsic, lurking, necessary, needful, nitty-gritty*, nub, primary, prime, primitive, radical, root, substratal, veiled, vital; SEE CONCEPTS *546,549*

undermine [v] *weaken*
attenuate, blunt, clip one's wings*, corrode, cripple, debilitate, dig, dig out*, disable, eat away*, enfeeble, erode, excavate, foil, frustrate, hollow out, hurt, impair, knock the bottom out of*, mine, poke full of holes*, ruin, sabotage, sandbag*, sap, soften, subvert, threaten, thwart, torpedo*, tunnel, undercut, wear, whittle away, wreck; SEE CONCEPTS *14,240*

underneath [adv/prep] *below*
beneath, bottom, covered, lower, neath, nether, under; SEE CONCEPTS *586,735*

underprivileged [adj] *poor*
badly off*, depressed, deprived, destitute, disadvantaged, down and out*, handicapped, hapless, hard up*, have-not*, ill-fated, ill-starred, impoverished, indigent, in dire straits, in need, in want, needy, unfortunate, unlucky; SEE CONCEPT *334*

underscore [v] *underline, emphasize*
accent, accentuate, call attention to, caption, draw attention to, feature, give emphasis, highlight, indicate, italicize, mark, point to, stress; SEE CONCEPTS *49,79*

understand [v1] *appreciate, comprehend*
accept, apprehend, be aware, be conscious of, be with it*, catch, catch on, conceive, deduce, discern, distinguish, explain, fathom, figure out, find out, follow, get*, get the hang of*, get the idea*, get the picture*, get the point*, grasp, have knowledge of, identify with, infer, interpret, ken*, know, learn, make out*, make sense of, master, note, penetrate, perceive, possess, read, realize, recognize, register, savvy*, see, seize, sense, sympathize, take in*, take meaning, tolerate; SEE CONCEPT *15*

understand [v2] *think, believe*
accept, assume, be informed, concede, conceive, conclude, conjecture, consider, count on, deduce, expect, fancy, feel for, gather, guess, hear, imagine, infer, learn, presume, reckon, suppose, surmise, suspect, take for granted, take it, think; SEE CONCEPT *12*

understanding [adj] *accepting, tolerant*
compassionate, considerate, discerning, empathetic, forbearing, forgiving, generous, kind, kindly, patient, perceptive, responsive, sensitive, sympathetic; SEE CONCEPTS *401,542*

understanding [n1] *comprehension, appreciation*
acumen, apperception, apprehension, assimilation, awareness, decipherment, discernment, discrimination, grasp, grip, insight, intellect, intelligence, intuition, judgment, ken, knowing, knowledge, mastery, penetration, perception, perceptiveness, perceptivity, percipience, perspicacity, prehension, realization, reason, recognition, savvy, sense, sharpness, wit; SEE CONCEPT *409*

understanding [n2] *belief*
acceptation, conception, conclusion, estimation, idea, import, impression, inkling, intendment, interpretation, judgment, knowledge, meaning, message, notion, opinion, perception, purport, sense, significance, significancy, signification, sympathy, view, viewpoint; SEE CONCEPTS *682,689*

understanding [n3] *informal agreement*
accord, common view, concord, deal, handshake*, harmony, meeting of minds*, pact; SEE CONCEPT *684*

understood [adj] *assumed, implicit*
accepted, appreciated, axiomatic, down pat*, implied, inferential, inferred, known, on to*, pat, presumed, roger*, tacit, taken for granted, undeclared, unexpressed, unsaid, unspoken, unstated, wise to, wordless; SEE CONCEPT *529*

understudy [n] *substitute*
alternate, backup, double, fill-in, pinch-hitter*, replacement, reserve, stand-by, stand-in, sub*, successor; SEE CONCEPTS *423,712*

undertake [v] *attempt, engage in*
address oneself, agree, answer for, bargain, begin, commence, commit, commit oneself, con-

un
un

tract, covenant, devote, embark, endeavor, enter upon, fall into, go about, go for, go in for, go into, guarantee, have a hand in*, have a try, hazard, initiate, launch, make a run at*, move, offer, pitch in, pledge, promise, set about, set in motion, set out, shoulder, stake, stipulate, tackle, take on, take the plunge*, take upon oneself, try, try out, venture, volunteer; SEE CONCEPTS *87,100*

undertaker [*n*] *funeral director*
embalmer, grave digger, mortician; SEE CONCEPT *304*

undertaking [*n*] *endeavor, attempt*
adventure, affair, business, deal, effort, engagement, enterprise, essay, experiment, game, happening, hassle, hazard, job, move, operation, outfit, play, project, proposition, pursuit, shop, striving, struggle, task, thing*, trial, try, venture, what one is into*, work; SEE CONCEPTS *87,324,349,362*

undertone [*n*] *suggestion, whisper*
association, atmosphere, buzz, connotation, feeling, flavor, hint, hum, implication, low tone, mumble, murmur, mutter, overtone, rumor, tinge, touch, trace, undercurrent; SEE CONCEPTS *65,682*

underwear [*n*] *clothing worn under outerwear*
bikini, boxers*, boxer shorts, bra, briefs, BVDs*, corset, drawers*, intimate things, jockeys, jockey shorts, lingerie, long johns, panties, shorts, skivvies*, smallclothes, underclothes, underclothing, undergarment, underpants, undershirt, underthings, undies; SEE CONCEPT *451*

underweight [*adj*] *thin*
angular, anorectic, bony, gangly, malnourished, puny, scrawny, shadow, skeleton*, skin and bones*, skinny, starved, stringbean*, undernourished, undersized; SEE CONCEPT *491*

underworld [*n*] *criminal activity, element*
abyss, Cosa Nostra, criminals, felonry, gangland, gangsters, Mafia, mob*, organized crime, racket*, riffraff*, syndicate; SEE CONCEPTS *412,645*

underwrite [*v*] *endorse, insure*
accede, agree to, angel*, approve, back, bankroll*, collateral, consent, countersign, endow, finance, float, fund, guarantee, help, initial, okay*, pay, provide, provide financing, sanction, seal, secure, sign, sponsor, stake, subscribe, subsidize, support; SEE CONCEPTS *50,88,110,341*

undesirable [*adj*] *offensive, unacceptable*
abominable, annoying, bothersome, defective, disagreeable, disliked, displeasing, distasteful, dreaded, icky, inadmissible, incommodious, inconvenient, inexpedient, insufferable, loathed, loathsome, objectionable, obnoxious, offensive, outcast, out of place, rejected, repellent, repugnant, scorned, shunned, to be avoided, troublesome, unacceptable, unattractive, unlikable, unpleasing, unpopular, unsatisfactory, unsavory, unsought, unsuitable, unwanted, unwelcome, unwished for, useless; SEE CONCEPTS *529,570*

undeveloped [*adj*] *immature*
abortive, backward, behindhand, embryonic, half-baked, ignored, inchoate, incipient, inexperienced, latent, potential, primitive, primordial, unactualized, underdeveloped, unevolved, unprogressive, untaught, untrained; SEE CONCEPTS *485,578,797*

undisciplined [*adj*] *uncontrolled*
defiant, disorderly, headstrong, inconsistent, insubordinate, lacking self controll, mischievous, naughty, noncompliant, ungoverned, unrestrained, unruly, untrained, wayward; SEE CONCEPT *401*

undisputed/undisputable [*adj*] *positive, accepted*
acknowledged, admitted, arbitrary, assured, authoritative, beyond question, certain, conclusive, decided, dogmatic, final, incontestable, incontrovertible, indisputable, indubitable, irrefutable, not disputed, positive, recognized, sure, tyrannous, unchallenged, uncontested, undeniable, undoubted, unequivocal, unerring, unquestioned; SEE CONCEPT *535*

undistinguished [*adj*] *ordinary*
average, characterless, common, commonplace, dull, everyday, fair, garden-variety*, generic, mean, mediocre, modest, no great shakes*, normal, nothing special, nothing to write home about*, pedestrian, plain, prosaic, routine, run-of-the-mill*, second-rate, so-so*, typical, uneventful, unexceptional, unexciting, uninspired, unmemorable, unnoteworthy, unremarkable, usual; SEE CONCEPTS *530,575*

undivided [*adj*] *whole*
absorbed, circumspect, collective, combined, complete, concentrated, concerted, continued, deliberate, detailed, diligent, engrossed, entire, exclusive, fast, fixed, full, intense, intent, joined, lock stock and barrel*, minute, rigid, scrupulous, single, solid, steady, thorough, unanimous, unbroken, uncut, undistracted, unflagging, united, unswerving, vigilant, wholehearted; SEE CONCEPTS *482,531*

undo [*v1*] *open*
disengage, disentangle, free, loose, loosen, release, unbind, unblock, unbutton, unclose, unfasten, unfix, unlock, unloose, unloosen, unravel, unshut, unstop, untie, unwrap; SEE CONCEPT *135*

undo [*v2*] *nullify, invalidate*
abate, abolish, abrogate, annihilate, annul, break, bring down, bring to naught*, cancel, cramp*, craze, crimp*, decimate, defeat, demolish, destroy, have*, impoverish, injure, make waves*, mar, negate, neutralize, offset, outfox, outmaneuver, outsmart, overreach, overthrow, overturn, quash, queer*, raze, reverse, ruin, screw up*, shatter, skin*, smash, spoil, stymie*, subvert, unbuild, undermine, unsettle, upset, vitiate, wipe out*, wrack, wreck; SEE CONCEPTS *7,19,121,252*

undoing [*n*] *destruction, misfortune*
accident, adversity, affliction, bad luck, bad omen, bane, blight, blow, blunder, calamity, casualty, catastrophe, collapse, curse, defeat, destroyer, difficulty, disgrace, doom, downfall, error, failure, fault, faux pas, flaw, fumble, grief, humiliation, last straw*, misadventure, miscalculation, mischance, mishap, misstep, omission, overthrow, overturn, reversal, reverse, ruin, ruination, shame, slip, smash, stumble, subversion, trial, trip, trouble, visitation, weakness, wreck; SEE CONCEPTS *230,674,679*

undoubtedly [*adv*] *certainly*
assuredly, beyond question, beyond shadow of a doubt*, definitely, doubtless, easily, indeed, of course, really, surely, truly, undeniably, unmis-

takably, unquestionably, well, without doubt; SEE CONCEPT *535*

undress [*v*] *take off clothes*
denude, disarray, dismantle, disrobe, divest oneself, doff, get off, get out of, husk, peel, shed, shock, slip off, slip out of, strip, unattire, uncloak, unclothe, unmask; SEE CONCEPTS *211,453*

undue [*adj*] *excessive, unnecessary*
disproportionate, exceeding, exorbitant, extravagant, extreme, forbidden, illegal, ill-timed, immoderate, improper, inappropriate, inapt, indecorous, inept, inordinate, intemperate, needless, overmuch, sinister, too great, too much, unapt, uncalled-for, unconscionable, underhanded, undeserved, unfair, unfitting, unjust, unjustifiable, unjustified, unmeasurable, unreasonable, unseasonable, unseemly, unsuitable, untimely, unwarrantable, unwarranted; SEE CONCEPTS *546,558,569*

unduly [*adv*] *excessively*
disproportionately, ever, extravagantly, extremely, illegally, immensely, immoderately, improperly, indecorously, inordinately, out of proportion, over, overfull, overly, overmuch, too, underhandedly, unfairly, unjustifiably, unjustly, unnecessarily, unreasonably; SEE CONCEPTS *544,546,569*

undying [*adj*] *never-ending*
constant, continuing, deathless, eternal, everlasting, immortal, imperishable, indestructible, inextinguishable, infinite, interminable, perennial, permanent, perpetual, persistent, unceasing, undiminished, unended, unending, unfading; SEE CONCEPT *798*

unearned [*adj*] *undeserved*
not deserved, not earned, not merited, not warranted, unmerited, unwarranted; SEE CONCEPTS *545,548,558*

unearth [*v*] *dig up*
ascertain, bring to light*, catch on*, delve, determine, discover, disinter, dredge up, excavate, exhibit, exhume, expose, ferret, find, find out, hear, hit upon, learn, reveal, root, see, see the light, show, spark, spotlight*, strike, stumble on, turn up, unbury, uncover, uproot; SEE CONCEPTS *178,183*

unearthly [*adj*] *supernatural; very strange*
abnormal, absurd, appalling, demoniac, devilish, eerie, ethereal, extraordinary, fiendish, frightening, funereal, ghastly, ghostly, ghoulish, hairraising, haunted, heavenly, hyperphysical, miraculous, nightmarish, not of this world, phantom, preternatural, ridiculous, scary, sepulchral, spectral, spooky*, sublime, superhuman, uncanny, ungodly, unholy, unreasonable, weird; SEE CONCEPTS *536,564,582*

uneasy [*adj*] *awkward, uncomfortable*
afraid, agitated, alarmed, all nerves*, anguished, anxious, apprehensive, bothered, constrained, discomposed, dismayed, disquieted, disturbed, edgy, fearful, fidgety, fretful, harassed, ill at ease, impatient, insecure, in turmoil, irascible, irritable, jittery, jumpy, nervous, on edge, on the qui vive, palpitant, peevish, perplexed, perturbed, precarious, restive, restless, shaken, shaky, strained, suspicious, tense, tormented, troubled, unquiet, unsettled, unstable, upset, vexed, worried, wrung; SEE CONCEPTS *403,548,690*

uneducated [*adj*] *lacking knowledge*
benighted, empty-headed, ignoramus, ignorant, illiterate, inerudite, know-nothing*, lowbrow*, uncultivated, uncultured, uninstructed, unlearned, unlettered, unread, unrefined, unschooled, untaught, untutored; SEE CONCEPT *402*

unemotional [*adj*] *not responsive*
along for the ride*, apathetic, blah*, callous, chill*, cold, coldhearted*, cool, deadpan, dispassionate, emotionless, flat, frigid, glacial, going with the flow*, hard-boiled*, hard-hearted*, heartless, impassive, indifferent, insensitive, laid-back*, listless, marble*, obdurate, passionless, phlegmatic, quiet, reserved, reticent, rolling with the punches*, thick-skinned*, uncompassionate, undemonstrative, unexcitable, unfeeling, unimpressionable, unresponsive, unsympathetic; SEE CONCEPTS *401,403*

unemployed [*adj*] *without a job*
at liberty*, between jobs*, closed down*, disengaged, down, fired, free, idle, inactive, jobless, laid off, leisured, loafing*, on layoff, on the bench*, on the dole*, on the shelf*, out of action*, out of a job, out of work, resting, unapplied, underemployed, unengaged, unexercised, unoccupied, unused, without gainful employment, workless; SEE CONCEPT *538*

unending [*adj*] *continuing*
amaranthine, ceaseless, constant, continual, continuous, endless, eternal, everlasting, immortal, incessant, infinite, interminable, never-ending, perpetual, steady, unceasing, uninterrupted, unremitting; SEE CONCEPTS *482,798*

unequal [*adj1*] *different*
differing, disparate, dissimilar, distant, divergent, diverse, incommensurate, like night and day*, mismatched, not uniform, odd, poles apart*, unalike, unequivalent, uneven, unlike, unmatched, unsimilar, variable, various, varying, weird*; SEE CONCEPT *564*

unequal [*adj2*] *not balanced; lopsided*
asymmetrical, disproportionate, ill-matched, inequitable, irregular, nonsymmetrical, off-balance, one-sided, overbalanced, unbalanced, uneven, unproportionate, unsymmetrical; SEE CONCEPT *480*

unequaled [*adj*] *supreme, pre-eminent*
alone, beyond compare, incomparable, inimitable, matchless, nonpareil, only, paramount, peerless, second to none*, surpassing, towering, transcendent, ultimate, unique, unmatched, unparagoned, unparalleled, unrivaled, unsurpassed, without equal; SEE CONCEPT *574*

unequivocal [*adj*] *definite, positive*
absolute, apparent, categorical, certain, clear, clear-cut, decided, decisive, direct, distinct, downright, evident, explicit, flat out*, incontestable, incontrovertible, indisputable, indubitable, manifest, no catch*, no fine print*, no holds barred*, no ifs ands or buts*, no strings attached*, obvious, open and shut*, palpable, patent, plain, straight, straightforward, straight out, unambiguous, uncontestable, undeniable, undisputable, univocal, unmistakable, unquestionable; SEE CONCEPT *535*

unerring [*adj*] *accurate*
certain, errorless, exact, faultless, impeccable, inerrable, inerrant, infallible, invariable, just, perfect, reliable, sure, true, trustworthy, unfailing; SEE CONCEPTS *535,574*

un
un

unessential [*adj*] *unnecessary*
avoidable, beside the point*, dispensable, expendable, futile, inessential, irrelevant, needless, nonessential, optional, uncalled-for, unimportant, unneeded, unrequired, useless, worthless; SEE CONCEPT *546*

unethical [*adj*] *dishonest, immoral*
cheating, corrupt, crooked, dirty*, dirty-dealing*, dishonorable, disreputable, double-crossing*, fake, fishy*, flimflam*, fly-by-night*, illegal, improper, mercenary, scam*, shady*, sharp*, slick*, slippery*, sneaky*, two-faced*, two-timing*, underhand, unfair, unprincipled, unprofessional, unscrupulous, wrong; SEE CONCEPT *545*

uneven [*adj*] *not smooth or balanced*
asperous, asymmetrical, broken, bumpy, changeable, craggy, differing, discrepant, disparate, disproportionate, fitful, fluctuating, harsh, ill-matched, intermittent, irregular, jagged, jerky, leftover, lopsided, nonsymmetrical, notched, not flat, not level, not parallel, odd, off-balance, one-sided, overbalanced, patchy, remaining, rough, rugged, scabrous, scraggy, serrate, spasmodic, spotty, unbalanced, unequal, unfair, unlevel, unsmooth, unsteady, unsymmetrical, variable; SEE CONCEPTS *480,566,606*

uneventful [*adj*] *monotonous, dull*
boring, common, commonplace, humdrum, inconclusive, indecisive, ordinary, prosaic, quiet, routine, tedious, unexceptional, unexciting, unfateful, uninteresting, unmemorable, unnoteworthy, unremarkable, unvaried; SEE CONCEPT *548*

unexceptional [*adj*] *ordinary*
average, characterless, common, commonplace, conventional, dull, everyday, fair, garden-variety*, insignificant, mediocre, modest, no great shakes*, normal, nothing special, nothing to write home about*, pedestrian, plain, prosaic, routine, run-of-the-mill*, second-rate, so-so*, typical, undistinguished, uneventful, unexciting, unimpressive, uninspired, unmemorable, unnoteworthy, unremarkable, usual; SEE CONCEPTS *530,575*

unexciting [*adj*] *dull*
big yawn*, blah, boring, common, dead, dreary, familiar, ho hum*, humdrum*, long-winded, monotonous, ordinary, plain, prosaic, routine, run-of-the-mill*, uneventful, unimaginative, uninspiring, uninteresting, usual, usual thing; SEE CONCEPTS *529,530*

unexpected [*adj*] *surprising*
abrupt, accidental, amazing, astonishing, chance, electrifying, eye-opening*, fortuitous, from left field*, impetuous, impulsive, instantaneous, not bargained for*, not in the cards*, out of the blue*, payback, prodigious, staggering, startling, stunning, sudden, swift, unanticipated, unforeseen, unheralded, unlooked-for, unpredictable, unpredicted, wonderful; SEE CONCEPTS *544,548*

unfailing [*adj*] *certain, unchanging*
absolute, assiduous, bottomless, boundless, ceaseless, come-through*, consistent, constant, continual, continuing, continuous, counted on, delivering, dependable, diligent, dyed-in-the-wool*, endless, eternal, faithful, inexhaustible, infallible, invariable, loyal, never-failing, persistent, reliable, rock solid*, same, solid, staunch, steadfast, straight, sure, surefire, there*, tried-and-true*, true, trustworthy, unflagging, unlimited, unrelenting; SEE CONCEPTS *534,535,538*

unfair [*adj*] *prejudiced, wrongful*
arbitrary, bad, base, biased, bigoted, blameworthy, cheating, criminal, crooked, cruel, culpable, discreditable, discriminatory, dishonest, dishonorable, foul, grievous, illegal, immoral, improper, inequitable, inexcusable, iniquitous, injurious, low, mean, one-sided, partial, partisan, petty, shameful, shameless, uncalled-for, undue, unethical, unjust, unjustifiable, unlawful, unprincipled, unreasonable, unrightful, unscrupulous, unsporting, unwarranted, vicious, vile, wicked, wrong; SEE CONCEPTS *544,545,548*

unfaithful [*adj*] *disloyal, adulterous*
adulterine, cheating, deceitful, double-crossing*, faithless, false, false-hearted, fickle, foresworn, inconstant, incontinent, moonlighting*, not true to, of bad faith, perfidious, philandering, recreant, shifty*, snaky*, sneaking, traitorous, treacherous, treasonable, two-faced*, two-timing*, unchaste, unreliable, untrue, untrustworthy, wicked; SEE CONCEPT *545*

unfaltering [*adj*] *steadfast*
abiding, bent on, bound, bound and determined*, dead set on*, enduring, firm, going all the way*, indefatigable, meaning business*, mulish*, never-failing, persevering, pigheaded, resolute, set, steady, stiff-necked*, stubborn, sure, tireless, unfailing, unflagging, unflappable, unflinching, unqualified, unquestioning, unswerving, untiring, unwavering, wholehearted; SEE CONCEPTS *403,535,538*

unfamiliar [*adj1*] *different, strange*
alien, anomalous, bizarre, curious, exotic, extraordinary, fantastic, foreign, little known, new, novel, obscure, original, outlandish, out-of-the-way*, peculiar, recondite, remarkable, remote, unaccustomed, uncommon, unexpected, unexplored, uninvestigated, unknown, unusual; SEE CONCEPT *564*

unfamiliar [*adj2*] *inexperienced; not knowing about*
ignorant, incognizant, inconversant, not associated, not versed in, oblivious, out of contact, unaccustomed, unacquainted, unaware, unconversant, uninformed, uninitiated, uninstructed, unknowing, unknown, unpracticed, unskilled, unversed, unwitting; SEE CONCEPTS *402,678*

unfathomable [*adj1*] *bottomless*
abysmal, boundless, deep, eternal, immeasurable, infinite, sounding, unending, unmeasured, unplumbed; SEE CONCEPTS *482,777*

unfathomable [*adj2*] *hard to believe; difficult to understand*
abstruse, baffling, clear as mud*, deep, enigmatic, esoteric, heavy, impenetrable, incognizable, incomprehensible, indecipherable, inexplicable, obscure, profound, too deep*, uncomprehensible, ungraspable, unintelligible, unknowable; SEE CONCEPT *529*

unfavorable [*adj*] *very bad*
adverse, antagonistic, calamitous, contrary, damaging, destructive, disadvantageous, discommodious, hostile, ill, ill-advised, improper, inadvisable, inauspicious, inconvenient, inexpedient, infelicitous, inimical, inopportune, late, low, malapropos, negative, objectionable, ominous, opposed, poor, regrettable, tardy, threaten-

ing, troublesome, unfit, unfortunate, unfriendly, unlucky, unpromising, unpropitious, unseasonable, unseemly, unsuited, untimely, untoward, wrong; SEE CONCEPTS *529,571*

unfeeling [*adj*] *hard-hearted, numb*
anesthetized, apathetic, asleep, benumbed, brutal, callous, cantankerous, churlish, cold, cold-blooded, cold fish*, cold-hearted, crotchety, cruel, deadened, exacting, feelingless, hard, hardened, heartless, icy, inanimate, inhuman, insensate, insensible, insensitive, iron-hearted, merciless, obdurate, pitiless, ruthless, sensationless, senseless, severe, stony, surly, thick-skinned*, tough, unamiable, uncaring, uncompassionate, uncordial, unemotional, unkind, unsympathetic; SEE CONCEPTS *314,403,542*

unfinished [*adj*] *not completed*
amateurish, bare, crude, cut short, dabbling, defective, deficient, dilettante, faulty, formless, found wanting, fragmentary, half-baked*, half-done*, immature, imperfect, incomplete, in the making, in the rough*, lacking, natural, not done, plain, raw, rough, roughhewn, shapeless, sketchy, tentative, unaccomplished, unadorned, unassembled, uncompleted, unconcluded, under construction, undeveloped, undone, unexecuted, unfashioned, unfulfilled, unperfected, unpolished, unrefined, wanting; SEE CONCEPTS *485,531*

unfit [*adj1*] *not appropriate or suited*
below par*, can't make the grade*, debilitated, decrepit, discordant, down, dragging, feeble, flimsy, ill-adapted, ill-equipped, ill-suited, improper, inadequate, inapplicable, inappropriate, incompatible, incongruous, incorrect, ineffective, inexpedient, infelicitous, inharmonious, laid low*, mistaken, not fit, out of element*, out of place, out of shape, poorly, rocky*, unbecoming, uncongenial, uncool, unhealthy, unlikely, unmeet, unpromising, unsuitable, unsuited, useless, valueless; SEE CONCEPT *558*

unfit [*adj2*] *not ready*
amateur, awkward, blundering, bungling, bush league*, butter-fingered*, clumsy, debilitated, disqualified, feeble, heavy-handed, ill-equipped, impotent, inadequate, incapable, incapacitated, incompetent, ineffective, inefficient, ineligible, inept, inexperienced, inexpert, maladjusted, maladroit, no good*, not cut out for*, not equal to, not up to*, unable, unapt, unfitted, unhandy, unpracticed, unprepared, unproficient, unqualified, unskilled, unskillful, untrained, useless, weak; SEE CONCEPT *527*

unflagging [*adj*] *persistent*
active, assiduous, constant, diligent, dynamic, energetic, fixed, indefatigable, inexhaustible, persevering, staunch, steady, tireless, unceasing, undeviating, unfailing, unfaltering, unrelenting, unremitting, unretiring, untiring, unwearied; SEE CONCEPTS *538,798*

unflappable [*adj*] *cool and calm*
collected, composed, deliberate, disimpassioned, easy, impassive, imperturbable, level-headed, nonchalant, relaxed, self-possessed, unruffled; SEE CONCEPTS *401,542*

unfold [*v1*] *spread out*
disentangle, display, expand, extend, fan, fan out, flatten, loosen, open, outspread, outstretch, reel out, release, shake out, spread, straighten,

stretch out, unbend, uncoil, uncrease, uncurl, undo, unfurl, unravel, unroll, untwist, unwind, unwrap; SEE CONCEPT *201*

unfold [*v2*] *make known*
announce, clarify, clear up, decipher, describe, disclose, discover, display, divulge, dope out, elucidate, explain, explicate, expose, figure out, illustrate, present, publish, resolve, reveal, show, solve, uncover, unravel; SEE CONCEPTS *55,261*

unfold [*v3*] *develop*
bear fruit, demonstrate, elaborate, evidence, evince, evolve, expand, grow, manifest, mature; SEE CONCEPT *704*

unforeseeable [*adj*] *unpredictable*
capricious, chance, chancy, changeable, fluky*, from left field*, incalculable, random, uncertain, unexpected, unknowable; SEE CONCEPT *534*

unforeseen [*adj*] *surprising*
abrupt, accidental, from left field*, not bargained for*, out of the blue*, startling, sudden, surprise, unanticipated, uncalculated, unexpected, unlooked-for; SEE CONCEPTS *544,548*

unforgettable [*adj*] *memorable*
catchy, distinguished, enduring, eventful, exceptional, extraordinary, famous, great, historic, illustrious, important, lasting, meaningful, monumental, notable, noteworthy, not to be forgotten, remarkable, rememberable, remembered, significant, super; SEE CONCEPTS *529,548*

unforgivable [*adj*] *inexcusable*
blameworthy, contemptible, deplorable, disgraceful, indefensible, inexpiable, not forgivable, outrageous, reprehensible, shameful, unallowable, unconscionable, unjustifiable, unpardonable, unpermissible, untenable, wrong; SEE CONCEPTS *545,570*

unfortunate [*adj*] *unlucky, bad*
adverse, afflicted, broken, burdened, calamitous, cursed, damaging, deplorable, desperate, destitute, disastrous, doomed, forsaken, hapless, hopeless, ill-fated, ill-starred, in a bad way*, inappropriate, infelicitous, inopportune, jinxed, lamentable, luckless, out of luck*, pained, poor, regrettable, ruined, ruinous, shattered, star-crossed*, stricken, troubled, unbecoming, unfavorable, unhappy, unpropitious, unprosperous, unsuccessful, unsuitable, untoward, wretched; SEE CONCEPTS *334,548,570*

unfounded [*adj*] *not based on fact*
baseless, bottomless, deceptive, fabricated, fallacious, false, foundationless, gratuitous, groundless, idle, illogical, mendacious, misleading, off-base, spurious, trumped up*, uncalled-for, unjustified, unproven, unreal, unsubstantiated, untrue, untruthful, unwarranted, vain, without basis, without foundation; SEE CONCEPTS *267,582*

unfriendly [*adj*] *nasty, hostile*
acrimonious, against, alien, aloof, antagonistic, antisocial, censorious, chilly, cold, combative, competitive, conflicting, contrary, disaffected, disagreeable, distant, estranged, grouchy, grudging, gruff, hateful, ill-disposed, inauspicious, inhospitable, inimical, malicious, malignant, misanthropic, not on speaking terms*, opposed, opposite, quarrelsome, sour, spiteful, surly, uncharitable, uncongenial, unfavorable, unneighborly, unpropitious, unsociable, vengeful, warlike; SEE CONCEPTS *401,548*

**un
un**

ungodly [*adj1*] *not accepting a religious doctrine; impious*
atheistic, blasphemous, corrupt, depraved, godless, improper, indecent, indecorous, indelicate, irreligious, malevolent, profane, rough, sinful, undecorous, unhallowed, unholy, unseemly, vile, wicked; SEE CONCEPTS *542,545*

ungodly [*adj2*] *outrageous*
atrocious, barbarous, dreadful, horrendous, horrid, intolerable, nasty, shocking, unbelievable, uncivilized, unconscionable, unearthly, unreasonable, unseemly; SEE CONCEPTS *529,548,570*

ungrateful [*adj*] *not appreciative*
careless, demanding, dissatisfied, faultfinding, forgetful, grasping, grumbling, heedless, ingrate, insensible, oblivious, self-centered, selfish, thankless, unappreciative, unmindful, unnatural, unthankful; SEE CONCEPT *401*

unguarded [*adj*] *thoughtless; unwary*
accessible, artless, candid, careless, casual, direct, foolhardy, frank, headlong, heedless, honest, ill-considered, impolitic, imprudent, impulsive, incautious, indiscreet, ingenuous, naive, offhand, rash, spontaneous, straightforward, unalert, uncircumspect, unconscious, undiplomatic, unpremeditated, unreflective, unthinking, unvigilant, unwatchful, unwise, vulnerable, weak; SEE CONCEPT *401*

unhappy [*adj1*] *sad*
bleak, bleeding*, blue*, bummed out*, cheerless, crestfallen, dejected, depressed, despondent, destroyed, disconsolate, dismal, dispirited, down*, down and out*, downbeat, downcast, down in the mouth*, dragged, dreary, gloomy, grim, heavy-hearted, hurting, in a blue funk*, in pain, in the dumps*, let-down*, long-faced, low, melancholy, mirthless, miserable, mournful, oppressive, put away*, ripped*, sad, saddened, sorrowful, sorry, teary, troubled; SEE CONCEPT *403*

unhappy [*adj2*] *unfortunate, unlucky*
afflicted, cursed, hapless, ill-fated, ill-starred, luckless, misfortunate, troubled, untoward, wretched; SEE CONCEPT *548*

unharmed [*adj*] *unhurt*
all right, free from danger, in one piece*, intact, not hurt, okay*, out of danger, out of harm's way*, protected, safe, safe and sound*, sound, undamaged, uninjured, unscarred, unscathed, unscratched, untouched; SEE CONCEPTS *314,587*

unhealthy [*adj1*] *sick*
ailing, below par, debilitated, delicate, diseased, down, dragging, feeble, frail, ill, in a decline, infirm, in ill health, in poor health, invalid, laid low*, out of action*, out of shape, peaked, poorly, run-down, shaky, sickly, unsound, unwell, weak; SEE CONCEPT *314*

unhealthy [*adj2*] *very bad in effect on well-being*
baneful, chancy, corrupt, corrupting, dangerous, degenerate, degrading, deleterious, demoralizing, detrimental, harmful, hazardous, insalubrious, jeopardous, morbid, nefarious, negative, noisome, noxious, perilous, perverse, poisonous, risky, rotten, treacherous, undesirable, unhealthful, unsanitary, unsound, unwholesome, villainous, virulent, wicked; SEE CONCEPTS *537,571*

unheard-of [*adj*] *unique, obscure*
exceptional, inconceivable, little-known, nameless, new, novel, outlandish, preposterous, rare, shocking, singular, unbelievable, undiscovered, unfamiliar, unknown, unlikely, unprecedented, unrenowned, unsung, unusual; SEE CONCEPTS *564,576*

unholy [*adj1*] *sacreligious*
base, blameful, corrupt, culpable, depraved, dishonest, evil, godless, guilty, heinous, immoral, impious, iniquitous, irreligious, irreverent, irreverential, profane, sinful, ungodly, unhallowed, unsanctified, vile, wicked; SEE CONCEPTS *542,548*

unholy [*adj2*] *outrageous*
appalling, awful, barbarous, dreadful, horrendous, shocking, uncivilized, unearthly, ungodly, unnatural, unreasonable; SEE CONCEPT *537*

unidentified [*adj*] *secret*
anonymous, mysterious, nameless, not known, pseudonymous, unclassified, unfamiliar, unknown, unmarked, unnamed, unrecognized, unrevealed; SEE CONCEPT *576*

unification [*n*] *joining together*
affinity, alliance, amalgamation, coalescence, coalition, combination, concurrence, confederation, connection, consolidation, coupling, federation, fusion, hookup, interlocking, linkage, melding, merger, merging, union, uniting; SEE CONCEPTS *230,388*

unified [*adj*] *united*
affiliated, allied, banded, collective, combined, consolidated, cooperative, incorporated, joined up, leagued, linked, one, pooled, tied in, together, undivided; SEE CONCEPTS *563,577*

uniform [*adj1*] *consistent*
compatible, consonant, constant, equable, even, fated, fateful, fixed, habitual, homogeneous, immutable, incorrigible, inflexible, invariable, irreversible, level, methodical, monolithic, normal, of a piece*, ordered, orderly, ossified, plumb, regular, reliable, rigid, smooth, stable, static, steady, straight, symmetrical, systematic, true, unalterable, unbroken, unchanging, undeviating, undiversified, unfluctuating, unmodifiable, unvarying, well-balanced, well-proportioned; SEE CONCEPT *534*

uniform [*adj2*] *alike*
agnate, akin, analogous, comparable, consistent, consonant, correspondent, ditto*, double, equal, identical, like, mated, monotonous, parallel, same, same difference*, self-same, similar, treadmill*, undifferentiated, unvaried; SEE CONCEPTS *487,573*

uniform [*n*] *coordinated outfit*
attire, costume, dress, garb, gown, habit, khaki*, livery, monkey suit*, OD*, olive drab*, regalia, regimentals, robe, stripes*, suit; SEE CONCEPT *451*

unify [*v*] *unite*
affiliate, ally, associate, band, become one, bring together, combine, connect, consolidate, cooperate, couple, gather together, hook up with, join, join forces, link, marry, merge, pool, pull together, stick together, wed; SEE CONCEPTS *113,193*

unimaginable [*adj*] *mind-boggling*
beyond wildest dreams*, doubtful, exceptional, extraordinary, fantastic, impossible, improbable, inapprehensible, incogitable, incomprehensible, inconceivable, incredible, indescribable, ineffable, not understandable, rare, singular, unbelievable, uncommon, unheard-of, unique, unknowable, unordinary, unthinkable; SEE CONCEPTS *529,548*

unimaginative [*adj*] *dull, predictable*
banal, barren, bromidic, common, commonplace, derivative, dime a dozen*, dry, dull as dishwater*, flat, hackneyed, ho hum*, lifeless, matter-of-fact, ordinary, pabulum, pedestrian, prosaic, routine, square*, tame, tedious, trite, uncreative, uninspired, unoriginal, unromantic, usual, vanilla*, well-worn, zero*; SEE CONCEPTS *542,547,548*

unimportant [*adj*] *of no real worth, value*
beside the point*, casual, frivolous, frothy, immaterial, inconsequential, inconsiderable, indifferent, insignificant, irrelevant, little, low-ranking, meaningless, minor, minute, negligible, nonessential, nothing*, nugatory, null, of no account, of no consequence, paltry, petty, picayune, second-rate*, shoestring*, slight, trifling, trivial, unnecessary, useless, worthless, zero*, zilch*, zip*; SEE CONCEPT *575*

uninformed [*adj*] *unaware*
blind, caught napping*, daydreaming, deaf, ignorant, inattentive, in the dark*, negligent, not informed, not told, oblivious, out of it*, out to lunch*, unbriefed, unconscious, uneducated, unenlightened, uninstructed, unknowing, unschooled; SEE CONCEPT *402*

uninhibited [*adj*] *free and easy; without restraint*
audacious, candid, cut loose*, expansive, fancy-free*, footloose*, frank, free, hanging out*, informal, instinctive, liberated, natural, no holds barred*, off the cuff*, open, relaxed, spontaneous, unbridled, unchecked, unconstrained, uncontrolled, uncurbed, ungoverned, unhampered, unrepressed, unreserved, unrestrained, unrestricted, unself-conscious, unsuppressed; SEE CONCEPTS *267,401*

uninspired [*adj*] *dull, unoriginal*
bromidic, commonplace, corny*, everyday, heavy-handed, humdrum, indifferent, old hat*, ordinary, phoned in*, ponderous, prosaic, stale, sterile, stock, uncreative, unexciting, unimaginative, unimpressed, uninspiring, uninteresting, uninventive, unmoved, yawn*; SEE CONCEPTS *542,547,548*

unintelligent [*adj*] *stupid*
brainless, deficient, dense, doltish, dumb, empty-headed*, foolish, half-witted*, idiotic, imbecilic, inane, meaningless, mentally deficient, mentally handicapped, mindless, moronic, not intelligent, pointless, senseless, simple, simpleminded, slow, thick-headed*, unthinking, witless; SEE CONCEPTS *402,548*

unintelligible [*adj*] *not understandable*
ambiguous, equivocal, fathomless, Greek*, illegible, impenetrable, inarticulate, incognizable, incoherent, incomprehensible, indecipherable, indistinct, inexplicit, jumbled, meaningless, muddled, obscure, opaque, tenebrous, uncertain, unclear, unexplicit, unfathomable, ungraspable, unknowable, unreadable, vague; SEE CONCEPT *267*

unintentional/unintended [*adj*] *not planned*
accidental, aimless, casual, chance, erratic, extemporaneous, fortuitous, haphazard, inadvertent, involuntary, purposeless, random, unconscious, undesigned, undevised, unexpected, unforeseen, unintended, unplanned, unpremeditated, unthinking, unthought, unwitting; SEE CONCEPTS *401,548*

uninterested [*adj*] *oblivious to*
aloof, apathetic, blasé, bored, bored stiff*, casual, could care less*, detached, disinterested, distant, going through motions*, hard-hearted*, impassive, incurious, indifferent, listless, remote, thick-skinned*, turned off*, unconcerned, uncurious, uninvolved, unresponsive, weary, withdrawn; SEE CONCEPTS *401,403*

uninteresting [*adj*] *boring, uneventful*
arid, banal, big yawn*, bromidic, common, commonplace, depressing, dismal, drab, dreary, dry, dull, dusty*, fatiguing, flat, ho hum*, humdrum, insipid, irksome, jejune, monotonous, nothing*, nowhere*, pedestrian, prosaic, prosy, soporific, stale, stupid, tedious, tired, tiresome, trite, unenjoyable, unentertaining, unexciting, uninspiring, wearisome; SEE CONCEPTS *529,548*

uninterrupted [*adj*] *continuing; unbroken*
ceaseless, consecutive, constant, continual, continuous, direct, endless, interminable, nonstop, peaceful, perpetual, steady, straight, straightforward, sustained, through, unceasing, undisturbed, unending, unremitting; SEE CONCEPTS *482,798*

uninvited [*adj*] *unwanted*
blackballed*, excluded, inadmissible, left out in the cold*, not in the picture*, not wanted, rejected, shut out, unasked, undesired, unpopular, unsolicited, unwelcome; SEE CONCEPTS *529,555, 570*

uninviting [*adj*] *disagreeable, not pleasant*
awful, bad, disgusting, displeasing, distasteful, nasty, nauseating, offensive, repulsive, rotten, sickening, sour, unappealing, unappetizing, unpalatable, unpleasant; SEE CONCEPTS *537,548*

union [*n1*] *merger, joining*
abutment, accord, agglutination, agreement, amalgam, amalgamation, blend, centralization, coadunation, combination, coming together, commixture, compound, concatenation, conciliation, concord, concurrence, confluence, congregation, conjunction, consolidation, correlation, coupling, fusion, harmony, hookup, incorporation, intercourse, joint, junction, juncture, meeting, melding, merging, mixture, seam, symbiosis, synthesis, tie-in, tie-up, unanimity, unification, unison, uniting, unity; SEE CONCEPTS *113,664,714*

union [*n2*] *group with shared interest, cause*
alliance, association, brotherhood, club, coalition, confederacy, confederation, congress, employees, federation, guild, labor union, league, local, order, sisterhood, society, sodality, syndicate, trade union; SEE CONCEPTS *325,381*

unique [*adj1*] *alone, singular*
different, exclusive, individual, lone, one, one and only*, onliest*, only, particular, rare, separate, single, solitary, solo, sui generis, uncommon, unexampled; SEE CONCEPTS *564,577*

unique [*adj2*] *one-of-a-kind; without equal*
anomalous, best, exceptional, extraordinary, far-out*, incomparable, inimitable, matchless, most, nonpareil, novel, only, peerless, primo*, rare, singular, something else*, special, standout, strange, uncommon, unequaled, unexampled, unimaginable, unmatched, unparagoned, unparalleled, unprecedented, unreal, unrivaled, utmost, weird*; SEE CONCEPTS *564,574*

unison [*n*] *harmony*
accord, accordance, agreement, alliance, com-

un
un

munity, concert, concord, concordance, conjunction, consent, consonance, cooperation, federation, league, reciprocity, sympathy, unanimity, union, unity; SEE CONCEPT *664*

unit [*n1*] *whole*
assemblage, assembly, bunch, complement, crew, crowd, detachment, entirety, entity, gang, group, mob, one, outfit, ring, section, system, total, totality; SEE CONCEPTS *432,837*

unit [*n2*] *part*
arm, block, component, constituent, detachment, detail, digit, element, factor, feature, fraction, ingredient, integer, item, joint, layer, length, link, member, module, piece, portion, section, segment, square, wing; SEE CONCEPT *834*

unite [*v*] *combine; join together*
affiliate, ally, amalgamate, associate, band, band together, become one, blend, close ranks*, coadjute, coalesce, commingle, concur, confederate, conjoin, connect, consolidate, cooperate, couple, embody, fuse, gather together, hang together*, harden, hook up with, incorporate, intertwine, join, join forces, keep together, league, link, marry, meet, merge, mix, pool, pull together, relate, solidify, stay together, stick together, strengthen, throw in with*, unify, wed; SEE CONCEPTS *113,193*

united [*adj*] *combined; in agreement*
affiliated, agreed, allied, amalgamated, assembled, associated, banded, coadunate, cognate, collective, concerted, concordant, confederated, congruent, conjoint, conjugate, conjunctive, consolidated, cooperative, corporate, federal, homogeneous, hooked up*, in accord, in cahoots*, incorporated, integrated, joined up, leagued, likeminded*, lined up*, linked, of one mind, of the same opinion, one, plugged in*, pooled, tied in, unanimous, undivided, unified, unitary; SEE CONCEPTS *563,577*

unity [*n*] *wholeness*
accord, agreement, alliance, coadunation, combination, concord, concurrence, confederation, consensus, consent, consonance, entity, federation, harmony, homogeneity, homogeneousness, identity, individuality, indivisibility, integral, integrality, integrity, interconnection, oneness, peace, rapport, sameness, singleness, singularity, soleness, solidarity, synthesis, totality, unanimity, undividedness, unification, uniformity, union, unison; SEE CONCEPTS *664,714,837*

universal [*adj*] *worldwide, entire*
accepted, all, all-embracing, all-inclusive, all-over, astronomical, broad, catholic, celestial, common, comprehensive, cosmic, cosmopolitan, customary, diffuse, ecumenical, empyrean, extensive, general, generic, global, multinational, mundane, omnipresent, planetary, prevalent, regular, stellar, sweeping, terrestrial, total, ubiquitous, undisputed, unlimited, unrestricted, usual, whole, widespread, worldly; SEE CONCEPTS *536,772*

universe [*n*] *everything in creation*
cosmos, everything, macrocosm, natural world, nature, world; SEE CONCEPTS *370,511*

unjust [*adj*] *not fair*
below the belt*, biased, fixed*, inequitable, influenced, low-down*, one-sided, partial, partisan, prejudiced, shabby*, underhand, undeserved, unfair, unforgivable, unjustified,

unmerited, unrighteous, wrong, wrongful; SEE CONCEPT *545*

unjustifiable [*adj*] *unwarranted*
baseless, foundationless, groundless, indefensible, inexcusable, uncalled-for, unconscionable, unforgivable, unfounded, ungrounded, unjust, unjustified, unmerited, unpardonable, wrong; SEE CONCEPTS *545,548,558*

unkempt [*adj*] *shabby, sloppy*
bedraggled, coarse, crude, dilapidated, dirty, disarranged, disarrayed, disheveled, disordered, grubby*, grungy*, messed up, messy, mussed up*, neglected, rough, rumpled, scruffy, shaggy, slipshod, slovenly, tousled, unclean, uncombed, unfastidious, ungroomed, unimproved, unneat, unpolished, untidy, vulgar; SEE CONCEPTS *485,621*

unkind [*adj*] *not nice*
barbarous, brutal, cold-blooded, coldhearted, cruel, hard-hearted, harsh, hateful, heartless, inconsiderate, inhuman, inhumane, insensitive, malevolent, malicious, malignant, mean, nasty, sadistic, savage, spiteful, thoughtless, uncaring, uncharitable, unfeeling, unfriendly, unsympathetic; SEE CONCEPT *401*

unknowing [*adj*] *unaware*
blank, blind, caught napping*, daydreaming, deaf, ignorant, inattentive, in the dark*, negligent, not informed, not knowing, not told, oblivious, out of it*, out to lunch*, unbriefed, unconscious, uneducated, unenlightened, uninformed, uninstructed, unschooled; SEE CONCEPT *402*

unknown [*adj*] *obscure, mysterious*
alien, anonymous, concealed, dark, desolate, distant, exotic, far, faraway, far-off, foreign, hidden, humble, incog*, incognito, little known, nameless, new, remote, secret, so-and-so*, strange, such-and-such*, unapprehended, unascertained, uncelebrated, uncharted, undiscovered, undistinguished, unexplained, unexplored, unfamiliar, unheard-of, unidentified, unnamed, unnoted, unperceived, unrecognized, unrenowned, unrevealed, unsung, untold, X*; SEE CONCEPT *576*

unlawful [*adj*] *against the law*
actionable, banned, bootleg*, criminal, flagitious, forbidden, illegal, illegitimate, illicit, improper, iniquitous, lawless, nefarious, outlawed, prohibited, taboo, unauthorized, under-the-counter*, unlicensed, wrongful; SEE CONCEPT *319*

unlike [*adj*] *different*
apples and oranges*, clashing, conflicting, contradictory, contrary, contrasted, discordant, disharmonious, disparate, dissimilar, dissonant, distant, distinct, divergent, diverse, far cry from*, heterogeneous, hostile, incompatible, incongruous, inconsistent, mismatched, not alike, offbeat, opposed, opposite, poles apart*, separate, unalike, unequal, unrelated, variant, various, weird; SEE CONCEPT *564*

unlikely [*adj*] *not probable*
absurd, contrary, doubtful, dubious, faint, implausible, improbable, inconceivable, incredible, not likely, out of the ordinary, outside chance, questionable, rare, remote, slight, strange, unbelievable, unconvincing, unheard-of, unimaginable, untoward; SEE CONCEPT *552*

unlimited [*adj*] *extensive, complete*
absolute, all-encompassing, all-out*, boundless,

countless, endless, full, full-blown*, full-out*, full-scale, great, illimitable, immeasurable, immense, incalculable, incomprehensible, indefinite, infinite, interminable, limitless, measureless, no end of*, no end to*, no strings*, numberless, total, totalitarian, unbounded, unconditional, unconfined, unconstrained, unfathomed, unfettered, universal, unqualified, unrestrained, unrestricted, untold, vast, wide open; SEE CONCEPT *772*

unload [v] *take off; empty*
break bulk, cast, clear out, disburden, discharge, discommode, disencumber, disgorge, dump, get rid of, jettison, lighten, off-load, relieve, remove, rid, slough, take a load off, unburden, unlade, unpack, void; SEE CONCEPTS *180,211*

unlock [v] *open; solve*
break in, crack, decipher, free, jimmy, liberate, open the door*, pop, release, set free, solve, unbolt, unbutton, uncork, undo, unfasten, unhook, unlatch, unravel, unseal, unshut; SEE CONCEPTS *135,250,469*

unlucky [adj] *unfortunate, doomed*
afflicted, bad break*, behind eight ball*, black, calamitous, cataclysmic, catastrophic, cursed, dire, disastrous, down on luck*, hapless, hard luck, ill-fated, ill-starred, inauspicious, luckless, miserable, ominous, out of luck, star-crossed*, tough luck, tragic, unfavorable, unhappy, unsuccessful, untimely, untoward; SEE CONCEPTS *529,548*

unmanageable [adj] *unruly, wild*
awkward, berserk, chaotic, crazy, disobedient, disorderly, hysterical, lawless, madcap, nuts, out of control, outrageous, riotous, rowdy, turbulent, unbridled, uncontrollable, uncontrolled, undisciplined, ungovernable, unrestrained, violent; SEE CONCEPT *401*

unmarried [adj] *not presently wed*
bachelor, eligible, husbandless, single, sole, spouseless, unattached, uncoupled, unwed, unwedded, widowed, wifeless; SEE CONCEPT *555*

unmask [v] *reveal*
acknowledge, admit, announce, bare, bring out into the open*, bring to light*, come out with, confess, disclose, display, divulge, exhibit, expose, leak, let cat out of the bag*, make known, make public, show, tell, unclothe, uncover, unearth, unveil; SEE CONCEPTS *60,138*

unmerciful [adj] *cruel*
bestial, bloodthirsty, brutal, coldhearted, hard, heartless, hurtful, implacable, inhumane, merciless, monstrous, pitiless, relentless, remorseless, ruthless, tyrannous, uncaring, unfeeling, unpitying, unrelenting, unsparing, vengeful, vindictive; SEE CONCEPT *401*

unmistakable [adj] *certain, definite*
apparent, clear, conspicuous, decided, distinct, evident, explicit, for certain, glaring, indisputable, manifest, no ifs ands or buts*, obvious, open and shut*, palpable, patent, plain, positive, pronounced, self-explanatory, straightforward, sure, transparent, unambiguous, unequivocal, univocal; SEE CONCEPT *535*

unmitigated [adj] *absolute, pure*
arrant, austere, clear-cut, complete, consummate, damned, downright, gross, intense, oppressive, out-and-out*, outright, perfect, persistent, rank, relentless, rigid, severe, sheer, simple, straightout*, thorough, thoroughgoing, unabated,

unabridged, unadulterated, unalleviated, unbending, unbroken, undiluted, unmixed, unqualified, unrelieved, utter; SEE CONCEPTS *531,535,569*

unmotivated [adj] *uninspired*
apathetic, dull, everyday, humdrum, indifferent, lazy, old hat*, ordinary, prosaic, stale, unambitious, uncreative, unexciting, unimaginative, uninspiring, uninteresting, unmoved; SEE CONCEPTS *542,547,548*

unnatural [adj] *not regular; artificial*
aberrant, abnormal, affected, anomalous, assumed, bizarre, concocted, contrary, contrived, ersatz*, extraordinary, fabricated, factitious, false, feigned, forced, freakish, freaky, imitation, incredible, insincere, irregular, labored, made-up*, make-believe*, odd, outlandish, outrageous, perverse, perverted, phony, preposterous, pseudo*, put-on*, queer, staged, stiff, stilted*, strained, strange, studied, supernatural, synthetic, theatrical, unaccountable, uncanny, unconforming, unorthodox, unusual; SEE CONCEPTS *564,582*

unnecessary [adj] *not required*
accidental, additional, avoidable, beside the point*, casual, causeless, chance, dispensable, excess, exorbitant, expendable, extraneous, extrinsic, fortuitous, futile, gratuitous, haphazard, inessential, irrelevant, lavish, needless, noncompulsory, nonessential, optional, prodigal, profuse, random, redundant, supererogatory, superfluous, surplus, uncalled-for, uncritical, undesirable, unessential, unneeded, unrequired, useless, wanton, worthless; SEE CONCEPT *546*

unnerve [v] *upset, intimidate*
agitate, bewilder, bowl over*, buffalo*, chill*, confound, daunt, demoralize, disarm, discombobulate, disconcert, discourage, dishearten, dismay, dispirit, distract, enervate, enfeeble, floor*, fluster, frighten, get to*, give a turn*, intimidate, needle*, perturb, psych out*, rattle, ride, sap*, shake, spook, throw, throw off*, uncalm, undermine, unhinge, unsettle, weaken; SEE CONCEPTS *7,14,19*

unnoticed [adj] *ignored*
disregarded, glossed over, hidden, inconspicuous, neglected, overlooked, passed by, pushed aside, secret, unconsidered, undiscovered, unheeded, unobserved, unobtrusive, unperceived, unrecognized, unremarked, unremembered, unrespected, unseen, winked at; SEE CONCEPT *529*

unobtrusive [adj] *keeping a low profile*
humble, inconspicuous, low-key, low-profile, meek, modest, quiet, reserved, restrained, retiring, self-effacing, soft-pedaled*, subdued, tasteful, unassuming, unnoticeable, unostentatious, unpretentious; SEE CONCEPTS *401,548*

unorganized [adj] *disorderly, disorganized*
all over the place*, chaotic, cluttered, confused, dislocated, disordered, jumbled, messed up, messy, mixed up, scattered, scrambled, sloppy, unarranged, unkempt, unsystematic, untidy; SEE CONCEPTS *485,535*

unorthodox [adj] *abnormal; other than accepted*
beatnik*, crazy*, different, dissident, eccentric, far-out, flaky*, heretical, heterodox, irregular, kinky*, nonconformist, off the beaten path*, schismatic, sectarian, unconventional, uncustomary, unusual, unwonted, way-out*, weird*; SEE CONCEPT *564*

unpaid [adj] *free, voluntary*
contributed, donated, due, freewilled, gratuitous,

honorary, unindemnified, unrewarded, unsalaried, volunteer; SEE CONCEPT 538

unpaid [adj2] *not settled; taken without remuneration*
delinquent, due, in arrears, mature, not discharged, outstanding, overdue, owing, past due, payable, undefrayed, unliquidated, unsettled; SEE CONCEPT 334

unparalleled [adj] *superlative*
all-time*, alone, beyond compare, champ*, champion, consummate, exceptional, greatest, incomparable, matchless, most, nonpareil, only, peerless, rare, single, singular, solid gold*, ten*, tops*, unequaled, unique, unmatched, unprecedented, unrivaled, unsurpassed, winner, without equal, world-class*; SEE CONCEPT 574

unpleasant [adj] *bad*
abhorrent, bad news*, bad scene*, disagreeable, displeasing, distasteful, fierce, grody*, gross, hard-time*, icky*, irksome, lousy, nasty, objectionable, obnoxious, poisonous, repulsive, rotten, sour, troublesome, unacceptable, unattractive, uncool*, undesirable, unhappy, unlikable, unlovely, unpalatable, yucky*; SEE CONCEPTS 529,570

unpopular [adj] *not liked or sought after*
abhorred, avoided, creepy*, despised, detested, disesteemed, disfavored, disliked, drip*, dumpy*, execrated, gross*, loathed, loser*, lousy, nerdy*, obnoxious, ostracized, out, out of favor, rejected, scorned, shunned, unaccepted, unattractive, uncared for, undesirable, unloved, unvalued, unwanted, unwelcome, weird, wimpy*; SEE CONCEPTS 529,555

unprecedented [adj] *exceptional, original*
aberrant, abnormal, anomalous, bizarre, eccentric, exotic, extraordinary, fantastic, freakish, idiosyncratic, marvelous, miraculous, modern, new, newfangled, novel, odd, outlandish, out-of-the-way*, outré, preternatural, prodigious, remarkable, signal, singular, sui generis, uncommon, unexampled, unheard-of, unique, unparalleled, unrivaled, unusual; SEE CONCEPTS 549,564,574

unpredictable [adj] *changeable*
capricious, chance, chancy, dicey*, doubtful, erratic, fickle, fluctuating, fluky*, from left field*, hanging by a thread*, iffy*, incalculable, inconstant, random, touch and go*, touchy, uncertain, unforeseeable, unreliable, unstable, up for grabs*, variable, whimsical; SEE CONCEPT 534

unprejudiced [adj] *fair*
balanced, dispassionate, equal, equitable, evenhanded, fair-minded, impartial, just, liberal, nondiscriminatory, nonpartisan, objective, openminded, straight, unbiased, unbigoted, uncolored, uninfluenced; SEE CONCEPTS 319,401,542

unprepared [adj] *not ready*
ad-lib*, caught off guard*, ill-considered, impromptu, improvised, napping, not prepared, offhand, off the cuff*, off the top of one's head*, played by ear*, spontaneous, surprised, taken off guard*, unaware, unexpected, unplanned, unready, unrehearsed, unschooled, unskilled, untrained, vulnerable, winged*; SEE CONCEPT 267

unpretentious [adj] *simple, honest*
discreet, down, down home*, easy-going, folksy*, free-spirited, homey*, humble, inelaborate, laid-back*, lowly, modest, plain, prosaic, straightforward, unaffected, unambitious, unassuming, unbeautified, uncomplex, unembellished, unimposing, unobtrusive, unostentatious, unpresumptuous, unspoiled, up front; SEE CONCEPTS 401,404

unprincipled [adj] *corrupt*
abandoned, amoral, bent*, cheating, conscienceless, crooked, deceitful, devious, dirty-dealing*, dishonest, dissolute, double-crossing*, doubledealing*, immoral, licentious, mercenary, praetorian, profligate, reprobate, shady, sly, stop-at-nothing*, tricky, two-faced*, two-timing*, unconscionable, underhand, unethical, unprofessional, unscrupulous, venal, wanton; SEE CONCEPT 545

unproductive [adj] *idle, nonproductive*
barren, empty, fruitless, futile, ineffective, infertile, pointless, sterile, trivial, unprofitable, useless, worthless; SEE CONCEPTS 267,560

unprofessional [adj] *not done well or skillfully*
amateur, amateurish, ignorant, improper, inadequate, incompetent, inefficient, inexperienced, inexpert, lax, negligent, nonexpert, unethical, unfitting, unsuitable, untrained, unworthy; SEE CONCEPTS 527,538

unprotected [adj] *defenseless*
caught, endangered, exposed, helpless, indefensible, in the line of fire*, like a sitting duck*, naked*, open, out on a limb*, powerless, pregnable, unarmed, unguarded, unsafe, vulnerable, weak, wide open*; SEE CONCEPTS 555,576

unqualified [adj1] *not prepared, incompetent*
amateur, bush, bush-league*, disqualified, ill-equipped, inadequate, incapable, incompetent, ineligible, inexperienced, not equal to, not up to*, unequipped, unfit, unfitted, unprepared, unskilled; SEE CONCEPT 527

unqualified [adj2] *outright, absolute*
abiding, blasted, blessed, categorical, certain, clear, complete, confounded, consummate, downright, enduring, entire, explicit, express, firm, flat out*, infernal, never-failing, no catch*, no ifs ands or buts*, out-and-out*, perfect, positive, rank, sheer, simple, steadfast, steady, sure, thorough, thoroughgoing, total, unadulterated, unalloyed, unconditional, unfaltering, unlimited, unmitigated, unreserved, unrestrained, unrestricted, utter, wholehearted, without reservation; SEE CONCEPTS 531,535

unquestionable [adj] *definite; beyond doubt*
absolute, accurate, authentic, bona fide*, certain, clear, cold, conclusive, dependable, down pat*, downright, established, faultless, flat*, flawless, for certain, genuine, incontestable, incontrovertible, indisputable, indubitable, irrefutable, manifest, no ifs ands or buts*, obvious, pat, patent, perfect, positive, real, reliable, self-evident, superior, sure, sure-enough, true, undeniable, undisputable, undoubted, unequivocal, unimpeachable, unmistakable, veritable, wellfounded, well-grounded; SEE CONCEPTS 529,535

unreadable [adj] *illegible*
cacographic, crabbed, difficult to read, hard to make out*, incomprehensible, indecipherable, scrawled, scribbled, unclear, undecipherable; SEE CONCEPTS 535,576

unreal [adj] *fake, make-believe; hypothetical*
aerial, artificial, chimerical, delusive, dreamlike, fabled, fabulous, false, fanciful, fictitious, fictive, figmental, hallucinatory, ideal, illusory, imaginary, imagined, immaterial, impalpable, insin-

cere, insubstantial, intangible, invented, legendary, misleading, mock, mythical, nebulous, nonexistent, notional, ostensible, phantasmagoric*, pretended, reachy, romantic, seeming, sham*, storybook*, suppositious, supposititious, theoretical, unbelievable, unsubstantial, visionary; SEE CONCEPT *582*

unrealistic [*adj*] *not believable or practical*
blue sky*, floating, gone*, half-baked*, impossible, impracticable, impractical, improbable, ivory-tower*, nonrealistic, nonsensical, not applicable, not sensible, on cloud nine*, quixotic, reachy, romantic, silly, starry-eyed, theoretical, unreal, unworkable; SEE CONCEPTS *552,560*

unreasonable [*adj1*] *not logical or sensible*
absurd, all wet*, arbitrary, biased, capricious, contradictory, erratic, fallacious, far-fetched, foolish, full of hot air*, headstrong, illogical, incoherent, incongruous, inconsequential, inconsistent, invalid, irrational, loose, mad, nonsensical, off the wall*, opinionated, preposterous, quirky, reasonless, senseless, silly, stupid, thoughtless, unreasoned, vacant, wrong; SEE CONCEPTS *401,548*

unreasonable [*adj2*] *extravagant; beyond normal limits*
absonant, arbitrary, costing an arm and a leg*, dear, excessive, exorbitant, extortionate, extreme, far-out*, illegitimate, immoderate, improper, inordinate, intemperate, out of bounds*, overkill*, overmuch, peremptory, posh, pricey*, senseless, steep*, stiff*, too great, too much, too-too*, uncalled-for*, unconscionable, undue, unfair, unjust, unjustifiable, unlawful, unrightful, unwarrantable, unwarranted, up to here*, way out*, wrongful; SEE CONCEPTS *334,762,771*

unrehearsed [*adj*] *spontaneous*
ad-lib*, extemporaneous, from the hip*, impromptu, improvised, impulsive, not rehearsed, off the cuff*, off the top of one's head*, spur of the moment, unpracticed, unprepared; SEE CONCEPTS *401,542,548*

unrelated [*adj*] *independent; different*
beside the point*, dissimilar, extraneous, inapplicable, inappropriate, irrelative, irrelevant, mismatched, nongermane, not germane, not kin, not kindred, not related, separate, unassociated, unattached, unconnected, unlike; SEE CONCEPTS *563,564*

unrelenting [*adj*] *merciless*
bound, bound and determined, brick-wall*, ceaseless, constant, continual, continuous, cruel, dead set on*, endless, grim, hanging tough*, hard-headed*, implacable, incessant, inexorable, intransigent, iron-fisted, mortal, perpetual, persistent, pitiless, relentless, remorseless, rigid, ruthless, set, steady, stern, stiff, stiff-necked*, tenacious, tough, unabated, unbending, unbroken, unflinching, unremitting, unsparing, unwavering, unyielding; SEE CONCEPTS *401,548,798*

unreliable [*adj*] *not trustworthy, not true*
capricious, deceitful, deceptive, delusive, disreputable, dubious, erroneous, fake, fallible, false, fickle, fly-by-night*, furtive, hallucinatory, hollow, implausible, inaccurate, inconstant, irresponsible, makeshift, meretricious, mistaken, pretended, pseudo*, questionable, sham, shifty, specious, treacherous, tricky, uncertain, unconvincing, undependable, underhand, underhanded, unfaithful, unsound, unstable, unsure, untrue, untrustworthy, vacillating, wavering, weak; SEE CONCEPTS *542,552,587*

unresolved [*adj*] *uncertain; not settled*
betwixt and between*, changing, doubtful, faltering, hesitant, hesitating, hot and cold*, incomplete, indecisive, irresolute, moot, open to question*, pending, problematical, pussyfooting*, unanswered, unconcluded, undecided, undetermined, unfinished, unsettled, unsolved, up in the air*, vacillating, vague, waffling; SEE CONCEPTS *529,534*

unrest [*n*] *state of agitation; disturbance*
altercation, anarchy, annoyance, anxiety, bickering, bother, chagrin, change, confusion, contention, controversy, crisis, debate, disaffection, discontent, discord, disease, disquiet, dissatisfaction, dissension, distress, dither*, ennui, grief, insurrection, irritation, malaise, moodiness, mortification, perplexity, perturbation, protest, quarrel, rebellion, restlessness, sedition, sorrow, strife, tension, tizzy*, trouble, tumult, turmoil, unease, uneasiness, uproar, upset, vexation, worry; SEE CONCEPTS *410,674*

unrestricted [*adj*] *free*
able, allowed, at liberty, free-spirited, independent, lax, liberal, liberated, on one's own*, open, relaxed, unbounded, uncommitted, unconditional, unconstrained, unlimited, unregulated; SEE CONCEPTS *401,542*

unrivaled [*adj*] *peerless*
best, beyond compare, champion, excellent, faultless, greatest, incomparable, matchless, outstanding, perfect, second to none*, super, superior, supreme, tops*, unequaled, unmatched, unparalleled, unsurpassed, without equal; SEE CONCEPT *574*

unruly [*adj*] *disobedient*
assertive, bawdy, disorderly, drunken, forward, fractious, headstrong, heedless, impervious, impetuous, imprudent, impulsive, incorrigible, inexorable, insubordinate, intemperate, intractable, lawless, mean, mutinous, obstreperous, opinionated, ornery, out of control, out of line*, perverse, quarrelsome, rash, rebellious, recalcitrant, reckless, refractory, restive, riotous, rowdy, turbulent, uncontrollable, ungovernable, unmanageable, unyielding, violent, wayward, wild, willful; SEE CONCEPT *401*

unsafe [*adj*] *dangerous*
alarming, chancy, erratic, explosive, fearsome, hanging by a thread*, hazardous, insecure, on a limb*, on thin ice*, perilous, precarious, risky, shaky, slippery, threatening, ticklish*, touch and go*, touchy*, treacherous, uncertain, undependable, unreliable, unsound, unstable, untrustworthy; SEE CONCEPT *587*

unsaid [*adj*] *not expressed or partially expressed*
implicit, implied, inferred, left to the imagination*, silenced, tacit, undeclared, understood, unexpressed, unspoken, unstated, unuttered, unvoiced, wordless; SEE CONCEPT *267*

unsanitary [*adj*] *dirty, unclean*
contaminated, dusty, filthy, foul, grimy, messy, muddy, polluted, rancid, rank, rotten, sloppy, soiled, stained, stinking, sullied, tarnished, unhealthful, unhealthy, unhygienic; SEE CONCEPT *621*

unsatisfactory [*adj*] *insufficient, inadequate*
amiss, bad, damaged, deficient, disappointing, disconcerting, displeasing, disquieting, distress-

un
un

ing, disturbing, for the birds*, junky*, lame, mediocre, no good, not good enough, not up to par*, offensive, poor, regrettable, rotten, schlocky*, second, thin, unacceptable, undesirable, unsuitable, unwelcome, unworthy, upsetting, vexing, weak, wrong; SEE CONCEPTS *529,558,570*

unsavory [adj] *revolting, sickening*
acid, bitter, bland, disagreeable, distasteful, dull, flavorless, gross*, icky*, insipid, lousy, nasty, nauseating, no good*, objectionable, obnoxious, offensive, rancid, rank, raunchy*, repellent, repugnant, repulsive, rough, sad, shady, sharp, shifty, sour, stinking, tart, tasteless, tough, unappetizing, unpalatable, unpleasant, wrong; SEE CONCEPTS *462,571,613*

unscathed [adj] *not hurt*
in one piece*, safe, sound, unharmed, unhurt, uninjured, unmarked, unscarred, unscratched, untouched, whole; SEE CONCEPT *314*

unscrupulous [adj] *immoral*
arrant, base, casuistic, conscienceless, corrupt, crafty, crooked, deceitful, degraded, degrading, disgraceful, dishonest, dishonorable, exploitative, illegal, improper, low-down*, mercenary, perfidious, petty, questionable, recreant, ruthless, scandalous, scheming, selfish, self-seeking, shady, shameless, shifty, sinister, slippery, sly, two-faced*, unconscientious, unconscionable, underhand, underhanded, unethical, unfair, unprincipled, unworthy, venal, wicked, wrongful; SEE CONCEPTS *401,545*

unseemly [adj] *improper; in bad taste*
cheap, coarse, crude, discreditable, disreputable, inappropriate, inapt, incorrect, indecent, indecorous, indelicate, inelegant, inept, in poor taste, malapropos, malodorous, out of keeping, out of place, poor, raffish, rough, rowdy, rude, ruffian, tawdry, unapt, unbecoming, unbefitting, undignified, ungodly, unrefined, unsuitable, untoward, vulgar, wrong; SEE CONCEPTS *401,558*

unseen [adj] *hidden*
concealed, curtained, dark, imaginary, imagined, impalpable, impenetrable, imperceptible, inconspicuous, invisible, lurking, not in sight, obscure, occult, out of sight, shrouded, undetected, undiscovered, unnoticed, unobserved, unobtrusive, unperceived, unsuspected, veiled; SEE CONCEPT *576*

unselfish [adj] *kind, giving*
altruistic, benevolent, charitable, chivalrous, denying, devoted, disinterested, extroverted, generous, helpful, humanitarian, incorruptible, indulgent, liberal, loving, magnanimous, noble, open-handed, self-effacing, self-forgetting, selfless, self-sacrificing; SEE CONCEPTS *401,404*

unsettle [v] *bother, upset*
agitate, confuse, dement, derange, disarrange, disarray, discommode, discompose, disconcert, disorder, disorganize, displace, disquiet, disrupt, disturb, down, flurry, fluster, fuddle, get to*, jumble, needle, perturb, psych out*, put off, rattle, ruffle, rummage, sicken, spook, throw, throw off*, trouble, turn, unbalance, unhinge*, unnerve; SEE CONCEPTS *7,19,242*

unsettled [adj1] *bothered, upset*
active, agitated, antsy*, anxious, busy, changeable, changeful, changing, complex, complicated, confused, disorderly, disturbed, explosive, fidgety, fluid, flustered, inconstant, insecure, ki-

netic, mobile, mutable, on edge*, perilous, perturbed, precarious, rattled, restive, restless, shaken, shaky, shifting, shook up*, tense, thrown, ticklish, troubled, unbalanced, uncertain, uneasy, unnerved, unpeaceful, unpredictable, unquiet, unrestful, unstable, unsteady, variable, wavering, wobbling; SEE CONCEPTS *401,403*

unsettled [adj2] *not decided, taken care of*
betwixt and between*, clouded*, debatable, doubtful, dubious, dubitable, due, immature, in arrears, moot, open, outstanding, overdue, owing, payable, pendent, pending, problematic, uncertain, unclear, undecided, undetermined, unfixed, unpaid, unresolved, up for grabs*, waffling; SEE CONCEPTS *334,535*

unsightly [adj] *not pretty*
deformed, disagreeable, drab, dull, hideous, homely, horrid, lackluster, repulsive, revolting, ugly, unattractive, unpleasant, unprepossessing, unshapely; SEE CONCEPT *579*

unskilled [adj] *untrained*
awkward, green*, inadequate, incompetent, inept, inexperienced, inexpert, inproficient, not up to*, raw*, unable, undeveloped, uneducated, unequipped, unhandy, unqualified, unschooled, untalented; SEE CONCEPT *527*

unsociable [adj] *unfriendly*
aloof, antagonistic, brooding, cold, cool, distant, easy-going, hostile, inaccessible, inhospitable, introverted, laid-back*, nongregarious, recessive, reclusive, reserved, retiring, secretive, sensitive, shy, standoffish*, stuck-up*, timid, unapproachable, unbending, uncommunicative, uncongenial, unforthcoming, unneighborly, unsocial, uppity*, withdrawn; SEE CONCEPTS *401,555*

unsolicited [adj] *unasked for*
free, freewilled, gratis*, gratuitous, offered, spontaneous, uncalled-for*, undesirable, undesired, unforced, uninvited, unrequested, unsought, unwelcome, voluntary, volunteered; SEE CONCEPT *538*

unsophisticated [adj] *natural, simple*
artless, authentic, bush-league*, callow, childlike, clean, cornball*, corny*, crude, folksy, genuine, green*, guileless, homey*, inexperienced, ingenuous, innocent, kid*, naive, plain, pure, raw, rookie, straightforward, unadulterated, unaffected, unartificial, uncomplicated, uninvolved, unrefined, unschooled, unstudied, untutored, unworldly, wide-eyed*; SEE CONCEPTS *401,548,562*

unsound [adj] *not well; flimsy*
ailing, crazed, dangerous, decrepit, defective, delicate, demented, deranged, diseased, erroneous, fallacious, false, faulty, flawed, fragile, frail, ill, illogical, inaccurate, incongruous, incorrect, infirm, in poor health, insane, insecure, insubstantial, invalid, lunatic, mad, not solid, rickety, shaky, specious, tottering, unbacked, unbalanced, unhealthy, unhinged, unreliable, unsafe, unstable, unsteady, unsubstantial, unwell, weak, wobbly; SEE CONCEPTS *314,403,587*

unspeakable [adj] *very bad; beyond description*
abominable, alarming, appalling, atrocious, awful, beastly, beyond words, calamitous, detestable, dire, disgusting, dreadful, evil, execrable, fearful, frightening, frightful, heinous, horrible, horrid, incommunicable, inconceivable, indefinable, indescribable, ineffable, inexpressible, inhuman, loathsome, monstrous, nameless,

obnoxious, odious, offensive, outrageous, overwhelming, preternatural, repellent, repugnant, repulsive, revolting, shocking, unbelievable, unimaginable, unutterable; SEE CONCEPTS 548,571

unspoiled [adj] *fresh*
clean, clear, crisp, just out*, latest, natural, new, original, pristine, pure, recent, refreshing, sparkling, uncontaminated, unpolluted, unprocessed, untainted, untouched, whole, young; SEE CONCEPTS 537,578,797

unstable/unsteady [adj] *doubtful, weak*
ambiguous, borderline, capricious, changeable, dizzy, dubious, erratic, fickle, fitful, fluctuating, giddy, inconsistent, inconstant, insecure, irrational, lubricious, mercurial, mobile, movable, moving, mutable, not fixed, precarious, rickety, risky, rocky, sensitive, shaky, shifty, slippery, suspect, teetering, temperamental, ticklish, tricky, uncertain, unpredictable, unsettled, unsteady, untrustworthy, vacillating, variable, volatile, wavering, weaving, wiggly, wobbly; SEE CONCEPTS 488,534,542

unsubstantiated [adj] *questionable, unproven*
arguable, controversial, debatable, disputable, doubtful, dubious, dubitable, fishy*, hard to believe, iffy*, indefinite, open to doubt, open to question, suspect, suspicious, uncertain, unconfirmed, uncorroborated, unsupported; SEE CONCEPTS 529,535

unsuccessful [adj] *failing*
abortive, defeated, disastrous, doomed, failed, foiled, fruitless, futile, ill-fated, ineffective, ineffectual, losing, thwarted, unlucky, useless, vain; SEE CONCEPTS 485,489

unsuitable [adj] *not proper, inappropriate*
clashing, disagreeable, discordant, discrepant, disparate, disproportionate, dissident, dissonant, ill-suited, improper, inadequate, inadmissible, inapposite, inappropriate, inapt, incompatible, incongruous, inconsistent, ineligible, infelicitous, inharmonious, interfering, irrelevant, jarring, malapropos, out of character*, out of keeping, out of place, senseless, unacceptable, unbecoming, unbefitting, uncalled-for, undue, unfit, unfitting, unmatched, unseasonable, unseemly, unsuited; SEE CONCEPT 558

unsung [adj] *uncelebrated*
anonymous, disregarded, forgotten, nameless, neglected, overlooked, unacclaimed, unacknowledged, undistinguished, unfamed, unglorified, unhailed, unhonored, unknown, unnamed, unrecognized, unrenowned; SEE CONCEPTS 267,576

unsure [adj] *doubtful, insecure*
betwixt and between*, borderline, distrustful, dubious, fluctuant, fly-by-night*, hesitant, iffy*, in a quandary, indecisive, indeterminate, irresolute, lacking, mistrustful, open, problematic, rootless, shaky, skeptical, suspicious, touch and go*, unassured, uncertain, unclear, unconfident, unconvinced, undecided, undependable, unreliable, unstable, untrustworthy, untrusty, up for grabs*, vacillating, wavering, weak, wimpy*, wobbly; SEE CONCEPT 535

unsurpassed [adj] *supreme*
absolute, best, culminating, excellent, final, first, foremost, greatest, highest, incomparable, leading, matchless, paramount, peerless, perfect, prevailing, superior, top, ultimate, unequaled,

unmatched, unparalleled, unrivaled; SEE CONCEPTS 568,574

unsuspecting [adj] *gullible*
confiding, credulous, easy, inexperienced, ingenuous, innocent, naive, off guard*, simple, swallowing, taken in*, trustful, trusting, unconscious, undoubting, unsuspicious, unwarned, unwary; SEE CONCEPTS 401,404

unsympathetic [adj] *without agreement in feeling*
aloof, antipathetic, apathetic, aversive, callous, cold, cold-blooded, cool, cruel, disinterested, frigid, halfhearted, hard, harsh, heartless, icy, indifferent, insensitive, lukewarm*, mean, nasty, obdurate, repellent, repugnant, stony, tough, uncompassionate, unconcerned, uncongenial, unemotional, unfeeling, unkind, unmoved, unpitying, unpleasant, unresponsive; SEE CONCEPTS 401,542

untamed [adj] *wild*
barbarian, barbaric, barbarous, feral, ferocious, fierce, native, overgrown, overrun, rampant, savage, uncivilized, uncontrollable, uncultivated, undomesticated, uninhabited, unmanageable, vicious; SEE CONCEPTS 406,583

untangle [v] *straighten out*
clear up, disembroil, disencumber, disentangle, explain, extricate, put in order, solve, unravel, unscramble, unsnarl, untwist, unweave; SEE CONCEPT 126

unthinkable [adj] *incredible, unusual*
absurd, beyond belief, beyond possibility, exceptional, extraordinary, illogical, implausible, impossible, improbable, incogitable, inconceivable, insupportable, outlandish, out of the question*, preposterous, rare, singular, unbelievable, uncommon, unimaginable, unique, unlikely, unordinary, unreasonable; SEE CONCEPTS 564,582

unthinking [adj] *careless*
blundering, brutish, feckless, foolish, heedless, impulsive, inadvertent, inconsiderate, indelicate, insensitive, instinctive, mechanical, napping, negligent, oblivious, outrageous, rash, rude, selfish, senseless, tactless, thoughtless, uncaring, unconscious, undiplomatic, unheeding, unintended, unmeant, unmindful, unpremeditated, unreasoning, untactful, unwise, vacant, witless; SEE CONCEPT 401

untidy [adj] *dirty, disorderly*
bedraggled, careless, chaotic, cluttered, disarranged, disarrayed, disheveled, dowdy*, frowzy*, in disorder, jumbled, littered, mess, messy, mixed up*, muddled, rumpled, slapdash*, slipshod*, sloppy, slovenly, snarled, tacky*, tangled, topsy-turvy, tousled, uncombed, unfastidious, unkempt, unneat, unorderly, unsettled, upset; SEE CONCEPTS 589,621

until [prep] *just before*
as far as, before, before the coming, continuously, down to, in advance of, in expectation, prior to, till, to, up till, up to; SEE CONCEPT 820

untimely [adj] *inappropriate*
a bit previous*, abortive, anachronistic, awkward, badly timed, bright and early*, disagreeable, early, early bird*, early on, ill-timed, improper, inappropriate, inauspicious, inconvenient, inexpedient, inopportune, intrusive, malapropos, mistimed, out-of-date, overearly, oversoon, premature, previous, soon, too early, too late, undue, unfavorable, unfit, unfortunate,

unlucky, unpropitious, unseasonable, unseemly, unsuitable, unsuited, wrong; SEE CONCEPTS 548,799

untiring [*adj*] *determined, persevering*
constant, continued, continuing, dedicated, devoted, dogged, eager beaver*, fireball*, firm, go-go*, grind*, hyper*, incessant, indefatigable, indomitable, inexhaustible, jumping, patient, perky, persistent, pertinacious, plodding, plugging, resolute, staunch, steady, strong, tenacious, tireless, unceasing, undeterred, unfailing, unfaltering, unflagging, unflinching, unremitting, unstinted, unswerving, unwavering, unwearied; SEE CONCEPT 538

untold [*adj*] *very many; enormous*
beyond measure, countless, gigantic, hidden, huge, immense, incalculable, indescribable, inexpressible, innumerable, innumerous, mammoth, manifold, many, measureless, mighty, monstrous, multiple, multitudinous, myriad, numberless, private, prodigious, staggering, suppressed, titanic, uncountable, uncounted, undreamed of, unexpressed, unimaginable, unknown, unnumberable, unnumbered, unspeakable, unthinkable, vast; SEE CONCEPTS 529,762,781

untouched [*adj*] *whole; not spoiled*
clear, entire, flawless, fresh, good, immaculate, incorrupt, indifferent, in good condition, intact, out of danger, perfect, pure, safe and sound*, sanitary, secure, shipshape, sound, spotless, unaffected, unblemished, unbroken, unconcerned, undamaged, unharmed, unhurt, unimpressed, uninjured, unmarred, unmoved, unscathed, unstained, unstirred, untried, virgin, virginal, without a scratch; SEE CONCEPTS 403,485,621

untoward [*adj 1*] *troublesome*
adverse, annoying, awkward, contrary, disastrous, disturbing, fractious, hapless, ill-starred, inauspicious, inconvenient, indocile, inimical, inopportune, intractable, irritating, luckless, misfortunate, perverse, recalcitrant, refractory, star-crossed, undisciplined, unfavorable, unfortunate, ungovernable, unhappy, unlucky, unmanageable, unpliable, unpropitious, unruly, untimely, unyielding, vexatious, wild; SEE CONCEPTS 542,548,570

untoward [*adj 2*] *improper; not suitable*
improprietous, inappropriate, indecent, indecorous, indelicate, malodorous, out of place*, rough*, unbecoming, uncouth, unfitting, ungodly*, unseemly; SEE CONCEPTS 401,558

untroubled [*adj*] *calm, peaceful*
composed, cool, halcyon, hushed, placid, quiet, serene, steady, still, tranquil, unagitated, unconcerned, undisturbed, unflappable, unflustered, unperturbed, unruffled, unstirred, unworried; SEE CONCEPTS 403,548,594

untrue [*adj*] *dishonest*
apocryphal, cheating, counterfactual, deceitful, deceptive, delusive, deviant, disloyal, dissembling, distorted, erroneous, faithless, fallacious, false, fictitious, forsworn, hollow, imprecise, inaccurate, inconstant, incorrect, inexact, lying, meretricious, misleading, mistaken, off*, out of line*, perfidious, perjured, prevaricating, recreant, sham*, specious, spurious, traitorous, treacherous, two-faced*, unfaithful, unloyal, unsound, untrustworthy, untruthful, wide, wrong; SEE CONCEPTS 267,545,582

untrustworthy [*adj*] *not dependable, unfaithful*
capricious, conniving, crooked, deceitful, devious, dishonest, disloyal, dubious, fair-weather*, faithless, false, fickle, fink*, fly-by-night*, guileful, irresponsible, questionable, shady, sharp, shifty*, slippery, sneaky, treacherous, tricky, trustless, two-faced*, two-timing*, unassured, undependable, unfaithful, unreliable, unsafe, unsure, untrue, untrusty; SEE CONCEPTS 401,542,545

untruthful [*adj*] *dishonest*
bluffing, cheating, corrupt, crooked, deceitful, deceiving, deceptive, disreputable, double-crossing, double-dealing, false, fraudulent, lying, misleading, shady, shifty, sneaking, sneaky, tricky, two-faced*, two-timing*, underhanded, untrustworthy; SEE CONCEPT 267

unusual [*adj*] *different*
abnormal, amazing, astonishing, atypical, awe-inspiring, awesome, bizarre, conspicuous, curious, different, distinguished, eminent, exceptional, extraordinary, far-out*, inconceivable, incredible, memorable, noteworthy, odd, out of the ordinary*, outstanding, phenomenal, prodigious, prominent, queer, rare, refreshing, remarkable, significant, singular, something else*, special, strange, surprising, uncommon, unconventional, unexpected, unfamiliar, unique, unparalleled, unwonted, weird*; SEE CONCEPT 564

unusually [*adv*] *extremely*
almighty*, awful*, awfully, curiously, especially, extra, extraordinarily, mighty, oddly, peculiarly, plenty, powerful, rarely, real, really, remarkably, right, so, so much, strangely, surprisingly, terribly, terrifically, too much, uncommon, uncommonly, very; SEE CONCEPTS 544,569

unvarnished [*adj*] *plain, honest*
bare, candid, clean, folksy*, for real*, frank, genuine, homey*, naked, open, open and shut*, pure, pure and simple*, simple, sincere, stark, straight, straightforward, unadorned, unconcealed, undisguised, undissembled, unembellished, vanilla*; SEE CONCEPTS 267,582

unveil [*v*] *reveal*
bare, betray, bring to light*, come out, disclose, discover, display, divulge, expose, give away, lay bare*, lay open*, let it all hang out*, make known, make public, open, open up, show, spring, tell, tip one's hand*, unbosom, uncover; SEE CONCEPTS 60,138

unwarranted [*adj*] *not reasonable or right*
baseless, bottomless, foundationless, gratuitous, groundless, indefensible, inexcusable, uncalled-for, unconscionable, undue, unfair, unfounded, ungrounded, unjust, unjustifiable, unjustified, unprovoked, unreasonable, unwarrantable, wrong; SEE CONCEPTS 545,548,558

unwary [*adj*] *thoughtless, heedless*
brash, careless, credulous, hasty, ignorant, ill-advised, impetuous, imprudent, incautious, inconsiderate, indiscreet, negligent, rash, reckless, unadvised, unalert, uncircumspect, unguarded, unprepared, unsuspecting, unsuspicious, unvigilant, unwatchful; SEE CONCEPTS 401,403

unwavering [*adj*] *consistent, unchanging*
abiding, brick-wall*, dead set on*, dedicated, determined, enduring, firm, fixed, intense, never-failing, pat, regular, resolute, set, set in stone*, single-minded, solid, staunch, steadfast, steady,

sure, undeviating, unfaltering, unflagging, unflappable, unqualified, unshakable, unshaken, unswerving, untiring; SEE CONCEPTS *488,535,542*

unwelcome [*adj*] *not wanted, desired*
blackballed*, disagreeable, displeasing, distasteful, exceptionable, excess baggage*, excluded, ill-favored, inadmissible, left out in cold*, lousy, not in the picture*, objectionable, obnoxious, rejected, repellent, shut out, thankless, unacceptable, unasked, undesirable, uninvited, unpleasant, unpopular, unsought, unwanted, unwished-for; SEE CONCEPTS *529,555,570*

unwell [*adj*] *sick*
ailing, bedridden, broken down, debilitated, diseased, feeble, feverish, frail, hospitalized, ill, impaired, incurable, infected, infirm, in poor health, invalid, laid-up, nauseated, not feeling well, run down, sick as a dog*, sickly, suffering, under medication, under the weather*, unhealthy, weak; SEE CONCEPT *314*

unwieldy [*adj*] *awkward, bulky*
burdensome, clumsy, cumbersome, cumbrous, encumbering, gross, hefty, inconvenient, lumbering, massive, onerous, ponderous, uncontrollable, ungainly, unhandy, unmanageable, weighty; SEE CONCEPTS *562,781*

unwilling [*adj*] *not in the mood*
afraid, against, against the grain*, averse, backward, begrudging, compelled, contrary, demurring, disinclined, disobliging, evasive, forced, grudging, hesitating, indisposed, indocile, involuntary, laggard, loath, malcontent, opposed, recalcitrant, refractory, reluctant, remiss, resistant, shrinking, shy, slack, slow, unaccommodating, uncheerful, uncooperative, uneager, unenthusiastic, uninclined, unobliging, unready, unwishful, wayward; SEE CONCEPTS *401,542*

unwind [*v1*] *undo, untangle*
disentangle, free, loose, loosen, ravel, separate, slacken, unbend, uncoil, unfurl, unravel, unreel, unroll, untwine, untwist, unwrap; SEE CONCEPT *158*

unwind [*v2*] *relax*
calm down*, ease off*, loosen up*, quiet down*, quieten, recline, rest, sit back*, slow down*, take a break*, take it easy*, wind down*; SEE CONCEPT *210*

unwise [*adj*] *stupid, irresponsible*
childish, foolhardy, foolish, ill-advised, ill-considered, immature, impolitic, improvident, imprudent, inadvisable, inane, inappropriate, indiscreet, inept, injudicious, misguided, naive, rash, reckless, senseless, short-sighted, silly, thoughtless, undesirable, unfortunate, unintelligent, unsound, witless; SEE CONCEPTS *401,402,548*

unwitting [*adj*] *without fully realizing*
accidental, aimless, chance, comatose, forgetful, haphazard, ignorant, inadvertent, incognizant, inconversant, innocent, involuntary, numb, oblivious, senseless, unacquainted, unaware, unconscious, undesigned, unfamiliar, uninformed, uninstructed, unintended, unintentional, unknowing, unmeant, unmindful, unplanned, unsuspecting, unthinking; SEE CONCEPTS *401,544,548*

unworldly [*adj1*] *spiritual*
abstract, astral, celestial, daydreaming, daydreamy, dreamy, ethereal, extraterrestrial, fantastic, incorporeal, metaphysical, nonmaterialistic, otherworldly, religious, supersensory, transcendental, unearthly, unreal, visionary; SEE CONCEPTS *536,582*

unworldly [*adj2*] *not sophisticated; inexperienced*
artless, babe in woods*, clean, corn-fed*, country, folksy*, green*, idealistic, ingenuous, innocent, naive, natural, raw*, simple, trusting, unaffected, unartificial, uncool, unschooled, unsophisticated, unstudied, wide-eyed*; SEE CONCEPTS *401,555,589*

unworthy [*adj*] *not of value*
base, beneath, blamable, contemptible, degrading, disgraceful, dishonorable, disreputable, good-for-nothing, ignoble, improper, inappropriate, ineligible, inexcusable, no-account*, no-good*, not deserving, not fit, not good enough, nothing, not worth, offensive, out of place*, recreant, reprehensible, shameful, unbecoming, unbefitting, undeserving, unfit, unmerited, unseemly, unsuitable, valueless, vile, wretched, wrong; SEE CONCEPTS *404,558,571*

unwritten [*adj*] *understood*
accepted, conventional, customary, oral, spoken, tacit, traditional, unformulated, unrecorded, unsaid, verbal, vocal, word-of-mouth; SEE CONCEPTS *267,533*

unyielding [*adj*] *steadfast, resolute*
adamant, dead set on*, determined, firm, fixed, hard, hard-core*, hardheaded, hard-line*, hard-nosed*, headstrong*, immalleable, immovable, implacable, impliable, inexorable, inflexible, intractable, locked in, merciless, mulish, obdurate, obstinate, pertinacious, pigheaded*, refractory, relentless, resolute, rigid, ruthless, single-minded, solid, staunch, stiff, stiff-necked, stubborn, tough, unbending, uncompliant, uncompromising, unmovable, unrelenting, unswayable, unwavering; SEE CONCEPTS *401,542*

up-and-coming [*adj*] *rising*
ambitious, climbing, coming on strong*, determined, eager, enterprising, get up and go*, go-getter*, high-reaching, hungry, promising, soaring, striving, succeeding; SEE CONCEPTS *326,542*

upbeat [*adj*] *cheerful*
buoyant, cheery, encouraging, favorable, fond, happy, heartening, hopeful, optimistic, positive, promising, rosy, sanguine; SEE CONCEPTS *403,572*

upbraid [*v*] *scold*
admonish, berate, blame, castigate, censure, chasten, chastise, chew out*, chide, criticize, give a talking-to*, jump on*, lay down the law*, lecture, light into*, put down, rake over the coals*, ream, reprimand, reproach, take to task*, tell off*; SEE CONCEPTS *44,52,54*

update [*v*] *bring up to date*
amend, modernize, refresh, refurbish, rejuvenate, renew, renovate, restore, revise; SEE CONCEPT *244*

upgrade [*v*] *improve*
advance, better, boost, elevate, enhance, increase, lift, make better, make strides, move up, progress, promote, raise; SEE CONCEPTS *244,700*

upheaval [*n*] *major change*
about-face*, alteration, cataclysm, catastrophe, clamor, commotion, convulsion, disaster, disorder, disruption, disturbance, eruption, explosion,

un
up

ferment, flip-flop*, new ball-game*, new deal*, outbreak, outburst, outcry, overthrow, revolution, shakeout*, stirring, switch, temblor, tremor, tumult, turmoil, turnaround, upturn; SEE CONCEPT *230*

uphill [*adj1*] *going up*
acclivous, ascending, climbing, mounting, rising, skyward, sloping upward, toward summit, up, uprising; SEE CONCEPT *581*

uphill [*adj2*] *difficult, laborious*
arduous, effortful, exhausting, grueling, hard, labored, operose, punishing, rugged, strenuous, taxing, toilsome, tough, wearisome; SEE CONCEPTS *538,565*

uphold [*v*] *maintain, support*
advocate, aid, assist, back, back up, bolster, boost, brace, buoy up, buttress, carry, champion, confirm, countenance, defend, elevate, encourage, endorse, help, hoist, hold to, hold up one's end*, justify, pick up, promote, prop, raise, rear, second, shore up, side with, stand by, stick by, stick up for*, sustain, take up, upbear, uplift, upraise, uprear, vindicate; SEE CONCEPT *110*

upkeep [*n*] *maintenance*
budget, conservation, costs, expenditure, expenses, keep, outlay, overhead, preservation, price, repair, running, subsistence, support, sustenance, sustentation; SEE CONCEPTS *117,344*

uplift [*v*] *elevate, inspire*
boost, brighten, bring up, cheer, elate, excite, exhilarate, improve, lift up*, perk up*, raise spirits; SEE CONCEPTS *7,22*

upper [*adj1*] *above*
high, higher, loftier, more elevated, overhead, top, topmost, uppermost, upward; SEE CONCEPT *583*

upper [*adj2*] *superior*
beautiful, elevated, elite, eminent, greater, important, more important; SEE CONCEPTS *555,567*

upper hand [*n*] *advantage*
benefit, break, control, dominance, edge, favor, gain, help, improvement, leverage, rule, superiority, supremacy; SEE CONCEPT *574*

uppermost [*adj1*] *top*
apical, culminating, highest, loftiest, most elevated, topmost, upmost; SEE CONCEPT *583*

uppermost [*adj2*] *most important; chief*
best, big, boss, dominant, executive, foremost, greatest, high-up*, leading, main, paramount, predominant, preeminent, primary, principal, supreme, the most*, tops*, winner, world-class*; SEE CONCEPTS *568,632*

uppity [*adj*] *arrogant*
audacious, bossy, bragging, cavalier, cheeky, cocky, conceited, egotistic, haughty, high and mighty*, high falutin*, know-it-all*, overbearing, pompous, presumptuous, pretentious, puffed up*, self-important, smug, snobbish, snooty*, snotty*, stuck up*, superior, vain; SEE CONCEPTS *401,404*

upright [*adj1*] *straight-up*
cocked, end on, end up, erect, on end, perpendicular, plumb, raised, sheer, standing, stand-up, steep, straight, upended, upstanding, upward, vertical; SEE CONCEPTS *581,583*

upright [*adj2*] *honorable, honest*
aboveboard, blameless, circumspect, conscientious, correct, equitable, ethical, exemplary, fair, faithful, good, high-minded, impartial, incorruptible, just, kosher*, legit*, moral, noble, princi-

pled, punctilious, pure, right, righteous, square, straight, straightforward, true, true-blue*, trustworthy, unimpeachable, up front*, virtuous; SEE CONCEPTS *404,545*

uprising [*n*] *disturbance*
insurgence, insurrection, mutiny, outbreak, rebellion, revolt, revolution, riot, upheaval; SEE CONCEPTS *106,674*

uproar [*n*] *commotion, pandemonium*
ado, babble, babel, bedlam, bickering, big scene*, brawl, broil*, bustle, chaos, clamor, clangor, clatter, confusion, din, disorder, flap*, fracas*, free-for-all*, furor, fuss, hassle, jangle, mayhem, melee, noise, outcry, racket, riot, roughhouse*, row, ruction, shivaree*, stink*, stir, strife, to-do*, turbulence, turmoil, violence; SEE CONCEPTS *46,65,106,674*

uproot [*v*] *destroy; rip out of a place*
abate, abolish, annihilate, blot out, demolish, deracinate, dig up, displace, do away with*, eliminate, eradicate, excavate, exile, exterminate, extirpate, extract, move, overthrow, overturn, pull up, remove, root out, tear up, weed, weed out, wipe out; SEE CONCEPTS *147,178,211,252*

upset [*adj*] *disturbed, bothered*
agitated, all torn up*, amazed, antsy*, apprehensive, blue*, broken up*, bummed out*, capsized, chaotic, come apart*, confused, disconcerted, dismayed, disordered, disquieted, distressed, disturbed, dragged*, frantic, grieved, hurt, ill, in disarray, jittery, jumpy, low, muddled, overturned, overwrought, psyched out*, rattled, ruffled*, shocked, shook up*, sick, spilled, thrown, tipped over, toppled, troubled, tumbled, unglued*, unsettled, unzipped*, upside-down, worried; SEE CONCEPTS *403,485,570*

upset [*n*] *problem*
agitation, bother, complaint, defeat, destruction, disorder, disquiet, distress, disturbance, free-for-all*, goulash*, hassle, illness, malady, overthrow, queasiness, reverse, reversion, screw-up*, shake-up*, shock, sickness, stew*, subversion, surprise, tizzy*, trouble, turmoil, worry; SEE CONCEPT *674*

upset [*v1*] *disorder; knock over*
capsize, change, derange, disarray, disorganize, disturb, invert, jumble, keel over, mess up*, mix up, muddle, overset, overturn, pitch, put out of order, reverse, rummage, spill, spoil, subvert, tilt, tip over, topple, tumble, turn, turn inside-out*, turn topsy-turvy*, turn upside-down*, unsettle, upend, upturn; SEE CONCEPTS *147,208,213*

upset [*v2*] *bother, trouble*
adjy*, afflict, agitate, ail, bewilder, bug*, confound, cramp, craze, debilitate, derange, discombobulate*, discompose, disconcert, dismay, disquiet, distract, distress, disturb, egg on*, fire up*, flip*, flip out*, floor*, flurry, fluster, get to*, give a hard time*, grieve, incapacitate, indispose, key up*, lay up, make a scene*, make waves*, perturb, pick on*, pother, psych*, rattle, rock the boat*, ruffle, sicken, spook, stir up, throw off balance*, turn, turn on, unhinge*, unnerve, unsettle; SEE CONCEPTS *7,19*

upset [*v3*] *defeat*
beat, be victorious, conquer, get the better of*, outplay, overcome, overpower, overthrow, overturn, topple, triumph over, win; SEE CONCEPT *95*

upshot [*n*] *end result*
aftereffect, aftermath, burden, climax, completion, conclusion, consequence, core, culmina-

tion, denouement, development, effect, end, ending, event, eventuality, finale, finish, gist, issue, meaning, meat*, outcome, payoff, pith*, purport, result, sense, sequel, substance, termination, thrust; SEE CONCEPTS *230,682*

upside-down [*adj*] *overturned, inverted*
backward, bottom-side up, bottom up, confused, disordered, downside-up*, haywire*, helter-skelter*, in chaos, in disarray, jumbled, mixed-up, on head, reversed, tangled, topsy-turvy*, upended, wrong-side-up, wrong way; SEE CONCEPT *583*

upstanding [*adj*] *honorable*
ethical, good, honest, incorruptible, moral, principled, straightforward, true, trustworthy, upright; SEE CONCEPT *545*

upstart [*n*] *newly rich*
name-dropper, nouveau riche, parvenue, social climber, status seeker; SEE CONCEPT *347*

uptight [*adj*] *nervous*
anxious, apprehensive, cautious, concerned, conventional, edgy, nervy, old-fashioned, on edge*, on the defensive*, restive, strict, tense, troubled, uneasy, withdrawn, worried; SEE CONCEPT *401*

up-to-date [*adj*] *current, modern*
abreast, advanced, a' la mode*, all the rage*, au courant, avant-garde, brand-new, contemporary, cutting edge*, dashing, expedient, faddish*, fashionable, fitting, hot*, in, in fashion, in-thing*, in vogue, modernistic, modish, neoteric, new, newest, newfangled, now*, opportune, popular, red-hot*, state-of-the-art*, stylish, suitable, timely, today*, trendy, up*, up-to-the-minute, with it*; SEE CONCEPTS *578,589,797,799*

urban [*adj*] *city*
burghal, central, citified, civic, civil, downtown, inner-city, metropolitan, municipal, nonrural, oppidan, popular, public, town, village; SEE CONCEPT *536*

urbane [*adj*] *civilized*
affable, balanced, bland, civil, cosmopolitan, courteous, cultivated, cultured, debonair, elegant, genteel, gracious, mannerly, metropolitan, obliging, poised, polished, polite, refined, smooth, sophisticated, suave, well-bred, well-mannered; SEE CONCEPT *401*

urchin [*n*] *mischievious youngster*
brat*, cub, dickens*, gamin, imp, juvenile delinquent, punk*, pup*, ragamuffin, waif; SEE CONCEPT *423*

urge [*n*] *very strong desire*
appetite, appetition, compulsion, craving, drive, druthers, fancy, fire in belly*, goad, impetus, impulse, incentive, itch*, longing, lust, motive, passion, pressure, stimulant, stimulus, sweet tooth*, weakness, wish, yearning, yen; SEE CONCEPTS *20,532*

urge [*v*] *beg, push for, encourage*
adjure, advance, advise, advocate, appeal to, ask, attract, beseech, champion, charge, commend, compel, conjure, counsel, countenance, drive, egg on*, endorse, entreat, exhort, favor, fire up*, force, further, goad, hasten, impel, implore, incite, induce, influence, insist on, inspire, instigate, maneuver, move, plead, press, promote, prompt, propel, propose, push, put up to*, rationalize, recommend, request, sanction, solicit, speak for, spur, stimulate, support, tempt, wheedle; SEE CONCEPTS *68,75*

urgent [*adj*] *needing immediate attention*
burning*, called-for, capital, chief, clamant,

clamorous, compelling, critical, crucial, crying*, demanded, demanding, driving, essential, exigent, foremost, heavy*, hurry-up, immediate, impelling, imperative, important, importunate, indispensable, insistent, instant, leading, life and death*, momentous, necessary, paramount, persuasive, pressing, primary, principal, required, salient, serious, top-priority, touch and go*, touchy*, vital, wanted, weighty*; SEE CONCEPTS *548,568*

usable [*adj*] *available, working*
accessible, adaptable, advantageous, applicable, at disposal, at hand, beneficial, consumable, convenient, current, employable, exhaustible, expendable, exploitable, fit, functional, good, helpful, in order, instrumental, open, operative, practicable, practical, profitable, ready, running, serviceable, subservient, unused, useful, utile, utilizable, valid, valuable, wieldy; SEE CONCEPTS *560,576*

usage [*n*] *habit, custom*
acceptance, control, convention, currency, form, formula, habitude, handling, management, matter of course, method, mode, operation, practice, praxis, procedure, regime, regulation, rote, routine, rule, running, tradition, treatment, trick, use, way, wont; SEE CONCEPTS *6,658*

use [*n*] *application; employment*
account, adoption, advantage, appliance, applicability, appropriateness, avail, benefit, call, capitalization, cause, convenience, custom, end, exercise, exercising, exertion, fitness, good, habit, handling, help, helpfulness, mileage, mobilization, necessity, need, object, occasion, operation, point, practice, profit, purpose, reason, relevance, service, serviceability, treatment, usability, usage, usefulness, utility, value, way, wear and tear*, wont, worth; SEE CONCEPTS *225,658,709*

use [*v*] *work with; consume*
accept, adopt, apply, avail oneself of, bestow, bring into play*, bring to bear*, capitalize, control, do with, draw on, employ, exercise, exert, exhaust, expend, exploit, find a use, govern, handle, make do with*, make the most of*, make use, manage, manipulate, operate, play on, ply, practice, press into service*, put forth*, put into action, put to use, put to work, regulate, relate, run, run through, set in motion, spend, take advantage of*, turn to account, utilize, waste, wield, work; SEE CONCEPTS *169,225*

used [*adj*] *secondhand*
hand-me-down, nearly new, not new, passed down, pre-owned, recycled, worn; SEE CONCEPTS *334,567,574*

used to [*adj*] *familiar with*
acclimated, accustomed, at home with*, common, commonplace, customary, everyday, knowing, known, old hat*, ordinary, plain, recognizable, routine, well-known; SEE CONCEPTS *530,547*

useful [*adj*] *beneficial, valuable*
advantageous, all-purpose, applied, appropriate, brave, commodious, convenient, effective, favorable, fit, fruitful, functional, good, handy, helpful, instrumental, meet, of assistance, of service, of use, practicable, practical, pragmatic, profitable, proper, propitious, purposive, salutary, serviceable, subsidiary, suitable, suited, toward, utile, utilitarian, workaday, worthwhile; SEE CONCEPT *560*

up
us

useless [*adj*] *not working; not valuable*
abortive, bootless, counterproductive, disadvantageous, dysfunctional, expendable, feckless, fruitless, futile, good-for-nothing*, hopeless, idle, impracticable, impractical, incompetent, ineffective, ineffectual, inept, inoperative, inutile, meaningless, no good, nonfunctional, of no use, pointless, profitless, purposeless, scrap, stupid*, unavailable, unavailing, unfunctional, unproductive, unprofitable, unpurposed, unusuable, unworkable, vain, valueless, waste, weak, worthless; SEE CONCEPT *560*

user-friendly [*adj*] *easily operated*
accessible, adaptable, convenient, easy to use, feasible, foolproof, handy, manageable, practical, simple, straightforward, uncomplicated, useful, wieldy; SEE CONCEPTS *560,576*

usher [*n*] *person who guides others to place*
attendant, conductor, doorkeeper, doorperson, escort, guide, herald, lead, leader, page, pilot, precursor; SEE CONCEPT *352*

usher [*v*] *guide*
bring in, conduct, direct, escort, herald, inaugurate, initiate, institute, introduce, launch, lead, marshal, open the door, originate, pave the way*, pilot, precede, preface, receive, set up, show around, show in, show out, steer; SEE CONCEPTS *187,221*

usual [*adj*] *common, typical*
accepted, accustomed, average, chronic, commonplace, constant, conventional, current, customary, cut-and-dried*, everyday, expected, familiar, fixed, frequent, garden variety*, general, grind, habitual, mainstream, matter-of-course, natural, normal, ordinary, plain, plastic, prevailing, prevalent, quotidian, regular, rife, routine, run-of-the-mill*, so-so*, standard, stock, typic, unremarkable, vanilla*, white-bread*, wonted, workaday; SEE CONCEPTS *530,547*

usually [*adv*] *for the most part*
as a rule, as is the custom, as is usual, as usual, by and large, commonly, consistently, customarily, frequently, generally, habitually, in the main, mainly, more often than not, mostly, most often, normally, now and again, now and then, occasionally, once and again, on the whole, ordinarily, regularly, routinely, sometimes; SEE CONCEPTS *530,541*

usurp [*v*] *take over*
accroach, annex, appropriate, arrogate, assume, barge in*, butt in*, clap hands on*, commandeer, cut out, displace, elbow in*, get hands on*, grab, grab hold of, highjack*, infringe upon, lay hold of, muscle in*, preempt, seize, squeeze in, supplant, swipe, take, work in, worm in*, wrest; SEE CONCEPTS *142,384*

utensil [*n*] *tool, usually for eating*
apparatus, appliance, contrivance, convenience, device, equipment, fork, gadget, implement, instrument, knife, silverware, spoon, tableware, ware; SEE CONCEPTS *493,499*

utilitarian [*adj*] *practical*
commonsensical, down-to-earth, effective, efficient, functional, hard, hardheaded, matter-of-fact, nuts and bolts*, pragmatic, pragmatical, realistic, sensible, serviceable, unidealistic, unromantic, useful; SEE CONCEPT *560*

utility [*n*] *serviceableness*
account, adequacy, advantage, advantageousness, applicability, appropriateness, avail, benefit, convenience, efficacy, efficiency, expediency, favor, fitness, function, point, practicality, productiveness, profit, relevance, service, serviceability, use, usefulness; SEE CONCEPT *658*

utilize [*v*] *make use of*
advance, apply, appropriate, avail oneself of, bestow, employ, exercise, exploit, forward, further, handle, have recourse to, profit by, promote, put to use, resort to, take advantage of, turn to account, use; SEE CONCEPT *225*

utmost [*adj*] *extreme, maximum*
absolute, all-out*, chief, complete, entire, exhaustive, farthest, final, full, furthermost, greatest, highest, last, last straw*, maximal, most, most distant, outermost, out of bounds*, outside, paramount, plenary, preeminent, remotest, sheer, supreme, thorough, thoroughgoing, too much*, too-too*, top, topmost, total, ultimate, ultra*, unconditional, undiminished, unlimited, unmitigated, unqualified, unreserved, uttermost, whole, worst case*; SEE CONCEPTS *531,574,772*

utopia [*n*] *ideal place and life*
Arcadia, bliss, dreamland, dreamworld, Eden, Elysian Fields*, Erewhon*, fairyland, Garden of Eden, heaven, land of milk and honey*, never-never land*, paradise, perfection, pie in the sky*, promised land*, seventh heaven*, Shangri-La*, wonderland; SEE CONCEPTS *370,689*

utopian [*adj*] *imaginary, ideal*
abstract, airy, ambitious, arcadian, chimerical, dream, fanciful, fantasy, grandiose, hopeful, idealist, idealistic, ideological, illusory, impossible, impractical, lofty, otherworldly, perfect, pie-in-the-sky*, pretentious, quixotic, romantic, transcendental, unfeasible, visionary; SEE CONCEPTS *572,574,582*

utter [*adj*] *outright, absolute*
all-fired*, arrant, blasted*, blessed*, blooming*, complete, confounded, consummate, downright, entire, flat-out*, infernal, out-and-out*, perfect, pure, sheer, stark, straight-out*, thorough, thoroughgoing, total, unmitigated, unqualified; SEE CONCEPTS *531,535*

utter [*v*] *say, reveal*
affirm, air, announce, articulate, assert, asseverate, blurt, bring out, chime, chin*, come out with*, declaim, declare, deliver, disclose, divulge, ejaculate, enunciate, exclaim, express, give words to*, go, jaw*, lip*, make known, modulate, mouth*, mutter, proclaim, promulgate, pronounce, publish, put into words, recite, say, shout, speak, spiel*, state, talk, throw out, verbalize, vocalize, voice, whisper; SEE CONCEPTS *47,55*

utterance [*n*] *revelation*
announcement, articulation, assertion, asseveration, declaration, delivery, discourse, ejaculation, expression, opinion, oration, peroration, pronouncement, rant, recitation, remark, reply, response, saying, sentence, speaking, speech, spiel, statement, talk, vent, verbalization, vocalization, vociferation, voice, word, words; SEE CONCEPTS *47,278*

utterly [*adv*] *completely*
absolutely, all, all in all, altogether, entirely, exactly, extremely, fully, in toto, just, perfectly, plumb*, purely, quite, thoroughly, totally, to the core*, to the nth degree*, well, wholly; SEE CONCEPT *531*

uttermost [*adj*] *extreme*
farthest, final, furthermost, furthest, last, outermost, outmost, remotest, utmost; SEE CONCEPTS *585,778*

V

vacancy [*n*] *opening*
abstraction, blankness, desertedness, emptiness, gap, job, lack, opportunity, position, post, room, situation, space, vacuity, vacuousness, vacuum, void, voidness; SEE CONCEPTS *513,516,693*

vacant [*adj1*] *empty; unoccupied*
abandoned, available, bare, clear, deserted, devoid, disengaged, free, idle, not in use, stark, tenantless, to let, unemployed, unengaged, unfilled, uninhabited, unlived in, untaken, untenanted, unused, void, without contents; SEE CONCEPTS *481,560,740,774*

vacant [*adj2*] *absent-minded; expressionless*
abstracted, blank, daydreaming, deadpan, dreaming, dreamy, empty-headed*, foolish, idle, inane, incurious, inexpressive, silly, stupid, thoughtless, unexpressive, unintelligent, unthinking, vacuous, vapid, witless; SEE CONCEPT *402*

vacate [*v*] *leave empty*
abandon, abrogate, annul, clear, depart, discharge, dissolve, empty, evacuate, give up, go away, leave, move out, move out of, part with, quash, quit, relinquish, renounce, rescind, retract, reverse, revoke, void, withdraw; SEE CONCEPTS *195,234*

vacation [*n*] *planned time spent not working*
break, breathing space*, day of rest, few days off*, fiesta, furlough, holiday, intermission, layoff, leave, leave of absence, liberty, long weekend*, R and R*, recess, recreation, respite, rest, sabbatical, spell, time off, two weeks with pay*; SEE CONCEPTS *363,807*

vaccinate [*v*] *give a shot to treat or prevent disease*
immunize, inject, inoculate, mitigate, prevent, protect, treat, variolate; SEE CONCEPT *310*

vaccination [*n*] *immunization*
inoculation, shot*; SEE CONCEPT *307*

vacillate [*v*] *go back and forth*
alternate, be indecisive, be irresolute, change, change mind, dither, fence-straddle*, fluctuate, hedge, hem and haw*, hesitate, hover, oscillate, pause, pussyfoot around*, reel, rock, run hot and cold*, seesaw*, shilly-shally*, stagger, straddle, sway, swing, waffle, waver, whiffle*, yo-yo*; SEE CONCEPT *13*

vacuous [*adj*] *empty; unintelligent*
airheaded*, birdbrained*, blank, drained, dull, dumb, emptied, foolish, half-baked*, inane, lamebrained*, minus*, shallow, silly*, stupid, superficial, uncomprehending, unreasoning, vacant, void; SEE CONCEPT *402*

vacuum [*n*] *emptiness*
exhaustion, free space, gap, nothingness, rarefaction, space, vacuity, void; SEE CONCEPTS *513,740*

vagabond [*adj*] *unsettled; vagrant*
aimless, destitute, down-and-out*, drifting, errant, fancy-free*, fly-by-night*, footloose*, idle, itinerant, itinerate, journeying, mendicant, migratory, moving, nomadic, perambulant, perambulatory, peripatetic, prodigal, rambling, roaming, rootless, roving, sauntering, shifting, shiftless, straggling, stray, strolling, transient, travelling, unsettled, wandering, wayfaring, wayward; SEE CONCEPT *539*

vagabond [*n*] *person who leads an unsettled life; traveler*
explorer, gypsy, haji, pathfinder, pilgrim, pioneer, rambler, rover, tourist, trailblazer, trekker, wanderer, wayfarer; SEE CONCEPT *423*

vagary [*n*] *caprice*
crotchet, fancy, fool notion*, humor, idea, impulse, inconsistency, inconstancy, notion, quirk, whim, whimsy; SEE CONCEPTS *13,410*

vagrant [*n*] *person with no permanent home and often with no means of support*
drifter, floater, homeless person, itinerant, rolling stone*, street person, transient, wanderer; SEE CONCEPT *423*

vague [*adj*] *not definite or clear*
ambiguous, amorphous, amphibological, bewildering, bleary, blurred, cloudy, dark, dim, doubtful, dreamlike, dubious, enigmatic, equivocal, faint, fuzzy, generalized, hazy, ill-defined, impalpable, imprecise, indefinite, indeterminate, indistinct, inexplicable, lax, loose, misunderstood, muddy, nebulous, obscure, perplexing, problematic, puzzling, questionable, shadowy, superficial, tenebrous, uncertain, unclear, undetermined, unexplicit, unintelligible, unknown, unsettled, unspecified, unsure; SEE CONCEPTS *267,485,529*

vain [*adj1*] *egotistical*
arrogant, big-headed*, boastful, cocky*, conceited, egocentric, egoistic, haughty, high-and-mighty*, inflated, narcissistic, ostentatious, overweening, pleased with oneself*, proud, puffed up*, self-important, stuck-up*, swaggering*, swollen-headed*, vainglorious; SEE CONCEPTS *401,404*

vain [*adj2*] *futile, useless*
abortive, barren, bootless, delusive, delusory, empty, frivolous, fruitless, going nowhere*, hollow, idle, inefficacious, insignificant, in vicious circle*, misleading, not a prayer*, no-win*, nugatory, on a treadmill*, otiose, paltry, petty, pointless, profitless, puny, senseless, shuck, slight, sterile, time-wasting, trifling, trivial, unavailing, unimportant, unnotable, unproductive, unprofitable, valueless, void, worthless; SEE CONCEPTS *552,575*

vainglorious [*adj*] *boastful, proud*
arrogant, blowing one's own horn*, boasting, bragging, cavalier, cocky*, conceited, egotistic, egotistical, haughty, high-and-mighty*, highhanded*, huffy*, overbearing, pompous, presumptuous, pretentious, puffed up*, self-important, snobbish, snooty*, strutting, stuck-up*, swaggering, vain; SEE CONCEPTS *401,542*

vainglory [*n*] *pride*
arrogance, big-headedness*, boastfulness, bragging, cockiness*, conceit, condescension, egoism, egotism, haughtiness, huff, overconfidence, patronage, presumption, pretension, self-importance, smugness, snobbery, strutting, swagger, swelled head*, vanity; SEE CONCEPT *633*

us
va

valedictory [*adj*] *farewell*
departing, final, goodbye, last, parting, terminal;
SEE CONCEPT *267*

valiant [*adj*] *brave*
adventurous, assertive, audacious, bold, brave,
chivalrous, courageous, dauntless, fearless, fire-
eating*, gallant, game, grand, great, gritty*,
gutsy*, gutty*, heroic, high-spirited, indomitable, intrepid, lion-hearted, magnanimous,
nervy*, noble, plucky*, powerful, puissant, redoubtable, self-reliant, spunky*, stalwart, steadfast, stout, stouthearted, strong-willed, unafraid,
undaunted, undismayed, valorous, venturesome,
venturous, vigorous, worthy; SEE CONCEPTS
401,404,538

valid [*adj*] *right, genuine*
accurate, attested, authentic, authoritative, binding, bona fide, cogent, compelling, conclusive,
confirmed, convincing, credible, determinative,
efficacious, efficient, good, in force, irrefutable,
just, kosher*, lawful, legal, legit*, legitimate,
logical, official, original, persuasive, potent,
powerful, proven, pure, solid, sound, stringent,
strong, substantial, telling, tested, true, trustworthy, ultimate, unadulterated, unanswerable,
uncorrupted, weighty, well-founded, well-
grounded; SEE CONCEPTS *319,545,582*

validate [*v*] *ascertain the truth, authenticity of
something*
approve, authenticate, authorize, bear out, certify, confirm, constitute, corroborate, endorse,
give stamp of approval*, give the go-ahead*,
give the green light*, give the nod*, John Hancock*, justify, legalize, legitimize, make binding*, make legal*, make stick*, okay*, ratify,
rubber-stamp*, sanction, set seal on*, sign off
on*, substantiate, verify; SEE CONCEPTS
50,88,317

validity [*n*] *genuineness, lawfulness*
authority, cogency, effectiveness, efficacy, force,
foundation, gravity, grounds, legality, legitimacy, persuasiveness, point, potency, power,
punch, right, soundness, strength, substance,
validness, weight; SEE CONCEPTS *645,691,725*

valley [*n*] *hollow in the land*
basin, bottom, canyon, channel, coulee, dale,
dell, depression, dingle, glen, gorge, lowland,
notch, plain, swale, trough, vale; SEE CONCEPTS
509,513

valor [*n*] *bravery*
backbone*, boldness, courage, dash*, defiance,
derring-do*, determination, fearlessness, fight,
firmness, fortitude, gallantry, grit*, guts*, hardihood, heart, heroism, indomitableness, intestinal
fortitude*, intrepidity, invincibility, mettle,
moxie*, nerve, pluck, prowess, resolution,
sand*, spirit, spunk, starch*, stomach*, tenacity,
valiance, valiancy; SEE CONCEPTS *411,633*

valorous [*adj*] *courageous*
adventuresome, adventurous, bold, brave, chivalrous, daredevil, daring, dauntless, fearless, gallant, game, gritty*, gutsy*, heroic, lionhearted,
nervy, plucky*, Spartan, stalwart, stouthearted,
strong, tough, unafraid, undaunted, valiant, venturous; SEE CONCEPTS *401,404*

valuable [*adj*] *very important; priceless*
admired, appreciated, beneficial, cherished, collectible, costly, dear, esteemed, estimable, expensive, heirloom, held dear, helpful,
high-priced, hot*, hot property*, important, in

demand, inestimable, invaluable, of value, precious, prized, profitable, relevant, respected,
scarce, serviceable, treasured, useful, valued,
worthwhile, worthy; SEE CONCEPTS *334,560,568*

valuable [*n*] *prized possession*
advantage, antique, asset, benefit, collectible,
commodity, heirloom, nugget*, plum*, treasure;
SEE CONCEPT *446*

value [*n1*] *financial worth*
amount, appraisal, assessment, charge, cost,
equivalent, expense, market price, monetary
worth, price, profit, rate; SEE CONCEPTS *335,336*

value [*n2*] *advantage, worth*
account, bearing, benefit, caliber, condition, connotation, consequence, content, denotation, desirability, distinction, drift, eminence, esteem,
estimation, excellence, finish, force, goodness,
grade, help, implication, import, importance, interpretation, mark, marketability, meaning,
merit, power, preference, profit, purpose, quality,
regard, repute, sense, serviceableness, significance, state, stature, substance, superiority, use,
usefulness, utility, valuation; SEE CONCEPTS
346,658,668,682

valued [*adj*] *costly; treasured*
admired, appreciated, beloved, cherished, dear,
esteemed, expensive, fancy, highly regarded,
high-priced, loved, precious, priceless, prized,
respected, valuable; SEE CONCEPTS *334,555,567*

values [*n*] *principles*
attitude, beliefs, character, code, conduct, conscience, ethics, ideals, integrity, morals, mores,
scruples, sense of duty, sense of honor, standards; SEE CONCEPTS *645,689*

valve [*n*] *on-and-off device*
cock, faucet, flap, gate, hydrant, lid, pipe, plug,
shutoff, spigot, stopper, tap; SEE CONCEPTS
445,464,499

vandal [*n*] *person who defiles property*
defacer, despoiler, destroyer, hoodlum, looter,
mischief-maker, pillager, pirate, plunderer, ravager, thief; SEE CONCEPT *412*

vandalism [*n*] *destruction*
defacing, grafitti, mischief, ravaging, ruin, sacking, smashing, trashing, wreckage, wrecking; SEE
CONCEPTS *230,252*

vandalize [*v*] *destroy*
annihilate, damage, deface, demolish, despoil,
disfigure, impair, mar, ravage, ravish, raze, ruin,
smash, spray paint, trash*, wreck; SEE CONCEPTS
246,252

vanilla [*adj*] *simple, unadorned*
austere, clean, elementary, folksy, homely, humble, inelaborate, modest, plain, pure and simple*,
rustic, uncluttered, uncomplicated, undecorated,
unelaborate, unembellished, unornamented, unostentatious, unpretentious, your basic; SEE CON-
CEPTS *562,589*

vanish [*v*] *disappear*
become invisible, be lost, clear, dematerialize,
die, die out, dissolve, evanesce, evaporate, exit,
fade, fade away, go away, melt; SEE CONCEPT
105

vanity [*n*] *conceit, egotism*
affectation, airs, arrogance, big-headedness*,
conceitedness, display, ego trip*, narcissism, ostentation, pretension, pride, self-admiration, self-
love, self-worship, show*, showing off*,
smugness, vainglory; SEE CONCEPT *410*

vanquish [v] *defeat soundly*
bear down, beat, conquer, crush, humble, overcome, overpower, overturn, overwhelm, put down, quell, reduce, repress, rout, subdue, subjugate, subvert, surmount, trample, triumph over; SEE CONCEPT *95*

vapid [adj] *flat, dull*
bland, boring, colorless, dead*, driveling, flat, flat tire*, flavorless, inane, innocuous, insipid, jejune, least, lifeless, limp, milk-and-water*, milquetoast*, nothing, nowhere, stale, tame, tasteless, tedious, tiresome, unimaginative, uninspiring, uninteresting, unpalatable, vacant, vacuous, watery, weak, wishy-washy*, zero*; SEE CONCEPTS *529,537,575*

vapor [n] *fumes, mist*
breath, condensation, dampness, dew, effluvium, exhalation, fog, gas, haze, miasma, moisture, reek, smog, smoke, steam; SEE CONCEPTS *437,524*

variable [adj] *changing, changeable*
capricious, changeful, fickle, fitful, flexible, fluctuating, fluid, iffy*, inconstant, irregular, mercurial, mobile, mutable, protean, shifting, shifty, slippery*, spasmodic, temperamental, ticklish, uncertain, unequable, unsettled, unstable, unsteady, vacillating, volatile, waffling, wavering, yo-yo*; SEE CONCEPT *534*

variance [n] *difference*
about-face*, argument, change, conflict, contention, deviation, difference of opinion, different strokes*, disaccord, disagreement, discord, discrepancy, dissension, dissent, dissidence, disunity, divergence, diversity, division, flip-flop*, fluctuation, incongruity, inconsistency, midcourse correction*, mutation, separation, severing, strife, sundering, switch, transmogrification, unharmoniousness, variation, variety; SEE CONCEPTS *388,665,697*

variant [adj] *different*
alternative, derived, differing, divergent, exceptional, modified, various, varying; SEE CONCEPT *564*

variant [n] *derived form*
alternative, branch, development, exception, irregularity, modification, result, spinoff, variation, version; SEE CONCEPT *665*

variation [n] *difference; alternative*
aberration, abnormality, adaptation, alteration, bend, break, change, contradistinction, contrast, curve, deflection, departure, departure from the norm*, deviation, digression, discrepancy, disparity, displacement, dissimilarity, dissimilitude, distinction, divergence, diversification, diversity, exception, fluctuation, inequality, innovation, modification, mutation, novelty, shift, swerve, turn, unconformity, variety; SEE CONCEPTS *665,697*

varied [adj] *different*
assorted, conglomeration, discrete, diverse, heterogeneous, indiscriminate, miscellaneous, mixed, motley, multifarious, separate, sundry, various; SEE CONCEPT *564*

variegated [adj] *diversified; varicolored*
assorted, changeable, checkered, diverse, kaleidoscopic, mixed, motley, mottled, multicolor, multicolored, particolored, patched, spotted, streaked, striped, varied, versicolor; SEE CONCEPTS *564,618,772*

variety [n1] *difference*
array, assortment, change, collection, combo*, conglomeration, cross section, departure, discrepancy, disparateness, divergency, diversification, diversity, fluctuation, heterogeneity, incongruity, intermixture, many-sidedness, medley, mélange, miscellany, mishmash, mixed bag*, mixture, modification, multifariousness, multiplicity, potpourri, range, shift, soup, stew, variance, variation; SEE CONCEPTS *432,665*

variety [n2] *type, sort*
assortment, brand, breed, category, character, class, classification, description, division, family, genus, grade, ilk, kidney, kind, make, nature, order, quality, race, rank, species, strain, stripe, tribe; SEE CONCEPT *378*

various [adj] *miscellaneous, differing*
all manner of*, assorted, changeable, changing, different, discrete, disparate, distinct, distinctive, diverse, diversified, heterogeneous, individual, legion, manifold, many, many-sided, multifarious, multitudinal, multitudinous, numerous, omnifarious, peculiar, populous, separate, several, sundry, unalike, unequal, unlike, variant, varied, variegated; SEE CONCEPTS *564,771*

varnish [v] *add a layer to; embellish*
adorn, coat, cover, decorate, enamel, finish, gild, glaze, gloss, japan, lacquer, luster, paint, polish, shellac, surface, veneer, wash, wax; SEE CONCEPTS *172,177*

vary [v] *change*
alter, alternate, assort, be unlike, blow hot and cold*, convert, depart, deviate, differ, digress, disagree, displace, dissent, divaricate, diverge, diversify, divide, fluctuate, hem and haw*, inflect, interchange, modify, mutate, part, permutate, range, separate, shilly-shally*, swerve, take turns, transform, turn, variegate, yo-yo*; SEE CONCEPT *697*

varying [adj] *variable*
alternating, changeable, changing, deviating, differing, flexible, fluctuating, inconstant, irregular, shifting, uncertain, unstable, unsteady, vacillating, volatile, waffling, wavering; SEE CONCEPT *534*

vast [adj] *very large; wide in range*
all-inclusive, ample, astronomical, big, boundless, broad, capacious, colossal, comprehensive, detailed, endless, enormous, eternal, expanded, extensive, far-flung, far-reaching, forever, giant, gigantic, great, huge, illimitable, immeasurable, immense, infinite, limitless, mammoth, massive, measureless, monstrous, monumental, never-ending, prodigious, prolonged, spacious, spread-out, stretched-out, sweeping, titanic, tremendous, unbounded, unlimited, voluminous, widespread; SEE CONCEPTS *772,773,781*

vault [n] *depository*
basement, box, can, catacomb, cavern, cellar, crib*, crypt, dungeon, grave, mausoleum, pit, repository, safe, safe-deposit box, sepulcher, strong room, tomb; SEE CONCEPT *494*

vault [v] *jump over; span*
arch, ascend, bend, bounce, bound, bow, clear, curve, hop, hurdle, leap, mount, negotiate, over, overleap, rise, soar, spring, surmount; SEE CONCEPTS *194,752*

veer [v] *change direction*
angle off, avert, bear, be deflected, bend, change, change course, curve, cut, deflect, depart, devi-

va
ve

ate, digress, dip, divagate, diverge, divert, drift, get around, make a left*, make a right*, pivot, sheer, shift, skew, skid, swerve, swing, swivel, tack, train off, turn, twist, volte-face*, wheel, whip, whirl; SEE CONCEPTS *148,150,213*

vegetable [n] *edible part of plant*
edible, green, greens, herb, herbaceous plant, legume, produce, root, salad, truck, yellow; SEE CONCEPT *431*

vegetate [v1] *be very passive*
be inert, decay, deteriorate, exist, go to pot*, go to seed*, hibernate, idle, languish, loaf*, pass time, stagnate, weaken; SEE CONCEPTS *210,698*

vegetate [v2] *grow, sprout*
bloom, blossom, bud, burgeon, germinate, shoot, spring, swell; SEE CONCEPTS *253,257*

vehement [adj] *passionate, opinionated*
angry, ardent, concentrated, delirious, desperate, eager, earnest, emphatic, enthusiastic, exquisite, fervent, fervid, fierce, fiery, forceful, forcible, frantic, furious, hearty, heated, hopped up*, hot*, hyper*, impassioned, impetuous, inflamed, intense, lively, on the make*, potent, powerful, pronounced, rabid, strong, terrible, vicious, violent, wild, zealous; SEE CONCEPTS *401,542*

vehicle [n1] *machine used for transportation*
agent, automobile, bicycle, boat, buggy, bus, cab, car, carrier, chariot, conveyance, crate*, jalopy*, jeep, mechanism, motorcycle, taxi, transport, truck, van, vector, wagon, wheels; SEE CONCEPT *503*

vehicle [n2] *means of attaining end*
agency, agent, apparatus, channel, expedient, implement, instrument, instrumentality, intermediary, means of expression, mechanism, medium, ministry, organ, tool, vector, way, ways and means*; SEE CONCEPTS *6,277,278,694,712*

veil [n] *disguise*
blind, cloak, coloring, cover, curtain, facade, false front, film, front, guise, mantilla, mask, screen, shade, shroud, veiling; SEE CONCEPTS *451,673*

veil [v] *hide*
beard*, blanket, camouflage, cloak, conceal, cover, cover up, curtain*, dim, disguise, drape, enclose, enfold, enshroud, envelop, finesse, invest, launder, mantle, mask, obscure, put up a front*, screen, secrete, shield, shroud, stonewall*, whitewash*, wrap; SEE CONCEPT *172*

veiled [adj] *disguised*
camouflaged, cloaked, concealed, covered, hidden, hooded, invisible, masked, screened, secret, shielded, shrouded, undercover, unexposed, unrecognizable, unrevealed; SEE CONCEPTS *547,576,619*

vein [n1] *mood, tone*
attitude, bent, character, characteristic, complexion, dash, disposition, faculty, fashion, fettle, hint, humor, line, manner, mind, mode, nature, note, spice, spirit, strain, streak, style, suggestion, suspicion, tang, temper, temperament, tenor, tinge, touch, trace, turn, wave, way; SEE CONCEPTS *411,673,682*

vein [n2] *blood vessel*
capillary, course, current, duct, follicle, hair, lode, nerve, seam, stratum, streak, stripe, thread, venation; SEE CONCEPTS *393,420*

velocity [n] *speed*
acceleration, celerity, dispatch, expedition, fleetness, gait, haste, headway, hurry, impetus, mo-

mentum, pace, quickness, rapidity, rapidness, rate, swiftness, tempo; SEE CONCEPTS *755,792*

venal [adj] *bribable, corruptible*
amoral, bent*, buyable, conscienceless, corrupt, crooked, dishonest, double-dealing, immoral, mercenary, on the take*, padded*, purchasable, unethical, unprincipled, unprofessional, unscrupulous; SEE CONCEPT *545*

vendetta [n] *feud*
argument, bad blood*, bickering, conflict, disagreement, discord, dispute, dissension, falling out*, family feud, fight, fracas, grudge, hostility, quarrel, revenge, rivalry, row, squabble, strife; SEE CONCEPTS *46,106,388*

vendor [n] *person who sells wares*
businessperson, dealer, hawker, huckster*, merchant, outcrier, peddler, pitcher, traveler, traveling salesperson; SEE CONCEPT *348*

veneer [n] *pretense, front*
appearance, coating, cover, covering, disguise, exterior, facade, face, finish, gloss, guise, layer, leaf, mask, overlay, semblance, show, surface, window dressing*; SEE CONCEPTS *633,673,716*

veneer [v] *cover, overlay*
blanch, coat, extenuate, face, finish, gloss, palliate, plate, shellac, sugarcoat, surface, varnish, whiten, whitewash; SEE CONCEPT *172*

venerable [adj] *respected*
admirable, aged, august, dignified, esteemed, estimable, experienced, grand, grave, honorable, honored, imposing, matriarchal, noble, patriarchal, philosophical, revered, reverenced, reverend, sacred, sage, sedate, serious, stately, venerated, wise, worshipful, worshipped; SEE CONCEPT *574*

venerate [v] *revere*
admire, adore, apotheosize, appreciate, be in awe of, cherish, deify, esteem, exalt, hallow, hold in awe, honor, idolize, look up to*, love, put on a pedestal*, regard, respect, reverence, think highly of, treasure, value, worship; SEE CONCEPTS *10,32*

vengeance [n] *retaliation for another's act*
avengement, avenging, counterblow, evening of score*, eye for an eye*, getting even*, repayment, reprisal, requital, retribution, return, revenge, settling of score*, tit for tat*, vengefulness, wrath; SEE CONCEPTS *29,384*

vengeful [adj] *retaliating; hating*
antagonistic, avenging, hostile, implacable, inimical, punitive, rancorous, relentless, retaliatory, revengeful, spiteful, unforgiving, vindictive; SEE CONCEPTS *401,542*

venial [adj] *pardonable*
allowable, all right, defensible, excusable, explainable, forgivable, justifiable, minor, not serious*, not too bad*, okay, permissible, slight, tolerable, trivial, understandable; SEE CONCEPT *558*

venom [n] *poison; hating*
acidity, acrimony, anger, bane, bitterness, contagion, gall, grudge, hate, hatred, ill will, infection, malevolence, malice, maliciousness, malignity, rancor, spite, spitefulness, spleen, taint, toxin, virulence, virus; SEE CONCEPTS *29,399*

venomous [adj] *poisonous; hateful*
accidentally on purpose*, antagonistic, baleful, baneful, catty*, cussed*, deadly, destructive, dirty, evil, hostile, lethal, malefic, malevolent, malicious, malign, malignant, mean, mephitic,

noxious, ornery*, poisonous, rancorous, savage, spiteful, toxic, toxicant, vicious, vindictive, viperish, viperous, virulent, waspish; SEE CONCEPTS 537,542,544

vent [n] *outlet*
aperture, avenue, chimney, drain, duct, exit, flue, hole, opening, orifice, pipe, split, spout, ventilator; SEE CONCEPTS 440,464

vent [v] *let out; express*
air, assert, come out with, declare, discharge, drive out, emit, empty, express, give, give off, give out, issue, loose, pour out, provide escape, put, release, state, take out on*, throw off*, unleash, utter, ventilate, verbalize, voice; SEE CONCEPTS 49,51,179

ventilate [v] *air out; make known*
advertise, air, bring into the open, bring up, broach, broadcast, circulate, debate, deliberate, discourse, discuss, examine, express, free, give, go into, introduce, moot, publish, put, scrutinize, sift, state, take up, talk about, talk of, talk over, thresh out, vent, verbalize; SEE CONCEPTS 51,60

venture [n] *gamble, attempt*
adventure, baby*, chance, deal, endeavor, enterprise, essay, experiment, exploit, feat*, hazard, header, investment, jeopardy, peril, pet project*, project, proposition, pursuit, risk, setup*, shot*, spec*, speculation, stab*, stake, test, thing*, trial, undertaking, wager; SEE CONCEPTS 87,675

venture [v] *take a chance*
advance, assay, attempt, bet, brave, challenge, chance, dare, dare say*, defy, endanger, essay, experiment, expose, feel, front*, gamble, get down*, go out on a limb*, grope, have a fling at*, hazard, imperil, jeopardize, lay open, make a stab at*, make bold, operate, play for, play the market*, presume, put in jeopardy*, put up*, risk, speculate, stake, stick one's neck out*, take a crack at*, take a flyer*, take a plunge*, try, try out, volunteer, wager; SEE CONCEPTS 87,330,363

venturesome [adj] *courageous*
adventurous, aggressive, audacious, bold, brave, daredevil, daring, enterprising, fearless, foolhardy, gutsy, intrepid, overbold, plucky, pushy, rash, reckless, resourceful, risky, spirited, spunky, stalwart, stout, sturdy, temerarious, venturous; SEE CONCEPTS 401,548

veracious [adj] *true*
accurate, credible, dependable, direct, ethical, factual, faithful, frank, genuine, high-principled, honest, just, kosher*, legit*, like it is*, on the level*, on the line*, on the up and up*, open, reliable, right, righteous, straight-arrow*, straightforward, strict, true-blue*, trustworthy, truthful, undeceptive, up front*, valid, veridical; SEE CONCEPTS 267,545,582

veracity [n] *truth*
accuracy, actuality, authenticity, candor, correctness, credibility, exactitude, exactness, fact, fairness, fidelity, frankness, genuineness, gospel*, honest-to-god truth*, honesty, honor, impartiality, integrity, like it is*, openness, precision, probity, reality, real McCoy*, rectitude, rightness, sincerity, straight stuff*, trueness, truism, trustworthiness, truthfulness, uprightness, verisimilitude, verity, word*; SEE CONCEPTS 278,645

verbal [adj] *spoken*
exact, expressed, lingual, literal, oral, rhetorical, said, stated, told, unwritten, verbatim, word-for-word*, word-of-mouth*; SEE CONCEPT 267

verbalize [v] *speak*
articulate, blab*, break silence, chat, communicate, converse, enunciate, express, gab*, make known, mouth, mumble, open one's mouth, pronounce, put into words, rap*, say, shout, sound, state, talk, tell, utter, vocalize, voice, whisper, yak*, yammer; SEE CONCEPTS 47,266

verbatim [adj] *exactly*
accurately, direct, directly, literally, literatim, precisely, sic, to the letter*, word-for-word*; SEE CONCEPTS 267,535

verbiage [n] *repetition, wordiness*
circumlocution, expansiveness, floridity, long-windedness, loquacity, periphrase, periphrasis, pleonasm, prolixity, redundancy, tautology, verbosity; SEE CONCEPTS 278,695

verbose [adj] *wordy, long-winded*
bombastic, circumlocutory, diffuse, flowery, full of air*, fustian, gabby*, garrulous, grandiloquent, involved, loquacious, magniloquent, palaverous, periphrastic, pleonastic, prolix, redundant, repeating, repetitious, repetitive, rhetorical, talkative, talky*, tautological, tautologous, tedious, tortuous, windy*, yacking*; SEE CONCEPT 267

verbosity [n] *wordiness*
garrulous, logorrhea, long-windedness, loquaciousness, loquacity, prolixity, talkativeness, verbiage, verboseness; SEE CONCEPT 267

verdant [adj] *green, blooming*
flourishing, fresh, grassy, leafy, lush, verdurous; SEE CONCEPTS 485,618

verdict [n] *law judgment*
adjudication, answer, arbitrament, award, conclusion, decision, decree, deduction, determination, finding, opinion, ruling, sentence; SEE CONCEPT 318

verge [n] *extremity, limit*
border, borderline, boundary, brim, brink, edge, extreme, fringe, hem, lip, margin, point, rim, selvage, skirt, terminus, threshold; SEE CONCEPT 484

verge [v] *come near*
abut, adjoin, approach, be on the edge*, border, bound, brink on, butt on*, communicate, edge, end, fringe, gravitate toward, hem, incline, join, lean, line, march, margin, neighbor, outline, rim, skirt, surround, tend, touch, trench, trend; SEE CONCEPTS 657,749

verification [n] *proof*
affidavit, attestation, authentication, averment, certification, confirmation, credentials, deposition, documents, endorsement, evidence, facts, information, record, scoop*, seal, signature, stamp, substantiation, testament, testimony; SEE CONCEPT 274

verify [v] *confirm, validate*
add up*, attest, authenticate, bear out, certify, check, check out, check up, check up on*, confirm, corroborate, debunk, demonstrate, document, double-check, establish, eye*, eyeball*, find out, hold up, justify, make certain, make sure, pan out*, peg*, prove, settle, size*, size up*, stand up*, substantiate, support, test, try; SEE CONCEPTS 291,317

verisimilitude [n] *authenticity*
color, credibility, genuineness, likeliness, likeness, plausibility, realism, resemblance, semblance, show, similarity, virtual reality; SEE CONCEPT 725

ve
ve

veritable [*adj*] *authentic*
actual, bona fide, factual, for real*, genuine, indubitable, kosher*, legit*, real, true, undoubted, unquestionable, very; SEE CONCEPT 582

vernacular [*adj*] *native, colloquial*
common, dialectal, domesticated, idiomatic, indigenous, informal, ingrained, inherent, local, natural, ordinary, plebian, popular, vulgar; SEE CONCEPTS 267,549

vernacular [*n*] *native language*
argot, cant, dialect, idiom, jargon, jive talk*, language, lingo*, lingua franca, native tongue, parlance, patois, patter, phraseology, slang, speech, street talk*, tongue; SEE CONCEPT 276

versatile [*adj*] *adjustable, flexible*
able, accomplished, adaptable, adroit, all-around, all-purpose, ambidextrous, conversant, dexterous, elastic, facile, functional, gifted, handy, ingenuous, many-sided, mobile, multifaceted, plastic, pliable, protean, puttylike*, ready, resourceful, skilled, skillful, talented, variable, varied; SEE CONCEPTS 527,542

verse [*n*] *written composition*
ballad, epic, jingle, lay, lyric, ode, poem, poesy, poetry, rhyme, rune, song, sonnet, stanza; SEE CONCEPT 282

versed [*adj*] *experienced, informed*
abreast, accomplished, acquainted, au courant*, au fait*, competent, conversant, familiar, in the know*, knowledgeable, learned, practical, practiced, proficient, qualified, savvy, seasoned, skilled, trained, tuned in*, up*, up on*, versant, veteran, well-informed; SEE CONCEPTS 402,403, 527

version [*n*] *account of a happening*
adaptation, chronicle, clarification, condensation, construction, exercise, form, history, interpretation, narrative, paraphrase, portrayal, reading, redaction, rendering, rendition, report, restatement, rewording, side, simplification, sketch, statement, story, tale, transcription, translation, variant; SEE CONCEPT 282

vertex [*n*] *top*
acme, apex, apogee, cap, cope, crest, crown, culmination, extremity, fastigium, height, peak, pinnacle, roof, summit, tip, upper extremity, zenith; SEE CONCEPT 836

vertical [*adj*] *upright*
bolt upright, cocked, erect, on end, perpendicular, plumb, sheer, steep, straight-up, up-and-down, upward; SEE CONCEPTS 581,583

vertigo [*n*] *dizziness*
disequilibrium, giddiness, lightheadedness, loss of balance, loss of equilibrium, shakiness, spinning head, unsteadiness, wobbliness, wooziness; SEE CONCEPTS 314,480

verve [*n*] *energy, enthusiasm*
activity, ardor, dash, drive, elan, endurance, fire, force, forcefulness, get-up-and-go*, go, gumption, gusto, hardihood, intensity, juice, liveliness, moxie*, passion, pep, pizzazz, pluck, power, punch, sparkle, spirit, spunk, stamina, steam, strength, toughness, vigor, vim, virility, vitality, zeal, zest, zing, zip*; SEE CONCEPT 411

very [*adj*] *real, exact*
actual, appropriate, authentic, bare, bona fide, correct, especial, express, genuine, ideal, identical, indubitable, mere, model, perfect, plain, precise, pure, right, same, selfsame, sheer, simple, special, sure-enough, true, undoubted, unquali-

fied, unquestionable, veritable, very same; SEE CONCEPTS 535,557

very [*adv*] *much, really; to a high degree*
absolutely, acutely, amply, astonishingly, awfully, certainly, considerably, dearly, decidedly, deeply, eminently, emphatically, exaggeratedly, exceedingly, excessively, extensively, extraordinarily, extremely, greatly, highly, incredibly, indispensably, largely, notably, noticeably, particularly, positively, powerfully, pressingly, pretty, prodigiously, profoundly, remarkably, substantially, superlatively, surpassingly, surprisingly, terribly, truly, uncommonly, unusually, vastly, wonderfully; SEE CONCEPTS 544,569,772

vessel [*n1*] *ship*
barge, bark, bateau, boat, bottom, bucket*, can*, craft, liner, ocean liner, steamer, tanker, tub*; SEE CONCEPT 506

vessel [*n2*] *container, bowl*
basin, kettle, pitcher, pot, receptacle, urn, utensil; SEE CONCEPT 494

vest [*v*] *authorize, entrust*
belong, bestow, confer, consign, empower, endow, furnish, invest, lodge, pertain, place, put in the hands of*, settle; SEE CONCEPTS 50,88

vestibule [*n*] *small room for arrivals*
antechamber, anteroom, doorway, entrance, entrance hall, entry, entryway, foyer, gateway, hall, hallway, lobby, narthex, porch, portal, portico; SEE CONCEPT 448

vestige [*n*] *sign, indication*
evidence, glimmer, hint, memento, print, relic, remainder, remains, remnant, residue, scrap, shadow, suspicion, token, trace, track; SEE CONCEPTS 260,284,673

veteran [*adj*] *experienced, seasoned*
adept, battle-scarred*, been around*, disciplined, exercised, expert, from way back*, hardened, inured, knows one's stuff*, long-serving, longtime, not born yesterday*, of the old school*, old, old-time, practical, practiced, pro*, proficient, skilled, sophisticated, steady, trained, up to speed*, versed, vet*, weathered, wise, wise to ways*, worldly; SEE CONCEPTS 402,527,678

veteran [*n*] *person with much experience; particularly in war*
expert, GI*, old guard*, old hand*, old pro*, old salt*, old soldier*, old-timer*, pro, shellback*, sourdough*, trouper, vet*, warhorse*; SEE CONCEPTS 358,423

veto [*n*] *refusal of permission*
ban, blackball*, declination, denial, embargo, interdict, interdiction, negative, nonconsent, prohibition; SEE CONCEPTS 81,121,298,685

veto [*v*] *refuse permission*
ban, blackball*, burn, cut, decline, defeat, deny, disallow, disapprove, discountenance, forbid, give thumbs down*, interdict, kill, negate, negative, nix*, not go for*, pass, pass by, pass on, prohibit, put down, refuse, reject, rule out*, shoot down*, throw away*, throw out*, thumbs down*, turn down; SEE CONCEPTS 50,81,88,121, 298

vex [*v*] *distress, bother*
abrade, afflict, aggravate, agitate, anger, annoy, be at, chafe, depress, displease, disquiet, disturb, eat*, embarrass, exasperate, fret, gall*, get in one's hair*, get under one's skin*, give a bad time*, give a hard time*, grate on*, harass,

harry, hassle, infuriate, irk, irritate, molest, needle, nettle, offend, peeve, perplex, pester, pique, plague, provoke, put out*, rasp, ride, rile, tease, tick off*, torment, trouble, turn off*, upset, worry; SEE CONCEPTS 7,19

vexatious [adj] *distressing, bothersome*
afflicting, aggravating, annoying, burdensome, disagreeable, disappointing, disturbing, exasperating, irksome, irritating, mean, nagging, pesky*, provoking, teasing, tormenting, troublesome, troublous, trying, ugly, unpleasant, upsetting, wicked, worrisome, worrying; SEE CONCEPTS 529,537

via [p, ep] *by way of*
along, as a means, by, by dint of, by means of, by this route, by virtue of, on the way, over, per, through, through the medium of, through this medium, with; SEE CONCEPT 544

viable [adj] *reasonable, practicable*
applicable, doable, feasible, operable, possible, usable, within possibility, workable; SEE CONCEPTS 552,560

vibrant [adj1] *alive, colorful*
active, animated, dynamic, electrifying, energetic, lively, peppy, responsive, sensitive, sound, sparkling, spirited, vigorous, virile, vital, vivacious, vivid, zesty*, zippy*; SEE CONCEPTS 401,618

vibrant [adj2] *throbbing*
aquiver, consonant, oscillating, palpitating, pulsating, pulsing, quaking, quivering, resonant, resounding, reverberant, ringing, sonorant, sonorous, trembling; SEE CONCEPT 584

vibrate [v] *shake, quiver*
beat, echo, fluctuate, flutter, jar, oscillate, palpitate, pulsate, pulse, quake, resonate, resound, reverberate, ripple, shiver, sway, swing, throb, tremble, tremor, undulate, wave, waver; SEE CONCEPTS 152,748

vibration [n] *shaking, quivering*
beating, fluctuation, judder, oscillation, pulsation, pulse, quake, quiver, resonance, reverberation, shake, shimmy, throb, throbbing, trembling, tremor, vacillation, wave, wavering; SEE CONCEPTS 152,748

vicarious [adj] *done or felt for, or on behalf of, another*
by proxy, commissioned, delegated, deputed, empathetic, eventual, imagined, indirect, pretended, secondary, substituted, substitutional, surrogate, sympathetic; SEE CONCEPTS 401,538

vice [n1] *bad habit; sin*
carnality, corruption, debasement, debauchery, decay, degeneracy, depravity, evil, evildoing, ill, immorality, indecency, iniquity, lechery, lewdness, libidinousness, licentiousness, looseness, lubricity, lust, maleficence, malignance, offense, perversion, profligacy, rot, sensuality, squalor, transgression, trespass, venality, wickedness, wrong; SEE CONCEPTS 372,645

vice [n2] *weakness*
blemish, defect, demerit, failing, fault, flaw, foible, frailty, imperfection, mar, shortcoming, weak point; SEE CONCEPTS 411,657,666

vice versa [adv] *contrary, oppositely*
about-face*, again, contra, contrariwise*, conversely, far from it*, in reverse, on the contrary, the other way around*, turn about; SEE CONCEPTS 544,564

vicinity [n] *local area*
around*, ballpark*, district, environment, environs, hood, locality, nearness, neck of the woods*, neighborhood, precinct, pretty near*, propinquity, proximity, purlieus, range, region, surroundings, territory, turf*, vicinage; SEE CONCEPTS 198,747

vicious [adj1] *corrupt, wrong*
abandoned, abhorrent, atrocious, bad, barbarous, base, contaminated, cruel, dangerous, debased, degenerate, degraded, demoralized, depraved, diabolical, faulty, ferocious, fiendish, flagitious, foul, heinous, immoral, impious, impure, indecent, infamous, iniquitous, insubordinate, lewd, libidinous, licentious, miscreant, monstrous, nefarious, perverse, profligate, putrid, reprehensible, reprobate, rotten, savage, sinful, unprincipled, untamed, vile, villainous, violent, wicked, wild, worthless; SEE CONCEPTS 401,545,571

vicious [adj2] *nasty, hateful*
backbiting*, beastly, bloodthirsty, brutal, cruel, cussed*, defamatory, despiteful, dirty*, evil, fierce, frightful, furious, horrid, intense, lousy*, malevolent, malicious, malign, mean, murderous, ornery*, poisonous, rancorous, rough, savage, slanderous, spiteful, tough, vehement, venomous, vindictive, violent, wicked; SEE CONCEPTS 267,401,542

vicissitude [n] *change*
about-face*, alteration, alternation, diversity, flip-flop*, fluctuation, innovation, mid-course correction*, mutability, mutation, novelty, permutation, progression, reversal, revolution, shift, sport, switch, switchover, transposition, turnaround, uncertainty, ups and downs*, variation, variety; SEE CONCEPT 697

victim [n] *someone or something sacrificed, preyed upon*
babe in woods*, butt, casualty, clown, dupe, easy make*, easy mark*, fatality, fool, gambit, gopher*, gudgeon*, gull, hireling, hunted, immolation, injured party, innocent, mark, martyr, patsy, pawn, pigeon*, prey, pushover*, quarry, sacrifice, scapegoat, sitting duck*, sitting target*, soft touch*, stooge*, sucker*, sufferer, underdog, wretch; SEE CONCEPTS 423,659

victimize [v] *cheat, fool*
bamboozle*, burn*, chisel*, clip*, con, cozen, deceive, defraud, discriminate against, dupe, exploit, fleece, flimflam*, gull, have it in for*, hoax, hoodwink, immolate, persecute, pick on, pigeon*, prey on, rope in*, screw*, set up*, snow*, stack the deck*, stiff*, sting*, sucker*, swindle, take advantage of, trick, use; SEE CONCEPTS 14,59,192

victor [n] *person who wins*
champ, champion, conquering hero*, conqueror, defeater, first*, gold medalist, greatest, hero, king, medalist, prizewinner, queen, subjugator, title holder, top*, top dog*, vanquisher, winner; SEE CONCEPTS 366,416

Victorian [adj] *prudish*
conservative, conventional, demure, genteel, priggish*, prim, prissy*, proper, puritanical, respectable, rigid, smug, square, starchy*, stiff*, strait-laced, stuffy, uptight*; SEE CONCEPT 401

victorious [adj] *successful, winning*
arrived, champion, conquering, on top, prizewinning, triumphant, vanquishing; SEE CONCEPT 528

ve
vi

victory [n] *win, success*
achievement, advantage, ascendancy, bull's-eye*, clean sweep*, conquest, control, defeat, defeating, destruction, dominion, feather in cap*, gain, grand slam*, hit, hole in one*, killing*, laurels, mission accomplished*, overthrow, prize, subjugation, superiority, supremacy, sweep, the gold*, triumph, upper hand*, upset, winning; SEE CONCEPTS *95,671,706,832*

victuals [n] *food supplies*
aliment, bread, chow*, comestibles, eatables, eats, edibles, fare, feed, foodstuff, goodies*, groceries*, grub, larder, meal, nourishment, provender, provisions, rations, refreshments, snack, supplies, viands, vittles; SEE CONCEPTS *457,460,461*

video [n/adj] *related to the televised image*
broadcast, canned*, music video, prerecorded, program, promotional film, recorded, taped, telegenic, television, TV; SEE CONCEPTS *277,293.*

videocassette [n] *magnetic tape on which video image is recorded*
cartridge, flick*, movie, recording, rental, vid*, videotape; SEE CONCEPTS *277,293,464.*

vie [v] *compete*
be rivals, buck, challenge, contend, contest, counter, go for*, go for broke*, go for the gold*, go for the jugular*, jockey for position*, match, oppose, pit, play, play off, push, rival, scramble for, strive, struggle, sweat; SEE CONCEPTS *92,363*

view [n1] *something that is seen*
appearance, aspect, composition, contour, design, field of vision, glimpse, illustration, landscape, look, opening, outline, outlook, panorama, perspective, picture, prospect, range of vision, representation, scene, seascape, show, sight, spectacle, stretch, tableau, vision, vista, way; SEE CONCEPT *628*

view [n2] *examination*
analysis, audit, check, contemplation, display, eyeball*, flash*, gander*, inspection, lamp*, look, look-see, perlustration, review, scan, scrutiny, sight, slant, squint*, survey, viewing; SEE CONCEPTS *24,103*

view [n3] *belief*
attitude, belief, close-up, concept, conception, consideration, conviction, deduction, eye*, feeling, impression, inference, judgment, judgment call*, mind, notion, opinion, persuasion, point of view, say-so*, sentiment, slant*, thought, twist, two cents' worth*, value judgment*, way of thinking; SEE CONCEPT *689*

view [v1] *look at*
beam, behold, canvass, check out*, check over, consider, contemplate, descry, dig*, discern, distinguish, eagle eye*, espy, examine, explore, eye*, feast eyes on*, flash*, gaze, get a load of*, inspect, lay eyes on, mark, notice, observe, perceive, pipe*, read, regard, rubberneck*, scan, scope, scrutinize, see, set eyes on, spot, spy, stare, survey, take in*, watch, witness; SEE CONCEPTS *623,626*

view [v2] *believe*
account, consider, deem, judge, look on, reckon, regard, think about; SEE CONCEPT *12*

viewpoint [n] *way of thinking*
angle, aspect, attitude, direction, estimation, eye*, frame of reference, ground, light, long view, outlook, perspective, point of observation, point of view, position, posture, respect, side, slant, stance, stand, standpoint, twist, two cents' worth*, vantage point, view; SEE CONCEPT *689*

vigil [n] *watch*
attention, awareness, duty, eagle eye*, guard, lookout, monitoring, nightwatch, notice, observance, observation, patrol, stake-out, surveillance, vigilance, watchfulness; SEE CONCEPTS *134,623*

vigilance [n] *carefulness*
acuity, alertness, attention, attentiveness, caution, circumspection, diligence, lookout, observance, surveillance, vigil, watch, watchfulness; SEE CONCEPTS *644,657*

vigilant [adj] *careful, watchful*
acute, agog, alert, anxious, attentive, aware, cautious, circumspect, guarded, keen, looking for, looking to, observant, on alert, on guard, on the ball*, on the job*, on the lookout, on the qui vive, on toes*, open-eyed*, sharp, sleepless, unsleeping, waiting on, wakeful, wary, wide-awake, with eyes peeled*, with weather eye open*; SEE CONCEPTS *401,542,576*

vigor [n] *power, energy*
ability, action, activity, agility, alertness, bang*, birr, bounce, capability, capacity, dash, drive, dynamism, endurance, enterprise, exercise, fire, force, get-up-and-go*, go*, hardiness, healthiness, intensity, juice*, kick*, liveliness, lustiness, might, motion, moxie*, muscle*, nimbleness, pep*, pith, potency, puissance, punch*, push, quickness, snap*, sock, soundness, starch*, steam*, strength, tuck*, urgency, vehemence, vim, vitality, well-being, zing*, zip*; SEE CONCEPTS *316,411,732*

vigorous [adj] *energetic, powerful*
active, athletic, ball of fire*, bouncing, brisk, dashing, driving, dynamic, effective, efficient, enterprising, exuberant, flourishing, forceful, forcible, hale, hard-driving, hardy, healthy, hearty, intense, lively, lusty, mettlesome, peppy, persuasive, potent, red-blooded*, robust, rugged, snappy, sound, spanking, spirited, steamroller*, strapping, strenuous, strong, strong as an ox*, sturdy, take-charge*, take-over*, tough, vital, zealous, zippy*; SEE CONCEPTS *314,404,489*

vile [adj] *offensive, horrible*
abandoned, abject, appalling, bad, base, coarse, contemptible, corrupt, debased, degenerate, depraved, despicable, dirty, disgraceful, disgusting, evil, filthy, foul, horrid, humiliating, ignoble, immoral, impure, iniquitous, loathsome, low, mean, miserable, nasty, nauseating, nefarious, noxious, perverted, repellent, repugnant, repulsive, revolting, shocking, sickening, sinful, sleazy*, stinking*, ugly, vicious, vulgar, wicked, worthless, wretched; SEE CONCEPTS *529,545,571*

vilify [v] *criticize very harshly*
abuse, asperse, assail, attack, bad-mouth*, berate, blister, call down*, caluminate, censure, curse, cuss*, damn, debase, decry, defame, denigrate, denounce, dig*, disparage, dress down*, dump on*, give a black eye*, jinx, knock*, libel, malign, mistreat, mudsling*, pan*, put a whammy on*, put down*, rag on*, rap*, revile, rip up*, roast*, run down, scorch, skin alive*, slam*, slander, slur, smear*, speak ill of, tear down*, tear into*, traduce, vituperate, voodoo*; SEE CONCEPTS *44,52*

villa [n] *country estate*
chateau, country house, large house, manor,

mansion, summer house, vacation home; SEE CONCEPTS *439,516*

village [*n*] *small town*
center, crossroads, hamlet, suburb; SEE CONCEPT *507*

villain [*n*] *evil person*
antihero, blackguard*, brute, caitiff, creep*, criminal, devil, enfant terrible*, evildoer, heel, libertine, lowlife*, malefactor, mischief-maker*, miscreant, offender, profligate, rapscallion, rascal, reprobate, scoundrel, sinner, wretch; SEE CONCEPT *412*

villainous [*adj*] *criminal*
atrocious, bad, corrupt, crooked, cruel, culpable, deplorable, depraved, diabolical, dirty, evil, felonious, hateful, ignoble, illegal, illicit, immoral, iniquitous, knavish, lawless, low, mean, nefarious, peccant, reprehensible, scandalous, shady*, sinful, unlawful, vile, wicked; SEE CONCEPT *545*

vindicate [*v*] *prove one's innocence*
absolve, acquit, advocate, argue, assert, bear out, claim, clear, confute, contend, corroborate, defend, disculpate, disprove, do justice to, establish, exculpate, excuse, exonerate, extenuate, free, free from blame, guard, justify, maintain, plead for, protect, prove, rationalize, refute, rehabilitate, second, shield, substantiate, support, uphold, warrant, whitewash*; SEE CONCEPTS *49,57,317*

vindictive [*adj*] *hateful, revengeful*
avenging, cruel, grim, grudging, implacable, malicious, malignant, merciless, rancorous, relentless, resentful, retaliatory, ruthless, spiteful, unforgiving, unrelenting, vengeful, venomous, wreakful; SEE CONCEPTS *401,542*

vintage [*adj*] *superior*
best, choice, classic, classical, excellent, mature, old, prime, rare, ripe, select, selected, venerable; SEE CONCEPTS *574,578,797*

vintage [*n*] *crop, especially of wine*
collection, epoch, era, generation, grapes, harvest, origin, wine, year; SEE CONCEPT *429*

violate [*v1*] *break a law, agreement*
breach, contaminate, contravene, defy, disobey, disregard, disrupt, encroach, err, infract, infringe, meddle, offend, oppose, outrage, profane, resist, sacrilege, sin, tamper with, trample on, transgress, trespass, withstand; SEE CONCEPTS *101,192*

violate [*v2*] *rape, defile*
abuse, assault, befoul, debauch, defile, desecrate, force, invade, outrage, pollute, profane, ravish, spoil; SEE CONCEPTS *246,375*

violation [*n1*] *breach; breaking of the law*
abuse, break, breaking, contravention, encroachment, illegality, infraction, infringement, misbehavior, misdemeanor, negligence, nonobservance, offense, rupture, transgressing, transgression, trespass, trespassing, violating, wrong; SEE CONCEPTS *101,192*

violation [*n2*] *rape, defilement*
assault, blasphemy, debasement, defacement, defacing, degradation, desecration, destruction, devastation, dishonor, invasion, mistreatment, outrage, pollution, profanation, rapine, ravishment, ruin, sacrilege, spoliation; SEE CONCEPTS *246,252,375*

violence [*n*] *extreme force, intensity*
abandon, acuteness, assault, attack, bestiality, bloodshed, blowup, brutality, brute force, clash, coercion, compulsion, confusion, constraint, cruelty, destructiveness, disorder, disturbance, duress, ferocity, fervor, fierceness, fighting, flap, foul play, frenzy, fury, fuss, harshness, murderousness, onslaught, passion, power, raging, rampage, roughness, ruckus, rumble, savagery, severity, sharpness, storm, storminess, struggle, terrorism, tumult, turbulence, uproar, vehemence, wildness; SEE CONCEPTS *29,641,669,675*

violent [*adj1*] *destructive*
agitated, aroused, berserk, bloodthirsty, brutal, coercive, crazy, cruel, demoniac, desperate, distraught, disturbed, enraged, fierce, fiery, forceful, forcible, frantic, fuming, furious, great, headstrong, homicidal, hotheaded*, hysterical, impassioned, impetuous, inflamed, intemperate, mad, maddened, maniacal, mighty, murderous, passionate, potent, powerful, raging, riotous, rough, savage, strong, uncontrollable, ungovernable, unrestrained, urgent, vehement, vicious, wild; SEE CONCEPTS *401,540,544*

violent [*adj2*] *severe, extreme*
acute, agonizing, biting, blustery, coercive, concentrated, devastating, excruciating, exquisite, forceful, forcible, gale force*, great, harsh, immoderate, inordinate, intense, mighty, outrageous, painful, potent, powerful, raging, rough, ruinous, sharp, strong, tempestuous, terrible, tumultuous/tumultuous, turbulent, wild; SEE CONCEPTS *525,569*

viperous [*adj*] *malicious, venomous*
bad-natured, baleful, bitter, evil, evil-minded, green-eyed*, jealous, malevolent, mean, nasty, ornery, poisonous, rancorous, resentful, spiteful, vengeful, vicious, vindictive, wicked; SEE CONCEPTS *267,401,542*

virginity [*n*] *celibacy, chastity*
abstinence, chasteness, cleanness, continence, honor, immaculacy, innocence, integrity, maidenhood, purity, restraint, sinlessness, spotlessness, virtue; SEE CONCEPT *633*

virgin/virginal [*adj*] *brand-new, unused*
first, fresh, idle, immaculate, initial, innocent, intact, modest, natural, new, original, primeval, pristine, pure, spotless, uncorrupted, undefiled, undisturbed, unmarred, unspoiled, unsullied, untapped, untested, untouched, untried, vestal; SEE CONCEPTS *372,560,578,797*

virile [*adj*] *potent, powerful*
driving, energetic, forceful, generative, lusty, macho*, procreative, red-blooded*, reproductive, robust, sound, strong, vibrant, vigorous, vital; SEE CONCEPTS *372,401,404*

virility [*n*] *masculinity*
forceful, machismo, macho*, maleness, manhood, manliness, muscularity, potency, power, ruggedness, strength, vigor; SEE CONCEPTS *371,372,408,648*

virtual [*adj*] *in essence*
basic, constructive, essential, fundamental, implicit, implied, in all but name*, in conduct, indirect, in effect, in practice, potential, practical, pragmatic, tacit, unacknowledged; SEE CONCEPTS *487,537,544,573*

virtually [*adv*] *for all practical purposes*
around, as good as, basically, effectually, essentially, for all intents and purposes*, fundamentally, give or take a little*, guesstimate*, implicitly, in all but name*, in effect, in essence, in substance, in the ballpark*, in the neighbor-

hood*, morally, nearly, not absolutely, not actually, practically, something like*, upwards of*; SEE CONCEPTS *487,544,573*

virtue [*n*] *honor, integrity*
advantage, asset, character, charity, chastity, consideration, credit, ethic, ethicality, ethicalness, excellence, faith, faithfulness, fineness, fortitude, generosity, goodness, good point*, high-mindedness, hope, ideal, incorruptibility, innocence, justice, kindness, love, merit, morality, plus*, probity, prudence, purity, quality, rectitude, respectability, righteousness, temper, temperance, trustworthiness, uprightness, value, worth, worthiness; SEE CONCEPTS *411,645*

virtuoso [*n*] *person who is an expert*
ace, adept, artist, artiste, authority, big league*, brain*, celebrity, champ*, champion, crackerjack*, dillettante, egghead, genius, hotshot*, hot stuff*, intelligent, magician, musician, natural*, no slouch*, old hand*, old pro*, performer, pro*, prodigy, professional, pundit, sharp*, star, superstar, whiz*, wizard; SEE CONCEPTS *348,352,416*

virtuous [*adj*] *good, ethical; innocent*
blameless, celibate, chaste, clean-living, effective, effectual, efficient, excellent, exemplary, faithful, guiltless, high-principled, honest, honorable, incorruptible, inculpable, in the clear*, irreprehensible, kosher*, legit*, moral, moralistic, noble, on the level*, on the up and up*, praiseworthy, principled, pure, regular, righteous, right-minded, spotless, straight, true-blue*, unsullied, untainted, untarnished, up front*, upright, wholesome, without reproach, worthy; SEE CONCEPTS *401,545*

virulent [*adj1*] *poisonous, lethal*
baneful, deadly, destructive, fatal, harmful, infective, injurious, malign, malignant, mephitic, pernicious, poison, septic, toxic, toxicant, unhealthy, unwholesome, venomous; SEE CONCEPTS *537,571*

virulent [*adj2*] *hostile*
acrimonious, antagonistic, bitter, cutting, hateful, malevolent, malicious, rancorous, resentful, scathing, sharp, spiteful, splenetic, stabbing, unfriendly, venomous, vicious, vindictive, vitriolic; SEE CONCEPTS *267,542*

virus [*n*] *bacterium, bug*
ailment, bacillus, disease, germ, illness, infection, microbe, microorganism, pathogen, sickness; SEE CONCEPT *306*

visceral [*adj*] *instinctive*
accustomed, automatic, congenital, habitual, inborn, ingrained, inherent, innate, instinctual, intrinsic, intuitional, intuitive, knee-jerk*, natural, reflex, rooted, second-nature*; SEE CONCEPT *544*

viscous [*adj*] *sticky, gummy*
adhesive, clammy, gelatinous, gluey*, glutinous, gooey*, mucilaginous, ropy, slimy, stiff, syrupy, tenacious, thick, tough, viscid; SEE CONCEPT *606*

visible [*adj*] *apparent, seeable*
arresting, big as life*, bold, clear, conspicuous, detectable, discernible, discoverable, distinguishable, evident, inescapable, in sight, in view, macroscopic, manifest, marked, not hidden, noticeable, observable, obtrusive, obvious, ocular, open, out in the open*, outstanding, palpable, patent, perceivable, perceptible, plain, pointed, pronounced, revealed, salient, seen, signal, striking, to be seen, unconcealed, under one's nose*,

unhidden, unmistakable, viewable, visual; SEE CONCEPTS *529,576,619*

vision [*n1*] *ability to perceive with eyes*
eyes*, eyesight, faculty, optics, perceiving, perception, range of view, seeing, sight, view; SEE CONCEPT *629*

vision [*n2*] *mental image, concept*
angle, aspect, astuteness, breadth of view, castles in the air*, conception, daydream, discernment, divination, dream, facet, fancy, fantasy, farsightedness, foreknowledge, foresight, head trip*, idea, ideal, ideality, imagination, insight, intuition, keenness, mental picture, muse, nightmare, outlook, penetration, perspective, phantasm, pie in the sky*, pipe dream*, point of view, prescience, retrospect, slant, standpoint, trip, understanding, view; SEE CONCEPTS *529,532,689*

vision [*n3*] *apparition*
apocalypse, chimera, delusion, ecstasy, fantasy, ghost, hallucination, haunt, illusion, mirage, nightmare, oracle, phantasm, phantom, phenomenon, presence, prophecy, revelation, specter, spirit, spook, trance, warlock, wraith; SEE CONCEPTS *370,529*

vision [*n4*] *very beautiful thing or person*
angel*, dazzler, dream, eyeful*, feast for the eyes*, perfect picture*, picture, sight, sight for sore eyes*, spectacle, stunner*; SEE CONCEPTS *424,529*

visionary [*adj*] *idealized, romantic*
abstracted, ambitious, astral, chimerical, daydreaming, delusory, dreaming, dreamy, exalted, fanciful, fantastic, grandiose, ideal, idealist, idealistic, illusory, imaginary, impractical, in the clouds*, introspective, lofty, musing, noble, otherworldly, pretentious, prophetic, quixotic, radical, speculative, starry-eyed*, unreal, unrealistic, unworkable, unworldly, utopian; SEE CONCEPTS *529,560,582*

visionary [*n*] *person who dreams, is idealistic*
castle-builder*, daydreamer, Don Quixote*, dreamer, enthusiast, idealist, mystic, prophet, romancer, romantic, seer, stargazer, theorist, utopian, zealot; SEE CONCEPTS *361,416*

visit [*n*] *social call upon another*
appointment, call, evening, holiday, interview, sojourn, stay, stop, stopover, talk, tarriance, vacation, visitation, weekend; SEE CONCEPTS *226,227*

visit [*v1*] *be a guest of*
call, call on, chat, come around, come by, converse, crash, drop by, drop in, drop over, dwell, frequent, go over to*, go to see*, hit, inspect, look around, look in on, look up, pay a call*, pay a visit to, play, pop in*, reside, see, sojourn, stay at, stay with, step in, stop by*, stop off*, swing by*, take in, talk, tarry, tour; SEE CONCEPTS *226,227*

visit [*v2*] *bother, haunt*
afflict, assail, attack, avenge, befall, bring down on, descend upon, force upon, impose, inflict, pain, punish, smite, trouble, wreak, wreck; SEE CONCEPTS *7,14,19*

visitor [*n*] *person temporarily in a foreign location*
caller, company, foreigner, guest, habitué, inspector, invitee, out-of-towner, transient, visitant; SEE CONCEPT *423*

vista [*n*] *view*
field of vision, glimpse, landscape, look, outline,

panorama, perspective, scene, scenery, seascape, sight, vision; SEE CONCEPT *628*

visual [*adj*] *able to be seen with eyes*
beheld, discernible, imaged, observable, observed, ocular, optic, optical, perceptible, seeable, seen, viewable, viewed, visible, visional; SEE CONCEPTS *485,576,619*

visualize [*v*] *make a picture of in the mind*
anticipate, apprehend, bring to mind, call to mind, call up, conceive of, conjure up, create, divine, dream up, envisage, envision, fancy, feature, foresee, get the picture*, image, imagine, object, picture, reflect, see, see in the mind's eye*, think, view, vision; SEE CONCEPTS *17,34*

vital [*adj1*] *essential*
basic, bottom-line*, cardinal, coal-and-ice*, constitutive, critical, crucial, decisive, fundamental, heavy*, imperative, important, indispensable, integral, key, life-or-death*, meaningful, meat-and-potatoes*, name, name-of-the-game*, necessary, needed, nitty-gritty*, prerequisite, required, requisite, significant, underlined, urgent; SEE CONCEPTS *546,567*

vital [*adj2*] *lively*
animated, dynamic, energetic, forceful, lusty, red-blooded, spirited, strenuous, vibrant, vigorous, vivacious, zestful; SEE CONCEPT *401*

vital [*adj3*] *alive*
animate, animated, breathing, generative, invigorative, life-giving, live, living, quickening; SEE CONCEPT *539*

vitality [*n*] *energy, spirit*
animation, ardor, audacity, bang, being, bloom, bounce, clout, continuity, drive, endurance, existence, exuberance, fervor, force, get-up-and-go*, go, guts*, intensity, life, liveliness, lustiness, pep, pizzazz*, power, pulse, punch, robustness, snap, sparkle, spunk*, stamina, starch*, steam, strength, stuff*, venturesomeness, verve, vigor, vim, vivaciousness, vivacity, zest, zing*, zip*; SEE CONCEPTS *407,411,633*

vitiate [*v1*] *cancel*
abate, abolish, abrogate, annihilate, annul, delete, deny, invalidate, negate, nullify, quash, recant, revoke, undermine, undo; SEE CONCEPTS *121,317*

vitiate [*v2*] *hurt, corrupt*
blemish, blight, brutalize, contaminate, damage, debase, debauch, defile, deprave, deteriorate, devalue, harm, impair, injure, mar, pervert, pollute, prejudice, spoil, sully, taint, tarnish, violate, warp, water down, weaken; SEE CONCEPTS *246,250*

vitriol [*n*] *bitterness*
acrimoniousness, contempt, disdain, hatefulness, hostility, malevolence, maliciousness, nastiness, sarcasm, venom, virulence; SEE CONCEPTS *410,633*

vittles [*n*] *food*
chow*, comestibles, eatables, eats, edibles, fare, foodstuff, goodies*, groceries*, grub, larder, meal, nourishment, provender, provisions, refreshments, snack, viands, victuals; SEE CONCEPTS *457,460,463*

vituperate [*v*] *criticize harshly*
abuse, accuse, asperse, bark at*, bawl out*, berate, blame, calumniate, castigate, censure, chew out*, condemn, curse, denounce, find fault, growl, insult, lambaste*, lash, malign, rail, rate, reproach, revile, rip into*, run down*, scold,

smear, tear into*, tongue-lash*, traduce, upbraid, vilify, yell at*; SEE CONCEPTS *44,52,54*

vituperation [*n*] *verbal attack*
bad-mouthing*, berating, blame, castigation, censure, criticism, defamation, insults, libel, obloquy, reprimand, reproach, scolding, slander, tirade, upbraiding, verbal abuse; SEE CONCEPT *54*

vivacious [*adj*] *lively, spirited*
active, alert, animate, animated, bouncy, brash, breezy, bubbling, cheerful, ebullient, effervescent, exuberant, frolicsome, full of life*, gay, happy, high-spirited, jolly, jumping, keen, light-hearted, merry, playful, rocking, scintillating, sparkling, sportive, sprightly, swinging, upbeat, vibrant, vital, zesty; SEE CONCEPTS *401,404*

vivid [*adj*] *intense, powerful*
active, animated, bright, brilliant, clear, colorful, definite, distinct, dramatic, dynamic, eloquent, energetic, expressive, flamboyant, gay, glowing, graphic, highly colored, lifelike, lively, lucid, meaningful, memorable, picturesque, realistic, resplendent, rich, sharp, shining, spirited, stirring, striking, strong, telling, theatrical, true-to-life, vigorous; SEE CONCEPTS *537,569,618*

vocabulary [*n*] *language of a person or people*
cant, dictionary, glossary, jargon, lexicon, palaver, phraseology, terminology, thesaurus, wordbook, word-hoard*, words, word-stock*; SEE CONCEPTS *276,280*

vocal [*adj1*] *spoken*
articulate, articulated, choral, expressed, intonated, lyric, modulated, operatic, oral, phonetic, phonic, pronounced, put into words*, said, singing, sonant, sung, uttered, verbal, viva voce, vocalic, vocalized, voiced, vowel; SEE CONCEPTS *267,594*

vocal [*adj2*] *extroverted about opinion*
articulate, blunt, clamorous, eloquent, expressive, facile, fluent, forthright, frank, free, free-spoken, glib, noisy, outspoken, plain-spoken, round, smooth-spoken, stentorian, strident, venting, vociferous; SEE CONCEPTS *267,404*

vocalize [*v*] *put into words or song*
belt out*, canary*, chant, chirp, communicate, convey, croon, emit, enunciate, express, give out*, groan, impart, let out*, moan, pronounce, say, shout, sing, sound, speak, talk, utter, vent, verbalize, voice, warble, yodel; SEE CONCEPT *77*

vocation [*n*] *life's work*
art, business, calling, career, craft, do*, dodge*, duty, employment, field, game, handicraft, job, lifework, line*, line of business*, métier, mission, nine-to-five*, occupation, office, post, profession, pursuit, racket*, role, thing*, trade, undertaking; SEE CONCEPTS *349,360*

vociferous [*adj*] *loud, insistent*
boisterous, clamant, clamorous, distracting, loud-mouthed, noisy, obstreperous, ranting, shouting, shrill, strident, uproarious, vehement, vociferant; SEE CONCEPTS *267,592,594*

vogue [*adj*] *fashionable*
faddy*, in*, latest, mod*, modish, now, popular, prevalent, rage*, state-of-the-art*, trendy, up-to-the-minute*, with it*; SEE CONCEPT *589*

vogue [*n*] *fashion; current practice*
chic, craze*, currency, custom, dernier cri, fad*, fashionableness, favor, in thing*, last word*, latest, mode, popularity, practice, prevalence, rage*, style, stylishness, thing*, trend, usage, use, way; SEE CONCEPT *655*

vi
vo

voice [*n1*] *expression, language*
articulation, call, cry, delivery, exclamation, inflection, intonation, modulation, murmur, mutter, roar, shout, song, sound, speech, statement, tone, tongue, utterance, vent, vocalization, vociferation, words, yell; SEE CONCEPTS 77,276

voice [*n2*] *opinion*
approval, choice, decision, expression, option, part, participation, preference, representation, right of free speech, say, say-so*, suffrage, vent, view, vote, vox populi, will, wish; SEE CONCEPTS 278,376

voice [*v*] *express opinion; put into words*
air, announce, articulate, assert, come out with*, cry, declare, deliver, divulge, emphasize, enunciate, give expression, give utterance, inflect, intonate, modulate, present, proclaim, pronounce, put, recount, say, sound, speak, talk, tell, utter, vent, verbalize, vocalize; SEE CONCEPTS 49,51

void [*adj1*] *empty*
abandoned, bare, barren, bereft, clear, deprived, destitute, devoid, drained, emptied, free, lacking, scant, short, shy, tenantless, unfilled, unoccupied, vacant, vacuous, without; SEE CONCEPTS 481,583,740,774

void [*adj2*] *nullified, meaningless*
avoided, bad, dead, forceless, fruitless, ineffective, ineffectual, inoperative, invalid, negated, not viable, nugatory, null, null and void, set aside, sterile, unconfirmed, unenforceable, unfruitful, unratified, unsanctioned, unsuccessful, useless, vain, voided, worthless; SEE CONCEPT 560

void [*n*] *emptiness, want*
blank, blankness, cavity, gap, hole, hollow, lack, nihility, nothingness, nullity, opening, space, vacuity, vacuum; SEE CONCEPTS 513,646,709

void [*v1*] *get rid of; empty*
clear, deplete, discharge, dispose, drain, dump, eject, eliminate, emit, evacuate, flow, give off, go, pour, relieve, remove, throw out, vacate; SEE CONCEPTS 179,180

void [*v2*] *nullify, cancel*
abnegate, abrogate, annul, black out*, bleep*, blue pencil*, clean up, cut, declare null and void*, discharge, dissolve, drop*, gut*, invalidate, launder, rescind, sanitize, sterilize, take out, trim, vacate; SEE CONCEPTS 50,88,121,211

volatile [*adj*] *explosive, changeable*
airy, buoyant, capricious, effervescent, elastic, elusive, ephemeral, erratic, expansive, fickle, fleeting, flighty, flippant, frivolous, fugacious, fugitive, gaseous, gay, giddy, impermanent, imponderable, inconsistent, inconstant, light, lively, lubricious, mercurial, momentary, playful, resilient, short-lived, sprightly, subtle, temperamental, ticklish, transient, transitory, unsettled, unstable, unsteady, up-anddown, vaporous, variable, whimsical; SEE CONCEPTS 401,534

volition [*n*] *free will*
accord, choice, choosing, conation, desire, determination, discretion, election, option, preference, purpose, resolution, selection, will, willingness, wish; SEE CONCEPTS 20,41

volley [*n*] *barrage*
battery, bombardment, burst, cannonade, crossfire, enfilade, firing, fussilade, gunfire, hail, round, salvo, shelling, shower, storm; SEE CONCEPT 320

voluble [*adj*] *talkative*
articulate, bigmouthed*, chattering, chatty*, fluent, full of hot air*, gabby, garrulous, longwinded*, loquacious, mouthy*, multiloquent, prolix, rambling, running on*, slick*, smooth*, talky, verbal, windy*, wordy; SEE CONCEPT 267

volume [*n1*] *capacity, measure of capacity*
aggregate, amount, body, bulk, compass, content, contents, cubic measure, dimensions, extent, figure, mass, number, object, quantity, size, total; SEE CONCEPTS 719,740,794

volume [*n2*] *loudness of a sound*
amplification, degree, intensity, power, sonority, strength; SEE CONCEPTS 65,792

volume [*n3*] *book*
album, edition, publication, tome, treatise, version; SEE CONCEPT 280

voluminous [*adj*] *big, vast*
abundant, ample, billowing, bulky, capacious, cavernous, comprehensive, convoluted, copious, covering, expansive, extensive, full, great, large, legion, many, massive, multifarious, multitudinous, numerous, prolific, roomy, several, simple, spacious, sundry, swelling, various; SEE CONCEPTS 773,781

voluntarily [*adv*] *of one's own free will*
at one's discretion, by choice, by preference, deliberately, freely, intentionally, of one's own accord*, on one's own, on one's own initiative*, optionally, spontaneously, willingly, with all one's heart*, without being asked, without prompting; SEE CONCEPTS 538,544

voluntary [*adj*] *willing*
autonomous, chosen, deliberate, designful, discretional, elected, free, freely, free-willed, gratuitous, honorary, independent, intended, intentional, opted, optional, spontaneous, unasked, unbidden, uncompelled, unconstrained, unforced, unpaid, unprescribed, volitional, volunteer, willed, willful, wished, witting; SEE CONCEPTS 538,544

volunteer [*v*] *offer to do something*
advance, bring forward, chip in*, come forward, do on one's own volition*, enlist, go in*, let oneself in for*, offer services, present, proffer, propose, put at one's disposal*, put forward, sign up, speak up, stand up, step forward, submit oneself, suggest, take bull by the horns*, take initiative*, take the plunge*, take upon oneself*, tender; SEE CONCEPTS 66,67

voluptuous [*adj*] *given to sensual pleasure; pleasurable to the senses*
appealing, attractive, delightful, desirable, enticing, erotic, fleshly, hedonist, hedonistic, indulgent, lubricious, luxurious, pleasing, salacious, self-indulgent, sensuous, sexy, sybaritic, wanton; SEE CONCEPTS 372,485

vomit [*v*] *disgorge*
be seasick*, be sick, bring up*, dry heave*, eject, emit, expel, gag*, heave*, hurl*, puke*, regurgitate, retch, ruminate, spew, spit up, throw up, upchuck*; SEE CONCEPTS 179,185,308

voodoo [*n*] *black magic*
abracadabra*, alchemy, black art, charm, conjuring, devilry, divination, enchantment, evil eye, hocus-pocus*, hoodoo, jinx, mumbo-jumbo*, necromancy, obeah, obi, sorcery, spell, witchcraft, witchery, wizardry; SEE CONCEPTS 370,689

voracious [*adj*] *very hungry, greedy*
avid, covetous, devouring, dog-hungry*, eda-

cious, empty, gluttonous, gorging, grasping, gross, insatiable, omnivorous, piggy*, prodigious, rapacious, ravening, ravenous, sating, starved, starved to death*, starving, uncontrolled, unquenchable; SEE CONCEPTS *20,401*

vote [*n*] *decision or right to decide representation*
aye*, ballot, choice, franchise, majority, nay*, plebiscite, poll, referendum, secret ballot, show of hands*, suffrage, tally, ticket, will, wish, yea*, yes or no*; SEE CONCEPTS *300,376*

vote [*v*] *decide on representation*
ballot, cast ballot, cast vote, choose, confer, declare, determine, effect, elect, enact, enfranchise, establish, go to the polls*, grant, judge, opt, pronounce, propose, put in office*, recommend, return, second, suggest; SEE CONCEPTS *41,300*

vouch [*v*] *give assurance*
act as a witness, affirm, answer for, assert, asseverate, assure, attest to, avert, avow, back, bear testimony, be responsible for, certify, confirm, contend, corroborate, cosign, declare, get behind*, give an affidavit, guarantee, maintain, okay*, predicate, profess, prove, put forth, rubber-stamp*, say so*, sign for, sponsor, stand up for*, substantiate, support, swear to, swear up and down*, testify, uphold, verify, vow, warrant, witness; SEE CONCEPTS *49,71,317*

voucher [*n*] *receipt*
certificate, check, chit, coupon, credential, debenture, IOU*, note, notice, proof of purchase, release, sales slip, slip, stub, ticket, token; SEE CONCEPTS *271,332*

vow [*n*] *promise*
affiance, assertion, asseveration, oath, pledge, profession, troth, word of honor; SEE CONCEPTS *278,689*

vow [*v*] *make a solemn promise*
affirm, assure, consecrate, covenant, cross one's heart*, declare, dedicate, devote, give word of honor*, pledge, plight, promise, swear, swear up and down*, testify, undertake solemnly*, vouch, warrant; SEE CONCEPTS *71,297*

voyage [*n*] *journey, often by water*
boating, crossing, cruise, excursion, hop, jaunt, junket, overnight, passage, sail, swing, tour, travel, travels, trek, trip, weekend; SEE CONCEPTS *155,224*

vulgar [*adj1*] *rude, offensive*
base, blue*, boorish, cheap, coarse, common, contemptible, crude, dirty, disgusting, dishonorable, filthy, fractious, gross*, hard-core*, ignoble, impolite, improper, indecent, indecorous, indelicate, inferior, low, malicious, nasty, naughty, obscene, odious, off-color, profane, raw, repulsive, ribald, risqué, rough, rude, scatological, slippery, smutty, sneaking, soft-core*, sordid, suggestive, tasteless, tawdry, uncouth, unmannerly, unrefined, unworthy, villainous, X-rated*; SEE CONCEPTS *267,372,545*

vulgar [*adj2*] *common, general*
colloquial, conversational, dime a dozen*, everyday, familiar, garden variety*, low, native, ordinary, plastic, plebeian, popular, public, run-of-the-mill*, unrefined, vernacular; SEE CONCEPT *530*

vulnerable [*adj*] *open to attack*
accessible, assailable, defenseless, exposed, liable, naked, on the line*, on the spot*, out on a limb*, ready, sensitive, sitting duck*, sucker*,

susceptible, tender, thin-skinned*, unguarded, unprotected, unsafe, weak, wide open*; SEE CONCEPTS *403,587*

W

wacky [*adj*] *acting crazy*
absurd, balmy, crazed, crazy, daft, demented, deranged, eccentric, erratic, foolish, hare-brained, insane, irrational, loony*, lunatic, mad, nuts*, nutty*, odd, preposterous, screwy*, silly, unpredictable, wild, zany*; SEE CONCEPTS *401,403*

wad [*n*] *ball of something*
back, block, boodle, bunch, bundle, chunk, clump, cushion, fortune, gathering, heap, hunk, lining, lump, mass, mint, nugget, packet, pad, pile, plug, pot, ream, roll, slew, stuff, tuft, wadding; SEE CONCEPTS *432,436*

waddle [*v*] *walk like a duck*
rock, shuffle, sway, toddle, totter, wiggle, wobble; SEE CONCEPT *151*

wade [*v*] *plod, often through water*
attack, attempt, bathe, drudge, fall to, ford, get feet wet*, get stuck in*, go for, initiate, jump in, labor, launch, light into, paddle, pitch in, set about, set to, splash, start, stumble, tackle, tear into*, toil, trek, walk, work through; SEE CONCEPTS *87,151*

waft [*v*] *carry*
bear, be carried, blow, carry, convey, drift, float, ride, transmit, transport; SEE CONCEPTS *147,217*

wag [*n*] *person who is very funny*
a million laughs*, card*, clown, comedian, comic, cutup*, droll*, farceur*, funny person, funster*, humorist, jester*, joker, jokester, kibitzer*, kidder, life of the party*, madcap*, prankster, punster, quipster, show-off*, trickster, wisecracker, wit, zany; SEE CONCEPTS *416,423*

wag [*v*] *wiggle back and forth*
beat, bob, fish-tail*, flutter, lash, move side to side, nod, oscillate, quiver, rock, shake, shimmy, stir, sway, swing, switch, twitch, vibrate, waggle, wave; SEE CONCEPTS *150,152*

wage [*v*] *carry on*
carry out, conduct, do, engage in, fulfill, make, practice, proceed with, prosecute, pursue, undertake; SEE CONCEPTS *91,100*

wager [*n*] *money or something gambled*
action, ante*, bet, challenge, chunk, fifty-fifty*, fighting chance*, flyer*, gamble, handle, hazard, hedge, hunch, long shot*, odds on*, outside chance*, parlay, play, pledge, plunge, pot*, risk, stake, toss-up, venture; SEE CONCEPTS *329,363,364*

wager [*v*] *bet money or something else in a gamble*
adventure, chance, gamble, game, hazard, hedge, hustle, lay, lay a wager, parlay, play, play the market*, pledge, plunge, put on*, put on the line*, put up, risk, set*, shoot*, shoot the works*, spec*, speculate, stake, take action, venture; SEE CONCEPTS *28,363*

wage/wages [*n*] *earnings for work*
allowance, bacon*, bacon and eggs*, bread*, compensation, cut, emolument, fee, hire, pay,

payment, price, receipts, recompense, remuneration, return, returns, reward, salary, share, stipend, sugar*, take*, take-home*; SEE CONCEPT *344*

waggish [*adj*] *playful*
amusing, blithe, bubbly, cheerful, clowning, comical, frolicsome, funny, gamesome, gay, humorous, jaunty, jesting, jocular, jocund, joking, jolly, joyous, kittenish, lighthearted, lively, merry, mirthful, snappy, spirited, teasing, whimsical, witty; SEE CONCEPTS *401,542*

waif [*n*] *lost or unclaimed person or thing*
castaway, dogie, drop*, fetch*, flotsam, foundling, homeless one, jetsam, orphan, ragamuffin, stray, urchin; SEE CONCEPT *423*

wail [*v*] *cry loudly*
bawl, bay, bemoan, bewail, carry on*, complain, cry the blues*, deplore, fuss, grieve, howl, jowl, keen, kick, lament, moan, mourn, repine, sob, squall, ululate, weep, whimper, whine; SEE CONCEPTS *77,185*

wait [*n*] *pause, delay*
down, downtime*, halt, hold*, hold-up, interim, interval, on hold*, rest, stay, time wasted*; SEE CONCEPT *807*

wait [*v*] *pause, rest*
abide, anticipate, await, bide, bide one's time*, cool it*, dally, delay, expect, fill time, foresee, hang*, hang around*, hang onto your hat*, hang out, hold back, hold everything*, hold on, hold the phone*, hole up*, keep shirt on*, lie in wait*, lie low*, linger, look for, look forward to, mark time*, put on hold*, remain, save it*, sit tight*, sit up for*, stall, stand by, stay, stay up for, stick around*, sweat it*, tarry, watch; SEE CONCEPTS *210,681*

wait on [*v*] *serve*
arrange, attend, care for, deal, deliver, help, minister, nurse, portion, ready, set, tend; SEE CONCEPTS *136,324*

waive [*v*] *give up; let go*
abandon, allow, cede, defer, delay, disclaim, disown, dispense with, forgo, grant, hand over, hold off, hold up, leave, neglect, postpone, prorogue, put off, refrain from, reject, relinquish, remit, remove, renege, renounce, reserve, resign, set aside, shelve, stay, surrender, suspend, table, turn over, yield; SEE CONCEPTS *121,234,317*

waiver [*n*] *giving up; letting go*
abandonment, abdication, disclaimer, foregoing, postponement, refusal, rejection, relinquishment, remission, renunciation, reservation, resignation, setting aside, surrender, tabling; SEE CONCEPTS *121,318,685*

wake [*n1*] *formal observance of a body before funeral*
deathwatch, funeral service, last rites, obsequies, rites, vigil, watch; SEE CONCEPTS *367,377*

wake [*n2*] *trail behind something*
aftermath, backwash, furrow, path, track, train, wash, wave; SEE CONCEPTS *753,824*

wakeful [*adj*] *alert, restless*
alive, astir, attentive, careful, heedful, insomniac, insomnious, observant, on guard, on the alert, on the lookout, on the qui vive, sleepless, unsleeping, vigilant, waking, wary, watchful, wide-awake; SEE CONCEPTS *539,542*

wake/waken [*v1*] *stop sleeping*
arise, awake, awaken, be roused, bestir, bring to life*, call, come to, get out of bed*, get up,

nudge, open one's eyes*, prod, rise, rise and shine*, roll out, rouse, shake, stir, stretch, tumble out*, turn out, wake up; SEE CONCEPT *105*

wake/waken [*v2*] *excite, stimulate*
activate, animate, arouse, awaken, challenge, enliven, fire, fire up*, freshen, galvanize, grasp, jazz up*, key up*, kindle, notice, pep up*, provoke, quicken, rally, renew, rouse, see, steam up*, stir up, switch on*, understand, whet, zip up*; SEE CONCEPTS *7,14,22*

walk [*n1*] *brief travel on foot*
airing, carriage, circuit, constitutional, gait, hike, jaunt, march, pace, parade, perambulation, peregrination, promenade, ramble, saunter, schlepp*, step, stretch, stride, stroll, tour, traipse, tramp, tread, turn; SEE CONCEPTS *149,224*

walk [*n2*] *pathway*
aisle, alley, avenue, boardwalk, boulevard, bricks, bypath, byway, catwalk, cloister, course, court, crossing, esplanade, footpath, gangway, lane, mall, passage, path, pavement, pier, platform, promenade, road, sidewalk, street, track, trail; SEE CONCEPT *501*

walk [*n3*] *discipline*
area, arena, bailiwick, calling, career, course, domain, dominion, field, line, metier, profession, province, sphere, terrain, territory, trade, vocation; SEE CONCEPTS *349,360*

walk [*v*] *move along on foot*
advance, amble, ambulate, canter, escort, exercise, file, foot, go, go on foot*, hike, hit the road*, hoof it, knock about*, lead, leg*, locomote, lumber, march, meander, pace, pad, parade, patrol, perambulate, plod, prance, promenade, race, roam, rove, run, saunter, scuff, shamble, shuffle, slog, stalk, step, stride, stroll, strut, stump, take a walk, toddle, tour, traipse, tramp, travel on foot, traverse, tread, trek, troop, trudge, wander, wend one's way*; SEE CONCEPT *149*

wall [*n*] *obstruction, divider*
bank, bar, barricade, barrier, block, blockade, bulwark, curb, dam, embankment, enclosure, facade, fence, fortification, hindrance, hurdle, impediment, levee, limitation, palisade, panel, paneling, parapet, partition, rampart, restriction, retainer, roadblock, screen, side, stockade, stop, surface; SEE CONCEPTS *440,666*

wallop [*n*] *strong hit*
bash, belt, blow, bop, bump, clash, collision, crash, haymaker*, impact, jar, jolt, kick, percussion, punch, shock, slam, slug, smack, smash, thump, thwack*, whack; SEE CONCEPT *189*

wallop [*v1*] *beat, hit*
bam, bash, batter, belt, blast, boff, bop, buffet, bushwhack*, clobber*, drub*, hide, lambaste*, paste, pelt, plant one*, pound, pummel, punch, slam, slog, slug, smack, smash, sock, strike, swat, take out, tan*, thrash, thump, whack, wham, whomp, zap*; SEE CONCEPT *189*

wallop [*v2*] *defeat soundly*
beat, best, clobber*, crush*, drub*, lambaste*, lick*, rout, shellac*, thrash*, trim*, trounce, vanquish, whip*; SEE CONCEPT *95*

wallow [*v1*] *slosh around in*
bathe in, be immersed, blunder, flounder, get stuck, immerse, lie, loll, lurch, move around in, reel, roll, roll about, roll around in, splash around, sprawl, stagger, stumble, sway, toss, totter, tumble, wade, welter; SEE CONCEPTS *149,201*

wallow [*v2*] *become very involved in*
bask, delight, enjoy, glory, grovel, humor, indulge oneself, luxuriate, pamper, relish, revel, roll, rollick, spoil, take pleasure; SEE CONCEPT *384*

wan [*adj*] *colorless, weak*
anemic, ashen, ashy, bilious, blanched, bleached, bloodless, cadaverous, dim, discolored, faint, feeble, forceless, ghastly, haggard, ineffective, ineffectual, livid, pale, pallid, pasty, peaked, sickly, washed-out, waxen, white, worn; SEE CONCEPTS *314,618*

wand [*n*] *rod*
baton, caduceus, scepter, sprig, staff, stick, twig; SEE CONCEPTS *470,499*

wander [*v1*] *move about aimlessly*
aberrate, amble, circumambulate, circumlocute, circumnutate, cruise, deviate, divagate, diverge, drift, float, follow one's nose*, gad*, gallivant*, globe-trot, hike, hopscotch*, jaunt, maunder, meander, peregrinate, ramble, range, roam, roll, rove, saunter, straggle, stray, stroll, take to the road*, trail, traipse, tramp, trek, vagabond, walk the tracks*; SEE CONCEPTS *151,224*

wander [*v2*] *digress; get lost*
babble, depart, deviate, divagate, diverge, err, get off the track*, get sidetracked*, go astray*, go off on a tangent*, lose one's way, lose train of thought*, ramble, rave, shift, stray, swerve, talk nonsense*, veer; SEE CONCEPTS *101,266,665*

wanderer [*n*] *person who travels aimlessly*
adventurer, beachcomber, bum, drifter, explorer, floater, gad*, gadabout, gallivanter, globe-trotter, gypsy, itinerant, meanderer, nomad, pilgrim, rambler, ranger, roamer, rolling stone*, rover, straggler, stray, stroller, traveler, vagabond, vagrant, voyager; SEE CONCEPT *423*

wane [*v*] *diminish, lessen*
abate, atrophy, decline, decrease, die away, die down, die out, dim, draw to a close*, drop, dwindle, ease off, ebb, fade, fade away, fail, fall, fall short, let up, moderate, peter out*, relent, shrink, sink, slacken, slack off, subside, taper off, waste away, weaken, wind down*, wither; SEE CONCEPTS *698,776*

want [*n1*] *desire*
appetite, craving, demand, fancy, hankering, hunger, longing, necessity, need, requirement, thirst, wish, yearning, yen; SEE CONCEPT *20*

want [*n2*] *lack, need*
absence, dearth, default, defect, deficiency, destitution, exigency, exiguousness, famine, impecuniousness, impoverishment, inadequacy, indigence, insufficiency, meagerness, neediness, paucity, pauperism, penury, poorness, poverty, privation, scantiness, scarcity, shortage, skimpiness; SEE CONCEPTS *646,709*

want [*v1*] *desire*
ache, aspire, be greedy, choose, could do with*, covet, crave, desiderate, fancy, feel a need, hanker*, have ambition, have an urge for*, have a passion for*, have a yen for*, have eyes for*, hunger, incline toward*, itch for*, long, lust, need, pine, prefer, require, spoil for*, thirst, wish, yearn; SEE CONCEPT *20*

want [*v2*] *lack, need*
be deficient, be deprived of, be found wanting, be insufficient, be poor, be short of, be without, call for, demand, fall short in, have need of,

miss, require, stand in need of, starve; SEE CONCEPT *646*

wanting [*adj*] *lacking, inadequate*
absent, away, bankrupt, bereft, burned out*, cooked*, cut off, defective, deficient, deprived, destitute, devoid, disappointing, empty, failing, faulty, gone, half-baked*, imperfect, incomplete, in default, inferior, less, minus, missing, needed, not good enough, not up to par*, omitted, out of gas*, patchy, poor, scant, scanty, scarce, short, shy, sketchy, substandard, too little too late*, unfulfilled, unsound; SEE CONCEPTS *531,546,560*

wanton [*adj1*] *extravagant, lustful*
abandoned, fast*, lax, lewd, libertine, libidinous, licentious, outrageous, profligate, promiscuous, shameless, speedy*, unprincipled, unscrupulous, wayward, X-rated*; SEE CONCEPTS *372,401,545*

wanton [*adj2*] *cruel, malicious*
accidentally on purpose*, arbitrary, contrary, double-crossing*, evil, gratuitous, groundless, inconsiderate, malevolent, malicious, mean, merciless, motiveless, needless, ornery, perverse, senseless, spiteful, unasked, uncalled-for*, unfair, unjust, unjustifiable, unjustified, unprovoked, vicious, wayward, wicked, willful; SEE CONCEPT *401*

wanton [*adj3*] *careless*
capricious, changeable, devil-may-care*, extravagant, fanciful, fickle, fitful, fluctuating, free, frivolous, heedless, hot and cold*, immoderate, inconstant, intemperate, lavish, outrageous, prodigal, profuse, rash, reckless, spendthrift, spoiled, thriftless, unfettered, unreserved, unrestrained, up and down*, variable, volatile, wasteful, whimsical, wild; SEE CONCEPTS *534,542*

wanton [*n*] *profligate person*
debauchee, libertine, rake; SEE CONCEPTS *412,415,419*

war [*n*] *armed conflict*
battle, bloodshed, cold war, combat, conflict, contention, contest, enmity, fighting, hostilities, hostility, police action, strife, strike, struggle, warfare; SEE CONCEPT *320*

war [*v*] *fight, battle*
attack, attempt, bombard, campaign against, challenge, clash, combat, contend, contest, differ, disagree, endeavor, engage in combat, go to war, kill, make war, march against, meet, murder, oppugn, shell, shoot, strive, struggle, take on, take the field against, take up arms, tug, wage war; SEE CONCEPTS *106,320*

ward [*n1*] *district*
area, canton, department, diocese, division, parish, precinct, quarter, territory, zone; SEE CONCEPTS *508,513*

ward [*n2*] *custody; person in one's custody*
adopted child, care, charge, child, client, dependent, foster child, godchild, guardianship, keeping, minor, orphan, pensioner, protection, protégé, protégée, pupil, safekeeping, trust; SEE CONCEPTS *414,691*

warden [*n*] *person who guards and manages*
administrator, bodyguard, caretaker, curator, custodian, deacon, dogcatcher, gamekeeper, governor, guard, guardian, jailer/jailor, janitor, keeper, officer, overseer, prison head, ranger, skipper, superintendent, watchdog, watchkeeper; SEE CONCEPT *347*

wa
wa

wardrobe [n] *clothes or furniture for storing clothes*
apparel, attire, buffet, bureau, chest, chiffonier, closet, clothing, commode, costumes, cupboard, drapes*, dresser, dry goods, duds*, ensembles, garments, locker, outfits, rags*, suits, threads*, toggery, togs, trousseau, trunk, vestments, weeds*; SEE CONCEPTS *443,451*

ward/ward off [v] *defend, guard*
avert, avoid, beat off, block, check, deflect, deter, divert, fend, foil, forestall, frustrate, halt, hold off, interrupt, keep at arm's length*, keep at bay*, keep off, obviate, parry, preclude, prevent, rebuff, rebut, repel, repulse, rule out, stave off, stop, stymie*, thwart, turn, turn aside, turn away; SEE CONCEPTS *96,134*

warehouse [n] *storage place*
barn, bin, depository, depot, distribution center, establishment, repository, shed, stash house, stockpile, stockroom, store, storehouse; SEE CONCEPTS *439,449*

wares [n] *merchandise for sale*
articles, commodities, goods, line, lines, manufactures, material, produce, product, products, range, seconds, stock, stuff, vendibles; SEE CONCEPT *338*

warfare [n] *armed conflict*
armed struggle, arms, battle, blows, campaigning, clash, combat, competition, contest, counterinsurgency, discord, emulation, fighting, hostilities, military operation, passage of arms, rivalry, strategy, strife, striving, struggle, tug-of-war*, war; SEE CONCEPT *320*

wariness [n] *caution*
alertness, attention, care, carefulness, deliberation, discretion, guardedness, heed, heedfulness, prudence, vigilance, watchfulness; SEE CONCEPT *410*

warlike [adj] *hostile, battling*
aggressive, attacking, bellicose, belligerent, bloodthirsty, combative, contending, contentious, contrary, fighting, gladiatorial, hawkish, inimical, martial, militant, militaristic, military, offensive, pugnacious, quarrelsome, ructious, soldierly, truculent, unfriendly, warmongering, warring; SEE CONCEPTS *401,548*

warlock [n] *sorcerer, wizard*
astrologer, augurer, clairvoyant, conjurer, diviner, enchanter, fortune-teller, magician, medium, necromancer, occultist, seer, soothsayer, thaumaturge, witch; SEE CONCEPT *361*

warm [adj1] *moderately hot*
balmy, broiling, clement, close, flushed, glowing, heated, hot, lukewarm, melting, mild, perspiring, pleasant, roasting, scorching, sizzling, snug, summery, sunny, sweating, sweaty, sweltering, temperate, tepid, thermal, toasty, warmish; SEE CONCEPT *605*

warm [adj2] *friendly, kind*
affable, affectionate, amiable, amorous, ardent, cheerful, compassionate, cordial, empathetic, fervent, genial, gracious, happy, heartfelt, hearty, hospitable, kindhearted, kindly, loving, pleasant, responsive, sincere, softhearted, sympathetic, tender, warmhearted, wholehearted; SEE CONCEPTS *267,401,404*

warm [adj3] *enthusiastic*
amorous, angry, animated, ardent, earnest, effusive, emotional, excitable, excited, fervent, fervid, glowing, gung-ho*, heated, hot*, intense,

irascible, keen, lively, nutty*, passionate, spirited, stormy, vehement, vigorous, violent, zealous; SEE CONCEPTS *401,542*

warm [v] *heat up*
bake, chafe, cook, fix, heat, melt, microwave, prepare, put on the fire, thaw, toast, warm over, warm up; SEE CONCEPTS *170,255*

warmhearted [adj] *compassionate, kindly*
all heart, benevolent, charitable, cordial, friendly, generous, genial, gentle, good-hearted, good-natured, gracious, hearty, kind, kindhearted, merciful, neighborly, pleasant, polite, softhearted, sympathetic, tenderhearted, thoughtful, warm; SEE CONCEPTS *401,403,404,542*

warmonger [n] *militarist*
combatant, fighter, hawk*, jingoist, militant; SEE CONCEPTS *358,359*

warn [v] *give notice of possible occurrence*
acquaint, address, admonish, advise, advocate, alert, apprise, caution, clue, clue in*, counsel, cry wolf*, deprecate, direct, dissuade, enjoin, exhort, fill in, forbid, forearm, forewarn, give fair warning, give the high sign*, give warning, guide, hint, inform, instruct, lay it out*, make aware, notify, order, post, predict, prepare, prescribe, prompt, put on guard, recommend, remind, remonstrate, reprove, signal, suggest, summon, tell, threaten, tip, tip off*, urge, wise up*; SEE CONCEPT *78*

warning [adj] *cautionary*
admonishing, admonitory, cautioning, exemplary, exhortatory, monitorial, monitory, ominous, premonitory, threatening; SEE CONCEPT *267*

warning [n] *notice of possible occurrence*
admonition, advice, alarm, alert, augury, caution, caveat, distress signal, example, exhortation, fore, foretoken, forewarning, guidance, handwriting on wall*, heads up*, hint, indication, information, injunction, intimation, lesson, look out*, Mayday*, notification, omen, portent, prediction, premonition, presage, recommendation, sign, signal, SOS*, suggestion, threat, tip, tip-off*, token, watch-it*, wink, word, word to the wise*; SEE CONCEPTS *78,274*

warp [v] *bend, distort*
bastardize*, brutalize, color, contort, corrupt, crook, curve, debase, debauch, deform, deprave, deviate, misrepresent, misshape, pervert, swerve, torture, turn, twist, vitiate, wind; SEE CONCEPTS *63,137,213,250*

warrant [n] *authorization*
accreditation, assurance, authentication, authority, basis, carte blanche, certificate, commission, credential, credentials, ducat, earnest, foundation, go-ahead*, green light*, guarantee, license, official document, okay*, pass, passport, pawn, permission, permit, pledge, right, sanction, security, shingle*, sticker, subpoena, summons, tag, testimonial, ticket, token, verification, warranty, word; SEE CONCEPTS *376,685*

warrant [v] *guarantee, justify, authorize*
affirm, answer for, approve, argue, assert, assure, attest, avouch, back, bear out, call for, certify, claim, commission, contend, declare, defend, delegate, demand, empower, endorse, ensure, entitle, excuse, explain, give grounds for, guarantee, guaranty, insure, license, maintain, necessitate, permit, pledge, privilege, promise, require, sanction, secure, sponsor, stand behind,

state, stipulate, swear, take an oath*, undertake, underwrite, uphold, vindicate, vouch for, vow; SEE CONCEPTS *50,57,71,88*

warranty [*n*] *promise*
assurance, bail, bond, certificate, contract, covenant, guarantee, guaranty, pledge, security, surety, written promise; SEE CONCEPTS *684,685*

warrior [*n*] *person who fights in combat*
battler, champion, combatant, conscript, enlisted person, fighter, fighting person, GI*, hero, serviceperson, soldier, trooper; SEE CONCEPT *358*

wary [*adj*] *careful, cautious*
alert, attentive, cagey, calculating, canny, chary, circumspect, considerate, discreet, distrustful, doubting, frugal, gingerly, guarded, handling with kid gloves*, heedful, keeping on one's toes*, leery, on guard, on the lookout*, on the qui vive, provident, prudent, safe, saving, sly, sparing, suspicious, thinking twice*, thrifty, unwasteful, vigilant, walking on eggs*, watchful, watching one's step*, watching out, wide-awake; SEE CONCEPTS *401,403*

wash [*n1*] *laundry, bath*
ablution, bathe, cleaning, cleansing, dirty clothes, laundering, rinse, scrub, shampoo, shower, washing; SEE CONCEPTS *451,514*

wash [*n2*] *wave; water movement*
ebb and flow, eddy, flow, gush, heave, lapping, murmur, roll, rush, spurt, surge, surging, sweep, swell, swirl, swishing, undulation; SEE CONCEPT *748*

wash [*n3*] *coloring*
coat, coating, film, layer, overlay, rinse, stain, suffusion, swab; SEE CONCEPT *475*

wash [*v1*] *bathe, clean*
bath, brush up, bubble, cleanse, clean up, dip, do the dishes*, do the laundry*, douse, drench, float, freshen up*, fresh up*, hose, imbue, immerse, lap, launder, lave, moisten, rinse, scour, scrub, shampoo, shine, shower, slosh, soak, soap, sponge, starch, swab, take a bath*, take a shower*, tub, wash up*, wet, wipe; SEE CONCEPT *165*

wash [*v2*] *be convincing*
be acceptable, bear scrutiny, be plausible, be reasonable, carry weight, convince, endure, hold up, hold water*, stand up*, stick*; SEE CONCEPT *676*

washed-out [*adj*] *faded*
bleached, colorless, discolored, drained, drawn, dull, etiolated, fatigued, lusterless, not shiny, pale, pallid, run-down, shopworn, tattered, threadbare, tired, worn; SEE CONCEPTS *560,617, 618*

washed-up [*adj*] *finished*
broken down, come to an end, concluded, done, done for, done with, ended, over and done*, over the hill*, shot*, through, useless; SEE CONCEPTS *528,531*

wassail [*n*] *celebration*
bash*, blast*, blowout*, carousal, ceremony, festival, festivity, frolic, gala, hoopla, hullabaloo*, joviality, jubilee, merriment, merrymaking, party, revelry, shindig*, spree, wingding*; SEE CONCEPT *377*

wassail [*v*] *celebrate, toast*
applaud, carouse, clink glasses, drink to, extol, feast, get drunk, honor, jubilate, let loose*, live it up*, make merry, party, pledge, raise one's glass to*, revel, salute; SEE CONCEPT *377*

waste [*n1*] *spending, use without thought*
decay, desolation, destruction, devastation, dilapidation, dissipation, disuse, exhaustion, expenditure, extravagance, fritter*, havoc, improvidence, lavishness, loss, lost opportunity*, misapplication, misuse, overdoing, prodigality, ravage, ruin, squander, squandering, unthriftiness, wastage, wastefulness; SEE CONCEPTS *156,252*

waste [*n2*] *land that is uncultivated*
badlands, barren, bog, brush, brushland, bush, desert, dust bowl, fen, jungle, marsh, marshland, moor, quagmire, solitude, swamp, tundra, void, wasteland, wild, wilderness, wilds; SEE CONCEPT *509*

waste [*n3*] *garbage, refuse*
debris, dreck, dregs, dross, excess, hogwash*, junk, leavings, leftovers, litter, offal, offscourings, rubbish, rubble, ruins, rummage, scrap, slop, sweepings, swill, trash; SEE CONCEPT *260*

waste [*v1*] *spend or use without thought; dwindle*
atrophy, be of no avail*, blow, burn up, consume, corrode, crumble, debilitate, decay, decline, decrease, deplete, disable, disappear, dissipate, divert, drain, droop, eat away, ebb, emaciate, empty, enfeeble, exhaust, fade, fritter away*, frivol away*, gamble away, gnaw, go to waste, lavish, lose, misapply, misemploy, misuse, perish, pour down the drain*, run dry, run through*, sap, sink, splurge, squander, thin, throw away, trifle away, undermine, wane, wear, wear out, wilt, wither; SEE CONCEPT *156*

waste [*v2*] *ruin, destroy*
depredate, desecrate, desolate, despoil, devastate, devour, lay waste, pillage, rape, ravage, raze, reduce, sack, spoil, spoliate, wreak havoc; SEE CONCEPT *252*

wasted [*adj1*] *emaciated*
anorexic, atrophied, attenuated, bony, famished, gaunt, haggard, lank, lean, scrawny, shrivelled, skeletal, skin-and-bones*, skinny, starved, thin, underfed, undernourished, withered; SEE CONCEPTS *490,491*

wasted [*adj2*] *high on drugs*
baked*, bombed*, boozed up*, buzzed*, doped, drugged, drunk, feeling no pain*, flying*, fried, inebriated, intoxicated, loaded, on a trip*, plastered, ripped*, sloshed*, smashed*, spaced out*, stewed*, stoned*, strung out*, tanked*, tipsy, totaled*, tripping*; SEE CONCEPT *314*

wasteful [*adj*] *not economical*
careless, cavalier, destructive, dissipative, extravagant, immoderate, improvident, incontinent, lavish, liberal, overdone, overgenerous, poundfoolish*, prodigal, profligate, profuse, reckless, ruinous, spendthrift, squandering, thriftless, uneconomical, unthrifty, wanton, wild; SEE CONCEPT *401*

watch [*n1*] *clock worn on body*
analog watch, chronometer, digital watch, pocket watch, stopwatch, ticker*, timepiece, timer, wristwatch; SEE CONCEPT *463*

watch [*n2*] *lookout*
alertness, attention, awareness, duty, eagle eye*, eye*, gander, guard, hawk, heed, inspection, notice, observance, observation, patrol, picket, scrutiny, sentinel, sentry, supervision, surveillance, tab, tout, vigil, vigilance, watchfulness, weather eye*; SEE CONCEPTS *134,623*

wa
wa

watch [v1] *look at*
attend, case, check out, concentrate, contemplate, eagle-eye*, examine, eye*, eyeball*, focus, follow, gaze, get a load of*, give the once over*, have a look-see*, inspect, keep an eye on*, keep tabs on*, listen, look, mark, mind, note, observe, pay attention, peer, pipe*, regard, rubberneck*, scan, scope, scrutinize, see, spy, stare, take in, take notice, view, wait; SEE CONCEPT *623*

watch [v2] *guard, protect*
attend, be on alert*, be on the lookout*, be vigilant*, be wary, be watchful, care for, keep, keep eyes open*, keep eyes peeled*, keep watch over, look after, look out, mind, oversee, patrol, pick up on, police, ride shotgun for*, superintend, take care of, take heed*, tend, wait; SEE CONCEPTS *134,623*

watchful [adj] *on the lookout*
alert, all ears*, attentive, careful, cautious, chary, circumspect, glued*, guarded, heedful, hooked*, keen, not missing a trick*, observant, on guard, on one's toes*, on the ball*, on the job*, on the qui vive, on the watch, open-eyed, prepared, ready, see after, see to, suspicious, unsleeping, vigilant, wakeful, wary, wide-awake, with eyes peeled*; SEE CONCEPT *401*

watchkeeper [n] *person who guards, is on lookout*
caretaker, curator, custodian, detective, flagger, guard, keeper, lookout, observer, patrol, picket, police officer, ranger, scout, security guard, security officer, sentinel, sentry, signaller, spotter, spy, ward, warden, watch, watcher; SEE CONCEPT *348*

water [n] *pure liquid hydrogen and oxygen*
Adam's ale*, aqua, aqua pura*, drink, H_2O, rain, rainwater, saliva, tears; SEE CONCEPT *467*

water [v] *dampen; put water in*
baptize, bathe, damp, dilute, doctor, douse, drench, drool, flood, hose, imbue, inundate, irrigate, moisten, saturate, soak, sodden, souse, spatter, spray, sprinkle, steep, thin, wash, weaken, wet; SEE CONCEPT *256*

waterfall [n] *cascade*
cataract, chute, fall, rapids, shoot, weir; SEE CONCEPTS *514,787*

waterlogged [adj] *saturated*
dank, drenched, dripping, drowned, soaked, soaking, sodden, soggy, sopping, soppy, soused, wet, wringing-wet; SEE CONCEPT *603*

waterloo [n] *final defeat, total defeat*
annihilation, beating, collapse, conquest, crushing defeat, drubbing*, failure, fall, licking, massacre, overthrow, rout, shellacking*, slaughter, thrashing, trashing, trouncing, vanquishment, waxing, whipping, whitewashing; SEE CONCEPT *95*

watery [adj] *liquid, diluted*
adulterated, anemic, aqueous, bloodless, colorless, damp, dilute, doused, flavorless, fluid, humid, insipid, marshy, moist, pale, runny, serous, sodden, soggy, tasteless, thin, washed, watered-down, waterlike, water-logged, weak, wet; SEE CONCEPTS *485,603,618*

wave [n] *sea surf, current*
bending, billow, breaker, coil, comber, convolution, corkscrew, crest, crush, curl, curlicue, drift, flood, foam, ground swell, gush, heave, influx, loop, movement, outbreak, rash, ridge, ripple,
rippling, rocking, roll, roller, rush, scroll, sign, signal, stream, surge, sweep, swell, tendency, tide, tube, twirl, twist, undulation, unevenness, uprising, upsurge, whitecap, winding; SEE CONCEPTS *147,436,514*

wave [v] *move back and forth; gesture*
beckon, billow, brandish, coil, curl, direct, falter, flap, flourish, flow, fluctuate, flutter, fly, gesticulate, indicate, motion, move to and fro, oscillate, palpitate, pulsate, pulse, quaver, quiver, reel, ripple, seesaw, shake, sign, signal, stir, stream, surge, sway, swell, swing, swirl, swish, switch, tremble, twirl, twist, undulate, vacillate, vibrate, wag, waggle, waver, whirl, wield, wigwag*, wobble; SEE CONCEPTS *74,147,149*

waver [v] *shift back and forth; be indecisive*
be irresolute, be unable to decide*, blow hot and cold*, change, deliberate, dilly-dally*, dither, falter, flicker, fluctuate, halt, hedge, hem and haw*, hesitate, oscillate, palter, pause, pussyfoot around*, quiver, reel, run hot and cold*, seesaw*, shake, stagger, sway, teeter, totter, tremble, trim, undulate, vacillate, vary, waffle, wave, weave, whiffle, wobble, yo-yo*; SEE CONCEPTS *18,147,410*

wax [v] *become large, fuller*
augment, become, build, come, develop, dilate, enlarge, expand, fill out, get bigger, get to, grow, grow full, heighten, increase, magnify, mount, multiply, rise, run, swell, turn, upsurge; SEE CONCEPTS *704,780*

way [n1] *method, technique*
action, approach, contrivance, course, course of action, custom, design, expedient, fashion, form, groove*, habit, habitude, hang-up*, hook*, idea, instrument, kick, manner, means, measure, mode, modus, move, outline, plan, plot, policy, practice, procedure, process, scheme, shot, step, stroke, style, system, tack, thing*, usage, use, vehicle, wise, wont; SEE CONCEPT *6*

way [n2] *direction, route*
access, admission, admittance, advance, alternative, approach, artery, avenue, bearing, boulevard, byway, channel, course, distance, door, drag*, elbowroom, entrance, entrée, entry, extent, forward motion, gate, gateway, headway, highway, ingress, journey, lane, length, line, march, movement, opening, orbit, passage, path, pathway, progress, progression, ride, road, room, row, space, stone's throw*, street, stretch, tendency, thataway*, thoroughfare, track, trail, trend, walk; SEE CONCEPTS *501,738,739*

way [n3] *characteristic, habit*
aspect, behavior, circumstance, condition, conduct, consuetude, custom, detail, fashion, feature, fettle, form, gait, groove, guise, habit, hook, idiosyncrasy, kick*, manner, nature, particular, personality, point, practice, praxis, respect, sense, shape, shot, situation, state, status, style, thing*, tone, trait, trick, usage, use, wont; SEE CONCEPT *411*

wayfarer [n] *traveler*
adventurer, barnstormer*, bum*, drifter, excursionist, explorer, gadabout*, globetrotter, gypsy, hiker, hitchhiker, hobo, itinerant, journeyer, nomad, peddler, pilgrim, rambler, roamer, rover, trekker, vagabond, vagrant, walker, wanderer; SEE CONCEPTS *348,423*

wayfaring [adj] *traveling*
drifting, gadabout, globe-trotting, itinerant, itin-

erate, jet-setting*, journeying, nomadic, perambulant, perambulatory, peripatetic, rambling, roving, rubbernecking*, vagabond, vagrant, voyaging, walking, wandering; SEE CONCEPT *401*

waylay [*v*] *intercept, ambush*
accost, ambuscade, assail, attack, box*, bushwhack*, catch, hold up, intercept, jump, lay for*, lie in wait, lurk, pounce on, prowl, set upon, skulk, slink, surprise, swoop down on*; SEE CONCEPTS *86,121*

wayward [*adj*] *contrary, unmanageable*
aberrant, arbitrary, balky, capricious, changeable, contumacious, cross-grained, delinquent, disobedient, disorderly, errant, erratic, fickle, flighty, fractious, froward, headstrong, immoral, inconstant, incorrigible, insubordinate, intractable, mulish, obdurate, obstinate, ornery*, perverse, rebellious, recalcitrant, refractory, restive, self-indulgent, self-willed, stubborn, uncompliant, undependable, ungovernable, unpredictable, unruly, unstable, variable, whimsical, willful; SEE CONCEPT *401*

weak [*adj1*] *not strong*
anemic, debilitated, decrepit, delicate, effete, enervated, exhausted, faint, feeble, flaccid, flimsy, forceless, fragile, frail, hesitant, impuissant, infirm, insubstantial, irresolute, lackadaisical*, languid, languorous, limp, makeshift, out of gas*, powerless, prostrate, puny, rickety, rocky*, rotten, senile, shaky, sickly, sluggish, spent, spindly, supine, tender, torpid, uncertain, undependable, unsound, unsteady, unsubstantial, wasted, wavering, weakened, weakly, wobbly; SEE CONCEPTS *314,488,489*

weak [*adj2*] *cowardly*
faint-hearted, fluctuant, frightened, hesitant, impotent, indecisive, ineffectual, infirm, insecure, irresolute, laid-back*, nerveless, nervous, palsied, powerless, shaky, soft, spineless, tender, timorous, uncertain, undependable, unreliable, unstable, unsure, vacillating, wavering, weak-kneed*, wimpy*, wishy-washy*, wobbly, zero*; SEE CONCEPTS *402,403,542*

weak [*adj3*] *faint, soft*
bated, dim, distant, dull, feeble, gentle, imperceptible, inaudible, indistinct, low, muffled, pale, poor, quiet, reedy, slight, small, stifled, thin, unaccented, unstressed, whispered; SEE CONCEPT *594*

weak [*adj4*] *deficient, feeble*
faulty, flabby, flimsy, forceless, green*, handicapped, hollow, immature, implausible, impotent, improbable, inadequate, incompetent, incomplete, inconceivable, inconclusive, incredible, ineffective, ineffectual, inept, invalid, lacking, lame, limited, pathetic, poor, raw, shaky, shallow, slight, slim, small, spineless, substandard, thick, thin, unbelievable, unconvincing, unprepared, unqualified, unsatisfactory, unsubstantial, unsure, untrained, wanting; SEE CONCEPTS *537,558,570*

weak [*adj5*] *exposed, vulnerable*
accessible, assailable, defenseless, helpless, indefensible, unguarded, unprotected, unsafe, untenable, wide-open*, woundable; SEE CONCEPTS *576,587*

weak [*adj6*] *watered-down*
dilute, diluted, insipid, milk-and-water*, runny, tasteless, thin, washy, waterish, watery, wishywashy*; SEE CONCEPTS *462,485*

weaken [*v*] *reduce the strength of*
abate, adulterate, break up, cripple, crumble, cut, debase, debilitate, decline, decrease, depress, devitalize, dilute, diminish, droop, dwindle, ease up, enervate, exhaust, fade, fail, faint, flag, give way, halt, impair, impoverish, invalidate, languish, lessen, limp, lose, lose spirit, lower, minimize, mitigate, moderate, reduce, relapse, relax, sap, slow down, soften, temper, thin, thin out, tire, totter, tremble, undermine, vitiate, wane, water down, wilt; SEE CONCEPTS *240,698*

weakling [*n*] *person who has no strength*
baby, chicken*, chicken heart*, coward, cream puff*, crybaby, dotard, invertebrate, jellyfish*, misfit, pushover, wimp*, yellow belly*; SEE CONCEPTS *412,423*

weak-minded [*adj*] *indecisive*
astraddle, changeable, hemming and hawing*, hesitant, hesitating, indeterminate, irresolute, on the fence*, spineless, tentative, uncertain, undecided, undetermined, waffling, wavering, weak-kneed*, wishy-washy*, without guts*, yellow-bellied*; SEE CONCEPTS *534,535*

weakness [*n*] *defect, proneness*
Achilles heel*, appetite*, blemish, chink in armor*, debility, decrepitude, deficiency, delicacy, enervation, failing, faintness, fault, feebleness, flaw, fondness, fragility, frailty, gap, impairment, imperfection, impotence, inclination, inconstancy, indecision, infirmity, instability, invalidity, irresolution, lack, languor, lapse, liking, passion, penchant, powerlessness, predilection, proclivity, prostration, senility, shortcoming, soft spot*, sore point*, taste*, vice, vitiation, vulnerability; SEE CONCEPTS *411,674,732*

wealth [*n*] *money, resources*
abundance, affluence, assets, belongings, bounty, cache, capital, cash, clover*, commodities, copiousness, cornucopia, dough*, estate, fortune, funds, gold, goods, hoard, holdings, lap of luxury*, long green*, lucre, luxuriance, luxury, means, opulence, pelf, plenitude, plenty, possessions, profusion, property, prosperity, prosperousness, revenue, riches, richness, security, stocks and bonds, store, substance, substantiality, treasure, velvet*, worth; SEE CONCEPTS *340,710*

wealthy [*adj*] *rich; having a lot of money*
affluent, booming, comfortable, having it made*, independent, in the money*, loaded, made of money*, moneyed, of independent means, opulent, pecunious, prosperous, rolling in it*, substantial, upscale, well-heeled*, well-off*, well-to-do*; SEE CONCEPT *334*

weapon [*n*] *arm, armament*
ammunition, anlace, arbalest, archery, arrow, assegai, atlatl, ax, axe, backsword, ballista, banderilla, barong, bat, baton, battle-ax, bayonet, bazooka, billy club, blackjack, blade, blowgun, bludgeon, bomb, boomerang, bow and arrow, bowie knife, brass knuckles, cannon, catapult, cleaver, club, crossbow, cudgel, cutlass, dagger, dart, dirk, firearm, flamethrower, gun, harpoon, hatchet, howitzer, hunting knife, knife, lance, machete, machine gun, missile, musket, nerve gas, nuclear bomb, nunchaku, pistol, revolver, rifle, saber, scythe, shotgun, slingshot, spear, spike, stiletto, switchblade, sword, tear gas; SEE CONCEPT *500*

wa
we

wear [*n*] *use, corrosion*
abrasion, attrition, damage, depreciation, deterioration, dilapidation, diminution, disappearance, employment, erosion, friction, impairment, inroads, loss, mileage, service, usefulness, utility, waste, wear and tear; SEE CONCEPTS *658,698*

wear [*v1*] *be clothed in*
array, attire, bear, be dressed in, carry, clothe oneself, cover, display, don, draw on, dress in, effect, exhibit, fit out, get into, get on, harness, have on, put on, show, slip on, sport, suit up*, turn out*, wrap; SEE CONCEPTS *167,453*

wear [*v2*] *corrode, use*
abrade, become threadbare, become worn, be worthless, chafe, consume, crumble, cut down, decay, decline, decrease, deteriorate, diminish, drain, dwindle, erode, exhaust, fade, fatigue, fray, gall, go to seed*, graze, grind, impair, jade, overuse, overwork, rub, scrape, scrape off, scuff, shrink, tax, tire, use up, wash away, waste, wear out, wear thin, weary, weather; SEE CONCEPTS *156,225,240,698*

wear [*v3*] *bother, undermine*
annoy, drain, enervate, exasperate, exhaust, fatigue, get the better of, harass, irk, pester, reduce, tax, vex, weaken, wear down, weary; SEE CONCEPTS *7,19*

wear [*v4*] *endure*
bear up, be durable, hold up, last, remain, stand, stand up; SEE CONCEPT *23*

weary [*adj*] *tired*
all in*, beat*, bone-tired*, bored, burned out*, bushed, dead*, dead tired*, discontented, disgusted, dog-tired*, done in*, drained, drooping, drowsy, enervated, exhausted, fagged, fatigued, fed up, flagging, had it*, impatient, indifferent, jaded, knocked out, out of gas*, overworked, pooped*, punchy*, ready to drop*, sick, sick and tired*, sleepy, spent*, taxed, wearied, wearing, wiped out*, worn out, zonked*; SEE CONCEPTS *314,403,485*

weary [*v*] *make tired*
annoy, bore, burden, cause ennui, cloy, debilitate, depress, disgust, dishearten, distress, drain, droop, drowse, enervate, enfeeble, exasperate, exhaust, fade, fag, fall off, fatigue, flag, glut, grow tired, harass, have had enough*, irk, jade, leave one cold*, lose interest, make discontented, nauseate, oppress, overwork, pain, plague, sap, sicken, sink, strain, take it out of*, tax, tire, tire out, try the patience of*, tucker out*, vex, weaken, wear down, wear out, weigh; SEE CONCEPTS *13,250,303*

weasel [*n*] *sneak*
betrayer, blabbermouth*, canary*, deceiver, deep throat*, double-crosser, fink*, informant, informer, narc*, nark*, rat*, sneak, snitch, snitcher, source, squealer*, stoolie*, stool pigeon*, tattler, tattletale, tipster*, turncoat, weasel*, whistle-blower; SEE CONCEPTS *348,354,423*

weasel [*v*] *avoid, evade*
balk, beat around the bush*, circumvent, cop out, dance around an issue*, dodge, duck, elude, equivocate, eschew, flee, get around, give the runaround*, hedge, hem and haw*, lay low*, pussyfoot, put off, renege, shirk, shuck, sidestep, slip out, sneak away*, tap dance*, waffle*, welsh, worm one's way out of*; SEE CONCEPTS *30,102*

weather [*n*] *atmospheric conditions*
climate, clime, elements; SEE CONCEPTS *522,524*

weather [*v*] *endure*
acclimate, bear the brunt of*, bear up against*, become toughened, brave, come through, expose, get through, grow hardened, grow strong, harden, make it, overcome, pull through, resist, ride out*, rise above*, season, stand, stick it out*, suffer, surmount, survive, toughen, withstand; SEE CONCEPTS *23,35,202*

weatherperson [*n*] *meteorologist*
climatologist, storm chaser, weathercaster, weather-forecaster, weatherman/woman; SEE CONCEPTS *60,292*

weave [*v*] *blend, unite; contrive*
braid, build, careen, complect, complicate, compose, construct, create, criss-cross, crochet, cue, entwine, fabricate, fold, fuse, incorporate, interfold, interlace, interlink, intermingle, intertwine, introduce, knit, knot, loop, lurch, make, make up, manufacture, mat, merge, mesh, move in and out, net, piece together, plait, ply, put together, reticulate, sew, snake, spin, splice, twine, twist, twist and turn, whip through, wind, wreathe, writhe, zigzag; SEE CONCEPTS *147,158*

web [*n*] *netting*
cobweb, complexity, entanglement, fabric, fiber, filigree, gossamer, interconnection, interlacing, involvement, labyrinth, lacework, lattice, mat, matting, maze, mesh, meshwork, morass, net, network, plait, reticulation, screen, skein, snarl, tangle, texture, tissue, toil, trellis, warp, weave, webbing, weft, wicker, woof; SEE CONCEPTS *260,473*

wed [*v1*] *marry*
become husband and wife, be married, couple, espouse, get hitched*, get married, join, lead to the altar, make one*, receive in marriage, say I do*, take in marriage, tie*, tie the knot*, unite; SEE CONCEPT *297*

wed [*v2*] *join, unite*
ally, associate, blend, coalesce, cojoin, combine, commingle, connect, couple, dedicate, fuse, interweave, link, marry, merge, relate, unify, yoke; SEE CONCEPTS *113,193*

wedding [*n*] *marriage rite*
bells*, bridal, espousal, hook, marriage, marriage ceremony, matrimony, nuptial rite, nuptials, spousal, union, wedlock; SEE CONCEPT *297*

wedge [*n*] *solid piece, often triangular*
block, chock, chunk, cleat, cotter, cusp, keystone, lump, prong, quoin, shim, spire, taper; SEE CONCEPTS *471,499*

wedlock [*n*] *marriage*
alliance, association, conjugality, connubiality, coupling, espousal, holy matrimony, mating, matrimony, nuptials, spousal, union, wedded bliss*, wedding; SEE CONCEPTS *297,388*

wee [*adj*] *very small, tiny*
bitsy*, bitty, diminutive, infinitesimal, insignificant, itsy-bitsy*, itty-bitty*, Lilliputian, little, microscopic, miniature, minuscular, minuscule, minute, negligible, pee-wee*, petite, pint-sized*, pocket-size*, puny, slight, teensy*, teensy-weensy*, teeny*; SEE CONCEPTS *762,773,789*

weep [*v*] *cry*
bawl, bemoan, bewail, blubber*, boohoo*, break down*, burst into tears*, complain, deplore, drip, grieve, howl, keen, lament, let go*, let it out*, mewl, moan, mourn, shed tears, snivel, sob,

squall, ululate, wail, whimper, yowl; SEE CON-
CEPTS *49,185*

weigh [*v1*] *measure heaviness*
counterbalance, have a weight of, heft, measure,
put in the balance, put on the scale, scale, tip the
scales at; SEE CONCEPT *103*

weigh [*v2*] *consider, contemplate*
analyze, appraise, balance, brainstorm*, deliberate, estimate, evaluate, examine, excogitate, give
thought to, hash over*, meditate, mind, mull
over, perpend, ponder, rate, reflect upon, rehash,
sort out, study, sweat*, think about, think out,
think over, track; SEE CONCEPT *24*

weigh [*v3*] *have influence*
be heavy, be important, be influential, be something, burden, carry weight, charge, count, cumber, cut, cut some ice, import, impress, lade,
matter, mean, militate, press, pull, register, saddle, show, signify, stack up against*, tax, tell;
SEE CONCEPTS *7,19,22,237,682*

weigh down [*v*] *depress*
bear down, burden, cumber, get down, hold
down, oppress, overburden, overload, press,
press down, prey on, pull down, sadden, task,
trouble, weight, weigh upon, worry; SEE CON-
CEPTS *7,19*

weight [*n1*] *heaviness*
adiposity, avoirdupois, ballast, burden, density,
G-factor*, gravity, gross, heft, heftiness, load,
mass, measurement, net, ponderosity, ponder-
ousness, poundage, pressure, substance, tonnage;
SEE CONCEPT *795*

weight [*n2*] *something used to measure heaviness*
anchor, ballast, bob, counterbalance, counterpoise, counterweight, mass, pendulum, plumb,
plumb bob, poundage, pressure, rock, sandbag,
sinker, stone; SEE CONCEPTS *290,470*

weight [*n3*] *importance*
access, authority, clout, connection, consequence, consideration, credit, effectiveness, efficacy, emphasis, forcefulness, forcibleness,
impact, import, influence, magnitude, moment,
momentousness, persuasiveness, pith, potency,
power, powerfulness, prestige, pull, significance,
signification, substance, sway, value, weightiness; SEE CONCEPTS *668,682*

weight [*n4*] *burden*
albatross*, ball and chain*, charge, cumber,
cumbrance, deadweight*, duty, encumbrance,
excess baggage*, load, millstone*, onus, oppression, pressure, responsibility, strain, task, tax;
SEE CONCEPTS *532,674,679,690*

weighty [*adj1*] *heavy*
burdensome, cumbersome, cumbrous, dense, fat,
fleshy, hefty, massive, obese, overweight, ponderous, porcine, portly, stout; SEE CONCEPT *491*

weighty [*adj2*] *serious, important*
big, big deal*, consequential, considerable, critical, crucial, earnest, forcible, grave, heavy*,
heavyweight, life and death*, material, meaningful, momentous, no-nonsense*, portentous, sedate, severe, significant, sober, solemn, somber,
staid, substantial, underlined; SEE CONCEPTS
548,568

weighty [*adj3*] *troublesome, difficult*
backbreaking, burdensome, crushing, demanding, exacting, exigent, grievous, onerous, oppressive, superincumbent, taxing, tough, worrisome,
worrying; SEE CONCEPTS *538,565*

weird [*adj*] *odd, bizarre*
awe-inspiring, awful, creepy*, curious, dreadful,
eccentric, eerie*, far-out*, fearful, flaky*,
freaky*, funky*, ghastly, ghostly, grotesque,
haunting, horrific, inscrutable, kinky*, kooky*,
magical, mysterious, occult, oddball*, ominous,
outlandish, peculiar, preternatural, queer, secret,
singular, spooky*, strange, supernal, supernatural, uncanny, uncouth, unearthly, unnatural; SEE
CONCEPTS *564,570*

weirdo [*n*] *freak, oddball*
case*, character, crackpot*, eccentric, flake*,
fruitcake*, geek*, misfit, nutcase, odd bird*,
screwball*, strange bird*; SEE CONCEPT *423*

welcome [*adj*] *gladly received*
acceptable, accepted, agreeable, appreciated,
cherished, congenial, contenting, cordial, delightful, desirable, desired, esteemed, favorable,
genial, good, grateful, gratifying, honored, invited, nice, pleasant, pleasing, pleasurable, refreshing, satisfying, sympathetic, wanted; SEE
CONCEPTS *555,572*

welcome [*n*] *greeting*
acceptance, entertainment, entrée, friendliness,
handshake, hello, hospitality, howdy*, key to the
city*, ovation, reception, red carpet*, rumble*,
salutation, salute, tumble*; SEE CONCEPT *278*

welcome [*v*] *receive gladly*
accept, accept gladly, accost, admit, bid welcome, embrace, entertain, flag*, greet, hail, hug,
meet, offer hospitality, receive, roll out red carpet*, salute, show in, take in, tumble*, usher in;
SEE CONCEPTS *266,384*

weld [*v*] *bind, connect*
bond, braze, cement, combine, fix, fuse, join,
link, solder, unite; SEE CONCEPT *193*

welfare/well-being [*n*] *health and prosperity*
abundance, advantage, benefit, contentment,
ease, easy street*, euphoria, felicity, good, good
fortune, happiness, interest, luck, profit,
progress, satisfaction, success, thriving; SEE
CONCEPTS *316,693,706*

well [*adj1*] *healthy*
able-bodied, alive and kicking*, blooming,
bright-eyed*, bushy-tailed*, chipper*, fine, fit,
flourishing, fresh, great, hale, hardy, hearty,
husky, in good health, in the pink*, right, right as
rain*, robust, sane, solid as a rock*, sound,
strong, strong as an ox*, together, trim, up to
par*, vigorous, whole, wholesome, wrapped
tight*; SEE CONCEPT *314*

well [*adj2*] *lucky, fortunate*
advisable, agreeable, bright, comfortable, fine,
fitting, flourishing, good, happy, pleasing, profitable, proper, prosperous, providential, prudent,
right, satisfactory, thriving, useful; SEE CON-
CEPTS *548,572*

well [*adv1*] *happily, pleasantly; capably*
ably, accurately, adeptly, adequately, admirably,
agreeably, attentively, capitally, carefully,
closely, commendably, competently, completely,
conscientiously, correctly, effectively, efficiently, excellently, expertly, famously, favorably, fully, in a satisfactory manner,
irreproachably, nicely, proficiently, profoundly,
properly, rightly, satisfactorily, skillfully,
smoothly, soundly, splendidly, strongly, successfully, suitably, thoroughly, with skill; SEE CON-
CEPTS *527,528,544*

we
we

well [*adv2*] *sufficiently*
abundantly, adequately, amply, appropriately, becomingly, by a wide margin, completely, considerably, easily, effortlessly, entirely, extremely, far, fittingly, freely, fully, greatly, heartily, highly, luxuriantly, plentifully, properly, quite, rather, readily, right, satisfactorily, smoothly, somewhat, substantially, suitably, thoroughly, very much, wholly; SEE CONCEPTS *558,772*

well [*n*] *water hole*
abyss, bore, chasm, depression, derivation, fount, fountain, fountainhead, geyser, hole, inception, mine, mouth, origin, pit, pool, repository, reservoir, root, shaft, source, spa, spout, spring, springs, watering place, wellspring; SEE CONCEPTS *509,513,514*

well-balanced [*adj*] *sensible; equal*
all there*, astute, aware, cognizant, discriminating, graceful, having all one's marbles*, informed, intelligent, knowing, level-headed, logical, mentally stable, practical, proportional, prudent, rational, reasonable, sane, sound, symmetrical, together, well-thought-out, wise; SEE CONCEPTS *402,542*

well-bred [*adj*] *mannerly*
aristocratic, blue-blooded*, civil, considerate, courteous, courtly, cultivated, cultured, gallant, genteel, gentle, noble, patrician, polished, polite, refined, taught, trained, upper-crust*, urbane, well-behaved, well-mannered; SEE CONCEPTS *334,401*

well-defined [*adj*] *clear*
apparent, audible, clear-cut, comprehensible, distinct, explicit, graspable, intelligible, legible, lucent, lucid, obvious, plain, precise, sharp, spelled out*, straightforward, transparent, unambiguous, unblurred, understandable, well-marked; SEE CONCEPTS *402,562*

well-known [*adj*] *familiar, famous*
acclaimed, big, big name*, celeb*, celebrated, common, conspicuous, eminent, illustrious, important, infamous, in the limelight*, in the public eye*, known, large, leading, name, notable, noted, notorious, outstanding, popular, prominent, public, recognized, renowned, reputable, somebody, splashy, star, superstar, VIP*, widely known, WK*; SEE CONCEPT *568*

well-off [*adj*] *successful, wealthy*
affluent, comfortable, easy, flourishing, flush, fortunate, loaded, lucky, moneyed, prosperous, rich, snug, substantial, thriving, well, well-to-do; SEE CONCEPT *334*

well-preserved [*adj*] *well-kept*
boyish, childish, fresh, girlish, gull of life, tender, unspoiled, young; SEE CONCEPTS *542,578, 797*

well-to-do [*adj*] *well-off*
affluent, comfortable, flourishing, loaded, moneyed, prosperous, rich, rolling in it*, set for life*, snug, successful, wealthy; SEE CONCEPT *334*

welsh [*v*] *renege, swindle*
bamboozle, beat around the bush*, bilk, cheat, con, cop out, deceive, defraud, dodge, duck, dupe, fleece*, flimflam, fool, gull*, hoodwink, pull a fast one*, rip off*, sandbag, scam, shaft, slip out, stiff*, sting*, take for a ride*, take to the cleaners*, trick, weasel*, worm one's way out of*; SEE CONCEPTS *59,139,192*

welt [*n*] *red mark*
bruise, contusion, injury, mouse, ridge, scar, streak, stripe, wale, weal, wheal, wound; SEE CONCEPT *309*

wet [*adj*] *damp, moist*
aqueous, clammy, dank, dewy, drenched, dripping, drizzling, foggy, humid, misty, moistened, muggy, pouring, raining, rainy, saturate, saturated, showery, slimy, slippery, slushy, snowy, soaked, soaking, sodden, soggy, sopping, soppy, soused, stormy, teary, teeming, water-logged, watery, wringing-wet; SEE CONCEPT *603*

wet [*n*] *dampness, moisture*
clamminess, condensation, damp, drizzle, humidity, liquid, rain, rains, water, wetness; SEE CONCEPT *607*

wet [*v*] *cause to become damp, moist*
bathe, damp, dampen, deluge, dip, douse, drench, drown, hose, humidify, imbue, irrigate, moisten, rinse, saturate, soak, sop, souse, splash, spray, sprinkle, steep, wash, water; SEE CONCEPTS *161,256*

whack [*n1/v*] *hit*
bang, bash, bat, beat, belt, biff, box, buffet, clobber, clout, crack, cuff, ding*, lambaste*, nail, rap, slap, slug, smack, smash, sock, strike, thrash, thump, thwack*, wallop, wham*; SEE CONCEPT *189*

whack [*n2*] *try, attempt*
bash, crack, fling, go, pop, shot, slap, stab, turn, whirl; SEE CONCEPT *87*

whammy [*n*] *spell*
abracadabra*, charm, conjuration, curse, double whammy*, evil eye, hex, hexing, hocus-pocus*, jinx, magic, mumbo-jumbo*, triple whammy*, voodoo; SEE CONCEPTS *370,673,689*

wharf [*n*] *boat storage*
berth, breakwater, dock, jetty, landing, landing stage, levee, pier, quay, slip; SEE CONCEPT *439*

wheedle [*v*] *talk into*
banter, blandish, butter up*, cajole, charm, coax, con, court, draw, entice, finagle, flatter, inveigle, kowtow*, lay it on*, oil*, persuade, seduce, snow*, soap*, soften up*, soft-soap*, spread it on*, sweeten up*, sweet-talk*, work on*, worm*; SEE CONCEPT *68*

wheel [*n*] *circle, revolution*
caster, circuit, circulation, circumvolution, cycle, disk, drum, gyration, gyre, hoop, pivot, pulley, ratchet, ring, roll, roller, rotation, round, spin, trolley, turn, twirl, whirl; SEE CONCEPTS *436,464,502*

wheel [*v*] *turn, rotate*
circle, gyrate, orbit, pirouette, pivot, reel, revolve, roll, spin, swing, swivel, trundle, twirl, whirl; SEE CONCEPT *147*

wheeze [*v*] *breathe roughly, heavily*
buzz, catch one's breath, cough, gasp, hiss, murmur, pant, puff, rasp, sibilate, snore, whisper, whistle; SEE CONCEPTS *163,308*

when [*conj*] *though*
albeit, although, at, at the same time, during, howbeit, immediately upon, just after, just as, meanwhile, much as, whereas, while; SEE CONCEPT *799*

where [*n*] *place*
location, locus, point, position, site, situation, spot, station; SEE CONCEPT *198*

where/wherever [*adv*] *at which point*
anywhere, everywhere, in whatever place, in

which, to what end, to which, whereabouts, whither; SEE CONCEPT *583*

whet [*v1*] *make sharp*
edge, file, finish, grind, hone, sharpen, strop; SEE CONCEPTS *137,250*

whet [*v2*] *arouse, excite*
animate, awaken, challenge, enhance, incite, increase, kindle, pique, provoke, quicken, rally, rouse, stimulate, stir, wake, waken; SEE CONCEPTS *7,11,22*

whiff [*n*] *smell of an odor*
aroma, blast, breath, dash, draught, flatus, fume, gust, hint, inhalation, odor, puff, scent, shade, smack, sniff, snuff, soupçon, trace, trifle, waft; SEE CONCEPTS *599,601,602*

while [*conj1*] *as long as*
although, at the same time, during, during the time, in the time, throughout the time, whilst; SEE CONCEPT *799*

while [*conj2*] *even though*
albeit, although, howbeit, much as, though, when, whereas; SEE CONCEPT *544*

while [*n*] *time interval*
bit, instant, interim, meantime, moment, occasion, period, space, spell, stretch, time; SEE CONCEPTS *807,822*

whim [*n*] *sudden idea*
caprice, conceit, craze, desire, disposition, dream, fad, fancy, fantasy, freak, humor, impulse, inclination, notion, passing thought, quirk, sport, thought, urge, vagary, vision, whimsy; SEE CONCEPTS *529,661*

whimper [*v*] *cry softly*
bleat, blubber, complain, fuss, mewl, moan, object, pule, snivel, sob, weep, whine; SEE CONCEPTS *77,185*

whimsical [*adj*] *playful, fanciful*
amusing, arbitrary, capricious, chancy, chimerical, comical, curious, dicey, droll, eccentric, erratic, fantastic, flaky*, freakish, funny, kinky*, mischievous, odd, peculiar, quaint, queer*, quizzical, singular, uncertain, unpredictable, unusual, waggish, wayward, weird*; SEE CONCEPTS *401,548*

whine [*n*] *complaint, cry*
gripe, grouse, grumble, moan, plaintive cry, sob, wail, whimper; SEE CONCEPTS *54,77*

whine [*v*] *complain, cry*
bellyache, carp, drone, fuss, gripe, grouse, grumble, howl, kick, mewl, moan, murmur, pule, repine, snivel, sob, wail, whimper, yowl; SEE CONCEPTS *54,77*

whip [*n*] *length of material for hitting*
bat, belt, birch, bullwhip, cane, cat-o'-nine-tails, crop, goad, horsewhip, knout, lash, prod, push, rawhide, rod, ruler, scourge, strap, switch, thong; SEE CONCEPT *499*

whip [*v1*] *hit repeatedly*
bash, beat, birch, bludgeon, cane, castigate, chastise, cudgel, drub, ferule, flagellate, flog, hide, larrup*, lash, lather*, punish, scourge, spank, strap, strike, switch, tan, thrash, trash, wallop, whale, whomp*; SEE CONCEPT *189*

whip [*v2*] *defeat soundly*
beat, best, blast, clobber, conquer, drub, hammer*, kill*, lambaste, lick*, mop up*, outdo, overcome, overpower, overrun, overwhelm, put away*, rout, run circles around*, settle, steamroller*, subdue, take apart*, thrash, top, trim*,

trounce, vanquish, wallop, wax*, whomp*, worst*; SEE CONCEPT *95*

whip [*v3*] *dash, dart*
avert, deflect, dive, divert, flash, flit, fly, jerk, pivot, pull, rush, seize, sheer, shoot, snatch, surge, tear, turn, veer, wheel, whirl, whisk; SEE CONCEPTS *150,152*

whip [*v4*] *agitate, stir up*
beat, blend, mix, whisk, work up; SEE CONCEPTS *152,170*

whipping [*n*] *beating*
caning, flogging, licking, pasting, pounding, pummeling, punishment, spanking, tanning, thrashing, trouncing, whalloping; SEE CONCEPT *123*

whipping boy [*n*] *scapegoat*
dupe, fall guy*, goat*, mark*, patsy*, sacrifice, sucker, target, victim; SEE CONCEPT *412*

whip up [*v*] *incite, excite*
abet, agitate, arouse, compel, disturb, drive, foment, goad, hound, inflame, instigate, kindle, prick, prod, provoke, push, raise, set, set on, spur, start, stir, stir up, urge, work up; SEE CONCEPTS *14,221*

whirl [*n1*] *spin, revolution*
circle, circuit, circulation, circumvolution, flurry, gyration, gyre, pirouette, reel, roll, rotation, round, spin, surge, swirl, turn, twirl, twist, wheel, whir, whirlpool; SEE CONCEPTS *152,738*

whirl [*n2*] *commotion, confusion*
ado*, agitation, bustle, clatter, daze, dither, ferment, flurry, fluster, flutter, furor, fuss, hubbub*, hurly-burly*, hurry, merry-go-round*, moil, pother, round, ruction, rush, series, spin, stir, storm, succession, tempest, tumult, turbulence, uproar, whirlwind; SEE CONCEPTS *230,388*

whirl [*n3*] *attempt*
bash, crack, fling, go, pop, shot, slap, stab, try, whack*; SEE CONCEPT *87*

whirl [*v*] *spin around*
circle, eddy, gyrate, gyre, pirouette, pivot, purl, reel, revolve, roll, rotate, swirl, swoosh, turn, turn around, twirl, twist, wheel, whir; SEE CONCEPT *152*

whirlpool [*n*] *spinning water*
eddy, maelstrom, stir, undercurrent, undertow, vortex, whirl; SEE CONCEPT *514*

whirlwind [*adj*] *very fast*
cyclonic, hasty, headlong, hurricane, impetuous, impulsive, lightning, quick, rapid, rash, short, speedy, swift, tornado; SEE CONCEPTS *588,798*

whisk [*v*] *brush quickly; hasten*
barrel, bullet, dart, dash, flick, flit, flutter, fly, hurry, race, rush, shoot, speed, sweep, tear, whip, whiz, wipe, zip; SEE CONCEPT *152*

whisper [*n1*] *rumor; information expressed in soft voice*
buzz*, confidence, disclosure, divulgence, gossip, hint, hum, hushed tone, innuendo, insinuation, low voice, mumble, murmur, mutter, report, secret, secret message, sigh, sighing, susurration, undertone, word; SEE CONCEPTS *274,278*

whisper [*n2*] *trace, suggestion*
breath, dash, fraction, hint, shade, shadow, soupçon, suspicion, tinge, touch, whiff; SEE CONCEPTS *529,673,831*

whisper [*v*] *speak softly*
breathe, buzz*, confide, gossip, hint, hiss, insinuate, intimate, mumble, murmur, mutter, say softly, say under one's breath*, sibilate, sigh,

we
wh

speak confidentially, spread rumor, susurrate, talk into someone's ear*, talk low, tell, tell a secret; SEE CONCEPTS *60,266*

whistle [v] *make sharp, shrill sound*
blare, blast, fife, flute, hiss, pipe, shriek, signal, skirl, sound, toot, tootle, trill, warble, wheeze, whine, whiz*; SEE CONCEPTS *65,77*

whit [n] *very tiny bit*
atom, crumb, dash, drop, fragment, grain, hoot*, iota, jot, little, mite, modicum, particle, piece, pinch, scrap, shred, speck, trace; SEE CONCEPTS *831,835*

white [adj] *extremely pale; lacking color*
achromatic, achromic, alabaster, ashen, blanched, bleached, bloodless, chalky, clear, fair, frosted, ghastly, hoary, immaculate, ivory, light, milky, neutral, pallid, pasty, pearly, silver, silvery, snowy, transparent, wan, waxen; SEE CONCEPT *618*

whiten [v] *make or become extremely pale*
blanch, bleach, blench, chalk, decolor, decolorize, dull, etiolate, fade, frost, grizzle, lighten, pale, silver, turn pale, white, whitewash; SEE CONCEPT *250*

whitewash [v] *cover up the truth*
blanch, camouflage, conceal, exonerate, extenuate, gloss over, launder*, liberate, make light of*, paint, palliate, sugarcoat*, suppress, varnish, veneer, vindicate, white, whiten; SEE CONCEPTS *49,63*

whittle [v] *cut away at; reduce*
carve, chip, consume, decrease, diminish, eat away, erode, fashion, form, hew, lessen, model, mold, pare, sculpt, shape, shave, trim, undermine, wear away; SEE CONCEPTS *176,184,236,247*

whiz [n] *very intelligent person*
adept, expert, genius, gifted person, marvel, pro*, prodigy, professional, star, virtuoso, wonder; SEE CONCEPT *416*

whiz [v] *move quickly by*
bullet, buzz, dart, flit, fly, hiss, hum, hurry, hurtle, race, speed, swish, whir, whirl, whisk, whoosh*, zip; SEE CONCEPT *150*

whole [adj1] *entire, complete*
accomplished, aggregate, all, choate, completed, concentrated, conclusive, consummate, every, exclusive, exhaustive, fixed, fulfilled, full, full-length, gross, inclusive, in one piece, integral, outright, perfect, plenary, rounded, total, unabbreviated, unabridged, uncut, undivided, unexpurgated, unqualified, utter; SEE CONCEPT *531*

whole [adj2] *unbroken, perfect*
complete, completed, developed, faultless, flawless, good, in good order*, in one piece*, intact, inviolate, mature, mint, plenary, preserved, replete, safe, ship-shape, solid, sound, thorough, together, undamaged, unharmed, unhurt, unimpaired, uninjured, unmarred, unmutilated, unscathed, untouched, without a scratch; SEE CONCEPTS *485,574*

whole [adj3] *healthy*
able-bodied, better, cured, fit, hale, healed, hearty, in fine fettle, in good health, recovered, right, robust, sane, sound, strong, well, wholesome; SEE CONCEPT *314*

whole [n] *total made up of parts*
aggregate, aggregation, all, amount, assemblage, assembly, being, big picture, body, bulk, coherence, collectivity, combination, complex, ensem-

ble, entirety, entity, everything, fullness, gross, hook line and sinker*, integral, jackpot*, linkage, lock stock and barrel*, lot, lump, oneness, organism, organization, piece, quantity, quantum, result, sum, summation, sum total*, supply, system, the works*, totality, unit, unity, whole ball of wax*, whole enchilada*, whole nine yards*, whole shebang*; SEE CONCEPTS *432,635,837*

wholehearted/whole-hearted [adj] *enthusiastic, sincere*
abiding, ardent, authentic, bona fide, candid, committed, complete, dedicated, determined, devoted, earnest, emphatic, enduring, fervent, frank, genuine, heartfelt, hearty, impassioned, never-failing, passionate, real, serious, steadfast, steady, sure, true, unfaltering, unfeigned, unqualified, unquestioning, unreserved, unstinting, unwavering, warm, zealous; SEE CONCEPTS *542,548,582*

wholesale [adj] *all-inclusive*
broad, bulk, complete, comprehensive, extensive, far-reaching, general, in bulk, indiscriminate, in quantity, in the mass, large-scale, mass, overall, quantitative, sweeping, total, wide-ranging, widespread; SEE CONCEPTS *771,772*

wholesome [adj] *healthy, decent*
all there, beneficial, clean, edifying, ethical, exemplary, fit, good, hale, healthful, health-giving, helpful, honorable, hygienic, in fine feather*, innocent, in the pink*, invigorating, moral, nice, normal, nourishing, nutritious, nutritive, pure, respectable, restorative, right, righteous, safe, salubrious, salutary, sane, sanitary, sound, strengthening, together, virtuous, well, worthy; SEE CONCEPTS *314,462,537,545*

wholly [adv1] *completely, entirely*
all, all in all*, all the way*, altogether, comprehensively, from A to Z*, fully, heart and soul*, in every respect*, in toto, one hundred percent*, outright, perfectly, quite, roundly, thoroughly, top to bottom*, totally, utterly, well; SEE CONCEPTS *531,772*

wholly [adv2] *exclusively*
individually, just, only, purely, solely, specifically, without exception; SEE CONCEPT *557*

whoop [n/v] *hurrah*
bellow, boo, cheer, cry, cry out, holler, hoot, howl, jeer, scream, shout, shriek, squawk, yell; SEE CONCEPT *77*

whopping [adj] *enormous*
big, colossal, extraordinary, gargantuan, giant, gigantic, great, huge, immense, large, mammoth, massive, mighty, monstrous, mountainous, prodigious, tremendous; SEE CONCEPTS *773,781*

whore [n] *prostitute*
call girl, escort, fallen woman, harlot, hooker*, hustler, lady of the evening*, pro*, slut, streetwalker, strumpet, tramp, working girl*; SEE CONCEPT *412*

whorehouse [n] *brothel*
bagnio, bawdy house*, bordello, call house*, cathouse*, den of iniquity*, house of assignation, house of ill fame*, house of ill repute, house of prostitution, house with red doors*, massage parlor, red-light district; SEE CONCEPT *449*

whorl [n] *spiral*
coil, corkscrew, curl, eddy, helix, swirl, twirl, twist, vortex, whirlpool; SEE CONCEPT *436*

wicked [*adj1*] *corrupt, bad*
abandoned, abominable, amoral, arch, atrocious, bad news*, base, contemptible, debased, degenerate, depraved, devilish, dissolute, egregious, evil, fiendish, flagitious, foul, gross, guilty, heartless, heinous, immoral, impious, impish, incorrigible, indecent, iniquitous, irreligious, lowdown, mean, mischievous, nasty, naughty, nefarious, profane, reprobate, rotten, scandalous, shameful, shameless, sinful, unethical, unprincipled, unrighteous, vicious, vile, villainous, wayward, worthless; SEE CONCEPTS *401,545*

wicked [*adj2*] *destructive, troublesome*
acute, agonizing, awful, barbarous, bothersome, chancy, crashing, dangerous, difficult, distressing, dreadful, fearful, fierce, galling, harmful, hazardous, injurious, intense, mean, mighty, offensive, outrageous, painful, perilous, pesky, risky, severe, terrible, treacherous, troublous, trying, ugly, uncivilized, unconscionable, ungodly, unhealthy, unholy, unpleasant, unsound, vexatious; SEE CONCEPTS *537,565,571*

wicked [*adj3*] *expert*
able, adept, adroit, au fait, capable, clever, competent, deft, good, masterly, mighty, outstanding, powerful, pretty, qualified, skillful, strong; SEE CONCEPT *527*

wide [*adj1*] *expansive, roomy*
advanced, all-inclusive, ample, baggy, broad, capacious, catholic, commodious, comprehensive, deep, dilated, distended, encyclopedic, expanded, extensive, far-ranging, far-reaching, full, general, immense, inclusive, large, large-scale, liberal, loose, open, outspread, outstretched, progressive, radical, scopic, spacious, splay, squat, sweeping, tolerant, universal, vast, voluminous; SEE CONCEPTS *772,773,796*

wide [*adj2*] *off-course*
astray, away, distant, far, far-off, inaccurate, off, off-target, off the mark, remote; SEE CONCEPTS *581,583*

wide-awake [*adj*] *alert*
active, all ears*, attentive, bright, bright-eyed and bushy-tailed*, fast on the draw*, heads up*, intelligent, lively, on guard*, on one's toes*, on the ball*, on the job*, on the lookout*, psyched up*, quick, ready, sharp, spirited, vigilant, watchful, wired*; SEE CONCEPTS *402,403*

widen [*v*] *open up*
add to, augment, broaden, dilate, distend, enlarge, expand, extend, grow, grow larger, increase, multiply, open, open out, open wide, ream, spread, spread out, stretch, swell, unfold; SEE CONCEPTS *236,245,780*

widespread [*adj*] *extensive*
across the board*, all over the place*, boundless, broad, common, comprehensive, current, diffuse, epidemic, far-flung, far-reaching, general, on a large scale, outspread, overall, pandemic, pervasive, popular, prevailing, prevalent, public, rampant, regnant, rife, ruling, sweeping, universal, unlimited, unrestricted, wall-to-wall*, wholesale; SEE CONCEPTS *530,536,772*

widget [*n*] *gadget*
apparatus, appliance, contraption, contrivance, device, doodad*, doohickey*, gizmo*, invention, object, thing*, thingamabob*, thingamajig*, tool, whatchamacallit*; SEE CONCEPTS *463,499*

width [*n*] *breadth, wideness of some amount*
amplitude, area, broadness, compass, cross measure, diameter, distance across, expanse, extent, girth, measure, range, reach, scope, span, squatness, stretch, thickness; SEE CONCEPTS *760,788,792*

wield [*v*] *control, use*
apply, brandish, command, conduct, employ, exercise, exert, flourish, handle, have, have at one's disposal, hold, maintain, make use of, manage, maneuver, manipulate, operate, ply, possess, put to use, shake, swing, throw, utilize, wave, work; SEE CONCEPTS *94,147,225*

wife [*n*] *married woman*
bride, companion, consort, helpmate, mate, monogamist, other half*, partner, roommate, spouse; SEE CONCEPTS *414,415*

wig [*n*] *hairpiece*
false hair, hair extension, hair implant, hairpiece, hair weaving, periwig, peruke, postiche, rug*, toupee; SEE CONCEPT *392*

wiggle [*n/v*] *shake back and forth*
jerk, jiggle, shimmy, squirm, twist, twitch, wag, waggle, wave, worm, wriggle, writhe, zigzag; SEE CONCEPTS *80,150,152*

wild [*adj1*] *untamed*
agrarian, barbarian, barbaric, barbarous, dense, desert, deserted, desolate, escaped, feral, ferocious, fierce, free, indigenous, lush, luxuriant, native, natural, neglected, overgrown, overrun, primitive, rampant, rude, savage, unbroken, uncivilized, uncultivated, undomesticated, uninhabited, untouched, vicious, waste; SEE CONCEPTS *406,583*

wild [*adj2*] *disorderly, rowdy*
avid, berserk, boisterous, chaotic, crazed, crazy, eager, enthusiastic, extravagant, flighty, foolhardy, foolish, giddy, hysterical, impetuous, impracticable, imprudent, incautious, irrational, lawless, licentious, mad, madcap, nuts, outrageous, preposterous, profligate, rabid, rash, raving, reckless, riotous, rough, self-willed, turbulent, unbridled, uncontrolled, undisciplined, unfettered, ungovernable, unmanageable, unrestrained, unruly, uproarious, violent, wayward; SEE CONCEPT *401*

wild [*adj3*] *intense, stormy*
blustering, blustery, choppy, disturbed, furious, howling, inclement, raging, rough, storming, tempestuous, turbulent, violent; SEE CONCEPTS *525,569*

wilderness/wilds [*n*] *uninhabited area*
back country, back of beyond*, badland, barrens, boondocks, bush, desert, forest, hinterland, jungle, middle of nowhere*, outback, primeval forest, sticks*, waste, wasteland, wild; SEE CONCEPT *517*

wile [*n*] *cunning*
angle, artfulness, artifice, cheating, chicane, chicanery, con*, contrivance, craft, craftiness, deceit, deception, device, dishonesty, dissimulation, dodge, feint, flimflam*, fraud, gambit, game, gimmick, guile, hoax, horseplay, imposition, little game*, lure, maneuver, monkey business*, monkeyshines*, plot, ploy, racket*, ruse, scam*, scheming, setup*, shenanigans*, skullduggery*, slant, slyness, stratagem, stunt, subterfuge, switch, trick, trickery, twist; SEE CONCEPTS *59,63*

wh
wi

will [*n1*] *personal choice*
aim, appetite, attitude, character, conviction, craving, decision, decisiveness, decree, design, desire, determination, discipline, discretion, disposition, fancy, feeling, hankering, heart's desire*, inclination, intention, liking, longing, mind, option, passion, pining, pleasure, power, preference, prerogative, purpose, resolution, resolve, self-control, self-discipline, self-restraint, temperament, urge, velleity, volition, willfulness, willpower, wish, wishes, yearning; SEE CONCEPTS **20,411,659**

will [*n2*] *last wishes; command*
bequest, bestowal, declaration, decree, device, directions, dispensation, disposition, estate, heritage, inheritance, insistence, instructions, legacy, order, property, testament; SEE CONCEPT **318**

will [*v1*] *cause*
authorize, bid, bring about, command, decide on, decree, demand, determine, direct, effect, enjoin, exert, insist, intend, ordain, order, request, resolve; SEE CONCEPT **242**

will [*v2*] *choose*
be inclined, crave, desire, elect, have a mind to*, incline, like, opt, please, prefer, see fit*, want, wish; SEE CONCEPT **20**

will [*v3*] *give, bequeath to another*
bequest, confer, cut off, devise, disherit, disinherit, leave, legate, pass on, probate, transfer; SEE CONCEPTS **108,317**

willful [*adj1*] *stubborn, obstinate*
adamant, bullheaded, contumacious, determined, dogged, fractious, froward, headstrong, inflexible, intractable, intransigent, mulish, obdurate, persistent, pertinacious, perverse, pigheaded, refractory, resolved, self-willed, stiffnecked, uncompromising, unyielding; SEE CONCEPTS **401,542**

willful [*adj2*] *voluntary*
conscious, contemplated, deliberate, designed, intended, intentional, planned, premeditated, purposeful, studied, unforced, volitional, willed, willing, witting; SEE CONCEPTS **401,535**

willing [*adj*] *agreeable, ready*
accommodating, active, amenable, cheerful, compliant, consenting, content, deliberate, desirous, disposed, eager, energetic, enthusiastic, fair, favorable, feeling, forward, game, go along with, happy, in accord with, inclined, in favor, intentional, in the mood, like-minded, obedient, one, pleased, predisposed, prepared, prompt, prone, reliable, responsible, tractable, unasked, unbidden, unforced, voluntary, well-disposed, willful, witting, zealous; SEE CONCEPTS **401,403,576**

willowy [*adj*] *graceful, slender*
adroit, agile, dainty, delicate, elastic, elegant, flowing, limber, lithe, lithesome, nimble, pliant, shapely, skinny, springy, svelte, thin, trim; SEE CONCEPTS **579,584,589**

willpower [*n*] *personal determination*
discipline, drive, firmness, fixity, force, grit, resolution, resolve, self-control, self-discipline, self-government, self-restraint, single-mindedness, strength, will; SEE CONCEPT **411**

wilt [*v*] *sag, fail*
become limp, break down, cave in, collapse, diminish, droop, drop, dry up, dwindle, ebb, fade, faint, flag, give out, languish, melt, mummify,

shrivel, sink, succumb, wane, waste, waste away, weaken, wither, wizen; SEE CONCEPTS **181,427,469,699**

wily [*adj*] *crafty, clever*
arch, artful, astute, cagey, crazy like a fox*, crooked, cunning, deceitful, deceptive, deep, designing, foxy, greasy*, guileful, insidious, intriguing, knowing, sagacious, scheming, sharp, shifty, shrewd, slick*, slippery*, sly, smooth, sneaky, streetwise, tricky, underhanded; SEE CONCEPTS **401,545**

wimp [*n*] *weakling*
baby, caitiff, chicken*, chicken heart*, chicken liver*, coward, cream puff*, crybaby, daisy*, featherweight*, fraidy-cat*, jellyfish*, lily liver, loser, milksop, momma's boy*, namby-pamby, pansy, pantywaist*, puppy*, pushover, scaredy cat*, schlemiel*, sissy, wuss*, wussy*, yellow belly*; SEE CONCEPTS **412,423**

win [*n*] *victory*
accomplishment, achievement, conquest, gain, gold*, gold star*, kill*, killing*, pay dirt*, score, slam, success, sweep, triumph; SEE CONCEPTS **95,141,832**

win [*v1*] *finish first; succeed*
achieve, beat, be first, be victorious, carry the day*, come in first, conquer, edge, finish in front*, finish off, gain, gain victory, overcome, overwhelm, prevail, run circles around*, shut out*, sink*, take the prize, triumph, upset, walk away with*, walk off with*; SEE CONCEPTS **95,141,363**

win [*v2*] *achieve, obtain*
accomplish, acquire, annex, approach, attain, bag*, bring in, catch, collect, come away with*, derive, earn, effect, gain, get, harvest, have, make, net, pick up, procure, rack up*, reach, realize, receive, score, secure; SEE CONCEPTS **120,706**

win/win over [*v3*] *influence, persuade*
allure, argue into, attract, bring around, carry, charm, convert, convince, disarm, draw, get, induce, overcome, prevail upon, prompt, slay, sway, talk into, wow*; SEE CONCEPTS **11,68**

wince [*v*] *draw back*
back off, blanch, blench, cower, cringe, dodge, duck, flinch, grimace, jib, make a face*, quail, recoil, shrink, shy, start, swerve, turn; SEE CONCEPTS **154,185**

wind [*n1*] *air currents*
air, blast, blow, breath, breeze, chinook, cyclone, draft, draught, flurry, flutter, gale, gust, mistral, puff, tempest, typhoon, wafting, whiff, whirlwind, whisk, zephyr; SEE CONCEPT **524**

wind [*n2*] *warning, report*
babble, clue, cue, gossip, hint, hot air*, idle talk, inkling, intimation, notice, rumor, suggestion, talk, tidings, whisper; SEE CONCEPT **278**

wind [*v*] *bend, turn*
coil, convolute, corkscrew, cover, crook, curl, curve, deviate, distort, encircle, enclose, entwine, envelop, fold, furl, loop, meander, ramble, reel, roll, screw, slither, snake, spiral, swerve, twine, twist, weave, wrap, wreathe, wriggle, zigzag; SEE CONCEPTS **201,738**

windbag [*n*] *bigmouth, chatterer*
bag of wind*, big talker*, blabberer, blowhard*, boaster, braggart, bragger, gasbag*, gascon*, jabberer, know-it-all, motor-mouth*; SEE CONCEPTS **412,423**

windfall [*n*] *jackpot, profit*
bonanza, bonus, find, fortune, gift from the gods*, godsend, gravy*, lucky find, money from heaven*, pennies from heaven*, stroke of luck; SEE CONCEPTS *337,679*

winding [*adj*] *bending, turning*
ambiguous, anfractuous, circuitous, convoluted, crooked, curving, devious, flexuous, gyrating, indirect, intricate, involved, labyrinthine, mazy, meandering, roundabout, serpentine, sinuous, snaky, spiraling, tortuous, twisting, wriggly, zigzag; SEE CONCEPTS *581,584*

wind up [*v*] *finish*
be through with, bring to a close, clean up*, close, close down, come to the end, complete, conclude, determine, do, end, end up*, finalize, finish up, halt, liquidate, settle, terminate, tie up loose ends*, wrap up*; SEE CONCEPT *234*

windy [*adj1*] *breezy*
airy, blowing, blowy, blustering, blustery, boisterous, brisk, drafty, fresh, gusty, raw, squally, stormy, tempestuous, wild, windswept; SEE CONCEPT *525*

windy [*adj2*] *talkative; boastful*
bombastic, diffuse, empty, garrulous, inflated, lengthy, long-winded, loquacious, meandering, palaverous, pompous, prolix, rambling, redundant, turgid, verbose, wordy; SEE CONCEPT *267*

wing [*n1*] *organ, device of flight*
aileron, airfoil, appendage, feather, pennon, pinion; SEE CONCEPTS *399,502*

wing [*n2*] *section; extension*
addition, adjunct, annex, arm, block, branch, bulge, circle, clique, coterie, detachment, division, ell, expansion, faction, group, part, projection, prolongation, protrusion, protuberance, section, segment, set, side, unit; SEE CONCEPTS *440,441,824,835*

wing it [*v*] *improvise*
ad-lib, concoct, devise, do offhand, do off the top of your head*, fake it, improv*, invent, make do*, make up, play it by ear*, speak off the cuff*, throw together*; SEE CONCEPTS *173,266*

wink [*n1/v*] *flutter, flick*
bat, blink, flash, gleam, glimmer, glitter, nictate, nictitate, sparkle, squinch, squint, twinkle; SEE CONCEPTS *185,624*

wink [*n2*] *moment*
flash*, instant, jiffy*, minute, second, shake*, split second*, twinkle*, twinkling*; SEE CONCEPTS *808,821*

winner [*n*] *someone or something that succeeds*
champ, champion, conquering hero, conqueror, first, hero, medalist, medalwinner, number one*, prizewinner, title-holder, top dog*, vanquisher, victor; SEE CONCEPTS *366,416*

winning/winsome [*adj1*] *attractive, charming*
acceptable, adorable, agreeable, alluring, amiable, bewitching, captivating, cute, delectable, delightful, disarming, enchanting, endearing, engaging, fascinating, fetching, gratifying, lovable, lovely, pleasing, prepossessing, sweet, taking; SEE CONCEPTS *401,404*

winning [*adj2*] *triumphant*
champion, conquering, leading, successful, victorious; SEE CONCEPTS *528,632*

wino [*n*] *drunk*
alcoholic, boozer*, bum*, carouser*, dipsomaniac, drinker, drunkard, guzzler*, hobo, inebriate, lush*, sot*, sponge*; SEE CONCEPT *423*

winsome [*adj*] *charming*
absorbing, alluring, appealing, attractive, captivating, charismatic, cute, dainty, delicate, delightful, desirable, elegant, enamoring, engaging, enthralling, eye-catching, fascinating, glamorous, inviting, irresistible, lovable, pleasant, pleasing, pretty, rapturous, ravishing, seducing, seductive, sweet, tantalizing, titillating, winning; SEE CONCEPT *404*

winter [*n*] *cold season of the year*
chill, cold, frost, Jack Frost*, wintertide, wintertime; SEE CONCEPT *814*

wintry [*adj*] *cold, snowy*
biting, bleak, brumal, chilly, cutting, desolate, dismal, freezing, frigid, frosty, frozen, harsh, hibernal, hiemal, icebox*, icy, raw, snappy, three-dog night*; SEE CONCEPTS *525,605*

wipe [*v*] *brush, swab*
clean, clean off, clear, dry, dust, erase, mop, obliterate, remove, rub, sponge, take away, towel, wash; SEE CONCEPT *165*

wipeout [*n*] *fall*
collapse, crash, destruction, dive, downfall, drop, spill, tumble, yard sale*; SEE CONCEPTS *116,230, 674,699*

wipe out [*v*] *destroy; get rid of*
abate, abolish, annihilate, black out, blot out, cancel, decimate, delete, efface, eliminate, eradicate, erase, expunge, exterminate, extinguish, extirpate, kill, massacre, obliterate, remove, root out, slaughter, slay, uproot, X-out*; SEE CONCEPT *252*

wiry [*adj*] *thin and strong*
agile, athletic, bristly, fibrous, lean, light, limber, muscular, ropy, sinewy, stiff, strapping, stringy, supple, tough; SEE CONCEPTS *490,491*

wisdom [*n*] *insight, common sense*
acumen, astuteness, balance, brains*, caution, circumspection, clear thinking, comprehension, discernment, discrimination, enlightenment, erudition, experience, foresight, good judgment, gumption*, horse sense*, information, intelligence, judgment, judiciousness, knowledge, learning, pansophy, penetration, perspicacity, poise, practicality, prudence, reason, sagacity, sageness, sanity, sapience, savoir faire, savvy*, shrewdness, solidity, sophistication, stability, understanding; SEE CONCEPT *409*

wise [*adj*] *intelligent, reasonable*
astute, aware, calculating, careful, clever, cogitative, contemplative, crafty, cunning, discerning, discreet, educated, enlightened, erudite, experienced, foresighted, grasping, informed, insightful, intuitive, judicious, keen, knowing, knowledgeable, perceptive, perspicacious, politic, prudent, rational, reflective, sagacious, sage, sane, sapient, scholarly, sensible, sensing, sharp, shrewd, smart, sophic, sound, tactful, taught, thoughtful, understanding, wary, well-informed, witty; SEE CONCEPT *402*

wisecrack [*n*] *joke*
antic, caper, clowning, dig, escapade, farce, frolic, gag, lark, laugh, mischief, monkeyshine*, one-liner*, parody, prank, put-on, quip, remark, retort, rib, shenanigan*, smart crack*, stunt, trick, witticism, yarn, zinger*; SEE CONCEPT *273*

wise guy [*n*] *smart-aleck; gangster*
bigmouth*, criminal, crook, hood, hoodlum, know-it-all*, Mafioso*, member of the family,

wi
wi

mobster, smart ass*, smarty-pants*, wiseacre, wiseass, wisenheimer; SEE CONCEPT *412*

wish [*n*] *desire*
ambition, aspiration, choice, disposition, hankering, hope, hunger, inclination, intention, invocation, itch, liking, longing, pleasure, prayer, preference, request, thirst, urge, want, whim, will, yearning, yen; SEE CONCEPTS *20,709*

wish [*v*] *desire*
aspire, beg, choose, command, covet, crave, desiderate, elect, entreat, envy, expect, fancy, hanker*, hope, hunger, invoke, itch, like, long, look forward to*, need, order, please, pray for, prefer, request, set one's heart on*, sigh for, solicit, spoil for*, thirst, want, will, yearn, yen; SEE CONCEPT *20*

wishful [*adj*] *desirous*
acquisitive, ambitious, aspiring, craving, daydreaming, desiring, greedy, hankering, hopeful, itchy*, keen, longful, longing, lustful, wishing, yearning; SEE CONCEPTS *403,529*

wishy-washy [*adj*] *bland, dull*
banal, characterless, cowardly, enervated, feeble, flat, flavorless, indecisive, ineffective, ineffectual, insipid, irresolute, jejune, languid, listless, mediocre, namby-pamby*, sapless, spiritless, tasteless, thin, vacillating, vapid, watered-down, watery, wavering, weak, weak-kneed*; SEE CONCEPT *404*

wisp [*n*] *strand*
bit, lock, piece, shock, shred, snippet, string, thread, tuft, twist; SEE CONCEPTS *392,831*

wistful [*adj*] *daydreaming, longing*
contemplative, desirous, disconsolate, dreaming, dreamy, forlorn, hopeless, meditative, melancholy, mournful, musing, nostalgic, pensive, plaintive, reflective, sad, thoughtful, wishful, yearning; SEE CONCEPT *403*

wit [*n1*] *humor*
aphorism, badinage, banter, bon mot, burlesque, drollery, facetiousness, fun, gag, jest, jocularity, joke, lark, levity, pleasantry, practical joke, prank, pun, quip, raillery, repartee, sally, satire, trick, whimsicality, wisecrack, wittiness, wordplay; SEE CONCEPTS *59,273,411*

wit [*n2*] *person who is very funny*
a million laughs*, banterer, card, comedian, comic, cutup*, epigrammatist, farceur, funster, gag person, humorist, jester, joker, jokesmith, jokester, life of the party*, madcap, punster, quipster, trickster, wag, wisecracker; SEE CONCEPTS *352,416*

witch [*n*] *person who casts spells over others*
conjurer, enchanter, magician, necromancer, occultist, sorcerer; SEE CONCEPTS *361,412,415*

witchcraft [*n*] *spell-casting, magic*
abracadabra*, bewitchment, black art, black magic, charisma, conjuring, divination, enchantment, hocus-pocus*, hoodoo*, incantation, jinx, magnetism, mumbo-jumbo*, necromancy, occult, occultism, sorcery, spell, thaumaturgy, voodoo, voodooism, whammy*, witchery, witching, wizardry; SEE CONCEPTS *367,370,689*

witch doctor [*n*] *shaman*
healer, medicine man, priest, sorcerer, wizard; SEE CONCEPT *361*

withdraw [*v1*] *remove something or someone from situation*
abjure, absent oneself, back out, bail out, blow, book, bow out, check out, depart, detach, disen-

gage, draw away, draw back, drop out, ease out, eliminate, exfiltrate, exit, extract, fall back, get away, get lost, get off, give ground, give way, go, keep aloof, keep apart, leave, make oneself scarce*, phase out, pull back, pull out, quail, quit, recede, recoil, retire, retreat, run along, secede, seclude oneself, shrink, switch, take a hike*, take away, take leave, take off, take out, vacate; SEE CONCEPTS *195,211*

withdraw [*v2*] *retract; declare void*
abjure, abolish, abrogate, annul, ban, bar, call off, disavow, disclaim, dissolve, forswear, invalidate, nullify, quash, recall, recant, renege, renig, repress, repudiate, rescind, retire, reverse, revoke, stamp out, suppress, take back, unsay; SEE CONCEPTS *50,88,121,697*

withdrawal [*n*] *removal; retraction*
abandonment, abdication, abjuration, alienation, departure, disavowal, disclaimer, disengagement, egress, egression, exit, exiting, exodus, extraction, marooning, palinode, recall, recantation, relinquishment, repudiation, rescission, resignation, retirement, retreat, revocation, revulsion, secession; SEE CONCEPTS *195,211,685*

withdrawn [*adj1*] *unsociable*
aloof, aseptic, casual, cool, detached, disinterested, distant, incurious, indifferent, introverted, nongregarious, offish, quiet, recluse, reclusive, remote, reserved, restrained, retired, retiring, retreated, shrinking, shy, silent, solitary, standoffish, taciturn, timorous, uncommunicative, uncompanionable, unconcerned, uncurious, undemonstrative, unforthcoming, uninterested; SEE CONCEPT *401*

withdrawn [*adj2*] *hidden, remote*
cloistered, departed, isolated, out-of-the-way, private, recluse, removed, retreated, secluded, solitary, taken out; SEE CONCEPT *583*

wither [*v*] *droop, decline*
atrophy, become stale, blast, blight, collapse, constrict, contract, decay, deflate, desiccate, deteriorate, die, disintegrate, dry, dry up, fade, fold, languish, perish, shrink, shrivel, wane, waste, waste away, wilt, wizen; SEE CONCEPTS *427,698*

withhold [*v*] *keep back*
abstain, bridle, check, clam up*, conceal, constrain, curb, deduct, deny, detain, disallow, dummy up*, hide, hold, hold back, hold down, hold out, hold out on, inhibit, keep, keep secret, keep to oneself*, keep under one's hat*, keep under wraps*, kill, refrain, refuse, repress, reserve, resist, restrain, retain, sit on, spike, stop oneself, suppress; SEE CONCEPTS *35,121,188*

within [*adv*] *inside*
in, in a period, indoors, inner, in reach, interior, inward, not beyond, not outside, not over; SEE CONCEPTS *586,772*

with it [*adj*] *cognizant; stylish*
alive, apprehensive, au courant, awake, aware, chic, conscious, cool*, familiar, groovy*, hep to*, hip to*, in, in fashion, informed, in on, in the know, in vogue, knowing, knowledgeable, latest, mod*, now*, observant, on to*, perceptive, plugged in, savvy, switched on*, trendy, tuned in*, turned on*, up on*, versed, wise to*; SEE CONCEPTS *402,579,589*

without [*adv*] *outside*
after, beyond, externally, left out, on the outside, out, outdoors, out-of-doors, outwardly, past; SEE CONCEPTS *586,772*

withstand [v] *endure, bear*
brace, brave, buck, combat, confront, contest, cope, cross, defy, dispute, duel, face, fight, fly in the face of*, grapple with, hang on*, hang tough*, hold off*, hold one's ground*, hold out*, oppose, prevail against, put up struggle*, put up with*, remain firm, repel, resist, ride out*, sit and take it*, stand, stand fast*, stand firm*, stand one's ground*, stand up against*, stand up to*, stick*, stick fast*, suffer, take, take it*, take on, thwart, tolerate, traverse, violate, weather, win out; SEE CONCEPTS *23,96*

witless [adj] *foolish*
absurd, asinine, birdbrained*, brainless, cockamamy*, crazy, daffy*, doltish*, dotty*, dumb, feebleminded*, half-baked*, half-witted*, harebrained*, idiotic, ill-advised, irrational, jerky*, kooky*, loony*, ludicrous, lunatic, mad, mindless, moronic, nonsensical, nutty*, ridiculous, senseless, silly, stupid, unintelligent, unwise, wacky*, zany*; SEE CONCEPTS *401,542,544*

witness [n] *person who observes an event*
attestant, attestor, beholder, bystander, corroborator, deponent, eyewitness, gawker, looker-on, observer, onlooker, proof, rubbernecker*, signatory, signer, spectator, testifier, testimony, viewer, watcher; SEE CONCEPTS *355,423*

witness [v1] *observe*
attend, be a witness, behold, be on hand*, be on the scene*, be present, eyeball*, flash on*, get a load of*, look on, mark, note, notice, perceive, pick up on, pipe*, read, see, sight, spot, spy, take in, view, watch; SEE CONCEPT *626*

witness [v2] *testify; authenticate*
affirm, announce, argue, attest, bear out, bear witness, be a witness, bespeak, betoken, certify, confirm, corroborate, countersign, depone, depose, endorse, give evidence, give testimony, indicate, say under oath, sign, stand for, subscribe, vouch for; SEE CONCEPTS *49,50,88,317*

witty [adj] *funny and clever*
amusing, bright, brilliant, campy*, crazy*, diverting, droll, entertaining, epigrammatic, facetious, fanciful, gay, humorous, ingenious, intelligent, jocose, jocular, joshing, keen, lively, original, penetrating, piercing, piquant, quick-witted, ridiculous, scintillating, screaming*, slapstick, sparkling, waggish, whimsical; SEE CONCEPTS *267,542*

wit/wits [n3] *judgment, intelligence*
acumen, acuteness, astucity, astuteness, awareness, balance, brainpower, brains*, cleverness, common sense, comprehension, depth of perception, discernment, discrimination, esprit, grasp, ingenuity, insight, keenness, lucidity, marbles*, mentality, mind, perception, perspicacity, practicality, prudence, rationality, reason, sagaciousness, sagacity, sageness, saneness, sanity, sapience, sense, shrewdness, soundness, understanding, wisdom; SEE CONCEPT *409*

wizard [n1] *person who can perform magic*
astrologer, augurer, clairvoyant, conjurer, diviner, enchanter, fortuneteller, hypnotist, magician, magus, medium, necromancer, occultist, palmist, seer, shaman, soothsayer, sorcerer, thaumaturge, warlock, witch; SEE CONCEPT *361*

wizard [n2] *person who is highly skilled*
ace*, adept, artist, authority, crackerjack*, expert, genius, hot shot*, pro*, prodigy, professional, proficient, shark*, star, virtuoso, whiz*, whiz kid*, wiz*; SEE CONCEPTS *348,423*

wizened [adj] *dried, shriveled up*
diminished, gnarled, lean, macerated, mummified, old, reduced, shrunk, shrunken, wilted, withered, worn, wrinkled; SEE CONCEPTS *485,603*

wobble [v] *stagger, quake*
be unsteady, careen, falter, flounder, lurch, oscillate, quiver, reel, rock, roll, seesaw, shake, shimmy, stumble, sway, swing, teeter, totter, tremble, vacillate, vibrate, waver, weave, wiggle; SEE CONCEPTS *150,152*

wobbly [adj] *shaky*
fluctuant, insecure, precarious, rattletrap, rickety, rocky, teetering, tottering, unbalanced, uneven, unsafe, unstable, unsteady, unsure, vacillating, wavering, wavy, weak, wiggling; SEE CONCEPT *488*

woe [n] *suffering*
adversity, affliction, agony, anguish, bemoaning, blues*, burden, calamity, care, cataclysm, catastrophe, curse, dejection, deploring, depression, disaster, distress, dole, drag, gloom, grief, grieving, hardship, headache*, heartache*, heartbreak, lamentation, melancholy, misadventure, misery, misfortune, pain, rain*, regret, rue, sadness, sorrow, tragedy, trial, tribulation, trouble, unhappiness, wretchedness; SEE CONCEPTS *410,532,690,728*

woebegone [adj] *depressed, troubled*
black, bleak, blue*, bummed out*, chapfallen, cheerless, crestfallen, dejected, despondent, disconsolate, dismal, dispirited, doleful, down, downcast, downhearted, down-in-the-mouth*, dreary, forlorn, gloomy, grief-stricken, grim, hangdog*, hurting, in pain*, long-faced*, low, lugubrious, melancholy, miserable, mournful, sad, shot down*, sorrowful, unhappy, woeful, wretched; SEE CONCEPT *403*

woeful [adj] *terrible, sad*
afflicted, agonized, anguished, appalling, awful, bad, calamitous, catastrophic, cruel, deplorable, disappointing, disastrous, disconsolate, disgraceful, distressing, doleful, dreadful, feeble, gloomy, grieving, grievous, grim, heartbreaking, heartrending, heartsick, hopeless, inadequate, lamentable, lousy*, mean, miserable, mournful, paltry, pathetic, piteous, pitiable, pitiful, plaintive, poor, racked, rotten, shocking, sorrowful, sorry, tortured, tragic, unfortunate, unhappy, wretched; SEE CONCEPTS *548,571*

wolf [v] *consume sloppily and fast*
bolt, cram, devour, gobble, gorge, gulp, guzzle, ingurgitate, pack, slop, slosh, stuff, swallow; SEE CONCEPT *169*

woman [n] *female human*
aunt, daughter, gentlewoman, girl, girlfriend, grandmother, matron, mother, Ms./Miss/Mrs., niece, she, spouse, wife; SEE CONCEPTS *414,415*

womanizer [n] *philanderer*
Casanova, Don Juan, gigolo, heartbreaker, ladies' man, lady-killer, lecher, libertine, lothario, lover, lover-boy*, rake, Romeo, seducer, skirt chaser, stud*, wolf*; SEE CONCEPT *423*

womanly [adj] *feminine*
female, girlish, ladylike, maidenly, matronly, motherly, womanish; SEE CONCEPTS *371,372,408,648*

wi
wo

wonder [*n1*] *amazement*
admiration, astonishment, awe, bewilderment, concern, confusion, consternation, curiosity, doubt, fascination, fear, incredulity, jar, jolt, marveling, perplexity, perturbation, puzzlement, reverence, shock, skepticism, start, stupefaction, stupor, surprise, suspicion, uncertainty, wondering, wonderment; SEE CONCEPTS *410,532,690*

wonder [*n2*] *something that is amazing*
act of God*, curiosity, cynosure, freak, marvel, miracle, nonpareil, oddity, phenomenon, portent, prodigy, rara avis, rarity, sensation, sight, spectacle, stunner*, wonderment; SEE CONCEPTS *529,687*

wonder [*v1*] *doubt; ponder*
ask oneself, be curious, be inquisitive, conjecture, disbelieve, inquire, meditate, puzzle, query, question, speculate, think; SEE CONCEPTS *17,21*

wonder [*v2*] *be amazed*
admire, be astonished, be awestruck, be confounded, be dumbstruck, be fascinated, be flabbergasted, be startled, be taken aback, boggle, gape, gawk, look aghast, marvel, stare; SEE CONCEPT *34*

wonderful [*adj*] *great, extraordinary*
admirable, amazing, astonishing, astounding, awe-inspiring, awesome, brilliant, cool*, divine*, dynamite*, enjoyable, excellent, fabulous, fantastic, fine, groovy*, incredible, magnificent, marvelous, miraculous, outstanding, peachy*, phenomenal, pleasant, pleasing, prime, remarkable, sensational, something else*, staggering, startling, strange, stupendous, super, superb, surprising, swell, terrific, too much*, tremendous, unheard-of, wondrous; SEE CONCEPTS *529,574*

wonderment [*n*] *astonishment*
amazement, astoundment, awe, bewilderment, curiosity, fascination, marvel, shock, stunner, surprise, wonder; SEE CONCEPTS *230,410*

wonk [*n*] *excessive studier*
bookworm, brain*, dweeb*, geek*, greasy grind*, grind*, grub*, nerd, poindexter, swotter*; SEE CONCEPT *350*

woo [*v*] *seek as romantic partner*
address, aim for, beg, bill and coo*, butter up*, caress, charm, chase, court, cultivate, curry favor*, date, entreat, go steady, importune, keep company, make advances, make love, press one's suit with*, propose, pursue, run after, rush, seek in marriage*, seek the hand of*, set one's cap for*, solicit, spark*, spoon*; SEE CONCEPTS *297,375,384*

wooden [*adj1*] *made of timber*
board, clapboard, frame, ligneous, log, peg, plant, slab, timber, timbered, woody; SEE CONCEPT *485*

wooden [*adj2*] *stiff, inflexible*
awkward, bumbling, clumsy, gauche, gawky, graceless, heavy, heavy-handed, inelegant, inept, maladroit, obstinate, ponderous, rigid, stilted, unbending, ungainly, ungraceful, unhandy, unyielding, weighty; SEE CONCEPTS *488,542*

wood/woods [*n*] *forest*
copse, grove, lumber, thicket, timber, timberland, trees, weald, woodland; SEE CONCEPTS *430,509,517*

woozy [*adj*] *dizzy*
befuddled, bemused, bewildered, confused, dazed, dazzled, dumbfounded, faint, gaga*, giddy, groggy*, hazy, light-headed, muddled, off

balance*, punch-drunk*, punchy*, puzzled, queasy, reeling, seeing stars*, shaky, slaphappy*, staggered, staggering, tipsy, unsteady, weak in the knees*, weak-kneed*, wobbly; SEE CONCEPTS *314,480*

word [*n1*] *discussion*
chat, chitchat*, colloquy, confab*, confabulation, consultation, conversation, discussion, talk, tête-à-tête; SEE CONCEPT *56*

word [*n2*] *statement*
account, adage, advice, announcement, bulletin, byword, comment, communication, communiqué, declaration, directive, discourse, dispatch, expression, gossip, hearsay, information, intelligence, intimation, introduction, message, news, notice, pronouncement, proverb, remark, report, rumble, rumor, saw, saying, scuttlebutt, speech, talk, tidings, utterance; SEE CONCEPTS *274,278*

word [*n3*] *unit of language*
concept, designation, expression, idiom, lexeme, locution, morpheme, name, phrase, sound, term, usage, utterance, vocable; SEE CONCEPT *275*

word [*n4*] *command*
behest, bidding, charge, commandment, decree, dictate, edict, go-ahead*, green light*, injunction, mandate, order, signal, ukase, will; SEE CONCEPT *685*

word [*n5*] *promise*
affirmation, assertion, assurance, commitment, declaration, engagement, guarantee, oath, parole, pledge, plight, solemn oath*, solemn word*, vow, warrant, word of honor; SEE CONCEPTS *71,278,689*

word [*n6*] *password*
countersign, slogan, watchword; SEE CONCEPTS *684,685*

wording [*n*] *way of expressing a thought*
choice of words, diction, language, locution, manner, mode, parlance, phraseology, phrasing, style, terminology, turn of phrase, wordage, words; SEE CONCEPTS *278,682*

wordy [*adj*] *talkative*
bombastic, chatty*, diffuse, discursive, flatulent, gabby*, garrulous, inflated, lengthy, longwinded, loquacious, palaverous, pleonastic, prolix, rambling, redundant, rhetorical, tedious, turgid, verbose, voluble, windy*; SEE CONCEPT *267*

work [*n1*] *labor, chore*
assignment, attempt, commission, daily grind*, drudge, drudgery, effort, elbow grease*, endeavor, exertion, functioning, grind, grindstone*, industry, job, moil, muscle, obligation, pains*, performance, production, push, salt mines*, servitude, slogging, stint, stress, striving, struggle, sweat*, task, toil, travail, trial, trouble, undertaking; SEE CONCEPTS *87,362,677*

work [*n2*] *business, occupation*
activity, art, calling, commitment, contract, craft, do*, duty, employment, endeavor, gig*, grind*, industry, job, line, line of business, livelihood, métier, nine-to-five*, obligation, office, practice, profession, pursuit, racket*, responsibility, skill, slot*, specialization, stint, swindle, task, thing*, trade, vocation, walk; SEE CONCEPTS *349,351,360*

work [*n3*] *achievement*
act, application, article, composition, creation, deed, end product, function, handicraft, handi-

work, oeuvre, opus, output, performance, piece, product, production; SEE CONCEPTS *260,706*

work [*v1*] *be employed; exert oneself*
apply oneself, be gainfully employed, buckle down*, carry on, dig, do a job, do business, drive, drudge, earn a living*, freelance, have a job, hold a job, hustle*, knuckle down*, labor, manage, manufacture, moil, moonlight*, nine-to-five it*, peg away*, plug away*, ply, punch a clock*, pursue, report, scratch, slave, slog*, specialize, strain, strive, sweat*, take on, toil, try; SEE CONCEPTS *100,351*

work [*v2*] *manipulate, operate*
accomplish, achieve, act, behave, bring about, carry out, cause, contrive, control, create, direct, drive, effect, execute, force, function, go, handle, implement, manage, maneuver, move, perform, ply, progress, react, run, serve, take, tick, use, wield; SEE CONCEPTS *94,117,199,204*

work [*v3*] *cultivate, form*
care for, dig, dress, farm, fashion, handle, knead, labor, make, manipulate, mold, process, shape, tend, till; SEE CONCEPTS *173,184,257*

workable [*adj*] *feasible*
applicable, breeze*, cinch*, doable, duck soup*, easy, easy as pie*, exploitable, functional, no sweat*, piece of cake*, possible, practicable, practical, simple as ABC*, snap, usable, useful, viable, working; SEE CONCEPTS *538,552,560*

worker [*n*] *person who is employed*
artisan, blue collar*, breadwinner, company person, craftsperson, employee, hand, help, laborer, nine-to-fiver*, operative, peasant, proletarian, serf, slave, stiff, toiler, trader, tradesperson, wage earner, white collar*, working person, working stiff*; SEE CONCEPT *348*

working [*adj*] *active, occupied*
alive, busy, dynamic, effective, employed, engaged, functioning, going, hot*, in a job, in force, in full swing, in gear, in process, laboring, live, moving, on fire*, on the job, on track*, operative, practical, running, useful, viable; SEE CONCEPTS *538,560*

workmanship [*n*] *craftsmanship*
artisanship, artistry, artwork, craft, design, expertise, handicraft, handiwork, know-how*, skill, skillfulness, technique; SEE CONCEPTS *259,409,630*

workout [*n*] *exercise, practice*
conditioning, constitutional, drill, rehearsal, routine, session, test, training, tryout, warm-up, work; SEE CONCEPTS *290,363*

work out [*v*] *solve; satisfy*
accomplish, achieve, arrange, attain, be effective, bring off, clear, come out, come to terms*, complete, compromise, construct, contrive, develop, devise, elaborate, evolve, figure out, find out, finish, fix, form, formulate, get something done*, go, go well, handle, happen, manipulate, pan out*, plan, prosper, pull off*, put together, reach agreement, resolve, result, succeed, swing*, turn out, up, win; SEE CONCEPTS *706,713*

work up [*v*] *stimulate*
agitate, animate, arouse, breed, cause, develop, engender, excite, generate, get up, hatch, improve, incite, induce, inflame, instigate, move, muster up, occasion, produce, rouse, spur, stir up; SEE CONCEPTS *14,242*

world [*n1*] *planet, globe*
cosmos, creation, earth, heavenly body, macro-

cosm, microcosm, nature, sphere, star, terrene, universe; SEE CONCEPTS *511,770*

world [*n2*] *class of existing beings*
class, division, everybody, everyone, group, humanity, humankind, human race, race, realm; SEE CONCEPTS *378,391*

world [*n3*] *person's environment, experience*
ambience, area, atmosphere, business, domain, field, life, matters, memory, province, pursuits, realm, sphere, system; SEE CONCEPT *678*

worldly [*adj1*] *material, nonreligious*
carnal, earthly, earthy, fleshly, human, lay, materialistic, mundane, natural, physical, practical, profane, secular, sublunary, telluric, temporal, terrene, terrestrial, ungodly; SEE CONCEPTS *536,582*

worldly [*adj2*] *sophisticated, materialistic*
avaricious, been around, blasé, callous, cool*, cosmopolitan, covetous, disenchanted, grasping, greedy, hardened, knowing, opportunistic, power-loving, practical, self-centered, selfish, unprincipled, uptown*, urbane, worldly wise; SEE CONCEPT *401*

worldwide [*adj*] *general*
catholic, common, comprehensive, cosmic, ecumenical, extensive, global, international, multinational, omnipresent, pandemic, planetary, ubiquitous, universal; SEE CONCEPT *536*

worn/worn-out [*adj*] *used, tired*
beat, burned out*, bushed*, busted*, clichéd, consumed, depleted, destroyed, deteriorated, drained, drawn, effete, exhausted, fatigued, frayed, gone, hackneyed, had it*, haggard, jaded, kaput*, knocked out*, old, out of gas*, overused, overworked, pinched, played out*, pooped*, ragged, ruined, shabby, shot, spent, stale, tattered, the worse for wear*, threadbare, timeworn, tired out, totaled*, used up, useless, wearied, weary, well-worn, wiped out, worn down, wrung out*; SEE CONCEPTS *485,560*

worried [*adj*] *anxious, troubled*
afraid, apprehensive, beside oneself, bothered, clutched, concerned, distracted, distraught, distressed, disturbed, fearful, fretful, frightened, hung up*, ill-at-ease, nervous, on edge*, on pins and needles*, overwrought, perturbed, solicitous, tense, tormented, uneasy, upset, uptight, worried stiff*; SEE CONCEPT *403*

worrisome [*adj*] *troublesome*
agonizing, alarming, annoying, anxious, apprehensive, bothersome, burdensome, disquieting, disturbing, inconvenient, irksome, irritating, nervous, taxing, tiresome, trying, uneasy, unnerving, upsetting, vexing, wearisome, worrying; SEE CONCEPTS *529,565*

worry [*n*] *anxiety, trouble*
anguish, annoyance, apprehension, bad news*, care, concern, disquiet, distress, disturbance, doubt, fear, headache*, heartache*, irritation, misery, misgiving, nag*, pain*, perplexity, pest, plague, presentiment, problem, torment, torture, trial, uncertainty, uneasiness, vexation, woe, worriment; SEE CONCEPTS *532,690*

worry [*v*] *be or make anxious, troubled*
afflict, aggrieve, agonize, ail, annoy, attack, bedevil, beleaguer, beset, bite one's nails*, bother, brood, bug*, chafe, concern oneself, depress, despair, disquiet, distress, disturb, dun, feel uneasy, fret, gnaw at, goad, go for*, harass, harry, hassle, have qualms, hector, importune, irritate, needle,

WO
WO

oppress, persecute, perturb, pester, plague, stew*, sweat out*, take on, tantalize, tear, tease, test, torment, torture, trouble, try, unsettle, upset, vex, wince, writhe, wrong; SEE CONCEPTS *7,14,19,410*

worsen [v] *diminish, decay*
aggravate, corrode, damage, decline, degenerate, depress, descend, deteriorate, disintegrate, exacerbate, fall off, get worse, go downhill*, impair, lower, retrograde, retrogress, rot, sink; SEE CONCEPTS *240,698*

worship [n] *honoring, glorification*
adoration, adulation, awe, beatification, benediction, chapel, church service, deification, devotion, exaltation, genuflection, glory, homage, honor, idolatry, idolization, invocation, laudation, love, offering, praise, prayer, prostration, regard, respect, reverence, rite, ritual, service, supplication, veneration, vespers; SEE CONCEPTS *69,367*

worship [v] *honor, glorify*
admire, adore, adulate, bow down to, canonize, celebrate, chant, deify, dote on, esteem, exalt, extol, idolize, laud, love, magnify, offer prayers to, pay homage to, praise, pray to, put on a pedestal*, respect, revere, reverence, sanctify, sing, sing praises to*, venerate; SEE CONCEPTS *69,367*

worth [n] *value, estimation associated with something*
account, aid, assistance, avail, benefit, caliber, class, consequence, cost, credit, desirability, dignity, equivalence, excellence, goodness, help, importance, mark, meaningfulness, merit, moment, note, perfection, price, quality, rate, significance, stature, use, usefulness, utility, valuation, virtue, weight, worthiness; SEE CONCEPTS *335,346*

worthless [adj] *of no use; without value*
abandoned, abject, barren, base, bogus, cheap, contemptible, counterproductive, despicable, empty, futile, good-for-nothing*, ignoble, inconsequential, ineffective, ineffectual, inferior, insignificant, inutile, meaningless, mediocre, miserable, no-account*, no-good*, nothing, nugatory, paltry, pointless, poor, profitless, sterile, trashy, trifling, trivial, unavailing, unessential, unimportant, unproductive, unprofitable, unusable, useless, valueless, waste, wretched; SEE CONCEPTS *560,570,575*

worthwhile [adj] *helpful*
advantageous, beneficial, constructive, estimable, excellent, gainful, good, important, invaluable, justifiable, lucrative, meritorious, money-making, paying, priceless, productive, profitable, remunerative, rewarding, serviceable, useful, valuable, worthy; SEE CONCEPTS *560,567,572*

worthy [adj] *honorable, respectable*
A-1*, aces*, admirable, best, blameless, choice, commendable, creditable, decent, dependable, deserving, desirable, divine, estimable, ethical, excellent, exemplary, first-class*, first-rate*, good, honest, incorrupt, invaluable, laudable, meritorious, model, moral, noble, pleasing, praiseworthy, precious, priceless, pure, reliable, reputable, righteous, right-minded, salt of the earth*, satisfying, sterling, top-drawer*, top-notch*, true, trustworthy, upright, valuable, vir-

tuous, winning, worthwhile; SEE CONCEPTS *545,567,572*

wound [n] *injury*
anguish, bruise, cut, damage, distress, gash, grief, harm, heartbreak, hurt, insult, laceration, lesion, pain, pang, shock, slash, torment, torture, trauma; SEE CONCEPT *309*

wound [v1] *cause bodily damage*
bruise, carve, clip*, contuse, cut, damage, ding*, gash, harm, hit, hurt, injure, irritate, lacerate, nick, open up, ouch*, pierce, rough up*, scrape, scratch, slash, slice, stick, total*; SEE CONCEPTS *137,246,313*

wound [v2] *cause mental hurt*
bother, cut to the quick*, distress, disturb, do in*, dump on*, get*, grieve, hurt, hurt one's feelings, mortify, offend, outrage, pain, put down*, shake up*, sting, traumatize, trouble, upset; SEE CONCEPTS *7,14,19*

wow [v] *amuse, delight*
bowl over*, break one up*, charm, cheer, crack up*, entertain, go over big*, kill*, knock dead*, knock someone's socks off*, make laugh, make roll in the aisles*, slay*, tickle, tickle pink*, tickle to death*; SEE CONCEPTS *7,9,22,292,384*

wrangle [n] *fight, argument*
altercation, battle royal*, bickering, blow-off*, blowup*, branigan*, brawl, brouhaha*, clash, contest, controversy, disagreement, dispute, exchange, falling-out*, flap*, fracas, hassle, knock-down drag-out*, quarrel, row, ruckus*, ruction, rumble, rumpus, scene, set-to*, squabble, tiff; SEE CONCEPTS *46,106*

wrangle [v] *fight, argue*
altercate, bicker, brawl, bump heads*, contend, cross swords*, disagree, dispute, fall out*, hassle, have at it*, have words*, lock horns*, pick a bone*, put up a fight, quarrel, quibble, row, scrap, spat, squabble, take on, tangle, tiff; SEE CONCEPTS *46,106*

wrap [n] *clothing that is worn over for warmth*
blanket, cape, cloak, coat, cover, fur, jacket, mantle, shawl, stole; SEE CONCEPT *451*

wrap [v] *surround with a covering*
absorb, bandage, bind, bundle, bundle up, camouflage, cloak, clothe, cover, drape, encase, encircle, enclose, enfold, envelop, fold, gift-wrap*, hide, immerse, invest, mask, muffle, pack, package, protect, roll up, sheathe, shelter, shroud, swaddle, swathe, twine, veil, wind; SEE CONCEPT *172*

wrap up [v] *finish*
bring to a close, close, complete, conclude, determine, end, halt, polish off, terminate, wind up; SEE CONCEPT *234*

wrath [n] *extreme anger*
acrimony, asperity, boiling point*, conniption*, dander, displeasure, exasperation, flare-up, fury, hate, hatefulness, huff, indignation, ire, irritation, mad, madness, offense, passion, rage, resentment, rise, stew*, storm, temper, vengeance; SEE CONCEPTS *29,410*

wrathful [adj] *very angry*
beside oneself, displeased, enraged, furious, heated, incensed, indignant, infuriated, irate, ireful, mad, on the warpath*, raging, storming; SEE CONCEPT *403*

wreak [v] *force, cause*
bring about, carry out, create, effect, execute, ex-

ercise, force upon, inflict, unleash, vent, visit, work, wreck; SEE CONCEPT *242*

wreath [*n*] *circular decoration*
band, bay, bouquet, chaplet, circlet, coronal, coronet, crown, festoon, garland, laurel, lei, loop, ring, ringlet; SEE CONCEPTS *259,260,429*

wreck [*n*] *severe damage or severely damaged goods*
collapse, crash, crate, debacle, debris, derelict, destruction, devastation, disruption, fender bender*, heap*, hulk*, jalopy*, junk*, junker*, litter, mess, pile-up*, rear-ender*, relic, ruin, ruins, shipwreck, smashup*, total*, waste, wreckage; SEE CONCEPTS *260,674*

wreck [*v*] *ruin, destroy*
bash, batter, beach, break, capsize, crack up*, crash, cripple, dash, decimate, demolish, devastate, dilapidate, disable, do in*, efface, founder, impair, injure, mangle, mar, mess up*, pile up*, put out of commission*, ravage, raze, run aground, sabotage, scuttle, shatter, shipwreck, sink, smash, smash up, spoil, strand, subvert, take apart, take out, tear up, torpedo*, total*, trash*, undermine, vandalize, wrack*, wrack up*; SEE CONCEPT *252*

wrench [*v*] *jerk, force violently*
bend, coerce, compel, contort, dislocate, dislodge, distort, drag, exact, extract, pervert, pinch, pull, rend, rip, screw, sprain, squeeze, strain, tear, tug, tweak, twist, wrest, wring, yank; SEE CONCEPTS *80,206*

wrestle [*v*] *struggle physically or mentally with something*
battle, combat, contend, endeavor, essay, exert, fight, grapple, grunt, scuffle, strain, strive, tangle, tussle, work; SEE CONCEPTS *17,191,208*

wretched [*adj*] *terrible, very bad*
abject, afflicted, base, bummed, calamitous, cheap, contemptible, dejected, deplorable, depressed, despicable, disconsolate, distressed, dolorous, down, down-and-out*, downcast, faulty, flimsy, forlorn, gloomy, hapless, hopeless, hurting, inferior, in the pits*, low, low-down*, mean, melancholy, miserable, paltry, pathetic, pitiable, pitiful, poor, shabby, shameful, sordid, sorrowful, sorry, spiritless, tragic, unfortunate, unhappy, vile, weak, woebegone, woeful, worthless; SEE CONCEPTS *403,571*

wriggle [*v*] *maneuver out of; wiggle*
convulse, crawl, dodge, extricate oneself, glide, jerk, jiggle, ooze, skew, slink, slip, snake, sneak, squirm, turn, twist, twitch, wag, waggle, worm, writhe, zigzag; SEE CONCEPTS *30,149*

wring [*v*] *twist, contort*
choke, coerce, compress, draw out, exact, extort, extract, force, gouge, hurt, pain, pinch, pry, push, screw, shake down, squeeze, strain, strangle, throttle, turn, wrench, wrest; SEE CONCEPTS *142,206,208*

wrinkle [*n*] *crinkle, fold*
contraction, corrugation, crease, crow's-foot*, crumple, depression, furrow, gather, line, pleat, plica, pucker, ridge, rimple, rumple, tuck; SEE CONCEPTS *418,513*

wrinkle [*v*] *crinkle, fold*
compress, corrugate, crease, crimp, crisp, crumple, furrow, gather, line, prune up, pucker, purse, rimple, ruck, rumple, screw up, scrunch, seam, shrivel, twist; SEE CONCEPTS *185,201*

writ [*n*] *court order*
command, decree, document, habeas corpus, mandate, paper, prescript, process, replevin, subpoena, summons, warrant; SEE CONCEPT *318*

write [*v*] *put language down on paper*
address, author, autograph, bang out*, chalk*, commit, communicate, comp*, compose, copy, correspond, create, dash off*, draft, draw up*, drop a line*, drop a note*, engross, formulate, ghost, indite, ink, inscribe, jot down, knock off*, knock out*, letter, note, note down*, pen, pencil, print, push a pencil*, put in writing, record, reproduce, rewrite, scrawl, scribble, scribe, scriven, set down, set forth, sign, take down, tell, transcribe, turn out, typewrite, write down, write up; SEE CONCEPTS *79,203*

write off [*v*] *devalue; forget about*
cancel, cross out, decry, depreciate, disregard, downgrade, give up, lower, mark down, shelve, take a loss on, underrate, undervalue; SEE CONCEPT *54*

writer [*n*] *person who composes with language*
author, biographer, columnist, contributor, correspondent, critic, dramatist, editor, essayist, freelancer, ghostwriter, journalist, newspaper person, novelist, person of letters, poet, reporter, screenwriter, scribbler, scribe, scripter, stenographer, stringer, wordsmith; SEE CONCEPTS *348,356*

writhe [*v*] *contort; toss back and forth*
agonize, bend, distort, jerk, recoil, squirm, struggle, suffer, thrash, thresh, twist, wiggle, wince, worm, wriggle; SEE CONCEPTS *80,150*

writing [*n1*] *printing on paper*
autograph, calligraphy, chirography, cuneiform, hand, handwriting, hieroglyphics, longhand, manuscription, print, scrawl, scribble, script, shorthand; SEE CONCEPTS *79,284*

writing [*n2*] *printed composition*
article, belles-lettres, book, discourse, dissertation, document, editorial, essay, letter, literature, manuscript, novel, ode, opus, pamphlet, paper, piece, play, poem, prose, publication, record, review, signature, theme, thesis, tract, treatise, work; SEE CONCEPT *271*

wrong [*adj1*] *incorrect*
amiss, askew, astray, at fault, awry, bad, counterfactual, defective, erratic, erring, erroneous, fallacious, false, faulty, fluffed, goofed*, inaccurate, in error, inexact, miscalculated, misconstrued, misfigured, misguided, mishandled, mistaken, not precise, not right, not working, offtarget*, on the wrong track*, out, out of commission*, out of line*, out of order*, perverse, rotten*, sophistical, specious, spurious, ungrounded, unsatisfactory, unsound, unsubstantial, untrue, wide; SEE CONCEPTS *571,582*

wrong [*adj2*] *immoral, dishonest*
amoral, bad, base, blamable, blameworthy, blasphemous, censurable, corrupt, criminal, crooked, debauched, depraved, dishonorable, dissipated, dissolute, evil, felonious, illegal, illicit, indecent, iniquitous, naughty, profane, profligate, reprehensible, reprobate, risqué, sacrilegious, salacious, shady, sinful, smutty, unethical, unfair, ungodly, unholy, unjust, unlawful, unrighteous, vicious, wanton, wicked, wrongful; SEE CONCEPT *545*

wrong [*adj3*] *inappropriate, not suitable*
amiss, awkward, bad, disproportionate, funny, gauche, ill-advised, improper, inapt, incongru-

ous, incorrect, indecorous, infelicitous, malapropos, misplaced, not done*, off-balance, rotten*, unacceptable, unbecoming, unconventional, undesirable, unfit, unfitted, unfitting, unhappy, unsatisfactory, unseemly, unsuitable; SEE CONCEPT *558*

wrong [*adj4*] *reverse, opposite*
back, inside, inverse, obverse; SEE CONCEPT *586*

wrong [*adv*] *astray*
afield, amiss, askew, badly, erroneously, inaccurately, incorrectly, mistakenly, unfavorably, wrongly; SEE CONCEPTS *544,548*

wrong [*n*] *offense, sin*
abuse, bad deed, bias, blunder, crime, cruelty, damage, delinquency, discourtesy, error, evil, faux pas, favor, foul play, grievance, harm, hurt, immorality, imposition, indecency, inequity, inhumanity, iniquity, injury, injustice, insult, libel, malevolence, miscarriage, misdeed, misdemeanor, misdoing, mistake, oppression, persecution, prejudice, sinfulness, slander, slight, spite, tort, transgression, trespass, turpitude, unfairness, vice, villainy, violation, wickedness, wrongdoing; SEE CONCEPT *645*

wrong [*v*] *hurt, mistreat another*
abuse, aggrieve, cheat, damage, defame, discredit, dishonor, harm, hurt, ill-treat, impose upon, injure, malign, maltreat, misrepresent, mistreat, offend, oppress, outrage, persecute, take advantage of; SEE CONCEPTS *7,19,246,313*

wrongful [*adj*] *evil, illegal*
blameworthy, criminal, dishonest, dishonorable, felonious, illegitimate, illicit, immoral, improper, lawless, reprehensible, unethical, unfair, unjust, unlawful, wicked; SEE CONCEPTS *319,545*

wry [*adj*] *sarcastic, distorted*
askew, aslant, awry, contorted, crooked, cynical, deformed, droll, dry, ironic, mocking, sardonic, twisted, uneven, warped; SEE CONCEPTS *267,581*

X

Xanadu [*n*] *utopia*
Arcadia, dreamland, dreamworld, Eden, heaven, land of milk and honey*, never-never land*, paradise, promised land*, Shangri-La*, wonderland; SEE CONCEPTS *370,689*

xerophagy [*n*] *fasting*
hunger strike, keeping fast, Lenten fast, strict fast, without food, xerophagia; SEE CONCEPT *169*

Xerox [*v*] *copy*
carbon, clone, counterfeit, ditto, duplicate, forge, mimeograph, photocopy, photostat, replicate, reprint, reproduce, trace; SEE CONCEPT *171*

X-rated [*adj*] *pornographic*
adult, bawdy, dirty, erotic, fleshy, hard-core, immoral, indecent, lascivious, lewd, obscene, off-color, offensive, porn*, porno*, raunchy, sensual, sexual, sexy, smutty*, steamy*; SEE CONCEPTS *267,372,545*

x-ray [*n*] *picture of inside a body*
actinism, cathode rays, encephalogram, fluoroscope, radioactivity, radiograph, refractometry, Roentgen rays, ultraviolet rays; SEE CONCEPT *311*

Y

yacht [*n*] *pleasure boat*
cabin cruiser, cruiser, ketch, racer, sailboat, sailing boat, sloop, yawl; SEE CONCEPT *506*

yak/yap [*n/v*] *talk a lot*
babble, blather, chat, chatter, clack, confabulate, gab, gossip, jabber, jaw*, prate, prattle, run on*, tattle, yammer; SEE CONCEPTS *51,266*

yammer [*v*] *whine*
bellyache, carp, complain, fuss, gripe, grumble, howl, moan, repine, wail, whimper, yowl; SEE CONCEPTS *54,77*

yank [*v*] *pull hard and fast*
draw, evulse, extract, hitch, jerk, lug, snap, snatch, tear, tug, twitch, vellicate, wrench; SEE CONCEPT *206*

yard [*n*] *grassy area around a structure*
backyard, barnyard, clearing, close, corral, court, courtyard, enclosure, fold, garden, grass, lawn, lot, patch, patio, playground, quadrangle, terrace; SEE CONCEPT *509*

yardstick [*n*] *gauge*
barometer, basis, benchmark, criterion, example, guide, guideline, indicator, mark, measure, meter, model, norm, rule, sample, scale, standard, tape measure, test; SEE CONCEPTS *647,680,688,792*

yarn [*n1*] *fiber for knitting*
cotton fiber, flaxen thread, fleece, spun wool, thread, twist, wool; SEE CONCEPT *473*

yarn [*n2*] *story, often long and made-up*
adventure, alibi, anecdote, fable, fabrication, fairy tale, lie, line, narrative, potboiler*, prose, sea story*, song*, song and dance*, string*, tale, tall story*, tall tale; SEE CONCEPT *282*

yawn [*v*] *open mouth wide, usually sign of fatigue*
catch flies*, divide, doze, drowse, expand, gap, gape, give, nap, part, sleep, snooze, spread, yaw, yawp*; SEE CONCEPTS *163,185*

yearly [*adj*] *every twelve months*
annual, annually, once a year, per annum, perennial, regularly, year by year, yearlong; SEE CONCEPTS *541,823*

yearn [*v*] *desire strongly*
ache, be desirous of, be eager for, be passionate, chafe, covet, crave, dream, hanker, have a crush on*, have a yen for, hunger, itch, languish, long, lust, pine, set one's heart on*, thirst, want, wish for; SEE CONCEPT *20*

yearning [*n*] *desire*
ache, ambition, appetite, aspiration, craving, craze, eagerness, fancy, fascination, hankering*, hunger, infatuation, liking, longing, love, need, passion, thirst, urge, want; SEE CONCEPTS *20,709*

years [*n*] *age; old age*
age, agedness, caducity, dotage, elderliness, generation, lifespan, lifetime, oldness, senescence, senility; SEE CONCEPT *715*

yell [*n/v*] *loud communication*
bawl, bellow, call, cheer, complain, cry, holler*, hoot, howl, lament, roar, scream, screech, shout, shriek, shrill, squawk, squeal, ululate, vociferate, wail, weep, whoop, yap, yelp, yip; SEE CONCEPTS *47,595*

yellow [*adj2*] *cowardly*
chicken*, craven, deceitful, gutless, lily-livered*,

low, offensive, pusillanimous, sneaking, treacherous, tricky, unethical, unprincipled; SEE CONCEPTS *267,401*

yellow [*n/adj1*] *sunny color*
amber, bisque, blond, buff, chrome, cream, gold, ivory, lemon, saffron, sand, tawny; SEE CONCEPTS *618,622*

yelp [*n/v*] *short, high cry*
bark, hoot, howl, screech, yap, yip, yowl; SEE CONCEPT *64*

yen [*n*] *strong want*
craving, desire, hankering, hunger, itch, longing, lust, passion, thirst, urge, yearning; SEE CONCEPTS *20,709*

yes [*adv*] *agreed*
affirmative, all right*, amen, aye*, beyond a doubt, by all means, certainly, definitely, even so, exactly, fine, gladly, good, good enough, granted, indubitably, just so, most assuredly, naturally, of course, okay*, positively, precisely, surely, sure thing*, true, undoubtedly, unquestionably, very well, willingly, without fail, yea*, yep*; SEE CONCEPTS *535,572*

yes-person [*n*] *sycophant*
apple polisher*, backscratcher*, backslapper*, bootlicker*, brownnoser*, doormat*, fan, fawner, flatterer, flunky*, groupie*, hanger-on*, lackey, minion, puppet, toady; SEE CONCEPT *423*

yesterday [*n*] *the day before today*
bygone, foretime, lang syne*, last day, not long ago, past, recently, the other day*; SEE CONCEPT *815*

yet [*adv1*] *up until now*
as yet, earlier, hitherto, prior to, so far, still, thus far, till, until now, up to now; SEE CONCEPT *820*

yet [*adv2*] *in spite of*
after all, although, at any rate, but, despite, even though, howbeit, however, nevertheless, nonetheless, notwithstanding, on the other hand, still, still and all, though, withal; SEE CONCEPT *544*

yet [*adv3*] *in addition*
additionally, along, also, as well, besides, further, furthermore, likewise, more, moreover, over and above*, still, still further, to boot*, too; SEE CONCEPT *548*

yet [*adv4*] *in the future*
after a while, at some future time, beyond this, even, eventually, finally, in due course, in the course of time, someday, sometime, sooner or later, still, ultimately; SEE CONCEPT *799*

yield [*n*] *production of labor*
crop, earnings, harvest, income, output, outturn, produce, profit, return, revenue, takings, turnout; SEE CONCEPTS *260,338*

yield [*v1*] *produce*
accrue, admit, afford, allow, beam, bear, blossom, bring forth, bring in, discharge, earn, furnish, generate, give, give off, hold out, net, offer, pay, proffer, provide, return, sell for, supply, tender, turn out; SEE CONCEPT *205*

yield [*v2*] *give in, surrender*
abandon, abdicate, admit defeat, back down, bend, bow, break, buy, call it quits*, capitulate, cave in, cede, collapse, come to terms*, crumple, defer, fold, fold up, give oneself over, give up, give way*, go, hand over, knuckle, knuckle under*, lay down arms*, leave, let go*, part with, relax, relent, relinquish, resign, sag, sub-

mit, succumb, suffer defeat, surrender, throw in the towel*; SEE CONCEPTS *14,18,35*

yield [*v3*] *grant, allow*
accede, accept, acknowledge, acquiesce, admit, agree, assent, bow, break, comply, concede, concur, consent, defer, fail, fit in, go along with*, go with the flow*, permit, play the game*, surrender, toe the line*, toe the mark*, waive; SEE CONCEPT *8*

yielding [*adj1*] *accommodating*
acquiescent, biddable, compliant, docile, easy, flexible, humble, nonresistant, obedient, passive, pliable, pliant, putty in one's hands, resigned, submissive, tractable; SEE CONCEPTS *401,404*

yielding [*adj2*] *soft, flexible*
elastic, malleable, mushy, pappy, plastic, pliable, pulpy, quaggy, resilient, spongy, springy, squishy, supple, tractable, tractile, unresisting; SEE CONCEPTS *488,606*

yoke [*n*] *bondage, bond*
burden, chain, coupling, enslavement, helotry, knot, ligament, ligature, link, nexus, oppression, peonage, serfdom, service, servility, servitude, slavery, tie; SEE CONCEPTS *513,677*

yoke [*v*] *bond together; join*
associate, attach, bracket, buckle, combine, conjoin, conjugate, connect, couple, fasten, fix, harness, hitch, link, secure, splice, strap, tack, tie, unite, wed; SEE CONCEPTS *85,160,193*

yokel [*n*] *person who is mired in local custom*
backwoods person, boor*, country cousin*, country person, hayseed*, peasant, rustic; SEE CONCEPT *413*

yonder [*adv*] *faraway*
away, beyond, distant, farther, further, remote, yon; SEE CONCEPTS *586,778*

young [*adj*] *immature*
adolescent, blooming, blossoming, boyish, boylike, budding, burgeoning, callow, childish, childlike, crude, developing, early, fledgling, fresh, girlish, girllike, green*, growing, half-grown, ignorant, inexperienced, infant, inferior, junior, juvenile, little, modern, new, newborn, newish, not aged, pubescent, puerile, punk, raw, recent, tender, tenderfoot*, undeveloped, undisciplined, unfinished, unfledged, unlearned, unpracticed, unripe, unseasoned, untried, unversed, vernal, youthful; SEE CONCEPTS *578,678,715,797*

young [*n*] *animate beings that are not mature*
babies, baby, brood, family, infants, issue, litter, little ones*, offspring, progeny; SEE CONCEPTS *394,414,424*

youngster/youth [*n*] *person before the age of maturity*
boy, chick*, cub*, fledgling, girl, junior, juvenile, juvenile delinquent*, kid*, lad, lass, pup, pupil, student, teenager, young person; SEE CONCEPTS *414,424*

youth [*n*] *early period in life of animate being*
adolescence, awkward age, bloom, boyhood, childhood, girlhood, greenness, ignorance, immaturity, inexperience, innocence, juvenescence, minority, prime, puberty, salad days*, springtide, springtime of life, teens, tender age*, youthfulness; SEE CONCEPT *817*

youthful [*adj*] *new, immature*
active, adolescent, boyish, budding, buoyant, callow, childish, childlike, enthusiastic, fresh, full of life, girlish, green*, inexperienced, infant, juvenile, keen, pubescent, puerile, tender, under-

wr
yo

age, vernal, vigorous, young; SEE CONCEPTS 542,578,797

yowl [n/v] *long, loud animate sound*
bawl, bay, caterwaul, cry, holler*, howl, mewl, scream, screech, squall, squeal, ululate, wail, whine, yell, yelp, yip; SEE CONCEPT 77

yucky [adj] *disgusting*
abominable, awful, beastly, crappy*, creepy, cruddy*, crummy*, detestable, distasteful, foul, funky*, grody*, gross, gruesome, hideous, icky*, loathsome, lousy, nasty, nauseating, odious, offensive, raunchy, repugnant, repulsive, revolting, rotten, scuzzy*, sickening, skanky*, sleazy*, stinking, vile, vulgar, yecchy*; SEE CONCEPTS 485,548

yummy [adj] *delicious*
ambrosial, appetizing, choice, delectable, delightful, divine, enticing, fit for a king*, good, heavenly, juicy, luscious, mouthwatering, nectarous, out of this world*, palatable, piquant, pleasant, rich, sapid, savory, scrumptious, spicy, succulent, super, sweet, tasteful, tasty, tempting, toothsome; SEE CONCEPTS 572,613

yuppie [n/adj] *young upwardly mobile professional*
button-down, clone, conspicuous consumer, suit, three-piecer, urban professional, white-collar worker; SEE CONCEPT 348

Z

zany [adj] *crazy, funny*
camp*, campy*, clownish, comical, dumb, eccentric, fool, foolish, goofy, hare-brained*, humorous, joshing, kooky*, loony*, madcap*, nutty*, sappy*, wacky*, witty; SEE CONCEPTS 267,401

zany [n] *person who is wildly funny*
buffoon, card*, clown, comedian, comic, cutup*, farceur, funny person, gag person, humorist, idiot, jester, joker, madcap*, moron, nut*, practical joker, prankster, screwball*, show-off, simpleton*, wag*, wisecracker*; SEE CONCEPTS 352,423

zeal [n] *enthusiasm*
alacrity, ardor, bustle, determination, devotion, diligence, dispatch, drive, eagerness, earnestness, enterprise, fanaticism, fervor, fierceness, fire, gusto, hustle, inclination, initiative, intensity, intentness, keenness, mania, passion, perseverance, push, readiness, sincerity, spirit, stick-to-itiveness*, urgency, vehemence, verve, warmth, what-it-takes*, yen, zest; SEE CONCEPTS 32,410,411

zealous [adj] *enthusiastic*
afire, antsy*, ardent, avid, burning, coming on strong*, dedicated, devoted, eager, earnest, fanatic, fanatical, fervent, fervid, fireball*, fired, frenetic, gung-ho*, hot*, impassioned, itchy*, keen, obsessed, passionate, possessed, pushy*, rabid, ripe, self-starting, spirited, wild-eyed*; SEE CONCEPTS 326,401,404

zenith [n] *top*
acme, altitude, apex, apogee, cap, capper, capstone, climax, crest, crown, culmination, eleva-

tion, eminence, height, high noon*, high point, meridian, payoff*, peak, pinnacle, roof, summit, tiptop*, topper*, vertex; SEE CONCEPTS 706,832,836

zero [n] *nothing*
aught, blank, bottom, cipher, insignificancy, love*, lowest point, nada*, nadir, naught, nil*, nix*, nobody*, nonentity, nought, nullity, oblivion, ought, rock bottom*, scratch, shutout, void, zilch*, zip*, zot*; SEE CONCEPTS 407,784

zero hour [n] *vital moment*
appointed hour*, climax, contingency, countdown, crisis, crossroad, D-day*, emergency, exigency, jumping-off point*, juncture, moment of truth*, pinch, strait, target, the time*, turning point*; SEE CONCEPTS 668,815,832

zest [n1] *taste, flavor*
bite, body, charm, flavoring, ginger, guts*, interest, kick*, nip, piquancy, punch*, pungency, relish, salt, savor, seasoning, smack*, snap*, spice, tang, zap*, zip*; SEE CONCEPT 614

zest [n2] *energy, gusto*
appetite, ardor, bliss, bounce, cheer, delectation, delight, eagerness, ecstasy, elation, enjoyment, enthusiasm, fervor, guts*, happiness, keenness, moxie*, passion, pep*, pleasure, relish*, satisfaction, zeal, zing*; SEE CONCEPTS 410,411

zigzag [adj] *moving side to side*
askew, awry, bent, crinkled, crooked, devious, diagonal, erratic, fluctuating, inclined, indirect, irregular, jagged, meandering, oblique, oscillating, rambling, serrated, sinuous, sloping, snaking, tortuous, transverse, twisted, twisting, undulating, waggling, winding; SEE CONCEPT 581

zilch [n] *nothing*
blank, diddly-squat*, goose egg*, hill of beans*, insignificancy, nada*, naught, not anything, nothingness, nought, void, zero, zip, zippo*; SEE CONCEPTS 407,707

zing [n] *liveliness*
brio, dash, drive, elan, energy, enthusiasm, get-up-and-go*, go, gusto, life, oomph*, pep, pizazz, punch, sparkle, spirit, verve, vigor, vim, vitality, zest, zip; SEE CONCEPTS 411,633

zip [n] *enthusiasm, energy*
brio, drive, get-up-and-go*, go*, gusto, life, liveliness, oomph*, pep, pizzazz*, punch, sparkle, spirit, verve, vigor, vim, vitality, zest, zing*; SEE CONCEPTS 411,633

zip [v] *move about quickly*
bustle, dash, flash, fly, hasten, hurry, run, rush, shoot, speed, tear, waltz, whisk, whiz, zoom; SEE CONCEPT 150

zippy [adj] *energetic*
active, animated, ball of fire*, brisk, chipper, dashing, dynamic, enterprising, full of energy, full of life, full of pep, high-powered, kinetic, lively, peppy, potent, powerful, snappy, speedy, spirited, sprightly, spry, strong, tireless, untiring, vigorous, vital, vivacious, zestful, zingy*; SEE CONCEPTS 404,542

zit [n] *pimple*
abscess, acne, blackhead, blemish, bump, carbuncle, excrescence, goober*, goophead*, papula, papule, putsule, whitehead; SEE CONCEPT 306

zone [n] *district*
area, band, belt, circuit, ground, realm, region,

section, sector, segment, sphere, territory, tract; SEE CONCEPTS *508,513*

zonked [*adj*] *drunk, intoxicated; stunned*
amazed, astonished, bashed, boozed up*, buzzed*, crocked*, dazed, dumbfounded, feeling no pain*, flying*, groggy, high*, inebriated, juiced*, laced*, liquored up*, lit*, plastered*, seeing double*, sloshed*, stewed*, stoned*, tanked*, three sheets to the wind*, thunderstruck, tipsy, totaled*, under the influence, under the table*, wasted*; SEE CONCEPTS *314,545*

zoom [*v*] *move very quickly*
buzz, dart, dash, dive, flash, fly, hum, hurtle, outstrip, rip, rocket, rush, shoot, shoot up, skyrocket, speed, streak, surge, tear, whirl, whiz, zip*; SEE CONCEPT *150*

ROGET'S 21ST CENTURY CONCEPT INDEX

HOW TO USE THE CONCEPT INDEX

Simply put, a thesaurus is a collection of words grouped according to idea. Appearing in the A to Z listings of *Roget's 21st Century Thesaurus, Second Edition* are about 20,000 words and 500,000 synonyms to choose from. This selection alone would seem generous enough to satisfy the lexicographer's expectation of what a thesaurus should contain. But a wealth of new alternatives is created when we begin to think about the higher connections that can be made between words and ideas in the language. This is the purpose of *Roget's 21st Century's* Concept Index.

The Concept Index not only helps writers and thinkers to *organize* their ideas but leads them from those very ideas to the words that can best express them. It is a semantic hierarchy of the most common concepts we use in American English as it is spoken and written today.

There are 837 concepts classified according to their subject and usage, and grouped under ten general categories of interest: Actions, Causes, Fields of Human Activity, Life Forms, Objects, the Planet, Qualities, Senses, States, and Weights and Measures.

All of *Roget's 21st Century Thesaurus's* 20,000 main entries are cross-referenced to related concepts. For example, when you look up the entry for "knowledgeable" in the A to Z listing, it is referenced to concept #402. Turning in the index to concept #402, "attribute of intelligence," you will see over 100 other main entries that are also related to this concept:

MAIN ENTRY

with synonym list as it appears in the A to Z listing

> **knowledgeable** [*adj*] *aware, educated*
> abreast, acquainted, alert, appreciative, apprised, au courant, au fait, brainy*, bright, brilliant, clever, cognizant, conscious, conversant, discerning, erudite, experienced, familiar, informed, insightful, intelligent, in the know, knowing, learned, lettered, omniscient, perceptive, plugged in*, posted, prescient, privy, quick-witted, sagacious, sage, savvy, scholarly, sensible, sharp, smart, sophic, sophisticated, tuned-in*, understanding, versed, well-informed, well-rounded, wise, with-it; SEE CONCEPT *402*

CONCEPT

with collection of main entry words referenced to it in the index

> **402 attribute of intelligence:** able, abreast, abstruse, academic, accident-prone, acquainted, acute, adept, alert, amenable, analytic/analytical, appreciative, apt, asinine, astute, awake, aware, backward, bewildered, blank, blind, bright, brilliant, calculable, canny, catatonic, cerebral, childish, clairvoyant, clear, clever, clumsy, cognizant, coherent, common-sense, complex, comprehensible, conscious, considered, contemplative, conversant, creative, cunning, dark, deducible, deep, delirious, dense, designedly, dexterous, dim, discerning, dizzy, dopey, down-to-earth, dull, dumb, eagle-eyed, educated, efficient, elevated, empty, empty-headed, enlightened, erudite, experienced, expert, familiar, far-sighted,

fatuous, feebleminded, forgotten, frivolous, gifted, gullible, harebrained, hazy, highbrow, idiotic, ignorant, illiterate, imbecile, impressionable, incisive, incomprehensible, inefficient, ineligible, inept, inexperienced, informed, ingenious, inquiring, inquisitive, insightful, insipid, intellectual, intelligent, intuitive, inventive, irrational, judicious, keen, knowing, knowledgeable, learned, literate, logical, lowbrowed, lucid, mental, mindful, mistaken, moronic, nimble, not born yesterday, oblivious, observant, obtuse, omniscient, on the ball, penetrating, perceptive, perspicacious, philosophical/philosophic, precocious, privy, professional, proficient, profound, psychic, quick, quick-witted, rational, ready, reasonable, resourceful, sagacious, sage, sane, sapient, savvy, scatterbrained, scholarly, searching, seasoned, senile, sensible, sentinent, shallow, sharp, shrewd, simple, skillful, slick, slow, smart, soft, stolid, studious, stupid, subtle, talented, thick, thoughtful, thoughtless, touched, unaware, uncoordinated, uneducated, unfamiliar, uninformed, unintelligent, unknowing, unwise, vacant, vacuous, versed, veteran, weak, well-balanced, well-defined, wideawake, wise, with it

Any of these main entry words appearing together as attributes of intelligence in the Concept Index—from "able" to "ingenious" to "perspicacious" to "wise"—may be the perfect word you are looking for. Or, intrigued by the associations the word "veteran" brings to mind, you could return to the A to Z listing to explore its synonyms:

veteran [*adj*] *experienced, seasoned*
adept, battle-scarred*, been around*, disciplined, exercised, expert, from way back*, hardened, inured, knows one's stuff*, long-serving, longtime, not born yesterday*, of the old school*, old, old-time, practical, practiced, pro*, proficient, skilled, sophisticated, steady, trained, up to speed*, versed, vet*, weathered, wise, wise to ways*, worldly; SEE CONCEPTS *402,527,678*

Even further possibilities exist, when you realize that "veteran" is referenced to two additional concepts: #527, the quality of "ability" and #678, the state of "experience." Many main entries are referenced to as many as three or four different concepts.

Simple to use, the Concept Index becomes invaluable in the effort to turn an idea into a specific word. By linking together the main entries that share similar concepts, but may not be direct synonyms, the index makes possible creative semantic connections between words in our language, stimulating thought and broadening vocabulary.

Whether you begin by browsing through the Concept Index for ideas, or in the A to Z listing with a particular word in mind, you will find that *Roget's 21st Century Thesaurus, Second Edition* goes beyond traditional thesauri and synonymfinders to offer thousands of word choices through access to its unique Concept Index.

QUICK REFERENCE GUIDE TO CONCEPTS

Actions

CLASS OF

1 **action:** act, action, activity, behave, doings, feat, spurt, step, tour de force
2 **event:** affair, anything, be, event, eventuate, experience, fact, incident, locomotion, milestone, move, movement, occasion, outbreak, pass, proceeding
3 **occurrence:** development, episode, occurrence, proceeding, recur, thing, transpire
4 **occurrence with one participant:** act, befall, behave, break, chance, coincidence, come, come off, deed, episode, fall out, fluke, go, happen, happening, intervene, occur, occurrence, result, return, rise
5 **occurrence with two participants:** boundary, guideline, limit, measure, obstruct, reinforce, restraint, test
6 **series of related actions:** channel, commit, disposition, elapse, esplanade, form, instrument, maneuver, manner, means, mechanism, method, methodology, mode, modus operandi, path, pattern, policy, procedure, process, routine, rule, rut, system, technique, touch, usage, vehicle, way

COGNITIVE

7 **affect:** abandon, abase, acerbate; affect, afflict, affront, aggravate, agitate, agonize, alarm, alienate, allay, alleviate, allure, anger, annoy, antagonize, appall/appal, appeal, appease, appeasement, arouse, arrest, assuage, attract, awaken, awe, baffle, bait, beckon, bedazzle, befuddle, beguile, beleaguer, bemuse, beset, besiege, bewitch, bias, bombard, bore, bother, brighten, bring down, bring on, bug, buoy (up), burden, captivate, chafe, chagrin, charm, cheer, chill, clear, cloud, comfort, complicate, compose, concern, console, content, cow, craze, cross, crucify, crush, dampen, dash, daunt, debase, deceive, deception, defame, deflate, defuse, degrade, delight, demean, demoralize, deprecate, depreciate, depress, depressant, disaffect, disappoint, disarm, discomfit, discomfort, discommode, discompose, disconcert, discountenance, disgust, dishearten, dismay, disoblige, disparage, displease, disquiet, distress, disturb, divert, double-cross, downgrade, draw, dwarf, electrify, elevate, embarrass, embitter, embolden, embroil, enamor, enchant, encourage, encouragement, encroach, endear, energize, enliven, enrage, enrapture, enthrall, entice, enticement, entrance, estrange, exacerbate, exasperate, excite, exercise, exhilarate, fail, fascinate, faze, ferment, flurry, fluster, fortify, freak, fret, frustrate, fulfill, gall, galling, galvanize, get, gladden, govern, grate, gratify, grieve, grip, gripe, harass, harm, harry, hearten, henpeck, hoodwink, horrify, hound, hurt, impress, inflame, ingratiate, inspire, instigate, interest, intimidate, intrigue, invigorate, irk, irritate, jar, kid around, kindle, let down, lighten,

lower, lull, madden, matter, menace, miff, mock, molest, mollify, mortify, move, nag, needle, nerve, nettle, nonaggression, occupy, offend, oppress, outrage, pacify, pain, pall, peeve, pep up, perk up, persecute, perturb, pester, petrify, pick at/pick on, pique, placate, plague, please, prejudice, pressure, prime, prod, provoke, puncture, put out, quell, quicken, rack, rally, rankle, rasp, reach, reassure, reduce, regenerate, register, remind, repay, repel, revolt, ride, rile, rouse, rub the wrong way, ruffle, sadden, salve, satisfy, scar, scare, seduction, send, settle, shake, shame, shatter, sink, slight, slur, smooth, solace, soothe, spook, stagger, startle, still, strain, strengthen, stress, strike, sugarcoat, support, sweeten, take down, tantalize, taunt, tease, temper, terrify, terrorize, threaten, thrill, tickle, titillate, torment, torture, touch, tranquilize, transport, trouble, try, turn, turn off, two-time, undo, unnerve, unsettle, uplift, upset, vex, visit, wake/waken, wear, weigh, weigh down, whet, worry, wound, wow, wrong
8 **agree:** accede, accept, acceptance, accession, accord, acknowledge, acknowledgment, acquiesce, acquiescence, agree, align, assent, avowal, back, bear, cleave, cohere, comply, compromise, concur, consent, conspire, contract, covenant, draft, encourage, enlist, follow, give in/give up, go, go along/go along with, go by, grant, league, negotiate, stipulate, unanimous, yield
9 **amuse:** amuse, bait, divert, entertain, humor, wow
10 **approve:** acquiesce, acquiescence, advocate, agree, applaud, appreciate, approbation, approval, approve, authorize, blessing, champion, concur, condone, countenance, defend, deference, endorse, envy, espouse, exalt, exculpate, excuse, exonerate, favor, go for, go to bat for, honor, idolize, league, nod, okay, overlook, pardon, pity, pride, prize, proselytize, recognition, recommend, regard, respect, revere/reverence, reverence, sanctify, subscribe, support, swear by, venerate
11 **attract:** attract, fascinate, grip, interest, intrigue, inveigle, kid around, lure, mesmerize, pull, ravish, seduce, send, snare, take, tantalize, tease, tempt, titillate, transfix, turn on, whet, win/win over
12 **believe:** accept, acceptance, acknowledge, appreciate, appreciation, assume, authenticate, bank on, bear, believe, bleed, consider, convert, count on/count upon, credit, deem, disagree, eat up, embrace, esteem, expect, extrapolate, feel, forgive, glorify, glory, hold, imagine, infer, make believe, misjudge, object, opine, overrate, postulate, predispose, presume, proselytize, rate, reckon, regard, rely, sanctify, see, suppose, swallow, think, trust, underestimate, understand, view
13 **change conception:** ache, alternate, awakening, caprice, catharsis, concession, conform, conformity, crack, crack up, fit, flare, flip out, fluctuate, give, go back, go back on, go crazy, oscillate, perish, recharge, repudiate,

resuscitate, reverse, revert, revive, sway, thaw, tire, vacillate, vagary, weary

14 compel: abet, ail, alarm, attraction, badger, bait, bewilder, bewilderment, bind, boss around, brainwash, browbeat, brutality, bulldoze, bully, burden, butt in, coerce, coercion, come between, compel, confusion, conjure, constrain, constraint, convert, corrupt, dare, debauch, defeat, demoralize, deprave, discourage, disgrace, dispel, distract, domineer, duress, embitter, engross, enrage, enslave, entrance, excite, fan, fire, foist, foment, force, freeze, frighten, galvanize, get back at, goad, grate, grind, harass, harassment, hassle, haunt, horrify, humble, humiliate, hurt, impel, impinge, imposition, incense, incite, inconvenience, inculcate, indoctrinate, induce, infest, inflame, infuriate, instill, interject, intimidate, intrude, inveigle, invigorate, jinx, jog, kindle, load, lumber, make, manipulate, meddle, mesmerize, mistreat, molest, motivate, nauseate, nerve, nettle, nonplus, oblige, offend, oppress, oppression, panic, paralyze, pervert, petrify, pique, plague, poison, pound, predispose, prejudice, press, pressure, prey on, provocation, push, put, put out, rankle, ride, ruffle, scourge, screw, sell/sell out, shake up, shame, sicken, sour, spoil, spook, spur, stimulate, stir, sway, tame, task, tax, terrorize, tire, transfix, undermine, unnerve, victimize, visit, wake/waken, whip up, work up, worry, wound, yield

15 comprehend: appreciate, appreciation, apprehend, assimilate, catch, comprehend, conceive, decipher, decode, deduce, deduction, derive, determine, differentiate, dig, digest, discern, discriminate, distinguish, do, draw, embrace, extrapolate, familiarize, fathom, feel, figure, follow, gather, get, grasp, have someone's number, hear, identify with, infer, inure, know, make, make out, misapprehend, misconstrue, mistake, misunderstand, outwit/outsmart, penetrate, perceive, realize, recognize, resolve, see, solve, take, take in, tell, understand

16 confuse: confound, confuse, daze, dazzle, decoy, derange, disconcert, disrupt, distract, dumbfound, floor, fluster, foul up, get, hassle, humble, jumble, mix up, muddle, mystify, nonplus, obfuscate, obscure, overwhelm, perplex, perturb, puzzle, rattle, snarl, stump, throw

17 consider: absorb, ache, balance, begrudge, bleed, brood, buckle down, cogitate, commune, concentrate, consider, consult, contemplate, cook up, cram, daydream, deliberate, deliberation, devote, dream, dream up, dwell on/dwell upon, engross, entertain, envisage/envision, excogitate, eye, fancy, fantasize, fixate, focus, gnaw, grieve, harbor, heed, hide, hindsight, immerse, marvel, meditation, meditate, mull, muse, occupy, picture, ponder, puzzle, reconsider, reflect, reflection, reminisce, retrospect, revolve, speculate, think, thought, treat, turn over, visualize, wonder, wrestle

18 decide: abnegation, adjudicate, adopt, adoption, appraisal, appraise, call off, cancel, circumscribe, classification, classify, conclude, convict, count, credit, date, decide, dedicate,

define, derive, destine, determine, disapprove, disavow, dispose of, distinguish, evaluate, falter, figure, fix, go along/go along with, go by, ground, group, have someone's number, hedge, impose, influence, intend, judge, make out, misjudge, moderate, ordain, plant, premise, provide, purpose, referee, resolution, resolve, rule, set, settle, solve, specify, stipulate, surmise, turn down, type, waver, yield

19 depress: abandon, abase, acerbate, affect, afflict, affront, aggravate, agitate, agonize, alarm, alienate, anger, annoy, antagonize, appall/appal, appeal, arouse, arrest, awaken, awe, baffle, bait, befuddle, beguile, beleaguer, bemuse, beset, besiege, bias, bombard, bore, bother, bring down, bring on, bug, burden, chafe, chagrin, chill, cloud, complicate, concern, cow, craze, cross, crucify, crush, dampen, dash, daunt, debase, deceive, deception, defame, deflate, degrade, demean, demoralize, deprecate, depreciate, depress, disaffect, disappoint, disarm, discomfit, discomfort, discommode, discompose, disconcert, discountenance, disgust, dishearten, dismay, disoblige, disparage, displease, disquiet, distress, disturb, divert, double-cross, downgrade, draw, dwarf, embarrass, embitter, embroil, encroach, enrage, enthrall, entice, enticement, estrange, exacerbate, exasperate, excite, exercise, fail, faze, ferment, flurry, fluster, freak, fret, frustrate, gall, galling, get, govern, grate, grieve, gripe, harass, harm, harry, henpeck, hoodwink, horrify, hound, hurt, impress, inflame, instigate, intimidate, irk, irritate, jar, let down, lower, madden, matter, menace, miff, mock, molest, mortify, move, nag, needle, nettle, occupy, offend, oppress, outrage, pain, pall, peeve, persecute, perturb, pester, petrify, pick at/pick on, pique, plague, prejudice, pressure, prime, prod, provoke, puncture, put out, quicken, rack, rankle, rasp, reach, reduce, register, remind, repay, repel, revolt, ride, rile, rub the wrong way, ruffle, sadden, scar, scare, seduction, shake, shame, shatter, sink, slight, slur, spite, stagger, startle, strain, stress, strike, support, take down, tantalize, taunt, tease, terrify, terrorize, threaten, torment, torture, touch, trouble, try, turn, turn off, two-time, undo, unnerve, unsettle, upset, vex, visit, wear, weigh, weigh down, worry, wound, wrong

20 desire: addiction, advance(s), affinity, aim, alcoholism, ambition, angle for, appetite, aspiration, aspire, avid, behest, burn, care, covet, crave, craving, crush, cupidity, curiosity, dependence/dependency, desire, drool, eagerness, envy, eroticism, expect, famished, fancy, fantasy, fascination, fish for, free will, gluttonous, goad, greed, hanker after/hanker for, hankering, hope, hunger, hungry, impulse, inclination, indulge, insatiable, interest, itch, lack, languish, lean, leaning, lechery, libido, like, liking, long, longing, lust, malnutrition, mania, mind, miss, moon, mope, motivation, motive, need, nostalgia, notion, obsession, one-track mind, pant, penchant, pine, pipe dream, please, pleasure, predilection, predisposition, prefer, preference, proclivity, propensity, purport, purpose, pursue, relish, require, sigh, stomach, substance abuse, taste, temptation, thirst, urge, volition, voracious, want, will, wish, yearn, yearning, yen

21 **doubt:** begrudge, break with, controvert, deplore, despair, disallow, disapprove, disbelief, disbelieve, discount, discountenance, discredit, dissent, distrust, doubt, frown, fume, grudge, hesitate, hesitation, lovelorn, lovesick, mind, misgiving, mistrust, object, objection, oppose, oppugn, query, question, regret, reject, rejection, repudiate, repulse, rue, scorn, scruple, segregate, skepticism, spurn, suspect, turn, wonder

22 **elated:** affect, allay, alleviate, allure, appeal, appease, appeasement, arouse, arrest, assuage, attract, awaken, awe, beckon, bedazzle, beguile, bemuse, bewitch, brighten, buoy (up), captivate, charm, cheer, clear, comfort, compose, concern, console, content, defuse, delight, depressant, disarm, divert, draw, elated, electrify, elevate, embolden, enamor, enchant, encourage, encouragement, endear, energize, enliven, enrapture, enthrall, entice, enticement, entrance, excite, exhilarate, fascinate, ferment, fortify, fulfill, galvanize, get, gladden, govern, gratify, grip, hearten, impress, inflame, ingratiate, inspire, instigate, interest, intrigue, invigorate, kindle, lighten, lull, matter, mollify, move, nerve, nonaggression, occupy, pacify, pep up, perk up, pique, placate, please, pressure, prime, prod, provoke, quell, quicken, rally, reach, reassure, regenerate, register, remind, rouse, salve, satisfy, send, settle, smooth, solace, soothe, still, strengthen, strike, support, sugarcoat, sweeten, tantalize, tease, temper, thrill, tickle, titillate, touch, tranquilize, transport, uplift, wake/waken, weigh, whet

23 **endure:** abide, accept, accommodate, acquiesce, bear, bear up, bear with, bite the bullet, bow, brave, brook, come in for, come through, condone, cope, descend, digest, do without, endure, face, face the music, go, go through, hang on, hang tough, have, keep at, keep up, linger, lump, make out, manage, mind, mourn, pay, persist, receive, reconcile, remain, resist, resistance, shoulder, stand/stand for, stick, stomach, submit, subsist, suffer, support, survive, sustain, sweat, take, take it, tolerate, undergo, wear, weather, withstand

24 **examine:** analysis, analyze, assay, assess, assessment, bury, canvass, check, chew, cogitate, compare, comparison, consider, consideration, debate, decompose, deduce, deduction, deliberate, deliberation, dissect, dissection, enquire, enquiry, evaluate, evaluation, examine, excogitate, experiment, go into, go over, inquire, inquiry, introspection, meditation, observe, ponder, pore, reflect, reflection, resolve, review, ruminate, scrutinize, scrutiny, soul-searching, speculate, speculation, turn over, view, weigh

25 **exclude:** abnegation, abstain, blackball, blacklist, boycott, count out, deactivate, decommission, disallow, disavow, disinherit, except, exception, exclude, exclusion, jump, omission, omit, ostracism, ostracize, oust,

parry, pass, pass by, pass over, proscribe, recant, retract, rule out, shut off/shut out, take back

26 **expect:** anticipate, anticipation, assume, await, bargain for, calculate, count, count on/count upon, demand, depend, expect, foresee, imagine, lean, look, mean, opine, plan, postulate, predispose, presume, propose, reckon, rely, think

27 **fear:** apprehension, blanch, cold feet, cowardice, dismay, dread, fear, funk, horror, mistrust, panic, phobia, terror, trepidation

28 **guess:** accounting, believe, bet, calculation, call, conjecture, deem, divine, estimate, estimation, forecast, gamble, guess, hazard, implication, lottery, presume, project, projection, speculate, speculation, suppose, surmise, suspect, wager

29 **hate:** abhor, abominable, abominate, abomination, aggression, anarchy, anger, animosity, antagonism, antipathy, atrocity, aversion, bad blood, bad manners, blow up, boil, burn, contempt, deplore, despise, detest, discrimination, disdain, disfavor, disinclination, dislike, disrespect, dissatisfaction, dissent, distaste, enmity, exasperation, execrate, execration, frown, fume, fury, grudge, hate, hatred, horror, ill will, incivility, indignation, inhumanity, lament/lamentation, loath, loathe, loathing,, look down on, malice, mind, odium, opposition, outrage, phobia, pique, rage, rancor, repulsion, resent, resentment, revulsion, scorn, seethe, sexism, spite, temper, umbrage, vengeance, venom, violence, wrath

30 **ignore:** abjure, abnegate, blink, break with, brush aside/brush off, bypass, cold shoulder, disallow, discount, disdain, disobey, dispense with, disregard, drop, eliminate, elude, eschew, evade, except, exception, exclude, exclusion, fence, forget, forsake, get off someone's back, give the cold shoulder, goof off, hedge, ignore, leave, lose, lovelorn, lovesick, neglect, negligence, overlook, parry, pass, pass by, pass over, rebuff, refuse, reject, rejection, relegate, renounce, renunciation, repel, repudiate, retreat, run-around, scorn, shirk, shun, skip, skirt, skulk, slight, sneer, sneeze at, snub, spurn, weasel, wriggle

31 **learn:** absorb, acquaint, ascertain, catch, decipher, decode, determine, dig, discover, discovery, edification, find out, get, glean, hear, learn, master, orientation, pick up, probe, research, see, study, turn up

32 **love:** acceptance, activity, admiration, admire, adoration, adore, adulation, affair, affection, affinity, amour, appetite, appreciate, appreciation, approval, attachment, attention, bag, bask, bathos, bewitched, bliss, canonize, care, charity, cherish, consideration, consolation, constancy, court, delight in, devotion, dig, discriminate, discrimination, dote on/dote upon, empathy, enamored, endear, enjoy, enjoyment, esteem, exaltation, exult, exultation, fall for, fancy, fascinated, fascination, favor, fidelity, flame, flirtation, fond, fondness, get a kick out of, go for, gratitude, homage, idolize, infatuated, leaning, liaison, like, liking, love, lure, mad, mania, mercy, partiality, passion, penchant, predilection,

predisposition, prize, proclivity, rapture, relish, respect, revere/reverence, reverence, savor, sentiment, taste, temper, thrill, transport, treasure, triumph, venerate, zeal

33 mental event: learn, sense, shock, stroke, think

34 mental perception: ascertain, attend, behold, beware, burn, come at, empathize, feel, gnaw, gravitate, grope, hallucinate, learn, mind, note, notice, observe, occur, pity, presage, seethe, sensation, sense, shudder, sorrow, sympathize, visualize, wonder

35 mental preparation: abide, accustom, adjust, bottle up, brainstorm, capitulate, center, centralize, comply, concede, conceive, condition, convert, cope, crawl, dare, deign, descend, design, determine, dismiss, dispel, face, forbear, get over, go straight, habituate, harden, look out, manufacture, melt, orient, plan, preparation, prepare, prime, quail, ready, reform, refresh, rehabilitate, rejuvenate, relent, renew, resist, rustle up, season, simmer, sink, smolder, steel, stew, stoop, strengthen, succumb, sulk, sweat, tarry, train, weather, withhold, yield

36 plan: arrange, assure, base, block out, book, brew, budget, calculate, chart, coin, concoct, connive, conspire, contemplate, contrive, cook up, coordinate, daydream, delineate, design, devise, draft, dream up, engineer, fabricate, finagle, finesse, fix, formulate, frame, hatch, intend, intrigue, invent, lay, lay out, machinate, maneuver, manufacture, mean, organize, outline, parlay, plan, plot, program, project, propose, purpose, pursue, rough out, schedule, shape, sketch, synchronize

37 reason: analyze, cipher, clear up, conclude, construe, crack, criticize, date, decipher, dialectic, do, educe, equate, estimate, figure, forecast, gauge, generalize, induction, infer, judgment, logic, make, mapmaker, overview, pollster, premise, project, rank, rate, reason, reasoning, reckon, solve, speculate, stock, survey

38 recognize: acknowledge, ascertain, come across, come upon, conjure up, crack, cut, detect, detection, diagnose, differentiate, discern, discriminate, distinguish, elude, encounter, familiarize, fathom, feel, identify, inure, know, mark, perceive, pinpoint, place, recognition, recognize, remark, salute/salutation, salute, spot, stereotype

39 relate: ascribe, associate, association, categorize, class, classification, classify, codify, compare, comparison, contrast, correlate, equate, identify with, implication, liken, pigeonhole

40 remember: block out, déjà vu, flashback, forget, hindsight, memorize, mind, recall, recollect, remember, remembrance, remind, reminisce, retain, retrospect, think

41 select: aim, allocate, allot, allow, appoint, appointment, assign, assignment, cast, choice, choose, cull, designate, designation, elect, election, excerpt, favoritism, finger, like, name, nepotism, nominate, nomination, opt, pick, prefer, recruit, relegate, screen, select, take, turn, volition, vote

42 surprise: alarm, amaze, appall/appal, aston-ish, astound, awe, backfire, baffle, bedazzle, befuddle, bewilder, bowl over, confound, daze, dazzle, deluge, dumbfound, dumbstruck, electrify, flabbergast, frighten, jolt, overwhelm, overwhelming, petrify, scare, shock, stagger, startle, stun/stupefy, surprise, terrify

43 think: count, design, devise, envisage/envision, fancy, imagine, mint, occur, originate, picture, proceed, see, theorize, think, thought

COMMUNICATIVE

44 accuse: accuse, admonition, affront, arraign, bastardize, betray, betrayal, blame, blow up, catcall, charge, condemn, condemnation, decry, denounce, discredit, forswear, gripe, groan, grumble, heckle, hoot, humble, humiliate, impeach, implicate, impute, incriminate, indict, indictment, invective, inveigh, malign, mouth off, persecute, profane, rant, rebuke, reprimand, reproach, reprove, revile, scold, slur, tax, tell off, tirade, upbraid, vilify, vituperate

45 answer: acknowledge, agree, answer, counter, decline, denial, disclaimer, fill in, give in/give up, react, reaction, reciprocate, repartee, reply, respond, retort, return

46 argue: ado, agitate, altercation, argue, argument, back talk, battle, beard, bicker, brawl, cause celebre, clash, conflict, confront, confrontation, confute, contend, contention, contest, contradict, contradiction, contravene, controversy, controvert, demur, deny, dicker, differ, difference, difficulty, disagree, disagreement, dispute, dissension, dissent, diverge, divide, donnybrook, double standard, encounter, expostulate, fall out, falling out, feud, fight, fracas, friction, fuss, haggle, hassle, hue and cry, hullabaloo, imbroglio, maintain, misunderstanding, negate, object, objection, protest, quarrel, quibble, reason, rebut, remonstrate, rift, rock the boat, row, run-in, rupture, sass, scrap, squabble, strife, tiff, uproar, vendetta, wrangle

47 articulate: articulate, call, catcall, cry, delivery, diction, elocution, enunciate, exclaim, expression, hail, heckle, holler, hoot, mumble, parrot, pipe, pronounce, put, sing, slur, speak, speech, stammer, talk, utter, utterance, verbalize, yell

48 ask: accost, apologize, apology, appeal, application, apply, approach, ask, beg, beseech, canvass, catechize, charter, conjure, consult, consultation, crave, crawl, cross-examine, debrief, desire, enquire, enquiry, entreat, examine, FAQ, grill, hearing, implore, inquest, inquire, inquiry, interrogate, interview, investigate, investigation, invitation, invite, invocation, invoke, pester, petition, plead, poll, pray, prayer, propose, proposition, pump, query, quest, question, quiz, repent, requisition, scrounge, seek, survey

49 assert: accredit, acknowledge, adduce, advance, advocate, affirm, affirmation, allegation, allege, announce, announcement, ascribe, assert, assertion, attest, avow, bemoan, blow up, bluster, boast, brag, bravado, bring out, color, come clean, corroborate, crow, debunk, declaim, declaration, declare, defend, deny, dramatize, drum into, embellish, emphasize, establish, exclaim, exclamation, exult, generalize, gloat, glory, gloss, go to bat for, gush, impress, impute, insinuate, insist, intimate, justify, lay, level, magnify, maintain, mock, mockery, notification, overrate, pass, play down, play up, plead, plug, point out, pound, proclaim, profess, promote, promotion, pronounce, puff, punctuate, purport, push, rant, rave, refuse, retract, review, rumor, show off, speak out/speak up, spout, state, stereotype, stress, substantiate, support, swagger, swear, take back, testify, testimonial, testimony, underline, underscore, vent, vindicate, voice, vouch, weep, whitewash, witness

50 **authorize:** accede, accord, accredit, acknowledge, acknowledgment, acquit, affirm, aggrandize, appoint, appointment, approve, arm, assign, authorize, back, ban, bar, bear out, bless, blessing, certify, charter, chicken out, commission, concession, consent, constitute, contract, countenance, countermand, crown, decree, dedicate, delegate, delegation, detail, disown, empower, enable, enact, endorse, enforce, enjoin, entitle, entrust, establish, exempt, fire, forgive, grant, induct, inflict, invest, invoke, lay, let, let off, license, make, negate, nod, nominate, nomination, notarize, nullify, okay, ordain, order, override, overrule, pardon, permission, permit, place, prescribe, prohibit, ratify, recall, receive, release, relieve, repeal, reprieve, revoke, sanction, spare, station, subscribe, underwrite, validate, vest, veto, void, warrant, withdraw, witness

51 **comment:** accost, acknowledge, add, air, annotate, aside, babble, badger, bemoan, brag, bravado, bring up, broach, circumlocution, comment, commentary, congratulate, conjecture, couch, critique, declaim, decline, deliver, discourse, editorial, enunciate, express, extemporize, fumigate, greet, greeting, harangue, hearsay, interject, interrupt, jabber, jaw, moralize, observation, observe, pontificate, preach, ramble, rattle, rave, remark, report, rhetoric, say, spout, state, talk, throw out, touch, vent, ventilate, voice, yak/yap

52 **criticize:** abuse, admonish, admonition, air, aspersion, assail, assault, attack, bad-mouth, barb, baste, beat up, beef, belittle, berate, blast, browbeat, carp, castigate, censure, chasten, chastise, chew out, chide, come down on, complain, complaint, condemn, condemnation, confront, correct, cow, criticism, criticize, crticize, cut, cut up, damn, darn, debase, decry, denigrate, denounce, denunciation, deny, deprecate, depreciate, deride, derision, detract, detraction, diatribe, disapprove, disparage, disparagement, dress down, excoriate, flak, flame, fulminate, fulmination, gainsay, gibe, gird, grievance, gripe, groan, grouch, grumble, hiss, humble, humiliate, impeach, impugn, insult, invective, inveigh, jaw, kick, knock, lambaste, lament, lash, lay into, lecture, malign, moan, mortify, mouth off, mug, mutter, nag, objurgate, offense, pan, pick at/pick on, profane, protest, quibble, rail, rant, rap, re-

buke, reflection, remonstrate, reprimand, reproach, reprove, review, revile, rock the boat, row, run down, sarcasm, scold, scorn, scourge, sit-in, slam, sneer, squawk, storm, sulk, swear, take down, tell off, thunder, upbraid, vilify, vituperate

53 **demand:** adjure, ask, beckon, beg, behest, bid, bidding, bribe, call, challenge, charge, claim, command, countermand, crave, cross-examine, dare, debrief, decree, demand, dictate, direct, duel, enjoin, entreat, exact, extort, extortion, FAQ, grease, grill, importune, impose, inflict, insist, instruct, interrogate, necessitate, obligate, order, panhandle, petition, pump, query, question, request, require, requisition, reserve, solicit, sponge, squeeze, summon, supplicate, take on

54 **deny:** abjure, abnegate, abuse, accusation, affront, aspersion, attack, backbiting, backstab, bad-mouth, barb, belie, belittle, blacken, blame, blemish, casuistry, confront, contradict, curse, damn, darn, debase, defamation, defame, defile, demean, demur, denial, denigrate, deride, detract, detraction, dig, diminish, disclaim, disclaimer, discountenance, discredit, disgrace, dishonor, disown, disparage, disparagement, downgrade, downplay, embarrass, explode, flame, flout, forswear, fulminate, fulmination, gainsay, gibe, gird, insult, invective, inveigh, jeer, lambaste, lament, laugh at, lecture, lip, malign, mimic, minimize, mortify, mouth, mudslinging, needle, oath, oppose, oppugn, protest, puncture, put down, put-down, rave, rebuff, rebut, refute, revile, remonstrate, renounce, renunciation, ridicule, run down, sarcasm, satirize, scoff, scold, scorn, show up, sit-in, slam, slander, slur, smear, smear campaign, snap, sneer, snub, squawk, squeal, stain, sully, swear, swearing, tattle, taunt, thunder, tirade, traverse, turn, turn down, underestimate, vituperate, vituperation, whine, write off, yammer

55 **describe:** articulate, articulation, blab, define, delineate, denote, describe, detail, mean, narrate, narration, outline, paraphrase, phrase, portray, recite, recount, relate, signify, spell, state, summarize, sum up, tell, translate, typify, unfold, utter

56 **discuss:** argue, bargain, belabor, canvass, communicate, confer, conference, consult, debate, deliberate, deliberation, dialogue/dialog, discourse, discuss, discussion, gossip, huddle, intercede, interchange, jabber, jaw, negotiate, negotiation, powwow, rap, reason, rehash, repartee, seminar, symposium, talk, treat, word

57 **explain:** account for, admission, admit, annotate, apprise, bring out, cite, clarification, clarify, clear up, come clean, comment, concede, confide, confirm, construe, corroborate, declare, defense, define, demonstrate, detail, dilate, elaborate, elucidate, emphasize, enlighten, enumerate, evidence, excuse, expand, explain, explicate, expound, gloss, illuminate, illustrate, interpret, itemize, justify, let on, own, palliate, paraphrase, plea, preface, prove, rationalize, recite, render, simplify, speak out/speak up, specify, spell out, translate, translator, vindicate, warrant

58 fabricate: aspersion, backbiting, belie, bluff, disprove, embroider, fabricate, impugn, profane

59 fool: adulate, affect, artifice, assume, bamboozle, banter, beguile, bilk, blow up, bluff, brownnose, burn, cajole, charade, cheat, chicanery, circumvent, color, con, copy, corner, counterfeit, cross, deceit, deceive, deception, decoy, default, defraud, delude, dirty tricks, disguise, dishonesty, dissemble, dissimulate, do, dodge, do out of, double-cross, double-dealing, dramatize, dupe, duplicity, elude, enmesh, ensnare, entangle, entrap, evasion, excuse, extort, fake, feign, fence, finagle, finesse, flatter, flatterer, flattery, fleece, flimflam, fool, fooling, forge, forgery, fraud, frolic, fudge, gag, game, garble, gimmick, goof off, grift, gyp, hanky-panky, have, hoax, hocus-pocus, humbug, impersonate, imposition, imposture, inveigle, invent, juggle, kid, legerdemain, make believe, maneuver, masquerade, mimic, mince, mislead, mock, outwit/outsmart, overplay, palliate, pander, parlay, parody, play dirty, play down, ploy, pose, posture, prank, pretend, pretense, pretext, put on, renege, ridicule, ruse, satirize, scam, scheme, sham, shift, shirk, shortchange, sidestep, simulate, skulk, spoof, sport, strategem, string along, swindle, take, take in, trap, trick, trickery, victimize, welsh, wile, wit

60 inform: acknowledge, acquaint, address, advance, advertise, advise, allow, allude, allusion, announce, apprise, avow, bare, betray, betrayal, bill, blab, break, breathe, brief, briefing, bring out, broadcast, buzz, chronicle, circulate, clue, come out, come out with, confess, confession, convene, convey, cover, debunk, declare, define, deliver, detail, develop, dictate, disclose, divulge, enlighten, expose, exposure, feature, fumigate, furnish, get across, give, give away, gossip, herald, hint, impart, inform, instruct, intimate, introduce, issue, leak, lecture, let on, newscaster, notify, orate, oratory, out of the closet, outing, pass, plug, post, prescribe, proclaim, program, promulgate, propagate, publication, publicize, publish, ready, release, report, reveal, revelation, show up, sing, speak, speech, spill, spread, squeal, stipulate, talk, tattle, tip, unburden, uncover, unmask, unveil, ventilate, weatherperson, whisper

61 instruct: bar, direct, educate, instruct, prescribe

62 label: attach, brand, call, christen, define, designate, dub, entitle, identify, label, name, stigmatize, style, tag, term, title

63 lie: backbiting, belie, bunk, cant, casuistry, color, default, detraction, distort, distortion, duplicity, embroider, equivocate, equivocation, evasion, exaggerate, exaggeration, fabricate, fabrication, falsehood, falsify, feign, fib, fiction, fudge, garble, gloss, hoax, humbug, hypocrisy, invent, invention, juggle, libel, lie, malign, misinform, mislead, misrepresent/misquote, misrepresentation, misstatement, mock, obscure, overstate, pad, perjure, perjury, pervert, play down, pose, pretend, pretense, prevaricate, profane, profess, renege, sell/sell out, sensationalism,

simulate, skew, slant, smear, twist, warp, whitewash, wile

64 noise, animal: bark, bay, call, cheep, chirp, howl, peep, roar, squawk, squeak, squeal, yelp

65 noise-making: bang, blare, blast, blow, boom, buzz, cadence, chant, chime, clank, clash, clatter, click, clink, clump, cough, crash, creak, crinkle, drone, drum, grumble, gurgle, harmony, honk, hue and cry, hullabaloo, hum, hush, inflection, intonation, jangle, jar, jingle, measure, meter, muffle, murmur, mute, patter, peal, pipe, pitch, play, quiet, racket, rattle, reflect, resonate, resound, reverberate, ring, roll, rumble, rustle, silence, sizzle, sound, squeak, still, stillness, stress, swing, talk, tempo, tenor, thud/thump, thunder, tick, tinkle, toll, tone, tranquility, tune/tune up, undertone, uproar, volume, whistle

66 offer: allude, extend, lay, offer, pose, present, proffer, propose, put, submit, volunteer

67 offer to give: amends, apologize, apology, bid, bidding, come forward, concession, expiate, extend, furnish, offer, pose, present, proffer, put, surrender, volunteer

68 persuade: advance, argue, argument, assure, bend, bring around, budge, cajole, carry, coax, coerce, coercion, convince, disarm, discourage, dissuade, draw, drive, drum up, egg on, elicit, eloquence, entice, enticement, forward, get, goad, hammer away/hammer into, impel, induce, inducement, influence, ingratiate, invite, lead, lobby, maintain, motivate, negotiate, negotiation, occasion, persuade, persuasion, pitch, predispose, prevail upon/prevail on, procure, prompt, push, reason, spearhead, spur, stress, sway, tempt, urge, wheedle, win/win over

69 praise: accent, acclaim, acclamation, accolade, accredit, adulate, adulation, aggrandize, apotheosis, applaud, applause, approbation, benediction, blarney, bless, brownnose, champion, cheer, citation, commemorate, commend, commendation, compliment, congratulate, congratulations, consecrate, credit, crown, dedicate, dedication, deify, distinguish, elevate, elevation, endorse, enshrine, eulogize, eulogy, exalt, exaltation, extol, felicitate, flatter, flatterer, flattery, further, glorify, hail, homage, kudos, laud, laurels, lionize, magnify, obsequy, ovation, plaudits, praise, puff, reference, salute, thank, thanks, tout, tribute, worship

70 predict: announce, anticipate, astrology, augur, augury, call, divination, forebode, forecast, foreordain, foresee, foreshadow, foretell, horoscope, oracle, precursor, predict, prediction, presage, prognosticate, project, prophecy, prophesy

71 promise: assurance, assure, avow, bear witness, commitment, covenant, ensure, escrow, go back/go back on, guarantee, oath, pledge, portend, promise, vouch, vow, warrant, word

72 read: leaf, look up, narrate, narration, peruse, pore, read, reading, recitation, recite, refer, skim

73 refer: attach, attribute, drive at, instance, intend, mean, mention, oppose, point out, refer

74 signal: beckon, beep, call, doorbell, flag,

gesture, gesture/gesticulate, hail, harbinger, hint, indicate, indication, nod, omen, page, ripple, sign, signal, spell, suggest, symbolize, wave

75 **suggest:** advice, advise, advocate, approach, ask, cajole, come up with, commend, connote, counsel, drum into, enlighten, exhort, exhortation, fish for, foreshadow, get at, guidance, guide, hint, imply, innuendo, insinuate, intimate, moralize, motion, move, nominate, nomination, pointer, pontificate, pose, preach, proffer, propose, raise, recommend, spell, suggest, swear by, urge

76 **thank:** appreciate, gratitude, thank

77 **vocalize:** accent, air, bark, bawl, bellow, blare, cackle, caterwaul, chant, cheer, chortle, chuckle, clamor, croak, cry, drawl, drone, exclamation, giggle, groan, growl, grumble, guffaw, hail, harmonize, hiss, howl, hum, laugh/laughter, laugh, locution, moan, mumble, murmur, mutter, outcry, parrot, pipe, roar, scream, shout, shriek, shut up, sing, snap, snarl, snicker/snigger/sniggle, snore, squawk, squeal, stutter, vocalize, voice, wail, whimper, whine, whistle, whoop, yammer, yowl

78 **warn:** admonish, admonition, alert, bluster, caution, cautionary tale, caveat, charge, defy, dissuade, enjoin, exhort, exhortation, forebode, foreboding, forecast, foretell, forewarn, page, portend, remind, threaten, warn, warning

79 **write:** abstract, address, annotate, autograph, brand, chronicle, compile, compose, correspond, correspondence, cover, depict, dot, draft, draw, draw up, edit, emboss, endorse, engrave, engraving, enroll, extract, fill in, fleck, font, graffiti, hand, inscribe, label, line, list, mark, notify, page, pen, picture, plot, point, proofread, punctuate, put down, quote, register, revise, revision, rough out, score, scratch, scrawl, scribble, script, sign, spot, stamp, stigmatize, trace, transcribe, type, underline, underscore, write, writing

GENERAL

80 **act abstractly:** freak, jerk, lurch, twist, wiggle, wrench, writhe

81 **act over an area:** decree, rule, tour, veto

82 **admit:** accede, accept, acquiesce, admit, allow, concede, concur, grant

83 **allow:** absolve, accord, acquit, admission, admit, allow, approve, authorize, capitulate, capitulation, contribute, defer, enable, entitle, excuse, exempt, get off someone's back, grant, have, leave, let, let off, liberate, license, overlook, patronage, permission, permit, pity, receive, reception, spell, suffer, tolerate

84 **arrange:** adjust, alphabetize, antedate, arrange, arrangement, array, center, centralize, codify, collate, collocate, compile, concentrate, configuration, coordinate, derange, dispose, disrupt, distribute, disturb, divide, file, graduate, group, index, jumble, line, marshal, muddle, order, organization, organize, organized, perplex, pile, place, pro-

gram, range, rank, reconstruct, remodel, sort, synchronize, systematize, tabulate, type

85 **attach:** adhere, adhesion, adjoin, affix, anchor, annex, append, attach, batten, bind, bond, cement, chain, clamp, clasp, cling, cohere, connect, engage, fasten, fix, gasket, hitch, juxtapose, knot, latch, lock, moor, nail, paste, peg, pin, screw, seal, secure, shut, stick, tack, tag, tape, tether, tie, yoke

86 **attack:** aggression, ambush, assail, assault, attack, bashing, beat up, besiege, blast, blindside, blitz, bomb, bombard, brutality, burst, charge, combat, come at, coup d'état, descent, embroil, encounter, encroach, engage, fire, fix, foray, fray, go for, incursion, infest, inroad, insurrection, invade, invasion, lambaste, lay into, maraud, mug, nuke, occupation, occupy, offensive, onset, onslaught, outbreak, overrun, overwhelm, pillage, plunder, pounce, prey on, raid, rampage, ravage, revenge, rush, sabotage, sortie, storm, subvert, surprise, waylay

87 **attempt:** acid test, adhere, angle for, answer, apply, assume, attempt, bid, bother, buckle down, campaign, chance, commit, counteract, counterbalance, crack, dabble, dare, defy, delve, dip into, direct, drill, drive, drudge, effort, elbow grease, electioneering, emulate, endeavor, engage, enterprise, essay, exercise, exert, exertion, experiment, fiddle, function, further, go, go for it, hammer away/hammer into, hazard, hush, imitate, keep at, keep up, labor, mess around, monkey, offer, overdo, overplay, persevere, persist, plod, practice, presume, probation, purpose, pursue, putter, represent, risk, scramble, seek, slave, slog, stab, strain, strive, struggle, substitute, tackle, take after, take a crack at, take on, tinker, trial, try, tussle, undertake, undertaking, venture, wade, whack, whirl, work

88 **authorize:** accede, accord, accredit, acknowledge, acknowledgment, acquit, affirm, aggrandize, appoint, appointment, approve, arm, assign, authorize, avowal, back, ban, bar, bear out, bless, blessing, certify, charter, chicken out, commission, concession, consent, constitute, contract, countenance, countermand, crown, decree, dedicate, delegate, delegation, detail, disown, empower, enable, enact, endorse, enforce, enjoin, entitle, entrust, establish, exempt, fire, forgive, grant, induct, inflict, invest, invoke, lay, let, let off, license, make, name, negate, nod, nominate, nomination, notarize, nullify, okay, ordain, order, override, overrule, pardon, permission, permit, place, prescribe, prohibit, ratify, recall, receive, release, relieve, repeal, reprieve, revoke, sanction, spare, station, subscribe, underwrite, validate, vest, veto, void, warrant, withdraw, witness

89 **borrow:** borrow, charter, lease, let, mooch, rent

90 **capture:** abducted, abduction, apprehend, apprehension, arrest, bag, besiege, capture, catch, collar, commandeer, confinement, conquer, corner, coup d'état, custody, enslave, ensnare, entangle, entrap, expropriate, fetch, foray, get, grab, grasp, hijack, hijacker, hog, imprison, incarcerate, kidnap, nab, nail,

net, occupation, occupy, pinch, pull in, seize, seizure, sequester, shanghai, snap, snare, snatch, tackle, trap

91 carry out: accomplish, action, actualize, application, assure, avail, clone, complement, complete, comply, conclude, contrive, discharge, do, duplicate, echo, effect, enact, execute, execution, fill, finalize, finish, follow, follow through, fulfill, get the lead out, hammer out, handle, hustle, implement, make, make out, manage, meet, mind, obey, observe, offender, operate, perfect, perform, perpetrate, persist, practice, proceed, prosecute, pull off, realize, redeem, render, repeat, resonate, resound, rush, serve, specialize, transact, wage

92 compete: bout, boxing, compete, competition, contend, contention, contest, opposition, pit, play, rival, rivalry, take on, tie, vie

93 contract: catch, come down with, contract, get, incur, waterloo

94 control: aegis, auspices, contain, contrive, deal/deal with, determine, deregulate, direct, discipline, dominate, domineer, harness, manage, moderate, monopolize, operate, order about, organized, overlook, predominate, preside, prevail, regulate, regulation, ride, stage, steer, systematize, wield, work

95 defeat: beat, best, confute, conquer, conquest, coup de grâce, crush, defeat, discomfit, drub, edge, extinguish, finish, floor, landslide, lick, outdo, overcome, overpower, overrun, overtake, overthrow, overwhelm, prevail, prostrate, put down, quash, quell, reduce, rout, smash, stamp out, subjugate, subvert, surmount, thrash, top, topple, trim, triumph, trounce, upset, vanquish, victory, wallop, whip, win

96 defend: beard, bite the bullet, bulwark, convoy, counteract, counterbalance, cover, defend, ensure, fend, fend off, fight back/fight off, guard, parapet, protect, repulse, resist, resistance, safeguard, save, screen, secure, shield, ward/ward off, withstand

97 demonstrate: advertising, bear out, demonstrate, establish, evidence, exemplify, give, illustrate, imply

98 divide: allocate, apportion, bestow, bisect, cleave, dichotomy, disconnect, dismember, disrupt, dissect, distribute, distribution, divide, division, divvy up, fork, fragment, halve, mete, part, partition, place, portion, punctuate, quarter, ramification, ration, rupture, sever, share, slice, snap, split

99 enable: allow, enable, implement, qualify

100 engage in: address, anticipate, apply, collaborate, dig in, drudge, elbow grease, embark on, exist, fall to, fare, fend for, fight, give, go about, go for it, go into, go on, grub, immerse, labor, make, participate, pitch in, plunge, ply, practice, pursue, reiterate, risk, share, spend, step in, tackle, take, toil, trouble, turn, undertake, wage, work

101 err: Achilles' heel, blunder, boo boo, boner, botch, bungle, butcher, compromise, err, error, fault, faux pas, flounder, fluff, frailty, fumble, gaffe, glitch, goof, guilt, impropriety, inaccuracy, indiscretion, lapse, malpractice, miscalculate, mishandle/mismanage, misjudge, miss, misstep, mistake, muff, ne-

glect, overlook, oversight, screw up, sin, slip, slip up, snafu, stray, stumble, transgression, trespass, trip, violate, violation, wander

102 escape: abscond, avoid, avoidance, bail out, break, break out, bypass, circumvent, close call, decamp, disappear, disappearance, dodge, duck, elude, equivocate, escape, eschew, evade, evasion, extricate, flee, flight, flinch, fly, getaway, get out, loophole, lose, make off, pussy foot, shake off, sidestep, skedaddle, skirt, throw off, weasel

103 examine: adjudication, analysis, analyze, assay, audit, authenticate, autopsy, case, check, compare, confirm, criticize, decompose, delve, dig, evaluate, evaluation, examination, examine, experiment, explore, follow up, go into, go over, go through, grade, graduate, hearing, inspect, inspection, investigate, investigation, judgment, look into, mapmaker, measure, nose, observe, overview, peer, peruse, pollster, pore, postmortem, probe, quantify, quest, ransack, reconnaissance, research, review, sample, scan, scout, scrutinize, scrutiny, sift, skim, spy, study, surveillance, survey, test, try, try on/try out, view, weigh

104 exchange: alternate, amends, barter, commute, exchange, interchange, reciprocate, redeem, replace, rotate, substitute, swap/swop, switch, transpose

105 existential change: age, arise, awaken, awakening, begin, come from, date, demise, disappear, disappearance, dissipate, dissolution, dissolve, emerge, fade, form, go, go out, languish, materialize, originate, pass, perish, peter out, run out, spring, succumb, vanish, wake/waken

106 fight: act up, ado, altercation, battle, bout, box, brawl, brush, clamor, clash, combat, conflict, confrontation, contend, contention, contest, contravene, dispute, donnybrook, encounter, engage, engagement, faction, ferment, feud, fight, fight back/fight off, fighting, fracas, fray, free-for-all, friction, fuss, grapple, hassle, imbroglio, mayhem, melee, misunderstanding, oppose, opposition, quarrel, racket, rebel, rebellion, resist, resistance, revolt, revolution, rift, riot, rise, row, run-in, scrap, scuffle, sedition, skirmish, slugfest, spat, strife, struggle, tilt, tussle, uprising, uproar, vendetta, war, wrangle

107 fuel: charge, feed, fill, fuel, supply

108 give: administer, afford, allocate, allot, allow, apportion, atone, bear, bequeath, bestow, cast, cede, commend, commit, compensate, confide, consign, consignment, contribute, deal, defray, deliver, delivery, descend, devote, disburse, disseminate, dole out, donate, drop off, emit, endow, entrust, finance, furnish, give, give away, hand out, hand over, impart, kick in, leave, mete, pass, pass off, present, provide, reach, render, return, reward, rustle up, sacrifice, satisfy, show, surrender, transfer, turn over, will

109 group: aggregate, alloy, amass, bank, blend, bunch, cluster, collect, collection, commingle, compilation, compile, compound, concentrate, confluence, congregate, consolidate, consolidation, cull, distribution, flock, garner, gather, get together, group, heap, herd, muster, pick, pile, rake, reap, recruit, reunion, round up, stack, store

110 **help:** abet, aid, alleviate, assist, assistance, attend, baby, backing, bail out, befriend, benefit, bolster, boost, break, care, chip in, coddle, commiserate, contribute, convoy, cooperate, cooperation, cover, cultivate, cultivation, cure, defend, dispense, doctor, do for, ease, empathize, encourage, encouragement, facilitate, favor, fawn, forward, foster, free, further, furtherance, go straight, guarantee, guide, hand, help, hold, indulge, intercede, intervene, invigorate, keep, kindness, lavish, liberate, lift, lighten, mind, minister, nurse, nurture, oblige, patronage, patronize, pitch in, play ball, profit, promote, promotion, provide, quell, reform, relieve, serve, service, shore, shower, simplify, soothe, speed, spell, sponsor, stabilize, synchronize, subsidize, support, sustain, sympathize, teamwork, temper, tide over, toady, truckle, underwrite, uphold

111 **imitate:** ape, imitate, mimic, mirror, mock, mockery, parallel, parody, pattern, pretend, repeat, reproduce, sham, simulate, takeoff, take off

112 **involve:** attack, coalesce, confuse, contain, cooperate, cooperation, count, devote, embody, embrace, encapsulate, enclose, encompass, enmesh, entangle, entrap, figure in, implicate, include, incorporate, interpolate, introduce, involve, mire, overdo, play ball, synchronize, tangle, task, teamwork

113 **join:** accompany, add, adhere, adjoin, affiliate, affix, alloy, amalgamate, annex, annexation, append, articulate, articulation, assemble, assembly, attach, band, bridge, butt, cleave, close, coalesce, cohere, combine, compound, connect, converge, couple, desegregate, dovetail, embody, engage, fasten, fix, fuse, fusion, get together, graft, hitch, incorporate, integrate, intermingle, intersect, intertwine/interweave, introduce, join, juxtapose, knit, knot, lace, link, meeting, meld, merge, mesh, mix, pair, piece, pool, reunion, swarm, synthesis, synthesize, unify, union, unite, wed

114 **join socially:** affiliate, align, assemble, associate, attach, attend, band, belong, bump into, cahoots, call, cavort, chaperon, collect, collusion, confluence, congregate, consort, consultation, convene, convention, converge, convocation, couple, dalliance, dally/dally with, date, desegregate, enroll, enter, escort, fraternize, gather, group, hang about/hang around/hang out, horse around, huddle, integrate, intermingle, intertwine/interweave, join, league, link, matriculate, meet, mix, register, session, swarm, take

115 **lend:** defray, finance, fund, hock, invest, lease, lend, let, loan, pawn, rent, trust

116 **lose:** deliver, fall, forfeit, forget, leak, lose, misplace, omission, sacrifice, wipeout

117 **manage:** adjust, administer, administration, boss, carry on, charge, compose, conduct, control, custody, deal/deal with, deregulate, direct, dispense, dispose, dominate, drill, economy, face, fare, farm, farming, fend for, get along, get by, get on, guide, handle, handling, head, lead, manage, management, marshal, monitor, officiate, operate, orchestrate, order about, organization, overlook, oversee, oversight, predominate, preside, rally, regulate, regulation, reign, rule, run, running, save, spearhead, subjugate, supervise, supervision, sway, treatment, upkeep, work

118 **manifest:** agree, comprehend, connote, embodiment, embody, emerge, evince, exemplify, exude, give, indicate, loom, manifest, mirror, point, presage, promise, prove, radiate

119 **modify an event:** abide, abrogation, advent, balk, birth, cancellation, cessation, close, closure, come on, come out, come up, coming, commence, complement, completion, conception, conclude, conclusion, culminate, dawn, desist, develop, discontinuance, disposal, embargo, end, ending, end up, ensue, entrance, expiration, expire, fall, finish, genesis, give in/give up, graduation, halt, knock off, lapse, lay off, matriculate, moratorium, pass, pause, pull out, pull up, quit, recess, relinquish, renaissance, resign, resignation, result, resurgence, resurrection, retract, revival, rout, secede, spurt, standstill, step down, stop, surrender, suspend, suspension, terminate, termination

120 **obtain:** acquire, acquisition, amass, attain, capitalize, earn, gain, get, get at, get back, land, lay up/lay by, make, obtain, pick up, possess, procure, pull in, realize, reap, recover, recruit, regain, repossess, retrieve, save, secure, strike, take, win

121 **prevent:** abolish, abolition, abort, abrogate, abstain, adjourn, adjournment, anticipate, arrest, asphyxiate, avert, avoid, avoidance, baffle, balk, ban, banish, bar, birth control, block, bog down, brake, break, bridle, censor, cheat, check, choke, circumvent, clog, close, confine, constrain, constraint, contravene, cop out, counter, cripple, cross, curb, cut short, dash, deactivate, decommission, defeat, defer, deferment/deferral, delay, deprivation, deprive, deter, discharge, discontinue, discourage, dispossess, disqualify, dissolve, drop, drop out, encumber, exclude, exclusion, foil, forbear, forbid, forgo, freeze, frustrate, gag, halt, hesitate, hesitation, hinder, hold back/hold off, hold up, impede, impound, incapacitate, inhibit, intercept, interfere, interference, interrupt, invalidate, jam, keep, keep one's cool, kill, localize, mire, muffle, muzzle, negate, negation, neutralize, nip, nullify, obstruct, obviate, occlude, omit, outlaw, override/overrule, paralyze, parry, pause, pigeonhole, preclude, preempt, prevent, privation, procrastinate, prohibit, prohibition, proscribe, pull out, pull up, pussyfoot, put off, quash, quell, recess, refrain, relegate, remove, repeal, repress, rescind, respite, restrain, retard, revoke, rule out, run-around, scrap, scratch, scrub, seclude, shelve, shut, shut off/shut out, slowdown, slowpoke, spite, squash, squish, stall, stay, stem, stifle, still, stop, stymie, subdue, suppress, suspend, table, terminate, thwart, traverse, turn off, undo, veto, vitiate, void, waive, waiver, waylay, withdraw, withhold

122 **punish:** avenge, chasten, chastise, correct, correction, discipline, evict, exile, expel,

fine, pay, penalize, punish, revenge, scourge, sentence

123 punishment: blackmail, damage(s), discipline, dressing-down, eviction, fine, forfeit, lesson, punishment, rap, reprimand, reproach, retribution, sanction, whipping

124 receive: accept, acceptance, acquire, acquisition, bring in, come by, come in for, fetch, find, gain, have, inherit, make, object, profit, realize, reap, receipt, receive, reception, recoup, regain, retrieve, take

125 record: enroll, enter, enumerate, itemize, list, record, register, schedule, score, take down, tally, tape, transcribe

126 rectify: accommodate, amend, appease, appeasement, arbitrate, arbitration, atone, atonement, avenge, break even, compensate, conclude, correct, correction, counteract, counterbalance, cover, cure, debug, do up, edit, emend, equalize, expiate, fix, get even, iron out, make up, mediate, mediation, mend, offset, overhaul, penance, placate, proofread, quiet, recompense, recoup, rectify, redeem, redress, reform, rehabilitate, remedy, requite, restore, retaliate, retribution, revise, revision, right, satisfy, settle, square, standardize, suit, tailor, temper, tune/tune up, troubleshooter, untangle

127 release: acquittal, cede, clear, deliver, delivery, discharge, disentangle, dismiss, dismissal, emancipate, exculpate, exempt, exonerate, extricate, free, loose/loosen, ransom, redeem, release, relinquish, save

128 replace: change, fill in, follow, needlework, replace, supersede, supplant

129 reserve: allocate, assign, assignment, assumption, claim, clear, come by, deserts, deserve, designate, earmark, earn, engage, enroll, entitle, gain, intend, merit, put away/put by, rate, reserve, save, spare, store, subscribe

130 restrict: bar, barricade, bind, block, bound, boycott, brake, check, circumscribe, clog, cocoon, confine, constrain, constraint, constrict, constriction, control, cramp, curb, curtail, dam, deaden, defer, deferment/deferral, delay, desensitize, disable, embargo, encumber, enjoin, enslave, expatriate, expel, expulsion, fetter, fetters, foil, forbear, forgo, gag, govern, grind, ground, hamper, hamstring, handicap, harness, hem/hem in, hinder, hobble, hold back/hold off, hold up, impair, impede, imposition, impound, inhibit, keep one's cool, limit, localize, matter, moderate, narrow, obligate, obstruct, ostracism, postpone, prohibit, prohibition, rein, repress, restrain, restrict, retard, set back, shackle, slow, slowdown, smother, squelch, stifle, strangle, stymie, subdue, suppress, suspend, thwart, tie/tie up

131 return: deliver, fetch, hand over, ransom, recall, redeem, regain, repay, requite, restore, retrieve, return

132 reward: award, commend, confer, decorate, reward

133 rule: abdicate, accession, command, depose, deposition, dictatorship, displace, enforce, enforcement, govern, impose, oppress, rule, subjugate, supremacy

134 save: cocoon, conservation, conserve, deliverance, deposit, ecology, guard, harbor, lay up/lay by, maintain, maintenance, pad, patrol, preservation, preserve, protect, put away/put aside/put by, rehabilitate, rescue, salvage, salvation, save, shelter, shield, spare, vigil, ward/ward off, watch

135 separate: abstract, analyze, appropriate, appropriation, assign, class, classification, classify, dedicate, detach, dichotomy, disaffect, disconnect, disengage, disentangle, dislocate, dismantle, dismember, disperse, disrupt, dissociate, divide, division, filter, fragment, gape, garner, glean, hoard, isolation, loneliness, open, part, partition, quarantine, schism, secession, seclude, seclusion, segregate, segregation, separate, separation, split, split up, strain, sunder, undo, unlock

136 serve: accommodate, administer, board, bondage, cater, mollycoddle, obey, oblige, pamper, pander, provide, quench, serve, spoil, spoon-feed, tend, wait on

137 shape change: beat, bisect, bruise, carve, chip, chisel, cleave, clip, compact, crimp, crinkle, cut, depreciation, desiccate, disfigure, disguise, distort, disturb, divide, do in, edge, elongate, enlarge, fatigue, file, flatten, fragment, gash, hack, hone, lacerate, lance, mow, mutilated, nick, notch, pierce, prune, puncture, reduce, roll, rumple, scar, score, sculpture, shape, sharpen, shave, shear, shorten, shrink, shrivel, skew, slash, slice, smooth, stiffen, stretch, taper/taper off, thicken, thin, trample, truncate, warp, whet, wound

138 show: advertising, bare, circulate, model, point, prove, represent, reveal, show, substantiate, symbolize, tout, trot out, unveil

139 steal: abduct, abducted, abduction, appropriate, appropriation, assume, bilk, break in, burglary, cheat, confiscate, copy, divest, do out of, embezzle, embezzlement, extort, extortion, filch, fleece, flimflam, grift, heist, hijack, hijacker, hold up, kidnap, knock off, larceny, lift, loot, maraud, milk, misappropriate, pilfer, pillage, pinch, piracy, plagiarism, play dirty, plunder, poach, pocket, purloin, ransack, rifle, rip off, rip-off, rob, sack, shanghai, shoplift, shortchange, snitch, steal, swindle, swipe, take, theft, unmask, welsh

140 supply: appoint, contribute, deal, deluge, dish out, dispensation, dispense, disseminate, distribute, distribution, divide, divvy up, dole out, equip, feed, foster, fuel, furnish, glut, hand out, infuse, issue, keep, kick in, larder, lend, maintain, make out, nourish, nurse, nurture, portion, provide, provision, publish, quarter, ration, receive, render, replenish, rig, satisfy, serve, stock, stockpile, supply, support, sustain

141 surpass: abound, beat, better, break, cap, conquer, eclipse, exceed, excel, flourish, get ahead, go by, hack it, lead, lick, outclass, outdistance, outdo, outflank, outfox, outweigh, overtake, pass, predominate, prevail, succeed, supersede, surmount, surpass, top, tower, transcend, triumph, win

142 take: acquire, acquisition, arrogate, assume, assumption, broach, burn, commandeer, compass, confiscate, cull, deplete, deprivation, deprive, disarm, disarmament, dispossess, divest, drain, draw, educe, elicit, exact, excerpt, exfoliate, expropriate, extract, filch, harvest, have, leach, milk, molt, nip, peel, pilfer, pocket, preempt, privation, pump, ransack, rob, sap, seize, take, tap, usurp, wring

143 **transfer abstractly:** afford, bear, bring, commit, consign, consignment, conveyance, delegate, delegation, infect, recall, refer, relay, release, relegate, transfer, turn over

MOTION

144 **be moved:** earthquake, elapse, flop, hang, lap

145 **change of place:** flicker, locomotion, motion, movement, onrush, passage, pop, rush, sway, sweep, swing, swirl, swivel, teeter, tremor

146 **flow:** flow, pour, run, secrete, seep, stream, surge, swamp, teem, torrent, trickle

147 **move:** bob, budge, careen, churn, circulate, circulation, contort, cruise, curl, curve, dandle, deflect, descend, descent, dislocate, dislodge, displace, dive, drift, drive, entwine, falter, fidget, flex, flourish, gyrate, haul, lean, loop, move, oscillate, overturn, paddle, pitch, pivot, pulsate/pulse, pulse, revolve, ripple, rock, roll, rotate, round, skirt, tilt, topple, toss, transport, traverse, tumble, turn, twine, twist, uproot, upset, waft, wave, waver, weave, wheel, wield

148 **move mechanically:** aviation, bank, carriage, carry, cart, drive, fly, haul, mobilize, navigate, operate, pack, park, ride, rocket, ship, skyrocket, soar, takeoff, take off, veer

149 **move oneself:** ascend, ascension, bend, constitutional, flap, flex, flounce, gad, gait, gallivant, gambol, go ahead, go for, gyrate, hike, jerk, lope, motion, mount, mountaineer, mountaineering, move, negotiate, pace, pad, pass, patter, progress, quail, ripple, rock, roll, round, stalk, stamp, step, stir, stray, stride, strut, stump, swagger, tilt, traipse, tread, trip, tumble, walk, wallow, wave, wriggle

150 **move oneself quickly:** barge in/barge into, beat, bolt, bounce, bustle, capsize, coast, course, dart, dash, decamp, dodder, flash, flee, flinch, flit, flutter, fly, gallop, get the lead out, glide, hasten, hurry, hurtle, hustle, jerk, jiggle, lurch, make off, march, plunge, pound, prance, race, rebound, recoil, ricochet, rocket, run, rush, scamper, scoot, scramble, scurry, shake, shoot, shudder, skate, skedaddle, skim, skip, skyrocket, slide, slip, slither, soar, speed, spin, sprint, start, storm, sweep, swerve, swoop, tear, trot, twirl, veer, wag, whip, whiz, wiggle, wobble, writhe, zip, zoom

151 **move oneself slowly:** amble, crawl, creep, cruise, dalliance, dally, decline, dilly-dally, drag, hobble, jog, knock about/knock around, lag, laggard, limp, linger, loiter, lumber, lurk, meander, mosey, plod, poke, prowl, pussyfoot, ramble, range, reel, roam, saunter, shuffle, slink/slither, slog, sneak, stagger, steal, straggle, stroll, sway, tarry, totter, tramp, trudge, waddle, wade, wander

152 **move quickly:** advance, advancement, agitate, bear down, capsize, convulsion, course, discharge, dispatch, dodder, ejaculate, fall, flicker, flourish, flutter, hasten, jerk, jiggle, jostle, keel over, lurch, palpitate, plunge, precipitate, quake, quiver, rattle, rush, shake, shiver, shoot, shudder, skate, skid, skim, slide, slip, slither, speed, spin, stampede, sweep, tear, throb, tremble, twirl, vibrate, vibration, wag, whip, whirl, whisk, wiggle, wobble

153 **move slowly:** dangle, float, lag, reel

154 **position oneself:** arise, bow, cant, duck, get down, get off, get up, hover, huddle, hunch, kneel, lie, list, loll, lounge, mount, nestle, obeisance, perch, poise, pose, ramble, recline, repose, rest, rise, seat, sit, slouch, wince

155 **travelling:** lift, navigation, procession, railroad, transit, transport, voyage

PHYSICAL

156 **abuse:** abuse, charge, consumption, cop out, corrode, defile, dissipate, dope, enervate, exploit, exploitation, force, frazzle, fritter, impinge, lose, malpractice, milk, misappropriate, mishandle/mismanage, mistreat, misuse, overdo, pervert, prostitute, riddle, run through, sap, spend, squander, strain, throw away, waste, wear

157 **anatomical change:** distend, flake, neuter

158 **arrange:** agitation, align, arrange, bundle, collate, coordinate, crease, deploy, dispose, file, group, indent, lay, lay out, located, mess up, mix up, muss, order, organize, position, range, rank, reverse, ruffle, rummage, separate, shuffle, snarl, sort, split up, spread, stack, stir, straighten, unwind, weave

159 **arrive:** admission, advent, alight, appear, appearance, approach, arrival, arrive, billow, board, butt in, come, come in, coming, cross, cruise, disembark, dock, embark, encroach, enter, entrance, foray, get, get back, get in, get on, go, go ahead, gravitate, immigrate, infiltrate, influx, insinuate, intrude, invade, invasion, jaunt, lance, land, light, loom, lunge, make, penetrate, permeate, pierce, pounce, progress, pull up, reach, report, return, show up, stalk, swarm, trespass, turn out, turn up

160 **attach:** adhere, adhesion, adjoin, affix, anchor, annex, append, attach, batten, bind, bond, cement, chain, clamp, clasp, cling, cohere, connect, engage, fasten, fix, gasket, hitch, knot, latch, lock, moor, nail, paste, peg, pin, screw, seal, secure, shut, stick, tack, tag, tape, tether, tie, yoke

161 **bathe:** ablution, bath, bathe, clean, decontaminate, wet

162 **beautify:** accessorize, adorn, adornment, bask, beautify, comb, decorate, decoration, doll up, embellish, emblazon, enhance, facelift, festoon, fix up, flatter, furbish, groom, ornament, primp, shave, spruce up, trim

163 **breathe:** breath, breathe, draw, exhale, expire, gasp, heave, huff, inhale, pant, puff, sigh, suffocate, wheeze, yawn

164 **catch:** catch, field, intercept, seize, tackle

165 clean: ablution, abrade, bath, bathe, brush, catharsis, clarify, clean, cleanse, clear, decontaminate, disinfect, distill, distillation, do up, exorcism, expurgate, filter, flush, furbish, gut, housework, lather, launder, mop, purge, purification, purify, rake, refine, refinement, rinse, scour, scrape, scrub, sift, sweep, wash, wipe

166 climb: arise, ascend, ascension, ascent, climb, get on, mount, rise, scale, surface

167 clothe: array, attire, clothe, deck, disrobe, doll up, dress, dress up, garb, get on, ornament, outfit, primp, rig, sport, spruce up, stuff, try on/try out, turn out, wear

168 construct: build, compose, construct, construction, dismantle, erect, establish, fashion, forge, form, found, frame, make, modernize, pave, pitch, put up, raise, rear, reconstruct, remodel, renovate, revamp, throw up, ultramodern

169 consume: absorption, bolt, chew, chug, consume, consumption, contract, corrode, crunch, demolish, deplete, devour, diet, digest, dig in, dine, dispatch, dissipate, draft, drink, eat, engulf, exhaust, fast, feast, feed on, finish, gargle, glut, gnaw, gobble, gorge, gormandize, go through, graze, gulp, guzzle, imbibe, ingest, munch, nibble, nip, nosh, partake, peck, pig out, polish off, potable, prey on, put away, quaff, satiate, sip, spend, stuff, swallow, take, taste, tear down, use, wolf, xerophagy

170 cook: agitation, bake, barbecue, baste, beat, boil, brew, broil, butcher, can, churn, coddle, cook, cure, distill, fix, flavor, foam, fry, grill, honeyed, housework, knead, mash, microwave, nuke, pickle, preservation, preserve, sear, season, simmer, sizzle, stir, sweeten, toast, warm, whip

171 copy: ape, clone, copy, counterfeit, duplicate, echo, emulate, follow, forge, forgery, imitate, imitation, mimic, multiply, parallel, parrot, pattern, pretend, quote, reconstruct, reflect, reiterate, repeat, reproduce, sham, simulate, simulation, take after, transcribe, xerox

172 cover: blanket, bury, camouflage, coat, cover, daub, disguise, dissimulate, drape, dress, dust, engulf, enshroud, envelop, face, finish, funeral, gild, glaze, insulate, inter, inundate, laminate, lap, line, mask, masquerade, morgue, muzzle, obscure, oil, overrun, paint, palliate, paper, pave, pervade, plate, sheet, smear, smother, spatter, spread, top, varnish, veil, veneer, wrap

173 create: bear, beget, brainstorm, breed, coin, come up with, compose, conceive, concoct, constitute, construct, contrive, create, creation, design, engineer, establish, establishment, fabricate, fashion, father, film, forge, form, formation, formulate, frame, generate, generation, hatch, improvise, institute, invent, make, make up, materialize, mint, mold, originate, piece, pioneer, procreate, produce, regenerate, reproduce, reproduction, spawn, wing it, work

174 create art: chart, compose, depict, dot, draw, engrave, engraving, etch, illustrate, impress, imprint, lay out, mount, outline, paint, photograph, picture, plot, portray, pose, pottery, print, printer, rough out, sculpture, sketch, stamp, trace

175 create with effort: beat, forge, mold

176 cut: amputate, ax/axe, behead, bisect, carve, chisel, chop, cleave, clip, crop, cut, cut up, decapitate, dent, dismember, dissect, dissection, engrave, engraving, etch, exfoliate, fell, gash, hack, knife, lacerate, lop, mangle, mince, molt, mow, mutilate, nick, notch, pare, peel, pierce, pink, prune, scar, score, scratch, sever, shave, shear, shred, skin, slash, slice, slit, split, trim, whittle

177 decorate: accessorize, adorn, adornment, decorate, decoration, embellish, embellishment, emblazon, embroider, enhance, enrich, festoon, furnish, gild, modernize, ornament, paper, refurbish, renovate, revamp, trim, ultramodern, varnish

178 dig: bore, burrow, claw, dig, dredge, embed, excavate, excavation, exhume, grub, hollow, inter, mine, plant, plow, rake, root, scoop, tunnel, unearth, uproot

179 discharge: blast, blowout, blow up, bubble, burst, cascade, come from, deliver, detonate, detonation, discharge, disgorge, drain, dribble, drop, effusion, ejaculate, eject, ejection, emanate, emanation, emission, emit, erupt, eruption, evacuate, excrete, exorcise, expel, explode, explosion, express, exude, fire, flare, flood, flow, flush, gag, give off/give out, go off, gush, heave, impregnate, infest, infiltrate, influx, infuse, inject, inundate, issue, jet, launch, leak, liftoff, mushroom, ooze, ouster, outbreak, outflow, overflow, overrun, pass, penetrate, percolate, permeate, pervade, pour, proceed, project, regurgitate, scatter, secrete, seep, shed, shoot, spatter, spew, spill, spit, spot, spout, spray, sprinkle, spurt, squirt, stream, surge, swamp, teem, throw up, torrent, trickle, vent, void, vomit

180 dispose: boot, buck, chuck, discard, disposal, dispose, dispose of, ditch, do away with, dump, elimination, jettison, kick out, reject, rejection, rid, scrap, shed, throw away, unload, void

181 drop: alight, clatter, crash, crumble, decline, descend, descent, dip, dive, drip, droop, drop, duck, dump, fall, fell, flop, founder, fumble, go down, go under, ground, keel over, land, light, lower, percolate, pitch, plumb, plummet, plunge, plunk, sag, set, settle, shed, sink, sling, slump, spill, stoop, stumble, submerge, subside, suspend, swoop, thud/thump, topple, tumble, wilt

182 equip: arm, armed, do up, equip, fit, furnish, gear, outfit, rig, stock, stockpile

183 find: come across, detect, detection, discover, discovery, ferret out, find, find out, learn, locate, meet, pick up, pinpoint, recover, repossess, spot, strike, stumble, track/track down, turn up, uncover, unearth

184 form: arch, bend, bloat, braid, carve, chisel, constitute, contort, crumple, curl, curve, fold, form, materialize, model, mold, pat, round, sculpture, shape, twist, whittle, work

185 gesture: bawl, beam, beat, belch, bite, bleed, blink, blow, chew, clap, disgorge, drag, dribble, drivel, drool, excrete, expire, frown, gesture, gnaw, grimace, grin, guffaw, gulp, hemorrhage, itch, kink, kiss, laugh/laughter, laugh, lick, munch, necking, nod, perspire, pucker, puff, pulsate/pulse, pulse, purse, regurgitate, scowl, shiver, slobber, smile, smirk, smooch, sob, spasm, spit, squint, sweat, tear/tears, throb, twitch, vomit, wail, weep, whimper, wince, wink, wrinkle, yawn

186 grind: abrade, abrasion, corrode, creak, crunch, file, frazzle, gnash, granulate, grate, grind, mash, mill, pound, powder, pulverize, rasp, scrape

187 guide: aviation, channel, conduct, convey, direct, divert, drive, ease, ferry, funnel, guide, infuse, inject, jockey, lay, lead, level, maneuver, marshal, mobilize, navigate, navigation, point, refer, round, route, row, see, show, sidetrack, sled, sleigh, steer, take, transport, usher

188 hide: ambush, balk, bury, cache, camouflage, cloak, conceal, concealment, cover, coverup, cower, cringe, cut, disguise, dissemble, dissimulate, eavesdrop, embed, encode, ensconce, enshroud, envelop, harbor, hide, isolate, isolation, loneliness, lurk, mask, masquerade, obscure, palliate, quarantine, screen, seclude, seclusion, secrete, sequester, shelter, shrink, shut off/shut out, smother, sneak, withhold

189 hit: applaud, applause, bang, bash, baste, bat, batter, battery, beat, belt, blind-side, blow, boot, box, buffet, bump, bunt, butt, chip, clap, clash, clatter, clip, clobber, clout, club, collide, collision, concussion, crack, crash, crown, cuff, dash, deflect, dent, drive, drum, flail, flog, glance, hail, hammer, hand, hit, impact, jab, jar, jostle, kick, knock, lash, lick, maul, nail, pat, peck, pelt, plaudits, poke, pound, pummel, punch, ram, rap, rough up, scourge, slam, slap, slug, smack, smashup, sock, spank, strike, swat, swipe, tan, tap, thrash, thud/thump, tick, tip, wallop, whack, whip

190 hold: anchor, cling, clog, clutch, cradle, cuddle, dandle, dangle, embrace, fondle, grab, hog, hold, hook, hug, nip, nuzzle, pin, prop, retain, retard, seize, shore, snuggle, support, suspend, sustain, tangle

191 hold forcefully: apprehend, brace, cage, captivity, clasp, clench, clinch, clutch, confinement, constrict, constriction, contain, cramp, dam, detain, detention, embrace, enfold, enslave, fetter, fetters, grapple, grasp, grip, gripe, harness, hold, imprison, incarcerate, leash, overpower, pen, press, restrain, shackle, snap, snatch, stifle, strangle, tackle, throttle, wrestle

192 illegal behavior: backstab, blackmail, bleed, breach, break, break in, bribe, bug, buy, cheat, conspire, contraband, contravene, crime, delinquency, depredation, disobey, entrench, extortion, fault, felony, fix, foul, fraud, graft, grease, hara-kiri, have, holdup, hold up, imposture, infraction, infringe, injustice, intrigue, jinx, kickback, knock off, larceny, libel, loot, mischief, misconduct, misdeed/misdemeanor, murder, offense, outrage, pick, pilfer, piracy, plagiarism, poach, racket, rape, ravish, rip off, rip-off, rob, robbery, screw, sexual assault, sham, shenani-

gans, slander, smear campaign, smuggle, speculation, squeeze, stick up, swindle, take, tamper, theft, transgression, treason, trespass, victimize, violate, violation

193 join physically: link, meld, merge, mesh, mingle, mix, piece, pool, splice, tie, tuck, unify, unite, wed, weld, yoke

194 jump: bounce, bound, clear, deflect, dive, flip, gallop, gambol, hop, hurdle, jump, leap, lunge, lurch, plunge, pounce, rear, rebound, recoil, ricochet, skip, spring, start, vault

195 leave: abandon, abscond, back, beat it, blow, board, bolt, brain drain, break, break away, break out, clear out, cringe, curtains, dart, defection, depart, departure, desert, desertion, deviate, diaspora, digress, disappear, disappearance, dismount, distance, diverge, draw back, drop, ebb, egress, embark, evacuate, exit, exodus, fall back, farewell, flee, flight, fly, forsake, get along, get off, get out, go, goodbye, go off, go out, jaunt, jilt, leave, light out, make off, maroon, part, parting, pull out, push off/push on, quail, quit, recede, recoil, renounce, renunciation, repair, resign, resignation, retire, retreat, run, schism, scram, secession, segregation, separation, shake off, shove off, shrink, step down, strike out, swerve, takeoff, take off, threads, throw over, trousers, turn, vacate, withdraw, withdrawal

196 lift: boost, dip, elevate, elevator, heave, hoist, lift, pick up, pry, raise, rear

197 measure: balance, figure, measure, quantify, survey

198 move living quarters: anyplace, anywhere, approach, arena, battlefield, camp, colonization, cover, defect, defection, deport, deportation, destination, dominion, element, emigrate, empire, encampment, evict, eviction, exile, expatriate, expel, hideout, jurisdiction, landmark, locale/locality, location, lookout, migrate, move, nest, neighborhood, oasis, outdoors, outside, point, position, post, premises, province, refuge, region, reign, rendezvous, resort, seat, setting, site, situation, soil, spa, spot, station, stop, surroundings, terminal, territory, turn, vicinity, where

199 perform: fan, hit, perform, type, work

200 physical action: application, apply, bash, clout, drop, hit, hold, lift, plunk, push, slug

201 position: aim, barricade, bow, button, cant, close, cock, coil, deposit, dial, dip, direct, disseminate, ensconce, entwine, fix, hang, indent, insert, install, installation, interpolate, intersperse, isolate, jut, lap, lay, lean, lie, list, located, lodge, loop, misplace, occlude, park, pile, pitch, place, plant, point, position, post, prop, put, quarantine, recline, roll, seat, separate, set, sit, slant, slope, slouch, snuggle, sprawl, spread, squat, stand, station, stick, stoop, swerve, tip, top, train, traverse, turn, twine, twist, unfold, wallow, wind, wrinkle

202 prepare physically: acclimate, acculturation, accustom, adjust, braid, brush, brush up, buff, bundle, burnish, coat, condition, disguise, doll up, domesticate, do up, dress, embalm, embattle, face, fine-tune, finish, fix up, formulate, fortify, freezer, gear, get, gild, glaze, gloss, grace, grease, groom, habituate, housework, knit, lubricate, make up, modernize, modulate, orient, overhaul, pack, pad, pare, plaster, plate, polish, preparation, prepare, preservation, preserve, prime, primp, ready, reform, refresh, refrigerate, refurbish, regenerate, rehabilitate, rejuvenate, renew, renovate, rig, round, season, set, shave, shine, slim, smear, spruce up, square, straighten, strain, tailor, toughen, train, training, weather

203 print: edit, print, printer, type, write

204 process: gnash, grind, process, work

205 produce: agriculture, fabricate, fabrication, film, forge, form, generate, generation, horticulture, lay, make, manufacture, mint, output, print, produce, production, synthesize, turn out, yield

206 pull: drag, draw, extract, gut, lug, pick, pluck, pry, pull, pump, schlep, shut, strain, tear, tow, tug, twist, twitch, wrench, wring, yank

207 pursue: chase, dog, dragnet, follow, hound, hunt, pursue, pursuit, shadow, steal, tag, tail, trace, track/track down, trail

208 push: advance, advancement, back, balloon, barge in/barge into, bear down, billow, bloat, blow up, boost, bulge, bulldoze, burst, compact, compress, cram, crowd, crumple, crush, dent, depress, dig, drive, elbow, extrude, fan, force, hit, indent, inject, insinuate, intrude, jam, jog, jolt, jostle, knead, level, mash, massage, mob, nick, notch, nudge, poke, press, prod, propel, protrude, pulp, pump, purse, push, ram, repel, repulse, roll, shoulder, shove, shut, slam, squash, squish, strain, tax, thrust, tip, topple, trample, upset, wrestle, wring

209 put in container: box, encapsulate, enclose, fill, flood, fold, glut, imbue, inject, insert, interpolate, introduce, load, pack, plug, pour, ram, replenish, stow, stuff, surfeit

210 relax: asleep, bask, dalliance, dally, dawdle, dilly-dally, drop off, kick back, loaf, loiter, loll, lounge, lull, nap, nod, putter, relax, relaxation, repose, rest, sit tight, slack/slacken, snooze, stay, tarry, trifle, turn in, unwind, vegetate, wait

211 remove: abstract, amputate, blot, bounce, break off, call off, cancel, cashier, clear, clear out, cut out, delete, denude, deport, deportation, disarm, disarmament, discharge, distill, divest, doff, download, drain, efface, eliminate, empty, eradicate, erase, evict, eviction, except, exception, excerpt, excise, excoriate, expatriate, expulsion, expunge, extirpate, extract, extraction, free, gut, hollow, leach, omit, oust, peel, pry, purge, relegate, remove, replace, rid, shed, skim, skin, strip, subtract, take, top, transport, unburden, undress, unload, uproot, void, withdraw, withdrawal

212 repair: adjust, compensate, debug, fine-tune, fix, overhaul, patch, remedy, repair, restore, right, tinker, touch up, troubleshooter

213 reposition: bank, bow, bump, crimp, crinkle, crook, crouch, curl, curve, deploy, descend, descent, dislocate, dislodge, displace, divert, drag, draw back, invert, jump, reverse, shift, sidetrack, sink, squirm, transplant, turn, upset, veer, warp

214 rip: claw, fray, lacerate, rip, snag, tear

215 rub: bite, buff, burnish, chafe, creak, efface, erase, excoriate, file, fret, friction, gall, glaze, gloss, grate, grind, polish, rasp, rub, scrape, smear

216 search: comb, delve, dig, exploration, explore, ferret out, forage, frisk, grope, grub, hunt, investigate, investigation, look up, nose, pan, plumb, probe, prospect, pry, quest, rake, ransack, refer, rummage, scour, scout, scrounge, search, seek, snoop, trace, track/track down

217 send: banish, carriage, carry, cart, channel, commit, consign, consignment, convey, deliver, delivery, deport, deportation, direct, dismiss, dismissal, dispatch, disperse, distribute, distribution, download, export, extradite, ferry, forward, funnel, mail, pack, pass, passage, pipe, radiate, remit, return, route, scatter, send, ship, sled, sleigh, take, transfer, transmit, transport, waft

218 sew: baste, embroider, embroidery, knit, line, patch, sew, spin, tack, tailor, tuck

219 squeeze: choke, clasp, clinch, constrict, constriction, crease, crush, distill, enfold, gripe, pinch, pucker, pulp, pulverize, rumple, screw, squash, squeeze

220 stab: claw, drill, gore, gouge, impale, knife, lacerate, penetrate, perforate, pierce, prick, punch, puncture, riddle, spike, stab, stick, sting, tap, transfix

221 start: actuate, boot, emanate, emanation, embark on, engage, engender, erect, establish, establishment, fall to, foment, found, go back to square one, impel, implement, inaugurate, incite, initiate, initiation, inspire, install, installation, instigate, instill, institute, introduce, invent, kindle, launch, lead, make, mobilize, onset, open, originate, pioneer, plant, preface, propel, provoke, raise, recharge, renaissance, renew, resume, resurgence, resurrection, resuscitate, revival, revive, set, set up, spark, start, stir, take on, take up, turn on, usher, whip up

222 throw: buck, cast, chuck, dart, dash, deliver, disseminate, dust, eject, erupt, extrude, fire, fling, flip, heave, hurl, intersperse, jettison, launch, liftoff, lob, ouster, pelt, pitch, powder, project, propagate, propel, scatter, slam, sling, splash, splatter, sprinkle, throw, thrust, toss

223 transfer of an object: download, give, send, transact, transaction, transfer

224 travel: accompany, commute, cover, cross, cruise, do, double back, drive, embark, excursion, expedition, exploration, explore, field trip, flight, fly, gad, gallivant, hike, jaunt, journey, knock about/knock around, make, migrate, mountaineer, mountaineering, navigate, navigation, negotiate, odyssey, outing, passage, pick up, pilgrimage, ramble, range, ride, roam, run, safari, sail, shuttle, sojourn, takeoff, take off, tour, traffic, tramp, transit, travel, trek, trip, turn, voyage, walk, wander

225 use: apply, avail, bolt, borrow, broach, consume, consumption, deplete, devour, dip, drain, draw on, eat, employ, employment, enervate, exercise, exert, exhaust, expend, exploit, exploitation, fatigue, finish, gormandize, jockey, maneuver, manipulate, milk, occupy, partake, ply, polish off, resort, run, spend, squander, take, telephone, turn, use, utilize, wear, wield

226 use living quarters: abide, accommodate, cohabit, dwell, exist, hang about/hang

around/hang out, inhabit, live, locate, lodge, occupy, reside, settle, situate, sojourn, stay, visit

227 visit: call, come by, drop in, frequent, see, sojourn, stay, stop, tour, visit

Causes

ABSTRACT

228 affect: affect, cause, change, evoke

229 event that causes another: account, beginning, cause, origin, precipitous/precipitate

230 state of causation: abortion, Achilles' heel, adaptation, aftermath, amazement, anticlimax, armistice, astonishment, awe, backlash, backwash, bang, bedlam, bereavement, bind, blessing, bliss, blot, blunder, boo boo, boner, boom, bottom line, break, buildup, by-product, catharsis, cease-fire, certainty, change, chaos, check, clincher, coincidence, collapse, collision, comfort, complication, compromise, congestion, consequence, consternation, contamination, corollary, culmination, decay, deception, decomposition, decoy, degeneracy, degradation, descent, destruction, deterioration, disadvantage, disappointment, disarray, disaster area, disorder, disposal, disrepair, dissipation, dissolution, effect, end, ending, entropy, error, event, eventuality, fall, flap, fluff, flurry, frailty, frenzy, fruit, fulfillment, furor, gaffe, give and take, glitch, goof, gridlock, headway, hubbub, huddle, humbug, impact, imperfection, implode, impression, improvement, impurity, inaccuracy, infection, irony, issue, jinx, jitters, lapse, lather, maelstrom, malarky, mess, miscarriage, mistake, mix-up, morass, muddle, muss, nonsense, occurrence, outcome, outgrowth, payoff, phenomenon, piffle, poppycock, portent, press, price, proceed, product, quantum leap, racket, ramification, rash, repercussion, resolution, result, rigmarole, rubbish, scare, scramble, settlement, shambles, shortfall, slipup, snafu, solution, stain, stalemate, stigma, stink, stir, storm, taint, tangle, tempest, therefore, to-do, toll, tomfoolery, trend, trip, tripe, truce, tumult, turmoil, turn, twaddle, undoing, unification, upheaval, upshot, vandalism, whirl, wipeout, wonderment

231 to be: alienate, animate, antagonize, awake, awaken, awakening, calm, cause, compound, endangered, energize, even, materialize, sanitize, sterilize, straighten, threaten

232 to change: adapt, adjust, alter, alternate, assimilate, attune, break even, cancel, change, commute, conversion, convert, co-opt, differentiate, distort, diversify, double back, equalize, expurgate, fashion, fit, fix, invert, modify, neutralize, offset, overturn, restore, shift, switch, tamper, transform, translate, transpose, turn

233 to change abstractly: demote, heighten, intensify, mitigate

234 to change an event: abbreviate, accelerate,

acceleration, activate, actuate, adjourn, approach, arrest, bed, begin, break off, break up, build, cancel, cease, close, commence, complement, conclude, consummate, continue, crown, cut in, cut off, cut short, desist, determine, disband, discontinue, dispatch, dispose of, disrupt, dissolve, end, enter, finish, floor it, foul up, graduate, halt, hurry, intervene, invalidate, kick, knock off, lay off, leave, leave off, lift, manipulate, nip, nullify, pause, pick up, preclude, preempt, put off, quash, quell, quench, quit, relinquish, remit, rescind, retire, reverse, revoke, round off, ruin, scoot, scrub, seal, slow, smother, stall, stop, terminate, turn off, turn out, vacate, waive, wind up, wrap up

235 to change cognitively: agree, change, concede, harden, lay

236 to change number or quantity: abbreviate, abridge, abstract, accumulate, add, addition, advance, aggrandize, alleviate, amplification, amplify, augment, blow up, boost, build, build up, bump, commute, compress, condense, contract, curtail, cut, cut back, deduct, deepen, deflate, detract, digest, dilate, discount, double, downsize, draw out, encapsulate, enlarge, epitomize, escalate, evolve, expand, extend, extension, fatten, hike, imbue, increase, inflate, jump, lengthen, lift, lop, lower, magnify, modify, narrow, pare, prune, raise, reduce, reinforce, shorten, slash, step up, summarize, supplement, swell, take, trim, truncate, whittle, widen

237 to change or affect an event: delay, procrastinate, protract, slowpoke, stop, weigh

238 to change state of being: dispatch, do for

239 to continue: abide, bear, broaden, carry on, come, come back, continue, create, drag on/drag out, draw, drawl, draw out, dwell on/dwell upon, eke out, elongate, endure, extend, fated, go, go on, hammer away/hammer into, hang on, hold, kill, lengthen, linger, perpetuate, persevere, persist, prolong, protract, pursue, remain, resume, scam, survive, take up

240 to diminish: abate, adulterate, aggravate, aggravation, alloy, attenuate, blot, blunt, break, canker, cheapen, compound, compromise, cool, corrupt, crackdown, cut, deaden, debase, debauch, debilitate, decay, decline, decrease, degrade, depress, desensitize, disarrange, disorder, doctor, downgrade, downplay, downsize, emasculate, enfeeble, fatigue, geld, impair, imperil, let up, lower, minimize, mitigate, moderate, modify, muffle, mute, pale, pick-me-up, prevention, provocation, qualify, reduce, relax, retard, rot, sap, shorten, slash, stimulant, stimulus, stop, tax, tone down, undermine, weaken, wear, worsen

241 to function: animate, begin, cause, go back to square one, start

242 to happen: accelerate, boomerang, breathe, bring, copy, engender, ensue, entail, eventuate, evoke, expedite, expedition, facilitate, floor it, follow, impel, incite, inconvenience, induce, inflict, influence, inspire, instigate, institute, intervene, make, motivate, move, muddle, necessitate, oblige, occasion, occur, orchestrate, pass, precipitate, prod, produce, prompt, provoke, put, recur, result, return, stimulate, trigger, unsettle, will, work up, wreak

243 to have: accent, download, give, push, transfer

244 to improve: advance, allay, ameliorate, amend, assuage, augment, augmentation, become, benefit, better, betterment, boost, brighten, bring about, brush up, civilize, confirm, contribute, cultivate, cure, dignify, enhance, enrich, freshen, garnish, help, improve, lift, lighten, magnify, mend, mollify, pad, perfect, perk up, polish, quench, quiet, raise, refine, relieve, restore, revise, revision, rouse, step up, strengthen, supplement, touch up, unburden, update, upgrade

245 to increase quantity: accumulate, add, addition, advance, aggrandize, amplification, amplify, augment, augmentation, blow up, boost, build, build up, bump, deepen, dilate, double, draw out, enlarge, escalate, evolve, expand, extend, extension, fatten, hike, imbue, increase, inflate, jump, lengthen, lift, magnify, raise, reinforce, step up, supplement, swell, widen

246 to injure: abuse, afflict, ail, asphyxiate, batter, battery, beat, blemish, bruise, chip, cost, cripple, crush, damage, debilitate, decay, deface, defile, deform, dent, desecrate, desecration, devastate, disable, disagree, discomfort, disfigure, endanger, expose, flail, fragment, get back at, gripe, hamstring, handicap, harm, hurt, impair, incapacitate, infect, injure, irritate, jeopardize, knife, lacerate, lay up, maim, mangle, mar, maul, mistreat, molest, mutilate, mutilated, outrage, pain, paralyze, persecute, poison, pollute, pummel, rack, repay, rough up, ruin, rupture, sabotage, sap, scar, sexual harassment, shatter, shiver, shoot, sicken, smart, smash, snap, splinter, spoil, sting, stress, suffocate, taint, tarnish, torture, trample, turn, vandalize, violate, violation, vitiate, wound, wrong

247 to reduce quantity: abbreviate, abridge, abstract, alleviate, commute, compress, condense, contract, curtail, cut, cut back, deduct, deflate, detract, digest, discount, downsize, encapsulate, epitomize, extenuate, lessen, lower, minimize, modify, narrow, pare, prune, reduce, shorten, slash, summarize, take, trim, truncate, whittle

PHYSICAL

248 to break: collide, crack, crash, crumble, dash

249 to burn: arson, blaze, burn, char, conflagration, fire, flame, flare, glow, ignite, inciner-

ate, inflame, kindle, lick, light, parch, scorch, sear, singe, smolder

250 to change physically: awake, bite, blacken, black out, bleach, blush, brighten, bruise, buttress, chip, color, compact, confirm, congeal, consolidate, corrode, crimp, crinkle, cross, darken, daub, debase, deepen, deform, dehydrate, desiccate, dilute, dim, disarrange, discolor, disfigure, disorder, disorganize, distort, disturb, do in, douse, dry, dye, eclipse, edge, elongate, emasculate, enervate, exhaust, fade, fatigue, fatten, ferment, file, flatten, flush, fog, foul, geld, gird, harden, heighten, hone, hypnotize, intensify, jell, lay, level, light, lighten, liquefy, loose/loosen, mark, melt, muzzle, neaten, neuter, numb, open, pacify, pale, petrify, prolong, prostrate, protract, quicken, ravel, redden, reinforce, roll, rouse, rumple, sanitize, set, shade, shadow, sharpen, shrivel, slop, slow, smooth, soften, solidify, sour, stabilize, stain, sterilize, stiffen, streak, strengthen, stretch, sully, tame, temper, thicken, thin, tidy, tighten, tinge, tint, toughen, turn, unlock, vitiate, warp, weary, whet, whiten

251 to create: bear, beget, breed, conceive, concoct, constitute, construct, create, engineer, establish, fabricate, forge, form, generate, hatch, materialize, mint, mold, originate, piece, procreate, produce, regenerate, reproduce, spawn

252 to destroy: ablate, abolish, abolition, annihilate, annul, assassinate, batter, blight, bomb, break, bring down, bulldoze, burst, bust, butcher, carnage, clobber, collapse, come unglued, consume, consumption, contaminate, coup de grâce, crucify, crumple, crush, cut down, damage, decimate, deface, deforestation, demolish, demolition, depredation, desecrate, desecration, desolate, despoil, destroy, destruction, devastate, disintegrate, dismantle, disorganize, dispatch, dissolve, do away with, do for, do in, drown, end, endanger, enfeeble, eradicate, erode, erosion, euthanasia, execute, execution, expunge, exterminate, extinction, extinguish, extirpate, finish, hang, genocide, gore, hara-kiri, holocaust, homicide, hunt, jeopardize, kaput, kill, killing, knock off, level, liquidate, lynching, mangle, manslaughter, massacre, mess up, murder, nuke, obliterate, overthrow, paralyze, pervert, pillage, plunder, poison, predator, prostrate, pull down, pulverize, purge, put away, put down, put out, quash, quench, ravage, raze, remove, ruin, sabotage, sack, shatter, shiver, shoot, slaughter, slay, smash, spoil, stamp out, strangle, subdue, subvert, suppress, tear down, undo, uproot, vandalism, vandalize, violation, waste, wipe out, wreck

253 to grow: cultivate, develop, farm, farming, flower, plant, raise, sow, till, vegetate

254 to make dirty: adulterate, blur, clutter, contaminate, dirty, litter, mess up, pollute, smudge, soil, stain, taint, tarnish

255 to make hot or cold: air, boil, chill, cool, freeze, freezer, heat, liquefy, melt, molten, numb, parch, refrigerate, scorch, shrivel, thaw, warm

256 to make wet: absorb, absorption, dampen,

deluge, dip, douse, drench, drivel, drool, drown, dunk, engulf, extinguish, immerse, marinate, moisten, oil, overflow, permeate, rinse, saturate, soak, souse, spatter, splash, splatter, spray, sprinkle, squirt, steep, submerge, water, wet

Fields of human activity

AGRICULTURE

257 action: agriculture, bed, bury, conservation, cross, cultivate, cultivation, culture, deforestation, ecology, erosion, fertilize, gather, graft, harvest, horticulture, preservation, raise, reap, roundup, round up, sow, sprout, tend, till, vegetate, work

258 organization: cowboy, farm, grange, plantation, ranch

THE ARTS

259 art object: antique, antiquity, canvas, classic, coat, collage, composition, creation, decal, decoration, depiction, design, dye, emblem, embroidery, enamel, etching, exhibit, figure, flourish, glaze, handicraft, illustration, image, insignia, knickknack, landscape, lattice, logo, masterpiece, medium, model, monument, ornament, pattern, picture, piece, piece de resistance, pigment, plaid, portrait, pottery, print, profile, pyramid, showpiece, silhouette, stamp, statue, trademark, workmanship, wreath

260 created object: alloy, amulet, apparatus, ash(es), badge, brew, by-product, camouflage, capsule, card, change, charlatan, cinder, composite, composition, compound, concoction, contrivance, creation, curiosity, debris, decoration, derivative, detritus, dip, discovery, dregs, droppings, dung, embers, enamel, essence, excrement, fabrication, fake, fence, fertilizer, filth, flotsam, foam, folder, formation, froth, fusion, fuzz, garbage, garland, gimmick, glass, grime, grit, grounds, half-breed, hash, hodgepodge, hook, huddle, hybrid, imitation, innovation, invention, jalopy, junk, knickknack, lather, leftover, litter, manure, mess, mishmash, mix/mixture, novelty, oddity, odds and ends, offshoot, original, outgrowth, output, pack, pad, paper, pastiche, patchwork, pennant, placebo, poker, potpourri, preparation, quantum leap, refuse, remainder, remnant, replica, residue, rest, rubbish, scum, sediment, sewage, simulation, slime, sludge, smashup, solution, spin-off, stationery, surplus, talisman, trash, vestige, waste, web, work, wreath, wreck, yield

261 exhibition: appear, appearance, boast, brandish, declassify, demonstrate, demonstration, develop, display, evince, exhibit, exhibition, exhibitionism, expose, exposure, flash, flaunt, foreshadow, glitz, grandstand, impress, look, loom, manifest, mark, mount, parade, peep/peer, personify, point out, portend, posture, pout, present, presentation, produce, record, reflect, register, render, represent, show, show off, showpiece, sight, simplify, spectacle, sport, spotlight, strut, transpire, typify, uncover, unfold

262 musical instrument: accompaniment, arrangement, baton, bugle, compact disc, elegy, harmony, hymn, measure, medley, melody, meter, note, piece, requiem, score, song, strain

263 performance: anthem, aria, ballet, broadcasting, burlesque, carol, chant, character, comedy, composition, concert, drama, dramatization, enactment, event, extravaganza, farce, impression, lampoon, manuscript, medium, motion picture, movie, music, music hall, opus, part, performance, piece, play, premiere, presentation, preview, program, recital, recitation, rendition, repertory, role, satire, scene, scenery, script, set, setting, show, skit, stage, takeoff, theater/theatre

264 performance part: act, chorus, encore, epilogue, ovation, plot, prelude, recital, refrain, rehearsal, scene, snatch, stunt, tune

265 photograph: observe, photograph, portray, print, proof

COMMUNICATIONS

266 communication: address, ad-lib, answer, arrogate, audience, babble, back down, beam, bewail, bid, build up, call, carry, censor, chat, chatter, circumlocution, colloquy, commune, communicate, communication, contact, conversation, converse, correspond, debrief, digress, discourse, divide, drivel, effusion, E-mail, emit, exult, falter, gab, get, give, hush up, improvise, indicate, interact, intercourse, interplay, intervene, intrude, lecture, magnify, mince, monologue, oration, patter, prattle, punctuate, quash, quiet, rap, reach, read, recant, recapitulate, recitation, recite, recount, refuse, rehearse, reiterate, render, repartee, say, secrete, shoot the breeze, signify, silence, slant, speak, speech, stammer, stray, talk, taunt, telephone, tell, tête-a-tête, transmit, transpire, verbalize, wander, welcome, whisper, wing it, yak/yap

267 communicative quality: abusive, acerbity, acid, acidulous, acrid, acrimonious, ad-lib, ambiguous, amusing, apologetic, articulate, artless, behind one's back, biting, bitter, bluff, blunt, boastful, bombastic, brazen, brief, broken, brusque, candid, captious, caustic, censorious, chatty, classified, close, closemouthed, colloquial, communicative, complimentary, confidential, confidentially, convincing, courteous, crisp, critical, crude, cryptic, curt, cutting, cynical, debatable, defamatory, degrading, demonstrative, derisive, derogatory, descriptive, destructive, diffuse, direct, directly, dirty, disconnected, discursive, dishonest, disjointed, disrespectful, doctrinaire, dogmatic, droll, dry, effusive, eloquent, embittered, emphatic, encyclopedic, erroneous, et cetera, evasive, even, exaggerated, expansive, explanatory, explicit, expository, expressive, extemporaneous/extemporary, facetious, fallacious, false, falsely, farcical, fault-finding, feeble, fictitious, figurative, filthy, firm, firsthand, flaming, flatulent, flimsy, florid, flowery, fluent, forceful, forcible, foreign, forensic, forthright, foul, fractious, frank, frankly, fresh, fulsome, funny, fustian, gabby, garrulous, genuine, glib, glowing, grandiloquent, graphic, gross, grouchy, groundless, gruff, guileless, hackneyed, hard-line, harsh, hateful, heartfelt, heated, highfalutin, hollow, honest, honorable, humorous, hypercritical, hypocritical, idle, illogical, illustrative, imperative, imperious, implicit, implied, importunate, impromptu, improvised, imprudent, inarticulate, incisive, incoherent, indescribable, indicative, ineffable, inelegant, inexplicable, inflated, informative, ingenuous, inoffensive, insincere, insistent, insolent, instructive, insulting, ironic/ironical, jerrybuilt, jocular/jocose/jocund, jolly, keen, laconic, laudatory, laughable, legendary, legible, lengthy, libelous, lip service, literal, literally, literary, long-winded. loose, loquacious, lurid, lying, malicious, malign, matter-of-fact, mean, meaningful, meaty, mendacious, metaphorical, misleading, mordant, mouthy, mushy, musty, mythical/mythological, naked, nameless, narrative, natural, negative, noncommittal, oblique, obnoxious, obscene, offensive, offhand, off the cuff, off the record, oily, open, openhearted, openly, opinionated, opprobrious, oracular, oral, ornery, outspoken, overblown, overrated, parting, pejorative, penetrating, peppery, persuasive, pithy, plain, poetic, poignant, pointed, pompous, ponderous, pornographic, pregnant, priceless, private, privileged, privy, profane, prophetic, prosaic, public, pulp, pungent, quick-witted, quizzical, racy, rambling, redolent, reticent, rhetorical, ribald, rich, risqué, rough, round, rude, sacrilegious, sarcastic, satirical/satiric, saucy, scathing, scurrilous, secretive, secretly, sensational, sentimental, sharp, sharp-tongued, short, sidesplitting, significant, silent, simple, sincere, sincerely, smut, smutty, snappy, sneaky, snippy, speechless, spicy, spoken, square, stale, stilted, straight, straightforward, strained, succinct, suggestive, summary, symbolic, symptomatic, taciturn, talkative, tart, telltale, terse, threadbare, tongue-in-cheek, tongue-tied, transparent, trenchant, trite, truculent, true, truly, trumped up, trustworthy/trusty, truthful, unabridged, unanimous, unattached, uncivil, uncommunicative, unfounded, uninhibited, unintelligible, unsaid, untrue, untruthful, unvarnished, unwritten, vague, valedictory, veracious, verbal, verbatim, verbose, verbosity, vernacular, vicious, viperous, virulent, vocal, vociferous, voluble, vulgar, warm, warning, windy, witty, wordy, wry, X-rated, yellow, zany

268 description: appellation, deconstructionist, denotation, depiction, description, design, exposition, expression, formula, gloss, hermeneutical, history, hyperbole, identification, illustration, kudos, label, legend, moniker, name, news, nickname, nom de plume, notation, notes, obituary, ode, outline, paraphrase, pen name, plan, poem, poetry, portrait, profile, prose, pseudonym, sketch, sobriquet, surname, translation

269 devices used for: alarm, artificial intelligence, calculator, computer, copy, data processor, distress signal, downlink, fax, fire alarm, foghorn, personal computer, photocopy, smoke detector, software, telegram, telephone, transcript

270 document, part: addendum, advertisement, amendment, appendix, article, banner, body, chapter, clause, codicil, condition, entry, epilogue, excerpt, extract, feature, foreword, introduction, item, label, leaf, legend, margin, obituary, passage, preface, prologue, provision/proviso, rider, sheet, slip, sound bite, specification, stipulation, story, supplement, tab, tag, terms, text

271 document, physical object: act, affidavit, agreement, album, analysis, annal(s), Annie Oakley, annual, archive, article, balance sheet, bill, blueprint, book, bulletin, card, caricature, catalog/catalogue, certificate, chronicle, circular, commitment, compact, composition, concord, constitution, contract, convention, corpus, credentials, criticism, critique, declaration, deed, deposition, digest, diploma, direction(s), directive, dispatch, dissertation, docket, document, documentary, dossier, draft, drama, enclosure, entente, epistle, escrow, essay, explanation, exposition, facsimile, fiction, file, form, green card, guarantee, guideline, history, identification, injunction, journal, ledger, letter, life, line, log, mail, manifesto, manuscript, material, memoir, memorandum/memo, message, missive, monument, narrative, note/notes, notebook, notice, obloquy, opus, pact, pamphlet, paper/papers, paper, pass, passport, patent, permit, petition, piece, placard, plan, poker, policy, poster, proceedings, proclamation, promotion, pronouncement, proposal, prose, pyramid, reading, receipt, record, reference, release, reminder, résumé, satire, schedule, scheme, script, sequel, sign, statement, survey, telegram, theme, thesis, ticket, timetable, treatise, voucher, writing

272 document quality: readable, short, summary, terse

273 humorous tale: banter, chaff, crack, jest, joke, kid, lampoon, levity, parody, pleasantry, pun, quip, spoof, sport, take off, travesty, trick, wisecrack, wit

274 information: ace in the hole, admonition, advice, allusion, analysis, annotation, announcement, answer, back door, bit, broadcast, bulletin, buzz, byte, calendar, caution, cautionary tale, caveat, charge, clarification, clue, command, commitment, communication, confession, conjecture, construction, counsel, cybernetics, data, data bank, declaration, definition, dictate, digital library, direction(s), directive, dirt, disclosure, dope, evidence, excerpt, exhortation, explanation, exposé, fact, facts, freeware, gossip, grounds, groundwork, guidance, guide, guideline, herald, hint, hypermedia, illumination, indicator, information, instruction, intelligence, intimation, key, knowledge, lead, learning, lesson, light, lore, manifesto, material, message, minutiae, multimedia, news, notice, notification, on-line, particular, plug, point, pointer, prescription, prognosis, program, prompt, pronouncement, proof, publication, publicity, quotation/quote, reading, rebuttal, recipe, recommendation, reference, rejoinder, report, resolution, revelation, rumor, scholarship, science, scoop, scuttlebutt, secret, sign, small talk, sound bite, statement, story, telecast, tidings, tip/tipoff, trivia, tutelage, verification, warning, whisper, word

275 **integral language parts:** adjective, adverb, antonym, aphorism, bad form, banality, barbarism, buzzword, byword, cant, catchword, clause, cliché, computerese, euphemism, expletive, figure of speech, gobbledygook, grammar, idiom, jargon, metaphor, neologism, nomenclature, parlance, phrase, proverb, psychobabble, term, word

276 **language:** adage, adieu, alphabet, argot, code, computerese, dialect, diction, expression, gobbledygook, grammar, jargon, language, lexicon, lingo, nomenclature, patter, slang, speech, spiel, style, swearing, tongue, vernacular, vocabulary, voice

277 **media:** advertisement, banner, correspondence, criticism, desktop publishing, dispatch, infomercial, memorandum/memo, obloquy, pen, perjury, prattle, rebuttal, rejoinder, rhetoric, rumor, sarcasm, sass, screen, scuttlebutt, sensationalism, small talk, sound bite, spiel, television, terminology, translation, tripe, vehicle, video, videocassette

278 **object used in:** address, advertisement, alert, analogy, anathema, answer, aphorism, approach, assertion, assurance, axiom, babble, back talk, banner, banter, breath, bunk, call, cant, catchword, cause celebre, chat, chatter, claim, cliché, comeback, comment, commentary, commonplace, compliment, congratulations, contact, contention, contradiction, controversy, correspondence, criticism, cry, cue, curse, decision, declaration, defense, definition, derision, dialogue/dialog, dibs, dictum, digression, dirt, disapproval, dispatch, disputation, dispute, dissension, dissidence, dissonance, divination, double entendre, double standard, double-talk, dressing-down, drivel, edict, editorial, eloquence, embellishment, epigram, epilogue, epitaph, equivocation, eulogy, euphemism, exaggeration, exaltation, fabrication, falsehood, falsity, farewell, feedback, fib, figure of speech, flak, fulmination, gab, gibberish, gibe, goodbye, gossip, grace, gratitude, grievance, gripe, groan, guidance, harangue, hearsay, hiss, hocus-pocus, hogwash, honor, implication, impropriety, indication, indignity, innuendo, instruction, insult, invective, invention, invocation, irony, issue, knock, lament/lamentation, laurels, lecture, legerdemain, letter, lie, line, lip, litany, malediction, maxim, meaning, memorandum/memo, mention, missive,

mockery, monologue, moral, motif, motion, motto, mouth, negation, negative, notice, oath, obscenity, obsequy, observation, offense, offer, omen, oracle, oration, order, outcry, overtone, overture, password, patter, phrase, pitch, platform, platitude, plea, pleasantry, pledge, portent, praise, precursor, prediction, pretension, proclamation, profanity, profession, projection, promise, pronouncement, propaganda, prophecy, proverb, puff, pun, put-down, quip, quotation/quote, rebuff, rebuke, recommendation, reference, refusal, regards, remark, reminder, rendition, reply, report, reprimand, respects, response, retort, return, rhetoric, rhyme, rot, rubbish, rumor, sarcasm, saying, scandal, sermon, shadow, slam, slander, slogan, slur, statement, story, suggestion, swearing, tale, talk, testimonial, testimony, thanks, theme, threat, tirade, toast, translation, trash, tribute, truth, utterance, vehicle, veracity, verbiage, voice, vow, welcome, whisper, wind, word, wording

279 **organization:** bandwidth, ghetto box, media, newsletter, newspaper, radar, radio, tabloid, television

280 **publication:** advertisement, almanac, anthology, article, authority, autobiography, bible, bill, biography, book, brochure, canon, cartoon, catalog/catalogue, daybook, dictionary, directory, edition, erotica, fiction, glossary, guidebook, handbook, issue, journal, journalism, ledger, lexicon, literature, magazine, manual, memoir, newsletter, newspaper, novel, organ, pamphlet, paper, periodical, press, print, publication, publicity, reference, release, review, romance, satire, tabloid, text, textbook, thesaurus, tome, treatise, vocabulary, volume

281 **record:** annal(s), archive, calendar, dossier, itinerary, list, program, record, register, roll, roster

282 **story:** account, allegory, anecdote, biography, chronicle, documentary, epic, fable, fib, fiction, folklore, legend, lore, memoir, mystery, myth, mythology, narration, narrative, ode, old wives' tale, parable, phenomenology, plot, poem, poetry, report, saga, scenario, story, tale, verse, version, yarn

283 **summary:** abbreviation, abridgement, abstract, agenda, annotation, bill, breakdown, brief, caption, census, citation, compendium, condensation, daybook, diagnosis, diary, directory, epitome, heading, inscription, inventory, menu, moral, precis, profile, program, prospectus, report, résumé, return, review, roster, rundown, scenario, schedule, sketch, summary, syllabus, synopsis, table, tally, timetable, title

284 **symbol:** arms, augury, autograph, badge, beep, brand, capital, character, charm, check, code, crest, cue, decal, device, dot, emblem, emoticon, ensign, exponent, flag, fleck, flourish, font, graffiti, hallmark, handwriting, harbinger, herald, impression, imprint, index, indication, insignia, John Hancock, label, landmark, lead, letter, line, logo, mark, notation, note, numeral, placard, script, seal, sign, signal, spot, stamp, stripe, symbol, tag, talisman, tick, token, trademark, tread, type, vestige, writing

EDUCATION

285 educate: address, break in, breed, care, catechize, coach, domesticate, drill, educate, education, form, ground, illuminate, inculcate, indoctrinate, initiate, instill, instruct, instruction, lesson, orate, orator, oratory, preach, preparation, school, speak, speech, talk, teach, teaching, train, training, tutelage, tutor

286 education level: class, grade, level, rating

287 objects used in: academia, class, college, course, dissertation, edification, education, erudition, lesson, lore, preschool, school, teaching, tenure, text, textbook, thesis, tuition

288 organization: academia, academy, alma mater, class, college, enrollment, faculty, institute/institution, school

289 place of: academy, alma mater, class, college, preschool, school

290 test: acid test, assay, audition, criterion, dissection, drill, examination, exercise, experiment, guinea pig, index, inquest, inquiry, inspection, investigation, probation, probe, quiz, reconnaissance, test, trial, weight, workout

291 testing: fiddle, grade, pace, plumb, survey, test, trial, try, try on/try out, verify

ENTERTAINMENT

292 action: act, acting, amuse, amusement, antic, appear, arrange, bet, bill, broadcast, cruise, dance, diversion, dramatize, emote, enact, enactment, entertain, featuring, feign, game, host, hype, impersonate, interpret, issue, overplay, pageant, parody, perform, play, prance, pretend, preview, produce, publication, publicize, put on, regale, rehearsal, rehearse, relaxation, revel, romp, score, sing, spotlight, stage, takeoff, take off, tape, televise, translator, transmit, travesty, trifle, weatherperson

293 object: absent-mindedness, auditorium, balloon, bet, broadcast, broadcasting, butt, cinema, circus, comedy, disco, distraction, drama, dramatization, elegy, extravaganza, farce, film, firecracker, fireworks, humor, lounge, medium, motion picture, movie, movie hall, news, nightclub, picture, publicity, red herring, sensation, sequel, show, sight, song, telecast, television, theater/theatre, video, videocassette

294 organization: band, cast, chorus, corps, ensemble, following, gallery, orchestra

FAMILY

295 child raising: au pair, baby, baby-sit, breed, bring up, care, coddle, cradle, cultivate, daycare, form, foster, mind, mollycoddle, nanny, nourish, nurse, nursemaid, nurture, pamper, raise, rear, spoon-feed, support, tend

296 family: aristocracy, birth, blood, bride, bridegroom, brood, clan, class, consanguinity, court, descendant, descent, doll, extraction, family, family tree, folk, folks, genealogy, heritage, house, household, issue, kin, kindred, kinship, line, lineage, mate, offspring, origin, pedigree, people, posterity, progeny, rank, relation, stock, strain, tribe

297 marriage: annul, annulment, betroth, betrothal, couple, desert, desertion, divorce, elope, engage, engagement, espouse, estrange, estrangement, jilt, marriage, marry, match, mate, matrimony, nuptials, part, parting, polygamy, propose, rupture, separate, separation, sever, split, vow, wed, wedding, wedlock, woo

GOVERNMENT AND POLITICS

298 government action: abdicate, abolish, abolition, accession, administer, administration, amnesty, bust, cease-fire, colonization, command, decriminalize, depose, deposition, dethrone, displace, dominate, enact, enforce, enforcement, exile, expulsion, filibuster, legalize, override/overrule, pass, reign, rule, run in, secede, second, surveillance, tax, truce, veto

299 government organization: administration, ally, cabinet, capitalism, capitol, chamber, confederacy, congress, cop, council, court, delegation, democracy, deregulation, dictatorship, direction, empire, fascism, government, house, jury, legislature, police/police officer, post, regime, rule, sovereignty, tribunal, tyranny

300 political action: amnesty, arbitrate, arbitration, ballot, campaign, canvass, crusade, demonstrate, demonstration, displace, drive, drum up, elect, election, endorse, lobby, mutiny, nominate, nomination, patronage, picket, politics, poll, protest, reaction, rebellion, revolt, revolution, riot, run, sedition, vote

301 political organization: alliance, ballot, caucus, commonwealth, communism, confederacy, delegation, faction, fascism, machine, party, politics, side, socialism, tyranny

HEALTH

302 birth: bear, birth, breed, childbirth, conception, delivery, spring

303 change in: ache, black out, come down with, faint, fit, look up, mend, pull through, recover, recuperate, remission, repel, swoon, weary

304 death: abort, abortion, curtains, death, decease, demise, die, dissolution, end, expiration, expire, fatality, mortician, mortuary, pass away, passing, perish, undertaker

305 deathplace: boneyard, cemetery, crypt, grave, graveyard, mausoleum, monument, necropolis, tomb

306 disease: abscess, affliction, AIDS, ailment, bacteria, blight, bug, cancer, canker, carpal tunnel syndrome, complaint, condition, contagion, contamination, cyst, diarrhea, disease, disorder, epidemic, germ, growth, illness, impurity, indigestion, infection, infirmity, inflammation, malady, microbe, microorganism, pest, pestilence, pimple, plague, rash, sexually transmitted disease, sickness, spell, swelling, symptom, syndrome, tantrum, virus, zit

307 drug: acid, amphetamine, analgesic, anesthetic/anaesthetic, angel dust, antibiotic, antidote, antiseptic, antitoxin, balm, capsule, cocaine, condom, contraceptive, cure, dope, dose, drug, elixir, hashish, herbicide, heroin, laxative, LSD, marijuana, medicine/medication, narcotic, nostrum, opium, painkiller, panacea, pick-me-up, pill, poison, pot, potion, prescription, remedy, sedative, stimulant, stimulus, tablet, tonic, toxin, vaccination

308 event: abort, abortion, ache, attack, cardiac arrest, catch, contract, convulsion, cough, cramp, crick, faint, gag, gargle, heal, heart attack, massage, nauseate, palpitate, paroxysm, pass out, perk up, rubdown, rupture, seizure, spell, spew, stroke, suffer, swoon, take, throw up, tic, vomit, wheeze

309 injury: abrasion, abscess, affliction, bite, blister, boil, boo boo, bruise, concussion, contusion, corrosion, cut, damage, defect, detriment, disability, disadvantage, disservice, fracture, gash, harm, incision, inflammation, injury, laceration, lesion, prick, puncture, rip, rupture, rust, scratch, shock, stab, swelling, welt, wound

310 medical action: alter, analyze, autopsy, bandage, castrate, cure, diagnose, dissection, doctor, dope, dress, drug, ease, examination, heal, inject, inoculation, malpractice, massage, operate, operation, plastic surgery, postmortem, practice, remedy, rubdown, therapy, tranquilize, transplant, treat, treatment, vaccinate

311 medical instruments: bandage, cure, elixir, emollient, injection, liniment, lotion, matter, moisturizer, nostrum, ointment, panacea, prescription, remedy, salve, staff, x-ray

312 medical organization: asylum, clinic, delivery room, emergency room, headquarters, hospital, laboratory, loony bin, madhouse, mental hospital, nursing home, nut house, office

313 pain: ache, afflict, anesthesia/anaesthesia, discomfort, distress, gripe, harassment, harm, hurt, itch, pinch, sting, strain, stress, suffer, torment, torture, wound, wrong

314 quality of: able-bodied, adaptive, ailing, anemic, bad, bedridden, benign, better, burning, catching, clean, communicable, congenital, contagious, convalescent, crippled, curable, curative, delicate, disabled, diseased, ditsy, dizzy, doddering, done in, drugged, drunk, dysfunctional, epidemic, excruciating, faint, febrile, fit, full-blooded, game, genetic, giddy, gory, green around the gills, groggy, haggard, hale, hardy, healthy, hearty, high, hurt, ill, immune, incapacitated, indisposed, inebriated, infectious, infirm, insane, invalid, irreparable, lame, light-headed, low, lusty, malignant, mental, morbid, nauseating, nauseous, neurotic, normal, out cold, palsied, paralytic, peaked, pestilent/pestiential, plastered, pooped, poor, poorly, queasy, queer, right, robust, rocky, rugged, rundown, safe, salutary, sane, senile, sick, sickly, sinewy, slaphappy, soft, solvent, sore, sound, soused, spent, squeamish, stoned, strong, sturdy, tender, terminal, tired, tough, trim, tuckered out, unconscious, unfeeling, unharmed, unhealthy, unscathed, unsound, unwell, vertigo, vigorous, wan, wasted, weak, weary, well, whole, wholesome, woozy, zoned

315 sleep: anesthesia/anaesthesia, asleep, awake, coma, doze, drop off, hibernate, insomnia, languor, lassitude, lethargy, nap, nightmare, nod, quiet, rest, sleep, sleepy, slumber, snooze, snore, somnolent, stupor

316 state of: ache, addiction, ailment, apoplexy, beat, collapse, complaint, condition, cough, debility, dementia, disability, dislocation, eating disorder, epidemic, faint, fatigue, fitness, form, gestation, hangover, headache, health, hurt, hygiene, ill, immunity, implode, insanity, lapse, madness, malaise, maternity, mental illness, nausea, neurosis, pain, paroxysm, pestilence, pink, shape, stupor, substance abuse, symptom, syndrome, tone, trim, trouble, tumor, vigor, welfare/wellbeing

LEGAL

317 legal action: absolve, acquit, acquittal, action, adjudicate, adopt, adoption, annul, annulment, apprehend, apprehension, arraign, arrest, bear witness, bequeath, book, bring, bust, charge, cite, collar, commute, condemn, condemnation, convict, conviction, counsel, covenant, cross-examine, cut off, decree, decriminalize, detain, detention, disinherit, enact, enforce, enforcement, evidence, excommunicate, exculpate, exonerate, extradite, hearing, impeach, imprison, incarcerate, indict, indictment, inherit, insure, jail, judge, leave, legalize, let off, lift, litigate, moderate, nab, nail, ordain, outlaw, override/overrule, pardon, pass, perjure, pick up, pinch, plead, practice, prohibit, proscribe, prosecute, pull in, put away, raid, rap, repeal, represent, reprieve, rescind, run in, sentence, sing, sortie, substantiate, sue, testify, transport, trial, try, validate, verify, vindicate, vitiate, vouch, waive, will, witness

318 objects used in legal practice: acquittal, act, affidavit, article, bail, bar, bench, bequest, bill, bond, brief, canon, case, claim, code, constitution, court, debenture, decree, deed, deposition, dibs, dictate, easement, enactment, entreaty, evidence, indictment, injunction, inquest, institute, insurance, jury, law, lawsuit, legislation, libel, litigation, mandate, measure, ordinance, paper/papers, pardon, passage, patent, plea, pledge, precept, prescription, principle, regulation, repeal, reprieve, ruling, sentence, statute, stipulation, subpoena, suit, terms, testament, testimonial, testimony, tribunal, verdict, waiver, will, writ

319 quality of law: administrative, authoritarian, authoritative, autocratic, canonical, clear, constitutional, contraband, democratic, effectual, egalitarian, exempt, forensic, free, high-handed, illegal, illegitimate, illicit, inadmissible, judicial, just, kosher, lawful, lawless, legal, legislative, legitimate, misbegotten, on the level, permissible, punitive, unauthorized, unconstitutional, unlawful, unprejudiced, valid, wrongful

MILITARY

320 military action: action, aggression, barrage, blitz, blow up, campaign, conflict, contest, coup d'état, defeat, deploy, depose, deposition, descent, dethrone, detonation, disarm, disarmament, draft, electioneering, engage, engagement, enlist, explode, explosion, fire, incursion, induct, induction, insurrection, invade, invasion, maneuver, mobilize, occupation, occupy, offensive, oppression, overthrow, rally, rebellion, recruit, revolt, revolution, salute, service, station, surrender, volley, war, warfare

321 object used by military: armory, barracks, battery, battlefield, citadel, defense, draft, fort/fortress, garrison, magazine, post, rampart, service

322 organization: ally, army, artillery, battalion, brigade, cavalry, corps, defense, detachment, detail, enemy, fleet, flotilla, force, legion, military, navy, ordnanace, platoon, squad, troop/troops

MONETARY AND FINANCIAL AFFAIRS

323 association: association, black market, board, cartel, conglomerate, establishment, federation, firm, grocery store, industry, mall, market/mart, merger, patronage, stock market, syndicate, trust

324 business action: advertise, advertising, annexation, appear, appointment, auction, aviation, cashier, commercialize, commission, conclave, conference, consultation, convene, convention, cry, cut a deal, deal, dealings, deficit spending, depression, dictate, discharge, dismiss, drudge, enterprise, exchange, export, farm, farming, fold, gathering, hold, hype, incorporate, intercourse, malpractice, management, manufacture/manufacturing, market, mediate, mediation, meet, meeting, merge, merger, monopolize, operation, patronage, patronize, pioneer, popularize, position, powwow, practice, produce, project, promote, promotion, proposal, publicize, puff, push, put up, sale, seal, second, seminar, service, session, shake up, shut, sit, slavery, specialize, step in, stock, symposium, table, trade, traffic, transact, transaction, truck, undertaking, wait on

325 business organization: agency, airport, association, bakery, bar, branch, bureau, bureaucracy, business, cartel, clientele, commerce, company, concern, conglomerate, corporation, council, department store, direction, dispensation, enterprise, establishment, exchange, field, firm, house, industry, labor, mall, management, operation, outfit, partner-

ship, personnel, practice, red tape, regime, ring, singles bar, staff, store, syndicate, trust, union

326 business quality: accomplished, ambitious, businesslike, busy, careful, concentrated, diligent, discipline, eager, earnest, enterprising, grasping, greedy, methodical/methodic, miserly, ordered, orderly, painstaking, penurious, persistent, possessive, practical, professional, proper, purposeful, rapacious, regular, relentless, stingy, tenacious, tightfisted, up-and-coming, zealous

327 buying: buy, charge, lavish, lay out, order, patronize, pay, procure, purchase, redeem, shop, shortchange, shower, splurge, spree, squander, take, trade, traffic, treat, truck

328 cost: appraisal, cost, expense

329 fee: amount, bet, bill, bribe, charge, commission, damage(s), debt, duty, excise, expense, fare, fee, invoice, levy, obligation, overhead, pay, price, rate, rent, revenue, stake, surcharge, tab, tariff, tax, toll, wager

330 financial action: assess, audit, bank, bargain, bet, bid, bidding, bill, bring, bring in, budget, bust, cash, charge, deduct, deficit, deficit spending, deposit, depress, depression, devalue, dicker, discount, earn, economize, economy, endorse, fail, frugality, gross, hock, insure, invest, investment, levy, liquidate, mutual fund, net, pawn, pay, pinch, price, profit, realize, return, salt away, save, scrape, scrimp, shop, skimp, speculate, speculation, stake, stint, subsist, trade, traffic, transact, transaction, truck, venture

331 financial document: account, agreement, book, coupon, entente, reckoning, return, statement

332 financial object: account, adjustment, arrears, assessment, asset(s), backing, bail, balance, balance sheet, bargain, bill, bonanza, budget, capital, cheap, draft, equity, fund, insurance, interest, investment, invoice, liability, loan, lucre, means, mortgage, mutual fund, order, overhead, patronage, pawn, pay, pay dirt, pension, pledge, principal, profit, quotation/quote, receipt, revenue, score, stock, tightfisted, treasure, voucher

333 financial organization: bank, board, grocery store, mall, market/mart, stock market

334 financial quality: affluent, balanced, bankrupt, behind, broke, bush league, charitable, cheap, close, comfortable, commercial, complimentary, costly, cushy, dear, depressed, destitute, disadvantaged, disadvantageous, down-and-out, due, economic, economical, exorbitant, expensive, extravagant, fat, financial, finished, fiscal, flush, free, frugal, gainful, generous, ghetto, gold mine, good, grasping, gratis, gratuitous, high, humble, impecunious, impoverished, improvident, indebted, indigent, inexpensive, insolvent, invaluable, lavish, liberal, liquid, low, lucrative, marketable, mean, miserly, modest, monetary, moneyed, moneymaking, munificent, narrow, needy, net, nominal, on the house, opulent, outstanding, overdue, owing, palatial, paltry, parsimonious, patrician, payable, pecuniary, penniless, penurious, plush, poor, posh, poverty-stricken, precious, priceless, privileged, prodigal, profitable, profligate, prohibitive, prosperous, provident, rich, second-rate/second-class, self-sufficient, skimpy, sleazy, sordid, sparing, splendid, squalid, steep, stingy, strapped, substantial, sumptuous, tawdry, thrifty, thriving, tight, underprivileged, unfortunate, unpaid, unreasonable, unsettled, used, valuable, valued, wealthy, well-bred, well-off, well-to-do

335 **financial state:** afford, arrears, avarice, bankruptcy, boom, bring, circumstances, credit, cutback, default, deficit, depression, devalue, discount, economy, extravagance, fail, fortune, frugality, hyperinflation, inadequacy, individual retirement account, inflation, IRA, living, misery, need, obligation, owe, pageantry, panic, paucity, pile, pomp, poverty, prosperity, recession, riches, savings, shortfall, slum, slump, squalor, substance, thrift, traffic, value, worth

336 **financial value state:** cost, decline, downturn, expense, value

337 **gift:** acquisition, allowance, alms, arrival, atonement, award, balm, benefit, bequest, bonanza, bonus, boon, booty, bounty, charity, citation, comfort, commendation, compensation, contribution, courtesy, decoration, diploma, dispensation, dividend, dole, donation, due, endowment, extravagance, find, freebie, fruit, fundraiser, gain, gem, gift, godsend, good, grant, gratuity, haul, heirloom, honor, indulgence, inheritance, laurels, legacy, loot, luxury, medal, memento, memorabilia, memorial, offering, philanthropy, plum, premium, present, presentation, prize, purse, recognition, remembrance, reparation, reward, scholarship, souvenir, spoils, subsidy, token, treasure, trophy, windfall

338 **merchandise:** bargain, cargo, commodity, consignment, contraband, fabrication, freight, goods, hardware, harvest, haul, inventory, line, load, merchandise, order, product, stock, truck, turnout, wares, yield

339 **monetary container:** bag, bank, purse, satchel, till, treasury

340 **money:** ace in the hole, advance, affluence, allowance, appropriation, asset(s), bill, bread, cash, change, chicken feed, chips, coin, contribution, currency, deposit, dollar, donation, dough, endowment, estate, finances, financing, fund, funds, income, individual retirement account, investment, IRA, loot, lucre, maintenance, means, mint, money, offering, opulence, pay, payback, pile, pool, recompense, refund, reserve, resource, resources, return, riches, savings, support, sustenance, wealth

341 **money giving:** advance, blow, buy, compensate, disburse, discharge, endow, expend, finance, fritter, fund, invest, lavish, lay out, misappropriate, patronage, patronize, pay, play, ransom, recompense, refund, reimburse, remit, remunerate, repay, requite, reward, satisfy, settle, shell out, spend, sponsor, square, subscribe, subsidize, support, underwrite

342 **money taking:** bill, blackmail, bleed, clear, collect, extort, extortion, fine, fleece, recoup, squeeze

343 **ownership part:** hold, owner, possession, proprietor

344 **payment:** advance, alimony, bounty, collateral, commission, compensation, consideration, cut, deal, debt, deficit spending, deposit, disbursement, discharge, dividend, dole, draft, dues, earnings, equity, expenditure, expense, fee, financing, gain, graft, grant, gratuity, gross, income, installment, interest, kickback, outlay, pay, pay dirt, payment, penalty, pension, perk, perquisite, pittance, premium, prize, proceeds, profit, purse, raise, ransom, rebate, receipts, recompense, redress, refund, reparation, restitution, revenue, reward, safety net, salary, satisfaction, scholarship, stake, stipend, subsidy, surcharge, take, tip, upkeep, wage/wages

345 **selling:** auction, bazaar, charge, handle, market, merchandise, peddle, sale, sell, solicit, trade, traffic, truck

346 **value state:** appreciation, benefit, decline, downturn, import, importance, mark, quality, value, worth

PROFESSIONS

347 **business manager:** administrator, banker, best shot, boss, bureaucrat, businessperson, capitalist, captain, chief, commander, conductor, dealer, director, distributor, emir, emperor, employer, empress, entrepreneur, establishment, executive, farmer, financier, flagship, founder, front runner, hawker, head, huckster, impresario, investor, landlord, leader, magnate, manager, master, merchant, mogul, mover and shaker, notable, officer, official, overseer, owner, pacesetter, peasant, president, prime minister, principal, professional, proprietor, ringleader, seller, shopkeeper, specialist, storekeeper, superintendent, superior, supervisor, taskmaster, tycoon, upstart, warden

348 **businessperson:** abettor, accountant, adjutant, adviser/advisor, agent, aid/aide, analyst, announcer, applicant, apprentice, arbitrator, archaeologist, architect, assistant, associate, astronaut, attendant, auditor, author, authority, aviator, baker, banker, barber, bean counter, bearer, body guard, broker, builder, businessperson, butcher, buyer, caregiver, caretaker, carpenter, cartoonist, cashier, chair, chairperson, chef, clerk, client, collaborator, colleague, commuter, computer geek, connection, conservator, consultant, consumer, cook, correspondent, courier, court, craftsperson, creator, critic, curator, custodian, customer, cyberpunk, dabbler, deputy, desk jockey, detective, developer, devil's advocate, disc jockey, drudge, emissary, employee, engineer, envoy, epicure, espionage, expert, explorer, farmer, fellow, financier, flier, floozy, flyer, fortune-teller, fountainhead, freshman, friend, gatekeeper, go-between, gofer, gourmet, groom, guard, guide, guru, hack, hacker, hairdresser, hand, harlot, hawker, help, helper, henchman, hooker, housekeeper, huckster, hussy, inferior, informant/informer, innovator, inspector, intermediary, interviewer, inventor, investigator,

jailer, janitor, journalist, labor, laborer, liaison, lobbyist, machine, mariner, maverick, mediator, messenger, middle person, miser, model, moderator, mole, monitor, narrator, navigator, negotiator, newsman/woman, novice, opposition, originator, page, partner, patron, peasant, peddler, peon, picket, pilot, pioneer, playwright, poet, porter, practitioner, private eye, prodigal, professional, protégé, proxy, rat, recruit, referee, reporter, representative, researcher, reviewer, rider, rival, rookie, sailor, salesperson, scout, seafarer, seaman/woman, secretary, seller, sentinel, serf, servant, shopper, skinflint, slave, sleuth, snitch, snoop, speaker, spendthrift, spokesperson, sponsor, spy, stool pigeon, subordinate, surrogate, tailor, tenant, tightwad, tool, traveler, umpire, underling, vendor, virtuoso, watchkeeper, wayfarer, weasel, wizard, worker, writer, yuppie

349 discipline: affair, anatomy, anthropology, appointment, archaeology, architecture, arithmetic, art, astronomy, board, botany, browser, bulletin board, career, chat room, cinema, communications, cybernetics, cyberspace, demography, department, discipline, domain, employment, ergonomics, field, geography, hermeneutics, journalism, lifework, line, livelihood, logic, mathematics, matter, metier, occupation, orbit, passion, phenomenology, philosopher, philosophy, poetry, position, press, project, province, psychology, pursuit, realm, research, scene, school, science, scientist, semiotics, specialty, sphere, stage, station, territory, trade, undertaking, vocation, walk, work

350 educator: academic, adviser/advisor, alumnus/alumna, brain, coach, college student, conductor, consultant, cretin, dean, disciplinarian, educator, egghead, expert, faculty, fountainhead, freshman, genius, graduate, guru, half-wit, instructor, intellectual, inventor, learner, maharishi, martinet, master, mastermind, mentor, monitor, novice, practitioner, principal, professor, pupil, rookie, sage, savant, scholar, school, student, swami, teacher, trainer, tutor, wonk

351 employment: ax/axe, bounce, can, collaborate, commission, demote, discharge, dismiss, dismissal, earn, elevate, elevation, employ, employment, engage, fire, gross, headhunting, hire, interview, job, kick out, labor, layoff, lay off, live, livelihood, living, make, metier, occupation, office, oust, pay, picket, post, promote, promotion, raise, reinstate, relieve, resign, resignation, retain, retire, rise, sack, situation, spot, station, strike, suspend, work

352 entertainer: acrobat, actor, actress, adherent, aficionado, artist, ballet dancer, buff, character, comedian, comic, connoisseur, creator, dancer, director, diva, fan, fanatic, fledgling, follower, freak, geek, groupie, hero/heroine, host, humorist, idol, inventor, joker, luminary, lyricist, magician, mimic, minion, musician, name, notable, originator, paparazzi, participant, personage/personality, photographer, player, prima donna, protagonist, singer, star, thespian, troubadour, usher, virtuoso, wit, zany

353 financier: accountant, banker, bean counter, bearer, broker, financier, investor, spendthrift

354 government officer: administrator, ally, ambassador, arbiter, authoritarian, authority, autocracy, autocrat, bureaucrat, conqueror, consul, cop, delegate, deputy, despot, dictator, diplomat, disciplinarian, emir, emperor, empress, envoy, establishment, executive, exile, expatriate, fascist, figure, figurehead, flagship, front runner, governor, informant/informer, inhabitant, intermediary, justice, leader, legislator, liaison, lobbyist, magistrate, martinet, master, minister, mogul, monarch, mouthpiece, negotiator, officer, official, oppressor, pacesetter, page, patrol, peacemaker, personage/personality, police/police officer, potentate, prime minister, rat, representative, ringleader, snitch, sovereign, spokesperson, stool pigeon, tyrant, weasel

355 legal practitioner: attorney, bench, beneficiary, consul, counsel, counselor, heir, investigator, judge, jurist, lawyer, notary, officer, party, proponent, successor, witness

356 media person: commentator, interviewer, journalist, narrator, newsman/woman, press, reporter, writer

357 medical practitioner: analyst, doctor, druggist, healer, nurse, paramedic, patient, pharmacist, physician, psychiatrist, researcher, specialist, therapist

358 military person: combatant, commander, conqueror, deserter, fighter, GI, gladiator, guerrilla, lookout, mercenary, militant, officer, patrol, private, recruit, sailor, scout, seafarer, seaman/woman, soldier, truant, veteran, warmonger, warrior

359 politician: advocate, ally, anarchist, apostate, apostle, applicant, arbitrator, backer, bigot, candidate, conservative, demagogue, diehard, diplomat, dissident, donor, extremist, fanatic, firebrand, free spirit, hostage, iconoclast, idealist, insurgent, militant, misfit, mouthpiece, nominee, nonconformist, partisan, patron, perfectionist, picket, politician, proponent, protagonist, racist, radical, reactionary, rebel, refugee, renegade, sectarian, spokesperson, warmonger

360 profession: business, calling, career, craft, employment, finance, hacker, job, labor, lifework, line, livelihood, mission, occupation, place, position, profession, psychology, science, situation, trade, vocation, walk, work

361 religious person: acolyte, agnostic, angel, apostle, atheist, believer, chaplain, clergyperson, conformist, convert, creator, cynic, deacon, disciple, doubter, doubting Thomas, dreamer, enchantress, evangelism, evangelist, father, femme fatale, genie, hermit, inventor, layperson, loner, magician, minister, missionary, monk, nun, pagan, parson, pastor, preacher, priest, prophet, saint, shaman, skeptic, sorcerer, visionary, warlock, witch, witch doctor, wizard

362 task: affair, assignment, bee, berth, chore, commission, concern, drudgery, duty, effort, enterprise, errand, exercise, exertion, function, grind, groove, job, labor, mission, office, part, picnic, post, project, province, realm, research, role, routine, scientist, spot, stint, sweat, task, tax, toil, undertaking, work

RECREATION

363 action: acrobatics, aerobics/aerobic, angle, athletics, basketball, boating, bowl, boxing, bunt, championship, chance, coach, competition, contest, cruise, dance, deal, defeat, dissipation, diversion, engage, event, exercise, fish, fishing, gamble, gambol, game, gymnastics, hike, hobby, hunt, keep up, lay, leisure, lottery, marathon, match, meet, meeting, mess around, oppose, pastime, pit, play, race, raffle, recreation, rehearsal, rehearse, relaxation, rivalry, rout, shuffle, speculate, speculation, sport, stake, swim, tournament, trifle, turn, vacation, venture, vie, wager, win, workout

364 objects used in: amusement, avocation, bicycle, club, equipment, field, game, gymnasium, hobby, holiday, lap, motorcycle, point, pool, raffle, recreation, round, score, standoff, tie, wager

365 organization: conference, field, league, side, squad, team

366 participants: abolitionist, adherent, aficionado, amateur, aspirant, athlete, aviator, champion, coach, competitor, contestant, dabbler, dark horse, doozy, entrant, entry, fan, fanatic, fighter, fledgling, follower, freak, geek, gladiator, groupie, hacker, jock, mariner, master, minion, moderator, name, observer, opponent, opposition, participant, pedestrian, pitcher, player, prima donna, referee, rival, sailor, spectator, star, umpire, underdog, victor, winner

RELIGIOUS

367 action: anoint, apotheosis, baptism, baptize, bless, blessing, burial, bury, canonize, christen, communion, consecrate, dedicate, dedication, defect, defection, deify, distillation, enshrine, entomb, excommunicate, exorcism, inter, interment, penance, pray, prayer, preach, purification, purify, wake, witchcraft, worship

368 objects used in: abbey, beads, bible, boneyard, casket, cathedral, cemetery, church, cloister, coffin, convent, deity, denomination, divinity, faith, grace, holiness, invocation, litany, liturgy, monastery, mosque, necropolis, nunnery, pulpit, religion, requiem, sanctity, sanctuary, sermon, service, shrine, synagogue, temple

369 organization: church, clergy, congregation, cult, Jewish, parish, priesthood

370 supernatural: abracadabra, alchemy, angel, apparition, black magic, bottomless, deep space, deity, demon, devil, divinity, Eden, elf, eternity, fairy, fat city, galaxy, ghost, ghoul, goblin, god, heaven, hell, hereafter, hex, hobgoblin, incantation, incubus, inferno, leprechaun, Lucifer, magic, monster, necromancy, paradise, perdition, phantom, pixie, poltergeist, presence, purgatory, saint, Satan, savior, shade, Shangri-la, sorcery, specter,

spell, spirit, universe, utopia, vision, voodoo, whammy, witchcraft, Xanadu

SEX AND REPRODUCTION

371 attribute of gender: female, femininity/feminine, he-man, machismo, macho, male, masculinity/masculine, virility, womanly

372 attribute of sexuality: AC-DC, adulterous, amatory, amorous, androgynous, aphrodisiac, bisexual, carnal, celibate, chaste, close, desirable, erotic, femininity/feminine, fertile, fertility, fleshly, gay, homosexual, horny, hot, kinky, lascivious, lecherous, lewd, libidinous, licentious, loose, lothario, loving, masculinity/masculine, nasty, naughty, obscene, passion, passionate, peccadillo, pornographic, pornography, potent, promiscuous, provocative, prurient, pure, raunchy, raw, salicious, seductive, sensual, sensuous, sexual, sexy, smut, smutty, spicy, suggestive, sultry, thought-provoking, torrid, vice, virgin/virginal, virile, virility, voluptuous, vulgar, wanton, womanly, X-rated

373 birth: bear, birth, breed, childbirth, conception, delivery, spring

374 child bearing: beget, deliver, delivery, fertilize, generate, generation, get, have, labor, multiply, procreate, produce, propagate, reproduce, spawn

375 sex act: affair, alter, assignation, birth control, caress, climax, cohabit, conception, copulate, coquet, couple, cuddle, dalliance, dally/dally with, debauch, deflower, enamor, fertilize, flirt, flirtation, fondle, foreplay, fornicate, fornication, hug, impregnate, intercourse, kiss, love, love affair, lovemaking, mate, molest, necking, pass, paw, pet, proposition, rape, ravish, romance, seduce, sex, sexual assault, sin, smooch, tryst, violate, violation, woo

SOCIAL INTERACTIONS

376 authority: aegis, agency, agent, ascendancy/ascendency, auspices, authority, blabbermouth, carte blanche, censorship, chair, chairperson, chief, choice, civil rights, claim, clearance, cogency, command, connoisseur, control, curb, custody, dominance, domination, dominion, duty, ease, empire, franchise, green card, immunity, impunity, independence, jurisdiction, justice, leadership, leave, office, option, permission, permit, power, prerogative, privilege, rate, reign, right, rule, station, supremacy, sway, title, trust, voice, vote, warrant

377 celebration: acclamation, affair, banquet, baptism, carnival, celebrate, celebration, commemorate, commemoration, commencement, entertain, fair, fanfare, feast, festival, festivity, fete, fiesta, gaiety, gala, have a ball, jamboree, keep, observance, observe, orgy, pageant, pageantry, parade, pomp, rally, revel, revelry, rite, sacrament, splurge, spree, wake, wassail

378 class: branch, brand, breed, caste, category, class, classification, cut, denomination, description, division, echelon, estate, family, folks, form, genre/genus, gradation, grade, ilk, kind, manner, mob, model, mold, nature, nobility, order, position, quality, rabble, rank, rating, riffraff, sort, species, stock, third world, tier, type, variety, world

379 community: colony, commune, community, constituency, country, folk, hoi polloi, neighborhood, people, population, public, society

380 ethnic group: nationality, people, race, strain, tribe

381 organization: affiliate, affiliation, agency, apparatus, assembly, bar, brigade, coalition, combination, commission, committee, council, crew, crowd, department, federation, foundation, fraternity, guild, institute/institution, Internet, league, membership, movement, network, organization, panel, partnership, party, ring, sect, society, union

382 part of a group: chapter, division, plurality, sect

383 party: affair, bash, blowout, dance, entertainment, festivity, gala, masquerade, orgy, party, reception, shindig, show business, tear

384 social action: abuse, accept, advance(s), adventure, amends, amuse, appeal, appointment, associate, befriend, betray, bite, blackball, blooper, booking, bounce, break the ice, caper, carouse, cavort, cohabit, collaborate, come upon, commemorate, compel, conclave, conduct, consort, cool, coquet, court, cower, cultivate, cut up, disaffect, discriminate, disgrace, disobey, disorganize, dissociate, encounter, endanger, engagement, enjoy, entertain, entertainment, escapade, escort, estrange, excursion, faux pas, fawn, fete, fight, flirt, flirtation, flock, fornicate, fornication, forsake, fraternize, frequent, frisk, frolic, get a kick out of, get even, go together/go with, grovel, hanky-panky, haunt, hold, horse around, host, hubbub, induct, induction, infringe, insinuate, interfere, interference, interrupt, introduce, invitation, invite, jilt, kick out, know, kowtow, lose, love, make up, maroon, mask, meddle, mediate, mediation, meet, meeting, mingle, mishandle/mismanage, mutiny, network, obeisance, oblige, observance, observe, ostracize, overture, pander, part, parting, pass, patch up, patronize, penance, pick up, play, poke, popularize, powwow, prance, prank, pretend, program, proposition, prostrate, pry, pursue, put up, rampage, rapprochement, reception, reciprocate, reconcile, reduce, regale, reinstate, rendezvous, repay, reprisal, requite, respond, retaliate, retribution, revel, revelry, revenge, riot, romance, romp, rupture, seat, secede, second, see, separate, sever, share, show, show business, shun, sit, slight, snoop, snub, socialize, soothe, spree, spurn, squire, stab in the back, step in, stoop, stunt, taint, tantrum, tear, throw over, toady, toy, treat, trespass, trick, truckle, tryst, usurp, vengeance, wallow, welcome, woo

385 social change: breakup, civilize, give in/give up, revert, succumb

386 social event: adventure, assignation, ball,

bee, bells and whistles, benefit, binge, blast, bustle, caper, caricature, carnival, ceremony, clamor, clown, come between, conference, date, debut, display, dissipation, diversion, entertainment, escapade, exhibition, exhibitionism, exposition, fair, feature, field trip, fiesta, fling, frolic, fun, function, funeral, gathering, horseplay, inauguration, initiation, memorial, merriment/merrymaking, morgue, occasion, outing, parade, picnic, rally, riot, rite, ritual, rumpus, sacrament

387 social organization: association, band, brotherhood, circle, clan, class, clique, club, congregation, congress, crowd, cult, fraternity, elite, entourage, faction, fellowship, following, gang, guild, high society, jet set, league, legion, order, society

388 social state: abasement, admittance, affirmative action, amity, association, attendance, awkwardness, bad luck, behind, belong, belonging, bigotry, bond, brand, breach, break, breeding, brotherhood, calm, camaraderie, care, caste, celebrity, celibacy, censorship, ceremony, circumstances, civilization, class, clutches, coherence, commotion, companionship, compatibility, complicity, concert, concord, conflict, conjunction, connection, consanguinity, consequence, contact, contempt, cooperation, correlation, courtesy, courtship, credit, crunch, culture, dalliance, degree, detachment, détente, difference, dignitary, dignity, diplomacy, disaffection, disagreement, discord, disfavor, disgrace, disharmony, dishonor, disorder, dissociation, dissolution, distinction, disturbance, division, duty, ease, echelon, elite, eminence, enrollment, entertainment, entrée, entry, equality, estate, estrangement, excitement, face, falling-out, fame, familiarity, favoritism, fellowship, feud, fidelity, footing, foreplay, friendliness, friendship, frivolity, fun, furor, fuss, gaiety, genre/genus, gentility, get along, get on, glory, harmony, height, high society, hit it off, hoopla, hospitality, housing, hubbub, humbug, humiliation, immortality, immunity, importance, infidelity, intimacy, intrigue, jet set, juncture, kick, laissez-faire, lapse, lather, league, level, liaison, liberty, love affair, luxury, malarky, marriage, match, men's movement, mirth, mortification, mourning, mutiny, name, nepotism, network, nobility, nonsense, nonviolence, notch, notoriety, obligation, odium, onus, opprobrium, pandemonium, partnership, peace, piffle, pink, place, platitude, pleasure, polish, polygamy, poppycock, popularity, position, predicament, presence of mind, prestige, privacy, rage, rank, rapport, rapprochement, rate, refinement, relationship, report, reproach, repulse, reputation, rift, ruckus, rupture, scramble, seclusion, separation, servitude, setback, shame, showdown, situation, slavery, society, solitude, sophistication, sphere, split, spotlight, standing, stardom, state, station, status, stigma, stillness, stimulating, stink, stir, support, sympathy, taint, taste, tedium, terms, tie, tomfoolery, twaddle, uncertainty, unification, variance, wedlock, whirl

Life forms

BEINGS

389 beings: being, body, cell, creation, creature, cur, egg, form, individual, life, organism, soul

390 former beings: body, cadaver, carcass/carcase, corpse

391 group of beings: band, flock, group, third world, world

392 limb or appendage of: ankle, arm, back, backside, beak, behind, branch, bust, butt/buttocks, calf, chest, claw, derriere, digit, duff, egg, extremity, eye, fanny, fiber, finger, flank, flesh, foot, freckle, germ, hair, hand, head, jaw, leg, limb, lip, member, microorganism, mop, mouth, nose, posterior, rug, rump, seat, skin, strand, tail, toupee, trunk, tuft, wig, wisp

393 organ: abdomen, abdominal, bacteria, belly, blood, bone, bowels, brain, dentures, entrails, false teeth, gut, heart, joint, mind, molecule, muscle, nucleus, seed, skeleton, spine, stomach, tummy, vein

BEINGS, ANIMAL

394 animal: adult, animal, beast, brute, buck, calf, cat, cattle, chicken, clam, cock, colt, cur, dad, father, fawn, frog, game, goat, halfbreed, hog, horse, hound, hybrid, leech, litter, mom, mongrel, monkey, monster, mother, parasite, pet, pig, prey, stock, young

395 bird: bird, chicken

396 fish: aquarium, aquatic

397 group of animals: drove, family, herd, horde, insect, litter, pack, roundup, stock, swarm, team

398 insect: bee, bug, grub, pest

399 limb or appendage of: bill, chin, coat, crest, feather, fertilizer, fur, hot dog, manure, meat, mop, paunch, pelt, pulp, scale, shell, trunk, venom, wing

400 mammal: cat, dad, dog, donkey, father, fawn, goat, hog, hound, mom, mother, pig

GENERAL CHARACTERISTICS

401 attribute of behavior: abstemious, accident-prone, acerbity, acid, acrid, acrimonious, active, adamant, adolescent, affable, affected, affectionate, agog, agreeable, agreeably, aimless, alive, aloof, amiable, amuck, animate, animated, antsy, anxious, apathetic, arbitrary, arch, ardent, argumentative, arrogant, artificial, ascetic, assured, attentive, audacious, austere, authoritarian, avid, babyish, backhanded, backward, bad, balky, barbarian, barbaric, barbarous, barefaced, beaming, beastly, belligerent, benevolent, big, bland, blindly, bloodthirsty, boisterous, bold, bossy, brash, brassy, brave, brazen, brittle, brusque, brutal, cagey, calculating, calm, cantankerous, capricious, carnivorous, casual, cautious, cavalier, chary, cheeky, childish, chill, chivalrous, chummy, civil, clumsy, coarse, cocky/cocksure, collected, combative, comic/comical, common, compassionate, complacent, complaisant, composed, compulsive, concerned, conciliatory, condescending, considerate, constructive, contemptuous, contentious, contrary, contumacious, convivial, cool, cordial, correct, corrupt, country, courageous, courteous, courtly, covetous, cowardly, coy, crabby/crabbed, crafty, cranky, crass, craven, cross, crotchety, crude, cruel, crusty, cunning, cutthroat, daring, dark, dauntless, deaf, debonair, deceitful, decent, deceptive, decided, decorous, defensive, deferential, defiant, deliberate, deliberately, delicate, delightful, delinquent, delirious, demonstrative, demure, desperate, detached, devious, diffident, diplomatic, disagreeable, disarming, discourteous, discreet, disdainful, disgruntled, disingenuous, disinterested, disloyal, disobedient, disobliging, disorderly, dispassionate, disputatious, disrespectful, disruptive, dissipated, dissolute, distant, distraught, ditsy, divisive, docile, doctrinaire, dogged, dolorous, domineering, doting, double-dealing, dour, draconian, duplicitous, eager, earnest, easy, ebullient, edgy, effeminate, effervescent, elfin, emotionless, enthusiastic, envious, epicurean, equable, equal, evasive, even, even-tempered, exacting, excitable, excited, exuberant, fainthearted, faithful, faithless, fake, fallow, false, falsely, fanatical, favorable, favorably, fawning, fearful, fearless, feigned, feral, ferocious, ferocity, fervent/fervid, feverish, fickle, fidgety, fiery, fighting, finicky, flagrant, flamboyant, flexible, flighty, flippant, flirtatious, flushed, foolhardy, foolish, foolishly, footloose, forceful, formal, forward, foxy, fractious, free, freely, fresh, fretful, frisky, frivolous, fulsome, fussy, fustian, gamely, genial, genteel, giddy, glacial, glowing, gluttonous, good, goody-goody, goofy, graceless, gracious, grandiose, grave, gritty, grouchy, gruff, grumpy, gung ho, halcyon, halfhearted, hard, hardhearted, haramscarum, haughty, headstrong, heartless, hearty, heedless, helpless, heroic, high and mighty, high-handed, high-strung, holier-than-thou, hostile, hot, hotheaded, huffy, humane, humble, hyperactive, hypocritical, icy, idle, ill at ease, ill-mannered, ill-natured, ill-tempered, immodest, impatient, impersonal, impertinent, impish, impolite, impolitic, importunate, impossible, impudent, impulsive, inactive, inclement, inconsiderate, inexorable, ingratiating, inhospitable, inhuman/inhumane, inimical, innocuous, insensitive, insidious, insolent, insubordinate, insurgent, intractable/intransigent, intrepid, introverted, intrusive, invidious, irascible, irreconcilable, irrepressible, irreverent, irritable, jaded, jaundiced, jaunty, jazzed-up, jittery, jovial, jubilant, jumpy, juvenile, keen, kind, kittenish, kosher, lax, lazy, lecherous, lenient, lethargic, level, liberal, licentious, lifeless, light, light-headed, listless, litigious, lively, lofty, loose, loquacious, lothario, loud, loud-mouthed, loving, lunatic, Machiavellian maladroit, malevolent, malicious, manageable, mannered, mannerly, martial, mawkish, mean, meat-eating, meek, menacing, mercenary, merciful, merciless, mercurial, mild, militant, mincing, mischievous, miscreant, miserly, modest, mousy, mulish, munificent, mutinous, naive, narcissistic, nasty, natural, naughty, nefarious, neglectful, negligent, neighborly, nerveless, nervy, noble, nomadic, nonchalant, noncompliant, nonconformist, nonviolent, nosy, obdurate, obedient, obeisant, obliging, obnoxious, obsequious, obstinate, obtrusive, odious, offhand, oily, on edge, on guard, on purpose, on the wagon, orderly, ornery, ostentatious, outlandish, overbearing, overconfident, overwrought, parental, parsimonious, partisan, passionate, pedantic, peevish, pent-up, peppery, peppy, perfidious, peripatetic, perky, permissive, persistent, pert, perverse, petulant, philosophical/philosophic, phlegmatic, phobic, pious, pitiless, placid, plaintive, playful, play it safe, plucky, polite, politic, politically correct, pompous, possessed, pragmatic, precious, precipitous/precipitate, precise, predatory, premature, presumptuous, pretentious, prickly, prim, prissy, prodigal, profane, profligate, prompt, proper, propitious, proud, provident, prudent, prudish, psyched, puerile, pugnacious, pumped, punctilious, puritanical, pushy, quarrelsome, querulous, quick-tempered, quiet, racy, radiant, raffish, rakish, rash, raucous, ready, rebel, rebellious, recalcitrant, reckless, refined, regardful, regardless, relentless, reluctant, remiss, remorseful, remorseless, remote, renegade, reprobate, repugnant, reserved, resigned, respectful, responsible, responsive, restful, restive, restrained, reticent, retiring, reverent, revolutionary, ribald, rocky, roguish, rollicking, rootin'-tootin', rough, rousing, rowdy, rude, rugged, runaway, rustic, ruthless, sacrilegious, safe, salty, sanctimonious, sass, sassy, saucy, savage, savvy, scintillating, scrupulous, secluded, seditious, self-conscious, self-righteous, sensual, sentimental, serene, serpentine, servile, severe, shabby, shameful, shameless, sheepish, shiftless, shifty, short, short-sighted, shrewd, shy, silly, simple, simpleminded, sincere, sinister, skittish, slick, slippery, slothful, sluggish, sly, small, smart, smooth, snaky, snappy, sneaky, snide, snobbish, snooty, snotty, sober, sociable, soft, softhearted, solid, sophisticated, sophomoric, sparing, spineless, spiteful, spontaneous, sporting/sportive, sporty, sprightly, spry, square, squeamish, staid, standoffish, starchy, stately, staunch, steadfast, stealthy, stern, stiff, stilted, stingy, stodgy, stoic/stoical, stolid, stony, stouthearted, strained, strait-laced, street smart, strenuous, strict, stringent, stubborn, stuck-up, stuffy, suave, subdued, submissive, subservient, subversive, sunny, supercilious, superior, supine, sure, surly, sweet, sympa-

thetic, taciturn, tactful, tactless, tame, tasteless, tearful, temperate, tempestuous, tenacious, tender, tenderhearted, tense, testy, thankful, thankless, theatrical, thieving/thievish, thoughtful, thoughtless, thrifty, tight, timid, tipsy, torpid, touchy, tractable, traitorous, treacherous, treasonous, tricky, truculent, true, true-blue, trusting, turbulent, two-faced, ugly, unaffected, unafraid, unasked, unassuming, unattached, unbending, unbridled, uncivil, uncivilized, uncompromising, uncontrollable, uncoordinated, uncouth, undaunted, undependable, undisciplined, underhand, understanding, unemotional, unflappable, unfriendly, ungrateful, unguarded, uninhibited, unintentional/unintended, uninterested, unkind, unmanageable, unmerciful, unobtrusive, unprejudiced, unpretentious, unreasonable, unrehearsed, unrelenting, unrestricted, unruly, unscrupulous, unseemly, unselfish, unsettled, unsociable, unsophisticated, unsuspecting, unsympathetic, unthinking, untoward, untrustworthy, unwary, unwilling, unwise, unwitting, unworldly, unyielding, uppity, uptight, urbane, vain, vainglorious, valiant, valorous, vehement, vengeful, venturesome, vibrant, vicarious, vicious, viperous, virile, virtuous, vital, vivacious, volatile, voracious, wacky, waggish, wanton, warlike, warm, warmhearted, wary, wasteful, watchful, wayfaring, wayward, well-bred, whimsical, wicked, wild, willful, willing, wily, winning/winsome, withdrawn, witless, worldly, yellow, yielding, zany, zealous

402 attribute of intelligence: able, abreast, abstruse, academic, accident-prone, acquainted, acute, adept, alert, amenable, analytic/analytical, appreciative, apt, asinine, astute, awake, aware, backward, bewildered, blank, blind, bright, brilliant, calculable, canny, catatonic, cerebral, childish, clairvoyant, clear, clever, clumsy, cognizant, coherent, common-sense, complex, comprehensible, conscious, considered, contemplative, conversant, creative, cunning, dark, deducible, deep, delirious, dense, designedly, dexterous, dim, discerning, dizzy, dopey, down-to-earth, dull, dumb, eagle-eyed, educated, efficient, elevated, empty, empty-headed, enlightened, erudite, experienced, expert, familiar, far-sighted, fatuous, feebleminded, forgotten, frivolous, gifted, gullible, harebrained, hazy, highbrow, idiotic, ignorant, illiterate, imbecile, impressionable, incisive, incomprehensible, inefficient, ineligible, inept, inexperienced, informed, ingenious, inquiring, inquisitive, insightful, insipid, intellectual, intelligent, intuitive, inventive, irrational, judicious, keen, knowing, knowledgeable, learned, literate, logical, lowbrowed, lucid, mental, mindful, mistaken, moronic, nimble, not born yesterday, oblivious, observant, obtuse, omniscient, on the ball, penetrating, perceptive, perspicacious, philosophical/philosophic, precocious, privy, professional, proficient, profound, psychic, quick, quick-witted, rational, ready, reasonable, resourceful, sagacious, sage, sane, sapient, savvy, scatterbrained, scholarly, searching, seasoned, senile, sensible, sentinent, shallow, sharp, shrewd, simple, skillful, slick, slow, smart, soft, stolid, studious, stupid, subtle, talented, thick, thoughtful, thoughtless, touched, unaware, uncoordinated, uneducated, unfamiliar, uninformed, unintelligent, unknowing, unwise, vacant, vacuous, versed, veteran, weak, well-balanced, well-defined, wideawake, wise, with it

403 attribute of mentality: aback, abashed, abscondere, absentee, absent-minded, absorbed, absorbing, abstracted, accustomed, addled, affected, affectionate, afraid, aggrieved, aghast, agonizing, alert, allergic, amatory, amorous, angry, anxious, apathetic, appreciative, apprehensive, aspiring, assumed, attention deficit disorder, attentive, automatic, averse, avid, bad, balmy, beaten, beholden, believable, bent, berserk, beside oneself, bewildered, bewitched, bigoted, black, bleak, blissful, blue, boiling, breathless, broad, broad-minded, broken, brokenhearted, buoyant, burning, calculating, captive, carnal, cautious, certain, cheerful, cheerless, chipper, circumspect, clairvoyant, clear, compassionate, complacent, concerned, confident, confused, conscious, contemplative, content, contented, contrite, crabby/crabbed, cranky, crazy, crestfallen, cross, crotchety, curious, cynical, daffy, daft, dearly, decided, dejected, delighted, delirious, demented, depressed, deranged, desolate, despairing, desperately, despondent, disaffected, disappointed, disbelieving, disconcerted, disconsolate, discontented/discontent, discouraged, discouraging, disenchanted, disgruntled, disgusted, disillusioned, disinclined, disinterested, disoriented, dispirited, dissatisfied, dissident, distraught, distressed, distrustful, doleful, dolorous, dotty, doubtful, down, downbeat, downcast, downhearted, dumbfounded, ecstatic, elated, elegiac, emotional, emotionless, enamored, engrossed, enraged, envious, excited, expectant, exultant, fascinated, fed up, festive, firm, flaming, flushed, foggy, forgetful, forgotten, forlorn, frantic, frenetic, fretful, frightened, frustrated, fulfilled, funereal, furious, gay, glad, gladly, gleeful, gloomy, glum, goofy, grateful, greedy, griefstricken, grumpy, gut, half-baked, hangdog, happily, happy, hard, hard-boiled, hardline, harried, haywire, headstrong, healthy, heartsick, heavy, high, homesick, hopeful, hot, huffy, hurt, hysterical, ill at ease, ill-tempered, impartial, impassioned, impressionable, inattentive, incensed, inconsolable, incredulous, indifferent, indignant, indiscriminate, infatuated, insane, insatiable, insecure, insular, intent, intently, interested, intolerant, intoxicated, invidious, irate, irrational, irresolute, irritable, jaundiced, jealous, jovial, joyful/joyous, joyless, jubilant, judicious, keen, lackadaisical, languid, lascivious, lethargic, levelheaded, livid, lonely, lonesome, longing, loony, lost, low, lucid, lukewarm, lunatic, mad, malcontent, malleable, manic/maniacal, melancholy, mental, merry, mindful, mindless, mirthful, miser-

able, mixed-up, moody, morbid, morose, mournful, narrow, narrow-minded, negative, nerveless, nervous, neurotic, neutral, new age, noncommittal, normal, nostalgic, numb, nuts/nutty, objective, objectivity, oblivious, observant, obsess, obsessed, off-guard, on edge, one-sided, on the ball, on the fence, opposed/opposing, overcome, overjoyed, overwrought, partial, penitent, pensive, pent-up, pessimistic, petrified, petty, phlegmatic, pissed off, platonic, play it safe, pooped, possessive, predisposed, preoccupied, prepared, prepossessed, profound, proud, provincial, prurient, psyched, psychic, psychological, psychotic, pumped, punch-drunk, purposeful, puzzled, queasy, rabid, racist, radical, raging, rapacious, rapt, realistic, reflective, regretful, resolute, restless, right, rigid, romantic, rueful, sad, salacious, sane, sanguine, sappy, saturnine, scared, sectarian, secure, self-assured, senile, sensitive, serious, sick, silly, skeptical, sleepless, small-minded, solemn, solicitous, somber, sore, sorrowful, sorry, soulful, sound, sour, spellbound, spiritless, steady, stout, strong, stunned, stupefied, subdued, sulky, sullen, susceptible, suspicious, tearful, temperamental, tender, tense, testy, thankful, thirsty, thoughtful, thoughtless, thunderstruck, tired, tolerant, torn, touched, tough, tuckered out, ugly, unadvised, unbalanced, unbelieving, uncaring, uncomfortable, uncommitted, unconcerned, undecided, uneasy, unemotional, unfaltering, unfeeling, unhappy, uninterested, unsettled, unsound, untouched, untroubled, unwary, upbeat, upset, versed, vulnerable, wacky, warmhearted, wary, weak, weary, wide-awake, willing, wishful, wistful, woebegone, worried, wrathful, wretched

404 attribute of personality: aboveboard, abrasive, adventurous, aggressive, airy, altruistic, amenable, amorphous, approachable, ardent, arrogant, artful, assertive, assuming, assured, audacious, august, avaricious, bashful, belligerent, belonging to, big, big-hearted, bitter, blasé, blessed, blithe, bloodless, boastful, bold, boorish, bossy, brash, bright, buoyant, busy, callous, calm, captious, carefree, catty, charitable, charming, chaste, cheeky, cheerful, childlike, chill, chilly, choosy, churlish, clean, clear, clement, clinical, close, cocky/cocksure, co-dependent, cold, colorful, colorless, combative, conceited, confident, convivial, cool, courageous, coy, credulous, culpable, cursed, cute, cutthroat, dainty, dashing, dastardly, decent, dedicated, deep, delicate, delightful, demonic/demoniac/demoniacal, demure, dependent, deserving, despicable, detached, determined, devious, dewy-eyed, die-hard, difficult, dignified, discriminating, dispassionate, disreputable, distant, docile, dynamic, easy, easygoing, effeminate, egocentric, egotistic/egoistic, elastic, embittered, enchanting, endearing, energetic, engaging, enterprising, even-tempered, exacting, exalted, excitable, exemplary, extroverted, feckless, feisty, finicky, finished, flatulent, flirtatious, forbearing, fortunate, forward, foxy, free, fresh, frigid, fussy, gallant, game, garrulous, gauche, generous, genial, genteel, gentle, glacial, glib, good, good-humored, good-natured, green, gregarious, gritty, gutless, gutsy, halcyon, happy-go-lucky, hardened, hardhearted, hard-nosed/hardheaded, hateful, hell-bent, heroic, high and mighty, highstrung, humble, hyperactive, hypercritical, icy, ill-natured, immaculate, immovable, impassive, imperturbable, impetuous, individual, indomitable, indulgent, inexperienced, infamous, inflexible, inherent, inhibited, innocent, insipid, insouciant, intolerant, intrinsic, introverted, inveterate, inviting, irresponsible, jaunty, jazzed-up, kind, kindhearted, kindly, kosher, laid-back, largesse, latent, lazy, liberal, lighthearted, likable, little, loutish, lovable, low, lowly, loyal, magnanimous, magnetic, manageable, matronly, mercurial, meritorious, mild, mincing, misanthropic, miserly, modest, mulish, narcissistic, native, natural, nice, noble, nonchalant, notorious, obedient, obliging, obsequious, obsessed, odd/oddball, odious, officious, openhanded, openhearted, open-minded, opinionated, opprobrious, optimistic, ossified, outgoing, outspoken, overbearing, particular, patient, peculiar, peppy, perfidious, perky, persistent, persnickety, personable, pert, philanthropic, picky, pigheaded, pliable, predictable, prepossessing, prim, prissy, proper, puritanical, pushy, queer, quick-tempered, receptive, recluse/reclusive, remote, reserved, responsible, rotten, ruthless, saintly, sanctimonious, Satanic, sedate, selective, self-assured, self-centered, self-confident, self-conscious, selfish, self-satisfied, self-sufficient, servile, shabby, shiftless, shifty, shy, slothful, smug, snotty, sophisticated, spick-and-span, spirited, spotless, sprightly, spunky, square, squeamish, stable, staid, stalwart, standoffish, stodgy, stoic/stoical, straight, stubborn, stuffy, suave, subservient, sweet, thick-skinned, treacherous, trustworthy/trusty, unaffected, unapproachable, unassuming, unpretentious, unselfish, unsuspecting, unworthy, uppity, upright, vain, valiant, valorous, vigorous, virile, vivacious, vocal, warm, winning, winsome, wishy-washy, yielding, zealous, zippy

405 essential property of life forms: allergy, awkwardness, body, complexion, dotage, fatigue, hygiene, physique, sense, sensitivity

406 essential quality of life forms: adult, alimentary, animal, athletic, awake, awkward, barefoot, bearded, blank, bodily, breathless, brunette/brunet, bushy, buxom, cadaverous, corpulent, curly, curvaceous, dark, deadpan, decrepit, drowsy, empty, exhausted, expectant, expecting, expressionless, fair, famished, fleshy, florid, full, gaunt, glassy, haggard, hairless, hairy, high, human, hungry, imperceptible, inborn/inbred, infertile, innate, insensitive, intestinal/intestine, intoxicated, intrinsic, jaded, light, limber, lumbering, piercing, predatory, pregnant, primitive, private, promising, prostrate, ravenous, raw, rich, sensitive, sensory, shapely, smooth, starving/starved, sweaty, thin-skinned, tight, tipsy, tired, untamed, wild

407 existential state: be, being, casualty, coexis-

tence, endangered, endure, exist, existence, fettle, flesh, gone, live, loss, manage, matter, mortality, nature, none, nothing/nothingness, oblivion, outlast, outlive, presence, reside, spirit, stand, subsist, survive, threaten, vitality, zero, zilch

408 gender: female, femininity/feminine, gender, he-man, machismo, macho, male, masculinity/masculine

409 intelligence: acquaintance, acumen, anticipation, appreciation, apprehension, aptitude, attention, awareness, bent, brain, capacity, clairvoyance, clarity, cleverness, cognizance/cognition, common sense, comprehension, conception, consciousness, craft, creativity, dark, darkness, delusion, depth, dexterity, education, efficiency, empathy, enlightenment, erudition, experience, expertise/expertness, extrasensory perception, familiarity, fancy, feeling, finesse, foresight, forte, genius, gift, grasp, grip, head, idiocy, ignorance, illumination, imagination, ingenuity, innocence, insight, intellect, intelligence, interpretation, intuition, invention, judgment, ken, knack, know-how, knowledge, learning, light, literacy, memory, mentality, mind, misconception, misunderstanding, nirvana, observance, observation, originality, perception, precognition, proficiency, reason, sagacity, sage, sanity, savvy, scholarship, sense, sensibility, sixth sense, skill, smarts, soul, thought, understanding, wisdom, wit/wits, workmanship

410 mentality: abhorrence, absent-mindedness, absorption, abstraction, accession, ache, afterlife, aggravation, agility, agonize, agony, alarm, alienation, allergy, alter ego, amazement, anger, angst, anguish, anticipation, anxiety, apathy, application, assurance, astonishment, attention, attitude, attrition, avarice, awe, bad time, bathos, beatitude, behalf, belief, belonging, bigotry, bitterness, blues, boast, boredom, bosom, breakdown, breast, bristle, buoyancy/buoyance, cabin fever, capitulation, caprice, care, caution, censure, chagrin, cheer, clairvoyance, clemency, cliffhanger, cogitation, collapse, comfort, compassion, complex, composure, compulsion, compunction, conception, concern, confusion, conquest, consideration, consolation, constancy, contemplation, content, contentment, contrition, conviction, corollary, creativity, credit, cult, curiosity, dark, darkness, daze, decision, defeat, deference, degradation, delight, delight in, delirium, delusion, dementia, dependence/dependency, depression, design, desolation, despair, desperation, difficulty, disability, disaffection, disappointment, discipline, discomfiture, discomfort, discontent, discouragement, discrimination, disgust, disinclination, dismay, disorder, displeasure, disquiet, dissatisfaction, distraction, distress, disturbance, doldrums, dolor, doubt, dumps, ease, ecstasy, Eden, elation, embarrassment, emotion, encouragement, enjoyment, ennui, envy, equanimity, esprit de corps, euphoria, exaltation, exasperation, excitement, exhaustion, exhilaration, expectancy, expectation, extrasensory perception, exultation, fallacy, fat city, feeling, felicity, fever, firmness, fluster, fog, folly, forbearance, force, foresight, forethought, forgetfulness, fortitude, frame of mind, frazzle, free will, frenzy, fret, fright, frustration, fume, funk, furor, fury, gladness, glee, gloom, gratification, gratitude, grief, grieve, happiness, health, heart, heartache, heartbreak, heat, heaven, hesitation, hoopla, hope, huff, humbug, humanity, humiliation, humor, hysteria, idiocy, imagination, impulse, indifference, indignity, insanity, insight, instability, introspection, ire, jealousy, jitters, joy, ken, kick, lament/lamentation, languor, letdown, lethargy, levity, lunacy, madness, malaise, mania, martyrdom, melancholy, mental illness, merriment/merrymaking, mindset, mirth, mistake, monotony, mood, mope, morale, mortification, mourn, mourning, muddle, nausea, negative attitude, neglect, nerves, nervous breakdown, nervousness, neurosis, nostalgia, objection, oblivion, observance, observation, obsession, offense, optimism, originality, outlook, pain, panic, paradise, paroxysm, passion, pathos, peace, penance, penitence, perception, perspective, pessimism, pique, pity, pleasure, Pollyanna, posture, pout, precaution, precognition, predisposition, premonition, presage, presence, presentiment, psyche, psychology, push, pussyfoot, qualm, quarter, rage, rancor, rapture, rave, red herring, regret, rejoice, remorse, repent, repentance, repose, repulse, resent, resentment, resignation, resistance, resolution, resolve, restlessness, retrospect, ruckus, rue, sadness, sanity, satisfaction, scare, security, self-satisfaction, sensation, sensibility, sensitivity, sentiment, seriousness, servitude, shame, simmer, skepticism, slump, sob, solace, solicitude, sorrow, soul, soul-searching, state, status quo, stew, strain, strength, stress, subconscious, surprise, suspense, sympathy, tedium, telepathy, temper, temperament, temperance, tension, thought, tolerance, torment, torpor, torture, trance, transport, triumph, turn, umbrage, uncertainty, unrest, vagary, vanity, wariness, waver, woe, wonder, wonderment, worry, wrath, zeal, zest

411 personality: aggression, ardor, arrogance, art, artifice, assumption, atrocity, attribute, audacity, backbone, bearing, being, best, bounce, bravery, buoyancy/buoyance, caliber, calm, candor, character, characteristic, charisma, charity, charm, complexion, compliance, conceit, confidence, constraint, courage, cultivation, dash, decision, dedication, demeanor, determination, dignity, disposition, disrepute, distinction, drive, effrontery, ego, egoism/egotism, élan, empathy, endowment, endurance, energy, enterprise, entity, esprit de corps, essence, eye, failing, fettle, fiber, fight, fire, foible, forte, fortitude, frailty, gall, gallantry, generosity, geniality, gentility, glint, go, goodness, good will/goodwill, greatness, grit, gumption, gusto, guts, hauteur, heart, heroism, honor, hubris, humor, identity, idiosyncrasy, ilk, inclination, individuality, infamy, inhibition, initiative, innocence, integrity, kind, kink, laziness, life, longevity, loyalty, magnetism,

makeup, manner, mark, martyrdom, mentality, mettle, mien, might, mold, monstrosity, mood, morale, morals, motivation, moxie, mystique, nature, nerve, notoriety, obedience, oddity, oomph, panache, patience, peculiarity, penchant, pep, perseverance, personality, pizzazz, pluck, point, possibilities, potency, presence, presence of mind, pride, prima donna, probity, proclivity, propensity, property, prowess, psyche, push, qualify, quirk, reputation, responsibility, savor, self-respect/self-esteem, sex appeal, shortcoming, sloth, soul, sparkle, spirit, sportsmanship, spunk, stability, stamina, stamp, staying power, style, taste, temerity, temper, temperament, tenacity, tend, thing, trait, trick, turn, twist, type, valor, vein, verve, vice, vigor, virtue, vitality, way, weakness, will, willpower, wit, zeal, zest, zing, zip

HUMANS

412 bad person: accessory, accomplice, accurser, addict, adversary, agent provocateur, aggressor, agitator, alarmist, anarchist, antagonist, apostate, ass, assailant, assassin, attacker, authoritarian, bandit, barbarian, beggar, bigmouth, blabbermouth, bottom feeder, braggart, bum, bungler, burglar, butterfingers, cad, cannibal, captive, character, charlatan, cheat, clod, clown, cold fish, confederate, conspirator, convict, criminal, critic, crook, crybaby, culprit, cur, deadbeat, defendant, delinquent, demagogue, demon, demonstrator, derelict, deserter, desperado, despot, devil, dimwit, dirty old man, ditz, dolt, do-nothing, doomsayer, dope, drag queen, dregs, drifter, drone, dullard, dumbbell, dummy, dunce, enchantress, enemy, escapee, espionage, evildoer, exile, expatriate, failure, fake, fall guy, felon, femme fatale, fiend, fighter, fink, firebrand, foe, fool, fraud, fugitive, gadfly, gangster, ghoul, glutton, good-for-nothing, goon, gossip, grouch, grump, harlot, hellion, hit man, hobo, hog, hot dog, hussy, hypocrite, idiot, imbecile, imp, impostor, incendiary, incubus, instigator, insurgent, interloper, intruder, joke, Judas, juvenile delinquent, killer, killjoy, klutz, know-it-all, kook, lawbreaker, leech, lemon, liar, loafer, looter, loser, Lucifer, lummox, lunatic, mad person, malingerer, maniac, marauder, menace, mercenary, misanthrope, miscreant, miser, mobster, mole, monster, mountebank, murderer, naysayer, ne'er-do-well, nitwit, nuisance, numbskull, nut, oaf, ogre, oppressor, organized crime, outlaw, parasite, patsy, pawn, pervert, pessimist, pest, pill, pirate, placebo, prisoner, prodigal, profligate, prostitute, prowler, psychopath, punk, quack, ragamuffin, rascal, rebel, renegade, robber, rogue, rowdy, ruffian, runaway, sap, Satan, scamp, scapegoat, schlemiel, scoundrel, Scrooge, scum, shirked, showoff, shyster, sight, simpleton, sissy, skinflint, slacker, sleazebag, smart aleck, sneak, sociopath, sourpuss, sponge, spy, strumpet, swindler, tattletale/tattler, thief, thug, tightwad, tool, tough, traitor, tramp, troll, troublemaker, truant, turncoat, tyrant, underworld, vandal, villain, wanton, weakling, whipping boy, whore, wimp, wise guy, witch

413 community group member: aborigine, citizen, denizen, emigrant, émigré, explorer, foreigner, hayseed, hick, hillbilly, immigrant, inhabitant, innovator, local, migrant, native, newcomer, nomad, outsider, patriot, pioneer, plebeian, proletariat, redneck, refugee, resident, rustic, stranger, subject, tenderfoot, yokel

414 family member: ancestor, ancestry, antecedent(s), babe, baby, broad, brother, child, conservationist, damsel, descendant, domestic partner, father, fetus, fiancé/fiancée, forebearer, forefather, forerunner, guardian, guy, heir, he-man, husband, hybrid, infant, issue, keeper, kid, kin, kindred, kinship, man, mother, newborn, nurse, occupant, offspring, orphan, owner, paramedic, parent, partner, predecessor, progeny, relation, relative, roots, scion, seed, senior, sister, spitting image, spouse, successor, surrogate, sweetheart, toddler, trustee, twin, ward, woman, young, youngster/youth

415 female: bachelor, bride, broad, damsel, dated, debutante, dish, doll, female, girl, girlfriend, housekeeper, Jezebel, mother, nymph, paramour, sister, wanton, wife, woman

416 good person: ace, angel, benefactor, do-gooder, doozy, dreamer, egghead, expert, genius, hero/heroine, humanitarian, idealist, intellect, intellectual, intimate, missionary, pacifist, peacemaker, perfectionist, pet, philanthropist, prodigy, prude, pundit, savior, victor, virtuoso, visionary, wag, whiz, winner, wit

417 group of people: anybody, anyone, army, assemblage, attendance, audience, band, beanpole, board, body, cadre, caucus, circle, civilization, class, clientele, clique, cloud, company, congregation, contingent, convention, corps, corpse, crew, crowd, crush, earthling, elite, enrollment, entourage, everybody/everyone, expedition, federation, field, flesh, following, force, gallery, gathering, hoi polloi, horde, host, huddle, human, humanity, humankind, legion, masses, member, membership, mob, mortal, mortality, multitude, muster, outfit, pack, party, people, person, personnel, platoon, practice, public, rabble, riffraff, set, society, squad, suite, swarm, team, throng, troop/troops, troupe, turnout

418 limb or appendage: ankle, beard, bosom, bottom, braid, breast, bristle, brow, can, cheek, coiffure, curl, elbow, features, pore, wrinkle

419 male: bachelor, boy, boyfriend, bridegroom, brother, escort, father, floozy, groom, guy, he-man, hooker, husband, Jezebel, lad, male, man, wanton

420 organ: backbone, blood, bone, brain, heart, muscle, spine, stomach, tummy, vein

421 racial group member: kin, kindred, relation, tribe

422 royalty: crown, monarch, noble, potentate

423 social group member: accurser, acquaintance, addict, admirer, adventurer, advocate, alarmist, alcoholic, alien, alliance, alter ego, another, apprentice, aristocracy, aristocrat, arrival, aspirant, assistant, associate, atheist, augur, auxiliary, bachelor, beatnik, beau, beggar, beginner, believer, beloved, benefactor, beneficiary, best-seller, bigmouth, bigot, big shot, birds of a feather, blabbermouth, black sheep, bohemian, boor, bore, boyfriend, braggart, brownnose, brute, buddy, buff, buffoon, bully, bum, bungler, busybody, butt, butterfingers, bystander, captive, casualty, celebrity, chaperon, character, chicken, chum, churl, civilian, clairvoyant, clod, clown, cohort, collaborator, colleague, comedian, comic, companion, company, competitor, comrade, confidant, conformist, connection, conquest, conservationist, consort, convoy, correspondent, couch potato, coward, craven, cretin, crony, cynic, darling, daredevil, dark horse, date, deadbeat, dear, derelict, deserter, devil's advocate, devotee, diehard, dilettante, disciple, disciplinarian, dissident, ditz, do-gooder, doll, dolt, Don Juan, donor, do-nothing, doomsayer, dope, doubter, doubting Thomas, drifter, driver, drunk/drunkard, dude, dullard, dumbbell, dummy, dunce, dupe, eccentric, elitist, emigrant, emissary, enthusiast, entrant, epicure, epicurean, equal, escort, exception, exile, expatriate, exponent, extraterrestrial, extremist, extrovert, eyewitness, failure, fan, father, favorite, fellow, fiancé/fiancée, fiend, figure, figurehead, fink, fisherman, flame, flirt, follower, fool, fop, forerunner, fortune-teller, founder, freak, friend, fuddy-duddy, gentleperson, gigolo, girlfriend, go-between, goon, gourmet, greenhorn, grouch, grump, guardian, guest, guide, half-wit, hanger-on, hedonist, helper, henchman, herald, hermit, hippie, hobo, homeboy, hostage, humanitarian, humorist, iconoclast, idealist, idol, inferior, informant/informer, interloper, intimate, introvert, intruder, jerk, jester, joke, joker, keeper, killjoy, know-it-all, kook, layperson, lemon, liaison, local, loner, loser, lout, love, lover, luminary, machine, mad person, marionette, master, mate, maverick, mediator, milksop, mind reader, miser, misfit, moron, mother, namby-pamby, name-dropper, naysayer, negotiator, neighbor, neophyte, newcomer, noble, nobody/nonentity, nonconformist, notable, notary, nouveau riche, novice, nut, observer, oddity/oddball, odds-on-favorite, old hand, onlooker, original, outcast, outsider, pagan, pal, pantywaist, paramour, pariah, participant, partisan, partner, passenger, patrician, patron, pauper, peer, personage/personality, pessimist, philanderer, philanthropist, pill, pillar, plebeian, poet, prey, prognosticator, proletariat, promoter, prophet, proponent, protagonist, protégé, pundit, puppet, pushover, racist, ragamuffin, rebel, recluse, rich, rival, scream, second, sectarian, seer, shirked, sidekick, simpleton, sissy, skeptic, slacker, snob, snoop, socialite, somebody, soothsayer, sourpuss, spectator, spendthrift, sponge, sponsor, sport, square, standby, stick-in-the-mud, stooge, stranger, subject, subordinate, substitute, suitor, support/supporter, surrogate, sweetheart, sycophant, target, tattletale/tattler, tenderfoot, tenant, toady, tool, tourist, trainee, traveler, trustee, tyro, umpire, underdog, underling, understudy, urchin, vagabond, vagrant, veteran, victim, visitor, wag, waif, wanderer, wayfarer, weakling, weirdo, wimp, windbag, wino, witness, wizard, womanizer, yes-person, zany

424 traits: adolescent, adult, babe, baby, beauty, beginner, boy, brat, child, childish, colossus, daughter, debutante, dish, doll, dwarf, elder, eyeful, fetus, fledgling, freak, giant, girl, gnome, grown-up, infant, invalid, juvenile, kid, lad, midget, minor, mossback, mutant, neophyte, newborn, nymph, old-timer, pipsqueak, runt, senior, teenager, toddler, trainee, tyro, vision, young, youngster/youth

PLANTS

425 flower: bloom, blossom, bouquet, flower
426 fruit: berry, fruit, produce
427 growth or death of: bloom, blossom, bud, develop, germinate, grow, growth, pregnancy, wilt, wither
428 part: bark, bough, branch, bud, cereal, fiber, flavoring, flower, foliage, fruit, grain, husk, juice, leaf, limb, log, nut, peel, pod, pulp, scion, seed, shell, skin, stalk, stem, trunk
429 plant: algae, bouquet, bramble, brush, bush, creation, crop, fertilizer, fossil, garland, grass, grove, harvest, hedge, hybrid, nature, organism, plant, produce, vintage, wreath
430 tree: timber, tree, wood/woods
431 vegetable: produce, salad, vegetable

Objects

ARTICLES, PHYSICAL

432 group of: accrual, accumulation, admixture, agglomeration, aggregate, amalgam, anthology, archive, armada, array, arsenal, assembly, assortment, backlog, bale, batch, battery, bevy, blend, body, bolt, bunch, bundle, cadre, canon, caravan, cavalcade, chain, clot, cloud, clump, cluster, clutter, collection, column, combination, compilation, complex, composite, compound, concentration, concoction, concourse, congestion, conglomeration, couple, crush, deluge, deposit, drift, drove, ensemble, everything, fleet, flock, flotilla, fusion, glob, gridlock, group, hash, heap, herd, hodgepodge, host, huddle, jumble, junk, knot, litter, load, lot, lump, many, mass, medley, mélange, miscellany, mishmash, mix/mixture, mixed bag, mob, motorcade, mound, mountain, multitude, muster, navy, number, odds and ends, oodles, pack, package, pair, parcel, party, patchwork, pile, pool, potpourri, press, queue, repertory, residue, row, scads, score/scores, scramble, set, stack, stew, store, stuff, sum, surge, swarm, throng, train, tuft, unit, variety, wad, whole

433 object: anything, article, entity, fact, individual, loser, matter, object, something, substance, tableware, thing

434 part of: aspect, barb, carcass/carcase, compartment, cubicle, pigeonhole

435 place: asylum, barrier, base, bottomless, center, depository, depot, dynasty, haunt, haven, heaven, hell, inferno, library, mecca, perdition, place, purgatory, repository, storeroom

436 shape: angle, arc, arch, ball, bead, bend, bulb, bulge, check, circle, coil, cone, contortion, contour, convolution, corner, crescent, curl, curve, disk, dogleg, dummy, effigy, elbow, globe, helm, kink, knot, labyrinth, lap, line, loaf, loop, maze, mold, orb, orbit, outline, rainbow, revolution, ring, ripple, rod, roll, round, shape, sphere, spiral, streak, wad, wave, wheel, whorl

ATMOSPHERE

437 air: air, atmosphere, billow, blast, breath, breeze, bubble, cloud, draft, dust, effervescence, firmament, fumes, lather, puff, sky, vapor

BUILDINGS, FURNISHINGS. POSSESSIONS

438 arena: aquarium, arena, bazaar, center, coliseum, dump, field, gymnasium, hall, landfill, mecca, stadium, stage
439 building: abbey, airport, architecture, archives, armory, arsenal, asylum, auditorium, bakery, bank, bar, barn, booth, building, cathedral, clinic, club, conservatory, construction, consulate, court, delivery room, department store, disco, dock, domicile, edifice, embassy, emergency room, enclosure, factory, flophouse, food court, fort/fortress, fortification, framework, garage, garrison, gin mill, greasy spoon, gymnasium, hacienda, hall, hangout, harbor, headquarters, hospital, hotel, house, inn, installation, institute/institution, jail, jetty, joint, laboratory, mall, mansion, marina, mental hospital, mill, monastery, mooring, mosque, motel, museum, nightclub, nursing home, nut house, office, outlet, pavilion, pen, penitentiary, pier, plant, post, prison, pub, rampart, reformatory, repository, restaurant, ruins, saloon, sanctuary, shop, shrine, singles bar, skyscraper, stage, stockade, store, storeroom, stronghold, structure, tavern, temple, theater/theatre, tower, treasury, villa, warehouse, wharf
440 building part: aisle, alcove, annex, archway, attic, awning, balcony, basement, bay, belfry, bleachers, booth, buttress, canopy, ceiling, cellar, chimney, chute, closet, column, concourse, corner, corridor, cranny, den, depart-

index

ment, dome, door, egress, entrance, entry, exit, fireplace, floor, flue, foyer, gallery, gate, gazebo, gutter, hall, lectern, locker, niche, nook, partition, passage/passageway, pillar, platform, pole, post, prop, recess, screen, stack, stay, step, support, threshold, tower, vent, wall, wing

441 business place: agency, annex, boutique, building, bureau, factory, foyer, hall, lobby, office, shop, skyscraper, store, suite, wing

442 foundation: backbone, base, basis, bed, bottom, core, cornerstone, easel, foot, footing, foundation, frame, groundwork, infrastructure, kiosk, nadir, nitty-gritty, rest, rock, root, seat, stand, support

443 furniture: altar, antique, banister, bed, bench, bleachers, booth, buffet, bunk, bureau, cabinet, can, chair, cot, couch, cradle, crib, cupboard, davenport, desk, dresser, fireplace, furnishings, furniture, futon, gazebo, jetty, kiosk, lectern, mirror, partition, pen, perch, pier, platform, podium, pulpit, rack, rail/railing, ramp, screen, seat, secretary, sofa, stand, table, wardrobe

444 furniture accessory: bedding, bedspread, candlestick, canopy, chandelier, curtain, cushion

445 furniture part: button, faucet, gate, handle, knob, latch, ledge, nozzle, picket, pivot, post, quilt, screen, shade, shelf, stay, step, support, tap, valve

446 personal item: adornment, album, amulet, backpack, beads, belongings, best-seller, bracelet, briefcase, brooch, cache, camera, cargo, chain, charm, condom, contraceptive, curio, disguise, doll, effects, emollient, equipment, eyeglasses, favorite, fetish, gem, gimcrack, glasses, goods, handbag, jewel, jewelry, keepsake, knickknack, lotion, luggage, makeup, marionette, memento, memorabilia, moisturizer, necklace, nest egg, novelty, object d'art, odds and ends, odds-on-favorite, pack, paraphernalia, plaything, pledge, pocketbook, possession, pouch, pride, property, puppet, purchase, purse, relic, resources, riches, ring, savings, souvenir, spectacles, stuff, subsistence, supplies, support, sustenance, thing/things, toy, trappings, treasure, trifle, trinket, valuable

447 recreation area: cabaret, casino, hangout, landmark

448 room: alcove, apartment, attic, auditorium, bath, bathroom, bedroom, bistro, boutique, cell, cellar, chamber, den, dormitory, enclosure, food court, foyer, gallery, gin mill, greasy spoon, hall, kitchen, lavatory, lobby, loft, office, outhouse, outlet, parlor, pub, restaurant, room, saloon, sanctuary, shop, shrine, stage, stockade, store, tavern, tenement, theater/theatre, vestibule

449 workplace: bakery, base, bazaar, bistro, brothel, bureau, business, cabaret, café, cafeteria, canteen, capitol, church, clinic, conservatory, consulate, dairy, delicatessen, depot, diner, dive, dump, dungeon, embassy, emporium, establishment, exchange, factory, farm, field, flophouse, food court, gallery, garage, hangout, hospital, hotel, inn, jail, joint, landfill, lounge, madhouse, mall, market/mart,

mill, mine, motel, museum, nightclub, office, orchard, outlet, penitentiary, plant, plantation, port, prison, pub, ranch, reformatory, restaurant, saloon, shop, store, synagogue, tavern, treasury, warehouse, whorehouse

CLOTHING

450 accessory: bag, bandanna, belt, boot, buckle, cap, collar, mask, pocketbook, pouch, purse, satchel

451 clothing: apparel, armor, array, attire, bathing suit, blouse, cape, cloak, clothes/clothing, coat, costume, disguise, dress, duds, dungarees, ensemble, falsies, finery, frock, garb, garment, gear, girdle, glove, gown, habit, hat, helmet, jacket, masquerade, negligee, nightgown, nylons, outfit, pajamas, panties, pants, poncho, quilt, robe, scarf, shoe, skirt, sneaker, suit, supplies, swimsuit, thing/things, threads, trappings, trousers, underwear, uniform, veil, wardrobe, wash, wrap

452 part: collar, crease, crown, patch, pocket, seam, strand, tiara

453 state of dress: bareness, doff, nudity, try on/try out, undress, wear

FOOD AND DRINK

454 beverage: alcohol, ale, beverage, brew, coffee, draft, drink, moonshine, potable

455 beverage, alcoholic: beer, liquer, liquor

456 change in: curdle, spoil, turn

457 food: appetizer, batter, bite, bread, brew, broth, bun, candy, casserole, comfort food, condiment, confection, cracker, delicacy, diet, dish, doughnut, fare, feed, fodder, food, frankfurter, frosting, game, grub, hamburger, helping, hero, hors d'oeuvre, hot dog, leftover, loaf, macaroni, maintenance, meat, morsel, nosh, nourishment, nurture, nutrient, nutrition, pancake, pastry, preserves, produce, ration, refreshment, sandwich, seasoning, snack, stew, submarine, subsistence, supplies, support, sustenance, sweet, tart, treat, victuals, vittles

458 food part: morsel, nibble, nip, pat, taste, tidbit

459 meal: banquet, barbecue, bite, board, buffet, cuisine, diet, dinner, fare, feast, meal, nosh, picnic, plate, repast, snack, spread, table

460 produced from animal: comfort food, dish, feed, fodder, food, frankfurter, frosting, game, grub, hamburger, hero, loaf, macaroni, meat, sandwich, stew, submarine, victuals, vittles

461 produced from plant: condiment, dish, doughnut, food, loaf, pancake, pastry, preserves, produce, seasoning, stew, sweet

462 quality of: acerbity, alcoholic, baked, crusty, done, eatable, edible, effervescent, mellow, natural, nourishing, nutritious, perishable, rancid, rare, raw, ripe, rotten, salty, salutary, short, sour, stale, straight, strong, succulent, sweet, tempting, unappetizing, unsavory, weak, wholesome

MACHINES

463 machine: accordion, alarm, apparatus, appliance, artificial intelligence, boom box, brake, calculator, camera, catapult, clock, computer, contraption, contrivance, dashboard, data processor, device, distress signal, doodad, doohickey, droid, electronics, engine, fan, fire alarm, fixture, foghorn, furnace, gadget, gadgetry, gizmo, incinerator, installation, instrument, jet, machine, machinery, mechanism, model, motor, personal computer, plant, printer, robot, smoke detector, software, stove, technology, television, terminal, watch, widget

464 machine part: anchor, antenna, axle, bank, cog, cushion, engine, faucet, gear, helm, motor, nozzle, pivot, pointer, tap, valve, vent, videocassette, wheel

MATTER, CONDITIONS OF

465 gas: fart, gas, jet, miasma

466 gel: balm, batter, clot, cream, dip, gum, liniment, lotion, ointment, ooze, paste, plaster, salve, sunscreen

467 liquid: alcohol, broth, cream, dew, drool, drop, enamel, eruption, essence, flow, fluid, froth, fuel, gasoline, gush, jet, juice, liquid, matter, milk, moisture, moonshine, ooze, paint, petroleum, potion, precipitation, saliva, shower, solution, spit, sunscreen, surge, sweat, tear/tears, water

468 liquid part: cream, drop, froth

469 physical change: ablate, attrition, bubble, clot, cloud, coagulate, coagulation, collapse, color, come unglued, congeal, consolidation, contraction, crack, crumble, cry, darken, decay, decompose, degeneracy, degenerate, dehydrate, die, discolor, disintegrate, dissipate, dissolution, dissolve, distend, dry, eat, erode, evaporate, evaporation, exhaust, fade, fester, fizz, flake, flare, flatten, fluctuate, flush, foam, foul, fragment, give, glow, go out, grow, growth, harden, heat, jell, languish, metamorphose, metamorphosis, open, ossify, perspire, putrefy, ravel, redden, revive, rot, rust, settle, sink, solidify, spoil, stiffen, tarnish, thaw, thicken, tighten, tire, turn, wilt

470 solid: band, bar, barricade, barrier, baton, block, blockade, bolt, brace, bulge, cake, cast, clot, club, clump, cord, dam, deposit, fossil, glass, glob, hedge, hunk, hurdle, ice, jump, lump, matter, mirror, monument, night stick, obstacle, obstruction, occlusion, partition, pill, pole, post, prop, rock, rod, stick, wand, weight

471 solid part: arm, attachment, back, bar, beam, block, bolt, branch, button, chunk, chute, closure, corner, deposit, flap, girder, hinge, hump, hunk, knob, knot, leg, ligature, link, lump, node/nodule, nub, nugget, outgrowth, patch, plug, powder, projection, protuberance, ridge, rung, seam, slab, sliver, splinter, stake, strap, strip, support, tuft, wedge

MATTER, DIVISIONS OF

472 chemical: alkali, alkaline, ammonia, antiseptic

473 fabric: apparel, awning, bedding, blanket, canvas, carpet, cloth, ensign, fabric, filigree, flag, lace, mesh, nap, napkin, net, pad/padding, pennant, quilt, rug, screen, web, yarn

474 gem: gem, jewel, rock, stone

475 material: appointment, binding, blanket, brace, cast, cement, cloak, coat, coating, glaze, glue, herbicide, lace, lacquer, lasso, leash, line, material, pad/padding, pad, page, paint, paper, patchwork, pipe, plaster, plate, poison, pole, poncho, rope, sheet, slip, standard, strand, stationery, strap, string, tab, tablet, tack, tag, tape, tether, toxin, trim, twine, wash

476 metallic: alloy, armor, badge, can, chain, fence, iron, medal, metal, ornament

477 mineral: rock, stone

478 natural element: allergen, blaze, bonfire, carbohydrate, cell, conflagration, embers, ferment, film, fire, flame, jewel, rock, substance

479 wood: beam, board, cane, coffin, fence, framework, girder, log, paddle, perch, picket, pier, pole, post, rack, rail/railing, rod, splinter, staff, stake, stick, timber

MATTER, QUALITIES OF

480 balance: asymmetrical, awkward, dizzy, even, inequitable, lopsided, odd, proportionate/proportional, pro rata, slaphappy, smooth, symmetrical, unbalanced, unequal, uneven, vertigo, woozy

481 capacity: brimming/brimful, capacious, capacity, close, compact, congested, crowded, empty, full, packed, spacious, stuffed, teeming, vacant, void

482 continuity: broken, connected, continuous, direct, disconnected, discontinuous, disjointed, dragging, durable, elongated, endless, entire, episodic, eternal, fitful, flowing, indelible, intermittent, lengthy, long, neverending, nonstop, numberless, old, ongoing, patchy, perfect, running, sequential, serial, solid, spacious, spasmodic, straight, through, throughout, timeless, together, unbroken, undivided, unending, unfathomable, uninterrupted

483 density: airtight, anemic, close, compact, concentrated, congested, cramped, crowded, dense, devoid, fraught, full, hollow, impenetrable, impermeable, packed, petrified, replete, solid, stuffed, teeming, thick, tight

484 exteriority: adjunct, adornment, annex, border, bound/bounds, boundary, brink, buffer, casing, circuit, circumference, compass, confines, corner, cover, crust, cushion, edge, exterior, extreme, extremity, face, fringe, hem, horizon, hull, husk, jacket, lip, margin, membrane, mug, outer, outermost, outside, peel, perimeter, periphery, pod, revolution, rim, scale, sheet, shell, skin, skirt, surface, verge

485 physical: abhorrent, ablaze, acid, acute,

adulterated, aesthetic/esthetic, agile, alimentary, antiseptic, atomic, austere, bad, bald, bare, barren, bearded, beautiful, bedridden, bland, blank, bloody, blunt, brawny, broken, bumpy, burning, caustic, chintzy, clean, combustible, comfortable, corrugated, corrupt, cozy, crippled, crumbly, cuddly, curable, damaged, decayed, decrepit, deformed, deserted, desolate, devoid, dilapidated, diluted/dilute, dingy, dirty, disgusting, disheveled, disordered, disorderly, disorganized, disrepair, distended, done in, drained, drawn, droopy, ducky, dusty, effervescent, enervated, erect, exhausted, expectant, expecting, exposed, failing, faint, fallow, fat, fatigued, fatty, featureless, fertile, filthy, fireproof, fit, flaccid, flaming, flammable, flexible, foamy, forked, formless, foul, fragile, frail, free, fresh, frothy, game, gaping, ghastly, ghetto, ghostly, gnarled, godforsaken, good, green, grimy, grubby, gruesome, grungy, hardy, haywire, immature, impaired, impalpable, impervious, impotent, inchoate, inconspicuous, incorruptible, incurable, indistinct, infirm, inflammable, insubstantial, intact, invisible, irreparable, knurled, laden, leafy, lean, lifeless, liquid, livable, loathsome, loose, lusty, magnificent, malleable, mangy, marked, material, mature, mean, messy, mild, miserable, misshapen, mixed, moth-eaten, muddy, muscular, naked, nasty, natural, neat, neutral, noxious, nude, oblique, obtuse, obvious, on-the-blink, open, open-and-shut, ordered, orderly, outstanding, pacific, palatial, palpable, palsied, paltry, paralytic, pathetic, peaceful, pendulous/pendent, perfect, perishable, perverted, physical, piteous, pitiful, placid, plain, pregnant, premature, prepared, prickly, primitive, prolific, prominent, prostrate, puffy, pure, putrid, quizzical, ragged, rambling, ramshackle, rank, raw, rocky, rotten, rough, run-down, rusty, savage, scenic, scraggly, scruffy, seedy, serene, shabby, shady, shaggy, shipshape, shoddy, sinewy, slack, sleazy, slimy, slipshod, slovenly, smoky, snug, soft, somber, sorry, speckled, spectral, splendid, spotty, squalid, stale, stark, sterile, stony, sumptuous, surface, swollen, symmetrical, synthetic, tacky, tattered, tense, thin, thorny, threadbare, tidy, tight, topsy-turvy, torn, tousled, trim, tumescent, unadorned, unblemished, unbroken, uncomfortable, undeveloped, unfinished, unkempt, unorganized, unsuccessful, untouched, upset, vague, verdant, visual, voluptuous, watery, weak, weary, whole, wizened, wooden, worn/worn-out

486 shape: angular, baggy, beaten, bent, billowy, blunt, checkered, circular, concave, conical/conic, convex, crescent, crooked, curly, curved, deformed, dull, elliptical, flabby, flat, flush, gnarled, grotesque, kinky, malformed, misshapen, oblong, obtuse, oval, round, serrated, shapeless, sharp, spiral, square, straight

487 similarity: akin, alike, analogous, approximate, closely, cognate, comparable, comparative, conformable, different, equal, equivalent, faithful, homogenous, identical,

interchangeable, like, like-minded, parallel, related, representative, same, seeming, similar, synonymous, tantamount, twin, uniform, virtual, virtually

488 stability: adhesive, adrift, brittle, carved in stone, choppy, doddering, ductile, durable, fast, firm, firmly, fixed, flexible, hard, immobile, immovable, insecure, limber, lissom, lithe, motionless, movable, moving, pliable, ramshackle, resilient, rickety, rocky, secure, set, shaky, situated, soft, solid, solvent, sound, stable, stationary, steady, sturdy, supple, sure, taut, tenacious, tractable, unbreakable, unstable/unsteady, unwavering, weak, wobbly, wooden, yielding

489 strength: able-bodied, adaptive, athletic, brawny, breakable, brute, durable, failing, feeble, firmly, flimsy, fragile, frail, full-blooded, full-bodied, hale, hardy, Herculean, impregnable, indestructible, indomitable, infirm, invincible, lame, leathery, lusty, mighty, muscular, potent, powerful, powerless, puny, resilient, robust, rocky, rugged, stalwart, stout, strapping, strong, sturdy, tenacious, tenuous, tight, tough, unbreakable, unsuccessful, vigorous, weak

490 structure: airtight, airy, amorphous, anorexic, baggy, bare, beaten, bleak, blind, budding, cavernous, clean-cut, clear, cleft, composite, conglomerate, craggy, crooked, curvaceous, curved, dainty, delicate, depressed, detached, diaphanous, ductile, elastic, emaciated, even, flabby, flat, flush, gangling, gaping, gaunt, hollow, incarnate, irregular, jagged, level, limp, oblique, plane, pointed, precipitous, rude, rugged, scrawny, shapely, sheer, skinny, slender/slim, slight, spare, springy, stout, stringy, sunken, svelte, trim, wasted, wiry

491 weight: anorexic, bantam, beaten, buoyant, cadaverous, chubby, chunky, corpulent, dainty, dumpy, emaciated, ethereal, fat, fine, fleshy, gangling, gargantuan, gaunt, giant, gigantic, haggard, heavy, hefty, lanky, lean, light, lightweight, lithe, meager, obese, overweight, plump, ponderous, portable, portly, pudgy, rangy, roly-poly, rotund, round, scrawny, skinny, slender/slim, slight, spare, squat, stocky, stout, stubby, svelte, tenuous, thick, thin, titanic, trim, tubby, underweight, wasted, weighty, wiry

TOOLS

492 cleaner: antiseptic, cleanser, deodorant, detergent, polish

493 cooking: barbecue, bowl, china, frying pan, pan, plate, scoop, utensil

494 container: bag, baggage, barrel, basin, basket, bottle, bowl, box, briefcase, bucket, cabinet, cage, can, canteen, carton, case, cask, casket, cell, chamber, chest, coffer, coffin, container, crate, cup, decanter, dish, envelope, flask, frying pan, glass, hamper, jar, jug, keg, kettle, kit, luggage, main, mug, ossuary, package, packet, pan, parcel, pitcher, portfolio, pot, pottery, pouch, purse, receptacle, store, trunk, vault, vessel

495 **cutting:** blade, chisel, dagger, knife

496 **equipment:** equipment, gear, harness, installation, kit, outfit, pack, paraphernalia, plant, rig, tackle, trappings

497 **grasping:** bond, bridle, catch, clasp, curb, manacle

498 **part:** ammunition, hinge, hook, munitions, pivot, pointer, round, shot

499 **tool:** accordion, apparatus, ax/axe, blade, brace, broom, brush, cart, chain, chisel, clamp, club, conduit, connection, contraption, contrivance, dagger, dashboard, device, dolly, doodad, doohickey, drill, electronics, fastener, gadget, gadgetry, gizmo, hardware, implement, instrument, key, knife, latch, lock, mop, night stick, organ, paddle, pen, pipe, rein, ruler, scoop, tableware, technology, tool, utensil, valve, wand, wedge, whip, widget

500 **weapon:** A-bomb, ammunition, armament(s), arms, arrow, artillery, atom bomb, baton, battery, bomb, bullet, cannon, catapult, cudgel, defense, dynamite, explosive, fetters, firearm, fission, gun, magazine, missile, munitions, nuclear weapon, nuke, ordnance, pistol, rocket, round, weapon

TRANSPORTATION

501 **object used for:** access, alley, approach, arcade, artery, avenue, boulevard, bridge, career, channel, circuit, concourse, conduit, conveyance, course, crossing, detour, diversion, drain, duct, esplanade, expressway, flume, freeway, heading, highway, intersection, lane, line, mall, passage/passageway, path, road, route, street, track, trail, trajectory, turnpike, walk, way

502 **part, vehicle:** anchor, bow, fender, handle, portal, trunk, wheel, wing

503 **vehicle:** camper, caravan, conveyance, jet, motorcade, railroad, transport, vehicle

504 **vehicle, air:** aircraft, airplane, armada, balloon, blimp, craft, dirigible, flying saucer, helicopter, plane, shuttle, spacecraft, UFO

505 **vehicle, land:** ambulance, automobile, bicycle, cab, car, cart, cherry-picker, coach, dolly, earthmover, excavator, hack, model, motorcycle, traffic, truck

506 **vehicle, water:** armada, barge, boat, canoe, craft, ferry, fleet, flying saucer, sailboat, vessel, yacht

The Planet

GEOGRAPHY

507 **city:** capital, center, city, hamlet, metropolis, municipality, town, village

508 **geographic division:** area, country, county, department, desert, district, dynasty, grounds, kingdom, land, outskirts, province, quarter, region, sector, state, suburb, terrain, territory, town, tract, ward, zone

509 **land:** abyss, acreage, avalanche, backwoods, bank, basin, bay, beach, bed, black hole, bluff, bog, campus, canyon, cape, cave, cavern, clay, cliff, coast, compost, court, cove, crevice/crevasse, culvert, dirt, ditch, downgrade, drop, dune, earth, elevation, eminence, estuary, excavation, expanse, farm, field, forest, fossil, frontier, garden, geography, glacier, glen, gorge, grassland, green, grotto, ground, gulch, gulf, gully, harbor, hill, hillock, horizon, inlet, island, knoll, land, landscape, landslide, lawn, levee, lot, marsh, marshy, meadow, menagerie, mesa, mine, mire, moat, morass, mound, mountain, mountainous, mud, nature, orchard, outlook, parcel, park, pass, patio, peak, pit, plain, plateau, playground, plaza, plot, porch, port, prairie, precipice, projection, promontory, property, prospect, quagmire, rampart, ravine, reef, ridge, rock, savanna, seashore, shelf, shore, soil, square, stack, swamp, table, terrain, trench, trough, tundra, tunnel, valley, waste, well, wood/woods, yard

510 **nation:** country, fatherland, home, kingdom, land, nation, nationality, native land, soil, state

511 **planet:** cosmos, deep space, Earth, environment, galaxy, globe, moon, nature, planet, soil, sphere, universe, world

512 **region:** capital, colony, commonwealth, community, quarter, realm, region, reservation, settlement, suburb

513 **section:** acreage, across-the-board, aisle, alcove, backyard, barrier, beat, bed, belt, berth, blank, border, breach, brink, canyon, cavity, cell, chasm, chink, clearance, clearing, cleavage, cleft, corner, country, county, court, crack, cranny, crevice/crevasse, crossing, deadline, den, depression, dip, ditch, edge, enclosure, excavation, expanse, footprint, fracture, frontier, furrow, gap, green, groove, gulch, gulf, gully, gutter, hem, hinterland, hole, hump, interstice, lawn, leak, ledge, limit, lip, margin, marginal, menagerie, moat, mouth, niche, nook, notch, opening, orifice, outlet, outskirts, parcel, park, pass, patch, patio, pit, playground, plaza, plot, pocket, porch, pothole, precinct, precipice, projection, prominence, puncture, ravine, recess, rent, repair, ridge, rift, rip, rupture, rut, scratch, shelf, side, sight, slack, slit, slot, split, subdivision, tear, threshold, track, tract, trench, trough, tunnel, vacancy, vacuum, valley, void, ward, well, wrinkle, yoke, zone

514 **water:** abyss, aquarium, aqueduct, arm, basin, bay, beach, billow, blackball, brine, brook, canal, cape, cascade, channel, coast, condensation, course, creek, current, deep, eddy, estuary, flume, fountain, geyser, gulf, harbor, heading, ice, inlet, lagoon, lake, maelstrom, oasis, ocean, pond, pool, promontory, race, reservoir, river, sea, seashore, spray, spring, strait, stream, tide, trajectory, wash, waterfall, wave, well, whirlpool

HABITATS

515 habitat: abode, asylum, ecosystem, environment, environmentalist, fatherland, habitat/habitation, hideout, harbor, haven, home, lair, land, native land, nest, oasis, paradise, place, premises, property, refuge, sanctuary, settlement, shelter, tent

516 habitat, human: accommodations, address, apartment, asylum, barracks, berth, cabin, camp, castle, cloister, condominium, convent, cottage, domesticity, domicile, dungeon, dwelling, element, embassy, encampment, environs, estate, flat, grange, grounds, hacienda, haunt, home, hotel, house, household, housing, hovel, hut, inn, jail, lodge, lodging, loony bin, madhouse, mansion, monastery, motel, neighborhood, nunnery, old country, pad, palace, penitentiary, prison, quarters, reservation, residence, resort, retreat, sanctuary, shack, shanty, spa, suite, tenement, vacancy, villa

517 habitat, rural: barn, belt, burrow, cobweb, conservatory, dairy, desert, desolation, farm, field, forest, garden, grange, grove, jungle, lawn, sanctuary, wilderness/wilds, wood/woods

518 state of: domain, eco-rich, entrench, occupancy, occupation, presence

NATURAL RESOURCES

519 electricity: beam, current, spark
520 energy: electricity, energy, fuel, gasoline, nuclear energy, nuclear reactor, petroleum, power

521 expression of energy: blast, blaze, bonfire, boom, chill, combustion, concussion, crash, discharge, explosion, fire, flame, flash, freeze, noise, thunder

522 natural event: eclipse, effervescence, meteorology, weather

523 resources: fuel, material, resource, resources, rock, substance

WEATHER

524 object connected with: avalanche, blast, breeze, chill, climate, cloud, cold, deluge, dew, drift, film, flood, flurry, fog, frost, gale, gust, hail, haze, humidity, hurricane, landslide, meteorology, mist, moisture, precipitation, puff, shower, thunder, vapor, weather, wind

525 quality of: breezy, bright, clear, clement, close, cloudy, crisp, dirty, dismal, dreary, fair, fierce, fiercely, filmy, fine, foggy, furious, gentle, gloomy, gusty, hazy, heavy, humid, inclement, intimidating, mild, misty, muggy, oppressive, overcast, raw, rough, rugged, sepulchral, soft, sticky, stormy, stuffy, sultry, sunny, temperate, tempestuous, thick, threatening, tranquil, tropical, turbulent, violent, wild, windy, wintry

526 type of: blizzard, blow, cloud, downpour, drizzle, earthquake, fog, gale, hail, hurricane, mist, precipitation, puff, quake, rain, shade, shower, storm, tempest, thunder, torrent, tremor

Qualities

ABSTRACT

527 ability: able, ably, accountable, adept, adroit, agile, all-around, amateurish, artistic, awkward, barren, capable, commendable, competent, deft, dexterous, dilettante, disabled, easy as pie, effete, efficient, eligible, executive, experienced, expert, facile, feeble, gifted, good, great, handy, Herculean, inapt, incapable, incapacitated, incompetent, inefficient, inept, inexperienced, master, masterful, neat, nimble, not born yesterday, powerful, powerless, practical, professional, proficient, qualified, raw, ready, rusty, seasoned, short, skillful, talented, unable, unaccustomed, unfit, unprofessional, unqualified, unskilled, versatile, versed, veteran, well, wicked

528 achievement: able, abortive, achievable, accomplished, ace, artful, attainable, banner, complete, consummate, crack, defensible/done, effectual, efficacious, feasible, fine, finished, flourishing, forward, fruitful, fruitless, futile, gifted, great, obtainable, operable, possible, potential, practical, professional, proficient, prosperous, successful, swimmingly, thriving, triumphant, unavailing, victorious, washed-up, well, winning

529 cognitive: academic, ad nauseum, affective, afraid, afterthought, alluring, alternative, amicable, anathema, appalling, attractive, axiomatic, bad, bag, balm, bane, bearable, belief, beta, black, boring, bothersome, breast, breathtaking, burdensome, charismatic, cheering, chimera, comforting, comic/comical, comparison, complex, comprehensible, conceivable, considered, considering, corollary, crazy, daydream, deducible, deep, déjà vu, demonstrable, deplorable, depressing, derivable, desirous, detestable, dialectic, difficult, discouraging, disputable, disquieting, dissatisfactory, distasteful, doleful, doubtful, dream, dry, dull, dullsville, elusive, enchanting, engrossing, enigmatic/enigmatical, enjoyable, entertaining, equivocal, esoteric, evident, exalted, exciting, exhilarating, explicit, eye-catching, fabulous, fanciful, fantasy, far-fetched, fascinating, favored, favorite, fearful, fetish, figment, flashback, flat, fleshly, forerunner, forgotten, foul, frightful/frightening, frightful, funny, ghastly, ghoulish, glad, golden, good, grating, groundbreaking, hair-raising, halfbaked, hallucination, harbinger, hard, harebrained, harrowing, haunting, hazy, heady, heartbreaking, heartrending, heinous, hellish, heretical, hilarious, homesick, hopeless, horizon, horrible/horrendous/horrid, humorous, hypnotic, hypothetical, idea, ideal, idealistic, idyllic, illogical, illusory/illusive, image, imaginable, imaginary, imaginative, impalpable, impenetrable, impression, inadvisable, incomprehensible, inconceivable, incredible, incredulous, indelible, indicator, inexplicable, inner, innovation, innovative, inscrutable, inside, insoluble, inspiration, instinct, insufferable, intelligible, interesting, intimate, intolerable, intriguing, inviting, inward, irksome, irrational, irrefutable, irresistible, itch, jocular/jocose/jocund, joy, knotty, knowledge, known, lamentable, leery, left, left-wing, liberal, liking, limit, loathsome, logical, loose, lucid, luminous, lure, mad, maddening, make-believe, mania, manifest, marvel, marvelous, matter, maudlin, maze, measurable, memorable, memory, metaphysical, miraculous, mirage, mistaken, mode, monotonous, moving, mutinous, mysterious, mystic/mystical, naked, nauseating, nauseous, nemesis, nettlesome, new age, nightmarish, nondescript, nostalgic, note, noticeable, notion, obscure, observable, obsession, obvious, offensive, on paper, on the fence, opaque, open, open-and-shut, optimist, otherworldly, painful, palatable, palpable, panorama, pathetic, pedagogic, pedantic, perceptible, perspicuous, pesky, phantom, phenomenon, phobia, pick, pipe dream, piquant, piteous, pitiful, plain, plaintive, poignant, pointless, politically correct, ponderous, portent, portentous, precious, preference, premise, premonition, preposterous, presage, problem, problematic, profound, provocative, psychedelic, pure, purposely, putative, puzzling, questionable, quixotic, radical, rather, ravishing, reactionary, readable, reasoning, rebellious, recall, recondite, redolent, remembrance, reminder, reminiscent, repulsive, reputed, reverie, revolting, revolutionary, rich, ridiculous, right, riveting, rosy, rot, sad, satisfactory, scary, scintilla, scintillating, scream, scrumptious, secret, secular, seditious, selection, self-evident/self-explanatory, sensation, shock, sickening, sidesplitting, sign, signal, simple, slight, slow, smidgen, snare, somber, soothing, sorry, sound, soupçon, spectacle, spectacular, speculation, speculative, spooky, stimulating, stirring, strain, subconscious, subject, subjective, suggestion, suggestive, surmise, surprise, suspect, suspicion, suspicious, tacit, tactile, tall, tame, tangible, taste, tasteful, tedious, temptation, tempting, tenor, theorem, theoretical, theory, thesis, thick, thing, thinkable, thought, thought-provoking, thrill, tinge, tiresome, token, tolerable, touch, touching, trace, treat, troublesome, unacceptable, unaccountable, unappetizing, unbelievable, uncertain, uncomfortable, undecided, understood, undesirable, unexciting, unfathomable, unfavorable, unforgettable, ungodly, unimaginable, uninteresting, uninvited, unlucky, unnoticed, unpleasant, unpopular, unquestionable, unresolved, unsatisfactory, untold, unwelcome, vague, vapid, vexatious, vile, visible, vision, visionary, whim, whisper, wishful, wonder, wonderful, worrisome

530 commonality: accidental, addictive, antiquated, antique, au courant, automatic, banal, bourgeois, common, commonly, commonplace, conventional, current, customarily, customary, diffuse, dogmatic, dull, everyday, fair, familiar, frequent, frequently, general, generally, generic, habitual, hackneyed, infrequent, lay, less, little, mainly, mainstream, much, musty, natural, now and then, occasional, occasionally, off and on, old, old school, on and off, once in a while, ordinarily, ordinary, pedestrian, popular, prevailing, prevalent, proverbial, public, rare, rarely, regular, routine, spasmodic, stereotyped, stock, time-honored, traditional, trite, typical, ubiquitous, undistinguished, unexceptional, unexciting, used to, usual, usually, vulgar, widespread

531 completeness: absolutely, all-out, almost, altogether, blank, bodily, capsule, clean, complete, completely, comprehensive, conscientious, crowning, dead, deeply, deficient, definitive, demonstrative, done, downright, entire, entirely, every, exhaustive, fatal, final, finished, fulfilled, full, full-scale, fully, halfway, holistic, incomplete, inseparable, intact, integral, intensive, out-and-out, outright, over, panoramic, partial, partially, partly, past, perfectly, piecemeal, plenary, practically, pretty, primarily, principally, profound, pure, purely, quite, rank, right, rough, round, rude, sheer, simply, sketchy, sloppy, solid, stark, superficially, sweeping, thorough/thoroughgoing, thoroughly, through, throughout, total, totally, unabridged, unconditional, undivided, unfinished, unmitigated, unqualified, utmost, utter, utterly, wanting, washed-up, whole, wholly

532 concerned with: about, albatross, angst, anxiety, appertain, apply, apropos, bad news, barrier, bear on/bear upon, beat, behalf, behind, belong, bother, bug, burden, business, can of worms, care, catch-22, challenge, charge, compulsion, concept, concern, consideration, conundrum, craze, debate, difficulty, discovery, disputation, disquiet, distraction, distress, duel, ear, encumbrance, enigma, fancy, fascination, feeling, fixation, focus, forbidden fruit, guilt, hallucination, hang-up, heed, horror, include, interest, issue, keynote/keystone, matter, millstone, mystery, notice, notion, object, obstacle, obstruction, occlusion, pain, paradox, part, particular, passion, peeve, pertain, pivot, place, presentiment, priority, problem, province, provocation, qualm, quandary, question, refer, regard, relate, reverie, riddle, scruple, subject, suspicion, taboo, temptation, topic, touch, toward/towards, trouble, urge, vision, weight, woe, wonder, worry

533 conformity: acceptable, adequate, admissible, befitting, classic, decent, formal, ideal, mediocre, medium, middle-of-the-road, moderate, old school, ordinary, orthodox, practical, proper, regular, so-so, standard, time-honored, traditional, typical, unwritten

534 constancy: adjustable, ambivalent, arbitrary, borderline, changeable, chronic, consistent, constant, continual, fickle, firmly, fitful, fluid, forever, formative, frozen, grim, halting, hesitant, immovable, immutable, impervious, incessant, inconsistent, inconstant, indecisive, indestructible, indomitable, inexorable, insistent, intermittent, intractable/intransigent, invariable, inveterate, iron, irregular, irrevocable, monotonous, on and on, relentless, rigid, same, severe, slippery, solid, spotty, static, staunch, steadfast, steady, tentative, unbending, unceasing, uncertain, unchangeable, unchanging, unfailing, unforeseeable, uniform, unpredictable, unresolved, unstable/unsteady, variable, varying, volatile, wanton, weak-minded

535 definiteness: absolute, absolutely, accurate, accurately, ad hoc, airtight, ambiguous, apparent, apparently, assured, automatic, canonical, categorical, certain, certainly, clean, clean-cut, clear-cut, clearly, close, complete, conclusive, concrete, conscious, controversial, dead-on, debatable, decided, decidedly, decisive, deep-seated, definite, definitely, definitive, demonstrable, designedly, desultory, dicey, discernible, disordered, disorderly, disputable, distinct, doubtful, doubtless, dubious, easily, elective, emphatic, entirely, equivocal, erratic, especial, especially, evident, evidently, exact, exactly, experimental, explicit, express, expressly, factual, fail-safe, final, finally, finite, fixed, flat, foolproof, formless, for sure, graphic, gross, guaranteed, haphazard, hard, hard-core, hesitant, hit-or-miss, illegible, impeccable, implicit, implied, inalienable, incalculable, incontrovertible, indecisive, indeed, indefinite, indeterminate, indisputable, indistinct, indubitably, inevitable, infallible, ingrained, intangible, in the bag, ironclad, irrefutable, irresolute, just, legible, limpid, main, marked, markedly, mere, moot, nebulous, necessarily, necessary, obviously, official, only, open, outright, overt, palpable, pat, peremptory, perfect, plain, political, positive, positively, precarious, precise, precisely, pronounced, pure, questionable, random, rank, really, reliable, right, rigid, rigorous, scientific, secure, seriously, set, shaky, sharp, sheer, simply, slippery, sound, specific, straight, straightforward, strict, stringent, strong, sure, surely, tenebrous, tentative, tested, thorough/thoroughgoing, thoroughly, tried, tried-and-true, true, truly, trustworthy/trusty, ultimate, unavoidable, uncertain, unconditional, undeniable, undependable, undisputed/undisputable, undoubtedly, unequivocal, unerring, unfailing, unfaltering, unmistakable, unmitigated, unorganized, unqualified, unquestionable, unreadable, unsettled, unsubstantiated, unsure, unwavering, utter, verbatim, very, weak-minded, willful, yes

536 domain: absolute, academic, administrative, agrarian, agricultural, aquatic, athletic, authoritative, autocratic, blessed, bridal, bucolic, captive, celestial, chemical, city, civic, civil, classical, clerical, commanding, commercial, communal, confederate, constituent, country, democratic, dismal, domestic, drab, earthly, ecclesiastical, economic, educational, egalitarian, endemic, fleshly, foreign, free, global, God-fearing, home, homegrown, homemade, homespun, household, industrial, infernal, internal, international, itinerant, literary, local, marine/maritime, metropolitan, military, multinational, municipal, national, native, nautical/naval, nomadic, oceanic, pedagogic, personal, prevalent, psychological, public, religious, social, sovereign, spiritual, supernal, technical, terrestrial, theatrical, theological, totalitarian, unearthly, universal, unworldly, urban, widespread, worldly, worldwide

537 effects: advantageous, advisory, aphrodisiac, awesome, awry, bad, baleful, baneful, beastly, benign, bitter, bleak, bracing, bright, burning, calamitous, charismatic, cogent, combustible, coming, consequent, convincing, corrective, corrosive, costly, cultural, curative, damaging, deadly, deathly, deep, defamatory, deleterious, demonstrative, desperate, destined, destructive, detrimental, dire, direful, disadvantageous, disagreeable, disastrous, disruptive, divisive, done for, doomed, dramatic, drastic, dread, dreadful, eclectic, ecumenical, eerie, effective, effectual, efficacious, embarrassing, emergent, entertaining, epidemic, exigent, expressive, extenuating, faint, fatal, fateful, favorable, favorably, fearful, fecund, fetching, fierce, fiercely, flat, food poisoning, fooled, forbidding, forcible, foreign, for kicks, formative, formidable, fortunately, foul, fresh, frightful/frightening, fruitful, fruitless, fun, funereal, funny, furious, general, gentle, ghastly, ghostly, gloomy, gold mine, good, gory, grateful, grave, greatly, grievous, grisly, gross, grotesque, harmful, harmless, harsh, haunting, healthful/healthy, heartbreaking, heartrending, heavenly, helpful, hideous, highly, histrionic, horrible/horrendous/horrid, hurtful, hypnotic, ill, ill-fated/ill-starred, imperceptible, imposing, incendiary, inconclusive, inconvenient, ineffective/ineffectual, inflammatory, influential, inimical, injurious, insipid, insufferable, insulting, intoxicating, invigorating, inviting, jazzy, juicy, lamentable, lethal, lovely, lucky, lurid, macabre, madly, magic/magical, magnetic, malign, memorial, menacing, mighty, mild, monstrous, morbid, mortal, moving, narcotic, nasty, nettlesome, neutral, nightmarish, noisome, nondescript, noticeable, nourishing, noxious, offensive, oppressive, outstanding, painful, pale, pallid, pallor, penetrating, peremptory, pernicious, persuasive, pesky, pestilent/pestilential, piercing, pleasing/pleasurable, poison/poisonous, prejudicial, prepossessing, productive, profitable, prosaic, provocative, psychedelic, remedial, right, rugged, ruinous, safe, satisfying, sedative, sensational, sensuous, sharp, sick, sickly, slow, soft, soporific, spectacular, spectral, spooky, star-crossed, stirring, strong, subtle, tangy, telling, therapeutic, tiresome, touching, toxic, trenchant, tyrannical, unbearable, uncanny, uncomfortable, unhealthy, unholy, uninviting, unspoiled, vapid, venomous, vexatious, virtual, virulent, vivid, weak, wholesome, wicked

538 efforts: amateurish, ambitious, applied, assiduous, automated, automatic, backbreaking, concerted, conscientious, cooperative, difficult, diligent, employed, gladly, go-ahead, hard, heavy, homicidal, idle, indolent, industrious, inexhaustible, jobless, labored, laborious, laden, light, lightly, mechanize, mindless, murderous, on duty, onerous, painstaking, persistent, religious, rugged, running, scrupulous, sedulous, serious, simple, slack, slow, softly, straightforward, strenuous, studied, studious, thankless, thorough/thoroughgoing, thoroughly, tireless, tiresome, together, toilsome, torpid, tough, unemployed, unfailing, unfaltering, unflagging, unpaid, unprofessional, unsolicited, untiring, uphill, valiant, vicarious, voluntarily, voluntary, weighty, workable, working

539 existential: alive, almighty, animate, comatose, conscious, consist, dead, deadly, deceased, defunct, departed, dormant, drowsy, dying, extant, extinct, fallen, fatal, immaterial, immortal, inanimate, incarnate, late, lifeless, live, living, lost, luxuriate, missing, moribund, nil, nonexistent, obsolete, out, out cold, perennial, present, sentient, sleepy, somnolent, soporific, street person, unconscious, vagabond, vital, wakeful

540 forcefulness: almighty, bang, blatant, bloody, brute, cumulative, desperate, driving, dynamic, effective, electric/electrical, fierce, fiercely, hard, high-powered, impregnable, insistent, invincible, invulnerable, madly, mightily, mighty, potent, powerful, powerfully, savage, stiff, strong, violent

541 frequency: annual, annually, casual, commonly, daily, hardly, nightly, now and then, occasional, occasionally, off and on, often, on and off, once in a while, periodic, rapid, rarely, recurrent, scarce, scarcely, seldom, spasmodic, sporadic, uncommonly, usually, yearly

542 inclination: abrupt, accommodating, acquisitive, active, addicted, adrift, adventurous, affirmative, aggressive, agog, agreeable, alive, all-around, allergic, aloof, ambitious, amicable, antithetical, anxious, apt, arbitrary, arid, assiduous, attention deficit disorder, avaricious, base, beastly, benign, big-hearted, blindly, brisk, busy, careful, carefully, careless, casual, characteristic, charitable, cheap, co-dependent, cold-blooded, competitive, conducive, confirmed, conflicting, conservative, conspicuous, constant, contentious, contradictory, corporal, corporeal, correct, cost-effective, crack, creditable, curious, decent, dedicated, deep, deliberate, deliberately, delicate, delicately, demanding, dependable, derelict, designing, determined, detestable, devoted, devout, dewy-eyed, dictatorial, die-hard, difficult, dilatory, diligent, dim, diplomatic, dirty, discriminating, disinclined, disingenuous, disposed, disputatious, distrustful, dog-eat-dog, dogged, dogmatic, domestic, doubtful, dour, downtrodden, dull, dutiful, dynamic, eager, eagle-eyed, earnest, earthy, easy, economical, effervescent, effusive, elusive, emotional, emotionless, energetic, engaged, engrossed, enterprising, enthusiastic, equable, equal, equitable, errant, erratic, evasive, even, even-handed, exact, exaggerated, exciting, execrable, exi-

gent, exotic, expeditious, explosive, factious, fail-safe, fair, fairly, fallible, farcical, fast, fastidious, feckless, feisty, feral, ferocious, ferocity, fervent/fervid, fiery, firm, firmly, flexible, fluid, fly-by-night, fond, foolish, foolishly, footloose, forbearing, forced, fortunate, frantic, free, frenzied, fresh, frisky, frolicsome, funereal, gaily, gallant, gay, generous, gentle, genuine, gingerly, given to, gladly, go-ahead, godless, godly, good, gracious, grandiose, grasping, gratuitous, greedy, gross, guarded, guileless, gullible, gung ho, gutless, gutsy, hair-raising, half-hearted, happily, happy-go-lucky, hard, hard-boiled, hard-core, hardened, hard-nosed/hardheaded, harsh, harum-scarum, hasty, headlong, heartless, heartwarming, hearty, hell-bent, helpless, hesitant, highfalutin, hooked, hospitable, hostile, hotheaded, humane, humanitarian, hurtful, hypocritical, hysterical, idle, ignoble, ignorant, imaginative, immersed, impartial, impassive, impatient, impersonal, impetuous, implacable, improper, improvident, imprudent, impulsive, inadvertent, inane, inattentive, incautious, inclined, indefatigable, indifferent, indignant, indiscreet, indiscriminate, indisposed, indolent, indulgent, inelegant, inert, inexhaustible, infant/infantile, inflammatory, ingenuous, inhibited, innocent, inoffensive, inquiring, insecure, insidious, insightful, insincere, insouciant, intent, intolerant, intractable/intransigent, intrusive, inventive, involved, irate, jaundiced, jealous, jolly, joyful/joyous, joyless, judicious, kind, kindhearted, kindly, kinky, lackadaisical, lackluster, languid, largesse, lax, left-wing, lenient, levelheaded, lewd, liable, liberal, lifeless, light, lighthearted, lip service, litigious, live, lively, livid, loath, loud, loving, low, low-key, lukewarm, magnanimous, malevolent, malicious, malign, materialistic, maudlin, mawkish, mean, melodramatic, merciful, merciless, meretricious, methodical/methodic, meticulous, mindful, mushy, naive, narrow, narrow-minded, neat, neglectful, negligent, nerveless, nervous, neutral, nice, nonchalant, noncommittal, noncompliant, nonconformist, nonpartisan, obdurate, objective, objectively, objectivity, oblivious, obnoxious, obstinate, obtrusive, occupied, odd/oddball, off-guard, offhand, one-sided, on purpose, open, openhanded, openhearted, opposed/opposing, oppressed, opprobrious, optimistic, ossified, overconfident, overrated, overwrought, pacific, pagan, parental, parochial, partial, particular, partisan, passionate, passive, patient, peaceful, peevish, penitent, peppery, perceptive, peremptory, perfunctory, persuasive, perverse, petulant, philanthropic, pigheaded, plastic, playful, pleasant, politically correct, pompous, ponderous, poor, portentous, practical, pragmatic, precipitous/precipitate, precise, predictable, premature, premeditated, prepossessed, presumptuous, pretentious, productive, progressive, prolific, prone, prostrate, protective, proud, prudent, pugnacious, punctilious, purposeful, quarrelsome, querulous, radical, raging, rambunctious, raunchy, reactionary, ready, realistic, rebellious, reckless, reliable, renegade, resigned, resolute, responsive, restive, restless, restrained, revolutionary, rival, romantic, rousing, sadistic, safe, sanctioned, sanguine, sappy, savage, scheming, scrupulous, scurrilous, sedate, sedentary, sedulous, selective, selfish, self-righteous, self-satisfied, sensible, sentimental, serious, seriously, serpentine, set, severe, short-sighted, silly, simple, sincere, slapdash, sleepless, sly, small-minded, smart, smug, sneaky, sober, softhearted, solemn, soulful, sour, spineless, spirited, spiritless, spiteful, spontaneous, sporty, sprightly, spunky, square, staunch, steadfast, steady, stern, stimulating, stout, straight, strenuous, strict, strong, subjective, sunny, susceptible, suspicious, sweet, sympathetic, tame, tardy, temperate, tempestuous, tenacious, tender, tenderhearted, tentative, tepid, testy, thick-skinned, thoughtful, thoughtless, tireless, together, tolerant, torn, touched, touchy, tough, tractable, tranquil, true, trusting, truthful, unaffected, unbiased, uncaring, uncommitted, uncompromising, unconcerned, unconscious, uncritical, understanding, unfeeling, unflappable, ungodly, unholy, unimaginative, uninspired, unprejudiced, unrehearsed, unreliable, unrestricted, unstable/unsteady, unsympathetic, untoward, untrustworthy, unwavering, unwilling, unyielding, up-and-coming, vainglorious, vehement, vengeful, venomous, versatile, vicious, vigilant, vindictive, virulent, voucher, wakeful, wanton, warm, weak, well-balanced, well-preserved, wholehearted/whole-hearted, willful, witless, witty, wooden, youthful, zippy

543 is an attribute of: appear, appearance, belong, minutiae, quality, savor, seem, sound, trivia

544 manner: abominable, absurd, advisedly, aimless, although, anyhow, anyway, as, backhanded, beautifully, blah, blind, breezy, broken, brutal, brutally, busily, businesslike, busy, by, by hand, calm, camp, casual, catchy, circuitous, circumspect, counter, covert, covertly, cumbersome, delicately, deluxe, despite, dreary, easy, eat high on the hog, equable, ergo, even, foolish, foolishly, for, forcibly, forthwith, fortunately, freely, frenzied, frequently, gradual, gradually, grievous, grim, grisly, hastily, helter-skelter, how, however, ill-advised, immediately, immoderate, impersonal, impolitic, inadvertent, incautious, incidentally, indelicate, indirect, individually, inequitable, instant, instantly, instinctive, intentional, intently, involuntary, irregularly, irresponsible, just, justly, kindly, lackadaisical, largely, leisurely, less, lightly, little, long, low-key, luckily, luxuriate, luxurious, madly, mainly, manual, markedly, mechanical, methodical/methodic, meticulous, mightily, misguided, misspent, moderately, monotonous, more, moreover, mortally, most, mostly, motorized, much, mutually, narrowly, naturally, necessarily, nevertheless, notwithstanding, objectively, of course, one by one, openly, otherwise, outwardly, over, overly, parenthetical, partially, pell-

mell, perfectly, perfunctory, per se, personally, piecemeal, poorly, positively, possibly, posthaste, powerfully, presumably, primarily, principally, progressive, promptly, providing/provided, punctual, purely, purposeless, purposely, quick, rampant, rapidly, rather, readily, recurrent, regardless, regular, relatively, reliable, revolutionary, ritzy, separately, seriously, sheer, simply, slightly, softly, solely, somehow, still, straight, strategic, subtle, summarily, superficially, surprising, swimmingly, tactical, though, through, thus, together, too, true, ulterior, unawares, unconditional, unconscious, undercover, underhand, unduly, unexpected, unfair, unforeseen, unusually, unwitting, venomous, very, via, vice versa, violent, virtual, virtually, visceral, voluntarily, voluntary, well, while, wrong, yet

545 morality: abandoned, above suspicion, answerable, arrant, astray, atrocious, bad, badly, bawdy, black, blasphemous, blue, broad, cagey, coarse, common, conscientious, contraband, corrupt, criminal, crooked, culpable, cunning, damnable, damned, dark, dastardly, debauched, decadent, degenerate, demonic/demoniac/demoniacal, depraved, devilish, diabolic, dirty, disorderly, dissipated, dissolute, drunk, egregious, elevated, elfin, equitable, erotic, errant, ethical, evil, faithful, faithless, fast, faultless, felonious, fickle, fiendish, filthy, flagrant, fleshly, fraudulent, frightful, God-fearing, good, gross, guileless, guiltless, guilty, heathen, heretical, high-minded, holy, honest, honorable, hood, hoodlum, hooligan, ignoble, ill, illegal, illicit, immaculate, immodest, immoral, impious, improper, impure, incorruptible, indecent, indefensible, indelicate, inexcusable, infamous, infernal, inhuman/inhumane, innocent, irreligious, insidious, insincere, involved, irreproachable, just, justifiable, justly, lawful, lawless, lewd, liable, libidinous, licentious, loose, loyal, Machiavellian, mischievous, miscreant, moral, nasty, naughty, nefarious, obscene, off-color, perversion, perverted, plastered, pornographic, pornography, prejudicial, pretended, profane, profligate, promiscuous, racy, rakish, rank, raw, religious, reprobate, reputable, responsible, right, righteous, rightful, risqué, roguish, rotten, sadistic, satanic, scandalous, scurrilous, seamy, secret, sensational, shady, shameful, shameless, sharp, sinful, smutty, sordid, sorry, soused, spicy, suggestive, true-blue, unconscionable, unconstitutional, unearned, unethical, unfair, unfaithful, unforgivable, ungodly, unjust, unjustified, unprincipled, unscrupulous, untrue, untrustworthy, unwarranted, upright, upstanding, valid, venal, veracious, vicious, villainous, vile, virtuous, vulgar, wanton, wholesome, wicked, wily, worthy, wrong, wrongful, zonked

546 necessity: absent, applied, auxiliary, backup, bereft, binding, capital, chosen, collateral, component, compulsory, controversial, deciding, dependent, dire, discretionary, dispensable, elementary, enough, essential, expendable, extra, extraneous, famished, fresh, fundamental, gratuitous, imperative, inadequate, inapplicable, indebted, indispensable, insatiable, insufficient, integral, intrinsic, introductory, lacking, main, mandatory, marketable, meager, necessary, needless, nonessential, obligatory, piddle, preparatory, prerequisite, providing/provided, provisional, radical, required/requisite, rudimentary, shy, staple, starving/starved, strategic, superfluous, ultimate, uncalled for, underlying, undue, unduly, unessential, unnecessary, vital, wanting

547 normality: aberrant, abnormal, accepted, accustomed, addictive, all right, amazing, anomalous, astonishing, atypical, average, bizarre, characteristic, classic, common, conventional, curious, customarily, customary, disguised, eccentric, everyday, exorbitant, extreme, familiar, flaky, formal, general, generally, gonzo, habitual, incidental, incongruous, irregular, lowly, macabre, maladjusted, mean, mediocre, medium, middle, middling, mind-blowing, mind-boggling, moderate, modest, mundane, natural, nondescript, normal, normally, ordinary, pedestrian, plain, prevalent, prosaic, reasonable, regular, routine, run-of-the-mill, screwy, spacey/spacy, stock, temperate, typical, unaccustomed, unimaginative, uninspired, unmotivated, used to, usual, veiled

548 occurrence: abhorrent, accidentally, accursed, amusing, asinine, astounding, atrocious, behind one's back, ceremonial, ceremonious, chaotic, chronological, closed, coincident, coincidental, consequent, covert, covertly, crowning, cumulative, cursed, dangerous, dangerously, dark, desperate, desultory, didactic, dire, disagreeable, disastrous, disgusting, dismal, downbeat, dramatic, droll, ducky, dull, dullsville, egregious, embarrassing, empirical/empiric, endurable, enjoyable, ensuing, eventful, exciting, excruciating, exhilarating, exigent, exposed, express, fated, feebleminded, festive, forbidden, forced, forcibly, forthcoming, fortuitous, foul, furious, furtive, futile, gala, ghoulish, gloomy, grateful, grave, grievous, gruesome, hairy, half-baked, hapless, happily, harrowing, hazardous, heartwarming, heavy, hectic, heinous, historic, historical, histrionic, hit-or-miss, homicidal, hopeful, hopeless, humdrum, hurried, ill-advised, ill-fated/ill-starred, ill-timed, imminent, impending, inane, inauspicious, incidental, inconclusive, inconvenient, incurable, indefensible, informal, insane, ironic/ironical, irregularly, intimidating, jolly, joyful/joyous, joyless, juicy, lackluster, lass, late, limit, lively, low-key, ludicrous, madcap, magic/magical, maiden, memorable, menacing, meritorious, merry, meteoric, miraculous, mirthful, misguided, misleading, moronic, mostly, much, murderous, nasty, nearing, necessary, nefarious, nerve-racking, nice, oafish, objectionable, offensive, ominous, oncoming, opportune, oppressive, outlandish, over, overall, overblown, overdue, partisan, peaceable, penal, pending, perilous, permissible, pernicious, pessimistic, pleasant, poignant, pointless, poor, predetermined,

predictable, premeditated, preposterous, pressing, primarily, privileged, promising, propitious, prospective, prosperous, queer, random, rather, realistic, regardless, regrettable, rewarding, ridiculous, riotous, risky, risqué, rollicking, romantic, rosy, routine, ruinous, sad, safe, scary, secretive, secretly, self-evident/self-explanatory, senseless, sequential, shocking, simpleminded, simultaneous, sinful, sinister, slow, someday, somewhat, soon, speedy, spontaneous, staggering, star-crossed, studied, stupid, sure, surprising, surreptitious, swell, taboo, tacit, tame, tardy, tedious, tender, tense, terminal, thankless, then, thick, threatening, thrilling, through, ticklish, tight, together, tolerable, topsy-turvy, touchy, tragic, trial, trying, tumultous/tumultuous, tyrannical, ugly, unadvised, unaffected, unauthorized, unavailing, unawares, unbelievable, unearned, uneasy, uneventful, unexpected, unfair, unforeseen, unforgettable, unfortunate, unfriendly, ungodly, unhappy, unholy, unimaginable, unimaginative, uninspired, unintelligent, unintentional/unintended, uninteresting, uninviting, unjustifiable, unlucky, unobtrusive, unreasonable, unrelenting, unsophisticated, unspeakable, untimely, untoward, untroubled, unwarranted, unwise, unwitting, urgent, venturesome, warlike, weighty, well, whimsical, wholehearted/whole-hearted, woeful, wrong, yet

549 original: aboriginal, ancestral, automated, automatic, bastard, belonging to, born, built-in, classical, colonial, congenital, constitutional, counterfeit, deep-seated, derivative, domestic, essential, ethereal, ethnic, exotic, extraneous, extrinsic, foreign, from, genetic, hereditary, human, humble, ignoble, illegitimate, implicit, imported, inborn/inbred, indigenous, ingrained, inherent, inherited, innate, intimate, low, lowly, mechanize, medieval, misbegotten, mortal, mystic/mystical, native, noble, organic, original, otherworldly, patrician, pedigree, plebeian, preliminary, premature, primary/prime, proper, provincial, racial, radical, royal, rudimentary, secondary, secular, strange, thoroughbred, underlying, unprecedented, vernacular

550 peculiarity: ablaze, adaptable, aggressive, airy, ashamed, austere, authoritative, babyish, born, characteristic, clement, closed, contemptible, continent, conventional, corny, craven, cultured, dead, defensive, dreadful, fastidious, forbidding, forceful, forgetful, gawky, gingerly, halting, hokey, laborious, laughable, leisurely, on guard, protective, punctual, shamefaced

551 permanency: abiding, always, carved in stone, chronic, endless, evanescent, fixed, fleeting, fly-by-night, forever, fugitive, invincible, invulnerable, irrevocable, lasting, long-standing, makeshift, passing, permanent, perpetual, standing, stationary, stopgap, temporary, tentative, unchanging

552 probability: absurd, accidental, accidentally, achievable, alleged, apparent, apparently, attainable, chance, chancy, clearly, conceivable, contingent, convincing, credible, definitely, dicey, disposed, doubtless, dubious, earthly, easily, eventual, eventually, far-fetched, fat chance, feasible, fishy, fluky, for sure, fortuitous, funny, groundless, hardly, hypothetical, ideal, iffy, illusory/illusive, imaginable, immune, implausible, impossible, impractical/impracticable, improbable, inclined, inconceivable, incredible, inevitable, insurmountable, intended, invalid, legendary, liable, likely, logical, marvelous, maybe, negligible, obviously, odd, off, operable, optional, ostensible, out, outside, perhaps, plausible, possible, possibly, potential, preposterous, presumably, probable, probably, prone, prospective, remote, ridiculous, slender/slim, so-called, sound, specious, starry-eyed, subject, tenable, tentative, unlikely, unrealistic, unreliable, vain, viable, workable

553 repetition: again, alternate, away, redundant, repeatedly, repetitious

554 restrictiveness: absolute, all, autonomous, beyond, binding, bound, bounded, boundless, captive, cloistered, concentrated, conditional, confined, dye-in-the-wool, exclusive, exclusively, exclusive of, exempt, finite, fixed, freelance, independent, independently, ironclad, limited, narrow, nonconforming, numbered, obligated, obliged, off-limits, oligarchic, permissible, prohibited, prohibitive, provisional, qualified, rampant, self-reliant

555 social: accommodating, allied, amorous, antisocial, aristocratic, awkward, bigoted, blameless, brotherly, burlesque, busy, chummy, civilian, clandestine, clannish, close, commemorative, companionable, compatible, congenial, conjugal, connubial, cooperative, cultural, dear, defenseless, degrading, depressed, difficult, dignified, disadvantageous, disaffected, disgraceful, dishonorable, elite, eminent, engaged, fallen, familiar, forsaken, friendless, friendly, frisky, gentle, homeless, hospitable, hot, important, inelegant, inglorious, intimate, lonely, lonesome, marital, matrimonial, matronly, meddlesome, near, noble, nuptial, palsy-walsy, platonic, popular, preferred, prestigious, racist, recluse/reclusive, refined, single, sociable, social, sole, solitary, thick, thoughtful, thoughtless, top-level, unaccompanied, unapproachable, unarmed, uninvited, unmarried, unpopular, unprotected, unsociable, unwelcome, unworldly, upper, valued, welcome

556 specialization: alone, circumstantial, express, expressly, finicky, respective

557 specificity: accurate, accurately, ad hoc, all right, approximate, careless, certain, closely, correct, definite, descriptive, detailed, exact, exactly, extra, fine, general, just, lax, limited, literal, literally, meticulous, minute, namely, nice, particular, particularly, pat, peculiar, perfect, photographic, precise, precisely, proper, punctilious, random, right, rigorous, rough, rude, sectional, separate, simply, skin-deep, smack, special, specially, specific, specifically, strict, such, superficial, systematic, thorough/thoroughgoing, thoroughly, topical, very, wholly

558 suitability: absurd, acceptable, accepted, ac-

cordant, accordingly, adequate, adequately, advantageous, agreeable, all right, ample, amply, applicable, appropriate, apropos, apt, awkward, becoming, befitting, best, conformable, congruous, correct, correctly, cut out for, decent, decorous, de rigeur, discordant, dissatisfactory, done, down-to-earth, due, duly, eligible, enough, excusable, exorbitant, expedient, extreme, favorable, favorably, feasible, felicitous, felicity, fit, fitted, fitting, full-grown/full-fledged, fully, germane, good, granted, happy, ill-suited, improper, inadmissible, inadvisable, inapplicable, inappropriate, inapt, incongruous, incorrect, ineligible, inept, inopportune, just, justifiable, kosher, lame, legitimate, livable, meet, nice, objectionable, okay, old, on the level, orthodox, passable, pat, perfect, pertinent, prehistoric, presentable, previous, proper, reasonable, relative, relevant, right, rightful, ripe, satisfactory, seasonable, seemly, senseless, sound, sufficient, suitable, tailor-made, tenable, timely, unacceptable, unasked, unbecoming, undue, unfit, unsatisfactory, unseemly, unsuitable, untoward, unwarranted, unworthy, venial, weak, well, wrong

559 transmission: infectious, passable, roundabout

560 usefulness: acting, adequately, barren, broken, convenient, damaged, dead, defective, defunct, dependable, derelict, desert, desirable, desolate, dilapidated, dissipated, drained, effective, effete, efficient, employed, enervated, excessive, exhausted, expedient, extravagant, faded, fallow, faulty, finished, fitted, fixed, fruitful, fruitless, functional, futile, futility, godforsaken, good, handy, helpful, hollow, idle, idealistic, impaired, impoverished, inactive, ineffective/ineffectual, inefficient, infallible, infertile, instead, instrumental, interim, invalid, irrelevant, leftover, live, living, lost, makeshift, misspent, neither here nor there, null, obsolete, occupied, old, on duty, on the blink, open, operational, operative, outmoded, practicable, practical, prehistoric, prepared, prodigal, productive, propitious, purposeless, quixotic, ready, residual, ripe, running, salubrious, satisfactory, serviceable, short, spent, starry-eyed, stopgap, subservient, subsidiary, substitute, sufficient, superfluous, supine, surplus, trashy, trial, tributary, under, unproductive, unrealistic, usable, useful, useless, user-friendly, utilitarian, vacant, valuable, viable, virgin/virginal, visionary, void, wanting, washed-out, workable, working, worn/worn-out, worthless, worthwhile

COMPARATIVE

561 compared with: contrast, mark, touch

562 complexity: abstruse, artless, backward, bare, baroque, bilateral, blank, civilized, clarion, clear, complex, complicated, crude, cursory, elaborate, elementary, exaggerated, fancy, folksy, graphic, high-flown, intricate, involved, modest, pell-mell, simple, simply, sophisticated, tortuous, tricky, ultra, unsophisticated, unwieldy, vanilla, well-defined

563 correspondence: accordant, akin, allied, applicable, close, commensurate, concerning, concurrent, conformable, congruent, congruous, consistent, consonant, corporate, duplicate, euphonious, harmonious, kindred, likewise, moderate, mutual, proportionate/proportional, pro rata, relative, sympathetic, truant, twin, unanimous, unified, united, unrelated

564 difference: against, alien, altered, alternative, ambivalent, another, assorted, atypical, avant-garde, averse, bizarre, contrived, converse, curious, deviant, diametric/diametrical, different, differently, discordant, discrepant, discrete, disparate, disproportionate, dissimilar, dissonant, distinct, distinctive, divergent, diverse, eccentric, especial, especially, exceptional, extraordinary, fantastic, flaky, freakish, funny, gonzo, heterogeneous, incompatible, inconsistent, individual, inverse, irreconcilable, manifold, miscellaneous, mixed, monstrous, motley, multiple/multifarious, nerd, new, novel, odd/oddball, offbeat, opposed/opposing, opposite, other, particular, peculiar, phenomenal, plural, polar, preternatural, quaint, queer, refreshing, remote, repugnant, rival, screwy, separate, several, single, singular, sole, spacey/spacy, special, specific, specifically, strange, sundry, suspicious, unaccountable, unaccustomed, uncanny, uncommon, unconventional, underground, unearthly, unequal, unfamiliar, unheard-of, unique, unlike, unnatural, unorthodox, unprecedented, unrelated, unthinkable, unusual, variant, varied, variegated, various, vice versa, weird

565 difficulty: agonizing, arduous, awkward, complicated, defective, deficient, delicate, demanding, easily, easy, easy as pie, effortless, facile, formidable, grueling, hard, heavy, inaccurate, insurmountable, knotty, laborious, maddening, mortally, murderous, nerve-racking, nothing to it, onerous, ponderous, prickly, rigorous, rugged, serious, seriously, severe, sticky, stiff, tall, taxing, thorny, ticklish, tight, tough, treacherous, troublesome, trying, uncomplicated, uphill, weighty, wicked, worrisome

566 equivalence: alike, alternate, approximately, asymmetrical, balanced, commensurate, comparable, comparative, coordinate, corresponding, disproportionate, duplicate, equal, equivalent, even, identical, indistinguishable, level, matching, mock, model, more or less, nearly, reciprocal, regular, same, uneven

567 importance: above, august, below, beneath, beneficial, big league, bush-league, central, chiefly, chosen, climactic/climacteric, collateral, component, conspicuous, costly, dear, dogmatic, elevated, essential, estimable, exclusive, front, fundamental, grave, high, holy, immediate, important, inferior, known, life-and-death, main, majestic, material, meaningful, newsworthy, noteworthy, noticeable, operative, precious, pregnant, primary/prime, prodigious, reputable, salient, second-rate/second-class, significant, special,

strategic, telling, top, towering, upper, used, vital, worthwhile, worthy

568 importance, extreme: acclaimed, acute, basic, basically, beloved, best, better, big, big league, blessed, bright, brilliant, burning, capital, cardinal, celebrated, chief, consequential, considerable, critical, crucial, deciding, dire, divine, dominant, earnest, eminent, exigent, fabled, famous, fatal, fateful, favored, favorite, first, foremost, glorious, grand, great, hallowed, head, high-class, historic, illustrious, immortal, influential, invaluable, key, larger than life, legendary, major, master, momentous, monumental, necessary, notable, noted, noteworthy, oligarchic, outstanding, overriding, paramount, pet, pivotal, praiseworthy, predominant, preeminent, premier, pressing, prestigious, priceless, principal, prominent, renowned, ruling, serious, seriously, signal, significant, sovereign, splendid, star, substantial, supreme, ultimate, unsurpassed, uppermost, urgent, valuable, weighty, well-known

569 intensity: acute, almighty, awfully, bad, badly, biting, blatant, bloody, concentrated, considerably, desperate, desperately, drastic, exceedingly, exquisite, extra, extreme, extremely, greatly, harsh, heavy, high, highly, immoderate, insanely, intense, mightily, most, notably, outrageous, powerfully, pretty, profound, quite, severe, severely, sharp, somewhat, stark, stiff, stringent, strong, substantially, terribly, terrific, too, ultra, unconscionable, undue, unduly, unmitigated, unusually, very, violent, vivid, wild

570 negative: adverse, affected, amiss, apocryphal, awful, awfully, bad, baleful, baneful, base, beside oneself, black, conflicting, creepy, cruel, damnable, damned, defiled, degenerate, deleterious, delinquent, deplorable, derogatory, despicable, detrimental, dire, direful, done for, egregious, empty, erroneous, evil, fallacious, false, faulty, fearful, filthy, grim, grisly, heinous, hellish, icky, ill, imperfect, inadequate, inauspicious, incendiary, incorrect, incorrigible, inexcusable, infamous, injurious, inordinate, insecure, lame, loathsome, miserable, misguided, misspent, negative, nerd, null, objectionable, off, poor, prejudicial, rancid, rotten, ruinous, rundown, seedy, slipshod, squalid, tasteless, terribly, threatening, trashy, trumped up, undesirable, unforgivable, unfortunate, ungodly, unpleasant, unsatisfactory, untoward, unwelcome, upset, weak, weird, worthless

571 negative, extreme: abject, abominable, accursed, ad nauseam, astounding, atrocious, awful, awfully, bad, badly, crappy, crummy, cursed, lousy, nasty, noisome, outrageous, pernicious, perverse, poorly, regrettable, reprehensible, repugnant, repulsive, rotten, shameful, shocking, shoddy, sick, sickening, sickly, sinister, sordid, staggering, terrible, tragic, ugly, unbearable, unfavorable, unhealthy, unsavory, unspeakable, unworthy, vicious, vile, virulent, wicked, woeful, wretched, wrong

572 positive: admirable, affirmative, agreeable, agreeably, all right, amazing, angelic, astonishing, auspicious, awesome, beloved, beneficial, benign, best, better, boss, comfort, comfortable, commendable, consummate, cool, decent, delicious, desirable, estimable, exceptional, exemplary, extraordinary, fabulous, fanciful, fantastic, far-out, faultless, favorable, favorably, for kicks, fortunate, fortunately, fun, good, grateful, groovy, heavenly, high-class, homey, idyllic, incredible, innocuous, interesting, intriguing, luckily, lucky, magnificent, majestic, meritorious, merry, mind-blowing, mind-boggling, miraculous, nice, nifty, noble, opportune, pleasant, pleasing/pleasurable, positive, prodigious, profitable, propitious, prosperous, proud, respectable, rewarding, right, salubrious, satisfying, terrific, thrilling, toothsome, upbeat, utopian, welcome, well, worthwhile, worthy, yes, yummy

573 similarity: akin, alike, analogous, approximate, closely, cognate, comparable, comparative, conformable, different, equal, equivalent, faithful, homogenous, identical, interchangeable, like, like-minded, parallel, related, representative, same, seeming, similar, synonymous, tantamount, twin, uniform, virtual, virtually

574 superiority: absolute, acclaimed, admirable, advanced, advantage, advisable, all right, all-time, arch, below par, capital, cardinal, champion, chief, choice, chosen, classic/classical, coarse, commanding, correct, crack, dandy, definitive, delectable, delicate, deluxe, dependent, deplorable, dignified, distinctive, distinguished, divine, dominant, elegant, elite, eminently, enviable, especial, especially, excellent, exceptional, exemplary, exquisite, fantastic, fine, first-class/first-rate, flat-out, flawless, glorious, gnarly, golden, grand, great, head, high-powered, holy, ideal, impeccable, imperative, imperfect, imperious, important, imposing, impressive, incomparable, ineffable, infallible, inferior, inimitable, irreproachable, irresistible, junior, laudable, leading, less, lofty, low, luscious, lush, luxuriant, luxurious, majestic, major, marvelous, matchless, maximum, menial, mint, model, omnipotent, optimal, optimum, outstanding, paramount, peerless, perfect, perfectly, pet, phenomenal, poor, poorly, powerful, praiseworthy, predominant, preeminent, preferred, premium, prevalent, primary/prime, principal, privileged, prize, prodigious, proud, rare, remarkable, renowned, reputable, ritzy, rotten, royal, ruling, sacred, sacrosanct, secondary, second-rate/second-class, select, senior, sensational, signal, solemn, spectacular, splendid, stately, sterling, striking, stunning, stupendous, sublime, substandard, sumptuous, super, superb, superior, superlative, supreme, swell, tasteful, top, top-level, top-notch, transcendent/transcendental, tremendous, ultimate, uncommon, unequaled, unerring, unique, unparalleled, unprecedented, unrivaled, unsurpassed, upper hand, utmost, utopian, venerable, vintage, whole, wonderful

575 unimportance: beside the point, empty, expendable, frivolous, hand-me-down, immaterial, inconsequential/inconsiderable, insignificant, irrelevant, lesser, lightweight, little, meaningless, menial, middle-of-the-road, minor, minute, moderate, needless, negligible, neither here nor there, nominal, nonessential, ordinary, peripheral, petty, picayune, piddling, puny, remote, second, secondary, side, slight, small, small-time, so-so, subject, subordinate, subservient, subsidiary, substitute, tenuous, trifling, trivial, under, undistinguished, unexceptional, unimportant, vain, vapid, worthless

PHYSICAL

576 accessibility: accessible, adaptable, approachable, arcane, arrant, available, bereft, blind, broad, clandestine, classified, close, closed, concealed, confidential, confidentially, cryptic, dark, defenseless, depleted, discernible, dissipated, distant, dubious, engaged, enigmatic/enigmatical, esoteric, exposed, far-flung, flagrant, furtive, glaring, graphic, hidden, hush-hush, illegible, impenetrable, inaccessible, incognito, inconspicuous, inner, inscrutable, inside, insoluble, known, latent, legible, lost, manifest, missing, mobile, mysterious, nameless, obscure, observable, obtainable, occult, off-course, off-limits, off the record, on call, open, optional, out, outward, outwardly, passable, patent, perceptible, permeable, plain, possible, private, privy, prohibited, pronounced, public, rare, ready, recondite, reserved, secluded, secret, stealthy, strange, tight, ulterior, unapproachable, unarmed, uncharted, uncovered, undercover, underground, unheard-of, unidentified, unknown, unprotected, unreadable, unseen, unsung, usable, user-friendly, veiled, vigilant, visible, visual, weak, willing

577 accompaniment: abandoned, again, alone, along, also, and, attendant, complementary, concomitant, connected, corporate, deserted, each, en masse, en route, ensemble, et cetera, except, furthermore, incidental, including, isolated, joint, jointly, left, lone, mutually, odd, one, only, parenthetical, per se, personally, reciprocal, related, separate, separately, single, single-handed, singly, singular, sole, solely, solitary, solo, stranded, unaccompanied, under, unified, unique, united

578 age: adolescent, advanced, afresh, aged, ancient, antediluvian, antiquarian, antiquated, antique, archaic, big, callow, childish, contemporary, crude, dated, doddering, elder, elderly, embryonic, fresh, full-grown/full-fledged, futuristic, green, groundbreaking, hoary, immature, immemorial, inchoate, infant/infantile, innovative, junior, juvenile, late, mature, medieval, mellow, mint, modern, modish, musty, new, newfangled, novel, old, older, old-fashioned, original, originally, outdated/out-of-date, outmoded, passé, puerile, quaint, recent, refreshing, ripe, secondhand, senior, stale, state-of-the-art, tender, undeveloped, unspoiled, up-to-date, vintage, well-preserved, young, youthful

579 appearance: adorable, aesthetic/esthetic, alluring, artistic, attractive, beautiful, becoming, comely, cosmetic, crisp, cute, dapper, deathly, decorative, delectable, desirable, disheveled, dressy, elegant, exquisite, eye-catching, fair, fancy, fashionable, fetching, fine, flawless, glamorous, glorious, good-looking, gorgeous, graceful, grotesque, grungy, handsome, hideous, hip, homely, imperfect, irresistible, lovely, natty, ornamental, ornate, picturesque, plain, presentable, pretty, ravishing, refreshing, repulsive, resplendent, scenic, seductive, snazzy, spiffy, statuesque, striking, stunning, stylish, symmetrical, ugly, unattractive, unbecoming, unsightly, willowy, with it

580 deformity: acne, birth defect, birthmark, blemish, blot, blotch, bug, chip, contortion, defect, deformity, dent, distortion, fault, flaw, frailty, freak, hip, malformation, misrepresentation, misstatement, mole, mutant, pockmark, scar

581 direction: about, across, adrift, along, around, askance, astern, astray, at, away, awry, backward, below, centrifugal, circuitous, counter, crooked, crosswise/crossways, devious, diagonal, diagonally, direct, directly, due, erect, errant, erratic, forked, forth, forward, haphazard, horizontal, indirect, inward, lateral, left, north, off-center, outgoing, outward, parallel, perpendicular, plane, plumb, ramble, right, rotary, roundabout, sharp, sheer, sideways, sinuous, snaky, steep, straight, thereabout, through, tortuous, uphill, upright, vertical, wide, winding, wry, zigzag

582 genuineness: abstract, actual, actually, airy, alias, allegorical, apocryphal, apparent, apparently, artificial, arty, assumed, authentic, authoritative, baseless, believable, beta, bogus, bona fide, certain, circumstantial, colored, concrete, conjectural, contrived, counterfeit, credible, dark, deceptive, de facto, delusive, dogmatic, dreamy, duplicitous, ecclesiastical, effective, empirical/empiric, enigmatic/enigmatical, erroneous, ersatz, esoteric, ethereal, extant, factual, fake, fallacious, false, fantastic, far-fetched, feigned, fictitious, figurative, foolproof, frank, fraudulent, genuine, good, groundless, hard, heartfelt, historical, honest-to-God, hypothetical, illusory/illusive, imaginary, imitative, inaccurate, indisputable, intangible, invisible, irrefutable, just, legitimate, lifelike, made-up, magic/magical, make-believe, matter-of-fact, metaphorical, metaphysical, mock, monstrous, mystic/mystical, mythical/mythological, nominal, nonexistent, occult, openhearted, ostensible, ostensibly, palpable, paranormal, phony, physical, plastic, positive, positively, pretended, pseudo, quack, quasi, quite, real, realistic, really, right, sham, sincerely, sound, specious, spiritual, spurious, substantial, supernatural, suspect, synthetic, tactile, tangible, temporal, true, truly, unearthly, unfounded, unnatural, unreal, unthinkable, untrue, unvarnished, unworldly, utopian, valid, veracious, veritable, visionary, wholehearted/whole-hearted, worldly, wrong

583 location: aboard, about, abroad, absconder, absent, absentee, advance, aerial, agricul-

tural, aground, airy, alone, ashore, askance, astride, at, beached, bucolic, center, central, civic, civil, cloistered, coastal, diffuse, down, everywhere, exterior, external, fixed, forward, from, front, here, horizontal, inside, insular, interior, isolated, lateral, leafy, left, lonely, low, middle, north, off, off-center, off-course, omnipresent, out, outdoor, outer, outermost, outlying, outside, outward, over, overseas, pastoral, penal, peripheral, perpendicular, polar, populous, posterior, precipitous, present, private, prominent, prone, prostrate, quiet, rear, recumbent, remote, restful, roomy, roughly, rural, rustic, secluded, sideways, single-handed, solitary, solo, somewhere, stray, subterranean, surface, supernal, through, top, topical, truant, uncomfortable, underground, untamed, upper, uppermost, upright, upside-down, vertical, void, where/wherever, wide, wild, withdrawn

584 movement: ambulatory, billowy, brisk, centrifugal, clumsy, destined, fleet, flowing, fluent, flying, frozen, fugitive, gawky, graceful, graceless, heavy, immobile, inactive, indolent, inert, itinerant, languid, leisurely, lethargic, lifeless, lightly, liquid, listless, lithe, lumbering, maladroit, migrant/migratory, mobile, motionless, movable, moving, nimble, nomadic, nonstop, oafish, outgoing, passive, pendulous/pendent, peripatetic, portable, quiet, restless, rotary, roundabout, running, sedentary, slack, slow, sluggish, speedy, stagnant, static, still, vibrant, willowy, winding

585 order: advance, advanced, alphabetical, avant-garde, bottom, center, chronological, collective, confused, consecutive, direct, disjointed, disorganized, first, following, fore, foregoing, foremost, former, formerly, forward, from scratch, front, hand-me-down, immediate, incipient, indiscriminate, initial, intermediate, internal, introductory, jumbled, lass, last, lastly, latter, leading, least, maiden, mean, median, methodical/methodic, muddled, neatly, next, older, on, onward/onwards, orderly, original, originally, past, pell-mell, pioneer, posterior, preceding, preliminary, premier, preparatory, previous, primary/prime, regular, second, senior, sequential, serial, shipshape, straight, subsequent, subsequently, succeeding/successive, systematic, tidy, together, topsy-turvy, uttermost

586 relative placement: abaft, about, abreast, adjacent, adjoining, after, ahead, ajar, almost, along, alongside, amid/amidst, among, apart, approximate, around, aside, askew, behind, below, beneath, beside, between, bottom, by, close, cockeyed, contiguous, convenient, direct, down, downhill, elsewhere, en route, far, faraway, farther, farthest, furthest, gone, halfway, handy, hard, immediate, lower, near, nearby, next, on, overhead, parallel, preceding, thereabout, toward/towards, under, underneath, within, without, wrong, yonder

587 safety: chancy, chary, perilous, precarious, sacred, safe, secure, treacherous, unharmed, unreliable, unsafe, unsound, vulnerable, weak

588 speed: agile, cursory, expeditious, express, fast, fleet, gradual, gradually, hastily, hasty, headlong, hurried, instant, instantly, one by one, on the double, posthaste, precipitous/precipitate, quick, quickly, rapid, rapidly, slow, snappy, speedy, swift, swiftly/swift, whirlwind

589 style: adorable, bald, baroque, beautiful, becoming, bedraggled, black, bland, bold, bourgeois, brassy, casual, cheap, chic, class, classical, classy, conglomerate, contemporary, cosmopolitan, country, crude, cultural, cursory, dashing, distasteful, dowdy, dressy, eat high on the hog, elegant, exquisite, fashionable, featureless, fitted, flamboyant, flashy, floral, florid, flowery, folksy, formless, frumpy, futuristic, gaily, garish, gaudy, gay, generous, glamorous, glaring, gorgeous, graceful, grand, grandiose, graphic, homely, hot, humble, improvised, incognito, informal, ingenuous, innovative, jazzy, kinky, lavish, loud, lovely, lush, luxuriate, luxurious, marked, mean, mere, meretricious, modern, modish, naked, neat, neatly, new, newfangled, obsolete, old-fashioned, opulent, orderly, original, ornamental, ornate, ostentatious, outdated/out-of-date, outmoded, palatial, passé, picturesque, plain, plush, popular, posh, pretentious, prevalent, provincial, quaint, quiet, refined, regal, resplendent, rich, rustic, salty, scruffy, shapeless, sharp, showy, simple, slack, sleazy, slipshod, smart, snappy, snazzy, sophisticated, spiffy, splendid, spruce, stale, stately, state-of-the-art, statuesque, stylish, swank/swanky, swish, tacky, tasteful, tasteless, tawdry, tousled, trendy, two-bit, unadorned, unbecoming, untidy, unworldly, up-to-date, vanilla, vogue

Senses

ASPECTS OF PERCEPTION

590 physical: burn, caress, hear, see, smell, taste, touch

AUDITORY

591 attribute of hearing: acoustic, audible, deaf, distinct

592 attribute of noise: blatant, brassy, cacophonous, clarion, deafening, discordant, dissonant, earsplitting, grating, loud, noisy, obstreperous, piercing, quiet, raucous, rough, shrill, soft, soft-spoken, sonorous, strident, vociferous

593 attribute of noise-making: dumb, mute

594 attribute of sound: acoustic, aloud, audible, blatant, brassy, cacophonous, clarion, deafening, deep, discordant, dissonant, dulcet, dull, earsplitting, faint, full, gentle, grating, gruff, guttural, high, hoarse, hollow, husky, inaudible, loud, low, lyric, lyrical, mellifluous, mellow, melodious/melodic, muffled, mum, musical, noiseless, noiseproof, noisy, obstreperous, off-key, piercing, quiet, raspy, raucous, resonant, rich, rough, round, shrill, silent, still, soft-spoken, sonorous, soundproof, strident, subdued, sweet, tight-lipped, tranquil, tuneful, untroubled, vocal, vociferous, weak

595 audible object: acknowledgment, acoustics, air, alert, anthem, aria, arrangement, ballad, bang, bell, blast, boom, buzz, carillon, carol, chant, clamor, clank, clap, clatter, click, clink, clump, crack, crash, delivery, din, dirge, discord, dissonance, ditty, drone, echo, gasp, groan, growl, gurgle, harmony, hiss, holler, howl, hymn, inflection, intonation, jangle, jazz, melody, murmur, music, noise, peal, pop, psalm, refrain, report, rhyme, rhythm, ring, roar, roll, rumpus, rustle, scream, shout, shriek, slam, song, sound, strain, thunder, tick, tune, yell

596 hearing: attend, bug, commiserate, eavesdrop, hear, listen, mind, monitor, regard

597 sound perception: hearing

OLFACTORY

598 attribute of odor: aromatic, astringent, fetid, fragrant, gamy, high, malodorous, musty, noisome, odorless, odorous, putrid, rancid, rank, scented, sharp, smelly, stale, stinking, strong, sweet, tangy

599 object that can be smelled: aroma, bouquet, breath, cologne, incense, odor, perfume, scent, smell, stench, stink, tang, whiff

600 odor: cologne, fragrance, fumes, incense, perfume, reek, smell, stench, stink, tang

601 olfactory perception: breathe, inhale, nose, scent, smell, sniff, whiff

602 smelling: scent, smell, sniff, whiff

TACTILE

603 attribute of dryness: absorbent, arid, balmy, clammy, damp, dank, dry, filmy, fluid, humid, juicy, liquid, misty, moist, moldy, muggy, musty, oily, parched, sloppy, soaked soggy, sopping, thirsty, waterlogged, watery, wet, wizened

604 attribute of hardness: adamant, concrete, downy, erect, firm, firmly, flaccid, flinty, hard, impenetrable, impermeable, impervious, inflexible, iron, limp, lissome, mushy, pavement, permeable, petrified, plastic, rocky, solid, stiff, supple, taut, tender, tense, unbending

605 attribute of temperature: ablaze, arctic, balmy, benign, biting, bland, boiling, bracing, brisk, broiling, burning, chill, chilly, close, cold, cool, cozy, crisp, febrile, feverish, fiery, freezing, frigid, frosty, frozen, glacial, heated, hot, icy, lukewarm, polar, sultry, sweltering, tepid, thermal, torrid, tropical, warm, wintry

606 attribute of texture: abrasive, adhesive, beaten, bias, breakable, brittle, bumpy, bushy, coarse, corrugated, cozy, craggy, creamy, crisp, crumbly, crunchy, crusty, dainty, delicate, diaphanous, diluted/dilute, downy, elastic, ethereal, fibrous, filmy, fine, firm, fleecy, flimsy, fluff, fluffy, fuzzy, gauzy, gelatinous, glassy, glossy, gooey, gossamer, greasy, gritty, icy, irregular, jagged, knurled, lacy, leathery, lubricant, lucid, matted, mottled, muddy, mushy, nappy, oily, opaque, paper, pasty, permeable, pointed, porous, powdery, rough, rugged, sheer, silky, sleek, slick, slippery, smooth, soft, spongy, springy, sticky, tenacious, tender, thick, thin, threadbare, transparent, uneven, viscous, yielding

607 dryness: drought, evaporation, humidity, wet

608 tactile perception: feeling, itch, touch

609 tactile quality: excruciating, numb

610 temperature: cold, fever, frost, glow, heat, temperature

611 texture: consistency, delicacy, feel, fiber, finish, gloss, grain, mesh, nap, polish, texture

612 touching: brush, caress, dab, feel, finger, flick, graze, grope, handle, itch, lick, manipulate, meet, monkey, nestle, nudge, nuzzle, pat, paw, pet, reach, stroke, tickle, tingle, toothsome, touch, yummy

TASTING

613 attribute of taste: acerbic, acerbity, acid, acidulous, acrid, appetizing, astringent, bad, bitter, bland, corrupt, delectable, delicious, distasteful, done, eatable, edible, full-bodied, hot, insipid, luscious, mouth-watering, palatable, peppery, piquant, poignant, pungent, racy, rancid, rich, robust, salty, savory, scrumptious, sharp, sour, spicy, succulent, sweet, tart, tasteless, tasty, unsavory, yummy

614 taste: acidity, bite, bitterness, flavor, savor, spice, tang, taste, zest

615 taste perception: taste

616 tasting: bite, gargle, sample, savor, taste

VISUAL

617 attribute of brightness: ablaze, beaming, bold, bright, brilliant, clear, colorful, crystal, dark, dazzling, dim, dingy, drab, dull, dusky, effulgent, faded, faint, glaring, gloomy, glossy, glowing, incandescent, lackluster, light, lucid, luminescent, luminous, lustrous, misty, murky, nebulous, obscure, opaque, radiant, resplendent, scintillating, sepulchral, shady, shiny, sunny, tenebrous, washed-out

618 attribute of color: amber, anemic, ashen, beige, black, blond/blonde, bloodless, blue, bold, bright, bronze, brown, brunette/brunet, buff, cadaverous, cherry, clear, colored, colorful, colorless, crystal, dappled, dark, deathly, deep, drab, dusky, faded, fair, florid, flushed, gaudy, gay, gloomy, glowing,

gold/golden, gray/grey, green, hoary, iridescent, jet, light, livid, mauve, milky, motley, mottled, mousy, muddy, multicolored, murky, neutral, opaque, orange, pale, pallid, pallor, pastel, pasty, peaked, pearly, purple, red, rich, rosy, ruddy, sable, sallow, sanguine, silver, smoky, soft, speckled, strong, swarthy, tan, translucent, transparent, variegated, verdant, vibrant, vivid, wan, watery, white, yellow

619 attribute of vision: appreciable, blind, clear, concealed, conspicuous, discernible, disguised, distinct, fuzzy, glaring, glassy, graphic, impalpable, invisible, lucid, myopic, nearsighted, prominent, pronounced, visible, visual

620 brightness: dark, darkness, gleam, glitter, gloom, gloss, glow, illumination, lamp, lantern, light, luster, murk, night, overshadow, pall, polish, radiance, radiate, shade, shadow, sheen, shimmer, shine, splendor

621 clean: grimy, grubby, hygienic, immaculate, impeccable, impure, mangy, messy, neat, pristine, pure, refined, sanitary, scraggly, slimy, sloppy, slovenly, spick-and-span, spotless, stagnant, sterile, straight, tidy, trim, unadulterated, unblemished, unclean, unkempt, unsanitary, untidy, untouched

622 color: auburn, beige, blush, cast, color, complexion, decor, fade, flush, gloom, glow, hue, orange, pigment, pink, purple, red, shade, shadow, stain, stripe, tan, tinge, tint, tone, yellow

623 looking: attend, avert, bear in mind, browse, contemplate, contemplation, dip into, eye, face, fix, fixate, focus, gape, gawk, gaze, glance, glare, glimpse, glower, heed, inspect, leaf, leer, look, lookout, look out, mind, monitor, ogle, patrol, peek/peep, peer, point, pry, regard, rubberneck, scan, scout, scrutinize, scrutiny, skim, snoop, spy, squint, stare, view, vigil, watch

624 occurrence of light: beam, blink, bolt, cast, eclipse, flash, flicker, glance, glare, gleam, glimmer, glint, glisten, glitter, glow, halo, illuminate, illumination, lamp, lantern, light, lighten, ray, reflect, shimmer, shine, spark, sparkle, spotlight, twinkle, wink

625 picture: arms, blueprint, caricature, cartoon, chart, design, diagram, drawing, emblem, engraving, facsimile, figure, flowchart, format, graphics, handwriting, impression, imprint, layout, map, model, outline, pattern, picture, plaid, plan, portrait, profile, reproduction, scene, scheme, silhouette, sketch, table, tableau

626 seeing: behold, distinguish, eye, gaze, make out, mark, meet, note, notice, observe, perceive, regard, remark, see, sight, spot, view, witness

627 visibility change: blur, clear, dim, fog

628 visible object: acknowledgment, alert, aspect, beacon, beam, blaze, buoy, cue, footprint, glance, glare, hallmark, halo, handwriting, light, mirage, model, outlook, panorama, prospect, ray, reflection, scene, scenery, sparkle, streak, track, view, vista

629 visual perception: blindness, eyesight, perspective, sight, vision

States

ABSTRACT

630 ability: ability, agility, artifice, artistry, awkwardness, bent, can, capability, capacity, competence, dexterity, disqualification, ease, efficiency, eloquence, endowment, expertise/expertness, facility, faculty, feebleness, flair, gift, hand, handicraft, head, inability, inclination, knack, know-how, league, literacy, master, mastery, mind, modus operandi, niche, performance, pizzazz, power, productivity, proficiency, promise, propensity, prowess, qualification, qualify, readiness, right stuff, skill, talent, technique, telepathy, touch, trick, turn

631 accessibility: access, back door, circulation, concealment, cover-up, privacy, seclusion, secrecy, secret

632 be ahead: ahead, first, front, uppermost, winning

633 behavior: abandon, abstention, abstinence, acquit, acrimony, act, act up, adultery, affectation, airs, alacrity, altruism, amenity, antithesis, apathy, arrogance, asperity, audacity, austerity, bad form, bad manners, balance, barbarism, barbarity, bearing, behave, behavior, benevolence, betrayal, bitterness, bluster, brass, bravery, carriage, carry on, chastity, cheek, chivalry, chutzpah, coarseness, cold shoulder, compassion, complaisance, condescend, condescension, condolence, conduct, continence, cordiality, correctness, corruption, countenance, courage, courtesy, cruelty, culture, custom, cut, debauchery, deceit, decency, decorum, deference, defiance, demeanor, deportment, desperation, detachment, diffidence, diplomacy, dirty tricks, dishonesty, disloyalty, disobedience, disregard, disrespect, dissidence, dissipation, distance, do, eagerness, earnestness, ebullience, effervescence, effrontery, endurance, enthusiasm, equanimity, equilibrium, etiquette, excess, excitement, exuberance, face, faithfulness, faithlessness, falderal, flare-up, fanaticism, feint, fervor, firmness, flightiness, flippancy, folly, foolishness, forbearance, formality, freedom, frivolity, fusillade, fuss, gall, geniality, grace, grit, grovel, haughtiness, hauteur, heroism, honesty, honor, hostility, hubris, humanity, humility, hypocrisy, impatience, impertinence, incivility, indecency, indiscretion, insolence, insubordination, irreverence, kindness, laziness, lethargy, license, lifestyle, longevity, lunacy, manhood/womanhood, manner, manners, mercy, misbehave, misbehavior, mischief, misconduct, misdeed/misdemeanor, moderation, modesty, monkey business, moxie, mutiny, naïveté, negligence, nonconformity, nonsense, obedience, oblivion, observance, order, ostentation, outburst, pep, perseverance, piety, poise, polish, pose, precaution, presumption, pretense, pretension, pride, propriety, prowess, punctilio, purpose, quarter, radiance, rancor, react, reaction, readiness, rebel, rebellion, refine-

ment, refusal, regress, reserve, responsibility, restraint, rigmarole, scene, self-control, serenity, shenanigans, show, simplicity, sincerity, sloth, sobriety, sophistication, spunk, steam, submission, sympathy, tact, technicality, temerity, temperance, treachery, treat, treatment, vainglory, valor, veneer, virginity, vitality, vitriol, zing, zip

634 commonality: diffusion, frequency, ritual

635 completeness: bulk, clincher, complement, culmination, deficiency, entirety, finality, fullness, integrity, whole

636 conformity: adequacy, adhere, archetype, cohere, fidelity, par

637 constancy: consistency, constancy, continuance, instability, monotony

638 definiteness: accuracy, ambiguity, certainty, clarity, correctness, exactness, finality, precision, rigor, sure thing, truth

639 exist in a condition: blame, condition, existence, state, status quo

640 extension: addition, continuation

641 forcefulness: clasp, clutches, dictatorship, efficacy, force, gravity, impact, impetus, impulse, intensity, kick, might, momentum, muscle, power, pressure, propulsion, push, swamp, violence

642 made of: compose, have, inclusion, manifestation

643 make up: accompany, comprise, consist of, cover, form, include, make up

644 mannerism: air, attention(s), austerity, characterize, clemency, courtesy, custom, earmark, entity, epitomize, fashion, foible, forgetfulness, habit, idiosyncrasy, manner, mannerism, mark, methodology, mien, mode, mores, propriety, purpose, quirk, regard, trait, vigilance

645 morality: abandon, accountability, affirmative action, atrocity, blasphemy, coarseness, conscience, corruption, craft, debauchery, decadence, degeneracy, delinquency, depravity, dirt, disservice, enormity, environment, equality, equity, ethics/ethic, evil, excess, fairness, faithfulness, faithlessness, falsity, foul play, favoritism, fraud, good, goodness, good will/goodwill, greatness, guile, guilt, guise, holiness, honesty, honor, ideals, imposition, imposture, indecency, infamy, infidelity, infraction, inhumanity, iniquity, injustice, innocence, justice, liability, license, loyalty, misbehave, misbehavior, mischief, misconduct, misdeed/misdemeanor, morality, morals, obligation, obscenity, organized crime, outrage, peccadillo, principle/principles, probity, profanity, prostitute, responsibility, right, sacrilege, sanctity, scandal, scheme, score, segregate, sin, transgression, treachery, treason, trespass, trick, trickery, trust, turpitude, underworld, validity, values, veracity, vice, virtue, wrong

646 necessity: absence, behoove, call for, dearth, defect, deficit, demand, do, do without, drought, enough, entail, essential, exigency/exigence, frill, go without, have, lack, mainstay, must, necessitate, necessity, need, obligate, oblige, paucity, prerequisite, provide, qualification, require, requirement/requisite, reservation, shortage, specification, subsistence, take, void, want

647 normality: aberration, abnormality, anomaly, average, eccentricity, gauge, norm, rule, rut, yardstick

648 origin: ancestry, birth, bottom, counterfeit, cradle, DNA, derivation, derive from, emanate, emanation, extraction, femininity/feminine, font, fountain, funny money, germ, geyser, hail, head, heredity, heritage, home, inception, issue, masculinity/masculine, matrix, mortality, origin, parent, precursor, root(s), seed, sex, source, spring, start, stem, threshold

649 permanency: constant, fixed, forever, permanent, perpetual, unchanging

650 probability: absurdity, chance, contingency, credibility, eventuality, liability, likelihood, must, odds, possibilities, possibility, potential, probability, promise, tend

651 range: area, breadth, circulation, compass, continuation, country mile, degree, diffusion, dissemination, dissipation, distance, diversity, expanse, extent, gamut, go, jurisdiction, latitude, length, matter, overrun, panorama, play, radius, range, reach, realm, room, run, scale, scope, spread, stretch, sweep

652 restrictiveness: abbreviation, abridgement, autonomy, bar, block, blockade, bondage, captivity, constraint, curb, exemption, flexibility, prohibition, qualification

653 specialization: alone, circumstantial, express, precise, select

654 specificity: accuracy, correctness, exactness, model, point, precision, property, rigor

655 style: appeal, approach, artistry, behavior, clash, classic, classicism, cultivation, cut, dash, dernier cri, discrimination, elegance, fad, fashion, finish, frill, frippery, genre/genus, glamour, glitter, grace, look, mode, ostentation, polish, pomp, popularity, rage, refinement, simplicity, sophistication, splendor, style, taste, tone, touch, trend, vogue

656 suitability: absurdity, adequacy, agree, awkwardness, blend, consistency, correctness, do, expediency/expedience, fitness, propriety, satisfy, serve, suit

657 tendency: acrimony, alacrity, alms, animation, aptitude, atrocity, cabin fever, care, charity, cultivation, dedication, defiance, determination, devotion, diligence, direction, discretion, dishonesty, disinclination, eagerness, earnestness, effervescence, enterprise, enthusiasm, equity, face, fairness, fashion, fervor, finesse, fundraiser, gallantry, generosity, grace, guile, gusto, guts, heat, hospitality, hostility, humility, hurry, hypocrisy, idleness, impatience, incline, indifference, indignation, indulgence, inertia, inhibition, initiative, kindness, liability, mind, moderation, monstrosity, naïveté, neglect, nervousness, nonconformity, patience, philanthropy, pity, posture, presence, pretension, rage, resignation, resolution, restlessness, seriousness, sincerity, streak, tenacity, tendency, thing, tolerance, trend, trick, truth, verge, vice, vigilance

658 usefulness: abend, agency, agent, convenience, efficiency, employment, expediency/expedience, good, help, makeshift, malfunction, medium, operation, practice, purpose, resource, serve, service, surplus, usage, use, utility, value, wear

COGNITIVE

659 goal: aim, ambition, aspiration, destination, dream, end, function, goal, intent/intention, mark, meaning, mission, object, objective, pleasure, point, prize, purport, purpose, quarry, reason, resolve, sake, target, taste, victim, will

660 plan: angle, approach, architecture, cahoots, calculation, channel, chart, chicanery, collusion, complicity, concoction, conspiracy, contrivance, craft, deceit, design, device, diagram, diet, dispensation, disposition, dodge, draft, expediency/expedience, expedient, feint, flowchart, form, format, freeware, gambit, game, gimmick, groundwork, idea, innovation, intrigue, invention, itinerary, layout, logistics, machination, maneuver, manner, method, move, plan, plot, policy, program, purport, purpose, route, scenario, schedule, scheme, shift, stratagem, strategy, tactics

661 reason: alibi, angle, asset, ax to grind, basis, benefit, blame, boon, cause, confirmation, essence, essential, excuse, explanation, footing, fuel, goad, grounds, groundwork, hypothesis, idea, impetus, incentive, inducement, inspiration, justification, keynote/keystone, lesson, meaning, message, motive, nub, occasion, origin, pretext, raison d'être, rationale, reason, root, sake, solution, spring, spur, stimulant, stimulus, whim

662 request: command, demand, desire, directive, edict, entreaty, petition, plea, prayer, proposal, proposition, query, recall, request, requisition, suit, ultimatum

COMPARATIVE

663 complexity: complexity, exaggeration, labyrinth, simplicity, snarl

664 correspondence: accord, answer, approximate, balance, clash, clone, community, conform, conformity, connection, consonance, consort, correspond, correspondence, double, dovetail, duplicate, fit, flatter, go, go together/go with, harmonize, harmony, identity, jibe, likeness, look-alike, make, match, mate, proportion, resemblance, resemble, solidarity, spitting image, square, sympathy, twin, union, unison, unity

665 difference: aberration, antithesis, assortment, backslide, contradict, contradiction, contrast, controversy, converse, depart, departure, deviate, deviation, differ, difference, digression, disagree, disagreement, discrepancy, disharmony, disparity, disproportion, dissension, dissent, dissimilarity, dissonance, distinction, diverge, divergence, diversity, eccentricity, exception, flip side, foil, gap, gradation, grade, inequality, innovation, miscellany, mismatch, mixed bag, multiculturalism, mutation, novelty, nuance, oddity, opposite, opposition, peculiarity, rent, reverse, shade, variance, variant, variation, variety, wander

666 difficulty: abomination, awkwardness, bottleneck, conundrum, deficiency, delay, disadvantage(s), downside, drawback, enormity, entanglement, facility, handicap, hindrance, hitch, impediment, labyrinth, limitation, matter, misery, muddle, obstacle, obstruction, plight, pressure, problem, quagmire, question, restraint, restriction, rigor, rub, shortcoming, snag, snarl, spot, stumbling block, task, tax, tribulation, trouble, vice, wall

667 equivalence: alternate, amount, balance, border on, cancel, clone, cohere, coincide, coincidence, come up to, copy, correlation, counterpart, disproportion, ditto, duplicate, equal, equality, equate, equivalence, equivalent, fax, image, make, match, model, par, parallel, parity, rival, sameness, standoff, tie, transcript

668 importance: accent, aspect, bearing, beauty, berth, best, celebrity, character, cipher, consequence, core, count, cream, crux, cutting edge, dignitary, dignity, dominance, element, elevation, eminence, emphasis, essence, flower, forefront/foreground, fundamental, glory, grandeur, gravity, greatness, height, honor, honorary, humdinger, immortality, import, importance, kernel, key, lead, magnitude, mark, matter, moment, name, nobility, nothingness, overshadow, peak, prestige, pride, priority, prominence, quality, renown, rudiments, sense, seriousness, significance, signify, situation, spotlight, stardom, stature, status, stress, stuff, style, tedium, top, trifle, value, weight, zero hour

669 intensity: intensity, strength, violence

670 similarity: affinity, agree, analogy, community, consistency, equivalence, equivalent, identity, likeness, parallel, parity, replica, reproduction, resemblance, resemble, sameness, second, similarity, tune, twin

671 superiority: ascendancy/ascendency, distinction, elegance, eminence, excel, excellence, hairsplitting, ideal, imperfection, importance, jewel, landslide, marvel, miracle, paragon, perfection, pick, power, precedence, preponderance, prodigy, rank, seniority, superiority, victory

OF BEING

672 abstraction: manifestation, oblivion

673 aura: abracadabra, air, allure, ambience, appeal, appearance, aspect, atmosphere, attribute, aura, background, being, blaze, celestial, charm, chorus, climate, cultivation, dash, dump, ease, environment, environmentalist, feel, feeling, flavor, glory, glow, hex, kind, look, medium, milieu, monotony, mood, orbit, presence, quiet, romance, semblance, serenity, sign, solitude, spell, spice, spirit, splendor, supernal, surroundings, texture, tone, tranquility, undercurrent, veil, vein, veneer, vestige, whammy, whisper

674 bad situation: abend, abortion, accident, act of God, adversity, affliction, anarchy, anticli-

max, apocalypse, atrophy, backwash, bad luck, bad scene, bad trip, bane, beaten, bedlam, bereavement, bind, blight, blooper, blow, bottleneck, brunt, bug, bum wrap, bummer, calamity, can of worms, casualty, cataclysm, catastrophe, catch, chagrin, chaos, clamor, clog, clutter, cobweb, collapse, collision, comedown, commotion, complication, conflict, contamination, contempt, corner, crisis, critical mass, crunch, curse, damage, dead end, deadlock, dearth, debacle, decay, decline, decomposition, deficiency, descent, detriment, devastation, difficulty, dilemma, disadvantage(s), disappointment, disaster, disaster area, discomfiture, discouragement, disorganization, disrepair, disservice, distress, disturbance, downer, downfall, downside, drag, drama, drawback, dud, duress, embarrassment, emergency, entanglement, error, exigency/exigence, eyesore, failing, fall, famine, ferment, fiasco, filth, fix, flap, flash point, flaw, flip-flop, flop, flotsam, frenzy, friction, frustration, gadfly, handicap, hang-up, hardship, harm, hassle, havoc, headache, hell, hindrance, histrionics, hitch, holdup, hole, hurdle, ill, impasse, imposture, impropriety, inadequacy, inconvenience, indiscretion, infirmity, injustice, jalopy, jam, jump, kink, lapse, liability, limitation, load, lose, loss, madhouse, maelstrom, malfunction, matter, maze, mess, mire, misadventure, misery, misfortune/mishap, misstep, mix-up, muss, neglect, nemesis, nightmare, nuisance, obstacle, obstruction, onus, oppression, ordeal, outrage, pall, pandemonium, pass, pellmell, pest, pickle, pinch, pitfall, pity, plague, plight, poison, predicament, press, pressure, problem, puncture, quagmire, quandary, question, repulse, restraint, restriction, reverse, rub, ruin, ruse, scandal, scourge, scrape, setback, shambles, shortcoming, showdown, slump, smash, snag, snare, snarl, spot, squeeze, storm, strait, strife, struggle, syndrome, tangle, tiff, to-do, tragedy, trap, trial, trouble, tumult, turmoil, tussle, undoing, unrest, uprising, uproar, upset, weakness, weight, wreck

675 danger: act of God, bad scene, bad trip, bête noire, calamity, carcinogen, cataclysm, corner, crapshoot, crunch, curse, danger, dilemma, disaster, emergency, fatality, hardship, hazard, ill, jeopardy, mayhem, menace, peril, poison, risk, scourge, seriousness, smash, threat, tragedy, trouble, venture, violence

676 effect: amount, attraction, because, cogency, combustion, cost, culmination, effectiveness, efficacy, feebleness, magnetism, potency, proceed, punch, sex appeal, splash, tell, therefore, wash

677 effort: concentration, cooperation, difficulty, diligence, direct, effort, exertion, force, go, groove, headache, idleness, industry, plod, sweat, toil, trouble, try, work, yoke

678 experience: background, callow, career, culture, heritage, history, ignorance, lead (a life), life, live, maturity, mellow, memory, naive, naïveté, phenomenon, practical, readiness, record, sustain, taste, training, unaccustomed, unfamiliar, veteran, world, young

679 fate: accident, blessing, break, bum rap, bummer, catch, chaff, chance, contingency, cost, damnation, demise, destiny, disadvantage, doom, downer, downfall, dues, duty, fate, flip-flop, fluke, fortune, freak, future, godsend, good, jinx, judgment, kismet, limbo, long shot, lot, luck, misfortune/mishap, oblivion, outlook, payoff, penalty, pitfall, plague, portion, predestination, reverse, setback, shortcoming, suspense, turning point, undoing, weight, windfall

680 function: application, avail, bar, begin, bolt, cloak, closure, cord, cushion, decoy, deterrent, disguise, dump, gauge, operate, operation, run, spray, tie, yardstick

681 inaction: abeyance, abide, asleep, bide, dalliance, dally, dawdle, doze, drag, fool around, forbear, forgo, hang, hesitate, hesitation, idleness, inertia, leisure, linger, loaf, loiter, lounge, neglect, nod, procrastinate, refrain, relief, remain, repose, respite, rest, shirk, sit tight, skip, slack/slacken, stay, wait

682 meaning: ambiguity, connotation, content, context, cryptic, denotation, denote, double entendre, drift, drive at, emphasis, express, fiber, gist, imply, import, importance, light, matter, mean, meaning, meat, message, motif, nature, nub, point, punch, purport, quintessence, represent, respect, sense, significance, signify, spirit, stand for, strain, strength, stuff, substance, suggest, symbolize, tenor, terminology, text, texture, theme, thrust, tone, typify, understanding, undertone, upshot, value, vein, weigh, weight, wording

683 name: alias, anonymous, appellation, denomination, designation, epithet, handle, moniker, name, nickname, nom de plume, nomenclature, pen name, pseudonym, sobriquet, surname, term, title

684 of agreement: accord, agreement, alliance, armistice, arrangement, assent, bargain, bond, charter, chorus, coherence, coincidence, communion, compact, compliance, compromise, concert, concord, consensus, consent, contract, convention, covenant, deal, debenture, faction, give-and-take, meeting, negotiation, okay, order, pact, protocol, provision/proviso, settlement, stipulation, terms, transaction, treaty, truce, understanding, warranty, word

685 of authorization: absolution, admittance, Annie Oakley, approval, authority, certificate, charter, confirmation, consent, credentials, decree, delegation, determination, dispensation, doorbell, easement, enactment, endorsement, enforcement, entrée, entry, exemption, fiat, finding, forgiveness, go-ahead, grace, guarantee, induction, leave, license, mandate, negation, nod, order, pardon, pass, passage, passport, patent, permission, permit, recall, release, remission, repeal, reprieve, sanction, seal, signal, ticket, treaty, veto, waiver, warrant, warranty, withdrawal, word

686 of being an example: archetype, case, classic, clout, embodiment, epitome, example, exemplar, exponent, guide, ideal, illustration, instance, lesson, light, measure, model, norm, original, paradigm, paragon, pattern, picture, precedent, prototype, replica, representative, sample, specimen, stereotype, type

687 of being an influence: bolt, contact, effect, effectiveness, fetish, forbidden fruit, gush, influence, instrument, leadership, leverage, mores, muscle, orbit, persuasion, philosopher, preponderance, pressure, rudiments, sphere, squeeze, sway, wonder

688 of being a rule: authority, axiom, ban, basis, benchmark, canon, code, condition, convention, creed, criterion, custom, democracy, dictate, doctrine, dogma, edict, essence, ethics/ethic, fact, form, formality, formula, fundamental, gauge, generality, ideology, institute, keynote/keystone, law, line, measure, model, morals, norm, observance, parameter, philosophy, policy, practice, precept, principle, protocol, regulation, ritual, rule, standard, taboo, tenet, theorem, tradition

689 of belief: absolution, activism, adjudication, advocacy, ageism, alchemy, allegiance, anticipation, apartheid, aphorism, apparition, archetype, assumed, assumption, atheism, attitude, attrition, axiom, ax to grind, basis, belief, bias, black magic, capitalism, case, cause, chauvinism, church, commonplace, complaint, concept, conception, conclusion, confidence, conformity, conjecture, connotation, conscience, consensus, contention, conviction, credence, creed, cult, culture, decision, deduction, definition, delusion, democracy, denomination, dependence/dependency, derision, determination, diagnosis, dictum, disapproval, disbelief, discrimination, dissent, dissidence, dissonance, distrust, divinity, doctrine, dogma, doubt, estimate, ethics/ethic, evaluation, expectancy, expectation, eye, fait accompli, faith, faithfulness, fallacy, fanaticism, fantasy, fascism, fatalism, favor, feeling, fetish, foreboding, forgiveness, frame of mind, generality, gospel, grievance, guess, heresy, honor, honorary, hunch, hypothesis, idea, ideals, ideology, illusion, image, impression, incantation, induction, inkling, instinct, intimation, intuition, judgment, leaning, line, logic, magic, make-believe, maxim, millstone, mind, mindset, miracle, misconception, misgiving, misogynist, motivation, motive, multiculturalism, necromancy, negative attitude, nihilism, nonconformity, notion, objection, obsession, old wives' tale, omen, opinion, optimism, oracle, outlook, patriotism, perception, perspective, persuasion, pessimism, philosophy, piety, platform, Pollyanna, position, preconception, prediction, prejudice, premise, premonition, presage, presentiment, presumption, pride, principle/principles, prognosis, prophecy, prospect, purport, purpose, racism, reaction, reality, recognition, regard, reliance, religion, reputation, resolve, respect, right, school, self-respect/self-esteem, self-satisfaction, sentiment, sexism, Shangri-la, side, sign, sixth sense, slant, sorcery, speculation, spell, stance, stand, standpoint, stigma, stock, subject, substance, suggestion, superstition, supposition, surmise, suspicion, taste, tenet, theme, theorem, theory, thesis, trust, understanding, utopia, values, view, viewpoint, vision, voodoo, vow, witchcraft, word, Xanadu

690 of concern: afraid, aghast, alarm, albatross, anxiety, anxious, apprehension, burden, concern, conundrum, craze, difficulty, dismay, disquiet, distraction, distraught, distress, doubt, encumbrance, fascination, feeling, fixation, foreboding, frightened, guilt, hallucination, hang-up, harried, horror, interest, jitters, jittery, jumpy, millstone, misgiving, mistrust, obsession, one-track mind, panic, passion, peeve, petrified, premonition, puzzled, quandary, question, scruple, suspicion, temptation, terror, thunderstruck, trouble, uneasy, weight, woe, wonder, worry

691 of law: abomination, annulment, autocracy, custody, détente, emancipation, exemption, foul, freedom, independence, justice, laissez-faire, liberation, liberty, nonviolence, offense, order, peace, prohibition, trespass, trial, validity, ward

692 on a course: career, pitch, ramble, tack, tendency, traverse

693 opportunity: big win, cinch, contingency, crapshoot, duck soup, facility, fluke, freedom, handicap, hazard, hearing, interest, juncture, lead, leverage, luck, merit, miracle, occasion, odds, opening, opportunity, outlet, picnic, plus, possibility, preference, prize, profit, prospect, pushover, recourse, remedy, resort, risk, sake, serendipity, shot, snap, start, strength, stumble, success, time, treat, turn, vacancy, welfare/well-being

694 purpose: application, employment, help, purpose, role, vehicle

695 repetition: boomerang, echo, repeat, repetition, return, verbiage

696 situation: case, circumstance, condition, context, ecosystem, environment, experience, instance, landmark, matter, medium, mystery, occurrence, point, position, situation, state, uncertainty

OF CHANGE

697 abstract: about-face, accommodation, adapt, adaptation, adjust, adjustment, back down, back out, backslide, balance, deepen, depart, departure, deviate, deviation, digress, digression, dip, diversify, fluctuate, flux, get, interchange, metamorphose, metamorphosis, movement, mutation, novelty, oscillate, range, reconcile, redress, refresh, replace, retract, reversal, reverse, revive, revolution, rig, rotate, shift, suit, switch, tighten, transform, transformation, transition, transpose, turn, turnabout, variance, variation, vary, vicissitude, withdraw

698 diminish: abate, atrophy, come down, cut, cutback, decline, decrease, degenerate, depreciate, deteriorate, deterioration, die, diminish, diminution, drain, drop, drop off, dwarf, dwindle, ebb, entropy, erosion, evaporate, evaporation, extenuate, fade, fester, flag, go, go down, lapse, lessen, let up, lull, mollify, peter out, plummet, qualify, recede, reduce, regress, relapse, relax, relent, remission, remit, revert, rot, sag, shrink, sink, slack/slacken, slump, stagnate, subside,

taper/taper off, vegetate, wane, weaken, wear, wither, worsen

699 fail: abortion, blow, blow over, bomb, comedown, crash, decline, default, disappoint, disqualify, downfall, droop, error, fail, failure, fall, fault, fizzle, flag, flop, flounder, fold, founder, go, go down, go under, miscarriage, misfire, miss, misstep, neglect, omission, overlook, run out, slump, wilt

700 improve: accession, advance, advancement, amendment, boom, boost, clear up, come along, correction, develop, development, dignify, edification, elevate, embellish, embellishment, energize, expansion, furbish, grace, improve, improvement, lift, look up, mend, pay, pick up, progress, pull through, rally, recoup, recover, recuperate, relieve, repair, revision, rise, upgrade

701 of state: acclimate, acculturation, aging, alteration, alternate, approach, assimilate, backfire, become, break out, change, come, come about, conversion, convert, co-opt, metamorphose, metamorphosis, state

702 of structure: buckle, collapse, degenerate, dissolve, flatten

703 organizational: adjournment, dissolution, expansionism, growth, merger

704 progress: advance, advancement, batten, boom, breakthrough, breeze, bring off, buildup, click, climax, coast, come on, consummate, course, develop, development, evolution, evolve, expansion, expansionism, fare, flourish, flower, form, fruition, furtherance, gestation, get along, get on, go, go ahead, go far, grow, growth, headway, inroad, jump, mature, mellow, mount, mushroom, natural selection, passage, precipitate, progress, progression, push off/push on, rise, score, spread, thrive, unfold, wax

705 unchanged: abeyance, calm, limbo, peace, quiet

OF NEED OR ACHIEVEMENT

706 achievement: ability, accomplish, accomplishment, achieve, achievement, acme, action, apex, arrive, art, attain, attainment, background, big win, bloom, blossom, bring about, bring off, carry, carry out, climax, clinch, come at, comeback, come through, compass, completion, conquer, conquest, consummate, consummation, coup, craft, crash, crown, deed, degree, discharge, distinction, doer, doing, draw, drive, dynamo, eager beaver, effect, efficacy, excel, execute, execution, exercise, exploit, extreme, extremity, failure, feat, find, finish, flair, flourish, fruition, fulfill, fulfillment, gain, get, get ahead, gift, gig, go far, go over, graduation, hack it, hairsplitting, hammer out, hit, land, manage, maximum, milestone, operate, orgasm, pan out, pass, perfect, perfection, performance, pinnacle, potential, prodigy, proficiency, progress, progression, prosper, prosperity, pull off, pull through, rack up, reach, record, score, smash, stroke, succeed, success, take, thrive, tour de force, transact, triumph, victory, welfare/well-being, win, work, work out, zenith

707 lack: lack, loss, nothing/nothingness, zilch

708 mutual possession: communal, joint, mutual

709 need: addiction, affinity, alcoholism, bait, call, charge, claim, craving, cupidity, dearth, default, dependence/dependency, deprivation, desire, eroticism, exigency/exigence, famine, hankering, hope, hunger, inadequacy, lack, lechery, libido, longing, lust, malnutrition, must, necessity, need, partiality, penchant, poverty, predilection, predisposition, preference, prerequisite, prize, propensity, requirement/requisite, shortage, slum, squalor, sustenance, temptation, thirst, use, void, want, wish, yearning, yen

710 possession: abundance, acquisition, asset(s), belongings, boast, booty, buy, cache, capital, cash, clutches, commodity, custody, deserts, desolation, division, domain, dominion, due, dynasty, effects, enjoy, enjoyment, entrench, estate, exuberance, finances, fortune, fund, funds, gain, get, grasp, have, hoard, hold, keep, legacy, lot, monopolize, monopoly, nest egg, occupancy, occupation, opulence, own, ownership, payback, plunder, possess, possession, presence, prize, profusion, property, purchase, reservation, reserve, reserved, resource, resources, retain, return, riches, savings, share, spoils, stake, store, subsistence, title, treasure, wealth

711 requirement: depend, hinge, larder, provision/proviso, provisional, reservation, rest, safekeeping, standby, stockpile, tent, understudy

712 resource: amenity, ballast, bastion, catalyst, comfort, convenience, edge, expediency/expedience, expedient, facility, find, guard, hoard, indulgence, luxury, mainstay, maintenance, makeshift, medium, mine, momentum, nurture, option, organ, pillar, plum, protection, provision, recourse, redress, relief, remedy, reparation, repertory, reserve, reservoir, resort, resource, resources, rock, safeguard, safekeeping, security, shelter, shield, solution, stockpile, stopgap, stronghold, substitute, supply, support, vehicle

713 satisfaction: afford, suffice, work out

PHYSICAL

714 accompaniment: attend, both, chaperon, coincide, coincidence, conjunction, escort, friendship, go, privacy, relation, relationship, solidarity, solitude, squire, tune, union, unity

715 age: antiquity, dotage, freshness, majority, manhood/womanhood, maturity, novelty, old age, years, young

716 appearance: appear, appearance, beard, blind, braid, cast, color, copy, countenance, decay, dissemble, ditto, double, dummy, duplicate, echo, expression, eyesore, facade, face, facsimile, favor, fax, forgery, front, glare, grimace, grin, guise, illusion, image, imitation, likeness, look, look-alike, mark, mask, match, mug, personify, pose, pout, presence, pretense, pretext, radiate, represent, reproduction, resemblance, resemble, rise, role, scowl, semblance, show, sound, stand out, strike, surface, swagger, symmetry, tableau, veneer

717 balance: awkwardness, poise, proportion, symmetry

718 beauty: Afro, beauty, coiffure, countenance, elegance, embellishment, fright, glamour, glory, grace, hairstyle, imperfection, pulchritude

719 capacity: content, fill, hold, volume

720 condition: abhorrence, allure, apoplexy, beat, calm, carriage, comfort, connection, corrosion, disability, disgust, dislocation, dissipation, distress, disturbance, emptiness, exhaustion, form, frazzle, health, maturity, peace, pollutant, pollution, repose, rust, satisfaction, shape, smog, smoke, state, stress, tangle

721 continuity: alignment, bridge, concatenation, continuity, durability, halt, length, run, sequence, series, spread, stretch

722 density: consistency, density, firmness

723 essential: austerity, brawn, corruption, decor, fat, fertility, fitness, grease, love handles, poke, posture, smudge, tension

724 force: combustion, effort, force, propulsion, push

725 genuineness: actuality, appear, certainty, counterfeit, credibility, fact, fait accompli, fallacy, falsity, feint, funny money, make-believe, reality, sure thing, truth, validity, verisimilitude

726 hardness: firmness, temper, tension

727 order: alignment, arrangement, chain, column, concatenation, configuration, confusion, cosmos, course, disarray, dislocation, disorganization, distribution, file, form, gradation, grade, head, hierarchy, introduction, line, mean, median, method, order, organization, pattern, pecking order, precede, precedence, precursor, priority, procession, queue, range, rank, round, row, run, seniority, sequence, series, stage, standing, streak, string, succeed, suite, tier, trail, train

728 pain: ache, affliction, agony, anesthesia/anaesthesia, bad news, bad time, bête noire, boo boo, cramp, crick, discomfort, distress, grief, harm, headache, heartbreak, hurt, injury, itch, kink, letdown, misery, ordeal, pain, pang, pinch, remorse, repentance, smart, spasm, sting, strain, stress, suffering, torment, torture, trauma, trial, tribulation, trouble, twinge, woe

729 safety: buffer, bulwark, fortification, parapet, precaution, protection, safekeeping, safety, security, shield

730 size: brevity, bulk, caliber, condensation, dimensions/dimension, enormity, extent, fullness, greatness, infinity, magnitude, measurement, miniature, proportion(s), size

731 stability: anchor, durability, equilibrium, firmness, flexibility, instability, spring, stability, traction

732 strength: brawn, durability, feebleness, firmness, infirmity, kick, might, potency, power, stamina, staying power, strength, tolerance, vigor, weakness

733 structure: anatomy, architecture, composition, delicacy, easel, emptiness, fabric, figure, frame, framework, mesh, ruins, skeleton, structure

734 **weight:** buoyancy/buoyance, fat, fatness, grease, love handles, obesity, pressure

SPATIAL

735 **below:** below, bottom, down, downhill, under, underneath
736 **containment:** capacity, contain, fill
737 **depth:** deep, depth, shallow
738 **direction:** ascent, circulation, crook, cross, current, curve, decline, descent, deviation, dip, direction, diverge, divergence, diversion, downgrade, fork, grade, gradient, inclination, incline, intersect, lean, level, line, list, meander, orbit, pitch, reverse, revolution, revolve, rise, rotate, run, slant, slope, swirl, tack, tendency, tilt, trend, turn, twist, undercurrent, way, whirl, wind
739 **distance:** altitude, bearing/bearings, country mile, distance, latitude, leeway, scope, space, way
740 **fill:** brim, charge, cloy, content, cram, crowd, flood, glut, hollow, overflow, packed, replete, satiate, surfeit, teem, vacant, vacuum, void, volume
741 **height:** dominate, dwarf, elevation, eminence, height, rear, stature
742 **inside:** contain, have, hold, interior, twine
743 **length:** extent, height, length, range
744 **level:** gradation, grade, layer, level, line, mesa, notch, plane, plateau, rank, row, rung, scale, stage, tier
745 **limits, physical:** abutment, boundary, confines, curb, deadline, demarcation, end, extent, extreme, extremity, frontier, hinterland, limit, perimeter, periphery, play, range, term, terminal
746 **location:** absence, absenteeism, bearing/bearings, dissemination, front, hang, junc-

tion/juncture, lie, look, median, middle, protrude, space, stretch
747 **location, relative:** adjoin, border, butt, contact, cross, detachment, face, join, near miss, precede, precedence, presence, project, proximity, vicinity
748 **motion:** activity, agility, convulsion, discharge, ejection, hurry, lassitude, lethargy, onrush, outflow, restlessness, rush, spin, stagnate, still, sweep, swing, traction, turn, vibrate, vibration, wash
749 **nearness:** abut, border on, intersect, stalk, succeed, surveillance, verge
750 **on:** casing, cover, on, pile, top, traverse
751 **outside:** band, edge, skirt, stick out
752 **over:** above, altitude, dominate, overhang, overlook, rise, tower, vault
753 **sequential:** line, trail, wake
754 **shape:** bag, conformation, curvature, cut, entwine, figure, fold, form, hollow, loop, pucker, shape, turn, twist
755 **speed:** celerity, dispatch, expedition, haste, hurry, pace, rapidity, rate, speed, velocity
756 **spread:** balloon, branch off/branch out, breadth, bridge, go, latitude, range, reach, room, space, span, sweep
757 **structure:** aperture, ascent, attitude, bag, beef, break, build, composition, condition, conformation, constitution, construction, crease, curvature, even, fabric, figure, fluid, form, frame, grade, gradient, makeup, physique, plane, ramp, set, shape, slope, stance, stoop
758 **surrounding:** circle, coil, compass, define, edge, encircle, enclose, encompass, fence, frame, gird, hedge, hem/hem in, mob, pen, ring, surround
759 **touching:** meet, neighbor, overlap
760 **width:** breadth, diameter, width
761 **within a group:** middle, range

Weights and measures

MATHEMATICS

762 **attribute of a number:** abounding, any, apiece, average, calculable, countless, dual, flat-out, immeasurable, infinite, innumerable, just about, legion, less, light, limitless, manifold, many, mathematical, maximum, minimal, minimum, more, multiple/multifarious, multitudinous, myriad, nil, numberless, numeric/numerical, numerous, one, plentiful/plenty, plural, plus, profuse, round, several, short, shy, single, skimpy, slight, sparse, steep, tidy, tiny, total, unreasonable, untold, wee
763 **change in number:** accrue, appreciate, appreciation, deduction, discount, increase, increment, inflation, jump, peak, plummet, raise, reach, slump
764 **mathematic reasoning:** accounting, add, addition, appraise, arithmetic, average, balance, calculate, calculation, cast, computation, compute, count, enumerate, estimate, figure, gauge, mathematics, measure, number, pace, page, reckon, scale, score, stock, subtract, tabulate, tally, tell, total, underestimate

765 **numeric symbol:** digit, fraction, number
766 **numeric value:** appraisal, count, couple, majority, maximum, peak, percentage, rate, scant/scanty
767 **quantity:** abundance, copiousness, enough, exuberance, greatness, overabundance, paucity, peak, plenty, plethora, preponderance, profusion, scant/scanty, shortage, superabundance
768 **ratio:** quota, rate, ratio
769 **series:** array, chain, range, series, set, string
770 **system:** apparatus, automation, board, browser, bulletin board, bureaucracy, business, capitalism, channel, chat room, circuit, commerce, communications, complex, cosmos, cyberspace, dispensation, file, finance, grammar, Internet, machinery, mail, mesh, method, net, network, pattern, post, red tape, routine, scale, system, traffic, world

QUANTIFIERS

771 **attribute of quantity:** about, additional, affluent, all, altogether, amply, below, best,

better, big, bountiful, brimming/brimful, copious, depleted, disproportionate, double, dual, elephantine, enough, excessive, exhausted, exiguous, extra, extravagant, extreme, extremely, few, flush, fraught, further, good, hardly, huge, inadequate, insufficient, just about, lacking, leftover, liberal, limited, limitless, lush, luxuriant, many, more, most, much, new, nil, other, outrageous, over, plus, residual, respectable, rich, rife, slender/slim, spare, spent, sufficient, supplementary, thick, thin, too, unreasonable, various, wholesale

772 **attribute of range:** abysmal, across-the-board, all, all-out, barely, besides, beyond, blanket, bodily, bounded, boundless, broad, capacious, catholic, chiefly, comprehensive, cosmic, dead, dearly, deeply, different, diffuse, diverse, eclectic, ecumenical, encyclopedic, exhaustive, expansive, extended, extensive, far, far-reaching, full-scale, fully, general, generally, global, greatly, inclusive, increasingly, indiscriminate, inexhaustible, international, largely, lower, mainly, mixed, moderately, more, moreover, most, mostly, motley, much, multinational, multiple/multifarious, only, overall, panoramic, pervasive, practically, primarily, principally, quite, rambling, rampant, rather, relatively, rife, slightly, somewhat, substantially, sundry, sweeping, too, universal, unlimited, utmost, vast, very, well, wholesale, wholly, wide, widespread, within, without

773 **attribute of size:** angular, atomic, baby, bantam, better, big, brief, broad, burly, capacious, capsule, cavernous, chubby, chunky, commodious, compact, compendious, concise, corpulent, cramped, cumbersome, dwarf, elephantine, enormous, extensive, fleshy, full, gargantuan, giant, gigantic, grand, great, gross, hearty, hefty, huge, hulking, husky, immeasurable, immense, imposing, impressive, incalculable, infinitesimal, inflated, laconic, large, little, major, mammoth, massive, microscopic, midget, mighty, miniature, minimal, miniscule/minuscule, minor, minute, monolithic, monstrous, monumental, narrow, petite, pocket, portable, prodigious, pudgy, puny, roly-poly, round, scrawny, short, small, small-time, squat, stocky, stout, strapping, stubby, stunted, substantial, teeny/teensy, thick, thin, tiny, titanic, tremendous, vast, voluminous, wee, whopping, wide

774 **capacity:** brimming/brimful, capacious, capacity, close, compact, congested, crowded, empty, full, packed, spacious, teeming, vacant, void

775 **change of quantity:** accession, allowance, develop, development, grow, growth

776 **decreasing:** attrition, contraction, cut, cutback, deduction, deflate, depreciate, diminish, diminution, drop, drop off, dwindle, fall, lessen, recede, relent, sag, shrink, sink, subside, taper/taper off, wane

777 **depth:** abysmal, deep, profound, shallow, skin-deep, superficial, unfathomable

778 **distance:** about, afar, away, beyond, contiguous, directly, distant, extreme, far, faraway, far-flung, farther, farthest, furthest,

immediate, last, near, nearby, off, onward/onwards, uttermost, yonder

779 **height:** alpine, elevated, elongated, giant, gigantic, high, lanky, lofty, long, low, midget, petite, precipitous, rangy, short, soaring, squat, statuesque, stubby, stunted, tall, towering

780 **increasing:** accretion, accrual, accrue, accumulation, amplification, boost, bulge, distend, enlarge, enlargement, expansion, gather, increase, increment, inflate, inflation, leap, mount, peak, proliferate, reach, rise, swell, wax, widen

781 **large:** abounding, abundant, aggregate, ample, appreciable, bulky, colossal, commodious, considerable, countless, excessive, extreme, extremely, exuberant, fantastic, far, generous, giant, gigantic, good, great, gross, handsome, handsomely, hulking, immeasurable, incalculable, infinite, inordinate, jumbo, large, lavish, legion, manifold, massive, maximum, mighty, monolithic, monstrous, much, multitudinous, myriad, numberless, numerous, opulent, plentiful/plenty, prodigal, prodigious, profuse, redundant, sizable, stupendous, substantial, surplus, tidy, tremendous, untold, unwieldy, vast, voluminous, whopping

782 **length:** extended, high, lengthy, low, short, soaring, tall

783 **measurement:** degree, extent, mark, proportion

784 **number:** amount, digit, estimate, figure, number, numeral, pair, percentage, point, quotation/quote, score, sum, trio/triple, zero

785 **portion:** among, apart, asunder, fractional, fragmentary, gross, half, sectional

786 **quantity:** agglomeration, all, amount, array, avalanche, average, backlog, barrage, batch, buildup, bundle, calculation, cascade, census, cipher, deal, deluge, dollop, duo, excess, extravagance, few, figure, flood, flow, glut, gust, heap, lot, many, mass, measure, minimum, mint, myriad, number, oodles, overabundance, pile, pittance, plenty, plethora, quantity, sum, surge, tally, total, trio/triple, turnout

787 **range:** bound/bounds, breadth, compass, confines, expanse, extent, gamut, latitude, length, range, scads, scale, scope, spread, superabundance, sweep, waterfall, width

788 **relative:** cumulative, empty, fairly, full, influx

789 **small:** compendious, diminutive, dinky, exiguous, few, handful, infinitesimal, least, less, light, little, low, marginal, meager, measly, microscopic, miniature, minimal, minimum, miniscule/minuscule, minor, minute, negligible, nominal, one, outside, petite, piddling, piddly, scant/scanty, scarce, scarcely, shy, skimpy, slight, small, sparse, teeny/teensy, tiny, trifling

790 **unit of distance measure:** depth, distance, foot, inch, mile

791 **unit of height measure:** altitude, foot, height, inch, mile

792 **unit of measure:** acre, area, degree, dimensions/dimension, gauge, mass, measure, measurement, perimeter, proportions, revolution, size, velocity, volume, width

793 **unit of scalar measure:** above, abysmal, lesser, low, over, under

794 **unit of volume measure:** capacity, fill, volume

795 **unit of weight measure:** ounce, pound, weight

796 **width:** broad, cavernous, wide

TIME

797 **attribute of age:** adolescent, advanced, afresh, aged, ancient, antediluvian, antiquarian, antiquated, antique, archaic, behind the times, big, callow, childish, contemporary, crude, dated, doddering, elder, elderly, embryonic, fresh, full-grown/full-fledged, hoary, green, immature, immemorial, inchoate, infant/infantile, innovative, junior, juvenile, late, mature, medieval, mellow, mint, modern, modish, moldy, musty, new, newfangled, novel, old, older, old-fashioned, original, originally, outdated/out-of-date, outmoded, passé, puerile, quaint, recent, ripe, secondhand, senior, stale, tender, undeveloped, up-to-date, vintage, young, youthful

798 **attribute of duration:** ad infinitum, all-time, always, annual, awhile, brief, ceaseless, chronic, compact, concise, confirmed, constant, continual, continuous, dragging, endless, ephemeral, eternal, eternally, evanescent, ever, everlasting, extended, fleeting, forever, for keeps, fugitive, immortal, incessant, indefinitely, infinite, interminable, inveterate, laconic, lasting, lifelong, limitless, long, long-standing, meteoric, momentary, never-ending, nonstop, old, on and on, ongoing, passing, perennial, permanent, perpetual, relentless, running, sanctioned, short, short-lived, soon, steady, temporary, through, throughout, timeless, transient/transitory, unbreakable, unbroken, unceasing, undying, unending, unflagging, uninterrupted, unrelenting, whirlwind

799 **attribute of time:** actual, advance, afterward/afterwards, again, almost, already, antediluvian, anterior, at, behind, behind the times, bottom, colonial, coming, concurrent, consecutive, dilatory, dire, due, duly, early, effective, ever, extemporaneous/extemporary, fast, felicitous, finally, foremost, forever, for keeps, forthcoming, forward, frequently, from scratch, gradual, gradually, hasty, hence, hereafter, hurried, immemorial, initial, instant, instantly, intermittent, irregular, irregularly, just about, last, lastly, late, later, latter, leisurely, meantime, meanwhile, meteoric, narrowly, never, next, nightly, nocturnal, old, old-fashioned, once, once and for all, oncoming, on the double, originally, overdue, pell-mell, periodic, perpetual, posterior, posthaste, postmortem, preceding, precipitous/precipitate, preliminary, previous, primal, primarily, primary/prime, primeval, primitive, primordial, pristine, prompt, promptly, punctual, quickly, rapid, rapidly, ready, right, rude, sharp, short, simultaneous, snappy, sudden, suddenly, summarily, swift, swiftly/swift, tardy, temporal, then, thereafter, timely, ultimate, unawares, untimely, up-to-date, when, while, yet

800 **date:** anniversary, date

801 **day:** afternoon, almanac, anniversary, daily, date, day, ephemeral, evening, journal, midnight, morning, night, nightly, nocturnal, noon, time

802 **definite period:** date, day, furlough, holiday, instant, leave, midnight, morning, noon, present, sabbatical, shift

803 **division of:** day, minute, second

804 **duration:** brevity, continuance, continuation, course, duration, endurance, endure, eternity, extent, go, halt, length, remain

805 **frequency:** rapidity, sometimes

806 **hour:** afternoon, evening, morning, night, noon, time

807 **indefinite period:** age, antiquity, anytime, bit, bout, break, breath, continuance, convenience, downtime, eon, epoch, era, furlough, future, generation, hiatus, history, infinity, interim, interlude, intermission, interruption, interval, lapse, leave, leisure, letup, lull, meantime, millenium, minute, moment, moratorium, past, pause, period, present, recess, remission, respite, rest, round, sabbatical, semester, slack, space, span, spell, stalemate, stint, stretch, suspension, term, tour, trick, vacation, wait, while

808 **minute:** flash, instant, jiffy, moment, tick, wink

809 **month:** almanac, calendar, gestation, lunatic, moon, time

810 **part of a day:** afternoon, dark, dawn, day, daybreak, daylight, dusk, evening, gloom, light, morning, night, nightfall, sunrise, sunset, tick, twilight

811 **past or future:** following, future, past, preceding, previous, prior, succeeding/successive

812 **proximity:** immediate, near, now, prior, succeeding/successive

813 **relative order:** follow, precede, succeed

814 **season:** autumn, season, spring, summer, winter

815 **specific:** anniversary, beginning, date, dawn, daybreak, for openers, instance, juncture, point, present, yesterday, zero hour

816 **stage of existence:** administration, age, childhood, cycle, day, era, generation, life, millenium, past, phase, prime, stage, tenure

817 **stage of life form:** adolescence, age, babyhood, childhood, cradle, cycle, landmark, life, lifetime, majority, maternity, old age, prime, puberty, spell, youth

818 **temporal association:** anachronism, clockwork, dispatch, elapse, eternity, fly, following, future, haste, pace, past, precede, precedence, preceding, previous, prior, rush, succeeding/successive

819 **temporal object:** anytime, clock, time

820 **time relative to present:** abaft, abrupt, after, ago, ahead, amid/amidst, anew, antecedent, au courant, back, before, beforehand, behind, belated, between, bygone, circa, coincident, contemporary, current, deferred, destined, directly, during, early, ensuing, erstwhile, eventual, eventually, fated, final, first, following, fore, foregoing, former, formerly,

forthwith, future, historical, immediate, immediately, imminent, impending, infant/infantile, instantaneous, just, lately, momentarily, near, nearing, new, newly, now, once, past, present, presently, previous, previously, prior, readily, recent, recently, shortly, someday, soon, straight, subsequent, subsequently, succeeding/successive, topical, ultimate, ultimately, until, yet

821 unit of time measure: day, flash, minute, second, wink

822 within a time period: epoch, interim, interval, period, semester, span, spell, stint, stretch, term, while

823 year: almanac, anniversary, annual, annually, time, yearly

WHOLENESS OR DIVISION

824 added part: arm, attachment, auxiliary, backup, complement, complementary, excess, extension, extra, fitting, flap, fresh, frill, frippery, furthermore, garnish, we, offshoot, outgrowth, protuberance, ramification, repair, sequel, spare, spin-off, superfluous, supplement, surplus, trim, wake, wing

825 bottom part: fringe, rear, rest, rump, seat, skirt, stub, stump, tail

826 core part: base, bosom, bottom, constituent, core, cornerstone, crux, element, essential, filling/filler, focus, foundation, fundamental, germ, heart, hub, infrastructure, inner, interior, internal, kernel, marrow, meat, nerve center, nub, nucleus, quintessence, root, trunk

827 end part: abutment, addendum, back, border, butt, end, point, posterior, rear, seat, stub, stump, tail

828 first part: appetizer, early, hors d'oeuvre, initial, introduction, lead, nucleus, overture, precursor, predecessor, preliminary, spark

829 main part: bells and whistle, body, bulk, capital, chief, element, feature, flower, focus, fundamental, hulk, hull, main, majority, nerve center, parcel, plurality, root

830 middle part: aisle, axis, axle, bowels, center, central, filling/filler, inner, inside, interior, intermediate, internal, joint, junction/juncture, mean, median, middle, midst, pivot

831 minor part: atom, bit, breath, cereal, chip, collateral, component, crumb, dandruff, dash, detail, dot, drop, drop in the bucket, factor, feature, fiber, flake, fleck, flicker, glimmer, grain, grit, handle, iota, item, joint, lick, ligature, minimum, modicum, molecule, morsel, mote, nibble, nip, node/nodule, particle, patch, peripheral, pinch, point, powder, scintilla, scrap, shred, sliver, smidgen, soupçon, spark, specimen, speck, splinter, spot, sprinkling, suspicion, tinge, touch, trace, trifle, whisper, whit, wisp

832 of an event: chapter, close, conclusion, crackdown, dawn, denouement, end, ending, finale, finality, finish, genesis, germ, head, height, highlight, inception, installation, interruption, last, leg, limit, meridian, onset, opening, orientation, origin, origination, outbreak, overture, particular, peak, period, preliminary, prelude, premiere, prevention, preview, prime, sequel, snatch, stalemate, standstill, start, stay, step, stop, stoppage, suspension, swan song, term, termination, threshold, touch, turning point, twilight, twist, victory, win, zenith, zero hour

833 of an order: back, beginning, end, for openers, front, middle

834 part: accessory, accompaniment, attribute, component, constituent, counterpart, feature, member, part, phase, piece, strip, thing, trait, trash, trimmings, unit

835 portion: accompaniment, addition, adjunct, allocation, allotment, ancillary, appendage, arm, bit, bite, branch, constituent, contents, dab, deal, division, dollop, dose, drop, end, excerpt, excess, extract, facet, factor, feature, fraction, fragment, front, half, ingredient, installment, interest, item, layer, link, little, lot, majority, mass, measure, member, morsel, parcel, pat, percentage, piece, portion, precinct, quarter, quota, ration, remainder, remnant, rest, sample, scrap, section, sector, segment, share, side, slab, slice, stake, subdivision, taste, tidbit, whit, wing

836 top part: acme, alpine, apex, barb, brim, ceiling, citadel, climax, crescendo, crest, crown, extreme, extremity, face, front, head, height, lid, maximum, meridian, orgasm, peak, pinnacle, plug, point, prominence, rim, summit, tip, top, vertex, zenith

837 whole: all, amount, entirety, everything, gross, synthesis, system, total, unit, unity, whole